WATERLOO PUBLIC LIBRARY
3 3420 00634 482 5
P9-DGV-917

Fourteenth-century manuscript illumination depicting the Virgin and Child with noblewoman, St. Dominic, and St. Bernadino of Siena.
(© Historical Picture Archive/CORBIS)

NEW
CATHOLIC
ENCYCLOPEDIA

NEW CATHOLIC ENCYCLOPEDIA

SECOND EDITION

2
Baa–Cam

Detroit • New York • San Diego • San Francisco • Cleveland • New Haven, Conn. • Waterville, Maine • London • Munich

in association with
THE CATHOLIC UNIVERSITY OF AMERICA • WASHINGTON, D.C.

The New Catholic Encyclopedia, Second Edition

Project Editors
Thomas Carson, Joann Cerrito

Editorial
Erin Bealmear, Jim Craddock, Stephen Cusack, Miranda Ferrara, Kristin Hart, Melissa Hill, Margaret Mazurkiewicz, Carol Schwartz, Christine Tomassini, Michael J. Tyrkus

Permissions
Edna Hedblad, Shalice Shah-Caldwell

Imaging and Multimedia
Randy Bassett, Dean Dauphinais, Robert Duncan, Leitha Etheridge-Sims, Mary K. Grimes, Lezlie Light, Dan Newell, David G. Oblender, Christine O'Bryan, Luke Rademacher, Pamela Reed

Product Design
Michelle DiMercurio

Data Capture
Civie Green

Manufacturing
Rhonda Williams

Indexing
Victoria Agee, Victoria Baker, Lynne Maday, Do Mi Stauber, Amy Suchowski

For more information, contact
The Gale Group, Inc.
27500 Drake Rd.
Farmington Hills, MI 48331-3535
Or you can visit our Internet site at
http://www.gale.com

LIBRARY OF CONGRESS CATALOGING-IN-PUBLICATION DATA

New Catholic encyclopedia.—2nd ed.
p. cm.
Includes bibliographical references and indexes.
ISBN 0-7876-4004-2
1. Catholic Church—Encyclopedias. I. Catholic University of America.
BX841 .N44 2002
282' .03—dc21
2002000924

ISBN: 0-7876-4004-2 (set)
0-7876-4005-0 (v. 1)
0-7876-4006-9 (v. 2)
0-7876-4007-7 (v. 3)
0-7876-4008-5 (v. 4)
0-7876-4009-3 (v. 5)
0-7876-4010-7 (v. 6)
0-7876-4011-5 (v. 7)
0-7876-4012-3 (v. 8)
0-7876-4013-1 (v. 9)
0-7876-4014-x (v. 10)
0-7876-4015-8 (v. 11)
0-7876-4016-6 (v. 12)
0-7876-4017-4 (v. 13)
0-7876-4018-2 (v. 14)
0-7876-4019-0 (v. 15)

Printed in the United States of America
10 9 8 7 6 5 4 3 2 1

Foreword

This revised edition of the *New Catholic Encyclopedia* represents a third generation in the evolution of the text that traces its lineage back to the *Catholic Encyclopedia* published from 1907 to 1912. In 1967, sixty years after the first volume of the original set appeared, The Catholic University of America and the McGraw-Hill Book Company joined together in organizing a small army of editors and scholars to produce the *New Catholic Encyclopedia.* Although planning for the *NCE* had begun before the Second Vatican Council and most of the 17,000 entries were written before Council ended, Vatican II enhanced the encyclopedia's value and importance. The research and the scholarship that went into the articles witnessed to the continuity and richness of the Catholic Tradition given fresh expression by Council. In order to keep the *NCE* current, supplementary volumes were published in 1972, 1978, 1988, and 1995. Now, at the beginning of the third millennium, The Catholic University of America is proud to join with The Gale Group in presenting a new edition of the *New Catholic Encyclopedia.* It updates and incorporates the many articles from the 1967 edition and its supplements that have stood the test of time and adds hundreds of new entries.

As the president of The Catholic University of America, I cannot but be pleased at the reception the *NCE* has received. It has come to be recognized as an authoritative reference work in the field of religious studies and is praised for its comprehensive coverage of the Church's history and institutions. Although Canon Law no longer requires encyclopedias and reference works of this kind to receive an *imprimatur* before publication, I am confident that this new edition, like the original, reports accurate information about Catholic beliefs and practices. The editorial staff and their consultants were careful to present official Church teachings in a straightforward manner, and in areas where there are legitimate disputes over fact and differences in interpretation of events, they made every effort to insure a fair and balanced presentation of the issues.

The way for this revised edition was prepared by the publication, in 2000, of a Jubilee volume of the *NCE,* heralding the beginning of the new millennium. In my foreword to that volume I quoted Pope John Paul II's encyclical on Faith and Human Reason in which he wrote that history is "the arena where we see what God does for humanity." The *New Catholic Encyclopedia* describes that arena. It reports events, people, and ideas—"the things we know best and can verify most easily, the things of our everyday life, apart from which we cannot understand ourselves" (*Fides et ratio,* 12).

Finally, I want to express appreciation on my own behalf and on the behalf of the readers of these volumes to everyone who helped make this revision a reality. We are all indebted to The Gale Group and the staff of The Catholic University of America Press for their dedication and the alacrity with which they produced it.

Very Reverend David M. O'Connell, C.M., J.C.D.
President
The Catholic University of America

Preface to the Revised Edition

When first published in 1967 the *New Catholic Encyclopedia* was greeted with enthusiasm by librarians, researchers, and general readers interested in Catholicism. In the United States the *NCE* has been recognized as the standard reference work on matters of special interest to Catholics. In an effort to keep the encyclopedia current, supplementary volumes were published in 1972, 1978, 1988, and 1995. However, it became increasingly apparent that further supplements would not be adequate to this task. The publishers subsequently decided to undertake a thorough revision of the *NCE,* beginning with the publication of a Jubilee volume at the start of the new millennium.

Like the biblical scribe who brings from his storeroom of knowledge both the new and the old, this revised edition of the *New Catholic Encyclopedia* incorporates material from the 15-volume original edition and the supplement volumes. Entries that have withstood the test of time have been edited, and some have been amended to include the latest information and research. Hundreds of new entries have been added. For all practical purposes, it is an entirely new edition intended to serve as a comprehensive and authoritative work of reference reporting on the movements and interests that have shaped Christianity in general and Catholicism in particular over two millennia.

SCOPE

The title reflects its outlook and breadth. It is the *New Catholic Encyclopedia,* not merely a new encyclopedia of Catholicism. In addition to providing information on the doctrine, organization, and history of Christianity over the centuries, it includes information about persons, institutions, cultural phenomena, religions, philosophies, and social movements that have affected the Catholic Church from within and without. Accordingly, the *NCE* attends to the history and particular traditions of the Eastern Churches and the Churches of the Protestant Reformation, and other ecclesial communities. Christianity cannot be understood without exploring its roots in ancient Israel and Judaism, nor can the history of the medieval and modern Church be understood apart from its relationship with Islam. Interfaith dialogue requires an appreciation of Buddhism and other world religions, as well as some knowledge of the history of religion in general.

On the assumption that most readers and researchers who use the *NCE* are individuals interested in Catholicism in general and the Church in North America in particular, its editorial content gives priority to the Western Church, while not neglecting the churches in the East; to Roman Catholicism, acknowledging much common history with Protestantism; and to Catholicism in the United States, recognizing that it represents only a small part of the universal Church.

Scripture, Theology, Patrology, Liturgy. The many and varied articles dealing with Sacred Scripture and specific books of the Bible reflect contemporary biblical scholarship and its concerns. The *NCE* highlights official church teachings as expressed by the Church's magisterium. It reports developments in theology, explains issues and introduces ecclesiastical writers from the early Church Fathers to present-day theologians whose works exercise major influence on the development of Christian thought. The *NCE* traces the evolution of the Church's worship with special emphasis on rites and rituals consequent to the liturgical reforms and renewal initiated by the Second Vatican Council.

Church History. From its inception Christianity has been shaped by historical circumstances and itself has become a historical force. The *NCE* presents the Church's history from a number of points of view against the background of general political and cultural history. The revised edition reports in some detail the Church's missionary activity as it grew from a small community in Jerusalem to the worldwide phenomenon it is today. Some entries, such as those dealing with the Middle Ages, the Reformation, and the Enlightenment, focus on major time-periods and movements that cut across geographical boundaries. Other articles describe the history and structure of the Church in specific areas, countries, and regions. There are separate entries for many dioceses and monasteries which by reason of antiquity, size, or influence are of special importance in ecclesiastical history, as there are for religious orders and congregations. The *NCE* rounds out its comprehensive history of the Church with articles on religious movements and biographies of individuals.

Canon and Civil Law. The Church inherited and has safeguarded the precious legacy of ancient Rome, described by Virgil, "to rule people under law, [and] to establish the way of peace." The *NCE* deals with issues of ecclesiastical jurisprudence and outlines the development of legislation governing communal practices and individual obligations, taking care to incorporate and reference the 1983 *Code of Canon Law* throughout and, where appropriate, the *Code of Canons for the Eastern Churches.* It deals with issues of Church-State relations and with civil law as it impacts on the Church and Church's teaching regarding human rights and freedoms.

Philosophy. The Catholic tradition from its earliest years has investigated the relationship between faith and reason. The *NCE* considers at some length the many and varied schools of ancient, medieval, and modern philosophy with emphasis, when appropriate, on their relationship to theological positions. It pays particular attention to the scholastic tradition, particularly Thomism, which is prominent in Catholic intellectual history. Articles on many major and lesser philosophers contribute to a comprehensive survey of philosophy from pre-Christian times to the present.

Biography and Hagiography. The *NCE,* making an exception for the reigning pope, leaves to other reference works biographical information about living persons. This revised edition presents biographical sketches of hundreds of men and women, Christian and non-Christian, saints and sinners, because of their significance for the Church. They include: Old and New Testament figures; the Fathers of the Church and ecclesiastical writers; pagan and Christian emperors; medieval and modern kings; heads of state and other political figures; heretics and champions of orthodoxy; major and minor figures in the Reformation and Counter Reformation; popes, bishops, and priests; founders and members of religious orders and congregations; lay men and lay women; scholars, authors, composers, and artists. The *NCE* includes biographies of most saints whose feasts were once celebrated or are currently celebrated by the universal church. The revised edition relies on Butler's *Lives of the Saints* and similar reference works to give accounts of many saints, but the *NCE* also provides biographical information about recently canonized and beatified individuals who are, for one reason or another, of special interest to the English-speaking world.

Social Sciences. Social sciences came into their own in the twentieth century. Many articles in the *NCE* rely on data drawn from anthropology, economics, psychology and sociology for a better understanding of religious structures and behaviors. Papal encyclicals and pastoral letters of episcopal conferences are the source of principles and norms for Christian attitudes and practice in the field of social action and legislation. The *NCE* draws attention to the Church's organized activities in pursuit of peace and justice, social welfare and human rights. The growth of the role of the laity in the work of the Church also receives thorough coverage.

ARRANGEMENT OF ENTRIES

The articles in the *NCE* are arranged alphabetically by the first substantive word using the word-by-word method of alphabetization; thus "New Zealand" precedes "Newman, John Henry," and "Old Testament Literature" precedes "Oldcastle, Sir John." Monarchs, patriarchs, popes, and others who share a Christian name and are differentiated by a title and numerical designation are alphabetized by their title and then arranged numerically. Thus, entries for Byzantine emperors Leo I through IV precede those for popes of the same name, while "Henry VIII, King of England" precedes "Henry IV, King of France."

Maps, Charts, and Illustrations. The *New Catholic Encyclopedia* contains nearly 3,000 illustrations, including photographs, maps, and tables. Entries focusing on the Church in specific countries contain a map of the country as well as easy-to-read tables giving statistical data and, where helpful, lists of archdioceses and dioceses. Entries on the Church in U.S. states also contain tables listing archdioceses and dioceses where appropriate. The numerous photographs appearing in the *New Catholic Encyclopedia* help to illustrate the history of the Church, its role in modern societies, and the many magnificent works of art it has inspired.

SPECIAL FEATURES

Subject Overview Articles. For the convenience and guidance of the reader, the *New Catholic Encyclopedia* contains several brief articles outlining of scope of major fields: "Theology, Articles on," "Liturgy, Articles on," "Jesus Christ, Articles on," etc.

Cross-References. The cross-reference system in the *NCE* serves to direct the reader to related material in other articles. The appearance of a name or term in small capital letters in text indicates that there is an article of that title elsewhere in the encyclopedia. In some cases, the name of the related article has been inserted at the appropriate point as a *see* reference: (*see* THOMAS AQUINAS, ST.). When a further aspect of the subject is treated under another title, a *see also* reference is placed at the end of the article. In addition to this extensive cross-reference system, the comprehensive index in volume 15 will greatly increase the reader's ability to access the wealth of information contained in the encyclopedia.

Abbreviations List. Following common practice, books and versions of the Bible as well as other standard works by selected authors have been abbreviated throughout the text. A guide to these abbreviations follows this preface.

The Editors

Abbreviations

The system of abbreviations used for the works of Plato, Aristotle, St. Augustine, and St. Thomas Aquinas is as follows: Plato is cited by book and Stephanus number only, e.g., Phaedo 79B; Rep. 480A. Aristotle is cited by book and Bekker number only, e.g., Anal. post. 72b 8–12; Anim. 430a 18. St. Augustine is cited as in the Thesaurus Linguae Latinae, e.g., C. acad. 3.20.45; Conf. 13.38.53, with capitalization of the first word of the title. St. Thomas is cited as in scholarly journals, but using Arabic numerals. In addition, the following abbreviations have been used throughout the encyclopedia for biblical books and versions of the Bible.

Books

Acts	Acts of the Apostles
Am	Amos
Bar	Baruch
1–2 Chr	1 and 2 Chronicles (1 and 2 Paralipomenon in Septuagint and Vulgate)
Col	Colossians
1–2 Cor	1 and 2 Corinthians
Dn	Daniel
Dt	Deuteronomy
Eccl	Ecclesiastes
Eph	Ephesians
Est	Esther
Ex	Exodus
Ez	Ezekiel
Ezr	Ezra (Esdras B in Septuagint; 1 Esdras in Vulgate)
Gal	Galatians
Gn	Genesis
Hb	Habakkuk
Heb	Hebrews
Hg	Haggai
Hos	Hosea
Is	Isaiah
Jas	James
Jb	Job
Jdt	Judith
Jer	Jeremiah
Jgs	Judges
Jl	Joel
Jn	John
1–3 Jn	1, 2, and 3 John
Jon	Jonah
Jos	Joshua
Jude	Jude
1–2 Kgs	1 and 2 Kings (3 and 4 Kings in Septuagint and Vulgate)
Lam	Lamentations
Lk	Luke
Lv	Leviticus
Mal	Malachi (Malachias in Vulgate)
1–2 Mc	1 and 2 Maccabees
Mi	Micah
Mk	Mark
Mt	Matthew
Na	Nahum
Neh	Nehemiah (2 Esdras in Septuagint and Vulgate)
Nm	Numbers
Ob	Obadiah
Phil	Philippians
Phlm	Philemon
Prv	Proverbs
Ps	Psalms
1–2 Pt	1 and 2 Peter
Rom	Romans
Ru	Ruth
Rv	Revelation (Apocalypse in Vulgate)
Sg	Song of Songs
Sir	Sirach (Wisdom of Ben Sira; Ecclesiasticus in Septuagint and Vulgate)
1–2 Sm	1 and 2 Samuel (1 and 2 Kings in Septuagint and Vulgate)
Tb	Tobit
1–2 Thes	1 and 2 Thessalonians
Ti	Titus
1–2 Tm	1 and 2 Timothy
Wis	Wisdom
Zec	Zechariah
Zep	Zephaniah

Versions

Apoc	Apocrypha
ARV	American Standard Revised Version
ARVm	American Standard Revised Version, margin
AT	American Translation
AV	Authorized Version (King James)
CCD	Confraternity of Christian Doctrine
DV	Douay-Challoner Version

ERV	English Revised Version	NJB	New Jerusalem Bible
ERVm	English Revised Version, margin	NRSV	New Revised Standard Version
EV	English Version(s) of the Bible	NT	New Testament
JB	Jerusalem Bible	OT	Old Testament
LXX	Septuagint	RSV	Revised Standard Version
MT	Masoretic Text	RV	Revised Version
NAB	New American Bible	RVm	Revised Version, margin
NEB	New English Bible	Syr	Syriac
NIV	New International Version	Vulg	Vulgate

B

BAADER, FRANZ XAVER VON

Social philosopher, lay theologian, and mining engineer; b. Munich, March 27, 1765; d. Munich, May 23, 1841. Baader was a leading member of the ''Munich circle'' of romantic Catholics who did so much to advance the renewal of Catholicism in the 19th century. Through his influence on SCHELLING, DÖLLINGER, E. von Lasaulx, KIERKEGAARD, SOLOV'EV, and BERDÎAEV, he affected intellectual developments extending well beyond his century.

Baader first studied medicine at Ingolstadt and Vienna. His intellectual formation was strongly influenced by J. M. SAILER and the French mystic L. C. Saint-Martin. Abandoning medical practice after a short time, he turned to the study of mining engineering at Freiberg (1788–92). While serving as an engineer in England and Scotland (1792–96) he studied at firsthand the impact of the industrial revolution, the liberal economic theory of Adam SMITH, and the sensational psychology of Hume. About the same time, he undertook the study and criticism of Kant and German idealistic philosophy. His rejection of rationalistic philosophy, liberal economics, and the revolutionary transformation of the social order were rooted in these experiences and studies. He distinguished himself in his profession from the time of his return to Bavaria in 1799 until his retirement from engineering in 1820. Then he began intensive work and publication in the field of speculative theology and in 1826 was appointed professor of philosophy at Munich. Here, in association with GÖRRES and the younger members of the ''Munich circle,'' he published the journal *Eos.* Although his literary style was cloudy and aphoristic, he was regarded as one of the most brilliant conversationalists and lecturers in Germany.

Baader, in the years between 1814 and 1822, laid the basis for modern ecumenicism. He was responsible for the establishment of the Holy Alliance, which he conceived as a bridge not only between political entities but between Protestantism, Orthodoxy, and Catholicism. In 1822 he founded an ecumenical academy in St. Petersburg. Although these ventures were failures, Baader's efforts at reunion lived on in the thought of Döllinger and the South German school.

Baader's theosophical thought, colored by Neoplatonism and gnostic tendencies, aimed at a reconciliation of reason and authority. On this account he is frequently described as a neoscholastic, although his fantastic thought structures frequently verged on heterodoxy. More immediately important was his social teaching, which, like his epistemology, was a return to authority. Highly critical of liberal politics and economics, he proposed a corporative social structure based upon principles of authority, hierarchy, subordination, and status. His corporativist ideas became commonplaces of European social thought in the century that followed his death.

Bibliography: *Sämtliche Werke*, ed. F. HOFFMANN et al., 16 v. (Leipzig 1850–60); newly repr. (Aalen 1963—); *Lettres inédites*, ed. E. SUSINI (Paris 1943). Literature. H. GRASSL, *Neue deutsche Biographie* 1:474–76, extensive bibliog. D. BAUMGARDT, *Franz von Baader und die philosophische Romantik* (Halle 1927). E. SUSINI, *Franz von Baader et le romantisme mystique*, 2 v. (Paris 1943). For an introduction to Baader's social theory, consult R. BOWEN, *German Theories of the Corporative State* (New York 1947) 46–53. For Baader's relationship to romantic Catholicism, consult T. STEINBÜCHEL, ''Romantisches Denken im Katholizismus mit besonderer Berücksichtigung der romantischen Philosophic Franz von Baaders,'' *Romantik: Ein Zyklus Tübinger Vorlesungen*, ed. T. STEINBÜCHEL (Tübingen 1948).

[S. J. TONSOR]

BAAL

Chief god of the Canaanites, son or grandson of the sky god EL, and consort of Asera (Asherah). Baal was the most popular god of the Canaanite pantheon, since he was the administrator of divine favors, the high god El being treated as a shadowy and distant figurehead. In the mythology of UGARIT, Baal was the champion of the gods in their fight against the sea Dragon Yam; when he killed

Baal with a Lance. (©Gianni Dagli Orti/CORBIS)

him, he was acclaimed king and hailed as Zabul, ''the exalted lord of the earth,'' and Baal Samen, ''lord of the heavens.'' He was likewise known as ''the rider of the clouds'' (an Old Testament title of Yahweh as well) and ''the lord of the storm,'' whose voice was thunder. Thus, he was the god who controlled the rain. Since the Canaanites were entirely dependent on rain for the growth of their crops, they fervently sought the good will of Baal. Later he was identified with the storm god Hadad (Adad). In Akkadian, Baal was pronounced as Bel.

The Canaanite word *ba'al* (lord, master, owner, husband) was originally one of Baal's titles, but by the 15th or 14th century B.C. it was used almost exclusively as his proper name. Since Yahweh was the lord and master (and even husband) of His people Israel, the early Israelites often called Him *ba'al;*, but when they indulged in the fertility cult of the Canaanite Baal, this appellation for Yahweh was forbidden (Hos 2.18–19). Before this time many Israelite names were formed with *ba'al* as a title for Yahweh, e.g., Meri-Baal, a son of Saul (2 Sam 21.8) and a son of Jonathan (2 Sm 4.4); Ish-Baal, another son of Saul (1 Chr 8.33); and Baaliada, a daughter of David (1 Chr 14.7). Later scribes changed *ba'al* in some of these names to *bōšct* (shame). Place names were likewise formed with *ba'al*, e.g., Baala in northern Juda (Jos 15.9), Baal-Gad (Jos 11.17), Baal-Hermon (Jgs 3.3), etc.; but most, if not all, of these place names went back to the Canaanites, and their full form was probably as in Beth-Baal-Maon (house, i.e., sanctuary of the Lord of Maon; cf. Nm 32.38 with Jos 13.17).

The Old Testament (Jgs 2.11; 8.33; 10.10) speaks of Baals (in the plural), not because there were many different Baals, but because the same god was worshiped at different sanctuaries, e.g., at Baal-Phogor (Dt 4.3; Hos 9.10) and at the temple of Baal-Berith (the lord of the covenant) in Shechem (Jgs 8.33; 9.4). The commingling of the Israelites with the Canaanites led to more and more religious syncretism. Even among the Israelites, Baal had his high places (Jer 19.5; 32.35), his altars (Jgs 6.25–30), his sacred STONES (2 Kgs 11.18; 2 Chr 23.17), and his prophets (1 Kgs 18.19, 22). The struggle between Yahweh and Baal came to a climax under King Ahab of Israel and his wife JEZEBEL, who built a temple in Baal's honor at Samaria and supported 450 of his prophets (1 Kgs 16.32). Elijah successfully challenged these prophets on Mt. Carmel (1 Kgs 18.20–40). Although almost eradicated by Jehu (2 Kgs 10.18–28), the cult revived and remained until the destruction of the Northern Kingdom of Israel (2 Kgs 17.10). Promoters of the Baal cult in Judah were Ahab's daughter Athalia, who was married to King Jehoram of Judah (2 Kgs 11.18), and King Manasse (2 Kgs 21.3). Although strenuously opposed by the Prophets Jeremiah (Jer 2.23; 11.13) and Ezekiel (Ez 6.4–6), the cult continued in Judah until the destruction of the Southern Kingdom. Many of the attributes of Baal are paralleled by those applied to Yahweh, and perhaps some of the Psalms were influenced by the cultic hymns of Baal worship [e.g., Ps 28(29)].

Bibliography: *Encyclopedic Dictionary of the Bible*, tr. and adap. by L. HARTMAN (New York 1963) 182–183. A. S. KAPELRUD, *Baal in the Ras Shamra Texts* (Copenhagen 1952). G. R. DRIVER, *Canaanite Myths and Legends* (Edinburgh 1956). J. GRAY, *The Legacy of Canaan: The Ras Shamra Texts and Their Relevance to the Old Testament* (*Vetid Testamentum* Suppl. 5; 2d ed. 1964). R. DUSSAUD, ''Le Vrai nom de Ba'al,'' *Revue de l'histoire des religions* 113 (1936) 5–20.

[H. MUELLER]

BABISM

An ultra-Shī'ite sect founded in Shiraz, Persia, in 1844 by a dissenting theologian, Muḥammad'Alī (1819–50), who assumed the title of al-Bāb (Ar., short for Bāb-al-Dīn, ''the gateway to religion''). Al-Bāb built on foundations laid in Persia by a native of eastern Arabia, al-Shaykh Aḥmad Aḥsa'i (d. 1828), whose followers (Shaykhis) held the 12 IMĀM descendants of 'ALI in excessive veneration and emphasized the cult of al-Mahdī [the (divinely) guided one]. The MAHDĪ, according to the major body of the SHĪ'ITES, is the 12th hidden imām who, in the fullness of time, will reappear and, messiah-like, lead his followers to a new era of justice and prosperity. When on a pilgrimage to Kerbela (Karbalā), Iraq, al-Bāb made the acquaintance of a Shaykhi missionary from whom he received instruction, and when he was on another pilgrimage to MECCA, he developed the doctrine that he was the door to esoteric knowledge and the inner veiled meaning of the scriptures.

His ideas were formulated in a "revealed" book *al-Bayān* (the manifestation), where Qur'ānic laws were abrogated and an allegorical interpretation (*ta'wīl*) was so applied to the QUR'ĀN and ḥadīth (ISLAMIC TRADITIONS) as to be viewed as a threat to Shī'ism, the state religion, as well as to the state itself. The new teaching abolished the veil, circumcision, and ritual ablution. The law on usury was likewise repealed, but not that against drinking. Furthermore, the innovator proclaimed himself the mirror in which God was reflected and in which his adherents could see Him. Following neo-Pythagorean precedent, he gave the number 19 a mystical meaning. The year was divided into 19 months and the month into 19 days; the daily reading of 19 verses from *al-Bayān*, written in the style of the Qur'ān, was enjoined on all believers. The name of God was to be prayerfully repeated 361 times a day.

As al-Bāb went from place to place preaching his new gospel, he was jailed, and his followers were persecuted. Among his disciples was a beautiful, intelligent poetess, Qurrat al-'Ayn (the satisfaction of the eye), whose missionary activity was especially successful. Despite civil and governmental opposition, adherents increased. The movement became a rallying center for political, economic, and spiritual malcontents. At the accession of Shah Nāṣir-al-Dīn (1848), the Bābis, fearing intensified persecution, took up arms. Disturbances spread in Mashhad, Zanjān, Tabriz, and other towns of Persia. In the capital, Teheran, the insurgents routed the first contingents sent against them, but were later surrounded, starved, and destroyed. In July 1850 al-Bāb was executed in the public square of Tabriz, and his body was thrown into a ditch. Two years later Bābis were charged with conspiring to murder the Shah. Another persecution followed in which Qurrat-al-'Ayn was strangled. In all about 20,000 lost their lives at the hands of the mob, religious leaders, or soldiers.

A disciple of al-Bāb was accepted as the manifestation of the Diety for whom the Bāb had prepared the way. He assumed the title of Bahā'-Allāh (splendor of God). The cycle of 19 years (1844–63), was completed. Shaykhism led to Babism, and Babism ended in BAHA'ISM. All three movements represented spiritual ferment and political turbulence in 19th-century Persia; but while Shaykhism remained within the fold of Islam, its outgrowths moved to the periphery.

Bibliography: C. HUART, *La Religion de Bāb* (Paris 1889). ALĪ MUHAMMAD, SHĪRĀZĪ, *A Traveller's Narrative Written to Illustrate the Episode of the Bāb*, tr. and ed. E.G. BROWNE (Cambridge, Eng. 1891). E. G. BROWNE, comp., *Materials for the Study of the Bābī Religion* (Cambridge, Eng. 1918). NABÍL-I-A'ZAM, *The Dawn Breakers*, tr. SHOGHI EFFENDI (2d ed. Wilmette, Ill. 1953).

[P. K. HITTI]

BABYLON, CITY OF

Capital of BABYLONIA and one of the most famous cities of antiquity. Its original name was perhaps the Akkadian term *bābu ellu* (holy gate)—which term had been transferred from its processional gate to the section of the city near the gate and then to the whole city—or it was a pre-Semitic, non-Sumerian word; but at an early period this name was changed by folk etymology to *bāb-ilim*^{ki} [gate of the god (MARDUK)]. The latter name appeared in Hebrew as *bābel* and was translated into Sumerian as *ká-dingir-ra*^{ki}. Other neo-Sumerian names of the city were *tin-tir*^{ki} (part of life) and *e*^{ki} (canal city). In Gn 11.9 the Hebrew name *bābel* is explained by folk etymology as if the city were thus called because Yahweh there "confused" (*bālāl*) the language of the builders of the TOWER OF BABEL. From the neo-Babylonian name of the city *bāb-ilāni* (gate of the gods) is derived its Greek name Βαβυλών.

The ruins of the ancient city lie about 60 miles south of Baghdad, near the Hilla Canal of the Euphrates. About 12 miles to the east are the ruins of the much more ancient Sumerian city of Kish, which was once on the Euphrates. When the Euphrates changed its bed westward (probably in the 3d millennium B.C.), Babylon took the place of Kish as the chief city of middle Mesopotamia. The Euphrates has since then moved further to the west and is now about ten miles west of the site of Babylon.

Despite the descriptions of the city given in cuneiform documents and by classical authors, its topography is not entirely clear. But the excavations made by German archeologists under the direction of R. Koldewey have revealed the main features of the ancient city, especially its walls, its chief temple (the *é-sag-illa*, "the house that raises high its head") and ziggurat, or temple tower (the *é-tem-an-ki*, "the house of the foundation of heaven and earth"), and its magnificent processional "Ishtar Gate."

Most of the surface ruins come from the neo-Babylonian period.

The earliest mention of Babylon comes from the time of the Dynasty of Akkad (2360–2180). But the city was not important until it was taken and made the capital of a small kingdom by the AMORRITE founder of the First Dynasty of Babylon, Sumu-abum (1830–1817). The sixth king of this dynasty, HAMMURABI (1728–1686), extended the sway of Babylon over all of Mesopotamia and made the city the capital of an empire. Thereafter the history of the city of Babylon is intimately connected with the history of Babylonia. (*See* MESOPOTAMIA, ANCIENT.) Although it always retained its cultural leadership, it did not regain its political hegemony until the time of the Neo-Babylonian Empire (626–539), when, especially under NEBUCHADNEZZAR, it reached its greatest glory. After it fell to Cyrus the Great in 539 B.C., it was merely one, and not the most important one, of the several administrative centers of the Persian Empire. With the founding of Seleucia-Ctesiphon (about 45 miles to the north) as the political center of Mesopotamia toward the end of the 4th century B.C., Babylon quickly decayed, so that by the end of the 2d century B.C., especially after it had been sacked by the Parthians (127 B.C.), it had become a heap of ruins.

In the Bible Babylon looms large with the rise of the Neo-Babylonian Empire, and several oracles of the Prophets predict its doom because of its wickedness and its hostility toward Israel (e.g., Is 13.1–14.23;21.1–10; Jer 50.1–51.64). In the NT the name Babylon is a symbolic term for Rome (Rv ch. 17–18;1 Pt 5.13).

Bibliography: R. KOLDEWEY, *Das wieder erstehende Babylon* (4th ed. Leipzig 1925). W. VON SODEN, *Die Religion in Geschichte und Gegenwart* 1:808–810. E. UNGER, *Reallexikon der Assyriologie* 1:330–339. H. JUNKER, *Lexikon für Theologie und Kirche*, ed. J. HOFER and K. RAHNER, 10 v. (2d new ed. Freiburg 1957–65) 1:1165–67. *Encyclopedic Dictionary of the Bible*, tr. and adap. by L. HARTMAN (New York 1963) 184–188.

[J. S. CONSIDINE]

BABYLON OF THE CHALDEANS, PATRIARCHATE OF

Patriarchate of the Chaldean Catholic Church, located in Baghdad, Iraq. The name Chaldean, of Western origin in the 15th century when the Syriac language was called Chaldean, has been used to describe those Christians of the ASSYRIAN CHURCH OF THE EAST who entered into communion with Rome.

The apostolate of St. THOMAS THE APOSTLE in the area was mentioned by ORIGEN (185–253), and a tradition attributes the evangelization to St. ADDAI and his disciples. The gospel is said to have come by way of EDESSA before the Sassanid dynasty (226), and the region thus had ties, however weak, with the Patriarchate of ANTIOCH. Bishop Mar Papa of Seleucia-Ctesiphon, the Sassanid capital, organized the relatively independent bishops of the region under Seleucia (*c.* 300). Persecution by the Sassanids (340– *c.* 380), who had made Zoroastrianism the state religion and were constantly at war first with Rome and then with Byzantium, claimed martyrs, including St. SIMEON BARSABAE (d. 344) and other bishops. The school of theology at NISIBIS, where the Persian clergy studied, moved to Edessa when Nisibis came under Persian rule (363). With Yazdegerd I (399–420) persecution ceased and a council in Seleucia under MARUTHAS OF MARTYROPOLIS, a Byzantine archbishop and ambassador, accepted the canons of the Council of NICAEA I and organized the Sassanid episcopacy under the CATHOLICOS of Seleucia-Ctesiphon (410). Persecution returned at the end of Yazdegerd's reign to last until peace with Byzantium (422). In 424 the Synod of Markabta decreed that the catholicos thenceforth was subject to judgment by Christ alone, and the Persian Church became independent of the ''Western Fathers.'' Nestorian influence entered the Persian Church from Nisibis, to which the school of theology returned in 457, and at the Council of Seleucia (486) the Persian Church became officially Nestorian. Councils in 497 and 544 strengthened Nestorianism further.

Christians in Persia, closer to the Arabs in race and language than to the Iranians, were relieved of religious persecution by the arrival of the Arabs (637). The seat of the catholicate moved to Baghdad (*c.* 777), which had become the seat of the Abbasid caliphate (*c.* 750). Nestorian clergy, notably Catholicos TIMOTHEUS I (780–823), served the Caliphs; and Nestorian Christianity spread to India, central Asia, and China. After the embassy of the Dominican William of Montferrat to the Nestorian catholicos in 1235, JOHN OF MONTE CORVINO, in 1289, brought from Pope Nicholas IV a letter for Catholicos Yaballaha III (1281–1317), a Mongolian, resident in Maragheh, who was favorable to Catholics. When the Mongol rulers of Persia became Muslim, however, Nestorian Christians there suffered severe persecution, and little is heard of them from the early 14th to the 16th century.

In 1553, when the Nestorian patriarchate was located in Mosul, John Sulaqa was proclaimed in Rome as patriarch of the Chaldeans. However, his successors subsequently moved the patriarchate to Kotchanes. A Chaldean patriarchate of Christians remained in communion with Rome and was confirmed by the Holy See (1681). These patriarchs, who took the name Joseph, resided in Diarbekr. From 1780 they were administrators rather than patriarchs, inasmuch as Rome still was seeking the conversion of the two Nestorian patriarchates (Kotchanes and Rabban-Hormizd). Metropolitan John IX Hormizd (d. 1838) of Mosul, who had become Catholic in 1778, was confirmed by Rome in 1830 as patriarch of Babylon of the Chaldeans, the only patriarchate of Chaldeans recognized by Rome; his seat was in Mosul. Patriarch Joseph V Audo (1847–78) gained many conversions and disputed with Rome about his jurisdiction in the SYRO-MALABAR CHURCH. In 1950, the patriarchal seat was moved from Mosul to Baghad.

Bibliography: R. ROBERSON, *The Eastern Christian Churches: A Brief Survey,* 6th ed (Rome 1999).

[J. A. DEVENNY/EDS]

BABYLONIA

Babylonia was an ancient country in southern Mesopotamia, on the lower courses of the Tigris and Euphrates Rivers (*see* MESOPOTAMIA, ANCIENT). It was so named by the Greeks of the Hellenistic period after its capital city, BABYLON; the Babylonians themselves called the land Sumer and Akkad, after its southern and northern portions, respectively. In the Old Testament the land is termed Sennaar (Gn 10.10; Is 11.11; Dn 1.2; Zec 5.11) or the land of the Chaldeans (Jer 24.5; Ez 12.13) after its later Aramaic-speaking conquerors. A richly fertile land, Babylonia was the site of the earliest civilization known, that of the Sumerians, and remained a cultural center of the Near East throughout the pre-Christian period. It rose to political dominance under HAMMURABI (HAMMURAPI) in the 18th century B.C., and again under NEBUCHADREZZAR and the other kings of the Neo-Babylonian Empire (626–539 B.C.). Besides Babylon, other famous cities of Babylonia were NIPPUR, UR, and Uruk. For a more detailed history of Babylonia, *see* MESOPOTAMIA, ANCIENT.

Bibliography: B. MEISSNER, *Babylonien und Assyrien,* 2 v. (Heidelberg 1920–25); *Reallexikon der Assyriologie,* ed. E. EBELING and B. MEISSNER (Berlin 1928–) 1:369–384. *Encyclopedic Dictionary of the Bible,* tr. and adap. by L. HARTMAN (New York 1963), from A. VAN DEN BORN, *Bijbels Woordenboek,* 187–191. M. A. BEEK, *Atlas of Mesopotamia,* tr. D. R. WELSH (London 1962).

[R. I. CAPLICE]

BACCILIERI, FERDINANDO MARIA, BL.

Diocesan priest, tertiary of the Servants of Mary, and founder of the Servants of Mary of Galeazza; b. Campodoso di Reno Finalese near Modena, Emilia Romagna, Italy, May 14, 1821; d. Galeazza, Bologna, Italy, July 13, 1893. Ferdinando Maria Baccilieri was temporarily assigned as administrator of Santa Maria de Galeazza parish in Bologna, but stayed for forty-one years. In his youth he had attended the Bolognese school of the BARNABITES and the Jesuit school at Ferrara, before joining the JESUITS at Rome (1838). Poor health forced him to return home. Upon recovering, Baccilieri studied for the priesthood at Ferrara and was ordained (1844). He dedicated himself to missions and to preaching until he lost his voice (1867). He also taught Latin and Italian at the seminary in Finale Emilia, and gave spiritual direction. He began doctoral studies in canon and civil law at the Pontifical University of Bologna in 1848, and in 1851, Cardinal Archbishop Oppizzoni of Bologna asked him to administer the troubled Santa Maria parish, where he became pastor. He served with a deep affection for the poor, a strong devotion to the Virgin Mary, and a commitment to sacramental ministry.

Father Baccilieri founded a women's religious order, the Servants of Mary, to provide education for poor girls of the parish. The order started as the Confraternity of the Sorrows of Mary, but became a more formal congregation as the members were clothed in the mantellate of the Servite Third Order (1856), began to live in community (1862), and adopted the constitution and rule of the Mantellate Servite Sisters in Rome (1866). The congregation, which was recognized by the archbishop of Bologna in 1899 and approved by the Vatican in 1919, now has members in Italy, Germany, Brazil, South Korea, and the Czech Republic. On April 6, 1995, Baccilieri was declared venerable. A miracle attributed to his intercession was approved by the Vatican, July 3, 1998, leading to his beatification by John Paul II on Oct. 3, 1999.

Feast: July 1 (Bologna).

Bibliography: M. G. LUCCHETTA, *Ferdinando Baccilieri* (St. Ottilien 1993).

[K. I. RABENSTEIN]

BACH, JOHANN CHRISTIAN

Preclassical composer, referred to as the ''Milan Bach'' and the ''London Bach''; b. Leipzig, Sept. 5, 1735; d. London, Jan. 1, 1782. He was the youngest son of J. S. BACH and his second wife, Anna Magdalena. Only 15 at his father's death, he was taken to Berlin by his half-brother, Carl Philipp Emmanuel Bach, who taught him for five years. In 1756 he went to Milan with an introduction to Count Litta, who financed further study with G. B. (''Padre'') MARTINI, under whose tutelage he composed several church works. In 1760 he was appointed Milan cathedral organist, but opera commissions from

Johann Christian Bach (Archive Photos)

Turin and Naples in the same year necessitated prolonged absence from his duties. The strained situation resulting was terminated by his appointment to the King's Theatre, London, for the opera season 1762 to 1763. *Orione* (1763) was so successful that Christian was appointed music master to Queen Charlotte and retained this post as long as he lived. His copious works in the rococo (late baroque) idiom exerted a strong influence on the Viennese classical style, conspicuously on the boy MOZART, who visited Christian in London in 1764 and profited immensely from his interest and generous, practical advice.

Christian's conversion to Catholicism soon after his arrival in Italy was resented by his brothers. Several biographers have judged it merely an expedient act to gain church posts, but the fact that he adhered to his faith in Protestant England argues his sincerity. His Catholic church music (1756–62) reflects the prevailing style of Neapolitan opera, each work consisting of arias, duets, and choruses, and accompanied by an orchestra of strings, oboes, organ, and horns (or trumpets). Among his church works are two Glorias and Magnificats, a Requiem, Lessons and Responsories, *Misere re,* and *Te Deum,* this last described by a contemporary poet and musician, C. F. D. Schubart (1739–91), as ''one of the most beautiful we have in Europe.''

Bibliography: C. S. TERRY, *John Christian Bach* (Oxford 1929). K. GEIRINGER, *The Bach Family* (New York 1954). H. WIRTH, *Die Musik in Geschichte und Gegenwart,* ed. F. BLUME (Kassel-Basel 1949–) 1:942–954. R. G. PAULY, *Music in the Classic Period* (Englewood Cliffs, N.J. 1965). W. S. NEWMAN, *The Sonata in the Classic Era* (Chapel Hill, N.C. 1963). P. H. LÁNG, *Music in Western Civilization* (New York 1941). D. J. GROUT, *A Short History of Opera,* 2 v. (2d, rev. and enl. ed. New York 1965). Modern eds. of several works are available. P. CORNEILSON, ''The Case of J. C. Bach's *Lucio Silla,*'' *Journal of Musicology,* 12 (1994) 206–218. L. A. DERRY, *The Pre-Classical Concerto of Johann Christian Bach: First Movement Design in the Eighteen 'London' Keyboard Concertos,* (Ph.D. diss. Indiana University 1993). U. LEISINGER, ''Der langsame Satz des Flötenkonzerts D–Dur von Johann Christian Bach,'' *Tibia: Magazin für Holzbläser,* 23 (1998) 113–118. W. LANDOWSKA, ''The Gallant Style: About Some of Mozart's Keyboard Works,'' in *Landowska on Music,* ed. and tr. D. RESTOUT (New York 1964) 323. J. MEYER, ''The Keyboard Concertos of Johann Christian Bach and Their Influence on Mozart,'' *Miscellanea Musicologica,* 10 (1979) 59–73. L. SALTER, ''Which Bach?,'' *Consort,* 42 (1986) 50.

[A. MILNER]

BACH, JOHANN SEBASTIAN

Preeminent composer who brought the baroque style in music to a close; b. Eisenach, Germany, March 21, 1685; d. Leipzig, July 28, 1750.

Life. Bach was the most illustrious member of a family of successful musicians, all of whom, until Sebastian's youngest son Johann Christian BACH became a Catholic, were Lutheran. Sebastian was only ten when his father, a musician in the Eisenach town band, died; thereafter he received most of his musical training from his elder brother, Johann Christof, in Ohrdruf. In 1703 he entered his first post as organist of the New Church at Arnstadt, transferring in 1707 to a similar post at St. Blasius, Mühlhausen, where he married his cousin Maria Barbara Bach. A year later he became court organist to the Duke of Weimar and was later (1714) promoted to the post of concertmaster (i.e., director of the orchestra). In 1717 he became *Kapell meister* (director of music) to Prince Leopold of Cöthen. His wife died in 1720, and a year later he married Anna Magdalena Wülcken. In 1723 he was appointed to one of the chief musical posts in Germany, music director in Leipzig at two principal churches, St. Thomas and St. Nicholas, as well as the Pauliner-Kirche of the university, and cantor (choir director) at the Thomasschüle. He retained this post until his death. Nine of his 20 children survived him, four sons possessing outstanding musical talent: Wilhelm Friedmann and Carl Philipp Emmanuel (children of Maria Barbara), and Johann Christoph Friedrich and Johann Christian (children of Anna Magdalena). Philipp Emmanuel and Johann Christian became more famous than their father during their lifetimes.

Religious Music. Sebastian's fame was chiefly that of a virtuoso organist and a learned but old-fashioned contrapuntist; his music never had the success of G. F. HANDEL's because it was not addressed to the public audiences of the opera houses and choral concerts. If, like Handel, he had depended on popular approval for his livelihood, he might have adopted more of the newer compositional techniques; but since he remained all his life a paid employee of either prince or town council, he was under no urgent compulsion to please the public ear. Whereas Handel's music looks outward, every note designed to make an immediate impression on its audience, Bach's is introspective, full of detail that can be perceived only through careful listening and sympathetic understanding. Though he wrote much instrumental music, he designed the bulk of his work for use in the Lutheran church. In notes on thorough-bass playing dictated to his student Niedt, he said: "The aim and final reason of all music should be none else but the glory of God and the recreation of the mind. Where this is not observed, there will be no music but only a devilish hubbub."

Johann Sebastian Bach. (Archive Photos)

Bach wrote 295 church cantatas (five yearly cycles of 59 each) during the first six years of his Leipzig cantorate, of which some 200 are extant. To study them profitably it is important to remember their intimate connection with the liturgy of the Lutheran Sunday morning or festal service: their texts frequently contain quotations from, or reference to, the Epistle and Gospel of the day, and the concluding chorale is always that of the particular Sunday or feast day. The music is full of symbolism, allusion, and word painting that become clear only when the works are viewed in their liturgical context. Most of the cantatas commence with a large-scale movement, frequently blended with the Italian concerto style; but where Handel would have a largely homophonic texture, Bach develops the chorus in elaborate counterpoint, e.g., in the Ascension cantata (No. 11). Sometimes this is combined with a chorale *cantus firmus* in the top chorus voice (*Wachet auf,* No. 140). The first movement may also be built on a French overture (No. 61) or preceded by it (No. 119). Several cantatas use a chorale melody as a thematic basis for all movements, but treated very freely. Only one of these preserves the melody intact throughout—*Christ lag in Todesbanden* (No. 4). Cantatas having two or more chorales are generally narrative cantatas, e.g., the six constituting the *Christmas Oratorio.* Similar variety of style and form is found in the solo arias, duets, and trios that form the middle section of cantatas.

The Mass in B minor is a composite work: the first two movements were heard as a Lutheran *missa* when the Elector of Saxony visited Leipzig in 1733. The *Gloria* uses material from an earlier cantata (No. 191). The other movements, from the *Credo* onward, are now known to date from the very last years of Bach's life as far as their present form is concerned: most of them are built on materials, sections, and movements from other works. As court composer to the elector (who was a Catholic), Bach compiled the Mass, but it was never intended for Catholic or for any liturgy in its complete form. Each of the sections has something of the plan of a cantata but also follows the shape of contemporary Masses by Austrian and Italian composers.

The Passions according to *St. John* (1724) and *St. Matthew* (1729) represent a compromise between the earlier "dramatic" and the newer "opera" forms of Passion composition. Bach retained the complete relevant Gospel portions in both works, adding chorales of his own selection. For the solo arias and accompanied recitatives of *St. John* he drew on a text by Heinrich Brockes, and for *St. Matthew* his libretto was prepared by a Leipzig poet, Picander. *St. John* is more obviously dramatic by reason of the fewer lyrical interruptions to the narrative and the extended "crowd" sections; *St. Matthew,* though it has dramatic moments, is more meditative and leisurely in its progress. Bach's treatment of the Gospel narrative is peculiarly his own: he abandoned every trace of the old chant intonations, substituting a vocal line ostensibly based on the *secco recitativo* but with a lyrical turn of phrase not to be found there, an effect that conformed entirely to the requirements of the German language and to the expressiveness required by the subject. In the Passions, as in all his religious music, Bach's devotion and deep feeling for religion are manifest.

Bibliography: *Werke,* ed. BACH-GESELLSCHAFT, 61 v. in 47 (Leipzig 1851–1926; repr. Ann Arbor 1947); *Briefe,* ed. E. H. MÜLLER VON ASOW (2d ed. Regensburg 1950). P. SPITTA, *Johann Sebastian Bach,* tr. C. BELL and J. A. FULLER-MAITLAND, 3 v. (London 1884; 2d ed. New York 1951). C. S. TERRY, *Bach* (2d ed. London 1933). A. SCHWEITZER, *J. S. Bach,* tr. E. NEWMAN, 2 v. (New York 1911; reissue London 1923), new Ger. ed. (Wiesbaden 1955). A. PIRRO, *Johann Sebastian Bach,* tr. M. SAVILL (London 1959). H. T. DAVID and A. MENDELS, eds., *A Bach Reader* (New York 1954). K. and I. GEIRINGER, *The Bach Family* (New York 1954). N. DUFOURCQ, *Jean-Sébastian Bach: Le Maître de l'orgue* (Paris 1948). J. B. CONNOR, *Gregorian Chant and Medieval Hymn Tunes in the Works of J. S. Bach* (Washington 1957). F. BLUME, *Die Musik in Geschichte und Gegenwart,* ed. F. BLUME (Kassel-Basel 1949–) 1:962–1047. H. C. COLLES, *Grove's Dictionary of Music and Musicians,* ed. E. BLOM, 9 v. (5th ed. London 1954) 1:293–321. M. F. BUKOFZER, *Music in the Baroque Era* (New York 1947). P. H. LÁNG, *Music in Western Civilization* (New York 1941). W. BREIG, "Zu den Turba-Chören von Bachs *Johannes- Passion,*" *Hamburger Jahrbuch für Musikwissenschaft,* 8 (1985) 65–96. M. DIRST, "Bach's French Overtures and the Politics of Overdotting," *Early Music,* 27 (1997) 35–45. U. KONRAD, "Aspekte musikalisch-theologischen Verstehens in Mariane von Zieglers und Johann Sebastian Bachs Kantate *Bisher habt ihr nichts gebeten in meinem Namen* BWV 87," *Archiv für Musikwissenschaft,* 3 (2000) 199–221. W. LANDOWSKA, "On the Interpretation of Johann Sebastian Bach's Keyboard Works: *The Goldberg Variations,*" in *Landowska on Music,* ed. and tr. D. RESTOUT (New York 1964) 209–220. R. LOUCKS, "Was the *Well-Tempered Clavier* Performable on a Fretted Clavichord?," *Performance Practice Review,* 5 (1992) 44–89. M. MARISSEN, *The Social and Religious Designs of J. S. Bach's Brandenburg Concertos* (Princeton, N.J. 1995). D. R. MELAMED, *J. S. Bach and the German Motet* (Cambridge, Eng. 1995). U. MEYER, *Biblical Quotation and Allusion in the Cantata Libretti of Johann Sebastian Bach* (Lanham, Md. 1997). L. ROBINSON, "Notes on Editing the Bach Gamba Sonatas (BWV 1027–1029)," *Chelys,* 14 (1985) 25–39. YO TOMITA, "Bach Reception in Pre-Classical Vienna: Baron van Swieten's Circle Edits the *Well-Tempered Clavier II,*" *Music and Letters,* 81 (2000) 364–391. C. WOLFF, *Johann Sebastian Bach: The Learned Musician* (Oxford 2000).

[A. MILNER]

BACHA, CONSTANTINE

Modern historian of the Melkhite Church; b. Douma (Batroun, Lebanon), Feb. 3, 1870; d. Holy Savior's Monastery (Saida, Lebanon), Oct. 12, 1948. After his early studies at Holy Savior's Seminary (Saida), Bacha (al-Bāša) became a Salvatorian religious in 1886 and was ordained in 1893. Wherever he served as pastor, teacher, or administrator, he devoted all his leisure time to research in Church history. He visited every library he could, especially those of Rome and Paris. In 1925 he retired to Holy Savior's Monastery, where he devoted the rest of his life to writing a history of the Melkhite Church.

Holy Savior's library lists 40 works as translated, composed, or published by him. His magistral work is the *Tārīḫ Tāifat ar-Rūm al-Malakîyat war Rahbānīat al-Muḫallisītat* (*History of the Catholic Melkhite Community and of the Salvatorian Order*) in two volumes. The first volume, published in 1938, is dedicated to Metropolitan Euthymios ṢAIFI, and the second, published in 1945, to Patriarch Cyril Ṭanas. The extensive and varied sources used make this work a rich mine of information as well as a history of note. The manuscripts gathered by him for his research are preserved in the archives department of Holy Savior's Monastery and continue to be the richest collection of material on this subject to be found anywhere.

Bibliography: L. MALOUF in *Ar-Risālat al-Muḫallisīat* (Sidon, Leb. 1948) 705–18. J. CHAMMAS, *Ḫulāṣat Tārîcḫ al-Kanîsat alMalakîyat,* 3 v. (Sidon, Leb. 1952) 231–37.

[L. MALOUF]

BACHIARIUS

Fourth-century monk and theologian; b. probably in Galicia, Spain, *c.* 350; d. time and place unknown. He became a monk, was suspected of PRISCILLIANISM, and had to leave Spain (*c.* 380). He was the author of two books: *Libellus fidei,* written probably in Rome in 383 or 384 as a profession of faith to refute the accusation of heresy; and *De reparatione lapsi,* in which he pleaded for a monk who had sinned but was now repentant, and in so doing gave an excellent presentation of the Spanish penitential system (*see* PENITENTIALS). His explanations of the Trinity, the Incarnation, and the perpetual virginity of Mary are admired for their clarity and orthodoxy. G. MORIN regards him as the author of two letters on asceticism. Bachiarius's style has been compared to that of JEROME, and GENNADIUS calls him a "Christian philosopher" (*De vir. ill.* c. 24).

Bibliography: J. MADOZ, *Revista Española de Teología* 1 (1941) 457–88. G. MORIN, "Pages inédites de deux Pseudo-Jérômes," *Revue Bénédictine* 40 (1928) 289–318. H. RAHNER, *Lexikon für Theologie und Kirche* (Freiburg 1957–65) 1:1180. F. X. MURPHY, "Bachiarius," *Leaders of Iberian Christianity,* ed. J. M. F. MARIQUE (Boston 1962) 121–26. A. LAMBERT, *Dictionnaire d'histoire et de géographie ecclésiastiques* (Paris 1912—) 6:58–68.

[S. J. MCKENNA]

BACKER, AUGUSTIN DE

Bibliographer; b. Antwerp, Belgium, July 18, 1809; d. Liège, Belgium, Dec. 1, 1873. He joined the JESUITS (1835), went to Louvain to study theology (1840), and was ordained (1843). With the encouragement of his religious superiors, he remained in Louvain and continued the bibliography of writings by Jesuits published by Pedro de Ribadeneira in 1608 and 1613, by Philippe de Alegambe in 1643, and by Nathaniel Southwell in 1676. With the help of his brother Alois (1823–83) from 1850, he published *Bibliothèque des écrivains de la Compagnie de Jésus* (7 v. 1853–61). With Charles Ruelens he edited *Annales Plantiniennes depuis la fondation de l'imprimerie jusqu' à la mort de Christophe Plantin* (1865–66). Aided by Carlos Sommervogel he published a second edition of his *Bibliothèque* (3 v. 1869–76), which contained 11,000 names of Jesuit writers, together with information about their lives, works, editions, translations, manuscripts, etc. After the death of the De Backer brothers, Sommervogel continued the work.

Bibliography: V. VAN TRICHT, *La Bibliothèque des écrivains de la Compagnie de Jésus et le P. Augustin De Backer* (Louvain 1875). C. SOMMERVOGEL, *Bibliothèque de la Compagnie de Jésus* 1:753–755. E. LAMALLE, *Dictionnaire d'histoire et de géographie ecclésiastiques* 6:73–75. L. KOCH, *Jesuiten-Lexikon: Die Gesellschaft Jesu einst und jetzt* 1:145–146. B. SCHNEIDER, *Lexikon für Theologie und Kirche* 2 1:1181–82. É. DE MOREAU, *Biographie nationale de Belgique*, v.29 (Brussels 1956) 176–178.

[M. DIERICKX]

BACON, DAVID WILLIAM

First bishop of Portland, Maine; b. Brooklyn, N.Y., Sept. 15, 1813; d. New York City, Nov. 5, 1874. He was the son of William and Elizabeth (Redmond) Bacon. After study at the Sulpician College, Montreal, Canada, and Mt. St. Mary's Seminary, Emmitsburg, Md., he was ordained by Archbishop Samuel Eccleston on December 13, 1838. Following parish assignments in northern New York and in New Jersey, he was sent to Brooklyn to organize the new parish of the Assumption of Our Lady, where he was pastor from 1841 to 1855. He was appointed bishop of Portland, and was consecrated by Archbishop John Hughes in St. Patrick's Cathedral, New York City, on April 22, 1855. His diocese, which included Maine and New Hampshire, was aided by Jesuits who served Catholics in central Maine and by priests from Quebec, Canada, who ministered to Franco-Americans in northern Maine. Educational and charitable needs were met by the Sisters of Mercy, who established their first house in Manchester, N.H. (1858), and extended their work in Maine to Bangor (1865), Whitefield (1871), and Portland (1873). Bacon was a notable pulpit orator. He built the Cathedral of the Immaculate Conception, and he attended Vatican Council I. By the time of his death, his diocese possessed 52 priests, and its Catholic population, mainly Irish-Americans and Franco-Americans, had doubled to about 80,000.

Sir Francis Bacon.

Bibliography: W. L. LUCEY, *The Catholic Church in Maine* (Francestown, N.H. 1957).

[W. L. LUCEY]

BACON, FRANCIS

Statesman and philosopher, b. London, Jan. 22, 1561; d. London, April 9, 1626. He was educated in the classics at Cambridge and in law at Gray's Inn. He sought and obtained public offices in range from that of member of Parliament to the lord chancellorship, and became a knight, Baron Verulam, and Viscount St. Albans. Another object of Bacon's ambition was the reform of human learning through the advancement of a nontraditional, anti-Aristotelian philosophy. This undertaking was impeded by large expenditures of time on political and legal tasks. Of the 30-odd writings on philosophical and scientific topics that were begun, only seven were developed sufficiently for publication by the author. These are the *Advancement of Learning* (1605) and a Latin version with amendments of the same (1623), critical examinations of ''ancient'' opinions, disputational practices, and ''bookish'' preoccupations within the universities; *De sapientia veterum* (1609), a statement by way of interpretation of poetic fables of the basic principles of a naturalistic philosophy; *Novum organum* (1620), a confessedly incomplete description of a ''new logic'' of induction; and, hastily compiled in the last years of the author's life, three inconclusive works on natural history.

Sciences and Causes. In expounding his ''new philosophy'' Bacon rejects Aristotle's classification of independent sciences with their several segregating axioms. He refuses to separate physics or the science of nature from knowledge in the arts, and denies mathematics an independent status. He also transfers certain of Aristotle's metaphysical and ethical subjects, including the being and the nature of God on the one hand and the governing rules for human conduct on the other, to the province of revealed theology. The base of Bacon's own scheme of science, or philosophy, is natural history; above this in a ''pyramid'' of knowledge lies physics, and at the apex metaphysics or universal physics. Physics contains the more limited axioms or principles of causal explanation, and metaphysics the more general. The primary task of science, for Bacon, is the discovery of forms, the components of and the causes within the particulars of nature. These forms are inseparable from matter, which is itself formed, active, and causal. All natural causes, then, are material causes—there are no final causes in nature.

Induction and Axioms. The sole method for discovering forms is an induction that relies on a constant and perpetual adduction of particulars. This induction begins with particulars sorted within natural history, in a preliminary response to a query put, as a ''prenotion,'' to nature, and ascends through the less inclusive to the more general axiom. It proceeds by the examination of three sorts of instance, those of ''presence,'' of ''absence,'' and of ''deviation.'' The first or affirmative sort are examples in which the form or cause or nature under investigation is present—form, cause, and nature are, for Bacon, convertible terms. The second or negative sort of instances are examples from which the form is lacking. The third are examples that manifest severally varied degrees of the form's activity—the degrees of deviation, comparable to deflection in the compass needle, being dependent upon the operations severally of other conjunct forms, as causes, within the particulars under observation and experiment. The negative instances, long disregarded in inductive theory, are of especial consequence because of their agency in refuting such misleading axioms as may be too hastily derived from an examination of positive instances alone.

All axioms, whether suggested by particulars or by lesser axioms, are established through sense observation. No explanation that asserts a wider range of causation within particulars than testing by experiments can verify is ever to be deemed true; and always it is sense that must try the experiment. There is to be no adding to the content of science by the employment of deductive, syllogistic devices or through the introduction, at any stage, of so-called ''first principles.'' The most general or metaphysical axioms or principles of science are inductive pronouncements upon causal operation within the whole of nature. And since whatever in science is cause is also in nature operation, metaphysical knowledge enables the scientist to produce inventions in great array for the ''relief of man's estate''; and this, indeed—and not Aristotle's ''meditation''—is both the supreme warranty and the final goal of inductive metaphysics.

Evaluation. Because of his stress on induction Bacon has often been hailed as the ''prophet'' of ''experimental discovery.'' He has provided, also, an example for those who would equate the findings of experimental science with the principles of metaphysics; but few of his followers in this regard have thought it possible to establish or to pursue a science of physical nature, let alone an ontology, by the sole use of his inductive method. Bacon's philosophy has long been recognized as a definite antithesis to Aristotelianism. Certainly the two are opposites that do not readily lend themselves either to compromise or to transformation within a synthesis.

See Also: INDUCTION; FIRST PRINCIPLES; PHILOSOPHY, HISTORY OF.

Bibliography: *Works*, ed. J. SPEDDING et al., 14 v. (London 1857–74); 15 v. (New York 1869); *Novum Organum*, ed. T. FOWLER (2d ed. Oxford 1889); *The New Organon and Related Writings*, ed. F. H. ANDERSON (New York 1960). F. H. ANDERSON, *The Philosophy of Francis Bacon* (Chicago 1948); *Francis Bacon, His Career and His Thought* (Los Angeles 1962). C. D. BROAD, *The Philosophy of Francis Bacon* (Cambridge, Eng. 1926). R. W. CHURCH, *Bacon* (London 1884). K. FISCHER, *Francis Bacon of Verulam*, tr. J. OXENFORD (London 1857). A. LEVI, *Il pensiero di Francesco Bacone* (Turin 1925). C. F. M. DE RÉMUSAT, *Bacon: Sa vie, son temps, sa philosophie. . .* (Paris 1857).

[F. H. ANDERSON]

BADIA, TOMMASO

Theologian and cardinal; b. Modena, 1493 (1483?); d. Rome, Sept. 6, 1547. He was a Dominican from the province of Lombardy, a brilliant professor in Ferrara, Venice, and Bologna, and Master of the Sacred Palace. Badia was strict in condemning heterodoxy but lenient with regard to persons. From 1536 he belonged to the reform group of Cardinal Gasparo CONTARINI. He endorsed the *Consilium de emendanda ecclesia* and the *Consilium quattuor delectorum* in 1537, and became a member of the commission for the proposed council at Mantua. Paul III approved the Society of Jesus in 1539 on his recommendation. Badia wrote a letter to Contarini in the diet of Worms of 1540 and the next year was advisor to the cardinal-legate at the diet of Regensburg. He was made a cardinal in 1542 and then a member of the Inquisition. Although in 1543 and 1544 he was a member of the deputation for the Council of Trent, he remained in Rome. Badia has been widely known for learning and virtue, but his writings, letters, and treatises on philosophy and theology have yet to be studied.

Bibliography: M. T. DISDIER, *Dictionnaire d'histoire et de géographie ecclésiastiques*, ed. A. BAUDRILLART et al. (Paris 1912) 6:145. A. WALZ, *Lexikon für Theologie und Kirche*, ed. J. HOFER and K. RAHNER (Freiburg 1957–65) 1:1187–88. A. DUVAL, *Catholicisme* 1:1161–62. A. WALZ, *I domenicani al concilio di Trento* (Rome 1961).

[A. M. WALZ]

BADIN, STEPHEN THEODORE

Missionary; b. Orléans, France, July 17, 1768; d. Cincinnati, Ohio, April 19, 1853. In 1792, because of the revolution, he left the Sulpician seminary in France for America and became one of the first students at St. Mary's Seminary, Baltimore, Md. He was ordained by Bishop John Carroll on May 25, 1793, the first priest ordained in the United States.

From 1793 to 1811 Badin was Carroll's vicar-general in the Old West. Generally alone, and never with more than six priests to aid him, he served the scattered Catholics of Kentucky, Ohio, Indiana, Illinois, Michigan, and Tennessee. He was chiefly responsible for the designation of the see at Bardstown, Ky., and the selection of Benedict J. Flaget as its first bishop.

Because of difficulties with Flaget over church property, Badin returned to France in 1819 and remained there, acting as agent for various American bishops until 1826. On his return to the United States, he joined the Cincinnati diocese and was sent by Bishop Edward D. Fenwick to the Pottawatomie Indian mission in Indiana. He founded the first orphan asylum in that state near South Bend and bought the land on which the University of Notre Dame now stands. After the Indian mission closed, he served the Irish laborers building the Wabash canal and purchased tracts for Catholic churches along this route. From 1835 on, he traveled over the Ohio Valley, assisting the bishops and pastors of the area.

Badin possessed a keen wit and a sharp sense of humor. Although tolerant with Protestants, he was very strict with his own flock. His writings included several Latin poems, religious tracts, and two books on Catholic doctrine. Martin J. Spalding's sketches on the missions of early Kentucky were largely based on Badin's notes and reminiscences.

After 60 years of missionary labors on frontier lands, Badin died in his 85th year and was buried in the cathedral crypt in Cincinnati. In 1904 his remains were transferred to Notre Dame University and are in the Badin chapel there. At this university Badin Hall is named after him; there is a monument to him at the motherhouse of the Sisters of Loretto in Kentucky, the location of his headquarters in that state. His work earned him the right to be called ''the Apostle of Kentucky.''

Bibliography: J. H. SCHAUINGER, *Stephen T. Badin* (Milwaukee 1956). M. J. SPALDING, *Sketches of the Early Catholic Missions of Kentucky, 1787–1827* (Louisville 1844). B. J. WEBB, *The Centenary of Catholicity in Kentucky* (Louisville, 1884).

[J. H. SCHAUINGER]

BAGHDAD

Center of the ancient Baghdad Caliphate, Baghdad is the capital of modern Iraq, and the city of residence for the Chaldean Catholic Patriarch. In A.D. 762 Mansur, second caliph of the 'Abbāsid dynasty, founded Baghdad on the west bank of the Tigris about 30 miles from the ancient Sassanid Seleucia–Ctesiphon, from which building materials were taken for the new city. Originally called Madinat as-Salam (city of peace), it was known also by its Greek name Eirenopolis; Baghdad is the popular name, meaning probably Garden of Dat. A village of Christians was already in existence in the near vicinity in 762.

Under the 'Abbāsids Baghdad became the intellectual and cultural center of the highly developed Arab Empire. Religious tolerance toward Christians, Jews, and Zoroastrians generally prevailed, although some caliphs, as ''deputies of God,'' occasionally harassed non-Muslims. Churches were built for Christians captured in campaigns against the Byzantine Empire. In the 11th century, Baghdad fell temporarily under the rule of the Seljuk Turks. In 1256 the Mongols under Hulagu captured and destroyed a great part of the city. The Persians conquered and rebuilt it (1517), and in 1638 Baghdad became part of the Ottoman Empire. At the end of World War I it became the capital of modern-day Iraq.

As early as 1628 some Capuchins arrived in Baghdad, and in 1632 the first titular Latin bishop of Baghdad was appointed, but he died before assuming office. A second titular bishop, designated in 1634, refused the appointment. On June 6, 1638, URBAN VIII issued the bull *Super universas* [*Bullarium Romanum* (Magnum), ed. H. Mainardi and C. Cocquelines, 18 folio v. (Rome 1733–62) 14:652–654] establishing the Diocese of Baghdad, which became an archbishopric (*Ecclesia Babylonensis Latinorum*) in 1848.

The Chaldean Catholic Church (*Ecclesia Babylonensis Chaldaeorum*) was established in Baghdad in 1834. Some Persian Christians had earlier united with the Apostolic See in 1553 and formed the Chaldean Church, but this communion came to an end about a century later. Efforts for reunion (begun *c.* 1783) were successful, and John Hormez was enthroned as patriarch of Babylon in 1834.

[H. DRESSLER/EDS.]

BAGSHAW, CHRISTOPHER

Priest and controversialist; b. Lichfield?, *c.* 1552; d. Paris?, *c.* 1625. From Oxford he received his B.A. (July 12, 1572) and M.A. (June 21, 1575) degrees; he became principal of Gloucester Hall in 1579, but resigned and went to France in 1582. After his conversion to Catholicism, he began his studies at the English College, Rome, on Oct. 1, 1583. In January of 1585 he was expelled as ''unwilling to take the oath'' (*Liber Ruber*). He ''did not behave well.'' Passing through Italy to France, he acquired a doctorate at Padua; hence his nickname ''Doctor per saltum.'' He arrived at Douai on April 2, 1585, and was sent to England on May 27. Captured upon landing, he was imprisoned in the Tower, and then in Wisbich (Wisbech, Wisbeach) from 1588? until November of 1601 when, with the approval of the bishop of London, and the Privy Council, he passed with other appellants to Paris en route to Rome. He remained in Paris, a controversial figure, difficult to friends, and irreconcilable to the Jesuits. He was the author, most probably, of *A True Relation of the Faction begun at Wisbich by Fa: Edmonds, alias Weston, a Jesuit, 1595. . .* (London 1601); *Relatio compendiosa Turbarum quas Jesuitae Angli una cum D. Georgio Blackwello . . . concivere* (Rouen 1601); *An Answer. . . to certain points of a libell called an Apologie of the subordination in England* (Paris 1601); and *A sparing discoverie of our English Jesuits, and of Fa: Parsons . . .* (London 1601).

Bibliography: A. À. WOOD, *Athenae Oxonienses,* ed. P. BLISS, 5 v. (London 1813–20) 2:389–90. T. G. LAW, ed., *The Archpriest Controversy,* 2 v. (Camden Society 56, 58; London 1896–98). ''Liber Ruber,'' ed. W. KELLY (*Publications of the Catholic Record Society* 37; 1940) 43. P. RENOLD, ''The Wisbech Stirs,'' (ibid. 51; 1958). A. H. BULLEN, *The Dictionary of National Biography from the Earliest Times to 1900* 1:872–73. J. GILLOW, *A Literary and Biographical History or Bibliographical Dictionary of the English Catholics from 1534 to the Present Time* 1:100–101.

[F. EDWARDS]

BAHA'ISM

A religion founded by Mīrzā Ḥusayn 'Alī Nūrū, called Bahā'Ullāh (the splendor of God), who was born in Teheran, Iran, in 1817. According to Baha'i tradition, Bahā'Ullāh received no formal education. He became one of the early disciples of 'Alī Muḥammad of Shīrāz, called ''al-Bāb'' (the gateway), who had proclaimed himself as ''al-MAHDĪ'' in 1844. Al-Bāb was executed in 1850 by the order of Nāṣir-al-Dīn Shah, who was determined to eradicate the Bābi sect because of the disorder that its propaganda had caused throughout Iran. Bahā'Ullāh was imprisoned in Teheran for four months in 1852–53, and while in prison he experienced his first call to a prophetic mission. He was banished to Iraq with other Bābis and lived in Baghdad for a year and then in Kurdistan as a dervish from 1854 to 1856. During the following years in Baghdad he increased his spiritual influence over the Bābi exiles, whose numbers had swelled, until the Persian government formally requested his exile to Constantinople. Shortly before his departure in April of 1863 he declared himself to a small number of followers as *man yuzhiruhu 'llāh* (he whom God shall manifest), whom al-Bāb had predicted.

Bahā'Ullāh and some of his followers spent a few months in Constantinople in 1863 before being transferred to Edirne. There he openly proclaimed his prophethood and sent letters to various sovereigns inviting them to accept Baha'ism. Most of the Bābis accepted Bahā'Ullāh's claim, but a minority group loyal to his half brother Mirzā Yaḥyā precipitated such disturbances within the sect that the Ottoman authorities decided to exile the Baha'is to Acre and Cyprus. Bahā'Ullāh and his family were imprisoned in Acre between 1868 and 1877, and during that time they were allowed to live under house arrest at nearby Mazra'a. From 1871 to 1873 Bahā'Ullāh was engaged in writing the fundamental scripture of his faith, *Kitāb-i Aqdas* (the most holy book). In 1880 he moved nearer Acre to Bahji, where he died on May 26, 1892.

The greatest apostle of Baha'ism was 'Abbās Effendi, Bahā'Ullāh's eldest son, who was known as 'Abd-al-Bahā'. He was born in 1844 and accompanied his father on his journeys and exile and was recognized by most Baha'is as the authoritative interpreter of his father's teachings. However, a rival party, gathered around his brother Muḥammad 'Alī and brought about his imprisonment in 1908. Two years later he was granted amnesty by the Young Turks and set out on three missionary journeys to Egypt (1910), Europe (1911), and America (1912–13). These journeys had the effect of discrediting his brother's organization and of winning an international following for Baha'ism. 'Abd-al-Bahā' returned to Palestine, was knighted by the British government in 1920 for his philanthropic services during the war, and died the next year. By his testament his oldest grandson Shoghi Effendi was named ''Guardian of the Cause of God.''

From 1923 on Shoghi Effendi made his home in Haifa, Israel, thereafter the principal center of the Baha'i religion. He had studied at Oxford and in 1936 married a Canadian, Mary Maxwell.

Baha'ism propounds a body of doctrine that clearly originated in SHĪ'ITE ISLAM, but is regarded by orthodox Muslims as syncretistic and universalist. It declares that God is unknowable except through His "manifestations" the prophets, including Bahā'Ullāh himself, who are the "mirrors" of God. It holds a doctrine of creation and at the same time the "eternal" world of Greco-Islamic philosophy. Its eschatology is regarded as entirely symbolic. It aims to establish a unity of the human race, of all religions, and of science and advocates universal education, world peace through social equality and opposition to all forms of prejudice, equal rights for the sexes, an international language, and an international tribunal. It follows a calendar that is a revision of the Bābi calendar and elects local assemblies, but there is no public ritual nor even private rites of a sacred character. Its temples are designed in such fashion as to symbolize the unity of the "great" world religions.

Bibliography: *Kitáb-i-íqán (The Book of Certitude),* tr. SHOGHI EFFENDI (Wilmette, Ill. 1950); *Selected Writings of Bahā'u'lláh,* tr. SHOGHI EFFENDI (Wilmette, Ill. 1942). NABÍL-I-A'ZAM, *Dawn Breakers,* tr. SHOGHI EFFENDI (2d ed. London 1953). SHOGHI EFFENDI, *God Passes By* (Wilmette, Ill. 1944). J. SAVI, *The Eternal Quest for God: An Introduction to the Divine Philosophy of 'Abdu'l-Bahá* (Oxford, Eng. 1989). P. SMITH and M. MOMEN, "The Baha'i Faith 1957–1988: A Survey of Contemporary Developments," *Religion* 19 (1989) 63–91. J. A. MCLEAN, "Prolegomena to a Bahá'í Theology," *Journal of Bahá'í Studies* 5 (1992) 25–67 (with extensive bibliographies). P. SMITH, *The Bahá'i Religion: A Short Introduction to Its History and Teachings* (Oxford, Eng. 1998).

[J. KRITZECK/EDS.]

BAHAMAS, THE CATHOLIC CHURCH IN THE

The Commonwealth of the Bahamas includes some 3,000 islands and cays covering an area of approximately 90,000 square miles in the North Atlantic. Located southeast of Florida and north of Cuba, the Bahamian islands—Grand Bahama, Great Abaco, Eleuthera, New Providence, Cat Island, Andros Island, San Salvador, Crooked Island, Acklins Island, Mayaguana, Long Island, Great Exuma, Great Inagua and others— terminate in the Turks and Caicos Islands. Since most of the land is of coral formation and consequently unsuitable for agriculture, the modern Bahamas has developed a major tourist economy.

Capital: Nassau.
Size: 5,386 sq. miles.
Population: 294,982 in 2000.
Languages: English; Creole is spoken by Haitian immigrants.
Religions: 94,398 Baptists (32%), 56,046 Catholics (19%), 17,693 Methodists (6%), 58,998 Anglicans (20%), 58,789 other (20%), 9,058 without religious affiliation.
Metropolitan See: Nassau, with suffragans Hamilton, Barbados. In addition, there are 27 parishes located throughout the islands, and a mission *sui juris* located in the Turks and Caicos Islands.

History. The Bahamas were originally inhabited by the aboriginal Lucayan people. On Oct. 12, 1492 explorer Christopher Columbus landed on San Salvador, or Guanahani, as the island was known to its native inhabitants, and claimed the area for Spain. The first Mass was offered on San Salvador in the New World. Possessing neither gold, silver, nor precious stones, the island itself was of little interest to the Spaniards, but they enslaved its population. The Lucayan natives were captured and shipped to Haiti and Cuba, where they were forced to work in the mines. Mistreated, they quickly died out. Meanwhile, the Bahamian islands became a popular haunt of pirates and buccaneers.

During the 16th century three attempts were made to wrest control of the Bahamas from Spain. In 1578 Elizabeth I of England granted to Sir Humphrey Gilbert (half brother of Sir Walter Raleigh) lands "not actually possessed of any Christian prince or people." In 1629 the English king Charles I granted to Sir Robert Heath the Lucayan Island of "Veajus (Abaco) and Bahama." Four years later, in 1633 through Cardinal Richelieu, France granted to Guillaume de Caen a barony that included part of the Bahamas, and especially Guanahani. In each of these cases circumstances prevented colonization of the islands, and the claims ultimately proved fruitless.

In 1647 British Captain William Sayle, former governor of Bermuda, obtained a grant from Charles II. Early the following year, accompanied by a small band of Puritans in search of religious freedom, Sayle landed on a Bahamian island, which he named "Eleuthera", from the Greek word *Eleutherios,* meaning freedom. Survivors of these first colonists settled the island of New Providence, on which Nassau is located, about 20 years later, and it became the seat of government. Proximity to the Spanish Main and shipping lanes as well as the region's many protected harbors, also attracted pirates and shipwreckers looking to elude pursuit; occasional treasure finds from wrecked Spanish galleons attracted this more adventurous element to the Bahamas. Among the most famous English pirates who frequented Bahamian waters were Sir Henry Morgan and Bill Teach, otherwise known as "Blackbeard."

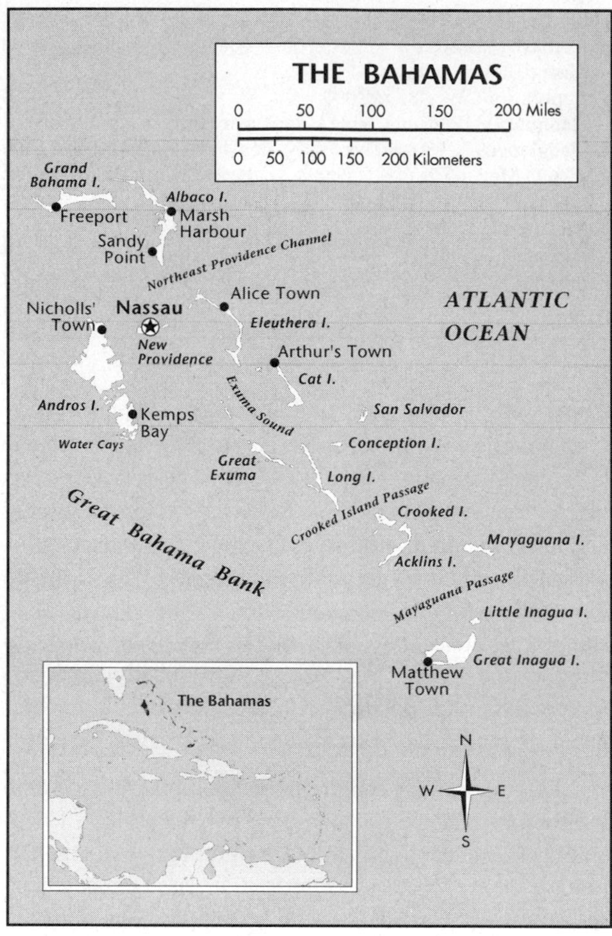

The Bahamian islands' colorful reputation changed in 1718, when Captain Woodes Rogers was appointed governor and given the backing of the British Navy in an effort to restore order. The motto "Expulsis Piratis, Restituta Commercia," incorporated in the Seal of the Bahamas, memorializes his efforts. Constitutional government was established in 1728 when King George II, by order-in-council, created the House of Assembly with powers similar to those of the British House of Commons. During the American War of Independence Nassau was captured and occupied by American forces for one day in 1776 and for three days in 1783. From May of 1782 to April of 1783 Spanish forces occupied Nassau. On Jan. 7, 1964, Great Britain granted a new constitution to the Bahamas, bestowing internal self-government within the British Commonwealth while retaining control of the region's civil service, internal security and foreign affairs.

The Church in the Bahamas. In 1858 Rome placed the Bahamas under the ecclesiastical jurisdiction of the Diocese of Charleston, South Carolina. Catholic priests visited Nassau sporadically until February of 1885, when Archbishop Corrigan of New York sent Rev. George O'Keefe to live on the islands. On July 28 of that same year Cardinal Simeoni of Rome's Congregation for the Evangelization of Peoples ("Propaganda") transferred the Bahamas to the ecclesiastical jurisdiction of New York. On Feb. 14, 1887, Archbishop Corrigan dedicated the island's first Catholic church under the patronage of St. Francis Xavier. This church, greatly enlarged, would eventually serve as a cathedral. The missions of the Church in the Bahamian Islands date from October of 1889, when Mother Ambrosia and four Sisters of Charity from Mt. St. Vincent on the Hudson in New York arrived in Nassau to establish St. Francis Xavier Academy. In January of 1890 the sisters opened the St. Francis Xavier Primary School.

At the invitation of Archbishop Corrigan, St. John's Benedictine Abbey, Collegeville, Minnesota, undertook responsibility for the mission. On Feb. 2, 1891 Chrysostom Schreiner, OSB, was appointed vicar forane by the archbishop of New York. Father Chrysostom, the "Apostle of the Bahamas," spent the rest of his life in the islands and died in 1928 at San Salvador, where he was buried. Although the non-Catholic population, with its established church, was militantly anti-Catholic, within a few short years Chrysostom had established the Sacred Heart church in Nassau and several mission churches at Andros. Gabriel Roerig, OSB, who spent his 56 years of priesthood in the Bahamas, received the decoration of M.B.E. from the government in recognition of his work. The decree *Constans apostolicae sedis* established the island as a prefecture apostolic on March 21, 1929. On Feb. 7, 1932, John Bernard Kevenhoerster, OSB, was installed as the first prefect apostolic. In 1941 the prefecture was raised to a vicariate apostolic and Bishop Bernard was named its first vicar. Paul Leonard Hagarty, OSB, was appointed vicar apostolic on June 25, 1950. On July 5, 1960, when the Bahamas was erected into the Diocese of Nassau, he was appointed its first bishop. On July 10, 1973, the Bahamas achieved independence from the United Kingdom as a constitutional democracy.

The Church Moves into the 21st Century. During the 19th and 20th centuries the Bahamas developed a predominately Protestant culture, in part because of generations of British influence. During the islands' history, no restrictions were placed on the practice of one's faith, and freedom of religion was confirmed via Bahamas' constitution in 1973. In the year 2000 the study of the Christian religion remained an integral part of all public-school education, despite the fact that no state church was sanctioned.

As one of several minority religions in the region in the 21st century, the Catholic Church focused on both native and tourist populations. Ethnically, residents of the

Bahamas are predominately of African origin, most descended from slaves or from Africans freed by the British navy while on their way to be sold into slavery. The Bahamians remained active in all phases of social, political and religious life within the islands, and it was among them that the missionary work of the Church proved most effective. By 2000 the Church claimed over 56,000 followers within the islands' population, a substantial increase over mid-1900 levels. In addition to the 13 secular priests attached to the archdiocese, 16 others were attached to religious orders; other active Catholics included a brother and 27 sisters. Eugenio Sbarbaro served as Papal representative for the region, and the Bahamas received a new archbishop in June of 2000.

Following its break from the United Kingdom, the growth of the island's tourist economy during the 1980s and 1990s proved to be a double-edged sword as drug trafficking became more common. The influx of wealthy tourists, as well as a growing off-shore banking industry, brought with it a host of social problems, from drug abuse to prostitution to AIDS. The support of the Church in battling such social ills reflected Bahamas' strong Christian heritage, despite the population's economic, ethnic and religious diversity.

Bibliography: J. H. LEFROY, *Memorials of the Discovery and Early Settlement of the Bermudas or Somers Islands,* 2 v. (Bermuda 1932). R. A. CURRY, *Bahamian Lore* (Paris 1930). M. MOSELEY, *The Bahamas Handbook* (Nassau 1926). C. J. BARRY, *Worship and Work: St. John's Abbey and University, 1856–1956* (Collegeville, MN 1956).

[B. F. FORSYTH/EDS.]

BAHIRA LEGEND

A tale widely circulated in medieval times concerning a meeting between MUḤAMMAD and a Christian monk or hermit named Bahira (Aramaic *baīrā*, ''the chosen''). The most common Muslim version of the legend is included in the principal biographies of Muḥammad by Ibn-Sa'd and Ibn-Isḥāq, confirmed by Ibn-Hishām and Al-Ṭabari and regarded as fact by most later Muslim biographers of Muḥammad. According to this version Muḥammad, when 12 years old, accompanied his uncle Abū Ṭālib (some accounts say Abū Bakr, Muḥammad's father-in-law and the first caliph) on a caravan trip to Syria. When the caravan was near or already in the town of Bosra, a Christian monk or hermit, noting what he regarded as a miraculous movement of a cloud (or branch) shading it, invited the caravan to dine with him. All accounts agree that the monk on that occasion foretold the young man's prophetic destiny. Some of them also assert that Bahira had foreknowledge of Muḥammad's advent, from certain ''unadulterated'' (*tabdīl*) Christian Scriptures in his possession; some mention an exchange of questions and answers between Bahira and Muḥammad; most include Bahira's admonition to Abū Ṭālib to preserve the lad against the malice of the Jews and the violence of the Byzantines. The name of the monk, Bahira, is lacking in the oldest versions of the legend, and is given in others as Sergius, Georgius, Nestor, or Nicholas. Within the Muslim tradition this legend supplied Islam with a prediction and guarantee of the prophet's mission, and had a considerable polemical value against Christianity.

On the other hand in its Christian form, the Bahira legend was regarded as confirmation of the falsity of Muḥammad's prophetic claim. Bahira was portrayed as a renegade heretic, most often a Nestorian, but in some cases a Jacobite (*Patrologia Graeca* 104:1446) or an Arian (*Patrologia Graeca* 108:192; 130:1333c), and an accomplice in or even an instigator of items of Islamic doctrine and the production of the QU'RĀN. Bahira is mentioned quite early in Byzantine historical and polemical literature under the name Sergius, and the two names were ultimately conjoined in that and other later Christian tradition. He is mentioned by Theophanes [ed. C. de Boor, 2 v. (Leipzig 1883–85) 333, 1209] with this name, but in such a way as to identify him more or less clearly with Waraqah ibn-Nawfal, a cousin of Muḥammad's wife, Khadījah. After the ninth century the name Bahira, with slight variations in form, was well known to Byzantine apologists such as Bartholomew of Edessa (*Patrologia Graeca* 104: 1429). The legend is included also in the famous Christian Arabic apology of 'Abd al-Masiḥ ibn-Isḥāq al KINDI. But the chief Christian form taken by the legend is that of the *Apocalypse of Bahira*, which, it is agreed, combines elements of earlier Christian literature of the same genre with some echoes of specifically Muslim lore and doctrine. In the Christian form of the legend, generally, Bahira is credited with having provided whatever authentic information from Scripture is to be found in the Qur'ān. A ''monastery of Bahira'' is still shown as a curiosity to travelers, at Bosra in Syria.

Bibliography: J. BIGNAMI-ODIER and G. LEVI DELLA VIDA, ''Une Version latine de l'Apocalypse syro-arabe de Serge-Bahira,'' *Mélanges d'Archéologie et d'Histoire* (École Française de Rome 1950) 125. R. GOTTHEIL, ''A Christian Bahira Legend,'' *Zeitschrift für Assyriologie* 13 (1898) 189–242; 14 (1899) 203–268. IBN-ISHÂQ, *Sîrat Rasûl Allâh* (*The Life of Muhammad*), tr. A. GUILLAUME (London 1955). A. ABEL, *Encyclopedia of Islam*[2] 1:922–923.

[J. KRITZECK]

BAHRAIN, THE CATHOLIC CHURCH IN

The State of Bahrain—in Arabic, Al Bahrayn or "the two seas"—is an independent emirate comprising the islands of Al-Bahrain, Al-Muḥarraq, Sitra and several smaller islands lying about 13 miles east of Saudi Arabia, in the Persian Gulf, although sovereignty over the Hawar island group remained in dispute between Qatar and Bahrain in 2000. Bahrain's low, flat desert plains rise to a central ridge, its climate arid with mild winters, and hot, humid summers. Natural resources include some oil reserves, while fishing, shrimping and the cultivation of fruits, vegetables and other agricultural crops support the regional economy.

In ancient times the main island, then called Tylos and later Awâl, was renowned for its pearls; Al-Muḥarraq was then called Arados. Prior to the discovery of oil in the early 20th century, pearls were the region's primary export. Oil, which was discovered in 1932, became the source of a continuously progressing modernization of the islands. The large islands, as well as the northern island of Al-Muḥarraq are home to most of the region's population, over 40 percent of whom are foreigners working in the country. Largely dependant upon petroleum refining, the region has also developed itself into a large-scale international banking center. The family ruling Bahrain in 2000 had been in power since 1782.

History. The region was discovered by Portuguese explorers in 1521 and occupied by them until the arrival of Arabs from Persia in 1602. While Catholic priests entered the region with the Portuguese, any influence they had was entirely eradicated when the islands came under Muslim rule. In 1782 a Kuwaiti family took control, supported in its administration by the British from 1820 to 1971. As Great Britain prepared to disengage from the region, Bahrain developed a council government in 1970, four decades after the discovery of oil had boosted its economy. The country remained almost wholly Muslim, and Islam was the state religion, although freedom of religion is protected within certain limits. Catholics living in the region are foreign workers, most from the Philippines, and by the year 2000 comprised a single parish, led by three priests and aided by fewer than 100 religious. Political interference by Church leaders is not tolerated, nor is proselytization. However, Bahrain Emir Sheikh Hamad bin Essa al-Khalifa met with Pope John Paul II in advance of his government's establishment of formal diplomatic relations with the Vatican in January of 2000.

Bibliography: *Bilan du Monde. Encyclopédie Catholique du Monde Chrétien*, 2 v. (Tournai 1964) 2: 119–120.

[A. JAMME/EDS.]

Capital: Manâma.
Size: 255 sq. miles.
Population: 634,137 in 2000.
Languages: Arabic, English, Farsi, Urdu.
Religions: 30,000 Catholics, Shī'a Muslims (75%), Sunni Muslims (24%)
Apostolic vicariate: Arabia.

BAILLY, VINCENT DE PAUL

Publisher, Assumptionist priest; b. Berteaucourt-les-Thennes, Dec. 2, 1832; d. Paris, Dec. 2, 1912. His grandfather had preserved the MSS of St. VINCENT DE PAUL during the Revolution, and his uncle and future mother had transported the body of the saint to Paris for interment. This heritage and the Christian atmosphere of his large family doubtless determined his vocation. His father, one of the founders of the Conférences St. Vincent de Paul, operated a boarding home for students in Paris and was active in all religious movements. Leading Catholics frequented the Bailly home, notably the Abbé Emmanuel d'ALZON, the founder of the Augustinian Congregation of the Assumption (the ASSUMPTIONISTS). Bailly entered the Paris École Polytechnique at 20, and after graduation he served for some years as a civil servant in the Post Office Department. In 1860, after a retreat at Nîmes, he decided to enter the Assumptionists. He was ordained at Rome in 1863 and became superior of the congregation's college at Nîmes (1863–67). He was chaplain to the French forces that defended the Holy See in 1867 and again at Metz during the war of 1870.

Bailly was deeply concerned with the welfare of the people. He aided in founding various Catholic associations and organized the first lay pilgrimages to La Salette, Lourdes, and Paray-le-Monial. In 1876 he took over the direction of *Le Pèlerin*, the journal devoted to promoting the pilgrimages, and transformed it into a lively popular weekly that was at the same time militantly Catholic. By 1879 *Le Pèrelin* had 80,000 subscribers and ably combatted the nonsectarian but anticlerical press. In 1883 he founded the daily *La Croix*, also designed as a popular and simple defense of the Church at a time when the successive governments of the Third Republic were either openly interdicting or rendering extremely difficult the existence of religious congregations.

The vigor of Bailly's polemics sometimes took him beyond a point sanctioned by Rome and incurred the hatred of his adversaries, but his sense of prayer and obedience balanced his excesses. In November 1899 the Assumptionists were suppressed by law, and Bailly left France for Rome, where he lived until 1906. He founded houses in Belgium and England and finally returned to

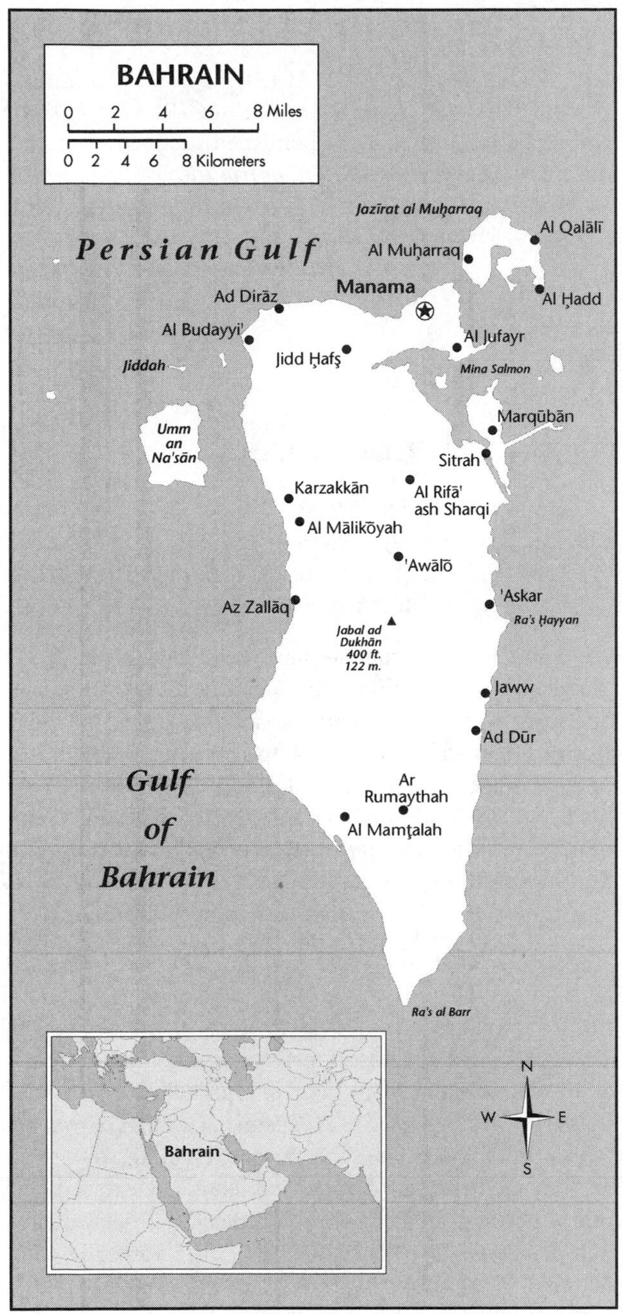

Paris. His achievement lay not only in the foundation of a great daily paper, a popular weekly, and a score of other publications connected with them, but more especially in the vision that led to the establishment of the publishing house, La Bonne Presse, at a time when such coordination of publishing was indispensable for the success of Catholic journalism.

Bibliography: E. LACOSTE, *Le Père Vincent de Paul Bailly* (Paris 1913). R. KOKEL, *Le Père Vincent de Paul Bailly* (Paris 1943).

[G. HOURDIN]

Vincent De Paul Bailly.

BAINBRIDGE, CHRISTOPHER

Cardinal archbishop of York, civil servant; b. Hilton, near Appleby, Westmorland, England, between 1462 and 1464; d. Rome, Italy, July 13 or 14, 1514. His family were gentry, and he was a nephew of Thomas Langton, bishop of Winchester. In 1479 he received a papal dispensation that allowed him to receive any benefice, with or without cure of souls, once he turned 16 years old. At Oxford he was a master of arts by 1486, after which he studied in Italy, at Ferrara (1487–88) and at Bologna, where he was admitted doctor of civil law (1492); by 1498 he was also a doctor of canon law. He incorporated as a doctor of civil law at Cambridge (1503–04); in 1505 he became a student of English common law at Lincoln's Inn. Meanwhile he had become provost of Queen's College, Oxford, in 1496 (until 1508); successively prebend in several cathedral churches; and dean of York in 1503. While dean he was concurrently master of the Rolls (1504–07) and then bishop of DURHAM by papal PROVISION (1507–08). In 1508 he was translated to YORK as archbishop, largely *in absentia.* HENRY VIII sent him in 1509 as his orator to Rome, where he remained until his death. Pope JULIUS II created him cardinal priest in 1511 and entrusted him with siege operations at Ferrara. An intense rivalry developed between Bainbridge, who was anti-French, and Silvestre Gigli, absentee bishop of

Worcester and resident English ambassador at Rome, who was pro-French. Possibly as a result of Gigli's machinations, Bainbridge was poisoned by one of his Italian chaplains, Rinaldo de Modena, who confessed under torture that he had acted on Gigli's orders. Bainbridge was buried in what has since become the English College at Rome, where his fine tomb with recumbent effigy remains.

Bibliography: A. B. EMDEN, *A Biographical Register of the University of Oxford to* A.D. *1500* 1:91–93. J. LENEVE, *Fasti Ecclesiae Anglicanae 1300-1541* v. 6. D. S. CHAMBERS, *Cardinal Bainbridge in the Court of Rome, 1509–14* (London 1965).

[H. S. REINMUTH, JR.]

BAINES, PETER AUGUSTINE

Titular bishop of Siga; b. Kirkby, Lancashire, Jan. 25, 1787; d. Prior Park, Bath, July 6, 1843. He was educated at the monastery in Lampspring, Germany (1798–1802) and at Ampleforth in England. After his profession in the BENEDICTINES (1804), he held many important offices at AMPLEFORTH ABBEY. He took charge of the Benedictine mission at Bath (1817) and was appointed (1823) coadjutor to Bishop Collingridge, vicar apostolic of the Western District of England, whom he succeeded (1829). Baines found that his district was the only one without a seminary, and in trying to remedy this, fell into acrimonious dispute with the Benedictines at DOWNSIDE ABBEY, because they were unwilling to agree to his plan, and resisted his coercive measures. Much bitterness ensued but the problem was eventually solved when four Ampleforth monks left the order, as did Baines, and put the seminary plan into effect at Prior Park, a magnificent mansion near Bath purchased by Baines. Lay students were also taught, and Baines indulged in dreams of a Catholic university. But the bishop was a man in advance of his times. Prior Park never achieved the success he had forecast.

Bibliography: J. S. ROCHE, *A History of Prior Park College and Its Founder Bishop Baines* (London 1931). J. GILLOW, *A Literary and Biographical History or Bibliographical Dictionary of the English Catholics from 1534 to the Present Time* 1:105–10.

[V. A. MCCLELLAND]

BAINVEL, JEAN VINCENT

Theologian; b. Plougoumelen, France, Aug. 4, 1858; d. Jan. 29, 1937. In 1877 he became a Jesuit, and in 1900 was named professor of fundamental theology at the Institut Catholique de Paris, where he worked until 1925. His works include the following: *La Foi et l'acte de foi* (Paris 1908), *La Vie intime du catholique* (Paris 1916), *La Dévotion au Sacré Coeur de Jésus* (Paris 1919), *Le Saint Coeur de Marie* (Paris 1919), *Naturel et Surnaturel* (Paris 1920), and *Marie, mère de Dieu* (Paris 1921). His courses at the Institut were published successively under the titles: *De magisterio vivo, et traditione* (Paris 1905), *De Scriptura Sacra* (Paris 1919), and *De Ecclesia Christi* (Paris 1925).

Bibliography: J. LEBRETON, *Catholicisme* 1:1168–69.

[G. MOLLAT]

BAIUS AND BAIANISM

Baius (de Bay, Michel), theologian; b. Mélin l'Évêque (Hennegau), Belgium, 1513; d. Louvain, Sept. 16, 1589. This article will present a summary of his life, an account of his doctrine, and a list of his chief errors.

Life. Baius began his philosophical studies at the University of Louvain in 1533, and became a master of arts in 1535. His theological studies occupied the years from 1536 to 1541. From 1544 to 1550, he taught philosophy at the University, and during this period received his licentiate (1545) and master's degree (1550) in theology. In 1551 he was named Regius Professor of Sacred Scripture.

With his friend, Jan Hessels, he inaugurated new methods in theology. Neglecting the doctrine on original sin and justification of the great scholastics and of the fifth (1546) and sixth (1547) sessions of the Council of Trent, they laid almost exclusive emphasis on Scripture, as they understood it in their interpretation of the anti-Pelagian writings of St. Augustine. Conflict arose between Baius and Hessels, on the one hand, and older colleagues such as Ruard Tapper and Josse Ravesteyn on the other. The new methods were combined with new doctrinal positions. On June 27, 1560, the Sorbonne condemned 18 theses extracted from notes taken by Baius's students. Baius's reply and defense broadened the conflict. The Cardinal Legate, Giovanni Commendone, sought the intervention of Rome, but Pius IV merely imposed silence on both sides. In 1563 Baius and Hessels were sent as theologians of the King of Spain to the Council of Trent, but did not exercise a prominent role.

Between 1563 and 1566 Baius published various opuscula that contain his essential doctrine and system. Excerpts from these works were condemned by the Universities of Alcalá and Salamanca. The Spanish condemnations caused grave concern in Rome. After a thorough examination of these writings, Pius V on October 1, 1567, condemned 79 propositions (H. Denzinger, *Enchi-*

ridion symbolorum 1901–79) in the papal bull EX OMNIBUS AFFLICTIONIBUS. These condemned theses are contained, for the most part, in Baius's works, but the bull did not mention him by name. The formal condemnation following the 79 theses was written without punctuation and proclaimed: ". . . quas quidem sententias stricto coram Nobis examine ponderatas quamquam nonnullae aliquo pacto sustineri possent in rigore et proprio sensu ab assertoribus intento haereticas erroneas . . . damnamus." According to whether a comma is placed after "possent" or after "intento," the condemnation has two quite different meanings. With the comma placed after "possent," it has the following meaning: "We condemn as heretical, erroneous, etc., in the sense intended by their authors and according to the strict use of the terms employed, the aforesaid opinions, after a close scrutiny of them has been conducted in our presence, even though some of them might in one way or another be defended." If the comma is placed after "intento," the clause ". . . in the sense intended by their authors and according to the strict use of the terms employed. . ." should be placed at the end of the whole sentence. This is the famous problem of the COMMA PIANUM, which has never been settled. Modern research tends to show that the pope, while certainly condemning the 79 theses, did not wish to embarrass Baius and to make his submission more difficult [cf. É. van Eijl, "L'Interprétation de la Bulle de Pie V portant condamnation de Baius," *Revue d'histoire ecclésiastique* 50 (1955) 499–542].

Baius at first submitted, but in 1569 he sent a protest to the pope. After a new hearing, Pius reiterated his first condemnation of the 79 theses. Baius was ordered not only to submit, but to express a formal disavowal of all the condemned propositions. In 1575 he became chancellor of the University. In 1580 Pope Gregory XIII published the bull *Provisionis nostrae* confirming the condemnation of Pius V. The new papal condemnation was promulgated solemnly at Louvain by Cardinal Toletus, March 21, 1580. Baius and the entire faculty of Louvain submitted. To put an end to any further controversy, the faculty, at the instigation of the papal nuncio, Bonomini, composed a document entitled *Doctrinae eius (quam certorum articulorum damnatio postulare visa est) brevis et quoad fieri potest ordinata et cohaerens explicatio* (1586). This document is a clear exposition of the positive doctrine opposed to the condemned propositions, and, after four centuries, still remains an excellent source for understanding correctly the exact meaning of the condemnation.

In the last years of Baius's life, the renowned controversy between the faculty of Louvain and the Jesuits arose. It is difficult to establish whether, or to what extent, Baius contributed to the composition of the faculty's censure against Leonard Lessius, SJ, in 1587, but he certainly had a share in its wide diffusion. Baius died in union with the Church.

Doctrine. An accurate understanding of the principal truths of Christianity depends, according to Baius, on a correct answer to two questions: (1) What was the nature of the first man's original integrity before his fall from original justice? (2) What is to be thought of the so-called virtues of sinners and infidels among Adam's posterity? For, without exact answers to these questions, one will neither recognize the corruption of human nature by original sin, nor will one be able to evaluate properly the restoration of human nature through Christ (*De prima hominis iustitia, Praefatio*).

Original Integrity. Baius answers that according to Sacred Scripture the first man was created in the image and likeness of God and was adorned with all virtues (*ibid.* ch. 1, 2). The integrity of Adam consisted not only in complete knowledge of the divine law and in full submission to his Creator, but also in the fact that the lower powers of man were subject to his higher faculties, and all the members of his body and their movements were submissive to his will, which was free with true liberty of choice (*ibid.* ch. 3). Furthermore, man's initial integrity was not an undue (i.e., supernatural) elevation of his nature. For, according to Baius, all perfections that pertain to any class of beings in their origin are natural (*ibid.* ch. 4). Thus he considers the lack of integrity in fallen man to be an evil; but evil in his view is the privation of what is natural. Hence the evils derived from original sin in Adam's posterity can be termed natural, but only in a very loose sense; namely, inasmuch as they are the result of the transmission through generation of a corrupt nature (*ibid.* ch. 5, 6). Conversely, if, and to whatever extent, the natural endowments, lost in Adam's sin, are restored to fallen human nature through Christ, they can be called supernatural, but again, only in the loose sense whereby one may designate as supernatural anything derived from a special benefit of God (for example, the miraculous restoration of sight to one who had been blinded), not however, in the sense that this restored integrity is itself supernatural (*ibid.* ch. 7–10).

Although Baius calls the endowments of man's original state natural, he does not mean that they emanate from the nature of man, considered as a composite of body and soul, as the faculties of intellect and will emanate from the soul; rather, they are communicated directly by God. Nevertheless, he maintains, they belong to man's nature and are demanded by man's natural constitution of soul and body, in this sense, that their lack would be an evil for human nature itself. They are, then, just as natural to man as his soul, which is not the product of the generative act of parents as efficient causes, but must be infused directly by God through creation (*ibid.* ch. 11).

Adam's Reward. Created in this state of natural integrity, Adam was obliged to obey his Creator, and thus to merit eternal life, i.e., the unending and immediate vision of God. Even as God's unchangeable wisdom established eternal death as the proportionate punishment of human disobedience and sin, the same wisdom established that the first man would have received eternal life as the natural and just recompense for his obedience to God. Thus, the reward of eternal life would have been man's natural end and would have been due solely to man's natural merit, and in no way to grace. Similarly the good angels after their trial received eternal life, not as a grace nor as in any wise unowed, but as the just reward of their obedience (*De meritis operum,* ch. 1–3).

From this, Baius concludes that God could not have created man without endowing him with integrity and without destining him uniquely to the beatific vision. He thus maintains that a state of pure nature, in which man would have been ordained by God to an end inferior to the direct and immediate vision of God and would have lacked the perfection of integrity, is impossible and chimerical. [See Pius XII, *Humani generis Acta Apostolicae Sedis* (Rome 1909–) 42 (1950) 570: ''Alii veram 'gratuitatem' ordinis supernaturalis corrumpunt, cum autument Deum entia intellectu praedita condere non posse quirt eadem ad beatificam visionem ordinet et vocet.'']

Original Sin. Through his sin, Adam lost his integrity, and thereby the possibility of attaining his unique end. His sin with these two consequences was transmitted to all his descendants by the vitiated and disordered generative act whereby all men are conceived (*De peccato originis,* ch. 1, 2). Original sin consists in the malice of a will that does not love God and His justice, in the rebellion of fallen man's lower nature against his spirit and in ignorance (*ibid.* ch. 3). Because of original sin, all men, even infants, are subject to the wrath of God and to eternal death. Even as Adam was created in God's favor through no merit of his own, so the newborn infant is the object of God's loathing; because of original sin alone, and not because of any personal commitment, the newborn baby stands in opposition to God and to His law (*ibid.* ch. 4).

Baius teaches that sin is essentially opposition to the law of God and disobedience to His commands. The question whether sin should be voluntary has nothing to do with its essence, but only with its origin. Whatever is contrary to the law of God is a sin in whomsoever it exists, and is justly imputed as sin by God, merely because it exists (*ibid.* ch. 7). In the state of integrity Adam could have fulfilled the law easily and with true freedom of choice (*De libero hominis arbitrio,* ch. 9). By original sin this power was lost completely (*ibid.* ch. 11).

Fallen Man. Nothing more deplorable than the moral condition of fallen man in the system of Baius can be imagined. Even man's indeliberate and inoperative desires, being infringements of the law of God *non concupisces* (Rom 7.7, ''Thou shalt not lust''), are actual sins worthy of eternal punishment (*De peccato originis,* ch. 2). Every sin deserves eternal punishment, because all sins are by their very nature mortal sins (*De meritis operum,* ch. 2). There is no certainty that God will give the power to perform what He commands. On the contrary, the opinion that God commands nothing impossible finds no support in Augustine, but derives from Pelagius (*De peccato originis,* ch. 12). The general conclusion, so well summed up in the words of the condemned proposition: ''All the works of unbelievers are sins'' (*Enchiridion symbolorum* 1925), is defended by Baius in his *De virtutibus impiorum:* there is, he says, only one possible end of man, which is the intuitive vision of God, and one way only of loving God, which is charity. Therefore without charity (which presupposes faith) there is only sin (*ibid.* ch. 5, 8).

Redemption and Justification. Christ came to restore to fallen man the spiritual state that was his due in creation, but which, owing to original sin, is now ''grace.'' Just as fallen man is wholly characterized and determined, before Redemption, by evil concupiscence, so that his every movement and impulse is sin, so redeemed man lives and merits the beatific vision by charity. Charity is ''. . . that motion of the soul whereby we love God and our neighbor'' (*De charitate,* ch. 2), and proceeds immediately from ''the touch of God, who is charity'' (*ibid.* ch. 3).

Justification in the sense of ''fulfilling all justice'' means no more than ''having charity,'' and this proceeds from actual grace; charity may also precede the remission of sins, which is conferred by the Sacraments of Baptism and Penance; charity bears no relation to a habitual state of formal, intrinsic, and permanent justification, as proposed by the scholastics (*ibid.* ch. 7). The scholastic insistence on charity as a permanent gift was quite mistaken. The origin of charity is a transitory impulse received from God, and this is all that matters, because such an impulse, indefinitely repeated, enables us to live in perfect justice (*ibid.* ch. 2). Perfect charity is not to be understood by reference ''to any sacrament or permanent state'' (*ibid.* ch. 9; cf. *Enchiridion symbolorum,* 1931–33). Similarly justification is really a continuous process, wherein man performs more and more good works under actual impulses of God, and overcomes more and more the evil desires of concupiscence, i.e., makes progress "toward the remission of sins" (*De justificatione,* ch. 1).

Merit. This denial of the significance, if not of the existence, of habitual or sanctifying grace, has an important bearing upon Baius's notion of merit, which is solely and exclusively the execution of God's commands, the fulfillment of the law of God. According to Baius, man's operation of itself and alone, i.e., apart from any freedom of choice and apart from the influx of habitual grace and of the infused virtues, merits heaven or hell: heaven if it proceeds from charity, i.e., from a transitory impulse of God, stronger than any opposing evil desire, which brings about the fulfillment of God's law; hell, if it proceeds from the evil desires of concupiscence, which effects the violation of God's law. The patristic and scholastic belief solemnly defined by the Council of Trent (*Enchiridion symbolorum* 1545–47), that it is our adoption by God as living members of Christ, sharing in His divine nature, which enables us to merit eternal life freely, with true freedom of choice (*ibid.* 1525–27, 1574), seemed to Baius to be entirely erroneous (*De meritis operum,* ch. 2). Consequently there is no need for man to be in the state of grace in order that his works be meritorious (*ibid.*).

The pharisaism of Baius's doctrine of justification and merit in fallen man is a sharp contrast to the Pelagianism of his doctrine on innocent man before the Fall, and reveals that extraordinary singularity that makes it impossible to call his system by any other name than his own. In endeavoring to set aside all subsequent tradition, even the authentic teaching of the Church, in order to rediscover the pure spirit of St. Augustine, he fell into a disastrous eclecticism.

Chief Errors. (1) Baius set up the anti-Pelagian treatises of Augustine, against the whole body of post-Augustinian thought, as the sole repository of orthodox teaching on grace. (2) He professed to mistrust any attempt to interpret, develop, or modify the doctrine of Augustine by the use of exegetical, historical, philosophical, or psychological progress in human intelligence. (3) He was not afraid, but rather glad, to arrive at conclusions, in matters of faith and morals, that were in open contradiction with all contemporary Catholic views.

The most important of his erroneous opinions are the following: (1) The state of pure nature is a useless fiction of scholastics and involves an insoluble contradiction. (2) The justice and merits of man in the state of original innocence were natural and did not proceed from grace. (3) Fallen man is determined to evil whenever he is not drawn by charity into holiness. (4) God may and does command man to do the impossible without any injustice. (5) Charity, which is the transitory impulse of God, is the only and infallible source of good works and of merit. (6) Man is not now free under the influence of grace.

It was the method of Baius and the conclusions just enumerated that laid the foundations for the much more important heresy of Jansenism.

See Also: AUGUSTINE, ST.; AUGUSTINIANISM; AUGUSTINIANISM, THEOLOGICAL SCHOOL OF; ELEVATION OF MAN; FREE WILL AND GRACE; GRACE; GRACE AND NATURE: JANSENISM; JUSTICE OF MEN; ORIGINAL JUSTICE; ORIGINAL SIN; PELAGIUS AND PELAGIANISM; PURE NATURE, STATE OF; SUPERNATURAL.

Bibliography: M. BAIUS, *Opera . . . studio A. P. theologi* (1696). N. J. ABERCROMBIE, *The Origins of Jansenism* (Oxford 1936). J. ALFARO, "Sobrenatural y pecado original en Bayo," *Revista española de teologia* 12 (1952) 3–75. X. M. LE BACHELET, *Dictionnaire de théologie catholique,* ed. A. VACANT, 15 v. (Paris 1903–50; Tables générales 1951–) 2.1:38–111. L. CEYSSENS, "Un Échange de lettres entre Michel Baius et Henri Gravius," *Ephemerides theologicae Lovanienses* 26 (1950) 59–86. F. CLAEYS-BOUUAERT, "Un Épisode peu connu de la procédure instituée contre le Baianisme à Louvain," *ibid.* 28 (1952) 277–284; "La soumission de Michel Baius, fut-elle sincère?" *ibid.* 30 (1954) 457–464. E. VAN EIJL, "Les Censures des Universités d'Alcalà et de Salamanque et la censure du Pape Pie V contre M. Baius, 1565–1567," *Revue d'histoire ecclésiastique* 48 (1953) 719–776. M. R. GAGNEBET, "L'Enseignement du Magistère et le problème du surnaturel," *Revue thomiste* 53 (1953) 5–27. R. GUELLUY, "L'Évolution des méthodes théologiques à Louvain d'Érasme à Jansénius," *Revue d'histoire ecclésiastique* 37 (1941) 31–144. F. X. JANSEN, *Baius et le Baianisme* (Louvain 1927). A. LANZ, "Dottrina di Michele Baio sul Romano Pontefice," *La civiltà cattolica* 90.2 (1939) 29–44, 507–521. H. DE LUBAC, "Deux Augustiniens fourvoyés, Baius et Jansenius," *Recherches de science religieuse* 21 (1931) 422–443; 513–540. F. X. LINSENMANN, *Michael Baius und die Grundlegung des Jansenismus* (Tübingen 1867). J. MARTÍNEZ DE RIPALDA, "Adversus Baium et Baianos," v. 5 and 6 of his *De ente supernaturali,* 8 v. (Paris 1871–72). M. J. SCHEEBEN, "Zur Geschichte des Baianismus," *Katholik* NS 19 (1868) 281–308. F. SUAREZ, *Opera Omnia,* v.7 *De gratia Dei, prolegomena* 6, ch. 2 (Paris 1857).

[P. J. DONNELLY]

BAKANJA, ISIDORE, BL.

Lay martyr; b. Boangi area of the Belgian Congo, *c.* 1885; baptized Mbandaka (Coquilhatville), May 6, 1906; d. Busirá, Congo, Aug. 8 or 15, 1909. Isidore Bakanja was baptized when he was about 18 years old. He was working as a mason's assistant when he was evangelized by Trappist missionaries from Westmalle Abbey, Belgium. Isidore wore a scapular to attest to his new faith, and so often shared his faith with others that many thought he was a catechist. He migrated to Ikile, in search of other Christians, where he was employed as a domestic servant by A. van Cauter, agent for the Belgium Anonymous Society that controlled the regional rubber plantations and ivory trade. Finding that many of the agents hated the missionaries, Isidore tried to return home, but was detained. On Feb. 2, 1909, Bakanja was scourged, beaten, and incarcerated in chains for refusing to remove his scapular. Later, he was banished from the village so that the company inspector would not discover the cruelty inflicted on him. En route Isidore met the inspector, who was horrified at the festering wounds and cared for him until Isidore died about six months later. A canonical inquiry was begun for Isidore's cause (1913–14), but dropped for political reasons. In 1976; the cause was reopened at the request of a Zairean lay group, known as the Catechists. He was beatified by John Paul II, April 24, 1994.

Feast: Aug. 15.

Bibliography: *Je meurs parce que je suis chrétien: le Conseil des laïcs catholiques médite sur la vie et le message qu'Isidore Bakanja adresse à ses frères zaïrois* (Kinshasa n.d.). C. DJUNGU-SIMBA K., *Bakanja Isidore: vrai zaïrois, vrai chrétien* (Kinshasa 1994). I. MATONDO KWA NZAMBI, *Le bienheureux Isidore Bakanja: la voix qui crie dans la forêt* (Limete, Kinshasa 1994). D. VAN GROENWEGHE, *Bakanja Isidore, martyr du Zaïre: récit biographique* (Brussels 1989). H. VINCK, *Bakanja Isidore: dossier pastoral* (Mbandaka, Zaire 1983).

[K. I. RABENSTEIN]

BAKER, DAVID AUGUSTINE

Benedictine spiritual writer; b. Abergavenny, Wales, Dec. 9, 1575; d. London, Aug. 9, 1641. He was brought up a Protestant, studied law in London, and became recorder of Abergavenny (1598). In 1600 a narrow escape from drowning turned his thoughts to religion from what was apparently a practical atheism. As a result he was received into the Church in 1603. He met some English Benedictine fathers of the Cassinese congregation, and in 1605 decided to join the order. In Padua, where he entered the novitiate at St. Justina's, his health suffered and he was sent back to England before making his profession. Early in 1607 he was professed on the English mission and subsequently joined the English congregation when it was refounded in 1619, and became a member of St. Laurence's, Dieulouard, now Ampleforth.

The outstanding feature of Baker's life as a religious was his great attraction for contemplative prayer, which appears to have been innate, for he tells that he received no instruction on it in his novitiate, and it was long before he discovered books on the subject. Soon after his profession, however, while at the house of Sir Nicholas Fortescue in Worcestershire, he gave himself up to the practice of internal prayer for as much as five or six hours a day. He reached what he considered his highest experience in it, which amounted apparently to some sort of intellectual vision. But so uninstructed was he that, when this was succeeded by a period of desolation, he gave up the practice of mental prayer and fell back into relative tepidity, which lasted for 12 years, until 1620. During this time he was ordained priest in France but lived mostly in England, where he did some notable historical research, which was afterward incorporated in the volume *Apostolatus Benedictinorum in Anglia* (1626). In 1620 he discovered the literature of contemplation and took up again the intensive practice of mental prayer, which he maintained for the rest of his life.

In 1624 he was recalled to France and made assistant chaplain to the English Benedictine nuns at Cambrai (now Stanbrook). There he gave spiritual conferences to the nuns and started to write his treatises on prayer. He left more than 60 treatises, though some of them were historical or were translations. He wrote without any idea of publication and in a style that is often diffuse and rambling, though sometimes attractively naïve. The treatises as a whole do not form any coherent treatment of the spiritual life; they reflect his reading, which was assiduous. His aim was always the achievement of contemplation, and he reacted against methodical meditation in favor of an affective prayer that tended to become purely contemplative. This reaction against meditation, then recently and highly developed, was resented by the official English Benedictine chaplain to the Cambrai nuns; and Baker was involved in something of a controversy over it. In the end his views were vindicated by the authorities of the congregation, but he was withdrawn to the monastery of St. Gregory at Douai (now Downside) in 1633, where he continued to write for another five years. In 1638 a difference of opinion with his superior led to his return to England.

Bibliography: Works. *Sancta Sophia,* ed. S. CRESSY (New York 1857); *Holy Wisdom*, ed. G. SITWELL (London 1964), not authoritative on higher forms of mystical prayer, but admirable on the mortifications and on the affective prayer of acts; *The Confessions of Venerable Father Augustine Baker*, ed. P. J. MCCANN (London 1922), his spiritual autobiography extracted from Baker's treatise on *The Cloud of Unknowing*, ed. P. MCCANN (5th ed. London 1947). Studies. P. J. MCCANN and R. H. CONNOLLY, eds., *Memorials of Father Augustine Baker* (*Publications of the Catholic Record Society* 33; London 1933). P. SALVIN and S. CRESSY, *The Life of Father Augustine Baker*, ed. P. J. MCCANN (London 1933). D. KNOWLES, *The English Mystical Tradition* (New York 1961). E. I. WATKIN, *Poets and Mystics* (New York 1953) 188–237.

[G. SITWELL]

BAKER, DIOCESE OF

Suffragan of the metropolitan See of Portland, Ore., the Baker diocese (*Bakeriensis*) comprises 18 counties of

Oregon east of the Cascade Mountain Range, an area of 66,826 square miles. In 2001, there were about 36,000 Catholics, approximately nine percent of a total population of 425,650.

The area, originally in the vicariate apostolic of Oregon and then part of the Diocese of Walla Walla (suppressed in 1850), later was placed under the care of the archbishop of Oregon City. It was erected a diocese by Leo XIII on June 19, 1903, and the first bishop, Charles J. O'Reilly, pastor of the Church of Mary Immaculate, Portland, was installed on Sept. 1, 1903. When Charles B. O'Reilly (Jan. 4, 1862–Feb. 4, 1923) was named bishop in 1903, he and a number of his priests were unsure whether this frontier diocese would survive. The territory was large but sparsely populated, with only 13 priests. In 1906 the Catholic Extension Society began to make contributions for churches and to provide subsidies for priests and seminarians. Irish Capuchins came in 1910.

In March of 1918, Bishop O'Reilly was transferred to the Diocese of Lincoln, Neb. His successor, Joseph F. McGrath (March 1, 1871–April 12, 1950), appointed Dec. 21, 1918, concerned that many children in the sprawling diocese had little religious instruction, established the Confraternity of Christian Doctrine. With help from what was then the Catholic Indian and Negro Bureau, new missions were initiated. Because of Bishop McGrath's advanced years, in 1948 the Holy See appointed Bishop Leo F. Fahey as coadjutor with right of succession, but he died March 31, 1950, just days before Bishop McGrath's own death.

Francis P. Leipzig (June 29, 1895–Jan. 17, 1981), pastor of St. Mary's Church in Eugene, Ore. and known for his administrative and public relations abilities, became bishop on July 18, 1950. Bishop Leipzig took the lead in constructing a new chancery office, establishing new parishes, and building churches and chapels with the aim of making it possible for Catholics to assist at Mass each Sunday, even in remote areas. The changes after Vatican II caused problems similar to those in Portland.

When Bishop Leipzig retired in May of 1971, he was succeeded by Thomas J. Connolly (July 19, 1922). Bishop Connolly accepted the challenged presented by the widespread diocese by becoming even more mobile than his predecessors. As school closures continued, including the last Catholic high school in the diocese; more effort went into religious education programs. Bishop Connolly encouraged lay ministry in response to the dwindling numbers of priests, and he developed methods for including the laity in decision-making. In 1987 he moved the diocese's administrative offices to Bend, although the Cathedral remained in Baker City.

Bishop Connolly retired in January of 2000 and was succeeded by Robert Francis Vasa, who was consecrated and installed Jan. 26, 2000.

An official diocesan newspaper, the *Catholic Sentinel,* is published weekly.

Bibliography: D. O'CONNOR, *Brief History of the Diocese of Baker City* (Baker 1930). W. P. SCHOENBERG, *A History of the Catholic Church in the Pacific Northwest 1743–1983* (Washington, DC 1987).

[P. BRANDT/EDS.]

BAKER, FRANCIS ASBURY

Paulist missionary; b. Baltimore, Maryland, March 30, 1820; d. New York City, April 4, 1865. Baker, the son of Sarah (Dickens) and Dr. Samuel Baker, both Methodists, joined the Episcopal Church shortly after his graduation from Princeton College (later University), and in 1846 was ordained to the ministry. At St. Paul's church, his first assignment, and later as rector of St. Luke's church in Baltimore, he was considered one of the city's outstanding preachers. Under the influence of the OXFORD MOVEMENT, he resigned his pulpit, and in 1853 he embraced Catholicism and entered the Redemptorist community. On Sept. 21, 1856, he was ordained in the Baltimore Cathedral (now basilica) and a month later joined four other American Redemptorist converts, Isaac Hecker, Augustine F. Hewit, George Deshon, and Clarence A. Walworth, in their missionary work throughout the United States. When Pius IX released the five missionaries from their Redemptorist vows in 1858, Baker united with Hecker, Hewit, and Deshon to form the Society of Missionary Priests of St. Paul the Apostle (*see* PAULISTS). While continuing his missionary career, he took a prominent part in inaugurating and establishing the Paulist tradition of ceremonial dignity in liturgical services.

Bibliography: J. MCSORLEY, *Father Hecker and His Friends* (2d ed. St. Louis 1953). V. F. HOLDEN, *The Yankee Paul: Isaac Thomas Hecker* (Milwaukee, WI 1958).

[V. F. HOLDEN]

BAKER, NELSON HENRY

Domestic prelate, servant of underprivileged; b. Buffalo, N.Y., Feb. 16, 1841; d. Lackawanna, N.Y., July 29, 1936. After his early education in public schools he went into business, but in 1868 resumed his education at Canisius College, Buffalo, as one of its first students. He entered Our Lady of Angels Seminary at Niagara

University, N.Y., in 1870, and was ordained on March 19, 1876. For five years he served as assistant pastor at Lackawanna, then as curate in Corning, N.Y. (then part of the Buffalo diocese). In 1882 he was recalled to Lackawanna to succeed Rev. Vincent Hines as superintendent of the institution destined to become Our Lady of Victory Homes of Charity, with an orphanage, industrial school, home for infants, and maternity hospital. Baker was named vicar general of the Buffalo diocese (1902), made a domestic prelate (1905), and later raised to the rank of prothonotary apostolic. The Basilica of Our Lady of Victory was consecrated in 1926, and, with the adjacent homes of charity, was administered by Baker for the rehabilitation of countless underprivileged men, women, and children.

Bibliography: F. ANDERSON, *Father Baker* (Milwaukee 1960).

[P. J. RIGA]

BAKHITA, GIUSEPPINA (JOSEPHINE), ST.

Also known as *Madre Moretta* (Black Mother), emancipated slave, religious of Daughter of Charity of Canossa (*Istituto delle Figlie della Caritá*); b. *c.* 1869–70, Darfur, the Sudan, North Africa; d. Feb. 8, 1947, at Schio near Vicenza, Venezia, Italy.

Although ''Bakhita,'' meaning ''lucky one,'' is treated as her surname, it was the name given to Giuseppina by the slave traders, who kidnapped the young (about age 7) Islamic girl. She was sold to various owners in the markets of El Obeid and Khartoum, where her fifth master, the Italian Consul Callisto Legnani, purchased her at about age 12. When Legnani returned to Genoa with Bakhita, the wife of his friend Augusto Michieli asked and received permission to keep the slave with her. Bakhita became the nanny to Mimmina Michieli and moved with the family to Zianigo in Venezia. The Michielis returned to Africa to manage a new hotel, but entrusted their daughter and Bakhita to the Canossian Sisters in Venice. There she was formally introduced to the faith. A few months later on Jan. 9, 1890, Bakhita was baptized Giuseppina, confirmed, and received her first Communion. Upon the return of the Michielis, Bakhita adamantly expressed her desire to remain with the Canossians. Signora Michieli claimed ownership but the cardinal archbishop of Venice and the king's procurator intervened to declare her a free woman. She entered the novitiate Dec. 7, 1893 and was consecrated Dec. 8, 1896. Sister Giuseppina served her sisters for 25 years as cook, seamstress, and portress at the houses of Venice, Verona (1896–1902), and Schio (1902–47). She was especially beloved by the students for her sweet nature and musical voice. Before her final illness, Giuseppina traveled throughout Italy to raise money for the missions.

The process for her beatification began 12 years after her death. She was declared venerable Dec. 1, 1978 and beatified by Pope John Paul II on May 17, 1992. After the required post-beatification miracle at Mother Giuseppina's intercession was approved Dec. 21, 1998, the consistory for her canonization was held July 2, 1999. John Paul II canonized this first Sudanese saint Oct. 1, 2000, as a witness to evangelical reconciliation and a model of freedom. The portrait of the former slave now hangs in the cathedral at Khartoum, Sudan. Additionally, the documentary *The Two Suitcases* was based on her life.

Feast: Feb. 8.

Bibliography: *M. Bakhita: Saintly Daughter of Africa Tells Her Story* (Harere 1997). *Bakhita,* (Kinshasa 1983). R. I. ZANINI, *Bakhita* (Milan 2000)

[K. I. RABENSTEIN]

BAKÓCZ, TAMÁS

Cardinal, prince primate of Hungary; b. Erdoed (Szatmar), *c.* 1442; d. June 15, 1521. He received his education in Hungary, Poland, and the Italian cities of Ferrara and Padua, where he obtained a doctor's degree. Returning to Hungary in 1470, he became secretary and confidant to King Matthias (Hunyadi). He was appointed bishop of Györ and member of the royal council in 1490, bishop of Eger and archbishop of Esztergom in 1497, cardinal in 1500, and titular patriarch of Constantinople ten years later.

Bakócz was Hungary's principal statesman until his death, and his policies were not free of the intrigue and bribery typical of Renaissance diplomacy. Invited by Julius II to attend the general Roman synod of 1512, he became influential in the committee for the reform of the Church and the Roman Curia. In the conclave in 1513 he was supported by Emperor Maximilian and by Venice, but his chance of election failed because the Italian cardinals feared that Bakócz as pope would devote his power exclusively to the destruction of the Ottoman menace. The new pope, Leo X, appointed him legate *a latere* for Hungary with a bull for a new crusade. George Dózsa was commissioned to form an army, but the opposition of the nobles turned the plan into a futile and bloody peasant revolt. Discredited, Bakócz retired from public life in 1516. He was a noted and generous patron of the arts, and built the famous Bakócz chapel, one of the few remaining masterpieces of the Hungarian Renaissance, in the original basilica of his primatial see in Esztergom.

Tapestry of St. Giuseppina Bakhita hung during her beatification ceremony, 1992. (AP/Wide World Photos)

Bibliography: V. FRAKÓI, *Ungarn vor der Schlacht bei Mohacs, 1524–26,* tr. J. H. SCHWICKER (Budapest 1886). S. DOMANOVSZKY, ed., *Magyar müvelödéstörténet,* 5 v. (Budapest 1939–42) v. 2, Magyar Renaissance. B. HOMAN and G. SZEKFÜ, *Magyar történet,* 5 v. (Budapest 1935–36). L. TOTH, *Dictionnaire d'histoire et de géographie ecclésiastiques* 6: 291–92. *Wetzer und Welte Kirchenlexicon,* v. 1 (2d ed. Freiburg 1882) 1862–67.

[G. C. PAIKERT]

BALAAM

Oriental seer summoned by Balak, king of Moab, to curse the invading Israelites who threatened to overrun Moab (Nm 22.1–7). Balaam came from ''the land of the Amauites,'' a region in northern Syria, to the west of the Euphrates, between Aleppo and Carchemish. The story of how Balaam's attempts to curse Israel were turned by Yahweh into blessings for Israel teaches the truth that even the pagan seer is subject to Israel's God; he is but the minister of God's word, and he can say only what God permits (Nm 23.12; 24.13). The OT concept of the intrinsic power of the spoken word in a CURSE or a BLESSING is taken for granted in the story. YAHWIST and ELOHIST traditions have been merged in the narrative, causing some discrepancies in the account.

A highlight in the story is the folk tale of Balaam's talking ass (Nm 22.22–35). The popular story makes the point that God's control over all nature, animate and inanimate, is so complete that He can use any form of nature as the instrument of His powerful revealing word. In this case He spoke through a harassed beast of burden, as later He would continue to utter His mighty word through a pagan diviner. Even a nonbeliever could serve temporarily as His prophet.

The hopes of King Balak were dashed when each attempt of Balaam to curse Israel misfired and turned into a blessing. The seer uttered three oracles at the request of the king, each time at a different location. But neither the new place nor the prepared ritual could thwart the protective care of Yahweh over His people. Balac finally gave up in despair and sent Balaam northward to his homeland.

The seer's fourth and final oracle, unsolicited by Balak, was a message to the enraged king predicting a smashing Israelite triumph over Moab. Part of this prophecy (Nm 24.17–18) was fulfilled in the Davidic triumph over Moab and Edom (2 Sm 8.2, 13–14), and it is possibly involved in the symbolism of the story of the Magi (Mt 2.1–12; *see* INFANCY NARRATIVES). It does not follow from this, however, that all the oracles of Balaam in Numbers 23–24 date from the 10th century B.C., the time of David. They are now ascribed by many competent scholars to the late 13th or early 12th century B.C., since they contain many archaic grammatical and stylistic features that are absent in later poetry.

Balaam is described in an entirely different light in Numbers 31.8, 16; Joshua 13.22. Here he is instrumental in leading the Israelites into infidelity and is executed by them. In the NT, therefore, he becomes a type for false teachers (2 Pt 2.16; Jude 11; Rv 2.14). Rabbinical sources have generally treated him with similar disdain.

Bibliography: *Encylopedic Dictionary of the Bible,* tr. and adap. by L. HARTMAN, (New York 1963), from A. VAN DEN BORN, *Bijbels Woordenboek,* 192–193. W. F. ALBRIGHT, ''The Oracles of Balaam,'' *Journal of Biblical Literature,* 63 (1944) 207–233.

[F. L. MORIARTY]

BALASSA, BÁLINT

Hungarian soldier-poet; b. Kékko, 1551; d. Esztergom, May 26, 1594. His education was supervised by Peter Bornemisza, court chaplain at the Balassas' baronial estate. Balassa's life was a succession of stormy adventures—of heroic deeds and audacious highway robberies. One day he was the ideal *miles christianus* practicing the vows of a monk, the next day he was accused of incest and was involved in endless lawsuits. In 1574 he fought against the Turks at Eger, and after an escape to Transylvania and Poland he resumed his personal war against them. In 1584 he married his cousin, Christine Dobó, but the marriage was nullified two years later when Balassa became a Catholic. In 1594 he fought at Esztergom, and almost in the midst of clashing arms he translated Edmund CAMPION's *Decem Rationes,* a pamphlet defending Catholic teaching. During the siege he received a mortal wound; his last words were ''My God, I have been Thy soldier.'' His poems fall into three categories: religious hymns, martial songs, and love poems. For beauty, sincerity, and expression of passion there is nothing to match them in 16th-century Hungarian literature. He was also the inventor of new verse forms.

Bibliography: B. BALASSA, *Minden munkái,* ed. L. DÉZSI, 2 v. (Budapest 1923). J. REMÉNYI, *Three Hungarian Poets: Bálint Balassa, Miklós Zrinyi, Mihály Csokonai Vitéz* (Washington 1955).

[O. J. EGRES]

BALAT, THÉODORIC, ST.

Franciscan priest, martyr, b. Oct. 28, 1858, St. Martin de Tours, Diocese of Albi, France; d. July 9, 1900, Taiyüan, Shansi Province, China. Théodoric, the son of Jean François Balat and Rose Taillefer, entered the minor seminary at Lavour at age 11 and became a member of the Third Order of St. Francis. While studying at the major seminary at Albi, Théodoric was inspired by a visiting Franciscan to take that Order's habit. He entered the novitiate at Pau (June 29, 1880), and made his first profession at Woodlands, England (June 30, 1881), where he remained several years. On July 2, 1884, he was solemnly professed. He made a pilgrimage to La Verna, Assisi, and the Holy Land prior to joining the Chinese mission (October 1884). During the course of his successful apostolate in Taiyüan (from December 1, 1885), he served Bp. Gregorio GRASSI as teacher in the minor seminary, novice master, mission promoter, and chaplain to the Franciscan Missionaries of Mary. At the outbreak of persecution, he refused to leave. He was arrested with the sisters to whom he gave his final blessing before being execution. He was beatified by Pope Pius XII (Nov. 24, 1946) and canonized (Oct.1, 2000) by Pope John Paul II with Augustine Zhao Rong and companions.

Feast: July 4; July 8 (Franciscans).

Bibliography: *Acta Apostolicae Sedis* 39 (1947) 213–221, 307–311. *Les Vingt-neuf martyrs de Chine, massacrés en 1900, béatifiés par Sa Sainteté Pie XII, le 24 novembre, 1946* (Rome 1946). P. X. MERTENS, *Du sang chrétien sur le fleuve jaune. Actes de martyrs dans la Chine contemporaine* (Paris 1937). L. MINER, *China's Book of Martyrs: A Record of Heroic Martyrdoms and Marvelous Deliverances of Chinese Christians during the Summer of 1900* (Ann Arbor 1994). J. SIMON, *Sous le sabre des Boxers* (Lille 1955). C. TESTORE, *Sangue e palme sul fiume giallo. I beati martiri cinesi nella persecuzione della Boxe Celi Sud-Est, 1900* (Rome 1955). *L'Osservatore Romano,* Eng. Ed. 40 (2000): 1–2, 10.

[K. I. RABENSTEIN]

BALDACHINO

Overhanging used as a mark of honor, named after Baghdad whence came the cloth originally used for this purpose. The more generic term for this covering is canopy. There are two chief forms of the fixed canopy: (1) the civory (*ciborium*), a structure in stone, metal, or wood consisting of four or more columns, united by an arch or architrave, roofed, highly decorated, and built over an altar; (2) the baldachin (*baldachino*) or tester, which is simpler in form and consists of a smaller, lighter structure of metal or wood (carved and gilded, and often adorned with textiles) either hung over an altar, or attached to the wall behind, like a bracket, or supported at the back by two pillars so that it juts over the altar like the canopy of a throne. A canopy of some form has been used as a mark of distinction over altars since the 4th century.

Another type of canopy is that placed over the throne of a ''greater prelate,'' i.e., a cardinal anywhere, or a nuncio, apostolic delegate, archbishop, bishop, or abbot in the place of his jurisdiction, as a mark of honor and a sign of authority.

In the medieval period, a portable canopy—a collapsible, ornamental awning of silk or other precious material—sustained by four, six, or eight poles, or in the form of a large ornamental umbrella, was borne as a mark of honor over the Blessed Sacrament in procession, as well as over the pope, a cardinal legate at his solemn entry into the place of his legacy, and a bishop for his first solemn entry into his cathedral or other church of his diocese.

Bibliography: J. B. O'CONNELL, *Church Building and Furnishing* (Notre Dame, IN 1955) 183–186. J. BRAUN, *I Paramenti sacri*, tr. G. ALLIOD (Turin 1914) 180–182, 215–217.

[J. B. O'CONNELL/EDS.]

BALDINUCCI, ANTONIO, BL.

Jesuit and preacher of popular missions; b. Florence, Italy, June 19, 1665; d. Pofio, Nov. 7, 1717. Baldinucci entered the famous Jesuit novitiate of Sant' Andrea, Rome, on April 21, 1681. He was ordained on Oct. 28, 1695. His precarious health led his superiors to refuse his repeated requests to labor as a missionary in India. Instead he was assigned in 1697 to mission work in the Italian provinces of Abruzzi and Romagna. During his remaining 20 years Baldinucci preached 448 popular missions, one to two weeks in length, traveling on foot (usually barefoot) from town to town. His preaching manner was dramatic, impassioned, and extraordinarily successful. He always carried with him a miraculous picture of the Madonna, and frequently preached laden with chains or bearing a heavy cross. At times he scourged himself publicly until blood flowed to obtain the conversion of hardened sinners. His techniques, while startling, were effective for the audiences of his day. He collapsed in October 1717 while serving the sick of his famine-stricken area. Leo XIII beatified him in 1893.

Feast: July 2 (Jesuits).

Bibliography: F. J. CORLEY and R. J. WILLMES, *Wings of Eagles: The Jesuit Saints and Blessed* (Milwaukee, WI 1941). F. M. GALLUZZI, *Vida del venerable padre Antonio Baldinucci, misionero apostolico de la Compañia de Jesus* (Mexico City 1760). J. N. TYLENDA, *Jesuit Saints and Martyrs* (Chicago 1998) 378–80. E. LAMALLE, *Dictionnaire d'histoire et de géographie ecclésiastiques,* ed. A. BAUDRILLART (Paris 1912–) 6:337–339. C. SOMMERVOGEL, *Bibliotèque de la Compagnie de Jésus,* 11 v. (Brussels-Paris 1890–1932) 1:828–829; 8:1733. *Acta Sanctorum* Nov. 3:723–742.

[F. A. SMALL]

Baldachino in Santa Maria Maggiore, built by Ferdinando Fuga, 1740s, Rome. (©Michael S. Yamashita/CORBIS)

BALDO, GIUSEPPE, BL.

Priest and founder of the Little Daughters of Saint Joseph; b. Puegnago (near Brescia), Lombardy, Italy, Feb. 19, 1843; d. Ronco all'Adige near Verona, Oct. 24, 1915. Son of the farmers Angelo Baldo and his wife Hippolita Casa, Baldo entered the seminary of Verona (1859) and was ordained with papal indult for the Diocese of Verona in 1865 at age twenty-two. After serving as a parish priest for a time, he was appointed vice-rector of the seminary. During his decade of teaching, Baldo wrote books on spirituality and pedagogy. In 1877, he asked for and received a parochial position at Ronco all'Adige. Although he was contemplative and devoted to the Eucharist, he was also active in social work for the poor and marginalized. He established a mutual benefit society, schools for adults and children, a nursery, and a farm loan bank. He organized the Servants of Charity of Our Lady of Succor to care for the homebound sick, then founded a hospital (1888) and the Little Daughters of St. Joseph to staff it (1894). Baldo also established an Archconfraternity of Christian Mothers, a Blessed Sacrament Confraternity, and a Society of the Forty Hours devotion. Baldo's holiness was especially evident in his patient endurance of illness during the last two years of his life. In 1950, his mortal remains were enshrined in his parish chapel. He was beatified by John Paul II, Oct. 31, 1989.

Bibliography: F. MALGERI, *Don Giuseppe Baldo Prete di Ronco all'Adige* (Turin 1995). E. VALENTINI, *Il messaggio pedagogico sociale del servo di Dio, Don Giuseppe Baldo* (Verona 1956).

[K. I. RABENSTEIN]

BALDWIN, KING OF JERUSALEM

Five kings of the Crusaders' Kingdom of JERUSALEM bore the name Baldwin.

Baldwin I, King of Jerusalem (1100–18). Born Baldwin of Boulogne, brother of GODFREY OF BOUILLON, founder of the first Crusaders' principality in Edessa (*see* CRUSADERS' STATES). On his brother's death he was welcomed in Jerusalem by the Lorraine party, and Godfrey's vassals swore allegiance. The Patriarch Daimbert of Pisa was constrained to crown him king (Dec. 25, 1100), and Daimbert's ambition to establish a churchstate were ultimately thwarted. Baldwin inherited a desperate economic and military situation, but within ten years, with the aid of the Genoese, whom he rewarded handsomely, he had occupied the ports of Arsuf, Caesarea, Acre, Beirut, and Sidon, the last-named with assistance from a Norwegian expedition. Meanwhile, he had beaten back Egyptian attacks, resisted pressure from the north and east, and aided in the capture of Tripoli (1109). Castles had been built at Toron in Galilee and Montréal (Shaubak), south of the Dead Sea, and the kingdom's boundaries had been extended to Ailah on the Gulf of Aqaba. Baldwin terrorized his enemies but was tolerant toward his native subjects. He died on April 2, 1118, the real founder of the feudal kingdom of Jerusalem.

Baldwin II, King of Jerusalem (1118–31). Formerly of Le Bourg, cousin of Baldwin I and count of Edessa. After Roger of Antioch's death in the great defeat of June 27, 1119, the new king, already an experienced crusader, was able to stabilize the military situation. Although he was captured in April 1123 and not released until Aug. 29, 1124, Tyre was taken (July 7, 1124) with the aid of a Venetian fleet, which the king had earlier requested. During Baldwin II's reign the feudal structure of the kingdom was further developed, the Knights TEMPLAR were established, and the Knights of St. John (KNIGHTS OF MALTA), militarized. An important Church council was held at Nablus in 1120. Under Baldwin II the authority of the King of Jerusalem over the other Crusaders' states reached a point not to be maintained afterward. His suzerainty was recognized, and he frequently acted as regent. In 1128 he took steps to prepare for the succession to the throne by sending to France. Fulk V of Anjou was selected and married the king's daughter, Melisend. Baldwin II was the last of the original crusaders. His death (Aug. 21, 1131) marked the end of an era in the Latin Orient.

Baldwin III, King of Jerusalem (1143–63). Son of King Fulk and Melisend. Since Baldwin was only 13 years old when his father died, the barons decided that he and his mother, Melisend, should be crowned jointly. The young ruler soon proved his courage and skill and grew to be a highly respected king of engaging personality, wide interests, and considerable administrative and diplomatic ability. His early years were troubled by the fall of Edessa (1144), the failure of the Second CRUSADE, in which he participated, and the rise of Nureddin. Since the joint rule with his mother had not worked well, Baldwin, acting on the advice of the barons, was crowned alone in 1151. In 1153 he achieved his greatest success, the capture of Ascalon, the last port still in Muslim hands. This operation foreshadowed a southward orientation of the kingdom's military effort, which coincided with the decline of the Fatimid caliphate in Egypt. The success was, however, somewhat offset by Nureddin's taking of Damascus in the following year and the largely ineffective countermoves on the part of the Crusaders. Another feature of Baldwin III's reign that foreshadowed future policies was the move toward rapprochement with Byzantium. In September of 1158 the king married Theodora, niece of Emperor Manuel I Comnenus. On April 12, 1159, the emperor entered Antioch with great ceremony. Plans for joint action against the Muslims did not materialize as Manuel, to the dismay of the Latins, accepted Nureddin's offer to negotiate. Nevertheless, the emperor did not then press the demands that he had previously made on Antioch or break with the Crusaders. In fact, on Dec. 25, 1161, he married Maria of Antioch. That the Latin kingdom had achieved a status in European affairs seems evident in Pope ALEXANDER III's seeking its declaration against the antipope. When Baldwin III died (Feb. 10, 1163) he was mourned by friend and foe alike. The historian WILLIAM OF TYRE eulogized him as the ideal king.

Baldwin IV, King of Jerusalem (1174–85), and Baldwin V. Nephew of Baldwin III, son of King Amalric I. He was only 13 years old at the time of his father's death. He had been tutored by William of Tyre, and he possessed a keen intelligence. Despite the affliction of leprosy, he displayed heroic fortitude in carrying on his duties. The state of his health necessitated frequent regencies, and these in turn gave rise to internal dissension just at the time SALADIN was completing the union of Egypt and Syria. In 1183 he had his five-year old nephew, Baldwin, crowned and shortly afterward arrangements were made for the guardianship in the event of his own death. Baldwin IV died early in 1185. The death of the boy king, Baldwin V, only a few months later in 1186 was the prelude to the fall of the kingdom.

Bibliography: For the early period, especially Baldwin I, consult *Historia Hierosolymitana*, ed. H. HAGENMEYER (Heidelberg 1913). For the later period, especially after 1127, consult WILLIAM OF TYRE, *Historia rerum in partibus transmarinis gestarum (Recueil des historiens des croisades: Historiens occidentaux* 1; Paris 1844); Eng. *A History of Deeds Done beyond the Sea*, ed. and tr. E. A. BABCOCK and A. C. KREY, 2 v. (New York 1943). J. L. LA MONTE, *Feudal Monarchy in . . . Jerusalem . . .* (Cambridge, Mass. 1932). S. RUNCIMAN, *A History of the Crusades*, 3 v. (Cambridge, Eng. 1951–54). K. M. SETTON, ed., *A History of the Crusades* (Philadelphia 1955—).

[M. W. BALDWIN]

BALDWIN OF CANTERBURY

Cistercian archbishop of Canterbury, canonist; b. Diocese of Exeter, England; d. Acre, Nov. 19 or 20, 1190. Born of humble stock, Baldwin was a learned product of the school of Exeter, perhaps a pupil of ROBERT PULLEN, and later himself a master of the school. Baldwin first emerges clearly as tutor to Gratian (the later *Cardinalis*), nephew of Pope INNOCENT II, at Ferentino (Italy) after November of 1150. Appointed archdeacon of Totnes (near Exeter) by BARTHOLOMEW OF EXETER, soon after the latter's consecration in 1161, he was much immersed in diocesan administration in the following years. The protégé of Bartholomew and a friend of the canonist Bishop ROGER OF WORCESTER and of JOHN OF SALISBURY, Baldwin was an emphatic supporter of Thomas BECKET in his dispute with King HENRY II from 1163. At the height of the conflict, he retired to the CISTERCIAN abbey of Ford (*c.* 1169) and by 1175 was its abbot. He succeeded Roger as bishop of WORCESTER (Aug. 10, 1180) and RICHARD OF CANTERBURY as archbishop of Canterbury (December of 1184). His rule at Worcester was marked by pastoral care and zealous administration, but that at Canterbury, while revealing similar characteristics, was marred by long and bitter strife with the monks in which he enjoyed the support of King Henry II, but lacked that of the popes (successively URBAN III, GREGORY VIII, and CLEMENT III). Baldwin visited the Welsh Church as legate in 1187 and preached the Third CRUSADE in Wales in 1188, having taken the cross at Geddington on February 11 of that year. He died while on the Crusade.

An ascetic and spiritual prelate, whose character and temperament have been variously assessed, Baldwin was a distinguished scholar. His works included *De commendatione fidei, De sacramento altaris*, and 16 extant sermons. An eminent canonist, he was appointed judge delegate by Pope Alexander III on several occasions while still at Ford, and later as bishop and archbishop he left a remarkable imprint in the primitive English decretal collections from *c.* 1179 (*see* DECRETALISTS).

Bibliography: Works. *Patrologia Latina* 204:401–774; 202:1533. *Chronicles and Memorials of the Reign of Richard I*, ed. W. STUBBS, 2 v. (*Rerum Britannicarum medii aevi scriptores* 38; 1864–65), v. 2. P. GUÉBIN, ''Deux sermons inédits . . . ,'' *Journal of Theological Studies* 13 (1911–12) 571–74. *Baudouin de Ford: Le Sacrement de l'autel*, ed. J. MORSON, French tr. E. DE SOLMS, 2 v. (Paris 1963), introd. J. LECLERQ. Literature. B. E. A. JONES, *The Acta of Archbishops Richard and Baldwin: 1174–90* (Doctoral diss. unpub. London 1964). W. HUNT, *The Dictionary of National Biography from the Earliest Times to 1900* 1:952–54. J. M. CANIVEZ, *Dictionnaire d'histoire et de géographie ecclésiastiques* 6:1415–16; *Dictionnaire de spiritualité ascétique et mystique. Doctrine et histoire* 1:1285–86. R. FOREVILLE, *L'Église et la royauté en Angleterre sous Henri II Plantagenet* (Paris 1943) 533–54. D. KNOWLES, *The Monastic Order in England 943–1216* (Cambridge, Eng. 1962) 316–22. C. DUGGAN, *Twelfth-Century Decretal Collections and Their Importance in English History* (London 1963) 110–15.

[C. DUGGAN]

BALES, CHRISTOPHER, BL.

Priest, martyr; *alias* Evers; b. ca. 1564, Coniscliffe near Darlington, Durham, England; hanged, drawn, and quartered in Fleet Street opposite Fetter Lane, London, March 4, 1590. Bales began his studies for the priesthood at the English College in Rome (1583), but he was sent to Rheims after contracting tuberculosis. He was ordained at Douay (March 28, 1587). Soon after his return to England (Nov. 2, 1588), he was arrested, racked, and tortured by Topcliffe (hung up by the hands for 24 hours at a time). He was condemned for high treason—for having been ordained abroad and coming to England to exercise his office. He asked Judge Anderson whether St. Augustine of Canterbury, apostle of the English, was also a traitor. The judge said no, but that the act had since been made treason by law. On the gibbet was set a placard: ''For treason and favoring foreign invasion.'' He spoke to the people from the ladder, showing them that his only ''treason'' was his priesthood. Executed on the same day was Bl. Nicholas HORNER for having made Bales a jerkin, and Bl. Alexander BLAKE for lodging him in his house. Bales was beatified by Pius XI on Dec. 15, 1929.

Feast of the English Martyrs: May 4 (England).

See Also: ENGLAND, SCOTLAND, AND WALES, MARTYRS OF.

Bibliography: R. CHALLONER, *Memoirs of Missionary Priests,* ed. J. H. POLLEN (rev. ed. London 1924; repr. Farnborough 1969). H. FOLEY, *Records of the English Province of the Society of Jesus,* 7 v. (London 1877–82). J. MORRIS, *The Catholics of York under Elizabeth* (London 1891). J. H. POLLEN, *Acts of English Martyrs* (London 1891).

[K. I. RABENSTEIN]

BALL, FRANCES MARY TERESA

Foundress of the Irish branch of the SISTERS OF LORETTO (Institute of the Blessed Virgin Mary): b. Dublin, Jan. 6, 1794; d. Dublin, May 19, 1861. Her father, a wealthy Dublin silk weaver, sent her to the Institute of the Blessed Virgin Mary, Micklegate Bar, York, England, for her education. In 1814 Bishop (later Archbishop) Daniel MURRAY of Dublin, hoping to introduce the institute into Ireland, arranged for her to make her novitiate at York. In 1822 Frances, now Mother Teresa, established Loretto House, the first Irish branch of the institute, at Rathfarnham, Dublin. After Catholic EMANCIPATION (1829), which afforded new opportunities for Catholic education, she opened boarding, day, and free schools in rapid succession. Guided by Peter Kenny, SJ, Tom Bourke, OP, and Archbishop D. Murray, she sent her sisters to India to found the first Loretto (or Loreto) foreign mission (1841). There were 34 Loretto convents in Ireland, England, Spain, Canada, India, Mauritius, and Gibraltar by 1861. Before 1900 the institute had spread to Australia and Africa.

Bibliography: H. J. COLERIDGE, *Life of Mother Frances Mary Teresa Ball* (London 1881). *Joyful Mother of Children* by a Loreto Sister (Dublin 1961).

[M. M. SHANAHAN]

BALL, JOHN

Priest, leader of the English Peasants' Revolt; d. Saint Albans, *c.* July 15, 1381. First heard of at York, where he was probably attached to the Benedictine abbey of St. Mary's, he later removed to Colchester. SIMON ISLIP, archbishop of Canterbury, excommunicated him sometime between 1362 and 1366, and Archbishops SIMON LANGHAM (1366) and SIMON OF SUDBURY (1376) confirmed the sentence, but Ball nevertheless continued to preach both in churches and out of doors and to circulate rhyming letters embodying radical views. Arrested in 1381, he was in the archbishop's prison at Maidstone, Kent, when the peasants' revolt started. Released by the rebels, he proceeded with them to Canterbury, Rochester, and Blackheath, where he incited them to murder nobles and lawyers, using the text, ''When Adam delved and Eve span, who was then the gentleman?'' His advocacy of complete social equality probably inspired some of the peasants' demands. Ball was among those who entered the Tower of London and murdered Sudbury. He was present at the young King Richard II's interview with Wat Tyler at Smithfield. Subsequently he fled, was captured at Coventry, brought before Richard, condemned for treason, and executed. Modern writers question Ball's sanity. His views were partly John WYCLIF's, especially on withholding TITHES from unworthy clergy, but his confession linking Wyclif with the revolt is unquestionably fraudulent.

Bibliography: THOMAS WALSINGHAM, *Historia Anglicana*, ed. H. T. RILEY, 2 v. (*Rerum Britannicarum medii aevi scriptores* 28.1; 1863–64) 2:32–34. *Fasciculi zizaniorum*, ed. W. W. SHIRLEY, (ibid. 5; 1858). J. GAIRDNER, *The Dictionary of National Biography from the Earliest Times to 1900* 1:993–94. H. B. WORKMAN, *Dictionnaire d'histoire et de géographie ecclésiastiques* 6:392. G. M. TREVELYAN, *England in the Age of Wycliffe* (new ed. London 1909; repr. 1948) 183–255. G. R. OWST, *Literature and Pulpit in Medieval England* (2d ed. New York 1961), *passim.* A. B. STEEL, *Richard II* (Cambridge, Eng. 1941; repr. 1963) 58–91. W. L. WARREN, ''The Peasants' Revolt,'' *History Today* 12 (1962) 845–53; 13 (1963) 44–51.

[R. W. HAYS]

BALLERINI, ANTONIO

Jesuit moral theologian; b. Medicina, near Bologna, Oct. 10, 1805; d. Rome, Nov. 27, 1881. He entered the Society of Jesus in 1826 and became professor of Church history at the Gregorian University in Rome in 1844 and then professor of moral theology in 1855. Among his early writing was *Sylloge monumentorum ad mysterium conceptionis Immaculatae Virginis Deiparae illustrandum* (2 v. Rome 1854–56), an historic work. Turning to moral theology, he published *De morali systemate s. Alphonsi M. de Ligorio* (Rome 1863) and then contributed annotations to the 17th edition of J. P. Gury's *Compendium theologiae moralis* (2 v. Rome 1866), which added to the value and to the further widespread use of that work. Ballerini was a strong defender of probabilism, and his interpretation of certain Alphonsian doctrines brought him into controversy with some of the Redemptorists. His last great work, *Opus theologicum morale in Busembaum medullam,* was nearly completed at the time of his death, and the last volume was written by D. Palmieri (7 v. Prato 1889–93). Ballerini was outstanding among his contemporaries for his contribution to the restoration and progress of moral theology.

Bibliography: C. SOMMERVOGEL et al., *Bibliothèquede la Compagnie de Jésus*, II v. (Brussels-Paris 1890–1932) 1:843–48, 8:1733–34. R. BROUILLARD, *Dictionnaire d'histoire et de géographie ecclésiastiques* 6:398–99. C. SOMMERVOGEL, *Dictionnaire de théologie catholique* 2.1:130–31. H. HURTER, *Nomenclator literarius theologiae catholicae* 5.2:1793–95.

[J. C. WILLKE]

BALLERINI, PIETRO AND GIROLAMO

Patristic scholars and theologians; Pietro, b. Sept. 7, 1698, d. March 28, 1769; Girolamo, b. Jan. 29, 1702, d. Feb. 23, 1781. The brothers, sons of a surgeon, were born and educated in Verona. Pietro was ordained in 1722 and became the principal of a classical school in Verona. Several propositions in his book on usury were condemned by Benedict XIV in the bull *Vix pervenit* (1745). But together with Girolamo (ordained 1725), Pietro opposed the Jansenists (*see* JANSENISM), and the Febronian party, which questioned the administrative power of the pope.

The Ballerinis' primary service to scholarship consisted in a close collaboration in editing ecclesiastical works, particularly the writings of several fathers of the Church. Between 1729 and 1732, they published four volumes of the historical and other writings of Cardinal Henry Noris, a Veronese compatriot. In quick succession, but with careful scholarship, they brought out *S. Zenonis, Episcopi Veronensis, Sermones* (with notes, 1739); *S. Antonini, Archiepiscopi Florentini, Summa Theologica* (with a life of the author, 4 parts, 1740–41); and *Ratherii, Episcopi Veronensis, Opera* (1765). At the request of Benedict XIV, they prepared a new edition of the works of St. Leo the Great to replace that of the Gallican-tainted Pasquier Quesnel (1675); theirs is still the standard edition (complete with notes, 3 v., Venice 1753–57; reprinted *Patrologia Latina* v. 54–56). Pietro published a history of probabilism, *Saggio della Storia del Probabilismo* (Verona 1736); *De vi et ratione Primatus Romanorum Pontificum* (1766); and *De Potestate Ecclesiastica Summorum Pontificum et Conciliorum Generalium* (1765).

Bibliography: A. DE MEYER, *Dictionnaire d'histoire et de géographie ecclésiastiques* 6:399–401. W. TELFER, ''The Codex Verona LX (58) Note B,'' *Harvard Theological Review* 36 (1943) 231–32. C. VERSCHAFFEL, *Dictionnaire de théologie catholique* (Paris 1903–50) 2.1:131–32.

[F. X. MURPHY]

BALMACEDA, FRANCISCO

Chilean ascetic; b. Ibscache, Oct. 2, 1772; d. Santiago, Nov. 2, 1842. He studied at the Convictorio Carolino and was ordained by Bishop Marán. Heir to a great fortune, he personally administered his hacienda in Ibscache. According to one of his biographers, ''He took special care of the moral and physical well-being of its tenants''; he taught them prayers, reading, writing, and arithmetic; he also provided them with seeds and farming tools. Many families in Santiago lived on the crops from his hacienda. Upon his mother's death, he gave away to the San Borja Hospital, among other smaller donations, his farm in Ibscache and a second one he had acquired for that purpose. He kept nothing for himself, except 1,000 pesos per year and the modest house in which he lived. A tall, strong man, inflamed with zeal, he had great self-control and practiced asceticism to the point of appearing strange. During hot weather he wore heavy garments; when it rained he used to walk in the middle of the street, unmindful of the rain. For many years he lived on boiled vegetables. On the morning of Nov. 2, 1842, on his way to the chapel of some neighboring nuns where he used to celebrate Mass, he collapsed in agony on his own doorstep. Some considered him an eccentric; yet the majority of the people of his time, particularly the poor, thought him a saint.

Bibliography: F. DE P. TAFORÓ, ''Don Francisco Balmaceda,'' *Revista de Sud-América* 3 (Valparaíso 1862) 735–41. E. BALMACEDA VALDÉS, *La familia Balmaceda* (Santiago 1919) 107–17.

[A. M. ESCUDERO]

BALMERINO, ABBEY OF

Former CISTERCIAN abbey on the south bank of the Tay in Fifeshire, Scotland, in the old Diocese of Saint Andrews. It was founded and richly endowed by King Alexander II and his mother, Queen Ermengarde, *c.* 1227 and colonized by monks from MELROSE on Dec. 13, 1229. The abbey was dedicated to St. Mary and St. Edward the Confessor. After it had been sacked and burned by the English under Admiral Wyndham on Dec. 25, 1547, and desecrated by Reformers in 1559, the abbey was erected into a temporal lordship by the royal charters of 1603 and 1607 for Sir James Elphinstone, first Lord Balmerino. Only ruins now remain.

Bibliography: W. B. TURNBULL, ed., *The Chartularies of Balmerino and Lindores* (Edinburgh 1841). J. M. CANIVEZ, ed., *Statuta capitulorum generalium ordinis cisterciensis ab anno 1116 ad annum 1786,* 8 v. (Louvain 1933–41) 2:63. J. WILKIE, *The Benedictine Monasteries of Northern Fife* (Edinburgh 1927). D. E. EASSON, *Medieval Religious Houses: Scotland* (London 1957) 62.

[L. MACFARLANE]

BALMES, JAIME LUCIANO

Spanish secular priest and philosopher; b. Vich, Catalonia, Aug. 28, 1810; d. there, July 9, 1848. He studied in the seminary at Vich (1817–26) and at the University of Cervera (1826–35). He was ordained in 1834 and received his degree in theology the following year. Returning to Vich, he taught mathematics in the seminary. The next eight years witnessed his prodigious expansion of activity devoted to the apologetical, philosophical, sociological, and political aspects of current problems. In Barcelona he founded and directed *La Civilización* (1841–43) and *La Sociedad* (1843–44). In Madrid he edited *El Pensamiento de la nación* (1844–46) and *El Conciliador* (1845). He made his entry into politics in 1840 by writing forcefully against the ambitions of General Espartero in *Consideraciones políticas sobre la situación de España* (Barcelona 1840). In answer to the general thesis of F. Guizot, he wrote *El Protestantismo comparado con el Catolicismo en sus relaciones con la civilización europea* (4 v. Barcelona 1842–44). This is actually a philosophy of history and, at the same time, a basic sociology that considers the various influences of Catholicism on society. Some of the very last works he published are also apologetical in character: *Cartas a un escéptico* (Barcelona 1864) and *Pio IX* (Madrid 1847).

His second and more philosophical period of development began with the bombardment of Barcelona, when, protected in the Prat de Dalt (1843), he spent a month and a half writing *El Criterio* (Barcelona 1845), in which the right use of reason is described as good sense and clear thinking. In *Filosofía fundamental* (4 v. Barcelona 1846) he tried to protect youth from the errors of modern philosophy, namely, sensism, materialism, rationalism, idealism, and skepticism. As a textbook for students, he provided *Filosofía elemental* (4 v. Madrid 1847); this was translated into many languages, including Latin. The basic qualities of his thought are realism, objectivity, order and clarity, and naturalness and simplicity. He eliminated useless questions and complicated technicalities. A sensitive observer and analyst, he considered also the totality of things. He was profoundly human, balanced, and independent in spirit.

Balmes thought highly of St. THOMAS AQUINAS, whose *Summa* he studied for four years at Cervera, but he himself was bound to no school. He did not accept fundamental Thomistic doctrines, such as the real distinction between essence and existence, potency and act, substance and accidents, hylomorphism, the agent intellect, and impressed species. Under the influence of P. Buffier, he treated the problem of certitude on a subjective and psychological level; this teaching would influence the school of Louvain. His confident intuitionism was rooted in ''common sense'' or an ''intellectual instinct,'' upon which were established three fundamental truths: a first fact (''that I think''), a first principle (contradiction), and a first condition (evidence).

Balmes prepared the way for the resurgence of Christian philosophy. Not so much a precursor of the scholastic revival, he is better enumerated among the Catholic apologists of the early 19th century as one who excelled in solidity of thought, in philosophical formation, and in historical erudition. LEO XIII, whom Balmes had known in Brussels, described him as ''the foremost political talent of the 19th century and one of the greatest in the history of political writers.''

Bibliography: *Obras Completas,* ed. I. CASANOVAS, 33 v. (Barcelona 1925–27); also in 8 v. in *Biblioteca de autores cristianos* (Madrid 1948–50). I. CASANOVAS, *Balmes: La Seva vida, el seu temps, les sevas obres*, 3 v. (Barcelona 1932); ''Balmes en el primer centenario de su muerte, 1848–1948,'' *Pensamiento* 3 (1947).

[G. FRAILE]

BALSAMON, THEODORE

Twelfth-century Byzantine canonist; b. Constantinople, *c.* 1105; d. there, *c.* 1195. Of a Constantinopolitan family, Theodore was a deacon in the church of HAGIA SOPHIA and served the patriarch as his chief legal adviser, or chartophylax. He was elected patriarch of Antioch in his eighties (between 1185 and 1191), but he remained in Constantinople until his death.

His chief work is his commentary on the Photian *Nomocanon* of 14 titles that he composed at the suggestion of Emperor Manuel I Comnenus and Patriarch Michael of Anchialos. This was an attempt to solve the difficulties raised by contradictory Church laws and conflicting ecclesiastical and civil legislation. Besides the 14 titles, he clarified the whole collection of Byzantine law, relying strongly on work of the earlier canonist Zonaras. His principal interest for the historian is the number of documents he cites, frequently verbatim, that would be otherwise unknown.

In 1195 Patriarch Marcus of Alexandria directed some 60 questions to the permanent synod (*synodos endemousa*) at Constantinople. Balsamon gave the answers; but recent investigation has shown that a second recension of these answers was most probably due to the Metropolitan John of Chalcedon, a contemporary of Balsamon.

A series of canonical monographs that clarify the inner organization of Byzantine ecclesiastical offices in relation to the patriarchate are also the work of Balsamon. He defended the position of the legal adviser to the patriarch against the encroachments of the protecticos, the curial official who presided over lesser legal cases. Balsamon aided the patriarch in composing a series of synodal acts, including that dealing with the translation of Patriarch Dositheus to the See of Constantinople (1190). Several manuscripts attribute to his authorship scholia on the Old Testament prophets; and Fabricius credits him with an account of the martyrdom of Saints Theodore and Claudius.

Bibliography: J. P. MIGNE, ed., *Patrologia Graeca* 119:904–909, 1162–1224, monographs; v. 137–38. G. A. RHALLES and M. POTLES, *Syntagma tōn theiōn kai hierōn kanonōn,* 6 v. (Athens 1852–59) in Greek. L. PETIT, *Dictionnaire de théologie catholique* (Paris 1903–50) 2.1:135–37. E. HERMAN, *Dictionnaire de droit canonique* (Paris 1935–65) 2:76–83. V. NARBEKOV, *Der Nomokanon des Photios mit der Erklärung Balsamons,* 2 v. (Kazan 1888–89), in Russ. S. P. LAMPROS, *Byzantinische Zeitschrift* 5 (1896) 565–66. V. GRUMEL, *Revue des études byzantines* 1 (1943) 239–49, tr. H. G. BECK, *Kirche und theologische Literatur im byzantinischen Reich* 70–73, 657–58, bibliog.

[F. X. MURPHY]

BALTHASAR, HANS URS VON

Theologian, author, publisher, priest; b. Aug. 24, 1905 of an ancient Catholic Swiss family of Lucerne; d.

Basel, June 26, 1988. Balthasar received a doctorate in German literature and philosophy in 1928 following studies in Zurich, Vienna, and Berlin. He entered the Society of Jesus in 1929, studied philosophy at Pullach, near Munich, and theology (1933–37) at Lyon (Fourvière), a companion to J. DANIÉLOU and H. Bouillard. He was ordained a priest in July of 1936. For a brief time he served as an associate editor of *Stimmen der Zeit* (1937–39). In 1940, when chaplain of students in Basel, he met Adrienne von SPEYR, introducing her to the Catholic Church and remaining her confessor until her death (1967). In 1945 he founded with her the secular institute Johannesgemeinschaft. Later he established Johannesverlag, a publishing house that issued major works on the Fathers of the Church and other ''Christian masters'' whom Balthasar regarded as foundational to Christian life and thought. Under his direction, Johannesverlag published some 60 volumes of von Speyr's writings, which she practically dictated to him in their entirety.

His departure from the Society of Jesus in 1950 dimmed his reputation for a while. He was not a *peritus* to the Second Vatican Council. Nevertheless, Pope Paul VI recognized Balthasar's brilliance and nominated him a member of the original INTERNATIONAL THEOLOGICAL COMMISSION in 1969, later reappointing him. Pope John Paul II also selected him for the commission in 1980 and 1986. In 1972 he launched in Germany and Italy the international Catholic review *COMMUNIO,* giving it both program and purpose; this review eventually appeared in 11 different languages. In 1984, Pope John Paul II recognized his achievement by personally giving him the ''Pope Paul VI'' prize. Although Balthasar was named a cardinal by Pope John Paul II, he died two days before receiving the red hat.

The Charism. While engaged in the spiritual exercises of St. IGNATIUS (1929), God unexpectedly called Balthasar to serve Him with the sole directive that he ''abandon everything and follow'' with a typically Ignatian indifference. This choice of God would determine his destiny, his thought, and his work. A priest who found himself at home in the Society of Jesus, Balthasar received through Adrienne von Speyr a theological and ecclesial mission, founded in the interrelated roles of Mary, John, and Peter, incarnated in the secular institute Johannesgemeinschaft, and founded to be an actualization of the charism of St. Ignatius under the form of a ''secular institute.'' Obliged as a result of his activities to quit the society, he would be broken like the Eucharistic bread. Passing beyond and reformulating the Lutheran idea of Good Friday and the Hegelian notion of a speculative Friday, he received the theology of Holy Saturday through von Speyr. It gave life and strength to his mission in a secular world. The most telling sign of the power of this charism, concealed in the invisible, was the colloquium he held in Rome (1985) that assembled several hundred friends of von Speyr from around the world.

His Writings. The books of Balthasar were written from within the interior of this charism. Under the influence of Erich Przywara (1889–1972), who exercised a decisive influence on him, Balthasar wrote the *Apokalypse der deutschen Seele* (3 vols., 1937–39), in which he attempted to unveil through ''the great modern spiritual figures of German history, the most recent religious attitude that, though it often remains hidden, is in a way that of 'confession'.'' Through Henri de LUBAC, whose disciple Balthasar became at Fourvière and with whom he maintained a lifelong friendship, Balthasar's thought found its ''Catholic'' basis. Balthasar was responsible for the German translation of Lubac's *Catholicism*, a work he held in high regard, and of many other of Lubac's works. Stimulated by such a master, Balthasar studied Origen, Gregory of Nyssa, and Maximus the Confessor (he had already compiled an anthology of the works of Saint Augustine). He also learned from Karl BARTH (1951), Romano GUARDINI (1970), Martin BUBER (1958), and Gustav Siewert.

Balthasar acknowledged the lasting influence of Adrienne von Speyr on his thought and publications. ''It was Adrienne von Speyr,'' he wrote, ''who pointed out the fulfilling way from Ignatius to John, and thus laid out the foundation for most of what has been published by me since 1940. Her work and mine is neither psychologically nor philosophically separable, two halves of a whole that, as center, has but one foundation'' (*Balthasar Reader,* 42). The experiences and theology of Adrienne von Speyr began to fulfill his hopes and to respond to questions, in particular, those concerning the final realities. He attributed to her his insights regarding the mystery of Holy Saturday ''and hence of hell and of universal redemption as well'' (ibid., 403).

Sometime about 1961, Balthasar elaborated a plan for a trilogy which he published in subsequent years as *Herrlichkeit, Theodramatik,* and *Theologik.* The multivolume work has the transcendentals—the Beautiful, the Good, and the True—as its foci; each concentrates on a different power of the human person: What can one perceive? For what should one hope? For what purpose has one intelligence? In fact, the trilogy is a theological synthesis that brings together Balthasar's vast knowledge of ancient and modern European literature and philosophy on the one hand, and the Christian tradition, including the Church fathers, scholastic and modem theology, exegesis, and mysticism on the other. In Balthasar's vision of things, the theological enterprise takes as its point of departure the mystery of revelation made known in the incarnate and crucified Word of God: made visible in Him is a glory or splendor (*Herrlichkeit*) integrating all natural beauty and surpassing all human attempts to order and shape the created universe.

The passage from ''aesthetic'' to ''dramatic'' takes place in the drama of the Incarnation and Crucifixion, whereby God gathers together and brings to perfection everything worthwhile in creation. Truth, which responds to every human question, is revealed in the kenosis of God in the Incarnation and the Crucifixion. According to Balthasar's scheme, *Theologik,* which concludes the trilogy, seeks to make intelligible the inner logic that underlies God's action in history. In the Truth that is Jesus Christ, every human question and all knowing is revealed.

The Form. ''To know as I am known'': the vertical of Revelation and of faith traverses and gives birth to the horizontal of history and human research. Theology cannot pass over anthropology, for ''man is the way of God'' (John Paul II) and in Christ man is completed as God loved and created him. All converges toward and in Christ, the Son of God who is delivered up for us and united with Mary the Church. Trinity, christology, soteriology, Mariology, ecclesiology, and anthropology are united as in the *Credo.* It is the same unity. Balthasar's ''catholic'' theology is aided by his musical and artistic gifts. It is not systematic, but ''symphonic.'' It finds coherence and dynamism in its ''return to the center,'' *(Einfaltung),* which is at the same time an unfolding *(Entfaltung).*

Balthasar contemplates a God who gives Himself by revealing who He is, thereby giving life to man's free response to Him. Because of this gift of freedom that God has given man, being is essential, for following Saint Thomas (in the manner in which G. Siewert had explained him), Balthasar regarded being as the gift of God to His creatures, in which they may participate in order to receive it in their own singularity. In considering this gift (being in the transcendentals) Balthasar did not forget the giver; in God the Beautiful is divine Glory, in which human beings are called to share; in God the Good is merciful love, by which humans hope for salvation (without excluding the possibility of Hell), and in God the True is the Word of the Father, communicated by the Spirit, through whom humans know the love that is beyond all knowledge. The transcendentals, without losing their own identity, are thereby theologically transmuted.

This transformation leads to several consequences, of which we shall consider a few. That which humans may see and sense has a profundity that goes beyond what constitutes them: Humans are called to contemplate the Glory of God. This intellectual act is also a sensible one, for there exist spiritual senses (cf. Origen). Correlatively Jesus is his own light; a manifestation of divine Glory in a union of spirit and body that sets aside all Platonism and demands an incarnated mystic.

The divine drama ''rests in part on the notion of mission that elevates and accomplishes the psychological and Christian notion of role . . . and in part on the confrontation of a created and finite freedom with the freedom of divine infinity.'' The divine mission, being the economic form of the procession, ''cannot be made one except with the theological notion of person.'' The confrontation of divine and human freedom leads, through Christ, to the abandoned state of the Son in death and to the separation of the Father and the Son, who are united without fail by the Spirit. Here Balthasar inserts a theology of Holy Saturday. These same notions of mission and person furnish the basis for an ecclesiology, wherein are illuminated the figures of Mary, John, and Peter.

Bibliography: For complete bibliography of Von Balthasar's work, see: *Hans Urs von Balthasar, Bibliographie: 1925–1990.* (Einsiedeln, Switzerland, 1990). M. KEHL and W. LOSER. *The Von Balthasar Reader,* translated by R. J. DALY and F. LAWRENCE (New York, 1982). HANS URS VON BALTHASAR. ''Discour du P. H. U. von Balthasar.'' *Hans Urs von Balthasar: Premio Internazionale Paolo VI 1984.* (Brescia, 1984); *First Glance at Adrienne von Speyr,* translated by A. LAWRY and S. ENGLUND (San Francisco, 1968); *My Work: In Retrospect* (San Francisco, 1993); *Our Task: A Report and a Plan,* translated by JOHN SAWARD (San Francisco, 1994). L.S. CHAPP, *The God Who Speaks: Hans Urs von Balthasar's Theology of Revelation* (Bethesda, Md. 1996). E. T. OAKES, *Pattern of Redemption: The Theology of Hans Urs von Balthasar.* (2d rev. ed. New York, 1997). DAVID SCHINDLER, ed., *Hans Urs von Balthasar: His Life and Work* (Notre Dame, Ind., 1991).

[G. CHANTRAINE]

BALTHASAR OF ST. CATHERINE OF SIENA

Discalced CARMELITE and mystical writer; b. Bologna, Aug. 24, 1597; d. Bologna, Aug. 23, 1673. He was a descendant of Niccolò Machiavelli. Balthasar was attracted to the Teresian Reform while taking part in the celebrations of St. TERESA's beatification. He took the habit at the novitiate of La Scala in Rome (Nov. 21, 1614), where he was later professed (Nov. 11, 1615). After his ordination, he was appointed professor at the Seminary for the Missions, then at St. Paul of the Quirinale. He filled various positions of administrative responsibility in his order: provincial, general definitor, procurator general.

The most important of his writings include a pastoral letter to the religious of his own Lombardy province; the Italian translation of the work of Father Joseph of Jesus

Mary (Quiroga), *Subida del Alma a Dios* (Rome 1664); his commentary on the *Mansions* of St. Teresa, titled *Splendori Riflessi di Gloria Celeste* (Bologna 1671–94), is representative of the Carmelite school (see Gabriel, bibliography). The work is important because he harmonized the teaching of St. Teresa, which prevailed in the Teresian carmel of the Italian congregation, with that of St. JOHN OF THE CROSS, then less known than St. Teresa in Italy. If these works have not been translated into other languages, it is primarily because the author's style is artificial and diffuse, after the fashion of his age. His interpretation of St. Teresa is, nevertheless, known among the representatives of the Teresian Carmelite school, and is often quoted.

Bibliography: GRAZIANO DELLA CROCE, ''Patrimonio espiritual de la Cong. de S. Elias,'' *El Monte Carmelo* 70 (1962) 228–229, 243–245. GABRIEL DE SAINTE MARIE MADELEINE, *Dictionnaire de spiritualité ascétique et mystique. Doctrine et histoire,* ed. M. VILLER et al. (Paris 1932–) 1.1:1210–17.

[O. RODRIGUEZ]

BALTIC RELIGION

The religion, typically agricultural, of the Baltic peoples (Latvians, Lithuanians, and Old Prussians). Among the high gods primacy was enjoyed by the gods of heaven. Dievs (Heaven), through etymology directly connected with Dyāus, Zeus, and Jupiter, was the most important of these. In his concrete form he was regarded as a great farmer who worked his fields in the same manner as the modern Latvian peasant. Generally, he was the arbiter of welfare and prosperity. Only Saule (the Sun, a goddess) could compete in importance with Dievs. She was usually regarded as the patroness of fertility, and numerous myths of the courtship of gods were associated with her. A prominent place was allotted also to Pērkons (Thunder), a god of fertility, and Mēness (Moon, a male deity), in whom one can discern traits of a god of war.

Much clearer in her functions was the earth goddess (called Mother Earth). She was patron of fertility, but, at the same time, seems to have been the source of a number of mythical figures of chthonic character. Of the feminine deities, however, Laima, the goddess of Fate, was the most fully developed. She belonged to the Indo-European group of arbiters of fate or destiny, and had a central place in Baltic religion.

Beside these higher deities there were numerous mythological figures who were generally connected with the different phases of agricultural life. The functions of these lower beings and those of the higher gods were not strictly delimited.

The higher gods received a definite cult, which was connected especially with important occasions in human life, and with annual feasts. There were birth and wedding rites; the summer solstice and the harvest were celebrated with special solemnity.

Bibliography: H. BIEZAIS, ''Baltische Religion,'' *Die Religion in Geschichte und Gegenwart* 3 1:856–859, with bibliog.; *Die Hauptgöttinnen der alten Letten* (Uppsala 1955); *Die Gottesgestalt der lettischen Volksreligion* (Uppsala 1961).

[H. BIEZAIS]

BALTIMORE, ARCHDIOCESE OF

The archdiocese of Baltimore (Latin title: *Baltimorensis*) is the senior metropolitan see of the United States, comprising Baltimore city and Baltimore, Allegany, Anne Arundel, Carroll, Frederick, Garrett, Harford, Howard, and Washington counties, an area of 4,801 square miles, with an estimated total population in 2000 of 2,850,000, including 485,000 Catholics. The diocese was established on Nov. 6, 1789; the archdiocese on April 8, 1808.

Origins. Catholicism was brought to Maryland (1634) by the first English settlers, among whom were three Jesuit missionaries whose successors continued the work of ministering to the colonists and converting the Native Americans. The area comprising the present Baltimore archdiocese was probably served by itinerant priests, including Benedict Neale, who visited Harford County in 1747. In 1755 a group of exiled French Catholic refugees from Acadia (Nova Scotia) settled in Edward Fotterell's abandoned house on Calvert and Fayette streets in Baltimore. From 1756 to 1763 Jesuits from the White Marsh mission, 25 miles southwest, periodically conducted services first in Fotterell's house and after 1775, in St. Peter's. This small church was built by laymen on a lot purchased by the Jesuit superior from Charles Carroll of Annapolis and located near the northwest corner of the later Charles and Saratoga streets. By 1784, when the first resident pastor, Charles Sewall, SJ, arrived, the church had been enlarged to more than twice its original size, and a rectory had been added. There the vicar apostolic of the new Republic, John CARROLL, took up residence in 1786 and remained until his death in 1815. By then, three more city churches had been added as the Catholic population increased to an estimated 10,000—St. Patrick's (1795); St. John's (1799), on the site of the later St. Alphonsus; and St. Mary's Seminary Chapel (1808), a Gothic structure designed by Maximilian Godefroy.

Ecclesiastical jurisdiction. From 1688 to 1784 the English colonies seemingly were under the jurisdiction of the vicar apostolic of the London District in the home

The nave of Baltimore Cathedral, designed by Benjamin Henry Latrobe, begun in 1806. (©G.E. Kidder Smith/CORBIS)

country. Before 1688 priests in the colonies (mostly Jesuits) apparently received all necessary faculties from the superiors of their religious communities. From 1784 to 1789 John Carroll as prefect apostolic exercised limited jurisdiction over the Church in the new Republic of the United States. After his appointment as bishop on Nov. 6, 1789, and his consecration in Lulworth Castle chapel, Dorset, England, on Aug. 15, 1790, Carroll assumed full responsibility for his vast Diocese of Baltimore, which was until 1808 the only see in the United States. It extended from the Atlantic Ocean to the Mississippi River and from Canada to Florida, an area of about 890,000 square miles, later comprising 25 states. The record of its territorial contraction as a diocese or archdiocese and as a province is, therefore, unique. In 1808, with the establishment of the suffragan sees of Boston, Mass., New York, N.Y., Philadelphia, Pa., and Bardstown (later Louisville), Ky., and the creation of Baltimore as a metropolitan see, the Archdiocese of Baltimore was confined to what are now the District of Columbia, Maryland, West Virginia, Virginia, North and South Carolina, Georgia, Alabama, and Mississippi, an area of 317,610 square miles. The archdiocese, which remained the only metropolitan see in the United States until 1846, was subsequently reduced in area by four main subdivisions. In 1820 it lost West Virginia and Virginia to the Diocese of Richmond, although the archbishops of Baltimore administered the see when it was vacant from 1822 to 1841. North Carolina, South Carolina, and Georgia also were separated in 1820 to form the Diocese of Charleston, S.C.; these divisions left the two remaining parts of the archdiocese separated by more than 500 miles. In 1825 Mississippi and Alabama were severed when each became a vicariate apostolic; the latter included Florida, recently ceded to the United States by Spain. When the Diocese of Wilmington, Del., was created in 1868, Baltimore lost all of Maryland's eastern shore counties (nine) to the new see. In 1939 the District of Columbia was

Cardinal William H. Keeler, Archbishop of Baltimore, leads 850 youths through the Baltimore streets to mark the beginning of Holy Week, April 15, 2000. (AP/Wide World Photos)

made an archdiocese, although its archbishop was simultaneously archbishop of Baltimore until 1947, when it was given its own archbishop and an additional five Maryland counties previously governed by Baltimore.

The Province of Baltimore was, in practice, coterminous with the Republic from 1808 to 1846, when Oregon City (now Portland, Ore.) became the second U.S. province. Between 1847 (when the Archdiocese of St. Louis, Mo., was erected) and 1850 (when the provinces of New York, New Orleans, La., and Cincinnati, Ohio, were set up) the senior province was greatly reduced in size, losing Alabama and Mississippi, once part of the Baltimore archdiocese, to the New Orleans province. Delaware, never a part of the archdiocese as such, remained in the province when the state of Delaware was detached from the Diocese of Philadelphia and made part of the new Diocese of Wilmington (1868). West Florida, which had become part of the province in 1819, was transferred to the New Orleans province in 1850, but East Florida remained in that of Baltimore. The state of Pennsylvania also remained part of the Baltimore province until 1875, when the Province of Philadelphia was erected. Since then Baltimore has lost the District of Columbia and the five Maryland counties (1947) included in the Archdiocese of Washington, which belongs to no province. In 1962 the establishment of the new Province of Atlanta took the states of Georgia, North and South Carolina, and the eastern part of Florida, leaving the Province of Baltimore with all of Maryland except five counties, and Delaware, Virginia, and West Virginia, with suffragan sees at Richmond, Va., Wheeling, W.Va., and Wilmington, Del.

Prominent leaders and developments. Baltimore's ordinaries, beginning with the renowned John Carroll, who ruled the see from 1789 to 1815, have included many outstanding prelates. Carroll's successor was his coadjutor, Leonard NEALE, whose brief administration terminated with his death in 1817. He was followed by the French-born Sulpician Ambrose MARÉCHAL (1817–28); English-born James WHITFIELD (1828–34); the Sulpician Samuel ECCLESTON, a native of Maryland (1834–51); Irish-born Francis Patrick KENRICK, who had served as bishop in Philadelphia, Pa., before his appointment to Baltimore (1851–63); Martin John SPALDING, born in Kentucky and auxiliary (1848–52) and bishop (1852–64) of Louisville, Ky., before his appointment as archbishop of Baltimore (1864–72); New York-born James Roosevelt BAYLEY (1872–77); James GIBBONS, who became the second U.S. cardinal (1877–1921); Michael Joseph CURLEY, Irish-born bishop of St. Augustine, Fla., when chosen for Baltimore (1921–47); Francis Patrick KEOUGH (1947–61); and Baltimore-born Lawrence Joseph SHEHAN, who was named auxiliary of the archbishop of Baltimore and Washington in 1945 while serving as pastor of St. Patrick's, Washington. In 1948 he became auxiliary to the archbishop of Baltimore, where he took up residence as pastor of SS. Philip and James. Made first bishop of Bridgeport, Conn., in 1953, he was named to Baltimore in July of 1961 as coadjutor archbishop and succeeded to the see upon Keough's death on December 8 of that year. In February of 1965 Shehan was raised to the College of Cardinals by Paul VI in recognition of his leadership in the areas of ecumenism and racial justice. William D. Borders succeeded Cardinal Sheehan as archbishop of Baltimore in 1974 and promoted lay involvement in the administration of the archdiocese. The 14th archbishop of Baltimore is William Cardinal Keeler, who was appointed to the see in 1989 and named a cardinal in 1994. In addition to his guidance of the archdiocese, Cardinal Keeler has a world-wide reputation as a leader in ecumenical affairs, particularly in the Church's relations with the Orthodox and with Jews.

Under its episcopal leaders, Baltimore assumed an important role in U.S. Catholic history that was both enhanced and reflected by the many important meetings of Church leaders held in the see city. As early as 1791, Carroll had called a meeting of his clergy (22 attended) at which a number of regulations were decreed for observance throughout the diocese. These decrees were reaffirmed and amplified in 1810, when Carroll met informally with Neale, his coadjutor, and his newly consecrated suffragans Michael Egan of Philadelphia, Jean Cheverus of Boston, and Benedict Flaget of Bardstown. The First Provincial Council of Baltimore was held in 1829, followed by others in 1833, 1837, 1840, 1843, 1846, 1849, 1855, 1858, and 1869. Of these, the first seven—like the meetings of 1791 and 1810—were nationwide in scope and hence plenary in effect. Three other Councils of Baltimore were plenary in the strict sense, since they were presided over by an apostolic delegate (in each case, the incumbent archbishop of Baltimore) and the nation had by then been divided into additional provinces, each headed by a metropolitan archbishop. Held in 1852, 1866, and 1884, these meetings were epochal in character (*see* BALTIMORE, COUNCILS OF). In addition, Baltimore was the site of nine diocesan synods (i.e., meetings of the archbishop and his diocesan clergy concerning strictly diocesan regulations), which besides the national synod of 1791 included those held in 1831, 1853, 1857, 1863, 1865, 1868, 1875, and 1886.

When the diocese was created, Baltimore had only one church, St. Peter's, which served as procathedral for Carroll, Neale, and Maréchal until 1821. The first synod in the United States was held there, as was also the first ordination (Stephen T. BADIN, 1793), and the first episcopal consecration (Leonard Neale, 1800). In use until 1841, it was razed the following year to make room for Calvert Hall, a boys' school conducted there (1845–91) by the Brothers of the Christian Schools. To carry on the name of St. Peter's, another city parish of that name was established in 1842. On land purchased from the estate of the Revolutionary war hero and Maryland governor, John Eager Howard, the old Cathedral of the Assumption of the Blessed Virgin Mary was begun on July 7, 1806, when Carroll laid the cornerstone. (Contrary to later development, this stone designated the church under the name of Jesus and Mary.) The Romanesque-Byzantine structure designed by the British-born non-Catholic Benjamin Henry Latrobe, one of the architects of the national capitol, was dedicated on May 31, 1821, but it remained in debt and unconsecrated until May 25, 1876. The building escaped the fires of 1873 and 1904; its location placed it (1964) on the northern edge of the city's 22-acre Charles Center redevelopment area. The old cathedral, important for its historical associations, became the nation's fourth minor basilica on Sept. 1, 1937. Within its walls all of Baltimore's great councils were solemnized. Beneath its altar lie all the archbishops of Baltimore except Neale, Bayley, and Keough. On Sept. 21, 1959, the basilica ceased to be the metropolitan cathedral, but it was accorded the status of a cocathedral. The Cathedral of Mary Our Queen was built from funds bequeathed by Thomas J. O'Neill (1849–1919), an Irish-born Baltimore merchant. Ground was broken by Keough on Oct. 10, 1954, and the cornerstone was laid the following May. The building was consecrated on Oct. 13, 1959, and solemnly opened November 15.

Religious communities. A number of religious communities established their first U.S. foundations under the ordinaries of Baltimore: the Carmelites in Port Tobacco, Md. (1790); the Sulpicians in Baltimore (1791); the Visitation nuns (1799) and the restored Jesuits (1806), both in Georgetown, D.C.; the Christian Brothers(1845), the Josephites (1871), and the Bon Secour Sisters (1881), all in Baltimore. In addition, three new communities for women were founded within the archdiocese. In 1809 the Sisters of St. Joseph, as they were originally called, founded by St. Elizabeth SETON, established St. Joseph's Academy in Emmitsburg, Md. The Oblate Sisters of Providence were founded in Baltimore in 1828 by Bl. Mary Elizabeth Lange. This community of African American Sisters is dedicated to the education of black children. The Mission Helpers of the Sacred Heart began in 1891, when Mary Cunningham (later Mother Demetrias) joined with a group of Baltimore women in helping the Josephites with their catechetical and missionary work among the black missions. With headquarters in Towson, Md., they engage in general and special catechetics.

Within the archdiocese the Sulpicians, Josephites, Pallottines, and Trinitarians have their national headquarters; Baltimore is also a center for the Friars Minor Conventuals, Jesuits, and Xaverian Brothers, as well as for the Daughters of Charity, Franciscan Sisters of Baltimore City, Franciscans Sisters of the Third Order, Good Shepherd Sisters, Notre Dame de Namur Sisters, Oblate Sisters of Providence, Religious Sisters of Mercy, and the School Sisters of Notre Dame.

Education. In the document establishing the diocese of Baltimore, the Holy See urged upon Carroll the necessity of establishing ''an episcopal seminary either in the same city [Baltimore] or elsewhere, as he shall judge most expedient.'' By the time the new bishop issued the nation's first pastoral letter in 1792, he was able ''to return God thanks for having conducted to our assistance a number of learned and exemplary clergymen, devoted by choice, and formed by experience to the important function of training young Ecclesiastics to all the duties of the ministry.'' These clergymen were the SULPICIANS, who had arrived in Baltimore in July of 1791. Three months after their arrival, and under the direction of Father Nagot, four Sulpicians and the five students who accompanied them from Europe had begun the pioneer U.S. Seminary, St. Mary's, Baltimore. The lack of native candidates to the priesthood during the Sulpicians' first 13 years nearly caused the closing of the seminary, and only the express wish of Pius VII saved the project. While continuing to prepare men from around the country for the priesthood, in recent decades it has also been offering training in theology to laymen and women.

Another training school for the diocesan priesthood, the seminary department of Mt. St. Mary's College, Emmitsburg, was established in 1808 by the Sulpician John Dubois, later third bishop of New York. Mt. St. Mary's was from the start both a seminary and a lay college. Since ending its association with the Sulpicians in 1826, the college has been directed by an association of secular priests from various dioceses, with the archbishop of Baltimore as ex officio president. Its graduates include many bishops and the first U.S. Cardinal, John McCloskey. Defying national trends, in the last two decades of the twentieth century Mt. St. Mary's Seminary has increased its enrollment as dioceses from around the country continue to send candidates for the priesthood there in ever greater numbers.

The archdiocese currently has three Catholic colleges. Mt. St. Mary's and Loyola, Baltimore (1852), are directed respectively by secular priests and Jesuits. A college for women, Notre Dame of Maryland (1873), was founded by the School Sisters of Notre Dame. These three colleges had a total enrollment of 11,428 students at the end of the millennium. In addition, there were 22 high schools (10,922 students) and 73 elementary schools (24,314 students) in the archdiocese under Catholic auspices in 2000.

Charitable works. In 2000 there were five general hospitals; these are Sacred Heart, Cumberland (Daughters of Charity, 1911), and four in Baltimore: St. Agnes (Daughters of Charity, 1862), St. Joseph (Sisters of St. Francis of Philadelphia, 1864), Mercy (Sisters of Mercy, 1874), and Bon Secours (Bon Secours Sisters, 1919). Rehabilitation centers and homes for the aged in the city of Baltimore include Dismas House East, Dismas House West, St. Elizabeth Rehabilitation and Nursing Center, St. Charles Villa, St. Joseph Nursing Home, and St. Martin's Home for the Aged. There are also the St. Agnes Nursing and Rehabilitation Center in Ellicott City, Villa St. Catherine in Emmitsburg, and Stella Maris Center in Timonium.

Catholic press. The short-lived *Metropolitan,* founded in Baltimore by Peter BLENKINSOP in 1830, is credited with being the pioneer Catholic magazine in the United States. In 1842 Rev. Charles I. WHITE of Baltimore began a monthly called the *Religious Cabinet.* Renamed the *U.S. Catholic Magazine* in 1843, in became a weekly in 1849 and was followed in 1850 by the *Catholic Mirror*, a weekly newspaper. Except for a brief period during the Civil War when its publisher was imprisoned for southern sympathies, it continued as Baltimore's archdiocesan paper until 1908. When White relinquished its editorship in 1853, he began another monthly under the old name of the *Metropolitan* and continued it until 1857. It died out shortly after a new editor took over in 1858. Since 1913 the official weekly organ of the archdiocese has been the *Baltimore Catholic Review.* Between 1944 and 1952 there were separate Baltimore and Washington editions. (Since then Washington has had its own paper.)

Other developments. The Third Plenary Council of Baltimore (1884) established a committee of bishops to draw up a catechism for use in elementary religious instruction throughout the United States. The first edition of the so-called Baltimore Catechism appeared in April of 1885; it was chiefly the work of Bp. John L. Spalding of Peoria, Ill., and Msgr. J. V. De Concilio of St. Michael's parish, Jersey City, N.J. This original edition became the No. 2 catechism, No. 1 being a simplified version and No. 3 an amplified one. In 1941 a considerably revised edition was published and remained a popular catechetical source until the Second Vatican Council encouraged new approaches to religious instruction. In 1995 the premier see of the United States welcomed Pope John Paul II to the city of Baltimore, where he offered a historic Mass at Camden Yards stadium.

Baltimore possesses a storehouse of documents ''ranking first among the archives of the Catholic Church in the United States,'' according to John Tracy Ellis, American Church historian. Located at St. Mary's Seminary, these documents are cataloged chiefly according to the administrations of the successive archbishops. A few documents antedate the American Revolution. There are autographed letters from ten popes (beginning with Pius VII in 1817) and sixteen American presidents (beginning with Washington in 1790).

The principal patron of the archdiocese is the Blessed Virgin Mary, Assumed into Heaven (synod of 1791); St. Ignatius Loyola was chosen as the secondary patron (synod of 1886), since the Jesuits established the first missions in Maryland (1634). His Spanish name still identifies one of the oldest towns in the state (St. Inigoes, St. Mary's county, 1634) and its historic church. In 2000 the archdiocese counted 155 parishes, 18 of which were without a resident pastor, served by 597 priests, of whom 291 were religious, 187 permanent deacons, 80 brothers, and 1212 women religious.

Bibliography: T. W. SPALDING, *The Premier See: A History of the Archdiocese of Baltimore, 1789–1989* (Baltimore, 1989). Partial sources include J. D. G. SHEA, *A History of the Catholic Church within the Limits of the United States,* 4 v. (New York 1886–92). M. E. STANTON, *A Century of Growth: The History of the Church in Western Maryland,* 2 v. (Baltimore, Md. 1891). M. J. RIORDAN, *Cathedral Records from the Beginning of Catholicism in Baltimore* (Baltimore, Md. 1906). P. K. GUILDAY, *Life and Times of John Carroll: Archbishop of Baltimore, 1735–1815,* 2 v. (New York 1927). J. T. ELLIS, *Life of James Cardinal Gibbons: Archbishop of Baltimore, 1834–1921,* 2 v. (Milwaukee, Wis. 1952). A. M. MELVILLE, *John Carroll of Baltimore* (New York 1955). By 1965 The Catholic University of America library contained studies of all Baltimore's archbishops from Carroll through Gibbons. Other valuable sources are the Archives of the Archdiocese of Baltimore, the Maryland Historical Society, and the Maryland Room of the Pratt Library.

[J. J. GALLAGHER/R. T. CONLEY]

BALTIMORE, COUNCILS OF

Although the Council of Trent (1545–63) decreed that diocesan synods were to be held everywhere each year and that provincial councils should meet every three years, this regulation was rarely, if ever, followed to the letter in any part of the world. The Code of Canon Law (1918) prescribes the holding of diocesan synods every ten years and of provincial councils every 20 years. Provision is also made in the Code for plenary councils, in which the bishops of more than one ecclesiastical province meet. In a plenary council, laws are promulgated that bind the dioceses in the area represented in the council; the decrees of a provincial council are binding within the territory of the province; and in a synod, diocesan statutes are laid down.

Regulations have been made for the Church in the United States in all three types of assembly. From 1789 to 1808, the whole territory of the United States belonged to the Diocese of Baltimore, Md., and from 1808 to 1846, the Province of Baltimore was the only one in the country. Although Oregon City became a metropolitan see in 1846 and St. Louis in 1847, the bishops who met in 1849 for the Seventh Provincial Council of Baltimore represented the entire nation. Since that time, three plenary councils of the U.S. Church have been held, all at Baltimore. Before the establishment of the first U.S. diocese in 1789, the clergy had met also in several general chapters at Whitemarsh, Md. Although these meetings did not fall within the strict canonical categories of synod and council, brief mention of them will be included in this article, which is divided as follows: (1) general chapters of the clergy (1783–89); (2) Baltimore diocesan synod (1791); (3) meeting of the American bishops (1810); (4) first seven provincial councils of Baltimore (1829–49); (5) the three plenary councils of Baltimore (1852–84).

General Chapters of the Clergy (1783–89). Until 1773 care of the Church in the English colonies on the Eastern Seaboard of the present United States was left almost entirely to missionaries of the Society of Jesus. There was no ecclesiastical organization except that which the internal Jesuit structure provided. From 1721 on, the colonies came under the tenuous supervision of the English vicar apostolic of the London district, a supervision that became more formal after 1757 but was never really effective. In 1773 the Society of Jesus was suppressed, but most of its missionaries in the English colonies continued their work there under the direction of the last superior of the mission, Rev. John Lewis. The American Revolution ended all possibility of ecclesiastical government from England, and for ten years no attempt at formal organization of the U.S. Church was made.

In 1782, Rev. John Carroll, one of the former Jesuits, proposed the creation of a provisional chapter of the clergy in order to preserve the property that had belonged to the Jesuit order and also to see to other problems of ecclesiastical administration. Three meetings of the General Chapter were held at Whitemarsh: in 1783–84, 1786, and 1789. Decisions were made touching on the preservation of the Jesuit estates, the foundation of an academy at

Third Plenary Council of Baltimore, 1884, from Clarke's "History of the Catholic Church in the United States," from negative by D. Bendann.

Georgetown (later Georgetown University, Washington, D.C.), the need for educating a native clergy, and the erection of the Diocese of Baltimore. In 1784, the chapter voted against the creation of a bishopric in the United States, but two years later the members changed their minds and petitioned the Holy See for the foundation of a diocese and the right to elect the first bishop. This was conceded by Rome. In 1789, Carroll, who had been superior of the mission by papal appointment since 1784, was chosen by the clergy as the first bishop in the United States. With the creation of the Diocese of Baltimore on Nov. 6, 1789, the general chapters of the clergy ceased to perform their quasi-conciliar function in the U.S. Church.

Synod of Baltimore (1791). When John Carroll was consecrated first bishop of Baltimore on Aug. 15, 1790, his jurisdiction extended over the entire area of what was then the United States. From Nov. 7 to 10, 1791, Carroll held a diocesan synod in St. Peter's procathedral, Baltimore. It was the only such formal meeting in his 18 years as bishop and seven years as archbishop (1790–1815). Twenty-two priests attended, most of them from Maryland and Pennsylvania. Boston was represented, but there were no delegates from New York, Philadelphia, Kentucky, the Northwest, or the South.

Twenty-four statutes were promulgated. The Blessed Virgin Mary was declared patroness of the diocese and August 15 was fixed as its principal feast day. In the remaining regulations, the administration of the Sacraments was standardized, the precept of paschal Communion was emphasized, mixed marriages were discouraged, and non-Catholic partners in such marriages were to be required to promise in the presence of witnesses that they would not oppose the education of their children in the Catholic faith. An order of Sunday services also was prescribed. Mass was to be preceded by the Litany of Loretto and followed by recitation of the prayer for the civil authorities that Carroll had composed, the Gospel of the day in the vernacular, notices, and a short sermon. Vespers and Benediction of the Blessed Sacrament were to be held in the afternoon. Provision was made also for catechism classes, to be conducted after Mass.

One of the principal problems confronting the infant U.S. Church was that of TRUSTEEISM. Although the decrees of the Baltimore Synod made no explicit reference to the efforts of some laymen to usurp control of various congregations, regulations were laid down concerning the collection and distribution of parish funds, and it was made clear that no priest could function in the diocese or change his place of residence without authorization from the bishop. Carroll also discussed with his priests the method to be adopted for electing future bishops. He issued two letters, one dealing with Christian marriage and the other a pastoral (May 28, 1792) that treated Catholic education, priestly vocations, support of pastors and the

Church, Mass attendance, prayers for the dead, and devotion to the Blessed Virgin Mary. The synodal statutes were submitted to Rome and, in 1794, were approved, with only minor changes, by the Congregation for the Propagation of the Faith.

Meeting of American Bishops (1810). On April 8, 1808, Pius VII made Baltimore a metropolitan see with suffragans at Boston, New York, Philadelphia, and Bardstown, Ky. Bp. Richard L. Concanen, OP, who was consecrated in Rome as first bishop of New York, died in Naples without ever reaching the United States. The three other bishops were consecrated in Baltimore between October 28 and November 4: John Cheverus, of Boston; Michael Egan, OFM, of Philadelphia; and Benedict J. Flaget, SS, of Bardstown.

After the consecration ceremonies, the new bishops met for two weeks with Archbishop Carroll and his coadjutor, Leonard Neale. Two series of resolutions were issued and made binding throughout the province. The bishops decided to defer calling a provincial council until 1812, and they resolved to advise the Holy See that the canonical prescriptions of annual synods and diocesan visitations were impractical in the United States and should be left to the discretion of each bishop. They also warned pastors and the faithful not to allow unauthorized priests to exercise the sacred ministry; discouraged frequent theater-going, dancing, and uncontrolled reading, particularly of novels; forbade the Sacraments to known Freemasons; ordered that Baptism should, as far as possible, be administered in church and not in private homes; and recommended that the same be done for Matrimony.

The bishops suggested to the Holy See that future episcopal nominations for their country be made by the U.S. hierarchy; they urged religious superiors not to transfer those of their subjects who held parochial offices without the consent of the local ordinary; and they ordered that the Douay Bible be used as the English version of Scripture in public worship and in devotional books. Although as early as 1787 Carroll had advocated introduction of a complete vernacular liturgy, the bishops' meeting of 1810 decreed that Latin should be used in the Mass and for the form of the Sacraments; all other prayers in the sacramental ceremonies might be in English. They promised to publish a ritual that would standardize liturgical practice. No pastoral letter was issued.

First Seven Provincial Councils. The War of 1812, the imprisonment of Pius VII by Napoleon, the difficulties of travel, and the lack of any outstanding problems demanding conciliar action were some of the factors that combined to postpone the council scheduled for 1812. Carroll had summoned the bishops to Baltimore in a letter sent out in June 1812, but the following September they were notified that the council would not be held. The archbishop died in 1815, and his successor, the ailing Leonard Neale, succumbed in 1817 without taking any action in regard to a council.

First Provincial Council (1829). Ambrose Maréchal, SS, third archbishop of Baltimore (1817–28), was unwilling to call a provincial council despite the insistent demands of Bp. John England of Charleston, S.C., that one be held. Maréchal remained convinced that there were no compelling reasons for a council; he also objected to the growing Irish influence in the U.S. Church and had no intention of giving Irish-born prelates like England a wider forum for their opinions.

Abp. James Whitfield succeeded Maréchal in 1828, and on December 18 of that year he announced that a provincial council would meet in October of 1829. After a preparatory meeting on September 30 in the archbishop's house, 13 private, 13 public, and three solemn sessions were held in the Baltimore cathedral (Oct. 3–18, 1829). Six bishops and the apostolic administrator of Philadelphia attended; three bishops were absent and Bishop Conwell was not admitted to a vote, a fact that he protested to the Congregation of the Propaganda. Three lawyers, including the future chief justice of the United States, Roger B. Taney, were invited as guests of the Council to advise on legal matters. Thirty-eight decrees were promulgated and sent to Rome for approval. The bishops also sent two letters to Pius VIII and another to the Society for the Propagation of the Faith at Lyons. These letters of gratitude to mission societies were to be a regular feature of all the Baltimore councils.

The first eight decrees of the First Provincial Council dealt with the stability of priests in the parishes assigned to them and with various aspects of trusteeism. Other decrees ordered the use of the Douay Version of the Bible and the Roman Ritual, although vernacular translations might be employed in administering the Sacraments after the Latin had been read. Several decrees called for a tightening of discipline in the administration of the Sacraments and in the life of the clergy. It was announced that a uniform catechism and ceremonial would be prepared, and the bishops asserted that it was ''absolutely necessary'' that Catholic schools be established. A tract society for publication of Catholic literature was established. Two pastoral letters were signed by the fathers of the Council, one to the clergy and one to the laity. Both were composed by Bishop England. The decrees of the Council were sent to Rome, where Bp. John Dubois of New York and Rev. Anthony Kohlmann, SJ, former administrator of the same diocese, were charged with their examination by the Propaganda. The decrees were finally approved by Pius VIII in 1830 and promulgated in 1831.

The net result of the First Provincial Council was a strengthening of ties with Rome and greater uniformity of practice among the several American dioceses.

Second Provincial Council (1833). The next council should have been held in 1832, but Whitfield was reluctant to issue the necessary summons. England, Bp. Joseph Rosati, of St. Louis, and Francis P. Kenrick, coadjutor of Philadelphia, enlisted the support of the Congregation of the Propaganda, and the archbishop was finally forced to call a council that met from Oct. 20 to 27, 1833, in the Baltimore cathedral. Nine bishops and the archbishop were present. Eleven decrees were adopted. Three of these dealt with the territorial distribution of the dioceses, another proposed that the selection of future bishops be kept in the hands of the hierarchy, and two assigned to the Jesuits the native American missions and the mission that it was hoped would be founded in Liberia. The presidents of St. Mary's Seminary, Baltimore; Mt. St. Mary's College, Emmitsburg, Md.; and Georgetown College were appointed to supervise publication of Catholic textbooks, and the bishops were encouraged to establish seminaries along the lines prescribed by the Council of Trent.

The bishops revoked an agreement made in 1810 according to which priests who had faculties in one diocese also had them in neighboring dioceses. A new edition of the Roman Ritual for the use of missionaries was also commissioned. England's suggestion of an American national seminary to be located in Ireland was not adopted. The pastoral letter of the Council, again composed by England, contained an appeal for a more vigorous sacramental life. It dealt also with Catholic education, priestly vocations, the laws of fast and abstinence, and, for the first time, with attacks that were being made on Catholics as the great tide of immigration to the United States began.

Third Provincial Council (1837). This was the first of five provincial councils presided over by Abp. Samuel Eccleston, SS. It met (April 16–23) at a time when Nativist anti-Catholic agitation was at its height. Nine of the fourteen American bishops participated. Eleven disciplinary decrees were enacted, including regulations on ordinations, provision for the care of aged and infirm priests, directions for safeguarding legal ownership of church property, and prohibitions against bringing ecclesiastical cases before civil courts and collecting alms without written permission from the bishop. In liturgical matters, the Ceremonial commissioned by the first provincial council (and approved in 1841 by the Holy See) was made normative. Sacred music was to be regulated, and vernacular hymns were forbidden at Mass and solemn Vespers.

The bishops also petitioned the Holy See for abrogation of the obligation to hear Mass on Easter and Pentecost Mondays, and of the fast on Wednesdays and Fridays in Advent. In a letter to Gregory XVI, the fathers asked that new dioceses be erected to cope with the flow of immigrants and that Rome support their requests for bishops from religious orders when it was found necessary to nominate them. The lengthy pastoral letter of 1837 outlined the persecution to which Catholics were being subjected, counseled patience and attention to religious duties, and included a ringing assertion of the loyalty of Catholics to the civil government. It also discussed trusteeism, the need for religious and clerical vocations, Catholic publications, education, and the support of the clergy.

Fourth Provincial Council (1840). John England, the father of the conciliar tradition in the U.S. Church, attended his last council in Baltimore from May 17 to 24, 1840. (He died in 1842.) The 12 U.S. bishops present at the Council admitted to their deliberations Bp. Charles de Forbin-Janson of Nancy and Toul, France, who was in the United States at the time. International affairs were given considerable attention. An unsuccessful plea was made that the prelates interest themselves in the educational controversy that was then occupying the Irish hierarchy. Gregory XVI's apostolic letter condemning the slave trade, *In supremo apostolatus*, was read. Letters of sympathy were sent to Archbishops Clemens von DrosteVischering of Cologne and Martin von Dunin of Gnesen-Posen, who were then engaged in the dispute with the Prussian government over mixed marriages. Previous conciliar decrees on Matrimony, preaching, and the catechism were reiterated, and temperance societies were commended.

The Protestant orientation of U.S. public schools was stressed, and Catholics were urged to assert their civil rights in the matter. Nothing was said about the establishment of parochial schools. Membership in secret societies was forbidden to Catholics. The final decree of the Council was an exhortation to the clergy to lead lives worthy of their vocation. The pastoral letter of 1840 touched upon the usual topics of anti-Catholicism, religious education, vocations, and marriage, but also included an exhortation to conscientious exercise of the right to vote in civil elections, and sections on secret societies, intemperance, and the dangers of wealth.

Fifth Provincial Council (1843). Sixteen bishops and the apostolic administrator of Charleston, S.C., met for the Fifth Provincial Council at Baltimore, from May 14 to 21, 1843. The Province of Baltimore then included 15 suffragan sees. Among those who attended the Council was the vicar apostolic of the Republic of Texas, Bp. Claude Dubuis. The 11 decrees dealt with matrimonial legislation, financial arrangements, ownership of church property, encouragement of Catholic printing houses, visitation of the sick, and the obligation to use the Latin prayers of the Roman Ritual, although prayers in English might be added. The pastoral letter treated Catholic education, secret societies, temperance, the missions in Liberia and among the native peoples, obedience to the civil government, the fruits in both England and the U.S. of the Oxford Movement, and the evils of divorce. One of the decrees of the Council imposed excommunication on those who attempted marriage after civil divorce.

Sixth Provincial Council (1846). Archbishop Eccleston and 23 bishops met in Baltimore from May 10 to 17, 1846. Although these were the peak Nativist years, neither the decrees nor the pastoral letter of the Council made any reference to the fact. Only four decrees were issued. The Blessed Virgin was declared patroness of the U.S., under the title of the Immaculate Conception; the Holy See was asked to forbid clerics in Sacred Orders from entering religious orders without the permission of their bishop; the proclamation of the banns of Matrimony was insisted upon; and priests were forbidden to administer Baptism and Matrimony to those who were not their proper subjects. The pastoral letter dealt with the same topics as in previous years, with the addition of a paragraph announcing the Council's action in naming the Mother of God, under the title of the Immaculate Conception, as patroness of the United States.

Seventh Provincial Council (1849). Oregon City had been made a metropolitan see in 1846, and one year later the same was done for St. Louis. By 1849 there were 29 U.S. dioceses. At the Council that met in Baltimore from May 6 to 13, 1849, Archbishops Eccleston and Peter R. Kenrick, of St. Louis, and 23 bishops were present. The archbishop of Oregon City and his suffragans did not attend. Despite the presence of Kenrick, Eccleston presided; the Council was not plenary in nature.

The fathers petitioned Pius IX to define the Immaculate Conception of the Blessed Virgin. They drafted regulations concerning the destination of alms, transfer of priests from one diocese to another, and the method of selecting bishops. They also asked permission to hold a national council in 1850 and petitioned the Holy See, unsuccessfully, to grant to the archbishop of Baltimore the title of primate. The pastoral letter dealt with only two topics: the pope and his office and the Immaculate Conception. Pius IX was at the time in Gaeta, a refugee from the Roman Revolution of 1848, and Bp. Michael Portier of Mobile, Ala., was commissioned to carry the acts and decrees of the Council to him there and to visit Lyons also to thank the Society for the Propagation of Faith for its help to the U.S. Church.

Three Plenary Councils. Although a plenary council had been planned for 1850, it did not meet until May 9, 1852.

First Plenary Council (1852). Six archbishops and twenty-seven U.S. bishops attended this Council, as did the Canadian bishop of Toronto. Its sessions lasted from May 9 to 20, with Francis P. Kenrick, the new archbishop of Baltimore, serving as apostolic delegate. Twenty-five decrees were promulgated. The first was a formal acknowledgment of the pope as successor of St. Peter, Vicar of Christ, head of the whole Church, and father and teacher of all Christians, with universal authority to rule and govern. The second decree expressly declared that the legislation of the seven Provincial Councils of Baltimore extended to all the dioceses of the United States. Some provisions of that legislation were explicitly restated in the decrees of the Plenary Council. Bishops were also urged to organize chancery offices and to appoint consultors and censors of books, and it was recommended that there be at least one major seminary in each province. The Council likewise urged the erection of parochial schools. The 19th decree included a tribute to the wise noninterference of U.S. civil authority in religious matters and urged bishops to see to it, prudently, that members of the Army and Navy were not required to attend non-Catholic services. Although the national crisis over slavery was mounting, the fathers made no statement on the subject. They petitioned once more that the primacy be granted to Baltimore, but it was not until 1858 that ''prerogative of place'' was granted to the occupant of that see.

The decrees of the Council were approved in Rome on Sept. 26, 1852, but a private letter was sent to Archbishop Kenrick in which he was warned that the asking of exceptions to general Church law should be kept to a minimum, lest the U.S. church take on the appearance of a national church. The pastoral letter of 1852, written by Kenrick, began with an explanation of the nature of episcopal authority and its relation to the papacy. Passages then followed on the administration of church property, obedience to ecclesiastical authority, the needs of the Church in the United States, Catholic education, vocations, and civil allegiance. The letter ended with separate exhortations to priests, sisters, and laity.

Second Plenary Council (1866). In the interim between the first two Plenary Councils, the slavery crisis had come to a head and the nation had undergone the Civil War. Martin J. Spalding had succeeded Archbishop Kenrick in Baltimore, and nearly half of the U.S. bishops had been appointed since 1852. There were in all seven metropolitan sees and 40 suffragan dioceses. On March 19, 1866, Spalding, as apostolic delegate, announced the forthcoming council and gave as the principal reason for it ''that at the close of the national crisis, which had acted as a dissolvent on all sectarian ecclesiastical institutions, the Catholic Church might present to the country and the world a striking proof of the strong bond of unity with which her members are knit together.''

An instruction on the agenda for the Council had been sent by the Propaganda on Jan. 31, 1866. It proposed as topics the care of the recently freed African Americans, the method of selecting bishops, the problem of unattached priests, the erection of seminaries, feasts, fasts and holy days of obligation, legal arrangements for the holding of church property, and the relation of bishops to religious orders in the same matter. The Congregation of the Propaganda asked the fathers to take up also the question of an increase in the number of dioceses. Spalding, one of the leading scholars in the Church, saw the 1866 assembly as an opportunity to include, for the first time in U.S. conciliar decrees, a doctrinal exposition on current heresies and errors, and to codify existing disciplinary legislation.

The Council met (Oct. 7–20, 1866) in the Baltimore cathedral and was the largest such meeting in the history of the U.S. Church to that time. Thousands of onlookers gathered for the opening procession, in which seven archbishops, 38 bishops, three abbots, and 120 theologians participated. The first order of business after the opening solemnities was the cabling of a greeting and good wishes to Pius IX.

The legislation of the Council was set down in 14 titles: on orthodox faith, hierarchy and government of the Church, ecclesiastical persons, church property, Sacraments, divine worship, promotion of disciplinary uniformity, regulars and nuns, education of youth, more efficacious promotion of the salvation of souls, books and newspapers, secret societies, erection of new sees and choice of episcopal candidates, and the more effective execution of the decrees of the Council. The decrees resumed previous U.S. legislation and included directives received from the Holy See, as well as ideas taken from other provincial councils that had been held in the U.S. and elsewhere. An entire chapter was devoted to the care of Negroes, and it was stated that segregated churches might be provided for them if the local situation demanded it. Although Spalding had hoped that a Catholic university might be authorized by the Council, the decree contented itself with a velleity on the point. Secret societies were condemned, but labor unions were specifically excluded from this prohibition. President Andrew Johnson attended the final solemn session of the Council.

The usual letters were sent by the fathers; the one to Pius IX was so phrased that it was later used at Vatican Council I (1869–70) in arguing that the Second Council of Baltimore had at least implicitly affirmed papal infallibility. This was denied by several of the signers, including Archbishops Kenrick and Purcell. The conciliar decrees were not approved until 1868, partly because several bishops, including Kenrick, had protested to Rome that insufficient time had been allowed for discussion, and that the text as adopted did not reflect accurately the wishes of the fathers. Nevertheless, the Council became a model for similar assemblies in other countries. A lengthy pastoral letter explained the conciliar legislation to the clergy and laity.

Third Plenary Council (1884). By 1884 the Church in the United States was increasing by about two million members every decade, largely as a result of immigration. The impetus for a council came chiefly from the West. The archbishops of the country were called to Rome in 1883 to plan the assembly. Since Cardinal John McCloskey of New York was too feeble to preside, Roman authorities intended to send an Italian archbishop as apostolic delegate. They were, however, persuaded to substitute Abp. James Gibbons of Baltimore, and it was he who organized and directed the Council.

Seventy-two prelates attended the sessions, which lasted from November 9 to December 7. The 12 titles of the conciliar decrees included Catholic faith, ecclesiastical persons, divine worship, Sacraments, clerical education, education of Catholic youth, Christian doctrine, zeal for souls, church property, ecclesiastical trials, and Christian burial. Much of the legislation repeated previous law, and it was stated that enactments of the Second Plenary Council remained in force unless revoked. In the first title, the decrees of Vatican Council I were explicitly accepted, and mention was made of errors condemned in the encyclicals of the reigning Pope, Leo XIII. Priests were given a voice in the choice of bishops, through diocesan consultors. One of a series of regulations on clerical discipline made the Roman collar obligatory. Relations between bishops and regulars were to be governed according to the constitution *Romanos pontifices* (1881). The Council once more urged erection of parochial schools, and a committee was set up to arrange for the creation of a Catholic university. Other committees were commissioned to prepare what became the Baltimore Catechism, to look after missions among African Americans and Native Americans, and to pass upon secret societies.

The Council had wide influence in the English-speaking world, especially because of the way in which it set up diocesan organization. The 1884 pastoral letter explained the decrees of the Council and exhorted clergy and laity to fulfillment of them. It was remarkable as a clear assertion of the fathers' belief that American institutions were most propitious to the growth of the Catholic Church.

From the Third Plenary Council of Baltimore until the formation of the National Catholic Welfare Conference, the archbishops of the United States met annually, but their discussions were not conciliar in form.

Bibliography: P. GUILDAY, ed., *A History of the Councils of Baltimore, 1791–1884* (New York 1932); *The National Pastorals of the American Hierarchy, 1792–1919* (Washington 1923). *Collectio Lacensis: Acta et decreta sacrorum conciliorum recentiorum,* ed. JESUITS OF MARIA LAACH, 7 v. (Freiburg 1870–90). J. D. BARRETT, *A Comparative Study of the Councils of Baltimore and the Code of Canon Law* (Washington 1932). *Concilia provincialia, Baltimori habita ab anno 1829, usque ad annum 1840* (Baltimore 1842). T. F. CASEY, *The Sacred Congregation de Propaganda Fide and the Revision of the First Provincial Council of Baltimore, 1829–30* (Analecta Gregoriana 88; Rome 1957). *Concilium plenarium totius Americae Septentrionalis Foederatae Baltimori habitum anno 1852* (Baltimore 1853). J. T. ELLIS, "The Centennial of the First Plenary Council of Baltimore," *Perspectives in American Catholicism* (Baltimore 1963). *Concilii plenarii Baltimorensis II . . . acta et decreta* (Baltimore 1868). J. L. SPALDING, *The Life of the Most Reverend M. J. Spalding* (New York 1873), for the Second Plenary Council. *Acta et decreta concilii plenarii Baltimorenis III* (Baltimore 1884, 1886). J. T. ELLIS, *The Life of James Cardinal Gibbons, Archbishop of Baltimore,* 1834–1921 (Milwaukee 1952), for the Third Plenary Council. T. W. SPALDING, *The Premier See: A History of the Archdiocese of Baltimore, 1789–1989* (Baltimore 1989).

[J. HENNESEY]

BALUFFI, GAETANO

First internuncio to South America; b. Ancona, Italy, 1788; d. Imola, Italy, Nov. 11, 1866. In 1835 Gregory XVI recognized the independence of New Granada and sent Baluffi, then bishop of Bagnorea, as his first internuncio there. In 1837 Baluffi began his mission to the government of General Santander, and then extended it to several South American countries, whose relations with the Holy See had previously been conducted through Madrid. His lack of knowledge of the environment led him into unfortunate attitudes, influenced by the sectarian Catholic Society. This society was hostile to Archbishop Manuel José Mosquera of Bogotá, whose policy was approved by Rome. Baluffi drafted a good proposal for a concordat, which was not approved. In 1841 he was named bishop of Camerino and apostolic administrator of Treja, and Pius IX named him bishop of Imola and a cardinal. He was the author of *La iglesia romana, conocida por su caridad al prójimo como verdadera iglesia de Jesucristo*, and *La América un tiempo española, considerada por su aspecto religioso, desde su descubrimiento hasta 1843.* The latter work was intended to make known to Europeans the political and religious situation of the republics that had won independence from Spain, but the work discussed only the causes of the revolution of 1810, and included nothing based on the author's personal experience. A book of history and apologetics, it is a bibliographical curiosity.

Bibliography: A. M. PINILLA COTE, *La internunciature de Mons. Cayetano Baluffi en Bogotá, primera en Hispanoamérica, 1837–42* (Rome 1953). J. RESTREPO POSADA, "La obra de Mons. B.," *Conferencias de la Academia Colombiana de Historia* (Bogotá 1947).

[R. GÓMEZ HOYOS]

BALUZE, ÉTIENNE

French bibliophile; b. Tulle, Nov. 24, 1630; d. Paris, July 28, 1718. At age 15 he was a cleric in a college in Toulouse, but he never went beyond tonsure. Ecclesiastical benefices permitted him to devote himself entirely to study. In 1652 and 1654 he had to retire to Tulle to regain his health. In 1652 he published an attack on P. Frizon's history of French cardinals (1638) that gained him scholarly recognition. He left Tulle in 1656 and went to Paris to be secretary and assistant to the archbishop of Paris, Pierre De MARCA, from whom he gained a rich knowledge of Church history and a sympathy for GALLICANISM. When De Marca died in 1662, Baluze served the archbishop of Auch briefly, leaving because he did not share the prelate's admiration of scholasticism. After sustaining nine theses of Canon Law, Gallican in sympathy, at the Sorbonne in 1665, he became librarian for J. B. Colbert in 1667. The library of rare MSS that Baluze collected for Colbert from all Europe later enriched the Bibliothèque Nationale. Baluze accurately transcribed about 80 volumes of material from MSS. In 1671 he had to stop work a third time because of an eye illness. Louis XIV made him professor of Canon Law at the Collège de France in 1689. Baluze resigned as librarian for Colbert in 1700 and withdrew outside Paris. In 1710 Louis XIV exiled him from the capital because Baluze had insisted on publicizing in his *Histoire généalogique de la maison d'Auvergne* in 1709 the descent of Cardinal BOUILLON from the Dukes of Aquitaine and the Counts of Auvergne, much to the displeasure of the king. In Tours, Baluze made copies of a wealth of documents later destroyed by fire. In 1713 he was allowed to return to Paris, but without position or pension. After his death the 10,000 printed works in his library were auctioned separately, but the king purchased the 1,500 MSS which are today in the Bibliothèque Nationale. Baluze was one of the greatest scholars of the age of Louis XIV.

The classification of Baluze's writings, mostly in Latin, is itself a task of historical research. His 1663 Latin version of a work of Cardinal de Marca, *De concordia sacerdotii et imperii seu de libertatibus ecclesiae gallicanae*, was put on the Index of Prohibited Books but went through five more editions. Baluze edited the works of Salvian of Marseilles; Vincent of Lerins; Lupus of Ferrières; Agobard, Leidradus, Amulo, and Florus of Lyons; Caesarius of Arles; Regino of Prüm; Antonio Agustin; Lactantius; letters of Innocent III (incomplete); and Cyprian of Carthage (completed 1726 by P. Maran). His capitularies of the French kings (2 v. 1677), in the 1780 edition of P. de Chiniac, was incorporated into Mansi's *Concilia.* In 1683 Baluze published the first volume of a new collection of councils but, perhaps fearing that his Gallican ideas might jeopardize his position, carried the work no further. In this volume he called attention to certain early councils not noted previously and, on the basis of manuscripts, published the most critical texts available. The mass of variant readings are useless, but the notes are exceptionally good. His lives of the Avignon popes (2 v. 1693), whom he accused of introducing immorality into Avignon, was put on the index. G. Mollat has re-edited the work (4 v. 1914–28) in line with later research and Baluze's own notes. Baluze's letters, many in French, are to important men about important matters, and some amount to official pronouncements.

Bibliography: Autobiography in *Capitularia regum Francorum* (Paris 1780). J. MARLIN, *Dictionnaire de théologie catholique,* ed. A. VACANT et al., 15 v. (Paris 1903–50; Tables générales 1951–), 2.1:138–139. G. MOLLAT, *Dictionnaire d'histoire et de géographie ecclésiastiques,* ed. A. BAUDRILLART et al. (Paris 1912–), 6:439–452. *Catholicisme. Hier, aujourd'hui et demain,* G. JACQUEMENT (Paris 1947–), 1:1197.

[W. E. LANGLEY]

BAMBER, EDWARD, BL.

Priest, martyr; *alias* Helmes, Reding, Reading, England; b. ca. 1600 at the Moor, Poulton-le-Fylde or at Carlton, Blackpool, Lancashire; d. Aug. 7, 1646, hanged, drawn, and quartered at Lancaster under Charles I. Many of the details of Bl. Edward's life are uncertain. He was educated abroad (Valladolid, Douai, or Seville and St. Omer). Following his ordination (1626), he was sent to England, where the governor of the castle observed him kneel down to thank God upon disembarkation at Dover. He was imprisoned, but soon released into exile.

He was probably chaplain at Standish Hall, near which he was arrested soon after his second return. En route to Lancaster Castle he was lodged at the Old-Green-Man Inn near Claughton-on-Brock, and managed to escape from his drunken keepers. A Mr. Singleton of Broughton Tower (who had been warned in a dream to help him), sheltered and assisted him during the next 16 years.

Arrested the third time (1643), Bamber was committed to Lancaster Castle, where he remained in close confinement for three years, escaped once, and was recaptured. At his trial with two other priests, BB. Thomas WHITAKER and John WOODCOCK, two former Catholics testified that Bamber had administered the sacraments, and he was condemned to die.

Bamber, who was known for his zeal and courage in pastoral work, instruction, and disputation, suffered with great constancy. He reconciled to the Church a felon executed with him, and encouraged his fellow martyrs to die bravely.

An ode composed on his death is still extant. He was beatified by Pope John Paul II on Nov. 22, 1987 with George Haydock and Companions.

Feast of the English Martyrs: May 4 (England).

See Also: ENGLAND, SCOTLAND, AND WALES, MARTYRS OF.

Bibliography: R. CHALLONER, *Memoirs of Missionary Priests,* ed. J. H. POLLEN (rev. ed. London 1924). J. H. POLLEN, *Acts of English Martyrs* (London 1891).

[K. I. RABENSTEIN]

BANDAS, RUDOLPH G.

Theologian and pioneer in the U.S. catechetical movement; b. Silver Lake, Minnesota, April 18, 1896; d. St. Paul, Minnesota, July 26, 1969. After seminary studies at St. Paul Seminary, St. Paul, he was ordained to the priesthood in 1921 and entered the University of Louvain. In 1924 he was awarded the degree of S.T.D. et M.

Bandas spent most of his priestly life as professor of dogmatic theology and catechetics and spent a period as rector of St. Paul Seminary. He taught one of the first formal courses in catechetics in the United States and authored a pioneer text on the subject, *Catechetical Methods* (1929). Throughout his life he wrote extensively in the field of religious education. Among his better known works are *The Master Idea of St. Paul's Epistles* (1925), *Religious Education and Instruction* (1938), and a series of booklets on biblical and catechetical problems for secondary schools. He was a long-time columnist for the *Wanderer.*

His most successful efforts were devoted to the Confraternity of Christian Doctrine. In the same year that the National Center of the CCD was organized in the United States (1935), he was appointed its first director for the Archdiocese of St. Paul—a position he held with distinction for nearly 30 years. He was chairman of the National Seminary Committee of the National Center in 1945, and he served as consultant to the Congregation of Seminaries and Universities in Rome. Pope Pius XII named him a domestic prelate in 1955. Bandas was a *peritus* at all sessions of the Second Vatican Council. He spent the final decade of his life as pastor of St. Agnes Church in St. Paul.

Bibliography: R. A. LUCKER, *The Aims of Religious Education in the Early Church and in the American Catechetical Movement* (Rome 1966).

[J. B. COLLINS]

BANDRÉS Y ELÓSEGUI, MARÍA ANTONIA, BL.

Religious; b. Tolosa, Guipúzcoa, Spain, March 6, 1898; d. Salamanca, Spain, April 27, 1919. María Antonia, born into a well-to-do family in the Basque country of north central Spain near the border with France, was the second of fifteen children born to the lawyer Ramón Bandrés and his wife Teresa Elósegui. María Antonia attended the local school run by the Daughters of Jesus, the congregation founded by Cándida María CIPITRIA (who was beatified with María Antonia). Despite her family's position in society, María Antonia provided assistance and catechesis to working women in the suburbs. Seeking greater perfection, she joined Mother Cándida's order at Salamanca (Dec. 8, 1915) and professed her religious vows (May 31, 1918). María Antonia's health failed when she was twenty years old. Her agnostic doctor, Filiberto Villalobos, with his friends Miguel de Unamuno and Indalecio Prieto, testified that her serenity and patient endurance inspired their conversion to faith. She was beatified in Rome by John Paul II, May 12, 1996.

Bibliography: E. ITÚRBIDE, *Antoñita Bandrés Elósegui, religiosa de Hijas de Jesús: fuego de holocausto que redime* (Pamplona 1960).

[K. I. RABENSTEIN]

BÁÑEZ AND BAÑEZIANISM

Domingo Báñez (originally Bañes or Vañez) was a Spanish Dominican theologian of major stature. The son of Juan Báñez of Mondragon, he was born on Feb. 29, 1528, in Valladolid. He moved with his family to Medina del Campo, at an early age, in what was then Old Castile and died there on Oct. 22, 1604. He began his studies in the arts and philosophy at Salamanca at the age of 15; and there, three years later, in the spring of 1546, he received the Dominican habit at San Esteban's, where, on May 3, 1547, he made his religious profession. He studied under such renowned theologians as Bartolomé de Medina and Melchior Cano at Salamanca; was for a time master of students and began his teaching career under Domingo de Soto as prior and regent. From 1561 to 1566 Báñez taught at Avila; in 1567 he occupied the chair of theology at Alcalá. He returned to Salamanca during 1572–73 and was regent of San Gregorio's at Valladolid from 1573 until 1577. When De Medina advanced to chief professorship, he assumed the so-called Durandus chair of theology at Salamanca from 1577 to 1580; on De Medina's death in 1580, Báñez was appointed his successor, a position he held for 20 years.

Relationship with St. Teresa of Avila. Of major significance in the life of Báñez is the influence he exerted upon St. TERESA OF AVILA. He first came in contact with her in 1562, and thenceforward, until her death in 1582, he served as her confessor and spiritual director. How meaningful this relationship was, St. Teresa suggests in her own words, saying of Báñez that ". . . it is with him that she has held, and still holds, the most frequent communication" [*The Spiritual Relations* 4, in *The Complete Works of St. Teresa of Avila,* 3 v., tr. E. A. Peers (New York 1946) 1:323–324]. Even before actually meeting the saint, Báñez alone defended her first reform foundation, that of San José in Avila, when civil and ecclesiastical authorities had summoned a *junta,* which was on the verge of recommending dissolution of the new convent. Teresa herself writes, "There was only one of them, a Presentado of the Order of St. Dominic, who was not opposed to the convent, though he objected to its poverty: he said that there was no reason for dissolving it . . ." (*Life of the Holy Mother Teresa of Jesus by Herself,* in *op. cit.* 1:254). Báñez's own words are quoted from the *Cronica carmelitana* by F. Martin, OP [*Santa Teresa y la Orden de Predicadores* (Ávila 1909) 275–2771].

Nearly all the correspondence between them has been lost; only four letters of the saint to Báñez and one of his letters to her are extant. He did carefully read over her *Vida,* or autobiography; and when years after its completion it was denounced to the Holy Office in Madrid in 1574, Báñez sent his own copy to the Holy Office with a vigorous vindication appended to the blank pages at the end of the volume, which judgment the Holy Office made its own. It was also at Báñez's suggestion that the saint wrote her *Way of Perfection.* He also gave deposition to the preparatory commission for Teresa's canonization. This holy association most probably accounts for a Thomistic cast of mind that underlies her spirituality. At any rate, Báñez did discern the work of God in her in spite of her exaggerated accounts of her own sins and his own acknowledged suspicions concerning her mystical visions and locutions. The image of him that emerges from St. Teresa's writings is of a learned man who was at the same time discreet and judicious, inclined to be firm and unbending with her and counseling above all patience and charity toward those who persecuted her.

Disputes on grace. The late 15th and the 16th centuries saw a revival of SCHOLASTICISM, especially in Spain, where Renaissance culture and the religious ferment of the Reformation were not strongly felt. The revival was dominated for the most part by illustrious Dominican theologians such as F. de Vitoria, M. Cano, D. de Soto, B. de Medina and finally Báñez. It received further impetus from the Council of Trent, summoned in 1545. In 1540 the Society of Jesus was founded, and after officially adopting the theological system of St. Thomas, the society soon entered into the academic life of the period. The first phase of an unrivaled theological controversy occurred in Salamanca in 1582. In a public disputation conducted by the Mercederian priest Francisco Zumel, Prudentius Montemayor, a Jesuit, defended the proposition that Christ, acting in obedience to His Father's command, died neither freely nor meritoriously. Supporting him on this was an Augustinian, Louis of León. This occasioned a strong reaction from the faculty at Salamanca, in particular from Báñez. Further debate resulted, culminating in the matter's being brought before the Inquisition, where on Feb. 3, 1584, judgment was pronounced against Montemayor and León. By this time the area of disagreement had broadened and 16 distinct propositions were condemned, among which were the following:

6. "God is not the cause of the free operation but only causes the cause to be."

9. "The providence of God does not determine the human will or any other particular cause to operate well, but rather the particular cause determines the act of divine providence."

13. "The impious man in his justification determines the sufficient help of God to actual use by his own will."

The second phase of the controversy occurred in 1588 with the publication in Lisbon of the first edition of the *Concordia liberi arbitrii cum gratiae donis, divina praescientia, providentia, praedestinatione et reprobatione* of Luis de MOLINA, SJ. The Inquisitor General of Portugal, Cardinal Albert of Austria, withheld distribution of the book pending the theological evaluation of Báñez, whom he had appointed as censor. It was the latter's opinion that Molina was giving restatement to six of the already condemned propositions of the preMolinists. Presented with these objections, Molina wrote a defense of himself and in August 1589 the *Concordia* was given an imprimatur and published with the defense as an appendix. The resulting agitations grew to alarming proportions, especially in the public debates between the Jesuits and Dominicans in March and May of 1594 in Valladolid, until in August of that year the papal nuncio at Madrid imposed silence on the disputants and related the matter to Rome. Molina sought to defend himself by denouncing Báñez to the Inquisition at Castile. Báñez replied with the publication in 1595 of *Apologia fratrum praedicatorum in provincia hispaniae sacrae theologiae professorum, adversus novas quasdam assertions cuiusdam doctoris Ludovici Molinae nuncupati,* in joint authorship with P. Herrera and D. Alvarez, both Dominicans. This was followed by the *Libellus supplex* in October of 1597, a letter (for text see De Meyer) addressed by Báñez to Pope Clement VIII seeking dissolution of the silence imposed in 1594. Cardinal C. Madruzzi writing on behalf of the pope to the nuncio granted this in a letter in February of 1598. Báñez's active participation ceased at this point; the *CONGREGATIO DE AUXILIIS*, begun in Rome in 1598, extended over two pontificates until 1607, three years after Báñez's death. It failed to resolve the dispute, choosing not to define either position as the true doctrine of the Church and granting each side freedom to teach in accord with its own interpretation.

The charge of Bañezianism. Molina's central doctrinal assertion was that God's graces are rendered efficacious (*see* GRACE, EFFICACIOUS) by the actual consent of the human will. God's infallible foreknowledge is safeguarded by recourse to a hypothesis, admittedly original with himself, namely, that there is in God a *SCIENTIA MEDIA*, or intermediate knowledge, whereby God foreknows what every man will choose in varying circumstances, before the will determines itself and independently of any divine PREDETERMINATION. Primary among the conclusions flowing from this is that God predestines those whom He foresees as consenting to His grace.

Báñez took immediate exception to this, seeing therein a rejection of the traditional teaching, founded in St. Augustine and St. Thomas, wherein grace is intrinsically efficacious as itself effecting the will's free consent, so that predestination is ultimately gratuitous rather than dependent upon foreseen merits. [*See* PREDESTINATION (IN CATHOLIC THEOLOGY)].

Historically, the countercharge was made that Báñez himself was an innovator; that such concepts as physical PREMOTION, intrinsically efficacious grace and predestination completely apart from foreseen merits represent but one interpretation of St. Thomas; and that such Thomism is in reality Bañezianism [cf, G. Schneemann, SJ, *Controversiarum de divinae gratiae liberique arbitrii concordia initia et progressus* (Freiburg 1881) and T. DE RÉGNON, SJ, *Báñez et Molina* (Paris 1883)]. This allegation has been rigorously refuted [cf. A. M. Dummermuth, OP, *Defensio doctrinae s. Thomae* (Louvain and Paris, 1895) and Cardinal T. Zigliara, OP, *Summa philosophica* (Paris 1898) 2:525]. The attribution to Báñez even among authors of the Molinist school is by no means universal; F. Suárez points rather to De Medina as the author of physical premotion (*De auxiliis* 7.2; Vivès 11:183), even at one point assigning the doctrine to St. Thomas (*De concursu Dei cum voluntate* 11.6; Vivès 11:50); Victor Frins, SJ, in his reply to Dummermuth traces the teaching back to F. de Vitoria.

With the waning of the controversy, there seems little doubt on the point of Báñez's fidelity to St. Thomas. His own intentions were very clear as is evident from his autobiographical prologue to his commentary on the *Prima pars.* The judgment of Cardinal Madruzzi corroborates this: "His teaching seems to be deduced from the principles of St. Thomas and to flow wholly from St. Thomas's doctrine, though he differs somewhat in his mode of speaking" (J. H. Serry, appendix 89). The equivalent of what he taught can be found in St. Thomas, as, for example, the intrinsic efficacy of grace (*De ver.* 6.2 ad 11). The very difficulties raised by the Molinist position and the new doctrines of the reformers, as well as Báñez's polemical intentions, account for the variations in language. Contemporary Thomistic thought does tend to mitigate somewhat the rigidity of his vocabulary [for example, F. Marín-Sola, OP, *Concordia tomista entre la mocion divina y la libertad creada,* 3 v. (Salamanca 1958) and F. P. Muñiz, OP, "Es posible una predestinación gratuita post praevisa merita?" *La ciencia tomista,* 73 (1947) 105–115], but this is a matter of emphasis and development, not rejection. Doctrinally, he stands in the main stream of Thomism linked both to his predecessors and to his successors.

Viewed from the vantage point of 400 years of history, two reflections suggest themselves: (1) that the disputes were excessively negative and partisan, perhaps hindering intellectual effort of a more positive nature; and (2) that, on the other hand, questions of great import and urgency were raised that had to be dealt with and that were profoundly clarified, if not resolved.

Báñez's writings. Báñez's depth and clarity earn him a deserved place in the forefront of St. Thomas's great commentators, a reputation that rests largely upon the following works. Scholastic commentaries: *In lam Partem divi Thomae,* qq. 1–64 (Salamanca 1584); qq. 65–119 (1588); *In 2am2ae Partem,* qq. 1–46 (1584); qq. 47–189 (1594). The following commentaries have been newly translated by V. Beltrán de Heredia, OP: *In lam2ae Partem—De fine ultimo et de actibus humanis, De vitiis et peccatis, De gratia* (Salamanca 1942–48); *In 3am Partem—De Verbo incarnato, De sacramentis* (Salamanca 1951–53). Other works: *Relectio de merito et augmento caritatis* (Salamanca 1590); *Institutiones minoris dialecticae* (Salamanca 1599); *Comment, in Libros de generatione et corruptione* (Salamanca 1585).

See Also: CONGRUISM; FREE WILL AND GRACE; FREE WILL AND PROVIDENCE; FUTURIBLE; GRACE, ARTICLES ON; GRACE, CONTROVERSIES ON; MOLINISM; OMNISCIENCE; PERSEVERANCE, FINAL; PREDEFINITION; REPROBATION, WILL OF GOD.

Bibliography: P. MANDONNET, *Dictionnaire de théologie catholique,* ed. A. VACANT et al., 15 v. (Paris 1903–50) 2.1:140–145. A. DUVAL, *Catholicisme,* 1:1202–04. C. VELECKY, *A Catholic Dictionary of Theology* (London 1962–) 1:227–228. L. DE MEYER, *Historia controversiarum de divinae gratiae auxiliis* (Venice 1742). N. DEL PRADO, *De gratia et libero arbitrio,* 3 v. (Fribourg 1907). R. GARRIGOU-LAGRANGE, *God: His Existence and His Nature,* tr., B. ROSE, 2 v. (St. Louis 1934–36), see app. T. DE LEMOS, *Panoplia gratiae,* 4 v. in 2 (Liège 1676). M. LÉPÉE, *Báñez et Ste. Thérèse* (Paris 1947). J. QUÉTIF and J. ÉCHARD, *Scriptores Ordinis Praedicatorum,* 5 v. (Paris 1719–23) 2.1:352–353. J. H. SERRY, *Historia congregationum de auxiliis divinae gratiae* (Venice 1740). D. BÁÑEZ, *Scholastica commentaria in primam partem* (Madrid 1934), prologue to 4 v. ed. of L. URBANO. V. BELTRÁN DE HEREDIA, *Lexikon für Theologie und Kirche,* ed. J. HOFER and K. RAHNER, 10 v. (2d, new ed. Freiburg 1957–65) 1:1219–20; in *La ciencia tomista,* 25–28 (1922–23); 37–39 (1928–29); 47 (1933).

[W. J. HILL]

BANGLADESH, THE CATHOLIC CHURCH IN

Encompassing the fertile delta of the Ganges and Brahmaputra rivers in the northeastern part of the Indian subcontinent, Bangladesh is bordered on the north, east, and west by India, on the southeast by Burma, and on the south by the Bay of Bengal. The cultivation of jute provides the country with its main economic base and rice is its main food crop; other resources include undeveloped coal, oil, and natural gas deposits. Each year, from June to October, Bangladesh is visited by monsoons that leave over one-third of its arable land flooded. Such routine flooding, augmented by violent cyclones, hampers agricultural productivity in this desperately poor country, and outbreaks of water-borne diseases have combined with food and water shortages to make the life expectancy for the average Bangladeshi only 60 years. Fewer than half of all adult Bangladeshi males can read and write; the country's overpopulation and poverty continue to invite foreign humanitarian aid.

Part of what is historically known as Bengal, the People's Republic of Bangladesh came into being in

1971. During the British colonial period it formed the province of East Bengal. In 1947 the Indian subcontinent was partitioned between India and Pakistan, and predominantly Muslim East Bengal became East Pakistan, one of the five provinces of Pakistan. East Pakistan's physical distance from the other four predominately Hindu provinces—1,100 miles across Indian territory— emboldened the region's Muslim agitators, and after the 1970 election civil war ensued. The people of Bangladesh belong to a number of ethno-linguistic groups that migrated into the area over the centuries; the largest of these are speakers of the Bengali language.

Ecclesiastically, Bangladesh is divided into six dioceses administered by native bishops. The archdiocese of Dhaka oversees suffragans Chittagong, Dinajpur, Khulna, Mymensingh, and Rajshahi.

Missionary Foundations. The early history of the Catholic Church in Bangladesh is closely linked to Portugese missionary activity in the rest of the Indian subcontinent. Originally the home of Buddhist and Hindu peoples, East Bengal came under Muslim rule in the 13th century. The first missionaries came to the area in 1517, making their headquarters at Hoogly in West Bengal (now India). Meanwhile, a large community of Portugese traders settled in East Bengal in the port city of Chittagong. In 1599 four Jesuit missionaries arrived in Chittagong to minister to this community, one of whom went on to Chandecan, near the present town of Sathkhira in the southwest of the country. There the first church was dedicated Jan. 1, 1600, as the Church of Jesus. The second church, established at Chittagong in 1601, was dedicated to St. John the Baptist.

When the Muslim Moghuls made Dhaka the capital city of Bengal in 1608, that city grew in trade and prominence, along with its Portuguese settlers and other foreign traders. In 1612 Portuguese Augustinian missionaries first introduced Christianity in Dhaka, and in 1628 they built the first church, the Church of the Assumption, at Narinda, the downtown area of Dhaka.

The first Catholic parish in East Bengal, Holy Rosary Church, was established in 1677 at Tejgaon in Dhaka. In 1695 the second parish was set up at Nagari, 20 miles northeast of Dhaka, named after St. Nicholas of Tolentino. The third church at Barisal, dedicated to Our Lady of Guidance, was built in 1764 in the present diocese of Chittagong. Other parishes were established in the 19th and 20th centuries in response to the gradual increase of the Christian population and migration of families from one part of the country to another.

In 1606, when Mylapore (Madras State, India) became a diocese, all the mission centers of undivided Bengal were brought under its jurisdiction. In 1834 Rome created the vicariate apostolic of Bengal under the jurisdiction of the Congregation for the PROPAGATION OF THE FAITH and in 1850 subdivided it into the vicariates apostolic of Western Bengal and Eastern Bengal. Two years later the vicariate of East Bengal, with headquarters at Dhaka, was entrusted to the newly founded Congregation of the Holy Cross. The first Holy Cross missionaries of the Canadian Province arrived in May 1853 and administered the vicarate until 1876, when they were called back to France. The vicariate was administered by Benedictine monks of the Anglo-Belgian province until the missionaries returned in 1889.

Catholic Diocese Established. On Sept. 1, 1886, Pope Leo XIII gave Dhaka the status of a diocese, the first in East Bengal. The new diocese included the territories of the present-day diocese of Chittagong (Bangladesh), Silchar (Assam, India), and Prome (Burma). However it was not until Nov. 12, 1890, that the secretary of the Congregation for the Propagation of the Faith announced the selection of Augustine Joseph Louage, CSC, as the first bishop of Dhaka; he arrived the following March. In September 1960, Pope John XXIII would name Theotonius Amol Ganguly the first native auxiliary bishop of Dhaka, delighting Bengalis. Ganguly was the archbishop of Dhaka from 1967 to his death in 1977.

On May 25, 1927, the dioceses of Chittagong and Dinajpur were created as new dioceses for better administration. Even after Great Britain relinquished its colonial power over the Indian subcontinent in 1947, Dhaka remained a suffragan of the archdiocese of Calcutta. However, in July 1950, a new ecclesiastical province was created when Dhaka was raised to an archdiocese and the dioceses of Chittagong and Dinajpur became its suffragans. On Jan. 3, 1952, Khulna Diocese (until 1956 called Jessore Diocese) became the fourth diocese in East Pakistan. Although the new diocese of Chittagong was initially entrusted to the Holy Cross missionaries, in 1952 the portion of the diocese in the Indian territory of Assam was detached to form the separate diocese of Silchar in India.

Due to massive migrations and social unrest between Muslims and Hindus following the partition of the Indian subcontinent, a major Church restructuring was eventually required. The present dioceses of Domka and Raigonj, as well as part of Jalpaiguri, were detached from the diocese of Dinajpur to join the Indian dioceses. Khulna Diocese was given to the St. Francis Xavier Foreign Mission Society, popularly known as the Xaverian Fathers.

The Church after Independence. On Dec. 16, 1971, after a nine-month war of independence in Pakistan, western Pakistan and eastern Pakistan were separated; East Pakistan became the independent state of Bangladesh. In 1988 Islam was declared the state religion, although freedom of religion was granted by the new constitution. Dhaka became the metropolitan see of this new country and grew in importance and greater responsibility. The ancient political capital also became the spiritual capital of Catholic Bangladesh.

On May 15, 1987, a year after visiting Bangladesh, Pope John Paul II created the diocese of Mymensingh and named Francis Anthony Gomes as the first bishop. And on May 21, 1990, the diocese of Rajshahi was canonically created, incorporating into its territory the southern portion of the greater diocese of Dinajpur. Patrick D'Rozario, CSC, was appointed as the first bishop of the new diocese.

Capital: Dhaka.
Size: 55,598 sq. miles.
Population: 129,194,200 in 2000.
Languages: Bangla (official language), English, Urdu, Bihari, and Hindi are also spoken.
Religions: 249,500 Catholics (.2%), 113,690,900 Muslims (88%), 14,211,300 Hindu (11%), 805,400 Buddhist (.6%)

In 1975, as a consequence of independence, a national major seminary was formally established in Dhaka to train candidates for priesthood as well as for the formation of native sisters, brothers, and laypersons. The Dhaka seminary resulted in an increase in the number of local priests, their numbers outstripping those of foreign priests by the early 1990s.

The Church Moves into the 21st Century. The majority of Bangladeshi Christians, a small fraction of the total population, were traditionally members of the Lushai tribe. Of these Christians, half were members of one of the country's 76 Catholic parishes in 2000. The Church continued to combat Bangladesh' high illiteracy rates through operation of two colleges, over 40 high schools, 190 primary schools and coaching centers, and four technical schools throughout the country. In addition, the Church provided much-needed humanitarian aid through its hospitals and dispensaries, leprosaria, orphanages, and homes for abandoned and disabled children and the destitute. In addition, Catholic-run Caritas Bangladesh gained international prominence for its involvement in human development issues, and Catholic organizations continued to be at the forefront in responding to the region's continuing struggle against natural disasters, such as the severe flooding that occurred in 1998.

By 2000 Bangladesh was cited as the most densely populated country in the world. Stresses caused by this extreme overpopulation, as well as by famine and continuing religious and ethnic differences flared in 1998, as Muslim extremists took credit for several attacks on both Catholic and Protestant churches and schools in Dhaka. In an effort to mitigate such actions, Bangladeshi bishops encouraged ecumenical programs and social outreach through all the country's parishes.

Bibliography: J. D'COSTA, *History of the Catholic Church in Bangladesh,* v. 1 (Dhaka 1988). S. D. ROZARIO, *The Catholic Directory of Bangladesh* (Dhaka 1992). J. J. A. CAMPOSE, *History of the Portuguese in Bengal* (Calcutta 1919).

[S. D. ROZARIO/EDS.]

BANGOR, ABBEYS OF

Three former Celtic abbeys of this name.

Bangor Fawr yn Arfon, on the eastern side of Menai Straits, Caernarvonshire, Wales, was founded by St. Deiniol in the 6th century and became the seat of the ancient See of Bangor.

Bangor-ys-coed, in Powys, Wales, on the river Dee, some 12 miles south of Chester, England, is noted for its abbot Dunot (Donatus), who was one of the seven native British bishops who met AUGUSTINE OF CANTERBURY in the second conference held between the Christian Britons and the missionaries from Rome. The meeting was a failure, and BEDE (*Hist. eccl.* 2.2) relates that the monks of Bangor were massacred by the Saxons under King Ethelfrid of Northumbria, in what was for the Britons the disastrous Battle of Chester (616). The number of monks slain is given at 1,200, which indicates a monastery of exceptional size and importance. However, it had a far more modest status in the succeeding centuries.

Bangor in the Ards of Ulster, County Down, Ireland, was founded *c.* 555 by St. COMGALL, who received his religious formation from St. Fintan of Clonenagh in Leix. The observance in Clonenagh was noted for its severity, and it was this exceptionally hard rule that, through Bangor and LUXEUIL, became the Irish rule known on the Continent of Europe. It was Comgall who helped (St.) COLUMBA OF IONA convert the Picts of Scotland and then sent (St.) Columban with 12 companions to help restore religious life in Merovingian Gaul. The writings of Columban and the liturgical manuscript known as the Antiphonary of Bangor (compiled 680–691), now in the Ambrosian Library, Milan, bear witness to the excellence of the monastic school. The Antiphonary contains *Sancti venite, Christi corpus sumite,* said to be the oldest Eucharistic hymn in existence. Comgall's vita claims that the Bangor community numbered 3,000, a statement repeated by BERNARD OF CLAIRVAUX in his life of St. MALACHY of Armagh (d. 1148). Bangor suffered severely at the hands of the Vikings; Malachy's revival met with only limited success. Later, Franciscans and Augustinians occupied the buildings. Only ruins remain.

Bibliography: *The Antiphonary,* ed. F. E. WARREN, 2 v. (Henry Bradshaw Society 4; 1893–95). *The Annals of Ulster,* ed. and tr. W. M. HENNESSEY and B. MACCARTHY, 4 v. (Dublin 1887–1901). R. GRAHAM, *Dictionnaire d'histoire et de géographie ecclésiastiques*, ed. A. BAUDRILLART et al. (Paris 1912–) 6:502. F. O'BRIAIN, *ibid.* 6:497–502.

[J. RYAN]

BANGOR, ANCIENT SEE OF

One of the four ancient Welsh dioceses growing out of the monastery of Bangor, Caernarvonshire, traditionally founded by St. Deiniol in the 6th century. Because WALES was converted by Celtic monk missionaries of the ''Age of Saints,'' Bangor, like other Welsh dioceses, was at first nonterritorial in character and depended on the affiliation of daughter churches to monastic mother churches in Gwynedd (northwest Wales). Chance very largely determined which of the leading Welsh monasteries should become permanent ecclesiastical sees. In 768 Elfodd, often called bishop of Bangor (more strictly, chief bishop of Gwynedd), took the lead in securing recognition of papal authority by the Welsh Church. After the Norman Conquest the boundaries of Bangor, which covered, broadly speaking, the modern counties of Anglesey, Caernarvon, and Merioneth, were delimited; and there were attempts to get Norman bishops elected and an oath of canonical obedience made to Canterbury. But the counter influence of the powerful native princes of Gwynedd usually sufficed to ensure the election of their own Welsh nominees. Even after the Edwardian Conquest (1282–83), and until late in the 14th century, the bishops chosen, often by papal PROVISION, were usually Welsh. Thereafter, the bishops were ordinarily royal nominees, frequently royal confessors and friars. The cathedral at Bangor was rebuilt by Bishop Anian (1267–1305), who cooperated closely with Abp. JOHN PECKHAM. A fine PONTIFICAL belonging to Anian is still preserved at Bangor, and bishops' registers survive from the 16th century. The cathedral was partly destroyed during the Glyn Dêr Rebellion (1400–10). It remained in ruinous condition for most of the 15th century, when successive bishops complained of the extreme poverty of the see, rated in *Valor ecclesiasticus* at £ 131—the poorest in England and Wales. Bp. Henry DEANE began the work of rebuilding, which was completed by Bishop Skeffington (1509–33). In 1558 Bangor's last Roman Catholic bishop-elect, Morys Clynnog, went into exile in Italy. Today Bangor is one of the six dioceses of the Church of Wales.

For information on the liturgical customs and usages of Bangor, *see* BANGOR USE.

See Also: LLANDAFF, ANCIENT SEE OF; SAINT ASAPH, ANCIENT SEE OF; SAINT DAVIDS, ANCIENT SEE OF.

Bibliography: *A Bibliography of the History of Wales* (2d ed. Cardiff 1962). J. C. DAVIES, *Episcopal Acts Relating to Welsh Dioceses, 1066–1272,* 2 v. (Cardiff 1946–48). G. WILLIAMS, *The Welsh Church from Conquest to Reformation* (Cardiff 1962).

[G. WILLIAMS/EDS.]

BANGOR USE

The first clear mention of a Bangor Use occurs in the introductory note prefixed by Cranmer to the *Book of*

Common Prayer, where he mentions that in the past "some followed Salisbury use, some Hereford use, and some the use of Bangor. . . ." But there seems to be no evidence now remaining to inform us what this use was. It has been supposed that its calendar was rich in Celtic, especially Welsh, saints, and that some Celtic practices were preserved, but this is no more than conjecture. William Maskell thought that he possessed a Bangor Missal, but this has proved to be nothing else than a Sarum Missal used (predominantly, at any rate) at Oswestry, and thus containing certain additional features like local feasts that led to his making the mistake. It certainly shows no characteristics that could lead us to suppose that it contained a number of specific local elements that would entitle it to be classed as a separate use. The Diocese of Bangor in Carnarvonshire, Wales (to be distinguished from Bangor in Ireland, *see* CELTIC RITE), according to tradition was founded by St. Deiniol (d. *c.* 584), but little is known of it until after the Norman Conquest. It can be supposed that the liturgy was revised at that time, probably on the general lines of the revision that took place elsewhere. That the calendar reflected local conditions is probable, but further than this it is impossible to conjecture without evidence.

Bibliography: W. MASKELL, *The Ancient Liturgy of the Church of England, According to the Uses of Sarum, Bangor, York and Herford, and the Modern Roman Liturgy* (3d ed. Oxford 1882). A. A. KING, *Liturgies of the Past* (Milwaukee 1959). W. H. ST. J. HOPE and E. G. ATCHLEY, *English Liturgical Colours* (London 1918). E. BISHOP, *Liturgica Historica,* ed. R. H. CONNOLLY and K. SISAM (Oxford 1918).

[L. C. SHEPPARD/EDS.]

BANNON, JOHN B.

Military chaplain, Confederate commissioner; b. Roosky, County Roscommon, Ireland, Dec. 28, 1829; d. Dublin, Ireland, July 14, 1913. Following his ordination at Maynooth, Ireland, in 1853, he came to St. Louis, Mo., where he served at St. Louis Cathedral and the Immaculate Conception Church. In 1858 he was made pastor of St. John's parish and immediately began the construction of a new church, which was completed in 1860. With the outbreak of the Civil War, St. Louis was divided in its loyalty. Many of Bannon's parishioners joined the Confederate forces under Gen. Sterling Price at Springfield, Mo. Without obtaining permission from his bishop, Bannon left his newly built church and in January of 1862 began serving as a chaplain to the Confederate forces under Price. He was on the battlefields of Pea Ridge, Iuka, Corinth, Fort Gibson, and Vicksburg, winning the respect of all religious groups. He was granted a commission as chaplain, on Feb. 12, 1863. Later in the same year, he was released from the Confederate army and appointed Confederate commissioner to Ireland. His task was to win friends for the South among the Irish. He enjoyed some success in explaining the Confederate cause as he wrote letters to the leading newspapers, prepared articles for magazines, and distributed thousands of handbills throughout Ireland. When Bishop Patrick Lynch of Charleston, S.C., visited Europe as Confederate commissioner in 1864, Bannon accompanied him to Rome. Their efforts to obtain papal recognition of the Confederacy were unsuccessful. After returning to Ireland, Bannon entered the Society of Jesus on Jan. 9, 1865, and made his final vows on Feb. 2, 1876. He served at St. Ignatius University College Church, Dublin, and St. Francis Xavier, Dublin, where for a while he was superior.

Bibliography: J. E. ROTHENSTEINER, *History of the Archdiocese of St. Louis,* 2 v. (St. Louis 1928). L. F. STOCK, "Catholic Participation in the Diplomacy of the Southern Confederacy," *American Catholic Historical Review* 16 (1930) 1–18.

[A. PLAISANCE]

BAOUARDY, MARÍAM, BL.

In religion, Marie de Jésus Crucifié, also known as Marie of Pau, Discalced Carmelite; b. Abellin (Zabulon, between Nazareth and Haifa), Cheffa-Amar, Galilee, Palestine (now Israel), Jan. 5, 1846; d. Bethlehem, Aug. 26, 1878. Miríam was born into a poor, Lebanese, Greek Melchite Catholic family headed by Giries (George) Baouardy and Maríam Chahyn. Her parents died when she was very young, and when she was three, an uncle in Alexandria, Egypt, took in the orphaned Maríam and her brother Boulos (Paul). At age 13, she refused an arranged marriage in order to consecrate her virginity to God and entered domestic service. She had never learned to read or write.

While working for families in Alexandria, Jerusalem, Beirut, and Marseilles, she discerned her vocation. In 1865, she entered the Sisters of Compassion, but was forced to leave because of ill health. For the next two years (May 1865 to June 1867) she was a postulant of the Institute of the Sisters of St. Joseph of the Apparition until she was judged unsuited for the cloister because of the unusual manifestations of her spiritual life, which included levitation, ectasies, and stimagtization (1867–76).

Together with her former novice mistress, Miríam joined the Discalced Carmelites at Pau, France (June 14, 1867). In 1870, she was sent with a group of founding sisters to Mangalore, India, where she made her profession (Nov. 21, 1871). Her spiritual director, Apostolic Vicar Ephrem M. Garrelon, believing her mystical experiences were a sign of demonic obsession, obliged her to return to France in 1872. In August 1875 she traveled to Palestine, where she died, to build a carmel at Bethlehem and to plan another for Nazareth. Maríam, patroness of prisoners, is best remembered for her humility and devotion to the Holy Spirit. Her cause was officially introduced in Rome on May 18, 1927, and she was beatified by John Paul II, Nov. 13, 1983.

Feast: Aug. 25 (Carmelites).

Bibliography: *Acta Apostolicae Sedis* 77 (1985): 5–8. *L'Osservatore Romano,* English edition, no. 48 (1983): 10. B. STOLZ, *Flamme der göttlichen Liebe* (3d ed. Gröbenzell 1970).

[K. I. RABENSTEIN]

BAPST, JOHN

Jesuit missionary and educator; b. LaRoche, Switzerland, Dec. 7, 1815; d. Baltimore, Md., Nov. 2, 1887. A prosperous farmer's son, Bapst attended St. Michael's College, Fribourg, Switzerland, entered the Society of Jesus in 1835, and was ordained in 1846. As one of a group of exiled Swiss Jesuits assigned to the United States, he arrived in New York in May of 1848. Although highly qualified for the classroom and disinclined to the missions, Bapst was immediately assigned to reside with the Indians on Indian Island in the newly established mission in north central Maine. He and a few companions organized a circuit covering 33 towns and serving, until recalled in 1859, about 9,000 people—Irish, Canadians, and the Indians on two reservations. The opposition of KNOW-NOTHINGISM in Ellsworth, Maine, ended in a brutal attack on him on Oct. 14, 1853, when he was tarred and feathered. Horrified Protestants of Bangor, Maine, honored him after his recovery. He was rector of the Boston, Mass., Jesuit seminary (1860–63), the first president of Boston College (1864–69), and superior of the New York/Canadian Mission (1869–73). His health had failed by 1881, and during the last years of his life his mind was haunted by the Ellsworth outrage.

Bibliography: Archives, Woodstock College, Md., J. Bapst correspondence. ''Fr. J. B., a Sketch,'' *Woodstock Letters* 17 (1888); 18 (1889); 20 (1891), contains many letters from the preceding reference. W. L. LUCEY, *The Catholic Church in Maine* (Francestown, N.H. 1957). D. R. DUNIGAN, *A History of Boston College* (Milwaukee 1947).

[W. L. LUCEY]

BAPTISM (IN THE BIBLE)

Described in the NT as the sacramental entrance into the people of God, baptism was foreshadowed in the OT by CIRCUMCISION and typified by the crossing of the RED SEA. Baptism into Christ, when received in faith, effects forgiveness of sin, bestows the Holy Spirit, and unites the believer to Christ's Mystical Body (*see* CHURCH, I [IN THE BIBLE]). As a providential preparation for the baptism instituted by Christ, a widespread use of ablutions and washings appeared in the religious sects of the pagan and Jewish world in the age preceding Christ; this preparation was climaxed in proselyte baptism of the Jews and the ministry of John the Baptist. This article treats baptism in three main sections: terminology, pre-Christian practices, and baptism in the NT.

Terminology. The name ''baptism'' came from the Greek noun βάπτισμα, ''the dipping, washing,'' less commonly βαπτισμός, stemming from the verb βάπτω, ''to dip'' or ''immerse.'' In the NT this verb is used only in the literal sense (Lk 16.24; Jn 13.26; Rv 19.13). From this form is derived the iterative form βαπτίζω, which, in classical Greek, was used in the literal sense of ''dipping'' and in the figurative sense of ''being overwhelmed'' with sufferings and miseries. The latter figurative meaning occurs in the NT where Christ and His Apostles are described as ''baptized'' with suffering (Mk 10.38–39). For the rest of the NT, however, the verb βαπτίζω has its technical sense signifying the religious ceremony of baptism. The nouns, also, are used in a technical religious sense: βαπτισμός designates the act of baptizing; βάπτισμα, used only in the NT and by later Christian writers, signifies baptism as an institution; and, ὁ βαπτιστής (the baptizer) became the title of John the Baptist. This development of technical terminology demonstrates that baptism was considered something special, something new; therefore, these technical terms were merely transliterated, not translated, into the Latin alphabet as *baptizo, baptisma,* and *baptista.*

Pre-Christian Practices. Christian baptism is an external rite that signifies what it effects. The rite of washing had long been used as a religious practice; the signification attributed to it in Christian times builds upon these earlier usages, and so an investigation of them will be useful to the present study.

In the Pagan World. In the ancient world the waters of the Ganges in India, Euphrates in Babylonia, and Nile in Egypt were used for sacred baths; the sacred bath was known also in the Hellenistic mystery cults. And in the Attis and Mithra cults sacred initiation included a blood bath. A twofold effect was attributed to these baths: first, a cleansing from ritual and, more rarely, moral impurities that, according to primitive notions, could be washed away like bodily dirt; second, a bestowal of immortality and an increase of vital strength. The latter idea developed especially in Egypt where a person who drowned in the Nile became divinized. Mystery baths and baptisms are only a further step; in symbolic rite the initiate dies, and his death results in divinization. Cleansing and vivification, however, are understood more in the merely ritual or magic than in the moral sense. This deficiency in their religion was sensed even by the pagans.

In the Old Testament and Judaism. The Hebrew verb *ṭābal,* which the Septuagint (LXX) regularly translates by βάπτω, means ''to dip'' into a liquid, e.g., a morsel into wine (Ru 2.14), the feet into the river (Jos 3.15), and ritually defiled objects into water. In the OT, *ṭābal* becomes a technical term connected with removal of ritual impurity: dipping (*ṭābal,* βάπτω) hyssop into blood and sprinkling it upon a leper who has been healed is part of the ritual by which he is pronounced clean (Lv 14.6–7). Later Judaism multiplied prescriptions of ritual purity referred to in the Gospels as ''washing [βαπτισμός] of cups and pots'' (Mk 7.4) and ''bathing [ἐβαπτίσθη] before eating'' (Lk 11.38).

Baths were prescribed also by the Torah for the removal of various kinds of ritual impurities; one must bathe after being cured of leprosy (Lv 14.8–9), after contracting personal uncleanness (Lv 15.11, 13, 16, 18,27), and after touching a corpse (Nm 19.19). But in all these instances, not the term *ṭābal,* but *rāhas* (*bammayim*), ''to wash (in water),'' is used, equivalent to a sort of sponge bath. Only once, in a clear case of immersion, does the LXX translate *ṭābal* with βαπτίζω: ''He [Naaman] went down, and washed in the Jordan seven times'' (2 Kgs 5.14). In later times, *ṭābal* and, therefore, βαπτίζω, became the technical terms for such bathing to remove ritual uncleanness: ''Each night she [Judith] went out to the ravine of Bethulia, where she washed herself [ἐβαπτίζετο] at the spring of the camp'' (Jdt 12.7). But these Jewish practices of washing and bathing were intended merely as ritual purifications and had no direct moral purpose.

An extension of the general custom of ritual washings and the simple bath of purification was proselyte baptism, which in later Judaism was prescribed for Gentile converts (*see* PROSELYTES [BIBLICAL]). Slowly it developed into a recognized rite of initiation consisting of three parts: circumcision, baptism, and sacrifice. It seems that this ritual rose from Jewish consciousness of the necessity for a Gentile proselyte to repeat the triple experience of the Israelites who had participated in the Sinaitic covenant: they were circumcised ''a second time'' (Jos 5.2), they were baptized in the desert (Ex 19.10 reads ''sanctify,'' but Jewish tradition understood this in a baptismal sense; cf. 1 Cor 10.2), and they shared the covenant sacrifice (Ex 24.3–8). Thus it was through circumcision and baptism that the non-Jew entered the covenant and became a full-fledged Israelite. All this, however, was concerned primarily with legal purity and juridical incorporation. As for the origin of proselyte baptism it must have been practiced in Judaism prior to Christianity; it is hardly likely that the Jews would have borrowed the practice of baptism from a sect they looked upon with animosity.

In the New Testament. By Christian baptism one enters into the kingdom of God and into the sphere of the saving work of Christ. John the Baptist proclaimed the advent of the kingdom and administered a baptism of penance by which those who received it proclaimed their willingness to enter the kingdom; his ministry, then, presents a good transition from earlier baptismal practices to those which were specifically Christian in character.

Baptism of John. From the middle of the 2d century B.C. until *c.* A.D. 300 there was a great deal of baptismal activity in Syria and Palestine, especially along the upper Jordan, among many different groups (see J. Thomas). But the different forms of ablution, whether the lustrations of Hellenistic syncretism, the baptism of the Mandaeans (a Gnostic sect of the Christian era; *see* MANDAEAN RELIGION), the bath of the ESSENES, or finally, proselyte baptism of late Judaism, are insufficient to account fully for the baptism of John; they fall short of the ethical and messianic implications of his baptism. Providentially, by the earlier baptismal movements, the people were disposed more immediately for John's baptism and ultimately for that of Christ. The fact that John came to be known as ''baptizer'' or the ''Baptist'' (even Flavius Josephus mentions him by this title in *Jewish Antiquities* 18.5.2 par. 116–117) shows that his activity must have been considered as something special and, at least partly, something new. This title was obviously first given him, not by Christians, but by pre-Christian popular consent.

In the mystery religions the lustrations and baptisms were conceived of as working magically; in Judaism proselyte baptism was derived from a legalistic conception of uncleanness; in contrast, John's baptism had an explicitly moral character. It was the visible sign of μετάνοια (repentance; *see* CONVERSION, I [IN THE BIBLE]), a change of heart necessary for the remission of sins (''There came John . . . preaching a baptism of repentance for the forgiveness of sins'': Mk 1.4; see also Acts 13.24; 19.4). Soon after John, the mightier One, the Messiah, was to come. John's baptism prepared for the eschatological kingdom: ''Repent, for the kingdom of heaven is at hand'' (Mt 3.1).

The Prophets had already used the symbolism of bathing to express the idea of interior, moral purification (Is 1.16; Ez 36.25; Zec 13.1; Ps 50[51].9). Although John's baptism was administered by divine command

(''Was the baptism of John from heaven or from men?'' Mk 11.30–33), it was a baptism with water lacking full messianic efficacy; it was a figure and a preparation for the baptism instituted by Christ, a symbol of the right disposition for the coming kingdom.

John's baptism posed a crisis for the piety of contemporary Judaism. His baptism implied that the law and all efforts to observe it could not produce the sanctity envisioned and foretold by the Prophets. One greater than John must come who would baptize ''with the Holy Spirit and with fire'' (Mt 3.11). The Messiah would pour forth the Holy Spirit and with that (according to the baptist) a coinciding eschatological judgment. In Acts it is emphasized that the baptism of John, in contrast to that of Jesus, did not confer the Spirit (Acts 1.5; 11.15–16; 19.1–6). The baptism of John, unlike proselyte baptism, was administered primarily to Jews (Mk 1.5). Between John and those he baptized, a community that lasted beyond his death was established (Acts 19.1–4).

The lustral practices of the Essenes attest to the widespread concern for ritual purity in later Judaism. The bath of the QUMRAN COMMUNITY shows similarities to John's baptism: both demand a conversion to God as a condition for the forgiveness of sin; both occur more or less in an eschatological context (see J. Gnilka, 205). John's baptism, however, stands more in the tradition of the Prophets both in its demand for moral reform and as the climactic preparation for the imminent messianic kingdom, whereas the bath of the Essenes is inspired more by the tradition of the law, especially in its emphasis on ritual purity as a precondition to participation in community cult. The practice of the Essenes was exclusive, whereas John's baptism was open to all. Moreover, the bath of Qumran neither symbolized nor effected entrance into the community; it is not regarded as an initiation rite by the *Manual of Discipline.*

Jesus also baptized during His public life (Jn 3.22), not personally, but through His disciples (Jn 4.2). In this pre-Passion baptism St. Augustine and St. Thomas saw the Christian Sacrament, but this is improbable (''The Spirit had not yet been given, since Jesus had not yet been glorified'': Jn 7.39).

Jesus Baptized by John. The Synoptic Gospels (Mk 1.9–11 and parallels) record and the Fourth Gospel (Jn 1.32–34) presumes that Jesus accepted baptism from the hands of John. In this baptism Jesus is symbolically and actually commissioned as Servant of Yahweh (*see* SUFFERING SERVANT, SONGS OF). Other Jews came to the Jordan to be baptized by John for their own sins. Jesus was baptized not for His own sins, but for those of the whole people; He is the one whom Isaiah prophesied must suffer vicariously for the sins of the people. The words ''Thou art my beloved Son; in thee I am well pleased'' (Mk 1.11) bring to mind Is 42.1, 4: ''Here is my servant [LXX παῖς] whom I uphold, my chosen one with whom I am pleased, upon whom I have put my spirit; he shall bring forth justice to the nations, . . . establish justice on the earth.'' The Greek term παῖς means both servant and son, two titles of Christ. And this allusion is meant to recall the wider context of the other Servant of Yahweh Oracles, especially Is 53.4–7: ''It was our infirmities that he bore, our sufferings that he endured. . . . The Lord laid upon him the guilt of us all. He was harshly treated . . . ; like a lamb led to the slaughter . . . , he opened not his mouth.'' Jesus was baptized in view of His death that effected the forgiveness of sins for all men. For this reason Jesus must unite Himself in solidarity with His whole people; ''all justice must be fulfilled'' (Mt 3.15). Thus the baptism of Jesus points forward to the cross, in which alone all baptism will find its fulfillment.

At His baptism in the Jordan Jesus also received the fullness of the Spirit. His full possession of the Spirit was to be joined to His redemptive suffering as the Servant of God: ''I have put my Spirit upon him [the Servant of God]; he shall bring forth justice to the nations'' (Is 42.1). Consequently, in Jesus' baptism in the Jordan, the prototype of every Christian baptism, the effects of the later Sacrament are foreshadowed, i.e., ''justice to the nations [forgiveness of sins]'' and possession of the Spirit. (*See* BAPTISM OF CHRIST.)

In the Apostolic Church. To Nicodemus Jesus clearly stated the necessity of baptism for salvation: ''Unless a man be born again he cannot see the kingdom of God,'' and more specifically, ''Unless a man be born again of water and the Spirit, he cannot enter into the kingdom of God'' (Jn 3.3, 5). The author of the Fourth Gospel viewed the washing of the feet of the Apostles by Jesus as a symbol of the cleansing of baptism; this is suggested by the words of Christ: ''If I do not wash thee, thou shalt have no part with me'' (Jn 13.8).

After His Resurrection Jesus gave His disciples the commission to preach the Gospel to all nations and to ''baptize them in the name of the Father, and of the Son, and of the Holy Spirit, teaching them to observe all that I have commanded you'' (Mt 28.19–20). To this, Mk 16.16 adds the necessary condition of faith for baptism and thus for salvation. Since the command to baptize is one of His most important commissions, Jesus refers to the eschatological Lordship that empowers Him to give such a command. Although the explicit formula of baptism in Mt 28.19 may derive from the liturgy of the Church, the central meaning of baptism and the command to baptize derive from Christ. It is to be noted, too, that the clearly formulated necessity of baptism found in the

Fourth Gospel is due to the fact that the final form of this Gospel reflects the actual experience and practice of the Apostolic Church. This does not contradict the teaching that Jesus spoke explicitly about the necessity of baptism and that He gave the commission to baptize. If He had not, one could not explain why, from the very outset, starting with Pentecost, the Apostolic Church preached the absolute need of baptism for salvation, admonishing all to do penance, to believe in Jesus, and to be baptized (Acts 2.38, 41; 8.12–13, 16, 36, 38; 9.18; 10.47; 19.3–5). References in the Epistles also prove that baptism was a well-established institution forming the climax of preaching and its acceptance by faith (Rom 6.3; 1 Cor 12.13). Although St. Paul says that Christ did not send him to baptize but to preach (1 Cor 1.17), this does not argue against the necessity of baptism. No writer in the NT stresses the need for baptism more than St. Paul; he knows no unbaptized Christian (Rom 6.3).

It is evident that baptism in the early Church was by immersion. This is implicit in terminology and context: ''Let us draw near . . . having . . . the body washed with clean water'' (Heb 10.22), and the account of the Ethiopian chamberlain, who, to be baptized, ''went down into the water'' and ''came up out of the water'' (Acts 8.38–39). St. Paul sees in baptism a burial with Christ and a rising with Him (Rom 6.3–4; Col 2.12). The term λουτρόν (Eph 5.26; Ti 3.5), finally, can mean only ''bath.'' The DIDACHE for the first time clearly advises baptism of infusion in case of necessity, ''If you have no running water . . . , pour water on the head'' (7.2–3). The NT does not explicitly mention infusion. Yet one might wonder if the Apostles did not use it in cases where a great number of people were baptized (3,000 on the first Pentecost: Acts 2.41), or when circumstances hardly allowed immersion, as in the case of the nocturnal baptism in Philippi of the jailer and his family (Acts 16.33). The NT defines neither the exact rite of baptism nor the exact formulas. That some formula was pronounced by the minister in baptism is certain from Christ's command (Mt 28.19) and is perhaps alluded to in Ephesians when St. Paul says that Christ shall sanctify His Church ''cleansing her in the bath of water by means of the word'' (Eph 5.26). Yet, possibly, ''the word'' may refer to the confession of faith of the one baptized. Despite baptismal traditions evident in 1 Peter, the exact reconstruction of the baptismal rite remains problematic, as attempts of H. Preisker, R. Perdelwitz, and M. E. Boismard show. Besides the formula of Matthew in explicit Trinitarian form (Mt 28.19), the NT refers also to baptism ''into Christ'' and ''into the name of Christ'' (Acts 2.38; 8.16; 10.48; 19.5). It is not clear whether either short phrase represents a formal, established baptismal formula. To baptize in the name of Jesus may mean to baptize by the authority of Jesus in distinction from any other baptism. The Didache in one place quotes the Trinitarian formula, ''baptize as follows: after first explaining all these points, baptize in the name of the Father, and of the Son, and of the Holy Spirit'' (7.3) and in another place states that only ''those baptized in the name of the Lord'' (9.5) shall eat and drink of the Eucharist. The frequent use of εἰς (into) in this context, however, probably expresses the new relationship into which one enters with Christ through baptism; one enters into the sphere of His saving activity, becomes His property.

The recipient of baptism made a profession of faith, as evidenced from Acts 22.16, which was essentially an expression of belief in Jesus as Son of God, Lord, and Messiah (see also Rom 10.9; 1 Cor 12.3; Phil 2.11), of belief in God as the one who raised up Jesus from the dead, and in the Holy Spirit as Him whom Jesus in His exaltation possesses and imparts (Acts 2.32–39). It seems that the phrase often occurring in the context of baptism, ''What prevents [i.e., baptism]''—τί κωλύει (Acts 8.36; 10.47; 11.17; see also Mt. 3.13) refers to the prebaptismal examination that sought to determine whether any hindrance existed and whether the candidate had really fulfilled the preliminary conditions. Texts treating baptism furnish primary sources for the profession-of-faith formulas used in the early Church (Rom 10.9; 1 Cor 10.1–6; Heb 6.2).

Theological Significance. Christian baptism is the NT fulfillment and replacement of circumcision (Col 2.11). Just as Jewish circumcision meant reception into the Old Covenant, so too Christian baptism means reception into the New Covenant. Circumcision was the seal (σφραγίς) of the faith of Abraham. Rightly understood, circumcision is of the heart (Rom 2.29) and leads directly to Christian baptism. Christian baptism is ''the circumcision of Christ'' (Col 2.11) by which the tyranny of ''the flesh'' is categorically repudiated; henceforth life is ''in the Spirit'' since the baptized is sealed (ἐσφραγίσθητε) with the Holy Spirit (Eph 1.13). Baptism is the seal, the climax of preaching and of the reception of preaching by faith. Faith is required for baptism and there is no true faith that does not lead to baptism (cf. Gal 3.25–27). Even the visible outpouring of the Holy Spirit does not remove the necessity of receiving baptism as a rite of initiation (Acts 10.48). Baptism is the initiation rite for all those who want to belong to Christ. They who ''have been baptized into Christ, have put on Christ'' (Gal 3.27), they have become a new man ''in Christ,'' and they are ''conformed'' (σύμμορφοι) to Christ (Rom 8.29). Baptism initiates into the Christian community: ''All [believers] are baptized into one body'' (1 Cor 12.13), i.e., into the body, which is Christ's Church (Eph 1.23). Baptism brings one into the community that knows no barriers between different nations (Eph 2.14); all are one in Christ, whether Jew or Greek, slave or free man, male or female (Gal 3.28). They are one body through the one Spirit (1 Cor 12.13), namely, the ''Body of Christ'' (1 Cor 12.27). Thus baptism has a great importance for both the local and world community since it symbolizes and at the same time brings about unity and harmony in society.

The full messianic efficacy of the baptism instituted by Christ became possible only through His death on the cross and His Resurrection. Only after Christ's death and Resurrection does the Church become the sphere of activity of the Holy Spirit (Jn 7.39). The baptismal rite of immersion suggests dying and rising with Christ. Being buried with Him means forgiveness of sins, and the emergence from this burial with Him means walking ''in newness of life'' (Rom 6.4; cf. Col 2.12), or walking ''in the Spirit'' (Gal 5.16). Both effects are essentially bound up with one another as is the death of Christ with His Resurrection. The baptism of John the Baptist was only an outward sign of contrition that cleansed according to the degree of contrition; Christian baptism, however, when received with faith, ''washes sins away'' (Acts 2.38; 3.19); it is a moral purification effected by the power of Christ's redemptive action (Heb 10.19–22). Thus it demands a decisive turning from evil and the reception of the gospel of Christ (Acts 2.38–41; 3.17–19).

Baptism effects justice, holiness, and sinlessness (Rom 6.1–14; 1 Cor 6.11; Eph 5.26–27) through the operation of the Holy Spirit, the eschatological gift of God (Acts 2.17–21, 33) given to all who are baptized (Acts 2.38). It makes man a child of God, forming him to the image of Christ (Gal 3.26–27), who is ''the firstborn among many brethren'' (Rom 8.29), and ''the firstborn from the dead'' (Col 1.18; see also 1 Cor 15.20). To have died to sin and to have risen with Christ to a new life imposes the obligation on the Christian of becoming morally what he is ontologically (1 Thes 4.3–8). Baptism does not magically effect sanctification, but requires conscious struggle against unruly passions (Rom 6.12–14, 19; Gal 5.24). The Christian life is a progressive laying hold of and appropriation of what was rendered accessible by baptism (Eph 5.6–14; Phil 2.15; Col 3.12–17).

In their endeavor to describe the baptismal mystery, the NT writers, besides drawing directly on Jesus' earthly career, have recourse also to the wonderful acts of God in the OT. St. Paul sees baptism as a new life, a second creation (Eph 2.10). Since the creation of light was most impressive and mysterious (Gn 1.3), it is fitting that the divine Word should be called ''the true light'' (Jn 1.4), and faith and baptism in His name an enlightenment (2 Cor 4.6; see also Heb 6.4–6). St. Peter saw baptismal symbolism in the waters of the flood and in the ark in which Noah was saved (1 Pt 3.20–21). The typology of the crossing of the Red Sea presents baptism as an incorporation by immersion, as it were, into Christ (1 Cor 10.1–5).

Bibliography: J. COPPENS and A. D'ALÈS, *Dictionnaire de la Bible,* suppl. ed. L. PIROT et al. (Paris 1928–) 1:852–924. A. OEPKE, G. KITTEL, *Theologisches Wörterbuch zum Neuen Testament* (Stuttgart 1935–) 1:527–543. J. THOMAS, *Le Mouvement baptiste en Palestine et Syrie* (Gembloux 1935). H. G. MARSH, *The Origin and Significance of the N. T. Baptism* (Manchester, Eng. 1941). F. J. LEENHARDT, *Le Baptême chrétien, son origine, sa signification* (Neuchâtel 1944). W. F. FLEMINGTON, *The N.T. Doctrine of Baptism* (New York 1949). J. CREHAN, *Early Christian Baptism and the Creed* (London 1950). R. SCHNACKENBURG, *Das Heilsgeschehen bei der Taufe nach dem Apostel Paulus* (Munich 1950). H. SCHWARZMANN, *Zur Tauftheologie des hl. Paulus in Röm. 6* (Heidelberg 1950). G. W. H. LAMPE, *The Seal of the Spirit* (London 1951). G. F. VICEDOM, *Die Taufe unter den Heiden* (Munich 1960). O. CULLMANN, *Baptism in the N.T.,* tr. J. K. S. REID (Studies in Biblical Theology 1; London 1961). G. R. BEASLEY-MURRAY, *Baptism in the N.T.* (New York 1962). A. GEORGE et al., *Baptism in the N.T.,* tr. D. ASKEW (Baltimore 1964). W. MICHAELIS, ''Zum jüdischen Hintergrund der Johannestaufe,'' *Judaica* 7 (1951) 81–120. N. A. DAHL, ''The Origin of Baptism,'' *Norsk Teologisk Tidsskrift* 56 (1955) 36–52. M. E. BOISMARD, ''Une Liturgie baptismale dans la Prima Petri,'' *Revue biblique* 63 (1956) 182–208; 64 (1957) 161–183. D. M. STANLEY, ''Baptism in the N.T.,'' *Scripture* 8 (1956) 44–57; ''The N.T. Doctrine of Baptism: An Essay in Biblical Theology,'' *Theological Studies* 18 (1957) 169–215. O. BETZ, ''Die Proselytentaufe der Qumransekte und die Taufe im N.T.,'' *Revue de Qumran* 1 (1958–59) 213–234. J. GNILKA, ''Die essenischen Tauchbäder und die Johannestaufe,'' *ibid.* 3 (1961–62) 185–207.

[H. MUELLER]

BAPTISM, SACRAMENT OF

''Baptism,'' derived from the Greek *baptizein* meaning ''to plunge or to immerse.'' The *Catechism of the Catholic Church* (CCC), quoting in part from the 1439 Council of Florence (DS 1314), describes baptism as ''the basis of the whole Christian life, the gateway to life in the Spirit, and the door which gives access to the other sacraments. Through Baptism we are freed from sin and reborn as sons of God; we become members of Christ, are incorporated into the Church and made sharers in her mission'' (CCC 1213). Drawing upon the insights of the Early Church, many theologians today often speak of baptism, along with the sacraments of confirmation and the Eucharist, as the Church's ''sacraments of initiation.'' Baptism is not a private affair between the individual Christian and God, for baptism establishes one as a member of the Universal Church and as a member of a particular faith community, enabling one to participate fully in the Church's sacramental life. Baptism is also the basis of all ministry within the Church. This entry surveys: (i) the history, and (ii) the sacramental theology of Christian baptism.

History

Baptism is discussed extensively in the Acts of the Apostles and Pauline epistles, and this sheds some light on the baptismal rite. That Baptism took place by immersion is evidenced by Paul's presenting it as a ''being buried with Christ'' (Rom 6.3–4; Col 2.12). The same is true of his description of Baptism as a bath (λουτρόν, Eph 5.26; Ti 3.5; see also Heb 10.22), which leaves open the question whether or not a complete submersion is meant so that the head must also disappear under the water. The form of the bath also manifests itself in the manner in which the Ethiopian was baptized (Acts 8.36–38), and finally in the word that is generally used for this, βαπτίζειν (A. Oepke, ''βάπτω'' G. Kittel, *Theologisches Wörterbuch zum Neuen Testament* 1:527–544).

According to the DIDACHE, pouring the water was permissible; if immersion was not feasible, one could ''pour water on the head three times, in the name of the Father and of the Son and of the Holy Spirit'' (7; J. Quasten, ed., *Monumenta eucharista et liturgica vetustissima* 10). It is clear from this that from the very beginning there was great freedom with regard to immersion. The activity of the minister was emphasized throughout; it seems to have consisted either in pouring water on the head of the candidate, or at least in touching the candidate with a slight pressure suggesting the motion of immersion.

Iconography seems to favor this latter notion. The pictorial representations of the baptism of Christ beginning with the 2nd century generally show John the Baptist placing his hand upon the Lord. However, this touch can also signify a washing with the moistened hand. By means of the pouring or sprinkling the (more or less complete) bath was made an ''immersion.'' Extant baptisteries from a few centuries later (see *Dictionnaire d'archéologie chrétienne et de liturgie*, ed. F. Cabrol, H. Leclerq, and H. I. Marrou, 2:382–409) show, by the very shallowness of the water receptacle, that an immersion for adults was no longer considered the general rule, and that therefore the pouring of water must have rounded out a partial bath. By comparison, the full immersion even for adults was still used by Otto of Bamberg (d. 1139), the apostle of Pomerania (*Vita* 2.15; *Dictionnaire d'archéologie chrétienne et de liturgie* 2.1:398–399). A complete immersion for infants must have remained in use longer, for St. Thomas Aquinas acknowledged it to have been the more common practice (*Summa theologiae* 3a, 66.7).

Formula. With regard to the formula used for Baptism in the early Church, there is the difficulty that although Matthew (28.19) speaks of the Trinitarian formula, which is now used, the Acts of the Apostles

St. Boniface baptizing a kneeling man. (Archive Photos)

(2.38; 8.16; 10.48; 19.5) and Paul (1 Cor 1.13; 6.11; Gal 3.27; Rom 6.3) speak only of Baptism ''in the Name of Jesus.'' It has been proposed that we assume that the one being baptized had to confess the name of Jesus and that then the minister pronounced a Trinitarian formula (Crehan 76, 81). This remains, however, an arbitrary conjecture.

While it is more obvious in the Matthaean formula (Mt 28.19) that Baptism establishes a relationship to the triune God, it is no less true when Baptism is given ''in the name of Jesus.'' Since Baptism is an incorporation into Christ, it bestows at the same time the Holy Spirit (Acts 2.38; Eph 1.13; Gal 3.14; 4.6) and makes us daughters and sons of the Father (Gal 4.6). It is also conceivable that ''in the name of Jesus'' meant nothing more than that the candidate was given over to Christ, consecrated to him, and submerged in him (in his death). Though there is no clear proof that this phase was really used as a liturgical formula, the possibility of its being used thus even as late as the 3rd century cannot be excluded (Stenzel

88–93). The validity of Baptism ''in the name of Jesus'' was still accepted in the age of scholasticism.

An explicit reference to the Trinitarian formula of Baptism cannot be found in the first centuries. The Didache, for instance, merely repeats Mt 28.19. In the East, St. John Chrysostom (d. 407) is the first to report it: ''N. is baptized in the name of the Father and of the Son and of the Holy Spirit'' [*Baptismal Instructions* 2.26; ed. P. Harkins, *Ancient Christian Writers*, ed. J. Quasten et al. 31 (Westminster, Maryland 1963) 52–53]. A similar form is also found in the *Apostolic Tradition* (21; B. Botte, *La Tradition aposolique de saint Hippolyte; Essai de reconstitution* 48–51). However, ancient Christian tradition until the 4th century (Western-Roman tradition until the 8th) shows that the baptismal formula was spoken as questions that the candidate answered.

It was natural to expect the candidate for Baptism to make a profession of his Christian faith—all the more necessary in view of the fact that at that time other groups had a baptism, e.g., the baptism of John (Acts 19.3). The Ethiopian chamberlain, for instance, had first to make a profession of his faith: ''I believe that Jesus Christ is the Son of God'' (Acts 8.37). The profession could be more or less explicit. As a matter of fact, the Christological part of the APOSTLES' CREED came into use first (1 Cor 15.3–4). Trinitarian formulas, however, also spread at an early time, and they could have appeared as an extension of Christological formulas (see the formula Paul uses for the greeting at the beginnings of his letters).

Around the 3rd or 4th century there is evidence that this profession of faith was the baptismal formula. Thus, the *Apostolic Tradition* reports that the minister places his hand on the candidate's head and asks: ''Do you believe in God, the Father almighty?'' The candidate answers: ''I believe.'' Then he baptizes (immerses?) him once. The minister asks again: ''Do you believe in Jesus Christ, the Son of God, who was born of the Holy Spirit and the Virgin Mary, suffered under Pontius Pilate, died, and on the third day arose from the dead?'' The candidate answers: ''I believe,'' and is baptized a second time. The minister once again asks: ''Do you believe in the Holy Spirit, the Holy Church and the resurrection of the body?'' The candidate replies: ''I believe,'' and is baptized the third time.

This baptismal formula in question form is found again and again in the West until the Gelasian Sacramentary [1.44]. But then a change occurs.

In the East, a 5th-century Syrian adaptation of the *Apostolic Tradition*, the *Canons of Hippolytus*, adds that the minister says each time he immerses the candidate: ''I baptize you in the name of the Father and of the Son and of the Holy Spirit'' (19.133 *Dictionnaire d'archéologie chrétienne et de liturgie* 2.1:262). This is the first time that a declarative formula accompanied the threefold immersion. Apparently in reaction to ARIANISM a single immersion was adopted in Spain, (Gregory the Great, *Epist.* 1.43; *Patrologia Latina*, ed. J. P. Migne, 77:497–498), and the Eastern use of a single declarative formula was followed, since it tied in so well with the single immersion (M. Andrieu, *Les 'Ordines Romani' du haut moyen-âge* 3:87–90).

The first Western books to report the declarative formula were the Gallican Sacramentaries [e.g., the 8th-century *Missale Gothicum* 260; ed. H. Bannister, Henry Bradshaw Society 52 (London 1917) 17]. From among the books of the Roman rite, the Hadrian recension (end of 8th century) of the Gregorian Sacramentary was the first to reproduce it [*Das Sakramentarium Gregorianum* 206.3; ed. H. Lietzmann (Münster 1921) 124]. While these documents do not indicate the number of times the immersion and formula were repeated, some manuscripts of this period seem to vacillate between the threefold interrogatory formula and the single declarative one. A Sacramentary written in Prague shortly before 794 contains the threefold interrogation and immersion but adds that the minister may say: ''I baptize you . . .'' without indicating whether this latter formula is to be repeated or not [*Das Prager Sakramentar*, ed. A. Dold and L. Eizenhöfer (Beuron 1949) 98.12]. On the other hand, other books, such as the Sacramentary of Gellone (end of 8th century), insist that the formula is spoken only once (P. de Puniet, *Dictionnaire d'archéologie chrétienne et de liturgie* 2.1:305).

A consideration of these historical facts forces us to conclude with De Puniet (*ibid.* 342) that the tradition of the Church until the 8th century was to accept the threefold Trinitarian question and answer as the baptismal formula.

Liturgical Rituals. The baptismal act has from ancient times been enlarged with preparatory and concluding rites. TERTULLIAN spoke of a renunciation of Satan, his pomps and his angels by means of three questions and answers [*De spect.* 4; *De corona militis* 3; *De anima* 35 (*Patrologia Latina* 1:635; 2:79; 2:710)].

According to the *Apostolic Tradition* (20–21; B. Botte, ed., *La Tradition apostolique de saint Hippolyte: Essai de reconstitution* 42–53), besides fasting and renunciation of Satan, there were also a preliminary anointing with oil that was exorcized beforehand (later, oil of catechumens) and an anointing after Baptism with oil over which a thanksgiving prayer had been spoken (later, chrism). The baptismal water was supposed to be blessed ahead of time (Tertullian, *De baptismo* 4; *Patrologia Latina* 1:1205).

A special practice, which lasted for but a few centuries, was the offering of a drink of milk and honey to the newly baptized before the reception of the chalice in the first celebration of the Eucharist on the part of the neophyte [Tertullian, *De corona militis* 3 (*Patrologia Latina* 2:99); *Apostolic Tradition* 21 (*La Tradition apostolique de saint Hippolyte: Essai de reconstitution* 56–57); Jerome, *Adv. Luciferianos* 8 (*Patrologia Latina* 23:172); John the Deacon, *Epist. ad Senarium* 12 (*Patrologia Latina* 59:405)]. This drink harkened back to the promise made to the Chosen People in the desert that they would inherit a land flowing with milk and honey, an inheritance that the candidate was now to enjoy. From the 4th century there is evidence of the white clothing received by the newly baptized to symbolize the innocence of his new life (Ambrose, *De mysteriis* 7; *Monumenta eucharista et liturgica vetustissima* 129). About the same time a presentation of a burning candle to the neophyte is reported (Pseudo-Ambrosius, *De lapsu virginis* 5; *Patrologia Latina* 16:372), a reminder of the purity of soul of the newly baptized. The anointing of the head of the newly baptized [*Apostolic Tradition* 21 (*La Tradition apostolique de saint Hippolyte: Essai de reconstitution* 51); Ambrose, *De sacramentis* 3.1.1 (*Monumenta eucharista et liturgica vetustissima* 151)] is to symbolize his configuration to Christ, the anointed priest.

The early Church took great care to bring out the fact that Baptism was the great event by which one is initiated into the Christian life. For this reason it was linked with the celebration of the Easter Vigil. The whole community, therefore, took part in it, not by being present during the baptismal act which took place in the form of an immersion in the baptistery, but by fasting beforehand with the candidates, and by bringing them into the church immediately after Baptism to celebrate the communal Eucharist. It was because reception into the Church is sealed with the Eucharist that the Communion of newly baptized infants was retained even as late as the 12th century.

While infants were baptized either immediately or on Holy Saturday without any preparation (Cyprian, *Epist.* 64; *Corpus scriptorum ecclesiasticorum latinorum* 3.1:720), adult candidates had to undergo a CATECHUMENATE of varying length before they could receive Baptism. The *Apostolic Tradition* calls for a period of instruction lasting three years, but does allow for a lesser time if the candidate proves especially zealous and trustworthy. The catechumens' instruction often preceded the community's celebration of the Eucharist, of which they could attend only the liturgy of the Word, and then in an area apart from the already-baptized. Because ''their kiss is not yet holy'' (*Apostolic Tradition*, 18), they could not exchange the kiss of peace either with the faithful or among themselves. This symbolic and physical separation continued until the day they were baptized.

At an early date the administration of the Sacrament was normally restricted to the Easter or Pentecost Vigil. LENT thus served as a period of final intensified instruction and interior preparation for reception of Baptism. Those catechumens who were ready to make the step were enrolled in the ranks of the *competentes,* those ''seeking'' Baptism; and exercises, called scrutinies, were held for them. The candidates on these occasions received many EXORCISMS, the exsufflation or blowing out of the devil, the IMPOSITION OF HANDS, salt; they were taught and had to repeat the Apostles' Creed and Our Father, the essential part of the rites for the *competentes.*

The *competentes* would fast on Good Friday and Holy Saturday, their last days as catechumens. On Saturday, the bishop called them together and imposed his hands on them, exorcising them of foreign spirits. An additional exorcism—the rite of exsufflation—would follow, as he breathed upon their faces. After making the sign of the cross on their ears and nose, he exhorted them to spend the entire night watching, listening to readings, and hearing further instruction.

The celebration resumed at dawn. A prayer was said over the water (which the *Apostolic Tradition* says should, if possible, be running or fountain water), and the bishop prayed over the oil of exorcism (oil of catechumens) and the oil of thanksgiving (chrism). A priest took each of the candidates aside and instructed them to face the west—the place of the setting sun and so, symbolically, the realm of darkness and sin. There they proclaimed, ''I renounce you, Satan, and all your undertakings and all your works.'' The priest then anointed each of them with the oil of exorcism and commanded Satan to depart.

Women and men were separated at this point. They removed their clothes and were brought to the bishop or priest standing near the baptismal waters. A deacon accompanied the men, a deaconess the women, as they proceeded into the water. (A specific mention of one in the ''office of deaconess'' performing this function is found in the *Didascalia Apostolorum,* ''The Teaching of the Apostles,'' written in North Syria circa 250.) The *Apostolic Tradition*'s baptismal formula consists of three questions, led by the one baptizing as he imposed his hands on the candidate's head: ''Do you believe in God, the Father Almighty? Do you believe in Jesus Christ, the Son of God, who was born of the Holy Spirit and the Virgin Mary, was crucified under Pontius Pilate, died, and on the third day rose from the dead; who ascended into heaven, sits at the right hand of the Father, and will come to judge the living and the dead? Do you believe in the Holy Spirit, the Holy Church and the resurrection of the body?'' Each candidate responded ''I do believe'' to these questions, and after each response the candidate was baptized either by complete or partial immersion or by water being poured over the head. *Apostolic Tradition* specifies the order in which the baptisms occur: children first, then men, and then women.

Emerging naked from the water, the *neophytes* (''newly enlightened'') were anointed by the priest with the oil of thanksgiving. They then dressed and entered the church. The bishop would impose his hands upon them, pray, anoint them again with the oil of thanksgiving, and mark their foreheads with the sign of the cross. Now one of the faithful, they would receive the kiss of peace from the bishop and would participate for the first time in the Liturgy of the Eucharist.

This second postbaptismal anointing by the bishop, taking place immediately after Baptism, was the sacrament of confirmation. As Christianity began to spread into rural areas and as infant baptisms increased in number—and, because of the danger of death, began to be practiced throughout the year—bishops were not always available to celebrate confirmation immediately after the child's baptism. The Eastern Churches maintained the original unity among the sacraments of initiation by allowing her priests to confirm and communicate infants and children when they are baptized. The Latin Church, preferring to preserve the notion that the bishop seals or completes the baptism through his anointing with chrism, allows infants or young children to be confirmed at their baptism only in emergency situations. *The Catechism of the Catholic Church* explains that ''The practice of the Eastern Churches gives greater emphasis to the unity of Christian initiation. That of the Latin Church more clearly expresses the communion of the new Christian with the bishop as guarantor and servant of the unity, catholicity and apostolicity of his Church, and hence the connection with the apostolic origins of Christ's Church'' (CCC 1292).

Baptismal instruction and catechesis did not conclude with the celebration of baptism. The neophytes continued to receive instruction about their faith and their new life in Christ for some days afterward. In many places they returned to the Church daily during the Easter Week to receive further instruction and exhortation by the bishop. Many of these post-baptismal instructions, known as Mystagogical Catecheses, have survived; among the more important are those of Ambrose (d. 397), Augustine (d. 430), and those attributed to Cyril of Jerusalem (d. 386). In addition, some pre-baptismal instructions of Theodore of Mopsuestia (d. 428) and John Chrysostom (d. 406) also survive. These works may be considered among the first ''textbooks'' of sacramental theology, for they explained to the neophytes the significance of the complex of symbols and ritual gestures they had just experienced, as well as instructing them further about other mysteries of the faith. From a pedagogical point of view the timing of these catecheses was effective in that they followed one's actual experience with the sacraments. Listening to the sacred mysteries being explained, the newly baptized could reflect upon what they had experienced, rather than attempting to fit an explanation onto a rite in which they had not yet participated and about whose details they knew little.

Subsequent developments. When at the start of the Middle Ages adult Baptism became more rare, the rites of the catechumenate were adapted somewhat clumsily for infant candidates. Although infant Baptism has been the usual form of Baptism for the majority of Christians since at least the eighth century, the first rite of Baptism designed specifically for infants was the post-Vatican II Rite of Baptism for Children (1969). In the Middle Ages, infant Baptism was even restricted to Easter and Pentecost; so strictly was this followed in Spain (Ildephonse, *De cognitione baptismi* 107; *Patrologia Latina* 96:156) and elsewhere that the baptistery was locked during Lent. Such a transfer to infant Baptism of customs designed for adults was impossible without abbreviations and loss of meaning.

Infant Baptism. The ritual for infant Baptism in the Middle Ages comprised a reception into the catechumenate by means of the sign of the cross, and exsufflation, the imposition of hands, and the giving of salt; the exorcism with the oration *Aeternam* coming from the catechumenate (*Ordo Romanus* 11.21, 24; *Les 'Ordines Romani' du haut moyen-âge* 2:423); and lastly, inside the church, the recitation of the Apostles' Creed and Our Father. There follows the threefold renunciation of Satan separated from the confession of faith, as was often done in ancient times, by the anointing with oil of catechumens. The threefold immersion, bound up in earlier times with the three baptismal questions, left its vestige in the triple pouring of water that now accompanies the single indicative Trinitarian formula.

Baptism of Adults. The ritual for Baptism of adults is basically nothing else but a more prolix rite for infant Baptism that originated in the later Middle Ages. Instead of the single exorcism a whole series of them was introduced. The ceremony for reception into the catechumenate was lengthened by mere repetition of already existing rites. An insufflation (breathing the Holy Spirit into the candidate) was added to the exsufflation. Finally the whole ritual was outfitted with an introduction consisting of psalms.

Defending the Church's teaching against the Protestant Reformers, the Council of Trent (1545–63) retained much of the medieval Baptism rite. The *Roman Ritual*, of 1614 established a theology and liturgical celebration of Baptism (and the other sacraments) that would remain essentially unchanged until the revisions called for by the Second Vatican Council three and a half centuries later. The baptismal liturgy and theology reflected the practice of the times: that those baptized were almost always infants, who should be baptized as soon as possible to remove the taint of original sin from their souls.

Vatican II. On April 16, 1962, the Holy See, wishing to make the ceremonies of adult Baptism a more meaningful introduction to the Christian life, published a new Ordinal allowing for the celebration of the rites of the catechumenate in a series of services prior to the actual conferring of the Sacrament [*Acta Apostolicae Sedis* 54 (1962) 310–338]. Vatican Council II also insisted on separating the adult baptismal rites into several distinct steps (*Constitution on the Sacred Liturgy* 3:64); but it went further and decreed a full revision of both adult and infant rites (3:64, 66–70).

In the ensuing years, the *Rite of Baptism for Children* (RBC) was promulgated in 1969, and a slightly emended version appeared in 1973; another revision is underway at the beginning of the 21st century. Notable aspects of the RBC include a refocusing and emphasizing of the ritual and post-ritual responsibilities of the child's parents and sponsors, as mandated by the Constitution on the Sacred Liturgy. It directs that baptism should be celebrated ''within the first weeks after birth'' (8.3). In order ''to fulfill the true meaning of the sacrament children must later be formed in the faith in which they have been baptized'' (3), the baptism is to be delayed ''in the complete absence of any well-founded hope that the infant will be brought up in the Catholic religion'' (8.3). The *Rite of Christian Initiation of Adults* (RCIA) first appeared in 1972; several revisions have led to the current 1988 edition. For more information, see also BAPTISM OF INFANTS and CATECHUMENATE.

Sacramental Theology

Baptism is necessary for salvation. As Christ himself said, unless one is born again of water and the Holy Spirit, one cannot enter the Kingdom of God (Jn 3.5). The Council of Trent declared: ''If anyone says that Baptism is optional, that is, not necessary for salvation, let him be anathema'' (H. Denzinger, *Enchiridion symbolorum*, ed. A. Schönmetzer 1618). Baptism incorporates all men and women into the mystery of Christ and into his body the Church. Baptism also confers a sacramental character upon the soul; once it has been validly received, therefore, baptism is not repeated. Baptism also confers the grace of justification, and effects the remission of all sins and their punishment. Adults must receive Baptism freely, and infants can and should be baptized. In the case of an emergency anyone (even a non-Christian) can baptize validly by using the proper matter (pouring of, or immersion into, water) and form (the Trinitarian formula).

From an individual point of view, the primary effects of Baptism are ''purification from sins and new birth in the Holy Spirit'' (CCC 1262), a new birth that makes one a co-heir with Christ (1 Cor 6.15; Rom 8.17) and a temple of the Holy Spirit (1 Cor 6.19). But Baptism also has communal or ecclesial effects: it makes us members of the Body of Christ (Eph 4.25) and so incorporates us into his Church (GIRM 2).

While the core meaning of baptism is expressed and effected by the action with water and the words of the minister, this essential matter and form has been ''clothed'' with numerous symbols and gestures that allow a fuller understanding and appreciation of the sacrament's significance. *The Catechism of the Catholic Church* observes that ''The different effects of Baptism are signified by the perceptible elements of the sacramental rite'' (CCC 1262). This applies to each of the Church's seven sacraments, but it is especially true of baptism, the liturgical celebration of which is among the most developed and richest of the Church's rituals. The following discussion complements the Church's teachings on Baptism by commenting upon seven additional, more conceptual or descriptive, effects of Baptism, and illustrating how these ''are signified by the perceptible elements of the sacramental rite.''

First, Baptism brings about *a change of ownership*. The passage 2 Cor 1.21–22 speaks of ''God, who establishes us with you in Christ and has anointed us, by putting his seal on us and giving us his Spirit in our hearts as a first installment'' of his promise (see also Eph 1.13–14). Through Baptism, we are claimed by God as one of God's own: we become God's property, God's instruments. That we are under new ownership is symbolized in the RCIA as those brought into the catechumenate are marked with the sign of the cross, ''the sign of [their] new way of life as catechumens'' (54–55). Similarly, in the Baptism of infants or children, this signing occurs near the beginning of the rite, after the parents and sponsors accept their responsibilities as Christian teachers (RBC 41). In both liturgies, those to be baptized are claimed for Christ in the name of the Christian community.

Second, Baptism effects a *change in our allegiance*. Throughout the Letter to the Romans, Paul insists that we neither live nor die to ourselves but to the Lord (Rom 6.15–18; 8.12–13; 14.7–9). This living and dying to the Lord involves real struggle in the lives of Christians, and the minor exorcisms in the RCIA ''draw the attention of the catechumen to the real nature of Christian life, the struggle between flesh and spirit.'' (90–94). In the RBC parents and sponsors—whose faith provides the reason and proper context for the Baptism of the child—renew their renunciation of sin and profession of faith (56).

Commenting upon the concept of Baptism as effecting in the baptized a ''change of ownership and allegiance,'' the *Catechism of the Catholic Church* describes the practical implications of these changes: ''From now on, he is called to be subject to others, to serve them in the community of the Church, and to 'obey and submit' to the Church's leaders [Heb 13.17], holding them in respect and affection [Eph 5.21 and other passages]. Just as Baptism is the source of responsibilities and duties, the baptized person also enjoys rights within the Church: to receive the sacraments, to be nourished with the Word of God and to be sustained by the other spiritual helps of the Church'' ([LG 37; *Codex iuris canonici* 208–223; *Codex Canonum Ecclesiarium Orientalium* 675:2] CCC 1269).

A third effect of Baptism is that of *stripping off* the old (man) and *putting on* the new man who is Christ: ''As many of you as were baptized into Christ have clothed yourselves with Christ'' (Gal 3.27; see also Col 3.9–11). In ancient days the newly baptized, laying aside their clothes before entering the font and then emerging naked to be clothed in their baptismal garment, reflected this ''putting on the new man'' in a striking way. Today, infants are ordinarily naked if they are baptized by immersion; in either case, they and adult initiates are clothed with a white garment after they are baptized, signifying the new creation they have become by being clothed in Christ (RBC 63; RCIA 229).

Titus 3.5 refers to a fourth understanding of Baptism, that the sacrament is the ''water of *rebirth and renewal* by the Holy Spirit.'' References to this rebirth and renewal abound in both infant and adult rites, concepts symbolized particularly effectively when Baptism is by immersion. The design of many baptismal fonts in the past and today, suggesting the maternal womb, lends itself well to this symbolism.

A fifth description of Baptism is that it is *enlightenment*. The passage 1 Pt 2.9, considered by many a baptismal homily or instruction, speaks of ''the new light into which we have been called.'' Indeed, technical names for the elect in the RCIA are *photizomenoi* or *illuminandi* (''those about to be enlightened''), while the newly baptized are called *neophytes* (''the newly enlightened''). The presentation of a lighted candle to newly baptized adults (RCIA 230) or to the parents and sponsors of an infant (RBC 64) symbolize this enlightenment.

Sixth, Baptism makes a person *a sharer in Christ, the anointed king and priest*. Both 2 Cor 1.21 and 1 Pt 2.9 speak of this priesthood. The postbaptismal anointing with chrism of infants (RBC 62) and of adults, when their confirmation is separated from their Baptism (RCIA 228), symbolically reflects this. When adults are confirmed following their Baptism, as is usually the case, the prayer introducing this sacramental anointing asks the Holy Spirit to ''make [them] more like Christ and help [them] to be witnesses to his suffering, death, and resurrection'' (RCIA 233).

Finally, through Baptism we are adopted as God's own children. Baptism is described as adoption several times in the *General Instruction to the Roman Missal* (1,2,5), drawing from Paul's use of the concept in Rom 8.14–17 and 8:23 (see also Eph 1.3). Paul is the only New Testament writer to use the word ''adoption'' which, in Greek, means ''the making or placing of a son.'' The notion of Baptism as adoption concisely describes the kind of relationship the baptized enjoy with God (his sons and daughters), how this relationship is made (through God's initiative), and the effects of the relationship (the baptized become co-heirs with Christ and are entitled to call God ''Abba, Father'').

Mutual Recognition of Baptism. Finally, the Second Vatican Council's call for a greater spirit of ecumenism among churches and ecclesial communities reflects the understanding that Baptism is the effecting and the sign of the fundamental unity of all Christians. The essential matter and form of Baptism is the action of water upon the person being baptized (immersion or pouring) while the minister pronounces the Trinitarian formula. The Catholic Church recognizes as valid baptisms performed by other churches and ecclesial communities if these two conditions are met, and if there is no serious reason to question either the intention of the minister (not the minister's faith) and the free acceptance of Baptism by the one baptized. In an emergency anyone (even a non-Christian) can validly baptize, so long as he or she intends ''to do what the Church does.''

Some of the non-Catholic churches whose baptisms are recognized as valid by the Catholic Church are those of Eastern non-Catholics, Adventists, Amish, Anglican, Assembly of God, Baptists, Congregational Church, Disciples of Christ, Episcopalians, Evangelical Churches, Lutherans, Methodists, Old Roman Catholics, Polish National Church, Presbyterian Church, Reformed Churches, and the United Church of Christ. Some of the churches whose baptisms the Catholic Church considers invalid are those of Christian Scientists, Jehovah's Witnesses, Pentecostal churches, Quakers, Salvation Army, and Unitarians. This list is by no means exhaustive. Masons have no baptism, and the Church considers ''doubtful'' the validity of Mormon baptism (Church of Jesus Christ of Latter-day Saints). A Mormon wishing to become a Catholic is *permitted* to be baptized conditionally; in the case of a Mormon desiring to marry a Catholic, the Mormon baptism is presumed valid.

Conditional Baptism is exceptional; its *private* celebration is allowed only if careful examination of the particular church's or ecclesial community's matter and form, the minister's intention, and the recipient's disposition has cast serious doubt about validity. Although called for in the preconciliar rite, the conditional Baptism of infants who are miscarried, stillborn, or killed in an abortion (''If you are still alive; if you are a human being, I baptize you . . .'') is *not* to be administered. Because ''sacraments are for the living,'' in these situations prayers for the deceased and the family are more appropriate than is the celebration of the sacrament.

Bibliography: J. H. CREHAN, *Early Christian Baptism and the Creed* (London 1950). J. QUASTEN, ''Baptismal Creed and Baptismal Act in St. Ambrose's 'De Mysteriis' and 'De Sacramentis,''' *Mélanges de Ghellinck,* 2 v. (Gembloux 1951) 1:223–234. A. STENZEL, *Die Taufe* (Innsbruck 1958). ANDRIEU and E. DICK, ''Das Pateninstitut im altchristlichen Katechumenate,'' *Zeitschrift für katholische Theologie* 68 (1939) 1–49. M. DUJARIER, *Le Parrainage des adultes aux trois premiers siècles de l'Église* (Paris 1962). T. MAERTENS, *Histoire et pastorale du rituel du catéchuménat et du baptême* (Bruges 1963). H. RAHNER, ''*Pompa Diaboli;* Ein Beitrag zur Bedeutungsgeschichte des Wortes πομπή-pompa in der urchristlichen Taufliturgie,'' *Zeitschrift für katholische Theologie* 55 (1931) 239–273. B. FISCHER, ''Formen gemeinschaftlicher Tauferinnerung im Abendland,'' *Liturgisches Jahrbuch* 9 (1959) 87–93; ''Formen privater Tauferinnerung im Abendland,'' *ibid.* 156–166. R. CABIÉ, ''Christian Initiation,'' 11–100, in ''The Sacraments,'' v. 3 of *The Church at Prayer*, ed. A. G. MARTIMORT (Collegeville 1988). A. J. CHUPUNGCO, O.S.B., ed. *Handbook of Liturgical Studies*, v. 4, ''Sacraments and Sacramentality,'' 3–90 (Collegeville 2000). P. JACKSON, ''Symbols in Baptism'' in *The New Dictionary of Sacramental Worship* (NDSW), 108–15, ed. P. E. FINK, S.J. (Collegeville 1990). M. E. JOHNSON, ed., *Living Water, Sealing Spirit: Readings on Christian Initiation* (Collegeville 1995). A. KAVANAGH, O.S.B., *The Shape of Baptism: The Rite of Christian Initiation* (New York 1978). K. B. OSBORNE, *The Christian Sacraments of Initiation: Baptism, Confirmation, Eucharist* (New York 1987). ''Rite of Christian Initiation of Adults,'' *Liturgical Ministry* 8 (Spring 1999). M. SEARLE, *Christening: The Making of Christians* (Collegeville 1980). L. G. WALSH, O. P., *The Sacraments of Initiation* (London 1988). E. C. WHITAKER, *Documents of the Baptismal Liturgy* Society for Promoting Christian Knowledge 1989 (1960). E. YARNOLD, S.J., *The Awe-Inspiring Rites of Initiation: The Origins of the R.C.I.A.* (2d ed. Collegeville 1994).

[J.A. JUNGMANN/K. STASIAK/EDS.]

BAPTISM OF INFANTS

The Baptism of Infants is a long-standing practice in the Church. Although the New Testament makes no specific mention of infant Baptism a number of Scripture texts seem to witness to the custom. St. Paul uses the example of circumcision to explain the significance of Baptism and thus implies that Baptism like circumcision could be administered to infants (1 Cor 7.14). He exhorts children to obey their parents ''in the Lord'' (Col 3.30; Eph 6.1), and at no time does Paul or any of the other N.T. writers suggest children will have to seek Baptism at some later date as they grow into adulthood.

In Mark's Gospel Jesus is pictured putting his arms around a child and saying, ''Whoever welcomes a child such as this for my sake welcomes me'' (9.37). Some scholars read into this passage a justification for infant Baptism. When as in the case of Lydia's (Acts 16.15), an entire ''household'' (*oikos*) was baptized, children are presumed to have been included along with the adults (see Acts 16.33; 18.8; and 1 Cor 1.16).

A century later evidence for infant Baptism becomes more definite. St. Justin speaks of Christians 60 or 70 years old who had ''from childhood been made disciples'' (Apol I,5). St. Irenaeus speaks of Christ as giving salvation to people of every age, and he expressly includes ''infants and little children'' (Adv Haer ii, 39). In the 3rd century Tertullian voices opposition to infant Baptism (the protest itself witnesses to the practice). He urged that the Baptism of children be deferred until they can ''know Christ.'' As he grew older Tertullian became stricter. His principal reason for postponing Baptism was that he felt the remission of sin after Baptism was difficult if not impossible. In the detailed account it gives of the baptismal rites *The Apostolic Tradition*, attributed by some to St. HIPPOLYTUS (d. 235) states, ''And they shall baptize little children first. And if they can answer for themselves, let them answer. But if they cannot, let their parents answer or someone from their family'' (N. xxii [Dix, 33]).

By the 4th century the catechumenate was no longer for a fixed period, and the practice of deferring Baptism was widespread. St. Ambrose (339–396), for example, was baptized only after he was acclaimed bishop of Milan at the age of 35. St. Jerome (345–420) was baptized at 19. As in the case of Ambrose and Jerome, the offspring of Christian families were frequently inscribed in the catechumenate as infants or small children and were given a Christian upbringing. The list of prominent churchmen of the period baptized as adults includes St. Basil the Great (d. 379), baptized at 26; St. Gregory Nazianzen, baptized at 28 or 29. (It has been suggested that the latter, living in a monastic community, deferred the sacrament until he could return home and be baptized by his father who was a bishop.) John Chrysostom's mother, widowed when he was a baby, put him under the tutelage of monks,

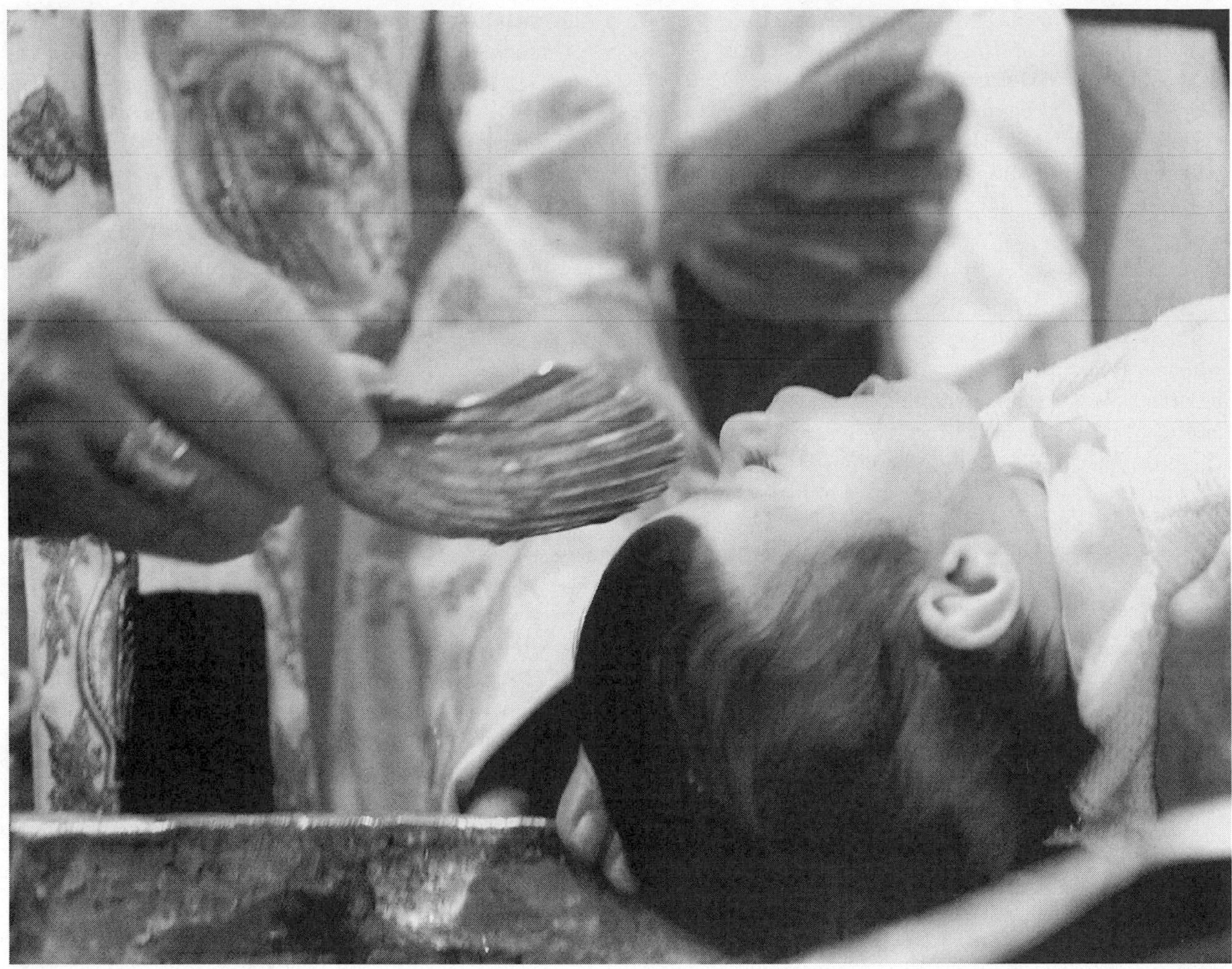

Pope John Paul II baptizes newborn Beatrice Boretta during a ceremony in the Sistine Chapel at the Vatican, January 7, 2001. The pope baptized 18 newborn babies in a ceremony to mark the Roman Catholic feast of the Baptism of Jesus. (©AFP/CORBIS)

was nearly 20 before he received baptism. Nonetheless in an Easter *Sermon to Neophytes*, c. 390, he said,

> You have seen how numerous are the gifts of baptism. Although many men think that the only gift it confers is the remission of sins, we have counted its honors to the number of ten. It is on this account that we baptize even infants, although they are sinless, that they may be given the further gifts of sanctification, justice, filial adoption, and inheritance, that they may be brothers and members of Christ, and become dwelling places for the Spirit.'' (N. 1) [H/H, p. 166]

The Eastern Churches, Orthodox and Catholic alike, follow the ancient custom of administering chrism (Confirmation) and Eucharist at the time of Baptism, even in the case of infants. (Infants received the Eucharist in the form of wine.) This was also the custom in the Roman Church until well into the Middle Ages.

Infant Baptism Questioned. In the course of time individuals and groups raised objections to the Church practice of infant Baptism. In broad outline, three periods can be distinguished: the period up to the Protestant Reformation, that of the Anabaptists at the time of the Reformation, and that of the present day.

Beginnings to Reformation. The first clash of any importance arose during the controversy over Pelagianism (*see* PELAGIUS AND PELAGIANISM) at the beginning of the fifth century. Although Pelagius denied original sin, he seems to have accepted the practice of infant Baptism. He asserted the necessity of Baptism to enter the kingdom of heaven, but not to obtain eternal life. The full meaning of this distinction still puzzles us today. At any rate, on the Pelagian controversy was the occasion for St. Augustine to reassert the Church's teaching that even infants are baptized for the ''remission of sin.''

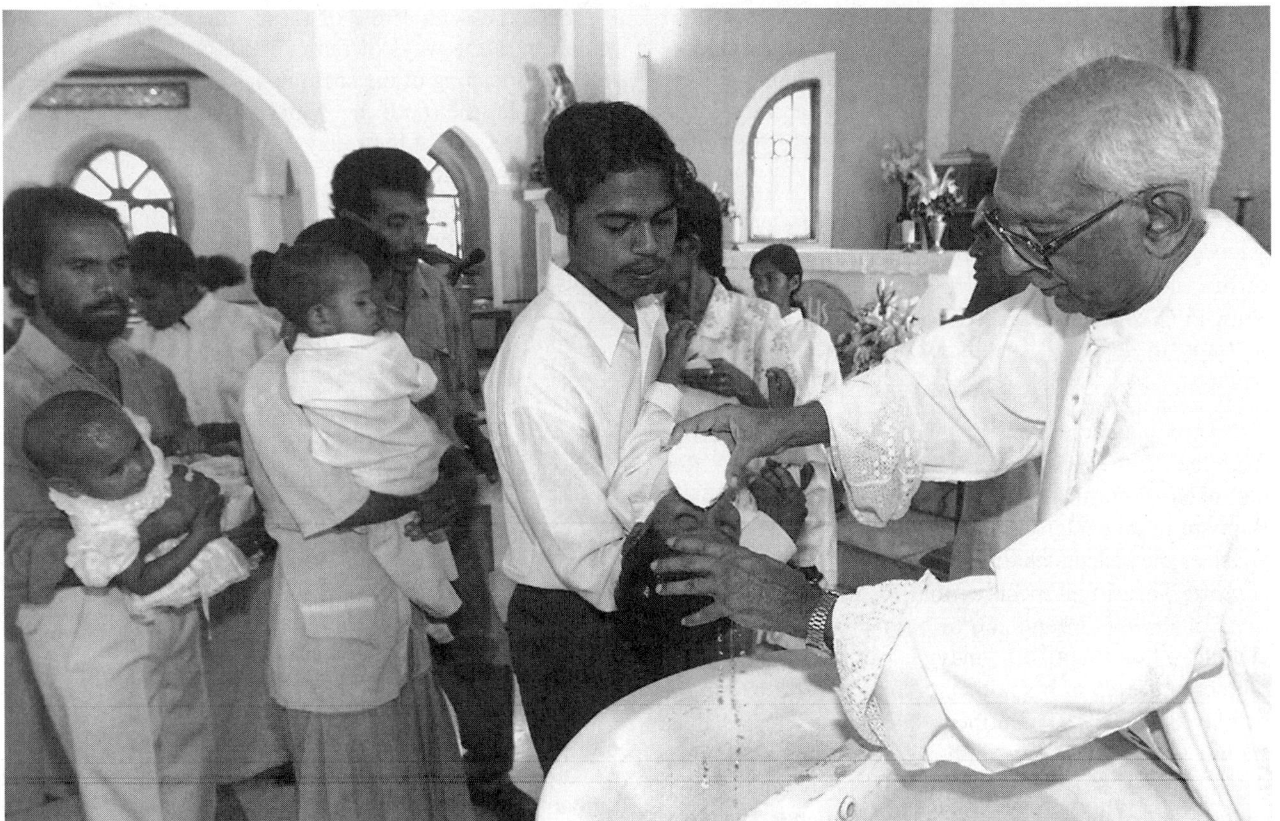

Father Monteiro baptizes small child during mass Baptism of 55 children at Becora Parish Church, Dili, East Timor. (AP/Wide World Photos)

Another denial appeared in the Middle Ages when certain sects such as the CATHARI rejected infant Baptism. Because of their dualist views on material things, all Sacraments were repulsive, but especially infant Baptism. In any other Sacrament the conscious assent of the recipient may mitigate the charge of materialism, but not in infant Baptism. In response Pope Innocent III defended infant Baptism by emphasizing the difference between original and actual sin. Original sin, which is contracted without consent, is in the case of infants ''remitted without consent by the power of the sacrament'' (H. Denzinger, *Enchiridion Symbolorum* 780).

In the early years of the Protestant Reformation, the meaning and purpose of the sacraments, especially Baptism, became a point of controversy. The Swiss Brethren held that Baptism is important because, in the words of the Schleitheim Confession (1527), it represents a public confession of ''repentance and amendment of life'' by those ''who believe truly that their sins are taken away by Christ.'' The Swiss Brethren, insisting that everyone make his or her own public profession of belief, rebaptized individuals who had been baptized as small children. Thus they became known (along with others who rejected infant Baptism) as ANABAPTISTS. ''Believer's baptism'' became the outward trait of the movement. In dissociating himself from the Anabaptists, Luther made a strong defense of infant Baptism. The Church, he says, could not have been permitted by God to remain in error for so long a time. He pointed out that the agreement of the entire Church about infant Baptism is a special miracle. To deny it is to deny the Church itself. The Confession of Augsburg, 1530, condemned the Anabaptists because they repudiated infant Baptism and asserted that children are saved without Baptism. The position of the Anabaptists was also clearly rejected by the Council of Trent (Denzinger 1514).

The issues raised by the Anabaptists persist in the Protestant communities and account for the diversity of practice in infant Baptism. Although lineally unrelated to the Anabaptists, those who do not practice infant Baptism—for example, the Seventh-day Adventists and Baptists—show doctrinal affinity with them. The Baptist position is that Baptism is a voluntary public profession of Christian faith and that only persons old enough to understand its significance and its symbolism should be accepted for Baptism.

About the time of World War II Karl Barth and Emil Brunner published harsh criticisms of the practice of infant Baptism. Joachim Jeremias and Kurt Aland were among those who examined at great length the evidence as to whether the Church baptized infants in her earliest days. (Jeremias answered ''yes,'' while Aland was more cautious stating that, *if* the Church did, it was very much the exception and not the rule).

Rite of Baptism for Children. The *Rite of Baptism for Children* (RBC), published in 1969, among the first of the sacramental rites to be revised after the Second Vatican Council (revised edition, 1973), is the first rite of Baptism designed specifically for infants and young children.

Three characteristics of the new RBC distinguish it from the 1614 *Roman Ritual*, ''adapted for infants'' that had been in common use. *First*, the RBC places infant Baptism in an ecclesial and Eucharistic context that emphasizes the paschal character of the sacrament. *Ecclesial context*: The ritual specifies that, unless necessity warrants otherwise, infants are to be baptized in the parish church so that [baptism] ''may clearly appear as the sacrament of the Church's faith and of incorporation into the people of God'' (10). Further, ''all recently born babies should be baptized at a common celebration on the same day'' (27). *Eucharistic context*: ''To bring out the paschal character of baptism,'' the RBC recommends ''that the sacrament be celebrated during the Easter Vigil or on Sunday, when the Church commemorates the Lord's resurrection. On Sunday, baptism may be celebrated even during Mass [occasionally], so that the entire community may be present and the relationship between baptism and eucharist may be clearly seen'' (9).

Second, the RBC makes a notable change in the focus of and ethos surrounding the sacrament. Previously, parents were required to baptize their infants *quam primum* (''as soon as possible'') after birth, even if the child's mother could not be present. The postconciliar RBC retains a sense of urgency, but put the onus on the parents who must *prepare* for the Baptism *quam primum*—even, as the RBC says, before the child is born (8.2). This preparation involves not only arranging for the liturgical celebration, but also, and especially, for examining and strengthening their own faith and participation in the life of the Church. The RBC even calls for the Baptism to be delayed ''in the complete absence of any well-founded hope that the infant will be brought up in the Catholic religion'' (8.3).

Third, the RBC highlights the parents' participation in the baptismal liturgy and their responsibilities afterwards, stressing the fact that the parents who, ''because of the natural relationships have a ministry and a responsibility in the baptism of infants more important than those of the godparents'' (5). The RBC, moreover, underscores the essential role of these ''first teachers of their children in the ways of faith'' (70). It states, ''To fulfill the true meaning of the sacrament, children must later be formed in the faith in which they have been baptized. . . . so that they may ultimately accept for themselves [that] faith'' (3).

Fate of Unbaptized Infants. Catholic teaching on the necessity of Baptism for salvation must be read in the context of the *Catechism of the Catholic Church.* The CCC states: ''*God has bound salvation to the sacrament of Baptism, but he himself is not bound by his sacraments*'' (1257). As for children dying without baptism, the Catechism says:

> The Church can only entrust them to the mercy of God, as she does in her funeral rites for them. Indeed, the great mercy of God who desires that all men should be saved, and Jesus' tenderness toward children which caused him to say: 'Let the children come to me, do not hinder them' (Mk 10:14), allow us to hope that there is a way of salvation for children who have died without Baptism. All the more urgent is the Church's call not to prevent little children coming to Christ through the gift of holy Baptism (1261).

In the past many Catholic theologians postulated that unbaptized infants, with no personal sin, were destined for a state they called LIMBO. In Limbo unbaptized infants were excluded from the joys of heaven, but they did not suffer the torments (*poena sensus*) of hell. It was never official Catholic teaching, and the *Catechism of the Catholic Church* does not mention it. Contemporary theology emphasizes that the Church baptizes infants in hope of what they are to become as children of God, and not, primarily, out of our fear of what might happen to them not baptized.

Bibliography: P. J. HILL, J. C. DIDIER, ed., *Le Baptême des enfants* (Paris 1959). K. ALAND, *Die Säuglingstaufe in Neuen Testament und in der alten Kirche* (Munich 1961). A. HAMMAN, ed. *Baptism: Ancient Liturgies and Patristic Texts* (Staten Island, NY 1967). CONGREGATION FOR THE DOCTRINE OF THE FAITH, ''Instruction on Infant Baptism'' *Acta Apostolica Sedis*, 72 (1980) 1137–56 (English translation in *Origins* 10 [1981] 474–480). P. COVINO, ''The Post-conciliar Infant Baptism Debate in the American Catholic Church,'' *Worship* 56 (1982) 240–260. G. HUCK, *Infant Baptism in the Parish: Understanding the Rite* (Chicago 1980). M. SEARLE, *Christening: The Making of Christians* (Collegeville, Minn. 1980). J.H,. MCKENNA, ''Infant Baptism: Theological Reflections,'' *Worship* 70 (1996) 194–210. L.L. MITCHELL, *Worship: Initiation and the Churches* (Washington, DC 1991). K. STASIAK, *Return to Grace: A Theology for Infant Baptism* (Collegeville, Minn. 1996).

[K. STASIAK/EDS.]

BAPTISM OF THE LORD

In both the biblical narrative and early post-biblical period the baptism of Jesus is a major mystery, worthy

"The Baptism of Christ," tempera painting by Pietro Perugino, 1490–1500, Kunsthistoriches Museum, Vienna. (©Archivo Iconografico, S.A./CORBIS)

to be included in the Creed. Jesus baptism is the original baptism, the icon of Christian salvation, the source of Christian baptism and cosmic redemption.

New Testament. In spite of the small scandal that Jesus' baptism must have created—what was the Sinless One doing having himself baptized?—it belonged to the earliest tradition, is recorded in all four gospels (Mt 3:13; Mk 1:9; Lk 3:21–22, Jn 1:29–34), and belongs undoubtedly to the events of the historical Jesus. In Mark it is the beginning of the gospel, and Luke has Jesus in the synagogue at Nazareth at the start of his ministry recalling his anointing with the Spirit at the Jordan. In the very short summary of the good news, Peter includes Jesus' baptism (Acts 1:22). In identifying who Jesus is, the biblical witness moves back from the resurrection (Rom 1:3–4), to the baptism of Jesus, to annunciation (Lk 1:26–38), to pre-existence (Jn 1:1). The Jordan event, therefore, is an important stage in this backward development in identifying Jesus.

Matthew and Luke, but above all Mark, arrange the ensemble of Christ's life according to the liturgical cycle of the year, beginning with the preaching of John the Baptist and the baptism of Jesus. John followed not the Jewish liturgical calendar, but the Jewish legal calendar, and therefore the baptism of Jesus, which began the liturgical year, came immediately after Easter. In both the Synoptics and John the baptism of Jesus opened the liturgical year. Both orthodox and heterodox Christians began the liturgical year at the Jordan.

Patristic Writings. The *regula fidei* of Ignatius of Antioch in Eph. 18.2 and Smyrn. 1.1–2 witness to the centrality of Jesus' baptism, which was the dominant model for Christian baptism. At the very earliest stage there was no evidence of the death and resurrection as a dominant model in the theology of Christian baptism, as in Rom 6:4. After Rom 6:4 appeared in Origen's theology of baptism at the beginning of the 3d century, it disappeared from that theology until almost the end of the 4th century.

The baptism of Jesus was an essential article in the early Armenian and Syriac Creeds. In the Syrian tradition Adam and Christ are fused, so the baptism of Jesus takes place on the first day of creation. The later Syrian tradition saw the baptism of Jesus as among the primary truths taught to catechumens. Whether citing the Creeds used in the Syrian baptismal rite, the eucharistic liturgy, or the Prayer of the Hours, the baptism of Jesus is a consistent and constitutive element, indicating that it is the primary, creative, normative manifestation of the Holy Spirit.

The earliest post-biblical witness turned to the baptism of Jesus as a way of speaking about the divine origins of Jesus. But adoptionism, holding that Jesus received his divine sonship and became the Anointed One at his baptism, brought the Jordan event into ill repute. Therefore, the baptism of Jesus as a way of identifying Jesus did not survive the early Christological controversies. The Arians used Jesus' need for baptism to support their Christology. Heterodox Christologies called the divinity of Christ into question and aided in the eclipse of the baptism of Jesus as theologically primary and normative.

Hilary of Poitiers held that the baptism of Jesus contained the "secret order" of the plan of salvation, namely, through the opening of the heavens, the visible descent of the Spirit, the Father's word attesting Christ's divine sonship one learns that the baptism of Jesus is the icon of salvation. The baptism of Jesus is both the order and image of our baptism, which has cosmic implications.

In Ephrem the Jordan event establishes the principle of identity, the Holy Spirit, as the finger of God, identifies who Jesus is. In Justin Martyr both the Spirit and the voice of the Father identifies Jesus. In the *Teaching of St. Gregory* the mutual knowing and mutual showing of Father, Son and Holy Spirit constitute the first full revelation of Jesus' identity as trinitarian communion. At the Jordan the Spirit comes down on the Son that he might reveal salvation to all, and teach believers how to attain the Father. Philoxenus of Mabbug sees the Jordan event as the place where one is "born of baptism, that is, of the Trinity." Those who imitate Jesus' baptism embrace the whole human/divine spectrum. Such communion in the Jordan event restores one's true, integral humanity ("everyone not born of it is not reckoned a man") at one end of the spectrum. At the other end of the spectrum, communion in the mystery places one on the road to "return" to the Trinity, the source, the beginning and goal of the Christian life.

The baptism of Jesus has strong ascetic overtones, especially for a life of poverty. Philoxenus exhorts "Observe the freedom in which Jesus went forth, and do thou thyself also go forth like him," and in the waters of baptism "put on freedom." Jesus was baptized in the Jordan and immediately took his baptism and gave it to us: his baptism is his, and his baptism is ours. Beyond this the seed of resurrection is planted in the waters of Jesus' baptism which is our baptism. In Ephrem and Jacob of Serugh, Christ went down into the waters of baptism to deposit there his robe of glory and Christians go down into the same waters to take up the same robe, the beginning of Christian resurrection. Theodore of Mopsuestia writes: "Know that you are baptized in the same baptism as that in which Christ our Lord in the flesh was baptized." For Philoxenus the Jordan event dominates the central two of the three stages in the history of salvation: 1) from birth of Jesus to baptism; 2) from baptism to the Cross; and 3) the Cross itself. Both Ignatius of Antioch and John of Apamea range the Jordan event among the four major mysteries of Jesus: Incarnation, baptism, death, and resurrection. John of Apamea noted that Jesus began to teach only after the witness of the Father and the Spirit. Philoxenus taught that the Jordan is "the beginning of the new order of the Spirit." Ephrem remarks that "many were baptized on that day, but the Spirit descended and rested only on One," and this was for the sake of Christian baptism and the beginning of the contemplative dimension of the Christian life.

There is a cosmic dimension to Jesus' baptism. At the Genesis moment the Spirit moves over the waters transforming chaos into cosmos, setting out the order of creatures. When Adam sinned the Spirit left him, but in the Jordan event all history and creation is renewed in power, according to Philoxenus. The baptism of Jesus is the inauguration of the new divine world, the first step in the eschatological consummation, where "mystically God [becomes] in all and all in God." Or again: "The return of all to God, that gathering up and the making new, that everything might be in him and he in all: these mysteries commenced at [Jesus'] baptism."

[K. MCDONNELL/R. E. MCCARRON]

Liturgical Feast. The liturgical celebration of the Baptism of Jesus was originally associated with the feast of the Epiphany, whose origins are in the East. Epiphany, observed on January 6, commemorated the appearance of Christ as Savior and the manifestation of God's glory to humankind. Local churches placed different emphases on various themes of manifestation and appearance: not only the Baptism of Jesus in the Jordan, but also the birth at Bethlehem with the visit of the Magi, the wedding feast at Cana, and others. The Epiphany feast was gradually adopted in the West beginning in Gaul, Northern Italy, and North Africa during the mid-4th century. The new context of the eastern feast in the West led to a reinterpretation of its central themes. The eastern Epiphany on January 6 may have been adopted in Rome during the pontificate of Damasus (366–84). The Roman church adapted the new feast in light of its December 25 celebration of the Nativity, leading to an accentuation of the theme of the visit of the Magi to differentiate it from the December 25 feast. Thus, the commemoration of the Baptism of the Lord was attenuated, though this theme remained viable. After the 8th century in the West, the feast of the Epiphany acquired an octave day (January 13), which soon absorbed the theme of the Baptism of the Lord, particularly in the offices. In the 18th century this octave day of Epiphany came to develop a distinct status as a commemoration of the Baptism of the Lord in certain local churches, primarily in France. This feast was adopted for universal celebration in the Roman Calendar in 1960 and fixed on January 13. The reform of the liturgical calendar in 1969 recovered the feast's association to Epiphany when it reckoned the Feast of the Baptism of the Lord on "Sunday falling after 6 January" (*General Norms of the Liturgical Year* [GNLY], no. 38), closing the Christmas cycle. In the East, the Baptism of the Lord remains the central theme of Epiphany (Theophany) to the present.

Bibliography: K. MCDONNELL, *The Baptism of Jesus in the Jordan: The Trinitarian and Cosmic Order of Salvation* (Collegeville 1996); "Jesus' Baptism in the Jordan," *Theological Studies* 56 (1995) 209–36. D. A. BERTRAND, *Le Baptême de Jésus* (Tübingen 1973). S. BROCK, "Baptismal Themes in the Writings of Jacob of Serugh," *Symposium Syriacum* 1976 (Rome 1978) 325–47. D. VIGNE, *Christ au Jordain* (Paris 1992). G. WINKLER, "A Remarkable Shift in the 4th-Century Creeds," *Studia Patristica* 17, pt. 3 (1982) 1396–401. A. GRILLMEIER, "Die Taufe Christi und die Taufe der Christen," *Fides Sacramenti: Sacramentum Fidei* (Assen 1981) 139–42.

[R. E. MCCARRON]

BAPTIST OF MANTUA (SPAGNOLI), BL.

Also called John Baptist Spagnuolo; Carmelite administrator and humanist; b. Mantua, Italy, April 17, 1447; d. there, March 20, 1516. As a youth he studied at Mantua and the University of Padua. He entered the CARMELITES at Ferrara in 1463 and completed his doctorate in theology at the University of Bologna in 1475. Early entrusted with teaching and administration, he was vicar-general of the Congregation of Mantua for six two-year terms from 1483 to 1513, and was prior general of the whole Carmelite order from 1513 until his death. LEO XIII declared Baptist blessed in 1885, and his relics are preserved in the cathedral at Mantua. The friar was a zealous advocate of reform, and his *Fastorum libri duodecim,* dedicated to LEO X, mentions the doom threatening the Church. Some of the Mantuan's strictures were so strong that LUTHER simply borrowed them. A poet of Christian humanism, he enjoyed the reputation of "the Christian Vergil" even in his lifetime. He corresponded with and counseled other humanists; Pico della Mirandola was his friend, and ERASMUS admired him, as did John COLET. His writings, all in Latin, had a phenomenal vogue in the sixteenth and seventeenth centuries; 179 *incunabula* have been catalogued, and there are more than 550 editions of his works printed after 1500. His poems include the famous *Eclogues,* written when he was 15 years old but later revised, and *Parthenice Mariana,* testimony to his

Baptismal font in Sacré Coeur church, Milhausen, France, 20th century.

tender devotion to the Blessed Virgin. His prose works include *De vita beata,* a Ciceronian dialogue with his father, first printed in 1474, and *De patientia.*

Feast: March 20.

Bibliography: *Opera omnia,* 4 v. (Antwerp 1576); *The Eclogues of Baptista Mantuanus,* ed. W. P. MUSTARD (Baltimore 1911). E. COCCIA, *Le edizione delle opere del Mantovano* (Rome 1960). L. M. SAGGI, *La congregazione mantovana dei Carmelitani* (Rome 1954) 116–152. E. MEUTHEN, *Lexikon für Theologie und Kirche*, ed. J. HOFER and K. RAHNER (Freiburg 1957–65) 1:1228. P. A. DE SAINT-PAUL, *Dictionnaire d'histoire et de géographie ecclésiastiques*, ed. A. BAUDRILLART et al. (Paris 1912) 5:525–527.

[E. R. CARROLL]

BAPTISTERIES AND BAPTISMAL FONTS

Baptisteries are the buildings, rooms, or otherwise defined spaces in which are located baptismal fonts. Baptismal fonts are pools or containers that hold the water for the celebration of the sacrament of Baptism.

Historical Developments In the earliest centuries of Christianity, Baptism was celebrated in natural bodies of water, such as rivers and lakes. In the second century AD, however, due to the persecution of Christians, Baptisms in North Africa, southern Europe, and some places in the East sometimes occurred in bathing rooms and courtyard fountains of private homes, and in the *frigidaria* (cold rooms) of small public baths. The oldest baptistery discovered was in DURA-EUROPOS, in what is now Syria, found in an adapted house church from the mid-third century. The rectangular font resembled basins in both the Roman baths and Roman and Syrian tombs (sarcophagi) in Dura. The walls of the baptistery were covered with frescoes depicting biblical scenes informing the meaning of baptism in particular, and of Christianity in general.

Around the fourth century, especially after the persecutions were ended, special buildings were constructed or adapted for the purpose of holding baptismal pools. Adult Baptism was the norm in many places, and evidence suggests that baptisms generally occurred during the Easter vigil—although there is also evidence of infant baptisms and of the sacrament being celebrated at times other than the Easter vigil.

In the earliest centuries, most baptisteries were located adjacent to cathedrals, since baptisms were administered by bishops. The baptisteries were separated from the cathedrals themselves, however, because the catechumens were baptized naked, and because the *disciplina arcani* during the third through fifth centuries required that major elements of the faith be kept secret for the nonbaptized. There is also evidence in some places that there may have been curtains surrounding the font itself.

The design and symbolism of many paleo-Christian baptisteries and fonts reflected the multivalent meanings of water that are reflected in baptismal theology prior to the fourth century when the paschal understanding (Rom. 6.3–5) of the sacrament gained prominence. Birth imagery was predominant in the East, but there are also mentions of it in the West, probably based on John 3.5. In the late second century, IRENAEUS of Lyon referred to the baptismal font as a womb. In the early third century, TERTULLIAN of Carthage wrote extensively of Baptism as birth. His imagery was echoed by AMBROSE of Milan as well as by a number of North Africans, including CYPRIAN of Carthage and AUGUSTINE. Some later theologians have suggested that the understanding of Baptism as birth gave rise to the round shape of the font, but this link remains to be established conclusively.

The earliest actual baptisteries in the West were in various locations not only juxtaposing the cathedrals, but also (later) parish churches. They were built in a variety of shapes and sometimes had more than one room; in some sites there is archaeological evidence that adjacent rooms were used for instruction and for conferring the sacrament of confirmation (chrismation). Niches in some of the baptisteries suggest the possibility of dressing areas for use before and after the water bath.

Ancient baptisteries and baptismal fonts had a variety of architectural antecedents in the Roman world. Some appear to have been influenced by baths; this seems to have been the case with the first Lateran baptistery in Rome. Others were influenced in design by burial places; such was the case with the fourth-century Ambrosian baptistery in Milan, modeled after an imperial mausoleum in the same city. It is not known whether using the plan of a mausoleum was to give architectural expression to the paschal understanding of Baptism, or whether the mausoleum's octagonal plan was simply a good structural design for a central space. Perhaps, both factors played a part in shaping the final design of the baptistery.

It does seem clear that Baptism's three major meanings—birth (Jn 3.5), washing or purification (1 Cor 6.11, Eph 5.26, 2 Pt 1.9), and death and resurrection (Rom 6.3–5, Col 2.12)—did influence the shapes of fonts, which in early centuries were generally pools in the ground at the center of the baptistery. These three meanings of birth, bath, and burial are not unrelated, however. The baptismal bath is in fact a drowning flood, and the new birth must be preceded by the death of the ''old'' person. Already in third-century Egypt, ORIGEN had reflected Romans 6 in writing of Baptism, referring to the font as a sepulcher, and this paschal understanding became the *cantus firmus* in the fourth-century mystagogical writings of CYRIL OF JERUSALEM and AMBROSE of Milan. This led to the primary design of baptismal pools as cruciform or variations thereof (such as the *quatrefoil*, a rounded cruciform shape), or even rectangular (the shape of sarcophagi), although shapes varied from place to place and from East to West.

Pisa Baptistery, 11th-13th century, Pisa, Italy. (©Angelo Hornak/CORBIS)

It was not only the meaning of Baptism that influenced the font shape; the mode of the sacrament—itself influenced by and expressive of the meaning—was also highly influential in the designs and sizes of fonts. *Submersion* (sometimes called ''total immersion'' or ''dipping'') involves pushing the person's entire body under the water, and for this the water must be quite deep, as is suggested by some remains from the sixth and seventh centuries. In *immersion*, the adult candidate stands or kneels in the water (usually between ankle- and waist-deep) while water is poured over the head or the head is lowered partially into the water. *Affusion* involves pouring water over the candidate's head. It began to replace immersion and submersion in cold regions of northern Europe, as infant Baptism became more common beginning in the medieval period in Europe. *Aspersion*, the most minimal mode, merely involves sprinkling water over the head. The more minimal the mode, the smaller the font required, so in-ground pools were gradually replaced by mere above-ground containers, eventually placed on one or more stone pedestals, in the medieval period often quite ornately carved. This became especially true as infant Baptism, often by parish priests, became more common, and as confirmation was separated from the water Baptism.

Shapes of Baptismal Fonts. The early in-ground fonts were often of startlingly large proportions. The first (fourth-century) circular baptismal pool of the Lateran Baptistery in Rome was 8.5 meters in diameter and sunk about one meter into the floor.

The rectangle is the most ancient font shape, as evidenced by the baptismal pool in the mid-third century Dura Europos house church. The rectangle was the common shape of ancient sarcophagi and burial niches, and it remains the shape of coffins in the twenty-first century. Early examples of rectangular fonts include the San Ponziano Catacomb in Rome, and the first stages of the fonts in Aquileia, Italy, and Geneva, Switzerland. A related shape is the square, of which Maktar, Tunisia, is a well-preserved example.

The octagon was a very common early font shape. It was interpreted as representing the Eighth Day, the day of Christ's Resurrection, into which candidates enter in baptism. In Milan, the baptistery constructed when Ambrose was bishop in the late fourth century contained an in-ground octagonal pool measuring almost five meters across and about 0.80 meters deep. Many other notable early pools were also octagonal, including those in Lyon, Fréjus, Aix-en-Provence, and Riez, France, and Castelseprio, Varese, and Cividale, Italy.

Also common were hexagonal fonts, beginning in fifth-century Italy and then in North Africa, often understood to represent the Sixth Day, the day of the Crucifixion (Rom 6.3–5). Important hexagonal pools have been excavated in Aquileia, Grado, Lomello, and Rome (San Marcello), Italy, Cimiez, France, and Carthage (Damous el-Karita), Tunisia. Much attention has been given to hexagonal fonts in octagonal baptisteries, such as in Grado and Lomello, and in the second font in Aquilea, all in northern Italy. Whether this was literally to reflect Rom 6.3–5 remains an open question.

Cruciform and *quatrefoil* quadrilobe (a rounded-lobe variant of the cruciform shape) fonts are common in North Africa and in the East. These shapes have long been interpreted as representing the paschal understanding of Baptism. A stunning mosaic-faced quadrilobe font from Kélibia, Tunisia, has been restored at the Bardo Museum in Tunis. Among the many cruciform pools are those in Tunisia, including Thuburbo Majus and Bulla Regia.

The round shape seems to have originated in fourth-century Rome, but was more common in the East than the West. In North Africa, ruins of circular fonts have been found more in Algeria than in Tunisia. The earliest font in the Orthodox Baptistery in Ravenna, Italy, was internally round, sunk about three meters below the present floor; the present medieval octagonal font was built on the foundations of the original circular plan. Other circular pools included the sixth-century font at Mustis, Tunisia; and certain stages of fonts in Aosta and Aquileia, Italy. There has been no clear agreement on the meaning of the circular pool; it may simply have derived from circular basins in Roman baths. Some scholars have interpreted the round shape in reference to the womb.

Most fonts were deep enough to require steps down into them, although the steps also were thought to serve the symbolic function of descending into death with Christ and then rising with him into new life.

Medieval and Modern Developments. In the late medieval period, in-ground pools were largely replaced by above-ground containers, and eventually by fonts on pedestals, thus minimizing the significance and understanding of Baptism. Originally they were large enough for both adult and infant submersion (*e.g.* the eighth-century above-ground font in Cividale, Italy), but they became smaller and smaller until finally they could accommodate only aspersion. Detached baptisteries became rare. By the late twentieth century in the West, and long before in many places in Europe, fonts were often located at the entrance to the nave, symbolizing Baptism as entrance into the community of the Church.

Only in the late twentieth century were the larger in-ground pools again constructed in liturgical churches in the West—they had been retained, usually in non-symbolic shapes, in Baptist and Anabaptist churches—as the ancient practice of the catechumenate and Christian initiation regained prominence in many churches across the ecumenical spectrum. Two documents were seminal in recovering a fuller understanding of Baptism: the *Roman Rite of Christian Initiation of Adults*, emanating from Vatican II and leading to the recovery of the adult catechumenate (first in the Roman Catholic Church and subsequently, to a lesser extent, in Lutheran and Episcopalian churches in North America); and the World Council of Churches Commission of Faith and Order 1982 document, *Baptism, Eucharist and Ministry*. The resulting renewal of baptismal theology resulted in the retrieval of ancient font shapes and designs in the construction of new baptisteries and fonts.

Notable examples of new fonts large and deep enough to enable adult and infant submersion include the in-ground cruciform pools set within octagons at St. Pius V Church in Pasadena, Texas, St. Charles Borromeo Church and Guardian Angel Church in London, Chiesa della Polomo in Madrid, Chiesa S. Maria del Buon Cammino in Naples, the large round pool (28 feet in diameter) at St. Benedict the African Church in Chicago, and the above-ground octagonal pools in the Cathedral of SS. Peter and Paul in Indianapolis and St. Monica Church in Chicago.

Font covers (which developed in the thirteenth century) have become very rare because most people in the present time are not inclined to take water from the font for the purpose of witchcraft. Some new fonts, however, do have covers, such as the two new cruciform fonts in London; the purpose of these covers is not to protect the water, however, but to allow for a coffin to be set on the font for a funeral, making very clear the relationship between Baptism and death and resurrection.

Bibliography: F. BOND, *Fonts and Font Covers* (London 1908 and 1985). F. CABROL, H. LECLERC, and H. MARROU, *Dictionnaire d' archéologie chrétienne et de la liturgie* (Paris 1924–1953). J. G. DAVIES, *The Architectural Setting of Baptism* (London 1962). A. KHATCHATRIAN, *Les baptistères paléochrétiens*. Paris, 1962. A. KHATCHATRIAN, *Origine et typologie des baptistères paléochrétiens* (Mulhouse 1982). R. KRAUTHEIMER, ''Introduction to an 'Iconography of Medieval Architecture,'' in *Studies in Early Christian, Medieval, and Renaissance Art* (New York 1969). R. KUEHN, *A Place for Baptism* (Chicago 1992). F. NORDSTRÖM, *Mediaeval Baptismal Fonts: An Iconographical Study* (Stockholm 1984). S. A. STAUFFER, *On Baptismal Fonts: Ancient and Modern* (Alcuin/GROW Liturgical Study 29–30; Cambridge 1994), extensive bibliography; *Re-Examining Baptismal Fonts: Baptismal Space for the Contemporary Church,* video (Collegeville, MN 1991).

[S.A. STAUFFER]

BAPTISTS

Protestant churches, congregational in ecclesial polity, greatly diverse in theological orientation, with a strong emphasis on autonomy and diversity. All Baptist congregations generally subscribe to a common core of beliefs, including: (1) the sovereign lordship of Jesus Christ, (2) Bible as divinely inspired, the sole rule of life; (3) the freedom of everyone to approach God directly; (4) salvation by one's faith and God's grace; (5) the two ordinances of baptism by immersion and the Lord's Supper, (6) independence of a local congregation, (7) the church as a group of regenerated believers baptized upon confession of faith in Christ, and (8) rejection of infant baptism as unbiblical.

A girl in Ms. Bert Atkin's sunday school class at Brick Baptist Church reads a book about Jesus Christ's crucifixion, March 1996. (©Jules T. Allen/CORBIS)

Distinctive Theological Emphases. Baptists differ from many Christians regarding the visible manifestation of church. Most Christian churches are territorial, indiscriminately embracing all believers within a given area regardless of spiritual qualifications, and level of faith commitment. Baptists, to the contrary, held that membership in visible churches should be limited to those who were members of the true people of God. In their own terms, ''Visible churches are made up of visible saints.''

Although Baptists conceded the impossibility of ascertaining perfectly who belonged to God's elect, they believed that there were signs that indicated whether a person were truly regenerate. Therefore, applicants for membership were required to relate their experience of God's grace before the entire congregation. When convinced of the authenticity of such a testimony, the church ''by a judgment of charity'' approved the person for baptism. Once admitted into the church, a member accepted covenant obligations and was subject to the discipline of the congregation. Baptists were not perfectionists, but they expected sincere commitment and an earnest attempt to be obedient to Christ.

Baptists also placed great importance upon each local congregation. Denying that the Universal Church is embodied in a single, concrete institution, they insisted that it is visible primarily in particular congregations. To every such "gathered church," they held, authority had been given to order its own affairs under the headship of Jesus Christ. All members were expected to participate in the worship and in the church meeting at which the will of Christ was sought on pertinent issues. The strong emphasis upon the local congregation was balanced by a recognition of the need for fellowship with other churches and for cooperation in common concerns. This sense of interdependence they acknowledged through forming associations.

In connection with their concept of the Church, Baptists had a strong conviction regarding religious liberty. Believing that congregations of disciplined Christians were a sensitive instrument for seeking the guidance of the Holy Spirit, they insisted that they should be free to obey the Lord's will. Therefore, they opposed interference from outside authorities, either civil or ecclesiastical.

Origin and Development in England. A late offshoot of the English Reformation, Baptists represented a variety of Puritanism. Although some have claimed for Baptists an unbroken succession from the 1st century, this view cannot be substantiated. Another theory relates Baptists to the Swiss Brethren of Zurich, via the Mennonite line; but if such a connection existed, it was very tenuous and had little significance for subsequent Baptist history (*see* ANABAPTISTS; MENNONITE CHURCHES). That Baptists emerged from English Congregationalism early in the 17th century is demonstrable, and there is no need to seek beyond this source to account for characteristic emphases of the Baptist faith (*see* CONGREGATIONAL CHURCHES).

At two distinct points, Baptist branches sprouted from the Congregationalist stalk. The first instance was that of an English refugee group of Congregationalists in Amsterdam, Holland, of whom John SMYTH was pastor. In about 1609 Smyth concluded that infant baptism was invalid, and he proceeded to baptize himself and the rest of his congregation, reconstituting the church on the basis of believer's baptism. Subsequently a part of that congregation returned to England to become the first Baptist church there. Two pastors of that church, Thomas Helwys and John Murton, published early pleas for religious freedom. Another separate emanation of Baptists occurred about 1638, when members of a Congregationalist church in London seceded to organize a new church that practiced believer's baptism. It appears that prior to 1641 Baptists practiced affusion, but after that date the rite was administered by the mode of immersion.

From these two churches the General and the Particular Baptists developed. In most respects they were alike, but they disagreed over the questions of predestination and human freedom. The General Baptists, stemming from Smyth's congregation, held that Christ's atoning death was *general.* This tinge of ARMINIANISM can be accounted for by their residence in the Netherlands when these issues were being fiercely debated. The Particular Baptists, arising from the London congregation of 1638, believed in a limited atonement. That is, since God had predestined those whom he would save, the atonement of Christ sufficed only for *particular* individuals who were of the elect.

Both General and Particular Baptists early declared their views in CONFESSIONS OF FAITH. Although they are frequently referred to as belonging to the "left-wing" variety of Puritanism, along with Quakers, Baptists placed much more importance upon objective authority of Scriptures, confessional statements, and procedural regularity than did the latter group (*see* FRIENDS, RELIGIOUS SOCIETY OF). The most important document of the General Baptists was the Orthodox Creed of 1678. Explicitly affirming acceptance of the Apostles', Nicene, and Athanasian Creeds, this document set forth the theological views of the General Baptists in detail. The classic formulation of Particular Baptists was the Second London Confession of 1677. For more than a century and a half it was used as a standard in both England and America.

Both groups had a similar understanding of baptism and the Lord's Supper, which they referred to as sacraments or ordinances. Baptism was regarded as the sign of engrafting into the body of Christ, of remission of sins, and of fellowship with Christ in his death and resurrection. Baptists differed with regard to the degree of authority that belonged to their respective general assemblies, and there were some differences in their church officers. In relationship to other Christians, they felt particularly close to Congregationalists and Presbyterians, but they refused to join in observing the Lord's Supper with any paedobaptists.

During the Civil Wars and Cromwell's Protectorate (1641–60), Baptists flourished. Many were in positions of leadership in the army and navy. Even after the Restoration (1660) they survived, although many of their number, such as John BUNYAN, were persecuted. In 1689 the Act of Toleration brought religious freedom to all Protestants, but in the ensuing years both General and Particular Baptists lapsed into a period of stagnation.

Renewal came toward the end of the 18th century. A new theological development, led mainly by Andrew Fuller, brought a breath of fresh air into the atmosphere of hyper-Calvinism that had stifled the Particular Baptists. This Fullerism provided a platform for an aggressive evangelistic stand in England and for a new era in foreign missions, launched by William CAREY and the Baptist Mission Society. Throughout the 19th century, the Particular Baptists were vigorous, but the General Baptists faded into obscurity; nevertheless, a revitalized movement known as the New Connection General Baptists sprang from them in 1770. In 1891 the Particulars merged with the New Connection group. Out of the British Baptists have come great preachers, such as Robert Hall, Charles Haddon SPURGEON, and John Clifford. They have also had renowned scholars, such as T. R. Glover, H. Wheeler Robinson, and H. H. Rowley. By mid-20th century British Baptists were diminishing in numbers, as they faced the secularism that has blighted both the Established Church and the Free Churches.

History in the U.S. In America, the first Baptist church was formed by Roger WILLIAMS in RHODE ISLAND. After his expulsion from Massachusetts Bay, he established a colony in which complete religious freedom was granted to all people. In 1638 he renounced infant baptism and formed a church of persons baptized upon a profession of faith. Soon thereafter, another Baptist church was organized at Newport by John Clarke. Before long both General and Particular Baptists were represented in Rhode Island, and at Newport in 1671 a Seventh Day Baptist church was constituted. Until about 1740 the General (Six-Principle) Baptists were predominant in New England, and in 1770 they organized an association. Their growth, however, was very slow.

Growth to 1800. The Particular Baptists were destined to become the mainstream of the denominational life in America as in Britain, and their earliest strength was in the Middle Colonies. In 1707 five churches in New Jersey and Pennsylvania organized the Philadelphia Baptist Association, which was to have great influence upon Baptist life in America. Delegates from churches met annually to discuss common interests, settle problems, and promote fellowship. Although each church retained its freedom of action, the association could eject churches that did not conform to the corporate will of the churches. By means of the association, doctrinal uniformity was long preserved, a ministry was provided, disputes were settled, and education was encouraged.

In keeping with the distinctive emphasis outlined earlier, each church was a close-knit fellowship. New churches were formed by means of a covenant that set forth the obligations of church members, and strict discipline was maintained by each congregation. Services of worship were simple, consisting of congregational songs, prayers, a Scripture lesson, and a lengthy sermon. Adornments and symbols such as candles, crosses, pictures, stained glass windows, and musical instruments were eschewed, and neither Christmas nor Easter was observed. Organization, too, was simple, vested in a pastor, deacons, clerk, and ruling elders. Ministers usually had little formal education, although a few attended colonial colleges and others were tutored by older ministers. The need of an educated ministry, however, was widely recognized, and many ministers achieved a surprising degree of learning by their own efforts. Ordination was kept in the power of each local church, but representatives from other churches were invited to help determine a candidate's fitness and to aid in the ordination service.

With the advent of the GREAT AWAKENING, Baptists began to grow. In New England, Baptists benefited by the accession of hundreds of New Light, or Separate, Congregationalists. It was in the South that Baptists experienced the greatest increase, as Separates from New England moved into that region. Beginning with Shubael Stearns and William Marshall, who came from New England to Sandy Creek, NC, a series of revivals produced numerous churches and pastors in a short time. From a handful of Baptists in the southern colonies in 1740, their number grew to more than 1,300 churches by 1800.

Baptists played an active role in the struggle for freedom. In the Revolutionary era they generally sided with the patriots, taking part in politics and serving as chaplains and soldiers. John Hart of New Jersey was a signer of the Declaration of Independence. In Massachusetts and Virginia, where they had suffered discrimination on religious grounds, Baptists carried on a vigorous campaign against the establishment. Isaac Backus, John Leland, and others made important contributions to the theory of religious liberty that became integral in American life.

Development after 1800. The early 19th century witnessed unprecedented activity in the churches, as interest in evangelism, missions, and education developed. In 1814 the Baptists organized a national society for foreign missions, when three Congregationalists became Baptists. Adoniram JUDSON, Ann Judson, and Luther RICE had been sent to India by the Congregationalists. but when they decided that infant baptism was unwarranted by the Scriptures, they became Baptists. Learning that the Judsons and Rice were available to serve as their missionaries, Baptists in America organized the Triennial Convention. Within a few years, they had also organized a publishing society, a home mission society, and a Bible society. Simultaneously, state conventions and educational societies were being established. All of these agencies were composed of interested persons who paid annual dues. The adoption of this ''society method'' for supporting missions and education was of great significance, for it meant that denominational organization would for a long time be based upon single-purpose voluntary societies that had no direct relationship to the churches. No national Baptist convention was formed in the North until the 20th century. Accompanying the rising interest in missions were other signs of vitality. Sunday Schools were organized rapidly after 1820, and academies and colleges were established in nearly every state. Newton Theological Institution, Mass., was founded in 1825. Colgate, Rochester, and Southern Baptist seminaries also were founded prior to the Civil War. And Baptists were active in reform movements, particularly the temperance cause.

Divisions. With rapid growth, diverse cultural influences, and increasing individualism, Baptists began to form separate groups. Out of the Great Awakening had come the Free Will Baptists, when Benjamin Randall sought to maintain an Arminian theology. In the 1830s, on the other hand, an Old School (Primitive) Baptist movement arose in protest against abandonment of the traditional predestinarianism of the Baptists. About 1850, under the leadership of James R. Graves, the Landmark Baptist movement started. Insisting that Baptists comprised the only true church, the Landmarkists (now the American Baptist Association) refused to recognize other churches. They held that the term "church" in the New Testament always refers to a local church, and thus they further encouraged particularistic tendencies among Baptists.

No division was more important than that which resulted over slavery. For years the home and foreign mission societies maintained neutrality on this issue, but in 1845 an open break occurred. Consequently, the Southern Baptist Convention was founded at Augusta, Ga. Instead of adopting the "society method" of supporting missions, the Southern Baptists organized a convention with integral boards responsible for home and foreign missions.

After the Civil War, Black Baptist churches flourished. Prior to that time blacks and whites had belonged to the same churches, but after the war the freed blacks preferred their own churches. These were at first affiliated with the regular associations and state conventions, particularly in the North. In 1880 the National Baptist Convention was organized, and in 1916 it divided into two parts, the National Baptist Convention of America and the National Baptist Convention, U.S.A., Inc. These two bodies comprise the bulk of the Black Baptist population.

Other Changes. Rapid industrialization, urban growth, and changing intellectual climate brought new challenges after 1865. Under the impact of new conditions, Baptists underwent further change. Social problems became more complex, as the gulf between rich and poor widened and city slums expanded. Among the Baptists who helped to awaken the social conscience of the churches were Walter RAUSCHENBUSCH, Shailer MATHEWS, Leighton Williams, and Samuel Zane Batten. Edward Judson developed a great institutional church in New York City, and Russell H. Conwell, in Philadelphia, PA, developed institutions to help the working classes. At the same time new scientific theories and Biblical criticism posed a threat for traditional theological systems. Baptists shared in the theological ferment, producing such leaders as William Newton Clarke and William Rainey Harper, who helped to popularize the new theological outlook.

As church memberships increased and organization became more complex, covenants fell into disuse and discipline declined. In the North, open communion (partaking the Lord's Supper with paedobaptists) became prevalent by World War I, and by mid-20th century open membership had become common (receiving paedobaptists without requiring that they be rebaptized). Worship services were tending toward greater formality, and there was much more use of symbolism in the sanctuaries. For the sake of efficiency, the Northern Baptist (now American Baptist) Convention was formed in 1907. Southern Baptists have been more reluctant to adopt open communion and open membership.

Many Baptists resisted the new social emphasis, the changing views of the Bible, and centralizing tendencies; but no party of protest was crystallized until about 1920. In the 1920s a "Fundamentalist" group within the Northern Baptist Convention sought to purge the schools and mission societies of unorthodox elements (*see* FUNDAMENTALISM). The flames were fed when Harry Emerson Fosdick, a Baptist minister, preached a sermon entitled "Shall the Fundamentalists Win?" By 1925 the Modernist-Fundamentalist controversy had reached a climax. Some of the more disaffected elements withdrew from the convention, and in 1932 the General Association of Regular Baptists was established. Dissatisfaction continued to smoulder within the convention, and in the 1940s the conflict was resumed, leading to a further exodus of churches to form the Conservative Baptist movement.

Southern Baptists were not as deeply affected by the SOCIAL GOSPEL movement or theological modernism in the 1920s. Evolution created a stir in some colleges, and a few professors were suspected of being unorthodox. In 1925 the Southern Baptist Convention voted to recommend the New Hampshire Confession of Faith to their churches, but the controversy did not reach major proportions as it had in the North. Four decades later, however, Southern Baptists were experiencing a tardy reaction to the changing views of Scripture that had penetrated at least some of their seminaries.

Membership and Organization. The growth rate of the various Baptist groups in the 20th century differed greatly. Black Baptists experienced considerable growth, but the American Baptist Convention remained nearly static after 1930. The newer, fundamentalist bodies also increased rapidly. It has been the Southern Baptists, however, whose expansion has been phenomenal. Not only did their number become nearly double in 30 years, but they had expanded into every state of the Union by 1960.

Of the many Baptist groups in the U.S. in 1964, about 90 per cent of them belonged to the four largest: the Southern, American, and two National Baptist Conventions. In underlying principles and general structure, the larger bodies are similar, although there are important differences in operation. On various levels are the associations, state conventions, and national conventions, each of which is directly related to the local churches. At the national level are boards that shape policy and program for missions, education, evangelism, publications, and pensions. Each board has a permanent staff of professional workers, which is responsible to trustees elected by delegates (or messengers) to the annual meeting of the national body. To coordinate the work of various boards, there is a national executive officer and some type of executive committee. State conventions may develop their own programs, but much of the time of their staffs is devoted to implementing policies national in scope. Associations seldom have permanent staffs, and their functions are usually confined to fellowship gatherings and cooperation in local matters.

Within this system juridical power is weak, and the authority of connectional bodies is not clearly defined. The associational principle implies that some authority resides in the wider fellowship, but there is disagreement as to how much authority belongs to associations and conventions. Individual churches cannot be coerced into conformity with a convention policy with which they disagree, although the latter body can withdraw fellowship from an uncooperative church. In general, cooperation depends upon agreement in purposes, moral suasion, and Christian unity.

The lack of a strong central jurisdiction affects the process of ordination to the gospel ministry. Authority to ordain has traditionally been claimed by the local church, but in practice others have always shared in the process. Other churches are asked to send delegates to examine candidates and to take part in the act of ordination, and conventions may set standards for their recognition of an ordination. There is considerable diversity in ordination practices and in the educational level of ministers in all of the conventions. In a congregational system, each church is responsible for securing a minister after a pulpit becomes vacant. Recommendations may come from seminaries, other ministers, or state secretaries; but a pastor is chosen by vote of the congregation. It should be noted that women may be ordained.

Bibliography: R. G. TORBET, *A History of the Baptists* (rev. ed. Valley Forge 1963). N. H. MARING and W. S. HUDSON, *A Baptist Manual of Polity and Practice* (Valley Forge 1963). W. L. LUMPKIN, *Baptist Confessions of Faith* (Chicago 1959); *Baptist Foundations in the South* (Nashville 1961). W. W. BARNES, *The Southern Baptist Convention, 1845–1953* (Nashville 1954). O. D. PELT and R. L. SMITH, *The Story of the National Baptists* (New York 1960). W. S. HUDSON, ed., *Baptist Concepts of the Church* (Chicago 1959). C. C. GOEN, *Revivalism and Separatism in New England, 1740–1800* (New Haven 1962). P. M. HARRISON, *Authority and Power in the Free Church Tradition: A Social Case Study of the American Baptist Convention* (Princeton, NJ 1959). *Baptist Advance: The Achievements of the Baptists of North America for a Century and a Half* (Nashville 1964). *The Chronicle* (Chester, PA 1938–57), a Baptist historical quarterly. Succeeded by *Foundations: A Baptist Journal of History and Theology* (New York 1958–), with important descriptive and interpretive articles. *The Review and Expositor* (Louisville, KY 1904–), a quarterly journal of the Southern Baptist Theological Seminary. A. GILMORE, ed., *Christian Baptism* (Chicago 1959). R. E. O. WHITE, *The Biblical Doctrine of Initiation* (Grand Rapids 1960). G. R. BEASLEY-MURRAY, *Baptism in the New Testament* (New York 1962). F. S. MEAD, S. S. HILL and C. D. ATWOOD, *Handbook of Denominations in the United States,* 11th rev. ed. (Nashville 2001).

[N. H. MARING/EDS.]

BAR, CATHÉRINE DE

Foundress of the Benedictine Nuns of the Blessed Sacrament; b. Saint-Dié, Vosges, France, Dec. 31, 1614; d. Paris, April 6, 1698. At the age of 17 Catherine joined the convent of the Annonciades at Bruyère, and she was professed in 1633. A year later she became superior. Violent fighting during the Thirty Years' War forced her to flee her convent, and in 1639 she found shelter with the Benedictines of Rambervillers. Attracted to the Benedictine form of life, she requested a transfer from the Annonciades. On July 11, 1640, she took her vows as a Benedictine. War again forced her to move, this time to Montmartre. There she assumed the name Mother Mechtilde of the Blessed Sacrament. She founded the Benedictine Nuns of the Blessed Sacrament to make reparation for outrages committed against Our Savior in the Eucharist. She was in contact with such renowned religious figures of her day as St. John Eudes and Jean-Jacques Olier; she also wrote on spiritual topics.

Bibliography: I. HERVIN and M. DOURLENS, *Vie de la très révérende Mère Mechtilde du Saint-Sacrement* (Paris 1883). R. SÉJOURNÉ, *Dictionnaire d'histoire et de géographie ecclésiastiques* 6:534–538.

[B. EGAN]

BAR-CURSUS (JOANNES TELLENSIS)

An exponent of the Monophysite Christology of Severus of Antioch; b. at Kallinikos, *c.* 483; d. Antioch, 538. He left the comfort of court life in order to enter monastic life. He became bishop of Tella in northern Mesopotamia in 519. In 533 he took part in the dogmatic discussions in Constantinople. He died a violent death in prison because of his convictions. He edited a collection of canons that is important for the history of liturgy and the Sacraments, especially for the Sacrament of the Holy Eucharist, e.g., the custom of giving Communion under one species.

Bibliography: T. J. LAMY, *Dissertatio de Syrorum fide et disciplina in re Eucharistia* (Louvain 1859). F. NAU, *Les Canons et les résolutions canoniques de Rabboula, Jean de Tella,* (Paris 1906). I. ORTIZ DE URBINA, *Patrologia syriaca.*

[L. R. KOZLOWSKI]

BAR-HEBRAEUS (GREGORIUS IBN AL-IBRI)

Jacobite Syrian theologian and writer; b. Melitene (modern Malatya, Turkey), Armenia, 1226; d. Maragheh, Iranian Azerbaijan, July 30, 1286.

Called Bar-Hebraeus (son of a Hebrew father), Gregory Abou'l Faradj received the name John at baptism. He was educated in philosophy, theology, and medicine by his father, a converted Jewish physician, and a coterie of scholars. He emigrated to Antioch in Syria with his family before the Mongol invasions and spent several years in solitude as a hermit. He traveled to Tripoli and studied logic and medicine under James the Nestorian. He took the name of Gregory when he was consecrated bishop of Gouba by the Jacobite Patriarch Ignatius II (Sept. 14, 1246). The next year he changed to the See of Laqabin and was promoted to the metropolitan See of ALEP by Patriarch Denis of Antioch, whose candidacy he supported (1252) against the claims of John Bar Madani.

When the Mongols conquered Baghdad and took possession of Syria, Gregory approached their chief, Hulagu, to negotiate the proper treatment of Christians. He was taken prisoner, however, and Alep was sacked. Before the martyrdom of Denis, Bar-Hebraeus had made peace with Patriarch Bar Madani; and he played a part in the selection of Ignatius III as patriarch of Antioch in 1264. Bar-Hebraeus was consecrated maphrian of Tagrit (the patriarchal vicar-general of the Jacobite Church, recognized by the Moslem governor) at Sis, Cilicia, in the presence of the Armenian king, Het'um; in 1273 he succeeded in healing a schism in the Jacobite Church caused by the influential physician Simon.

As maphrian, Bar-Hebraeus visited the various communities of the Jacobite Church in western Armenia and in Baghdad; he used their libraries, encouraged their pastors, and entered into amicable relations with the Nestorian leaders. In 1277 he visited his see at Tagrit, which had been sacked by the Tartars. It was the first time in 60 years that a maphrian had been able to visit the city. In 1282 he journeyed to Tabriz to give the new Mongol Prince Ahmed assurance of his loyalty and submission to the civil ruler.

In 1284 the partisans of the physician Simon elected him as the new patriarch without awaiting the arrival of Bar-Hebraeus; the latter accepted the *fait accompli* in the interest of ecclesiastical unity. He died at Maragheh while the Nestorian Patriarch Yabalaha was present in the city, and he was interred in the monastery of Mar-Mattai at Mosul with Byzantine, Nestorian, and Jacobite prelates in attendance.

Of vast erudition, Bar-Hebraeus won the respect of the various Christian churches and of the Mohammedans by his learning and amiability. Among his principal writings was a synthesis or encyclopedia of philosophy called the *Cream* or *Science of Sciences,* in which he commented on every branch of human knowledge in the Aristotelian tradition, with compendia on logic, physics, metaphysics, and practical philosophy culled from Aristotle and the Syrian and Arabic authors. He wrote voluminous commentaries on the Old and New Testament published under the title, *Storehouse of Mysteries,* utilizing the works of both Nestorian and Jacobite exegetes. He controlled the PESHITTA version of the Scriptures with Greek, Hebrew, Septuagint, Armenian, and Coptic versions; and he supplied materials for the recovery of the Hexapla of ORIGEN. In his *Lamp of the Sanctuary* he gave a systematic exposition of Jacobite doctrine: he wrote an *Ethics* whose moral philosophy was greatly influenced by Al Gazali. His ascetical treatise was called the *Book of the Dove,* a directory for monks, and he wrote a *Nomocanon* of ecclesiastical legislation that still plays a part in Oriental canon law.

As a historiographer, he produced a chronicle as a universal history whose first section, *Chronicon Syriacum,* dealt with secular events to the Mongol invasions; and whose second section, *Chronicon Ecclesiasticum,* in its first subdivision gave a history of the patriarchs of the Old Testament followed by those of the New Testament, namely the patriarchs of Antioch and the western Syrian Church. Its second subdivision covered the patriarchs of the Oriental Syrian Church to 1285. His brother Barsauma continued this account to 1288, and an anonymous author continued it to 1496.

Bar-Hebraeus followed the history of MICHAEL I the Syrian for the earlier centuries, but in both method and originality he surpassed his model, supplying first-class material for the later centuries. He made an Arabic synopsis of the work that he supplemented with information useful for a Moslem readership under the title *A History of the Dynasties.* He also composed a large grammar called the *Book of Splendors,* monographs on science and medicine, and liturgical, didactic, and polemical poetry that conformed to the artistic tastes of the Syrian culture. He wrote his own autobiography, and his death notice was supplied by his brother Barsauma.

Bibliography: E. HERMAN, *Dictionnaire d'histoire et de géographie ecclésiastiques* 6:792–94. J. S. ASSEMANI, *Bibliotheca orientalis* 2:244, 468. J. GÖTTSBERGER, *Bar-Hebraeus und seine Scholien zur heiligen Schrift* (Freiburg 1900). P. BEDJAN, *Barhebraei Ethicon seu Moralia* (Paris 1878); *Barhebraei Chronicon syriacum* (Paris 1890); *Barhebraei nomocanon* (Paris 1898). G. CARDAHI, *BarHebraeus's Book of the Dove together with Some Chapters of His Ethicon,* tr. A. WENSINCK (Leiden 1919). J. B. ABBELOOS and T. J. LAMY, *Chronicon ecclesiasticum,* 3 v. (Louvain 1872–77). P. SBATH, *Traité sur l'âme par Barhébraeus* (Cairo 1928). W. WRIGHT, *A Short History of Syriac Literature* (London 1894) 265–81. A. BAUMSTARK, *Geschichte der syrischen Literatur* (Bonn 1922) 312–20. I. ORTIZ DE URBINA, *Patrologia syriaca* 207–9.

[F. X. MURPHY]

BAR KOKHBA, SIMON (BAR COCHEBA)

The political leader of the second Jewish revolt against Rome (A.D. 132–35). From autograph letters written by him to various officers under his command and found in 1951, 1960, and 1961 in caves of the wadies Murabba'āt, Seiyâl, and Ḥabra in Jordan and Israel (*see* DEAD SEA SCROLLS), it is certain that his name was Simon ben Kosibah (*šm'wn bn kwsbh,* attested in a Greek letter as Σιμων Χωσιβα). In rabbinical writings (e.g., Babylonian Talmud, *Sanhedrin,* 11.1, 2, folio 93b) his name is given as *bar* (or *ben*) *Koziba,* "son of the lie." This form is probably the result of a wordplay on his name (Hebrew *kzb,* "to lie"), which originated with the Jews who either did not approve of his uprising or ironically reflected later on its ill-fated outcome. Rabbi AKIBA BEN JOSEPH, who approved of the revolt, regarded him as a messiah (Jerusalem Talmud, *Ta'anith* 4.68d) and applied to him the oracle of Balaam, "A star shall advance from Jacob" (Numbers 24.17). He was thus responsible for another wordplay on Simon's name, in which the patronymic *ben Kosibah* was changed to the Aramaic *bar Kokhba,* "the son of the star" (Aramaic *kôk^ebâ,* "star"). This name, which has clung to him in history, is found in a few Jewish writings. It is the only form used by Christian writers (Justin, *Apol.* 1.31; Eusebius, *Hist. Eccl.* 4.6.2).

Outbreak of the Revolt. Along with Rabbi Akiba, the intellectual leader of the time, and Eleazar the Priest, the spiritual leader, Bar Kokhba was the political and military commander of the Palestinian Jews in their second revolt against Rome. Coins minted during the first year of his uprising bear the title, "Simon, Prince of Israel" (*šm'wn nśy' yśr'l*), and the Murabba'āt documents preserve the fuller form, "Simon ben Kosibah, Prince of Israel" [*šm'wn bn kwsb' nsy' yśr'l* (*Mur.* 24 B 2–3)]. The coins and the documents reveal that the revolt was dedicated to the "liberation of Jerusalem" and the "redemption of Israel."

The causes of the revolt are not certain. Dio Cassius (*Roman History* 69.12.1–2) states that it was due to Hadrian's attempt to build a Greco-Roman city (Aelia Capitolina) on the site of Jerusalem and to erect a shrine to Jupiter on the ruins of the Temple of Yahweh. This is usually recognized as a major factor. The *Vita Hadriani* (14.2) cites another cause, relating the revolt to an imperial edict forbidding circumcision (*quod vetabantur mutilare genitalia*). Hadrian, who renewed a former prohibition of castration, so understood it as to include circumcision. It was not directed against the Jews in particular, for a later decree of Antoninus Pius (A.D. 138) specifically permitted them to circumcise their children, while still forbidding circumcision to others. Both causes would have vexed the Jews and probably contributed to their revolt.

The Murabba'āt contracts preserve a synchronism that shows that the era of the "redemption of Israel" coincided with a cycle of SABBATH YEARS (*Mur.* 24 B 1–10, E 1–10). From this synchronism the official date for the beginning of the era is calculated as 1 Tishri (October) A.D. 132. Another document (*Mur.* 30.8) is dated "21 Tishri, year 4," showing that the revolt at least began its fourth year (end of A.D. 135).

Bar Kokhba's Activity. Besides acting as a military leader, Bar Kokhba administered the land politically from his headquarters, probably in Jerusalem. He preserved the elaborate administrative machinery and division of Judea into toparchies that the Romans had set up. After liberating Jerusalem, he never met the Romans in open field battles, but he conducted a guerrilla-type warfare from many villages and outposts throughout the land. Chief among these were Herodium, Teqoa', 'Engedi, Meṣad Ḥasidin (Khirbet Qumran?), Beth-Ter. His local deputies rented out in his name farm lands in the fertile foothills and in southern Judea to lessees who were obliged to pay an annual rent in kind to the "treasury of the Prince of Israel at Herodium" (*Mur.* 24 D 17–18), that is, government granaries. His letters reveal his administrative concern for the observance of the SABBATH, the celebration of the Feast of BOOTHS (Tabernacles), the treatment of Galileans who had come to take part in the revolt, the arrest of certain individuals, and the seizure of the property of others.

At the beginning of the revolt, the Roman governor of Judea, Tineius Rufus, although in command of Roman garrisons resident in the province (*Legio X Fretensis, Legio VI Ferrata*), was helpless. The governor of Syria, Publicius Marcellus, came to his aid with further troops. Finally, Hadrian had to send his best general, Sextus Julius Severus, recalling him from Britain. He eventually put down the revolt after a slow process of starving out the Jews who had taken refuge in various strongholds and caves in the desert. Caves in the wadies Murabba'āt, Seiyâl, and Habra were used by whole families, who fled there with a few household belongings, biblical scrolls, and family archives. The officers from 'En-gedi fled to the Wadi Ḫabra cave, taking with them the letters of their commander-in-chief. The Romans set up camps in strategic positions around the caves to keep watch on them, lest the rebels escape.

End of the Revolt. After Jerusalem was once again taken by the Romans, Bar Kokhba withdrew and made his last stand at Beth-Ter (near modern *Bittîr,* about six miles west southwest of Jerusalem). The war reached its height there in Hadrian's 18th regnal year (A.D. 134–35). ''The siege lasted a long time before the rebels were driven to final destruction by famine and thirst, and the instigator of their madness paid the penalty he deserved'' (Eusebius, *Hist. Eccl.* 4.6.3). Subsequently Hadrian razed Jerusalem again to build Aelia Capitolina and decreed ''that the whole [Jewish] nation should be absolutely prevented from that time on from entering even the district around Jerusalem, so that not even from a distance could it see its ancestral home'' (ibid.). Ancient Christian writers were normally not sympathetic to Bar Kokhba, accusing him of persecuting and torturing the Christians who would not join his uprising (Justin, *Apol.* 1.31; Eusebius, *Chronicon* 283; *Die griechischen christlichen Schrift steller der ersten drei Jahrhunderte* 47.201).

Bibliography: E. SCHÜRER, *A History of the Jewish People in the Age of Jesus Christ* (175 B.C.–A.D. 135), 3 vols., rev. G. VERMES and F. MILLAR (Edinburgh 1973–1987), 1.514- 557. P. BENOIT et al., *Les Grottes de Murabba'ât* (*Discoveries in the Judaean Desert* 2; 1961). J. A. FITZMYER, ''The Bar Cochba Period,'' *Essays on the Semitic Background of the New Testament,* (London 1971; repr. Grand Rapids, Mich. 1997) 305–354. B. ISAAC and A. OPPENHEIMER, ''The Revolt of Bar Kokhba: Ideology and Modern Scholarship,'' *Journal of Jewish Studies* 36 (1985) 337–60. P. SCHÄFER, *Der Bar Kokhba-Aufstand* (*Texte und Studien zum antiken Judentum* 1; Tübingen 1981). Y. YADIN, *The Finds from the Bar Kokhba Period in the Cave of Letters* (Jerusalem 1963). N. LEWIS et al., *The Documents from the Bar Kokhba Period in the Cave of Letters* (Jerusalem 1989). A. OPPENHEIMER, ''Bar Kokhba, Shim'on,'' *Encyclopedia of the Dead Sea Scrolls* (2 vols.; ed. L. H. SCHIFFMAN and J. C. VANDERKAM; Oxford 2000), 1.78-83.

[J. A. FITZMYER]

BAR MITZVAH

The term for the religious rite by which a Jewish boy is formally initiated into the religious community and assumes the duties and responsibilities of a Jew. The words *bar mitzvah* (late Hebrew *bar miṣwâ*) literally mean, ''son of precept.'' Though the expression is found in the Talmud (Baba Meẓi'a 96a), it appears to have been used there simply to mean every adult Jew. The use of the word in the modern sense does not go back much beyond the 14th century. It was first so employed in the works of a German Jew, Mordecai ben Hillel.

Origin and Significance. Leopold Löw has established the fact that *bar mitzvah* was a fixed custom in Germany in the 14th century. Löw was of the opinion that the practice of *bar mitzvah* could not be traced beyond this point in time. There is, however, some probability that in a rudimentary form at least, *bar mitzvah* derives from an earlier period. With the solemnization of this rite, the Jewish boy is considered to have attained religious maturity. He may henceforth be called up to fill the *minyān,* i.e., the required number of 10 necessary for holding congregational worship. The *bar mitzvah* ceremony takes place on the Sabbath following a boy's 13th birthday (reckoned according to the Jewish calendar). As in Roman custom, the age of puberty is taken as the time for assuming responsibility.

Ceremony. There are three phases to the *bar mitzvah* ceremony. First, the boy must read in public from the Pentateuch and the Prophets. Meanwhile the boy's father prays in silence: ''Blessed be he who has taken the responsibility of this child's doing from me.'' This disavowal of the father's further responsibility for his son's sins is omitted by the Sephardim (Spanish and Portuguese Jews). Next follows an address given by the *bar mitzvah* boy. As a general rule, this talk is prepared by the rabbi or teacher and is memorized by the boy. Lastly there is the Se'udah or festive meal. It is customary at this celebration to give presents to the *bar mitzvah* boy. The *bar mitzvah* ceremony should be preceded by a period of training in which the boy is schooled in, among other things, the principal duties and observances of Jewish life.

Reform Judaism in the last century replaced *bar mitzvah* with Confirmation to which both boys and girls are admitted. This ceremony is held annually for all those of age at Shabuoth, the Feast of Weeks (Pentecost). In some Reform and Conservative congregations both Confirmation and *bar mitzvah* are held. In some synagogues too, *bath mitzvah* (''daughter of precept'') is observed. This is a rite developed for girls that generally corresponds to *bar mitzvah.*

"Pilate Liberating Barabbas and Crucifying Christ," from the "Predis Codex," by Cristoforo de Predis. (©Archivo Iconografico, S.A./CORBIS)

Bibliography: L. LÖW, *Die Lebensalter in der jüdischen Literatur* (Beiträge zur jüdischen Alterthumskunde 2; Szegedin 1875). National Association of Temple Educators, *Confirmation Practices* (Educational Research Survey 2; New York 1959). C. ROTH, "Bar-Mitzvah: Its History and Its Associations," *Bar-Mitzvah Illustrated,* ed. A. I. KATSH (New York 1955). I. LEVITATS, *Communal Regulation of Bar Mitzvah* (New York 1949). J. ARLOW, "A Psychoanalytic Study of a Religious Initiation Rite: Bar Mitzvah," *The Psychoanalytic Study of the Child* (New York 1945) 6:353–374.

[J. C. TURRO]

BARABBAS

The criminal who was released instead of Jesus. Barabbas (Βαραββᾶς, for Aramaic *bar-'abba',* "son of Abba") was his surname; according to some Greek MSS in Mt 27.16–17 his first name was Jesus. He is described in Jn 18.40 as a ληστής. Although this passage is commonly translated as "Barabbas was a robber," here the word ληστής does not mean a thief in the ordinary sense, but rather a bandit, a revolutionary, a meaning that the Greek word sometimes has also in the writings of Josephus. According to Mk 15.7 and Lk 23.19, Barabbas was an insurgent, a rebel against the Roman occupation forces. He was one of the rioters in an uprising in which someone was murdered, and he was arrested for the crime. In certain circles of the populace he was, no doubt, regarded as a local hero. Among such people he might even have aroused messianic expectations and hopes for the final unsheathing of the messianic sword.

According to Mt 27.20 and Lk 23.4, the Jewish authorities who accused Jesus before Pilate had with them a "crowd" or "crowds"; this has often been understood as a mob representative of the inimical attitude of the Jerusalem populace toward Jesus. Despite repeated assertions of popular support given Jesus in Jerusalem both before the Passion (Mk 11.18; 12.12, 37; 14.2) and even after it (Acts 2.41, 46–47; 3.11; 4.1–4, 21, 33; 5.13–14, 17, 26; 8.12; 9.31), this understanding has gone unquestioned for centuries. In Mk 15.7–8, however, the tight sequence of thought suggests that this "crowd" was actually composed of the followers or friends of Barabbas who came up to beg the paschal amnesty for their hero but had to fend off Pilate's attempts to release Jesus instead (see also Acts 3.14–15). After Barabbas had been released, the two λησταί between whom Jesus was crucified (Mk 15.27; Mt 27.38, 44) were presumably followers of the rebel leader.

Bibliography: J. J. TWOMEY, "Barabbas Was a Robber," *Scripture* 8 (1956) 115–119. D. M. CROSSAN, "Anti-Semitism and the Gospel," *Theological Studies* 26 (1965) 189–214. J. BLINZLER, *Lexikon für Theologie und Kirche,* ed. J. HOFER and K. RAHNER, 10 v. (2d, new ed. Frieburg 1957–65); suppl. *Das Zweite Vatikanische Konzil: Dokumente und Kommentare,* ed. H. S. BRECHTER et al., pt. 1 (1966) 1:1234. J. MÜLLER-BARDORFF, *Die Religion in Geischichte und Gegenwart,* 7 v. (3d ed. Tübingen 1957–65) 1:869. *Encyclopedic Dictionary of the Bible,* tr. and adap. by L. HARTMAN (New York 1963), from A. VAN DEN BORN, *Bijbels Woordenboek,* 206.

[D. M. CROSSAN]

BARADAI, JAMES

Monophysite bishop and founder of Jacobite Church; d. Romanos monastery of Kasion, Egypt, July 30, 578. James was Syrian by birth. He became a monk and priest at the Pesīltā monastery in the mountains of Izla, and *c.* 527 was sent to the Byzantine court in Constantinople, where he remained until 543 under the favor of the Empress THEODORA. Consecrated titular bishop of Edessa by the exiled Patriarch Theodosius of Alexandria, he was sent, at the request of the Arab prince Harith Ibn Gabala, to the eastern frontier of the empire to convert the Arabs. He consecrated a large number of Syrian Monophysites as bishops and priests, thus founding a new hierarchy that was organized by the Monophysite Patriarch of Antioch, Sergius (d. *c.* 560). The church thus established is still known as the Syrian Jacobite Church. Baradai left no authentic writings other than a few letters translated from Greek into Syriac.

Bibliography: E. HAMMERSCHMIDT, *Lexikon für Theologie und Kirche* 5:836. H. G. KLEYN, *Jacobus Baradaeus, de Stichter der syrische monophysitische Kerk* (Leiden 1882) 164–94. I. ORTIZ DE URBINA, *Patrologia syriaca* 153–54. W. WRIGHT, *A Short History of Syriac Literature* (London 1894). E. STEIN, *Histoire du Bas-Empire* 2:625–28, 684.

[I. ORTIZ DE URBINA]

BARAGA, FREDERIC

Pioneer missionary, first bishop of Marquette (MI) diocese; b. Mala Vas Castle, parish of Dobrinič, Carniola, a Slovene province later part of Yugoslavia, June 29, 1797; d. Marquette, Jan. 19, 1868. Baptized Irenaeus Frederic, he never used his first name. After receiving his preparatory education in Ljubljana, where his talent for languages was marked, he studied law at the University of Vienna, and during that period came under the influence of the Redemptorist, Clement Mary HOFBAUER. Upon graduation in 1821 he broke his engagement to marry, renounced his inheritance, and entered Ljubljana's seminary. He was ordained Sept. 21, 1823, and was sent first as curate to Šmartno, near Kranj, and in 1828 to Metlika, where he continued his pastoral zeal and literary activity. A prayer book, *Dušna Paša* (Spiritual Food), that ran to ten large editions, and two other devotional works are from this period.

Through the LEOPOLDINEN-STIFTUNG, founded in Vienna in 1829 to aid the American missions, Baraga volunteered for Cincinnati, thus realizing his ambition, inspired by Father Hofbauer, of laboring among the Native Americans. Shortly after arriving there, Jan. 18, 1831, he was dispatched to the Ottawas of Arbre Croche (now Harbor Springs), MI, where within 28 months he baptized 547 Native Americans and transformed a deteriorating mission into a model Christian community. Afterward followed his foundation of the Grand River (Grand Rapids) mission in September 1833, and in July 1835 his mission among the Lake Superior Chippewas at La Pointe, Madeline Island, where his church had to be twice rebuilt to accommodate his growing congregation. At L'Anse mission, which he established in 1843 on Keweenaw Bay, further success attended his efforts to convert pagans into Christians. Meanwhile, the development of copper mines on the Keweenaw Peninsula attracted pioneers and thus extended his labors and his territory, which he covered faithfully by foot and canoe.

In July 1853 Upper Peninsular Michigan became a vicariate apostolic, and on November 1 in Cincinnati Baraga was consecrated vicar apostolic with the title bishop of Amyzonia in *partibus infidelium.* His first act, after issuing pastorals in English and Native American, the latter an innovation, was to travel throughout Europe in search of funds and priests. He was responsible for most of the territory bordering Lake Superior and the northern area of the peninsula, as well as Native American sections of other dioceses ceded to him by neighboring bishops because of his zeal and competence. With the expansion of copper and iron mining, the pioneer population increased steadily and with it the need for more priests and churches; yet severe climatic and linguistic demands lessened the number of missionary candidates. During his three years as vicar apostolic, Baraga traveled constantly, preaching several times a day in various languages, building and maintaining churches and chapels. Though he lived frugally, his poverty was acute, especially during the Civil War when allotments from European societies, his chief source of income, shrank in purchasing power.

In 1857 his vicariate was raised to a diocese, and in 1866 Baraga transferred the see from Sault Ste. Marie to

Marquette, joyfully reporting that it was now well provided with priests and churches. His Native American missions were also firmly established. During the fall of that year, however, he suffered a stroke while attending the Second Plenary Council of Baltimore. Though critically ill, he insisted upon returning to Marquette to await his coadjutor and to fulfill his vow to die among the natives. Preliminary steps have been taken toward his beatification.

Baraga's writings include voluminous correspondence, records, diaries, and reports to European societies of great historical value. He also wrote: *Theoretical and Practical Grammar of the Otchipwe Language* (Detroit 1850); *Dictionary of the Ojibway Language* (Cincinnati 1853); *The History, Character, Life and Manners of the Indians* (in German and Slovene, Ljubljana 1837; in French, Paris 1837); *Animie-Misinaigan* (Ottawa prayerbook, later enl., rev., and tr., into Chippewa); *Jesus o Bimadisiwim* (''Life of Jesus'' in Ottawa; Paris 1837); *Gagikwe-Masinaigan* (sermon book in Chippewa, containing abstracts from Old and New Testaments, and Epistles and Gospels of the year; 1839, 1859); *Kagige Debwewinan* (''Eternal Truths''); *Nanagatawendamo-Masinaigan* (instructions on the Commandments and Sacraments); three devotional works for his friends and former parishioners in Slovenia, and many smaller items. His grammar and dictionary were the first published in the Chippewa and Ottawa languages and are still an aid to the study of Native American linguistics.

Bibliography: J. GREGORICH, *The Apostle of the Chippewas: The Life Story of the Most Rev. Frederick Baraga, D.D.* (Lemont, IL 1932). A. I. REZEK, *History of the Diocese of Sault Ste. Marie and Marquette*, 2 v. (Houghton, MI 1906–07). C. VERWYST, *Life and Labors of Rt. Rev. Frederic Baraga: First Bishop of Marquette, Mich.* (Milwaukee 1900). The Marquette diocesan library at Marquette contains holographs of the Journal (Diary) and of many letters, importantly those addressed to the Leopoldine Association, Vienna. Other materials are held by the Newberry Library (Ayer Collection), Chicago, the Notre Dame University archives, and private collectors.

[J. GREGORICH]

Bishop Frederic Baraga.

BARAT, MADELEINE SOPHIE, ST.

Foundress of the SACRED HEART SOCIETY; b. Joigny (Yonne), France, 12 Dec. 1779; d. Paris, 25 May 1865. She was the daughter of a Burgundy vine-grower and received her early education from her brother Louis, a priest. In 1800 her brother took her to Paris to continue her studies. There Joseph VARIN D'AINVILLE persuaded her to join a group of women living under religious rule. She followed this group to Amiens, where she became (1802) their superior general and head of their school for girls. In 1804 she founded the second house of the Society of the Sacred Heart in Grenoble, and there met Rose Philippine DUCHESNE, who later introduced the congregation into the United States.

For the next 60 years Mother Barat labored to extend her institute, which numbered 86 houses by 1865. Although she never engaged in teaching after leaving Amiens, she retained an interest in the intellectual training of her nuns. She also shaped the society's constitutions to guard against the mores of the court circles from which many of the pupils came. This, and a desire to reeducate in Christian principles children reared in a post-revolutionary society, inspired her to resist successfully the efforts of a chaplain of the Amiens house to reshape the constitutions. A similar reaction occurred in 1839, when a group of members tried to make the congregation resemble more closely the JESUITS. Although Mother Barat traveled much in order to establish and visit her foundations, her most fruitful years were spent at Grenoble with Philippine Duchesne; at Poitiers, where the first noviceship was founded; at Montet in Switzerland, where the novices were sent after the 1830 revolution; at Rome; and at Conflans, outside Paris, where the general noviceship of the society was situated at the time of her death. Her body reposes incorrupt in Jette, Belgium. She was beatified in 1908 and canonized in 1925.

St. Madeleine Sophie Barat.

Feast: May 25.

Bibliography: *Journal: 1806–1808*, ed. M.-T. VIRNOT (Poitiers 1977). C. E. MAGUIRE, *Saint Madeleine Sophie Barat* (New York 1960). A. BROU, *Saint Madeleine Sophie Barat,* tr. J. W. SAUL (New York 1963). M. WILLIAMS, *St. Madeleine Sophie* (New York 1965). P. KILROY, *Madeleine Sophie Barat* (Sterling, VA 2000).

[C. E. MAGUIRE]

BARBAL COSAN, JAIME (JAMES) HILARIO, ST.

Baptized Manuel, also known as Diego Barbal, Lasallian Christian Brother martyr; b. Enviny (Diocese of Urgel), Lérida Province, northern Spain, Jan. 2, 1898; d. Tarragona, Spain, Jan. 18, 1937. At age twelve Manuel Barbal Cosan began his studies for the priesthood in the minor seminary at La Seo de Urgel. When he developed a hearing loss and was advised to return home, he feared that he would be unable to fulfill his religious vocation. He attended the De la Salle training center at Mollerusa for seven months, then the brothers of the Christian Schools at Irun, Spain, accepted him into their novitiate (Feb. 24, 1917). For sixteen years (1918–34) he taught at De la Salle schools (Mollerusa, 1918–23, 1924–25; Manresa, 1923–24; Oliana, 1925–26; Pibrac near Toulouse, 1926–34), and became known for his professional competence as a teacher and catechist, as well as for his piety and adherence to the rule. When his hearing loss became too profound to continue teaching, he worked as cook in the school at Calaf (1934) and in the garden of Saint Joseph's novitiate at Cambrils, Tarragona (from December 1934), while he continued to write about French, Castillan, and Catalonian literature.

Upon hearing of the martyrdom of his religious brothers at Turón (with whom he was canonized), he expressed to his family his desire to die likewise. En route to visit them, he was recognized as a religious, arrested at Mollerusa (July 18, 1936), and imprisoned locally, then at Lérida (August 24); he was transferred to the prison ship *Mahon* at Tarragona (December 5). Refusing to win his release by denying his religious identity during the summary trial (Jan. 15, 1937), Jaime Hilario was taken to Monte de los Olivos cemetery for execution by firing squad. He was the first of ninety-seven Lasallian brothers of the District of Catalunia to die during the Spanish Civil War and in the first group of martyrs of the period to be canonized (Nov. 21, 1999), following his beatification by John Paul II on April 29, 1990. His cause was joined with that of the Martyrs of Turón, who had died three years before Barbal.

Feast: Jan. 18 (Lasallian Brothers).

Bibliography: V. CÁRCEL ORTÍ, *Martires españoles del siglo XX* (Madrid 1995). L. SALM, *The Martyrs of Turón and Tarragona: the De La Salle Brothers in Spain* (Romeoville, Ill. 1990).

[K. I. RABENSTEIN]

BARBANTINI, MARÍA DOMENICA BRUN, BL.

Foundress of the Pious Union of the Sisters of Charity and the Sister Servants of the Sick of St. Camillus; b. Lucca, Tuscany, Italy, Jan. 17, 1789; d. Lucca, May 22, 1868. Maria Domenica's husband, Salvatore Barbantini, died six months after they were married in 1811, and a short time later she gave birth to a son. A woman of boundless energy, she balanced motherhood and running her deceased husband's business while caring for those in need. Her own dedication and example attracted other women to the same work, and together they formed the Pious Union of the Sisters of Charity (1817). Following the death of her eight-year-old son, she abandoned herself completely to God. She lived for a time with the Sisters of the Visitation as she tested a contemplative vocation. Fr. Antonio Scalabrini, later superior general of the Order of St. Camillus, encouraged her to found the Sister Servants of the Sick of St. Camillus (1829). The archbishop of Lucca's approved of the rule in 1841 and authorized the organization as a diocesan religious institute. Pope John Paul II beatified Maria Domenica on May 7, 1995.

Bibliography: *Acta Apostolicae Sedis* (1995): 564. *L'Osservatore Romano,* English edition, no. 19 (1995): 2, 4.

[K. I. RABENSTEIN]

BARBARA, ST.

Virgin and martyr. Data of her vita and *passio* are from a legend composed in the 7th century, perhaps of Egyptian origin. Her father, Dioscorus, is said to have kept her in a tower so that her beauty would not be contaminated by the world; but on learning that she was baptized a Christian, he had her condemned by the prefect Martinianus and himself beheaded her, whereupon he was consumed by lightning. There is an 8th century fresco of Barbara in Rome. Her vita was taken from the *Menologion* of SYMEON METAPHRASTES and introduced into European MARTYROLOGIES in the 9th century. She is one of the FOURTEEN HOLY HELPERS and the patroness of those exposed to sudden death. The subject of many Flemish and Italian artists in the 15th and 16th centuries, she is portrayed with crown, palm, and sword, with tower and peacock, and with a chalice to symbolize a happy death.

Feast: Dec. 4.

Bibliography: V. SEMPELS, *Dictionnaire d'histoire et de géographie ecclésiastiques.* (Paris, 1912) 6:627–628. K. GROSS and H. BENDER, *Lexikon für Theologie und Kirche,* 10 v. (Freiburg 1957) 1:1235–36. G. D. GORDINI, *Bibliotheca Sanctorum* (Rome, 1961) 2:760–765.

[M. J. COSTELLOE]

BARBARIGO, GREGORY, ST.

Bishop and cardinal; b. Venice, Italy, Sept. 16, 1625; d. Padua, Italy, June 18, 1697. Gregory, the son of Giovanni Francesco BARBARIGO, of illustrious family, was educated in Padua. In 1648, he accompanied the Venetian embassy to Münster for the Treaty of Westphalia and met the papal nuncio, later Alexander VII. Gregory took a degree in law and was ordained in 1655. At Alexander's request he organized the care of the plague-stricken Roman Trastevere in 1656. As bishop of Bergamo in 1657, he promoted the reforms of the Council of Trent, visiting parishes, organizing the teaching of Christian doctrine, and raising the standards of the seminary and the clergy. He was made a cardinal in 1660, and bishop of Padua in 1667.

He adapted the curriculum of the seminary of Padua to contemporary needs, obtained books for its library throughout Europe, and wrote *Regulae Studiorum* (1690) for ecclesiastical studies. He set up a printing press with Latin, Greek, Hebrew, Syriac, Persian, and Slavonic types, preparing pamphlets for Christians under Moslem rule. His aid to Orthodox leaders was generous, and his death may have prevented negotiations for reunion with Rome. He took part in five papal conclaves and was a candidate in three, especially in 1691. His body is in the cathedral of Padua. He was beatified on Sept. 20, 1761, and canonized on May 25, 1960. John XXIII held him as a model during his seminary days. S. Serana has studied Gregory and his relations with mathematics, the Eastern Church, and his contemporaries (5 v., Padua 1932–40).

Feast: June 18.

Bibliography: John XIII, *Acta Apostolicae Sedis* 52 (1960) 437–462. A. MERCATI and A. PELZER, *Dizionario ecclesiastico* (Turin 1954–58) 2:263. H. RAAB, *Lexikon für Theologie und Kirche,* ed. J. HOFER and K. RAHNER (Freiburg 1957–65) 1:1236. C. BELLINATI, *S. Gregorio Barbarigo* (Padua 1960); *Pensieri e massime di S. Gregorio* (Padua 1962). G. BELTRAME, *Giovanni Chiericato, oratoriano padovano, ministro e biografo di S. Gregorio Barbarigo* (Padua 1976). S. SERENA, SEBASTIANO, *S. Gregorio Barbarigo e la vita spirituale e culturale nel suo Seminario di Padova; lettere e saggi editi dagli amici in memoria* (Padua 1963).

[M. O'CALLAGHAN]

BARBARIGO, MARC' ANTONIO AND GIOVANNI FRANCESCO

Cardinals, members of a prominent Venetian family.

Marc' Antonio. Cardinal; b. Venice, March 6, 1640; d. Montefiascone, May 26, 1706. Barbarigo, a member of the Venetian Council at age 25, left a promising political career for the priesthood and was ordained in 1671. When summoned to Padua by Gregory BARBARIGO, a distant relative, he became a canon in the cathedral and earned a degree *utroque jure* at the University of Padua. In 1676 he accompanied Cardinal Gregorio to the conclave that elected Innocent XI, and he remained in Rome at the new pope's request. He was appointed to the vacant episcopal See of Corfù in 1678 and was installed on September 24 of the same year. His peaceful and efficient administration lasted until 1685. On the first Sunday of Lent of that year, a controversy over a question of protocol arose between Barbarigo and Francesco Morosini, admiral of the Venetian fleet. Barbarigo fled to Venice to clear himself of charges brought against him. When denied a hearing and deprived of his possessions, he sought asylum in Rome. Having been cleared of the charges, he was made a cardinal by Innocent XI on Sept. 2, 1686. The following year he was appointed bishop of Montefiascone and Corneta, which he entered on Oct. 20, 1687. In this office, Barbarigo earned universal praise for his pastoral charity and his interest in education. Deeply concerned with the plight of underprivileged girls, he founded the institute of the Scuole e Maestre Pie for their care and education. In this work, he was assisted by Rose Venerini, foundress of similar schools in the diocese; one of the pupils, St. Lucy FILIPPINI, later became the superior of the Montefiascone institute. Barbarigo also promoted education and established a sound program of studies in the seminary "Barbarigo," which he generously endowed with a good library. He attended the conclaves that elected Alexander VIII, Innocent XII, and Clement XI. He is buried in the cathedral of Montefiascone. The process for his canonization is under way.

Giovanni Francesco. Cardinal, nephew of St. Gregory Barbarigo, cousin of Marc' Antonio; b. Venice, April 29, 1658; d. Padua, Jan. 26, 1730. Although ambassador of Venice at the court of Louis XIV, he renounced diplomacy for the priesthood. Bishop of Verona (1697) and of Brescia (1714), he was made cardinal by Clement XI in 1721, with the title of Saints Peter and Marcellinus. On Jan. 20, 1723, Innocent XIII named him bishop of Padua, where he distinguished himself for his piety and zeal, visiting hospitals, reorganizing ecclesiastical discipline, and promoting education. Barbarigo, munificent and learned scholar, published, at his own expense, the works of St. Zeno (1710) and of St. Gaudentius (1720). He is buried next to his uncle, Gregory.

Bibliography: M. A. Barbarigo. P. BERGAMASCHI, *Vita . . . del card. M. A. Barbarigo,* 2 v. (Rome 1919). G. MARANGONI, *Vita del card. M. Barbarigo* (Montefiascone 1930). A. ZERBINI, *Cultura e urnanesimo nell'Alto Lazio* (Rome 1955). H. RAAB, *Lexikon für Theologie und Kirche* (Freiburg 1957–65) 1:1237. G. F. BARBARIGO, *Lexikon für Theologie und Kirche*, 1:1236–37. C. EUBEL et al., *Hierarchia Catholica medii (et recentioris) aevi* 5:127, 309, 411. M. T. DISDIER, *Dictionnaire d'histoire et de géographie ecclésiastiques* (Paris 1912—) 6:578–79.

[E. J. THOMSON]

BARBARO

Noted Venetian family of humanists, statesmen, and churchmen.

Francesco, statesman and humanist; b. Venice, *c.* 1398; d. Venice, January 1454. A student of Manuel Chrysoloras, he was tutored in letters and Greek, and then studied at the University of Padua. He entered the Venetian senate in 1418 and was ambassador to Florence, Verona, Bologna, and other important Italian cities, as well as to the court of Pope MARTIN V. In 1438 he led the defense of Brescia against Filippo Maria VISCONTI, Duke of Milan, whose ambitions he considered the greatest danger to Venice. Francesco desired peace for all Italy. Active in negotiations for the Council of Basel-FERRARA-FLORENCE, he tried to effect religious unity with the Greek Church and urged that steps be taken to prevent Constantinople from falling to the Turks. He wrote *De re uxorio libri II* in 1415 and was acquainted with most of the Italian humanists of his time (*see* HUMANISM). His letters, *Orationum ac epistolarum libri XV,* were edited by A. Quirini (Brescia 1743), whose edition was improved by R. Sabbadini (Salerno 1884) and L. Frati (Venice 1888).

Nicolo (dates uncertain), Venetian ambassador to CONSTANTINOPLE, wrote a report of its siege and capture by the Turks in 1453, *Giornale dell'assedio di Constantinopoli,* which was published by both A. Sagredo (Venice 1856) and E. Cornet (Vienna 1856).

Ermolao the Elder, churchman and humanist, brother of Francesco; b. Venice, *c.* 1410; d. Venice, March 12, 1471. He became bishop of Treviso, Oct. 16, 1443, and of Verona, Nov. 16, 1453. In 1453 he wrote *Oratio contra poetas* objecting to excessive adulation of the ancient poets. His works are unpublished.

Ermolao the Younger, patriarch of AQUILEIA, humanist, churchman, diplomat, nephew of Ermolao; b. Venice, May 21, 1454; d. Rome, June 14, 1493. At the age of eight, he was sent to Rome to study under Pomponius Laetus; by 1477 he was professor of philosophy at the University of Padua. He served as Venetian ambassador to Milan in 1488 and to the court of Pope INNOCENT VIII in 1491. Though he was named patriarch of Aquileia by Innocent on March 6, 1491, the Venetians prevented him from taking possession of his see because he had accepted it without consent of the senate. He remained in Rome and died of the plague. His principal work is *Castigationes,* against Pliny the Elder; he also translated some of the writings of Aristotle into Latin. His *Epistolae, orationes et carmina* are edited by V. Branca, 2 v. (Florence 1943).

Daniele, statesman, patriarch of Aquileia; b. Venice, Feb. 8, 1513; d. Venice, April 12, 1570. He was a student and professor at Padua, who in 1548 became ambassador to England. Though named patriarch of Aquileia (Dec. 17, 1550) by Pope Julius III, he never governed it; the patriarchate continued to be administered by Giovanni Grimani in order to prevent a non-Venetian from obtaining the position. In 1562 Daniele began active participation in the Council of Trent. His works can be found in J. Morelli, *Codices manuscripti latini bibliothecae Nanianae* (Venice 1776) 4, 31–32, 198.

Francesco, patriarch of Aquileia, reformer; b. Venice; d. Venice, April 27, 1616. On Oct. 7, 1585, he became archbishop of Tyre, then vicar-general and coadjutor with right of succession to Giovanni Grimani, whom he succeeded on Oct. 3, 1593. He combatted heresy and, in his attempts to effect the reforms of Trent, opened a seminary at Udine in 1601.

Ermolao, patriarch of Aquileia; d. Venice, Dec. 22, 1622. He had been archbishop of Tyre and coadjutor to his brother Francesco whom he succeeded as patriarch, but because of wars of the Uscocchi he could never take possession of his see.

Bibliography: Francesco, statesman. G. M. MAZZUCHELLI, *Gli scrittori d'ltalia,* 2 v. (Brescia 1753–63) 2:264–69. P. GOTHEIN, *Francesco B.: Früh-Humanismus und Staatkunst in Venedig* (Berlin 1932). Ermolao the Elder. G. M. MAZZUCHELLI, *op. cit.* 2:253–56. Daniele. P. PASCHINI, ''I scritti religiosi di Daniele Barbaro,'' *Rivista di storia della Chiesa iri Italia* 5 (1951) 340–49. Francesco, patriarch. P. PASCHINI, ''Riforma e contro-riforma al confine nord-orientale d'Italia,'' *L'Arcadia* 4 (1922) 72-. Ermolao, patriarch. E. A. CICOGNA, *Iscriziòni veneziane,* 6 v. in 7 (Venice 1825–53) v.4. P. PASCHINI and M. T. DISDIER, *Dictionnaire d'histoire et de géographie ecclésiastiques* 6:582–90.

[W. H. WALLAIK]

Ermolao Barbaro (the Elder?), by an unknown 15th-century artist.

BARBASTRO, FRANCISCO ANTONIO

Franciscan prelate in northwest Mexico; b. Villa de Cariñena, Aragón, Spain, 1734; d. Aconchi, Sonora, Mexico, June 22, 1800. Barbastro took the habit at the Convento de Jesús in Zaragoza (1754), went to the Colegio of San Roque de Calamocha (1764), and from there to the Missionary College of Santa Cruz de Querétaro (1770). He was assigned to the missions of Sonora, of which he was made president. There he was the most outstanding of the missionaries because of his wisdom and his charity toward the Indians. He learned the languages of the various nations, particularly that of the Opatas, and preached in them. In 1783 he founded the school of Aconchi, the first in Sonora. On October 23 of that year the Custody of San Carlos was founded, and Barbastro governed it as vice custos until it was dissolved (1789) on his recommendation to Charles IV. Barbastro demonstrated that the custody was harmful to the missions. He wrote notes and reports for a history of the Province of Sonora as an *Apología* for the Franciscan provinces and colleges engaged in missions among the pagans.

[E. DEL HOYO]

BARBASTRO, MARTYRS OF

Felipe de Jesús Munárriz Azcona and 50 companions; martyrs; members of the Congregation of Missionary Sons of the Immaculate Heart of the Blessed Virgin Mary (Claretian Missionaries); d. August of 1936, Barbastro (Huesca), Spain; beatified by John Paul II, Oct. 25, 1992.

The first decades of the twentieth century found Spain mired in political upheaval and social unrest. Violent religious persecutions unfolded following the establishment of the Republic in 1931. During the Spanish Civil War (1936–39) there was a massive elimination of priests, nuns, and Catholic lay leaders throughout Spain. Fifty-one of those killed were Claretians, mostly young seminarians who had recently arrived at the Claretian house in Barbastro to complete the last year of their theological studies.

On July 20, 1936, the students, their professors and superiors, and some Claretian brothers were arrested and accused of harboring weapons. They were taken to the auditorium of the Piarist seminary, where they were subjected to various forms of psychological and physical abuse. Between August 2 and August 11, all 51 were executed.

In addition to the superior, Father Felipe Munárriz (b. Feb. 4, 1875 at Allo, Navarre, Spain), the following were also martyred on Aug. 2, 1936: Father Juan Díaz Nosti (b. Feb. 18, 1880 at Quinta de los Catalanes, Asturias); Father Leoncio Pérez Ramos (b. Sept. 12, 1875 at Muro de Aguas, Rioja).

The martyrs of Aug. 12, 1936 include Father Sebastián Calvo Martínez (b. Jan. 20, 1903 at Gumiel de Izán, Burgos); Wenceslao María Clarís Vilaregut (b. Jan. 3, 1907 at Olost de Llusanés, Barcelona); Father Pedro Cunill Padrós (b. March 17, 1903 at Vic, Catalonia); Brother Gregorio Chirivás Lacambra (b. April 24, 1880 at Siétamo, Huesca); Father José Pavón Bueno (b. Jan. 19, 1901 at Peral, Cartegena); Father Nicasio Sierra Ucar (b. Oct. 11, 1890 at Cascante, Navarre).

The martyrs of Aug. 13, 1936 include Javier Luis Bandrés Jiménez (b. Dec. 3, 1912 at Sangüesa, Navarre); José Brengaret Pujol (b. Jan. 18, 1913 at Sant Jordi Desvalls, Gerona); Brother Manuel Buil Lalueza (b. Aug. 31, 1914 at Abizanda, Huesca); Antolín María Calvo y Calvo at Gumiel del Mercado, Burgos); Tomás Capdevila Miró (b. May 5, 1914 at Maldá, Catalonia); Esteban Casadevall Puig (b. March 18, 1913 at Argelaguer, Gerona); Eusebio María Codina Millá (b. Dec. 7, 1914 at Albesa, Lérida); Juan Codinachs Tuneu (b. Feb. 12, 1914 at Santa Eugenia de Berga, Vic); Antonio María Dalmau Rosich (b. Oct. 4, 1912 at Urgell, Lérida); Juan Echarri Vique (b. March 30, 1913 at Olite, Navarre); Pedro García Bernal (b. April 27, 1911 at Santa Cruz de Salceda, Burgos); Hilario María Llorente Martín (b. Jan. 14, 1911 at Vadocondes, Burgos); Brother Alfonso Miquel Garriga (b. Feb. 24, 1914 at Prades de Molsosa); Ramón Novich Rabionet (b. April 8, 1913 at Sellera del Ter, Gerona); José María Ormo Seró (b. Aug. 18, 1913 at Almatret, Lérida); Father Secundino María Ortega García (b. May 20, 1912 at Santa Cruz de la Salceda, Burgos); Salvador Pigem Serra (b. Dec. 15, 1912 at Viloví de Onyar, Gerona); Teodoro Ruiz de Larrinaga García (b. Nov. 9, 1912 at Bargota, Navarre); Juan Sánchez Munárriz (b. June 15, 1913 at Malón, Zaragoza); Manuel Torras Saez (b. Feb. 12, 1915 at Sant Martí Vell, Gerona).

The martyrs of Aug. 15, 1936 include José María Amorós Hernández (b. Jan. 14, 1913 at Puebla Larga, Valencia); José María Badía Mateu (b. Sept. 30, 1912 at Puigpelat, Tarragona); Juan Baixeras Berenguer (b. Nov. 21, 1913 at Castelltersol, Barcelona); José María Blasco Juan (b. Jan. 2, 1912 at Játiva, Valencia); Rafael Briega Morales (b. Oct. 24, 1912 at Zaragoza); Brother Francisco Castán Messeguer (b. Feb. 1, 1911 at Fonz, Huesca); Luis Binefa Escalé (b. Sept. 18, 1912 at Fondarella, Lérida); José Figuero Beltrán (b. Aug. 14, 1911 at Gumiel del Mercado, Burgos); Ramón Illa Salvía (b. Feb. 12, 1914 at Bellvís, Lérida); Luis Lladó Teixidor (b. May 12, 1912 at Viladesens, Gerona); Brother Manuel Martínez Jarauta (b. Dec. 22, 1912 at Murchante, Navarre); Father Luis Masferrer Vila (b. July 9, 1912 at Torelló, Barcelona), who had saved the Eucharist from desecration; Miguel Massip González (b. June 8, 1913 at Llardecans, Lérida); Faustino Pérez García (b. July 30, 1911 at Baríndano, Navarre); Sebastián Riera Coromina (b. Oct. 13, 1913 at Ribas de Fresser, Gerona); Eduardo Ripoll Diego (b. Jan. 9, 1912 at Játiva, Valencia); Francisco Roura Farró (b. Jan. 13, 1913 at Sors, Gerona); José María Ros Florensa (b. Oct. 30, 1914 at Torms, Lérida); Alfonso Sorribes Teixidó (b. Dec. 17, 1912 at Rocafort de Vallbona, Lérida); Agustín Viela Ezcurdia (b. April 4, 1914 at Oteiza de la Solana, Navarre).

The martyrs of Aug. 18, 1936 include Jaime Falgarona Vilanova (b. Jan. 6, 1912 at Argelaguer, Gerona); Atanasio Vidaurreta Labra (b. May 2, 1911 at Adiós, Navarre).

Numerous testimonies remain that witness to the events, including those of two Argentinean Claretians who were spared. The martyrs' own testimony is found in the writings they left on scraps of paper, on bits of chocolate wrappers, and in the inscriptions they made on the back of a piano stool. To the end, they sang, forgave their persecutors, and proclaimed their faith with enthusiasm.

The cause of beatification of the 51 Claretians of Barbastro was introduced shortly after the end of the Spanish Civil War. Pope Paul VI put a moratorium on beatifications of Spanish Civil War victims that remained in effect until Pope John Paul II considered the situation in Spain changed and reopened the processes.

Speaking at the beatification in Rome, Pope John Paul II affirmed that "these Claretians died because they were disciples of Christ, because they would not deny their faith and their religious vows . . . with their blood they challenge us to live and die for the Word of God which we all have been called to announce."

Feast: Aug. 13.

Bibliography: GABRIEL CAMPO VILLEGAS, *The Claretian Martyrs of Barbastro, August 1936,* trans. J. DARIES (Rome 1992).

[L. BROWN]

BARBATIA, ANDREAS DE (ANDREAS SICULUS)

Lay canon lawyer; b. Messina, Sicily, *c.* 1400; d. Bologna, July 21, 1479. In 1425 he studied medicine at Bologna and then law. In 1438 he both taught and took his doctorate degree in canon law. From 1438 until 1442 he taught at Florence, then returned to Bologna and taught there until his retirement (1478). He was a renowned teacher and active practitioner of law. Among his students was Rodriquez Borgia, later Pope Innocent VI. His knowledge of both canon and civil law caused popes, kings, and civil leaders to seek out his advice. His works include *Lecturae seu Repetitiones,* on the Decretals, *Tractatus de Praestantia Cardinalium* (Bologna 1487), *Tractatus de Cardinalibus a latere legatis* (Lyons 1518), and *Tractatus de praetensionibus* (Bologna 1487).

Bibliography: A. AMANIEU, *Dictionnaire de droit canonique* 1:520–21. J. F. VON SCHULTE, *Die Geschichte der Quellen und der Literatur des kanonischen Rechts* 2:306–11.

[T. F. DONOVAN]

BARBATUS, ST.

Bishop and patron of Benevento; b. Cerreto Sannita, Italy, early seventh century; d. Benevento, Italy, Feb. 19, 682. Little is known of his life until he succeeded Hildebrand as bishop of Benevento in 663, but he devoted his attention both before and after his election to stamping out the remains of pagan superstitions in his diocese. It was reported that he won the support of his people by predicting both the calamities that would occur because of the invasion in 663 of the army of Emperor CONSTANS II and the later lifting of the siege. In 681 he attended the sixth general council, CONSTANTINOPLE III; he died not long after he returned from this meeting. He is especially venerated in Benevento, where his body is buried under the main altar of the cathedral. There is a tendentious life of Barbatus dating from the ninth century (ed. G. Waitz, *Monumenta Germaniae Historica: Scriptores rerum Langobardicarum* [Berlin 1826—] 556–563).

Feast: Feb. 19.

Bibliography: *Bibliotheca hagiograpica latina antiquae et mediae aetatis* (Brussels 1898–1901) 973–975. A. P. FRUTAZ, *Lexikon für Theologie und Kirche*, ed. J. HOFER and K. RAHNER (Freiburg 1957–65) 1:1238. G. CANGIANO, *Origini della chiesa Beneventana* (Benevento 1923) 40–51; "Sulla leggenda della 'vipera longobarda' e delle 'streghe,'" *Atti della Societá storica del Sannio* 5–7 (1927–29) 84–96. A. M. JANNACCHINO, *S. Barbato e il suo secolo* (Benevento 1902).

[R. E. GEIGER]

BARBEAUX, ABBEY OF

Former French abbey, Diocese of Sens. Barbeaux was founded in 1146 by CISTERCIANS of Preuilly on the site of an early hermitage (*Sacer Portus*), but in 1156 it was transferred to Barbeaux, donated by King Louis VII. The king continued to be a generous benefactor of the abbey and, according to his wishes, was buried there. In spite of royal patronage the monastery suffered during the Hundred Years' War and was deserted for 40 years. Reconstruction was hampered when Barbeaux came under commendatory abbots after 1498. When the 17 monks of the community embraced the Cistercian Strict Observance in 1643, there followed a period of financial and moral recovery. In 1768, there were ten monks in the abbey, while revenues amounted to 18,500 livres. The abbey was suppressed by the French Revolution. While under private ownership, the church and cloister were demolished. Other buildings housed an orphanage in the Napoleonic era.

Bibliography: C. RABOURDIN, *L'Abbaye royale de Barbeaux* (Melun 1895). U. CHEVALIER, *Répertoire des sources historiques du moyen-âge. Topobibliographie,* 2 v. (Paris 1894–1903) 1:307. J. M. CANIVEZ, *Dictionnaire d'histoire et de géographie ecclésiastiques,* ed. A. BAUDRILLART et al. (Paris 1912–) 6: 629–631. L. H. COTTINEAU, *Répertoire topobibliographique des abbayes et prieurés,* 2 v. (Mâcon 1935–39) 1:260–261.

[L. J. LEKAI]

BARBELIN, FELIX JOSEPH

Pastor and educator; b. Lunéville, Lorraine, France, May 30, 1808; d. Philadelphia, Pa., June 8, 1869. After education in French schools and seminaries, he became a Jesuit in Maryland in 1831, was ordained on Sept. 22, 1835, and taught at Georgetown University. He served as an assistant at St. Joseph's, Philadelphia, and became pastor there in 1844, remaining in that post until his death. He inaugurated the first parish sodality at St. Joseph's (1841) and established a St. Vincent de Paul conference and a free school for girls in Philadelphia. The Italian congregation he organized developed into the first Italian Catholic parish in Philadelphia. He gathered the first African American congregation in Philadelphia and established a school for African American children. He founded St. Joseph's Hospital and established St. Joseph's College, Philadelphia, serving as its first and third president. He also conducted a night school for adults.

Bibliography: J. M. DALEY, *St. Joseph's Church, Willing's Alley* (Philadelphia 1963). F. X. TALBOT, *Jesuit Education in Philadelphia* (Philadelphia 1927). *Records of the American Catholic Historical Society of Philadelphia. Woodstock Letters.*

[H. J. NOLAN]

BARBER

A prominent New England family converted to Catholicism in the early 19th century. *Daniel* (b. Simsbury,

Conn., Oct. 2, 1756; d. St. Inigoes, Md. March 24, 1834) was a soldier in the Continental Army and left the Congregational Church to become an Episcopal minister. In 1818 he terminated a 24-year career as resident Episcopal minister at Claremont, N.H., and entered the Catholic Church. He wrote *Catholic Worships and Piety Explained* (1821) and *The History of My Own Times* (1827). His son, *Virgil Horace* (b. Simsbury, Conn., May 9, 1782; d. Georgetown, D.C., March 27, 1847), was educated at Dartmouth College, Hanover, N.H. He entered the Episcopal ministry and became the highly regarded resident pastor (1807–14) of St. John's Episcopal Church, Waterbury, Conn. On June 1, 1814, Virgil resigned his position at Waterbury to become principal of an Episcopal academy at Fairfield, N.Y. After his conversion to the Catholic Church in 1816 with his entire family, Virgil and his wife received permission to enter religious societies, and he was ordained in the Society of Jesus at Boston, Mass., Dec. 3, 1822. While assigned to Claremont, N.H. (1823–24), Barber opened the first Catholic church and school in that area. After a period of missionary work in Maine, he returned to varied assignments at and in the vicinity of Georgetown, D.C., until his death. His wife, *Jerusha* (b. Booth, in Newtown, Conn., July 20, 1789; d. Mobile, Ala., Jan. 2, 1860), entered the Visitandines and made her vows at Georgetown, D.C., Feb. 2, 1820, selecting the name Sister Mary Austin (or Augustina). She served her community with distinction at Georgetown, Kaskaskia, Ill., St. Louis, Mo., and Mobile, Ala. It is fairly certain that the children of Virgil and Jerusha Barber, with the exception of the youngest, were born at Waterbury, Conn. All of them, four daughters and one son, eventually entered and achieved prominence in religious societies of the church. *Mary* (b. Jan. 31, 1810; d. Quebec, Canada, May 9, 1848) entered the Ursulines, as did her two younger sisters, *Abigail, Sister St. Francis Xavier* (b. Feb. 5, 1811; d. Quebec, Canada, March 2, 1880) and *Susan, Sister Mary St. Joseph* (b. 1813; d. Three Rivers, Canada, Jan. 24, 1837). *Samuel Joseph*, the only son (b. March 19, 1814; d. St. Thomas Manor, Md., Feb. 23, 1864), was a priest in the Society of Jesus. *Josephine*, the youngest child (b. Fairfield, N.Y., Aug. 9, 1816; d. St. Louis, Mo., July 17, 1888) was a Visitandine nun.

Bibliography: L. DE GOESBRIAND, *Catholic Memoirs of Vermont and New Hamspshire* (Burlington, Vt. 1886). H. MITCHELL, ''Virgil Horace Barber,'' *Woodstock Letters* 79 (1950) 297–334. F. J. KINGSBURY, *A Narrative and Documentary History of St. John's Protestant Episcopal Church. . . of Waterbury, Connecticut* (New Haven 1907).

[J. W. SCULLY]

BARBERI, DOMENICO, BL.

Born near Viterbo, Italy, June 22, 1792; d. Reading, England, Aug. 27, 1849. He was the youngest of the 11 children of Giuseppe, a tenant farmer, and Marie Antonia (Pacelli) Barberi. Without formal schooling, he entered the PASSIONISTS (1814), took the name Dominic of the Mother of God (Domenico della Madre di Dio), made his profession (Nov. 15, 1815), and was ordained at Rome (March 1, 1818). From 1821 to 1831 he lectured on philosophy and theology to Passionist clerics. After serving as superior of the new monastery at Lucca, Italy (1831–33), he became provincial for southern Italy (1833). Moving to England (1841), he opened the first British Passionist monastery at Aston in Staffordshire (1842). Despite his ugly, ungainly appearance, ridicule by Catholics, and persecution by Protestants, he was responsible for many conversions because of his saintly life. His greatest consolation was to receive John Henry NEWMAN into the Church. Barberi was beatified on Oct. 27, 1963.

Feast: Aug. 27.

Bibliography: *Acta Apostolicae Sedis* 55 (1963) 893–895, 996–1001, 1020–25. D. R. GWYNN, *Father Dominic Barberi* (London 1947; Buffalo 1948). J. MEAD, *Shepherd of the Second Spring; the Life of Blessed Dominic Barberi* (Paterson, N.J. 1968). A. WILSON, *Blessed Dominic Barberi* (London 1966); *Blessed Dominic Barberi; Supernaturalized Briton* (London 1967).

[D. MILBURN]

BARBERINI

Surname of an aristocratic Italian family whose members played leading roles in the government of the Church and the beautifying of Rome in the 17th century. The family traced its descent from a family in Ancona named Tafani that, after becoming rich by trade, changed its name to that of the castle Barberini located in the region of Siena. In the 14th century there were Barberinis living in Florence. During the pontificate of Paul III, *Francesco* Barberini was in Rome, where he held the offices of prothonotary apostolic and referendary to both Segnaturas. His nephew *Maffeo* Barberini, from Florence, profited from his uncle's help and rose in the Church to a position from which he was able to be elected pope on Aug. 6, 1623. He took the name URBAN VIII, and as pope he saw to it that the other members of his family were given important and lucrative positions in the Church and the government of the Papal States. One brother, *Carlo,* was named governor of the Borgo and a general of the Church. Two of Carlo's sons, *Francesco* (1597–1679) and *Antonio* (1607–71), were created cardinals at ages 25 and 20 respectively and appointed to high offices in the Church. Another son of Carlo, *Taddeo,* was married to Anne, the daughter of Filippo Colonna, by Urban VIII and became prince of Palestrina, castellan of S. Angelo, captain of the guard, and prefect of Rome. He succeeded his father as governor of the Borgo and a general of the Church. Another brother of Urban VIII, *Antonio* (1569–1646), was a Capuchin not very interested in possessions, but he too was made a cardinal in 1624 and became part of the governmental operations of the Church. Benefices were even assigned to two sisters of Urban VIII who were in the Carmelite convent of Florence.

The wealth amassed by Urban VIII's nephews during his pontificate was enormous. Like their uncle, however, they expended much of it in the service of art and literature. Francesco was the founder of the Barberini library, the richest library after that of the Vatican. Under Barberini patronage, Giovanni Lorenzo Bernini built the Palazzo Barberini on the slope of the Quirinal near the Quattro Fontane. Rome and its environs were beautified by the attention the Barberini paid to the rebuilding of churches, and the construction of fountains and piazzas; the three bees in their coat of arms could be found imprinted everywhere in Rome as a testimonial to their public spirit.

When INNOCENT X became pope, the nephews fled to France, where they were protected by Cardinal Mazarin. They had feared that an investigation begun by the pope into the way in which they had acquired their wealth might harm them, but eventually Innocent X pardoned them. As part of this reconciliation, Taddeo's son *Maffeo* married Olimpiuccia Giustiniani, Innocent X's niece. In 1690 *Francesco* Barberini, Urban VIII's great grandnephew, was made a cardinal; he died in 1738. The daughter and heiress of Maffeo's heir, *Urbano* (d. 1722), *Cornelia* Barberini, married Guilio Cesare Colonna di Sciarra in 1728.

Bibliography: P. PECCHIAI, *I Barberini* (Rome 1959). L. CÀLLARI, *I palazzi di Roma* (3d ed. Rome 1944). L. PASTOR, *The History of the Popes from the Close of the Middle Ages* (London-St. Louis 1938–61): from 1st German ed. *Geschichte des Päpste seit dem Ausgang des Mittelalters*, 16 v. in 21 (Freiburg 1885–1933; repr. 1955–) 29:439–447, 498–507. M. T. DISDIER and F. BONNARD, *Dictionnaire d'histoire et de géographie ecclésiastiques*, ed. A. BAUDRILLART et al. (Paris 1912–) 6:640–645.

[V. PONKO, JR.]

BARBIERI, CLELIA MARIA RACHEL, ST.

Co-foundress of the Congregation of Minims of the Sorrowful Mother; b. Le Budrie, San Giovanni, Persiceto

Domenico Barberi.

(diocese of Bologna), Emilia, Italy, Feb. 13, 1847; d. Le Budrie, July 13, 1870. Clelia was born into a working class family; the death of her father, Joseph, in 1855 left the family impoverished. Clelia assumed many responsibilities for the household so that her mother, Hyacintha (née Nanett), could support them. At age 14, Clelia became a catechist for her parish. Her pastor, Gaetano Guidi, suggested that she and Teodora Baraldi begin teaching young women secular subjects as well. Barbieri and Baraldi lived with two other friends in a small community called the Retreat of Providence. When she and Orsola Donati founded the Minims (Little Sisters) of Our Lady of Sorrows (1868) under the patronage of St. Francis of Paola, Clelia became the youngest founder in the history of the Church. Clelia's spirituality centered around contemplation of the Blessed Sacrament, which was her ''glorious inspiration'' (John Paul II). She was subject to mystical experiences and possessed the gift of reading hearts.

Following her sudden death from tuberculosis at age 23, she was buried in the Church of Santa Maria Annunziata in her hometown where she was venerated almost immediately. The Congregation of Minims of the Sorrowful Mother, which was given pontifical status in 1949 and attached to the Servites, has spread throughout Italy and into Tanzania and India where they operate hospitals, nursing homes, and elementary schools, and serve as catechists and catalysts of parochial charitable ministries. Clelia, patroness of those ridiculed for their piety, was beatified Oct. 27, 1968 by Paul VI and canonized April 9, 1989 by John Paul II.

Feast: July 13.

Bibliography: *Acta Apostolicae Sedis* 60 (1968): 680–684. *L'Osservatore Romano,* English edition, no. 32 (1968): 2, 8. P. BERTI, *Santa Clelia Barbieri* (Milan 1991). L. GHERARDI, *Il sole sugli argini. Testimonianza evangelica della b. Clelia Barbieri* (Bologna 1970). G. GUSMINI, *Beata Clelia Barbieri*, 4th. ed. (Bari, Italy 1968). C. ZAPPULLI, *The Power of Goodness: The Life of Blessed Clelia Barbieri* (Boston 1980).

[K. I. RABENSTEIN]

BARBOSA, AGOSTINO

Bishop and canonist; b. Guimarens, Portugal, 1589; d. Nov. 19, 1649. He studied canon law in Portugal and in Rome. He was noted for his sanctity, affability, and prodigious memory. In 1632 he went to Madrid and functioned as an ecclesiastical judge. In 1648 he was nominated as bishop of Ungento, in Otranto, by Philip IV. His many writings are noted for their erudition and familiarity with authors, sources, and controverted questions. His most important work is the *Historia iuris ecclesiastici universi libri tres* (Lyons 1633, 1645, 1718). He also published a commentary on the Council of Trent, which was later placed on the Index; a compendium of law; and a juridical lexicon. All his works were published at Lyons (1657–75) in 19 volumes, 16 volumes in folio, and again (1698–1716) 20 volumes, 18 volumes in folio.

Bibliography: J. RAFFALLI, *Dictionnaire de droit canonique* (Paris 1935–65) 2:203. A. VAN HOVE, *Commentarium Lovaniense in Codicem iuris canonici 1* 1:388, 536, 555–56. J. F. VON SCHULTE, *Die Geschichte der Quellen und der Literatur des kanonischen Rechts* 3:54, 746.

[J. M. BUCKLEY]

BARBOSA, JANUÁRIO DA CUNHA

Brazilian priest, journalist, and liberal politician; b. Rio de Janeiro, July 10, 1780; d. Rio de Janeiro, Feb. 22, 1846. Son of a Portuguese and a Brazilian woman, he lost both parents before he was ten years old. He was well educated by an uncle who, wanting a prominent place for his nephew in society, destined him to the priesthood. He studied in the Seminary São José in Rio. Ordained in 1803, he went to Europe to round out his studies. He returned to Brazil in 1805 and worked in a parish, where he gained a reputation as a preacher. In 1814 he was named professor of rational and moral philosophy in the seminary. He became one of the leaders of Brazilian independence and, with Joaquim Gonçalves Ledo, founded the *Revérbero Constitucional Fluminense.* Januário was a brilliant journalist, a terrible polemicist with a great sense of humor, and a preacher of amazing erudition. Frei Francisco do Monte Alverne, the greatest glory of the Brazilian pulpit, called him a ''Giant of Oratory.'' His 400 sermons are in the panegyrist style of the epoch. After a year's exile because of his opposition to the Andrada brothers, who controlled the government, Januário enjoyed all the privileges of a royal courtier: canon and royal preacher of the imperial chapel, imperial chronicler, director of the national library, and editor of the governmental daily. He became a Mason during the independence movement, as did many other clergymen of the time, because of the political influence of the lodges. A man of strong liberal ideas in his early political battles, Januário was also a regalist and later on turned to conservativism. He was always a defender of the anti-Roman policy of the imperial government. In 1826 he was elected deputy to the General Assembly for the Province of Rio de Janeiro, but his real field was journalism: He became a satirist, composing plays and poems to ridicule his political adversaries, and even founded a witty newspaper, *Mutuca Picante* (big biting fly). Januário was cofounder of the *Revista do Instituto histórico e geográfico brasileiro,* a monthly journal that has contributed greatly to the improvement of arts and sciences in Brazil.

Bibliography: A. DA CUNHA BARBOZA, ''Esboco biographico do conego Januário da Cunha Barboza,'' *Revista do Instituto histórico e geográphico brasileiro* 65.2 (1902) 197–284.

[T. BEAL]

BARCLAY, JOHN

Founder of a religious sect known as Bereans or Barclayites; b. Muthill, Perthshire, Scotland, 1734; d. Edinburgh, July 29, 1798. He studied for the Presbyterian ministry at St. Andrews University, where he supported the heterodox views of his professor, Dr. Archibald Campbell, ''that the knowledge of the existence of God was derived from revelation and not from nature.'' He was licensed as a preacher in the Church of Scotland in 1759 and held assistantships at Errol and Fettercairn; but while he gained a popular reputation as a preacher, his clerical brethren regarded his theological opinions as dangerous. Defying the censure of his theological opinions by the presbytery of Fordoun, he published his views in several books between 1766 and 1771. Since he was refused any appointment in the Church of Scotland, Barclay was ordained in 1773 at Newcastle, England, outside the jurisdiction of the Scottish church. Adherents of his views formed themselves into independent churches in Edinburgh, Fettercairn, and a few other places. These sectarians, while accepting the general Calvinist theology of the Church of Scotland, held that natural religion undermines the evidences of Christianity, that assurance is of the essence of faith, that unbelief is the unpardonable sin, and that the psalms refer exclusively to Christ. Their constant appeal to Scripture in vindication of their views was regarded as similar to the attitude of the Bereans mentioned in Acts 17.10. Barclay was given charge of the Edinburgh congregation.

Bibliography: *The Works of John Barclay,* ed. J. THOMSON and D. MCMILLAN (Glasgow 1852). R. CHAMBERS, *A Biographical Dictionary of Eminent Scotsmen,* ed. T. THOMSON, 3 v. (3d rev. ed. London 1868–70).

[D. MCROBERTS]

BARCLAY, ROBERT

Scottish Quaker theologian and apologist; b. Gordonstown (Elginshire), Dec. 23, 1648; d. Ury (Aberdeen), Oct. 3, 1690. His father, David (1610–86), had been a soldier in the army of Gustavus II Adolphus, and later served in the English parliament of Oliver CROMWELL) (1654 and 1656). He joined the Society of FRIENDS in 1666, and Robert, who was educated at the Roman Catholic Scottish College at Paris, followed his example the next year. Robert was imprisoned several times for his Quaker beliefs, but in his travels through Germany and Holland he won the sympathy of Elizabeth, Princess Palatine, and on his return to England found favor with the Duke of York (later James II). This friendship was instrumental in obtaining a patent of the province of East New Jersey for William PENN and 12 Quakers. Barclay was governor of this territory in 1683.

Barclay's learning is revealed in several publications: *A Catechism and Confession of Faith* (1673); *Theologiae verae christianae apologia* (Amsterdam 1676), translated into Dutch, French, Spanish, and entitled in English *An Apology for the True Christian Divinity: Being an Explanation and Vindication of the People Called Quakers* (1678); *The Anarchy of Ranters* (1676); *The Apology Vindicated* (1679); and *The Possibilty and Necessity of an Inward and Immediate Revelation* (1680). His *Apology* is organized on the basis of 15 propositions: (1) The true knowledge of God is the most necessary knowledge. (2) Divine inward revelations are absolutely necessary for building true faith. (3) The Scriptures give a faithful and historical account of God's acts, prophecies, and the principal doctrines of Christ. (4) All mankind fell with Adam. (5) Christ, the true Light, enlightens all (universal redemption). (6) This universal redemption must be placed in the evangelical principle of light and life. (7) Justification is ''Jesus Christ formed within us,'' producing good works. (8) Perfection does not rule out the possibility of sinning. (9) The possibility of falling from grace exists. (10) Human commission is not needed for preaching. (11) The Spirit moves inwardly and immediately for a true and acceptable worship of God. (12) Infant baptism is a human tradition. (13) Participation of the body and blood of Christ is inward and spiritual. (14) The civil magistrate cannot force the conscience of others. (15) Customs and habits, such as removing the hat, bowing, and recreations (sports), are to be rejected and forsaken. Barclay's writings are still regarded as authoritative together with those of William Penn, and Barclay's humanitarian and pacifist views are followed by the Society of Friends.

Bibliography: W. ARMISTEAD, *Life of Robert Barclay* (Manchester, Eng. 1850). M. C. CADBURY, *Robert Barclay* (London 1912). M. SCHMIDT, *Die Religion in Geschichte und Gegenwart* 1:870. F. L. CROSS, *The Oxford Dictionary of the Christian Church* 130. L. STEPHEN, *The Dictionary of National Biography from the Earliest Times to 1900* 1: 1087–90. A. SCHMITT, *Lexikon für Theologie und Kirche* (Freiburg 1957–65) 1:1241–42.

[C. S. MEYER]

BARDESANES (BAR-DAISĀN)

Christian astrologer and philosopher; b. Edessa, northwest Mesopotamia, 154; d. Edessa, 222. Bardesanes is often, though possibly erroneously, regarded as a leader of the Oriental school of GNOSTICISM founded by the Egyptian VALENTINUS. The many ancient and medieval accounts of the life and teachings of Bardesanes show little agreement about details. He was born of prominent pagan parents and educated by a pagan priest at Hierapolis (Mabog) in northern Syria. At age 25 he was converted to Christianity and was ordained a deacon or priest. Bardesanes wrote many works in Syriac that were later translated into Greek by his disciples. His many metrical hymns earned him the title of the father of Syriac poetry. His works on astrology and on India and Armenia are lost. Eusebius (H.E. 4.30) credits him with dialogues written against the Marcionites (*see* MARCION) and the Valentinians (*see* VALENTINUS). Bardesanes' personal doctrine is given by Philip, one of his disciples, in the *Book of the Laws of the Countries* (*Patrologia syriaca* 1.2:490–658), the oldest extant original composition in Syriac.

Bardesanes ranks as a heretical figure largely because his astrological and philosophical speculations were mingled with his Christianity. He taught explicit errors concerning the human body and the body of Christ. His influence as a teacher was widespread, however, and the sect continued by his disciples was vigorously opposed by St. Ephrem as a form of Gnosticism.

Bibliography: W. CURETON, ed., *Spicilegium Syriacum* (London 1855). R. GRAFFIN, ed., *Patrologia syriaca* 1.2:490–658. F. NAU, *Dictionnaire de théologie catholique*, 15 v. (Paris 1903–50) 2.2:391–401. E. BECK, ed., *Des Heiligen Ephraem des Syrers Hymnen contra Haereses Corpus scriptorum Christianorum orientalium* v. 169 and 170. F. J. A. HORT, *A Dictionary of Christian Biography* 1:250–60. L. CERFAUX, *Reallexikon für Antike und Christentum* 1:1180–86. J. QUASTEN, *Patrology* 1: 263–64.

[G. W. MACRAE]

BARDO OF OPPERSHOFEN, ST.

Archbishop of Mainz; b. Oppershofen, Germany, *c.* 980; d. Dornloh, near Paderborn, June 10, 1051. Born of a prominent family, he was sent at an early age to the monastery of Fulda, where he eventually became a monk and the director of the monastic school. In 1029 Bardo was made abbot of Werden, and two years later he assumed the leadership of the important monastery of Hersfeld. On June 29, 1031, he was consecrated archbishop of Mainz and energetically completed the construction of the cathedral, which he consecrated in 1036 when the emperor, CONRAD II, honored the occasion with his presence. The most important event during his episcopate was the synod held at Mainz in 1049 at which Pope LEO IX presided. In addition to having a great reputation for piety and humility, Bardo was highly regarded as an eloquent preacher and was frequently called another Chrysostom. If the sermon reported in his longer biography (*Monumenta Germaniae Historica: Scriptores* 11:330–35) can be taken as typical, the author was surprisingly familiar with Sacred Scripture. He was buried in the new cathedral at Mainz.

Feast: June 15.

Bibliography: *Monumenta Germaniae Historica: Scriptores* (Berlin 1826—) 11:317–342. *Acta Sanctorum* June 2:296–315. J. F. BOHMER and C. WILL, eds., *Regesten zur Geschichte der Mainzer Erzbischöfe,* 2 v. (Innsbruck 1877–86) 1:165–176. Literature. G. ALLEMANG, *Dictionnaire d'histoire et de géographie ecclésiastiques*, ed. A. BAUDRILLART et al. (Paris 1912) 6:775. P. ACHT, *Lexikon für Theologie und Kirche*, ed. J. HOFER and K. RAHNER (Freiburg 1957–65) 1:1243. A. M. ZIMMERMANN, *Bibliotheca sanctorum* 2:780–782; *Kalendarium Benedictinum* (Metten 1933–38) 2:297–299.

[H. DRESSLER]

BARDY, GUSTAVE

Patristic scholar, b. Belfort, France, Nov. 25, 1881; d. Dijon, Oct. 31, 1955. Educated at the Seminary of St. Sulpice (Issy), Bardy was ordained on June 30, 1906, attended the Institut Catholique of Paris until 1909, and lectured in theology at the University of Besançon. Called to military service in 1914, he was wounded and decorated for valor. In 1919, he joined the faculty of theology at Lille, remaining until 1927 when he transferred to the University of Dijon. He continued his patristic studies and edited the diocesan paper *Vie Diocésaine de Dijon* until his death.

His biography, *Didyme l'Aveugle,* appeared in 1910, and *S. Athanse* in 1914. He received doctorates in letters and in theology on the publication of his *Recherches sur . . . le texte . . . du 'De Principiis' d'Origène* and his magistral thesis, *Paul de Samosate,* in 1923. In the same year a study of the latter subject by the rationalist theologian Friedrich Loofs appeared. The two works demonstrated the difference in scholarly conclusions reached by men similar in competence and training, but divergent in belief and methods. Bardy's book was delated to the Holy Office, and in 1929 he brought out a thoroughly revised edition.

Bardy possessed a vast knowledge of the early Church and was abreast of diverse schools of investigation. He published more than 30 full-length books, edited several Greek texts, contributed major articles on patristic topics to the principal ecclesiastical encyclopedias, and wrote extensive articles on the theology of the early Church, monasticism, early Christian education, literary frauds, conversion, pagan survivals, Arianism, and the moral teaching of the Alexandrian Fathers. Encyclopedic in knowledge after the fashion of Louis Sébastien le Nain de TILLEMONT, Bardy was long regarded as the dean of French patrologists. He spent his last days completing an introduction to his translation of the *Church History of Eusebius* (*Sources Chrétiennes* v. 31, 41, 55, 73).

Bibliography: ''Mémorial Gustave Bardy,'' *Revue des études augustiniennes* (August 2, 1956) 1–37. J. LEBON, *Revue d'histoire ecclésiastique* 51 (1956) 348–49.

[F. X. MURPHY]

BARKING ABBEY

Essex, England, a Benedictine nunnery dedicated to Our Lady and St. Ethelburga, was founded by St. ERCONWALD, Bishop of London, *c.* 677; his sister ETHELBURGA was its first abbess. It was burnt by the Danes in 870 and restored by King EDGAR. The abbey numbered among its abbesses St. HILDELIDE (d. 717?), to whom ALDHELM addressed his *De virginitate,* and Mary, the sister of Thomas BECKET. The shrine of St. Ethelburga was a center of pilgrimage in medieval England. Tradition says that WIL-

LIAM I resided at Barking after his coronation until the Tower of London was built. Dame Dorothy Barley surrendered the house to Henry VIII, Nov. 14, 1539. Of this once magnificent abbey, nothing now remains.

Bibliography: W. DUGDALE, *Monasticon Anglicanum* (London 1655–73); best ed. by J. CALEY et al., 6 v. (1817–30) 1:435–446. J. B. L. TOLHURST, ed., *The Ordinale and Customary of the Benedictine Nuns of Barking Abbey,* 2 v. (Henry Bradshaw Society 65,66; London 1927–28). L. H. COTTINEAU, *Répertoire topo-bibliographique des abbayes et prieurés,* 2 v. (Mâcon 1935–39) 1:266. D. KNOWLES and R. N. HADCOCK, *Medieval Religious Houses: England and Wales* (New York 1953) 210.

[F. CORRIGAN]

BARKWORTH, MARK, BL.

Benedictine priest, martyr; *alias* Lambert; b. Searby, Lincolnshire, England, *c.* 1572; d. hanged, drawn, and quartered at Tyburn (London), Feb. 27, 1601. Following his conversion to Catholicism at Douai (1594), the Oxford-educated Barkworth studied for the priesthood at the English College in Valladolid (1596–99), where he was ordained. Thereafter he left for the English mission in the company of St. Thomas GARNET. During a stopover at the Benedictine Abbey of Hyrache in Navarre, he became a Benedictine Oblate (with the privilege of making profession at the hour of death). This was a great desire of his because of an earlier vision he had of St. Benedict. Although he escaped death at the hands of the Protestants in La Rochelle, France, he was arrested upon landing in England and imprisoned at Newgate for six months, then moved to Bridewell. The tall, burly priest staunchly defended the faith under examination. As a result he was condemned and thrown into Newgate's dungeon, where he remained cheerful, even singing en route to his execution. Dressed in the Benedictine habit, he told the crowd: "I am come here to die, being a Catholic, a priest, and a religious man, belonging to the Order of St. Benedict; it was by this same order that England was converted." After his quartering a witness held up one of Barkworth's legs with its knee hardened by constant kneeling and said, "Which of you Gospellers can show such a knee?" He was beatified by Pius XI on Dec. 15, 1929.

Feast of the English Martyrs: May 4 (England).

See Also: ENGLAND, SCOTLAND, AND WALES, MARTYRS OF.

Bibliography: B. CAMM, *A Benedictine Martyr in England* (London 1897). R. CHALLONER, *Memoirs of Missionary Priests,* ed. J. H. POLLEN (rev. ed. London 1924; repr. Farnborough 1969). J. H. POLLEN, *Acts of English Martyrs* (London 1891).

[K. I. RABENSTEIN]

BARLAAM OF CALABRIA

Italo-Greek monk, theologian, and bishop, opponent of HESYCHASM; b. Seminara, Calabria, *c.* 1290; d. Gerace, Calabria, 1350. Born of schismatic parents and educated in the Byzantine monasteries of southern Italy, Barlaam appeared first as a teacher in the Holy Savior monastery and the Imperial University in Constantinople from 1326 to 1327. After a public debate with Nicephorus Gregoras on the physical sciences, he taught at Thessalonica, where he had Demetrius Cydones as a pupil. In 1334 he was chosen to dispute with two Dominican bishops, envoys of Pope John XXII, on the issues of papal primacy and the procession of the Holy Spirit. Pamphlets that he wrote for the occasion were criticized by Gregory PALAMAS, and between 1334 and 1337 Barlaam engaged in a bitter dispute with the Hesychastic monks of Mt. Athos. He accused them of illuminism and a crude type of Messalianism and ridiculed their posture when engaged in contemplative prayer. He sarcastically called the monks *omphalopsychoi* (men-with-their-souls-in-their-navels) and ordered them to be delated to the patriarch John Calecas.

In 1339 the imperial court sent Barlaam to Pope Benedict XII at Avignon to solicit a crusade against the Turks and to discuss reunion. There he apparently taught Greek to Petrarch, who persuaded him to reconsider the Catholic position. On his return to Constantinople (1341), a synod condemned his attack on the Hesychasts, and he had to make a public retraction. He was in Calabria in July 1341 and at Avignon again in 1342. Upon his full conversion to Roman Catholicism with the aid of Petrarch, he was consecrated bishop of Gerace in Calabria by Pope Clement VI at Avignon in 1342. He is said to have influenced the Italian Renaissance through his contact with the Italian humanists. In 1346 he was sent to Constantinople to discuss reunion, but the project proved fruitless since the emperor was the Palamite, John Cantecuzenus. Barlaam returned to his diocese, where he died in 1350 (not 1348).

Barlaam seems to have denied the possibility of apodictic arguments in theology in his dispute with the Dominicans. He wanted to base reunion of the churches on the fact that the disputes between East and West were really unresolvable and should not be cause for separation. In his disagreement with Palamas, he accused him of dividing God by teaching that while God's nature was invisible, his energies could be apprehended as in the white light that shone on Mt. Thabor at the Transfiguration. Most of Barlaam's writings are still unedited. He wrote 21 tracts against the Latins (18 on the Holy Spirit and three on the Roman primacy); a *Contra Messalianos;* two books on Stoic ethics; and a number of letters sup-

Exterior of Barlaam Monastery, Meteoria, Greece. (©Kevin Schafer/CORBIS)

porting the Catholic position after his conversion. He wrote also a *Reasoned Arithmetic* and a commentary on the second book of Euclid.

Bibliography: J. P. MIGNE, ed., *Patrologia Graeca* 151:1243–1364. J. A. FABRICIUS and C. C. HARLES, *Bibliotheca Graeca* (Hamburg 1790–1809) 11:462–70. M. JUGIE, *Catholicisme* 1:1253–55; *Dictionnaire d'histoire et de géographie ecclésiastiques,* ed. A. BAUDRILLART et al. (Paris 1912) 6:817–34. J. MEYENDORFF, *A Study of Gregory Palareas,* tr. G. LAWRENCE (London 1964). K. M. SETTON, *Proceedings of the American Philosophical Society* 100 (1956) 1–76. J. S. ROMANIDES, *The Greek Orthodox Theological Review* 6 (1960–61) 186–205, Palamite controversy.

[H. D. HUNTER]

BARLAAM AND JOASAPH

The title of a curious novel found among the works of St. John Damascene. The tale, which is an adaptation of a Buddhist legend, relates how the monk Barlaam converted the Indian prince Joasaph against his father's wishes. There is much discussion of the meaning of Christianity, monasticism, and the truths of faith. Joasaph, becoming king, converts his entire realm and then dies a hermit. The author attributes the rise of monastic fasting and penance to the desire of ascetics to imitate the sufferings of the primitive martyrs, that ''becoming martyrs in intention they too might imitate the sufferings of Christ'' (12.102).

Barlaam and Joasaph have been venerated in the Roman MARTYROLOGY since 1583 on November 27 [see H. Delehaye et al., *Propylaeum ad Acta Sanctorum Decembris* (Brussels 1940) 551]. The cult became widely popular in the Middle Ages. P. Peeters [*Analecta Bollandiana* 49 (1931) 276] developed a strong case against the Damascene's authorship, suggesting that the novel was first translated into Greek from a Georgian source by Euthymius, abbot of Iviron, Mt. ATHOS (d. 1028), to whom the work is attributed in some late MSS. But the case for Damascene's authorship was effectively renewed by F. Dölger in 1953. In addition to parallels in doctrine and style with the works of Damascene, several MSS possibly antedate Euthymius; four of the oldest MSS attribute the work to John, and none of the numerous Iviron MSS attribute it to Euthymius. Dölger accepts the idea of its transmission from a Buddhist original—to a Pehlevi version—thence to a possible Syriac version, from which came two branches, the Arabic version on the one side and the Greek version of John with the Georgian version on the other. The Damascene parallels in the area of Christology, the Trinity, and other points of doctrine are impressive, but Dölger's position is still controverted.

Bibliography: *Barlaam and Joasaph,* ed. and tr. G. R. WOODWARD and H. MATTLINGLY (*Loeb Classical Library* 1914). B. STUDER, *Lexikon für Theologie und Kirche*, ed. J. HOFER and K. RAHNER, 10 v. (2d, new ed. Freiburg 1957–65) 1:1.246–47; *Die theologische Arbeitsweise des Johannes von Damaskus* (Ettal 1956). H. BACHT, *Reallexikon für Antike und Christentum*, ed. T. KLAUSER [Stuttgart 1941 (1950–)] 1:1193–1200. F. DÖLGER, *Der griechische Barlaam-Roman* (Ettal 1953). P. DEVOS, *Analecta Bollandiana* 75 (1957) 83–104. B. ALTANER, *Patrology*, tr. H. GRAEF from 5th German ed. (New York 1960) 639. G. DOWNEY, *Speculum. A Journal of Mediaeval Studies* 31 (1956) 165–168.

[H. MUSURILLO]

BARLOW, AMBROSE (EDWARD), ST.

English martyr; b. Barlow Hall, near Manchester, 1585; d. Lancaster, Sept. 10, 1641. Although born a Catholic, Barlow conformed to the Protestant church in his youth. At the age of 22, he returned to the faith and entered the English seminary at Douai. In 1613, on a visit to England, Barlow was imprisoned for several months; after his release he joined the English Benedictine monks at St. Gregory's, Douai, where his brother was prior. He took the name Ambrose in place of his baptismal name of Edward. He was professed in 1614 and ordained in 1617, after which he returned to England where, for 24 years, he labored in the Manchester and Liverpool districts. Resembling Thomas More in his wit and mildness, Barlow was greatly loved by the poor, whom he entertained at his house on the great feasts. There is a detailed account of his apostolate in a short contemporary work, *The Apostolical Life of Ambrose Barlow* (Cheetham Society).

Partially paralyzed by a stroke in 1641, on Easter day of that year he was captured at Leigh, Lancashire while preaching to his congregation. Sitting on a horse, with a man behind him to prevent his falling, he was taken to Lancaster Castle by an escort of 60 men. After four months in prison, where he passed most of his time in prayer, he was brought to trial; he at once acknowledged his priesthood. When the judge offered to release him if he agreed ''not to seduce any more people,'' he answered, ''I am no seducer, but a reducer of the people to the true and ancient religion. . . . I am in the resolution to continue until death to render this good office to these strayed souls.'' On September 8 he was condemned. Five days before this, a general chapter of the English Benedictine Congregation had accepted the resignation of his brother, Rudesind Barlow, as titular prior of Coventry, and had elected Ambrose in his place. He was executed at Lancaster on September 10. Ambrose's skull is preserved at Wardley Hall, near Manchester, and his left hand at Stanbrook Abbey, Worcestershire. He was canonized on Oct. 25, 1970 (*see* ENGLAND, SCOTLAND, AND WALES, MARTYRS OF).

Feast: Sept. 10; Oct. 25; May 4.

Bibliography: B. CAMM, *Nine Martyr Monks . . .* (London 1931). J. STONOR, *Ambrose Barlow* (Postulation pamphlet; London 1961). A. BUTLER, *The Lives of the Saints* (New York, 1956) 3:535–537. R. CHALLONER, *Memoirs of Missionary Priests*, ed. and rev. J. H. POLLEN (rev. ed. London, 1924). J. GILLOW, *A Literary and Biographical History or Bibliographical Dictionary of the English Catholics from 1534 to the Present Time* (London and New York 1885–1902; reprint 1961) 1:134–135.

[G. FITZHERBERT]

BARLOW, WILLIAM

Augustinian canon and successively bishop of St. Asaph, St. David's, Bath and Wells, and Chichester; said to have been born in Essex (date unknown); d. Aug. 13, 1568. He was a canon of St. Osyth's and became, successively, prior of several houses of Augustinian canons and, about 1524, prior of Bromehill, Norfolk. Its suppression in 1528 turned him into a violent enemy of Wolsey, and his enmity found expression in several pamphlets that were condemned as heretical in 1529. He recanted, but by 1535 he had become an ardent reformer. He was elected bishop of St. Asaph on Jan. 16, 1536 and soon afterward (April? 1536) he was translated to St. David's, where he quarreled frequently with his chapter, which denounced him as a heretic. In 1548 he was translated to Bath and Wells, but at the accession of Queen Mary he resigned his see and, after a short imprisonment, made his way to Germany. After Mary's death he returned to England and was nominated bishop of Chichester in 1559.

Bibliography: T. F. TOUT, *The Dictionary of National Biography from the Earliest Times to 1900* 1:1149–51. P. HUGHES, *The Reformation in England.* C. JENKINS, ''Bishop Barlow's Consecration and Archbishop Parker's Register,'' *Church Historical Society Publications* (London) NS 17 (1935).

[G. DE C. PARMITER]

BARLOW, WILLIAM RUDESIND

English Benedictine writer and administrator; b. Barlow Hall, Lancashire, 1584?; d. Douai, Sept. 19, 1656. He was the son of Sir Alexander Barlow and brother of Ambrose (Edward) BARLOW, the martyr. William entered Douai College in 1602, left to join the Benedictine Order in 1605, was professed in Spain in 1606, and was ordained in 1608. Barlow took doctorates in divinity at both Salamanca and Douai. From 1614 to 1620 and again from 1625 to 1629, he was prior of St. Gregory's, Douai. He served as president general of the English Benedictine Congregation (1621). He was for many years professor of theology at the College of St. Vedast, Douai. Equally renowned as a theologian and a canonist, he figured in two celebrated ecclesiastical quarrels: (1) with Richard SMITH, bishop of Chalcedon, whose claim to possess ordinary jurisdiction over Catholics in England he vigorously opposed in his *Epistola . . . ad RR. Provinciales et ad Definitores* . . . (1627–28), commonly known from its opening word as ''Mandatum,'' and (2) with Augustine Baker of his own order on the subject of conventual life. Baker drew an unflattering portrait of him in *An Introduction or Preparative to a Treatise on the English Mission* (1638).

Bibliography: T. B. SNOW, *Necrology of the English Congregation of the Order of Saint Benedict from 1600 to 1883* (London 1883). J. GILLOW, *A Literary and Biographical History or Bibliographical Dictionary of the English Catholics from 1534 to the Present Time* (London and New York, 1885–1902; reprint 1961) 1:136.

[A. F. ALLISON]

BARNABAS, EPISTLE OF

An anonymous Christian work dating from the late 1st or early 2d century. Clement of Alexandria knew it well and spoke of it as the work of ''the apostle Barnabas.'' This tradition was repeated by Origen, Jerome, and others, but finds no support in the text. Eusebius categorizes the epistle twice among the ''disputed'' books (*Hist. eccl.* 6.13.6; 6.14.1), once among the ''spurious'' (3.25.4).

Both author and audience are left unidentified, and the epistolary character of the writing has long been questioned. Many scholars have classified *Barnabas* as a theological treatise, others as a homily. The work evinces a tendentious theological agenda and a rambling style. Scriptural quotations are piled up and connected loosely with keywords, often relying on an interpretive logic that may escape the modern reader.

The author, almost certainly a Gentile, reads the Old Testament christocentrically, argues vigorously for a spiritualized understanding of Jewish cult practices, and views the golden-calf incident as the epochal transgression for which ancient Israel lost its claim to be God's people. He denies the literal significance of sacrifice (chap. 2), fasting (chap. 3), circumcision (chap. 9), the dietary laws (chap. 10), sabbath observance (chap. 15), and the temple (chap. 16). On the other hand, the author finds Jesus and the cross wholly foreshadowed in Scripture: in the scapegoat ritual (chap. 7), the rite of the red heifer (chap. 8), the naming of Joshua (=''Jesus'') as Moses' successor (chap. 12), and Moses' outstretched arms during the battle with Amalek (chap. 12). Many of the christological and cultic proof texts are similar to those adduced in Justin's *Dialogue with Trypho*. The closing chapters (18–20) offer a catechesis on the ''two ways'' that exhibits close affinities to chaps. 1 to 5 of the *Didache*. The content of *Barnabas* thus accords well with the emerging literary forms of the 2d-century Church.

The provenance of *Barnabas* remains disputed. Its frequent attestation among North African Fathers, especially Clement, and the author's use of the allegorical method of interpretation point toward Alexandria, but Syria and Asia Minor have also been suggested.

Bibliography: *Anchor Bible Dictionary* 1.611–14. J. N. B. CARLETON PAGET, *The Epistle of Barnabas: Outlook and Background* (Wissenschaftliche Untersuchungen zum Neuen Testament 2, 64; Tübingen 1994). R. HVALVIK, *The Struggle for Scripture and Covenant: The Purpose of the Epistle of Barnabas and Jewish-Christian Competition in the Second Century* (Wissenschaftliche Untersuchungen zum Neuen Testament 2, 82; Tübingen 1996). R. A. KRAFT, *Barnabas and the Didache*, vol. 3 of *The Apostolic Fathers: A Translation and Commentary* (New York 1965). F. R. PROSTMEIER, *Der Barnabasbrief* (Kommentar zu den Apostolischen Vätern 8; Göttingen 1999).

[J. N. RHODES]

BARNABAS, ST.

Missionary and traveling companion of Paul mentioned 23 times in the book of Acts and four times in the undisputed letters of Paul. The deutero-Pauline Epistle to the Colossians also mentions Barnabas in 4.10, where it identifies him as the cousin of (John) Mark.

According to Luke, Barnabas was a Levite from Cyprus whose given name was Joseph (Acts 4.36). His more familiar name ''Barnabas'' was bestowed upon him by the apostles, a name Luke explains as meaning ''son of encouragement.'' Luke's introductory vignette tells how Barnabas sold a field and laid the proceeds at the feet of the apostles. Barnabas thus serves as a foil for the figures of Ananias and Sapphira, who also sold a piece of land but conspired to withhold some of the proceeds (Acts 4:34–5:11). The Jerusalem church later sent Barnabas to Antioch of Syria after hearing that evangelists from Cyprus and Cyrene had made converts among the Greeks (Acts 11:20–24).

Luke highlights the relationship of Barnabas to Paul in several ways. It was Barnabas who brought Paul to the church at Antioch (Acts 11:25–26) where the two collaborated and were remembered among the ''prophets and teachers'' associated with that church (Acts 13:1). In Acts 13–14, Luke narrates the collaboration of Barnabas and Paul on a mission to Cyprus and Asia Minor, a mission that scholars have come to refer to as Paul's ''first missionary journey.'' Barnabas and Paul likewise represent the Antiochene church in Jerusalem when controversy arises over the Gentile mission (Acts 15:1–2).

More fundamentally, Luke identifies Barnabas as the one who facilitated the first meeting between the newly converted Paul and the apostles in Jerusalem (Acts 9:26–28). This may be an inference from their later collaboration at Antioch since this information stands in tension with Paul's own assertions about his first visit to Jerusalem (Gal 1:18–19). According to Luke, the collaboration of Barnabas and Paul came to an end when the two clashed over whether or not to take along John Mark on a follow-up mission in Asia Minor (Acts 15:36–40).

Apart from a passing reference in 1 Cor. 9:6, Paul mentions Barnabas only in his letter to the churches of Galatia (2:1, 9, 13). He does not mention the mediation of Barnabas when he describes his initial meeting with Cephas and James in Jerusalem (Gal. 1:18–19). If Barnabas did play such a role, Paul's desire to show his apostolic independence could explain his willingness to overlook it (Gal. 1:1, 11–17). Paul does, however, acknowledge the collaboration of Barnabas in the circumcision-free mission to Gentiles and the subsequent trip to Jerusalem to defend this activity (Gal. 2:1, 9). From Paul's point of view, Barnabas compromised his principles when he withdrew from table fellowship with Gentiles, following the example of Cephas (Gal. 2:13). Some see this as the real reason for the parting of ways between Barnabas and Paul, but such a conclusion is speculative.

Later tradition places Barnabas in such faraway places as Rome and Alexandria and ascribes to him a martyr's death on Cyprus. The so-called *Epistle of Barnabas* and apocryphal works known as the *Gospel of Barnabas* and the *Acts of Barnabas* add nothing to our historical knowledge of the missionary companion of Paul.

Bibliography: *Anchor Bible Dictionary* 1.610 11.

[J. N. RHODES]

St. Barnabas, detail of ''Virgin and Child with Angels and Saints,'' by Botticelli.

BARNABITES

The Clerics Regular of St. Paul (abbreviated: CRSP, Official Catholic Directory #0160), or Barnabites, founded in 1530 in Milan, Italy, by St. Anthony ZACCARIA, Ven. James Morigia, and Ven. Bartholomew FERRARI; the order was approved in 1533 by Clement VII. The founder's enthusiasm for St. Paul inspired the official name of the society and its Pauline spirit and tradition of studies; the popular name derives from the motherhouse built near the church of St. Barnabas in Milan.

At its founding, the Barnabites' primary objective was to reform the corrupt morals of the time by the example of their own penitent life and by missions among the people. Their apostolate began in Lombardy and Venetia, amid hardships and persecutions; later they found in St. Charles Borromeo a staunch protector and second father. He promulgated the constitutions in the general chapter of 1579. In 1608 the order was divided into provinces. Suppressed by Napoleon in 1810, the order was later reestablished and regained its vitality. By the end of the 20th century, it had established a presence in 17 countries—Afghanistan, Albania, Argentina, Belgium, Brazil, Canada, Chile, France, Italy, Philippines, Poland, Rwanda, Spain, Switzerland, Tanzania, United States, and Zaire.

Since the 17th century, the Barnabites have been principally engaged in education, chaplaincies, parishes, pastoral work and missionary outreach. The Barnabites' missionary activity was extended in the 18th century to Burma, where the order distinguished itself for its scientific study of the flora and fauna and the native languages. In the 19th century Barnabites went to Scandinavia and also worked for the healing of the schism between the Russian Orthodox Church and the Roman Catholic Church.

Three canonized saints were members of the order: St. Anthony Zaccaria, the founder (d. 1539); St. Alexander SAULI, bishop of Aleria and Pavia (d. 1592); and St. FRANCIS XAVIER BIANCHI (d. 1815). The order has had seven cardinals, including the philosopher Hyacinthe S. Gerdil; Francesco L. Fontana, the companion of Pius VII during his French exile; and Luigi Lambruschini, the secretary of state of Gregory XVI; 67 bishops; and numerous scholars, particularly in historical, liturgical, literary, and physical-mathematical studies.

Bibliography: G. BOFFITO, *Scrittori Barnabiti*, 4 v. (Florence 1933–37). G. CHASTEL, *Saint Antoine-Marie Zaccaria barnabite* (Paris 1930). A. M. GENTILI, S., *Antonio M. Zaccaria: appunti per una lettura spirituale degli scritti*, 2 v. (Rome 1980, 1983). V. MICHELINI, *I Barnabiti: chierici regolari di S. Paolo alle radici della congregazione, 1533–1983* (Milan 1983). R. L. DEMOLEN, ed., *Religious Orders of the Catholic Reformation: In Honor of John C. Olin on His Seventy-Fifth Birthday* (New York 1994). E. BONORA, *I conflitti della Controriforma: santità e obbedienza nell'esperienza religiosa dei primi barnabiti* (Florence 1998).

[U. M. FASOLA/EDS.]

BARNARD OF VIENNE, ST.

Archbishop; b. near Lyons, France, *c.* 778; d. Abbey of Saints-Severin-Exupère-et-Félicien, Valence, France, Jan. 22, 842. He was one of the outstanding figures of the Frankish episcopate during the CAROLINGIAN reform. He entered the army and, after seven years of married life, decided to renounce the world. He founded the BENEDICTINE monastery of Ambronay, where he became a monk in 803 and where four years later he became abbot. He was elected archbishop of VIENNE in 810, and in this office he played an important role in the synodal movement that attempted to reestablish peace and order in both Church and State. By taking part in the consecration of AGOBARD to the metropolitan See of Lyons before the death of the reigning prelate LEIDRADUS, who had entered a monastery, he incurred the hostility of his colleagues and was accused of violating Canon Law. Barnard enjoyed the favor of LOUIS I THE PIOUS, for a time; but when he sided with his son LOTHAIR against him, he was forced to escape to Italy after the victory of the emperor. Louis forgave the luckless intervention, and the archbishop was able to return to his see and found the monastery of Saints-Severin-Exupère-et-Félicien, where he retired to spend his last days and where he was buried. His cult was reconfirmed in 1903.

Feast: Jan. 23.

Bibliography: *Acta Sanctae Sedis* (Rome 1865–1908) 3:157–161. P. É. GIRAUD, *Essai historique sur l'Abbaye de saint Barnard de Romans*, 5 v. (Lyons 1856–69). A. M. ZIMMERMANN, *Kalendarium Benedictinum*, (Metten 1933–38) 1:118–120. A. M. ZIMMERMANN, *Lexikon für Theologie und Kirche*, ed. J. HOFER and K. RAHNER (Freiburg 1957–65) 1:1257. G. MARIÉ, *Dictionnaire d'histoire et de géographie ecclésiastiques*, ed. A. BAUDRILLART et al. (Paris 1912) 6: 858–859.

[T. C. CROWLEY]

BARON, VINCENT

Dominican theologian and preacher; b. Martres, Haute-Garonne, France, May 17, 1604; d. Paris, Jan. 21, 1674. Baron was born of a prominent family, and from his earliest years he showed clear signs of genius and integrity. At age 17, he left the Jesuit college at Toulouse and entered the Dominican convent of St. Thomas in the same city. He made his religious profession there on May 16, 1622 and went on to complete his philosophical and theological studies. As early as 1634 he was first professor in his priory and conventual doctor at the University of Toulouse. In time he came to be considered one of the leading theologians of France.

In addition to teaching, he delivered courses of Lenten sermons in the principal churches of Toulouse, Avignon, Bordeaux, and other cities of southern France. At the invitation of the bishops of Languedoc, he preached throughout their dioceses for ten years, laboring to revive the faith of Catholics, to better their morals, and to combat the errors of the Calvinists, with whose ministers he frequently joined in open debate, sometimes in their public synods. He published an abridgment of these controversies under the title *L'Hérésie convainçue*. Of his sermons to Catholic congregations, we have only those preached at Paris in 1658 and 1659. They were doctrinal discourses and panegyrics of intellectual merit, but composed in the forced style of his age.

From 1630 to 1659 he filled the office of prior in the convents of Toulouse, Rhodez, Castres, Albi, Avignon, and in the general novitiate in Paris. He strove to promote the reforms in study and religious observance inaugurated by Sebastian Michaelis in the first years of the century. Declining the office of provincial in Toulouse, he was sent by the master general in 1660 to make a canonical visitation of the Portuguese houses of the order.

After his return to Paris, he devoted the remaining 14 years of his life to the composition of theological works. His most important productions were written to satisfy the desire expressed by Alexander VII to the Dominicans assembled in a general chapter at Rome in 1656 that they should publish a course in moral theology conformable to the doctrine of St. Thomas, and thus correct the laxity of morals encouraged by certain casuists. These works were *Theologiae Moralis adv. Laxiores probabilistas pars prior*, *Manuductionis ad moralem theologian pars altera*, and *Theologiae moralis summa bipartita*. In these writings, while condemning opinions that seemed too lax and censuring others that appeared too rigorous, he ably defended the system of probabiliorism. He engaged in an extended controversy with Jean de Launoy regarding the authenticity of the *Summa theologica* of St. Thomas Aquinas. Another of his valuable works is *Libri V apologetici pro religione, utraque theologia, moribus ac juribus Ord. Praed.*

At the time of his death, he was engaged in writing a complete course in theology to be entitled *D. Thomas sui intepres.* This work, only half completed and never published, is not to be confused with the one bearing the same title by Antonin Massouli, OP.

Bibliography: P. MANDONNET, *Dictionnaire de théologie catholique* (Paris, 1903–1959) 2.1:425–426. J. QUÉTIF and J. ECHARD, *Scriptores Ordinis Praedicatorum* (Paris, 1719–1723) 2.2:655–656. A. TOURON, *Histoire des hommes illustres de l'ordre de Saint Dominique,* 6 v., v. 5.

[R. J. RUST]

BARONIUS, CAESAR, VEN.

Cardinal and church historian; b. Sora, in the Campagna, Oct. 31, 1538; d. Rome, June 30, 1607. Though descendants of noble families, his parents were of ordinary means. Having completed his elementary education at Veroli, he studied philosophy, theology, and law at Naples until a French invasion in 1557 forced him to continue his studies at Rome; he gained a doctorate in law *in utroque,* May 30, 1561. In Rome he met Philip NERI and placed himself under his spiritual guidance. Though Philip had not yet established the Congregation of the Oratory, he had begun the Oratory exercises. These meetings, open to the clergy and laity, aimed to draw souls closer to God through plain sermons and mental prayer.

The appearance of the *Centuriae Magdeburgenses,* a Lutheran polemical history of the Church, gave concern to Pius V and Gregory XIII (*see* CENTURIATORS OF MAGDEBURG). A refutation by a keen historian was needed, and Philip, detecting the germ of such scholarship in Baronius, directed him to deliver sermons on the history of the Church. The 20-year-old Baronius began the research that served as the foundation for the 12-volume *Annales ecclesiastici* (Rome 1598–1607). This work had great success, being often reedited and translated into Italian, French, Polish, and German; it extended to the accession of Innocent III and was continued to 1565 by

Caesar Baronius, 17th-century engraving.

Odorico RINALDI. After his ordination, May 27, 1564, Baronius lived at St. John of the Florentines with other priests who followed Philip. There he engaged in the ministry and continued his research. It was not until 1575 at the insistence of the pope that the Oratory was formally established with Philip Neri as its reluctant superior. Baronius then lived under the same roof with the saint who began to test his spirit. Knowing that a scholar needs great patience in sifting minute details, must resist discouragement, narrate events truthfully, and not succumb to pride when praised, Philip drove Baronius relentlessly. In addition to the tedious research, he insisted that Baronius preach, hear confessions, visit the sick, and even cook. Baronius had hoped to publish one volume of the *Annales* a year, but he soon saw this to be impossible. The first volume appeared in 1588; the last, the year he died. Thus a 12-year plan became a 19-year program.

As a scholar Baronius was most exact. He read innumerable sources, investigated coins, inscriptions, or whatever else yielded information. In the interest of accuracy he became involved in an endless correspondence with other scholars. The manuscript and all the corrections were done in his own hand. He used secretaries only for his correspondence. He welcomed criticism even of trifles that proved time-consuming.

The life of Baronius was far from that of a tranquil scholar. In 1593 he succeeded Philip Neri as provost of the Oratory. He also displayed diplomatic skill in furthering the reconciliation of Henry IV of France with the Church. Clement VIII made him his confessor and desired to confer honors on him. Baronius resisted, but on June 5, 1596, he was elevated to the cardinalate; he took as his motto ''Obedience and Peace.'' For two years Baronius not only manifested sorrow at being torn away from the Oratory, but appeared resentful of his dignities. It was not until an enforced idleness while on a special mission to Ferrara that Baronius came to accept the honors as God's will.

In addition to his constant labors on the *Annales,* Baronius found himself the confidant of popes, served on various commissions, undertook the revision and correction of the Roman Martyrology at the request of Guglielmo SIRLETO, and held the post of Vatican librarian. Constant study, lengthy correspondence, grave responsibilities, and adversities were ever present as the *Annales* were published. Over the years scholars have offered critiques of his work. Some believe Baronius was too intent on considering historical events from the point of view of papal primacy; they have also noted inaccuracies. However, they acknowledge that in such a pioneer work, the errors are far fewer than could have been expected. Baronius wrote also a life of St. Ambrose and the *Paraenensis ad rempublicam Venetam.* Of his numerous letters 451 were edited by R. Alberici, *Epistolae et opuscula inedita.* Twice in 1605 Baronius narrowly escaped election to the papacy, due to his own pleading, the use of the *exclusiva* by Spain, and his opposition to the MONARCHIA SICULA. On Jan. 18, 1745, he was declared venerable by Benedict XV.

Bibliography: *A. Cesare Baronio: Scritti Vari,* complete bibliog. of bks., manuscripts, articles on Baronius. A. KERR, *The Life of Cesare Cardinal Baronius of the Roman Oratory.* A. CAPECELATRO, *The Life of St. Philip Neri,* tr. T. A. POPE. G. DE LIBERO, *Cesarae Baronio.* L. PASTOR, *The History of the Popes from the Close of the Middle Ages* v. 1925. A. G. RONCALLI, *Il cardinale Cesare Baronio, Scuola cattolica* 13: 329. H. JEDIN, *Lexikon für Theologie und Kirche* (second edition) 1:1270-72. A. MOLIEN, *Dictionnaire d'histoire et de geéographie ecclésiastiques* 6:871-82, bibliog.

[J. WAHL]

BARONTUS, ST.

Merovingian monk of Lonray, Diocese of Bourges, France; d. *c.* 720. He has often been wrongly identified with a monk of the same name (commemorated in the Roman Martyrology on March 25) who was a hermit in Pistoia. The chief source for knowledge of Barontus is the *Visio Baronti monachi Longoretensis,* probably written by a contemporary. Barontus, after some years of married life, distributed his considerable possessions and entered the monastery of Saint-Pierre de Longoret in Lonray, together with his son, St. Desiderius. On March 25, 678, in the course of a violent fever, he had a vision which he later recounted. The fantastic journey through the otherworld recorded in the *Visio* witnesses to the eschatological curiosity of the time.

Feast: March 26 (Diocese of Bourges).

Bibliography: *Acta Sanctorum* March 3:565572. *Visio, Monumenta Germaniae Historica: Scriptores rerum Merovingicarum* (Berlin 1826–) 5:368–394. J. COIGNET, *Dictionnaire d'histoire et de géographie ecclésiastiques,* ed. A. BAUDRILLART et al. (Paris 1912) 6:882–885. G. RASPINI, *Bibliotheca sanctorum* 2:828–829.

[J. E. LYNCH]

BAROQUE, THE

The term is used strictly to designate an epoch in the history of the arts, roughly 1550–1750; loosely to designate a characteristic of a whole era of European culture; more specifically, a style of art marked by complexity and tension.

The Term. The word was applied in the 16th century to pearls irregular in shape (*perolas barrocas*) as distinct from well-shaped ones, in the Portuguese market at Goa. It has also been suggested that the term derives from *baroco,* the name of a syllogism in Scholastic philosophy.

The term was first used in a cultural sense by French writers in the 17th century. In the 18th century late baroque art became known as *rococo* because it was ''odd,'' in that it was a striking departure from the forms of symmetric classical art. In the 19th century scholars extended the term ''baroque'' to the late Renaissance. It generally connoted lack of taste, even when applied to artists such as Giovanni Lorenzo Bernini (1598–1680), Francesco Borromini (1599–1667), or Peter Paul Rubens (1577–1640).

A shift from a negative to a positive connotation owed something to French Impressionism of the 19th century, which recalled similar techniques of Diego Velázquez (1599–1660) and Rembrandt van Rijn (1606–69), while Richard Wagner's (1813–83) 19th-century ambition of unifying all the arts in opera was reminiscent of similar attempts in the 17th century. At the same time, relativists were beginning to deny any objective criteria for the evaluation of art. These trends enabled Heinrich Wölfflin to proclaim the baroque a different but no less beautiful art than that of the Renaissance.

Dissemination. The movement began in Italy, growing out of the RENAISSANCE and Mannerism, both a development of those styles and in some ways a dramatic departure from them. Mannerism, with its asymmetrical and generally crowded compositions, deliberately violated classical rules of proportion and thus developed into the baroque.

The baroque was an Italian creation both because Italy had been for well over a century the center of the greatest artistic creativity and because the papal project of rebuilding the city of Rome provided unparalleled opportunities for architects and artists.

The identification of the baroque with the COUNTER-REFORMATION is qualified somewhat by the fact that the vital center of religious reform, throughout most of the 16th century, was Spain, where baroque developed somewhat later than in Italy and was not as ubiquitous, thus showing that other styles were equally capable of expressing the new religious sensibilities. But a serious religious spirit and a propensity for paradox and exaggeration were already characteristic of the Spanish mentality and served as a basis for the new movement.

Although French classicism of the second half of the 17th century is sometimes juxtaposed to the pre-classicism or quasi baroque of the first half, many things in the culture of the times—costume, decoration, festivities, operas, public rituals—qualify as baroque, which logically developed into the rococo. But French baroque was more restrained in thought and form and more secularized than in other countries. Classicism subdued, but did not change, the baroque character of 17th-century France.

The French, who assumed the spiritual leadership of the Counter-Reformation soon after 1600, were somewhat reserved in their response to the baroque. In the early 17th century churches continued to be built in the gothic style, albeit often with baroque modifications, and there were few French buildings as unrestrainedly exuberant as some in Italy and elsewhere. The rococo style—less flamboyant, more attentive to exquisite detail—was a French invention.

Several factors combined to ensure this French reserve—a traditional commitment to the ideals of classical restraint and balance, the increasing influence of the monarchy over artistic production, and Jansenist austerity, which mistrusted display in general and in particular disapproved of the exuberant joyfulness of so much baroque religious expression.

Presumed portrait of "Beatrice Cenci," painting attributed to Guido Reni.

Initially Louis XIV sought the advice of BERNINI on remodeling the palace of the Louvre in Paris. But eventually the king lost interest in the project and concentrated his attention on his new palace at Versailles, a structure baroque in its grandeur but in many ways quite classical in design.

The movement came relatively late to Germany, possibly because of the disruptions of the THIRTY YEARS' WAR, but in the German lands it had its last, and in some ways most spectacular, flowering, in the great abbey churches of Bavaria and Austria and in the music of Johann Sebastian BACH (1685–1750) and George Frideric HANDEL (1685–1759).

By attenuating the term somewhat it has been possible to find baroque influences in the Protestant North as well, especially in England, less in the visual arts than in literature.

Baroque proved to be a truly international style, especially in Catholic lands, as it spread to Italy, America, the Philippines, Goa, and other territories beyond Europe itself. Spain was responsible for much of it, with strong influences visible in Central and South American churches.

"The Education of the Virgin". (©Francis G. Mayer/CORBIS)

Counter-Reformation. Although the origins of the baroque lay in the high Renaissance and the Mannerism that followed it, the Counter-Reformation (Catholic Reformation), beginning in the mid-16th century, gave the artistic movement its major impetus.

The sometimes worldly and critical spirit of the Renaissance, as well as the quite different spirit of the Protestant REFORMATION, in some ways blocked the spread of the renewed spirituality of the Catholic Church, an opposition that motivated the establishment of the Roman INQUISITION and the INDEX OF PROHIBITED BOOKS (1559), both of which scrutinized the faith and the conduct of writers and artists. Thus the artistic experiments of the baroque were achieved while remaining within the boundaries of religious orthodoxy. Despite obvious stylistic differences with both, the baroque might be said to have united the substance of medieval Catholicism with the forms of Renaissance classicism.

Sixtus V (pope 1585–90) put the statues of SS. Peter and Paul on the top of the columns of the Roman emperors Trajan and Marcus Aurelius, and erected anew the Egyptian obelisk of the emperor Caligula in St. Peter's square, together with the cross inscribed "Christus vincit." Urban VIII (pope 1623–44), during whose pontificate the Papal States reached their greatest extent, reopened St. Peter's Basilica (1626), the restored majestic sanctuary of Christendom.

In part the ecclesiastical influence on the baroque was through patronage, as various newly established religious orders, especially the Jesuits and Oratorians in Rome, later the Theatines in Germany, commissioned architects to build great churches in the new style. But the Counter-Reformation influence went much deeper, baroque art serving as perhaps the chief instrument for expressing the spirituality of the age.

The great ascetics and mystics of the time were also founders or reformers of religious orders, such as St. TERESA OF ÁVILA (1515–82) and St. JOHN OF THE CROSS (1526?–94). Most important was St. IGNATIUS LOYOLA (1491–1556) with his motto: "Omnia ad majorem Dei gloriam" (All for the greater glory of God). These saints forged the spirituality in which Christian feeling and thinking became radically theocentric, a concept that baroque ecclesiastical art incorporated by centering churches and whole cities around the tabernacle and the monstrance, symbolizing in a way the spiritual heliocentricity of the baroque age. The mystical experience described by St. Teresa and others was the highest expression of that human striving which was the heart of the baroque sensibility, the mystical experience the ultimate paradox, where human and divine met in all-engulfing love.

Torquato Tasso. (Archive Photos)

In France, St. FRANCIS DE SALES (1567–1622), Cardinal Pierre de BERULLE (1575–1629), St. John EUDES (1601–80), Bl. MARIE DE L'INCARNATION (1599–1672), and St. MARGARET MARY ALACOQUE (1647–90) developed devotions, such as the cult of the Sacred Heart, which might be called baroque, and St. Louis-Marie GRIGNION DE MONTFORT (1673–1716) promoted the heightened devotion to the Eucharist.

The baroque spirit did, however, present difficulties for Christianity, which since its inception had warned against the snares of the world, the danger of losing sight of the heaven amidst the distractions of Earth. The baroque awareness of disorder could seem almost antireligious, a repudiation of ancient verities. But the fact that Christians had a love of the world, yet were called upon to reject it, was precisely the kind of tension that was the root of baroque creativity. It was the uniquely appropriate style for the 17th century, which saw the simultaneous growth of both skepticism and piety.

In a sense the starting point for the resolution of this dilemma was the Christian doctrine of human sinfulness. Prone as they were to sin, people could not perceive the world except through the prism of their own experiences. The challenge was to enable them to transcend those experiences.

The facade of the Church of S. Agnese, Rome, designed by Francesco Borromini and constructed between 1645 and 1650.

Thus the exuberant, possibly even arrogant, baroque urge to break through existing boundaries served religious faith by its artistic transformation of restlessness into the search for infinity, the desire to rise above the mundane world without shunning it. The baroque often began with dense, complex renderings of worldly scenes, then led the eye higher and higher, as in domes painted to seem open to the sky, where human beings visibly escaped the bonds of Earth into the heavens, natural and supernatural yoked together in the same tableau. ''The baroque artist adopts a tactic of, first, negation, then strong affirmation, which gives a special illusion of release into 'distance' and 'infinity''' (Wylie Sypher).

The new churches were expected to provide worshippers with a foretaste of Paradise, although at first there was some tension between Counter-Reformation austerity and the exuberant new style. St. Philip NERI originally intended that the walls of the Chiesa Nuova in Rome should be whitewashed, and the original Jesuit plans for the Gesu Church were comparably restrained.

Rome itself, a city built on hills, supported this sense of triumph. Subjects in baroque art were often represented as looking up, and a favorite theme was the miraculous levitation of particular saints, along with gloriously triumphant scenes of entry into heaven, as on the tomb of St. Ignatius in the Gesu Church. Everywhere the style expressed energy barely held in, the urge to soar.

Although TRENT expressed a preference for relatively simple church music, such as plain chant, the creativity of the era expressed itself musically as well, especially in the masses of Giovanni Pierluigi da Palestrina (1526?–94). At the Chiesa Nuova, Philip Neri sponsored performances of a new genre outside the context of the Mass itself—the free musical composition called the oratorio, which reached its climax with Handel.

Another starting point of the baroque was the Catholic Church's teaching on the value of free will, in the face of the denial of that belief by Martin LUTHER, John CALVIN, and others. St. Ignatius was the great psychologist of the will, his Spiritual Exercises a guide whereby directors might teach people ways of mastering the self for the sake of God. The palpable tensions within baroque artistic creation, the conflicts and even contradictions that they embodied, could be taken as visible manifestations of the struggle to subdue the human will to the will of God. The self experienced itself as divided, which only the divinely guided will could unify. The path to heaven now became a strenuous one, with joyous rewards visible to those who dared look up.

Thus the Church was optimistic about its own future and, as contrasted with classic Protestantism, relatively optimistic about the human ability to achieve salvation. Baroque religious art tended to be highly celebratory, representing a series of great spiritual triumphs, the visible and the invisible, the finite and the infinite, which began as apparently contradictory of one another but in the end were gloriously united.

So also the reemphasized sacramentalism of the Counter-Reformation Church justified the baroque's dazzling rendition of material realities, the triumph of the eye over the mind, the act of faith itself made through the physical, especially the sacrament of the altar. Trent's affirmation of the sacredness of matter provided the theological justification for the entire Catholic baroque enterprise.

The ''pagan humanism'' of the Italian Renaissance, which tried to pattern life on the natural ideals of the ancients rather than on the morality taught by Christianity, was largely unacceptable to the later 16th century. Although the depth of this paganism has been exaggerated, even the Christian Humanism of Erasmus, who urged a return to the ancient sources both in religion and in secular learning, was often rejected by devout Catholics such as St. Ignatius.

The RATIO STUDIORUM of the Society of Jesus might be called baroque, in part because of the antihumanist reaction (although the Jesuits incorporated the study of the pagan classics into their curriculum), in part because of the severe Jesuit emphasis on disciplining the will. The humanism of the Jesuits and its underlying baroque spirit was a devout humanism, brought into harmony with Christianity on the basis of the principle ''Omnia ad majorem Dei gloriam.''

The development of the extravagant, almost unrestrained, baroque style has sometimes been understood as disregarding the Council of Trent's injunction that religious art should be austere and relatively simple. Trent's strictures in this regard, however, have been exaggerated, and in fact the conciliar decrees did not go much beyond insisting that religious art be instructive and edifying. Baroque art was often didactic, in its frank intention to convey religious messages, an artistic purpose that was scarcely new.

There was some debate at Trent as to whether the veneration of images should still be encouraged, since it sometimes led to superstitions that Protestantism had attacked to great effect. In the end, however, in this as in other things, the council chose to emphasize precisely what the Protestants had condemned, among them veneration of the saints as spiritual exemplars and as intercessors with God. The new baroque churches had many side chapels dedicated to particular saints, and baroque sculpture had no greater achievement than its statues of the saints.

Trent's sanctioning of religious images was part of its larger affirmation of the principle that the spiritual is mediated to human beings through the material, an affirmation that lay at the heart of much of baroque art and architecture, indeed the very charter of their existence. The task of the artist was, above all, to render palpable and visible the higher unseen realities.

The dogma of transubstantiation—that the bread and wine of the Eucharist are changed into the body and blood of Christ—was at the center of the new piety, the most important way in which the physical manifested the spiritual. The new emphasis on Eucharistic piety and adoration had profound effects on architecture, as the tabernacle was set on the high altar, the altar came to be the focus of the worshiper's attention (often highlighted by a magnificent canopy), and churches were built as large open spaces, without rood screens and with as few pillars as possible to interfere with the vista. (The rule of the Jesuits, who were among the most important early patrons of the new style, did not provide for the celebration of the Divine Office by priests in common, thereby dispensing with the choir stalls that had separated the laity from the high altar in many medieval churches.)

MICHAELANGELO's rendition of the ''Last Judgment'' in the SISTINE CHAPEL had been commissioned by Clement VII in reparation for the Sack of Rome (1527), the low point of the early modern papacy. But, as the baroque style developed, it became the vehicle of Roman triumph, marking a sense of partial victory over Protestantism and a successful reassertion of papal authority. The theme of the triumph of the soul over the heaviness of Earth—its flight to the heavenly realms—blended almost imperceptibly into the celebration of the triumph of the Church over its enemies, both triumphs experienced as a single event. The triumph of the Church was the victory of truth over falsehood, a victory that made possible the soul's triumph over evil. (Thus St. Ignatius's tomb shows not only his entry into heaven but heretics being cast into hell.)

Having rejected the Protestant doctrine of sinful depravity, the Church of the Counter-Reformation could rejoice in its own triumphs and in the triumphs of the souls to whom eternal reward was accessible after heroic effort, for which the great saints provided concrete examples.

Along with the religious orders, high-ranking churchmen were the chief patrons of the baroque, and these ecclesiastical princes often specified the subject matter for the artists, so that artistic creations were the result of some kind of negotiation between the patron and the artist. But, to the degree that church officials controlled baroque art, it was not simply through the exercise of coercive influence. Most of the artists of the age were themselves sincere believers, some of them quite devout.

Bernini made retreats under the guidance of the Spiritual Exercises. The poet Torquato Tasso (1544–95), still deeply entrenched in the chivalrous and amorous tastes of Renaissance epic, accused himself before the Inquisition of not being able to write a Christian epic and after many attempts succeeded in purifying his ''Gerusalemme Liberata'' into the ''Gerusalemme Conquistata''. The attractions of the world appeared diabolic in the new ascetic atmosphere, symbolized by the figure of Don Juan, who covered under a mask of gentleness his unbridled voluptuosity and ended in Hell. Lope de Vega, after a life of multiple adultery and public scandal, paid for by suffering and penance, became a priest, but at an advanced age fell again when he met an actress performing in his comedies.

In accordance with the admonitions of Trent, baroque art was consciously used to defend controverted Catholic beliefs and practices—devotion to the Virgin Mary, the primacy of Peter, the seven sacraments, acts of charity and other good works, the veneration of the saints and of relics, the union of the living and the dead. Martyrdom, often rendered with disconcerting vividness, was a favorite theme, intended especially to inspire apostolic zeal in priests who might go as missionaries to newly discovered lands. Baroque art freely made use of allegory, which Protestant biblical theology had rejected.

While the Church remained vigilant against heresy, it continued to tolerate benignly some of the devotional excesses of its own members, in a new kind of folk art. ''The great achievements of the Catholic Church lay in harmonizing, humanizing, civilizing the deepest impulses of ordinary people'' (Kenneth Clark).

Protestantism. The concept of Protestant baroque is problematical, given the Protestant rejection of religious images and its minimizing of the sacred character of church buildings. Protestantism removed all mediators between man and God, which obviated the commemoration of saints or the depiction of spiritual hierarchies stretching between Earth and heaven. Overall it minimized the sacramental principle itself, whereby the spiritual was manifest through the material.

To the degree that the baroque built on the Catholic affirmation of free will, making possible a sense of striving for God, Protestantism was also inhospitable to the baroque spirit, because of Protestant claims about fundamental human sinfulness that negated that freedom. It was a theology that lent itself to the baroque primarily, therefore, in its preoccupation with human bondage to sin and the means of escaping it.

Rembrandt has often been called a baroque painter, as he was also the greatest Protestant painter, in his rendition of biblical scenes. His baroque qualities were particularly manifest in his dramatic and spiritually revealing use of light and shadow and in the dynamic postures of his subjects in his illustrations of familiar biblical stories.

The baroque spirit could also express itself through literature in Protestant cultures. A major flowering were the Metaphysical poets of 17th-century England, of whom John DONNE (1573–1631), Andrew Marvell (1621–78), Richard Crashaw (1613?–49), and George Herbert (1593–1633) were the supreme examples, in their fascination with paradoxical, even daring imagery; their use of religious and sensual imagery almost interchangeably; and their preoccupation, in an almost Ignatian manner, with the discipline of the will, a preoccupation made possible by the Anglican adherence to Dutch ARMINIANISM, which affirmed freedom of the will in a qualified way and also opened the door to an appreciation of the ''beauty of holiness'' as it might be manifest visibly in church buildings and liturgy.

John MILTON (1608–74), however, was a Puritan, a movement that rejected Arminianism, and his *Paradise Lost* has been considered a baroque masterpiece in its dramatic rendering of rebellious men and angels breaking out of the boundaries placed around them by God.

The baroque style was born and matured within aristocratic, courtly societies, in contrast to the bourgeois culture of, for example, the Protestant Netherlands, and the exuberance of the baroque has been attributed not only to religion but to the aristocratic mentality that was disdainful of economic considerations and willing to spend lavishly for the arts. The bourgeois ideal was to ''maintain a high average standard,'' whereas ''the Baroque spirit lives in and for the moment of creative ecstasy. It will have all or nothing'' (Christopher Dawson).

Only in ''high church'' Anglicanism could the baroque spirit manifest itself architecturally in any way comparable to its Catholic creations, the greatest Protestant baroque church being Christopher Wren's (1632–1723) St. Paul's Cathedral, London, which was, however, less grand than St. Peter's in Rome.

Both the Anglican and Lutheran churches revered sacred music, and the culminating baroque expressions of that art form were Protestant, in Bach and Handel. The Catholic Church had its own baroque musical tradition, beginning with Palestrina, and baroque music can be called a truly ecumenical creation, the Lutheran Bach even composing Catholic masses.

Secular Uses. With patronage essential to almost all artistic activities, separation of religious from secular art was not always clear-cut, and the baroque style was also adopted by lay princes for palaces and other secular buildings, even as ecclesiastical princes, notably the great Roman papal families, commissioned works that reflected their own worldly importance.

The baroque lent itself to such purposes because its soaring and vast painted walls could be used to glorify princes as well as saints, its massive structures celebrating political power as well as salvation. The baroque became in a sense the preferred style of the ''absolute'' monarchs who were centralizing and regimenting government and society throughout the 17th and 18th centuries. Government patronage took control of artistic expression (as in the French Academy) in the same way as the Church of the Counter-Reformation.

If musically the earliest great baroque compositions were settings of the Mass, eventually the baroque spirit led to the creation of opera, an essentially secular genre that was primarily musical but brought into play all other aspects of baroque creativity—poetry, scenery, costumes, even the theater building itself. In opera the powerful emotions originally stirred by religion were permitted expression in secular ways.

The Rome of the late 16th century was itself a master example of harmonious town planning, and similar efforts were made by secular princes—capital cities where cathedral, castle, and opera were integrated into a whole, the streets laid out so as to draw the individual toward the town's major foci.

Typical of baroque luxury was the cult of the garden. In the South these featured cascades of water falling from rocky heights into sculptured basins, surrounded by grottos and pavilions. In the North they were turned into mazes and labyrinths of glades, clipped groves, shaded alleys with Greco-Roman statues, long latticed arbors, lakes, ponds, flower beds worked into various patterns, hedges, fountains with Nereids and nymphs spouting jets of water.

Spirit. The baroque began from the matrix of the Renaissance, but its impetus came from the urge to break out of the formal boundaries that Renaissance classicism honored. The baroque took as its starting point a restless, even chaotic world, on which order had to be imposed without doing violence to the richness of reality.

This imperative has been seen as the result of a profound cultural breakdown that occurred in the 16th and 17th centuries—the Reformation, which forever sundered the religious unity of the West; the consequent religious wars; a radically new perspective on the world, brought about by geographical discovery; and a radical new view of Earth itself in the context of the whole universe, as a result of the Copernican heliocentric theory. All of these rendered obsolete the measured, harmonious, finite world represented in medieval and Renaissance art.

Thus the baroque sensibility was characterized by restlessness, by nervous aspiring energy, by mass in motion, by a looming sense of power conveyed through sheer size. The universe itself, in accordance with the new astronomy, was now seen as an infinite and unbroken space with no true center. In baroque buildings the eye's inability to encompass the whole reinforced the sense of infinity. The baroque style valued the dynamic over the static, the restless over the peaceful. It reveled in contradictions, was immersed in fantasy and spectacle, and employed extravagant modes of expression. Love of paradox was thus at the heart of the baroque sensibility, conveying truth through artistic illusion, by means ostensibly designed merely to delight.

Certain central motifs of the baroque become discernable when contrasted to the motifs of the Renaissance—*memento mori* (remember death) over *carpe diem* (seize the day), the vanity of earthly pleasure over the enjoyment of life, instability over confidence in oneself, movement and change over a fixed untroubled attitude, dissimulation, disguise, confusion, madness and simulation of madness.

There was a clash between Christian mores and the values of aristocratic society. The frequency of duels, which were condemned by the Church, is an example. Ostentatious honor, generosity, and detachment for secular motives were pushed to the levels of heroism and virtue on the spiritual plane, as chastity, virginity, widowhood, suffering, martyrdom—saintly virtues little esteemed in the Renaissance—were exalted. These motifs were presented within the framework of larger tensions: duty versus passion, love versus renunciation, virtue versus intrigue, right versus might, hope versus despair, the finite versus the infinite, time versus eternity.

At the same time the contrast between Renaissance and baroque should not be exaggerated because, despite its violations of classical rules, the baroque adhered strictly to certain rules of its own, most readily seen in its more restrained French manifestations and in poetry. Part of the baroque exploitation of illusion was the fact that apparent confusion masked an often rigid order.

As with all art, the creations of the baroque cannot necessarily be taken as directly mirroring the interior state of their creators, a fact that imposes caution on any postulation that the artists of the age personally experienced some unique anxiety arising from social and cultural dislocations.

The ultimate undoing of the baroque style was perhaps its very fascination with display and illusion, so that it sometimes seemed that the spiritual had been turned into the material rather than the reverse. The striving for greater and greater dramatic effect eventually led to a shallow sensationalism, with religious statues encrusted with jewels or provided with human hair. The baroque style was the last great manifestation of truly religious art in Western civilization, but its excesses also led to the kinds of tasteless, sentimental popular religious art common in the 19th and 20th centuries.

Increasingly, especially as the style was adopted for political uses, the baroque sense of triumph was less a celebration of spiritual victories and more a vehicle for worldly display. In its multiplication of vivid images, its dramatic contrast of light and shadow, and its ability to convey a sense of motion, the baroque has been seen as anticipating the art of the modern film.

Specific Manifestations. *Architecture.* Among the earliest baroque buildings are the two great churches of the Society of Jesus in Rome. The interior of the Gesu is still almost a continuation of Renaissance style in its geometric and stereometric forms, together with the linear arrangement of the walls and the straight continuation of the longitudinal nave into the apse, the whole covered by a mighty but simple dome whose baroque interior was painted much later. The church of San Ignazio, on the other hand, is fullest baroque, with all forms picturesquely segmented and merged into a dream world where the flowing lines of the solid walls, the painted curtains and balustrades, the real windows and their painted sills and columns cannot be distinguished.

The same differences can be found in Renaissance and baroque church facades, for instance, Santa Maria Novella in Florence and Borromini's San Carlo alle Quattro Fontane in Rome. The former is seen as a plane, all decor arranged along the surface in a two-dimensional order, whereas the latter suggests a moving wave in its line of concave and convex forms, restless and recessional, and in its front with broad curves. A Renaissance church, as a building of ''closed'' form, fits into the house front of a city street, but a baroque church (such as the Val de Grace in Paris, the Stift Melk in Austria, and Santa Maria della Salute in Venice), as an ''open'' building, belongs to the landscape, where foreshortenings offer to the viewer, from various points of observation, towers and cupola, frontal and lateral walls in ever new aspects.

Sculpture. Baroque statues seem to leave their niches and to give the viewer an opportunity to see them from different angles, in this regard analogous to the ''open'' baroque of architecture. The spirit of the Council of Trent and the introduction of new Spanish saints to the whole Catholic world gave statuary a different flowering on monuments and tombs, as occured in secular ways through the adulation of princes of Church and state.

The religious statues of Europe and Latin America followed the ideal of polychrome sculpture as exemplified by Juan Martínez Montañés (1568–1649), a tradition in Spain that reached its peak in Alonso Cano (1601–67). The plastic clouds surrounding the Blessed Virgin on Bavarian and Austrian columns represent the same exuberance. In Italy the highest achievement of baroque sculpture was Bernini's marble statue of the almost trembling body of St. Teresa, her heart pierced by the golden arrow of a cherub, in Santa Maria della Vittoria in Rome.

Painting. If picturesqueness is a hallmark of baroque in architecture and sculpture, it is preeminently so in painting. Renaissance painters such as Raphael and Leonardo da Vinci stressed drawing almost too much to appear painterly. But the Mannerists painted so that contours were effaced and objects fused with their surroundings, as in Michelangelo's *Last Judgment.* Baroque painters included Pietro da Cortona (1596–1669), famous for effectual foreshortening; Guido Reni (1575–1642), known for the characteristic uplifted eyes of his figures; and the painters of elongated figures, culminating with El Greco (1541–1614) in Spain.

The High Renaissance in Italy gradually yielded to the colorful Venetian Renaissance of Paolo Veronese (1528?–88) and Titian (1488?–1576) and culminated in the naturalism of Caravaggio (1565–1609). Moreover, in accordance with the perspectivist compositions of Tintoretto (1518–94), Roman influences appear in the chiaroscuro murals of Federico Barocci (1526?–1612) and the Würzburg frescoes of Giovanni Battista Tiepolo (1696–1770).

What had, however, become mere technique in Italy reached a new height under the Flemish influence of Pieter Brueghel (1525?–69) and Rubens. Its powerful sensuality was expressed in theatrical groupings of nudes in grandiose environments. Spanish artists replaced colorfulness by the impressionistic brush strokes, color spots, and tonal gradations of the ingenious Velázquez, whose military and courtly subjects were to have technical parallels in the Madonnas of Bartolomé Murillo (1617–82) and the monks of Francisco de Zurbarán (1598–1664). Velázquez's subdued baroque also had certain parallels in the North. Closest in style to his interiors were those of Jan Vermeer (1632–75). Closest to the military display of his *Surrender of Breda* (1635) is the chiaroscuro *Night Watch* of Rembrandt (1641), with its stress on golden chains, fur, and feathered hats.

The same baroque impressionism is found in the dream-light atmosphere of the French stage landscapes of Claude Lorrain (1600–82).

Music. Historians of music use the term ''baroque'' when discussing the invention of opera, the oratorio, the instrumental concert, the cantata, sonata, fugue, prelude, and organ music, these ''novelties'' of the baroque era reaching from Claudio Monteverdi (1567–1643) to Henry Purcell (1659–95), Bach, and Antonio Vivaldi (1675?–1741). A line of Renaissance, exclusively vocal a cappella music culminating in Palestrina, was extended into the baroque by the ecclesiastical *stile antico.*

Theoreticians, however, understand by baroque music a certain secular *stile moderno.* Unlike the *musica gravis* of the Renaissance, where a clear line and axis of polyphonic harmony stressed by the tenor voices oriented all the contrapuntal voices, the baroque *musica luxurians* had recourse to another leading principle—that of the general basso or *bassus continuus,* in which the leading upper voices were reflected according to movement, chords, cadences, and even dissonances, while the middle voices merely filled out the harmony without any contrapuntal significance. The basso and soprano furnished the skeleton of the composition. The consequence of this novelty was a monodic polarity between fundamental and ornamental instruments, with the stress on the deep-toned cembalo, violoncello, viola da gamba, and viola da braccio.

Another baroque principle, comparable to the principle of openness in the graphic arts, was the combination of measured with free music as introduced by Giulio Caccini (1550?–1618) and Girolamo Frescobaldi (1583–1643). According to this principle the polyphonic choir followed the traditional preestablished measurement, while the two leading voices and the *bassus continuus* were free to hover (*senza battuta*) above the measured parts of the cantata or madrigal. This baroque novelty had a number of consequences: the recitative, or speech-song, as well as the strutting aria; the virtuosity of the coloratura and the dependence of minor and major keys on passions provided in the libretti; the hunting for castrati to combine in the voices boyish charm with virile decision; and the opportunity for mezzo-sopranos to match the new deep-toned instruments. The baroque combination of music and poetry in the opera is a parallel to the combination of baroque architecture and painting in church interiors.

Poetry. The baroque in poetry appeared as tension between the secularism of the Renaissance and new spiritual trends, manifest in conflicting attitudes of escape, revolt, and interior consent to the ideals of the Catholic reform. As early as 1550 a transformation of Renaissance love poetry was leading to the praise of a spiritualized, rather than a real, lady, as in the sonnets of the Portuguese poet Luís de Camões (1524–80). There is even the mystical shift to divine love, called in Italy *spirituale* and in Spain *a el divino.* The new baroque tendency was present in the poetical works of St. John of the Cross. The further shift, that of the central motif from love to death, resulted in remarkable poems of disillusionment by Francisco Quevedo (1580–1645), as well as in the English Metaphysical poets.

Sometimes a deeper insight into the destructive effects of human passion, thanks to the new spirituality, inspired a baroque lyricism of repentance, as in many poems of Lope de Vega (1562–1635) and Tasso. Baroque poetry culminated in the biblical and liturgical paraphrases and imitations of the Spaniard Fray Luis de León (1527–91), and in the French poets Pierre Corneille (1606–84) and Jean Racine (1639–99), as well as in the quasi-mystical alexandrines of the German Catholic convert Angelus Silesius (1624–77).

Prose. The secular-spiritual tension apparent in baroque poetry occurred also in prose. Within the pastoral novel *Diana* by Jorge de Montemayor (1521?–61) in Spain, as in *Astree* by Honoré d'Urfé (1568–1625) in France, appeared a love casuistry in which platonic friendship won out against sensuous relations. The type, taken up in France by Bishop Pierre Camus (1584–1652), led to the secularized but strictly moral psychological novel, which reached its zenith in *La Princesse de Cleves* by Marie de La Fayette (1634–93). Baroque novels, in a certain parallel to art, also exhibited formal innovations. The psychological questions discussed at length allowed a unified and open form, with a larger extension of the plot than had the short, multiple stories of the Renaissance, closed within an artificial frame.

The frame ostensibly burst under the impact of the interlocked and inseparable episodes of the *Don Quixote* of Miguel de Cervantes (1547–1616), imitated in Germany by Hans Jakob von Grimmelshausen (1620?–76) in his *Simplicius Simplicissimus.* Cervantes's novel also illustrated a tension, so characteristic of the baroque, between self-willed idealism and unrestrained materialism, neither of which can satisfy man, who is looking for something that transcends both, namely, sanctity. The baroque, particularly with Cervantes, created a new prose style. A preference for directness and terseness, a kind of Tacitean style, was applied to the vernacular in the *Essais* of Michel de Montaigne (1533–92), and both tendencies merged in Cervantes's rhythmic, Italianate, but popular style. At the same time, an elaborate pulpit eloquence was revived by the *Ars praedicandi* (1562) of Lucas Baglioni. Sacred oratory reached high peaks in the Spanish preacher Hortensio Felix Paravicino (1580–1633), in the Portuguese Jesuit Antonio Vieira (1608–97), and most of all in the ''Eagle of Meaux,'' the French court preacher Jacques-Benigne Bossuet (1627–1704), who transcended hackneyed themes in his famous funeral orations and sermons.

Literary Theory. A fundamental tension in literary theory was evident in a trend that, following strictly the ''rules'' of Aristotle's *Rhetoric* and *Poetics,* at the same time prepared for a break from them. Not only was the question of unity of action, place, and time raised, but under the new religious trends the problems of verisimilitude and decency appeared, especially the question whether literature ought primarily to instruct or delight. The question was summarized by the *Poetics* of Antonio Possevino, SJ (1595), and the answer given in the fusing of instruction and delight in a profitable higher pleasure.

On the question of how to achieve this fusion, literary theories differed. In Spain, Baltasar Gracián (1601–58), in his *Agudeza y arte de ingenio,* found the solution in a wholesale imagery that was required to reveal at the same time intelligence and wit. Nicolas Boileau (1636–1711) in France, in his *Art poetique,* and Martin Opitz (1597–1639) in Germany, believed that by following the great literary patterns of the past, one would find a dignified and sublime circumlocution in which reason prevailed, rather than a profusion of metaphors.

Drama. The baroque epoch was preeminently the age of drama, because of the tensions hitherto described.

The contrasts between virtue and sin, will and passion, were foremost in the minds of theologians. Discussions concerning grace, free will, and their mysterious interrelationships attracted Lope de Vega, William Shakespeare (1564–1616), Corneille, Racine, and the Dutchman Joost van den Vondel (1587–1679).

In the variegated baroque drama, man was always shown within the limitations of his condition, on the stage of the world, while God was the unseen stage director. The motif of life as a dream occurred in Pedro Calderón de la Baraca's (1600–81) *El gran teatro del mundo* but it was likewise discernible in Shakespeare's *Macbeth.* The dream motif became famous through Calderón's *La Vida es Sueflo,* but the convention is evident also in Shakespeare's *The Taming of the Shrew.* Tirso de Molina's (1571?–1648) hero in *El condenado por desconfiado* came to realize that a proud hermit, who tried to get to heaven by his own effort, could be surpassed by a fundamentally charitable robber who, aware of his own weakness, ultimately relied on God.

Racine's heroine in *Phedre* (1677), worn out by an adulterous love and feebly resisting, let her will be so weakened that she caused murder and committed suicide out of jealousy and despair. Thus in the age of casuistry the passions were tracked to their roots. The jealousy of suspicious husbands led to the killing of their innocent wives in Lope's and Calderón's versions of *El medico de su honra,* as well as in Shakespeare's *Othello.*

But the baroque drama also had a formal counterpoint. Progressive cutting of secondary actions from plays led, as in the visual arts, from multiplicity to unity. Dramatic unity was achieved through plots knit so tightly that they could end in catastrophe within the shortest imaginable time, a psychological time even less than the 24 hours thought to have been prescribed by Aristotle.

Stagecraft. The gigantic baroque opera stage featured the supernatural, the miraculous, the unusual, the bizarre, the sumptuous, the limitless, and the grandiose. Here, the illusion of space verging on infinity was created by showing only half the theater building to the spectators, who were enclosed in boxes, arranged in horizontal and vertical rows of great heights. The other half belonged to a deep platform where, with the help of mechanical devices, the same illusions of perspective could be produced as in the painted heavens of baroque churches. If a building could not house all the splendor of ballets and cavalcades, an open-air theater was created for such performances, and naval battles were enacted on artificial lakes. The baroque stage, with its illusions and surprises, was one of the typical creations of an age when ostentation played an enormous role, despite the fact that the dichotomy between outer show and inner worth was felt as a defect.

Language. Literary language centered around paradox as the supreme figure of speech: life is death and death is life; love of God is hatred of the world; martyrdom is sweet and freedom is bitter; one is dying from not dying; one is victorious in defeat; chaste in nakedness; proud in humility; desperate in hope; one receives the brightest light from the darkest night. The paradox metaphor became a myth-creating force—striking, fresh, eloquent, grandiose though artificial. Metaphor and paradox joined to create gigantic antitheses. The whole epoch might be said to stand between light and shade, night and day, reason and faith. Epigrammatic condensation vied with lush description. Playful, pleasant, and grotesque elements became counterparts of the grandiose, the majestic, and the magnificent, as when Blaise Pascal declared man to be a thinking reed and a beast that tries to play the angel and Don Quixote was called the "wise fool."

Another device was the impressionistic blurring and gradual clarification of an event. In Velázquez's *Las Lanzas* the movement was from the indistinct background of a military camp, to a middle ground of dim contours, and finally to the foreground of distinguishable soldiers and horses. In this way Cervantes and Luis de Góngora y Argote described the meetings of people, revealing personality by progressively clearer bits of conversation, until names and professions were clarified and the persons moved to a goal, for instance, a wedding feast first vaguely discussed; then apprehended from noises, illumination, and music; finally confronted in detailed reality.

Philosophy. The term "baroque" has been applied to 17th-century philosophy, in part because the century's discovery of an unshakable mechanism in the physical world, alongside the Catholic belief in moral liberty, set up a tension so difficult to bridge that it affected even the theological discussions on free will and predestination between Jesuits and Jansenists.

The oratorian Nicolas de MALEBRANCHE (1638–1715), a disciple of René DESCARTES (1596–1650), the most influential philosopher of the early part of the century, tried to overcome the dichotomy by a general principle of divine order that works differently in the material and the spiritual worlds, so that miracles follow a principle of order that the human mind is not able to discover.

The tension between matter and spirit offered itself in a quite different way to Gottfried Wilhelm von Leibniz (1646–1716), who started, in the medieval Scholastic way, from God as the immovable First Cause and Master of the material as well as of the moral-spiritual world. Both worlds are subject to His plan and purpose. There is a preestablished harmony between the macrocosm of creation and the microcosm of the human soul, which works out its destiny in liberty within the best imaginable of worlds, a world that pleads for the bounty of God (*Theodicy,* 1710).

Blaise PASCAL (1623–62), without achieving a philosophical system, was perhaps the 17th-century man who felt most acutely these tensions within himself. He rejected Descartes's approach and resolved his own tension by distinguishing three ''orders''—the world of geometry, of ''finesse'' (art, life), and of charity (religion).

Bibliography: K. CLARK, *Civilization* (New York 1969). G. MAIORINO, *The Cornucopia and the Baroque Unity of the Arts* (State College, Pa. 1990). J. N. STEADMAN, *Redefining a Period Style* (Pittsburgh 1990). A. D. WRIGHT, *The Counter-Reformation* (New York 1982). C. DAWSON, *The Dividing of Christendom* (New York 1958). C. NORBERG-SCHULZ, *Baroque Architecture* (New York 1971); *Late Baroque and Rococo Architecture* (New York 1974). L. L. MARTZ, *The Poetry of Meditation* (New Haven, Conn. 1954); *From Renaissance to Baroque* (Columbia, Mo. 1991). P. N. SKRINE, *The Baroque* (London 1978). V. TAPIE, *The Age of Grandeur* (London 1960). A. BLUNT, *Baroque and Rococo Architecture and Decoration* (New York 1978). J. BOURKE, *Baroque Churches of Central Europe* (London 1958). N. POWELL, *From Baroque to Rococo* (London 1959). E. K. WATERHOUSE, *Italian Baroque Painting* (New York 1962). R. WITTKOWER, *Art and Architecture in Italy, 1600–1750* (Baltimore and New York 1972). W. SYPHER, *Four Stages of Renaissance Style* (Garden City, N.Y. 1955). H. WÖLFFLIN, *Principles of Art History* (New York 1950). M. F. BUKOFZER, *Music in the Baroque Era* (New York 1947). E. CASTELLI, *Retorica e Barocco* (Rome 1955). A. CIORANESCU, *El Barroco O el descubrimiento del drama* (Laguna 1957). C. J. FRIEDRICH, *The Age of the Baroque* (New York 1952). I. A. LEONARD, *Baroque Times in Old Mexico* (Ann Arbor, Mich. 1959). G. BAZIN, *Baroque and Rococo Art* (New York 1964). J. POPE-HENNESSY, *Italian High Renaissance and Baroque Sculpture* (London 1963). J. LEES-MILNE, *The Baroque in Spain and Portugal* (New York 1960). H. B. SEGEL, *The Baroque Poem* (New York 1974). A. A. HAUSER, *The Social History of Art,* v. 1 (New York 1951).

[H. HATZFELD/J. F. HITCHCOCK]

BARRÉ, NICHOLAS, BL.

Pedagogue, founder of the Schools of Charity, the Congregation of Sisters of the Holy Infant Jesus (also known as the Ladies of St. Maur), and the Sisters of the Holy Infant Jesus of Providence of Rouen (France); b. Amiens, France, Oct. 21, 1621; d. Paris, May 31, 1686. Born into a well-to-do family, Nicholas chose to enter the Order of the Minims of St. Francis de Paul at age 18 and was professed at Amiens in 1641. Even before his ordination, Barré was given the chair of theology at Paris, which he held with honor for 20 years. At the convent of the Royal Square (Paris), he had as confreres illustrious men of science, of wide knowledge, and profound spirituality.

Although he trained many students in scholastic as well as spiritual matters, he spent the major part of his ministry in preaching, spiritual direction, and the great work of instituting free popular teaching. In Rouen first (1662) and later in Paris, he founded and directed those Schools of Charity of the Holy Infant Jesus that became models throughout France. To these schools he gave program, method, and teachers whose religious, cultural, and didactic preparation he had scrupulously supervised. The Institute of the Sisters of the Holy Infant Jesus had two distinct branches: one in Rouen, also called the ''Institute of Providence''; the other at Paris, called the ''Institute of the Dames of St. Maur,'' from the house of its foundation. Barré also considered a male branch of the Congregation: the ''Teachers.'' This, however, was accomplished in the foundation of the Brothers of the Christian Schools by St. John de la Salle, whom Barré had directed, advised, and encouraged.

Barré had a solid base of Thomistic theology and a sense of equilibrium that enabled him to avoid the excesses of rigorism and laxism. He fought both JANSENISM and QUIETISM. Humility, faith, charity, mortification, and personal encounter with Jesus in the Eucharist are the pillars of his spiritual doctrine. He was an advocate of frequent Communion, and often affirmed that Holy Communion is the best disposition for Holy Communion. His extant spiritual works are *Lettres spirituelles* (Rouen 1697; Toulouse 1876) and *Maximes spirituelles* (Paris 1694). His cause for beatification was introduced before the Sacred Congregation of Rites in 1931. On April 6, 1998, a miracle attributed to his intercession was approved, which led to his beatification by John Paul II, March 7, 1999.

Feast: Oct. 21.

Bibliography: *Œuvres complètes*, ed. T. DARRAS, M. T. FLOUREZ, and M. F. TOULOUSE (Paris 1994). *Acta Apostolicae Sedis* no. 7 (1999): 310–312. *L'Osservatore Romano,* English edition, no. 8 (1999): 2; no. 10 (1999): 1, 3, 6. C. FARCY, *Le Révérend Père Barré, religieux minime* (Paris 1942). B. FLOUREZ, *Marcheur dans la nuit: Nicolas Barré, 1621–1686,* 2d. ed. (Paris 1994). H. DE GRÈZES, *Vie du R. P. Barré . . .* (Barle-Duc 1892). G. MORETTI, *Un pedagogista santo* (Rome 1929). G. PAPÀSOGLI, *Nicola Barré, educatore di anime* (Rome 1975).

[A. BELLANTONIO]

BARRIÈRE, JEAN DE LA

Founder of the FEUILLANTS; b. Saint-Céré, France, April 29, 1544; d. Rome, April 25, 1600. His parents were nobles. After studying in Toulouse and Bordeaux, he was granted the Cistercian Abbey of Les Feuillans *in commendam* in 1565. He went to Paris to complete his studies and, influenced by Arnaud d'Ossat (a future cardinal), resolved to reform his abbey. In 1573 he became a Cistercian and was ordained. In 1577, after initial difficulties about the severity of his reforms, he became regular abbot with two novices and two professed clerics. Vocations multiplied until in 1587 there were 140 members. As an independent reform congregation, the Feuillants spread in France and Italy. Barrière became the first general superior but was deposed in 1592, unjustly accused for his part in the civil war raging in France. He bore the humiliation patiently, spending his last years in confinement in Rome. He was rehabilitated a few months before his death by the intervention of Cardinal Robert BELLARMINE. Pope Clement VIII, recalling the heroic nature of his asceticism, called him blessed.

Bibliography: J. M. CANIVEZ, *Dictionnaire d'histoire et de géographie ecclésiastiques* (Paris 1912—) 6:924926. S. LENSSEN, *Hagiologium cisterciense* (Tilburg 1948–49) 1:173176. E. G. KRENIG, *Lexikon für Theologie und Kirche* (Freiburg 1957–65) 2:2. M. STANDAERT, *Dictionnaire de spiritualité ascétique et mystique* (Paris 1932—) 5:274287.

[L. J. LEKAI]

BARRON, EDWARD

Missionary and bishop; b. Ballyneale, County Waterford, Ireland, June 28, 1801; d. Savannah, Georgia Sept. 12, 1854. As the youngest son of wealthy Pierse and Anna Barron, Edward had exceptional educational advantages. He successfully read a law course at Trinity College, Dublin, to qualify for the Irish bar. In 1825 he began studying for the priesthood and in 1829 was ordained in Rome, returning to teach at St. John's College, Waterford, Ireland. Despite delicate health, he accepted Bp. Francis Kenrick's invitation to be rector of the Philadelphia, Pennsylvania seminary. Too easily imposed upon, Barron was removed from the seminary. As pastor of St. Mary's Philadelphia and vicar-general, he volunteered to go to Liberia when Rome asked Kenrick to send priests to that difficult mission. Reluctantly, Kenrick released his talented vicar-general. While enroute Barron was named prefect apostolic of Upper Guinea; before his consecration in Rome on Nov. 1, 1842, his jurisdiction was extended to Sierra Leone and the whole western coast of Africa that was not under the care of other ecclesiastical authority.

In France, the bishop procured seven priests of the Congregation of the Immaculate Heart and three young laymen. Difficulties arose at Cape Palmas, where the French missionaries were suspected of being used as instruments by the French in an effort to extend the French West African empire. Barron consequently transferred all but one of his missionaries to French territories; however, the group of Frenchmen, who had been joined by two from Ireland, was ravaged by disease, and only the bishop and one priest reached Senegal alive. Barron made a fresh start at Goree, planning a seminary. Again the climate caused the death of nearly all his priests, and in 1845 the sickly bishop resigned. He returned to the United States and assisted Bp. Peter Kenrick of St. Louis, Missouri with his Indian missions. Although both Francis and Peter Kenrick wanted Barron as an auxiliary bishop, neither requests were ever honored.

Barron contracted advanced pulmonary tuberculosis and spent his final years as a missionary in Florida. In July of 1854, for health reasons, he left Florida for Philadelphia, but he hurried to Savannah when he heard of the yellow fever epidemic in Georgia. While administering to the sick, he succumbed to the fever himself.

Bibliography: M. J. BANE, *The Catholic Story of Liberia*; *Catholic Pioneers in West Africa*. R. K. MACMASTER, ''Bishop Barron and the West African Missions, 1841–1845,'' *Historical Records and Studies of the U. S. Catholic Historical Society of New York*, 50 83–129.

[H. J. NOLAN]

BARRUEL, AUGUSTIN DE

Jesuit polemicist; b. Villeneuve de Berg (Ardèche), Oct. 2, 1741; d. Paris, Oct. 5, 1820. He entered the JESUITS in 1756, was exiled (1762) with them, and returned to France on the occasion of their suppression (1774). In collaboration with Fréron on the *Année littéraire* from 1774, he attacked the *philosophes* in his *Helviennes ou Lettres provinciales philosophiques* (1781). He edited (1788–92) the *Journal ecclésiastique*, which he used to criticize the FRENCH REVOLUTION. He wrote pamphlets (1790–91) against the CIVIL CONSTITUTION OF THE CLERGY, and then gathered into one *Collection ecclésiastique* (13 v. 1791–93) all documents on this subject. From England he published his *Histoire du clergé pendant la Revolution* (1784). His most provocative work, *Mémoires pour servir à l'histoire du Jacobinisme* (London 1787) underscored the role of Freemasonry and secret societies in the French Revolution: his thesis, correct but too sweeping, precipitated a flood of refutations. Barruel returned to France at the fall of the Directory, and wrote in defense of the new political order. He upheld the CONCORDAT OF 1801 and the right of the pope to depose French bishops in *Du Pape et de ses droits religieux* (1803). He reentered the restored Society of Jesus (1815). His last years were spent preparing a refutation of Kant.

Bibliography: C. SOMMERVOGEL, *Bibliothèque de la Compagnie de Jésus* (Brussels-Paris 1890–1932) 1:930–945; 7:1767. J. J. DUSSAULT, *Notice sur la vie et les ouvrages d'Augustin de Barruel* (Paris 1825). R. DAESCHLER, *Dictionnaire d'histoire et de géographie ecclésiastiques* (Paris 1912—) 6:937.

[R. J. SEALY]

BARRY, COLMAN JAMES

Church historian, college president; b. Lake City, MN, May 29, 1921; d. Collegeville, MN, Jan. 7, 1994. Colman Barry entered the Order of St. Benedict of St. John's Abbey, Collegeville, Minnesota, in 1943 and was ordained a priest in 1947. A student of John Tracy Ellis at the Catholic University of America, he received his Ph.D. in 1953. His dissertation, *The Catholic Church and German Americans*, was later published; it was widely received and is a standard work in that vital area of American Catholic history. At St. John's he taught history from 1951 to 1966 and served as president from 1964 to 1971. As president of St. John's, Barry oversaw an extensive building program, gained the first local affiliate for Minnesota Public Radio, and opened the Center for Ecumenical and Cultural Research and the Hill Monastic Library, a microfilm collection of manuscripts from monasteries throughout the world.

As a church historian Barry's publications were wide-ranging, and include *American Nuncio: Cardinal Aloisius Muench* (1969); *Upon These Rocks: Catholics in the Bahamas* (1973); *Worship and Work. The Centennial History of St. John's Abbey and University* (1956; revised 1980, 1993); and three volumes of *Readings in Church History*. He was president of the American Catholic Historical Association (1977) and served as editor of *Benedictine Studies* and the *American Benedictine Review*.

As an indication of the widespread respect for his scholarship, he was appointed visiting professor of Church History at Yale University in 1973. His administrative leadership was evident during his four-year tenure as the first dean of the School of Religious Studies at the Catholic University of America. It was a challenging position, one that entailed incorporating constitutive departments into a new school and brokering a consensus on other foundational policy issues.

When he returned to St. John's in 1977, Barry became the first executive director of the Institute of Spirituality, well-known for its creative conferences in an ecumenical context. Concurrently, he was president of the Hill Monastic Library. Barry's richly diverse life marks him as an excellent teacher, a highly regarded historian, a creative administrator, a dynamic fund raiser, and a committed monk.

[C. J. KAUFFMAN]

BARRY, GERALD, MOTHER

Educator, administrator; b. Inagh, Ennis, County Clare, Ireland, March 11, 1881; d. Adrian, Mich., Nov. 20, 1961. Barry was one of 18 children. Her parents, Michael Barry, a traveled scholar and prosperous farmer, and Catherine Barry, a homemaker, had her christened Catherine Bridget. As a young woman, Barry immigrated to America. She engaged in business for several years before entering the Dominican Sisters of Adrian on Feb. 2, 1913. After making her vows, Barry served as teacher, principal, novice mistress, and prioress general. During her superiorship, community membership increased from 930 to 2,480, and two senior colleges, four high schools for girls, and a Sisters House of Studies (Washington, DC) were built. In addition, 70 parochial schools, a teachers college, and a residence for businesswomen were opened; an academy and two missions were established in Santo Domingo; and hundreds of sisters were assigned to study for baccalaureate and higher degrees. At the request of the Holy See, Barry acted as first executive chairman of the Sisters Committee for the National Congress of Religious in the U.S. (Notre Dame, Ind., August 1952). She was also appointed to preside at the meeting of superiors in Chicago, Ill., from which developed the permanent Conference of Major Superiors of Women's Religious Institutes. Barry was widely known as an energetic, humorous, and shrewd leader of her community.

Bibliography: M. GERALD BARRY, *The Charity of Christ Presses Us: Letters to Her Community*, ed. M. PHILIP RYAN. M. PAUL, Mother Mary Gerald, O.P., *Dominican Educational Bulletin* (Winter 1962).

[M. P. MCKEOUGH]

BARRY, JOHN

Second bishop of Savannah, Ga.; b. Oylegate, County Wexford, Ireland, July 1799; d. Paris, France, Nov. 21, 1859. He studied under Bp. John England of Charleston, S.C., and was ordained there Sept. 24, 1825. He then served as assistant at the cathedral and secretary to the bishop until July 1828, when he was made pastor of St. Marys Church, Charleston. Subsequently he was given charge of St. Peters Church, Columbia, S.C., and later assigned to Holy Trinity Church, Augusta, Ga. At its Barnwell, S.C., mission he built St. Andrews Church, the fourth Catholic church erected in the state. When the Irish Volunteers of Charleston, a company of militia, joined the active forces in Florida at the outbreak of the Seminole War, Barry was assigned as chaplain; he served with the unit throughout the campaign. During the yellow fever epidemic of 1839 in Augusta he turned his rectory into a hospital and obtained Sisters of Our Lady, of Mercy from Charleston to attend the sick. He was highly commended by the city officials for his action. After the epidemic he conducted an orphanage in his rectory and opened a school.

Karl Barth.

He served as vicar-general under England and his successor, Bp. Ignatius Reynolds; attended the Fourth Provincial Council of Baltimore as England's theologian; and was named vicar-general of Savannah when that diocese was erected. When Bp. Francis Gartland died in 1854, Barry was appointed administrator of Savannah and in that capacity attended the Eighth Provincial Council of Baltimore. He was selected as bishop of Savannah and consecrated Aug. 2, 1857, in Baltimore. However, he was already in poor health, and a year later, while traveling in Europe, he became seriously ill and died in the Paris hospital of the Brothers of St. John of God. Some years later his body was brought back to Georgia and buried in the crypt of St. Patricks Church, Augusta.

Bibliography: J. J. O'CONNELL, *Catholicity in the Carolinas and Georgia 1820–1878* (New York 1879).

[R. C. MADDEN]

BARTH, KARL

Preeminent proponent of neo-orthodox or dialectical theology; b. Basel, Switzerland, May 10, 1886; d. Basel, Dec. 10, 1968. The son of Swiss Reformed minister and New Testament scholar Fritz Barth, Karl was reared in Berne. In 1913 he married Nelly Hoffmann, with whom he had five children. From 1904 to 1909 Barth studied theology at the universities of Berne, Berlin, Tübingen, and Marburg. At first he adhered to the liberal Protestant theology of teachers such as Adolph von Harnack and Wilhelm Herrmann. He began his ministerial career in 1909 as a vicar in Geneva, then in 1911 was appointed pastor of the Swiss Reformed Church in Safenwil, Canton of Aargau. Barth's pastoral experience soon led him to question the adequacy of liberal theology and its confidence in the ultimate perfectibility of man. The outbreak of World War I in 1914 and the use of technology for inhumane purposes led Barth to further question the optimism of liberal theology. The decisive break occurred when he learned that many of his former teachers in Germany supported the war policies of Kaiser Wilhelm II. To assess his heritage and find a theological path, Barth turned to an intensive study of the Bible and in 1919 published *The Epistle to the Romans*. This powerful commentary, especially the completely rewritten second edition of 1922, launched a fresh theological movement dedicated to the recovery of a theology of the Word of God. Barth emphasized the sinfulness of humanity, God's absolute transcendence, and the human inability to know God apart from revelation.

Called to a professorship in 1921, Barth taught systematic theology at the universities of Göttingen (1921–25), Münster (1925–30), Bonn (1930–35), and Basel (1935–62). His illustrious career included theological leadership of the Confessing Church against Nazi influence in the German Protestant Church, chief authorship of the Barmen Declaration of 1934, expulsion from Germany by the Nazi government in 1935, delivery of the Gifford Lectures in 1937–38, participation in the Amsterdam Assembly of the World Council of Churches in 1948, an American tour in 1962, and a visit to the Vatican in 1966. A legacy of more than 600 writings is crowned by his monumental *Church Dogmatics* (1932–67), a Christ-centered theological *summa* that investigates the meaning of God and human redemption in the light of the Gospels.

Doctrine. Throughout the *Church Dogmatics* there is reflection on the implications of a Christocentric theological system. Barth's theological system, for which the name ''coherent Christology'' is quite apt, stands on the principle that a theological understanding of any subject is totally dependent on the penetration of that subject's relation to Christ. In general, that system begins with the dialectical Word of God which enters history vertically and contradicts human efforts to know God through religion or philosophy. Here, Barth singles out the analogy of being as a faithless attempt by sinful humanity at self-justification, i.e., through the analogy of being humanity seeks to establish continuity between a human word and a divine word.

In later volumes of the *Church Dogmatics* Barth's thought moved beyond dialectics and examined the consequences of the reconciliation between God and humanity that is accomplished in Jesus Christ. Barth moved increasingly toward a Christological doctrine of analogy that is grounded in the unity of two natures brought about by the incarnation of Jesus Christ. More fundamental than the human opposition to God in sin is the basic reality that in the incarnation of Jesus Christ creation itself has been assumed by God and justified. The human nature of Jesus Christ, as the humanity of God, becomes the basis for an analogy or continuity between God and creation that goes beyond any contradiction between the two; such is the analogy of faith. In the end, Barth speaks of human words and human lights shining forth from the one Word of God in Jesus Christ that dwells among us.

The unfolding of Barth's Christ-centered theological project can be seen, at least germinally, in the outline of the *Church Dogmatics*:

The Doctrine of the Word of God. In volume one, Barth works out a theory of the Word as divine activity present and revealed *solely* in Jesus Christ, to whom the Scriptures and the Church bear witness. It is also the occasion of his emphasizing the absolute gratuity of the Word's descent, to the degree that any attempt on man's part to prepare for or initiate this event (*Ereignis*) is impossible.

The Doctrine of God. In volume two, Barth takes up the problem of man's knowledge of God, affirming that God is known *only* in Jesus Christ. Barth consistently preserves divine initiative in the revelation in Jesus Christ, and thus denies the native power of reason to know even God's existence. Under this heading, Barth also discusses the language used in speaking of God, the mystery of predestination, i.e., Jesus Christ as the *sole* object of God's free election, and the nature of God's command over men.

The Doctrine of Creation. In volume three, Barth develops an understanding of Jesus Christ as the divine word through whom all of creation is maintained and controlled. As such, creation is transformed by God's work in the incarnation and redemption. God's reconciliation with creation is not to be seen as the completion of creation, but as an entirely new work of God, revelation transforms creation—and humanity—from without, even as God's grace works within creation.

The Doctrine of Reconciliation. In volume four, Barth treats the subject that he believes to be at the core of dogmatics and of the preaching of the Church. In it he discusses the covenant between God and man, grace and sin, and the atonement made by Jesus Christ. Barth also elaborates on the subjective appropriation of our redemption in Jesus Christ (justification) that is effected by the grace of God working in the world. Finally, Barth takes up the law of God, in so far as it punishes sin and restores us, with a view toward our eternal destiny with God.

Barth's reaction against liberalism must be judged as beneficial to Protestantism as a whole. His attempt to reinstate and systematically defend the transcendence of God as a theological principle is altogether praiseworthy; for it puts man in his true position in relation to God, that of utter receptivity.

When, however, Barth's entire system is viewed in light of Catholic tradition, some sharp divergences appear. Most evident—but perhaps only symptomatic of a more radical difficulty—is the compromise of the consistency of creation, especially of rational creatures. To give Jesus Christ the primacy in all things is quite valid. St. Paul does this. Barth, however, seems to so overstate this primacy as to make unnecessary and even impossible a true encounter between God and humanity at the level of nature. Scrutiny of his work evokes constantly the question of the reality of human receptivity to God's word.

Barth's effort to rehabilitate Protestant dogmatics, his partial success together with his evident exaggerations, points to a root difficulty in his thought. The exaltation of God's transcendent majesty by Calvin and of God's perfect freedom in the distribution of grace by Luther are fully comprehended only when complemented by the majesty of God's work in creation itself, as well as in the universality of grace. This balance Barth does not seem to have achieved in his *Church Dogmatics*.

Bibliography: Works. *Church Dogmatics*, tr. G. T. THOMSON (New York 1955–); *Dogmatics in Outline*, tr. G. T. THOMSON (New York 1949); *Evangelical Theology: An Introduction*, tr. G. FOLEY (New York, 1963). Complete list to 1955 in *Antwort: Karl Barth zum 70 Geburtstag* (Zurich 1956) 945–960. Continued list of complete works from 1956 in *Parrhesia: Karl Barth zum 80. Geburtstag* (Zürich 1966) 709–723. K. BARTH, *How I Changed My Mind,* intro. and epilogue J. D. GODSEY (Richmond, Va. 1966). G. CASALIS, *Portrait of Karl Barth* intro. and tr. R. MCA. BROWN (Garden City, N.Y. 1963). T. H. L. PARKER, *Karl Barth* (Grand Rapids, Mich. 1970). **Commentary.** G. W. BROMILEY, *Introduction to the Theology of Karl Barth* (Grand Rapids, Mich. 1979). H. U. VON BALTHASAR, *The Theology of Karl Barth*, tr. E. T. OAKES (San Francisco 1992). H. KUNG, *Justification: The Doctrine of Karl Barth and a Catholic Reflection* (New York 1964).

[J. GODSEY/M. B. SCHEPERS/J. BURNETT]

BARTHOLOMAEUS ANGLICUS

Encyclopedist (known as Bartholomew the Englishman); b. late 12th century in Oldengland, England, possi-

Folio from "De proprietatibus rerum" manuscripts, by Bartholomaeus Anglicus, c. 1400.

bly of the noble Norfolk family of Glanville. He studied at OXFORD before going to Paris (*c.* 1225–31), where he seems to have entered the French province of FRANCISCANS. He was a *baccalaureus biblicus* at the University of Paris in 1231 when Franciscan Minister General JOHN PARENTI sent him as lecturer to the Order's house of studies at Magdeburg (Salimbene, *Chronical, ad an. 1237*). Bartholomaeus' reputation as one of the great medieval encyclopedists rests on his *De proprietatibus rerum* (*On the Properties of Things*), a work devoted to the natural sciences, and intended as a tool for Biblical and theological students and preachers. It reflects the principles, methods, and scope of Oxford, where it was probably begun. Bartholomaeus, however, continued his work at Paris and finished it at Magdeburg (*c.* 1240–50). The encyclopedia is divided into 19 books: books 1–2, the spiritual substances, God and the angels; books 3–7, the mixed substances, man—the soul, the body, the members, his ages and infirmities; books 8–18, the corporeal substances; and book 19, the accidents—color, odor, taste, and liquidness. An appendix treats of numbers, weights, measures, and sounds. The books on medicine, geography, and ethnography are especially valuable. The encyclopedia has often been attributed to a mythical Bartholomaeus de Glanvilla of the 14th century.

Not always unoriginal but at times naive, the encyclopedia was largely a compilation of available scientific information, borrowed from the *Etymologies* of ISIDORE OF SEVILLE, ROBERT GROSSETESTE, ALFRED OF SARESHEL and others. The great diffusion of its manuscripts (F. Stegmüller *Repertorium biblicum medii aevi* n. 1564), early editions, and translations into French (e.g., by John Corbichon in 1372), into English (by John de TREVISA, 1495), and into Dutch and Spanish testifies to its wide usage. It also circulated in several abridged versions. The best Latin text is the Frankfurt edition of 1601. A critical edition is needed.

Other works attributed to Bartholomaeus are several scriptural writings (F. Stegmüller, *Repertorium biblicum medii aevi* nn. 1561–63) and a *Sermonum liber.* He is not the author of *Tractatus septiformis de moralitate rerum.*

Bibliography: M. C. SEYMOUR, *Bartholomaeus Anglicus and His Encyclopedia* (Brookfield, Vt. 1992).

[A. EMMEN]

BARTHOLOMEW, APOSTLE, ST.

The name Bartholomew appears in all four lists of ''the Twelve'' (Mk 3:16–19; Mt 10:2–4; Lk 6:14–16; Acts 1:13) always coupled with the name Philip (cf. Acts 1:13). Bartholomew, however, is not mentioned outside

''The Apostle Bartholomew,'' attributed to Rembrandt Harmensz van Rijn. (©Burstein Collection/CORBIS)

these lists in the New Testament, nor is he mentioned among those named as ''one of the Twelve'' in the Fourth Gospel. Instead one finds a disciple, unique to the Johannine tradition, named Nathanael. The discrepancy between the synoptic material and the Johannine material has been the cause of much speculation over the centuries. The question of Nathanael's identity has led many to explore further the identity of Bartholomew.

Among the early church fathers, including Augustine and Jerome, Nathaniel was not regarded as a member of the Twelve, but simply a disciple of Jesus. In contrast to this several early synaxaria (i.e., catalogues of saints) identified Nathanael with Simon the Zealot, a member of the Twelve. The association of these two names probably owes to the description of Simon as a Cananaean (Mk 3:18; Mt 10:4). The description of Nathanael one ''from Cana in Galilee'' (Jn 21:2) provides the basis for this identification. In the end, however, the identification of Simon with Nathanael is not well founded. The description of Simon as a Cananean (ὁ Καναναῖος) does not mean that he is from Cana, rather it is related to the Aramaic word *qan'ānā'* (''to be zealous''). The fact that the Lucan lists call Simon a Zealot (ζηλωτής — a member of a nationalistic anti-Roman party; Lk 6:15; Acts 1:13) precludes the possibility of identifying Simon with Nathanael.

Nathanael/Bartholomew The most tenable approach to the discrepancy was first posited by the ninth century Nestorian bishop Isho'dad of Merv, who identified Bartholomew with Nathanael. This solution, though not without its problems, has been adopted by most scholars today. Two factors seem to support this. First, the name Bartholomew in Aramaic is patronymic (*Bar-Talmai* means "son of Tholmai," see Josh 15:14 and Jos. *Ant.* 20.1.1§5) while Nathanael is a surname. Many biblical scholars today believe that the surname was preserved in the Johannine tradition, while the family name was preserved in the synoptic tradition. Second, Bartholomew is closely associated with Philip in the synoptic lists of the Twelve, while the name of Nathanael is closely associated with Philip in one narrative portion of the Fourth Gospel. Any theological or biographical details about Nathanael/Bartholomew comes to us from the Fourth Gospel.

In the Fourth Gospel Nathanael serves as a symbol of Israel coming to God. In Jn 1:35–51, the call of the first disciples, Nathanael makes his only appearance in the NT. Jn 1:3542 narrates the encounter between Andrew and Jesus, then after the account of the call of Andrew and Simon Peter there is the account in which Philip brings Nathaniel to Jesus. As a result of this, Nathanael acknowledges the messianic identity of Jesus. In this narrative Jesus describes Nathanael as "a true Israelite in whom there is no guile" (δόλος – deceit). This identification links Nathanael to the description of Jacob in Gn 27:35 and is complemented by the reference to Gn 28:12 in Jn 1:51. Nathanael's doubt regarding Jesus calls to mind the behavior of "the Jews" throughout the rest of the gospel. However, Nathanael's lack of "guile" or deceit makes him different for "the Jews" who come to Jesus only to seek his destruction. Nathanael's character is punctuated by his willingness to approach Jesus and see the one to whom Philip has borne witness. Nathanael's initial doubt also links him to the story of Thomas in Jn 20:24–29. The two accounts form a literary *inclusio* that places emphasis on the theme of testimony (both Nathanael and Thomas express doubt when presented with testimony regarding Jesus) as well as the theme of christology (both Nathanael and Thomas make faith proclamations regarding Jesus identity).

Early Christian tradition states that Bartholomew preached the gospel in India (Eusebius) and then Armenia where he was martyred (see *the Martyrdom of Bartholomew*). Several apocryphal works have been attributed to Bartholomew including "The Questions of Bartholomew," a work which probably represents a recession of the *Gospel of Bartholomew* mentioned by Jerome in his commentary on Matthew, and also mentioned by Bede. There also exist fragments of a Coptic work called *The Book of the Resurrection of Christ by Bartholomew the Apostle* which purports to be the record of the visions enjoyed by Bartholomew concerning the events surrounding Jesus' Resurrection.

Feast: Aug. 24.

Bibliography: R. E. BROWN, *The Gospel According to John,* 2 v. (Garden City, NJ 1966–1970). U. HOLZMEISTER, "Nathanael fuitne idem ac S. Bartholomeus Apostolus," *Biblica* 21(1940):28–39. E. LEIDIG, "Nathanael, ein Sohn des Tholomäus," *Theologische Zeitschrift* 36 (1980): 374–5. J. P. MEIER, "The Circle of the Twelve: Did it Exist During Jesus' Public Ministry?" *Journal of Biblical Literature* 116 (1997): 635–72.

[C. MCMAHON]

BARTHOLOMEW OF BRAGA, VEN.

Dominican theologian and archbishop of Braga; b. Lisbon, May 3, 1514; d. Viana, July 16, 1590. Though his surname was Fernandez, he was called Bartholomeus de Martyribus after the church of his baptism, S. Maria de Martyribus. He became a Dominican friar on Nov. 11, 1528; after the completion of his studies, he taught philosophy and then theology for 20 years. In 1558, against his inclination and at the wish of his provincial, Luis of Granada, he accepted the appointment to the archiepiscopal see of Braga. He was greatly influential in the reform activity of the Council of Trent in the sessions from 1562 to 1563. He promulgated the conciliar decrees and interpreted them strictly in his provincial council of 1566. He started a seminary in his palace, instituted chairs of moral theology in Braga and Viana do Castelo, composed a catechism, preached assiduously, and dedicated much time to the visitation of his nearly 1,300 parishes. Worn out from this pastoral activity, he resigned his bishopric in 1582 and retired to the Dominican priory of Viana do Castelo. Among his more than 30 works are the *Catecismo ou doutrina cristã* (1564), *Stimulus pastorum* (1565), and *Compendium spiritualis doctrinae* (1582).

Bibliography: P. DAMINO, *Il contributo teologico di Bartolomeo dé Martiri al Concilio di Trento* (Rome 1962). L. SOUSA, *Vida de D. Fr. Bartolomeu dos Mártires*, 3 v. (Lisbon 1946). A. WALZ, *Lexikon für Theologie und Kirche,* ed. J. HOFER and K. RAHNER, 10 v. (2d, new ed. Freiburg 1957–65) 2:12–13. F. DE ALMEIDA, *Dictionnaire d'histoire et de géographie ecclésiastiques,* ed. A. BAUDRILLART (Paris 1912–) 6:983–984.

[R. DE ALMEIDA ROLO]

BARTHOLOMEW OF BRESCIA

Canonist; b. second half of the 12th century; d. 1258. He studied Roman law and Canon Law in Bologna under

Hugolinus de Presbyteris and Tancred, and taught Canon Law there from *c.* 1234. That he did not have a creative mind is best demonstrated by his works, which are all more or less a revision of the works of other authors. He is important as a transmitter of traditional material and as a learned popularizer.

His *Casus Decretorum* was a revision of the work of the same name by Benencasa Aretinus; Bartholomew composed this work while still a student. It was printed in 1505 with the *Glossa ordinaria* of the Decretum of Gratian. *Historiae super libro Decretorum* was an early revision of a collection of the description of biblical events most frequently encountered in the glossaries on the Decretum. The author of the original is unknown. From 1505 the *Historiae* were printed also with the *Glossa ordinaria Brocarda*, the revision of a work of the same name by Damasus Ungarus undertaken shortly after 1234, which has been printed frequently. *Ordo iudiciarius*, a revision of a work of the same name by Tancred, was finished after Tancred's death (1236). *Quaestiones veneriales* and *dominicales*, written between 1234 and 1241, are now considered to be a revision of sources already in extensive circulation and present in other collections. *Repertorium Decreti,* a *Summarium* of the Decretum, is attributed by many to Bartholomew, but it is not known for certain to be his work.

The *Glossa ordinaria Decreti,* Bartholomew's chief work, entitles him to a place in the history of Canon Law literature; it is a revision of the work of JOANNES TEUTONICUS and was published between 1240 and 1245. In the prologue, Bartholomew writes, "Quoniam novis supervenientibus causis novis est remediis succurrendum . . . ," stating the reason for and essence of the revision: a recasting of the citations from the *Compilationes antiquae* to harmonize them with the Decretals of GREGORY IX, an insertion of omitted citations and of later decretals, and expansions and corrections of the doctrines of Joannes. This version of the *GLOSSA ORDINARIA* was appended to most manuscripts of the Decretum. When printed editions began to be published, they were often printed along with the text of the Decretum in the form of a marginal gloss.

Bibliography: J. F. VON SCHULTE, *Die Geschichte der Quellen und der Literatur des kanonischen Rechts* (Stuttgart 1875–1810) 2:83–88. S. KUTTNER, *Repertorium der Kanonistik* (Rome 1937). S. KUTTNER, "Bernardus Compostellanus Antiquus," *Traditio* 1 (1943) 292. A. VAN HOVE, *Commentarium Lovaniense in Codicem iuris Canonici.* (2d. ed. 1945) v. 1, see index. G. FRANSEN, "Tribunaux ecclésiastiques et langue vulgaire d'après les 'Quaestiones' des canonistes," *Ephemerides theologicae Lovanienses* 40 (1964) 409–412. G. LE BRAS, *Dictionnaire de droit canonique*, 7 v. (Paris 1935–65) 2:216–217. J. WENNER, *Dictionnaire d'histoire et de géographie ecclésiastiques* (Paris 1912—) 6:984–985. A. M. STICKLER, *Lexikon für Theologie und Kirche*, 10 v. (Freiburg 1957–65) 2:11.

[A. M. STICKLER]

BARTHOLOMEW OF EXETER

Bishop of Exeter, English canonist; b. Diocese of Coutances (Normandy) *c.* 1110; d. Dec. 15, 1184. An eminent master at Paris in the years 1140 to 1142, Bartholomew migrated to England, became a member of Archbishop THEOBALD'S *familia* at Canterbury for a while, and was archdeacon of Exeter by 1155. His rising influence was revealed at the London Synod of 1159 where he supported Pope ALEXANDER III against his schismatic rival. A friend of JOHN OF SALISBURY and later of ROGER OF WORCESTER, as well as Theobald's intimate, Bartholomew was the archbishop's choice for the EXETER SEE following the death of Robert Warelwast in March of 1160. Bartholomew was finally elected bishop of Exeter between February and April of 1161, after a protracted contest with a less worthy choice of the king; and he was consecrated a short time after Theobald's death on April 18, 1161.

A supporter in principle of Thomas BECKET in the archbishop's conflict with King HENRY II, Bartholomew nevertheless favored restraint and moderation in the crisis of 1164 (*see* CLARENDON, CONSTITUTIONS OF). Courted, and occasionally censured by both sides, he moved decisively to Becket's cause during the latter's exile, remained in correspondence with the exiled party, withheld himself from hostile actions, and finally withdrew in 1169 from public involvement in the affair. He retained Becket's favor to the end and played a leading and conciliatory role in the settlement following Becket's death in 1170 and after the agreement at AVRANCHES IN 1172.

Thereafter the central focus of Bartholomew's actions turned to pastoral and judicial functions. Highly esteemed by Alexander III, he received numerous commissions as papal judge-delegate, sometimes jointly with Roger of Worcester, these two being Alexander's *duo luminaria* of the English Church. Together with BALDWIN (later of Canterbury), Roger, and Abp. RICHARD OF CANTERBURY, he promoted the development of decretal law and codification and of judge-delegate jurisdiction from the mid-1170s. He was present at Archbishop Richard's council at Westminster in 1175, but not at the LATERAN COUNCIL III OF 1179. A scholar of versatility and wide reputation, and a bishop of spirituality and high moral integrity, Bartholomew composed a *Penitentiale,* the *De libero arbitrio,* the *Dialogus contra Judaeos,* and various sermons.

Bibliography: A. MOREY, *Bartholomew of Exeter: Bishop and Canonist* (Cambridge, Eng. 1937). D. KNOWLES, *The Episcopal Colleagues of Archbishop Thomas Becket* (Cambridge, Eng. 1951) 27–28, 102–104. C. DUGGAN, *Twelfth-Century Decretal Collections and Their Importance in English History* (London 1963).

[C. DUGGAN]

BARTHOLOMEW OF LUCCA

Called also Ptolomeo, Tolomeo, and de Fiadonibus, Dominican bishop of Torcello, historian and theologian; b. Lucca, Italy, *c.* 1236; d. Torcello (near Venice), 1327. He was born of a middle-class family and became a DOMINICAN IN LUCCA. A student and associate of THOMAS AQUINAS from 1261 to 1268, Bartholomew traveled with him and lived with him in Naples during the last year of Thomas's life. In the 1280s and 1290s Bartholomew was prior of various houses in Tuscany and was occupied with teaching and preaching. From 1309 to 1319 he was almost continuously at the papal court in Avignon (*see* AVIGNON PAPACY) engaged in research and writing, and, some think, acting as papal librarian. Appointed bishop of Torcello in 1318, he came into conflict with the patriarch of Grado, who imprisoned him. He was released on orders of Pope JOHN XXII. At Avignon in March of 1323, he was acquitted of all guilt; it is thought he was there for the canonization of Aquinas (July of 1323). He died in Torcello, aged 91 years.

His works include the following: *Determinatio compendiosa* (Turin 1924), written in 1280, a study on the limits of imperial jurisdiction in Italy; *Annales* (*Scriptores rerum Germanicarum. New Series.* 8), finished in 1307, a description of main events from 1061 to 1303; *Historia ecclesiastica* (L. A. Muratori, *Rerum Italicarum scriptores* 11:740–1242), a work in 24 books on the history of the Church from the birth of Christ to 1314, books 22 and 23 being one of the most important sources for the life of St. Thomas [tr. K. Foster, *The Life of St. Thomas* (Baltimore 1959)]; *Exaemeron* [ed. P. Masetti (Siena 1880)], a work showing his wide acquaintance with the natural science of his day; *Tractatus de jurisdictione ecclesiae super regnum Siciliae et Apuliae* (Mansi, *Miscellanea* 1). The *Historia tripartita* to which Bartholomew often referred is not extant. The completion of St. Thomas's *De regimine principum,* with which he used to be credited, is now questioned [I. T. Eschmann, *On Kingship* (Toronto 1949) ix–xxv].

Bibliography: J. QUÉTIF and J. ECHARD, *Scriptores Ordinis Praedicatorum* (Paris 1719–1723) 1:541. I. TAURISANO, *I Domenicani in Lucca* (Lucca 1914) 44–77; ed., *S. Tommaso d'Aquino, O.P.: Miscellanea storico-artistica* (Rome 1924) 163–170. Introduction, "Life and Works," in *Die Annalen des Tholomeus von Lucca*, ed. B. SCHMEIDLER (2d ed. *Scriptores rerum Germanicarum. New Series.* 8; Berlin 1955).

[P. F. MULHERN]

BARTHOLOMEW OF MARMOUTIER, ST.

Benedictine priest and abbot of MARMOUTIER near Tours from 1063 until his death on Feb. 24, 1084. He successfully resisted the claims of Geoffrey the Bearded, count of Touraine and Anjou, to spiritual and temporal dominion over the monastery. He then so improved the discipline at Marmoutier that lay and ecclesiastical reformers sought monks from his abbey to reform old monasteries and to found new ones. When WILLIAM I, the Conqueror, founded BATTLE ABBEY in thanksgiving for his victory at Hastings, he sought and received monks from Bartholomew's house. Under Bartholomew's rule, Marmoutier thus acquired several churches and monasteries in France and in England. His name was included in many medieval Benedictine martyrologies, but no cult in his honor has ever been approved.

Bibliography: P. CALENDINI, *Dictionnarie d'histoire et de géographie ecclésiastiques* (Paris 1912), 6:1014–15.

[J. C. MOORE]

BARTHOLOMEW OF ROME

Religious reformer, eminent preacher; b. Campo de' Fiori, Rome; d. monastery of San Benedetto Po, Mantua, 1430. He promoted religious reform in the territory of Venice and was among the principal members of the group that reformed the monastery of Santa Maria di Fregionaia near Lucca. Out of this movement emerged the Congregation of Canons Regular of St. John Lateran (*see* CANONS REGULAR OF ST. AUGUSTINE). He was elected prior by his companions in 1403 and held the office again from August 1407 to 1408. He seems not to have held any office permanently, but rather to have continued to carry on his preaching career. At his death he had a reputation for sanctity. He was not, as some historians have believed, a member of the Colonna family, nor was he the founder of the Congregation of St. George in Alga near Venice, established later by Pope Clement IX in 1668.

Bibliography: N. WIDLOECHER, *La congregazione dei canonici regolari Lateranensi* (Gubbio 1929). K. EGGER, *Für Gottes Haus und Herde* (Bolzano 1952) 17–22.

[R. H. TRAME]

BARTHOLOMEW OF SAN CONCORDIO (OF PISA)

Dominican theologian; b. San Concordio near Pisa, 1262; d. June 11, 1347, Pisa, Italy. One of the most erudite men of his time, a great preacher and writer, he lectured at Lucca, Florence, and Pisa. Of his major works, *De documentis antiquorum* is a collection of opinions by classical and ecclesiastical authors; his own translation, *Ammaestramenti degli antichi,* is a Tuscan classic. His

Summa de Casibus Conscientiae was very widely used during the 14th and 15th centuries. Besides a compendium of moral theology and a series of Lenten sermons, he also wrote treatises on the virtues and vices, on Latin pronunciation and orthography, and on the tragedies of Virgil and Seneca.

Bibliography: A. STEFANUCCI ALA, *Sulla vita e sulle opere di frate Bartolomeo da San Concordio* (Rome 1838). P. MANDONNET, *Dictionnaire de théologie catholique* (Paris 1903–1950) 2:435–436.

[J. R. COONEY]

BARTHOLOMEW OF SIMERI, ST.

Abbot and organizer of Basilian monasticism in southern Italy; b. Simeri, Calabria, Italy, mid-eleventh century; d. Rossano, Italy, Aug. 19, 1130. In his earliest youth, impelled by an urge to leave the world, Bartholomew became a disciple of the hermit Cyril. He built his first monastery in the mountains near ROSSANO with the help of the distinguished Christodoulos, possibly a converted Saracen and later an emir of SICILY, and also, through him, with the help of Count ROGER OF SICILY, brother of ROBERT GUISCARD, and other Norman barons. This monastery of Santa Maria Odigitria (she who shows the way), built toward the close of the eleventh century and before the death of Roger in 1101, was later called the Patirion to honor the saintly founder (Πατήρ); it became an important center of BASILIAN MONASTICISM in Calabria and Sicily.

After 1104, having received a charter for his foundation from Count Roger II, Bartholomew was ordained by the bishop of Belcastro, and in 1105 he journeyed to Rome to obtain from Pope PASCHAL II confirmation of immunity for his monastery. There is some evidence that Bartholomew visited Constantinople to obtain gifts of ICONS, liturgical books, and sacred vessels from Emperor ALEXIUS I COMNENUS and Empress Irene, as well as from Basil Kalimeris, a high official of the empire. The latter, as patron of the monastery of St. Basil the Great on Mount ATHOS, charged Bartholomew with the task of reforming that institution. After his return to Italy, Bartholomew founded a second monastery, San Salvatore de Messina, with 12 monks sent from Santa Maria of Rossano. His cult seems to have spread through the Basilian monasteries of southern Italy soon after his death.

Feast: Aug. 19.

Bibliography: *Acta Sanctae Sedis* Sept. 8:792–826. L. BRÉHIER, *Dictionnaire d'histoire et de géographie ecclésiastiques*, ed. A. BAUDRILLART et al. (Paris 1912) 6:968–970. P. BATIFFOL, "L'Archive du Saint-Sauveur de Messine," *Revue des questions historiques* 42 (1887) 555–567; *L'Abbaye de Rossano* (Paris 1891) 1–10. M. SCADUTO, *Il monachismo basiliano nella Sicilia medievale* (Rome 1947).

[P. L. HUG]

BARTHOLOMEW OF TRENT

Dominican hagiographer; b. Trent; d. Trent, *c.* 1251. He traveled widely in Italy (e.g., he was present at the first translation of St. Dominic's body, 1233) and visited France and Germany. Esteemed for piety and learning, he was also politically shrewd and was often at the papal and imperial courts. INNOCENT IV entrusted him with at least one peace mission to Frederick II. His chief work, the *Liber epilogorum* (1245–51), a series of concise, informative biographies of saints interlarded with ascetical and moral reflections, inaugurated a new type of hagiographic literature, intended not for liturgical use but to nourish the piety of the reader and to provide illustrative material for preachers. A *Summa theologica adversus sui temporis haereses* has also been ascribed to him.

Bibliography: J. QUÉTIF and J. ÉCHARD, *Scriptores Ordinis Praedicatorum* (New York 1959) 1:110. G. ABATE, "Il *Liber epilogorum* di fra Bartolomeo da Trento, O.P.," *Miscellanea Pio Paschini,* 2 v. (Rome 1948–49) 1:269–292.

[F. C. RYAN]

BARTHOLOMEW OF URBINO

Augustinian bishop, compiler of patristic compendia; d. 1350. He served the last three years of his life as bishop of his native city of Urbino. In papal documents he is called Bartholomeus Hominis de Taiuti (Ditaiuti or Dio ti aiuti), of which the name given by certain Augustinian historians, Bartholomeus Simonis de Carusis, may be a corruption. He was a student at the universities of BOLOGNA and PARIS and after 1321 was a teacher at Bologna, where no doubt he began his friendship with a fellow teacher, the canonist JOANNES ANDREAE. It was there, too, that he must have first met PETRARCH. From Petrarch's pen there is a letter to Bartholomew (*Fam.* 8.6), probably dating from 1348 or 1349, forwarding two alternate sets of verses for the embellishment of the Augustinian's principal work. This opus by Bartholomew, the widely used and still valuable *Milleloquium veritatis s. Augustini* (Lyons 1555), suggested by the *Hieronymianus* of Joannes Andreae, reveals in its compiler a knowledge of the writings of St. AUGUSTINE probably unmatched in his time. Dedicated to CLEMENT VI, the work is an orderly assembly of perhaps 15,000 citations from Augustine's works, under about 1,000 subject headings (Abel-Zizania). A *Distinctio librorum,* in which Bartholomew lists and identifies the letters (about 190), the books, and more than 600 sermons from which he quotes, all apparently consulted directly *in originali,* places Bartholomew among the prehumanist discoverers of Latin manuscripts. Similarly arranged is a less widely dispersed *Milleloquium Sancti Ambrosii* (Lyons 1556). Little is certain about Bartholomew's other writings.

Bibliography: R. ARBESMANN, ''Der Augustinereremitenorden und der Beginn der humanistischen Bewegung,'' first pt., in *Augustiniana* 14 (1964) 277–296; entire work to appear also as monograph. B. M. PEEBLES, ''The Verse Embellishments of the *Milleloquium Sancti Augustini,*'' *Traditio* 10 (1954) 555–566. G. POZZI, ''Il Vat. Lat. 479 ed. altri codici annotati da Roberto de' Bardi,'' *Miscellanea del Centro di studi medievali* 2 (1958) 142–145. A. ZUMKELLER, ''Manuskripte von Werken der Autoren des Augustiner-Eremitenordens in mitteleuropäischen Bibliotheken,'' *Augustiniana* 172–174; incomplete list of MSS of the two *Milleloquia,* also of a doubtful *De pugna spirituali.* F. DOLBEAU, ''Un sermon inédit de S. Augustin sur la santé corporelle, partiellement cité chez Barthélemy d'Urbino,'' *Revue des études augustiniennes* 40 (1994).

[B. M. PEEBLES]

BARTHOLOMEW OF VICENZA, BL.

Bishop, preacher, spiritual writer; b. *c.* 1200; d. 1270 at Vicenza (Breganze), Italy. Bartholomew was an active Dominican preacher, a disputant with heretics, and a civil peacemaker. In 1233 he founded the Militia of Jesus Christ for knights. He served as regent of the theological faculty at the papal Curia before becoming bishop of Limassol, Cyprus, in 1252. He was transferred to Vicenza in 1255. While serving as papal envoy to England and France, he received from LOUIS IX a thorn from the reputed CROWN OF THORNS. ''An Exposition of the Canticle of Canticles'' and ''The Search for Divine Love'' are his principal works, though none of his writings are published. His theology is affective rather than speculative, having been derived from RICHARD OF ST. VICTOR and PSEUDO-DIONYSIUS. His cult was approved in 1793.

Feast: Oct. 23.

Bibliography: *Année Dominicaine.* Oct. 2 (1902) 671–676. T. KÄPPELI, ''Der literarische Nachlass des sel. Bartholomäus von Vicenza,'' *Mélanges Auguste Pelzer* (Louvain 1947) 275–301. F. STEGSMÜLLER, *Repertorium biblicum medii aevi* 7 v. (Madrid 1949–61) 2:1576.

[J. F. HINNEBUSCH]

BARTHOLOMITES

Armenian monks from Tarsus who sought refuge in Italy when their land was invaded by the Egyptian sultan in 1296. This first group landed in 1307 in Genoa, where the church of St. Bartholomew was built for them, hence the name Bartholomites. Others of these persecuted monks soon followed, establishing themselves in Parma, Siena, Florence, Bologna, and Milan. They observed the Rule of St. Basil and the ARMENIAN liturgy. Soon they abandoned their national traditions and adopted the Roman liturgy, the Rule of St. Augustine, and a habit similar to that of the Dominicans. Innocent VI approved this change in 1356 and confirmed the union of the monasteries, previously autonomous, into one congregation. Boniface IX granted the congregation the privileges of the Dominican Order but prohibited it from joining any other orders, excepting that of the Carthusians. Superior generals, formerly elected for life, were ordered by Sixtus IV to have three-year terms. For about two centuries this Armenian congregation flourished; then regular observance declined. Their membership decreased until many of their houses had to be closed. In the last half of the 17th century, Innocent X authorized members either to enter another religious order or to become secularized, assuring the latter of a pension. In 1650 he suppressed the congregation, putting its houses and revenues to new uses. The congregation had several renowned preachers, such as Cherubini Cerebelloni of Genoa and Paul Costa of Milan. Among its celebrated writers was Gregori Bitio, who wrote the history of the order. In their church of St. Bartholomew in Genoa the celebrated portrait of Christ, ''The Holy Face of Edessa,'' is still preserved. The Armenian Bartholomites are not to be confused with the religious community of the same name founded in Bavaria in the 17th century by Bartholomew Holzhauser.

Bibliography: P. HÉLYOT, *Histoire des ordres monastiques,* 8 v. (Paris 1714–19) 1:243–248. M. VAN DEN OUDENRIJN, ''Les Constitutions des Frères arméniens de S. Basile en Italie,'' *Orientalia Christiania Anaectal* 126 (1946) 7–117; *Lexikon für Theologie und Kirche,* ed. J. HOFER and K. RAHNER (Freiburg 1957–65) 2:16.

[C. LYNCH]

BARTÓK, BÉLA

Composer, pianist, and ethnomusicologist; b. Nagyszentmiklós (now Romania), March 25, 1881; d. New York, N.Y., Sept. 26, 1945. After studying at the Royal Hungarian Academy of Music in Budapest, he became the principal piano teacher there (1907–34), simultaneously pursuing an international career as concert pianist. In 1905 he began collecting and systematizing Hungarian peasant music (of which little was then known) and subsequently published an important series of ethnomusicological studies of the music of Hungarians, Romanians, Slovakians, Turks, and North African

Arabs. His early compositions were strongly influenced by Brahms, Liszt, and Richard Strauss, but with the discovery of an authentic Magyar folk music he developed a highly personal style based upon its rhythmic and melodic elements, while not ignoring the influence of other folk music or that of Stravinsky, Schoenberg, and the French Impressionists. His works include six remarkable string quartets; three piano concertos; two violin concertos; an opera, *Duke Bluebeard's Castle;* two ballets; several important works for orchestra (among them the *Dance Suite; Music for Strings, Percussion, and Celesta;* and *Concerto for Orchestra*); the *Cantata Profana* for chorus, soli, and orchestra; and *Mikrokosmos,* a set of 153 didactic piano pieces providing a comprehensive introduction to 20th-century styles. His influence upon younger composers in Hungary, Western Europe, and America has been considerable.

Bartók was occupied at times with problems of philosophy and theology and in 1907 declared himself an atheist. In 1919, however, he and his family joined the First Unitarian Church in Budapest, where he was musical adviser, especially in compilation of the Hungarian Unitarian hymn book. In the U.S., where he had settled in 1940, he held an appointment for folk-song research and appeared frequently in concert. His autobiography, correspondence, and many writings on music (all edited by J. Demény) have been published in Budapest but are not yet translated.

Bibliography: *Hungarian Folk Music,* tr. M. D. CALVOCORESSI (London 1931). H. STEVENS, *The Life and Music of Béla Bartók* (rev. ed. New York 1964), extensive bibliog. D. BARTHA, *Die Musik in Geschichte und Gegenwart,* ed. F. BLUME (Kassel-Basel 1949–) 1:1345–50. N. SLONIMSKY, ed., *Baker's Biographical Dictionary of Musicians* (5th ed. New York 1958) 93–94. B. SZABOLCSI, *Bela Bartok: His Life in Pictures* (New York 1964). J. BOUËT and B. LORTAT-JACOB, ''Quatre-vingts ans après Bartók: pratiques de terrain en Roumanie,'' *Revue de Musicologie,* 81 (1995) 5–24. M. GILLIES, ed. *The Bartók Companion* (Boston 1993); ''Bartók and Boosey and Hawkes: The European Years,'' *Tempo,* 200 (1997) 4–7; ''Bartók and Boosey and Hawkes: The American Years,'' *Tempo,* 205 (1998) 8–11. E. GOLLIN, ''Transformational Techniques in Bartók's Etude op. 18, no. 2,'' *Theory and Practice,* 20 (1995) 13–30. E. LENDVAI, ''Duality and Synthesis in the Music of Béla Bartók (Part One),'' *Hungarian Music Quarterly,* 5/1 (1994) 5–14; ''Duality and Synthesis in the Music of Béla Bartók (Part Two),'' *Hungarian Music Quarterly,* 5/2 (1994) 8–16. V. RÜLKE, ''Bartóks Wende zur Atonalität: Die *Études* op. 18,'' *Archiv Für Musikwissenschaft,* 57 (2000) 240–263. D. E. SCHNEIDER, ''A Context for Béla Bartók on the Eve of World War II: The Violin Concerto (1938),'' *Repercussions,* 5 (1996) 21–68. L. SOMFAI, *Béla Bartók: Composition, Concepts, and Autograph Sources* (Los Angeles 1996).

[H. STEVENS]

Béla Bartók.

BARTOLO OF SASSOFERRATO

One of the most important jurists of the later Middle Ages; b. Sassoferrato, 1313; d. Perugia, 1357. He studied law under Cinus at Perugia and under James of Belvisio at Bologna, where he received his doctorate of law in 1334. After further private study, he became professor of law at Pisa in 1339, and later at Perugia, where he remained until his death. He is most famous for developing a method of applying Roman law to contemporary problems by use of the scholastic method. A group of jurists who followed his method were known as ''Bartolists.'' He wrote many important works, the most famous being a commentary on the Code of Justinian.

Bibliography: B. KURTSCHEID, ''Bartoli de Saxoferrato, vita, opera, momentum, influxus,'' *Apollinaris* 11 (1938) 110–117. A. VAN HOVE, *Commentarium Lovaniense in Codicem iuris canonici 1* (Mechlin 1945) 1:520–523. C. N. WOOLF, *Bartolus of Sassoferrato: His Position in the History of Medieval Political Thought* (Cambridge, Eng. 1913).

[J. M. BUCKLEY]

BARTOLOCCI, GIULIO

Eminent Hebraist; b. Celano, in the Abruzzi, April 1, 1613; d. Rome, Oct. 20, 1687. He made his profession as a Cistercian monk of the Italian congregation of the Feuillants (reformed Bernadines) at the monastery of St. Pudentiana in Rome. He studied theology at Mondovi and Turin, did extensive research in Jewish literature in the libraries of Italy, and taught Hebrew at Rome. He was named *Scriptor Hebraicus* at the Vatican Library, where he was assisted by convert from Judaism Jehudah JONAH BEN JISHAQ. He was appointed a consulter to the Congregation of the Index, served as superior of Cistercian houses in Brisighella and Rome, presided at their general chapter, was visitor for the Roman province, and became titular abbot of San Sebastiano ad Catacumbas. His chief work was the *Bibliotheca magna rabbinica de scriptoribus et scriptis hebraicis,* which appeared in four volumes in 1675, 1678 (dedicated to Pope Innocent XI), 1683, and 1694 (edited posthumously by his pupil Carlo Imbonati). Despite its shortcomings, this vast account of Jewish writers and literature was valued greatly by later compilers. Bartolocci's unpublished works include *Liber Tobiae,* a Hebrew version with interlinear Latin translation; *Defensio Christiana;* and *Collectanea de Trinitate, Messiae divinitate ac gentium vocatione.*

Bibliography: J. M. CANIVEZ, *Dictionnaire d'histoire et de géographie ecclésiastiques* (Paris 1912—) 6:1050–51. *Encyclopaedia Judaica: Das Judentum in Geschichte und Gegenwart* (Berlin 1928–34) 3:1102–03. C. J. MOROZZO, *Cistercii reflorescentis . . . chronologica historia* (Turin 1690) 123. J. OLIVIERI, *Dictionnaire de la Bible* (Paris 1895–1912) 1.2:1474–75. K. SPAHR, *Lexikon für Theologie und Kirche* (Freiburg 1957–65) 2:17–18.

[C. BERNAS]

BARTON, ELIZABETH

"The Nun of Kent"; b. *c.* 1506; d. London, April 20, 1534. In 1525 Elizabeth, a servant in the Aldington, Kent, household of Thomas Cobb, steward of William Warham, Archbishop of Canterbury, suffered an illness that gave rise to trances, religious ecstasies, and prophecies. A diocesan commission headed by Edward Bocking, OSB, examined her and pronounced her condition of divine origin. The "servant girl who spoke to angels" soon received much attention and renown. Removed to Saint Sepulchre Priory near Canterbury, Elizabeth became a nun and continued her warnings and prophecies, which found credence with high and low. Bocking and his fellow monks appear to have used her to revive pious devotions and to weaken heretical teachings. Miracles were attributed to her despite the skeptical attitudes of Thomas More and of the king himself. During the royal divorce proceedings, the nun more plainly admonished the king and his sympathizers. Elizabeth seems to have convinced Warham, her patron, and to have swayed even Wolsey to oppose the king's insistence on marrying Anne Boleyn. John Fisher, Bishop of Rochester, the Marchioness of Exeter, the Countess of Salisbury, and other supporters of Queen Catherine, consulted Elizabeth from 1528 to 1532, and she became a champion of Henry's opposition. Catherine never consulted Elizabeth. Elizabeth announced that Henry would die if he remarried and that he had forfeited his throne before God. In 1533 Thomas Cranmer succeeded to the See of Canterbury, and with Thomas Cromwell, used the nun to ensnare the enemies of Henrician reform. Cranmer skillfully extorted a confession in which Elizabeth admitted deceit and duplicity. Denounced as a fraud, Elizabeth, with a number of others, More and Fisher included, was eventually condemned by a bill of attainder. More's earlier skepticism won his exclusion from the action, but the nun and six others were condemned to death. Fisher and five others were imprisoned and their goods confiscated. Elizabeth was executed at Tyburn, publicly confessing her guilt and pride. Cromwell's methods undoubtedly raise some question as to the validity of the charges made by him. On the other hand, it seems clear that Elizabeth was exploited by Bocking and others for religious and possibly political reasons.

Bibliography: P. HUGHES, *The Reformation in England.* S. LEE, *The Dictionary of National Biography from the Earliest Times to 1900* (London 1885–1900) 1:1263–66. G. MATTINGLY, *Catherine of Aragon* (Boston 1941).

[P. S. MCGARRY]

BARUCH

Son of Nerias, friend and secretary of the Prophet Jeremiah. Jeremiah dictated several of his oracles to Baruch (Heb. *bārûk,* blessed, probably a shortened form of *b^erûkyâ,* blessed of Yahweh), who wrote them on a scroll and then read them before the people in the Temple and later before the authorities; when King Jehoiakim had heard the oracles, he burned the scroll, and Baruch wrote them down a second time at Jeremiah's dictation (Jer 36.4–32). Because of Baruch's loyalty, special blessings were promised to him by Jeremiah (Jer 45.1–5). After the fall of Jerusalem, the Jewish refugees took Jeremiah and Baruch along with them to Egypt (Jer 43.6). According to a tradition recounted by St. Jerome, Baruch died there. He is important not only because he served Jeremiah, but also because he is responsible for the biographical portions of that Prophet's book. Later generations credited him with the deuterocanonical Book of BARUCH and with two apocryphal books, the Syriac Apocalypse of Baruch and the Greek Apocalypse of Baruch.

Bibliography: *Encyclopedic Dictionary of the Bible,* tr. and adap. L. HARTMAN (New York 1963) 210–211. V. HAMP, *Lexikon* *für Theologie und Kirche*, ed. J. HOFER and K. RAHNER (Freiberg 1957–65) 2: 18–19. G. VON RAD, *Theologie des Alten Testaments,* 2 v. (Göttingen 1957–60) 2:218–220, Eng. tr. D. STALKER (New York 1962–). C. SCHEDL, *Geschichte des Alten Testament* (Innsbruck 1956–) 4:395–402.

[L. A. IRANYI]

BARUCH, BOOK OF

A deuterocanonical book of the OT whose title (Bar 1.1–2) attributes it to BARUCH, the erstwhile secretary of Jeremiah (Jer 36.4), writing in Babylon during the Exile.

Authorship, Unity, and Contents. It seems established, on the basis of a number of indications, that Baruch was not the author of this book: (1) in spite of the authority that the name of Baruch would have given to it, the book was never taken into the Hebrew Canon (*see* CANON, BIBLICAL) or even preserved in Hebrew, if it ever existed in the language; (2) there are good grounds for believing that parts of it were composed in Hebrew, but other parts were probably composed in Greek (see below); (3) the book is not a unified prophetic composition, but a combination of different literary forms; (4) finally, many of the historical inaccuracies would be incomprehensible if they came from an author contemporary with the events, as Baruch was. For example, the introduction (1.1–14) supposes that the Temple was still standing and the liturgy was performed in it, while, in fact, the Temple was in ruins; the incorrect supposition that BELSASSAR (BEL-SHAR-USUR) was the son of Nabuchodonosor is found (Bar 1.11–12), perhaps under the influence of Dn 5.2; and Jechonia is placed in the crowd of Jewish exiles (Bar 1.3), although at this time he was really in prison.

The book is, in fact, an artful combination of pieces of diverse origin. The first section (1.1–14) is an edifying unhistorical narrative intended to introduce the book as reading for the Feast of BOOTHS; then follows a penitential prayer placed in the mouths of the exiles (1.15–3.8), similar to the liturgy found in Neh 9.5–38 and based in part (1.15–2.19) on Dn 9.4–19; the third section (Bar 3.9–4.4), sapiential in character, is a Wisdom hymn; and the fourth section (4.5–5.9) is an anthology of poems in which Jerusalem speaks to her children (4.5–29), and her children speak to her (4.30–5.9). Note that 5.5–9 depends on Psalm of Solomon 11.2–7. *See* BIBLE, III (CANON). For details on ch. 6, appended to Baruch in the Vulgate but separate in the Septuagint, *see* JEREMIAH, LETTER OF.

Language and Time of Composition. While conservative opinion still retained Baruch as the author, it had to insist that the book was written in Hebrew and that its original was lost. Modern opinion (e.g., B. N. Wambacq), however, holds that the different parts of the book were written in different languages. It is suggested that 1.1–14 was written in Greek; 1.15–3.8, in Hebrew; 3.9–4.4, possibly in Hebrew but more likely in Greek; and 4.5–5.9, very probably in Greek.

It is most likely that the different parts of the book were written at different times. The following is the reconstruction suggested by Wambacq: 1.15–3.8 was written between 165 B.C. (about the time of the composition of Daniel) and A.D. 70, since it supposes that the Temple is still standing; 3.9–4.4 mirrors the doctrine of Sirach and presumably was written about the same time (160–130 B.C.); 4.5–5.9 depends on Psalm of Solomon 11 and therefore could not be earlier than 63 B.C. The final combination of these parts would have been *c.* 60 B.C., with 1.3–14 added at a later date. Extreme opinions hold that the book was written in Roman times and that Nabuchodonosor and Belsassar really stand for Vespasian and Titus. At the other extreme, A. Penna proposes that 1.1–3.8 was written by Baruch, but that 3.9–4.4 and 4.5–5.9 were written in the Persian and exilic era respectively. A. Gelin is of the opinion that 1.1–14 is from the Maccabean period and that the rest is contemporary with Sir 24.1–31; 36.1–17.

Doctrinal Character. The book's central theme is collective sin and resulting suffering. There is no mention of a resurrection, but only of Sheol and no individual judgment is mentioned. Wisdom is identified with the Law or Torah (Bar 4.1–4; cf. Sir 24.23), which is the source of joy and happiness. God is referred to as eternal (Bar 4.14), as is the covenant (2.35) and the Law (4.1). The author's interest in eternity derives from Deutero-Isaiah (*see* ISAIAH, BOOK OF). The book reflects the mentality of the late Diaspora (*see* DIASPORA, JEWISH), as does Tobit. *See* TOBIT (TOBIAS), BOOK OF. It speaks of adaptation to the host country (cf. the prayer for the kings in Bar 1.11–12), although there is an occasional outburst of hatred against the oppressor (4.25).

The book emphasizes fidelity to Yahweh through the service of the synagogue and, above all, through observance of the Law. It is not surprising that it is on the Feast of Booths, the day on which the Law was read and the covenant renewed, that the author wishes his book to be read in the Lord's Temple (1.14).

Bibliography: *Encyclopedic Dictionary of the Bible,* tr. and adap. by L. HARTMAN (New York 1963) 210–212, from A. VAN DEN BORN, *Bijbels Woordenboek.* A. GELIN, *Jérémie, Les Lamentations, Le Livre de Baruch* (*Bible de Jérusalem,* 23; Paris 1951). V. HAMP, J. HÖFER and K. RAHNER, *Lexicon für Theologie und Kirche,* (Freiburg, 1957–66) 2:18–19. A. PENNA, *Geremia* (Turin 1954). B. N. WAMBACQ, ''Les Prières de Baruch (1.15–2.19) et de Daniel (9.5–19),'' *Biblica* 40 (1949) 463–475; ''L'Unité littéraire de Bar. 1.1–3.8,'' *Sacra Pagina* 1 (1959) 455–460.

[L. A. IRANYI]

BARZYŃSKI, VINCENT

Missionary whose varied activities influenced Polish Catholic development in the United States; b. Sulislawice, Russian-held Poland, Sept. 20, 1838; d. Chicago, Ill., May 2, 1899. He was the son of Joseph and Mary (Sroczyńska) Barzyński and was baptized Michael. After studies at the diocesan seminary in Lublin, Poland, he was ordained there on Oct. 27, 1861. He participated in the unsuccessful Polish uprising in January of 1863 against Russia and then sought refuge in Austria and in France. At Paris he joined (1866) the recently founded Congregation of the Resurrection and was sent to the United States to work among Polish Catholics in the Diocese of Galveston, Texas. In 1874 he was appointed pastor of St. Stanislaus Kostka parish in Chicago, remaining there until his death. Besides administrating the largest Polish parish and grade school in America, he founded a publishing house that launched (1890) a Polish Catholic daily, *Dziennik Chicagoski,* still in existence. He established (1891) St. Stanislaus Kostka High School for boys, which he unsuccessfully planned to expand into a college. He was active in the Polish Roman Catholic Union; in the organization of several Chicago parishes and parochial schools; in the formation of a new Polish-American sisterhood, the Franciscan Sisters of Bl. Kunegunda; and in the building of an orphanage and home for the aged. After serving as a superior of the Chicago Resurrectionists, he became the first provincial of the congregation's American province (1898–99); he has been described as one of the most effective executors of the Resurrectionist concept of the modern parish as a barrier against the radical socialist influences of the times in which he lived.

Bibliography: W. KWIATKOWSKI, *Historia Zgromadzenia Zmartwychwstania Pańskiego na Stuletnią Rocznicę Jego Założenia 1842–1942* (Albano 1942). L. M. LONG, *The Resurrectionists* (Chicago 1947). S. SIATKA, *Krótkie Wspomnienie o Życiu i Działalności Ks. M. Wincentego Barzyńskiego CR* (Chicago 1901).

[J. V. SWASTEK]

BASALENQUE, DIEGO

Augustinian chronicler and linguist of colonial Mexico; b. Salamanca, Spain, July 25, 1577; d. Charo, Mexico, Dec. 11, 1651. His parents, Alonso Serrano and Isabel Cardona, emigrated to New Spain (Mexico) when Diego was a child. He joined the Augustinians when he was 15 years old and made his religious profession in Mexico City on Feb. 4, 1594. Recognized as a man of unusual talents, he was assigned after ordination to teach the students of his order in the province of Michoacán (created in 1602). He was later awarded the degree of master of theology and was chosen for various offices, including those of prior in the monasteries of San Luis Potosí and Valladolid (formerly Guayangareo, now Morelia), and provincial of Michoacán (1623). Though learned in many fields, Basalenque was probably best known for his skill in law, both civil and ecclesiastical, and in languages. He was proficient in Latin, Greek, and Hebrew, and in several Mexican tongues as well. He is reputed to be the author of numerous works on diverse subjects from theology to mathematics, but only three of his works are known to have been published. The most valuable for Augustinian history and biography is *Historia de la provincia de San Nicolás de Tolentino de Michoacán del orden de N. P. S. Agustín,* completed in three books in 1644 and published in Mexico City in 1673 (repr. Mexico City 1886). For the events of the 16th century, he copied much from the chronicle of Juan de GRIJALVA. Basalenque's style, typical of his time, was excessively rhetorical. Of his two known studies on native tongues, only one was published—*Arte de la lengua Tarasca* (Mexico City 1714, 1805, and 1886). A treatise on the spiritual life, *Muerte en vida y vida en muerte,* was published in part in various numbers of *Archivo agustiniano* from volume 33 (1930) to volume 43 (1935). A life of Basalenque, who was regarded by his contemporaries as a man of holiness as well as learning, was published by one of his confreres, Pedro Salguero, in Mexico City in 1664 (repr. Rome 1761).

Bibliography: G. DE SANTIAGO VELA, *Ensayo de una biblioteca ibero-americana de la orden de San Agustín,* 7 v. in 8 (Madrid 1913–31) 1:331–337. M. T. DISDIER, *Dictionnaire d'histoire et de géographie ecclésiastiques* (Paris 1912–) 6:1063–64. I. MONASTERIO, *Archivo agustiniano* 29 (1928) 408–417.

[A. J. ENNIS]

BASCIO, MATTEO SERAFINI DA

First vicar-general of the Friars Minor Capuchin; b. Bascio, near Pesaro, *c.* 1495; d. Venice, Aug. 6, 1552. Bascio joined the Friars Minor Observants of the Province of Ancona *c.* 1511 and was ordained *c.* 1520. Restless for reform, Matteo left his friary at Montefalcone secretly in 1525, went to Rome, and there obtained from Clement VII verbal permission to observe the Rule of St. Francis to the letter, to wear a habit more in accordance with the type thought to be worn by Francis, and to preach wherever he wished without any fixed residence, provided that he presented himself to his provincial once each year. Once when obeying the last injunction, Matteo was confined in the friary at Forano as a fugitive, but was freed through the intervention of Caterina Cibo, Duchess of Camerino.

The purely personal privilege that Matteo had obtained encouraged like-minded confreres to join him, and thus, unsuspectingly, he became the herald of a movement that resulted in the foundation of a new branch of the Franciscan family, the Friars Minor Capuchin. This new congregation received canonical approbation with the granting of the bull *Religionis Zelus,* July 3, 1528.

The following year, Matteo, elected first vicar-general of the new order, accepted office with reluctance, resigning shortly afterward. He then continued his wandering apostolate first as a Capuchin, then from 1536, apparently, under the minister general of the Observants. Preaching with great success, he played a notable part in the Italian Catholic reformation. In 1546 he accompanied the papal troops that Paul III sent to Germany to assist Charles V against the members of the SCHMALKALDIC LEAGUE. At Mühlberg in April 1547, Matteo, crucifix held aloft, encouraged the Catholic soldiers to a decisive victory. He then continued his apostolate in Venice, where he was venerated for his holiness.

Bibliography: FATHER CUTHBERT, *The Capuchins,* 2 v. (London 1928). M. A POBLADURA, ed., *Monumenta historica Ordinis Fratrum Minorum Capuccinorum,* (Assisi 1937–40; Rome 1950–). *Lexicon Capuccinum* (Rome 1951) 1075–76, gives general bibliog. F. SPRUCK, ''Matteo da Bascio,'' *Round Table of Franciscan Research* 7 (1941–42) 123–146. D. DA PORTOGRUARO, ''Il processo dei Miracoli del P. Matteo da Bascio,'' *Collectanea Franciscana* (Rome 1931–) 15 (1945) 92–116. G. ABATE, ''Fra' Matteo da Bascio e gli inizî dell'Ordine Cappuccino,'' *ibid.* 30 (1960) 31–77.

[C. REEL]

BASEL, COUNCIL OF

An ecumenical council announced in Siena on Feb. 19, 1423, and convoked at Basel, Switzerland, by Martin V on Feb. 1, 1431, and after his death confirmed by Eugene IV. In 1437, it was transferred to Ferrara; in 1439, to Florence (*see* FLORENCE, COUNCIL OF). The WESTERN SCHISM of 1378 to 1417 had provoked the cardinals into summoning the Council of PISA (1409) independently of the papacy. This practical CONCILIARISM had been given theoretical expression in the Council of CONSTANCE (1414–18), which declared that a general council was the highest authority in the Church with regard to heresy, peace, and reform of both head and members. The conciliarists focused on reform, especially reform of the head, i.e., the pope and the curia. The reform-minded conciliarists had been checked in the Council of Siena, but they asserted themselves at Basel. The events of the Basel Council fell into two periods: that of the council proper (1431–37) and the period of the *concil iabulum* (1437–49). The matters treated at the council proper can conveniently be described under the three headings of peace, reform, and heresy, which constituted the proper competence of a general council according to the conciliarists.

Peace or Unity. The council was inaugurated on July 23, 1431, but when its president, Cardinal Giuliano CESARINI, arrived on September 9 he found very few people present. On December 18, because of the sparse attendance, war, and the prospect of a council with the Greeks in Italy, Pope Eugene prorogued the assembly at Basel with the plan to meet in Bologna after 18 months; this was despite Cesarini's expostulation. The council Fathers refused to disperse, and in the second session (Feb. 15, 1432) adopted the principle of the Council of Constance on conciliar superiority with an even more stringent interpretation. New members joined the council, which they thought stood for much-needed reform against a resisting Roman Curia. Thirty-eight prelates were present by the end of April and Eugene was told firmly to withdraw his dissolution and to come to the council in person or by proxy. The cardinals began to desert him. The secular powers (except England, Venice, Florence, and SIGISMUND after his coronation as emperor, May 31, 1433) supported the council. Eugene began to make concessions, but not quickly enough for the growing sense of power of the council. With its membership increasing and Eugene yielding, the council became more imperious and threatening still. It refused to accept the five presidents nominated by the pope and imposed the text of a bull withdrawing the dissolution. Eugene, ill and very nearly without supporters, tried to evade the stringency of this proposed formula but finally promulgated the *Dudum sacrum* (Dec. 15, 1433) saying: ''We decree and declare that the said general council from the time of its inception has been and is being legitimately carried on . . . that it ought to be carried on . . . for the aforesaid ends [heresy, peace of the Church, reform].'' On Feb. 5, 1434 (16th session), seven cardinals, three patriarchs (Latin), 50 bishops, 30 abbots, and 422 other members declared themselves satisfied. But they received the five papal presidents only after they had taken the conciliar oath with a special addition asserting conciliar supremacy (April 26, 1434). In July, three Greek envoys arrived with whom it was agreed to hold a unionistic council in one of certain specified towns (September 7). Eugene, who was at the time an exile in Florence from rebellious Rome, acquiesced even though he had earlier made different arrangements with the Greeks. The next year, June 9, 1435, the council forbade the payment of ANNATES and steadily refused any form of compensation to meet necessary papal expenses. On April 14, 1436, it published a plenary indulgence in favor of the Greek-Latin council, but afraid of the prestige that would accrue to the pope if the council were held in Italy, it insisted on Basel or Avignon as the site, despite the repeated refusal of the Greeks and Eugene's opposition. The council's intransigent attitude on this issue, together with its fierce antagonism to the papacy, lost it its supporters. Cardinals returned to papal allegiance; secular governments, fearing a new schism, counseled moderation. The council itself split, for while the majority favored its being held at Basel or Avignon, a respectable minority voted for one of the towns named in the treaty. On May 7, 1437, both majority and minority parties promulgated decrees simultaneously. The minority, with the Greek delegates, took their decree to Eugene who was in Bologna and he agreed to implement it. Immediately hiring ships to transport the Greeks, Eugene transferred the Council of Basel to Ferrara by the bull *Doctoris gentium*, Sept. 18, 1437. This bull was confirmed December 30, whereupon the Council of Basel legally ceased to exist. The council, removed to Ferrara, lasted until 1439.

Reform. When the council met in 1431 the Church unquestionably needed reform, both in head and members. Members were plentifully represented at Basel but each section—bishops, princes, religious orders, cathedral chapters, universities—resisted reform of itself. Attention, therefore, was concentrated on the head. The reforms imposed, though few in number, were all theoretically good. Some, however, were impracticable, at least to the drastic degree envisaged by the council. On July 13, 1433, it limited papal PROVISIONS to benefices; on Jan. 22, 1435, it forbade clerical concubinage and regulated excommunication; on June 9 it banished every form of payment except bare administrative expenses upon the conferment of BENEFICES, including annates to the pope and, of course, SIMONY; on March 24, 1436, it established new norms for papal elections, and for the conduct, number, and qualities of cardinals. Those reforms advantageous for France and Germany survived for a time, but the rest lapsed. During its six years the council's main occupations were opposition to the papacy and reform of and controversy with the HUSSITES and the Greeks.

Extirpation of Heresy. The heresy of WYCLIF had been condemned both in England and in the Council of Constance where Hus and Jerome of Prague had died at the stake. But it was the basis of the Hussitism, intermingled with legitimate aspirations for reform, with which the Council of Basel was concerned. The Hussites insisted on four points: communion under both kinds, punishment of mortal sin by the secular power, unrestricted freedom to preach, and evangelical poverty for all clergy. Negotiations between the council and the Bohemians began with the ''Accord of Eger'' (May 18, 1432) making the Scriptures, councils, and doctors ''the most reliable and impartial judge.'' Fifteen Hussite delegates with a suite of 300 came to Basel on Jan. 1, 1433. Council envoys went to Prague with the delegates, returning to Basel with three Hussites in August. Subsequently, the Council of Basel sent its same long-suffering representatives to Prague (November 18), Regensburg (Aug. 21, 1434), Brünn (July 1, 1435), Stuhlweissenburg (Dec. 20), and Iglau. An agreement, the *Compacts*, had been reached in Prague in 1433 when the council conceded to the Bohemians the use of the chalice at Communion. Subsequent meetings were occupied with the interpretation of the four points, especially poverty. At Iglau (July 5, 1436), the *Compacts* were solemnly promulgated, largely because the Emperor Sigismund guaranteed their fulfillment. In spite of pressure the Czechs never joined the Council of Basel and did not loyally observe the *Compacts.* The agreement lapsed under Pius II in 1458.

Basel 1437–49: the Conciliabulum. With very reduced numbers, the ''Council of Basel'' defied Eugene's decree of translation to Ferrara. It sent its fleet to bring the Greeks from Constantinople, but they preferred the papal fleet. On Jan. 24, 1438, it declared Eugene suspended and deprived of all spiritual and temporal power. It sent strong delegations to the various French and German diets but resisted dissolution in favor of a third council. On May 16, 1439, it declared the principle of superiority of a council over the pope a truth of Catholic faith, and on June 25 it deposed Eugene. On November 5 it elected an antipope, Felix V. Thereafter it wrote long answers to papal bulls, but passed no legislation. In February of 1448 Frederick of Austria withdrew his safe-conducts and the council members joined Felix in Lausanne. Charles VII of France sponsored an arrangement whereby the ''Council of Basel'' would dissolve—Felix, who resigned, and its chief members being honorably treated. On April 19, 1449, the council elected the reigning NICHOLAS V to succeed Felix and solemnly reenacted the principle of conciliar supremacy. Then, on April 25, it decreed its own dissolution.

Significance of the Council. The council at its height had some 500 members, divided into four deputations. There were, however, never more than about 100 bishops and abbots present and they alone, by tradition, had a deliberative vote. But in Basel every member had a vote. Several of the most important measures were passed by relatively few bishops plus a mass of others. Basel signified the height and defeat of conciliarism, which, despite the sincere motivation of several of the leading conciliarists, degenerated in the circumstances into antipapalism. The duplication at Basel of most departments of the Papal Curia, the refusal to compromise over annates and the site of the council with the Greeks, and the determination to abase the pope and his office, alienated princes, cardinals, and the moderate-minded, and led to the reconciliation of Eugene and such one-time conciliarists as Cesarini and Nicholas of Cusa. When the Council of Basel broke its pact with the Greeks rather than allow a council in Italy, it made possible the Council of Ferrara-Florence whose success and definition of papal supremacy were a grievous blow to Basel and conciliarism.

Bibliography: Sources. *Monumenta conciliorum generalium saeculi decimi quinti,* 4 v. (Vienna-Basel 1857–1935). J. HALLER et al., eds., *Concilium Basiliense*, 8 v. (Basel 1896–1936). J. D. MANSI *Sacrorum Conciliorum nova et amplissima collectio* (repr. Graz 1960) v.19. *Conciliorum oecumenicorum decreta* (Bologna-Freiberg 1962). Literature. A. BAUDRILLART, A. VACANT et al, ed. *Dictionnaire de théologie catholique*, 1:113–129. N. VALOIS, *Le Pape et le Concile, 1418–1450,* 2 v. (Paris 1909). C. J. VON HEFELE, *Histoire des conciles d'après les documents originaux* (Paris 1907–38) v. 7.2. A. M. JACQUIN, *Dictionnaire d'histoire et de géographie ecclésiastiques* 6:356–362. B. TIERNEY, *Foundations of the Conciliar Theory* (Cambridge, Eng. 1955). J. B. VILLIGER, J. HÖFER and K. RAHNER *Lexikon für Theologie und Kirche,* 2:23–25. E. F. JACOB, "The Conciliar Movement . . ." *The Bulletin of the John Rylands Library* 41 (1958) 26–53. J. GILL, *Eugenius IV: Pope of Christian Union* (Westminster, Md. 1961). P. L. MCDERMOTT, "Nicholas of Cusa: Continuity and Conciliation at the Council of Basel," *Church History* 67 (1998): 254–273. G. CHRISTIANSON, "Nicholas of Cusa and the Presidency Debate at the Council of Basel, 1434," in *Nicholas of Cusa on Christ and the Church*, ed. G. CHRISTIANSON and T. M. IZBICK (Leiden 1996), 87–103. J. W. STEIBER, "Christian Unity from the Perspective of the Council Fathers at Basel and that of Eugenius IV," in *In Search of Christian Unity*, ed. J. A. BURGESS (Minneapolis 1991), 57–73. L. BILDERBACK, "Eugene IV and the First Dissolution of the Council of Basel," *Church History* 36 (1967): 243–253.

[J. GILL]

BASIC CHRISTIAN COMMUNITIES

Basic Christian communities (English term for *comunidades eclesiales de base, communautés de base*; also known as mini-parishes, life-communions, neighborhood churches, and grass-roots communities) are relatively small (in comparison with parishes), homogeneous groups of Christians who share common interests, values, and objectives; who search to emphasize primary, interpersonal, ongoing relationships; and who view themselves as ecclesial entities. Basic Christian communities are the form in which growing numbers of concerned peoples are structuring themselves as an alternative or a complement to the parish model of Church. Their common interests, their possibly living in the same area, and their limited numbers (from 8 to 40, some would say 100) allow members to develop close personal relationships. Generally these groups seek some concerted impact on the world and undertake apostolic options as a group. The rhythm of sacramental life varies according to group discernment and the availability of a priest or deacon. The purpose of basic Christian communities is not to be parish societies that provide services to the parish, to be study groups, or to be movements infusing church life with one special quality; but rather to hold their own identity as an ecclesial unit.

Such factors as discontent, the unavailability of a priest, impersonalism, and the great distances between the members of some rural parishes have been catalysts for the origin of some basic Christian communities. Among the positive features of these communities are: the experience of authentic community and close supportive relationships beyond the family; effective community supports and challenges to the members towards more meaningful service; a setting in which faith is deepened by the critique of the interaction between reading the Gospel and the struggle to live as Christians; promotion of involvement in contemporary society; rapid development of many and varied ministries or services among the members; and a questioning of the parish as the only model for Church.

In the late 20th century basic Christian communities became a major element of the pastoral practice of significant segments of the Catholic and Protestant Churches over the world. They are a cornerstone of much Latin American pastoral work. In many areas of Africa and Asia they are likewise a key for pastoral development.

See Also: PARISH (PASTORAL THEOLOGY).

Bibliography: T. G. BISSONNETTE, "Comunidades Eclesiales de Base: Contemporary Grass Roots Attempts to Build Ecclesial Koinonia," *Jurist* 36 (1976) 24–58. C. FLORISTAN, *Comunidad Christiana de Base* (San Antonio 1976). J. MARINS and T. TREVISAN, *Communidades Eclesiales de Base* (Bogotá 1975).

[T. G. BISSONNETTE]

BASIL, ST.

Bishop and Doctor of the Church, called Basil the Great of Caesarea; b. Pontus, Asia Minor, *c.* 329; d. Caesarea, Jan. 1, 379.

Life. Basil was the first Doctor of the Church to combine endowments that often recurred together in later Fathers: aristocracy of birth, refinement of culture, enthusiastic participation in the ascetical movement, and an episcopal ministry. His family were landowners of substance in Pontus, probably of the senatorial class, and had demonstrated heroic loyalty to Christianity during the persecutions; through GREGORY THAUMATURGUS they became attached to ORIGENISM. Basil's grandmother MACRINA, his parents Basil and Emilia, his sister Macrina, and his younger brothers GREGORY OF NYSSA and Peter of Sebaste are all venerated as saints. Basil was trained in rhetoric at Constantinople and Athens and became a close friend of GREGORY OF NAZIANZUS; he was baptized with him about 358 and gave up a brilliant administrative career to join his family in the life of ascetical retirement they were living at Annesi in Pontus, under the influence of EUSTATHIUS OF SEBASTE.

St. Basil.

Anyone belonging to the ascetical groups, which were then strongly deprecated by the ruling classes, could expect many difficulties; but Basil was admitted into the clergy of Caesarea, and divided his time between a retired ascetical life and priestly activity. He was ordained *c.* 365 and dedicated himself not only to the defense of Nicean orthodoxy but also to social work of Christian charity. After being elected bishop in the spring of 370, he relied heavily on the common people, who venerated his holiness and charity; his social standing gave him leverage for a vigorous opposition to the civil administration, which was protecting Arianism; but he was utilized by that administration to discipline the new forces and to develop mission activity in Armenia. He tried unsuccessfully to oppose the division of Cappadocia, which deprived him of some influence when a new ecclesiastical province was erected and centered in Tyana. His efforts to reunite all orthodox Christians divided by the schism of ANTIOCH extended to the whole of the East and were crowned with success, after his death, in the Synod of Antioch (379) and the Council of CONSTANTINOPLE I (381). In 372 he failed in his efforts to win over his old mentor Eustathius of Sebaste, who had become a leading Pneumatomachian. Immediately after Basil's death, his friend Gregory of Nazianzus and his brother Gregory of Nyssa eulogized him in terms already redolent of hagiography; but none of his contemporaries wrote a detailed biography of Basil. Two ancient biographies, one in Syriac and the other in Greek, are wrongly ascribed to his disciple Amphilochius; they contain no useful information. There is evidence of local veneration shortly after Basil's death. The high regard in which Basil was held by ATHANASIUS, AMBROSE, and RUFINUS OF AQUILEIA explains the rapid spread of this veneration to the other Churches, despite the scant sympathy of DAASUS I and JEROME. Basil's doctrinal authority is evident in the writings of AUGUSTINE and later of Pope LEO I and in the FLORILEGIA occasioned in such large quantities by the Council of CHALCEDON.

Works. With Gregory of Nazianzus Basil became from the beginning of his retreat in Annesi a disciple of ORIGEN and compiled an anthology of Origen's works, the *Philocalia,* apparently published posthumously. The *Moralia* is an anthology of 1,553 verses of the New Testament, with a preface, *On the Judgment of God;* a second preface, *On the Faith,* was added later by the author. The famous *Ad adolescentes, de legendis libris Gentilium,* on the reading of the pagan classics, must also be classed among the works of Basil's earlier years; it is an apology of asceticism addressed to a public with a highly developed Hellenistic culture. A final composition of his early maturity is the small treatise *On the Spirit,* probably authentic, inspired by PLOTINUS, who was a source for Basil's later writings. The two most important dogmatic works can be dated with some precision: in 364 he wrote three books *Contra Eunomium* (books 4 and 5 in the preserved text are by Didymus of Alexandria) that refuted the *Apologia* of EUNOMIUS OF CONSTANTINOPLE, the mouthpiece of the Anomoeans (361); the treatise *De Spiritu Sancto* (375), addressed to AMPHILOCHIUS OF ICONIUM, gives a report in its chapters 10 to 28 of a tense dialogue between Basil and Eustathius of Sebaste that took place in Sebaste in June 372.

The voluminous correspondence (366 letters) of Basil can often be dated with certainty and furnishes valuable documentation on the ecclesiastical politics of the age. The majority of the homilies are in all probability from the time of his sacerdotal ministry; but there are reasons for dating the nine homilies *On the Hexaemeron* at the end of Basil's career; these homilies contain a Christian explanation of the created universe, drawing heavily upon Greek science. The *Asceticon* consists of 55 Great Rules, or systematic regulations, for the cenobitic life and 313 Little Rules, or practical answers, to questions raised on the occasion of visitations to already established communities; they also contain elements from other occasions. The text translated into Latin by Rufinus of Aquileia (*c.* 400) contains only a rough draft of the first of the Great Rules and half of the Little Rules. This archaic version (Little Asceticon) enables us to grasp the institutions in their creative evolution (BASILIAN MONASTICISM).

Among the works of disputed authenticity should be listed the two books *De Baptismo,* written during the episcopate, and perhaps the *Commentary on Isaias,* the work of a 4th-century Cappadocian bishop, very well attested in the manuscript tradition. Basil probably did not put the finishing touches to these two works and is not entirely responsible for their style. The homily on Psalm 115 seems to be authentic, but not that on Psalm 37 (Eusebius of Caesarea) or on Psalm 132, or yet the second homily on Psalm 28 (the work of a disciple of Basil), or the homilies *On the Structure of Man* (probably by Gregory of Nyssa) and *On Paradise,* which claim to be continuations of the *Hexaemeron.* Certainly spurious are the treatises *On Virginity* (probably by Basil of Ancyra), *Consolation to One Lying Sick* (perhaps by Proclus), *On the Incarnation* (also probably by Proclus), and *On Virginity* (of Syrian orgin). The few homilies still not edited have scarcely any claim to authenticity.

Of the minor ascetical fragments, the Prologue (*Patrologia Graeca* 31:1509) is authentic, as are the Prologue (PG 31:881) and a list of penances (1305, n. 1–11 and 1313, n. 1–19), at least in the sense that they come from a Basilian environment. Some discourses (PG 31:619, 647, and perhaps 869) are from the 4th or 5th century. The *Constitutions* (with the exception of ch. 1, which comes from a semi-Messalian environment) and the *Exhortation to Renunciation* (PG 31:1321, 625) are later works and come from environments influenced vaguely by Basil. The *Admonitio ad filium spiritualem* and the *De consolatione in adversis* are ancient but of Latin origin. The *De laude solitariae vitae* is by St. Peter Damien (*Opusc.* 11, ch. 19).

Spurious letters are Nos. 8 (EVAGRIUS PONTICUS); 10, 16, and 38 (all three by Gregory of Nyssa); 39 to 45; 47 (Gregory of Nazianzus the Elder); 50, 166 to 167, and 169 to 171 (all six by Gregory of Nazianzus); 189 (Gregory of Nyssa), 197.2; 321 (Gregory of Nazianzus); 335 to 343 (though these may be authentic); 344 to 346 (likewise?); 347 to 356, 357, 359, 360, 365; 366 (taken from CLEMENT OF ALEXANDRIA); 361 to 364 seem to be authentic.

Doctrine. The Cappadocians resumed the tradition of Origen; Basil did this in a critical and highly personal fashion, but it was precisely the sureness of touch with which he succeeded in integrating Origen into orthodoxy that made it possible for the two Gregorys, and later Evagrius Ponticus, to give Origen such importance. Basil drew on Stoic and Platonic philosophy, especially that of Plotinus; Dehnhard's researches show that Basil's assimilation of these philosophical currents was thorough, based on the tradition of the Church. Basil placed supreme reliance on the Bible and was conscientious in referring to it as touchstone for everything; at one point, however, his native sincerity in dialogue with Eustathius of Sebaste made him admit that the orthodoxy of his day had had to define more precisely certain Biblical formulas, and he thus for the first time took clear note of the nature and importance of unwritten TRADITION (*De Spiritu Sancto,* c. 27).

Trinity. Basil was far more aware than Athanasius and the Westerners of the danger, represented by MARCELLUS OF ANCYRA, of not distinguishing sufficiently between the Divine Persons; that is why he adopted the formula ''three hypostases.'' In his assertion of the perfect resemblance of the Son (and the Spirit) to the Father, he sometimes came close to Tritheism; if he escaped this danger, it was because of his entirely spiritualized conception of the Divine Being and his respect for the incomprehensibility of God. Basil's ascetical training convinced him that only the purified spirit could know things divine. He tried to avoid multiplication of formulas and to induce contemplation in an attitude of adoration: this is the essence of his monastic theology.

In refuting the subtleties of the heretics, however, he did not hesitate to introduce nonscriptural distinctions between what is common in the Trinity, the *ousia,* and what is typical of each of the hypostases. As Doctor of the Holy Spirit, he excommunicated those who asserted that the Spirit is a creature, but he did not demand any more positive confession of faith on this point of the divinity of the Third Person. His friends themselves were astonished at this *oeconomia.* It must be seen not as pure adaptation or ''condescension'' but as a profound respect for the mystery involved and a desire not to go beyond the terms of the Biblical revelation. In the face of the incipient difficulties of CHRISTOLOGY, Basil initially attempted to adopt the same prudential line, but he finally had to condemn APOLLINARIS OF LAODICEA.

Ecclesiology. Basil's efforts to reconcile the various Churches were intimately connected with his specifically theological activity. CAESAREA was associated with Antioch, where Bishop Meletius was in conflict not only with an Arian faction but with a small intransigent group headed by Paulinus of Antioch and supported by Athanasius and Pope Damasus I.

Despite his attachment to the formula ''one single hypostasis,'' Paulinus did not deviate from the orthodox faith, and the schism was primarily a matter of personality clashes. Full of nostalgia for the happy days when the Churches acted in unity as members of the same Body of Christ and aware of the harm being done to the faith of the ordinary laity by the clumsy intervention of the West, Basil made superhuman efforts. He tried not to persuade Meletius to bow out in favor of the man being supported by the Westerners but rather to enlighten those Westerners and if possible to persuade them to come and see on the spot who was in the right, to open their eyes to the actual state of affairs in the East.

Despite the misunderstanding of Basil's position by certain Westerners, he is a very important witness to Catholic unity; his action as mediator implies that he was in communion with Athanasius and Damasus as well as with Meletius. It cannot be denied, of course, that his conception of the local Church and episcopal collegiality, based on faith and charity, is already in line with later orthodox ecclesiology. He had a very clear conception of the freedom of the Church with regard to the imperial power.

Asceticism and Social Christianity. The specific mark of Basil's ecclesiology is its bond with asceticism. The disciples of Eustathius of Sebaste took so seriously the demands for evangelical renunciation that they were in danger of constituting a sect opposed to the official Church, as can be seen at the Council of GANGRA (*c.* 340). Basil criticized this enthusiasm from the inside, carefully checking its motives against the Gospel, conferring upon it wisdom and respectability and enlightening it with his humanistic culture. He took care not to mistake exterior manifestations, such as virginity or spectacular poverty, for the essential. His own status in the hierarchy facilitated contacts. In fact the discipline he imposed on his brothers made of them, little by little, distinct communities within the Church; but he himself took care not to regard them as such.

Basil based his entire doctrine of renunciation on perfect obedience to the two commandments of the gospel rather than on the evangelical counsels. He made the same demands in his preaching to the people, when he proposed a sort of Christian communism with communal use, if not ownership, of property and with charity serving as the incentive to labor. His preaching was so demanding upon the rich that it may be asked whether it did not express an exaggerated idealism that refused to see the economic realities. But the historical studies of economists on the fall of ancient civilization show that its essential defects were the disparity between the social classes and the increase in unproductive expenses, i.e., precisely the evils that Basil was combating in the name of Christian poverty.

Ecclesiastical Discipline. Three canonical letters of Basil to Amphilochius of Iconium have been received into the code of the Byzantine Church; they give operational directions on the duration and modalities of excommunication for various faults. Basil was there merely systematizing and correcting the severe usages that he found in force. He was not expressing his personal conception of Christianity as freely as he did in the *Asceticon* or in his preaching; rather he was giving proof of a remarkable capacity for adaptation.

Liturgy. Basil took into the Church the monastic tradition of the East and canonized psalm-singing, thus contributing to the molding of the ecclesiastical Office of the Hours. A witness as early as Gregory of Nazianzus bears witness to Basil's liturgical activity. Many prayers bear his name. It is difficult to say if all these are genuine; but the Eucharistic Liturgy attributed to him certainly has some connection with him. It survived in two forms, one called the Alexandrine, the other and longer version called the Byzantine. Some of the alterations typical of the second form bear an unmistakable personal mark of Basil. This does not mean, however, that this Liturgy today retains the form he gave it. As for the first, it is still difficult to say whether it represents an earlier Liturgy that Basil inherited or whether it has also been retouched by his hand. He was under no obligation to use one single and identical formula.

Feast: June 14; Jan. 1, Jan. 30 in the East.

Bibliography: Biographical sources and editions of works. P. MARAN, ed., *Vita S. Basilii, Patrologia Graeca,* ed. J. P. MIGNE, 29:v-clxxvii (Paris 1857–66). M. M. FOX, *The Life and Times of St. Basil the Great* (Catholic University of America, *Patristic Studies,* 57). L. VISCHER, *Basilius der Grosse* (Basel 1953), ecclesiology. Annotated editions of ancient funeral orations. GREGORY OF NYSSA, *Discours funèbres,* ed. and tr. F. BOULENGER (Paris 1908); *Encomium of Saint Gregory, Bishop of Nyssa, on His Brother Saint Basil* ed. and tr. J. A. STEIN (Catholic University of America, *Patristic Studies,* 17); *Vita S. Macrinae,* ed. V. W. CALLAHAN in *Gregorii Nysseni opera,* ed. W. JAEGER, v.8.1 (Leiden 1952) 370–414. EPHREM THE SYRIAN, "Encomium in S. Basilium Magnum," in *Opera,* ed. S. G. MERCATI, V.1.1 (Rome 1915) 113–188. K. V. ZETTERSTÉEN, tr., "Eine Homilie des Amphilochius von Iconium über Basilius," *Oriens Christianus* 3d ser., 9: 67–98. A. VÖÖBUS, "Das literarische Verhältnis zwischen der Biographie des Rabbūlā und dem Pseudo-Amphilochianischen Panegyrikus über Basilius," *ibid.* 44 (1960) 40–45. *Opera omnia, Patrologia Graeca,* ed. J. P. MIGNE, v.29–32, reimpression with introd. and bibliog. by P. MARAN and J. GARNIER (Paris 1857–66). The introd. by J. GRIBOMONT to the 1960 repr. gives a complete bibliog. of the eds. and studies on each of his works. F. E. BRIGHTMAN, *Liturgies Eastern and Western* (Oxford 1896), v.1 *Eastern Liturgies,* 309–344, 400–401. J. DORESSE et al., *Un Témoin archaïque de la liturgie copte de saint Basile* (Louvain 1960). Ancient Latin version of the Hexaemeron, E. AMAND DE MENDIETA and S. Y. RUDBERG, eds., *Eustathius* (*Texte und Untersuchungen zur Geschichte der altchristlichen Literatur* 66). Homilies. M. HUGLO, *Revue Bénédictine* 64: 129–132. *Asceticon, Patrologia Latina,* ed. J. P. MIGNE (Paris 1878–90) 103:487–554. *De Spiritu Sancto,* ed. C. T. JOHNSTON (Oxford 1892); ed. B. PRUCHE, *Sources Chrétiennes,* ed. H. DE LUBAC et al. 17 (Paris 1947). *Letters,* ed. and tr. R. J. DEFERRARI, 4 v. (*Loeb Classical Library* [London-New York-Cambridge, Mass. 1926–34]) (as an app., *Address to Young Men,* ed. with M. R. P. MC-

GUIRE, *ibid.* 4:363–435); tr. A. C. WAY, ed. R. J. DEFERRARI, 2 v. (*The Fathers of the Church: A New Translation,* ed. R. J. DEFERRARI et al. 13, 28 [New York 1951–55]); ed. and Fr. tr. Y. COURTONNE, 2 v. (Paris 1957–61), v.3 still to appear, more critical text, insufficient annotation. *Exegetic Homilies,* tr. A. C. WAY, *The Fathers of the Church: A New Translation,* ed. R. J. DEFERRARI et al. 46 (Washington 1963). *The Ascetic Works of Saint Basil,* ed. and tr. W. K. L. CLARKE (Society for Promoting Christian Knowledge (London 1925). *Selected Works,* ed. and tr. B. JACKSON in *A Select Library of the Nicene and Post-Nicene Fathers,* 2d series, ed. P. SCHAFF and H. WACE 8 (1895). Textual criticism. M. BESSIÈRES, *La Tradition manuscrite de la correspondance de s. Basile* (Oxford 1923). A. CAVALLIN, *Studien zu den Briefen des hl. Basillius* (Lund 1944). J. GRIBOMONT, *Histoire du texte des Ascétiques de saint Basile* (Louvain 1953). S. Y. RUDBERG, *Études sur la tradition manuscrite de saint Basile* (Upsala 1953); ed. and tr., *L'Homélie de Basile Césarée sur le mot ''Observe-toi toi-même''* (Stockholm 1962). History of doctrine. E. IVÁNKA, *Hellenisches und Christliches im frühbyzantinischen Geistesleben* (Vienna 1948) 28–67. H. DEHNHARD, *Das Problem der Abhängigkeit des Basilius von Plotin* (Patristische Texte und Studien 3; Berlin 1964). W. M. ROGGISCH, *Platons Spuren bei Basilius dem Grossen* (Diss. Bonn 1949). J. F. CALLAHAN, ''Greek Philosophy and the Cappadocian Cosmology,'' *Dumbarton Oaks Papers,* Harvard Univ. 12 (Cambridge, Mass. 1958) 29–57. B. OTIS, ''Cappadocian Thought as a Coherent System,'' *ibid.* 95–124. W. A. TIECK, *Basil of Caesarea and the Bible* (Doctoral diss. microfilm; Columbia U. 1953). J. GRIBOMONT, ''Le Paulinisme de s. Baslie,'' *Studiorum Paulinorum,* 2 v. *Analecta biblica* 17–18; 2: 481–490; ''L'Origénisme de s. Basile'' in *L'Homme devant Dieu: Mélanges Henri du Lubac,* 3 v. (Paris 1963–64) 1:281–294. T. SPIDLÍK, *La Sophiologie de S. Basile Orientalia Christiana Analecta.* 162 (Rome 1961). Trinity. K. HOLL, *Amphilochius von Ikonium in seinem Verhätnis zu den grossen Kappadoziern* (Tübingen 1904), very incisive, but attributes to Basil letters 8 and 38. H. DÖRRIES, *De Spiritu Sancto: Der Beitrag des Basilius zum Abschluss des trinitarischen Dogmas* (Göttingen 1956). J. LEBON, ''Le Sort du 'consubstantiel' nicéen,'' *Revue d'histoire ecclésiastique* 48: 632–682. B. PRUCHE, ''Autour de traité sur le Saint-Esprit de s. Basile,'' *Recherches de science religieuse* 52: 204–232. G. L. PRESTIGE, *St. Basil the Great and Apollinaris of Laodicea,* ed. H. CHADWICK (Society for Promoting Christian Knowledge; London 1956). H. DE RIEDMATTEN, ''La Correspondance entre Basile de Césarée et Apollinaire de Laodicée,'' *Journal of Theological Studies* new series 7: 199–210; 8: 53–70. Ecclesiology. P. BATIFFOL, ''L'Ecclésiologie de s. Basile,'' *Échos d'Orient* 21 (Paris 1922) 9–30. V. GRUMEL, ''S. Basile et le Siège apostolique,'' *ibid.* 280–292. E. SCHWARTZ, ''Zur Kirchengeschichte des vierten Jahrhunderts,'' in *Gesammelte Schriften,* 4 v. (Berlin 1960) 39–88. M. RICHARD, ''S. Basile et la mission du diacre Sabinus,'' *Analecta Bollandiana* 67: 178–202, corrects the preceding work. E. AMAND DE MENDIETA, ''Basile de Césarée et Damase de Rome,'' in *Biblical and Patristic Studies in Memory of R. P. Casey,* ed. J. N. BIRDSALL and R. W. THOMSON (Freiburg 1963) 122–166, exaggerates failure of negotiations. G. F. REILLY, *Imperium and Sacerdotium according to St. Basil* (Washington 1945). Ethics and sociology. S. GIET, *Les Idées et l'action sociales de s. Baslie* (Paris 1941). B. TREUCKER, *Politische und sozialgeschichtliche Studien zu den Basilius-Briefen* (Munich 1961). Liturgy. A. RAES, ''Un Nouveau document de la liturgie de s. Basle,'' *Orientalia Christiana periodica* 26 (Rome 1960) 401–411. W. E. PITT, ''The Origin of the Anaphora of the Liturgy of St. Basil,'' *The Journal of Ecclesiastical History* 12: 1–13. H. ENGBERDING, ''Das anaphorische Fübittgebet der Basiliusliturgie,'' *Oriens Christianus* 14 (Leipzig-Wiesbaden 1963) 16–52; 49 (Leipzig-Wiesbaden 1965) 18–32. J. MATEOS, ''L'Office monastique à la fin du IVe siècle: Antioche, Palestine, Cappadoce,'' *Oriens Christianus* 47: 53–88. Culture. L. V. JACKS, *St. Basil and Greek Literature* (Catholic University of America, *Patristic Studies*; Washington D.C. 1922) A. C. WAY, *The Language and Style of the Letters of St. Basil* (*ibid.* 13; 1927). Y. COURTONNE, *Saint Basile et l'Hellénisme* (Paris 1934). W. HENGSBERG, *De ornatu rhetorico quem Basilius Magnus . . . adhibuit* (Diss. Bonn 1957).

[J. GRIBOMONT]

BASIL OF ANCYRA

4th-century bishop and writer; d. in exile, *c.* 364. A former physician, Basil became bishop of Ancyra (modern Ankara) when Marcellus was deposed for suspected Sabellianism in 336; and he soon became the leader of the moderate semi-Arian party at the Synod of Ancyra (358). In both his *Synodal Letter* and *Dogmatic Memoir* on the Trinity (preserved by Epiphanius, *Haer.* 73.2), Basil defended the homoiousian position, saying that ''the Son is in all things like the Father, in will as well as hypostasis, in existence and in being.''

Despite the efforts of Basil and his colleagues Eustathius of Sebaste and Eleusius of Cyzicus, the extreme Arian party, the Anomoeans, succeeded in winning over Emperor Constantius II, and both the Western synod held at Ariminum and the Eastern synod at Seleucia turned against the formula of Basil. He and his colleagues were sent to Constantius at Constantinople, where they signed the homoean formula of Ariminum in 359. As leadership of the group thus passed from Basil to Acacius of Caesarea, Arianism was at least temporarily in control. Acacius held a synod at Constantinople in 360, at which Basil and his friends were deposed and sent into exile. Basil was banished to Illyria; he apparently attempted to be reinstated under Emperor Jovianus, but died in exile *c.* 364 after recanting his consent to the formula of Ariminum.

Although EPIPHANIUS OF CONSTANTIA is harsh on Basil, claiming he was merely an Arian in disguise, HILARY OF POITIERS and Athanasius are far more just; Athanasius (*De synodis* 41) suggests that his doctrine, apart from his rejection of the *HOMOOUSIOS*, was nearly equivalent to the orthodox position, and such men ''must not be treated as enemies.'' Athanasius' moderate view accords with Basil's actions during his last years and is surely right.

Jerome (*De vir. ill.* 89) mentions two other works, *Against Marcellus,* which has been lost, and a treatise *On Virginity,* which is almost certainly to be identified with the treatise *On the True Purity of Chastity,* dedicated to Letoius, recovered from the works of Basil the Great by F. Cavallera [*Revue d'histoire ecclésiastique* 6 (1905)

5–14]. The physiological and anatomical details found throughout this work suit the tradition that Basil had been a physician. The angelic life of virginity can be achieved only on the foundation of bodily harmony, which must be fostered by fasting, austerities, the avoidance of condiments and wine, and care in the use of foods that arouse the passions and lend a foothold to the devil. Moderation and balance are always to be observed: the reins of the chariot must be neither too tight nor too loose. Basil's doctrine here is Neoplatonic and Alexandrian. The Slavonic text of the treatise has been edited by A. Vaillant (Paris 1943), who disputes the thesis of Cavallera.

Bibliography: F. CAVALLERA, *Dictionnaire de spiritualité ascétique et mystique: Doctrine et histoire* (Paris 1932–) 1:1283. J. JANINI CUESTA, "Dieta y virginidad," *Miscelánea Comillas* 14 (1950) 187–197. *Patrologia Graeca* (Paris 1857–66) 30:669–810. J. QUASTEN, *Patrology* (Westminster, Md. 1950–) 3:201–203.

[H. MUSURILLO]

BASILE OF SOISSONS

Theologian; b. Soissons, date of birth unknown; d. Paris, March 3, 1698. He entered the Capuchins on April 20, 1635. His apostolic and literary activities were aimed chiefly at the defense of the faith. He contributed to this cause a fundamental work of four volumes *I Fondement inébranlable* (Paris 1680–82). Employing the only criterion admitted by his adversaries, Sacred Scripture, he treated successively the Creed, Decalogue, Sacraments, and prayer. The Eucharist holds a major place in his *I Défense invincible* (Paris 1676). In *La Véritable décision* (Paris 1685) he shows that the only true judge in doctrinal and religious questions is the Catholic Church.

Bibliography: É. D'ALENCON, *Dictionnaire de théologie catholique* 2.1:464–465. A. TEETAERT, *Dictionnaire d'histoire et de géographie ecclésiastiques* 6:1157–58.

[M. DE POBLADURA]

BASILIAN MONASTICISM

The monastic development under Basil of Caesarea is usually placed in the line of development after the anchoritism of St. ANTHONY OF EGYPT and the CENOBITISM of the large communities under St. PACHOMIUS, leading toward the establishment of Benedictine monasticism (*see* MONASTICISM). This is an error in perspective. Basil was a successor in the tradition of the enthusiastic and sectarian asceticism of EUSTATHIUS OF SEBASTE; he aimed not at constituting an isolated group but at reforming the Church according to the demands of the gospel, without clashing with the bulk of the faithful.

The Asceticon. The chronological development of Basil's thought can be followed through the two successive editions of his I *Asceticon,* one in 202 questions (*Patrologia Latina*, ed. J. P. Migne, 103:487), the other in 55 great rules (which develop out of the 11 first questions of the first edition) and in 313 short rules (191 questions of the first edition with new ones added). When new brotherhoods began to develop, Basil in no way attempted to impose his own conceptions on them but, rather, sought to meditate with them on the New Testament, to put into practice the renunciation demanded by Baptism.

OBEDIENCE is understood in terms of the Biblical commandments, interpreted in the light of the need of one's neighbor. POVERTY is not a juridical convention but, rather, a generous devotion of the fruits of a conscientious toil to the service of the poor; and here Basil separates himself radically from Messalianism. Celibacy is taken for granted; in the second edition there is a requirement of a formal engagement in this matter, but it is never made a central point except when a virgin fails to honor her promises (*Epist.* 46).

Reference to the individual superior appears only in the latest texts; at the outset emphasis was placed on the group of those who had received the charisms of discernment of spirits; for each had his function and duties, expressing charity to the other members of the Body of Christ. Basil was a vigorous opponent of anchoritism. His stand must be understood in the light of the history of his day: he states that the tendency to isolation in one's environment is not healthy but, rather, is a self-willed anchoritism. Further, he shows little sympathy for the appeal of inwardness that so delighted his friend GREGORY OF NAZIANZUS. Basil stressed the objective aspect of prayer; he thought of prayer as liturgical, and readily mingled prayer with work and apostolic responsibilities: prayer was for Basil more a song than a silence.

Basilians. Basil never promulgated any precise rule, nor did he found a centralized order; there is no justification for calling Basilian even those Oriental monks who recognize him as one of their fathers. The idea of a Basilian order is a Latin one, a product of the Roman Curia's extension of Western categories. Following the curial practice, the Uniate Oriental monks from the Middle Ages on can in a certain sense be considered Basilians, and the Curia officially made them such when it reformed them. The Italo-Greek monks, who also had a Spanish Latin-rite congregation; the Ukrainian Basilians of St. Josaphat, with a few Rumanian monks; and finally the Melchites of Lebanon should be mentioned.

Italo-Greek. The Greeks who had been so flourishing an ethnic group in south Italy in antiquity had not entirely disappeared there when JUSTINIAN I in the 6th century reoccupied these provinces. Monasticism spread there despite the threat of Arab invasions. It prospered in

SICILY and especially in Calabria and Lucania, from the 9th to the 1lth century, based on a Studite tradition but with direct contacts with Palestine and Egypt. Numerous Italo-Greek manuscripts still witness to this culture. Although it was the first Byzantine province to be invaded by the Latins (Normans), south Italy did not, for all that, lose its characteristics; indeed the new dynasty relied on the monasteries for support and favored them in return. As many as 265 have been counted, most of them quite small. Confederations developed around S. Salvatore in Messina and St. Elias of Carbone. Leaders among the monks included St. Elias the Younger (d. 903), St. Elias Spelaiotes (d. 960), St. SABAS THE YOUNGER (d. 990 or 991), St. NICODEMUS OF MAMMOLA (d. 990), St. Luke of Armento (d. 993), St. NILUS OF ROSSANO (d. 1005), St. SIMEON OF POLIRONE (d. 1016), and St. Bartholomew of Rossano (d. 1020).

The influence of these spiritual centers on medieval spirituality (e.g., MONTE CASSINO, St. ROMUALD) and on the Greek culture in Rome itself should not be underestimated. Unfortunately the rule of the Angevins brought the beginning of a decline, and the Greek element disappeared little by little. When BESSARION tried to reform the monasteries in 1446, the majority of the houses had passed to Latin religious or disappeared. Cardinal Santoro pursued Bessarion's efforts, and 1579 was to become the official date of the foundation of a congregation of 38 monasteries. With these were associated the Basilians of Spain. The emigrations from Albania revived the Greek-language groups. In 1866 the government suppressed the monasteries with the exception of GROTTAFERRATA (outside Rome), whose traditions of scholarship, liturgy, and music experienced a brilliant revival.

In Spain, two groups of Latin religious and hermits adopted almost simultaneously the Rule of St. Basil at Orviedo and Tardon (the so-called reformed province, given more to manual labor) in 1561 and in 1568; in 1569 they were united to the Basilians of Italy. They were suppressed by the Spanish government in 1855.

Ruthenians, Rumanians, and Melchites. The Ruthenian Basilians of St. JOSAPHAT KUNCEVYČ were established shortly after the Union of Brest-Litovsk (1595), when St. Josaphat reformed about 30 Ukrainian monasteries, under the influence of the constitutions of St. IGNATIUS OF LOYOLA, and instituted an active congregation, which he called Basilian (1617). It played a crucial role in the Ruthenian Church, representing the cultural element and furnishing the bishops. It had provinces in Russia, Lithuania, Poland, and Austria. In the reform under Pope LEO XIII, the personality of Metropolitan A. SHEPTYTS'KYĬ gave the order a more Oriental character. In the wake of World War I the monks emigrated, especially to North and South America.

Rumanian Basilians consisted of a little congregation of monks around the monastery of Blaj, from 1750 to 1870; and another group, around Bixad from 1925 to 1945.

Among the Melchites, at the end of the 17th century, when a United Melchite Church was reconstituted, Euthymius Saifi organized the Congregation of Our Savior or Salvatorians (1684); and later, that of the Chouerites (1697), from which that of the Aleppans would branch off (1829). The three congregations are flourishing today in Lebanon.

Bibliography: D. AMAND, *L'Ascése monastique de saint Basile* (Maredsous 1949). J. GRIBOMONT, in *Théologie de la vie monastique* (Maredsous 1961) 99–113. C. KOROLEVSKIJ, *Dictionnaire d'histoire et de géographie ecclésiastiques*, ed. A. BAUDRILLART et al. (Paris 1912–) 6:1180–1236; *Le Métropolite A. Szeptickyj* (Rome 1964). M. SCADUTO, *Il monachismo basiliano nella Sicilia medievale* (Rome 1947). B. CAPELLI, *Il monachismo basiliano ai confini calabrolucani* (Naples 1963). A. GUILLOU, *Mélanges d'archéologie et d'histoire* 75 (1963) 79–110. R. DEVREESE, *Les Manuscrits grecs de l'Italie méridionale* (*Studi et Testi* 183; 1955). B. HAMILTON, ''The City of Rome and the Eastern Churches in the Xth Century,'' *Orientalia Christiana periodica* 27 (1961) 4–26. A. BENITO DURÁN, *Revista de la biblioteca* 20 (1951) 167–237. T. BORESKY, *Life of St. Josaphat* (New York 1955). *Analecta Ordinis S. Basilii Magni* (Zhovkua 1944) *passim.* J. GEORGESCO, *Dictionnaire de théologie catholique*, ed. A. VACANT et al., 15 v. (Paris 1903–50) 14.1:66–67 R. JANIN, *Dictionnaire de théologie catholique* 10.1:519–20.

[J. GRIBOMONT]

BASILIANS

Popular name for the Congregation of Priests of St. Basil (CSB, Official Catholic Directory #0170), a community of priests with simple vows who belong to the Roman Rite and whose principal work is the Christian education of youth.

Origin. The congregation had its origin in the Catholic movement for survival during the French Revolution. Abp. Charles d'Aviau (1736–1826) of Vienne appointed Joseph Bouvier Lapierre (1757–1838) pastor of the hamlet of Saint-Symphorien-de-Mahun in the Ardèche mountains and asked him to teach Latin to six aspirants to the priesthood. This rectory study group quickly grew into a school of 140 students that was transferred in 1802 to the city Annonay. Léorat Picansel (1741–1823), vicar-general of the Diocese of Viviers, drew up the first rule and guided the founders in the organization of a religious community. On Nov. 21, 1822, nine priest-teachers joined with Lapierre in forming a community of diocesan priests. Gregory XVI raised it to pontifical rank and bestowed on it the decree of praise on Sept. 15, 1837. Papal approbations were given by Pius IX in 1863, Pius X in 1913, and Pius XI in 1938.

Growth was gradual, and the work was limited to Annonay and a few neighboring towns, until 1850 when a graduate of the College of Annonay, Armand François, comte de Charbonnel (1802–91), was named bishop of Toronto, Canada. Before leaving France for his diocese, he obtained from his former teachers the services of a young Irish priest, Patrick Molony (1813–80). In 1852, the motherhouse of the Basilian Fathers in America, the University of St. Michael's College, was established in Toronto, with a staff of three priests and two seminarians. Under the direction of the first superior, Jean Soulerin (1807–79), a novitiate was opened, and soon vocations permitted expansion to other cities. The parish of St. Mary of the Assumption, Owen Sound, Canada, was taken over in 1863 with the mission field attached to it. In 1870, Denis O'Connor (1841–1911), later successively bishop of London and archbishop of Toronto, took charge of a school that later became Assumption University, Windsor. Attached to this institution is historic Assumption parish, which began as a mission to the Native Americans in 1728.

The first permanent Basilian foundation in the United States was made at St. Anne's Church, Detroit, Mich., in 1886, when Pierre Grand (1845–1922) became pastor of the parish, which dates back to 1701. Other foundations included St. Louis College, opened at Louisville, Ohio, in 1867 and closed in 1873; and St. Basil's College, Waco, Tex., undertaken in 1899 and given up in 1915. The first successful school in the United States was St. Thomas High School, Houston, Tex., established in 1900 by Nicholas Roche (1866–1932).

Growth. Expansion in the United States and Canada during the second half of the 19th century was paralleled by similar growth in Europe, which included the establishment of the College of Mary Immaculate at Beaconfield, England (1883), and three missions in Algeria. Unfortunately, this vitality did not last, partly because of a decrease in vocations after the Franco-Prussian War of 1870 and partly because of anticlericalism and the suppression of religious houses in France in 1902.

The canonical development of the Basilian fathers into a full religious community came about slowly. Founded as a community of diocesan priests, members first took the vows of obedience, chastity, and poverty on Oct. 1, 1852, although the constitutions retained the earlier practice of limited poverty. For several decades, modifications in the vow of poverty were a source of difficulty to those who wished to follow the religious life without reservation. On June 14, 1922, at the request of the French province, the Holy See erected the American and French provinces into distinct communities. The separation lasted until 1955, when a new decree united the two communities.

After separation, the Basilian fathers in America, under the leadership of Father Francis Forster (1873–1929), embraced the simple vow of poverty without any reservations. This step was followed by a notable increase in vocations, which made possible new foundations and the expansion of existing houses. In Canada, the congregation established houses in the Archdioceses of Ottawa, Toronto, and Vancouver; and in the Dioceses of Calgary, Hamilton, London, Saskatoon, and Sault Sainte Marie. Basilians conduct the Pontifical Institute of Mediaeval Studies, Toronto; the University of St. Michael's College, Toronto; Assumption University, Windsor; St. Thomas More College, Saskatoon; St. Mark's College, Vancouver; nine high schools; and eight parishes. They developed a system of cooperation with state universities that has been copied by other Catholic colleges in Canada. John Read Teefy (1848–1911) was author of the first such affiliation, between the University of Toronto and St. Michael's College in 1881.

In the United States, the congregation established the University of St. Thomas in Houston, Tex.; and St. John Fisher College, Rochester, N.Y. In 1961 the Basilians undertook the care of San Juan Crisóstomo parish in the suburbs of Mexico City, as an extension of their work with Latin Americans. By the time of the union in 1955, the once flourishing Basilian houses in France were reduced to the motherhouse in Annonay, L'Institution Secondaire du Sacré-Coeur. All others had been closed or taken over by diocesan priests after the suppression of religious houses in 1902.

Bibliography: *Basilian Annals* (Toronto, Canada 1943–). *Basilian Teacher* (Toronto, Canada 1956–).

[R. J. SCOLLARD]

BASILIANS (BYZANTINE)

Within the Eastern Catholic Churches, there are five branches of the order of St. Basil the Great (OSBM, Official Catholic Directory #0180): Grottaferrata, in the Italo-Albanian Catholic Church; St. Josaphat, in the Ukrainian and Romanian Eastern Catholic Churches; and St. Saviour, St. John Baptist, and Aleppo, in the Melkite Greek Catholic Church. Each of these groups follows basically the rule of St. BASIL the Great.

Basil, Archbishop of Caesarea in Cappadocia (modern Turkey), was the great legislator of Eastern monasticism. Beginning in 358, he composed a rule in two forms (a longer and a shorter series of articles) through which he became the founder of cenobitic monasticism. Although his teachings had their greater impact in the East, Basil exercised some influence also over the BENEDICTINE

RULE in the West. Characteristic of Basil's rule (or rules) was CENOBITISM (common life) in the strict sense, in contrast to the earlier eremitism of St. ANTHONY OF EGYPT and the mitigated cenobitism of St. PACHOMIUS. Another characteristic was the addition of social activity to the customary monastic prayer and work. Specifically, Basil recommended the founding of schools for boys. Basil's rule was further determined, in the late 8th century, by the *typikon* (constitutions) of (St.) THEODORE THE STUDITE at STUDION, the famous monastery in Constantinople. In this later form the rule was adopted by the monasteries of the Byzantine Empire, including the great laura on Mount ATHOS founded in the 10th century by (St.) ATHANASIUS THE ATHONITE.

Basilian Order of Grottaferrata. In the 7th and 8th centuries monasteries following the Basilian rule were founded in southern Italy and Sicily by Greek monks who fled from their native countries during the persecutions arising out of ICONOCLASM. In the 10th century (St.) NILUS OF ROSSANO established the Greek monastery of GROTTAFERRATA outside Rome. Many other monasteries were erected in Italy in the 11th century under the Norman regime. The rule of St. Basil was adopted also in Spain in the 16th century at a monastery in the Diocese of Jaén, upon the advice of Bp. Diego Tavera. The man designated to be the first superior, Bernardo de la Cruz, went to Grottaferrata where he made his profession. Pius IV then created (1561) the Spanish congregation, a Basilian group in the Latin Church. Not long afterward Gregory XIII first united all the Greek monasteries in Italy into one congregation and then, by the bull *Benedictus Dominus* (Nov. 1, 1579), erected the Italo-Spanish Basilian Congregation under one archimandrite. Over the subsequent years the Italian branch tended to adopt the Latin rite, a move that was opposed by the Holy See. Both branches of the congregation later went out of existence, the Spanish in 1855, and the Italian in 1866. Grottaferrata, however, was restored in its Greek tradition in 1880 under the leadership of its abbot, Giuseppe Cozza-Luzi (d. 1905). New constitutions were approved in 1900, and in 1937 Pius XI elevated the monastery to the exarchal rank. Grottaferrata has several dependent foundations in southern Italy and Sicily, including the ancient monastery of Mezzoiusso (Calabria).

Basilian Order of St. Josaphat. In 1072 the rule of St. Basil was introduced in the monastery Pecherska Lavra in Kiev, capital of the Ukraine, by (St.) Theodosius (d. 1074). Subsequently the rule became the model for other monasteries in the Ukraine, Belarus, and Russia. Following the union of the See of Kiev with Rome (1596) some monasteries of the Ukraine and Belarus formed in 1617 the Basilian Congregation of the Holy Trinity (also called the Lithuanian Congregation). Approval was given by Urban VIII in the brief *Exponi nobis,* Aug. 20, 1631. The initiators of this reorganization were the archbishop of Kiev, Velamin Rutski (1574–1637), and (St.) JOSAPHAT KUNCEVYČ. Gradually other monasteries joined the congregation, but some remained independent until, by order of the synod of Zamosc (1720), the Congregation of the Protection of the Holy Virgin (also called the Ruthenian Congregation) was formed in 1739. By decree of Benedict XIV (1742) both groups were joined in one order of St. Basil the Great, and in the general chapter at Dubno in 1743 two provinces were created, Lithuanian and Ruthenian. In 1780 the order was divided into four provinces because of the partition of Poland (1772).

In the 17th and 18th centuries the Basilians were engaged in various missionary, pastoral, and educational activities, especially for the promotion of the union of the Ukrainian Church with Rome. In the beginning their novitiate was at Wilno (Lithuania) under the direction of Josaphat; later it was moved to Byten (Belarus) in the care first of the Jesuits, and later, of the Basilians themselves. The young clerical students, after their novitiate and religious profession, usually pursued their philosophical studies at the monastery of Zhytrovytsi, a renowned place of pilgrimage. For theology they went to Western Europe where Urban VIII had established 22 scholarships for them in the pontifical schools of the following cities: four in Rome, two in Vienna, two in Prague, two in Olmütz (Moravia), six in Braunsberg (Prussia), and six in Graz (Austria). Basilians staffed the diocesan seminary at Minsk (Belarus), and many colleges for boys, among which the most notable was that of Vladimir-Volynski, the birthplace of Josaphat.

All the metropolitans of Kiev in the 17th and 18th centuries were Basilians. Velamin Rutski and his four immediate successors in the metropolitan see were also the superiors general of the order of St. Basil. Each of them held that office (protoarchimandrite) until death. After 1675 the two offices were separated and the protoarchimandrite (now simply a monk) was elected to a term of four years, later extended to eight in 1751. He made his residence in one of the order's monasteries, while the procurator general resided in Rome. Provinces were ruled by *protohegumeni* (provincials); monasteries, by either archimandrites constituted for life, or by *hegumeni* (local superiors) in office for four years. By 1772 Basilian monasteries in the Ukraine and Belarus numbered 144 with 1,225 religious (944 priests, 190 clerical students, and 91 lay brothers).

The work of the Basilians for the union of the Eastern Churches with Rome was almost totally destroyed by the further partition of Poland, the hostility toward union in the Russian empire, and the suppression of Basilian monasteries. Toward the end of the 19th century only one province remained, that of Galicia in the Austrian empire. Here too the Basilians suffered, along with other religious orders, from JOSEPHINISM. Leo XIII, in 1882, reorganized the remaining 14 monasteries of Galicia by placing them under the direction of the Jesuits in Dobromil. The members of the Dobromil reform gradually extended their activity among the following peoples: the Ukrainians in Galicia and, later, in the Carpathian Ukraine (Ruthenia); the Hungarians of the Eastern Christians; the Ukrainians, Croatians, and Macedonians in Yugoslavia; and the Romanians. The Basilians also followed the emigrants of these peoples to the United States, Canada, Brazil, and Argentina. The reform begun at Dobromil was brought to completion when a general chapter was held there in 1931. The superior general elected at that chapter, Dionysius Tkachuk (1867–1944), took up residence in Rome for the first time. Pius XI, on Feb. 24, 1932, approved the present name of the order, the Basilian Order of St. Josaphat.

Before the Soviet occupation of Eastern Europe the Basilians were organized in four provinces: Galicia, the Carpathian Ukraine, Hungary, and Romania. Their activity, as in the past, was diversified. They continued their traditional life, a combination of monastic prayer and active apostolate. In Galicia they conducted for a time three diocesan seminaries at Lvov, Peremyshl, and Stanislav; a boys' high school in Buchach; and a publications center in Zhovkva. In the Carpathian Ukraine there was a high school and publications' center at Uzhgorod. In Hungary the Basilians had charge of a pilgrimage church at Mariapocs, and in Romania they had a publications' center at Bixad. Two other seminaries were under their direction: a minor seminary at Zagreb, Yugoslavia, and the pontifical Ukrainian College of St. Josaphat in Rome. With the coming of the Communist governments many Basilians were arrested and sent to labor camps; some, however, continued to work in secret. The collapse of communism gave rise to a modest revival of the Basilians.

Outside of Europe the order of St. Basil has carried on its ministry among Eastern Catholic emigres peoples. In 1897 the Basilians established a presence in South America, where they have a province in Brazil and a vice province in Argentina, both erected in 1948. In 1902 they came to Canada where a province was created in 1932. The novitiate and house of studies were located in Mundare, Alberta, and a publications' center in Toronto, Ontario, where they conduct a school for boys. The U.S. branch began in 1926 and became a province separate from Canada in 1948.

Basilian Orders of the Melkite Greek Catholic Church. The Basilian Order of St. Saviour was founded by the archbishop of Tyre and Sidon (Lebanon), Euthymios Saifi, in 1684. Benedict XIV placed it under the rule of St. Basil in 1743. Before the occupation of Syria by the Egyptians in 1832, the Basilians were engaged in parochial ministry in Lebanon, Palestine, Egypt, and the city of Damascus.

The Basilian Order of St. John Baptist, also known as the order of Suwayr, or the Baladites, was begun in 1712 by two Syrian monks, Gerasim and Solomon, who had established themselves at the church of St. John Baptist in a valley near the village of Suwayr in Lebanon. The first superior of the group, Nicephore Karmi, prescribed four vows for the community in 1722. The vow of humility was added to the usual vows of poverty, chastity, and obedience. Efforts toward uniting this group with the Basilian Order of St. Saviour were not successful, and in 1743 Benedict XIV imposed the rule of St. Basil. The constitutions, approved by the same pope in 1757, were developed from those of the Maronite monks of St. Anthony. As in the case of order of St. Saviour, the canonical status of the Baladites was fixed by the Holy See in 1955. The motherhouse of the order is in Khonchara in Lebanon.

The Basilian Order of Aleppo is an offshoot of the preceding group; the separation took place in 1829 and was approved by the Holy See in 1832. Its canonical development was the same as that indicated for the aforementioned orders. The headquarters of the order is at the monastery of St. Saviour in Sarba, Djunieh, Lebanon. Acacius COUSSA, the Oriental canonist, was a member of this Basilian group.

Bibliography: *Analecta Ordinis S. Basilii Magni,* Ser. 1 (Zhovkva 1924–35) Ser. 2 (Rome 1949–). M. WOJNAR, *De regimine Basilianorum Ruthenorum a Metropolita J. V. Rutskyj instauratorum* (Rome 1949); *De capitulis Basilianorum* (Rome 1954); *De Protoarchimandrita Basilianorum* (Rome 1958). C. PUJOL, *De religiosis orientalibus ad normam vigentis iuris* (Rome 1957). M. KAROVETZ, *Velyka Revorma Chyna Sv. Vasyliia Velykoho,* 4 v. (Zhovkva 1933–38). A. SHEPTYCKYJ, *Pravyla dla monakhiv* (Zhovkva 1911); *Asketychni tvory Sv. O. N. Vasyliia V.* (Lvov 1929).

[M. M. WOJNAR/EDS.]

BASILIANS—SISTERS OF THE ORDER OF ST. BASIL THE GREAT (OSBM)

The Order of the Sisters of St. Basil the Great (*Ordo S. Basilii Magni*), a community of women dedicated to the spiritual and educational pursuits of the people of God, was founded in the fourth century by St. Basil the Great and his sister, St. Macrina. The order with foundations in Europe, North and South America, and Australia serves primarily people of the Eastern Catholic church. St. Basil and St. Macrina urged their followers to be co-workers with God in the task of developing the potential of each human being through education and development of the whole person. The Basilian tradition spread throughout Asia Minor and Europe, and by the 11th century, it had become centered in Ukraine.

The community's first foundation in the United States was established in 1911 when the Most Reverend Soter Ortynsky, the first Ukrainian Bishop in North America, invited the Sisters of St. Basil to come to Philadelphia and open an orphanage and school. Upon their arrival in Philadelphia, Mother Helena Langevich, at the time 32 years of age, and two companions, Sister Paphnutia and Sister Euphemia, met the needs of Ukrainian immigrants by teaching religion, language and culture. Evening classes gave way to the establishment of a parochial school. Under the direction of Mother Josaphat Theodorouych, the first American superior, the order purchased the property in Fox Chase, Pennsylvania, and continued to grow. In time the sisters established a printing house, an orphanage, a high school for girls (St. Basil Academy), Manor College, the only accredited college sponsored by the Eastern Catholic Church in the United States, and a Basilian Spirituality Center.

The Generalate of the Order is located in Rome. The Order has two provinces in the United States. The one with headquarters in Fox Chase Manor follows the Ukrainian Byzantine Rite and is represented in the Archeparchy of Philadelphia and the eparchies of Chicago, Parma, Ohio, and Stamford, Connecticut. The other with its motherhouse in Uniontown, Pennsylvania, follows the Ruthenian Byzantine Rite and is represented in the Archeparchy of Pittsburgh and the eparchies of Parma, Passaic, New Jersey and Van Nuys, California.

[M. M. WOJNAR/EDS.]

BASILICA

A large rectangular, hall-like building, fully covered with a roof and usually supported by interior columns. At Athens the *Stoa Basilikē* (royal stoa) was a building on the Areopagus, where official and other business was transacted. In its Latinized form, basilica referred to a public building, hall-like in form, such as the Basilica Julia, erected by Julius Caesar and reconstructed by both Augustus and Diocletian (285–305). It was rectangular in shape and had a series of double colonnades that divided it into four aisles with a central hall, at one end of which was an apse or rounded court where the praetor sat. The other end contained the single entrance, and above the main aisle there was a second story. The basilica was used for the transaction of both public and private business, particularly in inclement weather. In the later empire, every sizable city had one or more such buildings facing the forum.

Ruins of Phidia and Christian Basilica workshop, Olympia, Greece, 5th Century B.C. (©Michael Nicholson/CORBIS)

Christian House Church

The primitive Christians, following the example of Christ, who presided at the Last Supper in a *coenaculum,* or upper room (Mk 14.15; Lk 22.12), and that of the Apostles and Disciples, who gathered in prayer while awaiting the coming of the Holy Spirit on the first Pentecost in an upper room (Acts 1.13–14), held their assemblies in private houses where they received instruction, broke bread in the Eucharistic celebration, and prayed (Acts 20.7–9). The Christians of Jerusalem were gathered in the home of Mary, the mother of John Mark, praying at night when Peter was delivered from prison (Acts 12.12–17), and Paul refers several times to private homes

Basilica of Aquileia, central nave, Aquileia, Italy, early 9th century. (©Elio Ciol/CORBIS)

in which he preached and prayed (1 Cor 16.19; Rom 16.3, 5; Col 4.15; Plm 1.2–3).

At the end of the 1st century the DIDACHE describes the exhortation, the Eucharistic celebration, and preparation for Baptism in a private home (4.14; 14.1), and JUSTIN MARTYR alludes (*c.* 160) to a place for the ablution or Baptism (Apol. 1.65–67), again clearly in a private home where the Christian mysteries were celebrated. MINUCIUS FELIX uses the word *sacraria* to specify a special place where Christians gathered for worship (Octav. 9.1), but it was still in a private house (10.2).

Archeological Evidence. Archeological evidence from the 3d century confirms the fact that the so-called *domus ecclesia,* or house church, was the usual site of Christian liturgical gatherings. References to meetings in the cemeteries for the celebration of rites other than the commemoration of the dead before the middle of the 3d century are usually legendary, although Saints Chrysanthus and Daria, and Pope SIXTUS II and his companions, were surprised by the police in cemeteries and martyred respectively on the Via Salaria and the Via Appia outside Rome.

Evidence from the early 4th century presented by excavations beneath the Basilica of Saint CLEMENT, Rome, which have revealed several levels of construction, are not conclusive as to the presence or place of Christian cult before the 4th-century construction of the original church; the same must be said of the excavations beneath the Basilica of Saint ANASTASIA and the title church of San Martino ai Monti. However, those beneath the Basilica of Saints John and Paul do reveal a house church that existed during the late 3rd or early 4th century, when its walls were decorated with Christian figures. At DURA-EUROPOS, the house church (*c.* 232) contained several rooms, only a few of which were devoted to Christian cult. At Qirq-Bezin, Syria, however, the early 4th-century house seems to have been a primitive model of the later Syrian type of basilica with a hall-like room for ceremonies preceded by an atrium; a room for relics; a bēma, or bishop's chair; and a martyrion.

Funerary monuments and crypts in the cemeteries display evidence of Christian usage early in the 3rd century. The *tropaion,* or monument, erected over the grave of Saint Peter at the VATICAN goes back to *c.* 180; but the *hypogeum,* or crypt, of the Flavii and that of Ampliatus in the CATACOMB of Domitilla are later, as are the *cappella graeca* of the catacomb of Priscilla and the crypt of Lucina on the Via Appia near the catacomb of Callistus, in which many early popes were buried (*c.* 235). This evidence indicates Christian interest in construction that by the end of the 3rd century had manifested itself in the erection of churches such as that close to the palace of the emperor in Nicomedia, which was destroyed at the outbreak of the persecution of DIOCLETIAN.

Constantine I. Evidence for the existence of a Christian basilica (*c.* 306) has been discovered in Aquileia, but the first certain basilica-type construction must be credited to CONSTANTINE I. In 313 he gave Pope Miltiades a palace at the Lateran for the papal residence and began the construction of a church called later the Basilica of Saint John Lateran. He likewise transformed a hall of the Sessorian palace into a basilica-like church where Saint HELENA preserved a relic of the true cross (Santa Croce in Gerusalemme).

At the Vatican over the tomb of Saint Peter, Constantine began construction of the ancient Basilica of Saint Peter, and in Palestine he ordered the construction of the Basilicas of the Nativity at Bethlehem, the Annunciation at Nazareth, the Martyrion and Anastasis in Jerusalem, as well as basilicas at Capua, Antioch, Naples, Nicomedia, and Tréves and the Church of the Apostles at CONSTANTINOPLE. Constantine also authorized public funds for building churches in various parts of the Empire, and this work of construction provided all the large Christian centers with basilicas or greater churches in Africa and the Orient during the 4th century.

It was but normal that the Christian churches should have adopted the form of public buildings in the locale where they were constructed, and this was almost certainly the case of the basilicas that were built in Rome and Italy. From the beginning, however, the requirements of Christian cult dictated modifications.

The Christian Basilica

The classical type of Christian basilica was a rectangular building supported by four walls and divided by two or more rows of columns into a central nave and two or more aisles on each side of the nave (ambulatories). The roof of the nave was raised higher than the roof above the aisles. The roofs were of timber, the one above the nave being an isosceles triangle of fairly low altitude crossing the span. The roof timbering was usually hidden by a flat ceiling. The walls supporting the roof above the nave constituted a clerestory whose windows, formed of pierced stone slabs, provided air and a mellow, diffuse light. The exterior was subdued and unadorned so that no architectural extravagance might detract from the spiritual purpose.

Furnishings and Adornment. The only departure from the simple rectangular design was the semicircular apse (concha, tribune), in which stood the throne (cathedra) of the bishop, flanked by seats for the clergy. At the opposite end was the main doorway leading into the nave and smaller doorways leading to the aisles or ambulatories. Beyond the entrance was a quadrangular court (atrium) in the center of which stood a fountain or cistern (*cantharus, pluviale*), in which the worshipers washed their hands and lips in preparation for receiving Holy Communion.

At times, the atrium was surrounded by a colonnaded cloister (S. Clemente in Rome, S. Ambrogio at Milan, old Saint. Peter's), but it was often reduced to a narrow portico or vestibule (narthex) as the entrance portico was called in the Eastern Empire. In some basilicas, a transept extended in front of the sanctuary to facilitate the procession of the people to and from the altar. At the juncture of the nave and the transept was a triumphal arch that served to direct and concenntrate attention on the altar The rounded apse was decorated with scenes from the Bible or portrayals of Our Lord in glory surrounded by martyrs.

To the front of the apse, faced by the cathedra, stood the table-shaped altar covered by a permanent canopy (*ciborium*) supported on marble columns. Mass was celebrated facing the people. Relics of the saint to whom the church was dedicated were often placed beneath the altar and were visible through a small window (*fenestella confessionis*). In some cases, the relics were kept in a crypt opening under the apse and communicating with the altar. The altar was separated from the nave by low marble screens (*cancelli*) or by a chancel. The space reserved for the choir at the head of the nave was also railed off by *cancelli.* On each side of the nave screen were stone pulpits (*ambones*) for the reading of the Epistle and Gospel. The congregation occupied the aisles, the men on the

Transfiguration Basilica, designed by Antonio Barluzzi, Mount Tabor, Israel, 1924. (©Paul Almasy/CORBIS)

south side and the women on the north. The rear of the nave was reserved for the catechumens, and the penitents were confined to the portico.

Although the basilica was austere in its exterior, it was richly adorned within. The wall spaces above the columns of the nave were covered with glass mosaics. The floor was decorated with marble mosaics in the fashion familiar to the Roman. The baptistery was usually a small domed structure erected near the church and connected with it by a covered passageway. A large basin or pool for immersion (*piscina, fons*) was sunk in the floor and provided with steps. When infant Baptism became general, the baptismal font replaced the basin and Baptism was administered in the church.

Liturgical Meeting. An early Christian document, the Syriac *Didascalia Apostolorum,* presents a description of a liturgical meeting and place of worship and at the same time suggests the problems facing the early Christian architect:

> In your assemblies in the holy churches . . . arrange the places of the brethren carefully with all sobriety. Let a place be reserved for the presbyters in the midst of the eastern part of the house, and let the throne of the bishop be placed amongst them; let the presbyters sit with him; but also at the other, eastern side of the house let the laymen sit; for thus it is required that the presbyters should sit at the eastern side of the house with the bishops, and afterwards the laymen, and next the women: that when you stand to pray the rulers

> may stand first, afterwards the laymen, and then the women also . . .
>
> As for the deacons, let one of them stand constantly over the gifts of the Eucharist, and let another stand outside the door and look at those who come in; and afterwards when you make offerings, let them serve together in the Church. And if a man be found sitting out of his place, let the deacon who is within reprove him, and make him get up and sit in the place that befits him. [J. Quasten, *Patrology* (Westminster, Md. 1950–) 2.148.]

The practice of ''orienting'' the basilica took cognizance of a symbolism that was older than Christianity. The *Apostolic Constitutions* required that the throne of the bishop be turned to face the east and that the liturgy should be celebrated facing that direction. The Jews and the pagans prayed facing the east, though for different reasons. The pagans, who adored the sun, greeted it at its rising and its setting. Their temples also were oriented. The Jews in their synagogues turned toward the east in their public prayer in order to be facing the Temple of Jerusalem. For the greater number of Jews of the Diaspora, the Temple of Jerusalem was in the east.

By the 5th century, the custom of orienting the basilica had become almost a rule. Socrates the Church historian protested when the altar of a certain church faced the west (*Ecclesiastical History* 5.22). HAGIA SOPHIA at Constantinople and Saint Apollinaris at Ravenna have their apses turned toward the east. At Rome there was resistance to this usage, which appeared to have become obligatory. Pope LEO I (d. 461) rebuked Christians whom he observed turning toward the east and inclining toward the sun before entering the Basilica of St. Peter (*Serm.* 27.4). The custom persisted in spite of papal disfavor, and as late as the 9th century Walafrid Strabo noted that orientation was general in the West but not rigorously practiced.

At Rome the so-called Constantinian basilicas gave no indication of orientation; but when they were rebuilt, an effort was made to satisfy the wishes of the people, who had by now attached a mystic interpretation to the custom carried over from paganism. Nevertheless, there was no hesitation on the part of Christians to set orientation aside if there were sufficient reason for doing so. In the late 4th century, almost as many basilicas faced south and west as faced east.

The Christian basilica corresponded so closely to its sacred purposes that it has remained in essence the basis of church architecture. In it the Christian ceremonies attained a level of magnificence while the splendor of the interior satisfied the aesthetic needs of the Christian spirit. All the early basilicas, however, with the exception of Saint Mary Major, Saint Pudentiana, and Saint Sabina, have undergone such extensive changes that their original disposition is difficult to determine.

Bibliography: V. CHIRONE, *The House of God through the Ages,* tr. K. NOTTRIDGE, 3 v. (Rome 1960–61) v.1. A. MOLIEN, *Dictionnaire de droit canonique*, ed. R. NAZ, 7 v. (Paris 1935–65) 2:224–49. G. DOWNEY, ''The Architectural Significance of the Use of the Words *Stoa* and *Basilike* in Classical Literature,'' *American Journal of Archeology* (Concord, N.H. 1885–) 2d series 41 (1937) 194–211. V. MÜLLER, ''The Roman Basilica,'' *ibid.* 250–61. *Liber pontificalis*, ed. L. DUCHESNE, v.1–2 (Paris 1886–92) v.3 (Paris 1958) 170–304. R. C. DE LASTEYRIE DU SAILLANT, *L'Architecture religieuse en France à l'époque romane* (2d ed. Paris 1929). R. LEMAIRE, *L'Origine de la basilique latine* (Brussels 1911). W. L. MACDONALD, *Early Christian and Byzantine Architecture* (New York 1962). O. MARUCCHI, *Basiliques et églises de Rome* (Paris 1902). A. P. SHEEHAN, *The New Temple of God as Reflected in the Early Church Edifices* (Master's dissertation unpublished Catholic University of America 1964). P. TESTINI, *Archeologia cristiana* (Rome 1958). A. C. A. ZESTERMANN, *De basilicis* (Brussels 1847). L. VOELKL and A. P. FRUTAZ, *Lexikon für Theologie und Kirche*, ed. J. HOFER and K. RAHNER, 10 v. (2d, new ed. Freiburg 1957–65) 2:40–45. E. LANGLOTZ and F. W. DEICHMANN, *Reallexikon für Antike und Christentum*, ed. T. KLAUSER [Stuttgart 1941 (1950)–] 1:1225–29. T. F. MATHEWS, ''An Early Roman Chancel Arrangement and Its Liturgical Functions,'' *Revista di archeologia cristiana* (Rome 1924–) 38 (1962) 73–95. R. KRAUTHEIMER, *Corpus basilicarum christianarum Romae* (Vatican City 1937–). T.F. MATHEWS, *The Early Churches of Constantinople: Architecture and Liturgy* (University Park, Pa. 1970).

[M. C. HILFERTY/EDS.]

BASILIDES

Gnostic teacher, 2d-century founder of a Gnostic school in Alexandria. Of the life of Basilides little is known with certainty. Epiphanius (*Haer.* 1.23) reports that he was a fellow pupil of Saturnilus under Menander in Antioch. Basilides taught at Alexandria, most probably under the reigns of Hadrian and Antoninus Pius (*c.* A.D. 120–145). The most distinguished disciple in his heretical sect, still in existence in the 4th century, was his son Isidore. Basilides composed his own version of the Gospels, a commentary on this work in 24 books called the *Exegetica* (fragments in HEGEMONIUS, *Acta Archelai* 67.4–12 and CLEMENT OF ALEXANDRIA, *Strom.* 4.81–88), and some odes and psalms now lost.

It is difficult to determine precisely the doctrines of Basilides. According to IRENAEUS (*Adv. Haer.* 1.24) he began with a system of emanations starting with the Father, the Nous, the Logos, Phronesis, Sophia, and Dynamis, followed by 365 groups of angels and powers, each of which created a heaven, and the last of which created our world. Christ was the Nous who visited the world but was not really crucified. Salvation comes by knowledge of the Nous and the system, the acts of the body are a matter of indifference, magic and incantations have an important role. HIPPOLYTUS OF ROME (*Ref.* 7.20–27), however, describes a much more original doctrine involving a nonexistent God from whose seed arise a triple order of Sonship, a series of Archons, and upper and lower regions called the Ogdoad and the Hebdomad. A key feature of this presentation is the denial of the typically Gnostic doctrine of emanation. Despite the marked differences in their account of Basilides' teaching, it is possible that Irenaeus describes an earlier version of his doctrine and Hippolytus a later one. Hegemonius (*supra*) states that Basilides taught Persian dualism, though the other accounts present his system as monistic. Clement of Alexandria (*supra*) was chiefly concerned with ethical aspects of his teachings. Basilides seems to have been mainly a philosopher; his very subtlety may have impeded the spread of his sect beyond Egypt.

See Also: GNOSTICISM.

Bibliography: W. VÖLKER, *Quellen zur Geschichte der christlichen Gnosis* (Tübingen 1932) 38–57. A. S. PEAKE, *Encyclopedia of Religion and Ethics,* ed. J. HASTINGS (Edinburgh 1908–27) 2:426–433. J. H. WASZINK, *Reallexikon für Antike und Christemtum* 1:1217–25. J. QUASTEN, *Patrology,* 3. v. (Westminster, MD 1950) 1:257–259. R. M. WILSON, *The Gnostic Problem* (London 1958). J. DORESSE, *The Secret Books of the Egyptian Gnostics,* tr. P. MAIRET (New York 1960). R. M. GRANT, *Gnosticism: A Sourcebook* (New York 1961).

[G. W. MACRAE]

BASILIDES, SS.

Martyr; d. Alexandria, 202–203. A soldier, he protected St. Potamiaena from the crowd as he led her, after tortures, to her martyrdom under boiling pitch. She promised to repay him for his kindness, and when Basilides was imprisoned as a Christian for refusing to take an oath, she appeared to him, wreathed his head with a crown, and promised soon to take him to herself. Basilides was baptized and the next day beheaded, the seventh catechumen of ORIGEN to suffer martyrdom. His story, which is preserved by Eusebius (*Hist. Eccl.* 6.5), is one of the earliest testimonies in the Church to belief in the intercession of saints. In the martyrology of Jerome, he is commemorated on June 28 with Potamiaena and her martyred mother, Marcella.

Feast: June 30.

On June 12 the Roman martyrology commemorates a Basilides with Cyrinus, Nabor, and Nazarius. He was a Roman martyr buried at the twelfth milestone of the Via Aurelia, where there was a shrine to him in the seventh century. The three accounts of him are late and without historical value, and there is no connection between him and Cyrinus (probably Quirinus, bishop of Siscia) and Nabor and Nazarius (martyrs of Milan).

Bibliography: A. P. FRUTAZ and A. KREUZ, *Lexikon für Theologie und Kirche,* ed. J. HOFER and K. RAHNER (Freiburg 1957–65) 2:39–40. B. CIGNITTI and F. CARAFFA, *Bibliotheca Sanctorum* 2:904–906.

[M. J. COSTELLOE]

BASILISCUS, BYZANTINE EMPEROR

The Byzantine emperor Basiliscus (475–476) was brother-in-law of Emperor Leo I (457–474) through his sister Verina. It has been suggested that he was a relative of Odoacer, though this seems unlikely. Basiliscus was married to Zenonis and had several children, including a son, Marcus. He had a successful military career, serving in the Balkans as *magister militum per Thracias* (464–468) and was awarded a consulate in 465. In 468 he led the disastrous expedition against the Vandals, though his subsequent career in the Balkans was successful.

After the accession of Zeno in 474, Basiliscus seized power in Constantinople in January 475. Zeno fled. Once in power, Basiliscus restored as patriarchs Timothy Aelurus to Alexandria and Peter the Fuller to Antioch. He then issued his encyclical, rejecting the 451 Council of Chalcedon and the Tome of Leo. A revised version issued at Ephesus promising the removal of patriarchal authority from Constantinople led to strong support, but it also led to the rejection of the encyclical by Acacius, patriarch of Constantinople. Acacius received widespread support in Constantinople, especially from the monks, but also from Pope Simplicius in Rome. When Acacius induced Daniel the Stylite to descend from his pillar to lead a march of protest, Basiliscus was forced to meet the two men and admit his inability to resolve matters of faith. Basiliscus then issued his antencyclical, confirming Acacius's position as patriarch and retracting his encyclical. Military forces sent against Zeno were unsuccessful. Zeno was able to persuade their generals to return to supporting him. When Zeno arrived back at Constantinople in August 476, Basiliscus was left with little support. After taking refuge in Hagia Sophia, he surrendered to Zeno on a promise of no blood being shed. Zeno condemned Basiliscus and his family to imprisonment at Limnae in Cappadocia where the prisoners were starved to death.

Bibliography: W. BRANDES, ''Familienbände? Odoaker, Basiliskos und Harmatios,'' *Klio* 75 (1993) 407–437. S. KRAUTSCHICK, ''Zwei Aspekte des Jahres 476,'' *Historia* 35 (1986) 344–371. S. KRAUTSCHICK, ''Die unmögliche Tatsache: Argumente gegen Johannes Antiochenus,'' *Klio* 77 (1995) 332–338. M. REDIES, ''Die Usurpation des Basiliskos (475–476) im Kontext der aufsteigenden monophysitischen Kirche,'' *Antiquité Tardive* 5 (1997) 211–221.

[H. W. ELTON]

Basiliscus pushed into a cistern. (©Bettmann/CORBIS)

BASSIANUS OF EPHESUS

5th-century bishop; d. after 451. A popular and influential priest of Ephesus, Bassianus was forced by his bishop, Memnon, because of jealousy, to be consecrated bishop of Evaza (*c.* 431), but he refused to occupy his see. Memnon's successor, Basil, consecrated another bishop for Evaza and allowed Bassianus to return to Ephesus (*c.* 434). With the approval of Emperor THEODOSIUS II and Proclus, Patriarch of Constantinople, Bassianus was chosen to succeed Basil in Ephesus (444). Four years later, however, Bassianus was forcibly deposed, and Stephen was named his successor. Bassianus appealed to the emperor, who referred the matter to the Council of CHALCEDON. The fathers heard the testimony of both sides at the 11th session (Oct. 29, 451). Although many sided with Bassianus, no decision was reached until the 12th session on the following day. The council then decided that both Stephen and Bassianus were to be deposed, and a new bishop to be chosen by the bishops of the province. Bassianus and Stephen, however, were each to receive 200 gold solidi a year from the See of Ephesus. Little is known of Bassianus after that.

Bibliography: R. JANIN, *Dictionnaire d'histoire et de géographie ecclésiastiques* (Paris 1912–) 6:1274–75. J. D. MANSI, *Sacrorum conciliorum nova et amplissima collectio* (Graz 1960–) 7:273–300. F. X. MURPHY, *Peter Speaks through Leo* (Washington, D.C. 1952) 87–89. C. J. VON HEFELE and H. LECLERCQ, *Histoire des conciles d'après les documents originaux* (Mechlin 1945) 2.2:755–761.

[R. K. POETZEL]

BATAILLON, PIERRE MARIE

Pioneer Marist missioner in OCEANIA; b. Saint-Cyr-les-Vignes (Loire), France, Jan. 6, 1810; d. Wallis Island, April 10, 1877. He joined the MARIST FATHERS and was ordained. Leaving France with Bp. Jean POMPALLIER, (Dec. 24, 1836) he arrived at Wallis Island in the southwest Pacific (Nov. 1, 1837), where he and Brother Joseph Luzy began their apostolate in the face of privation and violent hostility. His courage, forcefulness, and charity so impressed the savage Polynesian chiefs that the entire population of about 2,700 was converted (1842). When Pompallier's Vicariate Apostolic of Western Oceania was divided (1842), Bataillon became the first vicar apostolic of Central Oceania, which included New Caledonia, New Hebrides, the Fiji Islands, the Tonga Islands, Samoa, the Tokelau Islands, and Wallis and Futuna Islands. Consecrated bishop (Dec. 3, 1843), Bataillon began with his slender forces an immediate evangelization of Fiji, Tonga, and Samoa, all three of which later became vicariates, and also of Rotuma. To train a native clergy he opened on Wallis the first seminary in Oceania (1874). The vicar was an extremely apostolic man of vision and perseverance, but such an exacting taskmaster to his missionaries that Marist superiors became disturbed and promulgated new directives defining mission administration. As Fiji and Samoa became established missions, Bataillon's Central Oceania vicariate was restricted to Wallis, Futuna, and Tonga (1873).

Bibliography: A. M. MANGERET, *Mgr. Bataillon et les missions de l'Océanie Centrale,* 2 v. (2d ed. Lyon 1895); *La Croix dans les îles du Pacifique: Vie de Mgr. Bataillon* (Paris 1932). N. WEBER, *Brief Biographical Dictionary of the Marist Hierarchy* (Washington, DC 1953).

[J. E. BELL]

BATH, ABBEY OF

Anglo-Saxon Benedictine monastery in Bath, England (patron, St. Peter). The early history of Bath is obscure and involved in the complicated politics of the Mercian hegemony. It was founded probably by the underking of the Hwicce in the last quarter of the 7th century as a convent of nuns. Apparently the nunnery did not prosper, if indeed it was ever a real community at all, and it came into the possession of the local bishop of WORCESTER. In the 8th century the great Mercian king Offa took it from the bishop of Worcester and soon after some kind of genuine monastic community was found there. Bath did not prosper for long, and during the Viking wars it again became derelict. In the 10th century King Edmund gave the estates to a group of secular clerks who had been expelled from a monastery in Flanders by the reformer GERARD OF BROGNE. The abbey was reformed again, probably by OSWALD OF YORK, and turned into one of the greatest English abbeys in King Edgar's reign. Although it is said that the martyr ALPHEGE OF CANTERBURY was abbot of St. Peter's in Bath, he was actually the abbot of a smaller, quite distinct community at Bath. After the Conquest, St. Peter's was largely destroyed in the rebellion following the death of William the Conqueror in 1087. At the same time it was decided to move the local see from Wells to Bath, and St. Peter's was rebuilt and henceforth became the seat of the bishops of BATH AND WELLS.

Bibliography: W. DUGDALE, *Monasticon Anglicanum* (London 1655–73); best ed. by J. CALEY et al., 6 v. (1817–30) 2:256–273. D. KNOWLES and R. N. HADCOCK, *Medieval Religious Houses: England and Wales* (New York 1953) 59, 253. D. KNOWLES, *The Monastic Order in England, 943–1216* (2d ed. Cambridge, Eng. 1962), *passim.* D. KNOWLES, *The Religious Orders in England,* 3 v. (Cambridge, Eng. 1948–60), *passim.*

[E. JOHN]

A statue of a Roman legionnaire overlooks the remains of the Roman baths in the city of Bath, southern England. The 16th-century abbey church lies beyond. (©Adam Woolfitt/CORBIS)

BATH AND WELLS, ANCIENT SEE OF

The ancient see of Bath and Wells was a medieval Catholic diocese coterminous with the County of Somerset, England, in the ecclesiastical province of CANTERBURY; it was formed by the union of the ancient Abbey of BATH and the church of canons regular at Wells, Somerset, England. The original Diocese of Wells was founded in 909 with the appointment of Aethelhelm as bishop; Bishop Gisa (1060–88) made an important contribution to its establishment in the transitional period from the Old English state to the early Norman settlement. But the transfer of the episcopal seat to Bath by John de Villula (John of Tours) in 1090 interrupted this development. A dispute between the canons of Wells and the monks of Bath reached a crisis under Bp. Roger of Lewes (1136–66) and was temporarily settled by a papal ruling that both places should thenceforth be episcopal sees, both chapters sharing in the bishop's election; but that the prior of Bath should formally announce the election, and the bishop's enthronement should take place in both churches, but first in Bath. This precedence for Bath continued, and Bp. SAVARIC OF BATH (1192–1205) set up a see in GLASTONBURY ABBEY in 1197, and for a short time the diocese was subsequently known as Bath and Glastonbury, until the arrangement was dissolved by Pope HONORIUS III in 1219. The death of Bp. JOCELIN OF WELLS in 1242 precipitated a final settlement, again by papal judgment, which reasserted the principle of joint election and established the title of Bath and Wells. This title survived the Reformation, though after the monastic dissolution the abbey church at Bath became a parish church and the Anglican episcopal seat was maintained at Wells alone. The last Catholic bishop was Gilbert BOURNE, who was deprived by Queen ELIZABETH I in 1559.

The abbey at Bath was rebuilt in the late Perpendicular style in the early 16th century. The Gothic cathedral at Wells evolved through several stages: the Norman cathedral of Robert of Lewes was replaced by Bp. Reginald Fitz Jocelin (1174–91), whose plans were brought to completion by Bp. Jocelin of Wells (1206–42); the tower with the famous inverted columns beneath it, the chapter house, and the lady chapel were added in the early 14th century.

Bibliography: F. M. POWICKE and C. R. CHENEY, eds., *Councils and Synods* (Oxford 1964) 2.1: 44–46, 586–626. *The Victoria History of the County of Somerset,* ed. W. PAGE, v. 2 (London 1911) 1–39. A. H. THOMPSON, *The Cathedral Churches of England* (London 1925). K. EDWARDS, *The English Secular Cathedrals in the Middle Ages* (Manchester 1949). D. FALCONER, *Bath Abbey* (Stroud 1999) H. E. REYNOLDS, ed. *Wells Cathedral: Its Foundation, Constitutional History, and Statutes* (Leeds 1881). L. S. COLCHESTER, *Wells Cathedral: A History* (Wells 1996).

[C. DUGGAN]

BATHILDIS, ST.

Queen of France; d. Chelles, Jan. 30 *c.* 680. A native of England, whence she had been kidnapped by pirates, she lived at the court of Neustria as a part of the household of Erchinoald, mayor of the palace, but refused to become his wife. She married Clovis II, king of Neustria and Burgundy, and bore him three sons: Chlotar, Childeric, and Theodoric. At the death of Clovis, she became queen regent under the nominal reign of her eldest son Chlotar, with such advisers as (St.) Ouen and Chrodobert, bishop of Paris. Before 673, the mayor of the palace Ebroinus deprived her of power and had her conducted to the abbey of Chelles, France (Department Seine-et-Marne), where she lived in all simplicity. Bathildis founded the abbeys of Corbie and Chelles and was lavish in endowing the churches and monasteries of her kingdom. Although not entirely vindicated for her part in the assassination of Bishop AUNEMUND OF LYONS (658), her memory is honored because of her struggle against slavery, simony, and abusive taxation. The *Vita prima s. Bathildis* is an excellent biography, written by a contemporary who used as a model the life of St. RADEGUNDA. A *Vita secunda* was composed at the end of the eighth century or at the beginning of the ninth century. Her cult began before 822.

Feast: Jan. 30.

Bibliography: *Monumenta Germaniae Historica: Scriptores rerum Merovingicarum* 2:475–508. O. ABEL, tr., *Die Chronik Fredegars und der Frankenkönige, die Lebensbeschreibungen des Abtes Columban, der Bischöfe Arnulf, Leodegar und Eligius, der Königin Bathilde* (Leipzig 1888). E. VACANDARD, *Vie de Saint Ouen* (Paris 1902). M. J. COUTURIER, *Sainte Bathilde, reine des Francs* (Paris 1909). A. BELLESSORT, *Sainte Bathilde, reine de France* (Paris 1941). J.-P. LAPORTE, *Sépultures et reliques de la reine Bathilde. . . .* (Chelles 1991). *La vie de sainte Bathilde*, ed. A. BENGTSSON (Lund, Sweden 1996). L. VAN DER ESSEN, *Dictionnaire d'histoire et de géographie ecclésiastiques*, ed. A. BAUDRILLART et al. (Paris 1912) 6: 1321–22. J. L. BAUDOT and L. CHAUSSIN, *Vies des saints et des bienhereux selon l'ordre du calendrier avec l'historique des fêtes* (Paris 1935–56) 1:616–619. *Histoire de l'église depuis les origines jusqu'à nos jours*, ed. A. FLICHE and V. MARTIN (Paris 1935) 5:350–352. R. AIGRAIN, *Catholicisme* 1:1194–95. E. EWIG, *Lexikon für Theologie und Kirche*, ed. J. HOFER and K. RAHNER (Freiburg 1957–65) 2:50. J. MARILIER, *Bibliotheca sanctorum* 2:971–972.

[É. BROUETTE]

BÁTHORY

Hungarian princely family stemming from the ancient Magyar clan of Gut-Keled.

Andrew (András), Bishop of Nagyvárad (1333), was the confidant of King Charles Robert of Hungary and builder of the famed Gothic cathedral of Nagyvárad, which was later destroyed by the Turks.

Ladislaus (László), Bl., a member of the Order of the Hermits of St. Paul, lived in the first half of the 15th century. He translated the Bible into Hungarian.

Stephen (István) (1533–86), an outstanding soldier and diplomat, was unanimously elected to the vacant sovereignty of Transylvania in 1571. In 1575 he was elected king of Poland, thus ending the interregnum following the abdication of the Polish King Henry III (Valois). Stephen's marriage to the Polish Princess Anne of Jagello strengthened his position. He fought the Muscovites with skill, repeatedly defeating Ivan the Terrible. His other triumphs over the invading Turks and Tartars restored Poland to a leading position in northeastern Europe. He gave strong support to the Catholic reform movement, encouraged the Jesuits, and abolished the edict that gave equal rights to the Protestants. He also introduced the Gregorian calendar into Poland. Upon the death of Ivan the Terrible in 1584, Báthory prepared for a possible Polish-Muscovite union, but he died unexpectedly in 1586.

Sigismund (Zsigmond) (1572–1613) was elected sovereign of Transylvania in 1581, assuming power at the age of 16. He was a talented statesman and general, and scored a decisive victory over the Ottoman general, Sinan Pasha, in 1595. Four years later, upset at the desertion of his wife, Maria Christina of Austria, and perhaps affected by an inherent eccentricity, he suddenly abdicated in favor of Emperor Rudolf II in exchange for the Duchy of Oppeln. His abdication was not approved by the Transylvanian estates; therefore in that year he offered the throne to his cousin Andrew, and it was accepted.

Andrew (András) (1566–99), cardinal bishop of Ermland. In 1599 he left his diocese to assume the sovereignty of Transylvania offered by his cousin Sigismund, but he died in battle.

Bibliography: I. ACSÁDY, *A magyar birodalom története,* 2 v. (Budapest 1903–04) 2. B. HÓMAN and J. SZEKFŰ, *Magyar történet,* 8 v. (Budapest 1928–34). I. LUKINICH, *Erdély területi változásai a török hódítás korában, 1541–1711* (Budapest 1918). POLSKA AKADEMIA UMIEJETNÓSCI, *Etienne Báthory, roi de Pologne, prince de Transylvanie* (Cracow 1935). S. SZILÁGYI, ed., *Monumenta comitialia regni Transylvaniae (1540–1699),* 21 v. (Budapest 1875–98). L. TOTH, *Dictionnaire d'histoire et de géographie ecclésiastiques* 6:1323–25.

[G. C. PAIKERT]

BATHS

This article is concerned primarily with baths and bathing in Christian antiquity.

General background. Baths and bathing were an important feature of Greek life from the age of Homer, but they played a much greater role among the Romans from the 3d century B.C. to the end of antiquity. The Romans developed elaborate heating arrangements for their baths and erected enormous bathing establishments (*thermae*), which included lounging rooms, lecture halls, and libraries, as well as the baths proper and their own complex of chambers, dressing rooms, etc. They corresponded in many respects to the modern social center. As early as 33 B.C., there were 170 public baths in Rome alone, and under the empire this number was greatly increased. The fee for admission was very small, thus making the baths accessible to the great majority of the population. All cities and towns throughout the empire had their public baths, and all men of wealth had elaborate private baths in their town houses and on their country estates. There were separate public bathing facilities for women as well as for men. Under the empire, however, the custom of mixed bathing was introduced and led to abuses that were severely condemned by pagan and later by Christian moralists. Physicians and moralists also denounced the tendency to spend long periods of time in the warm baths on the ground that this practice was enervating both physically and morally. On the other hand, they recommended bathing with moderation, especially in cold water, as beneficial for the mind as well as for the body.

Bathing and the baths were an essential part of everyday life and are referred to as such in casual terms by Christian writers such as Clement of Alexandria, Tertullian, and St. Augustine. The Christian Fathers, however, found it necessary to warn repeatedly against the dangers to morals in the public baths, and they were concerned in particular about the special moral dangers to which women bathers were exposed. As archeology has shown, rich Christians continued to erect and maintain elaborate baths in their own town houses and on their country estates to the very end of the empire in the West and in early Byzantine times.

In Christian asceticism. The attitude of the early ascetical writers and founders of monasticism is entirely different. While the immorality connected with public baths was a cause of hostility, the chief reason for the stern prohibitions regarding baths and bathing came from the spirit of asceticism itself. The body was to be chastised severely for the good of the soul by fasting and was to be deprived of all else, along with food and drink, that could give it comfort and pleasure. Hence the ascetical opposition to the pleasure derived from scrupulous cleanliness and bathing. It is not difficult for moderns to understand how acutely painful was the loss of the bath and bathing to men and women for whom they were such a normal part of everyday life in its social as well as in its hygienic aspects. The Rule of St. PACHOMIUS (d. A.D. 346) permits complete bathing of the body only in case of sickness, but some ascetics even refused the comfort of bathing when seriously ill. St. Jerome, ardent champion of asceticism, makes practically no concessions. St. Augustine (*Letter* 211.13) permits a community of religious women to visit the baths only once a month, and then only on condition that they go at least three together. He permits more frequent bathing only on the advice of a physician. St. Caesarius of Arles (d. A.D. 542) in his rule for nuns (ch. 31) permits baths only to those who are ill. The Rule of St. Benedict (ch. 36) is relatively mild, but it is couched in the same ascetical spirit. This monastic tradition passed on to the Middle Ages, sometimes in its most rigorous forms, and had its effects on general penitential discipline. A temporary prohibition from indulging in bathing was often given as a penance to laymen—in both East and West. Celtic monasticism in particular developed a special form of asceticism arising out of the idea of bathing, namely, the painful practice of standing for fairly long periods in water that was very cold or even icy.

It is hardly necessary to give more than passing mention to the legend that the years of the Middle Ages were bathless. The legend was undoubtedly based on the presumed application of the prohibitions of monastic rules and treatises, written for the guidance of ascetics, to all classes of society. In the later Middle Ages, even public baths were common in many cities and were very popular.

Bibliography: H. FLECKENSTEIN, *Lexikon für Theologie und Kirche* (Freiburg 1957–65) 1:1183–84. L. GOUGAUD, *Dictionnaire* *de spiritualité ascétique et mystique,* ed. M. VILLER (Paris 1932—) 1:1197–1200. J. JÜTHNER, *Reallexikon für Antike und Christentum,* ed. T. KLAUSER (Stuttgart 1941) 1:1134–43, with bibliog. J. ZELLINGER, *Bad und Bäder in der altchristlichen Kirche* (Munich 1928). P. GALLAND, *L'Église et l'hygiène en Moyen Âge* (Paris 1933). H. DUMAINE, *Dictionnaire d'archéologie chrétienne et de liturgie,* ed. F. CABROL, H. LECLERQ, and H. I. MARROU (Paris 1907–53) 2:72–117, with bibliog. M. C. MCCARTHY, *The Rule for Nuns of St. Caesarius of Arles* (Catholic University of America Studies in Medieval History NS 16; Washington 1960) esp. 122–123, 145–146.

[M. R. P. MCGUIRE]

BATIFFOL, PIERRE

Theologian, Church historian; b. Toulouse, Jan. 27, 1861; d. Paris, Jan. 13, 1929. He studied at the Seminary of St. Sulpice in Paris (1878–82), was ordained in 1884, and attended the Institut Catholique and the École des Hautes Études while serving as a curate in Paris. He was an early friend of the biblical scholar M. J. LAGRANGE, a protégé of the Church historian L. DUCHESNE, and also came under the influence of the archeologist G. B. ROSSI in Rome. He was chaplain at L'École de Ste. Barbe in Paris from 1889 until he was named rector of the Institut Catholique of Toulouse in 1898. Here he devoted himself to the history of penance, the agape, and the *disciplina arcani,* publishing the results in his *Études d'histoire et de théologie positive* (1902). Though he opposed the Modernist movement in his *L'Enseignement de Jésus* (1905), his *L'Eucharistie: la Présence réelle et la Transubstantiation* was put on the Index (1907). Thereupon he resigned his rectorship and returned to the chaplaincy in Paris, remaining there until his death. In 1913 he published a complete revision of the book on the Eucharist.

Batiffol's first important publications included *La Vaticane de Paul IV à Paul V* (1890), and *L'Abbaye de Rossano: Contribution à l'histoire de la Vaticane* (1891). His *Histoire du Bréviaire romain* (1893; Eng. tr. 1898) stimulated a revival of liturgical studies in France. Besides his *Studia Patristica* (1889–90) and editions of numerous texts, including the *Tractatus Origenis* (1900), he contributed studies on the Bible and on Byzantine historiography to leading German and French periodicals. His later works concerned with the early papacy include *L'Église naissante et le catholicisme* (1909; Eng. tr., *Primitive Catholicism,* 1911), *La Paix constantinienne et le catholicisme* (1914), *Le Catholicisme de S. Augustin* (1920), *S. Léon le Grand* (*Dictionnaire de théologie catholique* 9:218–301), and *S. Grégoire le Grand* (1928, Eng. tr. 1929). Batiffol advanced research in positive theology and introduced his colleagues to non-Catholic and foreign scholarship in his fields of study.

Bibliography: G. BARDY, ''L'Oeuvre de Mgr. Batiffol,'' *Recherches de science religieuse* 10 (1929) 393–400. *Dictionnaire de théologie catholique: Tables générales* (Paris 1960) 385–386. J. RIVIÈRE, *Mgr. Pierre Batiffol* (Paris 1929) incl. bibliog.; *Dictionnaire d'histoire et de géographie ecclésiastiques* (Paris 1912—) 6:1327–30.

[F. X. MURPHY]

BATISTA, CÍCERO ROMÃO

Brazilian priest, object of popular devotion; b. Ceará, Brazil, 1844; d. Rome, 1934. He was ordained in 1870 and had manifested mystic tendencies while still in the seminary. As pastor in Juazeiro, Ceará—a poor region, both geographically and culturally isolated, and of old messianic tradition—he worked to invigorate the religious faith of the inhabitants, preaching sermons in which he advised repentance and an ascetic life. The drought of 1877 to 1879 brought many more people to this parish, and his reputation and authority increased. In 1889 there occurred ''miracles'' with hosts that were transformed into blood. Religious fervor increased, and whole families migrated to Juazeiro. The diocesan bishop condemned the miracles (1891), prohibited the priest from preaching and confessing (1892), and from celebrating Mass (1896). Father Cícero traveled to Rome in 1898, where Leo XIII permitted him to celebrate Mass only in a private oratory. Meanwhile, the popular devotion increased as did the population of Juazeiro. Little by little it became dominated by local politics, and clashes with the governors of the state of Ceará reached the point of armed conflict in which the priest's followers considered themselves supernaturally protected by their ''padrinho,'' Father Cícero. The situation continued until his death. The city of Juazeiro even in 1963 continued to be one of the greatest centers of religious pilgrimage in Brazil because of the legends concerning this priest.

Bibliography: A. F. MONTENEGRO, *História do fanatismo religioso no Ceará* (Fortaleza, Brazil 1959).

[J. A. GONSALVES DE MELLO]

BATIZ SAINZ, LUIS, ST.

Martyr, pastor; b. Sept. 13, 1870, San Miguel del Mezquital, Zacatecas, Archdiocese of Durango, Mexico; d. Aug. 15, 1926, Puerto de Santa Teresa, near Zacatecas. At 12 he entered the seminary of Durango, where he was known for his piety. From his ordination (Jan. 1, 1894) until his death, he served as spiritual director of the seminary and parish priest at San Pedro Chalchihuites. His involvement with Catholic Action led him to found elementary and technical schools. After convening a meeting of the National League in defense of religious freedom before the bishops closed the churches, Batiz was denounced as a conspirator plotting to overthrow the government and forced into hiding. He was arrested Aug. 14. When the townspeople demanded his release, he was transferred to Zacatecas. En route he was executed together with three members of Catholic Action (SS. Manuel MORALES, Salvador LARA, and David ROLDÁN). Fr. Batiz was both beatified (Nov. 22, 1992) and canonized (May 21, 2000) with Cristobal MAGALLANES [*see* GUADALAJARA (MEXICO), MARTYRS OF, SS.] by Pope John Paul II.

Feast: May 25 (Mexico).

Bibliography: J. CARDOSO, *Los mártires mexicanos* (Mexico City 1953). V. GARCÍA JUÁREZ, *Los cristeros* (Fresnillo, Zac. 1990).

[K. I. RABENSTEIN]

BATON ROUGE, DIOCESE OF

The Diocese of Baton Rouge (*Rubribaculensis*) was created Aug. 14, 1961, by Pope John XXIII, who named as its first bishop Robert E. Tracy, formerly auxiliary bishop of Lafayette, La. The see city is the capital of Louisiana and is the locale of Louisiana State University, where Tracy had been chaplain of the Catholic Student Center (1946–59). He was installed Nov. 8, 1961, in St. Joseph's Cathedral, the oldest (1792) parish, and served until he retired in March of 1974 (d. April 4, 1980). He was succeeded by Bishop Joseph V. Sullivan, who had been auxiliary to the bishop of Kansas City-St. Joseph, Missouri since 1967. Bishop Sullivan died Sept. 4, 1982 and in January of 1983 Bishop Stanley J. Ott, who had been auxiliary bishop in New Orleans, was named the third bishop of Baton Rouge. Bishop Ott served until his death in 1992. His successor was Bishop Alfred C. Hughes, formerly auxiliary bishop in Boston. He served until he was named coadjutor with right of succession to Archbishop Francis B. Schulte of New Orleans in February, 2001. In March 2002, the Most Reverend Robert W. Muench, former bishop of Covington, Kentucky, assumed the pastoral leadership of the Diocese of Baton Rouge.

The diocese of Baton Rouge embraces 12 civil parishes (counties) Ascension, Assumption, East Baton Rouge, West Baton Rouge, Iberville, Pointe Coupee, East Feliciana, West Feliciana, St. Helena, Tangipahoa, Livingston and St. James, which had earlier formed part of the Archdiocese of NEW ORLEANS. About 30 percent of the population are Catholic, distributed across 70 parishes. The location of Baton Rouge on the Mississippi River, its oil refineries, and petrochemical and allied industries contribute to its economic importance.

[H. C. BEZOU/M. GUIDRY/EDS.]

BATTLE, ABBEY OF

Former BENEDICTINE monastery near Hastings, Sussex, England, founded 1067. To commemorate the Battle of Hastings (1066) and his victory over Harold, WILLIAM I the Conqueror founded on the site of the battle an abbey dedicated to the Holy Trinity, St. Mary, and St. Martin and endowed it with all the lands within a radius of a mile and a half, as well as with several other manors in Kent and Sussex. The original community was drawn from the famous Abbey of MARMOUTIER, near Tours, whose abbots also appointed the first two abbots of Battle, even though Battle was never a dependency of Marmoutier. Among the privileges of the abbey were the rights of sanctuary, of treasure trove, of free warren, of inquest, and of certain exemptions from episcopal jurisdiction. These exemptions led to a series of disputes with the bishop of CHICHESTER, settled finally by the *Compositio* of 1235. While the abbey was not exempt from the metropolitan visitations of the archbishop of Canterbury, the episcopal visitation occurred only triennially and had to be carried out by two monks, of whom one was elected by the bishop and the other by the community itself. From 1295 to 1538 the abbots of Battle sat in the House of Lords. The abbey was suppressed in 1539; its annual income amounted then to £900, and the community consisted of the abbot and only 16 monks.

Bibliography: *Chronicon monasterii de Bello,* ed. J. S. BREWER (London 1846). *The Chronicle of Battle Abbey, 1066–1176,* tr. M. A. LOWER (London 1851). W. DUGDALE, *Monasticon Anglicanum* (London 1655–73) best ed. by J. CALEY et al., 6 v. (1817–30) 3:233–259. *Custumals of Battle Abbey . . . , 1283–1312,* ed. S. R. SCARGILLBIRD (Camden Soc., NS 41; London 1887). H. W. C. DAVIS, "The Chronicle of Battle Abbey," *English Historical Review* 29 (1914) 426–434. R. GRAHAM, "The Monastery of Battle," in *English Ecclesiastical Studies* 29 (1929). *The Victoria History of the County of Sussex,* ed. W. PAGE (London 1905–) v. 2. *Descriptive Catalogue of the Original Charters . . .* (London 1835). *The Sussex Archaeological Collections* (Sussex Archaeological Society) v. 3, 17.

[J. BRÜCKMANN]

BATTLE STANDARDS, CULT OF

The early Roman army had a standard called the *signum* for each maniple, carried by the centurion who commanded the unit. When Marius established a professional army in Rome (about 100 B.C.), he reorganized the legion, making the cohorts the major tactical units, and giving it a standard, the eagle or *aquila.* This standard was regarded as the sacred emblem that personified the legion's existence. A chapel was built for it, and it was honored with a religious cult. The standard was made first of silver, later of gold. It was placed at the top of a

Battle Abbey. (©Charles and Josette Lenars/CORBIS)

long pole and variously ornamented. Its loss brought disgrace on the members of the legion and frequently led to the disbanding of the legion in question. In the period of the Roman Empire before Constantine, the image of the reigning emperor was carried also as a standard by various military units, and was likewise an object of worship. The cult of these standards created a formidable problem for Christian soldiers, and particularly for Christian officers.

Bibliography: M. MARÍN Y PEÑA, *Instituciones militares romanas* (Madrid 1956) 375–390. W. KUBITSCHEK, *Paulys Realenzyklopädie der klassischen Altertumswissenschaft,* ed. G. WISSOWA et al., 2.2:2335–44. H. LECLERCQ, *Dictionnaire d'archéologie chrétienne et de liturgie,* ed. F. CABROL, H. LECLERCQ, and H. I. MARROU, 15 v. (Paris 1907–53) 11.1: 1116–30.

[T. A. BRADY]

BAUCH, BRUNO

German philosopher of the Neo-Kantian school; b. Gross-Nossen, Silesia, Jan. 19, 1877: d. Jena. Feb. 27, 1942. He was formed in the school of W. Windelband and H. Rickert, which concerned itself primarily with problems of value and took its point of departure from Kant's *Critique of Judgment.* Bauch, in turn, devoted himself to the two main interests of this branch of the Neo-Kantian movement: the theory of value and of culture and the history of philosophy. In the latter field, his greatest achievement is his *Immanuel Kant* (Berlin 1917), which ranks among the best monographs on that philosopher, exhibiting complete mastery of his writings and interpreting them in the perspective of the Windelband school. Important also are his studies on the theory of knowledge in Greek thought and on the moral philosophy of Martin Luther. In the theoretical area, he expounded his own conception of philosophy as the interpretation of the cultural consciousness in a mature work: *Die erzieherische Bedeutung der Kulturgüter* (Leipzig 1930).

Bauch's intense interest in the theory of value and of culture engendered some tension in his adherence to Kant. He defended the ethics of Kant from the charges of formalism, but accused Kant of misprizing cultural values, confusing them with hedonic values and thus bringing them within range of moral censure. The values of culture are understood by Bauch as the content of the hypothetical imperative; consequently, the duties of individuals depend not exclusively on the universal law of the CATEGORICAL IMPERATIVE, but on the peculiar cultural circumstances of their action. In his most important theoretical work, *Grundzüge der Ethik* (Stuttgart 1935), he presented an extensive treatment of the general theory of value, relating value, on the one hand, to ethics, and on the other, to a general theory of reality. Reality is not value, but it is the matrix for the perception and realization of value. Baouch served for an extended period as editor of the journal *Kantstudien.*

See Also: KANTIANISM; NEO-KANTIANISM; VALUE, PHILOSOPHY OF.

Bibliography: *Blätter für Deutsche Philosophie* (1937) 351–440, studies in tribute to B. Bauch. P. R. FÄH, *Begriff und Konkreszenz bei B. B.* (Diss. Sarnen 1940).

[A. R. CAPONIGRI]

BAUDOUIN, LOUIS MARIE, VEN.

Religious founder; b. Montaigu (Vendée), France, Aug. 2, 1765; d. Chavagnes-en-Paillers (Vendée), Feb. 12, 1835. Educated by the Vincentians at the seminary of Luçon, he was ordained in 1789 and appointed assistant to his brother, who was pastor in Luçon. When the CIVIL CONSTITUTION OF THE CLERGY was legislated during the FRENCH REVOLUTION, the Baudouin brothers refused to take the required oath and were barred from priestly ministrations in the village church. The two emigrated to Spain in 1792. When his brother died (1796) Louis returned to France, where he became a refugee at Sables d'Olonne. Since the persecution against priests had been renewed, he exercised a hidden apostolate. In 1802, he became a parish priest in Chavagnes. There he founded a religious congregation known as the Sons of Mary Immaculate of Luçon, more commonly as the Priests of Chavagnes. Together with Gabrielle Charlotte Ranfray de la Rochette, a former religious, he founded a congregation of women devoted to the education of young girls, the Ursulines of Jesus. Named rector of the seminary of La Rochelle in 1812, he became vicar-general of the restored See of Luçon in 1822. He was proclaimed venerable in 1871.

Bibliography: M. MAUPILIER, *Louis-Marie Baudouin, prêtre et ses disciples: une famille religieuse dans l'Église* (Paris 1973). P. MICHAUD, *Life of the Ven. Louis Marie Baudouin,* tr. W. A. PHILLIPSON (London 1914). J. ROBIN, *Dictionnaire de spiritualité ascétique et mystique. Doctrine et histoire,* ed. M. VILLER et al. (Paris 1932) 1:1286–87.

[L. P. MAHONEY]

BAUDRILLART, HENRI MARIE ALFRED

Cardinal, scholar, educator, diplomat; b. Paris, Jan. 6, 1859; d. Paris, May 19, 1942. Trained in history, he received a doctor of letters degree in 1890. As a lay teacher he taught at schools in Laval, Caen, and Paris, and in 1883 became affiliated with the Institut Catholique. After joining the Oratory in 1890, he was ordained on July 9, 1893, and two years later he received his doctorate in theology and returned to the Institut Catholique as professor (1894–1907). In 1907 he became rector of the Institut Catholique, which he built into a first-class institution. He was made titular bishop of Himeria (1921), titular archbishop of Melitene (1928), and cardinal priest (1935). Baudrillart continued his scholarly researches and served as diplomatic representative of the Holy See. He was instrumental in the resumption of French diplomatic relations with the Vatican in 1921; in his diplomatic capacity he traveled in Europe, Africa, and North and South America, and twice he visited the United States. He was made a member of the Académie Française in 1918, a chevalier of the Légion d'Honneur in 1920, and commander of the Légion in 1935. Among his publications were *Philippe V et la cour de France* (5 v. Paris 1890–1901); *L'Église catholique, la Renaissance, le protestantisme* (Paris 1904), tr. into Eng. by Mrs. Philip Gibbs as *The Catholic Church, the Renaissance and Protestantism* (New York 1908); *Vie de Mgr. d'Hulst* (2 v. Paris 1912–14); *Lettres du duc de Bourgogne au roi d'Espagne* (2 v. Paris 1912–16); and *La France, les catholiques et le guerre* (Paris 1917). Perhaps his most important scholarly contribution was the initial organization and publication of the *Dictionnaire d'histoire et de géographie ecclésiastiques.*

Bibliography: V. CARRIERE, *Le Cardinal Baudrillart, 1859–1942* (Paris 1942). A. GUNY, *Catholicisme* 1:1316–17. V. L. SAULNIER, *Dictionnaire de biographie française* (Paris 1929—) 5:893–895.

[V. L. BULLOUGH]

BAUER, ANDRÉ, ST.

Franciscan brother, martyr, b. Nov. 24, 1866, Guebwiller, Alsace, France; d. July 9, 1900, Taiyüan, Shansi Province, China. André was the sixth of the eight children of Luc Bauer and Lucia Moser. He joined the Franciscan Third Order as a teenager. On Aug. 12, 1886, he was clothed as a Franciscan oblate in Clevedon, England. Recalled to France, he completed his mandatory three years of military service in the Cuirassiers Regiment, then he returned home for a time to aid his aging parents. In 1895, he received the Franciscan habit at Amiens before returning to the friary in England. On May 4, 1899, he arrived at the mission in Taiyüan, where he served in the infirmary until he was captured and decapitated by the Boxers 14 months later. En route to his execution, his joy was expressed by his chanting: ''Praise the Lord, all you nations!'' (Ps. 117). He was beatified by Pope Pius XII (Nov. 24, 1946) and canonized (Oct. 1, 2000) by Pope John Paul II with Augustine Zhao Rong and companions.

Feast: July 4; July 8 (Franciscans).

Bibliography: *Acta Apostolicae Sedis* 39 (1947) 213–221, 307–311. *Les Vingt-neuf martyrs de Chine, massacrés en 1900, béatifiés par Sa Sainteté Pie XII, le 24 novembre, 1946* (Rome 1946). P. X. MERTENS, *Du sang chrétien sur le fleuve jaune. Actes de martyrs dans la Chine contemporaine* (Paris 1937). L. MINER, *China's Book of Martyrs: A Record of Heroic Martyrdoms and Marvelous Deliverances of Chinese Christians during the Summer of 1900* (Ann Arbor 1994). J. SIMON, *Sous le sabre des Boxers* (Lille 1955). C. TESTORE, *Sangue e palme sul fiume giallo. I beati martiri cinesi nella persecuzione della Boxe Celi Sud-Est, 1900* (Rome 1955). *L'Osservatore Romano,* Eng. Ed. 40 (2000): 1–2, 10.

[K. I. RABENSTEIN]

BAUER, BRUNO

Protestant biblical critic and historian; b. Eisenberg, Germany, Sept. 6, 1809; d. Rixdorf, Germany, April 15, 1882. At Berlin he studied theology and philosophy, especially Hegel. He became an instructor at the University of Bonn in 1839 but was dismissed in 1842 when he abandoned his conservative HEGELIANISM and published his *Kritik der evangelischen Geschichte des Johannes* (1840) and *Kritik der evangelischen Geschichte der Synoptiker* (2 v. 1841–42). Denying both the historicity of Jesus and traditional belief in God, Bauer held that the Gospels were derived neither from facts nor from the imagination of the Christian community, but from the Evangelists' own minds. He became increasingly radical in his criticism, portrayed Philo, Seneca, and the Gnostics as the real forces of Christianity, whose framework alone was Jewish and whose spirit was Western. In *Christus und die Cäsaren* (1877), he placed the first Gospel in the time of Hadrian (118–138) and the genesis of the Christian religion as late as Marcus Aurelius (160–180). Friedrich NIETZSCHE, Wilhelm Wrede, and Karl MARX were among those influenced by Bauer's writings.

Bibliography: E. BARNIKOL, "Bruno Bauers Kampf gegen Religion und Christentum und die Spaltung der vormärzlichen preussischen Opposition,'' *Zeitschrift für Kirchengeschichte* 46 (1928) 1–34; *Die Religion in Geschichte und Gegenwart* (Tübingen 1957–65) 1:922–924. W. BUFF, *Neue deutsche Biographie* (Leipzig 1875–1910) 1:636–637. K. LÖWITH, *Von Hegel zu Nietzsche* (Stuttgart 1958). A. SCHWEITZER, *The Quest of the Historical Jesus,* tr. W. MONTGOMERY (New York 1956).

[L. J. SWIDLER]

BÄUMER, SUITBERT

Liturgist; b. Leuchtenburg, Rhineland, March 28, 1845; d. Freiburg im Breisgau, Aug. 12, 1894. He became a monk of Beuron in 1865, was ordained in 1869, and studied at Bonn and Tübingen. Sojourning in Belgium and England during the Kulturkampf (1875–90), he served as liturgical consultant to Desclée in Tournai for its editions of the Missal, monastic Breviary, the Vulgate, etc. He wrote numerous works on liturgy, patristics, and the history of monasticism. His most influential work was *Geschichte des Breviers* (Freiburg 1895), which was revised and enlarged in the French edition by R. Biron (2 v. Paris 1905).

Bibliography: S. MAYER, *Beuroner Bibliographie, 1863–1963* (Beuron 1963) 38–49. R. PROOST, *Dictionnaire d'archéologie chrétienne et de liturgie* (Paris 1907–53) 2:623–626. P. SÉJOURNÉ, *Dictionnaire d'histoire et de géographie ecclésiastiques* (Paris 1912—) 6:1474–81.

[S. MAYER]

BAUMSTARK, ANTON

Liturgist and Orientalist; b. Constance, Aug. 4, 1872; d. Bonn, May 31, 1948. As inheritor of physical and spiritual gifts from his father, Reinhold Baumstark, Anton showed extraordinary versatility in an age of extreme specialization. A married layman, he devoted his rich energies to scholarship. He was knowledgeable in literature, philology, theology, and religious and art history, both classical and Oriental. One of the few arts he failed to master was that of German style; his style was difficult to follow as a result of this.

In 1901 at Rome he began the journal *Oriens Christianus* with Anton de WAAL, and with but a short interruption edited it through 36 volumes. None of its issues appeared without a significant contribution from him. Into its pages he poured the results of his unique comprehensive grasp of the culture of the Mediterranean Basin. The journal stands as the most important monument of his life of scholarship. In the same field he published the *Geschichte der syrischen Literatur* (Bonn 1922).

With Odo CASEL, he began the *Jahrbuch für Liturgiewissenschaft*; to this he brought unusual qualifications. Since worship was the center of ancient culture, and Baumstark was by nature a very religious person, he made the study of the evolution of worship, especially the historical development of Christian liturgy, the object of his predilection. Although his ingenious hypotheses did not always prove to be correct, he nevertheless greatly stimulated research, and his own insights and discoveries have made irreplaceable contributions to liturgical scholarship. The results of the method of comparative liturgy, which Baumstark himself worked out, were published in *Liturgie comparée* [Chevetogne 1940; *Comparative Liturgy* (London 1958)]. He traced the laws of all liturgical evolution in *Vom geschichtlichen Werden der Liturgie* (Freiburg 1923). In numerous articles (his published works number 546) he tried to determine the exact relations of the Christian liturgy to the Jewish and Hellenistic world.

In keeping with his broad and profound knowledge, Baumstark taught at several centers of learning: classical and Oriental philology at the University of Heidelberg (1898), early Christian Oriental civilization at the University of Bonn (1921–30), Semitic languages and comparative liturgy at the University of Nijmegen (1923), the science of Islam and Arabic languages at the University of Utrecht (1926), and Oriental studies at the University of Münster (1930–35).

During his last years, Baumstark led an increasingly isolated life because of his involvement in Nazism; he was, unfortunately, naive in political matters. He nevertheless remained constantly devoted to scholarship and to the Church and her liturgy.

Bibliography: T. KLAUSER, *Ephemerides liturgicae* 63 (Rome 1949) 185–187. H. E. KILLY, *Ephemerides liturgicae* 63 (Rome 1949) 187–207, contains complete list of his works. G. GRAF, ''Zum Geleit und zum Andenken an Anton Baumstark und Adolf Rücker,'' *Oriens Christianus* 37 (Leipzig-Wiesbaden 1953) 1–5. R. TAFT, ''Comparative Liturgy Fifty Years after Anton Baumstark (d. 1948): A Reply to Recent Critics,'' *Worship* 73 (1999) 521–540. F. WEST, *The Comparative Liturgy of Anton Baumstark* (Bramcote, Nottingham, 1995).

[B. NEUNHEUSER]

BAUNY, ÉTIENNE

Jesuit moral theologian; b. Mouzon (Ardennes), June 1, 1575; d. Saint-Pol-de-Léon, Dec. 12, 1649. He entered the Society of Jesus in 1593 and at first taught humanities and rhetoric. He then became professor of moral theology and casuistry at the college of Clermont in Paris, a position that he held for 16 years. He later became superior at Pontoise and then spent the last years of his life at Saint-Pol-de-Léon, where he enjoyed the friendship and confidence of the bishop of Léon, René de Rieux.

Bauny enjoyed a reputation for great learning and holiness and was held in esteem by prominent prelates of his time. However, he came into difficulty with the publication of some of his works. His *Somme des péchés qui se commettent en tous états* (Paris 1640, many later eds.) was written to accommodate clerics whose knowledge of Latin was weak. It was followed by *Pratique du droit canonique au gouvernement de l'Église* (Paris 1633) and *De sacramentis ac personis sacris . . . Theologiae moralis* (*Pars prima* Paris 1640; *Pars altera* 1642). The first part of the latter work and the two publications in French were placed on the Index in 1640. His lenient interpretations had aroused the opposition of the Sorbonne and made him the target of Jansenist attack. This was in fact the beginning of the Jansenist campaign of accusing Jesuit theologians of laxism. Pascal was particularly severe in his attack on Bauny. Certain of the propositions advanced by Bauny were to find more precise and acceptable expression in the writings of St. Alphonsus; others were too vague, loose, or exaggerated. However, the personal orthodoxy of Bauny was never questioned. He later wrote *Tractatus de censuris ecclesiasticis* (Paris 1642) and *Libri tres quibus, quae in contractuum ac quasi contractuum materia videntur ardua ac difficilia, enucleantur* (Paris 1645).

Bibliography: R. BROULLIARD, *Dictionnaire d'histoire et de géographie ecclésiastiques* (Paris 1912–) 6:1497–98. H. FOUQUERAY, *Histoire de la compagnie de Jésus en France*, 5 v. (Paris 1910–25) 5:416–417. H. HURTER, *Nomenclator literarius theologiae catholicae* (Innsbruck 1926) 1:494. M. PETROCCHI, *Il problema del Lassismo* (Rome 1953). C. SOMMERVOGEL et al., *Bibliothèque de la Compagnie de Jésus* (Brussels-Paris 1890–1932) 1:1058–60.

[J. T. KELLEHER]

BAUR, FERDINAND CHRISTIAN

German Protestant ecclesiastical historian and founder of the new TÜBINGEN SCHOOL; b. Schmiden, near Stuttgart, June 21, 1792; d. Tübingen, Dec. 2, 1860. After studying at Tübingen, he taught at Blaubeuren (1817–26) and then spent the remainder of his life at Tübingen as professor of historical theology (1826–60). At first Baur seems to have been a disciple of the more ''orthodox'' Tübingen school, but his convictions concerning its positions were shaken by his study of SCHLEIERMACHER's *Glaubenslehre*. The radical change that came over his thought, however, depended much more on HEGEL's philosophy of religion. As a result Baur developed along Hegelian lines a theory of the history of the primitive Church. According to this theory, there existed in apostolic times two sharply divided factions, personified in St. Peter and St. Paul. These two groups differed on the doctrine of justification and on the nature of the Church's polity. During the 2d and 3d centuries a ''synthesis'' evolved from these two factions, thereby producing Catholicism. This theory also led Baur to reject the apostolic origin of most of the New Testament canon. Thus he claimed to perceive this compromise, indicative of a later date of composition, in all the Pauline Epistles except Romans, 1 and 2 Corinthians, and Galatians, which alone Baur admitted as Pauline in origin. Baur participated later in the controversy surrounding the work of David STRAUSS concerning the synoptic problem. Among his numerous writings were *Die christliche Lehre von der Versöhnung in ihrer geschichtliche Entwicklung (1838)*; *Die christliche Lehre von der Dreieinigkeit und der Menschenwerdung Gottes* (3 v. 1841–43); *Lehrbuch der christliche Dogmengeschichte* (1847); *Paulus der Apostel Jesu Christi* (1845, Eng. tr. 1873–75); and *Geschichte der christlichen Kirche* (5 v. 1853–63). Only two volumes of the last work appeared during Baur's lifetime. The first volume was translated into English as *Church History of the First Three Centuries* (2 v. 1878).

Bibliography: F. L. CROSS, *The Oxford Dictionary of the Christian Church* (London 1957) 142–143. J. SCHMID, *Lexikon für Theologie und Kirche* (Freiburg 1957–65) 2:72–73. H. SCHMIDT and J. HAUSSLEITER, in J. J. HERZOG and A. HAUCK, eds., *Realencyklopädie für protestantische Theologie* (Leipzig 1896–1913) 2:467–483, with complete list of Baur's writings. M. TETZ, *Die Religion in Geschichte und Gegenwart* (Tübingen 1957–65) 1:935–938.

[M. B. SCHEPERS]

BAUTAIN, LOUIS EUGÈNE MARIE

Philosopher and theologian; b. Paris, Feb. 17, 1796; d. Viroflay, Oct. 15, 1867. He went through stages of eclecticism and rationalism, but he regained the faith of his childhood in 1819 under the influence of Louise Humann and began studies for the priesthood. He was ordained in 1828 and became dean of the faculty of letters at the University of Strasbourg in 1838. In the same year he went to Rome to disprove the accusation of FIDEISM brought against him by his bishop, Le Pappe de Trévern. From 1842 to 1846 he gave many conferences to the Cercle Philosophique de Paris. He became vicar-general for Monsignor Sibour, archbishop of Paris in 1849, and was professor of moral theology at the Sorbonne from 1853 to 1863. He founded the Sisters of St. Louis, who have extended their teaching apostolate well beyond France (*see* ST. LOUIS, SISTERS OF).

His extreme reaction to rationalism made him one of the principal representatives of fideism. His bishop suspended him in 1834 because of his philosophical manifesto in 1833 that sustained the Augustinian thesis that "philosophy, which is the study of wisdom, is nothing else but religion." On April 26, 1834, however, he signed a profession of faith rejecting as erroneous these two propositions: Reason alone cannot demonstrate the existence of God; reason alone cannot establish the credibility of the Christian religion. His principal works were *La Philosophie du Christianisme* (1835), *Philosophie, psychologie expérimentale* (1839), *Philosophie morale* (1842), and *L'Esprit humain et ses facultés* (1859).

Bibliography: E. DE RÉGNY, *L'Abbé Bautain* (Paris 1884). W. M. HORTON, *The Philosophy of the Abbé Bautain* (New York 1926). P. POUPARD, *Un Essai de philosophie chrétienne au XIXe siècle: L'Abbé Louis Bautain* (Paris 1962). P. ARCHAMBAULT, *Catholicisme* 1:1322–23. M. A. MICHEL, *Lexikon für Theologie und Kirche* (Freiburg 1957–65) 2:73–74.

[P. POUPARD]

BAVO (ALLOWIN), ST.

Monastic founder and patron of Ghent; b. Hesbaye, Belgium, *c.* 600; d. at a hermitage near Ghent, Belgium, Oct. 1, 660. The oldest vita of the saint was composed in the ninth century, some 200 years after his death; it records that Bavo was descended from a noble Belgian family and was married to the daughter of a certain Count Adilion. After his wife's death, he decided to devote himself to the religious life and sought out the missionary AMANDUS, who was then at Ghent. He sold all his possessions and founded in that city a Benedictine monastery dedicated to St. Peter and later renamed Saint-Bavon. Bavo accompanied Amandus on a missionary journey through Flanders and on his return settled in a hermitage near the abbey he had endowed. He was buried at Ghent, and when the abbey church was destroyed in 1540, his relics were taken to the new cathedral. His name appears in the liturgy from the early ninth century.

Feast: Oct. 1.

Bibliography: *Acta Sanctorum* Oct. 1:199–302. *Monumenta Germaniae Historica: Scriptores rerum Merovingicanum* 4:527–545. J. MABILLON, *Acta sanctorum ordinis S. Benedicti* (Venice 1733–40) 2:396–403. *Bibliotheca hagiograpica latina antiquae et mediae aetatis* (Brussels 1898–1901) 1049–60. L. VAN DER ESSEN, *Étude critique et littéraire sur les vitae des saints mérovingiens de l'ancienne Belgique* (Louvain 1907) 349–357. É. DE MOREAU, *Saint Amand* (Louvain 1927) 220–223. A. M. ZIMMERMANN, *Kalendarium Benedictinum*, (Metten 1933–38) 3:122–124. J. VAN BRABANT, *Sint Bavo, edelman, boeteling en monnik* (Wilrijk, 1968). R. PODEVIJN, *Bavo* (Bruges 1945). R. AIGRAIN, *Catholicisme* 1:1323–24.

[B. J. COMASKEY]

BAWDEN, WILLIAM (BALDWIN)

Jesuit priest; b. Cornwall, 1563; d. Saint-Omer, Flanders, Sept. 28, 1632. After five years' study at Oxford, he arrived at Douai on Dec. 31, 1582, and at Rome on Oct. 1, 1583. He took the college oath on May 31, 1584, and was ordained on April 16, 1588. After a year as penitentiary at St. Peter's, he entered the Society of Jesus in Flanders in 1590. He taught moral theology at Louvain. Then he set out for Spain disguised as a merchant in the winter of 1594 and 1595. He was captured at sea and taken to England. The Privy Council failed to identify him and exchanged him for an English prisoner in Spain. Bawden ministered for six months in Hampshire and then functioned in Rome as minister at the English College. At Brussels, he was vice-prefect of the English mission from about 1600 to 1610, being accused unjustly of complicity in the Gunpowder Plot. An ineffective attempt was made for his extradition, but in 1610 he was recognized and taken while traveling incognito through the Palatinate; he was surrendered to the English government, which kept him in the Tower until June 15, 1618, when he was released at the insistence of Count Gondomar, the Spanish ambassador. In 1622, after a year as rector of Louvain, he became rector of Saint-Omer, governing the college successfully until his death.

Bibliography: H. CHADWICK, *St. Omers to Stonyhurst* (London 1962). T. COOPER, *The Dictionary of National Biography from the Earliest Times to 1900* (London 1885–1900) 1:959–960. H. FOLEY, ed., *Records of the English Province of the Society of Jesus,* 7 v. (London 1877–82) 3:501–520. J. GILLOW, *A Literary and Biographical History or Bibliographical Dictionary of the English Catholics from 1534 to the Present Time* (London–New York 1885–1902) 1:156–157. H. MORE, *Historia Provinciae Anglicanae Societatis Jesu* (Saint-Omer 1660) lib. 8:374–378. C. SOMMERVOGEL et al., *Bibliothèque de la Compagnie de Jésus* (Brussels-Paris 1890–1932) 1:830.

[F. EDWARDS]

BAXTER, RICHARD

Puritan divine; b. Rowton, Shropshire, England, Nov. 12, 1615; d. London, Dec. 8, 1691. His crude education under incompetent curates was compensated for by J. Owen at the Wroxeter free school and by a lifetime of private study. Baxter developed his theological views through scrupulous introspection. He entered the ministry in 1638, accepting the establishment's tenets despite private tendencies toward moderate PRESBYTERIANISM, which grew from his sympathy with NONCONFORMISTS. He favored latitudinarian views that might fuse Protestant sects into one national church based on fundamental doctrines in the Creed, Lord's Prayer, the Decalogue, and the Bible as revelation. He favored tolerance of Romanists if they worshiped privately. Baxter avoided political controversy in the civil war and supported the parliamentarians.

After 1653, he criticized Oliver CROMWELL and lamented the demise of legally constituted monarchy. Baxter cheered the Restoration but questioned the episcopacy. The Act of Uniformity of 1662 turned him from the state Church to the persecuted nonconformists with whom he suffered until the Toleration Act of 1690. Baxter spent most of his life, after 1653, in extensive literary productivity, virtually unequaled then in quality or quantity. Prominent among his more than 200 works are *Saints' Everlasting Rest* (1650), *The Reformed Pastor* (1656), and the autobiographical *Reliquiae Baxterianae* (1696).

Bibliography: R. BAXTER, *The Practical Works of the Late Reverend and Pious Mr. Richard Baxter,* ed. W. ORME, 23 v. (London 1830); *The Autobiography of Richard Baxter,* ed. J. M. LLOYD THOMAS (New York 1931); *Richard Baxter and Puritan Politics,* ed. R. SCHLATTER (New Brunswick, N.J. 1957). A. B. GROSART, comp., *Annotated List of the Writings of Richard Baxter* (London 1868); *The Dictionary of National Biography from the Earliest Times to 1900* (London 1885–1900) 1:1349–57. F. J. POWICKE, *A Life of the Reverend Richard Baxter* (London 1924).

[M. J. HAVRAN]

BAY PSALM BOOK

Popular title of the first book produced by English-speaking American authors on a British-North American press; published by Stephen Day(e) in Cambridge, Mass., 1640, under the official title of *The Whole Booke of Psalmes Faithfully Translated into English Metre.* This psalter was a new translation begun in 1636 by a group of Puritan divines—Richard Mather, John Eliot, and Thomas Weld, with some additions by the English poet Francis Quarles—who had become dissatisfied with the Sternhold and Hopkins translation being used in Massachusetts Bay Colony. The new psalter was immediately adopted by the congregations, but around 1647 the ministers of the Bay Colony felt that a revision of their initial effort was needed. The result was the third, and definitive, edition of 1651, entitled *The Psalms Hymns and Spiritual Songs of the Old and New Testament, Faithfully Translated into English Metre,* popularly known as the New England Psalm Book. The first known edition to contain examples of notated music was the ninth (1698). In its revised form the book was widely used for more than a century, not only in America but also among Puritan congregations in England and Scotland. It ranked among the most popular English psalters of its time.

See Also: HYMNS AND HYMNALS; MUSIC, SACRED (U.S.); PSALTERS, METRICAL

Bibliography: Z. HARASZTI, *The Enigma of the Bay Psalm Book* (Chicago 1956). G. CHASE, *America's Music* (New York 1955) 14, 19–21.

[A. M. GARRETT]

BAYEUX

City and diocese (*Baiocensis*) in Calvados, Normandy, France. In 1802 it incorporated part of the Diocese of

Encounter of King Harold II and William, Duke of Normandy, detail of the "Bayeux Tapestry." (© Gianni Dagli Orti/CORBIS)

LISIEUX and in 1855 became the See of Bayeux-Lisieux. Its Christian origins are unknown. As the capitol of the *civitas Baiocassium,* it is first mentioned in the late fourth century, the time of its first three bishops—Saints Exuperius, Rufinianus and Lupus. Bishop Vigor evangelized the pagans at the time of the Merovingian Childebert (511–558). Two nearby monasteries, Cerisy and Deux-Jumeaux, had early origins. The episcopal succession was disrupted by the invasion of the Normans, who slew Bishops Sulpicius (844) and Baltfrid (858). The disruption of the church lasted until Bishop Hugh (1015–49) began the religious restoration by building rural churches to combat paganism. The Norman barons began to donate their loot from elsewhere to local churches and under William the Conqueror, a reform of Normandy was undertaken by his half brother Bishop ODO, and LANFRANC by holding councils and building abbeys. In the 12th century churches multiplied. After Philip II incorporated Normandy into France (1204), synods at ROUEN worked diligently to improve ecclesiastical discipline. When the English evacuated the area in 1450 at the end of the Hundred Years' War, it was in material and moral ruin, and the clergy were at a very low status.

Lutheranism appeared by 1540 and Calvinist churches by 1555. Catholic worship was interrupted for months in 1562 when Huguenots sacked Bayeux, and Protestantism took a firm foothold in the area. The Holy LEAGUE again sacked the city in 1589. Bishops Édouard Molé (1647–52) and François Servien (1654–59) began the reform. St. John EUDES undertook missions and the COMPAGNIE DU SAINT-SACREMENT took the offensive against Protestants. Bishop François de Nesmond (1662–1715) founded the seminary and restored discipline among secular and religious clergy. Bishop François de Lorraine-Armagnac (1719–28) was an ardent Jansenist. There was an influx of religious orders into the diocese in the 17th century, as there had been in the 13th century. On the eve of the French Revolution there were 620 parish priests, 12 monasteries and two convents.

The cathedral was rebuilt by Bishop Odo in 1046 after a fire and again by Henry I of England after it was destroyed in 1105. In the 14th and 15th centuries it was enlarged and embellished. St. Jean Brébeuf, the apostle of the Hurons, canonized in 1930, was born in Bayeux. The distinctive and conservative liturgy of Bayeux, to which DURANDUS OF TROARN contributed in the 11th century, is preserved in many manuscripts of the 13th, 14th and 15th centuries. Since the 16th century the liturgy has been modified only slowly and gradually.

The Bayeux Tapestry is a linen roll of colored stitchwork, 231 feet long and 20 inches wide in its present state, representing in 72 scenes the events that led up to the battle of Hastings in 1066. It was made *c.* 1080, perhaps in England. Depicting 623 persons, 202 horses and mules, 55 dogs, 505 other animals, 37 buildings, 41 boats and ships and 49 trees, it is of value for the study of arms and armor, warfare, architecture, dress and the folklore of the period. The upper and lower borders are decorated with a series of animals, some of which are real, others imaginary.

Bibliography: S. E. GLEASON, *An Ecclesiastical Barony of the Middle Ages: The Bishopric of Bayeux 1066–1204* (Cambridge, Mass. 1936). E. DE LAHEUDRIE, *Bayeux, capitale du Bessin, des origines à la fin de la monarchie*, 2 v. in 1 (Bayeux 1945). E. JARRY and J. HOURLIER, *Catholicisme,* 1:1324–31.

[J. GOURHAND]

BAYLE, PIERRE

French skeptic who had an enormous influence on 18th-century thought; b. Carla, southern France, Nov. 18, 1647; d. Rotterdam, Dec. 28, 1706. Bayle, son of a Calvinist minister, attended the Protestant school at Puylaurens, and then the Jesuit college at Toulouse, where he converted to Catholicism and shortly thereafter back to Calvinism. His second conversion made him a *relaps*, subject to severe penalties during the persecutions of the Huguenots. Bayle fled to Geneva and studied philosophy and theology at the university. He then secretly returned to France and lived in disguise, earning his living as a tutor in Paris and Rouen and later as professor of philosophy at the Calvinist academy at Sedan, as the protegé of the fanatic Calvinist leader, Pierre Jurieu. In 1682, when the academy was closed by Louis XIV, Bayle and Jurieu became professors at the *École illustre* of Rotterdam. Here Bayle published his first work, his *Thoughts on the Comets of 1680,* a critical attack on superstition, intolerance, various philosophical and theological systems, historical inaccuracies, etc., followed by an answer to Father L. Maimbourg's *History of Calvinism* and a collection of defenses of CARTESIANISM answering the attacks of the French Jesuits. From 1684 to 1687 he edited the *Nouvelles de la République des Lettres,* reviewing all of the important writings then appearing. His famous work on toleration, the *Philosophical Commentary* on the words of Jesus, ''Constrain them to come in,'' appeared in 1686. Here Bayle offered a defense of toleration of all groups from Catholics to Muslims, Jews, Unitarians, and even atheists. His erstwhile supporter, Jurieu, then turned upon him and denounced Bayle as a secret atheist. Thereafter Bayle and Jurieu fought each other in a constant pamphlet warfare whose fruits included the termination of Bayle's academic career, which thus gave him time to write his most important and influential work, the *Historical and Critical Dictionary,* first published in 1697. Bayle's *Dictionary*, which grew to be between seven and eight million words long, consists of biographical articles on all sorts of people from the most obscure theologians to the most famous figures in the Old Testament, and the most notorious political figures. The ''meat'' of the *Dictionary* consists in the lengthy, digressive, erudite footnotes, and notes to the notes, attacking and dissecting every possible theory in philosophy, theology, and science, and retailing salacious tales about famous and infamous personages. Some of the articles (on David, the Manichaeans, Pyrrho, Rorarius, Spinoza, and Zeno) became major battlegrounds of the intellectual world for the next 50 years, eliciting replies from philosophers and theologians of every persuasion. Bayle spent his remaining years writing defenses and explanations of his views against attacks from conservative and liberal Protestants, from Catholics, and from such philosophers as G. W. Leibniz. Bayle died with pen in hand finishing off another rebuttal.

Throughout the *Dictionary* and his later works, Bayle argued that various theories in philosophy, theology, and science involve contradictions and absurdities that appear incapable of resolution. Over and over, Bayle contended that his massive skeptical barrage showed that rational endeavor in all areas is hopeless, and that man should abandon reason and turn to faith as the only source of true knowledge. He reinforced his FIDEISM by arguing that revealed truth was unintelligible, in conflict with reason, evidence, and morality. Heretical views such as Manichaeanism, he claimed, could be better defended rationally than could Christianity.

Many of Bayle's contemporaries assumed that his point was not the defense of religion, but its destruction. The *philosophes* saw the *Dictionary* as ''the Arsenal of the Enlightenment,'' and used it to undermine traditional religion, theology, and philosophy. Leibniz, G. Berkeley, and D. Hume wrestled with Bayle's arguments and sought new solutions. But the 18th century ultimately found its resolution in replacing Bayle's skeptical treasury with scientific studies. As his learned biographies became outdated, his endless doubts came to be ignored and forgotten, and his fideism seen as a covert rationalistic critique of religion and philosophy, preparing the way for the Age of Reason. Recent studies, aimed at placing Bayle in the context of his time, have led to a reconsideration of his fideism, and suggest that he was, perhaps, a serious, though puzzled and puzzling believer, struggling with the various religious and scientific tensions of his day. His doubts and religious concern may have more lasting value than the scientific optimism that emerged from taking his texts as the death knell of the pre-Newtonian age.

See Also: SKEPTICISM; ENLIGHTENMENT, PHILOSOPHY OF.

Bibliography: *Oeuvres diverses,* comp. P. DES MAIZEAUX, 4 v. (The Hague 1727–31; repr. 1964); *A General Dictionary, Historical and Critical,* 10 v. (London 1734–41); *Selections from Bayle's Dictionary,* ed. R. H. POPKIN (New York 1965). P. DIBON et al., eds., *Pierre Bayle, le philosophe de Rotterdam* (Amsterdam 1959). E. LABROUSSE, *Pierre Bayle* (The Hague 1963–64).

[R. H. POPKIN]

BAYLEY, JAMES ROOSEVELT

Eighth archbishop of the Baltimore, Md., Archdiocese; b. New York, N.Y., Aug. 23, 1814; d. Newark, N.J., Oct. 3, 1877. A descendant of long-established families of English and Dutch ancestry, he was the son of Dr. Guy Carleton and Grace (Roosevelt) Bayley and the grandson of Richard Bayley, physician, and James Roosevelt, a prominent merchant. Elizabeth Bayley SETON, foundress of the Sisters of Charity in the United States, was his aunt. He attended Mt. Pleasant Classical Institution and Amherst College in Amherst, Mass., and Trinity College, Hartford, Conn., from which he graduated in 1835. After a year in medicine, he studied for the Episcopal ministry under Dr. Samuel Farmar Jarvis, Middletown, Conn., and was ordained on Feb. 14, 1840, while rector of St. Andrew's Church, Harlem, N.Y.

Worried by doubts concerning the claims of his church, he resigned the rectorship and late in 1841 sailed for Europe. At the Church of the Gesù in Rome he was received into the Catholic Church by Bartholomew Esmonde, SJ, on April 28, 1842. Then, after a year at the Seminary of Saint-Sulpice in Paris, he finished his studies in New York and was ordained on March 2, 1844, in St. Patrick's Cathedral. After administrative posts at St. John's College (Fordham University), New York City, and some pastoral experience, he served as secretary to Bp. John HUGHES for seven years. During this time he became interested in the history of the Church in the United States.

In 1853 he was appointed the first bishop of the Diocese of Newark, covering the state of New Jersey. He was consecrated in St. Patrick's Cathedral on October 30, by Abp. Cajetan Bedini, Papal Nuncio to Brazil. The ensuing 19 years brought a great transformation in Newark as he organized and administered the growing diocese, founded a college, a seminary, and a community of Sisters of Charity, and brought in other religious communities of men and women. His attendance at Church councils, including VATICAN COUNCIL I in 1869, journeys to Europe and the Holy Land, and his writing and lecturing indicated widening spheres of action.

Bayley's *Brief Sketch of the Early History of the Catholic Church on the Island of New York* (1853, 1870) and the *Memoirs of the Rt. Rev. Simon Wm. Gabriel Bruté, D.D., First Bishop of Vincennes* (1860) appeared when Catholic historical scholarship was just beginning in the United States. Unfortunately, his duties left little time for his interest in Catholic history, literature, and bibliography. He was decided in his convictions and simple and direct in expressing them in the many pastoral letters he wrote and the many lectures he gave, especially on behalf of temperance. However, he believed in kindness and good example rather than controversy as the means of arousing interest in the Church. Against his wishes, he was appointed on July 21, 1872, as successor to Martin J. Spalding, Archbishop of Baltimore. He was harassed by frequent illness and burdened by the demands of an extensive province and the conservatism of an old, established see. His last pastoral letter in 1876 pleaded for greater zeal and generosity in support of archdiocesan institutions.

In addition to his interest in the Native American missions and the American College in Rome, which he had helped from its founding, he was called upon by the Holy See to help in the school question and in the erection of new metropolitan sees. He conferred the biretta upon the first U.S. cardinal, Abp. John MCCLOSKEY of New York. He had the satisfaction of consecrating the Baltimore cathedral 55 years after its dedication. By 1876 chronic illness induced him to ask for a coadjutor with the right of succession in the person of Bp. James GIBBONS of Richmond. The papal brief for this was received while Bayley was seeking relief from illness in Vichy, France. In August of 1877, he returned to New Jersey critically ill and died in Newark. Following the Requiem in Baltimore, he was interred as he had requested at St. Joseph's Convent, Emmitsburg, Md., beside his aunt, (Bl.) Elizabeth Seton.

Bibliography: M. H. YEAGER, *Life of James Roosevelt Bayley, First Bishop of Newark and Eighth Archbishop of Baltimore 1814–1877* (Catholic University of America, *Studies in American Church History* 36; Washington 1947).

[M. H. YEAGER]

Bibliography: S. KUTTNER, *Repertorium der Kanonistik*, (Rome 1937) index *s.v.* Bazianus. J. F. VON SCHULTE, *Die Geschichte der Quellen und der Literatur des kanonischen Rechts* (Graz 1956) 1:154–156.

[T. P. MCLAUGHLIN]

BAYS, MARGUERITE, BL.

Seamstress and member of the Third Order of Franciscans; b. La Pierraz, Siviriez, Fribourg Canton, Switzerland, Sept. 8, 1815; d. Siviriez, Switzerland, June 27, 1879. Marguerite, born into a farming family, led a simple life, working as a dressmaker. Active in her parish, she catechized children, established the Association for the Holy Childhood there, and helped to found a Catholic newspaper. Beyond the parish, she visited the sick and dying. She received the stigmata after being miraculously cured of intestinal cancer (Dec. 8, 1954). For the next twenty-five years, she mystically relived Christ's Passion each Friday. She died on the octave of the Feast of the Sacred Heart. Despite Rome's refusal of her cause, her mortal remains were exhumed in 1929 and enshrined in the convent of la Fille-Dieu at Romont, which was governed by Marguerite's goddaughter and great-niece, Mother Marie-Lutgarde Fasel. Finally her cause was accepted in 1953. Pope John Paul II beatified her on Oct. 29, 1995.

Feast: June 27.

Bibliography: R. LOUP, *Marguerite Bays*, 3d. ed. (Fribourg, Switzerland 1969).

[K. I. RABENSTEIN]

BAZIANUS

A 12th-century canonist whose *glossae* are variously designated by the sigla *B., Bar., Bac., Baç., Baça., Baz.* has been identified as Bazianus. He has frequently been confused with Joannes Bassianus, better known as a commentator on Roman law but also the author of some canonical literature. Bazianus has been called the first *doctor in utroque jure.* To which of the two does the distinction belong? Both seem to have worked in both fields. Further confusion has arisen from the use of the siglum *Bar.* and the later and better known BARTHOLOMEW OF BRESCIA. Bazianus belongs to the school of glossators and is certainly before JOANNES TEUTONICUS. If, as has been affirmed, he added glosses to the *Summa* of JOANNES FAVENTINUS, then his period of activity falls in the last half or even the last quarter of the 12th century. It is perhaps safe to say that he was attached to the school of Bologna.

See Also: DECRETISTS.

BAZIN, JOHN STEPHEN

Third bishop of Vincennes, Ind.; b. Duerne, France Oct. 15, 1796; d. Vincennes, April 23, 1848. He was educated in Lyons, France, and ordained there on July 22, 1822. Eight years later Bazin, then a seminary professor, volunteered for the American missions in the diocese of Bp. Michael Portier of Mobile, Ala. He left France on Oct. 8, 1830, and arrived two months later in Mobile, where he was assigned to the staff of Spring Hill College, a diocesan college-seminary founded by Portier in May of 1830. During the 17 years Bazin was associated with the college, he served first as professor of philosophy and theology, as well as procurator and superior of the seminary, and then as president (1832–36, 1839, 1842–44, 1846). He is credited with establishing the college on a permanent basis in 1847, when he negotiated the transfer of the properties and administration of the institution to the Jesuits.

As vicar-general of the diocese and pastor of the cathedral (1836–47), Bazin promoted pioneer building programs and furthered the organizational work involved in parochial and institutional expansion. In his pastoral apostolate, he gained recognition as a preacher and was known for his charity toward the sick and the orphans. He built a new cathedral, using his own personal wealth in an effort to meet some of the construction costs. On April 3, 1847, he was appointed third bishop of Vincennes and was consecrated there on Oct. 24, 1847, in the Cathedral of St. Francis Xavier, the first bishop to be consecrated in the see city. During his six-month episcopacy, Bazin restored peace and order in the diocese, where relations between his predecessor, Celestine de la Hailandière, and many of the clergy and religious communities had deteriorated. The new bishop initiated settlement of jurisdictional and property ownership issues where such lay at the root of the difficulties with religious communities. He tried to provide a stronger educational institution for the training of diocesan seminarians by merging the financially unsound St. Gabriel College with St. Charles diocesan seminary, assuming the financial debts of the college himself. Bazin also laid plans for the establishment of a diocesan orphanage. His Lenten pastoral letter (1848) exhorted the laity to be sensitive to the vocational needs of the diocese and outlined for them and for the clergy practical plans for the encouragement of vocations to the priesthood. He contracted pneumonia and died on Easter Sunday.

Bibliography: M. B. BROWN, *History of the Sisters of Providence of Saint-Mary-of-the-Woods,* v. 1 (New York 1949). M. KENNY, *Catholic Culture in Alabama: Centenary Story of Spring Hill College* (New York 1931). M. C. SCHROEDER, *The Catholic Church in the Diocese of Vincennes, 1847–1877* (Catholic University of America, *Studies in American Church History* 35; Washington 1946).

[M. C. SCHROEDER]

BEA, AUGUSTIN

Cardinal, biblical scholar, ecumenist; b. May 28, 1881, Riedböhringen, Baden; d. Rome, Nov. 16, 1968. Augustin Bea, the only son of Karl Bea and Maria Merk, completed his early education with the study of theology for two years at the University of Freiburg, and entered the Society of Jesus in 1902, and was ordained ten years later. He studied ancient Near Eastern philology for a semester at the University of Berlin. From 1917 to 1921 he taught the Old Testament in the German theologate at Valkenburg, Holland, where he was also prefect of studies until his nomination as provincial of Bavaria. As visitor to the Japanese mission he was influential in the founding of Sophia University, Tokyo. He went to Rome in 1924 to take charge of Jesuits assigned to graduate studies and taught in the Pontifical Biblical Institute, of which he was rector from 1930 to 1949.

He served on many Roman Congregations, including the PONTIFICAL BIBLICAL COMMISSION and the Congregation for the Doctrine of the Faith, was confessor to Pius XII (1945–58), and was chairman of the committee for the revision of the Latin psalter. After his creation as cardinal deacon of S. Saba, Dec. 14, 1959 (he was also made bishop), he headed the Secretariate for Promoting Christian Unity (1960–68) until his death.

Bea's service to the Church was chiefly carried out in three disparate areas: administration, biblical studies, and ecumenism. His exceptional talents for government were displayed within the Society of Jesus, and later given broader scope as rector of the Biblicum during 19 years and then as creator and leader of the Secretariate for Promoting Christian Unity. He established the principles for its *modus operandi,* chose and trained collaborators, and provided the initial impetus and orientation of this commission.

The list of his publications in Scripture is lengthy and impressive. The liberating views displayed in *La storicità dei Vangeli* (1964) on the vexing question of the historicity of the Gospels, originally circulated as a pamphlet for the fathers of Vatican Council II, are characteristic of his position on biblical issues.

His obituary in *Biblica,* a periodical of which he was editor 20 years, noted that "by his counselling, and especially by his recommendation of wide reading, he saw to it that his students were made aware that other less restricted positions might be equally, or more, defensible."

Bea made significant contributions to Roman documents, such as the defense of critical biblical scholarship composed by the Biblical Commission in 1941 (against the anonymous attacks of an obscurantist Italian cleric), the encyclical *Divino afflante Spiritu* (1943), the letter to Cardinal Suhard on the need for scientific exegesis (1948), the detailed progressive program for scriptural teaching in seminaries in 1950, and his role in the drafting of several documents issued by Vatican II, especially that on divine revelation, *Dei Verbum.*

His ecumenical achievements in the cause of Christian unity stemmed directly from his talents for friendship and his interest and competence in biblical studies. Already in 1935, with the express approval of Pius XI, his participation in the Old Testament congress of Protestant scholars at Göttingen established a precedent from which the present-day Catholic collaboration in common projects concerning the Bible derives.

Bibliography: S. SCHMIDT, ed., *Augustin Cardinal Bea: Spiritual Profile; Notes from the Cardinal's Diary, with a Commentary* (London 1971). J. HÖFER, "Das geistliche Profil des Kardinal Bea," *Catholica* 26 (1972) 50–63. H. BACHT, "Kardinal Bea: Wegbereiter der Einheit," *Catholica* 35 (1981) 173–188 K. H. NEUFELD, "Wirksame Ökumene: Kardinal Beas Einsatz für die Einigung der Christen," *Catholica* 353 (1981) 189–210. C. C. ARONSFELD, ed. "Augustin Cardinal Bea, 1881–1968: Thoughts on His Centenary," [thematic issue, with extensive bibliographies] *Christian Jewish Relations* 14:4 3–57. E. LANNE, "La contribution du Cardinal Bea à la question du baptême et l'unité des chrétiens," *Irénikon* 55 (1982) 471–499. S. SCHMIDT, *Augustin Bea: The Cardinal of Unity* (New Rochelle, N.Y. 1992). G. GRIESMAYR, *Die eine Kirche und die eine Welt: die ökumenische Vision Kardinal Augustin Beas* (Frankfurt am Main 1997).

[D. M. STANLEY]

BEASLEY, MATHILDA, MOTHER

Foundress; b. New Orleans, 1834; d. Savannah, 1903. Her mother was a Creole of African and European ancestry, her father was Native American. Orphaned at a young age, she came to live and work in Savannah, Georgia. She taught black children in her home, in secret, because instructing such children was against state law at that time. In Savannah, she married Abraham Beasley, a black Catholic and widower from Richmond, Feb. 9, 1869. She was baptized in the Catholic Church, at the Cathedral of Saint John the Baptist, March 27, 1869.

Abraham Beasley was a wealthy entrepreneur, whose business ventures had included running a restaurant, owning a saloon, operating a grocery store and dealing in slaves. Upon Abraham's death on Sept. 3, 1877, Mathilda inherited all his property. She, in turn, gave her inheritance to the Catholic Church. The only request she made in return was that some of the proceeds would be used to found a home for African American orphans.

When Mathilda decided to become a nun, she sailed to York, England, to enter a Franciscan novitiate in 1885, supported in part by Father Oswald Moosmüller, OSB, who had undertaken a ministry to freed slaves in Savannah after the Civil War. On her return to Savannah, she worked with the Poor Clares, a Franciscan order of sisters who taught impoverished black women and cared for orphans for a short time on Skidaway Island, near Savannah.

After Bishop Thomas A. Becker was transferred to Savannah in 1886, he became convinced of the need for ''an Orphan Asylum for the colored orphans.'' He noted that there were ''some twenty children under the charge of a mother, one of the colored women, who has spared no pains to teach these little folks.'' The teacher who ''spared no pains'' was Mathilda Taylor Beasley.

In 1887, Mrs. Beasley and Father Moosmüller cofounded the ''Saint Francis Industrial and Boarding School for Girls,'' a school for Black African girls. The school offered courses in dressmaking and music, in addition to other subjects.

In 1889, Mathilda Beasley founded the first religious community of African American women in Georgia, affiliated with the Third Order of Saint Francis. It consisted of three members. In 1891, Bishop Becker wrote to Mother Katharine Drexel, asking for financial aid for the Orphan Asylum and urging her to incorporate ''Mother'' Mathilda's community into her own Blessed Sacrament Sisters. Although no sisters ''from the north'' were forthcoming, Mother Drexel contributed financial support to the new venture.

When Mother Beasley's little community disbanded the next year, on account of dwindling numbers, she affiliated herself with the Missionary Franciscans. By 1901, her health was no longer good and she was given a little cottage on Price Street, which may have been part of the property she had previously donated to the Church. Mother Mathilda continued to minister to the orphans and to work as a seamstress in order to earn money for the poor.

On Dec. 20, 1903, Mathilda Beasley died while praying in the chapel of her small cottage. She was buried from Sacred Heart Church, in accordance with her wishes. Local newspapers of the time eulogized her, calling her ''a notable figure and foundress of Saint Francis Home for Colored Orphans.'' The papers likewise noted that Mother Beasley's ''unparalleled charities had made her the idol of the poor, especially among the Negroes.'' She was buried in the Savannah's Catholic Cemetery. Her orphanage survived her until the late 1930s or early 1940s.

Bibliography: T. J. PETERMAN, *The Cutting Edge: The Life of Thomas Becker* (Devon, PA 1982) 196–197.

[D. K. CLARK]

BEATA NOBIS GAUDIA

An office hymn in iambic dimeter by an unknown author; attributed to HILARY OF POITIERS with very slight probability; and found quite generally throughout the Western liturgy since the tenth century. Traditionally sung at Lauds on the feast of Pentecost, it relates poetically the two most important events of the feast, the descent of the Holy Spirit in tongues of fire, and the preaching of the Apostles with the gift of tongues to the community of Jerusalem, as described in Acts 2.2–4. A beautiful prayer follows, in which the Church requests that the gifts of the Holy Spirit be given to us also. Just as the time of the descent of the Holy Spirit upon the Apostles corresponded to the time of the Jewish jubilee, when debts were to be forgiven, so do we in this prayer beg forgiveness of our sins.

Bibliography: A. MIRRA, *Gl'inni del breviario romano* (Naples 1947). *Analecta Hymnica* 51:97–98. J. SZÖVÉRFFY, *Die Annalen der lateinischen Hymnendichtung* (Berlin 1964–65) 1:348.

[J. J. GAVIGAN]

BEATIFIC VISION

The supernatural act of the created intellect by which the beatified angels and souls are united to God in a direct, intuitive, and clear knowledge of the Triune God as He is in Himself. This direct, intuitive, intellectual vision of God, with the perfection of charity necessarily accompanying it, is the consummation of the divine indwelling in the sanctified spirit or soul, for by this vision the blessed are brought to fruition in such a union with God in knowledge and love that they share forever in God's own happiness (*see* GOD, INTUITION OF).

Faith seeks understanding of the beatific vision in terms of its possibility, its existence, its nature, its characteristics, and its relation to the other mysteries of salvation revealed by God. This article approaches the mystery under each of these facets.

POSSIBILITY OF THE BEATIFIC VISION

When the question arises as to the possibility of the beatific vision, a distinction must be made between the natural possibility of an intuitive vision of God by intellectual creatures and the supernatural possibility of such a vision.

Impossibility on the Natural Level. No creature can by its own natural powers alone attain to the intuitive vision of God. Sacred Scripture shows that the only knowledge of God possible to the natural powers of man is that drawn from creatures and is indirect, analogous knowledge (Wis 13.1–9; Rom 1.18–21). Intuitive knowledge of God as He is in Himself is proper only to the Blessed Trinity (Jn 1.18; 6.46; Mt 11.27; 1 Cor 2.11), and God is essentially invisible (1 Tm 1.17), dwelling in light inaccessible to man (1 Tm 6.16; Jn 1.18). Moreover, the intuitive vision of God promised to man after death is expressly said to be linked to the order of grace (1 Jn 3.2; Jn 17.2–3; Rom 6.23).

The Church has insisted in its ordinary and in its solemn magisterium that the vision of God transcends the natural power of man. Eunomius, the leader of one of the Semi-Arian sects of the 4th century A.D., taught that man by his own natural intellectual power can come to a comprehension of the divine essence as it is in itself. In their refutation of Eunomius, St. Basil the Great [*Eun.* 1.4; 12.14 (*Patrologia graeca*, ed. J. P. Migne 49:540, 544)] and St. Gregory of Nyssa (*Eun.* 12, PG 45:944; *Mort.*, PG 46:513; *V. Mos.*, PG 44:317) emphasized the eminently supernatural character of the intuitive vision of God and the incomprehensibility of God to any creature. The Council of VIENNE (A.D. 1311–12) condemned the teaching of the BEGUINES and the Beghards that the soul does not need the light of glory to elevate it to the vision of God but is able to attain to this happiness by its own powers (H. Denzinger, *Enchiridion symbolorum* 894, 895). N. MALEBRANCHE (1638–1715) and V. GIOBERTI (1801–52) both eliminated the supernatural character of the intuitive vision of God in their teaching that the first act of the intelligence is a natural intuition of being, which is so identified with God that the created intelligence knows God Himself intuitively and properly as object. Their philosophical-religious system, known as ONTOLOGISM, was condemned by a decree of the Holy Office in 1861 (Denzinger 2841–47). In their solemn definitions of the existence of the beatific vision, Pope Benedict XII and the Council of Florence both teach that only those who have been reborn supernaturally in grace see God after death (Denzinger 1000–02, 1304–06).

St. Thomas Aquinas points up the reason why the intuitive knowledge of God as He is in Himself is impossible on the natural level for any creature in the following argument. The knowledge of every knower is proportioned to the mode of being of the knower. Now God alone is self-subsistent being. Therefore to know self-subsistent being is natural only to the divine intellect. On the other hand, since neither angels nor men are self-subsistent beings, their created intellects cannot know God as He is in Himself by their natural powers (see Summa theologiae 1a, 12.4; 1a, 64.1 ad 2; 1a2ae, 5.5; *In 2 sent.* 4.1.1; 23.2.1; *In 4 sent.* 49.2.6; *C. gent.* 3.49, 52; *De ver.* 8.3; *De anim.* 17 ad 10; *In epist. 1 ad Tim.* 6 lect. 3).

Possibility on the Supernatural Level. The beatific vision is strictly supernatural in every aspect. Therefore, the very concept of the beatific vision so transcends the natural cognitive power of any created intellect that it can be known only through divine revelation, and after the existence of such vision has been revealed, its nature still remains impenetrable by the mind of man in this life, even by the mind enlightened by faith. Further, the beatific vision is a wholly gratuitous gift from God in no way demanded by the natural requirements of a created nature. Once God has revealed the mystery of the beatific vision as man's ultimate end, however, reason illumined by faith can contemplate the fittingness of such a vision in terms of man's intellectual openness to truth in general and of the human desire to see God.

Obediential Potency. The supernatural elevation of the intellects of men to the intuitive vision of God involves no contradiction, for the proper object of the created intellect is the intelligible. A being is intelligible, however, insofar as it is in act. Therefore, God, who is PURE ACT, is in Himself infinitely intelligible. That God is unknowable as He is in Himself to created intellects that do not have the light of glory is because the very perfection of His intelligibility is blinding to the unaided intellectual faculty of angel or man. Because this same intellectual power is spiritual, however, and so able mentally to abstract the form from the concrete existent and to consider the concrete form and its existence in abstraction, this same created intellect is open to being elevated by divine grace to the contemplation of God, who is subsisting existence. This is often referred to as an obediential potency for the beatific vision. That such a potency be actuated, however, depends entirely upon the divine omnipotence and initiative, and is above the natural exigency or active potency of any creature (see St. Thomas Aquinas, ST 1a, 12.1; 12.4 ad 3; 85.1; 86.2; 87.3; 1a2ae, 3.8; 5.1; 2a2ae, 8.1; *In 4 sent.* 46.2.1; *C. gent.* 3.51, 54, 57; *De ver.* 8.1; *Comp. theol.* 104; *In Mt.* 5.2; *In Joann.* 1.2).

Nature and Grace. The fittingness of the beatific vision as evidenced by man's natural desire to see God is a very delicate question because it concerns the relation between the natural and the supernatural. Michel de Bay (BAIUS) and the Jansenists claimed that in the state of original justice man's natural desire of the vision of God was efficacious in such a way that the beatific vision was due to human nature and natural for man (*see* JANSENISM). This erroneous position was condemned by Pope St. Pius V in 1567 (Denzinger 1903–05, 1921, 1923, 1926; *see EX OMNIBUS AFFLICTIONIBUS*) and Gregory XIII in 1580. Implicit in these papal condemnations is the affirmation of the Church's teaching that grace and its consummation in the beatific vision are always strictly supernatural and never due to the natural exigencies of any created nature.

St. Thomas Aquinas uses the argument of man's natural desire for the vision of God in support of the possibility of the beatific vision many times in his theological writings, but always in the context of the divine revelation that man is ordered to the beatific vision as his ultimate end, and that this end, which is supernatural to man in every way, is a matter of faith (see ST 1a, 12.1, 4–6; 38.1; 43.3–4, 6; 1a2ae, 5.5–6, 7 ad 3; 62.1–3; 63.3; 109.5; 110.1; 112.1–3; 114.2, 5; 2a2ae, 6.1;24.2–3; *C. gent.* 3.50–54; *Comp. theol.* 104–106; *In Mt.* 5.2; *In epist. 1 ad Cor.* 13 lect. 4; *In epist. ad Rom.* 5 lect. 1; *In epist. ad Heb.* 13 lect. 3). St. Thomas analyzes the God-given ultimate end of man in ST 1a2ae, 1–5. In question two, he approaches the problem of perfect happiness in terms of man's will, which necessarily desires happiness and seeks that which will perfect man and bring him happiness, although many err in regard to that in which their perfect happiness will be found. He shows that because the will is open to universal good, not all particular limited goods together will satisfy man's desires. Man can find perfect happiness only in God, who is infinite Goodness, for infinite goodness alone will so satisfy man's desire for good that nothing more can be desired. In question three, St. Thomas considers happiness in terms of that human operation by which man can attain God. Although the good that alone can satisfy all man's desires will be the uncreated goodness of God, still man's attainment of that good must be an operation of man if it is to be his happiness. Since God is a spirit, however, this operation can only be that of one of man's two spiritual faculties—intellect or will. The will is a blind faculty that never takes possession of the good it desires directly, but does so through some other faculty and then rests in the enjoyment of the good attained. Therefore, the will takes possession of infinite Goodness through an act of the intellect, and it will be in this act of the intellect that happiness will be found essentially. If man is to be perfectly happy, this act of the intellect must be the contemplation of the divine essence itself, for only such contemplation will satisfy man's desire to come to the knowledge of the first cause of the created effects that cause wonder in him. God, the creator of man, would not put in man a natural desire that could in no way be fulfilled. Without the contemplation of the divine essence, however, man would be left with an unfulfilled desire. St. Thomas is always insistent, nevertheless, that this desire can be fulfilled only by a gratuitous, supernatural elevation of man to the order of grace and glory. According to St. Thomas, the very existence of the beatific vision as man's ultimate end can be known only through divine revelation and must be believed by divine faith. His argument from the natural desire to see God is not given as proof of the existence of the beatific vision, but as an argument from reason to indicate the harmony existing between nature and supernature in the providence of that God who is the author of both the natural and the supernatural orders. Man's created openness to the supernatural gift of the vision of God involves no contradiction.

The meaning of this natural desire for the vision of God has been much debated. Some (e.g., Ferrariensis, D. Báñez, John of St. Thomas, and many modern Thomists) speak of a conscious, elicited desire, which is conditional and ineffective without grace. Others (e.g., Domingo de Soto, John Duns Scotus, Durandus, Gregory of Valencia, H. Noris, G. Berti, and an increasing number of moderns among Thomists) consider this desire to be an innate, natural, but inefficacious desire that is reducible to the desire for happiness, but without a realization that happiness will be found only in the vision of God; hence, no conscious desire for such a vision. The second opinion would seem to be closer to the truth.

EXISTENCE OF THE BEATIFIC VISION

Only through divine supernatural revelation could man know that he is ordained to the intuitive vision of God in heaven.

Vision of God in the Old Testament. "To see" and "to know" in Biblical terminology often express a relation of nearness to someone in which there is an experience of the other person's presence. Because the eye is the principal instrument of knowing, the theme of vision is used to express the ineffable experience of the presence of the hidden God in a THEOPHANY. In the Old Testament one reads that Jacob saw God (Gn 32.31) and Moses and the 70 elders beheld the God of Israel (Ex 24.10–11; Nm 12.8; Dt 34.10). Likewise it is asserted that Isaiah "saw the Lord" (Is 6.1). In every instance, however, the context indicates that a theophany is meant, not an intuitive vision of the divine essence. To Moses' plea of "Do let me see your glory," Yahweh answered "I will make all my beauty pass before you . . . but my face you cannot see, for no man sees me and still lives" (Ex 33.18–20). Both the Old and the New Testaments teach that man cannot see God in this life (Ex 33.20; Jgs 6.22–23; 13.22; Is 6.5; Jn 1.18; 5.37; 6.46; 1 Jn 4.12; 2 Cor 5.7).

Although the theme of happiness goes through the whole of Biblical revelation, from paradise lost to paradise regained, nowhere in the Old Testament is there an explicit revelation that man's ultimate happiness will be found in an intuitive vision of God. Nevertheless, two positive aspects are to be noted in Israel's expectation of the happiness reserved for those who are faithful to Yahweh. In the first place, this happiness will be real, involving the whole man. Second, this happiness will be found not only in the possession of terrestrial goods in a transfigured earth, but most of all in a life lived in the divine presence [see Ps 15(16).7–11; 16(17).15; 35(36).9–10; 48(49).16; 72(73).23–28; Is 2.1–5; 25.1–9; 35.1–10; 40.1–11; 60.1–22; Jer 31.31–40; Ez 36.26–36; Hos 2.20–25; Wis 4.4–17; 5.1–16].

In the measure that the messianic expectation develops, Israel desires to see the manifestation of God that brings salvation (see, e.g., Is 40.5; 52.10b; Mal 3.2), but in these texts one still has only the signs of God's presence. Intimations were given, however, that man was destined for a union with God that would transcend the happiness the just Israelite found in the presence of God in His temple in Jerusalem. Psalms 15 (16) and 72 (73) especially pose the problem of the permanence of the joy with Yahweh and voice the hope of being always in the divine presence. Ps 15 (16).11 would seem to indicate that one comes to the face of God in order to enjoy God alone. The faith of Israel in eternal life with God beyond the grave is expressed in Wis 4.7–17; 5.1–16; Dn 12.13; 2 Mc 7.9, 11, 14, 23, 36, and Psalms 15 (16) and 72 (73), but the revelation that the just man's happiness would be found in the intuitive vision of God was not given until the Word became incarnate.

Vision of God in the New Testament. When the Son of God, who is Himself the revelation of the Father (see Jn 1.18; 8.19; 10.30, 38; 12.45; 14.7, 9, 11; Col 1.15), became for men "God-given wisdom, and justice, and sanctification, and redemption" (1 Cor 1.30), He brought the good news that all who receive Him in faith and love become the sons of God (Jn 1.12–13;3.5; Rom 8.15–17; Gal 4.3–7; 1 Jn 3.1–2; 4.15). The revelation of the mystery of the beatific vision is an intrinsic part of this fuller revelation of the meaning of divine adopted sonship in and through the Son; for all who participate in the divine nature will share in the divine inheritance, which is the eternal life of the beatific vision (2 Pt 1.4; Rom 8.15–17; Eph 1.3–14; 1 Cor 13.12; 1 Jn 3.2).

Christ summed up His mission as the giving of everlasting life to all whom the Father had given to Him (Jn 17.2) and then epitomized the meaning of everlasting life with: "Now this is everlasting life, that they know thee, the only true God, and him whom thou hast sent, Jesus Christ" (Jn 17.3). That this knowing is the intuitive vision of God as He is in Himself is clearly expressed by St. Paul in the climax of his hymn to charity: "We see now through a mirror in an obscure manner, but then face to face. Now I know in part, but then I shall know even as I have been known" (1 Cor 13.12). St. Paul distinguishes two phases in the Christian economy of salvation, marked by the antithesis between "now" and "then." During this life, which is likened to a time of childhood (1 Cor 13.11), the Christian knows God only in part, obscurely, as in a mirror. When the Christian attains to adulthood in adopted sonship, however, he will know God as God knows him; that is, he will know God in His very being albeit not so much as God is knowable. The Apostle further clarifies this knowledge of God by contrasting the obscure, indirect vision in the mirror of his time with the clear vision that comes when the knower is "face to face" with the known. This deliberate juxtaposition of a knowing in part with a knowing as God knows, and of an indirect vision of God through His created manifestations as in a mirror with a direct "face to face" vision through no created medium, emphasizes the difference between "face to face" vision in 1 Cor 13.12 and the intimacy of Moses with God in Ex 33.11; Nm 12.8, which was not the vision of God (Ex 33.20). In 1 Cor 13.12 St. Paul can mean only the clear intuitive vision of the divine essence [cf. St. Augustine, *In evang. Ioh.* 34.9; 101.5 (*Corpus Christianorum* 36:315–316, 592–593); St. Ambrose, *De bono mortis* 11.49 (Patrologia latina, ed. J. P. Migne, 14:562–563); St. Thomas Aquinas, *In epist. 1 ad Cor.* 13 lect. 4; see also C. Spicq, *Agapè* . . . 2:94–107].

Charity, which leads to the vision of God, "never fails," so that in the end there will remain charity (v. 8) and the vision of God (v. 12). This bond between charity and the beatific vision is rooted in the mystery of divine adopted sonship, for the charity of God is poured forth into the hearts of His adopted sons by the Holy Spirit, who is given to them (Rom 5.5). Affective love for God becomes effective, however, only in the love of neighbor (cf. Mt 25.31–40; Jn 13.34–35; 1 Cor 13.4–7;1 Jn 4.7–21). Through love of God in neighbor, the Christian is gradually assimilated to Christ (2 Cor 3.18; Eph 2.1–10; 5.1–2; Phil 2.5–11) and is prepared for the perfection of sonship in the union of vision (1 Jn 3.2).

Writing of the beatific vision, St. Augustine, St. Thomas Aquinas, and many modern exegetes intertwine Jn 17.3; 1 Cor 13.12; Mt 5.8; 1 Jn 3.2–3; Heb 12.14; Mt 18.10–11; and Rv 22.4 [see, e.g., St. Augustine, *In evang. Ioh.* 34.9; 53.12; 101.5; 111.3 (*Corpus Christianorum* 36:315–316, 457–458, 593, 630–631); *Serm. de Vet. Test.* 38.3 (*Corpus Christianorum* 41:478); *In psalm.* 84.9.39–85; 97.3 (*Corpus Christianorum* 39:1168,

1373–74); St. Thomas Aquinas, *In Mt. 5.2; In Ioann.* 17.1.3; A. Gelin, "'Voir Dieu' dans l'Ancien Testament," *Bible et vie Chrétienne* 23 (1958) 11–12; A. George, "Heureux les coeurs purs! Ils verront Dieu!" *ibid.* 13 (1956) 78; L. Pirot, *Dictionnaire de la Bible,* suppl. ed. 1:937; C. Spicq, *Agapè* . . . 2:103; *La Sainte Bible,* see cross refs. for 1 Cor 13.12; 1 Jn 3.2; and Heb 12.14].

In His discourse at the Last Supper, Christ spoke of the mystery of the Trinity and of the divine indwelling in those who accept Him in faith and in love (John ch. 14–17). He promised that "he who loves me will be loved by my Father and I will love him and manifest myself to him" (Jn 14.21b). But the manifestation of the Son is also the manifestation of the Father, for to Philip's plea that He show them the Father, Christ replied: ". . . he who sees me sees also the Father" (Jn 14.8–9), for "I am in the Father and the Father in me" (Jn 14.10). The explicit revelation of the beatific vision in "Beloved, now we are the children of God, and it has not yet appeared what we shall be. We know that when he appears, we shall be like to him, for we shall see him just as he is" (1 Jn 3.2) is best understood in the context of this revelation of the mystery of the Trinity and of the divine indwelling in those who are made sons of God in and through the Son. Exegetes differ as to whether the Father or the Son is meant in "when he appears," but the revelation of the vision of God remains untouched by their difference. St. Augustine, who seems to consider this a reference to the appearance of the Father, insists that it also promises a vision of the Son in His divinity, because when "the one God is seen, the Trinity is seen—the Father and the Son and the Holy Spirit . . . There is no difference between the vision of the Son and the vision of the Father" (cf. *In psalm.* 84.9.55–85, *Corpus Christianorum* 39:1168–69; *Trin* 1.13.28, PL 42:840–841). Some modern exegetes are of the opinion that "when he appears" refers to the Son. Again, the revelation of the beatific vision remains the same, for the addition of the words "we shall be *like him, for* we shall see him *just as he is*" indicates that only those who are like him in divine sonship will see Him as He is. At least at the last judgment all the damned will see Christ in His glorious humanity. The vision promised in 1 Jn 3.2, therefore, is that of His Godhead, for it is reserved to those who are like Him in His divinity. Those who see Him in His divinity, however, see the Father and the Holy Spirit, too, for they see God.

Commenting on the sixth beatitude, "Blessed are the clean of heart, for they shall see God" (Mt 5.8), L. Pirot insists that this beatitude refers literally to the "face to face" vision of God. Christ beatifies interior purity. In Hebrew psychology the heart is the seat of thoughts, of emotions, of actions. This cleanness of heart, therefore, connotes a total submission to God in love and in obedience to His law (Pirot, 936). A. George refers to the sixth beatitude as "a summit of revelation" that goes further than all the other beatitudes, for this one announces the Ineffable Presence, the Supreme GOOD, as the reward of those who are faithful sons of God [78; cf. St. Aug., Civ. 20.21.44–50 (*Corpus Christianorum* 48:737); *In psalm.* 84.9.74–85; 85.21.557 (*Corpus Christianorum* 39:1168–69, 1193–94); St. Thomas Aquinas, *In Mt.* 5.2].

Teaching of the Church. The intuitive and beatifying vision of God already enjoyed by the Church triumphant is an essential part of the faith and of the eschatological hope of the Church militant [see Vatican Council II, *Dogmatic Constitution on the Church* 48–51; *Acta Apostolicae Sedis* 57 (1965) 53–58]. In its ordinary and in its solemn magisterium, the Church proposes the mystery of the beatific vision as the revealed ultimate end of man, to be believed by supernatural faith.

Ordinary Magisterium. The best witnesses to the teaching of the ordinary magisterium of the Church in regard to the beatific vision will be found in the writings of the Fathers, who were themselves a part of the Apostolic hierarchy and so of the magisterium. For St. Ignatius of Antioch, the hope of the vision of Christ in His divinity was the incentive for a life given in martyrdom (Rom. 6.2; PG 5:692). St. Theophilus of Antioch wrote that "one day God will be contemplated face to face in glory" (*Autol.* 1.7; PG 5:1036). Although St. Irenaeus of Lyons erred in thinking the beatific vision is not given to the just until their resurrection, still he did teach that eternal life comes to each one from the act of seeing God (*Haer.* 4.20.4–7; PG 7:1035–37). St. Hilary of Poitiers affirms that by the gift of God all the clean of heart will see God (*In psalm.* 118.38; PL 9:555). St. Basil the Great speaks of a gradual perfecting and strengthening of the mind supernaturally so that the day will come when it will approach the unveiled divinity itself, and says "our mind will be elevated and quickened to the height of beatitude when it sees the oneness of the Word" (*Epist.* 8.7; PG 32:257–259). In his funeral oration for his sister Gorgonia, St. Gregory of Nazianzus rejoices that she sees the vision of glory and the splendor of the most Holy Trinity, which she contemplates and possesses—"the whole of it by the whole mind and shining on your soul with the whole light of divinity" (*Or.* 8.23; PG 35:816). In his funeral oration for St. Basil, St. Gregory looks forward to the day when "together we may behold in greater purity and fullness the holy and blessed Trinity," which he now knows incompletely through images (*Or.* 43.82; PG 36:604–605).

St. John Chrysostom in his first letter to Theodore writes that if Peter was so enraptured in the vision of

Christ's glorious humanity, "what will happen when the full reality is presented . . . and it is permitted us to look upon the king Himself, no longer in an obscure manner, nor through a mirror, but face to face; no longer by faith, but by sight" (*Thdr.* 1.11; PG 47:292). St. Ambrose teaches that the just "have this as reward that they see the face of God and that Light which enlightens every man" (*De bono mortis* 2; PL 14:562–563). Pope St. Leo the Great preached that in the Transfiguration the Apostles saw the royal splendor that belongs in a special way to the nature of Christ's assumed manhood, but while they were in the flesh "they could not look upon and see the ineffable and inaccessible vision of the divinity itself, which is reserved for the eternal life of the clean of heart" (*Serm.* 51.2; PL 54:311). Pope St. Gregory the Great writes:

> We ought to mention that there were some who have held that even in the region of blessedness God is beheld in His glory, but is not seen in His nature. These persons are deceived by the very lack of logic in their investigations, for in that simple and unchangeable essence, glory is not one thing and nature another. God's nature is itself His glory, and His glory is itself His nature. Because one day the Wisdom of God would show itself to those who love Him, He Himself promises the vision of His essence when He says: "He who loves me will be loved of my Father, and I will love him and will manifest myself to him" (Jn 14.21). It is as if He said clearly: "You who perceive me in your nature shall yet see me in my own." He says again: "Blessed are the clean of heart, for they shall see God" (Mt 5.8). Hence Paul says: "We see now through a mirror in an obscure manner, but then face to face. Now I know in part, but then I shall know even as I have been known" (I Cor 13.12). [*Moralia* 18.54.90; PL 76:93–94.]

The book or sermon written by St. Augustine in which he did not mention the beatific vision is the exception, for the saint was absorbed in the mystery of the Trinity and on fire with the desire to contemplate God face to face. St. Augustine teaches that the reward of the just, after their purification, is the clear, intuitive, intellectual vision of the Triune God. By this vision they are made supremely happy forever. Although there are degrees in formal beatitude dependent upon the merits of the just, still all are filled with happiness and all see God as He is, even though none know Him as much as He is knowable [see, e.g., *In evang. Ioh.* 34.7–8; 53.12; 76.1–4 (*Corpus Christianorum* 36:314–315, 457–458, 517–519); *Epist.* 92.4–6 (PL 33:319–320); *Epist.* 147.8.20; 9.21; 23.51 (PL 33:605, 606, 620); *Serm.* 4.4–6; 23.16–18; 38.3 (*Corpus Christianorum* 41:21–23, 318–319, 477–478); *De videndo Deo* 15.37 (PL 33:612); Trin. 1.8.16–18; 1.13.28; 14.17–19.23–25 (PL 42:831–832, 840–841, 1054–56); *Civ.* 20.21.40–50; 21.24.125–152; 22.29.1–210; 22.30.99–152 (*Corpus Christianorum* 48:737, 792, 856–862, 864–866); *In psalm.* 75.5.32–42; 78.8.52–80; 85.21.1–59; 97.3.15–35 (*Corpus Christianorum* 39:1040–41, 1153–54, 1193–94, 1373–74); *In psalm.* 104.3.1–40; 109.12.2078; 123.2.12–47; 139.18.1–44 (*Corpus Christianorum* 40:1536–37, 1611–13, 1825–26, 2024–25)].

Solemn Magisterium. Implicitly the Council of Vienne taught the existence of the beatific vision in its insistence on the necessity of the light of glory for that vision (Denzinger 895). The first definition of the existence and nature of the beatific vision was occasioned by a dispute regarding the immediacy or the delay of the beatific vision for the souls of the just after death. Although the Church's faith in the existence of the beatific vision never wavered, an initial concentration upon the Parousia and the glorious resurrection of the elect tended for a time to obscure the realization of the glorification of the individual saint before the corporate triumph in Christ at the Last Judgment. The clear understanding that the vision of God is given at once to the soul that dies in grace and has been purified, matured only gradually. By the 14th century, however, the immediacy of the beatific vision for the just after death was the common teaching of the Church. Therefore, when in his advanced old age Pope John XXII espoused in several sermons St. Bernard's opinion that the souls of the just must wait until the final judgment to see God, a hot dispute ensued between certain Franciscans who supported the pope's opinion and the Dominicans who defended the traditional position. In the conclusion of his second sermon, Pope John XXII clearly indicated he was speaking as a private theologian, however, and stated that he was open to correction in the matter. He himself earlier, in the bull of canonization of Louis d'Anjou (1317), had said that the soul of Louis had entered heaven to contemplate his God face to face. On his deathbed in 1334, the Pope declared it his opinion that the souls of the just when purified see God and the divine essence face to face so far as the state and condition of a separated soul allows this.

The arguments continued after his death, however, and so, for the peace of mind of the faithful, his successor, Pope Benedict XII, settled the question once for all in the constitution BENEDICTUS DEUS, issued on Jan. 29, 1336. In the *Benedictus Deus,* Pope Benedict XII "defines by apostolic authority and with a constitution that shall be valid forever" that the souls of all the saints who departed this world before the Passion of Our Lord Jesus Christ, and the souls of all the saints who die after they have received the sacred Baptism of Christ and have been purified, should they need such purification,

> directly after their death and this purification in those needing such purification, even before the resumption of their bodies and the general judgment, after the Ascension of Our Lord and Savior Jesus Christ into heaven, have been, are, and will be in heaven, in the kingdom of heaven and the heavenly paradise, together with Christ . . . and that after the Passion and death of Our Lord Jesus Christ they have beheld and do behold the divine essence with intuitive and face-to-face vision, with no creature mediating in the manner of object seen, but the divine essence immediately showing itself to them without covering, clearly and openly; and that when they see in this way they have full enjoyment of that same divine essence. From this vision and enjoyment the souls of those who have already departed are truly blessed and have eternal life and rest; and the souls of those who will depart hereafter will also see that same divine essence and will have full enjoyment of it before the general judgment. This vision and this fruition of the divine essence do away with the acts of faith and hope in these souls insofar as faith and hope are theological virtues in the strict sense; and after this intuitive face-to-face vision and enjoyment has begun or begins to exist in these souls, the same vision and fruition exists continuously and will continue up to the last judgment and from then on through eternity. [Denzinger 1000, 1001.]

In its *Decree for the Greeks,* the bull *Laetentur coeli,* July 6, 1439, the Council of Florence added something to the clarity of the preceding definition in defining that

> the souls of those who after the reception of Baptism have incurred no stain of sin at all, and also those souls which after the contraction of sin have been purged, whether in their bodies or when delivered of these same bodies . . . are immediately received into heaven and see clearly the one and Triune God, just as He is, yet one more perfectly than another, in proportion to the diversity of merits. [Denzinger 1305.]

NATURE OF THE BEATIFIC VISION

A fruitful doctrinal study of the beatific vision requires that the supernatural character of this vision be emphasized, for the object of the beatific vision is God, the holy and undivided Trinity. Nevertheless, elevated and strengthened by the light of faith, reason is able to penetrate the mystery to some extent from the analogy of sensible and intellectual vision and from the relationship of the beatific vision to the other mysteries of the faith that have been revealed.

The beatific vision is revealed to men as a kind of seeing that is at the same time a supernatural knowing (1 Cor 13.12; 1 Jn 3.2). From the analogy of natural vision, both sensible and intellectual, some light is thrown on the act of vision by which the blessed see God. The vision given by eyesight is an act that, by the activity of the seer and without transforming the seer into the colored object he sees, effects in the seer an actualizing of a color that has its real existence in an external object. A necessary condition for the production of this act is the presence of light and its common action upon the colored object and upon the sense of vision. In fact, light is required for the reception of visual sensation and for the unity of the image produced in the act of seeing. Now the act of intellectual perception of truth is called vision by an analogy with bodily vision. Intellectual perception of truth is an act that, by the activity of the knower and without transforming the knower into the being that he knows, effects in the knower an actualizing intentionally of an essence that has its real existence in an external object. As light is necessary in bodily vision, so also something analogous to light is required in intellectual vision, namely, the "light of truth," which must exist and act not only in the mind but also in the object that the mind knows. Therefore, intellectual vision has a threefold requirement: (1) the intelligibility of that which is known; (2) the power of knowing in the knower; and (3) a union between the knower and the known. How are these three requirements fulfilled in the beatific vision?

Intelligibility of that Which Is Known. God, who is pure act, first truth in being, is most intelligible in Himself and so infinitely knowable. That God is unknowable as He is in Himself to created intellects on the natural level is because of the very excess of His intelligibility, which is blinding to the unaided intellectual power of angel or man.

Power of Knowing in the Knower. The intellectual power of the rational creature is a participated likeness of Him who is the first intellect (ST 1a, 12.2). The connatural object of this created power of intellectual vision, however, is not the divine essence, but created essences; hence, by its own unaided power neither the angelic nor the human intellect could ever see the divine essence. For the vision of God, the created intellect must be elevated and strengthened by a created supernatural gift, the light of glory. The light of glory, which is a new perfection of the intellect itself, replaces the light of faith and gives the created intellect a higher supernatural participation in the Divine Light. St. Thomas does not hesitate to say that by the light of glory the blessed are made deiform (ST 1a, 12.5). Not that the light of glory makes the essence of God intelligible, for He is always infinitely knowable, but rather this light perfects the created intellect for the act of vision in much the same way that a habit perfects a power for its most perfect act. Therefore, the light of glory is in no way a medium in which God is seen but rather one by which He is seen; and such a medium does not take away the immediate vision of God (cf. ST 1a, 12.5; *C. gent.* 3.53).

Union between the Knower and the Known. That God, who is the object known, be in the knower by His essence so that God becomes one with the knower is impossible, for even though God is present most intimately by His power, presence, and essence to all creatures, no creature can ever be so elevated as to be absorbed into the divine essence. Nor can God be known intuitively as He is in Himself by means of a created idea of God that is united with the mind of the beatified making it to know, for no created idea can be the uncreated as He is in Himself, or express Him as He is in Himself. Yet, God has revealed and the Church has defined that the just see God as He is in Himself. St. Thomas points out that there is a mode of union by way of likeness that makes possible a union between God and the created intellect, namely, that in which one and the same being is the principle of the power of knowing and is also the object known. This mode of union is uniquely possible in the vision of God, for God is the author of the intellectual power of man, and He is the object of vision present to the intellect in the beatific vision. In the beatific vision the divine essence is united with the created intellect in such a way that the act of vision terminates not in any created form, but in the divine essence itself. From this union of the divine essence and the supernaturalized intellect of the blessed one thing is understood, and that one thing is God as He is in Himself. St. Thomas explains the nature of this immediate union between God and the created intellect thus: ''The divine essence is existence itself. Hence as other intelligible forms, which are not their own existence, are united to the intellect according to a kind of mental existence by which they inform the intellect and make it in act, so the divine essence is united to the created intellect as the object actually understood, by Itself making the intellect actually understanding'' (ST1a, 12.2 ad 3). This is what M. De la Taille, SJ, most aptly called created actuation by Uncreated Act (cf. M. De la Taille, *The Hypostatic Union and Created Actuation by Uncreated Act* 30–33). In the beatific vision God is the quasi form of the act of vision, not as the act informing the human intellect, but rather as the Act terminating the act of the intellect (cf. ST 1a, 12.5; *Comp. theol.* 105; De ver. 8.1; ST 3a, suppl., 92.1 ad 8; also De la Taille, *op. cit.,* and K. Rahner, ''Some Implications of the Scholastic Concept of Uncreated Grace''325–346). For this act of vision the creature must be assimilated supernaturally to the Triune God in essence and in operation. In His very gift of Himself to His creature God brings about that assimilation if there is no resistance to Him. In order that His rational creatures attain Him in the beatific vision, God perfects the essence of the soul through the entitative habit of habitual sanctifying GRACE, which is a created participation in the divine nature that makes its possessor an adopted son of God and a member of the Divine Family. Likewise God elevates the spiritual faculties of intellect and will so that the rational creature may know and love God as He knows and loves Himself. The intellect is perfected by the light of glory, which is simultaneously the created effect of the Uncreated actuation of the intellect by the Object known and the disposition for the act of knowing the Uncreated. The will is perfected for the concomitant act of fruition by infused charity, which abides in heaven in one unending act of love of God. Although all the blessed know God as He is, not any know Him as much as He is knowable. The greater the love in the creature, the greater its participation in the light of glory; and the greater its participation in the light of glory, the greater the perfection of its act of vision (Council of Florence, Denz 1305; St. Thomas Aquinas, ST 1a, 12.6, 1a2ae, 5.2).

In the vision of God the elect participate in a finite way in God's own knowledge. For example, the mysteries of the faith are now known not by faith but by vision, albeit this clear knowledge by vision is never exhaustive of the mystery. In the beatific vision each of the blessed also perceives the exact nature of the divine dispensation pertaining to his own salvation and perfection. The saints in heaven know their dear ones in God even more perfectly than they have or will know them in themselves, and in their vision of God the blessed continue to know and to interest themselves in all that concerns the Church and their dear ones on earth. The blessed also know in the vision of God all that He has created that is of interest to them. Everything other than God as He is in Himself, however, everything that involves the relationship of a creature to God is only secondarily the object of the beatific vision. Man's ultimate end consists primarily in God Himself, and man's beatitude will be in the immediate vision of God and the joy concomitant with the personal possession in vision and love of the Triune God, whose nature is identical with the intelligibility of Himself and with the intellection of Himself.

CHARACTERISTICS OF THE BEATIFIC VISION

Happiness is found not only in the act by which the soul takes possession of God in knowing Him as it is known by Him, but also in all the concomitant properties that are consequent upon that act of vision. (1) Comprehension is the first of these consequences of the act of vision—comprehension in the sense of attaining God, to repose in His presence, not in the sense of knowing Him as much as He is knowable, which is possible only to God Himself (ST 1a2ae, 4.3). (2) The beatific vision causes perfect joy to the soul, which now rests in the beloved in an unending act of perfect charity (STla2ae, 4.1, 2; 2a2ae, 28.1, 3). (3) The beatific vision brings sinlessness as one of its effects, for since final happiness consists in an intellectual vision of Him who is infinite truth and beauty, and the will then reposes through that act in the possession of infinite goodness, it is psychologically impossible for the will to turn from its adequate object to a created good preferred to the uncreated good now possessed (ST 1a2ae, 4.4). (4) God has promised and the Church has defined that the beatific vision will last forever. Nothing less than eternal beatitude would be perfect beatitude (ST 1a2ae, 5.4). (5) The total person is beatified. Therefore, although it is the soul that alone can take possession of God, since God is a spirit, still the beatified soul will be substantially united to the body after the resurrection, and the joy of the soul will overflow into the body (ST 1a2ae, 4.6).

BEATIFIC VISION AND OTHER MYSTERIES OF FAITH

The mystery of the beatific vision is related to that of grace, for the intrinsic supernaturality of grace is pointed up by its term, the altogether supernatural act of knowing God as He is in Himself. But it is the Triune God who is known in this way; hence the mystery of the beatific vision is intrinsically related to the mystery of the Trinity and of the divine INDWELLING in the rational creature. Light is thrown on the mystery of the beatific vision by the mystery of the INCARNATION and REDEMPTION, for it is in and by the Son that men become sons of God; they are brought to the consummation of adopted sonship by sharing in the Son's inheritance. The beatific vision in turn casts light on the mystery of the Incarnation, for from the lesser created actuation by uncreated act in the vision of God the mind is helped, by analogy, to a deeper understanding of the grace of HYPOSTATIC UNION, that created actuation of the sacred-humanity of Christ by the uncreated Word of God. Since the beatific vision and the total beatitude of the human person is the goal of the sacramental life, the beatific vision gives a deeper understanding of that sacramental life (*see* SACRAMENTS, THEOLOGY OF). Likewise, the beatific vision gives some understanding of PURGATORY, for only after the soul has been detached from all inordinate affections and unified in its being (Mt 5.8) is it capable of the total gift of self to God in the beatific vision. The glorifying vision is the key to a glorious RESURRECTION OF THE DEAD, for the qualities of the glorified body are due to its life principle, the beatified soul. The beatific vision is also a key to a better understanding of the MEDIATION of the Blessed Virgin Mary, for it is her total interiority in God through the beatific vision—the vision that is hers in terms of her fullness of grace and charity and of her total maternal vocation—that is the source of her mediation of grace now [*see* MARY, BLESSED VIRGIN, II (IN THEOLOGY)]. Her maternal desires are united to the very power and love of God. And last of all, the perfection of the COMMUNION of saints will be found in their vision of God.

See Also: DEATH (THEOLOGY OF); DESIRE TO SEE GOD, NATURAL; DESTINY, SUPERNATURAL; ELEVATION OF MAN; ESCHATOLOGY, ARTICLES ON; GRACE, ARTICLES ON; HAPPINESS; HEAVEN (THEOLOGY OF); JESUS CHRIST, III (SPECIAL QUESTIONS); LIGHT OF GLORY; MAN; OBEDIENTIAL POTENCY; SUPERNATURAL; VOCATION TO SUPERNATURAL LIFE.

Bibliography: A. MICHEL, *Dictionnaire de théologie catholique*, ed. A. VACANT et al (Paris 1903–50) 7.2:2351–94. R. SCHNACKENBURG and K. FORSTER, *Lexicon für Theologie und Kirche*, 1:583–591. H. CAZELLES et al., *Catholicisme* 1:1342–54. *The Catechism of the Council of Trent* 132–140. F. CEUPPENS, *Theologia Biblica*, v.1, *De Deo uno* (rev. ed. Turin 1948) 103–125; *Quaestiones selectae ex epistulis s. Pauli* (Turin 1951). I. M. DALMAU, *Sacrae theologiae summa* 2.1:1–74. M. DE LA TAILLE, *The Hypostatic Union and Created Actuation by Uncreated Act*, tr. C. VOLLERT (West Baden, Ind. 1952). H. DE LUBAC, *Surnaturel: Études historiques* (Paris 1946). K. FORSTER, *Die Verteidigung der Lehre des heiligen Thomas von der Gottesschau durch Johannes Capreolus* (Munich 1955). R. GARRIGOU-LAGRANGE, *Beatitude*, tr. P. CUMMINS (St. Louis 1956) 33–129; *Life Everlasting*, tr. P. CUMMINS (St. Louis 1952) 205–255; *The One God*, tr. B. ROSE (St. Louis 1943) 306–381; ''La Possibilité de la vision béatifique peut-elle se démontrer?'' *Revue thomiste* 38 (1933) 669–688. T. GILBY, in ST. THOMAS AQUINAS, *Summa theologiae*, v.3 (1a, 12–13), ed. H. MCCABE (McGraw Hill; New York 1964) xix-xl. R. W. GLEASON, *The World to Come* (New York 1958) 129–169. G. HOFFMANN, *Der Streit über die selige Schau Gottes: 1331–1338* (Leipzig 1917). K. E. KIRK, *The Vision of God: The Christian Doctrine of the Summum Bonum* (London 1932, complete ed.). K. RAHNER, ''Current Problems in Christology,'' *Theological Investigations*, v.1, tr. C. ERNST (Baltimore 1961) 149–200; ''Concerning the Relationship between Nature and Grace,'' *ibid.* 297–317; ''Some Implications of the Scholastic Concept of Uncreated Grace,'' *ibid.* 319–346. H. RONDET, *Do Dogmas Change?* tr. M. PONTIFEX (New York 1961) 22–35. M. J. SCHEEBEN, *The Mysteries of Christianity*, tr. C. VOLLERT (St. Louis 1946) 613–665; *Nature and Grace*, tr. C. VOLLERT (St. Louis 1954). C. SPICQ, *Agapè dans le Nouveau Testament: Analyse des textes*, 3 v. (Paris 1958–59) 2:94–120; 3:204–222, 285–299. J. STAUDINGER, *Life Hereafter*, tr. J. J. COYNE (Westminster, Md. 1964) 115–168. P. VAN IMSCHOOT, *Théologie de l'Ancien Testament*, 2 v. (Paris Tournai 1954–56) 2:42–75. A. WINKLHOFER, *The Coming of His Kingdom*, tr. A. V. LITTLEDALE (New York 1963) 120–254. J. ALFARO, ''Trascendencia e inmanencia de lo sobrenatural,'' *Gregorianum* 38 (1957) 5–50. E. BRISBOIS, ''Le Désir de voir Dieu et la métaphysique du vouloir selon saint Thomas,'' *Nouvelle revue théologique* 63 (1936) 1103–05. R. BRUCH, ''Das Verhältnis von Natur und Übernatur nach der Auffassung der neueren Theologie,'' *Theologie und Glaube* 46 (1956) 81–102. A. BRUNNER, ''Gott schauen,'' *Zeitschrift für katholiche Theologie* 73 (1951) 214–223. P. DE LETTER, ''Created Actuation by the Uncreated Act: Difficulties and Answers,'' *Theological Studies* 18 (1957) 60–92. P. J. DONNELLY, ''The Supernatural: Father de Lubac's Book,'' *Review of Politics* 10 (1948) 226–232. A. GARDEIL, ''Le Désir naturel de voir Dieu,'' *Revue thomiste* 31 (1926) 381–410, 477–489, 523–527. F. M. GENUYT, ''Voir Dieu,'' *Lumière et vie* 10

(April–May 1961) 89–114. A. GEORGE, ''Le Bonheur promis par Jésus d'après le Nouveau Testament,'' *ibid.* 36–59. P. GRELOT, ''La Révélation du bonheur dans l'Ancien Testament,'' *ibid.* 5–35. D. J. LEAHY, ''St. Augustine and the Vision of God in Heaven,'' *American Ecclesiastical Review* 99 (1938) 128–142. L. MALEVEZ, ''La Gratuité du surnaturel,'' *Nouvelle revue théologique* 75 (1953) 561–586, 673–689.

[M. J. REDLE]

BEATIFICATION

The act by which the Church, through papal decree, permits a specified diocese, region, nation, or religious institute to honor with public cult under the title of Blessed a person who has died with a reputation for holiness. The cult usually consists of a Mass and Office in the person's honor, and it may even be permitted for the universal Church. However, beatification is limited in its effects, e.g., a blessed may not be the titular patron of a church.

Formal beatification is a positive declaration, following a canonical process, that a person did practice heroic virtue, or suffered a true martyrdom, and after death worked authentic miracles upon being invoked in prayer. Besides witnesses' testimony to his virtues, evidence of a first-class miracle is required, though this requirement may be waived in the case of a martyr. Equivalent beatification is the silent consent of the Church, aware of, yet not opposing, the public cult given one of its children over a long period of time.

In proclaiming a person Blessed the pope does not exercise his infallibility, for he does not declare definitively that the person is in glory. Beatification, then, does not demand faith yet gives moral certainty of its truth, and to deny it would be temerarious. It differs from canonization as permission to venerate differs from precept.

See Also: SAINTS, INTERCESSION OF; CANONIZATION OF SAINTS (HISTORY AND PROCEDURE); VENERABLE.

Bibliography: T. ORTOLAN, *Dictionnaire de théologie catholique*, ed. A. VACANT et al., 15 v. (Paris 1903–50) 2.1:493–497.

[A. E. GREEN/EDS.]

BEATITUDES (IN THE BIBLE)

The beatitudes in the Bible may be treated under three headings: as a literary form; as they are found in the Old Testament; as Our Lord used them in the SERMON ON THE MOUNT.

The beatitude is a literary form. It begins by pronouncing someone happy (Gr. μακάριος; Heb. *'ašrě*, literally, ''the happiness of''). It then states the reason for his happiness and sometimes goes on to mention the reward he will receive.

Beatification ceremony for new African saints inside St. Peter's Basilica, 1965, Vatican City, Rome. (©David Lees/CORBIS)

The Old Testament beatitudes are found mainly in the sapiential literature. They usually praise the man who enjoys God's friendship. At times, they cite God's initiative, e.g., ''Happy is he whose fault is taken away'' [Ps 31(32).1]. At other times, they stress the response a man gives to God, e.g., ''Happy are they who observe what is right'' [Ps 105(106).3]. The rewards are usually in terms of a full life on earth, although the nearness of God is the source of such happiness. In Proverbs, wisdom as a source of beatitude is praised: ''Happy the man who finds wisdom'' (Prv 3.13). Sirach has the only extended list of beatitudes, ten in number (Sir 25.7–11).

The most important beatitudes in the New Testament are the two large collections in Mt 5.3–12 and Lk 6.20–26, where they introduce the Sermon on the Mount.

In Matthew, the first beatitude, ''Blessed are the poor in spirit,'' sets the keynote for the whole group of nine. The Old Testament helps us to identify the poor, the *'ănāwîm* (Heb.). Since the poor, the materially destitute, were often unfortunate victims of the rich, the prophets taught that God would intervene in their favor. Especially in the Psalms, the concept gradually became spiritualized to represent those who acknowledged their deep need and dependence on God. These ''poor'' looked only to Him as a savior and not to men or material things. Consequently, the later prophets looked to the messianic times for God's intervention to save His *'ănāwîm* (Zep 3.12; Is 61.1, 2).

The first beatitude, then, announces that these last times have come: God has finally taken up the cause of His poor and will soon bring on the final stage of the messianic kingdom. ''Blessed are the meek . . .'' has the same sense as the first beatitude, but with emphasis on the patience of the poor. ''For they shall possess the land . . .'' [from Ps 36(37).11] is parallel to the possession of the kingdom in Mt 5.3, since the promised land is a symbol of messianic hopes. ''Blessed are they who mourn for they shall be comforted'' (the second and third beatitudes are in reverse order in most of the Greek texts) explains how those who are oppressed look for God Himself to be the consolation of the new Israel (cf. Lk 2.25). ''Blessed are they who hunger and thirst . . .''—hunger and thirst are often figures of intense desire for God [e.g., Ps 41(42).2–4]; ''for justice''—for God's coming regime of justice, a pure gift now anticipated in His grace and friendship; ''for they shall be filled''—the figure is that of the coming joyful messianic banquet, which will completely satisfy all the elect (cf. Is 25.6).

The next three beatitudes concern the Christian's response to God's mercy. ''Blessed are the merciful . . .'' who reflect to others the generosity they themselves have received from God. ''Blessed are the pure of heart for they shall see God''—Psalm 23(24) describes the single-hearted man in his relations to his neighbor; he alone can ascend to see Him, i.e., to experience the joy of His presence. ''Blessed are the peacemakers . . .''—peace is the totality of blessings, including especially harmony among men, that results from the gift of God's friendship. It will be a great characteristic of the messianic age (Eph 2.14). The blessing is on those who spread the messianic kingdom, not by violence, but by love: ''they shall be called children of God.'' In Hos 2.1 it is said: ''they shall be called children of the living God.'' This most intimate union with God, a loving Father, was to be the great privilege of the messianic era.

The last two beatitudes are addressed to the Church under persecution. They can rejoice and exult since they are undergoing the final sufferings of the last age that will precede the PAROUSIA, when their reward will be great.

In Luke, there are four beatitudes followed by four maledictions (6.20–26). While Matthew emphasizes the moral and eschatological viewpoint, Luke leans more to the present and social aspects: ''Blessed are you poor . . . , but woe to you rich! for you are now having your comfort'' (Lk 6.20, 24). The messianic community is composed of those who willingly share their goods with those in need, thus becoming poor in fact as well as in spirit.

Bibliography: J. DUPONT, *Les Beatitudes* (Bruges 1958), with extensive bibliography. *Encyclopedic Dictionary of the Bible*, tr. and adap. by L. HARTMAN (New York 1963) 215–217. N. J. MCELENEY, ''The Beatitudes of the Sermon on the Mount/Plain,'' *Catholic Biblical Quarterly* 43 (1981):1–13. U. LUZ., *Mathew 1–7: A Commentary* (Minneapolis 1989).

[J. A. GRASSI]

BEATITUDES (IN THE CHRISTIAN LIFE)

Beatitude properly, the state of blessedness achieved in the beatific vision, is the full possession of the only truly perfect good. The activities of human life that most efficaciously lead to this beatitude, and so deserve to share its name, are those in which the Holy Spirit takes over the supernatural life of the soul. Hence St. Augustine, and St. Thomas Aquinas following him, saw in the beatitudes declared by Jesus Christ in the Sermon on the Mount (Mt 5.3–10) the description of a soul living under the direction of the Holy Spirit. Thus the beatitudes came to be known as the highest acts of virtue that can be performed in this life by one in whom the gifts of the Holy Spirit predominate.

The supernatural acts the Lord described in the first seven affirmations of blessedness represent the activities proper to the seven gifts. The application is confirmed by the terms Christ used. Poverty of spirit, evangelical meekness, hunger and thirst for justice, tears, compassion, detachment of heart, and making of peace are effects that only absolute dependence upon God could achieve in the soul.

The beatitudes are the crowning achievement in the Christian's life on earth. They are acts of virtue that have been perfected to the highest possible degree by one who has become habitually docile to the Holy Spirit. So, while the beatitudes are acts of virtue, their activity is also the result of a life influenced by the gifts. They are the joint achievement of virtues and gifts. In reality they are the accomplishment of the greatest Gift, the Holy Spirit, who works in the soul, indirectly by way of the virtues, directly by way of the gifts.

According to St. Thomas, each beatitude corresponds to a gift. Poverty of spirit, for example, corresponds to fear. The virtue of temperance prompts a man to use what is delightful to the senses with moderation;

the gift of fear goes further and inspires him with a certain contempt for such goods. Thus, he reaches poverty of spirit and in that act he is blessed or beatified. And so it is with the others: the beatitude of meekness corresponds to the gift of piety; tears, to that of knowledge; justice, to fortitude; mercy, to counsel; cleanness of heart, to understanding; the beatitude of peacemaking, to the gift of wisdom. The eighth beatitude, which is the suffering of persecution, or the acceptance of martyrdom, is a summary and a consummation of all the others.

See Also: HOLY SPIRIT, GIFTS OF.

Bibliography: L. M. MARTÍNEZ, *The Sanctifier,* tr. M. AQUINAS (Paterson, N.J. 1957). B. FROGET, *The Indwelling of the Holy Spirit in the Souls of the Just,* tr. S. A. RAEMERS (Westminster, Md. 1950). B. JARRETT, *The Abiding Presence of the Holy Ghost* (2d ed. London 1934). THOMAS AQUINAS, *Summa theologiae* 1a2ae, 69–70. S. PINCKAERS, *The Source of Christian Ethics,* tr. M. T. NOBLE (Washington, D.C. 1995)

[P. MULHERN]

BEATON, JAMES (BETHUNE)

Primate and archbishop of Glasgow (1509–22) and St. Andrews (1522–39), one of the regents during the minority of James V, Chancellor of Scotland (1513–26); b. *c.* 1473; d. St. Andrews, 1539. Eleven years after receiving his M.A. from St. Andrews in 1493, James Beaton was made abbot of Dunfermline. In the next year he was appointed by the king to succeed his brother Sir David on the staff of the high treasurer. His whole career was similarly divided between affairs of Church and State. Elected to the See of Galloway in 1508, Beaton was then consecrated archbishop of Glasgow and in 1522 was appointed to the See of St. Andrews. In the struggles for the control of the young King James V, following the death of his father at the Battle of Flodden, Beaton was allied with the duke of Albany. The regency had been transferred to Albany at the marriage of the earl of Angus and Margaret Tudor, the queen mother and former regent. Angus's policy was generally pro-English, while Albany's was dedicated to maintaining and strengthening the ''auld alliance'' of the Scots with France. While in 1517 Albany began a four-year stay in France for this purpose, Beaton entered into correspondence with Cardinal Thomas Wolsey in England. Beaton professed hopes at preserving peace between the two countries, although Wolsey's schemes for Scotland were bound to clash with Beaton's. During Albany's absence Beaton was included in the Council of Regency. A long-standing feud between Angus and the earl of Arran for control of the king led to an outbreak in Edinburgh (1520), when Beaton was asked by Gawin Douglas, bishop of Dunkeld, to mediate. In a famous encounter, while James Beaton struck his breast and announced that on his conscience he knew nothing of the intentions of the opposing faction, his own armor rattled beneath his vestments. Gawin Douglas remarked: ''Faith, my lord, but yours is a poor conscience, for I heard it clatter.''

By 1526 Angus had gained control, and Beaton was dismissed as chancellor. Angus proceeded to consolidate his power by defeating Beaton's faction and placing James V in confinement. In 1528 the king escaped, and Angus was forced to flee to England. Although the Scots negotiated a treaty with Henry VIII in 1534, Beaton's influence remained sufficiently strong to help bring about the marriage of James V to Madeleine de Valois at Paris three years later. Madeleine died within a few months, and James married Marie de Guise-Lorraine the next year. Their daughter Mary, born in December of 1542, became MARY, Queen of Scots (on the death of her father) when she was but one week old.

From his castle at St. Andrews on a rocky headland near the cathedral, Beaton opposed the Protestantism that was gaining strength throughout the nation. Several advocates of the new religious doctrines were sentenced to death during his administration. The most notable was probably Patrick HAMILTON, who was burned at the stake in 1528 and became a protomartyr as the first native-born Scot to suffer death for the teachings that were to become those of the established church. Although Henry VIII's breach with Rome probably strengthened the Catholic sympathies of James V, the policies of James Beaton were nevertheless marked by a worldliness similar to that of many of his English ecclesiastical contemporaries. Despite the desperate need for radical reform within the Church of Scotland, Beaton too often acted as the astute politician guided by political expediency rather than as the churchman alert to the tragic ecclesiastical abuses within the realm. After his death he was succeeded in the archbishopric of St. Andrews by his nephew David Beaton, the first Scottish cardinal. James Beaton was interred at the cathedral church of St. Andrews, where he had held the primacy of Scotland for 16 years.

Bibliography: J. BAIN and C. ROGERS, eds., *Liber protocollorum M. C. Simonis* (London 1875). W. C. DICKINSON, *Scotland from Earliest Times to 1603* (*A New History of Scotland* 1; New York 1961) 379–388, select bibliog. W. C. DICKINSON et al., eds., *A Source Book of Scottish History,* 3 v. (2d ed. London 1958–61) v. 2. R. K. HANNAY, *The Letters of James IV,* ed. R. L. MACKIE and A. SPILMAN (Edinburgh 1953); *The Letters of James V,* ed. D. HAY (Edinburgh 1954). D. HAY, ed., *The Anglica Historia of Polydore Vergil* (London 1950). J. HERKLESS and R. K. HANNAY, *The Archbishops of St. Andrews,* 5 v. (Edinburgh 1907–15). M. MACARTHUR, *The Dictionary of National Biography from the Earliest Times to 1900* (London 1885–1900) 2:18–19. D. MCROBERTS, ed., *Essays on the Scottish Reformation, 1513–1625* (Glasgow 1962).

[J. G. DWYER]

BEATON, JAMES (BETHUNE)

Last pre-Reformation Roman Catholic archbishop of Glasgow, nephew of Cardinal David Beaton, and son of James Beaton of Balfarg; b. 1517; d. April 24, 1603. He received his early education chiefly in Paris. In 1552 he was consecrated archbishop of Glasgow at Rome. As adviser for Queen Mother Mary of Guise, he was a determined opponent of the new religious teachings. Provincial Councils of the Scottish Church in 1546, 1552, and 1559 had freely admitted the grave abuses in the Church. In April of 1559 Archbishop Beaton promulgated decrees for the improvement of preaching, the repair of churches, the condemnation of pluralism and concubinage among the clergy, and other disciplinary and administrative reforms in ecclesiastical policy. The 1560 meeting of the Scottish Estates at Edinburgh brought about the establishment of the newly reformed religious settlement. Several months earlier James Beaton had made good his escape to France. His departure at such a crucial moment has been questioned by many. However, his many years of loyal service to Mary Queen of Scots, as her ambassador in France and then to James VI, at least clear him of any suspicion of faintheartedness. When he fled to France, he took with him many of the treasures and documents of his diocese. These records were later deposited in the Scots College. A considerable number of the documents were returned to Scotland after the French Revolution, to St. Mary's Catholic College at Blairs, Aberdeenshire. During his years in France, he corresponded frequently with leading diplomats and churchmen, including Mary Queen of Scots, James VI, and the later Valois French kings. James Beaton died while James VI of Scotland was on his way to London to become James I, King of England. In his will Beaton stated that he died "as a true and faithful Catholic." He asked that all his debts be paid and then stipulated that the remainder of his legacy should be used to endow a Scots College at Paris, where poor scholars from Scotland could pursue their studies of classical learning and theology. James Beaton established a reputation for faithfulness and loyalty. No scandal is known to have blemished his private life. He was interred in Paris at Saint-Jean de Lateran.

Bibliography: *Calendar of State Papers Relating to Scotland . . .1547–1603,* ed. J. BAIN et al. (Edinburgh 1898–). J. B. BLACK, *The Reign of Elizabeth, 1558–1603* (2d ed. Oxford 1959) 507–509, good bibliog. on Anglo-Scottish relations. W. C. DICKINSON et al., eds., *A Source Book of Scottish History,* 3 v. (2d ed. London 1958–61) v. 2–3. G. DONALDSON, *The Scottish Reformation* (Cambridge, Eng. 1960). M. MACARTHUR, *The Dictionary of National Biography from the Earliest Times to 1900* (London 1885–1900) 2:19–20. D. MCROBERTS, ed., *Essays on the Scottish Reformation, 1513–1625* (Glasgow 1962). F. W. MAITLAND, "The Anglican Settlement and the Scottish Reformation," in his *Selected Historical Essays* (Cambridge, Eng. 1962) 152–210.

[J. G. DWYER]

BEATRICE D'ESTE, BL.

Name of two members of the D'Este family.

Beatrice d'Este I, Benedictine nun; b. *c.* 1191; d. Gemolo, Italy, May 10, 1226. Daughter of Azzo VI d'Este and Princess Leonara of Savoy, she entered the convent of St. Margaret at Solarola when she was 14 years old, but because of local political disturbances she and the women companions who had joined her at St. Margaret's moved to the deserted monastery of St. John the Baptist near Gemolo. They adopted the Benedictine Rule and gained a reputation for their holiness. Her body was translated to the church of St. Sophia in Padua (1578). Her cult was approved in 1763.

Feast: May 10.

Beatrice d'Este II, Benedictine nun, niece of Bl. Beatrice I; b. 1230; d. Jan. 18, 1262. The daughter of Azzo VII d'Este and Joan of Apulia, she emulated her aunt, but her family planned her marriage to Galeazzo Manfredi, Duke of Vicenza and Veradino. When he died of wounds shortly before the projected marriage, she entered the convent at St. Lazarus. The D'Este family built a convent for her group at Ferrara that was called first St. Stephen, then St. Anthony's. She was professed in 1254 and died less than 10 years later. Clement XIV approved her cult in 1774.

Feast: Jan. 18; Feb. 28 (Benedictines).

Bibliography: *Acta Sanctorum* May 2:597–602; Jan. 2:759. P. BALAN, *Memorie della vita della b. Beatrice d'Este* (Venice 1878). G. BARUFFALDI, *Vita della b. B. seconda d'E.* (New ed. Ferrara 1777). A. M. ZIMMERMANN, *Kalendarium Benedictinum: Die Heiligen und Seligen des Benediktinerorderns und seiner Zweige* (Metten 1933–38) 2:166–169; 1:263–265.

[C. L. HOHL, JR.]

BEATRICE OF NAZARETH, BL.

Cistercian nun and spiritual writer; b. Tirlemont, *c.* 1200; d. Notre Dame-de-Nazareth, near Lierre (Brabant), August 29, 1268. Beatrice (Beatrijs van Tienen) was only seven when her father placed her with the Beguines at Léau. Later, he transferred her to Bleomendael, a Cistercian abbey he had just founded. When she was about 17 years old, she was received into the religious life. A second foundation of the community was made at Maagdendael, and she was sent there. When a third house was opened at Notre-Dame-de-Nazareth, she was made its prioress and remained there until her death.

From an early age she kept notes on her ascetical and mystical experiences, and among these were included little treatises on spiritual topics. The autobiographical notes have been lost, but after her death they were abridged and translated into Latin by a Cistercian monk (perhaps Guillaume d'Affigham, abbot of Saint-Trond) in the form of a biography. Data contained in the biography have made it possible to recognize as the work of Beatrice a treatise entitled *De divina charitate et septem ejus gradibus,* or *Van seven manieren van Heiligher Minnen,* which survived in a collection of sermons entitled *Limburgsche Sermoenen* that appeared in the early fourteenth century. This is the oldest known essay in Old Flemish and treats experimentally the ascent of the soul toward union with God in a manner that causes the reader to think of St. Teresa's seven castles of the soul.

Beatrice had a special devotion to the Sacred Heart and with this she associated the idea of reparation. Often ill, she was given to excessive penances, and her writings are not free of certain morbid, pathological characteristics. Her importance lies in her description in the vernacular of the speculative mysticism practiced by Beguines at the beginning of the great flowering of Flemish spirituality.

Feast: July 29.

Bibliography: BEATRICE OF NAZARETH, *Seven Manieren van Minne,* ed. L. REYPENS and J. VAN MIERLO (Louvain 1926). *Vita Beatricis,* Dutch tr. as *Hoezeer heeft God mij bemind,* ed. H. W. J. VEKEMAN (Kampen, Netherlands 1993); Eng. tr. *The Life of Beatrice of Nazareth,* tr. R. DE GANCK and J. B. HASBROUCK (Kalamazoo, MI 1991). R. DE GANCK, *Beatrice of Nazareth in Her Context,* 2 v. (Kalamazoo, MI 1991). G. J. LEWIS, *Bibliographie zur deutschen Frauenmystik des Mittelalters* (Berlin 1989).

[J. VERBILLON]

BEATRICE OF TUSCANY

Noblewoman, identified with the GREGORIAN REFORM; b. Lorraine, *c.* 1015; d. Pisa, April 28, 1076. Her two marriages united the princely houses of Lorraine and Tuscany. She was the daughter of Frederick II, duke of Upper Lorraine, and Matilda of Suabia, and the niece of Empress Gisela, wife of CONRAD II, at whose court she was educated. About 1036 she married Boniface III of Canossa, margrave of Tuscany, by whom she had three children. After Boniface was murdered in 1052, she ruled his former marches of Tuscany and Lombardy-Emilia in her son's name. In 1054, without the knowledge of Emperor HENRY III, she married her cousin, Godfrey the Bearded, then duke of Upper Lorraine, who had twice rebelled against the emperor. Henry took immediate action in Italy, imprisoning Beatrice and her only surviving child MATILDA, and transporting them to Germany (1055). Released by Empress Agnes after Henry's death, Beatrice yielded much of her power in Tuscany to Godfrey, devoting her energies to the education of her daughter and the service of ecclesiastical reform. After Godfrey's death in 1069, she ruled the Canossan dominions jointly with Matilda until her own death in 1076. She collaborated closely with GREGORY VII, whose letters bear testimony to a relationship of mutual trust. In the INVESTITURE struggle her action was mediatorial, but her sympathies were clearly anti-imperial and pro-papal.

Bibliography: E. DUPRÉEL, *Histoire critique de Godefroid le Barbu, duc de Lotharingie, marquis de Toscane* (Ukkel 1904). A. FALCE, *Bonifacio di Canossa padre di Matilde,* 2 v. (Reggio-Emilia 1926–27). H. GLAESENER, "Un mariage fertile en conséquences (Godefroid le Barbu et B. de T.)," *Revue d'histoire ecclésiastique* 42 (1947) 379–416.

[C. E. BOYD]

BEATUS, ST.

Apostle of Switzerland; d. 112. An unauthenticated tenth-century legend says that he was of Gallic origin, had been ordained by St. PETER himself, and went to Switzerland to convert the heathen Helvetiae in the area around Lake Thun. The legend further relates that he killed a dragon there, lived in its cave until he died at the age of 90, and was buried on the site. His cult did not become popular until the thirteenth century, when the neighboring village of Beatenburg became the center of pilgrimage to him that lasted until the early sixteenth century. About 1300 an altar was dedicated to him in the Zurich Frauenmünster and a confraternity of St. Beatus was set up. In later medieval art he is portrayed as a hermit with staff and rosary in hand and with a dragon by his side. He was patron of central Switzerland and his assistance was invoked against plague, glandular diseases, and cancer. If he had a historical existence, it was probably as an English or Irish missionary of the sixth century, or else he has been confused with the ninth-century Beatus of Vendôme.

Feast: May 9.

Bibliography: H. MORETUS, "La légende de s. Béat, apôtre de Suisse," *Analecta Bollandiana* 26 (1907) 423–453. W. STAMMLER, *Lexikon für Theologie und Kirche*, ed. J. HOFER and K. RAHNER (Freiburg 1957–65) 2:86. A. M. JACQUIN, *Dictionnaire d'histoire et de géographie ecclésiastiques*, ed. A. BAUDRILLART et al. (Paris 1912) 7:86–87. J. STAMMLER, *Der hl. Beatus, seine Höhle und sein Grab* (Bern 1904). O. SCHEIWILLER, "Beatus-Frage," *Zeitschrift für schweizerische Kirchengeschichte* 5 (1911) 21–52. L. RÉAU, *Iconographie de l'art chrétien*, 6 v. (Paris 1955–59) 3:190.

[J. L. GRASSI]

BEATUS OF LIÉBANA

Monk and writer; b. Liébana, near Santander, Spain; d. Feb. 19, 798. He combated ADOPTIONISM and wrote a famous commentary on the Apocalypse in 12 books. ALCUIN mentioned him. In 784, he attacked the heretical proponents of adoptionism, Abp. ELIPANDUS OF TOLEDO and Bp. Felix of Urgel in two letters, *Ad Elipandum epistulae duae* (*Patrologia Latina* 96:894–1030), composed jointly with Bp. Etherius of Osma. As teacher and adviser to Queen Adosinda of León, Beatus wrote the first redaction of the *Commentary* in 776, reediting it in 784 and 786. Since it was drawn from similar works of the Fathers from Irenaeus to Isidore of Seville, it was ascribed to various authors. Ambrosio de Morales and MABILLON identified it as Beatus's work. FLÓREZ published it (Madrid 1770), as did H. A. Sanders (Rome 1930). But more important than the text are the illustrations in the 30 extant MSS (9th to 13th century), exemplifying the development of Spanish art. The geometric design and interlacing in the MSS are evidence of CELTIC (or COPTIC?) art influence; but the color, imagery, domed architecture, oriental flora and fauna are Mozarabic. The nimbus of red dots is Celtic, the ''carpet-page'' Coptic. The *Commentary* illustrations had an immense impact upon Romanesque sculptors at Vézelay, SAINT-BENOÎT-SUR-LOIRE, and especially at MOISSAC, where the tympanum shows 24 elders carrying, as viols, Spanish guitars identical with those in a Beatus MS of the same scene. Beatus probably wrote *O Dei verbum, Patris ore proditum,* a hymn for the feast of St. James.

Feast: Feb. 19 (Spain).

Bibliography: *Acta Sanctorum*, Feb. 3:149–150. M. R. JAMES, *The Apocalypse in Art* (London 1931). É. MÂLE, *L'Art religieux du XIIe siècle en France* (5th ed. Paris 1947). W. NEUSS, *Die Apokalypse . . . in . . . Bibel-Illustration* (Münster 1931). J. PÉREZ DE URBEL, *Dictionnaire d'histoire et de géographie ecclésiastiques* (Paris 1912—) 7:89–90. F. STEGMÜLLER, *Lexikon für Theologie und Kirche* (Freiburg 1957–65) 2:86–87.

[M. J. DALY]

BEATUS OF TRIER, ST.

Hermit; fl. seventh century. According to a tradition not rich in detail, Beatus and his brother Bantus were priests who lived as hermits near Trier when Modoald (d. between 647 and 649) was bishop of that city. The same local tradition reports that the brothers died with a great reputation for sanctity and that Beatus was buried in the church of St. Mary of the Martyrs. His relics were, after 1331, brought to Koblenz in the care of the CARTHUSIANS at Beatusberg (*Mons S. Beati*). The beginnings of the cult are shrouded in obscurity, and the earliest document to refer to Beatus as a saint is the tenth-century *Psalter of Egbert,* where his name is listed in a *laetania universalis.* Still later documents from the fifteenth century report how Poppo, archbishop of Trier (d. 1047), enclosed relics of the saint in the main altar of the abbey church of St. Mary, which he consecrated on Dec. 16, 1017 (*Monumenta Germaniae Historica: Scriptores* 15.2:1272).

Feast: Aug. 26; July 31 (Trier).

Bibliography: *Monumenta Germaniae Historica: Scriptores* (Berlin 1826—) 8:159. *Acta Sanctorum* 7 July (1868) 318–319. L. H. COTTINEAU, *Répertoire topobibliographique des abbayes et prieurés* (Mâcon 1935–39) 1:826; 2:3210–11. G. ALLEMANG, *Dictionnaire d'histoire et de géographie ecclésiastiques,* ed. A. BAUDRILLART et al. (Paris 1912) 6:518. J. L. BAUDOT and L. CHAUSSIN, *Vies des saints et des bienhereux selon l'ordre du calendrier avec l'historique des fêtes* (Paris 1935–56) 7:734. M. COENS, *Analecta Bollandiana* 59 (1941) 284–286. A. HEINTZ, *Lexikon für Theologie und Kirche*, ed. J. HOFER and K. RAHNER (Freiburg 1957–65) 2:87. G. FUSCONI, *Bibliotheca sanctorum* 2:747–748.

[H. DRESSLER]

BEAUCHAMP, RICHARD

Bishop of Salisbury; d. Oct. 18, 1481. He was the son of Sir Walter Beauchamp, sometime speaker for the Commons in Parliament, and his second wife, Elizabeth, daughter and coheiress of Sir John Roche. Possibly resident in Exeter College, Oxford, in 1440, he was a doctor of Canon Law by 1442. Having served as canon lawyer, chancery clerk, and royal chaplain, he became bishop of HEREFORD (1448), where he was the first to make good the episcopal claim to visit his cathedral officially. He was translated to Salisbury (1450), where his predecessor, Aiscough, had been murdered by a mob during Jack Cade's rebellion. There Beauchamp was a capable administrator, vigorous in defending episcopal jurisdiction over the city, with whose inhabitants he disputed (1465–74). The result, with royal support, was a complete capitulation of the citizens and a half-century of comparative tranquility in episcopal-city relations. In 1456 the cathedral chapter secured the canonization of OSMUND, the 11th-century episcopal founder of Old Sarum cathedral, partly through Beauchamp's efforts. He served as an emissary in the contemporary Lancaster-York struggle in England and later as an envoy to France. He was allowed to hold the deanship of Windsor (1478) concurrently with his bishopric; this reflects his lengthy connection with the Order of the Garter, which he served as first chancellor in 1475. As master and surveyor of St. George's Chapel, Windsor, Beauchamp was deeply involved in the construction of one of the supreme glories of Perpendicular architecture. He was buried in his own chantry chapel in Salisbury cathedral, since destroyed.

Bibliography: *Registrum Ricardi Beauchamp, Episcopi Herefordensis . . .*, ed. A. T. BANNISTER (Canterbury and York Society; London 1919). Beauchamp's unprinted register in 2 v. is in the Diocesan Registry, Salisbury. *The Victoria History of Wiltshire,* v. 3, ed. R. B. PUGH and E. CRITTALL (London 1956), v. 6, ed. E. CRITTALL (1962). A. B. EMDEN, *A Biographical Register of the University of Oxford to A.D. 1500* (Cambridge, Eng. 1963) 1:137–138.

[H. S. REINMUTH, JR.]

BEAUDUIN, LAMBERT

Liturgist; b. Rosouxlez-Waremme, Belgium, Aug. 5, 1873; d. Chevetogne, Jan. 11, 1960. Beauduin studied at the minor seminary of Saint-Trond, then at the seminary of Liège, where he came under the influence of Abbot Pottier, founder of the École Sociale de Liège. Beauduin was ordained in 1897 and rejoined the Aumôniers du Travail, a society of priests founded to care for workingmen, the next year. In 1906, he became a Benedictine at the Abbey of Mont-César, where he was initiated in the study of liturgy by Dom Joseph Columba MARMION. After his religious profession, Beauduin discovered the ecclesial importance of the liturgy while teaching a course in dogma. In 1909, he helped to begin the Liturgical Weeks; in the same year, he began *La vie liturgique* (since 1911, *Les questions liturgiques*). He also wrote *La piété de l'Eglise* (Louvain 1914) as the manifesto of the liturgical movement.

In 1921, Beauduin was named professor of theology at S. Anselmo in Rome, where he became interested in the Eastern liturgies. Pius XI wanted the Benedictine Order to mediate the work of reunion between East and West. As a result, Beauduin founded the monastery "de l'Union" in Amay (Liège) and the review *Irénikon,* both in September 1925. At the same time, he joined Cardinal D. J. MERCIER in the MALINES CONVERSATIONS. In a memoir of May 25, 1925, Beauduin originated the formula "The Anglican Church united to Rome, not absorbed" which aroused lively reactions.

The bold views of Beauduin in liturgy and ecclesiology shocked many people. In 1928, he had to leave Amay; in January 1931, when he returned from a visit to Bulgaria, he was brought before a Roman tribunal, condemned, and sent to the Abbey of En-Calcat. A retreat that he preached in 1942 was the origin of the future Centre de Pastorale liturgique in Paris. Thus, he became associated with the dominant figures of the Christian renewal in France. He visited numerous Protestants and members of the Orthodox Church, for whom he had sympathy and understanding.

In 1950, Beauduin was able to return to the monastery he had founded. In 1954, his spiritual sons celebrated his 80th birthday with the work *L'Église et les Églises* (2 v., Chevetogne).

When Cardinal Angelo Roncalli, formerly nuncio to France, became Patriarch of Venice, he said: "The true method of working for the reunion of the churches is that of Dom Beauduin." The "condemned" of 1931 had one last joy: JOHN XXIII, the former Roncalli, announced an ecumenical council for reunion in 1958.

Bibliography: O. ROUSSEAU, *Irénikon* 33 (1960) 3–28, 582. R. AUBERT, *Revue Nouvelle* 31 (1960) 225–249. T. BECQUET, *Revue Générale Belge* (April 1960) 109–117. A. G. MARTIMORT, "Dom Lambert Beauduin et le Centre de Pastorale Liturgique," *Maison-Dieu,* No. 62 (1960) 10–17. S. A. QUITSLUND, *Beauduin: A Prophet Vindicated* (New York 1973).

[N. HUYGHEBAERT]

BEAUFORT, HENRY

Cardinal and bishop of Winchester; b. Beaufort-en-Vallée, France, *c.* 1375; d. Winchester, England, April 11, 1447. He was the second of the illegitimate children of John of Gaunt (d. 1399) and Catherine Swynford (d. 1403), and therefore a half brother to King Henry IV (d. 1413) of England. He was eventually legitimated in 1396. Consecrated bishop of Lincoln in 1398, he was transferred to WINCHESTER in 1405 by papal provision, and for the next 30 years he was one of Europe's leading ecclesiastical politicians. As a reward for the part he played at the Council of CONSTANCE, Pope MARTIN V made Beaufort a CARDINAL without title in 1417, and then employed him in 1420 and again in 1427 and 1428 to manage crusades against the HUSSITES in Bohemia. For this purpose he was appointed legate to Germany, Hungary, and Bohemia and was made cardinal priest of Saint Eusebius. Beaufort's failure in Bohemia was due partly to the diversion of his troops to the service of England in France, a move that marked the end of Beaufort's influence on the continent and his hopes of receiving the papal tiara. Conversely, his influence on English politics increased. He had already been chancellor of England (1403–04, 1413–17, and 1424–26) and then became the chief and successful rival to Humphrey of Gloucester as the shaper of English policy during the reign of HENRY VI. Whereas his rival favored an aggressive foreign policy, Beaufort favored peace, an attitude determined by financial, not religious considerations, for he was the country's banker and the king's chief creditor, but an indifferent churchman. He was buried in Winchester Cathedral, whose construction he had seen completed.

Bibliography: A. B. EMDEN, *Biographical Register of the Scholars of the University of Cambridge before 1500* 46–49 or *A Biographical Register of the University of Oxford to A.D. 1500* (Cambridge, Eng. 1963) 1:139–142. K. B. MCFARLANE, "Henry V, Bishop Beaufort and the Red Hat, 1417–1421," *English Historical Review* 60 (1945) 316–348. L. B. RADFORD, *Henry Beaufort* (London 1908).

[D. NICHOLL]

BEAUFORT, MARGARET, LADY

Countess of Richmond and Derby, mother of King Henry VII, and benefactress of CAMBRIDGE University; b. May 31, 1443; d. 1509. She was the daughter and heiress of John Beaufort, duke of Somerset (d. 1444). Her marriage as a child to the duke of Suffolk's heir was later dissolved, and she became successively wife to Edmund Tudor, Earl of Richmond (d. 1456), by whom she bore Henry VII; to Sir Henry Stafford (d. 1471); and to Thomas Stanley, earl of Derby (d. 1504). She was noted for piety and devotion, and took monastic vows in 1504, but she never retired to a religious house. Under the influence of her confessor, John FISHER, she became in later life an active and munificent patron of education. By 1503 she had established the two Lady Margaret professorships in divinity in OXFORD and Cambridge, and in 1504 she founded the Lady Margaret preachership at Cambridge. She completed Henry VI's foundation of God's House, Cambridge, opened in 1505 as Christ's College, and in 1508 began the foundation of St. John's College, later completed by Fisher. She also endowed a school and chantry in the Beaufort seat of Wimborne Minster, Dorset.

Bibliography: JOHN FISHER, *The Funeral Sermon of Margaret, Countess of Richmond and Derby,* ed. J. HYMERS (Cambridge, Eng. 1840). C. H. COOPER, *Memoir of Margaret, Countess of Richmond and Derby,* ed. J. E. B. MAYOR (Cambridge, Eng. 1874). J. B. MULLINGER, *The University of Cambridge,* 3 v. (Cambridge, Eng. 1873–1911) 1:434–71. G. E. COKAYNE, *The Complete Peerage,* ed. V. GIBBS et al. (London 1910-) v. 10.

[C. D. ROSS]

BEAUTY

BEAUTY AS A TRANSCENDENTAL

The theory of the transcendental properties of being was formally expounded by Aristotle. Yet even before him thinkers had indicated the transcendentality of beauty, and later philosophers through the centuries have held the same view.

Ancient and Early Medieval Views. At least three pre-Aristotelian thinkers speak, more or less clearly, of the transcendentality of beauty, viz, Heraclitus, Socrates, and Plato. Of the three, HERACLITUS (H. Diels, *Die Fragmente der Vorwokratiker: Griechisch und Deutsch*, ed. W. Kranz, 22 B 102, 1:173) and SOCRATES (Xenophon., *Mem.* 3.8.5, 7) assert that everything is both good and beautiful. PLATO teaches the same doctrine in two ways: indirectly, by teaching that whatever is good is beautiful (*Lysis* 216D, *Tim.* 87C) and that everything participates in the good (*Rep.* 517C); and directly, by holding that everything is made both good and beautiful (*Tim.* 53B).

Expounding his theory, Aristotle lists unity (*Meta.* 1003b 22–23, 1054a 13–19), truth (*ibid.* 993b 31), and goodness (*Eth. Nic.* 1096a 23–24) as transcendental properties, but not beauty—a feature that has become just as characteristic of the Aristotelian tradition as the inclusion of beauty among the transcendentals is characteristic of the Platonic tradition. Among the Platonists, PLOTINUS (*Enn.* 5.8.9, 6.6.18, 6.7.31–32) adds beauty to the Aristotelian list of transcendentals, as do St. AUGUSTINE (*Civ.* 11.4.2; *Ver. relig.* 20.40) and Pseudo-Dionysius, all of them maintaining that every being is both good and beautiful. In contrast, the more Aristotelian thinkers, such as BOETHIUS and the medieval Arabian philosophers, give lists of transcendentals that do not contain beauty. This procedure is the more conspicuous because Avicenna adds two new transcendentals (*res* and *aliquid*) to those mentioned by Aristotle.

In two typically Platonic ways, PSEUDO-DIONYSIUS is an enduring model for medieval thought on transcendental beauty: indirectly, by stressing the real identity of beauty and goodness (*De div. nom.* 4.10, 7; *Patrologia Graeca*, ed. J. P. Migne, 3:705C–D, 704A–B) together with the goodness of God and all creatures; and directly, by teaching that God is beautiful by essence and every creature by participation (*ibid.* 4.7, 701C–704B; 4.10, 708A; *De cael. hier.* 2.3, 141C). See also John Scotus Erigena, *De div. nat.*, 4.16 and *Hier. coel.* 1.2 (*Patrologia Latina*, ed. J. P. Migne, 122:827D, 828C; 134), and HUGH OF SAINT-VICTOR, *In hier. coel.* 2.1, and *Didasc.* 7.4 (*Patrologia Latina* 175:943–944, 176:960–61,815A).

High and Late Scholastic Theories. The influence of Pseudo-Dionysius continued long after the turn of the 13th century. For instance, the *De bono et malo* (1228) of WILLIAM OF AUVERGNE stresses the identity of beauty and goodness at the level of both the divine and the creature, whereas THOMAS GALLUS OF VERCELLI, in his commentary on *De divinis nominibus* (1242), teaches both this identity and the participation of all creatures in God's beauty. On the other hand, one finds St. ANSELM OF CANTERBURY considering truth and goodness as fundamental notions (*De ver.* 7, 10, 13; *Patrologia Latina* 158:475B–C, 479A, 486B–C) and DOMINIC GUNDISALVI, a late 12th-century thinker strongly influenced by Boethius and by Arabian Aristotelianism, writing a treatise on unity, the third of Aristotle's transcendentals (*De unitate et uno*). Even PHILIP THE CHANCELLOR omits beauty from his *Summa de bono* (*c.* 1230), which lists all three Aristotelian transcendentals.

Compromise Solution. There existed in this period, then, an age-old Neoplatonic and a revived Aristotelian line of thought on the transcendentals. The meeting of the two by way of a genial compromise is to be found in the so-called *Summa fratris Alexandri*—a joint effort of ALEXANDER OF HALES, JOHN OF LA ROCHELLE, and other Franciscans. Their compromise consists of two seemingly clashing doctrines: an initial list of transcendentals containing only unity, truth, and goodness (*Summa theologiae* 1.1.2) and the proposal of a real identity and a merely conceptual difference between beauty and goodness (*ibid.* 1.1.3.3.1.1.2 sol.). The latter part of this Franciscan compromise clearly conformed to and continued the old Neoplatonic (i.e., Augustinian and Dionysian) position, whereas the omission of beauty from the list of transcendentals and its treatment only as related to goodness were a concession to the ever-growing Aristotelianism of the times. And, as if to symbolize the relative strength of Neoplatonism over the Aristotelianism then current, the compromise itself was made in the spirit of Plato's *Philebus,* where the idea of beauty is treated as a mere component of the idea of goodness (65A).

This compromise was eventually adopted by Alexander's contemporaries, such as ROBERT GROSSETESTE (unpub. commentary on *De div. nom.;* see Pouillon, 287–88), as well as by the leading thinkers within high scholasticism. Thus, both St. ALBERT THE GREAT (*Opusc. de pulchro et bono* 11; *Summa theologiae* 1.6.26.1.2.3; 2.11.62.1 sol.; *Summa de bono* 1.2.2 *sol.* 8, 9) and St. THOMAS AQUINAS (*In Dion. de div. nom.* 4.5; *Summa theologiae* 1a, 5.4 ad 1; 1a2ae, 27.1 ad 3) hold the real identity and virtual distinction of beauty and goodness, and imply thereby the transcendental coextension of beauty with being, although both (St. Albert in *Summa theologiae* 1.6 and St. Thomas in *De ver.* 1.1) omit beauty from their formal list of transcendental properties. St. Albert's disciple ULRIC OF STRASSBURG holds a similar position (*Summa de bono* 2.3.4).

Only a small group of Franciscans rejected the compromise formula. THOMAS OF YORK (unpub. *Sapientiale, c.* 1260) and St. BONAVENTURE unhesitatingly list beauty together with the other transcendentals (unpub. comm.; see Pouillon, 281), while also using traditional expressions for transcendental beauty (*In 2 sent.* 34.2.3.6a; *Itin.* 2.10). Thus their philosophies represent the culmination of high scholasticism's concern with transcendental beauty; they were to find an isolated follower a century later in DENIS THE CARTHUSIAN (*Tr. de venustate mundi et pulchritudine Dei* 1, 3).

Status as a Transcendental. In this light no one can contest that Thomas of York and St. Bonaventure held the transcendentality of beauty. But whether the users of the above-described compromise, i.e., Alexander of Hales, St. Albert, and even St. Thomas, really regarded beauty as a transcendental has been both denied (G. Sanseverino, J. J. Urráburu, D. J. Mercier, P. M. de Munninck, C. Boyer, etc.) and defended (J. Jungmann, J. Maritain, É. H. Gilson, G. B. Phelan, T. C. Donlan, C. A. Hart, J. Owens, etc.). What, then, is the truth?

The Aristotelian and high scholastic criteria for a transcendental property are three: predicability of every being; logical posteriority to being, i.e., by the addition of a logical note, or general mode, to being; and coextension and convertibility. Now, the *Summa fratris Alexandri* (1.2.1.3.6 ad 3; 1.2.1.1.2.1.2.3), St. Albert (*Summa theologiae* 2.10.39.1.1.2.2 ad 8; 2.11.62.1 sol.), and St. Thomas (*In Dion. de div. nom.* 4.5; *Summa theologiae* 1a, 36.2) agree that both God and creatures are beautiful. They all hold also that the beautiful is cognitively delightful and, as such, directly subsequent to the good (*Summa theologiae* 1.2.1.2.3; 1.1.3.3.1.1.2 sol.; St. Albert, *Summa theologiae* 1.6.26.1.2.3.8a and sol.; St. Thomas, *Summa theologiae* 1a2ae, 27.1 ad 3; 1a,5.4 ad 1; *De ver.* 21.3). Finally, they hold coextension and convertibility either implicitly, through the real identity and virtual distinction of beauty and goodness, or explicitly (St. Thomas, *In Dion. de div. nom.* 4.22; *De ver.* 22.1 ad 12; *Summa theologiae* 1a, 5.4 ad 1). Therefore, the only difference between them and Bonaventure is that they do not, whereas Bonaventure does, explicitly list beauty among the transcendentals. Some hold that this reasoning establishes that these thinkers held beauty to be a transcendental notion only and not a transcendental property of being (*see* THING). Yet any such distinction is of much later origin and is doctrinally difficult to maintain, since nothing but being itself can be the sufficient reason for any transcendental predicability.

John DUNS SCOTUS does not adopt St. Thomas's compromise treatment of transcendental beauty, nor does he share St. Bonaventure's deep concern with the same. Instead, he stands closest to St. Albert, for both of them add new transcendentals to the traditional list (St. Albert, *honestum* and *decorum;* Scotus, the disjunctive transcendentals), and both reject at least one of the Avicennian additions on St. Thomas's list. They differ, however, in their treatment of beauty: St. Albert often and clearly speaks of beauty as a transcendental, whereas Scotus never goes beyond some cryptic remarks (e.g., *Quodlib.* 18.1 schol.; *De prim. princ.* 3.19) that are difficult to evaluate.

This antitranscendentalist tendency concerning beauty is further strengthened by the interpretation proposed by Tommaso de Vio CAJETAN of a crucial text in St. Thomas's philosophy of beauty (*Summa theologiae* 1a2ae, 27.1 ad3) as meaning that beauty is a species of goodness. Since the SPECIES is less universal than its GENUS, the implication is clear: St. Thomas did not hold beauty to be a transcendental. Owing to Cajetan's great authority, this view became widely accepted, although it ignored such Thomistic texts as ''truth is the good of the intellect'' (*De ver.* 1.10 ad 4 in contr.; *Summa theologiae* 1a2ae, 57.2 ad 3) and ''truth is a kind of goodness; and goodness, a kind of truth'' (*De ver.* 3.3 ad 9; *De mal.* 6.1). Thus, F. de TOLEDO, commenting on a parallel text (*Summa theologiae* 1a, 5.4 ad 1), does not mention transcendental beauty as an obvious fourth conclusion of the text, and JOHN OF ST. THOMAS treats only of the three Aristotelian transcendental properties of being. In the meantime, F. SUÁREZ, himself an antitranscendentalist, introduced the distinction between transcendental notions and transcendental properties of being (*Disp. meta.* 3.2.1)—a doctrine that eventually became an additional basis for antitranscendentalist positions concerning beauty.

These, then, were the factors leading to the virtually universal rejection of transcendental beauty among the schoolmen of the Renaissance and modern times down to the rebirth of scholasticism after the encyclical *Aeterni Patris* (1879).

Neoscholastic Positions. Following the example of some isolated textbook authors (Sanseverino, D. Palmieri, T. Zigliara, etc.), the author of the first elaborate neoscholastic aesthetics, Josef JUNGMANN, declared beauty to be a transcendental property [*Ästhetik* (Freiburg im Breisgau 1884) 161]. Although his position was moderate on the question, it elicited a strong negative reaction lead by Urráburu [*Ontologia* (Vallisoleti 1891) 535–41]. Thus began the neoscholastic controversy over the transcendentality of beauty that divided contemporary schoolmen into the transcendentalists, the antitranscendentalists, and the undecided.

The antitranscendentalists are represented by at least three currents of thought. One version consists in explicitly rejecting transcendental beauty on historical (Urráburu, De Munninck), practical (S. Reinstadler, M. de Wulf, E. de Bruyne, C. Frick), or speculative grounds (T. Pesch, F. van Steenberghen, C. N. Bittle). A less immoderate version asserts that a list of transcendentals not including beauty is complete, without explicitly denying, however, the transcendentality of beauty (T. Harper, Mercier, J. Gredt). The most moderate version does not assert the completeness of the list of transcendentals not containing beauty, nor does it raise the question of transcendental beauty at all when treating other transcendentals or beauty itself (S. Tongiorgi, M. Liberatore, K. Gutberlet).

The second main group of modern schoolmen appreciate the arguments of both sides and, consequently, are undecided. Some of them raise the question of transcendental beauty but leave it unanswered or otherwise express their uncertainty over the true answer (J. Donat, A. G. Sertillanges, H. Carpenter, R. J. Kreyche). Others show their indecision by making statements some of which endorse, others reject, transcendental beauty (F. Egger, J. Rickaby). Others again resort to a compromise formula, referring to beauty as a quasitranscendental or something similar (E. R. Baschab, A. Dupeyrat).

The transcendentalists, who seem presently to constitute the majority, express their position either implicitly (J. S. Hickey, R. Spiazzi) or explicitly, and in the latter case, either with or without qualification. Those who qualify the transcendentality of beauty distinguish between fundamental and formal transcendentality (P. Coffey), transcendentality in the broad and strict sense (A. Rother), transcendental notion and transcendental property of being (H. Grenier, F. X. Maquart), transcendental properties not to be listed and those to be listed separately (Jungmann, H. J. Koren, Boyer, M. Vaske), essential or specific and accidental or individual (A. Stöckl, E. Hugon, L. Callahan), and metaphysical and sensible transcendentality (J. B. Lotz, R. E. McCall, Owens), and concede beauty to be a transcendental in the former but not in the latter senses. Another and much larger group of transcendentalists assert without further qualification that beauty is a transcendental property of being with a unique relation to the intellect and to the will (M. de Maria, V. Remer, L. Baur, P. J. Wébert, Maritain, Phelan, L. de Raeymaeker, E. Chapmann, J. F. McCormick, H. Renard, J. Aumann, G. Esser, G. P. Klubertanz, D. J. Sullivan, Hart, Gilson, J. A. Peter, etc.).

See Also: TRANSCENDENTALS.

Bibliography: L. DE RAEYMAEKER, *Metaphysica generalis,* 2 v. (new ed. Louvain 1935). H. POUILLON, ''La Beauté, proprieré transcendentale chez la scholastique (1220–1270),'' *Archives d'histoire doctrinale et littéraire du moyen-âge* 15 (1946) 263–314. F. J. KOVACH, ''The Transcendentality of Beauty in Thomas A.,'' *Die Metaphysik im Mittelalter,* ed. P. WILPERT (Miscellanea mediaevalia 2; Berlin 1963); *Die Ästhetik des Thomas v. A.* (Berlin 1961) 5–10, 20–24, 182–214.

[F. J. KOVACH]

BEAUTY IN AESTHETICS

Beauty is a QUALITY constituting the nonutilitarian value of a FORM, inhering in it as a subtle and hazardous union of the quantitative and qualitative elements, and discovered with increasing interest and adherence of the mind. Although the subtlety of its nature, the complexity and persistence of disputes regarding it, and the radical vicissitudes of the arts have led many of even the best aestheticians to abandon the word beauty, efforts to distinguish the phenomenon it denotes continue undiminished.

Distinctness from Other Values. Because beauty inheres in the organization of the elements of a beautiful object, many consider its value that of substantial rather than of accidental being. However, beauty is not the object organized, but a quality of its organization. Thus an object is not beautiful if its parts lack variety, if their interrelationships lack subtlety, etc. As value, beauty is desirable; but unlike the value that makes things useful or exchangeable, that of beauty is value as end and desirable for contemplation. Such value is said to be aesthetic. Values in the individuated object are suffused and qualify one another, but they can be abstracted by the mind and simplified for the sake of clear distinctions.

Beauty's distinctness from the GOOD appears in the fact that whereas a thing is beautiful through the internal ordering of its parts, it is good through their external ordering. Hence the good inclines the natural appetite, the sensitive appetite, or the will toward possessing it, whereas the desirability of beauty leads not to possession but only to contemplation. Beauty differs from TRUTH, for it depends on internal fitness of parts, whereas truth depends on conformity between what is in the mind and what exists in reality independently of the mind. Moreover, unlike beauty, truth qualifies the intellect, not the object known. Only metaphorically and hypothetically can beauty be said to be a ''sensuous manifestation of the Absolute.'' Taken literally, this assertion would make the condition of beauty a fitness between the beautiful object and the ultimate metaphysical reality ''behind'' appearances, instead of a fitness of part to part within the boundaries of the object itself. By implication it would make beauty a phenomenon of the supernatural rather than of the natural order.

Although the term beauty is sometimes loosely used as a synonym for all aesthetic value, more rigorous usage discriminates between aesthetic qualities. For example, although the sublime or the graceful or both may qualify an object characterized also by beauty, these two aesthetic values are distinguishable from beauty: they both tend, though in opposite ways, toward dynamic disequilibrium, whereas beauty imposes equilibrium. Disequilibrium is inequality between actual formal expression and the intuitive expectation of it in a receiver (viewer, listener, reader). If the sublime characterizes a structure (of meaning), the unexpressed potential seems, by the natural movement of the mind, to be multiplied, while the actual (expression) seems to advance toward relative annihilation. A new potentiality accrues to the scope of meaning. On the other hand, if grace qualifies the form, the actual expression—casually and without strain—exceeds the expectation of already superior expression, and inference is drawn of potential still unactualized. This potential accrues to the agent, who is suspected of an exciting superiority. By contrast with the sublime and the graceful, the beautiful reveals equality between the actual (interrelationship discovered) and the potential. Its potential is perceived as the threat to unity provided by delicate hazards, namely, qualitative and quantitative lures so subtle and various that they are, practically speaking, inexhaustible; thus, as relation is discovered, interest mounts increasingly. Its unactualized potential accrues to the perfection of the structure.

Nature of Beauty. Beauty qualifies both NATURE and art, and originates ultimately in the ''mind'' of God. More immediately, the beauty of an art object originates by the human agency of the artist. The concept of artistic agency is contradicted by the idea that an object is invested with beauty when ''touched by a ray of transcendent light.'' Taken metaphorically, as the familiar image of sunlight illuminating the surfaces of things and so making the world beautiful, it has validity; but this image is rather one of enormous complexity unified by a common reflection. Beauty qualifies structure, whether this organizes the relations among physical elements or among relations simply as such (incorporeal form). However, inquiry inclines usually toward the beauty of what is perceptible by the senses, particularly sight and hearing. Beauty is not imposed on matter as form is, but qualifies form itself. Multiple categorical dissimilarities naturally tend to confusion or to waste. But if in complex aspects of material and formal elements some native similarity is discoverable, the similar parts are perceived as unified, and in the recognition of this unity the mind is suffused with pleasure. The interest it awakens stimulates apprehension of further relationship, and thus heightens awareness and affectivity. The more profound and hazardous the relationships, the greater the excitement experienced. Relevancies seem privileged and original.

In a beautiful form relationships themselves are found related (proportion), by discoveries that occasion at each instant a pleasurable sense of their inevitability. Hence proportion is apprehended as ''due.'' The affective impulse of the mind as it finds subtle proportions drives it to enjoy relationship, and creates the illusion that unity is inviolable (organic). In the totality of arrangement, as complexity is constantly explored, the surprising new appearances of fitness announce that nothing due is missing (integrity); no incompatibility remains. The unique mode of the relation that unifies relationships specifies the hierarchies in the posture of elements.

Although related surfaces, sounds, aspects, etc., are perceived through the senses, their interrelationships are actualized by the mind. The more delicate these are, the more engaged is the mind—not analytically, but in immediate, primary perception of the whole. Subtlety effects a multiple beguiling of the notice that alternates between synoptic distribution over fields of relatedness and the sa-

Saint-Pierre Cathedral in Beauvais. (©Paul Almasy/CORBIS)

voring of individual parts of rare insistence. Beauty is both objective and subjective. It inheres in objects and, being distinguishable, can also provide an objective criterion; yet beauty depends for its appearance on the mind, since it is the mind that renders relation actual.

See Also: AESTHETICS.

Bibliography: ARISTOTLE, *Poetics,* ed. I. BYWATER (Oxford 1909). R. BAYER, *L'Esthétique de la grâce,* 2 v. (Paris 1933). M. BEARDSLEY, "Beauty and Aesthetic Value," *Journal of Philosophy* 59 (1962) 617–28. W. A. HAMMOND, ed., *A Bibliography of Aesthetics and of the Philosophy of Fine Arts from 1900 to 1932* (rev. ed. New York 1934). T. E. JESSOP, "The Definition of Beauty," *Proceedings of the Aristotelian Society,* new series 33 (1932–33) 159–772. *Journal of Aesthetics and Art Criticism* (Detroit-Cleveland 1941–), index to v.1–20. J. LAIRD, *The Idea of Value* (Cambridge, Eng. 1929). H. OSBORNE, *The Theory of Beauty* (New York 1953); *Aesthetics and Criticism* (New York 1955) 325–34, bibliography on aesthetics. *Proceedings of the 4th International Congress on Aesthetics,* ed. P. A. MICHELIS (Athens 1960) 29–36, 206–09, 458–64, 525–37. P. VALÉRY, *Aesthetics,* tr. R. MANHEIM, v.13 of *Collected Works* (Bollingen Series 45; New York 1964). W. WEIDLÉ, "Biology of Art," *Diogenes* 17 (Spring 1957) 1–5.

[M. F. SLATTERY]

BEAUVAIS

French town at the confluence of the Thérain and Avelon Rivers, 49 miles north of Paris. It is the seat of a diocese (*Bellovacensis*) suffragan to REIMS. The Roman *Caesaromagus,* capital of the Gallic *Bellovaci* tribe, was part of *Belgica II* and no earlier than the 4th century came to be called *Bellovacum* (Beauvais). The introduction of Christianity in the 3d century is traditionally attributed to the martyr Lucian, a Roman, whose 8th-century vita has little historical value. The process of Christianization was set back in the early 5th century by barbarian invasions. The 13th bishop, Maurinus (632), is the first who can be dated. The relies of St. Angadrisma, who entered a nearby monastery (*c.* 660), were translated to Beauvais (851), of which she and Lucian are patron saints.

Merovingian monasteries seem to have been abandoned during the Norman invasions (852–940). HINCMAR was elected archbishop of Reims in a council of Beauvais (845). By 900 the bishops were temporal lords; the last lay count appeared in 1035. In the 12th century the bishops were feudal lords; in 1789 they held 450 fiefs. The commune, which was full grown in 1099, probably received its rights from Bishop Guy (1063–85). LOUIS IX used an uprising of the commune as an excuse to violate the episcopal rights of Bp. Milo of Nanteuil (1217–34), who had been a crusader in the East (1218–19) and was with LOUIS VIII in southern France (1226). Although a council of NOYON condemned Louis (1233) and a compromise was achieved (1248), royal authority was entrenched in Beauvais. *Bourgeoisie* uprisings continued, however. During the Hundred Years' War, which devastated the diocese, Bp. Pierre Cauchon (1420–32) helped condemn Joan of Arc. In 1472 Beauvais valiantly withstood a siege by Charles the Bold of Burgundy. During the wars clerical morals declined, buildings were destroyed, and there was no attempt to rebuild. Abbeys were held in COMMENDATION. Beauvais's bishop Cardinal Odet de Châtillon, abjured Catholicism for Calvinism (1562), married, and took the title count of Beauvais (1564); it took until 1569 to depose him.

Claude Gouine, vicar-general of Bp. Nicholas Fumée (1575–92), administered the see until his death (1607), rebuilding churches, reforming religious houses, bringing in Capuchins (1603), and applying some of the decrees of the Council of Trent. The founders of the seminary, which opened in 1648, and Bp. Nicholas Choart de Buzanval (1650–79) were Jansenist, but Toussaint de Forbin-Janson (1679–1713) purged the see of Jansenists, including the erudite hagiographer Adrien Baillet (1649–1706). Bishop F. J. de LA ROCHEFOUCAULD died a martyr in Paris (1792), as did the Carmelites in COMPIÈGNE; but most of the clergy accepted the CIVIL CONSTITUTION OF THE CLERGY. The diocese, which is rural, was suppressed and incorporated into the See of AMIENS (1801) but was restored (1817–22).

The unfinished Gothic cathedral of St.-Pierre, begun *c.* 1240, has collapsed several times. It has a choir, transept, and seven chapels, and a vault 158 feet high; the 13th- to 16th-century stained glass of the windows is famous, as are the tapestries depicting the lives of SS. Peter and Paul. Beauvais's tapestry industry was stimulated by the royal establishment there in 1664.

Bibliography: E. JARRY, *Catholicisme* (Paris 1947–) 1:1361–64. J. BÉREUX, *Dictionnaire d'histoire et de géographie ecclésiastiques*, ed. A. BAUDRILLART (Paris 1912–) 7:255–302.

[E. P. COLBERT]

BEC (LE BEC-HELLOUIN), ABBEY OF

Benedictine foundation in Normandy, Diocese of Évreux, north France. It was founded by Herluin (1034) and eventually established by the stream Bec. After the arrival of LANFRANC (1041), a brilliant professor of law and grammar at Pavia and Avranches, the community developed with a cloister school for monks and an outside school for clerics and sons of Norman nobles. As prior, Lanfranc got Pope Nicholas II to grant a dispensation to Duke William of Normandy to marry his cousin Matilda of Flanders (1063); the duke named Lanfranc abbot of the new monastery of Saint-Étienne in CAEN, built in thanksgiving. After his conquest of England, WILLIAM made Lanfranc archbishop of CANTERBURY (1070) to reorganize the Church there and be his private counselor, as were later abbots of Bec. ANSELM (OF CANTERBURY), prior of Bec after Lanfranc (1059), was elected abbot after Herluin's death (1078) and, despite the opposition of the community, had to accept the See of Canterbury after Lanfranc's death (1093).

History. At first a poor monastery, Bec soon received many donations from Norman lords and Anglo-Norman kings, especially Henry I and Matilda: liturgical furnishings and relics (1134), many priories in Normandy and England (St. Walburga in CHESTER), churches, domains, and fiefs. In 1704 Bec had 87 possessions in the Diocese of ROUEN, 32 in ÉVREUX, 32 in Lisieux, 17 in PARIS, and 15 in CHARTRES. After Lanfranc and Anselm, THEOBALD became archbishop of Canterbury, Gondulf and Arnulf bishops of ROCHESTER, Hugh and GILBERT CRISPIN abbots of SAINT AUGUSTINE (CANTERBURY) and WESTMINSTER.

Bec was a ducal, then a royal abbey, the abbots being confirmed by the dukes, then by the kings of England. The archbishop of Rouen, who blessed the abbot and received the oath of obedience, made canonical visitations; Odo Rigaldus, who made 13 visitations (124–869), called Bec the best ruled monastery in Normandy. The kings of France intervened in the thirteenth century and, from the time of Louis XI, designated commendatory abbots; the first, Jean Boucart, was royal confessor and bishop of Avranches (1471–84); some were generous, some greedy.

Saint-Nicolas Tower at Le Bec-Hellouin Abbey, France. (©Paul Almasy/CORBIS)

In the fourteenth century there were frequent differences with nobles over tithes and the patronage of churches. Commendatory abbots disputed with the monks over revenue; Roger de la Rochefoucauld (1708–13) demanded an additional 13,000 livres but finally ceded all his holdings for an annual revenue of 48,000 livres. There were frequent and heavy levies by the popes (Syrian Crusade, 1307–12; rebuilding of MONTE CASSINO, 1369) and by the kings for war (Charles VI, 1412; Louis XI, 1471) and for levies on the clergy in 1567, 1588, and in 1710 for a final redemption of the head tax.

After an occupation by Anglo-Navarrese troops (1356), Bec was fortified with a French garrison (1358); the cloister and part of the dormitory were torn down and the church used to house refugees and their possessions. Geoffrey Harenc (1388–99) rebuilt the cloister, restored the chapter, and reclaimed the farmland. William of Auvillars (1399–1418) completed an immense wall on the order of the French king (1405–15). Bec sheltered a garrison and refugees when Henry V devastated Normandy. After a three-week siege, it surrendered to the English (May of 1418), who pillaged it and kept a large garrison there. Abbot Robert (1418–30) took an oath of fidelity to Henry V (1419). When a French coup almost regained the abbey (June of 1421), the monks were expelled and the abbot imprisoned; but Henry V did not hold the monks responsible and restored the temporal goods, ordering the fortress demolished. After his death (1422) anarchy and pillaging ensued. In 1563 Huguenots pillaged Bec, and two monks were slain.

Architecture. The first church burned down in 1158 and was rebuilt and consecrated by the archbishop of Rouen in the presence of the king of England and his sons (1178). After a partial collapse (1197), it was rebuilt under Richard of St. Leger with towers and a spire (1215–17); burned again (1263), it was rebuilt with the aid of a bull of Urban IV and taxes imposed on priories. The lantern tower collapsed, bringing with it the choir and transept (1274); transept and choir with apsidal chapels were rebuilt in grandiose style at a different height than the nave (1275–1327). Painted glass and 16 large statues of Apostles, Evangelists, and Latin Doctors of the Church that were painted and gilded in the fifteenth century gave added beauty. A square belfrey tower for large bells was completed in 1468. The nave collapsed (1591) and was rebuilt (1639–43), reduced from nine to two bays. The main portal was replaced with a classical façade, bells were recast, and liturgical furnishings renewed (1644–74). The monk architect-sculptor Guillaume de la Tremblaye did the main altar and side altars, the pulpit, a large jube, and a new tomb of Matilda (1684), which was transferred to Rouen (1847). The organs were of English make (1671). Nave vaulting was restored (1699), and choir and sanctuary pavement was done in black-and-white marble dalles (1710).

The first cloister buildings (1073) were enlarged by Roger I Bailleul (1159–79) with a large hostel, an infirmary and dormitory, and an aqueduct to a covered reservoir. Reconstruction took place under Geoffrey Harenc after 1392, Robert Valée from 1428, Geoffrey d'Epaigne (1452–76), Louis de Bourbon-Condé (1742–58), and recently under Abbot Grammont (1948).

Culture. Lanfranc (1042–63) was a lucid teacher, subtle, learned, and a skillful dialectician who disputed with BERENGARIUS. Anselm turned more to the soul, silence, and composure, and fixed the use of philosophy in theology. They had many famous disciples in the school of Bec: Archbishop William Good Soul of Rouen, IVO OF CHARTRES, Bishop Fulk of Beauvais, Hervé, dean of Canterbury, Gilbert and Miles Crispin (biographers of Herluin and Lanfranc), the prolific writer ROBERT OF TORIGNY, Stephen of Rouen (*Draco Normannicus,* a chronicle of Normandy), and Peter of Dives (*Gesta septem abbatum Beccensium,* in *Patrologia Latina* 181:1709–18).

Monastic laxity accompanied wars. The MAURIST reform was introduced (1626) by Abbot Dominic de Vic, archbishop of Auch. Peace and order brought prosperity and an increase in revenue; the monks' revenue increased from 30,000 livres (1654) to 48,000 (1685), but the riches benefitted the nobility. A theological school was installed (1651) with famous professors: René Massuet (1665–1716), editor of the works of St. Irenaeus, and Guillaume Bessin. A chronicle of Bec to 1331 by Thibaut and a collection by Jouvelin (both in manuscripts) are valuable historical works.

Lanfranc's library of 160 volumes, primarily on Holy Scripture and the Fathers, increased with bequests by Bishop Philip d'Harcourt of Bayeux (d. 1164; 113 volumes) and the priest and medical doctor Jean de Bessay (fourteenth century). But Estout d'Estouteville took away beautiful manuscripts in 1391. In 1421 there were 700 volumes besides liturgical books. Some 5,000 volumes were rearranged by the Maurists in 1677. A general inventory of 1671 divided charters into two charter rooms and three chartularies (thirteenth and fourteenth centuries). In 1789 there were 5,000 printed books besides pamphlets, and 220 manuscripts, of which 19 are extant (12 in the Paris Bibliothèque Nationale).

The tradition of generosity to the poor and strangers goes back to St. Anselm. In the thirteenth century 200 loaves of bread a week were distributed to the poor. Many refugees were cared for in crises (1358, 1417, 1418), and in 1693 some 10,000 were fed in time of need. The people were kindly disposed toward the abbey.

In 1792 the eight remaining monks had to leave. Ten bells and much silver work were sent to Rouen (1789) and BERNAY (1792) to be melted down. The furniture was sold for almost nothing. The lead roof of the church was pillaged. The church itself, fallen to ruin, was condemned and demolished (1810–24); the main altar, jube, statues, and the dalles of the sanctuary were obtained by the pastor of Sainte-Croix in Bernay. The chapter hall was demolished (1816–17). The buildings became a stud farm.

Olivetan Benedictines from Mesnil-Saint-Loup (Champagne) reoccupied Bec (1948), which with 20 monks and many visitors is expanding under Abbot Grammont. The old refectory has been made into a church.

Bibliography: GILBERT CRISPIN, *Vita Herluini,* in *Patrolgia Latina,* 217 v., ed. J. P. MIGNE (Paris 1878–90) 150:695–714; Eng. ed. in J. A. ROBINSON, *Gilbert Crispin* (Cambridge, Eng. 1911) 87–110. *Chronicon Beccense* (1034–1467), in *Patrologia Latina* 150:639–695. *Chronique du Bec . . .* (1149–1476), ed. A. PORÉE (Rouen 1883). J. BOURGET, *The History of the Royal Abbey of Bec, Near Rouen in Normandy,* tr. A. C. DUCAREL (London 1779), "Philosophe," admirer of Voltaire who ignores early authors because of miracles; brief. A. PORÉE, "L'Abbaye du Bec au XVIIIe siècle," *Congrès archéologique de France* (Paris 1881) 372–455; *L'Abbaye du Bec et ses écoles, 1045–1790* (Évreux 1892); *Histoire de l'abbaye du Bec,* 2 v. (Évreux 1901). E. VEUCLIN, *Fin de la célèbre abbaye du Bec-Hellouin* (Brionne 1885). B. HEURTEBIZE, *Dictionnaire d'histoire et de géographie ecclésiastiques,* ed. A. BAUDRILLART et al. (Paris 1912—) 7:325–335. G. NORTIER, "La

Bibliothèque de l'abbaye du Bec,'' *Revue Mabillon* (Paris 1957) 57–83. M. DE BOUARD and J. MERCET, ''La Remise en état de l'abbaye du Bec,'' *Monuments historiques de la France* 5 (Paris 1959) 149–173. M. P. DICKSON, ''Introduction à l'édition critique du Coutumier du Bec,'' *Spicilegium Beccense* 1 (Paris 1959) 599–632. M. M. MORGAN, *The English Lands of the Abbey of Bec* (New York 1946) J. TAIT, ed., *The Chartulary or Register of the Abbey of Saint Werburgh, Chester,* 2 v. (Manchester 1920–23). L. H. COTTINEAU, *Répertoire topobibliographique des abbayes et prieurés,* 2 v. (Mâon 1935–39) 1:316–319.

[P. COUSIN]

BECANUS, MARTIN

Jesuit theologian and controversialist; b. Hilvarenbeek (northern Brabant), Holland, Jan. 6, 1563; d. Vienna, Jan. 24, 1624. He received his degree in philosophy at the Jesuit college in Cologne, and in 1583 he entered the Society of Jesus. After teaching philosophy at Cologne, he taught theology for many years at Würzburg, Mainz, and Vienna. During these years he enjoyed great respect for his teaching and produced most of his important writing. In 1620 he became royal confessor to FERDINAND II, and he spent his remaining years in Vienna. There he advised the emperor on the difficult problems concerning relations with the Holy See and toleration of Protestants within the realm.

Becanus was one of the most highly esteemed theologians in Germany in his time and was a prolific writer. He devoted a large part of his work to refuting CALVINIST teachings and to presenting Catholic doctrine in a clear, logical fashion. In this respect his writing was unsurpassed, and the bitterness that characterized so much polemical writing of the day was singularly lacking in his work. His chief theological study, the *Summa theologiae scholasticae* (4 v. Mainz 1612), is for the most part a compendium of the commentary of SUÁREZ on St. THOMAS AQUINAS. The *Controversia anglicana de potestate regis et pontificis* (Mainz 1612) was placed on the Index in 1613, apparently not because it contained any gross error, but rather to prevent the faculty of the University of Paris from condemning it and at the same time adding their own declarations against papal authority. A short time later, the *Controversia* was published again in a corrected edition with a dedication to PAUL V. Another important work of Becanus was the *Manuale controversiarum* (Mainz 1623), which went through many editions and was translated into several languages.

Bibliography: C. SOMMERVOGEL et al., *Bibliothèque de la Compagnie de Jésus* (Brussels-Paris 1890–1932) 1:1091–1111; 8:1789–90. H. HURTER, *Nomenclator literarius theologiae catholicae* (Innsbruck 1903–13) 1:293–294. E. LAMALLE, *Dictionnaire d'histoire et de géographie ecclésiastiques* (Paris 1912–) 7:341–344. J. BRUCKER, *Dictionnaire de théologie catholique* (Paris 1903–50) 2.1:521–523.

[J. T. KELLEHER]

BECCARIA, CESARE BONESANA

Political economist credited with ushering in modern criminal law and penal practice; b. Milan, March 15, 1738; d. Milan, Nov. 28, 1794. Beccaria was of a noble family, attended the Jesuit college at Parma, and graduated in jurisprudence from the University of Pavia in 1758. Although diffident about his formal education, he was prompted by his association with the intellectual circle of Pietro and Alessandro Verri to write his *Tratto dei Delitti e delle Pene* (1764), first published anonymously, and translated into English as *Essay on Crimes and Punishments.* It was received so enthusiastically throughout the Continent that by 1770 it had appeared in three Italian editions, had been translated into French and English with prefaces attributed to Voltaire, and had received approbation from Catherine the Great, as well as from the monarchs of Naples and Austria. Beccaria acknowledged his debt to Jean Jacques ROUSSEAU, Charles de MONTESQUIEU, and the ENCYCLOPEDISTS, for he was in the mainstream of rationalist thought; his influence on Jeremy BENTHAM is clear, and they are linked as the founders of the classical school of CRIMINOLOGY. Although others had rebelled at the barbarity of prevailing penal practices, it was Beccaria who systematically set forth the principles that punishment should be proportionate to the crime and serve the sole purpose of societal protection.

Bibliography: E. MONACHESI, ''Pioneers in Criminology: Cesare Beccaria,'' *The Journal of Criminal Law, Criminology and Police Science* 46 (1955) 439–449.

[R. LANE]

BECERRA TANCO, LUIS

Mexican scholar whose writings are an important source of information about the apparitions of Our Lady of GUADALUPE; b. Taxco, 1602; d. Mexico City, 1672. He received the baccalaureate in liberal arts and Canon Law from the University of Mexico, where he was appointed to the chair of mathematics. He also distinguished himself in physics and chemistry. Becerra Tanco was regarded by his contemporaries as a marvel in the field of linguistics, for he mastered Hebrew, Greek, Latin, Italian, French, Portuguese, and English, and he taught the native tongues of Nahuatl and Otomi. He was renowned also as poet, preacher, philosopher, historian, and scientist. He was ordained under benefice in 1631, and he served in various curacies of the Archdiocese of Mexico. As a historian of the Church in Mexico, he is noted principally for his research on the apparitions of the Blessed Virgin at Tepeyac. His book *Origen milagroso del Santuario de Nuestra Señora de Guadalupe* (Mexico City 1666) was reissued in an enlarged posthumous edition in 1675 under the title *Felicidad de Mexico en la admirable aparición de la Vírgen María Nuestra Señora de Guadalupe* and has been reprinted many times.

Bibliography: BERISTAIN, *Diccionario universal de historia y de geografía,* 10 v. (Mexico City 1853–56) 1:520.

[J. A. MAGNER]

BECHE, JOHN, BL.

Abbot executed by Henry VIII, also known as Thomas Becbe or Marshall; b. *c.* 1500; d. Dec. 1, 1539. He received a B.D. at Oxford (1509). He was first a Benedictine monk at the Abbey of Chester. In 1533 he was elected abbot of St. John's Colchester, and he took the Oath of Supremacy in the following year. In 1538, however, he refused to surrender his abbey to the Crown, which in 1539 sought evidence of Beche's treason in order to secure his domain. He was indicted for denying the royal supremacy and sent to the Tower of London. He made a complete retraction of this denial but was tried for treason on Dec. 1, 1539, found guilty, and condemned. There is no evidence that he ever reasserted belief in the papal primacy, not even after condemnation.

Feast: Dec. 1.

See Also: ENGLAND, SCOTLAND, AND WALES, MARTYRS OF.

Bibliography: D. KNOWLES, *The Religious Orders in England* 3:376, 491. J. E. PAUL, ''The Last Abbots of Reading and Colchester,'' *Bulletin of the Institute of Historical Research* 33 (1960) 115–121.

[J. E. PAUL]

BECKER, CHRISTOPHER EDMUND

Salvatorian founder of the Medical Mission Institute of Würzburg; b. Elsoff, near Frankfort am Main, Oct. 22, 1875; d. Würzburg, March 30, 1937. He entered the Society of the Divine Savior in Rome in 1889 and obtained doctorates in philosophy and theology before his ordination in 1898. He was professor and then rector of the Salvatorian house in Merano until in 1905 when he was made first prefect apostolic of the Salvatorian mission field in Assam, India. He labored there until World War I interrupted mission activities. With his missionaries, Becker was first interned and then expelled from India. Since it was impossible to return, Becker resigned his position of prefect apostolic after the war. In 1922 he founded the Medical Mission Institute of Würzburg, the first of its kind to train qualified physicians for work in the foreign missions (*see* MEDICAL MISSIONS). He remained director of the institute until his death, and he also served as professor of missiology at the University of Würzburg. His writings include *Im Stromtal des Brahmaputra* (Munich 1927); *Indisches Kastenwesen und christliche Mission* (Aachen 1921); and *Missionsärztliche Kulturarbeit* (Würzburg 1928).

Bibliography: G. WUNDERLE, ''Professor C. E. Becker: Gründer des Missionsärztlichen Instituts,'' *Katholische Missionsärztliche Fürsorge: Jahresbericht* 14 (1937) 3–14. G. SCHREIBER, *Deutsches Reich und deutsche Medizin* (Leipzig 1926) 292ff.

[W. HERBST]

BECKER, THOMAS ANDREW

Theologian, writer, first bishop of WILMINGTON, Del., sixth bishop of SAVANNAH, Ga.; b. Pittsburgh, Dec. 20, 1832; d. Washington, Ga., July 29, 1899. The son of John and Susannah Becker, German Protestants, he attended Allegheny Institute and Western University, Pittsburgh, Pa. While studying at the University of Virginia, he became a friend of Joseph H. Plunkett, pastor of St. Joseph's Church, Martinsburg, W. Va., who probably interested him in Catholicism.

He was received into the Church on May 22, 1853, was accepted for the priesthood by Bp. John McGill of Richmond, Va., and in June of 1855 entered the College of the Propaganda in Rome, where he distinguished himself as a student and earned the degree of S.T.D. Following ordination at the basilica of St. John Lateran on June 18, 1859, he was temporarily assigned to St. Peter's Cathedral, Richmond, and in January of 1860, succeeded Father Plunkett as pastor at Martinsburg. There, his secessionist position resulted in his arrest for refusing to recite certain public prayers ordered by the provost-marshal for the Union cause. Archbishop Kenrick of Baltimore obtained his release and appointed him to Mt. St. Mary's College, Emmitsburg, Md., to teach dogma, Scripture, and Church history. A year later he became secretary to Kenrick's successor, M. J. SPALDING of Baltimore, with whom he collaborated on the *Catholic Miscellany,* and for whom he worked with other theologians on the agenda for the second Council of Baltimore (1866). At the council's close he returned to the cathedral staff in Richmond, and there he organized and directed a boys' school and prepared a prayerbook, *Vade Mecum.* When the see of Wilmington was erected on March 3, 1868, Becker was named its bishop and was consecrated (along with the future Cardinal Gibbons) in Baltimore that August 16. Despite the record of his accomplishments as founding bishop, he became discouraged at what he felt was lack of progress, and in September of 1879 submitted his resignation, which was not accepted. Meanwhile he worked with Gibbons on preparations for the Third Plenary Council (1884), produced the important chapter on clerical education, and delivered before the council a sermon on the Church and the promotion of learning. In May of 1886, he was transferred to the older see of Savannah, Ga. Eleven years later, incapacitated by malaria, he told Cardinal Gibbons of his intention to retire. He died at Washington, Ga., while substituting for one of his priests.

Though naturally reticent, Becker was a vigorous and original thinker. He was among the first to advocate the establishment of a national Catholic university, in two articles in *American Catholic Quarterly Review* in 1876: ''Shall We Have a University?'' and ''A Plan for a Proposed Catholic University.'' In discussing secret societies in the same review (1878), he confronted the then controversial topic of labor unions, upholding the right of labor to organize and pronouncing clearly upon the morality of labor practices.

Bibliography: J. T. ELLIS, *The Life of James Cardinal Gibbons*, 2 v. (Milwaukee 1952). J. G. D. SHEA, *The Hierarchy of the Catholic Church in the United States* (New York 1887). Archives of the Archdiocese of Baltimore, of the Diocese of Wilmington, of the Diocese of Richmond, of Mt. St. Mary's College, Emmitsburg, Md.

[E. B. CARLEY]

Martyrdom of St. Thomas Becket. (© Leonard de Selva/CORBIS)

BECKET, THOMAS, ST.

Archbishop and martyr; b. London, 1117–18; d. CANTERBURY, Dec. 29, 1170. He was educated at Merton Priory (Surrey) and at Paris. Thomas, of Norman bourgeois parents, became a merchant's clerk in London, but soon joined the household of Abp. THEOBALD OF CANTERBURY, and may subsequently have studied at BOLOGNA. Tall, handsome, vigorous, extroverted, intelligent but not intellectual, Thomas of London, as he was called, lived the life of an ambitious young cleric, ingratiating himself to the old archbishop, who made him archdeacon of Canterbury, and to other prospective patrons.

Chancellor. In 1154, on Theobald's recommendation, the young King HENRY II (b. 1132), to whom Thomas was bound by strong mutual affection, appointed him chancellor. His gifts of administration and initiative and his taste for magnificence together with his charm, his energy, and his efficiency were displayed fully. He amassed wealth and spent lavishly and generously; while archdeacon he even appeared in full armor at the siege of Toulouse. Yet he remained pure and even devout.

Archbishop. Theobald's death (1161) was followed by a long vacancy of the See of Canterbury. The king had begun his lifelong endeavor to gain complete control of his kingdom, with a program that included a submissive Church, and saw in his chancellor the perfect agent and ally. Passing over the respectable Gilbert FOLIOT, he pressed Thomas upon the unwilling monks and bishops (1162). The chancellor resisted sincerely, knowing both the king and his own conscience. Once elected, he completely changed his style of life to one of regularity, piety, and austerity, while retaining his magnificence, his generosity, and his commanding personality. He resisted with audacity all royal encroachments on ecclesiastical liberty, as well as attacks on the possessions and prerogatives of his see.

Conflict with Henry. Discord between king and archbishop came to a head in the matter of ''criminous clerks,'' the king asserting his traditional right of judgment, the archbishop maintaining the strictest canonical position of complete jurisdiction for the Christian courts. At a council at Westminster (1163) the king demanded from the bishops acceptance of all the ''ancient customs'' of the realm. They refused, but Thomas later submitted in private. The king repeated his demands at CLARENDON (WILTSHIRE) in January 1164, finally producing in writing the 16 celebrated Constitutions to which he demanded assent. The bishops submitted, but Thomas immediately repented.

Meanwhile Pope ALEXANDER III condemned some of the constitutions. In October 1164 the king, in a council at Northampton, demanded the condemnation of the archbishop for feudal insubordination. His colleagues demurred, but in the end yielded. Henry then pressed a series of frivolous and punitive demands, and there were threats of imprisonment and even of death. The bishops, forbidden by Thomas to judge him, appealed against him to the pope while the lay barons passed judgment. Anticipating his sentence, the archbishop fled and escaped to France, taking refuge in the Cistercian Abbey of PONTIGNY and devoting himself to penitential exercises and the study of canon law. His exile lasted until 1170; the king of France welcomed him, and the pope, then in France, proclaimed the justice of his cause. But Alexander III was himself in grave difficulties with the emperor and his antipope, and was unwilling to go to extremes with Henry, and the months and years passed while the king harassed and exiled the archbishop's relatives and allies, and the archbishop excommunicated and suspended his opponents. Negotiations, and even a meeting of the two in 1169, broke down.

At last Henry and some bishops made the grave error of crowning (June 14, 1170) ''the young king,'' Henry's son, in defiance of Canterbury's rights, which had been reaffirmed by the pope. The bishops were excommunicated, and the king felt it necessary to yield. A reconciliation, satisfactory to Thomas, took place at Fréteval (Orléanais) on July 22. Once more the king broke faith, supported by some bishops; once more Thomas excommunicated his enemies. His return to England was a triumph. But the injured prelates had inflamed the king's mind: he called for a riddance from his enemy and four knights crossed at once to Canterbury where, after a stormy interview, they murdered the archbishop in his cathedral (December 29). The atrocity shocked all Europe. Miracles were reported at the tomb; the pope excommunicated the king, who later did penance and abated his principal claims and was reconciled at Avranches (1172). In 1173 Thomas was canonized, and his tomb rapidly became a resort of pilgrims; churches were dedicated to him from Iceland to Spain.

Estimate of Becket's Career. The issue between king and archbishop was confused by clashes of temperament and emotion and embittered by the king's insincerity and the archbishop's pugnacity. Henry aimed at a complete control of the Church at a time when Europe had accepted the papal claims of GREGORY VII (*see* GREGORIAN REFORM). Thomas stood for those claims in their entirety. Had he not resisted, England might have become for a time a separated unit in Christendom. By his death he won for his cause an immediate victory, which gave place in time to a compromise in practice. His biographers all wrote to celebrate a saint, but there will always be disputes about his character and his cause. Worldly and ambitious for long, and retaining even as archbishop traits of impetuosity and harshness, he nevertheless showed in adversity a steadfast courage and devotion to principle that gained him a death he and others regarded with justice as a sacrifice for the freedom of the Church in England.

Feast: Dec. 29.

Bibliography: Sources. *Materials for the History of Thomas Becket,* ed. J. C. ROBERTSON, 7 v. (*Rerum Britannicarum medii aevi scriptores* 67; London 1875–85); for criticism. E. WALBERG, *La Tradition hagiographique de Saint Thomas* (Paris 1929). *The Correspondence of Thomas Becket*, ed. and tr. A. J. DUGGAN (New York 2000). Literature. E. ABBOTT, *St. Thomas of Canterbury* (London 1898, reprinted New York 1980). F. BARLOW, *Thomas Becket* (Berkeley 1986). C. BARONIO, *The Life or the Ecclesiasticall Historie of S. Thomas* (London 1639, reprinted Ilkley 1975). T. BORENIUS, *St. Thomas Becket in Art* (Port Washington, N.Y. 1970). J. R. BUTLER, *The Quest for Becket's Bones: The Mystery of the Relics of St. Thomas Becket of Canterbury* (New Haven, Conn. 1995). T. CORFE, *The Murder of Archbishop Thomas* (Minneapolis 1977). A. DUGGAN, *Thomas Becket: A Textual History of His Letters* (Oxford 1980). C. DUGGAN, *Canon Law in Medieval England: The Becket Dispute and Decretal Collections* (London 1982). G. W. GREENAWAY, tr. and ed., *The Life and Death of Thomas Becket, Chancellor of England and Archbishop of Canterbury, based on the account of William fitzStephen, His Clerk, with Additions from Other Contemporary Sources* (London 1965). GUERNES DE PONT-SAINTE-MAXENCE, *La vie de saint Thomas Becket*, tr. J.-G. GOUTTEBROZE and A. QUEFFELEC (Paris 1990). T. M. JONES, *The Becket Controversy* (New York 1970). D. KNOWLES, *The Episcopal Colleagues of Archbishop Thomas Becket* (Cambridge, Eng. 1951); *The Historian and Character* (New York 1963); *Thomas Becket* (Stanford, Calif. 1971). R. FOREVILLE, *L'Église et la royauté en Angleterre . . . 1154–1189* (Paris 1943), is full and scholarly, but biased. F. OZANAM, *Two chancellors of England*, tr. J. FINDLAY, ed. J. DAWES (Sydney 1967). W. URRY, *Thomas Becket: His Last Days* ed. P. A. ROWE (Stroud 1999). F. WATT, *Canterbury Pilgrims and Their Ways* (Philadelphia 1977).

[M. D. KNOWLES]

BECOMING

A philosophical term (Gr. γίγνεσθαι; Lat. *fieri*) that is not strictly definable but is understood by contrast with permanent BEING. Man's senses show him all things as coming-to-be and passing away. HERACLITUS made this process essential to physical bodies to the exclusion of any permanent being. The Heraclitean position was revived with some modification in modern philosophy by G. W. F. HEGEL and H. L. BERGSON. PARMENIDES declared becoming illusory and emphasized the absolute and unchangeable character of being, as conceived by the intellect. PLATO tempered this opposition with the distinction that becoming is perceived by opinion with the help of sensation, while being is perceived by reason (*Rep.* 508D). The reconciliation of becoming with being thus became the central problem of Greek philosophy. Aristotle distinguished the kinds of being—potential and actual, substantial and accidental—and thus was able to show that there is becoming with respect to each class of being (*Phys.* 201a 8, 225a 12–19). The term ''becoming'' in an unqualified sense came to be reserved for the coming-into-being of substances. The coming-into-being of accidents is called ''becoming with qualification.'' When an accident is changed from a less to a more perfect state, the process is called motion. Contemporary psychology, under the stimulus of existentialism, uses the term ''becoming'' to signify the development of PERSONALITY.

See Also: CHANGE; GENERATION-CORRUPTION; MOTION

[M. A. GLUTZ]

The Venerable Bede, detail of manuscript, 8th century. (©David Reed/CORBIS)

BEDE, ST.

Monk, priest, theologian, and Doctor of the Church; b. in the English kingdom of Northumbria in the region south of the River Tyne, probably 672 or 673; d. in his monastery in the same region, probably 735. Knowledge of the main facts of his life and work is solidly based on his own account at the end of his *Historia Ecclesiastica gentis Anglorum* (completed 731). Born on land that shortly afterward came to belong to the dual monastery of SS. Peter and Paul, with houses at Wearmouth and Jarrow, Bede was entrusted by relatives to that monastery. He spent the rest of his life there, being ordained deacon at the unusually early age of 19 and priest at 30. The ''Venerable'' by which he is commonly known was probably the title given to priests then (*see* JARROW, ABBEY OF; WEARMOUTH, ABBEY OF).

Scope of His Work. In the course of an outwardly quiet life, Bede used the considerable monastic library assembled by the founder and abbot, Benedict Biscop (*c.* 628–690), to become one of the great polymaths of the medieval Church. His works cover secular areas, such as grammar, metrics, and chronology; the latter a speciality of his, related both to his historical interests and to his concern with the controversy, still alive in his day, against those Celts who had not yet accepted Roman practice in computing the date of Easter (*see* EASTER CONTROVERSY). The *Ecclesiastical History* is commonly and rightly regarded as a decisive moment in the development of the art and science of historiography. Bede's voluminous commentaries on Scripture were highly valued by his contemporaries and throughout the Middle Ages. Here Bede seems to have aimed primarily at presenting clearly the opinions of the great Latin Fathers, mainly (but not exclusively) Augustine, Jerome, Ambrose, and Gregory; but he certainly knew Greek and probably some Hebrew. Some of Bede's letters, particularly one to his former student EGBERT (d. 766), Archbishop of York, are also of importance. Other of his historical works are the *History of the Abbots* (of his monastery) and a life of Cuthbert in verse and prose.

More specifically, literary works include Latin poems, homilies, and a poem on death in five alliterative lines in Northumbrian English. In general, present literary taste finds Bede at his best in the great sections of the *Ecclesiastical History* and in passages of a more personal character, such as prayers, scattered throughout his works.

Cuthbert of Lindisfarne, manuscript illumination from the "Life of St. Cuthbert," written by St. Bede, thought to have been produced at Durham, c. 1200.

The general image of Bede suggested by these passages is borne out by an account of his death written by a pupil who was present. Bede was a monk radiant with a holy joy in teaching and learning. All who come to know him in his work will understand why Plummer wrote in 1896: "We have not, it seems to me, amid all our discoveries, invented as yet anything better than the Christian life which Bede lived, and the Christian death which he died." Regard for the beauty of Bede's character, however, should not obscure appreciation of his intellectual acuity and of the originality of his contribution to the development of practice and thought in the Western Church. Bede had a sense for contemporary fact. His exegetical works show, in their precision and clarity, his feeling for the needs of the monastic students of non–Latin background who would use them. The letter to Egbert is full of sane, practical suggestions, including use of the vernacular in prayers, for improving the religious life of the Northumbrian laity.

Significance of the Work. Bede's own sense for the exigencies of time and situation sharpened his awareness of the same quality in others and hence contributed to the value of the *Ecclesiastical History*. The notable portrait of St. AIDAN (OF LINDISFARNE, d. 651) is a case in point. Almost everything known about Aidan is from Bede, and what Bede tells of the specific working of the Irish mission makes it possible to say that Aidan was one of the great missionary geniuses of all time. Knowledge of another practical genius, the Easterner, Theodore of Tarsus (602–90), who came to England well advanced in age, and, as archbishop of Canterbury, inaugurated a golden era of early English Christianity, is likewise derived mainly from Bede's pages. That golden age was coming to an end by the time of Bede's death, but it had fulfilled its purpose; it had brought to completion the long and demanding task, begun 300 years earlier by British and Irish Celts, of preparing Western Christianity to assimilate the unromanized and barbarous North.

With almost prophetic genius Bede saw and judged clearly the importance of what had been going on in the England of his own and the preceding generation. His *Ecclesiastical History* images forth great events in a way that reveals their significance. Therein lies its value as history; but more than historical insight is involved. It may well be that Bede's scriptural commentary is derivative and presents little in the way of theological development. The *Ecclesiastical History*, however, does represent a significant advance in theological insight. Here an opening to a new day in the life of the Church was recognized, even as it took place, and was preserved in a form that taught posterity to sense the theological significance of the contemporary.

Feast: May 25.

See Also: HISTORIOGRAPHY, ECCLESIASTICAL.

Bibliography: *The Complete Works,* ed. J. A. GILES, 12 v. (London 1843–44), latest complete ed. A new ed. meeting modern philological requirements is now appearing in *Corpus Christianorum. Series latina* (Turnhout, Belg. 1953–) v. 119 (1962) and v. 120 (1960), *Opera exegetica,* ed. D. HURST, and v. 122 (1955), *Opera homiletica,* ed. D. HURST, and *Opera rhythmica,* ed. J. FRAIPOINT, have appeared. *Ecclesiastical History,* ed. C. PLUMMER, 2 v. (Oxford 1896; repr. 1956), indispensable notes and best general account and appreciation of Bede. Trs. of *Ecclesiastical History,* T. STAPLETON (1565), rev. J. E. KI G (*Loeb Classical Library* (London–New York–Cambridge, Mass. 1912–); New York 1930), bilingual. *English Historical Documents,* ed. D. DOUGLAS (New York 1953–), to be completed in 12 v., v.1, *c. 500–1042,* ed. D. WHITELOCK, select bibliog. M. L. W. LAISTNER, *Thought and Letters in Western Europe, A.D. 500 to 900* (2d ed. New York 1957). *Bedae Venerabilis opera de temporibus,* ed. C. W. JONES (Studies in Medieval History NS 9; Cambridge, Mass. 1943). T. A. CARROLL, *The Venerable Bede: His Spiritual Teachings* (Washington 1946). B. WARD, *The Venerable Bede* (London 1998). L. L. J. R. HOUWEN and A. A. MACDONALD, *Beda Venerabilis: Historian, Monk & Northumbrian* (Groningen, Netherlands 1996). J. F. KELLY, "On the Brink: Bede [Christian Scholar 'Between two World,' 7th–8th Cent.]," *Journal of Early Christian Studies* 5 (1997): 85–103. B. P. ROBINSON, "The Venerable Bede as Exegete," *Downside Review* 112 (1994): 201–226. *Bede and His World: The Jarrow Lectures, 1958–1993* (Aldershot, England 1994). P. HUNTER BLAIR, *The*

World of Bede (Cambridge 1990). J. M. WALLACE–HADRILL, *Bede's Ecclesiastical History of the English People: A Historical Commentary* (Oxford 1988). G. H. BROWN, *Bede the Venerable* (Boston 1987). H. E. J. COWDREY, ''Bede and the 'English People,''' *Journal of Religious History* 11 (1981): 501–523. R. T. FARRELL, ed., *Bede and Anglo–Saxon England: Papers in Honour of the 1300th Anniversary of the Birth of Bede* (Oxford 1978). G. BONNER, ed., *Famulus Christi: Essays in Commemoration of the Thirteenth Centenary of the Birth of the Venerable Bede* (London 1976).

[C. J. DONAHUE]

BEDINGFELD, FRANCES

English religious and educator during penal times; b. Redlingfield, Norfolk, 1616; d. Munich, Germany, 1704. Frances, a member of a devout Catholic family of Norfolk, from which 12 daughters entered religion, joined the English Institute of Mary, known also as the Institute of English Virgins, at Munich and was professed in 1633. This society had been founded in 1603 for the Catholic education of young Englishwomen. Mother Bedingfeld succeeded her sister as superior of the motherhouse in 1666 and three years later was invited by Catherine of Braganza, Catholic consort of Charles II, to open a school in London. With several English companions, she founded an academy at Hammersmith; seven years later another school was established at Mickelgate Bar, York. Mother Bedingfeld's years in England coincided with the intensification of harassment of Catholics by the authorities. She was forced to adopt the alias of Mrs. Long and to wear secular dress, and she was repeatedly called before the local magistrates. During the hysteria of the ''Popish Plot,'' she was briefly committed to Ousebridge jail in York in 1679. In 1699 she returned to the convent at Munich, where she enjoyed a wide reputation for sanctity. She lived to see the rule of her order approved by Clement IX in 1703.

Bibliography: H. FOLEY, ed., *Records of the English Province of the Society of Jesus,* 7 v. (London 1877–82) 5.1:579–582. J. GILLOW, *A Literary and Biographical History or Bibliographical Dictionary of the English Catholics from 1534 to the Present Time* 1:166–168.

[H. F. GRETSCH]

BEDINI, GAETANO

Cardinal, priest, diplomat, administrator; b. Sinigaglia, Italy, May 15, 1806; d. Viterbo, Sept. 6, 1864. After his ordination at Sinigaglia on Dec. 20, 1828, by Cardinal Fabrizio Sceberas-Testaferrata, Bedini held a variety of posts. He was appointed secretary to Cardinal Ludovico Altieri, papal nuncio to Vienna (1838); then became apostolic internuncio to the Imperial Court of Brazil (1846); substitute secretary of state of the Vatican (1848); prolegate to Bologna (1849), and later extraordinary pontifical commissioner of the four legations of Bologna, Ferrara, Forti, and Ravenna. Raised to the rank of titular archbishop of Thebes and apostolic nuncio to Brazil (March 15, 1852), he was consecrated in Rome in May of 1852 by Cardinal Altieri. Supposedly on his way to Brazil, Bedini visited the United States (June 30, 1853 through Feb. 4, 1854). In June of 1856 Pius IX named him secretary of the Congregation of Propaganda Fide. On March 18, 1861, he was elevated to the See of Viterbo-Toscanella and in the consistory of Sept. 27, 1861, he was created cardinal priest with the title church of Santa Maria Sopra Minerva.

Bedini's trip to the United States secured his place in the history of the American Church. He came to investigate the Church in the United States and the possibility of establishing an apostolic nunciature in Washington. Rome needed more information about the missionary Church in the United States. Astounded at the continued increase in the number of Catholics and the resulting pressing need for more bishops, dioceses, priests, churches, and charitable institutions, the Holy See desired a firsthand report. The need for this knowledge was made sharply evident by Rome's failure to assess the rampaging anti-Catholicism in the United States at that time.

Almost as soon as he landed in New York, Bedini felt the sting of this anti-Catholicism, which was instigated by German and Italian revolutionaries and American nativists and encouraged by some of the press during his visit to more than 20 cities in the United States and Canada. In Philadelphia, Pa., and Buffalo, N.Y., he was unsuccessful in solving the trustee problems. There were disturbances in Pittsburgh, Pa., and a riot in Cincinnati, Ohio, while he was present, and he was constrained to sail secretly from New York.

When he returned to Rome, without going to Brazil, he inspired the foundation of the North American College. The first part of the report he submitted to the Vatican secretary of state gave a detailed description of the Church in the United States; the second part stressed the necessity, but also inopportuneness, of establishing an apostolic nunciature in Washington. The Bedini mission having failed, Rome waited until 1893 to act in this matter, and then erected an apostolic delegation.

Bibliography: J. F. CONNELLY, *The Visit of Archbishop Bedini to the United States of America* (Rome 1960).

[J. F. CONNELLY]

BEDJAN, PAUL

Missionary and Orientalist; b. Khusrawi, Iran, Nov. 27, 1838; d. Cologne-Nippes, Germany, June 9, 1920. He studied at the minor seminary of the French Vincentians in Khusrawi (1850–56), changed from the CHALDEAN to the Latin rite, and entered the Vincentian novitiate in Paris in 1856. He was ordained May 25, 1861, and returning to northwest Persia, did missionary work in Khusrawi and Rizaiyeh until 1880. It distressed him that only Protestants were printing books in Neo-Syriac, the vernacular of his people, and he returned to Europe to devote himself thereafter to the publication of texts in Syriac (36 v., Paris 1885–1912). Some of these were popular works of religious devotion, his own compositions or translations into Neo-Syriac, but most were carefully prepared editions of ancient Syriac texts based on MSS of libraries and museums in Europe and the Near East. With the approval of the Holy See, which made him a consultor on the Congregation of the Propaganda in 1886, he printed a new edition of the Breviary for priests of the Chaldean rite (3 v., 1886–87), but the Chaldean patriarch of Mosul, Abp. Elias Abolionan, rejected the Missal he had likewise prepared because of its innovations. Noteworthy are Bedjan's editions of the *Acts of Martyrs and Saints of the East* (7 v., 1890–97), the *Sermons of Jacob of Sarûg* (5 v., 1905–10), and the *Book of Heraclides of Damascus* (1910), an authentic but then unknown writing by NESTORIUS.

Bibliography: F. COMBALUZIER, *Dictionnaire d'histoire et de géographie ecclésiastiques* (Paris 1912–) 7:410–413. A. RÜKER, *Kulture* 31 (1912) 200–208. J. M. VOSTÉ, ''Paul Bedjan, le lazariste persan,'' *Orientalia Christiana periodica* 11 (1945) 45–102.

[L. F. HARTMAN]

BEDÓN, PEDRO

Ecuadorian Dominican painter and social worker; b. Quito, *c.* 1555; d. there, Feb. 27, 1621. Bedón was the son of the Asturian Pedro Bedón and Juana Díaz de Pineda of Quito, daughter of the conquistador and scribe, Gonzalo Díaz de Pineda. Bedón studied philosophy in Quito under professors who had come from the University of San Gregorio in Valladolid. He studied theology at the University of Lima, where he learned the art of painting under the Jesuit brother Bernardo BITTI. Returning to Quito in 1587, he taught philosophy and theology at the Dominican school. He devoted his free time to social service, through the Confraternity of the Rosary, which he organized with Spanish, Indian, and African American members. In addition, he founded a school of painting for the Indians, whom he put to work making copies of choral books with beautiful initial letters. He raised the question of the legality of the sales taxes and as a result was forced to go to Bogotá and soon afterward to Tunja. In both cities he left examples of his artistic skill. At Bogotá he held the chair of theology. In 1596 he returned to Quito, where he resumed his scholarly career and his social apostolate. He founded the convent of Riobamba and of La Recoleta in Quito, and one in Ibarra. Elected provincial, he traveled about the cities of the *audiencia,* examining not only the religious establishments but also the situation of the Indians. On behalf of the Indians, he negotiated with the authorities with a zeal worthy of LAS CASAS. Bedón is one of the most important representatives of Ecuadorian culture and of the social apostolate. He is considered the father of painting in Quito.

Bibliography: J. M. VARGAS, ''El venerable padre maestro fray Pedro Bedón, O.P.: Su vida, sus escritos,'' *El Oriente Dominicano* 8 (1935) 115–117.

[J. M. VARGAS]

BEDYLL, THOMAS

Clerk of Privy Council; b. unknown; d. London?, Sept. 1537. He received his education at New College, Oxford, and became secretary to William WARHAM, Archbishop of Canterbury, remaining in his service until the archbishop's death in August of 1532. He was then appointed clerk of the Privy Council. As such, he was engaged in securing the support of Oxford University for HENRY VIII's proposed divorce from CATHERINE OF ARAGON. When in May of 1533, Archbishop CRANMER declared the marriage invalid, Bedyll, who was present, wrote Thomas CROMWELL expressing his approval of the decision and assuring him that it would ''please the King's Grace very well.'' Throughout the next two years, he was occupied in administering the oath supporting the royal supremacy, in various religious communities. In 1536, after the trials of John FISHER and Thomas MORE, in which he had participated, Bedyll made a series of visits to confiscated monastery lands and was then appointed to a committee considering the validity of certain papal bulls. Bedyll's only surviving works are his letters that, despite his later change of allegiance, show him to have been on moderately friendly terms with More and ERASMUS in his youth.

Bibliography: P. HUGHES, *The Reformation in England* (New York 1963). C. T. MARTIN, *The Dictionary of National Biography from the Earliest Times to 1900* (London 1885–1900) 2:120–121. *The Epistles of Erasmus,* ed. F. M. NICHOLS, 3 v. (New York 1962).

[J. G. DWYER]

The Beecher family: Lyman sitting (center), Henry Ward standing (extreme right), Harriet sitting (second from right). Vintage photograph by Mathew Brady.

BEECHER

A prominent New England family headed by Lyman Beecher, whose 13 children included the well-known Harriet Beecher Stowe and Charles, Edward, Thomas, Catherine, and Henry Ward Beecher.

Lyman, Congregational preacher and first president of Lane Theological Seminary in Cincinnati, Ohio; b. New Haven, Conn., Oct. 12, 1775; d. Brooklyn, N.Y., Jan. 10, 1863. He was born just a year before the Declaration of Independence, and he died just after Lincoln's Emancipation Proclamation. During his undergraduate days at Yale University, New Haven, Conn., he was strongly influenced by its Pres. Timothy DWIGHT and became an ardent exponent of revivals, especially during his third pastorate (1826) at the newly organized Hanover Street Church in Boston, Mass. His earlier pastoral experience had been obtained at the Presbyterian Church at Easthampton, N.Y. (1799), and the Congregational Church at Litchfield, Conn. (1810). Beecher, a colorful personality, became famous for his sermons against dueling, intemperance, infidelity, disestablishmentarianism, and slavery. His *Six Sermons on Temperance* (1825) underwent several editions and translations. In 1832, with Dr. Leonard Bacon, Beecher formed an American Anti-Slavery Society, which focused the interest of churches on the antislavery movement. Although prosecuted for "heresy, slander, and hypocrisy," he was eventually cleared by his Synod, most of whom had "Old School" sympathies. His seven sons entered the ministry, and his two daughters became famous authors. In 1871 Yale University inaugurated the annual Lyman Beecher Lectures on Preaching in his memory.

Henry Ward, Congregational preacher, journalist; b. Litchfield, Conn., June 24, 1813; d. Brooklyn, N.Y., March 8, 1887. In 1834 he graduated from Amherst College, Mass., and entered Lane Theological Seminary, Cincinnati, Ohio. After pastorates near Cincinnati and in Indianapolis, Ind., he was called (1847) to the Plymouth Congregational Church of Brooklyn, N.Y., and preached there with unremitting zeal for 40 years. Accused of dallying with the affections of Elizabeth Tilton, wife of his good friend Theodore Tilton, who had succeeded him as editor of the *Independent,* he successfully weathered "the great scandal" of the 1870s and retained his position and influence. He was intensely opposed to slavery, favored woman suffrage, and supported the theory of evolution. In 1870 he became editor of the *Christian*

Union. As the most eloquent preacher of his day, he attracted thousands by his dramatic, warm, and Christocentric Gospel message. His published works include *The Life of Jesus the Christ* (1871) and *Evolution and Religion* (1885).

Bibliography: L. ABBOTT et al., *Henry Ward Beecher* (new ed. Hartford 1887). L. BEECHER, *Autobiography, Correspondence, etc.*, ed. C. BEECHER, 2 v. (New York 1864). R. SHAPLEN, *Free Love and Heavenly Sinners* (New York 1954).

[J. R. WILLIS]

BEELEN, JAN THEODOOR

Exegete and Orientalist; b. Amsterdam, Holland, Jan. 12, 1807; d. Louvain, Belgium, March 31, 1884. He made higher studies in Rome, where he received the doctorate in theology, and in 1836 he was appointed professor of Sacred Scripture and Oriental languages at the Catholic University of Louvain. In 1876 he relinquished his position to his pupil, T. J. Lamy. He was the author of many biblical works; his commentary on the Epistle to the Romans (Louvain 1854) was held in high regard. He also published works in the field of Oriental scholarship, including a useful *Chrestomathia rabbinica et Chaldaica* (3 v. Louvain 1841–43). He revived Oriental studies in Belgium, where he established an Oriental printing plant, for which he purchased complete fonts of Hebrew, Syriac, Arabic, and Ethiopic type. He was made domestic prelate of the pope, consultor of the Congregation of the Index, honorary canon of Liège, and Knight of the Order of Leopold.

Bibliography: F. BECHTEL, *The Catholic Encyclopedia*, ed. C. G. HERBERMANN et al. (New York 1907–14) 2:388. O. REY, *Dictionnaire de la Bible* (Paris 1895–1912) 1.2:1542–43.

[M. C. MCGARRAGHY]

BEELZEBUL

Beelzebul is a name used in the New Testament for "the prince of DEMONS" (Mt 12.24; Lk 11.15). The enemies of Jesus said that He was possessed by Beelzebul (Mk 3.24), that He was Beelzebul in person (Mt 10.25), and that it was by the power of Beelzebul that He cast out demons (Mt 12.24–26; Lk 11.15, 18–19). Although Beelzebub, rather than Beelzebul, appears in older Catholic translations of the Bible, Beelzebub is found only in the Latin and the Syriac versions; almost all the Greek manuscripts have Βεελζεβούλ (Beelzebul). The New American Bible (1970) has Beelzebul, reflecting the orthography of the Greek manuscripts. A comparison of Mt 12.24 with Mt 12.26 shows that this name, whatever its correct form may have been, was used interchangeably with that of SATAN or the DEVIL. Since both Satan in Hebrew (*śāṭān*) and devil in Greek (διάβολος) have the meaning of adversary, accuser, and slanderer, the peculiar Gospel name for the same evil spirit may rightly be surmised to have the same meaning. The form Beelzebub cannot be disconnected from the Aramaic word *bᵉʿ el-dᵉbābā,* which has precisely the same meaning as the above-mentioned Hebrew and Greek words (i.e., adversary, accuser, Satan) and is itself a loanword from the Akkadian term *bêl dabābi* (literally "master of speech," but in usage, "litigant, adversary in a lawsuit"). Both Beelzebub (Baal-Zebub) and Beelzebul (Baal-Zebul) draw upon divine epithets for non-Israelite deities. The explanations, in the Masoretic text, of Beelzebub (Baal-Zebub) to mean "lord of the flies" or "lord of the dung" reflect popular etymologies. If they are ancient, they would express Israelite disparagement of the Philistine deity of Ekron (2 Kgs 1:2–16) or of the Satan, the adversary in the heavenly court. Beelzebul probably means "lord of the temple" or "lord of the dwelling." It is likely that *zᵉbûl* in this term meant "dwelling, temple" (cf. Is 63.15; 1 Kgs 8.13), or it is to be connected with the Ugaritic word *zbl,* meaning prince, ruler. The rendering of *ba'al zᵉbûl* as Βεελζεβούβ (Beelzebub) by the Septuagint and Symmachus was probably due to its phonetic resemblance with the Aramaic word for Satan.

Bibliography: J. SCHNACKENBURG, *Lexikon für Theologie und Kirche,* ed. J. HOFER and K. RAHNER, 10 v. 2d, new ed. Freiburg 1957–65) 2:97. *Encyclopedic Dictionary of the Bible,* tr. and adap. by L. HARTMAN (New York 1963) 218. W. FOERSTER, in G. KITTEL, *Theologisches Wörterbuch zum Neuen Testament* (Stuttgart 1935–) 1:605–606.

[M. R. RYAN/EDS.]

BEESLEY, GEORGE, BL.

Priest, martyr; b. *c.* 1563 at The Hill in Goosnargh (Goosenoor) parish, Lancashire, England; d. July 2, 1591, hanged, drawn, and quartered on Fleet Street in London. As with the scions of many ancient Catholic families of England, he was sent to Rheims, where he was ordained in 1587. On Nov. 1, 1588, he returned to his native land, where he labored primarily in London and in the north of England. He was a strong, robust young man when captured by Topcliffe late in 1590, but reduced to a skeleton by torture. He endured all with invincible courage and could not be induced to betray his fellow Catholics. His last words were *"Absit mihi gloriari nisi in cruce Domini nostri Jesu Christi"* and, after a pause, "Good people, I beseech God to send all felicity." Beesley was beatified by Pope John Paul II on Nov. 22, 1987 with George Haydock and Companions.

Feast of the English Martyrs: May 4 (England)

See Also: ENGLAND, SCOTLAND, AND WALES, MARTYRS OF.

Bibliography: R. CHALLONER, *Memoirs of Missionary Priests,* ed. J. H. POLLEN (rev. ed. London 1924). J. H. POLLEN, *Acts of English Martyrs* (London 1891).

[K. I. RABENSTEIN]

BEETHOVEN, LUDWIG VAN

German composer; b. Bonn, Jan. 15 or 16, 1770; d. Vienna, March 26, 1827. The composer's grandfather, Louis van Beethoven, had been Kapellmeister in the chapel of the archbishop elector of Bonn (1761); his father, Johann, a member of the electoral chapel choir until 1789, was a teacher of clavier and violin. In 1767 Johann had married Maria Magdalena Laym; three children of this marriage survived infancy: Ludwig, Caspar Anton Karl (b. 1774), and Nikolaus Johann (b. 1776). In 1787 Maria Magdalena died; two years later Johann van Beethoven, for whom life had never been very smooth, was dismissed from his position. Thus at the age of 19 his son Ludwig was in fact the head of a family, with two younger brothers to support and guide.

Early Years. He had given early evidence of his musical talent, and, although his first music teachers were not particularly distinguished, Beethoven did have the opportunity sometime about 1781 to study under a competent composer, Christian Gottlob Neefe, who was organist at the electoral court. Under his tutelage Beethoven studied Bach and other composers so well that at the age of 12 he was permitted, in Neefe's absence, to supervise orchestra rehearsals for the court theater. At 14 he was appointed assistant court organist. In 1788 while still serving as organist, Beethoven was also playing viola in the orchestra for operatic performances at the court; this position helped him become familiar with operas by the leading composers of the day—Mozart, Cimarosa, Paisiello, Gluck, and others.

It is possible that Beethoven may have met Mozart in 1787, and had a few lessons in composition from him. He may have met Haydn in 1790; at any rate, Haydn, impressed by an original composition Beethoven had written, brought the young man to Vienna (1792) to continue his study of composition under him. These lessons ended sometime before early 1794. Among others with whom Beethoven studied were Albrechtsberger, known for his sacred music and his theoretical work on counterpoint; Johann Schenk, a composer of Singspiele; and Antonio Salieri, Kapellmeister at the Viennese court and a composer of Italian operas. The association with Salieri continued until 1802.

Ludwig van Beethoven.

In 1798 and 1799 Beethoven became aware of increasing difficulty in hearing. Doctors and treatments could not help him, and the inexorable progress of his deafness caused that great spiritual crisis that is reflected in the "Heiligenstadt Testament," a letter Beethoven wrote to his brothers in 1802.

Personal Traits. Beethoven seems to have been extremely careless about his physical appearance; he certainly was absentminded. As his hearing grew worse, he became more and more moody and irritable. He appears never seriously to have lacked money; his compositions, however much they may have been misunderstood by his contemporaries, were evidently very much appreciated. Beethoven's income had been derived from playing the piano before his deafness cut off this source of revenue; he also taught, and derived further income from dedicating works for a fee, and from the sale of rights to his compositions. In these negotiations he seems often to have been deplorably unscrupulous, selling the same rights to different persons at the same time. From 1809 on he received an annuity provided by the Archduke Rudolph, Prince Lobkowitz, and Prince Kinsky. Freed in these ways from economic and patronal pressure, Beethoven was able to compose his music to please no demands but those of his own genius.

In Bonn he was in the service of the archbishop, and among the dedications of his compositions there are several to the Archduke Rudolph, Beethoven's patron and former pupil who became archbishop of Olmütz in 1820. He was generous with his services for charity and more than once permitted his music to be used at a concert for the benefit of an Ursuline convent school at Graz.

Beethoven's relationships with his family were unhappy. He never married, and the two younger brothers, whose guardian he had become at 19, both made marriages of which he disapproved. His brother Caspar died in 1815, and Beethoven was declared sole legal guardian of Caspar's son, Karl (1819). The youth, who did not respond well to Beethoven's well-intentioned but often misplaced efforts, attempted suicide in 1826. Beethoven's relations with his youngest brother, Nikolaus Johann, were complicated by the composer's dislike for Nikolaus's wife. It was after a visit to their home with Karl in 1826, that, on the trip back to Vienna, he fell ill, and died several months later, after receiving the last rites of the Church.

His Music. Among his compositions are nine symphonies, 11 overtures, various concerti (including five for piano and one for violin), 16 string quartets and much other chamber music, 30 piano sonatas and numerous sets of variations for piano, the oratorio *Christus am Ölberg* (1802), the opera *Fidelio* (1804), and two Masses. The earlier of these, the Mass in C, Op. 86, was composed in the honor of Princess Esterhazy and was first performed on the Sunday after her name day, Sept. 13, 1807, in Eisenstadt—the same occasion and place for which in other years some of Haydn's Masses were composed. The other, the Mass in D, usually known as the *Missa solemnis,* Op. 123, was begun in 1819, and was to have been performed at the installation of the Archduke Rudolph as archbishop. The *Missa solemnis,* however, was not completed until 1823.

Beethoven's Masses, traditional in many respects, are scored for solo quartet, chorus in four parts, and orchestra. They feature word painting (rising lines on ''ascendit in caelos,'' for example), dramatic contrast (sharp difference in scoring, dynamics, and rhythm between the phrases ''Gloria in excelsis Deo'' and ''et in terra pax''), standard devices for setting certain words (rests between repetitions of the word ''non''), and the use of instrumental forms in some movements. These characteristics of Beethoven's Masses are similar to those to be found in the works of numerous other composers of the late 18th and early 19th centuries. At times, however, the scoring in Beethoven's Masses differs from that of other Masses of the classic period. Orchestral introductions and interludes are more prominent. Great attention is paid to orchestration: there are monumental, brilliantly written *tutti* passages (e.g., ''Gloria in excelsis Deo'' in the *Missa solemnis*). There are also passages where the use of sharply reduced orchestral forces produces very impressive effects (e.g., the beginning of the Benedictus in the same Mass, where there are only two flutes and a solo violin; the middle of the Agnus Dei, with only two trumpets and tympani). The solo singers often have highly dramatic and individual lines, which would be artistically impossible for a chorus to perform. A particularly striking example of this is in the Agnus Dei of the *Missa solemnis* where each of the soloists sings ''Agnus Dei, qui tollis peccata mundi'' in the style of operatic accompanied recitative to an ominous background of trumpets, drums, and strings *tremolo.* On the other hand, Beethoven sometimes has the solo quartet sing together unaccompanied in a homophonic style, similiar to that of the chorale; this happens, for example, in the Benedictus of the Mass in C.

A composer of Masses who wishes, as Beethoven did, to compose music reflective of the rhythm and the meaning of the words, has a particular problem with the long texts. If each new idea in the text is given its own theme, the work becomes too diffuse; if each of these themes is developed, the movement can become too long. The use of some sort of refrain is one way of solving this problem. In the Gloria of the *Missa solemnis,* Beethoven creats a vigorous rising figure for the opening line which he brings back on the phrases ''laudamus te'' and ''Domine Deus,'' as well as at the end, after the fugue, with its original text.

Missa Solemnis. However, if the movements with short texts are not to be dwarfed by the others, their texts must be repeated to expand the length of the movement. For example, in Masses of the classic period, the Benedictus is often a slow lyrical movement, with many repetitions of text, in binary form. It is preceded by a Sanctus set briefly and in homophonic style, a Pleni in a terse but brilliant style—sometimes polyphonic—and an Osanna similarly set. It is followed by a second Osanna section (sometimes a literal repeat of the first) and, in some cases, by a phrase of the Benedictus and a final Osanna. This basic form is found in the Sanctus of the *Missa solemnis* and also in that of the Coronation Mass (k. 317) of Mozart. The *Missa solemnis* Sanctus differs from the earlier work most conspicuously in its length. In such late works as the *Missa solemnis,* Beethoven writes very long lines, avoiding cadences through a variety of devices, and expanding the length of movements proportionately.

The *Missa solemnis* is gigantic in length, style, and emotional range. It is true that in Bach's Mass in B minor, for example, changes in scoring, range, rhythm, and texture dramatize the text: the ''Crucifixus'' sounds tragic, the ''Et resurrexit'' jubilant. But Beethoven explores the possibilities of text expression even further; he uses the changing emotions inspired by the Mass text as impulses toward the creation of a musical expression of the text. Further, he works and reworks his ideas so that in each movement there is a strong and compelling drive from one idea to the next, and an ending that is both overwhelming and inevitable.

The *Missa solemnis* contains two ponderous and extremely complex fugues that end the Gloria and the Credo; but it also has passages of serene lyricism, such as the Benedictus. This Mass is not an objective statement of the text, but an emotional expression of it resulting from a serious and highly personal reflection on the words. Its inappropriateness for the liturgy has not prevented it from affecting many listeners quite deeply.

Bibliography: W. M. MCNAUGHT, *Grove's Dictionary of Music and Musicians*, ed. E. BLOM 9 v. (5th ed. London 1954) 1:530–595. D. F. TOVEY, *Essays in Musical Analysis,* v.1 (London 1935) 21–67. *Thayer's Life of Beethoven,* rev. and ed. E. FORBES, 2 v. (Princeton 1964). E. AGMON, ''The First Movement of Beethoven's Cello Sonata Op. 69: The Opening Solo as a Structural and Motivic Source,'' *The Journal of Musicology* 16 (1998): 394–409. C. BASHFORD, ''The Late Beethoven Quartets and the London Press, 1836–ca. 1850,'' *The Musical Quarterly* 84 (2000): 84–122. D. B. DENNIS, *Beethoven in German Politics, 1870–1989* (New Haven 1999). R. DUNN, ''The Fourth Horn in Beethoven's Ninth Symphony,'' *Journal of the Conductors' League* 17 (1996):116–120. G. THOMAS EALY, ''Of Ear Trumpets and a Resonance Plate: Early Hearing Aids and Beethoven's Hearing Perception,'' *19th Century Music* 17 (1994): 262–273. R. KAMIEN, ''Non-Tonic Settings of the Primary Tone in Beethoven Piano Sonatas,'' *The Journal of Musicology* 16 (1998): 379–393. J. PARSONS, ''*Fidelio, oder Die eheliche Liebe* (*Fidelio, or Conjugal Love*)'' In *International Dictionary of Opera* 2 vols. ed. C. STEVEN LARUE, 436–438 (Detroit 1993). L. PLATINGA, *Beethoven's Concertos: History, Style, Performance,* (New York 1999). M. SHEER, ''Dynamics in Beethoven's Late Instrumental Works: A New Profile,'' *The Journal of Musicology* 16 (1998): 358–378.

[R. STEINER]

BEGA (BEE), ST.

Irish saint, sixth and seventh centuries. Although nothing certain is known of her life, legend says that she was a daughter of an Irish king, and that, having vowed virginity, she fled Ireland rather than marry a son of the king of Norway. Her name was early corrupted to Bee. She is thought to have been the founder (*c.* 650) of St. Bees in Cumberland, England, a cell later belonging to St. Mary's York. This and other indications of the presence of her cult in the northwest of England (e.g., the name of the town and headland, St. Bees) are evidence of early Irish influence in that area. Through the centuries her life became confused with that of Heiu of Hartlepool, the first Northumbrian woman to take the veil, receiving it from AIDAN OF LINDISFARNE (d. 651). Heiu founded the monastery of Hartlepool, which was later taken over by HILDA OF WHITBY. Both Bee and Heiu must be distinguished from St. Begu, an Anglo-Saxon nun who died on Oct. 31, 681, and whose feast is Sept. 6 or Oct. 10. Begu was a nun at Hackness in Northumbria, one of the houses under Hilda, and, according to BEDE (*Eccl. Hist.* 3, 4), it was Begu who had the vision of the soul of St. Hilda being received into heaven.

Feast: Sept. 6 or Oct. 31.

Bibliography: *Acta Sanctorum* Sept. 2:694–700. C. COTTON, *Dictionnaire d'histoire et de géographie ecclésiastiques*, ed. A. BAUDRILLART et al. (Paris 1912) 7:423–424, 449–450. A. M. ZIMMERMANN, *Kalendarium Benedictinum,* (Metten 1933–38) 3:19–21. J. L. BAUDOT and L. CHAUSSIN, *Vies des saints et des bienhereux selon l'ordre du calendrier avec l'historique des fêtes* (Paris 1935–56) 10:1012–13. A. BUTLER, *The Lives of the Saints*, ed. H. THURSTON and D. ATTWATER (New York 1956) 3:498.

[E. JOHN]

BEGGA, ST.

Widow, patron of BEGUINES; d. Andenne, Dec. 17, 693. She was the daughter of Pepin of Landen and St. IDUBERGA, and the older sister of St. Gertrude of Nivelles. Begga married the nobleman Ansegis and was the mother of PEPIN THE SHORT. After becoming a widow, she founded (in 691–692) a convent at Andenne, near Namur, Belgium. The first nuns came from Nivelles and introduced Irish monastic customs. Begga's remains are preserved at Andenne; her vita was written in the late eleventh century. She is invoked for the cure of hernias and of infants' diseases. Although she has been the patroness of the Beguines since the fourteenth century, she was not their foundress.

Feast: Dec. 17.

Bibliography: Sources. J. G. DE RYCKEL, *Vita S. Beggae* (Louvain 1631). P. SMET, *Acta Sanctorum Belgii selecta,* ed. J. GHESQUIÈRE et al., 6 v. (Brussels 1783–94) 5:70–125. Literature. L. VAN DER ESSEN, *Étude critique et littéraire sur les Vitae des saints mérovingiens* (Louvain 1907) 182–186. F. BAIX, *Dictionnaire d'histoire et de géographie ecclésiastiques*, ed. A. BAUDRILLART et al. (Paris 1912) 7:441–448. A. BUTLER, *The Lives of the Saints*, ed. H. THURSTON and D. ATTWATER (New York 1956) 4:579. J. L. BAUDOT and L. CHAUSSIN, *Vies des saints et des bienhereux selon l'ordre du calendrier avec l'historique des fêtes* (Paris 1935–56) 12:504–505. É. BROUETTE, ''Le Plus ancien MS de la *Vita Beggae,*'' *Scriptorium* 16 (1962) 81–84. H. PLATELLE, *Bibliotheca sanctorum* 2:1077–78.

[É. BROUETTE]

BÉGIN, LOUIS NAZAIRE

Cardinal archbishop of Quebec, Canada; b. Lévis, Canada, Jan. 10, 1840; d. Quebec, July 18, 1925. He was the son of Charles and Luce (Paradis) Bégin. After attending the minor seminary of Quebec, he completed his studies in Europe, was ordained in Rome (1865), and received a doctorate in theology. Back in Quebec, he taught theology, held various offices at the seminary, and published several works that merited him entrance into the Royal Society of Canada. In 1888 he was appointed second bishop of Chicoutimi, where he built a bishop's palace. He was transferred to Quebec as coadjutor (1891) and became, successively, administrator (1894), archbishop (1898), and cardinal (1914). He founded 70 parishes, welcomed several religious communities to the archdiocese, and sanctioned ecclesiastical and charitable institutions, as well as the work of the newspaper *L'Action Catholique* and a famous diocesan temperance campaign. He reestablished the cathedral chapter of canons in 1915. The First Plenary Council of Canada took place (1909) during his reign.

Bibliography: L. A. PAQUET in *The Royal Society of Canada, Proceedings* (Ottawa 1926), eulogy.

[H. PROVOST]

BEGUINES AND BEGHARDS

The feminine religious movement known as the Beguines and the masculine counterpart, the Beghards, belong to the blossoming and multiplicity of the religious life that, with the *vita apostolica* as the premise for reform, accompanied urbanization and the increasing articulation of laymen in spiritual matters during the high Middle Ages. The terms ''Beguine'' and ''Beghard'' occur persistently in contemporary literature, but they are often used loosely—sometimes as abusive epithets by opponents, through confusion with doctrinal aberrations, sometimes as synonyms for kindred lay movements. Possibly originating with a Catharist tinge (*see* CATHARI), *beghini* continued to denote, in Provence, the APOSTOLICI, FRATICELLI, and Franciscan SPIRITUALS. In the Rhineland they were identified with the heretical BROTHERS AND SISTERS OF THE FREE SPIRIT. However, if their way of life had much in common with that of the penitential associations, hospital orders, and the HUMILIATI of Lombardy, as well as the THIRD ORDERS, it also looked back to recluses, CISTERCIANS, and PREMONSTRATENSIANS and forward to the DEVOTIO MODERNA. Although Beguinal convents were common in German towns, it was above all in the Low Countries that they prospered. Beghards never achieved the same prominence (*see* SPIRITUALITY OF THE LOW COUNTRIES; SPIRITUALITY, RHENISH).

Way of Life. Beguines can best be described as extra-regulars, since they occupied a position midway between monastic and lay status. Although not bound by irrevocable vows, orthodox Beguines, particularly in Flanders, Brabant, and the Diocese of Liège, partook of the instruction and examples of older monachism, chiefly Cîteaux (J. Greven), the canons regular, and eventually the friars. As *congregationes beguinarum disciplinatarum,* they exemplified popular mysticism, guided by hierarchy and sacrament. They put a premium on geographical stability as long as they owed obedience to local statutes, the superior of the Beguinage, and ecclesiastical authority. In their espousal of the common life they dwelt either in small convents, as in Germany, or in a large, walled enclosure, known as a Beguinage (e.g., in Burges, Ghent). Beguines promised to observe chastity during their sojourn in the community, but they could freely leave to marry or to engage in ordinary lay pursuits. In place of a formal vow of poverty they retained possession of house and property; they emphasized manual work, whether caritative (education, nursing) or industrial (cloth- and lace-making). Whether in temporary or permanent retreat, they sought to leaven their daily life with religious practices.

History. To underscore their quasi-religious character the women were at first called *mulieres religiosae* or *sanctae, virgines continentes,* or *dilectae Deo filiae.* The fact that the term *beguina* in its earliest appearance in the north (CAESARIUS OF HEISTERBACH in *c.* 1199 and the *Chronica regia of Cologne* in 1209) is prejorative suggests that it may be a corruption of ''Albigeois'' (J. Van Mierlo). Derivation from St. BEGGA may be dismissed as a tradition rooted in regeneration in the 17th century. Although place and date of origin cannot be determined with certainty, Lambert le Bègue (d. 1177), a reforming priest in Liège, organized what might be called proto-Beguines. The Beguinage was one answer to socioeconomic problems—the *Frauen frage*—relating to widows and unmarried women, but to associate the inmates only with the dispossessed, at least in the beginning of the movement, begs oversimplification (Grundmann). Their infirmary not only served as a hospital, but, as a foundation for the indigent, it supplemented the Holy Ghost Table. However, the Beghards or Bogards, who were often fullers, dyers, and weavers in the Flemish cloth industry, reflect wider recruitment from the lower classes. This is even more true of the vagrants in the Rhineland who, dependent on mendicancy, were wont to shout *Brod durch Gott* (''Bread for the love of God''). That the feminine religious movement continued to be the object of disparagement is evident from JACQUES DE VITRY'S vita of MARY OF OIGNIES (*Acta Sanctorum* June 4:630–84), written shortly after her death (1213). His is an eloquent description of the spirituality of the coteries at Nivelles and Oignies. In spite of attempts of LATERAN COUNCIL IV to curb the proliferation of new orders and to exact submission to an approved rule (c. 13), Jacques obtained from Pope HONORIUS III in 1216 oral approbation for the *mulieres religiosae* in France and the empire (*tam in regno quam in imperio*), as well as in the Diocese of Liège, to live together under one roof and to exhort each other to perform good works [*Ep.* 1, ed. R. B. C. Huygens, *Lettres* (Leiden 1960) 74]. The crusade preacher saw in these women an antidote to the ALBIGENSES. Pope Gregory IX's bull *Gloriam virginalem* (1233) hastened the maturing of the Beguinages. If Jacques was their patron at the papal Curia, closer to home the *beguinae clausae* could expect protection from the episcopate as well as from the counts of Flanders and the dukes of Brabant. While they enjoyed in Paris the all-encompassing endowment for which King Louis IX was renowned, Rutebeuf included them in his vast indictment of ''pseudoreligious.''

Beguines continued to be suspected of heretical inclinations, and the brief career of Margaret Porete (d. 1310) or Bloemardinne of Brussels (d. 1336) seemed to substantiate the charges. But it was the Beguines and Beghards in Cologne and Strasbourg who gave the gravest concern. After many tentative steps at discipline, Henry II of Virnebourg, Archbishop of Cologne (1306–32), took action against the Beghards in 1307. But it remained for the two Clementine decrees, *Cum de quibusdam mulieribus* and *Ad nostrum qui desideranter,* promulgated at the Council of VIENNE in 1311, together with reenactments by JOHN XXII, to focus attention on the Beguine-Beghard issue and to enlist papal support in the efforts of the episcopate to crush heretical confraternities. Yet CLEMENT V had added a saving clause when he exempted the orthodox communities in the West from persecution. In his bull *Racio recta non patitur* (1318) John XXII acknowledged that many Beguines led a life in obedience beyond reproach and therefore should be tolerated. This statement was supplemented the following year by the bull *Sacrosancta romana,* which put the *beguinae clausae* of Brabant, together with their property, under papal protection. The sporadic prosecution of the extraregulars in the Rhineland during the 14th century was thus paralleled by the rehabilitation of those in Belgium and their incorporation into the ecclesiastical fabric through closer identification with approved religious orders, adoption of the Rule of St. AUGUSTINE, and parochial organization.

Modern Era. After a period of decay the 17th century witnessed a reform that assured the Beguinages fresh vitality. Although hard pressed during the French Revolution, Belgian Beguinages have continued to the present day to maintain something of the rich heritage of medieval spirituality. Beguine literary figures included the Flemish BEATRICE OF NAZARETH and the poetess HADEWIJCH (fl. 1240), and the German MECHTILD OF MAGDEBURG. To the Beguines and Beghards in Strasbourg Meister ECKHART delivered sermons.

Beguine nuns. (©Hulton-Deutsch Collection/CORBIS)

Bibliography: J. GREVEN, *Die Anfänge der Beginen: Ein Beitrag zur Geschichte der Volksfrömmigkeit und des Ordenswesens im Hochmittelalter* (Münster 1912); ''Der Ursprung des Beginenwesens,'' *Historisches Jahrbuch der Görres-Gesellschaft* 35 (1914) 26–58, 291–318. L. J. M. PHILIPPEN, *De Begijnhoven: Oorsprong, Geschiedenis, Inrichting* (Antwerp 1918). J. VAN MIERLO, *Dictionnaire d'histoire et de géographie ecclésiastiques*, ed. A. BAUDRILLART et al. (Paris 1912–) 7:426–41, 457–73; *Dictionnaire de spiritualité ascétique et mystique. Doctrine et histoire*, ed. M. VILLER et al. (Paris 1932–) 1:1341–52. F. VERNET, *ibid.* 1329–41. D. PHILLIPS, *Beguines in Medieval Strasburg: A Study of the Social Aspect of Beguine Life* (Stanford 1941). A. MENS, *Oorsprong en betekenis van de Nederlandse Begijnen en Begardenbeweging, Vergelijkende Studie: XIIde–XIIIde Studie* (Louvain 1947). E. W. MCDONNELL, *Beguines and Beghards in Medieval Culture, with Special Emphasis on the Belgian Scene* (New Brunswick, N.J. 1954). R. MANSELLI, *Spirituali e Beghini in Provenza* (*Istituto Storico Italiano per il Medio Evo. Studi Storici* 31–34; Rome 1959), E. G. NEUMANN, *Rheinisches Beginen- und Begardenwesen* (Meisenheim am Glan 1960). H. GRUNDMANN, *Religiöse Bewegungen im Mittelalter* (2d ed. Hildesheim 1961). G. KOCH, *Frauenfrage und Ketzertum im Mittelalter* (Berlin 1962).

[E. W. MCDONNELL]

BEHEIM, LORENZ

Humanist; b. Nürnberg, Germany, *c.* 1457; d. Bamberg, Germany, April 11, 1521. He studied theology, first in Ingolstadt and then at the University of Leipzig, where he obtained the degree of *magister artium.* He moved to Italy in 1480, where he obtained a doctorate in Canon Law. For 22 years he was in the service of Cardinal Rodrigo Borgia, the future Pope ALEXANDER VI, and had contact also with his son Cesare BORGIA. He held various posts in the Curia, and in 1505 he joined the chapter of St. Stephan in Bamberg. During his stay in Rome he transcribed, in a collection of Roman epigraphs, the inscriptions under the frescoes of Pinturicchio (d. 1513) that commemorate the main events of the pontificate of Alexander VI, thus preserving descriptions of masterpieces that have since been destroyed.

Bibliography: *Allgemeine deutsche Biographie* (Leipzig 1875–1910) 2:276. F. GREGOROVIUS, *History of the City of Rome in the Middle Ages,* tr. A. HAMILTON, 8 v. in 13 (London 1894–1902). K. PILZ, *Neue deutsche Biographie* (Berlin 1953–) 1:794. E. REICKE, ''Der Bamberger Kanonikus L. Behaim, Pirckheimers Freund,'' in *Forschungen zur Geschichte Bayerns* 14 (1906) 1–40. H. ROSENFELD, *Lexikon für Theologie und Kirche* (Freiburg 1957–65) 2:124.

[M. MONACO]

BEING

Being (Lat. *ens, esse;* Gr. τὸ ὄν, εἶναι) may be defined as what is; that which exists; REALITY. The term ''being'' signifies a CONCEPT that has the widest extension and the least comprehension. Being is the first thing grasped by the human INTELLECT, but it is also the principal interest of the philosopher in his capacity as metaphysician. It is necessary, therefore, to distinguish being as what everybody first knows from being as the subject of METAPHYSICS. Generally speaking, the transition from the former to the latter is made in virtue of the recognition that not every being is sensible and material. No attempt can be made here to trace the history of philosophical doctrines concerning being (*see* EXISTENCE; PARMENIDES; PLATO; ARISTOTLE; PLOTINUS; PROCLUS; HEGEL, GEORG WILHELM FRIEDRICH; BERKELEY, GEORGE; KANT, IMMANUEL). The emphasis here is on the teaching of St. THOMAS AQUINAS.

Being as what is first known. Being is the first concept the human mind forms; that is, if one knows anything at all he knows being. The concept of being is not simply chronologically prior to all others; it is also analytically prior, insofar as every subsequent concept is some modification of this first concept. This does not mean, of course, that ''being'' is the first word uttered by a child. Man's first concept formed on the basis of sense experience of the things of this world is of something there, what is, being; it is involved in every other concept and is a latent content of the meaning of the first word he employs. Intellectual life begins in dependence on sense experience, since the mind comes into play in an effort to understand what has been seen, heard, tasted, smelled, or felt. The recognition of the ''thereness'' of what is so sensed underlies the formation of the concept of what exists, what is there, what is present to the senses. This does not mean that to be is to be perceived (*esse est percipi*), as was proposed by BERKELEY, but that what is first called being is what is sensed. Things do not exist because they are sensed; rather they can be sensed because they exist.

The concept of what is, of what is there, thus enables the mind to embrace in a confused and universal manner whatever can be grasped by the senses. We can see from this why the concept of being is said to tell us the least about anything, but something of everything. As the first concept and the commencement of the intellectual life, it could hardly be otherwise. Man attains a more exact and precise knowledge the more he recognizes how one being differs from another. Being as first conceived is not the knowledge of the sensible singular as such, nor is it the knowledge of something apart from sensible singulars. The universality of the concept is in consequence of the way in which sensible things are grasped intellectually.

Being as the subject of metaphysics. Being as being is the subject of metaphysics. As the very name of this science indicates, it is after or beyond (μετά) the PHILOSOPHY OF NATURE (φυσικά), which is concerned with material and changeable being. If there were no immaterial beings, there would be no need for a science beyond natural philosophy. But if immaterial beings exist and if this is known, it becomes of interest to investigate the properties or characteristics and causes of being, not as material and mobile, but precisely as being. For reasons indicated below, this cannot mean that metaphysics is concerned with immaterial beings as a realm of entities other than physical entities; it particularly does not mean that God is the subject of metaphysics. Before these assertions can be justified, however, we must inquire into the various meanings of being.

Meanings of being. An investigation of the ways in which being is employed in philosophy will clarify the content of the first concept of the intellect as well as the subject of metaphysics.

Being and Essence. The term ''being'' sometimes designates positive being, sometimes propositional being (*ens ut verum*) and logical being. Consider the following statements: (1) Peter is; (2) Uncle Sam needs you; (3) Definitions abound. Only the subject of (1) can be said to be without qualification; it signifies positive or extramental being. Uncle Sam exists in the sense that he can figure in statements like (2), for if we asked where he could be found the reply would be that he does not "really" exist. So too, logical entities like DEFINITION—as in (3)— SPECIES, and the like, do not enjoy extramental existence. Thus, if there is a sense in which mythical or fictional as well as logical entities exist, in the full sense of the term they do not exist and are not beings. Only what enjoys positive or extramental existence has an ESSENCE, meaning by essence that whereby something can exist in the real order (*see* ESSENCE AND EXISTENCE). Since the concern of the metaphysician is with positive being, with what enjoys existence independently of man's knowing, he is concerned with whatever has essence.

Substance and Accident. All real or positive beings, however, do not have essence in the same sense. Although essence is that whereby real being has existence, men, MOTION, colors, and sizes do not exist in the same manner. Motion, color, and size exist as modifications of a more basic type of existent; their mode of being is one of inherence, of being in a subject. A man, on the other hand, does not exist in a subject. Rather he is a subject in which motion, color, and size inhere in order to enjoy the mode of existence that is theirs. In short, the kind of being that has essence, positive or real being, is subdivided into two types, substantial and accidental being, and essence means either that whereby a SUBSTANCE exists or that whereby an ACCIDENT exists. The doctrine of the CATEGORIES of being is founded on this distinction.

Primary and Secondary Senses. If both substance and accident are instances of real being, the term "being" is not predicated of them equally. Substance is what is chiefly and obviously meant by "what has essence" and "what exists extramentally"; accident is rather *in* what exists—it is a modification of what *is* in a more fundamental sense. The meaning of being as applied to accident therefore incorporates the meaning that is predicated directly of substance. In a precise sense, when predicated of accident, being takes on a secondary meaning. Thus Socrates, a dog, and a tree are said to be and to have essence in a primary and direct sense, while the activities of such beings, their colors and sizes, are said to "be" in the secondary sense that they exist in such beings as Socrates, a dog, and a tree.

Analogy of Being. That being is predicated unequally of substance and accident is emphasized in the traditional tenet that being is not a GENUS. A simple way of stating the grounds for this tenet follows: If being were a genus, substance and accident would have to differ in something other than being; but only NONBEING is other than being, and for substance and accident to differ in nonbeing is no difference at all (cf. Thomas Aquinas, *In 3 meta.* 8.433). Since being is not a genus, it cannot be predicated univocally of substance and accident. (A term is predicated univocally when said of several things with exactly the same meaning; it is predicated equivocally when said of several things with wholly different meanings; and it is predicated analogically when said of several things with meanings that are neither exactly the same nor wholly different.) Being is predicated analogically of substance and accident because its meaning as said of accident includes its meaning as said of substance, but not conversely. (*See* ANALOGY.)

Transcendental attributes of being. The division of being into substance and accident gives rise to words whose scope is less than that of being itself. For example, while every substance is a being, not every being is a substance. There are other terms, however, whose range and scope are equal to those of being itself. Since what they mean transcends the division into categories, they are called transcendental attributes of being. Their predicable community equaling that of being, these transcendental terms are common in just the way being itself is, namely, analogically. That is, their meaning may vary as they are predicated of different categories, but there is a controlling or focal meaning which gives proportional unity to their diversity of signification (*see* TRANSCENDENTALS).

One, true, and good are examples of such transcendental attributes. Whatever *is* is undivided in itself; that is, it is one. To say of something that it is one "does not add something real to being but only the negation of division, since 'one' means only a being which is undivided. From this it is clear that one is convertible with being, since every being is either simple or composed and what is simple is neither actually nor potentially divided. What is composed does not have being so long as its parts are divided but only when they constitute the composite. Thus it is clear that for a thing to be involves indivision" (*Summa Theologiae* 1a, 11.1). The primacy of substance is strikingly clear in this analysis of St. Thomas. So too, whatever *is* is said to be true insofar as essence is a principle of INTELLIGIBILITY as well as of existence. Whatever *is* is good insofar as its existence is perfective of it. This is first and most obviously seen in the case of composed beings that result from change, for the product is the goal, term, or good aimed at by the process (*see* UNITY; TRUTH; GOOD).

Abstraction and separation. It was mentioned earlier that if all beings were material and changeable, there would be no need for a science beyond physics. Yet God, who is the immaterial and unchangeable substance *par excellence,* is not part of the subject of metaphysics. To understand this, one must compare the subject of metaphysics with those of other theoretical sciences. Two criteria for the object of a theoretical science enter into the distinction of such sciences. Given the mode of operation of the mind, the object of knowledge must be immaterial; given the demands of SCIENCE, it must be necessary, that is, unchangeable. If, then, there are formally different references to MATTER and CHANGE in the definitions of objects, we can speak of different theoretical sciences. The objects of natural science include sensible matter in their definitions, but since such science studies mobile things in terms of common characteristics, there is a certain departure from the material singular. MATHEMATICS, in this context, is said to consider things in a way in which they do not exist extramentally. The geometrician's definitions of line, plane, etc., while doubtless suggested by the sensible world, do not refer to, nor are they verified of, physical things (*see* SCIENCES, CLASSIFICATION OF).

Metaphysics is possible to the degree that scientific objects can be defined without sensible matter and that such definitions can be verified extramentally. The objects of natural science and mathematics can be attained by ABSTRACTION; they leave aside, simply do not consider, certain aspects of physical things (singularity and sensible matter, respectively), while in no way implying that things exist without the aspects left aside. The objects of metaphysics are not simply more general characterizations of physical things; rather the implication is that things exist that verify metaphysical definitions because they exist independently of matter and motion. For this reason metaphysics presupposes what are called judgments of separation; for example, the truth of such statements as ''Not all being is material and mobile'' and ''Not every substance is physical.'' Since neither of these propositions is self-evident, they must be reached, if at all, by DEMONSTRATION. When we know that some beings are immaterial, we have a warrant for a science beyond physics but unlike mathematics.

Being as Being. Metaphysics takes its rise from the recognition that there is a realm of beings, of substances, beyond the physical. Does this mean that metaphysics has God and the angels for its subject? The whole thrust of philosophy, in the traditional sense, is in the direction of natural knowledge of the divine, and yet simple substance cannot be the subject of any human science. If metaphysics is to be THEOLOGY, this can only be indirectly. The only kind of being directly accessible to man is physical being, and it is to this that he turns when he sets out to do metaphysics. ''There are some objects of theoretical science,'' St. Thomas writes, ''which do not depend upon matter in order to exist because they can exist without matter whether because they are never in matter, like God and the angels, or because they are sometimes in matter and sometimes not, like substance, QUALITY, being, POTENCY, ACT, the one and many, and so forth . . .'' (*In Boeth. de Trin.* 5.1). The second class of names enumerated by Aquinas indicates the bridge the metaphysician builds between physical substance and immaterial substance, qualities of material things and those of immaterial things, and so forth.

This effort accents what has been called the grandeur and misery of metaphysics. From the point of view of physical things, the concept of substance that the metaphysician forms seems inadequate and abstract, for he constructs a definition free of matter, and physical substance is material. From the point of view of separate substance, immaterial substance, such a concept is also representationally poor. In discussing the view of AVEMPACE, who held that in order to get concepts appropriate to immaterial things all one has to do is abstract from, or drop the material notes found in concepts of physical things, St. Thomas observes, ''This would be cogent if immaterial substances were the forms and species of material ones. . . . If this is not granted and it is assumed that immaterial substances are of a quite different definition from the QUIDDITY of material things, no matter how much our mind abstracts the quiddity of the material thing from matter, it will never arrive at something similar to immaterial substance'' (*Summa Theologiae* 1a, 88.2). He concludes that any approach to immaterial substance from material substance falls short of perfect knowledge of the former. The difficulty is that no other approach is open to man. The metaphysician has no alternative to his attempt to ''purify concepts'' so that they provide him with an indirect, analogical, and always inadequate knowledge of immaterial substance.

God and Metaphysics. Metaphysics is often called theology because its principal concern is God. Psychological reasoning shows that God cannot be the subject of metaphysics. The proportionate object of the mind is the nature of sensible being; since man has no direct knowledge of God, God can enter into human science only as related to the subject of that science. A logical argument can also be given against immaterial substance's being the subject of a science. ''Given that in any question we ask something about something, for example, we seek the cause of matter, which is the formal cause, or the cause of form being in matter, namely the end and efficient cause, it is clear that with respect to simple substances, which are not composed of matter and form, no questions are relevant. For in every question, as has been shown, something must be known and something must be sought. Such substances, however, are either wholly known or wholly unknown. . . . Hence no question can be asked concerning them and because of this there is no doctrine like that of theoretical sciences concerning them'' (*In 7 Meta.* 17.1669–70).

Being and participation. Being is what has existence: ''Being is that which finitely participates existence'' (*In lib. de caus.* 6). From a logical point of view, one speaks of a common being (*esse commune*) that is shared by substance and accident analogically. But God, too, is spoken of as *esse commune,* not as predicably common to created beings but rather as something numerically one whose CAUSALITY extends to all creatures. God as common being is conceived of as the totality of perfections only partially reflected in each creature and indeed in the sum of creatures. By means of a subtle dialectical procedure, the metaphysician compares the real hierarchy to the logical one, but whereas in the latter the highest terms express the least, in the former God is conceived as a kind of limit, comprising all perfection (*see* PERFECTION, ONTOLOGICAL). Creatures are then seen as forming a hierarchy of being that reaches from the highest angel to the least material thing. This *via descensus,* which is considered the Platonic component of the Thomistic synthesis, is currently being explored and providing a deepening understanding of the achievement of Aquinas. In his metaphysics, Thomas is seen as the heir not only of ARISTOTELIANISM, but also of Proclus, PSEUDO-DIONYSIUS, and JOHN SCOTUS ERIGENA (*see* PARTICIPATION).

See Also: METAPHYSICS; ESSENCE; EXISTENCE; CATEGORIES OF BEING.

Bibliography: R. M. MCINERNY, *The Logic of Analogy* (The Hague 1961). J. BOBIK, ''Some Disputable Points Apropos of St. Thomas and Metaphysics,'' *The New Scholasticism* 37 (1963): 411–430. E. H. GILSON, *Being and Some Philosophers* (2d ed., Toronto 1952). J. MARITAIN, *A Preface to Metaphysics: Seven Lectures on Being* (New York 1945). T. C. O'BRIEN, *Metaphysics and the Existence of God* (Washington 1960). C. FABRO, *Partecipazione e causalita secondo S. Tommaso d'Aquino* (Turin 1960). B. MONTAGNES, *La Doctrine de l'analogie de l'être d'après saint Thomas d'Aquin* (Louvain 1963).

[R. M. MCINERNY]

BEK, ANTHONY

Bishop of Durham and titular patriarch of Jerusalem; b. *c.* 1240; d. Eltham, Kent, England, March 3, 1311. He and his brother Thomas (d. 1293), later bishop of SAINT DAVIDS, were sons of a Lincolnshire baron and were students at the University of OXFORD by 1267. Even before that time, however, Anthony Bek had begun his career in the royal service, which was to bring him from lowly messenger under HENRY III to chancellor of the realm briefly in 1274 under EDWARD I. He was one of the three principal councilors of Edward I and was frequently used by Edward on diplomatic missions. Although he fell into disfavor in 1297, Bek was again shown signs of royal favor by EDWARD II upon his accession in 1307. The suggestion of Edward I to the monks of DURHAM CATHEDRAL in 1283 that they elect Bek to the vacant bishopric was taken up readily by a chapter deep in dispute with the archbishop of YORK, their METROPOLITAN. Ironically enough, by asserting his right of VISITATION of the priory in 1300, Bek occasioned a dispute that lasted more than five years and saw appeals and counterappeals to the court of Rome. As temporal ruler of the palatinate of Durham, Bek urged its rights with vigor and ambition, but as a bishop he enjoyed a reputation for magnanimity and chastity among his contemporaries. Pope CLEMENT V named him patriarch of Jerusalem in 1305, but he was never able to assume the administration of the see, for the Latins had been expelled more than a century before. His body was buried in the east end of Durham Cathedral near the tomb of St. CUTHBERT OF LINDISFARNE.

Bibliography: *Records of Antony Bek, Bishop and Patriarch, 1283–1311,* ed. C. M. FRASER (London 1953). R. BRENTANO, *York Metropolitan Jurisdiction and Papal Judges Delegate, 1279–1296* (Berkeley 1959). M. CREIGHTON, *The Dictionary of National Biography from the Earliest Times to 1900* (London 1885–1900) 2:134–136. A. B. EMDEN, *A Biographical Register of the University of Oxford to A.D. 1500* (Oxford 1957–59) 1:151–152. C. M. FRASER, *A History of Antony Bek, Bishop of Durham, 1283–1311* (Oxford 1957). R. K. RICHARDSON, ''The Bishopric of Durham under Anthony Bek, 1283–1311,'' *Archaeologia Aeliana,* 3d ser., 9 (1913) 89–229. A. H. THOMPSON, *Dictionnaire d'histoire et de géographie ecclésiastiques* (Paris 1912–) 7:485–489.

[F. D. LOGAN]

BEKYNTON, THOMAS (BECKINGTON)

Reforming bishop, royal official, English humanist; b. Beckington, near Frome, Somerset, England; d. Wells, Jan. 14, 1465. Nothing is known of his parentage. He was admitted to Winchester College (1404) and to New College, Oxford (June 24, 1406), where he was a fellow (1408–20). He incepted as doctor of civil law (1418) and was subwarden (1419). There he probably attracted the notice of Humphrey, duke of Gloucester, whom he served (1420–*c.* 1438), principally as chancellor. As Gloucester's protégé, he quickly became an ecclesiastical pluralist. About 1438 he was appointed King HENRY VI's secretary, beginning four years of continuous royal service. He was one of the diplomats with Cardinal Henry BEAUFORT at Calais (1439) and led the abortive but lengthy Armagnac marriage negotiations at Bordeaux (1442–43). He was a valuable supporter of Henry's educational foundations, Eton College and King's College, Cambridge. While still in the royal service, as keeper of the privy seal (1443–44), he was appointed bishop of BATH AND WELLS, being consecrated on Oct. 13, 1443. Soon out of the royal service, he resided at Wells, where he proved an able and energetic administrator, making episcopal VISITATIONS of BATH ABBEY in 1449 and 1454 and of GLASTONBURY ABBEY in 1445 over the protestations of the aged abbot, Nicolas Frome, whose objections he treated with consummate contempt. His ordinances for the vicars choral of Wells (1450) are still largely in effect today. He was a munificent benefactor to Wells, where he spent some 6,000 marks on buildings, both in the cathedral precincts and in the city, where a fountain and conduit bear his name. The vicar's close that he built has been considered a splendid example of 15th-century domestic architecture.

Bekynton was a friend and correspondent of many contemporary Italian humanists such as Flavio BIONDO, who presented him with a copy of his *Decades.* In addition he encouraged younger English scholars such as Thomas Chaundler, who dedicated his Latin works to Bekynton. He changed the Latin style of diplomatic correspondence from the prolixities of previous medieval practice to the more restrained and direct Latin of the Italian humanists and so commenced a trend of humanistic Latin studies among later royal servants. What remains of his library bears eloquent testimony to his interest in theology and Canon Law and in contemporary Latin poetry and prose.

Bibliography: *Memorials of the Reign of King Henry VI. Official Correspondence of Thomas Bekynton, Secretary to King Henry VI, and Bishop of Bath and Wells,* ed. G. WILLIAMS, 2 v. (*Rerum Britannicarum medii aevi scriptores* 56; 1872), biog. in 1:xv-1viii. *The Register of T. B., Bishop . . . ,* ed. H. C. M. LYTE and M. C. B. DAWES, 2 v. (Somerset Record Society 49–50; London 1934–35). A. B. EMDEN, *A Biographical Register of the University of Oxford to A.D. 1500* (Oxford 1957–59) 1:157–159. A. JUDD, *Life of Thomas Bekynton* (Chichester 1961). *The Victoria History of the County of Somerset,* v. 2, ed. W. PAGE (London 1911). R. WEISS, *Humanism in England during the Fifteenth Century* (2d ed. Oxford 1957) 71–83, valuable refs. to works and articles on Bekynton.

[H. S. REINMUTH, JR.]

BEL

Title of the chief god of Mesopotamia. The word (Akkadian *bêl*) is a contraction of the older Semitic form *ba'al* (lord), which in West Semitic (Canaanite, etc.) retained its original form as BAAL, the Canaanite god of rain and fertility. In Babylonia the word Bel was first used as the Akkadian equivalent of Sumerian *e n* (lord) and in particular as the Akkadian name for Sumerian Enlil, the god of NIPPUR, the most sacred city of ancient Mesopotamia, where he had his main temple, the É-kur (house of the mountain). Associated with Enlil (lord of the air) were the other members of the supreme triad of the Sumerian pantheon, An or Anu (the sky) and En-ki (lord of the ground, i.e., the nether world and the subterranean waters). According to Sumerian mythology, Anu, the father of all the gods, bestowed on Enlil kingship over all the land. When HAMMURABI made Babylon the leading city of Mesopotamia, its local god MARDUK received Enlil's title of Bel, and as such took over Enlil's function as divine king of all the land; see J. B. PRITCHARD, *Ancient Near Eastern Texts Relating to the Old Testament* (2d, rev. ed. Princeton 1955) 164.

In the Bible, Deutero-Isaiah (Is 46.1) speaks of the downfall of Bel and the god NEBO (NABU); Jeremiah, too, announces the punishment inflicted on Bel by Yahweh (Jer 51.44); and Baruch ridicules Bel as a deaf and dumb idol (Bar 6.40). But the most devastating OT polemic against Bel is in Dn 14.1–22—the story of how Daniel showed that Bel's priests ate the food given to the god.

See Also: MESOPOTAMIA, ANCIENT.

Bibliography: *Reallexikon der Vorgeschichte,* ed. M. EBERT, 15 vol. (Berlin 1924–32) 2:282–390. *Encyclopedic Dictionary of the Bible,* tr. and adap. by L. HARTMAN (New York 1963), from A. VAN DEN BORN, *Bijbels Woordenboek,* 220–221.

[H. MUELLER]

BEL AND THE DRAGON

Bel and the dragon are two stories, now united as one, that constitute a deuterocanonical addition ending the Book of Daniel (Dn 14.1–42) in the Catholic canon [*see* BIBLE, III (CANON)]. The story of Bel (v. 1–22) tells how Daniel, Cyrus's court favorite, proved that the statue of BEL, i.e., MARDUK, was no true god and that the food offered it was consumed, not by the idol, as Cyrus believed, but by the priests. Through Daniel's clever detective work Cyrus was convinced, the priests were put to death, and the idol was handed over to Daniel, who destroyed it—Theodotion's text [*see* BIBLE, IV (TEXTS AND VERSIONS)] adds: "and its temple," i.e., the renowned Esagila. The story of the DRAGON (v. 23–42) tells how Daniel destroyed a living dragon (serpent?) worshiped at Babylon by feeding it cakes made from a mixture of pitch, fat, and hair, which caused it to burst asunder. The irate populace obliged the king to condemn Daniel to be thrown into a den of lions (a doublet of the story in Dn 6.2–25), where he was fed by Habacuc (Theodotion adds "the prophet"), who was brought through the air from Palestine, and where he was kept unharmed by God until his release. The king then put his accusers to death.

Both stories, in the manner of Wis 13.1–14.31, the Letter of JEREMIAH (Bar 6.1–72), and other Old Testament texts, ridicule idol worship. They were probably intended to strengthen Jewish faith against idolatry, particularly of the Babylonian type that experienced a reflorescence in the 3rd century B.C. Their popular, burlesque character explains the presence of such improbable elements as Cyrus's credulity and Habacuc's journey. Since there is no evidence of a cult of living serpents in Babylon, the dragon story may be another attack on Marduk, who was accompanied or symbolized by a dragon in the Babylonian art, and it may contain a remote reference to the myth of Marduk's victory over Tiamat (i.e., CHAOS represented as a sea monster) at creation. Preserved only in Greek, the stories were probably composed in Hebrew or Aramaic between the 3rd and 1st centuries B.C.

Bibliography: R. H. PFEIFFER, *History of N.T. Times* (New York 1949) 436–438, 455–456. F. ZIMMERMANN, "Bel and the Dragon," *Vetus Testamentum* 8 (1958) 438–440. E. D. VAN BUREN, "The Dragon in Ancient Mesopotamia," *Orientalia* 15 (1946) 1–45.

[M. MCNAMARA]

BÉLANGER, DINA, BL.

Known in religion as Marie Sainte-Cecile de Rome or Sister Cecilia, musician, mystic, religious of the Sisters of Jesus-Marie; b. Québec, Canada, April 30, 1897; d. Sillery, Québec, Sept. 4, 1929. Dina Bélanger was an accomplished pianist who received special training in Canada and New York, but unable to find satisfaction in the secular world, she desired to become totally united with God. When Dina joined the Sisters of Jesus-Marie (1920), she took the name of the Roman martyr who was the patroness of musicians, St. CECILIA. During the course of her life as a religious, Dina's devotion to the Blessed Sacrament transformed her into a woman of infectious joy despite an illness that was contracted soon after her profession. Her sanctity was also marked by a devotion to the Blessed Mother and saints, and she respected those in authority as representatives of God. Under obedience to her superiors, Dina wrote her compelling autobiography the *Canticle of Love*. Pope John Paul II beatified Dina Bélanger on March 20, 1993 because of her devotion to Jesus in the Blessed Sacrament.

Feast: Sept. 4 (Canada).

Bibliography: D. BÉLANGER, *Canticle of Love*, English tr. by M. SAINT STEPHEN (1945; reprint, Québec1984). B. GHERARDINI, *Negli abissi dell'amore: Dina Bélanger e la sua esperienza mistica; una valutazione teologica* (Rome 1991).

[K. I. RABENSTEIN]

BELARUS, THE CATHOLIC CHURCH IN

The Republic of Belarus is located in eastern Europe, and is bound on the north by Lithuania and Latvia, on the east by Russia, on the south by Ukraine and on the west by Poland. Although landlocked, it benefits from a strong agricultural region containing fertile plains, while other areas are marshy due to the runoff from several rivers. Natural resources include petroleum, peat moss and natural gas, while agricultural products consist of grains, potatoes, vegetables, sugar beets and flax. Strong livestock and dairy industries also operate in the region. Much of the country is forested.

Known previously as Belorussia (Byelorussia) or White Russia, Belarus was part of Lithuania and then Poland, before that country's conquest by Russian troops

Capital: Minsk.
Size: 80,134 sq. miles.
Population: 10,366,719 in 2000.
Languages: Belorussian, Russian.
Religions: 1,555,000 Catholics (15%), 8,293,375 Russian Orthodox (80%), 311,000 Protestants (3%), 70,000 Jews (.6%), 137,344 practice other faiths.
Archdiocese: Minsk-Mohilev, with suffragans Grodno, Pinsk, and Vitebsk.

under Catherine the Great in the late 18th century. A constituent republic of the USSR as the Belorussian Soviet Socialist Republic, the region gained its independence in 1991, following the fall of Moscow's Supreme Soviet. An authoritarian regime, elected during the country's first free elections in 1994, imposed increasing restrictions on individual and political liberty throughout the region, and by 2000 the Belarusian government was viewed internationally with increasing concern due to its growing intolerance to opposition and Western influences. Manufactured goods such as agricultural equipment, clothing and chemicals provided the basis of the region's economy, although the lack of raw materials remained problematic, forcing Belarus into an economic partnership with Russia by the late 1990s.

History. Inhabited by eastern Slavic tribes by the fifth century, the region came under the rule of Kiev from the ninth century, until that city fell to the Mongol invaders in the 1200s. Byzantine Christianity entered the region through the Vikings *c.* 1000, and had become highly influential by the 16th century. Lithuanian nobles took control of Belorussia, and it eventually became a part of the Grand Duchy of Lithuania, along with the Ukranian cities of Galicia and Kiev. During the split of the Church between Kiev and Moscow in 1459 that created the Russian Orthodox Church, Belorussia retained allegiance with Kiev and, under Kiev, Constantinople. When Lithuania merged with Poland in 1569, Poland gained Belorussia as well. During the partition of Poland in the late 18th century, Belorussia became part of the growing Russian empire under Catherine the Great and became subject to the incursions of the Russian Orthodox Church. In 1596 the Union of BREST, made between the Eastern Orthodox leaders of Belorussia and Ukraine, allowed these churches to retain their autonomy and local customs in exchange for their recognition of the authority of Rome, thus preserving them from the increasing domination of the Moscow patriarchate. From 1569 to 1680 the Belorussian Orthodox Church was transferred from Kiev to the Polish patriarchate, but as the power of the Eastern Orthodox metropolitans dwindled in the late 1600s, that leadership was usurped by the Moscow patriarchate, which thereafter claimed full authority over all Orthodox churches in Belorussia and Ukraine. By the time that it was banned in 1839 by the Russian government, the Orthodox Church counted 75 percent of Belarussians among its faithful adherents.

During the next century the Russian Orthodox Church controlled Belorussia, leaving Byzantine Catholics to worship in underground communities. A small Roman Catholic minority also existed in the country, composed mainly of Polish immigrants who had migrated to the region after the partitioning of the 18th century and were allowed to worship openly. All this would change following World War I.

In July of 1917, shortly after the Russian Revolution, a Bolshevik-led committee representing Belorussian nationalists proclaimed the region an independent republic, although its independence was short-lived. By February of 1918 the Communist support had pulled out troops in advance of incoming German/Polish forces, which set up a puppet government in Belorussia. The Polish-Soviet War that followed from 1918 to 1921 resulted in the Treaty of Riga, under which the western district was ceded to Poland and, in 1922, the eastern district became part of the USSR as the Belorussian Soviet Socialist Republic. The region was reunited in 1939 when the Soviet Union occupied the western district. In 1941 Belorussia was invaded by German troops and the war-torn years that followed witnessed a massive loss of life. In addition, thousands of Jews living in the region lost their lives after being shipped to Nazi concentration camps. Minsk was liberated from German occupation on July 3, 1944.

One of the primary goals of the new communist-controlled government was to undermine the traditional social and political order, which meant undermining the Russian Orthodox Church. Their first tact was to fragment the Church through the encouragement of breakaway sects and the introduction of Protestantism. Encouraged to increase its profile, the formerly outlawed Belorussian Orthodox Church proclaimed its independence from Moscow in July of 1922 as the Belorussian Autocephalous Orthodox Church. The Roman Catholic Church, meanwhile, adapted to the changing administration by going through a reorganization: in 1926 a papal commission authorized the formation of nine administrative regions, Mogilev-Minsk among them, each headed by an apostolic administrator. Unfortunately, as the phasing in of Communism continued, the relaxed attitude of the state that had permitted such religious proliferation and reorganization was shattered by a 1929 law banning ''religious propaganda'', and priests and other religious found themselves targets of the state through the 1930s. The Catholic apostolic administrator was imprisoned by the Soviet government, then banished from the region.

Between 1929 and 1932 most priests in the region were jailed, and the churches suppressed. In 1945 Belorussia joined the United Nations, and all ethnic Poles living in the western region, formerly part of Poland, were allowed to immigrate to their home country.

In 1986 the Chernobyl nuclear power-plant disaster shocked the world. The explosion and the resulting cover-up by the Soviet government had long-lasting repercussions for southern Belorussia, which received 70 percent of the nuclear fallout from the Ukranian-based nuclear power plant. For decades afterward, the Belorussian population experienced increased instances of cancer and other devastating disease. In 1996, a rally held in Minsk marking the tenth anniversary of the disaster turned into an anti-government march of 50,000 strong that was swiftly dispersed by local police forces. Two Eastern-rite Catholics, leaders of the march, were arrested and imprisoned, but ultimately released after a three-week hunger strike and a massive public outcry.

Break-up of USSR Creates Autonomous Church. The conflicting forces created by the break-up of the Communist system and the dissolution of the Soviet state ultimately threatened the Moscow patriarchate, which had suppressed nationalistic elements within the Soviet Orthodox sphere for many decades. In January of 1990 the bishop's council of the Russian Orthodox Church met in Moscow and decided to grant a certain measure of autonomy to the Orthodox churches in Ukraine and Belorussia. Consequently, the Belorussian Orthodox Church was made an exarchate of the Moscow patriarchate.

Following the August of 1991 coup and the fall of the Gorbachev government in Moscow, declarations of independence by Estonia, Latvia and Ukraine became a mobilizing force in Belorussia. The long-dormant stirrings of nationalism took the form of a massive general strike and the temporary suspension of the ruling Communist party. As early as July of 1990 the region declared itself a sovereign state, and the Supreme Soviet proclaimed Belarus independent on August 25, 1991. The name of the state was officially changed from the Belorussian Soviet Socialist Republic to the Republic of Belarus during the chaotic period that followed, as government restructuring began. In December of 1991, as the USSR dissolved, Belarus became a founding member of the Commonwealth of Independent States (CIS), headquartered in Minsk. A new constitution went into effect on March 30, 1994 that created a democratic government, granted freedom of religion and proclaimed the country's intention of being a non-nuclear, politically neutral state. Elected during the first free elections the following July, President Aleksandr Lukashyenko set about realigning his government with that of Russia in hopes of gaining economic advantages, a position that angered many, and signed an agreement with Russian president Boris Yeltsin to create an economic union between the two governments. Censorship of the media in the 1995 elections signaled the return to a strong central government in which political power was increasingly vested in the hands of Lukashyenko, who although not a communist was a totalitarian. By 2000 the region's planned market economy suffered due to a downturn in the Russian economy which provided the market for 70 percent of Belarus's goods.

Into the 21st Century. Belarus's transition from communism to democracy remained rocky in 2000, and restrictions on speech, the press and peaceful assembly were increasingly implemented despite the freedoms outlined in the 1995 constitution. The government effectively intimidated those who criticized its policies and personnel, while state ownership of most of the public presses guaranteed censorship of the media. In 1996 a referendum granted Lukashenko dictatorial powers, and three years later, by canceling the scheduled elections and altering the constitution, he retained the presidency.

Human rights abuses remained a major focus of the region's Catholic population, as they witnessed men and women who raised their voices in public opposition to the government either arrested and imprisoned, or reported missing. Even more tragic was the government's effort to divide the Orthodox faithful by supporting the Belorussian Orthodox Church (which was dependent on the Moscow Patriarchate) against the underground Belorussian Autocephalous Orthodox Church.

The preservation of Slav/Orthodox culture prompted several speeches by President Lukashenko in the late 1990s that rallied the government into prohibition of many Church functions, and in 1998 he pledged that Orthodoxy would be the major religion in the country. This position was reinforced by a 1996 constitutional amendment stating that the relationship between the state and religious entities be ''regulated with regard for their influence on the formation of spiritual, cultural, and country traditions of the Belarusian people.'' By refusing to register Catholic churches as legitimate, the practice of the Eastern-rite was forced underground and it was increasingly difficult for many parishes to retain ownership or even maintain church properties.

By 2000 there were 390 Roman Catholic parishes, tended by 112 diocesan and 132 religious priests. Other religious included approximately 12 brothers and 290 sisters, most of whom operated Catholic primary and secondary schools in the country and tended to the growing number of children who were tragically affected by the Chernobyl disaster. While the Roman Catholic Church benefited from tax-exempt status as a ''traditional religion'' under the constitution, it did not receive state subsidies for its work in the country, such subsidies being relegated exclusively to the Belorussian Orthodox Church controlled by Moscow. Under the leadership of Patriarchal Exarch Filaret, who was appointed at the creation of the Belorussian exarchate in 1989, the number of Orthodox parishes grew from fewer than 800 in 1995 to over 1,100 by 2000. Roman Catholicism remained the second largest religion, its faithful led by Cardinal Kazmierz Swiatek, archbishop of Minsk-Mogilev. Most Roman Catholics were of Polish ancestry and resided in the western part of the country. To avoid attracting the ire of the government, Swiatek refrained from involvement in internal political issues as much as possible, and encouraged the use of Belarusian rather than the Polish language in religious services. The Greek-rite Belorussian Autocephalus Orthodox Church continued to be banned by the government, and became increasingly associated with the Belarusian Popular Front, an opposition party.

Problems stemming from a lack of clergy were exacerbated by foreign religious—mostly from Poland—being denied work permits by the government. In addition, priests were arrested and deported with increasing regularity. 1997 saw a priest in Nyazvizh removed from his parish after his refusal to allow the government to turn his church's crypt into a museum, while in March of 2000 much-loved Polish priest Zbigniew Karoljak was arrested during a Mass in Brest for violation of visa regulations, having been denied authority to work in Belarus since 1995. Karoljak, who had worked in Belarus since 1990, was deported in June of 2000 over the objections of Archbishop Swiatek. Concurrent with his permission for the Church to open a seminary to train new priests, Lukashenko announced in 1999 that he would deny visa renewals in the future for the 130 foreign clergy then at work in the country, as well as enforce a prohibition on new foreign religious from entering. The president also publicly blamed the Roman Catholic Church's amicable relationship with the Church in neighboring Poland for his own failed efforts at improving diplomatic relations with Poland. Added to concerns resulting from the oppression of the Catholic Church were increasing worries about the rise of anti-Semitism in Belarus, as articles blaming Jews for the nation's economic woes appeared with increasing frequency in several government-controlled newspapers.

Bibliography: N. VAKAR, *Belorussia: The Making of a Nation.* P. MOJZES, *Religious Liberty in Eastern Europe and the USSR: Before and After the Great Transformation* (Boulder, CO 1992). I. LUBANCHKO, *Belorussia under Soviet Rule, 1917-1957.* J. ZAPRUDNIK, *Belarus: At a Crossroads in History.* S. P. RAMET, *Nihil Obstat: Religion, Politics, and Social Change in East-Central Europe and Russia* (Durham, NC 1998).

[P. SHELTON]

BELASYSE, JOHN

Soldier and English Catholic politician; b. Newburgh Priory, North Riding, Yorkshire, *c.* 1614; d. London, Sept. 10, 1689. It seems clear that Belasyse, second son of an ambitious country landowner of covert Catholic sympathies, conformed to Anglicanism at home, at Peterhouse, Cambridge, and while serving as Member of Parliament for Thirsk, from 1640 to 1642. During the first Civil War he emerged as a capable royalist general; he was present at the Edgehill, Newbury, Naseby, Selby, and Newark actions. He was created Baron Belasyse of Worlaby, Lincolnshire, by Charles I in 1645. His father, the first Viscount Fauconberg, eventually became a Catholic on his deathbed, but John Belasyse's nephew, the second Viscount Fauconberg, was resolutely Protestant and was married to Oliver Cromwell's daughter, Mary. After the Restoration of the monarchy in 1660, Belasyse became governor of Tangier and lord-lieutenant of the East Riding. By 1664 his refusal to take the anti-Catholic oaths of office for Tangier revealed a definite shift in his religious views, and in 1673 the House of Lords accounted him a papist. In 1678 he and four other Catholic peers were imprisoned in the Tower during the Popish Plot scare, and he was not released until the accession of James II in 1685. He was then aged and very lame. Though elevated by James to the Privy Council and made first Lord Commissioner of the Treasury, he was politically moderate and it seems played no major part in the politics of the reign.

Bibliography: V. GIBBS, ed., *The Complete Peerage* (London 1910–). J. GILLOW, *A Literary and Biographical History or Bibliographical Dictionary of the English Catholics from 1534 to the Present Time* (New York 1961) 1:178–179. F. C. TURNER, *James II* (New York 1948).

[H. AVELING]

BELAUNZARÁN, JOSÉ MARÍA DE JESÚS

Mexican bishop; b. Mexico City, Jan. 31, 1772; d. La Profesa, Mexico, Sept. 11, 1857. He received the Franciscan habit in 1789 in the monastery of Recollects of the Apostolic College of Pachuca. In 1796 he became a priest. Because he was so esteemed as a preacher, he was considered the apostle of Mexico City. Gregory XVI appointed him bishop of Linares, Monterey, on Feb. 28,

1831. Bishop Vázquez of Puebla consecrated him on November 28 in the church of San Diego in Mexico City; after that Belaunzarán undertook the visitation of his immense diocese. His active involvement in the struggle against the laws of Gómez Farías that persecuted the Church resulted in his exile from the country in 1834. Still later he made further petitions to General Santa Anna, asking for the repeal of Farías's laws, but without success. As a result of these difficulties and his failing health, he offered his resignation from the bishopric on various occasions. The third time (1839) it was accepted by Gregory XVI. Belaunzarán then withdrew to the monastery of San Francisco in Mexico City. Santa Anna bestowed on him the cross of Knight of the Order of Guadalupe and made him his honorary councilor. Among the bishops whom he consecrated was Francisco García Diego, bishop of the Californias.

Bibliography: M. CUEVAS, *Historia de la Iglesia en México,* 5 v. (5th ed. Mexico City 1946–47) 5:207. E. VALVERDE TÉLLEZ, *Bio-bibliografía eclesiástica mexicans (1821–1943),* 3 v. (Mexico City 1949) 1:159–164.

[L. MEDINA-ASCENSIO]

BELCOURT, GEORGE ANTHONY

Missionary; b. Quebec, Canada, April 22, 1803; d. Magdalen Islands, May 31, 1874. He was born of French parents. After attending the Petit Seminaire of Nicolet, Canada, he was ordained on March 10, 1827, and assigned to parish work in the District of Montreal. Four years later he accompanied Bp. Joseph Provencher to the Winnipeg-St. Boniface area, where they labored together for 17 years. Learning the native language, Belcourt compiled a Native North American dictionary and endeavored to make settled agriculturists out of the nomadic native hunters. There were frequent misunderstandings with Provencher, who could not agree that a priest should teach farming along with Christianity. When Hudson's Bay Company officials also expressed their disapproval, Belcourt was recalled to Quebec in 1848. The following year he was sent by Bp. Mathias Loras to Pembina in North Dakota. There among the native Americans he taught catechism, started schools, erected buildings, encouraged agriculture, and even accompanied them on buffalo hunts. But Belcourt again found himself unable to work successfully with other priests, and he was forced to leave the diocese in 1859. The sisters he had founded were disbanded, his buildings were neglected, and his settlement at St. Joseph (Walhalla) failed to prosper. He spent his remaining years in parishes on Prince Edward Island and the Magdalen Islands, where he lived in retirement until his death.

Bibliography: J. M. REARDON, *George Anthony Belcourt: Pioneer Catholic Missionary of the Northwest* (St. Paul 1955).

[P. ZYLLA]

BELGIUM, THE CATHOLIC CHURCH IN

Located in western Europe, the Kingdom of Belgium is bordered on the north by the NETHERLANDS and the North Sea, on the east by Germany and Luxembourg, and on the south and east by FRANCE. Brussels, the capital city, is the seat of both NATO and the European Union due to its location in the crossroads of Western Europe. The flat, coastal plains of Belgium's industrialized north rise to become rolling hills in the central region, then climb steeply as the country's southern regions encompass the deep forests of the mountainous Ardennes. Containing limited natural resources, which include coal and natural gas, Belgium relies on imports and its sophisticated transportation system to maintain its thriving industrial economy. Belgium's main exports include machinery, chemicals, and metals and metal products.

In antiquity Belgium was a part of the Roman Empire; in the Middle Ages, together with the Netherlands and Luxembourg, it became a part of the Low Countries. After passing under different dynasties, the country gradually began its unification in the 15th century, and its present frontiers date mostly from the 17th century. Belgium became an autonomous state in 1830, and was a charter member of the European Monetary Union in 1999. In 1993–94 Belgium was restructured into a federal system with three regions: Flanders, Wallonia and Brussels; with three communities: Flemish, French and German; and four linguistic areas: Dutch-, French-, German-speaking and bilingual (Dutch-French) Brussels.

The essay that follows is in two parts: Part I discusses the history of the Church in Belgium through World War II; Part II continues that history through the present.

Church History to the Modern Era

Although originally settled by the Celtic Belgae and conquered by Caesar in 57 B.C., by the 5th century Belgium had achieved a large German population due to migrations south- and eastward. Christianity entered the region—then part of Gaul—via merchants and soldiers who followed the Roman roads or descended the Rhine during these migrations. To the east, Tongeren formed a *civitas* whose first bishop was Servatius. In the western part of the country mention is made of Superior, Bishop of Bavai or CAMBRAI (*c.* 350), although Christianity in this region seems to have been effaced during the German

invasions, whereas the Church continued to exist to the east. Following the fall of the Roman Empire, Gaul reverted to the Frankish kings. CLOVIS (481–511), the first great king of the Frankish MEROVINGIAN dynasty, was baptized in 506. This led to the conversion of all his people, the FRANKS. Both Arras and Tournai had a bishop at the beginning of the 6th century, but for want of Christians, Arras was soon united with the See of Cambrai, and Tournai with that of Noyon.

Evangelization and Consolidation: 625 to 800. St. AMANDUS, a native of France, founded an abbey at Elnone *c.* 625. After converting the inhabitants of Ghent, Amandus became bishop of Tongeren and Maastricht, founded several other abbeys, and continued his evangelizing efforts in Antwerp. The region to the west was evangelized by St. ELIGIUS, Bishop of Noyon, and St. WILLIBRORD, Bishop of Utrecht, while conversions in eastern Gaul became the work of St. LAMBERT and St. HUBERT, bishops of Maastricht and LIÈGE. The present area of Belgium was completely converted *c.* 730.

From the 8th to the 10th century many rural parishes were founded. The earliest ones were PROPRIETARY CHURCHES (*Eigenkirchen*) built on the estate of the founder, who continued to be their proprietor and who could dispose of them as he saw fit. Because of the element of control—the proprietor could sell his church, cede it as a benefice, appoint the pastor, and take for himself church revenues—this system soon became corrupted.

During the Middle Ages the union of Church and State resulted in the spirit of Christianity permeating all aspects of Western culture. Frankish king and Holy Roman Emperor CHARLEMAGNE (742–814) demanded that bishops hold synods and visit their dioceses, supervised clerical training, reminded clerics of their obligation to the infirm, favored the multiplication of parishes and prescribed the payment of the tithe for the support of pastors. Through such demands, Charlemagne was instrumental in the cultural revival called the CAROLINGIAN RENAISSANCE, but by the late 9th century Norman invaders had partially depopulated the country, and had devastated the episcopal towns and abbeys that had engaged in this Christian-inspired cultural renaissance.

The Feudal Church: 900–1100. Part of German-ruled Eastern Gaul, LIÈGE became home to an imperial church, the bishop of which was made a prince-bishop by the German emperor. During the INVESTITURE struggle, Bishop WAZO OF LIÈGE (1042–48) was a principal supporter of the reformer Pope Gregory VII, although Wazo's successors would side with the emperors in their conflicts with the popes.

In the 10th century, although monastic and cathedral schools enjoyed great renown, monastic life fell into decadence, partly as a result of the Norman invasions. However, it was restored by reformers such as St. GERARD OF BROGNE, founder of a reformed abbey near Namur and appointed to reform several other abbeys, including those of St. Pierre and St. Bavon in Ghent. In the 11th century the Church persuaded warlike lords and knights to abide by the PEACE OF GOD, which protected women, religious, peasants and pilgrims; and also by the Truce of God, which forbade wars during Lent, Advent and other periods. The knights of the Low Countries joined the CRUSADES, while GODFREY OF BOUILLON, a mediator between the French and Germans, because of his character and knowledge of the two languages, became the first ruler of Jerusalem.

The Communes and the Dukes of Burgundy: 1200–1400. By 1200 the ecclesiastical division of the Low Countries had become defined. In the west were the Dioceses of Cambrai, Tournai, Arras and Thérouanne, all of which were suffragans to the ecclesiastical province of Reims in France. In the east was the See of Liège, and in the north the See of UTRECHT, both of which were suffragans of COLOGNE. Flourishing towns were also established in the Low Countries beginning in the 12th century, and Franciscan and Dominican settlers acquired profound influence a century later. The BEGUINES were a creation peculiar to the Low Countries and the Rhineland; although not nuns, they observed a vow of chastity during their residence and devoted themselves to prayer, manual works, care of the sick and teaching. St. Juliana of Liège, an Augustinian canoness of the Monastery of MONT-CORNILLON, helped in the first celebration of the Feast of Corpus Christi at Liège in 1251; it was prescribed for the whole Church in 1264 by Pope Urban IV. By far the most renowned mystic of the Low Countries was Blessed Jan van RUYSBROECK (1293–1381), a devout prior of the convent of Groenendaal, who was one of the promoters of the DEVOTIO MODERNA, which insisted on the interior life and methodical meditation and which produced a spiritual classic in the *IMITATION OF CHRIST* by THOMAS À KEMPIS.

The Reformation: 1500–1640. During the WESTERN SCHISM (1378–1417) the Low Countries had remained faithful to the Roman line of claimants, and in 1477 they passed by marriage to the Hapsburg emperor. By the 16th century the region's traditionally strong faith remained deeply rooted, although piety was sometimes difficult to discern. Many priests were ignorant, and their disordered private lives and lack of zeal caused scandals. The coming of the RENAISSANCE and the rise of HUMANISM began to foster religious indifference. ERASMUS, a leading humanist, was a native of the Low Countries.

Capital: Brussels.
Size: 11,781 sq. miles.
Population: 10,241,506 in 2000.
Languages: Flemish (Dutch), French, German.
Religions: 7,681,130 Catholics (75%), 97,400 Protestants (1%), 345,900 Sunni Muslim (3%), 1,171,186 other (11%), 945,890 without religious affiliation.
Archdiocese: Mechelen-Brussels, with suffragans Antwerp, Bruges, Ghent, Hasselt, Liège, Namur, and Tournai.

LUTHERANISM penetrated the Low Countries through Antwerp, where the convent of the Augustinians provided the first Lutheran center. King CHARLES V organized the INQUISITION and published severe edicts (*placards*) against the Lutherans. After 1530 Anabaptism began to spread, especially in Holland and in Antwerp. In putting into effect the *placards* during the 16th century, the civil authorities put to death nearly 2,000 heretics, mostly Anabaptists, a group seen to disturb social order.

A peace with France in 1559 opened southern Belgium to CALVINISM, which quickly made inroads in Tournai, Cambrai, Lille and in the textile centers of French Flanders; later they advanced toward Antwerp. PHILIP II, who succeeded Charles V in 1555 and who ruled the expanding Habsburg empire from Spain, was eager to apply the *placards* rigorously, but he did not comprehend the changes that had occurred in the distant Low Countries. The Compromise of the Nobles (1566), which demanded the cessation of the Inquisition and abolition of the *placards,* made the failure of a purely negative repression evident. At King Philip's request, Pope Paul IV reorganized the ecclesiastical hierarchy of the Low Countries by erecting 14 new sees and grouping the 18 bishoprics into three ecclesiastical provinces independent of Reims and Cologne. The decrees of the Council of TRENT were promulgated in the Low Countries in 1565–66, and seminaries were established that trained priests who were well educated and morally exemplary.

Unfortunately a revolution erupted in the region, its cause partly political and partly religious. Eighty years of war (1568–1648) ended with the permanent separation of the northern and southern section of the Low Countries. By 1600 the Protestant north had won its independence and began persecuting Catholics (who would continue to remain a minority in the Netherlands). The south—comprising for the most part present-day Belgium—remained subject to Spain and preserved its Catholic faith. Under Archduke Albert and Archduchess Isabella

(1598–1633) the region became one of the most Catholic in the world. Fervent bishops, aided by the nuncios at Brussels, trained an enlightened clergy and attacked abuses. Through their colleges, JESUITS oriented the laity toward a more profound piety and toward apostolic works, and also taught the catechism to thousands of children. The Capuchins (*see* FRANCISCANS, FIRST ORDER), who founded 41 convents between 1585 and 1629, were highly esteemed by the populace for their simplicity, their joyous abnegation and their simple, apostolic preaching.

The Age of Empires: 1640–1830. *Augustinus*, the posthumous work of Cornelius JANSEN, a professor at Louvain and former bishop of Ypres, appeared in 1640. During the second half of the 17th century JANSENISM gained fervent adherents among Louvain professors, bishops, clergy and educated laymen before it was finally subdued in the 18th century. Meanwhile it chilled the fervor of the Catholic restoration considerably.

In 1713 the Catholic Low Countries came under the control of Austria. During the next century the ENLIGHTENMENT made slight headway in Belgium except in Liège. In 1763 Johann Nikolaus von HONTHEIM, coadjutor bishop of Trier, published *De statu Ecclesiae,* which conceded to the State great power over the Church while reducing the papal primacy to a mere primacy of honor (*see* FEBRONIANISM). The ministers of Austrian Archduchess MARIA THERESA (1740–70) also manifested their anticlericalism. Thus, when the Society of Jesus was suppressed by Pope Clement XIV in 1773, they treated the Jesuits with special severity.

Emperor JOSEPH II (1780–90), an enlightened despot, believed he had a vocation to reform the Church in the Catholic Low Countries. In 1781 he published an edict of tolerance in support of the region's Protestant minority, and the following year suppressed contemplative orders and confiscated the property of the 2,600 contemplative religious. He also reorganized parishes and liturgical worship, and in 1786 ordered seminarians to study at the college of philosophy, that he instituted at Louvain and staffed with professors imbued with his own ideas (*see* JOSEPHINISM). These religious changes, together with administrative and judiciary reforms, incited a revolution to overthrow Austrian rule in 1789. Following a revolt in Liège the prince-bishop fled and the equality of all citizens was proclaimed. Unfortunately, the troops of the new emperor, Leopold II, would quickly reinstate the prince-bishop and reconquer the region.

In 1792, while in the midst of their own revolution, the French conquered Belgium. Religious persecution began in the region in 1796, and after the coup d'état of Fructidor 18 (Sept. 4, 1797) antireligious hatred was given free rein. When the oath of hatred for royalty and of submission to the laws of the republic was put into effect, 8,565 priests were condemned to deportation for refusing to subscribe to it, although only 865 were actually apprehended. Churches were closed and religious services celebrated only in secret. Ecclesiastical properties were sold, the University of Louvain was closed and all religious orders and congregations of religious were suppressed. The Flemish population to the north became exasperated by this persecution—as well as by compulsory military conscriptions demanded by Napoleon Bonaparte in his effort at world conquest—and began the wars of the peasants (*Boerenkrijg*) in 1798. Lack of organization caused the failure of that uprising, and Bonaparte eventually gained the good will of Belgian Catholics by the French CONCORDAT OF 1801 which permitted Catholic worship once again. However, that good will was rescinded after Bonaparte imposed the Imperial CATECHISM (1806), arrested and imprisoned Pope PIUS VII from 1809–14, interfered in religious matters and closed the seminaries in Ghent and Tournai. His downfall at Waterloo was hailed in Belgium with great joy.

After Waterloo, Belgium became a province of the Netherlands, and was ruled from 1815 to 1830 by King William I. The Fundamental Law the king imposed, which suppressed all the former privileges enjoyed by the clergy while proclaiming religious liberty, displeased many Catholics. Still more disquieting to them was William's determination to rule the Church as an enlightened despot. He subjected private education to severe restrictions, banished the Jesuits and Christian Brothers, and in 1825 imitated Joseph II by compelling seminarians to attend the college of philosophy at Louvain. Before 1825 Catholics aimed only to restore the privileges of the *ancien régime,* but from 1825 to 1830 they sought religious freedom. When negotiations for a concordat between the king and the Holy See failed in 1827, Catholics joined forces with the Liberals to demand both civil and religious liberties. This union created a climate favorable for the successful revolution of 1830.

1830 to World War II. In 1830 Belgium became an independent kingdom ruled by Prince Leopold of Saxe-Coburg. The constitution of 1831 accorded liberty of association, reunion, education, the press and worship. It deprived the government of all right to interfere in clerical appointments or to prevent clerics from corresponding with their superiors. It also provided that the State would assume the obligation of financially compensating clergymen. In regard to marriage, the constitution provided that the civil ceremony precede the religious one. The cults recognized by the constitution were the Catholic, Protestant and Jewish. The encyclical of GREGORY XVI *Mirari vos* (1832) reflected Rome's concern over this constitution.

From 1830 to 1847 political figures from the right and the left worked together to form the new Belgian state. This period also witnessed another Catholic restoration: a papal nuncio was established in Brussels, the Diocese of Bruges was reestablished and Belgium's reorganized seminaries soon provided sufficient priests to replace a thinly scattered and aged clergy. The number of religious increased from 4,791 in 1829 to 11,968 in 1846. Missions preached by Redemptorists, Jesuits and secular priests worked among the populace, and soon the country was covered with a network of Catholic primary and secondary schools. The Catholic University of Louvain reopened in 1834.

Belgium's Liberal party was organized in 1846 and held an almost constant majority in the Chamber until 1884. One of the crushing arguments of the Liberals was that the Catholic approval of the constitution was feigned. To be sure, suspicion at this liberal constitution was voiced by one Catholic group promoting ULTRAMONTANISM. However, Cardinal STERCKX, the Archbishop of Mechelen (1832–67), was a vigorous defender of the constitution. It was Pope LEO XIII who put an end to this dispute among Catholics by stating in March 1879: "The Belgian constitution consecrates some principles that I, as Pope, could not approve of; but the situation of Catholicism in Belgium, after the experience of half a century, demonstrates that in the present state of modern society, the system of liberty established in this country is most favorable to the Church. Belgian Catholics should not only abstain from attacking the constitution, they should also defend it."

As early as 1850 Liberals passed a law on secondary education that displeased Catholics; in 1879 they would instigate a five-year war over the school question, when laws were passed obliging each community to establish an official school wherein the teaching of the Catholic religion would only be permitted outside class hours. Catholic bishops reacted vigorously and the country was soon dotted with private schools. By 1881 the majority of Belgian students attended Catholic rather than public schools. In 1880 Liberals caused Belgium to sever diplomatic relations with the Holy See because of the Pope's refusal to disapprove the Belgian bishops. A Catholic government came into power after 1884 and restored educational freedom.

The Catholic party became a confessional party because of the activities of the anticlerical liberal government (1878–84), and between 1884 and 1914 it gained an absolute majority in the legislature. It lost this majority after the introduction of universal suffrage (1919) and was then obliged to form a coalition government.

During the late 1800s Catholic leaders attempted to remedy the social ills of the proletariat in an unfortunately paternalistic spirit. The encyclical RERUM NOVARUM (1891) finally set in motion a soundly conceived Catholic social movement. Around 1900 Christian trade unions were finally established, but in some cases it was too late; masses of workers had lost the faith. Wallonia, the most highly industrialized area, saw the greatest decline in Catholics, as the majority of the working class there quit the Church. In Flanders, which was industrialized later and which imbibed much less influence from French anticlericalism because of language differences, the faith was much better safeguarded.

Besides engaging in educational work, caring for the sick and devoting themselves to other social and charitable works, Belgian religious were second only to the French in the numbers who served in mission territories by 1900. Best known among these religious were Pierre Jean DE SMET, SJ, who labored among native tribes in North America and whose statue was erected in Washington, D.C.; Joseph DAMIEN, a Picpus priest and apostle of the lepers in Molokai; and Konstant Lievens, SJ, a defender of the aborigines in Chota-Nagpur, India. The conversion of nearly half the Africans in the Belgian Congo was due almost exclusively to the labors of Belgian missionaries, although the region would suffer under Belgian control. The work of Flemish priests was also noteworthy of special note. P. Meeus established a foundation that led thousands to monthly Confession and Communion. Edward Poppe established the Eucharistic Crusade to promote the reception of Communion by the very young. And in 1925 the Jeunesse ouvrière chretienne was organized by the parish priest Jozef Cardijn, created cardinal by Pope Paul VI in 1965.

In 1914 Germany invaded Belgium and World War I began. Occupation followed, during which time Catholic religious supported Belgian interests. In 1940 Belgium was again invaded, forcing King Leopold III to exile in London for the duration of World War II. With their country under Nazi occupation, Belgian bishops were firm in their opposition to the doctrines of National Socialism and in their protest against the deportation of workers. Between 1940 and 1945, 85 Belgian priests and religious were either put to death by the Germans or perished in concentration camps.

Bibliography: H. PIRENNE, *Bibliographie de l'histoire de Belgique,* rev. H. NOWÉ and H. OBREEN (3d ed. Brussels 1931). General. É. DE MOREAU, *Dictionnaire d'histoire et de géographie ecclésiastiques,* ed. A. BAUDRILLART et al., (Paris 1912–) 7:520–756; *Histoire de l'Église en Belgique,* 5 v. (Brussels 1945–52), 2 Suppl; *L'Église en Belgique* (Paris 1944). Special studies. A. CAUCHIE, *La Querelle des investitures dans les diocèses de Liège et de Cambrai,* 2 v. (Louvain 1890). U. BERLIÈRE, *Monasticon beige,* 3 v. (Maredsous-Liège 1890–1960). G. KURTH, *Notger de Liège et la civilisation au Xe siècle,* 2 v. (Brussels 1905). C. TERLINDEN, *Guillaume Ier, roi des Pays-Bas et l'Église catholique en Belgique, 1814–30,*

2 v. (Brussels 1906). A. PASTURE, *La Restauration religieuse aux Pays-Bas catholiques sous les archiducs Albert et Isabelle* (Louvain 1925). A. PONCELET, *Histoire de la Compagnie de Jésus dans les anciens Pays-Bas,* 2 v. (Brussels 1927–28). F. WILLCOX, *L'Introduction des décrets du Concile de Trente dans les Pays-Bas et dans la principauté de Liège* (Louvain 1929). L. J. VAN DER ESSEN, *De gulden eeuw onzer christianisatie VII*e *-VIII*e *eeuw* (Diest 1943). M. LOBET, *L'Épopée belge des Croisades* (Liège 1944). J. SCHEERDER, *De Inquisitie in de Nederlanden in de XVI*e *eeuw* (Antwerp 1944). A. MENS, *Oorsprong en betekenis van de Nederlandse Begijnen- en Begardenbeweging* (Louvain 1947). S. AXTERS, *The Spirituality of the Old Low Countries,* tr. D. ATTWATER (London 1954); *Geschiedenis van de vroomheid in de Nederlanden,* 4 v. (Antwerp 1950–60). L. WILLAERT, *Les Origines du jansénisme dans les Pays-Bas catholiques* (Brussels 1948). M. DIERICKX, *De oprichting der nieuwe bisdommen in de Nederlanden onder Filips II, 1559–1570* (Antwerp 1950). A. SIMON, *Le Cardinal Sterckx et son temps, 1792–1867,* 2 v. (Wetteren 1950); *Le Parti catholique belge, 1830—1945* (Brussels 1958). H. HAAG, *Les Origines du catholicisme libéral en Belgique, 1789–1839* (Louvain 1950); ''The Catholic Movement in Belgium,'' in *Church and Society,* ed. J. N. MOODY (New York 1953) 279–324. É. DE MOREAU, *Les Abbayes de Belgique, VII*e *-XII*e *siècles* (Brussels 1952). M. BECQUÉ, *Le Cardinal Dechamps,* 2 v. (Louvain 1956). P. HILDEBRAND, *Les Capucins en Belgique et au nord de la France* (Antwerp 1957). K. VAN ISACKER, *Het daensisme* (Antwerp 1959). V. MALLINSON, *Power and Politics in Belgian Education, 1815–1961* (London 1963).

[M. DIERICKX/EDS.]

The Church After World War II

Following World War II Leopold abdicated in favor of his son, Baudouin, who remained king until 1993. In 1977 the country was organized into three political regions—Flanders, Walloonia and Brussels—as a means of uniting regions that had ties due to language and cultural differences. Gradually the Church, too, followed the trend toward confederation. Most religious orders split along language lines. In 1967, the vast diocese of Liège was divided into the Dutch-speaking diocese of Hasselt and the French-speaking diocese of Liège. In 1982, the archdiocese of Mechelen-Brussels was subdivided along linguistic lines into three vicariates, Flemish Brabant, Walloon Brabant and bilingual Brussels, with four auxiliary bishops, one for each linguistic area, plus an auxiliary for French speakers and one for Dutch speakers in Brussels. In May of 1998 King Albert and Queen Paola visited the Vatican and received a private audience with Pope John Paul II, signaling the respectful relationship between the Holy See and the Belgian State.

Throughout the 20th century the government continued to support the church by paying the salaries, retirement and housing costs of priests and teachers in Church-run schools, and also provided financial assistance in renovating church buildings. While freedom of religion continued to be respected, the Belgian government became increasingly concerned about the rise in the number of ''harmful sects'' in the country, and by the late 1990s was singling out the Church of Scientology in particular. The Catholic Church sponsored nation-wide groups to maintain a dialogue between the various faiths in Belgium.

In the 1960s the central issue in Belgium became the splitting of the University of Louvain along linguistic lines into Flemish- and French-language universities. The situation became explosive in 1966 after the Flemish bishops' decision that the university, already bilingual at faculty level, should remain unified. The University of Louvain became a lever for those in support of the ''Frenchification'' of Flanders, while Flemish-speakers viewed it as an attack on their efforts to emancipate Flemish culture. All of Belgium's political parties became involved, and the government fell. Finally, in 1968, the Flemish bishops admitted they had erred, and in 1970 the University of Louvain was divided into the Katholieke Universiteit Leuven (KUL) and the Université Catholique de Louvain (UCL), the latter which moved to a new campus south of Brussels called Louvain-la-Neuve. The KUL eventually established an English-speaking faculty, and attracted students from all parts of the world. As a result of the division of the University of Louvain, Belgium developed into two ecclesiastical regions.

Influence of Vatican II. The vitality and organization of Church life in Belgium at mid-century was reflected in the contribution by Belgian bishops and theologians during the Second Vatican Council and in the openness of the faithful to the call for reform and renewal. Professors from the University of Louvain also had a decisive influence on the most important constitutions, *Lumen gentium* and *Gaudium et spes.* After the Council completed its work Louvain educators continued to play central roles in the implementation of Vatican II. Between 1967 and 1972 pastoral councils and priestly senates were created in all dioceses.

In 1970 an interdiocesan pastoral council was established for Belgium's Flemish region. Its influence in dealing with such subjects as prayer life, economic crisis, priestly ministry and celibacy, adult catechesis, immigration and care of the sick and the dying was impressive, and its status as a permanent consultative church parliament remained unique in Europe. However, social issues threatened to derail the council's progress; in 1968, for example, the nuanced position of Belgian bishops with regard to Humanae Vitae was met with objections from Christian women's organizations that accepted the use of contraceptives and polarization began to occur.

Beginning in 1938 the country's major Catholic charitable institutions were grouped in four sections under Caritas Catholica. The Fédération des Institutions Hospitaliéreres focused on hospitals, clinics, psychiatric institutions and homes for the aged. The Fédération des Services Médico-sociaux was concerned with home services and institutions for preventive medicine and small children. The Fédération des Institutions de l'Enfance Inadaptée supervised the care of mentally impaired children, while the fourth section, Caritas-Secours, provided aid in emergency situations, both in Belgium and elsewhere. In addition to the work of Caritas, many charitable works were performed by small, grassroots organizations.

Church Battles Increasing Secularization. Despite the reorganization following Vatican II, some in the Church began to express concern that an increasingly liberal Church leadership was growing indifferent to certain positions taken by the Holy See that were unpopular with the public at large. In one such example, during the late 1990s a Vatican directive not to participate in in-vitro fertilization procedures was disregarded by one Catholic-run Belgian hospital. The tendency of some priests to split with Vatican positions and preach a censured doctrine acceptable to an increasingly secular culture was condemned by one cardinal in attendance at the 1999 Synod for Europe as ''suicidal''.

The number of priests and religious decreased during the late 20th century, from 10,450 in 1961 to 6,832 by 1990, with more than half over the age of 65. The situation became so pronounced that Flemish and Walloon pastoral councils began to plead for the ordination of married men to the priesthood and of women to the diaconate, with a majority of people even supporting women's ordination to the priesthood. After 1970 an increasing number of laity were trained for pastoral responsibilities as volunteers, catechists, or part- and full-time pastoral workers. The decline in the number of priests had dramatic consequences: some celebrations were ''confederated'' with small teams of priests; parishes increasingly found themselves without a priest; and the laity were increasingly involved in preparations for baptisms, weddings and funerals. By 2000 the numbers of priests had begun to rise from 1990 levels, although the numbers still remained inadequate for the needs of a growing population.

While Catholicism remained Belgium's major faith, Christians as a community of believers found themselves in crisis and disarray by the late 20th century. As was the case elsewhere in Europe, church membership declined steadily, regular church attendance becoming a practice of the elderly only. Adherence to traditional Christian beliefs waned particularly among young people, while society as a whole increased its acceptance of such things as premarital sex, extramarital affairs, divorce and tax evasion. Active believers became increasingly conscious of being a ''minority Church'' in an atmosphere of religious indifference and viewed their central task as transmitting the faith to a younger generations. A somewhat effective pastoral strategy was eventually developed that focused on pastoral teams, base communities and Bible and prayer groups. Despite the continued statistical decline in church membership, a substantial proportion of Belgians continued to see the Church as a defender of major human values and as a source of spiritual guidance within a spiritual void. An important witness was the funeral of King Baudouin in Brussels' Cathedral in August 1993, which was followed on television by millions of people throughout Europe. A Christian who strongly opposed the decriminalization of abortion—in 1990 he temporarily resigned his throne rather than sign an abortion rights bill into law—Baudouin was honored as a leader in matters ethical and a man of faith. In 1995, 70 percent of all children born in Belgium were baptized in the Catholic Church.

Into the 21st Century. By the year 2000, the Belgian Church had 3,919 parishes tended by 5,442 secular and 3,366 religious priests. There were 1,497 brothers and 17,734 sisters also working in the country, as well as many more in missionary service around the world. Many religious continued to dedicate themselves to educating the young, and Belgium's Catholic primary and secondary school network remained among the strongest in Europe. In the mid-1990s the Catholic school system educated approximately half of all school-age children in Belgium, although the percentages varied between Flanders, Wallonia and Brussels. Eight Catholic universities also operated in Belgium.

Social issues continued to weigh heavily on Church leaders as they looked beyond the Jubilee Year 2000, with the realization that recent elections had relegated Catholics to the position of the opposition party in an increasingly liberal political climate. A consequence of Belgium's membership in the European Union was that its government abide by human rights provisions established by far more liberal nations, one of which was removing legal obstacles to women choosing abortion. The defense of the right to life by Belgian bishops in the face of abortion rights legislation was a position praised by the pope as ''strong and courageous'' in their insistence ''on the necessity to respect the intrinsic dignity of the human being from conception to natural death.'' In a related matter, concerns were raised that the legalization of euthanasia across Belgium's northern border would spill down into Flanders, supported by that region's liberal coalition government. It was estimated that by 1998, 40 percent of deaths in Flanders involved a medical decision to end life.

Bibliography: J. KERKHOFS and J. VAN HOUTTE, *De Kerk in Vlaanderen* (Tielt 1962). *Rapport annuaire de la Fondation Universitaire* (Brussels 1964). *Annuaire statistique de l'enseignement catholique, 1960–1961* (Brussels 1963). *Caritas, 1938–1963* (Brussels 1963). *Het Verbond der Verplegingsinstellingen van Caritas Catholica* (Brussels). E. DE SMET et al., *Atlas des élections belges, 1919–1954,* 2 v. (Brussels 1958), with app. for the elections of 1958. *Each One for All. All for Each: The Belgian Boerenbond* (Louvain 1958). *Mouvement ouvrier chrétien: Rapport d'activité, 21e congrès, Bruxelles 17–19 avril 1964* (Brussels). A. BRYS, *Comment est conçu et organisé le Mouvement ouvrier chrétien en Belgique* (Brussels 1960). R. AUBERT, 150 ans de vie des Eglises (Brussels 1980). *Kerkelijk leven in Vlaanderen anno 2000,* eds., J. BULCKENS and P. COOREMAN, (Leuven-Amersfoort 1989). A. DENAUX, *Godsdienstsekten in Vlaanderen* (Leuven 1982). *België en zijn goden/La Belgique et ses dieux,* eds., K. DOBBELAERE, L. VOYE and J. BILLIET (Leuven 1985). K. DOBBELAERE, "Secularization, Pillarization, Religious Involvement and Religious change in the Low Countries," in *World Catholicism in Transition,* ed. T. GANNON (New York and London 1988) 80–115. *Het 'volk Gods' de mist in? Over de Kerk in België* (Leuven 1988). M. ELCHARDUS and P. HEYVAERT, *Soepel, flexibel en ongebonden. Een vergelijking van twee laat-moderne generaties* (Brussel 1990). P. ESTER, L. HALMAN and R. DE MOOR, *The Individualizing Society, Value Change in Europe and North America* (Tilburg 1993). *Bilan du Monde* 2:124–142. *Annuaire catholique de Belgique, 1963–64* (Brussels 1964). R. C. FOX, "Is religion important in Belgium," Archives *européennes de Sociologie,* 23 (1982) 3–38. J. KERKHOFS and R. REZSOHAZY, *De stille Ommekeer* (Tielt 1984); *L'Univers des Belges* (Louvain-la-Neuve 1984); *De versnelde Ommekeer,* eds., J. KERKHOFS and L. VOYE (Tielt 1992); *Belges, heureux et satisfaits*(Brussels 1992); "L'Eglise en Wallonie," *La Foi et le Temps* (January 1992); "Les Protestants en Belgique," Centre de recherche et d'iformation socio-politiques (CRISP) 1430–1431 (Brussels 1994); *The Church in Belgium,* Pro Mundi Vita Dossiers, 18 (Brussels 1982). *Annuario Pontificio* has annual data on all dioceses.

[J. KERKHOFS/EDS.]

BELIEFS

Contemporary scholars find it necessary to distinguish sharply between "faith" and "beliefs." "Faith" is considered more basic, more personal; as having to do with one's fundamental orientation—if not in a religious sense to God—then in one's basic stance toward life. "Beliefs," on the other hand, are considered to be secondary, more intellectual; they have to do with the conceptualization of religious matters and their formulation as doctrines.

Until recent years "beliefs" and "faith" were nearly synonymous for Catholics. In its religious sense, "beliefs" has been taken to mean the teachings and formulas of the Church. The totality of "beliefs" has been called "the faith," while the act of belief has traditionally been considered to be the virtue faith made concrete through the acceptance of what God has revealed.

Historical Background. The tendency in Catholic theology to identify faith with the act of belief can be found in its classic form in the work of Thomas Aquinas. For Aquinas, faith, or *fides,* along with hope and charity, is one of the three theological virtues. These virtues result from sanctifying grace and direct one toward supernatural happiness. Hope and charity mutually perfect the will, the former enabling one to intend the will of God, the latter enabling one to become like God in one's heart. Faith specifically perfects the intellect by enabling one to give intellectual assent to the truths that God has revealed. "To believe," or *credere,* for Aquinas, is "an act of intellect assenting to the divine truth by virtue of the command of the will as moved by God through grace" (*Summa theologiae* 2a2ae, 2.9). It is with this sense of "belief" that Aquinas identified "faith."

In addition to the relationship between *fides* and *credere,* there is another classical distinction in Catholic theology that underlies the contemporary distinction between "faith" and "beliefs." This is the distinction between *fides qua creditur,* the faith by which one believes, and *fides quae creditur,* the faith that one believes. The difference is between "faith" taken as the virtue that empowers one to believe and "faith" taken as the beliefs that one accepts.

When the Protestant Reformers called for "faith alone," they used a meaning of "faith" different from that of Aquinas and more in line with the New Testament writings of Paul. "Faith," or *Glauben,* for Martin Luther, became an all-embracing category for describing one's relationship of trust with God. What Luther meant by "faith," was something like what Catholics meant by "faith," "hope," and "charity" combined. This semantic difference, along with the complaint that Catholic theology had become too intellectual by placing undue emphasis on the acceptance of correct doctrines, to the neglect of one's personal relationship with God, led the Reformers to stress the difference between "having faith" and "accepting doctrines."

Need for the Distinction. Several factors have led contemporary scholars, both Catholic and Protestant, to distinguish sharply between "faith" and "beliefs."

First, in English-speaking countries, the common use of the word "faith" corresponds more with the traditional Protestant meaning than with the traditional Catholic meaning. Protestant theologian Paul Tillich's view of "faith" as a centered act of the total personality that includes the emotions, the intellect, and the will, has gained much popular acceptance. Also popular is the view of liberation theologian Gustavo Gutierrez who insists that "faith" is not simply assent but must include commitment and action. Identifying "faith" with "beliefs" in

English is thus often more confusing than helpful. It should be noted, though, that the problem is not simply a semantic one confined to English; it is as well a conceptual matter that can be found in Latin, French, German, and potentially in any language.

Second, the need to distinguish between "faith" and "beliefs" can be seen in ecumenical and interreligious dialogue. In the work of Wilfred Cantwell Smith and Raimundo Panikkar, for example, "faith" is used to describe the most fundamental thing that all religious persons share. "Beliefs" is used to describe the intellectual areas concerning which religious persons tend to differ. Without a clear distinction between "faith" and "beliefs" interdenominational and interreligious dialogue would have less of an identifiable common basis.

Third, the need to distinguish between "faith" and "beliefs" has arisen in the social and natural sciences in these areas where they interface with religious studies. In the philosophy of science, F. R. Tennant finds in "faith" the common root between scientific "knowledge" and religious "belief." In psychology, James W. Fowler has constructed a theory of how faith develops in individuals through an identifiable sequence of measurable stages. Fowler attempts to measure the state of religious maturity of the individual in a way that is distinct from any particular set of beliefs. Contemporary studies in the sociology of knowledge by Thomas Luckmann, Peter Berger, and Robert Bellah indicate that beliefs comprise a major dimension of a socially-constructed reality that requires consideration apart from issues of "faith."

Fourth, the need to distinguish between faith and beliefs can be found in theological discussion surrounding the question of religious truth. Contemporary theologians, with the support of the Vatican II Decree on Ecumenism (*Unitatis redintegratio*), find that within beliefs there can be discovered a "hierarchy of truths." Some truths are more centrally related to the foundation of Christianity than are others. When beliefs are sweepingly identified as "the faith," such discriminate rankings are more difficult to make.

Furthermore, many scholars raise questions about the truth status of beliefs without wanting to call into question the truth of one's fundamental relationship with God or the transcendent. Some theologians, such as Wilfred Cantwell Smith, Raimundo Panikkar, James W. Fowler, and George Lindbeck, have displayed a tendency to emphasize the strictly secondary nature of beliefs in relation to faith and to stress the limitations of their truth claims. Other theologians, such as Bernard Lonergan and David Tracy, emphasize the nature of beliefs as public claims to truth. While agreeing that faith is more basic and more important, they stress that despite inadequacies of formulation and conceptualization an essential claim to truth is intended in "beliefs."

Fifth, the need to distinguish between faith and beliefs has arisen in a 20th century movement within Catholic theology to correct unfortunate tendencies toward intellectualism. Aquinas may have been readily able to distinguish between faith and the act of belief, but that did not mean that all who followed him could do so. From a Catholic point of view, the problem, was not so much one of allowing faith to be identified with the act of belief as it was of allowing faith to become detached from grace; that is, it seemed to become possible in Catholic theology to link faith with the act of belief in such a mechanical fashion that one could forget that faith is a gift from God that will transform one's very mode of perceiving. Theologians such as Pierre Rousselot and Roger Aubert tried to reaffirm the connection between faith and grace by describing faith as the "eye of love," as the mode of perception that flows from sanctifying grace. To stress the connection of faith with grace is necessarily to stress the way in which faith is distinct from beliefs, for it entails considering "seeing with the eyes of love" in a way that is prior to the acceptance of any particular set of doctrines.

Bernard Lonergan has drawn upon this approach in formulating the distinction between "faith" and "beliefs" that provides part of the underpinning of his outline of theological method. The distinction allows Lonergan to grant a high place to beliefs or doctrine while maintaining the ability to refer back to the religious experience in which doctrine finds its ground. This move away from intellectualism can also be found in contemporary catechetics in the distinction between formation in faith and the transmission of beliefs.

Today the distinction between "faith" and "beliefs" is commonplace among both Catholic and Protestant theologians, although there remain some areas in need of further clarification. Theologians generally agree that faith should describe one's fundamental relationship with God or the transcendent, yet there is some debate concerning whether faith should be considered to be more of a fundamentally human (Tracy) or a fundamentally religious (Lonergan) character. "Belief" is used by theologians to mean both the act of accepting religious doctrines and to refer to a particular doctrine that is accepted. In the latter sense, belief sometimes denotes a statement or a formula, sometimes a concept, and sometimes a formula or concept inclusive of the reality to which it is intended to refer.

Although both faith and beliefs have a wide range of meanings, the need to distinguish between them usually stems from the recognition that beliefs are cognitive while faith is more than cognitive. The contemporary distinction between "faith" and "beliefs" can generally be taken to mean that one's fundamental relationship with God should be confused neither with the act of believing (*credere*) nor with that which is believed (*fides quae creditur*).

See Also: FAITH.

Bibliography: J. W. FOWLER, *Stages of Faith* (San Francisco 1981). B. LONERGAN, *Method in Theology* (New York 1972). R. PANIKKAR, *The Intrareligious Dialogue* (New York 1978); *Myth, Faith, and Hermeneutics* (New York 1979). W. C. SMITH, *Belief and History* (Charlottesville 1977); *Faith and Belief* (Princeton 1979). D. TRACY, *Blessed Ridge for Order* (New York 1975); *The Analogical Imagination* (New York 1981). H. DE LUBAC, *The Christian Faith* (San Francisco 1986). W. KASPER, *An Introduction to Christian Faith* (New York 1980).

[D. M. DOYLE]

BELISARIUS

Sixth-century Byzantine general; b. Illyricum, *c.* 500; d. March 565. Belisarius had the historian Procopius as his juridical and administrative adviser from 527 to 540, while he was the faithful and efficacious instrument of the politics of JUSTINIAN I in the recovery of Italy from the Goths. He was implicated in the troubled events marking the passage of the pontificate from SILVERIUS (536–537) to VIGILIUS (537–555). According to the *Liber pontificalis*, the *Anecdota,* and the *Breviarium* of the Carthaginian deacon LIBERATUS, he acted as an unwilling executor of the intrigues of the Empress Theodora, who hoped that with Vigilius's accession she could recover the See of Constantinople for her protégé ANTHIMUS OF TREBIZOND. Belisarius campaigned successfully against the Persians (541–542), bringing them to submission after they dealt a surprise attack near Nisibis occasioned by Belisarius's pacificatory attitude. He served as the emperor's official representative in the negotiations with Pope Vigilius before and during the Council of CONSTANTINOPLE III (553). He fell into disfavor in 562 when unjustly accused of conspiracy against the emperor, but returned to favor before his death. Procopius described him at the height of his glory; and although he may have given him too much credit, Belisarius's campaigns were wholly successful. A gold cross, his gift for the tomb of St. Peter, is preserved in Rome, as is a hospice that he founded on the Via Lata. Legends about Belisarius can be traced to the Middle Ages.

Bibliography: L. BRÉHIER, *Dictionnaire d'histoire et de géographie ecclésiastiques* 7:776–787. E. STEIN, *Histoire du Bas-Empire* tr. J. R. PALANQUE, 2 v. in 3 (Paris 1949–59) 284–286, 312–324, 386, 494–498, 665–666, 719–720, 779.

[P. ROCHE]

BELIZE, THE CATHOLIC CHURCH IN

Located in Central America at the south of the Yucatán Peninsula, Belize is bound on the north by Mexico, on the east by the Caribbean, and on the south and west by Guatemala; the River Sarstoon flows along its southern boundary. A number of islets, reefs and cays are scattered along its coast. A tropical climate, frequent hurricanes during the fall months, and coastal flooding characterize much of the region, which has a swampy coastal plain rising to low mountains in the south. The region's most important exports are sugar, bananas and citrus; natural resources include timber, fish and hydropower. Tourism was on the increase by 2000, bolstering the Belizean economy despite a corresponding increase in crime due to the South American drug trade. Mayans, the original inhabitants of the region, are a minority population; the majority of Belizeans are descendants of early European settlers and African slaves. Formerly known as British Honduras, Belize gained its independence in 1981.

History of the Church. Evangelization efforts in Belize were concurrent with those in Guatemala, occurring during the 16th century. By the mid-1600s the region was home to British lumbermen who emigrated from Jamaica. In 1786 the region was made a superindependency of Great Britain, to which the Bay Islands were added in 1841. Belize received its first Catholic settlers in 1830. At the time Franciscan priest Fray Antonio arrived to serve the new immigrants, Belize was included in the vicariate of Trinidad. In 1836 it became a part of the vicariate of Jamaica. In 1851 Benito Fernández, a Franciscan and the first vicar apostolic, sent two Jesuit missionaries to tend the refugees of the native revolt in the Yucatán. The region was made a crown colony under Jamaica from 1862 to 1884. In 1888 communication difficulties with the vicariate of Jamaica caused the region, then known as British Honduras, to become a prefecture apostolic. Five years later the mission was made a vicariate apostolic and put under the direction of the Jesuits of the Missouri province. In November of 1956, the vicariate was raised to a diocese, and Vicar Apostolic David Hickey, SJ, was named the first bishop of Belize.

From 1899 to his drowning in 1923, Bishop Frederick Hopkins, SJ, oversaw great progress in establishing the faith, including the opening of a convent by the Pallottine Sisters at Benque Viejo. The blessing of the novitiate for the Pallottine Sisters occurred in 1931; the same year a hurricane devastated Belize City and took the lives of 11 Jesuits. Many of the mission's buildings, including those of St. John's College, were destroyed, although generous benefactors enabled the mission to continue.

Major hurricanes struck again during the 1940s, forcing the Church to undertake a large reconstruction program. In 1955 hurricane Janet destroyed many northern towns, including Corozal, which necessitated yet more reconstruction.

The main contribution of the Church in Belize occurred in the field of education, as the majority of the nation's schools were affiliated with a church. In the 1890s the Sisters of Mercy opened an academy for girls, while the Jesuits started a secondary school that would eventually become St. John's College. The Sisters of the Holy Family established elementary and secondary schools for girls, while a teacher training program began in July of 1947. An extension of St. John's College was established in 1947, and that of St. John's Teachers' College in 1954. The Lyman Agricultural College, established in 1954, anticipated the United Nations' *Development Plan for British Honduras,* which stressed agricultural improvements as a solution for the country's economic ills. At the grade-school level the government supported Church efforts by paying teachers' salaries and a percentage of the building and maintenance costs. In secondary schooling the diocese was aided by Papal Volunteers and the Peace Corps. Religion was part of the mandatory curriculum in both private and state-run schools in Belize.

Into the 21st Century. Rooted in the nationalization movement begun at the Jesuit-run St. John's College in the 1940s, the Belizeans implemented a new constitution in 1960 and were granted internal independence from Great Britain five years later. Full independence was achieved on Sept. 21, 1981, after which time the country operated as a parliamentary democracy within the British Commonwealth, with Queen Elizabeth II chief of state and a governor general acting for the Crown locally. Relations between Church and State remained amicable after independence was granted, and in 1991 a longstanding border dispute with Guatemala was finally resolved. Under the constitution of 1981, absolute freedom of worship prevailed, and no established church existed, although the country was founded ''upon principles which acknowledge the supremacy of God.'' The Catholic faith continued to predominate, despite the efforts of a number of evangelical Protestant movements.

As of 2000 Belize had 13 parishes, served by 15 diocesan priests, 23 religious priests, eight brothers and 71 sisters. Most government leaders were also Roman Catholic, and Church-affiliated organizations such as the St. Vincent de Paul Society and Catholic Relief Services aided in humanitarian efforts throughout the region. The Church operated 139 primary schools and six secondary schools in the country, instilling Catholic values in an estimated 35,000 young people each year.

Capital: Belmopan.
Size: 8,867 sq. miles.
Population: 249,183 in 2000.
Languages: Spanish, English; native dialects are spoken in various regions.
Religions: 154,493 Catholics (62%), 74,755 Protestants (30%), 14,950 other (6%), 4,985 without religious affiliation.
Archdiocese: Kingston, Jamaica, with suffragans Belize City-Belmopan, Mandevilla, and Montego Bay, Jamaica, as well as a mission sui juris at Turks and Caicos.

Bibliography: A. C. S. WRIGHT et al., *Land in British Honduras* (London 1959). S. L. CAIGER, *British Honduras: Past and Present* (London 1951). J. H. PARRY and P. M. SHERLOCK, *Short History of the British West Indies* (New York 1956). E. O. WINZERLING, *The Beginning of British Honduras*, 1506–1765 (New York 1946; 1960). F. C. HOPKINS, ''The Catholic Church in British Honduras, 1851–1918,'' *American Catholic Historical Review,* 4 (1918–19) 304–314.

[R. F. O'TOOLE/EDS.]

BELL, ARTHUR, BL.

Franciscan priest, martyr; *alias* Francis Bell; b. Jan. 13, 1590, at Temple-Broughton (near Worcester), England; d. Dec. 11, 1643, HDQ at Tyburn (London) under Charles I. At age eight Arthur was entrusted to the care of his maternal uncle, Francis Daniel, who sent Bell abroad to study at age 24. After completing the course at the English College in Valladolid, Spain, he was ordained a priest at Salamanca. He received the Franciscan habit at Segovia, Aug. 8, 1618.

He was one of the first members of the Franciscan community at Douai, where he subsequently fulfilled the offices of guardian and professor of Hebrew. Called to Scotland in 1632 as the first Franciscan provincial, his efforts to restore the order there proved unsuccessful, and he returned to England, where he labored until his arrest (Nov. 6, 1643) as a spy and was committed to Newgate Prison.

The record of his trial shows a man of singular devotion who did not shrink from suffering. When the death sentence was declared, he praised God and thanked his judges for allowing him to die for Christ.

Bell wrote *The History, Life, and Miracles of Joane of the Cross* (St. Omer 1625) and translated from the Spanish Andrew a Soto's *A brief instruction on how we ought to hear Mass* (Brussels 1624).

He was beatified by Pope John Paul II on Nov. 22, 1987 with George Haydock and Companions.

Feast of the English Martyrs: May 4 (England).

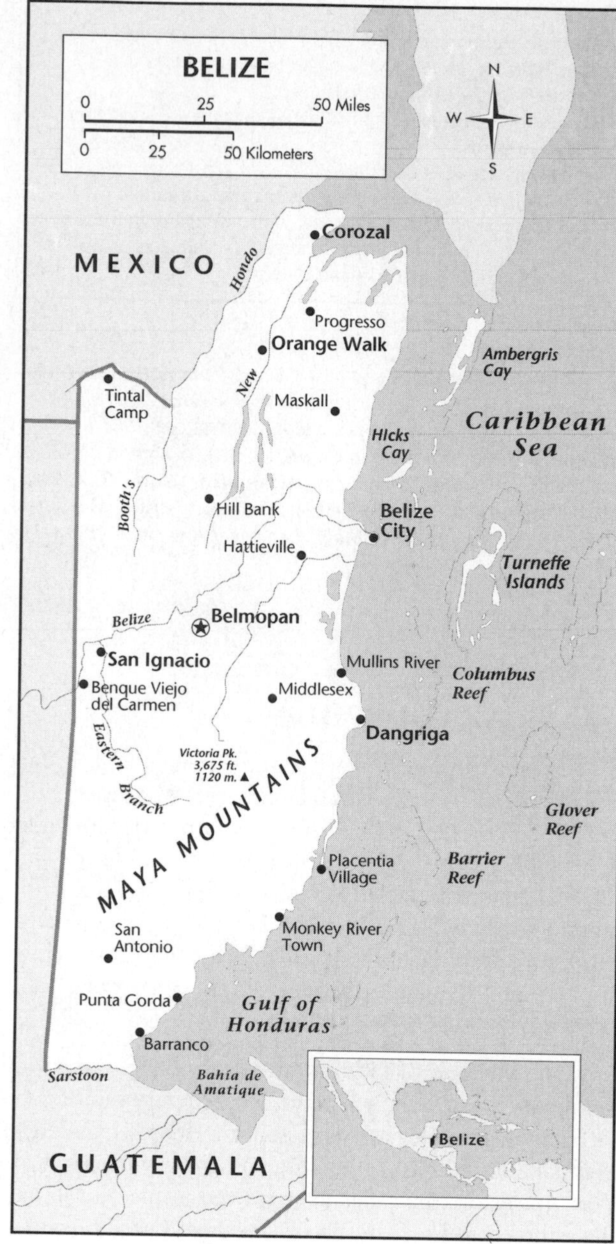

See Also: ENGLAND, SCOTLAND, AND WALES, MARTYRS OF.

Bibliography: R. CHALLONER, *Memoirs of Missionary Priests,* ed. J. H. POLLEN (rev. ed. London 1924). J. H. POLLEN, *Acts of English Martyrs* (London 1891). J. THADDEUS, *The Franciscans in England 1600–1859,* 15 v. (London, 1898).

[S. M. DONOVAN/K. I. RABENSTEIN]

BELL, JAMES, BL.

Marian priest, martyr; b. ca. 1520, Warrington, Lancashire, England; hanged, drawn, and quartered April 20, 1584. Bell, who studied at Oxford, was ordained to the priesthood during the reign of Queen Marty, but conformed to the Anglican Church at the ascension of Elizabeth I. Two decades later he could no longer minister in good conscience and was reduced to near destitution. He was finally reconciled to the Catholic Church. Once his faculties were restored, he worked for two years prior to his arrest Jan. 17, 1584. He was arraigned at Manchester and tried at the Lancaster Assizes in March 1584. At his sentencing he told the judge: ''I beg your Lordship would add to the sentence that my lips and the tops of my fingers may be cut off, for having sworn and subscribed to the articles of heretics contrary both to my conscience and to God's Truth.'' He was beatified by Pius XI on Dec. 15, 1929.

Feast of the English Martyrs: May 4 (England).

See Also: ENGLAND, SCOTLAND, AND WALES, MARTYRS OF.

Bibliography: BRIDGEWATER, *Concertatio ecclesi'Catholic'in Anglia* (n.s. 1588). R. CHALLONER, *Memoirs of Missionary Priests,* ed. J. H. POLLEN (rev. ed. London 1924; repr. Farnborough 1969). J. H. POLLEN, *Acts of English Martyrs* (London 1891). D. DE YEPES, *Historia Particular de la persecución de Inglaterra* (Madrid 1599).

[K. I. RABENSTEIN]

BELLARMINE, ROBERT (ROBERTO), ST.

Cardinal and Doctor of the Church; b. Montepulciano, Tuscany, Italy, Oct. 4, 1542; d. Rome, Sept. 17, 1621. Bellarmine's parents were Vincent Bellarmine and Cinthia Cervini; the latter was a sister of Marcellus II (d. 1555). In 1560, Bellarmine entered the Jesuits' Roman College, made his first vows as a Jesuit, and began a study of Aristotelian philosophy.

Career as Teacher. After a brief study of Thomistic theology at Padua, Bellarmine was sent in 1569 to Louvain, Belgium, where he became the first Jesuit professor at the University of Louvain. He was ordained in 1570. Bellarmine taught theology from the *Summa Theologiae* of St. THOMAS AQUINAS in the Jesuit house of studies, and began the groundwork for his major work, the *Controversies.* The University of Louvain was part of the Church's front-line defense against the Reformers. The atmosphere was one of practical defensive scholarship rather than calm speculation or reasoned development of dogmas that were held securely. Both the history of the Catholic Church and patristic studies were in a sad state of neglect. As if in answer to the needs of the time, Bellarmine devoted his energy to the study of Scripture,

Church history, and patristics in order to systematize Church doctrine against the attacks of the Reformers. He wrote a Hebrew grammar and compiled a patristic work, *De Scriptoribus ecclesiasticis.*

In 1576, GREGORY XIII requested that Bellarmine teach theology to English and German missionary students in the Roman College; Bellarmine continued teaching until 1588. The vast synthesis of Protestant and Catholic theology resulting from these lectures appeared in three volumes, *Disputationes de Controversiis Christianae Fidei adversus hujus temporis haereticos* (Igolstadt 1586-88-93). It is Bellarmine's largest and most important work, containing most of the ideas that he developed later. Particularly noteworthy are the sections on the temporal power of the pope and the role of the laity. Along with the *De translatione Imperii Romani* (Antwerp 1584), these constitute Bellarmine's earliest major writings on papal power. The *Controversies* are monumental because they put order into the chaotic argumentation of attack and defense waged between Reformers and Catholics. Bellarmine's criticism of reform theology was remarkably fair and just in that he pointed out its strengths as well as its weaknesses. This was in direct contrast to much of the polemic writing of the times. The *Controversies* were small enough to be carried by missionaries, yet afforded more than the excellent but sketchy catechism of St. Peter CANISIUS for warding off the attacks of scholarly disputants. They were so effective a weapon against reform theology that special chairs of learning were erected just to combat their influence, and they seem to have occasioned the return of many to the Church.

In 1588, Bellarmine became spiritual director of the Roman College. His catechetical lessons to lay brothers and students resulted in the small catechism for children *Dottrina cristiana breve* (Rome 1597) and the catechism for teachers *Dichiarazione più copiosa della dottrina cristiana* (Rome 1598). CLEMENT VIII (d. 1605) solemnly approved both manuals, which were often translated and widely used; they remained popular until Vatican Council I.

In 1590, Bellarmine experienced his first major difficulty over his theory of indirect papal power. Only the sudden death of SIXTUS V prevented the pope from putting the first volume of the *Controversies,* which contained this theory, on the Index.

Career as Churchman. Bellarmine served as rector of the Roman College (1592), provincial of the Jesuits' Neapolitan province (1594), and theologian to CLEMENT VIII (1597), who made him a cardinal in 1599. From that time on, Bellarmine served as a member of all of the Roman Congregations and of many commissions. One of Bellarmine's continual concerns was the discipline of bishops, e.g., their appointment, residency, and transfer.

At the turn of the century, Bellarmine became involved in the controversy over efficacious grace. He defended his disciple Leonard LESSIUS; wrote a report, *De Controversia Lovaniensi,* for the president of the *CONGREGATIO DE AUXILIIS*; and debated on paper with Domingo BÁÑEZ (*see* BÁÑEZ AND BAÑEZIANISM; GRACE, CONTROVERSIES ON).

In 1602, Clement VIII personally consecrated Bellarmine an archbishop and sent him to Capua, where he lived a pastoral life of charity, preaching, and reform. In 1605, PAUL V recalled him to Rome to serve the Church at large.

Bellarmine spent the next few years in controversies involving papal power: against the Republic of Venice over clerical immunities, 1606–07; against King JAMES I OF ENGLAND over the DIVINE RIGHT of kings and the English oath of allegiance, 1607 to 1609; against the GALLICANISM of William Barclay and Roger Widdrington, 1610, which occasioned Bellarmine's famous *Tractatus de potestate Summi Pontificis in rebus temporalibus adversus Gulielmum Barclaeum.*

Bellarmine is famous, not because he invented the theory of the indirect power of the pope in temporal affairs, but because he used it so effectively in the history of CHURCH AND STATE relations, clearly distinguishing between the temporal and the purely spiritual power of the pope. By applying Thomistic political philosophy to the confusions and exaggerations of his age, he emphasized the purely spiritual power of the Church, yet showed that because the spiritual power of the Church is primary and the temporal secondary, the pope may act regarding those temporal things affecting the spiritual. While Bellarmine is famous for defending the distinction and subordination of powers as part of Catholic doctrine, his practical applications of these principles manifest a confusion of what is permanent with what was contingent in the Church's actual use of her power. Perhaps this stems from the fact that he looked upon the state not as having an existence independent of the Church but as making up one society with the Church. In addition, Bellarmine seems to have failed to note that the Church intervenes in temporal affairs for two basically different reasons: either she has a divine right to act or she fills a vacuum left by the failure of political society to act. No doubt Bellarmine's understanding of history was greatly influenced by the sources available to him.

The last major controversy of Bellarmine's life came in 1616 when he had to admonish GALILEO, whom he admired: he gave the admonition on behalf of the Holy Office, which had decided that the heliocentric theory of Nicolaus COPERNICUS was contrary to Scripture. Although Bellarmine had served on commissions for the revision of the Vulgate and the Greek New Testament, there is some question whether he understood the Council of Trent's teaching on the interpretation of Scripture as well as Galileo did. Bellarmine also hesitated on the question of how to reconcile Scripture and science.

Bellarmine's ascetical works, such as *In omnes Psalmos dilucida esposito* (Rome 1611), *De gemitu columbae* (Rome 1615), and *De arte bene moriendi* (Rome 1620), appeared near the end of his life.

Bellarmine practiced self-sacrifice, poverty, disinterestedness, and devotion to duty. He fostered a special devotion to St. FRANCIS OF ASSISI. The process for his canonization, begun in 1627, was delayed for political reasons until 1930. In 1931, PIUS XI declared him a Doctor of the Church. Bellarmine's body lies in the Church of St. Ignatius in Rome.

Feast: Sept. 17.

Bibliography: Collected Works. *Opera omnis,* ed. J. FÈVRE, 12 v. (Paris 1870–74); *Epistolae familiares,* ed. J. FULIGATTI (Rome 1650): *Opera oratoria postuma,* ed. S. TROMP, 9 V. (Rome 1942–50). C. SOMMERVOGEL et al., *Bibliotheque de la Compagnie de Jésus* (Brussels-Paris 1890–1932) 1:1151–1254. X. M. LEBACHELET, *Bellarmin avant son cardinalat: Correspondance et documents* (Paris 1911). R. BELLARMINE, *Auctarium Bellarminianum,* ed. X. M. LEBACHELET (Paris 1913). J. BRODRICK, *Robert Bellarmine: Saint and Scholar* (London 1928, rep. London 1966). J. LEBRETON, *Catholicisme. Hier, aujourd'hui et demain,* ed. G. JACQUEMET 1:1379–84. S. MERKLE, "Grundsätzliche und methodologische Erörterungen zur Bellarminforschung," *Zeitschrift für Kirchengeschicte* 45 (1927) 26–73. F. Z. ARNOLD, *Die Staatslehre des Kardinals Bellarmin* (Munich 1934). R. J. BLACKWELL, *Galileo, Bellarmine, and the Bible* (Notre Dame, Ind. 1991). T. DIETRICH, *Die Theologie der Kirche bei Robert Bellarmin* (Paderborn 1999). P. GODMAN, *The Saint as Censor: Robert Bellarmine between Inquisition and Index* (Leiden 2000). T. HARDING, *A briefe answere: Thomas Harding. Apologia Cardinalis Bellarmini* (Ilkley, Eng. 1976). E. A. RYAN, *The Historical Scholarship of Saint Bellarmin* (New York 1936). J. C. MURRAY, "St. Robert Bellarmine on the Indirect Power," *Theological Studies* 9 (1948) 491–535. N. HENS, *Die Augustinusinterpretation des hl. Robert Bellarmin bezüglich der wirksamen Gnade und der Vorherbestimmung nach der Kontroverse* (Rome 1949). J. HARDON, *A Comparative Study of Bellarmine's Doctrine on the Relation of Sincere Non-Catholics to the Catholic Church* (Rome 1951). J. BEUMER, "Die Frage nach Schrift und Tradition bein Robert Bellarmin," *Scholastik* 34 (1959) 1–22. R. S. WESTFALL, *Essays on the Trial of Galileo* (Vatican City 1989).

[J. FRISKE]

BELLESINI, STEFANO, BL.

Priest; b. Trent, Italy, Nov. 25, 1774; d. Genazzano, Italy, Feb. 2, 1840. Aloisio Giuseppe Bellesini was the son of Giuseppe and Maria Ursula (Meichembeck) Bellesini. After joining the AUGUSTINIANS in 1790, he took the name Stefano. During his theological studies at Bologna, the forces of the French Revolution forced him home to Trent, where, as a deacon, he did much preaching. He was ordained in 1797. During the suppression of the religious orders, he lived as a secular priest and established free schools for the Christian education of youth. His success led to his appointment by the Austrian government as inspector of all schools in Trent. In 1817, when the Augustinians were reestablished in the States of the Church, Stefano went there, and became master of novices successively in Rome, in Città della Pieve, and in Genazzano at the basilica of Our Mother of Good Counsel, where he was appointed pastor in 1830. His zeal in caring for the sick during a typhoid epidemic led to his fatal contraction of the disease. He was beatified Dec. 27, 1904.

Feast: Feb. 3.

Bibliography: F. BALZOFIORE, *Della vita . . . Stefano Bellesini . . .* (Rome 1868). P. BILLERI, *Vita del Beato Stefano Bellesini* (Rome 1904). A. BORZI, *Un uomo per gli altri* (Genazzano, Italy 1973). D. RICCARDI, *Un santo tra poveri e ragazzi. Vita del beato Stefano Bellesini agostiniano* (Milan 1970). C. VIVALDELLI, *Trento fra siori e pezotéri: Stefano Bellesini e il primo risveglio sociale del Trentino* (Trent 1974).

[M. J. HALPHEN]

BELLINI

Surname of a father and his two sons, painters who worked principally in Venice. Their works exemplify the main currents of north Italian painting in the 15th century.

Jacopo; b. Venice, early 15th century; d. there, 1470 or 1471. He was probably trained in Florence by Gentile da Fabriano and his few autograph Madonnas (Venice, Accademia; Florence, Uffizi) show the influence of the international style in their soft modeling and delicate colors. The quiet poses, impassive faces, and bulky forms give them monumental dignity. Interesting aspects of Jacopo's work are revealed in two large volumes of his drawings (London, British Museum; Paris, Louvre). These contain studies of animals and costumes, compositional sketches, copies of antique monuments and inscriptions, and highly finished narrative compositions set in elaborate architectural perspectives. The books combine humanist preoccupations with the medieval tradition of model books.

Gentile; b. Venice, 1429; d. there, 1507. His early works (organ doors, Venice, San Marco) reveal his contact with Paduan art. The low vanishing point, elaborate "antique" architecture, and harsh plasticity are typical also of his brother-in-law Andrea Mantegna. In 1479 Gentile traveled to Constantinople, where he portrayed

Sultan Mohammed II (London, National Gallery). In this and in portraits of Venetian nobility he suggests character with precise lines and minute detail. Gentile is perhaps best remembered for a series of huge canvases depicting miracles that take place in panoramic Venetian cityscapes crowded with colorful processions (Venice, Accademia; Milan, Brera).

Giovanni; b. Venice, *c.* 1430; d. there, Nov. 20, 1516. Although also influenced by Paduan art (''Transfiguration,'' Venice, Correr), he early demonstrated his extraordinary gift for unifying a composition through rich and subtle use of color. By the 1470s Giovanni was painting on a monumental scale works that explore the possibilities of delicate oil glazes while retaining the crystal clarity of earlier works (''Coronation of the Virgin,'' Pesaro; ''St. Francis,'' New York, Frick). From the 1480s Giovanni's gradual loosening and softening of the color achieves greater effects of atmospheric luminosity, and the figures develop breadth and monumentality. He left a notable series of half-length Madonnas (Bergamo; Venice, Accademia) and altarpieces of the Madonna and saints (Venice, Accademia; Frari, 1488; and San Zaccaria, 1505). In these altarpieces the Madonnas are enthroned under hemispherical church apses. The architecture defines and unifies the space in which the figures are harmoniously arranged. Giovanni's work thus spans the era from mid–15th-century experimentation to the classic phase of the High Renaissance. His paintings are among the most beautiful and profound of the Venetian Renaissance.

Bibliography: L. DUSSLER, *Giovanni Bellini* (Vienna 1949). V. GOLOUBEW, *Les Dessins de Jacopo Bellini au Louvre et au British Museum,* 2 v. (Brussels 1908-12). G. GRONAU, *Die Künstlerfamilie Bellini* (Leipzig 1909). F. HEINEMANN, *Giovanni Bellini e i Belliniani,* 2 v. (Venice 1962). P. HENDY and L. GOLDSCHEIDER, *Giovanni Bellini* (New York 1945). M. MEISS, *Giovanni Bellini's St. Francis in the Frick Collection* (Princeton 1964). R. PALLUCCHINI, *Catologo illustrato della mostra di G.B.* (Venice 1949); *Giovanni Bellini* (Milan 1959). L. PLANISCIG, ''Jacopo und Gentile Bellini,'' *Jahrbuch der Kunsthistorischen Sammlungen in Wien* NS 2 (1928) 41–62. G. ROBERTSON, ''The Earlier Work of Giovanni Bellini,'' *Journal of the Warburg and Courtauld Institutes* 23 (1960) 45–59. M. RÖTHLISBERGER, ''Studi su Jacopo Bellini,'' *Saggi e memorie distoria dell'arte* 2 (1958-59) 41-89.

[L. A. ANDERSON]

BELLINI, VINCENZO

Renowned opera composer; b. Catania, Sicily, Nov. 3, 1801; d. Puteaux (near Paris), Sept. 23, 1835. He was the namesake of his grandfather, *maestro* at the Catania cathedral, who saw to his musical training. Bellini's first opera, *Adelson e Salvini* (1825), was produced while he was still a pupil of Zingarelli at the Naples Conservatory.

Giovanni Bellini.

He was soon composing with increasing popularity for the leading opera houses of Italy. His most celebrated works are *Montecchi e Capuletti* (*Romeo and Juliet;* Venice 1830); *La Sonnambula* and *Norma,* both produced in Milan in 1831; and his last opera, *I Puritani,* first performed in 1835 in Paris, where he had been residing since 1833. Although Bellini was gifted neither in comedy as was Donizetti nor in the grand manner as was Rossini, he, like Donizetti, continued and refined the *bel canto* vocal tradition associated with Rossini, and strongly influenced the singing style of Chopin's piano. Despite the threadbare sentiments and poor literary value of his libretti, coupled with the conventional harmony and thin orchestral accompaniments of the music, the abovementioned operas are often revived because of their graceful, elegiac melodies and because they serve admirably as vehicles for virtuoso singing. In his younger years Bellini composed some Masses and psalms that are now forgotten.

Bibliography: A. POUGIN, *Bellini* (Paris 1868). D. J. GROUT, *A Short History of Opera,* 2 v. (2d, rev. and enl. ed. New York 1965). A. EINSTEIN, *Music in the Romantic Era* (New York 1947). *La Revue musicale,* 66 (May 1935), special issue on Bellini. F. BONAVIA, *Grove's Dictionary of Music and Musicians,* ed. E. BLOM, 9 v. (5th ed. London 1954) 1:608–610. G. BARBLAN, *Die Musik in Geschichte und Gegenwart,* ed. F. BLUME (Kassel-Basel 1949–) 1:1611–16. N. SLONIMSKY, ed., *Baker's Biographical Dic-*

Vincenzo Bellini.

tionary of Musicians (5th ed. New York 1958) 123. P. CECCHI, "Temi letterari e individuazione melodrammatica in *Norma* di Vincenzo Bellini," *Recercare,* 9 (1997) 121–153. R. CELLETTI, "Il vocalismo Italiano da Rossini a Donizetti, Parte II: Bellini e Donizetti," *Analecta Musicologia,* 7 (1969) 215–223. J. A. FELDMAN, "*Norma,*" in *International Dictionary of Opera,* ed. C. S. LARUE, 2 v. (Detroit 1993) 941–943. C. GREENSPAN, "*I Puritani* (*The Puritans*)," in *International Dictionary of Opera,* ed. C. S. LARUE, 2 v. (Detroit 1993) 1070–1071; "*La Sonnambula* (*The Sleepwalker*)," in *International Dictionary of Opera,* ed. C. S. LARUE, 2 v. (Detroit 1993) 1264–1266. D. KIMBELL, *Vincenzo Bellini: "Norma"* (Cambridge, Eng. 1998). J. ROSSELLI, *The Life of Bellini* (Cambridge, Eng. 1996).

[R. W. LOWE]

BELLINZAGA, ISABELLA CRISTINA (LOMAZZI)

Author of a controversial book on the spiritual life; b. Milan, 1551; d. there, Jan. 26, 1624. Lomazzi was her family name; Bellinzaga, the name of the maternal uncle who adopted her. In 1584 she made a private vow to follow the spiritual direction of the Jesuits. Under the guidance of Achille GAGLIARDI, and perhaps with his collaboration, she wrote between 1584 and 1594 her little book, *Breve compendio intorno alla perfezione cristiana* (Brescia 1611), better known in its French translation as *Abrégé de la perfection* (Paris 1596). Its central thesis is that perfection consists principally in contempt of all created things, especially self, and in determination to die rather than offend God. That she makes three stages of perfection correspond to increasing passivity of the will caused the book to be suspected of QUIETISM; it was placed on the Index from 1703 until 1900. Going through numerous editions and translated also into German, Dutch, and Spanish, the *Breve compendio* exercised considerable influence on subsequent spiritual writers, including in France, Pierre de BÉRULLE, the Capuchin LAURENT DE PARIS, the Dominican Antoine du Saint-Sacrement, and the Jesuits Jean Joseph SURIN and Jean RIGOLEUC; in Italy, the Basiltan Giuseppe de Camillis and Miguel de MOLINOS.

Bibliography: H. BRÉMOND, *Histoire littéraire du sentiment réligieux en France depuis la fin des guerres de religion jusqu'à nos jours* (Paris 1911–36) 11:3-16. M. VILLER, *Dictionnaire de spiritualité ascétique et mystique: Doctrine et histoire* (Paris 1932—) 1:1940-42.

[M. S. CONLAN]

BELLOC, JOSEPH HILAIRE PIERRE

Historian, biographer, essayist, poet, writer of children's literature; b. La Celle'Saint-Cloud, France, July 27, 1870; d. Guildford, England, July 16, 1953. Hilaire (as he always called himself and under which name he wrote) was the son of Louis and Elizabeth Belloc; his only other sibling, Marie, also became a writer. The family moved to England in 1870, but Belloc spent much of his childhood in France. He attended the Edgbaston Oratory School (1880–87) and matriculated at Oxford in 1892; the previous year, he served his term in the French army. At the Oratory, he was grounded in classics: at Balliol, he read history, was awarded the Brackenbury scholarship, and gained a first class in the History Honours School. Having been unsuccessful in an attempt to secure an expected fellowship, he left Oxford in 1896 for a public career. In the same year, he married Elodie Hogan, a Californian whom he had met in England in 1889. In 1902, Belloc became an English citizen. His wife's death in 1914 left him with the responsibility of rearing their five children.

Belloc's first publication was *Verses and Sonnets* (1895). This was followed by a series of biographies—*Danton* (1899), *Robespierre* (1901), and *Marie Antoinette* (1909); in 1911, Belloc produced a short work on the French Revolution. His travel and critical essays *The Path to Rome* (1902) and *Averil* (1904) aroused considerable interest in his ideas and style. He was a Liberal Member of Parliament (1906–10) and wrote forcefully on political subjects in such works as *The Party System* (1911, with Cecil Chesterton), and *The Servile State* (1912). During World War I, Belloc wrote weekly military comments for the journal *Land and Water.* His son Louis was killed in action just before the armistice.

From 1920 to 1942, Belloc wrote voluminously and lectured in the U.S. and Europe, arousing as much controversy as admiration. His deep personal convictions led to dogmatism and to a myopic view of Germany and of Protestantism; no spark of ecumenism exists in his flaming apology for the Faith. In his handling of moot questions, his expository prose was not always as convincing as his earlier writings. Equally dubious in *Europe and the Faith* (1920) are the style and the thesis that ''the Church is Europe: and Europe is the Church.'' Likewise in *The Jews* (1922), the manner in which he proposed Jewish segregation was as offensive to many of his readers as was the long-standing suspicion that he was anti-Semitic. There is more foundation for the annoyance of readers of *The Jews* who try to discover whether Belloc means literally what he says.

Scholars received Belloc's four-volume *History of England* (1925–31) with coolness. Understandably, they expected documentation of this reinterpretation of history; his personal statement scarcely convinced serious readers that ''religion is the determining force of society,'' and that English institutions do not have Anglo-Saxon origins but instead stem ''from known and recorded civilization.'' The *History,* some commentators declared, was a good story written with force and lucidity, but it was not genuine history.

Belloc himself doubted that he was a historian. He never doubted that he was a writer, and a good one. He produced more than 150 books: history, essays, fiction, light verse, and poetry. He will be best remembered, it seems, for his poetry. The author of *Tarantella* and of rousing songs and ballads was a charming troubadour. He is also well known for his verse and mock cautionary tales for children.

After 1942, Belloc continued to write articles, but produced no new books. The death of his son Peter in 1941 was a shock from which he never recovered. After he suffered a stroke in 1942, Belloc's mind was frequently clouded. On July 12, 1953, he fell near an open fireplace and was fatally burned. His simple funeral was held at West Grinstead; a more elaborate memorial service took place later at Westminster Cathedral.

Bibliography: R. SPEAIGHT, *The Life of Hilaire Belloc* (New York 1957), contains the best bibliographical data on primary and secondary sources. M. A. LOWNDES, *I, Too, Have Lived in Arcadia* (New York 1942); *Young Hilaire Belloc* (New York 1956). E. and R. JEBB, *Testimony to Hilaire Belloc* (London 1956). J. B. MORTON, *Hilaire Belloc* (New York 1955). H. VAN THAL, ed., *Belloc: A Biographical Anthology* (New York 1970).

Joseph Hilaire Pierre Belloc.

[M. A. HART]

BELLOT, PAUL

Benedictine architect active in the modern renewal of church architecture; b. Paris, June 7, 1876; d. St.-Benoit-du-Lac, Canada, July 5, 1944. The son of an architect, he entered the École des Beaux-Arts in 1894 and received his architect's diploma in 1900. After he entered the novitiate at SOLESMES (1902), the monks were exiled from France (as all religious were) under the new law of 1903. The Solesmes monks moved to the Isle of Wight (England), where between 1907 and 1912 Dom Bellot built the abbatial church of QUARR ABBEY, which established his reputation. His earlier designs of 1906 for the Abbey of Oosterhout, Holland (where the monks of the Abbey of Wisque took refuge), had initiated his architectural career. In his monastic life he was professed on May 29, 1904, and ordained on June 10, 1911.

Having moved to Holland after World War I, he designed a number of brick churches both there and in Belgium; when the French monks returned to the Abbey of Wisque, he went with them and designed several new buildings there. Besides brick he began to employ cement and stone in churches he designed from 1930 to 1937; among those in France are the priory convent of Sainte-Bathilde, Vanves (1930-35); Nôtre-Dame des Trévoix, Troyes (1933); Saint-Joseph at Annecy (1936); and the Dominican convent at Montpellier. He also furnished plans for the church of Our Lady of the Conception at Porto, Portugal (1936).

After being called to Canada (1937) to work on the Oratory of Saint-Joseph, Montreal, he was invited in 1938 to lay plans for a definitive monastic structure at the Abbey of Saint-Benoit-du-Lac. With the collaboration of two Canadian architects, M. Félix Racicot and Dom Claude Côté, he made a master plan; construction began in 1939, and the first two new buildings were dedicated on July 11, 1941. His death followed a year of suffering with cancer.

Although his churches are clean and show a sensitive use of materials, in his efforts to create a religious architecture in the 20th century he was unable to break with a strong sentiment for the Middle Ages. Yet his considered use of light and shadow along with studied proportions and rhythms in arches, stairways, and fenestration have created works with a dignity superior to the popular work of his time.

See Also: CHURCH ARCHITECTURE.

Bibliography: *Abbaye Saint-Benoit-du-Lac* (Saint-Léger-Vauban 1962), 50th anniversary brochure. R. GAZEAU, *Catholicisme* 1:1391. J. PICHARD, *Les Églises nouvelles à travers le monde* (Paris 1962); Eng. *Modern Church Architecture,* tr. E. CALLMANN (New York 1960).

[J. PICHARD]

BELLOY, JEAN BAPTISTE DE

Cardinal archbishop of Paris; b. Moragles (Oise), Oct. 19, 1709; d. Paris, June 10, 1808. He studied in Paris, receiving his doctorate in theology in 1737. He was consecrated bishop of Glandèves in 1752. The famous Assembly of 1755 split the French clergy into moderates and zealots, the latter denying the Last Sacraments to all nonsubscribers to Clement XI's *Unigenitus* (1713). Henri BELSUNCE DE CASTELMORAN, Bishop of Marseilles, died during the Assembly, and Belloy, a supporter of the moderate party, was at once named to replace him. Belsunce's misguided zeal for *Unigenitus* had created the danger of schism. Belloy's conciliatory spirit won both sides and restored peace. In July 1790 the National Assembly suppressed the Marseilles diocese. Belloy protested, quietly withdrew to Chambly, and remained there during the French Revolution. In 1801, to help his concordat with Napoleon, Pius VII asked the French bishops to resign. Belloy quickly complied. In 1802 Napoleon named him archbishop of Paris. Belloy accepted the new order with its freedom of conscience and worship and urged Catholics to do the same. Despite his admiration for Napoleon he avoided politics.

Bibliography: A. LESORT, *Dictionnaire d'histoire et de géographie ecclésiastiques* 7:929–31. R. DE CHAUVIGNY, *Le Card. de Belloy e l'Église de Marseille de 1789 à 1802* (Avignon 1930). J. F. MICHAUD, *Biographie universelle ancienne et moderne*, 45 v. (Paris 1854–65) 3:593–594.

[W. E. LANGLEY]

BELLS

A medieval legend held that the bell was ''invented'' in Nola, in the Campania, Italy, and that St. PAULINUS OF NOLA was responsible for its adoption into the Church. Actually it was the fruit of primitive man's discovery that striking one hard object with another produced a sound that could mark the rhythm of his dances. Dried peas in a pod, forerunner of the rattle and the Egyptian sistra, induced man to form rattles of shell, wood, and later hammered metal (the crotal), enclosing hard pellets to produce the sound. When the rattle was opened on the bottom, a finger loop attached to the head, and a pellet hung on the inside to form a clapper, the bell came into being. With the progress of civilization, people became intrigued by bronze vessels whose resonant tone was soon explored. The deep cup was an ancestor of the Western bell and the Oriental barrel-formed bell, while the shallower dish developed into the cymbal. Small bells of one form or another (*tintinnabula* to the Romans) evolved several centuries before Christ. When the Church adopted the bell as a signal in its liturgy, the tinkling cymbal was gradually transformed into the campaniform object that the West knows today.

Early Use. In the early medieval period, churches used a small bell to mark solemn parts of the Mass. As communities grew larger and more people sought protection within monastery or town walls, greater and louder bells were needed. Larger bells meant larger housing—in belfry or campanile, the interesting new architectural form of the 10th and 11th centuries. As the use of bells spread, more and different-sounding bells were required to distinguish one announcement from another. Church and community often shared the bells of the same belfry, as they still do in parts of Europe. There were bells to announce the beginning of Mass, the ANGELUS, birth and death, wedding and feast, fire and flood, to warn of enemies or pestilence, to appease the storm, to call to work, and to cover the fires for the night (Fr. *couvre feu,* curfew). In the 14th century the great tower clocks evolved, marking the quarters on the smaller bells, the hours on the deepest bourdon.

The Musical Bell. As the number of bells hung from a given belfry increased, it became customary, early in the 15th century in the Low Countries and to some extent in the section of England just across the North Sea, to ring the bells together. Until that time it had been enough that the bell function as a signal; it did not have to be pleasing to the ear as well. However, since musicians of that region were on the threshold of evolving the science of harmony, this new development meant searching for forms that would allow the bell to sound euphonic, not only when ringing alone, but also when pealed with others. The bell then took on its characteristic campaniform aspect. The more experienced and musically educated bell-founders discovered that the bell produced not just one note, but a whole series of tones, the pitches of which played a determining part in the purity of the bell. They then developed a form that would embrace the most musical series and learned how to tune each of these partials to a desired pitch. It was found that it was possible to give the bell almost the same series of overtones as that produced by nature in the taut string and the pipe—with one exception: the bell has a minor third, quite contrary to nature. It is this tone that gives the bell its distinctive characteristic, its plaintiveness and appeal. If a bell does not possess this tonal series, or if any of the partials are not on pitch, the bell sounds false in direct measure to the deviation from the norms. Since the 15th century, one criterion of a good founder has been the success with which he tunes his bells. The string and the pipe are nature's instruments; human beings developed and perfected the bell.

Thereafter, in the Low Countries, in adjoining northern France and western Germany, and in parts of Switzerland, peals of three or more bells produced music more pleasing than even the purest single bell. In Flanders and Holland particularly the number of bells was augmented to cover a range of two octaves. After the Reformation, the English abandoned this practice, in the development of which they had participated with the Continent, and now demanded only that their bells occupy positions in the scale. From this time dates "change ringing"—pealing rings of from 5 to 12 bells in ever changing sequences, sometimes for hours at a time—the traditional practice of the Anglican Church. However, in Spain, most of Italy, Scandinavia, the Balkans, and Russia, no thought has been given to purity of bell tone, and any definite pitch is purely accidental. The Orient has never modified its barrel-formed bells, a form incapable of pitch or harmony.

The carillon bells of the "Nieuwe Kerk" or New Church in Delft, Netherlands. (©Michael John Kielty/CORBIS)

Great Bells. Some of the greatest bells in Christendom, installed either singly or as the bourdons (bass bells) of peals or carillons, are the 18,000-pound bell in the Basilica of St. Peter in Rome, the 55,000-pound bourdon of the peal of five bells in Cologne cathedral, St. Stephen's 4,000-pound bell in Vienna, the 40,000 pound bourdon of the carillon in the Riverside Church in New York, and the 38,000-pound bourdon of the carillon at the University of Chicago chapel, as well as the University of Notre Dame's 28,700-pound bell, Sacré Coeur de Montmartre's 44,000-pound bell in Paris, St. Paul's 11,500-pound bell in London, and Lincoln cathedral's 12,000-pound bourdon. In Moscow three bells (none of which is hung to swing) top all of these: one weighing 60,800 pounds; another at 120,000 pounds; and the Tsar Kolokol, the "King of Bells," which has never been used, at 443,772 pounds.

Bibliography: S. N. COLEMAN, *Bells* (New York 1928). J. S. VAN WAESBERGHE, ed., *Cymbala: Bells in the Middle Ages* (Amer. Inst. of Musicology. Studies and Documents 1; Rome 1951). W.

WESCOTT, *Bells and Their Music* (New York 1970). P. PRICE, *Bells and Man* (Oxford, 1983).

[A. L. BIGELOW/EDS.]

BELMONT, FRANÇOIS VACHON DE

Sulpician missionary; b. Grenoble, France, April 2, 1645; d. Montreal, Canada, May 22, 1732. He came from a family of judges and scholars and possessed both fortune and talents. In 1680 he was sent to Canada, where he worked as missionary among the indigenous people, rebuilding at his own expense the ''Mountain Mission'' burned down in 1694. In 1701 he was appointed superior of Saint-Sulpice in Montreal and played an important part in the affairs of the French colony, including the digging of the Lachine Canal, begun by Dollier de Casson, and the erection of the Jesuit Chapel and the façade of Notre Dame Church. He was the author of a history of Canada from 1608 to 1700, published (1840) by the Literary and Historical Society of Quebec in its first series of *Historical Documents.*

Bibliography: O. MAURAULT, *Le Fort des Messieurs* (Montreal 1925). H. GAUTHIER, *Sulpitiana* (Montreal 1926).

[J. LANGIS]

BELSON, THOMAS, BL.

Martyr; b. ca. 1565 at Brill, Aylesbury, Buckinghamshire, England; d. July 5, 1589, hanged at Oxford. He studied at Oxford, then for a time at the English College in Rheims (1584). On a visit to Oxford he was arrested with his confessor Fr. George NICHOLS, Fr. Richard YAXLEY, and Humphrey Pritchard, a servant. They were sent to London for examination by Walsingham and were repeatedly tortured in Bridewell and the Tower. Thereafter they were returned to Oxford for trial. Belson was found guilty of felony for assisting the priests. He was beatified by Pope John Paul II on Nov. 22, 1987 with George Haydock and Companions.

Feast: Feb. 12; Feast of the English Martyrs: May 4 (England).

See Also: ENGLAND, SCOTLAND, AND WALES, MARTYRS OF.

Bibliography: C. KELLY, *Blessed Thomas Belson* (Chester Springs, Penna. 1987). R. CHALLONER, *Memoirs of Missionary Priests,* ed. J. H. POLLEN (rev. ed. London 1924). T. F. KNOX, *First and Second Diaries of English College, Douai* (London 1878). J. H. POLLEN, *Acts of English Martyrs* (London 1891). D. DE YEPES, *Historia Particular de la persecución de Inglaterra* (Madrid 1599).

[K. I. RABENSTEIN]

BELSUNCE DE CASTELMORAN, HENRI FRANÇOIS XAVIER DE

Bishop of Marseilles, foe of Jansenism; b. Chateau de la Force, Périgord, 1671; d. Marseilles, 1755. He was the son of the Marquis de Castelmoran and Ann de Caumont de Lausun. After classical studies at the Collège de Clermont (Louis-le-Grand), he entered the Society of Jesus, but left to become vicar-general of Agen in 1699, and bishop of Marseilles in 1709. By his heroic care of plague victims in 1720–21, he earned the title of ''Good Bishop'' and mention in Pope's *Essay on Man.* Louis XV offered him the See of Laon, with first ecclesiastical peerage in France, and the office of metropolitan of Bordeaux. Both rewards Belsunce refused. As bishop, he fought Jansenism by participating in the synod of Embrun (1727), by ordering his priests to refuse absolution to appellants against *UNIGENITUS*, and by pastoral letters (although these may have been the work of the Jesuit Lemoire). His writings include a biography of his aunt, *Vie de Suzanne-Henriette de Foix* (Agen 1702); *Antiquités de l'Église de Marseille et la sucession de ses évèques* (Marseilles 1747–51); and translations of St. Augustine's *De agone christiano* and St. Robert Bellarmine's *De arte bene moriendi.*

Bibliography: *Oeuvres choisies*, ed. A. JAUFFRET, 2 v. (Metz 1822). T. BÉRENGIER, *Vie de Mgr. Henry de Belsunce, évèque de Marseille*, 2 v. (Lyon 1886–87). P. BARBET-MASSIN, *Éloge de Belzunce* (Paris 1821). P. CALENDINI, *Dictionnaire d'histoire et de géographie ecclésiastiques* 7:951–53.

[V. HEALY]

BELTRÁN, LUIS

Franciscan friar, collaborator of José de SAN MARTÍN and Bolívar; b. Mendoza, Argentina, Sept. 8, 1784; d. Buenos Aires, Dec. 8, 1827. In the course of his studies as a Franciscan, he became interested in mathematics, physics, and mechanics. He was at the motherhouse of the order in Santiago, Chile, when the revolution against Spain erupted. He volunteered in the Chilean army and served as chaplain under General Carrera. His interest in ordnance stood him in good stead, and when the Chilean army had to flee to Argentina in 1814, he was asked by San Martín to take charge of assembling cannon and munitions for the march across the Andes. An indefatigable worker, Beltrán worked near miracles with practically no resources. After the victory of the Army of the Andes over the Spaniards at Maipú in 1818, O'Higgins and San Martín gave Beltrán carte blanche to create the largest and best ordnance establishment in America and to assemble *matériel* for an army of 4,000 men. Beltrán accompanied the Argentine-Chilean expedition to Peru in

1820, supervising the loading of all military supplies on the ships. He served as arms director of the entire artillery in the Peruvian campaign, 1820 to 1824, gaining the rank of lieutenant colonel. After San Martín's withdrawal from Peru, Beltrán served under Bolívar for two years. He returned to Argentina in 1824 but soon left for the front along the Uruguay River, serving in the war against Brazil as chief of munitions under Gen. Martín Rodríguez. His rank of lieutenant colonel was recognized by the government of Buenos Aires in 1826, and to this honor was soon added the rank of sergeant major. He also supervised the provisioning of Admiral Brown's navy. With the victory over Brazil at Ituzaingó, in which Beltrán participated, he retired from the army for reasons of health and returned to Buenos Aires. He was buried in his friar's habit. Beltrán's services to his country can hardly be overestimated. An Argentine historian has said that "he knew how to convert into forge and anvil the very bosom of the Cordillera itself to assure the independence and liberty of the Continent . . . [making] possible, with Franciscan self-abnegation, the liberating movement of San Martín."

Bibliography: L. CÓRDOBA, *Fray Luis Beltrán: Reivindicación histórica del prócer* (Mendoza 1938). F. L. HOFFMANN, "A Franciscan Fighter for South American Independence," *Americas* 10 (1954) 289–300.

[F. L. HOFFMAN]

BÉNARD, LAURENT

Benedictine reformer and founder of the Congregation of Saint Maur; b. Nevers, France, 1573; d. Paris, April 20, 1620. Laurent entered the Monastery of St. Stephen, Nevers, then a dependency of Cluny. He studied at Bourges and Paris, becoming a doctor of the Sorbonne. After his ordination he devoted himself to preaching. As prior of the College of Cluny at Paris, he reintroduced cloister and other necessary reforms. He was associated with the founder of the Congregation of St. Vanne, Dom Didier de la Cour, in reforming French monasteries. Laurent was visitor for the Abbey of Fontevrault and helped to reestablish observance at the Abbey of Montmartre. In May of 1618, a general chapter of reformed Benedictines commissioned him to form a congregation independent of Lorraine. Six months later, the newly founded Congregation of Saint Maur held its first chapter at the Monastery of Blancs-Manteaux. Laurent had applied to Rome for a bull of erection, but he died before it was promulgated. His writings deal mainly with religious topics, especially with the Benedictine rule and life.

Bibliography: J. FRANÇOIS, *Bibliothèque générale des écrivains de l'Ordre de Saint Benoît,* 4 v. (Bouillon 1777-78; reprint Louvain 1961) 1:106–107. B. HEURTEBIZE, *Dictionnaire d'histoire et de géographie ecclésiastiques* (Paris 1912–) 7:1028-30. R. P. TASSIN, *Histoire littéraire de la congrégation de Saint-Maur* (Brussels 1770).

[B. EGAN]

BENAVIDES, ALONSO DE

Franciscan missionary in New Mexico; b. San Miguel, Azores, *c.* 1580; d. 1636. He joined the Franciscan Order in Mexico City, making his religious profession on Aug. 12, 1603. He worked in various parts of Mexico, carrying out functions of the Holy Office on several occasions. On Oct. 19, 1623, he was chosen as *custos,* or regional superior, of the Franciscan missions of New Mexico. He did not arrive there until the end of 1625, taking formal possession of his office on Jan. 24 and 25, 1626. He governed the activities of the Church in New Mexico until early 1629. In 1630 he was sent to Spain to give an account of the mission work in New Mexico to the king and the Franciscan minister general. In that year he presented to the royal court a report that gained the attention of both king and pope. Remaining in Spain, he publicized the work of the Franciscans in New Mexico and sought the appointment of a bishop for the area. On Feb. 12, 1634, he presented a revised Memorial on the missions of New Mexico to Pope Urban VIII. In late 1634 royal provision was made for his return to Mexico, but he stayed in Spain until February of 1636. He then went to Lisbon and soon afterward was appointed auxiliary bishop of the Diocese of Goa in India. He sailed for his new post in April of 1636 but died before reaching it.

Bibliography: B. H. MORROW, ed., *A Harvest of Reluctant Souls: The Memorial of Fray Alonso De Benavides, 1630* (Colorado 1996).

[F. B. WARREN]

BENAVIDES, MIGUEL DE

Dominican missionary and archbishop of Manila; b. Carrión de los Condes (Palencia), Spain, 1552; d. Manila, June 26, 1605, or July 26, 1607. Benavides studied under D. Bañez and taught at Valladolid. In 1586 he sailed for Manila, where he and his companions established the Dominican province of the Most Holy Rosary. He was the first of the missionaries to learn the Chinese language in order to instruct the Chinese living in Manila. In 1589 he went to China but was imprisoned there and later expelled. He was sent to Madrid in 1590 to act as procurator for the Dominican province of the Philippines and to carry on important negotiations with the Royal Council for the Indies. In 1595 he was named bishop of New Segovia in the Philippines and in 1597 became archbishop of Manila. Zealous for learning, he founded the Colegio de Santo Tomás in Manila, which later became a university.

Bibliography: J. QUÉTIF and J. ECHARD, *Scriptores Ordinis Praedicatorum* (New York 1959) 2:363–364. R. STREIT and J. DINDINGER, *Bibliotheca missionum* (Freiburg 1916) 4: 358–359. J. FERRANDO and J. FONSECA, eds., *Historia de los PP. Domenicos en las islas Filipinas* (Madrid 1870–72). R. D. FERRERES, *Enciclopedia de la Religión Católica* 1:1402.

[P. K. MEAGHER]

BENEDICAMUS DOMINO

The concluding formula that was historically prescribed in the Latin rite for the Divine Office. Before the liturgical reforms of Vatican II, it was also used as an alternate concluding formula for masses when the Gloria was not sung. The earliest traces of the *Benedicamus* as a concluding formula at Mass are to be found in the Gallican liturgy *c.* 800 (Bishop, *Liturgica historica* 323; Theodulf of Orleans, *Capitulare* 2; *see* GALLICAN RITES, CHANTS OF).

As a replacement for the *ITE, MISSA EST* in the Roman rite it appears, under Galilean influence, for the first time in the 11th century (Bernold of Constance, *Micrologus* 19, *Patrologia latina* 151:990). The criterion for its use to replace the *Ite* appears to have been twofold. First, it was used on days when the Mass did not have a *Gloria.* Thus, the idea developed that the *Ite* was an expression of joy to be used only on festive days, while the *Benedicamus* was substituted on days of a more penitential character. Similarly, the *Requiescant in pace* began to replace the *Ite* in Requiem Masses from about the 12th century. Second, it was used when the divine service continued, as at the midnight Mass of Christmas when Lauds followed, or on Holy Thursday when the procession with the Blessed Sacrament followed the evening Mass.

The medieval melodies for the *Benedicamus Domino* may be grouped in three basic categories: (1) those composed for the Divine Office (e.g., Lauds and Vespers); (2) those adapted from the *Ite, missa est* melodies for use at Mass; and (3) those composed especially for the Mass. The melodies composed for use at the Divine Office show the greatest sensitivity toward the characteristics of the Latin language: the adapted melodies for use at Mass are decidedly inferior in this regard. The *Benedicamus* TROPES, as found in early 12th-century MSS of the school of St. Martial in Limoges (Paris B.N. lat. 1120, 903, 887, nouv. acq. 1871), show the development of one of the most important structural devices in all medieval music: the *tenor*. Furthermore, the *Benedicamus* trope *Humane prolis*, also of the St. Martial school, has two simultaneously sung texts (the chief feature of the early motet). The *Benedi camus* trope *Congaudeant catholici* found in the Codex Calixtinus (c. 1140) of Santiago de Compostela is often cited as the oldest three-part composition known.

Bibliography: *Antiphonale monasticum* (Paris 1934). *Gradual Romanum* (New York 1961). J. HANDSCHIN, ''Trope, Sequence and Conductus,'' *New Oxford History of Music* 2:128–174. J. A. JUNGMANN, *The Mass of the Roman Rite*, tr. F. A. BRUNNER, 2 v. (New York 1951–55) 2:434–437. G. REESE, *Music in the Middle Ages* (New York 1940). W. APEL, *Gregorian Chant* (Bloomington, IN 1958).

[C. KELLY/EDS.]

BENEDICT, ST.

Monastic founder; b. *c.* 480, Nursia, Italy; d. *c.* 547, Monte Cassino, Italy. Author of the most celebrated of monastic rules, founder of the abbeys of Subiaco and Monte Cassino, patriarch of western cenobitic life, one of the patron saints of Europe, Benedict has given his name to an order and way of life that have influenced the Catholic Church and Western civilization profoundly in the centuries since his death. The source that provides details of Benedict's life is book two of the *Dialogues* of Pope Gregory the Great. Although written as a form of hagiography intended to edify the reader, the historical details contained in the work correspond with the figures and events of sixth-century Italy.

Life. Benedict was born of a distinguished family in the central Italian city of Nursia around 480. As a young man, he was sent to Rome to further his education. Rejecting what he saw as the corrupt and depraved environment of the city, Benedict retired first to the village of Affile, east of Rome, then to a cave in a rugged region near Subiaco, where he spent time in solitude and ascetical practice. A testament to Benedict's reputation for holiness of life came when a group of local monks asked him to serve as their superior in nearby Vicovaro. However after Benedict insisted upon a reform of their way of life, they attempted to kill him by placing poison in his drinking cup. The *Dialogues* relate how when Benedict blessed the cup, it shattered, a scene that has been preserved in Benedictine iconography. Benedict then moved back to the ancient villa of Nero near Subiaco, where he attracted a growing number of adherents and eventually oversaw the growth of twelve different monasteries. The success of his project prompted a local priest, Florentius, in his envy, to send Benedict a loaf of bread in which he

"Saint Benedict Supervising the Construction of Twelve Monasteries," 16th-century Italian fresco painting by Il Sodoma, Monte Oliveto Maggiore, Siena, Italy. (© Archivo Iconografico S.A./CORBIS)

had concealed poison. The *Dialogues* again relate how Benedict was given knowledge of the deed and ordered a raven that would come to feed at the monastery to take away the bread in its beak, another scene that has become a staple in artistic renderings of Benedict.

Benedict then left Subiaco with a band of his monks and went south of Rome to Monte Cassino, an elevated redoubt that had formerly been the site of a pagan temple to Apollo. Benedict destroyed the temple, replacing it with two oratories, dedicated to St. John the Baptist and St. Martin of Tours. It was at Monte Cassino that the large portion of the miracles and wonders recounted by Gregory the Great took place. One reads of secular rulers with whom Benedict interacted, such as the Gothic King Totila, as well as contemporaries such as Germanus of Capua and Sabinus of Canosa. One also learns of some of Benedict's more noted followers, foremost of whom are Maurus and Placid, sons of Roman nobility. One also discovers Benedict's sister, Scholastica, who established her own community of women at Monte Cassino and would eventually be buried there with her brother.

The time of Benedict's monastic experiment at Monte Cassino was one of intense social upheaval, with wars of the Goths and Lombards, famines and plagues, many of which are recounted in the *Dialogues*. It was at Monte Cassino that Benedict realized the final form of his rule for monks and where his death took place around the year 547.

Cult and Patronage. Even though Gregory the Great's *Dialogues* did much to enhance the reputation of Benedict, there is no indication of a devotion to St. Benedict before the destruction of Monte Cassino by the Lombards about 577. After the monastery's restoration under Abbot Petronax (*c.* 720) there is evidence to suggest a cult surrounding Benedict's tomb. The martyrologies and liturgical calendars of Monte Cassino, dating from the eighth century, mention a solemnity celebrated on March 21. This date was later observed as the feast of Benedict's transitus (death). Later the liturgical celebration for the wider Church was transposed to July 11, the date that marked the translation of the relics of Benedict to the abbey of Saint-Benoit-sur-Loire, Fleury. Monks of that abbey in France recovered the bones of Benedict from Monte Cassino after the abbey had been sacked in the late seventh century and brought them to Fleury. From that time a cult began to flourish, as well as a considerable literature occasioned by the presence of the relics in the monastery. The cult was soon picked up at Monte Cassino itself. Pope Zachary sent a copy of the Rule of Benedict to the monks of Monte Cassino at the time of the restoration of the monastery in the first half of the eighth century under Abbot Petronax.

Ancient iconography of Benedict includes frescoes in the eighth-century subterranean basilica of Hermes at Rome, the ninth-century monastery of Monte Civate, and the tenth-century lower church of St. Chrysogonus in Rome's Trastavere; a number of miniatures in tenth- and eleventh-century manuscripts; the antependium of the eleventh-century cathedral of Basel; capitals on the twelfth-century basilica at Fleury; and the frescoes on the thirteenth-century church at Subiaco's Sacro Speco.

Devotion to Saint Benedict in modern times has been popularized chiefly through the Benedictine medal. A manuscript dating back to the early fifteenth century, discovered at the Bavarian Abbey of Metten in the seventeenth century, provided a drawing with a representation of St. Benedict, as well as a detailed explanation of the letters found on the medal. Subsequent devotion led to two types of Benedictine medals. The first is found in various sizes and is known as the ''Ordinary'' medal. The second is known as the ''Jubilee'' or ''Centenary'' medal. It was struck in 1880 at Monte Cassino in commemoration of the 1400th anniversary of the birth of St. Benedict and has become the more popular.

The ''Jubilee'' medal depicts on one side Benedict holding in his hands a cross and his rule. On the other side there is a cruciform design with the letters C.S.P.B., which correspond to the Latin phrase ''Crux Sancti Patris Benedicti'' (Cross of our Holy Father Benedict). On the perpendicular bar of the cross are the letters C.S.S.M.L, which correspond to the Latin phrase ''Crux Sacra Sit Mihi Lux'' (May the holy cross be a light to me). On the horizontal bar are the letters N.D.S.M.D., which correspond to the Latin phrase ''Non Draco Sit Mihi Dux'' (Let not the dragon [devil] be my guide). Around the margin are the letters V.R.S.N.S.M.V.S.M.Q.L.I.V.B., which correspond to the Latin verse, ''Vade Retro Satana! Numquam Suade Mihi Vana. Sunt Mala Quae Libas; Ipse Venena'' (Get behind me, Satan! Do not persuade me with your vanities. The libation you offer me is evil; go drink your own poison). The motto of the Benedictine Order, ''Pax,'' is found above the cross. On the side of the medal depicting St. Benedict, there are scenes of the poisoned cup, shattered by the sign of the cross, as well as of the raven, ready to carry away the poisoned loaf of bread sent to him. Above the cup and the raven stands the phrase ''Crux S. Patris Benedicti'' (Cross of Holy Father Benedict). Around the border of one side stands the phrase ''Ejus in obitu nostro praesentia muniamur'' (May we be protected by his presence at our death).

Tradition has it that Benedict used these phrases when making the sign of the cross against anything having to do with the devil or temptation. Its power is affirmed by the fact that it is the only medal in the Catholic Church whose blessing has a special exorcism in the Roman Ritual.

Feast: July 11.

Bibliography: I. SCHUSTER, *Storia di san Benedetto e dei suoi tempi* (3d ed. Viboldone 1953); Eng. tr. G. J. ROETTGER, *Saint Benedict and His Times* (St. Louis 1951). K. HALLINGER, ''Development of the Cult and of Devotion to St. Benedict,'' *American Benedictine Review* 36:2 (June 1985) 193–215. T. KARDONG, ''A New Look at Gregory's Dialogues,'' *American Benedictine Review* 36:1 (March 1985) 44–64; *The Benedictines* (Collegeville, Minn. 1988). A. L. CONDE, *San Benito Y Los Benedictinos*, v. 1 (Braga, Portugal 1992). A. DE VOGUE, ''La Foi et le monde au temps de saint Benoit, pere de L'Occident,'' *Ecoute* 162 (February 1968); *The Life of St. Benedict-Gregory the Great* (Petersham, Mass. 1993).

[J. RIPPINGER]

BENEDICT I, POPE

Pontificate: June 2, 575 to July 30, 579. The successor of Pope JOHN III was very likely elected soon after his death but could not be consecrated until a year later, apparently awaiting imperial confirmation. The Lombards reached Rome and besieged the city (579). Help had been requested of the Emperor Justin II in the name of the pope and the Roman Senate, but the troops the emperor sent were inadequate, and the grain ships from Egypt provided only temporary relief for the city. The emperor and his wife Sophia probably gave to Benedict the precious reliquary in the form of a jeweled cross containing a piece of the true cross, which is still preserved in the treasury of the Vatican basilica, a masterpiece of Byzantine workmanship. He consecrated twenty-one bishops, including John III of Ravenna, thus extending papal influence to the center of Byzantine rule in Italy. Very little is known about his reign. Benedict I was buried in St. Peter's.

Bibliography: *Liber pontificalis*, ed. L. DUCHESNE (Paris 1886–92, 1958) 1:308; 3:92. R. U. MONTINI, *Le tombe dei papi*

(Rome 1957) 112. H. JEDIN, *History of the Church* (New York 1980), 2:629. J. N. D. KELLY, *Oxford Dictionary of Popes* (New York 1986) 64–65. J. RICHARDS, *Popes and Papacy the Early Middle Ages* (London 1979) 165–166.

[J. CHAPIN]

BENEDICT II, POPE, ST.

Pontificate: June 26, 684 to May 8, 685. He was elected soon after the death of Pope LEO II (July 3, 683), but because of delay in obtaining imperial confirmation, he was not consecrated until June 684. A Roman, he was trained in the urban *SCHOLA CANTORUM* and ordained to its priesthood. Two letters antedating his consecration designate him *electus*. Good relations between Emperor CONSTANTINE IV Pogonatus and Benedict are reflected in the former's sending the pope locks of his son's hair and in his remitting the mandate that papal elections be imperially ratified, though the exarch at RAVENNA still had to be notified. (The new procedures for installing a pope are recorded in the Roman *LIBER DIURNUS*, form. 82–85). Benedict's directive of 683–684 that WILFRID OF YORK be restored to the See of YORK, of which he had been deprived in 677, was partially honored in 686. Benedict's support of the acts of the Third Council of CONSTANTINOPLE was manifest in his futile effort to secure the recantation of MONOTHELETISM by Macarius, the deposed (since March 681) patriarch of Antioch and in his dispatching the notary, Peter, to Spain to secure its hierarchy's adherence to the acts of the Council. In November 684 the Council of TOLEDO XIV endorsed the anti-Monothelite decrees of Constantinople III, but the pope objected to two expressions in the *Apologia* forwarded by Abp. JULIAN OF TOLEDO.

Feast: May 7.

Bibliography: *Liber pontificalis,* ed. L. DUCHESNE (Paris 1886–1958) 1:363–365; 3:96. P. JAFFÉ, *Regesta pontificum romanorum ab condita ecclesia ad annum post Christum natum 1198* (Graz 1959) 1:241242; 2:699. F. DÖLGER, *Corpus der griechischen Urkunden des Mittelalters und der neueren Zeit* (Munich 1924–32) 252. J. D. MANSI, *Sacrorum Conciliorum nova et amplissima collectio* (Graz 1960) 11:1086–92; 12:10–12, 1035. H. K. MANN, *The Lives of the Popes in the Early Middle Ages from 590 to 1304* (London 1902–32) 1.2:54–63. F. BAIX, *Dictionnaire d'histoire et de géographie ecclésiastiques,* ed. A. BAUDRILLART et al. (Paris 1912) 8:9–14. O. BERTOLINI, *Roma di fronte a Bisanzio e ai Longobardi* (Bologna 1941). E. CASPAR, *Geschichte de Papsttums von den Anfängen bis zur Höhe der Weltherrschaft* (Tubingen 1930–33) 2:614–619, 673–676, 782–785. J. N. D. KELLY, *Oxford Dictionary of Popes* (New York 1986) 79–80.

[H. G. J. BECK]

BENEDICT III, POPE

Pontificate: July 855 to Apr. 17, 858. He was a Roman cardinal-priest of St. Calixtus when elected to the papacy. The party of the Emperor, LOUIS II, however, supported the anti-pope, ANASTASIUS THE LIBRARIAN, even though LEO IV had excommunicated him in 853. But Benedict won recognition because the clergy and people of Rome remained loyal. According to a 13th-century legend the popess JOAN governed the Church during this pontificate. In attempting to curb the licentiousness of the nobility, Benedict threatened to excommunicate Hubert, the brother of Queen Theutberga of Lorraine, for plundering monasteries; and insisted that Ingeltrude leave the court of LOTHAIR II OF LORRAINE and return to her husband, Count Boso. Benedict protested against the English who had deposed their bishops without trial and condemned the inaction of the French hierarchy in not removing clerical abuses. He refused to sanction the deposition of Gregory, the Archbishop of Syracuse, by IGNATIUS, the Patriarch of Constantinople, until he had examined the evidence. At the request of HINCMAR OF REIMS, Benedict approved the acts of the Council of Soissons (853), which upheld Hincmar's claim to the See of REIMS, provided that the rights of the Holy See were preserved.

Bibliography: P. JAFFÉ, *Regesta pontificum romanorum ab condita ecclesia ad annum post Christum natum 1198* (Graz 1956) 1:235–236. *Liber pontificalis,* ed. L. DUCHESNE (Paris 1886–1958) 2:140–150. F. BALX, *Dictionnaire d'histoire et de géographie ecclésiastiques,* ed. A. BAUDRILLART et al. (Paris 1912) 8:14–27. J. HALLER, *Das Papsttum* (Stuttgart 1950–53) v.2. H. K. MANN, *The Lives of the Popes in the Early Middle Ages from 590 to 1304* (London 1902–32) 2:308–329. J. BOUSSARD, "Le diplôme de Hugues Capet, de 988, pour l'abbaye de Corbie," *Journal des Savants* (Paris 1976) 54–64. P. H. DEPREUX, "Büchersuche und Büchertausch im Zeitalter der karolingischen Renaissance am Beispiel des Briefwechsels des Lupus von Ferrières," *Archiv für Kulturgeschichte* (1993) 290. C. LEONARDI, *Lexikon für Theologie und Kirche,* 3d. ed., (1995). J. N. D. KELLY, *Oxford Dictionary of Popes* (New York 1986) 105–106.

[S. MCKENNA]

BENEDICT IV, POPE

Pontificate: Jan.–April 900 to July 903. A Roman, ordained by Pope FORMOSUS, Benedict summoned a Lateran synod (900), which validated the consecrations and ordinations of Formosus. His generosity toward those in distress was praised by Frodoard the historian. This is evident in his support of Stephen, unjustly deprived of his see at Sorrento, Italy, and of an eastern prelate, Malacenus, who had been driven into exile by the Saracens. He formally excommunicated the murderer of Fulk, the Archbishop of Reims, and ordered the French bishops to promulgate this decree throughout the country. In February 901 he crowned Louis III, the Blind, King of Provence and Emperor of Italy. But Louis was defeated by BERENGAR I in 902 and forced to take an oath to leave Italy forever. At Benedict's death, the papacy became the object of party strife.

Bibliography: P. JAFFÉ, *Regesta pontificum romanorum ab condita ecclesia ad annum post Christum natum 1198* (Graz 1956) 1:306. *Liber pontificalis,* ed. L. DUCHESNE (Paris 1886–1958) 2:233. H. K. MANN, *The Lives of the Popes in the Early Middle Ages from 590 to 1304* (London 1902–32) 4:103–110. F. BAIX, *Dictionnaire d'histoire et de géographie ecclésiastiques,* ed. A. BAUDRILLART et al. (Paris 1912) 8:27–31. W. KÖLMEL, *Rom und der Kirchenstaat im 10. Und 11. Jahrhundert* (Berlin 1935). J. HALLER, *Das Papsttum* (Stuttgart 1950–53) 2:193, 546. R. BENERICETTI, *La cronologia dei Papi dei secoli IX–XI secondo le carte di Ravenna,* (1999) 31–32. J. N. D. KELLY, *Oxford Dictionary of Popes* (New York 1986) 117–118.

[S. MCKENNA]

BENEDICT V, POPE

Pontificate: May 964 to July 4, 964 or 965; d. Hamburg, Germany, July 4, 966?. He was a deacon of Rome, noted for virtue and learning. His election infuriated the emperor OTTO I, who regarded LEO VIII as lawful pope. The Romans tried to prevent the emperor's army from entering their city, but hunger forced their surrender. In a Lateran synod, convened by Otto and Leo VIII (June 23, 964), Benedict admitted, according to Liutprand, that he was an intruder. He was publicly degraded, reduced to deacon, and sent to Hamburg, where he was placed in the charge of Archbishop ADALDAG until death. According to the *Annuario Pontificio* (2001), "If Leo VIII was a legitimate pope, Benedict V . . . is an antipope." In 988, OTTO III transferred his remains to Rome.

Bibliography: *Monumenta Germaniae Historica: Scriptores* ser. 4, 3:626–627. P. JAFFÉ, *Regesta pontificum romanorum ab condita ecclesia ad annum post Christum natum 1198* (Graz 1956) 1:325. *Liber pontificalis,* ed. L DUCHESNE 2:251. H. K. MANN, *The Lives of the Popes in the Early Middle Ages from 590 to 1304* 4:273–281. F. BALX, *Dictionnaire d'histoire et de géographie ecclésiastiques,* ed. A. BAUDRILLART et al. (Paris 1912) 8:31–38. P. BREZZI, *Roma e l'Imperio medioevale* (Bologne 1947). J. HALLER, *Das Papsttum* (Stuttgart 1950–53) 2:213. H. ZIMMERMANN, "Die Deposition der Päpste . . . Benedikt V," *Mitteilungen des Instituts für österreichische Geschichtsforschung* 68 (1960) 209–225. J. N. D. KELLY, *Oxford Dictionary of Popes* (New York 1986) 128–9.

[S. MCKENNA]

BENEDICT VI, POPE

Pontificate: Dec. 972 to July 974. A Roman by birth and a member of the clergy, he was chosen as pope by OTTO I. When Otto died, May 7, 973, and while his son OTTO II was fully occupied with German affairs, the nobility of Rome rose against Benedict. Under the leadership of Crescentius I (*see* CRESCENTII) they made Benedict a prisoner (June 974) and chose as antipope a deacon named Franco, who called himself Boniface VII. All the evidence indicates that it was he who ordered Benedict to be strangled in prison, June 974. Surviving documents of Benedict's pontificate concerning the dispute between Archbishop Frederick of Salzburg and Bishop PILGRIM OF PASSAU over the jurisdiction in Noricum and Pannonia (Hungary) are forgeries.

Bibliography: P. JAFFÉ, *Regesta pontificum romanorum ab condita ecclesia ad annum post Christum natur 1198* (Graz 1956) 1:331, 2:707. *Liber pontificalis,* ed. L. DUCHESNE (Paris 1886–1958) 2:255–256, 568. H. K. MANN, *The Lives of the Popes in the Early Middle Ages from 590 to 1304* (London 1902–32) 4:305–314. F. BAIX, *Dictionnaire d'histoire et de géographie ecclésiastiques,* ed. A. BAUDRILLART et al. (Paris 1912) 8:38–43. J. HALLER, *Das Papsttum* (Stuttgart 1950–53) 2:217–255. J. N. D. KELLY, *Oxford Dictionary of Popes* (New York 1986) 130.

[S. MCKENNA]

BENEDICT VII, POPE

Pontificate: Oct. 974 to July 10, 983. Benedict was a Roman and former bishop of Sutri. He was chosen as pope by the emperor OTTO II. At his election, the antipope, Boniface VII (Franco), fled to Constantinople. Working in harmony with the emperor, Benedict granted many privileges to the churches and monasteries of Germany and concerned himself with the conversion of the SLAVS. But his decision to suppress the German See of Merseburg (981) was a setback in the conversion of Central Europe. Benedict published a strongly worded condemnation of simony (981). He allowed St. MAJOLUS of CLUNY to place his monastery under the special protection of the Holy See and granted the same privilege to the Abbey of SAINTVALÉRY, recently founded by Hugh Capet. This practice later became more common and prepared the way for the reform movement of the 11th century.

See Also: CLUNIAC REFORM; GREGORIAN REFORM.

Bibliography: P. JAFFÉ, *Regesta pontificum romanorum ab condita ecclesia ad annum post Christum natum 1198* (Graz 1956) 1:402–443, 2:707. *Liber pontificalis,* ed. L. DUCHESNE (Paris 1886–1958) 2:258. H. K. MANN, *The Lives of the Popes in the Early Middle Ages from 590 to 1304* (London 1902–32) 4:315–329. F. BALX, *Dictionnaire d'histoire et de géographie ecclésiastiques,* ed. A. BAUDRILLART et al. (Paris 1912) 8:43–61. G. SCHWAIGER, *Lexikon für Theologie und Kirche*, ed. J. HOFER and K. RAHNER (Freiburg 1957–65) 2:174–175. M. DE WAHA, "Sigebert de Gembloux faussaire? Le chroniqueur et les 'sources anciennes' de son abbaye," *Revue Belge de Philogie et d'Histoire* 55 (Bruxelles 1977)

989–1036. F. RONIG, ''Erzbischof Egbert von Trier (977–993),'' *Trierer Theologische Zeitschrift* (1994) 81–91. G. WOLF, ''Das Marienkloster zu Memleben,'' *Archiv für Diplomatik, Schriftgeschichte, Siegelkunde und Wappenkunde* (1995) 21–30. J. N. D. KELLY, *Oxford Dictionary of Popes* (New York 1986) 131–132.

[S. MCKENNA]

BENEDICT VIII, POPE

Pontificate: May 18, 1012 to April 9, 1024; b. Theophylactus. He was a brother both to that Alberic who became *consul et dux* of Rome and to the future Pope JOHN XIX, and was the first pope of the TUSCULANI. Benedict, and not the candidate of the CRESCENTII, the antipope Gregory VI, obtained the approval of HENRY II, whom he crowned emperor in Rome in 1014. Benedict was a statesman of stature. In 1016 the alliance of the pope, Genoa, and Pisa successfully liberated SARDINIA from the Spanish Saracens and freed the mainland from their incursions. Byzantine pressure in southern Italy was, however, too strong for the local forces to contain, and in 1020, Benedict journeyed to BAMBERG to solicit imperial support. While in Bamberg he consecrated St. Stephen's church, and Henry renewed the *Ottonianum* (*see* PAPACY), at the same time granting the bishopric of Bamberg as a fief to the Roman Church. The campaign of the emperor, accompanied by the pope, in southern Italy (1021–22), could do no more than restore the status quo. The most pressing problem of the age was REFORM IN THE CHURCH. Benedict followed the leadership of Henry II. The Roman synod of 1014 had issued decrees concerning irregular ordinations (*see* SIMONY) and the alienation of CHURCH PROPERTY. The great synod of Pavia, August 1020, which opened with the pope's address, decreed degradation for uncelibate clerics in higher orders and the reduction of their offspring to the status of slavery (*see* CELIBACY, HISTORY OF). The emperor approved these decrees and enacted them as the law of the empire.

Bibliography: P. JAFFÉ, *Regesta pontificum romanorum ab condita ecclesia ad annum post Christum natum 1198* (Graz 1956) 1:506–514. *Liber pontificalis,* ed. L. DUCHESNE (Paris 1886–1958) 2:61–92. P. F. KEHR, *Regesta Pontificum Romanorum. German Pontificia,* ed. A. BRACKMANN (Berlin 1911—). P. F. KEHR, *Regesta Pontificum Romanorum. Italia Pontificia* (Berlin 1906-35). H. K. MANN, *The Lives of the Popes in the Early Middle Ages from 590 to 1304* (London 1902–32) 5. F. BAIX, *Dictionnaire d'histoire et de géographie ecclésiastiques,* ed. A. BAUDRILLART et al. (Paris 1912) 8:61–92. W. KÖLMEL, *Rom und der Kirchenstaat im 10. und 11. Jahrhundert* (Berlin 1935). A. FLICHE and V. MARTIN, eds., *Histoire de l'église depuis les origines jusqu'à nos jours* 7. J. HALLER, *Das Papsttum* (Stuttgart 1950–53) 2:229–234. H. SCHMIDINGER, ''Die Palliumverleihung Benedikts VIII. für Ragusa,'' *Mitteilungen des Instituts für österreichische Geschichtsforschung* 58 (1950) 31–49. F. X. SEPPELT, *Geschichte der Päpste von den Anfängen bis zur Mitte des 20. Jh.* (Munich 1954–59) 2:402–408. R. BENERICETTI, *La cronologia dei Papi dei secoli IX–XI secondo le carte di Ravenna* (1999) 62–65. K. J. HERRMANN, *Das Tuskulanerpapsttum (1012–1046). Benedikt VIII, Johannes XIX, Benedikt IX,* (Stuttgart 1973). H. JAKOBS, ''Anmerkungen zur Urkunde Benedikts VIII für Bernward von Hildesheim,'' *Niedersächsisches Jahrbuch für Landesgeschichte* 66 (1994) 199–214. J. F. LEMARIGNIER, ''Paix et réforme monastique en Flandre et en Normandi autour de l'année 1023. Quelques observations:'' in *Droit privé et institutions régionales. Études historiques offertes à Jean Yver* (Paris 1976) 443–68. M. NIEDERKORN-BRUCK, *Der heilige Koloman: der erste Patron Niederösterreichs,* (Vienna 1992). T. STRUVE, *Lexikon des Mittelalters* 7 (Munich-Zurich 1992–93), s.v. ''Seligenstadt, Synode v. 1023.'' J. N. D. KELLY, *Oxford Dictionary of Popes* (New York 1986) 139.

[V. GELLHAUS]

BENEDICT IX, POPE

Pontificate: August or September 1032 to September 1044; b. Theophylactus; d. Grottaferrata, 1055?. He was a son of Alberic III, leader of the TUSCULANI, and he simoniacally succeeded his uncles, BENEDICT VIII and JOHN XIX. Though young (perhaps 30), Theophylactus was certainly not a boy of 12 when he became pope. His personal conduct was often not edifying. The first 12 years of Benedict's pontificate were peaceful, and he was free to meet CONRAD II AT CREMONA and Spello and to journey to Marseilles. There was no controversy with the emperor; and when Conrad uncanonically deposed Abp. Heribert of Milan, Benedict compliantly excommunicated him. In 1044 a revolt drove Benedict from Rome and installed Bishop John of Sabina as antipope Sylvester III. In March 1045 Benedict in turn drove out Sylvester. Then on May 1 Benedict sold his papal office to his baptismal sponsor, the reforming archpriest John Gratian, Pope GREGORY VI. In the fall of 1045 the reform-minded Emperor HENRY III entered the fray. Reform synods held at Pavia, Sutri, and Rome deposed Gregory, and Suidger of Bamberg was acclaimed Pope CLEMENT II. After Clement's untimely death in 1047, Benedict again controlled Rome, Nov. 8, 1047 to July 16, 1048, until Boniface of Tuscany, acting on Henry's orders, drove him out for good and installed the new pope, DAMASUS II. Benedict died probably at the end of 1055.

Bibliography: P. JAFFÉ, *Regesta pontificum romanorum ab condita ecclesia ad annum post Christum natum 1198* (Graz 1956) 1:519–523. P. F. KEHR, *Regesta Pontificum Romanorum. Italia Pontificia* (Berlin 1911) 6.2. *Liber pontificalis,* ed. L. DUCHESNE (Paris 1886–1958) 2:270–272. G. B. BORINO, ''L'elezione e la deposizione di Gregorio VI,'' *Archivio della Societa Romana di Storia Patria* 39 (1916) 142–252, 295–410; ''Invitus ultra montes cure domno Papa Gregorio abii,'' *Studi gregoriani,* 1 (1947) 3–46. R. L. POOLE, ''Benedict IX and Gregory VI,'' *Proceedings of the British Academy* 8 (1917–18) 199–235. H. K. MANN, *The Lives of the Popes in the Early Middle Ages from 590 to 1304* (London 1902–32) 6. F. BAIX and L. JADIN, *Dictionnaire d'histoire et de géographie eccle-*

siastiques, ed. A. BAUDRILLART et al. (Paris 1912) 8:93–105. A. FLICHE and V. MARTIN, eds., *Histoire de l'église depuis les origines jusqu'à nos jours* (Paris 1935) 7. T. SCHIEFFER, "Heinrich II und Konrad II," *Deutsches Archiv für Erforschung des Mittelalters* 8 (1951) 384–437. F. X. SEPPELT, *Geschichte der Päpste von den Anfängen bis zur Mitte des 20. Jh.* (Munich 1954–59) 2–3. T. BASIL, "La conversione di Bendetto IX dei conti di Tuscolo," *Castelli Romani* 21 (1976) 142–43. R. BENERICETTI, "La conversione di Benedetto IX dei conti di Tuscolo," *Castelli Romani* 21 (1976) 142–43. K. J. BENZ, "Kaiser Konrad II. (1024–1039) als kirchlicher Herrscher. Der Strassburger Adventisstreit und die Synode von 1038 im Kloster Limburg an der Haardt," *Archiv für Liturgiewissenschaft* 20–21 (1978–79), 56–80. L. L. GHIRADINI, *Il papa fanciullo Benedetto IX (1032–1948). La verità storica su un fatto straordinario* (Parma 1980). I. HEIDRICH, "Die Absetzung Herzog Adalberos von Kärnten durch Kaiser Konrad II. 1035," *Historisches Jahrbuch* 91 (1971), 70–9. J. N. D. KELLY, *Oxford Dictionary of Popes* (New York 1986) 142–144.

[V. GELLHAUS]

BENEDICT X, ANTIPOPE

Pontificate: April 5, 1058–January 1059 (when he renounced) or April 1060 (officially deposed). Born John Mincius, he was cardinal bishop of Velletri, and died sometime after 1073. His reign as antipope came early in the days of the Investiture Controversy, and represents a late attempt by the Roman aristocracy to control the papacy. Since the 1040s the German kings had intervened consistently in an effort to end such control (see Clement II, Boniface IX, Damasus II, Leo IX, Victor II, and Stephen IX), and a group of similarly reform-minded clerics had emerged in Rome. On March 24, 1058, only five days before his death, Pope Stephen IX (1057–58) had an assembly of Roman clergy and laymen swear an oath that if he died they would wait for the reforming subdeacon Hildebrand (soon to be Gregory VII) to return before electing a successor. Upon Stephen's death a group of nobles broke the oath and, under the leadership of Gregory of Tusculum and Gerard of Galeria, elected John Mincius to be Pope Benedict X.

Reaction within the curia was deliberate and consistent. Every cardinal except one fled Rome and threatened to excommunicate Benedict. Soon the cardinals met in Florence, which was controlled by Duke Godfrey the Bearded of Lorraine. Among them was Humbert of Silva Candida and the cardinal-bishop of Ostia, Peter Damian (1001–72). As bishop of Ostia, one of Peter's traditional functions was to concelebrate at the consecration of a new pope, but he refused to recognize Benedict's election. Thus Benedict was irregularly elected and irregularly consecrated. While Benedict functioned as pope in Rome (he is known to have sent the pallium to Archbishop Stigand of Canterbury), the cardinals met at various locations around Tuscany. Finally, in Siena and with the support of Duke Godfrey, they elected (December 1058) Bishop Gerard of Florence to be Pope Nicholas II (1059–61). This election was subsequently confirmed by the regent Empress Agnes, and the new emperor, Henry IV (1056–1106). Nicholas then convened a Synod at Sutri (early January 1059) that excommunicated Benedict X as a usurper and a perjurer because he broke the oath to Pope Stephen. (Though his opposition to Benedict is clear, Damian's precise view of these events may need revision due to the changes in our understanding of his letters brought about by K. Reindel's new edition. Reindel considers Letters 3 and 4 in the *Patrologia latina* edition—sometimes cited in relation to Benedict X—to be incorrectly numbered, with their recipients sometimes incorrectly identified.)

On Jan. 24, 1059 Pope Nicholas entered Rome accompanied by Duke Godfrey, the duke's troops, all of the cardinals, and the German chancellor for Italy, Guibert of Ravenna (later Antipope Clement III, 1080–1100). Benedict fled Rome, first for Passarano, and then for Gerard of Galeria's castle. The antipope was captured in the autumn of 1059 after a three month siege. He renounced his title and, after a month spent on a family estate, was imprisoned by Hildebrand. In April 1060, Hildebrand conducted a public trial at which Benedict was formally deposed and sentenced to confinement in the hospice of the church of St. Agnes on the Via Nomentana. It is not known when he died, but Hildebrand, as Pope Gregory VII (1073–85), allowed him to be buried in the church of St. Agnes; many scholars take this as evidence that he survived until at least 1073.

Bibliography: BONIZO OF SUTRI, *Liber ad amicum* 4 in *Monumenta Germaniae historica, Libelli de lite* 1.590–600. L. DUCHESNE, ed. *Liber Pontificalis* (Paris 1886–92; repr. 1955–57) 2.270–79, 334–356. P. JAFFÉ, *Regesta pontificum Romanorum* (Leipzig 1885–88; repr. Graz 1956) 1.556–57, 563. LEO OSTIENSIS, *Chronica monasterii Casinensis* 2.99 in *Monumenta Germaniae historica, Scriptores* 7.695. PETER DAMIAN, *Die Briefe des Petrus Damiani*, ed. K. REINDEL, in *Monumenta Germaniae historica, Briefe der deutschen Kaiserzeit* (Munich 1983ff); trans. O. BLUM, *The Letters of Peter Damian* (Washington, D.C. 1989ff). I. M. WATTERICH, *Pontificum Romanorum* (Leipzig 1862; repr. Aalen 1966) 1.203–05, 738. B. PLATINA, *De vita Christi ac omnium pontificum* 160 (155), ed. G. GAIDA, in *Rerum italicarum scriptores* 3.1, ed. L. A. MURATORI, (Città di Castello and Bologna 1913–32) 185–86. F. J. SCHMALE, in *Dictionnaire d'histoire et de géographie ecclésiastiques* (Paris 1935) 8.105–06. F. X. SEPPELT, *Geschichte der Päpste von den Anfängen bis zur Mitte des zwanzigsten Jahrhunderts* (Munich 1954–59) 2.36–44. O. CAPITANI, "Benedetto X," *Dizionario biografico degli Italiani* (Rome 1966) 8.366–70. H. ZIMMERMAN, *Papstabsetzungen des Mittelalters* (Graz, Vienna, Cologne 1968) 139–47. U. R. BLUMENTHAL, *The Investiture Controversy* (Philadelphia 1982) 84–105. J. N. D. KELLY, *The Oxford Dictionary of Popes* (New York 1986) 150–151.

[P. M. SAVAGE]

BENEDICT XI, POPE, BL.

Pontificate: Oct. 22, 1303 to July 7, 1304; b. Niccolo Boccasini, at Treviso, Italy, 1240; d. Perugia. The son of a notary, he entered the DOMINICANS in 1254 and studied at Venice and Milan, becoming lector for his fellow religious in 1268. He was distinguished both as a scholar, having written commentaries on the Psalms, Job, Matthew, and Revelations, and as a religious superior. After serving as subprior, prior, and provincial of Lombardy (1282–96), he was elected master general of the order in May 1296. He kept the Dominicans loyal to Pope BONIFACE VIII in the crisis of 1297; served on Boniface's peace embassy to England and France; and as cardinal (1300), acted as legate to Hungary in the mission in favor of Caroberf of ANJOU. He was one of two faithful cardinals with Boniface VIII at Anagni. The major reason for his first-ballot election as pope was the universal esteem for his sanctity and prudential administrative talents. Benedict proved to be a peace-seeking pontiff. Anxious to end the discord of Boniface's pontificate without sacrificing principle, he modified *CLERICIS LAICOS* and reconciled PHILIP IV OF FRANCE to the papacy. Benedict's acts should be interpreted as pastoral not appeasive. Furthermore, he did not absolve NOGARET and Sciarra COLONNA, the principal perpetrators of Anagni. While processing their case, Benedict died suddenly at Perugia, where his cult developed immediately. He was beatified by Clement XII, April 24, 1736.

Feast: July 7.

Bibliography: C. A. GRANDJEAN, ed., *Le Registre de Benôit XI* (Paris 1905). B. GUIDO, *Rerum italicarum scriptores, 500–1500* (Milan 1748–71) 3.1:672–673. L. JADIN, *Dictionnaire d'histoire et de géographie ecclésiastiques,* ed. A. BAUDRILLART et al. (Paris 1912) 8:106–116. G. BELTRAME, "La patria del b. Benedetto XI papa (1240–1304)," *Padova* 26 (1980) 11–17. J. H. DENTON, "Complaints to the Apostolic See in an Early Fourteenth-Century Memorandum from England," *Archivum Historiae Pontificiae* 20 (1982) 389–400. G. KASTNER, *Lexikon der christlichen Ikonographie* (Rome 1974). J. N. D. KELLY, *Oxford Dictionary of Popes* (New York 1986) 210.

[E. J. SMYTH]

BENEDICT XII, POPE

Pontificate: Dec. 20, 1334 to April 25, 1342; b. Jacques Fournier, at Saverdun (Ariège) France; d. Avignon. The talent of this CISTERCIAN for inquisitorial matters was used by JOHN XXII, who sought his advice concerning cases of heresy being appealed to the papal court. As bishop of Pamiers (1317) and of Mirepoix (1326), he freed the dioceses of any WALDENSES, CATHARI, and ALBIGENSES still infesting them. He was a zealous inquisitor, masterfully wresting confessions from the accused and never faltering in his integrity. A harsh man on occasion, he showed clemency to heretics who confessed their guilt: only four Waldenses and one relapsed Catharist died at the stake (*see* INQUISITION). He was made cardinal priest in 1327. A doctor of theology from Paris, he took part in the great controversies of the age centering on the poverty controversy and the BEATIFIC VISION; he wrote a treatise against the FRATICELLI; a refutation of the errors of JOACHIM OF FIORE and Meister ECKHART; a dissertation on the doctrines propagated by MICHAEL OF CESENA, WILLIAM OF OCKHAM, and PETER JOHN OLIVI; an explanation of the state of the holy souls before the Last Judgment and of questions concerning the theories of DURANDUS OF SAINT POURÇIN.

Pope Benedict XII, polychromed marble sculpture by Paolo da Siena (1342) in the grotto of the Vatican, Rome. (Alinari-Art Reference/Art Resource, NY)

Succeeding John XXII during the AVIGNON papacy, Benedict was crowned pope on Jan. 8, 1335. He quickly ended the discussion on the beatific vision, imprudently begun by his predecessor in 1331. John had stated that before the resurrection of the body the souls of the just would not enjoy the intuitive vision of God, but only after the Last Judgment, and that they would remain until then *sub altare Dei*, diverted by the view of the humanity of Christ. Benedict's bull *BENEDICTUS DEUS* of Jan. 29, 1336, held that just souls immediately see the divine essence with an intuitive and even facial vision. As a reformer, Benedict set up an inquest that confirmed the existence of many abuses in the papal court. He then decreed salutary regulations for his Curia.

As a former abbot of FONTFROIDE, Benedict was aware of the contemporary defects of discipline in the religious orders: the CISTERCIANS, the BENEDICTINES, and the FRANCISCANS were compelled to observe new severe constitutions, which regulated the question of the orders' temporal power, prescribed the regular holding of CHAPTERS and visitation of monasteries, demanded that young religious attend the universities, and repressed luxury and vagrancy. As for the secular clergy, Benedict's revocation of COMMENDATION, restriction of expectancies, insistence on RESIDENCE, tailoring on ANNATES, and encouragement toward sacred studies assured its proper behavior. In the STATES OF THE CHURCH, scrupulous inspections were a prelude to reforms. In the diplomatic domain the rigid character of the pope hardly predisposed him for compromise, and almost nothing but defeats are recorded. Instead of maintaining an armed force in Italy, he allowed himself to be duped by minor local tyrants; the temporal authority of the Church in the Romagna, the March of Ancona, and even in Bologna, practically ceased to exist. Such events made him little anxious to return to Rome, and he began building the papal palace at AVIGNON. Negotiations to reconcile Emperor LOUIS IV the Bavarian with the papacy were fruitless. On the one hand, Benedict was influenced by King Philip VI of France and the king of Naples, who, for private political reasons, were hostile to all compromise, while, on the other hand, Louis promulgated the edict *Licet juris* (1338), which sanctioned the decision of the electors at Rense to free the imperial dignity from the customary approval and sanction of the Holy See (*see* HOLY ROMAN EMPIRE). He was unable to curb Edward III and the nascent Hundred Years' War.

Bibliography: Sources. BENEDICT XII, *Lettres communes*, comment. J. M. VIDAL, 3 v. (Paris 1902–11); *Lettres . . . intéressant les pays autres que la France*, comment. J. M. VIDAL, 6 fasc. (Paris 1913–50); *Lettres . . . à la France*, comment. G. DAUMET, 3 v. (Paris 1899–1920). J. M. VIDAL, ''Notice sur les oeuvres . . . ,'' *Revue d'histoire ecclésiastique* 6 (Louvain 1905) 557–565, 785–810. É BALUZE, *Vitae paparum Avenionensium*, ed. G. MOLLAT, 4 v. (Paris 1914–27). Literature. U. BERLIÈRE, ''Les Chapitres généraux . . . ,'' *Mélanges d'histoire bénédictine*, ed. U. BERLÌERE, 4 v. (Maredsous, Bel. 1897–1902) 4:52–171; *Notes supplémentaires* (Bruges 1905), for Benedictine reform. J. B. MAHN, *Le Pape Benoit XII et les cisterciens* (Paris 1949). C. SCHMITT, *Un pape réformateur . . .* (Quaracchi-Florence 1959). L. PASTOR, *The History of the Popes From the Close of the Middle Ages*, (London-St. Louis 1938–61) 1:83–86. H. JENKINS, *Papal Efforts for Peace under Benedict XII* (Philadelphia 1933). H. OTTO, ''Zur politischen Einstellung Papstes Benedikts XII,'' *Zeitschrift für Kirchengeschicte* (Stuttgart 1877–) 62, (1943–44) 103–126. G. MOLLAT, *The Popes at Avignon*, tr. J. LOVE (New York 1963). B. GUILLEMAIN, *La Politique bénéficiale du Pape Benoît XII* (Paris 1952). F. WETTER, *Analecta Gregoriana: Die Lehre Benedikts XII vom intensiven Wachstum der Gottesschau* 92 (1958). S. BROWN, ''A Dispute between Archbishop Melton and the Dean and Chapter of York, c. 1336–8,'' *Bulletin of the Institute of Historical Research* 54 (London 1979) 110–119. T. H. GANDLAU, *Biographisch-Bibliographisches Kirchenlexikon* 12 (1997), s.v. ''Venturino 'von Bergano.''' G. GRESHAKE, *Lexikon für Theologie und Kirche* 2 (1995), s.v. '''Benedictus Deus': Bulle Benedikts XII.'' E. GRIFFE, *Le Languedoc cathare et l'Inquisition (1229–1329)* (Paris 1980). R. M. HAINES, ''An English Archbishop and the Cerberus of War,'' *Studies in Church History* 20 (Oxford 1983) 153–70. R. MANNO TOLU, ''La 'Domus pauperum scolarium Italorum' a Parigi nel 1334,'' *Archivio Storico Italiano* (1988) 49–56. P. MCDONALD, ''The Papacy and Monastic Observance in the Later Middle Ages,'' *The Journal of Religious History* 14 (Sydney 1985) 117–132. E. SABBADINI, ''Un pontefice avignonese riformatore della Chiesa: Benedetto XII (Cistercense),'' *Rivista Cistercense* (1985) 2:19–30. L. VONES, *Lexikon für Theologie und Kirche* 2 (1995). K. WALSH, ''An Irish Preacher at Avignon: Richard FitzRalph's Sermons to the Dominican Friars,'' *Xenia Medii Aevi historiam illustrantia oblata Thomae Kaeppeli* (Rome 1978) 1:401–15. J. N. D. KELLY, *Oxford Dictionary of Popes* (New York 1986) 217.

[G. MOLLAT]

BENEDICT XIII, POPE

Pontificate: May 29, 1724, to Feb. 21, 1730; b. Pietro Francesco Orsini, Gravina, Feb. 2, 1649; d. Rome. He was the eldest son and heir of the Duke of Gravina. The Orsini family, prominent in Rome for many centuries, had already seen two of its members become popes—Celestine III (1191–98) and Nicholas III (1277–80). Despite family opposition, Pietro abandoned his splendid inheritance to become Fra Vincenzo Maria of the Order of Preachers (1667). Like Aloysius Gonzaga, whom he later canonized, he gave all his rights of inheritance to his younger brother. Fra Vincenzo Maria proved to be an excellent religious and a dedicated student. He studied philosophy and theology at Naples, Bologna, and Venice. After these studies he taught philosophy at Brescia. But even if he had fled from his family's secular honors, his family saw to it that he received ecclesiastical honors. Clement X made him a cardinal at the age of 23. Three years later he became archbishop of Manfredonia, then of Cesena (1680), and then of Benevento (1686), where he remained for 38 years. In all his dioceses he strove to promote good discipline and morals in his flock. He loved Benevento and was charitable to its people. Living like a Dominican friar, he summoned two provincial councils and wrote three volumes of scholarly and spiritual works.

When elected pope after a conclave of more than two months, he accepted with the greatest reluctance, determined to preserve his monastic lifestyle. Benedict XIII was religiously well qualified for his lofty task, but he proved to have serious deficiencies in practical administration and diplomacy. While he fulminated against the use of wigs by the clergy and devoted himself to liturgical functions, a group of Beneventans made a good thing out of the pope's imprudent favors. The leader of these grafters was Niccolò Coscia, who had been Benedict's chancellor and secretary at Benevento. Coscia, later made a cardinal, had a great appetite for graft, a fact lost on the unworldly pontiff. Benedict XIII proved unsuccessful in his dealings with the powers. Although a great defender of Church rights in theory, he compromised on the *monarchia sicula* question and gave extensive privileges in ecclesiastical matters to the Court of Turin.

In matters more completely spiritual, Benedict XIII was eminent, taking delight in consecrating churches, administering the sacraments, and offering religious instruction. He took a firm stand against the Jansenists; fostered the progress of religious orders, approving, among others, the Institute of the Brothers of the Christian Schools; held a provincial council in Rome in 1725; and canonized many saints, including John of the Cross, the Latin Americans Turibius and Francis Solano, and the youths Stanislaus and Aloysius.

Bibliography: L. PASTOR, *The History of the Popes from the Close of the Middle Ages* (London-St. Louis 1938–61) 34:98–299. A. F. ARTAUD DE MONTOR, *The Lives and Times of the Popes,* 10 v. (New York 1910–11) 6:230–245. *Bullarium Romanum* (Magnum), ed. H. MAINARDI and C. COCQUELINES, 18 folio v. (Rome 1733–62) v.22. P. MIKAT, *Lexikon für Theologie und Kirche,* ed. J. HOFER and K. RAHNER, 10 v. (2d, new ed. Freiburg 1957–65) 2:177. H. HEMMER, *Dictionnaire de théologie catholique,* ed. A. VACANT et al., 15 v. (Paris 1903–50; Tables générales 1951–) 2.1:704–705. J. CARREYRE, *Dictionnaire d'histoire et de géographie ecclésiastiques,* ed. A. BAUDRILLAT et al. (Paris 1912–) 8:163–164. F. HEYER, *The Catholic Church from 1648 to 1870* (London 1969). A. D. WRIGHT, *The Early Modern Papacy: From the Council of Trent to the French Revolution, 1564–1789* (London 2000).

[J. S. BRUSHER]

Tomb of Pope Benedict XIII, designed by Carlo Marchionni, Church of S. Maria Sopra Minerva, Rome.

BENEDICT XIII, ANTIPOPE

Pontificate (Avignon obedience): Sept. 28, 1394 to July 26, 1417. Born Pedro de Luna in 1342 at Illueca, Aragon. His parents, both of important Aragonese families, were Juan Martínez de Luna and Maria Pérez de Gotor. He was elected pope Sept. 28, 1394, deposed by the Council of Pisa June 5, 1409, and again deposed at the Council of Constance (summer 1417). He considered himself to be the rightful pope until his death at Peñíscola (near Valencia) on Nov. 22, 1422. The date of his death is uncertain; according to some it was kept secret from his followers until the most commonly cited date of May 23, 1423.

Before pursuing the study of canon law, de Luna served in the court of Henry II Trastámara, who would become king of Castile (1369–79). In the 1370s he became a doctor of canon law at Montpellier, where he also taught. During this time he entered holy orders, was a canon in Vich, Tarragona, Huesca, and Majorca, and obtained prebends in the churches of Tarragona, Zaragoza, Valencia, and Tortosa. In December 1375, Pope Gregory XI made him cardinal deacon of St. Maria in Cosmedin. He was among the cardinals who returned to Rome with Gregory (ending the Babylonian Captivity), and was part of the conclave that elected Urban VI (1378–1389), for whom he voted. Nonetheless, he was later part of the faction that elected Clement VII pope, thus beginning the Great Schism.

De Luna was an important member of Clement's curia. As legate to Castile (1381), Aragón (1387), Navarre (1390), and Portugal he was central to securing those areas' allegiance to Avignon (though Portugal remained loyal to Urban). In 1393 Clement appointed de Luna legate to France, Flanders, England, Scotland, and Ireland. He was based in Paris, where he appeared to support the position that both popes should abdicate (the *via cessionis*), then popular at the University of Paris. However, most scholars question de Luna's devotion to the cause, especially in light of his later position. He returned to Avignon in 1394. When Clement died later that year there was pressure from the French crown to postpone an election in the hope that the schism could be ended. Instead, the 21 cardinals held an election and swore that whoever won would resign when the majority of their college determined it appropriate. Cardinal de Luna (still a deacon) was then unanimously elected pope on Sept. 28, 1394. On October 3 he was consecrated priest; on October 11 he was made a bishop and then took the name Benedict XIII.

Benedict was heavily involved in political and conciliar battles from the outset. After his election he sent a letter to Paris that referred vaguely to a desire for church unity, but at a synod in the spring of 1395 King Charles VI of France (1380–1422) and the University of Paris (over the objection of its chancellor, Pierre d'Ailly) demanded that Benedict resign as pope. Missions to Avignon from France, England, and some German territories followed over the next two years, but they could not bring Benedict actively to support a *via cessionis* policy. By 1398, France, its ally Castile, Navarre, and England supported such a policy. Benedict argued that a papal abdication was not canonical and may be sinful; he had been rightly elected, would work for compromise, but would not submit to king, university, or church council. On July 28, 1398 Charles VI formally proclaimed that France withdrew its obedience from Benedict; Navarre, Castile, and some smaller territories did the same. These moves significantly reduced Benedict's revenues and his political prestige. To make matters worse, on September 1 royal officials declared that any clergy in Benedict's curia would forfeit their French benefices if they remained at Avignon. At this, 18 of Benedict's 23 cardinals left for French territory, and Charles began a four and a half year siege of the papal palace at Avignon.

Benedict managed to escape from Avignon the night of March 11, 1403 and soon regained the backing of the French government and many cardinals. He was able to do this through the influence of his ally Louis, Duke of Orléans, the king's brother and an important French governmental advisor. In addition, there were others, including Jean Gerson and Nicholas de Clémanges, who questioned the validity of the French withdrawal of obedience. At this time Benedict also began negotiations with the Roman pope so that they might end the schism through papal compromise (the so-called *via discussionis*). Benedict sent a delegation to Rome in September 1404 to this end, but neither pope appears to have been truly interested in such a solution. Proposed meetings between Benedict and Gregory XII in Savona (1407) and in Tuscany (1408) never took place. In the meantime, Gregory's cardinals were losing confidence in his leadership; some deserted and even joined Benedict's cardinals. In 1408, after the murder of the duke of Orléans, France again withdrew its obedience from Benedict and all parties embraced their own vision of a council.

Benedict called a council in Perpignan (his new base in Aragón); the majority of cardinals (both Benedict's and Gregory's) called a council in Pisa; and Gregory XII held his own sparsely attended council in Cividale (near his Venetian power base). Of the three councils, Pisa was by far the most widely attended, but it lacked strong political support and thus only succeeded in creating a third pope, Alexander V (1409–10). Even though Pisa had deposed Benedict, Scotland, Aragon, Castile and Sicily continued to recognize him. In a few years, with the ascension of a new German king, Sigismund (1410–37), and a new Pisan pope, John XXIII (1410–15), there was broader political support for a new council to end the schism; it would meet in Constance. Sigismund negotiated with Castile and Aragon to pressure Benedict XIII to send representatives, but he never did. On July 26, 1417 the Council of Constance deposed Benedict. This council's decision had far greater effect on the antipope than Pisa because it was made with the cooperation of the Spanish kingdoms. No important political entity now recognized Benedict, and the council's new pope, Martin V (1417–31), was widely acclaimed and received cardinals from all three obediences.

For his part, Benedict had retired to a family castle at Peñíscola as early as 1415. He had four remaining cardinals, but they went over to Martin V soon after Constance. He nonetheless considered himself the legitimate pope, and created four new cardinals on Nov. 27, 1422. At his death his followers elected a successor who took the name Clement VIII (1423–29). Benedict's crosier and chalice can still be seen in the church at Peñíscola, but his grave in Illueca was desecrated in 1811 by French troops.

Benedict XIII was arguably the most qualified man to call himself pope during the Great Schism; he was immensely capable in political affairs and as a canon lawyer. In addition, he was widely considered a morally upright man of austere life and broad learning. Nicholas de Clémanges called him "a great, a laudable, indeed a holy man." St. Vincent Ferrer served in Cardinal de Luna's court, was at Benedict's papal court from 1395 to 1399, and remained a friend, even pleading with the antipope to abdicate after the Council of Constance. Pedro de Luna's written work in theology and canon law shows a man who thought carefully about a broad range of ecclesiastical and intellectual matters. His work includes treatises on church councils (*De concilio generali*), the schism (*De novo schismate*), and the controversial *Tractatus contra Iudaeos*, which has been connected to Spanish efforts to convert the Jews during his lifetime. The better-known *Speculum Sapientiae vel Libri XV de consolatione theologica* is now generally ascribed to John of Dambach.

Bibliography: L. DUCHESNE, ed. *Liber Pontificalis* (Paris 1886–92; repr. 1955–57) 2.507–40, 545, 554. PEDRO DE LUNA, *Libro de las consolaciones de la vida humana* ed. P. DE GAYANGOS (Madrid 1860). *Lettres de Benoit XIII (1394–1422)*, ed. J. PAYE-BOURGEOIS (Brussels 1983). DIETRICH OF NIEM, *De schismate* (Leipzig 1890). É. BALUZE, *Vitae paparum Avenionensium*, ed. G. MOLLAT (Paris 1914–1927) 1.421–542, 597–98; 2.699–711 and passim; 4.177ff, 254ff, 360, 367. MARTIN DE ALPARTIL, *Chronica actitatorum temporibus domini Benedicti XIII*, ed. F. EHRLE (Paderborn 1906). H. DENIFLE, ed., *Chartularium Universitatis Parisiensis* (Paris 1880–97) 4.1–164. É. AMMAN, *Dictionnaire de théologie catholique* (Paris 1903–50) 12.2020–9. S. PUIG Y PUIG, *Pedro de Luna: ultimo papa de Aviñón, 1387–1430* (Barcelona 1920). F. BAIX and L. JEDIN, *Dictionnaire d'histoire et de géographie ecclésiastiques* (Paris 1935) 8.135–63. G. PILLEMENT, *Pedro de Luna dèrnier Pape d'Avignon* (Paris Grasset, 1955). A. GLASFURD, *The Antipope Peter de Luna, 1342–1423* (New York 1965). H. JEDIN and J. DOLAN, eds. *Handbook of Church History* (New York 1965–81) 4.401–473 passim. C. M. D. CROWDER, *Unity, Heresy, and Reform: 1378–1460* (London 1977). A. CANELLAS, *Diccionario de Historia Eclesiastica de España* (Madrid 1972–75) 2.1368–1370. Also J. GOÑI, *Diccionario de Historia Eclesiastica de España, Suplemento I* (Madrid 1987) 128–58 for an overview of the Schism with an emphasis on Spain. F. MCGURK, *Calendar of Papal Letters to Scotlan of Benedict XIII of Avignon, 1394–1419* (Edinburgh 1976). W. BRANDMÜLLER, *Lexikon des Mittelalters* (Munich 1979) 1.1862–1864 for additional bibliography. O. CUELLA ESTEBAN, *Aportaciones culturales y artísticas del Papa Luna* (Zaragoza 1984). F. DE MOXÓ Y MONTOLIU, *El Papa Luna: un imposible empeño, estudio político-económico* (Zaragoza 1986). J. A. PARRILLA and J. A. MUÑIZ, *Benedicto XIII: la vida y el tiempo del Papa Luna* (Zaragoza 1987). M. H. J. DE POMMEROL, *La bibliothèque pontificale a Avignon et à Peñiscola* (Rome 1991). B. SCHIMMELPHENNIG, *The Papacy* (New York 1992) 219–236. A. SESMA MUÑOZ, *Benedicto XIII, el Papa Luna: muestra de documentación histórica aragonesa en conmemoración del sexto centenario de la elección papal de Don Pedro Martínez de Luna (Aviñón, 28 septiembre 1394): Sala Corona de Aragón, Edificio Pignatelli, 28 de septiembre–31 de octubre, 1994* (Zaragoza 1994). *Jornadas de estudio: VI Centenario del Papa Luna. Calatayud-Illueca, 1994* (1996). P. LINEHAN, ''Papa Luna in 1415, a proposal by Benedict XIII for the ending of the Great Schism,'' *English Historical Review* 113 (1998) 91–8. B. PEREIRA PAGÁN, *El Papa Luna: Benedicto XIII* (Madrid 1999). H. MILLET, *Encyclopedia of the Middle Ages*, ed. A. VAUCHEZ (Chicago and London 2000) 1.165.

[P. M. SAVAGE]

BENEDICT XIV, POPE

Pontificate: Aug. 17, 1740, to May 3, 1758; b. Prospero Lorenzo Lambertini, Bologna, March 31, 1675. He came of a noble Bolognese family. After an early education from tutors, he was sent to the Collegium Clementinum in Rome, where he studied for four years. In 1694 he received the doctorate in theology and law from the University of Rome.

''Monument of Pope Benedict XIV,'' sculptural group by Antonio Bracci, late 18th century, St. Peter's Basilica, Rome. (Alinari-Art Reference/Art Resource, NY)

He began his public career as an assistant lawyer in Rome during the pontificate of INNOCENT XII. Among the eleven offices he held under CLEMENT XI and INNOCENT XIII, the first two were of special significance. In 1701 Clement appointed him consistorial advocate for two canonizations and in 1708, Promoter of the Faith. In the latter office he had charge of all canonizations until 1727. Seeing the need for a record of such work, he wrote *De servorum Dei beatificatione et beatorum canonizatione,* (On the Beatification and Canonization of the Servants of God) which is still an important book.

In 1724, when nearly 50, he was ordained a priest. In 1728 Benedict XIII created him a cardinal, having appointed him archbishop of Ancona in 1727. Four years later Clement XII transferred him to Bologna as archbishop. In both archdioceses he showed zeal and devotion. He sought to improve the spiritual state of his people, for example, by visiting even remote villages and later checking to see that the proposed changes had been made. He held synods and from that experience published another important book, *De synodo diocesana* (The Diocesan Synod), in 1748.

When elected pope in one of the longest conclaves since the Middle Ages, he chose the name Benedict in honor of Benedict XIII, who had named him to the college of cardinals. He faced the aggressive monarchs who sent armies through the Papal States in the War of Austrian Succession, but he could only protest this violation of neutrality and distribute alms to his suffering people. During preceding pontificates rulers had also sought to gain supremacy over the Church in their kingdoms, but Benedict acted quickly regarding this problem. Before 1740 ended he had begun new negotiations with the kings of Savoy, Naples, and Spain. Because of his willingness to make concessions concordats were signed with Savoy and Naples in 1741. The negotiations with Spain proved more difficult. Finally the concordat was signed in 1753, with Benedict making concessions for which he has been criticized. However, a complete rupture, which he feared, would have hampered the spiritual work of the Church. Furthermore, only reluctantly did he make new cardinals on the basis of foreign pressure. Ranke praised Benedict's ability to understand how much he must concede and how much he must retain without weakening the papacy. This was particularly clear in his diplomatic handling of the crisis between the French bishops and the parliaments over the refusal of Sacraments to persons suspected of JANSENISM. When the government asked him to send instructions to the bishops in an encyclical rather than a bull, he complied in 1756.

In the Papal States he sought to reform the Administration. He improved living conditions by having granaries built in all villages and towns, roads repaired, and necessary commodities exported without fees. A great deal was done to preserve historic objects and buildings: statues were purchased for the Capitoline Museum and a picture gallery added; a Museum of Christian Antiquities was established in the Vatican Palace; and both major and minor churches in Rome and other cities were restored. According to Montesquieu he was ''the scholars' pope.'' He founded four academies where papers were read about the Church and Roman history, purchased manuscripts and books for the Vatican Library, and improved the University of Rome. At his suggestion new editions and books were published. Meanwhile, he replenished the treasure of Sixtus V in the Castel Sant' Angelo.

Above all he was a good pastor. Unlike his predecessor or his successor, Benedict did not succumb to nepotism. By instructions and by example he showed his great interest in the spiritual life. Two months after his election he established a congregation to select worthy bishops and a month later, another congregation to answer bishops' questions. His briefs to bishops emphasized their duties: the training of priests, visiting of parishes, and promoting of missions and other religious exercises. The bulls of 1742 and 1744 suppressed the pagan CHINESE and MALABAR rites used by natives who had been converted to Christianity; thus a long controversy was ended. A bull in 1745 answered arguments about usury; one in 1746 pertained to the residence of bishops in their dioceses; another in 1748, to mixed marriages. He set an example for spiritual growth by his simple living, humility, and charitable attitude toward others.

No pope before him left so full a written record about himself. There are extant 760 personal letters to Cardinal Tencin in France and many others to Italian friends. The letters reveal his sarcasm and humor, about which so much has been written, but the letters also show his good characteristics. There is no discrepancy between his own statements about his duties and the judgments of men who had seen his work, such as Charles de Brosses of France and Francesco Venier, the Venetian ambassador.

Bibliography: *Opera,* ed. J. SILVESTER, 17 v. (Prato, Italy 1839–47). L. PASTOR, The History of the Popes from the Close of the Middle Ages (London-St. Louis 1938–61) 35–36 L. VON RANKE, *The History of the Popes During the Last Four Centuries,* tr. MRS. FOSTER, ed. G. R. DENNIS, 3 v. v.23. F. L. CROSS, *The Oxford Dictionary of the Christian Church* (London 1957) 154. P. MIKAT, *Lexikon für Theologie und Kirche,* ed. J. HOFER and K. RAHNER, 10 v. (2d, new ed. Freiburg 1957–65) 2:177178. J. CARREYRE, *Dictionnaire d'histoire et de géographie ecclésiastiques,* ed. A. BAUDRILLAT et al. (Paris 1912–) 8:164167. T. BERTONE, *Il governo della Chiesa nel pensiero di Benedetto XIV* (Rome 1978). R. HAYNES, *Philosopher King: The Humanist Pope Benedict XIV* (London 1970). S. BORSI, ed. *Roma di Benedetto XIV* (Rome 1993). M. CECCHELLI, *Bendetto XIV* (Cento 1982).

[M. L. SHAY]

BENEDICT XV, POPE

Pontificate: Sept. 3, 1914, to Jan. 22, 1922; b. Giacomo Della Chiesa (''of the church''), Pegli, near Genoa, Italy, Nov. 21, 1854. His parents, the Marchese Giuseppe Della Chiesa and Giovanna Migliorati, were of the nobility, his mother related to Innocent VII (1404–06).

Early Life. As a child he was of delicate health and was first educated by tutors, his secondary schooling being at the Istituto Donavaro e Giusso. His father, insisting that even priests needed a profession in modern society, required him to delay his clerical studies, and he received a doctorate in civil law from the University of Genoa before going to Rome, where he resided at the Capranica College, studied at the Gregorian University, and was ordained Dec. 21, 1878. He subsequently received doctorates in theology and canon law.

He was small, stoop-shouldered, and very thin (dubbed ''the midget'' by some, even after he became pope), with the left side of his body higher than the right, and he limped. His personality was not prepossessing. Kindly, he nonetheless manifested occasional outbursts of temper of which he repented.

Papal Diplomat and Curialist. Teaching at the Accademia dei Nobili Ecclesiastici, he attracted the attention of Archbishop Mariano RAMPOLLA DEL TINDARO, who had Della Chiesa appointed to the staff of the papal Secretariat of State. When Rampolla became nuncio to Spain (1882), Della Chiesa became his secretary. Besides their official diplomatic work, the two clerics organized relief programs and nursed the victims of a cholera epidemic.

In 1887 Rampolla was named secretary of state and cardinal, and Della Chiesa returned to Rome with his patron. In 1901 he was promoted to undersecretary. With the accession of Pius X (1903), Cardinal Rafael MERRY DEL VAL became secretary of state, replacing Rampolla, who had been denied the papal throne after his candidacy was vetoed by the Austro-Hungarian emperor. Della Chiesa remained as undersecretary, although considered a member of the Rampolla group in rivalry with Merry del Val.

Ordinarily Della Chiesa might have become nuncio to Spain in 1907, but Merry del Val apparently wanted him removed from the papal diplomatic service, and Della Chiesa was made archbishop of Bologna and consecrated by Pius X in the Sistine Chapel (Dec. 22, 1907).

Archbishop of Bologna. His exile from the Vatican probably aided the career of the future pope, giving him the pastoral experience usually considered necessary for the papal office. Bologna was in one of the more secular and anti-clerical districts of Italy, with a good deal of social turmoil. The new archbishop visited every Catholic institution in his see, some of the rural parishes being reachable only on horseback. His priorities included catechizing the laity and raising the spiritual level of the clergy, both of whom he found deficient.

The condemnation of Modernism by Pius X had given rise to a high degree of vigilance against heresy. Although impeccably orthodox, Della Chiesa defended some of his seminary professors against what he considered unwarranted suspicions.

Bologna had long been a cardinalitial see, but Pius X did not confer the red hat on its archbishop until May of 1914, the delay undoubtedly due to Merry del Val, who among other things considered Modernism to be a greater danger than Della Chiesa judged it to be.

Election as Pope. Pius X died three months after the archbishop of Bologna's elevation. Della Chiesa led on each ballot in the conclave and was elected on the 10th (September 3). He probably took the name Benedict in memory of the last pope elected from the see of Bologna, Benedict XIV (1740–58). The coronation was held in the Sistine Chapel, because of the crisis of World War I.

Pope Benedict XV. (©CORBIS)

Merry del Val had been Benedict's chief rival in the conclave and was now replaced as secretary of state and transferred to the Holy Office. Both German and Austrian cardinals had spoken against Della Chiesa before the election, accusing him of pro-French partisanship, but the chief issue was probably INTEGRALISM, the militant orthodoxy which had led to what Benedict and others regarded as excessive zeal in searching for heretics.

The Search for Peace. From the beginning, the new pontificate was dominated by the pope's urgent attempts to end the war. Along with his sincere longing for peace, he was motivated by the need to avoid dangerous political shoals, as they affected the interests of the Church. Great Britain, Germany, and (later) the United States were predominantly Protestant countries, France and Italy anticlerical, Russia militantly Orthodox, and Ottoman Empire Muslim. Thus Vatican neutrality was dictated both by moral considerations and by the need to avoid becoming linked to the interests of any one country or to either of the two alliances. Austria alone was staunchly Catholic, and Benedict saw it as an essential buffer between Germany and Russia. However, he urged Austria to make territorial concessions to Italy, so as to keep Italy out of the war.

His formal peace proposal was made on Aug. 1, 1917. Its main provisions were: (1) substitution of the "moral force of right" for military force, (2) reciprocal decrease in armaments, (3) arbitration of international disputes, (4) freedom of the seas, (5) renunciation of war indemnities, (6) restoration of all occupied territories, (7) examination "in a conciliatory spirit" of rival territorial claims.

While publicly the belligerents made evasive replies, in private their response was almost wholly negative. The Central Powers called Benedict "der französische Papst" and the Allies "le pape boche," and both sides treated his intervention as presumptuous. Pressed to condemn atrocities, he did so with a conscious effort to be non-partisan. The failure of the peace effort was the greatest disappointment of his pontificate.

The sincerity of Benedict's humanitarianism was demonstrated in his untiring efforts to relieve the sufferings of the war, personal charity being perhaps his most conspicuous virtue. He established an international missing-persons bureau, persuaded Switzerland to give refuge to soldiers suffering from tuberculosis, assigned priests to visit the wounded and prisoners, and established relief agencies. So generous was he in such activities that at his death the Holy See was virtually bankrupt.

The Peace. Benedict wanted to participate in the peace conference at the end of the war. However, the Allies, at the behest of Italy, had secretly agreed that the Holy See should be excluded, even though Woodrow Wilson's Fourteen Points, the basis of the Versailles settlement, in many ways resembled Benedict's own plan. The pope deplored some aspects of the settlement, considering the reparations imposed on Germany too harsh and believing that the treaty contained the seeds of future wars. The Holy See was also excluded from the League of Nations, which Benedict thought would fail because it was not based on principles of justice. He was cool to nationalism, hence to Wilson's principle of "self- determination."

Postwar Diplomacy. Benedict remained diplomatically active until his death, activity which brought visible fruit in the fact that the number of countries represented at the Holy See rose from 14 to 26, with the Vatican now recognized as an important center of international intelligence.

Because of his dislike of nationalism he did not at first welcome Irish independence. He opposed the Balfour Declaration, which promised Jews a homeland in Palestine, fearing the major Jewish migration would threaten the status of Catholics in the Holy Land, even as he was fearful of Orthodox and Protestant influence there. He had some success in easing relations with France, the canonization of JOAN OF ARC (1920) contributing much to that improvement.

Cardinal Pietro GASPARRI, secretary of state, engaged in private discussions with Benito Mussolini, which helped prepare the way for the LATERAN PACTS of 1929. Benedict cautiously supported the new Partito Populare Italiano, founded by the priest Luigi Sturzo, which for the first time gave Catholics a vehicle for participating in Italian electoral politics. The pope also supported women's suffrage, on the grounds that women would offset the influence of radicals.

Strongly anti-socialist, he was planning an encyclical on Communism which he never completed. However, instead of condemning the Soviet Union publicly he authorized negotiations with the Bolshevik government, hoping that the lot of Catholics would be easier under Communism than it had been under Orthodoxy.

Internal Church Matters. Although curbing what he considered anti-Modernist excesses, he reaffirmed Pius X's condemnations and in 1922 issued an encyclical, *Spiritus paraclitus,* warning against modern biblical criticism. He envisioned a universal Catholic catechism but was unable to take steps toward that goal during his brief pontificate. Although generally anti-Protestant, he gave cautious permission for the MALINES CONVERSATIONS between Anglicans and Catholics.

The codification of Canon Law begun under Pius X was completed by Gasparri, with Benedict's strong encouragement.

In 1917 the pope established the Sacred Congregation for the Oriental Church, with himself as prefect, his concern for Eastern Catholics having been one of his principal motives during the war and after. *Maximum illud* ("That Greatest Thing") (1919) signaled a change in missionary attitudes, especially in calling for the development of native clergy.

Death. Benedict's final illness lasted only a few days, the result of influenza which turned into pneumonia. The Holy See had to borrow money to pay for the funeral, the conclave, and the coronation of Pius XI.

Bibliography: J. F. POLLARD, *The Unknown Pope* (London 1999). A. RHODES, *The Power of Rome in the Twentieth Century* (New York 1983). F. J. COPPA, *The Modern Papacy since 1789* (New York 1998). M. C. CARLEN, *Dictionary of Papal Pronouncements: Leo XIII to Pius XII, 1878–1957* (New York 1958). W. H. PETERS, *The Life of Benedict XV* (Milwaukee 1959). H. E. G. ROPE,

Benedict XV (London 1940). F. A. MACNUTT, *A Papal Chamberlain* (London 1936). D. R. ZIVOJINAVIC, *The United States and Vatican Policy, 1914–1918* (Boulder 1978). G. RUMI, *Benedetto XV* (Brescia 1990). C. FALCONI, *The Popes in the Twentieth Century* (London 1960). F. HAYWARD, *Un Pape Méconnu: Benoît XV* (Tournai 1955).

[J. HITCHCOCK]

BENEDICT BISCOP, ST.

Benedictine abbot, known also as Baducing, founder of the joint monasteries of SS. Peter and Paul at Wearmouth and Jarrow; b. *c.* 628; d. Jan. 12, 690. He was of noble birth, a thane of King Oswiu of Northumbria. In 653 he renounced the world, traveling to Rome to learn more about the Church's teaching and institutions. WILFRID OF YORK was his companion as far as Lyons, and thence he traveled alone, returning after some months filled with enthusiasm for Roman institutions, art, and learning. He revisited Rome in 665, later becoming a monk at Lérins; after two years he went back to Rome, just in time to conduct the newly consecrated Abp. Theodore of Canterbury to England. After acting temporarily as abbot of SS. Peter and Paul, Canterbury, he again visited Rome in 671, returning laden with books. Soon afterward he established a monastery at Wearmouth on land given by King Ecgfrith, building a stone church with the assistance of glaziers and masons from Gaul. At the new monastery he introduced the BENEDICTINE RULE, but with certain modifications. He was back in Rome in 678 with his kinsman Ceolfrith. This time he brought back John, precentor of St. Peter's, to instruct the English in Church music. In 682 he founded the monastery at Jarrow, returning to Rome in 687 to bring back more books and church furnishings. Back in Jarrow, he fell ill and died after a short time. He did much to bring England into contact with western European civilization, while the magnificent library he gathered made Bede's work possible.

Feast: Jan. 12.

Bibliography: BEDE, *Historia ecclesiastica* 4.18; 5.19, 24, and *Historia abbatum,* ed. C. PLUMMER, 2 v. (Oxford 1896). A. M. ZIMMERMANN, *Kalendarium Benedictinum,* (Metten 1933–38) 1:71–75. E. FLETCHER, *Benedict Biscop* (Jarrow, Durham 1981). W. LEVISON, *England and the Continent in the Eighth Century* (Oxford 1946). E. S. DUCKETT, *Anglo-Saxon Saints and Scholars* (New York 1947).

[B. COLGRAVE]

BENEDICT OF ANIANE, ST.

Benedictine reformer; b. Witiza, Lat. Euticius, *c.* 750; d. at the monastery of Kornelimünster near Aachen, Feb. 11, 821. He came from a Visigothic noble family of Aquitaine and entered court service under PEPIN III, but left to become a monk in 773 at the monastery of Saint-Seine near Dijon. In 779 he founded a monastery on his parental inheritance at Aniane (Diocese of Montpellier) and became its abbot. At first inspired by the ideals of ancient monasticism, he led a severe penitential life but gradually he changed and began to fight for a new interpretation of the BENEDICTINE RULE. Numerous monasteries in western France joined with him in observing the new rule that he introduced at Aniane. Benedict enjoyed the confidence of LOUIS THE PIOUS and became his advisor on monastic affairs. In 814, at the emperor's behest, Benedict became abbot of Marmoutier in Alsace, then at Inden (Kornelimünster), established in the vicinity of Aachen. He strove for recognition of a uniform rule for all monasteries and for a close federation of monasteries united under a superimposed jurisdiction. Louis made him superior over all the monasteries of his kingdom, which he likewise wished to observe the same customs (*una consuetudo*) as well as the same (Benedictine) rule.

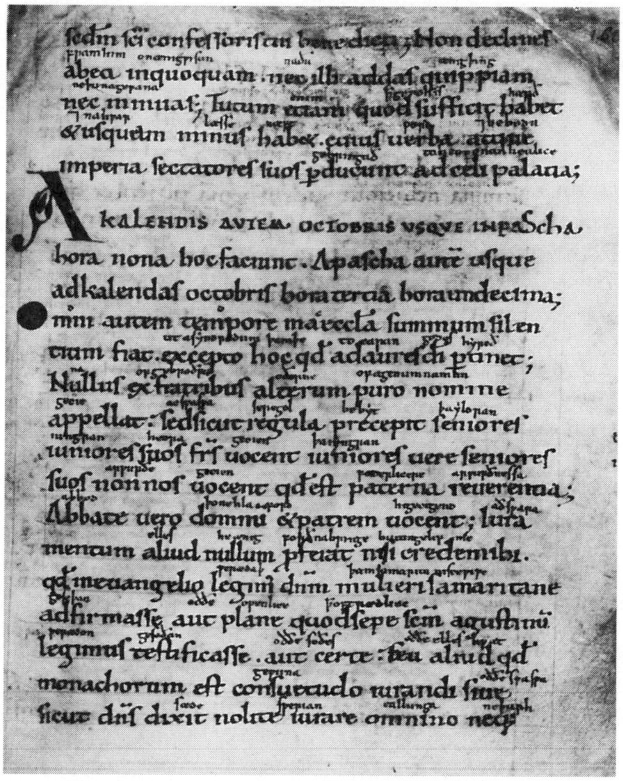

Manuscript page from "Epitome," by St. Benedict of Aniane (Cotton MS Tiberius III, fol. 164).

Toward that end the emperor convoked a meeting of abbots at Aachen in July 817, which was primarily the work of Benedict and issued in the *Capitulare institutum,* the first general code for all the monasteries of one area. Louis supported the capitulary by appointing royal *missi* as inspectors of monastic observance, a provision that guaranteed the ultimate unification in rule and custom observed by the monasteries of France.

Louis the Pious was generous in assessing the obligations of the monks but extremely cautious about according them any rights. Benedict secured—for some monasteries only—the right of free election of an abbot from within the monastic community. Even so, for each abbatial election permission had to be secured—and could, of course, be withheld.

Benedict has been adversely criticized for his prohibition against educating externs in the monastic schools. He aimed thereby to strengthen the contemplative character of the monasteries thus paving the way for Cluniac emphasis (overemphasis?) on the recitation of the Divine Office. Benedict is certainly responsible for the addition of 15 Psalms before the night Office and probably also for the daily recitation of the Office of the Dead. Benedict was a highly educated man and collected ancient monastic rules, which he harmonized in his *Concordia regularum.* He is possibly the author of a collection of homilies and of several works on doctrine. Some of his letters also are extant.

Feast: Feb. 11.

Bibliography: Sources. *Patrologia Latina*, ed. J. MIGNE (Paris 1878–90) 103:393–664, 703–1420, works. *Monumenta Germaniae Historica: Epistolae* (Berlin 1826–) 4:561–563, letters. J. LECLERCQ, ''Les *Munimenta fidei* de S. Benoit d'Aniane,'' *Analecta monastica* 1 (1948) 21–74. Conclusions from Abbots' conference of 817, ed. J. SEMMLER in K. HALLINGER, ed., *Corpus consuetudinum monasticarum* 1 (Siegburg 1963) 453–481; also the so-called *Regula Benedicti Aniani,* 503–536 and *Modus poenitentiarum,* 565–582. J. SEMMLER, ''Zur Überlieferung der monastischen Gesetzgebung Ludwigs des Frommen,'' *Deutsches Archiv für Erforschung des Mittelalters* 16 (1960) 309–388. *Vita, Monumenta Germaniae Historica: Scriptores* 15.1:200–220. Literature. A. HAUCK, *Kirchengeschichte Deutschlands* (Berlin-Leipzig 1958) 2:588–614. A. M. ZIMMERMANN, *Kalendarium Benedictinum,* (Metten 1933–38) 1:199–202. ARDO, *The emperor's monk: Contemporary life of Benedict of Aniane*, tr. A. CABANISS (Ilfracombe, Devon 1979). L. BARTHÈS, *L'abbaye et la cité d'Aniane de Saint-Benoît à la Révolution* (Aniane 1992). A. MERCATI and A. PELZER, *Dizionario ecclesiastico* (Turin 1954–58) 1:338–339. J. SEMMLER, *Lexicon für Theologie und Kirche*, ed. J. HOFER and K. RAHNER (Freiburg 1957–65) 2:179–180. E. BISHOP, *Liturgica historica* (Oxford 1918; repr. 1962) 211–218. S. DULCY, *La Règle de saint Benoit d'Aniane et la réforme monastique à l'époque carolingienne* (Nîmes 1935). P. SCHMITZ, *Histoire de l'ordre de Saint Benoît,* 7 v. (Maredsous 1942–56) v.1; *Dictionnaire d'histoire et de géographie ecclésiastiques*, ed. A. BAUDRILLART et al. (Paris 1912) 8:177–188; ''L'Influence de S. Benoît d'Aniane dans l'histoire de l'ordre de St. Benoit,'' *Il monachesimo nell' alto medioevo* (Spoleto 1957) 401–415. K. HALLINGER, *Gorze-Kluny,* 2 v. (Rome 1950–51) v.2. J. WINANDY, ''L'Oeuvre monastique de Saint Benoît d'Aniane,'' *Mélanges bénédictins* (Saint-Wandrille 1947) 235–258.

[S. HILPISCH]

BENEDICT OF BENEVENTO, ST.

Missionary and martyr; b. Benevento, Italy; d. near Gniezno, Poland, May 11, 1003. He was the leader of the five massacred brothers—himself, John, Isaac, Matthew, and Christian. Benedict had been a monk of San Salvatore in Calabria, and he later took up the life of a hermit. In 1001 he was persuaded by Bruno of Querfurt, who was eventually his biographer, to become a missionary in Poland. He and his companion John were well received by the duke, Boleslav I (d. 1025), who built a hermitage for them. Their work prospered, and they were joined by people of the district, among them Isaac, Matthew, and Christian. On a rumor that the duke had given them a great treasure, they were murdered one night by a former servant and his accomplices. They were buried in their hermitage, and the site soon became a center of pilgrimage. The cult of this group that is sometimes misleadingly called ''the Five Polish Brothers'' was popular in the Polish Church from an early date and was confirmed by Pope Julius II in 1508.

Feast: Nov. 12.

Bibliography: BRUNO OF QUERFURT, *Vita quinque fratrum,* ed. R. KALE in *Monumenta Germaniae Historica: Scriptores* (Berlin 1826—) 15.2:709–738. M. BARONIUS, *Vitae gesta et miracula sanctorum quinque fratrum* (Cracow 1610). J. DAVID, *Dictionnaire d'histoire et de géographie ecclésiastiques*, ed. A. BAUDRILLART et al. (Paris 1912) 8:3–5. A. M. ZIMMERMANN, *Kalendarium Benedictinum,* (Metten 1933–38) 3:291–294.

[J. L. GRASSI]

BENEDICT OF PETERBOROUGH

Abbot, chronicler of Thomas Becket; d. Peterborough Abbey, England, 1193. He was very probably a BENEDICTINE at Christ Church, Canterbury; hence his writings on Thomas BECKET are most likely eyewitness accounts. In 1174 he became chancellor to Becket's successor, Abp. RICHARD OF CANTERBURY, and in 1175, prior of Christ Church. In 1177 he was elected abbot at PETERBOROUGH ABBEY, a post vacant since Abbot Waterville was deposed, two years earlier. Though he found the abbey heavily in debt, Benedict was able during his 15 years as abbot to restore solvency. A notable builder, he completed a portion of the nave of the abbey church and built certain chapels as well as the great abbey gate. He was a friend of King RICHARD I, the Lion Heart, and, like most of the leading abbots of his day, was called on to play an active part in government service. In a somewhat enthusiastic biography (ed. J. Sparke, *Historiae Anglicanae scriptores varii,* 1723), Robert Swafham, a monk of the abbey, describes Benedict's efforts to build up the Peterborough library by having the monks copy a number of manuscripts. Undoubtedly one of these was the valuable *Gesta Henrici II* (London B.M., Cotton MS Julius A.xi), a chronicle of the reigns of Kings HENRY II and Richard I long ascribed to Benedict's pen but now generally recognized as the first draft of Roger of Hoveden's *Chronica* (ed. W. Stubbs, 2 v., *Rerum Britannicarum medii aevi scriptores* 49). Benedict wrote a *passio* of the martyrdom of Becket; and although the complete work is lost, substantial portions of it were incorporated by the compiler of the *Quadrilogus* (*Materials . . . T. Becket* 4:386–408 or 2:1–20). As the second section of the *passio,* Benedict composed an account of the *Miracula* of Becket, but this has survived as a separate work (*ibid.* 2:21–281).

Bibliography: *Bibliotheca hagiographica latina antiquae et mediae aetatis* (Brussels 1898–1901) 8170–75. *Materials for the History of Thomas Becket,* ed. J. C. ROBERTSON and J. B. SHEPPARD, 7 v. (*Rerum Britannicarum medii aevi scriptores* 67; 1875–85) 2:xix–xxi. D. M. STENTON, ''Roger of Howden and 'Benedict,''' *English Historical Review* 68 (1953) 574–582. E. M. THOMPSON, *The Dictionary of National Biography from the Earliest Times to 1900* (London 1885–1900) 2:213–214.

[M. J. HAMILTON]

BENEDICT THE LEVITE

Also known as Deacon Benedict, the name of the unknown author of a collection of forged capitularies (1,319 specimens) belonging to the group of the FALSE DECRETALS (Pseudo-Isidorian forgeries). The collection is appended as books five to seven to the four books of the genuine collection of Ansegis. The last of the additions may have been written at the time of the Pseudo-Isidorian Decretals, but all the rest must be dated earlier, about 850, and come probably from Le Mans. About one-fourth of them are genuine, as such, but forged in this text. The majority reproduce genuine, notably ecclesiastical, sources falsified into Frankish imperial laws and in the process subjected to repeated interpolations. Benedict sought to give the impression that the laws were the product of a collaboration between state and ecclesiastical authorities. The collection embraces almost all areas of Canon Law. It was calculated to remedy the sad state of the Frankish Church. Dominant principles are freedom of the Church and independence of its hierarchy.

Bibliography: Editions. F. H. KNUST, *Monumenta Germaniae Historica: Leges* (Berlin 1826–) 2.2:17–139. *Patrologia Latina,* ed. J. P. MIGNE, 217 v. (Paris 1878–90) 97:698–912. Literature. E. SECKEL, ''Studien zu B. L.,'' pts. 1–8.3 *Neues Archiv der Gesellschaft für ältere deutsche Geschichtskunde* 26 (1900) 37–72; 29 (1904) 275–331; 31 (1905) 59–139, 238–239; 34 (1909) 319–381; 35 (1910) 105–191, 433–539; 39 (1914) 327–431; 40 (1915) 15–130; 41 (1916) 157–263; pts. 8.4–5, ed. J. JUNCKER, *Zeitschrift der Savigny-Stiftung für Rechtsgeschichte, Kanonistische Abteilung* 23 (1934) 269–377; 24 (1935) 1–112; ''B. L. decurtatus et excerptus'' in *Festschrift für Heinrich Brunner* (Munich 1914) 377–464. P. FOURNIER and G. LEBRAS, *Histoire des collections canoniques en occident depuis les fausses décrétales jusqu'au Décret de Gratien,* 2 v. (Paris 1931–32) 1:145–171, 190–192, 202–209. F. BAIX, *Dictionnaire de droit canonique*, ed. R. NAZ, 7 v. (Paris 1935–65) 2:400–406. S. WILLIAMS, ''The Pseudo-Isidorian Problem Today,'' *Speculum. A Journal of Mediaeval Studies* 29 (1954) 702–707. R. GRAND, ''Nouvelles remarques sur l'origine du Pseudo-Isidore source du Décret de Gratien,'' *Studia Gratiana* 3 (1955) 1–16. R. BUCHNER, *Die Religion in Geschichte und Gegenwart*, 7 v. (3d ed. Tübingen 1957–65) 1:1032–33. G. MAY, ''Die Infamie bei B. L.,'' *Österreichisches Archiv Für Kirchenrecht* 11 (1960) 16–36. H. FUHRMANN, ''Die Fälschungen im Mittelalter,'' *Historische Zeitschrift* 197 (1963) 529–554.

[G. MAY]

BENEDICT THE MOOR, ST.

Franciscan lay brother, patron of blacks of North America; b. San Fratello, near Messina, Italy, 1526; d. Palermo, Italy, April 4. He was the son of Christopher and Diana Manasseri, slaves converted to Christianity after they had been brought to Sicily from Africa. As a field hand, he was given his liberty when he attained the age of 18, and thereafter he earned his living as a day laborer. He generously shared his small wages with the poor and spent much of his leisure time caring for the sick. Among the beneficiaries of his charity he became known as ''The Holy Negro.'' But there is also evidence that he was often the object of ridicule because of his race and origin. While still a young man he joined a company of hermits who lived in the hills near San Fratello under the direction of Jerome Lanza, a nobleman who had forsaken the world for the solitary life. When Jerome died, his followers chose Benedict as their new superior, and under his leadership the group prospered. When in 1562 Pope Pius IV ordered independent groups of hermits to be incorporated into the established religious orders, Benedict chose to enter the Order of Friars Minor of the Observance as a lay brother. For some years after his reception into the order, he was employed as cook at the Friary of St. Mary of Jesus in Palermo. Although he could neither read nor write, he was chosen in 1578 as guardian of the Palermo friary. After serving one term in this office, he was appointed master of novices. An austere man, he was granted extraordinary gifts of prayer; his counsel was sought by persons of every class; and the fame of his sanctity spread throughout Sicily. Toward the end of his life he asked to be relieved of all offices in the order and he resumed his duties as cook. At the age of 63 he contracted a severe illness, and after receiving the Last Rites with intense fervor, he died at the exact hour he had predicted. He was buried in the friary church in Palermo. In 1611 King Philip III of Spain provided in the same church a new shrine to which the saint's incorrupt remains were transferred and where they are still venerated by the faithful. Immediately upon Benedict's death, a vigorous cult developed. His veneration became especially popular in Italy, Spain, and Latin America; and the city of Palermo chose him as its heavenly protector. He was beatified by Pope Benedict XIV in 1743 and canonized by Pope Pius VII in 1807.

Feast: April 4; April 3 (Franciscans).

Bibliography: ''Bulla canonizationis beati Benedicti a S. Philadelphio laici professi Ord. minorum,'' *Acta Ordinis Fratrum Minorum* 26 (1907) 214–222. M. ALLIBERT, *Life of St. Benedict the Moor* (London 1895). G. CARLETTI, *Life of St. Benedict*, tr. M. ALLIBERT (Freeport, N.Y. 1971). E. ELTON, *São Benedito* (Vitória-ES, Brazil 1988). LEON DE CLARY, *Lives of the Saints and Blessed of the Three Orders of St. Francis,* 4 v. (Taunton, Eng. 1885–87) 2:14–31. *Three Studies in Simplicity*, tr. M. CARROLL of POL DE LEON ALBARET *Sainte Benedict l'Africain* (Chicago 1974). B. NICOLOSI, *Vita di San Benedetto di San Fratello* (Palermo 1907).

[C. LYNCH]

BENEDICTINE ABBEYS AND PRIORIES IN THE U.S.

Unlike other religious orders, the Benedictines for most of their existence have maintained a decentralized and highly autonomous structure. It was only in the last years of the nineteenth century, under the urging of Pope Leo XIII, that Benedictines began to organize themselves into a worldwide confederation of congregations. These different congregations constituted a network presided over by an abbot primate, whose role was largely to facilitate communication between individual Benedictine communities and their respective congregations. The diverse congregations that constituted the confederation were organized largely around linguistic or national lines, each with its own constitutions and customs, as well as an abbot president. Each congregation was established as autonomous in its governance, similar to the system of self-sufficiency and self-governance found in the individual monasteries.

Those Benedictine houses designated by the title ''abbey'' are completely independent entities, whose superior is an abbot. Those designated as priories are generally foundations of a particular abbey that still maintain some link of financial or canonical dependence on the mother house. Their superiors are called priors. The term ''archabbey'' is a purely honorific title, used in the United States to designate the first two monasteries of the two major United States Benedictine congregations, Saint Vincent Archabbey and Saint Meinrad Archabbey respectively.

The American Cassinese Congregation. The Benedictines came to the United States to serve the needs of the increasing tide of new German-speaking Catholic immigrants in the first half of the nineteenth century. American Catholic bishops, faced with the challenge of how to minister to this new population, sent requests for pastoral assistance to religious houses in Germany, Austria, and Switzerland.

These requests coincided with the emerging vision of a young Bavarian monk from the German abbey of Metten, Boniface Wimmer. Wimmer elaborated a plan to establish a permanent Benedictine community in the United States. Its main purposes were to be the sacramental care of the German-speaking Catholics and the education of immigrant children. Though he was initially discouraged from carrying out his plan by his abbot and other community members, Wimmer secured approval from Rome for the venture in 1845. In addition, he was able to receive financial aid from the *Ludwig Missionsverein*, a Munich immigrant aid society.

Wimmer set out for North America in 1846. With him were 18 recruits, 14 lay brothers and four candidates for the priesthood, none of whom had any prior experience in Benedictine life. On arrival, the group went to Pennsylvania. After investigating several sites, Wimmer accepted an offer to take land near Latrobe, in the diocese of Pittsburgh. The first monastic community was given the title of Saint Vincent. Within a decade of its foundation, in 1855, it was recognized by the Holy See as an abbey and Boniface Wimmer became its first abbot. Wimmer also was designated as the first president of the newly established American Cassinese Congregation. ''Cassinese'' was the name of a nineteenth-century Italian reform congregation, deriving its name from the abbey of Monte Cassino in Italy, founded by Saint Benedict. The American congregation came into being as a direct result of other Benedictine communities that had been founded from Saint Vincent. Saint John's Abbey in Minnesota was founded in 1856. One year later, the monastery of Saint Benedict in Atchison, Kansas, was established.

Before Wimmer's death in 1887, he was instrumental in making foundations in the cities of Newark and Chicago, which became the basis for the present abbeys of Saint Mary's (1884) and Saint Procopius (1894). Two other abbeys were founded in the American South, Belmont, North Carolina (1884) and Saint Bernard, Alabama (1891). Wimmer also started a monastic house in Savannah, Georgia, that remains today as Benedictine Priory. He also initiated foundations that later became Saint Leo Abbey, Florida (1902) and Mary Mother of the Church Abbey in Richmond, Virginia (1989).

In the twentieth century the congregation continued its expansion. In addition to Saint Bede Abbey, Peru, Illinois (1910), the American Cassinese Congregation was petitioned to absorb the abbeys of Sacred Heart (now Saint Gregory), Oklahoma (1929) and Saint Mary's (now Assumption), North Dakota (1932). It extended its growth in the western United States with Holy Cross Abbey in Canon City, Colorado (1925) and Saint Martin's Abbey in Lacey, Washington (1914). Subsequent foundations of houses in the eastern United States included Saint Anselm Abbey in Manchester, New Hampshire (1927), Saint Andrew Abbey, Cleveland, Ohio (1934), the Byzantine Rite Monastery of Holy Trinity, Butler, Pennsylvania (1955) and Newark Abbey, New Jersey (1968). Monasteries founded outside the United States included Saint Peter's Abbey in Saskatchewan, Canada (1911), Tepeyac Abbey in Mexico City (1971) and Saint Anthony the Abbot Abbey in Humacao, Puerto Rico (1984). Other foreign foundations in the twentieth century include Benedicitne and Wimmer Priories in Taiwan, Holy Trinity Priory in Fujimi, Japan, Saint Augustine Priory in the Bahamas, and Saint Joseph Priory in Mineiros, Brazil.

The Swiss-American Congregation. The second major aggregate of American Benedictines is that of the Swiss-American Congregation. Their origin is associated with the monastery of Saint Meinrad in southern Indiana in 1854, a foundation of the Swiss Abbey of Einsiedeln. This house became an abbey in 1871 and an archabbey in 1954. Under the leadership of their first two abbots, Martin Marty and Fintan Mundwiller, they founded a succession of new houses. These include Subiaco Abbey in Subiaco, Arkansas (1891) and Saint Joseph Abbey in Saint Benedict, Louisiana (1903). The other major branch of the Swiss-American Congregation came from the Swiss Abbey of Engelberg. Fathers Frowin Conrad and Adelhelm Odermatt came to the United States in 1873 to found a monastery in northwest Missouri that later became Conception Abbey (1881), with Conrad as its first abbot. That same year the Swiss-American Congregation was established in a papal brief. A year later Odermatt founded a monastery in Oregon that became Mount Angel Abbey (1904). Almost a half of a century later, after World War II, another set of American houses came into being. Foundations from Saint Meinrad included Marmion Abbey, Aurora, Illinois (1947), Blue Cloud Abbey in Marvin, South Dakota (1954) and Prince of Peace Abbey, Oceanside, California (1983). Foundations from Conception were Saint Benedict's Abbey, Benet Lake, Wisconsin (1952) and Mount Michael Abbey, Elkhorn, Nebraska (1964). Westminster Monastery, Mission, British Columbia, Canada, became an abbey in 1953 as a foundation of Mount Angel. A later foundation of Mount Angel was Ascension Priory, Jerome, Idaho (1998). Corpus Christi, a Texan foundation of Subiaco Abbey, became an independent abbey in 1961. During this period a number of new communities outside the United States sprang up. The monastery of Jesus Christ Crucified in Esquipulas, Guatemala, was started by Saint Joseph Abbey in 1959. It became an abbey in 1982. The monastery of Our Lady of the Angels in Cuernavaca, Mexico, was started by Mount Angel Abbey in 1966. In Guatemala two other foundations were made in the 1960s. Marmion Abbey founded the Priory of San Jose (Solola and Quetzaltenango) in 1967. Blue Cloud Abbey's Resurrection Monastery in Coban became a priory in 1970. Subiaco Abbey founded Holy Family Monastery in Belize in 1971. A foundation in Peru by Saint Meinrad, in Nigeria by Subiaco Abbey, and in Denmark by Conception Abbey, and several small communities from Saint Benedict's Abbey, Benet Lake, in El Salvador and Nicaragua were later closed. Two houses in Massachusetts affiliated with the Swiss-American Congregation were Our Lady of Glastonbury Abbey, Hingham, Massachusetts (1973) and Saint Benedict Abbey, Still River, Massachusetts (1993). Monasteries in Richardton, North Dakota (Saint Mary's) and Pecos, New Mexico (Our Lady of Guadalupe Abbey), originally under the aegis of the Swiss-American Congregation, later joined other monastic congregations. Two foundations made by Conception Abbey in Cottonwood, Idaho and Pevely, Missouri, subsequently closed.

Other Monastic Congregations. A third congregation of Benedictines, the English Benedictine Congregation, was represented in the twentieth century with the monastic foundation of Saint Anselm in Washington, D.C. Saint Anselm's became a priory in 1949 and an abbey in 1961. Two other communities also took root, one in 1919 near Newport, Rhode Island, originally under the jurisdiction of Downside Abbey, which became Portsmouth Abbey (1969) and one that was a foundation of Ampleforth Abbey, begun in Saint Louis in 1955, which became Saint Louis Abbey (1989).

The French Solesme Congregation made their first North American foundation in 1912 in Quebec. It became the Abbey of Saint Benoit-du-Lac. The same congregation was responsible for the Monastery of Our Lady of Clear Creek, Hulbert, Oklahoma (2000).

A number of other European Benedictine houses came to the U.S. after World War II. From China came monks of the Congregation of the Annunciation, who founded the community of Saint Andrew in Valyermo, which became an independent house in 1965. Another group of monastic refugees from Hungary founded Woodside Priory, California, in 1957. Earlier German monks from the Missionary Congregation of Saint Ottilien settled in Newton, New Jersey, in 1924, which became Saint Paul's Abbey (1947).

The Italian Camaldolese Congregation founded the Monastery of the Immaculate Heart in Big Sur, California (1958). The Italian Sylvestrine Congregation had their sole foundation of Saint Benedict Monastery, Oxford, Michigan (1960). The Italian Olivetan Congregation originally made a foundation in Louisiana but then took over the Abbey of Our Lady of Guadalupe, Pecos, New Mexico (1973), as well as the monastic communities of Holy Trinity, Saint David, Arizona (1974), and the Monastery of the Risen Christ, San Luis Obispo, California (1992).

The Subiaco Congregation took over the monastery of Christ in the Desert, New Mexico (1996) and subsequently made foundations in Veracruz and Guanajusto, Mexico and in Chicago at Holy Cross Monastery (2000). Saint Mary's Monastery in Petersham, Massachusetts (1987) is also a member of the Subiaco Congregation.

Two independent Benedictine foundations in the United States were also made after the war. Father Damasus Winzen was the founder of Mount Saviour Monastery, Pine City, New York (1950). Father Leo Rudloff founded Weston Priory, Weston, Vermont (1952). Both of these communities remain under the jurisdiction of the abbot primate.

Bibliography: C. BARRY, *Worship and Work* (revised ed. Collegeville, Minn. 1993). T. KARDONG, *The Benedictines* (Collegeville, Minn. 1988). A. KESSLER, *Benedictine Men and Women of Courage* (Yankton, S.D. 1992). J. OETGEN, *Saint Vincent in Pennsylvania: A History of the First Benedictine Monastery in the United States* (Washington, D.C. 2000); *An American Abbot: Boniface Wimmer, O.S.B.* (Washington, D.C. 1997). J. RIPPINGER, *The Benedictine Order in the United States: An Interpretive History* (Collegeville, Minn. 1991).

[J. RIPPINGER]

BENEDICTINE NUNS AND SISTERS

Benedictine women trace their origin to the sixth century monastic rule attributed to (St.) BENEDICT of Nursia. His sister (St.) Scholastica was a consecrated virgin who participated in Benedict's spiritual teaching. In the early days of monasticism, both men and women used rules that were localized and often were composed of concepts from different sources; thus to speak of a Benedictine order or a date of its foundation would be misleading. Under the influence of Pope GREGORY THE GREAT, the Benedictine rule spread through Europe. With its introduction into monasteries early in the seventh century, as well as the increased restriction upon other forms of monastic life, the *Rule of St. Benedict* gradually supplanted other rules, remaining the standard guide for most women's communities until the twelfth century, although adapted and interpreted in a variety of ways.

Early Growth. With the Benedictine missions in England, foundations of nuns began at FOLKSTONE (630) and Thanet (670). Under the influence of the monks of Canterbury, these monasteries probably observed the *Rule of St. Benedict* from their beginning. Other important monasteries were founded at ELY (673), BARKING (675), WILTON (800), and RAMSEY (967). In 657, St. HILDA founded Whitby and participated in the famous synod there in 664. The synod's adoption of the Roman rite in preference to the Celtic observance further reinforced the supremacy of Benedictine monasticism. Coldingham (673), ruled by St. CUTHBURGA, was another important monastery in Northumbria. Contemporary writings reveal the interest of these early English nuns in theological, scriptural, and patristic studies, as well as their skill in the arts of illumination, gold lettering, and needlework. Although practically all these monasteries, with the exception of Barking, were destroyed during the Danish invasions of the ninth and tenth centuries, some were subsequently restored and many others were founded in England after the Norman Conquest of 1066.

In Germany the first monastery to adopt, at least basically, the *Rule of St. Benedict*, was probably NONNBERG in Salzburg, founded about the year 700 by St. RUPERT. Among other early monasteries were four founded by St. BONIFACE: Tauberbischofsheim, Kitzingen, Ochsenfurt, and Schornsheim, all under the direction of St. LIOBA, who came from WIMBORNE ABBEY. Lioba, St. Thecla, St. WALBURGA, and other Anglo-Saxon nuns succeeded in imparting to Teutonic women not only the faith and the Christian heritage, but also a tradition of learning that continued through the Middle Ages. This was a marked characteristic of St. Hildegarde's monasteries at Rupertsberg and Bingen, and of the monastery of HELFTA, the home of St. GERTRUDE THE GREAT and other thirteenth century mystics.

The role of women in these monasteries mirrored the role of noble women in the culture. These women and others attest to the influence exercised not only in the spiritual and liturgical life, but in other areas of education and culture as well. The nuns devoted themselves also to the care of the sick and the needy, the study of science, literature and the arts.

In France during the seventh and eighth centuries the rules most widely used by women were those of Saints CAESARIUS and COLUMBAN. About 629 LUXEUIL, the center of Celtic monasticism, adopted a rule combining those of Saints Benedict and Columban and REMIREMONT be-

Benedictine nuns from the Convent of Perpetual Adoration in Kansas City make communion wafers for distribution in the lower midwest. (©Ted Spiegel/CORBIS)

came for the nuns what Luxeuil had been for the monks. Among the more important monasteries that followed a mixed observance were Sainte-Marie in Soissons, Rebais, Saint-Martial in Paris, FAREMOUTIERS, JOUARRE-EN-BRIE, and Chelles. The Council of Aix-la-Chapelle in 817 made the *Rule of St. Benedict* obligatory for all monasteries. One of the most famous during the Middle Ages was the Abbey of Notre-Dame at Angers (1028), which had under its jurisdiction a large number of other priories.

Benedictine women's monasteries were similarly founded in Italy in the seventh and eighth centuries and became so numerous during the Middle Ages that practically every city had one. By the early eleventh century, Benedictine communities were established also in Spain, Portugal, and the Scandinavian countries.

Reform Congregations. When the various invasions threatened European monastic life, the houses were reduced in number and greatly impoverished. During the CLUNIAC REFORM movement, St. Hugh founded a community for the nobility of France at Marcigny. Under the centralized government of Cluny, affiliated women's houses were directly under the control of its abbot and were obliged to observe its constitutions. However, many monastic communities not belonging to the congregation were influenced by its spirit and adopted some of its customs.

Changes in cultural and Church attitudes towards the role of women and of monastics in general resulted in a restriction of the activities and movement of women. Beginning in the thirteenth century, a series of ecclesiastical documents encouraged the ideal of separation from the world as essential to the monastic life. In keeping with this model of monastics as withdrawn from the world and devoted to liturgical prayer and contemplation, reforms like that of CÎTEAUX superseded the Cluniac model. Their

Benedictine nuns from Kylemore Abbey, on the Connemara Peninsula, load a wagon with peat. (©Hulton-Deutsch Collection/ CORBIS)

affective form of prayer, with its mystic tendencies, had a special attraction for women. This integration of liturgy and personal encounter with the divine is manifested in the life and writings of St. Gertrude the Great, St. MECHTILD OF HACKEBORN, MECHTILD OF MAGDEBURG and other mystical writers.

Women also participated in new Benedictine congregations, such as the Camaldolese, the VALLOMBROSANS, and, somewhat later, the Olivetans. Other reform movements of the fourteenth and fifteenth centuries, such as that later known as the Cassinese Congregation, as well as the Bursfeld Congregation in Germany, and the congregation of Claustrales in Spain, likewise had branches for women.

Post-Reformation Development

The restriction of the monastic role in culture, the popularity of new forms of religious life and the decline in quality of life within the monasteries all contributed to a decrease in Benedictine vocations after the Middle Ages. New legislation demanded that the lifestyle of Benedictine women become enclosed and strictly contemplative while other types of religious took up the activities of external ministry. The vows of the more recent orders focused on the evangelical counsels of poverty, chastity and obedience, and these came to be seen as the norm. Likewise, the larger and more visible population of apostolic sisters, identified with the Church's ministries, became a new model for women religious.

The Protestant Reformation of the sixteenth century dealt monastic life a further blow. Houses were suppressed in England, Germany, Denmark, and the Scandinavian countries. The practice of COMMENDATION, a form of secular control of monasteries, and the religious wars in France weakened monastic life there. Eventually, however, as the legislation of the Council of Trent (1545 to 1563) became effective, monastic life began to flourish again all over Europe.

France was one of the first countries to respond to the renewal. Although two of the most influential foundations of men, Saint-Vanne and Saint-Maur, refused to admit nuns into their congregations, old monastic houses were revived and new ones established. In the general renewal of this period, the monasteries at Montmartre, Beauvais, Val-de-Grace, and Douai played an important part. The new spirituality also influenced the foundation of the Benedictine nuns of Calvary and the Benedictine nuns of the Blessed Sacrament and Perpetual Adoration. Both congregations stressed the interior motive of reparation and enjoined severe penitential observances. The French Revolution and subsequent secularization decrees resulted in another setback for Benedictine life, but developments in the later ninteenth century included a resurgence of monasticism, marked by a renewal of the contemplative aspect of the Benedictine vocation and a remarkable expansion of missionary activity.

German participation in the post-Reformation renascence of Catholic life was evidenced in the new statutes drawn up for the monasteries at Hohenwart, Fulda, Nonnberg, Chiemsee, and Eichstätt, in which emphasis was placed on the Divine Office. England benefited from the French Revolution, which brought a return of English nuns to their native land. From Brussels, where the first post-Reformation English women's monastery was organized in 1597, the nuns escaped to Colchester, England. The community of Cambrai (1623) returned to England to establish what became STANBROOK ABBEY in Worcester. A member of the Cambrai community, Dame Gertrude More, great-great-granddaughter of Thomas More, became a significant figure under the direction of Dom Augustine BAKER. Her writings included the *Spiritual Exercises and Practices in Divine Love*.

Both Abbot Prosper GUÉRANGER of Solesmes and Archabbot Maurus Wolter of Beuron, nineteenth century monastic reformers, were convinced that nuns, unhampered by priestly duties, were in a better position to live the Benedictine life than were the monks. Thus Solesmes and Beuron fostered the liturgy among the nuns, and Guéranger founded the monastery of Sainte-Cécile, near Solesmes, while the Beuronese Congregation erected a women's monastery in Prague. There was a flourishing liturgical life in monasteries such as Eibingen, Herstelle, Fulda, and Maredret as well. The writings of Jenny H. Cécile BRUYÈRE, abbess of Sainte-Cécile, clearly reflect the liturgical spirit of the times.

Missionary activity brought about the establishment of new congregations, such as the Sisters for Foreign Missions, founded in Tutzing, Bavaria, and the Missionary Benedictine Nuns, founded in France. In the mid-ninteenth century there began also the establishment of monasteries in Australia, North America, and South America and, in the twentieth century, Benedictine life began to fluorish in Africa and Asia as well.

Benedictines in the United States. At the invitation of Boniface WIMMER, monk of METTEN Abbey in Bavaria the first three nuns from Eichstätt, Bavaria, arrived in the United States in 1852 and, with Mother Benedicta Riepp as foundress, opened St. Joseph's Convent and School at St. Marys, Pa. During the next century, more than 30 houses were founded, directly or indirectly, from the original community. Three other motherhouses in Switzerland, Maria Rickenbach, Sarnen, and Melchthal also began North American monasteries in the later nineteenth century. French communities sponsored United States foundations as well.

At the time of the American missionary efforts, Benedictine nuns generally led an enclosed life with the primary ministry of contemplative liturgical prayer, although Eichstätt was among those which had an attached school. The hierarchy of the United States, which was a mission territory, forbade the establishment of communities of enclosed contemplatives by a decree of the Second Council of Baltimore in 1865. This led to a confusion of roles for the Benedictine women who valued the praying of the Divine Office and the autonomy and local nature of their communities. Canon law distinguished between NUN (*monialis*), a member of the older orders with their solemn vows and enclosed contemplative lifestyle, and religious SISTER (*soror*), one who belonged to an apostolic order. A 50-year struggle led to the approval of Benedictine monasteries without enclosure as the nuns took up increasingly more external ministries expected of them by bishops and local needs.

Eventually, as new congregations of non-enclosed Benedictine sisters were established elsewhere, the canonical distinctions among religious became less specific, and the attitude towards contemplative life changed. Nevertheless, the American lifestyle has remained somewhat unique. The United States Benedictines continued to maintain their autonomy, with their own local membership, novitiate, and administration, as is common to Benedictine nuns. Instead of the evangelical vows, Benedictine women retain the ancient rite of monastic profession in which they commit themselves to ''conversatio'' or fidelity to the monastic way, obedience to the rule and its life of attentiveness, and stability to the particular women of that community. Most Benedictine women's communities in the United States were eventually placed under pontifical jurisdiction, in contrast to Europe, where more communities remained subject to the local ordinary.

A majority of the American foundations have grouped together into federations which provide mutual support and supervision. Women's houses use the term "federation" in order to distinguish their monastic congregations from the different structure of apostolic congregations of women.

Among the American monastic congregations of pontifical status, the Federation of St. Scholastica is the oldest and largest, the roots of which were initiated in 1881. Because of the difficulties over the question of the classification of American Benedictines, final approval of the congregation was delayed until 1930. Subsequently the path was clear for the formation of other federations, the Federation of St. Gertrude the Great, approved in 1937, and the Federation of St. Benedict in 1956.

Federation of St. Scholastica [0230, I]. At the beginning of the twenty-first century, the Federation of St. Scholastica had over 1,000 sisters in 22 monasteries in the United States and Mexico. All these monasteries were descended from the original foundation at St. Mary's, Pennsylvania. Members are: Mount St. Scholastica (Atchison, Kansas), St. Scholastica's (Boerne, Texas), St. Benedict (Bristow, Virginia.), St. Scholastica (Chicago, Illinois), Benet Hill (Colorado Springs, Colorado), St. Walburg (Covington, Kentucky), Sacred Heart (Cullman, Alabama), St. Walburga (Elizabeth, New Jersey), Mount St. Benedict (Erie, Pennsylvania), St. Lucy's (Glendora, California), Queen of Angels (Liberty, Missouri), Sacred Heart (Lisle, Illinois), Emmanuel (Lutherville, Maryland), San Benito (Mexico City, Mexico), Red Plains (Piedmont, Oklahoma), St. Benedict (Pittsburgh, Pennsylvania), St. Gertrude (Ridgely, Maryland), Holy Name (St. Leo, Florida), St. Joseph (St. Marys, Pennsylvania), Pan de Vida (Torreon, Mexico), St. Joseph (Tulsa, Oklahoma), and Queen of Heaven-Byzantine Rite (Warren, Ohio).

Federation of St. Gertrude [0230, II]. The Federation of St. Gertrude consists of 17 houses, also with approximately 1,000 sisters. Members come from both the German and Swiss nineteenth century foundations. They are: Our Lady of Grace (Beech Grove, Indiana), Queen of Peace (Belcourt, North Dakota), Our Lady of Peace (Columbia, Missouri), St. Gertrude (Cottonwood, Idaho), Mount St. Benedict (Crookston, Minnesota), Immaculate Conception (Ferdinand, Indiana), St. Scholastica (Fort Smith, Arkansas), Holy Spirit (Grand Terrace, California), St. Benedict Center (Madison, Wisconsin), Dwelling Place (Martin, Kentucky), Queen of Angels (Mt. Angel, Oregon), House of Bread (Nanaimo, British Columbia, Canada), St. Martin (Rapid City, South Dakota), Sacred Heart (Richardton, North Dakota), Mother of God (Watertown, South Dakota), St. Benedict (Winnipeg, Manitoba, Canada), and Sacred Heart (Yankton, South Dakota).

Federation of St. Benedict [0230, III]. The Federation of St. Benedict consists of daughterhouses of the original St. Marys group, mostly foundations from the community at St. Joseph, Minnesota. There are 900 sisters in 11 monasteries in several countries. The monasteries are: St. Benedict's (St. Joseph, Minnesota), Annunciation (Bismarck, North Dakota), St. Scholastica (Duluth, Minnesota), St. Bede (Eau Claire, Wisconsin), St. Placid (Lacey, Washington), St. Martin (Nassau, Bahamas), St. Mary (Rock Island, Illinois), Mount Benedict (Ogden, Utah), St. Paul's (St. Paul, Minnesota), St. Benedict's (Sapporo, Japan) and St. Benedict's (Tanshui, Taiwan).

The sisters of these federations engage in a wide variety of ministries both within their monasteries and in external locations. Wherever they are and whatever they do, the daily Liturgy of the Hours and the witness of life in a contemplative and supportive community remain primary. Besides these three federations, there are also other Benedictine sisters in the United States in some other affiliations or jurisdictions.

The Congregation of Benedictine Sisters of Perpetual Adoration [0220]. This congregation was founded in 1874 by five sisters from Maria Rickenbach in Switzerland and its constitutions were approved in 1925. Consisting of a motherhouse in Clyde, Missouri, and several interdependent priories, the congregation observes the rule of St. Benedict with a primary dedication to the Eucharist. Its members serve the Church through a ministry of contemplative prayer and offer hospitality and retreats to guests in a shared environment of monastic peace. The liturgy of the hours is offered daily in each monastery and other works of the community are consistent with a contemplative life-style. Formation for new members is centered in Clyde, while the vow of stability, made to the congregation, allows transfer to other of the priories, located in Dayton, Wyoming, Sand Spring, Oklahoma, and Tucson, Arizona.

There remain a very few monasteries in this country which are outside of the major federations. These are usually associated with some other international federation or motherhouse in another country. The Congregation of Missionary Benedictine Sisters of Tutzing [0210], a congregation of pontifical jurisdiction, originated in 1885 in Bavaria and has missions throughout the world. The generalate is located in Rome and the general motherhouse remains at Tutzing, Germany. In 1923 a house was established in the United States at Norfolk, Nebraska, where the sisters engage in a variety of ministries.

Holy Angels, Jonesboro, Arkansas, [0240] is a diocesan community affiliated with the Olivetan Congregation. It was begun in 1887 by sisters from Clyde, Missouri, and became a member of the Benedictines of Mount Olivet in Rome, Italy, in 1893. There is a foundation of Camaldolese hermits at Windsor, New York [0235] and cloistered communities at Regina Laudis (Bethlehem, Connecticut.) [0180] and at St. Scholastica, of the Subiaco Congregation, (Petersham, Massachusetts) [0233]. The nuns of Eichstätt, after the acceptance of contemplative communities in this country, made two further foundations. Conditions in Germany in the 1930s led to the establishment of St. Emma's (Greensburg, Pennsylvania) and St. Walburga (Virginia Dale, Colorado) [0190]. The Sisters of Jesus Crucified, O.S.B., are an enclosed community in Branford, Connecticut.

Because of the unique canonical conditions in the United States, Benedictine life developed very differently than in other areas of the New World. Today, traditional enclosed communities exist in Latin America and Canada, along with communities which were originated as missions of United States monasteries and maintain the American model. In Australia, besides the contemplative communities, missionary sisters were organized by Bishop Polding according to the congregational model. With a single central generalate, the Sisters of the Good Samaritan of the Order of St. Benedict live throughout the country and now in several other countries. Other communities with external ministries and a Benedictine contemplative focus have been formed in other places as well. Meanwhile, many communities in Europe maintain the tradition, often in monasteries hundreds of years old. In Asia and Africa, as well as in Eastern Europe and elsewhere, monastic life is being established or re-founded. The longevity and continuity of the Benedictine way of life, its diversity around the world, and its ability to adapt to many times and cultures give witness to the wisdom and timelessness of St. Benedict's teaching.

Bibliography: R. BASKA, *The Benedictine Congregation of Saint Scholastica: Its Foundation and Development* (Washington 1935). J. CHITTISTER et al., *Climb Along the Cutting Edge: An Analysis of Change in Religious Life* (New York 1977). D. DOWLING, *In Your Midst: The Story of the Benedictine Sisters of Perpetual Adoration* (St. Louis 1988). G. ENGELHART, trans., *Spring and Harvest* (St. Meinrad, Indiana 1952). I. GIRGEN, *Behind the Beginnings* (St. Joseph, Minnesota 1981). E. HOLLERMANN, *The Reshaping of a Tradition: American Benedictine Women, 1852–1881* (St. Joseph, Minnesota 1994). P. JOHNSON, *Equal in Monastic Profession* (Chicago 1991). J. KLIMISCH, *Women Gathering: The Story of the Benedictine Federation of St. Gertrude* (Toronto 1993). *Medieval Women Monastics: Wisdom's Wellsprings*, eds., L. KULZER and M. SCHMITT (Collegeville, Minnesota 1996). J. RIPPINGER, *The Benedictine Order in the United States* (Collegeville, Minnesota 1990). J. T. SCHULLENBURG, *Forgetful of Their Sex: Female Sanctity and Society, CA 500–1000* (Chicago 1998). J. SUTERA, *True Daughters: Monastic Identity and American Benedictine Women's History* (Atchison, Kansas 1987). H. VAN ZELLER, *The Benedictine Nun* (Baltimore 1961). B. WALTER, *Sustained by God's Faithfulness: The Missionary Benedictine Sisters of Tutzing*, trans. M. HANDL (St. Ottilien 1987.)

[T. A. DOYLE/J. SUTERA]

BENEDICTINE RULE

The Rule of St. Benedict was composed in the 6th century by St. Benedict of Nursia when he was abbot of Monte Cassino. It is a relatively short document, comprising a prologue and 73 chapters. Many scholars maintain that ch. 67 to 73 are additions to an earlier version of the rule. Its directions for the formation, government, and administration of a monastery and for the spiritual and daily life of its monks have been found valid and practical for almost 15 centuries. It gives advice to the abbot and other officials and outlines the principal monastic virtues such as obedience (ch. 5), silence (6), and humility (7). The rule provides for an autonomous, self-contained community (66) and gives instructions for the election of an abbot (64); for the reception, training, and profession of novices (58–60); and for the appointment and duties of prior (65), cellarer (31), novice master (58), guestmaster (53), and councillors (3). Psalmody and prayers at the Divine Office (*opus Dei*) are regulated in detail (8–19). Food (39–41, 56), sleep (22), clothing (55), and daily work (48) have their chapters. The monastery described in the rule is a microcosm containing members of every age and condition, from children and boys to old men (37), oblates (59), converted adults (85), former serfs (2), clerics (60 and 62), monks from other houses (61), and sons of men of means and position (58–59). The waking hours are divided almost equally between three occupations: prayer in common (*opus Dei*), religious reading (*lectio divina*, 48), and manual work of domestic, craft (57), and horticultural (48) character.

A unique feature of the rule is the space given to practical and spiritual advice. In many ways it is a sapiential document. The prologue and chapters on humility and obedience, and the chapters outlining the abbot's duties (2, 27, and 64), are recognized masterpieces of wisdom. Though strictly impersonal, the rule has impressed readers from the time of Gregory the Great as the reflection of a wise, holy, firm, and paternal character in an author who can combine strict principles with moderation and humanity. His use of common sense and natural inclination as criteria of moral goodness is notable in an age influenced by the more rigorous teaching of St. Augustine. St. Benedict indeed deprecates extreme severity more than once, and in the course of centuries, his authority has been invoked, not always validly, on the side of conde-

"Saint Benedict Presents the Rule of the New Order," by Turino di Vanni. (©Arte & Immagini srl/CORBIS)

scension to human weakness. Among the virtues, humility, obedience, and stability stand out; the monk's life is a return from disobedience in sin to obedience in the service of God under an abbot who teaches and follows the rule. No works, pursuits, or ends outside the monastery are considered; there is no connection with any other establishment or superior save the local bishop. The lack of strict disciplinary sanctions and constitutional machinery, inevitable in a document of the 6th century, has sometimes been seen as a weakness in the rule. Yet it has served to maintain abbatial authority and the autonomy of the individual monastery throughout the ages. It has been well said that the rule presupposes and needs for its viability an abbot of unassailable virtue. No provision is made for new foundations, but varied climatic conditions are envisaged (55). The regulations for recruitment and profession, and the integration of Prime and Compline into the Office, passed from the rule into universal practice (although Prime has been excluded by most monasteries since Vatican Council II). As sources, St. Benedict used Eastern rules, patristic maxims, the work of John Cassian, and contemporary codes. He is recognized as having given to the West the wisdom of the desert adapted to a fully cenobitical life and to the capabilities of normal Western men and women.

Authorship. The attribution of the rule to St. Benedict was unquestioned until 1938, when Dom Augustine Génestout, a monk of Solesmes, argued that the rule was closely based on the anonymous *Regula Magistri*, of which the prologue and chapters one through ten are almost identical with the prologue and chapters one through seven of the Rule of Benedict, with many further resemblances. Numerous studies have been devoted to the problem. Today the weight of evidence is strongly in favor of the priority of the Rule of the Master; no prominent expert holds that the Rule of Benedict is earlier than the Rule of the Master. The genesis and development of the Rule of the Master and the form in which it was known to Benedict are still matters of dispute. In any case, the firm outline of the liturgical, administrative, and spiritual life are certainly the achievement of Benedict alone. The Rule of Benedict, and not the Rule of the Master, is the document that gave form to European monasticism and has been found valuable by every generation of Benedictine monks, nuns, and sisters.

Text. The rule was written in the vernacular Latin of the 6th century and is preserved in hundreds of manuscripts. Except for biblical literature, probably no other ancient text was copied in the Middle Ages as often as the Rule of Benedict. Since the first printing at Venice in 1489, more than a thousand editions have been published, including either the Latin text or translations into various vernacular languages or both together in bilingual versions.

The pioneer in the critical work on the text was Daniel Haneburg, a Benedictine scholar of Munich. After collating a number of manuscripts he turned over his material to Dom Edmund Schmidt of Metten who in 1880 published the first critical edition based on 15 manuscripts. The next critical edition was done by Eduard Wölfflin, an authority on Low Latin, who produced an edition in 1895 based on four manuscripts. In 1898 the German philologist Ludwig Traube reconstructed the history of the text of the rule in such a way that has determined its subsequent study. Critical editions produced in the 20th century followed Traube's principles. First was that of Dom Cuthbert Butler, monk and later abbot of Downside, which appeared in 1912. Intended for practical use, Butler normalized the grammatical irregularities and provided a text based on sound textual criticism; he did pioneer work in the investigation of the sources of the Rule of Benedict. In 1922 Bruno Linderbauer, a monk of Metten, produced a more accurate text, accompanied by philological notes; he provided a fuller apparatus than Butler's in a 1928 edition. Additional useful Latin editions were produced by Anselmo Lentini of Monte Cassino in 1947, with an Italian translation and commentary; by Justin McCann of Ampleforth in 1952, with an English translation and notes; and by Gregorio Penco of Finalpia in 1958, the first edition to indicate the Rule of the Master parallels and include the readings of the Rule of the Master manuscripts in the apparatus, together with an Italian translation and a commentary on the common and parallel passages.

The task of producing the definitive edition of the Rule of Benedict, which was to reconstruct the original text and trace the history of the text tradition, was entrusted by the Vienna Academy to Heribert Plenkers, one of Traube's pupils. After 30 years of work on the project, he died in 1931 without completing the task. In 1951 the work was taken up by Rudolph Hanslik, who produced his Vienna Corpus edition in 1960. He collated 300 manuscripts and retained 63 for his edition, but his work was strongly criticized both for its methodology and many errors (some of which were corrected in the second edition of 1977). Nevertheless, his edition contains the fullest apparatus so far assembled and provides useful tools for study in its extensive indices.

The most recent edition, appearing in 1972, is that of Jean Neufville of Pierre-qui-Vire. It is the first edition to adopt the priority of the Rule of the Master as a working principle for the establishment of the text. It is accompanied with a French translation, notes, and extensive commentary, all by the distinguished monk and prolific scholar of Pierre-qui-Vire, Adalbert de Vogüé. The definitive edition has yet to appear and is not thought to be imminent.

There are numerous commentaries on the Rule of Benedict, some learned, some devotional. That by Paul the Deacon (778–780) is an invaluable witness to the early tradition; that of Dom Augustin Calmet (1732) sums up the learning of the Maurists and others. Also to be noted is the commentary of Abbot Paul Delatte of Solesmes. Especially valuable is the excellent work of a number of United States's scholars, *Revue biblique 1980: The Rule of St. Benedict with Notes,* edited by Timothy Fry. More recently, Terrence G. Kardong has produced his own translation and extensive commentary, *Benedict's Rule: A Translation and Commentary.* Other authors who have written excellent commentaries on the rule include Aqinata Böckmann, André Borias, Michael Casey, Georg Holzherr, Eugene Lanning, Basil Steidle, and Ambrose Wathen.

Bibliography: E. C. BUTLER, *Benedictine Monachism* (repr. Cambridge, Eng. 1961). *Revue biblique 1980: The Rule of St. Benedict in Latin and English with Notes,* ed. T. FRY (Collegeville 1981). T. G. KARDONG, *Benedict's Rule: A Translation and Commentary* (Collegeville 1996). A. BÖCKMANN, *Perspektiven der Regula Benedict* (Münsterschwarzach 1986). G. HOLZHERR, *Die Benediktus Regel: Eine Anleitung zu Christlichem Leben* (Einsiedeln 2d ed. 1982). H. ROCHAIS and E. MANNING, *Règle de Saint Benoît* (Rochefort 1980). P. SCHMITZ, *Règle de Saint Benoît* (Turnhout 1987). B. STEIDLE, *Die Benediktusregel* (Beuron 1975). A. DE VOGÜÉ, *La Règle de Saint Benoît* (Paris 1977).

[M. D. KNOWLES/R. K. SEASOLTZ]

BENEDICTINE SPIRITUALITY

The word ''Benedictine'' is relatively modern; it scarcely existed before the 17th century. It evokes the name of St. Benedict, who lived in the 6th century, together with all those who have been inspired by the Rule of Benedict and associate themselves with the Benedictine spiritual tradition. Since Benedict was a monk, the spirituality which is based on his rule, is fundamentally monastic.

Monastic Spirituality. The thing that distinguishes monks from other religious in the Catholic Church is not primarily a matter of governmental structures or observances; all of these are found in other forms of consecrated life. It is rather the fact that monastic existence is a form of religious life having not secondary or ministerial purpose. It is specified solely by a commitment to God sanctioned by public vows. Tradition assigns no other end to monastic life than to ''seek God'' or ''to live for God alone,'' an ideal that can be achieved only by a life of conversion and prayer. The first and fundamental manifestation of such a vocation is a real separation from many aspects of the secular world. All monks are by definition ''solitaries,'' for this is the original meaning of their name, which comes from the Greek word *monachos*, derived from *monos*, to which corresponds the Latin *solus* (alone). The second characteristic of the monastic vocation is that it demands a life of which a privileged part is given to prayer. Personal or private prayer is traditionally exercised under the form of meditative reading of Holy Scripture and of authors who explain and reflect on it, according to the three phases designated by the words ''reading'' (*lectio*), meditation (*meditatio*), and ''prayer'' (*oratio* or *contemplatio*). In monastic life public prayer is only one observance among those which help the monk seek God. It is not one of the distinguishing characteristics of early monastic life. Only in later centuries and especially since the 19th century has it occupied a more important place in monastic life than in the observance of the majority of non-monastic religious congregations, with the consequence that it is usually considered a special feature of monastic life and spirituality.

The ascetic and contemplative orientation of the monastic life was accompanied historically by such cultural activities and manifestations as were compatible with a separation from the secular world, conversion, and a life of personal prayer.

Benedict's Rule and Spirituality. Christian monasticism had been in existence for a long time before Benedict wrote his rule. In the East it dates back to the 3rd century with St. Anthony, and in the West to the 4th century with St. Martin and other founders of monasteries. It was not founded by a particular saint. It appeared little by little wherever the Church took root, a spontaneous manifestation of the Holy Spirit urging Christians to become monks in response to the counsel given by Jesus in the Gospel: ''If you wish to be perfect, go, sell your possessions . . . , follow me . . .'' (Mt 19.21). Thus when St. Benedict appeared, monasticism was already solidly implanted in Egypt, Syria, Palestine—the whole East—and in Ireland, Gaul, Italy, Spain, and Africa in the West. The term was applied to two principal types: the hermits who lived alone or in small unorganinzed groups, and the cenobites who lived in community. There were also other forms of monastic life, but they were more or less eccentric in comparison with the two main types and sometimes led to abuse. Hence the spirituality that we find implicit in the Rule of Benedict was dependent in many ways on earlier sources, though he was certainly wise in what he incorporated and what he left behind.

What gives the Rule of Benedict its exceptional quality has commonly been called its ''discretion,'' in the double sense of the word: discernment and moderation. It sets up a framework of life, an institution, of which the essential and constitutive elements are firmly determined: life in common under the government of a superior called an abbot, who has the help of a prior and other officials and takes counsel of the whole assembly of monks, even the youngest in the community. As for details, Benedict left much to the discernment and initiative of the superior. Furthermore, he avoids anything that would be excessive or beyond the capacity of the average monk. He neither innovated nor broke with tradition. He simply organized a form of cenobitic life in complete conformity with the demands of the monastic vocation, which is but integral Christian life. Thus the rule refers frequently to the ''divine commandments'' and often cites the Bible, particularly the gospel. Its principal source is the Word of God and its model is Christ.

The diffusion of the Rule of Benedict in the West was slow. It acted and penetrated not as a legislative text imposed from without by authority but rather as a leaven by virtue of its intrinsic power. In the 7th and 8th centuries it was often combined with other rules, especially that of St. Columban (d. 615). Little by little, however, the Rule of Benedict became the principal rule, particularly in the Anglo-Saxon countries and in Italy. Where it was adopted, it was looked upon as a venerable text but not necessarily requiring observance in all its prescriptions. It was considered as proposing a spiritual program, while daily life was regulated by ''customaries,'' to which succeeded, from the beginning of the 16th century, ''Declarations'' and ''Constitutions'' as well as the ''Ceremonial.'' Even the Cistercians, who in the 12th century had intended to return to a faithful observance of the rule itself, added numerous statutes.

The rule did not become a text of the past or a dead document; rather it continued to live and to vivify, but its very fecundity, its inexhaustible youth—fruits of its discretion—explain how it was able to inspire different realizations. More than a founder in the juridical sense of the word, its author had been an educator, or better, a spiritual father, and he aimed at forming consciences capable of spiritual liberty. He did not intend to impose uniformity; he foresaw and intended diversity and reserved to each monastery the possibility of adapting the rule's prescriptions to various circumstances, provided the essential values of monasticism were safeguarded. The principles of evolution just enumerated enable us to understand why within one and the same Benedictine spiritual tradition there could appear and subsist different tendencies. Prosperity and ties with temporal society often led monasteries, especially the larger ones, to depart more or less from certain fundamental observances required by the rule, notably separation from secular society, real simplicity of life, and manual labor. Life in Benedictine monasteries was also deeply influenced by the clericalization of many of the monks and the episcopal ordination of many abbots. From the middle of the 20th century there appeared in Europe, America, Africa, and elsewhere monastic foundations that, drawing their inspiration from ancient sources, tended to return to forms of monastic life that are simpler and more contemplative.

Benedictine spirituality is essentially contemplative even though many who follow the rule are deeply involved in intellectual or manual work as well as in ministerial service to others. The Benedictine tradition has frequently presented examples of spiritual men and women, many of them venerated as saints, who in the line of their monastic vocation have sought to unite themselves to God by the eremetical or solitary life, normally in dependence on their superior and in the neighborhood of their monastery. The Cistercian Order reinforced the eremetical character of the cenobitical life itself. But for all, the ideal has remained ''solitude of heart'' with God, guaranteed by the ''order of charity'' in the community institution. From the 13th century, Benedictine monasteries have often felt the influence of spiritual movements coming from non-monastic sources. The *devotio moderna* is an example. In this, affective piety and the contemplative study of the mysteries of God were no longer so strictly united as in the preceding centuries, in which the patristic tradition had been preserved. Benedictine writers often appealed to methods of prayer and asceticism that were foreign to the monastic tradition.

Characteristics of Benedictine Spirituality. The Rule of Benedict opens with the word ''listen'' (*ausculta*). This is the key to Benedict's whole spiritual teaching. A monk should be above all a good listener. One of the primary functions of the various monastic structures is to provide conditions in which the monks can concentrate on learning the art of listening. Monks are to listen ''to the precepts of the master'' but their primary and ultimate master is God. It is only in a secondary sense that Benedict himself, speaking through the rule, and the abbot of the community are masters. The whole spiritual life of the monk consists in listening to God by ''inclining the ear of the heart.'' This listening is not merely an intellectual or rational activity; it is intuitive, springing from the very core of the monk's being where he is most open to God and most open to the word of life that God speaks. God speaks to the monk through Christ, but the monk is called to see Christ not only in the superior but also in the guests, in the sick, in the young, and in the old. In a very special way God speaks through the Scriptures, through the liturgy of the hours (*opus Dei*), and through personal prayer. This means that the monk must be very quiet and still within himself, but also very alert and attentive if the word of God is to resonate properly within his innermost depths so that he is enlightened and nourished by it. Benedict calls the monastery a ''school'' because it is the place where the monk is to be taught by God. This invitation to listen came to Benedict from the heart of the Old and New Testament traditions. The monk's listening is to be modeled after the prayer of Jesus who spent long hours listening and attentive in the presence of his heavenly Father.

Humility is also a dominant theme in Benedictine spirituality; in fact it is closely related to contemplation. It is humility that takes the monk beyond the myth of his own grandeur to the grandeur of God. If he gets the grandeur of God in place, he is apt to get the rest of monastic life in place too. Humility enables the monk to stand in awe before the world and to receive the gifts of God and others. In Benedict's rule, humility is not the same as humiliations, for humiliations degrade the person. The rule is marked by a strong sense of the individual monk's personal worth and dignity. Humility is the ability to recognize one's rightful place in the universe and to see oneself as a mysterious combination of strengths and weaknesses. The rule invites the monk to recognize the presence of God in his life, a presence which is neither gained or won or achieved but simply given.

Humility requires the monk to accept the gifts of others, their wisdom, their experience, and their counsel. But it also requires that he let go of false expectations concerning others. When a monk is aware of his own littleness, he is not driven to satisfy his own ego more than his true needs. He does not harbor illusions of grandeur but senses that all of his life is simply gift. Hence he is able to receive others in the community, including guests, with kind consideration. Through contemplative prayer, the monk becomes an emptiness so there is space for God as well as space for others.

A monk spends his whole life becoming humble. St. Benedict speaks of steps in humility, comparing them to the rungs of a ladder which we climb one by one—an image that implies not a strict order of ascent but a more general sense of movement growth. Humility demands that the monk take God seriously, that he take others seriously, but that he never take himself too seriously.

Closely related to both listening and humility is the virtue of obedience. Benedict's treatment of obedience must be understood in light of his understanding of authority. It is God who is the primary author of life for Benedict's disciples; hence the monk's obedience is above all to God and God's word which the monk finds mediated into his life through a wide variety of persons and experiences—in the rule, in the abbot, in the community as a whole, in the young and the old, in the sick and in guests, in the liturgy of the hours and in personal prayer, in sacred reading, in work, and in silence. One of the great challenges in the rule is that the monk obey others not only in their strengths but also in their weaknesses, for it is tempting to see others in their weakness as simply burdens rather than as gifts.

Benedict's community might well be called a formation community in which all, including the abbot and other superiors in the community, are in the process of being formed all of their lives into the likeness of Christ by attentive listening to the word of God, and a loving response to that word mediated into the life of the community by Christ's own offer of friendship through the communication of the Holy Spirit. Hence, conversion to Christ and response to his love through the power of the Holy Spirit are the goals of obedience. It is likewise through that response that one becomes free to be and develop as the person one is called to be. The ideal of this pattern of conversion is meant to be incarnated in a special way for the community in the abbot, who is expected to be a symbolic center exercising a centripetal force that draws individuals into a truly Christian community of life for God and others in Jesus Christ through the power of the Holy Spirit.

Simplicity of life and a sense of stewardship are also characteristics of Benedictine spirituality. The monk is called to discern how the Benedictine tradition speaks to the basic human condition, often characterized by blindness and greed. At the heart of his contemplative tradition are values which are directly opposed to blindness, materialism, and greed. Poverty of spirit, simplicity, sharing and giving, self-denial prompted by love, freedom of heart, gratitude, care for persons, and sound judgment with regard to created things should proceed from exposure to God in prayer. Certainly the rule does not see material privation as an end in itself; it is in no way part of the Benedictine tradition to assess everything economically by materialistic standards or to override aesthetic or other values for the sake of cheapness or squalor, for such a mentality narrows the monk's horizons and even creates those very evils accompanying destitution which all Christians have duty to banish from the earth. Benedictine simplicity of life is understood properly with the reality of Christ and his mission in mind. It is rooted in faith, and like Christ's own simplicity of life must be an outward expression of trustful dependence on God.

Of all creatures, the human person is in fact the neediest. But the monk's development, like that of all human beings, requires both material resources and the help of other people. One of the sure signs of monastic maturity is the honest acceptance of one's need for other people in community. Hence the monk must be poor psychologically because he realizes his dependence on others. Consequently he accepts the services and ideas of others, the gifts of life, and community. He is called to live in the rhythm of alternating between receiving and giving, accepting the gifts of God and others, while sharing generously jut as others share generously with him. This pattern of sharing is a basic characteristic of a cenobitic community.

The monk's own attitude toward his life then is one of stewardship. Instead of being possessive and manipulative, he is called to grow in detachment which manifests itself in the constructive and creative use of things. He realizes that attachment to oneself and one's talents or goods brings anxiety, a bondage that ties the human spirit down to the earth and allows no enlargement of either one's horizons or one's heart. Benedictine detachment does not imply a disparagement of good things, nor a fear of their power, but rather a just appreciation of all things as gifts of God.

Being poor with the poor has characterized many religious from the time of the Middle Ages, but Benedictines, because of their cenobitic life and their cultural inheritance, are often rich. But if they are rich communally, they must be rich for the many people who are poor not only materially but also intellectually, culturally, spiritually, and humanly. Benedictine monks have often received freely from their families and educators, from the rich Benedictine tradition, from the abundant life of their own communities, and from the many mercies of God. Hence they are rich compared with many who come to the monastery for help. That is why the ministry of hospitality is such an important part of the Benedictine heritage.

On a personal level the rule calls the monk to live a life marked by frugality, simplicity, and gratitude for the many gifts of God. He is called to witness in a materialistic world to the dependence of all men and women on God, and to their need and destiny for a happiness that lies beyond material fulfillment.

In chapter 72 of the rule, Benedict encourages his monks to be zealous, ''supporting with the greatest patience one another's weaknesses of body and behavior, and earnestly competing in obedience to one another. No one is to pursue what he judges better for himself, but instead, what he judges better for someone else.'' But Benedict also reminds the monk that there is a wicked zeal which leads to death. If a monk's life is not grounded in God, he is tempted to put himself in the place of God. To be empowered by anything less than the God of love is to risk evil zeal in the name of vengeance. When the monk has zeal for God, he will come to see that he is consumed not only with love for God but for everything and everyone else that God has created.

It is the balanced spirituality that one finds in the Rule of Benedict that has made it attractive to many men and women throughout the ages. It is that same balance that has made it attractive today to those countless lay men and women who are not living vowed lives in a monastery but who are associated with Benedictine monasteries as oblates attempting to live their lives in the secular world according to the spiritual values set out in the rule.

Bibliography: *Marked for Life: Prayer in the Easter Christ* (London 1979). J. CHITTISTER, *The Rule of Benedict: Insights for the Ages* (New York 1992). D. REES et al., *Consider Your Call: A Theology of Monastic Life Today* (Kalamazoo 1978). C. SMITH, *The Path of Life* (Ampleforth, England 1995). K. VERMEIREN, *Praying with Benedict: Prayer in the Rule of St. Benedict* (Kalamazoo 1999). A. DE VOGÜÉ, *The Rule of Saint Benedict: A Doctrinal and Spiritual Commentary* (Kalamazoo 1983). E. DE WAAL, *Seeking God: The Way of St. Benedict* (Collegeville 1984).

[J. LECLERCQ/R. K. SEASOLTZ]

BENEDICTINES

The Order of St. Benedict signifies not a centralized religious institute but the confederated congregations of monks, nuns, and sisters following the Rule of St. Benedict (*see* BENEDICTINE RULE). Each monastery is an autonomous community, bound by strong or weak links to other monasteries of the same congregation but no juridical ties to the rest of the confederation.

St. Benedict of Nursia, in his 6th-century rule, legislated for a cenobitic monastery, which should constitute a community under its abbot, elected for life by the monks. The vow of stability bound the monk to the monastery of his profession; that of *conversatio morum* obliged him to follow a monastic way of life according to the Rule of Benedict; and obedience bound him to follow the directives of the rule under his abbot. The daily life consisted of the public celebration of the liturgy of the hours, serious reading (*lectio divina*), and manual labor. Everything, including ascetical practices, was subject to the abbot's discretion. The spiritual program, grounded on obedience, silence, and humility, and flexible enough to take account of diverse strengths and weaknesses among the brethren, was intended to promote a faithful following of the gospel. Benedict is known to have founded only Subiaco, Monte Cassino, and Terracina, but his reputation may have induced other Italian monasteries to adopt his rule. Whether or not Cassiodorus introduced it at Vivarium, his program of intellectual work quickly grafted itself onto Benedictinism throughout Europe.

The Lombard invasion of 568 virtually destroyed monasticism in Italy. Monte Cassino was taken about 577, but the community escaped to Rome, thereby enabling the future Pope Gregory the Great, recently become a monk, to make acquaintance with the Benedictine rule, which he then adopted for the monasteries under his direction. Through his *Dialogues* Gregory promoted Benedict's reputation in the West and the adoption of his rule. The wisdom and moderation of the rule itself, as well as the missionary zeal of the monks and papal patronage, were the chief factors contributing to the preeminence so quickly acquired by the Rule of Benedict in Latin Christendom. By 800 it had supplanted most other monastic observances. By the same date most monks were priests and many of them had become bishops. Intellectual work came more and more into favor, while manual labor was left to the uneducated. The very numerous monasteries were centers for the civilizing of the neighborhoods as well as houses of worship; hence they were rich sources of the Western Christian civilization that was coming to birth.

Earliest Expansion (596–814). In 596 Gregory sent some 40 monks to convert the Anglo-Saxons. Their superior, Augustine, became the first archbishop of Canterbury. Despite numerous setbacks, the work progressed, and sees and monasteries were founded. Saint Paulinus was among the second group of monks sent by Gregory to help Augustine. In 625 he became a bishop and moved to the north of England where he eventually undertook the evangelization of the people. There was tension between the monks following the Rule of Benedict and those following Irish customaries, especially those who came from Iona. By 663 the tension was resolved in favor of the Roman Benedictine tradition. By 685 the Anglo-Saxon kingdoms had embraced Christianity. Flourishing schools became the source of a brilliant culture, which reached its zenith in the life and writings of Bede. En route to Britain, Augustine's mission of 596 had made the Rule of Benedict known in the Frankish kingdom, where the predominant monastic influence was that of the Irish monk Columban. His harsh observance diminished in prestige after his death in 615, and from 629 it was supplemented and eventually supplanted by the Rule of Benedict. The transfer of Benedict's relics from the desolate site of Monte Cassino to Saint-Benoît-sur-Loire (*c.* 672) gave the latter monastery an unrivaled renown among the increasingly numerous Frankish monasteries.

Anglo-Saxon Benedictinism was marked by a strong attraction toward missionary activity. The evangelization of Frisia, undertaken by Wilfrid, Bishop of York, in 678, was resumed in 690 by Willibrord, who in 696 established the See of Utrecht as his base. His plans for Denmark were premature, but in southern Frisia he was

Benedictine monks at prayer. (©Ted Spiegel/CORBIS)

highly successful. Beyond the Rhine, Benedictinism was first planted at Reichenau, founded by a Frankish monk, Pirmin, in 724. At least eight other houses quickly developed in Alamannia, all under his jurisdiction. Farther north, Kaiserswerth, established by the Anglo-Saxon Swithbert, became a center of the apostolate in its region. Central Germany was the field of another Anglo-Saxon, Boniface, whose missionary methods became a model for subsequent evangelization. He assisted Willibrord in southern Frisia from 719 to 722, when he was ordained bishop by Pope Gregory II and commissioned to evangelize Hesse and Thuringia. While being careful to keep in close contact with Rome, he developed a number of monasteries, the most important being Fulda (744). He organized the Church in the newly converted lands, reinvigorated and reorganized the Bavarian Church, persuaded the Bavarian monasteries to adopt the Rule of Benedict, and inaugurated the urgently needed reform of the Frankish Church. In 753 he proceeded to the still pagan area of northern Frisia, where he was martyred in 754.

The gradual conversion of the Lombards permitted the revival of Benedictinism in Lombard Italy. The first agents of the restoration were Franks and Lombards, who founded Farfa in 705 and St.-Vincent-on-the-Volturno about 710. Petronax of Brescia gathered about himself some hermits living at Monte Cassino; from 729 they were instructed in the Rule of Benedict by the Anglo-Saxon Willibald (later bishop of Eichstätt). South of the Pyrenees the rule was followed only in the March of Spain, erected by Charlemagne in 795.

Reform and Centralization (814–1125). The Carolingian period witnessed serious abuses because kings and magnates, with no concern for the true spirit of monastic life, had delivered many monasteries into the hands of lay abbots who were often crude soldiers. Benedict of Aniane instituted a reform. In his own foundation at Aniane (*c.* 780) he insisted on the literal observance of the rule. His ideas, more severe than the letter of the rule, spread to other houses in Aquitaine, thanks to the support of Louis the Pious. When in 814 Louis succeeded Charlemagne as emperor, he installed Benedict of Inden as superior general of all monasteries of the empire. At Aachen in 817 the Frankish abbots adopted a uniform discipline, and inspectors were appointed to enforce it. In an effort to protect each monastery from abusive lay abbots, the property of each house was divided into the *abbatia* and the *mensa conventualis;* the abbot had no control over the latter. In addition, the reform gave to public worship a predominance not envisaged by the rule; thereafter the liturgy became more elaborate and more solemn, while manual labor declined in importance among the monks, especially those who were ordained.

The absolute uniformity insisted on by Benedict of Aniane was foreign to the spirit of the rule and too dependent on imperial patronage. Only the Italian abbeys maintained the more rigorous tradition. Nevertheless, the first half of the 9th century was characterized by regularity of discipline in the Frankish houses and by serious scholarship, nourished in numerous schools. The fruit of such intellectual work was manifested in the writings of Smaragdus, Paschasius Radbertus, Ratramnus, Lupus of Ferrières, Rabanus Maurus, and Walafrid Strabo. Missionary zeal was exemplified in the life of Ansgar, monk of Corbie, who in 826 undertook the evangelization of Denmark and Sweden. His successor, Rembert, continued his work until his death brought the enterprise to a close.

The dismemberment of the empire in 843 and the succeeding fratricidal wars, in which kings distributed monastic property to their allies as guarantees of fidelity, the forcible assimilation of monasteries to benefices, and the attacks of Vikings, Muslims, and Magyars all but engulfed Benedictinism in total ruin. The monks who survived were constrained to beg their livelihood, and discipline collapsed. When they were once again able to recover their houses, they had to place themselves under the protection of the local magnate, who arrogated to himself the abbatial election or even the abbacy itself. Thus, for sheer survival, monasteries took their place in nascent feudalism. Abbots became vassals of the territorial prince, from whom they held in fief the monastic lands and often a more extensive domain. They were also lords, exercising public authority over their fiefs. Functions not proper to ecclesiastics were performed within each fief by the abbot's advocate, a layman who was commissioned to protect the monastery's property, but who often became its pillager, especially when a king, duke, or count assumed the office. Such a situation in no way promoted the monastic life, and by 900 it was extremely difficult to discover a house where the rule was observed even reasonably well.

The violent 10th century, however, witnessed a strong revival of Benedictine life almost simultaneously in Burgundy and Lotharingia. The recovery, not dependent upon royal favor or enforced by any general legislation, was more lasting than the reform of the preceding century. It began by relieving monasteries from every external influence, thus freeing them to live the rule. The earliest and most influential reform center was Cluny, founded in 910 by William of Aquitaine, who placed it exclusively under papal authority. Three long-lived and extremely capable abbots directed Cluny's destiny during 154 years with remarkable consistency of policy: Majolus (954–994), Odilo (994–1048), and Hugh (1049–1109). They organized the new foundations and the reformed houses into an "order," which in the 12th century included some 1,450 monasteries; most of them were ruled by priors, and all were subject to the abbot of Cluny. In the 11th and 12th centuries, the abbot of Cluny was one of the most important and influential personages in the Church, ruling monasteries in France, Germany, Italy, England, and elsewhere. For two centuries Cluny's profound fervor was maintained. Stern centralization was foreign to the Benedictine idea, but in the 10th and 11th centuries it seemed to be the only solution to the problem of monastic independence and freedom. More pernicious was the gradually increasing overemphasis on an ever more elaborate liturgy, which left neither time nor energy for work, study, or even personal prayer, and eventually prompted a fatal lowering of admission standards. Eventually empty formalism took over, but Cluny had, meanwhile, reinvigorated monasticism and freed it from external control.

Saint-Benoît-sur-Loire, reformed by Cluny in 930, retained its autonomy and became a secondary reform center for France, Lotharingia, and England. Entirely independent of the Cluniac influence were Brogne in Lower Lotharingia, founded about 919 by Gerard of Brogne, and Gorze in Upper Lotharingia, restored in 933. The Brogne observance extended into Flanders, Normandy, and the German Empire; that of Gorze covered Lotharingia. These movements did not long survive their authors, but they were reactivated later by Richard of Saint-Vanne (d. 1046) and Poppo of Stavelot. The Cluniac observance penetrated very early into Italy. In 936 Odo of Cluny was made superior of all abbeys in the Papal State; he and his successors reformed old houses and established new ones. In the 9th century the Danes had totally ruined the once numerous Anglo-Saxon monasteries. From 943 monasticism was restored in England by Dunstan, Ethelwold, and Oswald of York, the chief influences coming from Fleury and Brogne. The

Rule of Benedict entered the slowly expanding Spanish principalities from 895, and Sancho III of Navarre introduced the Cluniac observance in 1022. Most Spanish abbeys were in some degree dependent on a distinguished French or Italian monastery.

The Benedictine recovery in the 10th century was accompanied by a fresh zeal for evangelization, whereby the rule, too, was spread. The work of Ansgar in Denmark and Sweden was resumed in 934 by Unni, monk of Corvey. Anglo-Saxon monks were soon active throughout Scandinavia. In the 11th century Denmark, Sweden, Norway, and Iceland had Benedictine abbeys. In 933 the first monastery was opened in Bohemia at Brevnov, built by Adalbert of Prague; the 11th century witnessed numerous foundations. The conversion of Poland, begun about 967, was largely the work of Benedictines from Fulda; Adalbert of Prague also gave Poland its first monastery, Meseritz (*c.* 996). The apostles of the Wends were monks from German houses. Adalbert of Prague in 997 and Bruno of Querfurt in 1009 were martyred while seeking to evangelize the Prussians. Hungary owes its faith in large measure to Benedictines; the first missionary was Wolfgang of Regensberg. The first monastery, Pannonhalma, was founded in 996. Dalmatia's attachment to the Latin Church was the work of Benedictines, first sent there from Monte Cassino in 986. In the 12th century the Rule of Benedict was implemented also in the Crusader Kingdom of Jerusalem.

The monastic reform of the 10th century deeply stirred the conscience of Europe and contributed in important ways to the general reform of Christian society after 1049. The popes fostered the monastic revival by granting numerous houses exemption from episcopal control. In turn, monasticism cooperated actively in the reform by supplying both ideas and leaders, notably Popes Stephen IX, Gregory VII, Victor III, Urban II, Paschal II, and Gelasius II. Cluny's vast monastic family as well as other reform groups incessantly reminded clergy and laity of the claims of the moral law and in most cases actively implemented the papal program. Among the most influential centers were Saint-Victor in Marseilles, Saint-Benigne de Dijon, Tiron, Chaise-Dieu, Bec, and Sauve-Majeur, in France; Saint-Vanne (Verdun-sur-Meuse), in Lotharingia; Sankt Blasien, Reichenau, Einsiedeln, Sankt Emmeram, Fulda, and Hirsau, in Germany; and Monte Cassino, Farfa, Fruttuaria, and La Cava, in Italy.

The foremost German center was Hirsau. About 150 monasteries, new and old, followed its observance in a union that left them their autonomy. The institute of lay brothers, sketched by John Gualbert at Vallombrosa, was organized in the 11th century by William of Hirsau, who prescribed a special mode of life for religious assigned to menial tasks and to the management of distant estates. The Norman Conquest of 1066 meant the internal strengthening of Benedictine monasticism in England and its flowering there. French abbeys, including Cluny, founded priories in England. Queen Margaret, wife of Malcolm III, introduced the Rule of Benedict in Scotland. The first Benedictine houses in Ireland were established in the 12th century.

It is not known precisely when the monks and nuns living under the Rule of Benedict began to call themselves ''Benedictines,'' a name that tended to align them with the centralized orders such as the Cistercians and Franciscans. Before the 13th century Benedictines, apart from those in the Cluniac system and other special reforming movements, had no form of centralized government controlling the monasteries and imposing uniformity on them. Each monastery was free to respond to the demands made upon it by its social, economic, and religious environment. Nevertheless this pluralism was kept from degenerating into mere heterogeneity by the common inspiration of the rule, which not only established in essential matters an objective way of life but also provided criteria by which adaptation to the environment could be assessed. Above all it was the common spirituality inspired by the rule that united the various monasteries. But the existence of many varying interpretations meant that most of the communities lacked a stable structure or depended too much on the personality of the abbot. Excess of organization and overemphasis on a particular element in the life eventually stifled the spirit; nevertheless, from the 9th to the 12th century the Benedictine family virtually monopolized religious life in the West. This predominance ended around 1125. Though the houses continued to be powerful and wealthy, they were more respectable than vigorous. The history of Benedictine monasticism for the next three centuries was one of decadence, sterility, and false starts.

The 11th century, which witnessed Cluny's splendor, witnessed also a strong reaction against Cluny's onesidedness through return to the letter of the rule, manual labor, corporate poverty, and even the eremitical and penitential ideal of primitive monasticism. Thus several shoots from the main line grew into new institutes. The Camaldolese, the Vallombrosans, and the monks of Grandmont, in the 11th century, provided for the eremitical life in a greater or lesser degree. Similarly, there developed in the 13th century the Celestines and Sylvestrines, and in the 14th century, the Olivetans (*see* BENEDICTINES, OLIVETAN; BENEDICTINES, SYLVESTRINE). The Cistercians (1098) retained the cenobitic life and aimed to restore the rule's wise balance and more or less complete withdrawal from the secular world.

Decadence (1125–1408). The feudal system had undermined not only the rule but the vows themselves, since not only the abbacy but the several claustral offices became fiefs, belonging to their holders. Before long the individual monk had his own pecuniary benefice, and monasteries came to be regarded as suitable places for locating persons undesirable elsewhere. Some monasteries reserved admission to nobles, who continued their former way of life. Hence the Benedictine houses were avoided by persons seriously in search of holiness. Few abbeys escaped this moral decay, and the failure to gain recruits had disastrous effects on the liturgy, intellectual life, and external influence.

Although the monasteries had traditionally been havens of stability and security as well as sources of leadership for missionary activity, in the case of Benedictine nuns chastity and the freedom for service took second place to the value of enclosure as women often entered monasteries for a variety of nonreligious reasons. Benedictine nunneries became refuges for widows, undowried and therefore unmarriageable daughters, captives who had been abused by soldiers, women seeking sanctuary when they refused to marry, and even children. As the number of nunneries multiplied, they competed for economic support via dowries, legacies, and other benefactions. Like their male counterparts, women's communities were an integral part of a complex system of landholding and other obligations that was the hallmark of feudalism. Consequently they were often involved in disputes over inheritances and the alienation of family property. Their vulnerability to secular influences easily led to abuses such as the diversion of revenues by a lord to support family members or to meet military obligations, or the imposition of secular abbesses. In the 12th century, women determinedly emulated new male communities such as the Cistercians and Premonstratensians, adopting their rule, following their style of life, and even adopting their name. Most of these male orders, however, wanted little or nothing to do with providing sacramental services and pastoral care to communities of women. The responsibility for the *cura mulierum* continued to be a cause of strife for male monasteries until the Reformation.

The dangers that come from the isolation of monasteries have always been real. When there is no authority structure to ensure correction and support among individual monasteries, decadence tends to be widespread. In the 13th century those seeking reform had recourse to a Cistercian institution, the general chapter. Popes Innocent III, Honorius III, and Gregory IX took vigorous steps to correct abuses but not always with consideration for the essential autonomy of Benedictinism; hence their efforts were not always successful. Innocent III prescribed general chapters, restored free abbatial elections, and insisted on simplicity of life and control of finances. The Fourth Lateran Council in 1215 established triennial provincial chapters, which were to elect visitators to supervise the execution of legislated reforms. The first Benedictines to implement the Lateran decrees were the English monks; the present English Congregation ranks as the oldest Benedictine congregation. Honorius III (1216–27) required annual chapters, and Gregory IX (1227–41) extended the powers of visitators. Other councils, papal legates, and local bishops also sought to raise the moral tone of the monasteries.

In 1336 Benedict XII undertook a further monastic reform by gathering all the monasteries into 32 provinces, prescribing a triennial chapter and visitation in each, and demanding the raising of the intellectual level of the communities. In 1338 he ordered an inquiry by special agents into the condition of every monastery. This legislation remained in force for two centuries, but there was no effective organ of enforcement. Princes, fearing the loss of their claims, hindered the holding of chapters, popes mitigated the regulations, and the system of papal reservations too often meant the naming of unfit abbots. The notorious *commenda,* whereby the abbacy of a monastery was given to a secular ecclesiastic as his benefice, grew rapidly. The commendatory abbot reserved for himself the lion's share of the income, frequently leaving the monks an insufficient portion. In France the community continued to control the *mensa conventualis,* but elsewhere the commendatory abbot took what he wanted; to increase his income he often hindered recruitment. Only England and Germany escaped this evil. The Hundred Years' War (1337–1453), the Black Death (1348), and the Western Schism (1378–1417) brought about the depopulation and demoralization of monastic houses. Not all monasteries, however, fell into complete decline; a good abbot was often able to preserve discipline or restore fervor, and many monasteries were exemplary. But, in general, too many monks forgot their ideals and became worldly.

Reform Congregations (1408–1815). The 15th century saw the development of a new institution, the congregation, which more efficaciously guaranteed a disciplined life according to the rule. Luigi Barbo (d. 1443) became the abbot of Santa Giustina at Padua in 1408 and instituted regular discipline in that decadent house. Recruits were so numerous that he was able to found new monasteries and reform existing ones, all of which were united in a congregation in 1419. To avoid the *commenda,* the office of local superior was made temporary, and all authority was concentrated in the annual general chapter. All monks made their profession for the congregation, and the chapter could move them about.

All the monasteries of Italy and Sicily eventually joined the congregation, which, with the accession of Monte Cassino in 1504, became known as the Cassinese Congregation. A high level of intellectual and moral life was maintained so the monks were able to exert a salutary influence on the neighborhood. The reform movement was adopted in the monasteries of Catalonia, Poland, and Dalmatia; it also inspired the congregation of Chezal-Benoît, Sainte-Vanne, Saint-Maur, and Valladolid.

The Council of Constance (1414–18) influenced the spread throughout south Germany of the reforms introduced at Kastl and at Melk, but weak organization made these unions too dependent on individual abbots. More enduring, because better organized, was the Congregation of Bursfeld, approved in 1446 by the Council of Basel. Under Abbot John Dederoth, Bursfeld Abbey adopted an observance that spread so rapidly in northern Germany that in the 16th century the congregation numbered 200 houses. In 1514 the Hungarian abbeys united in a congregation, with the statutes of Monte Cassino and Melk. The Congregation of Valladolid (1489), with temporary abbots, embraced the monasteries of Castile and some in Catalonia, and eventually spread to Mexico and Peru. The Congregation of Portugal (1566) united all the houses of the kingdom and those of Brazil. In France the reform efforts of the abbot of Cluny were obstructed by the political disorders, the *commenda,* and the resistance of many monks. In 1481 renewed efforts were more successful. At the same time the houses of the Tiron observance accepted reform, as did Chezal-Benoît, which founded its own congregation. In England, Scotland, Denmark, Sweden, Norway, Iceland, Holland, and much of Germany monasticism was swept away. In Switzerland, France, and Belgium it endured a cruel ordeal. Of some 3,000 Benedictine monasteries, about 800 ceased to exist.

The Council of Trent (1545–63) legislated for the restoration and maintenance of discipline, defined the conditions of admission and profession, the choosing of superiors, and the administration of property, and ordered all monasteries to unite in congregations, with triennial general chapters and visitations. Thereby the congregational system became ecclesiastical law, enforced by the Holy See, and exempt from episcopal authority. The exempt Congregation of Flanders and that of the Presentation (1629) were organized in the Belgian Netherlands. In France, the earliest was that called the Exempt (1580). The Congregations of Brittany (1604), Saint-Denis (1607), and Allobroges (1622) were short lived. In 1604 Didier de la Cour (d. 1623) founded the Congregation of Saint-Vanne de Verdun. At its head was a president, annually appointed by the general chapter, which exercised sovereign authority. It was outstanding for the spiritual and intellectual formation of its members, and included houses in Lorraine and Franche-Comté. In 1621 the Congregation of Saint-Maur was constituted of those French monasteries that had adopted the Saint-Vanne reform. It absorbed the Breton Congregation in 1628, that of Chezal-Benoît in 1636, and eventually all French monasteries except the Cluniac. Grégoire Tarisse (d. 1648) reorganized the congregation in 1645, giving it an effective government. The Maurists were celebrated for scholarship, and at the same time they were exemplary monks. Cardinal Armand Richelieu in 1629 decided to unite the Cluniac Congregation to Saint-Maur, but the Holy See disapproved. Many of the Cluniacs had been won over to a strict observance and in 1646 became a distinct congregation.

English Benedictines lived in various monasteries on the Continent or in residences at Douai and Dieulouart in France, and elsewhere. Some English monks joined the Valladolid and Cassinese Congregations, but in 1619 Paul V united all of them in the English Congregation.

In 1592 Clement VIII reformed the Spanish Congregation of Claustrales, founded in 1336. In Germany about a dozen poorly organized and isolated congregations were eventually formed, the most important being the Swiss (1602), the Alsatian (1624), the Austrian (1630), and the Bavarian (1684).

By 1700 the Benedictine family was, in general, in a healthy state, thanks to the new congregations. The 18th century, however, witnessed a new decline and virtual extinction under the attacks of the Enlightenment, the French Revolution, and wholesale secularization. Of 410 French Benedictine houses, 122 were suppressed by 1768. The revolution completed the task by 1792 and extended it to Belgium (1796), Switzerland (1798), the left bank of the Rhine (1802), and Central Italy (1810). Monasteries under Hapsburg rule had been subjected to interference since 1754 and Joseph II suppressed many of them. Bavaria, Württemberg, and Prussia—141 monasteries—disappeared. By 1815 only about 30 monasteries were still in existence. Those of Portugal and Spain were swept away in 1834 and 1835.

Recovery and Expansion (1815 to the Present). Despite the Prussian Kulturkampf, the suppressions in Portugal, Spain, France, Italy, and Switzerland, and the Brazilian prohibition of receiving novices, the 19th century was an age of vigorous renewal and worldwide expansion. Hungary led the way in 1802 by reopening monasteries for the sake of education; Austria quickly followed suit, and in Spain and Italy monks were able to recover some of their houses. English monks, refugees from revolutionary France, were welcomed in England, where Ampleforth (1802) and Downside (1814) were established (*see* BENEDICTINES, ENGLISH). English and Spanish monks transplanted Benedictinism to Australia, where New Norcia was founded in 1846.

In France Benedictine monasticism was restored at Solesmes by Prosper Guéranger in 1833, and the French Congregation came into existence four years later. Ludwig I of Bavaria reopened Metten in 1830, and then other houses, and the Bavarian Congregation was approved in 1858. From Metten the rule was brought to the United States in 1846 by Boniface Wimmer, founder of the American Cassinese Congregation. The Swiss-American Congregation (1881) originated with Saint Meinrad Archabbey in Indiana and Conception Abbey in Missouri. Placidus and Maurus Wolter established themselves at Beuron, Germany, in 1863; the Beuronese Congregation (1868) modeled itself on that of Solesmes except in regard to its more active life. In 1872 Beuron founded Maredsous in Belgium; in 1920 four Belgian abbeys were separated from Beuron to constitute the Belgian Congregation, now known as the Annunciation Congregation. The Brazilian Congregation, erected in 1827 and nearly obliterated by hostile laws in 1853, revived with the help of Maredsous. In 1904 the Congregation of Sankt Ottilien was founded for work in the foreign missions. The reform of Subiaco, Italy, in 1851 was to give birth in 1872 to the Congregation of the Primitive Observance, now known as the Subiaco Congregation and divided into nine provinces. Two Austrian Congregations, both established in 1889, were united in 1930. In 1945 six Slavonic houses were organized to form the Congregation of Saint Adalbert.

In 1888 Leo XIII revived in Rome the Collegio Sant' Anselmo, originally founded in 1687 by the Cassinese Congregation, as an international college for monks of all congregations. In 1893 he created the office of abbot primate to head the confederated Benedictine congregations. In 1952 Pius XII approved the *Lex Propria* governing the confederation. Substantial changes were made in the government of the confederation and the Collegio Sant' Anselmo at the Congress of Abbots in 1967. Although many Benedictines originally resisted the establishment of the office of abbot primate, experience has shown that his moral authority has been a source of encouragement to the individual congregations and monasteries, and the office itself has been an effective agency through which the values of monasticism have been represented before the Holy See. Since the abbot primate's authority is moral rather than disciplinary, his office in no way interferes with the individual communities and their relations with the Holy See.

In 2000 there were 21 congregations of monks in the Benedictine Confederation. That includes the Olivetans who joined in 1960, the Vallumbrosians who joined in 1966, the Camaldolese who joined in 1966, and the Sylvestines who joined in 1976. Benedictine nuns and sisters were late in forming congregations or federations. In 2000 there were 61 congregations or federations of nuns and sisters, most of which were founded in the 20th century.

In addition to their pursuit of monastic life through prayer, manual labor, and *lectio divina,* most Benedictines today are engaged in educational, parochial, scholarly, or missionary work. The oblate institution, whereby both clerical and lay persons are affiliated to a particular monastery, is very popular.

Bibliography: P. SCHMITZ, *Histoire de l'Ordre de Saint-Benoît,* 7 v. (Maredsous 1942–56). S. HILPISCH, *Benedictinism through Changing Centuries,* tr. L. J. DOYLE (Collegeville, Minn. 1958). H. VAN ZELLER, *The Benedictine Idea* (Springfield, Ill. 1960). B. C. BUTLER, *Benedictine Monachism* (2d ed. 1924; repr. New York 1961); *Catalogus Monasteriorum O.S.B. Monachorum,* editio XIX (Rome 2000); *Catalogus Monasteriorum O.S.B. Sororum et Monialium,* editio I (Rome 2000).

[A. G. BIGGS/R. K. SEASOLTZ]

BENEDICTINES, ENGLISH

The English Congregation of the Order of St. BENEDICT (OSB) traces its origin back to the early Middle Ages. Monasticism was brought to England in 597 by the monk, (St.) AUGUSTINE OF CANTERBURY, sent from Rome to convert the Anglo-Saxons. The first monastery was established at Canterbury in Kent. Monastic communities gradually took root in other parts of the Heptarchy, and a brilliant period of missionary and cultural activity followed. Outstanding figures of this period were the saints BENEDICT BISCOP, WILFRED OF YORK, BEDE, and BONIFACE, and the scholar ALCUIN. The Danish invasions arrested this initial development, and by the time of the reign of ALFRED THE GREAT (871–899), monasticism was practically extinct. In the 10th century (St.) DUNSTAN, with royal assistance initiated a restoration that was so successful that Benedictine monasticism from that time until its extinction in the 16th century enjoyed uninterrupted development and expansion. The Norman Conquest brought only new vigor to this growth, drawing the greater houses into the feudal pattern. Abbots sat with the bishops, as barons, in the councils of the realm. As landlords the monks enjoyed a reputation for benevolence.

In 1215 a decree of the Fourth Lateran Council initiated the gradual association of the autonomous monastic communities into congregations by means of general chapters with defined rights of legislation and visitation. In 1218 the first Benedictine general chapter convened at

Oxford, but not all the English monasteries were united to the congregation until the 4th century. Monasteries following the Benedictine Rule continued to spread throughout the kingdom. Central to the life and activities of the Benedictine monk was the *Opus Dei,* the daily and reverent performance of the sacred liturgy. Work in the beginning was largely manual, but in time intellectual activities came to predominate, and the monks provided a substantial cultural contribution through scholarship, instruction of the young, and the practice of the fine arts.

In the 16th century the monastic communities were dissolved by HENRY VIII, and their property was confiscated. During the years of persecution that followed, English Catholics who wished to be monks had to make their profession in communities abroad. English monks had established themselves in Lorraine and the Netherlands. Later the French Revolution compelled these monks in exile to seek refuge in their native England, and from these returning communities has developed the present English Benedictine Congregation. In 1919 a property was acquired at Portsmouth, R.I., for the purpose of bringing English Benedictinism to America. The Abbey of St. Gregory the Great, Portsmouth, is now a flourishing community. Five years later St. Anselm's Abbey was established as a priory in Washington, D.C.; it became an abbey in 1961. A third American foundation, the Abbey of St. Mary and St. Louis, was made at Creve Coeur, Mo., in 1955; it became an abbey in 1989.

Bibliography: O.S.B., Official Catholic Directory #0200. D. KNOWLES, *The Monastic Order in England, 943–1216* (Cambridge, Eng. 1962). BEDE, *A History of the English Church and People,* tr. L. SHERLEY-PRICE (Baltimore 1955). B. WELDON, *Chronological Notes Containing the Rise, Growth and Present State of the English Congregation of the Order of St. Benedict* (London 1881). J. MCCANN, "The English Benedictine Revival 1588–1619," *American Benedictine Revue* (1951) 261–286. W. W. BAYNE, "Thirty-Three Years of Portsmouth History," *ibid.* 3 (1952) 315–339.

[W. W. BAYNE/EDS.]

BENEDICTINES, OLIVETAN

A monastic order whose Latin title is *Congregatio Sanctae Mariae Montis Oliveti Ordinis Sancti Benedicti.* The Olivetan Benedictine monks, who have belonged to the Benedictine Confederation since 1959, were established in the 14th century when Bl. Bernard Tolomei and his followers withdrew (1313) to a place of solitude called Accona (about 12 miles from Siena, Italy), where Bernard later founded the Abbey of Mount Olivet. The congregation was approved by Clement VI (Jan. 21, 1344). The monks, most of whom are priests, profess solemn vows and pursue a semicontemplative, monastic life, giving special attention to liturgical solemnities. They also engage in active ministry, particularly in teaching and retreat work. The monasteries of the congregation, each ruled by an elected abbot or a prior, are independent of one another, but are subject to the abbot general, who is also the abbot of the motherhouse, the Abbey of Mount Olivet.

The Olivetans came into existence during a period of decline in Benedictine monasticism, adopted a form of government suitable for the correction of abuses, and restored a rigorous observance of the rule. The reform spread rapidly, first in Tuscany, then in all of Italy, where, by the end of the 14th century, some 50 Olivetan monasteries were flourishing under the protection of popes and bishops. While the growth of the congregation continued into the 17th century, when there were nearly 2,000 monks in about 100 monasteries, monastic discipline deteriorated, especially because noblemen entered the monasteries without true vocations. The political disturbances and suppressions of the 18th and 19th centuries brought grave harm to the order, but from these misfortunes there emerged some outstanding monks who worked for a restoration of the congregation in Italy. Foundations, never before successful, were established outside of Italy, first in France (late 19th century), then in Austria, Brazil, and Lebanon (early 20th century). Houses were founded in Belgium, England, and Mexico. The U.S. foundations include Holy Trinity Monastery (St. David, AZ), Our Lady of Guadalupe Abbey (Pecos, NM) and the Benedictine Monastery of Hawaii (Waialua, HI).

Bibliography: OSB, Official Catholic Directory #0200. M. SCARPINI, *I monaci benedettini di Monte Oliveto* (Alessandria 1952). G. PICASSO, "Aspetti e problemi della storia della Congr. Benedettina di Monte Oliveto," *Studia Monastica* 3 (1961) 383–408. V. CATTANA, "La preghiera alle origini della tradizione olivetana," *La preghiera nella Bibbia e nella tradizione patristica e monastica* (Rome 1964) 703–731.

[G. PICASSO/EDS.]

BENEDICTINES, SYLVESTRINE

A monastic congregation, originally named *Ordo Sancti Benedicti de Monte Fano,* and now designated *Monachorum Silvestrunorum, OSB.* The Sylvestrines, as they are commonly called, were founded by St. SILVESTER GUZZOLINI (1177–1267) in 1231 at Montefano, near Fabriano (Ancona), Italy. Silvester led a reform movement at a time when the BENEDICTINES were in decline, and when the MENDICANT ORDERS appeared to be supplanting the monastic orders. The followers of Silvester lived in caves, in huts, and in poor, cramped monasteries. They restored the primitive spirit of the BENEDICTINE RULE by alternating prayer with manual labor and apostolic work among the simple people of the countryside. Innocent IV issued a bull of approval (June 27, 1227), despite the decrees of the Fourth Lateran Council (1215), which aimed to consolidate the various monastic institutes, and to prevent the birth of new ones. Papal approval was more easily granted because of the Sylvestrines' organized juridical structure with its centralization of authority under a prior or abbot general.

In the 14th century the order counted more than 1,000 monks and dozens of monasteries, among which was the celebrated San Marco in Florence, which later passed to the Dominicans. Meanwhile, the original eremitical ideal gave way to a cenobitic form of monastic life. In time much of the vitality of the movement was sapped by poverty, by the evils of the system of COMMENDATION, and by the sizable contribution of 300,000 *scudi* requested by Alexander VII in 1664 for the support of Christian armies. After the Holy See had suppressed about 15 of the smaller monasteries, the Sylvestrines were ordered (1662) to unite with the VALLOMBROSANS in one congregation. Five years later, however, the union was ended, and in 1690 Alexander VIII approved the constitutions of the Sylvestrine congregation. These critical circumstances rendered ineffective the attempts to expand into Portugal, Brazil, and Vietnam. Not until 1845 was a mission opened in Ceylon (Sri Lanka).

In the 19th century the suppression by Napoleon I, and later, by the Piedmontese government, reduced the order to a few dozen members. In the middle of the 20th century a recovery was under way. Foundations were established in India, Australia, and Canada. In the U.S., where they arrived in 1910, the congregation has established three monasteries: St. Benedict Priory (Oxford, Mich.), St. Sylvester Monastery (Detroit, Mich.) and Holy Face Monastery (Clifton, N.J.).

In art and culture Sylvestrines won renown with their papermill in Fabriano (1276), one of the oldest in Europe. Fra Bevignate, sculptor and architect, designed the great fountain (*fontana grande*) in Perugia (1278), and developed the first plan for the cathedral in Orvieto (1290). Varino Favorino, Bishop of Nocera (1514) and humanist (d. 1538), composed the *Magnum et perutile dictionarium,* the first printed Greek lexicon.

Bibliography: OSB, Official Catholic Directory #0200. A. M. CANCELLIERI, *S. Silvestro Abate e l'opera sua* (Milan 1942). G. PAGNANI, *I codici dell' Archivio di Montefano* (Picena 1958). G. PENCO, *Storia del monachesimo in Italia* (Rome 1961). M. PAPI, *La voce della selva* (Rome 1962); *Il poema figurativo di Fra' Bevignate* (Casamari 1965).

[M. PAPI/EDS.]

BENEDICTION OF THE BLESSED SACRAMENT

Historically, benediction probably developed from the showing of the Host at the various stations of the Corpus Christi procession. The first known example of benediction similar to that common today was at Hildesheim in the 15th century. It was a response to the growing desire on the part of the faithful to look upon the Host, a desire enhanced by the earlier theological disputes over transubstantiation and the exact moment of consecration. Concurrent with the strengthening of this desire was the gradual introduction of an evening service for the faithful centered around the Salve Regina, which had been composed in the 11th century. By 1221 it had been joined to Compline in the Dominican monastery in Bologna. As early as 1250 it was part of a popular evening devotion in France. During the next two or three centuries the two devotions, one to the Blessed Mother, the other to the Blessed Sacrament, were combined, whence benediction is still known in France as Le Salut.

The rite of benediction given in the document *Holy Communion and Worship of the Eucharist Outside Mass* (Congregation of Divine Worship, June 21, 1973) is simple; it consists of a Eucharistic hymn or song, incensation (if the sacrament is exposed in a monstrance), a brief period of silence, prayer, a blessing of the people with the monstrance (or ciborium) in the form of a cross (the priest or deacon wearing a humeral veil), reposition of the sacrament, and concluding acclamation (HCWE 97–100).

[M. BURBACH/N. D. MITCHELL]

BENEDICTUS (CANTICLE OF ZECHARIAH)

The first word of the Latin text of the Canticle of Zechariah, ''Benedictus Dominus Deus Israel'' (''Blessed be the Lord, God of Israel,'' Lk. 1:68–79). It may be divided into two parts. The first part is closely related to the theme of the MAGNIFICAT, because Zechariah praises and gives thanks to God, who through the Incarnation has already begun to fulfill the promises of messianic salvation made to the patriarchs and prophets. In the second part he addresses his son as the Messiah's prophet and precursor.

As a liturgical canticle, the Benedictus is sung daily in the Office of Lauds (Morning Prayer) in the Catholic Church, after the 9th ode of the canon in the Byzantine morning Office of Orthros (it replaces this ode during Eastertide), and before the Nicene Creed at the Office of Mattins (Morning Prayer) in the Anglican tradition. Its liturgical use probably stemmed from the verses 78b–79 (''by which the daybreak from on high will visit us to shine on those who sit in darkness and death's shadow . . .'').

Bibliography: F. ROUSSEAU, ''Les structures du Benedictus (Luc 1:68–79)'' *New Testament Studies,* 32 (1986) 268–282. R. F. TAFT, *The Liturgy of the Hours in East and West: The Origins of the Divine Office and Its Meaning for Today,* 2d rev. ed. (Collegeville 1993). G. GUIVER, *Company of Voices: Daily Prayer and the People of God* (New York 1988). P. F. BRADSHAW, *Daily Prayer in the Early Church: A Study of the Origin and Early Development of the Divine Office* (London 1981).

[S. D. RUEGG/EDS.]

BENEDICTUS DEUS

Title of a constitution of Benedict XII issued Jan. 29, 1336. It was occasioned by the activity of his predecessor, John XXII, who had preached that it is only at the resurrection of the body on the last day that the just will begin to enjoy the beatific vision and sinners suffer the pains of hell; the day before he died, however, John retracted these views in the bull *Ne super his.* Benedict had as a cardinal written a full account of the condition of the disembodied souls prior to the general judgment; he had this book thoroughly inspected by theologians and then made the infallible pronouncement contained in *Benedictus Deus.* This document states that in the ordinary plan of God all who after death have undergone whatever purgation is necessary immediately (i.e., prior to the recovery of their bodies at the general judgment) enjoy the beatific vision and do so continuously. It further states that in God's ordinary plan all who die in actual mortal sin immediately suffer the pains of hell (i.e., prior to their appearance at the general judgment).

Bibliography: J. D. MANSI, *Sacrorum Conciliorum nova et amplissima collectio,* 31 v. (Florence-Venice 1757–98); reprinted and continued by L. PETIT and J. B. MARTIN, 53 v. in 60 (Paris 1889–1927; repr. Graz 1960–) 25:985–987. H. DENZINGER, *Enchiridion symbolorum,* ed. A. SCHÖNMETZER (32d ed. Freiburg 1963) 1000–02.

[B. FORSHAW]

BENEDIKTBEUERN, ABBEY OF

Benedictine abbey founded in the Bavarian Alps by Count Huosi, between 739 and 740, and consecrated by St. Boniface on Oct. 22, 742. Although pillaged by invading Magyars (955), Benediktbeuern (Buron, Beweren, Benedictoburum) was restored by the priest Wolford and staffed with a community of canons regular by St. ULRIC OF AUGSBURG (969). Benedictine rule was reinstated in 1031 by Abbot Ellinger and 11 monks from the neighboring Abbey of TEGERNSEE. During the long term of Ellinger's successor, Abbot Gothelm (1032–62), the abbey was fully repaired, and its library was reorganized. In spite of fires (1248, 1377, 1378, 1490), it prospered and became a center of learning and also of pilgrimage, since it possessed a relic of St. Benedict given by Charlemagne, as well as a relic of St. Anastasia brought there by St. GOTTSCHALK in 1053. It received privileges from popes and kings and acquired princely status from Rudolph of Hapsburg; Abbot Ortholph II (1271–84) begins the list of prince-abbots. The abbey was depleted by the plague of 1611 and ransacked by the Swedes who invaded Germany under Gustavus Adolphus in 1632. At this time the monk Simon Speer was tortured and slain for refusing to surrender the goods of the monastery. Much of Benediktbeuern's fame rests with its impressive library. When catalogued (1736) by M. Ziegelbauer (d. 1750), it numbered 338 MSS and 30,000 volumes; 40,000 at the time of its suppression. It is here that the scholarly historian of the Bavarian Benedictines, C. Meichelbeck, worked. The church, rebuilt by Abbot Placidus (1672–90), is an example of Bavarian high baroque style and has frescoes by H. G. Asams (1649–1711). Benediktbeuern was suppressed by the government in 1803 and became successively a barracks and a military hospital; it is now a theological seminary for Salesian students.

Bibliography: O. L. KAPSNER, *A Benedictine Bibliography: An Author-Subject Union List,* 2 v. (2d ed. Callegeville, Minn. 1962) 2:190. P. VOLK, *Dictionnaire d'histoire et de géographie ecclésiastiques,* ed. A. BAUDRILLART et al. (Paris 1912–) 7:1235–36, list of abbots. K. MINDERA, *Lexikon für Theologie und Kirche,* ed. J. HOFER and K. RAHNER, 10 v. (2d, new ed. Freiburg 1957–65) 2:183–184. L. H. COTTINEAU, *Répertoire topobibliographique des abbayes et prieurés,* 2 v. (Mâcon 1935–39) 1:340–341.

[E. D. MCSHANE]

BENELLI, GIOVANNI

Vatican reformer; b. Paggiole de Vernio, near Pistora, Italy, May 12, 1921; d. Oct. 26, 1982. As *sostituto* (or deputy) to the Vatican Secretary of State, he played a key but controversial reforming role in the pontificate of Paul VI. One of three children of middle-class parents, he entered the seminary at Pistora, was ordained at 22, and did further studies at the Gregorian University and the Ecclesiastical Academy or school for diplomats.

In 1947 he entered the Roman Curia as secretary to Giovanni Battista Montini, the future Paul VI, who remained his 'patron.' He rose steadily in the Vatican diplomatic service through successive appointments: Dublin 1950, Paris 1953, Rio di Janeiro 1960, and Madrid 1962, where he was credited with recommending bishops who

Benediktbeuern Abbey. (©Gregor Schmid/CORBIS)

could live happily in a post-Franco world. This diplomatic posting meant that he missed the first-hand experience of Vatican II. In 1965 Paul VI named him Observer to UNESCO in Paris but, after a brief spell in West Africa, brought him back to Rome in 1967 as his chief executive.

Pope Paul summoned him back to Rome to serve as *sostituto* to the Vatican Secretary of State, Amleto Cardinal Cicognani (d. 1969). As *sostituto* he was responsible for carrying out the reform of the Curia announced in August 1967. Since one of its features was that the Secretariat of State was made responsible for the overall 'coordination' of the work of all curial departments, his influence was considerable. A glutton for work himself, he expected others to be the same. He was a practical reformer, and put a stop to abuses and nepotism in the Vatican administration.

His loyalty to the reforming aims of Paul VI was unchallenged. In particular he sought to ensure a balance between the 'new curia' (the Secretariats for Christian Unity, Non-Believers, and Non-Christian Religions) and the traditional Roman dicasteries. This meant that both groups regarded him on occasion with suspicion. He was the man in the middle. The buck tended to stop with Benelli. He became known as the '*Gauleiter*' or the 'Berlin Wall' for the brusque directness of his management style. He supervised the work of the International Justice and Peace Commission very closely, and he took a keen interest in the activities of the Italian Episcopal Conference. Very little escaped his notice. His attentions were not always welcomed by those for whom they were intended. He was charged with abusing his closeness to the by now enfeebled Paul VI, and in particular, he was said to 'go over the head' of the French Secretary of State, Cardinal Jean VILLOT.

His critics thought they had won a victory in 1977 when Benelli became Archbishop of Florence and a cardinal. But this was a mistaken reading of the event. In the August 1978 conclave Benelli was the king-maker and his candidate, Albino Luciani, came through with remarkable swiftness. In the October conclave, however, Benelli was himself a contender and came very close to the two-thirds plus one needed to be elected. But supporters of Cardinal Giuseppe Siri would not yield. With the two Italians dead-locked, the way was open for this first non-Italian pope since Hadrian VI in 1523.

Benelli did not repine. He no longer expected to return to Rome as Secretary of State, and was content to be the first Tuscan to be Archbishop of Florence in over a hundred years. He determined to make Florence the cultural and spiritual capital of the European community, and to provide the European Common Market with a soul (as he put it). But the new pope, John Paul II, was more concerned about the 'wider Europe' which included the Slavs. Benelli's world was changing.

Bibliography: ''Benelli, Giovanni Cardinal,'' *Current Biography* 1987 (New York 1987) 48–50.

[P. HEBBLETHWAITE]

BENEVENTAN CHANT

The chant of the extinct Beneventan liturgical rite. Like the Beneventan rite itself, Beneventan chant was a distinct repertory, different from but sharing a common origin with the Gregorian and Ambrosian repertories. Since the Beneventan rite and chant had been superseded by the Roman rite and Gregorian chant by the beginning of the 9th century, a full century before the earliest liturgical books with notation, it is only by chance that anything of the rite or its music is preserved. Two graduals, however, manuscripts VI. 38 and VI. 40 of the Capitular Library in Benevento, have a Beneventan-rite Mass proper (consisting of a Milanese-like ingressa instead of an introit, gradual, alleluia, offertory, and Communion) following the Roman proper on certain major feasts. Both manuscripts have Beneventan chants for Holy Saturday, Easter, St. Michael (May 8), Ascension, Pentecost, St. John Baptist, SS. Peter and Paul, Assumption, and St. Andrew; VI. 40 has in addition Holy Thursday, St. Laurence, Twelve Brothers (September 1), Exaltation of the Holy Cross, SS. Simon and Jude, All Saints, and St. Martin. Manuscript VI. 38 alone preserves Palm Sunday and an offertory for the finding of the holy cross. A single fragment of what may have been an exclusively Beneventan rite book was bound into the manuscript Benevento VI. 35 as the rear flyleaf; it contains portions of the Masses of Christmas and St. Stephen. Finally, Beneventan chants for some of the Holy Week ceremonies appear in the gradual Vat. lat. 10673.

The arrangement of manuscripts VI. 38 and VI. 40 suggests that an attempt was made in Benevento to preserve the ancient local liturgical and musical heritage, but a comparison of Beneventan with Gregorian chant shows readily enough why the local product did not survive. The Beneventan melodies tend to be long-winded and repetitious; indeed some consist of a single rather florid phrase repeated over and over. Except for the St. Stephen fragment, all the surviving alleluia verses are set to a single melody. When a reciting tone occurs, as in a tract, the Beneventan chant employs, instead of the single pitch of Gregorian chant, an ascending second (notated by a podatus) reiterated on each syllable, an especially tedious effect. Interestingly, while the region of Benevento (from Monte Cassino to Bari) continued to exhibit a degree of liturgical independence after the adoption of the Roman rite, so that, for instance, a distinct Romano-Beneventan dialect of Gregorian chant may be identified, the latter shows no points of contact with the old Beneventan chant. Connections with Milan are equally tenuous; although the term ''Ambrosian'' does appear in Beneventan manuscripts, it only means non-Roman, i.e., Beneventan, and in fact never refers to pieces common to the Beneventan and Milanese repertories.

Bibliography: B. BAROFFIO, ''Benevent,'' *Die Musik in Geschichte und Gegenwart*, ed. F. BLUME (Kassel-Basel 1949–). R. J. HESBERT, ''L'*Antiphonale missarum* de l'ancien rit bénéventain,'' *Ephemerides liturgicae* 52 (1938) 28–66, 141–158; 53 (1939) 168–190; 15 (1945) 69–95; 60 (1946) 103–141; 61 (1947) 153–210. T. F. KELLY, ''Palimpsest Evidence of an Old-Beneventan Gradual,'' *Kirchenmusikalisches Jahrbuch 67 Jahrgang—1983* (Köln 1985) 5–23. T. F. KELLY, *The Beneventan Chant* (Cambridge 1989). P. SALMON, ''Nouvelle liste de manuscrits en écriture bénéventaine,'' *Studia Codicologica, Texte u Untersuchungen z Geschichte d altchristlichen Literatur v. 124* (Berlin 1977) 401–405. B. BAROFFIO, ''Liturgie in beneventanischen Raum,'' *Geschichte der katholischen Kirchenmusik*, ed. K. G. FELLERER (Kassel 1972) 204–8. J. MALLET and A. THIBAUT, *Les manuscrits en ecriture beneventaine de la Bibliotheque capitulaire de Benevent* (Paris 1984–). M. HUGLO, ''L'ancien chant beneventain,'' *Ecclesia orans* (1985) 265–93. N. ALBAROSA and A. TURCO, eds., *Benevento, Biblioteca capitolare 40 Graduale* (Padua 1991).

[A. DOHERTY/EDS.]

BENEVENTAN RITE

A Benedictine archbishop, B. Bonazzi (d. 1915), was the first to recognize that Benevento once had a rite of its own. It appeared that a liturgical rite had existed in southern Italy before the Lombard invasions of the 6th century, vestiges of which remain as liturgical anomalies in later liturgical manuscripts. The Beneventan rite and its chant evolved together with the rise of the Lombards, reaching its peak in the 8th century. The Beneventan rite would have been practiced in an area coterminous with the orbit Terracina-Chieti, Salerno-Bari. Some scholars think that it probably ceased under Prince Arechis II (d. 787), a ruler preoccupied with Church affairs. When the relics of St. Bartholomew arrived in Benevento (808), the rite was Roman, and there was no Mass of the saint in the old repertory. The sanctoral had included St. Michael, SS. Simon and Jude, Twelve Brothers (Apulian martyrs), and All Saints. All Saints was the last Beneventan entry. Complete liturgical texts of the Beneventan rite are no longer extant. Scholars have identified fragments of the rite and its chant in about 90 manuscript sources no earlier than the 10th century. Of these, the most important is the ancient Beneventan Holy Week liturgy, portions of which are preserved with full rubrics in century manuscripts dating no earlier than late 10th century. Elements of Beneventan Holy Week ceremonies, together with the ancient Beneventan texts and chants of the Exsultet survived as popular practices long after the rite was suppressed.

See Also: BENEVENTAN CHANT

Bibliography: D. ANDOYER, "Ancienne Liturgie de Bénévent," *Revue du chant grégorien* 20–24 (1911–14, 1919–21). R. J. HESBERT, "L'*Antiphonale missarum* de l'ancien ritbénéventain," *Ephemerides liturgicae* 52 (1938) 28–66, 141–158; 53 (1939) 168–190; 15 (1945) 69–95; 60 (1946) 103–141; 61 (1947) 153–210. A. A. KING, *Liturgies of the Past* (Milwaukee 1959). T. F. KELLY, "Palimpsest evidence of an old-Beneventan gradual," *Kirchenmusikalisches Jahrbuch 67 Jahrgang—1983* (Köln 1985) 5–23. T. F. KELLY, *The Beneventan Chant* (Cambridge 1989). P. SALMON, "Nouvelle liste de manuscrits en écriture bénéventaine," *Studia Codicologica, Texte u Untersuchungen z Geschichte d altchristlichen Literatur v. 124* (Berlin 1977) 401–405. B. BAROFFIO, "Liturgie in beneventanischen Raum," *Geschichte der katholischen Kirchenmusik*, ed. K. G. FELLERER (Kassel 1972) 204–8. J. MALLET and A. THIBAUT, *Les manuscrits en ecriture beneventaine de la Bibliotheque capitulaire de Benevent* (Paris 1984–). M. HUGLO, "L'ancien chant beneventain," *Ecclesia orans* (1985) 265–93. N. ALBAROSA and A. TURCO, eds., *Benevento, Biblioteca capitolare 40 Graduale* (Padua 1991).

[A. A. KING/EDS.]

BÉNÉZET, ST.

Patron of bridge builders; initiator and promoter of the bridge across the Rhone at Avignon; b. perhaps at Hermillion-en-Maurienne (Savoie), *c.* 1165; d. Avignon, *c.* 1184. Arriving as a young man in Avignon in 1177, Bénézet (Benedictus) convinced the Avignonais that God willed them to build the first bridge across the turbulent Rhone. For seven years he collected funds and organized a group of laymen (*donati*) as the *fratres pontis* to carry on his work. The bridge was completed in 1188. Documents in 1202 refer to him as blessed, in 1237 as saint. His relics are in St. Didier in Avignon.

Feast: April 14.

Bibliography: *Acta Sanctorum* April 2:254–263. F. LEFORT, "Histoire d'un manuscrit du 13e siècle relatif à la construction des premiers ponts sur le Rhône," *Travaux de l'Académie Nationale de Reims* 86 (1884–85) 206–227; "La Légende de saint Bénézet," *Revue des questions historiques* 23 (1878) 555–570. N. MARMOTTAN, *Le pont d'Avignon, le petit pâtre Bénézet* (Cavaillon, France 1964). P. PANSIER, "Histoire de l'ordre des frères du pont d'Avignon (1181–1410)," *Annales d'Avignon et du Comtat Venaissin* 7 (1920–21) 5–74. J. GARIN, *Dictionnaire d'histoire et de géographie ecclésiastiques*, ed. A. BAUDRILLART et al. (Paris 1912) 7:1292–93.

[M. N. BOYER]

BENIGNI, UMBERTO

Italian ecclesiastical historian, journalist, integralist; b. Perugia, March 30,1862; d. Rome, Feb. 26, 1934. After ordination (1884) he became secretary to the archbishop of Perugia and then professor of ecclesiastical history in the diocesan seminary. As a result of his interest in Catholic journalism and in social problems, he acted also as editor of a local journal until he founded (1892) *La Rassegna Sociale*, the pioneer Catholic periodical of this type in Italy. He went to Genoa in 1893 to edit *L'Eco d'Italia* and later to Rome as a collaborator in *La Voce della verità.* One fruit of a stay in Germany to study the language and the social situation was a polemical book on papal grain policies, *Die Getreide politik der Päpste* (1898). While holding the chair of ecclesiastical history at the Apollinaris in Rome (1901–04), he was noted for his lectures, delivered in Italian rather than in the traditional Latin, which were vivacious but lacking in order, precision, and depth. For the use of his students he published *Historiae ecclesiasticae repertorium* (1902), which incorporated his earlier *Propedeutica.* In 1904 he entered the Congregation for the Propagation of the Faith as a secretary (*minutante*). He transferred in 1906 to the secretariat of state, where he worked until 1911 as an undersecretary connected with the press office in the section dealing with extraordinary affairs. There he came into contact with Cardinal Rafael MERRY DEL VAL, papal secretary of state. From 1911 he taught at the Academy of Noble Ecclesiastics. His useful *Manuale di stilo diplomatico* (1920) represented the content of his lectures there.

Monsignor Benigni's opposition to Modernism made him a leading figure in INTEGRALISM. Because of the clandestine nature of many of his activities, his role in the anti-Modernist movement, though central, remains shrouded in considerable mystery and controversy. Until the necessary documents are brought to light, this situation is likely to continue. When *Correspondenza di Roma*, which he founded in 1907, changed its title to *Correspondance de Rome* in 1908, it served as a kind of international news agency, particularly for the dissemination of information concerning Modernism. In this publication appeared many denunciations of scholars and others who were thought to bear a Modernist taint. After leaving the secretariat of state in 1911, Benigni devoted himself to the SODALITIUM PIANUM, which he founded in 1909 and in which he remained the key figure until its dissolution by order of Benedict XV (1921). From this date until his death as a poor man, he continued to favor ACTION FRANÇAISE.

The most important of Benigni's several books was *Storia sociale della Chiesa* (5 v. in 7, 1906–33). This study, which was carried to the 14th century, contains considerable source material of a heterogeneous kind, but it suffers from a defective critical sense and an imprecise notion of the proper scope of this subject. He contributed numerous articles to the *Catholic Encyclopedia.*

Bibliography: *Dizionario biographico degli Italiani*, ed. A. M. GHISALBERTI, s.v. ''Benigni, U.'' (Rome 1960–). N. FONTAINE (pseud. for L. CANET), *Saint-Siège: Action française et catholiques intégraux* (Paris 1928). J. SCHMIDLIN, *Papstgeschichte der neuesten Zeit, 1800–1939*, v. 3 (Munich 1933–39).

[T. P. JOYCE]

BENIGNUS OF DIJON, ST.

Early martyr. According to the unhistorical legend from the sixth century, he came from Asia Minor as a disciple of St. POLYCARP and a missionary to Burgundy. He is supposed to have suffered martyrdom at the order of the Roman Emperor MARCUS AURELIUS. He was venerated as a saint even before the sixth century and was recognized as the patron of Dijon. The basilica and the Abbey of Saint-Bénigne were built over his tomb in Dijon.

Feast: Nov. 1.

Bibliography: *Acta Sanctorum* Nov. 1:134–194. E. EWIG, *Lexikon für Theologie und Kirche*, ed. J. HOFER and K. RAHNER (Freiburg 1957–65) 2:203–204. G. BARDY, *Dictionnaire d'histoire et de géographie ecclésiastiques*, ed. A. BAUDRILLART et al. (Paris 1912) 7:1314–15. A. BUTLER, *The Lives of the Saints*, ed. H. THURSTON and D. ATTWATER (New York 1956) 4:236.

[P. VOLK]

BÉNILDE, BL.

Educator; b. Thuret, near Clermont-Ferrand (Puy-de-Dôme), France, June 14, 1805; d. Saugues (Haute-Loire), France, Aug. 13, 1862. Bénilde was the name in religion of Pierre Romançon. From 1817 to 1820 he attended the school in Riom conducted by the CHRISTIAN BROTHERS, and then he entered the novitiate of this congregation after being refused admission in 1819 because of his short stature. He taught at Aurillac, Limoges, and Clermont-Ferrand until 1842, when he was assigned to a school newly opened in Saugues. There he spent the remainder of his life as head of the school and superior of the religious community. Under his direction the school became noted for its large number of vocations to the priesthood and brotherhood. Despite his unprepossessing appearance, Bénilde had little difficulty in exercising authority over boys. During his externally uneventful life, his reputation for sanctity became widespread. His sanctification came through the perfect accomplishment of everyday duties, as Pius XII pointed out on the occasion of Bénilde's beatification on April 1, 1948.

Feast: April 4.

Bibliography: G. RIGAULT, *Un Instituteur sur les autels: Le bienheureux Bénilde* (Paris 1947). A. J. LIDDY, *Chalk-Dust Halo: Life of Blessed Benildus* (London 1956). L. SALM, *Brother Benilde Romançon, FSC: The Teacher Saint* (Romeoville, Ill. 1987).

[W. J. BATTERSBY]

BENIN, THE CATHOLIC CHURCH IN

The Republic of Benin is a largely agricultural country located in West Africa that is bordered on the north by Niger, on the east by Nigeria, on the south by the Bight of Benin and the Gulf of Guinea, on the west by Togo and on the northwest by Burkina Faso. More than half the population dwells in the tropical coastal region. The landscape rises to hills in the northwest, while agricultural plains stretch through the east and the semi-arid north, a region visited by dry harmattan winds during the winter months. Agricultural products include cotton, Palm, corn, yams and cassava. In addition to limestone, marble and stands of timber, oil reserves are located off Benin's coast. Because of an underdeveloped economy, most Beninese rely on subsistence agriculture for their survival, although the newly seated government's transition to a market economy bodes well for the country's future. In 2000 one-third of Benin's citizens lived below the poverty line.

Once part of Upper Guinea and made a territory of French West Africa in 1895, Benin achieved self-rule in 1960 as the independent republic of Dahomey, and retained membership in the French Community. In 1976 the region changed its name to Benin after becoming a socialist state, but returned to a democratic republic in 1991. Like many African nations, the spread of AIDS continued to threat the Beninese population, and by 2000 the average life expectancy stood at 50 years. In 2000, Cardinal Bernardin Gantin, a native of Benin and the dean of the College of Cardinals in Vatican City, called AIDS ''a menace to the lives of scores of millions of Africans, and an obstacle to the development of all Africa.''

History. Benin was part of one of the most sophisticated states in Africa prior to the coming of Europeans, and had its chief city in Abomey. Entering the region in 1485, the Portuguese built a chapel at Ouidah in 1680, but during the 16th, 17th and 18th centuries, attempts at evangelization were sporadic and ineffectual. In about 1830 Catholicism in Benin consisted of about 2,000 Portuguese and former slaves repatriated from Brazil who dwelt along the coast and who were under the jurisdiction of the bishop of São Tomé. In 1860 the territory was made part of the Vicariate Apostolic of the Two Guineas,

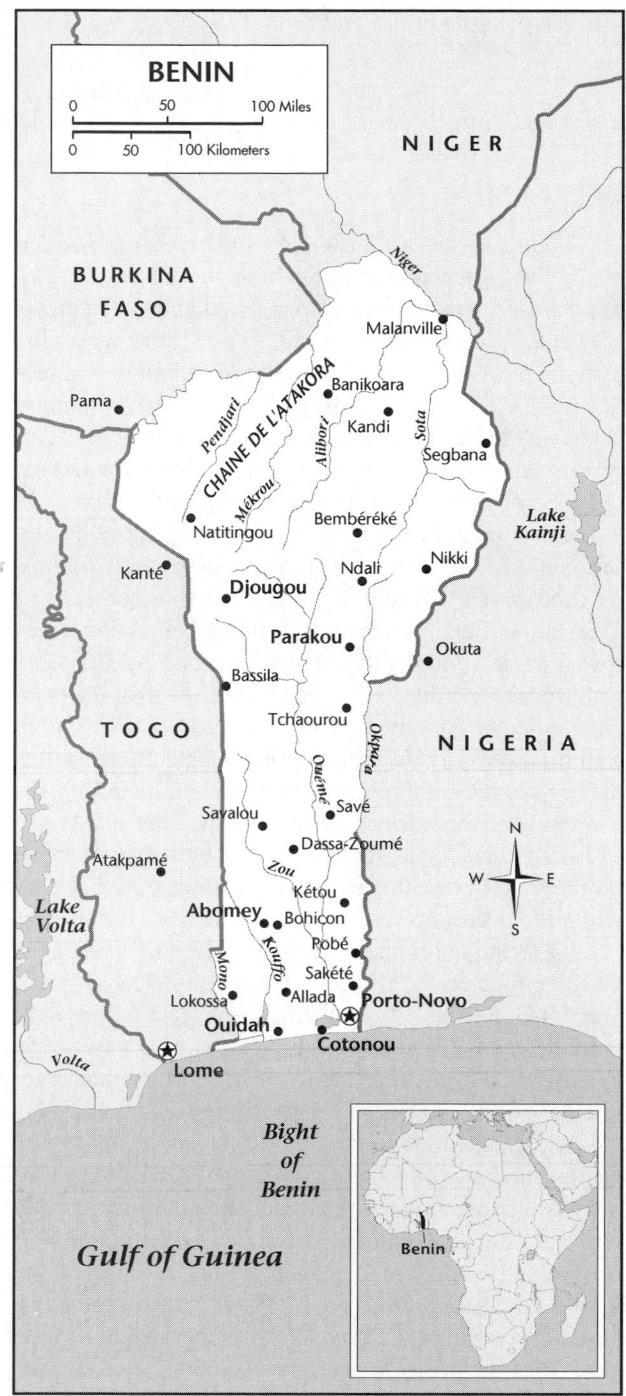

Capital: Porto Novo; Cotonou is the seat of government.
Size: 44,695 sq. miles.
Population: 6,395,919 in 2000.
Languages: French; Fon, Yoruba, and other tribal languages are spoken in various regions.
Religions: 1,151,240 Catholics (18%), 767,510 Muslims (12%), 192,075 Protestants (3%), 4,285,094 practice indigenous beliefs (67%).
Archdioceses: Cotonou, with suffragans Abomey, Dassa-Zoumé, Lokossa, and Porto Novo; Parakou, with suffragans Djougou, Kandi, and Natitingou.

and was confided to the Society of the AFRICAN MISSIONS (SMA). Two priests arrived at Ouidah in 1861, but their efforts were restricted to working among foreigners. The Prefecture Apostolic of Dahomey was established in 1883 and briefly included Togo.

Following the successes of a French military expedition, which overthrew the native government in 1892, freedom to evangelize was granted in 1894, when the region became a French colony. In 1901 Benin/Dahomey became a vicariate apostolic, and its jurisdiction was extended northward to include Niger. A native congregation of women, the *Petites Servantes des Pauvres de Cotonou,* was founded in 1912, and a seminary was opened at Ouidah in 1913. A separate prefecture apostolic, embracing northern Benin, was established at Niamey, Niger, in 1942; but in 1948 northern Benin became the Prefecture Apostolic of Parakou (diocese in 1964), and the Vicariate of Dahomey became the Vicariate of Ouidah. Another vicariate was created in 1954 for the southeast at Porto Novo (diocese in 1955). The hierarchy was established in 1955, when Cotonou (formerly the Vicariate of Ouidah) became an archdiocese and metropolitan see for the country.

An overseas territory of France since 1946, the region became the self-governing Republic of Dahomey and received full independence on Aug. 1, 1960. Following the rise to power of a Marxist government in 1974, the country's name was changed from Dahomey to Benin, and atheistic policies were adopted. All churches were nationalized. Visas of foreign missionaries were revoked, forcing them to leave the country, while local priests were threatened with jail for any actions viewed as threatening to the state.

In December of 1989 the Marxist government was abolished, and the following February Cotonou Archbishop Isidore de Souza led the conference that drafted the country's new constitution. Democratic elections followed in 1991.

Into the 21st Century. By 2000 Benin had 172 parishes, 250 diocesan priests and 107 religious priests. Religious included 53 brothers and 689 sisters who operated clinics, hospitals and ran Benin's 22 primary and 18 secondary Catholic schools. The regional seminary of St. Gall, in Ouidah, was under the direction of the Sulpicians, while the Christian Brothers maintained a normal school at Bohican. The Trappists established a house in 1959 and the Cistercian nuns in 1960. In December of 1997 the Vatican opened a campus of the John Paul II Institute in Cotonou, a school in Rome that focused on the study of marriage and family life. A Catholic radio station, Rado Immaculate Conception, broadcast services and other Church-related programming. Most Catholics resided in the south, in or near the cities of Porto-Novo and Cotonou.

As part of the country's Christian minority, one of the challenges faced by the Church was the development of programs to promote relations with Benin's other faiths. Most Beninese were adherents of animist faiths such as vodoun, although elements of the Christian and Muslim doctrines often found their way into such indigenous religions. Although religious groups were required to register with the government, they were also given tax-exempt status and Church-based holidays were recognized by the state. Another issue of growing concern among Church leaders was the persistent trafficking in child slavery, and the Archdiocese of Cotonou established a counseling center to deal with this evil. Estimates put the number of children trafficked in West Africa at over 200,000 per year, many of whom were put to work on plantations, as domestics, or were forced into prostitution.

Bibliography: *Bilan du Monde,* 2:299–303. *Annuario Pontificio* has data on all diocese. For additional bibliography, *see* AFRICA.

[J. BOUCHAUD/EDS.]

BENINCASA, URSULA, VEN.

Foundress of the Theatine Sisters; b. Naples, Oct. 20, 1547; d. St. Elmo's Mount, Naples, Oct. 20, 1618. At the age of 10 she received mystical gifts. In 1579, when refused admission to the Capuchinesses, she retired as a solitary to the nearby St. Elmo's Mount. There she built a church in honor of the Immaculate Conception. After a vision on March 12, 1582, Ursula went to Rome to interest Gregory XIII in her plans for assisting in Church reform. Again in Naples in 1583, she founded the Oblates of the Immaculate Conception, whose members consecrate themselves to God in the education of youth. In 1617 Ursula founded the Contemplative Hermit Sisters, an order with solemn vows and strict enclosure. Gregory XV approved its rules on June 23, 1623, and put this institute and the Oblates under the direction of the Theatine Fathers. To Ursula's vision of Feb. 2, 1617 is attributed the origin of the Blue Scapular of the Immaculate Conception. Pius VI proclaimed the heroicity of her virtues on Aug. 7, 1793.

Bibliography: A. VENY BALLESTER, *Ursula Benincasa* (Zaragoza 1967). M. HEIMBUCHER, *Die Orden urd Kongregationen der katolischen Kirche*, 2 v. (3d. ed. Paderborn 1932–34) 2:104–106. F. M. MAGGI, *Compendium vitae venerabilis matris Ursulae de Benincasa* (Brussels 1658).

[A. SAGRERA]

BENJAMIN

Youngest son of JACOB and a full brother of Joseph; his mother, Rachel, died at his birth (Gn 35.16–19, 24). The Joseph narratives depict Benjamin (Hebrews *binyāmîn,* ''son of the right hand,'' i.e., southerner) as the instrument of the estranged Joseph in reuniting and reconciling Jacob's family in Egypt (Gn 39–50). Little more is known of him than that he had ten sons (Gn 46.21). According to the census recorded by the PRIESTLY WRITERS, the tribe of Benjamin had 35,400 males of military age at the beginning of the 40 years of wandering in the desert, and 45,000 at its end; on the value of these figures, *see* CENSUS (IN THE BIBLE). At the Israelite conquest of Canaan, the Benjaminites received as a possession a narrow tract of central hill country bounded by Ephraim, Dan, Judah, and the Jordan, containing some of the principal cities of Israelite history (Jos 18.11–28). A barren territory, naturally defensible and strategically located at the heart of the chief routes of communication in Canaan, it determined the warlike character of the tribe and its role in Israelite history as reflected in the blessings of Jacob (Gn 49.27). During the period of the Judges, Aod, a Benjaminite. overthrew a Moabite oppressor, Eglon (Jgs 3.12–30), and under the leadership of Debora and Barac, Benjamin joined the tribal coalition that defeated Sisera (Jgs 5.14). Because of an attempt to protect fellow Benjaminites guilty of a heinous crime, the tribe was nearly exterminated by the reprisal of all Israel. The remnant abducted wives to restore their decimated ranks (Jgs 19–21). Benjaminite martial glory reached its zenith against the Philistine aggression of the 11th century B.C., a crisis that precipitated the establishment of the monarchy and Israelite unification. SAUL, a Benjaminite warrior, rallied Israel and was anointed its first king (1 Sm 9.1–12.25). At his death (*c.* 1000 B.C.) a power struggle ensued between Saul's son IS-BAAL, supported by Abner, general of the army, and David, the newly elected king in Judah (2 Sm 2.1–11). Most Benjaminites remained faithful to Saul's house against Judah until Abner's break with Is-Baal and his pact with David (2 Sm 2.12–3.21). Upon Is-Baal's death David was acknowledged as king by all Israel and shifted his capital from Hebron in Judah to Jerusalem in Benjaminite territory, a neutral location (2 Sm 4.1–5.10). Benjaminite dissatisfaction with David manifested itself in the two abortive rebellions of Absalom and Seba (2 Sm 15–18; 20). Benjamin seems initially to have joined the northern kingdom under Jeroboam I at Solomon's death (*c.* 922 B.C.; 1 Kgs 12.20), only to become and remain annexed to Juda when Roboam occupied its territory in order to keep Jerusalem as his capital (1 Kgs 11.29–36; 2 Chr 11.1, 5–12, 23; 14.8). Subsequently, Benjamin became a buffer state in the internal wars for supremacy between the northern and southern kingdoms (1 Kgs 15.17–22; 2 Chr 13.19; 15.8). With the destruction of the north in 721 B.C., Benjaminite fortunes became linked with those of Judah. Elements of the tribe are mentioned in the post-Exilic tribal lists of Nehemiah's time (1 Chr 8.1–40). The most famous of the later Benjaminites was Saul of Tarsus, the NT Apostle of the Gentiles (Phil 3.5).

Bibliography: *Encylopedic Dictionary of the Bible,* tr. and adap. by L. HARTMAN, (New York 1963), from A. VAN DEN BORN, *Bijbels Woordenboek,* 225–226. J. BRIGHT, *A History of Israel* (Philadelphia 1959).

[R. BARRETT]

BENNO II OF OSNABRÜCK, BL.

Bishop; b. Böhningen, Swabia, *c.* 1020; d. Iburg, Germany, July 27, 1088. Benno was the student of HERMANNUS CONTRACTUS and headed the cathedral school of Hildesheim, which he revitalized. He was cathedral provost, served in the imperial administration at Goslar and was coadjutor of Abp. ANNO OF COLOGNE before being elected bishop of Osnabrück as the candidate of Emperor HENRY IV (1068). In the investiture struggle, he was excommunicated by Pope GREGORY VII for participating in the Synod of Worms (1076). He thereafter attempted mediation, interceding for Henry IV at Canossa (1077), at Rome (1078–79), and during Henry's siege of Rome (1082–84). He skillfully retained the trust of both parties. Benno was a noted architect and worked on the imperial residence at Goslar, Speyer Cathedral, the imperial fortifications in Saxony, Hildesheim Cathedral, and his own foundation, the Abbey of Iburg.

Feast: July 22, Nov. 20.

See Also: INVESTITURE STRUGGLE.

Bibliography: *Vita, Monumenta Germaniae Historica Scriptores* (Berlin 1826–) 12:58–84. L. THYEN, *Benno II: Bischof von O.* (Osnabrück 1869). ABBOT NORBERT OF IBURG, *Vita Bennonis II, episcopi Osnabrugensis* (Hannover 1977). G. MEYER VON KNONAU, *Jahrbücher des deutschen Reiches unter Heinrich IV. und Heinrich V.,* 7 v. (Leipzig 1890–1909) v.1 and 4. I. HINDENBERG, *B. II. . . . als Architekt* (Strasbourg 1921). A. FLICHE, *La Ré forme grégorienne,* 3 v. (Louvain 1924–37) v.3. A. BUTLER, *The Lives of the Saints,* rev. ed. H. THURSTON and D. ATTWATER (New York 1956) 3:165–166. G. BÖING, *Lexikon für Theologie und Kirche,* ed. J. HOFER and K. RAHNER (Freiberg 1957–65) 2:206–207. E. N. JOHNSON, ''Bishop Benno II of Osnabrück,'' *Speculum* 16 (1941) 389–403.

[D. ANDREINI]

BENNO OF MEISSEN, ST.

Bishop; b. according to legend, Hildesheim, Germany, 1010; d. *c.* 1106. Benno, son of a noble Saxon family, became a canon attached to the imperial collegiate church in Goslar and then bishop of Meissen (1066). He was imprisoned by Emperor Henry IV in 1075 and 1076, apparently for not supporting the emperor during the revolt of the Saxon nobles, but was later released. In 1077, when Henry IV was excommunicated and deposed by Pope GREGORY VII during the INVESTITURE STRUGGLE, Benno took part in the election of Rudolph of Swabia as German king in Henry's stead. He was removed from his see by the prelates of the imperial party at the synod of Mainz in 1085, but restored in 1088 on the recommendation of the antipope GUIBERT OF RAVENNA (Clement III), to whom he had appealed on a trip to Italy (1085–86). After 1097 he recognized URBAN II as legitimate pope. He seems to have earned the title ''Apostle of the Wends'' by preaching to the Slavonic tribes in his diocese. His cult was established in 1285, when his relics were honored in the reconstructed cathedral of Meissen. Contemporary chronicles record many miracles at his tomb. His canonization in 1523 and the solemn exposition of his relics in 1524 evoked much protest, including a brochure by Martin Luther entitled ''Wider den neuen Abgott und alten Teufel, der zu Meissen soll erhoben werden'' (Against the New Idol and the Old Devil about to be set up at Meissen). To prevent desecration, his relics were transferred to Bavaria in 1576. Since 1580 they have been in the cathedral of Munich. Benno is patron of Munich, of the bishopric of Meissen, and of old Bavaria. In iconography he is represented with a fish holding in its mouth the keys of the cathedral of Meissen. He is patron of fishermen and drapers, and is invoked for rain.

Feast: June 16.

Bibliography: *Acta Sanctorum* June 4:121–186. For more reliable information see articles by O. LANGER in *Mitteilungen des Vereins für Geschichte der Stadt Meissen* 1.3 (1884) 70–95; 1.5 (1886) 1–38; 2.2 (1888) 99–144; 7.1 (1906) 122–125. A. HAUCK, *Kirchengeschichte Deutschlands* (Berlin-Leipzig 1958) 3:841–850. A. BIGELMAIR, *Dictionnaire d'histoire et de géographie ecclésiastiques,* ed. A. BAUDRILLART et al. (Paris 1912) 7:1363–65. A. M. ZIMMERMANN, *Kalendarium Benedictinum* (Metten 1933–38) 2:320.

[M. F. MCCARTHY]

BENNO OF METZ

Bishop; d. Aug. 3, 940. Benno came from a noble Swabian family. While still a young man he was made a canon at Strassburg. In 906, he retired to the hermitage that had formerly housed St. Meinrad. He rebuilt the chapel and the dwelling and soon gathered a group of disciples. Benno was named bishop of Metz in 927 by King Henry I, who opposed the locally elected candidate; but in 929 Benno was attacked by his enemies and blinded. Although the attackers were excommunicated and banished at the Synod of Duisburg (929), Benno renounced his episcopal office and returned to his former hermitage. In 934 he was joined by Eberhard, provost of Strassburg Cathedral, who developed the hermitage into the celebrated monastery of EINSIEDELN. Benno's cult has never been formally recognized, and he should properly be titled venerable.

Bibliography: A. BIGELMAIR, *Dictionnaire d'histoire et de géographie ecclésiastiques* (Paris 1912–) 7:1361–62. A. M. BURG, *Lexikon für Theologie und Kirche* (Freiburg 1957–65) 2:206.

[F. BEHRENDS]

BENOÎT, MICHEL

Astronomer; b. Autun or Dijon, Oct. 8, 1715; d. Peking, Oct. 23, 1774. He entered the Society of Jesus at age 22 at Nancy and was sent to the China missions at age 25. For this he studied astronomy in Paris under Delisle, Lacaille, and Le Monnier. Upon his arrival in Peking, he was assigned to a group of missionary mathematicians of the court. For all his astronomical preparation, Emperor Kien Lung asked him to landscape his gardens. He built in them European houses and a monumental water clock. He prepared a 12.5 by 6.5 foot map of the world, incorporating astronomical as well as geographical data. He also engraved in copper a map of the Chinese empire, creating for this task a group of native specialists in copper engraving. He wrote many of the letters in *Lettres édifiantes* and translated the *Imitation of Christ* into Chinese. From 1762 to 1772 Benoît was superior of the Jesuit mission in Peking. He died of a stroke a few days after being notified of the suppression of the Society of Jesus.

Bibliography: R. STREIT and J. DINDINGER, *Bibliotheca missionum* (Freiburg 1916–).

[E. T. SPAIN]

BENOIT, PIERRE

Bible scholar, archaeologist, and editor; b. Aug. 3, 1906; d. Jerusalem, April 23, 1987. Maurice Benoit entered the DOMINICAN Order in 1924 and received the religious name Pierre. At the conclusion of his studies at the Collège Théologique des Dominicains, Kain, Belgium, he was awarded the Lectorate in Theology (1932), and was assigned to the École Biblique et Archéologique Française, Jerusalem.

After earning his Licentiate in Sacred Scripture in 1933, he began a teaching career that was to span half a century. He taught the New Testament until he reached retirement age in 1976, but he continued his famous course on the topography of Jerusalem until he was incapacitated by cancer in the spring of 1984. He served as the director of the École Biblique (1965–72) and as the editor of the *Revue Biblique* (1953–68).

In recognition of his scientific contributions, POPE PAUL VI appointed him to the PONTIFICAL BIBLICAL COMMISSION (1972–87), and the French government made him first a Chevalier (1959) then an Officer de la Légion d'Honneur (1974). The Catholic Biblical Association of America (1964) and the Society of Biblical Literature (1963) elected him to honorary life membership, and the universities of Munich (1972) and Durham (1977) awarded him honorary doctorates. A founding member of the Society for New Testament Studies, he was its first Roman Catholic president (1962–63).

Benoit played a key role in the conception and execution of the pioneering *Bible de Jérusalem,* the first modern Roman Catholic Bible to be translated from the original languages. The layout invited the reader to approach it as literature, and the detailed notes constituted a critical and theological commentary accessible to nonspecialists. In addition to acting as New Testament editor, he translated and annotated the Gospel of Matthew and the four Captivity Epistles, on which he was a noted authority. He actively collaborated with Dom Henry Wansbrough, OSB, on the completely revised second edition of the *Jerusalem Bible.*

Having had the good fortune to begin his career at a time when scholars could still be polymaths, and with such wide-ranging geniuses as M.-J. LAGRANGE, L.-H. Vincent, F.-M. Abel, and W. F. ALBRIGHT to guide and inspire him, Benoit developed an abiding interest in archaeology, although he never considered himself an excavator. Well aware of the archaeologist's preference for the trowel rather than the typewriter (about 90 percent of the material excavated in Palestine has never been published), in 1954 he instituted the ''Chronique archéologique'' in the *Revue Biblique* in order to provide reports on current excavations.

Jerusalem Archaeology. His own specialty was the archaeology of JERUSALEM, which he knew in a detail that is unlikely ever to be surpassed. His principal concern was the light that topography could throw on the biblical text. His major contribution was to demonstrate that during the trial of Jesus, Pontius Pilate must have resided in the palace at the present Jaffa Gate rather than in the Antonia Fortress on the other side of the city. Since the Antonia Fortress is the starting-point of the traditional

Via Dolorosa, his study created a certain stir when it was first published in 1952.

In what is unusual for one so committed to text and monument, Benoit also did significant work in speculative theology. Invited to annotate the treatise on prophecy for a French version of the *Summa Theologica* of St. THOMAS AQUINAS (1947), he produced a series of studies that developed a sophisticated concept of biblical inspiration. He limited inerrancy to what is formally taught by the sacred writers, and thus opened the way to critical investigation of historical details. This combination of exegetical expertise and speculative creativity won him nomination as a theological expert for the last two sessions of VATICAN II (1963–65), where he contributed to the formulation of the conciliar documents on divine revelation, the Church, religious freedom, and non-Christian religions.

Dead Sea Scrolls. Benoit edited the Greek and Latin documents found in the caves of the Wadi Murabba'at. After the death of Roland de Vaux, OP, in 1971, he assumed the general editorship of the unpublished fragments of the Dead Sea Scrolls during a very difficult period. Dilatory scholars had put the project disastrously behind schedule, and complaint was mounting. In addition, as a result of the invasion of East Jerusalem in 1967, the Israelis had physical possession of the scrolls, which belonged to Jordan. By adroit diplomacy Benoit won the consent of both governments to continue the publication, and thereafter spent many exhausting hours trying to persuade recalcitrant editors to finalize their commitments. In the year before he died he facilitated the transfer of the general editorship to Prof. John Strugnell of Harvard University.

A very productive scholar, Benoit wrote articles on theology, archeology, and exegesis that when collected filled four volumes. His gifts of great erudition, theological insight, and historical judgment were to a great extent frustrated by a perfectionism that made large-scale projects impossible. He employed yoga exercises to keep himself extremely fit, and on field trips in his seventies could outwalk students a third of his age. A model religious, he made exacting demands on himself and found his only recreation in listening to classical music and playing the organ. His austerity and self-discipline often gave an impression of coldness, but behind the facade was a warm and generous personality, whose helpfulness to his students and colleagues was the norm. They learned from him a rigor of method, a clarity of thought, and a commitment to truth that came to represent a lived ideal of scholarly integrity.

Bibliography: P. BENOIT, *Somme théologique de saint Thomas d'Aquin; La prophétie. 2a–2ae, questions 171–178* (Paris 1947); Eng. *Prophecy and Inspiration. A Commentary on the Summa Theologica II–II, Questions 171–178* (New York 1961); *Exégèse et théologie* I-II (Paris 1961) III (Paris 1968) IV (Paris 1982); Eng. *Jesus and the Gospel. A Translation of Selected Articles from Exégèse et Théologie* I (London 1973) II (London 1974); *Synopse des quatre évangiles en français, avec parallèles des Apocryphes et des Pères,* with M.-E. BOISMARD (Paris 1965); *Passion et résurrection du Seigneur* (Paris 1966); Eng. *The Passion and Resurrection of Jesus Christ* (London 1969).

[J. MURPHY-O'CONNOR]

BENTHAM, JEREMY

Philosopher, legal theorist whose writings stimulated the rise of UTILITARIANISM in England; b. London, Feb. 15, 1748; d. London, June 6, 1832. Bentham, the son of a wealthy attorney, studied, but never practiced, law and devoted his life to legal reform. Faced with a prevailing interpretation of English common law so closely related to natural law that ''law as it is'' was almost indistinguishable from ''law as it ought to be,'' he sought a way to put legal and social criticism on a scientific basis. In certain views of T. Hobbes, J. Locke, D. Hume, J. Priestley, W. Paley, C. A. Helvetius, and C. B. Beccaria, he found hints of a solution, and these he developed into a form of HEDONISM known as utilitarianism.

Adam SMITH argued that the wealth and prosperity of a nation could be best promoted by permitting maximum individual freedom of action, limited only by government as a referee. Bentham agreed but believed that the referee often followed rules that could be justified only as ancient practice or as what was ''natural,'' with the result that the wrong people were rewarded or punished. We judge machines only on the basis of their utility, why not laws? The effect of Bentham's critique was to show how—in the spheres of civil, penal, and constitutional law—government could so lay down rules that the prospect of painful consequences would lead individuals (acting freely out of self-interest) to act for the public good, equivalent for Bentham with the greatest happiness of the greatest number.

Bentham's ethical theory, found in his *Introduction to the Principles of Morals and Legislation* (1789) and his *Deontology* (1834), was developed for the purpose of finding the springs of human conduct that could be tapped by the legislator. It is open to objection on a number of grounds: as a form of EGOISM, as a form of psychological and ethical hedonism, and also on the ground that Bentham failed to show why one morally ought to seek the happiness of everybody. Further, Bentham vastly overrated the practicality of his balance-of-pleasure-over-pain criterion for judging individual acts and laws. Again, although Bentham's influence on modern legal reform in

"Cardinal Guido Bentivoglio," detail of a portrait by Anthony Van Dyck.

England is perhaps second to none, the lack of a notion of GOOD more ultimate than quantity of "pleasure," together with an inadequate notion of justice, permits his philosophy to justify any of a broad range of socioeconomic systems from laissez-faire LIBERALISM to egalitarian SOCIALISM.

Bibliography: *Works,* ed. J. BOWRING, 11 v. (Edinburgh 1843). C. M. ATKINSON, *Jeremy Bentham: His Life and Work* (London 1905). G. KEETON and G. SCHWARZENBERGER, eds., *Jeremy Bentham and the Law: A Symposium* (London 1948). D. BAUMGARDT, *Bentham and the Ethics of Today* (Princeton 1952).

[R. L. CUNNINGHAM]

BENTIVOGLIO

A Bolognese family that originated from the castle of that name near Bologna. It claimed descent from Enzio (1224?–72), King of Sardinia. The family belonged to a guild of workingmen at Bologna during the 14th century and became powerful in the 15th. It contracted alliances with Aragon, Milan, and later, Ferrara. The following members are prominent:

Guido, cardinal; b. Ferrara, Oct. 4, 1579; d. Rome, Sept. 7, 1644. He studied law at Padua, where he was also taught by Galileo Galilei. He was named private chamberlain by Clement VII in 1587. Paul V sent him as nuncio to Flanders (1607) and to France (1617) and appointed him cardinal in 1621. Louis XIII of France made him protector of French interests in Rome. Guido also served in the Curia as the head of the Inquisition. A very trusted friend of Urban VIII, he would perhaps have succeeded him, had he not died in the conclave. He served at various times as bishop of Bologna, Rhodes, and Palestrina, to which he was appointed in 1641. His writings were a chronicle of the curial life of his time and were published at Venice in 1688. Among the more noted are *Della guerra di Flandria* and *Lettere diplomatiche di Guido Bentivoglio.* His portrait by Van Dyck hangs in the Pitti Palace in Florence.

Annibale, archbishop; date of birth unknown; d. April 21, 1663. Of the poetry in his native tongue that he produced, only *Applausi poetici in lode di Lionara Barroni* remains. He was nominated titular archbishop of Tebe in 1644.

Marco Cornelio, cardinal; b. Ferrara, March 27, 1688; d. Rome, Dec. 30, 1732. After holding various offices in the Roman Curia he was sent as nuncio to France on Oct. 21, 1711, by Clement XI. There his dealings with the Jansenists were unsuccessful because of his insistence upon the propositions of the bull *Unigenitus* (Sept. 8, 1713). He was recalled at the death of Louis XIV, calumniated, it is said, by the regime. He was created a cardinal (Nov. 29, 1719) and Spanish minister plenipotentiary at Rome (July 1726), which post he held until his death.

Domenico, soldier; b. Bologna, July 3, 1781; d. Rome, Dec. 26, 1851. He was admitted to the guard of honor of Eugene Beauharnais in 1805 as a lieutenant, and then as captain he took part in the Napoleonic campaigns from 1800 to 1814. He entered pontifical service after the fall of the Empire and was made a colonel for the gallant defense of Rieti against Sercognani.

Bibliography: R. BELVEDERI, *Guido Bentivoglio e la politica Europea del suo tempo, 1607–1621* (Padua 1964). L. PASTOR, *The History of the Popes from the Close of the Middle Ages* v. 23, *passim* (London–St. Louis 1938–61). R. D. TUCCI, *Il Cardinale Guido Bentivoglio e i suoi Rapporti con la Repubblica di Genova* (Genoa 1934). J. WODKA, *Lexikon für Theologie und Kirche*[2] 2:208.

[R. L. FOLEY]

BENTIVOGLIO, MARIA MADDALENA

POOR CLARE foundress in the United States; b. Rome, July 29, 1834; d. Evansville, Ind., Aug. 18, 1905. Born Anna Maria Bentivoglio (nicknamed "Annetta"), twelfth of sixteen children of Angela Sandri and Count Domenico Bentivoglio, a lieutenant-colonel and eventual general in the papal carabinieri. Annetta received her initial education in the convent school of the Religious of the Sacred Heart at the Trinita dei Monti, Rome. In 1842 she traveled to Turin with Madeleine Sophie Barat and continued her studies until the 1848 revolution when the members of the convent were forced to flee. Returning to Rome with her sister, Agata, a member of the Society of the Sacred Heart, Annetta followed her father and her family into exile as the revolutionary forces captured the city. Domenico died in 1851, Angela, her mother, in 1860. In 1862 Annetta and two of her sisters, Constanza and Matilda, took up residence in Rome at the monastery of the cloistered Dominican Sisters at Santa Caterina da Siena. Constanza entered the Roman convent of the Poor Clares, San Lorenzo in Panisperna, and Annetta followed on July 16, 1864, taking the name Maria Maddalena. After a one year novitiate, Maddalena professed on Oct. 4, 1865, and in the following years was decisively influenced by Bernardino da Portogruaro who was her spiritual director and, after 1869, the Minister General of the Order of Friars Minor.

Intensely religious and desirous of following the ideals of the primitive Rule of Saint Clare, Maddalena and Constanza, under Bernardino's direction, began to return to a rigorous observance of evangelical poverty. Commissioned by Pius IX to establish the primitive rule of St. Clare in the United States, Maddalena, accompanied by her sister, left for America on Aug. 12, 1875. After searching for examples of the observance of the rule in Assisi and Marseilles, she arrived in New York on October 12, but Cardinal John McCloskey refused the pilgrims' admittance into the archdiocese of New York because of the overwhelming need for active, not cloistered contemplative, religious. The two wandering sisters attracted several aspirants and after a brief settlement in New Orleans were invited by the Provincial of the Franciscan Observants to come to Cleveland. They suddenly departed that city after only six months (August 1877–February 1878) when the Provincial placed the new home under the authority of Poor Clare Colettines from Germany.

On Aug. 15, 1878, Maddalena arrived with two novices in Omaha, Nebraska, where they had been accepted by Bishop James O'Connor. With the philanthropic help of John Creighton, the sisters found a permanent convent and formalized canonical enclosure on July 5, 1882. Outside of a trip to establish a foundation in New Orleans in 1885 and early 1886, Maddalena remained in Omaha until July 1897 when she went to a third new monastery in Evansville, Indiana. She remained there until her death. In subsequent decades, her foundations became the sources of numerous other Poor Clare monasteries in the United States and abroad. The archive of her writings is housed at the Poor Clare monastery in Evansville.

Bibliography: M. FIEGE, *The Princess of Poverty* (Evansville, Ind. 1900). M. ZARRELLA, *I Will God's Will, Life of Mary Maddalena Bentivoglio, O.S.C., Foundress of Poor Clares in the United States* (Evansville, Ind. 1975). A. KLEBER, *A Bentivoglio of the Bentivoglio, The Servant of God Mary Maddalena of the Sacred Heart of Jesus, Countess Annetta Bentivoglio, 1834–1905, Poor Clare Abbess, Foundress of the Order of St. Clare of the Strict Observance in the United States of America* (Evansville, Ind. 1984).

[J. P. CHINNICI]

BENTLEY, RICHARD

Distinguished English classical scholar and Christian apologist; b. Oulton, Yorkshire, Jan. 27, 1662; d. Cambridge, July 7, 1742. After taking his B.A. at Cambridge at age 18, he served as tutor to the son of E. Stillingfleet, Dean of St. Paul's and later bishop of Worcester (1689–99). In Stillingfleet's house he had access to one of the best private libraries of the time, and when he accompanied his pupil to Oxford, he was able to make full use of the Bodleian. In 1690, he was ordained to the Anglican ministry and was appointed chaplain to Stillingfleet. In 1694, he was made keeper of Royal Libraries, and in 1700 he became master of Trinity College, Cambridge. Despite bitter feuds occasioned in part by his efforts at reform and in part by his own personality, he retained his mastership until his death, 42 years later.

His *Letter to Mill* (London 1691), published as an appendix to John MILL's edition of the chronicle of the Byzantine historian, John Malalas, revealed his profound knowledge and his brilliant critical powers. It was the first of a series of epoch-making contributions to Greek and Latin textual criticism, metrics, literary history, and historical criticism. Bentley's involvement in a controversy with Sir William TEMPLE over Temple's claim that the *Epistles of Phalaris* was an authentic work led to the writing of his *Dissertation on the Epistles of Phalaris* (London 1697; rev. and enl. ed., 1699). By a critical use of chronological, historical, literary, and linguistic evidence, he proved that the work did not date from the 6th century B.C., but was a forgery of the Hellenistic age. In this work, his masterpiece, he founded higher literary and historical criticism.

Bentley's activity in religious controversy and in biblical studies is important also and deserves more attention than it usually receives. As the first preacher appointed under the Boyle foundation at Cambridge, he delivered eight sermons on the *Folly of Atheism* (London 1692), making full use of the latest discoveries of Isaac

Newton in his apologetic. In 1713, under the pseudonym, Phileleutherus Lipsiensis, he published his *Remarks,* a strongly worded refutation of the *Discourse of Free-Thinking* by deist Anthony Collins (1676–1729). His *Proposals for the Edition of the Greek Testament* (London, 1720) is a pioneer work that anticipates in many respects the method of biblical textual criticism developed by Lachmann and other 19th-century biblical scholars. Through his own achievements and through his influence, Bentley is universally recognized as one of the greatest representatives of classical scholarship.

Bibliography: A. T. BARTHOLOMEW, *Richard Bentley, D.D.: A Bibliography of His Works* (Cambridge, Eng. 1908). R. C. JEBB, *The Dictionary of National Biography from the Earliest Times to 1900* 2:306–314. M. L. W. LAISTNER, "Richard Bentley, 1742–1942," *The Intellectual Heritage of the Early Middle Ages: Selected Essays by M. L. W. Laistner,* ed. C. G. STARR (Ithaca, N.Y. 1957) 239–254. J. E. SANDYS, *History of Classical Scholarship,* 3 v. (Cambridge, Eng. 1903–08) 2:401–410.

[M. R. P. MCGUIRE]

BENVENUTUS SCOTIVOLI, ST.

Bishop; d. Ancona, Italy, March 22, 1283. Having studied law at Bologna, he returned to his Diocese of Ancona, was ordained, and became archdeacon there. In 1263 he was appointed administrator, and in 1264 bishop, of the Diocese of Osimo, vacant since 1239. He was also made governor of the March of Ancona. Buried in the cathedral of Osimo, he became the city's patron saint in 1755. An earlier inspection of his tomb had revealed a gray capuche sewn to a lambskin, and this led the popular biographer Jean Baldi (1620) to assert that this bishop had been a Franciscan. L. Wadding accepted the evidence and F. Diaz obtained the concession of a Mass and Office (1697) for the new edition of the Franciscan Breviary. In 1765, D. Pannelli, a priest of Osimo, contended that Benvenutus had not been a Franciscan, opening a lively controversy with Flaminio da Latera. Although da Latera could not establish his position, the feast of St. Benvenutus was nevertheless retained in the Franciscan calendar on March 22.

Bibliography: A. DU MONSTIER, *Martyrologium franciscanum* (2d ed. Paris 1753). *Acta Sanctorum* March 3:390–393. L. WADDING, *Scriptores Ordinis Minorum* (Lyons 1625–54) 4:246; 5:4–5. D. PANNELLI, *Memorie istoriche de'santi Vitaliano e Benvenuto, vescovi d'Osimo,* 2 v. (Osimo 1763). D. FILLARETI, *Lettere . . . a un Padre Minorita* (2d ed. Osimo 1765). L. OLIGER, "Discussiones della vita e degli scritti del P. Flaminio Annibali da Latera, O.F.M.," *Archivum Franciscanum historicum* 7 (1914) 577–620, esp. 596–598. L. JADIN, *ibid.* 8:292–293. L. DE CLARY, *Lives of the Saints and Blessed of the Three Orders of St. Francis,* 4 v. (Taunton, Eng. 1885–87) 1:517–519. J. L. BAUDOT and L. CHAUSSIN, *Vies des saints et des bienhereux selon l'ordre du calendrier avec l'historique des fêtes* (Paris 1935–56) 3:497–498.

[J. CAMBELL]

BENZIGER

A family associated with the publication of Catholic books in Europe and the United States. The founder of the publishing house was Joseph Charles Benziger (1762–1841), who had started a small business in religious articles in Einsiedeln, Switzerland in 1793. When the French invaded Switzerland during the French Revolution, he and his family were forced to abandon the enterprise and flee the country. On returning home, he set up as a bookseller. In 1833, when Charles and Nicholas Benziger succeeded their father, they began printing and publishing books. In 1853 a sales branch of the firm was opened in New York, and it became a publishing house in 1860, under the direction of J. N. Adelrich Benziger (d. 1878) and Louis Benziger (d. 1896). In 1897, the American branch separated from the Swiss firm.

When Louis Benziger retired, he was followed by Louis G. Benziger and Nicholas C. Benziger. In 1912, 1919, and 1923, respectively, Xavier N., Bernard A., and Alfred F. Benziger were admitted to membership in the firm, their father, Nicholas, having retired. In 1964, Bernard C. Benziger, a member of the family's sixth generation, was president of Benziger Brothers, Inc., with headquarters in New York City. The publishing house also maintained branch stores in Cincinnati (1860), Chicago (1887), San Francisco (1929), and Boston (1937). In 1968, the company was acquired by Crowell Collier Macmillan, and its headquarters were moved to California.

Bibliography: K. J. BENZIGER, *Geschichte der Familie Benziger von Einsiedeln, Schweiz* (New York 1923).

[W. C. SMITH/EDS.]

BENZO OF ALBA

Bishop, Gregorian polemist; b. northern Italy, early 11th century; d. *c.* 1086–89. There is little certain knowledge about Benzo. He first appears at a Roman council (1059) where he signed himself as bishop of Alba. An extreme imperial partisan and bitter papal enemy, he vigorously supported Cadalus, the imperial antipope Honorius II, against Pope ALEXANDER II (1061). After Cadalus's deposition (May 1064), Benzo continued to attack the papacy in his writings until the PATARINES drove him from his see (1076). About 1086 he collected all his writings into a single volume, which he dedicated to Emperor HENRY IV under the title *Libri VII ad Heinricum IV.* At this point he disappears from history. His verse and prose prove Benzo well grounded in the classics and a skillful parodist.

See Also: INVESTITURE STRUGGLE.

Bibliography: A. FLICHE, *Catholicisme* 1:1456. A. HAUCK, *Kirchengeschichte Deutschlands*, 3:707 and *passim* (9th ed. Berlin-Leipzig 1958). M. MANITIUS, *Geschichte der lateinischen Literatur des Mittelalters* (Munich 1911–31) 3:454–457. H. K. MANN, *The Lives of the Popes in the Early Middle Ages from 590 to 1304* (London 1902–32) 6:242 and *passim*. C. MIRBT, in J. J. HERZOG and A. HAUCK, eds., *Realencyklopädie für protestantische Theologie* (3d ed. Leipzig 1896–1913) 2:605–606. K. PERTZ, *Monumenta Germaniae Historica: Scriptores* (Berlin 1826—) 11:591–597. T. SCHIEFFER, *Lexikon für Theologie und Kirche*, ed. J. HOFER and K. RAHNER (2d new ed. Freiburg 1957–65) 2:210–211.

[S. WILLIAMS]

Nicholas Benziger.

BEOWULF

The greatest surviving Old English poem, an epic that recounts two main events in the life of the legendary hero, Beowulf, with some digressions on apparently historical matters. In the first episode, Beowulf slays Grendel and Grendel's mother, demons who, in human form, are terrorizing the court of the Danish king; in the second, he kills a marauding dragon with the help of his kinsman Wiglaf, but is himself mortally wounded.

The poem exists in only one manuscript, the Cotton MS Vitellius A XV, 129a–198b, in the British Museum, London. This text dates from *c.* 1000, but scholars now generally date the poem's composition in the late 8th century. Some German critics (e.g., Ettmüller, Möller, Boer) in the 19th century insisted that it was the work of several authors. Further, such scholars held that it was substantially a pagan poem into which Christian interpolations had been introduced much later. Both these notions have been almost universally discounted. The author is, of course, anonymous. He was, however, familiar not only with the rich pagan Scandinavian and Germanic heroic legends but also, as F. Klaeber, R. W. Chambers, and C. W. Kennedy have shown (see bibliography), well instructed in the Christian virtues that permeate the poem. Its language is predominantly West Saxon with an admixture of other, particularly Anglian, elements. This combination of language and the poem's substantially Christian spirit would suggest that it was written either by a monk of West Mercia (known today as the West Midlands) or by a court poet.

Saga Elements. Much of the old Nordic tradition is unquestionably evident in the epic. The loyalty of thane to lord, the chief bond of early Germanic society, is prominent. Emphasis on gift giving, the lord's way of recognizing and rewarding the loyalty of his thane, is also important. The old element of fate or Wyrd that so permeated the old Nordic tales is still present but far less pervasively. The blood feuds that disrupted families and kingdoms in primitive northern society have a place as well, but it is significant that they are alluded to in the historical episodes or asides rather than made prominent in the main action of the poem. The character of Beowulf himself, with his fabulous handgrip, owes something to the bear-man motif that runs through many of the old Norse sagas, and, in general, a great deal of the physical detail of the story comes from the same source. The struggles with man-monsters, with water trolls in mysterious caves at the bottom of the sea, and with fire-breathing dragons all had a history in older Nordic legend, and practically all the details of the burial ceremonies for Beowulf are derived from pagan Nordic custom.

Distinctive Features. Despite these many similarities, *Beowulf* is remarkably and fundamentally different from the pagan sagas. In the first place, the character of Beowulf himself has undergone a substantial transformation. He is no longer the ruthless, self-centered pagan hero in pursuit merely of his own glory. He is eager for fame, as he frequently tells us, but performs all his exploits in a spirit of Christian humility and charity: he frequently acknowledges his dependence upon God for his prowess and in each episode dedicates his powers to help others.

Christian Allegory. Moreover, a deeper transformation has taken place. It intends to the whole substance and movement of the poem, to such an extent that it may be considered an allegory of the Christian story of salvation. In the story of Beowulf saving the kingdom of Hrothgar from the depradations of Grendel and his dam, and his own people from the ravages of the dragon, the Beowulf poet, it seems clear, was adapting the familiar legends of the North to allegorize for a Christian audience man's fall from the state of innocent happiness into the power of Satan and his absolute need of savior who came to him through the Incarnation. Sufficient clue for such an audience to identify Beowulf with the Savior would be the clear identification of Grendel and his dam in the first episodes with the powers of darkness or the forces to be overcome by the Savior, and, in the last episode, the parallel, which Klaeber has pointed out, between the circumstances that precede the death of Christ and Beowulf.

Relationship to the Harrowing of Hell. Particularly striking is the parallel between the second episode and Christ's harrowing of hell that had become a literary tradition before the time of the *Beowulf* poet. Beowulf descends into a mere to a burning cave, slays Grendel's dam, cuts off the head of the dead man-monster Grendel, and then ascends through the waters triumphantly bearing the magic sword and severed head. It was an Anglo-Saxon tradition (as Anglo-Saxon illuminated manuscripts reveal) to represent hell as a lake infested by man-monsters and serpents. Hence the *Beowulf* audience would readily have associated Beowulf's descent into the mere with Christ's descent into hell to signalize His triumph over Satan—a medieval tradition based on apocryphal Gospel of Nicodemus. The exorcism pronounced over the baptismal water in the Holy Saturday liturgy would also have lent significance to the symbolism of demon-infested waters as a symbol of hell.

It would seem that the *Beowulf* poet was writing in the spirit of Pope St. Gregory, who had cautioned St. Augustine of Canterbury not to make a clean sweep of the old, native Anglo-Saxon customs, myths ceremonies, and traditions but to adapt them to the new Christian message. It would seem further that the *Beowulf* poet was proceeding in manner exactly opposite to that of the authors of poems like *Andreas.* In that work an explicitly Christian subject matter is handled in the language and literary conventions of the old Norse sagas, whereas in *Beowulf* the pagan sagas are subtly reshaped and reorganized to bring forth the essential facts of the new story of salvation.

Bibliography: R. W. CHAMBERS, ed., *Beowulf: With the Finnsburg Fragment* (2d ed. New York 1932); ''Beowulf and the Heroic Age in England,'' *Man's Unconquerable Mind* (London 1952). F. KLAEBER, ed., *Beowulf and the Fight at Finnsburg* (Boston 1950). C. L. WRENN, ed., *Beowulf: With the Finnesburg Fragment* (London 1953). C. W. KENNEDY, tr., *Beowulf: The Oldest English Epic* (New York 1940). M. B. MCNAMEE, ''Beowulf: An Allegory of Salvation,'' *The Journal of English and Germanic Philology* 59 (1960) 190–207; ''Beowulf: Christian Hero,'' *Honor and the Epic Hero* (New York 1960). A. CABANISS, ''Beowulf and the Liturgy,'' *The Journal of English and Germanic Philology* 54 (1955) 195–201. J. R. R. TOLKIEN, ''Beowulf: The Monsters and Critics,'' *Proceedings of the British Academy* 22 (1936) 245–95. L. E. NICHOLSON, ed., *An Anthology of Beowulf Criticismm* (pa. Notre Dame, Ind. 1963).

[M. B. MCNAMEE]

BERAKHOT

The first tractate of the first order of the MISHNAH. The Mishnah contains the oral law transmitted together with the written Law at Mt. Sinai and passed down through the generations until Rabbi JUDAH HA-NASI compiled it into a set written text comprising six orders. The order Zeraim (Seeds) contains laws pertaining to the cultivation of the land and the produce of the soil. Its opening tractate, Berakhot (Blessings), specifies the benedictions for various foods and also discusses two sources of spiritual nourishment—the Shema [Hear (O Israel)], with its strong declaration of faith, and the Tephillah (Prayer), with its focal point in man's reliance on divine assistance.

The 64 folios (double pages) of the tractate are divided into nine chapters, each named after the opening words. The first three chapters deal with the Shema, consisting of the three passages of the Pentateuch (Dt 6.4–9; 11.13–21 and Nm 15.37–41) that are recited twice daily, morning and evening. Chapter one opens with the question: ''From what time may the Shema be read?'' and then designates the time for its recitation in the evening and the morning, and the proper manner of recitation.

Chapter two discusses the dedicated intention to fulfill a divine command. Valid and invalid recitations are listed, and reasons are given for the sequence in which the sections of the Shema are recited. Special occasions are enumerated when an individual may be excused from reciting the Shema.

Chapter three provides for further exemptions from the recitation of the Shema and also from the duty of reciting the Tephillah and putting on the PHYLACTERIES.

Chapters four and five deal with the Tephillah. The first of these prescribes the three periods during the day when the Tephillah has to be recited, as well as the time for the recitation of the Musaph (the additional prayer) on the Sabbath, New Moon, Festivals, and Holy days. Chapter five discusses preparation for prayer to ensure devoted concentration and to guard against error or deviation from the set prayer. It also outlines prayers for special purposes, e.g., for rain or for the termination of the Sabbath.

The last four chapters deal with blessings. Chapter six contains blessings for enjoyment of food, drink, and scent, since ''if one enjoys aught of this world without reciting a benediction over it, it is as if he robbed the Almighty'' (*Ber.* 35b). The question is raised whether one benediction may serve for a number of foods. The closing portion of the chapter begins the subject of grace after meals. Chapter seven outlines the procedure for grace when three or more persons are present and one leads in the recitation of grace. Chapter eight discusses laws and ceremonies regarding Kiddush (sanctification) and Havdalah (''distinction,'' a ceremony marking the end of the Sabbath), as well as additional laws regarding the saying of grace.

Chapter nine contains a variety of blessings giving praise and thanksgiving for unusual occasions, as on beholding a place where miracles have been wrought; on seeing lightning or mountains or hearing thunder; on entering and leaving a strange town. The last Mishnah of this chapter enjoins a benediction over evil tidings as well as over what are considered good tidings; the outcome of events is hidden from mortals by a veil, so that they are not in a position to pass an accurate final judgment. The closing words of advice are that the spiritual influence of faith should govern daily human relations.

HALAKAH (law) and HAGGADAH (related legends) are intertwined throughout. Haggadic material is abundant in Berakhot, proportionately more so than in any other of the 63 tractates of the Mishnah.

Bibliography: I. EPSTEIN, ed. and tr., *Hebrew-English Edition of the Babylonian Talmud,* 4 v. (London 1960). J. D. HERZOG, ed. and tr., *The Mishnah: Berakoth, Peah, Demai* (New York 1946). A. COHEN, tr., *The Babylonian Talmud: Tractate Berakot* (Cambridge, Eng., 1921). A. VIVIAN, ''Il trattato mishnico Berakhot e la sua concettualizzazione,'' in *Biblische und Judaistische Studien* (Frankfurt am Main 1990) 383–534. A. HOUTMAN, *Mishnah and Toseft: A Synoptic Comparison of the Tractates Berakhot and Shebiit; and, Appendix Volume: Synopsis of Tosefta and Mishna Berakhot and Shebiit* (Tübingen 1996).

[E. SUBAR/EDS.]

BERAN, JOSEF

Archbishop of Prague, Primate of Bohemia; b. Plzeu, Dec. 29, 1888; d. Rome, May 17, 1969. He studied in a classical gymnasium in Plzeu (1899–1907) and graduated with distinction in June of 1907. He was then sent to Rome to study theology (1907–11), was ordained on June 10, 1911, and graduated with the degree of doctor of sacred theology in 1912. After returning to his native country he was assigned to parish work (1913–15). He became the spiritual director in the Institute in Krč and from 1917 to 1929 was director of the Teachers Institute of St. Ann, conducted by the Congregation of School Sisters. His biography of the late Gabriel Schneider, a founder of the Congregation, was later accepted as his *thesis habilitations* at the Theological Faculty of Charles University in Prague. He began his academic career in 1928, in the department of pastoral theology. During this time his pastoral interests covered all fields of spiritual life—adviser, retreat master, organizer, and leader in all aspects of CATHOLIC ACTION.

Archbishop Kašpar made him rector of the major seminary in September of 1932. In 1936 he was made a papal prelate. On June 6, 1942, the German Gestapo took him to prison in Prague. He spent the rest of the war in concentration camps, first Teresin, then Dachau. Upon his return to Prague after the war, he continued to act as rector of the major seminary; and on Nov. 4, 1946 he was appointed archbishop of Prague to the great joy of the nation.

With the communist takeover of Czechoslovakia in February of 1948, persecution of the Catholic Church began. On June 19, 1949, Beran was put under house arrest in his palace in Prague. After resisting the government's pressure to resign as archbishop, he endured repeated transferrals from one place to another calculated to destroy every trace of his actual whereabouts. He was freed by the president's amnesty in October of 1963 and was transferred to the village of Mukařov and then to Radvanov near Tabor, where he remained until Feb. 17, 1965; at that time he was made cardinal by Pope Paul VI and went to Rome, where he was forced to remain in exile.

Beran, speaking at the fourth session of Vatican Council II, became a champion of the *Declaration on Religious Freedom.* On Sept. 20, 1965, he spoke of the principle of the independence of the Church and received a standing ovation. As cardinal he made a trip to the United States in 1966, where he received several honorary academic citations and was enthusiastically accepted by the hierarchy and the people. His headquarters during his exile was the Pontifical Nepomucene College in Rome, where he died and was buried in the crypt of St. Peter by the pope himself.

Bibliography: L. NEMEC, *Church and State in Czechoslovakia* (New York 1955); ''The Communist Ecclesiology during the Church-State Relationship in Czechoslovakia, 1945–1967,'' *Proceedings of the American Philosophical Society* 112, 4 (Aug. 1968) 245–276. D. O'GRADY ''A Meeting with Archbp. Beran,'' *U.S. Catholic* (Dec. 1965) 34–36. ''Cardinal Beran's 15-year Ordeal,'' *Herder Correspondence* 2, 8 (Aug. 1965) 260–261. F. ANDERSON, ed., *Council Daybook Vatican II, Session 4, Sept. 4, 1965, to Dec. 8, 1965* (Washington D.C. 1966) 35–36. *Velka Mse* (the Great Mass, Rome 1970).

[L. NEMEC]

BERARD OF CARBIO AND COMPANIONS, SS.

Franciscan protomartyrs; d. Morocco, Jan. 16, 1220. At the Franciscan General Chapter of 1219, FRANCIS OF ASSISI decided to send friars to the missions and six were chosen for Morocco: Vitalis, Berard, Peter, Adjutus, Accursio, and Odo. Vitalis, who became ill, remained in Aragon. The others went to Coimbra, then to Alenquer, and thence to Seville. To free himself from their proselytizing, the Moorish governor Aboul Ala banished them to Morocco into the charge of Pedro Fernandez, a Christian. In Marrakech, the missionaries stayed at the home of Dom Pedro, exiled brother of Alfonso II of Portugal. Berard, who alone knew Arabic, insisted on preaching. Sultan Aboidile (Abou Yacoub) in vain ordered the friars to leave the country; he then imprisoned them for 20 days without food. But as soon as they were free, they resumed their apostolate in the city. During an expedition led by Dom Pedro against bandits, Berard, who was serving as a chaplain for the prince, gained the good will of the prince's Moorish troops. Upon returning to the capital, Berard persisted in preaching, until the sultan himself encountered the friars on the road. During the interrogation—in which Prince Abou Said tried to save them—Odo drew attention by his fearless answers, and the sultan, exasperated, ordered their execution. Dom Pedro collected the relics of the martyrs in two silver reliquaries and, upon his return to Portugal, brought them to Ceuta, to Seville, and then to Coimbra, where they were deposited at Santa Cruz. The career of these martyrs and the presence of their relics in the church of the CANONS REGULAR of St. Augustine in Coimbra determined the Franciscan vocation of ANTHONY OF PADUA. The cult of Berard and his companions was approved by Sixtus IV on Aug. 4, 1481.

Feast: Jan. 16.

Bibliography: *Chronica XXIV Generalium Ordinis Minorum, Analecta Franciscana* 3 (1897) 579–596. JORDAN OF GIANO, *Chronica fratris Jordani,* ed. H. BOEHMER (Paris 1908) 7, n. 1. GILES OF ASSISI, *Dicta* (Quarracchi-Florence 1905). LÉON DE CLARY, *Lives of the Saints and Blessed of the Three Orders of St. Francis,* 4 v. (Taunton, Eng. 1885–87) 1:99–111. H. KOEHLER, *L'Église chrétienne du Maroc . . .* (Paris 1935). E. LONGPRÉ, *Catholicisme* 1:1457–58. *Bibliotheca Sanctorum* 2:1271–72.

[J. CAMBELL]

BERCHARIUS, ST.

B. Aquitaine; d. 685 or 696. Bercharius was educated perhaps at Reims and then entered the Benedictine Abbey of Luxueil, possibly during the abbacy of Waldebert (629–670). Nivard, bishop of Reims, asked his help for the foundation of Hautvillers, making him its first abbot. He built churches in honor of St. Peter and of the Virgin Mary and founded two monasteries in the forest of Der, one for women, Puellemontier, and one for men, the more famous Montier-en-Der, where he was buried. The *Vita* states that Bercharius died of wounds inflicted by a monk, Daguinus, whom he had been moved to correct. His cult began soon after his death and is well attested in the ninth and tenth centuries.

Feast: Oct. 16.

Bibliography: W. LEVISON, ''Die Merowingerdiplome für Montier-en-Der,'' *Neues Archiv der Gesellschaft für ältere deutsche Geschichtskunde* (Hanover 1876–1936) 33 (1908) 757. *Vita Bercharii,* J. MABILLON, *Acta sanctorum ordinis S. Benedicti* (Venice 1733–40) 2:797–826, late-tenth-century life by ADSO, Abbot of Montier-en-Der. *Vita Nivardi, Monumenta Germaniae Historica: Scriptores rerum Merovingicarum* 5:164–168, foundation of Hautvillers. M. MANITIUS, *Geschichte der lateinischen Literatur des Mittelalters* (Munich 1911–31) 2:432–442. E. DE MOREAU, *Dictionnaire d'histoire et de géographie ecclésiastiques,* ed. A. BAUDRILLART et al. (Paris 1912) 8:343–344. J. VAN HECKE, Preface to *Vita* in *Acta Sanctorum* Oct. 7.2: 986–1010. A. BUTLER, *The Lives of the Saints,* ed. H. THURSTON and D. ATTWATER (New York 1956) 4:128–129.

[V. I. J. FLINT]

BERCHMANS, JAN (JOHN), ST.

Scholastic of the Society of Jesus; b. Diest, Belgium, March 13, 1599; d. Rome, Aug. 13, 1621. He was the oldest of the five children of John Berchmans and Elizabeth van den Hove. He grew up in a tumultuous atmosphere caused by a religious war between the Catholic (southern) part and the Protestant (northern) part of the Netherlands. His piety was early directed to devotion to the Eucharist and to the Virgin Mary, so characteristic of the Counter Reformation. He was a student for three years at the public gymnasium at Diest. To continue his studies he worked as a servant in the household of Canon Froymont in Malines, where he enrolled at the ''Great School'' in 1612. When the Jesuits opened a college in July of 1615, Berchmans enrolled there to complete his course in rhetoric. As a very enthusiastic student, an excellent actor and orator, and an energetic member of the school, he had an unquestionable influence on his schoolmates.

The readings of the life of ALOYSIUS GONZAGA and the accounts of the apostolic works of the English Jesuit martyrs influenced Berchmans to decide on a vocation in the society. In September of 1616 he entered the novitiate at Malines, which was under the directorship of Father Antoine Sucquet. His spiritual doctrine was that sanctity consists less in unusual, dramatic actions than in the loving practice of fidelity to God in day-to-day living. This realistic appreciation of the value of ordinary things that one finds again and again in the grand tradition of the Flemish school—in all its mystical, aesthetic, and artistic forms—is also the distinctive mark of the sanctity of Berchmans. In Rome, where he went in 1619 to study philosophy, he requested a chaplaincy in the Catholic army, hoping to find martyrdom on the battlefield. He died, however, of a contagious disease. His last year was marked by trials and mystical graces. He was beatified by Pius IX on May 9, 1865 and canonized by LEO XIII, Jan. 15, 1888. His body lies in the church of St. Ignatius in Rome, and his heart is venerated at Louvain in the Jesuit church. The profession of faith in the Immaculate Conception of Mary, signed with his blood, is preserved in Brussels.

Feast: November 26.

Bibliography: V. CEPARI, *Vita di Giovanni Berchmans* (5th ed. Rome 1751). A. S. FOLEY, *A Modern Galahad, St. John Berchmans* (Milwaukee 1937, repr. Mobile 1973). A. SÉVERIN, *S. Jean Berchmans: Ses écrits* (Brussels 1931). A. PONCELET, ''Documents inédits sur Saint Jean Berchmans,'' *Analecta Bollandiana* 34–35 (Brussels 1915–16) 1–227. A. BUTLER, *The Lives of the Saints,* rev. ed. H. THURSTON and D. ATTWATER, 4:427–429 (New York 1956). K. SCHOETERS, *Jan Berchmans van Diest* (4th ed. Brussels 1962); ''War Johannes Berchmans Mystiker?'' *Zeitschrift für Aszese und Mystik* 13 (Würzburg 1938) 239–265. J. N. TYLENDA, *Jesuit Saints & Scholars* (Chicago 1998) 401–405.

[K. SCHOETERS]

BERDÎAEV, NIKOLAĬ ALEKSANDROVICH

Apocalyptic and existential-personalist philosopher; b. Kiev, March 6, 1874; d. Clamart, France, March 24, 1948. He was the second child of a military family dating to Louis VI of France. He entered Kiev university (1894) where he met L. Chestov and engaged in Marxist activities, was arrested, and finally exiled (1898) to Vologda. With S. Bulgakov he edited (1904) a social-religious periodical, *Novy Put'* (The New Way). After serving two years as professor of philosophy at Moscow, he was deported by the Leninists (1922) and established the Religious Philosophical Society in Berlin but transferred its activities (1924) to Paris; there, as leading Russian *emigré* spokesman and critic of communism, he edited the religious-philosophical review, *Put'* (1925–40). He also organized interconfessional meetings of Orthodox, Protestant, and Catholic figures, but he himself tended to the ''left'' of Orthodox positions. Cambridge awarded him an honorary doctorate in divinity (1947).

Berdîaev's mature philosophy, combining Alexandrine-Cappadocian GNOSTICISM, medieval EXEMPLARISM, Rineland MYSTICISM, German IDEALISM, and Russian religious thought, is designated ''eschatological metaphysics,'' a term that represents ''the maximum experience of human existence'' as revealed by the Christian promise of an ultimate transfiguration of creation. Discontent with the given world and hope for its renewal prompted Berdîaev to forswear logic for a prophetic and mystical language. He held that man's destiny is to create his personality as a unique and universal theandric image, despite the objectivizations of legalist ethics, culture, and society. Creativity is realized in ''existential time'' that ultimately prepares the human community (*Sobornost*) for the coming of God's Kingdom. As the Philo of his age, Berdîaev speaks a ''profoundly Christian'' language employing many Catholic elements, but he has been inaccurately described as a Manichaean and, possibly because of an anti-Thomistic bent, an opponent of Christian philosophy. *See* EXISTENTIALISM.

Bibliography: Works. *Dream and Reality: An Essay in Autobiography*, tr. K. LAMPERT (New York 1951). *The Divine and the Human*, tr. R. M. FRENCH (London 1949). *The Beginning and the End, id.* (London 1952). *The Destiny of Man*, tr. N. DUDDINGTON (New York 1960). Literature. B. SCHULTZE, *Lexikon für Theologie und Kirche*, 10 v. (2d, new ed. Freiburg 1957–65) 2:213. L. MÜLLER, *Die Religion in Geschichte und Gegenwart* 1:1041–42. D. A. LOWRIE, *Rebellious Prophet* (New York 1960). M. SPINKA, *Nicolas Berdyaev: Captive of Freedom* (Philadelphia 1950). E. PORRET, *Berdiaeff: Prophète des temps nouveaux* (Neuchâtel 1951).

[D. A. DRENNEN]

BERENGARIUS OF TOURS

Author of Eucharistic heresy; b. Tours, *c.* 1000; d. Saint-Cosmas Island, near Tours, 1088. His writings initiated the first clear-cut heresy in the history of Eucharistic theology; they gave occasion to the Berengarian controversy, in which a series of opposing monographs clarified and substantially developed the Eucharistic doctrine (*see* EUCHARISTIC CONTROVERSIES).

Life and Work. Berengarius studied under FULBERT at Chartres. He became *scholasticus* at St. Martin's school at Tours in 1031 and was appointed archdeacon of Angers in 1041. His Eucharistic teachings first came under ecclesiastical notice at a council held in Rome in 1050. There his doctrine was condemned, along with that of a 9th-century monk, RATRAMNUS OF CORBIE, though the council wrongly attributed the work of Ratramnus to JOHN SCOTUS ERIGENA. Further condemnations took place at Vercelli (1050), Paris (1051), Rome (1059), and again at Rome (1079), where Berengarius signed a formula in which the words *substantialiter converti* appear for the first time in an ecclesiastical document (*Dictionnaire de la Bible* 355). He retired from public life and died at peace with the Church. Berengarius seems to have been a chaste and upright man, charitable to the poor; but the evidence of his writings points to intellectual pride.

Direct knowledge of the teachings of Berengarius is derived from four sources: some early correspondence; extracts surviving from a lost *opusculum,* written shortly after the Roman Council of 1059 and cited by LANFRANC OF BEC in his own treatise, which is a reply to this lost *opusculum;* the lengthy *De sacra coena,* a polemic against Lanfranc; and finally a brief memorial of the events of 1078–79, written by Berengarius shortly after the Roman Council of 1079. Berengarius's major work, the *De sacra coena,* is an extremely rare work discovered in 1770 in a single extant MS. Considered entirely apart from the doctrine it presents, the *De sacra coena* is extremely lengthy and prolix, written in bad Latin without any semblance of order or consecutive development, lacking chapter headings and even paragraphs, and worst of all, made entirely tedious by the repetition of its themes.

Controversy. The three great works of anti-Berengarian controversy are the treatises of Lanfranc, GUITMUND OF AVERSA, and ALGER OF LIÈGE. Other writers contributed, but these three are traditionally cited. The controversy had its roots in the PASCHASIUS RADBERTUS-RATRAMNUS controversy of the 9th century. There is no doubt that Berengarius based his Eucharistic theology on that of Ratramnus, although he thought Ratramnus's work to be that of John Scotus, while the adversaries of Berengarius followed Paschasius Radbertus. This is not to say that the views of Berengarius would necessarily have been accepted by Ratramnus. However, it is generally held that Berengarius and Ratramnus can be reconciled in substance, if not on every point.

Berengarius approached the Eucharistic mystery as a rationalist and dialectician, not as a believer. He had only contempt for the common belief, which he called the opinion of the mob. He cited the Fathers where it suited him in support of his views, but he emphatically proclaimed the ''incomparable superiority'' of reason over traditional authority. He rejected scornfully (''council of vanities, a hub-bub'') the authority of the Church when it was brought to bear upon his teachings. Yet the ''reason'' upon which he built was an immature philosophical system, the dialectics of the prescholastic schools. Berengarius did not know metaphysics; yet his basic Eucharistic error was in the metaphysical order. He believed that the senses grasp not only the appearances of an object but also its essence, in a direct and immediate manner. Thus the distinction between substance and accident was lost on him, and he regarded as absurd a doctrine that held for a change of substance while the accidents remained.

Berengarius's inability to understand the traditional teaching of a Real Presence of the Body and Blood of Christ *in specie aliena* led him to adopt a crude and materialistic interpretation of the doctrine of substantial conversion. Finally, he criticized the realist formulas with arguments that amounted to mere logic-chopping and playing with words. ''If bread is called the Body of Christ,'' he said, ''then bread must remain.'' But Berengarius had to take account of the realistic language of the Fathers, and thus he built up a positive theory of the Eucharist as mere sign and symbol. He held that through the Consecration a conversion occurs, not of the Eucharistic elements themselves, but of the sentiment of the believer with respect to them. The elements remain what they had been before, but they become the Body and Blood of Christ in the contemplation of the recipient, and are endowed for him with the value of Christ's passion and death. Thus the conversion is purely in the moral order, and the Eucharistic activity begins and ends within the consciousness of the believer himself.

The opponents of Berengarius clarified and organized the revealed teaching and carried it to a point of development considerably in advance of the Fathers and postpatristic writers. Most important, they brought to an end the series of prescholastic discussions of the *veritas* and the *figura,* by saying that there is in this Sacrament both the reality and the symbol: the reality, because Christ's Body is actually present; the symbol, because He is present under the sign of bread and wine. Thus the Holy Eucharist is the true Body and Blood of Christ; but as a Sacrament, under the sacramental symbols, it is the sign of many things: of the Lord's Passion, of the union of the faithful with Christ, and of the unity of the Mystical Body, of the bond of love which should unite all who partake of the one spiritual bread.

Bibliography: ALGER, *De sacramentis corporis et sanguinis dominici, Patrologia Latina*, ed. J. P. MIGNE, 180:739–854 (Paris 1878–90). *Berengarii Turonensis de sacra coena adversus Lanfrancum liber posterior* (Berlin 1834), ed. W. H. BEEKENKAMP (The Hague 1941). M. CAPPUYNS, *Dictionnaire d'histoire et de géographie ecclésiastiques*, ed. A. BAUDRILLART et al., (Paris 1912–) 8:385–407. J. GEISELMANN, *Die Eucharistielehre der Vorscholastik* (Paderborn 1926). GUITMUND, *De corporis et sanguinis Christi veritate, Patrologia Latina*, ed. J. P. MIGNE, 149: 1427–94. R. HEURTEVENT, *Durand de Troarn et les origines de l'hérésie bérengarienne* (Paris 1912). LANFRANC, *De corpore et sanguine Domini, Patrologia Latina*, ed. J. P. MIGNE, 150:407–442. A. J. MACDONALD, *Berengar and the Reform of Sacramental Doctrine* (New York 1930). E. MARTÈNE and U. DURAND, *Thesaurus novus anecdotorum* (Paris 1717) 4:103–109. C. E. SHEEDY, *The Eucharistic Controversy of the Eleventh Century* (Washington 1947). F. VERNET, *Dictionnaire de théologie catholique*, ed. A. VACANT et al., (Paris 1903–50) 2.1:722–742.

[C. E. SHEEDY]

BERGIER, NICOLAS SYLVESTRE

Theologian, the best apologist the Church in France produced during the second half of the 18th century to oppose the RATIONALISM of VOLTAIRE, J. J. ROUSSEAU, P. H. D. HOLBACH, and their disciples; b. Darnay, Dec. 31, 1718; d. Versailles, April 9, 1790. From Besançon, he was called to Paris by Abp. Christophe de Beaumont as defender of the faith. His *Le Déisme réfuté par lui-même* (1765) is a serious attempt to expose the errors of Rousseau, particularly in his *Émile.* Indefatigably, often intemperately, Bergier reduced Rousseau's theology to its main tenets and denounced the contradictions in the profession of faith of the celebrated vicar. A modern theologian might use more finesse but would reach identical conclusions. In 1782 a second edition of Diderot's *Encyclopédie* appeared, entitled *Encyclopédie méthodique.* Bergier had agreed to contribute some 700 articles on theology, provided he was allowed to revise the 1,800 appearing in the original edition. Although criticized for lending his name to this rationalistic enterprise, he was nonetheless supported by his superiors, who saw the apologetic value of his contribution. These articles were published separately in his *Dictionnaire théologique* (3 v., 1788). He also wrote *Certitude des preuves du Christianisme* (1767), *Examen du matérialisme* (2 v., 1771), and *Traité de la vraie religion* (2 v., 1780). The apologetic nature of his works led him to emphasize the polemic aspect of theology—hence a certain haziness in his treatment of grace, the supernatural, and revelation, where at times he himself betrays the influence of rationalism. Yet this same influence led him to abandon the contemporary exegesis of the *compelle intrare* in favor of one completely acceptable to modern theologians.

See Also: ENCYCLOPEDISTS.

Bibliography: L. CROCKER, *An Age of Crisis: Man and World in Eighteenth-Century French Thought* (Baltimore 1959). E. DUBLANCHY, *Dictionnaire de théologie catholique*, ed. A. VACANT et al., (Paris 1903–50) 2.1:742–745. R. R. PALMER, *Catholics and Unbelievers in Eighteenth-Century France* (Princeton 1939).

[A. R. DESAUTELS]

BERGSON, HENRI LOUIS

Henri Louis Bergson.

French philosopher who overthrew the exaggerated scientism and mechanistic evolutionism of the 19th century and advanced a new theory of evolution acknowledging the spiritual dimension of man; b. Paris, Oct. 18, 1859; d. Paris, Jan. 4, 1941. Educated at the Lycée Condorcet and the École Normale Supérieure, where he distinguished himself in mathematics and physics, Bergson turned to philosophy, receiving the *agrégé* in 1881. After teaching at Angers and Clermont-Ferrand, he returned to Paris in 1888 to teach at the Lycée Henri Quatre and the École Normale Supérieure. At the Collège de France he held the chair of the history of philosophy from 1900 to 1921, attracting huge crowds to his lectures by the beauty and eloquence of his language and by the extraordinary appeal of his message. He became a member of the Académie Française in 1918, was elected president of the International Commission for Intellectual Cooperation after World War I, and received the Nobel prize for literature in 1927. Although born of Jewish parents, Bergson grew up without religion and began his philosophical career as an enthusiastic follower of Herbert SPENCER. However, his attempts to give a full and accurate account of reality led him to abandon Spencer's evolutionary theory, and the subsequent development of his thought brought him closer and closer to Catholicism. In his will he confessed his moral adhesion to the Catholic Church and revealed that he would have become a convert had he not felt obliged to remain with his Jewish brethren, then being persecuted under Hitler. Shortly before his death he arose from his sickbed to appear for the registration of Jews in Paris. A Catholic priest said the prayers at his funeral, as he had requested.

Philosophy. Although deeply influenced by EVOLUTIONISM and EMPIRICISM, Bergson rejected the narrow conception of man and of the world characteristic of scientific POSITIVISM, and sought to continue the metaphysicospiritualist tradition of MAINE DE BIRAN and Félix Ravaisson (1813–1900). His philosophy constitues a defense of spirit against MATERIALISM, intuition against RATIONALISM, freedom against DETERMINISM (both physical and biological), creativity against MECHANISM, and philosophy against SCIENTISM. Setting out from the "intuition of duration," which is the dominant idea in his philosophy, Bergson offered a renovated empiricism and a new and profoundly original doctrine of evolution.

In a thoroughgoing critique of science Bergson showed why, in his opinion, science does not and cannot give a true picture of life or of reality as a whole. Science is the product of intelligence, which evolved solely to assure man's physical survival and to make possible his dominion over nature. Intelligence views all reality as solid, timeless, and spatial. Since its function is the manipulation of matter for practical purposes, it seeks exact formulas for things and expresses them in ready-made concepts that serve as substitutes for the real. A mechanistic explanation of the universe results. All reality is described as static, homogeneous, discontinuous, and predictable; nothing vital, dynamic, novel, or unforeseeable is admitted. The very structure of intelligence renders it incapable of comprehending LIFE, BECOMING, SPIRIT, and FREEDOM. The refusal to admit the existence of GOD, the human SOUL, or FREE WILL is the consequence of recognizing as real only what can be grasped by intelligence.

Although Bergson held that intelligence is man's natural mode of knowing, he believed that the human mind is also capable of INTUITION—a direct contact or coincidence with things. To think intuitively is to think in duration, thereby experiencing the inner dynamism of being. Bergson regarded intuition as the kind of knowledge proper to philosophy, and attributed the failures of most philosophers to their having ignored intuition and based their metaphysics on abstraction, generalization, and reasoning. The true philosophy dispenses with all ready-made concepts in order to achieve an inner view of being. To communicate his intuition the philosopher must invent new words and employ those images best suited to suggest the inexpressible. According to Bergson, philosophy must be both empirical and intuitive. Although he rejected the prevailing empiricism, it was not because it placed too high a value on EXPERIENCE. Bergson believed that all philosophical problems must be solved according to the experimental method, since it is only experience that can give one certitude. An integral empiricism, however, must admit not only the knowledge of matter, but also all that man knows through INTROSPECTION all the vague suggestions of CONSCIOUSNESS, all that is revealed in the intuition of duration.

To start with the intellect's view of reality meant for Bergson to attempt a reconstruction of life and movement out of concepts appropriate only to inert matter. He sought to reverse the order and to start with life and movement grasped in intuition. Life (or consciousness) is then seen to be the primordial reality, and matter but its degradation or descending motion. From this fresh perspective reality appears to be ever moving and growing, a ceaseless flux. It is essentially dynamic, qualitative, creative, and unpredictable. To know existing things as they really are is to grasp them intuitively, that is, *sub specie durationis.* The implications of this approach to reality so impressed William JAMES that he hailed it as a new Copernican revolution comparable in its significance for philosophy to that of G. BERKELEY or I. KANT.

Principal Works. Bergson's leading ideas are encompassed in four principal works. In *Time and Free Will* he showed that free will is the most evident of facts and that its denial follows upon the confusion of succession with simultaneity, duration with intensity, and quality with quantity. In *Matter and Memory* he proved that spirit as well as matter exists. By demonstrating that consciousness is not identical with cerebral activity, he paved the way for a proof of the survival of the soul after death. In *Creative Evolution,* his most famous work, he showed that the mechanistic interpretation of evolution is not justified by the facts. Viewing the data of evolution in the light of his intuition of duration, he described the evolutionary process as the forward thrust of a great spiritual force, the life impulse (*élan vital*), rushing through time, insinuating itself into matter, and producing the various living forms culminating in man. Its movement is not predetermined but creative, ever generating novel and unpredictable forms. *The Two Sources of Morality and Religion* represents the full flowering of Bergson's thought. Morality and religion are traced back to their double source in the evolutionary process. Bergson distinguished two separate moralities and religions—the open and closed moralities, the static and dynamic religions. Closed morality pertains to social cohesion. It is static and rooted in social pressure, the morality of a group enclosed upon itself. It represents a halt in the evolutionary process. Open morality transcends the group to unite all mankind in a common brotherhood. It is progressive and creative, a forward thrust of the *élan vital.* Whereas closed morality and static religion originate in the instinct for survival, open morality and dynamic religion are inspired by the moral heroes, saints and mystics, those superior representatives of the human race who, like a new species, foreshadow the future condition of man. They draw man upward to a higher spiritual level by their vision of human destiny and of God, the source of all love. It is in the experience of the mystics that Bergson found the most convincing evidence for the existence of God.

Influence and Critique. Bergson's manner of philosophizing—his repugnance for definition and for a technical vocabulary and his method of attacking each problem separately—did not lend itself to the formation of a Bergsonian school. Yet his influence on 20th-century thought has been profound. Among the philosophers whose works reflect a strong Bergsonism are Édouard LE ROY, Maurice BLONDEL, Max SCHELER, and Maurice Pradines. Many Catholic scholars, notably Jacques Maritain, Étienne Gilson, and Gabriel Marcel, though voicing disagreement on certain points of doctrine, have acknowledged with gratitude his great inspiration. Bergson's influence is also discernible in the thought of numerous scientists, including Alexis CARREL, Pierre LECOMTE DU NOÜY, and Pierre TEILHARD DE CHARDIN; in many literary works, including those of Marcel PROUST and Charles PÉGUY; and in some schools of painting and music. From the start his books gained unprecedented fame. Appealing to a wide reading public, they were translated into many languages and have been reprinted again and again.

Acclaimed by many of his contemporaries as the long-awaited liberator from the tyranny of materialism, mechanism, and determinism, Bergson was criticized by some for stopping short of the Christian conception of God, creation, the human soul, and free choice. From the viewpoint of Christian doctrine, Bergson's philosophy remains at best—and in spite of his intentions perhaps—ambiguous and incomplete. For the primacy of BEING as a reality accessible to intellect, he substituted the primacy of becoming as a reality accessible only to intuition. His depreciation of reason necessitated the denial that the existence of God can be rationally demonstrated. Man's approach to God can be only through the intuitive experience of the mystic, he said. God is described as Love and Creative Energy; but since the relationship between Creative Energy and the *élan vital* is never clearly defined, the distinction between God and creatures remains blurred. The depreciation of rational knowledge also led Bergson to base morality on the infrarational faculty of instinct and the suprarational faculty of intuition. He allowed to reason no essential rôle in moral obligation; its function is merely to formulate and coordinate moral rules and to assure their logical consistency.

Furthermore, having identified being with becoming, Bergson was forced to deny the substantiality of the soul and to define soul as a duration or participation in the *élan vital.* While upholding the distinction between soul and body, he was unable to avoid a dualistic position in fixing their mutual relationship. A champion of free will, Bergson rejected all forms of determinism; yet he regarded freedom not as the rational determination of a human act but as the spontaneous bursting forth of vital energy from the depths of the self, a creative but nonrational act expressive of the total personality. To the Catholic philosopher or theologian such points of criticism, together with a misunderstanding of the supernatural character of Christian mysticism, represent important deficiencies in Bergson's thought. Yet no evaluation of his philosophy that is limited to pointing out its metaphysical inadequacies will render it full justice. It must also be seen as the sincere and arduous endeavor of a great soul to discover the truth, a spiritual itinerary from materialistic mechanism to the God known and loved by the Christian mystics.

See Also: TIME; LIFE PHILOSOPHIES.

Bibliography: Works. *Oeuvres,* ed. H. GOUHIER and A. ROBINET (Paris 1959), critical ed. of Bergson's major works; *Time and Free Will* (*Essais sur les Données Immédiates de la Conscience* 1889) tr. F. L. POGSON (New York 1910; repr. 1950); *Matter and Memory* (*Matière et Mémoire* 1896), tr. N. M. PAUL and W. S. PALMER (New York 1911); *Creative Evolution* (*L'Évolution créatrice* 1907) tr. A. MITCHELL (New York 1911); *Mind-Energy: Lectures and Essays* (*L'Énergie Spirituelle* 1920), tr. H. W. CARR (New York 1920); *The Two Sources of Morality and Religion* (*Les Deux Sources de la morale et de la religion,* Paris 1932), tr. R. A. AUDRA and C. BRERETON (New York 1935); *The Creative Mind* (*La Pensée et le Mouvant* 1934), tr. M. L. ANDISON (New York 1946), collected essays. Studies. I. W. ALEXANDER, *Bergson: Philosopher of Reflection* (New York 1957). J. CHEVALIER, *Henri Bergson,* tr. L. A. CLARE (New York 1928). É. LE ROY, *The New Philosophy of Henri Bergson,* tr. V. BENSON (New York 1913). L. ADOLPHE, *La Philosophe religieuse de Bergson* (Paris 1946). L. HUSSON, *L'Intellectualisme de Bergson* (Paris 1947). R. M. MOSSÉBASTIDE, *Bergson éducateur* (Thèse; Paris 1955), contains 90 pages of bibliog. M. T. L. PENIDO, *La Méthode intuitive de M. Bergson* (Paris 1918). B. A. SCHARFSTEIN, *Roots of Bergson's Philosophy* (New York 1943). For evaluation of Bergson's thought from the Catholic viewpoint, see esp. J. MARITAIN, *Bergsonian Philosophy and Thomism,* tr. M. L. and J. G. ANDISON (New York 1955) and É. H. GILSON, *The Philosopher and Theology,* tr. C. GILSON (New York 1962).

[I. J. GALLAGHER]

BERINGTON, CHARLES

Vicar apostolic of the English Midland district (1795–98) and controversialist; b. Stock Hall, Essex, 1748; d. Longbirch, Staffordshire, June 8, 1798. He was the third son of Thomas Berington of Moat Hall, Salop, and Anne Bates, heiress of Stock Hall, Essex. Educated at Douay College from 1761 to 1765 and St. Gregory's College, Paris, from 1765 to 1776, he was ordained in 1775, and won his doctorate at the Sorbonne the following year. He worked in the English mission at Ingatestone, Essex, and later became the tutor to the son and heir of Peter Giffard of Chillington, Staffordshire. On

Aug. 1, 1786 he was consecrated titular bishop of Hierocaesarea at Longbirch, and appointed coadjutor to Bp. Thomas Talbot, vicar apostolic of the Midland district. At Talbot's death, he succeeded to the vicariate. His membership in the ''Gallican'' Catholic Committee (founded in 1783), whose sympathies were nationalistic and anti-papal, placed him strongly at variance with the other vicars apostolic and with the policy of the Holy See toward England. This brought him the dislike of most of the clergy, though personally he was amiable, learned, and kindly. On his accession to the vicariate, Rome refused him faculties unless he recanted his views. After three years of difficult negotiations, he gave way under protest, but he died as the result of an accident before his faculties could reach him.

Bibliography: W. M. BRADY, *The Episcopal Succession in England, Scotland, and Ireland, A.D. 1400 to 1875,* 3 v. (Rome 1876–77) v. 3 *passim.* C. BUTLER, *Historical Memoirs Respecting the English, Irish and Scottish Catholics from the Reformation to the Present Time,* 4 v. (London 1819–21) v. 4. *The Dictionary of National Biography from the Earliest Times to 1900* (London 1885–1900) 2:337. B. N. WARD, *The Dawn of Catholic Revival in England, 1781–1803,* 2 v. (London 1909) 1:123, 2:131.

[B. WHELAN]

BERKELEY, GEORGE

Anglican bishop of Cloyne, divine, and philosopher; b. Kilcrene, near Kilkenny, Ireland, March 12, 1685; d. Oxford, Jan. 14, 1753.

Life. Berkeley was educated at Kilkenny College and at Trinity College, Dublin, which he entered as a ''pensioner'' in 1700. He studied mathematics, languages (Latin, Greek, French, and Hebrew), and philosophy, taking his B.A. degree in 1704. In 1707 he was elected to a junior fellowship and graduated as M.A. Earlier in the same year he published (anonymously) two short works, *Arithmetica* and *Miscellanea Mathematica.* In 1709 he was ordained deacon, and in 1710, a priest of the Anglican Church. From 1709 to 1713 he was a tutor at the College and held various academic posts, including that of junior Greek lecturer.

It was during these early years at Trinity that Berkeley's philosophy was born and grew rapidly to its final shape. Between 1704 and 1707 he read J. Locke, S. Clarke, I. Newton, and N. Malebranche, and sought a remedy against skepticism, materialism, atheism, and the waning influence of religion. Between 1707 and 1708 he made a collection of private notes—jottings of ideas as they occurred to him. There one can follow the progress of his discovery of the principle, *esse est percipi et percipere*, with which he launched his attack on a hidden, nonsensible substance existing ''absolutely,'' or independently of mind. Out of these notes Berkeley prepared his two first philosophical works: *An Essay towards a New Theory of Vision* (Dublin 1709), and *The Principles of Human Knowledge* (Dublin 1710). In 1713 he went to London, where in 1714 he published the *Three Dialogues between Hylas and Philonous.*

During the next eight years Berkeley traveled in France and Italy. In 1720 he wrote a short treatise *De motu* on his immaterialism and the principles of mechanics for the Royal Academy of Sciences at Paris, which offered a prize for an essay on the causes of motion. Berkeley did not receive the prize, but he published his treatise in London in 1721. He returned to Dublin in the same year and resumed his work as a tutor at Trinity. He had been co-opted senior fellow in his absence in 1717, took his B.D. and D.D. in 1721, and was thereupon appointed divinity lecturer and preacher. In 1724 he was appointed dean of Derry, and resigned his fellowship at Trinity.

Berkeley's thoughts then turned to the foundation of a college in Bermuda for the training of clergy for missionary work in America. He obtained a charter for the foundation of St. Paul's College and set sail for Rhode Island in 1728, settling at Newport early in the following year. As he realized that his scheme would fail, he devoted several months of enforced leisure to writing *Alciphron, or the Minute Philosopher,* which he published in London in 1732 on his return. Because he designed it as a vindication of the Christian revelation against current disbelief rather than as a purely philosophical work, he refrained from making use of his principle of immaterialism.

In 1734 Berkeley was appointed bishop of Cloyne and wrote *The Analyst, or Discourse addressed to an Infidel Mathematician,* in which he attacked Newton's theory of fluxions. Two years later he replied to an attack on this work by a Dr. Jurin in *A Defence of Free-Thinking in Mathematics.* Berkeley then devoted much time to spreading his ideas on the virtues of tar water in curing diseases. He set them forth, with his views on metaphysics and theology, in *Siris* (London 1744), in its day the most celebrated of all his works. Its publication provoked some controversy about the medicinal properties of tar water, which Berkeley defended with energy to the end. His last work, *Farther Thoughts on Tar-Water,* formed the opening paper of his Miscellany, published in 1752.

In 1752 Berkeley left Ireland to settle with his family in Oxford, where he died in his house in Holywell Street in January of 1753. He was buried in the chapel of Christ Church, the Anglican cathedral of Oxford.

Teaching. Berkeley has suffered both from the seemingly incurable habit of historians of seeing him as little more than one of the leading empiricists, linking Locke with Hume, and from the misjudgment of Kant, who regarded him as a subjective idealist. He was unquestionably an empiricist of a kind; he was certainly not a thoroughgoing subjective idealist.

To appreciate his work as a philosopher one must understand his intentions, and to understand his intentions one must, as Ardley has shown (10–11) regard him primarily as ''one of the company of Anglican divines and reformers'' that includes such men as Stillingfleet and Butler, and recognize that ''his excursion into philosophy was ancillary to the proper business of his calling.'' His constant aim in all his work was to revivify Christian THEISM, to meet the challenge of the contemporary rationalist DEISM, and to check the rising tide of the new empirical philosophy toward skepticism. At the roots of all the evils he fought, Berkeley saw the currently accepted philosophy of physics—a philosophy that had shaped the metaphysics of Descartes and the EMPIRICISM of Locke. He set himself the task of making a critique of the metaphysical assumptions of the new philosophy of ideas. The ''new physics'' assumed, for the purpose of safeguarding its own method of work, that the universe is a vast mechanical system of purely extended particles that move without purpose in space and time; and that both the particles and their movements are purely quantitative, so that the physical order of things can be expressed adequately by mathematical laws. Berkeley realized that if this postulate of the total mathematicization of nature came to be accepted as more than a rule of method for correlating mathematical abstractions, and as constituting a metaphysics of nature, the world of ordinary human experience would have to be set aside. This would become one vast illusion concealing from man's mind an unknowable, but supposedly real, world of matter or hidden substances. Such a universe could never be known as the work of God. Berkeley claimed to show that the world of the ''new physics'' is not a real, existent world of things but an artificial construction fabricated out of unreal abstractions, and that the world of common sense, the world of particular things rich in their individual qualities, is the one and only real world that man ought to designate when talking of material things.

Abstraction. The capital error of the 17th-century philosophers lay in their unwarrantable assumption that unthinking, inert matter exists on its own, ''absolutely,'' or independently of mind. They fell into this error because they thought in a world of bogus abstractions, which their fanciful theories of abstraction led them to regard as the sole realities. Berkeley rejected the theory expounded by Locke—that the mind can form a positive,

George Berkeley.

universal idea of the nature of a thing, or of a triangle, for example, which is no particular triangle but which enables man to think of all particular triangles. The abstract nature of a sensory object is not anything, and what is not cannot help one think of concrete particulars. But though he rejected abstract universal ideas, Berkeley realized that man cannot think without general ideas, for generality is involved in meaning. Man has, he held, general ideas that are not abstract. Such ideas are formed, not by abstracting or separating, but by the mind's considering a particular aspect or ''idea'' of a thing and relating it to like particular aspects of other things. Man can, he argued, fix the attention on one aspect of a thing, e.g., its squareness, and then use this ''idea'' that he sensibly perceives in one object as the sign or symbol of all other square shapes in other objects. Generality is, in other words, not a denial of the singularity of things, but a purely functional relation of a particular idea—the result of regarding it as the representative sign of other like ideas.

Esse est percipi et percipere. Matter, pure extension, and passive substances are unreal abstractions. What, then, is a material thing? It is a purely sensible thing. A tree, for example, is just what it is perceived to be; it is that, all that (not merely its primary mathematical qualities), and nothing other than that (not something concealed by its qualities and serving as their support). It is the individual thing a person perceives sensibly to be of a certain size, mass, solidity, shape, volume, of various colors, degrees of hardness, softness, etc. The real apple is the thing one eats, tastes, handles, and smells, and not some insensible substrate of these qualities. As a natural thing is wholly sensible, a material substance is nothing but the assemblage of its sensible properties. But since sensible qualities can exist only in being perceived, or dependently on mind, it follows that the whole being of a sensible thing consists in its being perceived. The primary qualities of extension and motion, being inseparable from the secondary qualities, must be as mind-dependent as the secondary. Sensible qualities need a ''support''; however, this must be found not in inert, passive substances (which could neither support anything nor produce any impressions on one's senses), but in active mind, the very nature of which is to perceive sensible qualities and thereby maintain them in existence. Berkeley did not say that material things are modes of mind, as an idealist would say; he denied this categorically: ''These qualities are in the mind only as they are perceived by it, not by way of *mode,* or *attribute,* but only by way of *idea*' (*Principles* 1.49; also 34).

Matter and Mind. Berkeley's universe comprises the world of sensible things that are neither substances nor material but ''ideas of sense,'' and the world of men who are finite spirits or minds, active substances that think, will, and perceive, and thereby exist. God is infinite spirit or mind, whose creative activity of mind and will set before men's minds the world of sensible things in law and order.

Critique. Berkeley's most enduring contribution to philosophy lies in a field overlooked by historians, namely, his philosophy of science. His critique of the philosophy of the new mathematico-physics, which he likened to a grammar of nature (*Principles* 1.108), anticipated many of the findings of P. DUHEM and A. N. WHITEHEAD. Berkeley's metaphysics has often been presented and criticized out of its historical setting, and the justifiable criticisms that have been made against his principle of immaterialism and his theory of nonabstract, general ideas have made all too familiar the weaker aspects of his system. Furthermore, the conventional associations of Berkeley with Locke and Hume, as well as with subjective IDEALISM, have hidden from view the import of Berkeley's constructive efforts to remedy the very ills empiricism and idealism brought about. He saw the need to restore man to his central place in the universe; to restore man's esteem for the order of nature, which he considered to have been dismissed as illusory by Descartes and Locke; and to display the universe in its dependence on God, making known His being and providence. In setting man at the heart of his metaphysics, and in highlighting the particularity of existent things, Berkeley is closer in his empiricism to the Christian existentialist philosophers of the 1960s than to the classical empiricists of his day. His pioneering efforts to harmonize the work of the sciences, philosophy, and theology should have won for him a place among the foremost divines and Christian humanists of the 18th century.

Bibliography: *The Works of George Berkeley, Bishop of Cloyne,* ed. A. A. LUCE and T. E. JESSOP, 9 v. (London 1948–57). A. A. LUCE, *The Life of George Berkeley, Bishop of Cloyne* (London 1949); *Berkeley's Immaterialism* (London 1945); *Berkeley and Malebranche* (London 1934). G. W. R. ARDLEY, *Berkeley's Philosophy of Nature* (Auckland 1962). J. WILD, *George Berkeley: A Study of His Life and Philosophy* (Cambridge, Mass. 1936). A. L. LEROY, *George Berkeley* (Paris 1959), N. BALADI, *La Pensée réligieuse de Berkeley et l'unité de sa philosophie* (Cairo 1945). E. A. SILLEM, *George Berkeley and the Proofs for the Existence of God* (New York 1957). C. D. BROAD, *Berkeley's Argument about Material Substance* (London 1942). *British Journal for the Philosophy of Science* 4 (1953–54) 13–87, George Berkeley bicentenary issue. *Revue Internationale de Philosophie* 7 (1953) 3–156, George Berkeley issue. G. STAMMLER, *Berkeleys Philosophie der mathematik* (Berlin 1921).

[E. A. SILLEM]

BERLIÈRE, URSMER

BENEDICTINE medievalist and editor; b. Gosselies, Hainaut, Belgium, Sept. 3, 1861; d. Maredsous Abbey, Aug. 27, 1932. Berlière, who was baptized Alfred, was educated by the Jesuits at Charleroi and entered the minor seminary at Tournai. He was professed a Benedictine in 1881 at the Abbey of MAREDSOUS, where he later (1885–92) taught after two years of study at SECKAU (1883–85). He was ordained in 1886. From 1894 to 1912 he directed the *Revue bénédictine.* He wrote the monumental *Monasticon belge* (1890–1929), which treated the history of monasticism in the Low Countries; a perceptive history, *L'Ordre monastique des origines au XII*e *siècle* (Maredsous 1912); and also *L'Ascèse bénédictine des origines à la fin du XII*e *siècle* (Paris 1927). Berlière held the posts of president of the Royal Historical Commission of Belgium and curator of the Royal Belgian Library (1912–14). He organized (1902) the Institut Historique Belge de Rome and launched the collection (1906) of Belgian-Vatican correspondence, *Analecta vaticano-belgica.* In 1930 he was named consultor for the historical section of the Congregation of Rites.

Bibliography: J. CUVELIER, ''Dom U. B.,'' *Annuaire de l'Académie Royale de Belgique* 105 (1939) 111–171, with Berlière's bibliog. R. GAZEAU, *Catholicisme* 1:1470–71. H. DE MOREAU, ''Dom U. B.,'' *Studien und Mitteilungen zur Geschichte des Benediktinerordens und seiner Zweige* 50 (1932) 31–32. P. H. PIRENNE et al., *L'Hommage à dom U. B.* (Brussels 1931).

[B. F. SCHERER]

BERLIOZ, LOUIS HECTOR

Romanticist composer whose works and ideas were decisive in the evolution of modern music; b. La Côte Saint-André (near Grenoble), France, Dec. 11, 1803; d. Paris, March 8, 1869. His father was a dedicated physician with Voltairian ideas and, like his wife, of high social rank in the region. The child's musical gifts were soon evident, and long before his formal training he was setting songs from which he later rescued some of his most haunting melodies. His nonmusical studies were supervised by his father, who hoped he would become a doctor. To that end Berlioz went to Paris in 1821 to master the basic sciences. When he began studying with J. F. LeSueur (Napoleon's favorite composer) with a view to enrolling at the Paris Conservatory, Hector's allowance was cut off, and he survived by doing hackwork for music publishers and by singing in comic-opera choruses. He studied at the conservatory and, more importantly, at the Opera (then still dominated by the GLUCK and SPONTINI repertory), but his teachers were slow to grasp his genius. Four times he was denied the Prix de Rome; when the prize was finally his, on the eve of the 1830 revolution, he had already performed his first masterpiece, *Symphonie Fantastique.*

Louis Hector Berlioz. (Archive Photos)

In 1833 began what he called his "Thirty Years' War against the pundits, the routineers, and the tone-deaf." This crusade consisted of (1) "campaigns" of conducting in Europe's great cities, which set a new standard of orchestral musicianship; (2) tireless exposition, through brilliant writings in journals of opinion, of his beliefs on the current music-drama question—in essence, that music should be inherently expressive, not the handmaiden of text or program, but relying for dramatic effect on deployment of musical means (melody, rhythm, harmony, orchestration) within musical forms; and (3) composition of large- and small-scale works, which gave form to his ideals. Chief among these are the early dramatic symphonies: *Fantastique* (1830), *Harold in Italy* (1834), *Romeo and Juliet* (1839), and *Symphonie Funèbre et Triomphale* (1840); the dramas *per musica: Benvenuto Cellini* (1838), *Damnation of Faust* (1846), *The Trojans* (1858), *Beatrice and Benedict* (1862); and the religious "dramas": *Requiem* (1837), *Te Deum* (1852), and *L'Enfance du Christ* (1854).

Although never a church composer, Berlioz was repeatedly drawn to religious subjects, and his intimate knowledge of the religious experience is reflected in his contemplative, ecstatic passages. His First Communion, which took place at an Ursuline convent to the accompaniment of the nuns' choir, became for him an ineffaceable experience of the ancient Catholic music tradition. Later, when he could no longer accept the Church's dogma, he never lost his aesthetic sympathy and respect for its forms or his humility before its wisdom. All his works, sacred and secular, are characterized by dazzling variety in atmosphere, structure, and orchestral texture. His method of development and his harmonic progressions bewildered most of his contemporaries, and it is only since World War II that a more perceptive scholarly outlook has combined with the advantage of long-playing recordings to set Berlioz in proper perspective; the figure of an extraordinary artist and theorist is emerging.

Bibliography: L. H. BERLIOZ, *Memoirs,* ed. E. NEWMAN, tr. R. and E. HOLMES (rev. ed. New York 1935); *New Letters,* ed. and tr. J. BARZUN (New York 1954); *Grand traité d'instrumentation et d'orchestration* (Paris 1844). R. ROLLAND, *Musicians of Today,* tr. M. BLAIKLOCK (New York 1915). T. S. WOTTON, *Hector Berlioz* (London 1935). W. J. TURNER, *Berlioz: The Man and His Work* (London 1934). B. VAN DIEREN, in *Down among the Dead Men* (New York 1935). J. BARZUN, *Berlioz and the Romantic Century,* 2 v. (Boston 1950); *Berlioz and His Century* (New York 1956), contains complete list of literary pubs. A complete edition of his works is in preparation. E. BAECK and H. BAECK-SCHILDERS, "Antoine Bessems en het manuscript van Hector Berlioz' *Messe Solennelle,*" *Musica Antiqua,* 10 (1993) 77–80; "The Bessems Brothers and the Autograph of Berlioz's *Messe Solennelle,*" *Revue Belge de Musicologie,* 53 (1999) 151–157. P. BLOOM, "Episodes in the Livelihood of an Artist: Berlioz's Contacts and Contràcts with Publishers," *Journal of Musicological Research,* 15 (1995) 219–273. M. E. BONDS, "*Sinfonia anti-eroica:* Berlioz's *Harold en Italie* and the Anxiety of Beethoven's Influence," *Journal of Musicology,* 10

(1992) 417–463. J. A. BOWEN, ''Mendelssohn, Berlioz, and Wagner as Conductors: The Origins of the Ideal of 'Fidelity to the Composer,''' *Performance Practice Review,* 6 (1993) 81–85. G. BURGESS, ''Berlioz und die Oboe (Teil 1),'' *Tibia: Magazin für Holzbläser,* 21 (1996) 81–93; ''Berlioz und die Oboe (Teil 2),'' *Tibia: Magazin für Holzbläser,* 21 (1996) 161–167. L. GOLDBERG, ''Aspects of Dramatic and Musical Unity in Berlioz's *Les Troyens,*'' *Journal of Musicological Research,* 13 (1993) 99–112. J. LANGFORD, ''The Byronic Berlioz: *Harold en Italie* and Beyond,'' *Journal of Musicological Research,* 16 (1997) 199–221. J. RUSHTON, ''The Overture to *Les troyens,*'' *Music Analysis,* 4 (1985) 119–144; ''(Louis-) Hector Berlioz,'' in *International Dictionary of Opera,* ed. C. S. LARUE, 2 v. (Detroit 1993) 125–129. T. SCHACHER, ''Geistliche Musik als 'drame sacré': Über den Einfluß Le Sueurs auf Berlioz' kirchenmusikalisches Werk,'' *Hamburger Jahrbuch für Musikwissenschaft,* 8 (1985) 203–221. A. P. SIMCO, ''Performing the Timpani Parts to *Symphonie Fantastique,*'' *Percussive Notes: The Journal of the Percussive Arts Society,* 36/2 (1998) 62–65.

[J. BARZUN]

BERMUDEZ, JOÃO

Pseudo-patriarch of Ethiopia, adventurer; d. S. Sabastião de Pedreira, Lisbon, 1570. Bermudez was a barber or surgeon in the Portuguese embassy, under Rodrigo de Lima, from Goa to the Ethiopian port of Massawa in 1520. He was in the suite of the negus of Ethiopia, David Lebna Dengel, for five years. When the Portuguese left the country in 1527, he remained behind. In 1535 when the negus was attacked by Muslims of Somalia and Galla under Ahmed Granye, Bermudez was sent to Portugal for help. In Rome in 1538–39, he claimed that he had been ordained as his successor by the schismatic Ethiopian patriarch, Marcos. When Bermudez returned to Ethiopia in 1541 with a Portuguese force under Cristovão, the son of Vasco da Gama, he claimed he had been confirmed by the pope. Although suspect in Rome and in Ethiopia, Bermudez succeeded in occupying the Ethiopian patriarchate until 1555, when he was expelled by Negus Galawdewos and replaced by a Jesuit from Portugal. He was back in Portugal in 1559 and later (Lisbon 1565) published an account of his embassy to Portugal.

Bibliography: E. CERULLI, *Lexikon für Theologie und Kirche,* ed. J. HOFER and K. RAHNER (2d new ed. Freiburg 1957–65) 2:233–234. S. EURINGER, ''Der Pseudopatriarch Johannes Bermudes,'' *Theologie und Glaube* 17 (1925) 226–256. I. ORTIZ DE URBINA, *Dictionnaire d'histoire et de géographie ecclésiastiques,* ed. A. BAUDRILLART et al. (Paris 1912–) 8:542–543.

[C. VERLINDEN]

BERNADOT, MARIE VINCENT

Author, editor, and publisher; b. Escatalens, June 14, 1883; d. Labastide Lévêque, June 25, 1941. Born in southern France, Bernadot was of peasant stock. He studied at the Grand Seminary at Montauban and was ordained in 1906. After serving as a parish priest, Bernadot entered the Order of Preachers (the Dominicans) in 1912; made his noviceship at Fiesole, Italy; and studied at Rome. He returned to France during World War I, where he resided at the priory of Saint-Maximin. Bernadot wrote several books on the spiritual life, of which *De l'Eucharistie à la Trinité* was most influential. His *L'Ordre des Frères Prêcheurs* (1917–18) remains an authentic interpretation of the ideals and achievements of the Dominicans. In 1919, Bernadot founded the journal *La Vie spirituelle,* which helped enormously in the spiritual rebirth of France. Within a year, its circulation had reached 3,300, and the revenues enabled the editor to launch *La Vie intellectuelle* in 1928. His purpose was to enrich the interior life by this monthly commentary on current events—political, religious, social, and artistic—and to this end he attracted the talent of such authors as Jacques Maritain, François Mauriac, Paul Claudel, Étienne Gilson, Henri Daniel-Rops, and Pierre Henri Simon. In 1928, Bernadot moved to a new priory at Juvisy, near Paris, and founded the publishing house L'Éditions du Cerf, which later moved to Paris. He inaugurated a weekly, *Sept* (1934), which soon had a circulation of 50,000. His editorial policy became increasingly involved in current political events (e.g., he advocated collaboration with the socialists and declared that the Spanish Civil War was not a ''holy crusade'') and occasioned some shock and scandal. In August 1937, Bernadot had to give up his work on the weekly that he had created. However, some of his lay friends, among them Mauriac and Maritain, continued its publication under the name *Temps présent,* with the approbation of the hierarchy. Bernadot returned to his religious studies and wrote *Notre Dame dans ma vie* (1937). He also started the journal *La Vie chrétienne avec Notre Dame,* which developed after the Second World War into *Fêtes et saisons* and *La Vie catholique illustrée.*

Bibliography: *La Vie spirituelle* (Aug. 1941, Nov. 1944). M. V. BERNADOT, *Lettres de direction* (Paris 1946).

[G. HOURDIN]

BERNANOS, GEORGES

French novelist, playwright, and essayist; b. Paris, Feb. 20, 1888; d. Neuilly, July 5, 1948. A family legend, doubtless based on the sound of the name, ascribed to Bernanos a Spanish ancestry. It told of ancestors who had lived in Santo Domingo until 1787, and hinted that one of these could have been a corsair during the time of Jean Bart. This picturesqueness, fitting as it may have been to the writer's temperament—his haughty air, love of the sun, and pugnacious vitality—is pure fiction. As far back as one can trace, Bernanos's roots are entirely French: Lorrainese on the side of his father Émile, from the vicinity of Metz; natives of Berry on the side of his mother, Hermance Moreau, a daughter of countryfolk of Pellevoisin, where the writer is buried near his parents. Bernanos's true native soil, however, is Artois. His home was in this province at Fressin (Pas de Calais). Since the meetings of the clergy of the deanery took place there, the child met many priests. After attending several colleges and minor seminaries at Paris and Bourges, he received his decisive character molding at the College of Saint Mary at Aire-sur-la-Lys. Finally, he chose Artois as the site of all his novels.

As a student at the Sorbonne (where he took degrees in the arts and in law), he was in the thick of the political struggle in which Catholics were opposing the monarchists of the ACTION FRANÇAISE under Charles MAURRAS and Léon DAUDET, and the democrats of the Sillon organization, led by Marc SANGNIER. On the eve of World War I, for which he volunteered as a *poilu,* he was a journalist at Rouen. On May 11, 1917, he married Jeanne Talbert d'Arc, a direct descendant of a brother of Jeanne d'Arc (*see* JOAN OF ARC, ST.). She bore him six children. The necessity to support this large family without giving up his independence as a writer was not the least of the reasons for his nomadic existence. He never knew material security, though he sought it in various parts of France and then in Majorca, where the Spanish Civil War overtook him. On July 20, 1938, he embarked with his family for Paraguay, but he had to settle in Brazil. He stayed there until July 1945, when he returned to France at the call of General de Gaulle. He resumed his nomadic habits and while in Tunisia (1947–48) he became ill, at a time when he had vowed to write nothing more except *La Vie de Jesus.*

Literary Career. Bernanos came into literary prominence rather late. His first book, the novelette *Madame Dargent,* was published in 1922. He was an insurance inspector when his novel *Sous le soleil de Satan* (1925) brought him immediate fame. The novel of Catholic inspiration owes its revitalization in France to this book—those that followed could only plumb somewhat deeper, and the influence of Bernanos's priest character on the agnostic writers of the period was profound. The hero of *Sous le soleil de Satan* was indeed a priest, the Abbé Donissan, another Curé of Ars (*see* VIANNEY, JEAN BAPTISTE MARIE, ST.). A priest is the principal character in nearly all the Bernanos novels, and the significant factor of Bernanos's portrayal is that it is not a matter, as it so often is in other fiction, of depicting a social specimen (however edifying) of the same category as a doctor or a lawyer, but of creating a being consecrated to and engaged body and soul in the spiritual drama. Bernanos tried to present these priests from an internal viewpoint, as if he and they were kindred spirits of the same calling; he succeeded so well that the critic Albert Béguin could style him ''the priestly novelist.''

Marie Vincent Bernadot.

Novelist of Holiness. Of course the Bernanos priest does not conform to plain reality. He represents a special ''case'' each time. Abbé Donissan, devoid, one might say, of armor, struggles with the demon and suffers the ''temptation of despair'' in ransoming those souls he saves. Abbá Cénabre (*L'Imposture,* 1927), who has lost his faith but keeps up outward appearances, is taken in charge by Abbé Chevance, who on his deathbed passes the burden on to a young woman, Chantal de Clergerie (*La Joie,* 1929), herself subject to some rather ecstatic phenomena. The parish priest of Ambricourt (*Le Journal d'un curé de campagne,* 1938, a novel of most classic construction, which won the Grand Prix of the Académie Française) is a hereditary alcoholic suffering from cancer, a condition that common sense would accept as an explanation of his apostolic ''imprudences.'' But it is necessary, in dealing with the tumultuous and tormented genius of Bernanos to renounce what one ordinarily calls common sense. What animates this writer is a ''supernatural sense.'' François Mauriac has written that Bernanos was very close to being ''the novelist of holiness''; at the very least he suggests the mystery of holiness, and those contemporaries furthest removed from the faith were fascinated by the all-pervading presence of the supernatural in a literary work.

Georges Bernanos. (Archive Photos)

The Supernatural in Bernanos. Bernanos believed that ''the supernatural cannot be set apart,'' meaning that human life is not lived in two compartments, one profane, the other sacred. The characters of his novels are at the extremes in their choices between good and evil, or perhaps it would be better to say that they play to the hilt the game of God or devil, and at all hazards. Bernanos disdained the middle ground, the ''average man,'' of whom he did not think except, in a polemical vein, as an imbecile or a coward (*La Grande peur des bien pensants,* 1931). More important, he portrayed in his novels the unhealthy unrest, even the crime and decay, that surrounds those who claim the supernatural does not affect them one way or the other, whose position is neither a clear ''Yes'' nor ''No'' (*M. Ouine,* 1943) and thus make of a town—drawn as an image of a great part of the contemporary world—a ''dead parish.'' In thus embracing the absolute, the romance of Bernanos enhances the tragedy of life, but in it destiny bears the name of vocation. The calamity is never such, nor is the obvious Manicheism such, that love cannot prevail over it. The confrontation of good and evil is made concrete in the struggle of ''a soul for a soul'' as expressed by the little parish priest of Ambricourt (*Le Journal d'un curé de campagne*), whose last words, borrowed from St. Thérèse de Lisieux, are well known: ''What matter? All is grace.''

In Bernanos's novels the champions of God never stop until they have snatched away the devil's prey; the strong pick up the burdens of the weak, as in the drama *Dialogues des Carmélites* (1948), where the ignoble death of a prioress, during the French Revolution, ensures the glorious martyrdom of a young religious overtaken by morbid cowardice. There is a constant illumination of the dogma of the Communion of Saints ''whose majesty fills us with wonder,'' in the author's own words; no less constant is the illustration of what Bernanos called ''the eternal youthfulness of the Beatitudes.'' These stances explain, in their somewhat extreme evangelical viewpoints, a certain reversal of some current values: the characters for whom Bernanos showed the greatest affection, to begin with the priests (just as in Dostoievskiĭ), are the most humble, indeed the most disinherited, humanly speaking. He showed deep compassion and a veritable tenderness toward the young woman in *La Nouvelle histoire de Mouchette* (1937), where it is evident that the heroine's suicide is an appeal from the deceit of this world to the justice of the kingdom of heaven. In this supernatural vision of the human soul, ''psychology,'' in the usual sense of the word, plays no part. Bernanos, who in more than one novel (notably in *La Joie*) evidenced his detestation of psychiatrists and psychoanalysts, excelled at ''confessing'' the essential reality of the soul. For him, this reality is demonstrated by the faithfulness of the young, and by that ''spirit of youth'' that is candor, honor, generosity, and courage. He associated it strongly with ''the spirit of Christianity,'' which sustains all his polemical works.

Polemical Works. Considered apart from the situations that occasioned them and from their contemporary French relevance, and making allowance for the vehemence and extremism of his writing, his polemical works manifest in general the same uncompromising spirituality as his novels. Bernanos possessed a sort of ''gift of prophecy''; a number of his statements concerning the lot of peoples during and after World War II are now seen to have been amazingly correct. But the most interesting and most fundamental of these essays, some of them single self-contained pieces (*Les Grands cimitières sous la lune,* 1938; *Scandale de la vérité,* 1939; *Lettre aux Anglais,* 1942), others in the form of diaries or journalistic contributions (*Les Enfants humiliés,* 1949; *Le Chemin de la Croix des âmes,* 1942), concern the demands of the Christian for his rights. The essayist, like the novelist, refused to accept a radical separation between the supernatural and the temporal; he grew indignant if the former came to terms with the latter, or if the latter guarded itself unduly against the requirements of the former; an obedient son of the Church, he did not hesitate to belabor ecclesiastical diplomacy when he judged that it had bargained with the ''honor of Christianity''; he wanted to ''reconcile morals with politics''; he believed that countries—but not ''nations''—are individuals, that each has its proper calling, and that they, too, run the risk of losing their souls.

In short, Bernanos dreamt of the Sermon on the Mount as the master plan for that ''kingdom of the meek on earth.'' This role of the ''great objector'' is inseparable from the personality of Bernanos himself, although it is the novelist who will best evidence this to posterity. Isolated, dragged this way and that by opposing camps, the author on various occasions made himself heard as the voice of the Catholic conscience; in a sense, he was a living apologetic.

Bernanos's other works are: novels—*Un crime* (1935), *Un mauvais rêve* (posthumous, 1950); essays—*Saint Dominique* (1926), *Jeanne relapse et sainte* (1934), *Noël à la maison de France* (1931), *Nous autres Français* (1942), *La France contre les robots* (1944); novelettes—*Une Nuit* (1928), *Dialogues d'ombres* (1928); articles—*Ecrit de combat* (1944), *La liberté pour quoi faire?* (collected 1953).

Bibliography: G. BERNANOS, *Bernanos par lui-même,* ed. A. BÉGUIN (Paris 1954). L. ESTANG, *Présence de Bernanos* (Paris 1947). W. M. FROHOCK, ''Georges Bernanos and His Priest-Hero,'' *Yale French Studies* 12 (1953) 54–61; ''The Vocation of Georges Bernanos,'' *Catholic World* 168 (March 1949) 448—452. H. HATZFELD, ''Georges Bernanos, 1888–1948, A Bibliography,'' *Thought* 23 (1948) 405–424; ''Georges Bernanos and Henri Bremond,'' *Renascence* 3 (1951) 120–127. P. MACCHI, *Bernanos e il problema del male* (Varese 1959). T. MOLNAR, *Bernanos: His Political Thought and Prophecy* (New York 1960). G. PICON, *Georges Bernanos* (Paris 1948). H. U. VON BALTHASAR, *Le Chrétien Bernanos,* tr. M. DE GANDILLAC (Paris 1956).

[L. ESTANG]

BERNARD GUI

Also known as Bernardus Guidonis, historian, inquisitor, bishop; b. Royère, Roche l'Abeille (Limousin), *c.* 1261; d. Lodève, Hérault, France, Dec. 30, 1331. Bernard became a DOMINICAN and was professed at Limoges on Sept. 16, 1280. A student of philosophy (1283), he lectured on logic at Brives (1284). He studied theology at Limoges (1285–88) and at Montpellier (1289–90). He was appointed sublector at Limoges (1291); lector at Albi (1292–93) and at Castres (1294); then prior at ALBI (1294–97), at Carcassone (1297–1301), and at Castres (1301–05); and then lector at Carcassone (1305). By August he was prior at Limoges (1305–07) and then inquisitor at Toulouse from Jan. 16, 1307, to 1323 or 1324, at the same time serving as procurator general (1317–21) under Master General Hervé de Nedellec. Bernard served on a peace embassy to Lombardy and Tuscany in 1317 and 1318 and to Flanders in 1318. He was later made bishop of Túy in Gálicia (Spain) on Aug. 26, 1323. On July 20, 1324, he was transferred to Lodève and died at the castle of Lauroux and was buried by his own wish in the Dominican church at Limoges.

As a historian and compiler Gui showed love for research, exceptional precision, and a sound and selective appreciation of the sources. The lack of any literary elegance in his writings is compensated for by his preservation of numerous documents and much information, whose original sources have since been lost. His most important work is the *Flores chronicorum* (no crit. ed.), a universal chronicle. His numerous other works include *Reges Francorum* and *Priores Artigiae,* the *De quatuor in quibus Deus Praed. Ord. insignivit* [ed. T. Kaeppeli, *Monumenta Ordinis Fratrum Praedicatorum historica* 22 (1949)], the *De fundatione et prioribus conv. prov. Tolos. et Provinciae O.P.* [ed. P. A. Amargier, *Monumenta Ordinis Fratrum Praedicatorum historica* 24 (1961)], his hagiographical work called *Sanctorale,* and the *De actibus fidei* and *De peccato originali.* His writings on heresy and the INQUISITION include *Practica officii inquisitionis* [ed. C. Douais (Paris 1886)] and the *Liber sententiarum inquisitionis Tolosanae* [ed. P. a Limborch (Amsterdam 1692)].

Bibliography: J. BREQUET, ''Aux origines du prieuré de l'Artige . . . ,'' *Bulletin de la Société archéologique et historique du Limousin* 90 (1963) 85–100. L. DELISLE, ''Notice sur les manuscrits de Bernard Gui,'' *Notices et extraits des manuscrits de la B. N. et autres bibliothèques* 27.2 (1879) 169–455. *Histoire littéraire de la France* 35:139–232, list of works. G. MOLLAT, *Dictionnaire d'histoire et de géographie ecclésiastiques,* ed. A. BAUDRILLART et al., (Paris 1912–) 8:677–681; *Dictionnaire de droit canonique,* ed. R. NAZ, (Paris 1935–65) 2:779–781. J. QUÉTIF and J. ÉCHARD, *Scriptores Ordinis Praedicatorum* (New York 1959) 1:576–580.

[S. L. FORTE]

BERNARD LOMBARDI

French Dominican theologian; fl. 1323 to 1333. He entered the order at Perpignan in southern France. In 1323, when he was prior of the house in Avignon and vicar provincial, he was elected seventh provincial of Provence. At the general chapter of the order in 1326, he was assigned to read the *Sentences* at Paris the following year, but he was not relieved of his administrative office. At the request of certain brethren, JOHN XXII absolved him from administrative duties during his academic term at Paris. He lectured on the *Sentences* in 1327–28, becoming master during the academic year 1331–32. He was regent for at least one year; one of his *quodlibets* is still extant. Avignon Manuscript 320 contains a number of his sermons (*collationes*). His unpublished commentary on the *Sentences* gives full details of the three commentaries on the *Sentences* composed by DURANDUS OF SAINT-POURÇAIN. In it he expresses clearly his own views on the Thomistic doctrines questioned by Durandus. This stand was prompted by the strong legislation of the general chapter of the order in 1329 regarding adherence to the teaching of St. THOMAS AQUINAS.

See Also: THOMISM.

Bibliography: J. QUÉTIF and J. ÉCHARD *Scriptores Ordinis Praedicatorum* (Paris 1719–23) 1.2:560–561. P. GLORIEUX, *La Littérature quodilbétique* (Paris 1935) 2:64–65. J. KOCH, *Durandus de Sancto Porciano, O.P., Beiträge zur Geschichte der Philosophie und Theologie des Mittelalters* 25 (Münster 1927) 314–340. F. STEGMÜLER, *Repertorium commentariorum in Sententias Petri Lombardi*, 2 v. (Würzburg 1947) 1:52, 103. E. FILTHAUT, *Lexikon für Theologie und Kirche*, ed. J. HOFER and K. RAHNER, 10 v. (2d, new ed. Freiburg 1957–65) 2:245.

[P. GLORIEUX]

BERNARD OF AOSTA, ST.

Known also as Bernard of Menthon, of Mont-Joux, restorer and patron of two famous Alpine hospices in the passes that bear his name; b. probably Italy (not Savoy); d. Novara, June 15, 1081(?). Archdeacon of Aosta for 40 years, his renown for holiness was consequent on the long years spent as a tireless, itinerant preacher through much of Piedmont, where his cult has always been popular. But his worldwide reputation today is chiefly linked with the hospices he reestablished and placed under the care of clerics and laymen who later became CANONS REGULAR OF ST. AUGUSTINE. The same order still conducts the hospices. According to a fifteenth-century document, Bernard was canonized by Richard, bishop of Novara (1115–21). In 1923, Pius XI proclaimed him patron of mountain climbers.

Feast: May 28, June 15.

Bibliography: *Acta Sanctorum* June 3:547–564. *Acta Apostolicae Sedis* 15 (1923) 437–442. A. DONNET, *Saint Bernard et les origines de l'Hospice du Mont-Joux* (Saint-Maurice 1942), critical. A. LÜTOLF, *Theologische Quartalsschrift* 61 (1879) 179–207. A. PONCELET, *Analecta Bollandiana* 26 (1907) 135–136. B. DE GAIFFIER, *ibid.* 63 (1945) 269–270. A. BUTLER, *The Lives of the Saints*, ed. H. THURSTON and D. ATTWATER (New York 1956) 2:411–413.

[N. M. RIEHLE]

BERNARD OF AUVERGNE (ALVERNIA)

French Dominican theologian; fl. 1294 to 1307. Originally from Gannat, he entered the Dominican Order at Clermont in the province of Auvergne. Known as *Malleus* (hammer) to his contemporaries, he taught at Paris as a bachelor of theology (1294–97) and commented on the *Sentences* (ed. Lyons 1519). Although direct evidence is lacking, it is probable that he became a master in theology, for five *Quaestiones disputatae* of his are extant and some manuscripts attribute that title to him. He was prior of Saint-Jacques in 1303, when he and the entire priory signed the appeal against BONIFACE VIII. Four sermons that he preached between 1301 and 1305 are extant. As an ardent defender of the doctrines of St. THOMAS AQUINAS, he vigorously opposed the views of HENRY OF GHENT, GODFREY OF FONTAINES and JAMES OF VITERBO. Thus, Bernard was one of the earliest theologians who contributed to the spread and development of THOMISM. Although the bulk of his extant writings is polemical in nature, he did not reply to the *Correctorium* of WILLIAM DE LA MARE (*see* CORRECTORIA). After the death of PETER OF AUVERGNE toward the end of 1304, Bernard was elected bishop of Clermont by the cathedral chapter, but CLEMENT V annulled this election in 1307. It is certain that Bernard never took possession of the see.

Bibliography: M. GRABMANN, "Bernhard von Alvergne, O.P., ein Interpret und Verteidiger der Lehre des hl. Thomas von Aquin aus alter Zeit," *Divus Thomas*, 10 (1932) 23–35. F. J. ROENSCH, *Early Thomistic School* (Dubuque 1964). E. FILTHAUT, *Lexicon für Theologie und Kirche*, ed. J. HOFER and K. RAHNER, 10 v. (2d, new ed. Freiburg 1957–65) 2:242. A. D'AMATO, *Enciclopedia filosofica* 4 v. (Venice-Rome 1957) 1:660.

[P. GLORIEUX]

BERNARD OF BESSE

An early Franciscan chronicler; fl. in France *c.* 1283. Little is known of his life beyond the fact that he was a member of the Franciscan custody of Cahors in the Province of Aquitaine and was a secretary of the Minister General, BONAVENTURE. In January 1250 he was probably residing at the convent of Limoges. His writings include a lost *Life of Brother Christopher of Romagna*, who died at Cahors in 1272, inserted in the *Chronicle of the 24 Generals* [*Analecta Franciscana* 3 (1897) 161–173]; the *Speculum disciplinae*, called also *Libellus de proposito regulae*, intended for the formation of novices (Quaracchi, *S. Bonaventurae opera omnia* 8:583–622); a letter, *Ad quendam novitium insolentem et instabilem* (*ibid.* 663–666); *De laudibus b. Francisci* [*Analecta Franciscana* 3 (1897) 666–679, 687–692]; *De triplici statu religionis b. Francisci* (ibid. 679–687); and a *Catalogus generalium ministrorum OFM* (*ibid.* 693–707; *Monumenta Germaniae Historica: Scriptores* 32:657–674), ending with Bonagratia Tielci (1283). Moderation and zeal characterize all his writings; the ascetical works—intended for the young—contain practical advice useful even for non-Franciscans. The prologue of the *De laudibus* discusses the biographers of St. FRANCIS (not mentioning Brother Leo of Assisi, however); the first chapter is the oldest Franciscan hagiographic catalogue. It should be noted that in certain chapters Bernard drew inspiration not only from THOMAS OF CELANO but also from the *Anonymus Perusinus*.

Bibliography: *Chronica XXIV generalium O.F.M.*, *Analecta Franciscana* 3 (1897) 161, 225, 228, 241, 262, 349, 361, 377. MARIAN DE FLORENCE, *Compendium chronicarum Fratrum Minorum*, *Archivum Franciscanum historicum* 2 (1909) 463; 4 (1911) 569. J. DE DIEU, *Dictionnaire de spiritualité ascétique et mystique. Doctrine et histoire*, ed. M. VILLER et al. (Paris 1932—) 1:1504–05. A. VAN DEN WYNGAERT, *Dictionnaire d'histoire et de géographie ecclésiastiques*, ed. A. BAUDRILLART et al. (Paris 1912—) 8:594–595.

[J. CAMPBELL]

BERNARD OF CHARTRES

Platonist, subdeacon, master and chancellor of Chartres, renowned teacher of grammar and philosophy; b. Brittany, c. 1160; d. between 1124 and 1126.

Little is known of Bernard's upbringing or educational background. From 1108 and probably earlier, he was subdeacon at Chartres cathedral, and he remained a subdeacon for the rest of his life. Some time Between 1110 and 1115 Bishop Ivo of Chartres appointed him master of the cathedral school, where his fame as a teacher drew many students to Chartres, including some of the most important figures in the intellectual life of the next generation. Bernard was the chancellor by 1124 and perhaps as early as 1119, which was the date of the death of the previous chancellor, Vulgrin. He signed documents as chancellor in 1124 and died between then and 1126, when Gilbert of Poitiers, his student, became the new chancellor. He bequeathed 24 volumes to the cathedral library.

The little we know of Bernard comes to us third hand from John of Salisbury's *Metalogicon,* where he waxes nostalgic about his education in the schools of France. John presents Bernard as the ideal philosopher/teacher in opposition to the Cornificians, educational reformers whom John despised. Three of Bernard's students, Gilbert of Poitiers, William of Conches, and Richard the Bishop were all teachers of John, and they instilled in him their deep sense of admiration for Bernard, whom John calls the "old man of Chartres." Of the few sayings of Bernard that John recounts, none is more famous than his description of contemporary thinkers as "dwarfs seated on the shoulders of giants" who had gone before them. John also describes in some detail the method by which Bernard taught grammar and about his insistence on instilling a sense of morals and faith. John also develops to some length certain aspects of Bernard's Platonism and his desire to reconcile Plato and Aristotle. Of note is Bernard's use of the term *formae nativae* which he uses to describe the way that the ideas of the divine mind, which are eternal but not co-eternal with God, are present in the things of the world. They are secondary forms distinct from the ideas that forever reside in the divine mind. Both John and Hugh of St. Victor (*Didascalicon* 3.12–19) record what is believed to be a short poem by Bernard concerning the "Six Keys of Learning." Paul Dutton has edited what he believes is Bernard's gloss on Plato's *Timaeus*. Scholarly opinion is still divided on the attribution. Opinion is also divided on whether or not Bernard was the brother of Thierry of Chartres.

Bibliography: BERNARD OF CHARTRES *Glosae super Platonem*, ed. P. DUTTON (Toronto 1992). P. DUTTON, "Uncovering the Glosae super platonem of Bernard of Chartres,"in *Medieval Studies* XLVI (1984): 192–221. D. LUSCOME, "Bernard of Chartres," in *The Encyclopedia of Philosophy* 1 (New York 1967) 305. L. MERLET and R. MERLET, *Les dignitaires de l'église Notre-Dame de Chartres: Listes chronologiques. Archives du diocèse de Chartres* 5 (Chartres 1900). E. JEAUNEAU, "Bernard of Chartres," in *Dictionary of Scientific Bibliography* 2 (New York 1970) 19–20. R. GIACONE, "Masters, Books and Library at Chartres According to the Cartularies of Notre Dame and Saint Père," *Vivarium* 12 (1974) 30–51. E. GILSON, "Le platonisme de Bernard de Chartres," in *Revue Néo-scholastique de philosophie* 25 (1923) 5–19. A. CLERVAL, "Bernard of Chartres," in *Les lettres chrétiennes* 4 (Paris 1882), 390–397; *Les écoles de Chartres au Moyen Age du Ve au XVIe siècle* (Paris 1895). See also the introduction and appendices of P. Dutton's critical edition above.

[P. ELLARD]

BERNARD OF CLAIRVAUX, ST.

Abbot, monastic theologian, and Doctor of the Church; b. Fontaines-les-Dijon, a village near Dijon, 1090; d. Clairvaux, August 20, 1153.

Life. Bernard's family was of noble lineage, both on the side of his father, Tescelin, and on that of his mother, Aleth or Aletta, but his ancestry cannot be clearly traced beyond his proximate forebears. The third of seven children, six of whom were sons, Bernard as a boy attended the school of the secular canons of Saint-Vorles, where it is probable that he studied the subjects included in the medieval trivium. In 1107 the early death of his mother, to whom he was bound by a strong affective tie, began a critical period in his life. Of the four years that followed, little is known but what can be inferred from their issue. In 1111 Bernard left the world and withdrew to the locality of Châtillon, where he was soon joined by all his brothers and a number of other relatives. He so distin-

Saint Bernard of Clairvaux.

guished himself in following the rule of the Cistercians, the strictest rule of the time, that after only three years he was chosen as abbot for a new foundation. For it, he with his 12 companions chose a solitary valley not far from the Aube, which they called Clara Vallis or Clairvaux. He was ordained by William of Champeaux, Bishop of Châlons-sur-Marne. In 1115, at 25 years of age, he was already at the juridical summit of his career, but he was to go on growing in the esteem of his contemporaries and in the effectiveness of his activity until he became the center of unity and the forward impetus for the ecclesiastical life of his time.

The first years of his abbacy were spent dealing with problems of monastic life—the organization and strengthening of the community at Clairvaux and the making of new foundations, the number of which was to reach 68 by the time of Bernard's death.

Controversy with Cluny. But if Clairvaux was to become a model of strict observance, Cluny, which was still a greater power in the Benedictine world, followed an adaptation of the Rule of St. Benedict. The beginning of Bernard's polemic against the disciplinary decadence of the Cluniacs occurred in 1119. [See Bernard's letter of 1119 or 1120 to his cousin Robert and the famous *Apologia ad Guillelmum S. Theodorici abbatem* of 1124 or 1125, *S. Bernardi opera, ed. Leclercq–Rochais* (Rome 1963) 3.81–108; hereafter, *Opera.*] In these writings the zeal of the saint expressed itself hotly at times and with some asperity, but in the warmth of debate a good fruit ripened, namely, the friendship between Bernard and PETER THE VENERABLE, Abbot of Cluny. Because of the contrast of temperament between the two, they were not by nature inclined to look upon each other sympathetically, but the vicissitudes of their relationship made each respect the holiness of the other, and they overcame the difficulty of temperament by their charity and mutual esteem.

Bernard was troubled about the relationship of his to other forms of the monastic life, and he had views of his own with regard to *transitus* or the transfer of a monk or a canon regular from one observance to another. Bernard was guided by his conviction of the superiority of the Cistercian life to every other manner of pursuing evangelical perfection and thought that when a soul sought a higher way of life, it was moved *duce spiritu libertatis,* and, such being the case, the matter transcended the disposition of the Rule of St. Benedict (ch. 61), or the agreements existing between orders, or papal privileges, and it even escaped the line of reasoning Bernard himself took in his *Liber de precepto et dispensatione* (*Opera* 3.283–288).

Schism. The ardent charity of the saint went beyond the horizons of the world of monks and canons and reached out to all the members of the Church. His qualities as a man of action were brought to light in the schism that took place in the Church in consequence of the election of two popes in 1130, Innocent II and Anacletus II, representatives of opposing factions, whose rivalry was reflected in the division of the College of Cardinals into two parties. Those who supported the Curia and were traditionalist in their conception of ecclesiastical life and methods of reform espoused the cause of Anacletus. The monastic party, of more recent formation, supported Innocent. Throughout the schism Bernard devoted himself strenuously to the task of securing the recognition of Innocent, on whose side he had stood from the beginning.

Abelard, Gilbert de la Porrée, and Arnold of Brescia. Successful in this battle, Bernard did not retire to the peace of the cloister for long. In 1140 he conducted the delicate operation that led to the condemnation of Abelard. Bernard's part in this was not unlike the part he played in the attempted condemnation of GILBERT DE LA

PORRÉE in 1148 at the Council of Reims. Many have been puzzled by his passionate involvement in these affairs. His polemical vehemence is impressive, even when due allowance is made for the peculiarities of that kind of literary genre (*see Tractatus ad Innocentium II pontificem contra quaedam capitula errorum Abaelardi, Patrologia Latina,* ed. J. P. Migne 217 v., indexes 4 v. (Paris 1878–90) 182.1053–57; *Epistolae* 188–189, 191–193, 331–338). There is no doubt that he was sincerely convinced that the teaching of Abelard constituted a grave danger for the faith, and his reaction was harsh and precipitate and showed little concern for literal exactitude or for distinguishing between the written and the spoken word or between the teaching of the master and the interpretation of his disciples. The same can be said of his reaction to Gilbert [see John of Salisbury, *Historia pontificalis,* ed. M. Chibnall (Edinburgh 1956) ch. 8–12; Otto of Freisingen, *Gesta Friderici imperatoris, Monumenta Germaniae Historica: Scriptores rerum Germanicarum* (Berlin 1826–), ed. G. Waitz–Von–Simson, 48, 61].

Between 1144 and 1145 Bernard was opposed to Arnold of Brescia, whose preaching against the wealth and luxury of the Church favored a movement of rebellion among the Roman people whom Bernard strove to win to the obedience of Lucius II and later of Eugene III. The election of the latter, a disciple of Bernard at Clairvaux, to the pontificate in 1145 further increased Bernard's influence upon ecclesiastical life at the center of Christendom, which reached its zenith in the first years of Eugene's pontificate.

The Crusades. In 1146 and 1147 Bernard was officially in charge of the preaching of the Second Crusade. Although the crusade itself ended in failure—a fact that saddened Bernard's last years—his success in winning support for it stood as evidence of the profound resonance evoked in the Christian West by the words and the personal charm of the saint. The war against the infidels was not Bernard's only cause in his popular preaching. Certain heresies then flourishing at home evoked his eloquence. Against the heretics he depended chiefly upon persuasion, but without neglecting, in cases of pertinacity, recourse to the secular arm.

At the hour of Tierce, August 20, 1153, Bernard died, consumed by sickness and austerity. He was canonized by Alexander III, Jan. 8, 1174, and proclaimed a Doctor of the Church by Pius VIII in 1830. The most recent act of the Holy See with regard to St. Bernard was the encyclical *Doctor mellifluus* of Pius XII on the occasion of the eighth centenary of his death.

Personality. Those of his contemporaries who spoke of Bernard agreed in attesting to the spiritual charm that emanated from him; the more analytical sought to trace it to his fascinating eloquence, fed by a rare combination of natural gifts and by a continuous and skillful use of the Scriptures, sustained by a life in conformity with his words, and strengthened by charismatic graces. Nevertheless, Bernard's behavior could be looked upon from different points of view, and it provoked discordant judgments.

Otto of Freisingen, in the most penetrating appraisal of the personality of Bernard made by a contemporary (*Gesta* 1.49), singled out certain traits that help to clarify attitudes indicated above: the ardent zeal that made him quick to intervene when he perceived a danger to the integrity of the faith and the facility, peculiar to impulsive temperaments, in accepting evidence without properly evaluating it. Nevertheless, a historically accurate reconstruction of the saint's personality does not lessen but puts into clearer relief the essential greatness of the man. He was perhaps the most authentic and complete representative of the monastic tradition in the current of medieval civilization. The life of Bernard remains an example of the Christian ideal, realized with total service and self-sacrifice, without egoism or personalism. The difficulty of the struggle he had to face because of his temperament, and the humility with which he recognized his own defects should not be undervalued. [See *Epist.* 70 and its appraisal by Dimier, *Revue d'histoire ecclésiastique* (Louvain 1900–) 50 (1955) 550–551.]

Theology. St. Bernard was a typical exponent of what has been called monastic theology by certain modern scholars. It is a theology that aims at a clear, orderly, warm exposition of truth, such as will serve to dispose the soul to prayer and contemplation. Bernardine theology was not distinguished by the discovery of new modes of thought or the achievement of new conclusions but by its continual permeation with a rich interior experience. Bernard's sources were principally the Scriptures, then the Fathers of the Church, works concerned with the regulation of monastic life (especially the Rule of St. Benedict), and finally the liturgy. The whole design of his theology can be reduced to a few lines: God, that is charity, created man by love and by love redeemed him. The supreme proof of that love is the Incarnation of the Word and the Redemption. Another exquisite proof of that love is the presence of a Mother, who is also the Mother of God, in the great picture of the Redemption.

It would be erroneous to attribute the detailed attention Bernard gave to the Blessed Virgin to reasons of pure sentiment. If the influence of his delicately sensitive spirit, sharpened by the sad loss of his own mother, cannot be denied, it must nevertheless be noted that Bernard exhibited a profound theological understanding of the function of Mary in Catholic dogma and particularly in the work of the Redemption.

Three points in his Mariology have been much commented upon. (1) With regard to the Immaculate Conception, there is his famous letter (n. 174), from which it can be certainly deduced that he did not admit that truth. (2) As to the dogma of the Assumption, clear texts are wanting, although a passage from the sermon recently published by J. Leclercq [''Études sur St. Bernard et le texte de ses écrits,'' in *Analecta S. Ordinis Cisterciensis* 9 (1953)] seems to point in the direction of that truth. (3) The mediation of Mary is one of the themes upon which Bernard insisted with great effectiveness, for example, in his well–known *Sermo de aquaeductu* (*Patrologia Latina,* ed. J. P. Migne 217 v., indexes 4 v. (Paris 1878–90) 183.437–448).

Apologetic and polemic considerations led Bernard to certain points in sacramental theology in his *Tractatus de baptismo.* He maintained, for example, that baptism of water was not absolutely necessary, and it could be substituted for that of blood or desire. He also held the justification of unbaptized infants in virtue of the faith of their parents.

Ascetical Doctrine. The theology of Bernard was so closely bound to personal experience of ascent to God that it is impossible to draw a clear dividing line between his dogmatic and his ascetical teaching. His fundamental ascetical treatises were three. (1) *De gratia et libero arbitrio* (*Opera* 3.165–203) is important because it provides the dogmatic and historical premises of Christian *ascesis* and describes the state of fallen but repaired human nature. Bernard insisted upon the primacy of the will, whose freedom from sin is actuated in Christ and through Christ. He strongly affirmed the necessity of grace, taking the strictly antipelagian position of St. Augustine. (2) The *De gradibus humilitatis et superbiae* (*Opera* 3.13–59) shows the fundamental importance that humility had for Bernard as the indispensable premise of charity. For him, humility was truth and was based in men on the humility-truth that is Christ, which takes possession of men and fills them with the gifts of His love. In the first part of the treatise are described the three degrees of humility; in the second, the 12 degrees of pride. This work, strongly marked by St. Bernard's personal experience, reveals his singular capacity for penetrating the human soul. (3) His brief *Liber de diligendo Deo* (*Opera* 3.119–154) is important for an understanding of his ascetical doctrine, but it is useful also for his mystical teaching, because it is centered upon the love of God and explains its motives. The first motive for loving God is the gifts He has given to mankind in general (ch. 2) and more especially those given to the Christian (ch. 3–4); the second is the good of man, who in God alone can satisfy his thirst for happiness. In the development of this meditation one encounters the central and vital function that the mysteries of the humanity of the Word have in Bernardine ascetical doctrine and piety. In a well-known passage of *Sermo 43 super cantica* (*Opera* 2.43) Bernard returns to the mysteries of the life and Passion of Jesus as the only wisdom and salvation and presents the Crucified as ''mea subtilior, interior philosophia''—a statement that reveals the Christocentric nature of his theology as well as the strongly affective character of his piety.

There is also ascetical doctrine of importance in the *De consideratione libri quinque ad Eugenium III* (*Opera* 3.393–493). The ''consideration'' in question is, at least in part, mental prayer, and the whole treatise, although divided into points strictly connected with the high office of the one to whom the work was addressed, still contains a development of the theme capable of broader application. Book 1 brings out the necessity of meditation as an essential element of piety (ch. 7–8). In book 2 Bernard proposes four series of themes for meditation: *te, quae sub te, quae circa te, quae supra te sunt* (ch. 3). Books 3 and 4 are concerned with the duties of the pontiff. In book 5, after having declared that meditation finds its fullness and high point in mystical contemplation (ch. 2), Bernard suggests many motives for meditation.

Mystical Doctrine. Bernard left no systematic exposition of mystical theology, but the *Sermones in cantica* and numerous passages in his other works contain the fruit of a genuine mystical experience, and in them, in spite of the lack of a systematic exposition, certain fundamental lines can be discerned. The ultimate and culminating development of theology for Bernard consisted in mystical experience. It represents the apex of all the works of God. Love wants to unite the soul to itself by charity even to the extent of mystical nuptials or spiritual marriage. In the stage of mystical union Bernard always presented the Word as the spouse of the soul, according to the characteristic Christocentricity of his thought.

His mystical teaching reveals another striking characteristic of the saint, his need to communicate his religious experience to others. In dispensing the riches of his interior life, he uncovered the whole grandeur of his mystical life. Few indeed even of the great mystics have had the ability to describe the mystical states so effectively. His truly great talent as an artist and a stylist was helpful to him in this, as can be seen in the descriptions of the visit of the Word to the soul in ch. 5 and 6 of *Sermo 74 in cantica.* To be noted are the limpid simplicity with which Bernard succeeds in expressing the ineffable; the paratactic construction permitting the period to proceed more rapidly and brokenly, thus giving more effective expression to the sighing of the soul; the exquisite use of rhythm extending to groups of phrases and giving rise to strophes and hymnic passages [*see* C. Mohrmann, ''Le Stile de St. Bernard'' in *S. Bernardo* (Milan 1954) 170–184].

St. Bernard must be ranked among the saints who have had a most profound influence by their doctrine and spirituality upon the life of the Church. The Franciscan school received some of its Christocentric orientation from St. Bernard. The author of the *Imitation of Christ* shows signs of having been abundantly nourished by the reading of the works of Bernard, and the French school of the 17th century manifests a notable affinity with certain fundamental lines of Bernardine theology (*see* Le Bail, 1.1492–98).

Culture and Art. Bernard was one of the most notable exponents of the monastic culture of the Middle Ages. He achieved a mastery of prose, despite his lack of direct acquaintance with the classics. Recent investigations by J. Leclercq of the manuscripts tradition appear to show that although Bernard dictated with facility and without much fussiness, he nevertheless took some care with the revision and polishing of his works.

His style, besides its well-known use of rhythm, was characterized by parallelism, antithesis, alliteration, and assonance, all of which are evidence of the influence of St. Augustine. One of his most admirable qualities as a stylist was his brilliant and fascinating ability to adapt the sacred text to the exigencies of artistic expression and to weave the passages of Scripture, which he had assimilated so well, into ever new designs (*see* JOHN OF SALISBURY, *Historia pontificalis* 12).

Bernard was hostile to the scholastic culture of his time, which was characterized by a growing sense of the function and autonomy of reason in the sphere of its competence. Nor did he look with favor upon the related demand for a theology that, although deduced from revealed premises and with all the reverence due to mystery, nevertheless built itself up with the exercise of reason and assumed the dignity of a science. Bernard could not see the need for such a theology. For him the search for truth simply out of a desire for truth was not a positive value, nor did he clearly recognize a field reserved to reason, although the beginning of such recognition can be found in certain passages of his writings.

In general, however, it can be affirmed that he had an awareness of the part study and knowledge can play in the ascent of the soul to God. But he valued knowledge only in that context. He was acutely conscious of the dangers involved in intellectual investigation, and he distrusted all that could give nourishment to pride. This attitude is to be explained in large part by his own inner experience that enabled him to draw supreme certitude from the joys of contemplation and from his own experience of the fecundity of grace. He felt no need for much reasoning and subtlety. He was inclined rather to be bored with it, and he viewed it as an obstacle. Nevertheless, within the limits he would set, Bernard valued study. At Clairvaux he laid the foundations of one of the best monastic libraries of the Middle Ages and maintained relations with William of Champeaux, Hugh of Saint-Victor, John of Salisbury, and Peter Lombard.

Feast: Aug. 20.

Bibliography: The four ancient lives of St. Bernard are in *Patrologia Latina,* ed. J. P. MIGNE, 217 v., indexes 4 v. (Paris 1878–90) 185:225–368. Biog. sources. E. VACANDARD, *Vie de Saint Bernard* (5th ed. Paris 1920). J. M. CANIVEZ, *Dictionnaire d'histoire et de géographie ecclésiastiques,* ed. A. BAUDRILLART et al. (Paris 1912–) 8:610–611. *The letters of St. Bernard of Clairvaux*, tr. B. S. JAMES (Chicago 1953, reprinted New York 1980). *Lettres*, ed. J. LECLERCQ, H. ROCHAIS, and H. TALBOT, tr. H. ROCHAIS (Paris 1997). Bernardine bibliog. L. JANAUSCHEK, *Bibliographia bernardina* (Vienna 1891). J. BOUTON, *Bibliographie bernardine* (Paris 1958). J. LECLERCQ, ''Les Études bernardines en 1963,'' *Bulletin de la société internationale pour l'Étude de la philosophie médiévale* 5 (1963) 121–138. Bernardine apocrypha and disputed writings. F. CAVALLERA, *Dictionnaire de dpiritualité ascétique et mystique. Doctrine et histoire,* ed. M. VILLER et al. (Paris 1932–) 1:1499–1502. Information on the critical ed. of the text. J. LECLERCQ, ''L'Édition de St. B.,'' *Revue d'histoire ecclésiastique* 45 (1950) 715–727. H. M. ROCHAIS, ''L'Édition critique des oeuvres de St. B.,'' *Studi medievali* 1 (1960) 701–719. Biog. studies. The biog. by Vacandard, mentioned above, was the first attempt at a truly hist. reconstruction of the personality of St. B. Hist. Commission of the Order of Citeaux, *Bernard de Clairvaux* (Paris 1953). *Bernard of Clairvaux: A Saint's Life in Word and Image*, ed. M. B. PENNINGTON, Y. KATZIR, and N. JOHNSTON (Huntington, Ind. 1994). A. H. BREDERO, *Bernard de Clairvaux: Culte et histoire* (Turnhout, Belgium 1998); Eng. tr. *Bernard of Clairvaux: Between Cult and History* (Grand Rapids, Mich. 1996). W. W. WILLIAMS, *Saint Bernard of Clairvaux* (Westminster, Md. 1952). J. CALMETTE and H. DAVID, *Saint Bernard* (Paris 1953). G. G. COULTON, *Two Saints, St. Bernard & St. Francis* (Norwood, Pa. 1976). P. DINZELBACHER, *Bernhard von Clairvaux: Leben und Werk des berühmten Zisterziensers* (Darmstadt 1998). B. P. MCGUIRE, *The Difficult Saint* (Kalamazoo, Mich. 1991). T. MERTON, *The Last of the Fathers* (New York 1981, *c.* 1954); *Thomas Merton on Saint Bernard* (Kalamazoo, Mich. 1980). M. RAYMOND, *The Family that Overtook Christ* (Boston, Mass. 1986). B. SCOTT-JAMES, *Saint Bernard of Clairvaux* (London 1957). Special studies. *Bernardus Magister*, papers presented 10–13 May 1990 at Institute of Cistercian Studies, ed. J. R. SOMMERFELDT (Spencer, Mass. 1992). É. GILSON, *Mystical Theology of St. Bernard* (2d ed. New York 1955). *St. Bernard théologien: Actes du Congrès de Dijon* (Rome 1953). E. C. BUTLER, *Western Mysticism* (New York 1975). M. CASEY, *A Thirst for God: Spiritual Desire in Bernard of Clairvaux's Sermons on the Song of Songs* (Kalamazoo, Mich. 1988). G. G. COULTON, *St. Bernard, his Predecessors and Successors* (Cambridge 1923, reprinted New York 1979). C. DUMONT, *Pathway of Peace*, tr. E. CONNOR of *Au chemin de la paix* (Kalamazoo, Mich. 1999). G. R. EVANS, *Bernard of Clairvaux* (New York 2000). M. K. HUFGARD, *Bernard of Clairvaux on*

Being and Beauty (Lewiston, N.Y. 2000). J. LECLERCQ, ''Un Guide de la lecture pour St. B.,'' *La Vie Spirituelle* 102 (1960) 440–447; *Saint Bernard mystique* (Paris 1948). *Festschrift zum 800 Jahrgedächtnis des Todes Bernhards von Clairvaux* (Vienna 1953). *Mélanges St. Bernard,* 24e Congrès de l'Assoc. bourguignonne des sociétés savantes (Dijon 1954). M. B. PRANGER, *Bernard of Clairvaux and the Shape of Monastic Thought* (Leiden 1994). C. RUDOLPH, *The ''Things of Greater Importance:'' Bernard of Clairvaux's Apologia and the Medieval Attitude Toward Art* (Philadelphia 1990). C. STERCAL, *Il ''Medius adventus:'' saggio di lettura degli scritti di Bernardo di Clairvaux* (Rome 1992). M. STICKELBROECK, *Mysterium venerandum: der trinitarische Gedanke im Werk des Bernhard von Clairvaux* (Münster 1994). D. E. TAMBURELLO, *Bernard of Clairvaux* (New York 2000); *Union with Christ: John Calvin and the Mysticism of St. Bernard* (Louisville, Ky. 1994). *The Joy of Learning and the Love of God* (Kalamazoo, Mich. 1995). J. LECLERCQ, *A Second Look at Bernard of Clairvaux* (Kalamazoo, Mich. 1990). G. R. EVANS, *The Mind of Saint Bernard* (Oxford 1983). M. BASIL PENNINGTON, *Saint Bernard of Clairvaux: Studies Commemorating the Eighth Centenary of His Canonization* (Kalamazoo, Mich. 1977). *Bernard of Clairvaux: Studies Presented to Dom Jean Leclerq,* ed. H. ROCHAIS (Spenser, Mass. 1973).

[P. ZERBI]

BERNARD OF CLUNY

Benedictine monk and poet; fl. mid-12th century, known also as Bernard of Morlas. Nothing is known for certain about his early years, although later unsubstantiated tradition describes him as a native of England or Brittany who entered religious life at the Abbey of Saint-Sauveur d'Aniane, transferring to the great BENEDICTINE foundation at CLUNY in the time of Abbot Pons de Melgueil (d. 1126). It is certain, however, that he was a monk at Cluny under PETER THE VENERABLE (1122–57), for he dedicates his major work to that abbot. Bernard is best known for his *De contemptu mundi,* a Latin poem of about 3,000 lines in dactylic hexameter, written *c.* 1140. It is a bitter satire against the moral disorders of his time, and the author did not flinch from protesting the vices of the leading churchmen of the day and the abuses that he saw in Rome itself. In his somewhat discursive fashion, he enlarged upon the transitory nature of all material things and the permanence of spiritual values. His vivid descriptions of heaven and hell might be compared with those of DANTE, and the whole work ends on an apocalyptic note. Bernard also produced a number of sermons and is usually credited with the authorship of the *Mariale*, a poem in praise of the Blessed Virgin, as well as the *Constitutiones cluniacenses,* a compilation of the early monastic customs that had been the basis of the CLUNIAC REFORM.

See Also: OMNI DIE DIC MARIAE.

Bibliography: Works. *De contemptu mundi by Bernard of Morval,* ed. H. C. HOSKIER (London 1929); *Constitutiones cluniacenses,* ed. B. ALBERS in *Constitutiones cluniacenses antiquiores* (Monte Cassino 1905). *Mariale, Analecta hymnica* 50:423–483. **Literature**. L. BERGERON, *Dictionnaire de spiritualité ascétique et mystique: Doctrine et histoire* (Paris 1932–) 1:1506–07. M. DISDIER, *Dictionnaire d'histoire et de géographie ecclésiastiques*, ed. A. BAUDRILLART et al., (Paris 1912–) 8:699–700. G. J. ENGELHARDT, ''The *De contemptu mundi* of Bernardus Morvalensis: A Study in Commonplace,'' *Mediaeval Studies* 22 (1960) 108–135. *Histoire littéraire de la France* (Paris 1814–1941) 12:236–246. M. MANITIUS, *Geschichte der lateinischen Literatur des Mittelalters* (Munich 1911–31) 3:780–783. *The Rhythm of Bernard of Morlaix,* ed. and tr. J. M. NEALE (5th ed. London 1864). R. C. PETRY, ''Medieval Eschatology and Social Responsibility in Bernard of Morval's *De contemptu mundi,*'' *Speculum* 24 (1949) 207–217. F. J. E. RABY, *A History of Christian-Latin Poetry from the Beginnings to the Close of the Middle Ages* (2d ed. Oxford 1953) 315–319. J. SZÖVÉRFFY, *Die Annalen der lateinischen Hymnendichtung: Ein Handbuch* (Berlin 1964–65) 2:86–89. A. WILMART, ''Grands poèmes inédits de Bernard le Clunisien,'' *Revue Bénédictine* 45 (1933) 249–253.

[B. J. COMASKEY]

BERNARD OF COMPOSTELLA, THE ELDER

Spanish canonist at Bologna in the early 13th century, dates and places of birth and death unknown. He held the dignity of archdeacon of Compostella, and some time before 1210 he was perhaps employed in a judicial or consulting capacity by the papal Curia. He may at some time have been also a member of the short-lived (1204–09) law school of Vicenza. At Bologna, where many Spaniards were active in the schools at that period, he apparently associated in particular with his fellow countrymen Melendus (later bishop of Osma, d. 1225), Pelagius (later cardinal-bishop of Albano, d. 1232), and Petrus Hispanus. After *c.* 1217, no further traces of his academic activities have been found. Bernard (Bernardus Compostellanus Antiquus) was particularly remembered at Bologna as the DECRETALIST who put together the so-called *Compilatio Romana* (1208), a compilation of decretals from the first ten years of Innocent III; but the work was criticized by the Curia because it included papal letters not meant to be used as binding precedents. It was soon replaced by an official collection (known as *Compilatio III antiqua*), which the pope sent to the schools. The failure of Bernard's *Compilatio Romana* probably explains why his achievements as a glossator received little recognition by the leading masters of his time in both the decretist and decretalist fields at Bologna.

Modern manuscript research has established that, apart from the decretal compilation, he wrote (1) an apparatus of glosses on the *Decretum* of GRATIAN (*c.* 1206), until recently known only from citations in other commentaries; (2) additions to and annotations on the *glossa ordinaria* of Joannes Teutonicus (*c.* 1217); (3) glosses on the *Compilatio I* of decretals (*c.* 1205–06; but no evidence has been found for his glosses on the *Compilatio II,* which were still known in the 14th century); and (4) *Quaestiones disputatae* (*c.* 1204–09, at Vicenza?).

Bibliography: S. KUTTNER, ''Bernardus Compostellanus Antiquus,'' *Traditio* 1 (1943) 277–340, with full bibliog. Edition of the *Compilatio Romana* (in the form of a calendar, except for the texts not elsewhere transmitted), ed. H. SINGER in *Sitzungsberichte der Akademie der Wissenschaften in Wien*, Philos-hist. Klasse 171.2 (1914). R. WEIGAND, in ''Bulletin of the Institute of Research and Study in Medieval Canon Law'' in *Traditio* 21 (1965) 482–485, on a MS of the *apparatus decretorum.*

[S. KUTTNER]

BERNARD OF COMPOSTELLA, THE YOUNGER

Bishop, canonist; d. Rome, 1267. He was dean of Lisbon in 1252. He is called ''the Younger'' to distinguish him from Bernard of Compostella ''the Elder'' (early 13th century), with whom, as Joannes Andreae testifies, he was being confused as early as the first part of the 14th century.

In a very busy lifetime he found time for only three works: (1) a *Margarita* or analytical table to Innocent IV's *Apparatus in quinque libros decretalium,* (2) a commentary on Innocent's own decretals—both of these were minor works written about 1250—and (3) a *Lectura* or commentary on the decretals of Gregory IX (which was begun about 1260 and had reached only as far as bk. 1, tit. 6 by 1267). For all its lack of originality, the fragmentary *Lectura* is of value, chiefly because it is the product of a writer who not only endorsed but also was perfectly familiar in practice with Innocent IV's ideas on centralization. Thus, drawing at one point on his own experience as an auditor, Bernard adds *Notabilia* to *Corpus iuris Canonici* X 1.3.30 (*De rescriptis*), which provide a fascinating glimpse of the century-old system of provisions at the very moment when the canonist-pope was giving it a juridical framework that would endure for centuries.

Bibliography: G. BARRACLOUGH, ''Bernard of Compostella,'' *English Historical Review* 49 (1934) 487–494; *Dictionnaire de droit canonique*, ed. R. NAZ, (Paris 1935–1965) 2:777–779. BERNARD OF COMPOSTELLA, *Lectura aurea,* in *Perillustrium tam veterum quam recentiorum in libros decretalium aurei commentarii,* v. 1 (Venice 1588). G. DURANTIS, *Speculum iuris,* glossed by JOANNES ANDREAE et al., 4 pts. in 3 (Venice 1576) pt. 3, lib. 3, p. 28, ''De inquisitione,'' gloss k. Schulte 2: 118–120. F. GILLMANN, *Zur Lehre der Scholastik vom Spender der Firmung und des Weihesakraments* (Paderborn 1920) 88–90, 226–227. P. G. KESSLER, ''Untersuchungen über die Novellen-Gesetzgebung Papst Innozenz' IV,'' *Zeitschrift der Savigny-Stiftung für Rechtsgeschichte, Kanonistische Abteilung* 32 (1943) 316–354. S. KUTTNER, *Repertorium der Kanonistik* 318; ''Bernardus Compostellanus antiquus,'' *Traditio* 1 (1943) 277–278. A. VAN HOVE, *Commentarium Lovaniense in Codicem iuris cononici 1* (Mechlin 1945) 1:477–478, 480–481.

[L. E. BOYLE]

BERNARD OF CORLEONE, BL.

Baptized Philip (Filippo) Latini; Capuchin lay brother; b. Corleone, Sicily, Feb. 6, 1605; d. Palermo, Sicily, January 12, 1667. Bernard was the third of six children born to Leonard and Frances (Xaxa) Latini, who owned a small vineyard. Bernard supported his widowed mother as a cobbler. He received no formal schooling but, in a town garrisoned by mercenaries employed by Spain, he learned swordsmanship so well that his name became a legend throughout Sicily. He wielded the sword, however, only in what he called ''Christian'' causes, especially the defense of women and poor peasants oppressed by the town's soldiers. His conversion to the religious life was occasioned when at the age of 27, he gravely wounded an adversary who had repeatedly provoked him to a duel. He entered the novitiate of the Capuchin Order at Caltanissetta, Dec. 13, 1632, as a lay brother. Although endowed with gifts of contemplation and miracles, Bernard is best remembered for heroic penance. His fasts and macerations recall the desert fathers. He is frequently pictured burning his mouth with a brand snatched from the kitchen fire, a penalty inflicted on himself for an unkind word to a confrere. Bernard was beatified by Clement XIII, April 29, 1768. On July 1, 2000 a miracle attributed to his intercession was approved, opening the way for his canonization.

Feast: Jan. 19.

Bibliography: D. DA GANGI, *Dalla spada al cilicio: Profilo del beato Bernardo da Corleone* (Tivoli 1934). B. VON MEHR, *Lexikon für Theologie und Kirche,* ed. J. HOFER and K. RAHNER, 10 v. (2d, new ed. Freiburg 1957–65) 2:243. A. TEETAERT, *Dictionnaire d'histoire et de géographie ecclésiastiques,* ed. A. BAUDRILLART (Paris 1912–) 8:647–648. A. BUTLER, *The Lives of the Saints,* ed. H. THURSTON and D. ATTWATER, 4 v. (New York 1956) 1:124. *Lexicon Capuccinum* (Rome 1951).

[T. MACVICAR]

BERNARD OF FONTCAUDE

PREMONSTRATENSIAN theologian; d. *c.* 1192. He seems to have been first abbot of Fontcaude in the former Diocese of Saint-Pons-de-Thomières, which he governed in 1172 and which Pope LUCIUS III in 1184 placed under the jurisdiction of the archbishop of Narbonne. In 1182 Bernard signed a charter in favor of the Abbey of AN

IANE, and in 1188, a document concerning the monastery of Combelongue. He wrote polemical tracts against the WALDENSES, published by Gretzer, together with two similar works in *Tria scriptorum adversus Valdensium sectam: Ebruardus Bethunensis, Bernardus abbas Fontis Calidi, Ermengaudus* (Ingolstadt 1614; *Patrologia Latina* 204:793–840). Bernard had been present at a disputation between Waldenses and Catholics and afterward undertook to edit and summarize the various points presented by both sides. His work is therefore considered to be an important source on the origins of the sect and the basis of their doctrinal position.

Bibliography: A. BORST, *Lexikon für Theologie und Kirche*, ed. J. HOFER and K. RAHNER (2d new ed. Freiburg 1957–65) 2:243. J. B. BOSSUET, *The History of the Variations of the Protestant Churches,* 2 v. (New York 1836) bk. 9, ch. 75–79. C. DE VIC and J. VAISSETE, *Histoire générale de Languedoc,* 16 v. in 17 (rev. ed. Toulouse 1872–1904) 6:218. L. E. DUPIN, *Histoire des controverses et des matières ecclésiastiques,* 9 v. (Paris 1694–98) 5:599. J. A. FABRICIUS, *Bibliotheca latina mediae et infimae aetatis,* 6 v. in 3 (Florence 1858–59) 1:213. *Gallia Christiana* (Paris 1856–65) 6:267. *Histoire littéraire de la France* (Paris 1814–1941) 15:35. L. VERREES, *Analecta Praemonstratensia* 31:5–35.

[J. DAOUST]

BERNARD OF MONTMIRAT

Abbot and canonist; b. Montmirat (southern France), *c.* 1225; d. Monte Cassino, 1296. It is not known whether he was already a Benedictine monk when he studied in Bologna under Peter of Sampson, whom he followed to Avignon. Subsequently he taught Canon Law at Béziers, and it is now known that he was a professor also at Toulouse. Appointed abbot of Montmajour in 1266 and rector of the March of Ancona in 1277 and 1278, he continued as abbot until 1286, when Pope Honorius IV appointed him bishop of Tripoli in Syria. Unable to take possession of his see because of political circumstances, he was employed on various missions, notably on legations to England and Sweden (1291–92) in connection with the projected crusade of Nicholas IV. In 1295 he was appointed administrator of the abbey of Monte Cassino. His canonical works were very successful: his *Lectura* (1259–66; printed Strasbourg 1510, Venice 1588) on the Decretals of GREGORY IX and his commentary (unprinted) on the *Novellae* of Innocent IV are famous; parts of his *Distinctiones* have survived also. These writings display a remarkable knowledge of classical Canon Law and are on a level with the works of other great doctors of the 13th century. Bernard was known at first as Abbas, and later called ''Abbas antiquus'' to distinguish him from the great abbot-canonist of the 15th century, Nicolaus de TUDESCHIS (''Abbas Modernus'').

Bibliography: S. KUTTNER, ''Wer war der Dekretalist 'Abbas Antiquus'?'' *Zeitschrift der Savigny-Stiftung für Rechtsgeschichte, Kanonistische Abteilung* 26 (1937) 471–489. A. VAN HOVE, *Commentarium Lovaniense in Codicem iuris cononici 1* (Mechlin 1928–) 1:456. A. VILLIEN, *Dictionnaire de droit canonique*, ed. R. NAZ (Paris 1935–65) 1:1–2. J. F. VON SCHULTE, *Die Geschichte der Quellen und der Literatur des kanonischen Rechts* (Stuttgart 1875–80) 2:130–132.

[P. LEGENDRE]

BERNARD OF OFFIDA, BL.

Capuchin lay brother famed for his sanctity and charity (baptized Domenico Peroni); b. Lama, Italy, Nov. 7, 1604; d. Offida, Aug. 22, 1694. He was born of peasant folk and received little education. He entered the Capuchin Order at Corinaldo on Feb. 16, 1626, and made rapid progress in the spiritual life. When sent to Fermo, he served as cook and infirmarian. Transferred to Offida at the age of 65, he became porter and questor. A plague in that area gave him occasion to devote his energies to the sick and poor, and this became his apostolate for the rest of his life. He worked many miraculous cures and brought many into the Church. His reputation for holiness spread throughout that region. In the bull of his beatification on May 25, 1795, Pope Pius VI cited his charity to the poor and needy and his profound humility. His cause for canonization is no longer active.

Feast: Aug. 26.

Bibliography: *Lexicon Capuccinum* (Rome 1951) 212. *Bernardo da Offida: atti del convegno storico sul beato cappuccino,* ed. R. LUPI and P. MARANESI (Rome 1996). A. TEETAERT, *Dictionnaire d'histoire et de géographie ecclésiastiques,* ed. A. BAUDRILLART (Paris 1912–) 8:709. *Bullarium O.F.M. Cap.*, v.1–7 (Rome 1740–52), v.8–10 (Innsbruck 1883–84) 10:771. PELLEGRINO DA FORLI, *Annali dell'Ordine dei FF. Minori Cappuccini,* 4 v. (Milan 1882–85) 3:505–516.

[B. SMITS]

BERNARD OF PARMA, ST.

Important canonist and glossator; b. Parma, *c.* 1200; d. Bologna, *c.* 1264. He studied under TANCRED at BOLOGNA, where he later taught. While at Bologna he received an ecclesiastical benefice (*canonicatus*) and became a chaplain to the pope. He wrote several works that are important in the history of decretal law. His *glossa* (*c.* 1245) on the *Decretals of GREGORY IX* became the standard commentary (*GLOSSA ORDINARIA*) on that collection of decretals. Bernard's *glossa* was the result of his life's work. His glosses are noted for their clarity and juridic precision; their understanding of Roman law in addition to Canon Law; and their comprehension of the ideas of the earlier glossators (especially those of the *QUINQUE COMPI-*

Episode from the Life of St. Bernard of Parma, painting by Andrea del Sarto, 1528.

LATIONES ANTIQUAE). Bernard also produced a compilation of juridic cases (known as the *Casus longi*) contained in papal decretals; several MSS and editions of this work still exist. His *Summa super titulis decretalium* is a short study on the material contained in each chapter of the *Decretals of Gregory IX;* it follows closely the works of Tancred and Bernard of Pavia. The *Summa* was used extensively by later jurists.

Bibliography: S. KUTTNER, *Repertorium der Kanonistik.* P. OURLIAC, *Dictionnaire de droit canonique*, ed. R. NAZ (Paris 1935–65) 2:781–782. A. VAN HOVE, *Commentarium Lovaniense in Codicem iuris cononici 1* (Mechlin 1928) 1:473 and *passim.* J. F. VON SCHULTE, *Die Geschichte der Quellen und der Literatur des kanonischen Rechts* (Stuttgart 1875–80; repr. Graz 1956).

[J. M. BUCKLEY]

BERNARD OF PARMA, ST.

Vallombrosan, cardinal, bishop of Parma, Italy; b. Florence *c.* 1055; d. Cavanna Abbey, near Parma, Dec. 4, 1133. According to tradition he was born of the noble Uberti family. He entered the newly founded VALLOMBROSAN order at San Salvi (*c.* 1075), where he became abbot (*c.* 1093) and then abbot general of the order (1098). Because of his unceasing zeal for the order's welfare he is considered its second founder. Shortly after becoming abbot general he was called to Rome and created cardinal by Pope URBAN II. The INVESTITURE STRUGGLE was then at its height: Bernard was sent to Lombardy by Pope PASCHAL II with powers of legate and with the mission of liberating the Lombard cities from the dominion of Emperor HENRY IV; Bernard won the friendship of Countess Matilda of Tuscany; he was at Canossa in 1102. Insulted and imprisoned by schismatics in Parma, he was liberated after three days through Matilda's intervention. Before 1106 he was elected bishop of Parma, where he proved a zealous pastor. He founded several monasteries, including that of Cavanna. He assisted Matilda on her death bed. At the Council of Piacenza, held under Pope Innocent II, he met Bernard of Clairvaux. He was frequently the subject of Renaissance painters, e.g., of Correggio (the cupola of Parma's cathedral), of Perugino, and of Andrea del Sarto.

Feast: Dec. 4.

Bibliography: *Acta Sanctorum* Dec. (Propylaeum) 566. *Monumenta Germaniae Historica: Scriptores* 30.2:1314–27, vita. F. BONNARD, *Dictionnaire d'histoire et de géographic ecclésias-*

Ceiling frescoes in the abbey of Saint-Savin-sur-Gartempe created c. 1060–1115. (Vanni Archive/CORBIS)

tiques, ed. A. BAUDRILLART et al. (Paris 1912) 8:718–721. N. PELICELLI, *I vescovi della chiesa parmense*, v. 1 (Parma 1936) 137–154.

[T. C. CROWLEY]

BERNARD OF TIRON, ST.

Benedictine reformer; b. Abbeville (Somme), France, *c.* 1046; d. April 14 or 25, 1117. He studied grammar and dialectics until he was 20 years old and then entered the Benedictine Abbey of Saint-Cyprien in Poitiers. He soon transferred to Saint-Savin-sur-Gartempe, where he was prior for 20 years. When Abbot Gervais died, Bernard fled the abbey to avoid succeeding as abbot and became a hermit. However, in 1100 he was made abbot of Saint-Cyprien; but when he, like ROBERT OF ARBRISSEL, fell into disagreement with Cluny's claims on the abbey, Bernard again retired to the forest. Forced to return as abbot, he undertook a trip to Rome and upon his return he reformed the lax discipline of his own abbey with the full approval of the pope. With the help of IVO OF CHARTRES and of King Louis VI, he founded (1114) the Abbey of Tiron (Eure-et-Loir), France, which enjoyed great prosperity (500 monks). From France and elsewhere came requests for these religious living the strict Benedictine Rule. The new congregation soon numbered 10 abbeys and 40 priories in France alone. Bernard's life was written by his disciple, Geoffrey the Fat, between 1131 and 1148.

Feast: April 14.

Bibliography: *Acta Sanctorum* April 2:220–254. *Patrologia Latina*, ed. J. P. MIGNE (Paris 1878–90) 172:1363–1446. C. CLAIREAUX, *Saint Bernard de Thiron* (Bellême, Fr. 1913). P. CALENDINI, *Dictionnaire d'histoire et de géographie ecclésiastiques*, ed. A. BAUDRILLART et al. (Paris 1912) 8:754–755. A. M. ZIMMERMANN, *Kalendarium Benedictinum*, (Metten 1933–38) 2:54–57. J. B. MAHN, *L'Ordre Cistercien et son gouvernement, des origines au milieu du XIIIe siècle* (1098–1265) (new ed. Paris 1951) 29–34. R. AIGRAIN, *Catholicisme* 1:1482–83.

[É. BROUETTE]

BERNARD OF TRILLE

Also called Bernard of Trilia, or de la Treille, Dominican Thomistic philosopher and theologian; b. Nîmes, southern France, *c.* 1240; d. Avignon, Aug. 4, 1292. After lecturing in various Dominican houses in Provence between 1266 and 1276, he was sent to the University of Paris in 1279 to lecture on the *Sentences.* He taught as master in Paris (1284–87). His unfinished *quodlibets,* as well as the greater part of his writings, date from the period of his mastership. Active in the internal affairs of the order, he was elected provincial of Provence in 1291, but he was removed in 1292 because of his defense of the master general, F. Munio, who had been deposed by NICHOLAS IV. He then retired to Avignon. Highly esteemed as a teacher and writer, he applied strictly Thomistic doctrines to problems of his day. Among his works are a commentary on the *Sentences, Quaestiones 18 de cognitione animae coniunctae, Quaestiones de differentia esse et essentiae, Quaestiones de spiritualibus creaturis et de potentia Dei,* three *Quodlibets,* postils on several books of the Bible, two sermons, and questions on the *De sphera* of JOHN DE SACROBOSCO. Only a few of his works are printed and many are incomplete or lost.

Bibliography: M. GRABMANN, "Bernhard von Trilia, O.P.," *Divus Thomas* 13 (1935) 385–399; in P. GLORIEUX, *Répertoire des maîtres en théologie de Paris au XIIIe siècle* (Paris 1933–34) 1:155–157. J. QUÉTIF and J. ÉCHARD, *Scriptores Ordinis Praedicatorum* (New York 1959) 1.1:432–434. F. STEGMÜLLER, *Repertorium biblicum medii aevi* (Madrid 1949–61) 1739–45. E. FILTHAUT, *Lexikon für Theologie und Kirche*, ed. J. HOFER and K. RAHNER (Freiburg 1957–65) 2:249. F. J. ROENSCH, *Early Thomistic School* (Dubuque 1964).

[J. F. HINNEBUSCH]

BERNARD SILVESTER

Lat. Bernardus Silvestris (Bernard of Tours), poet, philosopher, and teacher; born *c.* 1100; died *c.*1160. The earliest in a long series of medieval and Renaissance mythic poets who sought to use the language of metaphor and symbol to express theological and philosophical truths. Bernard simultaneously promoted the dignity of humanity, the dignity of nature and science, and the power of divine grace.

Life. Little is known of Bernard's life, even the dates of his birth and death are based only on the approximate dates of works attributed to him. Bernard seems to have spent most of his life teaching at the Cathedral school of Tours. He dedicated his most famous work, the *Cosmographia*, to Thierry of Chartres, who was still alive at the time, and it is possible that he studied under Thierry at Paris or at Chartres. He also shows profound knowledge of William of Conches, with whom he either studied or whom he read extensively. Because of this he has long been associated with the Chartrian tradition. The only sure date we have for Bernard is 1147, when he read his *Cosmographia* before Pope Eugene III. Bernard, we are told, won the pope's favor.

Thought. Bernard Silvester wrote commentaries and imaginative poetry in the great tradition of Boethius' *Consolation of Philosophy* and Plato's *Timaeus*. He sought to demonstrate the compatibility of pagan and Arabic thought with Christian teaching, and he saw classical literature as the outside wrapping (*integumentum*) of the inner kernel of divine truth. The task of the philosopher was to unlock the interpretative key and to reveal the truth that lay within, but Bernard moved from philosophical commentator to creator of mythic poetry. He saw himself as the poet inspired by God to reveal God's marvelous plan through the creative use of language. The legacy of his groundbreaking work can be found in Matthew of Vendome, Alan of Lille, and Dante. Fate played a large role in his writings, as did the power of God revealed in the created world and life of humanity. He is a poet who demonstrates a deep knowledge of the Aristotelian corpus as it was understood through mid-twelfth century Latin translations, as well as through Islamic philosophical and scientific works.

Works. Bernard's most celebrated work is the *Cosmographia* (1147). It is divided into two parts, the "Megacosmos," which deals with the creation of the universe, and the "Microcosmos," which discusses the creation of humanity. Natura, a goddess who personifies the spirit of nature, calls on Noys, another allegorical figure who represents the Platonic equivalent of the divine mind and wisdom, to grant form to Silva, the undifferentiated and unformed chaos. Noys, who also represents the Second Person of the Trinity, obliges by creating the universe, which Natura can then shape. Noys sends Natura to consult with Urania and Physis, the personifications of reason and the physical cosmos, on the creation of a human body and soul, which Natura then binds together. The three goddesses traverse the cosmos, momentarily passing outside the bounds of the celestial spheres to glimpse the abode of the Trinity. Not only does Bernard affirm the value and power of the creativity of the natural world, but humanity is also shown to be a co-creator along with Natura and the Divine Noys. The sciences and philosophy are the tools that humanity uses to participate fully in the sacred created and creating cosmos. However, human frailty is also stressed to the point of pessimism, since in Bernard's view the human condition is rife with instability, temptation, and sin. Fate looms large, and life is desperate when it is devoid of grace. This recognition of human frailty is responsible for the sad tone of the ending passage.

Fate is also one of the central themes of the *Mathematicus* (*c.* 1150), a long poem based on one of the *Declamations of pseudo-Quintilian*. In the *Mathematicus* an astrologer reveals to a mother that her son, Patricida, will grow up and kill his righteous father. Distraught, she has him raised elsewhere. After both father and son learn of fate's plan, they each offer their own lives so that the other may live. While his father appears to be following the guidance of fate, the Christ-like Patricida, who is now the king of his land, refuses to accept fate and offers himself. His suicide is a solution that prevents an almost inevitable act of violence against his father and a reaction against a blind adherence to the power of fate. Bernard again creatively reworks the poetic tradition and offers his own Christian theological vision hidden within the rhetoric of the metaphor. The poem cuts off before its ending, perhaps inviting the reader into the moral dilemma.

Bernard also appears to be the author of an introduction to the *Experimentarius*, (date uncertain) a book of divination. Once again the dominant theme is that of fate. The author writes in an apologetic that he—he uses the third person plural—does not worship the planets or the stars or see them as having inert power over the affairs of humanity. However, in the Christian Platonic tradition, he does insist that God, who alone is worshiped, has created the cosmos in such a way that God's power is filtered through the planets and the stars. This divine power is the power of fate, or perhaps better phrased as the power of divine providence.

Commentaries on Virgil's *Aeneid* (*c.*1125–30) and Martianus Capella's *De nuptiis* (*c.* 1130–35) have long been thought to be by Bernard, but a scholarly consensus has not been achieved. His commentary on Plato's *Timaeus* has of yet not been identified.

Bibliography: *Cosmographiai* ed. P. DRONKE (Leiden 1978); English trans. W. WETHERBEE (New York 1973). *Mathematicus*, ed. B. HAUREAU, *Le Mathematicus de Bernard Sylvestris* (Paris 1895). *The Commentary on the First Six Books of Virgil's Aeneid*, eds. J. W. JONES and E. F. JONES (Lincoln 1977). *The Commentary on Martianus Capella's De nupiis Philologiae et mercurii*, ed. H. H. WESTRA (Toronto 1986). *Experimentarius*, ed. M. BRINI SAVORELLI, ''Un manuale di geomanzia presentato da Bernardo Silvestre da Tours, XII secolo: l'Experimentarius,'' *Rivista Cristica di Storia della Filosofia XIV* (1959) 283–342. Literature. W. WETHERBEE, *Platonism and Poetry in the Twelfth Century. The Literary Influence of the School of Chartres* (Princeton 1972). C. S. F. BURNETT, ''What is the Experimentarius of Bernardus Silvestris? A Preliminary Survey of the Material'' *AHDLMA* xliv:79–125. T. SILVERSTEIN, ''Elementatum: Its Appearance among the Twelfth-Century Cosmogonists'' *Mediaeval Studies 16* (1954): 156–62; ''The Fabulous Cosmogony of Bernardus Silvestris: Cornifician Attack on the Liberal Arts'' *Viator 3* (1972): 219–73. B. STOCK, *Myth and Science in the Twelfth Century: A Study of Bernard Silvester* (Princeton 1972). E. GILSON, ''La Cosmogonie de Bernardus Silvestris,'' *AHDLMA* 3 (1928) 5–24. R. B.WOOLSEY, ''Bernard Silvester and the Hermetic Asclepius'' *Traditio 6* (1948): 340–44.

[P. ELLARD]

BERNARD TOLOMEI, BL.

Founder of the Olivetan Benedictines; b. Siena, May 10, 1272; d. Siena, August 20, 1348. As a youth, Bernard wanted to become a religious, but could not obtain his father's consent. He served in the armies of King Rudolph I, studied law, and became *podestà* (magistrate) of Siena. In 1313, with two companions, he withdrew into solitude at Accona, and in 1319 Bishop Guido of Arezzo gave the little community a white habit and the Benedictine Rule. At Accona, Bernard founded the monastery of Our Lady of Monte Oliveto, from which developed the strongly centralized Olivetan Benedictine Congregation (*see* BENEDICTINES, OLIVETAN). The primitive penitential observance exercised a strong appeal and for a while the institute grew rapidly. Bernard died caring for victims of the Black Death.

Feast: August 21.

Bibliography: S. M. AVANZO, *Fratello Bernardo: ''vester sum totus''* (Siena 1990). A. DONATELLI, *Il beato Bernardo Tolomei* (Siena 1976); *Giovanni Bernardo Tolomei, padre e maestro di monaci* (Siena 1977). P. LUGANO, ''La causa . . . B. Bernardo . . . ,'' *Rivista Storica Benedettina* 17 (1926) 204–289. B. HEURTEBIZE, *Dictionnaire d'histoire et de géographie ecclésiastiques*, ed. A. BAUDRILLART, et al. (Paris 1912–) 8:728–730. P. SCHMITZ, *Histoire de l'ordre de Saint-Benoît,* 7 v. (Maredsous 1942–56) 3:22–23. A. BUTLER, *The Lives of the Saints*, rev. ed. H. THURSTON and D. ATTWATER (New York 1956) 3:379–380.

[A. G. BIGGS]

BERNARDES, MANOEL

Oratorian writer and scholar; b. Lisbon, Aug. 20, 1644; d. there, Aug. 17, 1710. After studying canon law and philosophy at the University of Coimbra, he entered the Oratorians at Lisbon and dedicated himself to a life of study and preaching. He is remembered principally for his numerous writings, which rank among the classics of Portuguese literature, and as a foremost representative of Oratorian mysticism. Written with a simplicity of language, an elegance of style, and a vivid imagination, his spiritual treatises reveal a breadth of knowledge and deep religious inspiration. Among his works are *Exercicios espirituaes e meditaçôes* (2 v. Lisbon 1686); *Luz e calor* (Lisbon 1696); *Nova floresta* (5 v. 1706–28); and *Os últimos fins do homem* (Lisbon 1728).

Bibliography: P. AUVRAY, *Dictionnaire de spiritualité ascétique et mystique: Doctrine et histoire* (Paris 1932–) 1:1514. A. F. DO CASTILLO, *Manoel Bernardes* (Rio de Janeiro 1865). L. A. REBELO DA SILVA, ''O Padre Manoel Bernardes,'' *Bosquejos historico-literaros* 2 (1909) 93–139.

[J. C. WILLKE]

BERNARDIN, JOSEPH LOUIS

Cardinal, archbishop of Chicago; b. April 2, 1928, Columbia, South Carolina; d. Nov. 16, 1996, Chicago, Illinois. Bernardin was the oldest of two children born to Joseph and Maria Simion Bernardin. His father, a stonecutter who came to America from the province of Trent in Northern Italy, died when Joseph was six. His father's death drew him closer to his mother and his sister, Elaine. He studied for the priesthood at St. Mary's College in Kentucky and at St. Mary's Seminary and University in Baltimore, where in 1948 he received an A.B. degree in philosophy before going to the Catholic University of America for a master's in education in 1952. Ordained a priest for the Diocese of Charleston on April 26, 1952, he served as vice chancellor (1954–56), chancellor (1956–66), vicar general and diocesan consultor (1962–66), and administrator (1964–65). Pope Paul VI named him auxiliary bishop of Atlanta on March 9, 1966. As auxiliary bishop Bernardin also served as pastor of Atlanta's Christ the King Cathedral from 1966 to 1968.

In 1968 Bishop Bernardin was elected general secretary of the National Conference of Catholic Bishops (NCCB) and the United States Catholic Conference (USCC) in Washington, D.C. The newly established NCCB responded to the Second Vatican Council's call for national episcopal conferences and the USCC succeeded the National Catholic Welfare Conference as the permanent secretariat of the U.S. bishops.

Bernardin was installed as archbishop of CINCINNATI Dec. 19 1972. During his decade in Cincinnati he was host to his good friend, Karol Cardinal Wojtyła of Krakow, Poland. It is said that after Cardinal Wojtyła became Pope JOHN PAUL II he told the then-archbishop of Chicago, John Cardinal Cody, that his eventual successor would be Bernardin. Following Cody's death Bernardin was installed (August 25, 1982) and the next year John Paul II named him a cardinal, with the titular church of Gesù Divin Lavoratore.

The first American cardinal created by Pope John Paul II, Bernardin became a leading spokesman for the Church in the United States, with a reputation as a conciliator and mediator. He published several books, but most of his writing took the form of pastoral letters. He was also active on the international level, serving as a member of the permanent council of the Synod of Bishops from 1974 to 1994.

In the early 1980s Bernardin chaired an ad hoc NCCB committee to examine war and peace questions. The result of the committee's work was the pastoral letter *The Challenge of Peace: God's Promise and Our Response*, issued by the bishops in 1983, which led to Cardinal Bernardin receiving the Albert Einstein International Peace Prize. In a lecture at Fordham University that same year, he spoke of the pastoral letter as providing a starting point for developing a "consistent ethic of life." The

Joseph Louis Cardinal Bernardin. (Catholic News Service)

"dominant cultural fact" in increasing the modern awareness of the fragility of life, he said, is technology; and a consistent ethic of life is necessary to address the moral questions that arise in this context. Over the next few years Cardinal Bernardin repeatedly adverted to the theme of a "consistent ethic of life" as an essential element of the Catholic approach to a variety of moral questions, including abortion, euthanasia, capital punishment, nuclear war, poverty, and racism. In a lecture at St. Louis University in 1984, he referred to the linkage of these ideas as a "seamless garment," an expression that quickly became the popular way to refer to the concept.

In 1993 a former seminarian charged that he had been sexually abused in the 1970s, naming Bernardin as an abuser. The cardinal strongly denied the charge. He met and prayed with his accuser, who recanted. After June 1995, when Bernardin was diagnosed with pancreatic cancer, he reached out to cancer patients and the dying in his personal ministry. Pope John Paul spoke of Bernardin's "witness of dignity and hope in the face of the mystery of suffering and death." He died in Chicago of pancreatic cancer on Nov. 14, 1996. It was, his doctor said, a heroic death of one who loved life. He was interred in the mausoleum at Mount Carmel Cemetery in suburban Hillside. Several months later, a book of his re-

"St. Bernardine of Siena," center panel of a predella, tempera painting on panel by the Sienese artist Pietro di Giovanni.

flections on his last years, *The Gift of Peace*, was published and quickly became a bestseller.

Bibliography: Cardinal Bernardin's extensive personal papers are in the Joseph Cardinal Bernardin Archives and Records Center, 711 W. Monroe, Chicago.

[A. E. P. WALL]

BERNARDINE OF SIENA, ST.

Franciscan preacher and propagator of devotion to the Holy Name; b. Massa Marittima, in the territory of Siena, Sept. 8, 1380; d. Aquila, May 1444.

Life. When Bernardine was three years of age his mother (Nera degli Avveduti) died, and three years later the death of his father (Tollo degli Albizzeschi) left him an orphan. He was confided to the care of a maternal aunt, but at the age of 11 he was taken by paternal relatives to Siena, where he attended school and studied the humanities and philosophy (1391–97), and for another three years he studied Canon Law at the university in that city. Bernardine was devoted to the Latin classics, but he gave himself with no less enthusiasm to the study of Scripture and theology and to practices of piety. During the pestilence of the jubilee year 1400 he spent four months ministering to the plague-stricken in the hospital of Santa Maria della Scala until he himself became ill. He entered the Friars Minor when he was 22, was professed in 1403, and was ordained the following year. In 1405 he was commissioned to preach, and he continued in that work until his death.

Little is known of the first 15 years of his religious life. No doubt he spent them gathering his abundant knowledge of scholastic writings. During this period he transcribed or caused to be transcribed various books, two of which, entirely in his own hand, were discovered in 1962–63 (Codex 102 in the library of the University of Budapest and Codex VI. A. 19 of the National Library of Naples). He also began to attract attention as a preacher. For three years (1414–17) he held the office of vicar provincial of the Observants of Tuscany, at the completion of which he gave himself completely to the evangelization of Lombardy. The years 1417–29 were the most important period of his preaching. During this time he was engaged without remission in preaching throughout central and northern Italy. In the last 15 years of his life Bernardine continued his apostolic journeys, but these became more slowly paced because of the infirmities of age and his administrative responsibilities (he was vicar general of the Observants of Italy, 1438–1442) and because of his repeated and increasingly prolonged stays in the Sienese convent of Capriola, his ordinary place of residence, for the purpose of writing down and revising his treatises and sermons. In 1444, after completing his Lenten preaching in his native city of Massa, and in spite of his age and infirmity, Bernardine set out to evangelize the Kingdom of Naples. Some miles from Aquila in the Abruzzi he was stricken with a fever and could not go on. He was taken to Aquila and received in the convent of St. Francis, where he died peacefully on the vigil of the Feast of the Ascension. The city gave him the honor of a funeral of unprecedented splendor, and he was buried in the church of St. Francis. He was canonized by Nicholas V, May 24, 1450. His body was transferred May 17, 1471, to the nearby basilica erected in his honor and put in a magnificent shrine, where it is still preserved in an incorrupt state.

Preaching. The apostolate of Bernardine was singularly fruitful. He was the greatest preacher of his time. Cities everywhere invited him to come and preach, and when he did appear, churches were too small to contain the throngs that gathered to hear him, so that he was obliged to preach in the open. It is said that his audience sometimes numbered as many as 30,000. The reason for his success was, above all else, his holiness of life. St. Francis was his model of virtue, and he was like the holy patriarch also in his zealous concern to maintain a high standard of religious observance in the Franciscan community and to labor tirelessly for the moral reformation of the people. He was Franciscan—persuasive, fervent, joyous, and sometimes even merry. Other factors contributing to his success were: his acute intelligence, coupled with an intuitive understanding of the needs of his time and the mental and spiritual condition of his hearers; his superb gift of eloquence; the clarity and vivacity of his language; his use of a kind of dialogue form in the development of his argument; and his practicality in confining himself to themes of general interest. He disapproved of the practice, common at the time among preachers, of inveighing against the vices of ecclesiastics. He considered it better to inspire the people with reverence for the priestly state, and it was his wont to speak to the clergy separately at the conclusion of his ''missions.'' He was temperate when touching upon political matters and strove to rise above factionalism and differences of government.

Devotion to the Holy Name. St. Bernardine is especially remembered for his zeal in promoting devotion to the Holy Name. This devotion was not a new thing in the Church, but he contributed greatly to its spread, and he devised a symbol to help people appreciate its profound theological basis. This was the trigrammatic abbreviation ''yhs,'' in minuscule Gothic letters, of the name of Jesus. The trigram was set in the midst of a blazing sun, to whose spreading rays he attributed a mystical significance. He desired that this emblem should displace superstitious symbols and the insignia of factions. Through the apostolate of Bernardine and his disciples the cult of the Holy Name spread rapidly, and its symbol began to appear in churches, homes, and public buildings. Certain humanists and theologians of the time viewed this with distrust and considered the devotion a dangerous innovation. Three attempts were made to induce ecclesiastical authority to take action against Bernardine (in 1426 under Martin V, and in 1431 under Eugene IV, and in 1438 an appeal was made to the Council of Basel). St. Bernardine's vindication was such that no shadow of suspicion remained upon his orthodoxy, the rightness of his intentions, or the holiness of his life. Perhaps by way of amends and reward he was offered, successively, the bishoprics of Siena (to which he was elected), Ferrara, and Urbino, but he declined these honors.

Writings. Bernardine's literary work is almost entirely homiletic. A distinction should be made between the sermons, etc., edited by himself for the use of preachers, and true theological treatises, compiled with acumen and discernment from the writings of the great scholastic doctors, from the *Expositio super Apocalypsim* of Matthias of Sweden (of Linköping), from the *Arbor vitae crucifixae* of UBERTINO OF CASALE, and from the writings of PETER JOHN OLIVI. Of notable importance are the sermons and treatises on the name of Jesus, the Passion, and St. Joseph. Of special value, also, are the 11 sermons on the Madonna, which, taken together, constitute a complete Mariology. For their novelty and originality of method the sermons met with great success, which explains the considerable number of codices (about 300), all transcribed within the span of about 40 years, until they were all printed in various incunabula editions (1470–1501) or reprinted in sequence in *S. Bernardini Sen. Ord. Min. opera quae exrant omnia* (4 v. Venice 1591; Paris 1635; Lyons 1650; Venice 1745). These editions, however, contain certain works now known to be spurious. A critical edition of St. Bernardine's works is published by the Franciscan Fathers of Quaracchi.

Bernardine's sermons taken down by others do not have the same authority as those the saint edited himself, because it is improbable that his words were always put down in shorthand with absolute fidelity. Nevertheless, they are of considerable interest, especially those preached in Siena in 1427 (whose word-for-word accuracy is better authenticated), because of the biographical and historical data they provide and because of the light they throw upon the real personality of Bernardine and upon his abilities as a popular preacher.

Feast: May 20.

Bibliography: *S. Bernardini Sen. O.F.M., Opera omnia, studio et cura PP. Collegii S. Bonaventurae ad fidem codicum edita,* 9 vols. (Quaracchi-Florence 1950–1965). *Enciclopedia bernardiniana,* 2 v., v. 1. ed. E. D'ANGELO; v. 2 ed. M. A. PAVONE and V. PACELLI (Aquila 1980–1981). M. H. ALLIES, *Three Catholic Reformers of the Fifteenth Century* (Freeport, N.Y. 1972). F. MORMANDO, *The Preacher's Demons: Bernardino of Siena and the Social Underworld of Early Renaissance Italy* (Chicago 1999). C. POLECRITTI, *Preaching Peace in Renaissance Italy: Bernardino of Siena and His Audience* (Washington, D.C. 2000). R. DE ROOVER, *San Bernardino of Siena and Sant'Antonino of Florence* (Boston 1967). D. PACETTI, *L'Expositio super Apocalypsim di Mattia di Svezia,* 1281–1350: *Precipua fonte dottrinale di S. Bernardino da Siena, Archivum Franncíscanum historicum* 54 (1961), 274–302; ''Le postille autografe sopra l'Apocalisse di S. B. da S. recentemente scoperte nella Biblioteca Nazionale di Napoli,'' *ibid.* 56 (1963), 40–70; ''Le fonti dottrinali di S. B. a servizio del suo fecondo apostolato,'' *Studi Francescani* 60 (1963), 3–19. M. BERTAGNA, ''Vita e apostolato senese di S. B.,'' *ibid.* 20–99.

[D. PACETTI]

BERNARDINO OF FELTRE, BL.

Franciscan preacher; b. Feltre, in Venezia, Italy, 1439; d. Pavia, Sept. 28, 1494. He was born Martin Tomitano. After proving himself an excellent student in his early years, he was sent to the University of Padua. Impressed by the preaching of JAMES OF THE MARCHES, he joined the Franciscan Observants in May of 1456, taking his religious name after BERNARDINE OF SIENA, who had just been canonized. Ordained in 1463, he began his public preaching some six years later. He soon became immensely popular, and crowds flocked to hear his sermons (*Sermoni del beato Bernardino da Feltre,* ed. Carlo da Milano, Milan 1940) as he journeyed through the towns of northern Italy. Like his contemporary SAVONAROLA, he denounced the numerous abuses of the day and often ended his preaching with the burning of various vanities on a bonfire. Bernardine has become almost equally well known through his connection with Barnabas of Terni (d. 1472) and the establishment of the *MONTES PIETATIS*, a scheme whereby the poor could borrow money at low interest rates on the pledge of various goods, thus avoiding the clutches of usurious bankers, who were the contemporary scandal of Italy. Although he met much opposition from the bankers, as well as from those who objected to his charging even a reasonable rate of interest (*see* USURY) to make the operation self-supporting, Bernardine helped to establish some 30 *montes pietatis* during the last years of his apostolate. He was buried at S. Maria del Carmine in Pavia, and his cult was recognized in 1654. He is honored by the FRANCISCANS and is the patron of pawnbrokers.

Feast: Sept. 28.

Bibliography: A. LUISE, *Alza la voce come una bella tromba: aspetti della predicazione del beato Bernardino da Feltre* (Belluno, Italy 1994). V. MENEGHIN, *Iconografia del b. Bernardino Tomitano da Feltre* (Venice 1967). G. PALUDET, *Bernardino da Feltre: piccolo e poverello* (Venice 1993). O. PAMPALONI, *Storia di conventi e nobili famiglie* (San Casciano 1993).

[B. J. COMASKEY]

BERNARDINO OF LAREDO

Physician, Franciscan laybrother, ascetical and mystical writer whose works influenced St. Teresa; b. Laredo, Spain, 1482; d. 1540, near Seville. Bernardino came from a distinguished family, probably originating at the small fishing port of Laredo on the Cantabrian coast. As a boy he was placed as a page in the household of a Portuguese nobleman, the Conde de Gelves. Before he was 12 he had a desire to join the Franciscan order and thought of applying to the Capuchin province of Los Angeles in southern Spain. However, he was dissuaded from giving effect to this desire by the majordomo of the Gelves household. Continuing to cherish his longing for perfection, Bernardino then devoted himself to study, following an arts course and afterwards studying medicine, possibly at the University of Seville. He graduated and later obtained a doctor's degree. When Bernardino found that one of his friends, a doctor in law, had become a Franciscan laybrother, he determined to follow his example. He asked for the laybrother's habit at the Convento de San Francisco del Monte, a house of Franciscans of Regular Observance near Seville. There he lived a life of great austerity, fasting on bread and water on Mondays, Wednesdays, and Fridays, and on other days of the week eating the friars' leavings. He was eventually made infirmarian, and his medical knowledge was much sought after. Among the many patients he treated successfully was John II, king of Portugal, who, when the illness from which he was suffering took a dangerous turn, sent for the Franciscan laybrother.

Laredo found time and opportunity for writing, however. Besides two medical treatises, he wrote a work on asceticism and contemplation, the *Subida del Monte Sion.* Contemplation, Laredo says, can be achieved only through the Cross. Contemplative prayer is for all who are prepared to pay the price, for layfolk and married people as well as for friars and priests. He attaches considerable importance to fasts and vigils; it would seem that his own health was robust. At the same time he stresses the need for discretion. In a second edition of his book, Laredo's teaching on contemplation shows modification. He there emphasizes that contemplation is the work of the will rather than of the mind and puts forward the theory of love without knowledge, later taken up in Spain by John of the Angels and Jerónimo Gracián.

Bibliography: Works. BERNARDINO DE LAREDO, *Metaphora medicinae* (Seville 1522 and 1546); *Modus faciendi cum ordine medicandi* (Seville 1527, 1534, 1542, 1627); *Subida del Monte Sion* (Seville 1535). **Studies**. BERNARDINO DE LAREDO, *The Ascent of Mount Sion,* tr. and ed. E. A. PEERS (New York 1952) book 3 only of the treatise. FIDÈLE DE ROS, *Le Frère Bernardin de Laredo: Un inspirateur de sainte Thérèse* (Paris 1948). *Enciclopedia universal ilustrada Europeo-Americana* (Barcelona 1908–30) 29:824.

[K. E. POND]

BERNAY, ABBEY OF

Benedictine monastery in Lower Normandy, France, formerly in the Diocese of Lisieux (today Évreux). It was founded by Judith, wife of Duke Richard II of Normandy (1010–15), with the counsel of Abbot William of Dijon, who sent the first monks from FÉCAMP. On Judith's death (1017) her husband confirmed the donations in a charter signed also by their three sons and by bishops and lords of Normandy (1025). Thierry and Ralph were guardian priors who administered the abbey after 1028. The first abbot, Vital of Fécamp, was promoted to abbot of WESTMINSTER (1075). Begon of Murat was rector of the Cluniac college of St. Martial in Avignon, procurator general, vicar of Abbot John of Cluny, and visitor for the reform of Cluniac monasteries (1384–95). François Bo-hier, dean of Tours and provost of Normandy, was the delegate of the Regent Louise of Savoy to the comitia of Normandy (1525–26) and became bishop of Saint-Malo (1535–69). Drogon Hennequin de Villenoce, canon of Paris and commendatory abbot (1598–1651), rebuilt church and buildings and introduced the Maurist reform (1628). Léon Potier de Gesvres (d. 1744) was abbot of Bernay (1666) and AURILLAC (1679), archbishop of Bourges (1693), cardinal (1719), and abbot of SAINT-AMAND-LÈS-EAUX (1720) and SAINT-REMI (1729). Bernay was pillaged by both sides in the Hundred Years' War. In the Wars of Religion, Calvinists took it, killed the priests, burned the charter room and treasury, and left it in ruins (1562–63). Rebuilt, it was burned by the League (1590–96).

The abbey church (220 feet by 64 feet by 54 feet) was built in three stages (1020–55), determined by the style of the capitals. The nave had seven bays with aisles and a prominent transept topped by a massive tower; the transept had cross aisles terminated by apsidal chapels. In the 16th century the oven-shaped apse was replaced by a five-sided chevet; and its apsidal chapels, by straight walls pierced by windows with flamboyant tracery. The Maurists replaced two bays with a monumental façade and redid the vaulting. Chevet and tower were destroyed in the French Revolution; the church, an interesting Romanesque monument of Normandy, noteworthy for capitals influenced by those of the Burgundian Saint-Benigné in Dijon, continues to be secularized.

Bibliography: *Gallia Christiana* (Paris 1715–85) 11:830–834. J. BILSON, ''La Date et la construction de l'église abbatiale de Bernay,'' *Bulletin Monumental* 75 (1909) 403–422. A. A. PORÉE, ''L'Église abbatiale de Bernay,'' *Congrès archéologique de France* 75 (1910) 588–614. G. BONNENFANT, *Histoire générale du diocèse d'Evreux,* 2 v. (Paris 1933), *passim.* L. GRODECKI, ''Les Débuts de la sculpture romane en Normandie: Bernay,'' *Bulletin Monumental* 108 (1950) 7–67. P. CALENDINI, *Dictionnaire d'histoire et de géographie ecclésiastiques,* ed. A. BAUDRILLART et al. (Paris 1912–) 8:812–815.

[P. COUSIN]

BERNETTI, TOMMASO

Cardinal, papal secretary of state; b. Fermo, Italy, Dec. 29, 1779; d. there, March 21, 1852. After studying philosophy and law at the University of Fermo, he went to Rome (1800) and soon became secretary to the Rota. He accompanied the papal court to France (1808) and joined Cardinal Brancadoro, his uncle, in Reims, where Napoleon I exiled him (1810). There he acted as intermediary between the captive Pius VII, the cardinals, and the Belgian Catholics. Following Bernetti's return to Rome (1814), Pius VII sent him to persuade Austria to evacuate the Legations (1815). After serving as papal legate to Ferrara, governor and head of the police of Rome (1820–26), and papal representative at the coronation of Czar Nicholas I in Moscow (1826), he became a cardinal (1827), but he was not ordained priest until 1832. He succeeded DELLA SOMAGLIA as secretary of state from June 17, 1828, until the death of LEO XII on Feb. 10, 1829, after which Cardinal Giuseppe ALBANI assumed the office under Pius VIII (1829–30), who sent Bernetti as legate to Bologna. GREGORY XVI appointed Bernetti as prosecretary of state (Feb. 10, 1831) and secretary from Aug. 10, 1831, to Jan. 20, 1836. Revolution in the STATES OF THE CHURCH (1831), followed by intervention of the great powers who submitted a memorandum (May 21, 1831) demanding civil reforms, taxed Bernetti's abilities. He upheld papal independence, sternly repressed continuing disorders, organized a voluntary local militia, obtained Austrian military aid, and thereby preserved the state. When the French occupied Ancona (1832), Bernetti procured their evacuation by his diplomatic skill and patience. His unwillingness to become dependent on Austria, while seeking its military help, led Metternich to have LAMBRUSCHINI named secretary of state. Pius IX named Bernetti, together with Cardinal Gizzi and Lambruschini, a member of a consultative commission to help govern the States of the Church (1846). During the Roman uprising in 1848 Bernetti suffered a brief arrest, then joined the Pope at Gaeta. Ill health caused his retirement to Fermo (1850). He was an active, cultured, and good man, although the revolutionaries considered him intransigent and reactionary.

Bibliography: L. JADIN, *Dictionnaire d'histoire et de géographie ecclésiastiques,* ed. A. BAUDRILLART et al. (Paris 1912–) 8:828–830. E. MORELLI, *La politica estera di Tommaso Bernetti* (Rome 1953). L. PÁSZTOR, ''I Cardinali Albani e Bernetti e l'intervento austraico nel 1831,'' *Rivista di storia della Chiesa iri Italia* 8 (1954) 95–128.

[A. RANDALL]

BERNGER, BL.

Abbot; d. Oct. 29, 1108. He was the first abbot of the BENEDICTINE monastery of Formbach near Passau in Bavaria, having been brought there in 1094 by Bp. Ulric of Passau (d.1121) from the reforming monastery of Schwarzach am Main. He was succeeded as abbot by his friend, Wirnt, in 1108. He was known for his personal sanctity, his capable rule, and his generosity to widows, orphans, and the poor. At his order, the first collection of the customs of Formbach was begun.

Feast: Oct. 29.

Bibliography: *Vita Wirntonis,* ch. 1, *Monumenta Germaniae Historica: Scriptores* 15.2:1127–28; *Patrologia Latina* 194:

1427–28. A. M. ZIMMERMANN, *Kalendarium Benedictinum: Die Heiligen und Seligen des Benediktinerorderns und seiner Zweige* 3:231, 233. K. HALLINGER, *Gorze-Kluny,* 2 v. (StAnselm fasc. Rome 1950–51) v.1. J. OSWALD, *Lexikon für Theologie und Kirche*[2] 2:237.

[J. C. MOORE]

BERNIER, ÉTIENNE ALEXANDRE

Bishop of Orléans, prominent in politico-ecclesiastical affairs; b. Daon (Mayenne), France, Oct. 31, 1762; d. Paris, Oct. 1, 1806. After ordination (1786) he became a doctor of theology (1787), professor at the University of Angers, and pastor of St. Laud's parish in that city. During the French Revolution he refused to take the oath (1790) in support of the CIVIL CONSTITUTION OF THE CLERGY. For this he was replaced by the constitutional pastor Yves Besnard, but Bernier's opposition made the intruder's position unbearable. After the taking of Saumur, Bernier joined the army in the Vendée. By his ability, valor, and intrigues, he became one of the leaders of the insurrection, although lacking official title. He sided with Stofflet against Charette, and negotiated the peace of Saint-Florent with the generals of the Republic. After the deaths of Stofflet and Charette, Louis XVIII named him *agent général* of the Catholic and royal armies. But Bernier, realizing that the Vendée was incapable of continuing the battle, remained aloof from the final uprising in 1799.

Unable to deal with the Directory, he bided his time in order to begin a new career as a negotiator. The Coup d'État of Brumaire (Nov. 9, 1799) supplied a favorable opportunity, which he hastened to seize by offering his services to NAPOLEON. He duped the last Vendean leaders and concluded (Jan. 19, 1800) with General Hédouville the Peace of Montfaucon, which granted religious liberty to the Vendeans. Crowned with this success, he went to Paris, where Bonaparte frequently received him and listened to his counsels. The first consul also chose him to negotiate a concordat with SPINA, the papal representative, promising to reward him with the see of Paris and a cardinal's hat. Bernier, a very capable but somewhat unscrupulous diplomat, revealed his skill by defending to the best of his ability the interests of the Holy See. Once the CONCORDAT OF 1801 was concluded, Bernier helped put it into effect, and also acted as an intermediary between Portalis and the papal legate CAPRARA. His double role resulted in his composing both the notes of the French government and Cardinal Caprara's replies to them, in order to make more certain their agreement. This, plus his doubtful attitude at the time of the pretended retractation of the constitutional bishops promoted to new sees under the Concordat, led to his disgrace. Instead of obtaining the archdiocese of Paris, he had to content himself with the bishopric of Orléans (1802). If Pius VII named him cardinal, it was merely *in petto.*

TALLEYRAND had further recourse to his tact, having him negotiate the Italian and German Concordats and the imperial coronation of Napoleon. Bernier was the one who drafted the famous note that convinced the pope to come to Paris for the imperial consecration. He also regulated the entire ceremonial of this event in conjunction with Pius VII, who agreed to let Napoleon crown himself. In vain did he try to reestablish his personal position by having himself appointed nuncio to Germany. Confined to his diocese, Bernier proved a remarkably good administrator and an exemplary bishop. Ambitious, crafty, but exceptionally intelligent, he performed great services in his own fashion without succeeding in raising himself to the highest level, or in dissipating the very mixed impression created by his enigmatic character and his overclever manner.

Bibliography: J. LEFLON, *Étienne-Alexandre Bernier, évêque d'Orléans,* 2 v. (Paris 1938); *Étienne Bernier: Lettres, notes diplomatiques, mémoires, rapports inédits* (Reims 1938).

[J. LEFLON]

BERNIÈRES-LOUVIGNY, JEAN DE

Mystic; b. Caen, France, 1602; d. there, May 3, 1659. Son of Baron Pierre de Louvigny and Marguerite de Lion-Roger, Bernières-Louvigny came of one of the most distinguished houses of Normandy. Little is known of his early life or education. He did not become a priest or religious but lived devoutly as a layman. He had part in the establishment of a center of the celebrated COMPAGNIE DU SAINT-SACREMENT, through which he engaged in many charitable works. He assisted, financially and otherwise, in the foundation of many religious houses, hospitals, and seminaries. One of his charitable works was the erection of the Ursuline convent at Caen, where his sister, Jourdaine, was foundress and superior. He placed himself under the direction of a well-known Franciscan, Père Jean-Chrysostome, and following his advice built a hermitage in the outer courtyard of the Ursuline convent, to which he retired with a few companions.

In 1647 he made a private vow of poverty, giving his possessions to his nephews and charity. He led a life of celibacy, and as a layman was noted for austerities commonly associated with the most strict religious life. He acquired a singular reputation as a spiritual director, and after the death of Jean-Chrysostome took over the direction of a number of souls who had been dependent on the friar. He entered into correspondence and was associated with many other contemporary ascetics, particularly St. John Eudes, Marie des Valles, and Mère MARIE DE L'INCARNATION. Bernières-Louvigny was associated with Mère Marie and a Madame de la Peltrie in the foundation of the Ursuline community at Quebec. He seems to have attended to much of the financial and business negotiations connected with the support of the foundation.

Bernières-Louvigny published nothing himself; but he left notes he had dictated on spiritual topics, and a number of his letters were preserved. Some of his notes were published the year of his death under the title *L'Intérieur Chrétien*, and others soon after under the title *Le Chrétien Intérieur*. Both editions were very popular, and there were at least a dozen other publications, all anonymous and some rather dubious. In 1670 his sister brought out *Les oeuvres spirituelles de M. de Bernières-Louvigny*, which also became popular. *Le Chrétien Intérieur* was placed on the Index in 1689 and *Les oeuvres* in 1692, both cited for QUIETISM. There is some doubt that he was really responsible for the objectionable doctrine, because the MSS may have been tampered with. Corrected editions have since been issued.

Bibliography: P. POURRAT, *Catholicisme* 1:1491–92. R. HEURTEVENT, *L'oeuvre spirituelle de Jean de Bernières* (Paris 1938); M. VILLERS, *Dictionnaire de spiritualité ascétique et mystique* 1:1522–27.

[A. J. CLARK]

BERNINI, GIOVANNI LORENZO

The greatest sculptor and architect of the Italian baroque; b. Naples, 1598; d. Rome, Nov. 28, 1680. A child prodigy, Bernini learned the rudiments of his art from his father, Pietro, a Florentine late mannerist sculptor. In 1605 the family moved to Rome, where Bernini remained, except for a six-month sojourn (1665) at the court of Louis XIV in Paris. He was named architect to St. Peter's, where for more than 50 years he directed vast enterprises in the area of the Vatican (*see* ST. PETER'S BASILICA). Throughout the city he renovated and designed churches, squares, chapels, tombs, palaces, and fountains; he invented the full baroque portrait bust; he officiated in a gamut of civic undertakings from the planning of illuminations, carnival floats, fireworks, and catafalques to the presentation of operas and comedies for which he created the costumes and stage machinery. Bernini was one of the last of the "universal men." He gave Rome its baroque character and Europe a new sculptural style that reigned for several centuries.

Bernini's early reputation was made with three life-size marble groups (1618–24): "Aeneas and Anchises," "Pluto and Proserpina," and "Apollo and Daphne," as

Giovanni Lorenzo Bernini.

well as with "David," executed for Cardinal Scipione Borghese. He divided his attention equally between antique sculpture and contemporary painting; his astonishing craftsmanship delighted in technical feats of realism until then considered outside the realm of sculpture. The Roman Curia, notably Popes URBAN VIII, INNOCENT X, and ALEXANDER VII were Bernini's principal patrons. Among his achievements in St. Peter's are some of the most opulent expressions of the *Ecclesia triumphans:* the "Baldacchino" (1624–33); the decoration of chapels and nave; the "Scala Regia" (1663–66); the "Cathedra Petri" in the apse (1657–66); and the design for St. Peter's Square (1656–67). As in all Bernini's churches, S. Andrea al Quirinale (1658–67) combines architecture, sculpture, and ornamentation to form an indivisible unity whose purpose is to illumine the mystery of St. Andrew's salvation. So, too, in the Cornaro Chapel (1645–52, S. Maria della Vittoria), with the altar of St. Teresa in ecstasy (*see* TERESA OF AVILA, ST.), and in the Altieri Chapel, with Bl. Lodovica Albertoni (1671–74, S. Francesco a Ripa), a theatrical setting is used to transport the faithful to the realm of exultant mystical reality. A fervent practitioner of the spiritual exercises of St. Ignatius of Loyola, Bernini summoned every resource of his stupendous baroque rhetoric to deny the barrier between the real and imagined, the better to celebrate the spirit of 17th-century

Interior of the Church of S. Andrea al Quirinale, Rome, built 1658–67, designed by Giovanni Lorenzo Bernini. (Alinari-Art Reference/Art Resource, NY)

Catholicism.

See Also: BAROQUE ART; CHURCH ARCHITECTURE, 7.

Bibliography: Sources. F. BALDINUCCI, *Vita di Bernini* (Florence 1682), ed. S. S. LUDOVICI (Milan 1948). P. F. DE CHANTELOU, *Journal du voyage en France du chevalier Bernin,* ed. L. LALANNE (Paris 1930). See also the *Vitae* of G. BAGLIONE (1642), L. PASCOLI, 2 v. (1730–36), and G. B. PASSERI (1772). **Literature**. E. BENKARD, *G. L. Bernini* (Frankfurt a.M. 1926). L. GRASSI, *Disegni del Bernini* (Bergamo 1944); *Bernini pittore* (Rome 1945). V. MARTINELLI, ed., *Bernini* (Milan 1953). A. MUÑOZ, *G. L. Bernini: Architetto e decoratore* (Rome 1925). R. PANE, *Bernini architetto* (Venice 1953). M. REYMOND, *Le Bernin* (Paris 1911). M. VON BOEHN, *Lorenzo Bernini, seine Zeit, sein Leben, sein Werk* (2d ed. Bielefeld 1927). R. WITTKOWER, *G. L. Bernini, the Sculptor of the Roman Baroque* (New York 1955).

[R. M. ARB]

BERNIS, FRANÇOIS JOACHIM DE PIERRE DE

French cardinal and statesman; b. Saint–Marcel de l'Ardèche, Diocese of Viviers, May 22, 1715; d. Rome, Nov. 2, 1794. François, descendant of a noble but impoverished family, was educated in the humanities by the Jesuits and then studied theology at Saint-Sulpice. Through his cousin, the Baron de Montmorency, he was introduced to the Parisian court, where his charm and gallantry became well known. In 1744 in recognition of his poetical writings he was admitted to the French Academy, and under the patronage of Mme. de Pompadour he received a pension of 1,500 livres and apartments in the Tuileries. Louis XV appointed him ambassador to Venice in 1751. There he learned much of diplomacy and intrigue and earned the gratitude of Pope Benedict XIV for his intervention in papal differences with the Venetian government. In 1755 he returned to Paris, where he was ordained to the priesthood, and the next year he was sent to Vienna to secure an Austrian alliance with MARIA THERESA against England and Prussia in the maneuvers that later led to the Seven Years' War (1756–63). On his return (June 27, 1757) he replaced Pierre Rouillé as minister of foreign affairs, but the adverse course of the war lost him popular favor and the support of Mme. de Pompadour. His office was given to Étienne François, Duke de Choiseul in November 1758, and Bernis retired in disgrace to his abbey of Saint-Médard near Soissons. He had received the cardinal's hat from Clement XIII on October 2 of that year, and after regaining the friendship of Louis XV in 1764, he was made archbishop of Albi and five years later, ambassador to Rome. He was a powerful influence in selecting a candidate sympathetic to the French crown in the conclaves of 1769, which elected G. Vincenzo Ganganelli as Clement XIV, and 1775, which chose Angelo Braschi as Pius VI. He represented Louis XV in the negotiations for the suppression of the Jesuits, and though he seems to have found the mission distasteful, he terminated it successfully through the pressure of the Bourbons of France, Spain, and Naples. When he refused to take the constitutional oath demanded by the Revolutionary government on March 3, 1790, he lost his rich incomes. He spent his last years taking care of French exiles in Rome. He was buried in the French church of St. Louis in Rome.

Bibliography: *Memoirs and Letters of Cardinal de Bernis*, tr. K. P. WORMSLEY, 2 v. (Boston 1902). R. CHALUMEAU, *Catholicisme* 1:1492–93. M. DES OMBIAUX, *Éloge du Card. de Bernis* (Paris 1944). P. CALENDINI, *Dictionnaire d'histoire et de géographie ecclésiastiques* 8:847–849. S. SKALWEIT, *Lexikon für Theologie und Kirche* [2] 2:257–258. M. CHEKE, *The Cardinal de Bernis* (New York 1959).

[E. D. MCSHANE]

BERNO, BL.

First abbot of CLUNY; b. Burgundy, *c.* 850; d. Jan. 13, 927. He entered the BENEDICTINES at St. Martin of Autun. Later he was sent to reform the Abbey of Baume-Les-Messieurs. About 890 he founded Gigny and remained its superior. On Sept. 2, 909, the duke of Aquitaine, William the Pious, officially handed over to him the territory of Cluny, where he established a new monastery dedicated to SS. Peter and Paul. It was placed under the immediate authority of the Holy See (*see* CLUNIAC REFORM). Several houses were placed under Berno's care, notably Déols and SOUVIGNY. Before his death, he had provided for the election of (St.) ODO OF CLUNY as his successor.

Feast: Jan. 13.

Bibliography: *Acta Sanctorum* 2:106–112. J. MABILLON, *Acta sanctorum ordinis S. Benedicti,* 9 v. (Paris 1668–1701; 2d ed. Venice 1733–40) 7:66–88. M. MARRIER and A. DUCHESNE, eds., *Bibliotheca cluniacensis* (Paris 1614 repr. Mâcon 1915) 1–12 (*Patrologia Latina,* 133:843–858). A. BRUEL, ed., *Recueil des chartes de l'abbaye de Cluny,* 6 v. (Paris 1876–1903) 1:124–129. E. SACKUR, *Die Cluniacenser,* 2 v. (Halle 1892–94) 1:36–69. A. BUTLER, *The Lives of the Saints,* ed. H. THURSTON and D. ATTWATER, 4 v. (New York 1956) 1:75. R. AIGRAIN, *Catholicisme* 1:1493–94.

[R. GRÉGOIRE]

BERNO OF REICHENAU

Orator, hymn writer, musician, and liturgist; b. Prüm, near Trier, Germany; d. REICHENAU, June 7, 1048. He was educated at SANKT GALLEN. From the Benedictine monastery of PRÜM, where he was a monk, Berno was named abbot of Reichenau (1008–48) by HENRY II to replace Abbot Immo, whose zeal for the CLUNIAC REFORM had caused defections among his monks. A strong adherent of the reform, Berno, by adapting its spirit to the Reichenau tradition, was able to renew religious fervor in the monastery. He twice accompanied Henry II to Rome, once for Henry's coronation in 1014. After the latter's death, Berno supported Conrad the Young for emperor. When the rival candidate took the throne as CONRAD II, Berno gave him unswerving loyalty, despite the losses sustained by Reichenau during Conrad's struggle against the feudal princes, notably Duke Ernest of Swabia. When Conrad died in 1038, Berno gave his allegience to the emperor, HENRY III. In 1043 he took an active part in the Synod of Constance. He was buried in the St. Mark's choir, which he had built in the church of Reichenau. His grave was rediscovered in 1929. As abbot, Berno maintained cordial relations with persons and monasteries on both sides of the Alps. His writings (some of which are preserved, though with many interpolations, in *Patrologia Latina* 142:1055–1210) include liturgical works: *Liber qualiter adventus celebretur, quando nativitas Domini feria secunda advenerit; Dialogus qualiter quattuor temporum jejunia per sua sabbata sint observanda; De quibusdam rebus ad officium missae pertinentibus;* and musical works: *De consona et tonorum varietate,* and *Tonarius.* A collection of letters, sermons, and the *Vita Udalrici* by Berno are also extant.

Bibliography: R. MOLITOR, ''Die Musik der Reichenau,'' *Die Kultur der Abtei Reichenau,* ed. K. BEYERLE, 2 v. (Munich 1925) 2:802–820. H. ENGEL, *Die deutsche Literatur des Mittelalters: Verfasserlexikon,* W. STAMMLER and K. LANGOSCH, eds. 1:204–208 with critical bibliog. H. OESCH, *Berno und Hermann von Reichenau als Musiktheoretiker* (Bern 1961).

[M. F. MCCARTHY]

BERNOLD OF CONSTANCE

Noted chronicler (known also as Bernold of St. Blaise); b. *c.* 1050; d. Schaffhausen, Sept. 16, 1100. He was educated in the cathedral school of Constance, attended the 1079 Lenten synod in Rome, and was ordained in Constance in 1084 by Cardinal Legate Otto of Ostia. As an opponent of Emperor HENRY IV in the INVESTITURE STRUGGLE, he presumably took part in 1085 in the Quedlinburg Synod of anti-Emperor Hermann of Salm and certainly was at the battle of Pleichfeld in 1086. After 1085 Bernold called himself *ultimus fratrum* of SANKT BLASIEN, and from about 1091 he lived in All Saints monastery in Schaffhausen.

In his first treatise, written in 1074, Bernold came out strongly against the married clergy (*see* CELIBACY, CLERICAL HISTORY OF), and he later composed a number of polemical tracts as a partisan of GREGORY VII. In the *Apologeticus* he defended the authority of the papal decrees against all other sources of Canon Law. Bernold's chief work was his chronicle (MS Munich, Clm 432), accepted as his own work. After extracts from older chroniclers, this work presents Bernold's own account of historical events beginning from 1075 and extending to Aug. 3, 1100. It is strongly slanted against Henry IV. Bernold also wrote a liturgical work called the *Micrologus* and compiled a treatise on the Eucharist from texts used in the condemnations of BERENGARIUS OF TOURS.

Bibliography: J. AUTENRIETH, *Neue deutsche Biographie* 2:127–128; *Die Domschule von Konstanz zur Zeit des Investiturstreits* (Stuttgart 1956); *Lexikon für Theologie und Kirche*, ed. J. HOFER and K. RAHNER (2d new ed. Freiburg 1957–65) 2:259. J. R. GEISELMANN, *Bernold von St. Blasien: Sein neuentdecktes Werk über die Eucharistie* (Munich 1936). *Patrologia Latina*, ed. J. P. MIGNE (Paris 1878–90) 151:978–1022, *Micrologus. Monumenta Germaniae Historica: Libelli de lite* (Berlin 1826—)

2:1–168;3:601–602. *Monumenta Germaniae Historica: Scriptores* (*ibid.*) 5:385–467, chronicle. W. WATTENBACH, *Deutschlands Geschichtsquellen im Mittelalter: Deutsche Kaiserzeit*, ed. R. HOLTZMANN (Tübingen) 1:521–528. H. WEISWEILER, *Studi gregoriana* 4:129–147.

[L. KURRAS]

BERNOLD OF OTTOBEUREN, BL.

Priest, monk, and ascetic; fl. probably 11th century. A BENEDICTINE monk of the Abbey of OTTOBEUREN, he was especially noted in life for his dedicated spirit of mortification and heroic practice of penance. The annals of his abbey report that after Bernold's death miracles were performed through his intercession. On Dec. 25, 1189, Bl. Udalschalk solemnly translated his remains to the choir of the chapel of St. Michael; a second translation occurred in 1553. Since 1772 his body has rested in the chapel of St. John Nepomuc in the basilica of Ottobeuren.

Feast: Nov. 25.

Bibliography: M. FEYERABEND, *Des ehem. Reichsstiftes Ottenbeuren . . . sämtliche Jahrbücher,* 4 v. (Ottenbeuren 1813–16) 2:218–219; 4:400. A. M. ZIMMERMANN, *Kalendarium Benedictinum: Die Heiligen und Seligen des Benediktinerorderns und seiner Zweige* 3:354, 356. F. ZOEPFL, *Lexikon für Theologie und Kirche*[2] 2:259.

[O. J. BLUM]

BERNULF, ST.

Known also as Bernhold, Bennon, and Bernold; bishop of Utrecht; d. July 13, 1054. The opinion that Bernulf's appointment to his see was the result of strife over electing a successor to Adelboldus and of an accidental meeting with CONRAD II is probably groundless. Conrad always appointed the bishops, choosing imperial officials who continued to work for him even after consecration. Bernulf's friendship with Henry III resulted in notable gifts of land to his diocese (e.g., March 1040; Sept. 1042; May 22 and Aug. 23, 1046). He devoted himself energetically to the work of reform, participating in synods, building churches, and renewing monastic vigor even at the expense of reducing the privileges of his see over the monastery of Hohorst. His body lies in St. Peter's church in Utrecht. He is patron of the Netherlands' guild for Christian art (estab. 1870).

Feast: July 19.

Bibliography: *Acta Sanctorum* June 4:654–656. S. MULLER and A. C. BOUMAN, *Oorkondenboek van het sticht Utrecht tot 1301,* v.1 (Utrecht 1921) 173–193, 231, 302. G. J. LIEFTINCK, ''De herkomst van Bischofs van Utrecht,'' *Jaarboeke van ''Oud-Utrecht''* (Utrecht 1949) 23–40; *Bisschop Bernold en zijn geschenken aan de Ultrechtse kerken* (Groningen 1948). G. BÖING, *Lexikon für Theologie und Kirche*, ed. J. HOFER and K. RAHNER (Freiburg 1957–65) 2:260. P. POLMAN, *Dictionnaire d'histoire et de géographie ecclésiastiques*, ed. A. BAUDRILLART et al. (Paris 1912) 8:856–857.

[R. BALCH]

BERNWARD OF HILDESHEIM, ST.

Bishop and art patron; b. *c.* 960; d. Nov. 20, 1022. Bernward was the scion of a noble Saxon family; his maternal grandfather, Adalbero, was Count Palatine in Saxony. His uncle Volkmar, bishop of Utrecht (d. 990), brought Bernward to the cathedral school of Hildesheim, where he studied under THANGMAR sometime before 975. In Mainz, Archbishop Willigis (d. 1011) ordained him and later introduced him at court. In 978 Empress Theophano (d. 991) made him tutor of her son, OTTO III, who later arranged his election to the Diocese of Hildesheim in January of 993. Once there, Bernward built castles against the invading Danes and Slavs, introduced the system of archdeaneries, and established an annual diocesan synod. In 996 he called monks from Sankt-Pantaleon in Cologne under Abbot Goderamnus to form the first monastery of men in the diocese at the Abbey of Sankt-Michael, and he endowed their chapel with a relic of the true cross. In his struggle with Willigis over the Abbey of Gandersheim, he went to Rome (1000–01), where his rights over the abbey were confirmed, and in 1007 the archbishop finally abandoned his claims. Bernward consecrated the unfinished church of Sankt-Michael (Sept. 29, 1022) and accepted the habit of the Benedictine Order (Nov. 11, 1022) shortly before his death. He was buried in the crypt of Sankt-Michael's, and Pope CELESTINE III canonized him (December 21, 1192).

His biography was begun by Thangmar (*Monumenta Germaniae Historica: Scriptores* 4:757–786). Bernward played an outstanding role in the spiritual and political life of his period. His intellectual clarity and power of abstraction as well as his artistic sensitivity are reflected in the rich production of his workshop. He is the patron of goldsmiths and an important figure in his own right in the development of eleventh-century art. Today his name is most commonly associated with the bronze doors cast for Sankt-Michael *c.* 1008 to 1015 and the bronze column from *c.* 1018 to 1020. The unity of the door reliefs, which develop the theme of man's fall and redemption, lies not in the narrative sequence, but in the symbolic structure. Geometric clarity and harmony of proportions, already visible in the true cross reliquary, a *crux gemmata,* reach their perfection in Sankt-Michael itself. In this greatest of Ottonian churches, the classical tradition for the first time is translated completely into the medieval language of symbolic order.

Feast: Nov. 20.

Bibliography: *Bernward von Hildesheim und das Zeitalter der Ottonen*, ed. M. BRANDT and A. EGGEBRECHT (Hildesheim 1993). *Bernwardinische Kunst*, proceedings from a symposium (October 10–13, 1984) organized by the Kommission für Niedersächsische Bau- und Kunstgeschichte of the Braunschweigische Wissenschaftliche Gesellschaft in Hildesheim (Göttingen 1988). F. J. TSCHAN, *St. Bernward of Hildesheim,* 3 v. (Notre Dame 1942–52). H. BESELER and H. ROGGENKAMP, *Die Michaeliskirche in Hildesheim* (Berlin 1954). B. GALLISTL, *Die Bernwardsäule und die Michaeliskirche zu Hildesheim* (Hildesheim 1993); *Die Bronzetüren Bischof Bernwards im Dom zu Hildesheim* (Freiburg 1990). R. WESENBERG, *Bernwardinische Plastik* (Berlin 1955). W. VON DEN STEINEN, ''Bernward von Hildesheim über sich selbst,'' *Deutsches Archiv für Erforschung des Mittelalters* 12 (1956) 331–362. R. DRÖGEREIT, *Lexikon für Theologie und Kirche*, ed. J. HOFER and K. RAHNER (Freiburg 1957–65) 2:260–261. H. JANTZEN, *Ottonische Kunst* (2d ed. Hamburg 1959). K. ALGERMISSEN, *Bernward und Godehard von Hildesheim* (Hildesheim 1960). A. M. ZIMMERMANN, *Kalendarium Benedictinum* (Metten 1933–38) 3:335–338.

[A. A. SCHACHER]

BEROSSUS

Author of a three-volume history of Babylonia in Greek called Βαβυλωνιακά (in Latin, *Babyloniaca*); b. Babylon, *c.* 340 B.C.; d. Cos (island off the southwestern coast of Asia Minor), *c.* 270 B.C. His name Βηρωσός probably represents the Akkadian name *Bēl-rē'ušu* (Bel is his shepherd). He was a priest of the god BEL (MARDUK) in Babylon. At an advanced age he wrote his book and dedicated it to the Seleucid King Antiochus I Soter (281–261 B.C.). There seems to be no reason to doubt the statement of Vitruvius (first century B.C.) that Berossus, some time after the completion of his work, went to the island of Cos, where he established a school of astrology. This move from the Seleucid to the Ptolemaic sphere of influence may have been due to a loss of Antiochus's favor. Probably the purpose of Berossus's history of Babylonia (then a part of the Seleucid kingdom) had been the glorification of the Seleucid dynasty, just as his contemporary Manetho had written a history of Egypt in Greek for the purpose of glorifying the Ptolemies.

Berossus's work is not extant, but fragments of it have been preserved in citations of later Greek historians, principally Flavius JOSEPHUS, CLEMENT OF ALEXANDRIA, EUSEBIUS OF CAESAREA, and GEORGE SYNCELLUS. None of these, however, was directly conversant with Berossus's work; they knew it only through other writers, of whom the most important was Alexander Polyhistor (first century B.C.). In the course of such citation and recitation, even those fragments of the original work that remain have inevitably been subject to corruption; nonetheless, they are of great importance in the study of Babylonian mythology and history.

The first book recounts in mythic form the origins of man and of human civilization. Beginning with the latter, Berossus tells of the emergence of the monster Oannes, half fish and half man, from the Red Sea, and of his arrival in Babylonia, where he taught men, as yet living like beasts, the elements of civilized life—''literature and mathematics and all kinds of arts,'' including the construction of cities and temples, the use of legal institutions, and the practice of geometry and agriculture.

The story of the creation of world order and of mankind that follows was evidently placed in the mouth of Oannes. In the beginning the world was a chaos peopled by monstrous beings uniting the characteristics of men and animals, and ruled by a woman named ''Sea.'' Into this chaos the god Bel introduced order, overcoming ''Sea'' and cleaving her body into two parts, from which he formed heaven and earth. He then created the first men, fashioning them from earth and the blood of the gods. As related by Berossus, this story is clearly derived from the Babylonian creation epic *ENUMA ELISH*. Elements of the myth, such as the use of the sea to represent a primeval chaos that was reduced to order by divine intervention, were a common possession of the ancient Near East.

The second book contains the history of Mesopotamia from the first kings to the period of Nabonassar (747-728 B.C.). Its form, according to Eusebius, was essentially a mere listing of kings' names with the duration of their reigns. Similar documents are well known from Babylonian cuneiform archives, and it was undoubtedly from cuneiform records that Berossus derived his material. Noteworthy is the list of ten antediluvian kings. Comparing this list to the corresponding section of the Sumerian King List [Pritchard *Ancient Near Eastern Texts Relating to the Old Testament* (second edition), 265–66; T. Jacobsen, *The Sumerian King List* (Chicago 1937)] of the early second millennium B.C., one finds that Berossus's list, though it has grown from eight to ten names, is similar to that of the earlier document. The mythical regnal periods assigned by the King List, averaging some 30,000 years for each king, have been further increased to an average 43,200 years. Berossus's list has often been compared to Genesis' list of ten antediluvian patriarchs, and it is possible that there is some historical connection between them; the life spans assigned to the biblical patriarchs, though exaggerated, are modest by comparison with the Babylonian tradition.

The Babylonian story of the Flood was evidently used in Berossus's second book. Berossus's account differs only in detail from the 11th Tablet of the GILGAMESH EPIC; both compositions show a striking similarity to the parallel narrative in Genesis.

It is only in the third book of Berossus's work that one enters the realm of true history, with a detailed discussion of events and a realistic and generally accurate chronology. For this section of the work, Berossus evidently had access to a cuneiform chronicle source or sources reaching back to 747 B.C.; the information given agrees with Babylonian chronicles known from the cuneiform inscriptions and supplements them in several particulars.

Several fragments concerned with astrological lore have been attributed by Greek writers to Berossus. Though some modern scholars have been inclined to postulate a professedly astrological work as the source of these, there is no evidence of such a work, and it seems most probable that they were culled from the *Babyloniaca.* Interest in the subject was natural for a Babylonian scholar of Berossus's day, and undoubtedly his comments were welcomed by the Hellenistic readers for whom his book was intended.

Bibliography: C. MÜLLER, ed., *Fragmenta historicorum graecorum,* 5 v. (Paris 1878–85) 2:495–510. E. SCHWARTZ, *Griechische Geschichtschreiber* (Leipzig 1957) 189–197. C. F. LEHMANN-HAUPT, *Reallexikon der Assyriologie* 2:1–17. F. M. T. DE LIAGRE BÖHL, *Lexikon für Theologie und Kirche* (2d ed. Freiburg 1957–65) 2:261–62. W. VON SODEN, *Die Religion in Geschichte und Gegenwart* (3d ed. Tübingen 1957–65) 1:1069.

[R. I. CAPLICE]

BERQUIN, LOUIS DE

French royal counselor and humanist; b. Passy, 1490; d. Paris, April 17, 1529. He was a member of the circle of Margaret of Valois in the 1520s, and he translated Erasmus' *Enchiridion* and other works, and treatises of Hutten, Luther, and Melanchthon. He wrote a defense of Luther and a treatise, *De Sacerdotio*. Arrested, he was rescued in 1523, 1525, and 1526 from the wrath of Parlement and the Sorbonne by Francis I's intervention. It is uncertain whether he adhered to Luther's doctrines, but he was attracted by Luther's early boldness. At the end of the decade, Berquin was arraigned again during the French alliance with Rome and outbreaks of iconoclasm in Paris. He was condemned and burned as a heretic on the same day. Efforts were redoubled to unmask ''secret Lutherans,'' and the ''Meaux Group'' under Margaret's protection dispersed.

Bibliography: W. G. MOORE, *La Réforme allemande et la littérature française* (Strasbourg 1930). A. BAILLY, *La Réforme en France* (Paris 1960). J. CADIER, ''Luther et les débuts de la réforme française,''*Positions Lutheriennes* 6 (1958). J. VIÉNOT, *Histoire de la réforme française* 2 v. (Paris 1926–34). R. NÜRNBERGER, *Die Religion in Geschichte und Gegenwart* 3 1:1069. J. RATH, *Lexikon für Theologie und Kirche* 2 2:262.

[R. H. FISCHER]

BERRUYER, ISAAC JOSEPH

Jesuit exegete; b. Rouen, France, Nov. 7, 1681; d. Paris, Feb. 18, 1758. Berruyer's most noteworthy exegetical work was the ill-fated ''History of the People of God.'' The first part, entitled *Histoire du peuple de Dieu depuis son origine jusqu'à la venue du Messie,* appeared in seven volumes in 1728; by 1736 seven editions and four translations of the work had been published. The second part, *Histoire du peuple de Dieu depuis la naissance du Messie jusqu'à la fin de la Synagogue,* followed in 1753; a revised edition was published at Antwerp in 1754. Berruyer's name appears on few copies of the second part, which was published without the knowledge and against the will of his Jesuit superiors in Paris, and, possibly, of Berruyer himself. The third part, *Histoire du peuple de Dieu, ou paraphrase des épîtres des apôtres,* was printed at Lyons in 1757.

As the various parts of the work appeared, controversy grew increasingly bitter. Berruyer was denounced for cavalier treatment of the sacred texts, and some critics felt that his attitudes were dangerously Nestorian; but the chief complaint seems to have been that he was influenced by the eccentricities of Father Jean Hardouin. The *Histoire* was condemned by many French bishops, the superiors of the Society of Jesus, the Sorbonne, and the Parlement of Paris. The three divisions of the work were consigned to the Index in 1732, 1754, and 1758, but an approved revision of part one was issued at Besançon in 1828.

Bibliography: C. SOMMERVOGEL et al., *Bibliothèque de la Compagnie de Jésus,* 11 vol. (Brussels–Paris 1890–1932; v. 12 suppl. 1960) 1:1357–70. L. BOPP, *Lexikon für Theologie und Kirche,* J. HOFER and K. RAHNER, eds., 10 vol. (2d new ed. Freiburg, 1957–65) 2:262. J. BRUCKER, *Dictionnaire de la Bible,* suppl. ed. L. PIROT et al. (Paris 1928–) 1.2:1627–29. E. LAMALLE, *Dictionnaire d'histoire et de géographie ecclésiastiques,* A. BAUDRILLART et al., eds. (Paris 1912–) 8: 890–891. P. DELATTRE, *Catholicisme. Hier, aujourd'hui et demain,* G. JACQUEMET (Paris 1947–) 1:1495–96.

[J. B. DONNELLY]

BERSE, GASPAR (BARZEO)

Jesuit missionary in India and associate of St. Francis Xavier; b. Goes, Netherlands, 1515; d. Goa, Oct. 18,

1553. In his youth he studied philosophy at Louvain and, among other things, served for a time in the army of Charles V. He entered the Society of Jesus at Coimbra and was ordained shortly thereafter. The following year he left Lisbon for the missions in India, arriving in Goa in 1548. After teaching philosophy and Sacred Scripture for a short time at the college in Goa, he was deputed by Francis Xavier to evangelize Ormuz in Persia. For two and one half years (May 1549 to November 1551) Berse worked among the Moslems and Jews of the coastal city, earning their respect and achieving notable results. He was called back to Goa by Xavier, who appointed Berse rector of the college there and vice provincial of the entire foundation. Xavier left Berse with detailed directives for the discharge of his duties while Xavier was in China; but without a prudent superior to moderate his activities, Berse expended himself with more zeal than caution. A year later he was dead. Throughout his brief career on the mission, Berse took the spirit and methods of Xavier as his ideal. Like his master, Berse was able to move souls by his preaching and to inspire them by his zeal and holiness.

Bibliography: *Monumenta historica Societatis Jesu, passim.* G. SCHURHAMMER and J. WICKI, *Epistolae s. Francisci Xaverii*, 2 v. (Rome 1945–46), *passim.* R. STREIT and J. DINDINGER, *Bibliotheca missionum* (Freiburg 1916–) 4:155–156. C. SOMMERVOGEL et al., *Bibliothèque de la Compagnie de Jésus*, 11 vol. (Brussels–Paris 1890–1932; vol. 12 suppl. 1960) 1:906–937; 7:1772. E. LAMALLE, *Dictionnaire d'histoire et de géographie ecclésiastiques,* A. BAUDRILLART et al. (Paris 1912–) 6:1059–61, with extensive bibliog.

[J. C. WILLKE]

BERTHA OF BLANGY, ST.

Benedictine abbess; b. Arras, France, second half of seventh century; d. *c.* 725. She appears to have been married to a certain Sigfrid and to have had five daughters; her biography, written about two centuries after her death, is somewhat unreliable. It is certain, however, that she founded the monastery of Blangy *c.* 686 and retired there with two of her daughters, Gertrude and Deotila. Her body was transferred from Blangy *c.* 895 to the monastery of Erstein in Alsace, but it was returned after 1032, by which date BENEDICTINE monks again occupied Blangy.

Feast: July 4.

Bibliography: *Acta Sanctorum* July 2:47–60. *Bibliotheca hagiograpica latina antiquae et mediae aetatis* (Brussels 1898–1901) 1:1266–70. L. VAN DER ESSEN, *Étude critique et littéraire sur les vitae des saints mérovingiens de l'ancienne Belgique* (Louvain 1907); *Dictionnaire d'histoire et de géographie ecclésiastiques*, ed. A. BAUDRILLART et al. (Paris 1912) 8:944–945. A. M. ZIMMERMANN, *Lexikon für Theologie und Kirche*, ed. J. HOFER and K. RAHNER (Freiburg 1957–65) 2:263. R. AIGRAIN, *Catholicisme* 1:1499. A. M. ZIMMERMANN, *Kalendarium Benedictinum* (Metten 1933–38) 2:399–401.

[P. BLECKER]

BERTHA OF VAL D'OR, ST.

Foundress and abbess of Avenay, France (near Reims); d. *c.* 690. By mutual consent she lived in a state of virginity with the saintly Gombert, the founder of the convent of St. Peter at Reims. When he was murdered on a missionary journey, Bertha founded a convent at Avenay in a place once called Val d'Or and was made its first abbess. She is said to have been murdered by two nephews of her husband. The chief sources for her life are the chronicler FLODOARD OF REIMS (d. *c.* 966) and a later and largely worthless vita, which may contain, however, some material from the earlier vita used by Flodoard, but subsequently lost. Bertha and Gombert are honored together as saints and martyrs in the Proper of Reims for May 1.

Bibliography: A. M. ZIMMERMANN, *Kalendarium Benedictinum* (Metten 1933–38) 2:132–133. *Acta Sanctorum* May 1 (1866) 115–120. Flodoard, *Monumenta Germaniae Historica: Scriptores* 13:416–548, 595–596. F. BAIX, *Dictionnaire d'histoire et de géographie ecclésiastiques*, ed. A. BAUDRILLART et al. (Paris 1912) 8:943–944. P. SÉJOURNÉ, *ibid.* 5:1016–18.

[M. R. P. MCGUIRE]

BERTHARIUS, ST.

Abbot and martyr; b. Lombardy, Italy, early ninth century; d. Teano, Campania, Italy, Oct. 22, 884. He was received into the BENEDICTINE order at MONTE CASSINO by Bassacio, whom he succeeded as abbot in 848. He enriched the abbey church with precious vessels and Gospel Books, and when he entertained Emperor Louis II in 866, he obtained many privileges for his monastery. From Pope JOHN VIII he secured the exemption of Monte Cassino from episcopal jurisdiction. Bertharius encouraged the development of sacred studies and saw many of his students raised to the episcopate. Although he was in his own time a well-known author and medical writer, most of his writings have not survived; but a homily on St. SCHOLASTICA (d. 543) and a poem on the life, death, and miracles of St. BENEDICT (*Patrologia Latina*, 217 v. [Paris 1878–90] 126:975–990) do exist. When the Saracens overran southern Italy, Bertharius and a group of monks were martyred in the abbey church at Teano, where they had sought refuge. In 1514, after several transfers, his remains were placed under the altar of a chapel constructed in his honor at Monte Cassino. Pope BENEDICT XIII approved his cult on August 26, 1727.

Feast: Oct. 22.

Bibliography: *Acta Sanctae Sedis* Oct. 9:663–682. *Bibliotheca hagiograpica latina antiquae et mediae aetatis* (Brussels 1898–1901) 1107–09, 1271. *Biblioteca Casinensis,* 5 v. (Monte Cassino 1873–94). E. CARUSI, ''Il Memoratorium dell'abate Bertario,'' *Casinensia* 1 (1929) 457–548. G. PENCO, *Storia del monachesimo in Italia* (Rome 1961).

[B. D. HILL]

BERTHIER, GUILLAUME FRANÇOIS

Jesuit spiritual writer and teacher; b. Issoudun, France, April 7, 1704; d. Bourges, Dec. 15, 1782. He entered the Society of Jesus in 1722 and taught philosophy at Rennes and Rouen and theology at Paris. From 1745 to 1749 he published volumes 13 to 18 of the *Histoire de l'Église gallicane* begun by J. Longueval. As editor of *Mémoires de Trévoux* from 1745 to 1762, he maintained a spirited defense against the caustic attacks of Voltaire and the Encyclopedists. Upon the suppression of the Jesuits in France in 1762, he became court librarian and tutor to the sons of the dauphin (the future Louis XVI and Louis XVIII), but after 18 months he was forced to join other Jesuits in exile in Germany. While there he refused an invitation from Maria Theresa to take up residence in Vienna, for he preferred to devote himself to study and meditation. After the accession of Louis XVI in 1774, he returned to France and spent his remaining years in retirement at Bourges. His works were published posthumously by Y. M. Querbeuf. They include *Les Psaumes traduits en français avec des notes et des réflexions,* with a biographical notice by Querbeuf (8 v., Paris 1785), which was frequently reprinted; *Isaïe traduit en français avec des notes et réflexions* (5 v., Paris 1788–89); and *Reflexions spirituelles* (5 v., Paris 1790).

Bibliography: C. SOMMERVOGEL et al., *Bibliotèque de la Compagnie de Jésus,* 11 vol. (Brussels-Paris 1890–1932; v. 12 suppl. 1960) 1:1377–86. E. LAMALLE, *Dictionnaire d'histoire et de géographie ecclésiastiques,* ed. A. BAUDRILLART et al. (Paris 1912—) 8:954–955. M. VILLER, *Dictionnaire de spiritualité ascétique et mystique. Doctrine et histoire,* M. VILLER et al. (Paris 1932—) 1:1528–30. H. HURTER, *Nomenclator literarius theologiae catholicae,* 5 vol. in 6 (3d ed. Inssbruck 1903–13); v. 1 (4th ed. 1926) 1 4.1:411–413.

[J. C. WILLKE]

BERTHIER, JACQUES

Catholic layman, liturgical music composer and Organist, Jesuit Church of St. Ignace, Paris; b. Auxerre, 1923; d. Paris, June 27, 1994; was known internationally for the music he wrote for the Taizé ecumenical community.

Early years. His father, Paul Berthier was an accomplished church musician and composer who studied with Vincent d'Indy at the Schola Cantorum, and founded the *Petits chanteurs à la croix de bois* (Little Singers of the Wooden Cross) in 1907. Jacques' first music teachers were his parents, who taught him piano, organ and composition. From an early age, he served as a chorister and assisted as organist at Auxerre Cathedral, where his father was organist for more than 50 years. His early years were devoted to composing mostly secular works, writing his first serious composition at age 15, and a four-part motet for mixed voices at age 17. In 1945, he enrolled at the Ecole César Franck, where he studied organ, fugue and counterpoint with Edouard Souberbielle, and composition with Guy de Lioncourt, whose daughter he married. In 1960, he became the organist at St. Ignace in Paris, an appointment he held until his death.

Collaboration with Taizé. Berthier's collaboration with Taizé came about through his association with the French Jesuit liturgist and composer, Joseph Gelineau, whom he first met at the Ecole César Franck. As a result of Gelineau's introduction in 1955, the brothers of Taizé invited Berthier to compose liturgical music for their fledging community. The project included settings of the Office for Christmas, a setting of the Ordinary of the Mass, Propers for the Sundays after Christmas and for Epiphany, and the responses for Christmas week. Beginning in 1974 and continuing until his death, Berthier collaborated closely with Brother Robert Giscard (1922–1993) to create the corpus of music known today as ''Music from Taizé.'' Under Berthier's creative compositional genius, Brother Robert's arrangements of texts were transformed into simple, restrained yet extraordinary music that has been translated into more than 20 languages, and sung widely throughout the world.

Other music. Berthier continued to compose organ, instrumental and orchestral music, Masses for Catholic parishes, monastic communities and large gatherings, and a Mass for the visit of Pope John Paul II at Lyon in 1986, a project in which he collaborated with Didier Rimaud. These Masses include: *Messe francaise* (1964), *Que tes oeuvres sont belles* (1983), *Comme une aurore* (1984), *Du Christ roi* (1985), *Au coeur de ce monde* (1986), *Vienne la paix* (1986), *Messe de Brabant-Vallon* (1987), *Pour la gloire de Dieu* (1989), *De St Jean Baptiste* (1990), *Des amis de Dieu* (1991), and *Missa pro Europa* (1993). As a classically trained musician who devoted his life to liturgical music, he was totally committed to Vatican II's vision of the assembly's active participation in the liturgy. Well-respected by his contemporaries, including Olivier Messiaen and Jean Langlais, he was able to compose what other classically trained composers could not—quality liturgical music for congregational use. His greatest love remained Gregorian chant, which formed the foundation for his many improvisations. His conception of the Taizé melodies was inspired by his knowledge and love of chant.

See Also: TAIZÉ, MUSIC FROM.

Bibliography: J. BERTHIER, ''Jacques Berthier: Un serviteur de la musique liturgique,'' interview by Pierre Faure and Didier Rimaud, *Célébrer* 236 (Janvier 1994) 3–16. M.-P. FAURE, ''Jacques Berthier, a Friend of God.'' *Liturgy: Cistercians of the Strict Observance* 29 (1995) 93–86. J. M. KUBICKI, *Liturgical Music as Ritual Symbol: A Case Study of Jacques Berthier's Taizé Music* (Leuven 1999).

[J. M. KUBICKI]

BERTHIER, JEAN BAPTISTE

Missionary of Our Lady of la Salette, founder of the Institute of the Holy Family (Missionaries of the Holy Family) for late priestly vocations, and ascetical writer; b. Chatonnay, Isère (France), Feb. 24, 1840; d. Grave, Holland, Oct. 16, 1908. Berthier made his great impact through his 36 ascetical and theological works, the dominating theme of which is that sanctity is possible in any walk of life through imitation of the Holy Family and constant fidelity to the duties of one's state. Among his greatest works are *La Mère selon le coeur de Dieu* (Lyon 1866), which has been translated into five languages; *Le Prêtre dans le ministère* (Paris 1883); *Breve compendium theol.* (Grenoble 1887); *Le Sacerdoce* (Paris 1894); and *Des États de vie chrétienne et de la Vocation* (Rome 1875). He considered infused contemplation as ''ordinary'' and not to be ranked with ecstasies and visions and taught his followers how to dispose themselves to contemplation, ''the short-cut to sanctity.'' Few writers have sought to influence so wide a range of people.

Bibliography: P. J. RAMERS, *Bonus miles Christi Jesu* (Betzdorf 1931); *Le R. P. J. Berthier, missionaire de la Salette* (Fribourg 1925). J. M. DE LOMBAERDE, *La vie et l'esprit du Tr. R. P. Jean Berthier* (Grave 1910). A. BALLANDIER *Annuaire pontifical catholique* (Paris 1909). P. J. RAMERS, *Dictionnaire de spiritualité ascétique et mystique. Doctrine et histoire.* M. VILLER et al. (Paris 1932—) 1:1530–32. M. T. DISDIER, *Dictionnaire d'histoire et de géographie ecclésiastiques*, ed. A. BAUDRILLART et al. (Paris 1912—) 8:955–956.

[M. J. BARRY]

BERTHOLD OF CHIEMSEE (BERTHOLD PÜRSTINGER)

Bishop and theologian; b. Salzburg, 1465; d. Saalfelden, July 16, 1543. Berthold, a fine sensitive person of high character and a skilled writer, was a late medieval ecclesiastical reformer. He studied canon law in Perugia, became a priest at Schnaitsee and Stellung, and was made prince-bishop of Chiemsee (1508) and suffragan bishop of Salzburg. He mediated between the burghers of Salzburg and the archbishop in 1511, and between the rebellious peasants and Cardinal Matthäus Lang, the Archbishop (1524–26). Depressed by the outrages of the revolutionaries, he resigned on May 11, 1526, and withdrew to the Cistercian monastery at Raitenhaslach and then to a hostel and chapel in Saalfelden, which he had built (completed 1541) for a brotherhood of retired priests and for poor laymen. He wrote a *Tewtsche Theologey* (Munich 1528), the first German dogmatics based on scripture and St. Thomas Aquinas, for the education of priests and laymen. His *Tewtsche Rational über das Ambt heiliger Mess* and his *Keligpuechl* (both 1535) defended the Mass and Communion under one species against the Protestant reformers.

Bibliography: R. BAUERREISS, *Lexikon für Theologie und Kirche*, ed. J. HOFER and K. RAHNER, 10 vol. (2d new ed. Freiburg, 1957–65) 2:265–266. K. EDER, *Neue deutsche biographie* (Berlin 1953—) 2:162, with good bibliog. *Allgemeine deutsche Biographie* (Leipzig 1875–1910) 2:519.

[L. W. SPITZ]

BERTHOLD OF GARSTEN, BL.

Benedictine, first abbot of Garsten (Germany); d. July 27, 1142. He was descended from a family of *ministeriales,* probably Swabian. He became a monk at SANKT BLASIEN and rose to position of subprior. He was prior at GÖTTWEIG (1107) and abbot of Garsten (1111–42); the abbey flourished as a center of reform under his guidance. He was a strict but loving master in enforcing monastic observances. Humble, much given to prayer and the ascetical life, he was noted for charity to the poor and much sought as a wise and helpful confessor. Miracles at his grave in the monastery church made it a place of pilgrimage; a decree of canonization was issued by the bishop of Passau, July 16, 1236. Hearings on the recognition of his cult began in Rome in 1951; the cult was approved as a beatus.

Feast: July 27.

Bibliography: *Acta Sanctorum* July 6:469–494. F. X. PRITZ, *Kurzgefasste Lebensgeschichte des heiligen Berthold* (Linz 1842). W. NEUMÜLLER, ''Berthold von Garsten: Ein Kremsmünster Beitrag zur Geschichte seiner Verehrung,'' *Kremsmünster ober-Gymnasium Jahresbericht* 94 (Wels 1951). J. LENZENWEGER, *Berthold: Abt von Garsten* (Linz 1958), includes vita and rich bibliog.

[D. ANDREINI]

BERTI, GIOVANNI LORENZO

Theologian; b. Sarravezza, Tuscany, May 28, 1696; d. Florence, March 26, 1766. A Hermit of St. Augustine, he taught philosophy and theology and held high offices in his order. His superior general, A. Schiaffinati, directed him to write an exposition of the doctrine of St. Augustine. Berti's detractors found this eight-volume work, entitled *De theologicis disciplinis* (Rome 1739–45), to be Jansenistic. In defense of his doctrine, Berti wrote several works, chief of which was *Augustinianum systema de gratia vindicatum* (Rome 1747). His writings were examined in Rome under Benedict XIV and declared orthodox. He also wrote a widely used work on Church history, which was entitled *Ecclesiasticae historiae breviarium* (Pisa 1760).

Bibliography: H. HURTER, *Nomenclator literarius theologiae catholicae,* 5.1:1–4. E. PORTALIÉ, *Dictionnaire de théologie catholique* (Paris 1903–50) 1.2:2485–2501. P. STELLA, ''Fecerunt civitates duas amores duo (De civitate Dei XIV, 28) dall'agostinismo dell '600 all Rivoluzione francese,'' in E. CAVALCANTI, *Il ''De civitate Dei,'' l'opera, le interpretazioni, l'influsso* (Rome 1996) 447–467.

[A. ROCK]

BERTIERI, GIUSEPPE

Theologian; b. Ceva, in Piedmont, Nov. 9, 1734; d. Pavia, July 5, 1806. A Hermit of St. Augustine, he was a professor of theology at the University of Vienna. He published *De rebus theologicis* (3 v. Vienna 1774) and *Theologia dogmatica in systema reducta* (Vienna 1778). Though useful in their time, his writings are of little value today. He was considered sympathetic to Josephinism and was named bishop of Como in 1789. Though criticized as excessively submissive to the emperor, he was named bishop of Pavia (1792), where he courageously defended the Church's rights during the French invasion. He was elected a deputy to the assembly at Bologna in 1802.

Bibliography: A. SIEGFRIED, *Katholische Aufklärung und Josephinismus, hrsg. Im Auftrag der Wiener Katholischen Akademie von Elisabeth Kovács* (Versamelwerk; Munich 1979) 259–260. G. PIGNATELLI, ''Bertieri, Giuseppe, OSA, 1734–1804,'' *Dizionario biografico degli Italiani* 9 (1967).

[A. ROCK]

BERTILLA OF CHELLES, ST.

Benedictine abbess; b. near Soissons, first half of the seventh century; d. Chelles, Nov. 5, 705–713. Following the advice of St. OUEN OF ROUEN, she became a nun at Jouarre-en-Brie, *c.* 659. Bertilla distinguished herself by her virtues, especially obedience. At the request of Queen BATHILDIS, she left Jouarre to become the first abbess of Chelles, where Bathildis later lived in her enforced retreat. There, too, Bertilla was a model of religious life. Her relics are preserved at Chelles-Saint-André, except for her head, which is at Jouarre. The anniversary of the elevation and translation of her relics in 1185 is May 26.

Feast: Nov. 5.

Bibliography: *Monumenta Germaniae Historica: Scriptores rerum Merovingicarum* 6:95–109. *Acta Sanctorum* Nov. 3: 83–94. J.-P. LAPORTE, *Sépultures et reliques de la reine Bathilde et de l'abbesse Bertille* (Chelles 1991). A. M. ZIMMERMANN, *Kalendarium Benedictinum* (Metten 1933–38) 3:262–263. L. VAN DER ESSEN, *Dictionnaire d'histoire et de géographie ecclésiastiques*, ed. A. BAUDRILLART et al. (Paris 1912) 8:1004–05. J. L. BAUDOT and L. CHAUSSIN, *Vies des saints et des bienhereux selon l'ordre du calendrier avec l'historique des fêtes* (Paris 1935–56) 11:175–177. A. BUTLER, *The Lives of the Saints*, ed. H. THURSTON and D. ATTWATER (New York 1956) 4:268–269. R. AIGRAIN, *Catholicisme* 1:1503.

[É. BROUETTE]

BERTINUS, ST.

Benedictine abbot; b. Orval near Coutances, France, *c.* 615; d. Sithiu, France, Sept. 5, *c.* 709. Like his mentor, St. OMER OF THÉROUANNE, Bertinus came from Normandy and was trained at Luxeuil. Omer called him to Morinia (modern Pas-de-Calais), which was still only semiconverted. There he succeeded Momelin as abbot of SS. Peter and Paul on the island of Sithiu, when Momelin was elevated to the episcopal see of Noyon-Tournai in 660. At that time the abbey on Sithiu (later called Saint-Bertin) and the church of Sainte-Marie on the hill were under the same abbot. Bertinus wisely administered the temporal domain of the monastery, and an exchange of property with Momelin is recorded. During his tenure four men came from Armorica (Brittany), asking to be received as monks: Quadanoc, Ingenoc, Madoc, and St. Winnoc. Bertinus accepted them and built for them a *cella,* or small monastery, at Wormhout, on property he had received from a Flemish noble, Heremarus. When Bertinus began to fail, he called upon Rigobert to help him, and the latter built the church of Saint-Martin on Sithiu. Five years later Bertinus retired and was succeeded by Erlefrid. Almost 100 years old at the time of his death, Bertinus was buried at Saint-Bertin.

Feast: Sept. 5.

Bibliography: *Acta Sanctorum* Sept. 2:549–630. *Monumenta Germaniae Historica: Scriptorum rerum Merovingicarum* 5:729–769. *Bibliotheca hagiograpica latina antiquae et mediae aetatis* (Brussels 1898–1901) 1:763, 1290–98. O. BLED, ''Les Reliques de saint Bertin . . .'' *Mémoires de la Société des Antiquaires* *de la Morinie* 32 (1914–20) 1–112. L. VAN DER ESSEN, *Dictionnaire d'histoire et de géographie ecclésiastiques*, ed. A. BAUDRILLART et al. (Paris 1912) 8:1006–07. A. BUTLER, *The Lives of the Saints*, ed. H. THURSTON and D. ATTWATER (New York 1956) 3:493–494. V. REDLICH, *Lexikon für Theologie und Kirche*, ed. J. HOFER and K. RAHNER (Freiburg 1957–65) 2:269–270.

[G. COOLEN]

BERTONI, GASPARE (CASPAR) LUIGI DIONIGI, ST.

Diocesan priest of Verona, founder of the Congregation of the Priests of the Holy Stigmata of Our Lord; b. Verona, Venetia, Italy, Oct. 9, 1777; d. Verona, June 12, 1853. The son of a prosperous lawyer, Francesco Bertoni, and his wife Brunora Ravelli, Gaspare was educated at home with his sister, who died in childhood. Later he attended St. Sebastian's, where he became acquainted with the then suppressed Jesuits. The first of his many mystical experiences occurred on the day of his first communion, when he also discerned his vocation. He entered the seminary (1795), joined the Gospel Fraternity for Hospitals during the French occupation to care for war victims, and was ordained in 1800. His early years in the priesthood were divided between teaching in the seminary and working as a parish priest.

Aware of the need to salvage youth from the moral breakdown of society, he began to devote his energies to education. Gradually other priests joined him, and on Nov. 4, 1816, the group adopted a rule of life under the leadership of Bertoni. This was the foundation of the Stigmatine Congregation, which took its name from their residence, *Le Stimate*, formerly owned by a pious confraternity but given to Bertoni for his work.

In addition to founding the Stigmatines, Bertoni acted as spiritual director to the Daughters of Charity of Canossa, established Marian oratories, and promoted devotion to the Espousal of Mary and Joseph and to the Five Wounds of Christ. From 1812, following an ecstasy, he endured physical troubles that entailed numerous operations prior to his death. His grave is in the Stigmatine church at Verona. He was beatified Nov. 1, 1975 by Pope Paul VI and canonized by Pope John Paul II, Nov. 1, 1989.

Feast: June 12.

Bibliography: *Epistolario del Venerabile servo di Dio Don Gaspare Bertoni*, G. STOFELLA (Verona 1954); ''Memoriale privato'' in *Collectanea Stigmatina 4*, ed. G. STOFELLA (Rome 1962). *Acta Apostolicae Sedis* 68 (1976): 486–489. *L'Osservatore Romano,* English edition, no. 45 (1975): 1–4; no. 45 (1989): 1–2. *Symposium Bertonianum*, proceedings of Oct. 28, 1989 (Verona 1990). I. BONETTI, *La grammatica di Don Gaspare: meditazioni quotidiane dagli scritti di San Gaspare Bertoni* (Bologna 1993). G. CERESATTO, *Il volto e l'anima del venerabile Gaspare Bertoni* (Verona 1951). G. FIORIO, *Lo spirito del venerabile servo di Dio Don Gaspare Bertoni* (Verona 1914); *Vita del venerabile servo di Dio Don Gaspare Bertoni* (Verona 1922). G. GIACOBBE, *Vita del Servo di Dio Don Gaspare Bertoni* (Verona 1858). L. MALAMOCCO, *Quando senti il grillo cantare* (Udine 1996). G. MATTEI, *Il venerabile Gaspare Bertoni* (Verona 1924). L. MUZII, *Voglia di santità* (Rome 1989). E. RADIUS, *Gaspare Bertoni* (Verona 1975). N. DALLE VEDOVE, *Il venerabile Don Bertoni*, 2 v. (Rome 1962); *La giovinezza del venerabile Gaspare Bertoni e l'ambiente veronese dell'ultimo '700* (Rome 1971); *San Gaspare Bertoni, Fondatore degli Stimmatini* (Verona 1989); *Un modello di santo abbandono* (Verona 1951); *Vita e pensiero del beato Gaspare Bertoni agli albori dell '800 veronese* (Rome 1975). L. ZAUPA, *Gaspare Bertoni: un santo per il nostro tempo* (Verona 1994).

[J. E. MULLEN/EDS.]

BERTONIO, LUDOVICO

Jesuit missionary and linguist; b. Rocca Contrada, Ancona, Italy, 1557; d. Lima, Peru, Aug. 3, 1625. He entered the Jesuit province of Rome on Oct. 29, 1575. Assigned to Peru, he arrived in Lima in 1581 and taught humanities there. He was sent to the mission of Juli in the department of Puno, Peru, in 1585 ''because he much desired to concern himself with the Indians and he is an angel and has much aptitude for helping them.'' He made his profession on Nov. 1, 1593. For 40 years he served as a missionary in that Aymara parish. Then, suffering from arthritis, he was transferred to Arequipa and then to Lima. In addition to his extraordinary virtues, he was distinguished for his specialization in the Aymara language and for his devotion to the principle of adaptation, even when it ran counter to certain directives of the civil power. He composed two dictionaries, one Spanish-Aymara and one Aymara-Spanish, plus a grammar ''with a forest of phrases,'' a treatise for confession in both languages, and a life of Christ published in Peru and Chile in 1613. His work as a linguist is an indispensable source for the history of linguistic evolution that occurred in Upper Peru.

Bibliography: A. DE EGAÑA, *Monumenta Peruana* (Rome 1954). J. E. DE URIARTE and M. LECINA, *Biblioteca de escritores de la Compañía de Jesús . . .*, 2 v. (Madrid 1925–30) 1:477–479.

[A. DE EGAÑA]

BERTRAM OF LE MANS, ST.

Bishop; b. near Rouen, France, *c.* 550; d. June 30 *c.* 626. The son of a rich land owner, he received the TONSURE at Tours and major orders from GERMAIN, bishop of Paris, who appointed him archdeacon. In 586 Bertram (or Bertrand) became bishop of Le Mans and, as a loyal supporter of Chlotar II (d. 629), courageously bore imprisonment and harassments during the regime of Theodebert II (d. 612). Upon Chlotar's return to power, Bertram was restored to his see. In 614 he attended the Synod of Paris, and his name appears sixteenth in the list of prelates who signed the acts of the council (*Monumenta Germaniae Historica: Conciliae* 1:191). His last will and testament, dated March 26, 616, bears eloquent testimony to his lifelong fatherly concern for the poor and afflicted of his diocese; its churches, especially that dedicated to SS. Peter and Paul which he erected; and also his own serfs and slaves, whom he manumitted at his death. He was buried in the basilica of SS. Peter and Paul.

Feast: June 30.

Bibliography: *Acta Sanctorum* June 1:699–714. *Analecta Bollandiana* 26 (1907) 467–468. H. LECLERCQ, *Dictionnaire d'archéologie chrétienne et de liturgie*, ed. F. CABROL, H. LECLERCQ, and H. I. MARROU (Paris 1907–53) 10.2:1490–1520. P. GAMS, *Series episcoporum ecclesiae catholicae* (Graz 1957) 562. L. CALENDINI, *Dictionnaire d'histoire et de géographie ecclésiastiques*, ed. A. BAUDRILLART et al. (Paris 1912) 8:930–932. J. L. BAUDOT and L. CHAUSSIN, *Vies des saints et des bienhereux selon l'ordre du calendrier avec l'historique des fêtes* (Paris 1935–56) 6:523–524. E. EWIG, *Lexikon für Theologie und Kirche*, ed. J. HOFER and K. RAHNER (Freiburg 1957–65) 2:270. J. VANDAMME, *Bibliotheca sanctorum* 3:136–137. M. WEIDEMANN, *Das Testament des Bischofs Berthramn von Le Mans vom 27. März 616* (Mainz 1986).

[H. DRESSLER]

BERTRAND, LOUIS, ST.

Dominican preacher and missionary; b. Valencia, Spain, Jan. 1, 1526; d. there, Oct. 9, 1581. He entered the Dominican Order at the convent in Valencia on Aug. 26, 1544 and was ordained in October 1547. More distinguished for his extraordinary sanctity than for his scholarship, he spent much of his life as master of novices, first serving in that position in Valencia from 1553 to 1555. During the plague of 1557 he went into the city to care for the sick and help bury the dead. His preaching became so famous that the cathedral could not accommodate the crowds and he began preaching in the public squares. In 1562 he went to America as a missionary, working first in the kingdom of New Granada in the Turbará, Palauto, and Turbaco missions. Later he worked in the Diocese of Santa Marta in the area of Tenerife and Tamalameque, and he also visited several of the West Indian islands. His love and concern for the native peoples brought remarkable results to his missionary work wherever he went. After seven years in the mission area, just as he was named prior of Santa Fe, he was recalled to Spain. There he became prior of the convent of San Onofre, then master general, and he eventually went back to the convent in Valencia as master of novices and prior. Louis Bertrand was distinguished by his edifying penitential spirit and by the remarkable wonders that accompanied his preaching. Everywhere he was admired for his prudence and his religious spirit. He received extraordinary graces, including the gift of prophecy. He was beatified by Pope PAUL V and canonized by CLEMENT X in 1671. He was named patron of the New Kingdom of Granada (now Colombia) in 1690.

Feast: Oct. 9.

A namesake of St. Louis, Bl. Louis Bertrán, died as a Dominican martyr in Omura, Japan (1629) and was beatified in 1867.

Feast: July 29.

Bibliography: V. GALDUF BLASCO, *Luis Bertrán: El santo de los contrastes* (Barcelona 1961). A. DE ZAMORA, *Historia de la provincia de San Antonio,* ed. C. PARRA and A. MESANZA (Caracas 1930).

[J. RESTREPO POSADA]

BERTRAND, PIERRE

Cardinal and canonist; b. Annonay (southern France), 1280; d. 1349. He was a canon of Notre–Dame du Puy in 1296 and dean in 1314; he taught canon law in Avignon, Montpellier (1307), and Paris (after 1312); and in 1312 he was also professor of Roman law in Orléans. From 1314 he was immersed in juridical or political activities, both at the Parlement of Paris (1315) and as a member of King Philip V's Council of State (1318); in 1320 he became chancellor of Queen Joan of Burgundy. When appointed bishop of Nevers in January of 1320, he refused the see, accepting instead that of Autun some four months later. In 1329 in the famous memorandum *Super jurisdictione ecclesiastica et temporali,* which is his only work to be printed (Paris 1495), he upheld the Church's jurisdiction at a royal consultative assembly at Vincennes. He was subsequently named archbishop of Bourges (1330). In 1331, at the request of the king and queen, he was made a cardinal. He was entrusted with various papal diplomatic missions. Although a fervent polemicist, he had a taste for erudite works and compiled in the manner of the period a *Tabula super Decretum* and a *Scrinium iuris.* As a canonist, he has left two important works: an *Apparatus* on the *LIBER SEXTUS* and one on the *CLEMENTINAE*. He also added a fourth part to the *De origine jurisdictionum* of DURANDUS OF SAINT-POURÇAIN, OP. His teaching is very informative on the Church's constitutional problems in the 14th century.

Bibliography: F. DU CHESNE, *Histoire de tous les cardinaux français,* 2 v. (Paris 1660). O. MARTIN, *L'Assemblée de Vincennes* *de 1329 et ses conséquences* (Paris 1909). M. DÉRUELLE, *Dictionnaire de droit canonique*, R. NAZ ed., 7 v. (Paris 1935–65) 2:789–792. P. FOURNIER, *Histoire Littéraire de la France* 37 (1938) 85–120. A. VAN HOVE, *Commentarium Lovaniense in Codicem iuris canonici 1*, 5 v. (Mechlin 1928—) 1:458, 462. A. M. STICKLER, *Lexikon für Theologie und Kirche*, J. HOFER and K. RAHNER eds. (2d new ed. Freiburg, 1957–65) 8:351.

[P. LEGENDRE]

BERTRAND DE GARRIGA, BL.

Early Dominican; b. southern France, *c.* 1172; d. Toulouse, after 1230. An early follower and friend of St. DOMINIC, he joined the DOMINICANS at Toulouse in 1215. On Dominic's frequent journeys, Bertrand, if not taken as a companion, was left in charge of the brethren. He was an eyewitness to many of Dominic's miracles, which he kept secret in obedience to the saint's wishes, and revealed only at the insistence of JORDAN OF SAXONY. In 1217, Bertrand was sent to Paris; he returned to Toulouse in the following year as prior of St. Romanus, where he remained until his death. He became provincial of Provence, 1221. He was described as prayerful, humble, and austere. Many miracles were performed at his tomb, and 23 years after death his body was reported to be intact. Leo XIII approved his cult in 1881.

Feast: Sept. 6.

Bibliography: I. TAURISANO, *Catalogus hagiographicus ordinis praedicatorum* (Rome 1918) 9. B. ALTANER, *Der hl. Dominikus* (Breslau 1922). A. TOURON, *The First Disciples of Saint Dominic,* ed. and tr. V. F. O'DANIEL (Washington 1928). V. DE WILDE, *Dictionnaire d'histoire et de géographie ecclésiastiques,* ed. A. BAUDRILLART (Paris 1912–) 8:1060–61. G. GIERATHS, *Lexikon für Theologie und Kirche,* ed. J. HOFER and K. RAHNER, 10 v. (2d, new ed. Freiburg 1957–65) 2:272.

[L. M. SCHIER]

BERTRAND OF AQUILEIA, ST.

Patriarch of Aquileia; b. probably at Château de Saint-Géniès near Montcuq, France, *c.* 1260; d. near Spilimbergo, Italy, June 6, 1350. By 1314 Bertrand was licensed in both civil and canon law, having studied at the University of Toulouse. There he was a professor for a time while also holding many benefices. In 1318 he became a pontifical chaplain and heard pleas at the Roman Rota under JOHN XXII. He was employed also on diplomatic missions and was rewarded by nomination as patriarch of Aquileia on July 4, 1334. Bertrand immediately set about reconquering the lands and reestablishing the privileges of his patriarchate. He recaptured the town of Sacile and certain fortresses from the count of Goritz (Gorizia) and then successfully waged war with Venice. His increasing strength alarmed the city of Florence, which turned BENEDICT XII against him, and the pope brought about an alliance between the Florentines and Venetians, causing Bertrand to lose the ground he had gained. In another attempt to stop the encroachment of the nobles on Church property and their intimidation of its officials, a provincial synod at Aquileia, meeting on April 25, 1339, decreed that grave punishments be meted out to those who threatened the life and liberty of prelates. Bertrand wanted the proscription renewed at the Synod of Padua in 1350, but the cardinal-legate, Guy of Boulogne (d. 1373), preferred to reconcile the patriarch with his enemies. He failed, however, and as Bertrand left the synod, his escort was attacked by the retainers of the count of Goritz, and he was mortally wounded. Many miracles were attributed to his intercession, and his cult was officially recognized by Pope CLEMENT VIII on April 27, 1599.

Feast: June 6.

Bibliography: *Bibliotheca hagiograpica latina antiquae et mediae aetatis* (Brussels 1898–1901) 1:1301–03. G. MOLLAT, *Dictionnaire d'histoire et de géographie ecclésiastiques*, ed. A. BAUDRILLART et al. (Paris 1912) 8:1075–78. C. TOURNIER, *Le Bx. Bertrand de Saint-Géniès* (Paris 1929). C. SCHMITT, *Un Pape réformateur et un défenseur de l'unité de l'eglise: Benoît XII et l'Ordre des frères mineurs,* 1334–1342 (Florence 1959) 241–243, 301–302. J. L. BAUDOT and L. CHAUSSIN, *Vies des saints et des bienhereux selon l'ordre du calendrier avec l'historique des fêtes* (Paris 1935–56) 6:121–124. P. ALBERS, *Lexikon für Theologie und Kirche,* ed. J. HOFER and K. RAHNER (Freiburg 1957–65) 2:271.

[C. R. BYERLY]

BERTRAND OF COMMINGES, ST.

Bishop; b. Isle-Jourdain (then in the Diocese of Toulouse), France, *c.* 1050; d. Oct. 16, 1123. He was born of a noble family, educated in the Abbey of La Chaise-Dieu, and chosen canon and archdeacon of Toulouse. In 1073 he was elected bishop of Comminges (now included in the Toulouse Diocese) and energetically served his see for 50 years. He reorganized his ravaged diocese, visiting every section of it. Several times he faced opposition to his preaching, but after one such incident the penitent men of Azon offered to his see in perpetuity all their butter produced during the week before Whitsunday. Apparently this pledge was paid annually until the French Revolution. The story called the ''Great Pardon of Comminges,'' which relates Bertrand's deliverance of a certain thieving lord from Moorish exile and the apparition of the bishop to this prisoner who once vigorously opposed him, is commemorated locally every May 2.

Feast: Oct. 16.

Bibliography: *Acta Sanctorum* Oct. 7.2:1140–84. L. ANDRÉ-DELASTRE, *Saint Bertrand de Comminges, qui nous appelle sur la montagne* (Paris 1974). P. BEDIN, *Saint Bertrand, évêque de Comminges, 1040–1123* (Toulouse 1912). L. DE FIANCETTE D'AGOS, *Vie et miracles de saint Bertrand: avec une notice historique sur la ville et les évêques de Comminges* (Nîmes 1994). L. MÉDAN, *Dictionnaire d'histoire et de géographie ecclésiastiques*, ed. A. BAUDRILLART et al. (Paris 1912) 8:1050–51. J. ROCACHER, *Saint-Bertrand de Comminges* (Paris 1982).

[E. J. KEALEY]

BERTULF OF BOBBIO, ST.

Benedictine abbot; d. Aug. 19, 640. A member of a prominent pagan Frankish family, Bertulf was converted to Christianity by ARNULF OF METZ, a near relative, and became a monk at Luxeuil under Abbot EUSTACE (620). A few years later he accompanied Abbot Attala to Bobbio and succeeded him as abbot there (627). In 628 a conflict with the bishop of Tortona over jurisdiction took him to Rome to discuss the matter with HONORIUS I, who, in the first known instance of this procedure, granted Bobbio complete EXEMPTION from episcopal jurisdiction. The account of this mission is found in the life of Bertulf written (642) by JONAS OF BOBBIO, who accompanied Bertulf to Rome.

Feast: Aug. 19.

Bibliography: E. DE MOREAU, *Dictionnaire d'histoire et de géographie ecclésiastiques*, ed. A. BAUDRILLART et al. (Paris 1912) 8:1111. A. BUTLER, *The Lives of the Saints*, ed. H. THURSTON and D. ATTWATER (New York 1956) 3:356–357. E. EWIG, *Lexikon für Theologie und Kirche*, ed. J. HOFER and K. RAHNER (Freiburg 1957–65) 2:273. *Bibliotheca hagiographica latina antiquae et mediae aetatis* (Brussels 1898–1901) 1:1311–15. *Acta Sanctorum* Aug. 3:750–754. J. MABILLON, *Acta sanctorum ordinis S. Benedicti* (Venice 1733–40) 2:150–157. *Monumenta Germaniae Historica: Scriptores rerum Merovingicarum* 4:143–152. P. JAFFE, *Regesta pontificum romanorum ab condita ecclesia ad annum post Christum natum 1198*, ed. P. EWALD (Graz 1956) 1:224. C. CIPOLLA and G. BUZZI, eds., *Codice diplomatico del monastèro di S. Colombano di Bobbio*, 3 v. (Fonti per la storia d'Italia 52–54; 1918).

[C. P. LOUGHRAN]

BERTULF OF RENTY, ST.

Abbot; b. Germany, mid-seventh century; d. Renty, France, Feb. 5, *c.* 705. It is fairly certain that Bertulf (Bertoul or Bertulphus) founded the Abbey of Renty near Saint-Omer, but little else is known of his life, since his biography dates from the late eleventh century and appears to depend on material that can be traced no farther back than the tenth century. According to this account, he was born a pagan in Germany, went to Gaul, was baptized, and became the *economus* of a count whose properties at Renty he inherited. He later entered the monastic foundation he had made, became abbot, and died there. His relics were transferred from Renty to Boulogne, then to Harlebeke, Belgium (after 935), and finally (955) to Saint-Pierre-de-Gand. They disappeared during the course of the religious wars of the sixteenth century.

Feast: Feb. 5.

Bibliography: *Acta Sanctorum* Feb. 1:681–694. J. FERRANT, *Esquisse historique sur le culte et les reliques de saint Bertulphe de Renty en l'Église d'Harlebeke* (Bruges 1898). *Analecta Bollandiana* 17 (1898) 373–374. L. VAN DER ESSEN, *Étude critique et littéraire sur les vitae des saints mérovingiens de l'ancienne Belgique* (Louvain 1907) 422–423. E. DE MOREAU, *Dictionnaire d'histoire et de géographie ecclésiastiques*, ed. A. BAUDRILLART et al. (Paris 1912) 8:1112–13. A. M. ZIMMERMANN, *Kalendarium Benedictinum*, (Metten 1933–38) 1:170–172. R. AIGRAIN, *Catholicisme* 1:1511.

[P. BLECKER]

BÉRULLE, PIERRE DE

Cardinal, diplomat, theologian, mystic, spiritual writer, founder of the French Oratory, leading figure in the French school of spirituality; b. Chateau de Sérilly, between Sens and Troyes, France, Feb. 4, 1575; d. Paris, Oct. 2, 1629. Born of an old and distinguished family, Bérulle was brought up from infancy in a deeply religious environment in which he developed with such remarkable precocity that at the age of 17 he was considered a master of the spiritual life. He was educated by the Jesuits and at the Sorbonne and was ordained June 5, 1599. That same year he was named honorary almoner of King HENRY IV. In 1607 the king proposed to make him tutor to the Dauphin, but Bérulle declined. He also refused repeated and pressing offers of commendatory prelacies and bishoprics, preferring to devote himself entirely to spiritual direction, controversy with Protestants, and the promotion of reform among religious communities. The AUGUSTINIANS, BENEDICTINES, and FEUILLANTS were among the beneficiaries of his efforts in this last sphere. In his zeal for a spiritual restoration, Bérulle undertook long and difficult negotiations to introduce the CARMELITE nuns of the Teresian reform into France. He, together with André Duval and Jacques Gallemant, was put in charge of these religious by PAUL V, but in spite of his spiritual influence upon them, he encountered difficulties and resistance with regard to disciplinary matters and the vow of servitude.

After 1605 Bérulle took an interest in the decrees of the Council of TRENT concerning the education of the clergy. This led him to found in Paris the Oratory of Jesus, usually known as the French Oratory, modeled after the Oratory of St. Philip Neri. This undertaking was a great success, and the Oratory quickly spread to other places. By the time of Bérulle's death he had established 17 colleges, and his engagement in this work brought him into much disagreeable conflict with the university and the Jesuits.

As confidant and counselor of Queen Marie de Médicis and as friend of Louis XIII, he was a powerful influence for good at court. Besides his work as peacemaker (he effected a reconciliation between the queen and her son, Louis XIII, in 1620), he engaged in political activity of importance and conducted a number of diplomatic missions for the king. In this he was motivated chiefly by religious rather than nationalistic considerations. He desired to reunite Christians in an effective struggle against Protestantism. Hoping for the conversion of England, Bérulle supported the marriage of Henriette, sister of Louis XIII, to the Prince of Wales, the future CHARLES I of England, conducted the negotiations with Rome for the dispensation for the marriage, and accompanied the queen to Great Britain. He refused in 1629 to sign the treaty of alliance with England and the Low Countries because he could not abide the thought of France entering into a compact with Protestants against Catholic Spain. Nevertheless, the policy of alliance with the Protestants prevailed, and this put an end to Bérulle's political activity. He fell into disgrace, and Cardinal RICHELIEU wanted to have him sent from France.

Although he was deeply involved in political affairs, Bérulle remained essentially a contemplative, as is apparent in the many spiritual works that he composed. For the most part these were composed for the occasion, were hastily written, and have the appearance of being unfinished drafts. They are discourses and effusions that express the ardor of his faith rather than treatises in the strict sense. He was eminently a man whose orientation was spiritual; his speculation was joined with prayer in an indistinguishable act of adoration (*see* M. Dupuy, *Bérulle, une spiritualité d'adoration*, Tournai 1964). His principal works were *Discours de l'état et des grandeurs de Jésus* (1623, 2e partie 1629); *Élevations à Jésus-Christ sur sa conduite . . . vers S. Madeleine* (1625); *Bref discours de l'abnégation intérieure* (1597); and *Oeuvres de piété* (184 opuscula, ed. G. Rotureau, Paris 1944).

Bérulle was created cardinal in 1627 and died with a reputation for holiness. To his intercession 45 miracles were attributed. At the petition of François BOURGOING, superior general of the French Oratory, Innocent X introduced the process for Bérulle's beatification, but this was interrupted by JANSENIST intrigues.

See Also: SPIRITUALITY, FRENCH SCHOOL OF.

Bibliography: *Oeuvres complètes*, ed. J. P. MIGNE (Paris 1856); *Correspondance*, ed. J. DAGENS, 3 v. (Paris 1937–39). J. DAGENS, *Bérulle et les origines de la restauration catholique* (Bruges 1952) 383–387, a complete list of Bérulle's works and MSS; 379–383, of his biographies. J. F. NOURRISSON, *Le Cardinal de Bérulle: Sa vie, ses écrits, son temps* (Paris 1856). M. HOUSSAYE, *M. de Bérulle et les carmélites de France* (Paris 1872); *Le Père de Bérulle et l'Oratoire de Jésus* (Paris 1874); *Le Cardinal de Bérulle et le cardinal de Richelieu* (Paris 1875). A. MOLIEN, *Le Cardinal de Bérulle*, 2 v. (Paris 1947); M. VILLERS, *Dictionnaire de spiritualité ascétique et mystique* (Paris 1932—) 1:1539–81; *Dictionnaire d'histoire et de géographie ecclésiastiques* (Paris 1912—) 8:1115–35. A. GEORGE, *L'Oratoire* (Paris 1928). C. TAVEAU, *Le Cardinal de Bérulle, maître de la vie spirituelle* (Paris 1933). B. KIESLER, *Die Struktur des Theozentrismus bei Bérulle und de Condren* (Berlin 1934). R. BELLEMARE, *Le Sens de la créature dans la doctrine de Bérulle* (Ottawa 1959). P. COCHOIS, *Bérulle et l'École française* (Paris 1963). J. MOIOLI, *Teologia della devozione B. al Verbo Incarnato* (Varese 1964). J. H. CREHAN, *A Catholic Dictionary of Theology* 1:263–266. J. ORCIBAL, *Le Cardinal de Bérulle: Évolution d'une spiritualité* (Paris 1965).

[A. LIUIMA]

BERYLLUS OF BOSTRA

Died after 244. As an intellectual and the bishop of Bostra in Arabia, Beryllus was the most important person in the Arabia of his day. He was a Monarchian who believed that after the Incarnation the divine nature of the Father entered Jesus Christ. Eusebius tells us that *c.* 244 ORIGEN disputed with Beryllus and converted him to orthodoxy (*Hist. Eccl.* 6.33.1–4). According to Eusebius (*ibid.* 6.20.2) and Jerome (*De vir. ill.* 60), Beryllus wrote several letters concerning this episode; however, they are no longer extant.

Bibliography: P. GODET, *Dictionnaire de théologie catholique*, A. VACANT ed., 15 vol. (Paris 1903–50) 2.1:799–800. H. RAHNER, *Lexikon für Theologie und Kirche*, J. HOFER and K. RAHNER eds. (2d new ed. Freiburg, 1957–65) 2:286. J. QUASTEN, *Patrology* 2:40, 62. K. BIHLMEYER and H. TÜCHLE, *Kirchengeschichte* 1:162.

[R. K. POETZEL]

BESCHI, COSTANZO GIUSEPPE

Italian Jesuit missionary in South India and the foremost Christian poet in the Tamil language; b. Castiglione, Italy, Nov. 8, 1680; d. Manapar, India, Feb. 4, 1747. During studies at Rome he mastered Greek, Latin, French, Portuguese, and other European languages. He joined the Society of Jesus in 1698 and left for India; after some time in Goa, he reached Tirunelveli in the extreme south (1711) and later proceeded to Madura (1716). He became expert in Tamil under the guidance of a noted scholar, Supradīpa Kavirāyar, and learned Sanskrit, Telugu, and other South Indian languages, as well as Persian and

Urdu. He composed poems, dictionaries, grammars, and manuals on religious, didactic, and medical themes, and he wrote Tamil grammars in Latin; he also translated the *Kural* into Latin verse.

Like another Italian Catholic missionary in the South, Robert de NOBILI, Beschi adopted the customs of the Tamils in diet and dress and won their affection and trust. During his long ministry of about 35 years, he built many churches, and he spread the gospel through his Tamil writings. It is said that he won the confidence of the Muslim ruler of Trichinopoly (1736) and indeed served as his *diwan* (prime minister); but when the Marathas took over (1741), Beschi went to Ramnad and Tirunelveli and retired a few years before his death.

Beschi is more popularly known in southern India as Vīramāmunivar (The Heroic Sage) and Dhairyanāthar (Lord of Courage). As the author of the first Tamil dictionary, *Chaturaharāthi,* he is called the father of Tamil lexicography; as the author of the Tamil grammar, *Tonnūl Vilakkam,* he seems to have advocated certain innovations in Tamil orthography; his Tamil prose writings—religious as well as secular—like those of de Nobili, have helped to lay the foundations of modern Tamil prose. Among his poems are the hagiological *Kittēriammāl Charitram* (*On the Martyr St. Quiterea*) and *Tēmbāvani* (1726, *Unfading Garland*), his magnum opus. This epic is divided into three parts, 36 cantos, and 3,615 stanzas. The reference in the opening verse to "three worlds" and the fusion of philosophy and theology with a drama that is both human and divine have led critics to hail Beschi as the Tamil Dante. Beschi was obviously steeped in the ancient Tamil classics—for example, the *Jīvakachintāmani* and the *Rāmāyana* of Kamban—and he naturally followed the Tamil epic tradition when he composed this work on the life of Joseph and Mary, set in the background of the Old and New Testament world. *Tēmbāvani* has been described as "the noblest poem in honor of St. Joseph written in any literature East or West."

Bibliography: C. G. BESCHI, *Tembavani* (Madras 1849). C. SOMMERVOGEL et al., *Bibliothèque de la Compagnie de Jésus*, 11 v. (Brussels–Paris 1890–1932; v. 12 suppl. 1960) 1:1402–09. R. STREIT and J. DINDINGER, *Bibliotheca missionum* (Freiburg 1916—) 6:30–41, 53, 55, 64, 83, 84, 88, 92, 106. M. LEDRUS, *Dictionnaire d'histoire et de géographie ecclésiastiques*, A. BAUDRILLART et al. (Paris 1912—) 8:1167–70. M. S. VENKATASĀMI, *Christianity and Tamil* (Madras 1948), in Tamil. L. BESSE, *Father Beschi of the Society of Jesus: His Times and His Writings* (Trichinopoly 1918).

[K. R. SRINIVASA IYENGAR]

BESSARION, CARDINAL

Fifteenth-century Greek bishop, theologian, and humanist; b. Trebizond, Jan. 2, 1403; d. Ravenna, Italy, Nov. 18, 1472. Originally of a modest family, Bessarion was apparently adopted by the Metropolitan Dositheus of Trebizond and educated in rhetoric, philosophy, and asceticism at Constantinople, where he had Manuel Chrysococcus for a master and Filelfo and George Scholarius (GENNADIUS II SCHOLARIUS) as fellow students. Under the guidance of the archbishop of Selymbria, he took the monastic habit (Jan. 30, 1423), changed his name from Basil (not John) to Bessarion, and wrote an encomium in honor of the 5th-century saint thus chosen as his patron. He became a deacon in 1426. Ordained in 1431, he traveled to Mistra in the Peloponnesus, studied with George Gemistos, PLETHON, and wrote a series of *monodia,* or panegyrics, for the court. He settled a dispute between the emperor and his brother, the despot Theodore II of Morea (1436), and was recalled to Constantinople and made hegumen, or abbot, of the monastery of St. Basil.

In preparation for the Council of FLORENCE, he was created archbishop of Nicaea (1437), and he sailed with the emperor and Greek delegation to Venice. At the Council, both in Ferrara and Florence, he served with Mark EUGENICUS OF EPHESUS as spokesman for the Greeks; eventually he accepted the Roman position on the FILIOQUE and procession of the Holy Spirit and helped win over most of the other Byzantine delegates. He signed the decree of union (June 6, 1439) and, despite an offer to remain in the Roman Curia, returned to Constantinople (Feb. 1, 1440), where he wrote three public letters of consolation to the emperor on the death of his wife, and took part in the election of the new patriarch of Constantinople, Metrophanes II (March 1, 1440).

When created a cardinal by Pope EUGENE IV, Bessarion returned to Florence (Dec. 10, 1440); signed the decree of union with the Jacobites (Feb. 5, 1442); and consecrated the Franciscan church of the Holy Cross. He returned to Rome with the Curia (Sept. 28, 1443) and took up residence close to his title church of the 12 Apostles. Bessarion quickly achieved a perfect knowledge of Latin and Italian. He was charged with the beatification process for St. Bernardine of Siena (1449), and he served as papal legate to settle a peace between Venice and Milan (September 1449). He was made papal governor of Bologna (1450–55) and went on embassies to Naples (1457), Germany (1460–61), Venice (1463), and France (1472), in the vain hope of stirring the rulers of these lands to join a crusade against the Turks. On his return from an unsuccessful mission to King Louis XI of France he died at Ravenna; his body was returned to his title church in Rome, and Nicholas Capranica delivered his panegyric.

Bessarion's early writings were mainly court elegies, panegyrics, and letters. Before the Council of Florence, influenced by the doctrine of Thomas Aquinas concerning essence and existence in God, he had rejected the doctrine of Gregory PALAMAS in a defense of the writings of JOHN XI BECCUS. At the council he delivered a *Dogmatic Oration* in favor of union, helped compose most of the Greek speeches, and wrote the treatises on the Eucharist and the epiclesis. After the council he published a refutation of the Syllogisms of Mark Eugenicus against the council; a ''Justification of the Union'' addressed to Alexis Lascaris Philanthropinus (*c.* 1444); and a *Letter to the Despot Constantine* on the defense of Greece. Appointed protector of the Greek monks in Italy, he wrote an epitome of the rule of St. Basil, reorganized their government, held a general chapter for the Basilians (1446) and supervised visitations. He was endowed with numerous benefices and used the revenue in aiding the Italian humanists and Greek émigrés, both princes and scholars. After the fall of Constantinople (1453) he determined to collect all the extant Greek literature, both classic and patristic, and before his death he bequeathed a library of over 30 cases of manuscripts to St. Mark's in Venice (1468).

He had secured the patronage of Popes Nicholas V, Paul II, and Pius II for having both the classic and patristic Greek literature translated into Latin. He aided and protected such humanists as POGGIO BRACCIOLINI, Laurenzo VALLA, and Bartolomeo Platina, who also wrote a panegyric in his honor. Bessarion had translated some of Aristotle's works, and he wrote a *De natura et arte* and turned most of his own Greek writings into Latin. With his *In calumniatorem Platonis* Bessarion defended the Greek philosopher's reputation and provided the West with a good knowledge of Plato's philosophy, demonstrating its reconcilability with both Aristotle and Christianity. On the death of ISIDORE OF KIEV he was made patriarch of Constantinople (1463) and sent an encyclical to the Greeks living under Turkish rule. In 1470 he wrote an *Oration to Princes* calling them to a crusade; it was spread in northern Europe by William Fichet of Paris. Bessarion had encouraged L. Valla in his application of philological principles to textual criticism of the Bible, and composed a tract on the pericope in the Gospel of John (21.22). A man of deep piety and universal scholarly interests, he played a crucial part in the development of the Italian RENAISSANCE.

Cardinal Bessarion, 18th-century engraving.

Bibliography: *Patrologia Graeca,* ed. J. P. MIGNE (Paris 1857–66) 161:137–746. J. D. MANSI, *Sacrorum Concilliorum nova et amplissima collectio* (repr. Graz 1960) 31:893–966. L. MOHLER, *Kardinal Bessarion,* 3 v. (Paderborn 1923–42), v.2 *In Platonis calumniatorem,* v.3 *circle of scholars,* v.1 *chronology of life and works*; to be corrected according to R. LOERNERTZ, *Orientalia Christiana periodicalo* 10 (Rome 1944) 116–149. E. CANDAL, *Orientalia Christiana periodica* 4 (1938) 329–371, Thomas Aquinas; *ibid.* 6 (1940) 417–466, council; ed., *Oratio dogmatica* (Rome 1958). G. HOFMANN, *Orientalia Christiana periodica* 15 (1949) 277–290, letters. H. VAST, *Le Cardinal Bessarion* (Paris 1878). P. JOANNOU, *Analecta Bollandiana* 65 (1947) 107–138, *St. Bessarion.* L. BRÉHIER, *Dictionnaire d'histoire et de géographie ecclésiastiques* A. BAUDRILLART et al (Paris 1912–) 8:1181–99. A. PALMIERI, *Dictionnaire de théologie catholique* A. VACANT et al. 15 vol. (Paris 1903–50) 2.1:801–807. H. G. BECK, *Kirche und theologische Literature im byzantinischen Reich* (Munich 1959) 767–769. A. G. KELLER, *Cambridge Historical Journal* 11 (1955) 343–348. J. GILL, *The Council of Florence* (Cambridge, Eng. 1959), index 435. B. KOTTER, *Lexikon für Theologie und Kirche* J. HOFER and K. RAHNER eds., 10 vol. (2nd new ed. Freiburg, 1957–65) 2:301.

[F. X. MURPHY]

BESSARION OF EGYPT, ST.

Fifth-century Egyptian monk. He is known as a miracle worker and founder of a pilgrim shelter in Jerusalem and of a monastery on Mt. Sion. Bessarion (Passarion) is to be distinguished from a number of similarly named saints in the synaxarions and menologies. He is mentioned in the vita of St. Euthymius by CYRIL OF SCYTHOPOLIS and is said to have accompanied Bishop Juvenal of Jerusalem when he consecrated the laura of Euthymius in 429. He is also thought to have presented the

Emperor Theodosius II (425–450) with the hand of St. Stephen the protomartyr as a relic. An encomium on him was written by Cardinal Bessarion.

Feast: June 17.

Bibliography: *Acta Sanctorum* June 4:240–243. F. DELMAS, *Échos d'Orient* 3 (1899–1900) 162–163. E. SCHWARTZ, ed., *Kyrillos von Skythopolis* (TU 49.2; 1939) 26–27, 90. P. JOANNOU, *Analecta Bollandiana* 65 (1947) 107–138, encomium and details of life. O. VOLK, *Lexikon für Theologie und Kirche*, ed. J. HOFER and K. RAHNER (Freiburg 1957–65) 2:301–302.

[F. X. MURPHY]

BESSETTE, ANDRÉ, BL.

Baptized Alfred; thaumaturgist and member of the Brotherhood of the Holy Cross; b. Saint-Gregoire d'Iberville (southeast of Montréal), Québec, Canada, Aug. 9, 1845; d. Montréal, Jan. 6, 1937. Alfred, the eighth of twelve children of Isaac Bessette and Clothilde Foisy, was sickly and left orphaned by the age of twelve. He unsuccessfully attempted various occupations as a smith, cobbler, and baker. During the U.S. Civil War, he did manual labor in mills and on farms in New England, where he learned English. He returned to Montréal in 1867 and was accepted as a Holy Cross postulant despite his precarious health and illiteracy. With the help of Bishop Bouget of Montréal, Brother André professed his vows on Dec. 27, 1870.

Bessette gained a reputation as a healer during his many decades as porter of Notre Dame College. His devotion to St. Joseph, patron of the Universal Church, led him to build St. Joseph's Oratory atop Mont Royal in Montréal. The first small chapel (15' by 18') erected in 1904, was enlarged in 1908 and 1910. The cornerstone for a new crypt church—to hold 1,000 people—was laid in 1917, but the roof was not added until 1936. The oratory, where Blessed André served as guardian for thirty years and is buried, was solemnly dedicated as a minor basilica in 1955. He was beatified by Pope John Paul II on May 23, 1982.

Feast: Jan. 6 (U.S.A.).

Bibliography: L. BOUCHER, *Brother André: The Miracle Man of Mount Royal* (Montréal 1997). K. BURTON, *Brother André of Mount Royal* (Notre Dame, Ind. 1952). J. G. DUBUC, *Le frère André* (Saint-Laurent, Québec 1996), Eng. tr. R. PRUDHOMME, *Brother André* (Quebec 1999). H. GRENON, *Le frère André* (Montréal 1981). A. HATCH, *The Miracle of the Mountain: The Story of Brother André and the Shrine on Mount Royal* (New York 1959). M. LACHANCE, *Le frère André* (Montréal 1979). C. B. RUFFIN, *The Life of Brother André: The Miracle Worker of St. Joseph* (Huntington, Ind. 1988). S. T. STEIN, *The Tapestry of Saint Joseph: Chronological History of St. Joseph and His Apostle, Blessed Brother André* (Philadelphia, Pa. 1991). *Acta Apostolicae Sedis* 75 (1983): 14–16. *L'Osservatore Romano,* English edition, 24 (1982): 6–7.

[K. I. RABENSTEIN]

BESTIARY

A type of short medieval beast allegory of didactic purpose, written in verse or prose. One may trace the bestiary to the *PHYSIOLOGUS* (4th century) and treat rather as natural history those traditions that derive from Aristotle. During the Middle Ages, the bestiaries fused myth and legend with characteristics of certain regions; with religious symbols; or later, with practical problems of the training, breeding, and medical care of domesticated animals. The genre varied with the dominant preoccupations of given periods, and its golden age extended through the 13th and 14th centuries. Importance is attached to bestiaries by the fact that literatures of many countries derived a vast amount of beast lore and legendary material from their sources.

Early Types. Until about 1230, progress of a scientific kind was not widespread, and variations in natural science resulted from arbitrary rearrangements of animal lore to fit certain projects. If we consider Pliny's *Historia naturalis* an objective survey of the field, Solinus's *Collectanea rerum memorabilium* appears to have been a reaction against rationalism and objective science, and St. Isidore's *Etymologiae* a return to the encyclopedic type of objectivity. Running concurrently with these works, the *Physiologus* maintained an immutable form and scope, with strong Christian symbolism; the characteristics of these works mingled in the vast compilations of Bartholomeus Anglicus and Vincent of Beauvais.

Pliny had given a vast repertory of mammals (Book 8), fishes (Book 9), and birds (Book 10), either briefly described as a catalogue, or developed in some detail. He classified fish according to shape and other traits (9.36, 43–44), and as polyps (9.46–48) or crustaceans (9.50–52); but classifications were implicit in the groupings of domestic animals (8.69–77); birds were categorized as having claws or webbed feet, or as being able to speak or transmit omens (10.13). Pliny was interested particularly in animals that have some immediate relationship to man; and he noted anecdotes relative to customs and to the faithful services of dogs, horses (8.61, 64–69), and dolphins (9.7–10) and wrote of animals that had been seen in Rome. His most extensive information came from Africa and Asia; northern animals, such as the Scythian elk (8.15–16), were rare; the detailed chapter on the bear (8.54) is noteworthy. Of the few fabulous creatures that he treated, the basilisk and mantichora—a man-headed lion—(8.33, 45), the Indian whale and the phoenix (9.2, 10.2) reappeared in bestiaries.

Exotic Developments. The Plinian formula yielded to the irrational and exotic presentation of the *Collectanea rerum memorabilium* of Solinus, who introduced details basic in the later bestiaries and whose colorful accounts appealed strongly to medieval compilers. Insofar as the *Collectanea* was a survey of geography, it was based in part on Mela's *De Situ orbis.* Solinus, however, reduced the classical and archeological content of his model and developed the treatment of animals and stones as the principal noteworthy exotic curiosities in specific countries—Greek partridges and Numidian bears; and beavers, dolphins, cranes, and such fabulous monsters of Africa and India as the mantichora and the monoceros; he boldly passed from legend to generalities and included a multiplicity of sphinxes and gorgons.

The picturesque and the exotic were counteracted by St. Isidore's *Etymologiae* (*Patrologia Latina* 82). This book, tending strongly to offer objective fact, was one of the principal prototypes of the later encyclopedias. Isidore made extensive use of Solinus without in any way reducing the esteem held for this source. His Book 12 gathered the animals by categories, domestic and familiar (ch. 1), beasts of prey (ch. 2), *De minutis animantibus* (ch. 3), *De serpentibus* (ch. 4), *De vermibus* (ch. 5), *De piscibus* (ch. 6), and *De avibus* (ch. 7–8). The *Etymologiae* was popular among the revisers of the *Physiologus* as well as the encyclopedists for its verisimilitude and its incisive presentations.

Among Isidore's sources was the *Hexaemeron* of St. Ambrose (PL 14), constructed according to the ''days'' of Creation. The presentation of fishes and birds is exactly that of the *Physiologus,* with mention of a few physical or moral traits, and a Christian moralization for each. In Book 5 of the *Etymologiae* the birds (ch. 12–23) correspond well with those in the *Physiologus*, with the noteworthy terminal addition of the ''gallus.'' Book 6, hastily compiled, treats the animals pell-mell and without formal moralizations, and quite inappropriately, after the fox, includes the partridge as equally ''fraudulent,'' with some 50 words copied verbatim from the Latin *Physiologus.*

Influence of the *Physiologus*. The *Physiologus* was in fact the other major formative tradition of the bestiaries. This 4th-century Latin text, preserved intact in very few copies, was enriched in several steps by the use of Solinus and of Isidore, and had finally become the massive *De Bestiis et aliis rebus,* in turn expanded to four books (PL 177). Transpositions and eliminations in Books 2 and 3 hide the origins. Book 3, which should open with a prologue (*''Bestiarum vocabulum . . .''*) and the chapter on the lion, is an amplification of *versio L* (in 27 chapters) attributed to Chrysostom; it is extant in more than 20 MSS, and was published by M. R. James as *The Bestiary* (Oxford 1928), in 112 chapters, but 13 more should be added, e.g., from MS Harley 3244, etc. The innovations included the tiger, bear, and bee; dogs were presented as in Pliny. The compiler copied verbatim from the *Etymologiae* the treatment (ch. 43–54) of snakes and worms (*Etym.* 12.4–5), fish, precious stones, and trees (*Etym.* 17.7); the last mentioned is traceable ultimately to Dioscorides or Vitruvius. Book 1 dwells at great length on a few birds, especially doves, geese, chickens, and peacocks (ch. 1–55), and the domestic Accipiter (ch. 13–16). Book 2 deals with 36 creatures, of which the *crocodilus, ibex, canis, lupus,* and *draco* alone are not derived from the *Physiologus;* they are developed by the addition of moralizations. Book 4 is a convenient dictionary covering the names found in the preceding sections; of the 400 or more names, 300 appear in Book 3.

Flowering of the Genre. The 13th century brought the flowering of the bestiaries, either in the older pattern used by Solinus, according to regions and as a function of geography, or in massive forms convenient for reference. *L'Image du monde,* composed in French about 1250, and attributed to Gossouin or Gautier of Metz, is a *mappe-monde* or survey of the world, more realistic than that of Solinus; it was translated into English and published several times before 1500; it included dragons, elephants, the mantichora, and several magic stones. *De Proprietatibus rerum,* by Bartholomeus Anglicus, was translated into Italian in 1309 and into French in 1372, and printed more than 15 times from 1482. In Book 12, Bartholomeus presented the birds mentioned in the Bible, and cited Isidore, Ambrose, and Aristotle's *De Animalibus;* Book 18, dealing with 115 animals, proposed such classifications as carnivorous, nocturnal, domestic, and more or less intelligent; he discussed physiological traits, explaining all such variations in the light of moral and religious criteria. The immense *Speculum naturale* of Vincent of Beauvais consisted of notes.

Falconry. Books on hunting birds and their care and training suddenly appeared early in the 13th century and seem to have been derived from technical manuals of Persian origin. The visit of the Emperor Frederick II to the East in 1230 sets a probable date. The many tracts were interrelated and appeared both in Sicily and in Provence. Their source is sometimes identified as one ''Moamin,'' who used an Arabic model; some scholars consider Theodorus, named in 1239, the source; another person frequently credited was an anonymous author involved in the *Libro del Gandolfo Persiano,* a book devoted primarily to medical treatment and training. By the mid-century, a tract attributed to a King Dancus, and Daude de Pradas's *Dels auzels cassadors* appeared. These treatises were not, strictly speaking, bestiaries, but were so closely related as to deserve mention.

The most significant medieval book on falconry was the *Tractatus de arte venandi cum avibus* of Frederick II, revised by his son Manfred, and translated into French late in the 13th century. Frederick presumably composed this book himself shortly before 1250, after a decade of research and observation, and he may have directed the preparation of the fine illustrations. He used Aristotle as a point of departure, noting many of his errors and questionable hypotheses, and undoubtedly he knew other books of Eastern origin, such as the *De scientia venandi per aves* of Moamin, which he had translated around 1240. His principal source, however, beyond the practical knowledge from the falconers he brought to Italy in about 1230, was his own experience. After *De arte venandi,* the principal medieval treatises on falconry were the *Deduiz de la chasse* of Gaston Phébus, composed by 1370 and often printed, and the *Livre de la chasse du roi Modus.*

Later Developments. One may illustrate the status of the bestiaries in about 1260 by the contents of Brunetto Latini's *Li Livres dou Tresor.* Latini compiled and translated from a wide range of Latin sources. Intending his encyclopedia as a manual for the well-informed ruler, he selected rather than accumulated and used a well-organized plan. In his first book he surveyed general knowledge, including history (according to St. Isidore); geography (according to Solinus); and natural science, with a short tract on farming (based on that by Palladius) and a bestiary dealing with 70 animals, each developed in some detail and in symmetrical form.

Latini's basic source was the expanded *Physiologus* as found in Book 3 of *De Bestiis et aliis rebus,* further enriched from the *Etymologiae,* the *Collectanea,* and St. Ambrose. The moralizations disappeared along with almost all of the fabulous creatures and mystic stones. The animals were fairly well grouped as fish, birds, and mammals, each in its own alphabetical series. From *De Bestiis* Latini borrowed the mole and the peacock; from Solinus, the parrot, dog, and bear; and from Palladius, in part as an aspect of husbandry, a group of chapters on domestic animals, chickens, geese, cattle, horses, and sheep. Latini's chapters on hunting birds alone were gathered in a special group out of alphabetical order, and reflected the same kind of interest that one finds in *Dels auzels cassadors* and in the *Libro del Gandolfo Persiano.* Latini added no new information, but his selective method reflected a rational didactic purpose and a tendency to avoid sheer accumulation of detail.

Use of Semitic Lore. As a last step in compilation of intriguing and exotic creatures, we may mention the introduction of medieval Semitic lore through Bochart's *Hierozoicon,* about 1660. In methodical fashion, Bochart enriched a broad classical bibliography on the whale (Aelian, Aristotle, Homer, Nearchus, Philostratus), not only with the full Old Testament documentation on large fish (including the Leviathan), but also with that of the Hebrew *Porta caeli* and of the 12th-century *Miracula rerum creaturarum,* by Alkazuinus. He included also a work of Muhammad ad-Damir, which was his main source for *De dubiis vel fabulosis* (tragelaphus, myrmecoleon, gryphes) and *Aves fabulosae apud Arabes;* in it we find an echo of the *Zend-Avesta* in the Simorgh-Anka, a kind of ''coq d'or.''

See Also: ANIMALS, SYMBOLISM OF; ART, EARLY CHRISTIAN; SYMBOLISM, EARLY CHRISTIAN.

Bibliography: F. CARMODY, ''De Bestiis et aliis rebus and the Latin Physiologus,'' *Speculum* 13 (1938) 153–159. B. LATINI, *Li livres dou Tresor,* ed. F. J. CARMODY (Berkeley 1948). FRIEDRICH II, *The Art of Falconry,* tr. and ed. C. A. WOOD and F. M. FYRE (Stanford 1943), critical translation of Friedrick's *De arte venandi* with bibliographies for Daude de Pradas, Dancus, etc. S. BOCHART, *Opera omnis,* 3 v. (4th ed. Utrecht 1712), sources listed in 2:62–63. F. T. MCCULLOCH, *Medieval Latin and French Bestiaries* (Chapel Hill, N.C. 1960).

[F. CARMODY]

BETANCUR (BETHANCOURT), PEDRO DE SAN JOSÉ, BL.

Franciscan tertiary, missionary, and founder of charitable institutions and the Hospitaler Bethlehemites; b. Villaflores, Chasna, Tenerife Island, Spain, May 16 (or September 18), 1619; d. Guatemala City, Guatemala, April 25, 1667. Although he was descended from Juan de Bethancourt, one of the Norman conquerors (1404) of the Canary Islands, his immediate family was very poor and his first employment was as shepherd of the small family flock. In 1650, he left for Guatemala where a relative had preceded him as secretary to the governor general. His funds ran out in Havana, and Pedro had to pay for his passage from that point by working on a ship. He landed in Honduras and walked to Guatemala City, arriving there on February 18, 1651. He was so poor that he had to join the daily bread line at the Franciscan friary. In this way he met Fray Fernando Espino, a famous missionary, who befriended him and remained his lifelong counselor. Through Fray Fernando, Pedro was given work at a local textile factory, which enabled him to support himself, but which also employed culprits condemned by the court. In 1653, he entered the local Jesuit college of San Borja in the hopes of becoming a priest, but he lacked the ability to study and was soon forced to give up this dream. In the college, however, he met Manuel Lobo, SJ, who was his confessor throughout the rest of his life.

Fray Fernando invited him to join the Franciscan Order as a lay brother, but Pedro felt that God called him to remain in the world. Hence, in 1655, he joined the Third Order of St. Francis and took the tertiary habit as his garb. By this time his virtues were widely recognized in the city. In 1658, María de Esquivel's hut was given to him, and Pedro, remembering the experiences of his first desperate days in Guatemala, immediately began a hospital (Nuestra Señora de Belén) for the convalescent poor, a hostel for the homeless, a school, an oratory, and a nursing community known as the Bethlehemites. From then on, all his time was spent in alleviating the sufferings of the less fortunate. He begged alms with which to endow Masses to be celebrated by poor priests; he also endowed Masses that were to be celebrated at unusually early hours so that the poor might not have occasion to miss Mass because of their dress. He also had small chapels erected in the poorer sections where instruction was given to the children. On August 18, he would gather the children and have them sing the Seven Joys of the Franciscan Rosary in honor of the Blessed Mother, a custom that passed to Spain, but today remains only in Guatemala. On Christmas Eve he inaugurated the custom of imitating St. Joseph in search of lodgings for the Blessed Mother.

The gentle, kind man known as ''St. Francis of the Americas'' died peacefully in his hospital, hoping that his companions would carry on the many works he had begun. He is entombed in the Church of San Francisco in the old section of Guatemala City. Interest in his cause was renewed by the 1962 publication of his biography by Vázquez de Herrera, which led to his beatification by John Paul II on June 22, 1980. On July 7, 2001, a second miracle attribute to his intercession was approved. Upon his canonization Betancur will become Guatemala's first saint.

Feast: April 25 (Franciscans).

Bibliography: *Acta Apostolicae Sedis* 73 (1981): 253–258. *Gracias, Matiox, Thanks, Hermano Pedro: A Trilingual Anthology of Guatemalan Oral Tradition*, ed. & tr. M. C. CANALES and J. F. MORRISSEY (New York 1996). *L'Osservatore Romano,* English edition, no. 26 (1980): 10–11. J. ARRIOLA C., *Los milagros del venerable siervo de Dios, hermano Pedro de San José de Betancourt, efectuados en su vida y después de su muerto py su digno sucesor fray Rodrigo de la Cruz* (Guatemala 1983). A. ESTRADA MONROY, *Breve relación de la ejemplar vida del venerable siervo de Dios, Pedro de San Joseph Betancur* (Guatemala 1968). T. F. HALL DE ARÉVALO, *El apóstol de la campanilla* (Guatemala 1980). F. A. DE MONTALVO, *Vida admirable y muerte preciosa del venerable hermano Pedro de San José Betancur . . .* (Guatemala 1974). M. SOTO-HALL, *Pedro de San José Bethencourt, el San Francisco de Asís americano,* 3d. ed. (Guatemala 1981). F. VÁZQUEZ DE HERRERA, *Vida y virtudes del V. Hermano Pedro de San José de Betancur,* ed. L. LAMARDRID (Guatemala City 1962). D. DE VELA, *El Hermano Pedro (en la vida y en las letras)* (Guatemala City 1935 & 1961).

[L. LAMADRID]

Pedro de San José Betancur, 18th-century engraving.

BETANZOS, DOMINGO DE

Dominican missionary in Española and Mexico, inquisitor in Mexico, founder and first provincial of the province of Santiago de Mexico; b. León, Spain, *c.* 1480; d. Valladolid, Spain, September 1549. He earned a licentiate in civil law at the University of Salamanca, and then was a hermit for five years on the island of Ponza. According to Cuervo, Betanzos was professed at the Convent of San Esteban, Salamanca, May 30, 1511, and he was ordained in Seville on his way to America. According to Biermann, Betanzos and seven other Dominicans, on Oct. 8, 1513, were registered as passengers on Capt. Juan de Medina's vessel. Betanzos arrived at Española about the beginning of 1514 and was one of 12 Dominicans who went to Mexico in 1526. Within a year five died, and four returned to Spain. Betanzos, a priest, Gonzalo Lucero, a deacon, and Vicente de las Casas, a novice, were the only Dominicans left in Mexico. Twenty-four more Dominicans arrived in 1528, and Betanzos went with his companions to Santiago, Guatemala, in 1529. About January 1531 he was recalled to Mexico. The same year he made a trip to Naples, Italy, hoping to discuss with the ailing general the matter of the formation of an independent Mexican province. The general died in October 1531, and at Rome in 1532 Betanzos saw the new general. By the authority of Pope Clement VII, on

July 11, 1532, the province of Santiago de Mexico was instituted independent of the Dominicans of Española. By July of 1534 Betanzos had obtained all the necessary documents and by the end of 1534 he reached Mexico, with the title of vicar-general. On Aug. 24, 1535, Betanzos was elected provincial, and he served from 1535 to 1538.

Bibliography: J. CUERVO, *Historiadores del convento de San Esteban de Salamanca*, 3 v. (Salamanca 1914–15). F. R. DE LOS RÍOS ARCE, *Puebla de los Angeles y la Orden dominicana* 2 v. (Puebla 1910–11). A. M. CARREÑO, *Fray Domingo de Betanzos* (Mexico City 1924). B. BIERMANN, ''Die Anfänge der Dominikanertätigkeit in Neu–Spanien und Peru,'' *Archivum Fratrum Praedicatorum* 13 (1943) 5–58. J. J. DE LA CRUZ Y MOYA, *Historia de la santa y apostólica Provincia de Santiago de Predicadores de Mexico en la Nueva España*, 2 v. (Mexico City 1954–55).

[A. B. NIESER]

BETANZOS, PEDRO DE

Franciscan missionary; b. place and date unknown; d. near Chómez, Costa Rica, *c.* 1570. He came to New Spain in 1542. After a few months in Mexico, he mastered the Mexican language. In 1543 Toribio MOTOLINÍA took Betanzos to Guatemala, where he quickly learned the three native languages, Kiche, Tzutuhil, and Cakchiquel, so perfectly that the natives said he knew them as well as they did. He composed a grammar of Cakchiquel in cooperation with Francisco de Parra, who introduced several symbols for sounds not found in Spanish. He translated a group of prayers, which became the basic prayer formula for the natives, and with Juan de Torres he prepared a catechism in their language. His work was criticized by the Dominicans because he insisted on retaining the Spanish word *Dios* for God rather than using the indigenous word, which he considered tainted with idolatry. His usages were eventually accepted. In the 1550s he moved on with the conquerors into Honduras-Costa Rica, where with four other friars he laid the foundations for the province of Honduras.

Bibliography: F. VÁZQUEZ, *Crónica de la privincia del Santisimo nombre de Jesús de Guatemala*, ed. L. LAMADRID, 4 v. (Guatemala 1937–44) 1:119–128; 2:171–178.

[F. B. WARREN]

BETHARRAM FATHERS

Betharram Fathers is the popular name for the *Prêtres du Sacre-Coeur de Jesus* (PSCJ), founded 1832 at Bétharram in the Department of Basses Pyrénées in southwestern France, near Lourdes, by St. Michael GARICOÏTS. Members who are clerics or brothers follow the rule of St. Augustine, taking three simple vows. Under the leadership of Father Auguste Etchécopar (1830–97), third superior general, the institute received papal approbation on Sept. 5, 1877.

During the founder's lifetime the congregation spread into South America, to Buenos Aires (1856) and Montevideo (1861). Until the 20th century, growth was slow. The persecutions of 1903, which forced religious from France, resulted in the congregation embracing an international presence.

By the end of the 20th century, the congregation had communities in Europe (France, Italy, Great Britain, and Spain), Latin America (Argentina, Uruguay, Brazil, and Paraguay), Africa (the Ivory Coast and the Central African Republic), the Middle East (in the Holy Land) and Asia (Thailand and India). In 1989, associations of laity were established, enabling lay associates to collaborate with the professed religious. In addition to the congregation's traditional ministries of foreign missionary work, schools and colleges, chaplaincies and parishes, the congregation now operate centers for immigrants, refugees, and AIDS victims, and engage in youth ministries, pastoral ministry, retreats, and spiritual direction.

Bibliography: F. VEUILLOT, *Les Prêtres du Sacré-Coeur de Bétharram* (Paris 1942).

[P. DUVIGNAU]

BETHEL

Bethel is an ancient city and sanctuary on the site of the modern town of Beitîn, 12 miles north of Jerusalem. Archeology has determined that Luza, as the city was originally called (Gn 28.19), was first occupied *c.* 2200 B.C. When Abraham visited its vicinity about four centuries later (Gn.12.8), it was a flourishing Middle Bronze Age city with heavy fortifications and elaborate buildings. Though it was probably the site of an ancient Canaanite sanctuary, its continuance as an Israelite one was connected with a tradition that both Abraham and Jacob (Gn 35.1–7) had set up altars there to Yahweh. Jacob was credited (Gn 28.19) with renaming the place (Heb. *bêt'ēl,* house of God; but originally, house of the god El). After a silence of several centuries, the quiet and prosperity of Bethel were shattered by the invading Israelites (Jgs 1.22–25). Clear archeological evidence of a devastation of the Canaanite town toward the end of the 13th century B.C., overlaid by a much less developed occupation, proves the substantial historicity of the account of the Israelite capture of the place as given in Jgs 1.22–25. Modern research has relegated the parallel account of the destruction of Hai as given in Jos 8.129 to an etiologic explanation of the extensive but much more ancient ruins near Bethel. Samuel's annual tour of towns included Bethel (1 Sm 7.16). Bethel's location, so close to Judah's expansion into Benjamin's territory (Jos 16.1–2; 18.12–13; 1 Kgs 14.30), made it a constant object of strife in the divided kingdom (2 Chr 13.19). Added to this was the fact that Jeroboam I of Israel chose Bethel as the chief northern sanctuary and the rival of Jerusalem. The temple and golden calf that he established there (1 Kgs 12.26–13.32) were the object of severe censure by Hosea (Osee) (Hos 4.15–19; 10.5). Amos had already accused this sanctuary of luxurious and hypocritical worship (Am 4.4–5; 5.21–25) and had been expelled from it (Am 7.12). The people of Judah often referred to Bethel as Bethaven (bêt 'āwen), ''house of wickedness'' (Hos 5.8; Jos 7.2; 18.12; etc.). During the Assyrian occupation (after 721 B.C.), Bethel escaped destruction. The conquerors even dispatched one of the exiled priests to care for its sanctuary (2 Kgs 17.28). When Josiah controlled Bethel, its altar and High Place were included in the general destruction of all sanctuaries except the Temple in Jerusalem (2 Kgs 23.14). Bethel escaped the common destruction in 587, when the Babylonians ravaged all of Judah. During the exilic period, however, the town experienced rapid decline, and only a few Benjaminites were mentioned as peopling it in the reconstruction period (Ezr 2.28). It regained its former prosperity in Hellenistic (1 Mc 9.50) and Roman times and flourished until late in the Byzantine period. The excavations carried out at Bethel in 1934 by W. F. Albright and J. L. Kelso, and again in the 1950s by the latter, were very successful and fruitful in illuminating the problems and background of the Old Testament.

Bibliography: F. M. ABEL, *Géographie de la Palestine,* 2 v. (Paris 1933–38) 2:270–271. *Encyclopedic Dictionary of the Bible,* tr. and adap. by L. HARTMAN (New York 1963) from A. VAN DEN BORN, *Bijbels Woordenboek* 229230. H. HAAG, *Lexikon für Theologie und Kirche,* ed. J. HOFER and K. RAHNER, 10 v. (Freiburg 1957–65) 2:307–309. L. HENNEQUIN, *Dictionnaire de la Bible,* suppl. ed. L. PIROT et al. (Paris 1928–) 3:375–377. *The Bulletin of the American Schools of Oriental Research* 29 (1928) 9–11; 55–58 (1934–35); 74 (1939) 17–18; 137 (1955) 5–10; 151 (1958) 3–8; 164 (1961) 5–19. J. L. KELSO, ''Excavations at Bethel,'' *The Biblical Archaeologist* 9 (1956) 36–43.

[T. KARDONG]

BETHESDA

Name of a pool near the Sheepgate in Jerusalem where Jesus cured a man infirm for 38 years (Jn 5.2–9). Excavations have revealed the outlines of a large oblong pool in the location; this pool was provided with five porches (as in St. John's description—see 5.2), four lateral and a fifth central to divide the pool into two parts. A Hebrew graffito found there proves that the building existed before the time of Hadrian (A.D. 118), and it has been concluded that the complex was the work of Herod the Great (37–4 B.C.). At the site may now be seen a reconstructed pool and the foundations of a 5th-century Byzantine church.

The reading and derivation of the name of the pool are disputed. Bethesda (Βηθεσδά) is usually derived from the Aramaic *bêt ḥesdā',* ''house of mercy.'' Many, however, prefer the MS reading Bethzatha [Βηθζαθά, from Aramaic *bêt zētā'*, ''house of olives'' (?)]. J. T. Milik, however, believes that both readings and their derivation can be explained with the aid of a topographical reference in the Copper Scroll (11.12) found among the DEAD SEA SCROLLS. The reading *byt 'šdtyn* he understands to mean a rectangular double (note the dual ending) reservoir; Bethesda, then, would transliterate the singular form of the word, Bethzatha the emphatic plural.

It is to be noted that the reference to the angel who regularly ''went down into [or, according to some MSS, ''washed himself in''] the pool'' to stir up the water is probably not part of the original Gospel text. Textual evidence suggests that these words were originally a marginal gloss containing the popular explanation of the movement of the water referred to in Jn 5.7 (probably caused by an intermittent underground stream) and the healing properties attributed to it, which was later incorporated into the text by a copyist.

Bibliography: *Encyclopedic Dictionary of the Bible* 231. L. HEIDET, *Dictionnaire de la Bible* 1.2:1723–32. C. KOPP, *Lexikon für Theologie und Kirche*, 10 v. (2d, new ed. Freiburg 1957–65) 2:332. L. H. VINCENT and F. M. ABEL, *Jérusalem nouvelle,* 2 v. in 4 (Paris 1912–26) 2:669–684. J. JEREMIAS, *Die Wiederentdeckung von Bethesda, Johannes 5, 2* (Göttingen 1949). J. T. MILIK, *Revue biblique* 66 (1959) 347–348.

[J. E. WRIGLEY]

BETHLEHEM

Modern Bethlehem is located six miles south of Jerusalem. It is situated on a limestone ridge of the Judean highland, running east-northeast, overlooking to the west the main highway from Jerusalem to Hebron. The ridge is about 2,500 feet in elevation and forms a sort of semicircle with two little elevations at the ends. The Basilica of the Nativity is located on the southern end (*see* PALESTINE). Originally the spot was more isolated from the village proper. Many of the streets are narrow and lined with substantially built, cubical, flat-roofed stone houses revealing how the city may have looked at the time of Our Lord.

Several Canaanite cities bore the name Bethlehem, which is thought by some scholars to have meant ''Sanc-

Christmas procession in Manger Square, Bethlehem. (©Hanan Isachar/CORBIS)

tuary of Lahm (god of grain),'' although it has almost certainly no connection with the god Laḫmu or the goddess Laḫamu of the Sumerians. Others prefer not to go further than the obvious meaning of the Hebrew form of the name *bêt-leḥem*, ''house of bread.'' The modern Arab name for the town is Beit Laḫm, ''house of meat.'' Ephrata, another name of the place, means ''fruitful.'' All these names seem to be a reflection on the natural fertility of the environs.

Bethlehem is already mentioned before the Israelite conquest in the Amarna Letters (14th century B.C.) as belonging to the district of Urusalim (Jerusalem). After the conquest, the Calebite (1 Chr 2.19, 24, 50) clan of Ephrata settled in the vicinity of Bethlehem (1 Sm 17.12; Ru 1.2). Later the name Ephratah was applied to Bethlehem itself (Jos 15.59; Ru 4.11; Mi 5.1). Bethlehem was the native town of the Levite who became Micah's officiating priest (Jgs 17.7–13) and of the unfortunate wife of the Levite from Ephraim (Jgs 19). It was also the setting for the love idyll of Ruth, the Moabite, and Boaz, David's ancestor, as told in the book of RUTH. Other famous Bethlehemites were Jesse, David's father, and the sons of Zeruiah, David's sister (2 Sm 17.25). These nephews of David were Joab, Abishai, and Asahel (2 Sm 2.18; one Chr 2.16). Loyal but ruthlessly cruel, they became at once a protection and a menace to their royal relative. Young David roamed the hills and fields around Bethlehem as a shepherd boy (1 Sm 17.15) and later was anointed king of a new dynasty there by Samuel (1 Sm 16.1–13). In the early years of David's reign Bethlehem fell for some time to the Philistines. This was the occasion for the courageous errand to a Bethlehem well, narrated in 2 Sm 23.13–17; 1 Chr 11.16–19. Rehoboam, son and successor of King Solomon, fortified Bethlehem to guard the approach to Jerusalem (2 Chr 11.6). After the fall of Samaria (721 B.C.) and the consequent end of the kingdom of Israel, the prophet Micah (5.1–3) announced the future birth of the Messiah, the new David, at Bethlehem. The village was repeopled after the Exile (Ezr 2.21; Neh 7.26), but it remained in obscurity until the birth of Our Lord (Mt 2.1, 5–8, 16; Lk 2.4, 15; Jn 7.42).

Bibliography: F. M. ABEL, *Géographie de la Palestine*, 2 v. (Paris 1933-38) 2:276. R. LECONTE, ''Bethlehem aux jours du roi Herode,'' *Bible et Terre Sainte* 15 (1958) 4–9; *ibid.* 42 (1961) a whole number on Bethlehem with excellent photos. C. KOPP, *The Holy Places of the Gospels*, tr. R. WALLS (New York 1963) 1–48.

[E. LUSSIER]

BETHLEHEM FATHERS

Bethlehem Fathers is the popular name for the *Bethlehem Mission Immensee* (SMB), founded in 1921 in Immensee, Switzerland by Pietro BONDOLFI for foreign missionary work. From Switzerland, the society sent missionaries to Africa and Asia. The society's missions in Manchuria, established in 1926, and in Beijing (1946) ceased because of Communist pressure in 1954. Missionary refugees from China, arriving in Colorado in December 1948, established a mission two years later at Cheyenne Wells. The rapid extension of the enterprise prompted Urban J. Vehr, archbishop of Denver, to sanction the transfer of the establishment to his see city in 1955. Land was purchased for the development of the existing foundation into a future regional residence with adequate school facilities. In 1988, the society withdrew from the U.S. to focus on more pressing needs in Africa and Asia.

In the wake of Vatican II, the society opened its ranks to lay missionaries, male and female, single and married, who collaborate with the fathers and the brothers in various mission projects. At the end of 2000, the society had an active presence in Africa (Kenya, Mozam-

Children lighting candles in Church of Nativity, Bethlehem, which was constructed by crusaders on the site were Jesus was born. Sixty thousand people visit the site every year. (AP/Wide World Photos)

bique, Tanzania, Chad, Zambia, and Zimbabwe), South America (Bolivia, Colombia, Ecuador, Peru, and Haiti), Asia (China, Japan, the Philippines, and Taiwan) and Europe (Switzerland, Germany, Austria, France, and Italy).

Bibliography: A. RUST, *Die Bethlehem-Missionare, Immensee* (Fribourg 1961).

[A. J. BORER/EDS.]

BETHLEHEMITES

A former hospital order of men and women under the rule of St. AUGUSTINE. Its presence in England is attested by MATTHEW PARIS in 1257, but his account is vague and probably confused. The order's only well-known foundation was the hospital of St. Mary of Bethlehem in London, established in 1247; St. Mary's housed mental patients well before the Dissolution under HENRY VIII. In 1547 it became a royal establishment for the care of lunatics, and its unenviable reputation gave the word ''bedlam'' to the language. A few other hospitals and churches are known (there was one in Scotland, one in Pavia, Italy, and one in Clamécy, in the Diocese of Auxerre). All were under the direction of the bishop of Bethlehem, whose see was transferred to Clamécy in the 14th century, where he built on a site previously given (like the site of the London hospital) to the bishop and chapter of Bethlehem; the Clamécy house survived to the French Revolution. The habits worn by the brothers and sisters attached to the order's hospitals featured a red star, and this design has led to unfortunate confusion with a quite distinct, but equally obscure, Bohemian hospital order, the *Cruciferi cum stella,* established in Prague in the 13th century.

See Also: HOSPITALS, HISTORY OF.

Bibliography: *Gallia Christiana,* v. 1–13 (Paris 1715–85), v. 14–16 (Paris 1856–65) 12:686–699. *The Register of John Le*

Romeyn, Lord Archbishop of York, part 1 (*Publications of the Surtees Society,* 123; Durham 1913) xviii, 1–2. D. E. EASSON, *Medieval Religious Houses: Scotland* (London 1957). For several other groups, see M. T. DISDIER, *Dictionnaire d'histoire et de géographie ecclésiastiques,* ed. A. BAUDRILLART et al. (Paris 1912–) 8:1253–54.

[R. W. EMERY]

BEURON, ABBEY OF

Benedictine archabbey on the Danube River, 20 miles west of Sigmaringen, Diocese of Freiburg im Breisgau, southwest Germany; dedicated to St. Martin. An earlier foundation of Augustinian canons (1077), confirmed by Urban II (1097), had few canons and little property, and became an abbey only in 1687; in 1802 it was suppressed and became part of the Hohenzollern-Sigmaringen estate.

Beuron was restored as a Benedictine cloister in 1863 from SAINT PAUL-OUTSIDE-THE-WALLS by Maurus and Placidus Wolter, its first abbots, thanks to the widowed Princess Catherine von Hohenzollern (d. 1893). An abbey in 1868 and an archabbey in 1884, Beuron became the head of the Beuron Congregation (approved by the Holy See in 1884), with daughterhouses in Belgium, England, Austria, and Germany. The Prussian KULTURKAMPF drove the community to Volders in the Tirol (1875–87) but could not stop the growth of the Congregation, which included monks in Emmaus (Prague), SECKAU, Maria Laach, St. Joseph (Gerleve), NERESHEIM, WEINGARTEN, Grüssau, Neuburg (Heidelberg), and Las Condes (Santiago, Chile); and nuns in Bertholdstein, Eibingen, Herstelle, and Kellenried. Belgian and English abbeys left the Congregation (1920) as did Mount Sion in Jerusalem and Emmaus in Prague (1945). In 1895 Beuron undertook the restoration of Brazilian Benedictines at the request of the Holy See.

Under the Wolters, Beuron became the center of a liturgical monastic revival in Germany (Anselm SCHOTT, Suitbert Bäumer). Gregorian chant was studied and used. Hildebrand Höpfl was a noted exegete. The school of theology is devoted to scholarship and offers monks of the Congregation a four-year course. Alban DOLD (d. 1960) founded the series *Texte und Arbeiten,* 57 v. (1917–64) for texts and studies of the liturgy. Studies of the Old Latin Bible are pursued under Bonifatius Fischer at the Vetus Latina Institute, to which is attached the Palimpsest Institute. Since 1919 Beuron's press has published *Benediktinische Monatschrift.* Pastoral care of the many pilgrims to Beuron's miraculous image (a 15th-century Pietà), retreats, excursions, the training of lay catechists, and youth work are in the hands of the monks. Clergy and laity work closely together in Beuron's Secular Oblate Institute.

The 17th- and 18th-century buildings have had additions for the school of theology, the library (235,000 volumes), and the Vetus Latina; the church is baroque (1732–38). Beuron's school of art which began in 1894 with Desiderius LENZ was opposed to naturalism; it gained followers, including Willibrord Verkade, but declined after 1913 (*see* BEURONESE ART).

Bibliography: *Konstitutionen der Beuroner Kongregation von 1884* (*Archiv für katholisches Kirchenrecht* 54; 1885). K. T. ZINGELER, *Geschichte des Klosters Beuron* (Sigmaringen 1890). H. S. MAYER, *Benediktinisches Ordensrecht in der Beuroner Kongregation,* 4 v. (Beuron 1929–36). U. ENGELMANN, *Beuron* (Munich-Zurich 1957); *Lexikon für Theologie und Kirche,* ed. J. HOFER and K. RAHNER, 10 v. (2d, new ed. Freiburg 1957–65) 2:324–325. *Beuron, 1863–1963: Festschrift zum hundertjährigen Bestehen der Erzabtei St. Martin* (Beuron 1963). P. VOLK, *Dictionnaire d'histoire et de géographie ecclésiastiques,* ed. A. BAUDRILLART et al. (Paris 1912–) 8:1279–82. R. GAZEAU, *Catholicisme. Hier, aujourd'hui et demain,* ed. G. JACQUEMET (Paris 1947–) 2:5–7. L. H. COTTINEAU, *Répertoire topobibliographique des abbayes et prieurés,* 2 v. (Mâcon 1935–39) 1:370–371. O. L. KAPSNER, *A Benedictine Bibliography: An Author-Subject Union List,* 2 v. (2d ed. Collegeville, Minn. 1962) 2:190–191. S. MAYER, *Beuroner Bibliographie, 1863–1963* (Beuron 1963).

[U. ENGELMANN]

BEURONESE ART

A school founded in the Benedictine archabbey of BEURON by Desiderius LENZ, sculptor and architect. Beginning in 1864, Lenz developed his concepts in actual art projects and still more in sketches and theoretical treatises. Work was carried on from 1894 by the Beuron school, after G. Wüger and L. Steiner had associated themselves with it. Lenz aimed at an integral, liturgically inspired ecclesiastical art. Rejecting the dominant tendency of the period toward naturalism, he reverted to primitive Christian, early Greek, and especially Egyptian art. A more immediate influence was that of the German Nazarene school. He developed an aesthetic geometry in order to discover the primordial dimensions in nature and those of the human body. In looking to ancient sources as a starting point for modern religious art and architecture, the monastic artists of the Beuron school envisioned a religious art that was to be ordered and serene, hieratic in conception and style. The principal Beuronese monument is the St. Maur Chapel near Beuron (1868–71). In the last quarter of the 19th century, extensive projects of decoration were carried out in Monte Cassino and in churches in Prague. After the decoration of the Monte Cassino crypt church in 1913, Beuronese art suffered a steady decline that terminated in extinction. Despite its fate, however, the Beuronese school may be considered one of the forerunners in the movement for renewal of Church art and architecture in the twentieth century.

Crypt in the Abbey of Montecassino, Cassino, Italy. (©Archivo Iconografico, S.A./CORBIS)

Bibliography: Benedictine Abbey of Maredsous, Bel., *S. Benedictus* (Ghent 1880), pls. Benedictine Abbey of Emmaus, Prague, *Leben und Regel des heiligen Vaters Benedictus* (Prague 1901), illus. A. PÖLLMANN, *Vom Wesen der hieratischen Kunst* (Beuron 1905). G. PREZZOLINI, *La teoria e l'arte di Beuron* (Siena 1908). S. M. VISMARA, *La nuova arte di Beuron* (Rome 1913). J. KREITMAIER, *Beuroner Kunst: Eine Audrucksform der christlichen Mystik* (5th ed. Freiburg 1923). D. LENZ, *Zur Aesthetik der Beuroner Schule* (Vienna 1927). C. KNIEL, *Leben und Regel des heiligen Vaters Benediktus* (Beuron 1929), pls. G. MERCIER, *L'Art abstrait dans l'art sacré* (Paris 1964) 30–32.

[U. ENGELMANN]

BEZA, THEODORE

John CALVIN's chief assistant and successor as leader of Reformed PROTESTANTISM; b. Vézelay, France, June 25, 1519; d. Geneva, Oct. 13, 1605. Beza was born of a minor Burgundian noble family and received an excellent education in classical literature and law at Orléans, Bourges, and Paris; he was awarded several benefices while a student. In 1548 he moved to Geneva, announced his conversion to Protestantism, and married. Beza served the Reformed Church as professor of Greek at the Lausanne Academy (1549–58), professor of theology (1559–99) and first rector (1559–63) of the Geneva Academy, and pastor of the Geneva church (1559–1605) and moderator of its company of pastors (1564–80). He also served his church in a number of diplomatic missions to Protestant Germany, Protestant Switzerland, and France. He headed the Protestant delegation at the Colloquy of POISSY (1561), an attempt to reconcile Catholics and Protestants under royal auspices, and saw it founder over disagreements on eucharistic theology. He was an adviser to the princes who led the HUGUENOT armies in the French wars of religion. He fought successfully for tighter ecclesiastical discipline at several national synods of the French Reformed Church, over one of which he presided (La Rochelle, 1571). Beza probably served his church most effectively, however, with his voluminous and varied publications, many of them distinguished by substantial erudition and an elegant Latin style. His writings include (1) several editions of an annotated New Testament, based on an important manuscript Greek text (the Codex Bezae), rather freely translated into Latin, with extensive notes providing a Calvinist interpretation of the text; (2) translations of the Psalms into French, prepared jointly with Clément Marot, widely used in Reformed liturgies then and since; (3) polemical tracts, vehemently defending key Calvinist doctrines on such issues as double predestination, the Eucharist, and the necessity of persecuting heretics, against adversaries of Catholic, Lutheran, and Sacramentarian persuasions; (4) popular works, including anti-Catholic satirical pieces and short biographies, such as one of Calvin; (5) political tracts, notably *Du droit des magistrats,* a defense of the right to resist and even overthrow governments for religious reasons; (6) collections of Latin poems, some of them quite secular in tone; and (7) manuals for the study of Greek and French. Many of these works were published in both Latin and French, and a good number were also translated into other vernacular languages. They provide further evidence of Beza's great contemporary influence not only in his native France and in Switzerland, but also in England, the Protestant Netherlands, parts of Rhenish Germany, and parts of central Europe. Altogether he made the Reformed movement more tightly organized, more active in politics, more intellectual, and more rigid.

Bibliography: T. BEZA, *Correspondence,* ed. F. AUBERT et al. (Geneva 1960—). M. H. VICAIRE, *Lexikon für Theologie und Kirche,* J. HOFER and K. RAHNER eds., 10 v. (2d new ed. Freiburg, 1957–65) 2:331–332. O. E. STRASSER, *Die Religion in Geschichte und Gegenwart,* 7v. (3d ed. Tübingen 1957–65) 1:1117. H. M. BAIRD, *Theodore Beza* (New York 1899). P. F. GEISENDORF, *Théodore de Bèze* (Geneva 1949). F. GARDY and A. DUFOUR, *Bibliographie des oeuvres . . . de Théodore de Bèze* (Geneva 1960).

[R. M. KINGDON]

BHUTAN, THE CATHOLIC CHURCH IN

The Kingdom of Bhutan is located in the Himalayas, and is bordered on the north and northwest by Tibet and on the south, southwest, and east by India. A rugged, mountainous country, Bhutan has control of several important passes through the Himalayan mountain range. The region, which is known for violent storms and landslides during its rainy season, is predominately forested, and timber is one of Bhutan's primary industries.

Initially ruled by regional spiritual governors, Bhutan fell under Chinese domination in the late 18th century. In 1774 it signed a treaty with the British East India Company, which transferred external control of the region to Great Britain a century later. A British protectorate from 1910 until India was granted independence in August 1949, Bhutan successfully defeated claims against its territory by communist China in the 1950s. A hereditary monarchy, established in Bhutan in 1907, continued to successfully weather the tiny country's political changes. By 2000 much of Bhutan's trade was with India, which, due to its political relationship with its northern neighbor, also provided the underdeveloped nation with humanitarian aid.

Most Bhutanese, of Mongolian descent, practice Lamaist BUDDHISM, and numerous Buddhist monasteries exist.

Christianity first made its appearance in Bhutan when two Jesuit missionaries on a journey from Bengal across the Himalayas to Tibet entered the country in 1626. Detained by the nation's religious leader, the Dharma-Raja, at Paro for several weeks, they studied Tibetan with a Tsaparang lama. No other Catholic missionaries were recorded as having succeeded them, with the consequence that Catholicism never gained a following.

Over three centuries later, the Catholic presence reappeared in Bhutan, when the Bhutanese government, on the recommendation of Catholic educators in Darjeeling, India, invited Father William Mackey and a fellow Canadian Jesuit into the country in 1963 to establish a primary education system. Mackey remained until his death in 1995. A small group of Salesian missionaries were similarly welcomed two years later, but were expelled by the government in early 1982 on charges of proselytism. Buddhism remained the state religion; while freedom of individual worship was tolerated, missionary activities were prohibited by the government.

Initially part of the Diocese of Tezpur in India, care of Bhutanese Catholics was transferred to the Diocese of Darjeeling on Jan. 21, 1975. The Darjeeling Diocese ordained the first native Bhutanese priest in 1995; although the country had as yet no parishes, ten resident sisters administered to Bhutan's approximately 500 Catholic faithful by 2000. While the country modernized during the 20th century, abolishing the caste system, granting certain rights to women, and eliminating slavery, political parties remained illegal and the government continued to prohibit public dialogue in matters of religion. Despite efforts to preserve its traditional way of life, Bhutan exhibited the first sparks of social unrest in the 1990s as its Nepalese minority demanded political recognition. Such events were seen as possible signals of an increasing tolerance for—or an increasing repression of— religious diversity in the years to come.

Bibliography: C. A. BELL, *Tibet, Past and Present.* C. WESSELS, *Early Jesuit Travellers in Central Asia, 1603–1721* (The Hague 1924).

[E. R. HAMBYE/EDS.]

Capital: Thimphu.
Size: 16,000 sq. miles.
Population: 2,005,000 in 2000 (approx.).
Languages: Dzongkha; Tibetan and Nepalese dialects are spoken in various regions.
Religions: 500 Catholics (.02%), 1,503,840 Lamaistic Buddhists (75%), 500,660 Hindu (24.9%).

BIANCHI, FRANCESCO SAVERIO MARIA, ST.

B. Arpino, Italy, Dec. 2, 1743; d. Naples, Jan. 31, 1815. Because of parental opposition to his religious vocation, he studied law at the University of Naples before joining the BARNABITES. Almost all his priestly life was spent in Naples, where he was superior in the College of Portanova, and from 1778, professor of theology at the university. He was a member of several academies and soon gained a reputation as a learned man, but his writings have not been published, except for a few sermons. Charitable and pastoral labors, aid to the poor, and contemplation kept gaining more ascendancy over his studious activities, especially after his mysterious ecstasy on Pentecost of 1800. A strange and terrible disease afflicted his legs and immobilized him from 1804 until his death. Bianchi was the spiritual guide of St. Maria Francesca GALLO and many other elect souls. His fame for performing miracles was widespread, especially because of his prophecies and his arrest of the lava flow from Vesuvius in 1804 and 1805. Characteristic of his spirituality was a mystic ardor joined to a joyous serenity and a lively devotion to the Mass. His remains are in the church of S. Giuseppe a Pontecorvo in Naples.

He was beatified on Jan. 22, 1893, by Leo XIII, and canonized on Oct. 21, 1951, by Pius XII.

Feast: Jan. 31.

Bibliography: A. BARAVELLI, *Vita del b. F. S. M. Bianchi.* F. T. MOLTEDO, *Vita del b. F. S. M. B.*. F. M. SALA, *LApostolo di Napoli.* J. M. SISNANDO, *São Francisco Bianchi, sacerdote barnabita, apóstolo de Nápoles* (Belo Horizonte 1968). G. R. ZITAROSA, *Tre benefattori* (Naples 1967). G. BOFFITO, *Scrittori Barnabiti,* 1 212–217.

[U. M. FASOLA]

BIBER, HEINRICH JOHANN FRANZ VON

Baroque church composer influential in the development of violin technique; b. Wartenberg, Bohemia, Aug. 12, 1644; d. Salzburg, Austria, May 3, 1704. Biber was raised to the nobility by Emperor Leopold I, and spent many years with the archbishop of Salzburg, in whose service he composed Masses, Requiems, litanies, and Vespers in the *concertato* style prevalent in the late baroque era. His *Missa Sti. Henrici* (1701), e.g., is scored for five-part chorus and orchestra of strings, brass, timpani, and organ. The text is set with care, though there are many textual repetitions. The voice parts contain florid operatic sections, but only to dramatize specific words.

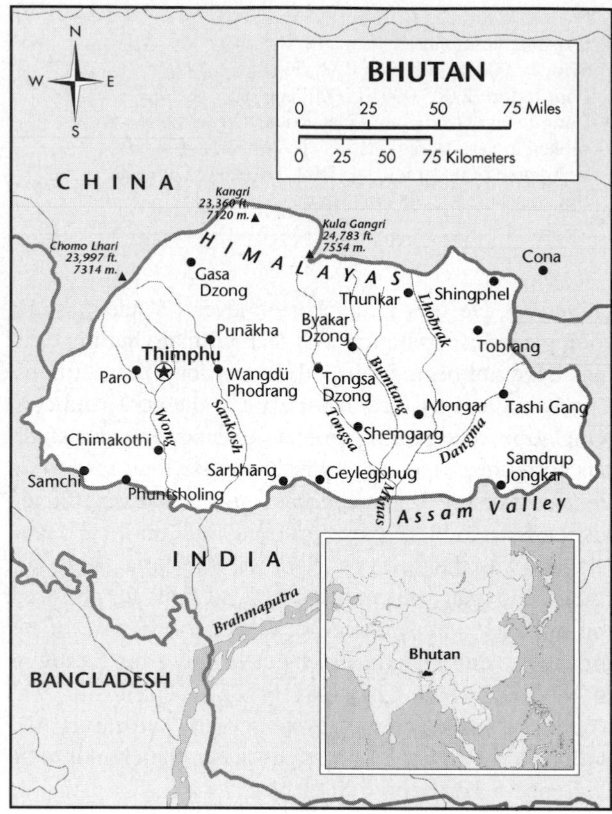

Biber revolutionized violin playing in Germany through his virtuoso violin writing, which employs such innovations as double stops, wide skips, and *scordatura* (the tuning of the strings to other than usual pitches for special effects), as exemplified in his sonata cycle honoring the ''15 Mysteries of the Life of Mary'' (1674).

Bibliography: *Selected Works* in *Denkmäler der Tonkunst in Österreich* vols. 11, 25, 49, 59, 92, 97, see introd. to each volume. P. NETTL, *H. F. von Biber* (Reichenberg 1926). T. RUSSELL, ''The Violin *Scordatura*,'' *Musical Quarterly* 24 (1938) 84–96. A. LEISS, *Die Musik in Geschichte und Gegenwart*, ed. F. BLUME (Kassel-Basel 1949–) 1:1827–31. C. BREWER, ''The Songs of Biber's Birds,'' *17th Century Music* 3/1 (1993) 1, 6–11. S. DAHMS, ''Bibers Oper *Chi la dura la vince*,'' *Österreichische Musik Zeitschrift* 49 (1994) 107–113. D. GIÜXAM, ''Die *Rosenkran-Sonaten* von H. J. F. Biber: ein Zyklus mit Vorgeschichte,'' *Österreichische Musik Zeitschrift* 54 (1999) 14–22. W. JAKSCH, ''*Missa Alleluia*: Quellenlage und einordnung einer mehrchörigen messe des Salzburger domkapellmeisters H. I. Fr. Biber (1644–1704),'' *Kirchenmusikalisches Jahrbuch* 70 (1986) 45–49. E. KUBITSCHEK, ''Bibers Instrumentalschaffen,'' *Österreichische Musik Zeitschrift* 49 (1994) 97–105.

[W. C. HOLMES]

BIBLE

The term ''Bible'' is derived, through the Latin *Biblia* (originally a neuter plural, but treated since the early Middle Ages as a feminine singular), from the Greek τὰ βιβλία, literally ''the books,'' with the word ἱερά (sacred) expressed or understood. The singular of this Greek word, βιβλίον (a diminutive in form, but with the diminutive force lost), occurs in Lk 4.17 in reference to the ''SCROLL'' of Isaiah from which Jesus read in the synagogue at Nazareth. The earlier form ἡ βιβλος (the book, i.e., the Bible), which occurs in 2 Mc 8.23, as does its plural, αἱ βιβλοι, in the Septuagint of Dn 9.2, comes from an original form, ἡ βύβλος, designating Egyptian papyrus, first known to the Greeks as writing material imported from the Phoenician city of BYBLOS. Synonymous terms for the sacred book(s) are αἱ γραφαί (the writings, the Scriptures) and ἡ γραφή (the writing, Scripture, the Bible as a whole), which are used in Mt 21.42; 22.29; 26.54; etc. and Acts 8.32; Rom 4.3; 9.17; etc., respectively.

The use of the singular number in these terms to designate the many writings that constitute the Bible comes from the regarding of the collection as a single unit that, despite its many human authors, has God as its chief author. Therefore, all who regard the Bible as a sacred book consider it, in some way, as written under divine inspiration and as establishing a norm of religious faith, whether alone or, as Catholics do, together with divine tradition [*see* TRADITION (IN THEOLOGY)].

The whole Bible possesses both its sacredness and its unity also by reason of its subject matter, which is SALVATION HISTORY (*Heilsgeschichte*). From beginning to end the Bible is concerned primarily with the acts of God for man's salvation, wrought through His covenants with man, particularly His covenant with Israel, through the mediatorship of Moses, whereby He assured Israel of ultimate salvation; and His covenant with the new people of God, the Christian Church, through the mediatorship of Jesus Christ, whereby He achieved this definitive salvation. Those who do not accept this New Covenant, i.e., the Jews, have a Bible consisting only of the books of the Old Covenant or Old Testament, whereas Christians have a Bible made up of the books of both the Old and the New Testament. *See* COVENANT (IN THE BIBLE); TESTAMENT (IN THE BIBLE).

Bibliography: B. HESSLER, *Lexikon für Theologie und Kirche*, ed. M. BUCHBERGER (Freiburg 1930–38) 2:335–336. *Encyclopedic Dictionary of the Bible*, tr. and adap. by L. HARTMAN (New York 1963) 238–241. A. ROBERT and A. TRICOT, *Guide to the Bible*, tr. E. P. ARBEZ and M. P. MCGUIRE (Tournai–New York 1951–55) 3–6. G. SCHRENK, *Theological Dictionary of the New Testament* (Grand Rapids, MI 1964—) 1:613–617. H. HÖPFL, *Dictionnaire de la Bible*, suppl. ed. L. PIROT, et al. (Paris 1928—) 2:457–465.

[L. F. HARTMAN]

BIBLE (TEXTS)

TEXT OF THE OLD TESTAMENT

The received Hebrew text of the OT as it appears in modern printed Bibles includes a basic consonantal text in ''square-letter'' Aramaic characters that was stabilized with entirely minimal variations by about A.D. 100. This basic text was already provided with its own verse and paragraph divisions, indicated exclusively by intervals of varying width within the text itself. No other markings, headings, colophons, or numberings of any kind are a part of this text. Though a spacing arrangement was known that would set off visually the hemistichs (half-line units) of Hebrew verse, most OT poetry is transmitted in the same format as that used for prose; exceptions are made always for Ex 15.1–18 and Dt 32.1–43 and often for Job, Psalms, and Proverbs.

This basic text is accompanied in modern Bibles by a traditional apparatus for its pronunciation and public reading, which reached its standard form in the days of Aaron ben Moses Ben Asher of Tiberias in Palestine, *c.* A.D. 930. Other Masoretic systems were developed both in Palestine and in Babylonia between the 8th and 10th centuries, but these are now mainly of historical interest. The few parts of the OT transmitted in Aramaic (in Gn 31.47; Jer 10.11; Ezr 4.8–6.18; 7.12–26; Dn 2.4–7.28) share in all respects the textual history of the Hebrew books. The OT books composed in Greek (Wisdom and 2 Maccabees) or preserved complete primarily in that language (Sirach, Tobit, Judith, Baruch, 1 Maccabees, and parts of Esther and Daniel), share in the distinctive history of the Septuagint. The Semitic evidence for Sirach and Tobit will be mentioned below; see also the articles on the books named, individually. What follows traces back the Hebrew text through the various stages of transmission for which evidence is available, namely (1) printed editions of the OT; (2) collations of manuscript materials; (3) medieval manuscripts and Origen's second column; (4) Sirach and Tobit; (5) the Samaritan Pentateuch; (6) the oldest MSS, from the 3rd century B.C. to the 2nd Christian century.

(1) Printed Editions of the Old Testament. The first Hebrew Biblical book to be printed was the Psalms, with D. Ḳimchi's commentary (Bologna 1477); the first complete printed OT in Hebrew was that from Soncino (1488). The text of the Alcalá Polyglot of 1521 (*see* POLYGLOT BIBLES), somewhat marred by typographical errors, was nevertheless based in part on two excellent 13th-century Spanish MSS and on another MS now lost that seems to have had Babylonian connections. The prototype for most editions of the Hebrew Masoretic text (MT) is the second RABBINICAL BIBLE published by Daniel BOMBERG in Venice (1524–25); its editor was the Jewish

Woodcut from a German Bible printed by Gunther Zainer at Augsburg, the first illustrated printed Bible, 1475 or 1476.

scholar Jacob ben Chayyim. Separated by six centuries from the fixing of the Ben Asher tradition, he dealt in eclectic fashion with the Masoretic data available to him, accepting, from Ashkenazi manuscript sources, a number of over-refinements and inconsistencies in details. Fine control of the Ben Asher system is reflected in the critical apparatus *minhat šay* of Shlomo Yedidiah de Norzi (d. 1626) printed in an OT from Mantua (1742). The later undertakings of S. Baer, sponsored by Franz Delitzsch, between 1869 and 1895, and of C. D. Ginsburg in OT editions (1894, 1908–26) failed to provide a sounder basic MT than the Ben Chayyim form of it.

Two current editions deserve notice: the *Biblia hebraica,* third and later editions (Stuttgart 1929–37 and later dates) with the text prepared under the supervision of Kahle and a critical apparatus by various scholars under the leadership of R. KITTEL; and the 1958 edition by N. H. Snaith for the British and Foreign Bible Society of London. The critical apparatus of the Kittel-Kahle edition has been roundly criticized, with a good deal of rea-

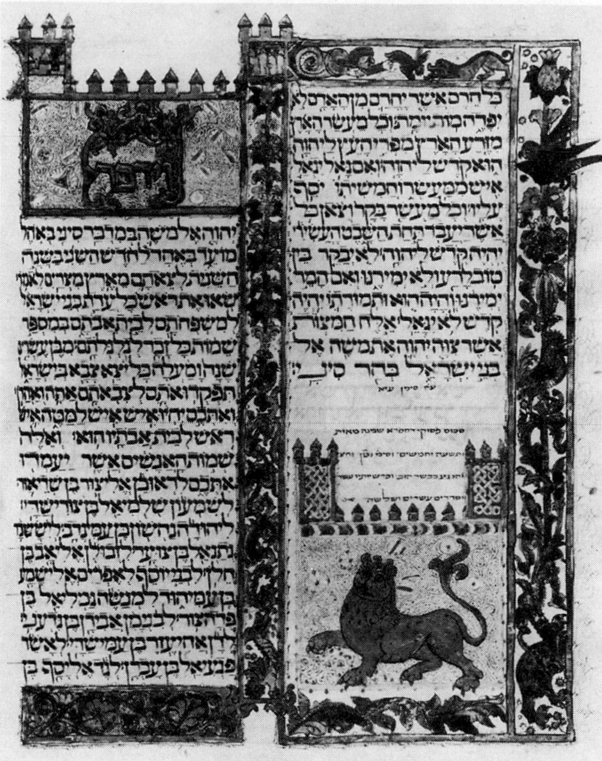

Illuminated folio from Hebrew Bible, c. 1491.

son, for its treatment of Septuagint (LXX) evidence in particular; its actual Hebrew text, based on a Leningrad MS [see (3) (i) (c) below] is quite successful in recovering the Ben Asher Masoretic tradition in a consistent form close to the source. A fully revised edition is actively being prepared. In its disposition of the text on the printed page, the Stuttgart OT abandons the traditional prose arrangement for the modern editors' judgment of poetic structure; this can be, and often is, a valuable aid, but it is also sometimes quite misleading. The Snaith edition, taking its start from Norzi's results, follows a carefully selected but much later MS [see (3) (i) (f) below] and presents, on its editor's testimony, a text very close to the Kahle text, in the standard prose arrangement with Psalms, Proverbs, and Job printed as verse. An undertaking now in progress at the Hebrew University in Israeli Jerusalem proposes to issue an OT text based on the Aleppo Codex [see (3) (i) (a) below] and other good MSS, with an apparatus of variants from all pertinent sources. An earlier Israeli edition bearing the name of M. D. Cassuto was issued by others after that scholar's death and has little to recommend it.

(2) Collations of Manuscript Materials. Three systematic compilations of some size for variants within the MT tradition exist, besides narrower collations from smaller MS groups (e.g., by J. H. Michaelis, 1720). The earliest, *Vetus Testamentum hebraicum cum variis lectionibus,* ed. B. Kennicott (2 v., Oxford 1776–80) concerns the consonantal text only. Its collating base is derived through E. van der Hooght's 1705 OT from the Ben Chayyim text of 1524–25; it provides variants from more than 600 MSS and 50 editions of the OT or its parts. In the Pentateuch it supplies also the Samaritan text [see (5) below] from the London Polyglot, with a collation of 16 Samaritan MSS. The next, *Variae lectiones Veteris Testamenti . . .* ed. Giovanni Bernardo de Rossi (4 v. Parma 1784–88), with a supplement, *Scholia critica in V.T. libros . . .* (Parma 1798), presumes, but does not print, the same collating base as Kennicott. De Rossi controlled a collection of some 800 MSS not included in the Kennicott collation. He presented not an exhaustive, but a selective listing of variants. For those that he did take into account he repeated Kennicott's evidence, added his own, and supplemented the Hebrew collation with data from the versions both supporting and differing from the received MT. Variants bearing not on the consonants, but on the vowel pointing, are also selectively cited. Though the versional evidence always needs rechecking in the light of later critical study, this is the most instructive compilation of variants antedating the discovery of the DEAD SEA SCROLLS [see (6) below]. Ginsburg's collation of more than 70 MSS, largely from the British Museum's collection, and of 19 early printed editions of the MT, in *The Old Testament. . . . Diligently Revised* (3 v. in 4 London 1908–26) goes over some of the same ground as the earlier compilations and is generally disappointing in its presentation and in its results.

(3) Medieval Manuscripts and Origen's Second Column. Here are included (i) the basic witnesses to the Ben Asher tradition; (ii) MSS with divergent vocalization from the Tiberian; and (iii) Origen's transcription of the OT Hebrew text into Greek letters.

(i) Basic Witnesses to the Ben Asher Tradition. Noteworthy MSS that contain the MT with the standard Ben Asher Tiberian vocalization are the following:

(a) The Aleppo Codex (known as A), originally a complete OT furnished with its vowel pointing and accents by Aaron ben Moses BEN ASHER (*c.* A.D. 930). It was donated to the Karaite Jewish community in Jerusalem and subsequently endorsed for its accuracy by MAIMONIDES; it is known to have been in Aleppo at least as early as 1478. During the Arab-Jewish hostilities in 1947 it disappeared for a time and was thought destroyed; the recovery of the MS in a badly truncated state was announced in Israel in 1958. It now lacks all of the Pentateuch to Dt 28.17; 2 Kgs 14.21–18.13; Jer 29.9–31.33; 32.2–4, 9–11, 21–24; Am 8.12-Mi 5.1; So 3.20–Za 9.17; 2 Chr 26.19–35.7; Ps 15.1–25.2 (MT enumeration); Sg

3.11 to the end, and all of Ecclesiastes, Lamentations, Esther, Daniel, and Ezra-Nehemiah. Never before available for systematic collation, it is under intensive study as part of the *Textus* project of the Hebrew University in Jerusalem and is to be employed, when possible, as the foundation for a new critical edition of the MT, as stated above [see (1)].

(b) The Cairo Prophets (known as C), the oldest dated Hebrew MS, written and pointed by Moses ben Asher in 895. Originally, like A, the property of the Karaite community in Jerusalem, it was seized during the First Crusade, then restored by King Baldwin at the instance of the Karaites of Cairo, among whom it is still preserved. It contains the prophetic portion of the Jewish canon, hence the so-called Earlier Prophets (Joshua, Judges, 1 and 2 Samuel, 1 and 2 Kings) in addition to the so-called Later Prophets (Isaiah, Jeremiah, Ezekiel, and the 12 MINOR PROPHETS; *see* PROPHETIC BOOKS OF THE OLD TESTAMENT). This MS was collated for the Kittel-Kahle OT apparatus and also by Cassuto. It is now alleged to conform rather to Ben Naphtali readings than to those of Aaron ben Moses ben Asher in the subsequent generation.

(c) The Leningrad Codex (known as L), dated 1008, MS B 19a of the Russian Public Library in Leningrad, brought originally from the Crimea by A. Firkowitsh in 1839. A colophon to this MS affirms that it was equipped with vowels and Masora from books corrected and annotated by Aaron ben Moses ben Asher. The pointing shows evidence of some reworking in the direction of conformity with what is otherwise known of Ben Asher practice. It was chosen as the best available base for the Kittel-Kahle edition, and its claim to transmit Ben Asher readings was cross-checked with the 10th- or 11th-century treatise of Mishael ben Uzziel on the differences between the Ben Asher and Ben Naphtali traditions; by this criterion it is trustworthy, but Mishael's list is of uncertain date.

(d) British Museum or. 4445, in London, a Pentateuch of which Gn 39.20–Dt 1.33 survives with brief lacunae in Nm 7.47–73 and 9.12–10.18; from the first half of the 10th century, referring in its margin to the scholar (Aaron) ben Asher in a manner that supposes he was still alive. This codex was used by Ginsburg, who dated its consonantal text a century earlier than the pointing; according to Kahle, text and pointing are contemporaneous.

(e) An OT in Parma, copied in Toledo in 1277, used by de Norzi for his critical work and later collated by De Rossi (his number 782).

(f) British Museum or. 2626–28, a complete and richly illuminated OT copied in Lisbon in 1483; the foundation, along with De Norzi's treatise and some supple-

Armenian Gospel, 10th century. (©Bojan Brecelj/CORBIS)

mentary MSS, for Snaith's edition. Like most good Sephardic MSS, it has been subsequently reworked to bring its pointing into agreement with the Ben Chayyim text; it is the unrevised readings of the first punctator that Snaith has followed.

(g) The second Firkowitsh collection, in Leningrad, contains 10th-century MT materials, notably a Pentateuch from the year 930.

(ii) Manuscripts with Divergent Vocalization from the Tiberian. Not all, but a large part of what is known about medieval Hebrew MSS outside the Ben Asher tradition is derived from the contents of the GENIZA (repository for disused religious texts) of the Ezra synagogue in Old Cairo (which before A.D. 969 was the Melchite church of St. Michael). The Biblical MSS from this source, scattered among libraries at Cambridge, Oxford, Paris, New York, and elsewhere, were studied especially by Kahle and his pupils, and more recently by A. Díez Macho. They include:

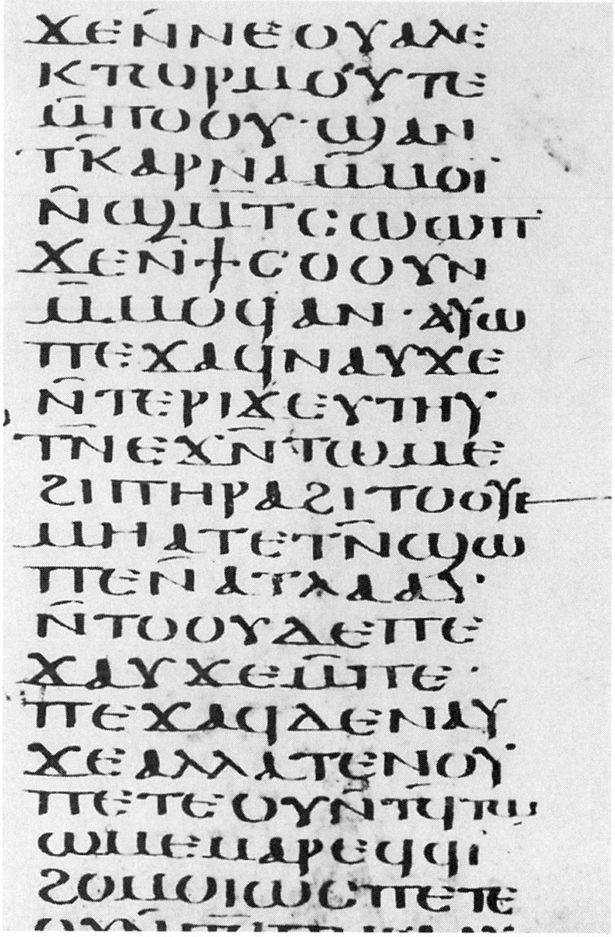

Coptic manuscript in Sahidic, written in Egypt, 6th century; text is Lk 22.34–36.

(a) Fragments with a Palestinian vowel-pointing older than that of the competing schools of Tiberias; the MSS that contain it often provide consonantal variations also.

(b) Manuscripts ascribed by Kahle to the Ben Naphtali school, rivals of the Ben Asher family. A number of these MSS are now seen by Díez Macho and others as transitional between the Palestinian and the full-fledged Tiberian systems. To this category seem to belong, in addition to various geniza fragments, the *Codex Reuchlinianus* of 1105, now in Karlsruhe; also a Pentateuch and a complete OT in Parma (De Rossi's codices 668 and 2, respectively). Díez Macho distinguishes three stages: a tentative proto-Tiberian form, the elaborated divergent form in the codices mentioned, and a later accommodation to the victorious Tiberian system in most features of the text. The difference between the Ben Asher and Ben Naphtali schools is narrowed according to this interpretation to some 900 small details, largely in the use of a single accent mark (the *meteg*).

(c) Manuscripts with a Babylonian vowel-apparatus written above the consonants of the text, hence called supralinear. The Cairo geniza yielded texts of this class in some profusion: the introduction to the Kittel-Kahle edition enumerates more than 120 such MSS, and Díz Macho has since enlarged the count. These fall into two classes, one with an early, simpler, and the other with a later, more developed, vowel system; the range in time is from about the 8th to the 10th century. Parallel to the geniza materials in this class is the firsthand vocalization in MS Berlin or. qu. 680, from the Yemen, of which (including seven leaves in New York) some 101 leaves are wholly or partially preserved. The St. Petersburg codex of the Later Prophets (known as P), dating from 916, already shows the use of the Babylonian symbols to record what is in fact an accommodation to the Tiberian Masoretic system.

(*iii*) *Origen's Second Column.* The principal current interest in the divergent vowel systems so far described lies in the opportunity they give for testing the Ben Asher vocalization, late and in many respects artificial, against other traditions and tendencies reaching back closer to the period of spoken Hebrew. The endeavor has also been made to exploit for this purpose the traditional Hebrew pronunciation among the Samaritans [see (5) below]; and the fuller consonantal orthography of some Qumran texts [see (6) below] is pertinent evidence on certain points. Transliterations of Biblical proper names into Greek or Latin letters are of interest in the same regard; and in the so-called Theodotionic recension of the LXX, for reasons not fully understood, there is a sprinkling of transcriptions into Greek letters of ordinary Hebrew words. The most notable single source of this kind is, however, the preserved evidence, mainly from the Ambrosian Library's palimpsest Psalter published by Cardinal G. MERCATI, for the second column of ORIGEN's *Hexapla.* This systematic transposition of the Hebrew text into Greek letters presents, within the limitations of the Greek alphabet, a sampling of the way the text was pronounced in the first half of the 3rd century at the latest. On the basis of the uniformity of this transcription and its variance from proper name forms in the LXX, Mercati sees it as contemporary with Origen; Kahle would make it Jewish in origin, like everything else in the *Hexapla*, and therefore, presumably, earlier. In any case it reflects the standardized Hebrew (consonantal) text subsequent to *c.* A.D. 100.

The materials listed up to this point pertain strictly to the Jewish canon of the OT and to the consonantal text as stabilized for the future by about the end of the 1st Christian century. Although that text has authentic roots in pre-Christian Judaism, the evidence of the LXX, the NT, Josephus, the Samaritan Pentateuch, and the Qumran and other discoveries combine to indicate that both the scope and the form of OT literature as it circulated among the Jews was somewhat more fluid and varied before that time. The textual evidence for this is discussed in what follows.

(4) Sirach and Tobit. The Cairo geniza contained not only MSS of the OT books received in the Jewish canon, but also five fragmentary Hebrew MSS of Sirach, dating from the 10th to the 12th century. Of these, four were published between 1897 and 1901, the first direct evidence for the original text of the book apart from dubious and undependable scattered citations in rabbinic literature. The fifth MS was brought to light in 1931, and again in 1958 and 1960 additional leaves of two of the known MSS appeared in print. Controversy over the authenticity of these materials sprang up with their initial publication, and skepticism on the part of Jewish scholars in particular has been somewhat widespread in recent years. There can, however, be no doubt, either of the basic authenticity of the text or of the fact that a certain amount of retroversion from the Syriac, done in the period when these copies were made, has been introduced. An added anomaly in the history of this book is that, although the citations of the earlier rabbis are nearly all vague and inaccurate, Gaon SA'ADIA BEN JOSEPH al-Fayyumi (d. 942) quotes Sirach in Hebrew quite exactly in 25 cases out of 26. A clue to this situation seems to be afforded by the Qumran discoveries and related research. From cave two at Qumran come late 1st-century B.C. fragments of Sir 6.20–31 (2Q18), published by M. Baillet, which are just large enough to show a coincidence of wording and a similarity of stichometric arrangement with the geniza copies (though the wording relates to geniza MSS A and C, while it is MS B, not extant for this portion, that is stichometric in the Cairo group). Also in 11QPs^{a} cols. 21–22, edited by J. A. Sanders, copied in the 1st Christian century, stand the first half and the last two words of the acrostic poem in Sir 51.13–30, this time in an authentic text where the geniza form has long been recognized as secondary to the Syriac. The 1963–64 excavations at Masada (near the southwest end of the Dead Sea) yielded fragments of 13 columns of a scroll of Sirach in a Hebrew script of the first half of the 1st century B.C. They contain portions of Sir 39.27–44.17 written stichometrically, two hemistichs to a line. It is reported by Y. Yadin [*Yediot* 29 (1965) 120–122, in Hebrew] to be in general agreement with the text of MS B from the Cairo geniza and to put the authenticity of the medieval copies beyond dispute. When one combines these facts with the indications from Christian, Jewish, and Muslim sources that MSS from a ''cave'' sect turned up near Jericho shortly before A.D. 800, it seems possible to identify both the occasion for recovery of an incomplete text of Sirach before Sa'adia and a part

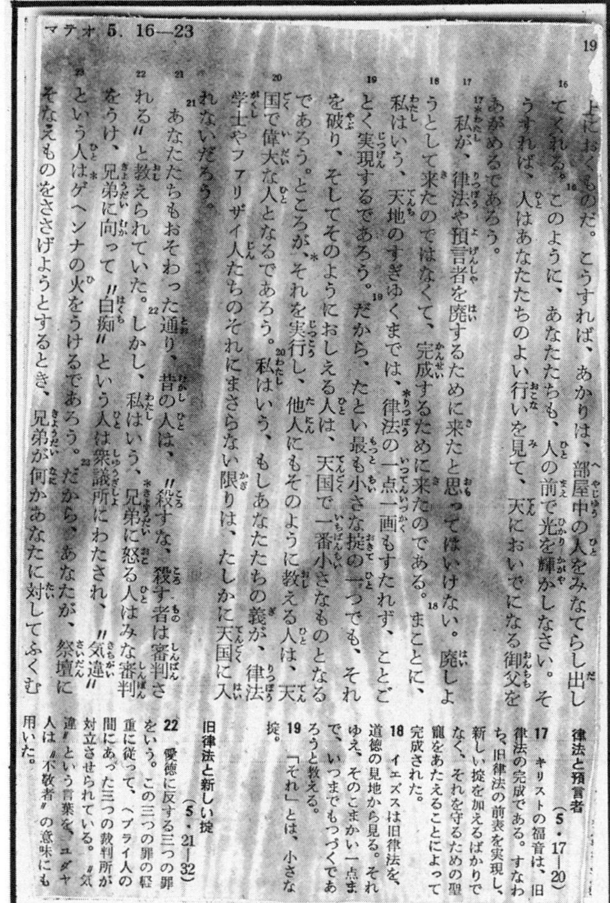
マテオ 5．16—23　19

上におくものだ。こうすれば、あかりは、部屋中の人をみなてらし出してくれる。16このように、あなたたちも、人の前で光を輝かしなさい。そうすれば、人はあなたたちのよい行いを見て、天においでになる御父をあがめるであろう。

17＊私が、律法や預言者を廃するために来たと思ってはいけない。廃しようとして来たのではなくて、完成するために来たのである。18まことに、私はいう、天地のすぎゆくまでは、＊律法の一点一画もすたれず、ことごとく実現するであろう。19だから、たとい最も小さな掟の一つでも、それを破り、そしてそのようにおしえる人は、天国で一番小さなものとなるであろう。ところが、＊それを実行し、他人にもそのように教える人は、天国で偉大な人となるであろう。20私はいう、もしあなたたちの義が、律法学士やファリザイ人たちのそれにまさらない限りは、たしかに天国に入れないだろう。

21あなたたちもおそわった通り、昔の人は、″殺すな、殺す者は審判される″と教えられていた。22しかし、私はいう、＊兄弟に怒る人はみな審判をうけ、兄弟に向って″白痴″という人は衆議所にわたされ、″気違″という人は＊ゲヘンナの火をうけるであろう。23だから、あなたが、祭壇にそなえものをささげようとするとき、兄弟が何かあなたに対してふくむ

律法と預言者（5・17—20）

17 キリストの福音は、旧律法の完成である。すなわち、旧律法の前表を実現し、新しい掟を加えるばかりでなく、それを守るための聖寵をあたえることによって完成された。

18 イエズスは旧律法を、道徳の見地から見る。それゆえ、そのこまかい一点まで、いつまでもつづくであろうと教える。

19 「それ」とは、小さな掟。

旧律法と新しい掟（5・21—32）

22 愛徳に反する三つの罪をいう。この三つの罪の軽重に従って、ヘブライ人の間にあった三つの裁判所が対立させられている。″気違″という言葉を、ユダヤ人は″不敬者″の意味にも用いた。

Page from a New Testament Bible (Mt 5.16–23) in modern Japanese (tr. F. Barbaro), with additional notes.

of the impetus to textual study among the Karaites that accompanied the activity of the several schools of Masoretes—the more so as the *Damascus Document* of the Qumran group also first came to light in the Cairo geniza.

In this connection may be mentioned the Qumran cave four fragments of Tobit, from four MSS in Aramaic, the original language, and one in Hebrew. J. T. Milik, who is publishing these, affirms that they support in all cases the longest available form of the book, usually represented by the Greek Codex Sinaiticus and by the Old Latin Version. The medieval Aramaic and Hebrew texts of this book, however, are all entirely secondary; none has appeared from the geniza. Of Baruch ch. six (the ''Letter of Jeremia''), which was certainly composed in Hebrew, only a Greek fragment (7Q2, published by Baillet) is known from Qumran.

(5) The Samaritan Pentateuch. This is a pre-Christian Palestinian Hebrew recension of the Mosaic books, transcribed in an archaic script derived from the paleo-Hebrew form of the Canaanite alphabet. The earli-

Spanish version of Bible. (©Richard Cummins/CORBIS)

est copy of it to reach western Europe was secured in Damascus by Pietro della Valle in 1616. It was published in the Paris and London polyglots, and its critical significance became the focal point of controversy. It is an expanded, repetitious form of the text, with a limited number of specifically sectarian details. The fact that in a large number of individual readings it coincides with the LXX against the MT has made it a continuing stimulus to text-critical study of the OT. It is now represented in European libraries, notably the John Rylands Library in Manchester, England, and the Russian Public Library in Leningrad, by a large number of copies, some dating from the 12th and 13th centuries. The famous ''scroll of Abisha,'' kept by the Samaritans at Nablus and ascribed by them to the 13th year after the conquest of Canaan by Josue, is in its oldest part a MS of the 11th Christian century. Having been twice photographed and its oldest part having been published by F. Perez Castro, it has proved to be a factitious piecing together of materials of varying ages. Kennicott was able to collate 16 MSS of the Samaritan text; a hand edition with variants was published by B. Blayney in 1790. A. von Gall issued (1914–18) from Berlin an edition with ambitions to be critical; it describes and collates a number of significant MSS; but since others of equal or greater importance were not available to the editor, a definitive edition (now promised by Perez Castro) remains to be produced.

In the light of the new evidences from Qumran [see (6) below], it is clear that the point of departure of the specifically Samaritan text from the earlier Palestinian recension on which it depends is to be sought in about the days of John Hyrcanus (134–104 B.C.). The Samaritan text and script, as well as history, converge on this result. Critical evaluation of this text will now be in a new setting, since it is henceforth only one of several witnesses to the state of the text in Palestine at the end of the 2nd century B.C. Transmission of this consonantal text in its older copies has, however, been remarkably faithful, as is proved by comparison with 4QpaleoEx^{m} [see (6) below]. In general, the expanded, transposed, and reworked features of this text are of no great moment from the standpoint of the textual critic, though the Palestinian recension represented is of historical importance; but its witness to specific ancient Palestinian readings divergent from those of the MT continues to be instructive and significant.

Study of the Samaritan pronunciation of Hebrew has been carried forward by several scholars from a variety of sources: oral dictation by Samaritans of portions of the Pentateuch transcribed into a Western phonetic orthography by Europeans; a vocalization contained in four Samaritan Pentateuch MSS; and grammatical and lexical treatises of Samaritan authors published in Hebrew and Arabic. Whether the evidence from these sources can be integrated with other (Qumran, Hexaplaric) materials to furnish a coherent impression of earlier pronunciation of Biblical Hebrew remains to be seen.

There is a Samaritan Aramaic Targum to the Pentateuch, not to be confused with the Hebrew text just described. This Targum has origins going back to the 4th Christian century and varies greatly from one MS to the next. Published editions of it are inadequate; but when fully known, it seems likely to be of much greater interest for the history of Palestinian Aramaic than for Biblical studies as such. On the other hand, the survival, mostly from the Hexapla, of a number of passages out of the *Samaritikon,* or Greek translation of the Samaritan Pentateuch, forms a useful link between the earliest Samaritan MSS and the older Palestinian recension from which they were ultimately derived.

(6) The Earliest Manuscripts. These come from the 3rd century B.C. to the 2nd Christian century. For the period before Origen, direct evidence of the Hebrew OT text was almost nonexistent up to 1947; the unique exception was the Nash papyrus, *c.* 150 B.C., from Egypt, containing Dt 6.4–6 and the Ten Commandments. Since that time, distinct discoveries of 2nd-Christian-century materials from the Wadi Murabba'āt and of still earlier texts from Khirbet Qumran and other, thus far less productive sites (the wadies west of Engeddi, and Masada) have yielded copies of some OT books (Ecclesiastes and Daniel) scarcely more than a century later than the composition of the books themselves. By the end of 1964 the number of separate OT MSS of which at least some fragments are extant from these various sources stood at about 180; ten are from 2nd-Christian-century contexts (Wadi Murabba'ā, Wadi Khabra) and the rest all antedate A.D. 68 (Qumran) or A.D. 73 (Masada) at the latest.

All these MSS, on leather or papyrus, were written in columns on one side only of the material; no Hebrew text of the 2nd century or earlier in codex (book) form is known. The complete scroll of Isaiah (1QIs[a]) from Qumran is made up of 17 strips of carefully prepared leather sewn end to end to a length of 24 ½ feet, 10 ½ inches high, meant to be kept rolled up when not in use. In it the text is disposed in 54 vertical columns, with an intentional main division after col. 27, the end of the present ch. 33 (of 66 ch.). This arrangement is suggestive for the format of any large biblical book at this period; nevertheless, from Qumran there are MSS with as few as nine lines of text to the column, and others with more than 60, whereas 1QIs[a] averages 30 lines to the column.

To take first the 10 MSS left by refugees after the Second Jewish Revolt (A.D. 132–135), the evidence includes fragments of Genesis, Exodus, and Numbers by one scribe; of Genesis in a different hand; of three other MSS of Numbers, two of Deuteronomy, and one each of Psalms, Isaiah, and the Minor Prophets. Only the MS of Psalms from the Wadi Khabra (fragments in Jordan, some few in Israel) is actually of 1st century date and exhibits some variation from the MT. The rest show the fixity of script, format, orthography, and content that constitutes the basic MT text. This might be expected for the Pentateuch and Isaia. The Minor Prophets (Mur 88), however, is preserved in very substantial portions representing ten of the 12 books; there are only three meaningful variants in it from the MT consonants, and only one of these is notable, though not an improvement.

Quite different are about 170 MSS from the 1st century and before. They include some archaic texts (4QExr[f], Sam[b], Jer[a]) dated from *c.* 250 to 200 B.C. by F. M. Cross on paleographical grounds. A somewhat larger number of 2nd-century B.C. texts is followed by the bulk of the MSS, dating from the 1st century B.C., with texts of the 1st Christian century also present in quantity. All books of the full Catholic OT canon are somehow represented (although 1 and 2 Chronicles by one isolated fragment with about five incomplete lines of text), except Esther, Judith, Wisdom, 1 and 2 Maccabees, Baruch ch. 1–5, and the LXX additions to Daniel. A limited number of these early MSS are in the paleo-Hebrew script descended from preexilic forms; besides Pentateuch MSS, surprisingly, there is one of Job. The orthography is not so consistent as in the MT. Although some of the oldest MSS have narrowly consonantal spelling, perhaps a third of the Biblical MSS show in varying degrees a much fuller orthography with lavish use of the weak consonants *h, w, y* and ʾ (*aleph*) to mark the place of vowels in the word. This usage, common also in extra-Biblical texts from Qumran, parallels that of Syriac and differs from medieval Hebrew practice, in that all "o" and "u" vowels are represented by *w,* regardless of their length, whereas only long "î" or "ê" vowels are indicated by *y.*

Unknown individual readings that are not mere vagaries of the particular copyist are on the whole somewhat rare. But textual tendencies in Palestine that could be envisaged only doubtfully and obscurely from the LXX and Samaritan evidence can now be studied directly in these texts. Far from proving the overall superiority of the LXX, these Hebrew MSS help to endow that version with a continuous history of development that makes the jumbled evidence in extant Greek MSS more adequately subject to control.

At the present stage of investigation, the incidence of fuller Palestinian readings coinciding with the LXX or the Samaritan, and the identifiable Palestinian tendency to an expansionist technique in copying and editing Biblical texts, from an early postexilic date until the reaction that is represented by the MT, have led Cross to posit for the Pentateuch (at least Exodus through Deuteronomy) and Samuel in the received text a Babylonian origin that would have kept them apart from the development in Palestine. For Samuel in particular, where the MT represents a surprisingly truncated and defective recension, some such explanation is surely called for. The MT of the Pentateuch is a sound, tightly organized, unexpanded text of a quite different character; but again, it is doubtful that such a text can be directly filiated to the fuller and less stabilized forms evidenced for Palestine from the proto-Lucianic LXX, the Samaritan, and now the Qumran sources.

Of individual MSS thus far published, only brief mention can be made. The complete Isaiah scroll (1QIs[a]) dates from *c.* 100 to 75 B.C. It is a reworked text of Isaiah, disclosing—beneath the very full orthography of its second half especially and beneath its harmonizations of related passages, simplified readings, and borrowings from other OT books—a basic text quite close to the MT tradition, with which all other (at least 14) Qumran MSS of Isaiah coincide more closely still; however, the degree of nearness of 1QIs[b], a later and more fragmentary MS, to the MT has in fact been overstated in the literature. An early 2nd-century B.C. copy of Exodus in the old script (4QpaleoEx^m) contains all the expansions known previously from the Samaritan Pentateuch [see (5) above], except that about the unhewn altar on Mt. Garizim after Ex 20.17. It proves the Samaritan recension quite faithful to a pre-Christian Palestinian form of text; but there are now a number of Qumran MSS that evidence, in varying degrees, these same Palestinian tendencies to expansion in Exodus through Deuteronomy, of which the Samaritan text is no longer the prime witness. In general, Qumran MSS of the historical books tend to coincide with the LXX evidence, especially that of a proto-Lucianic type; very remarkable in this regard is 4QSam^a (1st century B.C.), in which a notable amount of the text of 1 and 2 Samuel is preserved. The short recension of Jeremiah hitherto known only from the LXX is present in 4QJer^b, one of four MSS of that Prophet at Qumran. The compilation in 11QPs^a (1st Christian century), which combines 35 canonical Psalms in an irregular order with eight other compositions, seems to show special interest in David as a person and as author; various considerations suggest that the standard canonical order of the Psalms is presupposed by this unique collection.

In addition to the strictly Biblical MSS, the several hundred extra-biblical texts from the same sources will have to be studied extensively for biblical *lemmata* (formal citations of biblical verses as a basis for commentary in the *pesharim*), incidental quotations and allusions, before the full contribution of the discoveries since 1947 to an understanding of the history of the OT text can be assessed.

Bibliography: O. EISSFELDT, *The Old Testament: An Introduction,* tr. P. ACKROYD (New York 1965) sections 115–118, 126. P. E. KAHLE, *The Cairo Geniza* (2nd ed. New York 1960); *Der masoretische Text des A. T. nach der Überlieferung der babylonischen Juden* (Leipzig 1902); *Masoreten des Ostens* (Leipzig 1913); *Masoreten des Westens,* 2 v. (Stuttgart 1927–30); *Der hebräische Bibeltext seit Franz Delitzsch* (Stuttgart 1961). M. GREENBERG, "The Stabilization of the Text of the Hebrew Bible, Reviewed in the Light of the Biblical Materials from the Judean Desert," *The Journal of the American Oriental Society* 76 (1956) 157–167. G. E. WEIL, "La Nouvelle édition de la Massorah (BHK iv) et l'histoire de la Massorah," (*Vetus Testamentum* Suppl 9; 1963) 266–284. *Textus: Annual of the Hebrew University Bible Project,* ed. C. RABIN (1960–63), v.1–3. A. I. KATSH, *Ginze Russiyah* (New York 1958), fac. of Heb. MSS preserved in the U.S.S.R. A. DÍEZ MACHO, "A New List of So-Called *Ben Naftali* Manuscripts . . . ," *Hebrew and Semitic Studies presented to G. R. Driver. . . ,* ed. D. W. THOMAS and W. D. MCHARDY (Oxford 1963). G. MERCATI, *Psalterii hexapli reliquiae* (Vatican City 1958); "Il problema della colonna II dell' Esapla," *Biblica* 28 (1947) 1–30, 173–215. F. PEREZ CASTRO, *Séfer Abiša'* (Madrid 1959), see the important review by E. ROBERTSON, *Vetus Testamentum* 12 (1962) 228–235. N. H. SNAITH, "New Edition of the Hebrew Bible," *ibid.* 7 (1957) 207–208. M. BAILLET, "La Récitation de la Loi chez les Samaritains d'après Z. Ben-Hayyim," *Revue biblique* 69 (1962) 570–587. B. J. ROBERTS, "The Hebrew Bible since 1937," *Journal of Theological Studies* 15 (1964) 253–264. D. BARTHÉLEMY and J. T. MILIK, *Qumrân Cave I* (*Discoveries in the Judean Desert* 1; 1955). P. BENOIT et al., *Les Grottes de Murabba'āt* (*ibid.* 2; 1961). M. BAILLET et al., *Les "Petites Grottes" de Qumran* (*ibid.* 3; 1962). J. A. SANDERS, ed., *11Q Ps^a* (*ibid.* 4; 1965). M. BURROWS, *The Dead Sea Scrolls of St. Mark's Monastery,* 2 v. (New Haven 1950–51). E. L. SUKENIK, *The Dead Sea Scrolls of the Hebrew University* (Jerusalem 1955), in Heb. Y. YADIN, "The Expedition to the Judaean Desert, 1960: Expedition D," *Israel Exploration Journal* 11 (1961), 40 and plate 20D, a MS of Psalms. J. T. MILIK, *Ten Years of Discovery in the Wilderness of Judaea,* tr. J. STRUGNELL (Studies in Biblical Theology 26; Naperville, Ill. 1959). A. A. DI LELLA, *The Hebrew Text of Sirach: A Text-Critical and Historical Study* (The Hague 1965). F. M. CROSS, JR., *The Ancient Library of Qumran and Modern Biblical Studies* (rev. ed. 1961); "The Development of the Jewish Scripts," *The Bible and the Ancient Near East,* ed. G. E. WRIGHT (Garden City 1961); "The History of the Biblical Text in the Light of Discoveries in the Judaean Desert," *Harvard Theological Review* 57 (1964) 281–299. P. W. SKEHAN, "Qumran and the Present State of O.T. Studies: The Masoretic Text," *Journal of Biblical Literature* 78 (1959) 21–25; "Exodus in the Samaritan Recension from Qumran," *ibid.* 74 (1955) 182–187; "The Qumran Manuscripts and Textual Criticism," (*Vetus Testamentum* Suppl 4; 1957) 148–160; "A Psalm Manuscript from Qumran (4Q Ps^b)," *The Catholic Biblical Quarterly* 26 (1964) 313–322; "The Biblical Scrolls from Qumran and the Text of the Old Testament," *The Biblical Archaeologist* 28 (1965) 87–100. Y. YADIN, *The Ben Sira Scroll from Masada* (Jerusalem 1965).

[P. W. SKEHAN]

TEXT OF THE NEW TESTAMENT

This article will treat in chronological order the forms in which the Greek text of the NT has appeared from the earliest extant manuscripts (MSS), discussing printed editions and indicating projects to reproduce the text more adequately.

The autographs of the 27 canonical books of the NT, written or dictated by several inspired authors over a period of two generations, were lost before almost any extant manuscript (MS) was penned. After having been produced on papyrus scrolls, the autographs had been copied by hand, and these MSS had circulated among individual Christian communities until they in turn were replaced. In the course of transmission both scribal errors and conscious alterations modified the form of the original text. Short clarifications, modification of unfamiliar words, omissions, and harmonizations appeared in MSS. Those in ancient languages into which the NT was translated for Christians who did not speak Greek indicate some modifications not found in any extant Greek MS. In addition, homilies and commentaries of early ecclesiastical writers at times present other textual variations. The Greek text of the NT, as it appears in modern printed editions, is reconstructed on the basis of study and evaluation of all such witnesses, which are only a fraction of its many forms in history. This article deals with the Greek witnesses and modern critical presentations.

Extant Greek New Testament Manuscripts. The first attempt at a complete listing of all extant Greek NT MSS was made by C. R. Gregory (1847–1917) in the *Prolegomena* of the great 8th edition of C. von Tischendorf's *Novum Testamentum Graece* (Leipzig 1894). Gregory later completed this list in what is accepted as the official list and method of identifying NT Greek MSS (*Die griechischen Handschriften des Neuen Testaments.* [Leipzig 1908]). Supported by authority of the *Kommission für spätantike Religionsgeschichte* of the German Academy of Science in preference to proposals of Hermann von Soden, Gregory's list has been continued by E. von Dobschütz, J. Schmidt, and K. Aland through notices in *Zeitschrift für die neutestamentliche Wissenschaft und die Kunde der älteren Kirche.* The notice by Aland in 1957 brought the number to 67 papyri, 241 uncials, 2,533 cursives, and 1,838 lectionaries, although many of these 4,689 MSS contain only small parts of the Greek text. To keep information accurate, Aland founded the Institute for New Testament Textual Research at Münster in Westphalia in 1959 and inaugurated a series called the *Arbeiten zur neutestamentlichen Textforschung* in 1963. Of the large number of MSS, Gregory could list only one uncial, the Codex Sinaiticus, and about 35 cursives as having the entire NT.

With regard to the material on which the text is written, NT manuscripts are of papyrus, vellum or parchment, and paper. Since paper MSS are late and relatively unimportant, the official list divides the MSS into papyri, uncial vellum, and cursive vellum MSS. The use of vellum became common only from the time of Constantine, who ordered 50 copies on vellum for the churches of his empire. Since it was expensive and limited in quantity, usable parts of worn vellum codices were salvaged to be used again. Thus parts of the NT have been preserved in later writing on such PALIMPSEST MSS. The following is a brief description of the most important NT MSS in each of the three groups. Since the dates proposed depend upon paleographic evidence, they are at times only tentative (*see* PALEOGRAPHY, GREEK).

Principal NT Papyri. Significant progress has been made in knowledge of early forms of the NT text because of discoveries of papyri, some of which were written as early as 150 years before the oldest vellum MS (*see* PAPYROLOGY). In the official list they are designated by a capital P followed by the Arabic numeral indicating the order in which their discovery was reported. By 1964 some 77 papyri containing parts of the Greek text had been announced, dating from the 2nd to the 8th century. Although most of these are fragmentary, about half of the Greek NT is now extant on papyrus, parts of every book except 1 and 2 Timothy. Four of these fragments are from SCROLLS, the rest from codices (MS books). The oldest (P 52, John Rylands Library Gr. 457) contains parts of Jn 18.31–34, 37–38, written during the first half of the 2nd century in a text type like that of the Codex Vaticanus.

The most complete descriptive list of Greek NT papyri appears in the article "Papyrus Biblique" by B. Botte [*Dictionnaire de la Bible,* suppl. ed. 6 (1960): 1109–20]. It gives content, date, location, publication, and text type of each papyrus to P 72, except for P 38, erroneously omitted. P 38 (University of Michigan C. 1571) is a 3rd-century fragment of a popular, i.e., unrevised, text of Acts 18.27–19.6 and 19.12–16. Botte's article fails to give information on photographic facsimiles. The papyri most important for NT study have been found in this century and form part of the Chester Beatty and Bodmer collections.

Chester Beatty Papyri. In 1930 an Irish businessman, A. Chester Beatty, purchased in Egypt a collection of 11 Biblical papyri, including three of the NT. All these were edited by Sir Frederic George Kenyon with photographic facsimiles as *The Chester Beatty Biblical Papyri* (7 v. and pl. London 1933–37). From the NT are: (1) P 45 (Chester Beatty I). This consists of 30 mutilated leaves of a 3rd-century codex about 10 by 8 inches. Extant are fragments of all the Gospels and Acts in a popular text with no particular Western characteristics. This papyrus revolutionized understanding of the NT text by showing so-called Caesarean readings at a date much earlier than had previously been suspected. (2) P 46 (Chester Beatty II plus University of Michigan Inv. 6238). This early 3rd-century single-quire codex measures about 9 by 5 ½ inches. The 86 extant leaves of the original 104 contain parts of almost all the Pauline Epistles and the Epistles to the Hebrews, which follows immediately after Romans. About half of Romans, most of 1 Thessalonians, and all of 2 Thessalonians are missing, and Ephesians precedes Galatians. G. Kuntz has shown that this is an extremely valuable witness of the proto-Alexandrian text type, despite its many scribal errors. The University of Michigan owns 40 leaves but permitted Kenyon to edit them with the rest of the codex. Independently H. A. Sanders also studied the Michigan leaves in *A Third-Century Papyrus Codex of the Epistles of Paul* (Ann Arbor 1935). (3) P 47 (Chester Beatty III). This 3rd-century codex, consisting of ten leaves of Rv 9.10–17.2 with lacunae, is the earliest MS of this book and presents a text similar to that of the Codex Sinaiticus.

Bodmer NT Greek Papyri. These form part of the collection of classical, Biblical, and apocryphal texts in Greek and Coptic acquired by the Swiss industrialist whose name they bear, for his private library in Cologny near Geneva. Of the 19 published, the following six are

Greek NT texts: (1) P 66 (Bodmer II). This is the extant 108 pages in a codex of five quires about 6 ½ by 5 ½ inches containing most of Jn 1.1–14.26, except for a lacuna of 6.11–35, and fragments of the remainder of John V. Martin edited the first 14 chapters in 1956 and part of the fragments in 1958. Shortcomings of this edition and the lack of photographic reproductions were remedied in a second edition of the fragments, which includes a facsimile of the entire papyrus [V. Martin and J. W. B. Barnes, *Papyrus Bodmer II. Supplément. Evangile de Jean XIV–XXI* (Bibliothèque Bodmer, Cologny-Geneva 1962), 54 pp. and 154 plates]. The first editor dated this codex earlier than A.D. 200, and H. Hunger says that it is no later than A.D. 150. However, J. Duplacy refers to two unnamed papyrologists who place it in the 4th century [*Recherches de science religieuse* 50 (1962) 251]. It omits the pericope of the woman taken in adultery (Jn 7.53–8.11) and of the moving of the waters at the pool of Bethesda (Jn 5.4). Carelessly written, it is often corrected by the original and by later scribes. The text, which fluctuates in its agreements with classical text-types, shows clear resemblances to the Old Latin. (2) P 72 (Bodmer VII and VIII). This 3rd-century codex contains the Epistles of Jude and 1 and 2 Peter. M. Testuz, curator of the Bodmer library, edited these in 1959 and found the text much like that of Codex B and the Bohairic version, especially for 2 Peter. A complete collation of 1 Peter by E. Massaux indicates that it bears greatest similarity to the cursives 104, 424, 326, and 81 and reveals one of the many popular texts of the 2nd and 3rd centuries [*Ephemerides theologicae Lovanienses* 39 (1963) 616–71]. (3) P 74 (Bodmer XVII). This is a 6th- or 7th-century codex containing all of Acts and fragments of all the Catholic Epistles. Since the back part of the codex was severely damaged, the fragments decrease rapidly in size. R. Kassar edited this papyrus for the Bodmer library in 1961. (4) P 75 (Bodmer XIV and XV). This is the extant part of a 144-page codex from about A.D. 300 originally containing Luke and John. Extant are 25 full pages, 26 pages almost complete, and fragments of others. These were edited for the Bodmer library in two volumes with 98 plates by V. Martin and R. Kassar in 1961. Bodmer XIV contains Luke 3–17 and 22–24 in a text similar to Codex B. It contains the long text in Lk 22.19–20; 24.12, 40, 51b and omits the bloody sweat of Christ (Lk 22.43–44), also omitted by the Vaticanus and the first hand of Sinaiticus. Bodmer XV is the text of John 1–15, similar to that of Codex B. (5) P 73 is a fragment of Mt 24.43 and 26.2–3 that was found between leaves of P 74 and is unedited.

Principal NT Uncials. Most NT vellum MSS copied between the 4th and 10th centuries were without separation of words, had little punctuation, and were written in large, unconnected letters called uncials, a Latin word meaning ''one-twelfth,'' i.e., of a line of letters. In general these are the most highly esteemed witnesses of the text because of their careful composition. They are identified by a capital letter or by 0 plus an Arabic number, known as a siglum. Uncials fundamental for the study of the NT text are listed below.

Codex Vaticanus. The Vatican codex Gr. 1209, siglum B or 03, is a 4th-century MS originally containing the entire Bible in Greek, but Gn 1.1–46.27, Ps 106 (107)–138(139) and Heb 9.14 to the end of the NT are now missing. Since the Catholic Epistles are before Paul, they are extant, but the Pastoral Letters and the Apocalypse are lost. Although this codex was in the Vatican Library when it was first catalogued in 1475, it was published completely only in 1857. The splendid photographic edition of the Vatican Library appeared in 1889–90 in seven volumes. Although the entire NT seems to have been copied by one scribe, this is uncertain because the letters were inked over by a monk in the 12th century. Codex B offers the best example of the refined text existing in Egypt in the early 3rd century and, except in Paul, is free from the readings of the widely diffused popular 2nd-century texts. Codex B is the chief witness for the text type called ''neutral'' by Hort, ''Hesychian recension'' by von Soden, ''text B'' by Lagrange, ''proto-Alexandrian'' by Zuntz, and ''Beta'' by many recent critics. Westcott and Hort used it as the fundamental text for their edition, and through them it has played the decisive role in many manual editions. Its chief defects are mechanical, such as doubling or omission of letters, syllables, or lines.

Codex Sinaiticus. This is the Codex Frederico-Augustanus plus British Museum Add. MS 43725, siglum S or Hebrew aleph. K. von Tischendorf found this MS on two of his expeditions to the monastery of St. Catherine at Mt. Sinai, part of the OT in 1844 and the NT plus the Letter of Barnabas and the Shepherd of HERMAS in 1859. His second find of 199 leaves was sold by the Soviet government to the British Museum in 1933. In their study, *Scribes and Correctors of the Codex Sinaiticus* (London 1938), H. J. M. Milne and T. C. Skeat date the codex from the 2nd half of the 4th century and attribute it to three scribes writing from dictation. It has many mistakes, especially in the part executed by the third scribe, and was corrected in different ages by nine hands. Its place of origin seems to have been Caesarea. Kirsopp Lake and Helen Lake edited a photographic facsimile (Oxford 1911).

Codex Alexandrianus. This is an early 5th-century MS (British Museum, Royal MS 1 D V–VIII; siglum A or 02) that once contained the entire Bible. Now the NT begins with Mt 25.7 and lacks Jn 6.50–8.22 and 2 Cor

4.13–12.6. A photographic edition begun for the museum by K. Lake in 1909 was completed only in 1957 by T. C. Skeat in five volumes. This codex, noteworthy for its frequent substitution of synonyms, presents a text of unequal quality. The Gospels belong to the inferior Byzantine type, Acts and the Epistles to the Alexandrian type.

Codex Ephraemi Rescriptus. This is in the Paris National Library, Codex Gr. 9; siglum C or 04. The extant 209 leaves of this 5th-century palimpsest were employed in the 12th century for a Greek translation of the sermons of Ephraim. The 145 leaves from the NT preserve passages from all books except 2 Thessalonians and 2 John. In 1845 Tischendorf published as much as he could read of it. Fundamentally the text is Alexandrian, but it contains mixed readings. After Codex C the list of Gregory uses the same letter for more than one uncial because the rest contain only limited parts of the NT. Four of these demand mention here.

Codex Bezae. A MS of only Gospels and Acts; siglum D or 05. It is commonly known by the name of its 16th-century owner, Theodore BEZA, and is now preserved at Cambridge University. This 5th- or 6th-century uncial is the oldest extant Greek and Latin codex. The order of the Gospels is that of most Latin MSS, Matthew, John, Luke, and Mark. Its text, which is complex, is the leading witness of the Western text and the oldest MS with the pericope of the woman taken in adultery.

Codex Claromontanus. This 6th-century Greek and Latin Codex (siglum D or 06) of the National Library, Paris, contains 533 leaves written in sense lines of unequal length. The text type is also Western.

Codex Washingtonianus. This MS (siglum W or 032) of 187 leaves, now in the Freer Gallery, Washington, D.C., presents a modified uncial script of the 5th century except for the quire containing Jn 1.1–5.11, written by another scribe and offering an early Egyptian form of text. Mark often agrees with P 45, but other parts exhibit a variety of types. After Mk 16.14 is found the so-called Freer logion, a 16-line addition partly quoted by St. Jerome as being found in many MSS.

Codex Koridethi. This codex (siglum Θ or 038), found in a monastery on the Black Sea, was published by Gregory and Beerman in 1913. It cannot be dated exactly because its writing is unique, but it is placed between the 7th and the 9th centuries. It is related to families 1 and 13 mentioned below, and is a witness of the Caesarean text of the Gospels.

Principal NT Cursives. During the 9th century a cursive or miniscule book-hand began to replace the uncial style of writing, and this prevailed until the introduction of printing. Cursive MSS are generally of lesser value as witnesses, but some of them preserve early readings otherwise lost. They are identified simply by an Arabic number. The "queen of the cursives" is 33, a 9th-century codex containing most of the NT except Revelation in an Alexandrian text. The large number of cursives has enabled critics to trace relationships between "families," that is, groups of MSS originating from the same archetype. Two of these are described below.

Family 13. The collection is known also as the Ferrar family, after an Irish clergyman, W. H. Ferrar, who first established a relationship between four cursives in 1868. After his death a collation of these, 13, 69, 124, 346, was published by his collaborator, T. K. Abbot, in 1877. Further research, especially by Von Soden and K. Lake, enlarged this family to 13 medieval codices including one lectionary, all containing only the Gospels except 69, which includes the entire NT. The most striking feature of this family is the position of the pericope of the woman taken in adultery (Jn 7.53–8.11) after Lk 21.38. They preserve the Caesarean text-type and were copied in monasteries in southern Italy. J. Geerlings has continued research on this family in the series *Texts and Studies.* In v. 19–21 he published the hypothetical archetype of the Ferrar family text for Matthew, Luke and John.

Family 1. This is a designation for a group known also as the Lake family. Kirsopp Lake, in *Codex 1 and its Allies* (Cambridge 1902), identified four cursives, 1, 118, 131, and 209, as members of the same family. After relationship had been established between these, the Ferrar family, and the Codex Koridethi, B. H. Streeter, in *The Four Gospels* (London 1924; rev. 1930; repr. 1953), postulated the existence of a local, so-called Caesarean text of the Gospels. K. Lake, R. P. Blake, and S. New made a brilliant corporate effort to recover this text in "The Caesarean Text of the Gospel of Mark" [*Harvard Theological Review* 21 (1928) 207–404], in which they published a reconstruction of Mark ch. 1, 6, and 11 in this form. However, the discovery of P 45 showed that the "Caesarean" text had roots in Egypt. In projected studies on Family II, Geerlings hoped to shed more light on this intricate phase of the history of the NT text.

Greek NT Lectionaries. For the convenience of monks and clerics, volumes of liturgical readings from the Gospels and Epistles, called lectionaries, were compiled as early as the 6th century. Of the 1,838 of these in Gregory's list, fewer than 200 are uncials, and more than 1,200 contain readings from the Gospels only. Since most of them have not been investigated critically, their value as witnesses to the NT text is still unknown. To remedy this neglect, E. C. Colwell and D. W. Riddle inaugurated the series *Studies in the Lectionary Text of the New Testament* with their *Prolegomena to the Study of the Lection-*

ary Text of the Gospels (Chicago 1933). This series reached its fifth study with the monograph of William D. Bray, *The Weekday Lessons from Luke in the Greek Gospel Lectionary* (Chicago 1959). Since these researches have reached only the preliminary stages, results are not conclusive. Indications are that the lectionaries may belong predominantly to the Byzantine text-type but may at times support ancient readings.

Patristic Citations. Additional information about the text of the NT can be gleaned also from citations of ecclesiastical writers and Fathers of the Church, especially those who wrote before the widely diffused Byzantine text began to prevail in the 7th century. Gathering and evaluating this information is extremely difficult because of the lack of reliable critical editions and uncertainty about the accuracy of citations. Up to the 1960s, evidence had often been inconclusive. In his introduction to the pioneering study of P. M. Barnard, *The Biblical Text of Clement of Alexandria in the Four Gospels* (*Texts and Studies* 5; Cambridge 1899), F. C. Burkitt weakened Hort's theory of a neutral text by concluding that Clement was a witness for the Western text-type, related to the Sinaitic Syriac version of the Gospels. In the Pauline Epistles G. Zuntz cites Clement as having made use of a proto-Alexandrian text.

In three articles in the *Journal of Theological Studies* from 1935 to 1937, R. V. G. Tasker presented evidence to show that the text of ORIGEN (d. *c.* 254) usually follows the Alexandrian type but offers Caesarean readings in parts of Matthew and John. Although no critical edition of St. John Chrysostom is available, those who have investigated NT citations in his writings are agreed that he is not the father of the Byzantine text and that his text differed from that of any extant MS. He evidently combined readings from more than one source for greater clarity. In his study *The Gospel Text of Cyril of Jerusalem* (Copenhagen 1955) J. G. Greenlee indicated that Cyril's text was ''pre-Caesarean'' with similarities to Sinaiticus for the synoptics but a popular type for John. Among contemporary critics, M. E. Boismard places great stress upon the testimony of early ecclesiastical writers, and in his work on John he has shown that at times they witness to readings that may be original, although not found in any extant Greek MS.

PRINTED EDITIONS OF THE NEW TESTAMENT

The use of printing gradually brought to an end the multiplication of textual variants of the NT.

Early Editions. Desiderius ERASMUS published the first printed edition of the NT in a hurried and faulty Greek and Latin edition at Basel in 1516. The Greek text had already been printed in 1514 in the text of D. L. Stunica for the Complutensis POLYGLOT BIBLE of Cardinal XIMÉNEZ, but this edition did not actually appear until 1520. Erasmus used it to improve his 4th edition of 1527.

Critical notations of alternate readings were first added in the margins of the text published by R. ESTIENNE, who edited the text four times from 1546 to 1551. His final edition, which introduced the present division of the text into verses, was often reprinted. Another edition destined to have marked influence upon the diffusion of the NT text for 200 years was produced by the brothers B. and A. Elzevir (Leiden 1624). They introduced their second edition of 1633 as the *textus receptus,* ''the text received'' by all. Although this represents the official text of the Greek Church and is based on the largest number of uncials, e.g., N, Y, V, K, Π, Ω for the NT as a whole and A, E, F, G, H for the Gospels, and the vast majority of cursive manuscripts, this text type is of an inferior critical quality.

Preliminary research to improve the quality of printed editions was made by Richard SIMON, who pointed out the insufficiency of the *textus receptus* in his *Critical History of the NT Text* (London 1689), translated from the French edition of the same year. In 1734 J. A. Bengel made a positive contribution toward an improvement of printed editions by dividing MSS into ''families, tribes and nations,'' thus facilitating a more accurate critical evaluation of their text [*Novum Testamentum graecum* (Tubingen 1734)]. A major improvement in the presentation of MSS in the critical apparatus was introduced by J. J. Wettstein, whose edition was based on 330 MSS. He was the first to designate uncials by capital letters and cursives by Arabic numerals in his sigla, anticipating the system of Gregory [*Novum Testamentum graecum,* 2 v. (Amsterdam 1751–52; photographic reproduction Graz, Austria 1961)]. For his edition of the received text, J. J. Griesbach divided the Gospel MSS into the three classes that were to be commonly accepted, to which he gave the misleading names Western, Alexandrian, and Constantinopolitan recensions (Halle 1777; 2d ed., Leipzig 1796–1806).

Later Improved Editions. Only in 1830 did a NT editor depart from the custom of editing the received text. This was the distinction of the small but revolutionary edition of Karl Lachmann, who published also a larger edition (Berlin 1842–50). His goal was to reproduce the text current in the 4th century, and he limited his edition to a small number of witnesses. The English editor S. P. Tregelles, whose edition was completed after his death by Hort in 1879, likewise concentrated on a limited number of older witnesses. Most famous of all NT editors was Konstantin von TISCHENDORF, who collated and published more than 40 Biblical MSS and produced eight critical editions of the NT with four widely divergent texts. His final text, the 8th *editio critica major* (Leipzig 1865–72), was marred by his excessive preference for the readings of Codex Sinaiticus, which he had recently discovered. The lengthy introductory volume, which his pupil C. R. Gregory worked 22 years to write, is still a fundamental source of information about NT MSS, although surpassed and antiquated in many ways.

The 19th-century text that proved most decisive for NT studies was the result of 28 years of collaboration between Brooke Foss WESTCOTT, later an Anglican bishop, and Fenton John Anthony Hort [*The New Testament in Greek,* 2 v. (London 1881; 2nd ed. 1898)]. In contrast to Tischendorf, who refused to rely on the classification of MSS, this edition insisted that the history of the text must be considered in order to arrange the MSS according to their exact critical value. Hort's introductory volume, which is a treatise on NT textual criticism, explains that their text is based on "the best documentary evidence." To find this, MSS were divided into four classes, neutral, Western, Alexandrian, and Syrian. Internal criticism was to remain supplementary (see paras. 76 and 82). Critics found fault with the narrow basis for choosing the text, and the editor of the second edition, Francis Crawford BURKITT, acknowledged this fault (additional note to para. 170), because the discovery of the Old Syrian palimpsest of the Gospels by Mrs. Agnes Lewis in 1892 had emphasized the possibility that other combinations of witnesses, such as agreement of versions, could command more critical reliability than the primary Greek witnesses. As early as 1904, K. Lake called the edition by Westcott and Hort "a failure, though a splendid one." A generation later, comparing the work of Westcott-Hort with that of Marie Joseph LAGRANGE, he commented that perhaps no thesis more subjective than that of Hort ever existed [*Revue biblique* 48 (1939) 498]. The edition was attacked also because of its hypothesis of a neutral or uncontaminated text in Codex B and because the editors used internal criticism in a way incompatible with their stated principles. An effort to make greater use of all MS witnesses including the ancient versions appears in the edition of Bernard Weiss (Leipzig 1894–1900; 2nd ed. 1905), but it also depends chiefly upon Codex B.

The fruits of the critical researches on the NT text by Tischendorf, Westcott-Hort, and Weiss have been widely diffused chiefly through the frequently edited manual edition of Eberhard Nestle [*Novum Testamentum graece* (Stuttgart 1898)]. Its fourth edition was used also as the text of the first edition of the NT by the British and Foreign Bible Society. During its 24 editions the Nestle publication has incorporated new information on the text as far as possible in its present format. K. Aland, who along with Erwin Nestle is the current editor, is preparing an entirely new edition in a new format that will represent a major revision.

The last complete critical edition was prepared by a staff of 40 under the direction of H. von Soden [*Die Schriften des neuen Testaments in ihren ältesten erreichbaren Textgestalt,* 2 v. (Berlin-Göttingen 1902–13)]. After a thorough examination of the Greek MSS, he divided them into three recensions: H (Eta) by Hesychius in Egypt; I (Iota or Jerusalem) by Pamphilius of Caesarea, and K (Kappa) by Lucian of Antioch. Although Von Soden's text and new system of sigla were severely criticized, his introductory studies on the MSS contain information of great value. His critical researches influenced the manual editions of three Catholic editors. These were Heinrich Joseph Vogels, *Novum Testamentum graece* (Düsseldorf 1920; 3rd ed. Herder, Freiburg 1950); J. M. Bover, *Novi Testamenti Biblia* (Madrid 1943; 3rd ed. 1953), and Augustin Merk, *Novum Testamentum graece et latine* (Rome 1933; 8th ed. by J. P. Smith 1957). A revised edition of the last mentioned has been announced.

In an attempt to provide an edition of the NT with a more complete and accurate critical apparatus than was available, a committee of English scholars undertook the project and entrusted editorship to S. C. E. Legg. Severe criticism of the two volumes that appeared, Mark in 1935 and Matthew in 1940 (Oxford), caused a modification of plans. To prepare this complete critical apparatus an international committee was set up with M. M. Parvis as American secretary; the British secretary, G. D. Kilpatrick, was also editor of the second edition of the Greek NT of the British and Foreign Bible Society (London 1958). Another smaller international NT project was begun in 1956 under the direction of the American Bible Society and similar groups in other countries. The editorial committee undertook to prepare a new critical text with a limited apparatus of variants having theological and exegetical importance, and an accompanying supplement to explain the choice of readings adopted.

Bibliography: V. TAYLOR, *The Text of the NT: A Short Introduction* (New York 1961). F. G. KENYON and A. W. ADAMS, *Our Bible and the Ancient Manuscripts* (5th ed. rev. New York 1958). B. BOTTE, "Manuscrits grecs du NT," *Dictionnaire de la Bible,* suppl. ed. L. PIROT et al. (Paris 1928–) 5:819–835. G. ZUNTZ, *The Text of the Epistles* (New York 1953). W. H. P. HATCH, *The Principal Uncial Manuscripts of the NT,* with 76 plates (Chicago 1939). K. and S. LAKE, eds., *Dated Greek Minuscule MSS to the Year 1200,* with 150 tables (Boston 1934–38). M. M. PARVIS and A. P. WIKGREN, eds., *NT Manuscript Studies* (Chicago 1950). B. M. METZGER, *The Text of the New Testament* (New York 1964). L. VAGANAY, *An Introduction to the Textual Criticism of the NT,* tr. B. V. MILLER (St. Louis 1937). *Encyclopedic Dictionary of the Bible,* tr. and adap. by L. HARTMAN (New York 1963) 2419–22.

[J. M. REESE]

BIBLE, IRISH VERSIONS

That Irish scholars busied themselves with Biblical translation from very early times can be deduced from the many Latin manuscripts of Holy Scripture that are glossed with Irish words. Homilies contain many fragments of translation from both the OT and NT, but there is no complete translation of the Bible in Old or Middle Irish.

Protestant. In 1571 Queen Elizabeth I sent a font of type and a press to Dublin for the printing of the Bible in Irish, with the prayerful hope "that God in His mercy would raise up someone to translate the New Testament in Irish." In 1573 the translation was begun, and William O'Donnell, a Fellow of Trinity College, Dublin, signed the preface to the complete work in 1602. However, the sheets were not folded for the binder before the Queen died, and a dedication to King James was prefixed to the work. In 1629 William Bedell was consecrated bishop of Kilmore, and at 58 he began to study Irish with a view of producing a complete Irish Bible. He engaged Murtagh O'Conga, an excellent Irish scholar, to help him translate the NT. This Irish Bible was translated from the English version, and there were some misunderstandings of the original at times. Robert Boyle, the physicist, was greatly interested in the Irish Scriptures and paid for the printing in 1685. Fifty copies of the OT were sent to Scotland for the use of the Gaelic-speaking Highlanders, and eventually, by 1767, a translation into Scottish-Gaelic was published, based on the Irish translation. Whitley Stokes, a Trinity College professor of physics and grandfather of the great Celtic scholar of the same name, published a new translation of the Gospel of Luke and the Acts of the Apostles in 1799, and the four Gospels and the Acts in both Irish and English in 1806. In 1817 the British and Foreign Bible Society published the complete Irish Bible.

Catholic. In 1858 Abp. John MacHale of Tuam began a translation of the Vulgate Bible into Irish, but it did not go beyond the Pentateuch, although the title page called for the translation as far as Josue. It was published in 1861 with an English version from the Douay and some notes. Father Peter O'Leary, one of the founders of the Society for the Preservation of the Irish Language, published a translation of the Gospels in 1904. The late Msgr. Padraig de Brun, Rector of University College, Galway, published a new translation of the NT from the Greek in 1929.

Bibliography: *Bibliography of Irish Philology and of Printed Irish Literature* (Dublin 1913) 243–244. R. I. BEST, *Bibliography of Irish Philology and Manuscript Literature: 1913–1941* (Dublin 1942) 2047–48. T. K. ABBOTT, "On the History of the Irish Bible," *Hermathena* 17 (1912) 29–50. E. R. M. DIX, "The First Printing of the N.T. at Dublin," *Proceedings of the Royal Irish Academy*, sec. C. no. 6, 29 (1911) 180–185; "The N.T. in Erse," *Acts of Privy Council of England (sub anno 1587) in Printing in Dublin prior to 1601* (2d ed. Dublin 1932) 32.

[R. T. MEYER]

BIBLE CYCLES IN ART

By Bible cycle is meant an organic complex of visual representations intended to illustrate either various phases or aspects of one Biblical subject, or many Biblical subjects bound together by a single "thematic" idea.

EARLY CHRISTIAN

The decorations found in the catacombs and on the earliest Christian tombs are the first examples of Bible cycles in art. These date from the 2d and 3d centuries A.D. and are based upon themes of a symbolical nature. A few isolated exceptions, such as the 2d-century frescoes in the cemetery of Priscilla (Rome) of the "Virgin, the Child and Isaia" and the "Breaking of the Bread," are of a more concrete narrative character. The cycles of symbolical reference are interpreted according to the taste and style of composition characteristic of contemporary late Imperial painting. With only a few strokes of striking visual concreteness, the figures are depicted either alone or in groups on a white background, skillfully arranged in the allotted spaces and unified by the symmetry of the composition. The pictorial cycle of this "impressionistic" type succeeds, despite its sketchlike quality, in evoking with immediacy people and events from the Bible stories. Presented, as they are, in a single organic unit, the figures are gradually transformed into "symbols," sensible images of transcendent values.

Sepulchral Art. Early Christian catacomb and tomb art, especially in Rome, provides typical examples of the Bible cycles. The frescoes in a cubicle of the Roman catacomb of Saints Peter and Marcellinus have figures of Lazarus, Moses, Noah praying, and the three Magi on the walls; on the ceiling, in the center, is the Good Shepherd between four scenes where the stories of Jonah alternate with *ORANS* figures. These Biblical representations are clearly symbolic of faith in the divinity of the Redeemer risen from the dead. Also typical are the representations of Daniel in the lions' den in the catacomb of Lucina, or those of Noe in the ark in the catacomb of Domitilla, both symbolizing the mystery of the Resurrection. This kind of cycle was created to present the Biblical incidents to viewers with an adequate spiritual preparation. The depicted events recall facts or ideas that were well known and whose transcendent meaning could be evoked from the images presented.

A similar aim is seen in the early Christian tombs. Here, the plastic figuration tends to acquire a conscious artistic autonomy, and in addition there is greater interest in the narrative as such, over and above the idea that it symbolizes (sarcophagus of Jona, no. 119, Lateran Museum, Rome). The general theme of the Resurrection of Christ, recalled in a series of episodes from the Old and New Testaments, is overshadowed by the capricious ornament, laden with Hellenistic accents. Analogous in spirit but more typically Roman in style and dating from the height of the 4th century, is the sarcophagus of Junius Bassius (Grottoes of the Vatican). Lastly, of decidedly narrative character and showing a conscious intent to celebrate the mystery, is the sarcophagus of the Passion (no. 171; Lateran, Rome). Here the emphasis is on the cross in the central panel, surmounted by the monogram of Christ within a triumphal crown. There are many other contemporary examples similar in spirit and emphasis in which, however, the youthful and triumphant figure of Christ usually appears on a throne in place of the cross.

4th and 5th Centuries. Bible cycles found in the basreliefs of sarcophagi of the 4th and 5th centuries are clearly narrative in character and have a strong dramatic unity (nos. 135, 125, 155, and 183, Lateran Museum, Rome; sarcophagus of Adelfia, Syracuse Museum). They have a figurative quality that is free of the mannerisms of late classical art, and is founded on a previously unknown historical understanding of religious truths. Later, this conception became a strong determining force in neo-Latin art and civilization.

Among the earliest exemplifications of this tendency are the mosaics of the nave of St. Mary Major in Rome, depicting stories from the Old Testament, and those of the triumphal arch, with the glorification of Mary and stories of the childhood of Christ. The cycle was executed during the pontificate of Sixtus III (432–40). The mosaics of the nave are clearly in the Western tradition; they are constructed with a dramatic power and a solid sense of volumes, as if they had been produced by "tachist" brush strokes. In the triumphal arch, on the other hand, the symmetrical rows of flat-frontal figures produce an effect of hieratic solemnity.

Only a few decades later, the mosaics of the triumphal arch of the Roman basilica of St. Paul-Outside-the-Walls, created by order of Galla Placidia in the last years of her reign, show the fulfillment of the early Western style. The 24 Elders of the Revelation are represented in a rhythmic procession in two parallel lines. Clad in white robes, they stand out majestically against a gold background, which emphasizes the strikingly tragic and severe face of Christ the Judge in the center. The face of Christ is placed in even stronger relief by a radiant halo of sharply contrasting color.

Art of this period suggested intimate and profound sensitivity that was to strengthen the historical consciousness of the neo-Latin world. Foreshadowings of the coming changes of values can be seen in fundamental works of the 5th century: the wooden doors of St. Sabina in Rome, with events from the life of Christ and of Moses, and those of St. Ambrose in Milan, with episodes from the life of David; also (though in the 6th century) the Evangeliary of St. Augustine at Cambridge (Corpus Christi College, MS 286), and the mosaics of the chapel of S. Vittore in Ciel d'Oro in Milan.

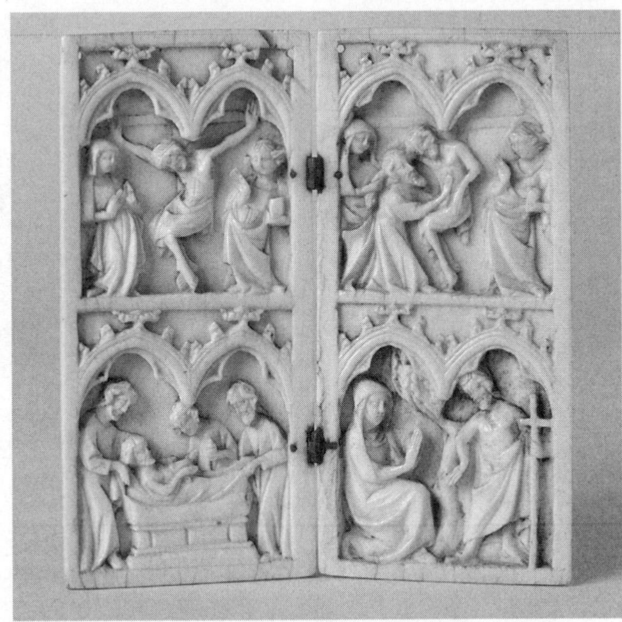

Ivory diptych showing four scenes from "The Passion of Christ": the "Crucifixion," "Deposition from the Cross," "The Entombment of Christ": "Noli Me Tangere (Don't Touch Me)." (©Arte & Immagini srl/CORBIS)

Ravenna. In Italy the passing of the early style tradition is evident in the mosaics of Ravenna, especially in the New Testament series of the nave of S. Apollinare Nuovo, which dates from the period of Theodoric. A highly refined culture is evident in the pictures filled with Christological scenes, on the upper parts of the walls, where the serene balance of the composition and the softly blended colors give the story depicted an unreal and dreamlike distance. The dramatic austerity of the mosaics of St. Paul is exhibited through silent, linear figures of far greater rhythmic rigor—in the series of the Prophets, on a golden background between the windows; as in the two "Theophanies" around Mary and Christ below. In the mosaics of S. Apollinare in Classe, the most subtle harmonies of color and composition envelop in an immobile silence scenes depicted with a striking descriptive power. There is in them an almost surrealistic clarity.

The same values are continued with more consistency in the mosaic cycles of the presbytery and the apse of

"Finding of Moses," detail, one of several depictions by Tintoretto, 16th century. (©Francis G. Mayer/CORBIS)

S. Vitale at Ravenna (6th century), which celebrate the prefiguration of the Eucharistic Sacrifice in the deeds of Moses, Abraham, and Melchizedek.

EARLY MEDIEVAL

A complicated theological program guided the development of the Biblical cycles in mosaic work, which superseded the earlier abstract type of decoration, in the basilicas of the Holy Apostles and of Hagia Sophia in Constantinople, of the Dormition of the Virgin in Nicaea (destroyed 1921–22), and of St. Demetrius at Salonika. The mosaics of the latter closely resemble contemporary work in S. Vitale.

Byzantine. The initial golden period of Byzantine civilization, from the beginning of the 6th century to the iconoclastic crisis, presents the triumph of the Biblical cycle, especially in the field of illumination work, of which authentic masterpieces are still extant: the Vienna Genesis and the Paris Gospel of St. Matthew from Sinope (Bibliothèque Nationale); the so-called Purple Codex of Rossano (Treasury of the Cathedral), whole pages of which are decorated with miniatures in which the almost complete disappearance of landscape elements and nervous proportions accompany the abstract theological theme of the typological relation between the prophecies of the Old Testament and the events of the New Testament; the 6th-century Syrian Codexes of Paris (Bibliothèque Nationale) and the Gospel Book of Rabbula (Laurentian Library, Florence).

In Rome the principal monumental cycles of the 7th and 8th centuries are characterized by fidelity to the classical tradition (frescoes of S. Maria Antiqua and those in the catacomb of Commodilla; mosaics in the oratory of John VII) and by the presence of a Greek stylistic manner analagous, for example, to that of the mosaic cycle of St. Catherine at Sinai (7th century). Thus Christian art, both Eastern and Western, reflected the consequences of the iconoclastic crisis whose effects persisted even after its official end in 843. Only in this period did Biblical cycles of great importance reappear, in general, in European painting, sculpture, and illumination work, and not only in art of Byzantine inspiration. More ancient examples of cycles had appeared in Rome or within its sphere of influence, for instance in the mosaics of the triumphal arch, of the apse, and of the chapel of St. Zeno in S. Prassede in Rome (early 9th century), and the frescoes of the church of S. Vincenzo of Volturno (826–43).

"The Epiphany" and "The Adoration of the Magi," part of a cycle by Hieronymus Bosch, c. 1510. (©Francis G. Mayer/CORBIS)

In the Byzantine world during the middle decades of the 9th century, after more than a century there was, on the whole, a resumption of the forms and artistic preferences of the period immediately preceding the iconoclastic crisis. Important examples are the Vatican copy (MS gr. 699) of the *Cosmographia Cristiana* of Cosma Indicopleuste, dating from the second half of the century, and the collection of the *Sermons* of St. Gregory of Paris (Bibliothèque Nationale, gr. 510) executed in Constantinople around 880 for Basilius I, founder of the Macedonian dynasty.

Several great Italian mosaic cycles of a later date also belong to the sphere of Byzantine artistic culture; these include the cycles of Martorana and of the Cappella Palatina in Palermo (*c.* 1150); New Testament mosaics in the cathedral of Cefalù (*c.* 1150); mosaics of the cathedral of Monreale (*c.* 1776–89); those of the nave (*c.* 1150) and the porch (early 13th century) in St. Mark's, Venice; and mosaics of the cathedral of Torcello (*c.* 1210–20).

Carolingian. In Western Europe, the artistic renaissance under CHARLEMAGNE (emperor 800–14) was accompanied by a revival of interest in history that was manifested in the triumphal return of cycles of religious, and especially Biblical, subjects regarded as histories valid in themselves over and above any symbolism. The admirable frescoes of S. Maria Foras Portas at Castelseprio belong to the Carolingian period, even though their style springs from an Oriental culture, and they were probably executed by Greek artists. The frescoes depict the story of Mary and the childhood of Jesus according to the apocryphal gospels of the Oriental tradition. Local artists were responsible for the almost contemporary frescoes of St. John at Münster (in a high valley of the Grisons), which narrate with stiff forms in the Byzantine style, but with expressionistic vigor, the stories of David and of Christ along the walls of the nave. The exaltation of the Redeemer is depicted in the three apses, with the Last Judgment on the inner facade. Such an arrangement

Frontispiece to Thomas Heskyn's "The Parliament of Christe (Upon the matter of the B. Sacrament)," published at Antwerp in 1566.

became common in western Europe during the Middle Ages.

Manuscript Illumination. From this period on, there was an immense flowering of Biblical cycles in the illuminated manuscripts of the Gospels, of the Psalters, and, in general, of religious books. There was a resurgence of classic influences in the sphere of Byzantine art, beginning before the 9th century and continuing into the succeeding centuries (Paris *Psalter,* Bibliothèque Nationale, gr. 139; the Vatican Bible, Reg. Svev. gr. I; the *Joshua Roll,* Vatican Library, Palat. graeco. gr. 431), characterized by very conservative tendencies both in style and in iconography. Only in the 11th century, for example, does a *Book of the Gospels* of Paris (Bibliothèque Nationale, gr. 74) offer one of the first examples of the insertion of the Gospel parables into an iconographic setting of strictly Byzantine origin. Analogous conservative characteristics and tendencies appear also in 11th-century monumental cycles such as that of the church of St. Luke in Phocis, the mosaics in Hagia Sophia in Constantinople, and the mosaic cycles of the church of Nea Moni of Chios and the church at Daphni. In these last two, however, the New Testament iconography is relatively renewed by themes from the apocryphal gospels and above all by themes freed from their traditional liturgical references.

Biblical illumination of German manuscripts by the school of Ada (9th century) limits figurative art almost entirely to the frontispieces, full-page illuminations, and small scenes contained within the capital letters. Several characteristic cycles of the Passion done in ivory can be attributed to the influence of the school of Ada; scenes are carved in a closely fitted series of squares surrounding the central figure of Christ Crucified, as in the ivory cover of the Codex at Munich (*c.* 870; Clm. 4452) and the ivory of Narbonne (9th to 10th century; Cathedral Museum). Throughout the 10th and 11th centuries, under the influence of the Ottonian civilization, the German illumination work of the school of Reichenau, fresco cycles of St. George at Oberzell, St. Sylvester at Goldbach and of Echternach display a taste for narrative that displays complete stylistic freedom; its fundamental roots are classical and early Christian in origin, but to it have been added the influences of the Carolingian renaissance. Among the best examples are: *Codex Egberti,* of Trier; the Evangelistary of Otto III, at Munich (Clm. 4453); the Golden Evangelistary of Henry III, at the Escorial; *Codex aureus Epternacensis* at Nuremberg; Book of the Pericopes of Henry II, at Munich (Clm. 4452); and the Evangelistary of Otto at Aquisgrana.

English illumination work is related also to the school of Reichenau. The principal centers in England, Winchester and Canterbury, produced the Benedictional of St. Aethelwold by Godeman, School of Winchester, 975 to 980 (British Museum); the Evangelistary of Grimbald (British Museum, Add. 34890, London); Caedmon's *Poem* (Bodleian Library, Oxford). The same influence is apparent in other sectors of the figurative arts: the Biblical cycles of the Milanese and Spanish ivories; the ciborium of St. Ambrose and the Arca Santa of Orvieto; the bronze doors of Bernward in the cathedral of Hildesheim; and the cathedrals of Augusta and of Novgorod.

HIGH MEDIEVAL

The Bible cycles of the Romanesque and Gothic periods manifest an increased complexity in their arrangement and give evidence of new artistic and spiritual values.

Romanesque. From the 11th century to the beginning of the 12th, Romanesque sculpture was almost entirely devoted to Biblical figures, arranged in true, organic cycles. French sculpture was the guiding source of European taste. The leading schools were those of Aquitaine (St. Saturnin in Toulouse and the abbey church of Moissac); of Burgundy (the abbey church of Cluny, the priory of Anzy-le-Duc, and St. Lazare at Autun); of Provence (St. Gilles at Saint-Gilles-du-Gard and St. Trophîme at Arles); and of Auvergne (Saint-Foy at Conques). In Italian sculpture, in addition to schools such as the Lombardian and Emilian, there are individual artists of primary importance. Among them was WILIGELMO, who created (*c.* 1099–1106) one of the noblest Biblical bas-reliefs of Genesis in the cathedral of Modena. In the intimate dialogue between our first parents and a very human God, as in the tragedy of Cain, Wiligelmo exalts human energy, for the first time in medieval Europe, with a force equal to the dolorous physical appearance of the bodies, which seem almost to burst forth from the confines of the limited space.

Gothic. The cycles of the Old and New Testament by Benedetto Antelami in the baptistery of Parma, at Borgo S. Donnino, and S. Andrea at Vercelli (*c.* 1196–1225) display a dynamism of genuinely Gothic inspiration. Parallels to the work of Antelami may be found in the oldest examples of the French *Bible moralisé* and the German *Biblia pauperum.* The sculpture of the Gothic Biblical cycles of France and northern Europe in the 13th and 14th centuries is dramatic and moving. The important masterworks include the reliefs of the Old Testament of the north portal of the cathedral of Chartres; the sculptures of the ''Master of Nuremberg'' at Magonza and Nuremberg; the Biblical reliefs of the choir of Nôtre-Dame of Paris; and the portals with New Testament cycles around the ''Crucifixion'' of St. Gilles, Strasbourg, and Reims.

Stained-glass windows presented Bible cycles in the 13th, 14th, and 15th centuries, reaching extraordinary mastery in the New Testament windows of the south nave of the cathedral of Chartres and those of Saint Remi at Reims. The tradition of the Bible cycle in manuscript illumination was continued by the celebrated miniaturist Jean de Berry, and by Bohemian miniaturists, especially those of the court of Charles IV of Prague.

The 13th-century Italian artist Niccolò Pisano created the Biblical cycles of the pulpits of the baptistery of Pisa and of the cathedral of Siena, and collaborated with his son Giovanni on the sculptures of the fountains of Perugia. He combined the unity characteristic of classic Latin art with lively action and sensitivity of style. The Nativity and the Crucifixion at Pisa and the Massacre of the Innocents and the Last Judgment at Siena are revivals of classical sculpture.

The work of Arnolfo di Cambio, and of Giovanni Pisano, and their collaborators was inspired by the art of Niccolò Pisano. In the cycles from the Old and New Testament in the pulpits of the cathedral of Pisa and in S. Andrea at Pistoia, as well as on the façade of the cathedral of Siena, Giovanni Pisano expressed power in clear Gothic style.

Influence of St. Francis. The effect upon 13th-century Italian art of Franciscan spirituality, in particular with reference to the iconography of the New Testament, was visible in a new interpretation of the humanity of Christ. A new version of the ''suffering Christ'' replacing the medieval conception of the Crucified Christ as the Judge, or King, is exemplified by the ''Crucifixion'' of Giunta Pisano in S. Domenico, Bologna.

The New Testament cycles in mosaic of the life of the Virgin by Pietro Cavallini in S. Maria in Trastevere (*c.* 1291) and the frescoes of St. Cecilia in Rome, though in a certain sense parallel to the classical revival of Niccolò Pisano, reflect also the new iconography of Franciscan origin. The same may be said for the work of Torriti and the so-called ''Master of Isacco,'' who produced the frescoes in the church of St. Francis in Assisi, and, above all, for the Old and New Testament cycles created by Cimabue in the upper church of St. Francis in Assisi. In paintings of the ''Assumption'' and the ''Crucifixion'' the Florentine artist combined ancient iconography with a fresh human concreteness.

New Testament iconography was given a new expression in the same period in the cycle of stories of Mary and Christ painted by the Sienese artist Duccio in a series of paintings for the front and back of the altar, comprising his famous ''Majesty'' (Museum of the Cathedral, Siena). Duccio's pictorial invention is equal to that of Cimabue in exquisiteness of style.

EARLY RENAISSANCE

At the beginning of the 14th century, GIOTTO painted the life of Christ and of Mary in fresco (1303–1305) in the chapel of the Scrovegni in Padua. Giotto's psychological insight underlines in the divine history the essential motives of the soul and of human action, presenting them with an almost violent clarity and showing a masterly disposition of the figures in space. A revolution in the relations between man and his natural surroundings foreshadowed the humanistic arrangement achieved in the 15th century in the Florentine Renaissance.

Representative of the continuing transition in Bible cycles are the bas-reliefs of Andrea Pisano on the doors of the baptistery and the bell tower of Florence; Ghiberti's doors for the same baptistery; the sculptures of the baptismal font of the cathedral of Siena; and the Biblical bas-reliefs of Jacopo della Quercia in the portal of St. Petronius at Bologna.

Masaccio and Donatello. The frescoes of Masaccio in the Brancacci chapel of the Carmine of Florence, including the ''Banishment of Adam and Eve'' and the ''Stories of St. Peter'' (1424–1427), emphasize in principal figures like Christ and St. Peter an emotion that binds the landscape and the men into a ''perspective'' unity at once both physical and spiritual, and of striking epic power.

In the cycle of the Passion sculptured by Donatello in the pulpits of S. Lorenzo in Florence, moral suffering is rendered in a tormented style. In the ''Deposition'' the important figures and all three crosses are in dramatic high relief; moreover, the center perspective toward which all the architectural and construction lines lead, is placed outside the limits of the composition. In this way the artist represented the tragic human events of the scene centered on Mary and the dead body of Christ as a ''fragment'' of a much greater picture whose limits cannot be measured by human means.

But formal balance was retained in the cycles of frescoes of Fra Angelico portraying scenes from the life of Mary and Christ in the convent of San Marco in Florence and the stories of Saints Stephen and Lawrence from the Acts of the Apostles in the chapel of Nicholas V in the Vatican. The interpretation from a humanistic viewpoint given by the Florentine Renaissance to Biblical subjects virtually dominated European art until the beginning of the 17th century. Thereafter, new interpretations affected the form of the Bible cycles.

Northern Symbolism and Italian Rationalism. One case, however, of striking independence stands out in painting in the ''Mystical Lamb'' of Ghent, painted in 1439 by Van Eyck. This is a huge complex of the greatest themes of the Old and New Testament, skillfully bound together by light and by symbolical elements, the whole center of interest being the Lamb. In effect the densely populated background is flooded with the sunlight of a bright morning hour.

Flemish art continued through the 15th and 16th centuries to express religious themes in a symbolic manner. The use of symbols was sometimes almost obsessive and in strong contrast to the clear, analytical, concrete use of pictorial material. Works of this kind include the ''Seven Capital Sins,'' the ''Parables,'' the ''Garden of Delights,'' and the many aspects of the Passion by Hieronymus Bosch; and the ''Triumph of Death'' and the ''Parables'' of Pieter Brueghel.

Italian Renaissance painting, on the other hand, was marked by a rational interpretation of Biblical themes. The emotional content was not diminished, but there was clearer harmony in the forms and more concrete employment of human elements. Among the most important Italian cycles around the turn of the 15th century were the frescoes with parallel scenes of the Old and New Testaments executed by PERUGINO, Pinturicchio, Signorelli, Ghirlandaio, Botticelli, C. Rosselli, and Piero di Cosimo on the lower part of the walls of the SISTINE CHAPEL in the Vatican; the fresco cycle of the ''Novissima'' by Signorelli in the cathedral of Orvieto (*c.* 1499); the New Testament ceramics of the DELLA ROBBIAS in the sanctuary of Alvernia; and the frescoes of Fra Lippo Lippi in the cathedral of Prato and of Gozzoli in the chapel of the Medici. The subject of Piero della Francesca's fresco cycle of the ''Legend of the Cross'' in the church of St. Francis in Arezzo was a derivation from the sacred history recorded in the New Testament. Piero's cycle, as well as the frescoes executed in the 16th century by Raphael in the Vatican stanze, synthesize the artistic and religious culture both of the artists and of the civilization in which they lived. The ''Last Supper'' of Leonardo da Vinci was the culmination of the synthesis.

HIGH RENAISSANCE TO MODERN

From the late 15th century to the 17th century the Bible cycles in European painting occurred in various and rich succession under the inspiration of earlier art.

Michelangelo. The cyclical works of MICHELANGELO include ''Genesis'' on the ceiling (1508 to 1512), the ''Last Judgment'' behind the altar (1536 to 1541) of the Sistine Chapel, and the frescoes of the Pauline Chapel in the Vatican (1546). They are the greatest works of their kind. The artist penetrates the depths of religious mysteries. The ceiling seems so molded by the painting that the cornices around the gigantic scenes appear real and firmly constructed. They bind the composition together and repeat the vibrant movement in the groups of Prophets, Sibyls, and naked figures that animate the interior of the structures. By contrast, in the ''Last Judgment'' no linear frames obstruct the whirling movement of the bodies, either tossed down or upraised as if by the power in the arm of Christ, who is at the center of a composition marked by continuous vertical ascending and descending movement. The frescoes of the Pauline Chapel show a new contrast. A silent landscape spreads out beyond the tightly knit human group surrounding Peter's inverted cross. The Apostle's figure, with eyes glaring at the viewer, produces a dramatic complement to the rearing, isolated horse in the center of the ''Conversion of St. Paul'' that serves to measure the distance from the deserted horizon.

Tintoretto and Others. The artistic productions that appeared in the wake of Michelangelo's supreme effort exhibit the widest ranging imagination; they include the colossal and intensely moving cycle of huge canvases of the Old and New Testaments painted by Tintoretto for the Scuola of S. Rocco in Venice (1564 to 1587) and the numerous Biblical paintings of Titian, Veronese, Lotto, and Jacopo Bassano. The spectacular Bible cycles by the ''Sacri Monti'' of the 16th, 17th, and 18th centuries, especially the work of Varallo, are in every sense of the word sacred representations from the plastic, pictorial, and architectural viewpoint.

New Trends. The work of Caravaggio is symptomatic of the progressive decline of interest in the creation of organic Biblical cycles after the Renaissance. Although Caravaggio was a brilliant painter his attention was centered on brief fragments of reality, and then was concentrated in compositions of extreme formal purity, with light audaciously used against solidly dark backgrounds. It was the beginning of a new age in European art, which—with an intensification of impassioned, personal research, and the vivid awareness of the value of the individual—lost contact with the sense of history as a series of universal events in which the individual had a part.

Two fundamental lines of development can be discerned in the 17th and 18th centuries. First, there was a tendency to paint sumptuous, superficial canvases on sacred themes, sometimes for their scenic effects, as in the work of Carracci, Gaulli, Pozzo, Piazzetta, Ricci, and Tiepolo; sometimes for their episodic value, as in the elaborate, affected type of sacred painting produced by Flemish, Dutch, and German artists, as well as those of Brescia and Bologna, which gave rise to genre painting; and sometimes for purely decorative effect, as in Tiepolo's cycle in the cathedral of Udine or that of Guardi in St. Raphael in Venice.

The second line of development tended to render the Biblical theme subjective, either by a tormented, personal search or by a fragmentary view of reality from which the specific sense of the sacred was banished, even though generalized spiritual values remained. The highest point in the art of personal search was reached in the throbbing luminosity of Rembrandt's paintings, which shifted the focus to the human and immeasurable vastness of dark spaces. In the art of generalized spiritual values, while Velázquez made decisive advances, the greatest developments were made in the 18th, 19th, and 20th centuries in the social interpretations of Goya and Millet, the chromatic transfigurations of Van Gogh, Gauguin, and Matisse, and the torturous personal testimonies of Emil Nolde and the German expressionists. In his cycle of the "Passion," Rouault attempted to constitute an organic cycle in the precise sense.

After World War II numerous works of art in cycles appeared, though rarely of purely Biblical subjects. Illustrations for the Bible by Marc Chagall (1956) have a quality of dreamlike, pictorial lightness. The "Door of Death" was created by Manzù for St. Peter's, Rome (1963). In it eight stupendous bas-reliefs suggest by broken rhythms the relation between Biblical and present-day events. It is a vertically oriented composition of utmost purity, crowned by the soaring movement of the "Death of the Virgin" and of the "Crucifixion."

Bibliography: E. STEINMANN, *Die Tituli und die kirchliche Wandmalerei* (Leipzig 1892). J. TIKKANEN, *Die Psalterillustrationen im Mittelalter* (Helsingfors 1895). J. REIL, *Die altchristlichen Bildzyklen des Lebens Jesu* (Leipzig 1910). A. DE LABORDE, *La Bible moralisée*, 4 v. (Paris 1911–21). G. MILLET, *Recherches sur l'iconographie de l'Évangile* (Paris 1916). E. B. SMITH, *Early Christian Iconography* (Princeton 1918). H. CORNELL, *Biblia pauperum* (Stockholm 1925). K. KÜNSTLE, *Ikonographie der christlichen Kunst*, 2 v. (Freiburg 1926–28). E. PANOFSKY, "Imago pietatis," in *Festschrift M. J. Friedländer* (Leipzig 1927). H. SCHRADE, *Zur Ikonographie der Himmelfahrt Christi* (Vorträge der Bibliothek Warburg 1928–29). H. VON CAMPENHAUSEN, *Die Passionssarkophage* (Marburg 1929). E. SANDBERG VAVALÀ, *La Croce dipinta italiana* (Verona 1929). H. SCHRADE, *Ikonographie der christlichen Kunst* (Berlin 1932). É. MÂLE, *L'Art religieux de la fin du XVIe siècle, du XVIIe siècle et du XVIII e siècle: Étude sur l'iconographie après le concile de Trente* (2d ed. Paris 1951). A. WALZER, *Das Bildprogramm an den mittelalterlichen Kirchenportalen Frankreichs und Deutschlands* (Leipzig 1938). F. GERKE, *Christus in der spätantiken Plastik* (3d ed. Mainz 1948). K. WEITZMANN, *Die Illustration der Septuaginta* (Munich 1952). *Lukasbücherei zur christlichen Ikonographie* (Düsseldorf 1949–). J. KOLLWITZ, *Das Christusbild des 3. Jahrhunderts* (Münster 1953). L. RÉAU, *Iconographie de l'art chrétien*, 6 v. (Paris 1955–59). A. PIGLER, *Barockthemen,* 2 v. (Budapest 1956), v.1. A. KATZENELLENBOGEN, *The Sculptural Programs of Chartres Cathedral* (Baltimore 1958). E. FRANCESCHINI, "La Bibbia nell'alto Medioevo," in *Nel Bibbia nell'Alto Medioevo* (Spoleto 1963) 13–38. A. GRABAR, "Les Sujets bibliques au service de l'iconographie chrétienne," *ibid.* 387–411. K. HOLTER, "Das Alte und Neue Testament in der Buchmalerei," *ibid.* 413–71.

[A. M. ROMANINI]

BIBLE MORALISÉE

The most complete and systematic commentary of the Bible, both visual and literary; it appeared in the 13th century. The original consists of 5,000 scenes, inscribed in roundels and featuring some 30,000 characters. It is believed to have been dedicated to King Louis IX (1226–70). The manuscript is scattered among the Bodleian Library, Oxford (270b), the Bibliothèque Nationale, Paris (lat. 11560), and the British Museum (Harl. 1526–27). A copy, kept in the library of Vienna, was presented to King Louis IX, and another one is exhibited in the treasure room of the cathedral of Toledo, Spain. There exist various French translations of the Latin original. The scenes are disposed in medallions assembled by pairs in two columns of four, with grounds of alternating color. The chromatic pattern of the ground also alternates between two consecutive folios. The disposition, which is reminiscent of certain stained-glass windows in the Ste-Chapelle of Paris (1248), was used also in the *Psalter of Saint Louis* (The Pierpont Morgan Library). The arrangement was adopted in the 12th century for illustrating the Souvigny Bible, and it was repeated toward the end of the 13th century in the *Albenga Psalter*. The formal connection of the layout of the illustrations in the *Bible Moralisée* with that used in a Psalter from Artois (Bibliothèque Nationale, lat. 10425) suggests that the main artist responsible for planning the decoration of the *Bible Moralisée* may have come from northern France. The illustrations are accompanied by iconographical comments, stressing the parallelism between the "figures," or events, of the Old Testament and the "mysteries" of the New Testament: the life of Christ and the Sacraments. According to an allegorizing exegesis, four meanings are distinguished in the Holy Scripture: *sensus litteralis, sensus allegoricus, sensus tropologicus, sensus anagogicus* (*see* EXEGESIS, BIBLICAL). The scenes illustrate, in preference to the three other meanings, the *sensus tropologicus*; that is, the symbolic imagery of the Old Testament (type) is explained *verbatim*, word for word and image for image, by the revelations of the New Dispensation (antitype). The method is in line with typological art of the 12th century, which originated in the Meuse Valley and was adopted in the abbey church of Saint-Denis by Abbot Suger. On the other hand, the *Bible Moralisée* follows strictly the *Concordantiae* of the Bible by HUGH OF SAINT-CHER and the Dominicans (second quarter of the 13th century). Like Hugh's *Postilla*, the written comments of the medallions in the *Bible Moralisée* expatiate particularly on the moral and disciplinary implications to be derived from the verses of the Bible.

See Also: MANUSCRIPT ILLUMINATION.

Bibliography: A. DE LABORDE, *La Bible Moralisée*, 4 v. (Paris 1911–21).

[P. VERDIER]

BIBLE AND PIETY

The relationship between the written Word of God and Christian spirituality.

Bible and Life. The Bible, since it contains the living Word of God, is the principal source of Christian spirituality and a guide for Christian living, as was already recognized by the biblical writers themselves (2 Tm 3.14–17). The men of the patristic period were particularly conscious of the role of the Word of God in Christian formation. After a period of neglect since the Counter Reformation, the Bible is again assuming its normative function in the lives of the faithful due to the 20th-century biblical revival. The Bible is not a collection of abstract propositions regarding religion and morality, but a sacred history that approaches the relationship between God and man in a concrete, dynamic, and existential manner (Heb 4.12). It is the record of God's revealing Himself in action to His people and summoning them to share in His own happiness. Its precepts and counsels, which are presented in a variety of interlocking themes, must be understood within the framework of this historical context. Despite the variety of materials of which it is composed, the Bible has a unity that confers a Christian meaning upon the entire revelation and supplies a concrete norm for Christian life.

Bible and Prayer. Since prayer is the principal activity of the spiritual life, the influence of the Bible is felt principally in this sphere. The Church makes extensive use of the Bible in her liturgical prayer, which is the model for private prayer. Prayer, the fundamental attitude toward God, is exemplified in the lives of the great figures of the Bible; and it is by steeping himself in the mentality of the Bible that the Christian can best dispose himself for prayer. This requires a meditative reading of the Scriptures, through which man assimilates the living Word of God and thus prepares himself to respond actively to it in personal prayer. Through contact with the Bible, the Christian takes his place in the development of sacred history by passing through the same stages recounted in the scriptural narrative.

Bibliography: A. LEFÈVRE et al., *Dictionnaire de spiritualité ascétique et mystique. Doctrine et histoire,* ed. M. VILLER et al. (Paris 1932–) 4.1:128–278. G. BRILLET, *Guide to the Bible,* ed. A. ROBERT and A. TRICOT, tr. E. P. ARBEZ and M. P. MCGUIRE, 2 v. (Tournai–New York 1951–55; v. 1, rev. and enl. 1960) 2:533–546. N. PETERS and J. DÉCARREAUX, *Notre Bible: Source de vie* (Bruges 1950). C. CHARLIER, *The Christian Approach to the Bible,* tr. H. J. RICHARDS and B. PETERS (Westminster, Md. 1958). L. LELOIR, *La Bibbia, scuola di preghiera* (Quaderni della rivista ''Bibbia e Oriente'' 1; Milan 1959). K. CONDON, *Word of Life* (Westminster, Md. 1960) 112–123. ''Bible, Life and Worship,'' *Proceedings of the 22nd Annual North American Liturgical Week* (Washington 1961). PAUL MARIE OF THE CROSS, *Spirituality of the Old Testament,* tr. E. MCCABE, 3 v. (St. Louis 1961–63).

[C. J. PEIFER]

BIBLIA PAUPERUM

One of the small, late-medieval picture books (*biblia picta*) for religious instruction of the poor in spirit (*pauperes spiritu*); used also by clerics who could not afford a complete Bible or expensive handbooks, such as historiated and moralized Bibles for preaching and catechism. The layout of the material differs according to the quality of the book. In principle, a central roundel or rectangular, picturing one of the most important events of the New Testament (the Annunciation, the Assumption of the Virgin, or the Last Judgment), is surrounded by four half-length figures of Prophets and flanked, on either side, by a roundel or rectangular with typological incidents from the Old Testament. Textual instruction is given in a general title, in an explanation of each of the Old Testament scenes and, on scrolls, in prophetic sayings. The name *Biblia pauperum* occurs only in late manuscripts, but the content of the work is derived from an ancient Christian method of teaching by means of typological picture cycles. It was prepared by an unknown late-13th-century theologian; the oldest manuscripts suggest Bavarian origin. It was particularly popular in Germany, France, and the Low Countries. More than 70 manuscripts (from *c.* 1300), blockbooks (*c.* 1450–80), and incunabula (1st ed., Albert Pfister, Bamberg 1462–63) exist. Together they give about 65 New Testament scenes; texts are in Latin or German. Illustrations differ widely; the usual pen-drawings with washes hardly ever have artistic value.

Bibliography: *Gesamtkatalog der Wiegendrucke* (Leipzig 1925–) 4:4325–27. *Reallexikon zur deutschen Kunstgeschichte*, ed. O. SCHMITT (Stuttgart 1937–) 1:1072–84. P. HEITZ and W. L. SCHREIBER, *Die Entstehung . . . der Biblia pauperum* (Strasbourg 1903). P. KRISTELLER, *Biblia pauperum* (Berlin 1906). H. CORNELL, *Biblia pauperum* (Stockholm 1925). H. ROST, *Die Bibel im Mittelalter* (Augsburg 1939). G. SCHMIDT, *Die Armenbibeln des 14. Jahrhunderts* (Graz-Cologne 1959).

[S. J. P. VAN DIJK]

BIBLICAL ARCHEOLOGY

Biblical archaeology is that branch of Biblical studies that uses the results of relevant archaeological research to illuminate the historical and cultural setting of the Bible. The development of this discipline in the late 20th century was affected by the evolution and refinement of archaeological techniques and the expanding of interests on the part of its practitioners.

Recent Developments. Until the late 20th century Biblical archaeology was almost exclusively interested in reconstructing the political history of ancient Israel. The objective of most excavations was to establish the chronology of sites in order to support the historical value of the Bible—particularly the Hebrew Scriptures. Under the influence of New World archaeology, Biblical archaeology broadened its concerns beyond chronology to the sociology, economy, politics, ecosystems and population patterns in order to reconstruct the entire culture of ancient Palestine from the prehistoric era down to the end of the Byzantine period (7th century A.D.).

Accompanying this shift in interest, Biblical archaeologists employed substantially improved techniques of retrieval, recording and analysis of data. The stratigraphic method of excavation developed in the 1950s was supplemented by photogrammetry and computer graphics. Earlier dating techniques were replaced by scientifically more sophisticated procedures such as chronometric dating, atomic absorption spectrometry, and dendrochronology. One result of this scientific sophistication is the interdisciplinary approach of archaeology. In addition to field archaeologists, excavation projects often employ specialists from the natural and social sciences to retrieve and interpret data.

This development in the technical side of archaeological method was accompanied by important changes in the presuppositions with which Biblical archaeologists have approached their work. Archaeology deals with the material remains of antiquity. The Bible is one of antiquity's literary legacies. In the past, data that came from the former were seen as providing an independent and objective support for the latter with the implication that faith was either dependent upon or perhaps enhanced by a demonstration that the events narrated in the Bible actually happened. Today, Biblical archaeologists see the complementary relationship that exists between the literary and nonliterary sources of knowledge of the Biblical era and its people. They excavate not to prove the historicity of Biblical narratives but to elucidate the meaning of these texts by understanding the people who produced, received, and transmitted them. This understanding is provided by the interpretation of the material remains which these people left behind.

Because of the narrower interests of early archaeologists, sites with connections to the Hebrew Scriptures were once the prime focus of attention. Because of the theological concerns that have characterized NT research it was believed that archaeology could have little more than tangential value for understanding the beginnings of the Christian movement; as a result, NT archaeology scarcely qualified for the status of an academic discipline. Similarly the wealth of literary sources from early Judaism seemed to make excavation of Jewish sites an unnecessary luxury. Today some of the most productive archaeological research being done is connected with sites from the Roman and Byzantine periods.

These excavations can help reconstruct the culture and history of the early Jews and Christians. The historian of early Judaism and Christianity can no longer depend solely on written sources since so much new data have been provided by archaeology. The new information must be evaluated and studied as seriously as have been the literary sources. Similarly, the broader, more humanistic goals of contemporary archaeologists have led to greater concern for remains from later periods which sometimes were ignored and discarded. This includes material from the Byzantine period to the modern period. It is especially important that remains from the Islamic period in Palestine be recovered and interpreted since this period has not always received the attention it deserves from earlier Biblical archaeologists.

Dever's Thesis. The most noteworthy area of disagreement among archaeologists in recent years has been focused on the very nature of the discipline. W. G. Dever has called for an end to what he considers the domination of archaeology by Biblical studies. Dever believes this is necessary in order for archaeology to develop its own identity as an academic discipline and thereby be in a position to achieve its own wider goals without having its agenda set by Biblical studies. He further suggests that the term "Biblical archaeology" be abandoned in favor of "Syro-Palestinian archaeology" so as to eliminate any possible misunderstanding of the archaeological enterprise as serving to enhance the Bible's credibility. The latter term carries no theological freight.

Dever defines Syro-Palestinian archaeology as that brand of general archaeology that deals with the geographical, cultural, and chronological entity that gave the distinctive land bridge between Egypt and Mesopotamia a succession of cultures from the middle of the fourth millennium B.C. to the end of the Byzantine period (7th century A.D.). He considers archaeology to be a secular, academic discipline whose assumptions, methods, and goals are determined by archaeology itself rather than by the concerns of religious belief or even Biblical scholarship. While some of Dever's colleagues consider his suggestion regarding the name of their enterprise to be merely a semantic exercise, Dever considers it vital to insure that archaeology achieve an independence necessary to the scholarly maturation of the discipline whose purpose, he feels, should be to understand the phenomenon of cultural process and change.

Although Dever calls for the end to what he sees as Biblical studies' domination of archaeology, he nonetheless believes that archaeology has much to contribute to Biblical studies. Dever describes five general areas within which archaeology can make significant contributions: by recovering the remains of many ancient Near Eastern peoples archaeology provides numerous opportunities for cross-cultural comparison; archaeology can provide a cultural context for events narrated in the Bible in a way that these narratives cannot do themselves; archaeology's recovery of the material remains of ancient cultures provides a supplement to the literary remains already available; archaeology sometimes provides a perspective different from the literary texts making possible a more balanced view of events narrated in the Bible; and it sometimes provides data which can aid the interpretation of an obscure text.

Important Projects. Biblical archaeology came into its own in the 1950s. From that time on many major surveys and excavations were initiated. What follows does not attempt to list and describe all these, but singles out some of the more noteworthy ventures.

A very significant project was one initiated by G. E. Wright at SHECHEM. The project began in 1956 and continued until 1973. Besides the systematic excavation of this important Biblical site, the principal contribution of the Shechem excavation was the successful combination of two archaeological techniques: the Wheeler-Kenyon method of stratigraphic excavation and the ceramic analysis developed by W. F. ALBRIGHT. K. Kenyon of the British School of Archaeology in Jerusalem first adapted R. E. M. Wheeler's method of stratigraphic excavation to the Palestinian scene during her excavations at Jericho (1952–58). This transformed archaeology from mere treasure hunting to a genuine scientific discipline. Wright combined Kenyon's method with the principles of ceramic typology developed by W. F. Albright that made more accurate dating of individual strata possible on the basis of the pottery found in them.

In 1964 Wright, W. G. Dever, and J. D. Seger began work at Gezer. They applied the methodology developed at Shechem to another significant Biblical site. The Gezer project, which continued until 1974, proved to be a training ground for a fair number of archaeologists who went on to direct their own excavations in Israel, Jordan, and elsewhere. Among such projects are those as Tell elHesi (the Biblical Eglon) under the direction of J. Worrell, L. E. Stager, and G. L. Rose begun in 1970, Tell Heshban (1968–78) in Jordan directed by L. T. Geraty, and Carthage (1973–1979) in Tunisia directed by L. E. Stager. These projects were carried out by American archaeologists who have been responsible for a significant number of important projects in Israel and Jordan under the aegis of the AMERICAN SCHOOLS OF ORIENTAL RESEARCH (Israel) and the American Center for Oriental Research (Jordan). Another important innovation of the Gezer project was the use of student volunteers who did the manual work connected with excavating the site. In the process, they learned the techniques of retrieval and recording of data. Their field experience was supplemented by lectures and seminars in the field school operated by the Gezer dig. The students contributed their services, which helped the project financially. In exchange, they received academic credit from sponsoring institutions. Today, most excavations depend upon the services of student volunteers.

The Israeli School. The Israeli approach to archaeology has not placed as much emphasis on stratigraphic excavation and ceramic typology as have the methods employed by the Americans and British. The Israelis have been more interested in the larger structures that excavation reveals. They believe that these provide a clearer picture of a site than that provided by analysis of the layers of occupation, though the differences between the American and Israeli approaches are not as pronounced as they once were.

The Israeli school of archaeology came into its own during the 1960s with the outstanding work of Y. Yadin at Hazor (1955–58, 68–69) and Megiddo (1960–71). The project at Hazor became the training ground for a number of Israeli archaeologists who learned how to conduct an excavation with both scientific precision and scholarly teamwork under the guidance of Yadin. In addition to these two important Biblical sites, Yadin excavated the HERODIAN and ZEALOT fortress of Masada (1963–64). Other important projects of the period include those of M. Dothan at Ashdod (1962–72), Y. Aharoni and R. Amiran at Arad (1962–78), A. Biran at Dan (1975–), and Y. Aharoni at Beersheba (1969–75). The excavation at Dan is notable for the intact Bronze Age city gate that was found in the course of its excavations. The mud brick gate was found intact with the monumental entranceway that led up to it. Work at this important site continues and results so far are quite promising.

Following the annexation of the Old City of JERUSALEM by the State of Israel in 1967, the Israelis began intensive excavations there. N. Avigad supervised excavations in the Jewish Quarter from 1969 to 1979. B. Mazar and M. Ben-Dov undertook a project near the southern and western walls of the Temple Mount

(1968–83) and in 1978 Y. Shiloh began work on the City of David located on the Ophel hill just south of the Temple Mount. Shiloh's excavation attempted to resolve some of the questions around David's city, which was actually outside the walls of what is today called the "Old City." Shiloh exposed the Israelite city and its complex water system.

Excavations in the Jewish Quarter of the Old City brought to light remains from the Israelite (8th century B.C.) to the Byzantine (7th century A.D.) periods. Excavators uncovered a portion of the 8th century B.C. city wall, which probably was built by Hezekiah when the population of Jerusalem spread beyond earlier city walls. Near the Temple Mount, remains from homes destroyed in the course of the First Revolt against Rome were found. One of these homes was preserved quite well and gives testimony to the intensity of the struggle that resulted in the destruction of Jerusalem in A.D. 70. These same excavations brought to light portions of the New Church dedicated to Mary under the title of Theotokos built by Justinian in A.D. 543 and destroyed by an earthquake in the 8th century. This church was depicted on the Medeba mosaic map and described in diaries of early pilgrims. Excavations revealed part of its western wall and southern apse. Another important feature of Jerusalem in this period depicted on the Medeba map and revealed by recent excavation is the Cardo Maximus, the main north-south artery of Byzantine Jerusalem.

Archaeologists would like to have the opportunity to begin other projects in the Old City, such as the excavation of the Temple Mount itself, but digging in Jerusalem is problematic because of the political and religious sensitivities of both Jews and Arabs who either reside there or consider excavation of religious sites inappropriate.

Roman Catholic School. Two Roman Catholic institutions have made significant contributions to Biblical archaeology over the years. The first is L' ÉCOLE BIBLIQUE et Archéologique Française which was established in 1890 by M.-J. LAGRANGE, OP (8:322a) in Jerusalem. It is perhaps most famous for the excavation of QUMRAN (1949–67) directed by R. deVaux, OP. In recent years, the principal project sponsored by this oldest of archaeological institutes in Palestine has been Tell Keisan. Work on this site was initiated by deVaux in 1971 and was carried on by P. Prignaud (1972–74) and J.-B. Humbert, OP (1975–80). Other projects of the École include new excavations of Rihab and Khirbet es-Samra in Jordan. Archaeological excavation has also been an important activity of the Studium Biblicum Franciscanum located in the Old City of Jerusalem. Most of the projects undertaken by the Franciscans, who have custody of the Holy Places that are related to the Christian presence in Palestine. Recent excavations include the synagogue and church of Capernaum excavated by V. Corbo, OFM, and S. Loffreda, OFM, from 1970 to 1975, the church and related structures at Nazareth supervised by B. Bagatti, OFM (1970) and the Byzantine period church atop Mt. Nebo (Khirbet el-Mukhayyet) in Jordan, which is a continuing, project undertaken by M. Piccirillo, OFM (1973–). The excavation of the synagogue at Capernaum proved to be the most controversial since its results have required a reassessment of historical, architectural and archaeological presuppositions that have guided scholars for more than 50 years. On the basis of their excavations, Corbo and Loffreda date the synagogue at Capernaum to the 4th and 5th centuries A.D. Many of their colleagues, principally the Israelis, do not accept these conclusions and continue to date the synagogue to the 2nd and 3rd centuries A.D. Bagatti's work at Nazareth and elsewhere in Palestine has led him to describe a phenomenon, which he calls Jewish Christianity, that he asserts existed in Palestine during the first centuries of the Christian era. For example, he maintains that graffiti and other remains found at Nazareth confirm the use of a synagogue for Christian worship.

Meiron Project. Significant progress has been made in the excavation of early Jewish sites in part because of the efforts of the Meiron Excavation Project. In the course of ten years (1971–81), E. Meyers, J. F. Strange and C. Meyers excavated synagogues at Khirbet Shema, Meiron, Gush Halav, and Nabratein. Their excavations not only shed new light on Judaism in Galilee during the Roman and Byzantine periods but also help set the standard for careful excavation and insightful interpretation. The published results of the Meiron Excavation project have demonstrated how a broadened archaeological approach can help shed new light on historical issues and the interpretation of ancient texts. One of the most important artifacts discovered in the process of excavation at these sites was the pediment of an ark (the shrine within which the Torah scrolls were kept) found in the ancient synagogue at Nabratein in 1980. It was the first and only such object ever found in Palestine.

Another important site from Roman and Byzantine Palestine is Caesarea Maritima. It is an immense site that has been excavated almost continuously since 1970. The ancient city was founded by Herod the Great and it served as the political capital for Roman and Byzantine Palestine. The harbor that Herod built is being excavated using underwater technology that is complicated and expensive. Most of the remains that have been uncovered (a theatre, hippodrome, civic complex, Mithraeum) date to the Byzantine Period, though work is continuing in order to reveal the Caesarea of Herod.

Islam. Excavations of places associated with the Islamic period have been largely confined to two important sites. M. Rosen-Ayalon and A. Eitan (1965–76) excavated at Ramla, the only city in Palestine founded by Muslims. The goal of the project was to trace the beginnings of city to its founding by the Umayyads. The most impressive remains from the Islamic period come from Jerusalem and were identified during the excavation of the area near the southern wall of the Temple Mount. Structures found there were once identified as Byzantine: however, the complete excavation of the area supervised by B. Mazar and M. Ben-Dov have confirmed that the magnificent buildings in the area formed an Umayyad palace complex that was an imposing architectural achievement in its day. Most of the other finds from the Islamic period have not been integrated into a coherent portrait of this era of the region's history. This is one of the most pressing tasks of Palestinian archaeology.

The study of archaeological remains from the Crusader period had been the domain of the Catholic scholars from L'École Biblique and the Studium Biblicum Franciscanum. Recently, Israeli archaeologists have been involved in both surveys and full-scale excavations of Crusader sites. A number of Crusader fortresses have been excavated and reconstructed in recent years: Acco (M. Kesten and G. Goldman, 1964–74), Qal'at Nimrud (A. Grabois, 1968–81), Caesarea (A. Negev, 1960), and Kochav Hayarden [Belvoir] (M. Ben Dov).

The Future. The future of Biblical archaeology depends in part on the climate of Middle Eastern politics. As long as there is no overall settlement of the political issues in the region, archaeologists, both native and foreign, will have to be ready to deal with the inevitable difficulties that are a consequence of these unresolved problems. Secondly, the rising costs of archaeological research will require creative attempts at cooperative ventures so that available resources can be used to their best advantage. Finally, Biblical archaeologists will have to become more scrupulously professional in their preparation, research design, fieldwork, and publications. The richness of the Middle East's cultural heritage is beyond calculation, and much of it still waits to be revealed. There is enough archaeological work in the Middle East to engage several future generations.

Bibliography: M. AVI-YONAH, ed., *Encyclopedia of Archaeological Excavations in the Holy Land* 4 v. (Englewood Cliffs 1974). B. BAGATTI, *The Church from the Circumcision* (Jerusalem 1971). W. G. DEVER, ''Syro-Palestinian and Biblical Archaeology,'' D. A. KNIGHT and G. M. TUCKER, eds., *The Hebrew Bible and Its Modern Interpreters* (Chico 1985) 31–74. L. J. HOPPE, ''Archaeology and Politics in Palestine.'' *The Link* 20 (1987) 1–14. P. J. KING, *American Archaeology in the Mideast* (Philadelphia 1983). J. A. SAUER, ''SyroPalestinian Archaeology, History, and Biblical Studies,'' *Biblical Archaeologist* 45 (1982) 201–209. H. SHANKS, ed., *Recent Archaeology in the Land of Israel* (Washington 1983). E. K. VOGEL, *Bibliography of Holy Land Sites* Parts I–II (Cambridge 1974, 1982).

[L. J. HOPPE/EDS.]

BIBLICAL LANGUAGES

Biblical languages consist of the tongues used by the inspired authors in writing the sacred Scriptures. All the protocanonical books of the Old Testament were written in Hebrew, except about one-half of Daniel (Dn 2.4b–7.28) and two sections of Ezra (Ez 4.8–6.18; 7.12–26), which were composed in Aramaic. Of the deuterocanonical books of the Old Testament, two (2 Maccabees and Wisdom) were composed in Greek; the others were written originally in Hebrew or Aramaic, but have been preserved only in ancient translations (especially Greek), except that about two-thirds of Sirach has been preserved in its original Hebrew. All the books of the New Testament were composed in Greek. On the nature of these tongues as used in the composition of the sacred Scriptures, *see* HEBREW LANGUAGE; ARAMAIC LANGUAGE; GREEK LANGUAGE, BIBLICAL.

[L. F. HARTMAN]

BIBLICAL THEOLOGY

All theology, if it is true to itself, is biblical, for it is defined as a discourse about God. This God, who ''dwells in light inaccessible'' (2 Tm 6.16), has revealed Himself; and the Bible is the record of this revelation. In the sense that any true theology's point of departure and primary datum is the Bible, it is of necessity biblical. But, if all theology is biblical, not every theology is biblical theology. This term, which might have sounded tautological to the Fathers and surprising to the scholastics, is of relatively recent coinage even as the sacred discipline it designates is still in quest of sharper definition. It is the purpose of this article to study the meaning of the term ''biblical theology'' mainly by tracing the general lines of its development and by considering its formulations in recent theologies of the OT and the NT. This, at the present stage in the progress of biblical theology, is as near a definition of the science as one can come; for no satisfactory definition has yet been formulated. There is, however, nothing surprising in this. Often in the history of the Church a reality is lived for centuries before its definition is formulated; and the newness of a term to designate such a reality is no argument against either its verity or its validity (an example from the mid-20th century is the term ''collegiality'').

Early Period

Sacred Scripture is God's word to man; theology is man's word about God. This word of man about God, in its prophetic, sapiential, priestly, evangelical, or apostolic formulation, was and remains a theology. To understand God's word—to expound its meaning, elucidate its content, and interpret its message—has been the task of the Church from its very inception. This task has ever been conditioned by the needs and circumstances of successive generations.

Patristic Age. In the first centuries of the Christian Era, patristic exegesis was determined by the vital needs of a nascent Church. Early controversies and scripturally founded apologetics, whether with Trypho the Jew or with the pagan CELSUS, paved the way for a progressive elaboration of orthodox expressions of dogma and the attempt to synthesize in a systematic theology the datum of revelation with human knowledge. This was not simply the preference of a so-called Greek bent of mind, but the response to a conscious need to grow in the understanding of the faith. The world in which the Church was born and the very circumstances of its early growth conditioned the formulation of its message and oriented its theological speculation for centuries.

The Fathers put the rational speculations of their culture at the service of the faith. In their orthodox expressions of dogma and their systematic formulation of a theology they used Sacred Scripture, not merely as a support for their tenets, but also as a norm for their formulas and as a source for their theological vocabulary. But the expanding needs of their culture exerted pressures that caused their exegetical methods to multiply into an ever-increasing number of so-called senses. In their interpretation of the OT they followed, and greatly enlarged upon, the method already discernible in the NT: the quest for the ''spirit'' behind the ''letter,'' projection of the mystery of Christ, and recourse to typology as its foundation for allegory. In exploring the action of the mystery of Christ upon the Christian soul and in reflecting upon its eschatological consummation, the Fathers sought to see what the facts of Christ's life symbolized. As, in principle, their exegetical interpretation of the OT was justified by the NT, so their understanding of the NT received its general guidelines from the Fourth Gospel. Thus the cultural milieu of Hellenism favored a systematic development of Pauline allegory and Johannine symbolism. While the mystery of Christ was and remained the unique object of biblical revelation, its elucidation was conditioned by the day-to-day needs of the Church. Pastoral care and the liturgy required a preponderance of allegory and symbolism; apologetics and controversies necessitated a stress on the historic and literal sense of the Scriptures.

Medieval Age. In the Middle Ages, as long as the pastoral care of souls predominated, the patristic method was followed both by compilers, such as St. BEDE, the Venerable, and by creators, such as St. BERNARD OF CLAIRVAUX. But from the 13th century on, a double trend, systematic (starting with the *lectio* of the *pagina sacra* and terminating in the *summae*) and apologetic (refuting the claims of the Jews and the Muslims) became evident. In both trends a strongly rational reflection was discernible, for Aristotelian dialectic had furnished theology with an instrument that was then judged to be adequate. Consequently, whereas in the early Middle Ages, in the use of Sacred Scripture, the principles of St. AUGUSTINE were adhered to and the practice of St. GREGORY I THE GREAT was followed, in the later Middle Ages it was St. JEROME's authority that was in the ascendancy. Jerome's attention to the original text, care to translate well, effort at literary analysis, and regard for the historical references of the biblical narrative made his work most valuable for the theologizing of men, such as HUGH OF SAINT-VICTOR and St. ALBERT THE GREAT. But it was left to the great genius of St. THOMAS AQUINAS to achieve a new synthesis between biblical revelation and rational speculation. He stressed the literal sense of Scripture as that alone on which a theologian can base his work. His exegetical method still remained faithful to the principles found in the NT and followed by the Fathers. His theology, like that of the scholastics and the Fathers, drew its inspiration from the Bible, rested its arguments upon it, and attempted to interpret and systematize its message. In that sense it was biblical.

Thus, from its earliest days, confronted by the need both of apologetics and controversies with the enemies without and of the pastoral care for its members within, the Church's use of the Bible followed lines of development that increasingly came to regard it as an arsenal for its polemics, a storehouse of premises for its dogmatic syntheses, and a rich mine of wisdom for its pastoral ministry. The drift away from the Bible as an integral entity that merited study by itself and for itself was accentuated in post-Tridentine times, whether by the instinctive reaction against the Reformers' *sola scriptura* or by the very educational system of the clergy. It was to culminate in the reduction of the Bible to ciphers cited as proof texts that had priority of place over patristic references and Denzinger numbers. The biblical message thus underwent the myriad procrustean coercions to which minds sharply honed in Aristotle's *Organon* chose to subject it in the defense of the faith (e.g., justification, predestination, Redemption) and the codification of Christian morals (e.g., divorce, the Sabbath rest, mental reservation).

17th to 19th Centuries. The term ''biblical theology'' was not always used with the same technical connotations and nuances that it possesses today. One of the first to use it, Abraham CALOV (1612–86) in his *Systema locorum theologicorum* (12 v. Wittenberg 1655–77), employed it to describe the whole field of biblical and exegetical studies. But it was Johannes Cocceius (1603–69) who first attempted to ''theologize in a purely biblical manner,'' to formulate a theology drawn from the Bible alone. His *Summa doctrinae de foedere et testamentis Dei* (Leipzig 1648) belongs to a school that came to be known as ''Federal theology.'' This school was a reaction against the aridities of scholasticism not unlike the reaction evident in the PIETISM of that age, which was exemplified in the work of Philipp Jakob SPENER (1635–1705). Toward the end of the 18th century Gottlieb Christian Storr (1746–1805) published his *Doctrinae christianae e solis sacris libris repetitae pars theoretica* (1793), in which he too attempted to develop a system of theology drawn solely from the Bible. Though these theologies foreshadowed future trends, they exerted no direct influence on the development of the discipline of biblical theology.

This discipline, ironically enough, owes its beginnings much more to the *collegia biblica,* the collections of scriptural proof texts that were then used in dogmatic theology. Although the texts were accompanied by exegesis and appropriate comment to facilitate their use, there was very often no attempt to distinguish the OT from the NT, or to differentiate various authors and modes of composition. The traditional order of subjects was followed in such *collegia* as Sebastian Schmid(ius)'s *Collegium biblicum . . . iuxta seriem locorum communium theologicorum* (1671). But the biblical theology of that era, which most approximated what modern usage understands by the term, was Carl Haymann's *Biblische Theologie* (1768).

New Hermeneutics. There was, however, no real possibility for the rise of biblical theology in the modern sense until a revolution in hermeneutics took place, allowing a less rigid understanding of the principles of *analogia fidei* and *analogia scripturae.* Two 18th-century scholars, Johann Salomo Semler (1725–91) and Johann August Ernesti (1707–81), did much to bring this revolution about by stressing the need to interpret the Sacred Scriptures in a purely grammatical and historical way. From that time on, books began to appear that used the classical proof texts with greater independence of dogmatic tracts and their structure. It was Anton Friedrich Büsching (1724–93) who gave, in his *dissertatio inauguralis* at Tübingen in 1755, what has been considered a first sketch of pure biblical theology. He followed it in 1757 with his work *Epitome theologiae e solis literis sacris concinnatae.* In 1785 and 1789 Wilhelm Hofnagel published the two volumes of his *Handbuch der biblischen Theologie* that sought to discover the meaning intended by the original author through an examination of the classical proof texts arranged in a theology-anthropology-soteriology pattern. But the man whose work ''seems to stand at the point of transition between the old dogmatic interest in the proof texts and the science of biblical theology which was shortly to be born'' (Dentan, 21) was Gotthilf Traugott Zachariae (d. 1772). His *Biblische Theologie* (1772–75) attempted the study of the Bible as a whole according to a plan derived from the Bible itself and not limited simply to the study of isolated *dicta probantia.*

Biblical Distinguished from Dogmatic Theology. Opinion is almost unanimous in crediting Johann Philipp Gabler's *Oratio de justo discrimine theologiae biblicae et theologiae dogmaticae regundisque recte utriusque finibus,* which was his inaugural lecture at the University of Altdorf, March 30, 1787, with being the starting point of the modern discipline of biblical theology. Gabler (1753–1826) set up a distinction between dogmatic theology and biblical theology: whereas dogmatic theology is a philosophizing on divine things (''theologia dogmatica e genere didactico, docens, quid theologus quisque pro ingenii modulo, vel temporis, aetatis, loci, sectae, scholae similiumque id genus aliorum, ratione super rebus divinis philosophetur,'' *Opuscula Academica,* ed. T. A. and I. G. Gabler, 2 v. [Ulm 1831] 2:183–184), biblical theology is basically historical, setting forth the thoughts of the inspired writers on divine things (''e genere historico tradens quid scriptores sacri de rebus divinis senserint'' [*ibid.* 183]). The method advocated by Gabler for the study of biblical theology consisted of (1) the interpretation of the scriptural passage on purely grammatical and historical grounds; (2) comparison of passages with each other to note both similarities and differences; and (3) the formulation of *notiones universae,* but without distorting them.

The biblical theologians who followed in Gabler's wake were, like Gabler himself, rationalists. This is perhaps why they could make such a break with dogmatic traditions and traditional modes of theologizing. Among them was Georg Lorenz Bauer (1755–1806), who was the first really to follow Gabler's distinction and write a biblical theology that broke away from the proof texts and was independent of dogmatic theology. His *Theologie des A.T. oder Abriss der religiösen Begriffe der alten Hebräer* (1796) not only separated the OT from the NT, but clearly distinguished persons, periods, and books of the former. It comprised two parts—theology (God's relation to man) and anthropology (man's relation to God)—and was intended as a preparatory step toward the study of NT theology. What had hitherto been a study of the literary, exegetical, and historical questions raised by the

Scriptures would henceforth also be a study of the religion of the Bible, of its ''religious ideas.'' Shortly after Bauer's work there appeared the three volumes of G. P. C. Kaiser's *Die biblische Theologie* (1813–21), which was the first work to apply systematically the *Religionsgeschichtlich* method to biblical interpretation. This work was followed by D. G. C. von Cölln's *Biblische Theologie* (1836), which insisted on the need of treating the biblical ideas ''genetically'' and conceived biblical theology as but the first chapter in the history of dogma.

Adoption by Conservatives. Rationalism and *Religionsgeschichte* (history of religion or comparative religion), however, were not the only factors operative in the formative years of biblical theology. Hegelian dialectic in the philosophy of religions was bound to be applied to the study of the religion of the Bible. Care to present the matter chronologically was, of course, quite characteristic here as is seen, for example, in *Die biblische Theologie* (1835) of J. K. Wilhelm Vatke (1806–62). To this triple threat to biblical orthodoxy the conservative reaction furnished a necessary and needed counterweight. As often happens initially, the opposition to the methods and the principles behind them led to a rejection of the discipline; but as happens no less often, the initial opposition yielded to a moderated tolerance and ended in the adoption of biblical theology by the conservative circles, which were by no means slow to recognize that it was not incompatible with devoted acceptance and orthodox interpretation of Sacred Scripture.

A representative work of the conservative circles was the *Vorlesungen über die Theologie des A.T.* (1840) of J. C. F. Steudel (1779–1837), which, using a strictly grammatical-historical method, attempted to show the content of the OT in such a way as to make it possible to understand the religious notions of a particular period in history. Steudel's student G. F. Oehler published a work that dealt exclusively with the theory and method of OT theology. His *Prolegomena zur Theologie des A.T.* (1845) stated that the function of OT theology was to discover the ''idea'' that formed the basis of OT religion, namely, ''the divine Spirit.'' ''Old Testament religion,'' Oehler wrote, ''is rather mediated through a series of divine acts and commands and through the institution of a divine state'' (quoted by Dentan, 45).

Methodological Refinement. In the latter half of the 19th century there was another clash of opinions that proved both illuminating and fruitful. In 1878 Julius WELLHAUSEN published his *Prolegomena zur Geschichte Israels,* which for a while at least seemed to have dealt the death blow to all OT theology. By insisting that Israel's religion was but another instance in the field of *Religionsgeschichte,* it reduced OT theology to an erudite history of the religion of Israel, to one more instance of a general pattern of religious development discernible in any of the religions of the ancient Near East. But reaction to this trend was not slow in coming. The *Handbuch der alttestamentlichen Theologie* of August Dillmann (1823–94; posthumously edited and published by Rudolf KITTEL in 1895) pointed out the inadequacy of Wellhausen's approach by underlining the uniqueness of Israel among its neighbors as well as the uniqueness and incompleteness of the OT ''religion of holiness.'' It was, however, Hermann Schultz who produced the greatest work on OT theology in the 19th century. His *Alttestamentliche Theologie: Die Offenbarungs-religion auf ihrer vorchristlichen Entwicklungsstufe* went through five editions between 1869 and 1896 and was translated into English (*OT Theology* [Edinburgh 1892]). Schultz pointed out that the method of biblical theology is historical; its function, to supply material needed by systematic theology and furnish a rule against which to measure later development; and its unifying principle, the kingdom of God on Earth. Consequently, as the subtitle of his work indicates, OT theology without its NT counterpart is one-sided and incomplete, while NT theology without an OT theology remains unintelligible. Fortunately the great work of Schultz on OT theology was paralleled by the *Lehrbuch der Neutestamentlichen Theologie* (1896–97) of Heinrich Julius Holtzmann (1832–1910) and the *Über Aufgabe und Methode der sogenannten neutestamentlichen Theologie* (1897) of William Wrede (1859–1906).

Incomplete Success. From the early beginnings of biblical theology, the theology of the OT and that of the NT were closely linked together. The successes and failures, the merits and shortcomings of the various biblical theologies inevitably influenced later theologies of both Testaments. Throughout the various periods, the Augustinian principle of *Novum in Vetere latet, Vetus in Novo patet* was never very far from the minds of those who attempted to write a biblical theology. Many of the authors saw in their theologies of the OT but a first step toward the formulation of a NT theology. In the study of the NT, no less than in that of the OT, the influence of the ENLIGHTENMENT and the effects of rationalism, *Religionsgeschichte,* and Hegelianism were in evidence (*see* HEGELIANISM AND NEO-HEGELIANISM). Both the literary-critical and the historical methods, in OT and NT theologies alike, were greatly enriched by the improved understanding of biblical languages and the extensive contributions of archaeology to the history of the biblical period. Both methods shed light on the progress of biblical revelation and its successive steps. As G. L. Bauer had divided his biblical theology into a study of the religion of the Jews before Christ, the religion of Jesus, and the religion of the Apostles, so similarly, Wilhelm M. L.

De Wette, *Biblische Dogmatik des A. und N.T.* (1813), distinguished two steps in the OT, the religion of Moses and the religion of the Jews, and two levels in the NT, the religion of Jesus and its interpretation in the message of the Apostles.

In both OT and NT theologies the influence of Wellhausen was greatly felt, and with the triumph of his school, theological interest declined in favor of the historical. The contributions of *Religionsgeschichte* were numerous, but its failure to evaluate the matter of both Testaments theologically was serious and damaging. The influence of G. W. F. HEGEL was greatly felt in both Testaments also, and here too a serious failure threatened to bring biblical theology to a halt. Hegelian dialectic might have succeeded in analyzing phenomena, but it failed to comprehend the living experience underlying them. There were some not wanting those who carried Hegelian dialectic to absurd extremes, e.g., Eduard Zeller (1814–1908) and Albert Schwegler (1819–57) in the NT and Wilhelm Vatke and Bruno BAUER in the OT. Thus they did great disservice both to the method they employed and the science in which they employed it.

Modern Period

Varied though the attempts were, both in method and in achievement in the biblical theology of the 18th and 19th centuries, the discipline began its growth into maturity only in the period that preceded and followed World War II. Apart from the many trends in thought and the reactions to them, solid scientific contribution in a variety of fields contributed a great deal toward the maturation process of biblical theology. The work of Sir James George Frazer and W. Oesterly in anthropology; of Max Weber in sociology; of Gustav Dalman (1855–1941) in geography; of A. Alt, W. F. Albright, and M. Noth in history and archaeology; of Emil Schürer, Wilhelm BOUSSET, and Richard Reitzenstein (1861–1931) in the background of Christianity—all were contributions that made the study of biblical theology not only possible but necessary. That biblical theology is a modern discipline owes as much to these various contributions as to the fact that the orientation of thought and interest in theology before the 18th century lay elsewhere.

Old Testament Theologies. In the period between the two world wars biblical theology received a fresh and new start along a path that has proved most rewarding and rich in possibilities. The number of works on the theology of either Testament has been so great since the 1920s as to preclude anything resembling even a quick survey of the field. The most that can be hoped for in this brief space is to mention some indicative works in a field that has produced much of lasting worth and interest. The aggregate of biblical and allied sciences continues to widen scholars' knowledge of, and increase their acquaintance with, the biblical world. The school of *Formgeschichte,* or biblical FORM CRITICISM, and its application to the literature of the OT, the better understanding of Israel's cult and worship as well as the various influences operative therein, and the growing appreciation of the Prophets and their function in the life of Israel all made, and continue to make, the study of OT theology more fruitful and rewarding.

Eissfeldt and Sellin. Otto Eissfeldt's article ''Israelitisch-jüdische Religionsgeschichte und alttestamentliche Theologie'' (*Zeitschrift für die alttestamentliche Wissenschaft* 44 [1926] 1–12) could well be taken as a starting point of the most recent and the richest period in the development of OT theology. Eissfeldt insisted that OT theology has religious faith as its only organ of knowledge and divine revelation as its subject. Accordingly, after a historical investigation of Israelite religion, OT theology must undertake a systematic presentation of the timeless truths of OT revelation. It was Ernst Sellin who first elaborated an OT theology according to Eissfeldt's conception. His *Alttestamentliche Theologie auf religionsgeschichtlicher Grundlage* (2 v. Leipzig 1933) was divided into two parts: the first treated the religion of Israel; the second presented OT theology according to the categories of God, man, and eschatology. The ''holiness of God'' was seen as the central and ruling idea throughout.

Eichrodt. Though Walther Eichrodt's ''Hat die alttestamentliche Theologie noch selbständige Bedeutung innherhalb des alt. Wissenschaft?'' (*Zeitschrift für die alttestamentliche Wissenschaft* 47 [1929] 83–91) challenged Eissfeldt's conception of OT theology three years after its publication, it was not until 1933 that the first volume of Eichrodt's monumental *Theologie des A.T.* (3 v. Leipzig 1933–39; Eng. tr. of v. 1, London 1961) appeared. The work was completed in three parts: God and People, God and the World, and God and Man—a plan that Eichrodt derived from his teacher, Otto Procksch, whose own *Theologie des A.T.* did not appear until 1949 (Gütersloh). Eichrodt was consciously engaged in describing a living process. He described his work as ''taking a cross section [*Querschnitt*] of the realm of OT thought''; hence it had to maintain throughout a constant interplay between a historical survey and a theological synthesis. Eichrodt sought to delineate the religion of the OT as a ''self-contained entity'' that, despite the mutability of historic conditions, manifests ''a constant basic tendency and character.'' The operative principle of this constancy is covenant theology, which, as T. C. Vriezen pointed out later, underscored the communion aspect rather than the contract aspect of the relation between

Yahweh and His people. Moreover, even though the Prophets often seem to have avoided the term ''covenant,'' it must be realized that for them ''election'' was but the beginning of a permanent intercourse between Yahweh and His people. Thus they too could make their valuable contribution to covenant theology. The work of Eichrodt, which has gone through several editions, will always remain a major milestone in the development of OT theology.

Vriezen. T. C. Vriezen's *Hoofdlijnen der Theologie van het Oude Testament* (Wageninen, Holland 1950), Eng. tr., S. Neuijen, *An Outline of OT Theology* (Oxford 1958), stresses, more than Eichrodt did, the OT as an integral part of the Christian Scriptures. For Vriezen biblical theology is not a purely descriptive and historical science, nor is it sufficient to present it systematically by taking a cross section through the history of the religion of Israel. The OT, first and foremost, is a book bearing witness to a divine revelation. This witness is not systematic, nor can it be forced into a system. To present it efficiently and faithfully, a thematic exposition of the most representative themes of Israel's faith and their interrelations would be required. Accordingly, Vriezen presents his *Theology* in themes of God; man; intercourse between God and man, between man and man; and God, man, and the world present and to come. This loose thematic pattern allows Vriezen to include Israel's cult and piety into his OT theology, two basic elements of OT life and thought that many another OT theology has not succeeded in including.

Von Rad. Since Eichrodt's, several other OT theologies have appeared (by the Protestant scholars Otto J. Baab, Edmond Jacob, George A. F. Knight, and G. Ernest Wright; and by the Catholic scholars Paul Heinisch, Albert Gelin, Jacques Guillet, and P. van Imschoot); but one of the most important among them is Gerhard von Rad's *Theologie des A.T.* (2 v. Munich 1957–60; Eng. tr., Edinburgh 1962–65). It is important, not simply because of the respect commanded by its author in the field of OT studies, but because it embodies an approach and a point of view that are bound to leave their mark on the evolution of biblical theology. Von Rad objects to Eichrodt's approach to the OT because of the fact that Israel's witness is primarily to what Yahweh has done in history. This witness is not a structured pattern of religious concepts; and consequently, biblical theology cannot be limited to a *Begriffsuntersuchung* (investigation of concepts) that, of its nature, tends to abstraction and generalization. SALVATION HISTORY (HEILSGESCHICHTE) dominates the OT, and biblical theology must elaborate this sacred history within a theological framework. OT theology must assume a historical form; it must be a retelling of the narrative (*Nacherzählung*) of Yahweh's redemptive acts. (See G. E. Wright, *God Who Acts: Biblical Theology as Recital* [Chicago 1952].)

New Testament Theologies. Theologies of the NT have kept pace with those of the OT. Here, however, apart from the theologies as such, one major phenomenon stands as a unique accomplishment in the field: Gerhard KITTEL's *Theologisches Wörterbuch zum N.T.* (Stuttgart 1935– ; abbreviated Kittel ThW or TWNT), which has as yet no comparable counterpart for the OT. Of course, Kittel's dictionary itself gives due attention to the vocabulary of the OT, and several recent biblical dictionaries (by J. J. von Allmen, X. Léon-Dufour, and A. Richardson) that treat OT concepts are available; but none treats the OT vocabulary with the thoroughness with which Kittel's monumental opus treats the NT. Whatever may be said in criticism of the method used in Kittel ThW, it will long remain an indispensable tool of far-reaching consequences in NT theologies, however diverse their approaches and their points of view.

Moreover, there are two opposing points of view that have been expounded in the realm of NT interpretation. Their protagonists are the Swiss theologian Karl Barth and Marburg's Professor Rudolph Bultmann. Their main concern, and it is a crucial one, is the role of reason vis-à-vis the divine message: whether a philosophy is necessary to make the categories of this message meaningful, and, if so, which philosophy? Bultmann responds affirmatively and opts unequivocally for Heideggerian existentialism as the philosophy best suited to achieve self-understanding by encounter with the message.

Special Problems. Still another factor in contemporary NT theology is the result of the method of *Redaktionsgeschichte* (investigation of the editorial work done by biblical authors on earlier material). After the work of W. Marxsen on Mark and H. Conzelmann on Luke, not only has the Synoptic question changed radically, but the individual theological genius of each Synoptist has come to the fore. If previously there were Pauline and Johannine theologies, henceforth there should be Marcan, Matthean, and Lucan theologies as well. Another factor operative in the NT and one of far greater complexity here than in the OT is the passage from the doctrine of the NT to the dogmatic formulations of the Council of CHALCEDON. The intertestamental period has, in recent times, been brought into sharper focus both through a better knowledge of later Judaism and rabbinic literature and through the epoch-making discoveries at Qumran. (*See* DEAD SEA SCROLLS.) But the period immediately following NT times is far more complex and problematic both because of the controversies that are discernible even in the evangelical and apostolic formulations of the NT itself and because of the introduction of categories other than the Semitic into the formulation of the message in post-Apostolic times. All these factors must be taken into account in NT theology; but beyond all this, it must be remembered that, even more than for the OT, NT theology is theology within the Church, of the Church, and for the Church. With this in mind, not the least important of the problems that must be confronted in NT theology is that of the canon. (*See* Stendahl, 428–430.)

Modern Studies. To see what has been done concretely in NT theology, only a few examples can be given here. Bultmann's *Theology of the N.T.,* tr. K. Grobel (2 v. London 1952–55) for all the shortcomings noted even by its favorable critics (such as extreme critical positions, failure to take the Synoptists as serious theologians, a somewhat too rigid adherence to lexicographic method, and insufficient attention to the influence of the OT on the NT) is an important landmark in the evolution of NT theology. Of two possibilities of presenting NT writings, "as a systematically ordered unity" or in their variety in which they can then "be understood as members of an historical continuity" (2:237), Bultmann chooses the latter. His rejection of the first alternative raises the question of the possibility of presenting NT theology as a single system composed of the ideas of the different writers, a NT "system of dogmatics."

Ethelbert Stauffer's *N.T. Theology,* tr. J. Marsh (London 1955) first appeared in Germany in 1941 and antedates Bultmann's by more than 10 years. In it Stauffer follows precisely the alternative rejected by Bultmann. Accordingly, he divides his *Theology* into three parts: the development of primitive Christian theology, the Christocentric theology of history in the NT, and the creeds of the primitive Church. The dominant theme of the theology is well summed up by the title of the second part: the NT presents a theology of history, a redemptive history of God's redemptive acts centered in Christ. Bultmann objects that this method "transforms theology into a religious philosophy of history."

The differences between the two approaches are as yet not resolved. NT theologies have appeared using one or the other alternative in their elaboration: Richardson and Oscar Cullmann, for example, favor the "synthetic" approach, whereas the two major Catholic contributions to the field, Joseph BONSIRVEN's and M. Meinertz's, opt for the other. The differences between the two are crucial, not because either approach would deny the evident Christocentricity of the NT or its historical element, but because ultimately they differ on what precisely NT theology in particular, and biblical theology in general, is all about.

Complexity and Unity of Biblical Revelation. Differences in method and in object both in the theology of the NT and of the OT are due ultimately to the complexity of the subject of biblical theology itself. It is not sufficient to classify it either as the first chapter in the history of dogma or an intermediary step between exegesis and dogmatic theology; nor is it enough to say its task is merely descriptive or merely systematic; nor is it accurate to characterize it either as a historic science or a theological discipline. Biblical revelation is in history, and thus historical; it is the revelation of a personal God, and thus theological; and it is addressed to man in a community, and thus anthropological and sociological. This revelation inexorably moves toward its climax and plenitude in the revelation of Christ; hence it is both Christological and Christocentric. But in revealing Christ to man God revealed man to himself; therefore, in this profounder sense it is anthropological. Moreover, through all the periods of *Heilsgeschichte,* through the endless succession of events, civilizations, cultures, and languages, there is both a community of spirit and of expression among the sacred authors and a unity of purpose and direction in the sacred books. The unity of the Bible, an essential datum of faith, is verified at the concrete level of language at the same time that it is, in essence, theological.

Because of this unity of the Bible it is possible to have a biblical theology that strives to be a direct echo of the immediate content of the inspired message in it. Such a theology can assume any of the various points of view that mark the principal moments in the development of revelation: Yahwist or Deuteronomic history, priestly or sapiential tradition, the Synoptic Gospels, Pauline doctrine, apocalyptic frescoes, or Johannine mystique. But beyond all this, a biblical theology can assume a broader point of view, seek to comprehend the unity of the Bible as an integral whole, and attempt to grasp the organic continuity and intelligible coherence that guarantees the profound unity of all the moments of the history of salvation. Then, and perhaps only then, can one hope to formulate a strict definition of biblical theology, its function, and its purpose.

Vatican Council II and Biblical Theology. Under the heading "The Revision of Ecclesiastical Studies" the council's "Decree on Priestly Formation" directed that "Dogmatic theology should be so arranged that the biblical themes are presented first" (*Optatam totius* 16). According to this statement, dogmatic theology is to begin the consideration of doctrine from Scripture and (methodologically speaking) from Scripture alone. The approach is to consist in an organic presentation of the meaning of the biblical passages that have bearing upon a particular doctrine so that a comprehensive grasp of the content and the actual state of the doctrine in Scripture is achieved. Only then is tradition (i.e., the later comprehension of biblical doctrine as it has occurred historically in the Church) to be considered. Finally, the contemporary understanding of the doctrine is to be taken up.

This conciliar directive on Scripture as the methodological starting point for dogmatic theology logically emerges from the council's comprehension of the Bible's place in the totality of divine Revelation, outlined in the ''Dogmatic Constitution on Divine Revelation''. Scripture itself attests to a variety of ways in which God has made Himself and His will known: in historical events; in the divinely inspired understanding and communication of the religious meaning of these events; in the choice of the OT patriarchs as vehicles through whom an initial understanding of His existence and of His plan for the human race was made known; in the activity and teaching of Jesus of Nazareth, and especially in His death on the cross and His resurrection (*Dei Verbum* 1–6). In this context of variety in God's communication of Himself and His will Sacred Scripture has arisen, willed by God as a perpetual record of His self-communication and in itself another form of that communication (*ibid.* 7). The origin of Scripture is not an accident of human history, but one of the ways in which God chooses to manifest Himself and His will. Just as the OT Scriptures arose to enshrine and to continue God's self-communication to the people of Israel, so the NT Scriptures arose, again at the inspiration of God, to enshrine and continue the divine self-communication in and through Jesus Christ and through the Apostles (*ibid.* 7–8).

The grasp of the religious content of Scripture in terms of totality, whether the totality be fully developed doctrine or doctrine on its way to completion or contained in Scripture only inchoately, lies among the general aims of biblical theology. Vatican II accepted this particular function of the discipline and directed that it be employed in dogmatic theology.

The methodological separation of the Bible from tradition and from contemporary theology possesses evident values. The acceptance of Scripture as the starting point of doctrine helps to prevent the distortion of the meaning of the biblical text that occurs when theological conceptions and understandings of a later time are introduced into it. Second, the idea of tradition as development in the understanding of biblical doctrine becomes clearer and, at least in its positive aspect, is legitimated. Third, the foundational importance of Scripture opens the way to interaction among the various branches of theology: biblical, patristic, historical, dogmatic, moral, liturgical, and pastoral. The whole of theology, including exegesis and biblical theology, has constantly to reevaluate itself in terms of its relationship to Scripture; each branch can illumine the other out of its own experience with Scripture. Finally, seeing Scripture in its totalities provides a balanced view of its religious content and better enables those who have teaching functions in the Church to convey its meaning to their contemporaries.

The Nature of Biblical Theology. When the terms ''Bible'' and ''theology'' are merged to create the term ''biblical theology,'' a question of meaning automatically arises. Historically, biblical theology originated out of the desire to bring the religious thought of Scripture into clear focus. Throughout its history the discipline has stood as a reaction to the inadequate relationship between dogmatic theology and Scripture, to the reduction of the content of Scripture to the phenomenon of religion as such by ''the history of religion school,'' and to a biblical exegesis that became primarily preoccupied with linguistic, historical, archaeological, and literary considerations raised in the material of the Bible. The historical origins of biblical theology, however, do not shed effective light on the nature of the discipline. The terms ''Bible'' and ''theology,'' and not historical origins, are of essential significance in the determination of the discipline's nature.

The Bible is God's Word to man. It contains both His self-communication as well as the inspired writer's reflection upon that communication. Theology is the science of faith. As a science it consists in the methodological reflection upon the content of faith. In the context of this understanding of the nature of the Bible and the nature of theology, biblical theology may be understood as the methodological reflection, undertaken in the light of faith, upon the religious content of Scripture. Since the discipline has the religious content of the Bible as the object of its study, it is biblical; since it reflects upon the content of Scripture in a methodological way, it is theological: hence the term ''biblical theology.'' As a discipline it makes the claim that methodological reflection on the religious content of Scripture for the purpose of understanding its thought in an organic manner is feasible and illuminating. It is in this claim, inherent in the discipline itself, that both the strength and weakness of biblical theology lie.

Strength of Biblical Theology. For the materials with which it works biblical theology has necessarily to depend on exegesis. It is the science of exegesis, and not biblical theology, that achieves direct contact with the thought of the biblical author, the actual meaning the inspired writer wished to convey to his contemporary listener or reader (the literal sense of Scripture). Since the biblical writers did not present their religious conceptions in a systematic fashion, their understanding of religious themes (e.g., faith, hope, love, resurrection, judgment) must be gleaned from the results of the exegesis of those passages where these themes occur or in which they play a part. One cannot understand, for example, faith in St. Paul from single passages in his letters but only from the totality of his writings. The task of the biblical theologian is to penetrate and organize the results of exegesis so as to arrive at the totality of the Apostle's conception of faith as he has bequeathed it to us.

When biblical theology has pursued the study of individual themes in the various authors and books of the NT as well as in the OT to the extent that the themes are present there, it has been at its fruitful best. The articles on biblical themes in modern encyclopedias of the Bible attest to the success of the discipline when it takes this approach to Scripture. In the field of the NT the discipline has enjoyed a similar success in studying the theological thought of Paul, John, and to a limited extent, the Synoptic Gospels. The letters of Paul, the Johannine literature (1–2 Jn, Jn, Rv), and the Synoptic Gospels readily lend themselves to an organic grasp of their thought, since each group of writings possesses fairly constant perspectives, ideas, and aims. The literature of the OT, however, does not contain groupings of material that derive from a single author or circle. Accordingly, in terms of literary units the theological thought of the OT has to be ascertained book by book and in the case of the Pentateuch with the help of the different sources that lie behind it.

The Problematic for a Biblical Theology. The strength of biblical theology consists in the tracing of individual themes throughout the Bible and in coming to grips with the thought of its literary units. In performing these functions it aims at a descriptive presentation of biblical thought, organized in a logical way, couched in modern language and resting solidly on the results of exegesis. These successful approaches to Scripture, however, arrive at the conclusion that it contains different types of methodological reflection on God's self-communication. Materially speaking, it is not a unified but a divergent presentation of thought, even on the same themes. St. Paul's conception of faith, for example, and the theological use he makes of it differ from the conception of faith and the use to which it is put in the Fourth Gospel and in the Synoptic Gospels. The same differentiation exists on many themes among authors and between books in the Bible.

This factor of different ''theologies'' in Scripture creates a serious difficulty for the ultimate goal of biblical theology: to create a theology of the OT, of the NT, and finally of the entire Bible. As long as the discipline works with themes and literary units in Scripture, its organic presentation of the thought of Scripture remains attached to the biblical books and authors, for it bases itself on the results of exegesis. But once it attempts to overcome the factor of differentiation in the theological methodologies in Scripture, its work takes a step away from biblical books and authors to biblical categories of thought (e.g., God, man, creation, grace, sin). Although it adheres to the results of exegesis, it places these results in new contexts. Thus it creates a personal construction of the theology in the Bible. The aphorism that there are as many biblical theologies as there are biblical theologians becomes verified. How this difficulty is to be overcome, if it can be overcome, constitutes a challenge to biblical theologians. Many NT scholars simply prefer to present its theological thought in terms of its principal literary units: the Synoptic Gospels, Paul, and John. In their view the factor of differentiation simply has to be accepted as a reality in the theological methodology of Scripture.

Biblical Theology and Hermeneutic. As far as Scripture is concerned, hermeneutic involves the question of communication and understanding. The Bible is a divinely inspired, religious communication through the written word. By the very fact that it is written word it is, like all literature, confined to time, place, culture, and a particular set of addressees. The original audiences for whom it was written could normally understand it as communication more easily than people of a later time. For the latter it is communication in a translation from Hebrew and Greek, which limits understanding, and it employs thought-patterns and types of literature no longer in vogue, at least in the Western world. Therefore it requires interpretation beyond translation that will bridge the gap between ancient communication and contemporary understanding.

Exegesis and biblical theology both have a role to play in bridging the gap. The first step belongs to exegesis. It is its task to establish the original meaning of the biblical text in its own time, place, and circumstances. The second step belongs, quite naturally, to biblical theology. It organizes the results of exegesis into a total focus that brings the necessary balance to the comprehension of biblical thought. In the performance of its role in the process of the interpretation of Scripture, however, biblical theology is as historical a discipline as is exegesis. In seeking a totality in the understanding of a biblical theme or of a biblical book or author, it must adhere faithfully to the original meaning of Scripture. Exegesis is the criterion by which biblical theology is fundamentally judged. No more than exegesis may it introduce later theological conceptions or religious views into scriptural thought.

Biblical theology makes its contribution directly to those whose knowledge of the Bible has been achieved through exegetical study or through sound exegetical instruction, for they are already in position to appreciate the thematic approach to scriptural understanding as well as the approach in terms of literary units. Finally, both exegesis and biblical theology are stimulated to reexamine their assessment of scriptural data by contemporary questions having a bearing upon biblical teaching, e.g., divorce and remarriage, social responsibility, the meaning of resurrection. The biblical theologian is in good position to consider such questions from his vantage-point in order to contribute to their contemporary solution from the theological implications of Scripture. In this role the biblical theologian joins with the patristic, historical, and contemporary, systematic theologian to contribute to the mature judgment of the magisterium of the Church.

Bibliography: V. HAMP et al., *Lexikon für Theologie und Kirche,* ed. J. HOFER and K. RAHNER, 10 v. (2d, new ed. Freiburg 1957–65) 2:439–451. J. HEMPEL and H. RIESENFELD, *Die Religion in Geschichte und Gegenwart,* 7 v. (3d ed. Tübingen 1957–65) 1:1256–62. K. STENDAHL, *The Interpreter's Dictionary of the Bible,* ed. G. A. BUTTRICK, 4 v. (Nashville 1962) 1:418–432. O. BETZ, *ibid.* 1:432–437. X. LÉON-DUFOUR, ed., *Vocabulaire de théologie biblique* (Paris 1962) xiii–xix. J. ALONSO, ''La Teología Bíblica a través de la historia: Consideración de lagunas tendencias,'' *Miscelanea Comillas* 29 (1958) 9–27. F. M. BRAUN, ''La Théologie biblique,'' *Revue thomiste* 53 (1953) 221–253. S. LYONNET, ''De notione et momento Theologiae Biblicae,'' *Verbum Domini* 34 (1956) 142–153. R. A. F. MACKENZIE, ''The Concept of Biblical Theology,'' *Catholic Theological Society of America. Proceedings* 10 (1955) 48–73. C. SPICQ, ''L'Avènement de la théologie biblique,'' *Revue des sciences philosophiques et théologiques* 35 (1951) 561–574; ''Nouvelles réflexions sur la théologie biblique,'' *ibid.* 42 (1958) 209–219. P. S. WATSON, ''The Nature and Function of Biblical Theology,'' *Expository Times* 73 (1961–62) 195–200. J. GRAY, ''Towards a Theology of the O.T.: The Contribution of Archaeology,'' *ibid.* 74 (1962–63) 347–351. N. W. PORTEOUS, ''The Present State of O.T. Theology,'' *ibid.* 75 (1963–64) 70–74. C. K. BARRETT, ''Ethelbert Stauffer's Theology of the N.T.,'' *ibid.* 72 (1960–61) 356–360. J. C. FENTON, ''Rudolph Bultmann's Theology of the N.T.,'' *ibid.* 73 (1961–62) 8–11. K. GRAYSTON, ''Alan Richardson's Theology of the N.T.,'' *ibid.* 73 (1961–62) 45–50. C. L. MITTON, ''A. M. Hunter's Theology of the N.T.,'' *ibid.* 73 (1961–62) 77–80. A. RICHARDSON, ''Present Issues in N.T. Theology,'' *ibid.* 75 (1963–64) 109–113. R. C. DENTAN, *Preface to O.T. Theology* (rev. ed. New York 1963), with bibliographies: before A.D. 1787 (127–128); 1787–1949 (128–135), and 1949–63 (135–144). R. SCHNACKENBURG, *N.T. Theology Today,* tr. D. ASKEW (New York 1963), with copious bibliog. H. VORGRIMLER, ed., *Dogmatic va. Biblical Theology* (Baltimore 1965). G. S. GLANZMAN and J. A. FITZMYER, *An Introductory Bibliography for the Study of Scripture* (Westminster, Md. 1961) 79–86. W. J. HARRINGTON, *The Path of Biblical Theology* (Dublin 1973). G. HASEL, *Old Testament Theology: Basic Issues in the Current Debate* (Grand Rapids, Mich. 1972); *New Testament Theology: Basic Issues in the Current Debate* (Grand Rapids, Mich. 1978). J. L. MCKENZIE, *A Theology of the Old Testament* (New York 1974). R. H. SCHELKLE, *Theology of the New Testament,* v. 3, tr. W. A. JURGENS (Collegeville, Minn. 1973). H. SCHLIER, *The Relevance of the New Testament,* tr. W. J. O'HARA (New York 1968) 1–25. Biblical theologies: W. G. KÜMMEL, *The Theology of the New Testament,* tr. J. E. STEELY (Nashville, Tenn. 1973). J. L. MCKENZIE, *op. cit.* H. RIDDERBOS, *Paul: An Outline of His Theology,* tr. J. R. DEWITT (Grand Rapids, Mich. 1975). K. H. SCHELKLE, *Theology of the New Testament,* 4 v., tr. W. A. JURGENS (Collegeville, Minn. 1971–76). Current Protestant discussion: K. STENDAHL, *The Interpreter's Dictionary of the Bible,* ed. G. A. BUTTRICK, 4 v. (Nashville, Tenn. 1962) 1:418–432. J. BARR, *The Interpreter's Dictionary of the Bible,* supp., ed. K. CRIM et al. (Nashville, Tenn. 1976) 104–111. B. S. CHILDS, *Biblical Theology in Crisis* (Philadelphia 1970).

[S. B. MARROW/C. P. CEROKE]

BICHIER DES AGES, JEANNE ÉLISABETH, ST.

Cofoundress of the Daughters of the Holy Cross of St. Andrew; b. Le Blanc, near Poitiers, France, July 5, 1773; d. Paris, Aug. 26, 1838. She was the daughter of a public official and was educated at Poitiers. Her early spiritual formation was influenced by an uncle, Abbé de Moussac. After her father's death (1792), she successfully conducted a protracted lawsuit with the revolutionary government to save the family property from confiscation. With her mother she settled at La Guimetière, near Bethines, Poitou, and followed a regular routine of prayer and good works.

Jeanne became the center of the local resistance to the Constitutional clergy. In 1797 she met St. André FOURNET, a priest of nearby Maillé, who had continued his pastoral labors despite his refusal to take the oath supporting the CIVIL CONSTITUTION OF THE CLERGY. Fournet became her spiritual director and advised against her emigration to join the Trappistines. After her mother's death (1804), Jeanne wore peasant clothing and gathered others to aid in her works. When Fournet presented her with a plan to establish a religious congregation to care for the sick and to educate the poor of the district, Jeanne entered the novitiate of the Carmelites at Poitiers to prepare for her superiorship. In 1805 Jeanne and five companions began the first community at La Guimetière. It moved closer to Maillé in 1806, and in 1811 to Rochefort. Jeanne made her religious profession in 1807. The bishop of Poitiers approved the community in 1816 as the Daughters of the Holy Cross of St. Andrew. ''La Bonne Soeur,'' as she was popularly known, guided the new community through rapid growth, despite some misunderstanding with Fournet. By 1820 there were 13 convents, and by 1830 more than 30. When a convent was opened in the Basque country at Ignon, Jeanne came to know St. Michael GARICOÏTS, who became spiritual director of the congregation after Fournet's death in 1834. Jeanne traveled frequently to establish new houses and to carry out her tasks as superior general, but ill health forced her to curtail her activity and to retire to Paris after 1834. She was beatified on May 13, 1934 and canonized with Michael Garicoïts on July 6, 1947.

Feast: Aug. 26.

Bibliography: G. BARRA, *Vive ancora; biografia di sant' Elisabetta Bichier des Ages* (Turin 1961). J. SAUBAT, *Élisabeth Bichier des Ages* (Paris 1942). PIUS XII, ''Plus d'une fois'' (Allocution, July 7, 1947). *Acta Apostolicae Sedis* 39 (1947) 401–408. A. BUTLER, *The Lives of the Saints*, ed. H. THURSTON and D. ATTWATER (New York 1956) 3:410–413.

[T. P. JOYCE]

BICKERDIKE, ROBERT, BL.

Martyr; b. at Low Hall (near Knaresborough), Farnham, Yorkshire,England; hanged, drawn, and quartered at York, Oct. 8, 1586. He was arrested for giving apriest, St.John BOSTE, a glass of ale. At his trial he was alsoaccused ofusing treasonable words, i.e., of defending the reputation of Bl. Francis INGLEBY en route to the latter's execution. Bickerdikewasacquitted, but Judge Rhodes, determined to have his blood, had him removed from thecity jail to York Castle, retried, and condemned for being reconciled to Romeand fortreasonable opinions. He was beatified by Pope John Paul II on Nov. 22, 1987with George Haydock and Companions.

See Also: ENGLAND, SCOTLAND, AND WALES, MARTYRS OF.

Bibliography: R. CHALLONER, *Memoirs of Missionary Priests,* ed. J. H.POLLEN (rev. ed. London 1924). J. MORRIS, *The Catholics of York under Elizabeth* (London,1891).J. H. POLLEN, *Acts of English Martyrs* (London 1891).

[K. I. RABENSTEIN]

BIDDLE, JOHN

Polemicist, pamphleteer; b. Wotton, Gloucestershire, 1615; d. London, 1662. As a grammar school boy, he ''outran his instructors and became tutor to himself,'' translating Vergil and Juvenal. Upon graduating from Magdalen Hall, Oxford (1638), he became master of the Free School, Gloucester, where he wrote ''Twelve Arguments against the Deity of the Holy Ghost.'' For this he was imprisoned and his manuscript seized. It was published in 1647 and ordered to be burnt publicly as blasphemous. Despite a penalty of death (1648) on all who denied the Trinity, he published two tracts against the doctrine. He was saved by friends in Parliament and withdrew to Staffordshire in extreme poverty, preaching and editing the Septuagint. Cromwell's Act of Oblivion (1652) enabled Biddle to gather his followers for public Sunday worship but, on publishing two scriptural catechisms, he was indicted before Parliament (1654). After periods in several prisons, he was banished to close custody in the Scilly Isles. He wrote with pathos and power for release, and he was brought for trial to Westminster and discharged by Lord Chief Justice Glynn. Biddle at once restarted his Bible classes. Again he was tried, fined, and put in prison; he died of disease contracted in the foulness of conditions there.

Bibliography: J. TOULMIN, *A Review of the Life, Character and Writings of the Rev. John Biddle, M.A.* (London 1791). A. B. GROSART, *The Dictionary of National Biography From the Earliest Times to 1900* (London 1885–1900) 2:475–478.

[G. ALBION]

BIEL, GABRIEL

Scholastic theologian and principal representative of late medieval NOMINALISM, sometimes referred to as *Doctor profundissimus;* b. Speyer, Germany, *c.* 1410; d. Einsiedel, Tübingen, Dec. 7, 1495. About 1460, after several years of study at the Universities of Heidelberg, Erfurt, and Cologne, he became principal preacher and vicar at Mainz. Having entered the Brothers of the Common Life *c.* 1468, he became propst of the brotherhouse in Butzbach (Hessen) in 1470 and in Urach (Württemberg) in 1479. In 1484 he took over the chair of theology to teach the *via moderna* at the University of Tübingen (founded in 1477); he was invested as its rector in 1485 and again in 1489. In theology and philosophy, Biel professed to follow the teachings of WILLIAM OF OCKHAM, but he also adopted certain views of St. BONAVENTURE, of St. THOMAS AQUINAS, of RICHARD OF MIDDLETON, and, above all, of John DUNS SCOTUS. Characteristic of his thought are his logic of suppositions, his interpretation and evaluation of intuitive knowledge, and his strong emphasis on the simplicity, omnipotence, and freedom of God. Particular notice should be paid to his development of an ethics covering social and economic questions: property, commerce, a just price (he favored authorized price control, since the formation of a monopoly could endanger the maintenance of a just price), fair taxation, interest rates, monetary operations, currency fluctuation, and the like. His commentary on the *Sentences* serves as the classical handbook of nominalism; it reveals a thorough, systematic, practically serviceable, and Church-oriented attitude, which sets him above any other theological spokesman of his time. Luther received his scholastic orientation through Biel and reflects his influence in both a positive and a negative manner.

Bibliography: Works. Systematic Writings. (1) *Collectorium super IV libros Sententiarum* (Tübingen 1501 and later), bk. 4 is incomplete (to d. 23). Extracts. *De potestate et utilitate monetarum* (bk. 4, Sent. d. 15, q. 9; Offenbach 1516), Eng. tr. R. B. BURKE (Philadelphia 1930); *Quaestiones de iustificatione,* ed. C. FECKES (Münster 1929); *In primam Quaestionem Prologi,* ed. P. BÖHNER (Paterson, N.J. 1939). (2) *Sacri canonis missae expositio* (Reutlingen 1488 and later); a critical ed. (Weisbaden 1963—), 2 v. pub. to 1965. Extracts. *Epitoma expositionis sacri canonis missae* (Tübingen 1499 and later); *Expositio brevis et interlinearis sacri canonis missae* (Tübingen *c.* 1500). Preaching. *Sermones I–IV: De festivitatibus Christi, B.V. Mariae, de sanctis, de tempore* (Tübingen 1499–1500 and later). *Sermo historialis passionis dominicae* (Tübingen 1489 and later). *Sermones medicinales contra pestilentiam,* ed. with *Sermones I–IV.* Shorter writings. *Regula puerorum* (Urach 1483). *Ars grammatica* (Urach *c.* 1483 and later). *Dictata varia de dialectica* (MS; Giessen), Cod. 1250, B.G. 16:86–199. *Defensorium obedientiae apostolicae ad Pium papam II,* ed. in *Sermones III. De communi vita clericorum,* ed. W. M. LANDEEN, in *Research Studies* 28 (1960) 79–95. Three academic addresses (MS; Giessen) Cod. 853, fol. 285–288. Literature. C. FECKES, *Die Rechtfertigungslehre des Gabriel Biel* (Münster 1925). J. HALLER, *Die Anfänge der Universität Tübingen,* 2 v. (Stuttgart 1927–29) 1:153–172; 2:54–64. W. M. LANDEEN, "Gabriel Biel and the Brethren of the Common Life in Germany," *Church History* 20 (1951) 23–36; "Gabriel Biel and the *Devotio Moderna* in Germany," *Research Studies* 27 (1959) 135–214; 28 (1960) 21–45, 61–79. L. GRANE, *Contra Gabrielem. Luthers Auseinandersetzung mit Gabriel Biel* in *Disputatio contra scholasticam theologiam, 1517* (Gyldenal 1962). H. A. OBERMAN, *The Harvest of Medieval Theology: Gabriel Biel and Late Medieval Nominalism* (Cambridge, Mass. 1963).

[V. HEYNCK]

BIFFI, EUGENIO

Member of the Milan Institute of Foreign Missions and bishop of Cartagena, Colombia; b. Milan, Dec. 22, 1829; d. Barranquilla, Colombia, Nov. 8, 1896. He studied at the seminary of Monza and was ordained in Milan on May 21, 1853. He entered the seminary of Foreign Missions of Milan that same year. He was sent to Cartagena (1856) but was expelled in the persecution of Tomas C. de Mosquera. He worked with the Jesuits in the mission of Belize, British Honduras. In 1867 he was named apostolic prefect of Eastern Birmania, residing in Toungoo, where he organized the mission. In 1882 Leo XIII named him bishop of Cartagena at the request of the city, and he was consecrated in Milan on Feb. 19, 1882. In Cartagena he reorganized the seminary and entrusted it to Eudist fathers from France. He founded schools and social welfare agencies, and he restored the church of St. Peter CLAVER and spread the veneration of this saint. He frequently visited his vast diocese and through his kindness gained the love of his people.

Bibliography: P. A. BRIOSCHI, *Un apóstol de dos continentes: Vida del excelentísimo Sr. Eugenio Biffi, de las misiones extranjeras de Milán* (Cartagena 1940).

[J. M. PACHECO]

BIHLMEYER, KARL

Catholic theologian and church historian; b. Aulendorf, Germany, July 7, 1874; d. Tübingen, March 27, 1942. Bihlmeyer studied theology at the University of Tübingen and was ordained in 1897. After a period of pastoral work, he became an instructor at Wilhelmstift, Tübingen, and later succeeded his master, F. X. Funk, as professor of church history at Tübingen University, where he lectured from 1907 to 1940. He revised the sixth edition of Funk's *Kirchengeschichte* (*Manual of Church History*), expanding it to three volumes and bringing out five successive editions based on new historical research and discoveries between 1911 and 1940. The most recent revised editions have been prepared by H. Tüchle [1951–64; Eng. tr., *Church History,* 3 v. (Westminster, Md. 1958–65)]. Bihlmeyer's early interest centered on the ancient Church, and he produced *Die syrischen Kaiser in Rom und das Christum* (Tübingen 1916); "Das Erste Allgemein Konzil zu Nizäa," *Analecta Sacra Tarraconensia* 2 (1926) 199–218; and an edition of Funk's *Die Apostolischen Väter* (Tübingen 1924). His interest extended also to medieval German mysticism, and he published *Heinrich Seuse, Deutsche Schriften* (Stuttgart 1907). He wrote articles for the *Tübinger Theol. Quartalschrift.* In his teaching and writing, Bihlmeyer exhibited a strictly scientific spirit, unconditional adherence to the truth combined with a discriminatory critical sense, and deep loyalty to the Church.

Bibliography: F. X. SEPPELT, *Historisches Jahrbuch der Görres–Gesellschaft* 62–69 (1942–49) 906–908. J. R. GEISELMANN, *Theologische Quartalschrift* 123 (1942) 73–78. H. TÜCHLE, *Lexikon für Theologie und Kirche*, J. HOFER and K. RAHNER 10 v. (2d new ed. Freiburg, 1957–65) 2:457; *Neue deutsche Biographie* (Berlin 1953–) 2:234–235.

[F. DE SA]

BIJNS, ANNA

Flemish poet and Catholic apologist; b. Antwerp, 1493; d. there, 1575. There is little biographical material available. She was a teacher and remained unmarried. Her first collection of poetry was published in 1528; the following year Eligius Eucharius of Ghent translated that work into Latin and published it at Antwerp. Two other published collections of her poems appeared in 1548 and in 1567. Many of her other poems were preserved in 16th- and 17th-century manuscripts, the two most important of which were published in 1886 and in 1902. Some historians believe she was the author of many popular tales and even of the miracle play *Mariken van Nieumeghen* (*Mary of Nimmegen*), but this ascription is doubtful. Bijns' lyrics are cast as "Refereinen," a form roughly similar to the French *ballade* of the *rhétoriquers;* their verse technique resembles that of the *Meistersinger* genre in German literature.

Her poems, striking in imagery and stirring in rhythm, are concerned chiefly with religion, education, friendship, and love. Much of Bijns' religious poetry had a controversial temper: she began writing shortly after Luther's original attacks on the Catholic church, and her passionate defenses, while often partisan, were eloquent, and were convincing at least to the popular mind. Her noncontroversial verse, even when occasionally marred by overt moralizing, reflects both her deep love of Christ and Mary, and a moving filial attachment to the Church. Other lyrics reveal her trust in God, especially in the face of death, a theme she handled with delicacy and power. Her love poems, also somewhat moralistic, are to an extent in the medieval tradition of COURTLY LOVE; they are alive with deep feeling but are less carefully and sensitively wrought than the best of her religious poems.

She was one of the first writers in Low Country literature to describe the beauty of nature, but she rejected the worldly spirit of the Renaissance. Notwithstanding her fervent interest in the religious events that announced the modern age, she might well be considered one of the last representatives of the Middle Ages.

Bibliography: A. BIJNS, *Refereinen,* ed. W. L. VAN HELTEN (Rotterdam 1875); *Nieuwe refereinen* (Ghent 1886); ''Onuitgegeven gedichten van Anna Bijns,'' *Leuvensche Bijdragen* 4 (1902) 199–368. L. ROOSE, *Anna Bijns: Een rederijkster uit de Hervormingstijd* (Vlaamse Academie voor Taal-en Letterkunde, 6th ser. Bekroonde Werken 93; Ghent 1963), with full bibliog.

[L. ROOSE]

BILHILD, ST.

Abbess, foundress of Altmünster near Mainz; fl. early eighth century. She is listed in a Fulda calendar of the ninth century, but details of her life are known only through legends written down in the twelfth century. These have her born of noble parents at Veitshöchheim near Würzburg (probably confused with Hocheim near Mainz) and married at age 17 to Hetan I, duke of Thuringia. During a war in which he died, she fled to her uncle, Bp. Rigibert of Mainz, became a nun, and founded the cloister, which in the twelfth century possessed property at Veitshöchheim and Hettstadt.

Feast: Nov. 27.

Bibliography: J. MABILLON, *Annales ordinis s. Benedicti,* 6 v. (2d ed. Lucca 1739–45) 2:90. G. KARCH, *Die Legende der hl. Bilhildis* (Würzburg 1869). M. STIMMING, ''Die heilige B.,'' *Mitteilungen des Instituts für österreichische Geschichtsforschung* 37 (1917) 234–255, with text of a falsified foundation charter from the twelfth century. J. BRAUN, *Tracht und Attribute der Heiligen in der deutschen Kunst* (Stuttgart 1943).

[W. E. WILKIE]

BILIO, LUIGI,

Italian cardinal; b. Alessandria (Piedmont), March 25, 1826; d. Rome, Jan. 1, 1884. He came from a poor family and entered the BARNABITES in Genoa. After ordination he taught philosophy for some years in various Barnabite colleges. In 1857 he went to Rome to teach theology in the Barnabite house of studies. He became a consultor of the Holy Office (1864) and of the Congregation of the Index (1865). In 1866 he was named cardinal. He served as bishop of the suburbicarian Diocese of Sabina, as prefect of the Congregations of Rites and of the Index, and as *penitenziere maggiore* in the Sacred Penitentiary. At the conclave in 1878 he was *papabile* but declined election. Bilio participated in the definitive drafting of the SYLLABUS OF ERRORS, whose composition was accelerated and completed after his appointment as consultor of the Holy Office and as head of the commission that prepared the document. His courteous and conciliating character would indicate that he exercised a moderating influence on the contents of the Syllabus. He was one of the presidents at VATICAN COUNCIL I, where his action was always moderate and considerate toward the arguments of the minority group in the discussion concerning papal infallibility and in the preparation of the constitution *Pastor aeternus.* Bilio's very valuable diary of Vatican Council I has been preserved but not published.

Bibliography: G. BOFFITO, *Biblioteca barnabitica,* 4 v. (Florence 1933–37) 1:220–227. C. BUTLER, *The Vatican Council,* 2 v. (New York 1930). G. MARTINA, ''Osservazioni sulle varie redazioni del *Sillabo,*'' in *Chiesa e stato nell'Ottocento: Miscellanea in onore di P. Pirri,* ed. R. AUBERT et al., 2 v. (Padua 1962) 2:419–523. U. BETTI, *La costituzione dommatica ''Pastor aeternus'' del Concilio Vaticano* (Rome 1961) 554, *passim.*

[A. MARTINI]

BILLERBECK, PAUL

Specialist in the theology of Judaism; b. Bad Schönfliess, Neumark, Province of Brandenburg, April 4, 1853; d. Frankfurt an der Oder, Dec. 23, 1932. After serving as pastor of the Evangelical Church successively in Zielensieg and Heinersdorf, Billerbeck lived in retirement at Frankfurt an der Oder from 1914 to 1932. His lifework, composed entirely by himself, is his *Kommentar zum NT aus Talmud und Midrasch* (4 v. Munich 1922–28; 2d ed. 1956 with 2 index v. by K. Adolph, 1956–61), a collection of everything that Jewish, particularly rabbinical, literature has to offer for an understanding of the *New Testament,* with a comprehensive grasp of all the material. With this contribution Billerbeck lastingly influenced and gave a new direction to *New Testament* studies throughout the world.

St. Julie (Marie Rose) Billiart.

Bibliography: J. JEREMIAS, *Theologische Blätter* 12 (1933) 33–36.

[J. SCHMID]

BILLIART, JULIE (MARIE ROSE), ST.

Religious foundress; b. Cuvilly, Picardy, France, July 12, 1751; d. Namur, Belgium, April 8, 1816. Daughter of an owner of a small shop, Julie resided in what is now the French department of the Oise. After hardships occasioned by the failure of her family's small business and the shock of witnessing the attempted murder of her father, Julie became unable to walk for 22 years. During her illness she developed her contemplative and apostolic interests by counseling and teaching those who visited her. During the French Revolution she gained a reputation for harboring nonjuring clergymen and refusing the services of constitutional priests. Her life imperiled, she was forced to take refuge in Amiens. There she met Françoise Blin de Bourdon, later Mother St. Joseph. The two, under the direction of Joseph VARIN D'AINVILLE, undertook the foundation of a religious community that developed into the Notre Dame de Namur Sisters. In 1809 the motherhouse was transferred to Namur, Belgium, where Mother Julie, as superior general, established sound ascetical and educational traditions. She also started seven other houses. The Sisters of Notre Dame of Amersfoort, Netherlands, whose first postulants were trained by Mother St. Joseph, regard Mother Julie as their foundress. So do the Sisters of Notre Dame of Coesfield, Germany. Mother Julie was beatified May 13, 1906 and canonized by Paul VI June 21, 1969.

Feast: April 8.

Bibliography: J. CLARE, ed., *The Life of Blessed Julie Billiart* (2d ed. St. Louis 1909). M. G. CARROLL, *The Charred Wood: The Story of Blessed Julie Billiart* (London 1952). F. CHARMOT, *In the light of the Trinity; the Spirituality of Blessed Julie Billiart* (Westminster, Md. 1964). M. F. MCMANAMA, *As Gold In the Furnace: The Life of Blessed Julie Billiart* (Milwaukee 1957). M. HALCANT, *Educational Ideals of Blessed Julie Billiart* (New York 1922). MOTHER SAINT JOSEPH, *The Memoirs of Mother Frances Blin de Bourdon*, tr. SISTER M. GODFREY (Westminster, Md. 1975). R. MURPHY, *Julie Billiart, Woman of Courage: The Story of the Foundress of the Sisters of Notre Dame* (New York 1995). A. RICHOMME, *L'appel de la route* (Paris 1968).

[J. BLAND]

BILLICK, EBERHARD

Theologian of the Catholic Reformation; b. *c.* 1499; d. Cologne, Jan. 12, 1557. Having entered the Carmelite Order at Cologne in 1513, he received a doctorate in theology and was professor (1540–52) and dean (1545–46) of the theology at the faculty of Cologne. A zealous defender of the Catholic faith, he was deeply concerned with the internal reform of the Church and his order, as well as with the urgent questions raised by the Reformation. Hermann von Wied, the Archbishop of Cologne, used him as theological consultant for the question of reform and sent him as his representative to the religious discussions held at Hagenau (1540) and at Worms and Regensburg (1540–41). However, when Hermann himself joined the Reformation forces (1542–43) and took the reformer Martin Bucer into his archdiocese, Billick at once sharply opposed him. During the struggle for the preservation of the Catholic faith in the Archdiocese of Cologne, he became, with J. Gropper (d. 1559), the center of resistance to Protestantism. His importance as a theologian shows in his polemical and controversial writings: *Judicium deputatorum universitatis et secundarii cleri Coloniensis de doctrina et vocatione M. Buceri ad Bonnam* (Cologne 1543); *Judicii universitatis et cleri Coloniensis defensio* (Cologne 1545); *De ratione summovendi praesentis temporis dissidia* (Cologne 1557); and *De dissidiis Ecclesiae componendis* (Cologne 1559), as well as in his participation as the emperor's representative at the negotiations for reconciliation at Regensburg (1546) and Augsburg (1548) and in his appointment (1551–52) as the theologian of Adolf von Schaumburg, archbishop of Cologne, at the Council of Trent.

Bibliography: A. POSTINA, *Der Karmelit Eberhard Billick* (1901), v. 2.2–3 of *Erläuterungen und Ergänzungen zu Janssens Geschichte des deutschen Volkes,* 4 v. (Freiburg im Br. 1899–1902). P. FERDINAND, *Dictionnaire d'histoire et de géographie ecclésiastiques,* ed. A. BAUDRILLART et al. (Paris 1912–) 8:1480–81. H. JEDIN, ''Die deutschen Teilnehmer am Trienter Konzil,'' *Theologische Quartalschrift* 122 (1941) 252–253. *Neue deutsche Biographie* (Berlin 1953–) 2:238–239.

[A. FRANZEN]

BILLOT, LOUIS

Theologian; b. Sierck (Moselle, France), Jan. 12, 1846; d. Galloro (near Rome), Dec. 18, 1931. He studied at Metz and Bordeaux and at the major seminary in Blois, where he was ordained in 1869. In the same year, he entered the Society of Jesus. He then preached in Paris (1875–78) and at Laval (1878–79). He began to teach dogmatic theology first at the Catholic University of Angers (1879–82), then at the Jesuit scholasticate on the Isle of Jersey (1882–85), and finally at the Gregorian (1885–1910), with a brief stay in Paris (1886). Leo XIII, most eager to promote a return to Thomistic doctrine, had him called to Rome. In 1910 he was named consultor to the Holy Office, and in 1911 he was created a cardinal by Pius X. Because of his sympathies for the movement Action Française, which was condemned by Pius XI in 1927, he was persuaded to renounce his cardinalitial dignity. His obedience was irreproachable, and he prevailed upon the members of the movement to sacrifice their ideas and conform to the orders of the pope. He then left for the novitiate of the Jesuit Roman province at Galloro and remained there until his death.

His works consist chiefly in theological treatises: *De Verbo Incarnato* (Rome 1892); *De Ecclesiae sacramentis* (2 v. Rome 1894–95); *Disquisitio de natura et ratione peccati personalis* (Rome 1894); *De peccato originali* (Rome 1912); *De Deo uno et trino* (Rome 1895); *De Ecclesia Christi* (2 v. Rome 1898–1910); *De virtutibus infusis* (Rome 1901); *Quaestiones de novissimis* (Rome 1902): *De Inspiratione Sacrae Scripturae* (Rome 1903); *De Sacra Traditione* (Rome 1904); *De gratia Christi* (Rome 1912). Added to these are several articles in the review *Gregorianum,* and two series of 10 articles each: ''La Parousie,'' *Etudes* 54–56 (1917–19), edited in one volume (Paris 1920); and ''La Providence de Dieu et le nombre infini d'hommes en dehors de la voie normale du salut,'' *Etudes* 56–60 (1919–23).

Following the directives of Leo XIII, Billot gave primary importance in his teachings to the fundamental theses of St. Thomas's metaphysics, especially the analogy of being, the distinction between act and potency, and the real distinction between essence and existence. He viewed the last distinction as one of greatest importance: *essentia* and *esse* are really distinct in creatures, and one and the same in God. Here is what the whole of metaphysics hinges upon, the very root of the assertion that nothing univocal can be ascribed to God and creatures. Billot used this distinction in the treatise on the Incarnation to explain the distinction between person and nature; having recourse to and renewing Capreolus's opinion, he defined the person of Christ as *Esse Verbi.*

His treatise on the Trinity is of special merit because of his subtle analysis of the concept of relation; it exemplifies a theological treatise, the rational explanations of which are systematically constructed with admirable logic upon a metaphysical notion. In his treatise on the infused virtues, he stressed the rational basis of the judgment of credibility. In the treatise on the Eucharist, he insisted on the notion of conversion as characterizing transubstantiation. He also developed a theory of the Mass according to which the sacrifice is to be understood as essentially a mystical immolation.

His thesis on the salvation of infidels was somewhat less acceptable. He held that a very great number of adults remain children from a moral point of view and, therefore, upon death go to Limbo. This was a solution that was generally rejected by theologians.

Among the doctrines or movements that he fought against especially were Modernism and Liberalism. He denounced Modernism with vigor, and in the encyclical *PASCENDI* his ideas, his formulas, and even excerpts from his works can be recognized. In Liberalism he saw a heresy that had issued from the ideas of the French Revolution and that was founded on an atheistic philosophy; he strove to refute the error that claims that individual liberty is man's supreme good. He did not conceal his hostility toward democratic ideas, and he vividly criticized the *Sillon* movement (*see* SANGNIER, MARC). Billot is justly praised for possessing a remarkable ability to speculate dogmatically and for his concern in giving a vigorous philosophical structure to theology. On the other hand, it must be admitted that he showed almost no interest at all in positive theology, and that at times he even mistrusted it.

Bibliography: H. LE FLOCH, *Le Cardinal Billot* (Paris 1947). J. LEBRETON, *Catholicisme* 2:61–63. A. MICHEL, *Dictionnaire de théologie catholique,* A. VACANT et al., eds. 15 v. (Paris 1903–50) Tables générales 1:444–446. E. HOCEDEZ, *Histoire de la théologie au XIXe siècle* (Brussels-Paris 1947) v. 3. F. COPLESTON, *A Catholic Dictionary of Theology* (Westminster, Md. 1950) 1:268–270.

[J. GALOT]

BILLUART, CHARLES RENÉ

Dominican theologian and controversialist; b. Revin, Belgium, Jan. 28, 1685; d. there, Jan. 20, 1757. He received his early education from the Jesuits at Charleville. At the age of 16, he took the Dominican habit at the priory in Revin and was ordained in 1708. After two years of graduate study at Liège, he became professor of philosophy at Douai. At various times he held positions of responsibility in his province, of which he was three times provincial, but his chief interests were theological and academic. He engaged in much controversy on matters of contemporary interest, especially Jansenism and quietism, and the Thomistic position with respect to both. His major work, however, was his *Summa S. Thomae hodiernis academiarum moribus accomodata* (Liège 1746–51), in which he attempted to present the ideas and even the order and letter of St. Thomas Aquinas, together with certain questions from ecclesiastical history. The provincial chapter of the Belgian province had requested such a work in 1733, and the master general had entrusted its composition to Billuart. Its success is indicated by the publication of 13 editions. Billuart later abridged this work in his *Summa Summae Sancti Thomae sive compendium theologiae* (Liège 1754), of which seven editions were made.

Billuart stated that his primary sources would be St. Thomas and his principal disciples. His references to Cajetan, John of St. Thomas, and the Salmanticenses are relatively infrequent. He depended chiefly upon Francis SYLVIUS, also a native Belgian and a professor at Douai, but not a Dominican. Billuart borrowed from GONET's *Clypeus theologiae thomisticae* for his method and proofs from scripture and tradition. For historical materials he turned to Alexander Natalis. Billuart was no eclectic, however, for in making use of many authors he was selective and accepted only those conclusions that corresponded with his own thought. His writings have exerted a considerable influence upon subsequent Thomism, an influence clearly discernible in the works of many contemporary Thomists.

Bibliography: P. MANDONNET, *Dictionnaire de théologie catholique,* A. VACANT et al., eds. 15 v. (Paris 1903–50) 2.2:890–892. C. R. BILLUART, *Supplementum Cursus Theologiae,* ed. D. LABYE, 20 v. (new ed. Paris 1827–31), ''Vita auctoris.'' L. FLYNN, *Billuart and His Summa Sancti Thomae* (London, Canada 1938).

[R. P. STENGER]

BILLY, JACQUES DE

Benedictine monk and patrologist; b. Guise (Aisne), 1535; d. Paris, Dec. 25, 1581. Educated in the humanities at Paris, Billy studied law at Orléans and Poitiers, and after the death of his parents, devoted himself to Greek and Hebrew letters at Lyon and Avignon. He succeeded his brother as abbot of St-Michel-en-l'Herm (Vendée) and of Notre Dame des Châtelliers (île de Ré). Driven from his abbey by religious wars, he lived at Nantes, Laon, and Paris, and studied, edited, commented on, and translated (into Latin or French) the Greek Church Fathers. His interest centered on Gregory of Nazianzus, John Damascene, Isidore of Pelusium, Epiphanius, and John Chrysostom; but he contributed also studies on Augustine, Gregory I, Irenaeus, Basil, Nicetas, Serronius, Psellos, Nonnus, and Elias of Crete. His Greek dictionary, *Locutiones graecae*, achieved a quick success. He published also books of sermons and spiritual verses; his letters are still in MSS at Sens and Troyes.

Bibliography: R. METZ, *Lexikon für Theologie und Kirche* [2] 2:478. P. SCHMITZ, *Dictionnaire d'histoire et de géographie ecclésiastiques* 8: 1488–90. R. GAZEAU, *Catholicisme* 2:63–64. *Gallia Christiana* 2:1296, 1421–22. B. HEURTEBIZE, *Dictionnaire de théologie catholique* 2.1:888–889.

[P. ROCHE]

BILOCATION

The location of one body in two places at the same time. This presents a special difficulty in scholasticism, where the Aristotelian notions of LOCATION (*ubi*) and PLACE are applied to events of the supernatural order. The difficulty is usually resolved by distinguishing between true bilocation, or simultaneous location in two places commensurately, and apparent bilocation, where the second supposed location is noncommensurate.

F. SUÁREZ and his followers maintain that, because of the Catholic doctrine of the Eucharist, true bilocation is both possible and necessary to hold. The argument for this rests ultimately on Suárez' understanding of location as absolute and independent of external place. St. Thomas Aquinas and scholastics in general hold the contrary. If location means that a body is completely surrounded by its place, then to admit a second location at the same time is to say the body is both surrounded and not surrounded—a contradiction. These authors explain the Eucharist as a noncommensurate presence in place. Similarly, they answer difficulties raised by reputed bilocations of the saints by maintaining that these also are only apparent bilocations—the second apparent location being explained miraculously.

See Also: BILOCATION, MYSTICAL; MIRACLES (THEOLOGY OF)

Bibliography: R. MASI, *Cosmologia* (Rome 1961). P. H. J. HOENEN, *Cosmologia* (5th ed. Rome 1956).

[P. R. DURBIN]

BILOCATION, MYSTICAL

An extraordinary mystical phenomenon in which the material body seems to be simultaneously present in two distinct places at the same time. Since it is physically impossible that a physical body completely surrounded by its place be present in another place at the same time, this could not occur even by a miracle. Therefore, bilocation is always an apparent or seeming bilocation. The most noteworthy cases among the saints are those of Clement, Francis of Assisi, Anthony of Padua, Francis Xavier, Joseph Cupertino, Martin de Porres, and Alphonsus Liguori. When bilocation occurs, the true and physical body is present in one place and is only apparently present in the other by means of a representation of some kind. This representation could be caused supernaturally, diabolically, or by means of a natural power or energy as yet unknown. If the apparent bilocation is caused supernaturally, the body is physically present in one place and represented in the other place in the form of a vision, i.e., through the instrumentality of angels or through an intellectual, imaginative, or sensible vision caused by God in the witnesses. Another possible explanation is that the body of the mystic was transported instantaneously, through the gift of AGILITY, from one place to another and was returned in the same manner. In this case, the apparent bilocation would be reduced to the phenomenon of agility.

Bibliography: R. OMEZ, *Psychical Phenomena*, tr. R. HAYNES (New York 1958). A. ROYO, *The Theology of Christian Perfection*, tr. and ed. J. AUMANN (Dubuque 1962). J. G. ARINTERO, *The Mystical Evolution in the Development and Vitality of the Church*, tr. J. AUMANN, 2 v. (St. Louis 1949–51). A. TANQUEREY, *The Spiritual Life*, tr. H. BRANDERIS (2d ed. Tournai 1930; reprint Westminster, Md. 1945). A. WIESINGER, *Occult Phenomena in the Light of Theology*, tr. B. BATTERSHAW (Westminster, Md. 1957).

[J. AUMANN]

BILOXI, DIOCESE OF

At the time that the diocese of Biloxi (*Dioecesis Biloxiiensis*) was established in 1977, it covered 17 counties with 42 parishes, 28 schools, and 48,000 Catholics. As early as 1970 Bishop Joseph Brunini of Jackson approached Rome about creating a second diocese in MISSISSIPPI. Brunini successfully pressed his case and in 1977, Rome created the diocese of Biloxi in the southeastern part of the state along the Gulf coast. Like Jackson, it is a suffragan see of the Archdiocese of NEW ORLEANS. Its first bishop, Most Reverend Joseph L. Howze, was no stranger to Mississippi, having served as auxiliary bishop in the Jackson diocese since 1973.

Howze was the first African American bishop to head a diocese in the 20th century. Born in Daphne, Alabama, he was 53 at the time of his appointment to Biloxi. A convert to Catholicism, he earned his B.S. from Alabama State University at Montgomery, and for a time taught high school. He studied for the priesthood at Epiphany College in Newburgh, NY, the Diocesans Preparatory Seminary in Buffalo, NY, and St. Bonaventure University. Ordained for the diocese of Raleigh, NC, he served as a parish pastor for a time, and in 1973 was appointed Brunini's Auxiliary Bishop.

Serving from the beginning of the diocese in 1977 until his retirement in 2001, Howze concentrated his efforts on building up the diocese in parishes and the number of Catholics while addressing prominent issues such as the role of the laity, the growing influence of women, race, suppression of a short-lived Lefebvre movement, and the promotion of peace. Historically, the area has been the home to people of different ethnic backgrounds: French, Spanish, African Americans and more recently Asian immigrants. Bishop Howze established a parish in D'Iberville, MI for Vietnamese Catholics. Its economy and the counties covered by the diocese depend on the fishing industry, shipbuilding (the famous Ingalls Shipbuilding company), and importing/exporting. In the year 2000 the diocese spanned 11 counties with a Catholic population of 68,000 out of a total population of 737,000, 41 priests and a representative number of brothers and sisters, along with 18 schools and 44 parishes.

On May 15, 2001, Rome announced that Thomas Rodie, vicar-general of the Archdiocese of New Orleans, was chosen as Howze's successor. Bishop Rodie was officially installed as the second ordinary of the diocese of Biloxi in July, 2001.

Bibliography: C. ELLINGTON, *Christ: The Living Water, The Catholic Church in Mississippi.* (Jackson, 1989). M. V. NAMORATO *The Catholic Church in Mississippi, 1911–1984* (Westport, CT, 1998).

[M. V. NAMORATO]

BINCHOIS, GILLES

Polyphonic composer of the Burgundian school; b. Mons (Hainaut), Belgium, *c.* 1400; d. Soignies (near Mons), Sept. 20, 1460. After a military service in his youth, Binchois served from *c.* 1430 as chaplain at the Burgundian court. He composed motets, hymns, Magnificats, and Mass sections that employ with distinction the technical devices of his day. One motet is isorhythmic; another, in honor of the Holy Cross, uses ''*fermata*-marked block chords'' to emphasize the important words; and several call for added voices in faux bourdon. The Magnificats are often characterized by faux bourdon-like

Guillaume Dufay and Gilles Binchois. (©Bettmann/CORBIS)

writing (perhaps an effect of English influence). Plainsong melodies are paraphrased in some Masses, and one *Agnus Dei* is noteworthy for its use of the lower range of the bass voice. Despite his excellent sacred music, he was known chiefly for his chansons. Many of these became the basis of later compositions, notably *De plus en plus* and *Comme femme desconfortée,* used, respectively, by OKEGHEM in a Mass and by DESPREZ in a *Stabat Mater.* Binchois is mentioned by TINCTORIS and others as among the most distinguished musicians of his era, and Okeghem wrote a *Déploration* on his death.

Bibliography: J. MARIX, ed., *Les Musiciens de la cour de Bourgogne au XVe siècle, 1420–1467 . . .* (Paris 1937), 10 Mass parts, 4 Magnificats, 17 sacred and 36 secular works. Modern reprs. in *Trienter Codices,* ed. G. ADLER and O. KOLLER, *Denkmäler der Tonkunst in Österreich* (1893– ; repr. Graz 1959–) 14, 15, 22, 53. J. SCHMIDT-GÖRG, *Die Musik in Geschichte und Gegenwart,* ed. F. BLUME (Kassel-Basel 1949–) 1:1853–57. C. VAN DEN BORREN, *Études sur le XVe siècle musical* (The Hague 1941). G. REESE, *Music in the Renaissance* (rev. ed. New York 1959). *Histoire de la musique,* ed. ROLAND-MANUEL, 2 v. (Paris 1960–63) v. 1; v. 9, 16 of *Encyclopédie de la Pléiade.* C. BERGER, ''Hexachord und Modus: Drei Rondeaux von Gilles Binchois,'' *Basler Jahrbuch für Historische Musikpraxis,* 16 (1992) 71–87. J. A. BOUCHER, ''The Religious Music of Gilles Binchois'' (Ph.D. diss. Boston University 1963). D. FALLOWS, ''Gilles de Bins Binchois,'' in *The New Grove Dictionary of Music and Musicians,* ed. S. SADIE, v. 2 (New York 1980) 709–722. A. KIRKMAN and D. SLAVIN, eds. *Binchois Studies* (Oxford 2000). D. M. RANDEL, ed., *The Harvard Biographical Dictionary of Music* (Cambridge, Mass. 1996) 79–80. D. SLAVIN, ''Some Distinctive Features of Songs by Binchois,'' *Journal of Musicology* 10 (1992) 342–361. N. SLONIMSKY, ed., *Baker's Biographical Dictionary of Musicians* (8th ed. New York 1992) 184.

[C. V. BROOKS]

BINDING AND LOOSING

This couplet occurs in the New Testament only in Matthew, where Christ promises to PETER (16.19) and to the DISCIPLES (18.18) that whatever they bind or loose on earth will also be bound or loosed in heaven. In most of the examples of the rabbinic usage given by Strack-Billerbeck (*Kommentar zum Neuen Testament,* 1:738–741), *'ăsar* and *šerā'* mean to declare something forbidden or allowed by the Law; there are a few examples of their meaning to exclude someone from the community or to readmit him. According to J. Jeremias (*Theological Dictionary of the New Testament* 3:751), the technical meanings that the couplet had in the rabbinic schools are particular applications of the original sense, which was to pass judgment, whether of condemnation or of pardon. While Peter and the Disciples are to exercise this power ''on earth,'' their acts will be ratified ''in heaven,'' that is, by the divine judgment. The exegesis of this phrase has been much influenced by the immediately preceding context (Mt 18.15–17), where is given the rule of fraternal correction, leading up to the excommunication of the obdurate offender. In the light of this context, v.18 has been taken to refer to the power to excommunicate or to absolve from excommunication, and hence to the power to retain or forgive sin. It is now generally agreed, however, that the connection between these verses is not original, and that from the context one can only conclude that the Evangelist, along with the community for which he wrote, saw the power to excommunicate as an application of the power to bind and loose. Most modern Catholic exegetes understand the terms in a broader sense: of the authority to pass judgments, both doctrinal and disciplinary, which are binding in conscience on the members of the Church. Vatican Council II clearly took the terms in this broad sense when, in reference to the supreme and universal power of the whole episcopate, it declared [*Dogmatic Constitution on the Church* 22; *Acta Apostolicae Sedis* 57 (1965) 26]: ''It is certain that that office of binding and loosing which was given to Peter (*Matth.* 16, 19) was also granted to the college of the Apostles, joined with its head (*Matth.* 18, 18; 28, 16–20).''

See Also: KEYS, POWER OF.

Bibliography: F. BÜCHSEL, *Theological Dictionary of the New Testament* 2:60–61. J. JEREMIAS, *Theological Dictionary of the*

New Testament 3:749–53. O. MICHEL, *Reallexikon für Antike und Christentum*, ed. T. KLAUSER (Stuttgart 1950—) 2:374–380. H. THYEN and J. HEUBACH, *Die Religion in Geschichte und Gegenwart* (Tübingen 1957–65) 5:1449–53. A. VÖGTLE, *Lexikon für Theologie und Kirche*, ed. J. HOFER and K. RAHNER (Freiburg 1957–65) 2:480–82. J. A. EMERTON, ''Binding and Loosing—Forgiving and Retaining,'' *Journal of Theological Studies* 13 (1962) 325–31. G. BORNKAMM, ''The Authority to 'Bind' and 'Loose' in the Church in Matthew's Gospel,'' *Perspective* 11 (1970) 37–50. W. G. THOMPSON, *Matthew's Advice to a Divided Community* (Rome 1970) 188–194. J. D. M. DERRETT, ''Binding and Loosing,'' *Journal of Biblical Literature* 102 (1983) 112–117.

[F. A. SULLIVAN]

BINET, ÉTIENNE

Jesuit preacher and spiritual writer; b. Dijon, 1569; d. Paris, July 4, 1639. He entered the Society of Jesus at Novellara, Italy. After Henry IV had authorized the reestablishment of the society within his realm in 1603, Binet returned to France, where he played an important part in Jesuit affairs. He was rector of the Jesuit colleges at Rouen and Paris and provincial of the provinces of Paris, Champagne, and Lyons, successively. He had a widespread reputation as a preacher, and his finest writing from a literary point of view, *Essai des merveilles de la nature* (Rouen 1621), was written as an aid for preachers.

He is remembered chiefly as an important figure in the renewal of religious life in France in the 17th century. A close friend of St. Francis de Sales and St. Jane Frances de Chantal, Binet had a cheerful sort of piety closely resembling that of the Salesian school. He was the author of many popular spiritual works that went through countless editions in various languages. One of the most striking is *La Grand chef-d'oeuvre de Dieu et les souveraines perfections de la sainte Vierge* (Paris 1634). He also wrote the lives of various saints, including SS. Ignatius Loyola, Francis Xavier, and Louis Gonzaga. Binet's testament as an eminent religious superior was contained in *Quel est le meilleur gouvernement, le rigoureux ou le doux?* (Paris 1636). He was one of the outstanding religious figures of his day, one who contributed notably to the popularization of the devout life among the people.

Bibliography: C. SOMMERVOGEL, *Bibliothèque de la Compagnie de Jésus* 11 vol. (Brussels-Paris 1890–1932; v. 12 suppl. 1960) 1:1487–1506. M. OLPHE-GALLIARD, *Dictionnaire de spiritualité ascétique et mystique. Doctrine et histoire*, ed. M. VILLER et al. (Paris 1932–) 1:1620–23. R. DAESCHLER, *Dictionnaire d'histoire et de géographie ecclésiastiques*, ed. A. BAUDRILLART et al. (Paris 1912–) 8:1504–05.

[J. T. KELLEHER]

BINGHAM, JOSEPH

English clergyman and scholar whose dedication to ecclesiastical antiquities enriched the literature of the English Church; b. Wakefield, Sept. 1668; d. Havant, Hampshire, Aug. 17, 1723. He won renown as a student at University College, Oxford, receiving his B.A. in 1688 and a fellowship in 1689. Two years later he was made a college tutor. In 1695, when the Trinitarian controversy was at its height, Bingham was accused of preaching unsound doctrines and was forced to withdraw from the university. Assigned immediately to the rectory of HeadbournWorthy, he began his scholarly work *Origines ecclesiasticae,* or *The Antiquities of the Christian Church* (10 v. 1708–22), which remains a valuable treatment on the customs and exercises of the Church during the first 500 years. He was the father of ten children by Dorothy Pocock, daughter of R. Pocock, bishop of Winchester. Pocock assigned Bingham (1712) to the rectory at Havant, near Portsmouth, where, less impoverished, he was enabled to complete his monumental *Antiquities.* Among his lesser works were *The French Church's Apology for the Church of England* (1706) and *The Scholastical History of Lay Baptism* (1712–14).

Bibliography: *Works,* ed. R. BINGHAM, 10 v. (new ed. Oxford 1855), with biography. J. H. OVERTON, *The Dictionary of National Biography from the Earliest Times to 1900,* (London 1885–1900) 63 vol. 2:510–512. D. CARTER, *Die Religion in Geschichte und Gegenwart,* 7 v. (Tübingen 1957–65) 1:1294. F. L. CROSS, *The Oxford Dictionary of the Christian Church* (London 1957) 173. N. SYKES, *Dictionnaire d'histoire et de géographie ecclésiastiques*, ed. A. BAUDRILLART et al. (Paris 1912–) 8:1506–08. H. ARMBRUSTER, *Lexikon für Theologie und Kirche*, ed. J. HOFER and K. RAHNER, 10 v. (2d new ed. Freiburg, 1957–65) 2:483.

[M. A. FRAWLEY]

BINIUS, SEVERIN

Editor of conciliar texts; b. Randerath, near Aachen, Germany, 1573; d. Cologne, Feb. 14, 1641. His career was centered in Cologne, where he was rector of the university from 1627 to 1629, and vicar–general of the diocese from 1631 to 1641. He published the histories of SOCRATES, THEODORET, SOZOMEN, and EVAGRIUS SCHOLASTICUS (Cologne 1612). In his main work, *Concilia generalia et provincialia* (4 v., Cologne 1606), he made use of the work of L. SURIUS, A. CARAFA, and Gracia de Loaisa's 1593 edition of Spanish councils, but he printed no Greek texts. The second edition (9 v., 1618) included Greek texts and made use of the Roman edition of Paul V (1608–12). But Binius abandoned the typographical distinction which had been used in the Roman edition in favor of 17th-century Latin versions of ancient Greek and Latin texts, and the resulting confusion persists to the present. A third edition in 11 volumes appeared in Paris in 1636.

Bibliography: J. B. MARTIN, *Dictionnaire de théologie catholique*, A. VACANT et al, 15 v. (Paris 1903–60) 2.1:900–901. A. FRANZEN, *Lexikon für Theologie und Kirche*, ed. J. HOFER and K. RAHNER, 10 v. (2d new ed. Freiburg, 1957–65) 2:483–484.

[B. L. MARTHALER]

BIOLOGY, I (HISTORY OF)

Biology is the experimental science that studies living things and their vital activities. It takes its origin from the natural human desire to know what living things are and what they do, but also, and more generally, from a practical interest in acquiring food, clothing, shelter, and protection, and in curing sickness. People sometimes tried to obtain these things, and especially cures, by supplicating the gods and having recourse to magic. People often also used a pragmatic approach, however, to determine things such as what foods were edible and where game was most likely to be found. In this way empirical knowledge about diet, medicinal herbs, and the raising of crops and animals gradually accumulated. Around the 7th century B.C. a new mentality manifested itself among the Greeks. The Greek quest for knowledge was motivated by wonder, a desire to know the causes of things, a desire satisfied only though observation and logical reasoning. The spirit and achievement of such research were embodied in the works of the father of medicine, HIPPOCRATES (fl. 400 B.C.). Most of the 60 or 70 separate treatises attributed to him were written over a period of several centuries. In these treatises are found not only remedies for different illnesses that are the fruits of empirical observation, but also an attempt to understand what the causes of illnesses are, and why the remedies work. The attempts at causal explanation were often far from the mark, but still represent a step beyond pragmatic generalizations.

Greek Period. The origin of biology as a science seeking knowledge of living things for its own sake, rather than for the sake of contributing to human well-being, is found above all in the works of ARISTOTLE (*c.* 384–322 B.C.). Aristotle founded biology as a school and was the foremost biologist of antiquity.

Aristotle's studies of living things can be divided into three kinds. He regarded living things as composed of matter and form, and he regarded the soul being the natural form distinguishing living natural things from other natural things. His treatise *On the Soul* treats the soul in itself. The second kind of treatise studies those activities of living things that are explained in terms of both soul and body, but chiefly in terms of the soul (e.g., *On Memory, On Sense and Sensation*). The final group of treatises examine those aspects of living things that are understood chiefly in terms of the body (e.g., *Parts of Animals, Generation of Animals*). In these latter treatises Aristotle first seeks to establish what the facts are, and then to seek causal explanations for them. His insistence on observation, his search for causes behind observed facts, his emphasis on seeking the final causes of organisms' parts and activities, along with his use of biological methods such as dissection and even (some limited) experiment, and his development of biological concepts, such as that of classification, have merited him the title of Father of Biology.

In addition to his contribution to the development of biology as a science, Aristotle made numerous observational contributions to biology. In many of his writings on natural history he faithfully extended the Hippocratic tradition of making generalizations from collected observations. Acquainted with the characteristic features of mammals, he was able to recognize whales, dolphins, and porpoises as properly belonging to this group and not to the fishes. He knew that some fish bring forth their young alive, and that one in particular approaches the mammals even more closely in that its young develop within the uterus of the female and are attached to a type of placenta. The existence of the placental dogfish and other facts unearthed by Aristotle were not substantiated until the 19th century. In an incubating hen's egg, Aristotle followed the day-by-day development of parts from a relatively homogeneous mass. None of Aristotle's botanical treatises have survived, but a few works by Theophrastus, his pupil, successor, and the father of botany, have come down to us. In his description of the parts of plants (plant anatomy), Theophrastus sought to devise a technical terminology. He valued developmental study (embryology) and distinguished various modes of plant reproduction.

After Aristotle and Theophrastus interest in biology as a scientific understanding of living nature for its own sake waned, and practical concerns regained center stage. From around 300 to 150 B.C. some discoveries were made in anatomy and physiology, two of the more noteworthy contributors being Herophilus and Erasistratus.

Roman Period. About the middle of the 2d century B.C., Greece succumbed to the Roman legions. The Romans made contributions in politics—but their interest in science was primarily in its application. Thus, in biology, both medicine and agriculture were encouraged because of their importance to the welfare of the army and the empire. Of note are Pliny, Dioscorides, and Galen.

Pliny the Elder (A.D. 23–79) put together a natural history of 37 volumes. This work influenced the development of biology and natural history throughout the Middle Ages in chiefly a negative way. In this encyclopedia of nature, Pliny mixed fact and fancy, and did not use scientific standards as a guide as can be seen from the anecdotes he recounts, such as the bear licking its cubs into shape. Soon after Christian authors, taking inspiration from Pliny, composed stories about animals to convey moral and religious messages. The medieval bestiaries were the continuation of this tradition of combining wonderful stories of birds and beasts with miracle and allegory.

Dioscorides (*c.* A.D. 40–90) was a Greek who worked under Nero as an army surgeon. He originated the pharmacopoeia, tersely describing plants of value to medicine and frequently including their habits and habitats. Annotated copies of this *materia medica* formed the chief source of pharmocological knowledge for the next 1,500 years.

The 2d century A.D. saw the last great biologist of antiquity, Galen of Pergamum, who standardized anatomy and physiology for the next 15 centuries. Court physician to Marcus Aurelius, he composed voluminous works containing the ideas of his predecessors as well as his own contributions. He described from dissections, and performed experiments on living animals. By severing the spinal cord of living animals at different levels he gained knowledge of nerve functions. Galen also distinguished between motor and sensory nerves. His knowledge of physiology and anatomy allowed him to effect cures when other physicians failed. Posing an obstacle to Galen's investigation was his inability to procure human cadavers for dissection. Consequently he relied chiefly on his dissections of the Barbary ape for an understanding of the human body, which resulted in his making a number of errors. Galen's brilliance had as an unfortunate side effect that he was taken as an absolute authority for many centuries.

Middle Ages. From many and varied causes that had been building up for centuries, the Western Empire crumbled in the 6th century. With the barbarians invading from the north, scientific progress came to a standstill. The few important links with the learning of the past were the hand-copied manuscripts carefully guarded in the monasteries of Britain and Italy. Although this period of the Middle Ages was not a time of scientific progress and experiment, men were trained to think. The habit of definite, exact thought was implanted in the European mind by theologians and philosophers of the late Middle Ages. With the spread of Islam after the death of Muhammad, the almost forgotten culture of the Greeks and the Near East was reintroduced into Western Europe. From the 9th to the 11th centuries this transmission vivified medieval thought with Arabic translations of Plato, Aristotle, Theophrastus, and others. During this period Avicenna (980–1037) wrote his famous ''Canon'' of medical science, which remained for centuries the principal authority in medical schools in both Europe and Asia.

By the 13th century the translations of Aristotle's zoological works provided an alternative to the bestiaries with their fabulous accounts, opening people's eyes to what true biological inquiry consisted in. Albert the Great's (1206?–1280) commentaries on Aristotle's zoological works include his personal observations of animals.

Renaissance. During the Renaissance, the sciences flourished. Biology did not, however, develop quite so rapidly as physics did. The reasons for this are that the object studied by the biologist is much more complex, and also that mathematics, a powerful tool for the physicist, is of relatively little use in biology. Moreover, it was oftentimes knowledge of physics that was behind the development of biological instruments such as the microscope. Indirectly, however, physics also had a negative impact on the development of biology. Thinkers such as René Descartes promoted the notion that organisms were merely machines, the study of which was to be reduced to physics. This retarded the development of an autonomous method in biology for quite some time, and limited the study of psychology to human beings.

The restlessness, probing curiosity, and many-sided learning of the Renaissance are epitomized in Leonardo da Vinci (1452–1519). Known primarily as an artist, he was also a talented engineer, inventor, observer of nature, and anatomist. Had his notes and drawings in human anatomy been published when made, anatomy might have been advanced by a century. He made scientific studies of the action of the eye, the mechanisms of various joints, and of the flight of birds. Embryological and comparative anatomical studies alike came within the compass of his work.

Biology in the 16th century is represented in the herbals, encyclopedias of nature, and monographs of the period. The German fathers of botany produced herbals that ranged from annotated texts of Dioscorides, like that of Otto Brunfels (1489–1534), to the beautifully illustrated manual of Leonhard Fuchs (1501–66), which was intended as a guide for the collection of medicinal plants in Western Europe. The encyclopedias attempted to gather together in one work all of the available knowledge about living things. The most influential of these was the *History of Animals* by Konrad Gesner (1516–65) of Switzerland, probably the most learned zoologist of the period. Some of Gesner's less ambitious contemporaries confined their efforts to treatises or monographs on special groups of organisms.

Human anatomy in the Renaissance was studied through a slavish interpretation of Galen by the teacher, while an attending barber's assistant crudely made the actual dissections. By his own skilled and careful dissections, however, Andreas Vesalius (1514–64) of Belgium showed his anatomy students at Padua that Galen, great as he was, could be wrong. In 1543 he published his wonderfully illustrated book, *On the Structure of the Human Body,* which marked the end of the servile adherence to the authority of the past.

Until the functioning of the heart and blood was understood it was impossible to grasp the natural ordering of the bodies of the higher animals. The publication in 1628 of William Harvey's (1578–1657) treatise *On the Motion of the Heart and Blood in Animals* was a large step forward in understanding anatomy. Numerous observations, carefully planned and executed experiments, and quantitative calculations led Harvey inductively to the conclusion that the heart is a muscular pump that propels the blood in a closed circuit throughout the vertebrate body. John Ray (1627–1705) is noted for his work in taxonomy. Ray sought to establish a system of classification of both plants and animals in which species sharing characteristics are shown to be related by their classification and nomenclature. Ray made careful studies of comparative anatomy, and used them as basis for his animal taxonomy. His work represents a huge step forward from the previous alphabetical lists of species, and it provided direction to later taxonomists such as Carolus Linnaeus.

In the 17th century the compound microscope was added to the apparatus of the biologist. As used by such men as Nehemiah Grew (1641–1712) in England and Marcello Malpighi (1628–94) in Italy to study the fine structure of living things, it led to the development of a new branch of biology called histology. The world of microbes was first seen by Antoni van Leeuwenhoek (1632–1723) through his homemade lenses, and microbiology was born. The microscope allowed biologists to observe entities that previously were only hypothetical, e.g., disease agents such as bacteria.

18th Century. In the 18th century new impetus was given to biology by the comparative method applied to anatomy and embryology. The classification (taxonomy) of living things as well as a system of naming them (nomenclature) were standardized. Georges Cuvier (1769–1832), the founder of modern comparative anatomy and paleontology, was able with his knowledge of animal structures and by the application of the theory of the ''correlation of parts'' to place many fossil forms in their correct systematic positions in the animal kingdom. He surmised that each species was specially created and that the existence of dissimilar fossils in series of rock strata could be explained by catastrophism. According to this theory, wide expanses of the earth were from time to time subjected to great cataclysms (floods, quakes, etc.), which obliterated all life in those areas. Later, such territory would be populated by different animal species, which migrated into the denuded areas from distant parts. These would eventually leave some descendants in the fossil record that would contrast with the fossils in the lower strata of sedimentary rocks.

The most important figure in 18th-century biology was Carolus Linnaeus (1707–78) of Sweden. From his youth, he had displayed a passion for classification and an extraordinary genius for accurate and detailed observation. He visited and collected plant specimens in Lapland, Norway, France, Germany, Holland, and England. As an outcome of these travels and studies he wrote his famous *Systema naturae,* published in Holland in 1735, in which he attempted to describe and classify every known animal and plant. In so doing he set standards for describing animals and plants with accuracy and succinctness.

During most of his life, Linnaeus firmly adhered to the idea that all of the present-day species of plants and animals were the unchanged linear descendants of original species individually created. When Linnaeus observed how plants of different species hybridize, however, he was led to revise his initial conceptions. In his *Fundamenta fructificationes* (1762) he conceded that perhaps there was a common stock for all of the species of a single genus, or even perhaps of a single order. The direct work of the Creator was confined then to the genera, or to the orders, the diversification of which was accomplished as a result of crossing or hybridization.

19th Century. Advances far-reaching in their effects were made in biology in the 19th century. The enunciation of the theory of evolution colored the thought of the period in many fields extraneous to biology. The germ theory of disease affected our entire civilization, as did the discovery of the basic laws of inheritance. Slightly less notable were the formulation of the cell theory and the advances in embryology and physiology. In this period the method of testing hypotheses through controlled experiment is spoken of explicitly by the biologist Claude Bernard (1813–78) and begins to be more widely used.

The term ''cell'' in its biological sense comes down from the 17th-century work of Robert Hooke (1635–1703), who thus described the tiny divisions that he saw in thin slices of cork under the microscope. The formulation of the cell theory was, however, a gradual development of the early 19th century. In brief, the cell theory states that all organisms are composed of cells (or a single cell) that are essentially alike in their composition and formed in the same fundamental manner by division of a preexisting cell. The basic points of the cell theory were stated and confirmed with clear-cut observations by Matthias Schleiden (1804–81) and Theodor Schwann (1810–82), in 1838 and 1839, respectively. The study of cells, cytology, became a distinct branch of biology in the 20th century.

Although crude ideas of evolution can be found among the Greek philosophers, it was not until the 19th century that a definite theory of evolution was presented. ''Theory of evolution'' is an ambiguous expression. It sometimes names the notion that species of living things took their origin from priorly existing species, instead of appearing without any reproductive continuity with them, as supported by evidence from different areas of biology. At other times theory of evolution names the various causative explanations offered for how species could originate one from another over time. J. B. de Lamarck (1744–1829) proposed as causal mechanism the inheritance of acquired characteristics. He believed that a felt need on the part of an organism might give rise to new organs and suggested that the use of an organ or part strengthens and develops it, while a lack of its use leads to a gradual atrophy, diminution, and eventual disappearance.

Evolution, however, has become almost synonymous with the name of Charles DARWIN (1809–82). No other publication has exerted so profound an influence on biology as his book *The Origin of Species by Means of Natural Selection* (1859). In *Origin of Species* Darwin both presents evidence that species have evolved, and presents a causal explanation for evolution, namely, chance variation subjected to natural selection. Darwin had spent 20 years gathering facts to substantiate his views. Although the same ideas were arrived at independently by Alfred Wallace at the same time, Wallace had not the same wealth of observational data to support them as had Darwin. Each had published a short presentation of his views in the same issue of the *Proceedings of the Linnean Society* the previous year. The first edition of *The Origin of Species* was sold out on the first day of its publication, and it brought forth a storm of controversy in the fields of religion and sociology, which continues to this day. (*See* EVOLUTION.)

In the 16th century, the Italian physician Girolamo Fracastoro (1483–1553) had contended that infection of all kinds, including fermentation, was the work of minute ''seeds'' or germs. This was proven by Louis Pasteur (1822–95) on experimental grounds. Though Pasteur was a chemist, his great discoveries were in microbiology and preventive medicine. He showed that such diseases as rabies and anthrax could be prevented by inoculation with the attenuated or even dead germs causing the disease.

Genetics is that branch of biology concerned with the phenomena of inheritance and the origin of heritable variations. Although genetics did not emerge as a full-fledged science until well into the 20th century, the basic laws of inheritance upon which it is founded were discovered by an Augustinian monk, Gregor MENDEL (1822–84); his work marks the beginning of precise knowledge of genetics. Working principally with garden peas, he combined the experimental breeding of pedigreed strains of plants and the statistical treatment of the data secured in regard to the inheritance of sharply contrasting characteristics, such as short and tall plants, or white and red flowers. His work, published (1866) in an obscure journal, remained almost wholly unnoticed until 1900.

August Weismann (1834–1914), who opposed the theory of the inheritance of acquired characteristics, published (1892) a volume entitled *The Germ Plasm.* He identified the chromosomes found in every cell nucleus as the bearers of hereditary traits and emphasized a sharp distinction between germ cells and somatic cells.

20th Century. One of the three men who had independently discovered Mendel's work in 1900 was a Dutch botanist, Hugo de Vries (1848–1935). His work in plant breeding had convinced him of the significance of the distinction between heritable and nonheritable variations. Among his plants he found variations in some individuals that marked them distinctly from the parent generation, and he discovered further that these bred true. In his book *The Mutation Theory,* he proposed that evolution proceeded by means of rather large mutations or saltations. This contrasted with Darwin's concept that natural selection had acted upon small, continuous, heritable variations. T. H. Morgan (1866–1945) showed that mutations occur constantly and range from minute, barely perceptible changes in structure and function to the large, discontinuous variations of the type considered by de Vries, but most were in the category of minute changes.

Morgan actually followed up the work of another American experimental zoologist, E. B. Wilson (1856–1939), who had opened the way with his studies in cellular biology—particularly those dealing with the chromosomes and their relation to heredity. H. J. Muller (1890–1967), who received the Nobel prize for his investigations in genetics, showed that the frequency of gene mutations is affected by temperature, age, and the stocks used. He discovered that ionizing radiations would speed up the mutations that normally occur at a relatively slow rate.

In the beginning of the 20th century it was still unknown what the hereditary material was. Proteins were the most likely candidates for this role. Nevertheless, evidence slowly began accumulating that chemically simpler DNA was in fact the hereditary material. In the 1920s Frederick Griffiths discovered that he could transform nonvirulent bacteria into virulent bacteria by mixing live nonvirulent bacteria with dead virulent bacteria. Apparently the live nonvirulent bacteria had taken up some chemical transforming principle from the dead virulent bacteria. In 1944 Oswald T. Avery, Colin MacLeod, and MacLyn McCarty isolated DNA from an extract containing the transforming principle, and showed that it alone of the substances in the extract caused bacteria to transform. Another experiment performed in 1952 by Alfred D. Hershey and Martha Chase gave further support to the notion that DNA is the carrier of hereditary information. The structure of DNA was elucidated in 1953 by James D. Watson and Francis Crick. DNA is a double helix composed of two strands held together by hydrogen bonds between complementarily paired bases. A great deal of subsequent research was devoted to understanding how DNA replicates and how the information contained in it is ultimately translated into the proteins that serve constitutive and other functions in the body. Some recent advances include the sequencing of the genomes of a variety of organisms including *homo sapiens,* the cloning of higher organisms, and genetic engineering, a process whereby genes are inserted into organisms allowing them to produce substances they normally would not produce.

The other dominant area of biology at the beginning of the 21st century, one that shares close ties to genetics, is cell biology. The interest in these areas lies in the possibility of discovering knowledge that can be used for developing cures for disease. Both genetics and cell biology seek an understanding of life processes in molecular terms. The crude earlier understanding of a cell as protoplasm along with a nucleus contained by a membrane has been replaced by a continually expanding knowledge of the specific constituents and chemical reactions going on in the cell.

Alongside modern genetics and cellular biology that try to understand life processes in physico-chemical terms are three other disciplines that adopt a more global approach: evolutionary biology, ecology, and ethology. Evolutionary biology drew profit from the work of geologists who, rejecting the catastrophism of Cuvier, developed new principles for relative age dating of rocks and devised reliable absolute dating techniques. Much work is currently being done in an attempt to trace the evolutionary history of the various species. Refinements have also been made in the area of evolutionary theory. The most prevalent theories are referred to as ''neo-Darwinian'' since they integrate the key notions of Darwin's theory with the discoveries made in genetics. There is disagreement among neo-Darwinians, but it is slight compared to that which exists between the neo-Darwinians and those in the Intelligent Design movement. Proponents of the latter group maintain that random variation sorted out by blind natural selection cannot adequately explain the order found in the organs and activities of living things.

Ecology deals with the relationships between living things and their natural environment in both its physical and biotic aspects. This sort of study is already found in the natural history of Aristotle. The science, however, took on new life at the end of the 19th century with the work of F. A. Forel (1841–1912) and E. A. Birge (1879–1941), among others. Emphasis was placed on studying populations, communities, and habitats. Increasing use was made of quantitative and statistical methods.

Ethology or the study of animal behavior has its origin in observations made early on by humankind. Modern ethology took a new beginning with the work of Konrad Lorenz (1903–89) and Niko Tinbergen (1907–88). These scientists sought to understand not only why animals perform certain actions, but also the causal mechanism behind the behavior (e.g., what hormones must be produced for a bird to be able to learn its song). Present-day ethology also has as its goal determining the evolutionary history of animal behavior.

Bibliography: G. A. SARTON, *A Guide to the History of Science* (Waltham, Mass. 1952); G. SARTON, *Introduction to the History of Science,* 3 v. in 5 (Baltimore 1927–48) v. 1. A. N. WHITEHEAD, *Science and the Modern World* (New York 1925). L. THORNDIKE, *Science and Thought in the Fifteenth Century* (New York 1929); L. THORNDIKE, *A History of Magic and Experimental Science,* 8 v. (New York 1923–58). E. NORDENSKIÖLD, *The History of Biology* (new ed. New York 1935). ARISTOTLE, *Works,* tr. W. D. ROSS, 12 v. (Oxford 1908–52) v. 4 Biological treatises: E. RÁDL, *History of Biological Theories,* tr. E. J. HATFIELD (London 1930). C. J. SINGER, *Greek Biology and Greek Medicine* (Oxford 1922); *History of Biology to about the Year 1900* (3d ed. rev. New York 1959). F. J. COLE, *History of Comparative Anatomy* (London 1944). A. R. HALL and M. B. HALL, *A Brief History of Science* (Toronto 1964). J. L. GOULD, *Ethology: The Mechanisms and Evolution of Behavior* (New York 1982).

[P. STOKELY]

BIOLOGY, II (CURRENT STATUS)

This essay intends to address the status of biology as science today, and how biology relates to philosophy and to the other natural sciences.

Biology, like the other natural sciences, initially had close ties with natural philosophy. ARISTOTLE, the father of biology, saw his biological investigations in continuity with his studies of the soul and of the psychic faculties of sensation and memory. Many later biologists of note, such as Galen and Harvey, were very much influenced by Aristotle's natural philosophy, e.g., by the doctrine of the four causes, and of the special importance of the final cause.

The doctrine of ''vitalism'' illustrates in another fashion the close ties originally present between philosophy and biology. Although vitalism is in fact a misinterpretation of Aristotle, it was one that influenced biology for a significant portion of its history. The vitalists shared in common with the Aristotle the view that living things and nonliving things differ in kind, and not simply in complexity. The vitalists and Aristotle parted ways when it came to explaining the reason for this difference. There are a variety of vitalist positions, but they are all variations on the basic idea that living things differ from nonliving things in that living things are composed of constituents or forces that cannot be produced or cannot be active outside of the living thing. In this context some vitalists made reference to known substances, whereas others called upon some as yet unidentified vital fluid or principle. As the chemists gradually found ways of synthesizing the various known substances supposedly unique to living things, and as no additional unique motive substance or force was ever come across, the notion of a special life material or life force eventually died out.

Aristotle did not regard the difference between living and nonliving to lie chiefly in their material constituents, but in the formal principle which unifies the material constituents so that they form a whole and act as a whole. For Aristotle, every individual natural thing has a substantial form. The soul is simply a higher type of substantial form that is present in certain natural things giving them the capacity for self-motion. The soul is not some added physical substance or force. It is true that Aristotle talks about ''pneuma,'' a physical substance primarily responsible for movement in living things, and one which is not found in nonliving things (*Movement of Animals* 703a4–27). Thus, the later thinkers who attempted to distinguish living from nonliving in terms of some vital fluid or vital force may well have derived this notion from reading Aristotle. It is also the case that Aristotle not only maintained that the soul is the substantial form of the body, but also held that it played an active role in controlling physical forces responsible for the processes of development and growth. Some biologists pondered how this might be and tried to incorporate this notion in their scientific explanations (e.g., Hans Driesh [1867–1941]), but the eventual trend was to leave such problems to the philosophers, and to look to chemistry and physics to unveil the immediate causes responsible for specific motions within the body. The growing success in the latter enterprise in stark contrast to the difficulty of the philosophical issues regarding body-soul relations were in part responsible for the eventual dichotomy between philosophical and biological inquiry regarding living things.

The other major factor that led to the present-day division of biology from philosophy was a change in the methodology which gained impetus starting with the Renaissance. The gradual development of the hypothetico-deductive method as the method of science marked a significant break between natural philosophy and the natural sciences. This method first gained widespread usage in physics. The hypothetico-deductive method starts from a question raised by the observation of facts. The next step is to interrelate and generalize the facts in the form of laws. A hypothetical cause is then posited for why the laws obtain, and then deductions are made in light of the supposed cause of other phenomena which should occur. These deductions are then tested through observations that are most often made in the context of experiment. The logic of the situation is such that while incorrect predictions establish that one's hypothesis is mistaken, correct predictions can never prove, but can only corroborate one's hypothesis. Hypotheses are thus always subject to being revised in light of new facts. Since proceeding by hypotheses and experiments is very different from proceeding by formulating definitions, making divisions, and using dialectic, the growing use of the scientific method widened the gap between biologist and philosopher.

While biology in some sense emancipated itself from philosophy by adopting the scientific method, by the same token it now had to establish itself as a genuine science alongside physics and chemistry. The fact that the scientific method was first used to any great extent in physics put a certain slant on what came to be regarded as the criteria for what was scientific and what was not, criteria that biology did not always meet. These criteria are as follows. First, control is crucial when performing experiments. It is needed in order to achieve precision, for one can only isolate a specific aspect of a phenomenon by holding the other aspects constant. Control is also needed in order for an experiment to be repeatable. If a scientist does not define the precise parameters under which the experiment is performed, other scientists cannot check the accuracy of the results. Second, experimental results are to be obtained through measurement (reflecting again a concern for precision), and scientific generalizations are to be arrived at by formulating experimental results into laws of a mathematical character. Experimental results and laws are to be expressed in unambiguous terms, namely, in terms of numbers and symbols. Third, in science complex wholes are regarded as fully explicable through an analysis of their parts.

Biology for some time was regarded as ''soft'' science because it does not completely meet the criteria elaborated in physics. This, however, is not to biology's discredit. After all, there are important differences between the things studied in the two areas. Living things in contrast to nonliving things are characterized by variety, variability, and manifest orientation to goals. There is a much wider variety of species than of atomic particles and chemical elements, and individuals within a species differ more from one another than do samples of chemicals of the same type. Living things develop through time (they have life cycles), and new species have developed in the course of the history of our planet. Organisms pursue recognizable goals, and have organs by which they do so. Moreover, they are only adequately understood in relation to other living things and to the environment.

Biologists are capable of performing experiments under controlled conditions, granted that in areas such as animal behavior the ability to exercise control is not as great as in those areas where biochemistry plays a greater role. Claude Bernard's work *An Introduction to the Study of Experimental Medicine* (1865) is noteworthy for explicitly addressing how the experimental method is to be applied in biology so that the control and repeatability that is the hallmark of science can be obtained.

As for the role of measurement and mathematical formulas, biology does not meet the physicists' expectations. Experimental results in biology are not always precise, and thus they cannot always be expressed in rigorous mathematical terms. The weight of an individual cow is not a constant as is the weight of a chemical element. Moreover, many important facts about living things cannot be expressed mathematically, including the behavior of an organism as a whole, the function of organs, and the relation of an organism to other organisms in its environment. And this affects the formulation of biological laws. Regularities between phenomena certainly have been discovered in biology, e.g., growth is stunted in poorly nourished children. However, regularities of this sort are often not called laws either due to their relatively narrow scope, or because they are not precise and mathematical, or because they admit of many exceptions, or a combination of these factors. For example, the flowering of different species of plants is stimulated by different external conditions and internal factors (such as hormones), and so the description of what happens in one species may vary considerably from what happens in another. There are no ideal laws of plant blooming, as there are ideal gas laws (though one may question how well the ideal gas laws apply to reality). Biology is not to be faulted in such cases because it cannot be more precise and cannot give exact formulae. To be more precise would result in inaccuracy rather than science. Accordingly, in biology books one find more models than equations (genetics being a partial exception), and more descriptions than symbolic representations.

To a large extent biology has adopted the reductionist approach of physics and chemistry whereby complex wholes and their activities are understood by understanding the workings of their constituent parts. The reductionist approach of explaining life processes in terms of the molecular constituents upon which they depend has proven itself to be a very powerful approach. Some biologists consider the philosophical question that naturally arises as to whether such reductionism is merely methodological or whether it is ontological, i.e., whether living things can be fully understood in terms of their material parts and their interactions. The debate becomes especially acute when it comes to determining how to explain phenomena such as consciousness. What is sometimes overlooked is that the reductionist approach is not the only approach that is currently used in biology. Another approach that is used is historical. It attempts to explain the parts and behavior of organisms in terms of their evolutionary ancestry, as in, for instance, the explanation of the presence of vestigial organs. Biology also sometimes proceeds in a way similar to natural philosophy, taking rather common observations as starting points, and trying to give some explanation of these well-known phenomena in terms of causes, especially in terms of the final cause. For example, biologists inquire why some trees lose their leaves in autumn. This sort of question is not answered in terms of material constituents, but in terms of what the part or process contributes to the well-being of the individual organism or to its reproductive success.

The practical applications of biology are what define it against physics and chemistry in the minds of many biologists. Physics sends people to the moon, whereas biology cures diseases and genetically alters organisms. Biologists approaching the question in a theoretical manner distinguish biology from physics and chemistry to a greater or lesser degree corresponding to the type of reductionism they embrace. One widespread view is that biology differs from the other natural sciences to the extent that it deals with the unique ways in which physical and chemical reactions are organized within living systems. Another popular view maintains that there are different levels of biological organization, and that the higher levels bring with them emergent properties that are not found at the lower levels. However, there are many other views as well, views which could only be completely enumerated and categorized by examining in detail all the different forms of reductionism.

Biology and Philosophy. An important area of debate, especially among evolutionary biologists, regards the nature and role of teleological explanation in biology. There is a strong current among contemporary biologists and philosophers of biology to eliminate any mention of final causality, either by a type of reduction of the final cause to the efficient cause, or by redefining it in some other way and renaming it (e.g., calling it teleonomy). Certainly what constitutes a proper biological explanation is at stake. However, oftentimes there is another underlying issue, namely, the philosophical question of whether natural causes alone can explain the order found in living things. Biologists often shy away from or reject any acknowledgement that organisms manifest finality or design, because they are concerned that they will have to follow the reasoning articulated by William Paley which concludes that there is a supernatural designer. At the same time, biologists cannot help asking when they see a structure or process for the first time: What is it good for? E.g., biologists seek to determine not only how the flying fish fly, but why. The majority of evolutionary biologists who acknowledge the importance of ''why?'' questions, and who address the philosophical question of whence the origin of the ordering to an end found in living things, maintain that the observed finality is due to the blind forces of chance and necessity. Chance provides new variations, and necessity (commonly referred to under the name of natural selection) determines which variants are reproductively successful. This view is contested by the proponents of the Intelligent Design movement who argue that the order found in living things requires an intelligent agent outside of nature to adequately explain it.

There are other issues in evolutionary biology as well which are either essentially philosophical or which take their point of reference from philosophical discussions, e.g., the questions of what constitutes a biological species and what constitutes the proper manner of classifying organisms. In other parts of biology, as well, philosophical issues arise, such as, for instance, neuroscience questions concerning the nature of consciousness and emotion. There is one philosophical issue that comes up in biology, however, which merits special mention because of its very general scope: namely, the question of certitude. The widespread notion among biologists is that certitude can never be achieved; everything in biology is subject to revision. This skepticism arises in part from the influence of philosophers such as Descartes, Hume, and Kant. It also has roots in the claims of certain philosophers of science.

The philosopher of science Thomas Kuhn (1922–1996) promoted the view that all observation is theory-laden, i.e., that what one sees always involves interpretation in light of a theoretical framework, and thus all observation lacks objectivity. This view when taken to the extreme denies the possibility of genuine scientific progress. Consider, for example, the historical case of biologists who, using a microscope, claimed to see miniature fowl in unincubated eggs and miniature humans (the ''humunculus'') in human sperm. It is reasonable to think that the scientists in question made these inaccurate observations because they were influenced by the preconceived notion that the parts of the adult were already present in the germ cell and only needed to grow (the notion of ''preformation''). However, when later scientists determined that these observations were inaccurate, it was not the case that it was simply a change in preconception that accounted for why they did not observe miniature parts, but it was also because there were no miniature parts to be observed. Even Charles Bonnet, an advocate of the doctrine of preformation who gives a forced explanation of why there is an observed lack of part-to-part correspondence between the early embryo and adult, nonetheless did not fail to note that under the microscope no such correspondence is observed.

The philosopher of science Karl POPPER (1902–1994) insisted upon the logical point that one can only falsify a hypothesis; one can never prove it. Correct deductions from a hypothesis serve to corroborate it, but not prove it, since some other hypothetical cause might account for the very same phenomena. Biology, however, unlike the other natural sciences, is sometimes capable of replacing hypotheses with observation. Dissection can reveal structures and their activities that were previously hidden. For instance, Galen refutes erroneous notions about the function of the ureters by doing experiments which involved cutting an animal open (*On the Natural Faculties*, bk. I, c. 13). Microscopes, from the light microscope to the electron microscope, have been a tremendous aid to the biologist by making visible structures that formerly could only be hypothesized to exist. For instance, while Harvey could only hypothesize that there existed vessels connecting arteries with veins, later on Malphighi, using a microscope, actually saw the capillaries that link the two. Facts discovered in these ways are not subject to revision (e.g., there is no doubt that the heart is an organ the function of which is to circulate blood in the body). The biologist is not so bound to formulating hypotheses as the physicist is because the objects the biologists observes are sometimes either macroscopic or at least visible with a microscope. Thus, in some cases biology attains a high degree of certitude, and one that excels that which is achieved in physics.

Biology today on the whole looks as if it were an entirely different enterprise than philosophy, especially due to the use it makes of the scientific method. However, closer examination reveals that the moment biologists begin to reflect upon methodological issues, such as whether the reductionist approach is sufficient or what constitutes a proper understanding of teleology or what kind of certitude can be achieved, they are engaging in philosophical reflections. Aside from these very general issues, philosophy is also important in certain discussions which come up in the context of particular parts of biology, questions ranging from the definition of "consciousness" to what role, if any, chance, necessity, and mind play in the evolutionary process. Certainly the tremendous advances that have been made in biology in understanding the workings of the cell and of heredity, as well as in understanding and curing various diseases—advances which make it perhaps fair to call biology the ruling science of the day—were due to the application of the scientific method, and not to philosophical discourse. At the same time, biology will always have ties with philosophy to the extent that a full understanding of the nature and origin of living things, as well as of the status of biology as science, are objects of philosophical reflection. Also not to be forgotten is the utility of moral philosophy for biologists faced as they are with difficult moral choices regarding the development of new technologies, experimentation on human and animal subjects, and other moral issues that arise while doing research.

[M. I. GEORGE]

BIONDO, FLAVIO

Humanist, historian of Roman antiquity, and secretary at the papal Curia; b. Forlì, Italy, November or December 1392; d. Rome, June 4, 1463. He usually signed himself Blondus. His literary education seems to have included little Greek, for he relied on translations of Greek literature. He was secretary for various people in many places in north Italy (1420–32), entered the papal service by early 1433, and, despite the fact that he was not trained in Canon Law, served as scriptor of apostolic letters under Popes Eugene IV, Nicholas V (except 1449–53), Callistus III, and Pius II from 1436 to his death. In 1423 he married, and by 1440 he was the father of ten children, one of whom, Gaspar (d. 1493), succeeded him as scriptor. Biondo lived and died poor, seeking no riches. His scholarly, methodical work contributed more to knowledge of the Middle Ages than that of his Renaissance colleagues, who disparaged his unrhetorical style. His *Historiarum ab inclinatione Romanorum imperii decades,* which imitates Livy, was intended as the contemporary history (1401–40) of Decades III and IV and was completed in 1453; this was supplemented with Decades I and II (410–1400), the whole being published in Venice in 1483. Both his *Roma instaurata,* a descriptive catalogue of ruins and monuments of Rome, completed in 1446 and published in 1471, and his *Italia illustrata,* an archeological and historical account of Italy from the Alps to Salerno, completed in 1453 and published in Rome in 1474, offer valuable data on monuments extant in 15th-century Italy. *Romae triumphantis libri X* (1460), a manual of Roman antiquities, sacerdotal and private rather than public, was the basis for much subsequent antiquarian interest. Biondo is important in the development of the idea of a "Middle" Age inasmuch as he thought the barbarian invasions ushered in a new period. He held that the Rome of the popes was at least the equal of that of the emperors and that Christians should unite against the new barbarians, the Turks, who took Constantinople in 1453. Biondo wrote other lesser works; many of his letters are lost.

Bibliography: *Opera omnia* (Basel 1531). *Scritti inediti e rari di Biondo Flavio,* ed. B. NOGARA [*Studi e Testi,* 48 (1927)]. A. MASIUS, *Flavio Biondo, sein Leben und seine Werke* (Leipzig 1897). B. NOGARA, *Enciclopedia Italiana di scienzi, littere ed arti,* 36 v. (Rome 1929–39) 7:56. L. MOHLER, *Lexikon für Theologie und Kirche,* ed. M. BUCHBERGER, 10 v. (Freiburg 1930–38) 2:363–364. F. BAIX, *Dictionnaire d'histoire et de géographie ecclésiastiques,* ed. A. BAUDRILLART et al. (Paris 1912–) 8:1513–19.

[E. P. COLBERT]

BIRETTA

A square cap with three peaks or ridges on top. A pompon in the center usually ornaments it. By the Middle Ages, the hood of the cope was rarely worn because it had become tight-fitting and richly ornamented. Some other protection from the cold was necessary for the head of the tonsured cleric. A skullcap was used, but more often a cap of soft material was worn with a tuft on top by which it could be removed easily. This cap was known as a pileus or *birettum.* By the 16th century, the *birettum* was reinforced with an interlining of stiff canvas to give it a neat appearance. The mortarboard used in academic dress seems to be a flattened *birettum* and a skullcap combined.

Bibliography: A. A. KING, *Liturgy of the Roman Church* (Milwaukee 1957). H. NORRIS, *Church Vestments: Their Origin and Development* (New York 1950).

[M. MCCANCE]

BIRINUS, ST.

Bishop, apostle of the West Saxons; d. between 648 and 650. He was commissioned by Pope HONORIUS I as a missionary to England and consecrated by Asterius, archbishop of Milan (not Genoa as is commonly said). A contemporary of Aidan of Lindisfarne, Birinus arrived in Wessex *c.* 634. He originally intended to work in the remoter parts of England, but finding the West Saxons still heathen, he stayed there. He baptized the West Saxon King Cynegils in the presence of King OSWALD, the Christian overlord of Britain, and was given Dorchester for his see (635). His patron King Cynegils died in 643, and his successor Cenwalh lapsed into paganism but was soon sent into exile. Cenwalh was finally converted and restored *c.* 648, and when Birinus died about a year later, the Church was securely established in Wessex.

Feast: Dec. 5.

Bibliography: Bede, *Ecclesiastical History* 3, ed. C. PLUMMER (Oxford 1956). *Three Eleventh-century Anglo-Latin Saints' Lives*, ed. and tr. R. C. LOVE (Oxford 1996). J. E. FIELD, *St. Berin: The Apostle of Wessex* (London 1902). T. VARLEY, *St. Birinus and Wessex* (Winchester, Eng. 1934). F. M. STENTON, *Anglo-Saxon England* (2d ed. Oxford 1947) 102, 117–118. R. GRAHAM, *Dictionnaire d'histoire et de géographie ecclésiastiques*, ed. A. BAUDRILLART et al. (Paris 1912) 8:1530–31.

[E. JOHN]

BISHOP, EDMUND

Historian, liturgist; b. Totnes, Devon, England, May 17, 1846; d. Barnstaple, Devon, Feb. 19, 1917. The youngest child of a country innkeeper, he went to school at Ashburton, Exeter, and Vilvorde (Belgium). He served Thomas Carlyle as amanuensis (1863) and joined the British civil service as a clerk in the Education Department in 1864. He spent all his spare time in historical research, working initially from documents in the British Museum. He was received into the Catholic church on Aug. 16, 1867, and through his friendship with Dom (later Cardinal) Gasquet and his associates, he was attracted by the attempted revival of monastic ideals at Downside Priory. Retiring from the Civil Service in 1885, he went to Downside as a postulant in 1886 but was disappointed by the initial failure of efforts to revitalize the English Benedictine congregation. Although he left the Benedictines in 1889, he never wavered in his affection for Downside, where he spent a substantial part of the last 15 years of his life and was buried with the monks. His earliest learned work, and especially his discovery in 1877 of the *Collectio Britannica* (an important document in the history of canon law), had by 1880 earned Bishop a high reputation as a medieval historian. In collaboration with Dom Bäumer of Beuron Abbey (d. 1894), around 1891 he began to publish brilliantly original work on the history of the missal and breviary, sharply at variance with the positions adopted and popularized by P. BATIFFOL and L. DUCHESNE, but nonetheless commanding respect. Bishop showed unequaled knowledge of the printed and manuscript literature in the libraries of western Europe and used profound scholarly judgment. He collaborated with Gasquet in more polemical work on the history and position of the Catholic church in England, particularly of the Black Monks.

From about 1900 Bishop lived in increasing retirement, intellectually in sympathy with many of the ideas associated with the Modernist movement. Nevertheless, his occasional publications, and still more his generous contributions to other scholars' work, continued to advance the frontiers of knowledge of the origins and early development of Western liturgies. Much of his most significant work was collected and revised by him in his *Liturgica Historica*, published posthumously in 1918. Apart from these specialized studies, his lifelong interest, by example, exhortation, and encouragement, was to stimulate English Catholics to greater intellectual activity and a more scientific approach to history. This was reflected in many of his articles in Catholic periodicals, and in a voluminous private correspondence. Bishop was the foremost English-speaking liturgist of the late 19th and the early 20th centuries.

Bibliography: E. C. BUTLER, *The Dictionary of National Biography from the Earliest Times to 1900,* 63 v. (London 1885–1900) 47–48. H. LECLERCQ, *Dictionnaire d'archéologie chrétienne et de liturgie* (Paris 1907–53) 9.2:1735–36. N. ABERCROMBIE, *Life and Work of Edmund Bishop* (London 1959).

[N. ABERCROMBIE]

BISHOP, WILLIAM

Bishop of Chalcedon; b. Warwickshire, England, *c.* 1554; d. on the English mission, April 13, 1624. Brought up a Catholic, he apparently went to Oxford, but did not take a degree. He trained for the priesthood at Reims and Rome, was ordained in 1583, and came back to England. He spent part of the next few years on mission and part in Paris where he received his doctorate in divinity.

Bishop was a prominent member of the Appellant party among the English secular clergy and one of the 13 priests who, in 1603, signed a declaration of allegiance to Queen Elizabeth repudiating the pope's power to depose her. However, after 1606 he refused to sign the oath of allegiance that Paul V had condemned. He was imprisoned but was released in 1611 and joined the little community of controversial Catholic writers at Arras College, Paris.

When Gregory XV decided to restore a measure of local episcopal rule to the Catholics in England in 1623, he appointed William Bishop as bishop for the whole country, with the titular See of Chalcedon in Asia Minor. Bishop proceeded to act on the assumption that he possessed the full rights and privileges of an ordinary. He created a dean and chapter (*see* OLD CHAPTER), along with other canonical offices, and embarked on a major reorganization of the Roman Church in England. He died before the full effects of his radical changes were felt. His successor was Richard SMITH.

Bibliography: T. COOPER, *The Dictionay of National Biography from the Earliest Times to 1900* (London 1885–1900) 2:558–559. *Publications of the Catholic Record Society* (London 1910–) v. 10. J. GILLOW, *A Literary and Biographical History or Bibliographical Dictionary of the English Catholics from 1534 to the Present Time* (London and New York, 1855–1902) 1:218–223. P. HUGHES, *Rome and the Counter-Reformation in England* (London 1942). A. F. ALLISON, ''Richard Smith, Richelieu and the French Marriage,'' *Recusant History* 7.4 (1963–64). A. F. ALLISON and D. M. ROGERS, *A Catalogue of Catholic Books in English . . . 1558–1640*, 2 v. (London 1956).

[A. F. ALLISON]

BISHOP, WILLIAM HOWARD

Founder of the Glenmary Home Missioners; b. Washington, D.C., Dec. 19, 1885; d. Glendale, Ohio, June 11, 1953. His mother, Ellen Teresa Knowles, was a Catholic; his father, Francis Besant Bishop, a rural doctor, was received into the Church by Cardinal Gibbons. Bishop was educated in Washington public schools, attended Harvard College from 1907 to 1908, and St. Mary's Seminary, Baltimore. He was ordained for the Archdiocese of Baltimore on March 27, 1915, and was sent to study at the Catholic University of America in Washington, D.C. In 1917 he became pastor of St. Louis parish, Clarksville, Maryland. With the approval of Abp. Michael J. Curley he founded the Archdiocesan League of the Little Flower to aid needy rural pastors. In 1925 he organized the Archdiocesan Rural Life Conference of Baltimore, the first of its kind in the United States. He became president of the National Rural Life Conference in 1928 and served in that capacity until 1933.

In the 1930s, when the unemployed were looking to the national government for relief, Bishop took courses in agriculture and studied the complex economic problems associated with it. Concern for the spiritual malaise of the country led him to compile statistics that he set forth on his ''No-Priest Land'' map; they showed that nearly half the counties of the United States were without resident priests.

In March of 1936 Bishop published a plan for a society of Catholic home missions to operate in rural sections where Catholics numbered as few as one-tenth of 1 percent of the population (*see* GLENMARY HOME MISSIONERS). The following year he was invited to the Archdiocese of Cincinnati by Abp. John T. McNicholas to found such a society. Within two years he had acquired six students and a priest; by 1949 he had started a theological seminary at Glendale, Ohio. The Glenmary Lay Brothers Society and the Glenmary Home Mission Sisters were also organized by Bishop and received approval from the Holy See before his death.

Bibliography: H. W. SANTEN, *Father Bishop, Founder of the Glenmary Home Missioners* (Milwaukee 1961). C. J. KAUFFMAN, *Mission to Rural America: The Story of W. Howard Bishop, Founder of Glenmary* (New York, 1991).

[C. F. BORCHERS]

BISHOP (IN THE BIBLE)

A title applied in the NT to the higher officers in the early Christian communities. The Greek word ἐπίσκοπος, from which the English word bishop is derived (through the Latin *episcopus*), means etymologically inspector, overseer, superintendent.

New Testament Usage. The word ἐπίσκοπος, occurs five times in the NT. It is used once of Christ, in 2 Pt 2.25, where, like the Good Shepherd of Jn 10.11–16, Christ is called ''the shepherd and guardian (ἐπίσκοπος,) of your souls''; cf. Wis 1.6, where God is called the inspector (ἐπίσκοπος,) of man's heart. In Phil 1.1, Paul greets the Christians at Philippi ''with their bishops and deacons''; since there were several such ''overseers'' in this single community, the term here cannot have the later technical meaning attached to the monarchical episcopate. In Acts 20.28 Paul says to the πρεσβύτεροι (PRESBYTER) of Ephesus who had assembled at Miletus (20.17–18), ''Take heed to yourselves and to the whole flock in which the Holy Spirit has placed you as bishops to rule the Church of God''; here again, the fact that there were several bishops in one community excludes the monarchical concept of the term, and the fact that the term is here synonymous with presbyters shows that at this time no clear distinction was made between bishops and priests—a term derived from πρεσβύτεροι.

In the PASTORAL EPISTLES the term occurs twice: in 1 Tm 3.2 and Ti 1.7. After stating in 1 Tm 31 that the ἐπισκοπή (office of bishop—the only NT occurrence of this word in such a technical sense) is a noble occupation, the passage (3.2–7) goes on to describe the qualities that should be found in a good bishop; but nothing is said here of his functions. Similarly, in Ti 1.7–9 there is a description of qualities to be found in one who is to be appointed bishop, with no mention of his functions; moreover, this passage follows immediately after an order to appoint presbyters, again showing that no distinction is made here between the two terms.

Therefore, since there is no clear evidence in the NT for a monarchical episcopate, this office, which was firmly established by the early decades of the 2nd century, must have been based on oral apostolic tradition going back ultimately to Christ [*see* BISHOP (IN THE CHURCH)].

Term and Office Outside the New Testament. In the pagan Hellenistic world the term ἐπίσκοποι was applied to men who held various offices, both secular and religious, such as state and city officials, stewards, and business managers of cult associations. Although the term as used of these officials in cult associations may have influenced the NT choice of the term for Christian officials, the influence would extend only to the terminology; in its functions the NT office of men''who rule the Church of God'' (Acts 20.28) is entirely different.

In the so-called Damascus Document of the DEAD SEA SCROLLS the *m*ᵉ*baqqēr* (examiner, inspector) is described as a teacher, preacher, financial manager, and authorized leader of his community. It has therefore been suggested that the NT ἐπίσκοπος is to be connected in some manner with the *m*ᵉ*baqqēr* of the QUMRAN community. However, in the Septuagint this Greek word is used almost always for words formed on the Hebrew root *pqd* (to visit), whereas the root *bqr* is rare in the Hebrew OT. But what is more important, the *m*ᵉ*baqqēr* of Qumran clearly appears as a monarchical leader of his community; if Christianity borrowed the office of the ἐπίσκοπος, directly from the Qumran community, it would be difficult to explain why the NT office of the episcopacy does not appear as monarchical from the beginning.

Bibliography: L. MARCHAL, *Dictionnaire de la Bible,* suppl. ed. L. PIROT, et al. (Paris 1928) 2:1297–1333. J. LÉ CUYER, *Dictionnaire de spiritualité ascétique et mystique. Doctrine et histoire,* ed. M. VILLER et al. (Paris 1932) 4.1:879–884. J. GEWIESS, *Lexicon für Theologie und Kirche* (Freiburg, 1957–66) 2:491–492. G. A. BUTTRICK, ed. *The Interpreters' Dictionary of the Bible* (Nashville 1962) 1:441–443. *Encyclopedic Dictionary of the Bible,* tr. and adap. by L. HARTMAN (New York 1963) 249–250. J. COLSON, *L'Évêque dans les communautés primitives* (Paris 1951); *Les Fonctions ecclésiales aux deux premiers siècles* (Bruges 1956). E. SCHWEIZER, *Church Order in the New Testament,* tr. F. CLARKE (Naperville, Ill. 1961). K. G. GOETZ, ''Ist der *m*ᵉ*baqqēr* der Genizafragmente wirklich das Vorbild des Christlichen Episkopats?'' *Zeitschrift für die neutestamentliche Wissenschaft und die Kunde der älteren Kirche* 30 (1931) 89–93. J. DANIÉLOU, ''La Communauté de Qumràn et l'organization de l'Église ancienne,'' *Revue d'histoire et de philosophie religieuses* 35 (1955) 104–116. R. MARCUS, ''*M*ᵉ*baqqēr* and *Rabbim* in the Manual of Discipline 6.11–13,'' *Journal of Biblical Literature* 75 (1956) 298–302.

[J. J. O'ROURKE]

BISHOP (IN THE CHURCH)

If we center our attention on the diocesan bishop (or *ordinarius loci*) as distinct from auxiliary bishop or coadjutor bishop, we may define a bishop as one who in unity with and with due dependence on the supreme pontiff possesses in a local Church, or diocese, proper and complete power, priestly, doctrinal, and pastoral. His power is said to be proper because, though it is exercised in the name of Christ, it is not exercised in the name of, or as vicar of, the Roman pontiff. And, while subordinate to the supreme power in the Church, it is complete in the sense that ordinarily without the consent of other persons or groups it is adequate and valid for all ecclesiastical acts. The bishop is, then, the high priest, the teacher, the shepherd of the faithful within the diocese.

Diocesan Bishops in the Early Church. The first documented examples we have of church leaders whose role corresponds to that of diocesan bishops as described above, are found in the letters of St. Ignatius of Antioch, which in the judgment of most scholars were written about the year 115. In these letters, Ignatius of Antioch, Polycarp of Smyrna, Onesimus of Ephesus, Damas of Magnesia, Polybius of Tralles, and the unnamed bishop of Philadelphia, are clearly described as bishops who have the pastoral care of the whole Christian community of a city, assisted by a council of presbyters and a number of deacons, all of whom, along with the faithful, are subject to the authority of the bishop. Ignatius strongly affirms that bishops receive their authority from God, but he nowhere explains this authority as derived from the mandate which Christ gave to the apostles. There is no hint in his letters of the notion of apostolic succession in the episcopate, nor does he tell us how he or any other bishop was chosen or installed in his office. From his observation that the presbyters of the church of Magnesia had not taken advantage of the youthfulness of their bishop, it is clear that a young man could be chosen bishop. This might indicate that the choice could be based on the presence of charismatic gifts in a candidate. Ignatius speaks of his own gift of prophesy in his letter to the Philadelphians, 7. In a number of places he associates the presbyters with the bishop in such a way as to show that there was still a strong collegial element in the governance of the local church. In the judgment of most scholars today, the system whereby the Christian community of each city was led by one bishop was preceded by a system of collegial leadership exercised by a group of men sometimes called *episkopoi* but more often called *presbuteroi.* This is what we find in the later books of the New Testament and in some documents of the very early church.

St. Paul began his letter to the Philippians with a greeting to the community along with the *episkopois* and *diakonois*. Here the word *episkopois* in the plural is correctly translated ''overseers'' rather than ''bishops,'' since a bishop is the individual leader of a local church. In his account of the farewell address of Paul to the lead-

Bishops (l to r) Piero Marini, Stanislaw Dziwisz, and James Harvey at ordination ceremony, St. Peter's Basilica, Vatican City. (AP/ Wide World Photos)

ers of the church of Ephesus, Luke refers to them as ''presbyters,'' but he has Paul say that the holy Spirit has appointed them *episkopous* in the church of God (Acts 20:17.28). That the same persons could be called by either of these names is also indicated in the letter to Titus, 1:5–7. The fact that the word *episkopon* is in the singular both in Ti 1:7 and in 1 Tim 3:2 does not indicate the presence of a single bishop in the Pastorals, since in both cases the construction is rightly understood as a generic singular. While in the New Testament there is considerable variety in the terms used of those who are left in charge of local churches, what is consistent is the use of the plural in referring to them. Examples of this, in addition to those just mentioned, are: ''those who are laboring among you and are over you in the Lord'' (1 Thes 5:12); ''the household of Stephanas'' (1 Cor 15:15); ''your leaders'' (Heb 13:17); ''presbyters in each church'' (Acts 14:23); ''the presbyters among you'' (1 Pt 5:1); ''presbyters who preside well'' (1 Tm 5:17); ''appoint presbyters in every town'' (Ti 1:5). There is no evidence in the New Testament that any apostle or evangelist who founded a local church left one individual as ''bishop'' in charge of it.

That the church of Corinth continued to be led by a college of presbyters rather than by a single bishop in the last decade of the first century, is attested by the Letter of the Romans to the Corinthians, also known as 1 Clement, usually dated to about 96. This letter attributes to the apostles not only the appointment of the first generation of *episkopoi* and *diakonoi*, but also the provision for regular succession in this ministry. However, this did not mean a succession of single bishops in each church, as there is no evidence of the presence of such a bishop in the church of Corinth at this time. The letter consistently refers to the leaders of that church as presbyters, urging those guilty of schism to submit to them, and ''let the flock of Christ be at peace with its duly appointed presbyters.'' (1 Clement 54). Some have taken the authorship of this letter by Clement (attested by Dionysius, bishop of Corinth around 170) as proof of the presence of a single bishop in the church of Rome at this time, but it is also possible that he was a presbyter deputed to correspond with other churches. Most scholars now think that the leadership of the church of Rome would have resembled that of Corinth at the time this letter was written.

An early Christian writing known as the *Shepherd of Hermas* provides evidence that the church of Rome continued to be led by a group of presbyters for some decades of the second century. There is general agreement among scholars that the author of this work was a lay member of the Roman church who wrote it over an extended period during the first half of the second century. When he referred to those in charge of the church he consistently used the plural, sometimes speaking of ''bishops,'' but also of ''the presbyters who preside over the church, ''the leaders of the church'' and ''those who occupy the first seats.'' From the absence of any reference to one bishop, and the several references in the plural to leaders and presbyters, most scholars conclude that at the time this work was written the church of Rome still had collegial leadership.

One of the bishops with whom Ignatius of Antioch stayed on his way to Rome, and to whom he wrote one of his letters, was Polycarp of Smyrna. Not long after Ignatius had gone on to his martyrdom, Polycarp wrote a letter to the church of Philippi, in response to one he had received from there. It is noteworthy that whereas Ignatius had consistently exhorted the Christian communities to be subject to their bishop as to God and Christ, Polycarp urged the Philippians to be obedient to their presbyters and deacons as to God and Christ. His letter also contains a fairly lengthy description of the pastoral ministry incumbent on the presbyters, but no mention of a bishop. One can hardly explain the complete absence of any reference to the bishop of Philippi if there had been one there at the time this letter was written. (One cannot so argue from the absence of any reference to a bishop in Ignatius' letter to the Romans, since the theme of that letter is so different from that of all the others).

From the *Shepherd of Hermas* and the letter of Polycarp, most scholars conclude that around the year 120 the churches of Rome and Philippi were still led by a group of presbyters, at a time when the churches in Syria and western Asia Minor each had a bishop clearly distinct from the presbyters. However, about 50 years later a Christian writer named Hegesippus described a journey he made from the East to Rome, during which he spent some days with the bishop of Corinth. He says that in Rome he made a list of the bishops who had led that church up to the time of Anicetus, Soter and Eleutherus, whose episcopates are calculated to span the years from 155 to 189. St. Irenaeus also describes a visit which Polycarp of Smyrna made to Rome while Anicetus was bishop there. From the testimony of Hegesippus, cited by Eusebius (*Hist Eccl.* 4:22), along with the writings of Irenaeus and Tertullian, and *The Apostolic Tradition* attributed to Hippolytus, there can be little doubt about the fact that by the end of the second century the church in each city was being led by a single bishop, assisted by a council of presbyters.

Consecration of a bishop, Gothic painting. (©Archivo Iconografico, S.A./CORBIS)

The conclusion to which this evidence has led most scholars is that during the course of the second century, but at different rates of speed in different regions, there was a development from the leadership of local churches by a college of presbyters, to the leadership of a single bishop. They are convinced that such a development took place also in the church of Rome, despite the fact that Irenaeus names the men who had succeeded one another as bishops of that church, beginning with Linus, who he says was appointed by its founding apostles, Peter and Paul (*Adv. Haer.* III:3,3). However, just as scholars have good reason to question the description of Peter and Paul as founders of the church of Rome, they also have good reason to question the use of the term ''bishops'' of those who were remembered late in the second century for their role of leadership in the church of Rome a century before. It seems more likely that at that early period these men had been the outstanding teachers and presiders among the Roman presbyters.

In any case, from the writings of Irenaeus, Tertullian and Origen it is certain that by the third century orthodox Christian communities everywhere recognized their bishops as the successors to the apostles in their role as pastors and teachers. On the other hand, there is no solid evidence to support a notion of apostolic succession according to which the apostles ordained a bishop for each of the churches they founded, and provided for a succession of such bishops. Rather, there are good grounds for the opinion held by most scholars today, that the episcopate was the result of a development that took place during the second century, in response to the need for stronger leadership to counter the threat to the faith and unity of the church posed by Gnosticism. The question on which churches are divided is whether this development should be understood as a purely human response to the contemporary need for stronger leadership, or should rather be seen as so evidently guided by the holy Spirit that the episcopate must be recognized as corresponding to God's design, and therefore as a divinely-willed element of the permanent structure of the church. For a presentation of the latter view, which is that of the Catholic, Orthodox and Anglican churches, see APOSTOLIC SUCCESSION.

Diocesan Bishops in Vatican II Documents. The theology of the episcopacy as refined at the Second Vatican Council is found chiefly in two documents: *Lumen gentium*, the ''Constitution on the Church'' (chapter III) and *Christus Dominus*, the ''Decree on the Bishops'Pastoral Office in the Church'', the second closely related to the first. The Constitution has as it basic premise that Christ established the Apostles as a collectivity (''college''), and that this college continues to subsist in the college of bishops—who are successors to the Apostles insofar as they form and are participants in this college, continuing its functions in the world.

Bishops are the successors of the apostles as pastors of the Church (*LG* 20) and vicars and legates of Christ (*LG* 28). Although the Constitution does not speak of bishops as vicars of the Roman Pontiff (*LG* 27), the Second Vatican Council developed a theology of the episcopacy that balances and complements the teaching on the universal primacy of the papacy defined at the First Vatican Council (1870). Vatican II confirmed the teaching of Vatican I regarding the institution, the permanence, the nature and import of the sacred primacy of the Roman Pontiff and his infallible teaching office (*LG* 18). *Lumen gentium* teaches that the Roman Pontiff is the visible source and foundation of the unity of the Church both in faith and in communion, but it situated this teaching within a theology of the episcopacy that balances and complements the teaching on the papacy of Vatican I by its emphasis on collegiality. Thus the teaching on the episcopacy provides a context for the teaching on the pope and yet is itself interpreted within a teaching on papal authority.

Bishops are the successors of the apostles as pastors of the Church (*LG* 20) and vicars and legates of Christ (*LG* 28). Although the Constitution does not speak of bishops as vicars of the Roman Pontiff (*LG* 27), the Second Vatican Council developed a theology of the episcopacy that balances and complements the teaching on the universal primacy of the papacy defined at the First Vatican Council (1870). Vatican II confirmed the teaching of Vatican I regarding the institution, the permanence, the nature and import of the sacred primacy of the Roman Pontiff and his infallible teaching office (*LG* 18). *Lumen gentium* teaches that the Roman Pontiff is the visible source and foundation of the unity of the Church both in faith and in communion, but it situated this teaching within a theology of the episcopacy that balances and complements the teaching on the papacy of Vatican I by its emphasis on collegiality. Thus the teaching on the episcopacy provides a context for the teaching on the pope and yet is itself interpreted within a teaching on papal authority.

Bishops represent an historical continuation of the apostolic office and therefore are essential to the Roman Catholic understanding of the apostolicity of the church. The early church spoke of bishops as ''vicars of Christ,'' but the title had come to be reserved to the pope since about the eighth century. Vatican II restores it to all bishops, thus indicating the spirit in which they are to undertake their office.

Collegiality. The episcopacy is considered to be a hierarchical office in the church by divine institution (*LG* 20), meaning that the office of the episcopacy is a necessary element in the church.

By virtue of their episcopal consecration and hierarchical communion with the Bishop of Rome and other bishops, they constitute a college or permanent assembly whose head is the Bishop of Rome (*LG* 19, 22). If a bishop refuses the apostolic communion, he cannot be admitted to office (*LG* 24). A bishop represents his own church within this college and all the bishops, together with the pope, represent the whole church (*LG* 22). The college of bishops does not constitute a legislative body apart from the pope, but includes the pope as member and head of the college.

As a member and head of the college of bishops, the Roman Pontiff is infallible when he proclaims in a definitive act a doctrine on faith or morals. The church's infallibility is also present in the body of bishops when, in union with Peter's successor, they exercise the supreme teaching office in ecumenical council. Although an individual bishop does not possess the prerogative of infallibility, bishops teach infallibly "even though dispersed throughout the world, but maintaining the bond of communion among themselves and with the successor of Peter, when in teaching authentically matters concerning faith and morals they agree about a judgment as one that has to be definitively held" (*LG* 25).

The episcopal college exercises its collegiality in a preeminent way in an ecumenical council. All bishops who are members of the episcopal college have the right to take part in an ecumenical council (*Christus Dominus* 4). The bishops as a college together with the pope and never apart from him have supreme and full authority over the universal Church (*LG* 22). This is exercised in an ecumenical council. However, they can also exercise collegiate power even while living in different parts of the world if the head of the college summons them to this collegiate action or at least approves or freely admits the corporate action of the unassembled bishops (*CD* 4). Bishops chosen from different parts of the world may also serve in a council called the Synod of Bishops where they act on behalf of the whole catholic episcopate (*CD* 5). Since the Second Vatican Council, the Synod of bishops has acted in a consultative capacity to the Pope.

Episcopal conferences usually are another form of collegial activity. An episcopal conference "is a kind of assembly in which the bishops of some nation or region discharge their pastoral office in collaboration, the better to promote the good which the church offers to people, and especially through forms and methods of apostolate carefully designed to meet contemporary conditions" (*CD* 38.1). The decisions of an episcopal conference have binding force in law provided that: 1) "they have been made legitimately and by at least a two-thirds majority of the votes of the prelates who are members of the conference with a deliberative vote"; 2) "that these decisions have been approved by the apostolic see;" and (3) "that they apply only to matters that have been prescribed by common law or enacted by special mandate of the apostolic see acting on its own initiative or in response to a petition made by the conference itself" (*CD* 38.4). The decisions of episcopal conferences are implemented on the conjoint authority of the bishops.

Collegiality is also exercised by the solicitude of the bishops for all the churches. This care for the other churches is exercised by contributing financial resources, by training lay and religious ministers for the missions, and contributing the services of diocesan priests to regions lacking clergy (*CD* 6).

Threefold Office: Priest, Prophet, and King. The episcopal office is described according to the threefold designation of priest, prophet and king that *Lumen Gentium* also uses to describe the people of God in Chapter 2 of Lumen Gentium and the laity in Chapter 4. It is significant that Vatican II first describes the church in its threefold relationship to Christ and then its ministers. However, the image of shepherd replaces that of king when this threefold office is applied to bishops (*LG* 20) Bishops are teachers of doctrine (prophet), ministers of sacred worship (priest) and holders of office in government (shepherd) (*LG* 20).

Vatican II teaches that the fullness of the sacrament of Orders is conferred by episcopal consecration (*LG* 21, 26; *CD* 15). The bishop is "the steward of the supreme priesthood," especially in the eucharist (*LG* 26). All priests share in and exercise the one priesthood of Christ (*CD* 28). Priesthood is a sharing in the office of Christ the one mediator (see 1 Tm 2:5) (*LG* 28).

The bishop has the responsibility of regulating the sacraments, especially every legitimate celebration of the Eucharist. He is the original minister of Confirmation, the dispenser of sacred orders, and the director of penitential discipline.

The bishop is the one primarily responsible for the life of the Church in his diocese. As an individual bishop he exercises his pastoral office of this church and not over other churches nor the church universal. By virtue of this ordination, a bishop's authority is proper, ordinary, and immediate (*LG* 27), meaning that a bishop possesses authority by virtue of his ordination that is not juridically delegated by the Bishop of Rome. The exercise of their authority, however, is ultimately controlled by the supreme authority of the Church and can be confined within certain limits if the pastoral care of the church requires this (*CD* 8a).

In Roman Catholicism the basic unit of the church is a particular church, usually a diocese, defined as an "altar community under the sacred ministry of the bishop" (*LG* 26). The bishop is responsible for the unity and communion of this church with the other churches. He exercises his pastoral office of this church and not over other churches or the church universal (*LG* 23), although he has a responsibility to have care and solicitude for the whole Church (*LG* 23). Administratively the particular church is a diocese, "a section of the People of God entrusted to a bishop" (*CD* 11). The "one, holy, catholic and apostolic Church of Christ is present and active" in the particular church (*CD* 11).

Episcopal Duties. Among principal tasks of bishops, the preaching of the gospel is pre-eminent (*LG* 25, CD 12). The duties of bishops are described with reference to his prophetic, priestly, and pastoral office.

Prophetic office. In their teaching function they must:

Pursue their apostolic work as witnesses of Christ to all people (*CD* 11).
Give themselves wholeheartedly to those who have wandered from the path of truth or who know nothing of the gospel of Christ and his saving mercy (*CD* 11).
Call all people to faith or strengthen them in living faith (*CD* 12).
Expound the mystery of Christ in its entirety, including those truth ignorance of which is ignorance of Christ (*CD* 12).
Point out the way divinely revealed for giving glory to God and thereby attaining eternal happiness (*CD* 12).
Show that the material things of life and human institutions can also be directed to the salvation of humanity and contribute substantially to building up the body of Christ (*CD* 12).
Expound in accord with the teaching of the church the inestimable value of the human person; her or his freedom and bodily vitality; the family and its unity and stability; the betting and educating of children; social structures with their laws and professions; labour and leisure, arts and technology; poverty and affluence (*CD* 12).
Propose methods for finding an answer to questions of the utmost gravity: the ownership, increase, and just distribution of material wealth; peace and war; the effective fellowship of all peoples (*CD* 12).
Present the doctrine of Christ in a manner suited to the needs of the times. Such teaching should deal with the most pressing difficulties and problems which weigh people down. Preserve this doctrine and teach the faithful themselves to defend it and spread it (*CD* 13).
Make evident the maternal solicitude of the church for everyone whether they are believers or not (*CD* 13).
Take particular care to further the interests of the poor and the underprivileged to whom the Lord has sent them to preach the gospel (*CD* 13).
Make an approach to people, seeking and promoting dialogue with them. If truth is constantly to be accompanied by charity and understanding by love, in such salutary discussions they should present their positions in clear language, unaggressively and diplomatically. Likewise they should show due prudence combined with confidence, for this is what brings about union of minds by encouraging friendship (*CD* 13).
Employ the various means of communication which are at hand at the present time to make known christian doctrine. This applies especially to preaching and catechetical instruction, which clearly come first in order of importance (*CD* 13).
Ensure that catechetical instruction is given to children, adolescents, young people and even adults. They should also ensure that in giving this instruction a suitable order and method are followed, accommodated not only to the subject matter but also to the disposition, aptitude, age and environment of the hearers. Let hem also ensure that this instruction is based on sacred scripture, tradition, liturgy, the teaching authority and life of the church (*CD* 14).
See that catechists are properly trained for their work (*CD* 14).
See to it that the instruction of adult catechumens is restored or improved (*CD* 14).

Priestly Office. In their office of sanctification, bishops are the principle stewards of the mysteries of God as well as directors, promoters and guardians of the whole liturgical life in the church which has been entrusted to them (*CD* 15). They should:

Make it their constant endeavor that the faithful acquire a deeper knowledge of the paschal mystery, and so live through the eucharist that they may form one closely-knit body unity in the love of Christ (*CD* 15).
Make a real effort to bring about that all those who have been entrusted to their care are of one mind in prayer and grow in grace through the reception of the sacraments, becoming faithful witnesses to the Lord (*CD* 15).
Be zealous in promoting the holy living of their clergy, religious and laity according to each one's particular vocation, bearing in mind that they themselves are obliged to show an example of holiness in charity, humility and simplicity of life (*CD* 15).
Let them so sanctify the churches entrusted to them that in these churches will be fully sensed the enlightening presence of the whole church of Christ (*CD* 15).
Encourage in every way vocations to the priesthood and to religious life, giving special attention to vocations to missionary work (*CD* 15).

Pastoral Office. In their paternal and pastoral function, bishops should:

Be in the midst of their flock as those who serve, be good shepherds who know their own sheep and whose sheep know them, be true fathers who manifest a spirit of love and care for all. Form their flock into a union of charity (*CD* 16).
Hold priests in special regard and treat them like sons and friends, listening to them in an atmosphere of mutual trust. Look after their spiritual,

intellectual and material wellbeing (*CD* 16, PO 7). Support courses of study and arrange special conferences. Take care of priests who are in danger of any kind or who have failed in some way (*CD* 16). "Their chief and most serious responsibility is the holiness of their priests: so they should take the utmost trouble over the continuing formation of their body of priests" (*PO* 7).

Be better prepared to give guidance for the welfare of the faithful according to the circumstances of each. Strive to acquire an accurate knowledge of their needs in the social conditions in which they live. Show themselves to be concerned for all. Respect the place proper to their faithful in the affairs of the church, acknowledging also their duty and right to work actively for the buildings up of the mystical body of Christ.

Cultivate friendly relations with separated fellow Christians and urge the faithful to treat them with real warmth and kindness. Foster ecumenism as understood by the church. Have a friendly regard for the non-baptized (*CD* 16).

Encourage and direct different forms of apostolate (*CD* 17).

Urge the laity to exercise their apostolate according to each one's capacity and circumstances (*CD* 17).

Adapt forms of the apostolate to the needs of the day, having regard to the conditions in which people live, not only spiritual and moral but also social, demographic and economic. Social and religious research is strongly recommended (*CD* 17).

Show special care for those who, because of the conditions in which they live, can get little or no benefit from the general pastoral care of parish priests: immigrants, exiles, refugees, sailors, people in aviation, gypsies, holiday-makers temporarily living outside their own region (*CD* 18).

See Also: BISHOP (IN THE BIBLE); BISHOP (SACRAMENTAL THEOLOGY OF); BISHOP, DIOCESAN (CANON LAW); APOSTOLIC SUCCESSION; AUTHORITY, ECCLESIASTICAL; EPISCOPAL CONFERENCES; INFALLIBILITY; OFFICE, ECCLESIASTICAL; PRIMACY OF THE POPE.

Bibliography: K. E. KIRK, ed., *The Apostolic Ministry* (London 1946). J. COLSON, *L'Évêque dans les communautés primitives* (Paris 1951). K RAHNER and J. RATZINGER, *The Episcopate and the Primacy* (New York 1962). J. COLSON, *L'Épiscopat catholique: Collegialité et primauté dans les trois premiers siècles* (Paris 1963). H. BOUËSSÉ and A. MANDOUZE, *L'Évêque dans l'Église de Christ* (Bruges/Paris 1963). W. ONCLIN et.al., *La charge pastorale des évêques* (Paris 1969). R. E. BROWN, *Priest and Bishop. Biblical Reflections* (Mahwah 1970). J. DELORME, *Le ministère et les ministères selon le N.T.* (Paris 1974). A. LEMAIRE, *Ministry in the Church* (London 1977). H. CHADWICK et al., *The Role of the Bishop in the Ancient Society* (Berkeley 1980). E. G. JAY, "From Presbyter-Bishops to Bishops and Presbyters: Christian Ministry in the Second Century," *Second Century* 1 (1981) 125–62. U. BETTI, *La dottrina sull'episcopato del Concilio Vaticano II* (Rome 1984). A. CUNNINGHAM, *The Bishop in the Church* (Wilmington 1985). F.A. SULLIVAN, *From Apostles to Bishops* (New York/Mahwah 2001). J. BEAL, J. CORIDEN, T. GREEN, eds.,*New Commentary on the Code of Canon Law.* (New York/Mahwah 2000). E. CAPARROS, M. THERIAULT, J. THORN, eds., *Code of Canon Law Annotated (English)* (Montreal 1993). G. SHEEHY, et al., eds. *The Canon Law: Letter and Spirit* (Collegeville, Minn. 1995). *A Manual for Bishops: Rights and Responsibilities of Diocesan Bishops in the Revised Code of Canon Law* (Washington 1992).

[F. A. SULLIVAN/S. K. WOOD]

BISHOP (SACRAMENTAL THEOLOGY OF)

The Dogmatic Constitution on the Church (1964) teaches that episcopal consecration constitutes the fullness of the sacrament of Orders, that fullness called the high priesthood (*Lumen gentium* 21). This theology of the sacramentality of episcopal consecration is reflected in the 1990 *Editio Typica Altera* of the rite of ordination. The 1990 *Pontificate Romanum* begins with the rite for the ordination of a bishop and then follows with the rites for presbyters and deacons in a descending order. The implication is that the bishop has the fullness of the sacrament and that the other orders are related to that fullness. What was formerly a prayer of consecration for a bishop is now designated as a prayer of ordination.

Pius XII in *Sacramentum Ordinis* (Nov. 30, 1947) and Paul VI in *Pontificalis Romani recognitio* (June 18, 1968) stipulated the matter and form of the sacrament, the imposition of hands and the central portion of the prayer of ordination calling on God to pour out upon the ordinand "that power which is from you, the governing Spirit." In accord with ancient custom, the principal ordaining bishop is joined by two other bishops in celebrating the ordination. All the bishops present join the principal ordaining bishop in laying hands on the bishop-elect, thus witnessing to the collegial nature of the Order of the episcopate.

History of the Question Before Vatican II. The status of the episcopacy as an order remained a disputed question in the Western Church. The superiority of bishops to priests had been affirmed in the early 2d century (St. Ignatius, *Ad. Phil.* 4; *Ad Smyrn.* 8), but some early writers such as Ambrosiaster, St. John Chrysostom, and St. Jerome emphasized the elements of equality between priests and bishops to counter an attempt by deacons to be accepted as superior to priests (see F. Prat, *Dictionnaire de théologie catholique,* 5:2:1661–63). The Protestant Reformation followed this opinion in the 16th century.

St. Thomas Aquinas denied that episcopal consecration confers a sacramental character since he did not see how a bishop could consecrate the eucharist any more intensively than a priest (*IV Sent., D. 24, q. 2, a. 1, sol. 2; Summa contra Gentiles*, l. IV. c. 74; *Summa Theologiae,* Suppl. 40.5). He interpreted episcopal consecration as imparting power over the Mystical Body, and thereby as imparting jurisdiction. He distinguished this from power over the eucharistic body which the sacrament of orders conferred.

The Council of Trent insisted that ecclesiastical hierarchy is of divine institution and that *de facto* it is composed of bishops, priests, and other ministers without, however, defining the *de facto* composition of bishops, priests, and other ministers. The Second Vatican Council confirmed that the church is a hierarchically constituted society (LG 20) and described this hierarchy as consisting of bishops, priests, and deacons.

Vatican II describes the effects of ordination as conferring a threefold office of sanctifying, teaching, and ruling. This language of the threefold office tends to replace the categories of sacramental power and jurisdiction that dominated sacramental theology prior to Vatican II. Within the threefold office governance is more than jurisdiction delegated from another authority; it is an office inherent to the sacrament. Thus *Lumen gentium* speaks of a bishop's authority as ''proper, ordinary, and immediate'' (LG 27). A bishop's authority is not delegated by the pope, but one he possesses by virtue of his ordination.

Identifying the ''Fullness'' of Orders. The teaching on the sacramentality of episcopal consecration raises the question of the difference between episcopal ordination and presbyteral ordination. In what does the fullness of the sacramental of Order consist? Since Vatican II did not identify this, various explanations represent theological speculation rather than official church teaching.

One explanation has been that bishops have certain sacramental powers not possessed by presbyters. The Council of Trent asserted that episcopal consecration conveys a power over the sacrament of confirmation and Holy Orders that does not belong in the same way to a priest. The history of sacramental theology has shown that bishops were the original ministers of Baptism, postbaptismal chrismation (Confirmation), the Eucharist, and Reconciliation. They delegated priests as the ministers of these sacraments at various times and in various circumstances. Priests, particularly mitered abbots, have at times been commissioned to confer the priesthood. The one power that has not been delegated to presbyters is the consecration of a bishop. This history makes it difficult to locate the essential difference between bishops and presbyters in the sacramental powers each possesses.

Traditionally, the sacramental effect of ordination was seen as the ordinand's configuration to Christ, which empowered the ordinand to teach, to govern, and to act in Christ's name in the administration of the sacraments. Here both presbyter and bishop signify Christ. The ordained person is *vicarious Christi*, a vicar of Christ, who acts *in persona Christi*, in the place of the person of Christ. Vatican II continues this teaching that ''through that sacrament priests by the anointing of the Holy Spirit are signed with a special character and so are configured to Christ the priest in such a way that they are able to act in the person of Christ the head'' (PO 2). Configuration to Christ so as to act in his name in the sacraments does not explain the difference between a bishop and a presbyter or give a complete account of the sacramentality of ordination, for a bishop does not act any more intensively or represent Christ more fully within the sacraments.

The difference, however, can be essentially located in the ecclesial signification of ordination, specifically in the representative function of the bishop. This is related to configuration to Christ precisely as head of his body, the Church. The sacrament of Orders creates a bond between a bishop and a particular eucharistic community. A bishop is never ordained absolutely, but within a church, even if this church is a historic one, as in the case of titular bishops. He represents the Church in its prayer to the Father, particularly in the Eucharist, and so acts *in persona ecclesiae*. According to this interpretation of the sacrament, the ordained person is ''ordered'' to Christ in a recapitulative relationship to the Church. The ordained person represents Christ in a relationship of headship while the baptized are configured to Christ as members of his body. This relationship to Christ is important since it is Christ who acts in the sacraments. The ordained person's relationship to Christ is thus inseparable from his relationship to the Church.

Orders also creates a bond of communion between a bishop and the other bishops, including the bishop of Rome and the college of bishops. A bishop becomes a member of the college of bishops by his sacramental consecration and communion with the other bishops and the bishop of Rome. The sacrament of Orders effects and signifies these relationships which both constitute and manifest the order of the Church as a communion of communions.

The bishops are the visible source and foundation of unity in their own particular churches. As a college they visibly represent the unity among the particular churches. A particular bishop represents and manifests a particular church. He represents this church within the communion of particular churches. As a college, all the bishops in their relationship to one another signify the relationship among the particular churches, namely, the communion of communions. The college of bishops sacramentalizes the communion of churches insofar as it makes visible these ecclesial interrelationships within the personal communion of the bishops. The ''fullness'' represented in the episcopacy is none other than this communion within the episcopal college.

A bishop differs essentially from a presbyter in his representative function. A bishop represents his particular church within the communion of churches while a presbyter does not. A presbyter cannot represent a particular church and is not a member of the college of bishops. This representative function is inseparable from governance, but here governance is seen through the lens of sacramentality rather than the lens of jurisdiction. Pastoral leadership, liturgical presidency, and authoritative teaching—the kingly, priestly, and prophetic roles of the bishop—are functions of the bishop's *ordo* in the community. This ecclesial relationship is signified and constituted by the sacrament of ordination. Thus there is both a Christological and an ecclesial referent to the sign of the sacrament of ordination, and the fullness of the sacrament of Orders refers to the bishop's ability to represent a particular church in the communion of particular churches.

Bibliography: E. BOULARAND, ''La consécration épiscopale est-elle sacramentelle?'' *Bulletin de litérature ecclésiastique* 54, (no. 1, 1953) 3–36; E. J. KILMARTIN, ''Apostolic Office: Sacrament of Christ,'' *Theological Studies* 36 (1975) 243–264; J. LÉCUYER, ''Orientations présentes de la théologie de l'épiscopat,'' in Y. CONGAR and B. D. DUPUY, eds., *L'Episcopat et l'église universelle* (Paris 1962) 781–811; G. NICOLUSSI, ''La sacramentalità dell'episcopato nella '*Lumen gentium*,' Cap. III,'' *Ephemerides theologicae Lovanienses* 47 (1971) 7–63; S. K. WOOD, Sacramental Orders (Collegeville, Minn. 2000).

[S. K. WOOD]

BISHOP, AUXILIARY

When pastoral needs of a diocese recommend it, one or more auxiliary bishops may be appointed at the request of the diocesan bishop. The general role of the auxiliary is clear: he assumes such duties and functions within a diocese that the diocesan bishop, because of the size of the diocese or ill health cannot adequately fulfill, especially functions that require the sacramental power of a bishop.

Auxiliary bishops, given their episcopal status in the particular church, are dealt with in a separate section in article 3 of Chapter II of the *Code of Canon Law*. The *Code of Canons of the Eastern Churches* deals specifically with auxiliary bishops in canons 212–218.

Auxiliary bishops may be appointed by the Holy See with or without special faculties. They are dependent upon the authority of the diocesan bishop. Because they should share in a special way with the diocesan bishop the general pastoral governance of the diocese, an auxiliary bishop who is appointed by the Holy See with special faculties is given special consideration in the law and is to be made a vicar general by the diocesan bishop. Auxiliary bishops without special faculties also should be made vicar generals or episcopal vicars. Vicar generals and episcopal vicars exercise vicariously the ordinary power of executive governance as defined by law.

Auxiliary bishops are titular bishops in that they hold title to some ancient Christian center in the Near or Middle East where a particular church once flourished but has long since disappeared. An auxiliary bishop has no power in this titular diocese.

Diocesan bishops are to consult in collaborative fashion with their auxiliary bishops in matters of major importance. Auxiliaries, on the other hand, are called to perform their duties with solicitude and in a spirit of harmony and unity with the diocesan bishop.

Auxiliary bishops have the right and duty to participate in ecumenical councils with a deliberative vote. They must be called to particular councils where they also have a deliberative vote. Auxiliaries belong to the conference of bishops and have a consultative vote or deliberative vote depending upon the statutes of the conference. Auxiliaries, however, may not serve as presidents of a conference of bishops.

Like diocesan bishops, auxiliary bishops are obliged to reside in the diocese to which they are appointed. They are not to be absent from the diocese except for brief periods of time and an annual vacation not exceeding a month.

An auxiliary bishop does not enjoy the right of succession, and they are asked to submit to the supreme pontiff their resignation at age 75 or sooner when they are unable to attend to their duties due to illness or some other grave cause. Their retirement does not become effective until it is accepted by the supreme pontiff. After retirement, the diocese they serve has the primary obligation for their support.

Bibliography: J. BEAL, J. CORIDEN, T. GREEN, eds., *New Commentary on the Code of Canon Law* (New York 2000). E. CAPARROS, M. THERIAULT, J. THORN, eds., *Code of Canon Law Annotated (English)* (Montreal 1993). V. J. POSPISHIL, *Eastern Catholic Church Law* (2d rev. ed. Staten Island, N.Y. 1996).

[A. J. QUINN]

BISHOP, DIOCESAN (CANON LAW)

Existing ecclesiastical law that delineates the office, duties and rights of bishops in general incorporates the teaching and directives of the Second Vatican Council found in *Christus Dominus*, the ''Decree on the Bishops' Pastoral Office in the Church.'' The norms and obligations governing the life and ministry of diocesan bishops, coadjutors and auxiliary bishops appears in Book II, Chapter II, canons 375–411 of the *Code of Canon Law*. The Eastern code treats eparchies (dioceses) and bishops in Title VII, canons 177–218 of the *Code of Canon Law*.

Bishops in General. The office of bishop originates from divine institution and confers power to teach, govern, and sanctify, powers that are to be exercised only in hierarchical communion with the head and members of the college of bishops. Bishops are successors to the apostles and pastors in the Church. As such, they are teachers of doctrine, priests of worship and ministers of governance. Bishops become members of the episcopal college through episcopal ordination and hierarchical communion with the head and other members of the college. Episcopal ordination confers an ontological share in the sacred functions of Christ (teach, govern, sanctify). By canonical mission the bishop is appointed to a particular church or assigned to certain persons for whom he exercises these functions.

Under the primacy of the Supreme Pontiff there exists a true and basic equality among bishops. Bishops act in communion with the whole of the episcopal body, not in an independent or autonomous manner.

All bishops belong to one of two categories, diocesan or titular. The care of a diocese is entrusted to the diocesan bishop.

The supreme pontiff appoints bishops or confirms those legitimately elected. Papal appointment or confirmation of a candidate legitimately proposed safeguards the communion which must exist between the universal Church and the particular church. The Apostolic See, therefore, makes the definitive judgment on a candidate's suitability for the office of bishop. Before being ordained the bishop-elect must take an oath of fidelity to the Apostolic See.

Every three years bishops of a province propose a confidential (secret) list of priests suitable for the office of bishop. This list is sent to the Apostolic See through the pontifical legate. Also, each diocesan bishop may propose to the Apostolic See the names of priests he judges worthy to become bishops.

A candidate for bishop must be at least 35 years of age and ordained to the priesthood for at least five years. He must enjoy a good reputation; that is, the candidate must be outstanding in faith, good morals, piety, zeal for souls, prudence, wisdom and virtue. Lastly, he must possess a doctorate or licentiate in scripture, theology or canon law . . . or be expert in these same disciplines.

Powers of a Diocesan Bishop. The diocesan bishop has the ordinary, proper, and immediate power to exercise his office. His jurisdiction is called *ordinary* because it is vested in him by reason of his office and not by delegation. It is proper in that it is exercised in his own name, not vicariously in the name of another. It is *immediate* because the power is directed toward all in the diocese without mediation of another.

Lumen Gentium and *Christus Dominus* explain that the diocesan bishop exercises this power personally in the name of Christ. In addition to his ordinary power, the bishop possesses further power that is delegated to him by the Apostolic See.

The diocesan bishop may exercise his role only after he has taken canonical possession of his office. A priest named a bishop is obligated to receive episcopal ordination within three months of the apostolic letter of appointment. The episcopal ordination must precede his taking canonical possession of the diocese. A bishop takes canonical possession of a diocese when he shows the apostolic letter to the college of consultors in the presence of the chancellor of the curia of the diocese who then records the event. If the bishop is appointed to a newly erected diocese, the bishop shows the apostolic letter to the clergy and people in the cathedral church and the senior priest present records the event.

Bound by the law of personal residence, a diocesan bishop is not to be absent from his diocese beyond a month without reasonable cause and his making provision that the diocese suffers no detriment from his absence. Moreover, except for grave and urgent reason, he is not to be absent from the diocese on Christmas, during Holy Week, on Easter, Pentecost and the Feast of the Body and Blood of Christ.

The Bishop as Pastor, Teacher and High Priest. A diocesan bishop is to show himself concerned for all the Christian faithful, as well as for the non-baptized, entrusted to his care. He is charged with fostering ecumenism in accordance with the mind of the Church (*Lumen Gentium* and *Christus Dominus*). The bishop is to proclaim the Gospel to non-believers since they, too, are subjects of his pastoral care.

The bishop is to show special solicitude for his priests and deacons and listen to them as counselors, not only as individuals but in groups such as the presbyteral council and the college of consultors. The college of consultors assists the bishop in specific areas identified in canon law, most of which concern temporal administration. The presbyteral council exists to help promote the pastoral good of the diocese.

Every diocesan bishop is the principal teacher of Catholic doctrine. He is obligated to explain truths of faith and morals and take care that the ministry of the word, especially homilies and catechetical instruction, is provided for all the faithful throughout the diocese. The diocesan bishop issues norms for catechetics and fosters catechetical formation.

It is incumbent upon bishops to foster vocations to ordained ministry as well as vocations to consecrated life and the missions. All bishops have the right to preach the Gospel everywhere unless the local bishop in a particular case has forbidden this.

The bishop is held to be watchful over writings and communications that could be harmful to the faith and morals of the Christian faithful. Writings pertaining to faith and morals should be submitted for approval before publication, and the bishop must himself be prepared to disapprove writings harmful to faith and morals.

It is the obligation of the bishops to promote the holiness of the faithful not only through teaching but by the charitable and simple humility of their personal lives. Since bishops are the high priests and the principal dispensers of the mysteries of God, bishops must encourage their people to grow in grace through the sacraments, especially through the Eucharist. Bishops, indeed, are the directors, promoters and guardians of liturgical life in the diocese entrusted to their care. Within the scope of their competence, then, bishops issue liturgical regulations to keep the worship life of the diocese within the norms of the church.

Each diocesan bishop is obliged personally to offer a Mass for the people of his diocese (particular church) each Sunday and holy day of obligation.

A diocesan bishop must preside frequently at celebrations of the Eucharist in the cathedral and other churches of his diocese. However, outside of his own diocese, a bishop may perform pontifical functions only with the expressed or reasonably presumed consent of the local diocesan bishop.

The diocesan bishop governs with legislative, executive, and judicial powers according to the norms of law. He himself exercises legislative power. However, he exercises executive power either personally or through vicars general or episcopal vicars. Also, he exercises judicial power either personally or through the judicial vicar and appointed judges. As the diocesan legislator, he is competent to interpret the diocesan laws he promulgates. He can abrogate or derogate from diocesan laws. He also can issue penal laws and penalties.

A bishop is held to promote the discipline of the whole Church and, therefore, must urge observance of all ecclesiastical laws by guarding against abuses, especially as they relate to the ministry of the word, the celebration of the sacraments and sacramentals, the worship of God, and administration of ecclesiastical goods. The diocesan bishop is the agent who represents the diocese in all its juridic affairs.

Episcopal Vitations and Reports. Because the faithful should see the bishop as their teacher, shepherd, and high priest, the bishop is obliged by law to visit his diocese annually in whole or in part, in such manner that he visits the entire diocese at least every five years. While a bishop may visit members of religious institutes of pontifical right and their houses only in cases allowed by law, he is encouraged to visit all churches and oratories, schools, and other places and works of religion or charity where the faithful habitually attend.

Every five years each diocesan bishop is bound to make a report to the supreme pontiff on the state of the diocese entrusted to his care. This quinquennial report is to be sent six months before the time set for the *ad limina* visit. The bishop also forwards an annual statistical report to the Offices of the Secretariat of State.

During the year the diocesan bishop is obligated to submit the quinquennial report to the supreme pontiff, the bishop is to go to Rome personally to venerate the tombs of Peter and Paul and to present himself to the Holy Father. If legitimately impeded, he may satisfy the obligation through another, e.g. his coadjutor, auxiliary, or suitable priest.

In these *ad limina* visits the Holy Father confirms and supports his brother bishops in faith and love. Bonds of hierarchical communion are strengthened and the catholicity of the church and unity of the episcopal college are manifested. These visits also engage bishops in dialogue with the dicasteries of the Roman Curia wherein information can be exchanged and mutual understanding deepened.

A diocesan bishop who has completed his 75th year is requested by canon law to tender his resignation from office to the supreme pontiff. Moreover, if a bishop becomes less able or unable to fulfill his office because of ill health or other grave cause, he is requested to offer his resignation from office. Canon law requests voluntary resignation. The resignation, then, must be accepted by the supreme pontiff. A diocese does not become vacant when a diocesan bishop tenders his resignation, but only when the supreme pontiff accepts the resignation.

A diocesan bishop whose resignation from office has been accepted retains the title of bishop *emeritus* of his diocese and can maintain a place of residence in that diocese. While recognizing that primary obligations fall upon the diocese the retiree has served, the conferences of bishops are obligated to issue guidelines for the suitable and decent support of retired bishops.

Retired bishops continue to be members of the college of bishops. They are pastors and teachers, priests of sacred worship, and ministers of governance. They may take part in an ecumenical council with a deliberative vote. Retired diocesan bishops can be elected by a conference of bishops as members of the synod of bishops.

Bibliography: J. BEAL, J. CORIDEN, T. GREEN, eds., *New Commentary on the Code of Canon Law* (New York 2000). E. CAPARROS, M. THERIAULT, J. THORN, eds., *Code of Canon Law Annotated (English)* (Montreal 1993). G. SHEEHY ET AL., eds. *The Canon Law: Letter and Spirit* Collegeville, Minn. 1995). V. J. POSPISHIL, *Eastern Catholic Church Law* (2d rev. ed., Staten Island 1996). *A Manual for Bishops: Rights and Responsibilities of Diocesan Bishops in the Revised Code of Canon Law* (Washington, D.C. 1992).

[A. J. QUINN]

BISHOP, MONASTIC

According to BEDE, speaking of Iona (*Eccl. Hist.* 3.14), ''This isle is wont always to have an abbot who is a priest as ruler, to whom the whole province and the bishops themselves by an unusual arrangement, are expected to be subject, a situation that goes back to the first teacher (St. COLUMBA) who was not a bishop but a priest and a monk.'' Iona was so much part of the Irish Church that Bede's statement has been given universal application. It has also been rigidly interpreted to mean that in the Irish Church all jurisdiction was in the hands of the abbots of the great monasteries.

The situation in Ireland was in fact much more complex. Priest-abbots were the ultimate in authority within their monasteries, and it is probable that they were the highest authority in the *paruchia,* the lands, often scattered, which each monastery held by gift as private property. The very possession of great holdings would give the abbot a position comparable to that of a noble or prince and would account for such titles as ''Abbot of Rome'' for the pope and ''Abbot of the Blessed'' for Christ himself.

In Ireland the title came to connote high ecclesiastical authority. Nevertheless, the abbot in Ireland was always inferior to the bishop in dignity. This is evident not merely in ecclesiastical documents, e.g., the *Collection of Canons* and the *Lives of the Saints,* but also from native secular law. Every Irish noble had his ''honor-price,'' and the honor-price of a bishop was equivalent to that of a king, while the abbot's was on a lower level, depending on his personal prestige and not on his professional status. In the *Old Irish Litanies* bishops had a place of special honor; they were invoked in groups of seven and even in greater numbers.

According to the *Rigail Pátraic,* the so-called rule of St. PATRICK (*c.* 8th century), every *tuath,* or state, should have a chief-bishop (prím-epscop) to ordain clergy and act as confessor and spiritual father to princes and nobles. It was the duty of the bishop to see that the *tuath* had worthy priests to celebrate Mass, to administer the Sacraments, and to bury the dead. The care of all priests rested with the bishop, whose duty it was to supervise priests in giving due and conscientious service to the laity. Obviously, the bishop was by far the most important ecclesiastic in the state. He might live in a monastery, but he was certainly not subject to its abbot. It may be taken as certain that a monk, once raised to the episcopate, ceased to owe obedience to any abbot. The nearest parallel to the Irish monastic bishop is the modern mission bishop of regular orders. All his clergy belong to the same order and have as their immediate head a superior nominated by the order. Thus the bishop would appear to depend utterly on the order, yet he is not subject to its superior general. Similarly, the Irish bishop might depend on the monastery in various ways, but as a bishop he would not be subject to its abbot. It is noteworthy that, when the Synod of Rathbresail (1111) divided Ireland into dioceses on the continental model, more than 50 bishops were present.

In Britain, after the destruction of towns by the Anglo-Saxon invaders, bishops had their sees in monasteries, which at the same time they ruled as abbots. On the Continent bishops might be found living in exempt monasteries, but that did not conflict with a diocesan system already well established.

Bibliography: BEDE, *Ecclesiastical history* 3.4, with note by C. PLUMMER, in *Opera Historica,* 2 v. (Oxford 1896) 2:133–134. ADAMNAN, *Life of Saint Columba,* ed. W. REEVES (Edinburgh 1874), with note 198f. C. PLUMMER, comp., *Vitae sanctorum Hiberniae,* 2 v. (Oxford 1910), introd. xxxi, n.3; ed. and tr, *Irish Litanies* (Henry Bradshaw Society 62; 1925). *Ancient Laws of Ireland,* ed. W. N. HANCOCK et al. 6 v. (Dublin 1865–1901) 1:16, 40, 202; 3:408; 5:22, 234, 412. J. G. O'KEEFFE, ''The Rule of Patrick,'' *Ériu* 1 (1904) 216–224. E. MACNEILL, ''Ancient Irish Law. The Law of Status or Franchise,'' *Proceedings of the Irish Academy, Section C* 36 (1923) 265–316. H. FRANK, *Lexikon für Theologie und Kirche,* ed. J. HOFER and K. RAHNER, 10 v. (2d new ed. Freiburg 1957–65) 6:346–347.

[J. RYAN]

BISMARCK, DIOCESE OF

The diocese of Bismarck (*Bismarckiensis*) is the suffragan of the metropolitan See of St. Paul, Minn., embracing 34,268 square miles in the western half of North Dakota. Established on March 21, 1910, the diocese earlier formed part of the Vicariate Apostolic of Dakota

Annunciation Priory, Bismarck, North Dakota. (©G.E. Kidder Smith/CORBIS)

(1879–89) and the Diocese of FARGO (1889–1910). The first bishop, Vincent Wehrle, OSB (1910–39), as founder of the mission centers of St. Gall's monastery at Devil's Lake (1894) and St. Mary's Abbey at Richardton (1899), had done much to preserve the faith of the German-speaking immigrants from Russia and Austria-Hungary, who formed part of his flock of 25,000 Catholics. Wehrle's episcopate was characterized by missionary conditions, but prosperity and great building activity coincided with the episcopacy of his successor, Vincent J. Ryan (1940–51). When the third bishop, Lambert A. Hoch (1952–57), was transferred to Sioux Falls, South Dakota, Dec. 5, 1956, he was succeeded by Hilary B. Hacker in 1957. Upon the retirement of Hacker in 1982, John F. Kinney, auxiliary bishop of Saint Paul was appointed as the fifth bishop of Bismark. In 1995, Kinney was transferred to the Diocese of Saint Cloud, Minn., and was succeeded by Paul A. Zipfel, auxiliary bishop of St. Louis.

The population of the diocese has remained fairly constant for several generations, but it has shifted from rural to urban to a large degree. This has meant the closing and consolidation of many small rural parishes and the growth of new urban parishes. By the end of 2000, Catholics comprised about one-fourth of the Bismarck region. A small but significant number of Catholics are Native Americans of the Standing Rock and Fort Berthold Reservations in western North Dakota. Their pastoral needs are provided by the diocese and the Benedictines of Assumption Abbey.

There is a Benedictine monastery, Assumption Abbey in Richardton, and two Benedictine monasteries for women, Annunciation Priory in Bismarck and Sacred Heart Monastery in Richardton.

University of Mary. The University of Mary in Bismarck is the sole Catholic university in the diocese. Founded in 1955 by the Benedictine Sisters of Anunciation Priory as Mary College, a two-year college for women, it turned coed, subsequently became a four-year degree-granting institution in 1955, and attained full university status in 1986.

Cathedral. The Cathedral of the Holy Spirit in Bismarck is perhaps the only art deco cathedral in country. It was built during World War II, and was dedicated in August 1945. It was renovated in 1993, and is a fine example of art deco church architecture.

Bibliography: T. G. KARDONG, *The Prairie Church: The Diocese of Bismarck, 1910–1985* (Bismarck 1985).

[L. PFALLER/T. KRAMER/EDS.]

BISTRITA, ABBEY OF

Name of two abbeys in Romania.

The one in Moldavia, district of Neamt, was founded in 1420 by Prince Alexander the Good and richly endowed with land and privileges by him and his wife, both of whom are buried there. The bell tower was built by Stephen the Great in 1498; it contains a small chapel, where beautiful 16th-century frescoes of pure Moldavian art were discovered in 1924. The principal church was completely reconstructed by Alexander Lapusneanu in 1554, with the help of Venetian architects and painters. Traces of ancient frescoes may still be seen in its cupola and vestibule.

The Abbey of Bistrita in Wallachia, district of Vilcea, was built in 1487 in a Serbo-Byzantine style by the brothers Craiovescu (Barbu, Pârvu, Danciu, Radu, Preda, and Mircea), sons of a boyar from Craiova. Radu purchased and transferred there the relics of St. Gregory the Decapolite. The monastery was restored in 1600 by the Moldavian Prince George Brâncoveanu. Having fallen into ruins, the church was demolished and completely rebuilt by German architects in 1856. An inscription with the name of the original architect, *Mane mester,* is preserved in the sculptured frame of its main entrance. The abbey had been a great center of Slavic studies and possessed many manuscripts; those preserved are now in the museum of Bucharest.

Bibliography: N. IORGA, *Istoria bisericii românesti,* 2 v. (2d ed. Bucharest 1929–32); and G. BALS, *Histoire de l'art roumain ancien* (Paris 1922). *Enciclopedia româniei,* 4 v. (Bucharest 1936–43) 2:305–306, 506.

[T. FOTITCH]

BITTI, BERNARDO

Jesuit painter; b. Camerino, Italy, 1548; d. Lima, Peru, 1610. Bitti took up painting at an early age. When he was 20, he joined the Society of Jesus in Rome as a brother. In 1568 the Jesuits went to Peru, where there was a need for religious who were skilled in trades and crafts. When word reached Rome from Lima that a painter was needed, Bitti, who was the best one available, was sent to Peru. He arrived in Lima in 1575 and went to work there. In 1583 he traveled to Cuzco as a painter, and later, to La Paz, Potosí, and Chuquisaca. He did most of his work in Juli, Peru, a town on Lake Titicaca, where the Jesuits had established missions to convert the Aymara people.

Bitti's work is representative of Italian mannerism. He painted in tempera with the delicacy of the followers of Michelangelo and Raphael. In his paintings, considered to be very fine, line and cool colors predominate and show a shared influence with Vasari. His work was a major influence in South America, especially in Cuzco and the Audiencia of Charcas (Bolivia). In fact, the painters of Peru and Bolivia were faithful to mannerism for many years after that style had disappeared in Europe. Bitti also influenced the Quito school through the Dominican painter Pedro BEDÓN.

At his death Bitti was esteemed for both his virtue and his talent. Among his surviving works are the canvasses of a retable dedicated to San Ildefonso in the church of San Miguel, Sucre. A number of examples of his paintings exist in Juli. His paintings of the ''Coronation of the Virgin'' are in both Cuzco and Lima. One of his followers was Gregorio Gamarra, who worked in Potosí and Cuzco from 1601 to 1628.

Bibliography: J. DE MESA and T. GISBERT, *Bernardo Bitti* (La Paz, Bolivia 1961); *Historia de la pintura cuzqueña* (Buenos Aires 1962). M. S. SORIA, *La pintura del siglo XVI en Sudamérica* (Buenos Aires 1956).

[J. DE MESA/T. GISBERT]

BLACK, WILLIAM

Methodist elder and missionary, known as the Father of Methodism in Nova Scotia, Canada; b. Huddersfield, West Yorkshire, England, 1760; d. Halifax, Nova Scotia, Sept. 6, 1834. In 1775, Black's parents emigrated with him to Nova Scotia, where they settled in the Amherst–Fort Cumberland district. About 1779 a revival began among the Methodists in the district; Black became a convert at age 19 and a lay preacher at age 20. In this capacity he traveled the length and breadth of Nova Scotia, laying the foundations of organic Methodism.

In 1786 at a conference in Halifax, he was placed in charge of the Nova Scotia mission. Three years later in

Philadelphia, Pennsylvania, which he had visited in 1785, he was ordained deacon and, the next day, elder. Upon his return to Nova Scotia, he became superintendent of the Methodist societies in British North America, and shortly afterward he visited the Windward Isles and Bermuda. In 1791 he appealed to England for more lay preachers; the response was good, and the work of consolidating the missions progressed well. In 1827 Black's first wife and both his children died; he remarried the following year.

Bibliography: M. RICHEY, *A Memoir of the Late Rev. William Black* (Halifax, 1839). J. E. SANDERSON, *The First Century of Methodism in Canada* (Toronto, 1908).

[J. F. REED]

BLACKMAN, JOHN

Carthusian biographer of Henry VI; b. Bath and Wells diocese, 1407–08; d. January 1485(?). Blackman was educated at Merton College, Oxford; he was a fellow of the college *c.* 1439 and subwarden *c.* 1443. From 1444 to 1452 he was precentor of Eton College, and in December of 1452 he was nominated warden of King's Hall, Cambridge. He had received an M. A. from Oxford by 1439 and a bachelor of theology by 1452. In July of 1457, he resigned his post as warden and subsequently entered the London Charterhouse, possibly as a *clericus redditus* rather than as a monk. Later he moved to WITHAM CHARTERHOUSE in Somerset; it is probable he died there.

As a secular priest, Blackman was closely associated with Henry VI, and *c.* 1480 he composed a brief essay in praise of the king's virtues. Blackman also owned a large collection of manuscripts, some written in his own hand, consisting of patristic, academic, and devotional texts. He gave most of them to the Witham Charterhouse.

Bibliography: J. BLACKMAN, *Collectarium mansuetudinum et bonorum morum regis Henrici VI*, first printed by Coplande *c.* 1510, ed. and tr. M. R. JAMES, *Henry the Sixth* (Cambridge, Eng. 1919). E. M. THOMPSON, *The Carthusian Order in England* (New York 1930) 316–322. A. B. EMDEN, *Biographical Register of the Scholars of the University of Cambridge before 1500* (Cambridge, Eng. 1963) 670–671.

[R. LOVATT]

BLACKWELL, GEORGE

First archpriest of England; b. Middlesex, *c.* 1545; d. Clink prison, Jan. 25, 1612. Although educated at Oxford (M.A., 1567), Blackwell left and went to Douai College, where he was ordained in 1576. For 22 years he worked in England. In March of 1598, four years after Cardinal William ALLEN's death, Clement VIII appointed Blackwell archpriest over the hitherto unorganized seminary priests in England. Though generally approved, he soon had difficulties with a minority of insubordinate priests who reprobated the new office, especially the provision in his instructions for consultation with the Jesuits. He was also accused of misusing his powers, and two appeals were prosecuted in Rome. Though thrice confirmed in office, a brief of Oct. 5, 1602, restricted his powers and severed Jesuit connections. Despite papal condemnation of the Oath of Allegiance, devised by Parliament after the Gunpowder Plot, Blackwell advocated that Catholics should take the oath. Deposed in 1608, he died without retracting his error. So much unpublished material exists that the following references and other works should be consulted with caution.

Bibliography: J. GILLOW, *A Literary and Biographical History or Bibliographical Dictionary of the English Catholics from 1534 to the Present Time* (London and New York, 1885–1902) 1:225–231. J. H. POLLEN, *The Institution of the Archpriest Blackwell* (London 1916). T. COOPER, *The Dictionary of National Biography from the Earliest Times to 1900* (London, 1885–1900) 2:606–608.

[P. RENOLD]

BLAINE AMENDMENT

The Blaine Amendment is the common title for a proposed amendment to the United States Constitution that would have forbidden the states to devote directly or indirectly any public money or land to schools having any religious affiliation. The history of this amendment shows both the political expediency and bigotry of the men who sponsored it.

One year before the disputed election of 1876, as an opening gun in the campaign to nominate a Republican candidate for the presidency, President Ulysses S. Grant told an encampment of Civil War veterans that the government of the United States had a serious obligation to educate all its citizens to preserve them from the dangers of "demagogery and priestcraft." Between Sept. 29, 1875, when this speech was delivered in Des Moines, Iowa, until the final decision that Rutherford B. Hayes had been elected over his Democratic opponent, Samuel J. Tilden, in March 1877, the issues suggested by Grant remained prominent. Grant's sketchy proposal was incorporated by James Gillespie Blaine, member of Congress from Maine, into a constitutional amendment presented to the House of Representatives on Dec. 14, 1875. Blaine then participated in the maneuvering in Congress while the measure was debated, and wrote to influential editors and politicians to secure support for his proposal.

Education and a Needed Issue. Like Grant, the incumbent president, and Hayes, then governor of Ohio but soon to be the candidate for the presidency, Blaine knew that issues marking a clear distinction between the two major parties were not abundant. The Republican party had emerged as the party of strength (after a brief period of immaturity) only when the Civil War began. Democratic party commitments to attitudes popular in the defeated South had materially decreased that party's effectiveness, but accusations of disloyalty had little impact a decade after the Civil War had ended. The Democrats had shown new strength, moreover, by winning a large number of mid-term elections in 1874. Some states theretofore regarded as certainly Republican had become Democratic; more were showing signs of disaffection from a party that had furnished evidences of corruption during the Grant administrations. The old device of the bloody shirt could hardly be flourished again.

Dissatisfaction of Voters. Republican leaders understood that other appeals, formerly successful in winning large numbers of votes, could no longer be regarded as reliable. Between 1865 and 1875, veterans of the Union Army had returned to their prewar occupations. Their primary interests centered in these activities, in their families, and in local concerns. Impassioned campaign speeches stressing military service of a decade before were proving ineffective in securing Republican victories. Equally disappointing were the efforts aimed at securing votes from an agricultural bloc. Farming regions differed too much, one from the other; the presence of a substantial number of farmers did not argue the existence of any agreement on what should constitute national farm policy. This decade, furthermore, witnessed an extraordinary growth in city dwelling and organization.

Present always in the minds of the party leaders of the 1870s was the possibility that the South might again decide to withdraw from the Union, or might at least participate in some rebellious activity. The ''bloody shirt'' issue could no longer unite the North and might further disaffect the South; neither veterans' nor farmers' votes could be relied on to ensure a Republican victory. Furthermore, public attention had to be distracted from the sorry record of the Grant years. Some new issue had to be found; and Grant's own speech, together with the letters of leaders within his party, make it clear that the school issue was the one accepted.

Personal Convictions. The unanimity with which Grant, Hayes, and Blaine seized upon this issue was attributable in part to their personal convictions and needs. All three might safely be described as committed to certain policies associated with the American democratic ideal as it was understood in the 19th century. An integral feature of this ideal was the furnishing of educational opportunity to all children in public elementary schools at public expense. Although the concept was introduced into America comparatively late, the idea of universal education had secured widespread support. The three chief figures in the presidential race of 1875 could rely on having chosen a ready-made issue of considerable appeal. Each of them could also associate this issue with his own hopes.

Grant was not yet convinced that a third term might not be his. If he could capitalize on the issues he suggested as vital in his annual message of 1875, he might yet secure sufficient support in the nominating convention to become the first third-term president. Hayes, often defeated for public office during a career of more than 30 years in Ohio politics, needed an appealing issue to carry his name before the national electorate. Neither of these leaders, however, had the deeply personal and strongly political needs of James G. Blaine.

Blaine and Catholicism. Originally a Pennsylvanian, Blaine had won political prominence in his adoptive state of Maine, and had served in the national House of Representatives through three terms. He had secured the speakership and used its then great power to decided effect. In all his actions, he gave evidence not only of great ability but of unusual political ambition. If he could make his name familiar to voters outside his home state, then he might well hope to secure the Republican nomination for the presidency and that office itself. Blaine began to work toward this end almost as soon as the lame duck Congress of 1875 began its sessions, although he must have been aware that a major inconsistency in his proposal could well appear if all the voters knew his entire background.

Family Ties. At a time when nativism continued to be a strong force within state and local politics, when Know-Nothingism frequently called attention to the presence of large numbers of Catholic immigrants in American cities Blaine had to keep hidden his affiliations with the Catholic Church or risk alienating his own constituents and possible future supporters throughout the country. Without losing the admiration and affection of his Catholic cousins, Ellen Ewing Sherman, wife of General William T. Sherman, and Mother Angela GILLESPIE, CSC, American foundress of her order, Blaine managed to keep hidden his own close connection with their Church. Newspaper stories frequently mentioned Blaine's Catholic mother, Maria Gillespie Blaine, but the vehemence with which Blaine denied any personal allegiance to the Church, together with the reverence he declared he felt for it, since it had been his mother's consolation, preserved him from the political harm he feared.

A Baptized Catholic. In actuality Blaine's ties to the Church were far more binding than he would admit. He had been baptized a Catholic and probably had received some Catholic instruction during early youth. His denial of this charge can hardly be accepted as convincing. He concealed the fact that his father, Ephraim, had been received into the Catholic Church on his deathbed, and had been buried in a Catholic cemetery. If these details became known, Blaine would incur the wrath of the urban Irish-Catholic voters, who would regard him as a traitor to their faith. If he could not maintain his public position as an adherent to some established variety of Protestantism—he claimed both Presbyterian and Congregational ties—he would lose large segments of the voting public elsewhere in the country and would incur, as well, the anger of other Republican chieftains. Hence he pleaded for newspaper stories that would show him as a worshipper in the "church of his fathers," the Presbyterian congregation of Carlisle, Pennsylvania.

Amendment and Debate. Blaine's private motives thus gave added urgency to his astute appeals to the electorate during the winter of 1875 to 1876. Without going directly to the voters, since he retained his House membership until July, Blaine could hope to work through his fellow Republicans to secure passage of the proposed amendment. The measure would forbid states to devote public monies or lands to schools under control of any religious sect. A favorable two-thirds vote of each chamber of Congress would send this measure to the states for their consideration. Adoption would mean that Blaine would be most favorably placed for political advancement; even consideration would ensure national political prominence for him.

Goals. Offered originally as a joint resolution, the Blaine amendment capitalized on Grant's message of a week earlier, which had stressed the desirability of such an amendment. The *Congressional Record* discloses that Grant had not only emphasized the need for an amendment, but that three of the five points appearing in the recapitulation of his message mentioned the need for public school education; the desirability of eliminating sectarian influences through the taxation of church properties; and the withholding of public funds from denominational schools, orphanages, hospitals, or other institutions.

Religious Prejudice. The debate touched off by Blaine's proposed amendment included references to nativism, bigotry, treason, and political intrigue. States like New York, Ohio, and Missouri had already adopted constitutional amendments respecting public schools; there was the question now merely of using the most persuasive arguments to place other states in the same column. Hayes had suggested that the Democrats be "crowded" on school and other state issues; Blaine's initial reaction to this suggestion had been to hope that elimination of denominational schools would mean the abolition of all sectarian strife. Since some of his fellow Republicans believed that the growth of the Democratic party was the work of the Roman Catholic hierarchy, however, appeals to religious prejudice as well as to party allegiance might be expected.

Debate over the terms of the amendment centered in conventional issues: the rights of states to determine their own educational policies—a strong Democratic position; the privilege of city-dwellers, many of them Catholics and of foreign origin, to secure religious instruction in schools attended by their children—a popular urban position; and the allegations of politicians distrustful of Blaine's ambitions. The Senate Judiciary Committee reported the amendment to the whole Senate in a fashion that seemed to cast doubts on Blaine's intelligence and honesty. Possibly the clinching arguments against the proposal were that the national government would be left free to give to any private, nonreligious corporation any amount of land or money, but could give nothing to any charitable cause, and that the states would likewise be crippled in their efforts to support worthy projects. Such an argument had the added merit of allowing a graceful retreat from support of the bill; it failed to win the necessary two-thirds majority by the middle of August 1876, and never again secured the essential support.

Lasting Effects. Despite this failure, however, the Blaine amendment had performed important services. It had called attention to the flimsiness of earlier political appeals, and pointed out quite accurately that there were deeper issues having greater interest for the electorate. For Blaine himself, it had served to make his name a national one, even though he would wait eight more years for the presidential nomination. In its own right, the amendment had demonstrated clearly that profound differences of opinion on educational, religious, and political questions existed in divisive fashion among native-white-Protestant and foreign-white-Catholic groups; that the urban and rural voters of the country could be separated into factions or grouped into voting blocs over matters not purely economic; and that a party's choice of an issue combining political with religious and intellectual implications was sure to attract attention. Even in its failure, then, the Blaine amendment proved a potent political force in 1875 to 1876, and surely helped to suggest the similar amendments of the 1890s and 1920s (*see* OREGON SCHOOL CASE).

Bibliography: Archives of The Catholic University of America, Lambert Papers. Library of Congress, Division of Manuscripts, Blaine, Harrison, Hayes, Whitelaw Reid Papers. *Congressional Record,* 44th Congress, 1875–76. A. P. STOKES, *Church and State in the United States,* 3 v. (New York 1950). M. C. KLINKHAMER, "The Blaine Amendment of 1875: Private Motives for Political Action,"

American Catholic Historical Review 42 (April 1956) 15–49; ''Historical Reasons for Inception of the Parochial School System,'' *The Catholic Educational Review* 52 (February 1954) 73–94.

[M. C. KLINKHAMER]

BLAISE OF SEBASTE, ST.

Bishop and martyr under the Emperor Licinius; b. Sebaste, Armenia; d. *c.* 316. According to legend, during persecution he withdrew from his bishopric of Sebaste to a cave, remaining until he was discovered in a hunt for beasts. Agricolaus, Governor of Cappadocia and Lesser Armenia, had him tortured and later beheaded for his faith. In prison he healed a boy with a fishbone stuck in his throat. Blaise had become the patron of throat diseases in the East by the 6th century, and in the West by the 9th century. He became one of the FOURTEEN HOLY HELPERS. The blessing of throats with candles began in the 16th century, when his cult was at its peak. He is the patron of the city of Ragusa and also of many tradesmen, including woolcarders (the iron comb was an instrument of his tortures). He is invoked to protect animals against wolves and to bring fair weather. His feast day was observed in the West on February 15 until the 11th century; it is celebrated on February. 11 in the East, bringing winter to a close.

Feast: Feb. 3

Bibliography: R. JANIN, *Dictionnaire d'histoire et de géographie ecclésiastiques,* ed. A. BAUDRILLAT et al. (Paris 1912–) 9:69. P. WIERTZ, *Lexikon für Theologie und Kirche,* ed. J. HOFER and K. RAHNER, 10 v. (2d, new ed. Freiburg 1957–65) 2:525–526. M. C. CELLETTI, *Biblioteca sanctorum* (Rome 1961–) 3:158–165.

[M. J. COSTELLOE]

BLAKE, ALEXANDER, BL.

Lay martyr; d. March 4, 1590, hanged at Gray's Inn Lane, London, England. He was arrested, sentenced, and died with Bl. Nicholas HORNER for having harbored Fr. Christopher BALES. All three were beatified by Pope John Paul II on Nov. 22, 1987 with George Haydock and Companions.

Feast of the English Martyrs: May 4 (England).

See Also: ENGLAND, SCOTLAND, AND WALES, MARTYRS OF.

Bibliography: R. CHALLONER, *Memoirs of Missionary Priests,* ed. J. H. POLLEN (rev. ed. London 1924). J. H. POLLEN, *Acts of English Martyrs* (London 1891). D. DE YEPES, *Historia Particular de la persecución de Inglaterra* (Madrid 1599).

[K. I. RABENSTEIN]

BLAKE, WILLIAM

Engraver, painter, and mystical poet; b. London, Nov. 28, 1757; d. London, Aug. 12, 1827. Blake's parents, Catharine Harmitage and James Blake, a hosier, encouraged his talent for visualization; at the age of 10, he was sent to a drawing school in the Strand, and at 14 he began his apprenticeship (1772–79) to the line engraver James Basire, for whom he copied royal effigies from Gothic tombs. At 21 he began exhibiting historical and poetical watercolors at the Royal Academy.

In 1782, he married Catherine Boucher, daughter of a market gardener. The following year, some of his friends printed a volume of his works entitled *Poetical Sketches,* containing superb lyrics and ironic dramatic fragments revealing disapproval of the American war. In 1784, he wrote *An Island in the Moon,* a satiric medley showing the author as ''Quid, the Cynic,'' among philosophizing, artistic, and egocentric friends who were interested in Voltaire, Locke, graveyard meditations, Chatterton, the perhaps uncontrollable chemical discoveries of Priestley, and the obtuseness of the Platonizing Thomas Taylor.

In 1788, he began to publish illustrated manifestoes and songs and prophetic poems utilizing an etching process he called ''illuminated printing.'' His small tractates *There is No Natural Religion and All Religions are One* were probably the earliest of these; *The Book of Thel* and *Songs of Innocence* were published in 1789; and *The Ghost of Abel* (1822) was the last.

Blake was now reading LAVATER and SWEDENBORG; he attended a London conference of Swedenborgians in April 1789. Soon events in France inspired him to write an epic on *The French Revolution;* of the seven parts he announced, only the first, printed in 1791, survives. He produced two great series of illuminated works in 1795: three historical prophecies called *America, Europe,* and *The Song of Los* (comprising ''Africa'' and ''Asia''), that announced a revolutionary apocalypse in Britain to complete those in America and France; and a philosophical series including *The Marriage of Heaven and Hell,* that replaced Swedenborg's vision of a balanced universe with a manifesto of revolutionary Christian humanism, *Visions of the Daughters of Albion,* probing the psychological roots of slavery, and *The Book of Urizen* with its sequels *Ahania* and *Los,* depicting the imaginative inadequacy and collapse of the exterior and interior worlds of Newton and LOCKE.

His other works of this period include the emblems called *The Gates of Paradise* (1793), *Songs of Innocence and of Experience: Shewing the Two Contrary States of the Human Soul* (1794), and an outpouring of color-printed symbolic pictures. For an ambitious edition of Edward Young's *Night Thoughts* in 1797, Blake made 537 drawings, but only 43 of them were engraved. He next began a symbolic epic as a unique illuminated manuscript. It's first title was *Vala,* later changed to *The Four Zoas,* concerning the generation and regeneration by resurrection of Everyman or "Albion."

During this period, Blake was painting a series of illustrations of the Bible for Thomas Butts. In 1800, he moved to Felpham, Sussex, to work near a new patron, William Hayley, but after 3 years of "slumber" and vexation, he returned to London to live out a busy but unprosperous life. The date 1804 on the title pages of *Milton* (etched about 1808) and *Jerusalem* (1818–20) may mark the beginning of his new dedication to the kind of artist's life he considered Jesus to have lived. In 1809, he held an exhibition of 16 "Historical and Poetical" paintings, including "apotheoses" depicting Lord Nelson and William Pitt as angels of war, the former in contention with a militant Christ. Pictorial series of his late period, each constituting a prophetic work, include his illustrations of *The Grave, The Canterbury Pilgrims,* the Book of Job, *Pilgrim's Progress,* and *The Divine Comedy.* In 1818, his poem of fiercely didactic lyric fragments, *The Everlasting Gospel,* affirmed the essential unity of his life's preaching.

Blake died at age 69, followed by his devoted wife, at the same age, four years later. He was buried in an unmarked grave in Bunhill Fields. A member of no church, Blake thought of himself as a Christian, but his savior was the creative genius in every man whose gospel was mutual forgiveness. At Blake's Judgment Day, fools perish, the "dark religions" depart, and "sweet Science reigns"—total imaginative consciousness attained through art. As all Blake's literary and philosophical "sources" were transformed to his own idiom, even the Bible, his greatest source, became in his painting and poetry a philosophical, psychological, historical prophecy—"the Great Code of Art."

See Also: MYSTICISM IN LITERATURE.

Bibliography: *Complete Writings,* ed. G. KEYNES (New York 1957–). *The Poetry and Prose of William Blake,* ed. D. V. ERDMAN, commentary by H. BLOOM (New York 1965). *Illustrations to the Bible: A Catalogue,* comp. G. KEYNES (Clairvaux 1957). A. GILCHRIST, *Life of William Blake* (New York 1942). J. LINDSAY, *William Blake: His Life and Work* (New York 1979). D. V. ERDMAN, *Blake: Prophet against Empire* (3d. ed.; Garden City, N.Y. 1977). N. FRYE, *Fearful Symmetry* (2d ed. Princeton 1958). P. E. FISHER, *The Valley of Vision: Blake as Prophet and Revolutionary* (Toronto 1961). H. BLOOM, *Blake's Apocalypse* (New York 1963). D. BINDMAN, *William Blake: His Art and Times* (New York 1982).

[D. V. ERDMAN]

William Blake.

BLAKELY, PAUL LENDRUM

Jesuit, editorial writer; b. Covington, Kentucky, Feb. 29, 1880; d. New York City, Feb. 26, 1943. Blakely's parents were Laurie John Blakely, a Confederate officer, and Lily (Hudson Lendrum) Blakely. He was tutored at home until the age of 11, and later he attended St. Xavier College, Cincinnati, Ohio. He entered the Jesuit novitiate at Florissant, Missouri, on July 30, 1897 and was ordained on June 27, 1912.

In 1914 he joined the editorial staff of *America,* a weekly review published by the Jesuits. For many years, under three editors-in-chief, Blakely was the principal editorial writer of the review. It has been estimated that he wrote more than 1,100 signed articles and 3,000 short unsigned pieces on the subjects of education, American history, the Federal Constitution, and social problems.

In the 1920s he opposed the creation of a federal department of education (Smith-Towner Bill) and defended the rights of parents in education. His editorials formed part of the background for the U.S. Supreme Court's 1925 decision in the Oregon School Case. Blakely, guided by the encyclicals of Leo XIII, fought against the abuses of capitalism and for the right of labor to organize. In his later years, he became a critic of Franklin D. Roosevelt's administration. His firm belief in states' rights was the basis of much of his writing.

[T. N. DAVIS]

BLANC, ANTHONY

First archbishop of New Orleans, Louisiana; b. Sury, France, Oct. 11, 1792; d. New Orleans, June 20, 1860. Blanc was ordained in Lyons, France, by Bp. Louis W. Dubourg of Louisiana on July 22, 1816 and accompanied the prelate on his return to the United States in 1817.

First appointed a missionary for Vincennes, he labored in Indiana until February of 1820. He spent the next 40 years in Louisiana, first as a parish priest with his brother, Rev. John Baptist Blanc, in Pointe Coupee, the Felicianas, and Baton Rouge (1820–30); then as vicar-general to his immediate predecessor, Bp. Leo de Neckère, with residence in New Orleans (1830–33). There, he served as administrator of the diocese (1833–35), bishop (1835–50), and finally archbishop (1850–60).

During Blanc's tenure as ordinary, New Orleans more than tripled its population. He established 18 parishes for Creole, German, Irish, and English-speaking congregations in the see city and its environs, and 30 in rural Louisiana. Until Natchez (now Natchez-Jackson) and Natchitoches (now Alexandria) were created dioceses in 1837 and 1853 respectively, his jurisdiction embraced both Mississippi and Louisiana. For a time (1838–40) he had charge of the Church in Texas.

Lay TRUSTEEISM at St. Louis Cathedral, New Orleans, and elsewhere, the threat of schism, the recrudescence of NATIVISM in the 1850s, the anti-Catholic bias of KNOW-NOTHINGISM, and the imminence of secession by the South were among his most grievous ordeals. The challenge by the trustees of the bishop's right to appoint pastors was checked by the Louisiana Supreme Court on June 8, 1844, but only after the cathedral had been interdicted (1842). The court decision vindicated the bishop but failed to uproot lay trusteeism in the state.

On July 19, 1850, New Orleans became an archdiocese, and Blanc its first archbishop. He received the pallium in St. Patrick's Church on Feb. 16, 1851. Despite a leg fracture suffered while engaged in yellow fever relief work in 1858, he remained active until his death, which came suddenly a few hours after he had offered Mass in his chapel.

Bibliography: R. BAUDIER, *The Catholic Church in Louisiana* (New Orleans 1939).

[H. C. BEZOU]

BLANCHET, FRANCIS NORBERT

Pacific Northwest missioner, first archbishop of Oregon City (now PORTLAND), Oregon, archdiocese; b. St. Pierre, Quebec, Canada, Sept. 3, 1795; d. Portland, June 18, 1883. Son of Pierre and Rosalie Blanchet, whose families had given distinguished leaders to Church and State in Canada, Blanchet attended the local parish school and the minor and major seminaries of Quebec. After ordination on July 18, 1819, he was stationed first at the cathedral in Quebec City. In October of 1820, in answer to an appeal for a French-speaking priest, he was sent by Bp. Joseph Signay to minister to the Acadians and the Micmac Indians living under primitive conditions in New Brunswick. Early in 1827 he became pastor of St. Joseph de Soulanges parish in Montreal. When Signay was pressed to supply priests for white settlers in the Pacific Northwest, mostly retired Hudson's Bay Company employees, he chose Blanchet as vicar-general for the Oregon country. With an assistant, Modeste Demers, a Quebec missionary who had worked under Bp. Joseph Provencher at Red River, Blanchet set out in May of 1838 with the annual brigade of Hudson's Bay Company, arriving on November 24 at Fort Vancouver, the western headquarters of the company. Eagerly welcomed by whites and Indians, Blanchet and Demers visited the principal posts of Hudson's Bay Company, established missions at Cowlitz and later among the French Canadians in Willamette Valley, and explored the possibility of working among the indigenous tribes. In addition to the difficulties to be expected in a wilderness, they also experienced frustrations and petty opposition from American Methodist missioners who were already well established and had gained converts even among the French Canadians.

In 1842 Blanchet met Pierre Jean De Smet, SJ, and with him and Demers drew up a plan for the ecclesiastical organization of the Oregon country. This plan was eventually approved by the Canadian and American bishops and presented by them to the Holy See. In December of 1843, a vicariate apostolic was erected in Oregon with Blanchet at its head as titular bishop of Philadelphia (later changed to Adrasus to avoid confusion with Philadelphia, Pennsylvania). He received the announcement of his appointment in November of 1844, and in December he embarked on a long sea journey to Montreal for his consecration by Bp. Ignatius Bourget, which took place on July 25, 1845. Before returning to his post, he sailed for Europe to seek funds and candidates for the missions. Reaching Rome in January of 1846, he had several audiences with Gregory XVI and successfully petitioned the Congregation for the Propagation of the Faith for the erection of an ecclesiastical province from his vicariate, with an archbishop and suffragan bishops, and further divisions to be made as the area developed. He was named archbishop of Oregon City, with his brother Augustin Magloire as bishop of Walla Walla, Washington, and Demers as bishop of Vancouver Island. After leaving Rome he appealed effectively in the major cities of Europe for assistance in his apostolate. When he sailed for home in February of 1847, he was accompanied by 21 missionaries, including 8 priests and 7 sisters.

Bright prospects for the new province were rudely shattered by the Whitman massacre on Nov. 29, 1847. The event practically ended missionary work among the Indians and was the signal for a new and virulent outbreak of bigotry that strained relations with many whites who clung to the belief, long since refuted, that the priests had been responsible for the massacre. Then, too, the discovery of gold in California drew many French Canadians from Oregon; priests and nuns, deserted by those to whom they ministered, went elsewhere.

In the face of all this, Blanchet convened the first Provincial Council of Oregon on Feb. 28, 1848. Again and again during the next decade he sought help for his work. In 1855, with the approval of Rome, he visited South America and was well received in Peru and Bolivia and especially in Chile, where he had published a pamphlet describing his province. He returned home in 1857 with sufficient money to meet the debts of his diocese. In 1859 he collected funds in eastern Canada and brought back 31 more helpers, among them Sisters of the Holy Names of Jesus and Mary to staff his schools. He also attended the First (1852) and Second (1866) Plenary Councils of Baltimore, and in 1869 Vatican Council I, at which he strongly favored the declaration of papal infallibility.

These years were marked by continuous development in Oregon. With the growth of the city of Portland, Blanchet established his residence there in 1862, and he chose Immaculate Conception Church for the procathedral. Schools and other facilities opened. A diocesan paper, the *Catholic Sentinel,* appeared in 1870. Even the Indian missions were reopened, though never on the scale that Blanchet had planned. After initiating his coadjutor, Bp. Charles J. Seghers (appointed Dec.10, 1878), into the work of the archdiocese, he resigned in 1880, retiring to St. Vincent's Hospital.

Essentially a man of action, Blanchet published only his *Historical Sketches of the Catholic Church in Oregon. . . .* (Portland, Ore. 1878). His "Catholic Ladder," a pictorial device for teaching Indians the life of Christ, Christian doctrine, and Church history, was copyrighted in 1859. His interest in the Native Americans never flagged. His last effort for them was to represent the hierarchy in protesting the injustice of a government policy that placed many Catholic reservations under Protestant control. In the course of protracted controversy, the need for the continual presence in Washington of an authorized representative of Catholic Indian missions became evident, and the Bureau of Catholic Indian Missions was organized in 1874.

Bibliography: L. M. LYONS, *Francis Norbert Blanchet and the Founding of the Oregon Missions, 1838–1848* (Washington 1940). C. B. BAGLEY, *Early Catholic Missions in Old Oregon,* 2 v. (Seattle 1932). H. H. BANCROFT, *History of Oregon,* 2 v. (San Francisco 1886–88). F. N. BLANCHET, *Historical Sketches of the Catholic Church in Oregon*, reprint (Fairfield, Wash., 1983). A DRIES, *The Missionary Movement in American Catholic History* (Orbis 1998). H. MUNNICK, *Priest's Progress* (Portland, Oreg. 1989). E. O'HARA, *Pioneer Catholic History of Oregon* (Paterson, NJ 1939).

[L. M. LYONS]

BLANDINA OF LYONS, ST.

Martyr at Lyons under Marcus Aurelius in 177. She was a young slave arrested with her mistress; she showed extraordinary constancy under torture, repeating again and again, "I am a Christian, and nothing wicked happens among us." She was later tied to a stake in the amphitheater, but the wild beasts did not touch her. On the last day of the games, she and Ponticus, a boy of 15, were brought to witness the tortures of the other Christians. Blandina, the last to be martyred, was put in a net to be tossed by a bull. The pagans confessed that never had they seen a woman suffer so long and so much. Information about Blandina and her companions derives from a Letter of the Churches of Lyons and Vienne quoted at some length by Eusebius (*Hist. Eccl.* 5.1). Blandina is usually the first of the 48 martyrs mentioned in the martyrologies. They are included because of the influence Lyons has had on their development.

Feast: June 2.

Bibliography: R. AIGRAIN, *Catholicisme* 2:77–78. H. PLATELLE, *Bibliotheca Sanctorum* 3:202. *Les Martyrs de Lyon*, proceedings of the international colloque of the Centre national de la recherche scientifique, Lyon, Sept. 20–23, 1977 (Paris 1978).

[M. J. COSTELLOE]

BLANDRATA, GIORGIO

Physician, lay leader in the anti-Trinitarian Minor Church of Poland and of the Unitarian Church of Transylvania; b. Saluzzo (Piedmont) 1515; d. Gyulafehérvár *c.* 1588 or 1590. Blandrata (Biandrata) studied in Pavia and became court physician abroad. Returning to Italy, he came under the theological influence of the equivocally anti-Trinitarian jurisconsult Matteo Gribaldi and fled from the Inquisition in 1556, becoming an elder in the Italian Reformed Congregation of Geneva. After coming into conflict with Calvin on the doctrine of the Trinity, he left for Zurich (1558), going on to Poland to become an influential elder and formulator of doctrine and church law in the synods of the Minor Church.

From 1563 he was physician to the king of Transylvania, John Sigismund, whom, with the Reformed court preacher Franz DÁVID, he won over to anti-Trinitarianism. When Dávid moved on to the still more extreme position of not praying to Christ (non-adorantism), Blandrata urged Faustus Socinus to come to his aid, lest the nascent Unitarian Church in Transylvania, by further innovations, imperil its status as one of the four recognized religions of the religiously and ethnically pluralistic realm. Blandrata, under Stephen BÁTHORY, lost interest in the Unitarian Church and associated with the Jesuits of the court, but he died a Unitarian.

Bibliography: I. RÉVÉSZ, *Magyar református egyhaztorténet,* v. 1 (1520–1608) (Debrecen 1938); abr. Eng. tr. G. A. F. KNIGHT, *History of the Hungarian Church* (Washington 1956). E. M. WILBUR, *A History of Unitarianism,* 2 v. (Cambridge, Mass. 1945–52).

[G. H. WILLIAMS]

BLANES GINER, MARINO, BL.

Lay Franciscan, martyr; b. Sept. 17, 1888, Alcoy (Alcoi), Alicante (Archdiocese of Valencia), Spain; d. there, Sept. 8, 1936.

The persecution of the Church began in Alcoy March 31, 1936—several months before the start of the civil war in July. On that day the San Mauro parish was closed by mandate. The following day it was demolished in order to build a store on the site. Thereafter other parishes suffered the same fate. Monasteries and convents were sacked, altars destroyed, bells melted down, parish records burned, and religious images and sacred objects profaned or disappeared. Soon the celebration of the Mass was forbidden, but priests continued their ministry covertly. During the period that followed, 15 priests and more than 300 lay people from two parishes in Alcoy were executed for being Christians. Five of whom were beatified, including Marino Blanes Giner, José María Ferrándiz Hernández, Amalia Abad Casasempere, Florencia Caerols Martíínez, and María Jordá Botella.

From the time of his baptism in St. Mary Church two days after his birth, Marino's parents, Jaime Blanes Reig and Josefa Giner Botella, ensured he received a Christian formation. He was confirmed Aug. 8, 1902 by Bp. Juan Benlloch. On Sept. 26, 1913, Marino married the 22-year-old Julia Jordá Lloret, who bore him nine children of whom four were instrumental in his beatification process: Julia Isabel, María de los Desamparados, María del Milagro, and Marino Francisco.

As a layman, Blanes exercised his evangelical spirit as an employee of the Banco Español de Crédito and as an alderman on the city council. He was a member of various Catholic groups, including among others the Third Order of St. Francis, St. Vincent de Paul Society, Apostles of Prayer, and the Nocturnal Adoration Society of which he was president. Additionally, he founded the Center for Catholic Instruction and served as a catechist. His charity exceeded monetary donations, which took him to the point of bankruptcy: on Sundays he personally attended the sick in the Hospital Oliver.

He was described as a peace-loving man of justice, a passionate defender of human and Christian values, honorable, hard-working, considerate of others, and a husband and father. Nevertheless, his close association with the Church marked him as a threat to the new order.

Although Marino was aware of the danger, he continued his catechetical activities following the onset of the revolution. He told his daughter that ''one cannot be considered a good Christian without being persecuted.''

Blanes was arrested in his home on July 21, 1936, together with his neighbor, Juan Torregrosa. They were taken to the town hall. Torregrosa was released, but Blanes was imprisoned for seven weeks in the municipal jail. Throughout his incarceration he remained optimistic and tranquil. His prison mates related that he treated the humblest and most unlovable among them with the same affection as the greatest and that he always remained pleasant, affable, and prayerful. He daily recited the rosary with Fr. Juan Bautista Carbonell, who was imprisoned with him.

About 3:00 A.M. on September 8, he was taken from the prison. When his son brought his breakfast the following morning, he was told that his father had been released. Another said that he had been taken to Alicante. It was later learned that he had been taken to the ''Paseo'' and executed. His body was never recovered. He was beatified by Pope John Paul II with José Aparicio Sanz and 232 companions on March 11, 2001.

Feast: Sept. 22.

Bibliography: V. CÁRCEL ORTÍ, *Martires españoles del siglo XX* (Madrid 1995). W. H. CARROLL, *The Last Crusade* (Front Royal, Va. 1996). J. PÉREZ DE URBEL, *Catholic Martyrs of the Spanish Civil War*, tr. M. F. INGRAMS (Kansas City, Mo. 1993). R. ROYAL, *The Catholic Martyrs of the Twentieth Century* (New York 2000). L'Osservatore Romano, Eng. no. 11 (14 March 2001) 1–4, 12.

[K. I. RABENSTEIN]

BLARER

The Blarer (Blaurer) family was prominent in 16th-century Church reform and in the politics of Southern Germany and the cantons of Switzerland.

Ludwig, BENEDICTINE, Catholic reformer; b. *c.* 1480; d. Feb. 26, 1544. Ludwig became a monk of the Abbey of SAINT GALL in Switzerland, where he served as cellarer. In 1528 Clement VII confirmed his appointment as administrator of the Abbey of EINSIEDELN and, in 1533, instated him as abbot. Because of the religious upheavals, the pope later granted Ludwig the right to administer the Sacrament of CONFIRMATION and to consecrate churches. In modern Church history Ludwig is considered a transitional a figure who strove to reform the Church from within.

Ambrosius, Protestant reformer in southern Germany and Switzerland; b. Constance, April 4, 1492; d. Winterthur, Dec. 6, 1564. Ambrosius entered the Benedictine Abbey of ALPIRSBACH in the Black Forest, but while pursuing further studies at Tübingen, he made the acquaintance of MELANCHTHON and other humanists, and he retained contact with Melanchthon after returning to the monastery. The spirit of LUTHER's writings so impressed him that he left the abbey in 1522 and returned to Constance, where he preached with zeal for the new movement. He was active later in Württemberg and Switzerland.

Gerwig, Benedictine, Catholic reformer; b. Constance, May 25, 1495; d. Weingarten, Aug. 30, 1567. Gerwig made profession in the Abbey of Weingarten in 1513, then studied Church law in Freiburg im Breisgau, Vienna, and Ferrara. In 1520 he was elected abbot of Weingarten, and in 1547, at the insistence of Emperor Charles V, he also became abbot of Ochsenhausen. Gerwig, always conservatively inclined, not only resisted energetically the efforts of the Protestant Reformers, but also became engaged in conflicts with the Jesuits. The preservation of the Catholic religion in Swabia is in part due to his political activity.

Thomas, politician and Protestant reformer; b. Constance, after 1492; d. Gyrsburg (Thurgau), March 19, 1567. After completing law studies in Freiburg im Breisgau, Thomas studied theology in Wittenberg where he sided with Luther. He was influential in inducing his brother, Ambrosius, to leave the monastery. Upon returning to Constance, Thomas entered political life, serving as mayor from 1537 to 1547, but was compelled to leave the city in 1548. He was an important influence in discussions among the Reformers who were attempting to reach an agreement about the teaching of the Lord's Supper.

Diethelm, Benedictine, religious reformer; b. 1503; d. Saint Gall, Switzerland, Dec. 18, 1564. Diethelm became a religious in 1523 and was elected abbot of Saint Gall in 1530. While in exile in Mehrerau, where he became abbot in 1532, he made arrangments with the civil authorities of Saint Gall to restore the famous abbey. At Mehrerau and Saint Gall he instituted sound spiritual life, and he extended the same spirit to the secular clergy, effecting the restoration of many religious houses for women in Switzerland.

Jakob Christoph, bishop of Basel, Catholic reformer; b. Rosenberg, May 11, 1542; d. Prunktrut (Canton Bern), April 18, 1603. When appointed bishop of Basel in 1575, Jakob Christoph found the diocese spiritually and materially impoverished. He resisted the inroads of the Protestant Reformers and carried out the instructions of the Council of Trent; he also erected a Jesuit college in his residential see of Prunktrut. He ranks as one of the foremost figures in the COUNTER REFORMATION in Switzerland.

Bibliography: Ludwig. R. HENGGELER, *Professbuch der fürstlichen Benediktinerabtei Unserer Lieben Frau zu Einsiedeln,* v. 3 of *Monasticon-Benedictinum Helvetiae,* 3 v. (Einsiedeln 1930–34). R. TSCHUDI, *Das Kloster Einsiedeln unter den Aebten Ludwig II Blarer und Joachim Eichorn 1526–69* (Doctoral diss. unpub. Fribourg U. 1946); *Lexikon für Theologie und Kirche*, ed. J. HOFER and K. RAHNER, 2:523. **Ambrosius**. P. STÄRKLE, "Zur Familiengeschichte der Blarer," *Zeitschrift für Schweizer Kirchengeschichte* 43 (1949) 100–131, 203–224. O. FEGER, *Neue deutsch Biographie*. (Berlin 1953) 2:287–288. O. VASELLA, *Lexikon für Theologie und Kirche*, ed. J. HOFER and K. RAHNER, 2:523. **Thomas**. P. STÄRKLE, *op. cit.* O. FEGER, *Neue deutsch Biographie* (Berlin, 1953) 2:288. O. VASELLA, *Lexikon für Theologie und Kirche*, ed. J. HOFER and K. RAHNER, 2:523–524. **Gerwig**. *Briefe und Akten,* ed. H. GÜNTHER, 2 v. (Stuttgart 1914–21). H. GÜNTHER, "Abt Georg Blarer von Weingarten und die Gegenreformation," *Festschrift Georg von Hertling* (Kempten 1913) 342–349. R. REINHARDT, *Lexikon für Theologie und Kirche*, ed. J. HOFER and K. RAHNER, 2:523. **Diethelm**. A. BAUMANN, *Die Fürstabtei St. Gallen unter Abt Diethelm Blarer 1530–64* (Doctoral diss. unpub. Fribourg U. 1948). G. THÜRER, *St. Galler Geschichte* (St. Gallen 1953—) v. 1. O. VASELLA, *Lexikon für Theologie und Kirche*, ed. J. HOFER and K. RAHNER, 2:524. **Jakob Christoph**. B. BURY, *Geschichte des Bistums Basel und seiner Bischöfe* (Solothurn 1927). W. BROTSCHI, *Der Kampf Jakob Christoph Blarers . . . um die religiöse Einheit im Fürstbistum Basel 1575–1608* (Studia Friburgensia, ns 13; Fribourg 1956). A. CHÈVRE, *Lexikon für Theologie und Kirche*, ed. J. HOFER and K. RAHNER, 2:524.

[O. L. KAPSNER]

BLASPHEMY

Any expression by word, sign, or gesture that is insulting to the goodness of God. Blasphemy is to be carefully distinguished from PROFANITY, which is without contempt or insulting intent and does irreverence to God simply by a careless, too frequent, or inappropriate use of sacred names or reference to sacred things. Some theologians list blasphemy among the sins opposed to the virtue of RELIGION, for it is the object of that virtue to give to God the reverence that is His due, whereas blasphemy, on the contrary, treats Him with positive irreverence and contempt (see B. Häring, *The Law of Christ,* 2.205). The 1917 *Code of Canon Law* also considered blasphemy a sin against religion (1917 *Codex iuris canonici* [Rome 1918; repr. Graz 1955] c. 2323). St. Thomas Aquinas, however, preferred to consider it as a sin opposed to the virtue of faith inasmuch as the blasphemer asserts some error contrary to a truth of faith that he should confess (*Summa theologiae* 2a2ae, 13.1). Without doubt blasphemy is an offense against both faith and religion, but to see it primarily in its opposition to faith serves to center attention on what is more radical in the transgression as well as to underline its malice, for, other things being equal, sins against the theological virtues are graver than those against the moral virtues.

Blasphemy is a single species of sin, but it can be committed in many ways. Theologians commonly distinguish between heretical and nonheretical blasphemy. It is heretical if it openly asserts something contrary to faith, as when it denies God's mercy, providence, or justice. It is nonheretical if it openly asserts nothing contrary to faith but consists simply in imprecations or contumelious speech against God. Even the latter type of blasphemy, however, implicitly contains some error with respect to faith, for it assumes that God is worthy of contumelious treatment. Theologians distinguish also between blasphemy that is directed immediately against God in His person or attributes and that which is directed against His saints, angels, men, or creation generally, in their relations to Him.

Blasphemy has always been considered to be among the gravest of sins from the point of view of objective malice. The degree of subjective malice in any particular occurrence depends on the greater or lesser willful involvement of the blasphemer in the sin. Although every form of blasphemy supposes a malicious will, in its gravest and most ''perfect'' form it is a deliberate and direct attack upon the honor of God with intent to insult Him. But blasphemy is also possible without a direct intent to insult the divine goodness, as when one gives expression to what does in fact derogate from the divine goodness. In this sense, expressions of formal heresy or infidelity are always blasphemous. So also are expressions, commands, or invocations calling upon God to do what is unworthy of Him, such as to curse another or to remove him from the sphere of divine love and favor. Hence if one attends simply to the literal meaning of the words, expressions calling upon God to damn something are objectively blasphemous. But words have meaning in ordinary usage according to the way in which people generally understand them. In many cases they become denatured through overuse and come to have a sense quite different from their literal meaning. The regrettable English expression ''God damn'' appears to have undergone such a transformation, and its use in ordinary circumstances, when one does not advert to or intend to apply the literal sense, is to be classified as profanity rather than blasphemy.

The Code of Justinian (6th century) prescribed the death penalty for blasphemy, and the crime was listed as capital throughout much of both pre- and post-Reformation Europe. Since the Enlightenment, however, secular authorities have looked upon it as a crime against the sensibilities of citizens rather than against God, and its punishment has been mitigated. Present canon law says that it is to be punished with ''a just penalty'' (*Codex iuris canonici* c. 1369).

Bibliography: CAJETAN, *Commentarii in* Summa theologiae 2am2ae 13. Adequate treatments of blasphemy may be found in most handbooks of moral theology, e.g., B. HÄRING, *The Law of Christ,* tr. E. G. KAISER, v. 1 (Westminster, Md. 1961) 205–207. B. H. MERKELBACH, *Summa theologiae moralis,* 3 v. (8th ed. Paris 1949) 1:610–616. J. A. MCHUGH and C. J. CALLAN, *Moral Theology,* rev. E. P. FARRELL, 2 v. (New York 1958) 1:347–356. V. OBLET, *Dictionnaire de théologie catholique,* ed. A. VACANT et al., 15 v. (Paris 1903–50; Tables générales 1951–) 2.1:907–910.

[G. A. BUCKLEY/EDS.]

BLASPHEMY (IN THE BIBLE)

Blasphemy in the OT involved any word or action offensive to God. The Mosaic Law ordered the stoning of anyone who cursed (*qillēl*) God, or blasphemed (*nāqab,* connected with *qābab,* ''curse'' [?]) His name (Lv 24.10–16; Ex 22.27). The defiant sinner insulted (*giddēp*) God (Nm 15.30), so also did Israel's rebellion against God (Ez 20.27), and the disparagement of God's power by Israel's enemies (2 Kgs 19.6, 22). Israel's enemies and wicked men are also said to taunt or mock (*ḥērēp*) God (Is 37.4, 17, 23; 65.7; Ps 73[74].10, 18; Prv 14.31). To oppress God's people is to despise or spurn or revile (*ni'ēṣ*) His name (Is 52.5). *Ni'ēṣ* appears frequently in connection with God (Nm 14.11; Dt 31.20; 2 Sm 12.14; Ps 9b[10].3,13; Is 1.4). Taking the name of God in vain or falsely is a form of blasphemy (Ex 20.7). Later Judaism refrained from even pronouncing God's sacred name, substituting ''Heavens,'' or ''the Name,'' etc.

In the NT βλασφημία (also in verbal and adjectival form) means ''revilement,'' ''slander,'' or ''railing'' with men as object (Ti 3.2; Rom 3.8; 1 Cor 4.13; 10.30; Acts 13.45; 18.6, Paul's teaching; Rv 2.9; see also the lists of vices in Mk 7.22; Eph 4.31; Col 3.8; Mt 15.19; 1 Tm 6.4; 2 Tm 3.2). It also denotes a sin against God. The Jews take Jesus' claim to the divine prerogative of forgiving sin (Mt 9.3 and parallels) and to be the Son of God (Jn 10.33, 36; cf. 5.18) as blasphemy. The Sanhedrin condemned Him to death for blasphemy (cf. His use of Ps 190[110].1 and Dn 7.13 in Mt 26.63–66 and parallels). The Jews accused St. Stephen of blasphemy because of his teaching on God, Moses, the Temple, and the Law (Acts 6.11, 13; 7.58; cf. Lv 24.10–16). Unrepentant men blaspheme God (Rv 16.11, 21). His name is also blasphemed (Rv 16.9; 13.6, by the beast of the sea; see also Rv 13.1; 17.3). The Jews by transgressing the law caused the name of God to be blasphemed among the Gentiles (Rom 2.24; St. Paul here uses Is 52.5, LXX, with his own inspired purpose). Rebellion of Christian slaves would cause blaspheming of the name of the Lord and His teachings (1 Tm 6.1). Since Christ's miracles are done by the power of the Holy Spirit, to attribute them to the devil is blasphemy against the Holy Spirit. This SIN AGAINST THE HOLY SPIRIT is unforgivable. A hardened blindness to the coming of the Spirit in power, it totally excludes the divine light of repentance. Other blasphemies, even those against the Son of Man whose divinity is veiled, are forgivable (Mt 12.25–32 and par.; Heb 6.4–6; 10.26–28). Christ is reviled (ἐβλασφήμουν) on the cross (Mt 27.39 and par.). The rich of this world blaspheme His name in their ill treatment of the poor (Jas 2.7). To deny Christ is blasphemy (1 Tm 1.13; Acts 26.11). Immoral conduct leads to blaspheming the Christian message (2 Pt 2.2; Ti 2.5; see also Rom 14.16). Evil men blaspheme angels (2 Pt 2.10; Jude 8, 10).

See Also: CURSE.

Bibliography: *Encyclopedic Dictionary of the Bible,* tr. and adap. by L. HARTMAN (New York 1963), from A. VAN DEN BORN, *Bijbels Woordenboek* 251–253. G. A. BUTTRICK, ed., *The Interpreter's Dictionary of the Bible,* 4 v. (Nashville 1962) v. 1.

[J. A. FALLON]

BLASTARES, MATTHEW

14th-century Byzantine canonist and monk. Little is known of his life other than that he was a monk and priest first on Mt. Athos, then in the Isaia monastery at Thessalonika. In 1335 he completed his *Syntagma,* an encyclopedic compilation of ecclesiastical and civil laws to which he added his own commentaries and those of his predecessors, especially Zonaras and the illustrious Theodore BALSAMON.

The *Syntagma* groups the laws, not according to subject matter, but according to the Greek alphabet. There are 24 main headings, and within each main section the items are arranged in alphabetical order. The work is completed with a short lexicon of Latin legal terms. Widely translated, the *Syntagma* influenced the legal codes of late Byzantium and the surrounding nations.

Blastares also entered into his work the theological controversies of his time, wrote against the Latin use of Azymes, composed a Description of the Error of the Latins (unedited), and enscribed a letter to Guy of Lusignan. He is also the probable author of five books written against the Jews, and several liturgical tracts and hymns are attributed to him.

Bibliography: *Patrologia Graeca*, ed. J. P. MIGNE, (Paris 1857–66) 144:960–1400. H. G. BECK, *Kirche und theologische Literatur im byzantinischen Reich* (Munich 1959) 786–787. L. PETIT, *Dictionnaire de théologie catholique* (Paris 1903–50) 2.1:916–917. R. JANIN, *Lexikon für Theologie und Kirche*, ed. J. HOFER and K. RAHNER (Freiburg 1957–65) 7:173; *Dictionnaire d'histoire et de géographie ecclésiastiques* (Paris 1912–) 9:160–161. J. HERMAN, *Dictionnaire de droit canonique* (Paris 1935–65) 2:920–925. A. SOLOVIEV, *Studi bizantini e neoellenici 5* (1939) 698–707.

[H. D. HUNTER]

BLENKINSOP

Irish-American family that contributed to the development of the Church in the United States.

Peter, publisher; b. Dublin, Ireland, toward the close of the 18th century. Peter was descended from a Catholic family originally from the north of England. He married Mary Kelly, a sister of Abp. Oliver Kelly of Tuam. In 1826 the family immigrated to America and settled in Baltimore, Maryland where Blenkinsop became a publisher and published Charles Constantine Pise's *A History of the Church* (5 v. Baltimore 1827–29). In 1830 he issued the first Catholic monthly periodical in the United States, the *Metropolitan,* which existed only briefly, from January to December of 1830. Peter then reverted to bookselling. His three children, William A., Peter J., and Catherine, entered religious life.

Peter J., educator; b. Dublin, April 19, 1818; d. Philadelphia, Pennsylvania, Nov. 5, 1896. Peter J. attended St. Mary's College, Baltimore (1830–33), entered the Society of Jesus at Frederick, Maryland (1834), and taught at Georgetown College (later University), in Washington, D.C. After his ordination in 1846, he was assigned to the College of the Holy Cross in Worcester, Massachusetts where he served as instructor and treasurer and, from 1854 to 1857, as its fifth president. He made frequent missionary journeys to the scattered Catholics of central New England, south as far as Norwich, Connecticut and west to Springfield, Massachusetts. After pastoral service at St. Joseph's Church in Philadelphia, he returned to Holy Cross in 1873 and cared for the mission in Leicester, Massachusetts until 1880, when he left for Georgetown. From 1882 until his death, he was stationed at the Church of the Gesu, in Philadelphia.

William A., missionary; b. Dublin, 1819; d. Boston, Massachusetts, Jan. 8, 1892. William A. studied at St. Mary's College, Baltimore (1833–39), received his M.A. there, and joined the faculty. After his ordination in 1843, he served for seven years in the missions of the Diocese of Natchez, Mississippi. He became pastor at Chicopee, then part of the Boston diocese, and continued the pioneer labors of Revs. James Fitton and John D. Brady by making monthly missionary trips through an extensive territory in western Massachusetts, including the towns of Holyoke, Ware, Greenfield, and Amherst. In a time of bitterness exacerbated by the excesses of KNOW-NOTHINGISM, he fostered an ecumenical spirit between Catholics and Protestants. He built the Church of the Holy Name of Jesus (dedicated in 1859) to care for the expanding Catholic population in Chicopee. In 1864 he was named pastor of SS. Peter and Paul, a parish then embracing the entire area of South Boston.

Catherine, educator; b. Dublin, April 18, 1816: d. Emmitsburg, Maryland, March 18, 1887. Catherine took the name of Euphemia when she entered the Sisters of Charity of Emmitsburg in 1831. After serving at St. Joseph's school in New York and at St. Peter's school and St. Mary's Asylum in Baltimore, she was appointed assistant for the motherhouse in Emmitsburg (1855) and directed the institutions of the Sisters of Charity in the Southern states during the Civil War. In 1866 Mother Euphemia became superior of the Sisters of Charity in the United States and in subsequent years opened charitable establishments in various cities.

Bibliography: R. H. LORD et al., *History of the Archdiocese of Boston, 1604–1943,* 3 v. (New York 1944). J. J. MCCOY, *History of the Catholic Church in the Diocese of Springfield* (Boston 1900).

[W. J. GRATTAN]

BLESSED

In the language of the Church, ''blessed'' refers to the just in heaven, those who after a life here below enjoy eternal happiness. St. Paul in 1 Cor 2.9 considers their happiness a mystery. Theologians treat the happiness of the saints in heaven as an aspect of the supernatural, beatific vision, which consists essentially in seeing and loving God without fully comprehending Him. According to Scripture and tradition this happiness is substantially the same for all, but varies according to the merits of the individual.

The title blessed is given by the Church to those whose cause has successfully passed through the process of beatification. After completion of these proceedings it is established that a person practiced heroic virtue and that this fact is miraculously confirmed. The blessed may be venerated. However, the cult given them is restricted.

As the translation of the Greek μακάριοι, blessed means happy, fortunate, blissful, and is the opening word of the eight solemn blessings, the Beatitudes (Mt 1.5–10), which are the first part of the Sermon on the Mount.

See Also: HEAVEN (THEOLOGY OF); CANONIZATION OF SAINTS (HISTORY AND PROCEDURE); BEATITUDES (IN THE BIBLE).

[O. A. BOENKI]

BLESSED SACRAMENT, SERVANTS OF THE

Societas Ancillarum Sanctissimi Sacramenti (SSS) is a contemplative congregation of women religious founded at Paris in 1858 by St. Pierre Julien (EYMARD) with papal approval (1871, 1885). The purpose of the community, whose members are cloistered and take perpetual vows, is devotion to the Blessed Sacrament and the promotion of that practice among the laity. Retreats for women are conducted in some of the larger convents. When Marguerite Guillot and a small group of ladies came under Eymard's direction, he was able to realize his intention of founding a congregation of sisters similar in scope to that of his BLESSED SACRAMENT FATHERS. The French government's antireligious policy (1903) occasioned the spread of the community to Chicoutimi, Quebec, Canada. In 1947 a convent was opened in Waterville, Maine, and a novitiate was established there. From Waterville the sisters established a second convent at Pueblo, Colo.

At the end of 2000, the congregation had communities in Europe (France, Italy, and The Netherlands), North America (Canada and the U.S.), South America (Brazil), Asia (the Philippines and Vietnam) and Australia. The generalate is in Rome.

[J. ROY/EDS.]

BLESSED SACRAMENT, SISTERS OF THE

(Abbreviation: SBS, Official Catholic Directory #0260); formerly known as the Sisters of the Blessed Sacrament for Indians and Colored People; a congregation of women religious founded by American-born Saint Katharine Mary DREXEL on Feb. 12, 1891. As defined by the foundress, the special purpose of the Sisters of the Blessed Sacrament consists in ministering to the needs of the African-Americans and Native-Americans.

During a personal audience with Leo XIII, Miss Drexel represented the need for sisters to staff schools for Blacks and Native Americans. In reply the Pope challenged Katharine to give herself as well as her wealth to this cause. In 1889, under the direction of Bishop James O'Connor of Omaha, Nebraska, and later under Archbishop Patrick Ryan of Philadelphia, Pennsylvania, the 31-year-old Katharine began a two-year novitiate with the Sisters of Mercy of Pittsburgh, Pennsylvania.

On July 16, 1890, Leo XIII sent his apostolic blessing to Sister Mary Katharine and her companions, the nucleus of the new congregation. When she made her vows on Feb. 12, 1891, Mother Katharine was named by Archbishop Ryan foundress and first superior of the community. During the construction of a motherhouse, the old Drexel home at Torresdale, near Philadelphia, served as a temporary novitiate. St. Elizabeth's Convent, the new motherhouse, was officially opened on Dec. 3, 1892.

The decree of praise for the constitutions came on Feb. 16, 1897; temporary approbation followed on July 11, 1907; and final approval was given by Pius X on May 25, 1913. On June 24, 1961, the Congregation for Religious approved a general revision of the constitutions.

Mother Katharine did not confine her efforts to her own institute but used the income from the vast family estate to support many other apostolic undertakings. The Drexel family built churches and schools, supported missionary priests and sisters, and gave bountifully to teachers on Black and Native American missions throughout the United States and in many foreign countries. When Mother Katharine survived her two sisters, the congregation she founded enjoyed the benefit of her increased income during her lifetime. After her death in 1955, the principal on which Mother Katharine's income had been based was distributed to various charities throughout the United States.

Bibliography: K. BURTON, *The Golden Door: The Life of Katharine Drexel* (New York 1957).

[H. J. SIEVERS/EDS.]

BLESSED SACRAMENT FATHERS

(SSS, Official Catholic Directory #0220); founded in France in 1856 by Pierre Julien EYMARD as a religious society of men who would devote themselves entirely to the glorification of the Holy Eucharist. The members of the congregation consist of both priests and lay brothers. Eymard had been ordained for the Diocese of Grenoble in 1834 and later joined the Society of Mary. After 17 years as a Marist, he founded the Congregation of the Blessed Sacrament for which he obtained formal approbation from Pius IX in 1863. From 1856 until his death Eymard worked on the constitutions of the congregation. He called this his only book although a collection of his sermons has been published in book form. Definitive approbation for the constitutions was obtained from Rome in 1895. At the time of his death in 1868 the society maintained seven houses, five in France and two in Belgium, and included 50 religious, of whom 16 were priests.

The congregation engages also in all forms of apostolate that spread the glory of the Holy Eucharist. The specific works have varied since the days of its foundation. Eymard devoted himself to the preparation of adults for their first Holy Communion, a great need in his day. The fathers have since promoted affiliated societies for different categories of persons who participate in the eucharistic vocation of the religious themselves.

The congregation was first divided into provinces in 1930. The U.S. provincialate is in Cleveland, Ohio. The generalate is in Rome.

Bibliography: E. NUÑEZ, ed., *Commentaire des constitutions de la Congrégation du Très Saint Sacrement* (Rome 1958—), with bibliographies. *Centenaire de la Congrégation du Très Saint Sacrement, 1856–1956* (Rome 1956). E. TENAILLON, *Venerable Pierre Julien Eymard* (New York 1914). F. TROCHU, *Le Bienheureux Pierre-Julien Eymard: . . . d'après ses écrits, son procès de béatification, et de nombreux documents inédits* (Lyons 1949).

[J. ROY/EDS.]

BLESSING (IN THE BIBLE)

The Old Testament contains only a few traces of a primitive belief in the magical efficacy of the spoken word, either to bless or to CURSE. Some older narratives contain vestiges of superstition, but in their final editing they always make it clear that blessings come ultimately from the Lord. Thus, the YAHWIST indicated that Isaac's blessing of Jacob, which according to the primitive belief could not be annulled, was due ultimately to God's choice of Jacob (Gn 25.23; 27.33–38). The actual formula of blessing is a prayer to the Lord without any suggestion of magical efficacy (Gn 27.28). The narrative about Jacob's struggle with God (Gn 32.24–30) was based upon older material that probably suggested that a blessing had been wrested from a numinous being. In the reshaping of the material, the Yahwist made clear that God imparted His blessing freely (Gn 32.29).

Roman Catholic sanctuary of the renaissance type, installed for the Church of St. Jean Baptiste (Fathers of the Blessed Sacrament) New York, 1922. (©Bettmann/CORBIS)

The loyal Israelite had a profound sense of dependence upon the Lord as the source of all blessings. A customary greeting was a prayer to the Lord for blessing (Gn 24.31; Ruth 2.4), so that the common verb for ''to bless,'' *bērak,* often meant ''to greet'' (Gn 47:7, 10; 1 Sm 13.10). God blessed living things with the special power of generation (Gn 1.22, 28). His blessing of Abraham was also connected with generation (Gn 12.2–3). Certain individuals possessed special authority to call down God's blessings upon men: a father, upon his children (Gn 9.26; 27.28; 49.25–26, 28); a king, upon his subjects (2 Sm 6.18; 1 Kgs 8.14, 55–61); and priests, upon the people (Nm 6.22–27).

The conception that one could strengthen one's God by blessing Him did not exist in Israel. By blessing Yahweh the Israelite solemnly acknowledged Him as Lord and King and the source of all blessings. In such a context, the verb *bērak* meant to praise or thank [Gn 24.48; Dt 8.10; Ps 65(66).8; 102(103).1–2] and is the antonym of *qillēl* (to curse), the verb predicated of a man who in his bitterness repudiated his parents, king, or God.

The place of blessing in the New Testament is typified in St. Luke's Gospel, where Christ ascends to the Father while blessing His disciples and the disciples return to Jerusalem ''praising and blessing God'' (Lk 24.51–53). These two aspects of the Old Testament blessing, namely, the calling down of God's bounty upon men and thanksgiving returned to God, found their perfect realization in the Eucharist. Christ's blessing at the Last Supper was both a prayer of thanksgiving to the Father and a calling of His sanctifying power (Mt 26.26; Lk 24.30). The New Testament term εὐλογέω is most often meant to invoke God's blessing, but it sometimes signified to give thanks (e.g., Luke 1.64; 1 Cor 14.16). The word εὐχαριστέω corresponded less perfectly to *bērak* since it meant only to give thanks. The words of the

Roman Canon, *Gratias agens benedixit* (giving thanks, He blessed), the result of a conflation of Mark 14.22 and 1 Corinthians 11.24, accurately describe the double aspect of the perfect Christian blessing.

Bibliography: J. SCHARBERT, *Lexikon für Theologie und Kirche*, eds., J. HOFER and K. RAHNER, 10 v. (2d, new ed. Freiburg 1957–65) 9:590–592. F. HORST and H. KÖSTER, *Die Religion in Geschichte und Gegenwart*, 7 v. (3d ed. Tübingen 1957–65) 5:1649–52. *Encyclopedic Dictionary of the Bible*, tr. and adap. by L. HARTMAN (New York 1963) 253–254. S. H. BLANK, ''Some Observations concerning Biblical Prayer,'' *Hebrew Union College Annual*, 32 (1961) 75–90. A. MURTONEN, ''The Use and Meaning of the Words *l[e]barek* and *b[e]'rakah* in the O.T.,'' *Vetus Testamentum*, 9 (1959) 158–177.

[J. V. MORRIS]

BLESSINGS, LITURGICAL

The chief sacramental actions of the Church next to the sacraments themselves are her blessings. As SACRAMENTALS they are sacred signs that render holy various occasions in life (see Vatican Council II, *Constitution on the Sacred Liturgy* 60). Like the sacraments, blessings are acts of worship of the Church. In keeping with the Biblical notion of blessing they have a twofold direction: (1) that of humanity's joyous praise and glorification of God, and (2) that of God's sanctifying action on all of humanity. Those members who are involved in such specific blessings are called to participate in the Church's praise and glorification of God, in addition to calling upon God's sanctifying action. In this sense, the recipients of blessings, as they are sometimes called, might better be described as participants in the prayers of blessing. While it seems that the external participation of those other than the minister is materially slight (perhaps no more than saying ''Amen''), this is no indication that its significance is of minor importance. Any tendency to regard the blessings as affording those who receive them only a passive part reflects a misunderstanding of these actions of the whole Church.

For this very reason, i.e., their ecclesial nature, the blessings of the Church are intended in the first place for her members. This term is not to be interpreted too strictly, however. Catechumens are subjects of blessings; those prior to Baptism are meant directly for them. In addition, those whose relationship to the Church is less than complete may on occasion receive these, e.g., ashes and palms.

In the Early Church. There are formulas of blessing in the earliest post-Apostolic documents. Especially significant are those within the celebration of the Mass as seen in Hippolytus's *Apostolic Tradition.* Here we find blessings of oil for the sick, milk, honey and water (to be taken at Communion by the newly baptized), lights, new fruits [5, 6, 21, 25, 32; B. Botte, ed., *La Tradition apostolique de saint Hippolyte: Essai de reconsitution* (*Liturgiegeschichtliche Quellen und Forschungen* 39; 1963) 19, 57, 65, 78]. Serapion attests to the blessing of the people, especially the sick, and that of oil and water [*Euchologion* 4, 6, 8, 17; F. X. Funk, ed., *Didascalia et constitutiones apostolorum* (Paderborn 1905) 2:163, 165, 167, 179].

The inclusion of such blessings in the Mass itself by the early Church teaches an important truth concerning the relation of blessings to the Eucharist. Most probably, the fruits of the earth were blessed at this particular point in the Mass to show the relationship of such blessings to the greatest of all God's blessings, Christ himself and his work of redemption.'' J. Jungmann suggested that in the final blessing at the end of the eucharist, the Church drew the faithful to herself and imparted a blessing as source of grace and strength for them. This was a practice not limited to the eucharist but carried out on other devotional occasions as well. (See Jungmann, *The Mass of the Roman Rite* 1:173–174).

Types of Blessings. Among her sanctifying actions some constitute a person or object to service in the Church. These are known as constitutive blessings and result in a permanent deputation to worship. Some constitutive blessings are more solemn than others, indicated by the use of the holy oils in their celebration; these are called consecrations in contra-distinction to simple constitutive blessings. The consecration of an altar, a church, or a chalice are examples of this same type of blessings for objects.

In addition to these there are many blessings that call on God to bless the persons who make use of objects or who are in certain needs. In these the person or object is not permanently changed. They are known as invocative blessings. The prayers seeking God's protection for a home or a sick person are of this class. Since the blessings she imparts consist primarily in her impetration, these (blessings) are what one means first of all in speaking of her sacramentals. The term is used in a secondary sense of the objects to which she gives her blessing.

Minister. Until the provision for laity as ministers of sacramentals in some cases by Vatican Council II (*Constitution on the Sacred Liturgy* 79) only clerics could fulfill this function. Vatican Council II's Constitution on the Sacred Liturgy requested that ''reserved blessings be few in number and only in favor of bishops or ordinaries: provision is also to be made that some blessings, at least in special circumstances and at the discretion of the ordinary, be given by qualified lay persons'' (*Sacrosanctum*

Concilium 79). This proviso has been implemented in the Book of Blessings, which provides both clerical and lay blessings in various contexts. Thus, the Book of Blessings contains blessings to be used within a domestic setting (e.g. the blessing of children, of the family, of food, of the Advent wreath in a home).

The Roman Pontifical contains those blessings and consecrations either strictly reserved to the bishop or whose ordinary minister is the bishop. The Roman Ritual contains those blessings given by the priest either as an ordinary minister or as an extraordinary minister delegated by the bishop or by special indult. Traditionally, there were three types of reserved blessings in the Roman Ritual: (1) those reserved to bishops and other Ordinaries and to priests with special faculties; (2) blessings given by priests having an apostolic indult; and (3) blessings proper to certain religious communities (Chapter XI). The 1964 *Inter oecumenici*, Instruction on the Proper Implementation of the Constitution on the Sacred Liturgy permits all priests to bestow the majority of these blessings. The recent revision of the sacramental and other liturgical rites has also extended to priests certain blessings once reserved to the bishop. Thus in case of necessity any priest may bless the oil used in the Anointing of the Sick. The 1977 Rite of a Dedication of a Church and Altar allows the priest to consecrate a chalice or paten.

Blessings given by the deacon have also been extended. ''It pertains to the office of a deacon, in so far as it may be assigned to him by competent authority, to administer Baptism solemnly, to be custodian and distributor of the Eucharist, in the name of the Church to assist at and to bless marriages, to bring Viaticum to the dying . . . to administer sacramentals, and to officiate at funeral and burial services'' (*Lumen gentium* 29). Thus the deacon, whether permanent or transitional, may give the blessings contained in these sacramental rites. When he is an ordinary minister for the exposition of the Eucharist, he may bless the people with the Sacrament. He may also preside at the celebration of the Liturgy of the Hours and bestow its concluding blessing.

Bibliography: A. G. MARTIMORT, *L'Église en prière* (Tournai 1961). *Book of Blessing Approved for Use in the Dioceses of the United States of America by the National Conference of Catholic Bishops and Confirmed by the Apostolic See* (Collegeville, Minn. 1990).

[L. J. JOHNSON/J. R. QUINN/EDS.]

BLONDEL, MAURICE

French Catholic philosopher; b. Nov. 2, 1861, Dijon; d. June 4, 1949, Aix-en-Provence.

L'Action. Blondel established himself as a philosopher in French university circles with a ground-breaking dissertation on *Action* in 1893, in which he crashed through two intellectual barriers common at the time: the confining of philosophy to a consideration of abstract ideas and the exclusion of religion from the scope of legitimate philosophical inquiry. Starting from the question, does human life make sense and does the human being have a destiny?, he argued for a strict necessity of raising the philosophical question of action (vs. dilettantism), a strict necessity of answering it in positive terms (vs. pessimism), and a strict necessity of considering it in subjective as well as objective terms (vs. positivism).

Through critical reflection on the origin of action in consciousness, Blondel distinguished between a willed will, which focuses on determinate objects of willing, and a willing will, which entails an infinite power of willing in search of an object that will be the equal of this power. From this he argued that it is necessary that the will go out of itself into the body, into co-action with others, to the very confines of the universe in search of an object that will be the equal of its infinite power. He showed how, in superstitious action, the will tends to attribute such an infinite value to certain things in the immanent order of human experience, whether it be a totem, a ritual, or even its own subjectivity.

From this reflection on the total phenomenon of action and from his criticism of superstition Blondel came to a twofold conclusion: that it is necessary for action to go out beyond its own immanent order and that it is impossible for it to do so left to its own resources. Hence he argued for the necessity of affirming a totally transcendent Necessary Being and for the necessity of coming to a choice in the face of this Necessary Being. The human being ultimately wants to be God. The choice is to be God with God or to be God without God. Both alternatives have consequences: in the former case, finding fulfillment of one's most intimate desire; in the latter, being totally deprived of any fulfillment. At the core of every human action lies this option which denotes a properly religious attitude, whether for or against God.

In this necessary religious attitude, however, philosophy can only grasp the necessity of saying yes or no to God, not the content of what God might will on His part or how He might choose to fulfill the human being's desire. This is why philosophy cannot replace religion, which has to be from God. Philosophy understands action only from the human standpoint. If it tries to replace religion in answering the question of how human destiny can ultimately be fulfilled, it becomes another form of superstition or immanentism. Philosophy may nevertheless still entertain the idea of a fulfillment that would be strictly from God and yet fulfilling according to the exigencies of human action. Hence the idea of the supernatural is hypothetically necessary for philosophy. As supernatural it is not bound by any necessity of nature in human action. It depends totally on God's free initiative, which ever remains a mystery for philosophy. Yet, if such an initiative is taken by God, even if it be supernatural, it becomes obligatory for human being or necessary as a condition of fulfillment. One cannot say no to it without going against one's most fundamental human desire.

Controversy. In *L'Action* Blondel went directly to the question of the supernatural as obligatory or necessary for man, as this had always been understood in the Catholic tradition, without passing through any idea of natural religion, which he regarded as another form of superstition based on abstract metaphysical concepts fabricated by man. He managed to convince his examiners of the philosophical validity of his argument, even though they were reluctant to accept any of his conclusions with regard to the necessity of supernatural religion and consequently to grant him status in the university.

On the other hand, Blondel ran into trouble in Catholic circles because he criticized the standard approaches to religion in apologetics as inadequate and as failing to get to the essential point of religion as something supernatural or free on the part of God and yet as necessary or obligatory on the part of human being. It was important for Blondel to show that this was a matter of philosophy and not just a matter of religious conviction, as too many French Catholic apologists supposed at the time. With this end in view he wrote a series of articles in 1896, while he was still looking for a post in the university, under the heading of a *Letter on the Exigencies of Contemporary Thought in the Matter of Apologetics and on the Method of Philosophy in the Study of the Religious Problem.* It reassured many of his stance as a philosopher but also antagonized many Catholics who began to realize that Blondel was not defending their particular conception of religion.

Thus Blondel found himself in a philosophical noman's land, having to show that his philosophy of religion was indeed a philosophy and not a theology, and having to defend himself against the misunderstanding of those believers who could not accept what appeared to them as an illegitimate intrusion on the part of philosophy into a realm reserved for faith or mysticism. Eventually he was accepted by the university and received the chair in philosophy in Aix-en-Provence (where he spent the rest of his academic career and came to be known as the Philosopher of Aix), but he was left with the problem of having to explain himself in the matter of Christian apologetics and to defend himself against attacks from those Catholics who had no concern with meeting the exigencies of contemporary thought.

Blondel spent the first fifteen years of his career at Aix, from 1898 until World War I, doing battle on two fronts, one with philosophers like BRUNSCHVICG and BERGSON, whose idealism or intuitionism he could not agree with, and the other with mainly theologians who also claimed to be philosophers, at least in the matter of apologetics. Many did try to have his work put on the Index of Forbidden books, during the time of the Modernist crisis, but they did not succeed. Blondel was among the first to spot the problem of MODERNISM and to write against it in an important article on *History and Dogma* in 1904. The article reemphasized the importance of tradition as something living in the Church and opened the way to a more positive discussion of development in dogma.

Later Philosophical Work. Blondel's interest was always philosophy, not theology nor even apologetics as such. Even while he was addressing the problem of apologetics he published a number of important articles in dialogue with Descartes, Spinoza, Malebranche, Pascal, etc., in which he discussed problems in the philosophy of religion. Early in his career he conceived of a grandiose project in philosophy that would set forth his thought in a more complete way than he had been able to do within the constraints of his dissertation on *Action*, for he was not satisfied with being thought of as only a philosopher of action. He worked on this project, which was clearly outlined in his mind under the three headings of *Thought*, *Being*, and *Action*, during most of his teaching career, but he was unable to publish any of it before he had to retire from his Chair in Philosophy in 1927 for reasons of blindness. It was only then, under the handicap of blindness, that he was able to complete what he thought of as his philosophical legacy with the collaboration of his faithful and devoted secretary, Nathalie Panis.

In the early 1930s Blondel published several articles on Augustine, on the occasion of the 1500th anniversary of the saint's death. He insisted on the philosophical import of Augustine as a Catholic thinker. This provoked a reaction against the idea of Christian philosophy, not only among non-Christians, but also among many Catholics like Etienne GILSON and most Thomists at the time. Blondel defended this idea of Catholic philosophy at some length because he saw that his own philosophy was at stake in it in the same way as his own original philosophy of action had been at stake in the refusal to consider religion as a philosophical problem. He still had a long struggle to organize his thoughts on paper, since he could no longer read the copious notes he had written over the years for the project. Family and friends tried to help, but only when Mlle Panis finally came on the scene in December 1931, did things begin to fall into place. Five volumes followed in quick succession between 1934 and

1937, two on *Thought*, one on *Being*, and two more on *Action*. Blondel also had in mind a three-volume work on *Philosophy and the Christian Spirit*, two volumes of which appeared before his death while the third remained unfinished. On the day before he died he signed a contract for another volume of essays written earlier on the *Philosophical Exigencies of Christianity*, bringing out once again certain Catholic dimensions of philosophy that should not be overlooked.

Above all Blondel was a philosopher, something he insisted on all his life, even in the midst of his controversies over apologetics, but a philosopher who had a tremendous positive influence in Christian theology as well as philosophy, not only in France but in many other countries as well, especially Italy, Germany, Spain, Portugal, and Latin America, where his work has long existed in translation. He has also been translated into Japanese and English, albeit at a later date.

Bibliography: R. VIRGOULAY and C. TROISFONTAINES, *Maurice Blondel: Bibliographie Analytique et Critique*, vol. 1: works by M. B. 1880–1973; vol. 2: studies on M. B. 1893–1975 (Louvain 1975–1976); continuation of secondary literature from 1976 to 1994 in A. RAFFELT, P. REIFENBERG, and G. FUCHS, *Das Tun, der Glaube, die Vernunft*, 216–238 (Echter 1995). *Oeuvres Complètes*, vol. 1, 1893. *Les Deux Thèses* (PUF 1995); vol. 2, 1888–1913. *La Philosophie de l'Action et la Crise Moderniste* (PUF 1997). Major works translated into English: *Action* (1893), tr. O. BLANCHETTE (Notre Dame 1984); *The Letter on Apologetics & History and Dogma*, tr. A. DRU and I. TRETHOWAN (Grand Rapids 1994).

[O. BLANCHETTE]

BLONDIN, MARIE-ANNE SUREAU, BL.

Foundress of the Congregation of the Sisters of St. Anne; baptized as Marie Esther Blondin; b. April 18, 1809, Terrebonne, Quebec, Canada; d. Jan. 2, 1890 at the motherhouse of Lachine near Montreal. Born to the poor, illiterate farmers Jean-Baptiste Blondin and Marie-Rose Limoges, Esther learned to read and write in her 20s while a domestic, then boarder, at the local convent of the Notre Dame Sisters. She began her novitiate there but was forced to leave due to ill health in 1833. During her tenure as a parochial school teacher in Vaudreuil, she came to understand that the Church mandate for sexually segregated education contributed to the high rate of illiteracy, especially among girls. In 1848, she sought and received permission from Bp. Ignace Bourget to found a religious congregation to establish coeducational country schools. Blondin became the first mother superior of the six sisters of St. Anne at its founding (Sept. 8, 1850), although she was asked to resign on Aug. 18, 1854 due to a conflict with the community's chaplain, Fr. Louis-Adolphe Marechal. Under obedience to the bishop, she refused to accept re-election in 1854, 1872, and 1878. For a time she was directress of the St. Geneviève Convent, until recalled in 1858 to the motherhouse at St. Jacques de l'Achigan (now St. Jacques de Montcalm near Joliette). There and at Lachine (to which the motherhouse was transferred in 1964) she was served as laundress (1859–1890). She was a continual example to her community of charity and humility, punctuated by her request to make her final confession to and forgive her persecutor, Fr. Marechal. Blondin's cause was opened in 1950 by Abp. Paul-Émile Leger. She was declared venerable (May 14, 1991) and beatified (April 29, 2001) by Pope John Paul II.

Bibliography: *L'Osservatore Romano,* Eng. Ed. 18 (2001), 1, 6–8; 19 (2001), 7, 10. C. MAILLOUX *Esther Blondin: prophète pour aujourd'hui* (Montreal 1987). M. J. DE PATHMOS *A History of the Sisters of Saint Anne*, tr. SR. MARIE ANNE EVA (New York 1962).

[K. I. RABENSTEIN]

BLOOD, RELIGIOUS SIGNIFICANCE OF

''Blood'' is from a Germanic root with the basic meaning of ''bloom.'' The Greek term αἷμα, in the sense of something which ''arouses awe or reverence,'' belongs much more closely to the vocabulary of religion (see ''Blut,'' *Reallexikon für Antike und Christentum*, ed. T. Klauser, 2:459).

In Mythology. In Norse myths, the *skalds* characterize blood as an intoxicant on the basis of the myth of Odin's drink of the poets (*Edda, Skáldskaparmál* 27). Blood itself is not personified, probably because, unlike water, it did not appear prominently as a great natural force or power. However, it was brought into numerous mythical relations with other things, and especially with the sun. In Egypt Ra (the Sun) was said to have originated from drops of blood. The association, blood and fire, is self-evident, but in Mexico it plays an especially significant role in Aztec religion. On the other hand, the blood of menstruation turned the imagination to the moon. The Bambuti, for example, call menstrual blood ''moon-blood'' [P. Schebesta, *Die Bambuti. Pygmäen* (4 v., Brussels, 1938–50) 3:190]. Practically the same idea is present in the Egyptian hieroglyph signifying the blood of Isis. Since this blood was shed to restore the dead Osiris to life, there is a clear association here of blood and life. The ideas of the connection between blood, fertility, and earth are firmly anchored in ancestor-worship. A Papuan group has a myth in which this combination is associated with that of blood and fire. Belief in the vampire is not found in this complex. It has perhaps a special origin, being found to some extent perhaps in animism. E. Rohde made animism the basis for his detailed exposition of the relations between blood and the soul in Greek religion (see E. Rohde, *Psyche,* English tr., H. B. Hillis, London 1925). In totemism, the blood of circumcision is regarded as a totem, at least in isolated instances [see *Zeitschrift für Ethnologie* 76 (1951) 63].

Sociological, Cultic, and Magical Aspects. Incest is generally forbidden even in preethnic groups, the prohibition being based on a feeling of fear or dread. At the same time, in all such groups the duty of blood revenge is already in evidence. It originated out of the barbarous experiences of wanton bloodshed in the kinship group. An extension of the kinship group by the mingling of the blood of men of different family origins—a procedure that may be described as a kind of primitive peace ritual (see König, RelHdbch, ''Friedensritualien,'' 263)—is realized through the blood brotherhood.

The blood dance of the Bushmen has less of the religious in itself than the practice of sprinkling themselves with their own blood found among the Pygmies and the Pomo, for this procedure approaches the central concept of SACRIFICE. But in such practices, even if animals are killed to secure blood, as among the Yukaghirs, there is not yet question of a cultic act. It is only when such killing is thought of as an essential part of worship that blood sacrifice, including human sacrifice, especially to the sun, enters upon its development. Blood magic likewise enters only at this stage. It serves especially to give greater strength or power to implements, vessels, actions, or persons, playing a special role in bier ordeals.

In the Bible. The Biblical significance of blood is summed up in Leviticus 17.11: ''The life of a living body is in its blood.'' This basic principle governs the Biblical theology of blood. Life belongs to God, and so blood belongs to Him. This explains both the moral and the cultic practices in which blood has a part. Some texts that refer to blood evoke also the idea of death. Hence, some scholars make blood the symbol of death. But blood is a sign of death only when it is poured out. This is precisely how blood came to stand for life. Once blood has gone out of a body, death follows. Because of this symbolism, the Biblical concept of blood affected the moral and cultic life of the Israelites.

Moral Life. Men were forbidden to eat the blood of animals (Lv 3.17). Although the prohibition may have had its origin in hygienic considerations of the ancient world, the Mosaic Law assigned it a religious context. Because all life belonged to God, the blood of slain animals had to be poured on the altar, given to God (Lv 17.11). Those who lived too far from the sanctuary expressed their faith in God as the sole Lord of life by pouring the blood on the ground and covering it with earth (Dt 12.24; Lv 17.13).

Men are forbidden to shed the blood of other men. Those ''who shed the blood of the innocent'' incur bloodguilt, a crime punishable by death (Nm 35.1634). A ''brother's blood'' shed unjustly cries to heaven for vengeance (Gn 4.8–16). ''Men of blood,'' i.e., men who unjustly shed blood, are wicked, and the anger of God falls on them. The punishment of the offender rests with the avenger of blood (Nm 35.19; *see* BLOOD VENGEANCE) and with the whole community (Dt 21.8–9). God demands the punishment of the murderer because no one but God has the claim on blood, the life of another.

Cultic Life. Blood held the central place in animal sacrifice. It signified the flow of life between God and man. Poured out on the altar (representative of God), it joined the offerer to God because he had placed his hand on the animal and had become one with it. The blood was not a substitute for that of the offerer but a ritual expression of the total surrender to God. God received the blood and returned it to the offerer in the form of divine life. Thus the desired effect of sacrifice, communion with God, was achieved.

The covenant sacrifice of Sinai was especially significant in underlining blood as the sign of a flow of life between God and man (*see* COVENANT [IN THE BIBLE]). There God set up a special bond between Himself and His people. Moses took the blood of the sacrificial victims and sprinkled it partly on the altar and partly on the people, declaring, ''This is the blood of the covenant'' (Ex 24.8). The blood ratified the covenant and expressed externally what had happened. God and man had been joined together in an agreement of friendship, and the blood sprinkled on the altar and the people was a forceful expression of the union that had taken place.

Closely associated with the covenant of Sinai was the slaying of the PASSOVER LAMB and the sprinkling of the doorposts with its blood (Ex 12.1–13, 21–23). The blood of the lamb saved the Israelites from the death of their firstborn (Ex 12.26–30). The sacrifice of the lamb on the feast of the Passover became a ritual reminder that the people had been redeemed by the blood of the lamb. Thus blood entered the theology of redemption. It became a symbol of liberation (from slavery) and of acquisition (by God). The blood of the paschal lamb was witness to the faith that God does enter into contact with man to bestow the divine favor that the blood ritual signified.

Another significant sacrifice was that of the Day of Atonement (Leviticus chapter 16). The blood rite was especially elaborate on this day. The high priest entered the

Holy of Holies and sprinkled the propitiatory (the top of the ARK) with blood. The altars of incense and of holocausts also were sprinkled. These rites underlined the special power of blood in expiating sin. In fact, its special value in expiatory sacrifices generally came to be highlighted: ''It is the blood, as the seat of life, that makes atonement'' (Lv 17.11). The blood of the victim should not be viewed as a punishment for sin. It forgave sins because it liberated life. The life poured out on the altar was received by God, who returned it to the repentant sinner in the form of divine life. This restored him to a state of friendship with God.

The blood rite illumines the vocabulary of expiation—propitiation, atonement, justification. Blood is a propitiation for sin because it makes God propitious to the sinner. He looks favorably on him because the blood poured out symbolizes so well the broken heart of the sinner. Blood achieves the justification of the sinner because it makes him just or holy by bringing God's own life to him. Because it restores a relationship of friendship with God, it is blood of ''atonement''; the sinner is set ''at one'' with God (*see* EXPIATION [IN THE BIBLE]).

Sacrificial blood played a large part also in the ordination to Old Testament priesthood. The blood was used to anoint the ear, hand, and foot of those ordained (Exodus 29.20). The anointing of these extremities of the body together proclaimed that the whole man was dedicated to God. Surely this is the meaning of the final anointing in which the blood mixed with oil was sprinkled on the priests and their vestments. This made them ''sacred'' (Ex 29.21). The blood was the bearer of God's life to the priests. Ordination made them holy because they were totally immersed in God's own life.

On the religious significance of blood in the New Testament, *see* PRECIOUS BLOOD.

See Also: SACRIFICE.

Bibliography: F. RÜSCHE, *Blut, Leben und Seele* (Paderborn 1930). C. M. SCHRÖDER, *Blutglaube in der Religionsgeschichte* (Munich 1936). T. SCHIFNER, *Blutzauber und Anderes* (2d ed. Leipzig 1930). H. TEGNAEUS, *Blood-Brothers* (Uppsala 1951). L. MORALDI, *Espiazione sacrificale e riti espiatori . . . (Analecta biblica* 5; 1956). S. LYONNET, *De peccato et redemptione,* v.2 (Rome 1960) R. DE VAUX, *Les Sacrifices de l'Ancien Testament* (Paris 1964). E. F. SIEGMAN, ''Blood in the Old Testament,'' *Proceedings of the Precious Blood Study Week* (Rensselaer, Indiana 1957) 33–64. L. DEWAR, ''The Biblical Use of the Term Blood,'' *Journal of Theological Studies* 4 (1953) 204–08.

[A. CLOSS/R. T. SIEBENECK]

BLOOD VENGEANCE

Blood vengeance is a primitive form of the law of retribution according to which a kinsman must vindicate the rights of a relative whose blood has been shed. Even in civilized societies the force of this primitive law could still be felt. According to the ancient Greek concept every act of bloodshed, even when committed in self-defense, created a certain defilement that required purification (Plato, *Laws* 916). Not only the criminal but also his family was defiled until the slain man's life was appeased by exacting vengeance. The initial crime could easily lead to a series of mutual crimes, a blood feud, or vendetta. In primitive societies a whole family or even a whole clan was annihilated for a murder committed by one of its members.

Ancient Israel, too, had the practice of blood vengeance based on the law of talion according to which, to restore the loss suffered by a crime, repayment had to be made strictly in kind: ''Life for life, eye for eye, tooth for tooth'' (Ex 21.23–25). This law rests on both the principle of the sacredness of blood (Lv 17.14) and that of clan solidarity. In Israel's primitive way of thinking, life resides in the blood; when a man loses his blood, his life is extinguished (*see* BLOOD, RELIGIOUS SIGNIFICANCE OF). Blood, therefore, as the seat of life, belongs to Yahweh, and its wanton shedding demands the life of him by whom it is shed (Gn 9.5–6). Blood spilled on the ground cries to heaven for vengeance (Gn 4.10; Jb 16.18; Ez 24.6–8; 2 Mc 8.3), and an account is demanded from him who shed it (Gn 4.11; 9.6; 2 Sm 4.11; Ez 23.37, 45) by a near relative or avenger acting in Yahweh's name.

Clan solidarity, the second aspect of blood vengeance, is realized in the person of the avenger, who represents the interest of the family or clan of the one slain. The duty of blood vengeance was based on the theory that the family, clan, or tribe was a sacred unity. When the blood of any one member was shed, it was the community's blood that was shed; thus, it fell upon a representative of the community to atone for the crime by shedding the blood of the murderer.

Israel, however, endeavored to restrict the evils connected with blood vengeance. According to Israelite law only the murderer himself, not his family or clan, was to be punished for the crime (Dt 24.16; 2 Kgs 14.6; 2 Chr 25.4). Whereas earlier Israelite custom made no distinction between premeditated and unintentional killing (Gn 9.6), the more benign interpretation of the Deuteronomic law allowed a man who killed another unintentionally to seek refuge in certain designated cities of ASYLUM (Ex 21.13; Nm 35.9–29; Dt 19.1–13; Jos 20.3–9). If, after a fair trial, the slayer was judged guilty, the punishment was still the prerogative of the avenger of blood (Dt 19.12); he was not free to pardon the slayer or accept a monetary compensation in exchange.

Bibliography: W. E. MÜHLMANN, *Die Religion in Geschichte und Gegenwart,* 7 v. (3d ed. Tübingen 1957–6) 1:1331–32. W.

KORNFELD, *Lexikon für Theologie und Kirche,* ed. J. HOFER and K. RAHNER, 10 v. (2d, new ed. Freiburg 1957–65) 2:546. *Encyclopedic Dictionary of the Bible,* tr. and adap. by L. HARTMAN (New York 1963), from A. VAN DEN BORN, *Bijbels Woordenboek* 258–259. M. GREENBERG, in *The Interpreters' Bible,* ed. G. A. BUTTRICK, 4 v. (Nashville 1962) 1:321; 449–450. J. P. E. PEDERSEN, *Israel: Its Life and Culture,* 4 v. in 2 (New York 1926–40; repr. 1959) 378–392, 420–425. R. DE VAUX, *Ancient Israel, Its Life and Institutions,* tr. J. MC HUGH (New York 1961) 10–12.

[E. J. CIUBA]

BLOSIUS, FRANCIS LOUIS (DE BLOIS)

Benedictine abbot and spiritual writer; b. Donstienne (Flanders), 1506; d. Liessies, Jan. 7, 1566. Blosius was of the lesser nobility and, for a time, a page at the court of the Emperor Charles V, but at the age of 14 he entered the Benedictine abbey of Liessies in the Austrian Netherlands.

Discipline in this abbey was more or less relaxed, in a manner characteristic of the times. Blosius was regarded as an outstanding young man, and his old and well-meaning but weak abbot picked him as his successor. He was made coadjutor abbot in 1527, and in 1530 succeeded as abbot. Blosius found himself faced, not with the problem of extirpating grave scandals, but with that of revitalizing the whole spirit of the monastic life. Perhaps in his youthful ardor, he demanded too much too soon, but he seems to have come to terms with his community and turned it into a fervent one.

Blosius belonged to the contemplative tradition of the late Middle Ages; the ideal he held out before the soul was a continual sense, as far as was possible, of the presence of God. He did not as much lay stress upon achieving the ultimate union as is usual for writers in this tradition, but he was aware of it and described it in terms of Dionysian mysticism, as represented by the German school—Tauler and Suso. His program for the soul is meditation in a wide sense, interior conversations with the soul itself and with God—affective prayer. He knew that this depended on detachment from self-will in all its ramifications and conformity to the will of God. In the contemplative tradition, he made mortification consistent with this, and his teaching is excellent on that subject. As befits one whose life work was to turn a relaxed community into a fervent one, he understood the weakness of human nature.

Bibliography: *Works,* tr. B. A. WILBERFORCE, 7 v. (London 1925–30), comprises all his original spiritual writings, although he also made florilegia and wrote a few small controversial works. A complete list of the many editions would be lengthy and difficult to compile. *Acta Sanctorum* Jan. 1:430–456. G. DE BLOIS, *A Benedictine of the Sixteenth Century: Blosius,* tr. LADY LOVAT (London 1878).

[G. SITWELL]

BLOY, LÉON HENRI MARC

Novelist and pamphleteer; b. Périgueux, France, July 11, 1846; d. Bourg-la-Reine, Nov. 3, 1917. Bloy was of French-Spanish parentage and was imbued at an early age with anticlericalism in the Masonic atmosphere of his home. When he moved to Paris, he fell under the influence of the novelist Barbey d'Aurevilly, and soon, as a young and passionate disciple, he joined a coterie of writers who gathered around Villiers de l'Isle-Adam and Huysmans. An obscure mystical experience restored his Catholic faith, of which he claimed to be one of the last loyal defenders. His piety was both humble and haughty, and the violence of his literary language created a void around him. ''I travel before my exiled thoughts on a great pillar of silence,'' he said bitterly. In 1890 he married the convert daughter of a Danish professor. His subsequent life was spent with his family in work and poverty, for his writings won only a limited number of readers. Only after his death did his work become somewhat more widely known.

Bloy was romantic, sometimes mystical, and sometimes truculent. At times he wrote of the purest regions of the love of God and of exultant hope. He had a firm pen, and although his style was sometimes grandiose, it could also be sneering or grave; but he was always original. His temperament drew him to extreme positions. He was not interested in politics, social questions, or science, but he did not hesitate to castigate those he judged inferior to their tasks: the rich, the writers, the priests. His books reveal the need he felt for sanctity, and a horror of spiritual mediocrity. As different and remote as he was from PÉGUY, from Francis Jammes, and from CLAUDEL, Bloy nevertheless is included with them in the company of writers who rejuvenated French Catholic literature at the beginning of the 20th century. Besides his two novels, *Le Désespéré* (1887) and *La Femme Pauvre* (1890), he wrote his *Journal* (1892–1917), edited in four volumes with notes by his biographer, Joseph Bollery. His other works are *Le Sang du Pauvre* (1909), *Le Salut par les Juifs* (1892), and *Le Pélerin de l'Absolu* (1914).

Bibliography: J. BOLLERY, *Léon Bloy,* 3 v. (Paris 1953) contains some unedited documents. M. J. LORY, *La Pensée religieuse de Léon Bloy* (Paris 1951). R. MARITAIN, *Adventures in Grace,* tr. J. KERNAN (New York 1945). H. COLLEYE, *L'âme de Léon Bloy* (Paris 1930). P. TERMIER, *Introduction à Léon Bloy* (Paris 1930). P. ARROU, *Les Logis de Léon Bloy* (Paris 1946). A. BÉGUIN, *Léon Bloy: A Study in Impatience,* tr. E. M. RILEY (New York 1947).

[P. ARROU]

B'NAI B'RITH

Jewish service organization, founded in New York City in 1843. The Independent Order of B'nai B'rith (''sons of the covenant'') engages in educational and philanthropic programs in the areas of youth work, adult education, veterans' services, civic projects, international affairs, and aid to Israel, among others. There are also lodges in Latin America, Europe, Asia, and Africa. The Supreme Lodge is located in Washington, D.C. It claims to represent Jewish public opinion in the U.S. because of the breadth of its membership. Its Anti-Defamation League was established in 1913, and the Hillel Foundations in 1923. In 1990 B'nai B'rith International admitted women into full membership.

Bibliography: E. E. GRUSD, *B'nai B'rith; the Story of a Covenant* (New York 1966). D. MALKAM, *La fantastique histoire du B'nai B'rith: la plus importante organisation humanitaire juive mondiale* (Paris 1993).

[J. J. DOUGHERTY/EDS.]

BOBADILLA, NICOLÁS ALFONSO DE

One of the first companions of IGNATIUS OF LOYOLA; b. Bobadilla, León, Spain, *c.* 1509; d. Loreto, Italy, Sept. 23, 1590. He studied rhetoric and logic in Valladolid, philosophy and some theology at Alcalá, and more theology under the Dominicans in Valladolid, then went to Paris in 1533 to complete his studies. He joined Ignatius there and went to Italy, being ordained in Venice on June 24, 1537. In Italy he traveled through more than 70 dioceses as a preacher and missionary. He worked also in Germany (1541–48), in the Valtelline (1558–59), and in Dalmatia (1559–61). As he writes in his autobiography, he had dealings with eight popes, three emperors, numerous electors and German princes, and cardinals and prelates through all of Italy. He was a man of much talent and great contrasts, independent and impulsive, outstanding for both accomplishments and imprudences. The pope kept him from participating in Jesuit deliberations in Rome in 1539 and 1541, Charles V expelled him from Germany in 1548; after the death of Ignatius, Bobadilla's unsuccessful demands for modifications in the society caused papal intervention. His autobiography is an unburdening of his soul and contains many important notices for the early history of the Jesuits. He left a list of his own works, which are concerned with preaching, exegesis, and theology. His important plan of reform of the Church, presented to Paul IV in 1555, has been studied by P. de Leturia [*Estudios ignacianos*, v.1 (Rome 1957) 447–459]. His work on frequent and daily Communion was the only one of his works published during his lifetime.

Bibliography: J. F. GILMONT, *Les Écrits spirituels des premiers Jésuites* (Rome 1961). M. SCADUTO, *Storia della Compagnia di Gesù in Italia* (Rome 1964). R. BROIULLARD, *Catholicisme* 2:99100. E. LAMALLE, *Dictionnaire d'histoire et de géographie ecclésiastiques* 9:270–272.

[I. IPARRAGUIRRE]

BOBBIO, ABBEY OF

Founded by Irish monks, a well-known Benedictine center in the diocese of the same name, Province of Pavia, northern Italy, located on the Trebbia River. St. COLUMBAN, exiled from LUXEUIL, crossed the Alps and founded the abbey with several of his companions. The community was organized under the Rule of St. Columban; it adopted a part of the Benedictine observance in 643, but not until the 10th century did the BENEDICTINE RULE replace that of the founder. The monastery, soon dedicated to Columban, enjoyed the favor of the Lombard King Agilulf, even though it took a leading part in the struggle against ARIANISM in northern Italy. Columban was followed by other outstanding abbots who strengthened the spiritual and temporal resources of Bobbio, especially ATHALA, BERTULF, and Bobolenus (d. 652). Bobbio was the first monastery to be granted papal EXEMPTION (628), and the abbots were given pontifical rights in 643. Emperors from CHARLEMAGNE to FREDERICK I BARBAROSSA made liberal grants of land and revenues to the community, and abbots such as WALA and Gerbert of Aurillac (the future Pope SYLVESTER II) were important figures in their time. In 1014 Emperor HENRY II, on the occasion of his own coronation in Rome, persuaded Pope BENEDICT VIII to create Bobbio an episcopal see, and Abbot Petroaldus (d. 1027) became first bishop; for some time his successors were chosen from among the monks and continued to reside in the abbey. The next few centuries saw a gradual decline in the spiritual and intellectual work of the abbey as conflicts arose between the bishops and the monks over jurisdiction. The abbey was a part of the congregation of St. Justina from 1449 until it was seized and secularized by the French army in 1803. What remains of the monastery buildings is used as a school, and the abbey church, with the tomb of Columban, now serves the local parish. The bishopric of Bobbio, also suppressed in 1803, was reestablished by PIUS VII in 1817, and St. Anthony GIANELLI held the see from 1838 to 1846. In 1965 the diocese had about 25,000 Catholics in 70 parishes. It is suffragan to Genoa.

In the early Middle Ages the abbey was especially well known for its library. Columban brought the traditions of Irish scholarship with him when he came to northern Italy, and later abbots encouraged studies and acquired books. In the middle of the 8th century the learned DUNGAL left his library, including the *Antiphonary of Bangor,* to the abbey, and a 10th-century catalogue [ed. L. Muratori, *Antiquitates italicae* (Milan 1740) 3:817–824] shows the broad scope of the library's holdings. It was such libraries as that at Bobbio that preserved much of classical literature during the so-called DARK AGES. The Bobbio Missal was produced in the monastic SCRIPTORIUM in the early 10th century. A great number of the library's books were lost in the 17th and again in the 19th century, although some can still be found in the Ambrosian Library at Milan, the VATICAN LIBRARY, and the National Library at Turin.

Bibliography: Sources. C. CIPOLLA, ed., *Codice diplomatico del monastero di S. Colombano di Bobbio . . . ,* 3 v. (Rome 1918). G. S. M. WALKER, ed., *S. Columbani opera* (Scriptores Latini Hiberniae 2; Dublin 1957). Literature. L. H. COTTINEAU, *Répertoire topobibliographique des abbayes et prieurés,* 2 v. (Mâcon 1935–39) 1:400–402. A. WILMART, *Dictionnaire d'archéologie chrétienne et de liturgie,* ed. F. CABROL, H. LECLERCQ, and H. I. MARROU, 15 v. (Paris 1907–53) 2:935–962. F. BONNARD, *Dictionnaire d'histoire et de géographie ecclésiastiques,* ed. A. BAUDRILLART et al. (Paris 1912–) 9:275–284. P. VERRUA, *Bibliografia bobbiese* (Piacenza 1936). P. COLLURA, *Studi paleografici: La precarolina e la carolina a Bobbio* (Milan 1943); *San Colombano e la sua opera in Italia* (Bobbio 1953). G. PENCO, "Sull' influsso Bobbiese in Liguria," *Benedictina* 9 (1955) 175–181; *Storia del monachesimo in Italia dalle origini alla fine del medio evo* (Rome 1960), *passim,* but esp. 100–110. *Annuario Pontifico* (1965) 67.

[B. J. COMASKEY]

BOBOLA, ANDREW, ST.

Polish Jesuit missionary and martyr; b. Palatinate Province of Sandomir, Poland, 1591; d. Janow, May 10, 1657. From an old and distinguished family, he was educated in the Jesuit Academy at Vilna (1606–11). He entered the Society of Jesus in 1611 and studied classics and philosophy at Vilna, taught for two years at Grunsberg, studied theology at Vilna, and was ordained there in 1622. As pastor at Nieswiez he worked heroically among the plague-stricken in 1624. Except for a period of temporary retirement because of ill health (1643–49), he spent his life in missionary and pastoral work at Vilna and in the countryside, bringing whole villages of Orthodox believers back to communion with Rome. In the political, social, and religious wars between Poland and Russia involving the Eastern and Western Churches, Bobola was a marked man because of his religious activities. In the devastation of East Poland, he was cruelly martyred by Ukrainian Cossacks at Janow. Devotion to Bobola spread rapidly in Poland and Lithuania when his inexplicably incorrupt body was discovered 40 years after burial in the crypt under the ruins of the Jesuit church in Pinsk. The cause of beatification was at first delayed by the suppression of the Society of Jesus and then by the death of Pius VIII, who had summoned a congregation for the advance of the cause in 1830. He was beatified in 1853. Marshal Józef Pilsudski sent a postulatory letter for canonization to Benedict XV in 1920. Canonization finally occurred in 1938. Over a period of 280 years the body of Andrew Bobola endured many translations. Having been buried in Pinsk in 1657, the body was removed to Polotsk in White Russia in 1808 and in 1922 taken to Vitebsk and to Moscow, where it was concealed by the Bolshevik government until 1923. Upon the third request of Pius XI, it was released and taken to Rome in October of 1923. Shortly after canonization in 1938, it was conveyed through Slavic countries via Budapest and Cracow to Warsaw. During the German invasion of Poland in 1939, the body was removed from the cathedral to the Church of St. Andrew Bobola at Mokotow in Warsaw, where it may still be seen. The first church in America named for St. Andrew was consecrated in Dudley, Mass., Diocese of Worcester, on Feb. 21, 954.

Feast: May 16 (Jesuits).

Bibliography: C. MARESCHINI, *The Life of Saint Andrew Bobola of the Society of Jesus, Martyr,* tr. and ed. L. J. GALLAGHER and P. V. DONOVAN (Boston 1939); *Santo Andrea Bobòla, martire, della Comp. di Gesù* (Isola de Liri 1938). L. ROCCI, *Vito del B. Andrea Bobòla, martire polacco* (2d ed. Rome 1938). C. SOMMERVOGEL et al., *Bibliothèque de la Compagnie de Jésus* (Brussels-Paris 1890–1932) 11:1402–04. J. DOBRACZYNSKI, *Mocarz: opowiesc o św. Andrzeju Boboli* (2d ed. Warsaw 1993). P. BERNARD, *Dictionnaire d'histoire et de géographie ecclésiastiques,* ed. A. BAUDRILLART et al. (Paris 1912) 2:1641–44. J. N. TYLENDA, *Jesuit Saints and Martyrs* (Chicago 1998) 136–138.

[L. J. GALLAGHER]

BOCCACCIO, GIOVANNI

Poet and prose writer; b. probably Florence or Certaldo, Italy, July 1313; d. Certaldo, December 21, 1375. Legend has falsely portrayed the earliest circumstances of his life. Using pseudoautobiographical confidences, vague and mysterious to the point of enigma, that were scattered throughout the youthful works, the 19th century set out to construct an entrancing *vie romancée,* in which Boccaccio was thought to have been born in Paris of the love of a merchant and a gentlewoman, or even a princess, and later to have been the chosen lover of the beautiful illegitimate daughter of King Robert of Anjou, Fiammetta. If his father, Boccaccio di Chellino, representative of the powerful trading company of the Bardi, was actually in Paris during 1313, then Giovanni was born of an illegitimate affair of his mother at Certaldo or, more likely, at Florence.

He passed his infancy in the San Pier Maggiore section of Florence, in his father's house, where Margherita

Giovanni Boccaccio.

de' Martoli had come as wife; she was related to the Portinari (Beatrice's family), and perhaps directly from her or from his first teacher, Giovanni Mazzuoli da Strada, sprang the earliest indications of that Dantean cult that grew throughout his life. When hardly out of boyhood (perhaps about 1325), he was sent into business at Naples with the Bardi Bank, which controlled the finances of the Angevin court. This commercial experience was unhappy and was followed by an equally disappointing study of Canon Law. Boccaccio thereupon turned completely to literature, under the direction and with the advice of the most learned men of the Neapolitan court (e.g., Paolo VENETO, Paolo da Perugia, Andalò del Negro) and of such friends as Cino da Pistoia, Dionigi da San Sepolcro, Barbato da Sulmona, and Giovanni Barrili, who held up to him the example of Petrarch. The carefree and lordly life of the Angevin court and city, necessary meeting place of the Italo-French and the Arab-Byzantine cultures, also deeply influenced his formation.

Fiammetta Period. Against such a background, dominated by both avid cultural interests and easygoing pleasure, Boccaccio desired to weave his great romance of love, centering on the fickle and fascinating figure of Fiammetta and the various heady adventures that had brightened his youth. Though Fiammetta is missing from the elegant portrayal of the aristocratic Neapolitan society within the mythological setting in his first poem, *Caccia di Diana* (1334?), and from the flowing ottava rima of *Filostrato* (1335?), which deals with the Troilus-Cressida story, she dominates, directly or indirectly, Boccaccio's other works up to the eve of his masterpiece.

Filocolo, the romantic story of the adventures of Florio and Biancofiore—made all the more valuable by the digressions in which the self-taught young man shows his scholarly enthusiasm, by the autobiographical allusions, and by the storytelling techniques that foreshadow the *Decameron*—appears to have been produced about 1336 at the direct request of Fiammetta. *Teseida* (written about 1340–41, perhaps partly in Florence), which tells the story of the love of Arcita and Palemone for Emilia, inserts lyric motifs and love laments that seem to echo and develop the notes in the dedicatory letter to Fiammetta into his ambitious plan for a first Italian epic poem. The *Commedia della Ninfe* (entitled *Ninfale d'Ameto* by 14th-century scribes and editors) and the *Amorosa visione* (one form in 1341–42 alternating prose and verse, the other in 1342–43 in Dantean *terza rima*) seem to wish to elevate, by the allegorical literary forms of the prevailing Tuscan tradition, the figure of the beloved to a superhuman level. The *Elegia di Madonna Fiammetta* (composed between 1343 and 1344), the first modern psychological novel, inverts the roles of the two lovers and blends the subtlest motivations with the innermost impulses of an enamored feminine heart.

Thus, nearly all the youthful work of Boccaccio (and even more clearly the *Rime* of this period), though patently autobiographical, gives evidence of becoming dominated and almost paralyzed by the experiences of love and enthusiasm for culture. But the immediacy of the first writings gradually gives way to a psychological analysis more detached from the sorrowful matter of love, under an interpretative effort sometimes almost allegorical.

The failure of the Bardi Bank forced Boccaccio to return to Florence in 1340 to meet painful domestic difficulties that are reflected in the laments that crop up in the works and letters of those years. Far from alienating him from literary pursuits, however, these harsh realities put him into immediate contact with his city and the life of the mercantile society to which he belonged. After brief periods in Ravenna at the court of Ostasio da Polenta (1345–46) and at Forlì with Francesco Ordelaffi (1347), he was again at Florence in 1348, where he witnessed the terrible plague described in the introduction to his masterpiece.

The Decameron. Shortly before 1348, Boccaccio had sung in ottava rima in *Ninfale fiesolano* (1344–46?) the story of a fresh and gentle love in the enchanted environs of the Fiesolan countryside. In 1348 he began to prepare and lay out the *Decameron* (1348–51?), the work that splendidly crowns his youthful experiences and sums up his narrative and romantic preludes in a superb *summa* of medieval storytelling. The setting is this: to escape the horrors of the plague of 1348, seven young ladies and three young men retire to a Fiesolan hillside; to pass away the time, each one is to tell a story every day, except Friday and Saturday, on a theme and in the order decreed by the one in charge for that day. A hundred *novelle,* interspersed with depictions of the group's aristocratic way of life, are thus recounted in ten days. In this powerful and multiform narrative work, Boccaccio displayed the "human comedy" of a society captured in both daily and extraordinary battles against ill-fortune. It is, in other words, the extraordinary epic of Boccaccio's own mercantile class.

According to the most acceptable aesthetic canons of his time, moreover, Boccaccio attached to his varied and iridescent images a didactic value beyond the mere story. Through the ten days into which his 100 stories are arranged he wished to display the extent of man's capacity for good and evil. To this end he pictured man on an imaginary journey that begins with a bitter condemnation of vice (First Day) and concludes with an exaltation of virtue (Tenth Day), after being tested by the three great forces that, as instruments of Providence, are at work in the world (Fortune, Second and Third Days; Love, Fourth and Fifth; Genius, Sixth, Seventh, Eighth; the Ninth Day is a transitional episode).

External Trouble; Interior Growth. His father's death in 1349 plunged Boccaccio even more deeply into family difficulties, but his established literary fame impelled his fellow citizens to entrust him with various civic tasks. In 1350 they sent him as ambassador to the Lords of Romagna and—a more pleasant duty—to present ten gold florins to Sister Beatrice, the nun daughter of Dante, as indemnity for damages sustained by her family. He was named chamberlain for the commune in 1351 and then representative of the republic (in the negotiations for the acquisition of Prato) and ambassador to Ludwig of Bavaria; in 1354 and 1365 he was ambassador to Innocent VI and Urban V at Avignon and in 1367 presented the homage of Florence to Urban V on his return to Rome. But these honorable missions failed to extricate him from the deplorable condition into which the Bardi bankruptcy had cast him. In the hope of bettering his affairs, and prompted by the pleasant memories of his youthful years and the friendship of Niccolò Acciaiuoli who had become the real arbiter of the Angevin court, he betook himself to Naples in 1355, 1362, and again in 1370–71. Nothing came of these ventures, and he returned disillusioned and embittered to Certaldo, where he had withdrawn probably as early as 1361–62.

The material and temporal circumstances of these years, however, are of far less importance than his humanistic development, his cultural interests, and the religious evolution of his thought. These attitudes were already present in the poems and letters of about 1350, but they emerge clearly after his encounter with PETRARCH, the most fortunate and decisive encounter for Italian and European culture of the 14th century.

Petrarch's Influence. Boccaccio met Petrarch for the first time in 1350, having eagerly gone some miles outside Florence to greet him and invite him to be his house guest. Boccaccio spent weeks of unforgettable, animated discourse at Petrarch's home in Padua in the spring of 1351; he was again his guest in 1359 at Milan, in 1363 at Venice, and in 1368 at Padua. They engaged in a voluminous correspondence, constantly exchanged books and literary information, and from 1350 on were generally *seiuncti licet corporibus unum animo* (though physically separated, one in spirit) as Petrarch wrote. After 1360 especially, Boccaccio's house became one of the chief centers of early Italian humanism, the retreat wherein Coluccio Salutati, Giovanni Villani, Luigi Marsili, and many other early humanists received inspiration, the scriptorium from which flowed marvelous literary discoveries (from Varro to Martial, from Tacitus to Apuleius) and the new interest in Greek that Boccaccio first, among the literary men of the time, had mastered through his dogged, industrious relationship with Leonzio Pilato (1360–62).

These early humanistic attitudes continued to characterize the works of his maturity, which he corrected and recorrected to his death, and established in various editions. The *Genealogia Deorum gentilium* (1350–75) is a great dictionary of mythology, a monument of prehumanistic culture; the *Bucolicum carmen* (1351–66?) is a collection of eclogues that are allegorical or allusive to contemporary political events, on the model of Dante and Petrarch. *De montibus, silvis, fontibus* (1355–74?) is an inventory of classical and contemporary geographical culture; *De casibus virorum illustrium* (1356–74?), is designed to show the transience of earthly goods and the ruin in store for those who climb too high, with examples drawn from all epochs. *De mulieribus claris* (1360–75?) sketches the lives of the most noted heroines of antiquity and the Middle Ages up to Queen Giovanna of Naples.

Zeal for the Vernacular. Boccaccio's early humanism, both for these works and in his activity in promoting classical culture, seems less concerned with stylistic and rhetorical principles than does Petrarch's. It is less refined and tends to eclecticism; but it is always supported by a zealous love for poetry, so much so that he feels himself "wholly intended for poetry from as far back as the maternal womb'' (*Genealogia,* 15:10). Better than Petrarch, he—the first apostle of the Dantean cult—synthesizes the wonderful and uninterrupted tradition of the intellectual life, of poetry and culture, from antiquity to his own days. Though he was a chief discoverer of the treasures of ancient Hellas, his vision was not confined within the boundaries of the classics; it encompassed Christian authors, certain medieval writers, and poets who wrote in the vernacular. It is not without significance that the *Teseida,* the most ambitious of his youthful works, was modeled both on the great Latin epics and on the typically medieval *cantari;* that in the *Decameron* classical and later sources were drawn upon; that in the description of the plague that opens this masterpiece he mixes Lucretian facts, gained at second hand, with a page from Paolo Diacono; that his prose rhythms favor Livy more than Cicero, and even more the currently accepted rhetorics and *artes dictandi.*

It is further significant that, as in his youthful years he had constantly juxtaposed experiments in the vernacular with the required employment of Latin, so precisely during the most characteristically early humanistic years, when he became more directly involved with Greek literature, Boccaccio did not abandon his fond relationship with the muses of the new language and new literature. In witness of this stand the *Epistola consolatoria a Pino de' Rossi,* (1361–62), addressed to a friend exiled for political reasons; that harsh invective against women that stands out in the *Corbaccio* (1366?); the *Trattatello in laude di Dante* (1358–63?); and many vernacular letters to friends. In the same period, too, he undertook to correct and rework the *Amorosa visione* (which occasioned the *Trionfi* of Petrarch) and the final version of the *Decameron* (the Hamilton autograph). All of Boccaccio's activity, whether as writer or as forceful promoter of humanistic studies, is constantly marked by this notable bilingualism that is not merely verbal but mental and cultural, by this vigorous and vital mixture of ancient and contemporary methods and experiments, by this passion, not rhetorical but human, for poetry, for all poetry.

Precisely because of this profound passion, Boccaccio in those years gathered up and defined in the last two books of the *Genealogia Deorum* his aesthetic doctrine, a synthesis of the leading poetic ideas of the Middle Ages and of earlier discussions by the men of the generation before that—discussions that heralded the rapidly approaching debates during the chivalric years between 1300 and 1400. Against the doubts and uncertainties of many, Boccaccio shows the complete propriety and high mission of poetry *ex sinu Die procedens,* of poetry as the *anima mundi.*

Religious Maturity. Tactfully helped by the serene and profound Christianity of Petrarch, Boccaccio during these years also resolved into a firm religious sensibility the emotional instability of his youth. To consecrate this achievement he received minor orders and in 1360 permission to become a director of souls; he dedicated himself enthusiastically to the study of Dante, on whose ''sacred poem'' he began to lecture at the church of San Stefano di Badia (1373–74). Just as he was publicly exalting the genius of Dante, the death of Petrarch (July 19, 1374) left a void in his heart. All his writings from then on only repeat the lament for the loss of his great friend, for his own spiritual loneliness. In these final years Boccaccio repudiated the worldliness of his Decameron and even tried to destroy the work's manuscripts. Despite such attempts, he remained for his contemporaries almost hieratically fixed in the role of last survivor of the ''three crowns,'' the last champion of Italian letters.

Bibliography: *Opere,* ed. V. BRANCA (Milan 1964–); *Decameron,* ed. V. BRANCA (4th ed. Florence 1965); Eng. tr. J. M. RIGG, 2 v. (London 1947); *The Filostrato,* tr. N. E. GRIFFIN and A. B. MYRICK (Philadelphia 1929); *Amorous Fiametta,* tr. B. YOUNG, ed. K. H. JOSLING (London 1929); *The Nymph of Fiesole,* tr. D. J. DONNO (New York 1960); *The Life of Dante,* tr. P. H. WICKSTEED (San Francisco 1922); *Concerning Famous Women,* tr. G. A. GUARINO (New Brunswick, NJ 1963). Three basic but old bibliographies are: A. BACCHI DELLA LEGA, *Serie delle edizioni delle opere di Giovanni Boccaccio latine, volgari, tradotte e trasformate* (Bologna 1875). G. TRAVERSARI, *Bibliografia Boccaccesca* (Città di Castello 1907). V. BRANCA, *Storia della critica al ''Decameron'' con bibliografia boccaccesca..* (Rome 1939). On the MSS: see V. BRANCA, *Tradizione delle opere di Giovanni Boccaccio* (Rome 1958); ed., *Studi sul Boccaccio* (Florence 1963–). The biographies by G. BILLANOVICH, *Restauri boccacceschi* (Rome 1945) and V. BRANCA, *Schemi letterari e schemi autobiografici nell'opera del Boccaccio* (Florence 1946) are in strong reaction to the romance built up, on presumed autobiographical confessions, especially by V. CRESCINI, *Contributo agli studi di Boccaccio* (Turin 1887), A. DELLA TORRE, *La giovinezza di G. Boccaccio (1313–1341) proposta d'una nuova cronologia* (Città di Castello 1905), and H. HAUVETTE, *Boccace* (Paris 1914). T. C. CHUBB, *The Life of Giovanni Boccaccio* (New York 1930) C. CARSWELL, *The Tranquil Hearth: Portrait of Giovanni Boccaccio* (New York 1937). A. C. LEE, *The Decameron: Its Sources and Analogues* (London 1909). E. G. PARODI, *Lingua e Letteratura,* 2 v. (Venice 1957). U. BOSCO, *Il Decameron: Saggio* (Rieti 1929). B. CROCE, *Poesia popolare e poesia d'arte* (Bari 1933). V. BRANCA, *Boccaccio medievale* (Florence 1956). H. G. WRIGHT, *Boccaccio in England: From Chaucer to Tennyson* (London 1957). G. GETTO, *Vita di forme e forme di vita nel Decameron* (Turin 1958). A. D. SCAGLIONE, *Nature and Love in the Late Middle Ages: Chiefly an Essay in the Cultural Context of the Decameron* (Berkeley 1963). R. WITT, *In the Footsteps of the Ancients* (Leiden 2000). E. H. WILKINS, *Studies on Petrarch and Boccaccio* (Padua 1978).

[V. BRANCA]

BOCCARDO, GIOVANNI MARIA, BL.

Diocesan priest and founder of the Congregation of the Poor Daughters of Saint Cajetan; b. Testona di Moncalieri (near Turin), Italy, Nov. 20, 1848; d. Pancalieri, Italy, Dec. 30, 1913. Giovanni Boccardo studied at the diocesan seminary of Turin and was ordained (1871). For the next eleven years he provided spiritual direction to seminarians in Chieri and Turin. His first parochial appointment was to Pancalieri in 1882, and he remained there until his death. Although he enjoyed the seminary, he viewed his parochial assignment as an opportunity for evangelization. When cholera struck the village (1884), he personally tended the sick. Afterwards he established the Hospice of Charity to care for those left abandoned or homeless by the epidemic, including orphans and the poor elderly. He founded the Poor Daughters of St. Cajetan to continue the work of the hospice. Within a few years the congregation spread throughout Italy. He was beatified in Milan, by John Paul II, May 24, 1998.

Bibliography: G. COSTA, *Ma chi è stato Giovanni M. Boccardo?* (Pinerolo 1976).

[K. I. RABENSTEIN]

BOCCHERINI, LUIGI

Rococo composer who helped crystallize the classical style, baptized Ridolfo Luigi; b. Lucca, Italy, Feb. 19, 1743; d. Madrid, May 25, 1805. His father, Leopold, a contrabass player, gave him his first violoncello lessons, and Luigi was playing professionally at 13. Further work with local teachers led him in 1757 to Rome, where he was exposed to the Palestrina style. Publication of his first collection of string quartets (1764) and recital tours with violinist Filippo Manfredi so impressed the Spanish ambassador to Paris that in 1768 he was named composer and virtuoso to the Infante Don Luis of Spain. After Luis's death in 1785, Boccherini joined Friedrich Wilhelm II of Prussia, an amateur cellist to whom he dedicated his celebrated Cello Concerto. The king's death (1797) freed him to return to Madrid, where in late 1800 his momentary patron was Lucien Bonaparte, French ambassador. Thereafter he supported his family with such hackwork as scoring his works for guitar *aficio nados,* but still maintaining his creative pace undaunted by poverty, intrigues, or family sorrows. He died as he had lived, a gentle Christian. Ceremonial return of his body to Lucca in 1927, plus the onset of long-play recording, triggered a thorough reappraisal of his music. Current research has refuted the ''wife of [F. J.] Haydn'' canard, and Boccherini is now regarded as the peer of pre-Mozart classicists. Although he was too much the lyricist and too timidly the contrapuntist to achieve stature as a symphonist, his chamber and other instrumental works reveal a perfection of form, instrumental inventiveness, and a civilized, contemplative beauty that is heightened by its unique infusion of autochthonous Spanish idioms. Of some 370 known works, the religious group includes a Mass for four voices and instruments; a cantata, villancicos, and motets for Christmastide; a pair of oratorios; and a *Stabat Mater* for three voices and strings that proves richer and more mature than PERGOLESI's, with which it is often compared.

Bibliography: L. PICQUOT, *Notice sur la vie et les ouvrages de Luigi Boccherini, suivie du catalogue raisonné . . .* (Paris 1851). G. DE SAINT-FOIX, *Boccherini: Notes et documents nouveaux* (Paris 1930), contains and updates Picquot. A. BONAVENTURA, *Boccherini* (Milan 1931). G. DE ROTHSCHILD, *Luigi Boccherini: Sa vie, son oeuvre* (Paris 1962). K. STEPHENSON, *Die Musik in Geschichte und Gegenwart,* ed. F. BLUME (Kassel-Basel 1949–) 2:1–6. C. F. POHL, *Grove's Dictionary of Music and Musicians,* ed. E. BLOM, 9 v. (5th ed. London 1954) 1:778–779. ''Lucca a Luigi Boccherini,'' *Lucchesia,* 5 (Oct. 9, 1927) special issue. A. BONACCORSI, ''Boccherini e il *Stabat,*'' *La rassegna musicale,* 19 (April 1949) 92–97. P. H. LÁNG, *Music in Western Civilization* (New York 1941). A. BROUDE, ''More about Luigi Boccherini: A Virtuoso Cellist-Composer,'' *Violoncello Society, Inc. Newsletter,* fall (1983) 1–5. P. GRIFFITHS, *The String Quartet: A History* (New York 1983) 24–26. D. HEARTZ, ''The Young Boccherini: Lucca, Vienna, and the Electoral Courts,'' *Journal of Musicology,* 13 (1995) 103–116. T. P. NOONAN, ''Structural Anomalies in the Symphonies of Boccherini'' (Ph.D. diss. University of Wisconsin at Madison 1996). J. A. BOCCHERINI SÁNCHEZ, ''Los testamentos de Boccherini,'' *Revista de Musicología,* 22 (1999) 93–121. J. TOTELLA, ''Líneas alternativas de investigación musicológica: El caso de Luigi Boccherini cerca del Banco de San Carlos,'' *Revista de Musicología,* 21 (1998) 531–552; *Luigi Boccherini y el Banco de San Carlos: un aspecto inédito* (Madrid 1998).

[M. E. EVANS]

BOCKING, EDWARD

English Benedictine, one of the chief associates of Elizabeth BARTON, the Nun of Kent; b. *c.* 1490; d. Tyburn, April 20, 1534. Bocking was educated at Oxford (D.D., 1518), and elected prior of Canterbury College there. Later, he became cellarer at the Benedictine cathedral priory of Christ Church, Canterbury, and in 1525 he headed a commission to inquire into Elizabeth Barton's prophecies. The result favored her, and Bocking was appointed her spiritual adviser after she had joined the Benedictine convent of St. Sepulchre's, Canterbury. The nun's reputation for sanctity grew, but trouble arose when her prophecies took on a political complexion at the time of the divorce, and the government was forced to take action in 1533. Dr. Bocking, in his dealings with Elizabeth Barton, had probably acted imprudently, but it is unlikely that he practiced willful deceit. His fate was inevitably linked with hers; and when she was condemned with others by attainder in 1534, after probably having made some sort of confession about her revelations, Bocking suffered with her and the rest. They were all executed at Tyburn on April 20, 1534.

Bibliography: D. KNOWLES, *The Religious Orders in England* (Cambridge, Eng. 1948–60). H. A. L. FISHER, *History of England 1485–1547* (London 1906).

[J. E. PAUL]

BODEY, JOHN, BL.

Layman, martyr, b. Somersetshire, England, 1550; d. Andover, Nov. 2, 1583. The son of a devout Catholic mother and a wealthy merchant and mayor of Wells, he attended Winchester College and New College, Oxford. He received an M.A. in February 1576; that year he was deprived of his Oxford fellowship by Bishop Horne of Winchester because of his Roman Catholicism. He left Oxford and began the study of civil law at Douai, returning to England in February 1578. He seems to have acted as a schoolmaster until 1580, when he was arrested with John Slade and imprisoned at Winchester. Two of the jailers were converted by them, and tradition says that their edifying behavior won many to Catholicism. For some reason not clear, John Slade and John Bodey were tried twice, once at Winchester and then again at Andover in August 1583. They were sentenced to death for denying that the queen had any supremacy over the Church in England; yet they publicly acknowledged the queen as their lawful sovereign. Bodey was declared venerable by Leo XIII in 1886, and beatified by Pius XI in 1929.

Bibliography: R. CHALLONER, *Memoirs of Missionary Priests,* ed. J. H. POLLEN (new ed. London 1924). J. H. POLLEN, *Acts of English Martyrs* (London 1891).

[B. C. FISHER]

BODHISATTVA

In Pāli *bodhisatta,* a term meaning "Wisdom Being," first applied to an incarnation of a candidate to Buddhahood, similar to the previous incarnations of Buddha narrated in the *Jātakas* (Birth Stories). In early BUDDHISM only a few zealous and persevering beings could be saved. But from the 1st century A.D., partly under Zoroastrian, Hellenic, and Christian influences, MAHĀYĀNA made Buddhahood accessible to all conscious beings with a mind for the truth (bodhicitta). "Bodhisattva" took on a dual meaning. On a lower level, the term applied to the ordinary believer who took the vow to gain supreme enlightenment for the sake of all suffering beings (in fact, an early term for the nascent Mahāyā movement was "bodhisattvayāa," the "vehicle of the bodhisattva "). Above the ordinary bodhisattvas are a divine compassionate savior who, upon developing Buddhahood through the practice of the perfections (*pāramitā*) of charity, morality, patience, zeal, meditation, and wisdom, along with accommodation, vows, determination, and understanding, postponed *nirvāna* and underwent endless rebirths until all conscious beings who invoked him with faith could be saved. Inspired by this merciful soteriological teaching, all good Mahāyāanists strove after the bodhisattva ideal. Above the ordinary bodhisattvas are the great bodhisattvas (mahābodhisattvas), who, on becoming Heavenly Buddhas, save the faithful by the transference (*parināma*) of their merit. The most popular Heavenly Buddha is Amitabha, assisted by Avalokiteśvara (Chinese, Kuan-yin; Japanese, Kannon), the God or Goddess of Mercy, Mañjuśri, the Begetter of Wisdom, and Maitreya, the Forthcoming Savior.

See Also: ZOROASTER (ZARATHUSHTRA).

Bibliography: H. DAYAL, *The Bodhisattva Doctrine in Buddhist Sanskrit Literature* (London 1932). NARADA THERA, *The Bodhisattva Ideal* (Colombo, Ceylon 1944). YÜ CHÜN-FANG, *Kuan Yin: The Chinese Transformation of Avalokiteśvara* (New York 2001). P. WILLIAMS, *Mahāyā Buddhism: The Doctrinal Foundations* (London 1989).

[A. S. ROSSO/C. B. JONES]

BOEHM, JOHN PHILIP

German Reformed mininster; b. Höchstädt, Germany, 1683; d. Whitpain, Pennsylvania, April 29, 1749. Boehm was the son of a Reformed minister and became a schoolmaster at Worms, Germany, before coming to the United States in 1720. After serving Reformed congregations in Montgomery Co., Pennsylvania as a lay reader (1725–29), he was ordained at the Dutch Reformed Church in New York City in 1729. In 1730 he became pastor of churches in Philadelphia and Germantown, Pennsylvania. He resisted the efforts of Count Nicholas Zinzendorf to unite the Reformed congregations with the Moravians from 1741 to 1743. With Rev. Michael Schlatter, Boehm formed the Synod of the Reformed Church in Pennsylvania, the first synod of this church in America, in 1747.

Bibliography: J. P. BOEHM, *Life and Letters,* ed. W. J. HINKE (Philadelphia 1916). H. DOTTERER, *Rev. John Philip Boehm* (Philadelphia 1890).

[R. K. MACMASTER]

BOEHM, MARTIN

Cofounder of the Church of the UNITED BRETHREN in Christ; b. Conestoga, Pennsylvania, Nov. 30, 1725; d. Conestoga, Pennsylvania, March 23, 1812. Boehm was the son of a German-born blacksmith and Mennonite

The Bodhisattva Kannon sits in contemplation on an island off the coast of southern India, the traditional home of the Buddhist deity Avalokitesvara. Kannon, who carried the soul of the dying believer to paradise, was the best loved deity of the Pure Land sect of Buddhism in Japan. (©Asian Art & Archaeology, Inc./CORBIS)

elder. After becoming a Mennonite preacher in 1756, he came under the influence of the Great Awakening through disciples of George Whitefield. In 1767 Boehm met Philip William Otterbein, a minister of the Reformed Church, and their association led to the formation of the Church of the United Brethren. Boehm was also closely associated with Bp. Francis Asbury and other early Methodists, with whose theology he agreed. He was a preacher of religious revival among German settlers in Pennsylvania, Maryland, and Virginia for more than 50 years, and he was made bishop of the Church of the United Brethren in 1800.

Bibliography: B. E. FOGLE, *Martin Boehm* (Dayton 1956). H. BOEHM, *Reminiscences . . . of Sixty-four Years in the Ministry* (New York 1866). A. W. DRURY, *History of the Church of the United Brethren in Christ* (Dayton 1924).

[R. K. MACMASTER]

BOEHNER, PHILOTHEUS HEINRICH

Medievalist, philosopher, and botanist; b. Lichtenau (Westphalia), Germany, Feb. 17, 1901; d. St. Bonaventure, New York, May 22, 1955. Boehner entered the Holy Cross (Saxonia) Province of the Order of Friars Minor in 1920 and was ordained in 1927. He began his career as a medievalist by translating into German É. Gilson's studies: *Der heilige Bonaventura* (Hellerau 1929), *Der heilige Augustin, Eine Einführung in seine Lehre* (Hellerau 1930), *Die Mystik des heiligen Bernhard von Clairvaux* (Wittlich 1936); and coauthored their *Die Geschichte der christlichen Philosophie* (Paderborn 1937). Majoring in botany and minoring in philosophy at the University of Münster (1929–33), he published as a doctoral dissertation *über die thermonastischen Blütenbewegungen bei der Tulpe [Zeitschrift der Botanik* 26 (1933) 65–107]. He taught philosophy and biology at the Franciscan studium in Dorsten (1933–39); then he went to the Pontifical Institute of Mediaeval Studies (Toronto) to edit the logic of William of Ockham. At the outbreak of World War II, he entered the U.S. and was naturalized. Noted for text editions and studies in 14th-century logic and Ockham's philosophy, he became first director of the Franciscan Institute research center at St. Bonaventure University; there he initiated the new series of *Franciscan Studies* (1941), *Franciscan Institute Publications* (1944), and the *Cord*, a review for Franciscan spirituality (1950).

Bibliography: G. GÁL, "Philotheus Boehner," in H. DAMICO, ed., *Medieval Scholarship. Biographical Studies on the Formation of a Discipline. Volume 3: Philosophy and the Arts.* (Garland, N.Y. 2000) 119–130. E. BUYTAERT, "Bibliography of Fr. Philotheus Boehner, O.F.M.," *Franciscan Studies* 15 (1955) 321–331. "In Memoriam," *Franciscan Studies* 15 (1955) 101–105. Franziskanische Studien 37 (1955) 292–298. *Cord* 5 (1955) 206–215.

[A. B. WOLTER]

BOETHIUS

Anicius Manlius Torquatus Severinus Boethius, philosopher and statesman; b. Rome, *c.* 480; d. near Pavia, *c.* 524. Educated in Athens and Alexandria, Boethius has been called a founder of the Middle Ages because of his lasting influence on the formation of medieval thought. His father was a consul in 487 under the Arian king of the Ostrogoths, Theodoric the Great (475–526), and in 510 he himself held the consulship. Accused of treason, Boethius was later imprisoned and put to death. During his long imprisonment, he wrote the *Consolation of Philosophy*, a work read by every educated man for more than 1,000 years. In it he describes the pursuit of wisdom and the love of God as the true source of human happiness.

Works. While one of his students, CASSIODORUS (*c.* 485– *c.* 580), employed the translator Epiphanius to make the Greek Fathers available to Latin readers, Boethius planned to translate into Latin the entire body of writings by Aristotle and Plato and to show their basic agreement in philosophy. It seems that only a small part of this farsighted project was carried out, however. Still extant is his translation (510) of Aristotle's *De Interpretatione*, which he explains in two commentaries, one for beginners (511) and one for more advanced students of logic (513). Also still in existence is his translation of Aristotle's *Categories* with a commentary written in 510. Before 505 he had already composed a commentary on Porphyry's *Isagoge*, translated by MARIUS VICTORINUS. Later (509) he decided to make his own translation of the *Isagoge* and comment on it (509–510). He mentions a translation of Aristotle's *Topics* and *Prior Analytics* (*Patrologia Latina*. 64: 1173C; 1216D; 1184D), perhaps still extant in MS Oxford, Trin. Coll. 47 (*Topics*) and MSS Chartres 497–498 (excerpts from the *Analytics*). The translations of Aristotle's two *Analytics,* his *Topics* and *Elenchi*, published under Boethius's name (*Patrologia Latina*. 64:639–762; 909–1040), date back to James of Venice (*c.* 1128).

Between 513 and 515, he wrote a commentary on Cicero's *Topics,* part of which is lost (*Patrologia Latina*. 64:1039–1174). In addition, Boethius wrote *An Introduction to Categorical Syllogisms* (*Patrologia Latina*. 64:761–94), two books each *On the Categorical Syllogism* (*Patrologia Latina*. 64:793–832) and, in 514, *On the Hypothetical Syllogism* (*Patrologia Latina*. 64:831–876).

While the book entitled *De divisione* (*Patrologia Latina*. 64: 875–92) is authentic, the *De definitione,* attribut-

"Boethius and Philosophy Personified." (Bettman/CORBIS)

ed to him (*Patrologia Latina.* 64:891–910) is the work of Marius Victorinus. Also spurious are the attributions to Boethius of the *De unitate et Uno* (*Patrologia Latina.* 63:1075–78), written by DOMINIC GUNDISALVI, and of the *De disciplina scholarium* (*Patrologia Latina.* 64: 1223–38), whose unknown author lived in the 13th century. It is believed that about 520 Boethius composed the *Theological Tractates,* known as *Opuscula sacra,* which were to establish him as a theological authority almost equal to St. Augustine in questions concerning the Blessed Trinity and the Incarnation.

Teaching. Boethius's literary activities began in the field of logic, which is a necessary tool for all the sciences, especially philosophy. The famous definition of PHILOSOPHY as ''love of wisdom,'' found in his first commentary on Porphyry's *Isagoge,* is interpreted by him as the quest for God, the root of all being and knowledge (*Patrologia Latina.* 64:10D–11A).

Division of Philosophy. Boethius divides philosophy into two kinds: practical and speculative (or theoretical). Practical philosophy is subdivided into three parts: ethics, which teaches man as an individual how to direct his moral actions; politics, which teaches how the state is to be governed in accordance with the four cardinal virtues; and economics, which concerns the proper conduct of family life (*Patrologia Latina.* 64:11D–12A). Speculative philosophy is likewise subdivided into three parts: natural philosophy, also called physiology, which studies the nature of physical bodies as they exist in reality; mathematics, which deals with the forms of physical bodies by way of abstraction from matter and motion; and theology, which studies forms existing without matter and motion, such as God and souls (*Patrologia Latina.* 64: 11B–C). Natural philosophy deals with objects as presented by the senses. Mathematics studies the many forms abstracted by the intellect from such objects, to distinguish between the various forms that cause a physical body to be quantitative (large, small) or qualitative (red, warm, soft, etc.). Theology rises above these material objects and contemplates God as the immaterial Form that is the source of all other being,''for everything owes its being (*esse*) to Form'' (*De Trin.* 2).

Liberal Arts. To the people living during the Middle Ages, Boethius transmitted the Roman concept of education comprised of the seven LIBERAL ARTS known as the trivium (logic, grammar, rhetoric) and the quadrivium (arithmetic, geometry, astronomy, music), the ''quadruple road to wisdom''. He himself wrote *On Arithmetic* (*Patrologia Latina.* 63:1079–1168) and *On Music* (*Patrologia Latina.* 63:1167–1300), though not the two works titled *On Geometry* that have been attributed to him (*Patrologia Latina.* 63:1307–52 and 1352–64).

Universals. The Middle Ages inherited from Boethius a keen interest in the problem of UNIVERSALS. In his endeavor to reconcile ARISTOTELIANISM and PLATONISM, he dealt at length with general ideas, or universals, as discussed in logic by PORPHYRY. His blending of the two different conceptions accounts for the confusion reflected in the divergent interpretations that divided medieval scholars from the days of ABELARD. Boethius himself leaned toward Plato; the question whether universals are real or simply conceptions of the mind he answered in the sense that universals (GENUS, SPECIES) are not only conceived separately from bodies, but also exist outside of them.

This view is based on the nature of being as understood by Boethius. Each thing owes its being to a number of forms that determine it to be the kind of thing it is. God is the Supreme Form, a pure form without matter. Lacking all composition, He is absolutely one. Creatures, on the other hand, are composed of parts or of a plurality of forms. An individual thing is a SUBSTANCE because it underlies accidents. If such a substance is of a rational nature, it is called a PERSON. A substance becomes a substance by means of a subsistence, a term applicable to all created substantial forms. Numerical difference is the result of a variety of accidents.

Theology. It used to be disputed widely whether or not Boethius was a Christian. The fact that he has been venerated as a Christian martyr at Pavia was officially recognized by Rome in 1883. Doubts were raised in view of the apparent absence of specifically Christian teaching in his most popular and final work, *Consolatio philosophiae.* It is, however, generally admitted that toward the end of his life Boethius turned his attention to theology and produced then the *Opuscula sacra.* He tells us that before writing his first tract, *De Trinitate*, he had studied the writings of Augustine and that he deliberately adopted ''new and unaccustomed words'' in the exposition of the mystery. Characteristic of his thoroughness is the analysis of the Aristotelian categories and the statement: ''But when these categories are applied to God they change their meaning entirely'' (*De Trinitate.* 4). The explanation culminates in the summary conclusion: ''So then, the category of substance preserves the Unity, that of relation brings about the Trinity'' (*De Trinitate.* 6). Boethius addressed this work to his father-in-law and former consul Quintus Aurelius SYMMACHUS.

To John the Deacon he addressed a shorter tract on the Trinity and a treatise against Eutyches and Nestorius, often called the *Liber de persona et duabus naturis*, in which he clarifies the various meanings of the term *nature* and defines *person* as ''an individual substance of a rational nature'' (*C. Eutych.* 3).

More philosophical than these tracts is his brief exposition generally known as *De hebdomadibus*. In it, the conclusion is reached that the being of all existing things is good because God, who gave them being, is good. Boethius answers the objection that by parity of reason all things ought to be just because God, who willed them to be, is just, by saying that to be good involves being, while to be just involves an act. In God, being and action are identical, but they are not identical in creatures.

There is no general consensus concerning the authenticity of the tract entitled *De fide catholica;* most historians, however, hold that Boethius wrote it. The tract summarizes such doctrines as that of the Trinity and rejects the tenets of Arius, the Sabellians, and the Manichaeans. Speaking of the Church, the author declares, ''This Catholic Church spread throughout the world is known by three particular marks: whatever is believed and taught in it has the authority of the Scriptures, or of universal tradition, or of local and more restricted Regulation'' (*De fide*, *Patrologia Latina*. 64:1338A). He teaches that all corruptible things shall pass away, that men shall rise for future judgment, that each shall receive reward according to his deserts, and that the reward of bliss will be the contemplation of the Creator. The author finally speaks of the heavenly city ''where the Virgin's Son is King and where will be neverending joy, delight, food, achievement, and unending praise of the Creator'' (*ibid.* 1338B).

Influence. The doctrinal influence of Boethius reached its peak in the 12th century in the commentaries written by scholars of the school of Chartres. But only one of them, GILBERT DE LA PORRÉE, wrote commentaries on all four *opuscula sacra* (1, 2, 3, 5) generally accepted as authentic. THIERRY OF CHARTRES and his disciple, CLARENBAUD OF ARRAS, are known to have commented on the first and third *Tractates*. Clarenbaud openly accuses both Abelard and Gilbert of erroneous doctrines based on their misunderstanding of Boethius. The earliest commentary on the first *Tractate* was written by the Carolingian philosopher REMIGIUS OF AUXERRE. Many marginal and interlinear glosses are still found in the libraries of Europe. In the 13th century St. THOMAS AQUINAS commented on the first *Tractate*.

The *Tractates* were first translated into English in 1926 by H. F. Stewart. However, translations of the *Consolation* have a much longer history: King Alfred the Great (849–899) translated it into Anglo-Saxon; Notker Labeo (*c.* 950–1022) made the first German translation; the Greek monk Maximos Planudes (1260–1310) translated it into Greek; and the French rendition by Jean (Clopinel) de Meung (*c.* 1240–*c.* 1305) is well known. While in prison, Albert of Florence (*floruit* 1323–32) wrote an outstanding Italian translation, Geoffrey Chaucer (*c.* 1340–1400) translated it between 1372 and 1386, and even Elizabeth, Queen of England (1533–1603), translated what the English historian Edward Gibbon (1737–94) called ''a golden volume, not unworthy of the leisure of Plato or of Tully.'' The English translation in vogue at present dates back to the 17th century. Only the initials (I.T.) of the translator's name are known.

See Also: SCHOLASTICISM, 1.

Bibliography: A list of editions is found in E. DEKKERS and A. GAAR, *Sacris eruditi* 3 (1951) 153–156. E. DEKKERS, ed. *Clavis Patrium latinorum* (Steenbrugge 1961) 196–198. F. L. CROSS, *The Oxford Dictionary of the Christian Church* (London 1957), 181–182. Studies and Bibliographies. É. H. GILSON, *History of Christian Pilosophy in the Middle Ages* (New York 1955). A. A. MAURER, *Medieval Philosophy,* v.2 of *A History of Philosophy,* ed. É. H. GILSON, 4 v. (New York 1962–). Copleston 2:101–104. D. KNOWLES, *The Evolution of Medieval Thought* (Baltimore 1962). H. R. PATCH, *The Tradition of Boethius* (New York 1935). H. M. BARRETT, *Boethius: Some Aspects of His Time and Works* (Cambridge, Eng. 1940). P. GODET, *Dictionnaire de théologie catholoque.* 2.1:918–922. M. CAPPUYNS, *Dictionnaire d'histoire et de géographie ecclésiastiques* 9:348–380. P. COURCELLE, *Les Lettres grecques . . . à Cassiodore* (rev. ed. Paris 1948); ''Étude critique sur les commentaires de la Consolation de Boèce,'' *Archives d'histoire doctrinale et littéraire du moyen–âge* 14 (1939) 5–140. J. P. MINGE, ed. *Patrologia Latina.* (Paris 1878–90).

[N. M. HARING]

BOETHIUS OF SWEDEN (DACIA)

Aristotelian philosopher; b. probably Denmark, first half of the 13th century; place and date of death unknown. The theory that he was of Swedish origin and a canon of the Diocese of Linköping has been seriously questioned by S. S. Jensen [''On the National Origin of the Philosopher Boetius de Dacia,'' *Classica et Mediaevalia* 24 (1963) 232–41]. As a secular cleric he taught philosophy in the faculty of arts at Paris, where he was associated with SIGER OF BRABANT in the Averroist movement condemned at Paris in 1270 and 1277. Later he probably became a Dominican of the province of Dacia. Boethius staunchly defended the freedom of philosophy from religion, teaching the eternity of the world and of the human species and denying creation and the Resurrection. However, he did not abandon the Christian faith but tried unsuccessfully to reconcile it with his philosophy. He claimed that faith teaches the truth, though reason sometimes contradicts it. Boethius wrote many commentaries on Aristotle, some of which are lost. His only published works are *De summo bono, De sompniis,* and *De aeternitate mundi.*

See Also: AVERROISM, LATIN

Bibliography: M. GRABMANN, *Neuaufgefundene Werke des Siger von Brabant und Boetius von Dacien* (Munich 1924); ''Die

Opuscula De Summo Bono sive De Vita Philosophi und De Sompniis des Boetius von Dacien,'' *Archives d'histoire doctrinale et littéraire du moyen-âge* 6 (1931) 287–317; *Mittelalterliches Geistesleben,* 3 v. (Munich 1925–56) 200–24. G. SAJÓ, ''Boetius de Dacia und seine philosophische Bedeutung,'' *Die Metaphysik im Mittelalter,* ed. P. WILPERT (Miscellanea Mediaevalia, 2; Berlin 1963) 454–63; ed., *De Aeternitate Mundi* (Berlin 1964). É. H. GILSON, *History of Christian Philosophy in the Middle Ages* (New York 1955) 399–402, 725.

[A. MAURER]

BOGARÍN, JUAN SINFORIANO

Paraguayan archbishop and patriot; b. Mbuyapey, Paraguay, Aug. 21, 1863; d. Asunción, Feb. 25, 1949. Bogarín, son of Juan José Bogarín and Mónica de la Cruz González, was outstanding among the prelates who governed the Church in Paraguay after its independence from Spain, not only for the length of his episcopate (54 years), but especially for the great work of national reconstruction that he accomplished. For 35 years he was the only bishop of the country and was its first archbishop.

As a young man, Bogarín studied in the seminary of Asunción under the Lazarist Fathers; he was ordained on Feb. 24, 1887. For several years he was assigned to the cathedral as curate and diocesan secretary and chancellor. Only seven years after ordination, he was appointed bishop of Paraguay by Pope Leo XIII (Sept. 21, 1894) and consecrated on the feast of San Blás (Feb. 3, 1895) by the Salesian Bishop Luis Lasagna.

The diocese covered 450,000 square kilometers of territory without means of communication and had barely recovered from the war of the Triple Alliance. The bishop visited the whole diocese at least three times, covering 48,425 kilometers, mainly on horseback. In organizing the diocese, he formed a curia and established parishes. He gave the only seminary in the republic strong leadership, a firm spiritual foundation, and an imposing edifice. He brought many religious orders to Paraguay, founded Catholic Action there, and created a Catholic press and radio.

In 1899, Bogarín participated in the First Plenary Council on Latin America, called in Rome by Pope Leo XIII. He was also named first president of the council of state created by the constitution in 1940. He lived to the full his episcopal motto—*Pro aris et focis.* He was an apostle, a tireless preacher, and a patriot. He was his country's outstanding pioneer, builder, spiritual leader, and peacemaker.

[A. ACHÁ DUARTE]

BOGOMILS

Adherents of a medieval Balkan sect that came into being in Bulgaria, but whose origins go back to MANICHAEISM via Paulicianism. In the 8th century the Byzantine emperors resettled a number of PAULICIANS in Thrace, and under the influence of these immigrants the heresy called Bogomilism after its founder, Pope Bogomil (''pleasing to God''), was eventually introduced into the Balkans. The first account of this heresy is found in a reply of Patriarch Theophylactus to the Bulgar Czar Peter (*c.* 950), stating that it was ''Manichaeism mixed with Paulicianism'' (Μανικαΐσμος γάρ ἐστι, Παυλικιανισμῷ συμμιγής). About 972, the Bulgarian priest Cosmas wrote his *Treatise on the Bogomils,* denouncing these heretics and emphasizing their refusal to obey any authority, civil or ecclesiastical.

For the Bogomils, the world and the human body were works of Satan; only the soul was a creation of God. The true Christian conquered matter by abstaining from all physical contacts, by abstaining from meat and wine, and by forgoing all earthly possessions. This monastic-type ideal was, in practice, possible only for the ''Perfect''; the ordinary faithful could sin but they were under obligation to obey the Perfect; they could receive ''spiritual baptism'' on their deathbeds. The Bogomils accepted only the New Testament and the Psalms, translated into the vernacular. They were Docetists, holding that Christ did not have a human body but only the appearance (δόκησις) of one. Like the Paulicians, they rejected Sacraments, churches, and relics, tithing and church property, but retained a hierarchy of their own.

Bogomilism spread rapidly in the Balkans and even in Asia Minor in the 11th century (as indicated in the *Epistola invectiva* of Euthymius of Peribleptos). At the same time it spread into Italy and in France, where its adherents were called PATARINES or CATHARI (καθαροί in German, *Ketzer*). Recruits came largely from among the artisans and peasants oppressed by feudalism, but the nobility, in Provence as in Bosnia, also adhered to this ''bargain church'' that permitted them to appropriate to themselves the goods of the Catholic Church. About 1110, Emperor John II Comnenus discovered a Bogomil organization in Constantinople headed by a physician, Basil by name, and 12 ''Apostles.'' Basil was burned at the stake, and the monk Euthymius Zygabenus included a description of the heresy in his *Panoplia dogmatica.* In Serbia Prince Stephen Nemania took stern measures against the Bogomils *c.* 1180, ordering the burning of their leaders and their books. In Bulgaria, the heresy was crushed by Czar Boril, whose *Synodicon* of 1211 censures and condemns the Bogomils. But the movement continued to grow in Dalmatia (where it is mentioned

Bogomil Cemetery, dating from 13th century. (©Hulton-Deutsch Collection/CORBIS)

from 1167 on) and in Bosnia, which later became the center of Bogomilism in Europe.

In 1203 the Bogomil leaders of Bosnia allegedly recanted their heresy before the legate of Pope Innocent III (Act of Bolinopolje), but the movement soon spread throughout the entire country, and Pope Honorius III preached a crusade against Bosnia. In 1237 a crusade by Hungarians scored some success, but after the Tatar invasions of Hungary, the whole of Bosnia went into heresy for two centuries. With substantial support coming especially from the nobility, Bogomilism became a national religion. Beginning in 1340, however, the Franciscans preached the Catholic faith in Bosnia and founded friaries there. The barons and kings of Bosnia reconverted to Catholicism, but were for a long time unable to combat the heresy, headed by a *dijed* (bishop), and by *gosti* and *starcy* (elders). At length, in 1450 King Thomas required his subjects to accept Catholicism; 40,000 recalcitrants took refuge with their *dijed* in Herzegovina, which remained the final bastion of Bogomilism. But in 1463 the Turks easily took Bosnia and in 1482, Herzegovina. Thereafter many of the local population preferred to abandon their superficial Catholicism and adopt Islam, as they found in it some resemblance to their old faith. Such Islamized Bosnians and Herzegovinians were dubbed *poturi* (those who became Turkish). Some *poturi* preachers worked among the remaining Paulicians in Bulgaria, evidenced by Bulgarian 17th-century Slavic books that had been written in Bosnia. As late as 1660 the *poturi* often read the Gospel side by side with the Qur'ān.

No traces of the Bogomils remain in the Balkans, except tombstones—quite numerous in Bosnia and Herzegovina—that bear symbolic decorations (sun and moon, Christ the Vine, the anthropomorphic cross) that hark back to Manichaeism.

Bibliography: M. JUGIE, *Dictionnaire de spiritualité ascétique et mystique. Doctrine et histoire*, ed. M. VILLER et al. (Paris 1932–) 1:1751–54. S. RUNCIMAN, *The Medieval Manichee: A Study* *of the Christian Dualist Heresy* (Cambridge, Eng. 1947, repr. 1955). D. OBOLENSKY, *The Bogomils: A Study in Balkan Neo-Manichaeism* (Cambridge, Eng. 1948). A. SCHMAUS, "Der Neumanichäismus auf dem Balkan," *Saeculum* 2 (1951) 271–299. A. BORST, *Die Katharer* (Schriften der *Monumenta Germaniae Historica* 12; Stuttgart 1953). E. WERNER, "Die Bogomilen in Bulgarien Forschungen und Fortschritte," *Studi medievali* 3rd ser. 3 (1962) 249–278. A. V. SOLOVIEV, "Bogomilentum und Bogomilengräber in den südslawischen Ländern," *Völker und Kulturen Südosteuropas* (Munich 1958) 173–199.

[A. V. SOLOVIEV]

BOGUMIŁ OF GNIEZNO, ST.

Archbishop of Gniezno; date of birth unknown; d. Dubrow, near Koło, Poland, 1092. Quite probably Bogumil (a.k.a. Theophilus) resigned his see in 1080 after five years in office and became a hermit until his death 12 years later. There is a puzzling divergence of opinion and lack of accurate information about him. He was venerated as a saint from the Middle Ages, and his cult was approved by the Holy See in 1925.

Feast: June 10.

Bibliography: Z. KOZŁOWSKA-BUDKOWA, in *Polski Słownik biograficzny*, v. 2 (Cracow 1936) 200–201. P. DAVID, *Dictionnaire d'histoire et de géographie ecclésiastiques*, ed. A. BAUDRILLART et al. (Paris 1912) 9:417–418. J. PRUS and W. SNIEWSKI, *Bogumil Piotr; arcybiskup Gnieznienski* (London 1973). Z. SZOSTKIEWICZ, "Katalog Biskupów obrz. łac. Przedrozbiorowej Polski," *Sacrum Poloniae Millennium* 1 (1954) 417, 535. For a different version, see A. BUTLER, *The Lives of the Saints*, ed. H. THURSTON and D. ATTWATER (New York 1956) 2:519–520. B. STASIEWSKI, *Lekicon für Theologie und Kirche*, ed. J. HOFER and K. RAHNER (Freiburg 1957–65) 2:558.

[L. SIEKANIEC]

BOHEMIA MANOR

An important early Jesuit school in Maryland. Around 1741 the growth of religious intolerance in the Maryland colony induced the Jesuits to move the center of their activities, at least for a time, to a remote location in Cecil County, not far from the Pennsylvania border. Here at Bohemia Manor (or Bohemian Manor) they opened a boarding school for boys. Although there is no record of the opening date, among the more likely ones are 1742 and 1745. Thomas Poulton, SJ, under whose jurisdiction the school was established, is mentioned as being at Bohemia Manor in 1742. Other indications make 1745 the more probable opening year. For example, it is believed that one of the school's most outstanding pupils, "Jacky" Carroll, later Abp. John Carroll, was about 11 years old when he came to Bohemia Manor, which would be in 1745 or 1746.

The organization and curriculum of the school at Bohemia Manor was quite simple but no doubt similar to that of its European predecessors. The duration of the school is uncertain; it was probably discontinued shortly after Poulton's death in 1749. According to the financial account of Mr. T. Wayt, the schoolmaster, there were apparently two courses available: a classical course for which he received 40 shillings as tuition, and an English course, probably a type of commercial course, for which he received 30 shillings. On the other hand, there may have been two programs: college preparatory and elementary. The scantiness of the records, however, gives us no complete answer to their exact nature. It would seem that the program was not limited to the three "Rs," for it certainly prepared students to be admitted to St. Omer's College in Flanders on completion of their studies at Bohemia Manor. Besides Carroll, among the early students were the three Neale brothers, Benedict, Edward, and Leonard, founder of the GEORGETOWN VISITATION Convent; James Heath; George Boyes; and Robert Brent.

Whatever the courses offered at Bohemia, the school, like Newtown Manor in St. Mary's County, was of great importance in the early educational endeavors of Maryland. Both schools were of significance to the future of the Church in the U.S., for they were to prepare many students for entrance into European colleges, whence these young men would return to be leaders of the Church in Maryland and the U.S.

Bibliography: T. A. HUGHES, *The History of the Society of Jesus in North America: Colonial and Federal*, 4 v. (New York 1907–17) v.2. J. M. DALEY, *Georgetown University: Origin and Early Years* (Washington 1957).

[J. M. DALEY]

BOHEMIAN BRETHREN

Members of the Unity of Brethren (*Jednota bratrská, Unitas fratrum*) in Bohemia and Moravia, almost all Czech-speaking, and including a later branch in Poland. With the Bible as their rule, interpreted according to the community, they followed a simple, humble life, renouncing violence and recognizing Christ as the only mediator. They held that the sacraments were valid only if administered by a worthy priest to a believer. They denied transubstantiation, having no cult of the Eucharist but admitting the presence of Christ when communion was given. Public faults were to be publicly confessed. The religious songs of the Unity were assigned importance.

The Unity originated in Prague in the early 1450s in the group around the UTRAQUIST Archbishop-elect John

Rokycana and was led by his nephew Řehoř. Rokycana brought the Brethren into contact with Peter Chelčický, who in a number of writings in Czech (e.g., The Net of Faith) called for a return to primitive Christianity. He viewed the functions of ruler, judge, and soldier as incompatible with the Christian calling; and he rejected oaths, serfdom, and town life. His doctrines were taken over by Rehor's followers, who in 1457–58 settled at Kunvald in northeastern Bohemia. A church discipline was promulgated in 1464. In 1467, at a meeting at Lhotka (near Rychnov), the group broke with the Utraquists when they drew lots to choose three priests from their midst; these were confirmed by a Waldensian elder. The step brought renewed persecution for nearly 150 years.

At first most Brethren were countryfolk or artisans. But in the 1490s pressure from younger, university-educated priests led by LUKÁŠ OF PRAGUE and difficulties due to the Brethren's position toward secular authority caused the Unity to reject this social radicalism. A small minority who split off soon disintegrated.

Lukáš reorganized the Unity, strengthened church discipline, reformulated theology, and wrote constantly in its defense. Soon after his death, Lutheran doctrines found acceptance in the Unity. Their main protagonist was John Augusta. Brethren nobles, who now played an increasingly important role in the Unity, participated in the resistance of the Czech estates in 1547 and provided Ferdinand I with an excuse to suppress the Unity in Bohemia. Some Brethren went into exile in East Prussia and Poland. The Polish Unity worked closely with other Polish Protestants, e.g., the Union of Koźminek (1555) and the Consensus Sandomiriensis (1570). It died out in the 18th century.

In the early 1550s pressure on the Bohemian Unity relaxed. During Augusta's imprisonment (1548–64) John Blahoslav, historian, humanist, and Biblical scholar, rose to prominence. His Czech version of the NT and that of the OT carried out after his death, together known as the Kralice Bible (1579–94), is a landmark in Czech literature. The Brethren had now emerged from their cultural isolation. While Augusta strove for Protestant union, Blahoslav believed the Brethren should preserve an independent testimony. Yet by 1575 the Unity had virtually gone over to a Calvinist doctrinal position. As a result of renewed Catholic activity, Brethren and Lutheran-minded neo-Utraquists drew together and composed a common statement of faith: the *Confessio Bohemica* (1575). In 1609 the Unity obtained full religious freedom with the Letter of Majesty. After the Czech defeat at the White Mountain in 1620, the Unity was suppressed in 1627–28. Among those who went into exile was the theologian John Amos COMENIUS. Two bodies claim the heritage of the Unity: the MORAVIAN CHURCH, whose episcopacy derives from the Unity's Polish branch and whose earliest members included descendants of German-speaking Brethren in Moravia; and the Evangelical Czech Brethren Church in the Czech Republic.

Bibliography: R. ŘÍČAN, *Dějiny Jednoty bratrské* (Prague 1957), abr. as *Die Böhmischen Brüder*, tr. B. POPELÁŘ (Berlin 1961), with bibliog. J. T. MÜLLER, *Geschichte der Böhmischen Brüder*, 3 v. (Herrnhut, Ger. 1922–31). P. BROCK, *The Political and Social Doctrines of the Unity of Czech Brethren . . .* (The Hague 1957). M. SPINKA, "Peter Chelčický, Spiritual Father of the Unitas Fratrum," *Church History* 12 (1943) 271–291. M. S. FOUSEK, "The Pastoral Office in the Early Unitas Fratrum," *Slavonic and East European Review* 40 (1962) 444–457. Y. CONGAR, *Catholicisme* 2:109–111. J. WEISSKOPF, *Lexikon für Theologie und Kirche*, ed. J. HOFER and K. RAHNER, 10 v. (2d new ed. Freiburg 1957–65) 2:563–565. H. RENKEWITZ, *Die Religion in Geschichte und Gegenwart* (3d ed. Tübingen 1957–65) 1:1435–39.

[P. BROCK]

BÖHM, HANS

Shepherd, religious enthusiast; b. near Helmstadt, *c.* 1450; d. Würzburg (lower Franconia), July 19, 1476. Nicknamed Hansel the Drummer or the Piper, Böhm entertained the peasants with kettledrums and bagpipes. Suddenly, on Laetare Sunday, 1476 (March 24), he burned his drum in front of the pilgrimage church of Niklashausen on the Tauber (Baden) and proclaimed that it was the will of Mary, revealed to him in a vision, that she be especially venerated at that place.

Inspired by stories of St. JOHN CAPISTRAN's success, the unlearned enthusiast began to preach penance. Eventually he demanded revolutionary social changes that were a combination of radical communism and hatred for the clergy and for the authorities. WALDENSIAN and HUSSITE influences, with which his name is linked, hardly touched him directly; his visions of Mary and his Marian devotion are the best proof of that. The influence of some unknown nobles and priests still remains uncertain.

His sermons and alleged miracles attracted thousands of people from central and southern Germany. When he called for an armed meeting, Bp. Rudolf of Würzburg, in agreement with the archbishop of Mainz, had him arrested. After a disorganized attempt by his followers to free him, he was burned as a heretic. The "Niklashausen pilgrimage" lived on in the memory of the people, and the church had to be destroyed (1477) to prevent the continuation of the movement, one of many isolated outbreaks antecedent to the PEASANTS' WAR (1524–25).

Bibliography: Sources. *Die Rats-Chronik der Stadt Würzburg,* ed. W. ENGEL (Würzburg 1950), n. 117. Literature. F. A.

REUSS, "H. B. und die Wallfahrt nac Niklashausen im Jahre 1476," *Archiv des Historischen Vereines von Unterfranken* 10 (1850) 300–318. A. K. BARACK, *ibid.* 14 (1858) 1–108, basic study. W. E. PEUCKERT, *Die grosse Wende* (Hamburg 1948). A. MEUSEL, *Thomas Müntzer und seine Zeit* (Berlin 1952) 7–40, 185–187. O. GRAF, *Neue deutsche Biographie* (Berlin 1953–) 2:382. A. BIGELMAIR, *Lexikon für Theologie und Kirche*, ed. J. HOFER and K. RAHNER (Freiburg 1957–65) 2:559. G. FRANZ, *Der deutsche Bauernkrieg* (4th ed. Darmstadt 1956). W. BRÖL, *Dictionnaire d'histoire et de géographie ecclésiastiques* (Paris 1912–) 9:388–389.

[H. WOLFRAM]

BÖHME, JAKOB

German Lutheran mystic and writer (known also as Boehmme, Behmen); b. Alt-Seidenber near Görlitz, 1575; d. Görlitz, Nov. 17, 1624. Böhme's parents were poor peasants who apprenticed him to a shoemaker at Görlitz. Jakob became a master in 1599 and married the daughter of a master butcher. They had four sons and two daughters, and he prospered as a shoemaker. As he grew older, his tendency toward mystical experiences, already apparent in his youth, became more pronounced. He finally gave up his business and began to write.

About 1612 he published his first work, *Aurora oder die Morgenröthe im Anfang.* In it he attempted to clarify certain knowledge of God and the universe hitherto unknown causing his Lutheran pastor, Gregorius Richter, to declare him heretical and have him banished from town. However, the town fathers reversed the decision on condition that Böhme cease his writing. In the years that immediately followed, he suffered much from the criticisms of his more orthodox fellow religionists. Five years later, he again published his ideas, only to meet with renewed persecution. In 1624 he went to Dresden where he lived peacefully for a short while, then returned to Görlitz where he died. Though he was given Christian burial by the protesting clergy, the ornate cross placed on his tomb by friends was torn down by one of his enemies.

Böhme was, in spirit, a devout Lutheran who, throughout his religious experiences, clung to the traditional doctrine of the Trinity, Incarnation, Redemption, and the Sacraments of Baptism and the Lord's Supper. It was in attempting to explain the doctrine of the Trinity that he went astray. When he identified God with heaven, hell, and the material world he was approaching pantheism. When he tried to explain the problem of good and evil, he posited a sort of dualism in the divine nature. He continued to attend church services, although he put much emphasis on the church as it existed in the hearts of men. He believed that by self-renunciation, prayer, and contemplation man can hasten the time of his union with God. Böhme had little formal education, and this deficiency as well as the nature of his writings produced a "dazzling chaos" that to the present day has confused even his admirers. Nevertheless, he had an impact not only on religious thinkers, such as George Fox, Antoinette Bourgignon, and Philip Spener, but also on philosophers, such as Hegel and Schelling.

Bibliography: J. BÖHME, *Sämtliche Werke,* ed. K. W. SCHIEBLER, 7 v. (Leipzig 1832–60). J. J. STOUDT, *Sunrise to Eternity: A Study in J. Boehme's Life and Thought* (Philadelphia 1957). H. A. GRUNSKY, *Jakob Böhme* (Stuttgart 1956). P. HANKAMER, *Jakob Böhme* (Hildesheim, Ger. 1960). A. KOYRÉ, *La Philosophie de Jacob Boehme* (Paris 1929). L. LOEVENBRUCK, *Dictionnaire de théologie catholique.* 2.1:924–926. F. W. DEBELIUS, *The New Schaff-Herzog Encyclopedia of Religious Knowledge,* ed. S. M. JACKSON et al., 13 v. (Grand Rapids 1951–54) 2:209–211.

[H. J. MULLER]

BOISGELIN DE CUCÉ, JEAN DE DIEU, RAYMOND DE

Archbishop and cardinal; b. Rennes, France, Feb. 27, 1732; d. Angervilliers, Aug. 22, 1804. As a member of an old family of Brittany, Boisgelin De Cucé entered the service of the Church. Promotion was assured, and at the age of 33 he became bishop of Lavour. Five years later he was nominated to the See of Aix in Provence.

As archbishop he was concerned for the material as well as the spiritual well-being of his flock and proved himself an enlightened and effective administrator. His reputation merited for him election to the French Academy in 1776. With the coming of the Revolution, the prospects for a new order in France appealed to the archbishop of Aix. He was elected a deputy to the Estates-General and demonstrated his ability as a leader.

In the early months of the deliberations of the Assembly, he showed that he was willing to accept change, and the Assembly honored him by electing him president for a two-week term. In the months that followed, the archbishop joined the opposition when the majority voted for the confiscation of the Church's property and passed the CIVIL CONSTITUTION OF THE CLERGY. He was a vigorous spokesman in defense of the Church's rights and refused to take the oath supporting the Civil Constitution.

For the following ten years he resided in England. When Napoleon came to power and settled the problem of Church-State relations with the CONCORDAT OF 1801, the archbishop returned to France. In 1802 he was appointed to the See of Tours and received the cardinal's hat from Pope Pius VII. His many contributions to literature have not had much enduring influence.

Bibliography: E. LAVAQUERY, *Le Cardinal de Boisgelin*, 2 v. (Paris 1920). C. CONSTANTIN, *Dictionnaire de théologie catholique*

Jakob Böhme. (Archive Photos)

(Paris 1903–50) 2:942–944. P. CALENDINI, *Dictionnaire d'histoire et de géographie ecclésiastiques* (Paris 1912–) 9:575–576. F. REIBEL, *Lexikon für Theologie und Kirche*, ed. J. HOFER and K. RAHNER (Freiburg 1957–65) 2:566.

[H. L. STANSELL]

BOJANOWSKI, EDMUND WOJCIECH STANISLAS, BL.

Layman and founder of the Sister Servants of the Mary Immaculate (SSMI); b. Grabonóg (near Poznán), northwestern Poland, Nov. 14, 1814; d. Gorka Duchowna, Poland, Aug. 7, 1871. Born into a landed family of nobility, Bojanowski studied literature at the universities of Breslau (Wrocław) and Berlin. Although he contracted tuberculosis in his 20s, he walked more than a mile daily to attend Mass, and personally responded to the misery he encountered by teaching literacy and opening reading rooms for the poor, particularly in rural areas. During the cholera epidemic of 1849, he not only founded an orphanage and hospital, but himself tended to the victims of the disease, both in these institutions and in their country homes. Bojanowski also founded a daycare nursery in Gostyn. In 1850, three young girls and a widow committed themselves to running the nursery. In 1855 they became the nucleus of the Sister Servants of Mary Immaculate (originally called the Little Servants of the Mother of God), which now has branches in Europe, Africa, and America working in a variety of apostolates, including daycare centers for children. Bojanowski also organized a passive resistance to Prussian repression. He entered the seminary in 1869, but was forced to leave because of ill health and died two years later.

Bojanowski was declared venerable July 3, 1998; a miracle attributed to his intercession was approved Dec. 21, 1998 leading to his beatification in Warsaw, Poland, by John Paul II on June 13, 1999. During the beatification homily, Pope John Paul II said that Bojanowski ''anticipated much of what the Second Vatican Council said about the apostolate of the laity.''

Feast: Aug. 7.

Bibliography: M. WINOWSKA, *Edmond Bojanowski: précurseur de Vatican II* (Paris 1979).

[K. I. RABENSTEIN]

BOLAÑOS, LUIS DE

Founder of the first reductions in Paraguay; b. Marchena, Spain, *c.* 1550; d. Buenos Aires, Oct. 11, 1629. Bolaños became a Franciscan in his native town. In 1572, while still a deacon, he left with the Juan Ortiz de Zárate expedition, and he arrived in Asunción in February 1575. With his friend and patron Fray Alonso de San Buenaventura, Bolaños began almost at once to visit the native people of Guayrá and Villa Rica and to found pueblos, or reductions, which were later transferred to the Jesuits. Since these provinces were later devastated by the fearsome Mamelukes and the territory now belongs to Brazil, there are no records of these pueblos destroyed by the slave raiders from São Paulo. In 1580 he began the reduction of Pacuyú to the north of Asunción, the first reduction begun by Bolaños of which the name is now known. In 1585, while guardian of the Franciscan friary of Asunción, Bolaños was ordained. In that same year, to the south of Asunción, he founded the famous reductions of San Bias de Itá and San Buenaventura de Yaguarón. Hampered by a lack of help, Bolaños spent the years 1585 to 1607 in caring for the pueblos already founded. In 1607 he began to found another series of reductions to the south of Asunción beginning with San José de Caazapá, still a flourishing city, and ending in 1616 with Baradero near Buenos Aires. In 1623 Bolaños retired to the Franciscan house in Buenos Aires, where he died and where his tomb is still honored.

Bolaños was not only an imaginative missionary but also a true scholar in Amerindian languages and customs and in theology. His Guaraní catechism, approved by the synod of Paraguay in 1603, was used in all the missions of the region, even those of the Jesuits. His grammar and vocabulary in the same tongue were considered the best of their kind. As a theologian, Bolaños defended the validity of the Guaraní pagan marriages and defended them against the colonists. His hymns and poems in Guaraní have passed into the common domain of folklore. As a man Bolaños was beloved by all. Perhaps this is his best testimonial. Few regions of Spanish America were beset with more dissensions than Rio de la Plata. Yet Bolaños was esteemed by none more than by the Jesuits, who worked so closely with him.

Bibliography: A. MILLÉ, *Crónica de la Orden Franciscana en la conquista del Perú, Paraguay, y el Tucumán y su Convento del antigno Buenos Aires 1212–1800* (Buenos Aires 1961). B. ORO, *Fray Luis de Bolaños, apóstol del Paraguay y Río de la Plata* (Córdoba 1934). R. A. MOLINA, ''La obra franciscana en el Paraguay y Rio de la Plata,'' *Missionalia hispánica* 11 (1954), esp. 335–336.

[L. G. CANEDO]

BOLIVIA, THE CATHOLIC CHURCH IN

The Republic of Bolivia, one of two landlocked countries in South America, is also the poorest. It is bounded on the north and the east by Brazil, on the west by Peru and Chile, on the south by Argentina, and on the southeast by Paraguay. The low, hot lands of the east are dominated by tropical rain forests; the west by the cordillera of the Andes mountains, which traverses one-third of Bolivia. The Andean section includes a high plateau known as the Altiplano Boliviano, and a sierra broken by small protected valleys. This region contains the principal centers of population and economic activity: La Paz, the seat of government; Potosí, the mining center; Cochabamba; and Sucre. Natural resources include tin, natural gas, copper, and lead, tin being the country's largest export after natural gas. The northern and eastern plains are used for tropical farming and forest industries, yielding crops such as barley, wheat, rice, sugar cane, coffee, and coca leaves, the last of which is smuggled to Colombia for processing into cocaine. The rich petroleum fields of eastern Bolivia have been exploited by government agencies and U.S. oil companies.

Made part of the Incan civilization in 1200, Bolivia eventually came under the jurisdiction of the Audiencia de Charcas, which lasted almost 300 years under the colonial rule of Spain. In 1809 a revolt against this regime started a bloody war that lasted until 1825, when Bolivia proclaimed independence. As a result of the War of the Pacific, Bolivia lost its sea coast to Chile in 1880, and territorial disputes continued to shadow its history into the 20th century. Over half the region's population are descendants of pre-Columbian inhabitants: Quechua, Aymará, Guarani, and other ethnic groups; of the remainder 30 percent were mestizos, and an additional 15 percent white.

Capital: Sucre; La Paz houses the seat of government.
Size: 424,162 sq. miles.
Population: 8,152,620 in 2000.
Languages: Spanish, Quechuan, and Aymaran.
Religions: 7,541,175 Catholics (92.5%), 407,630 Evangelical Protestants (5%), 203,815 Baha'i (2.5%).

THE CHURCH IN BOLIVIA TO 1900

Catholicism came to South America with the first Spaniards, who were attracted to the silver and other rich mineral deposits abounding in Bolivia's mountainous region and who founded the urban communities of La Plata (modern Sucre), Potosí, and La Paz. Created a dependency to the Charcas, Bolivia (then called Upper Peru) was annexed to the Viceroyalty of Buenos Aires in 1776. The growth of a nationalist movement prompted the fight for independence, which was granted on Aug. 6, 1825. The country is named after famed revolutionary leader Simon Bolivar, who worked to free Hispanic America from Spain.

Ecclesial Organization. With Hernando Pizarro, who conquered the region in 1538, came Catholic priests entrusted with the parochial ministry among the Spaniards and the evangelization of the native peoples. A bishopric was erected at La Plata in 1552, with jurisdiction over most of South America, and the Dominican Tomás de San Martin was appointed the first bishop. The dioceses of La Paz and Santa Cruz were erected in 1605, and four years later La Plata became an archdiocese, forming a new ecclesiastical province that included, besides La Paz and Santa Cruz, the bishoprics of Asunción, Buenos Aires, and Tucumán. The first synod held in Bolivia was convoked in 1629.

For the most part, priests, both secular and religious, were of European origin; most were born in Spain but some were of mixed race. One exception was the bishop of La Plata, Fernando Arias de Ugarte (1626–30), who said he was an aborigine and signed his pastoral documents ''Fernando indio arzobispo.'' Mestizos were usually admitted to religious orders as lay brothers.

Development of the Missions. Within a few years of arriving in Bolivia, both secular and religious priests traveled to the Amerindian Aymará and Quechua communities on the Altiplano and in the mountains. They learned the languages and won the natives over to Christianity, although some aspects of their indigenous religions—such as rituals and superstitions surrounding harvests and luck—remained entwined in their spiritual beliefs. Unlike the Aymaras and Quechuas, the natives on the plains were warlike nomads who resisted foreign domination. It took many years of work by Jesuit missionaries working among the Moxos and Chiquitos and Franciscans working among the Chiriguanos to bring them into the missions. Among the early missionaries were the Jesuits Pedro Marbán and Cipriano Barace, founders of the Reductions among the Moxos in the middle of the 17th century; José de Arce, first to catechize the Chiquitos, and his successor, Lucas Caballero; the Franciscan brother Francisco del Pilar, who founded missions among the aboriginal Chiriguanos; and the Mercedarian Diego de Porres.

About the middle of the 18th century, evangelization among the Moxos and Chiquitos reached its peak with 22 missions, under the care of 45 missionaries. When the Spanish crown expelled the Jesuits in 1767 and secular priests took charge, the missions declined. Whites and mestizos came to live in the communities, which were transformed into diocesan parishes. The Franciscan missions among the Chiriguanos reached their acme in about 1800, with 16 towns. Unfortunately, during the war of independence that soon began, guerrilla bands, opposed to

Metropolitan Sees	Suffragans
Cochabama	Oruro, as well as the prelature of Aiquile
La Paz	Coroico and El Alto, as well as the prelature of Corocoro
Santa Cruz de la Sierra	San Ignacio de Velasco
Sucre	Potosí and Tarija
Apostolic vicarates: El Beni, Pando, Cuevo, El Ñuflo de Chávez, and Reyes	

everything Spanish, destroyed the missions. By the close of the fighting in 1825 only a few missions remained and the diocesan authority converted them into ''curatos doctrineros.''

The missions among the Chiriguanos were reestablished from 1840 to 1850 by Franciscans from Spain, Italy, and Austria. They also established new missions in the region, and extended their efforts into the territory of the Guarayos and in the regions of the northwest among the Amerindians of the forest. The mission of the Chiriguanos in the province of Cordillera was secularized in 1915, and that among the Guarayos in 1937, thus ending the accomplishment of centuries of work. Many natives returned to the forests, and the old mission towns disappeared. By the 1960s, the few missions left were attended by Austrian and Spanish friars.

Religious Orders. During Spanish rule, monasteries and residences were established by Franciscans, Mercedarians, Dominicans, Augustinians, Jesuits, and the Hospitallers of St. John. The Franciscans and Jesuits worked mainly in the Amerindian missions, while the Mercedarians and Augustinians cared for parishes among the Quechuas and Aymaras in the cities and rural towns. The Dominicans took as their main work the parishes among the people of European origin, while the religious of St. John of God served in hospitals. Jesuits in urban residences took up the work of education and established the Universidad Mayor de San Francisco Xavier in La Plata in 1624.

Congregations of women were restricted to nuns living the cloistered life, as the Franciscan sisters or Poor Clares, and the Augustinian nuns, who were then called Mónicas. In the 17th century the Carmelites of the Teresan reform entered the region, and convents were established in La Plata, La Paz, Potosí, and Cochabamba. The nuns' special function was to provide the churches with furnishings and liturgical vestments, to sew and embroider, and to make fine pastry. In the 18th century some of these congregations took charge of the education of children and the care of orphans.

Special Devotions. In colonial times two sanctuaries were prominent in the religious life of the country, and these became centers of national pilgrimage. In the town of Copacabana, situated in the Altiplano on the shores of the historic lake Titicaca, is venerated the image of the Virgin Mary, carved by Tito Yupanqui in the middle of the 17th century in circumstances that bordered on the miraculous, as popular legend has it. On the eastern plains in the town of Cotoca, a small image of the Mother of God is venerated. Legend says that the image was found in a dense forest within the trunk of a tree by some humble farmers in the middle of the 18th century. Both sanctuaries draw large crowds of the devout, especially on their respective feast days. Though people of all classes come there, the poor are in the majority.

INDEPENDENCE FROM SPAIN

In Bolivia, revolutionary outbreaks in opposition to Spanish rule occurred earlier than they did in neighboring regions, but those taking place before 1780 were unsuccessful. Also unlike the rest of Spanish America, the Church made no official pronouncement on the independence movement when it grew in strength at the turn of the 19th century. In general the hierarchy and the higher ranks of clergymen remained loyal to the Spanish government, while the majority of priests took part in the struggle for independence. The priests José Antonio Medina, José Andrés Salvatierra, and Juan Bautista Oquendo incited the popular movements of 1809 and 1810. Father Muñecas was a leader of a band of guerrillas, and Fathers Polanco and Mercado, and Fray Justo acted as chaplains for the guerrillas.

One year following José de Sucre's victory at the battle of Ayacucho in 1824, the sovereign state of Bolivia was created. After a brief alliance with Peru, Bolivia battled Chile over rights to a coastal region, then lost this land altogether in the War of the Pacific in 1884. After a succession of military coups, a stable democratic regime lasted through the first decades of the 20th century. This state of flux of political affairs did not bring a substantial change in the Church. The PATRONATO REAL, which had been exercised by the king of Spain, was passed on to the president; eventually, through the Concordat of 1951, the right to regulate church-state relations would be granted to the Holy See.

Focus of Church Outreach. Religious vocations, which had been numerous during the colonial period, diminished somewhat during the first century of independence. Still, during the 19th century a number of

charitable institutions were founded in the newly independent Bolivia, growing to more than 50 by 1900. Most were in the charge of religious congregations of women, such as the Sisters of the Good Shepherd, Sisters of St. Vincent de Paul, the Adoration Sisters, the Missionary Crusaders of the Church, and the Servants of Mary. Lay institutes and religious congregations maintained hospitals, homes for the aged and for foundlings, and first aid stations. The commitment to education also increased notably in the course of the republic, particularly religious orders or congregations such as Jesuits, Christian Brothers, Franciscans, Sisters of St. Ann, and Sisters of the Sacred Hearts. Most of the grammar schools were free, particularly those in rural areas.

In the mid-19th century a press was established in La Plata. The periodical *El Cruzado* was published in Sucre under the direction of eminent religious writers, and *La Cátedra* was edited in La Paz up to the 1930s. Among the ecclesiastical authors of books or pamphlets on religious subjects may be mentioned Juan de Dios Bosque, in theology and Canon law; Jacinto Anaya, in Canon law; Francisco María del Granado, famous preacher; and Cayetano de la Llosa, author of commentaries on the devout life. José María Izquierdo in *Carta abierta a Flam*

Village church on the shore of Lake Titicaca, Bolivia. (©Wolfgang Kaehler/CORBIS)

marión refuted rationalism; Primo Arieta wrote a remarkable polemic in defense of religion; Pedro Arístides Zejas was the author of instructive catechisms; and Facundo Quiroga was a famous teacher.

[H. SANABRIA FERNÁNDEZ]

THE MODERN CHURCH

The effects of the sectarian and anti-Catholic liberalism that had first made its appearance in Bolivia during the late 19th century began to show themselves in concrete ways after 1900. The law of Oct. 11, 1911, instituted civil marriage, while another law of April 15, 1932, allowed absolute divorce. Catholic universities established during the colonial period were by now integrated into the national system of state universities by liberal politicians who severed their ties with the Church and closed the faculties of theology and canon law. Such policies drew increasing opposition from a vigorous group of Catholic-based thinkers by the early 1900s. Among these intellectuals were Donato Vázquez, Aurelio Beltrán, José Santos Machicao, Luis Paz, and Mariano Baptista, the last of whom was elected president of the republic during the government's pendulum-like swing between liberal and conservative regimes. In 1936 a military coup ousted the last of the liberal presidents, reformist Daniel Salamanca, and installed a military regime. In 1952 a second coup occurred, leading to the deaths of 1,000 people and bringing to power the left-wing Movimento Nacionalista in the person of President Victor Paz Estenssoro. Estenssoro nationalized the tin mines, extended voting rights to all adults, and distributed large blocks of formerly Spanish-owned lands among the lower classes. A military government ousted him from power in 1962.

Poverty Prompts Civil Unrest. During the 1940s and 1950s Church-run charitable institutions such as hospitals and medical stations reached deeply into the life of the country and sought to combat the appeals of communism, which had taken root in Central and South America. The effect was especially visible in mining centers, such as Catavi, Llallagua, and Corocoro, where communist agitators were most active. In 1967 the economic situation in Bolivia prompted South American revolutionary leader Ché Guevara to move to Bolivia and attempt to mobilize tin miners to rise up against the country's military government. Guevara's efforts were unsuccessful, and he was executed within the year.

The pressure for change and social justice in Bolivia and throughout Latin America from the mid-1960s on-

Laja, Bolivia, church built in commemoration of Spanish victory over Incas. (©David Johnson)

wards coincided with efforts to implement reforms called for by the Second Vatican Council. The conciliar awakening among Catholics heightened the sense of responsibility of service to the poor and the native peoples and gave direction to social reform. On Feb. 2, 1967, a new constitution was put into place in Bolivia that reflected some of these attitudes. This document recognized as official the Catholic religion and granted the Church state support. Religious education was made obligatory in primary and middle schools, and the teachers received special income.

Resurgence Follows Vatican II. Missionaries from North America and Europe had a significant role in the postconciliar renewal. Maryknoll priests and sisters from the United States had begun their first mission to assist the Bolivian Church in 1942, and they were soon joined by others from not only the United States but Italy and elsewhere in Europe. Lay men and women joined in the mission efforts through such programs as the Papal Volunteers. In all, over 30 countries and dozens of religious communities sent missionaries to Bolivia in the years after Vatican II, although by the 1980s their numbers would be reduced as the reforms took root in the Bolivian Church and new theologies of mission began to develop. The CELAM meeting at SANTO DOMINGO in 1992 signaled a new direction for Latin America and Bolivia with its emphasis on relating the faith to local cultures and ending missionary colonialism. In another effort toward renewal, the Holy See sponsored a program by Church leaders to translate the Bible into Quechua, an Andean native language, as part of Jubilee 2000.

After Vatican II the bishops, who had met periodically during the 1950s, formalized their gatherings. As the Bolivian Bishops' Conference they began to exert a more active presence. Because of their pastoral emphasis, they avoided the doctrinal and theological conflicts that beset other Latin America countries. The Bolivian Bishops' Conference stressed renewal through various pastoral planning guidelines that emphasize the development of Basic Christian Communities, the preferential option for the poor (especially indigenous ethnic groups), lay formation programs, family life programs, and the promotion of vocations to the priesthood and religious life. The new vitality, strength, and influence brought by the forces for social change and Vatican II's renewal of Catholicism to the Bolivian Church were evidenced in 1992 by the national consultation of Bolivian Catholics by their bishops that resulted in a highly praised study of pastoral priorities presented to the bishops of Latin America in preparation for Santo Domingo.

In 1952, a group of lay Catholics began publishing the daily secular newspaper *Presencia.* which went on to play an invaluable role as the Church's voice against the excesses of torture, exile, and human rights abuses of the succession of military dictators during the 1960s and 1970s. By the late 20th century it had become an influential voice for the poor and indigenous peoples of Bolivia. Catholic radio stations grew in numbers and prestige after Vatican II and broadcast regional programming in each of Bolivia's variety of native languages.

In 1966 the Catholic University was founded by the Bishops' Conference. With its center in La Paz, the school had branches in Cochabamba and Santa Cruz. It opened a department of religious studies to offer graduate and postgraduate degrees not previously available in the country. The archdiocese of La Paz and the archdiocese of Santa Cruz also began campus ministry programs at state universities and teacher colleges around the country to instruct Catholic students in higher education. Church-run primary and secondary schools were estimated to educate 14 percent of the entire student population by the 1990s. Catholic religious instruction continued to be provided in all the country's public schools.

Moral Leadership. From the mid-1960s onward, military governments succeeded each other in quick succession, a situation that would continue until 1982, when exiled former president Paz Estenssoro returned to Bolivia and took power. This period was characterized by repression, violence, and religious repression, as governments attempted to hold onto political power in a nation with severe economic problems.

In 1978, a small group of miners' wives, protested their poverty and the military repression that, under the regime of General Hugo Banzer Suarez, caused hundreds to be killed, exiled, or ''disappeared''. On their hunger strike to restore democracy they were joined by Luis Espinal, SJ, as well as many other priests, religious, and lay people. President Banzer relented and called for free elections. However, on March 22, 1980, Espinal was murdered by paramilitary forces. His death had a tremendous influence on young people; 70,000 people of all walks of life attended his funeral, and many schools, institutes, libraries, and youth centers now bear his name. The Church became a target of particular repression a few months later, during the July 1980 coup of General Louis Garcia Meza, when over 50 priests, women religious, and lay missionaries were put in prison, exiled, or expelled from the country.

After the downfall of Meza's regime, Paz Estenssoro regained the presidency of Bolivia in 1982. He remained in the office until 1989, when the civil unrest resulting from a sustained economic downturn prompted voters to seek a new approach. Beginning in the 1990s the results of Bolivia's transition to a market-oriented economy, the increase in trafficking in illegal drugs, and concerns over government corruption continued to demand the attention of the country's democratically elected presidents.

By the 1990s radical feminists within Bolivia were actively lobbying for abortion rights, reflecting a worldwide move toward a liberal social agenda. Much to the dismay of Church leaders, the government moved in the same direction, attempting to stem the tide of the country's 50,000 annual illegally performed abortions by permitting legal abortions. Bishops also spoke against another 20th century social ill, materialism, by warning the faithful to guard against the culture of violence and consumerism that was coming on the heels of the nation's economic advancement.

In the early 1990s thousands of native peoples marched on La Paz seeking to reclaim their rights to land, language, and culture. The Church supported their demands and mediated the conflicts with peaceful results, although not always with significant legal changes. Such social and religious ferment continued to inspire Catholics across the region to seek reform and, in some cases, even revolution. Nonetheless the continuing economic, political, and social tensions cast the Church in a leadership role mediating disputes about land reform, workers' rights, indigenous people's rights to their territories and their culture, education reform, health care, and welfare reforms required by the modernization process. Continuing their tradition of providing input into government policy-making, in 1997 Church leaders came out in support of President Barzer's economic reform proposals, although they did express criticisms regarding other facets of his political agenda.

Into the 21st Century. At the beginning of the 21st century, the Church oversaw over 300 hospitals, clinics, and parish health centers, mostly in poor or rural areas. Because of the national extension of these Church programs, there were many projects of technical and financial collaboration between church and state. In many poor rural and urban areas the Church was the principal agent for government-subsidized social programs and projects, and Catholic-run schools provided the only education in many remote areas of the country. However, the majority of Church pastoral, educational, and social programs were funded by Church sources with a continued heavy dependence on mission collections from other countries.

While religious liberty prevailed in Bolivia, the privileged position of the Catholic Church began to come under question, as the activity of some of the over 250

Christian sects operating in the country—Pentecostals, Mormons, Assemblies of God, and Jehovah's Witnesses among them—increased during the late 20th century. While missionaries from the major Protestant faiths became increasingly active in entering communities, dispensing economic aid, and proselytizing, they remained without significant influence in the life of the country, and in 1999 the Church initiated an interfaith dialogue with representatives of the country's Pentecostal churches as well as members of its Jewish minority. However, so-called ''dissident'' and ''pseudoreligious'' sects were seen as more problematic, causing Bishop Jesus Juarez of the Bolivian Bishops' Conference to observe that such groups were ''causing the loss of the sense of history, damaging the native culture, and creating division within communities.''

In 2000, there were 29 bishops in Bolivia. The clergy numbered 1,058 priests, 664 of whom were religious. The figures for religious totaled 2,104 sisters and 198 brothers, the majority of whom were missionaries. Despite predictions that Catholicism would wane during the 20th century, in 2000 the country remained among those South American nations most strongly committed to the Church.

Bibliography: E. DUSSEL, ed., *The Church in Latin America, 1492–1992* (Maryknoll, N.Y. 1992). CONFERENCE OF BOLIVIAN BISHOPS, *Guía Eclesiastica* (La Paz 1994); *Mensajes y Exhortaciones de la Conferencia Episcopal de Bolivia,* 2 vols. 1963–78, 1979–92 (La Paz) *Presencia* (La Paz 1952—). GOVERNMENT MINISTRY OF PLANNING AND COORDINATION, Censo Nacional de Población-1992 (La Paz). N. PAZ, *My Life for My Friends* (New York 1978).

[M. GILLGANNON/EDS.]

BOLLANDISTS

A small group of Jesuits in Antwerp, Belgium, organized into a society in the 17th century by Jean Bolland for the critical study and publication of the lives of the saints. Although named after the first of their number, the group got inspiration from the learned Leribert Rosweyde (1569 to 1629), who conceived the idea of purging the lives of the saints of the innumerable apocryphal and legendary details that encumbered them by the publication of a scholarly *Acta sanctorum.* In a short treatise, *Fastes des saints,* he explained his intention of dealing with the deeds of the saints whose lives are recorded in the manuscripts collected in Belgian libraries (1607). Rosweyde did not succeed in completing this project, but laid the foundation for the *Acta sanctorum* by editing the oldest texts of the Lives of the Desert Fathers in his *Vitae Patrum* (1615). Charged with continuing the work of Rosweyde, Jean Bolland (b. Julémont, Diocese of Liège, Aug. 13, 1596; d. Antwerp, Sept. 12, 1665) modified both the plan and the method. He decided to deal with all the known saints in the Church's calendar, gathering all the information known about each and publishing it with notes and comments. Each volume of the *Acta* would be furnished with a table of reference and an index. In 1635 Bolland was given Godefroid Henschenius (1601 to 1681), a student of his, as collaborator. Henschenius's suggestions caused him to enlarge the conception of the enterprise, to the extent that he recalled some of his own work that was already in print, and both men turned attention to the saints in the calendar for January. The appearance of the *Acta sanctorum* for January (1643) and February (1658) elicited the admiration of scholars. In 1659 Daniel van Papenbroek, or Papebroch (b. Anvers, 1628; d. 1714), whom H. Delehaye has called ''le bollandist par excellence,'' joined the group and proved to be one of the most learned men of his time, an indefatigable worker, and great discoverer of documents, who combined a firm judgment with the courage of his scientific opinions and was responsible for the publication of 19 volumes. The munificence of Pope ALEXANDER VII made it possible for the first two companions of Bolland to embark on a journey of study and investigation, the first of a long tradition. They discovered many manuscripts in Germany, Italy, and France, copies of which were sent to the Bollandist collection.

Papebroch enlarged the field of interest of the *Acta* to include both the chronology of the popes and the evaluation of false documents. This latter study, the fruit of a month of forced leisure at Luxemburg, was based on insufficient evidence and brought him into controversy with the Benedictine scholar Jean MABILLON, whose representations Papebroch finally accepted. His intellectual honesty and the admirable letter of acquiescence in his opponent's opinion, gained for the Bollandists the friendship of the Benedictine scholar. Since the Bollandists refused to acknowledge the prophet Elijah as founder of the Carmelites, they were savagely attacked by certain members of that order. The Bollandists became the victims of a violent pamphlet warfare, and their work was condemned by the Spanish Inquisition; they had to send Father Janninck to Rome to avoid greater difficulties, and Papebroch himself lost much time in refuting the charge of the Carmelite Sebastian de St. Paul. Although condemnation in Rome was avoided, the Bollandists continued to be victims of malevolent insinuations until Pope BENEDICT XIV intervened and put an end to the unfortunate quarrel.

The golden age of the society was constituted by Bolland, Henschenius, and Papebroch, whose successors did not always have their scientific competence. Among them, Du Sollier and J. Stilting showed signs of timidity and prolixity.

With the suppression of the Society of Jesus in 1773, the Bollandist Collection, which had arrived at the third volume for October, was subjected to great difficulty; and although volumes four and five were published in Brussels (1780, 1786), and volume 6 in Tongerloo (1794), the work had to be abandoned as the result of the disturbance that followed the French Revolution (1789). The library was dispersed and many of its precious manuscripts lost.

In 1837 the society was reconstituted and began republication of the *Acta* in 1845. V. de Buck (d. 1876), C. de Smedt (d. 1911), A. Poncelet, and H. DELEHAYE (d. 1941) brought to their study the assistance of philology and other subsidiary historical disciplines; Delehaye opened new perspectives, and P. Peeters concentrated attention on the hagiography of the Eastern Churches.

Besides the *Acta sanctorum,* which now consists of 67 folio volumes (January 1 to November 10), including a Commentary on the Martyrology of St. Jerome (1931) and a *Propylaeum ad Acta SS. Decembris* dealing with the Roman Martyrology (1940), the Bollandists publish a review, the *Analecta Bollandiana,* begun in 1882 and completed with a bulletin of hagiographical publications (since 1891). They produce also a collection of *Subsidia hagiographica* (since 1886) with a control listing of sources for the lives of the saints in alphabetical order, called the *Bibliotheca hagiographica latina* (BHL), the *Bibliotheca hagiographica graeca* (BHG), and the *Bibliotheca hagiographia orientalis* (BHO).

Bibliography: B. DE GAIFFIER, *Lexikon für Theologie und Kirche*, ed. J. HOFER and K. RAHNER (2d, new ed. Freiburg 1957–65) 2:571–72. H. DELEHAYE, *L'Oeuvre des Bollandistes à travers trois siècles* (*Subsidia hagiographica* 13a.2; 2d ed. 1958), with bibliography. P. PEETERS, *Analecta Bollandiana* 55 (1937) v–xlix; *Figures bollandiennes contemporaines* (Brussels 1948); *L'Oeuvre des Bollandistes* (new ed. Brussels 1961); *Analecta Bollandiana* 60 (1942) i–lii, FR. DELEHAYE. P. DEVOS, *ibid.* 69 (1951) i–lix. R. AIGRAIN, *L'Hagiographie* (Paris 1953) 329–50.

[P. ROCHE/EDS.]

BOLOGNA, UNIVERSITY OF

A coeducational state institution of higher learning in Italy, enjoying administrative autonomy and financially supported by the state and by student tuition.

Early History. The origin of a school at Bologna is so closely linked to the rebirth of the study of law after the 11th century that it is just as impossible to fix a precise date for its foundation as it is to fix a date for the philosophical movements that are identified with it.

The tradition of the commentators (those masters who labored over the interpretation of the text of Roman law—in particular the *Digest,* the most important part of the Justinian collection, which came to their hands by ways no less mysterious than their reasons for meeting in Bologna) refers to a certain Pepo, the predecessor of IRNERIUS, who according to tradition headed a school in Bologna around 1080. It was only in the first part of the 12th century, however, that the Bolognese school is thought to have assumed, under Irnerius, that distinctive feature that would remain peculiar to it—the isolation of the study of law from the study of the other arts. This was a decisive step in the history of the school, the fame of which was already so widespread at the middle of the 12th century that it attracted the attention of the emperor Frederick I. He called the four famous Bolognese doctors, Bulgaro, Martino, Ugo, and Jacopo, to Roncaglia to decide the prerogatives of the emperor in regard to the cities. Again, according to tradition, each of the masters had a different approach to philosophy and juridical research. Nevertheless, if they and their assembly at Roncaglia can be considered as part of the myth that surrounds the Bolognese school, the famous privilege granted to the students there by Frederick I in 1158 is certainly not a myth. This privilege granted students the right to be judged by their masters (*privilegium scholasticum*), a privilege that spread from Bologna and was later inserted in the code of Roman laws, where it is still referred to as the *Habita.*

Organization. By the middle of the 12th century students were flocking to Bologna not only from the various regions of Italy but even from the farthest parts of Europe. The organization of the school, although originally dependent on the name and worth of its masters, really depended on the student organizations, which chose the masters and paid their fees. In its earliest organization the school consisted of groups of students gathered around a master who taught in his home and was recompensed by a collection taken up among his disciples. The city later taking notice of the importance of the school tried to interfere in education—the first step being taken in 1180 when the city of Bologna obliged all masters to swear they would not teach outside the city. The students then organized both to facilitate their living problems and to protect their interests and privileges in dealing with the city and civil authority. In this manner, there arose two great organizations, the so-called cismontanes and the ultramontanes, each headed by a rector who was a student. Later the associations subdivided into nations according to the nationality of the single groups. In 1217 the cismontanes (the Italians) split into three groups: Lombards, Tuscans, and Romans, the last of which also included students from Sicily and Campania, later called *Illi de regno.* In 1265 the nations of the ultramontanes (the foreigners) were 13 in number with students from France, Spain, Pro-

Manuscript illumination of "A Lecturer at the University of Bologna." (©Gianni Dagli Orti/CORBIS)

Bologna University, the oldest surviving university in world. Alumni include Dante Alighieri, Petrarch, and Torquato Tasso. (©Hulton Getty/Liaison Agency)

vence, England, Picardy, Burgundy, Poitou, Tours, Maine, Normandy, Cataluna, Hungary, Poland, and Germany. In 1432 with the growth of the school the number of nations increased to 16.

Contrasts and strife between masters and groups of students and between students and the civil authorities led to an increase in the network of new university centers outside Bologna. Universities arose in France, in Montpellier and Orléans; in Spain, in Salamanca; and in Italy, in Vicenza (1204), Arezzo (1215), Padua (1222), Vercelli (1228), Siena (1321), Florence, Pisa, Modena, Perugia, Rome (1303), Pavia (1361), Ferrara (1391), Parma, Turin, Messina, and Catania.

Canon and Civil Law. In the meantime, in the mid-12th century, instruction in canon law was introduced by Gratian, a monk of the Bolognese monastery of SS. Felix and Nabor. About the year 1140 he worked to unify canon law in the *Decretum* that was to be the basis of Church legislation in the 13th century. (*See* GRATIAN, DECRETUM OF.) As the genius of Irnerius appeared in the separation of the study of civil law from that of the other arts, so the genius of Gratian was manifested in the distinction he introduced between canon law and theology. This work completes and perfects the plan of medieval studies with the union of Roman law and canon law in a unique system—*l'utrumque ius,* an ideal form for the new civilization advancing toward the second millennium of Christianity.

These two great branches of 13th-century medieval culture are found distinct at the Bolognese school in two colleges—the *Ius Canonicum,* composed of 12 members, and the *Ius Civile sive Casesareum,* with 16. These groups gathered together the masters or their representatives from the various colleges for the final examination of a candidate or in exceptional cases held a common meeting.

Expansion. The restoration of Aristotelian philosophy in the 13th century gave a new impulse to the teaching of mathematical, liberal, and mechanical arts, a fact confirmed by the establishment of a third college—*Collegium artistarum et medicorum*—for instruction in philosophical and technical subjects.

These three colleges, which unite the masters, canonists, lawyers, artists, philosophers, and doctors, can be compared to the ancient student organizations of cismontanes, ultramontanes, and nations. The course of study lasted six years for canon law, eight years for civil law, and four years for arts and medicine. The doctorate was obtained by successfully carrying on a discussion on a topic assigned on the eve by the professors who themselves held the opposition. Those who were successful could obtain the doctorate by giving a lecture in the presence of the academic body, the rectors of the universities, and their colleagues. Since 1219 the formal conferring of the doctorate has been the prerogative of the archdeacon of the Cathedral of Bologna, acting as papal delegate. This formality made the doctorate received at Bologna not simply a *licentia docendi* (an authorization to teach) but rather a *licentia ubique docendi* (an authorization to teach anywhere).

The organization of the university based on three colleges of masters and three ''universities'' of students remained unchanged until the end of the 18th century. In the late 16th century the various schools were united in one building, the Palazzo dell'Archiginnasio, provided by the city, in keeping with the civil authorities' plan to assume authority over the university.

During the French Revolution and especially during the Napoleonic era (1800–15), the ancient organization of the university was transformed. It emerged from this period as a modern state university. The Palazzo dell'Archiginnasio was abandoned, and the university moved to the Palazzo Poggi where it still functions.

The bull of Leo XIII, *Quod divina sapientia,* of Aug. 28, 1824, raised the University of Bologna to the status of a Pontifical University, placing it side by side with the University of Rome with the right to confer both the licentiate and the doctorate. Since 1860 (when it was annexed to the Kingdom of Italy) the University of Bologna has conformed to the organization of institutes of higher learning in the new Italian State.

Bibliography: A. SORBELLI, *Enciclopedia Italiana di scienzi, littere ed arti,* 36 v. (Rome 1929–39;) 7:347–348. S. D'IRSAY, *Histoire des universités,* 2 v. (Paris 1933–35) v. 1. H. RASHDALL, *The Universities of Europe in the Middle Ages,* ed. F. M. POWICKE and A. B. EMDEN, 3 v. (Oxford 1936). *Chartularium studii Bononiensis,* 13 v. (Bologna 1909–40). *Studi e memorie per la storia dell' Università di Bologna,* ser. 1, 18 v. (Bologna 1907–50); NS 1–2 (1956–61).

[G. ORLANDELLI]

BOLSEC, JÉRÔME HERMÈS

Writer and physician; b. Paris, date unknown; d. Lyons, France *c.* 1585. As a Paris Carmelite, Bolsec was suspected of heresy, so he fled to Italy and the sympathetic protection of Duchess Renée of Ferrara (1545). There he renounced his religious vows and Catholicism, studied medicine, and married.

By 1550 he was in Geneva where he differed publicly with Calvin over predestination. Bolsec maintained that if faith was the consequence rather than the condition of election, God must be charged with partiality. He called Calvin's position illogical and absurd, saying that it manifested a fundamental weakness in the reformer's theological system. In consequence, Bolsec was arrested, imprisoned, and banished from Geneva.

He went to Bern, but was soon expelled from there as well. In 1551 he returned to France and sought a pastorate from the Reformed Church, but was rejected because of unorthodoxy. In 1563 he sought asylum at Lausanne; but when Theodore BEZA insisted that he first sign the *Confession of Bern* as proof of orthodoxy, Bolsec refused, returned to France, abjured his errors, reembraced the Catholic faith, and retired to Lyons to practice medicine and write. His biographies, *Histoire . . . de Jean Calvin* (1577) and *Histoire . . . de Th. de Beze* (1582), are highly controversial.

Bibliography: C. DE SAINT ÉTIENNE DE VILLIERS, *Bibliotheca carmelitana,* ed. P. G. WESSELS, 2 v. in 1 (Rome 1927) 637–639. J. DEDIEU, *Dictionnaire d'histoire et de géographie ecclésiastiques* (Paris 1912–) 9:676–679, bibliog. H. LIEBING, *Die Religion in Geschichte und Gegenwart* (Tübingen 1957–65) 1:1349–50.

[J. W. ROONEY, JR.]

BOMBERG, DANIEL

Dutch Christian printer and publisher of Hebrew books; b. Antwerp, Holland, *c.* 1470–80; d. Venice, Italy, 1549. In 1515 Bomberg established a printing press in Venice, where he published more than 200 Hebrew books. In 1516–17, he published the first Hebrew Bible, edited by Felix PRATENSIS, that embraced not only the Hebrew text, but also the Aramaic Targums and Rabbinical commentaries. A second important edition of the Hebrew Bible published by Bomberg was that of Jacob ben Chayyim in 1524–25. In 1519–22, with the permission of Pope LEO X, Bomberg published the first complete Babylonian TALMUD; his edition of the Palestinian Talmud appeared *c.* 1522–23. During this period he also published law books, grammatical works, and important books on various rites.

Bibliography: D. W. AMRAM, *Makers of Hebrew Books in Italy* (Philadelphia 1909) 146–148. M. SCHWAB, *The Jewish Encyclopedia* (New York 1901–06) 3: 299–300. E. KÜMMERER, *Die Religion in Geschichte und Gegenwart* (Tübingen 1957–65) 1:1351. E. L. EHRLICH, *Lexikon für Theologie und Kirche* (Freiburg 1957–65) 2:578.

[C. H. PICKAR]

BOMBOLOGNUS OF BOLOGNA

Italian Dominican theologian; fl. 1265 to 1270. A contemporary of THOMAS AQUINAS, although not a Thomist, he lectured on the *Sentences* at the Dominican priory of San Domenico in Bologna. His is the earliest-known commentary on the *Sentences* composed by an Italian Dominican in Italy. The autograph copy containing the commentary on the first book of the *Sentences* is preserved in Bologna, Bibl. Univ. 753. Two other manuscripts, Bologna, Bibl. Univ. 755, and Assisi, Com. 155, contain his commentary on the third book. Although Parisian influences are not altogether lacking, the work fundamentally represents Italian traditions. Bombolognus upheld universal hylomorphism on the authority of AVICEBRON. He described the thesis of the IMMACULATE CONCEPTION in clear terms, but he himself rejected it in favor of Mary's sanctification before birth. He was familiar with some of the writings of Aquinas, of St. BONAVENTURE, and of Peter of Tarentaise (later INNOCENT V).

Bibliography: M. GRABMANN, *Mittelalterliches Geistesleben*, 3 v. (Munich 1926–56) 1:339–340. F. PELSTER, "Les Manuscrits de Bombolognus de Bologne, O.P.," *Recherches de théologie ancienne et médiévale* 9 (Louvain 1937) 404–412. O. LOTTIN, *Psychologie et morale aux XIIe et XIIIe siècles*, v.3 (Louvain 1949) 235–239, 418–421. A. D'AMATO, "B. de Musolinis da B. notizie biografiche e bibliografiche," *Sapienza* 1 (1948) 75–90, 232–252. A. WALZ, *Lexicon für Theologie und Kirche*, ed. J. HOFER and K. RAHNER, 10 v. (2d, new ed. Freiburg 1957–65) 2:578.

[P. GLORIEUX]

BON SECOURS, SISTERS OF (CBS)

Officially known as the Congregation of Bon Secours (CBS), a pontifical institute founded on Jan. 24, 1824, when 12 young women pronounced their vows at Saint-Sulpice in Paris, dedicating themselves to the care of the sick in their homes in the aftermath of the trail of destruction that followed the French Revolution. Josephine Potel was the first superior. Hyacinthe de QUÉLEN, archbishop of Paris, had deliberated long in granting approbation to such an endeavor since it was then a novel form of apostolate. Soon other houses were opened throughout France, and the sisters added the tasks of caring for orphans, operating a school, opening clinics, and providing meeting places for school girls on their days off. The congregation spread to Ireland, England, and later to Scotland.

Through the request of James Gibbons (later cardinal), three sisters went to Baltimore, Md., in 1881 for the first U.S. foundation. In Baltimore, the sisters answered the calls of the sick in their homes, setting up the first modern in-home healthcare service in the U.S. Other innovative healthcare achievements included the establishment of the first daycare center (1907) for children of working mothers who would otherwise be placed in orphanages, and St. Edmond's Home for Crippled Children (1916), the first Catholic-run facility for disabled children in the U.S. In 1919, the sisters opened their first hospital, the Bon Secours Hospital in Baltimore.

By the end of 2000, the congregation operated healthcare facilities in Europe (France, Ireland, and Great Britain), the U.S., and South America (Peru and Ecuador). In the U.S., the congregation operates the non-profit Bon Secours Healthcare system that comprises hospitals, hospices, retirement and assisted care facilities, and clinics. The generalate is located in Paris, France, and the congregation's U.S. headquarters is in Marriottsville, Maryland.

Bibliography: M. BADIOU, *Les Soeurs du Bon Secours de Paris* (Lyon 1958). J. M. HAYES, *The Bon Secours Sisters in the U.S.* (2d ed. Washington 1931). R. C. CONNELLY and N. TAYLOR, *Bon Secours Centennial: 1881–1981: Tributes to Medical Pioneers.* (Grosse Pointe, Mich. 1982). M. C. O'SULLIVAN, *The Sisters of Bon Secours in the United States, 1881–1981: A Century of Caring* (Marriottsville, Md. 1982).

[M. L. NUGENT/EDS.]

BONA, ST.

Patroness of travel hostesses; b. Pisa, Italy, *c.* 1156; d. Pisa, May 29, 1207. Distinguished by her piety as a child, Bona was received as a young woman into the CANONS REGULAR OF ST. AUGUSTINE and henceforth lived in a house near the Canons who served St. Martin's church in Pisa. As a result of a vision of Our Lord, she made a pilgrimage to the Holy Land. There a hermit Ubald instructed her about the holy places she was to visit and eventually told her when to return to Pisa. On the way home she was wounded by Saracens and molested by robbers. Henceforth she lived as a recluse in Pisa, except for her nine pilgrimages to SANTIAGO DE COMPOSTELA and frequent visits to St. Peter's tomb in Rome. She is buried in St. Martin's, Pisa. In 1962 Pope John XXIII named her the patroness of Italian travel hostesses.

Feast: May 29.

Bibliography: *Acta Sanctorum* May 7:141–161, 858. *Bibliotheca hagiograpica latina antiquae et mediae aetatis* (Brussels 1898–1901) 1:206–207. J. L. BAUDOT and L. CHAUSSIN, *Vies des saints et des bienhereux selon l'ordre du calendrier avec l'historique des fêtes* (Paris 1935–56) 5:569–572. F. BARTORELLI, *Santa B. da Pisa* (Bari 1960). B. MATTEUCCI, *Bibliotheca sanctorum* 3:234–235. *Acta Apostolicae Sedis* 54 (1962) 707–708.

[M. J. HAMILTON]

BONA, GIOVANNI

Cardinal, Cistercian monk, liturgist, and ascetical writer; b. Mondovi, Piedmont, Oct. 10, 1609; d. Rome, Oct. 28, 1674. Bona took the habit of a Cistercian monk of the Congregation of Feullants in Italy when he was 16 years old. He pursued studies in Rome and became a successful professor of theology (1633–36). He was appointed prior, abbot, and abbot general of his congregation (1651), and, finally, was created cardinal in 1669.

Bona's liturgical writings, the fruit of vast research and soberly critical judgment, place him among the founders of modern liturgical studies. The scope of his work on the Divine Office, *De Divina Psalmodia,* is suggested by its earlier title, *Psallentis Ecclesiae harmonia, Tractatus historicus, symbolicus, asceticus de divina psalmodia eiusque causis, mysteriis et disciplina, deque variis ritibus omnium Ecclesiarum in psallendis divinis officiis* (1653). His work on the Mass, *Rerum liturgicarum libri duo* (1671), is simpler and clearer. In explaining the origins of the Mass, its different ways of celebration, its structure and constituent elements, he keeps surprisingly free, for a man of his time, of symbolic interpretation and polemic tone. Another work, *De sacrificio missae tractatus asceticus* (1658), offers pious considerations in aid of the priest's devotion as he offers the sacrifice of the Mass.

Bona's ascetical works are not original. Drawing from extensive readings in the Fathers, St. Thomas, and more recent spiritual writers, such as St. Francis de Sales and St. Ignatius, his teaching is simple, solid, and traditional. In his *Manuductio ad Coelum* (1658), after explaining the ultimate end of man and insisting on the need for a spiritual director, he treats his subject according to the familiar three ways (*see* THREE WAYS, THE). In his *Via compendii ad Deum per motus anagogicos et orationes jaculatorias* (1657), he explains how union with God is perfected in actual loving attention to Him, and proposes ejaculatory prayer as a means to this. His *De discretione spirituum* (1671) is usually discussed in modern treatments of the discernment of spirits.

Bibliography: G. BONA, *Hortus Coelestium Deliciarum,* ed. M. VATTASSO (Rome 1918). H. DUMAINE, *Dictionnaire d'archéologie chrétienne et de liturgie* (Paris 1907–53) 2:992–1002. J. M. CANIVEZ, *Dictionnaire do spiritualité ascétique et mystique. Doctrine et histoire* (Paris 1932–) 1:1762–66. L. BERTOLOTTI, *Vita Ioannis Bona* (Asti 1677). "Si può sperare la canonizzatione del Cardinale Giovanni Bona?" *Rivista storica Benedettina* 5 (1910) 253–268, 321–364. PIUS X, "Il Cardinale Giovanni Bona a Mondovì," *ibid.* 418–422. A. CORSI, "La feste centenarie di Mondovì pel Cardinale Giovanni Bona," *ibid.* 535–540. A. MICHELOTTI, "Musica e poesia nell'opera del cardinale Giovanni Bona," *ibid.* 6 (1911) 5–35.

[T. BOYD]

BONAL, FRANÇOIS DE

French prelate; b. Bonal, near Agen, France, May 9, 1734; d. Munich, Sept. 5, 1800. He was director general of the Carmelites, and became bishop of Clermont in 1776. He led an austere, apostolic life. He played an important role in the French Revolution. As deputy to the Estates General of 1789, he was named president of the ecclesiastical committee of the assembly and fought anticlerical measures until he was forced to resign. He took the oath of loyalty to the civil constitution in February 1790, but not to the CIVIL CONSTITUTION OF THE CLERGY in January 1791. His letter of April 1791 advising Louis XVI not to receive the Sacraments from the civil clergy, was introduced later in the trial of the king. Bonal immigrated to Brussels and The Hague (1794). He was captured by French troops, and condemned to deportation. Impoverished, he went to Altona in Prussia, then to Fribourg in Switzerland, and finally to Munich.

In April 1798, he signed the *Instruction sur les atteintes partées à la religion*, published by French refugee bishops in Germany, and before his death he dictated a spiritual testament giving his last instructions to his diocese. He was buried in the Capuchin monastery in Munich.

Bibliography: ABBÉ BOEUF, *Mgr. de Bonnal* (Paris 1910). G. WAGNER, *Catholicisme* 2:120. R. LIMOUZIN-LAMOTHE, *Dictionnaire de biographie française* 6:903.

[W. E. LANGLEY]

BONAL, RAYMOND

Founder of the Congregation of the Priests of St. Mary (Bonalists); moral theologian; b. Villefranche–de–Rouerque, Aug. 15, 1600; d. Agde, Aug. 9, 1653. Bonal did his classical, philosophical, theological, and legal studies in Cahors at the Jesuit college and the university. He was ordained at Lombes in 1624 and received a doctorate in theology from the University of Toulouse in 1626.

He exercised the ministry at Villefranche, where his spiritual energy attracted other priests to work with him. This was the nucleus of the congregation whose spirit was that of St. Francis de Sales. They followed the common life as early as 1631 at the chapel of Our Lady of Pity in Villefranche. Vincent de Paul, Father Bourdoise, and Jane Frances de Chantal advised Bonal in the drawing up of the Constitutions, which were completed in 1637 and given episcopal approval in 1648. Papal and royal approval came in 1665 and 1678. Mission preaching, retreats for laity and priests, and seminary teaching constituted the congregation's apostolate. The activities of the community spread during Bonal's lifetime to Foix, Aleth, and Toulouse, where he established a seminary-college called Caraman in 1651. The following year a seminary project at Agde was frustrated by an epidemic. At the same time episcopal approval of his rule was given by Charles Augustus de Sales, third successor and nephew of Francis de Sales.

After Bonal's death in 1653, his work was carried on successfully for another 60 years, but vocations became so meager that in 1723 the seminary at Villefranche was entrusted to the Lazarists; the Toulouse seminary suffered the same fate in 1752. This process continued until the congregation was finally absorbed by the Congregation of the Mission.

Bibliography: There is a MS biography of Bonal by a priest of his congregation in the seminary of Sainte-Sulpice. É. M. FAILLON, *Vie de M. Olier* 2 v. (4th ed. Paris 1873) 362–364. L. BERTRAND, *Bibliothèque Sulpicienne* (Paris 1900) 1:214–215. B. MAYRAN, *Raymond Bonal dans les Diocèses de Pamier et d'Alet* (Foix 1914). E. MANGENOT, *Dictionnaire de théologie catholique* (Paris 1903–50) 2:956–957.

[J. J. SMITH]

BONALD, LOUIS GABRIEL AMBROISE DE

French statesman and social and political theorist, whose writings not only epitomized TRADITIONALISM but also influenced significantly the development of sociological theory; b. Le Monna, near Millau (Rouergue, Aveyron), France, Oct. 2, 1754; d. Paris, Nov. 23, 1840. His family, Catholic and of the ''nobility of the robe'' (magistrates), had him educated by the Oratorians of Juilly, where he came under the influence of Malebranche's philosophy. He emigrated during the French Revolution but later found favor with Napoleon and returned to France. Under the Restoration monarchy, he was elected to the Académie Française (1816) and named vicomte (1821) and peer (1823). As the leading theorist of the ultraroyalists, he opposed all liberal tendencies. After the Revolution of 1830, he resigned his peerage and retired to Le Monna.

The purpose Bonald set for himself in his writings was to overcome the effects of Enlightenment rationalism by establishing, after the manner of a geometrician proving a series of theorems, the principles upon which a well-ordered society would be founded. To him these included a union of an absolute political power with an absolute religious power in a hierarchical society ordering every aspect of life according to immutable principles arrived at by deduction. Bonald argued first that since man cannot have invented language, God must have revealed it to the first man, and with it all religious, social, and moral truths. It followed that tradition and not individual human reason was the necessary means of attaining truth. The argument embodied all the basic elements of traditionalism, including a failure to distinguish between the natural and supernatural orders of reality, but when the traditionalist position—as a kind of FIDEISM—was condemned by the Catholic Church, Bonald's works were not specifically included in the condemnation (cf. Denz. 2811–2814, 3026). His principal writings are *La Théorie du pouvoir politique et religieux* (1796), which sets forth his main thesis regarding the nature of society; and *La Législation primitive . . .* (1802) and *Recherches philosophiques . . .* (1818), which together embody most of his arguments.

Bonald's originality lay in his ability to construct an internally consistent system that could treat politics, social organization, religion, the arts, education, and, in theory, all elements in a culture as interacting functions within a closed order. An a priori explanation was applicable to all. His ideas were assimilated in such varied intellectual traditions as those represented by Henri de Saint-Simon, Félicité de Lamennais, Auguste Comte, Hippolyte Taine, and Charles Maurras; the explanation lies principally in the fact that Bonald, grappling with the problem of the relationship between the individual and society, resolved it in favor of man's being, and being only, a product of society. Thus, both the authoritarian and the positivistic implications of Bonald's work have assured it a place in the history of ideas.

Bibliography: *Oeuvres complètes*, ed. J. P. MIGNE, 3 v. (Paris 1859). C. CONSTANTIN, *Dictionnaire de théologie catholique* 2:958–961. H. MOULINIÈ, *De Bonald: La Vie, la carrière politique, la doctrine* (Paris 1916). R. SPAEMANN, *Der Ursprung der Soziologie aus dem Geist der Restauration: Studien über L. G. A. de Bon-*

ald (Munich 1959). M. H. QUINLAN, *The Historical Thought of the Vicomte de Bonald* (Washington 1953).

[M. H. QUINLAN]

BONAVENTURE, ST.

Franciscan saint, scholastic, seventh general minister of the Lesser Brothers (*friars minor*), cardinal bishop of Albano, Doctor of the Church; b. Bagnoregio, 1217; d. Lyons, July 15, 1274.

LIFE

Bonaventure is the religious name of Giovanni di Fidanza (John of Fidanza) who was born in 1217 in Bagnoregio near Viterbo in Tuscany, Italy. His parents were John di Fidanza, a physician, and Maria di Ritello. Bonaventure tells the story of how as a boy he fell deathly ill and was miraculously saved through the intercession of St. FRANCIS OF ASSISI (8.579; references refer to the volume and page number of the Quarrachi *opera omnia* listed at the end of this article). This event occurred sometime after Francis's death in 1226. No other details of his youth have survived.

Early Years. After receiving his early education in Bagnoregio (1225–1235), Bonaventure continued his studies at the University of Paris *c.* 1235, becoming a bachelor of arts in 1241 and a master of arts in 1243. Shortly thereafter, probably following the lead of his teacher ALEXANDER OF HALES (d. 1245) who had just established the new Franciscan school at Paris, Bonaventure joined the Franciscans in Paris (1243–44). In addition to Alexander, his ''master and father,'' Bonaventure also studied under the masters JOHN OF LA ROCHELLE (d. 1245) and the Dominican Guerric of Saint-Quentin (d. 1245). Following their deaths, he continued his studies with Odo Rigaud (d. 1275) and WILLIAM OF MELITONA (d. 1260).

After becoming a bachelor of Scripture under William in 1248 he lectured on Scripture until 1250. Then he became a bachelor of the Sentences, taught Lombard's *Sentences*, and wrote his massive *Commentaries on the Sentences* (1250–52). These commentaries contain all the basic principles of his theology, illustrate his mastery of the Christian tradition, and systematically outline his understanding of the nature of theology. Afterwards, at the request of the general minister Bl. John of Parma (1247–1257), he began lecturing on Scripture and wrote several commentaries which he reworked from his earlier studies on Scripture (1253–54). Of his five exegetical works surviving, the most notable are his writings on the Gospels of John and Luke which contain reflections on the mystery of the Incarnation and Christ's mediation.

Saint Bonaventure. (Archive Photos)

The latter was rewritten and polished to help in the formation of future Franciscan preachers. He probably reworked his *Sentence Commentary* into its final form during this same period (1253–1256).

In 1253 he was ordained a priest and was ready to become a regent master (*magister regens*), but due to the opposition to the mendicants on the part of the secular clergy who were masters at the University of Paris, he may not have been formally approved as a *magister* until Oct. 23, 1257. Nevertheless, it is clear that he functioned as a regent master before this date. In 1253 he occupied the Franciscan chair of theology and from this position he taught, preached, and delivered at least three disputed questions: *On Christ's Knowledge, On the Mystery of the Trinity, and On Evangelical Perfection* (1254–1257). In 1257, at the request of his students, he wrote the *Breviloquium* as a compendium of his theology. The prologue presents his scriptural methodology and the chapters provide a concise summary of his scholastic theology. Shortly after this, drastic changes would end his formal academic career at the University of Paris.

In 1254, with the support of Pope Innocent IV (1243–1254) and under the leadership of William of Saint-Amour (d.1272), the secular masters argued that the poverty promoted by the mendicants was against gos-

Title	Volume/Page	Date
Commentarius in librum Ecclesiastes (Commentary on the Book of Ecclesiastes)	6.1-103	1248-1254
Commentarius in librum Sapientiae (Commentary on the Book of Wisdom)	6.105-233	1248-1254
Commentarius in Evangelium Ioannis (Commentary on the Gospel of John)	6.237-532	1248-1254
Collationes in Evangelium Ioannis (Collations on the Gospel of John)	6.533-634	1248-1254
Commentarius in quatuor libros Sententiarum Petri Lombardi (Commentary on the Four Books of Sentences of Peter Lombard)		1250-1252 rewritten
Book I: The Trinity and Unity of God	1.88-861	1252-1254
Book II: God the creator, grace, original and actual sin	2.12-1016	
Book III: The Incarnation and redemption, on virtue and the commandments	3.10-896	
Book IV: The sacraments in general, the seven sacraments, the last things	4.8-1054	
Commentarius in Evangelium Lucae (Commentary on the Gospel of Luke)	7.1-604	1253-1254
Quaestio disputata de scientia Christi (Disputed Questions on the Knowledge of Christ)	5.3-43	1254-1256
Quaestio disputata de mysterio Trinitatis (Disputed Questions on the Mystery of the Trinity)	5.45-115	1254-1256
Quaestio disputata de perfectione evangelica (Disputed Questions on Evangelical Perfection)	5.117-198	1254-1255
Sermo de triplici testimonio sanctissimae Trinitatis (Sermon on the Triple Testimony of the Most Holy Trinity)	5.535-538	1254-1256
Epistola de tribus quaestionibus ad magistrum innominatum (Letter on Three Questions to an Unknown Master)	8.331-336	1254-1255
Epistola (First Encyclical Letter to the Order)	8.468-69	1257
Sermo Christus unus omnium magister (Sermon on Christ the One Teacher of All)	5.567-574	1257
Breviloquium	5.199-291	1257
Itinerarium mentis in Deum (Journey of the Mind into God)	5.293-316	1259
De perfectione vitae ad sorores (On the Perfection of Life addressed to Sisters)	8.107-127	1259
De triplici via (The Triple Way)	8.1-18	1259-1260
Soliloquium de quatuor mentalibus exercitiis (Soliloquy on Four Spiritual Exercises)	8.28-67	1260
Tractatus de praeparatione ad missam (Tract on the Preparation for Mass)	8.99-106	1260
Lignum vitae (The Tree of Life)	8.68-86	1260
De quinque festivitatibus pueri Jesu (On the Five Feasts of the Child Jesus)	8.88-95	1260-63?
Regula novitiorum (Instructions for Novices)	8.475-490	1260
Constitutiones Generales Narbonenses (The Constitutions of Narbonne)	8.449-467	1260
Sermo de regno Dei descripto in parabolis evangelicis (Sermon on God's Reign described in the Gospel Parables)	5.539-553	1256-61?
Legenda major sancti Francisci (Major Life of St. Francis)	8.504-565	1261-1263
Legenda minor sancti Francisci (Minor Life of St. Francis)	8.565-579	1261-1263
Officium de passione Domini (Office on the Passion of the Lord)	8.152-158	1263
De sex alis Seraphim (On the Six Wings of the Seraph)	8.131-151	1263
Vitis mystica sive Tractus de passione Domini (The Mystical Vine; authenticity disputed)	8.159-189	1263?
Sermo de sanctissimo corpore Christi (Sermon on the Most Holy Body of Christ)	5.553-566	1264
Epistola (Second Encyclical Letter to the Order)	8.470-71	1266
De regimine animae (On the Regimen of the Soul)	8.128-130	1266-68?
Collationes de decem praeceptis (Collations on the Ten Commandments)	5.505-532	1267

Title	Volume/Page	Date
Collationes de septem donis Spiritus sancti (Collations on the Seven Gifts of the Holy Spirit)	5.455-503	1268
Apologia pauperum (Apology for the Poor)	8.232-330	1269
De reductione artium ad theologiam (On the Reduction of Arts to Theology)	5.319-325	1269-70?
Tractatus de plantatione paradisi (Tract on the Planting of Paradise)	5.574-579	1270-1273
Collationes in Hexaëmeron (Collations on the Six Days)	5.327-454	1273
Epistola de imitatione Christi (Letter on the Imitation of Christ)	8.499-503	?
Epistola continens viginti quinque memorialia (Letter Containing Twenty-Five Points to Remember)	8.491-498	?
Epistola de sandaliis apostolorum (Letter on the sandals of the Apostles)	8.386-390	?
Quare Fratres Minores praedicent et confessiones audiant (Why Lesser Brothers Should Preach and Hear Confessions)	8.375-385	?
Sermo super regulam Fratrum Minorum (Sermon on the Rule of the Lesser Brothers)	8.438-448	?
Sermones (Sermons; the sermons span his entire life and are from numerous locations)	9.23-731	various

pel teaching and subverted church authority. They fiercely opposed the two mendicant orders (Franciscan and Dominican) and attempted to have them excluded from their university positions of teaching publically. Bonaventure responded with a *Letter to an Unknown Master* and *On Evangelical Perfection.* The latter argues that humility itself is the foundation of evangelical perfection, that is, a life of poverty, chastity, and obedience conformed to the love of Christ. This heated confrontation was finally settled by the new pope, Alexander IV (1254–1261), who sided with the mendicants and condemned William's views in 1255. Following this papal intervention, Bonaventure was formally raised to regent master in 1257, six months after he had already been elected general minister of the Franciscan Order.

His election as general minister was in part a response to the wounds sustained by the Franciscans during the mendicant controversy. In 1254 the apocalyptic-minded Franciscan Gerard of Borgo San Donnino (d. 1276–77), reinterpreting the apocalyptic theology of Joachim of Fiore (d. 1202), published his radical book the *Eternal Gospel.* This book prophesied that the new age of the Spirit would begin in 1260. It was quickly condemned by Alexander on Oct. 23, 1255. Nevertheless, many other Franciscans embraced Gerard's views of Joachim's apocalyptic theology. Most notable was the general minister John of Parma who, at the suggestion of the pope, resigned in January 1257. When the brothers asked who could best serve as leader, John himself recommended that Bonaventure replace him. Thus, on Feb. 2, 1257, at the General Chapter of Rome, Bonaventure was elected the seventh general minister of the Franciscan Order. He was 40 years old. Upon resigning from his academic post in Paris, Bonaventure delivered his powerful sermon *Christ the One Teacher of All.* It identifies Christ as the source of all knowledge and provides insight into the heart of his theological synthesis.

Middle Years. Bonaventure's election as general minister radically impacted his life and career. He dedicated his efforts to this office which he held for the remaining 17 years of his life. He inherited an expanding order of over 30,000 brothers suffering internal divisions regarding the practice of Francis's ideals, especially regarding poverty. He quickly issued his first encyclical letter to the entire order on April 23, 1257. It sternly addresses the condition of the order, laxity in the practice of poverty, and the need for spiritual renewal through prayer. In May of the same year, he traveled to Italy where he was officially conferred general minister by Pope Alexander IV. In late summer, he returned to his usual residence at the ''grand couvent des cordeliers'' in Mantes-sur-Seine near Paris.

For the next two years he visited the order throughout Europe (Italy, France, England, Germany) personally learning its problems and needs. This activity resulted in an almost complete hiatus in his writing. However, in 1259 this changed and his new writings signal a significant transition. While remaining a theologian, he began to compose spiritual/mystical/ascetical writings on prayer devised for the needs of his brothers. His masterpiece the *Journey of the Mind into God,* which presents six levels of illumination modeled on Francis's vision of a seraph and subsequent reception of the stigmata, leads the contemplative wayfarer in a spiraling ascent from creation upward into God, ending with a mystical death paralleling Francis's own seraphic experience with Christ. This text inaugurated a new period in Bonaventure's literary production. For the next four years his works involved a combination of texts on spirituality, hagiography, and governance.

His spiritual writings of this period include the widely popular *The Triple Way* which follows Pseudo-Dionysius's formulation of mystical theology as a process of purgation, illumination, and perfection/union. Following the examples of AUGUSTINE and HUGH OF SAINT VICTOR, he also wrote the *Soliloquy on Four Spiritual Exercises*, devised as a psychological introspection leading the mind to contemplation. Likewise, his meditations on the life of Christ in *The Tree of Life* and *On the Five Feasts of the Child Jesus* present a form of imaginative prayer that calls upon the mind to recollect the mysteries of Christ. With these writings, one can sense that Bonaventure discerned the order's need to undergo a spiritual reform, return to the path of prayer, and embrace a life in the footsteps of St. Francis. Moreover, throughout his travels, and for the entire span of his ministry as general minister, he preached frequently and many of his sermons survive. The extent of his preaching activity is evidenced by the entire ninth volume of his *Opera omnia*, which consists of sermons integral for understanding his spirituality. They are also very helpful in reconstructing his travels. Two of his main travel companions were his secretary Bernard of Besse and his friend Mark of Montefeltro who recorded many of his sermons.

His two hagiographical works are *The Major Legend of St. Francis* and the shorter *The Minor Legend of St. Francis*, devised for liturgical use. The term *legenda* indicates that these works were intended for public reading by the brothers and the wider Christian community. Both works are the result of the request that he write a new life of St. Francis in order to bring the large body of earlier hagiography into a deeper synthesis. Although most modern studies claim that this request was made by the General Chapter of Narbonne in 1260, it is more probable that it came from the General Chapter of Rome in 1257. With this mandate, he repeatedly traveled to Italy to visit Assisi (1259–1263) where he interviewed the living companions of Francis. During his visit of 1260, he attended the consecration of the church at Mount La Verna and the transfer of St. Clare's body from San Damiano to the new Basilica. It is likely he provided an update of this major project at Narbonne in 1260.

The Major Legend is faithful to the Chapter mandate by integrating the earlier tradition, especially Thomas of Celano, Julian of Speyer, and material from the *Assisi Compilation*, into a hagiographical, spiritual, and theological masterpiece. Bonaventure recasts the earlier materials about Francis into the framework of his theology of grace: the visible events of Francis's life reveal the invisible presence of God's grace which purifies, illumines, and perfects Francis. *The Minor Legend* was also significant in disseminating the image, message, and spirituality of Francis while emphasizing the importance of prayer, via the liturgical medium, for following Francis's life of evangelical perfection. According to tradition, these two hagiographies were finished by 1261 and Bonaventure later presented them to the brothers at the General Chapter of Pisa (1263). While in Italy that year, he attended the translation of the body St. Anthony from Arcella to the new basilica in Padua, and he also likely presided over the trial of John of Parma, who continued his adherence to Joachimism.

During this intense activity, he compiled for the General Chapter of Narbonne (1260) the *Constitutions of Narbonne*, which codify the order's earlier existing legislation into a systematic collection of regulations, divided into12 headings corresponding to the 12 chapters of the Rule. While the codification adds little to the already existing laws, it is of major importance in the history of Franciscan legislation. Additions are found in the *Statutes Issued by the Chapter of Narbonne*. The *Determinations of Questions Concerning the Rule of the Lesser Brothers* and *Exposition on the Rule of the Lesser Brothers* are spurious works attributed to Bonaventure and should not be included when assessing his administration of the Order.

Approximately the same time, he wrote *Instructions for Novices* (1260). This provides a defined structure for the critical task of initial formation since the novitiate year was the only ''explicit formation'' a new brother received. This text envisions a total transformation of the novice through disciplinary practices enabling him to discern and understand the movement of the Spirit better. Two years later, he wrote *On the Six Wings of the Seraph* for use by religious superiors so they could better serve their brothers. All Bonaventure's authentic works regarding the order reveal his concern for the brothers' proper interpretation of, formation within, and ministerial service toward a life of evangelical perfection as expressed within the Rule approved by Pope Honorius III (1216–1227) in 1223.

In addition to accepting and disseminating Bonaventure's two *Legenda* of St. Francis, the General Chapter of Pisa (1263) also issued several statues addressing Franciscan liturgical practices. Again, a concern for the formation of the brothers through the liturgy is evident. Subsequently, he made several trips throughout Italy and France, and in 1265 visited England. The same year, Pope Clement IV nominated him archbishop of York, but he humbly refused, preferring instead to continue his ministry to the brothers. In 1266, he presided over his third General Chapter, in Paris, which responded to several questions concerning the interpretation and observance of the recently approved *Constitutions of Narbonne*. His even harsher *Second Encyclical Letter*, possibly delivered there, reveals that the observance of poverty was a persistent problem plaguing the brothers. This chapter is famous for its decree that ''all the legends of St. Francis that have been made should be removed'' (*Miscellanea francescana* 72, 247). The Chapter of Narbonne had done the same with earlier copies of the general constitutions (*Archivium franciscanum historicum* 3, 491). Thus, *The Major Legend* and the new Constitutions of Narbonne attempted a new beginning for the order's interpretation of Francis and implementation of the way of life he inspired. Around this time Bonaventure also wrote *On the Regimen of the Soul* which presents a concise summary of his spiritual doctrine and its practical exercises.

Later Years. Following the death in 1268 of the pro-Franciscan Clement IV (1265–1268), a three-year vacancy in the papacy ensued. This vacancy signals a significant shift in the historical climate that impacted Bonaventure's life and writings until his death. The previous year, the decade-long uneasy truce between the seculars and mendicants at the University of Paris began to dissolve and new threats faced the Franciscans. Since the mendicants had lost the protection of the Holy See, the secular masters, led by Gerard of Abbeville (d. 1272), again increased their attacks against the mendicants. Also, through the influence of SIGER OF BRABANT (d. 1281), the secular masters supported the rise of Averroistic Aristotelianism and the related claims that philosophy is self-sufficient. Thus, from around 1266 to 1274, these two heated issues engaged Bonaventure in a battle on two fronts. Again he defended the ideals of mendicancy, this time attacking radical Aristotelianism as well. Most of his longer works from this period are in the form of *collations* which he did not write himself; rather, they are the records of scribes who copied his lectures as they were delivered at the University of Paris. From 1267 to 1274 he delivered three such lectures along with his *Apology for the Poor* which he wrote in his own hand.

In 1267 Bonaventure's anti-Aristotelianism first appears in his *Collations on the Ten Commandments*. The very first collation rejects two errors: the eternity of the world and the unicity of the agent intellect. Throughout he emphasizes the primacy of Christ over the philosophy of Aristotle. His polemic is not against Aristotle per se, but against the Aristotelian philosophers of his day. The following year (1268), his *Collations on the Gifts of the Holy Spirit* vehemently refutes Averroistic Aristotelianism. He reemphasises his previous objections, increases his references to other related errors like ethical determinism, and explicitly renounces Gerard of Abbeville and other rationalistic philosophers who were reviving their attacks against the mendicants at the university. Bonaventure juxtaposes faith in Christ (the good teacher) against radical Aristotelianism, arguing that one only receives the Spirit's seven gifts through and in Christ who is the foundation and fruition of each gift. In short, he follows Augustine's definition of Christian philosophy as ''the cause of being, the basis of understanding, and the order of living'' (*De civitate Dei*, 8.4), and argues that the eternity of the world contradicts the first, the unity of the intellect violates the second, and the necessity of fate subverts the third (*On the Gifts of the Holy Spirit*, 5.497).

In 1269 Gerard of Abbeville countered with *Against the Adversary of Christian Perfection* which assails the ecclesial status of the mendicant faculty. The same year, Bonaventure responded with *Apology for the Poor* (sometimes called *Defense of the Mendicants*), which is his most articulate and ardent defense of Franciscan mendicancy as an authentic expression of evangelical perfection. He marshals tradition, canon law, ecclesiastical decrees, the example of the saints, and the authority of Scripture as he constructs his defense around the Rule of 1223, claiming that the brothers, in their life of evangelical perfection, are true disciples of Christ who is their true master. Considering the related issue of the self-sufficiency of Aristotelianism, it is likely that he wrote at this time (1269–70?) *On the Reduction of the Arts to Theology*, a mature and compact expression of his synthesis of retracing all knowledge and philosophy to a Christian wisdom-theology based on Scripture. A precise date for this text remains elusive, and some scholars date it around 1256. In December 1270, the positions of the secular masters were condemned at the University of Paris.

With this controversy still raging at the university, Bonaventure traveled from Paris to Italy and presided over his fourth General Chapter, in Assisi (1269). The attacks against the Franciscans, along with the possibility of the election of a new pope less sympathetic to the order, prompted the chapter to clean house by issuing several disciplinary and liturgical degrees. The issue of mendicancy was solved, at least temporarily, by the election of the pro-Franciscan Gregory X in 1271 (1271–1276). Once again the Franciscans had a strong ally in the pope. During his travels, Bonaventure worked his way to his fifth General Chapter in Lyon in 1272, which attended to constitutional and liturgical matters, and further defined the relations between the brothers and the Poor Ladies of St. Clare. After the Chapter, he continued his tour of the order.

In 1273, his last journey to Paris resulted in his extraordinary *Collations on the Six Days*, his final synthesis. Again, the Aristotelianism crisis forms the backdrop for this series of lectures, and the entire university community came to hear him. His message is unambiguous: Christ, not Aristotle, is the metaphysical center for all knowledge, understanding and wisdom (*On the Six Days* 1.10–39; 3.2ff.). On one level, he rejects the errors of the Aristotelian philosophers by explaining how christocentric exemplarism is the true foundation for Christian metaphysics. He subtly counters the issues of the eternity of the world, the unicity of the agent intellect, and ethical determinism with his theology of the threefold Word: the uncreated Word refutes the first, the incarnate Word the second, and the inspired Word the third. On another level, he organizes his lectures within an eschatological framework thereby emphasizing, against the same errors, that time begins with God, proceeds through Christ the center, and returns to the Father in a grand circular dynamic. Throughout, his insights and associations are veiled in a fusion of analogical and scriptural symbolism, making it a unique masterpiece of mystical theology.

This last work remained unfinished. Before its completion Gregory X, who urged him not to refuse, nominated him cardinal in preparation for the upcoming Second Council of Lyon (May-July 1274). After traveling with the pope to Lyon, Bonaventure was consecrated bishop of Albano; Gregory also consecrated the Dominican Bl. Peter of Tarantaise (future Pope Innocent V, 1276) as archbishop of Lyon. The two served as the pope's chief legates at the council, which sought to reunify the Greek and Latin churches. Bonaventure remained general minister until he resigned at the General Chapter held in conjunction with the council. The pope presided over the chapter's election of his successor. The unanimous choice was Jerome of Ascoli (future Pope Nicholas IV, 1288–1292) who was not present because he was accompanying the Greek envoys from Constantinople. Thus, under the direction of the pope, Bonaventure guided the chapter to issue several decrees regarding the interpretation and observance of poverty so as to alleviate antimendicant sentiments within ecclesiastical ranks. Bonaventure's resignation brought his extended generalate to a close, and his 17 years of leadership earned him in modern times the title ''second founder of the Franciscan Order.''

The Greek delegates arrived at the council on May 24, and Bonaventure probably presided over several meetings regarding reunification. Shortly after preaching a sermon celebrating the brief reunion of both churches on June 29, he suddenly became ill, and died on the morning of July 15, 1274, two days before the end of the council. He was buried on the same day in the Franciscan Church at Lyon before the entire council. On April 14, 1482 he was canonized by the Franciscan pope Sixtus IV (1471–1484). A century later another Franciscan pope, Sixtus V (1585–1590), made him the sixth Doctor of the Church on March 14, 1588 with the title Seraphic Doctor (*Doctor Seraphicus*). In 1890, Pope Leo XIII (1878–1903) named him the prince of mystical theology.

THOUGHT

The prologue to the first book of the *Sentence Commentary* defines the task of theology as the teaching of salvation. It involves the study of how God creates everything and how everything returns to God through grace as if by an intelligible circle (1.639, 5.148, 5.177, 5.253, 5.322, 5.332–33), with Scripture as the point of departure. Scripture is like a great river irrigating all of Bonaventure's thought. The prologue to the *Breviloquium* uses the terms *sacra scriptura* and *theologia* interchangeably (5.201–08). Thus, theology/Scripture, based on faith and assisted by human reason, orders everything back to God in a grand circular dynamic of exit and return. While he saw a continuity between the goals of philosophy and theology (1.84, 2.716, 5.210, 5.305–06, 5.473–76, 5.320–21, 5.368–87), Bonaventure never developed a distinct philosophy; rather, his philosophy serves and ultimately culminates in his theology (5.319–25). Like philosophy, theology is a science because it organizes knowledge, thereby making reality intelligible. Yet, theology is the highest science because, avoiding idle curiosity (2.5, 5.73, 5.330–32, 5.413–14, 5.420, 5.636), it attempts to integrate all knowledge into the spiritual journey leading to loving union with God (5.210). Hence, theology is not simply speculative. It must also be practical, so that the theologian arrives at wisdom by way of both knowledge and love (3.774). Ultimately, the true aim or end of theology is ''to become good'' (1.13, 5.574), and this orients Bonaventure's entire theological synthesis toward mystical union with God in love.

PRINCIPLES

Bonaventure's thought is simultaneously Trinitarian and Christological. His theology of the Trinity is christocentric, and his Christology is Trinitarian. They are two manifestations of the same mystery. Bonaventure's metaphysics of the Trinity and Christology both operate according to the threefold dynamic of emanation (*emanatio*: how things come from God), exemplarity (*exemplaritas*: how things reflect God) and consummation (*consummatio*: how things return to God) (5.332). Bonaventure explains the interconnection between the Trinity and Christology by considering the mystery of the Trinity as forming the circle of emanation, exemplarity, and consummation in both the divine and created orders, while Christ is the center of the circle who holds the divine and created orders together. On one level, the self-communication of the Trinity is the basis for the entire circular process of emanation, exemplarity, and consummation both within the divine order (Father-Son-Spirit) and as expressed in the created order (creation-history-salvation). The mystery of God's unity and plurality provides Bonaventure with his basic insight into the metaphysical substructure of all reality. On another level, God's self-communication as Trinity is especially focused in Christ who is the self-expression of the entire Trinity, and so Christ is the metaphysical center of emanation, exemplarity, and consummation in both the divine and the created orders. In the divine order Christ is the center who joins the Father and the Spirit; in the created order Christ is also the center because creation issues forth through Christ, is perfected by Christ, and returns to God in Christ.

Bonaventure holds these two mysteries—circle and center, Trinity and Christ—as the two roots of Christian faith upon which all knowledge, understanding, and wisdom depend (5.370). The mystery of Christ reveals the Trinity, and the mystery of the Trinity is the transcendent horizon to the mystery of Christ. Everything that exists is in relationship with both the Trinity and Christ. The inner self-communication of the Trinity forms a corresponding circular dynamic in God, in creation, in understanding, and in salvation. Simultaneously, this divine self-communication is fully revealed in Christ who is the same center in God, in creation, in understanding, and in salvation.

While Bonaventure borrows from many sources to construct his theology, it is ultimately St. Francis of Assisi who provides him with the key insights of his systematic synthesis. Bonaventure translates Francis's emphasis on God's goodness and the centrality of Christ in his spirituality into a theological system based on the idea of God's self-diffusive good within the Trinity and the correlative idea of Christ the center. From Francis, Bonaventure constructs a truly Franciscan theology, and, like Francis, he sees the thrust and goal of theology to be union with the Triune God through Christ. Accordingly, to understand Bonaventure's theology, the interrelationship between the Trinity and Christology must be understood.

Trinity. The inner logic of Bonaventure's thought is Trinitarian. The Trinity forms the structural foundation for his metaphysics by which he constructs his entire theological system and all its interconnecting parts according to the circular dynamic of emanation, exemplarity, and consummation. His basic insight into the mystery of the Trinity is the ''firstness'' (*primitas*) of the Father (1.53–57, 1.215, 1.469–72, 5.114–15) who is the ultimate source and origin of all emanation, first within the divine order of persons, and then freely extended to the created order of the world. Nowhere does Bonaventure develop an independent treatment of the divine nature separated from a consideration of the divine persons. Rather, he consistently approaches God's existence (1.67–80, 1.153–56, 5.45–51, 5.308–09) by considering how the unity of the divine nature and the plurality of the divine persons are ultimately reconciled and explained by the firstness of the Father who is the fecund source of both. In approaching the mystery of the Trinity in this manner, he significantly adjusts the Augustinian model which begins with the unity of the divine nature (*de deo uno*) by following the Eastern approach of beginning with the divine persons (*de deo trino*).

Based on the New Testament view of God as love (1 Jn 4.8–16) and goodness (Mk 10.18, Lk 18.19) (5.308, 5.310), Bonaventure's theology of the internal emanations in the Trinity (*ad intra*) follows Richard of St. Victor and Pseudo-Dionysius (1.53–57, 5.70, 5.310–11, 5.381–82). From Richard, he explains the mystery of the Trinity according to an analysis of the nature of love which illustrates the necessity of three persons within the Godhead. He fuses this analysis of love into Pseudo-Dionysius's concept of the self-diffusive good (*bonum diffusivum sui*), and develops a Trinitarian metaphysics that is essentially based upon the Father's primacy (*primitas*) and the related notions of God's fontal plenitude (*plenitudo fontalis*) and fecundity (*fecunditas*) (1.139, 5.114). Starting with the Father as the eternal origin and fontal plenitude of goodness that is intrinsically self-communicative, he explains the eternal emanations of the Son and Spirit according to two modes: the Son according to nature (*per modum naturae*), and the Spirit according to will (*per modum voluntatis*) (1.128, 5.211, 5.311). The first reflects the Dionysian principle that the good is naturally self-diffusive, thereby explaining the necessary self-communication within God. The second reflects the Victorine principle that divine love is free, thereby showing the free self-communication within God. By combining both principles, Bonaventure arrives at a unique synthesis that views the Trinity as a mystery of the necessary and free self-communication of love (*circumincessio*).

The internal emanations of the divine *circumincessio* follow a circular dynamic based on the order of origin (*ordo originis*) (5.75–76, 5.210, 5.114–15). The Father, who is first (*primitas*), is the inaccessible (*innascibilitas*) origin who only gives love. The Son, who is the center (*medium*), has an origin (Father) and is an origin for another (Spirit) who both receives love (Father) and gives love (Spirit). The Spirit, who is the consummation (*ulti-*

mum), has both the Father and Son as origin, is not an origin for another, and therefore only receives love.

This circular dynamic depicts the inner constitution of the divine order of persons and forms Bonaventure's simple but profound insight into the metaphysical basis of all order: everything must have a beginning (emanation), a middle (exemplarity), and an end (consummation) (1.57–58, 2.41, 2.277, 5.332, 5.381). As first (*primitas*), the Father's fecundity overflows into the emanations of the Son and Spirit according to the metaphysics of Good; as center (*medium*), the Son's exemplarity mediates the entire reality of the Godhead according to the metaphysics of Being; and, as last, the Spirit's unity or bond (*nexus*) joins the Father and Son according to the metaphysics of Love. The Good, not Being, is the fontal source of Bonaventure's whole metaphysics, and both are united in Love. This insight into the mystery of the Trinity makes Bonaventure's entire theological synthesis distinctive. In sum, everything in both the divine and created orders overflows from the fecundity of the Father, flowing through the Son, and into the Spirit. Likewise, everything returns in the Spirit, through the Son to unity with the Father. Ultimately, all creation has its origin in Good; its constitutive being is an expression of Good, and its finality is love for Good.

While the Father is first within the divine order, the entire Trinity, as divine essence, is first in relation to the created order (5.115). Thus, Bonaventure constructs his entire system within the dialectical framework of exit (*exitus/emanatio*) and return (*reditus/reductio*) with the exemplarity of Christ as the universal center in both the divine and created orders.

Christology. Bonaventure's Christology emerges from the circular dynamic within the inner life of the Trinity. His basic Christological insight is the simple fact that Christ is the center (*medium*) (1.486, 3.32, 5.242, 5.269, 5.309–12, 5.330–35) of the circular dynamic of exit and return in both the divine and created orders. For this reason, his theology is rightfully identified as christocentric since the two closely related doctrines of exemplarism and salvation emerge from his vision of Christ. On the one hand, Christ is the center as *exemplar* in the emanation from the Father; on the other hand, Christ is the center as *mediator* in the consummation of all things in return to the Father (5.324–25).

Exemplarism. Bonaventure roots his exemplarism in a threefold understanding of Christ: as Son, as Image, and as Word of God (3.29–33). The Son's emanation from the Father is the ontological basis for his exemplarism. Since the Father's self-communication to the Son is absolute and perfect, all the Father can express is expressed in the Son. Yet, as perfect expression, Christ is also the true Image who only reflects/imitates the Father, and as perfect likeness, co-emanates the Spirit with the Father within the Trinity. As the Father's perfect expressed likeness, Christ is also truly the Word of God, and Bonaventure prefers this title (6.247) because it is through the Word that the Father freely creates. Thus, the Word is God's all inclusive self-knowledge encompassing the inner relationships of Father-Son and Trinity-Image as well as God's external relationship with creation. In sum, everything that God creates first exists in the Word; thus, the Word is the exemplar of everything that exists (1.485, 5.331–32, 5.343, 5.372–73, 5.426). The Word is both the self- expression of the divine order within and the exemplar of the created order without.

Exemplarism explores how all things are a copy (*exemplatum*) of the original model or exemplar. To understand fully the *exemplatum*, the exemplar must be known. If everything exists through the Word, then everything must be known in the Word. Bonaventure explains this with the doctrine of the divine Ideas/eternal Reasons which reside within the Word or eternal ''Art'' of the Father (5.301, 5.343, 5.426). Following Augustine, he understands the divine Ideas as eternally existing within the Word as God's omniscient self-knowledge of everything that actually or potentially exists. The one infinite Idea within God contains the multiplicity of everything in creation as well as all that God is in relation to creation. Thus, as the inner self-expression of the Trinity, the Word is the center of the unity and plurality within God; as the external expression of the Word, the unity and plurality of creation also finds its center in Word. The Word is the universal center who contains/reflects the Trinitarian exemplarism of the divine order and communicates it to the created order in the act of creation. Thus, the mystery of reality is unlocked by the Word, and Bonaventure teaches that the threefold Word is the key to contemplation.

With the threefold Word, Bonaventure's doctrine of exemplarism receives its fullest expression (5.241, 5.306, 5.343, 5.457–59, 8.84). The uncreated Word relates to the emanation of all things from the Father, the incarnate Word relates to the restoration of all things in the eternal/temporal exemplar of the Son, and the inspired Word relates to the revelation of all things in the consummation of the Holy Spirit. The threefold Word is the one center that joins creation, knowledge, and salvation with the Trinity according to the circular dynamic of exit/return. Thus, Bonaventure interconnects all reality in the exemplarism of the Word, the very center of all reality.

Salvation. Bonaventure's theology of redemption emerges from his trinitarian exemplarism. At the center of the threefold Word is the mystery of the Incarnation, and this mystery grounds Bonaventure's soteriology. In the return to God, the center (*medium*) becomes the *mediator* of salvation within the circular dynamic of exit/return (3.20). The Incarnation reveals the hidden center where the divine and created orders meet, and the two extremes are reconciled (1.2, 5.330–33, 7.356, 9.107). Bonaventure understands the Incarnation's role in salvation in a twofold sense that can be called ''redemptive-completion.'' On the one hand, Bonaventure approaches the mystery of the Incarnation from the historical and existential perspective of sin (3.706), and so, the actual mode of redemption is through the Incarnate Word by which redemption from sin is achieved through Christ's death on the cross (3.431, 3.427–28). Thus, he writes, ''The principal reason of the incarnation was the redemption of the human race.'' (3.23–24). Salvation is through the redemptive *reductio* of Christ's death and resurrection (3.30). On the other hand, the Incarnation perfects and completes creation (3.20, 5.324, 5.241, 9.109–10). Bonaventure writes, ''For the Incarnation makes for the perfection of the human — and consequently for the perfection of the entire universe.'' (3.23, 3.29). Since the Word is the prior ontological basis for all creation (3.254), from the beginning, God willed the Incarnation as the perfection of an otherwise incomplete universe (3.26–27).

The two positions of ''redemptive-completion'' are not contradictory, rather, they give complimentary emphasis to the one mystery of the Incarnation as *medium*. Christ is *medium* in the exit from God, and the *medium* in the return to God, and this would be true whether sin had disrupted the original created order or not. Thus, the Incarnation is the consummation of the created universe because it closes the intelligible circle and completes the order of creation. However, this perfection of order also repairs the broken order caused by sin. Because of sin, there is no completion without redemption. Thus, redemption is the principle reason for the Incarnation, but sin is not the ultimate cause of the Incarnation. Rather, God's love and mercy is the supreme cause of the Incarnation (3.22–23, 3.27, 3.706). God willed the Incarnation as a free gift for the perfection of the human person and all of creation, not simply as a response to sin. With or without sin, God willed the Incarnation because without Christ creation remains incomplete. In sum, Christ the center (*medium*) both perfects and redeems creation and *vice versa*. Christ's *mediatio* is the salvific *reductio* of all creation to the Father (3.410, 5.243, 5.325). Thus Bonaventure's soteriology of ''redemptive-completion'' develops beyond Anselm's legal/moral categories of satisfaction. It is also within the context of Christ's mediation of salvation that Bonaventure's Mariology should be interpreted (5.237, 5.487, 7.27, 7.179, 8.79, 8.315, 9.422, 9.612, 9.633–721).

Bonaventure applies his Trinitarian theology and Christology to explain how the created order of the universe reflects, relates, and returns to the divine order within God.

Universal Analogy. Bonaventure's basic insight into the relationship between God and creation is his theory of universal analogy by which he considers how creation manifests God's presence and thus is capable of returning to God through participation (2.44, 5.575–77). Though this manifestation is natural, the complete return is only possible through faith and grace (5.298). The same circular dynamic of exit/return emerges with the existence of created things standing in the middle according to the exemplarity of the Word.

Bonaventure writes, ''Every creature proclaims God's existence'' (5.229), and ''the divine Word is every creature because God speaks'' (6.16). Every created thing receives its inner constitution from the Word of God, and since the mystery of the Trinity is reflected in the mystery of the Word (5.331), every created thing is a reflection of the Trinity (1.72, 5.389). Thus, every particular thing in the created order reflects the divine order of the creative Trinity. Universal analogy is simply the process of discovering the Trinitarian reflections throughout reality. To explain this, Bonaventure describes creation as a book or mirror that reflects, represents, and describes the creative Trinity (5.55, 5.230, 5.297, 5.386–90). As book or mirror, all of creation is an external sign, symbol, and sacrament of God's own internal self-expression. Thus, the created order is a sacred order manifesting the overflowing goodness and love of the divine order. Through the Word, the internal self-communication of God overflows into creation as the external self-communication of God. Universal analogy explains this dynamic by intertwining the ultimate meaning of the universe deep within the mystery of the Trinity. Yet, while every creature reflects the Trinity (5.389), not all reflect the Trinity in the same way. Rather, creation reflects the Trinity in three degrees of intensity: as vestige (*vestigium*), as image (*imago*), or as similitude (*similitudo*) (5.229–30). These degrees define a thing's proximity to and cooperation with God (2.394, 5.24).

The vestige reflects God from a distance. Every creature has God as its efficient, exemplary, and final cause (1.74, 5.219, 5.571), and so every creature is a vestige reflecting the Trinitarian appropriations of power (Father), wisdom (Son), and goodness (Spirit). Thus the inner constitution of all things, as determined by triple causality, is an analogy of God's power, wisdom, and goodness (5.302–03). The image has a greater similarity and closer relation to God. It refers to the human person who, as possessing memory, intellect, and will, reflects God not only as cause, but also as the ultimate object of its knowledge and love (1.80, 2.395, 5.55, 5.305). Memory is analogous to the Father, intellect to the Son, and will to the Spirit (1.81, 2.394–95, 5.305, 9.447). Thus the unity, distinction, and interrelatedness of the soul's powers correspond to the unity, distinction, and interpersonal relations within the Trinity. The creation of the human person in God's image is the basis of Bonaventure's anthropology. Image conveys the necessary and utterly dependent relationship of the human person to God, and the soul's powers of memory, intellect, and will are what make union with God possible. Similitude is the closest relation and highest cooperation with God; it refers to the infused gift of sanctifying grace (5.252–53) or God's indwelling presence (5.214) within the soul whereby the image becomes an expressed similitude through the theological virtues of faith, hope, and love (1.71, 5.230, 5.256, 5.306). Through the graces conferred by Christ and the Spirit, faith reforms memory, hope transforms the intellect, and love conforms the will into a true similitude of the Father, Son, and Holy Spirit. Thus the image not only knows and loves but also participates in God's life through grace. As an expressed similitude, the human person becomes God-like (*deiform*) (1.58, 1.852, 4.915–17, 5.252–263, 5.288–91, 5.428–34). Just as the Word, as Image, is the expressed similitude of the Father, the true identity of the human person, as image, is to be an expressed similitude of the Word (2.407, 3.29). To conform to Christ is to conform to the Trinity. Likewise, just as the Word is the center of the divine hierarchy of the Trinity, the human person, as image of the Word, is the center of the created hierarchy of the universe (2.418–19, 3.38, 5.221–28, 5.289). With the Incarnation, Christ joins both in one center.

Closely related to Bonaventure's theory of universal analogy are the doctrines of creation from nothing, the composition of things, and the illumination of the mind.

Creation. God freely creates the world from nothing (*ex nihilo*) and in time (2.16–17, 2.33–35, 5.92, 5.219, 5.350, 5.379, 5.498). Bonaventure vehemently opposed the doctrine of the eternity of the world because he believed that it destroys the fundamental and distinctive relationship of order between God and creation (1.788, 5.497). Time must be seen in the perspective of creation's emanation from God (2.68, 5.219). If the world is eternal, then the created circular dynamic of exit and return is no longer distinct from the uncreated circular dynamic. The created order is then no longer an unnecessary, free and gratuitous self-expression of the divine order. This is why he argued that an eternal world contains a self-contradiction (1.788) and is contrary to the essential principles of causality (5.497). Time and space are essential to the created order just as eternity and infinity are essential to the divine order. If the world is eternal then the world has no beginning, and thus no middle or end (2.332), and so any analogy between the divine order and the created order becomes impossible. Unintelligibility results. Thus, Bonaventure never confuses the two orders. Since creation is *ex nihilo*, its emanation is not necessary but according to God's free act. Everything, including time, is radically distinct from God and therefore radically dependent on God; and so time itself is a vestige of eternity (5.90). Not only are created things reflecting God, created time itself reflects God. Thus, as an analogy of God (5.203, 5.307, 5.395–96), the unfolding of salvation history within time reflects the circular movement from God and to God.

Plurality of Forms. The succession of time implies the question of change. To explain how things change Bonaventure explains the composition of all created physical and spiritual beings according to the theory of universal HYLOMORPHISM (matter/form) (2.89–101, 2.413–425, 5.221). He adopts Aristotle's theory of matter and form, but adapts it significantly by arguing for a plurality of forms and by combining this altered hylomorphism with Augustine's theory of seminal reasons. Following Aristotle, a form refers to the actuality or existence of a thing, while matter refers to the potentiality or essence of a thing. However, rejecting the theory of a unity of form, Bonaventure opts instead for a plurality of forms. Since only God is pure actuality, all creatures (physical and spiritual) possess potentiality (matter). Matter is simply the name for the principle of potentiality and does not necessarily refer to something physical. Thus there is spiritual matter (angels, human soul) and physical matter (corporeal bodies) and both are potentialities that can be informed by the actualities of either spiritual or physical forms. Ultimately, all created things have at least two forms, the created form which is a copy (*exemplatum*), and the eternal Form (*exemplar*) within the divine Ideas of the Word. By arguing for the plurality of FORMS, Bonaventure again clearly distinguishes between the divine order (PURE ACT) and the created order (plural composition of matter and form) as he explains how things change within time. Yet he did not conceive matter and form as being in a static relationship; rather, matter is an ''active'' potentiality that naturally inclines to unite with a form thereby emerging into existence (5.324). Reciprocally, a form not only unites with matter to constitute a new thing, but also infuses matter with new potentialities that can again join with more forms — in effect, a virtual chain reaction approaching infinity. Bonaventure explains this powerful inner dynamism according to Augustine's theory of seminal reasons (*ratio seminalis*) (2.198, 2.206–07, 2.375, 2.436–42). Potencies (matter) are latent acts (form) that exist in a dormant or germinal state. All forms, except the human soul (5.351) which is directly created by God, were created along with and imbedded into matter (potency) when the world was created. Thus all that exists, and all that can exist, exists from the beginning in the seminal reasons. Material realty is not passive but innately evolving and expanding with active powers resulting in an intrinsically dynamic universe bursting with "potential." When forms are drawn from the potency of the seminal reasons, they exist according to the efficient, formal and final causality of the creative Trinity (5.219) and thus are analogies of the power, wisdom and goodness of God.

Illumination. In a world of dynamic change, Bonaventure employs his theory of illumination to explain how there can be certainty in human knowledge (5.17–27, 5.295–313, 5.567–74, 9.441–44). Again following Aristotle, he rejects the theory of innate ideas by arguing that knowledge is dependent on sensation. Yet, he modifies Aristotle's epistemology by combining it with Augustine's theory of illumination to explain how the mind judges according to an implicit awareness of the divine Ideas or eternal Reasons. Bonaventure combines Aristotle and Augustine as he explains the mind's twofold orientation: one external through the senses, and the other internal through illumination (5.54, 5.229–30, 5.496, 5.570). On the external level, the mind can turn outward to the macrocosm of the world and receive innumerable data from the senses (5.299–302). However, not all that is in the intellect is first in the senses. Rather, on the internal level, the mind can turn inward into itself, the microcosm, and discover itself as an image of God, and arrive at certitude through "full analysis" (*plene resolvens*) by reducing (*reductio*) all knowledge to elementary principles found in the divine Ideas (1.504, 5.23–24, 5.302–305, 5.569). Consequently, the human mind is not totally and exclusively dependent on the external sense world; rather, since the mind is the image of God, all external sense knowledge can be illumined by the "light" of the divine Ideas that are internally present to the mind. However, the mind does not "see" the divine Ideas directly but must know them through contuition (*contuitio*) of finite objects that are known through the senses. Since the external finite object and the internal knowing subject are both ontologically rooted in the exemplarism of the divine Word, *contuitio* is a simultaneous knowing of the created order and the divine order (2.542, 3.298, 3.778, 5.22–24, 5.312, 5.324, 5.569–72). In effect, all human knowing is rooted in the Word, God's own self-knowledge.

Thus, the eternal light of divine Ideas within the uncreated Word illumines the mind through memory, regulates it through the intellect and motivates it through the will (5.24, 5.302–05). Illumination, therefore, is possible precisely because the mind's powers of memory, intellect and will are an analogy of the Trinity which is the light of all understanding (5.112, 5.382). And because the entire Trinity is expressed in the Word, Christ is the "fontal principle of all cognitive illumination" (5.567) and the "root of all understanding" (5.343–44). Christ the center is both the ground of being (emanation of creation) and the ground of knowing (source of certitude) (5.331). In Christ, who is the eternal exemplar of the Word, all things find their most real and true identity (1.622–26), and so Bonaventure can write "I will see myself better in God than in myself" (5.386), and "God is closer to you than you are to yourself" (8.31). In effect, knowledge of creation (vestige, image, similitude) can not be separated from a subtle, innate knowledge of God. Knowledge of the external world simultaneously opens to a mystical epistemology of God. All human knowledge naturally moves toward the mystical. This means the return (*reductio*) of creation through universal analogy and the return (*reductio*) of knowledge through illumination *both* converge in Christ the center who is the *reductio* to God, not only in an ontological and metaphysical sense, but especially in the spiritual and existential sense of personally following Christ in his return to the Father.

GOAL

The end or goal of Bonaventure's theology is the return or *reductio* of all things to God, and his understanding of the *reductio* is decidedly christocentric (1.2, 5.332, 5.343). Bonaventure's logic is again circular and illustrates his theory of emanation, exemplarity and consummation. Since everything exists through the Word (emanation) and according to the Word (exemplarity), all reality can be led back or reduced by the Word (consummation) to its ultimate end, that is, to its origin within the uncreated Word. However, Bonaventure's basic insight into the *reductio* is not an abstract theological principle but the person of St. Francis of Assisi. Francis perfectly imitated Christ the incarnate Word who stands in the center of creation recapitulating everything to the Father in the Spirit. If Christ is the *reductio*, then imitation of Christ is an intimate participation in his *reductio*, a participation that manifests itself as the mystery of freely giving and receiving personal love. Thus, Bonaventure's spirituality of the *reductio* is a spirituality of love, a love that is fully given and received on the cross.

Imitation of Christ. Bonaventure frequently describes the imitation of Christ (8.12, 8.246, 8.272, 8.285, 8.499–503). Imitation of Christ is nothing less than an embrace of Christ's poverty, humility and charity. For example, Bonaventure describes Francis in this way at the end of the *Legenda major*: "O truly the most Christian of men, who strove by perfect imitation to be conformed while living to Christ living, dying to Christ dying, and dead to Christ dead, and deserved to be adorned with an expressed likeness'' (8.346). Francis's *expressed* likeness or perfect conformity to Christ is most fully manifested in the *impressed* stigmata upon his flesh (5.441, 8.505, 8.545). The dialectic of expression-impression unites Francis's burning love for Christ crucified with Christ's humble, poor, self-giving love of the cross. And so, the *stigmatized* Francis is the model of Christian perfection since, ''In all things [Francis] wished without hesitation to be conformed to Christ Crucified'' (8.346). Bonaventure never tires of exploring the mystery of the stigmata (5.295, 5.312, 8.246–48, 8.542–45, 8.549–51, 8.575–77, 9.534–35, 9.573–75, 9.575–82, 9.585–90, 9.590–97). He interprets the stigmata as a divine seal authenticating St. Francis's life of evangelical perfection (8.247, 8.505, 8.542, 8.569, 8.573–76, 9.593), that is, his life of poverty, humility and charity is truly an illustration of and participation in Christ's *reductio* to God. Thus, Bonaventure calls Francis, ''the mirror of holiness and the exemplar of all Gospel perfection'' (8.547, 9.515).

In the stigmata, Francis ''is totally transformed into the likeness of Christ crucified'' (8.542). To imitate Christ is to be conformed to his cross, and to be conformed to the cross is to be transformed by cruciform love (4.783, 7.225–30, 8.171, 8.252, 8.542–43, 8.575–76). With cruciform love, the created order joins the Trinitarian order, and this is the *reductio* of salvation. Christ crucified is the center of both orders, the greatest expression of God's love, and the fullest manifestation of Christian wisdom, because the cross is the reciprocal self-emptying of the divine into the human and the human into the divine. Just as God fully comes to humanity through the cross, fallen humanity must return to God through the cross. Thus Francis, burning with the love of Christ crucified (5.312), emptied himself and returned to God through the cross of Christ.

For Bonaventure, the logic of the cross is the logic of love which is both poor and humble: poor because the cross manifests the absolute self-emptying of God's love, humble because the cross reveals the radical condescension of God's love. Bonaventure sees the two virtues of poverty and humility as the source of Christian perfection which can only be fully realized in charity/love (8.242–45). Again the Trinitarian dynamic of Bonaventure's spirituality emerges. Within the divine order, poverty is ultimately rooted in the self-diffusive goodness of the Father who gives entirely everything to the Son. Humility is supremely revealed in the exemplarity of Christ who obediently receives everything from the Father and does not grasp at divine status. Charity is perfectly shared in the bond of the Holy Spirit who unites the self-communication between the Father and Son in the mystery of divine love. Likewise, within the created order, poverty especially relates to the ontological status of being created *ex nihilo* which signifies the absolute dependency of everything upon God's self-diffusive goodness. Humility refers to the awareness of sin and to the grateful acceptance of God's gifts of creation and grace whereby the true identity of the human person is regained through conformity with Christ, the incarnate exemplar. Charity reveals the power of the Holy Spirit that conforms the human person to Christ leading to union with God. In sum, the self-gift of poverty, humility and charity originate within the divine life of the Trinity itself. Christ's life, death and resurrection exemplify this same mystery, and Francis's vision of evangelical perfection embodies the same virtues which are fulfilled and confirmed in the divine seal of the stigmata.

The emphasis upon the stigmata as perfect conformity to Christ crucified indicates that Bonaventure focuses his entire spirituality of the *reductio* upon his theology of the cross (3.20, 5.295, 5.312, 5.324, 5.332–33, 5.387, 7.573–86, 8.12–14, 8.40–41, 8.68, 8.77–78, 8.120–23, 8.168, 8.499–500, 9.107–09). Since creation is fallen, it must be redeemed by the poverty, humility and charity of the Incarnation which is most fully realized on the cross. Cruciform love is selfless love that freely returns what is freely given by God. All is gift and Christ crucified is the ultimate *reductio* because the cross is a perfect expression of love that redeems the created order by returning it to the divine order of humble, self-giving charity. Thus, the love of the cross repairs the *reductio* destroyed by sin.

Sin. Originally the human person was fit for perpetual contemplation of God (2.1–6, 5.229, 5.297–98, 5.390). However, sin ruptures the human's *reductio* to God and so creation's circle of exit and return is also broken. Sin is the great disorder alienating the divine order from the created order (2.838–39, 2.960–66, 5.235–40) resulting in the corruption of the order within the individual soul, the social order within humanity, and the cosmic order of the universe (9.61). For Bonaventure, the root cause of sin is pride (5.232–33, 5.238), which manifests itself as the love of things over the love of God, the turning away from the divine light toward darkness (5.298), and the desire for self will instead of God's will. Pride is an illicit desire in which the sinner not only rejects God (2.5), but deforms itself as the image of the Trinity (5.240). The sin of pride is ultimately a sin against the Son who alone shares perfect equality and similitude with God. (3.29.30). Sin perverts a person's core identity by distracting the memory with anxiety, clouding the intellect with ignorance and infecting the will with concupiscence (2.3–6, 2.528, 5.234–35, 5.306, 5.540). Sin, therefore, corrupts the human capacity for wisdom (5.230, 5.340) and love (5.231). The soul's sinful disorder is a deformation that Bonaventure depicts as being bent over (*incurvatus*) (2.636, 5.253, 5.297–98, 5.325, 7.342; see Lk 13.11–13). This imagery suggests a person doubled over upon himself unable to straighten up and gaze upon the divine light. As *incurvatus*, humans can no longer stand upright and fulfill their function as mediator between heaven and earth (2.5) and so all of creation is unable to complete the *reductio* back to God (5.285–86, 5.390).

However, the grace of Christ the center heals the effects of sin and reorders the human into an image of the Trinity (5.253–54, 5.298, 5.306–08). The sins of pride, selfishness and concupiscence are overcome and replaced by Christ's poverty, humility and charity (3.776, 5.175, 5.348, 5.370, 7.141, 7.148, 7.175, 7.228, 7.244, 8.272, 9.90, 9.102, 9.148, 9.232, 9.372, 9.443). While not all Christ's actions can be imitated, Christ is the exemplar and model of all Christian perfection (8.243). Any authentic relationship with Christ must historically and concretely manifest the humility, poverty and charity of Christ. True imitation of Christ begins in humility, expresses itself in poverty, and comes to perfection in charity (5.120–21, 8.242–48). Humility and poverty are always inseparable from the love of self, neighbor, and God, and *vice versa* (5.460–61). Moreover, only in humility and poverty can a human person truly discern his or her true identity which is both incomplete in the natural order and fallen in the moral order (5.117–24). Thus, creation's ontological incompleteness as existing *ex nihilo* and the historical alienation of sin are both reconciled by the poverty, humility and charity of the Incarnation and Crucifixion. In effect, Christ's reconciliation is the *reductio* of the human person to God. This *reductio* is intrinsically intertwined with the ongoing process of conformity to Christ. Only by descending with Christ and embracing his poverty and humility can one ascend to God in love (5.297, 5.442–46, 9.534). Bonaventure describes this dynamic of the descent-ascent with the concept of hierarchy which, through the grace of Christ, reorders the soul's sinful *incurvatus* into a hierarchical spirit.

Hierarchy. Influenced by Pseudo-Dionysius, Bonaventure calls the re-ordering of the human image into its original state the hierarchization of the soul. Hierarchization is a technical term which means the total transformation and re-ordering of the soul according to the triple way of purgation, illumination and perfection/union (2.635, 5.205, 5.222, 5.252, 5.306–07, 5.429–49, 7.349) which is accomplished by the grace of Christ who is the Hierarch (4.508, 5.205–07, 5.341–437, 8.83, 9.388). Bonaventure simply defines mystical theology as the acquisition of ecstatic love through the hierarchic power of purgation, illumination and perfection/union (7.349). Purgation relates to the removal of sin, illumination to the imitation of Christ, and perfection to the contemplation of God's presence in all things. All three activities work concurrently and in unison to make the human spirit hierarchic by reordering the image into conformity with Christ, the divine Hierarch. The entire triple way is present in every step of the soul's spiritual journey. This mutually inclusive process is the focus of the widely influential *De triplici via* (8.1–18) which details the soul's process of transformation according to the integration of the triple way with the three spiritual practices of prayer, meditation and contemplation whereby the soul receives the gifts of peace, truth and love.

The effects of the soul's hierarchization is simultaneously transformative and unitive. On one level, Christ is the inner teacher of the soul (5.327, 5.429) who purges, illumines and perfects the human image into an expressed similitude of the Trinity whereby the memory, intellect and will are re-ordered into proper relationship through faith, hope and love (5.256, 5.306–07) and the related beatitudes, habits, virtues and gifts (3.737, 5.256–60).

The hierarchic re-ordering of the human body, soul, and spirit results in the re-ordering of the entire human person/image into its proper position as intermediary within the physical, spiritual and transcendent hierarchy of creation. The individual, societal and cosmic disorder caused by sin are reversed by the soul's hierarchization according to the grace of Christ who is the center of each order (5.297, 5.306, 5.312, 5.345, 5.370–71). Thus, on another level, Christ is simultaneously the Hierarch who unites the inner hierarchy of the soul, the outer hierarchy of the earthly church, the transcendent hierarchy of the heavenly church and the divine hierarchy of the Trinity (5.225–26, 5.429–37). Through and in the grace of Christ, the reformed image fully participates in the church on earth, becomes like the heavenly church and is continually becoming a fuller expressed similitude of the Trinity. Throughout, Christ is the one Hierarch who is the center of each hierarchy beginning in the highest hierarchy of the Trinity through the intermediate hierarchies of the angels and church into the lowest hierarchy of the human soul. Likewise, since Francis's imitation of and conformity to Christ was perfect, Bonaventure calls Francis a ''hierarchic man'' (5.577, 8.504) and portrays him as the perfect model of purgation, illumination and perfection, and therefore the true model of contemplation (5.440–41).

Contemplation. For Bonaventure, contemplation is the fullest *reductio* possible while still on earth. While he frequently discusses contemplation (2.545–46, 3.530–31,

3.778–79, 5.39–42, 5.258–60, 5.312–13, 5.570–72, 7.230–39, 8.16–17, 9.162–63, 9.228–29, 9.268–69, 9.509–10), he never offers a precise definition. Rather, rooted in the idea of hierarchization, he upholds contemplation as the highest form of knowledge through and in which the human person glimpses the continuity of all reality, that is, the internal-external, physical-spiritual, and divine-created all converging in one unifying vision (5.424–49). Contemplation is the fullness of *contuitio*.

Bonaventure arrives at this unifying vision of God's presence by way of two distinct but related forms of contemplation (3.531, 5.38–42, 5.259, 5.358, 5.575–76, 8.16–17): one derived from Augustine and another from Pseudo-Dionysius (7.232). From Augustine, he teaches a form of contemplation that follows the ''affirmative way'' (*via affirmativa*) which turns toward creatures and discovers God's presence through and in all creation (1.74, 5.297). It achieves its fullness in the gift of understanding. This form of ''cataphatic'' contemplation is more active, emphasizes the speculative way of understanding God's truth, especially as revealed in Scripture, and culminates in the ecstacy of the intellect (5.42–43, 5.313). From Pseudo-Dionysius, he teaches a form of contemplation that follows the ''negative way'' (*via negativa*) which turns away from creatures, and in a state of ''darkness'' turns exclusively and completely toward God. Here the gift par excellence is wisdom. This form of ''apophatic'' contemplation is more passive, emphasizes the affections (*affectus*) over the intellect, focuses on the experience of God's love, and culminates in the ecstacy of the will (3.292, 3.531, 5.306, 5.344, 5.434). In sum, the ecstacy of understanding renders the soul conformed to God, while the ecstacy of love transforms the soul into unity with God (2.916, 5.313, 5.436).

The *Itinerarium mentis in Deum* is an excellent example of the two forms of contemplation. Therein Bonaventure presents St. Francis as ''an example of perfect contemplation'' (5.312) whose vision of the crucified seraph accompanying the reception of the stigmata ''represents our father's suspension in contemplation and the way to reach it'' (5.295). For Bonaventure, Francis's vision of the six wings of the ''Seraph in the form of the Crucified'' reveals both the goal and the means of contemplation. On the one hand, each of the seraph's six wings symbolizes an illumination (means) which begin with creatures and lead up to God according to the affirmative way. On the other hand, the crucified body of the seraph itself (5.312) symbolizes mystical union with God (goal) in apophatic darkness. By constructing the *Itinerarium* in this way, Bonaventure sets forth Francis's stigmata, symbolically represented by the seraph, as the perfect mirror of contemplation through which one can discover the divine presence in all things and receive mystical union with God through Christ crucified.

Union with God. Bonaventure describes union with God as a mystical death (*mors mystica*) or passing over (*transitus*) (5.312–13, 5.429, 6.590, 6.619, 8.49–51). Mystical union transcends the mind's intellectual activities (2.544–46, 5.260, 5.312, 5.340–42), subsuming the mind into a transformed state of ''affective knowing'' which is more like a feeling than knowledge (6.256). At this point, intellectual knowledge becomes insufficient and gives way to the experiential knowledge of God's love. In this state, the soul becomes passive and is totally transferred and transformed into God by the unifying love of the Holy Spirit (1.41, 5.40, 5.254, 5.312). Specifically, it is in the ''most burning love of the Crucified'' (5.260, 5.295, 5.113, 8.121) that one experiences union with God by mystically participating, like Francis, in Christ's death upon the cross. Bonaventure describes this loving embrace as an absolute self-emptying and total self-giving of love. Here, in the love of the cross, one shares in the mystery of Christ's loving return to the Father in the unity of the Spirit. In sum, union with God is through and in union with Christ crucified. Furthermore, Bonaventure distinguishes between two types of union with God (3.744, 5.259, 5.347–48): ecstacy (*excessus/ecstasis*) which is open to everyone through the grace of contemplation (2.546, 3.531, 5.19–21, 5.259), and rapture (*raptus*) which is reserved for very few through an act of divine glory (2.544–46, 4.160, 5.24, 5.455–56, 5.347–48, 9.229). For Bonaventure, Francis is a new model for both, and for this reason, he signifies a new age in salvation history.

Eschatology. While contemplation focuses on the *reductio* of the individual Christian to God, eschatology focuses on the *reductio* of the entire church and all of history to God. In reality the two are inseparable. In his last unfinished work, the *Collationes in Hexaëmeron*, Bonaventure combines them by paralleling and associating six levels of illumination with the six days of creation and the six ages of salvation history (2.338–39, 5.205–06, 5.245, 5.269, 5.321, 5.388–89). Bonaventure thus situates the significance of St. Francis and the Franciscan Order within a symbolically rich ''apocalyptic eschatology'' which anticipates a new age of spiritual/prophetic understanding of Scripture and perfect conformity to Christ through contemplation. To explain this monumental transition in salvation history, Bonaventure adopts Augustine's traditional theology of history which envisions a correspondence between the seven days of creation and the seven ages from Adam to Christ (5.388, 5.392–402). Bonaventure adapts this schema by combining it with the apocalyptic theology of Joachim of Fiore (5.388–400, 5.405–08). While rejecting certain key aspects of Joachim's apocalypticism (1.121, 5.403), he employs, possibly indirectly, Joachim's exegetical method of exact historical parallels between the seven ages of both the Old and the New Testaments. Thus, Bonaventure conceives salvation history according to a twofold parallel between the Old Testament, spanning seven ages from Adam to Christ (Augustine), and a corresponding schema in the New Testament, spanning seven ages of the church from Christ until the end of the World (Joachim).

Within this eschatological framework, Bonaventure interprets both Francis and his order as appearing at the end of the sixth age of the New Testament (5.440–41). Francis is the prophetic figure signifying, especially in the miracle of the stigmata, the advent of the seventh age after Christ, namely, an age of revelation (5.338–39, 5.408, 5.430) and peace (5.401–02) preparing the way for the kingdom of God. To highlight Francis's eschatological significance, Bonaventure identifies Francis as the Angel of the Sixth Seal (Rv 7.2) who both embodies and signals the coming of a new age of contemplation before the end of the world (5.164, 5.405, 5.408, 5.509–10, 5.445, 5.447, 8.247, 8.504, 8.516, 8.545, 9.587). Thus, during the crisis of the false uses of Aristotelian philosophy (5.360–61, 5.418–19, 5.422–23) and the continued attacks against mendicancy, Bonaventure looks to Francis as an eschatological figure of hope. Francis, in perfect conformity to Christ in the stigmata, establishes a new order of contemplatives (5.402, 5.449) in the church that can be embraced by anyone who follows Francis's example by embracing Christ crucified (5.437–44). In effect, Bonaventure interprets the stigmata to have eschatological-prophetic meaning as well as mystical-contemplative meaning.

Bonaventure's emphasis on Francis as an eschatological figure always leads back to conformity to Christ, who in turn, leads everything back (*reductio*) to the Father. In effect, Bonaventure sees Christ as the center of his double seven schema of salvation history. Just like the rest of his theology, Bonaventure's eschatology is christocentric. It is within this eschatological and christocentric framework that Bonaventure situates his theology of the church (4.602–607ff, 5.431–44) and the Sacraments (4.8–46ff, 5.265–80). In sum, all of salvation history is engaged in a grand circular dynamic of exit and return with Christ as its universal center uniting the divine order of the Trinity with the created order of history.

WORKS

The critical edition of Bonaventure's works was published as *Opera Omnia: Doctoris Seraphici S. Bonaventurae opera omnia*, 10 vols. (Quaracchi: Collegium S. Bonaventurae, 1882–1902). The table accompanying this essay lists these works in chronological order, giving their volume and page numbers in this edition.

Feast: July 15.

Bibliography: Works. *Collationes in Hexaëmeron et Bonaventuriana quaedam selecta*, ed. F. DELORME (Quarachi 1934); *Sancti bonaventurae sermones dominicales*, ed. J. G. BOUGEROL (Grottaferrata 1977). B. DISTELBRINK, *Bonaventurae Scripta: Authentica dubia vel spuria critice recensita* (Rome 1975). I. BRADY, "The Opera Omnia of St. Bonaventure," *Archivum Franciscanum Historicum* 70 (1977) 352–76. **English Translations.** *Works of Saint Bonaventure*, 7 v., ed. G. MARCIL and Z. HAYES (St. Bonaventure, N.Y. 1956–). *The Works of Bonaventure*, tr. J. DE VINCK, 5 v. (Quincy, IL. 1960–1970). *What Manner of Man: Sermons on Christ by St. Bonaventure*, tr. Z. HAYES (Chicago 1989). *Bringing Forth Christ: Five Feasts of the Child Jesus*, tr. E. DOYLE (Quincy, IL. 1984). *Francis of Assisi: Early Documents*, v. 2, ed. R. ARMSTRONG, J. A. HELLMANN, and W. SHORT (New York 2000). *Bonaventure: The Soul's Journey into God, The Tree of Life, The Life of St. Francis*, tr. E. COUSINS (New York 1978). *Bonaventure: Mystic of God's Word*, ed. T. JOHNSON (New York 1999). **Collected Essays.** *Sancta Bonaventura 1274–1974*, ed. J. G. BOUGEROL, 5 v. (Grottaferrata 1974). *Bonaventuriana: Miscellanea in onore di Jacques Guy Bogerol*, ed. F. BLANCO, 2 v. (Rome 1988). *San Bonaventura Maestro di vita francescana e di sapienza cristiana*, ed. A. POMPEI, 3 v. (Rome 1976). *The Medieval Heritage: A Colloquy on the Thought of Aquinas and Bonaventure*, ed. D. TRACY (Chicago 1989). *S. Bonaventura Francescano*, Covegni del Centro di Studi sulla Spiritualità Medievale XIV (Todi 1974). *Proceedings of the Seventh Centenary Celebration of the Death of Saint Bonaventure*, ed. P. FOLEY (St. Bonaventure, N.Y. 1975). **English Studies.** J. G. BOUGEROL, *Introduction to the Works of Bonaventure*, tr. J. DE VINCK (Paterson 1963). C. CARPENTER, *Theology as the Road to Holiness in Bonaventure* (New York 1999). E. COUSINS, *Bonaventure and the Coincidence of Opposites* (Chicago 1978); "Bonaventure's Mysticism of Language," in *Mysticism and Language*, ed. S. KATZ (New York 1992) 236–57. I. DELIO, *Crucified Love: Bonaventure's Mysticism of the Crucified Christ* (Quincy, IL. 1998); *Simply Bonaventure: An Introduction to His Life, Thought and Writings* (New York 2001). P. FEHLNER, *The Role of Charity in the Ecclesiology of St. Bonaventure* (Rome 1965). E. GILSON, *The Philosophy of St. Bonaventure*, tr. I. TRETHOWAN and F. SHEED (Paterson 1965). J. HAMMOND, *Seeking Peace Through Prayer: Bonaventure's Journey of the Mind into God* (Quincy, IL. 2002). Z. HAYES, *The Hidden Center: Spirituality and Speculative Christology in St. Bonaventure* (New York 1981); *Bonaventure: Mystical Writings* (New York 1999); "Bonaventure: Mystery of the Triune God," in *The History of Franciscan Theology*, ed. K. OSBORNE (St. Bonaventure, N.Y. 1994) 39–126. J. A. HELLMANN, *Divine and Created Order in Bonaventure's Theology*, tr. J. HAMMOND (St. Bonaventure, N.Y. 2001). T. JOHNSON, *The Soul in Ascent: Bonaventure on Poverty, Prayer and Union with God* (Quincy, IL. 2001). B. MCGINN, "Bonaventure's Mystical Synthesis," in *The Flowering of Mysticism* (New York 1998) 87–112. R. PRENTICE, *The Psychology of Love According to St. Bonaventure* (St. Bonaventure, N.Y. 1992). J. QUINN, *The Historical Constitution of St. Bonaventure's Philosophy* (Toronto 1973). J. RATZINGER, *The Theology of History in St. Bonaventure*, tr. Z. HAYES (Chicago 1971). A. SCHAEFER, *The Position and Function of Man in the Created World According to Saint Bonaventure* (Washington 1965). G. TAVARD, *Transiency and Permanence: The Nature of Theology according to St. Bonaventure* (St. Bonaventure, N.Y.1954).

[J. M. HAMMOND]

BONDOLFI, PIETRO

Founder of the BETHLEHEM FATHERS; b. Rome, April 10, 1872; d. Immensee (Schwyz), Switzerland, June 27, 1943. Bondolfi, who had been orphaned in 1882, was ordained in 1896 after seminary studies in Chur, Switzerland. He gained a doctorate in Canon Law after studies at Innsbruck and Rome. At Louvain, he won a licentiate in economics (1898). He was appointed archivist of the Diocese of Chur, and in 1900 served in the parish of St. Moritz. In 1904 Bondolfi was named canonical visitor of the apostolic school of Bethlehem in Immensee, founded by Peter Barrall to educate priests for missions and poor dioceses. During a financial crisis in 1907 Bondolfi was appointed director of the school. In this position he placed the school on a sound financial basis, dedicated it to the Sacred Heart, and infused it with a new spirit. Pius X suggested that the school become a missionary institute, but the plan was not put into effect until 1921 when Bondolfi became the first superior general of the Bethlehem Fathers. He served in this office until his death. Throughout Switzerland he promoted interest in the missions, especially through the monthly periodical *Bethlehem.* In 1924 he sent his first missionaries to China. At his death the institute had four foundations in Switzerland. Bondolfi revealed his spirituality in the booklet *Der Geist des Kindes von Bethlehem* (1938).

Bibliography: *Bethlehem* (1946) 7–87, biog. of Bondolfi; an Eng. monthly issued by the Bethlehem Fathers. A. RUST, *Die Bethlehem-Missionare Immensee* (Fribourg 1961).

[A. J. BORER]

BONET, NICHOLAS

Theologian; b. Tours, France, *c.* 1280; d. perhaps Malta, before Oct. 27, 1343. Bonet was a Franciscan, and a disciple of John DUNS SCOTUS at Paris, where Bonet taught for many years. Philip VI made him his private chaplain and authorized him to examine JOHN XXII'S teaching on the beatific vision. Benedict XII sent him as his legate (1338) to Kublai, the Great Khan of the Tartars, and Clement VI named him bishop of Malta (1342). He was not able to complete his term as legate and was bishop of Malta for but a short time. His influence was greatly felt through his writings: *Theologia naturalis* (Venice 1505) and *Formalitates in via Scoti* (Venice 1489).

Bibliography: F. O'BRIAIN, *Dictionnaire d'histoire et de géographie ecclésiastiques* (Paris 1912–) 9:849–852. T. BARTH, *Lexikon für Theologie und Kirche*, ed. J. HOFER and K. RAHNER (Freiburg 1957–65) 7:982.

[G. ODOARDI]

BONFRÈRE, JACQUES

Biblical scholar; b. Dinant, now in Belgium, April 12, 1573; d. Tournai, now in Belgium, May 9, 1642. In 1592 he became a Jesuit, and he taught for many years at Scots College, DOUAI, now in France. He wrote commentaries on the Pentateuch (Antwerp 1625) and on Joshua, Judges, and Ruth (Paris 1631). In the latter volume as an appendix he added his edition of Jerome's translation of Eusebius's *Onomasticon urbium et locorum S. Scripturae,* which was republished by R. J. de Tournemine in his edition of Menochius's commentary (Paris 1719). The *Praeloquia* (introduction) to his commentary on the Pentateuch, treating the Bible as a whole, was selected by J. P. MIGNE as the most suitable introduction for his *Scripturae S. Cursus* [(Paris 1839) 1:5–242]. Although scientific methodology was unknown to him and the selection of his topics was largely governed by then current controversies, his erudition was extensive and included a good grasp of Hebrew and biblical geography. He did not, however, distinguish clearly between inspiration and revelation, and certain of his ideas, e.g., on the possibility of inspiration subsequent to composition, did not find favor with other theologians.

Bibliography: C. SOMMERVOGEL et al., *Bibliothèque de la Compagnie de Jésus*, 11 v. (Brussels-Paris 1890–1932) 1:1713–15. H. HURTER, *Nomenclator literarius theologiae catholicae*, 5 v. in 6 (3d ed. Innsbruck 1903–13) 3:1033–35. A. PONCELET, *Histoire de la Compagnie de Jésus dans les anciens Pays-Bas* (Brussels 1928).

[L. F. HARTMAN]

BONIFACE, ST.

Archbishop of Mainz, apostle of Germany; b. Wessex, England, between 672 and 675; d. Dokkum, Frisia, June 5, 754. According to Willibald of Mainz (*Vita* 1.1), Winfrid (Wynfrid, later Boniface) was entrusted at first to BENEDICTINES at Exeter as a result of the serious illness of his father and was later sent to Nursling between Winchester and Southampton, where the learned Wynbercht was abbot. Here Winfrid imbibed ANGLO-SAXON monastic ideals: love for learning, for Rome, and for missionary activity (*peregrinatio pro Christo*). He entered the monastic school. Willibald claims that Winfrid was an orator (*ibid.* 1.4), undertook a mission for King Berchtwald of CANTERBURY (692–731), and was called upon to attend several synods (*ibid.*). Winfrid wrote a Latin grammar and numerous poems (Manitius 1:149–).

Missionary Career. When Winfrid was about 40 he secured the permission of his abbot to evangelize in Frisia (716), a part of the Frankish kingdom since its conquest in 689 by Pepin II. After Pepin's death Frisia became the scene of a revolt led by Duke Radbod and of a widespread rejection of Christianity. WILLIBRORD OF UTRECHT, apostle of Frisia (690–739), withdrew temporarily, and it was under these unfavorable conditions that Winfrid attempted an apostolate, even visiting Radbod, who did not actually forbid missionary activity. But Winfrid realized that the time was not ripe and returned to Nursling probably in the same year (716). On the death of his abbot in 717, he was elected to succeed him but relinquished the office in 718 for the purpose of visiting Rome to beg for a mission from the pope; his request was backed by a letter of recommendation from Bp. Daniel of Winchester. He journeyed from London to La Canche, Quentovic (in Frisia), and thence with a group of pilgrims to Rome, where he was received several times by GREGORY II (715–731). On May 15, 719, the pope gave him a letter assigning to him broad missionary jurisdiction among the pagans and urging the Roman formula of baptism and recourse to Rome in every difficulty. At the same time Gregory changed Winfrid's name to Boniface in honor of the martyr whose feast had been celebrated the day before. (Willibrord's name had been similarly changed to Clement.)

Boniface went first to Thuringia, where he preached to the leaders of the people and tried to reform the incontinent and partly pagan clergy. The death of Radbod in 719 and Boniface's desire to familiarize himself with Willibrord's missionary methods attracted him again to Frisia, where he worked for several years (719–722?). Willibrord would gladly have made him his auxiliary bishop, but Boniface wanted an independent sphere of activity in view of his Roman commission. Probably in 721 he left Frisia for Hesse, the most pagan area he evangelized. Assisted by two Christian nobles, Dettic and Deorulf, he established a monastery at Amöneburg. Winning the pagan Hessians by his kindness to the unfortunate, he baptized a large number on the Feast of Pentecost 722; his biographer speaks of thousands of converts on this occasion (*ibid.* 1.7). Boniface reported his success to Rome and sought the advice of the pope on several questions. The pope invited him to Rome, where he consecrated him bishop (Nov. 30, 722) after receiving his profession of faith. He gave him a collection of canons, probably that of DIONYSIUS EXIGUUS, and letters of recommendation to all religious and civil rulers in Germany, including CHARLES MARTEL. In a letter to the German clergy dated Dec. 1, 722, the pope summarized the instructions he had given to the new bishop. Boniface went from Rome to Charles Martel, successor to Pepin II as mayor of the palace (714–741), and that prince in 723 granted him a letter of safe conduct, without which Boniface admitted his work would have been impossible.

St. Boniface baptizing a man. (Archive Photos)

Return to Germany. The bishop returned for a second mission to Hesse (723–725), where converted Hessians advised him to overwhelm the remaining pagans by felling the sacred oak at Geismar near the Abbey of Fritzlar; Boniface used planks sawn from this tree to erect a chapel to St. Peter. From Hesse he returned to Thuringia (725–735), an area conquered by the Franks under Thierry I and already somewhat Christianized since the recent immigration and the efforts of Frankish and Irish missionaries, such as KILIAN OF WÜRZBURG. In 724 Gregory II reproached Gerold of Mainz for his failure to further extend Christianity and to defend his episcopal rights, and the pope later recommended Boniface to the Thuringians. Boniface's task was complicated by ignorant and even vicious priests, poorly prepared catechumens, and pagan admixtures in Christian ceremonies. His ten-year apostolate, however, was fruitful in conversions and reform. He established a monastery at Ohrdruf, near Gotha.

The pope died in 731 and was succeeded by GREGORY III (d. 741), to whom Boniface immediately offered his homage and services. Gregory replied in 732 by elevating

Boniface to the rank of archbishop, sending him the PALLIUM, and bidding him consecrate missionary bishops. In 734 Boniface made a short trip to Bavaria, which had been evangelized earlier by RUPERT OF SALZBURG with the aid of Irish monks. There Duke Hubert I offered his assistance.

Boniface made his third and last visit to Rome in the fall of 737, remaining there a year. The pope urged him to evangelize the Old Saxons, a mission dear to Boniface. Gregory also commissioned Boniface to organize the German Church, and he wrote supporting letters to bishops, abbots, and magnates of Hesse, Thuringia, and Bavaria. During this visit Boniface attracted to his apostolate a number of Romans, Franks, and Bavarians, such men as WINNEBALD and WILLIBALD OF EICHSTÄTT, who came to him from MONTE CASSINO, and probably also at this time LULL, later bishop of Mainz.

Returning in 738 as papal LEGATE to Germany, Boniface established three new bishoprics in Bavaria in addition to Passau, already ruled by Bishop Vivolo; they were: Salzburg, which under Arno was eventually to become an archbishopric in 798, Regensburg, and Freising. The first Bavarian synod was held in Boniface's presence in 740, and the following year several other dioceses were set up: Buraburg for Hesse under the Anglo-Saxon WITTA, Erfurt for Thuringia under Dadanus(?), Würzburg for Franconia under BURCHARD, a pupil of Boniface in England, and Eichstätt under the Anglo-Saxon Willibald. Nearby Heidenheim was the site of an important abbey, the only double MONASTERY in Germany, organized and ruled by Winnebald and then by WALBURGA, brother and sister of Bishop Willibald. The establishment of bishoprics and abbeys did not solve all problems, for Bishop VIRGILIUS OF SALZBURG (745–784) worried Boniface, who reported what he considered to be his heretical views to the pope. In 744 Boniface founded the most celebrated of his monasteries at FULDA. Its purpose, like that of all Boniface's monasteries, was to consolidate the progress already made in the evangelization of upper Bavaria, and it was placed directly under Roman jurisdiction by Pope ZACHARY in 751. STURMI, a young Bavarian noble who had joined Boniface at Fritzlar, became its first abbot. Fulda was a place of spiritual renewal for Boniface and the center of Germany's religious and intellectual life, where the annual conference of German bishops is still held.

The Reform of the Frankish Church (742–747). The Frankish Church had suffered a decline for over a century largely as a result of lay interference in episcopal elections and consequent worldliness among the clergy, PROPRIETARY CHURCHES, exempt monasteries churches, exempt monasteries (*see* EXEMPTION, HISTORY OF), and CARLOMAN, Austrasian mayor of the palace (741–747), cooperated with Boniface by calling councils to reform the Church in his domain: one, called the *Concilium Germanicum,* was held April 21, 742, at an unknown place, and another, at Liftina or Liptina (modern Estinnes in Hainaut, Belgium) on March 1, 743. Bishops, priests, and lay magnates attended, but final approval of the conciliar decrees was reserved to Carloman, who legislated for annual synods; in 743 and 744 these were held in early March, probably to coincide with the *campus Martius.* In 744 PEPIN III held a council at Soissons that adopted the Austrasian decrees; a council for the whole kingdom, which Boniface probably attended, was held the following year. Archbishops were consecrated for Rouen, Reims, and Sens; Rouen received the pallium, but it is not certain whether the other two sees were similarly favored. The council condemned two wandering bishops: the Frank, Aldebert, who claimed to be a saint, and a heretical Irishman, Clement; both escaped imprisonment. Gewiliob, bishop of Mainz, was deposed by the council for having killed his father's murderer, and Boniface was appointed to his place, for, although archbishop since 742, he had been assigned neither see nor suffragans. At first he hoped to establish his metropolitan see in COLOGNE, a plan approved by the council of 745 and by the Pope, but he was forced to abandon the idea in face of opposition from the Frankish bishops. Later, in 752, when Boniface resigned, Lull succeeded him, but as a bishop, and Mainz became an archbishopric permanently only *c.* 781. Implementation of the decrees of 745 was difficult because lay lords opposed the restoration of CHURCH PROPERTY, and clerics sometimes resisted reform. In 747 a council was held to which all the bishops of the kingdom were invited, but only 13 attended. Boniface tried to unite them to Rome by professions of faith and loyalty. In the same year Carloman retired to a monastery, and Pepin became sole mayor of the palace. Boniface's authority declined, and it is not certain whether he even attended Pepin's coronation. Boniface feared that his collaborators, mostly Anglo-Saxons, would suffer after his death, so he wrote on their behalf to Fulrad, Abbot of SAINT-DENIS.

Last Mission and Martyrdom. Boniface undertook a final mission to the Frisians, accompanied by EOBAN, archbishop of Utrecht, and others. He was very successful for about a year and was preparing a group of neophytes for Confirmation near Dokkum when attacked at sunrise by pagan Frisians. Boniface would not permit a struggle. An old woman later declared on oath that she saw him protect himself with a Gospel Book (now at Fulda). Boniface and 53 companions were massacred. His remains, which he had asked to have interred at Fulda, rested en route at Utrecht and Mainz, and his cult developed immediately in all three places. Fulda became a center of pilgrimage. Except for the top of his skull, the remains of Boniface are now enshrined in a baroque tomb from which the recumbent statue of the bishop appears as emerging with the assistance of two cherubim. Pope PIUS IX extended his feast to the entire Church in 1874.

Characteristics of Boniface's Missionary Activity. Boniface organized the German Church in closest union with Rome, he himself having recourse to the popes for authorization, protection, and guidance. At the same time he depended on his monasteries to give permanence to his work in rural areas. The *ingens multitudo* of Anglo-Saxon monks and nuns who followed him to the Continent peopled his houses and established new ones. Boniface introduced Benedictine nuns into the active apostolate of education, anticipating by many centuries the work of religious women in that field.

Feast: June 5.

Bibliography: *Vita,* ed. W. LEVISON, Scriptores rerum Germanicarum v.57. *Die Briefe,* ed. M. TANGL, Epistolae selectae v.1, tr. as *The letters of Saint Boniface*, tr. E. EMERTON (New York 1940, 2000). *Die Gedichte,* Poetae 1:3–23. H. HAHN, *Bonifaz und Lul* (Leipzig 1883). Hauck 1:418–552. J. M. WILLIAMSON, *Life and Times of St. Boniface* (London 1904). G. F. BROWNE, *Boniface of Credition and His Companions* (London 1910). P. KEHL, *Kult und Nachleben des heiligen Bonifatius im Mittelalter* (Fulda 1993). M. MOSTERT, *754, Bonifatius bij Dokkum vermoord* (Hilversum 1999). L. VON PADBERG, *Studien zur Bonifatiusverehrung* (Frankfurt am Main 1996). J. C. SLADDEN, *Boniface of Devon* (Exeter, Eng. 1980). D. TRAUTWEIN, *Heil von den Inseln: Bonifatius und die Iroschotten* (Constance 1993). WILLIBALD, *The Life of Saint Boniface,* tr. G. W. ROBINSON (Cambridge, Mass. 1916). *The English Correspondence of St. Boniface,* ed. and tr. E. KYLIE (London 1924). W. LEVISON, *England and the Continent in the Eighth Century* (Oxford 1946) 70–93. E. S. DUCKETT, *Anglo-Saxon Saints and Scholars* (New York 1947, rep. Hamden, Conn. 1967) 337–455. D. PONTIFEX, *St. Boniface* (London 1954). *The Greatest Englishman*, ec. T. REUTER (Exeter 1980). T. SCHIEFFER, *Winfrid-Bonifatius und die christliche Grundlegung Europas* (Freiburg 1954). *Sankt Bonifatius: Gedenkgabe zum 1200. Todestag* (Fulda 1954). A. ERDLE and H. BUTTERWEGGE, eds., *Bonifatius, Wanderer Christi* (Paderborn 1954). G. W. GREENAWAY, *Saint Boniface* (London 1955). H. LÖWE, ''Bonifatius und die bayerisch-fränkische Spannung,'' *Jahrbuch für fränkische Landesforschung* 15 (1955) 85–127; ''Vom Bild des Bonifatius in der neueren deutschen Geschichtschreibung,'' *Geschichte in Wissenschaft und Unterricht* 6 (1955) 539–555.

[S. HILPISCH/C. M. AHERNE]

BONIFACE I, POPE, ST.

Pontificate: Dec. 28 or 29, 418 to Sept. 4, 422. Boniface was Roman-born, the son of the priest Iocundus, and had been INNOCENT I'S legate to Constantinople on several occasions. While Pope ZOSIMUS was being buried, the archdeacon Eulalius returned to the Lateran where he was acclaimed bishop of Rome. The rest of the presbyterium and the people waited till the next day and elected the aged priest Boniface in the basilica of Theodora. The following Sunday (December 29) both candidates were consecrated and installed. Boniface was consecrated at St. Marcellus and installed in St. Peter's, because the Lateran was held by the faction of Eulalius. The pagan prefect of Rome, Symmachus, attempted to settle the quarrel, intervening on behalf of Eulalius, but was overruled by the imperial court where Boniface had powerful support. The question was debated inconclusively by several synods.

Pope St. Boniface I. (Archive Photos)

Meanwhile, both contenders were ordered to leave Rome pending a final solution, and the bishop of Spoleto was delegated to preside at the Easter celebrations (419). Eulalius attempted to prevent this, caused a riot, and was considered to have forfeited his rights, whereupon the emperor declared Boniface the lawful bishop. When Boniface became ill shortly afterward, he feared a repetition of the schism if he should die and wrote to the Roman Emperor HONORIUS in the name of the clergy requesting assurances that peace would be maintained. The imperial rescript replied that if a double election occurred again, the government would remove both candidates and recognize only an election that was morally unanimous, a strong assertion of imperial rights in papal elections and which the pope did not challenge.

The case of the African priest Apiarius, who had appealed to Pope Zosimus, was considered at a plenary council in Carthage on May 25, 419, attended by Faustinus and another papal legate. It was decided to verify the acts of Nicaea to which Zosimus had appealed by comparing them with copies kept at Constantinople, Antioch, and Alexandria, since the African version did not correspond to the Roman. Meanwhile the African bishops were willing to abide by the decision of the pope; Apiarius was to be released from excommunication and transferred to another diocese if he begged pardon for his misdeeds. In their reply to Boniface the African bishops maintained a moderate and dignified tone, though they expressed their annoyance at the arrogance of Faustinus. Boniface also became involved in a second African dispute when the bishop Antoninus of Fussala appealed to the pope concerning his deposition for theft by an African council that was organized by Augustine of Hippo. To Augustine's outrage, Boniface agreed to hear the appeal and sent a Roman investigative commission to Africa, but when Boniface died shortly thereafter, the papal emissaries deferred to an African council, which repated the condemnation of Antoninus.

In dealing with the Pelagians, Boniface acquiesced to Emperor Honorius, who issued an edict (June 9, 419) requiring all the bishops to sign the *Tractoria* of Pope Zosimus; Boniface likewise deferred to St. AUGUSTINE and the African bishops, persuading Augustine to write his *Contra duas epistulas Pelagianorum.* The controversy was prolonged in Italy, however, by a few bishops led by JULIAN OF ECLANUM, who refused to sign the imperial edict.

Under Boniface the vicariate of Gaul, which Pope Zosimus had conferred on Patroclus of Arles, was not renewed. But when the Byzantine Emperor THEODOSIUS II issued an edict (July 14, 421) ordering the Praetorian prefect for Illyricum not to allow ecclesiastical matters affecting his prefecture to be decided without the knowledge of the bishop of Constantinople "because the latter enjoys the prerogative of Old Rome," Boniface persuaded Honorius to obtain from Theodosius II the revocation of his edict. He wrote to Rufus of Thessalonica as his vicar, and to the other Illyrian and Macedonian bishops insisting that they respect the rules of the vicariate. The law of Theodosius was nevertheless retained in both the Theodosian and Justinian Codes despite papal opposition.

Boniface was buried in a chapel or oratory that he built in the cemetery of St. Felicitas on the Via Salaria, the exact location of his tomb being unknown. The date of his death is correctly noted in the MARTYROLOGY OF ST. JEROME, but wrongly given as October 25 in the Roman MARTYROLOGY, which follows the *Liber pontificalis.*

Feast: Sept. 4.

Bibliography: *Clavis Patrum latinorum,* ed. E. DEKKERS (2d. ed. Streenbrugge 1961) 1648–49 and *Patrologiae cursus completus, series latina;* ed. A. HAMMAN 1:1032–34, editions. *Patrologia Latina,* ed. J. P. MIGNE (Paris 1878–90) 20:749–792. *Liber pontificalis,* ed. L. DUCHESNE, 1 (Paris 1886–92) 227–229; 3:84. H. LECLERCQ, *Dictionnaire d'éologie chrétienne et de liturgie,* ed. F. CHABROL, H. LECLERCQ, and H. I. MARROU, 15 v. (Paris 1907–53) 13.1:1203. R. U. MONTINI, *Le tombe dei Papi* (Rome 1957) 98. G. SCHWAIGER, *Lexikon für Theologie und Kirche,* ed. J. HOFER and K. RAHNER, 10 v. (2d, new ed. Freiburg 1957–65) 2:587–588. G. BARDY, *Dictionnaire d'histoire et de géographie ecclésiastiques,* ed. A. BAUDRILLAT et al. (Paris 1912–) 9:895–897. J. P. BURNS, "Augustine's Role in the Imperial Action against Pelagius," *Journal of Theological Studies* 30: 67–83. A. DIBERARDINO, *Patrology* (Westminister, MD 1986) 4:586–587. E. FERGUSON, ed., *Encyclopedia of Early Christianity* (New York 1997) 1:190. D.FRYE, "Bishops as Pawns in Early Fifth–Century Gaul," *Journal of Ecclesiastical History* 42: 349–361. H. JEDIN, *History of the Church* (New York, 1980) 2:261–263. J. N. D. KELLY, *Oxford Dictionary of Popes* (New York 1986) 40–41. J. MERDINGER, *Rome and the African Church* (New Haven 1997) 114–120, 149–153. C. OCKER, "Augustine, Imperial Interests, and the Papacy in Late Roman Africa," *Journal of Ecclesiastical History* 42: 179–201. C. PIETRI, *Rome Christiana* (Rome 1976), 1254–1270. O.WERMINGLER, *Rome und Pelagius* (Stuttgart 1975). P.J. CAREFOTTE, "Pope Boniface I, the Pelagian Controversy and the Growth of Papal Authority," *Augustiniana* 46: 261–89.

[J. CHAPIN]

BONIFACE II, POPE

Pontificate: Sept. 20 or 22, 530 to Oct. 10, 532; b. Rome, date unknown; d. Rome. Boniface, the first pope of German lineage, was an archdeacon under Pope FELIX IV, who was determined to avoid contention and schism by designating his successor in the papacy and preferred a cleric who was favorable to the imperial court at Ravenna. Shortly before his death, Felix summoned the Roman clergy and several Roman senators and conferred the pallium of papal sovereignty on Boniface, proclaiming him his successor as pope.

On the death of Felix IV, a large majority of the Roman clergy refused to accept Boniface as bishop and proceeded to elect the deacon Dioscorus of Alexandria. Opposition to Boniface stemmed also from the Romans' fear of Ostrogothic domination. Dioscorus and Boniface were consecrated bishops on the same day (Sept. 22,

530), giving rise to the seventh antipapal schism, which lasted only 22 days since Dioscorus died on Oct. 14, 530. The leaderless Dioscoran faction then reconciled themselves with Boniface II. He convened a Roman synod and forced the submission of his opponents, who had to pledge obedience to him as pope and condemn in writing the memory of Dioscorus (Dec. 27, 530). Having made his point, Boniface wisely avoided avenging himself on his opponents and tried to live in peace with all his clergy.

In 537, Boniface convoked a second synod, at which he proposed a constitution granting the pope the right to appoint his successor. Since the Roman clergy subscribed and pledged their support, Boniface nominated the deacon Vigilius as his successor; and the choice was ratified by the Roman priests and people. In a short time, however, resentment grew; and after an imperial protest against such action, a third synod was convoked in 531. In the presence of the Roman Senate, Boniface rescinded the former arrangement and personally burned the document.

During his pontificate Boniface II confirmed the acts of the Second Council of Orange (529), which under the leadership of CAESARIUS OF ARLES terminated the controversies over SEMI-PELAGIANISM. He was esteemed by the populace for his charity, particularly during a famine in Rome. In a jurisdictional dispute in Illyria, Boniface intervened, upholding the election of Stephen of Larissa against the jurisdictional encroachment of Epiphanius of Constantinople, who still insisted on his rights in that area. Boniface was buried in St. Peter's, where a fragment of his epitaph is still visible.

Bibliography: A. SCHWAIGER, *Lexikon für Theologie und Kirche*, ed. J. HOFER and K. RAHNER (Freiburg 1957–65) 2:588. C. J. VON HEFELE, *Histoire des conciles d'après les documents originaux* (Paris 1907–38) 2.2:1115–19, 1358–65. E. FERGUSON, ed., *Encyclopedia of Early Christianity* (New York 1997) 1:190. H. JEDIN, *History of the Church* (New York 1980) 2:626. J. N. D.KELLY, *Oxford Dictionary of Popes* (New York 1986) 57. J. RICHARDS, *Popes and Papacy the Early Middle Ages* (London 1979) 122–125.

[A. H. SKEABECK]

BONIFACE III, POPE

Pontificate: Feb. 19 to Nov. 10, 607. A Roman in the service of the Holy See as *primus defensor,* Boniface was appointed *APOSCRISIARIUS* to the court of the Byzantine Emperor Phocas in 603 by GREGORY THE GREAT. Boniface was a more successful diplomat than SABINIAN, who had preceded him as *apocrisarius* as he was to precede him as pope, and he won the support of the imperial court for the papacy and obtained from Phocas a decree repeating the Novella (*Corpus iuris civilis, Novellae* 131.2.14) of Justinian, whereby the Roman pontiff was recognized as head of all churches. This pronouncement contradicted the title ''ecumenical partiarch'' then recently assumed by the Partriarch of Constantinople, JOHN IV the Faster, and his successor, Cyriacus—a title Pope Gregory had felt challenged the unity of the Church under the pope. The most noteworthy legislation of Boniface's short pontificate was the decree of a Roman council whereby anathema was pronounced on anyone who would propose the successor to a pope or bishop before the third day after his death.

Bibliography: *Liber pontificalis,* ed. L. DUCHESNE (Paris 1886–1958) 1:316. *Gregori Registrum epistolorum XIII,* 41, ed. P. EWALD and L. M. HARTMANN, *Monumenta Germaniae Historica: Epistolae* 1–2. C. J. VON HEFELE, *Histoire des conciles d'après les documents originaux* (Paris 1907–38) 3.1:247. H. K. MANN, *The Lives of the Popes in the Early Middle Ages from 590 to 1304* (London 1902–32) 1.1:259–267. *Cambridge Medieval History* 4.1:440. P. JAFFÉ, *Regesta pontificum romanorum ab condita ecclesia ad annum post Christum natum 1198* (Graz 1956) 1:220; 2:698. A. FLICHE and V. MARTIN, eds., *Histoire de l'église depuis les origines jusqu'à nos jours* (Paris 1935) 5:71, 393. J. N. D. KELLY, *Oxford Dictionary of Popes* (New York 1986) 68.

[P. J. MULLINS]

BONIFACE IV, POPE

Pontificate: Aug. 25, 608 to May 8, 615. Boniface proved to be pious, industrious, and devoted to the poor, a worthy successor of GREGORY I. The most remarkable event of his pontificate was the consecration of the basilica Sancta Maria ad Martyres on the site of the Pantheon (609). The Emperor Phocas had acceded to the pope's request for the conversion of the ancient pagan monument into a Christian church, and Boniface translated there a number of relics from the catacombs. In 610 Boniface held a synod at Rome for the restoration of monastic discipline. MELLITUS, the first bishop of London, was present. He returned to England with the synodal decrees and papal letters to LAWRENCE, ARCHBISHOP OF CANTERBURY, to King ETHELBERT OF KENT, and to the people of England.

During his pontificate the heresy of MONOPHYSITISM was a cause of much ecclesiastical and political confusion. The success of the Persian invasion of many provinces of the Byzantine Empire was aided by the cooperation of heretical bishops. HERACLIUS, exarch of Africa, took advantage of the disorder to lead a revolt against Phocas and to seize the throne. Although victorious against the Persians, Heraclius did not succeed in restoring the Monophysites to the unity of the Church.

In northern Italy several of the Lombard bishops persisted in the Istrian schism, which rejected the condemnation of the THREE CHAPTERS by the Second Council of

CONSTANTINOPLE (553). The Irish monk COLUMBAN of Bobbio reprimanded him for his support of the Council's action. No reply of the pope is extant, but subsequent letters seem to indicate that the ill-informed Columban in no wise diminished by this imprudence the relation of his mission to the Holy See.

Bibliography: P. JAFFÉ, *Regesta pontificum romanorum ab condita ecclesia ad annum post Christum natum 1198* (Graz 1956) 1:220–222; 2:698, 739. *Liber pontificalis,* ed, L. DUCHESNE (Paris 1886–1958) 1:317–318. BEDE, *Ecclesiastical History* 2.4. H. K. MANN, *The Lives of the Popes in the Early Middle Ages from 590 to 1304* (London 1902–32) 1:268–279. H. LECLERCQ, *Dictionnaire d'archéologie chrétienne et de liturgie*, ed. F. CABROL, H. LECLERQ, I. MARROU (Paris 1907–53) 10:2:2062–68; 13.1:1063–67. E. CASPAR, *Geschichte de Papsttums von den Anfängen bis zur Höhe der Weltherrschaft* (Tubingen 1930–33) 2:517–522. G. SCHWAIGER, *Lexicon für Theologie und Kirche*, ed. J. HOFER and K. RAHNER (Freiburg 1957–65) 2:588–589. J. N. D. KELLY, *Oxford Dictionary of Popes* (New York 1986) 69.

[P. J. MULLINS]

BONIFACE V, POPE

Pontificate: Dec. 23, 619 to Oct. 25, 625. A Neapolitan, consecrated pope after the war-torn pontificate of DEUSDEDIT I, Boniface was noted for his organizing ability. In Rome he endeavored to conform ecclesiastical usage to civil law in the matter of bequests; he established the principle of right of asylum and issued laws over the liturgical function of various orders of clerics. Concerned with England, Boniface sent the PALLIUM as a symbol of honor and jurisdiction to JUSTUS, Archbishop of Canterbury, with a letter encouraging him to consecrate other bishops for the spread of the faith in England (624). The pope also wrote directly to King EDWIN OF NORTHUMBRIA, urging him to study the Catholic faith, and to Queen ETHELBURGA, a Christian, encouraging her to procure the Christianization of Edwin and his subjects. Some years later the Queen's confessor, PAULINUS OF YORK, baptized Edwin and founded the Archdiocese of YORK. At the opposite end of Christendom, Boniface and his successor witnessed the capitulation of the three ancient Patriarchates of JERUSALEM, ANTIOCH, and ALEXANDRIA to the rule of ISLAM as they became, in effect, "Christian caliphates." Constantinople remained the sole patriarchate of the East (*see* PATRIARCHATE).

Bibliography: *Liber pontificalis*, ed. L. DUCHESNE (Paris 1886–92) 1:321–322. P. JAFFÉ, *Regesta pontificum romanorum ab condita ecclesia ad annum post Christum natum 1198* (Graz 1956) 1:222–223; 2: 698. BEDE, *Ecclesiastical History* v.2. H. K. MANN, *The Lives of the Popes in the Early Middle Ages from 590 to 1304* (London 1902–32) 1:294–303. F. M. STENTON, *Anglo-Saxon England* (2d ed. Oxford 1947). P. BERTOLINI, *Dizionario biografico delgi italiani,* 12 (Rome 1971). P. H. BLAIR, *Anglo-Saxon Northumbria,* (London 1984). P. CLASSEN, "Der erste Römerzug in der Weltgeschichte. Zur Geschichte des Kaisertums in Westen und der Kaiserkrönung in Rom zwischen Theodosius der Groß, und Karl der Groß" *Ausgewäthe Aufätze* (1983) 23–43. J. N. D. KELLY, *Oxford Dictionary of Popes* (New York 1986), 69–70.

[P. J. MULLINS]

BONIFACE VI, POPE

Pontificate: April 11, 896 to April 26, 896; b. Rome; d. there. He was the son of Adrian, a bishop, and was elected pope almost immediately after the death of his predecessor, FORMOSUS, on April 4, 896. A struggle for control of Rome was then going on between the partisans of Arnulf, the German emperor, and those of LAMBERT OF SPOLETO. In the ensuing popular tumult, the latter group accomplished the election of Boniface, but later a Roman synod under JOHN IX (898) deplored his election since he had been twice suspended, as a subdeacon and again as a priest, because of unworthy conduct, and had not been canonically reinstated. Afflicted with gout, he died 15 days after his election and was buried in the portico of the popes in the Vatican.

Bibliography: F. BAIX, *Dictionnaire d'histoire et de géographie ecclésiastiques*, ed. A. BAUDRILLART et al. (Paris 1912) 9:899–900. P. JAFFÉ, *Regesta pontificum romanorum ab condita ecclesia ad annum post Christum natum 1198*, ed. S. LÖWENFELD (2d ed. Leipzig 1881–88; repr. Graz 1956) 439. F. X. SEPPELT, *Geschichte der Päpste von den Anfängen bis zur Mitte des 20. Jh.* (Munich 1955) 2:341. G. SCHWAIGER, *Lexikon für Theologie und Kirche*, ed. J. HOFER and K. RAHNER (Freiburg 1957–65) 2:589. P. BERTOLINI, *Dizionario biografio delgi italiani* (Rome 1970). J. N. D. KELLY, *Oxford Dictionary of Popes* (New York 1986) 115.

[A. J. ENNIS]

BONIFACE VII, ANTIPOPE

Pontificate: June–July 974; summer 980–March 981; April 984–July 20, 985. Born into a Roman family and named Franco (his father's name was Ferrucius), he was a cardinal deacon when Crescentius I de Theodora led a revolt against Pope Benedict VI (973–74). Benedict was imprisoned in the Castel Sant' Angelo, and Franco was consecrated Pope Boniface VII. The imprisoned pope had the support of Emperor Otto II (973–83), who sent Count Sicco from Spoleto to demand the pope's release. Boniface had Benedict VI strangled in order to maintain his position. This led to riots in the city and Boniface had to retreat to the Castel Sant' Angelo. He escaped with part of the papal treasury and fled to Byzantine-controlled southern Italy before Sicco could take him. The antipope was excommunicated at a synod (October, 974) called by the new pope, Benedict VII (974–983). Thus ended Boniface's first attempt at being pope. Boniface, however, kept his eyes on Rome. In the summer of 980, while Benedict was not in the city, he brought about another coup and installed himself in the Lateran. Benedict appealed to Otto and returned in March 981 with troops led by the emperor himself. Boniface fled to Constantinople, ending his second reign as antipope.

Pope Benedict's successor, John XIV (983–84), was not popular in Rome, and after the death of Otto, Boniface took the opportunity to return yet again. Financed by the Byzantines, and with the help of Crescentius' sons, John and Crescentius II, Boniface had Pope John deposed and imprisoned in April of 984. In August the pope was murdered, which again made Boniface the only remaining pope. Little is known of his reign, except that he died suddenly on July 20, 985. Assassination is a possibility, but one that cannot be confirmed in the sources. There was, however, obviously strong factionalism within the city. Some referred to the antipope as ''Malefatius'' (a play on his Latin name Bonifatius) and as a ''horrendum monstrum.'' Additionally, upon his death, Boniface's corpse was dragged through the streets and mutilated. Finally it was left in front of the Lateran Palace, to be buried the next morning.

Bibliography: L. DUCHESNE, ed. *Liber Pontificalis* (Paris 1886–92; repr. 1955–57) 2.255–60. P. JAFFÉ, *Regesta pontificum Romanorum* (Leipzig 1885–88; repr. Graz 1956) 1.485; 2.707, 747. J. F. BÖHMER, *Regesta Imperii* (Graz, Vienna, Cologne 1969) 211–56. B. PLATINA, *De vita Christi ac omnium pontificum* 139 (138), ed. G. GAIDA, in *Rerum italicarum scriptores* 3.1, ed. L. A. MURATORI (Città di Castello and Bologna 1913–32) 172–73. H. K. MANN, *The Lives of the Popes in the Early Middle Ages* (London 1902–32) 4.339–42. F. BAIX, *Dictionnaire d'histoire et de géographie ecclésiastiques* (Paris 1937) 9.900–04. P. BREZZI, *Roma e l'impero medioevale, 774–1252* (Bologna 1947) 148–57. F. X. SEPPELT, *Geschichte der Päpste von den Anfängen bis zur Mitte des zwanzigsten Jahrhunderts* (Munich 1954–59) 2.378–83. H. ZIMMERMAN, *Papstabsetzungen des Mittelalters* (Graz, Vienna, Cologne 1968) 99–103. H. ZIMMERMAN, *Das dunkle Jahrhundert* (Graz, Vienna, Cologne 1971) 202–27. J. N. D. KELLY, *The Oxford Dictionary of Popes* (New York 1986) 130–31. R. SCHIEFFER, *Lexikon des Mittelalters* (Munich 1982) 2.414.

[P. M. SAVAGE]

BONIFACE VIII, POPE

Pontificate: Dec. 24, 1294, to Oct. 11, 1303; b. Benedict Gaetani, Anagni, *c.* 1235; d. Rome. His reign is remembered especially for the fierce conflict of Church and State between the papacy and the French monarchy that broke out in 1296. Boniface has been accused of committing the papacy to novel and extravagant claims in the temporal sphere in the course of that struggle. It is true that he was a pope of grand ambitions, determined to uphold all the prerogatives of his office. He was also a man of autocratic temper, impatient of opposition, given to hot outbursts of rage (which were perhaps caused in part by the painful disease of ''the stone'' from which he suffered). But it is not true that his own dominating personality led him to propound new doctrines of papal might. The claim that the pope's ''plentitude of power'' included a right to depose secular rulers and to act in the last resort as a supreme judge set over all men and all their affairs had already been formulated by Boniface's predecessors, especially by INNOCENT IV. The defeats that marked Boniface's reign did not, then, result from any aggressive new demands on his part, but rather from his stubborn defense of long-established claims of the PAPACY in the political order at a time when they had become totally unacceptable to the new monarchies.

Pope Boniface VIII, manuscript illumination.

Election. A member of the noble GAETANI family, Benedict studied Roman and Canon Law at BOLOGNA and subsequently entered the service of the Roman Curia, serving in a minor capacity with embassies to France in 1264 and to England in 1265. He became cardinal deacon in 1281 and cardinal priest in 1291. At the Council of Paris in 1290 Benedict played a leading role as papal legate. He vehemently defended the rights of the MENDICANT ORDERS against attacks from the secular masters of the University of Paris and, in the diplomatic sphere, succeeded in negotiating a peace between France and Aragon. In 1294 he was active in persuading the holy but incompetent CELESTINE V to relinquish the papal office and was himself elected pope at the conclave that followed. From the beginning Boniface had bitter enemies. His part in encouraging Celestine's abdication earned him the hatred of the Franciscan SPIRITUALS and their patron, Cardinal James COLONNA, who soon found another motive for opposition in the frank NEPOTISM that the new Pope displayed in enriching his own Gaetani kin with offices and lands in the Papal States.

Sicily and Northern Europe. Celestine V had been a mere tool of King Charles II of Naples in whose territory he resided. Boniface promptly moved the Curia back to Rome and resumed the conduct of an independent papal diplomacy. There were many problems to claim his attention. The most pressing one was the struggle between JAMES II of Aragon and Charles II of Anjou for the throne of Sicily. In 1295 Boniface achieved a settlement, which seemed at first a brilliant stroke of diplomacy, by persuading James to relinquish his claim; but the people of Sicily subsequently offered the kingship to James's brother Frederick, and in 1302 Boniface reluctantly had to acknowledge Frederick as independent King of the island of Sicily. Boniface was much concerned with the diplomatic affairs of northern Europe. In 1299 he tried unsuccessfully to mediate between Scotland and England. In 1298 he excommunicated King Eric of Denmark for imprisoning the archbishop of Lund and, in 1303, obtained the King's submission. Boniface at first opposed the election of Albert of Austria as emperor, but in April 1303, at the climax of his conflict with France, he recognized Albert's claim. The Pope took advantage of the occasion to restate the old theory that all national kings were subordinate to the emperor and that the emperor's power in turn came from the pope. (In 1955 PIUS XII referred to this assertion of Boniface as "a medieval conception, conditioned by the period.")

Struggle with Philip the Fair. The great struggle with France began in 1296. Edward I of England and PHILIP IV of France were engaged in a war arising out of feudal disputes and commercial rivalries, and both of them had imposed heavy new taxes on their clergy to help finance the campaigns. A canon of the Fourth LATERAN COUNCIL (1215) laid down that clerics were not to be taxed without consent of the pope, but the papacy had acquiesced in such levies in the past, especially when they were intended to support a "just war." In 1296, however, two Christian Kings each claimed to be waging a "just war" against the other, and both were determined to tax the clergy with unusual severity. The situation seemed to Boniface intolerable, and he determined to end it. His bull *CLERICIS LAICOS* (1296) opened with the assertion that "the laity have always been hostile to the clergy" and went on to describe the recent exactions as an example of this hostility. In the future, Boniface decreed, any lay ruler who demanded taxes from his clergy without prior papal permission would incur automatic excommunication, and so would any cleric who yielded to such demands. The promulgation of the bull was bitterly resented by the Kings whose policies had provoked it. In England the steadfast ROBERT OF WINCHELSEA, Archbishop of Canterbury, bore the brunt of Edward's anger. Philip of France found a way of striking directly at the Pope himself. He issued an order forbidding all export of treasure and negotiable currency from France, a move that created serious financial embarrassment for Boniface, who relied heavily on revenues from the French Church. In September 1296 Boniface sent an indignant protest to Philip (*Ineffabilis amor*), declaring that he would rather suffer death than surrender any of the liberties of the Church; but he explained in conciliatory fashion that his recent bull had not been intended to apply to customary dues from the feudal lands of the Church. He added that Philip was being deluded by evil counselors and that he was rash to pick a quarrel with the papacy, especially when the pope was the rightful judge of the political disputes in which Philip was involved—for the King's enemies alleged that Philip had sinned against them, and judgment on matters of sin belonged to the Roman see.

Struggle with Colonna. Unfortunately Boniface threw away any chance there might have been of carrying the whole issue to a successful conclusion by choosing this time to force a final breach with the Colonna family. In May 1297 a relative of the Colonnas plundered a convoy of papal treasure. Boniface summoned the two cardinals of the family to his presence and commanded that they hand over to him three strategic Colonna castles. The cardinals refused and withdrew to their fortress at Longhezza, where they were joined by JACOPONE DA TODI, a leader of the Franciscan Spirituals. From there they issued a manifesto declaring that Boniface was no true pope since the abdication of Celestine V had been illegal. Subsequently they accused Boniface of heresy and simony and also of murdering the aged Celestine, who had indeed died in a papal prison. It was the first public statement of charges—always unproved—that was to harass Boniface to the end of his reign. When Philip IV's minister, Pierre Flotte, traveled south to negotiate with Boniface, he met with representatives of the Colonnas, and his hand was greatly strengthened by the possibility that Philip might support their charges. In July 1297 Boniface capitulated completely. His bull *Etsi de statu* conceded that in time of necessity the King could tax the French clergy without consulting the Pope and that it was for the King himself to determine when a state of necessity existed.

Resumption of Struggle with Philip. By 1300 Boniface's fortunes seemed to be reviving. To mark the centennial he proclaimed a year of JUBILEE, the first such occasion in the history of the Church, and tens of thousands of pilgrims from many lands poured into Rome to worship at the shrines of the Apostles. When the Pope, encouraged by the enthusiastic devotion of the pilgrims, heard of new encroachments on the liberties of the Church in France, he was prepared to challenge Philip again. The occasion of this second dispute was the King's treatment of a French bishop, Bernard of Saisset. In 1301 Philip accused Saisset of treason and had him arrested, tried before a royal court, and thrown into prison. In defiance of the universal jurisdiction of the pope over all bishops, Philip was asserting total sovereignty over the persons as well as the property of the French episcopate. Boniface protested in the bull *AUSCULTA FILI* (December 1301), which was considered and approved in a consistory of cardinals. The bull accused Philip of subverting the whole state of the Church in France by abuse of royal rights of patronage and illicit extensions of royal jurisdiction. It declared, "Let no one persuade you that you have no superior or that you are not subject to the head of the ecclesiastical hierarchy, for he is a fool who so thinks." When the bull arrived in Paris, its contents were not publicized, but a crude forgery was put into circulation by the King's agents in which Boniface was alleged to have written, "Know that you are subject to us in spiritualities and in temporalities."

At the end of 1301 Boniface also commanded the French bishops to attend a council to be held at Rome in November 1302 to consider the reform of the French Church. Philip forbade them to attend and in April 1302 summoned an assembly of his own at Paris—a meeting of nobles, burgesses, and clergy. Pierre Flotte harangued this first French Estates-General and apparently accused Boniface of claiming to be feudal overlord of France. The nobles and burgesses then wrote to the cardinals denouncing Boniface and refusing to recognize him as pope. The clergy wrote to Boniface himself addressing him as Pope but protesting against his "unheard-of assertions." When Boniface received the envoys of the French Estates he denied angrily that he had ever claimed to be feudal overlord of France, but he declared that his predecessors had deposed three French kings and that he was quite prepared to depose Philip if necessary.

There was a lull during the summer of 1302. Philip was distracted from his feud against Boniface by a major defeat inflicted on his forces by the Flemings at the battle of Courtrai, in which the King's chief minister Flotte was killed. But Philip still refused to permit his bishops to attend the Pope's council in Rome. When the council met, fewer than half the French bishops were present, and no measures for the reform of the French Church were agreed upon. Immediately after this abortive council (November 1302) Boniface issued the bull *UNAM SANCTAM*, the most famous medieval document on spiritual and temporal power. The bull was essentially a theological treatise on the unity of the Church, a unity threatened, as Boniface well saw, when national hierarchies of bishops hesitated between allegiance to their king and obedience to their pope. But it also emphasized, perhaps more explicitly than any earlier papal pronouncement, the power of the pope to "institute" and to judge temporal kings.

Attack on Pope's Person; His Death. Philip's reply to this claim was an extraordinarily brutal and unscrupulous attack on the Pope's reputation and even on his person. At an Estates-General held in March 1303 the King's new minister, Guillaume de Nogaret, presented a series of accusations against Boniface and demanded that a general council be assembled to sit in judgment on him. The charges were presented in more detail at another meeting held in June. Boniface was accused of usurping the papal office, of heresy, blasphemy, murder, simony, and sodomy. (After all this it is something of an anticlimax to read that "he does not fast on fast days.") Meanwhile Nogaret had left Paris for Italy in an attempt to settle the whole issue by brute force.

In the summer of 1303 Boniface drew up a solemn bull of excommunication directed against Philip (*Super Petri solio*) and moved from Rome to Anagni, from where he intended to promulgate it. Before he could do so (September 7), the little city was seized by a band of mercenaries led by Nogaret and Sciarra Colonna. After a day of fighting they broke into the papal palace and confronted Boniface, who was waiting for them arrayed in his pontifical robes. Nogaret demanded that Boniface renounce the papacy. When he refused, Sciarra Colonna wanted to kill him on the spot, but Nogaret hoped to carry him off to be condemned by some sort of council. They left Boniface under guard for the night. As he saw the soldiers looting the palace, he murmured only "The Lord gave and the Lord taketh away." On the second day Nogaret and Sciarra Colonna still disagreed about their next move. By the third day the whole town and countryside was roused against them, and they had to flee from Anagni leaving Boniface at liberty. But the Pope had collapsed after facing Nogaret, and he never recovered in mind or body. He was carried back to Rome and died a few weeks later. Philip continued to hound his memory after his death and succeeded in extracting from a later Pope, CLEMENT V, an acknowledgment that, in their proceedings against Boniface, Philip and his councilors had "acted out of an estimable, just and sincere zeal and from the fervor of their Catholic faith."

Evaluation of Boniface's Reign. The tragedy of Boniface's reign lies in the disproportion between the ends he set himself and the resources of his own personality. All his diplomacy aimed at establishing peace and concord in a Christendom guided and led by the pope.

But his inability to comprehend the new forces of nationalism that were stirring into life, his excessive preoccupation with the advancement of the Gaetani family, his impatient and irascible disposition, all made the attainment of such an end impossible. He was a great lawyer; and the *LIBER SEXTUS*, the third volume of the *CORPUS IURIS CANONICI*, which was promulgated in 1298 at Boniface's command, stands as a monument to his juristic acumen.

Bibliography: *Les Registres de Boniface VIII,* ed. G. A. L. DIGARD et al., 4 v. (Paris 1884–1939). T. S. R. BOASE, *Boniface VIII* (London 1933). G. A. L. DIGARD, *Philippe le Bel et le Saint-Siège de 1285 à 1304,* 2 v. (Paris 1936). H. DENIFLE, "Die Denkschriften der Colonna gegen Bonifaz VIII. und der Cardinäle gegen die Colonna," H. DENIFLE and F. EHRLE, eds., *Archiv für Literatur- und Kirchengeschichte des Mittelalters,* [(Berlin) Freiburg 1885–1900] 5:493–529. P. DUPUY, *Histoire du différend d'entre le pape Boniface VIII. et Philippe le Bel* (Paris 1655). H. FINKE, *Aus den Tagen Bonifaz VIII* (Münster 1902). J. RIVIÈRE, *Le Problème de l'église et de l'état au temps de Philippe le Bel* (Paris 1926). R. SCHOLZ, *Die Publizistik zur Zeit Philipps des Schönen und Bonifaz' VIII* (Stuttgart 1903). G. DE LAGARDE, *La Naissance de l'esprit laïque au déclin du moyen âge* (Vienna 1934–). L. E. BOYLE, "The Constitution *Cum ex eo* of Pope Boniface VIII," *Mediaeval Studies* 24: 263–302. A. FRUGONI, "Il giubileo di Bonifacio VIII," *Bollettino dell'Istituto storico per il Medioevo* 62: 1–121. E. DUPRE THESEIDER, *Dizionario biografico degli Italiani* 12 (1970). J. MULDOON, "Boniface VIII's Forty Years of Experience in the Law," *The Jurist* 11 (1971) 449–477. R.-H. BAUTIER, "Le jubilé romain de 1300 et l'alliance franco-pontificale au temps de Philippe le Bel et de Boniface VIII," *Moyen Age* 86: 189–216. T. SCHMIDT, *Libri rationum Camerae Bonifatii papae VIII* (Vatican City 1984). T. SCHMIDT, *Der Bonifaz-Prozess* (Cologne-Vienna 1989). A.SOMMERLECHNER, "Die Darstellung des Attentats von Anagni," *Römische Historische Mitteilungen* 32/33: 51–102. T. SCHMIDT, "Papst Bonifaz VIII. als Gesetzgeber," *Proceedings of the Eighth International Congress of Medieval Canon Law,* ed. S. CHODOROW (Vatican City 1992) 227–245.

[B. TIERNEY/L. SCHMUGGE]

BONIFACE IX, POPE

Pontificate: Nov. 2, 1389 to Oct. 1, 1404; b. Pietro Tomacelli, Naples, *c.* 1355. Descended from an old Neapolitan family, he was created cardinal deacon of St. George while still a young man, and in 1385, cardinal priest of St. Anastasia by Pope URBAN VI. Little else is known of his life until his election as pope in Rome in the midst of the WESTERN SCHISM. On Urban VI's death, the Avignon antipope, CLEMENT VII, had hoped that through the diplomacy of King Charles VI of France the 14 Roman cardinals would elect him Urban's successor and end the schism. Instead they elected Tomacelli as Boniface IX. In contrast to his bitter, intolerant, and imprudent predecessor, Urban, the handsome Boniface was amiable, kindly, and practical. Convinced, however, of his papal rights, Boniface immediately excommunicated Clement, declared (1391) sinful the proposal to end the schism through a general council, refused to abdicate (1396–98) despite Anglo-French and German pressure, and rejected (1404) the embassy of Clement's successor at Avignon, antipope BENEDICT XIII. Boniface's pontificate had two major problems: the establishment of his political position and the raising of money. Urban had alienated much of Italy. To strengthen his position in Rome, Boniface supported the claims of Ladislaus to the Kingdom of Naples against his Clementine rival, Louis II of Anjou; won back the allegiance of Rome; and established his authority in the STATES OF THE CHURCH. Although France withdrew its commitment (1398–1403) to his Avignon rival, Benedict XIII, Boniface was unable to increase his European sphere of influence. England remained faithful but disturbed; Sicily and Genoa actually withdrew their allegiance. Boniface was forced to take the side of Prince-elector Rupert of the Palatinale against King WENCESLAS in Germany, and of Ladislaus of Naples against Emperor SIGISMUND in Hungary. These essentially secular activities forced Boniface to exploit old sources of revenue and tap new ones. In 1392 he insisted on *medii fructus* from every cleric whom he appointed to a benefice (*see* ANNATES). He gave preferments to the highest bidder, sold exemptions, and in the HOLY YEARS of 1390 and 1400 used indulgences, especially *ad instar,* for financial gain. He was assisted in his monetary troubles by Baldassare Cossa, later antipope JOHN XXIII, whom he raised to the cardinalate in 1402. Boniface did not profit personally from these simoniacal practices, but the Church suffered severely. His pontificate was a troubled one; it deserves the phrase "the crooked days of Boniface IX."

Bibliography: L. PASTOR, *The History of the Popes from the Close of the Middle Ages* (Freiburg 1955) v.1, *passim.* H. HEMMER, *Dictionnaire de théologie catholique,* ed. A. VACANT et al. (Paris 1903–50) 2:1: 1003–05. E. VANSTEENBERGHE, *Dictionnaire d'histoire et de géographie ecclésiastiques*, ed. A. BAUDRILLART et al. (Paris 1912) 9:909–922. J. B. VILLIGER, *Lexicon für Theologie und Kirche*, ed. J. HOFER and K. RAHNER (Freiburg 1957–65) 2:591. G. BRUCKER, *The Civic World of Early Renaissance Florence* (Princeton, NJ 1977). K. DALE, *The Rise of the Medici* (Oxford 1978). M. L. DE WEESEN, *A Study on Decision Making in France During the Reign of Charles VI. (The Rejection of the Avignon Papacy 1395)* (London-Ann Arbor 1973). S. FODALE, *Documenti del pontificato di Bonifacio IX. Documenti sulle relazioni tra la Sicilia e il Papato fra Tre e Quattrocentro* (Palermo 1983). R. LEFEVRE, "Tre 'ethiopes nigri de India' a Roma nel 1404," *Strènna dei Romanisti* 49 (1988) 237–44. L. PALMERO, "L'anno santo dei mercanti: dibattio storiografico e documenti economici sul cosidetto Giubileo del 1400," in *Cultura e società nell'Italia medioevale. Studi per Paolo Brezzi* (Rome 1988), 605–18. C. L. STINGLER, *Humanism and Church Fathers: Ambrogio Traversari (1386–1439) and Christian Antiquity in the Italian Renaissance* (Albany 1977). R. N. SWANSON, "A Survey of Views on the Great Schism, C 1395," *Archivum Historiae Pontificiae* 21 (1983) 79–103. J. N. D. KELLY, *Oxford Dictionary of Popes* (New York 1986) 230.

[E. J. SMYTH]

BONIFACE OF SAVOY, BL.

Carthusian monk, archbishop of Canterbury; b. *c.* 1207; d. Sainte-Hélène, Savoy, July 14, 1270. The son of Thomas I, count of Savoy, Boniface entered La Grande-Chartreuse at an early age. In c. 1232 he became bishop of Belley in Burgundy, serving as administrator of the Diocese of Valence as well in 1239. As uncle of Eleanor of Provence, Henry III's queen of England, he was elected archbishop of Canterbury in 1241 to succeed Abp. Edmund of Abingdon, but he was confirmed only in 1243. In 1244 he arrived in England, was involved in the governmental crisis of that year, and made the first of his two metropolitan visitations. At the Council of Lyons (1245), he succeeded in gaining for Canterbury province the first fruits, or annates, of vacant benefices for the next seven years. When he returned to England in 1249, he was finally enthroned. Also in 1249 he made his second reforming visitation, during which he was opposed by the chapter of Saint Paul's Cathedral and the priory of St. Bartholomew in the Diocese of London. This led to excommunications, which Rome annulled in 1251. In 1254 he accompanied Prince Edward I when he married Eleanor of Castile. Boniface was involved in the governmental crises of 1258 to 1265, the so-called Barons' War. In 1258 he compiled constitutions for reform—in the tradition of ROBERT GROSSETESTE—which were later used by Abp. JOHN PECKHAM. When his reform measures were published in 1261, Henry III caused Pope Urban IV to refuse them confirmation. In 1263 and 1264 Boniface pleaded for Henry III at the court of Louis IX of France. Boniface spent his last years in Savoy. His cult was approved in 1838 by Pope Gregory XVI.

Feast: July 14 (Savoy, Sardinia, and Carthusians), formerly on July 15 and 21.

Bibliography: MATTHEW PARIS, *Historia Anglorum . . . Historia minor,* ed. F. MADDEN, 3 v. (*Rerum Britannicarum medii aevi scriptores* 44; London 1866–69) v. 3. INNOCENT IV, *Register . . .*, ed. E. BERGER, v. 2 (Bibliothèque des Écoles françaises d'Athènes et de Rome, 2d ser.; Paris 1885). C. W. PREVITÉ-ORTON, *The Early History of the House of Savoy* (Cambridge, Eng. 1912). G. STRICKLAND, ''Ricerche storica sopra il B. Bonifacio de Savoia,'' *Miscellenea di storia Italica,* 3d ser. 1 (1895) 349–432. F. M. POWICKE, *The Thirteenth Century* (2d ed. Oxford 1962). R. FOREVILLE, ''L'Élection de B. de S. au siège primatial de Canterbury . . . ,'' *Bulletin philologique et historique (jusqu'à 1610) du Comité des travaux historiques et scientifiques* 1 (1960) 435–450.

[V. I. J. FLINT]

BONILLI, PIETRO, BL.

Parish priest and founder of the Sisters of the Holy Family of Spoleto; b. San Lorenzo (di Trevi), Umbria, Italy, March 15, 1841; d. Spoleto, Umbria, Jan. 5, 1935. Pietro, son of Sebastian Bonilli and Maria Allegretti, attended the diocesan seminary and was ordained priest in 1863. From 1863 to 1898 he served San Michele Arcangelo Parish in Cannaiola di Trevi, the most depressed area of the Diocese of Spoleto. There he founded the Little Orphanage of Nazareth (1884) and the Congregation of Sisters of the Holy Family (1888) to staff it and expand his ministry to the poor. He also opened (1893) a hospice for the deaf and blind, which the sisters moved to Spoleto. He followed them and was appointed canon of Spoleto cathedral and rector of the regional seminary. Before his death he was honored (1908) by Pope St. PIUS X. Bonilli's tomb is in his church of San Michele Arcangelo. He was beatified by John Paul II, April 24, 1988.

Bibliography: *L'Osservatore Romano,* English edition, no. 16 (1988): 12.

[K. I. RABENSTEIN]

BONINO, GIUSEPPINA GABRIELLA, BL.

Foundress of the Sisters of the Holy Family of Savigliano; b. Savigliano, Piedmont, Italy, Sept. 5, 1843; d. Savona, Liguria, Italy, Feb. 8, 1906. Raised in a religious family, Bonino moved to Turin when she was 12. Her spiritual director, discerning her true vocation, encouraged her to make a temporary vow of virginity when she was 18. In 1869 she moved back to Savigliano to care for her ailing father until his death. During a pilgrimage to Lourdes in 1877, in thanksgiving for a successful back surgery, she was given to understand that her vocation was to return God's gift of a good family by becoming a mother to numerous infants and children with no family. Twice she sampled the cloistered life before realizing that her service would be better undertaken in an active religious community. She founded and became the superior of the Sisters of the Holy Family, an institute dedicated to serving orphans and the elderly poor (1881). She founded four other houses before her death.

During his homily at her beatification on May 7, 1995, John Paul II proclaimed, ''Her charism was family love, learned and practiced above all while living with her parents until adulthood and then by following the Lord's call in consecrated life. From the family as the domestic church to the religious community as a spiritual family: this is the summary of her humble journey, hidden but of incalculable value, that of the family, the environment of extraordinary love in ordinary things.'' She is one of the patronesses of families.

Feast: Feb. 8.

Bibliography: *L'Osservatore Romano,* English edition, no. 19 (1995): 2, 4. G. MINA, *Quando l'amore chiama: una vita pre-*

sente nell'oggi: Madre Giuseppina Gabriella Bonino, fondatrice delle Suore della Sacra Famiglia di Savigliano (Cavallermaggiore 1993).

[K. I. RABENSTEIN]

BONITUS OF CLERMONT, ST.

Bishop and ascetic; b. Auvergne, France, *c.* 623; d. Lyons, Jan. 15, 706. His life is known through an anonymous contemporary biography by a monk of the abbey of Manglieu in Auvergne. Bonitus (Bont) was born to a Roman senatorial family and educated in grammar, rhetoric, and Roman law. He was attached to the court of Sigebert III (634–656) and then made rector of the Prefecture of Marseilles under Pepin of Heristal. He succeeded his older brother, St. Avitus, as bishop of Clermont sometime after 690. Concerned over the form of his election, he resigned (or, as it has been suggested, was forced to resign) and retired to the abbey of Manglieu. After a leisurely pilgrimage to Rome, he returned to France and reached Lyons in 702. The translation of his relics in 712 was accompanied by miracles, and his remains became the object of fervent veneration in Auvergne and surrounding provinces.

Feast: Jan. 15 (Clermont, Autun, Lyons, Marseilles, Moulins, and Saint-Flour).

Bibliography: J. MABILLON, *Acta sanctorum ordinis S. Benedicti* (Venice 1733–40) 3:78–89. *Monumenta Germaniae Historica: Scriptores rerum Merovingicarum* 6:110–139. L. BRÉHIER, *Dictionnaire d'histoire et de géographie ecclésiastiques*, ed. A. BAUDRILLART et al. (Paris 1912) 9:843–847. J. L. BAUDOT and L. CHAUSSIN, *Vies des saints et des bienhereux selon l'ordre du calendrier avec l'historique des fêtes* (Paris 1935–56) 1:312–314.

[P. BLECKER]

BONIZO OF SUTRI

Bishop, canonist, and publicist under Gregory VII (known also as Bonitho, Bonitus); b. perhaps in Cremona, Italy, *c.* 1045; d. probably before 1095, but possibly as late as 1099. A native Lombard, Bonizo devoted his life to the reform of the Church in north Italy and to the GREGORIAN REFORM in general, a program for which he was an extreme and uncompromising advocate. As a subdeacon leading the PATARINES in Piacenza, he came to the attention of Pope GREGORY VII, who made him bishop of the strategic See of Sutri (1075 or 1076) and employed him as legate (1078).

During the INVESTITURE STRUGGLE he was captured by Emperor HENRY IV (1082), but he escaped and took refuge with MATILDA OF TUSCANY. While there, he wrote his most famous work, the *Liber ad amicum* [*Monumenta Germaniae Historica* (Berlin 1826) Libelli de lite, 1:568–620], designed to rally all reformers after Gregory's death in 1085. Partisan, polemical, and panegyric, it is a personal and unreliable memoir of Gregory, although its distortions do not seem to be deliberate.

Around 1086 Bonizo was elected bishop of Piacenza, but the citizens expelled him from the city (1089), whereupon he resigned and devoted his last years to the *Liber de vita christiana* [ed. E. Perels (Berlin 1930)], a compilation of canonistic extracts with commentary. The exact date of his death is unknown.

Bibliography: P. FOURNIER and G. LEBRAS, *Histoire des collections canoniques en occident depuis les fausses décrétales jusqu'au Décret de Gratien* (Paris 1931–32) 2:139–150. L. JADIN, *Dictionnaire d'histoire et de géographie ecclésiastiques* (Paris 1912–) 9:994–998. E. NASALLI ROCCA DI CORNELIANO, ''Osservazioni su Bonizione vescovo di Sutri et di Piacenza come canonista,'' *Studi gregoriani* 2 (1947) 151–162.

[R. KAY]

BONNE-ESPÉRANCE, MONASTERY OF

Premonstratensian monastery near Binche, Belgium, in the province of Hainault, Diocese of Tournai; founded 1125 or 1126 by Rainaud de la Croix and his wife Béatrice. The property at Ramignies originally given to St. Norbert proved unsuitable. Odo (d. 1125 or 1126), the first abbot, moved the community to Sart-Richevin and finally to Vellereille-le-Brayeux in 1130. In 1140 a cloister of nuns was erected by Bonne-Espérance (Bona Spes) at Rivreulle as a daughterhouse of the Abbey of PRÉMONTRÉ. The monastery gained new prominence when the second abbot of Bonne-Espérance, the noted exegete and hagiographer, Philippe de Harvengt (d. 1183), incorporated a number of parishes during his term of office. But the abbey suffered severe damage during the religious wars. It was pillaged in 1543 at the siege of Binche, burned in 1568 by the Prince of Orange and again devastated in 1577, at which time Abbot Jean Trusse (d. 1580) was imprisoned. In 1792, during the Battle of Jemmapses, the abbey was besieged once more, and Abbot Bonaventure Daublain (d. 1797) and his community dispersed. In 1794 it was suppressed, and the buildings, acquired by the Diocese of Tournai, were converted into a seminary.

Bibliography: N. BACKMUND, *Monasticon Praemonstratense,* 3 v. (Straubing 1949–56) 2:361–364. A. VERSTEYLEN, *Dictionnaire d'histoire et de géographie ecclésiastiques,* ed. A. BAUDRILLART (Paris 1912–) 9: 1030–32. É. POUMON, *Abbayes de Belgique* (Brussels 1954). L. H. COTTINEAU, *Répertoire topobibliographique des abbayes et prieurés,* 2 v. (Mâcon 1935–39) 1:424. É. BROUETTE,

Obituaire de l'abbaye de Bonne-Espérance de l'ordre de Prémontré (Louvain 1964).

[E. D. MCSHANE]

BONNECHOSE, HENRI MARIE GASTON DE

Cardinal, archbishop of Rouen; b. Paris, May 30, 1800; d. Rouen, Oct. 28, 1883. He was the son of a Norman of gentle birth and a Dutch Protestant mother, and made his First Communion at the age of 18. After occupying many posts in the magistrature, he studied for the priesthood, was ordained (1833), and was for some time a member of the Society of St. Louis, established by Abbé Louis BAUTAIN. He became superior of the community at Saint-Louis des Français in Rome (1844), bishop of Carcassonne (1847) and then of Evreux (1854), archbishop of Rouen (1858), and cardinal (1863). As a member of the French senate from 1863 he intervened perseveringly and eloquently in that body and before Emperor Napoleon III, whom he highly esteemed, in favor of the papal temporal power and in defense of religion. At VATICAN COUNCIL I he served on the committee on *postulata* and headed the "third party" among the members, which favored the definition of papal infallibility in a more mitigated form than MANNING and his group sought. During the Franco-Prussian War, Rouen found him a generous protector and an efficacious advocate with the conqueror. He was an energetic and charitable administrator, and continued his religious work diligently under the Third Republic. He was one of the episcopal founders of the Institut Catholique de Paris.

Bibliography: L. BESSON, *Vie du cardinal de Bonnechose, archevêque de Rouen*, 2 v. (Paris 1882). R. EUDE, *Histoire religieuse du diocèse de Rouen au XIXe siècle* v.1 *Les Archevêques de Rouen 1802–1915* (Rouen 1954). C. BUTLER, *The Vatican Council* 2 v. (New York 1930). M. PREVOST, *Dictionnaire de biographie française* 6:996–997. C. LAPLATTE, *Dictionnaire d'histoire et de géographie ecclésiastiques* 9:1027–28.

[C. LEDRÉ]

BONNER, EDMUND

English Reformation bishop and legist; b. probably 1500; d. Marshalsea prison, London, Sept. 5, 1569. Although it is still debated, Bonner is believed to have been the illegitimate son of George Savage, rector of Daneham, Cheshire, and Elizabeth Frodsham, who later married Edmund Bonner, a long-sawyer of Hanley, Worcestershire. At Pembroke College, Oxford, Bonner obtained a baccalaureate in Civil and Canon Law (1519) and a doctorate in Civil Law (1525). He was ordained around 1519.

In 1529 he became a chaplain to Cardinal Thomas Wolsey and took part in negotiations between the cardinal and Thomas Cromwell, remaining with Wolsey after his fall from power. Enjoying the favor of Cromwell, Bonner was employed by Henry VIII from 1532 to 1540 on several diplomatic missions on the Continent to Clement VII, Charles V, Francis I, and the Lutheran princes. At Marseilles he argued Henry's case for annulment so truculently before Clement VII that it infuriated him; on another occasion Bonner's overbearing manner gave offense to Francis I.

Although appointed by Henry to the See of Hereford (1538), he was not yet consecrated when he was translated to London (1539). He was consecrated there in April of 1540. A vigorous defender of Henry's marriage to Anne Boleyn, he accepted the royal supremacy. He showed his zeal by writing a very antipapal preface to the Hamburg (1536) edition of the *De Vera Obedientia,* Stephen GARDINER's defense of Henry's claim to be head of the English Church.

Bonner also facilitated the printing of Tyndale's Bible that was intended for distribution in England. Nevertheless, he was just as strongly opposed to Protestant doctrines as were Cuthbert TUNSTALL and Stephen Gardiner. In later years, he openly attributed his acceptance of the royal supremacy to his fear of retaliation by the king.

After Edward VI's accession (1547), Bonner was imprisoned on several charges, such as refusing to recognize the right of the King's Council to make innovations in religion during the royal minority, but essentially for refusing to accept the introduction of Protestantism. As a result of charges brought by John Hooper and Hugh Latimer, and after examination by Archbishop Cranmer, Bonner was deprived of his bishopric in October of 1549.

Restored by Mary, he took a leading part in the return to the papal allegiance and orthodox doctrine. As bishop of London he presided over the trials of a great many heretics, since his see was the chief center of Protestantism. His position in this connection laid him open to the taunt of having been formerly a belligerent foe of the papacy. He took a more positive attitude to Protestantism by writing and distributing in his diocese *A Profitable and Necessary Doctrine for Every Christian Man,* a simple statement of Catholic doctrines that Philip Hughes has described as "a singularly warmhearted guide to a better life."

For opposing Elizabeth's changes in the Mass and refusing to recognize her claim to supremacy, he was deprived of his see and committed to the Marshalsea in May of 1559. His legal acumen enabled him to rebut charges of a more obviously criminal nature, such as the violation of *Praemunire,* thereby discouraging the government from executing other bishops. He died while still in prison.

Bonner was accused by Protestant contemporaries, notably John Bale and John Foxe, of being a bloodthirsty persecutor of Protestants, so that his name was reviled in English histories until late in the 19th century. As a result of more objective writings on the Reformation, particularly the works of such (Protestant) scholars as S. R. Maitland and James Gairdner, Bonner's reputation has been freed from this charge. It is now generally agreed that in the light of royal policy and the standards of the time, he was neither cruel nor overzealous in the punishment of heresy.

Bibliography: P. HUGHES, *The Reformation of England.* 3 v. in 1 (New York, 1968). L. B. SMITH, *Tudor Prelates and Politics* (Princeton 1953). G. L. M. J. CONSTANT, *The Reformation in England,* tr. R. E. SCANTLEBURY and E. I. WATKIN, 2 v. (New York 1934–42). G. E. PHILLIPS, *The Truth about Bishop Bonner* (London 1910). J. GAIRDNER, *The Dictionary of National Biography from the Earliest Times to 1900* (London 1885–1900) 2:818–822. H. O. EVENNETT, *Lexikon für Theologie und Kirche*, ed. J. HOFER and K. RAHNER (Freiburg 1957–65) 2:600–601. J. GILLOW, *A Literary and Biographical History or Bibliographical Dictionary of the English Catholics from 1534 to the Present Time*, 5 v. (London–New York, 1885–1902) 1:260–266.

[M. R. O'CONNELL]

BONNETTY, AUGUSTIN

Philosopher and historian; b. Entrevaux, France, April 9, 1798; d. Paris, March 26, 1879. Although Bonnetty spent four years at the major seminary of Digne, he decided not to embrace the priesthood. He went to Paris to live and become part of the circle of Catholic intellectuals that included O. P. GERBET and H. F. de LAMENNAIS. In 1830 he founded the review *Annales de philosophie chrétienne,* which he edited until his death. He also collaborated in editing *Université catholique,* begun by Gerbet in 1836, completely assumed its direction in 1840, and in 1855 fused it with his own *Annales.* In these two reviews, Bonnetty dedicated his rich talents entirely to the service of the Church, particularly by propagating what he considered to be Christian philosophy.

Unfortunately, he vigorously defended FIDEISM and TRADITIONALISM, although his system was not as extreme as that of Louis G. A. de BONALD and Louis E. M. BAUTAIN. Originally, he had no intention of discussing the theoretical limits of human reason. He felt it was useless even to pose the question because, according to him, man had never been left on a merely natural level, but from the very beginning was instructed by God in the necessary moral and religious truths. The only problem real to Bonnetty was the origin of man's rational and religious beliefs. In his opinion, all man's knowledge is traceable to a revelation made by God to our first parents. Bonnetty went beyond this historical question, however, in maintaining that man is incapable of discovering truth without the help of revelation. This led him to condemn the scholasticism that upheld the demonstrative power of the human intellect.

Because of these opinions, on June 11, 1855 the Congregation of the Index insisted that Bonnetty subscribe to four propositions (H. Denzinger, *Enchiridion symbolorum* [Freiburg, 1963, 2811–14]) maintaining the distinction, but harmony, between faith and reason and exonerating scholasticism from the accusation of rationalism. He submitted to the judgment of the Holy See without reserve and remained faithful to the Church.

Beside his many articles in the *Annales,* Bonnetty also published *Morceaux choisis de l'Église,* 2 v. (Paris 1828), which appeared again in 1841 under the title *Beautés de l'histoire de l'Église; Documents historiques sur la religion des romains,* 4 v. (Paris 1867–78); and an annotated translation of the Jesuit De Prémaré's work, *Vestiges des principaux dogmes chrétiens, tirés des anciens livres chinois* (Paris 1879).

Bibliography: E. DUBLANCHY, *Dictionnaire de théologie catholique* (Paris 1903–50) 2.1:1019–26. J. DOPP, *Dictionnaire d'histoire et de géographie ecclésiastiques* (Paris 1912—) 9:1058–60.

[J. H. MILLER]

BONOMELLI, GEREMIA

Bishop, writer; b. Nigoline di Franciacorta (Brescia), Italy, Sept. 12, 1831; d. there, Aug. 3, 1914. Bonomelli came of a peasant family. He was ordained in 1855, and continued his theological studies at the Gregorian University in Rome. He taught at the seminary in Brescia until 1866, became pastor in Lovere, and was made bishop of Cremona (1871–1914). He was a very zealous, pious bishop, deeply interested in pastoral needs, the ROMAN QUESTION, social problems, and the reconciliation of science and religion. He was impulsive and intransigent, but never a Modernist. When queried by Leo XIII (1882), he suggested that Catholics should participate in political elections; in 1904 he counseled Pius X to withdraw the *NON EXPEDIT*.

Convinced that the STATES OF THE CHURCH could not be restored and that a miniature papal state should instead be created, he anonymously wrote a periodical article in 1889, *''Roma e l'Italia e la realtà delle cose,''* soon published separately as a booklet, that was placed on the

Index on April 13, 1889. Courageously Bonomelli admitted his authorship and submitted publicly and without delay to the judgment of the Holy See. In 1929 the LATERAN PACTS reached a solution along the lines proposed by Bonomelli.

He published numerous periodical articles and books on a variety of topics, but mostly on current religious and socio-economic problems. Many of his pastoral letters, sermons, and conferences also appeared in print. He carried on an extensive correspondence with many eminent contemporaries. His concern for the difficulties of Italian emigrants led him to found the Opera di assistenza agli operai italiani emigranti in 1900, better known as the Opera Bonomelli.

Bibliography: P. GUERRINI, ed., *Geremia Bonomelli* (Brescia 1939). C. BELLÒ, *Geremia Bonomelli* (Brescia 1963). G. ASTORI, ''Mons. Geremia Bonomelli: L'opera sua per la conciliazione,'' *Vita e pensiero* 30 (1939) 574–581; ''S. Pio X ed il vescovo G. Bonomelli,'' Rivista di Storia della Chiesa iri Italia (Rome 1947–) 10 (1956) 212–266. S. FURLANI, *Enciclopedia cattolica*. 2:1887–90. P. PISANI, A. Mercati and A. Pelzer, *Dizionario ecclesiastico*, 3v. (Turin 1954–58) 1:411–412.

[E. A. CARRILLO]

BONONIUS, ST.

Abbot; b. Bologna, Italy, *c.* mid-tenth century; d. Lucedio, Italy, Aug. 30, 1026. He first became a BENEDICTINE monk in the monastery of San Stefano in his native city. Later he set out for Cairo with the intention of becoming a hermit at Mt. Sinai, and thus he is often called the apostle of Egypt. In 990 he was recalled to Italy by Bp. Peter of Vercelli (d. 997) and became abbot of Lucedio in Piedmont, where he applied himself to the work of monastic reform until his death. He was canonized by Pope John XIX. There is another tradition concerning the life of Bononius, propagated by the CAMALDOLESE, in which he is said to have been a student of ROMUALD, the founder of that order.

Feast: Aug. 30.

Bibliography: *Vita. Monumenta Germaniae Historica: Scriptores* 30.2:1026–30. G. B. MITTARELLI and A. COSTADONI, *Annales Camaldulenses,* 9 v. (Venice 175573) 1:396–399. *Bibliotheca hagiograpica latina antiquae et mediae aetatis* (Brussels 1898–1901) 1:1421–24. *Analecta Bollandiana* 48 (1930) 411–412.

[K. NOLAN]

BONSIRVEN, JOSEPH

NT exegete and Rabbinic scholar; b. in Lavaur, Diocese of Albi, France, Jan. 25, 1880; d. Toulouse, Feb. 12,

Geremia Bonomelli.

1958. After his education at the Sulpician seminary in Paris, Bonsirven was ordained on Sept. 19, 1903, and immediately thereafter he was assigned to teach Scripture at the major seminary of Albi. In 1906 he studied at the École Biblique under Père Lagrange, and in 1909 he received his licentiate in Sacred Scripture from the Pontifical Biblical Commission.

The following year his doctoral thesis on rabbinic eschatology, for reasons that had little to do with its scientific merit, was not accepted, and he was forbidden to teach Sacred Scripture. Bonsirven humbly accepted the decision and returned to his diocese for pastoral work, but this was interrupted by his service and subsequent imprisonment during World War I. While a prisoner of war, he was appointed by Benedict XV to teach dogmatic theology and Sacred Scripture to imprisoned seminarians.

After the war he entered the Society of Jesus (Sept. 9, 1919). Following his noviceship and his theological studies, he taught fundamental and dogmatic theology at Enghien, Belgium. In 1928 he finally returned to teaching

NT exegesis: in Enghien (1928–40 and 1946–47) and in Lyon–Fourvière, France (1941–46). In 1948 he joined the faculty of the Pontifical Biblical Institute in Rome, where he remained until 1953, when ill health forced him to seek his native climate.

Among his numerous published works are ''Bulletins du Judaïsme ancien,'' in *Revue des sciences religieuses* from 1929 to 1938; a commentary on Hebrews (Paris 1943); the *Johannine Epistles* (Paris 1935, 2d ed. 1954) and the Apocalypse volumes for the *Verbum Salutis* Series (Paris 1951); *Le judaïsme palestinien au temps de Jésus-Christ* (Paris 1934–35) in two volumes, later abridged into one (Turin 1950); *Exégèse rabbinique et exégèse paulinienne* (Paris 1939); *Théologie du NT* (Paris 1951); *Textes rabbiniques des premiers siècles chrétiens pour servir à l'intelligence du NT* (Rome 1955); and *Le Règne de Dieu* (Paris 1957).

Bibliography: S. LYONNET, *Biblica* 39 (1958) 262–268.

[S. B. MARROW]

BONZEL, MARIA THERESIA, MOTHER

Foundress of the Poor Sisters of St. Francis Seraph of Perpetual Adoration; b. Olpe, Germany, Sept. 17, 1830; d. Olpe, Feb. 6, 1905. Aline was the elder of two daughters of Friedrich Edmund Bonzel, a wealthy industrialist and philanthropist, and Maria Anna (Liese) Bonzel. After studying under the Ursulines at Cologne, she became a Franciscan tertiary (1851) and took the name Theresia, which she retained in religion. Her desire to join the Salesian Sisters was frustrated for more than five years after 1852, first by her inability to gain her mother's consent, and then by a protracted illness. She founded her congregation (July 20, 1863) at Olpe to care for poor and neglected children, an apostolate later extended to the education of children and nursing the sick, especially the poor. During Theresia's lifelong term as superior general, she saw the institute spread to the United States (1875) and Austria, and increase to 700 members (*see* FRANCISCAN SISTERS).

Bibliography: S. ELSNER, *Mutter Maria Theresia Bonzel und ihre Stiftung* (Werl 1926), Eng. *From the Wounds of St. Francis*, tr. M. F. PETERS and M. H. HAU (Mishawaka, Ind. 1955).

[M. F. PETERS]

BOOK, THE ANCIENT

Books may be discussed with regard to their composition and dissemination. Their composition involves writing materials, book forms, the art of copying, and format of the book; the knowledge of dissemination of books includes their publication, authentication, literary information, and preservation.

COMPOSITION

The composition of the book in antiquity entailed the solution of difficulties no longer met today because of basic techniques developed then.

Writing Materials. The oldest material used for literary purposes and classifiable as a book was the clay tablet, in use in ancient Babylonia and Sumeria. Originally square (but later elongated), smooth on top and concave below, they could be kept in series. The lettering was done while the clay was still soft in one or three columns with a stylus similar to a pencil (Jer 17.1). When baked, the tablet retained its contents indelibly. For cataloguing the tablets the series, number, initial words of the text, and a summary were indicated in captions. These tablets constituted the first attempt to preserve important writings in libraries. More practical were the waxed boards on which characters were engraved with the sharp point of a stylus. The flattened end of the stylus was used to smooth the wax again. Wax tablets were difficult to handle and store but convenient for outlines, bills, letters, and school work, in which they could be corrected and used again (Tibullus 4.7.7; Propertius 3.23; Jerome, *Epist.* 8.1; Augustine, *Epist.* 15.1). In Greece Homer (*Iliad* 6.168) was the first to mention the ''folded slate,'' a wooden tablet covered with a white substance (Euripides, *Alc.* 968), which was used also in ancient Palestine (Ez 37.15–22) and Italy (Gaius, *Inst.* 2.104). In Italy public registers of wood, iron, or ivory were engraved with a heated stylus (Tacitus, *Ann.* 13.28; Jerome, *In Ier.* 3.17; PL 24.786). Authors quoting such documents called them books (Cicero, *Verr.* 1.36).

Papyrus, called βύβλος in Greek, after the Syrian city of Byblos, was made from the pith of the papyrus plant. Extant papyri show that upon a vertical layer of narrow strips was placed a horizontal layer. When these were pressed, the fibers were united by the glue in the plant, or glue added thereto, and formed a smooth writing surface. Different qualities were produced, from packaging material to the fine white paper called *Augustea Regia* (Pliny, *Nat.* 13.74–76, 82; Isidore, *Orig.* 6.10.2). Despite its high cost, four drachmas per roll in the 2d century A.D., many sheets of papyrus had defective strips, bad joinings, or layers that did not stick together firmly. If papyrus was scarce, the writing could be erased with a sponge and the papyrus used again (Martial 4.10). Outlines, notes, letters, records, and literary works of leisure were written on papyrus. Used in Egypt in earliest times, it was exported from there as early as the 11th century B.C., and was

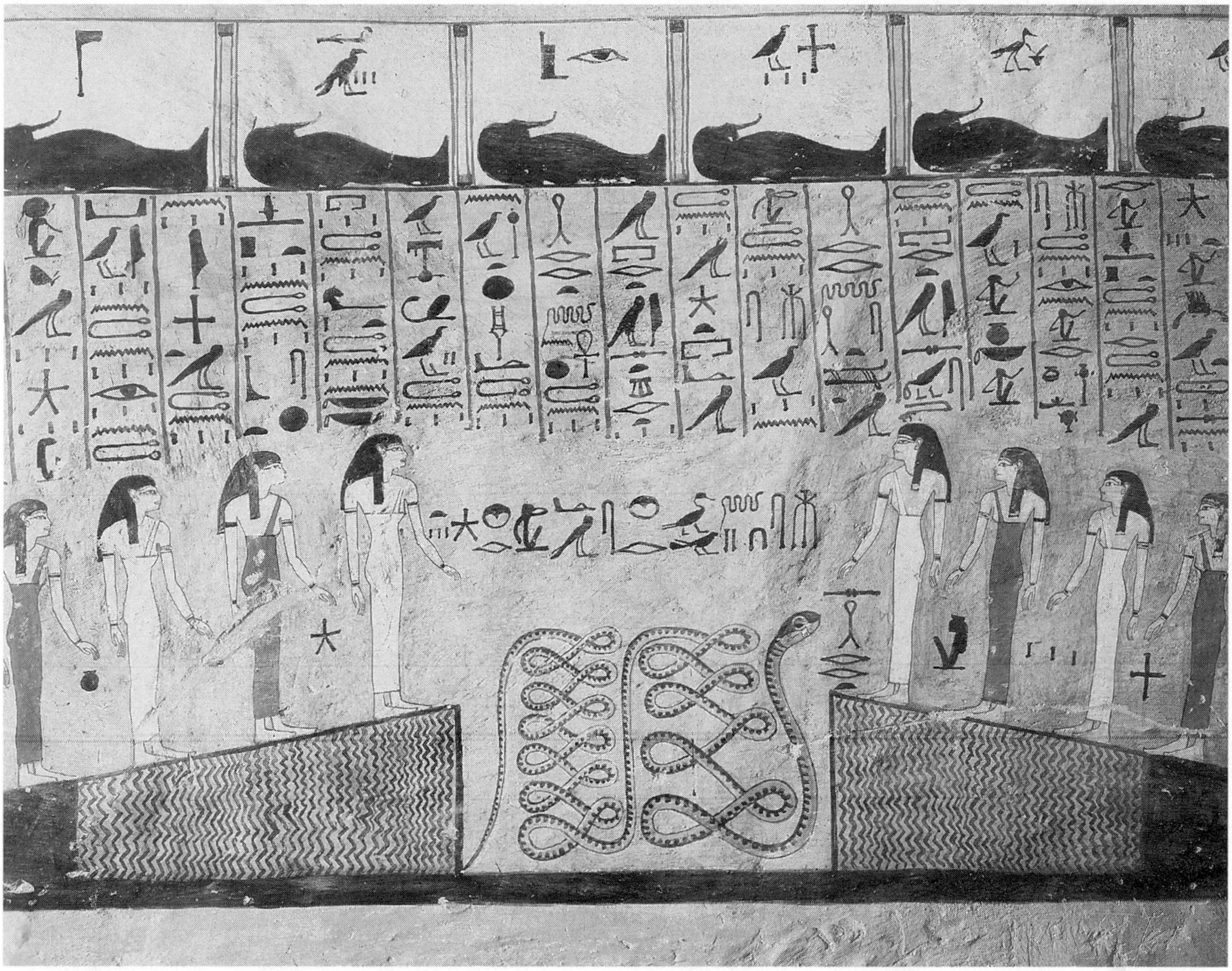

Illustration from the "Book of Portals," ca. 1295–1294 B.C., Egyptian. (©Gianni Dagli Orti/CORBIS)

sold in Alexandria until the end of antiquity (Jerome, *Epist.* 72.2). From the 7th century B.C., Ionia imported it into the Greek world. Solon's decree that Homer's entire epic be declaimed during the Panathenian feasts led to a more general use, for written copies were made. At the end of the 5th century Aristophanes could affirm that every person of culture possessed books (*Frogs* 1114). The tombs and the dry sands of Egypt have preserved most of the known papyri, some of which are of great value, e.g., the *P 66* (Bodmer 2) of the 2d century, which contains a good part of the Gospel of St. John.

Parchment derives its name, according to an ancient tradition that lasted until the 6th century A.D., from Pergamum, a city in Asia Minor that first flourished *c.* 300 B.C. The material was used for writing in 2000 B.C., however. Although less common than papyrus, parchment was known to the Greek world in the 6th century B.C. (Herodotus 5.58.3), the Dorians being the first Greeks to write on the skins of goats and sheep. Proof for the early use of parchment in Rome is seen in the legend that during the period of the kings, treaties of peace were permanently recorded on the skins of sacrificed animals (Dionysius Halicarnassensis, *Antiq. Rom.* 4.58.4). But as late as the 3d century A.D. it was necessary for Ulpian to determine for jurists that animal skins were as valid for testaments as was papyrus (*Dig.* 37.11.1). Little is known about the preparation of parchment. The hair was scraped off and the hides were dressed and smoothed for long strips, both sides of which could be written upon. Smaller pieces prepared for private and public archives, when stacked on top of one another and fastened together, would later form the "codex," the forerunner of the modern book. Parchment was not prized for literary compositions, because it was crude in comparison with light and elegant papyri, but by the 5th century it had replaced papyrus. It appealed to the circles of Christian ascetics, and Bibles written on it would last longer (Jerome, *Vir. ill.* 113). It was used for correspondence, however, only when papy-

Tablet impressed with cuneiform script, Baghdad Museum, Iraq. (©David Lees/CORBIS)

rus became scarce. As a result, the letters published in antiquity, more than any other genre, have perished. Valuable pagan and Christian works have been preserved thanks to Christian writers of the 4th century and after who wrote on parchment.

Book Forms. The scroll (Latin *volumen,* from *volvere,* ''to roll'') suggests the unrolling of a long MS. The scroll was the usual form for books in Babylonia and Assyria in the 9th century. From there it may have passed to the Phoenicians and Aramaeans. Reference to it in the 7th century B.C. (Jer 36.2) suggests that it was then in common use. Strips of papyrus or parchment already inscribed were overlapped and glued or sewn together. The seams were visible, although great care was taken with them. In Athens the pioneer in the trade of gluing merited a statue, and in Rome an epitaph has immortalized a gluer [*Dictionnaire d'archéologie chrétienne et de liturgie*, ed. F. Cabrol, H. Leclercq, and H. I. Marrou (Paris 1907–53) 9.1760]. Isidore observes that the length of the scroll depended upon the type of composition (*Orig.* 6.12), a small scroll for the lyric, a longer one for epic and history. Very long rolls were rare. Pliny says that ''A good book is all the better, the longer it is'' (*Epist* 1.20.4), but for him one of Cicero's discourses was a large book. For Martial 300 epigrams was a volume of insufferable length (*Epigr.* 2.1). The four Gospels, even Mark or Luke alone, would constitute a ''scroll'' (Jerome, *Epist.* 121.6). Even when codices had replaced rolls, Sacred Scripture was often copied on rolls. Copies of the ''Exsultet'' on great rolls that were annotated and illuminated solemnized the Easter Vigil liturgy until the Middle Ages. The scroll was held in the right hand and unrolled with the left, the text being in perpendicular columns. If, as happened infrequently, the text ran continuously down the scroll, it could be held under the chin and unrolled with both hands (Martial, *Epigr.* 1.66). The *Logia Jesu,* found at Oxyrhynchos (*P. Oxy* 4.454), and the scriptural texts found at Qumran near the Dead Sea are examples of books preserved in scrolls.

The codex or loose-leaf manuscript, although based on the old Oriental device of attaching tablets to one another, seems to have been of Roman origin. It was made of parchment and papyrus, or alternating folia of each, and revolutionized bookmaking. In the 3d century A.D. it was disputed whether codices constituted books according to Roman law. Profane authors would not use them. Of the 3d-century MS fragments extant, there is only one codex for every 15 scrolls. Among Christian writers of the same period there are four codices for each scroll. Christians copied profane works as well as their own works in codices (Rufinus, *Apol. adv. Hier.* 2.8; Jerome, *Epist.* 22.30). Christian calligraphers continued the tradition of artistic ornamentation in gold, purple, and precious gems, particularly in Bibles, in competition with secular and heretical books. Manes, founder of the Manichees, asserted, ''The Apostles did not portray wisdom through paintings as I painted her'' (*Kephalaia* 154). Augustine speaks of the costly books of the Manichees, ''so many and such large and such sumptuous codexes'' (*C. Faust.* 13.6). Arians and other adversaries of the Church followed suit. MS *P. Oxy* 30 dates probably from A.D. 100. A few Greek codices date from the 2d century. The 13 codices discovered in Nag' Hammâdi, Egypt, in 1946–47, comprising about 1,000 leaves of papyrus, date from the 3d century to *c.* 400. Of these leaves, 749 are well preserved. Codex X, measuring 21 by 27 centimeters with 37 lines per page, is the largest and most beautiful of the 13. From the 4th and 5th centuries the codex was the usual book form.

Art of Copying. Black ink (*atramentum*) made of charcoal and gum was used. Red ink (*rubrum*) served for titles. Costly MSS were written in gold letters. The copyist held his parchment or papyrus over a narrow board or inclined table and wrote with a stylus across the column. For the sake of elegance, lines ran continuously down the roll. Each line contained, at most, 18 syllables, a hexameter. To judge from the MSS extant, the number of syllables in a line was not rigidly determined. The columns were narrow enough for the eye to pass from one line to the next without losing the thread of thought. Division into columns (Latin *paginae,* Greek σελίδες) made it possible for Origen to attempt the first critical edition of the Bible, the HEXAPLA, six texts in parallel columns. Codices Vaticanus and Sinaiticus, both of the 4th century, are in three and four columns, respectively. Normally only one side of the page was written on. Pliny, to prove that his uncle Pliny the Elder wrote prodigiously, asserts that he wrote opisthographs, i.e., he filled both sides of the scroll (*Epist.* 3.5.17). Ironical allusions of the poets indicate that the reverse side served only for outlines and school work (Martial, *Epigr.* 4.86). The Revelation, however, refers to the sealed scroll, written within and without (Rv 5.1).

Dictation of their works by authors, classical as well as Christian, and especially public officials, was the rule. The stenographers used three devices: suspension [Anc(ient)], contraction [B(oo)k], and the substitution of conventional signs [&]. In Rome a shorthand system, *notae tironianae,* using 13,000 elements was employed. A professor of stenography in A.D. 301 received a salary 50 percent larger than that of a teacher on the primary level or a professor of penmanship. In the 5th century a slave skilled in shorthand cost two and a half times more than an unskilled slave (*Cod. lust.* 6.43.3.1; 7.7.1.5). The stenographic copy was transcribed upon papyrus or upon vellum. No one succeeded, even in the classical period and in the periods of greatest literary production, in establishing an organization for the purely technical task of copying books. But there was training, and schools existed for perfecting the skill of copyists, an art that the Christians preserved. Although the *First Rule* of the cenobitic monks, that of St. Pachomius of the 4th century, does not mention copyists, they were represented before long in the monasteries. Jerome recognized the job of copyist as a means of livelihood and as a stimulus for reading (*Epist.* 125.11). The only evidence that groups of copyists wrote in a workshop while someone dictated to them is a single Egyptian drawing. To say nothing of inevitable errors in dictation, the technical part of copying lent itself very little to team work. A group can hardly trace lines, begin new columns, maintain elegant penmanship, paint, and illumine at the same rate of speed. The copy used as a model, like modern plates, remained with the author, the bookseller, or in the library for further copies.

Format of the Book. ''Book,'' Latin *liber,* originally designated bark on which uncivilized men wrote (Pliny, *Hist. nat.* 13.21.69; Jerome, *Epist.* 8.1). Later it signified a complete literary work or a part thereof. In the first leaf or column appeared the title, index, division, and author's name. These data, indispensable for identification or consultation, sometimes appeared in more complete form at the end of the work where they were better protected. The title could be repeated elsewhere in the work, and the table of contents might appear separately. Many ancient books are known and classified by their initial words, the *incipit,* even in 19th-century editions, just as encyclicals and papal bulls today are identified. Dedications, frequent in pagan and Christian antiquity, might be directed to some divinity, an important person, or a pupil. They included the homage, the first few notes about the book, the author's method, an exposition of difficult points, and at times invectives. Prefaces, ever the same, appear in all periods. To receive a dedication among the ancients was to be immortalized, for they still believed in the immortality of the book. The modern form of chapters and paragraphs were unknown to the ancients although the terms were used. The reader oriented himself by means of brief summaries or captions in the margin of the scroll or page. To cite a passage one referred to these summaries with an indication of its position in the book. Because it might be difficult for the reader to find the passage, or even the work cited, important passages were preferably transcribed or, more often, cited from memory. Critical signs to indicate lacunae, corrections, doubts, and interpolations existed from the days of early Alexandria until the end of antiquity (Isidore, *Orig.* 1.21). Those used by Origen in the Hexapla are well known. To these Jerome added the colon to signify the end of a quotation.

At the end of a book the Hebrews wrote *Amen, Sela,* or *Salom,* ''So be it! Pause! Peace!'' to confirm the assertions of the book, while promising it survival and expressing joy on the completion of copying (Jerome, *Epist.* 28.4). The Latins, besides *Amen,* used the more functional term *Explicuit* (The End), *Explicuit feliciter* (Thank goodness it's finished!), or other phrases expressing the copyist's relief. In the classical period one finds formulas, inherited from the ancient Orient, that guarantee the fidelity of the copy. Jerome has transmitted the formula of St. Irenaeus (d. 202): ''You who will transcribe this book, I charge you, in the name of our Lord Jesus Christ and of His glorious Second Coming, in which He will come to judge the living and dead, compare what you have copied against the original and correct it carefully. Furthermore, transcribe this adjuration and place it in the copy'' (*Vir. ill.* 35). To prevent papyrus copies from tearing, the ancients reinforced them at both ends of the roll for a width of five centimeters. This part was called significantly *cornu,* ''horn.'' At the end of the reading when the scroll was completely unrolled, it was held by the horns.

DISSEMINATION

The dissemination of the book was laborious and expensive. Forgeries and inaccuracies were difficult to control.

Publication. The terms for publication were in Greek, ἐκδίδωμι, διαδίδωμι; Latin, *librum edere, publicare, divulgare,* and others; *editio* signifies both the process and the result of publication. Unless the author himself provides it, the date of publication can hardly be determined from the various hand-copied MSS. During the classical period publication in large centers normally began with a public reading before friends and distinguished persons. After the session and applause, the book was handed over for distribution. Further advertising, even in handbills and posters, was not neglected (Suetonius, *Ep.* 5.11.3). Authors under the protection of sovereigns or patrons advertised through official channels. This was the procedure with works destined to celebrate great feats or to solemnize religious and civil assemblies or even festive reunions, e.g., the declamations of Homer, Pindar, Herodotus, the Greek tragedies, and until the end of the Roman Empire, the imperial panegyrics. The protection of the poets Vergil, Horace, and Propertius by Augustus and his minister Maecenas was proverbial. Genuine workshops for the dissemination of MSS arose with the libraries of the 5th century B.C. and municipal and court archives, especially with the library at Alexandria *c.* 300 B.C. which later held 700,000 scrolls. In Pergamum, in the libraries of Augustus and Trajan in Rome, and in the more important cities of the empire originals were sought for reproduction. Ten copies a year of Tacitus's works were made for the archives by order of the Emperor Tacitus (d. 276). Booksellers, *bibliopolae,* reproduced and sold books of interest to the public. The authors, who received the fame but not the money, frequently made allusions to this exploitation. The copies were expensive, and ordinarily each copy was made as the demand arose, although a few might be kept on hand. The 1,000 copies of M. Regulus's panegyric (Pliny, *Epist.* 4.2.7) were singular.

Influential men maintained their own copyists to meet their needs. St. Clement of Alexandria (d. *c.* 215) indicated Anaxagoras (5th century B.C.) as the first such publisher. Atticus in Cicero's time was another (*Att.* 2.1.2). Among the Christians Origen, Jerome (*Vir. ill.* 61, *Hom. Orig. in Ier.* prologue), and Augustine (*Epist.* 44.2) maintained up to seven copyists for their own works and those of others. Paulinus of Nola, himself an author, disseminated the books of Ambrose (Augustine, *Epist.* 31.8); requested the books of Augustine not only for his personal instruction "but for the good of many churches" (Paulinus, *Epist.* 25.1); and created publicity for Sulpicius Severus (Sulpicius Severus, *Dial.* 3.17 A), Jerome, Rufinus, and others. Generations of monks would later undertake the reproduction of these authors. In the monastery of Martin of Tours this was the only skill allowed (Sulpicius Severus, *Mart.* 10.6). Clerics carried works from India to Alexandria (Jerome, *Vir. ill.* 36), and within their lifetimes Christian authors might be read from one end of the known world to the other (Sulpicius Severus, *Dial.* 1.8).

The author, or others, sometimes published improved, revised, or abbreviated texts, e.g., the longer original text of the Rule of St. Pachomius (*c.* 318) and the shorter text composed after the 5th century. A new edition might offer only the slightest modifications or a complete revision. When an author died his work became public property, and changes were made freely and with impunity. From the 4th to the 6th century the distribution of books without the author's consent became more and more audacious, as did the corruption of texts, the falsification of signatures, and the theft of MSS.

Authentication. Introduced from Syria, authentication by signature appeared in Greece by the 5th century B.C. Signatures to the copy could be forged, however (Jerome, *Epist.* 105.3). Another means of identification was the signet ring possessed by persons of distinction and used on official documents and to authenticate messages, letters, and even entire works. If an authentic copy of a text could be found in an archive or a library, it was easy to authenticate a text in hand. Otherwise authentication had to be accomplished by an internal criticism or by a comparison of data in copies.

Literary Information. In antiquity data about literary works were transmitted with little method. Children in school came to know famous authors through copies of their verses, extant in many papyrus fragments. In the schools of great masters, as in Athens and Rhodes, privileged youths broadened their knowledge of names and books. Once in public life, they kept themselves informed through conversations, meetings, correspondence, and public readings. There were attempts at systematic instruction, similar to modern manuals of the history of literature, such as Plutarch's *Lives* in Greek, Cicero's *Brutus* for Roman eloquence, and especially Suetonius's *De viris illustribus,* which introduced readers to poets, grammarians, rhetoricians, and philosophers. In Christian times Jerome compiled the first manual of literary information in his *De viris illustribus,* a work continued by Gennadius of Marseilles at the end of the 5th century, by Isidore of Seville at the beginning of the 7th, and by Ildefonsus of Toledo (d. 667). The uncertainty of literary information can be seen in expressions like "As someone said recently," "As I myself inquired," and "They say that he produced" (Jerome, *Vir. ill.* 126, 128).

Preservation. When stored, books were bound with leather thongs, *constrictus liber,* and at times inserted into a stronger parchment or papyrus cover, *sittybos.* Scrolls gathered together, especially in a collection, were newly bound and placed in a cylinder or box, Greek κιβωτός or χαρτοφυλάκιον Latin *scrinium, chartarium, arca, armarium, cista, capsa.* The titles were hung outside the container on strips of leather, *pittac ia* (Cicero, *Att.* 4.4b.1; Ovid, *Trist.* 1.1.109). Humidity and insects were a real danger. Cedar oil was used against worms and decomposition (Ovid, *Trist.* 1.1.7; Martial 5.6.14). Catalogs antedate the library at Alexandria, but the systematic collecting of books began there. Smaller libraries also assembled books for particular subjects, especially for the divine services (*Acta purgationis Felicis ep. Autumnitani,* CSEL 26).

Precious scrolls were rolled on wooden rods or bones, which were sometimes decorated or gilded. The elaborateness of the internal ornamentation and the external appearance of books were points of pride for amateur book collectors and the newly rich. Wooden chests, boxes of iron or a more precious metal, and even ivory containers, protected literary works for later generations.

Bibliography: J. DE GHELLINCK, *Patristique et moyen âage,* v.1–3 (Gembloux 1946–). F.G. KENYON, *Books and Readers in Ancient Greece and Rome* (2d ed. Oxford 1951). E. ARNS, *La Technique du livre d'aprèes saint Jérôme* (Paris 1953), bibliography. A. BATAILLE, *Les Papyrus* (Paris 1955). W. NEUSS, *Lexikon für Theologie und Kirche,* ed. J. HOFER and K. RAHNER (Freiburg 1957–65) 2:746–748. W. MATTHIAS, *Die Religion in Geschichte und Gegenwart,* 7 v. (Tübingen 1957–65) 1:1459–61. *Reallexikon für Antike und Christentum,* ed. T. KLAUSER [Stuttgart 1941 (1950–)] 2:664–772. C. H. ROBERTS and T.C. SKEAT, *The Birth of the Codex* (London 1985). A. BLANCHARD, ed., *Les Débuts du Codex* (Turnhout 1989). H-J MARTIN and R. CHARTIER, eds., *Histoire de l'édition française* (Paris 1983).

[E. ARNS]

BOOK, THE MEDIEVAL

The medieval book par excellence is the codex, though the rotulus or roll (which must be distinguished from the roll of antiquity) also was in use. The triumph of the parchment codex over the papyrus roll (*see* ROLL AND CODEX), together with the accompanying change in copying procedure of the 4th century, led to the rapid disappearance of papyrus, hitherto dominant. From then on papyrus was used but rarely except for documents (e.g., in the papal chancery into the 11th century). When early medieval codices are compared with the unexcelled quality of the parchment codices of late antiquity (4th to the 6th century), they represent a clear regression, although the method of making them (for which instructions have been preserved from the 8th century) can scarcely have been substantially altered.

"Book of Hours of the Duchess of Burgundy: February." (©Archivo Iconografico, S.A./CORBIS)

Parchment. Parchment was called διφθέρα in Greek and *membrana* in Latin; as early as A.D. 301 there is mention of *membrana pergamena,* and Jerome refers variously to *membrana* and *pergamena.* In the Middle Ages the word *charta,* or charter, was often modified by such words as *ovina, vitulina,* and *pergamena.* The parchment was prepared for writing by a *membranarius, pergamenarius,* etc. The untanned animal skin was first coated with caustic lime for several days, then bleached in limewater. The hair, epidermis, and any remnants of flesh were scraped off. The hide was once again cleaned in a lime bath, stretched on a frame, dried, and finally scraped smooth with pumice. Whiting was then poured over the hide and rubbed in. The inner or flesh side (F) of the parchment and the outer or hair side (H) differed in that the former would be whiter and smoother, the latter rather yellowish or gray, rough, and porous. The difference could be almost eliminated, but only by very special treatment, especially by oxidation. In charters, which usually carried writing on only one side (documents with writing on both sides, called opisthographs, are rare), the difference between F and H is more apparent than in books, since care was taken by bookmakers to render the contrast less noticeable. In southern Europe a finer sort of parchment, whose F is clearly whiter and smoother than its H, was used, whereas in the north a thicker, coars-

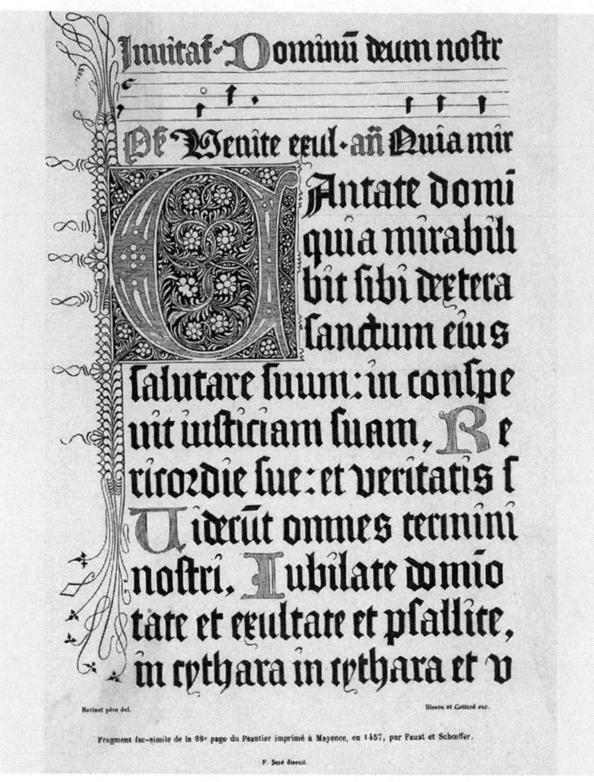

Page Of Psalm book, with decorative type. (©Bettmann/ CORBIS)

er, and more yellowish parchment predominated. However, it should be noted that the drastic difference between F and H of parchments can be easily discerned only down to the 10th and 11th centuries; from then on both sides tend to be more evenly oxidized. Vellum made from sheepskin by a special method is typical of the British Isles. Southern Europe preferred sheepskins and goatskins; the north often used calfskin as well. The finest parchment came from the skin of newborn or unborn lambs; it was called *charta virginea* or *charta non nata.* The writing surface of deluxe MSS or single pages would sometimes be dyed, generally purple. This ancient custom (used in, e.g., the Codex Argenteus, the Codex Rossanensis, and the Vienna Genesis) came into vogue again under the Carolingians (having been used, e.g., in the Ada MS, the Gottschalk Gospel Book, and the Coronation Gospel Book of Vienna) but died out again in the 11th century. Blue and black parchment is very rare and a collector's item.

Parchment was better suited for repeated use than was papyrus. Hence, when it was in short supply, MSS that were expendable because their content was out of date, no longer valued, or objectionable, or because the script had become ''old-fashioned,'' were often used again. This happened especially from the 7th to the 9th century, at which time many MSS from the 5th to the 7th century were reused. The original writing was erased by first scraping the parchment with a knife (*rasorium*), then rubbing it with pumice (*pumex,* hence *pumicare*), then soaking it in milk and washing it with a sponge (*spongium* or *peniculus,* hence the German *Pinsel*). When modern scholars first tried to read these twice-inscribed pages (called PALIMPSESTS), they used reagents (gallnut ink, Gioberti ink) to bring out the original text; but too often this resulted in the total destruction of the text. Today the quartz lamp is used, as is also palimpsest photography. Until the 12th century various European monastic centers—which were the chief consumers—manufactured their own parchment and even sold it. After that time parchment preparation became a secular craft.

Paper. Parchment was employed for books until the 16th or 17th century, but after the 14th or 15th century its use was generally restricted to precious liturgical books and collectors' items. It began to be replaced in the 13th century by paper (called *charta bombycina,* or in 1077 *bambycina,* then *charta papyri* in 1231, and then *papirus* in 1311). Paper had been a Chinese invention dating from the early 2d century B.C., allegedly of the minister of agriculture Ts'ai Lun. It had been used since A.D. 751 by the Arabs, first in Samarkand, and then throughout the Caliphate. In the East, paper replaced papyrus without a transitional parchment stage, but it came to Europe only in the 11th century via Spain, where the oldest paper mill in the West was established in Játiva before 1150, and via northern Italy as an Arab article of trade. In 1276 the first paper mill in Italy was built in Fabriano, in 1337 the first French mill was in Troyes, and in 1390 the first German mill appeared in Nuremberg. Paper first replaced parchment in the chanceries, where it was used for registers, communications, minute books, protocols, letters, etc. It was utilized for books earlier or later according to regions; e.g., in Spain paper was used before 1036, but it was not common before 1300.

Once the rags, the raw material for paper, were chopped into small pieces, they were soaked in water and underwent a decomposition process. The fiber was given more water and was then pulped by a stamping mill into half stuff. This was placed in storage chests and 24 hours later was stamped into paper pulp, or full stuff. The pulp was stored in vats, from which the vat assistant extracted a thin layer with a screen, i.e., a rectangular wooden frame strung with seven bronze wires. Gentle shaking of the screen matted the fibers and drained off the excess water. The leaves of paper thus obtained were then couched, i.e., each leaf was laid between two mats, piled one on top of the other, and pressed so that the water was sucked up by the mat. After a second pressing, this time without mats, the sheets were hung up to dry, often on a clothesline, and then dipped into a solution of glue or gelatinous material, made out of animal offal, to glaze the sheets. Lastly, from the 13th century on, the sheets were always marked with figures, symbols, letters, etc., and together with the imprints of the bottom and binding wire of the frames they formed the ''watermark'' or filigree. Two journeymen always worked together with a pair of frames: the dipper drew the pulp from the vat with a frame; the coucher pressed the dipped sheet off the frame onto the mat. Further preparation of any codex—as pictured in the 10 medallions on the title page of the 12th-century Michelsberg MS of St. Ambrose in Bamberg—was the business of the scribe.

Assembling the Book. The medieval book was usually of an elongated rectangular shape; some few (of an early date) were almost square, and occasionally an oblique shape appeared (but this was an insular idiosyncrasy). The size, however, varied to an extraordinary degree, depending on contemporary, local, and personal taste, on the book's purpose (e.g., a pocket-size prayerbook, a large choir book), the size of the available hides, the instructions of the client, etc. Thus there are codices of the tiniest size and almost all intervening sizes up to and including the large folio volume. The number of pages likewise varied from that of the slim little volume to that of a ponderous tome.

The scribe first had to cut the parchment given him into the desired size. For this he used a sharp curved knife (*novacula, rasorium*) and a ruler (*regula, linula, norma, canon, praeductale*). The basic unit of any book was the double sheet (*diploma, plicatura,* rarely *arcus*); the single sheet was called a *folium.* The scribe often had to glue tears in the parchment, repair damaged spots, smooth out rough places with the *plana,* and sew up holes with catgut or twine; this was sometimes done in artistic form by skilled women using varicolored silk threads. The trimmed double sheet was then folded together into an individual gathering. If there were a considerable difference between F and H, further care was taken so that similar sides faced each other (F to F, H to H). When the difference was negligible, this rule was less strictly observed. Gatherings were formed by placing folded double sheets inside each other; thus two double sheets formed a binion (II); three, a ternion (III); four, a quaternion (IV); five, a quinternion (V); and six, a sexternion (VI). Until the 12th century, quaternions were most often used in books on the Continent, though often IIs, IIIs, and Vs were intermingled. The Irish (like the ancients) preferred quinternions. From the 13th century on, however, the form and size of the gatherings became irregular, influenced perhaps by the paper codices, in which sexternions often occurred, as did gatherings of up to 10 and more double sheets.

For ruling the page, a compass (*circinus, punctorium*) was used; fine punctures were made at the edge of the sheet at intervals as regular as possible. These punctures are called prickings. A standard scale for ruling seems to have been plotted on the edge of the writing desk, to judge from miniatures. Vertical and horizontal lines were then drawn with a ruler, and a meticulous scribe gave his most careful attention to the accuracy of this operation. Down to the 10th century horizontal lines were ideally framed by double vertical lines; later scribes contented themselves, as a rule, with one vertical line. If there were to be columns, they were similarly separated by vertical lines down the center. In the late Middle Ages the uppermost line (usually not written on), and the bottom line (or several at the top and bottom and occasionally one in the middle) were drawn from the outer left to the outer right edge over both open pages so that the two sheets would not become displaced. Until the 12th century a blunt, or dry, stylus (*stilus, graphium, graphius, graphiarium, ligniculum, sulcare,* i.e., to draw lines) was generally used to make concave and convex ''blind'' lines on the recto and verso side of the sheet, respectively. By the 12th century, however, the pages were rather generally being ruled with lead pencil or crayon (*plumbum*); and from the 13th century, increasingly with ink. For the earlier, pre-12th century period several variations are worthy of note: in the British Isles, after each gathering had been formed, the folded sheet was punctured with prickings at the inner and outer edge and ruled up; but on the Continent (up to the 10th or 11th century) proper procedure called for the double sheet, not yet folded, to be spread out and then for two, three, or all sheets of the future gathering to be laid on top of it so that when the top sheet was ruled up, the scribe pressed hard enough with the stylus to leave impressions on the sheets below. Only then were the sheets folded and made into a gathering. But from the 12th century on (to some extent even in the 11th) ruling was done after the sheets had been folded into a gathering. Then the two open pages were ruled at a time, skipping the next two, so that in each case the convex impression of the verso side served as lines. Early medieval scribes numbered the gatherings for the bookbinder, generally on the last page of each gathering using Roman numerals, often preceded by a Q (for quaternion). This practice was continued to the 12th century, although most such numbering was lost when the book was trimmed by the bookbinder. In the later Middle Ages the scribe tended to number the first page of the gathering, the last, or both. He might use letters, capital and minuscule, as well as Roman numerals, often with characteristic decoration. A further aid for the bookbinder when putting the gatherings together was the catchword; it guaranteed an accurate sequence of individual gatherings and is still of importance today for arranging the text in its right order. The catchwords were always located on the last page of a gathering, usually at the bottom inside edge. They consisted of the first word or words of the first page of the next gathering. Aside from isolated examples from the 8th and 9th centuries, the catchwords—which were forerunners of the signature marks of old printed books—came into use only in the 12th century. As opposed to the Egypto-Greek and Coptic custom of numbering pages, spaces, or lines, the Middle Ages produced only isolated instances of folio numbering between the 8th and the 12th or 13th century. But in the 12th century, foliation was used in Missals; and by the 13th century, it was already fairly widespread, and was customary by the 14th century. Arabic numbers were used as well as Roman numbers. By contrast, pagination was never generally employed in the Middle Ages. In the 15th century some MSS—like the earlier printed books—numbered only from the first to the middle sheet of the gathering, with letters and figures, e.g., a1, a2, a3, a4 in the first gathering (quaternion), and b1, b2, b3, b4 in the second gathering, etc.

Writing Instruments. After preliminary work of preparing his materials the scribe (Latin, *antiquarius, librarius, scriptor, scriba, notarius, clericus,* etc.) could begin writing—usually copying rather than taking dictation or composing. In addition to the reed pen (*calamus*), the pen (*penna, pennula*) had gained popularity in the Roman Empire (isolated bronze and silver pens have been preserved). From the 4th century the quill pen, made from the tail and wing feathers of geese and swans, competed with the reed pen. This is understandable since parchment was becoming predominant, and the pen wrote better than the reed on parchment. However, since the words *calamus* and *penna* occur side by side and are often synonymous, the exact date at which the reed pen was abandoned cannot be fixed. It is possible that it was used down to the 11th century in individual instances, and it is known that the Renaissance humanists used it again in their antiquarian enthusiasm. The reed pen was kept in a cylindrical holder of wood or metal (Greek καλαμοθήκη, καλαμίς, κανών Latin *theca calamaria, theca cannarum, calamarium*); the pen was stored in an elongated penholder suited to its shape (*theca libraria, but also calamarium*). These containers might also hold an inkwell (*atramentarium, incausterium,* and by metonymy, *calamarium*); but the buckhorn (*cornu*) also was used, one for red and one for black ink, either hung on the wall or placed in an opening of the writing desk. For sharpening both instruments as well as for erasing, the scribe had a broad knife with bowed back (*scalprum librarium, cultellus scripturalis, scalpellum, temperatorium, artavus;* the process was called *acuere, temperare*). It was very important for the writing process how the pen was cut, whether symetrically or obliquely, i.e., whether the left or right edge was cut. A pen was tested by the scribe before he began to copy, hence the many *probationes pennae* in medieval MSS, which give interesting clues to the scribe's educational status, etc.

The Ink. Ink used in the Middle Ages was black, but in the course of time it took on shades of brown, gray, and green, by virtue of its chemical composition and atmospheric influences. Codices of late antiquity and generally those of Ireland were written in a deep black ink. Continental codices down to the 11th century often shade from light brown to black; in the 12th and 13th centuries they show deep black tints; in the 14th century, more often green (because of the addition of copper substances); and in the 15th, brown and gray tones, as well as black. The ink was called μέλαν, μελάνιον in Greek, and *atramentum librarium* in Latin, after its black color, to distinguish it from shoeblack, *atramentum sutorium.* When it was manufactured by cooking, it was called *encaustum, incaustum.* Less frequent is the designation *tincta, tingta, tinctura,* from *tingere*, to dye. The earliest inks were made of lampblack and gum and could be washed off with a sponge. Obviously this would not adhere well to parchment, and at least from the 4th or 5th century there was a shift to the manufacture of inks from metallic salts (e.g., iron sulfate or copper sulfate) and from gallnuts dissolved in wine, with admixtures of vinegar (or beer) and gum (or water). The metal content in this ink, or acids, or both together have not only caused the ink to turn color but, what is worse, have occasioned serious damage in the older MSS by corrosion (ink erosion). Today research is being devoted to the repair of such damage.

Red ink was made from red lead (*minium*) or cinnabar. It was used by the scribe, an illuminator specialist, or a rubricator to accentuate certain passages, especially at the beginning of a codex, by little red strokes affixed to the letters (red dots in Irish MSS), by writing on top of individual letters or whole lines with red, or by simply writing in red (Latin, *miniare, rubricare*). Red was generally used to decorate and to distinguish any titles, as well as for the *incipit* and *explicit,* for labeling, for initial capitals in chapters and sentences, for initials, etc. With the Carolingian period gold and silver ink was used in writing on purple parchment and in accentuating individual initials and illuminations. For this the scribe used a brush (*peniculus, penicillus*).

The Writing. Writing (Greek γραφεῖν hence the Latin *graphiare* to the extent that this word is not derived from *graphium* or slate-pencil, or the Greek χαράττειν and Latin *charaxare, scribere;* to make a simple copy or *exemplar* was *exemplare,* but to write elaborately and artistically was *formare,* hence the phrase *littera formata*) was executed by the scribe sitting at a desk with a sloping top (*SCRIPTORIUM*). Numerous representations show the scribe sitting before the desk, holding the knife in his left hand to erase or to hold down the sheet, while he writes with the pen in his right hand, often with the index and middle finger on the pen and the other fingers under it, without supporting his wrist on the desk. When the scribe was finished with his work, the rubricator or illuminator was called upon to execute any decoration the codex might require.

Bookbinding. When the scribe and rubricator had finished, the MS went to the bookbinder. Several papyrus codices from the 2d and 3d centuries are extant (e.g., the Nag-Hammādi), consisting of one rather large signature made up of many sheets of papyrus, bound in leather-covered boards. For multisignature codices, chain stitching was used in Coptic Egypt, the individual signatures being bound together by loop stitches in such a way that a chainlike pattern—which often served as ornamentation—was formed on the back of the cover, which had been laced to the signatures in the same process. Knowledge of bookbinding technique in late antiquity is very incomplete. The bound codex may have developed out of the Diptych. By the 8th century at the latest (from the earlier periods only the 7th-century, deluxe-bound Theodelinda Gospel Book in Monza, Italy, has been preserved) the signatures were sewn together. But with certain exceptions (including three Fulda MSS), the earliest bindings preserved are from the 9th century. It is possible that many books before that time were simply wrapped in parchment sheets, as may be seen in codices preserved in SANKT GALLEN. Such MSS encountered in contemporary catalogues are designated as *in quaternionibus* and the like.

The typical method of binding in the Middle Ages was to stitch the individual signatures to several bands or cords running crosswise at the back with whose help the assembled book was laced to the covers. The stitching thread originally ran over the whole length of the back and was allowed to extend out above and below in order to bind the signatures to one another. To prevent the threads from tearing the signatures at top and bottom, a parchment or leather strip was added; this strip was sewn all around and thus formed the headband. After the assembled book had been laced to the cover, the outer edges were cut or planed smooth; in the later Middle Ages the edges were then painted or inscribed, especially if the volumes were displayed with the cut edges facing the user.

Book covers (in contrast to archive volumes, which often had no hard covers) were usually of wood up to the 16th century, but this was gradually supplanted in the Renaissance by pasteboard, which had appeared much earlier in Islamic bindings. Less frequent were covers made of parchment, leather, or woven fabric without boards. Wooden covers were made of beech, maple, or oak and covered with fabric, or more usually with leather made from skins of sheep, goat, deer, antelope, calf, cow; or pig. The leather was stretched moist over the wooden boards. After the boards were covered, the leather that overlapped was glued to the front and back inside cover, and an endpaper was glued over it. Up to the 12th or 13th century the first leaf of the first signature and the last leaf of the last signature of the book were so used, but later wastepaper (parchment or paper) was more often employed. The first free or unattached sheet (often missing at the back) is the end paper in the strict sense, the so-called fly leaf. In older volumes the fly leaf was usually a part of the first signature (i.e., the second sheet of that signature), but later it was often pasted-in wastepaper. Until the 11th century the binding most often had a smooth back, i.e., no back bands were visible; the headband, however, stood out sharply. The leather of the cover was usually decorated only with vertical, horizontal, or diagonal, simple or multiple parallel lines, etc.; only seldom did the cover bear figured ornamentation (cf. the early bindings of Fulda, Sankt Gallen, Schaffhausen, etc.). But from the 12th century book covers began to appear with beveled edges and with metal corner and center pieces (studs, bosses, bands, borders) of iron, copper, or brass, and with decorative and protective clasps (*clausurae*). Strips of leather, similarly cut and applied, were used, but rarely, in place of these. Metal strips were applied to the outer edges of covers for heavy folio books. Books that were to be chained usually had the chain fastened with a ring through the upper edge of the back cover, though sometimes through the front cover; a ring at the other end of the chain fastened it to a rod on the reading desk. The covers of a book were held together in front by hasps or clasps (*clausurae, fibulae*) made of metal, leather, plaited straps with hinges, etc.

Variations of the simple binding used generally throughout the Middle Ages were the pouch book, the girdle book, and book with jacket, all easy to carry or readily attachable to the belt. The covering material of the pouch and girdle bookbindings was allowed to extend far beyond the bottom edge of the cover (rather than being folded over into the inside of the cover). A book with a jacket binding had another material (leather, silk, velvet) that covered the book's regular binding; since the jacket binding extended some length beyond the edges of the book, it provided protection from dust.

Many bindings incorporated bookmarkers of leather, plaited hemp, or ribbons made of some fabric (*corda, cordula, registrum*), which were fastened to the upper headband. In very large tomes there was sometimes a set of leather bookmarkers fastened to a free, or loose, diagonal strip (*tenaculum*) located on the upper edge. There are some rare volumes that had a wooden box with sliding lid that was affixed to the top edge of the back cover and that contained a wooden reading-stick. Parchment strips called *misericordiae* were often attached to the outside edge of certain pages in the late Middle Ages; sometimes they were dyed red, inscribed, and made to protrude from the edge to facilitate the finding of certain passages or texts. Besides the simple, generally prevalent bindings (*ligatura, coopertorium*), there is also a group of deluxe bindings, many of which date from as early as the 8th century. These are made with ivory covers, exemplified by the consular diptychs of antiquity and by books of Byzantine and medieval western making. Other deluxe bindings were embossed with gold or silver, such as the *Codex Argenteus* and the *Codex Aureus.* Still others were enamel, particularly from Limoges, or adorned with precious stones or filigrees. In the 12th century, leather bindings came to be enhanced with carving (e.g., some Codices of Engelberg), and later, plate and roller stamps were popular. Bookbinding became a secular craft in the 12th or 13th century, and subsequent bindings show that it became a highly developed art form.

See Also: BOOK, THE ANCIENT; BOOK, THE PRINTED.

Bibliography: S. DAHL, *History of the Book* (New York 1958), revision of original Ger. ed. (1928). E. P. GOLDSCHMIDT, *Gothic and Renaissance Bookbindings,* v.1 (New York 1928). R. DELBRÜUCK, *Die Konsulardiptychen* (Studien zur spätantiken Kunstgeschichte 2; Berlin 1929). J. DESTREZ, *La Pecia dans les manuscrits universitaires du XIII e et du XIV e siècle* (Paris 1935). *Lexikon des gesamten Buchwesens,* ed. K. LÖFFLER and J. KIRCHNER, 3 v. (Leipzig 1935–37). P. LEHMANN, ''Blätter, Seiten, Spalten, Zeilen,'' *Zentralblatt für Bibliothekswessen* 53 (1936) 333–361, 411–442; repr. in *Erforschung des Mittelalters,* 4 v. (2d ed. Stuttgart 1959–61) 3: 1–59. L. W. JONES, ''Pricking Manuscripts: The Instruments and Their Significance,'' *Speculum* 21 (1946) 389–403. *Scriptorium* (Antwerp 1946–). F. G. KENYON, *Books and Readers in Ancient Greece and Rome* (2d ed. Oxford 1951). K. LÖFFLER and P. RUF, ''Allgemeine Handschriftkunde,'' *Handbuch der Bibliothekswissenschaft,* ed. F. MILKAU and G. LEYH, v.1 *Schrift und Buch* (2d ed. Wiesbaden 1950) 106–162. A. BOECKLER and A. A. SCHMID, ''Die Buchmalerei,'' *ibid.* 249–387, with important bibliogs. E. VON RATH and R. JUCHHOFF, ''Buchdruck und Buchillustration bis zum Jahre 1600,'' *ibid.* 388–533. M. J. HUSUNG and F. A. SCHMIDT-KUNSEMÜLLER, ''Geschichte des Bucheinbandes,'' *ibid.* 782–848. E. KUHNERT and H. WILMANN, ''Geschichte des Buchhandels,'' *ibid.* 849–1004. A. RENKER, ''Geschichte des Papiers,'' *ibid.* 1047–68. D. DIRINGER, *The Hand-produced Book* (New York 1953). G. PICCARD, ''Die Wasserzeichenforschung als historische Hilfswissenschaft,'' *Archivalische Zeitschrift* 52 (1956) 62–115. W. WATTENBACH, *Das Schriftwesen im Mittelalter* (3d ed. Leipzig 1896; 4th ed. repr. Graz 1958). D. DIRINGER, *The Illuminated Book, Its History and Production* (New York 1958). *L'Histoire et ses méthodes,* ed. C. SAMARAN (Paris 1961), with important methodological articles by select authors, with bibliogs. B. BISCHOFF, *Latin Palaeography: Antiquity and the Middle Ages* (Cambridge, Eng. 1990). A. PETRUCCI, *Writers and Readers in Medieval Italy: Studies in the History of Written Culture* (New Haven 1995). R. H. ROUSE, *Preachers, Florilegia and Sermons* (Toronto 1979). M. B. PARKES, *Pause and Effect: An Introduction to the History of Punctuation in the West* (Berkeley 1993). P. SAENGER, *Space Between Words: The Origins of Silent Reading* (Stanford 1997).

[A. BRUCKNER]

BOOK, THE PRINTED

The book printed from moveable type represents a relatively late development in history. In tracing its progress in the West from the 15th century, this article focuses on those aspects of the printed book that are relevant to the fine arts, that is, the effect of its appearance as produced by type face, page design, and illustration.

Printed Books and Manuscripts. Although the printed book can be considered a mechanical product, its physical format in the first stages of development in the 15th century differed little from the medieval manuscript book. Of the similarities between them, perhaps the most significant was the parallel between script and its position on the page and printed type and its position. The decoration of manuscripts, including rubrication, initial lettering, and elaborate marginal treatment, often served as inspiration for similar decoration in the printed book. At first these elements were added by hand; later they were produced by woodcut, metal-cut, and type forms such as printers' flowers. The printers were quick to use woodcut illustrations, which corresponded to the illuminations in manuscript. Finally, common to both the printed book and the illuminated manuscript was the protection provided by binding.

Throughout their history, handwritings in manuscripts assumed characteristic forms that are comparable to styles in the history of art. Beginning with the square capital derived from formal stone-cut letters, such as those on Trajan's Column in Rome, the manuscript letter in Europe underwent various changes in design, resulting finally in the 15th-century gothic pointed letter (called also ''black letter'') used in the north, and a humanistic rounded letter (''roman''), lighter in weight, that was characteristic of the south. On these two basic MS hands the first type faces were modeled.

A Benedictine Missal printed at Bamberg in 1481 by Johann Sensenschmidt exemplifies the typical gothic type face. The angular letters, somewhat condensed in width, perpendicular and rigid in structure, and black in color, result in a magnificent effect of solemnity, dignity, and formality. This lettering was intended primarily for folio volumes to be used in Offices of the Church. A work such as Cicero's *Epistles,* printed by Nicholas Jenson in Venice (1471), may serve to illustrate the Renaissance round hand. Beautifully designed letters, each in perfect relation to all the others, give a sense of ease and movement in the lines of the page. The two styles of type face corresponded to the prevailing architectural styles of Europe at the time—the pointed Gothic of northern Europe and the round-arched Renaissance style characteristic of Italy.

The Discovery of Printing. How printing was invented in the Western world in the 15th century and who was responsible for it have long been matters of controversy among scholars. It seems to have been a matter of the cumulative solution, at a propitious time, of certain technical problems, rather than the discovery of any new principles. In China moveable wood characters were used for printing by the 11th century, and in Korea cast metal characters were in use in the 14th century. In the West the invention of printing with moveable type has been claimed for Laurens Jansoon Coster from Haarlem in the Netherlands and Procopius Waldfoghel from Avignon in southern France. However, it was Johann Gutenberg of Mainz, Germany, who first devised the most satisfactory method of printing books, using metal type cast in molds that adjusted to exact dimensions for the separate characters, a workable linseed oil varnish ink, and a press with a sliding bed. Historical records show that Gutenberg was carrying out experiments in printing as early as 1439.

The earliest known example of printing in Germany is a part of a leaf of a Sibylline poem known as the "Fragment of the World Judgment." This work, together with a Latin grammar and an astronomical calendar, were probably printed on an experimental basis in Gutenberg's Mainz workshop between 1444 and 1447. The type face is a pointed gothic letter, not very skillfully handled. The earliest dated piece of printing is a collection of papal indulgences with the date 1454; it contains receipts requested of Pope Nicholas V by the King of Cyprus for donors of money to oppose the invasion of the Muslim Turks and the attendant threat to Christianity. However, the first complete book—and a supreme achievement in printing—is the famous Gutenberg or Forty-Two-Line Bible. By 1450 the Bible was being planned by Gutenberg; with the assistance of Peter Schoeffer, a calligrapher and later one of the most skillful of 15th-century printers, he completed it in 1456. The Bible is folio in size, and its 1286 pages are arranged in two columns of type printed in the pointed black letter (*lettre de forme*) similar to the letters in manuscripts written in the Mainz area in the early 15th century. Border and marginal decorations were added by hand. A copy preserved in two volumes in the Bibliothèeque Nationale contains an inscription by the rubricator, Heinrich Cremer, a curate of St. Stephen's Collegiate Church in Mainz, stating that it was finished before Aug. 15, 1456. Of the 47 copies known to be in existence, it is thought that the most beautiful is the one in the Library of Congress, Washington, D.C.

Two other important books printed in Mainz have been connected with Gutenberg. The rare Thirty-Six-Line Bible was begun *c.* 1450 but not finished until 1460–61. This Bible was probably set up from the printed Forty-Two-Line Bible as copy and has perhaps more valid claim to the title "Gutenberg Bible." The *Catholicon,* a Latin dictionary compiled by Joannes Balbus in the 13th century, was printed at Mainz in 1460 in a small rounded gothic type face, with Lombard capitals for initial letters and with the text arranged in two columns to the page. It has been suggested that Gutenberg himself was the author of its colophon (a statement at the end of a book giving information pertaining to its printing).

With the completion of the Forty-Two-Line Bible in 1456, Gutenberg seems to have given up his activities in printing, leaving Johann Fust and Peter Schoeffer as the major practitioners. The Psalter of 1457, the first dated and signed book and one of the most beautiful ever printed, is credited to them (*see* PRAYER BOOKS). Its handsome typography is enhanced by red and blue floriated initials printed individually from large metal type after the book was printed, rather than drawn in by hand. Of the 10 copies known to be in existence, that in Vienna is the only one in which the printer's device of the double shield appears in the colophon.

Printing soon flourished in other cities in Germany, such as Strassburg, Bamberg, Augsburg, Nuremburg, and Ulm. The subject matter of the books was primarily religious. In general there came to be three type faces in common use: the *lettre de forme* or pointed gothic letter reserved for formal publications such as service books for the Church; the less formal *lettre de somme* or rounded gothic; and the *lettre batarde,* a cursive influenced style used chiefly for works in the vernacular. The *lettre de forme* was elaborated in the 16th century with many flourishes into the *fraktur* style, most spectacularly expressed in the *Theuerdanck* printed by Hans Schonsperger in 1517 for Emperor Maximilian. A pure roman type face was first used in Germany by Adolf Rusch at Strassburg in 1464 in the *Rationale divinorum officiorum,* a popular work by Duranti the Elder on the origin and meaning of ecclesiastical ceremonies. In the 16th century, Johann Froben of Basel used a roman face almost exclusively.

Early Printed Illustration. Woodcut illustration became a concern of the 15th-century printer as early as 1460 in the books printed by Albrecht Pfister at Bamberg.

Among the most famous of the early illustrated books is the *Nuremberg Chronicle* printed by Anton Koberger in 1493. This volume, compiled by Hartmann Schedel, is a world history up to 1492 in which, obligingly, three pages were left blank for the recording of what might happen after that date. Its 1,809 illustrations, designed chiefly by Michael Wohlgemuth, were made from only 645 separate woodblocks by repeating the same view for many cities and the same portrait for many kings. Stefan Fridolin's *Schatzbehalter,* published by Koberger two years before the *Chronicle,* with almost 100 cuts of biblical subjects, is of greater aesthetic value. Another illustrated book of importance, the extremely popular Narrenschiff, of Sebastian Brant, was printed by Johann Bergmann at Basel in 1494. Albrecht Dürer is credited with the illustrations of this satire on the foibles of mankind. Both Dürer and Holbein the Younger gave considerable impetus to book illustration. Of the illustrated Bibles of the period, the Cologne Bible of 1478, printed by Heinrich Quentell, and the Lübeck Bible of 1494 are outstanding. Bernhard Breydenbach's *Peregrinations to the Holy Land* is one of the most interesting of these early illustrated books. The artist Erhard Reuwich accompanied the author on his travels and is thought to have made drawings of scenes as he actually observed them, even though one of the illustrations of animals is a representation of a unicorn. An outstanding work from the Netherlands is the *Chevalier Délibéré,* printed at Gouda (1486–90).

An interesting variation of the illustrated book was the blockbook, with both letter text and illustration cut from wood blocks. Like those of moveable types, blockbooks existed in China long before they made their appearance in the West. The earliest known Chinese example is the *Diamond Sutra* of 868, printed as an aid to popular devotions. Blockbooks became popular in Europe in the mid-15th century and are significant as an early indication of the great social changes that were to result from the development of the printing press. Their purpose was to dramatize pictorially legends, miracle stories, and teachings of the Scriptures for semiliterate people; the printed text played a minor role. In style and design they were derived from contemporary manuscripts. One of the most delightful is the *Canticum canticorum,* illustrating the Song of Solomon as an Old Testament prefiguration of the history of the Virgin (*see* SONG OF SONGS). Others of interest are the *ARS MORIENDI* and the *BIBLIA PAUPERUM*; the popularity of these two books is attested by the great number of their editions. Blockbooks may have been made as early as 1420, and they continued to be produced after books were printed from moveable type.

The Spread of Printing. As the result of religious difficulties in Mainz and conditions that were unfavorable to the guilds, many printers left that city in the 1460s to practice the newly learned craft elsewhere throughout Europe—Italy, France, Spain, and England. Printing in each of these countries, however, early assumed an unmistakably national character.

In Italy, through the encouragement of Cardinal Juan de Torquemada, Conrad Sweyenheym and Arnold Pannartz of Mainz began printing in the monastery of Santa Scholastica, at Subiaco, near Tivoli. One of their earliest works was St. Augustine's *De civitate Dei,* printed in 1467 in a transitional type face that retained the heavy blackness and narrow proportions of the gothic but also anticipated the rounded forms of the roman humanistic hand. A year later Sweyenheym and Pannartz moved to Rome, where they printed under the patronage of the Massimi family.

Venice became the great printing center in Italy. John and Wendelin de Spire were the first to practice the craft there. Another successful printer, Erhard Ratdolt, specialized in printed decoration. His edition of Appian's *Historia Romana* (1477) shows how readily the printer could adjust his craft to the needs of the printed book. Printing reached its zenith in Venice with Nicholas Jenson, whose roman type has been the model for type faces ever since. An excellent example of his work is Pliny's *Historia naturalis,* printed in 1476. Jenson showed consistently in his work a sensitivity for appropriate marginal ratio.

Aldus MANUTIUS was, after Gutenberg, perhaps the most famous among printers. He was the inventor not only of a beautiful roman type face but also of the italic letter, which he used for his pocket-size editions of the classics, comparable to Loeb or Everyman editions of recent times. The well-known printing device of Aldus consists of a dolphin, supposedly a symbol of speed and activity, entwined around an anchor, representing firmness and stability. The most beautiful work printed by Aldus was the *Hypnerotomachia Poliphili* (1499), a dream allegory written by the Dominican Francesco Colonna, in a mixture of Italian, Greek, Latin, and Hebrew. This masterpiece of typography is remarkable for the harmonious relationship between outline woodcut illustrations, attributed to various Renaissance artists, and the handsome roman text type and initial letters.

In France the most notable examples of early printing are to be found in the Book of Hours, the layman's manual of devotion. Artists, illuminators, and printers all devoted their skills to this type of book, which was frequently embellished with illustrations of religious scenes, printed from relief-engraved metal plates. In general, early French printing was characterized by elaborate decoration combined with graceful type face designs. A good example is *La Mer des Hystoires,* printed in Paris in 1478 by Pierre La Rouge. This book reflects its derivation from Merovingian manuscripts of the 7th and 8th centuries in the type face and the full-page initials ending in fantastic animal heads. The full-page calligraphic letters, which were characteristic of French printing, may be seen in the title page of another edition of the same book printed in Lyons in 1491 by Jean du Pré. The type face favored by the French was the gothic *lettre batarde,* with a spirited delicacy of design. Other important printers and publishers in France include: Philippe Pigouchet, Simon Vostre, Antoine Verard, and Guy Marchand.

The delight and charm of the medieval spirit of the 15th-century book in France continued into the 16th. There were many scholarly printers as well, especially the Estienne family, who produced Greek and Hebrew classics and scientific works. An important figure representing the new Renaissance ideal in France was Geoffroy Tory. The type and ornamentation of his printed Books of Hours reveal the Italian influence that Francis I had made fashionable at the French court. The *Champfleury,* his greatest work, incorporates his theories of letter design based on the proportions of the human body, a subject that intrigued such artists as Albrecht Dürer, Fra Pacioli, and Leonardo da Vinci.

Printing in Spain in the 15th and 16th centuries was marked by a splendor of effect with heavy black decoration, reflecting the intensity of much Spanish painting. Among the important printers were Pablos Hurus at Saragossa, Fadrique of Basilea at Burgos, and Lambert Palmart and Nicolaus Spindeler at Valencia.

William Caxton, the first important English printer, was as much a scholar as a craftsman. He designed several types and produced at least 100 books, some of which were the first books to be printed in the vernacular. Caxton was followed in the 16th century by Wynkyn de Worde and Richard Pynson. Johann Froben was another scholarly printer who worked in Basel. He is remembered for his association with Erasmus and for his employment of Hans Holbein the Younger to decorate many of his publications.

From the 17th Century to the Present. In the 17th century, production of the luxurious book reflected the baroque style of the period. Book design became architectural with the elaboration of bordered title pages, and illustrations were printed from copper line-engravings designed by such artists as Peter Paul Rubens. The style was exemplified by the *Opera* of Justus Lipsius printed in 1637 at the Plantin-Moretus Press, in Antwerp. Despite the frequent aesthetic deficiencies of the printed book in the 17th century, the period was important for book production. The Imprimerie Royale in France published handsome volumes, its first product being the *De imitatione Christi* of Thomas à Kempis in 1640.

In the 18th century the printed book was marked by the same classical tendencies that one finds expressed in literature, painting, and architecture. John Baskerville in England is important for his type designs and his experiments in papermaking. William Caslon, an English typefounder, designed a handsome old-style type face that has been in continuous use for more than 200 years. The printed book reached its culmination at this time in the simple restrained work of Giambattista Bodoni in Italy and the Didot family in France. Their modern-style type faces, with thick and thin lines sharply defined, and the open spacing of a page resulted in a classical dignity that was also somewhat cold and forbidding. Typical of what may be called the ''neoclassical'' in printing are the works of Horace printed by Bodoni at Parma in 1793.

In the 19th century, printing underwent a certain decline as a result of innovations in machine-printing. Those who were interested in fine printed books groped for a new aesthetic pattern. At the end of the century an interest in the handpress was revived through the activities of William Morris. The most impressive and ambitious undertaking of his Kelmscott Press was the printing of the works of Chaucer in 1896. In folio format, the book was printed in one of Morris's gothic types, decorated with elaborate borders and initials designed by him, and illustrated with woodcuts based on drawings by Edward Burne-Jones. Although Morris sometimes violated his own stated principles of good bookmaking in his extravagant decoration and typography, he succeeded in creating a new interest and enthusiasm for fine printing and careful craftsmanship. The private press movement to which he gave impetus has left its mark in raised standards of book design. In this as in other areas, Morris's work was a protest against the ugly, the mediocre, and the indifferent. The first book published by the Kelmscott Press in accordance with the function of the private press as it was originally conceived was one of Morris's own works, *The Story of the Glittering Plain,* printed in his ''golden'' type. Of the numerous private presses that subsequently came into existence, the most important were the Ashendane, established by C. H. St. John Hornby, and the Doves, founded by Emery Walker and T. J. Cobden-Sanderson. The *Doves Bible* (1903–05) is one of the most beautiful examples of fine printing from any period, marked by a sophisticated simplicity of typography reminiscent of Jenson's work in Venice. Among more recent influential private presses was the late Laboratory Press, established in 439 1923 at the Carnegie Institute of Technology. This press was experimental in approach; most of its imprints were student projects, worked out as individual solutions to typographical problems posed by the director, Porter Garnett. The private press has flourished also in Germany. The Janus Press, founded by Walter Tiemann, has published works of simple design and high quality. Wilhelm Wiegand's Bremer Press in Munich is especially notable for the use of handsome initial letters designed by Anna Simons. More recent is the distinguished work in type and book design carried out at the Bauhaus.

Bruce Rogers is the most important figure in fine printing of the 20th century in the United States. His work shows versatility and an instinct for propriety. He has worked with almost impish delight with printers' flowers, yet always in restrained good taste, as in his *Rime of the Ancient Mariner* by Coleridge, printed in 1931. His *Holy Bible,* published by Oxford University Press, is set in the Centaur type face, of Rogers' own creation. In it he has demonstrated the basic tradition of the maker of fine printed books, a sensitivity for the material to be printed.

Considerable interest has been shown in recent times for handsome publications illustrated in fine print media by artists of distinction, such as Rouault, Odilon Redon, Picasso, Braque, and Chagall. The French publisher and art dealer Ambroise Vollard has been an important influence in this area. Similar to the *livre de luxe* of the 17th century, these books show a great freedom of imagination and interpretation for the artist. One of the most impressive is the *Cantiques Spirituels de Saint Jean de la Croix,* illustrated with lithographs by Alfred Manessier, whose style is uniquely expressive of the mysticism pervading the writings of the Carmelite theologian. With the recent emphasis on the artist as illustrator and with the technical knowledge gained over the centuries, the printed book continues in the tradition in which it began, that of being both functional and beautiful.

Bibliography: *Biblia Latina,* 2 v. (Leipzig 1913–14; repr. New York 1961), fac. ed. of Gutenberg Bible. P. GARNETT, *The Fine Book* (Pittsburgh 1934). F. WEITENKAMPF, *The Illustrated Book* (Cambridge, Mass. 1938). G. P. WINSHIP, *Printing in the Fifteenth Century* (Philadelphia 1940). D. C. MCMURTRIE, *The Book: The Story of Printing and Bookmaking* (3d ed. New York 1943). S. MORISON, *Art of Printing* (New York 1945). P. HOFER, *Baroque Book Illustration* (Cambridge, Mass. 1951). C. EDE, ed., *The Art of the Book* (New York 1951). D. BLAND, *A History of Book Illustration* (Cleveland 1958). D. C. NORMAN, *The 500th Anniversary Pictorial Census of the Gutenberg Bible* (Chicago 1961). S. H. STEINBERG, *Five Hundred Years of Printing* (2d ed. Baltimore 1962). R. BELLM, *P. Stephan Fridolin: Der Schatzbehalter,* 2 v. (Wiesbaden 1962). J. C. HARRISON, *Five Hundred Years of the Printed Bible* (Pittsburgh 1964). R. CHARTIER and G. CAVALLO, eds., *A History of Reading in the West* (Amherst 1999). H-J MARTIN, *The History and Power of Writing* (Chicago 1994). L. FEBVRE and H-J MARTIN, *L'Apparition du Livre* (Paris 1999). P. SAENGER, "The Impact of the Early Printed Page on the History of Reading," *Bulletin du Bibliophile* (1996) 237–301.

[V. E. LEWIS]

BOOK OF COMMON PRAYER

Since the middle of the sixteenth century, The Book of Common Prayer (BCP) has served as the title of an entire family of books that contain the authorized canonical rites for each province of the Anglican Communion. The title originated in the Church of England, but was applied to later adaptations of the English BCP as autonomous provinces emerged with the expansion of Anglicanism around the world. For the first four hundred years of its development, the various versions of the BCP depended heavily upon the English sources. However, more recent versions, beginning in the middle of the twentieth century, contain newer liturgical materials reflecting the increased ethnic diversity of the Anglican Communion and an increased ecumenical consensus with regard to common liturgical texts.

The source editions of the BCP were issued in England during the reign of King Edward VI, namely, the books of 1549 and 1552 that were imposed upon the English Church by parliamentary Acts of Uniformity. These two books were primarily the work of Archbishop Thomas Cranmer, the Archbishop of Canterbury from 1533 to 1556. Cranmer took as his primary source the medieval Sarum Use, the Latin Rite as it was celebrated in the majority of English dioceses during the late Middle Ages. Other sources were the Greek liturgies of Basil the Great and John Chrysostom, medieval Gallican rites, and early forms of the Lutheran Church Orders. In his development of the Anglican Offices of Morning and Evening Prayer, perhaps his greatest work, Cranmer was influenced by the breviary published in 1535 by Cardinal Francisco de Quinones.

The first Book of Common Prayer (1549) was a conservative adaptation of the old Latin rite, but with pressure from more radical reformers, and in conformity with his own developing theological convictions, Cranmer imparted to the second Book (1552) a more decidedly Protestant emphasis, especially in his reconstruction of the Holy Communion rite and in the elimination of many traditional ceremonies. Queen Mary proscribed the Prayer Book on her accession in 1553, but a new Act of Uniformity in 1559, under Elizabeth I, restored the 1552 Prayer Book, albeit with certain modifications that made it more patient of a Catholic interpretation of the Real Presence in the Eucharist. During the Commonwealth (1645–60) public use of the Prayer Book was again forbidden, but following the restoration of the monarchy and episcopacy in 1660, the Prayer Book was revised, after unsuccessful attempts in conference to win dissident Puritan and Presbyterian groups to accept it, and issued under a new Act of Uniformity in 1662.

The BCP of 1662 has continued as the officially authorized book until the present time, but just as local provincial adaptations of the book began to take into account the growth of liturgical knowledge, so also in England there was increasing demand for Prayer Book reform. The proposed revision of 1928–29 was not approved by Parliament, but nevertheless had considerable influence upon worship in the Church of England.

In the latter half of the twentieth-century, significant changes in the texts written by or adapted from Archbishop Cranmer came to be incorporated in Prayer Book revisions in various provinces of the Anglican Communion. Among those revisions, the BCP of the American Church was issued in 1979 and replaced the earlier book of 1928, *The Alternative Service Book* (ASB) was approved in England for use in tendem with the BCP of 1662, and in Canada *The Book of Alternative Services* was published in 1985 with the intention that it would not replace the earlier book of 1962. Beginning in Advent 2000, the ASB was superseded by *Common Worship*, a consolidation and revision of the ASB, together with specially commissioned material. All thhese books continued to embod a respectful priority to the classical texts of Cranmer.

The most innovative departure thus far from the inherited sources is *A New Zealand Prayer Book (He Karakia Mihinare o Aotearoa)*, authorized for use in the Province of New Zealand in 1989. Not only does this book include a substantial quantity of new ritual material, but it also offers parallel texts in the Maori language in many parts of the book. In spite of the fact that this book is only canonically authorized for use in New Zealand, its experimental character and directness of style have commended it for use in many parts of the Anglican Communion.

The particular genius of the BCP tradition is that each version contains in one volume all the fundamental ritual texts and sacramental rites for the public worship in Anglican communities. Thus, in one volume both laity and clergy have the texts needed for Morning and Evening Prayer, for the Eucharist, for particular ministrations of priests— such as rites for baptism and marriage, penance and reconciliation, rites for the sick, and the rites of Christian burial—, and for the particular ministrations of bishops, such as ordinations and the Consecration of Churches.

The Prayer Book has served as an important symbol of Anglican unity, and so when local provinces began to move beyond the Cranmerian texts, this was frequently met with anxiety about the erosion of this unity. By the time of the Lambeth Conference of Anglican bishops in 1958, it was generally recognized that liturgical unity did not so much require identical texts as it did a common structure, especially for the eucharistic rite. In the decades since that time, it has become increasingly common

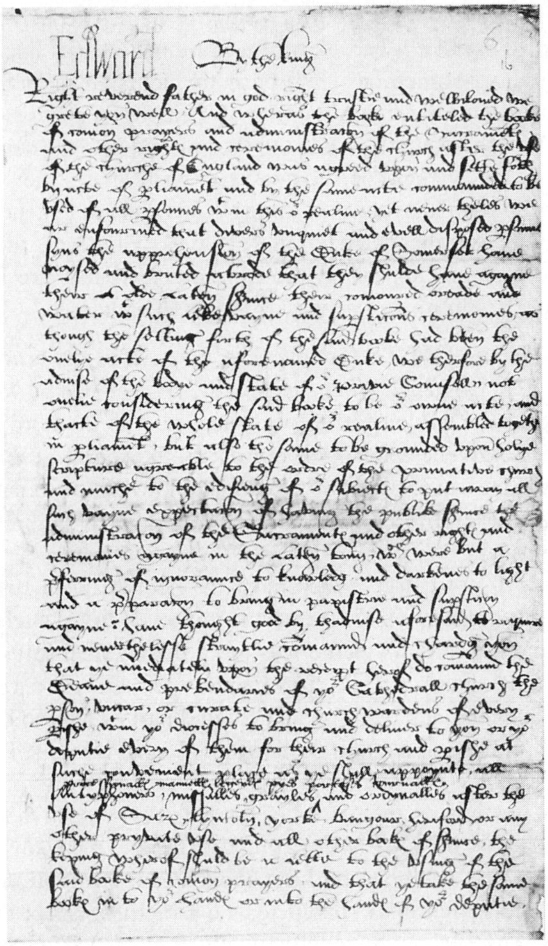

Letter from King Edward VI and council ordering use of "Book of Common Prayer," and to collect and abolish old service books (Stowe MS 142, fol.16).

at major Anglican liturgical celebrations to embrace the ethnic and ritual diversity of the Communion as a providential development in its history.

Bibliography: F. E. BRIGHTMAN, *The English Rite*, 2 v. (London 1915). G. J. CUMING, *A History of Anglican Liturgy*, 2nd. ed. (London 1982). M. J. HATCHETT, *Commentary on the American Prayer Book* (New York 1980). P. V. MARSHALL, *Prayer Book Parallels, 2 v.* (New York 1989). R. A. MEYERS, *A Prayer Book for the 21st. Century* (Liturgical Studies Three; New York 1996). C. P. PRICE & L. WEIL, *Liturgy for Living*, Revised edition (Harrisburg, PA 2000). M. H. SHEPHERD, *The Oxford American Prayer Book Commentary* (New York 1950).

[M. H. SHEPHERD/L. WEIL]

BOOK OF LIFE

Term found in both the Old Testament and the New Testament for an imaginary record of the members of the people of God and of those destined for eternal happiness. The idea of a record or book of names kept by the Lord most likely had its origin in human census lists in antiquity. Sometimes, reference to inclusion in such a book is simply a figurative way of speaking of one's natural life; for example, when the Psalmist adds to the curses upon his wicked persecutors the wish that ''they be erased from the book of living'' [Ps 68(69).29], he is praying for the death of his enemies. However, those whose names appear on the Lord's census lists are His elect, His intimate friends, or at least His people.

In the Old Testament. The first use of the term is found in Ex 32.32. After the Israelites had sinned by worshiping the golden calf, Moses pleaded with the Lord for their forgiveness in words similar to those that St. Paul would later use when he wrote, ''I could wish to be anathema myself from Christ for the sake of my brethren'' (Rom 9.3). With great boldness Moses demanded, ''If you will not (forgive the sin of the people), then strike me out of the book that you have written.'' In the ancient Near East, a man's name was more than a label suitable for distinguishing him from others. In Egypt, e.g., a man's name, his *ren*, was an essential part of him; to blot it out was equivalent to destroying the man himself. This view explains the zeal shown by the native Egyptian kings in erasing the names of the hated Hyksos invaders from every monument in Egypt after their expulsion. The notion that obliteration of the name meant devastation to the one named was shared by the Israelites, a fact that makes Moses' act of generosity all the more magnificent.

Isaiah, speaking of the messianic blessings of the future under the figure of a lush harvest, announces their possession by the remnant of Israel, which will consist of those ''marked down for life in Jerusalem'' (4.3), i.e., God's list of his chosen ones. Malachi speaks of a ''record book . . . of those who fear the Lord'' (Mal 3.16). Daniel says that ''everyone who is found written in the book'' shall escape in the ''time of unsurpassed distress'' (Dn 12.1–2). In Ps 138(139).16 the book is envisioned as one that contains not only names but deeds that constitute material for judgment, an idea found also in the New Testament Book of Revelation.

In the New Testament. The notion that God keeps a record in the ''book of life'' of those who are destined for heaven is found in Phil 4.3 (Paul's ''fellow workers whose names are in the book of life''; cf. Lk 10.20; Heb 12.23). But the figure is especially frequent in Revelation: in 3.5 it is said of him ''who overcomes'' that Christ ''will not blot his name from the book of life''; in 13.8 the book is called the ''book of life of the Lamb''; in this passage and in 17.8 those not destined for salvation are called those ''whose names have not been written in the book of life''; in 20.12, 15 ''anyone not found written in the book of life'' is cast into the pool of fire; in 21.27 the inhabitants of the heavenly Jerusalem are those ''who are written in the book of life of the Lamb.''

See Also: LIFE, CONCEPT OF (IN THE BIBLE); PREDESTINATION.

Bibliography: *Encyclopedic Dictionary of the Bible*, tr. & adap. L. HARTMAN 261–263. C. KOPP, *Lexicon für Theologie und Kirche* [2] 2:738–739. J. DUPONT, *Essais sur la christologie de saint Jean* (Bruges 1951), 157–162. L. KOEP, *Das himmlische Buch in Ankike und Christentum* (Bonn 1952).

[W. N. SCHUIT]

BOOK OF THE COVENANT

The collection of laws extending from Exodus 20.22 to 23.19 is so named because of the designation in Exodus 24.7; it is generally attributed to the ELOHIST (E) tradition of the PENTATEUCH. This law code, undoubtedly Israel's oldest after the Decalogue, is presented in its present literary context as part of the terms of the Sinai Covenant (Ex ch. 19–24).

General Character. The laws of the covenant code point, like the Decalogue, to man's duty toward God, his fellow man and society as a whole; but they follow no orderly plan of presentation. Enclosed between an initial cultic section (20.22–26) and a final exhortation (23.20–33) are laws regulating cult (22.28–29; 23.10–19), determining man's moral responsibility to God and neighbor (22.15–27) and upholding the interests of justice within society (21.1–22.14; 23.1–9). The form of the laws themselves is twofold: casuistic, a type commonly found in ancient law codes, using a conditional clause (''if,'' ''when,'' ''whoever'') to express the case, followed in the main clause by the determined sanction or action to be pursued, for example, 21.26–27; and apodictic, a type more specifically Israelite, expressing the law succinctly either as a positive command (22.30; 23.11–12) or as a prohibition (22.17, 20; 23.1–3) (*see* LAW, MOSAIC).

Date and Background. Despite evidence of some editing done as late as the eighth century B.C., the substance of the code reflects the period of Israel's transition from a seminomadic to a settled agricultural existence during the period immediately preceding or concomitant with the occupation of Palestine at the end of the Late Bronze Age, with at least some of its laws attributable to Moses himself. The time of its codification, according to scholars favoring this early date, ranges from the period of the Transjordanian sojourn before entrance into the Promised Land (Dt 28.69) to the time of Joshua's assembly of the tribes at Sichem (Jos 24.25–26). Its clearly premonarchical tone argues against any date later than the time of the Judges, a period favored by some scholars.

A comparison of the covenant code with the more ancient Mesopotamian codes, for example, those of Lipit-Ishtar, Eshnunna, Hammurabi (*see* LAW, ANCIENT NEAR-EASTERN), while warranting no conclusions regarding direct dependence, gives ample evidence of a common legal milieu. The fact of the Israelites' Mesopotamian origins coupled with the spread of the Sumero-Babylonian culture in the Oriental world of the second millennium makes this wholly understandable. In addition, the code evidences Assyrian and Hittite influences. But what makes the Exodus laws truly distinct is the sacred character with which they are permeated, their intimate connection with the covenant that they are intended to safeguard, and above all, their being presented as given by God Himself.

While granting the code's antiquity, critical scholarship generally maintains that it has been linked artificially with the actual Sinai event. One cannot overlook its concern with the cares of a recently settled community. Moreover, references in Deuteronomy to the covenant law clearly refer to the Decalogue alone (Dt 4.12–14; 5.2–22). If the code is to be identified with the final stages of the Israelite journey, it may have originally stood where Deuteronomy now stands. Displaced by the more developed Deuteronomic Code, it was then incorporated into the covenant account.

Contents. The worship laws of the code were those in force during the early period of tribal federation. Monolatry is strongly emphasized (20.22–23; 23.13b); altar construction at local sanctuaries is specified (20.24–26), with directives given for the firstborn and first-fruit offerings (22.28, 29; 23.19), the observance of the weekly SABBATH, the SABBATH YEAR and the three pilgrimage feasts, namely, Unleavened Bread, Weeks and Booths (23.10–17) [*see* FEASTS, RELIGIOUS; BOOTHS (TABERNACLES), FEAST OF; PASSOVER, FEAST OF; PENTECOST].

Moral precepts (22.15–27) regulate conduct toward God (v. 19, 27a), tribal chiefs (v. 27b), unmarried women (v. 15–16), resident foreigners (vv. 20–23) and fellow Israelites (v. 24–26). In the matter of justice, an unbiased attitude is required of a witness or judge in a lawsuit and respect must be shown for the property of others (23.1–8).

The book's central section (21.1–22.14), comprised mainly of casuistic laws, designates the rights of slave and master, setting limits on the former's length of service (21.1–11) and indicating the penalty to be meted out to those inflicting personal injury (21.12–32). Restitution is demanded for property damages (21.33–22.5); it is to be noted that the "gored ox" case (21.35–36) is closely paralleled in the centuries older Code of Eshnunna (par. 53). Restitution is to be made also for the loss of entrusted goods, the amount to be restored depending on the degree of guilt (22.6–14).

Bibliography: H. CAZELLES, *Études sur le code de l'alliance* (Paris 1946). A. ALT, "Die Ursprünge des israelitischen Rechts," *Kleine Schriften zur Geschichte des Volkes Israel,* v.1 (Munich 1953) 278–332. R. DE VAUX, *Ancient Israel, Its Life and Institutions,* tr. J. MCHUGH (New York 1961) 143–163. J. VAN DER PLOEG, "Studies in Hebrew Law," *The Catholic Bible Quarterly,* 12 (1950) 248–259, 416–427; 13 (1951) 28–43, 164–171, 296–307. G. E. MENDENHALL, "Ancient Oriental and Biblical Law," *The Biblical Archaeologist,* 17 (1954) 26–46.

[R. J. FALEY]

BOOK OF THE DEAD

A body of Egyptian texts on death and the afterworld, written on papyrus and placed in the tombs. The name Book of the Dead is generally applied to the texts of the New Kingdom and later, but their origin can be traced back to the mortuary literature of earlier periods: the Coffin Texts and Pyramid Texts.

The Pyramid Texts are the oldest heterogeneous compositions inscribed on the walls of the inner chambers of the Fifth- and Sixth-Dynasty pyramids for the benefit of the deceased kings. They include rituals, mythological allusions, incantations, and magical spells. Most of them are associated with the solar cult center at Heliopolis, but some reflect the basically different Osirian complex, and others can be explained only as remnants of predynastic fetishism. Some sections of the Pyramid Texts were later included in the mortuary texts of Egyptian nobility of the Middle Kingdom and were inscribed on coffins; hence they are known as the Coffin Texts. Through the Coffin Texts these sections made their way into the New Kingdom Book of the Dead, which was considered beneficial to anyone who could afford to purchase a copy and place it in his tomb.

The Book of the Dead contains, according to the different recensions, from about 150 to 190 chapters, not all of equal value, equal popularity, or equal length. They include: magical spells of much variety; prayers and hymn to the gods RA (RE), Osiris, etc.; ritual recitations with instructions for priests; theological instructions; and a guidebook to the other world. Almost every chapter had its own title, such as, Chapters of Coming Forth by Day (ch. 1–2), Chapter of Opening of the Mouth (ch. 23), Chapter of Not Dying for a Second Time (ch. 44), Chapter of Not Being Tripped Up in the Underworld (ch. 51), Chapter of Changing into a Divine Hawk (ch. 78).

Among the most important and interesting are chapters 17 and 125. Chapter 17 consists of questions and answers on theological subjects, such as:

Deceased making an offering before Horus, illustration from the Egyptian Book of the Dead. (©Gianni Dagli Orti/CORBIS)

> "I am the great god who came into being by himself." Who is he? "The great god who came into being by himself" is water; he is Nun, the father of the gods. Another version: He is Ra . . . .
>
> "I am yesterday, while I know tomorrow." Who is he? As for "yesterday," that is Osiris. As for "tomorrow," that is Ra on that day on which the enemies of the All-Lord are annihilated and his son Horus is made ruler . . . . [Translation of J. A. Wilson.]

Chapter 125, which concerns the judgment of the soul before Osiris and 42 divine judges, includes the so-called Negative Confession or, more correctly, Declaration of Guiltlessness, containing statements such as these:

> I have not made anyone weep . . . . I have not killed . . . . I have neither increased nor diminished the grain measure . . . . I have not taken milk from the mouths of children . . . . [Translation of J. A. Wilson.]

The Book of the Dead was primarily a book of rituals, as has been recently demonstrated; it often mentions the reciting priest and the ritual objects. The kind of ritual was generally indicated in the title of each chapter. However, it was apparently intended, not for the priests, but for the deceased, so that his soul could participate in his own funerary service. A large portion of these rituals had to be performed in front of the eternal gods by the soul itself in the netherworld.

Beyond the ritual requirements and overwhelming magic, employed here as a protective force, the Book of the Dead contains the fundamental belief in personal responsibility of each soul before the divine judgment and in ultimate justice in the afterlife.

Bibliography: Pyramid Texts. K. H. SETHE, *Die altägyptischen Pyramidentexte,* 4 v. (Leipzig 1908–22); *Übersetzung und Kommentar zu den altägyptischen Pyramidentexten,* 6 v. (Hamburg 1935–62), no more pub. S. A. B. MERCER, *The Pyramid Texts in Transslation and Commentary,* 4 v. (New York 1952). Coffin Texts. A. DE BUCK, *The Egyptian Coffin Texts,* 7 v. (Chicago 1935–61), the Egyptian text without tr. Book of the Dead. E. A. T. W. BUDGE, tr., *The Book of the Dead: The Hieroglyphic Transcript of the Papyrus of Ani . . .* (London 1895; repr. New Hyde Park, N.Y. 1960), somewhat out of date. T. G. ALLEN, ed., *The Egyptian Book of the Dead: Documents in the Oriental Institute Museum . . .* (Chicago 1960). C. MAYSTRE, *Les Déclarations d'innocence: Livre des morts,* chap. 125 (Cairo 1937). J. A. WILSON, *The Burden of Egypt: An Interpretation of Ancient Egyptian Culture* (Chicago 1951) 116–118. J. B. PRITCHARD, *Ancient Near Eastern Texts Relating to the Old Testament* (2d, rev. ed. Princeton 1955) 3–4, 10–12, 34–36.

[B. MARCZUK]

BOONEN, JACQUES

Archbishop of Malines (Belgium) and protector of Jansenism in its initial stages; b. Antwerp, Oct. 11, 1573; d. Brussels, June 30, 1655. Boonen was born into a family of jurists, studied law at the University of Louvain, received his licentiate, and became a lawyer at the Council of Brabant in 1596. He then entered upon an ecclesiastical career. He became a canon in 1604 and was ordained in 1611. He was made *officialis* of Malines in 1608; ecclesiastical counselor to the Great Council in 1611; dean of the cathedral of Malines in 1620; member of the Estates of Brabant in 1621; and counselor to the Council of State in 1626. He generously served the interests of his country and the Church.

Boonen, imbued with the spirit of Charles BORROMEO, was one of a succession of prelates who fought for the application of the decrees of the Council of Trent and the restoration of the Church. He was a rigorist who fought laxism in all its forms. Some of the propositions censured by the University of Louvain at his command were afterward condemned by Rome.

As a friend and admirer of his suffragan Cornelius JANSEN, he petitioned Rome untiringly, even calling upon the good offices of the king of Spain, in order to bring about a reversal of Rome's condemnation of Jansenism. He was misunderstood and severe censures were imposed upon him; however, these were soon lifted (1653). His historical reputation continues to be controversial.

Bibliography: P. CLAESSENS, *Histoire des archévêques de Malines,* 2 v. (Louvain 1881) v. 1. L. CEYSSENS, "La Publication officielle de la bulle 'In eminenti,'" *Augustiniana* 9 (1959) 161–182, 304–338, 412–430; 10 (1960) 77–114, 245–296, 365–423; "Les Dernières années de Boonen," *ibid.* 11 (1961) 87–120, 320–335, 564–582. V. SEMPELS, *Dictionnaire d'histoire et de géographie ecclésiastiques* (Paris 1912–) 9:1144–60.

[L. CEYSSENS]

BOOTH, LAWRENCE

Archbishop of York, chancellor of England; b. Lancashire; d. Southwell, May 19, 1480. Booth became master of Pembroke Hall, Cambridge, in April of 1450, a position he held for life. Soon after succeeding his half brother William BOOTH as chancellor to Henry VI's wife, Queen Margaret, in 1452, he received rapid preferment with court patronage, becoming archdeacon of Richmond (1454) and dean of St. Paul's, London (November 1456). On Aug. 22, 1457, he was provided to the See of DURHAM and on September 25, consecrated.

As keeper of the privy seal from September of 1456 to July of 1460, he was closely associated with the queen and the court party in Henry's later years, but the political importance of his northern palatinate brought him into favor with Yorkist King Edward IV, to whom he became confessor (1461). His loyalty was later suspected; his temporalities were confiscated (December 1462 to April 1464), and he seems to have lived chiefly in his Cambridge College between 1462 and 1466.

Restored to favor in 1471, he was chancellor of England from July of 1473 to May of 1474. In July of 1476, he was provided to the archbishopric of YORK, which he held until his death. Little is known of his diocesan administration, but it is doubtful whether he was an active pastor, politics being his chief concern.

Bibliography: A. B. EMDEN, *Biographical Register of the Scholars of the University of Cambridge before 1500* (Cambridge, Eng. 1963) 78–79. A. H. THOMPSON, *Dictionnaire d'histoire et de géographie ecclésiastiques* (Paris 1912–) 9:1164-65.

[C. D. ROSS]

BOOTH, WILLIAM

Archbishop of York; b. Lancashire; d. Sept. 12, 1464. Booth was one of the few English prelates of his age not to receive a university education, but had as a young man practiced law at Gray's Inn, London. He became a prebendary of Southwell (York diocese) in 1416, chancellor of St. Paul's, London (1421–23), and archdeacon of Middlesex (1429–41). He first became prominent in 1445 as chancellor to Henry VI's queen, Margaret of Anjou; court influence procured his provision to the See of Coventry and Lichfield on April 26, 1447, and his subsequent succession to Cardinal John KEMP at YORK, by papal bull of July 21, 1452. His half-brother, Lawrence BOOTH, succeeded William as chancellor.

Although less active in politics thereafter and holding no high office under the crown, William still did not turn his energies to pastoral work. In January 1450, Pope CALLISTUS III had dispensed him for life from personally making the episcopal visitation of his diocese, and the diocesan administration of York remained in the hands of competent subordinates. His contemporary Thomas Gascoigne unfairly criticized the avarice, lack of learning, and nepotism of this *indignus episcopus Cestriae.* Booth undoubtedly promoted the advancement of his kinsmen, three of whom became bishops, but they seem to have been men of ability. At York he was remembered as a benefactor of the lesser clergy.

Bibliography: A. H. THOMPSON, *Dictionnaire d'histoire et de géographie ecclésiastiques* 9:1166-67. MS Register in Borthwick Institute, St. Anthony's Hall, York.

[C. D. ROSS]

BOOTH, WILLIAM

Founder of the SALVATION ARMY; b. Nottingham, England, April 10, 1829; d. near London, Aug. 20, 1912. Booth was from a working-class family, partly Jewish in origin, and had an unhappy youth. As a pawnbroker's apprentice (1842), he learned urban misery. He abandoned nominal Anglicanism for Methodism at age 15 when he was stirred by Feargus O'Connor and experienced ''conversion.'' When he was 17 years old, influenced by an American evangelist, Booth preached in the Nottingham slums. He went to London (1849), worked as a pawnbroker's assistant to support his mother, and acted as a lay preacher.

Booth thought about joining the Wesleyans and the Congregationalists, but he disliked the Wesleyans' individualism and the Congregationalists' doctrine of predestination, so instead he entered the Methodist New Connexion (1854). After briefly attending a London seminary, he became an outstanding evangelist and was ordained in 1858.

In 1855 he married Catherine Mumford (1829–90), who shared his outlook. Their preaching success intensified Booth's view that God intended them to be roving revivalists. When ordered to a pastorate (1861), he left his denomination, became an independent evangelist, and gained some financial support.

In 1865, while preaching in a tent in London, Booth began the movement that became the Salvation Army in 1878. For the remainder of his life he was its general. Horrified by the plight of the homeless, he collaborated with W. T. Stead and wrote *In Darkest England and the Way Out* (1890). Booth sought the material rehabilitation of the poor to effect their spiritual regeneration. In this, as in his evangelizing, Booth met opposition, but by his persistence he triumphed. He died a national hero. Booth was a Biblicist, and stressed the sacrifice of Christ, instantaneous conversion, and Christian perfection.

Bibliography: ST. JOHN G. ERVINE, *God's Soldier: General William Booth,* 2 v. (New York 1935). H. C. STEELE, *I Was a Stranger: The Faith of William Booth* (New York 1954). R. HATTERSLEY, *Blood and Fire: William and Catherine Booth and Their Salvation Army* (New York 2000).

[E. E. BEAUREGARD]

BOOTHS (TABERNACLES), FEAST OF

An agricultural feast of Canaanite origin celebrated at the conclusion of harvest and upon adoption by the Israelites, soon transferred to local sanctuaries and ulti-

Jews in Brooklyn observe the festival of Sukkot by spending time in succahs, or temporary dwellings. (©David H. Wells/CORBIS)

mately to Jerusalem, where it became the greatest of the three pilgrimage feasts. With the passage of time, the Feast of Booths was ''historicized'' by symbolic connection with the desert sojourn of the Exodus. It also became an occasion for reading the Law to the assembled people. This article treats the Feast of Booths in its origins, in the Old Testament, in Rabbinic literature, in its messianic symbolism, in the New Testament and in the Christian Era.

Origins. The Hebrew appellation of the feast, *ḥag hassukkôt,* indicates a ''pilgrimage feast'' (*ḥag*) that is ''of the booths'' (*hassukkôt*). The term ''booths'' (Lat. *tabernacula,* hence Eng. Tabernacles) originally signified the temporary, leafy structure, supported by branches, built in the vineyard or field to accommodate the busy farmer during the harvest season (Gn 33.17; Jb 27.18; 38.40; Is 1.8). Jews call the feast simply ''Sukkot.'' Evidence indicates that Booths was, in its origins, an agricultural feast connected with harvest booths. It has always been celebrated during Tishri (September–October) in connection with the grape and olive harvest. Its most ancient appellation is the ''feast of ingathering'' (*āsîp;* Ex 23.16; 34.22); and it is noteworthy that the Gezer calendar mentions with this same word the season of ''ingathering.'' The ''hut'' feature, plainly agricultural, has never been dropped from the solemnities of the feast. Finally, the texts show confusion in fixing the date for the celebration of the feast, partially because in Palestine, as elsewhere, the harvest season varies slightly from place to place and from year to year [Ex 34.18-23 (J); Ex 23.14-17 (E); Dt 16.13-15 (D); Lv 23.33-36, 39-43 (P); De Vaux 498–500]. Although S. Mowinckel agrees that the Feast of Booths had its harvest aspect, according to his hypothesis it was not a simple harvest feast that later became historicized, but rather the great, ancient New Year's Festival that in preexilic times had the enthronement rites of Yahweh as king, analogous to Babylonian cult; also, this great feast began with purification rites that were later separated to form the distinct cultic celebration of Yom Kippur. H. J. Kraus sees the origin of the feast in an ancient, nomadic ''feast of tents'' that celebrated a covenant renewal; this nomadic feast assimilated the indigenous Canaanite harvest feast. G. MacRae discusses and concedes the plausibility of Kraus's hypothesis. However, R. de Vaux rejects both Mowinckel's hypothesis of the elaborate New Year's enthronement feast and the hypothesis of nomadic origins. He considers the feast purely agricultural in its origins, pointing out that in the earlier sources the feast is always connected with the *sukkâ* (booth), while only in later, secondary sources is it connected with the desert tent of the Exodus (Lv 23.43) or with the Sabbatical-year reading of the Law (Dt 31.9-3).

In the Old Testament. The feast was originally celebrated in the vineyards at the conclusion of the grape and olive harvest, accompanied by dancing, merrymaking and even some licentiousness [Jgs 9.27; 21.19; (prophetic censures in) Am 5.21–27; Hos 9.1; Is 28.7-8]. Unlike the feasts of PASSOVER and PENTECOST, which were connected with such farm work as mowing and threshing, Booths was held after the harvest. This leisure facilitated the eventual transfer of the festivities to neighboring and more decorous sanctuaries. Shiloh assumed a certain importance in connection with this feast (1 Sm 1.3). The celebration at the sanctuaries may, later on, have included a covenant renewal ceremony; the reading of the Law every seventh year in connection with Booths was prescribed in Dt 31.10-12. Solomon dedicated his Temple on the occasion of this feast (1 Kgs 8.1-3, 65-66; 2 Chr 5.2-7.10) and Jerusalem became more and more the center for Booths, as well as for the other feasts. The meaning of the feast shifted accordingly and as it became more a Temple festivity, new and more complicated rites were introduced. After the destruction of the Temple, some people continued to come up to the ruined city to keep the feast (Jer 41.5). The Jews who returned after the Exile restored the ancient feast (Neh 8.13–18; cf. Ezr 3.4) in keeping with the prescription of Dt 31.10-13.

In Rabbinical Literature. According to the Talmud the feast lasted seven days (15th to 21st of Tishri), with an eighth ''day of conclusion'' (*šᵉmînî ʿăṣeret;* cf. Neh 8.18) added. And rabbinical custom added a ninth day, ''the joy of the Law'' (*śimḥat tôrâ*), on which the yearly cycle of Scripture readings was completed. The tractate *Sukkah* of the Talmud, which treats of this feast, delineates the salient characteristics of the celebration that prevailed around the time of Our Lord. The hut had to be of a temporary nature and the participants were to eat and sleep in the hut during the celebration. Together with myrtle and willow branches, the *lûlāb* (palm) and *'etrôg* (citron) were carried in procession. These two items, as important to Sukkot as the evergreen is to Christmas, have remained prominent to the present day. Two other features of the Temple celebration, water drawing and illumination, are treated in the Talmud. The priests went each day to the pool of Siloam, where they drew water in large silver ewers. Upon their returning, in joyous procession through the Water Gate to the Temple confines, a libation was poured on the southwest corner of the altar. Rain comes to Jerusalem from the southwest and a primitive rainmaking rite is perhaps at the basis of this ceremony. On the eve of the first day of the feast, a massive illumination was held in the women's court of the Temple and the huge candelabra were witness to joyful dancing and much festivity. The seventh day featured the singing of the great Hosanna (cf. Jn 7.37; ''the great day of the festival''). Booths, accepted as the greatest of all feasts, was often referred to simply as ''the Feast'' (Lv 23.39; Ez 45.25; Josephus, *Ant.* 8.4.1). Rabbinical tradition considered Booths the ''time of our joy.''

Messianic Symbolism. The great feast acquired messianic overtones, and the Prophets taught that its observance by the faithful ''remnant'' and the Gentiles would herald messianic days (Zec 14.16; 8.20–23; Mi 4.1-3; Is 56.6-7). Zechariah especially stresses the messianic details of the coming feast. The illumination aspect will blossom into perpetual light (14.7), and the water drawing will evolve into the eschatological streams of living water that will flow from Jerusalem to the ends of the earth (14.8).

In the New Testament. In John ch. 7, Jesus is presented as going up to Jerusalem for the feast of σκηνοπηγία (literally, ''booth-building''; Jn 7.3), that is, Booths. A messianic discussion develops, and Jesus says, ''If anyone is thirsty, let him come to me and drink . . . I am the light of the world'' (Jn 7.37; 8.12). Note also the three booths and the bright cloud in the Transfiguration accounts (Mt 17.1-8; Mk 9.2-13; Lk 9.28-36), as well as the palm and hosanna details of the triumphant entry into Jerusalem for the Passover (Lk 19.35–38). The description of the New Jerusalem in the Revelation juxtaposes water and light once again in a messianic context (21.23–26 and 22.1-2). Finally, it is of interest that light and water figure prominently in the Easter vigil service, the messianic feast par excellence, although a relationship of dependence upon Booths is improbable here.

In the Christian Era. Post-Biblical Judaism has considered the hut that is erected for the feast a tearful reminder of the splendorous Temple. Orthodox Jews, who build their booths in their gardens or yards, keep the first, second, eighth, and ninth days of the feast as full holidays, while the Reformed Jews observe only the first and eighth in this way. The Reformed also stress, once again, the agricultural aspects of the feast. This is the approach (somewhat secularized) to the feast also in the modern state of Israel. The Passover has overshadowed Sukkot in importance since the period of the second Temple, but the note of deep joy and messianic expectancy has proved durable and surrounds the feast to this day.

Bibliography: R. DE VAUX, *Ancient Israel, Its Life and Institutions,* tr. J. MCHUGH (New York 1961) 495–502. *The Interpreters' Dictionary of the Bible,* ed. G. A. BUTTRICK, 4 v. (Nashville 1962) 1:455458. *Encyclopedic Dictionary of the Bible,* tr. and adap. by L. HARTMAN (New York 1963) 265–270. H. J. KRAUS, *Gottesdienst in Israel: Studien zur Geschichte des Laubhüttenfestes* (Munich 1954). H. SCHAUSS, *The Jewish Festivals* (Cincinnati 1938; repr. New York 1958). J. VAN GOUDOEVER, *Biblical Calendars* (2d ed. Leiden 1961). G. W. MACRAE, ''The Meaning and Evolution of the Feast of Tabernacles,'' *The Catholic Bible Quarterly,* 22 (1960) 251–276.

[W. F. BARNETT]

BORDA, ANDRÉS DE

Mexican theologian; b. Mexico City, date unknown; d. there, 1723. The problems that accompanied the conquest and conversion of Mexico in the 16th century challenged the philosophers and theologians to produce books of enduring value. The humanistic revival of 18th-century Mexico called forth works that were prized by the 20th century because of the similarity in point of view prevalent in the two centuries. Mexican authors of the 17th century are ignored not because they were less learned, but because there is little interest in their problems and solutions. Andrés de Borda is one of these authors, greatly appreciated in his lifetime and almost completely forgotten since. He was trained in the Franciscan houses of study of Mexico City. As the first Franciscan to receive a doctor's degree from the University of Mexico (1697), he ended a period of estrangement begun at the time of the founding (1553), when the Franciscans were intent on building a university for the native converts at their college of Santa Cruz de Tlaltelolco. In 1688 he had been given the Scotistic chair at the University of Mexico, and he retained it until his retirement in 1711. In 1701 he was named to go to Spain to defend the university against the pretension of the Colegio de los Santos. In 1708, with Juan Ignacio de Castorena y Ursúa, later editor of the *Gaceta de México*, he drew up the official response to the 14 doubts presented to the university by the Bethlehemites. After retirement from the university, Borda became theological consultant to the Inquisition of Mexico City and prepared the verdict in the important case, pending since 1702, against Francisco Figueroa, disciple of the ex-Jesuit Francisco Davi. At the request of the university, Borda wrote also a series of philosophical treatises that remain in manuscript. All his works show that he was an author of his time; yet, he was calm; he searched for the truth, and prized the value of human dignity; and he had an objective sense that gave him an advantage over his contemporaries. Most highly valued among his spiritual works is his *Práctica de confesores de monjas* (1708), a work marked by its clarity, kindness, and objectivity.

Bibliography: J. M. BERISTAIN DE SOUZA, *Biblioteca hispano americana septentrional*, 5 v. in 2 (Colección Daniel; 3d ed. Mexico City 1947).

[R. BECERRA]

BORDONI, FRANCESCO

Theologian, canonist, historian: b. Parma. April 25, 1595; d. Aug. 7, 1671. At the age of 15, Bordoni joined the Franciscan Third Order Regular. He studied philosophy and theology in the Studium Parmense, where he received the doctorate and taught theology for 20 years. He was chosen master of novices, prior, and provincial in the Province of Bologna; from 1653 to 1659, he governed the Order as minister general. His first literary production appeared in 1630, and from then until his death his writing was prolific. Forty-one printed works and almost as many unprinted works remain extant. The most important are *Sacrum Septenarium lmmaculatae Conceptionis* (Palermo 1644), *Propugnaculum Opinionis Probabilis* (Lyon 1666), *De Miraculis* (Parma 1703), *Contraversiae Morales* (Lyon 1665-66), *Cronologium Fratrum et Sororum Tertii Ordinis S. Francisci* (Parma 1658), and the *Archivium Bullarum Tertii Ordinis* (Parma 1658).

Bibliography: R. PAZZELLI, *Il Terz'Ordine Regolare di S. Francesco* (Rome 1958). F. O. MANCINI, *Brevis historia gestorum P. Francisci Bordoni Parmensis* (Parma 1703).

[V. PETRICCIONE]

BORGESS, CASPAR HENRY

Bishop; b. Addrup, Oldenburg, Germany, Aug. 1, 1826; d. Kalamazoo, Michigan, May 3, 1890. At the age of 12, Borgess immigrated to the United States with his parents; he entered St. Mary's Seminary in Cincinnati, Ohio and was ordained on Dec. 8, 1845. After 11 years as pastor of Holy Cross parish in Columbus, Ohio and a year at Immaculate Conception parish in Cincinnati, he was appointed chancellor of that archdiocese (1860). On Feb. 14, 1870, Pius IX named him coadjutor and administrator of DETROIT, Michigan, a diocese left vacant by the departure for Germany of Frederic Résé, its first bishop. Borgess was consecrated titular bishop of Calydon on April 24 in the Cincinnati cathedral, and he arrived in Detroit on May 8, 1870; he succeeded to the see at Résé's death the following year.

The main portal of the Borghese Palace at Rome. (Alinari-Art Reference/Art Resource, NY)

During his administration, Borgess worked to develop an indigenous clergy, to reduce nationalistic tensions among immigrant groups, and to extend Catholic education, especially by inviting the Jesuits (1877) to establish what later became the University of Detroit and to improve the administrative structure of the diocese. In 1881, he petitioned the Holy See for a division of his see; a year later the Diocese of Grand Rapids was established, reducing Detroit to the 29 counties of southern Michigan. Ill health, aggravated by several unpleasant experiences with recalcitrant priests, caused Borgess to resign on April 16, 1887, three years before his death. A hospital and nursing school in Kalamazoo were named in his honor.

[F. X. CANFIELD]

BORGHESE

A Sienese patrician family noted from the start of the 13th century for its jurists and municipal officials. *Agostino* was made a knight by Emperor Sigismund (1410–37) and granted the privilege of carrying the eagle on his escutcheon. During the pontificate of Leo X (1513–21), *Pietro* served as a Roman senator. *Giambattista* defended Clement VII (1523–34) during the sack of Rome (1527) by the mutinous imperial army of Charles V. *Niccolò* is remembered for his biography of Catherine of Siena, whom he claimed was a Borghese. *Galgano* represented Siena at the Roman court of Nicholas V (1447–55) and later became ambassador to Naples (1456).

Upon the election of *Camillo* Borghese (1552–1621) as PAUL V (1605–21), the family acquired great wealth and distinction. Paul's cousin, *Camillo,* was made bishop of Castro (1594) and *Montalcino* (1600) and archbishop of Siena (1607). One of the Pope's nephews, *Marcantonio,* on whom the continuation of the family line would depend, was created Prince of Sulmona (1610), then married to Princess Camilia Orsini (1619), and the next year appointed general of the Church. Another nephew, *Scipione* (1576–1633), son of Francesco Caffarelli and Ortensia Borghese, sister of Patti V, was invested as cardinal of San Grisogono (1606), given the Borghese coat-of-arms, and made cardinal nephew (secretary of state). He was also appointed legate to Avignon (1607), archpriest of the Lateran, prefect of the Congregation of the Council, abbot of San Gregorio on the Coelian (1608), librarian of the Roman Church (1609), head of the Grand Penitentiary, archbishop of Bologna (1610), *Camerlengo* of the Roman Church, and prefect of Briefs (1612). Through his large annual income (90,000 scudi in 1609; 140,000 scudi in 1612) Scipione was able to buy extensive estates in Latium and the suburbs of Rome and become a generous patron of the arts. Affable and indulgent, but shrewd, he lived as a Maecenas in the Villa Borghese, which he built outside the Porta Pinciana to house his great collections of art and books and to serve as a setting for fêtes and theatrical performances. At Paul V's death, his prominence in Roman public life decreased, but his building projects and renovation of Roman monuments continued until his own death.

Among other prelates bearing the Borghese name are: *Ippolito,* a Benedictine monk who became abbot general of the Congregation of Olivetans (1617–18) and bishop of Montalcino (1619) and Pienza (1636); *Pier Maria,* grandnephew of Paul V, created cardinal of Santa Maria in Cosmedin (1626) and San Grisogono (1633); *Enrico,* prior general of the Servites (1652), then bishop of Alife in the Kingdom of Naples (1658); *Girolamo,* Benedictine scholar and bishop of Pienza (1668); *Lucio,* Bishop of Chiusi (1682); *Francesco,* titular Archbishop of Trajanopolis (1728) and Cardinal of San Pietro in Montorio (1729), San Silvestro in Capite (1732), and Santa Maria in Trastevere (1743), as well as Bishop of Albano (1752) and of Porto (1759); *Scipione, maestro di camera* of Clement XIII (1766), Archbishop of Theodosia (1766), created cardinal of Santa Maria della Minerva by Clement XIV (1770); and, finally, *Tiberio,* Bishop of Soana in Tuscany (1762) and Archbishop of Siena (1772)

In the 19th century the Borghese were prominent in the politics affecting the Papal States. *Camillo* (1775–1832) married Marie Pauline, sister of Napoleon Bonaparte and widow of Gen. Jacques Leclerc. He was made a brigadier general, the duke of Guastalla (1806), and governor of the French provinces of Piedmont and Genoa. When he died childless, the princely Borghese title passed to his brother *Francesco* (1776–1839). Because of previous intermarriage, the Borghese by this time also carried the family names of the Salviati and Aldobrandini. Accordingly, Francesco divided the titles among his three sons; Marcantonio (1814-86) as firstborn was Prince Borghese, and married Catherine Gwendolyn, daughter of the last Catholic Duke Talbot Shrewsbury—both were known for their humanitarian interest in supporting schools, asylums, and bettering the lot of the underprivileged—; *Camillo* (Borghese) Aldobrandini (1816–1902) became a colonel of the papal guard (1848) and war minister in the cabinet of Giacomo ANTONELLI; *Scipione* (Borghese) Salvati (1823–92) married Arabella Fitz-James, and after 1870 was a leader of Catholic interests in the strained relations of the Church with the Italian State—together with his wife he founded the hospital of the Child Jesus in Rome. The Borghese line was again divided by Marcantonio for his two sons: *Paolo,* (1845–1920) with the cognomen Borghese and the titles of prince of Montecompatri, prince of Vivaro, duke of Bomarzo, and prince of Nettuno; and *Giulio,* (1847–1914) with the cognomen Torlonia, and titles of prince of Fucino, duke of Ceri, and marquis of Romavecchia.

The splendor of the Borghese family came to an abrupt halt with the great bankruptcy of 1891 when their wealth fell into the hands of speculators. The palace of Paul V became an emporium and housed a Freemason's lodge. The art collection and library were auctioned. Leo XIII bought the MSS and the family archives for 300,000 francs. The MSS (300) are in the Vatican Museum; the archives, known as the *fondi Borghese,* became part of the Secret Vatican Archives. In 1902 the state acquired the Villa Borghese and converted it into a public park.

Bibliography: For the early history: G. GIGLI, ed., *Diario Sanese* 2 v. (Lucca 1723)) v.1. J. H. DOUGLAS *The Principal Noble Families of Rome* (Rome 1905). P. E. VISCONTI, *Città e famiglie nobili e celebri dello stato pontificio,* 3 v. (Rome 1847) 3:913–985. E. RE, *Enciclopedia Italiana di scienzi, littere ed arti* (Rome 1929–39) 7:468–469. L. PASTOR, *The History of the Popes from the Close of the Middle Ages* (London-St. Louis 1938–61) v.25. G. WAGNER, *Catholicisme* 2:167–68. G. MORONI, *Dizionario de erudizione storico-ecclesiastica* (Venice 1840–61) 6:37–45. P. PASCHINI, *Dictionnaire d'histoire et de géographie ecclésiastiques* 9:1213–17.

Cesare Borgia.

[E. D. MCSHANE]

BORGIA (BORJA)

A number of persons with the surname Borja (later Italianized as Borgia), originally from the Aragonese city of that name, settled in the kingdom of Valencia after the reconquest in 1238. In the 14th century there was a branch of the Borjas, of the lesser nobility, living in Valencia and Alzira with a manor house in Xàtiva. Gonçal-Gil de Borja was military magistrate (*jurat militar*) in 1346. He was the father of Rodrigo-Gil (testament 1375) who, after his marriage with Francesca Fenollet, had two children, Rodrigo-Gil, junior, and Francesc (?) de Borja. The latter became the father of two children also, Francesca and Francesc de Borja. But this last Francesc has been considered since the 16th century to have been the illegitimate son of Alfons de Borja, who later became Pope CALLISTUS III. Francesc was bishop of Teano and archbishop of Cosenza and was elevated to the cardinalate in 1500 by Pope ALEXANDER VI.

Rise to Prominence. The Borjas' social standing dated from the War of Union between Pedro IV of Ara-

Lucrezia Borgia.

gón and the feudal nobles, when the Borjas fought on the King's side. Rodrigo-Gil, junior, married Sibília (d'Oms). From this union were born Joan-Gil; Rodrigo, Bishop of Barcelona (d. 1478); Galceran-Gil (testament 1435); Joana, childless wife of Bartomeu Serra; and Jofré-Gil de Borja, Master of Adzeuva and Albuixa (testament 1430). Another branch of the family included Domingo, Master of Canals, who was father of Catarina. She married Joan del Milà, Baron of Masalavès. Their children were Joan-Lluís del Milà, cardinal under Callistus III and founder of the line of the counts of Albaida; Joana, who married Bartomeu Martí and left no children; Alfons (Callistus III); and Isabel. Isabel married the Jofré-Gil mentioned above. Their son Rodrigo de Borja became Alexander VI. Their other children were Pere-Lluís, Duke of Spoleto under Callistus III (d. 1458 without heirs); Tecla (d. *c.* 1462); Beatriu (d. 1503), and Joana, who in her second marriage with Pere-Guillem Llançol de Romaní, Baron of Vilallonga (d. 1489) had a son, Jofré de Borja-Llançol. This son changed the order of his last names, married Joana de Montcada, and went to Rome. His children all served Pope Alexander VI: Rodrigo as a military man; Joan as bishop of Melfi, governor of Perugia, archbishop of Capua and Valencia, and cardinal in 1496 (d. 1500); Pere-Lluís as his brother's successor as archbishop of Valencia and cardinal in 1500 (d. 1511); their sister Jeronima was married first to Fabio Orsini and then to Tiberio Carafa; the other sister, Angela, married to Alessandro Pio, was lady-in-waiting to Lucrezia in Ferrara (see below). Alexander VI's nepotism gave the cardinal's hat to other Borjas: in 1492 to Joan de Borja, senior, son of Galceran, who in turn was the son of the above mentioned Galceran-Gil and Tecla Navarro d'Alpicat; in 1493 to his own son Cesare (see below); in 1503 to Joan Castellar, son of Bernadona de Borja (who was the daughter of the same Galceran-Gil) and her husband, Galceran de Castellar, Master of Picassent: and finally to Francesc de Lloris, son of Isabel de Borja (sister of Cardinal Joan de Borja senior) and Ximèn Pérez de Lloris. Other relatives of the Pope also made cardinals were Giuliano Cesarini (named in 1493), Bartomeu Martí, the Catalan Joan de Castro (1496), and Jaume Serra (1500). Family friends included the Valencians Joan Llopis, datary (1496), Joan de Vera (1500), Jaume Casanova (1503), and another Catalan, Francesc Remolins (1503). The cardinals Luigi d'Aragona, illegitimate son of Ferrante I of Naples (1494), and the Sicilian Pietro Desvalls or d'Isvaglies (1500) were of Catalonian-Aragonese origin. The only Castilian cardinals were Bernardino López de Carvajal (1493) and Diego Hurtado de Mendoza (1500).

Children of Rodrigo Borgia. Critical value is lacking in the pseudo-apologetic efforts made to deny Alexander VI's paternity of a number of children. The mothers of the first three children are unknown. The children were Pere-Lluís (see below); Girolama (d. *c.* 1484), who married Gianandrea Cesarini in 1482 but left no children; and Isabella, who married Piergiovanni Mattuzzi (d. 1519). The other four children (see below), Cesare, Joan, Lucrezia, and Jofré, were born of Vannozza Cattanei, possibly from Mantua, who was married successively to Domenico d'Arignano, Giorgio de Croce, and Carlo Canale, all employees of the Roman Curia. It has not been proved that Alexander VI was the father of Orsino Orsini or Laura Orsini (b. 1492), daughter of Giulia Farnese, who was the mistress of Rodrigo de Borja at the end of his cardinalate. Giulia was married to Orsino Orsini, who was the son of Ludovico Orsini and Adriana del Milà, daughter of Pere del Milà, brother of the abovementioned Cardinal del Milà. However, it is certain that Alexander VI was the father of Joan de Borja, Duke of Camerino and Nepi (1498–1546). The documents are contradictory as to whether Lucrezia was Joan's mother. Also sufficiently proved was Alexander's paternity of Rodrigo de Borja (b. 1502 or 1503), whose mother is unknown.

Pere-Lluís, first Borgian duke of Gandia; b. Rome, *c.* 1468; d. Rome, 1488. He was the son of Cardinal Rodrigo de Borja (Alexander VI). In 1483 his father gave him 50,000 ducats and the barony of Llombai and sent him to Spain. He was arrested in 1484 by Ferdinand II, King of Aragón, because of dissension between the King and the cardinal. Pere-Lluís took part in the seizure of Ronda and on May 28, 1484, the King recognized his nobility along with that of his younger brothers, Cesare, Joan, and Jofré. On December 3 Ferdinand, acting as procurator for his son Don Juan de Aragón sold Pere-Lluís the city and lands of Gandia and the next day gave him the title of duke. In 1486 the Duke became engaged to María Enríquez, first cousin of the King. Before the marriage could take place, the Duke died in Rome in August of 1488, leaving his holdings to his brother Joan.

Cesare, cardinal and condottiere; b. Rome, Sept. 1475; d. Viana, Navarre, March 12, 1507. He was the son of Cardinal Rodrigo (Alexander VI) and Vannozza Cattanei. Ferdinand II legitimized him in 1481. The year before Sixtus IV had dispensed his illegitimacy so that he could obtain ecclesiastical benefits. After having received only the tonsure, he was successively apostolic protonotary, canon of Valencia, archdeacon of Xàtiva, sacristan of Cartagena, bishop of Pamplona in 1491, and archbishop of Valencia in 1492. In spite of all that, Ferrante I of Naples offered his illegitimate daughter Lucrezia d'Aragona to Alexander VI as a wife for either Cesare or Jofré. On Sept. 20, 1493, Cesare was made a cardinal. Although he had received the diaconate on March 26, 1494, his unrestrained life and his ambitions took him back to the lay state on the grounds of reverential fear of ordination (1498). Alexander VI forbade him to marry Carlotta d'Aragona, daughter of Federico III of Naples, but accepted for Cesare the hand of Charlotte d'Albret, sister of Juan II, King Consort of Navarre. Named duke of Valentinois by Louis XII of France, Cesare saw in the campaign against Milan in 1499 the chance to establish a feudal state in Romagna with small feudal holdings belonging to the Holy See. Cesare took over Forli, Cesena, and Faenza, plotted with Giovanni Bentivoglio of Bologna, called himself master and duke of Romagna, invaded Tuscany, and took over Piombino. In the War of Naples in 1501, which ended in the division of the kingdom between Ferdinand the Catholic and Louis XII, Cesare fought on the side of the King of France. He attacked Urbino, Camerino. and Senigaglia and invaded Umbria in 1503. But the death of Alexander VI prevented Cesare's keeping his holdings. Cesare, taken prisoner by Julius II, escaped and fled to Naples. When this kingdom was conquered by Ferdinand, Cesare was arrested, sent to Spain. and imprisoned in the Castillo de la Mota (Medina del Campo). Escaping to France, he went into the service of the King of France in his wars against Ferdinand. Cesare died in the Battle of Viana.

Joan (Juan), second duke of Gandia; b. Rome, 1476; d. Rome, July 14 or 15, 1497. He was the son of Cardinal Rodrigo de Borja (Alexander VI) and Vannozza Cattanei. In 1493 he married María Enríquez, who had been betrothed to his brother Pere-Lluís, from whom he inherited the dukedom. Joan stayed in Valencia and Gandia and consolidated his holdings, although Ferdinand and Isabella did not make good their promises to him. Named captain-general of the Church, he returned to Italy. His military losses in the war against Charles VIII of France and his allies drove him back to Rome, where he was assassinated and thrown into the Tiber. It is uncertain whether his brother Cesare was the instigator of the crime.

Lucrezia (Llucrècia), duchess of Ferrara; b. Subiaco, April 1480; d. Ferrara, June 24, 1519. She was the daughter of Cardinal Rodrigo de Borja (Alexander VI) and Vannozza Cattanei. She lived in Rome with her relatives Adriana del Milà and Joana de Montcada. After unsuccessful plans for marriage with Querubí de Centelles, Gaspar de Próxita, and the Count of Prada, she was betrothed by Alexander VI in 1492 to Giovanni Sforza, Count of Cotignola and Master of Pesaro, in order to consolidate an alliance with the Sforzas of Milan. Later the alliance of Charles VIII of France with Milan brought about a divorce on the grounds that the marriage had not been consummated. In 1498 Lucrezia, having given birth to an illegitimate son, was prevailed upon by Alexander for political reasons to marry Alfonso d'Aragona, Duke of Bisceglie, who was the illegitimate son of Alfonso II of Naples (d.1495). The couple had a son, Rodrigo d'Aragona (1499–1512). On Aug. 18, 1500, Alfonso was assassinated in Rome by a henchman of Cesare. On Dec. 30, 1501, Lucrezia married Alfonso d'Este in the Vatican. He was the son and heir of Hercules II, Duke of Ferrara (d. 1504). In spite of her secret affairs with Pietro Bembo and with her brother-in-law Francesco Gonzaga, Duke of Mantua, and of the scandals involving her lady-in-waiting, Angela Borja, Lucrezia was seriously religious, especially in her later years. She gave her husband, Alfonso, seven sons, three of whom died in infancy. The survivors included the future Hercules III, Cardinal Ippolito, and Francesco.

Jofré, prince of Squillace; b. Rome, 1481; d. Squillace, 1517. He was the son of Cardinal Rodrigo de Borja (Alexander VI) and Vannozza Cattanei. Alexander, although he legitimized Jofré, doubted that he was really Jofré's father. In 1494 Jofré married Sancha d'Aragona, sister of the Duke of Bisceglie. Alfonso II of Naples gave Jofré and Sancha the principality of Squillace, which gift was confirmed by Ferdinand the Catholic in 1502. When Sancha died after an irregular life, leaving no children,

Jofré married Maria del Milà. Their children were Lucrezia, Marina, and Francesco, heir to the title.

Bibliography: Sources. M. OLIVER, "D. Rodrigo de Borja," *Boletín de la Real Academia de la Historia* 9 (1886) 402–447. "S. Franciscus Borgia," *Monumenta historica Societatis Jesu* I (1894), *passim.* J. BURCHARD, *Liber notarum,* Eng. tr. G. PARKER (London 1963). M. MENOTTI, *Documenti inediti sulla famiglia e la corte di Alessandro VI* (Rome 1917). J. SANCHIS Y SIVERA, *Algunos documentos y cartas privadas que pertenecieron al segundo Duque de Gandía, don Juan de Borja* (Valencia 1919). P. DE ROO, *Material for a History of Pope Alexander VI, His Relatives and His Time,* 5 v. (New York 1924). M. BATLLORI, *Epistolari dels B.* (Barcelona 1966); and L. CERVERÓ, *Genealogía documentada de los B.* (Rome 1967). Literature. F. A. GREGOROVIUS, *Lucrezia Borgia* (4th ed. Stuttgart 1906), Eng. *Lucrezia Borgia,* ed. L. GOLDSCHEIDER, tr. J. L. GARNER (London 1948). C. E. YRIARTE, *Les Borgia: César Borgia* (Paris 1889), Eng. *Cesare Borgia,* tr. W. STIRLING (London 1947). P. D. PASOLINI DALL'ONDA, *Caterina Sforza,* 4 v. (Rome 1893–97). F. FERNÁNDEZ DE BÉTHENCOURT, *Historia genealógica y heráldica de la monarquía española,* 10 v. (Madrid 1897–1920) 4:3–389. W. H. WOODWARD, *Cesare Borgia* (London 1913). M. BELLONCI, *Lucrezia Borgia,* tr. B. and B. WALL (New York 1957). G. PEPE, *La politica dei Borgia* (Naples 1946). M. BATLLORI, *Vuit segles de cultura catalana a Europa* (2d ed. Barcelona 1959) 51–83; "De ortu Iohannis, tertii ducis gandiensis, sancti Francisci Borgiae patris, monumenta quaedam," *Archivum historicum Societatis Jesu* 26 (1957) 199–211. A. LUZIO, "Isabella d'Este e i Borgia," *Archivio storico lombardo,* 5 ser. 1 (1914) 469–553; 5 ser. 2 (1915) 115–167, 412–464. M. MENOTTI, *I Borgia, storia ed iconografia* (Rome 1917).

[M. BATLLORI]

BORGIA, FRANCIS, ST.

Third general of the Society of Jesus; b. Gandía, Spain, Oct. 28, 1510; d. Rome, Sept. 30, 1572. He was the first son of Juan Borja, third duke of Gandía, and of Joanna of Aragón. At the age of ten, after the death of his mother, he was sent to Zaragoza, where his uncle Juan of Aragón was archbishop. Later he went to Tordesillas as page to the sister of Emperor Charles V, Princess Catherine, who in 1525 became the wife of John III of Portugal. In 1528 Francis was in the service of the emperor at the Court of Spain. In the next year he married Leonor de Castro, and they had eight sons. On July 7, 1530, his barony of Lombay was raised to the category of marquisate by Charles, and he was nominated first hunter of the court and head of the stables of the Empress Isabella. His wife became her lady-in-waiting. Deeply moved by the death of the empress on May 1, 1539, he accompanied her remains to Granada and assisted at the ceremonies of identification and burial on May 17. On June 26 of that year, Francis was named viceroy of Catalonia, an office that he kept until 1543. After his father's death on Dec. 17, 1542, he went to Gandía to claim his inheritance and his rights as successor in the dukedom. In Barcelona he had met the Jesuits Antonio de Araoz and (Bl.) Peter FABER (Lefèvre), and he determined to build them a college in Gandía. Faber laid the cornerstone of this first college of the society on May 4, 1546. Pope Paul III elevated it to the rank of university on Nov. 4, 1547.

In 1546, after the sudden death of Doña Leonor, Francis took his first vows in the society; he made his solemn profession on Feb. 1, 1548. He kept this a secret and continued to wear secular clothes in order to administer his estates and settle his children. He also studied theology at his new university, receiving a doctorate on Aug. 20, 1550. On the 26th of the same month, Francis started a pilgrimage to Rome, ostensibly to gain the Jubilee indulgences of the Holy Year, but mainly to arrange with (St.) Ignatius of Loyola for his official entrance into the society. He remained in Rome until Feb. 4, 1551, and on May 23, he was ordained in Oñate, celebrating his first Mass at Loyola on August 1. Following his ordination, he preached and taught catechism to children throughout Guipúzcoa and practiced severe austerities until curbed by his superiors. On April 1, 1554, he became commissary general of the society in Spain, and in the following year he went to Tordesillas to assist Queen Joanna in her last illness. Charles V, who in 1556 abdicated and retired to Yuste, often relied on Borgia for advice and made him and Philip II the executors of his will. In 1559 a book entitled *Las Obras del Duque de Gandía* was placed on the list of forbidden books for Spain. It included some treatises of his but also writings not of his authorship. In order to avoid further embarrassment, Borgia retired to Portugal until called to Rome by Pope Pius IV in 1561. There he was received kindly and three years later was appointed assistant general for Spain and Portugal.

In 1565, after the death of the General Diego Laínez on January 19, Francis was nominated vicar-general, and on July 2 of that year he was elected general of the society. His seven years in office were noted for activity and the expansion of the Society of Jesus. He started new missions in the Americas, strengthened the organization of those already existing in the East Indies and Far East, and furthered the training of priests at the German College in Rome for the lands lost to Protestantism. He established new colleges in France, erected the province of Poland, and planned others. The Roman College continued to receive his special interest, and the Gesù, the church of Sant' Andrea, and a novitiate were erected. He is noted, too, for his interior mystical life, which seems to have thrived in the surroundings of business. He was beatified on Nov. 24, 1624, by Urban VIII and canonized on April 12, 1671, by Clement X.

Feast: Oct. 10 (general), Oct. 3 (Jesuits).

Bibliography: His writings are ed. by C. DE DALMASES and J. F. GILMONT, *Archivum historicum Societatis Jesu* 30 (1961)

125–179; *Evangelio meditado,* ed. F. CERVÓS (Madrid 1912); *Meditaciones sobre los evangelios para las fiestas de los santos,* ed. J. M. MARCH (Barcelona 1925); *Monamenta Borgiae,* 5 v. (*Monumenta historica Societatis Jesus,* Madrid 1894–1911); *Tratados espirituales,* ed. C. DE DALMASES (Barcelona 1964). Literature. A. CIENFUEGOS, *La heroyca vida, virtudes, y milagros del grande S. Francisco de Borja, antes duque quarto de Gandia, y despues tercero general de la Compañia de Jesus* (Barcelona 1754). C. DE DALMASES, *Francis Borgia: Grandee of Spain, Jesuit, Saint,* tr. C. M. BUCKLEY (St. Louis 1991). F. W. ROLFE, *A History of the Borgias* (Westport, Conn. 1975). P. SUAU, *St. François de Borgia 1510–1572* (Paris 1905). O. KARRER, *Der Heilige Franz von Borga 1510–1572* (Freiburg 1921). H. DENNIS, *St. Francis Borgia* (Madrid 1956). C. SOMMERVOGEL et al., *Bibliothèque de la Compagnie de Jésus* (Brussels-Paris 1890–1932) 1:1808–17, 8:1875–76.

[C. DE DALMASES]

BORIS I OF BULGARIA

First Christian ruler of Bulgaria 852 to 889; d. May 7, 907. During the reign of Boris I of Bulgaria, Christianity was introduced among the Slavs and Bulgars of BULGARIA and the Bulgarian Church was first established. An ambitious and energetic ruler, Boris realized the importance of bringing his people within the community of Christian nations, but he hesitated to accept Christianity from the Byzantine PATRIARCHATE under the auspices of the Byzantine Empire, the traditional rival of Bulgaria. Instead, he wanted to secure complete independence from the jurisdiction of Constantinople for the Bulgarian Church, and with this in view, he began negotiations with Rome and the Frankish Empire.

In 864, Byzantine military pressure compelled him to accept Baptism from Constantinople with the Emperor MICHAEL III as godfather, but Constantinople's refusal to grant autonomy to the Bulgarian Church prompted Boris to turn to Pope NICHOLAS I in Rome in 866 to ask for bishops and missionaries. In 870 he returned to Constantinople, and in 880, Rome and Constantinople reached an agreement that recognized Roman jurisdiction over the Bulgarian Church.

Political events and the remoteness of the area prevented Rome from exercising effective authority over missionary activities in Bulgaria, and they remained largely in the hands of the Byzantine clergy. In 885 Boris welcomed to Bulgaria the clergy of the Slavic rite expelled from Moravia after the death of Methodius in 884 (*see* CYRIL AND METHODIUS, SS.). Their missionary work, conducted in the vernacular, was very successful among the Bulgarian Slavs and was an effective counterpoise to Byzantine influence.

In 889 Boris resigned the throne in favor of his son Vladimir (889–893), but the pagan reaction with which Vladimir seems to have been in sympathy forced Boris to return to power. Having suppressed the rebellion and deposed Vladimir, he replaced him with his other son, Symeon (893–927). After that Boris returned to his monastery, where he died in 907.

St. Charles Borromeo.

Bibliography: V. N. ZLATARSKI and N. STANEV, *Geschichte der Bulgaren,* 2 v. (Leipzig 1917). S. RUNCIMAN, *A History of the First Bulgarian Empire* (London 1930). F. DVORNIK, *Les Slaves, Byzance et Rome au IX*e *Siècle* (Paris 1926); *The Slavs: Their Early History and Civilization* (Boston 1956).

[O. P. SHERBOWITZ-WETZOR]

BORROMEO, CHARLES, ST.

Cardinal, archbishop of Milan, and prominent figure in the Tridentine Reform; b. Rocca d'Arona, near Lago Maggiore, Oct. 2, 1538; d. Milan, Nov. 3, 1584. The second son of Count Giberto Borromeo and Margherita de'Medici, sister of Pius IV, he was intended for the service of the Church, and received the clerical tonsure and the title of the abbacy of San Gratiniano when 12 years old. He was tutored at Milan by Francesco Alciati, and studied law at the University of Pavia (1552–59) where he earned a doctorate *in utroque.* Three weeks later (Dec. 25, 1559) Cardinal Gian Angelo de'Medici succeeded Paul IV, taking the name of PIUS IV. The new pope called his young nephew to Rome and advanced him rapidly through a brilliant ecclesiastical career.

Curial Responsibilities. Borromeo held several posts in the Roman Curia, and was created a cardinal in 1560 with the title of SS. Vitus and Modestus (changed in 1564 to St. Praxedes). He was cardinal protector of Portugal, the Low Countries, and the Catholic cantons of Switzerland, and of six religious orders (Franciscans, Carmelites, HUMILIATI, Canons Regular of the Holy Cross of Coimbra, Knights of Malta, and Knights of the Holy Cross of Christ in Portugal); administrator of the Legations of Bologna, Romagna, and the Marches; and commendatory abbot of several monasteries. His most responsible office as cardinal nephew was that of prefect of the Secretariate of State, in which he was his uncle's most valued assistant, especially during the third period of the Council of TRENT (1562–63). Grief at the death of his elder brother, Federigo, on Nov.19, 1562, turned him to a more austere manner of living as well as to his ordination to the priesthood (July 17, 1563). The literary academy of the *Noctes Vaticanae,* which he had founded, was transformed and adopted for its spiritual meetings rather than literary and philosophical themes. He took steps to raise the moral tone of the people of Rome by promoting the *Catechismus romanus ad parochos* and collaborating in projects for the completion of the work of the Council of Trent, such as the Roman Seminary, reforms in the Missal, Breviary, and sacred music, and the edition of the writings of the Church Fathers.

Archbishop of Milan. In the year of his promotion to the cardinalate, Borromeo was named also perpetual administrator of the Archdiocese of Milan, of which he would be titular archbishop for the remainder of his life. Because of his multiple duties in Rome, he was at first represented by a vicar-general, Niccolò Ormaneto, but in October 1565 he came to Milan to preside over the first provincial council, and from April 1566 he remained in permanent residence. His pastoral activities during these years were of considerable influence upon the whole Catholic world and affected the many important facets of the post-Tridentine Church. To his credit are: (1) the reorganization of diocesan administration into subordinate offices and functions; (2) the calling of six provincial councils and 11 diocesan synods; (3) regular and systematic pastoral visits to all parts of his diocese; (4) the opening of a seminary entrusted to the Jesuits (1564–79) and later to the Oblates of St. Ambrose, as well as similar institutions for candidates for the priesthood (Collegio Helvetico); (5) a considerable use of existing religious groups, as the Jesuits and Capuchins, and the foundation of a new diocesan religious society, the OBLATES OF ST. CHARLES (1578), for which he wrote the *Institutiones* (1581); (6) various cultural and social institutions that include the Collegio Borromeo at Pavia (1564–68), the University of Brera at Milan (1572), shelters for wanderers, homes for neglected or abandoned wives (Casa del Soccorso), refuges for reformed women, orphanages, *montes pietatis* (lending houses), and hospitals; and (7) the noteworthy promotion of the Confraternity of Christian Doctrine for the teaching of catechism, which in 1595 had grown to more than 20,000 pupils.

Pastoral Ideal. Borromeo's pastoral awareness was inspired by his high ideal of the responsibility of a bishop. To him, each pastor was obliged to have a detailed knowledge of the conditions of his flock. This ideal made astonishingly severe demands in its successful implementation and showed constructive characteristics that were hierarchic, systematic, kerygmatic, and sacramentarian. The amazing results are described in the *Acta ecclesiae Mediolanensis,* whose many editions published since 1582 have become the patrimony of the whole Church. There are found the records of the provincial councils and diocesan synods; numerous instructions, edicts, decrees, pastoral letters; and the rules and constitutions for a score of congregations, confraternities, and other charitable, cultural, or pious groups that Borromeo founded or encouraged. These documents treat the subjects regarded by Borromeo as most useful in promoting religious renewal in his archdiocese along the lines of the Council of Trent. They include preaching, reception of the Sacraments, presence at Mass, liturgical feasts, funerals, the exercise of Eucharistic devotion, exact clerical deportment, the building and equipping of churches, meetings of the diocesan clergy, Lenten regulations, relations with heretics, and preparation of the *Liber status animarum* and similar tracts on parochial administration. Much was written in Italian, and certain rules were prescribed for pulpit reading at least once a year. A great part of Borromeo's effectiveness and popularity was due to his interest in social problems. A well-known episode, frequently illustrated by artists, is the plague of 1576 (Plague of St. Charles) during which he proved his heroic dedication.

Reform and Opposition. Borromeo's resolve to promote Catholic reform and to protect the prerogatives of his office brought opposition both from the civil power over questions of jurisdiction and from clerical communities over his disciplinary demands. He struggled with the Spanish governors of Milan, Gabriel de la Cueva, Duke of Alburquerque, Luis de Requesens, and Marquis Antonio di Ayamonte; peace was restored only through the intervention of Philip II and the pope. Twice his life was endangered. The first occasion involved his right to episcopal visitation of the collegiate church of Santa Maria della Scala, which claimed an exemption from the jurisdiction of the archbishop of Milan granted by Clement VII in 1531. The exemption had been given but was provisional upon the consent of the archbishop, which had not been obtained. When Borromeo attempted to enter the church in September 1569, he was prevented by the canons and by soldiers of the Duke of Alburquerque who opened fire and damaged the cross in his hands. In October 1569 he was again in danger. Some of the Humiliati resisted his reform programs and conspired to take his life. A hired assassin, Girolamo Donato, known as ''Farina,'' fired at him point-blank while he knelt in prayer with his household. The wound was slight, but civil authorities later condemned Farina to death by hanging.

Borromeo also undertook reform activities outside his diocese. He made apostolic visits to the Dioceses of Cremona (1575), Bergamo (1575), and Brescia (1580), and four missionary journeys into pastorally neglected Alpine valleys, where he worked vigorously against sorcery and the infiltration of Protestantism. Three times he traveled even into German areas of Switzerland (Altdorf, Unterwalden, Zug, Sankt Gallen, Schwyz, and Einsiedeln), where his influence led to the establishment of a papal nunciature at Lucerne. Other trips took him to Rome, to Loretto, to the Holy Shroud of Turin, and to his favorite place of pilgrimage at the Sacro Monte at Varallo. At the end of October 1584, on his return from Milan after making the Spiritual Exercises, he was stricken with fever. He was brought into the city on a stretcher, and died on November 3. He was canonized by Paul V on Nov. 1, 1610. His body rests at the foot of the main altar in the cathedral of Milan. His popular cult spread rapidly, especially in Italy, Germany, and the Spanish Netherlands. A statue 100 feet tall was erected on a hill near his birthplace, and many works of art recall episodes in his career of reform. Several cultural and religious associations were founded under his patronage. One of the last acts of Cardinal Giovanni Battista Montini before he left Milan to become Paul VI was the creation of the ''Accademia di san Carlo Borromeo'' to promote scientific research and study of the life and writings of this saint.

Feast: Nov. 4.

Bibliography: Manuscript sources. The principal collections are found in Milan (Archiepiscopal Curia, Ambrosian Library and the archives of the Borromeo family), Rome (Archives of the Vatican and Congregation of Rites, and the Library of the Barnabites), and Brussels (Library of the Bollandists). Printed sources. *Opere complete di S. Carlo Borromeo,* ed. G. A. SASSI, 5 v. (Milan 1747), 2d ed., 2 v. (Augsburg, 1758). *S. Caroli Borromaei Orationes XII* (Rome 1963), ed. at request of Paul VI for the Fathers of Vatican Council II. A. RIVOLTA, ''Epistolario giovanile di S. Carlo Borromeo,'' *Aevum* 12 (1938) 253–280; ''Corrispondenti di S. Carlo Borromeo,'' *ibid.* 556–619; 13 (1939) 65–116. G. GALBIATI, *I duchi di Savoia Emanuele Filiberto e Carlo Emanuele I nel loro carteggio con S. Carlo Borromeo* (Milan 1941). A. G. RONCALLI [JOHN XXIII] and P. FORNO, comp., *Gli atti della visita pastorale di S. Carlo Borromeo a Bergamo, 1575,* 5 v. (Florence 1936–57). *Acta Ecclesiae Mediolanensis,* ed. A. RATTI [PIUS XI] (Milan 1890–92) v.2–3. Contemporary biographies. A. VALIERO, *Vita Caroli Borromaei* (Verona 1586). C. BASCAPÉ (Basilica Petri), *De vita et rebus gestis Caroli card. S. Praxedis* (Ingolstadt 1592; Brescia 1610). G. P. GIUSSANO, *Istoria della vita, virtu, morte e miracoli di Carlo Borromeo* (Milan 1610), annotated copiously by B. OLTROCCHI (Milan 1751), tr. into Eng. with pref. by H. E. MANNING, 2 v. (London 1884). Recent biographies. More than 60 exist, of which the principal are A. SALA, *Biografia di S. Carlo Borromeo,* 3 v. (Milan 1857–61), numerous documents. C. SYLVAIN, *Histoire de St. Charles Borromée,* 3 v. (Lille 1884). L. CELIER, *St. Charles Borromée* (Paris 1923). C. ORSENIGO, *Vita di S. Carlo Borromeo* (Milan 1929), Eng. tr. R. KRAUS (St. Louis 1943). A. RIVOLTA, *S. Carlo Borromeo, note biographiche. Studio sulle sue lettere e suoi documenti* (Milan 1938). M. YEO, *A Prince of Pastors: St. Charles Borromeo* (London 1938). P. GORLA, *S. Carlo Borromeo* (Milan 1939). G. SORANZO, *S. Carlo Borromeo* (Milan 1944). A. DEROO, *Saint Charles Borromée, Cardinal réformateur, docteur de la pastorale* (Paris 1963), bibliog. G. ALBERIGO, *Karl Borromaus* (Münster 1995). F. BUZZI and D. ZARDIN, eds., *Carlo Borromeo e l'Opera della ''Grande Riforma''* (Milan 1997). H. JEDIN, *Carlo Borromeo* (Rome 1971). S. A. RIMOLDI, *Bibliotheca sanctorum* (Rome 1961–) 3:812–850, with bibliog. A. BUTLER, *The Lives of the Saints,* rev. ed. H. THURSTON and D. ATTWATER, 4 v. (New York 1956) 1:255–262. F. VAN ORTROY, *Analectta Bollandiana* (Brussels 1882–) 39 (1921) 338–345. A. DUVAL, *Catholicisme* 2:992–994. C. CASTIGLIONI, *Dictionnaire de spiritualité ascétique et mystique. Doctrine et histoire,* ed. M. VILLER et al. (Paris 1932–) 2:692–700, with bibliog. L. RÉAU, *Iconographie de l'art chrétien,* 6 v. (Paris 1955–59) 3.1:298–300. R. MOLS, *Dictionnaire d'histoire et de géographie ecclésiastiques,* ed. A. BAUDRILLART et al. (Paris 1912–) 12:486–534, with bibliog.

[R. MOLS]

BORROMEO, FEDERIGO

Cardinal and leader of Catholic reform; b. Milan, Aug. 18, 1564; d. Milan, Sept. 22, 1631. Federigo, son of Giulio Cesare and Margherita Trivulzio, was orphaned early in life and oriented toward an ecclesiastic career by his renowned cousin, Charles BORROMEO, in whose footsteps he followed. Having completed his studies at Bologna and Pavia with a doctorate in theology (1585), he resided in Rome in the service of Sixtus V, who made him a cardinal (December 1587). He was friendly with Caesar BARONIUS, Robert BELLARMINE, JOSEPH CALASANCTIUS, and Philip NERI.

After being appointed to the See of Milan, he resided there as a leader of reform and patron of learning from 1601 until his death. He held a provincial council and 14 diocesan synods, made regular visits to the parishes, constructed churches, established colleges and academies, and built a picture gallery and, one of his most important achievments, the Ambrosian library (1609). At the conclave of 1623, he received 18 votes, but was opposed by the Spanish party.

His interest in mystical problems and his correspondence with certain sisters, such as Caterina Vannini, a former courtesan who entered the convent, caused diverse comment. Borromeo was highly regarded because of his courage and generosity during the famine of 1627–28 and the plague of 1630. His writings, though unpublished, are listed by C. Cantù—*La Lombardia nel secolo XVII* (Milan 1832, appendix D).

Bibliography: F. RIVOLA, *Vita di Federigo Borromeo* (Milan 1656), contemporary and detailed. P. BELLEZZA, *Federigo Borromeo* (Milan 1931). M. PETTROCHI, *Omaggio a Federigo Borromeo: L'uomo e la storia* (Bologna 1940). P. MISCIATTELLI, *Caterina Vannini: Una cortegiana convertita senese e il card. Federigo Borromeo alla luce di un epistolario* (Milan 1932), and the reply by A. SABA, *Federigo Borromeo e i mistici del suo tempo. Con la vita e la corrispondenza inedita di Caterina Vannini da Sienna* (Florence 1933). G. GALBIATI, *Federigo Borromeo, studioso umanista e mecenate* (Milan 1932); *Enciclopedia Italiana di scienzi littere ed arti* (Rome 1929–39) 7:512–513, with bibliog. G. MORONI, *Dizionario de erudizone storico-ecclesiastica* (Venice 1840–61) 6:60–62. C. EUBEL et al., *Hierarchia Catholica medii (et recentioris) aevi.* 3:52, 240; 4:237. P. PASCHINI, *Dictionnaire d'histoire et de géographie ecclésiastiques* (Paris 1912–) 9:1281–83.

[R. MOLS]

BOSATTA, CHIARA (CLARE) DINA, BL.

Baptized Dina, also known as Chiara de Pianello, religious of the Daughters of St. Mary of Providence; b. Pianello Lario near Como, Lombardy, Italy, May 27, 1858; d. Pianello Lario, April 20, 1887. Dina and her sister Marcellina Bosatta were among the first to support the work of Blessed Luigi GUANELLA. Living as a religious at home, Dina served the poor of her parish, from whom she contracted a disease that afflicted her the rest of her life. In 1886, she formally joined the congregation Guanella had founded, taking the name Chiara (Clare), and she served as superior of the community for a time. A contemplative, she offered God her own life to protect, raise, and educate children and young people in difficulty. Chiara died at the age of twenty-nine and was beatified by John Paul II, April 21, 1991.

Feast: April 20.

Bibliography: *Acta Apostolicae Sedis* 83 (1991): 369–71. *L'Osservatore Romano,* English edition, no. 16 (April 22, 1991): 10.

[K. I. RABENSTEIN]

BOSBOOM-TOUSSAINT, ANNA LOUISA GEERTRUIDA

Dutch novelist; b. Alkmaar, Dec. 16, 1812; d.'s Gravenhage, April 13, 1886. Bosboom-Toussaint is the best-known Dutch author of historical novels in the tradition of Walter Scott, but she did not have the passion that gave Scott his impulse to tell stories in relation to a historic past. Her passion was to recapture religious experiences, especially in times of great spiritual and social upheaval, such as the rise of the Reformation in the Netherlands.

In Bosboom-Toussaint's novels, historical facts, diligently researched and often given in too much detail, serve only as the background for emotional involvement. The attractiveness of the dominant characters in her best novels is striking, such as Paul in *Het Huis Lauernesse* (1840, The House of Lauernesse), Gideon Florensz in the *Leycester Cycle* (1846–56), and Jan Jacobsz in *De Delftsche wonderdokter* (1870, The Wonder-doctor of Delft). They are well-balanced people who, passionately devoted to the new religious ideas, stimulate others to emulate their high religious ideals. These ideals are the author's own and based on an evangelical belief in the Bible.

Bosboom-Toussaint was prejudiced against Catholicism, as represented by Capuchins, Dominicans, and Jesuits in her novels, but dealt with Catholics sincerely and honestly in daily life. Her novels are frequently ambiguous because she tried to combine the techniques of the picaresque novel with those of the novel of character. Her peculiar talent, and her greatest achievement, lies in the second field, wherein she exhibits deep psychological insight. This develops in her later novels and reaches a peak in the best, *Major Francis* (1874), a psychological study of an unconventional young woman who is molded into a fine character by love.

Bibliography: A. L. G. BOSBOOM-TOUSSAINT, *Romantische Werken,* 25 v. (The Hague 1885–88). G. KNUVELDER, *Handboek tot de geschiedenis der Nederlandse letterkunde van der aanvang tot heden,* 4 v. (Hertogenbosch 1948–53). J. M. C. BOUVY, *Idee en werkwijze van Mevrouw Bosboom-Toussaint* (Rotterdam 1935).

[P. LUKKENAER]

BOSCARDIN, MARIA BERTILLA, ST.

Nursing sister; b. Brendola, near Vicenza, Italy, Oct. 6, 1888; d. Treviso, Italy, Oct. 20, 1922. Baptized Anna Francesca, as a young girl she was pious, obedient, and quiet. She suffered because of her father's excessive drinking. At school, where she was diligent but slow to learn, she was derisively called ''the goose.'' In 1901 she took a private vow of virginity, and in 1905 she joined the DOROTHEANS at Vicenza. While a novice, she was sent to the local hospital in Treviso to work as a kitchen maid. When she made her religious profession (1907), she took the name Maria Bertilla. Returning to the hospital at Treviso, she cared for children stricken by diphtheria. Outwardly her life was not out of the ordinary. During the bombardment of Treviso after the collapse of the Italian troops at Caporetto (1917), however, her courage sustained the wounded soldiers. The advance of the German troops forced the transfer of the hospital to Viggiù, near Como, but after the armistice she returned to Treviso. She was beatified on June 8, 1952, and canonized May 11, 1961.

Feast: Oct. 20 (formerly Oct. 22).

Bibliography: *Acta Apostolicae Sedis* 44 (1952) 522–527; 53 (1961) 289–295. L. CALIARO, *La Beata M. B. B.* (Vicenza 1952). E. FEDERICI, *Santa M. B.* (Vicenza 1959). L. X. AUBIN, *Ste. Marie Bertilla* (Montreal 1963). C. DE VITO, *The Cinderella of the Gospel* (Bombay n.d.) A. BUTLER, *The Lives of the Saints*, ed. H. THURSTON and D. ATTWATER (New York 1956) 4:161–162.

[F. G. SOTTOCORNOLA]

St. Maria Bertilla Boscardin.

BOSCO, JOHN, ST.

Founder of the SALESIANS and the SALESIAN SISTERS and commonly referred to as Don Bosco; b. Becchi, near Turin, Italy, August 16, 1815; d. Turin, January 31, 1888. John's father died in 1817, and John was reared in poverty by his pious, hard-working mother, Margaret (Occhiena) Bosco. St. Joseph CAFASSO encouraged the boy's ambition to become a priest and to work with youths and directed him to enter the major seminary in Turin (1835), where John was ordained (1841). On December 8, 1841, his main work began when he met, in the sacristy of Cafasso's Institute of St. Francis, a poor orphan, Bartolomeo Garelli, and decided to prepare him for his first Communion. Soon he gathered a group of young apprentices to teach them the catechism. Through Cafasso he was introduced to the Marchesa di Barola and became chaplain at her hospice of St. Philomena for working girls. In order to devote himself completely to working with boys, he opened, in the Valdocco section of Turin, his own hospice, which grew into the Oratory of St. Francis de Sales. His mother served as housekeeper there until her death. Don Bosco gained powerful patrons, such as Abp. Franzoni of Turin and Count Camillo CAVOUR. By 1850 two workshops for shoemaking and tailoring were added to the hospice, and by 1856 there were 150 boys in residence. Later Don Bosco obtained a printing press, and he wrote and printed catechetical and pious pamphlets for youths. His reputation as a preacher became widespread, and miracles were attributed to his intercession. So successful was his work among homeless youth that even the bitterly anticlerical politician Urbano Rattazzi encouraged him.

Don Bosco experienced so much difficulty in retaining the services of young priests that from 1850 he began training his own helpers. By 1854 a group of these bound themselves together informally under the patronage of St. Francis de Sales. With Pious IX's encouragement, Don Bosco gathered 17 of them and founded (1859) a religious congregation that received papal approval in 1868. The Salesians spread quickly throughout Italy. When the founder died, there were 1,039 members and 57 houses in Italy, Spain, France, England, Argentina, Uruguay, and Brazil. The apostolate came to include work on the missions as well as the education of boys. Together with St. Maria MAZZARELLO, Don Bosco founded (1872) the Salesian Sisters for a similar apostolate among girls. In 1964 there were more than 40,000 Salesian priests, lay brothers, and sisters in all parts of the world. Don Bosco also established a kind of third order, the Salesian Cooperators, to assist in this work.

Don Bosco was preeminently an educator whose characteristic approach is known as the Salesian preventive system of education. It rejected corporal punishment and strove to place youths in surroundings that removed them from the likelihood of committing sin. Frequent confession and Communion, thorough catechetical training, and fatherly guidance were the pillars of this system of spiritual formation that also sought to unite the spiritu

St. John Bosco, painting by Giuseppe Rollini, 1888.

al life of youths with their study, work, and play. Don Bosco's insistence that boys be taught trades made him a pioneer in modern vocational training.

Don Bosco had special devotion to Mary Help of Christians and was responsible for the construction of a basilica in Turin with that title (1868). He also began the erection of the Basilica of the Sacred Heart in Rome and traveled to France in 1883 to raise funds for it. PIUS XI, who as a young priest had known Don Bosco, beatified him June 2, 1929, and canonized him April 1, 1934. He has been named patron saint of Catholic publishers and of young apprentices.

Feast: January 31.

Bibliography: Works. *Don Bosco educatore: scritti e testimonianze*, ed. P. BRAIDO, A. DA SILVA FERREIRA, F. MOTTO, and J. M. PRELLEZO (3d. ed. Rome 1997). *Il sistema preventivo nella educazione della gioventù*, ed. P. BRAIDO (Rome 1985). *Memoirs of the Oratory of Saint Francis de Sales from 1815 to 1855: The autobiography of Saint John Bosco*, tr. D. LYONS, ed. E. CERIA, L. CASTELVECCHI, and M. MENDL (New Rochelle, N.Y. 1989). *St. Dominic Savio*, tr. P. ARONICA (2d ed. New Rochelle, N.Y. 1979). *Scritti pedagogici*, ed. A. L'ARCO (Naples 1967). *Scritti spirituali*, ed. J. AUBRY (Rome 1976), Eng. tr. as *The Spiritual Writings of Saint John Bosco*, tr. J. CASELLI (New Rochelle, N.Y. 1984). Literature. P. STELLA, *Don Bosco Life and Work,* trans. J. DRURY (2d rev ed New Rochelle, N.Y. 1985). A. AUFFRAY, *Bl. John Bosco,* tr. W. H. MITCHELL (London 1930). H. GHEON, ''The Secret of Don Bosco,'' *The Secrets of the Saints,* tr. F. J. SHEED and D. ATTWATER (New York 1944). N. BOYTON, *The Bl. Friend of Youth, St. John Bosco* (2d ed. New York 1943). F. A. M. FORBES, *St. John Bosco* (Tampa, Fla. 1941). L. C. SHEPPARD, Don Bosco (Westminster, Md. 1957). E. B. PHELAN, *Don Bosco, A Spiritual Portrait* (Garden City, N.Y. 1963).

[E. F. FARDELLONE]

BOSNIA-HERZEGOVINA, THE CATHOLIC CHURCH IN

Located in the Balkan Peninsula of southeastern Europe, Bosnia-Herzegovina is bordered on the west and north by Croatia, on the east by Serbia and on the southeast by Montenegro. The country is landlocked except for a few miles of coastline along the Adriatic Sea to its south. A heavily forested region, Bosnia-Herzegovina is also mountainous. Natural resources include coal, iron, copper and manganese, while agricultural crops consist of cereals, fruits, tobacco and citrus. The steel and mining industries make up much of the region's export.

Originally under Croatian control, the region was incorporated into the former Yugoslavia until the early 1990s, when it declared independence. The poorest of the Yugoslav republics, Bosnia-Herzegovina suffered from its feudal past, and many of its citizens, after losing their landholdings through the land reforms of the interwar period, either engaged in small-scale farming, became tradesmen, craftsmen or traveled outside the region to work. Bosnia's poor economy fueled ethnic unrest which was transformed into religious intolerance due to the close connection between ethnicity and religious background. In 1991 Bosnia-Herzegovina became the site of ethnic violence as Orthodox Bosnian Serbs, with support from Serbia to the east, fought Catholic Croats and Bosniaks (ethnic Muslims) in an effort to divide the region along ethnic lines. In 1995 an accord was reached in which the region was divided between the Federation of Bosnia and Herzegovina and the Bosnian Serb Republika Srpska. NATO forces remained in the region through 2000, although no further violence was reported.

Early History. Using the Drina and Zeta rivers as lines of demarcation, Roman Emperor GRATIAN divided the area then known as Illyricum into eastern and western regions in 379. Eastern Illyricum was ruled by the Eastern Roman Empire, where Greek Byzantine culture predominated. It belonged ecclesiastically to the Patriarchate of Rome until 732, when Emperor Leo III made it subject to the Patriarchate of CONSTANTINOPLE. Western Illyricum was assigned to the Western Roman Empire in 395, and Latin culture predominated. The border between eastern and western Illyricum, passing almost through the center of what would become the kingdom of Yugoslavia, became the source of the historical unrest in the Balkan region.

Slavs entered the region in the 7th century, and by 1150 Bosnia was an independent principality under Hungarian rule. The medieval heresy of Bogomilism in the Balkans was persecuted, and the BOGOMILS, banished from Bulgaria, Serbia and Hungary, sought refuge in Bosnia where rulers received them. Bogomilism became the Bosnian national religion during the 13th and 14th centuries. Although the Holy See sent legates and organized crusades against these heretics, Bogomilism endured until the Turkish occupation of Bosnia in 1463. Under the Turks many Bogomils converted to Islam, and their descendants constituted the region's main Muslim population by the 20th century.

Orthodox Serbs settled in Bosnia-Herzegovina mostly after their country was defeated and occupied by the Turks in 1389. Priests accompanied them, and an Orthodox hierarchy was soon established. In the early 14th century, as Catholic bishops left the country due to the Bogomils, an autonomous church developed, neither Roman nor Orthodox. From 1684 to 1735, during the Turkish occupation, Bosnia had neither Catholic bishops nor diocesan clergy. Franciscans cared for those Catholics that remained, and through their active evangelizing won over many in the nobility as well as in the peasant classes. In 1735 Bosnia-Herzegovina became a vicariate apostolic, entrusted to the Franciscans. After the Turks were obliged to leave Bosnia-Herzegovina in 1878, Austria annexed the area, assuming full control in 1908. Leo XIII restored the hierarchy (July 5, 1881) in one ecclesiastical province, with the archdiocese of Sarajevo, or Vrhbosna, as the metropolitan see, and Banjaluka and Mostar as suffragan dioceses. The Orthodox were organized in 1880 as an autonomous metropolitan, with four dioceses.

Tensions between Serbia and the Austro-Hungarian empire escalated during the first decade of the 20th century, culminating in the assassination of Archduke Franz Ferdinand and his wife in Sarajevo in 1914. This murderous act by a Serbian terrorist sparked World War I, after which Bosnia was integrated into a united kingdom of Balkan nations.

Under Yugoslavian Control. Yugoslavia (South Slavia) came into being on Dec. 1, 1918, as the Kingdom of the Serbs, Croats and Slovenes. Its 95,576 square miles included Serbia, Macedonia, Croatia, Slovenia, Dalmatia, Montenegro and Voivodina. Under its constitution, dated June 28, 1921, it was a constitutional monarchy, but an absolute monarchy was established in early 1929 as the Kingdom of Yugoslavia. During World War II the region was divided through invasions by Germany and Italy, whereupon Croatia proclaimed its independence and Serbia remained nominally independent while still under German control.

Capital: Sarajevo.
Size: 19,741 sq. miles.
Population: 3,853,777 (est.) in 2000.
Languages: Croatian, Serbian, Bosnian.
Religions: 655,150 Catholics (17%), 154,000 Protestants (4%), 1,194,760 Orthodox (31%), 1,695,600 Muslims (44%), 154,267 practice other faiths.
Diocese: Vrhbosna (Sarajevo), with suffragans Mostar-Duvno and Trebinije-Mrkan, as well as a bishopric at Skopje-Prizren, located in Skopje, Macedonia.

In the Kingdom of Yugoslavia Serbs dominated the political realm, extending their power into social, cultural and religious matters despite protests by Croat and Bosnian minorities. Although the constitution of 1921 guaranteed freedom and equality to all religions, the Orthodox Serbian Church received favoritism, thereby attracting new members, and between 1918 and 1938, the Roman Catholic population decreased markedly in Yugoslavia as a whole. Although the newly established government began negotiations with the Holy See for a concordat in 1922 that would have regularized the Catholic Church's organization so that diocesan and state borders would correspond, the Orthodox Church influenced the Yugoslavian parliament into refusing the ratification of the agreement in 1935. In retaliation, during World War II, nationalist Croat priests forced Orthodox Serbs living in western Bosnia to convert to Catholicism, a factor that would have serious repercussions by the end of the 20th century.

The Church under Communism. In 1945 Bosnia-Herzegovina fell to communism with the rest of Yugoslavia when the Federal People's Republic of Yugoslavia was proclaimed under Josip Broz Tito. Although the constitution of Nov. 30, 1946 guaranteed religious liberty, the government promoted its anti-religious sentiment by open persecution. Bishop Peter Čule of Mostar was sentenced to 11 years in prison in 1948, sharing the fate of many other Catholic, as well as Muslim, leaders. All Catholic schools, except for a few minor seminaries, were closed, and religious instruction in state schools was prohibited. Church-owned property was confiscated, the Catholic press was abolished and Catholic associations were suppressed. The number of professed atheists in Yugoslavia was estimated at two million by 1953.

Fortunately for the Church, by 1948 political differences between Tito and Soviet leaders had surfaced, forcing Yugoslavia to look to Western powers for support.

Persecution of religious groups consequently diminished and by 1956 the communists had inaugurated a policy of limited cooperation. The Holy See was allowed to appoint new bishops, charges against the clergy were dropped, some religious presses resumed operation and several minor seminaries opened. In 1962 Bosnian bishops received permission to attend Vatican Council II.

In Bosnia-Herzegovina, perhaps more than in other regions of Yugoslavia, no single religion predominated: Muslims of Slav descent as well as Serbian Orthodox lived alongside Croatian Catholics. By 1961, with a population of 3,274,886—18 percent of the Yugoslav total—the region boasted one of the highest rate of sustained believers in Yugoslavia at 84 percent. While the Roman Catholic Church was able to create a stable relationship with the communist government, area Muslims, isolated from the Islamic world, had their special religious courts suppressed after 1946, and their difficulties with the communist government were exacerbated by confusion between religion and ethnicity. The communists also sought to promote Muslim solidarity as a way of preventing either Serbs or Croats from gaining supremacy, and the region's Muslim majority was denied first-class citizenship status until 1966.

Independent Once Again. With Tito's death in 1980 the government's policy toward religion became less doctrinaire, and regional governments developed policies which promoted peaceful relations within their own particular sphere of influence. By the late 1980s this liberalization allowed all faiths to be practiced openly, and a religious revival was underway by 1990, as Easter services were televised nationwide. While Yugoslavia crumbled in the early 1990s, the Muslim majority in Bosnia-Herzegovina agitated for a referendum to vote for independence.

In October of 1991 Bosnia and Herzegovina declared their independence from the former Yugoslavia. The Muslim-dominated government, established in April of 1992, was immediately confronted by violence as ethnic Serb and Croat minorities resisted the formation of a nation along non-ethnic lines. The desire of Serbs was to ignore the boundary formed by the Drina River and become annexed to Serbia to the east. During the next three years over 450,000 Catholics living in predominately Serbian areas were forced to flee, some to Croatia. Meanwhile, ethnic disputes between Bosniaks and Croats ended in 1994 with the formation of a joint Bosniak/Croat Federation and the agreement that this federation would be joined by Serbs. While Serbs agreed to the federation concept in theory, there was no consensus as to where boundary lines should be drawn, and fighting escalated to the point that by 1993 Serbs controlled most of the region. Thousands of civilians were massacred, many of them Muslims who were the target of ethnic cleansing by Bosnian Serbs. The homes of those fleeing Serbian-held areas in the north and east were destroyed to ensure that they did not return. After three years of violence UN and NATO bombing raids proved convincing and on Nov. 21, 1995, Serbs and Bosniaks met in Dayton, Ohio, to sign a peace accord creating two separate regions: a Bosniak-Croat federation in the west and a Serb-governed Republika Srpska in the north and east. The newly elected tripartite government immediately set about to privatize the economy, which had suffered during the civil war, although the trial of war criminals, the recovery of land mines, the return of church property confiscated by the Yugoslav government under communism and the relocation of refugees continued to be dealt with into the 21st century. In 1999, as fighting still raged in the republic of Kosovo, Bosnia provided refuge to many ethnic Albanians fleeing Serb violence. NATO forces, which had remained in Bosnia following the peace accord, were reduced to minimal levels by 2000.

By 2000 Bosnia-Herzegovina contained 281 parishes, tended by 210 secular and 340 religious priests, as well as 14 brothers and 540 sisters. In the Republika Srpska the Serbian Orthodox Church was considered the state church and was materially supported by the regional government, while in Bosnia-Herzegovina neither Islam nor Catholicism enjoyed special privilege. By 1999 the diocese of Banja Luka, located in the Republika Srpska, was closed, 98 percent of its churches destroyed and 412 of its parishioners killed during the violence preceding the 1995 peace. Classes in religion were offered in Bosnia's public schools, the religion taught based on the local demographics. Bosnian bishops, while taking responsibility for the retaliatory violence committed by some Croatian Catholics, called for the safe return of all Catholics to the region. Problems that erupted in 1999 after seven parishes in Mostar were given by the Vatican to Franciscans showed that ethnic tensions remained close to the surface into the 21st century. However, a return to the faith was exhibited by Croats, particularly young people, in the aftermath of the region's difficulties, and by 2000 political trends signaled a move toward multi-ethnic parties. In 2001 the Vatican backed the formation of an international tribunal to prosecute violators of human rights in the former Yugoslavia.

Bibliography: *Monumenta spectantia historiam Slavorum meridionalium* (Zagreb 1868—) 46 v. to 1951. M. SPINKA, *A History of Christianity in the Balkans* (Chicago, IL 1933). R. RISTELHUEBER, *Histoire des peoples balkaniques* (Paris 1950). P. D. OSTROVÍC, *The Truth about Yugoslavia* (New York 1952). W. MARKERT, *Jugoslawien* (Cologne 1954). F. DVORNIK, *The Slavs: Their Early History and Civilization* (Boston 1956); *The Slavs in European History and Civilization* (New Brunswick, NJ 1962). K. S. LATOURETTE, *Christianity in a Revolutionary Age: A History of Christianity in the Nineteenth and Twentieth Centuries,* 5 v. (New York 1958–62) v.1, 2, 4. F. MACLEAN, *The Heretic: The Life and Times of Josip Broz-Tito* (New York 1957). D. MANDIČ, *Bosna i Hercegovina,* 2 v. (Chicago 1960–62). S. P. RAMET, *Nihil Obstat: Religion, Politics, and Social Change in East-Central Europe and Russia* (Durham, NC 1998). J. MATL, *Lexikon für Theologie und Kirche*, eds., J. HOFER and K. RAHNER, 10 v. (2d, new ed. Freiburg 1957–65) 5:1191–94. B. SPULER and H. KOCH, *Die Religion in Geschichte und Gegenwart*, 7 v. (3d ed. Tübingen 1957–65) 3:1054–60. *Bilan du Monde,* 2:914–928. *Annuario Pontificio* has annual data on all dioceses.

[P. SHELTON]

BOSO, CARDINAL

Papal chamberlain; d. Rome, 1178. Boso was probably an Englishman who made a career for himself at the papal Curia. A Bologna necrology calls him English (the sole evidence for this), though it has been argued that he was of Lombard origin. A papal clerk and scriptor, he was made a chamberlain by ADRIAN IV in 1154–55. In this office he was responsible for the Lateran treasury and the papal finances, and he drew up a revision of an earlier book of dues, the *LIBER CENSUUM*. He became a cardinal in 1156 and was sent by Adrian on a mission of uncertain purpose to Portugal. In the disputed papal election of 1159, he held the CASTEL SANT' ANGELO in Rome for ALEXANDER III against the antipope Victor IV. He wrote useful biographies of Adrian and Alexander.

Bibliography: F. GEISTHARDT, *Der Kämmerer Boso* (Berlin 1936). G. ALBION, *Dictionnaire d'histoire et de géographie ecclésiastiques* (Paris 1912–) 9:1319–20. M. PACAUT, *Alexandre III* (Paris 1956). J. SYDOW, *Lexikon für Theologie und Kirche*, ed. J. HOFER and K. RAHNER (Freiburg 1957–65) 2:621.

[H. MAYR-HARTING]

BOSSILKOV, EVGENIJ, BL.

Bishop, first blessed of Bulgaria, and first martyr of the Communist era; b. Belene, Bulgaria, Nov. 16, 1900; d. Sofia, Bulgaria, Nov. 11, 1952. Given the name Vincent at birth by his Latin-rite family, he took the name Evgenij (Eugene) after receiving the habit of the Passionist congregation in Ere (Belgium) in 1919 where he had gone for novitiate and further seminary studies after his minor seminary years in Oresh and Rousse in Bulgaria. He was ordained to the presbyterate in 1926 and sent to Rome for further education at the Pontifical Institute for Eastern Church Studies (P.I.O.S.) where he received a doctorate after defending the thesis ''The Union of the Bulgarians with the Church of Rome at the beginning of XIII Century'' (1931). Bossilkov returned to Bulgaria where he was assigned first to the office of Bishop Damian Theelen of Nicopolis (Rousse) and later put in charge of St. Joseph's parish in the large Catholic village of Bardarski Gheran (1934). Bossilkov initiated a new style in dealing with parishioners, often going well beyond strictly spiritual needs, reaching out toward non-Catholics, especially among the intellectual and professional leaders throughout the country. He played soccer with the youth (for which petition has been made to name him patron of soccer) and hunted in the countryside with the adults.

After the Communist takeover in September of 1944, Bossilkov suffered the limitations imposed by the atheistic regime on the country and on the Church in particular. Documents indicate that he was shadowed by the intelligence service of the Communist underground long before the end of the war. When Bishop Theelen died in 1946, Bossilkov was appointed an administrator of the diocese. The following year he was named bishop. During this period, he worked closely with the apostolic delegate, Francesco Galloni, until the latter's expulsion from the country in December of 1948. At that point, persecution of the Church was escalated; all Catholic institutions were separated from the Church, religious orders were disbanded, and many priests and religious were arrested, questioned, and sent to prison. In 1952 a series of trials, some behind closed doors, deprived the Church of practically all able clergy.

In one of the trials, held September 30 to October 4, 37 ecclesiastics were sentenced to prison, while four—Kamen Vichev, Pavel Djidjov, Josaphat Shishkov, and Bishop Bossilkov—received death sentences. The evidence brought up during the examination of Bossilkov's cause shows that the real grounds for his harsh sentence was his refusal to head a schismatic national church. Half a century elapsed before documents could be produced (1992) that proved the execution had been carried out late in the night of Nov. 11, 1952. Bossilkov's grave is unknown, though his blood-stained shirt and pectoral cross were later returned to his family.

The canonization process was initiated in the West by the order of the Passionist Fathers in 1985. However, the regime in Bulgaria, not having recovered from the international uproar over their alleged connection with the attempt on the life of the pope (May 13, 1981), put great pressure on the Bulgarian bishops in the country. They in turn convinced church authorities in Rome to suspend the process (December 1985). When the political climate changed and normal diplomatic relations were established between Bulgaria and the Holy See in the summer of 1991, Bishop Samuil Djoundrin of Bossilkov's native diocese made formal petition that the process be resumed. Bossilkov was beatified March 15, 1988 by Pope John Paul II.

Bibliography: *Canonizationis seu Declarationis Martyrii Servi Dei Eugenii Bossilkov, C.P. Positio super Martyrio* (Rome 1993). PIERLUIGI DI EUGENIO, *Beato Eugenio Bossilkov. Morire per la fede* (Teramo 1998). GIORGIO ELDAROV, *Bossilkov*. Collection of articles in: *Abagar* (*Bulgarian Catholic Journal*) 3 and 4 (1998) (in Bulgarian).

[G. ELDAROV]

BOSSUET, JACQUES BÉNIGNE

French writer, bishop and orator; b. Dijon, France, Sept. 27, 1627; d. Paris, April 12, 1704. He was the seventh child of Bénigne Bossuet, a judge in the parliament of Dijon, and Madeleine Mochet. For more than half a century his ancestors, both paternal and maternal, had occupied judicial posts. He began his classical studies at the Jesuit college in Dijon and, when his father was appointed to the parliament of Metz, remained in Dijon under the care of an uncle. He made remarkable progress, at the same time becoming thoroughly acquainted with the

Bible, which always remained his principal source of inspiration. Destined for the Church, he received the tonsure at the age of eight and at 13 obtained a canonicate in the cathedral of Metz. Moving to Paris in 1642, he continued his classical studies adding philosophy and theology, at the Collège de Navarre. He defended his theses for the Bachelor in Theology (*tentativa*) in 1648, was ordained subdeacon the same year, deacon the next, and began to preach at Metz. His theses for the Licenciate were defended in 1650 and 1651, after which he prepared for the priesthood under St. Vincent de Paul (1576–1660). He was ordained March 18, 1652, and received the degree of doctor of theology a few weeks later. He then resided at Metz for seven years, engaged in preaching, study of the Bible and the Fathers, discussion with Protestants, and activities as a member of the Assembly of the Three Orders. He was associated also with the Compagnie du Saint-Sacrement.

In 1659 Bossuet returned to Paris on business for his chapter, but was induced to remain there as a preacher, largely through the influence of Vincent de Paul and the Queen Mother, Anne of Austria. He retained his connection with Metz and was appointed dean when his father, a widower, became a priest and canon at the same cathedral. In 1670 Bossuet was consecrated bishop of Condom. Although he was not obliged to reside in his diocese, his convictions in this matter caused him to resign a year later, at which time also he was elected to the French Academy. He was named tutor to the Dauphin in 1670 and threw himself energetically into his functions, even composing books for his pupil's instruction (see below). After the Dauphin's marriage in 1681, Bossuet was assigned to the bishopric of Meaux. He administered his see in residence, following the Assembly of the French Clergy in 1682, but was called away more and more frequently to Paris or to wherever the court might be staying. His health was failing by 1700, but he continued to defend his principles to the end, dictating letters and polemical essays to his secretary from his bed.

Court Orator. Bossuet's eminence as an orator is uncontested. He has been called the voice of France in the age of Louis XIV and is a perfect exemplar of the period's classicism. His simple but facile vocabulary well served the intensity of his thought, often expressed in the deep sonority of periodic sentences. His thought turned normally to terms of universality, majesty, balance, order, and *raison* in the 17th-century sense. He was passionately devoted to unity and considered its attainment possible only in absolutism. He believed in the divine right of kings and in a hierarchy involving both Church and State; and if he was himself somewhat authoritarian, this resulted probably from his conviction that it was his duty to demand from inferiors and those he directed the same obedience that he himself must render to superiors. Yet he was remarkably human, and, until his last years, conciliatory to the point of being accused of weakness.

Jacques Bossuet.

With unfailing courage—and with some success—he preached and counseled against the King's adulterous liaisons. When Louis bridled, insisting that monarchs are above the law of men, Bossuet conceded this much but insisted that even kings are not above the law of God. Although this stand was clearly taken, Bossuet continued to admire the great ruler who, with all his faults, could unify and glorify France. Inspired by St. Vincent, Bossuet pleaded the cause of the poor against the extravagance of the court, but at the same time he felt that the proper discharge of his own role demanded a certain wealth, used with detachment of spirit. He also frankly enjoyed position and power, but most biographers find no justification for the charge that he actively sought them. He remained at court probably because he was convinced that his presence there acted as a Christian leaven in the midst of corruption.

Bossuet was physically and mentally robust and usually convinced that he was right. He was sometimes sanguine to the point of naïveté. Thus he approved the revocation of the Edict of Nantes (1685), while neither approving nor expecting the use of force, because he was convinced that Protestants would be amenable to the new ruling and would collaborate for Christian unity. (*See* NANTES, EDICT OF.)

Writer and Preacher. Bossuet's first published work, *Réfutation du catéchisme du sieur Paul Ferry, ministre de la religion prétendue réformée* (1655), was directed against a Protestant pastor at Metz. During this early period he began also to compose and preach panegyrics on the saints. Those on St. Francis of Assisi (1652), St. Bernard (1653), St. Paul (1657), and the Apostle Peter (1661) are among the best. The studies served as bases for moral lessons; he employed the same tactic in his masterpieces, the *Oraisons funèbres.* The first of these was preached at Metz, but the more highly perfected ones came later, notably those for Henriette de France (1669), for Henriette d'Angleterre (1670), and for le Prince de Condé (1687).

Bossuet's ordinary sermons, not composed for publication, were scattered in manuscript and note form and have been recovered only gradually and incompletely. His greatest preaching period extended from 1659 to 1670. He was invited to give the Lenten sermons at the Louvre in 1662 and his stern commentary on the wicked rich, the efficacy of Penance, death, and so on, sometimes leveled at the King personally, and accompanied by threats of damnation, was little calculated to improve its author's welcome, although it was recognized that a genuine orator had emerged from a host of preachers. Soon, however, he became involved in the Jansenist controversy (*see* JANSENISM). The degree of his sympathy with PORT-ROYAL is debated. While he undoubtedly favored the austere Jansenist morality and condemned what he considered the ''easy devotion'' of the Jesuits, he agreed with full conviction that five propositions drawn from *AUGUSTINUS* were to be found in Port-Royal doctrine and should be condemned. His own spirituality was Bérullian (*see* BÉRULLE, PIERRE DE), influenced by St. Vincent de Paul and by the works of St. Francis de Sales (1567–1622).

Three of Bossuet's most important works were composed primarily for the instruction of the Dauphin: *Traité de la connaissance de Dieu et de soi-même* (1677), *Politique tirée de l'Écriture Sainte* (1679), and the *Discours sur l'histoire universelle* (1681). He considered the *Discours* his most important written work; he published two revisions, and was working on another at the time of his death. In what was one of the first ''philosophies of history,'' Bossuet conceived the whole of history as directed by Providence, and in relation to a single event, the Incarnation. In philosophy as such, Bossuet was partially Thomist, but he taught the Dauphin the ideas of Descartes, which he later repudiated. In the Assembly of the Clergy called by the King to deal with jurisdiction over vacant episcopal sees, the whole question of papal authority and the rights and liberties of the Gallican church came up for debate (*see* GALLICANISM). Although Bossuet was Gallican by family tradition and patriotism and did not believe in papal infallibility, he had no thought of renouncing due submission to Rome. He sought a compromise and was chosen to draw up the Four Articles (1682) that Pope Innocent XI rejected. An act of submission from the French bishops in 1693 ended the troubles, and it was chiefly Bossuet's loyalty and spirit of moderation that recalled France from the brink of schism.

Severity of His Later Years. To the period of Meaux belongs his *Histoire des variations des églises protestantes* (1688); in 1691 he began a correspondence with LEIBNIZ, a kindred spirit who, from the Protestant point of view, also dreamed of a Christian unification of the world. Their rapprochement failed and their hopes were soon abandoned. So many reverses in Bossuet's grandiose plans began to weaken the patience that had always characterized him, and a certain harsh and sometimes unjust insistence marked his final controversies. He was a ruthless foe of any innovations in Biblical or historical criticism and strongly opposed the works of R. Simon and L. Ellies do Pin's *Bibliothèque des auteurs ecclésiastiques.* He began furiously to blame the classics and the theater for relaxed morality, and condemned all poetry and amusement. These ideas are expressed in his *Traité de la concupiscence* (1693) and *Maximes sur la comédie* (1694). Most 17th-century moralists tended to frown upon the theater, but Bossuet's frown was as grim as the Jansenists'. In this period the great quarrel over QUIETISM arose (especially *c.* 1694–1700). Bossuet, neither conversant with mysticism nor drawn to it by temperament, worked hard to grasp its meaning when asked to examine Mme. GUYON, whom FÉNELON defended. Bossuet recognized in Mme. Guyon an unbalanced personality and a false mysticism. He had a hand in the Articles of Issy that condemned propositions drawn from Mme. Guyon's writings. Bossuet wrote during this affair the *Instruction sur les états d'oraison* (1696) and *Relation sur le quiétisme* (1698). His remaining years were troubled by the resurgence of Jansenism; his death however reflected the calm and majesty of his great works.

Bibliography: *Oeuvres complètes,* ed. E. N. GUILLAUME, 10 v. (Bar-le-Duc 1877); *Oeuvres oratoires,* ed. J. LEBARQ et al., 7 v. (Paris 1922–27); *Correspondance,* ed. C. URBAIN and E. LEVESQUE, 15 v. (Paris 1909–25). J. CALVET, *Bossuet: L'Homme et l'oeuvre* (Paris 1941); *Histoire de la littérature française,* v.5 (Paris 1939) 259–319, good bibliography 450–453. A. RÉBELLIAU, *Bossuet* (Paris 1900). J. TRUCHET, *La Prédication de Bossuet* (Paris. 1960), A. LARGENT, *Dictionnaire de théologie catholique,* ed. A. VACANT et al. (Paris 1903–50; Tables générales 1951–) 2:1049–89. P. DUDON, *Dictionnaire de spiritualité ascétique et mystique. Doc-*

trine et histoire, M. VILLER et al., 1:1874–83. W. J. SIMPSON, *A Study of Bossuet* (New York 1937). D. O'MAHONY, ed., *Panegyrics of the Saints: From the French of Bossuet and Bourdaloue* (St. Louis 1924), also contains parts of other works of Bossuet. A. G. MARTIMORT, *Le Gallicanisme de Bossuet* (Paris 1953).

[L. TINSLEY/J. M. GRES-GAYER]

BOSTE, JOHN, ST.

One of martyrs of Durham; b. Dufton, Westmoreland, *c.* 1543; d. Dryburn, near Durham; July 24, 1594. John Boste (Boast, Bost) was educated at Queen's College, Oxford, and after receiving his M.A. took the Oath of Supremacy. However, he was converted to Catholicism in 1576 and four years later began his studies for the priesthood at the English College at Rheims. He was ordained in 1581 and returned to England to an active apostolate among the English Catholics. Traveling disguised as a servingman in the livery of Lord Montacute, he visited Norwich, Maidenhead, Colnbrook, and Gloucestershire. Most of his missionary years were spent in the northern counties—Westmoreland, Cumberland and the Border, Durham, and Yorkshire. Because of his energy and success, he was sought after by both his Catholic friends and the English government. He was betrayed by a Catholic apostate, Francis Ecclesfield, and arrested near Durham, September 1593. He was conveyed to York, and thence to the Tower of London. Several times he was tortured in an effort to make him reveal his associates and was finally sent back to Durham for trial in July 1594, together with Father John Ingram and George Swallowell, both later beatified. Boste was charged under the statute of 1585 with having been ordained abroad as a Roman priest and with having returned to England to further the Catholic faith. He refused to plead to the indictment, saying he would not have a jury guilty of his blood. When accused of having had foreknowledge of the attempt at a Spanish invasion he answered: ''It is our [priests'] function to invade souls, and not to meddle with these temporal invasions.'' He was condemned for high treason and sentenced to be hanged, drawn, and quartered. His trust and tranquility in the face of death inspired Swallowell, who in his fear was near apostatizing, to persevere. Boste endured his martyrdom with heroic resolution, joy, and fortitude, forgiving his executioners and inspiring a multitude of spectators. He was beatified in 1929 and canonized in 1970. (*See* ENGLAND, SCOTLAND, AND WALES, MARTYRS OF.)

Feast: July 24; Oct. 25; May 4.

Bibliography: R. CHALLONER, *Memoirs of Missionary Priests,* ed. J. H. POLLEN (new ed. London 1924). J. MORRIS, ed., *The Troubles of Our Catholic Forefathers Related by Themselves,* 3 v. (London 1872–77) v.3. *Publications of the Catholic Record Society* 1 (1905); 5 (1908). T. COOPER, *The Dictionary of National Biography from the Earliest Times to 1900* (London 1908–09), 2:884.

[A. M. C. FORSTER]

BOSTIUS, ARNOLD

Carmelite theologian and humanist (known also as Arnold van Vaernewijck); b. Ghent, 1445; d. Ghent, April 4, 1499. Bostius, subprior and possibly prior at Ghent, served as a spiritual director to Carmelite nuns. He was greatly influenced by the Carmelite reformer Bl. John SORETH (D. 1471). Keenly interested in the humanistic movement, Bostius promoted classical studies within his order and was in contact with such leading humanists as ERASMUS, Sebastian TRITHEMIUS, Robert BRANT, GAGUIN, and Bl. BAPTIST OF MANTUA. He was a proponent of the Immaculate Conception and wrote about the Virgin Mary's patronage of the Carmelites (*De patronatu et patrocinio Virginis Mariae*). Bostius also composed works on the history of his order (*De illustribus viris; Speculum historiale;* and *Breviloquium tripartitum*).

Bibliography: ''Epistolae Arnoldi Bostii Gandavensis,'' *Monumenta historica Carmelitana,* ed. B. ZIMMERMANN (Lérins 1907) 511–522. P. S. ALLEN, ''Letters of A. B.,'' *English Historical Review* (London 1886) 34 (1919) 225–236. C. DE VILLIERS, *Bibliotheca carmelitana* (Orléans 1752); ed. G. WESSELS, 2 v. in 1 (Rome 1927) 1:198–200. A. DE SAINT PAUL, *Dictionnaire d'histoire et de géographie ecclésiastiques* (Paris 1912–) 4:555–558. G. MESTERS, *Lexikon für Theologie und Kirche,* ed. J. HOFER and K. RAHNER (Freiburg 1957–65) 1:892–893. E. R. CARROLL, *Doctrina Mariologica Arnoldi Bostii, 1445–1499* (Doctoral diss. unpub. Pontifical Gregorian U. 1951); *The Marian Theology of Arnold Bostius, O.Carm., 1445–1499* (Rome 1962).

[K. J. EGAN]

BOSTON, ARCHDIOCESE OF

The Diocese of Boston (Bostoniensis) was formed April 8, 1808 as one of four subdivisions of the original U.S. Diocese of Baltimore, and was raised to the rank of archdiocese in 1875. In 2001, the Archdiocese of Boston extended over five counties in Eastern Massachusetts, Suffolk, Essex, Middlesex, Norfolk, and Plymouth (with the towns of Mattapoisett, Marion, and Wareham excepted, in order to connect Cape Cod and the Islands with the mainland portion of the Fall River Diocese). Catholics numbered 2,038,032, 53 percent of the total population of 3,857,751. Suffragans of the Ecclesiastical Province of Boston, in addition to the Dioceses of Massachusetts, Fall River, Springfield, and Worcester, include the sees of Burlington, Vermont, Manchester, New Hampshire, and Portland, Maine.

Early History The explorer Samuel de Champlain mapped the coast of New England in two successive voy-

The wedding of Mary Curley, and Lt. Col. Edward C. Donnelly, inside the Cathedral of the Holy Cross, performed by William Cardinal O'Connell, 1935, Boston. (©Bettmann/CORBIS)

ages, 1604 and 1605, while he was a colonist at Sainte Croix, Maine; a priest Nicholas Aubry was chaplain for the colony established in 1604. In this same period an Englishman named Waymouth also planted the cross in the region in preparation for the attempt under Lord Thomas Arundel to establish an English Catholic colony, a venture that proved unsuccessful. The French colonists were attacked by the English from Virginia in 1613, and all but a few left Sainte Croix for Cape Sable. On Nov. 3, 1620, the English crown granted a patent for a colony between 40 and 48 degrees North Latitude in the region to be called New England. Plymouth was settled in 1620, and Salem, and Boston in the following decade.

Colonial Anti-Catholicism. The only priests in the region at the time were beyond the Kennebec River. Although the Massachusetts Bay Colony had passed a law in 1647 to ban the presence of any priest in the colony, Gabriel Druillettes, SJ, was allowed to visit Boston in December 1650 to discuss trade proposals between Canada and the English colony. The antipriest law was reenacted in 1700, with a penalty of life imprisonment for offenders and death for a priest who might escape confinement. From 1685 the observance of Pope's Day (November 5) gave public expression to hatred of the Catholic Church. Recurring battles between the colonists and the combined French and Native American forces to the north culminated in the Norridgewok raid on Aug. 23, 1724, and the death, among others, of the Native Americans' chaplain, Sebastian RALE, SJ. The victorious Boston captain brought the priest's scalp and those of 27 natives to Boston to claim the bounty of £100 from the Massachusetts Council. A peace treaty signed Aug. 6, 1726, assured the Native Americans religious freedom.

Meanwhile Massachusetts maintained a hostile attitude toward Catholicism, evidenced in the annual Dudleian Lectures at Harvard and the continued observance of

Pope's Day. The latter custom was checked only during the Revolution by the action of General Washington, who ordered an end to its observance among his troops. On the eve of the Revolution, the Quebec Act, which in 1774 granted religious freedom in Canada, was resented in Boston, but hostility had to give way to the practical considerations of trying to win the cooperation of Canada. In addition, the aid given by France in the war and valiant military service of Catholics in the cause of liberty led to the granting of religious freedom in the Massachusetts constitution of June 15, 1780.

Beginning of Organized Church. French naval chaplains said Mass in Boston during the war years. The French officer Chevalier de St. Sauveur, killed in a riot in Boston, was buried in King's Chapel in September 1778, and before a parish was established Mass was offered by the occasional French visitors. The first native Bostonian to become a priest was John THAYER, a convert in 1783 from Congregationalism and a Yale graduate, who was ordained in Paris, June 2, 1787. The first foundation of the Church in Boston was the work of a renegade French naval chaplain, Claude Florent Bouchard, who called himself Abbé de la Poterie. Born in 1751 at Craon and ordained for the Diocese of Angers in 1777, he served two terms as a naval chaplain before leaving the fleet when it sailed from Boston, Sept. 28, 1788. He offered the first public Mass in Boston, Nov. 2, 1788, in a church formerly used by Huguenots and Congregationalists. The relic of the true cross brought to Boston by the abbé is still preserved in the Cathedral of the Holy Cross. The superior of the Catholic Church in the U.S., John Carroll, extended faculties to Poterie until, after several months, the abbé's debts, troubles with the French consul, and damaging letters from French ecclesiastical authorities dictated that he be suspended. To replace the abbé, Carroll sent Father Louis de Rousselet, who found it difficult to work in harmony with Thayer. The latter's pastorate in Boston (1790–92) was troubled by controversies with Protestants as well as by disputes with Rousselet that led to open schism. The situation was settled by the departure of both under the direction of Carroll, now bishop, and the assignment to Boston of the French refugee priest, Francis Anthony MATIGNON.

Arriving in Boston, Aug. 20, 1792, Matignon found only a few Catholics attending Mass because of the factional strife of the preceding years. He quickly healed the division, and Catholics in New England soon numbered 500. His appointment as Carroll's vicar-general for New England was followed by the arrival on Oct. 3, 1796, of his former student Jean Lefebvre de CHEVERUS. Like Matignon, Cheverus had refused the oath supporting the civil constitution of the clergy in France and had escaped to England, where he received Matignon's invitation to Boston. There he aided the pastor in constructing Holy Cross Church according to plans drawn up by Charles Bulfinch. Cheverus was subjected to court trials over his right to perform marriages and to counsel people who were taxed to support local ministers. Despite these difficulties, when the new church was dedicated on Sept. 29, 1803, the Catholic flock in New England numbered 1,000. Indefatigable mission tours of the vast area invigorated religious life and attracted Protestants and Catholics alike. Father Cheverus was active in the process of conversions. He knew Dr. Stephen Cleveland Blyth of Salem who, after extensive study, was baptized in 1809, followed by Thomas Walley in 1814. The Barber family of Claremont, N.H., was responsible for scores of conversions, leading with their own turning to the faith and religious life, and the English consul in Boston requested Baptism on his deathbed. Elizabeth SETON wrote to the Boston priests for guidance in her early years as a Catholic.

Establishment of the Diocese On April 8, 1808, Pope Pius VII erected a diocese for New England, which was to be a suffragan of Baltimore, and named Cheverus the first bishop of Boston.

Cheverus. The consecration of the new bishop was delayed for two years by the blockade of Papal States' ports. After authentic copies of the bulls reached Baltimore, he was solemnly consecrated there on Nov. 1, 1810. He then conferred with his brother bishops, visited Mother Seton at Emmitsburg, and returned to Boston. The War of 1812 impaired the commerce of the city and hurt Cheverus's efforts to establish schools. Catholic groups helped build fortifications when the city was threatened by British troops. A legacy of Thayer, who died in Ireland, Feb. 17, 1815, provided for the foundation of an Ursuline school in the city. By 1820 the first nuns had arrived. Cheverus suffered a crushing loss in the death of Matignon on Sept. 19, 1818, a loss scarcely lightened by the tributes of the newspaper and the signs of public mourning.

Immigration brought Catholics to all parts of New England, where by 1820 political liberty for Catholics was fully realized. In 1823, although he had refused to accept nomination to the See of Montauban, Cheverus was commanded by the King of France to return. With great reluctance and over the protests of Catholics and Protestants in New England, he departed on Sept. 26, 1823. In 1826 he was named archbishop of Bordeaux and shortly before his death (July 19, 1836) was raised to membership in the College of Cardinals. Boston, numbering five priests and 4,000 Catholics, was administered by William Taylor, vicar-general, until a successor was named.

Fenwick. The second bishop of Boston, Benedict Joseph FENWICK, was a native American of a Colonial Maryland family, who entered the Society of Jesus and was ordained June 11, 1808. Thereafter he served in New York for nine years, was twice president of Georgetown College, vicar-general for Georgia and the Carolinas, and pastor in Maryland. He was consecrated on Nov. 1, 1825, in Baltimore by Abp. Ambrose Maréchal and took possession of his diocese on December 4. He found that the number of priests had fallen to three, the number of Catholics had increased to 7,000, and that he had only eight churches in addition to the cathedral to serve them.

The bishop set about building more churches to meet the needs of immigrants attracted to New England by the development of manufacturing centers and the building of canals and railroads. In 1826 he moved the Ursuline school to Mount Benedict in Charlestown. He brought students into his own house to prepare them for the priesthood. Meanwhile, at Claremont, N.H., the convert Barber family led a flood of conversions. New churches sprang up to the south of Boston and in Vermont, with continued attention given to the Native Americans in Maine. Cheap rates of passage brought great numbers of Irish to New Brunswick and thence to New England. In 1833 Bishop Fenwick began his Catholic colony at Benedicta, Aroostook County, Maine, planning to have mills, homes, and schools. Two members of the new community of the Sacred Hearts of Jesus and Mary were obtained and aid for the growing diocese came from the Society for the PROPAGATION OF THE FAITH and the Austrian Leopoldine Society.

Fenwick's era counted many physicians as converts; as well as such ministers as George Haskins and William Hoyt; the artist David Claypoole Johnson; Ruth Charlotte Dana; and such members of the Brook Farm colony as Isaac Hecker and Mrs. George Ripley. Orestes Brownson was perhaps the most distinguished convert of the period. Unfortunately, however, the rapid growth in the number of Roman Catholics caused grave anxiety among native Bostonians, and led to sporadic episodes of violence. The revival of evangelical Protestantism after 1820 intensified attacks on the Church, both verbal and physical. Boston witnessed bloody street riots during the 1830s and 1840s, and the Ursuline Convent was burned to the ground on Aug. 11, 1834.

In 1843 Hartford was made a diocese, encompassing Connecticut and Rhode Island. Plagued by such troubles as TRUSTEEISM, nationalism, and bigotry (*see* NATIVISM), Fenwick continued to expand his diocese. At his death in 1846 there were 39 priests, 48 churches, and 70,000 Catholics. He took special pride in the foundation of the Jesuit College of the Holy Cross at Worcester, Mass., June 21, 1843. To him goes the credit for the first clergy retreat in Boston and the first synod in 1842; regular catechism for the children of the diocese (four hours weekly); the establishment of homes for orphan boys and girls (the latter cared for by Sisters of Charity from 1832); the inauguration of a Catholic newspaper in 1829 (first called the *Jesuit* continued as the *Pilot* in 1836); approximately 2,000 conversions; and a significant role in the first five Provincial Councils of Baltimore. His death on Aug. 11, 1846, after an episcopate that was the turning point in the history of the Catholic Church in New England, was followed by a procession through the streets of Boston.

Fitzpatrick. Fenwick had consecrated his successor, Boston-born John Bernard Fitzpatrick, March 24, 1844, in the chapel of the Visitation nuns at Georgetown. During his two years as coadjutor of Boston, Fitzpatrick made visitations to Maine and Vermont and administered Confirmation in all parts of the diocese, where his charity made him a beloved figure, known to all as Bishop John. Gifted and urbane, he also won entry into the society of the Cabots and the Lodges. Five trips to Maine and two to Vermont led him to propose the separation of the northern states into two new dioceses in 1853, Burlington for Vermont, and Portland for the states of Maine and New Hampshire. This division gave eight churches to Burlington and 24 to Portland, leaving Boston with 63 churches. Fitzpatrick's schoolmate, Louis de Göesbriand, was named first bishop of Burlington, and until the choice of a bishop for Portland was settled in 1855, Fitzpatrick administered that diocese. He opposed as premature the proposal that Boston be raised to an archdiocese.

In 1854 he was the first Boston bishop to make the *ad limina* visit. In Rome he discussed with the Jesuit general and his council his hope of opening a college in Boston; and in Paris he obtained a renewal of aid from the Society for the Propagation of the Faith. With 57 priests in the diocese by 1854, the bishop named as the first chancellor and secretary, an African American priest, Father James Healy, who later became bishop of Portland. A clergy society was formed to aid sick and aged members of the clergy, and to parish life were added such new organizations as the Sodality, Propagation of the Faith, and the Association of the Holy Childhood. Generous contributions were made to relieve famine victims in Ireland, and the generosity of Yankee neighbors increased the total to $150,000. At home the needs of increasing numbers of immigrants were met. Hundreds of homeless children were sheltered in St. Vincent's Orphan Asylum and the House of the Angel Guardian. Through the generosity of Andrew Carney, the hospital that bears his name was opened (1863). Schools multiplied, and Boston College was established by the Jesuits in 1863. Bishop Fitzpatrick's prominence in the Boston community led to a number of significant conversions including George M. Searle, later Paulist general and director of the Vatican Observatory; Paul Revere's grandson; Nathaniel Hawthorne's daughter; and Longfellow's niece, Marion.

The remarkable influx of Irish-Catholic immigrants during the late 1840s and early 1850s as a result of the Great Famine produced a strong and angry reaction from native Bostonians, who resented the demands the newcomers placed on their social services and who feared the impact of their Catholic faith on their democratic institutions. During the mid-1850s, nativists formed the American Party—popularly known as the Know-Nothing Party—designed to preserve America from the "insidious wiles of foreigners." Hoping to put their political candidate in the White House in 1856, they planned to strengthen the national immigration laws, while keeping present immigrants in subservient positions. Nativists insisted that Catholic children read a Protestant version of the Bible in public schools, and refused to allow Catholic priests to minister to Catholics in public institutions. Bishop Fitzpatrick responded by avoiding public violence, and by regular appeals to the laws and to the courts, as well as a determined insistence on the constitutional rights of American Catholics.

During the Civil War, Boston Catholics fought proudly for the preservation of the Union. Three priests of the diocese served as military chaplains, and the patriotism of Boston Catholics, particularly in the 9th and 28th Regiments at Bull Run, Antietam, Gettysburg, and the Wilderness, scored a victory over bigotry in Massachusetts. In 1861 Harvard University conferred an honorary doctor of divinity degree on Fitzpatrick. Under his supervision plans were drawn by Patrick Keeley for a new cathedral; however, it could not be constructed until after the war. Fitzpatrick, an invalid during his last years, died Feb. 13, 1866, four days after the papal bulls arrived naming John J. WILLIAMS his coadjutor with right of succession.

Williams. The fourth bishop of Boston and its first archbishop had served as pastor of St. James in Boston and vicar-general before his nomination as coadjutor *cum iure* Jan. 8, 1866. During the 40 years following his consecration (March 11, 1866, at St. James Church) churches and schools multiplied beyond any expectation. Diocesan synods were held in 1868, 1872, 1879, and 1886; the last was mistakenly numbered the fourth, when in fact it was the fifth synod in Boston. At Vatican Council I, Abp. Martin J. Spalding's proposal for a compromise solution of the debate on infallibility was endorsed by Williams. At his suggestion, the Diocese of Springfield was created June 14, 1870, embracing five counties of central and western Massachusetts and taking from Boston 52 churches, 40 priests, and 100,000 people. Two years later, when Rhode Island was separated from the Diocese of Hartford as the Diocese of Providence, Williams gave up four counties in southeastern Massachusetts and three towns in Plymouth County to assure sufficient population for the new diocese. Fifteen churches, as many priests, and 30,000 Catholics were affected by this transfer.

Establishment of the Archdiocese The rapid growth of the Church in New England was recognized on Feb. 12, 1875, when the New England states were constituted a province, with Boston as the archdiocesan see. Williams received the pallium from Cardinal John McCloskey May 2, 1875. Following the dedication of the new Cathedral of the Holy Cross Dec. 8, 1875, the archbishop built St. John's Seminary, Brighton, blessing the first building on Sept. 18, 1884, and staffing it with Sulpicians headed by the Abbé John Baptist Hogan. A second building was opened in 1890, and the Romanesque chapel was completed in 1899. In response to the constant growth of his flock, which now included immigrants from Portugal (the Azores and Cape Verde Islands), Poland, Lithuania, Germany, Italy, and the Near East, Williams set up a matrimonial tribunal in 1893 and named a superintendent for archdiocesan schools in 1897. Through its branches of the Society for the Propagation of the Faith, Boston by 1904 led the entire world in its contributions to the missions.

Carmelites were brought to Boston in 1890 and Franciscan Poor Clares, in 1899. The Little Sisters of the Poor established their apostolate, the Sisters of St. Joseph undertook teaching duties, and the Sisters of the Good Shepherd came with their protective mission. Hospitals were built in Cambridge (Holy Ghost), Lowell (St. John's), and Boston (St. Elizabeth's). When he was 82, Williams asked for a coadjutor with the right of succession. In 1906 Rome named Bp. William H. O'CONNELL of Portland, Maine, who became second archbishop of Boston at Williams's death, Aug. 30, 1907.

O'Connell. Boston's fifth ordinary and second archbishop brought to his task not only experience as an ordinary in Portland, but Roman training and a worldwide comprehension of the Church. During his 37-year rule he undertook the reorganization of the archdiocese, an intensification of apostolic activities, and an adjustment of relations with the community. The centenary of the diocese was observed in 1908, the fifth synod was held Feb. 11, 1909, the duties of the chancellor were broadened, 32 new parishes were set up in four years, and annual retreats for the clergy ordered. The *Pilot* was purchased as a diocesan journal, Boston College moved from its original location in the South End to a new campus in suburban Newton, and the seminary was transferred from

Sulpician to diocesan management. Several institutions were saved from bankruptcy. Father James Anthony WALSH was released from the archdiocese to establish the MARYKNOLL FATHERS, the American foreign mission society. Passionists and the Religious of the Cenacle came to Boston to direct retreats. On Nov. 27, 1911, O'Connell was created cardinal priest, with the title church of St. Clement; he took part in the election of Pius XII in 1939, having failed twice before to arrive in Rome in time to vote in the conclaves that ended in the elections of Benedict XV and Pius XI. During World War I he issued frequent messages on behalf of the war effort and gave over diocesan facilities in the influenza epidemic of 1918. The sixth synod, April 7, 1919, resulted in the naming of rural deans, synodal judges, and a diocesan building commission. Between 1907 and 1944, the number of churches grew from 248 to 375; parishes, from 194 to 322; priests, from 598 to 1,582; brothers, from 140 to 356; and sisters, from 1,567 to 5,469. Religious communities of men increased from 13 to 21; those of women, from 29 to 44. O'Connell remained well and active, without need of a coadjutor or more than one auxiliary bishop, until his death April 22, 1944.

Cushing. At O'Connell's death, his auxiliary, Richard James CUSHING, was named administrator and became archbishop of Boston Sept. 25, 1944. Born in Boston Aug. 24, 1896, he attended Boston College and St. John's Seminary, was ordained May 26, 1921, and consecrated bishop June 10, 1929. He was raised to the College of Cardinals Dec. 15, 1958, as cardinal priest, with the title church of Santa Susanna. Under his direction the number of colleges in the archdiocese doubled, from three to six: Boston (Newton), Cardinal Cushing (Brookline), Emmanuel (Boston), Merrimack (Andover), Regis (Weston), and Newton College of the Sacred Heart (Newton). Social works were inaugurated to meet the needs of the aged, the handicapped, and the homeless. The vast building program reached every corner of the archdiocese from seminary and chancery to hospitals, schools, catechetical centers, churches, convents, and rectories. An ecumenical committee was organized in 1963 to promote dialogue with Protestants and Jews. The Sacramental Apostolate of the Archdiocese offered lectures and information on liturgical topics. The Holy Name Society, the Sodality of Our Lady, and the Confraternity of Christian Doctrine expanded their influence to all parishes. The program of lending priests to other dioceses, which Cushing began soon after his installation, developed into the MISSIONARY SOCIETY OF ST. JAMES THE APOSTLE. Established, July 1958, the Society sent English-speaking diocesan priests from Boston and from elsewhere to Peru, Bolivia, and Ecuador. Cushing's apostolate included recitation twice daily of the Rosary by radio, televised Mass on Sunday, the first television channel allotted to a diocese in the U.S. (WIHS), local and long-distance pilgrimages, and personal visits to Protestant and Orthodox audiences. In 1952 the seventh synod was held. A year later the separation from Hartford left Boston a province with six suffragans. The Sons of Mary, a medical mission community of diocesan status, was founded by Edward Garesché, SJ, at Framingham in 1952. The first national seminary for late vocations, named for Pope John XXIII, with a capacity of 100 seminarians opened in Weston, Mass., in 1964.

Medeiros. In 1970, after a period of declining health, Cardinal Cushing resigned, and was succeeded by Humberto S. Medeiros, Bishop of Brownsville, Tex. Born in 1915 in the Portuguese Azores, Medeiros and his family moved to America in 1931 and settled in the town of Fall River, some 50 miles south of Boston. Ordained a priest in 1946, he pursued graduate theological studies, graduating with a doctorate in sacred theology from Gregorian University in 1949. Medeiros became the second bishop of Brownsville in 1966, before succeeding Cushing as Archbishop of Boston in 1970. In 1973, Pope Paul VI named him to the College of Cardinals. One of the first things that Medeiros addressed was the reduction of the archdiocesan debt of some $40 million, reducing it to a manageable level by 1977. Medeiros also reorganized the archdiocesan administrative bodies. He created three episcopal regions: the North Region, the South Region, and the Central, or Greater Boston Region. The number was later increased to four, with the addition of a West Region. Each region was under the supervision of a regional bishop who reported directly to the archbishop. To promote vocations and to stimulate greater lay involvement, Cardinal Medeiros restored and revitalized the office of the permanent diaconate. In May 1976, the first class of permanent deacons was ordained in the Cathedral of the Holy Cross. Medeiros also drew up new guidelines to reinvigorate the various campus ministries in the numerous colleges and universities in the Boston-Cambridge area. It was also Medeiros who brought the Catholic Church even closer to the laity by authorizing the appointment of eucharistic ministers in all parishes in the archdiocese. After trying in vain to come up with an equitable resolution to the bitter racial conflict over school desegregation and court-ordered busing that divided the city of Boston during the mid-1970s, Cardinal Medeiros died unexpectedly on Sept. 17, 1983.

Law. On Jan. 24, 1984, the Holy See announced that the Most Reverend Bernard F. Law, bishop of Springfield-Cape Girardeau, would succeed Medeiros as the eighth bishop and the fourth archbishop of Boston. Born in Torreon, Mexico, Nov. 4, 1931, Law graduated from Harvard University in 1953, and pursued theological studies at The Pontifical College Josephinum at Columbus, Ohio, before his priestly ordination in May 1961. In 1973, Pope Paul VI appointed him bishop of the Diocese of Springfield-Cape Girardeau, Mo. In 1984, Law became archbishop of Boston, and a year later named to the College of Cardinals. As Archbishop of Boston, Law retained the system of four episcopal regions established by his predecessor, and also added a fifth episcopal region, Merrimack, incorporating parishes from the West, the South, and the Central region. He established a special committee to suggest ways to further modernize diocesan operations and reduce expenditures. On the basis of its recommendations, he created a cabinet system for the archdiocese, with a series of cabinet secretaries incorporating the work of some 87 agencies which had formerly operated as independent units. In place of a previous system of multiple archdiocesan collections throughout the year, Law established a single major fundraising event called the Cardinal's Appeal that provided the basis for an annual diocesan budget. Several firsts occurred under Law's episcopacy, including the appointment of a layman as chancellor of the archdiocese; a woman religious as judge on the archdiocesan marriage tribunal; and lawyers, business leaders, and physicians as cabinet secretaries. Law was a major influence in the publication in 1994 of the new *Catechism of the Catholic Church*, and he promoted a Catholic health-care network called Caritas Christi within the archdiocese. Law also took a keen interest in the affairs of the Church throughout Latin America, but especially in Cuba where, in January 1998, he led a group of pilgrims in support of the historic visit of Pope John Paul II to that country. In light of rapid demographic changes, Law was forced to close a number of old churches that were either in depopulated areas or had been serving older European national groups. At the same time, he created new parishes in suburban areas with younger families, as well as in urban districts where new Asian, Haitian, and Latin American residents had settled. The last years of Law's tenure were clouded by a major scandal over his handling of pedophiles in the priesthood.

Bibliography: R. H. LORD et al., *History of the Archdiocese of Boston . . . 1604 to 1943,* 3 v. (New York 1944; Boston 1945). T. H. O'CONNOR, *Boston Catholics: A History of the Church and Its People* (Boston 1998). W. H. O'CONNELL, *Recollections of Seventy Years* (Boston 1934). A. M. MELVILLE, *Jean Lefebvre de Cheverus, 1768–1836* (Milwaukee 1958). T. H. O'CONNOR, *Fitzpatrick's Boston, 1844–1866* (Boston, 1984). J. E. SEXTON and A. J. RILEY, *History of St. John's Seminary, Brighton* (Boston 1945). D. G. WAYMAN, *Cardinal O'Connell of Boston* (New York 1955). J. M. O'TOOLE, *Militant and Triumphant: William Henry O'Connell and the Catholic Church in Boston, 1859–1944* (Notre Dame, 1992).

[T. F. CASEY/T. H. O'CONNOR]

BOSTON COLLEGE

A Jesuit coeducational university in Chestnut Hill, Mass., on the borderline of Newton and Boston. Its origins and history are closely allied to the pastoral ministry of the Society of Jesus in Massachusetts that began in 1825 when Benedict Joseph Fenwick, SJ, was named bishop of Boston. In 1847 Fenwick's successor, Bp. John B. Fitzpatrick, invited members of the Jesuit society to take charge of St. Mary's Church in Boston's North End.

Boston was one of the principal East-Coast cities inundated, during the late 1840s and early 1850s, with Irish Catholic immigrants seeking sanctuary from the potato famine and from political oppression. Since the majority of these newcomers had little formal education and the demands of a hostile community frequently caused hardship to many young students, there was pressing need for parochial schools in Boston. While Fitzpatrick's most immediate concern was for elementary schools, John McElroy, SJ, at St. Mary's, was considering the possibility of a Catholic college in the city. Following his appointment by President James K. Polk as a chaplain in Zachary Taylor's army during the Mexican War, in 1847 McElroy was assigned to Boston where he continually urged the establishment of a Catholic college. Although the difficulties involved in establishing, financing, and staffing such a college made the prospects discouraging, McElroy pressed forward with determination.

After a long struggle, McElroy obtained a tract of land in a residential area in Boston's South End where he constructed the Church of the Immaculate Conception and the red-brick building that was the nucleus of Boston College. In March 1863, while the Civil War was at its most critical phase, the Massachusetts Legislature approved the university charter. When Boston College formally opened as an institution of advanced learning in September 1864, the first president, John Bapst, SJ, presided over a faculty of six Jesuits and a student body of 22 young Bostonians.

New Location. The modern history of Boston College begins in January 1907 with the appointment of Thomas I. Gasson, SJ, as its 13th president. Shortly after his accession he began the search for a new location to accommodate the growing student body and make room for expansion. He chose the Lawrence farm, a rolling hillside overlooking the Chestnut Hill Reservoir. The architect Charles Donagh Maginnis laid elaborate plans for a campus to be constructed in the English Collegiate Gothic style. The original edifice, the Gasson tower building, completed in 1913, continues to dominate the campus.

The period after World War II was a time of further growth with the influx of returning veterans and the financing of the GI Bill. In 1948 enrollment passed the 5,000 mark. Under college president Rev. Michael P. Walsh, SJ, the property was extended, new academic buildings were constructed, student dormitories were built, and a professional faculty was recruited. From a small, all-male, liberal arts commuter college, Boston College had evolved into one of the largest coeducational Catholic universities in the United States. It expanded into dozens of magnificent structures spread over three campuses covering some 200 acres.

The main or middle campus, with gothic-style buildings clustered around the Gasson tower, contains the Jesuit residence, the university libraries, the administrative buildings, and most of the classroom buildings for the College of Arts and Sciences, the graduate school, the Carroll School of Management, the Lynch School of Education, the Graduate School of Social Work, and the College of Advancing Studies. Adjacent to the Bapst Library is the Burns Library of Rare Books and Special Collections, with an Irish collection composed of rare Irish first editions and manuscripts, as well as works of art by contemporary Irish artists. The newer Thomas P. O'Neill Library, named after the long-time speaker of the U.S. House of Representatives, serves as the main research facility on the campus.

To the east of the middle campus of Boston College is the lower campus, which is the site of several undergraduate dormitories, the university's Robsham Theater, and the University Church of St. Ignatius Loyola. It is also the location of the university's major athletic facilities. West of the middle campus is the upper campus, the location of housing for freshmen and sophomores. In 1974, Boston College acquired Newton College of the Sacred Heart, about a mile-and-a-half west of the main campus. The Newton Campus became the location of the Boston College law school and the Boston College alumni association, as well as several residence halls.

In 1972, Rev. J. Donald Monan, SJ became the 24th president of Boston College, and under his direction the university streamlined its fiscal management, broadened its academic programs, attracted an enrollment of students representing 40 states and 27 foreign countries, and established a national reputation. It was during his tenure in office that the College acquired the property of Newton College of the Sacred Heart. By the end of Monan's twenty-four year presidency—the longest in the history of the institution, Boston College had a total enrollment of some 12,500 students—8,500 undergraduates and 4,000 graduate students. The number of full-time faculty members had risen to more than 500 lay professors, and 130 Jesuits, many of whom came from Third World countries to pursue graduate study. In the 1980s, the Jesuit community at Boston College established a multimillion-dollar foundation to support the Jesuit Institute, a research center of Catholic theology and thought.

When Father Monan was named chancellor of the university in 1996 he was succeeded in the presidency by the Rev. William P. Leahy, SJ. Under Leahy's direction Boston College continued the 400-year-old tradition of education according to the principles of the Jesuit RATIO STUDIORUM.

Bibliography: C. DONOVAN, et al., *History of Boston College: From the Beginnings to 1990* (Chestnut Hill 1990). R. DUNIGAN, *A History of Boston College* (Milwaukee 1947). W. E. MURPHY, "The Story of Boston College," *The Catholic Contribution to Religion and Education* v.5 of T. H. O'CONNOR, *Boston Catholics: A History of the Church and Its People* (Boston 1998). W. S. BENSON et al., *Catholic Builders of the Nation,* ed. C. E. MCGUIRE, 5 v. (Boston 1923). E. BOYLE, *Father John McElroy, the Irish Priest* (Washington 1878). R. H. LORD et al., *History of the Archdiocese of Boston in the Various Stages of Its Development, 1604–1943,* 3 v. (New York 1944). O. HANDLIN, *Boston's Immigrants, 1790–1880: A Study of Acculturation* (rev. ed. Cambridge, Mass. 1959). M. L. HANSEN, *The Atlantic Migration, 1607–1860* (Cambridge, Mass. 1940). M. P. HARNEY, *The Jesuits in History* (Chicago 1962).

[T. H. O'CONNOR]

BOSWELL, JAMES

Scottish man of letters, convert to Roman Catholicism; b. Edinburgh, Oct. 29, 1740; d. London, May 19, 1795. Boswell was the eldest son of Lord Auchinleck, of an old and staunchly Presbyterian family. Though he studied law and was admitted to the bar, he was always more attracted to literature. He visited Corsica in 1766 and first distinguished himself as a writer with his *Account of Corsica* (1768) and *Essays in Favour of the Brave Corsicans* (1769). Hero-worship stimulated his best writing and was the inspiration for his famous *Life of Samuel Johnson* (1791). As Johnson's guide he made the tour through Scotland that provided material for *Tour to the Hebrides* (1785). His copious journals, unpublished during his life, were discovered 135 years after his death.

Boswell was an eccentric and remarkable character, often vehemently attacked for his sycophancy, his conceit, and his immorality. His severest critics, however, are constrained to praise the charm and lucidity of his style and his gift for capturing the personalities of his acquaintances and the flavor of their conversations. Shrewd judgment and conscientious art underlie the deceptive ease of his narration. His writing is full of humor and captures unique pictures of life in Scotland and London in the 18th century.

At the age of 17 Boswell ran away to London and was received into the Catholic Church. As a Catholic in penal times he would have been prevented from following any professional career and from succeeding to the family estates. He accordingly concealed his conversion and did not live as a Catholic, although his journals contain many references to attending Mass. He avoided any formal abjuration of his beliefs, and on occasion argued with Dr. Johnson in defense of them. He left in his will a request for prayers for his soul, but this was suppressed by his heirs, who held no belief in purgatory.

Although devoted to his wife, Boswell was frequently unfaithful to her. He constantly expresses contrition for his marital lapses and for his bouts of drunkenness; he laments his weakness of character, which plunged him into periods of terrible despondency. He writes even of his own conceit and pretentiousness with candor and humility. The affection he inspired in men of high principle and discrimination is a tribute to his capacity for loyalty and friendship.

Bibliography: J. BOSWELL, *Note Book, 1776–1777,* ed. R. W. CHAPMAN (London 1925); *Private Papers of J. Boswell from Malahide Castle,* ed. G. SCOTT and F. A. POTTLE, 18 v. (London 1928–34); *Letters,* ed. C. B. TINKER, 2 v. (London 1924); D. B. WYNDHAM LEWIS, *The Hooded Hawk* (London 1946). The Yale edition of the Private Papers of James Boswell, ed. F. A. POTTLE et al. (New York): *London Journal, 1762–1763,* ed. F. A. POTTLE (1950); *Boswell in Holland, 1763–1764* (1952); *Boswell on the Grand Tour* 2 v. (1953–55); *Boswell in Search of a Wife, 1766–1769* (1956); *Boswell for the Defence, 1769–1774* (1960); *The Ominous Years, 1774–1776* (1963).

[G. SCOTT-MONCRIEFF]

James Boswell, engraving by E. Finden of a Joshua Reynolds painting. (Archive Photos)

BOTSWANA, THE CATHOLIC CHURCH IN

The Republic of Botswana is an arid, mostly agricultural country in the interior of Africa, bordered on the west and north by Namibia, on the northeast by Zimbabwe, and on the south and southeast by the Republic of South Africa. The terrain is flat, rising to gently rolling hills and the southwest is encompassed by the Kalahari Desert. Although Botswana's natural resources include diamonds, copper, nickel, salt and silver, large-scale diamond mining only began in the 1980s. Agricultural crops include sorghum, corn, millet, nuts, beans and livestock. One of Botswana's principal exports has traditionally been human labor, as many citizens went to work in South Africa or Zimbabwe, sending much of their earnings home to support the family left behind.

Known as Bechuanaland from 1884 to 1966, the region was a British protectorate administered by a high commissioner together with Swaziland and Lesotho (formerly Basutoland). Most of the population lives along the eastern border. Commercial developments in the country operate in the Western capitalistic model, while the tribal, communal system of property ownership prevails elsewhere.

History. The Holy Ghost Fathers established the first Catholic missions *c.* 1880, but were ultimately unsuccessful. In 1889 the territory was confided to the Oblates of Mary Immaculate, and the German Oblates began laboring in the southern section in 1923, establishing a mission near Gaborone five years later. In 1930 Mariannhill Missionaries began to labor in the northern parts. The Prefecture Apostolic of Bechuanaland, created in 1959 and entrusted to the Passionists, included the entire country.

Although the Church supported the country's policy of harboring refugees from South African apartheid policies during the latter half of the 20th century, by the 1990s the strain of supporting refugee populations from both South Africa and violence-torn Rhodesia (now Zimbabwe) had proved detrimental. While for some more affluent refugees, Botswana served as a stopping-off point to acquire air transportation to another refuge, for thousands of others, it served as a temporary home during

Capital: Gaborone.
Size: 225,000 sq. miles.
Population: 1,576,470 in 2000.
Languages: English, Setswana.
Religions: 236,470 Catholics (15%), 39,460 Muslims (2.5%), 614,815 Protestants (39%), 47,310 Anglicans (3%), 638,415 follow other Christian or indigenous faiths or are without religious affiliation.
Diocese: Gaborone, suffragan to Bloemfontein, South Africa. An apostolic vicariate is located in Francistown.

their wait for the return of political and social stability in the country from which they had fled. International aid met the needs of refugees to some extent, but the increasing number of clients and the delay in the arrival of aid caused considerable suffering among the new arrivals.

By 2000, the Catholic Church remained a minority faith in Botswana, and had 42 parishes, seven diocesan and 40 religious priests, and approximately five brothers and 40 sisters. The Church operated nine primary schools and six secondary schools in the country. Due to the increasing wealth of the region as the diamond mining operations expanded in the 1990s into 2000, the Church was able to turn from issues of survival to deal with such matters as unemployment, family life and countering the negative effects wrought by rising affluence. The government supported full religious freedom, and provided no financial subsidy to any religious group. One challenge addressed by the Church in Botswana was adapting the teachings of the Church to the region's African culture. Another was the spread of HIV/AIDS, which was estimated to have infected a third of the population by 2000—the highest rate of infection of any nation in the world.

Bibliography: W. E. BROWN, *The Catholic Church in South Africa* (New York 1960). *Bilan du Monde,* 2:123–124. *Annuario Pontificio* has information on the diocese.

[J. E. BRADY/EDS.]

BOTULPH OF ICANHOE, ST.

Abbot and monastic founder; fl. 7th century. Very little is known about him, for the *Anglo-Saxon Chronicle* states merely that in 654 ''Botulf began to build a minster at Ycean-ho,'' and the anonymous *Historia abbatum,* once mistakenly attributed to BEDE, mentions him as ''a man of distinguished achievement and learning, dedicated to the spiritual life,'' who was already famous in his own lifetime. It was only in the 11th century that Folcard, Abbot of THORNEY, recorded the historically unreliable and legendary life. According to this legend, Botulph was the brother of St. Adulph, an alleged bishop of Utrecht, of whose existence at Utrecht there is no record. The two brothers left their native England to become monks on the Continent, but Botulph returned and founded a BENEDICTINE monastery at Icanhoe, a location now generally identified with Boston (Botulphstown). He is said to have died *c.* 655 and to have been buried with Adulph in the sanctuary of his foundation, which, however, was destroyed in the Danish invasions. His cult was widespread, especially in Norfolk, and the brothers share the same feast day in most calendars.

Feast: June 17.

Bibliography: Sources. ''The Anglo-Saxon Chronicle,'' ed. H. PETRIE et al., in *Monumenta historica britannica* (London 1848) 1:312. ''Historia abbatum auctore anonymo,'' in *Venerabilis Baedae opera historica,* ed. C. PLUMMER, 2 v. (Oxford 1896) 1:389. J. MABILLON, *Acta sanctorum ordinis S. Benedicti,* 9 v. (Paris 1668–1701; 2d ed. Venice 1733–40) 3.1:3–7. *Acta Santorum,* June 4:324–330. Literature. F. WORMALD, ed., *English Kalendars before A.D. 1100,* v.1 (Henry Bradshaw Society 72; London 1934) 161, 203, 245, 259. F. S. STEVENSON, *Proceedings of the Suffolk Institute of Archaeology and Natural History* (Ipswich 1922) 29–52. A. M. ZIMMERMAN, *Kalendarium Benedictinum: Die Heiligen und Seligen des Benediktineorderns und seiner Zweige,* 4 v. (Metten 1933–38) 2:322, 324–325. F. O'BRIAIN, *Dictionnaire d'histoire et de géographie ecclésiastiques,* ed. A. BAUDRILLAT et al. (Paris 1912–) 9:1433–34. S. BRECHTER, *Lexikon für Theologie und Kirche,* ed. J. HOFER and K. RAHNER, 10 v. (2d, new ed. Freiburg 1957–65) 2:625–626.

[J. BRÜCKMANN]

BOTURINI BENADUCI, LORENZO

Historian and collector of Mexican antiquities, devotee of Our Lady of Guadalupe; b. Sondrio, Lombardy, Italy, 1702; d. Madrid, Spain, apparently in 1755. Little is known of Boturini's early life. He studied in Milan and spent some time in Vienna and Lisbon. In Madrid, he met the Countess of Santibáñez, a descendant of the Aztec Emperor Montezuma, who in 1735 ceded to Boturini a yearly stipend of 1,000 pesos paid her from the royal treasury of Mexico City. By February of 1736 he was in Mexico City collecting the pension. Boturini became interested in the pilgrimages to the shrine of Our Lady of GUADALUPE at Tepeyac and in the tradition that the Virgin Mary had appeared there in December of 1531. To find documentary evidence of this miracle, he began intensive research into the native North American past. He learned Nahuatl so that he could converse with the natives in their own tongue and collected native codices of historical events. In his enthusiasm, he spent six years accumulating a fine collection of documents, even though few of them bore direct testimony to the apparitions. By then he planned to use the material to write a new history of colonial Mexico.

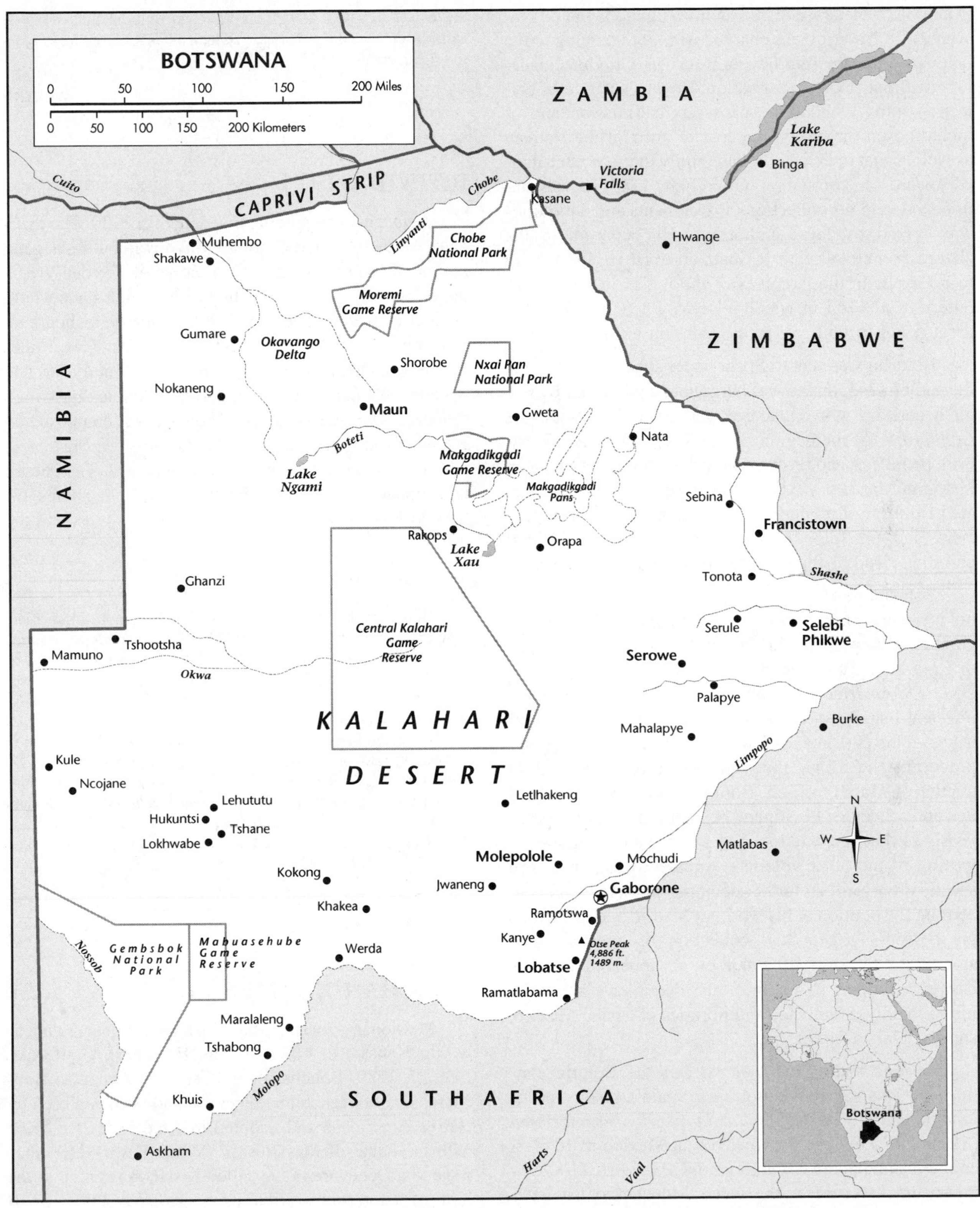

In the meantime, he wished to contribute to the devotion to Our Lady of Guadalupe by placing a golden crown over her head on the miraculously painted image. In July of 1740 he obtained permission from ecclesiastical authorities in Rome to do so, and he began to solicit funds for the coronation. Late in 1742 the new viceroy, the

Count of Fuenclara, ordered an investigation, and on November 28 Boturini was charged with both coming to the colony and promoting devotion to Our Lady of Guadalupe without royal authorization. He was accused of collecting alms without the necessary permission and of including on the crown the coat of arms of the Vatican as well as that of a noble Italian family that had contributed toward the coronation. On Feb. 4, 1743, he was imprisoned, and his collection of documents and antiquities was seized by local authorities. His answers to the charges, sent to officials in Spain on April 16, 1743, were to no avail. In the Archives of the Indies in Seville are letters from 1743 in which Viceroy Fuenclara wrote in great detail to Philip V of the Boturini affair.

Boturini was sent to Spain under special vigilance at the end of 1743, but he was put ashore at Gibraltar by English corsairs who plundered and sunk his vessel, the *Concordia*. At the beginning of 1744, he arrived in Madrid, penniless, and received assistance from the Mexican historian Mariano Veytia. The Council of Indies exonerated Boturini of all charges. He was given a yearly pension, and on July 10, 1747, he was named official chronicler and historian of the New World.

Boturini never returned to Mexico and therefore did not repossess his collection of antiquities. He did, however, attempt to write the history of the Indies, and by April of 1749 he had finished the first volume of *Historia general de la América septentrional.* It was an account of the physical features of the valley of Mexico, its indigenous tribes, their customs, and way of life. Even though approved by the crown, the work was never published. In a letter of March 6, 1755, Boturini reminded officials of this and asked that his stipend be increased to 5,000 pesos yearly so that he could return to Mexico and continue the writing of the other volumes. Apparently Boturini died shortly afterward; no further documentation is found concerning the petition or his work. In Madrid and in Mexico his personal papers and collection of ancient MSS, amounting to some 40 volumes, disappeared in time. However, copies of many of the documents are to be found mainly in archives and libraries of Spain, Mexico, and the United States.

Besides writing his *Historia general,* Boturini outlined the general division of New Spain's history in the *Idea de una historia general de la América septentrional* (Madrid 1746). This was reedited in Mexico in 1871. It contains an appendix, *Catálogo del Museo Histórico Indiano,* that lists some of the materials the author had gathered when he lived in Mexico. Boturini also wrote a short treatise in Latin on the apparitions of Our Lady of Guadalupe.

Bibliography: J. GARCÍA ICAZBALCETA, *Diccionario universal de historia y de geografia,* 10 v. (Mexico City 1853–56) 1:676–677. J. TORRE REVELLO, ''Lorenzo Boturini Benaduci y el cargo de cronista de las Indias,'' *Boletín del Instituto de Investigaciones Históricas* 5 (1926–27) 52–61.

[N. F. MARTIN]

BOTVID, ST.

Active in evangelizing Sweden; d. *c.* 1120. The exact dates of his birth and death are unknown, but his legend seems fairly reliable. Botvid, a native of Sweden, was a pious layman, and he was killed by a foreign slave whom he had converted and freed. His relics were honored, probably from 1129 and translated in 1176. Two offices are known; the older was found in a 13th-century MS and is composed partly in prose, partly rhythmically, with a sequence *Almi patris merita.* The later was composed by Bp. Nicolaus Hermanni (d. 1391) as a *historia rhythmica,* with the sequence *Celi chorus esto gaudens.* The church and village of Botkyrka (Botvidskyrka) are named for him. In iconography he is symbolized by the ax and the fish.

Feast: July 28.

Bibliography: *Scriptores rerum Suecicarum medii aevi,* ed. E. M. FANT et al., v.2 (Uppsala 1828) 377–387. *Analecta hymnica* (Leipzig 1886–1922) 25:179–181; 42:180–181; 43:104–105. I. G. A. COLLIJN, *Redogörelse för på uppdrag af Kungl. Maj:t i Kammararkivet och Riksarkivet verkställd undersökning angående äldre arkivalieomslag* (Stockholm 1914); ed., *Acta et processus canonizacionis beate Birgitte* (Uppsala 1924–31) 81, 486, 619, issued in 10 pts. BRIDGET OF SWEDEN, *Revelationes,* Extravagantes, ch. 72. T. SCHMID, ''Eskil, Botvid och David,'' *Scandia* 4 (1931) 102–114. H. JÄGERSTAD, *Lexikon für Theologie und Kirche,* ed. J. HOFER and K. RAHNER, 10 v. (2d, new ed. Freiburg 1957–65) 2:626. A. BUTLER, *The Lives of the Saints,* rev. ed. H. THURSTON and D. ATTWATER, 4 v. (New York 1956) 3:204.

[T. SCHMID]

BOUCHARD, JAMES

Missionary, orator; b. Muskagola, near Leavenworth, Kansas, *c.* 1823; d. San Francisco, California, Dec. 27, 1889. Bouchard's mother, also surnamed Bouchard, was of French ancestry; she had been captured by Native Americans and adopted into the Delaware Tribe with the name of Monotowan (White Fawn). Her marriage to a Delaware brave called Kistalwa resulted in the birth of a son whose tribal name was Watomika (Swift Foot). After his father's death in a skirmish with the Sioux in 1834, Watomika was taken by a Protestant missionary to Marietta College, Ohio, where he studied for the Presbyterian ministry. While visiting St. Louis, Missouri in late 1846 or early 1847, he was converted to Catholicism by the Jesuit missionary Arnold Damen. Bouchard entered the Jesuits at Florissant, Missouri on July 29, 1848, and was ordained on Aug. 5, 1855, in St. Francis Xavier's College Church, St. Louis. He was the first Native American to be ordained in the United States. After several years of ministry in the Midwest, he was assigned to California. He arrived in San Francisco on Aug. 16, 1861, and was soon in demand as a retreat master, pulpit orator, and lecturer. He was asked to preach at the dedications of St. Vibiana's Cathedral, Los Angeles (1876), and the Cathedral of the Blessed Sacrament, Sacramento (1889), and also spoke on public issues such as the Chinese question in California. In addition to his speaking engagements, he devoted himself to missionary activity in the mining camps and towns of the Mother Lode section of California.

Bibliography: J. B. MCGLOIN, *Eloquent Indian: The Life of James Bouchard, California Jesuit* (Stanford 1949).

[J. B. MCGLOIN]

BOUILLON, EMMANUEL THÉODOSE DE LA TOUR D'AUVERGNE

French diplomat, prelate; b. Turenne, Aug. 24, 1643; d. Rome, March 2, 1715. He was educated at the College of Navarre in Paris, and received the doctorate in theology at the Sorbonne in 1667. In 1669 he was created a cardinal at the request of Louis XIV, and two years later was named Louis's chief almoner. However, he became involved in court intrigue through his efforts to further his family's fortunes, and was removed from office and exiled to the abbey of Cluny by the king in 1685. Eventually he was back in favor and for a time was the royal representative in Rome. Again Bouillon irritated Louis XIV by failing to demand the condemnation of Fénelon at Rome and by refusing to answer the king's summons back to France. Despite the royal displeasure, Bouillon functioned in Rome as dean of the cardinals, and directed the conclave that elected Clement XL. Finally he submitted and accepted retirement, first at Cluny (1701–09), and then in Holland (1709–13). In 1713 he returned to Rome, died there, and was buried at the Jesuit novitiate.

Bibliography: L. DE ROUVROY SAINT-SIMON, *Mémoires*, ed. A. DE BOISLISLE, 41 v. (Paris 1879–1928) v.7, 26. F. REYSSIÉ, *Le Cardinal de Bouillon 1643–1715* (Paris 1899). A. DE BOISLISLE, "La Désertion du cardinal de Bouillon en 1710," *Revue des questions historiques* 84 (1908) 420–471; 85 (1909) 61–107, 444–491.

[C. B. O'KEEFE]

BOULAY, CÉSAR ÉGASSE DU (BULAEUS)

Educator and historian; b. Saint-Elier (Mayenne), *c.* 1600; d. Paris, Oct. 16, 1678. Boulay's early career was that of teacher of humanities and rhetoric, first at Poitiers, then at the College of Navarre. In 1661 he was named rector of the University of Paris. In 1662 he was made registrar of the University. He is best known as an historian of the University of Paris. Between 1665 and 1673 he published a six-volume history of the University in Latin, entitled *Historia Universitatis Parisiensis*, covering the period from its origins to the time of its reformation by Henry IV. Boulay also wrote an abridged version in French, *Histoire de l'université*, as well as seven separate works in French on the organization and history of the university. His work is less a conventional history than a collection of documents to support his interpretation of the origins of the University. According to Boulay the University was founded by Charlemagne and consisted originally only of the faculty of arts and the four nations. This interpretation, which gave to the faculty of arts exclusive rights to name the rector and to the four nations equal status with the faculties of theology, medicine, and law, was challenged by the interested parties. He was also accused of misappropriating funds for the writing of his books. He died before the latter charge was investigated.

Bibliography: C. H. JOURDAIN, *Histoire de l'Université de Paris au XVIIe et XVIIIe siècle* (Paris 1862). A. TUILIER, *Histoire de l'Université de Paris et de la Sorbonne* (Paris 1994). J. M. GRES-GAYER, *Le Gallicanisme de Sorbonne, 1656–1688* (Paris 2001).

[J. W. BUSH/J. M. GRES-GAYER]

BOUQUILLON, THOMAS JOSEPH

Educator, moral theologian; b. Warneton, Belgium, May 16, 1842; d. Brussels, Belgium, Nov. 5, 1902. Bouquillon had a brilliant career as a student in the Collège of Saint-Louis in Menin, and later in the preparatory seminary at Roulers and the major seminary at Bruges, Belgium. He entered the Capranica in Rome and was ordained in 1865. Two years later, he received his doctorate from the Gregorian University and returned to the seminary in Bruges, where he was appointed professor of moral theology. In 1877 he was appointed to the Catholic University of Lille, France where he taught moral theology until 1885. He spent four years (1885–89) with the Benedictines of the Abbey of Maredsous, Belgium, and then accepted the invitation of Bp. John J. KEANE, first rector of The Catholic University of America in Washington, D.C., to join the original faculty as professor of moral theology.

Bouquillon's theological knowledge was exceptionally wide, encompassing more than is usually included within the limits of moral theology. He was an expert on the theologians of 16th– and 17th–century Spain and the Netherlands. His influence on the academic development of the new university in Washington was considerable; he planned and selected a basic theological library of 30,000 volumes. He cultivated in his students a critical sense of history as the context for their theological understanding. A prodigious author and commentator on the subjects of the day, he published a pamphlet on education (1891) that aroused great opposition throughout the United States and Europe (*see* BOUQUILLON CONTROVERSY). In addition to more than 50 scholarly articles in several languages in such journals as *Revue des sciences ecclésiastiques, Nouvelle revue théologique, Revue Bénédictine, American Catholic Quarterly Review,* and *The Catholic University Bulletin,* his published works include *Theologia Moralis Fundamentalis* (1903), *De Virtutibus Theologicis* (1890), and *De Virtute Religionis* (2 v. 1880). He completed, but did not publish, three other works: ''De Justitia et Jure,'' ''De Eucharistia,'' and ''De Penitentia.'' He edited and added critical notes to the following: *De Magnitudine Ecclesiae Romanae* of Thomas Stapleton (1881), *Leonis XIII Allocutiones, Epistolae, Aliaque Acta* (first 2 v. 1887), the *Catechismus ad Parochas* (1890), the *Dies Sacerdotalis* of Dirckinck (1888), *L'Excellence de la très sainte eucharistie* of Luis de Granada, and *Synopsis Cursus Theologiae* by Platel.

In June of 1902 Bouquillon left Washington for Europe, where he became ill and died in Brussels.

Bibliography: J. FORGET, *Dictionnaire de théologie catholique* (Paris 1903–50) 2.1:1093–94. *The Catholic University of America Bulletin* 9 (1903) 152–163. C. G. HERBERMANN, ''The Faculty of the Catholic University,'' *American Catholic Quarterly Review* 14 (1889) 701–715. J. T. ELLIS, *The Formative Years of the Catholic University of America* (Washington 1946).

[J. P. WHALEN]

BOUQUILLON CONTROVERSY

An educational dispute precipitated in the U.S. in 1891 by the FARIBAULT PLAN, a compromise school arrangement effected by Abp. John Ireland with the public school boards of Faribault and Stillwater, Minn. Its name came from Rev. Thomas BOUQUILLON, professor of moral theology at The Catholic University of America, Washington, D.C., whose theory granting the state a special and proper right to educate engendered contradictory reactions.

Cause. Concomitant with the rise of the public school system in the U.S. between 1820 and 1870 was a growing tendency to secularize tax-supported schools. The American hierarchy, urged by the Congregation of Propaganda Fide in 1875, passed laws at the Third Plenary Council of Baltimore in 1884 discouraging attendance at public schools and pressing the construction of parochial schools. The hierarchy, however, were not unanimous in the execution of the laws. In 1890 Archbishop Ireland of St. Paul, Minn., and other bishops pleaded poverty as an excuse from building and maintaining parochial schools, and proposed giving daily religious instructions to Catholic students in public schools outside class hours as an alternative solution. Abp. Michael A. Corrigan of New York and certain Jesuit writers championed parochial schools as envisioned by the decrees of the Third Plenary Council of Baltimore.

In the midst of this practical debate over constructing parochial schools, Bouquillon published his pamphlet, *Education: To Whom Does It Belong?* Although he claimed that his tract was ''a purely abstract exposition of principles independent of circumstances of time and country,'' the arguments presented so buttressed the position championed by Ireland and his party that Bouquillon was accused of knowingly offering the theoretical basis for Ireland's solution to the school question. The publication date, Nov. 18, 1891, ten days before the American hierarchy was to meet in St. Louis, Mo., to debate the issue, seemed to confirm that suspicion.

Bouquillon held that education ''belongs to the individual, physical or moral, to the family, to the state, to the church; to none of these solely and exclusively, but to all four combined in harmonious working . . . .'' By ceding this right to an individual and equating the rights of the family, the State, and the Church, Bouquillon offered a new view for Catholics on the right to educate.

Regarding the State's power in this area, moreover, he maintained that ''the state has been endowed by God with the right of founding schools that contribute to its welfare.'' Based on this prerogative, therefore, the State has the further right to pass compulsory education laws, determine the minimum of obligatory instruction, establish schools, appoint capable teachers, prescribe branches of knowledge, and inspect hygiene and public morality.

The Rejoinder. It was incumbent on Catholic educators favoring establishment of parochial schools to answer these arguments, especially the seeming equality of State and Church in conducting schools. René Holaind, SJ, Professor of Ethics at the Jesuit seminary, Woodstock College, Md., prepared an answer within a week of Bouquillon's publication and before the bishops' meeting. Holaind's main objections were: (1) teaching is essentially the duty of the Church and the parents; the State, which has no proper right to educate, enters the field of education at the bidding of the family and/or the Church; (2) the State enters the field of education only when it is entirely necessary and not merely when it is useful to contribute to the State's welfare; (3) the State has no right to control instruction in non-State schools since this would abrogate the rights and duties of parents and Church to open schools and control instruction.

Ecclesiastical Intervention. The two pamphlets generated such a heated public discussion in the religious and secular press that both sides appealed to Rome to settle the problem. In November 1892 Abp. Francesco Satolli, a special representative of Rome, presented to the assembled hierarchy ''Fourteen Propositions Designed for the Settling of the School Question,'' which, since they were more practical than theoretical, left the basic issue unsolved. Rome, in fact, had intended that the hierarchy debate the propositions secretly among themselves, and then by majority vote, reach an agreement emanating from Catholic principles. The propositions, however, were leaked to the secular press and the controversy could not be solved in the heat of the ensuing public debate.

In view of this impasse, Leo XIII asked all the bishops to submit their views to Rome and permit the Holy See to settle the question. On May 31, 1893, Leo XIII addressed his answer to Cardinal James Gibbons for the American hierarchy, stating that the Holy See supported the propositions of the Third Plenary Council of Baltimore and encouraged the construction of Catholic schools, but granted to the local ordinary the power to decide under what conditions Catholics might attend public schools. The meeting of the American hierarchy in September 1893 unanimously adopted a resolution declaring that the controversy over the ''School Question'' had ended. Privately both sides claimed victory, although the problem is still unsolved.

Bibliography: D. F. REILLY, *The School Controversy, 1891–1893* (Washington 1943). T. BOUQUILLON, *Education: To Whom Does It Belong?* (Baltimore 1891); *Education: To Whom Does It Belong? A Rejoinder to Critics* (Baltimore 1892); *Education: To Whom Does It Belong? A Rejoinder to the Civiltà Cattolica* (Baltimore 1892). R. I. HOLAIND, *The Parent First* (New York 1891). F. SATOLLI, *For the Settling of the School Question and the Giving of Religious Education* (Baltimore 1892).

[E. G. RYAN]

BOURDALOUE, LOUIS

French Jesuit preacher who brought the classic sermon to its most perfect oratorical technique; b. Bourges, France, Aug. 20, 1632; d. Paris, May 13, 1704. Bourdaloue, of a distinguished, although not wealthy, family, en-

Louis Bourdaloue.

tered the Society of Jesus in 1648 at the age of 17. After completing his studies, he became a professor of philosophy and later, of moral theology. When he showed special talent for oratory, he was asked to dedicate himself to preaching. He began preaching in Amiens in 1665 and later went to Orléans and Rouen. In 1669 he was sent to Paris where he preached for 34 consecutive years, each year with greater success, until the end of his life.

In eloquence, Bourdaloue ranked with the great masters of style in the most splendid part of Louis XIV's reign. He was hailed as the ''king of orators and the orator of kings.'' Bourdaloue used two exordiums: the first, more general, beginning adroitly with the text of the subject matter of the sermon and ending with a Hail Mary; the second, more detailed and specific, presenting the doctrine in three different manners. The body of the discourse was divided into three points: exposition of the doctrine found in Scripture and the Fathers of the Church, the moral to be drawn from the doctrine, and the portrayal of worldly Christians whose lives were at variance with the moral doctrine with which he was concerned. Each of these three points was further subdivided into three parts. Fénelon and La Bruyère vigorously criticized Bourdaloue's method as rigidly and arbitrarily mechanical, but admitted that it was useful as a memory aid for the speaker and the listeners.

Bourdaloue was most effective in the moral sermons in which he manifested a remarkable delicacy of balance. For him, Christian morality was just as free from excessive rigors as it was from any culpable indulgence. Sainte-Beuve considered his sermons the best refutations of Pascal's *Lettres Provinciales.*

He was masterly in his analysis of the human heart and was able to draw strikingly true word portraits. No doubt the 17th century taste for moral analysis accounted for much of his success. His reasoning was rigorous, and he habitually sought to convince his auditors. In this, he was adapting himself to an audience that, though irresponsive to other appeals because of its worldliness and frivolity, showed great esteem for reason. His personal saintliness and gentleness contributed to his influence. While always duly respectful to the great, he was also simple and devoted to the poor. He was always ready to hear confessions and exerted a wonderful power at deathbeds, especially those of hardened sinners.

Bourdaloue won a place for himself in French literature. Fénelon said that his style ''had perhaps arrived at the perfection of which our language is capable in that kind of eloquence.'' Sainte-Beuve wrote, ''He was a good orator and is a good writer.'' Voltaire claimed that he was superior to Bossuet.

Bibliography: L. BOURDALOUE, *Sermons*, ed. F. BRETONNEAU, 16 v. (Paris 1707–21); *Pensées*, ed. F. BRETONNEAU, 2 v. (Paris 1734), together the authoritative source of Bourdaloue's complete works. They were published together in 4 v. (Bar-le-Duc 1864). C. A. SAINTE-BEUVE, *Causeries du lundi*, 15 v. (Paris 1851–62). H. CHÉROT, *Bourdaloue inconnu* (Paris 1898); *Bourdaloue: Sa correspondance et ses correspondants* (Paris 1899); *Dictionnaire de théologie catholique*. 2.1:1095–99. A. A. L. PAUIHE, *Bourdaloue, d'après des documents nouveaux: Les maitres de la chaire en France au XVII 'siècle* (Paris 1900). C. H. BROOKE, ed. and tr., *Great French Preachers*. 2 v. (London 1904), sermons of Bourdaloue. E. BYRNE, *Bourdaloue moraliste* (Paris 1929). R. DAESCHLER, *Bourdaloue: Doctrine spirituelle* (Paris 1932). T. J. CAMPBELL, *The Catholic Encyclopedia* 2:717–719.

[R. B. MEAGHER]

BOURGCHIER, THOMAS (BOURCHIER)

Archbishop of Canterbury, cardinal; b. *c.* 1410; d. Knole manor, Kent, England, March 30, 1486. A younger son of William Bourgchier, count of Eu, by Anne, daughter of Thomas, duke of Gloucester, Bourgchier's high birth marked him out for rapid advancement. An M.A. from Oxford (by 1433) and chancellor of the University (1434–37), he was made dean of St. Martins-le-Grand, London before taking orders and held canonries in Lichfield, Wells, Lincoln, and York (1428–35). In 1433 Cardinal Henry BEAUFORT and the court party pressed him on Pope Eugene IV for the See of WORCESTER, notwithstanding Bourgchier's lack of canonical age, although the pope had already provided Thomas BROUNS. The dispute lasted until March 9, 1435, when Bourgchier was appointed by a reluctant pope. By 1437 Bourgchier had become a royal councilor, and he spared little attention to either Worcester or ELY, to which he was translated on Dec. 20, 1443. On June 21, 1454, he succeeded Cardinal John KEMP as archbishop of Canterbury. Prominent as a mediator in the party struggles between 1452 and 1458, he supported the Yorkists in 1460 and became a loyal servant of King Edward IV, who persuaded Pope Paul IV to make Bourgchier a cardinal in September of 1467. Bourgchier held high office only briefly (as chancellor of England, March 1455–October 1456), but was active in the court and council of Edward IV. As archbishop he crowned Edward IV in 1461, Richard III in 1483 (albeit with reluctance), and Henry VII in 1485. He was not regarded as merely serving his time, but won his contemporaries' respect, although his busy political life made him a negligent archbishop; in 32 years as primate he performed no ordinations and relied heavily on suffragans and officials in his diocesan administration.

Bibliography: *Registrum Thome Bourgchier,* ed. F. R. H. DU BOULAY, 2 v. (Canterbury and York Society 54; Oxford 1957). C. L. SCOFIELD, *The Life and Reign of Edward the Fourth*, 2 v. (New York 1923). A. B. EMDEN, *A Biographical Register of the University of Oxford to A. D. 1500* (Oxford 1957–1959) 1:230–232.

[C. D. ROSS]

BOURGEOYS, MARGUERITE, ST.

Foundress and first superior of the Sisters of the Congregation de Notre Dame; b. Troyes, France, April 17, 1620; d. Montreal, Canada, January 12, 1700. The daughter of a prosperous merchant, Marguerite grew up in a quiet corner of Champagne. In 1653, after several unsuccessful attempts to enter the cloister, she sailed for Canada with Paul de C. Maisonneuve, governor of Montreal, a frontier garrison in New France, founded only twelve years before. There, in 1658, she opened the first school in Montreal in an abandoned stone stable. Within a few years she had established a school for native people, a native mission, a boarding school for the daughters of merchants, and a training school for the poor. As the scope of her work grew, she brought assistants from France; later, Canadian-born girls and two Natives joined her in her work. The group developed into a new kind of religious community, not bound to the cloister, but free to go, dressed in the costume of the poor, wherever their zeal and the needs of the people demanded. In 1698, two years before her death, the Congregation de Notre Dame won ecclesiastical approval.

The foundress consistently refused endowments, dowries for her companions, and gifts of money that would have made her life less directly dependent on God. She and her religious supported themselves by sewing, and lived frugally so that they could give alms to the poor. They began needed buildings without the money to complete them, and offered the work of their hands in exchange for the services of carpenters and masons. After a disastrous fire in December of 1683, the community was left destitute. As soon as the ground thawed in the spring, they began, totally without resources, the construction of a new school. With alms, Marguerite built a chapel as a place of pilgrimage to Our Lady, Notre Dame de Bon Secours; she and her companions carried stones and poured mortar for the masons. Marguerite spent her last years writing an autobiography. She was beatified in 1956; John Paul II canonized her, April 2, 1982.

Feast: Jan. 12 (Canada).

Bibliography: C. M. BOURGEOYS, *Les Écrits de Mère Bourgeoys. Autobiographie et testament spirituel* (Montreal 1964). E. MONTGOLFIER, *La vie de la vénérable Marguerite Bourgeoys dite du Saint-Sacrement, institutrice, fondatrice* (Montreal 1818). É. M. FAILLON, *Vie de la soeur Bourgeoys,* 2 v. (Villemarie 1853). A. JAMET, *Marguerite Bourgeoys,* 2 v. (Montreal 1942). Y. CHARRON, *Mère Bourgeoys,* tr. SISTER ST. GODELIVA (Montreal 1950). K. BURTON, *Vahant Voyager* (Milwaukee 1964). P. SIMPSON, *Marguerite Bourgeoys and Montreal 1640–1665* (Montreal 1997).

[V. M. COTTER]

St. Marguerite Bourgeoys (Archive Photos)

BOURGET, IGNACE

Second bishop of Montreal, Canada; b. Saint-Joseph-de-Lévis, Canada, Oct. 30, 1799; d. Montreal, June 8, 1885. Bourget attended secondary school in Quebec and began his work in theology there, finishing it in Montreal under J. J. Lartigue, the auxiliary bishop to whom he was secretary. When Montreal became a diocese (1836), Bourget was named vicar-general; the following year he was consecrated coadjutor bishop, and in 1840 he succeeded to the see.

His first concern was to obtain the priests and institutions Montreal needed. He entrusted the direction of its Grand Seminary to the Sulpicians. In 1841, he went to Europe and obtained the services of several Oblates of Mary Immaculate (1841), Jesuits and Sisters of the Sacred Heart (1842), and nuns of the Good Shepherd from Angers (1844). He also made arrangements for the coming of other religious institutes: the Clerics of St. Viator and the Fathers, Brothers, and Sisters of the Holy Cross (1847). He founded two institutes of charity—the Sisters of Providence (1843) and the Sisters of Mercy—and two institutes of instruction—the Sisters of the Holy Names of Jesus and Mary (1844) and the Sisters of St. Anne (1848). He also welcomed into the diocese the Brothers of Charity of Gand (1865).

Although a man of action himself, Bourget was a great believer in prayer; he collaborated in the foundation of a Canadian contemplative institute, the Sisters of the Precious Blood (1861), and he established the Carmelites of Reims in Montreal (1875). His zeal was not limited to his own diocese, and he sent out to the poorest of the dioceses, and especially to the missions of the Pacific Coast, numerous secular priests, monks, and nuns. ''The best means of preserving the Faith,'' he said, ''is to propagate it far and wide.''

In concord with many bishops of his time, he favored ULTRAMONTANISM, or papal supremacy, and he had to withstand heavy attacks from liberals and the supporters of GALLICANISM of the period. Ten years after the foundation of Laval University at Quebec (1852), he tried to obtain an independent Catholic university for his episcopal city. Although his 15-year effort was unsuccessful, he advanced all the arguments that ultimately led to the establishment of the independent University of Montreal (1920).

No less important was the struggle he waged for the spiritual well-being of Montreal. By virtue of a privilege dating from the 17th century, which he himself had confirmed in 1843, the Seminary of Montreal was empowered to minister in perpetuity to the entire city as a single parish. Because of the rapid increase in the city's population (to 100,000 in 1860), this privilege became more burdensome than useful. In 1865 Rome granted Bourget the right to establish new parishes in the city in accordance with the needs of the faithful, thus enabling the Diocese of Montreal to progress at the same rate as the rest of the country during the second half of the 19th century. The prestige and the reputation for sanctity that accrued to him during his lifetime did not cease with his death; in 1903 a monument was erected to him in front of the basilica, and his remains are interred in a marble tomb in the center of the bishops' funeral chapel.

Bibliography: A. LEBLOND DE BRUMATH, *Monseigneur Bourget, archévêque de Marianapolis ancien, évêque de Montréal* (Montreal 1885). F. LANGEVIN, *Mgr. Ignace Bourget, deuxième évêque de Montréal* (Montreal 1931). L. POULIOT, *Monseigneur Bourget et son temps,* 5 v. (Montreal 1955–1977).

[L. POULIOT]

BOURGOING, FRANÇOIS

Oratorian spiritual writer; b. Paris, Mar. 18, 1585; d. Paris, Oct. 28, 1662. Born of a noble family, Bourgoing was the *curé* of Clichy until 1611, at which time he resigned that position in favor of Vincent de Paul and became one of the first six priests of the Oratory founded by Pierre de BÉRULLE. He taught in various seminaries, including those of Paris, Rouen, and Nantes, and preached extensively in Auvergne, Brittany, and Lyons. In 1626, at the request of the archbishop of Malines, he went to Flanders and established Oratorian houses in Louvain, Maubeuge, and Mons. He preached the funeral oration for Cardinal Bérulle at Louvain, and then presided at the assembly of the Oratory that elected Charles de CONDREN as Bérulle's successor.

Bourgoing returned to France in 1630, and on Condren's death in 1641, became the third superior general of the Oratory. He initiated vigorous regulations for his community and drew up a plan of studies for seminaries. His subordinates criticized him for his authoritarian manner, and the assembly of 1661 indirectly reproached him for accepting the office of confessor to the duke of Orleans by legislating that no superior could accept a position at court. Nevertheless, the prosperity of the Oratory under his direction proved his wisdom and competence as an administrator.

In 1656 he suffered a stroke from which he never fully recovered, and after 1660 his health and spirit failed. Bousset preached the funeral oration for Bourgoing. A close disciple of Bérulle, Bourgoing was a fierce opponent of Jansenism and one of the leading figures in the religious renaissance in France in the 17th century. A prolific writer, he published many works of piety that went through numerous editions and were translated into other languages. Among his principal works are *Lignum vitae* (Mons 1629), *Institutio spiritualis ordinandorum* (Paris 1639), *Méditations sur les vérités et excellence de Jésus Christ* (6 v. Paris 1636), and *Exercises de retraites* (4 v. Paris 1648). He edited the works of Bérulle as well as other collections of homilies on the gospel and meditation on the Blessed Virgin and the saints,.

Bibliography: C. E. CLOYSEAULT, *Généralats du P. François Bourgoing,* 2 v. (Paris 1880) 2:1–26. L. BATTEREL, *Mémoires domestiques pour servir à l'histoire de l'Oratoire*, 5 v. (Paris 1903–11) 2: 285–329. A. MOLIEN, *Dictionnaire de spiritualité ascétique et mystique. Doctrine et histoire*. (Paris 1932–) 1: 1910–15. E. LEVESQUE, *Dictionnaire d'histoire et de géographie ecclésiastiques* (Paris 1912–) 10: 226–228.

[J. T. KELLEHER]

BOURGUEIL-EN-VALLÉE, ABBEY OF

Former Benedictine house in the former Diocese of Angers, now Indre-et-Loire, France (patron, St. Peter). It was founded in 989 by Emma, wife of Count William IV of Poitiers, and confirmed by Pope John XV in 990 and by King Hugh Capet in 994. The first abbot, Gausbert, ruled simultaneously the Abbeys of Bourgueil, Saint-Julien of Tours, MARMOUTIER, and La Couture at Le Mans. Baudry of Bourgueil, the seventh abbot (1079–1107), was the most notable prelate to come from the abbey. He was archbishop of Dol in Brittany and one of the most important Latin poets of the 12th century. At its height the abbey directed 42 priories and 64 parish churches; it had properties throughout western France, as well as some important vineyards in the Loire Valley. The abbey was placed under commendatory abbots after 1475 but was reformed by the MAURISTS in 1630. It was suppressed in 1791. The buildings, which were mostly destroyed during the French Revolution, included the Gothic church (built 1246–93), a cloister of the 15th century, and the conventual dwellings dating from 1658 to 1672.

Bibliography: There is a copy of the unedited cartulary of Bourgueil at the Bibliothéque Municipale of Tours, MS 1338, 1339. *Gallia Christiana,* v. 1–13 (Paris 1715–85), v. 14–16 (Paris 1856–65) 14:654–667. P. CALENDINI, *Dictionnaire d'histoire et de géographie ecclésiastiques,* ed. A. BAUDRILLART et al. (Paris 1912–) 10:229–234. L. MUSSET, "Les Plus anciennes chartes normandes de l'abbaye de B.," *Bulletin de la société des antiquaires de Normandie,* 54 (1957–58) 15–54; "Deux nouvelles chartes normandes de l'abbaye de B.," *ibid.,* 56 (1961–62) 5–41. M. DUPONT,

"Monographie du cartulaire de B., des origines à la fin du moyen âge" (Mémoires de la soc. archeol. de Touraine 56; Tours 1962).

[L. MUSSET]

BOURNE, FRANCIS

Cardinal, fourth archbishop of Westminster, England; b. Clapham, London, England, March 23, 1861; d. Westminster, Jan. 1, 1935. Bourne was the son of Henry, a convert and post office clerk, and Ellen (Byrne) Bourne. He was educated in England at Ushaw College, Durham; St. Edmund's, Ware; and Hammersmith. After completing his theological studies at Saint-Sulpice, Paris, he was ordained (June 11, 1884). He held several brief curacies before becoming rector of a house of studies at Henfield Place, Sussex (1889), and of the diocesan seminary at Wonersh (1891). In 1896 he was consecrated as coadjutor to the bishop of Southwark, whom he succeeded in the same year. In 1903, he was transferred to the Archdiocese of Westminster where he was elevated to the cardinalate (1910). His achievements as archbishop included a successful defense of Catholic voluntary schools against government restriction, organization of the International Eucharistic Congress in London (1908), and progress in the construction of Westminster Cathedral, consecrated in 1910.

Francis Bourne. (The Catholic University of America)

Bibliography: E. OLDMEADOW, *Francis Cardinal Bourne,* 2 v. (London 1940–44). W. J. WOOD, *The Dictionary of National Biogrpahy From the Earliest Times to 1900* (1931–40) 92–93.

[D. MILBURN]

BOURNE, GILBERT

Last Catholic bishop of Bath and Wells, noted orator and disputant; b. place and date unknown; d. Silverton, Devonshire, Sept. 10, 1569. Bourne's father was Philip Bourne of Worcestershire. Gilbert entered the University of Oxford in 1524 and was a fellow of All Soul's College in 1531. In 1541 he became prebendary of the king's new foundation at Worcester. Dr. Bourne must have conformed to the religious changes under Edward VI because he was prebend at St. Paul's, London, rector of High Ongar in Essex, and archdeacon of Bedford. However, he remained loyal to his patron, Bishop Edmund BONNER, during the latter's trial in 1549.

With Mary's accession, Bourne returned to the old religion. Mary utilized his great gifts as a preacher, and as royal preacher, he caused a tumult among the enraged reformers with a sermon in defense of Catholic doctrine and Bonner, delivered on Aug. 13, 1553 at Paul's Cross, London. His eloquence and courage, together with the influence of his uncle, Sir John Bourne, principal secretary of state, won him election as bishop of Bath and Wells on March 28, 1554. After his consecration by Bishop Bonner, Bourne zealously restored Catholic practices and worship.

Bourne was especially noted, even among Protestants, for his kindness. There is no record of any execution in his diocese. Queen Mary showed her esteem by appointing him lord president of the Council of Wales, from which he was removed by Elizabeth in 1558. His refusal to participate in a commission for consecrating Matthew Parker as archbishop of Canterbury and to take the oaths of supremacy and allegiance (Oct. 18, 1559) brought his deprivation and imprisonment in the Tower. In September of 1563, he was removed to house arrest, first with the bishop of Lincoln, and then with Dean Carey of Exeter, where he died.

Bibliography: W. M. BRADY, *The Episcopal Succession in England, Scotland, and Ireland, A.D. 1400 to 1875,* 3 v. (Rome 1876–77). H. TOOTELL, *Dodd's Church History of England,* ed. M. A. TIERNEY, 5 v. (London 1839–43). P. HUGHES, *The Reformation in England.* (New York 1963). RE. W. HUNT, *The Dictionary of National Biography from the Earliest Times to 1900* (London 1885–1900) 2:936–937.

[J. D. HANLON]

BOUSSET, WILHELM

Protestant NT scholar; b. Lübeck, Germany, Sept. 3, 1865; d. Giessen, Germany, March 8, 1920. He taught Scripture at Göttingen from 1896 to 1916 and at Giessen from 1916 until his death. At Göttingen he was one of the cofounders of the school of comparative religion, and together with W. Heitmüller he successfully applied its method in the field of NT studies. He opened new paths with his commentary on the Apocalypse [*Offenbarung Johannes* (*Meyer Kommentar* 16; Göttingen 1896, 6th ed, 1906)], his *Die Religion des Judentums im ntl. Zeitalter* [Göttingen 1902; rev. ed., H. Gressmann, ed., *Die Religion . . . im späthellenistischen Zeitalter* (Göttingen 3d ed. 1926)], his *Die Hauptprobleme der Gnosis* (Göttingen 1907), and his chief work, *Kyrios Christos* (Göttingen 1913, 4th ed. 1935; new ed. in preparation in 1965). In these works he endeavored to show that so-called late Judaism was influenced by Iranian and especially Hellenistic ideas and that Hellenistic GNOSTICISM borrowed religious concepts from the Near East. While A. von HARNACK regarded the history of dogma as a history of the Hellenization of Christianity, according to Bousset, primitive Christianity had been deeply influenced by Hellenism, and the decisive turning point in the history of Christianity lay not at the end of the NT period, but was the transitional period when the faith of the primitive Judeo-Christian community of Palestine in the Son of Man with its expectation of His Parousia changed into the faith of Gentile Christianity of the Hellenistic world with its veneration of Kyrios already present. Thus the inner bond between the theology of the NT and that of the early Church could be explained. Bousset's ideas continued to affect NT scholars in the 20th century, particularly R. Bultmann and his disciples.

Bousset founded the *Theologische Rundschau* (1897), which he edited together with W. Heitmüller until 1917. With H. GUNKEL he published the *Forschungen zur Religion und Literatur des Alten und Neuen Testamentes* (1901–20). With Heitmüller he prepared the third edition of *Die Schriften des Neuen Testaments neu übersetzt und für die Gegenwart erklärt* (Göttingen 1917–19).

Bibliography: H. GUNKEL, *Evangelische Freiheit* 42 (1920) 141–162. L. THOMAS, *Dictionnaire de la Bible,* Suppl. ed., (Paris 1895–1912) 1:989–992. H. SCHLIER, *Lexikon für Theologie und Kirche,* (Freiburg 1957–65) 2:632. E. KAMLAH, *Die Religion in Geschichte und Gegenwart* (Tübingen 1957–65) 1:1373–74.

[O. KAISER]

BOUTEILLER, MARTHE LE, BL.

Baptized Aimée Adèle, nicknamed ''Soeur Cidre'' or ''Sister Cider,'' religious; b. La Henrière (near Percy), Manche, France, Dec. 2, 1816; d. Abbey of Saint-Sauveur-le-Vicomte, France, March 18, 1883. Aimée, third of the four children of André and Marie-Française le Bouteiller, was raised on a small farm and attended a local religious school. Her school mistress, Sister Marie-Française Farcy, inspired the young girl's religious vocation. She joined the Sisters of St. Madeleine POSTEL (1842) and served the Abbey of Saint-Sauveur-le-Vicomte in the kitchen, fields, and laundry for the rest of her life. Her constant cheerfulness and devoted service radiated the love of God through ordinary tasks. She was beatified by John Paul II on Nov. 4, 1990.

Bibliography: M. CLÉVENOT, *Adèle l'obscure: soeur Marthe* (Paris 1989).

[K. I. RABENSTEIN]

BOUTROUX, ÉTIENNE ÉMILE MARIE

French philosopher of science; b. Montrouge, July 28, 1845; d. Paris, Nov. 22, 1921. Boutroux succeeded J. LACHELIER as conference master at the École Normale, and exercised a great influence over a whole generation of French philosophers and philosophers of science, including H. BERGSON, M. BLONDEL, P. Duhem, and J. Henri Poincaré.

His doctoral dissertation, *De la contingence des lois de la nature* (1874), was hailed as a landmark in the philosophy of nature. It was an attack on the doctrinaire determinism of academic rationalists and positivists who allowed no contingency in the laws of nature. Scientific laws are abstract figures of an ideal necessity that can never be fully equated with the concrete, physical reality they symbolize; first, because one can never know all of the influences that condition a fact or event, and second, because the human mind, due to its limitations, necessarily eliminates differences in order to stress what is common. Hypotheses, then, are but partial views that are reformable, and in no sense absolute or necessary. They tell little about nature itself, whose behavior is unpredictable and not subject to the scientific formulas man invents to describe it. It is a mistake, then, to absolutize nature or man's way of thinking about nature.

In addition, quite apart from the multiplicity of external factors that condition scientific facts, the constructions of science are influenced by, and in turn have only a limited application to, human life, thought, and freedom. In sympathy with E. Zeller, whose lectures he heard in Germany, Boutroux extended his criticism of determinism in his later works to those neo-Hegelians who viewed history as a deductive science subject to iron laws of necessity. Man's freedom breaks into the closed world of historical and scientific determinism, resisting all attempts to subject the course of progress to an absolute rule.

Yet, man's quest for an absolute and his attachment to the noncontingent reveal a deeper necessity whose complement lies in the area of morality and religion. He is confronted with the fact of duty and the need for a faith, and science itself shows the importance of cooperative enterprise that should engage all men in the common task of wresting from nature her secrets and working toward the universal brotherhood of man. It is the Christian Gospel that outlines what should be the fullest realization of unity among men. Not only does it offer the hope of reconciling freedom and necessity, and the aspirations of the person with the needs of the community, but it also places science and history within the larger framework of a reality that transcends the limits of the contingent order of creation.

Bibliography: Major works translated into English. *Science and Religion in Contemporary Philosophy,* tr. J. NIELD, (London 1909); *Historical Studies in Philosophy,* tr. F. ROTHWELL (London 1912); *William James,* tr. A. and B. HENDERSON (London 1912); *Natural Law in Science and Philosophy,* tr. F. ROTHWELL (London 1914); *The Contingency of the Laws of Nature,* tr. F. ROTHWELL (London 1916). Studies. A. P. LA FONTAINE, *La Philosophie d'É. Boutroux,* v. 1 of *La Culture française,* 3 v. (Paris 1920–26). M. SCHYNS, *La Philosophie d'Émile Boutroux* (Paris 1924). A. BAILLOT, ''La Philosophie et la religion selon Émile Boutroux,'' *Revue thomiste* 39.1 (1934) 313–352. J. BENDA, *De quelques constantes de l'esprit humain* (Paris 1950).

[J. M. SOMERVILLE]

BOUVET, JOACHIM

Mathematician and missionary; b. Le Mans, France, July 18, 1656; d. Beijing, China, June 28, 1732. At the age of 17 he entered the Society of Jesus. One of six Jesuits selected by Louis XIV to further French influence in China by the advancement of religion and science, Bouvet arrived at Beijing on Feb. 7, 1688, where he was received and retained at court as royal mathematician by the Emperor Hsüan-Yeh. He made a visit to France from 1697 to 1699 to carry presents between emperor and king and to recruit more Jesuits for the mission. From 1708 to 1715, he prepared a geographical survey of China. His services to the emperor did much to facilitate the religious ministry of the Jesuits. He cooperated with four fellow missionaries to obtain from Hsüan-Yeh an official pronouncement that certain Chinese ceremonies in honor of Confucius and the dead were without religious significance. Besides his works on mathematics, he compiled a Chinese dictionary. His unpublished letters include correspondence with Leibniz. His most well-known work, *Portrait historique de l'Empereur de Chine* (Paris 1697), was subsequently translated into English, Dutch, German, Italian, and Latin, the last by Leibniz in 1699.

Jean Baptiste Bouvier.

Bibliography: C. SOMMERVOGEL, *Bibliothèque de la Compagnie de Jésus* (Brussels-Paris 1890–1932) 2:54–58; 8:1896; 12:970. A. DE BIL, *Dictionaire d'histoire et de géographie ecclésiastiques* (Paris 1912–) 10:275–276. A. H. ROWBOTHAM, *Missionary and Mandarin: The Jesuits at the Court of China* (Berkeley 1942). C. CARY-ELWES, *China and the Cross: A Survey of Missionary History* (New York 1957). K. S. LATOURETTE, *A History of Christian Missions in China* (New York 1929).

[J. V. MENTAG]

BOUVIER, JEAN BAPTISTE

Bishop and theologian; b. Saint-Charles-la-Forêt, Mayenne, Jan. 16, 1783; d. Rome, Dec. 29, 1854. The son of a carpenter, he entered the seminary of Angers in 1805 and was ordained in 1808. After teaching philosophy at the College of Château Gonthier, he became professor of philosophy and moral theology at the seminary of Le Mans in 1811 and was made rector there in 1819. After 1820 he was vicar-general of the diocese until he was consecrated bishop of Le Mans in 1834. During his episcopate he was known for his learning, piety, and apostolic zeal. The Sisters of Providence of St. Mary-of-the-Woods (Ind.) are particularly indebted to Bouvier for his support and assistance in the foundation of their community. Pius IX held him in such high esteem that he invited Bouvier to be present at the definition of the dogma of the Immaculate Conception.

The principal work among his many writings was the *Institutiones theologicae* (Le Mans 1817), which went through 15 editions and was used in almost all the seminaries of France, the U.S., and Canada. First issued in separate theological treatises comprising 13 volumes, the work was reduced to six volumes in 1834. Although Bouvier tried to improve his work in the course of succeeding editions, he never succeeded in removing completely the traces of Gallicanism that had influenced his early formation. He readily submitted to the corrections of the theologians selected by Pius IX. Their revision resulted in the eighth edition (1853). After Bouvier's death, the professors at Le Mans seminary eliminated many imperfections not noted by the papal revisers.

As a manual, the *Institutiones theologicae* was well adapted to the period of transition (1830–70) in ecclesiastical studies, during which they were recovering ground lost in the Gallican and Jansenist disturbances in the French Church. A mélange of history, liturgy, canon and civil law, and casuistry, the work contained serious weaknesses. However, clerical studies had become so disorganized in the course of the 18th century that the reestablishment of a solid curriculum was a very difficult problem. Moreover, the scarcity of vocations, the urgent need for priests, and limited financial resources had reduced seminary training to three years. Despite its faults, Bouvier's work served to free clerical education from the errors and the lethargy of the preceding period, and thereby opened the way to reforms achieved during the latter part of the 19th century.

Bibliography: A. L. SÉBAUX, *Vie de mgr. J. B. Bouvier, évêque du Mans* (2d ed. Paris 1889). F. DESHAYES, *Dictionnaire de théologie catholique,* 2.1:1117–19. L. CALENDINI, *Dictionnaire d'histoire et de géographie ecclésiastiques,* 10:276–277. M. B. BROWN, *History of the Sisters of Providence of Saint-Mary-of-the-Woods,* v. 1 (New York 1949).

[F. C. LEHNER]

BOVA, ST.

Benedictine abbess, 7th century. She was the first abbess of Saint-Pierre, Reims, where she introduced the BENEDICTINE RULE. According to FLODOARD OF REIMS, she was the daughter of SIGEBERT, King of Austrasia, and therefore would have been the sister of St. Baudry of Montfaucon, but the place and date of her birth are not known. Her feast is observed with that of her niece, Doda, who became a religious in the same monastery and probably succeeded her as abbess.

Feast: April 24.

Bibliography: *Acta Santorum,* April 3:285–293. J. BOUETTE DE BLÉMUR, *L'Année bénédictine,* 6 v. (Paris 1667–73). P. DE BEAUVAIS, *Le Tableau . . . de sainte Bove et sainte Dode* (Reims 1655). J. L. BAUDOT and L. CHAUSSIN, *Vies des saints et des bieheureux selon l'ordre du calendrier avec l'historique des fêtes,* ed. by the Benedictines of Paris, 12 v. (Paris 1935–56); v. 13, suppl. and table générale (1959) 4:615–616. W. GRUNDHÖFER, *Lexikon für Theologie und Kirche,* ed. J. HOFER and K. RAHNER, 10 v. (2d, new ed. Freiburg 1957–65) 2:633. A. D'HAENENS, *Biblioteca sanctorum* (Rome 1961–) :377–378.

[O. L. KAPSNER]

BOVILLUS, CAROLUS (CHARLES DE BOUELLES)

Humanist, philosopher, and theologian; b. Saucourt near Amiens, *c.* 1470; d. Noyon, *c.* 1553. A disciple of Jacques LEFÈVRE D'ÉTAPLES, Bovillus traveled widely and came to know many of the intellectuals of his day. Some time after ordination, he became canon and professor of theology at Noyon. His interests were almost universal; he composed valuable works on geometry, physics, linguistics, philosophy, theology, and spirituality. His most important and most characteristic philosophical work is *De sapiente* [new ed. in E. Cassirer, *Individuum und Kosmos in der Philosophie der Renaissance* (Leipzig 1927)], a typical Renaissance document placing the concept of man at the center of reality. In his philosophico-theological system, Bovillus unites elements from the Aristotelian-traditional school, from PICO DELLA MIRANDOLA, and from NICHOLAS OF CUSA. He is particularly indebted to Nicholas not only for his writings on philosophy and theology, but also for his works on spirituality. On the subject of prayer, Bovillus emphasized the necessity of internal dispositions [*De indifferentia orationis* (Paris 1529)] and the importance of the element of praise. He explained ecstasy as the overflow of the soul into God and the overflow of God into the soul. Though not immune from a certain rationalism, his synthesis, founded on the principles of Nicholas of Cusa, is Catholic in spirit.

Bibliography: F. STEGMÜLLER, *Lexikon für Theologie und Kirche* (Freiburg 1957–65) 2:627. A. VANSTEENBERGHE, *Dictionnaire de spiritualité ascétique et mystique* (Paris 1932–) 1:1894–95.

[M. A. ROCHE]

BOWES, MARMADUKE, BL.

Lay martyr; b. possibly at Ingram Grange (near Appleton), Welbury, Cleveland in Yorkshire, England; d. Nov. 26, 1585, hanged at York. Both Marmaduke and his wife were imprisoned at York and released, but required under bond to appear in York at the assizes beginning Nov. 23, 1585. Upon his arrival, he found that Bl. Hugh TAYLOR was about to be arraigned. Previously Bowes had offered food and drink in his home to Fr. Taylor, which had been observed by his children's former tutor, an apostate Catholic. Bowes, though always a Catholic at heart, had outwardly conformed to the Anglican Church; the tutor provided the sole evidence against Bowes, leading to his condemnation for harboring and assisting an unlawful priest. Bowes boldly confessed his faith as a Catholic before his death. He was beatified by Pope John Paul II on Nov. 22, 1987 with George Haydock and Companions.

Feast of the English Martyrs: May 4 (England).

See Also: ENGLAND, SCOTLAND, AND WALES, MARTYRS OF.

Bibliography: R. CHALLONER, *Memoirs of Missionary Priests,* ed. J. H. POLLEN (rev. ed. London 1924). J. H. POLLEN, *Acts of English Martyrs* (London 1891).

[K. I. RABENSTEIN]

BOWET, HENRY

Archbishop of York, civil servant; b. probably *c.* 1350; d. Cawood Castle, Yorkshire, Oct. 20, 1423. He was a doctor of canon and civil law by 1386. As a young man of knightly family, he accompanied Henry DESPENSER, bishop of Norwich, on his crusade to Flanders (1382). From *c.* 1385 to the mid-1390s he was an official of the Roman Curia. During the parliamentary crisis under Richard II, Bowet was accused by the Appellants in 1388 and was excluded from pardon. But with the restoration of Richard II to real power, he was back in royal grace. Through John of Gaunt's good offices, he was made constable of Bordeaux (1396). When Bolingbroke (later King Henry IV) was banished, Bowet joined him in exile. Although he was subsequently condemned to death by a parliamentary commission set up by Richard II, his sentence was later commuted to perpetual exile and confiscation of all domains and benefices. But upon Henry IV's return to England and coronation, Bowet's possessions were returned, and Henry added new benefices. An integral part of the new regime, Bowet was made bishop of BATH AND WELLS in 1401 and was briefly treasurer of England (1402). He was charged to defend Carmathen during Owain Glyndwr's rebellion. In 1407, despite his mismanagement of the Diocese of Bath and Wells (he left debts to his successor), he was translated to the archbishopric of York, succeeding the executed Abp. Richard SCROPE. After his appointment to York, his interest and involvement in state matters declined. In 1411 the king remitted Bowet's debts in consideration of his diplomatic and state services.

Bibliography: Register from Bath and Wells, ed. T. S. HOLMES (Somerset Record Society 13; London 1899). T. F. TOUT, *The Dictionary of National Biography from the Earliest Times to 1900* (London 1885–1900) 2:971–973. A. H. THOMPSON, *Dictionnaire d'histoire et de géographie ecclésiastiques* (Paris 1912–) 10:304–306. A. STEEL, *Richard II* (Cambridge, Eng. 1941; repr. 1963). A. H. THOMPSON, *The English Clergy and Their Organization in the Later Middle Ages* (Oxford 1947). *Biographical Register of the Scholars of the University of Cambridge before 1500* (Cambridge, Eng. 1963) 83–84.

[V. MUDROCH]

BOWMAN, THEA

Religious sister, educator, lecturer, vocalist, evangelist; b. Bertha Bowman in Yazoo City, Mississippi, Dec. 29, 1937; d. Canton, Mississippi, March 30, 1990. In August of 1953, at the age of 15, Bowman entered the formation program of the Franciscan Sisters of Perpetual Adoration in La Crosse, Wisconsin. She graduated from Viterbo College in La Crosse and then pursued graduate studies in English literature and linguistics at the Catholic University of America in Washington, DC. She wrote her dissertation on St. Thomas MORE's Dialogue of Comfort and received her doctorate in 1972.

Sister Thea taught in elementary schools in La Crosse and Canton; from 1971 to 1978 she taught English literature at Viterbo College. During this period, she began offering programs and workshops to foster cultural and racial awareness and openness, working especially with international students and the Winnebago Native American people. In 1978, the bishop of Jackson, Mississippi, Joseph Brunini, asked her to return to Mississippi and work with the diocesan intercultural program.

In 1980, Sister Thea helped establish the Institute for Black Catholic Studies at Xavier University in New Orleans. The first of its kind, the summer graduate institute sought to meld the Catholic tradition with the burgeoning scholarship of the African American community. Sister Thea brought to the institute her expertise in linguistics and aesthetics, as well as a profound knowledge of African American culture and tradition. As a faculty member she created a series of courses and liturical celebrations that helped form numerous pastors, pastoral ministers, religious education directors, and theology students from diverse ethnic and cultural groups. For almost a decade before being incapacitated by cancer, she traveled throughout the country, preaching and singing, giving workshops, lectures, and programs, and urging people to celebrate their own heritage, their own gifts, and their own beauty. Turning to African Americans of all ages but especially to children, she stressed the need for them to celebrate their ethnicity, their ancestors, and their faith. She celebrated her own Catholic faith and made contributions to the emerging consciousness of black Catholics by calling them to be both true to their heritage and their Catholic faith. A high point was the address she delivered from her wheelchair to the United States bishops assembled at Seton Hall University in June of 1989, in which she spoke to them of their need to reach out to all peoples but especially to African Americans, and to value the distinctive cultural gifts of all peoples.

Two years before her death she made her second and last trip to Africa. She continued to travel, to speak, and to sing, despite her exhaustion and frailty. Vocalist as well as lecturer, she was extremely ill when she made two audiocassette recordings: *Sister Thea: Songs of My People* (1988) and *Round the Glory Manger* (1989) (Krystal Records, Daughters of St. Paul). In her final days she drew upon her reserves of strength and joy to become a living testimony to courage in the face of death and love in the face of divisions. She was posthumously awarded the Laetare Medal by the University of Notre Dame in the spring of 1990.

Bibliography: T. BOWMAN, "Spirituality: The Soul of the People," in *Tell It Like It Is: A Black Catholic Perspective on Christian Education* (Oakland 1983) 837–95. T. BOWMAN, ed., *Families: Black and Catholic, Catholic and Black* (Washington 1985); "Black History and Culture," *U.S. Catholic Historian* 7 (1988) 307–310. C. CEPRESS, ed., *Sister Thea Bowman Shooting Star: Selected Writings and Speeches* (Winona, MN 1993). C. KOONTZ, ed., *Thea Bowman: Handing on Her Legacy* (Kansas City, MO 1991).

[C. DAVIS]

BOY BISHOP

The name given in the Middle Ages to the leader of the revels of the choirboys on Holy Innocents' Day (December 28). The revels can be traced to the 10th century; their initial motive seems to have been the exaltation of the innocent and lowly. For the duration of the festival, the choirboys took over the senior positions in all the cathedral ceremonies and offices except the Mass. In these activities they were led by a boy bishop, or *episcopus puerorum,* whom they elected well in advance, often on December 6, the Feast of St. Nicholas. The custom, originally confined to the cathedrals, spread to large monastic and scholastic establishments, and to nearly all parishes throughout Europe, flourishing particularly in France, Germany, and England. In England the feast proved far more popular and enduring than the FEAST OF FOOLS. It is amply recorded from the 13th century to the 16th, with full details for the ministry of the boy bishop provided by the Sarum breviary and processional.

The central rite was the great procession between Vespers and Compline on the Eve of Holy Innocents, after which the boys took the higher stalls and kept them until Vespers of the feast. On the Continent, at First Vespers, the *baculus* (staff of office) was handed over to the boy bishop while the *Deposuit potentes* of the Magnificat was being sung. In various places in England the boy bishop preached at Mass. Several church councils attempted to abolish or to restrain the abuses, which crept in probably through contamination by the revels of the subdeacons. The boy bishop was, however, less subject to criticism than the lord of fools, and the feast certainly preserved for a longer period the integrity of the original religious tradition. The custom was prohibited by the Council of Basle in 1435, but was too popular to be entirely suppressed. In England it was finally abolished by Elizabeth I; on the Continent traces of the feast survived into the 19th century.

See Also: FEAST OF ASSES.

Bibliography: E. K. CHAMBERS, *The Medieval Stage,* 2 v. (Oxford 1903) 1:336–371, 2:282–289. K. YOUNG, *The Drama of the Medieval Church,* 2 v. (Oxford 1933) 1:106–111, 552.

[M. N. MALTMAN]

BOYLE, ABBEY OF

Former Cistercian abbey on the river Boyle, within the Diocese of Elphin, County Roscommon, Ireland (Latin, *Monasterium Buellense;* Gaelic, *Mainistir na Búille*). Originally the Celtic foundation Áth Da Loarg of Bishop Mac Cainne, it was taken over by CISTERCIAN monks from MELLIFONT (in 1161), who had first established themselves at Greallach Da Iach in 1148. Many of its abbots became bishops; four of its monks died for the faith between 1580 and 1585. There is no evidence that the famous poet Donnchadh Mór Ó Dálaigh was abbot there. From it were founded Assaroe (1178) in the Diocese of Raphoe and Knockmoy (1190) in the Diocese of Tuam. At the time of its suppression (before 1569) it consisted of a church (consecrated in 1218), a belfry, a cloister, a hall, a dormitory, a cemetery, and a round tower (a survival of the Celtic foundation), and extensive lands (frequently mentioned in state papers dating from the end of the 16th and the beginning of the 17th centuries).

Bibliography: J. M. CANIVEZ, *Dictionnaire d'histoire et de géographie ecclésiastiques,* ed. A. BAUDRILLART et al. (Paris

Boyle Abbey. (©Michael St. Maur Shell/CORBIS)

1912–) 10:315–316. M. V. RONAN, *Irish Martyrs of the Penal Laws* (London 1935) 199, 201. M. O'FLANAGAN, ed., *Letters Containing Information Relative to the Antiquities of the County of Roscommon,* 2 v. in 1 (Bray, Ire. 1927) 1:204–206, 224–236. G. MACNIOCAILL, *Na manaigh liatha in Éirinn, 1142–c.1600* (Dublin 1959).

[C. MCGRATH]

BRACCO, TERESA, BL.

Lay woman and martyr; b. Santa Giulia in Sanvarezzo (Diocese of Acqui), Savona, Italy, Feb. 24, 1924; d. Zerbi (near Sanvarezzo), Aug. 28, 1944. The formation of Teresa Bracco began under the tutelage of her parents, Giacomo Bracco and Anna Pera, who were humble farmers with a strong devotion to the Eucharist and the Blessed Mother. Throughout her short life, Teresa attended daily Mass and had great devotion for the Eucharist. She became known for her modesty in dress and speech. Her spiritual maturity prepared her to resist the threat of rape by a Nazi soldier who shot her twice, then crushed her skull. Her death was declared a martyrdom on July 7, 1997. During her beatification on May 24, 1998, in the Piazza Vittorio, Turin, Italy, Pope John Paul II proclaimed that in Teresa Bracco ''the virtue of chastity shines out . . . she was its champion and witness to the point of martyrdom.''

Feast: Aug. 28 (Italy).

Bibliography: C. SICCARDI, *Martire a vent'anni* (Rome 1998).

[K. I. RABENSTEIN]

BRACTON, HENRY DE

English cleric and jurist (known also as Henry of Bratton); b. Bratton Fleming, Devon, England, *c.* 1210; d. by September 1268. He came from a well-to-do family from Devon and quite possibly studied at the University of Oxford. He was in orders and held various ecclesiastical benefices, becoming canon, prebendary, and eventually (1264) chancellor of the Diocese of EXETER. Bracton was trained in law and devoted much of his career to its administration and study, first entering the service of a noted judge, William Raleigh (d. 1250). When Raleigh was nominated bishop of Norwich in 1239, Bracton transferred to the service of King Henry III and became a judge himself in 1244, serving for the most part in the southwestern counties. He was a member of the King's

Council in 1255–56 and after the Barons' War was named a special commissioner to settle the claims of the disinherited supporters of Simon de Montfort in February, 1267. He was buried in the nave of Exeter Cathedral, where he founded a chantry for two chaplains.

Bracton's fame rests chiefly on his writings, *De legibus et consuetudinibus Angliae* (ed. G. E. Woodbine, New Haven 1915—) and a *Note Book* (ed. F. W. Maitland, 3 v. London 1887), which together form one of the most important attempts to organize and rationalize English medieval common law, which had evolved from classical prototypes. The *De legibus et consuetudinibus Angliae* may have been begun as early as 1239, and Bracton was still revising it at the time of his death. Surviving MSS are often corrupted by interpolations of later editors. It begins with an analysis of the principles of English law and then cites some 450 cases exemplifying the practice and procedure of the courts. The *Note Book* contains some 2,000 cases Bracton heard during his years on the bench. The complex interrelationship of *rex* and *lex*, king and law, is treated but not completely resolved. The work of this English churchman had an impact on later constitutional development, especially with regard to appeal to legal precedent. Not until Blackstone was there a more comprehensive treatment of common law.

Bibliography: H. U. KANTOROWICZ, *Bractonian Problems* (Glasgow 1941). C. H. MCILWAIN, "The Present Status of the Problem of the Bracton Text," *Harvard Law Review* 57 (1943) 220–240. F. SCHULTZ, "Critical Studies on B.'s Treatise," *Law Quarterly Review* 59 (1943) 172–180; "A New Approach to B.," *Seminar* 2 (1944) 41–50; "B. on Kingship," *English Historical Review* 60 (1945) 136–176. G. POST, "A Romano-Canonical Maxim Quod omnes tangit in B.," *Traditio* 4 (1946) 197–251. G. T. LAPSLEY, "B. and the Authorship of the *addicio de cartis*," *English Historical Review* 62 (1947) 1–19. S. J. T. MILLER, "The Position of the King in B. and Beaumanoir," *Speculum* 31 (1956) 263–296. W. S. HOLDSWORTH, *A History of English Law* 2:239–290. E. KANTOROWICZ, *The King's Two Bodies* (Princeton 1957) 143–192. A. B. EMDEN, *A Biographical Register of the University of Oxford* 1:240–241. T. F. T. PLUCKNETT, *Early English Legal Literature* (Cambridge, Eng. 1958) 61–79. B. TIERNEY, "B. on Government," *Speculum* 38 (1963) 295–317. H. G. RICHARDSON, "Tancred, Raymond and B.," *English Historical Review* 59 (1944) 376–384; "Azo, Drogheda and B.," *ibid.* 22–47; "Studies in B.," *Traditio* 6 (1948) 61–104; *Bracton: The Problem of His Text* (Seldon Society Supplementary Series 2; London 1965).

[B. J. COMASKEY]

BRADFORD, WILLIAM

Pilgrim father and governor of Plymouth Colony, Mass.; b. Austerfield, Yorkshire, England, 1590; d. Plymouth, 1657. Although he was only 16 years old when the Puritans organized their church at Scrooby, his piety and knowledge soon made him one of the leaders of the congregation. With the rest of the Scrooby congregation he went to Holland (1609–20), where he developed a deep knowledge of theology. He arrived in Plymouth (1620) on the *Mayflower*; and, following the death of the first governor, was elected his successor (April 1621), remaining governor for 30 of the next 36 years. Although Calvinist in theology, he was in practice quite liberal for the period. He took part in legislation against the Quakers, but declared "it is too great arrogance for any man or church to think that he or they have so sounded the word of God to the bottom." His famous *History of Plymouth Plantation,* not intended for publication but probably only for the use of his family, was begun in 1630 and completed probably in 1650. It was printed in full for the first time in 1856, although the manuscript was available to historians before that time.

Bibliography: V. H. PALTSITS, *Dictionary of American Biography* (New York 1928–36) 2:564–566. P. G. E. MILLER and T. H. JOHNSON, eds., *The Puritans,* 2 v. (New York 1938). B. SMITH, *Bradford of Plymouth* (Philadelphia 1951).

[E. DELANEY]

BRADLEY, DENIS MARY

Bishop; b. County Kerry, Ireland, Feb. 25, 1846; d. Manchester, N.H., Dec. 13, 1903. His mother brought the family to Manchester after the father's death in Ireland. Denis was taught by Thomas Cochran, a pioneer Catholic educator, and in 1864 entered Holy Cross College, Worcester, Mass. He subsequently attended Georgetown College (now University), Washington, D.C., and St. Joseph's Seminary, Troy, N.Y. After ordination on July 3, 1871, he was appointed curate at the cathedral in Portland, Maine, and he later became chancellor of the diocese and rector of the cathedral. His interest in the temperance movement gained him support from the non-Catholics of Portland. In 1884, after serving as pastor of St. Joseph's church in Manchester, he was appointed to the new Diocese of Manchester and consecrated by Abp. John J. Williams of Boston, Mass. Bradley helped to revitalize Catholicism in New Hampshire. In addition to administering his diocese and sponsoring a building program, he dealt successfully with problems created by NATIVISM and labor dissatisfaction. He also helped to promote the growth of Catholic schools in the state.

Bibliography: M. H. DOWN, *Life of Denis M. Bradley* (Manchester, N.H. 1905).

[J. L. MORRISON]

BRADLEY, FRANCIS HERBERT

A major English philosopher of the post-Hegelian school of monistic idealism; b. Clapham, Jan. 30, 1846;

d. Sept. 18, 1924. Bradley was the fourth child of Rev. Charles Bradley, a popular evangelical preacher, by his second wife, Emma Linton. A. C. Bradley, the noted literary critic and scholar, was F. H. Bradley's younger brother.

Life. Bradley was educated at Cheltenham (1856–61) and Marlborough (1861–63), where his half brother, George Granville Bradley, was headmaster. In 1865 he went to University College, Oxford, where he achieved a first in classical moderations in 1867 but dropped to a second class in *literae humaniores* in 1869. This reversal may have been due to his increasing disenchantment with the empiricist orthodoxy, stemming from J. LOCKE, G. BERKELEY, and D. HUME and continued in J. S. MILL, which then dominated philosophical England and Oxford and whose hegemony Bradley was to overthrow during his lifetime. In spite of the 1869 setback, the next year saw him appointed to an exclusively research fellowship at Merton College, Oxford, with no teaching or lecturing duties, which he held for the rest of his life. In 1871 Bradley was the victim of a kidney inflammation, which became chronic; for the remainder of his long life he was never fully well and was often in pain. He wintered usually on the Riviera or the English coasts, but conscientiously returned to all college meetings. Chronic illness and later deafness combined to make Bradley something of a recluse, although within a small circle of friends he was both liked and a little feared. He is said to have been intolerant of stupidity; indeed, he became one of the greatest masters of philosophical polemic in history. The poet T. S. Eliot considered him one of the most perfect stylists in the English language. The increasing influence of his writings led to many honors, both at home and abroad, culminating in the Order of Merit in 1924.

Thought. Bradley's first book, *Ethical Studies,* was published when he was 30. It is an all-out attack against the reigning doctrines of English Utilitarianism, especially in the famous criticism of HEDONISM in the third essay. *Ethical Studies* is the most Hegelian of Bradley's works, not only in its exploitation of the notion of the ''concrete universal'' but in its dialectical structure, ranging particular and partial moral views against each other as theses and antitheses and seeking their correctives in higher viewpoints. For Bradley, morality is self-realization, and the inadequacies in this respect of hedonism, of the Kantian identification of self-realization with activity of a purely formal will, and even of the self as equated with the social organism, are all exposed. Bradley goes on to maintain that morality involves a collision between self-assertion, in the interest of comprehensiveness and system, and self-sacrifice, in the interest of higher ends. The contradictory demands of morality call for transcendence in religion, in the assertion of a higher divine will. But Bradley is unwilling to identify God, understood as personal, with ultimate, Absolute Reality. Thought about God, like all thought, is inexorably relational, and to be in relationship is to have only a compromised, an appearance mode of existing that, when analyzed, exhibits contradiction.

The later works of Bradley develop, in the contexts of logic, epistemology, and metaphysics, the schism between appearance and reality. Negatively, Bradley was devoted, like PARMENIDES and ZENO OF ELEA, to showing the self-destructive implication of any pluralism, whether of externally or internally related entities. Beginning with a felt unity of experience beneath relations, thought, separating always the ''what'' and the ''that,'' seeks hopelessly to reunite existence and formal content by endlessly extending the system of relations. Bradley's idealism does not identify thought and reality, but it finds Absolute Reality in an experience that transcends thought and that is beyond all relation. The content of the experience that is Absolute Reality is not other than the content of the experience of finite centers that appear only, but the mode of synthesis or fusion is nonrelational.

The absolute monism of Bradley's doctrine is clearly unacceptable to Christian theists. But the dialectical power of his thought can teach all philosophers much.

See Also: IDEALISM.

Bibliography: Works. *Ethical Studies* (Oxford 1876; 2d ed. 1927); *The Principles of Logic,* 2 v. (London 1883; 2d ed. rev. New York 1922); *Appearance and Reality* (London 1893; 2d ed. 1897); *Essays on Truth and Reality* (Oxford 1914); *Collected Essays,* 2 v. (Oxford 1935), detailed bibliography of Bradley's writings in v. 1. **Study.** R. WOLLHEIM, *F. H. Bradley* (Baltimore 1959).

[L. J. ESLICK]

BRADLEY, RITAMARY

Scholar, author, educator and pioneer in the Religious Formation movement; b. Jan. 30, 1916 in Stuart, Iowa; d. Davenport, Iowa, March 20, 2000.

The daughter of James and Mary (Muldoon) Bradley, Ritamary joined the Congregation of the Humility of Mary of Ottumwa, Iowa, in 1933, and in 1972, the Sisters for Christian Community. A graduate of Marygrove College in Detroit, Mich. (1938), she received a doctorate in English from St. Louis University in 1953. After teaching at Marycrest College in Davenport, Iowa, from 1940 to 1956, she joined the English department at St. Ambrose in 1965, where she was professor emerita at the time of her death.

Sister Ritamary was a powerful force in the origins and development of the Sister Formation Conference.

From 1951 to 1964 she served as Associate Executive Secretary with Sister Annette Walters, C.S.J., the Executive Secretary of the Conference. She was well in advance of major superiors in grasping the changes taking place in the church and the world, and the consequent demands upon religious-apostolic communities of sisters. Her most outstanding contribution came as founder and editor of the Sister Formation Bulletin (1954–1964). In this role, she empowered women religious of the United States by providing an open forum in which sisters could express their opinions and have them published without censorship from male editors.

With the advance of the electronic age, Bradley seized the opportunity to facilitate communication lines among all women religious and established SISTER-L, an e-mail discussion group for those interested in the history and contemporary concerns of Catholic women religious. In addition to her interest in the lives of women religious, Bradley involved herself in numerous civic and humanitarian issues. She was a member of the Davenport Civil Rights Commission; the Iowa Humanities Board program committee, and the Religion and Literature Advisory Board at the University of Notre Dame. She was a volunteer chaplain at the Scott County Jail and received the Volunteer Service Award in 1990.

Among her extensive writings are two books on the fourteenth century mystic Julian of Norwich. She cofounded the *Fourteenth-Century English Mystics Newsletter*, now the *Mystics Quarterly*.

[M. R. MADDEN]

BRADY, IGNATIUS CHARLES

Franciscan philosopher; b. May 9, 1911, Detroit, Michigan; d. Aug. 4, 1990, Cincinnati, Ohio. Charles Brady was the oldest son of five children of Hubert John Brady and Agnes McSweeney. Both his parents were children of Irish immigrants from Counties Cavin and Clare. Charles entered the Friars Minor in 1929 when he was given the religious name, Ignatius, and in 1937 he was ordained to the priesthood. The following year Brady began graduate studies at the Pontifical Institute of Medieval Studies, Toronto, Canada, where in 1940 he received a Master of Arts Degree, in 1941 a Licentiate in Medieval Studies, and in 1948 a Doctorate in Philosophy. He began teaching at Duns Scotus College, Southfield, Michigan (1942–1952), then at Mary Grove College, Detroit, Michigan (1945–1946), St. Francis College, Ft. Wayne, Indiana (1955–1956), and the Catholic University of America, Washington, D.C. (1959–1961).

In 1956, Brady joined the research center of the Friars Minor at Collegio San Bonaventura, Quarrachi, Italy. Five years later the friars appointed him prefect of the center's theological section. In that role, he helped lay the solid foundation for a renewal of Franciscan spirituality after the Second Vatican Council. His enormous literary output covered a variety of subjects, from the writings of Saints Francis and Clare of Assisi to those of Saint Bonaventure and Blessed Duns Scotus. The later years of his life were devoted to the critical edition of the writings of Peter Lombard. Brady spent every summer at the Franciscan Institute of St. Bonaventure University, and preached and traveled extensively in the promotion of Franciscan values.

He died at St. Clare Retirement Community in Cincinnati, Ohio, after a long struggle with illness. To generations of Franciscans from all branches of that family, he was living witness to the wisdom, humility, and graciousness of their founder.

[R. J. ARMSTRONG]

BRADY, MATTHEW FRANCIS

Bishop and educator; b. Waterbury, Conn., Jan. 15, 1893; d. Burlington, Vt., Sept. 20, 1959. He was the son of John and Catherine (Caffrey) Brady. After early education in the public schools of Waterbury, he attended St. Thomas Seminary, Bloomfield, Conn.; the American College, Louvain, Belgium; and St. Bernard Seminary, Rochester, N.Y. He was ordained in Hartford, Conn., on June 10, 1916, and served as assistant pastor at Sacred Heart, New Haven, until 1922, except for eight months as U.S. Army chaplain during World War I. From 1922 to 1932 he taught English, French, and Sacred Scripture at St. Thomas Seminary, Bloomfield, returning then to pastoral work at St. Rita's, Hamden. In 1934 he was appointed to the archdiocesan staff of Hartford, where, as director of the Confraternity of Christian Doctrine (CCD), he organized the Fourth National Catechetical Congress, held in Hartford in October of 1938.

Appointed bishop of Burlington on July 30, 1938, he was consecrated in his cathedral on October 26 by Abp. Amleto Cicognani, then U.S. apostolic delegate. In Burlington, Brady established the CCD, a diocesan school department, a bureau of information, the Catholic Boy Scouts, and the Junior Catholic Daughters of America. He gave strong leadership to Catholic Charities and was host to the First New England Regional Congress of the CCD, which was held in Burlington. During World War II he established centers for servicemen and women. On Nov. 11, 1944, Brady was transferred to the See of Manchester, N.H., as fifth ordinary. Besides founding Catholic Charities (1946) and a diocesan labor institute, he established 30 parishes, built 47 churches, 11 grammar schools, 5 high schools, 3 homes for the aged, 2 large summer camps, 11 convents, 29 rectories, and 18 parish halls.

On the national level, Brady served as episcopal chairman of the department of education, National Catholic Welfare Conference (1950–56), and president general of the National Catholic Educational Association (1957–58). In 1945 he became a member of the episcopal committee of the CCD, and at the death of Abp. E. V. O'Hara, replaced him as its chairman (October 1956), an office Brady held until his own death three years later.

[W. H. PARADIS]

BRADY, WILLIAM MAZIERE

Irish ecclesiastical historian; b. Dublin, Ireland, Jan. 8, 1825; d. Rome, March 19, 1894. Brady, who came from a distinguished Protestant-Irish family, entered Trinity College, Dublin (1842), and received there an M.A. (1853) and a D.D. (1863). After taking orders in the Church of Ireland (1848), he served as curate in Maynooth and then as rector and vicar in the Dioceses of Dublin, Limerick, Cloyne, and Meath. He also served as chaplain to liberal lords lieutenant of Ireland, such as Clarendon, St. Germans, Carlisle, and Spencer. In 1851 he married a widow, Frances (Walker) O'Reilly. Brady published *Clerical and Parochial Records of Cork, Cloyne and Ross* (3 v. 1863–64), the preparation of which convinced him of the unhistorical nature of the Church of Ireland's claim to continuity from Celtic times. Later works, notably *The Alleged Conversion of the Irish Bishops at the Succession of Queen Elizabeth* (1866) and *State Papers Concerning the Irish Church* (1868), received a hostile reception from his coreligionists. His argument for the disestablishment of the Church of Ireland, which appeared in books and in articles in *Fraser's Magazine* and *The Contemporary*, contained massive factual information that materially assisted William Ewart GLADSTONE in carrying disestablishment through Parliament (1869–71). Brady pursued his researches on the Irish Church in the Vatican Archives in Rome, where he and his wife were received into the Catholic Church (1873). Subsequent publications included *Episcopal Succession in England, Scotland and Ireland* (3 v. 1867–77), a work impressive in its day, but lacking in meticulousness by present standards. Brady's studies and publications altered substantially the accepted English identification of the Church of Ireland with the early Irish Church and strengthened the links between Irish national tradition and the Roman Church. But his later works, notably *Rome and Fenianism* (1883) and *Anglo-Roman Papers* (1890), were uncritical in sifting sources. Pius IX and Leo XIII honored Brady by making him a private chamberlain.

[R. D. EDWARDS]

BRAGAN RITE

The origins of the ancient liturgical rite of the archiepiscopal see of Braga, the primatial see of Portugal, are very obscure; it is most difficult to trace the history of any particular practice or custom. Little is known of liturgical practices before the 6th century when Bishop Profuturus consulted Rome about the rite of BAPTISM, the formula of CONSECRATION, and the date of EASTER. Even though there exists documentation of Pope VIGILIUS's (6th century) reply touching Baptism and the Canon of the Mass according to the Roman usage, it is not known to what extent the Roman usages were subsequently followed at Braga. Vigilius sent only suggestions; he did not impose the Roman usage. A century later the MOZARABIC liturgy became common in most of the Iberian peninsula, prescribed as it was by the Visigoths. In contrast, the Roman rite was imposed by Rome in the 11th century. But since the Roman rite was brought to the peninsula at this time by the monks of CLUNY, it was well mixed with Gallican customs. The Bragan rite was rooted in this varied background and there is no evidence with which to relate with certitude its special practices to any historical moment. The ancient roots and character of the rite have always been stressed by official documents confirming its continuance. As late as 1918 it was necessary for a diocesan synod to insist that the liturgical books of the rite were of obligation. A new edition of the Breviary was approved by the Holy See in 1919, and a new Missal in 1924. The Bragan rite was one of the exceptions cited by Pius V in 1570 in the bull *Quam primum* imposing the Roman Missal on the churches of the West. In the wake of the liturgical reforms of Vatican II, the use of the Bragan rite is now restricted to a few special occasions.

There are few particulars to be pointed out concerning the historical Bragan rite. The preparations for Mass and the final prayer after Mass included Marian elements. The Calendar was closely patterned after that of the Roman rite, the greatest variations being in the feasts of the saints. In the Mass ritual, the chalice was prepared with wine and water before the introductory prayers at the low Mass, while at the high Mass it was prepared between the Epistle and Gospel at the bench. Offerings from the people were received after the incensations in the Offertory rite. The rubrics prescribed the sermon at the same place, between the incensations and the washing of the hands. There were three Elevations, one after the

Consecration, a second at the beginning of the Lord's Prayer, and a third just before the Communion of the celebrant. Not surprisingly, many scholars regard the Bragan rite as a mere variant or ''use'' of the Roman Rite.

The most reliable sources for the rite of Braga are the Missal of Mateus, discovered in 1925, and a Pontifical that dates from the 12th century. The Missal of Matous is of 15th-century usage and dates probably from the 10th or 11th century.

Bibliography: A. A. KING, *Liturgies of the Primatial Sees* (Milwaukee 1957) 155–285. J. A. FERREIRA, *Estudos históricolitúrgicos: Os ritos particulares das Igrejas de Braga e Toledo* (Coimbra 1924). A. G. RIBEIRO DE VASCONCELOS, *Notas Litúrgico-Bracarenses: Congresso litúrgico nacional* (Braga 1927) 177–255.

[R. F. LECHNER/EDS.]

BRAHMAN

Originally meaning ''sacred utterance,'' Brahman came to signify the ''sacred power'' believed to reside in the ancient Vedic sacrifice in Hinduism, and then by a natural transition of thought the sacred power that sustains the universe. In the Upanishads and in all later Hindu thought, the word is used to signify the Supreme Being or the Absolute. The Brahman is conceived as pervading the universe in such a way that it can be said, ''All this [world] is Brahman.'' Again, it is said, ''As a spider comes out with its thread or as small sparks come forth from a fire,'' so all this world comes forth from the Brahman. At the same time, lest this be taken in a material sense, it is said, ''Brahman is not this, not this'' (*neti, neti*); it is beyond all material forms. It is described as ''consisting of nothing but knowledge,'' and again, as ''knowledge and bliss.'' Hence, in later philosophy it came to be defined as ''being-knowledge-bliss'' (*saccidānanda*). Conceived as knowledge and bliss, Brahman is not the object of thought, but the subject; it is ''that by which all things are known''; it is the ''Knower,'' the ''Ruler within,'' the ''immortal Person'' (*puruṣa*). Thus, Hindu philosophy was led to its great affirmation: ''The Brahman is the Atman,'' or Self. That is, the ultimate ground of the soul or self is identical with the ultimate ground of the universe. This, in one form or other, is the basic doctrine of Hindu philosophy.

See Also: INDIAN PHILOSOPHY; HINDUISM.

[B. GRIFFITHS]

BRAHMS, JOHANNES

Eminent composer of the late 19th century; b. Hamburg, Germany, May 7, 1833; d. Vienna, April 3, 1897. The standard biographies have traced the influences of poverty and sordid childhood circumstances on the composer's youth, character, and creative intuitions. It is clear that his lifelong friendships and correspondence with Clara Schumann (*see* SCHUMANN, ROBERT) and the music *amateur* Theodor Billroth, among others, testify to his capacity for warm personal loyalties; and that in matters of musical opinion he remained true to the inner necessities of personal conviction, despite strong opposition from partisans of LISZT, WAGNER, and BRUCKNER. (Brahms was championed by the critic Eduard Hanslick, whose reviews kept the musical world of that day in a lively ferment of pro- and anti-Brahms debate.) From a religious point of view, however, still to be settled are (1) the relation, if any, between Brahms's ''form-consciousness'' and his ethical background, and (2) the influence of his type of Protestant piety on such works as *A German Requiem,* a nonliturgical setting of texts from Luther's translation of the Bible (1857–63). ''The chaste Johannes,'' as Wagner called him, may, in rejecting the symphonic poem of Liszt and the music drama of Wagner, have been motivated by ethical convictions that favored the ''orderliness'' of Beethovenian sonata-form over the more amorphous cyclic utterances of BERLIOZ and Liszt, although the *idée fixe* of Berlioz and the ''motivic cell'' of Liszt, like the *leitmotiv* of Wagner, led to a ''formlessness'' that was more apparent than real. Brahms, too, offered a contemporary and personal yet basically traditional solution to the problem of form in his four symphonies, four concertos (of symphonic proportions), and some two dozen major works in varying chamber combinations, as well as in more than 250 songs and a rich legacy of piano pieces. It may perhaps still be argued whether he should be labeled as a ''classical romanticist'' or a ''romantic classicist'' within his own compellingly expressive but rigorously disciplined personal idiom. Schoenberg saw in Brahams's epiclyric mastery of structural techniques a ''development of the musical language'' unequaled since Mozart.

The attitude of professional musicology toward the philosophical discipline of aesthetics hardly admits, yet, of a style-critical analysis that could ''prove'' the point of Brahms's Protestant piety as a tangible factor in the *Requiem.* One may instinctively sense, nevertheless, not only the presence of the elegiac, but also of the pessimistic in this and corresponding works, noting with Geiringer that in the *Requiem* ''all mention of the name of Christ is expressly avoided.'' An early *Missa canonica* (*c.* 1855) survives in only its brief *Benedictus.* Settings of *O bone Jesu, Adoramus te,* and *Regina coeli* (Opus 37) are among the composer's somewhat unjustly neglected minor works. Eleven Chorale Preludes for Organ (Opus 122) brought his *oeuvre* to a close (1896) with a setting of "O Welt, ich muss dich lassen" (Oh world, I must leave you).

Bibliography: *Briefwechsel,* ed. DEUTSCHE BRAHMS-GESELLSCHAFT, 16 v. (Berlin 1907–22). E. EVANS, *Historical, Descriptive, and Analytical Account of the Entire Work of Johannes Brahms,* 4 v. (London 1912–36). M. KALBECK, *Johannes Brahms,* 4 v. (Berlin 1904–14). K. GEIRINGER, *Johannes Brahms: His Life and Work,* tr. H. B. WEINER and B. MIALL (2d ed. New York 1947). P. C. LANDORMY, *Brahms* (Paris 1948). P. MIES, "Brahms und die katholische Kirchenmusik," *Gregoriushlatt,* 53.4 (Düsseldorf 1930). S. KROSS, *Die Chorwerke von Johannes Brahms* (Berlin 1958). A. SCHOENBERG, "Brahms the Progressive," in *Style and Idea* (New York 1950). R. GERBER, *Die Musik in Geschichte und Gegenwart,* ed. F. BLUME (Kassel-Basel 1949–) 2:184–212; "Das Deutsche Requiem als Dokument Brahmscher Frömmigkeit," *Deutsche Musikleben* (1959) no. 7–10. P. F. RADCLIFFE, *Grove's Dictionary of Music and Musicians,* ed. E. BLOM, 9 v. (5th ed. London 1954) 1:870–903. P. M. YOUNG, *The Choral Tradition* (New York 1962). P. H. LÁNG, *Music in Western Civilization* (New York 1941). P. ACKERMANN, "*Liebeslieder:* Brahms und der Wiener Walzer," *Musiktheorie,* 10 (1995) 11–20. R. ATLAS, "Text and Musical Gesture in Brahms's Vocal Duets and Quartets with Piano," *Journal of Musicology,* 10 (1992) 231–260. D. BELLER-MCKENNA, "How *Deutsch* a Requiem? Absolute Music, Universality, and the Reception of Brahms's *Ein deutsches Requiem,* op. 45," *19th Century Music,* 22 (1998) 3–19. W. EBERT, "Brahms und Joachim in Siebenbürgen," *Studien zur Musikwessenschaft,* 40 (1991) 185–204. B. VON HAKEN, "Brahms und Bruckner: Zur Verbindung von Theorie und Geschichte in Hugo Riemanns *Musik-Lexikon,*" *Musiktheorie,* 10 (1995) 149–157. A. LINDMAYR-BRANDL, "Johannes Brahms und Schuberts *Drei Klavierstücke* D. 946: Entstehungsgeschichte, Kompositionsprozess und Werkverständnis," *Die Musikforschung,* 53 (2000) 134–144. M. MUSGRAVE, *Brahms: "A German Requiem,"* (Cambridge, Eng. 1996). B. D. SHERMAN, "Tempos and Proportions in Brahms: Period Evidence," *Early Music,* 25 (1997) 462–477. H. C. STEKEL, "Johannes Brahms und der Katholizismus," *Musik und Kirche,* 67 (1997) 84–89.

[F. J. BURKLEY]

Johannes Brahms.

BRANCATI, LORENZO

Theologian; b. Giovanni Francesco in Lauria, Calabria, Italy, April 10, 1612; d. Rome, Nov. 30, 1693. He entered the Conventual Franciscans in 1630, taking the name Lorenzo. After his profession in 1631, he studied at Lecce, Bari, and the Roman College of St. Bonaventure; he was ordained in 1636, and awarded the doctorate in theology in 1637. He taught at Aversa, Naples, and was regent of studies for his order in Florence, Ferrara, and Bologna. Later, he was professor at the Sapienza University, Rome, where he earned his great reputation as a Scotist; and for many years he was prefect of studies at the Propaganda, Rome. From 1655 he held numerous posts in the Roman Curia as consultor to ten Congregations, and was prefect of the Vatican Library. In 1681 he was created cardinal by Innocent XI (d. 1689), and was named librarian of the Holy Roman Church. Brancati also played a considerable role in the Jansenist and quietist controversies of his day.

His chief work is the *Commentaria in III et IV Librum Sententiarum J. D. Scoti* (8 v. Rome 1653–82). With the 12 volumes of the *Sacrae Theologiae Summa* of A. VULPES, Brancati's commentary forms one of the most complete expositions of Scotus's teaching. This work treats nearly all subjects pertaining to special dogmatic theology. Part of the tract "De Fide" of the commentary is devoted to a treatise on the missions. The first part is a historical survey of the missionary activity of the Church to the 16th century. The second part is doctrinal and concerns the missionary vocation, its requisites, purpose, and the methods to be employed by the missionary. By formulating the general principles of the missionary apostolate Brancati made a distinctive contribution to mission science. Publication of the treatise by the Propaganda is indication that the mission doctrine of the author was in conformity with the mind and practice of the Congregation at that time.

His penchant for positive theology is apparent in the commentaries on the third book of Scotus's Sentences, as well as in his *Opuscula Tria de Deo* (Rome 1687). As a result of his teaching experience at the Propaganda College, he was the first and for a long time the only theologian to include a systematic study of the missions as an integral part of theology. His *Opuscula Octo de Oratione Christiana* (Romc 1685), written because of the quietist

Lorenzo Brancati.

controversy, remains a classic. Benedict XIV (d. 1758) drew much on Brancarti in the composition of his work on beatification and canonization of saints. In general, Brancati was a faithful disciple of Scotus, except on questions of grace, in which he followed St. Augustine.

Bibliography: H. Hurter, *Nomenclator literarius theologiae catholicae*, 5 v. in 6 (3d ed. Innsbruck 1903–13) 4:351–355. É. D'ALENÇON, *Dictionnaire de théologie catholique,* 9.1:13–15. J. HEERINCKX, *Dictionnaire de spiritualité ascétique et mystique,* 1:1921–23. R. HOFFMAN, *Pioneer Theories of Missiology* (Washington 1960). C. TESTORE, *Enciclopedia cattolica,* 3:23. J. H. SBARALEA, *Supplementum et castigatio ad scriptores trium odinum S. Francisci A Waddings*, 2 v. (Rome 1806; new ed. in 4 v. 1906–36) v.3:267–268.

[P. D. FEHLNER]

BRANCH THEORY OF THE CHURCH

A theoretical, ecclesiological teaching devised by theologians of the19th-century OXFORD MOVEMENT in the Church of England that, while excluding communion with the Roman Catholic Church, attempted to explain the meaning of the UNITY OF THE CHURCH and the relation of this unity to different Christian bodies fulfilling the definition of Catholicism as understood by Anglicans. The classical formula of this teaching was set down by William Palmer of Worcester College, Oxford (1838). It became more general and popular later through the writings of Edward B. PUSEY (1800–82), who in 1865 wrote his famous letter to John Keble, *Eirenicon: The Church of England a Portion of Christ's One Holy Catholic Church, and a Means of Restoring Visible Unity.* However, one finds a sign of this teaching in the writings of the 16th-century Catholic Henrician Bp. Stephen GARDINER (*c.* 1490–1555), aswell as in the theory of James I, distinguishing between "the Church" and "communions." This position is still held today, although with slight adjustments of categories and labels that emphasize the pragmatic nature of the theory.

Accordingly, the Catholic Church is alleged to be one through a deep unity of life and profession of the faith of the Apostles in the one, original, undivided Church, while maintaining the apostolic order and succession of its bishops, celebrating the same Sacraments, and adhering to its ecclesiastical institutions. Through schism the Church is *de facto* although not *de jure* divided as to belief and ecclesiastical communion into three great bodies separated from one another: the EasternChurch, the Roman Church, and the Anglican Church. The proponents of the branch theory do not identify their teaching with the constitution of the Church, but with the vital unity underlying its divisions in its actual state. The substantial unity of the Church is that of a family bound by a common life and a common origin. Confessional differences and breaches of ecclesiastical communion do not involve the *esse* of the Church and hence are normal and inevitable. The unity is not broken by this schism: the same Catholic Church is Anglican in England, Gallican in France, Roman in Italy. These particular Churches are but one Catholic Church, indeed one visible body, and although the *diversum sentire* creates external barriers, yet it is united by the essential principles of its oneness (*salvo jure communionis;* cf. Rosenthal's distinction between unity and union). This is actually the basis of the Anglican Reformation as seen in *The King's Book* (1543). Consult therein"The Creed, Article 9." Similarly compare *The Anglican Canons of 1603,* revised in 1865.

These schismatic branches, according to the theory, will eventually be united into the future "ecumenical" Church, a synthesis of all of the confessional Churches at present separated in practice but united in origin and substance with the reality of apostolic Catholicism. (See *The Lambeth Appeal,* pars. 4 and 9.) This ecumenical Church will be one in essentials although, in the Anglican mystique, broadly diversified as to doctrine and discipline in nonessentials all broadly conceived in relation to "fundamental doctrines." This would permit the variety of the customs and rites and dogmatic formulas as already expressed by the Roman, Greek, Anglican, Lutheran, and Presbyterian liturgies no less than the confessions of each particularChurch—e.g., the WESTMINSTER CONFESSION, the Confession of AUGSBURG, the Formula of CONCORD. All these would be considered as valid differentiations of the one Christian revelation.

See Also: ANGLICANISM; UNICITY OF THE CHURCH; UNITY OF FAITH.

Bibliography: T. SARTORY, *Lexicon für Theologie und Kirche* (Freiburg, 1957–66) 2:643–644. W. PALMER, *A Treatise on the Church of Christ,* 2 v. (New York 1841). E. B. PUSEY, *An Eirenicon,* 3 v. (Oxford 1865–70). J. H. NEWMAN, *Parochial and Plain Sermons,* 8 v. (new ed. London 1877–88) 3:191–192. ''The Lambeth Quadrilateral (1888–1920),'' in *Documents on Christian Unity,* ed. G. K. A. BELL, 2 v. (London 1924–30) 2:47–49, The Lambeth Appeal (1920). G. D. ROSENTHAL,*The Unity of the Church: Report of the Anglo-Catholic Congress 1930* (London 1930). H. DENZIGER, *Enchiridion symbolicorum,* ed. A. SCHÖNMETZER (32nd ed. Freiburg 1963) 2885–88. Y. M. J. CONGAR, *Chrétiens désunis* (Paris 1937) 218–247, with best criticism. A. GATARD, ''Anglicanisme,'' *Dictionnaire de théologie catholique* (Paris 1903–50) 1.2:1298–1302.

[A. H. AMADIO]

BRANDSMA, TITUS, BL.

Bl. Titus Brandsma.

Baptized Anno Sjoerd, Carmelite priest, martyr for the freedom of the Catholic press, philosopher, historian of mysticism; b. Feb. 23, 1881, Oegeklooster in Bolsward, Friesland, The Netherlands; d. July 26, 1942, Dachau Concentration Camp near Munich, Germany.

One of six children of Tjitsje Postma and her husband Titus, Brandsma took the name Titus when he entered the Carmelite Order in 1898. His activities in the novitiate served as the foundation for much of his later work: he published a Dutch translation of selected writings of works of St. TERESA OF AVILA (1901), acted as literary agent for his religious brothers, and began an inhouse magazine that was eventually available to all Dutch Catholics.

Ordained in 1905, Brandsma earned a doctorate in philosophy at the Gregorian University in Rome (1909). Returning to The Netherlands, he lectured in the Carmelite major seminary at Oss founded *Carmelrozen,* a journal of Carmelite spirituality and organized scholars to translate the works of St. Teresa. Meanwhile he promoted the study of Frisian language and culture, engaged in various civic and religious projects such as editing the local paper and establishing an apostolate for the reunification of the Oriental Churches.

In 1923, he took up a post as professor of philosophy and the history of mysticism at the newly founded Catholic University of Nijmegen and in 1932 became rector. In addition to distinguishing himself in the study of medieval Dutch mysticism, he wrote on sociology and gained a reputation as a journalist. In 1935, he lectured in the U.S. In that same year he was appointed spiritual director of the union of Dutch Catholic journalists and began his campaign to denounce the anti-Semitic laws passed in Germany. After the Nazis occupied Holland in 1940, he vigorously defended the Catholic schools and refused to dismiss Jewish children from them. In the name of the Dutch bishops, and with full knowledge of the likely consequence for himself, Brandsma induced Catholic newspaper editors to reject Nazi propaganda.

On Jan. 19, 1942, Brandsma was imprisoned at Scheveningen where he composed poetry, meditations on the Way of the Cross, and two booklets (*My Cell* and *Letters from Prison*). Beginning in April he was transfered from prison to prison, arriving at Dachau on June 19. A month later Brandsma was taken to the camp hospital, where he became the subject of medical experiments. He gave his Rosary to the nursing aid who prepared the injection of carbolic acid which killed him ten minutes later. His body was cremated and the ashes deposited in a common grave. He was beatified Nov. 3, 1985, by Pope John Paul II.

Feast: July 27 (Carmelites).

Bibliography: *Acta Apostolicae Sedis* (1985): 1151. J. ALZIN, *A Dangerous Little Friar* (Dublin 1957). H. W. F. AUKES, *Het leven van Titus Brandsma* (Utrecht 1963). R. M. VALABEK, ed., *Essays on Titus Brandsma: Carmelite, Educator, Journalist, Martyr,* (Rome 1985). B. HANLEY, *No Strangers to Violence, No Strangers to Love* (South Bend, Ind. 1983). H. KLEIN, *Liebender ohne Mass. Titus Brandsma* (Trier 1967). B. MEIJER, *Titus Brandsma* (Bussum 1951). F. MILLAN ROMERAL, "Carmelitas en Dachau: las cartas del P. A. Urbanski, desde el lager, en el 50 aniversario de la liberación," *Carmelus* 42 (1995): 22–43. *L'Osservatore Romano,* English edition, nos. 44 & 46 (1985). J. REES, *Titus Brandsma: A Modern Martyr* (London 1971). E. RHODES, *His Memory Shall Not Pass* (New York 1958). S. SCAPIN, *Tito Brandsma: maestro di umanitá, martire della libertá* (Milan 1990). R. TIJHUIS, "Met Pater Titus Brandsma in Dachau," *Carmelrozen* nos.31–32 (1945/46): 18–21, 53–58, 80–85. Eng. tr. *Dachau Eye–witness,* in: AA.VV., Essays on Titus Brandsma, ed. R. VALABEK (Rome 1985): 58–67.

[A. STARING/K. I. RABENSTEIN]

BRANN, HENRY ATHANASIUS

Writer, pastor; b. Parkstown, County Muth, Ireland, Aug. 15, 1837; d. New York City, Dec. 28, 1921. His parents brought him to the United States in 1849, settling in Jersey City, N.J., where Brann attended public and parochial schools. He graduated from St. Francis Xavier College, New York City, in 1857; studied at St. Mary's Seminary, Wilmington, Del., and at Issy, France; and entered the North American College in Rome in October of 1860. On June 14, 1862, he was ordained for the Diocese of Newark, N.J., and he became vice president and professor of metaphysics (1862–64) at Seton Hall College (now University), South Orange, N.J. Following pastorates in Jersey City and Fort Lee, N.J., he became director (1868) of the diocesan seminary in Wheeling, W.Va. In 1870 he went to New York, where Abp. John McCloskey assigned him to form St. Elizabeth's parish in the Fort Washington area. He built a church there in 1871 and one at Kingsbridge in 1877. From January of 1890 until his death he was pastor of St. Agnes Church, New York City, where he built a school, church, and rectory; bought a convent; and raised funds to endow a boys' high school. In 1910, he was made a domestic prelate by Leo XIII. Brann was a popular speaker and an ardent controversialist. He contributed regularly to leading Catholic newspapers and periodicals, and was noted for the articles against the FARIBAULT PLAN that he wrote in support of Abp. Michael A. Corrigan's position during the school controversy in 1897. Among his published works are *Age of Unreason* (1880), a reply to Robert Ingersoll and other rationalists; *Life of Archbishop Hughes* (1892); and *History of the American College, Rome* (1912).

[F. D. COHALAN]

BRANT, SEBASTIAN (BRANDT)

German humanist author and satirist; b. Strassburg, 1457; d. there, May 10, 1521. He was the son of an innkeeper and entered the University of Basel (1475), where he taught Roman and Canon Law (1489–99). When Emperor Maximilian I ceded Basel to Switzerland, Brant returned to his birthplace and through the intercession of Geiler von Kaisersburg (1445–1510), a famous scholar and powerful preacher, became Syndikus (1500) and three years later city clerk of Strassburg and was named an imperial councilor and Count Palatinate. Although born in a time of transition, Brant adhered to the old faith and to the medieval traditions of the German Empire.

Apart from judicial treatises, Brant wrote religious and politico-historical poems; he translated Vergil, some writings of the Church Fathers, the complete works of Petrarch, and Latin hymns and aphorisms by Cato, Facetus, and others. He also reedited Freidank's (d. *c.* 1233) didactic *Bescheidenheit* (1508). None of these works, however, attained the fame of his first work, *Das Narrenschiff* (1494), which was reprinted, reedited, revised, plagiarized, imitated, and translated many times. A Latin version by Jacob Locher, *Stultifera navis* (1497), was translated into English by Alexander Barclay (1509). The original had been composed in Brant's native Alsatian dialect at a time when most chanceries and individual authors used modern High German, and the language—in versification as well as in the choice of expression—betrays clumsiness, but the theme and its verse treatment apparently charmed readers of that time.

Das Narrenschiff is a satire on all the sins, crimes, and foibles of mankind, which are treated, after the humanist fashion, with ridicule as being follies. There are 112 categories of "fools" on board the ship that is to take them to Schlaraffenland (Utopia) on their way to Narragonia. But the ship is wrecked and all perish. Brant's treatment of an old theme is new in that he does not gravely judge and admonish his readers, but holds a mirror up to them (the text was accompanied by explanatory woodcuts) so that they may recognize themselves, be ashamed, and abjure the evil that springs from a lack of self-knowledge. His gentle hints are fortified by learned allusions to the Bible, Vergil, Ovid, the Fathers of the Church, and the *Corpus Iuris*, and to idioms and popular proverbs. Thus the satire becomes a treasure trove of practical wisdom. This first bourgeois satire received high praise: Brant's friend Geiler modeled more than 100 sermons on the different categories of fools, and another contemporary, the Swiss Franciscan Thomas MURNER (*c.* 1475–1537), an outspoken adversary of Martin Luther, followed its style in his *Die Narrenbeschwörung* and *Die Schelmenzunft* (1512).

Bibliography: S. BRANT, *Das Narrenschiff*, ed. F. SCHULTZ (Strassburg 1913), new fac. ed. with an epilogue. W. KOSCH, *Deutsches Literature-Lexikon*, 4 v. (2d ed. Bern 1947–58) 1:210, with bibliog.

[S. A. SCHULZ]

BRASK, HANS

Swedish bishop and opponent of Lutheranism; b. 1464; d. Danzig, July 30, 1538 or 1539. He studied in Rostock and Griefswald. In 1510 he was provost of the cathedral and then (1513) bishop of Linköping, where he was exceptionally able and zealous, promoting scholasticism, and writing chronicles (now lost). In the national revolt against Denmark he supported Gustavus Vasa, but he opposed the introduction of Lutheran doctrines by the Petersson (Petri) brothers. In 1522 he threatened to excommunicate anyone bringing in Luther's writings, in 1523 he accused Olaus PETRI of heresy, and he continued to denounce Petri, despite the king's displeasure. After breaking with Rome over annates (1524), the impecunious Gustavus in 1526 attacked church property, particularly Brask's wealthy see, and he gave Uppsala's press to Petri. The climax came at the diet of Västerås (1527). As spokesman for the bishops, Brask refused to surrender clerical properties or to authorize a doctrinal disputation. Nevertheless, the diet deprived the bishops of power and property, subjected the Church to royal control, and virtually established Lutheranism. Brask preferred exile at Danzig to submission.

Bibliography: *Svenskt biografiskt lexikon*, ed. J. A. ALMQUIST et al. (Stockholm 1917—) 6:45–65. H. JÁCERSTAD, *Lexikon für Theologie und Kirche* (Freiburg 1957–65) 2:653.

[J. T. GRAHAM]

BRAULIO, ST.

Bishop and writer; b. probably *c.* 585; bishop of Zaragoza 631–651; d. Zaragoza 651.

Braulio was the outstanding figure of an ecclesiastical dynasty in northeastern Spain. His father, Gregory, was a bishop, possibly of Osma. (At this time it was acceptable for married men of high standing to join the clergy, leading a celibate life after ordination.) John, Braulio's elder brother, preceded him as bishop of Zaragoza, the most important see in the Ebro valley, from 619–631. There is evidence for another brother, Fronimian, who rose to be an abbot, but no real justification for the claim that Basila and Pomponia, with whom Braulio corresponded, were his sisters.

Little is known of Braulio's early life. His education probably started within his family. At some point he moved to Seville where he studied for several years with St. Isidore, the towering figure of Visigothic Spanish culture. The two men developed a close and lasting friendship as is shown in their surviving correspondence. Braulio encouraged Isidore to compile his great encyclopaedia, the *Etymologies*, and was responsible for its division into books, although he was to complain at his friend's apparent evasiveness in failing to send him a copy (epp. 3, 5). As an addition to Isidore's own 'On Famous Men,' Braulio composed a brief encomium of the author and a list of his literary work, with 17 items, which serves as the basic corpus of Isidoran writing. Braulio's education gave him a thorough grounding in scriptural and theological matters as well as a familiarity with some classical authors, if only through their use by later Christian writers. An enthusiastic collector of books, he developed an extensive library.

Around 619 Braulio returned to Zaragoza. It is most likely that he became an archdeacon there, possibly in connection with the episcopate of his brother John. At this time, following John's suggestion, Braulio began writing a *Life of St. Aemilian*, which was completed during his own episcopate. After succeeding John as bishop of Zaragoza, Braulio served as an influential figure in the life of Visigothic Spain. He participated in three national church councils held at Toledo: IV (633), V (636), VI (638), but was not present at VII (646). Braulio was evidently a respected figure within the Spanish church although it is not possible to assess his precise role. On behalf of his colleagues at VI Toledo, Braulio sent a dissenting but respectful reply to a letter from Pope Honorius I (625–638), rejecting papal criticisms of the lax attitude towards Jews shown by Spanish bishops (ep. 21). Braulio was involved in secular politics, holding office under several Visigothic kings and corresponding with two of them on various matters. He urged Chindaswinth (642–653) to share the throne with his son, Recceswinth (649–672), as a way to avoid problems of succession. Overall, Braulio's relations with Recceswinth seem to have been warmer and it may be that he was asked to draft the *Liber Iudiciorum*, a law code promulgated during that king's reign.

As many of Braulio's letters have survived, it is possible to discern something of his personality, which appears as firm, friendly and learned. His writings establish him as second only to Isidore and alongside Julian of Toledo as a figure of outstanding influence and prestige in seventh-century Spain. In Zaragoza, Braulio transmitted Isidoran traditions to Taio, his successor as bishop, and Eugenius, the future metropolitan of Toledo. Following the death of Braulio, Zaragoza came to be eclipsed by Toledo as the intellectual centre of Visigothic Spain. The cult of St. Braulio developed in the thirteenth century. He is honoured as the patron saint of Aragon.

Braulio's writings. *The Life of St. Aemilian* was begun at the request of his brothers, John and Fronimian, and completed during Braulio's own episcopate, it is essentially a collection of miracle stories relating to the life of a hermit who lived in the upper Ebro valley in the second half of the sixth century. All three brothers promoted the cult of St. Aemilian, perhaps suggesting a family origin in the district of La Rioja where the saint had been active. Besides *The Life*, Braulio also wrote a hymn in honour of St. Aemilian and urged the deacon Eugene, later metropolitan in Toledo (636–646), to compose a mass for the saint.

Epistolary: A single manuscript from Leòn preserves a collection of 44 letters sent to and by Braulio. It far exceeds what has survived from any comparable figure in Visigothic Spain. Besides revealing their author's sympathetic personality, the letters invoke over twenty men and women in covering matters as varied as grief-counseling, theological questions and the royal succession.

List of the Books of Isidore of Seville: This is a short work, praising Isidore of Seville and naming his literary output. It is always found in association with his book, *On Famous Men.*

Hymn of St. Aemilian: Although Braulio was a noted hymn-composer who wrote in honour of the saint, his authorship of this particular work has been questioned.

Feast: March 26.

Bibliography: BRAULIO, *Vita s. Aemiliani*, ed. L. PARGA (Madrid 1943); tr. *Life of St. Emilian* in C. W. BARLOW, *Iberian Fathers* v. 2 (Washington 1969) and *The Life of St. Aemilian the Confessor* in A. T. FEAR, *The Lives of the Visigothic Fathers* (Liverpool 1997). *Epistolario de San Braulio*, ed. L. TERRERO (Seville 1975), tr. *Letters of Braulio* in C. W. BARLOW, *op.cit. Patrologia Latina: Renotatio librorum divi Isidori* 80, 699–714, tr. C. W. BARLOW, *op.cit.* Hymn of St. Aemilian, ed. *Patrologia Latina* 80, 713–716. C. H. LYNCH, *Saint Braulio, Bishop of Saragossa* (Washington 1938); Span. ed. rev. P. GALINDO, *San Braulio, Obispo de Zaragoza* (Madrid 1950).

[J. WREGLESWORTH]

BRAUN, JOSEPH

Archeologist and liturgist; b. Wipperfürth, Rhineland, Jan. 31, 1857; d. Pullach near Munich, July 8, 1947. He was ordained in 1881 and entered the Society of Jesus in 1890. After much travel and study, he taught archeology and the history of art in the theological scholasticates of his order at Valkenburg, Frankfurt, and Pullach. He was for a long time a collaborator on the *Stimmen aus Maria Laach.* Without opening essentially new vistas of knowledge, he produced many voluminous works basic to a knowledge of Christian archeology, iconography, and liturgy; they are indispensable to students because of their massive material and their description of literary sources. The monumental two-volume *Der christliche Altar in seiner geschichtlichen Entwicklung* (Munich 1924) is without doubt his most significant contribution to modern scholarship. His other works, however, are not less important: *Die liturgische Gewandung im Occident und Orient nach Ursprung und Entwicklung, Verwendung und Symbolik* (Freiburg 1907), *Sakramente und Sakramentalien* (Regensburg 1922), *Liturgisches Handlexikon* (2d edition, Regensburg 1924), *Das christliche Altargerät in seinem Sein und seiner Entwicklung* (Munich 1932), *Die Reliquiare des christlichen Kultus und ihre Entwicklung* (Freiburg 1940), *Tracht und Attribute der Heiligen in der deutschen Kunst* (Stuttgart 1943).

Bibliography: *Lexikon für Theologie und Kirche* (Freiburg 1957–65) 2:655. *Neue deutsche Biographie* (Berlin 1953–) 2:553.

[B. NEUNHEUSER]

BRAUWEILER, ABBEY OF

Former BENEDICTINE monastery near Cologne, Germany, Archdiocese of Cologne (patrons, SS. Nicholas and Medard). It was founded in 1024 by the Count Palatine Erenfrid (Ezzo) of Lorraine and his consort Matilda. Abbot POPPO OF STAVELOT supplied the first monks; the first and third abbots, Ello and Bl. WOLFHELM (1065–91), came from Sankt Maximin at Trier. The abbey sided with the emperor in the INVESTITURE STRUGGLE. It is thought that Wolfhelm may have adopted the CLUNIAC REFORM from Fruttuaria-Siegburg, but the reform may have been introduced later on. Monks from Brauweiler collaborated with Count Burkhard, who wanted to convert his castle into a monastery, and thus was founded the Abbey of Komburg, which also took St. Nicholas as patron. In 1467 monks from St. Martin the Great in Cologne went to Brauweiler, which then became part of the BURSFELD reform congregation. In 1802 Brauweiler was secularized. The abbey church, a late Romanesque columned basilica whose west towers and nave date from *c.* 1140 and whose east end and choir are early 13th century (six towers in all), is now a parish church. Its portals are richly sculptured with signs of the zodiac. Today the monastery buildings (dating from 1760–80 except for the chapter room, which has late 12th-century Biblical frescoes) serve as the provincial house of correction.

Bibliography: P. CLEMEN, ed., *Die Kansldenkmäler der Rheinprovinz,* v.4 (Düsseldorf 1897). L. H. COTTINEAU, *Répertoire* *topobibliographique des abbayes et prieurés*, 2 v. (Mâcon 1935–39) 1:480. W. BADER, *Die Benediktinerabtei Brauweiler bei Köln* (Berlin 1937). P. VOLK, *Dictionnaire d'histoire et de géographie ecclésiastiques*, ed. A. BAUDRILLART et al. (Paris 1912–) 10:457–458. P. SCHMITZ, *Histoire de l'Ordre de Saint-Benoît*, 7 v. (Maredsous, Bel. 1942–56). K. HALLINGER, *Gorze Kluny*, 2 v. (*Studia anselmiana* 22–25; 1950–51). E. WISPLINGHOFF, in *Jahrbuch des kölnischen Geschichtsvereins* 31–32 (1956–57) 6273.

[G. SPAHR]

BRAZIL, MARTYRS OF, BB.

Also known as André de Soveral (b. ca. 1572, São Vicente, Brazil), Ambrósio Francisco Ferro, and 28 companions, or the Martyrs of Rio Grande do Norte, protomartyrs of Brazil; d. 1645 in northern Brazil, July 16, 1645 in Cunhaú and Oct. 3, 1645 in Uruaçu (both near Natal).

The martyrdom of André, Ambrósio, and their companions took place in the context of anti-Catholic persecution by Dutch Calvinists who had invaded the Rio Grande do Norte region of Brazil in 1630. The Gospel had been brought to Natal, Brazil, by two Portuguese Jesuits and two Franciscans on Dec. 25, 1597, who catechized the indigenous people. The following century the Dutch Calvinists overtook the region and restricted Catholic practice.

The Massacre at Cunhaú occurred on Sunday, July 16, 1645. Sixty-nine parishioners were worshiping together in the Chapel of Our Lady of the Candles. Dutch soldiers barred the church doors and launched an attack against unresisting civilians. The Massacre at Uruaçu (Oct. 3, 1645) was led by a convert to Calvinism. Dutch troops and armed natives attacked Father Ambrósio Francisco Ferro and some of his parishioners. One of them, Mateus Moreira, was particularly remembered by Pope John Paul II, both at the closing of the National Eucharistic Congress in Natal (1991) and during the beatification homily for refusing to deny the Real Presence of Jesus in the Eucharist.

The martyrs include André de Soveral, native Brazilian priest, and Ambrósio Francisco Ferro, Portuguese priest; and the laymen Antônio Baracho; the Spaniard Antônio Vilela Cid; Antônio Vilela and his son, slaves; Diogo (James) Pereira; Estêvão Machado de Miranda and his two children; Francisco de Bastos; the son of Francisco Dias, a young slave; Francisco Mendes Pereira; João da Silveira; the Frenchman João Lostau Navarro; João Martins, a youth, and his seven young friends; José do Porto; Manuel Rodrigues de Moura and his wife; Mateus (Matthew) Moreira; Simão Correia; and Vicente de Souza Pereira.

On Dec. 21, 1998, John Paul II declared that the thirty died as martyrs for the faith, and on Mar. 5, 2000, he beatified them.

Bibliography: P. HERONCIO, *Os holandêses no Rio Grande* (Rio de Janeiro 1937). *L'Osservatore Romano,* English edition, no. 10 (2000): 2.

[K. I. RABENSTEIN]

BRAZIL, THE CATHOLIC CHURCH IN

The largest and most populous country in South America and the largest Catholic nation in the world, Brazil is situated along the Atlantic coast. Straddling the equator, it borders Venezuela, Guyana, Suriname and French Guiana on the north, the North and South Atlantic on the east, Uruguay on the south, and Argentina, Paraguay, Bolivia, Peru and Columbia on the west. From the southern plain, the terrain rises to an upland dotted by many lakes, then to the Mato Grosso plateau and a mountainous region. To the far north is the Amazon basin, which is crossed by many tributaries. Natural resources include the third largest bauxite reserve and the largest high-grade iron ore reserve in the world, as well as tin, beryllium and nickel. Agricultural crops consist of coffee, soybeans, wheat, rice, corn and sugarcane. Brazil's commercial center, São Paulo, ranks among the largest metropolitan areas in the world.

Brazil declared its independence on Sept. 7, 1822, and by the time of World War II, it had become a world power and was governed by a democratic constitution. Economic chaos and political discord, however, led to a coup in 1964 that brought a rightist military regime to power. A stable democratic government was restored in the late 1980s, and a new constitution was promulgated on Oct. 5, 1988 under which freedom of religion was guaranteed but no state religion was designated. The traditionally rural profile of the country underwent a drastic transformation after World War II; by the year 2000 more than 75 percent of Brazilians lived in urban areas. Of concern to the world was the continued destruction of the Amazon rainforest, which by 2000 had been reduced by millions of acres through slash and burn methods to obtain farmland. In 1999 Brazilian President Fernando Cardoso signed legislation that made deforestation a criminal act.

Early History. The region, home to the Tupí peoples, was discovered on April 22, 1500, by Portuguese explorer Pedro Álvares Cabral, then on his way to India. The only activity following discovery was purely commercial, as Portuguese expeditions went in search of the

Capital: Brasília.
Size: 3,288,240 sq. miles.
Population: 172,860,370 in 2000.
Languages: Portuguese, Spanish, English, French; Amerindian languages are spoken in various regions.
Religions: 129,645,370 Catholics (75%), 210,000 Muslims (.1%), 28,572,070 Pentecostal and other Protestants (20%), 346,000 Jews (.2%), 10,371,620 follow spiritist or indigenous faiths (6%), 3,715,310 without religious affiliation.

brazilwood used in making dyes. Forts were established along the coast, but only a few had resident priests.

Between 1500 and 1521 a group of Portuguese Franciscans were present at Pôrto Seguro. The culture of the Tupí made conversion difficult. Their religion was a naturalistic pantheism, and they were extremely well adapted to their environment, although polygamy, cannibalism and continuous wars of vengeance also figured in their culture. From the Tupí the Portuguese learned many things, such as the use of manioc as food, the hammock as a bed and the slash-and-burn system of cultivation. Unfortunately, this first group of missionaries, as well as several other white colonists, were captured and eaten by the natives shortly after their arrival.

In 1530 the king divided the land into captaincies, to be administered in a semi-feudal manner by donataries, each with absolute power in his region, subordinate only to the monarch. There was no centralized government in the colony and only sporadic priestly activity. Franciscans again ventured into the region about 1538, at the founding of the captaincy of Pôrto Seguro. The Franciscan Frei Pedro Palacios, a Spanish member of the Portuguese province, after helping the Jesuits catechize the native people for some time, founded the sanctuary of Penha in modern Espirito Santo sometime in the 1560s. The early Jesuits, especially José de ANCHIETA, speak of the local people so well catechized by these early friars that they spontaneously presented themselves as Christians to the Jesuits when the latter arrived in 1549.

With the failure of the captaincy system to colonize Brazil, the Portuguese king, John III created a central government in 1549, naming Tomé de Sousa as governor-general and Salvador as the capitol. Four Jesuit priests and two lay brothers, under the direction of Manuel da NÓBREGA, accompanied the governor to the New World. Some secular priests were also sent. The Jesuits fell to work immediately, both among the colonists and among the natives. After founding a church and school in Salvador, they moved into the neighboring villages, and within a year had baptized about 1,000 people. The Jesuits created crude grammars and catechisms in the so-called ''lingoa geral'' a sort of lingua franca more or less understood by most of the native people in the region (*see* ALDEIAMENTO SYSTEM IN BRAZIL).

From 1514 to 1551 Brazil was under the nominal jurisdiction of the bishop of Funchal, but was separated from Funchal and the diocese of Salvador was created and declared a suffragan of Lisbon. The first bishop of Bahia and commissary general of all Brazil was Dom Pedro Fernandes SARDINHA, who took possession of his diocese in 1552, bringing with him several secular clerics to form his cathedral chapter. In 1553 the Jesuit general superior in Rome separated the missions of Brazil from Portugal and founded an independent province of Jesuits in the new land. Nóbrega was named provincial and Luis de Grã his alternate. By the following year the province had 26 members.

In 1553 Duarte da Costa was named governor (1553–57), and arrived with 16 Jesuits. Among them was José de ANCHIETA, the ''Apostle of Brazil.'' Difficulties soon arose between Jesuit missionaries and Bishop Sardinha. On his way to an audience with the king regarding this situation, Bishop Sardinha was shipwrecked, captured and finally eaten by cannibals. The following year Duarte da Costa resigned from the governorship, throwing the colony into complete disorder.

The new governor, Mem de Sá (1557–72), consolidated central government, pacified the native tribes and corrected some of the most flagrant abuses of the colonists, which had caused the native revolts in the first place. He promoted the work of the Jesuits, helping them erect schools and missions throughout Brazil. However, in 1563 disease swept many of the villages, causing thousands of deaths. Many people fled to the wilderness, and it was only with difficulty that the missionaries persuaded them to return to the *aldeias*, or mission villages, after the plagues had passed.

When Governor Mem de Sá asked to be relieved of his position, Luis Fernandes de Vasconcelos was sent in 1570. Unfortunately, on the voyage to Brazil he and his companions, including 40 Jesuits, were captured by French Huguenot pirates and forced to walk the plank, leaving Mem de Sá at his post until his death in 1572.

Missions Threaten Colonial Interests. On July 19, 1576 Pope Gregory XIII created the prelacy of Rio de Janeiro, which included the captaincies of Pôrto Seguro, Espirito Santo, Rio de Janeiro and São Vicente, extending southward to the Rio de la Plata. The new prelate traveled throughout his vast territory and attempted a reform in customs and religious instruction of his people. Unfortunately, since he openly and strenuously defended the native people, he was persecuted by slaveholding col-

Archdioceses	Suffragans
Aparecida	Lorena, São José dos Campos, Taubaté
Aracaju	Estância, Popriá
Belém do Pará	Abaetetuba, Bragança do Pará, Macapá, Marabá, Ponta de Pedras, Santarém, Santíssima Conceição do Araguaia
Belo Horizonte	Divinópolis, Luz, Oliveira, Sete Lagoas
Botucatu	Araçatuba, Assis, Bauru, Lins, Marília, Ourinhos, Presidente Prudente
Brasília	Formosa, Luziânia, Paracatu, Uruaçu
Campinas	Amparo, Bragança Paulista, Limeira, Piracicaba, São Carlos
Campo Grande	Corumbá, Dourados, Jardim, Três Lagoas
Cascavel	Foz do Iguaçu, Palmas-Francisco Betrão, Toledo
Cuiabá	Barro do Garças, Diamantino, Guiratinga, Juína, Rondonópolis, Sáo Luís do Cáceres, Sinop
Curitiba	Guarapuava, Paranaguá, Ponta Grossa, São João Batista em Curitiba
Diamantina	Almenara, Araçuaí, Guanhães, Janaúba, Januária, Montes Claros, Teófilo Otoni
Florianópolis	Blumenau, Caçador, Chapecó, Critiúma, Joaçaba, Joinville, Lages, Rio do Sul, Tubarão
Foraleza	Crateús, Crato, Iguatu, Itapipoca, Limoeiro do Norte, Quixadá, Sobral, Tianguá
Goiânia	Anápolis, Goiás, Ipameri, Itumbiara, Jataí, Rubiataba-Mozarlândia, São Luís de Montes Belos
Juiz de Fora	Leopoldina, São João del Rei
Londrina	Apucarana, Cornélio Procópio, Jacarezinho
Maceió	Palmeira dos Índios
Manaus	Alto Solimões, Cruzeiro do Sul, Parintins, Rio Branco, Roraima, São Gabriel da Cachoeira
Mariana	Caratinga, Governador Valadares, Itabira-Fabriciano
Maringá	Campo Mourão, Paranavaí, Umuarama
Natal	Caicó, Mossoró
Niterói	Campos, Novo Friburgo, Petrópolis
Olinda e Recife	Afogados da Ingazeira, Caruaru, Floresta, Garanhuns, Nazaré, Palmares, Pesqueira, Petrolina
Palmas	Miracema do Tocantins, Porto Nacional, Tocantinópolis
Paraíba	Cajazeiras, Campina Grande, Guarabira, Patos
Porto Alegre	Bagé, Cachoeira do Sul, Caxias do Sul, Cruz Alta, Erexim, Frederico Westphalen, Novo Hamburgo, Osório, Passo fundo, Pelotas, Rio Grande, Santa Cruz do Sul, Santa Maria, Santo Ângelo, Uruguaiana, Vacaria
Porto Velho	Guajará-Mirm, Humaitá, Ji-Paraná

Archdioceses	Suffragans
Pouso Alegre	Barretos, Campanha, Guaxupé
Ribeirão Preto	Barretos, Catanduva, Franca, Jabticabal, Jales, Rio Preto, and São João da Boa Vista
São Luís do Maranhão	Bacabal, Balsas, Brejo, Carolina, Caxias do Maranhão, Coroatá, Grajaú, Imperatriz, Pinheiro, Viana, Zé Doca
São Paulo	Campo Limpo, Caraguatatauba, Guarulhos, Mogi das Cruzes Osasco, Santo Amaro, Santo André, Santos, São Miguel Paulista
São Salvador da Bahía	Alaginhas, Amargosa, Barra, Barreiras, Bom Jusus da Lapa, Bonfim, Caetité, Eunápolis, Feira de Santana, Ilhéus, Irecê, Itabuna, Jequié, Juazeiro, Livramento de Nossa Senhora, Paulo Afonson, Ruy Barbosa, Teixeira de Freitas-Caravelas, Vitório da Conquista
São Sebastão do rio de Janeiro	Barra do Piraí-volta Redonda, Duque de Caxias, Itaguaí, Nova Iguaçu, Valença
Sorocaba	Itapetininga, Itapeva, Jundiaí, Registro
Teresina	Bom Jesus do Gurguéia, Campo Maior, Oeiras-Floriano, Parnaíba, Picos, São Raimundo Nonato
Uberaba	Ituiutaba, Patos de Minas, Uberlândia
Vitória	Cachoeiro de Itapemirim, Colatina, São Mateus.

The Maronite Catholic Church has a diocese at Nossa Senhora do Líbano em São Pulo; the Greek Melkite Church has a diocese at Nossa Senhora do Paraíso em São Paulo; and the Ukranian-Byzantine rite has a diocese at União de Vitória. There are 14 prelatures, two abbeys nulluis, and a military ordinariate in the country, as well as an ordinariate for the Byzantine rite.

onists, as were all his successors until the creation of a bishopric in 1676.

The missions made great strides with the arrival of new missionaries from Portugal, and soon the Jesuits had colleges in Bahia, Rio de Janeiro and Pernambuco. In the captaincy of Bahia alone there were 62 churches and chapels, 16 of which were parishes. In 1584 the Franciscans began organized work under Frei Melquior de Santa Catarina, beginning in Olinda and expanding to Bahia in 1587, Iguaraçu in 1588, and Paraíba in 1589. Within 70 years the Franciscans had more than 20 monasteries, with many native missions. The Benedictines, headed by Dom Antônio Ventura, founded an abbey in Salvador in 1584, and within 80 years had monasteries in Rio de Janeiro, Olinda, Paraíba do Norte, São Paulo, Santos and Sorocaba. The Carmelites arrived in Pernambuco in 1589 and led by Frei Domingos Freire, spread to Salvador, Santos, São Paulo and Rio de Janeiro, and cared for many people in their missions, especially in the Amazon region.

At the end of the 16th century a push was made towards the north, partly to combat French efforts to colonize there and partly in response to the desire of restless adventurers who wanted to conquer new lands. A French attempt in 1594 failed to found a settlement on the island of Maranhão, but within 20 years the French returned, with four French Capuchins under Claude d' ABBEVILLE. The Capuchins, who expanded to 21 in 1614, studied the native tribes and their customs, but French efforts were ultimately doomed by Portuguese efforts to expel them. These efforts succeeded in 1615, and the work of the Capuchins was taken over by the Jesuits and the Franciscans.

In 1624 Brazil was divided into two states, with capitals at Salvador and São Luiz. With the new governor came Frei Cristóvão de LISBOA, who was sent with quasi-episcopal powers to the newly named state of Maranhão e Grão Pará. Cristóvão attempted to set up orderly tribal-colonist relations, but was met by colonial disobedience and his results proved meager. This experience was repeated throughout Brazil, as missionaries' encountered opposition from both colonists and government officials due to a need for enslaved natives to work the plantations. Feliciano de Coelho, governor of Paraíba, expelled the Jesuits in 1593 and the Franciscans three years later. Governor General Diogo de Botelho (1602–07) forbid the founding of any new monasteries in Brazil; both he and his successor, Diogo Menezes (1607–12), were involved in almost continual quarrels with Bishop Dom Constantino Barradas (1600–18) and with local religious regarding the question of tribal protection from slavers.

In parts of Brazil the arrival of African slaves in the mid-1600s freed the native populations from slave hunters, but in the Amazon colonists who could not pay the exorbitant prices charged for blacks continued to hunt the rainforest tribes. At issue was who would administer and control the natives, laymen or religious? As early as 1624 Frei Cristóvão de Lisboa had attempted to effect Franciscan control of indigenous people, but the crown was forced by colonial opposition to suspend the execution of such efforts. So began a series of vacillations of the Portuguese crown: sometimes it protected the tribes and allowed them to be Christianized, while at other times colonists gained influence. During the 17th century militant Jesuit Antônio Vieira obtained adequate authority to missionize and thus protect the tribes to a greater extent than ever before. However, insurrection in Maranhão in 1661 forced the Jesuits from Brazil. Effective missionizing was renewed two decades later, when new laws unpopular with plantation owners passed control over native tribes to the missions and forbid enslavement.

Boa Vontade Church, Brasilia, Brazil. (©Diego Lezama Orezzoli/CORBIS)

While there continued to be vacillation on the part of the government in the face of colonial interests, the golden age of the missions in the Amazon region was 1680 to 1750.

Influence of Changing Balance of Power. One consequence of the Spain-Portugal alliance (1580–1640) was that the Dutch resolved to conquer part of Brazil. Bahia was taken after token resistance in May 1624; Governor Diogo de Mendonça Furtado, along with many Jesuits, Benedictines and Franciscans, was removed under guard to Holland. Other religious fled to Pernambuco, while some priests along with Bishop Dom Marcos Teixeira went into the interior. The cathedral was transformed into a Calvinist temple, the Jesuit College into a barracks and churches into warehouses. The Portuguese retook Salvador in 1625, but the Dutch returned in 1630, secured Olinda and Recife in Pernambuco, and built a colonial empire extending northward to Pará. Catholics there experienced repression and bigotry: Franciscans were allowed use of only four of their six monasteries, Carmelites one of their ten monasteries, while Jesuits were forbidden altogether. After Franciscans and Carmelites planned sedition, priests were imprisoned. Dutch governor Maurice of Nassau ended the persecution for a short time and restrained the Calvinist ministers in their anti-Catholic zeal, although he later exiled and killed friars found to be working for their mother country. A series of battles from 1648–49 crushed the Dutch, thus ending the strongest Protestant threat to colonial Brazil.

Although the Portuguese revolted successfully against Spanish rule in 1640, a peace treaty was not signed until 1668. With this peace, Pope Innocent XI raised Bahia to an archdiocese, with suffragan sees in Rio de Janeiro, Olinda and Maranhão. Meanwhile, regalism kept the number of dioceses and bishops in Brazil small, as the government avoided the cost of supporting new dioceses and paying clerics' salaries. Besides Salvador (1551) and Rio de Janeiro (1676), only five more dio-

The Corcovado statue, Rio, Brazil. (Archive Photos)

ceses were created during the entire colonial period: São Luiz do Maranhão (1677), Olinda-Recife (1678), Belém do Pará (1719), São Paulo (1746) and Mariana (1748). Although the Portuguese government had accepted without modification the decrees of the Council of Trent that made diocesan seminaries obligatory, the results were meager; the first quasi-conciliar seminary was begun in Rio de Janeiro only in 1739, followed by seminaries in Belém (1749), Mariana (1750), Olinda (1800) and Salvador (1815). Most did not endure long, and their purpose was not served because the majority of students were simply taking advantage of the only institutions of higher learning in Brazil.

Because of royal restrictions issued in 1603, 1609 and 1683, convents of nuns were not founded in Brazil until late in the colonial period. Ursulines of the Sacred Heart of Jesus, of the Roman Union, founded the Colégio das Mercês (1735) and the Colégio da Soledade (1739) in Bahia and later expanded their work to the south. The Carmelites of St. Theresa established themselves in Rio de Janeiro in 1742. The Conceptionist sisters entered Bahia in 1744, founding at first a retreat house and then the monastery of Lapa. In 1750 they founded the monastery of Ajuda in Rio de Janerio in the institution originally established by Capuchin sisters in 1705. The retreat house of the Macaúbas, Santa Luzia do Rio das Velhas in Minas Gerais, founded in 1715, eventually became a Conceptionist monastery (1933) as did a number of similar foundations. In 1720 there was also a convent of Poor Clares in Bahia. The social contribution of these cloistered communities was principally educational for they usually conducted boarding schools.

The Age of Enlightenment. The Church began to encounter immense difficulties in the late 1700s, as religious idealism was replaced, even among ecclesiastics, by gold and diamond fever. The irreligious spirit of the age of Enlightenment culminated in the suppression of the Society of Jesus in 1782 and in the ensuing control over education by the state. The treaty of Madrid of 1750 gave Sacremento (present-day Uruguay) to Spain, while Spain ceded to Portugal the Jesuit missions in the present state of Rio Grande do Sul with their population of 30,000 Guaraní natives. The fact that some Jesuits working among these tribes disregarded the command of the Jesuit general to abide by the treaty presented an opportunity for the Marquês de Pombal, Minister of State in Portugal (1750–77). Desirous of breaking the power of the church, Pombal used this evidence of noncompliance to

José de Anchieta, missionary and linguist, called the "Apostle of Brazil."

campaign against the society. A joint Spanish-Portuguese expedition defeated the Guaraní and expelled them in 1756. When the governor of Rio de Janeiro refused to take over the mission lands or to cede Colônia to Sacramento, the treaty was annulled and the Guaraní allowed to return to their ruined villages in 1761. Next Pombal used the delimiting expedition in the Amazon region, under the command of his brother, Francisco Xavier de Mendonça Furtado, with the bishop of Belém Dom Miguel de Bulhões as his willing ally, to attack the northern Jesuits. For real or imagined insults to the royal prerogative, the Jesuits were deprived of their royal salary, their missions, their lands and finally their freedom. Sent under guard to Portugal, many of them spent long years in prison, while ecclesiastics or laymen who defended them were subject to exile. Religious of other orders were also exiled from Brazil at the same time.

The loss of hundreds of religious at one time was a blow from which the Church would not recover from until well into the 20th century. Now without temporal power, those religious who stayed and continued work among the natives were powerless, after the so-called "law of liberation of 1755," to stop the depredations of slavers against their native parishioners. They were reduced to parish priests in parishes the size of European countries. There was in the late 18th century a growing move to repress religious orders of both sexes, generally through the very effective means of controlling or prohibiting the reception of novices for years at a time.

At the end of the colonial period the principle that priests were civil servants had been firmly established. Education was completely under governmental control and the so-called "Reforms of Coimbra," which stressed the positive sciences at the expense of scholastic or spiritual philosophy, were taught in every school beginning with the primary grades. The texts used in philosophy and theology were controlled by the state, and Jansenist and regalist texts predominated. The paucity of bishops and the immense traveling distances within their dioceses made inspection difficult, and ecclesiastical subjects had the right of recourse to the civil courts, which made discipline difficult to uphold. While dedicated bishops were not always lacking, little could be done against the all-pervading *padroado* (*see* PATRONATO REAL). While many churchmen were already becoming politicians, it remained for the empire after independence (1822–89) to perfect regalistic control over the Brazilian Church and, in the process, bring the Church to the lowest condition it ever suffered.

The Church in Independent Brazil. Under pressure from French emperor Napoleon Bonaparte, the royal family fled Portugal and arrived in Rio de Janeiro in March of 1808, whereupon the colony became the metropolis of the Portuguese Empire through the return of King John VI to Lisbon in 1821. Although the Church officially did not take sides in the growing struggle for independence, many churchmen played prominent parts. Freemasonry, making its own the ideas of independence and republicanism, found many adherents, lay and ecclesiastic. An unsuccessful republican revolution in Pernambuco in 1817 had so many priests among the agitators that it became known as the "revolution of the padres." Most churchmen and laymen involved in this revolution had been educated in the seminary of Olinda, which taught the special species of Jansenistic regalism inculcated by Pombal in his reform of the University of Coimbra. The influence of the seminary at Olinda continued to be felt through most of the 18th century.

Brazil declared its independence from Portugal on Sept. 7, 1822, and its new government was dominated by ultraliberal republican ideas. With few exceptions, the 23 clergymen appointed to the constituent assembly in 1823 expressed uniformly regalistic ideas. However, the constitution unilaterally promulgated by the Portuguese king John VI's son, Emperor Pedro I (1822–31), following the dissolution of the assembly, proclaimed Catholicism as the official state religion. The treatment of the Church at this juncture was owing mainly to the efforts of José da Silva Lisboa, who led the Catholic cause.

After independence diocesan reorganization was undertaken. The prelacies of Goiás and Cuiabá were raised to the category of bishoprics in 1826. Two years later the dioceses of Maranhão and Pará were separated from the archdiocese of Lisbon and made suffragans of Salvador, Bahia. In 1826 an apostolic nunciature was also created, but in 1832 it was reduced to the rank of a simple internunciature.

During the reign of Pedro I and the regency (1831–40) that followed, interference by the crown was rampant. Pontifical messages required the imperial placet; religious orders were subjected to unwarranted interference, even in internal affairs, as were dioceses and diocesan seminaries. The government suppressed the Augustinians in Bahia in 1824 and the discalced Carmelites and Capuchins in Pernambuco in 1830. The government gave hundreds of permissions to religious, male and female, to reside outside the convents for long periods of time, thus fostering decadence in the religious orders. The regency period saw the introduction of many anti-Church and antireligious measures, inspired by liberalism and freemasonry. The bishops frequently complained of the flood of decrees that restricted their liberty and independence of action.

The Cathedral Metropolitana, Belem, Brazil. (©Wolfgang Kaehler/CORBIS)

Questions of the confirmation of bishops and of celibacy muddied relations with the Holy See for years. Noted antipapal ultraregalist priest Antônio de Moura was deliberately proposed by the state as the bishop of Rio de Janeiro. When the Holy See refused this nomination, Father Diogo FEIJÓ, the regent, resolved in the name of the crown to deny any Brazilian recourse to the Holy See until Moura's confirmation was granted. The stalemate finally terminated when Moura withdrew his candidacy. The crown also demonstrated its intention to control the economy of the Church and reduce it to a department of civil administration. Happily a champion arose: Dom Romualdo Antônio de SEIXAS, archbishop and primate of Bahia.

Against the onslaughts of the crown, monastic life in the 19th century declined dramatically, with some religious communities dying out completely. Others were forced to sell monastic property and convents to support themselves. All suffered from a lack of vocations and from the growing ease with which the civil government and the papal internuncios gave briefs of exclaustration or secularization to religious. The crown determined that it would take over the property of the orders upon the death of the respective last member and, to expedite this eventuality, in 1855 José Tomás Nabuco de Araújo, minister of justice, decreed that no novices could be accepted in any religious order ''until a concordat about to be presented by the crown to the Holy See be resolved.'' No concordat was presented during the rest of the empire, although a few half-hearted attempts were made. Cynically, the government continued to speak piously of the ''reform'' of the religious orders.

The Franciscans, who had replaced the Jesuits in the missions after 1759, now found themselves without power to protect native Brazilians. Moreover, that task became increasingly impossible as their numbers decreased and no new members were allowed. In 1825 Italian Capuchins were called in to work among the tribes, and their efforts continued throughout the empire. Ironically, the very government attempting to extinguish local orders paid for foreign friars to continue the same work. A few Vincentians, Salesians, Redemptorists and Sisters of Charity also were allowed to come into the country during this century, but their numbers were too small to stem the tide of religious decadence.

Since colonial times *irmandades*, or ecclesiastical brotherhoods, were founded along class lines for social, economic and religious purposes. These brotherhoods built their own churches and were always difficult for local bishops to control. In the 19th century Freemasonry penetrated these confraternities, able to do so because of

The Church of Santo Domingo, Salvador, Brazil. (©Stephanie Colasanti/CORBIS)

the common opinion that Brazilian Masonry was, unlike world Masonry, favorable to religion and was therefore open even to clergy memberships. The clergy joined the lodges with distressing regularity.

The Religious Question: 1872–75. Antagonism between the Church and Masonry came to a head in 1872, when Bishop Dom Pedro María de Lacerda of Rio de Janeiro suspended Almeida Martins, who was going to celebrate a solemn Mass of Thanksgiving on the anniversary of the founding of the local Masonic lodge. The Viscount Rio Branco, minister of state and grand master of the Grand Orient of Lavradio, decided to ''smash the episcopate with a double condemnation, civil and religious,'' so that never again would a Catholic bishop dare to question the rights of all Brazilians to be Freemasons and Catholics at the same time. The other local lodge, the Grand Orient of the Vale dos Beneditinos, joined in the attack on Bishop Lacerda, who allowed the suspension to stand but was afraid to take any more steps.

Only two bishops entered openly into this battle against regalism: Dom Vital María GONÇALVES DE OLIVEIRA, bishop of Olinda and Dom Antônio de MACEDO COSTA, bishop of Belém, both of whom stated in pastorals that Brazilian Masonry was identical with that of Europe. Brotherhoods in these dioceses published lists of members, including priests, who were Masons and members in good standing in the brotherhoods. When the two bishops ordered priests to sever all connection with these brotherhoods, the clergy obeyed, with one or two exceptions. When the brotherhoods would not expel Masonic members, the bishops placed them under interdict, which edict was appealed to the emperor. Pedro II, following the advice of Minister Rio Branco, sent a message to the bishops ordering them to lift the censures, which they refused.

The crown, hoping to gain a double condemnation of the bishops by both Church and State, sent the Baron of Penedo in August of 1873 as special envoy to Rome. In talks with the Secretary of State Cardinal Antonelli, the baron stressed the need to restore peace to the Brazilian Church and insinuated that the conflict could have been avoided if the bishops had acted with less precipitation. He made no mention of the fact that the bishops had already been apprehended. Both Pius IX and Cardinal Antonelli likely believed the envoy; without further verification they dispatched a letter on Dec. 18, 1873, to the two bishops. The letter praised the zeal of the bishops but mildly censured them for the rapidity of their actions; it ordered them to lift the interdict and concern themselves with the purification of the brotherhoods. Within a few days word reached Rome of the imprisonment of the bishops, who were now awaiting trial.

On trial before the supreme court, the bishops refused to defend themselves and did not recognize the legitimacy of the secular tribunal. Although three distinguished Catholic laymen, Zacarías de Góis e Vasconcelos, Cândido Mendes de Almeida and Antônio Ferreira Viana, voluntarily presented a brilliant defense, both bishops were condemned to four years at hard labor. While the emperor refused amnesty, he reduced the sentence to simple imprisonment.

A flood of protests reached the emperor from every side. Pope Pius IX wrote a personal letter to Pedro II, decrying the violence and duplicity of the government and approving all actions of the two bishops. He also reiterated the condemnation of Brazilian Masons. The Holy Father also ordered the nuncio to destroy the ''fatal letter'' of Cardinal Antonelli.

Even after being imprisoned, the two bishops did not lift their interdicts. Their substitutes in the two dioceses, some of who went to prison, also refused to do so. With the Brazilian bishops so united, a Catholic revival set in. Churches were crowded with people pledging their allegiance to the two condemned bishops. Under political pressure, Pedro II pardoned the bishops in September 1875. Pius IX, in a communication to the bishops, commanded them to lift the interdicts immediately upon their release. They did so but could not then insist on the purification of the brotherhoods, leaving their control over the more influential brotherhoods tenuous.

Abolition Heralds New Republic. By 1870 the movement to abolish slavery had gained ground, in part because of its support among members of the new republican party. Clergymen had little to do with abolition, although some religious orders and bishops had freed all their slaves many years before. While decrees in 1871, 1885, and 1888 destroyed slavery gradually, the ''golden law'' of 1888 served a severe blow to Brazil's plantation economy. A year later, on Nov. 15, 1889, Pedro II quietly went into exile, and on Jan. 7, 1890, the provisional government declared extinct ''all patronage with all its institutions, recourses and prerogatives.''

The new constitution of 1891 decreed the complete separation of Church and State, while also granting complete liberty of cults, secularization of cemeteries, the laicization of education in public schools, civil marriage as the only legal marriage, denial of all political rights to religious, exclusion of Jesuits and the absolute prohibition against new convents of religious. The mode of attack was different, but the purpose was still the same: to crush the Church and keep her powerless.

In March of 1890 the bishops issued a pastoral letter protesting the new decrees and their action had some success. The Church gained the right of self-government and the law against Jesuits was abolished. Official government persecution also ceased. Foreign members of religious orders living in Brazil were allowed to revive these venerable groups. The Franciscans, Carmelites and Benedictines were able to rebuild their provinces. Jesuits and Redemptorists once again entered the region. Pope Leo XIII now divided the country into two provinces: Bahia, with seven suffragan sees, and Rio de Janeiro, with nine. Pius X raised the number of archbishoprics to seven and created many new bishoprics and prelacies. Benedict XV, Pius XI and Pius XII continued to increase the number of dioceses. Relations with Rome continued to improve after 1890, and in 1919 Brazil's representation at the Holy See was raised to the rank of embassy.

In addition to the renewed freedoms granted to the Catholic Church, other faiths were now allowed to practice unrestrained. Among its many religions, Brazil developed a small cult connected with Kadecismo, a pretended communication with departed spirits that entered Brazil in 1865 and coalesced in 1884 in the Federação Espírita Brasileira, which from that point on directed the Brazilian Spiritist movement. Other movements included Candomble, Xango, Macumba and Umbanda, the last an African-inspired cult that claimed to practice communication with the spirits of the dead, although in a boisterous way and with ceremonies unknown among the Kardecists. These spiritist cults continued to remain active into the 21st century, although their membership would decline after the mid-20th century.

Because of the secularistic contents of the 1891 constitution, the Church had very little influence in the public schools. Little by little the prohibition against the teaching of religion in public schools broke down. Minas Gerais became the first state to introduce religious education into the schools; it was followed by the state of São Paulo. A strong fight against these changes was made by the ultraliberals and Freemasons, but in the constitution of Nov. 10, 1937, it was ordained that the teaching of religion be allowed if the parents so wished. In 1939 the first Brazilian council of bishops was held, coinciding with the opening of the Catholic University of Rio de Janeiro. In 1930, the first Catholic newspaper in Portuguese was published.

See Also: MISSION IN COLONIAL AMERICA, II (PORTUGUESE MISSIONS).

Bibliography: F. A. DE VARNHAGEN, *História geral do Brasil,* 5 v. (4th ed. São Paulo 1948–53). R. SOUTHEY, *History of Brazil,* 3 v. (London 1810–22). J. L. MECHAM, *Church and State in Latin America* (Chapel Hill 1934). H. VAN DER VAT, *Princípios da igreja no Brasil* (Rio de Janeiro 1952). J. DORNAS, *O padroado e a igreja brasileira* (São Paulo 1938). F. DE AZEVEDO, *Brazilian Culture,* tr. W. R. CRAWFORD (New York 1950). G. FREYRE, *The Masters and the Slaves,* tr. S. PUTNAM (2d ed. New York 1956). C. HARING, *Empire in Brazil* (Cambridge, MA 1958). C. R. BOXER, *The Dutch in Brazil, 1624–1654* (Oxford 1957). M. C. KIEMEN, *The Indian Policy of Portugal in the Amazon Region, 1614–1693* (Washington 1954). R. DE OLIVEIRA, *O conflito maçônico-religioso de 1872* (Rio de Janeiro 1952). F. GUERRA, *A questão religiosa do segundo império brasileiro* (Rio de Janeiro 1952). B. KLOPPENBURG, *O espiritismo no Brasil* (Petrópolis 1960); *A umbanda no Brasil* (Petrópolis 1961); *O reencarnacionismo no Brasil* (Petrópolis 1961). D. KALVERKAMP and B. KLOPPENBURG, *Acão pastoral perante o espiristismo* (Petrópolis 1961). C. P. DE CAMARGO, *Aspectos sociológicos del espiritismo en São Paulo* (Fribourg 1961).

[M. C. KIEMEN/B. KLOPPENBURG]

The Modern Church. During the worldwide depression of the 1930s, Brazil suffered economic decline and the political chaos that followed the elections of 1930 was resolved by a military coup that brought Getúlio Vargas into power. During subsequent governments, efforts were made to restore the stability of the national economy through development of both the capital city and the interior. By 1960 rising inflation and a heavy international debt had taken its toll, particularly on the poor. As peasants agitated for land reform—the redistribution of unused land for agriculture—their actions threatened Brazilian industrialists, which were estimated to own 80 percent of the nation's acreage. An industrialist-backed coup in 1964 ousted the democratically elected president, ushering in a series of hard-line military leaders who suspended all constitutional guarantees. Rural and urban guerilla movements spread rapidly, followed by a period of violent repression, arbitrary arrests, torture, assassination and exile of many who opposed the regime, including student leaders, union organizers and several priests.

The Influence of Vatican II. During the turbulent decade preceding the Second Vatican Council (1962–65), Catholic Action groups such as Catholic Action and the Young Catholic Workers pioneered initiatives in the areas of basic education and the unionizing of rural workers. The rapid growth of the Catholic Action movement in the 1950s not only developed lay leaders who became a force of change in society and the Church, but it was also a source of bishops, many of whom were former Catholic Action chaplains who encouraged pastoral and social experimentation. The National Conference of Brazilian Bishops was created in 1952. The spirit of reform generated by Vatican II further influenced and pastoral action in Brazil.

Faced with an increasing number of Protestant missionary groups and millions of rural migrants moving to the large cities, the Church became a more visible presence among the poor, developing a massive program of basic education, directed principally to the illiterate masses in the northeast. The Basic Education Movement, sponsored by the Brazilian Episcopal Conference and funded by the federal government, reached half a million peasants by radio by 1964, whereupon the new military regime all but snuffed it out.

Liberation Theology. Political amnesty was declared in 1979 under President Figueiredo, whereupon new political parties were formed and a new constitution promulgated in 1988. Within an atmosphere of increased freedom, the bishops published numerous documents addressing such topics as Sacraments, the Church and the Land Question, basic values and the position of the Church in society, while also encouraging the faithful to engage in improving society. On the outskirts of urban areas, grassroots social movements were organizing as early as 1972, directing attention to the lack of adequate housing, health care, education, public transportation and public security.

Although the country experienced an economic upturn during the 1970s, this temporary prosperity was rooted in heavy international investments, resulting in a rapidly increasing foreign debt. By the late 1970s Brazil experienced recession, rising inflation and a decline in the quality of life of the poor and the working classes. The growing concentration of land and wealth in the hands of industrialists drove millions of poor to the subsistence level. From 1978–80 workers in heavily industrialized São Paulo participated in massive strikes that transformed the union structure and led to the formation of the Workers' Party and the combative national Confederation of Workers' Unions. Rural unions were also reorganized, motivated by the struggle for land, and during the 1980s sugar cane cutters of the northeast gained significant advances.

In response to the nation's economic hardship, Church leaders undertook several bold initiatives, some of which met strong opposition from both the Brazilian government and Vatican officials who considered such initiatives theologically or pastorally unfounded. Undergirding these hotly debated initiatives was LIBERATION THEOLOGY, a doctrine developed by Franciscan theologian Leonardo Boff and others.

Social ministries of the Church, such as Catholic Action, were congenial to the development of liberation theology. Conceived within an ecumenical horizon that already existed in embryo within the evangelical churches from the early 1960s, Catholic theologians began relating the sufferings of the poor in their struggles for liberation to the Word of God, convinced that the Spirit was active in the world and that Jesus of Nazareth was identified with the poor and marginalized in history. In Brazil liberation theology came to examine the relationship of the church to the nation's economy, ecology and culture. It also gave an impetus to feminist theology, highlighting the experiences of women in the social movements as well as in the more inculturated forms of religious life. The Holy See moved from an initial attitude of encouragement and approval of this consideration toward one of restraint and even, on occasion, direct intervention. Pope John Paul II, visiting Brazil in July 1980, confirmed his support for the cause of justice as well as for the practical pastoral position of Church leaders in responding to poverty in Brazil. By 1985 however, the position of the Church was somewhat mixed. A number of Brazilians had joined other Latin American theologians in writing a ''summa'' of liberation theology; their aim to rethink Catholic theology from the perspective of liberation. The Roman Magisterium expressed reservations regarding this project, and in 1986 Pope John Paul II condemned the theology's Marxist underpinnings while stating that ''liberation theology is not only opportune but also useful and necessary.'' Strong in their convictions, Brazilian bishops led the fight for land reform through the Pastoral Land Commission, facing violence and sometimes even death. In rural communities, 1,800 people lost their lives while advocating for the redistribution of landed wealth.

Into the 21st Century. By the year 2000 there were 8,243 parishes tended by 8,210 diocesan and 7,375 religious priests. Other religious included approximately 2,270 brothers and 35,900 sisters, who engaged in humanitarian works and operated Brazil's 2,333 primary and 1,059 secondary schools (Catholic education was eliminated from the public school system in 1997). Greatly due to the efforts of religious, by 2000, 83 percent of Brazilians could both read and write. Through participation in such organizations as the Indigenous Missionary

Council, Catholics continued their longtime advocacy on behalf of Brazil's native tribes, while maintaining a crucial advocacy role in numerous other social programs. The Child Pastoral Commission's 140,000 volunteers provided much-needed health care and food to the children of Brazil's poor. In addition, efforts were made to aid the Church in the former Portuguese colony of East Timor. Church leaders remained outspoken on the domestic front, issuing a statement in 1997 criticizing the economic policy of then-President Cardoso as beneficial only to ''businessmen, bankers, big land owner, and [certain] politicians.'' In addition, an increasingly liberalized government broke with Church teachings through such legislation as allowing abortions when fetuses exhibited genetic defects and reducing the punishment for euthenasia. While Brazil remained an overwhelmingly Catholic country, it was estimated that only 20 percent of all Catholics regularly practiced their faith.

Bibliography: P. E. ARNS, *Brasil, Nunca Mais: um relato para a história* (Petrópolis 1985). M. AZEVEDO, *Comunidades Eclesiais de Base e Inculturação* (São Paulo 1986). J. O. BEOZZO, *A Igreja do Brasil: de João XXIII a João Paulo II, de Medellin a Santo Domingo* (São Paulo 1994); ''Historia da Igreja Catolica no Brasil,'' in *Curso do Verão, Ano III* (São Paulo 1989) 120–176. S. BERNAL, *CNBB: Da Igreja da Cristandade à Igreja dos Pobres* (São Paulo 1989). L. BOFF, *Eclesiogênese: as Comunidades Eclesiais de Base Reinventam a Igreja* (Petrópolis 1986). P. CASALDÁLIGA, *Na Procura do Reino: antologia de textos 1968–1988* (São Paulo 1988). J. COMBLIN, *O Espírito Santo e a Libertção* (Petrópolis 1987). J. B. LIBÂNIO, *A Volta à Grande Disciplina* (São Paulo 1983). S. MAINWARING, *Igreja Catolica e Política no Brasil: 1916–1985* (São Paulo 1989). C. MESTERS, *Flor Sem Defesa: uma Explicação da Bíblia a partir do Povo* (Petrópolis 1984). D. REGAN, *Church for Liberation, a Pastoral Portrait of the Church in Brazil* (Dublin 1985). J. M. SUNG, *Teologia e Economia: Repensando a Teologia da Libertação e Utopias* (Petrópolis 1994).

[W. T. REINHARD/EDS.]

BREAD, LITURGICAL USE OF

By divine institution, bread is one of the two essential elements of the Eucharist. The Eastern Churches (except the Armenians) make use of leavened bread, while the Western Churches, since the 11th century, have used unleavened bread. Unleavened bread came into use in the West for pragmatic reasons: they kept fresh longer, and clergy were prevented from using scraps of bread from the dining table for the Eucharist. Only bread made of wheat is recognized by the Catholic Church as a valid element of the Eucharist. In the beginning, the faithful took bread from their domestic supply and brought it for divine service; consequently, the Eucharistic bread did not differ from the shape of bread used for domestic purposes. By the Middle Ages, the altar breads assumed a round form of moderate thickness; and, in the Western Church, they took the light, waferlike form now so common.

Another liturgical use of bread is the traditional distribution of blessed bread at the end of the Eucharist, a custom that survives in Eastern liturgies and in parts of France and French Canada. In Eastern liturgies, the blessed bread is called *antidoron* (ἀντίδωρον), while the French call it *pain bénit.* At the end of the liturgy, bread that has been specially blessed is distributed to the faithful who are present. Centuries ago, this blessed bread was considered to be a substitute for Holy Communion and was distributed only to noncommunicants. This conception, however, gradually disappeared; the blessed bread is distributed to everyone present.

Bibliography: J. A. JUNGMANN, *The Mass of the Roman Rite,* tr. F. BRUNNER, 2 v. (New York 1951–55) 2:31–37, 452–455.

[E. J. GRATSCH/EDS.]

BREAKING OF BREAD

An early technical term used in Acts 2.42, 46; 20.7, 11; 1 Cor 10.16 for the celebration of the Eucharist. The Jews were accustomed to beginning their common meals with a prayer of grateful praise to God (the Semitic idea behind εὐχαριστία, εὐλογία) spoken over a loaf of bread, which was then divided among the participants (e.g., *Berakhot* 46a–b). Although foreshadowed at least linguistically in the Old Testament (Is 58.7; Jer 16.7; perhaps Lam 4.4), this breaking of bread, as a special rite with fraternal and religious significance, was unknown in the Greek and Roman world; *fractio panis* is itself an expression of Christian Latinity.

Jesus had used this ordinary Jewish rite during the meals of His public ministry (Mk 6.41 and parallels). The accounts of the Last Supper in Mk 14.22 (and parallels) and 1 Cor 11.24 indicate the place the rite had in the institution of the Eucharist and why the Judaeo-Christians used the breaking of bread as a technical term to describe the reenactment of the LORD'S SUPPER. In Acts 2.42–47 the breaking of bread is mentioned as parallel to temple worship in a liturgical context: the Christians of the primitive Jerusalem community were faithful to fraternal union, the breaking of bread, and common prayer—all characteristic of a liturgically communal life (Acts 4.32). The sorrow of the Last Supper had given way to the joy of the meals eaten with the risen Lord (Acts 2.46; Lk 24.30, 41–43; Jn 21.9–13). As in the DIDACHE (14.1), the Christians of the Pauline church at Troas met on Sunday precisely for the breaking of bread (Acts 20.7–11). Paul's words (1 Cor 10.16; 11.23–29) related the breaking of bread to the Body of the Lord, conceived of as a sacred meal.

Pope John Paul II consecrates the Host at a Mass in Central Park, New York. (©Robert Maass/CORBIS)

In Lk 24.13–35, the two disciples at Emmaus recognized Jesus in the breaking of bread. It appears that Luke used this term with a eucharistic meaning. Perhaps his intention was to show that, while the Scriptures lead to Christ, only the Eucharist permits Christians to recognize and possess Him fully. A similar purpose can be discerned in Acts 27.33–38: Paul's action in taking ordinary food is described in eucharistic terminology (took bread; gave thanks to God; broke it) to remind the readers that the Eucharist is the true ''food for your safety'' (or ''salvation,'' σωτηρία has both meanings). Writing about 25 years later, St. Ignatius of Antioch described the broken bread as ''the medicine of immortality'' (*Ephesians* 20.2). The multiplication of loaves in Jn 6.1–13 not only served as a prelude to the great discourse on the bread of life, but like the Synoptic accounts (Mk 6.41; 8.6 and parallels) was described in terms reminiscent of the Last Supper, thus showing how the early church saw in this miracle a foreshadow or type of the eucharistic banquet.

Bibliography: J. DUPONT, ''Le Repas d'Emmaüs,'' *Lumière et vie* 6 (Bruges, Belg. 1957) 77–92. B. E. THIERING, ''Breaking of Bread and Harvest in Mark's Gospel,'' *Novum Testamentum* 12 (1970) 1–12. E. LAVERDIERE, *The Breaking of the Bread: The Development of the Eucharist according to the Acts of the Apostles* (Chicago 1998).

[C. BERNAS/EDS.]

BRÉHIER, LOUIS

Byzantine scholar; b. Brest, France, Aug. 5, 1868; d. Reims, Oct. 13, 1951. Bréhier studied at the Sorbonne, where he received the licentiate in 1890, was declared agrégé in 1892, and received the doctorate in 1899. After teaching in four lycées, he was appointed to the chair of ancient and medieval history at the University of Clermont-Ferrand in 1898, remaining there until his retirement in 1938. Bréhier lived and worked in isolation at Clermont-Ferrand and, after his retirement, at Reims. An extraordinarily prolific scholar, he wrote some 30 books and hundreds of articles. His interests centered on the history of Greek-Latin relations during the Middle Ages. The first of his published studies was *Le Schisme oriental du XI*[e] *siècle* (Paris 1900). His essay on the papacy and the Crusades, *L'Église et l'Orient au moyen-âge,* has passed through many editions and is one of his best-known works. Bréhier wrote much on the history of art, including *L'Art chrétien* (Paris 1918), *L'Art byzantin* (Paris 1924), *La Sculpture et les arts mineurs byzantins* (Paris 1936), and *Le Style roman* (Paris 1946). His crowning achievement was a three-volume synthesis of Byzantine history and civilization, *Le Monde byzantin* (Paris 1947–50).

Bibliography: P. LEMERLE, *Revue historique* 208 (1952) 380–382. R. DUSSAUD, *Syria* 28 (1951) 362–363. P. GUILLAND, *Byzantinoslavica* 12 (1951) 287.

[J. A. BRUNDAGE]

BREMOND, HENRI

Spiritual writer; b. Aix-en-Provence, France, 1865; d. Arthez d'Asson, France, Aug. 17, 1933. He received his early education at Aix-en-Provence, and in 1882 entered the Society of Jesus. He was sent for his novitiate and studies to England, where he spent ten years. During this time he ''discovered'' John Henry NEWMAN, who, after Maurice BLONDEL, had the greatest influence on his thought. Bremond was ordained in 1892. Though a professor and an editor of *Études,* he still found time to devote to extensive research, unwittingly preparing himself for the great work he was to publish from 1916 to 1933. During this earlier period his books, characteristically, were studies of religious thought: *L'Inquiétude religieuse* (1900); *Âmes religieuses* (1902); *Thomas More* (1904); *Newman: Essai de biographie psychologique* (1906); *Gerbet* (1907); *La Provence mystique au XVIIème siècle* (1908); *Nicole* (1909); and *Apologie pour Fénélon* (1910), a book that, though brilliant, was unfair to Bossuet.

Bremond's chief work is *L'Histoire littéraire du sentiment religieux en France, depuis la fin des guerres de religion jusqu'à nos jours.* The title indicates that he intended to study religious thought not in the actions that provokes, but in the literary expression that men of talent had given it. He did not include the Middle Ages, because his purpose was the study of the religious life of modern man, the product of the Renaissance. He intended to extend his investigations to works of the 20th century, but at his death his study had progressed only to the end of the 17th century. His central idea was that French religious thought in the 17th century had been revivified by the influence of the Italian, Spanish, and Flemish mystics, thus reaching a sort of perfection of its own and becoming a truly original expression. The French had ignored the riches of their spirituality: the studies of Bremond were for them a revelation.

The writing of this work did not keep Bremond from making literary excursions according to his fancy. He explored widely, returning always, as to a focal point, to the thought of Pascal: ''God is apprehended and felt by the heart, which has its reasons that the mind knows not of.'' Thus he came to relate mysticism with poetry, not to confound them, but to show that they spring from the same faculty ''outside of reason.'' In the course of these researches he coined the term ''pure poetry,'' which had immediate popularity and which represented poetry stripped of its rational elements and reduced to its essence. Among his works should be mentioned *Poésie et prière* (1925), *Dans les tempêtes* (1926), *Introduction à la Philosophie de la prière* (1929), *Divertissements devant l'Arche* (1930), and *La Poésie pure* (1933).

In 1904 Bremond left the Society of Jesus ''because of incompatibility of temperament,'' as he said. He had a volatile and independent nature, which he showed by maintaining his friendly relations with George TYRRELL and Alfred LOISY, even to the point of compromising himself and throwing doubt on the sincerity of his own faith, which was, however, incontestable. He was elected a member of the French Academy in 1923. He spent little time in Paris, making his home at Arthez d'Asson, near Pau, in the Pyrenees.

Bibliography: A. AUSTIN, *Henri Bremond* (Paris 1946). J. DE GUIBERT, *Dictionnaire de spiritualité ascétique et mystique* (Paris 1932–) 1:1928–38. A. BREMOND, ''Henri Bremond,'' *Études* 217 (1933) 29–53. J. JACQUEMET, *Catholicisme* 2 (1948) 239–242. H. HOGARTH, *Henri Bremond: The Life and Work of a Devout Humanist* (London 1950).

[J. CALVET]

BRENDAN, SS.

The name of several Irish saints: Brendan of Clonfert, Irish abbot, patron of the Diocese of Kerry; b. Annagh on Tralee Bay, *c.* 486; d. 578. He is said to have been fostered by St. ITA OF KILLEEDY before further studies with Bishop Erc at St. Finian's Clonard and with St. Jarlath of TUAM. Later, Brendan took charge of the monastery at Ardfert, making a number of new foundations in both Ireland and Scotland. Of these his principal monastery was Clonfert, County Galway, founded in 561. Brendan was a great traveler—he is mentioned in the Hebrides with COLUMBA OF IONA (Colmcille) in ADAMNAN'S biography of Columba; he may also have visit-

Map showing St. Brendan's Island, Ireland, 1367, by Pizzigani.

ed Wales and perhaps Brittany. He is associated with Mt. Brandon, County Kerry, Ireland's second highest mountain, on the summit of which a ruined oratory and cells are claimed to mark the saint's hermitage. It was once among the most famous places of pilgrimage in Ireland. Probably in the first half of the 10th century, an unknown Irish resident on the Continent chose Brendan of Clonfert as the hero of a voyage romance. Such romances were an Irish literary form, conveniently linking adventures on several islands into a unified story. Of these, the *Voyage of Brendan* is the most famous and has been translated into all the languages of Europe. St. Brendan's Island continued to be marked on charts into the 18th century. The author drew on what he knew of world geography, and on mythological and adventure themes from many sources. C. Selmer considers the work to be a deliberately Christianized Aeneid. Voyage romances were also attached to other Irish saints beside Brendan, but they have not been preserved in their entirety. Any idea that Brendan's voyage represents a historical reality, happening to a historical person, must be dismissed.

Brendan of Birr, Irish abbot. He was a contemporary of Brendan of Clonfert, known only from references to him in accounts of other saints. He would appear to have been an important individual, famous enough to be called "the chief of the prophets of Ireland." His principal monastic foundation was at Birr, County Offaly.

Feast: (Brendan of Clonfert) May 16. (Brendan of Birr) Nov. 29.

Bibliography: BRENDAN, *Navigatio sancti Brendani Abbatis,* ed. C. SELMFR (Notre Dame, IN 1959). J. F. KENNEY, *The Sources for the Early History of Ireland* 1:406–420. F. O'BRIAIN, *Dictionnaire d'histoire et de géographie ecclésiastiques,* ed. A. BAUDRILLART et. al. 10:532–534. C. PLUMMER, comp., *Vitae sanctorum Hiberniae,* 2 v. (Oxford 1910) 1:98–151; 2:270–294; ed., *Bethada náem nÉrenn,* 2 v. (Oxford 1922) 1:44–102; 2:44–98. L. GOUGAUD, *Les Saints irlandais hors d'Irelande* (Louvain 1936). K. HUGHES, "On an Irish Litany of Pilgrim Saints Compiled c. 800," *Analecta Bollandiana* 77 (1959) 305–331. G. A. LITTLE, *Brendan the Navigator* (Dublin 1945). G. ASHE, *Land to the West: St. Brendan's Voyage to America* (New York 1962).

[D. D. C. POCHIN MOULD]

BRENNAN, FRANCIS

Cardinal, dean of the Roman Rota; b. Shenandoah, PA, May 7, 1895; d. Philadelphia, July 2, 1968. He was one of six children born to James and Margaret Connor

Brennan. By nature and preference a laconic and unassuming man, he nonetheless served in offices of considerable canonical and curial prestige.

Brennan attended the public schools of Shenandoah; Saint Charles Borromeo Seminary in Overbrook, PA, which he entered in 1910; the Pontifical Roman Seminary, from which he was ordained by Cardinal Pompili on April 3, 1920; and the Juridical Seminary of Saint Apollinaire, from which he received the doctoral degree in civil law and Canon Law (JUD) in 1924. Upon his return to Philadelphia, Brennan served for four years as assistant pastor and taught high-school Latin. While professor of moral theology and Canon Law at Saint Charles Borromeo Seminary (1928–40), he worked on the tribunal of the Archdiocese of Philadelphia and became officialis on Jan. 1, 1938.

On Aug. 1, 1940, at the insistence of his former teacher, Archbishop Ameleto Cicognani, then apostolic delegate to the United States, Brennan became the first American to be assigned to the Roman Rota. He fulfilled the duties of auditor of the Rota from the time of his appointment until 1959, and he subsequently served as dean of the Rota from 1959 until 1967. During the years of Vatican Council II, Brennan served on conciliar preparatory commissions.

Brennan was designated a cardinal by Paul VI on June 27, 1967. The preceding day he had been consecrated bishop in the church of S. Anselmo in Rome and given the titular diocese of Tubune in Mauritania. His titular church in Rome was that of S. Eustachius. In the same year Brennan was designated an assistant on the Cardinals' Commission for the Prefecture of Economic Affairs of the Holy See. In January of 1968 he was appointed prefect of the Congregation for the Discipline of the Sacraments.

During his 28 years in Rome, Brennan served in various additional capacities: the Vatican Court of Appeal, of which he was president; the Congregation of the Council; the Congregation for the Propagation of the Faith; and the Congregation of Sacred Rites.

[F. A. CARBINE]

BRENT, CHARLES HENRY

Charles Henry Brent.

Protestant Episcopal bishop and pioneer in the ecumenical movement; b. Newcastle, Ontario, Canada, April 9, 1862; d. Lausanne, Switzerland, March 27, 1929. He received his B.A. (1884) from Trinity College, Toronto, Canada, and was ordained in 1887. After serving in several parishes he was elected bishop of the Philippines in 1901, a post he held until 1918, when he became bishop of western New York. In 1926 he was chosen bishop-in-charge of the Episcopal churches in Europe for a term of two years.

Brent's experience as a missionary in the Philippines convinced him of the need for Christian unity. In 1910 he attended the World Missionary Conference at Edinburgh, Scotland, considered the beginning of the modern ECUMENICAL MOVEMENT. The harmony and zeal evidenced at the Edinburgh meeting convinced him that cooperation among the various denominations was possible, and he urged an international meeting for the discussion of religious differences. En route to the Philippines, he attended the 1910 general convention of the American Episcopal Church in Cincinnati, Ohio, where his words in praise of the Edinburgh meeting resulted in the formation of a commission for the purpose of organizing an international meeting of Christian churches. World War I and its aftermath delayed the planning, but representatives of 108 churches finally met at Lausanne in 1927 under the presidency of Bishop Brent. Doctrinal differences were discussed, and a continuation committee was appointed to meet annually with Brent as chairman. From these and other independent meetings later developed the WORLD COUNCIL OF CHURCHES.

Brent believed in a religious unity analogous to the unity that bound together the dissimilar sections of the British Empire, i.e., a unity of essential principles that would at the same time respect the traditions of the various groups. He looked to a future united church to which every Christian communion would contribute something from its own particular insight or experience.

Bibliography: A. ZABRISKIE, *Bishop Brent: Crusader for Christian Unity* (New York 1948). G. WEIGEL, *A Catholic Primer on the Ecumenical Movement* (Westminster Md. 1957).

[E. DELANEY]

BRENT, MARGARET

Maryland pioneer; b. England, *c.* 1601; d. Virginia, *c.* 1671. Her parents, Richard, Lord of Admington and Larkstoke, Gloucester, England, and his wife, Elizabeth (Reed), had 13 children. With her sister Mary and her brothers Giles and Foulke, Margaret immigrated to St. Mary's, Md., in November of 1638, bringing letters from Lord Baltimore ordering Gov. Leonard Calvert to grant them as large a portion of land and as great privileges as had been given to the first settlers. To the initial grant of 70 1/2 acres of townland and 1,000 acres outside the town, Margaret gradually added extensive holdings; she was the first woman in Maryland to hold land in her own right, and she played an important part in the affairs of the colony. During Claiborne's rebellion she raised a small body of volunteers in defense of the Calvert government and property. Subsequently, as executrix of Governor Calvert and as attorney for the proprietary interests, she engaged in a multiplicity of lawsuits. In January of 1648 she asked the Maryland assembly to give her voice and vote in her double capacity as executrix and attorney. Although her request was refused, the assembly later came to her defense when the heirs contested her handling of the Calvert estates. Her brother Giles, an ardent royalist, made over his Maryland property to her (1642); and when he moved to Virginia (1646), he made her his attorney. Margaret stayed in Maryland until 1650, when, having made George Manners attorney for her own and her brother's interests, she joined Giles in Virginia. Her will, dated Dec. 26, 1663, and admitted to probate on May 19, 1671, left her land in Maryland and Virginia to her brother Giles and his heirs.

Bibliography: Maryland Historical Society, *Transcripts from the Public Records: References to Mistress Margaret Brent, 1638–1644. Archives of Maryland* (1883–) v. 1, 4, *passim.* W. B. CHILTON, ''The Brent Family,'' *Virginia Magazine* 13–21 (1903–13), *passim.* A. REPPLIER, ''The Elusive Lady of Maryland,'' *Catholic World* 138 (1933–34) 660–669.

[J. DE L. LEONARD]

BRENTANO, FRANZ

German philosophical psychologist influential in the development of PHENOMENOLOGY; b. Marienberg, near Boppard, June 16, 1838; d. Zürich, Switzerland, March 17, 1917. Brentano's parents were devout Catholics; his uncle, Clemens Brentano, was a noted romantic poet; his brother, Lujo, was a political economist and professor at the University of Munich. Franz entered the Dominican Order in his youth but left as a novice. In 1864 he was ordained and in the same year was attached to the University of Würzburg, first as a lecturer in philosophy, later as a full professor (1872). Though he was deep in doubt concerning certain dogmas of the Church, he was asked to prepare a brief on papal infallibility for a meeting of the German bishops before VATICAN COUNCIL I. When the dogma of infallibility was proclaimed, Brentano resigned his professorship and abandoned his priesthood. In 1874 the University of Vienna offered him a professorship, which he surrendered in 1880 when he married. He remained in Vienna for 15 years as an unsalaried lecturer, until approaching blindness forced him to retire. He spent his remaining years traveling in Italy and Switzerland.

Thought. Three major influences were operative in Brentano's thinking. First, he became acquainted with the philosophies of Aristotle, St. Thomas Aquinas, and the scholastics during his seminary training. From these Brentano adopted many principles, as well as his orderly, analytic approach to philosophy. Second, he refused to accept the a priori principles of German idealists, being opposed to any form of dogmatism. Third, impressed with the discoveries of the physical sciences, he attributed progress in science to empirical methodology and urged that such methodology be adopted by the philosopher. Under these influences, Brentano set out to construct a ''scientific'' philosophy that would start with no ''categories'' or ''forms.'' On the analogy of mathematics' being basic to the physical sciences, he sought to determine a similar science that would be basic to philosophy, and settled upon psychology.

Arguing that psychological phenomena can be objectively studied only in their proper setting, which is experience, Brentano proposed to construct a ''psychology from an empirical standpoint.'' He avoided the subjectivist extreme of studying experience through introspection alone; rather, he proposed that in each man there is an experience of ''inner perception,'' an awareness that is both immediate and infallible. By analyzing this ''inner perception,'' Brentano hoped to describe and categorize the contents of experience.

For Brentano, all psychological phenomena possess an ''intentionality,'' a property not found in physical phenomena. His was not the Thomistic theory of an idea's ''intentional inexistence'' in the mind (*see* INTENTIONALITY; SPECIES, INTENTIONAL). Instead, Brentano merely stated that psychological phenomena have a ''reference-to-an-object''; ideas, desires, feelings are essentially concerned with things external. By his ''inner perception,'' man is immediately aware that each psychic phenomenon refers to or ''intends'' an outside object. Thus every such phenomenon must be conscious; unconscious phenomena are self-contradictory.

In Brentano's view, psychic phenomena are of three types: (1) mere representations, (2) judgments, and (3) feelings of love and hate. These phenomena are not static concepts; Brentano saw them all as ''activities'' that refer differently to objects. An analysis of each type uncovers a basic truth. (1) Representations are the primary phenomena; thus every psychological phenomenon is, at least originally, a representation. (2) Judgments are objectively true or false; yet certain judgments are experienced by all men as self-evident. (3) All acts of love and hate possess the value of good or evil; analogously, certain of these volitional acts are experienced as naturally good or evil. It was on this analogy of self-evident value that Brentano based his ethics.

Influence. Brentano prepared the ground for phenomenology by enlarging the scope of empiricism: man not only viewed the elements of experience; he was aided by a certain intuition. His notion of ''intentional reference'' is his most important contribution to the philosophy of E. HUSSERL, who called Brentano ''my one and only teacher in philosophy.'' His analogue of self-evidence applied to moral philosophy is at least indirectly reflected in the value-qualified beings of M. SCHELER. However, his impact on philosophy was as a teacher, not as an author. His major works are *Psychologie des Aristotles* (1867), *Psychologie vom empirischen Standpunkt* (Leipzig 1874), and *Vom Ursprung sittlicher Erkenntnis* (Leipzig 1889).

Bibliography: C. ROSSO, *Enciclopedia filosofica,* 4 v. (Venice-Rome 1957) 1:796–799. A. SCHOLZ, *Lexikon für Theologie und Kirche,* ed. J. HOFER and K. RAHNER (Freiburg 1957–65) 2:670. H. SPIEGELBERG, *The Phenomenological Movement* (The Hague 1960–) v. 1. A. KASTIL, *Die Philosophie Franz Brentanos* (Bern 1951). B. SMITH, *Austrian Philosophy: The Legacy of Franz Brentano* (Chicago 1994). R. M. CHISHOLM, *Brentano and Intrinsic Value* (Cambridge 1986).

[C. P. SVOBODA]

BRENZ, JOHANN

Lutheran reformer of Württemberg; b. Weil der Stadt, 1499; d. Stuttgart, Sept. 11, 1570. Brenz saw Luther at Heidelberg in 1518 and became his follower. For 24 years he served as an evangelical minister in Schwäbisch-Hall, writing a small catechism for youth in 1529, composing an influential order of service, and publishing sermons and scriptural commentaries. In the Sacramentarian controversy with the Swiss REFORMED CHURCHES, he held to the doctrine of the real presence of Christ, his *Syngramma suevicum* being one of the best statements of the Lutheran doctrine. As the Protestant reformer of Württemberg he assisted Duke Ulrich, after his restoration in 1534, and his successor Duke Christopher. Brenz fled to Switzerland during the Schmalkaldic War when the imperial chancellor Antoine Perrenot De GRANVELLE put a price on his head. In Württemberg he established schools, orphanages, homes for the poor, and proseminaries; helped reform Tübingen University; and developed a church order (1559), used as a model in other parts of the empire. He even composed a ''Swabian Confession'' for the Council of Trent, which was, however, flatly rejected.

Bibliography: J. HARTMANN and K. JÄGER, *Johann Brenz,* 2 v. (Hamburg 1840–42). G. BAYER, *Johannes Brenz, der Reformator Württembergs* (Stuttgart 1899). A. BRECHT, *Johannes Brenz* (Stuttgart 1949). W. KÖHLER, *Bibliographia Brentiana* (Berlin 1904; repub. Nieuwkoop 1963). H. FAUSEL, *Die Religion in Geschichte und Gegenwart* (Tübingen 1957–65) 1:1400–01.

[L. W. SPITZ]

BREST, UNION OF

An agreement concluded in 1596 uniting the Ruthenian Orthodox and Roman Catholic Churches of Poland. The Union had both political and religious aspects. Fearing the continued influence and danger arising from the independent Orthodox Patriarchate of Moscow founded in 1589, the Polish government was eager for the elimination of Russian religious and political institutions and traditions. The Orthodox clergy in Ruthenia (the Polish Ukraine) were at this time engaged in an effort to reform and revive the religious, moral, and social life of their discouraged coreligionists. A number of leading Orthodox nobles also supported reform, among them Prince Constantine Ostrogski, who favored reunion with Rome as well. The idea of reunion with the Latin rite along the lines of the Union of Florence (1439) gained strength among members of the Ruthenian hierarchy. Led by Michael Rahosa, Metropolitan of Kiev, and the bishops of Łuck (Terlecki), Lvov (Balaban), Pŕzemyśl (Kopýstenski), Pinsk (Pełczyński) and Chelm (Zbirujski), the first overtures were made to Catholic authorities. Among the latter, King Sigismund III, John Zamoyski, Chancellor of the Kingdom, John Solikowski, Archbishop of Lvov, Bishop Bernard Maciejowski of Łuck (later bishop and cardinal of Cracow), and members of the Jesuit Order, especially Piotr SKARGA and Antonio POSSEVINO, were most favorable to reunion. In 1590 Metropolitan Rahosa convoked an Orthodox synod at Brest. A few days before it opened on June 24, Bishops Terlecki, Balaban, Pełczyński, and Zbirujski drew up a document agreeing to "submit their will and intelligence to the Pope of Rome." The synod subsequently approved this statement, which was secretly sent to King Sigismund, who promised to grant the Ruthenians the rights and privileges enjoyed by the Latin rite. Progress was slow, however; finally, in June 1594, the Ruthenian hierarchy once again advanced the proposals of 1590. A year later Rahosa, assisted by three bishops, met at Brest and drew up two petitions, one to Clement VIII and one to Sigismund III, requesting a reunion based on the Union of Florence, except for the retention of Eastern rites and customs. After Ruthenian consultations with royal delegates and the papal nuncio, King Sigismund on Aug. 2, 1595, proclaimed equal rights, privileges, and guarantees for both Ruthenian and Latin Churches, pending papal sanction. Eventually Clement VIII issued *Magnus Dominus et laudabilis nimis,* confirming and approving the rites, customs, and Julian calendar of the reunited Ruthenian Church.

Despite the devious behavior of Rahosa, who now attempted to hinder the Union, and Prince Ostrogski, who denounced and opposed it, the reunion movement proceeded. In keeping with the pope's request, a synod was held at Brest in October 1596. Although there was opposition and division, a majority of the Ruthenian bishops led by Rahosa accepted the Union proclaimed at Brest. Bishops Balaban and Kopýstenski dissented, however, and were deposed and excommunicated. Ostrogski became the leader of the opposition, which won strong support among the lower clergy and peasantry. The optimistic expectations of both parties failed to materialize. Rome believed that the Union would be a stepping stone toward unity with Moscow, but the strong opposition in Ruthenia itself portended the failure of this hope. Instead of a united Church based on peace and cooperation resulting, distrust and fear created hostile and separated brethren.

In 1995, Pope John Paul II observed the fourth centenary of the Union by issuing an apostolic letter. He highlighted both the right of the Ukrainian Greek Catholic Church to exist and its responsibility within the contemporary ecumenical movement.

See Also: UKRAINIAN CATHOLIC CHURCH.

Bibliography: E. LIKOWSKI, *Die ruthenisch-römische Kirchenvereinigung, gennant Union zu Brest,* tr. P. JEDZINK (Freiburg 1904). J. WOLINSKI, *Polska Kościol prawoslawny* (Lvov 1936), Poland and the Orthodox Church. *The Cambridge History of Poland,* ed. W. F. REDDAWAY et al., 2 v. (Cambridge, Eng. 1941–50). J. OSTROWSKY, *Dictionnaire d'histoire et de géographie ecclésiastiques,* ed. A. BAUDRILLART et al. (Paris 1912–) 10:615–618.

[F. J. LADOWICZ]

BRETHREN

Brethren is a term used in the names of several Protestant denominations, signifying fellowship and the unity of the believing Christians in Christ and with one another. In most cases the name originated from the circumstances of a small persecuted group, forced to rely on its own inner spiritual resources and sense of community. The followers of John HUS represented such a group in Moravia. Under the patronage of Count Nicholas Zinzendorf, a remnant of the HUSSITES was invited to settle on the Count's estate at Herrnhut in southern Germany. From this nucleus, the *Unitas Fratrum,* or Church of the Moravian Brethren, developed. The present MORAVIAN CHURCH in America grew from the settlements made by Zinzendorf at Bethlehem, Pa., in 1741. The ANABAPTIST movement in Germany and Switzerland in the 16th century resulted in the dispersion of all but a few minority groups, the Swiss Brethren, the HUTTERITES, and the MENNONITES, who continued to insist on faith before baptism. Despite intermittent persecution, a number of Hutterian communities (*Bruderhofs*) developed in Moravia, Hungary, and Transylvania. Persecution drove the Hutterian Brethren to Russia and finally to the U.S. (1874–77). Two other small groups of German immigrants to Pennsylvania were spiritual descendants of the Anabaptists. The CHURCH OF THE BRETHREN (DUNKERS) was formed in 1708 at Schwarzenau, Germany, and a majority of its members had settled in Pennsylvania by 1729. A similar group of German origin had settled in York County, Pa., along the banks of the Susquehanna River. From this circumstance, their fellowship became known as the RIVER BRETHREN. A religious revival among the Mennonite and Reformed churches in Pennsylvania resulted in the formation of a church of essentially Methodist faith and polity among the German settlers. It took its name from the phrase used by M. BOEHM and P. W. OTTERBEIN on their first meeting in 1767 ("We are brethren") and is now known as the EVANGELICAL UNITED BRETHREN Church. The PLYMOUTH BRETHREN share the common note of origin as a small group met for fellowship and prayer, but otherwise have nothing in common with the other groups of brethren. Their congregations, formed (1827) in Plymouth, England, are only centers of Bible study and do not form a separate church in the eyes of their adherents.

Bibliography: J. T. HAMILTON, *A History of the Moravian Church* (Bethlehem, Pa. 1901). J. HORSCH, *The Hutterian Brethren,*

1528–1931 (Goshen, Ind. 1931). D. F. DURNBAUGH, comp. and tr., *European Origins of the Brethren* (Elgin, Ill. 1958). F. MALLOTT, *Studies in Brethren History* (Elgin, Ill. 1954). M. G. BRUMBAUGH, *A History of the German Baptist Brethren in Europe and America* (Mt. Morris, Ill. 1899; new ed. North Manchester, Ind. 1961).

[R. K. MACMASTER]

BRETHREN OF THE COMMON LIFE

A religious society in the Netherlands from the fourteenth to the sixteenth century; it differed from religious orders in that its members did not take vows. During the lifetime of Gerard GROOTE (1340–84) the first community of Brethren of the Common Life, priests and laymen, lived in the house of Florent Radewijns in Deventer. They led a life in community without specific religious vows or joining any definite religious order, although they did renounce the world. The task the Brethren set themselves was to live in the presence of God a life of total dedication to Him and to prepare themselves for eternal life. They also strove to arouse true and fervent religious life in others by means of pastoral care and preaching. It was the preaching of Gerard Groote that had inspired the organization of such a free community.

Origin. It is still a question how the first community in Deventer actually came into being. A theory based on information furnished by THOMAS À KEMPIS seems most probable: that the community developed gradually because of the fact that men, sympathetic to the efforts of Gerard Groote, met regularly in the house of Groote's fellow worker, Florent Radewijns, and that some of them stayed there and lived from the revenues accruing from their work as copyists, which they put into a common fund. Florent Radewijns took over the direction after Gerard Groote's death (1384). Among the earliest Brethren were John of Höxter, John Brinckerinck, John Vos of Heusden, Amilius van Buren, Gerard Zerbolt of Zutphen, and several others. Their way of life, as described in shorter or longer vitae, was presented to later members of the community as an example worthy of imitation. These biographies, written in Latin or occasionally in the vernacular, aimed at a lively picture of pious predecessors whose lives had been filled with fervent love for Christ and the desire to imitate him; they may be found in the *Chronicon Windeshemense* of John Busch, in Rudolph Dier of Muiden, Thomas à Kempis, Peter Hoorn, in the *Narratio de incohatione domus clericorum in Zwollis* of James de Voecht, and in the anonymous Frenswegen manuscript. It may be assumed that they were read to the Brethren during mealtimes.

Growth and Expansion. The Deventer community became an example for houses of the Brethren in other cities, and later the Brethren settled also outside the cities in solitary places of the countryside.

In the Netherlands. During Gerard Groote's lifetime a community was started in Zwolle itself, but as the Brethren soon moved to the monastery of Mount St. Agnes in the neighborhood of Zwolle, a second foundation was launched in Zwolle, the St. Gregory House. Together with the Deventer House it became an important center of the DEVOTIO MODERNA and a base for new foundations in the neighborhood, for example, Albergen (1406) and Hulsbergen (1407). Houses were also founded in Hoorn (1384), Amersfoort (1395), and Delft (1403). Although some of these establishments had little or no success, others were founded throughout the fifteenth century, in Brussels (1422), Hertogenbosch (1424), Doesburg (1426), Groningen (1435), Harderwijk (1441), Gouda (1446), Geerardsbergen (1452), Emmeri (1467), Nijmegen (1470), Utrecht (1475), Berlicum (1482)—all in the Netherlands.

In Germany. The Brethren of the Common Life spread also into the neighboring German regions. From Deventer Henry of Ahaus founded a house in Münster (1401), with which were associated foundations in Osnabrück (1410), Osterberg (1410), Cologne (1417), Herford (1426), Wesel (1435), and Hildesheim (1440). In the second half of the fifteenth century, the Brethren spread to southern Germany. Some of the German houses amalgamated into the *Colloquium* of Münster (1431). Outside Westphalia and the Rhenish territories, several German houses were of an intermediary sort, somewhat resembling monasteries of Canons Regular, in which, under the influence of the Devotio Moderna, the common life of the canons was revived after it had been abandoned during the High Middle Ages. Most of the houses of the Brethren in the Netherlands confederated into the *Colloquium* of Zwolle, but it is not known exactly which ones these were.

Decline. The development was rather slow; some communities collapsed, and others constituted themselves as monasteries soon after their foundation. The number of houses of the Brethren that were founded in the course of a century and managed to maintain themselves was not very large, and the number of Brethren in each house was also often very modest. In Albergen, for example, there were only about five brothers at the outset, and this number increased somewhat only later. Exactly the same situation prevailed in Emmerich and several other houses; only in such houses as Deventer, Zwolle, and Münster was the number larger. There were many reasons for this: first, the Brethren were by no means desirous of exerting much pressure to build up their houses. Furthermore, they were initially regarded with suspicion and were even opposed later on, especially by the mendicant orders.

Opposition was aroused among the regular clergy by the fact that the Brethren united into a common life without forming a monastic community and that they gave to these free (that is, canonically unrecognized) communities a certain organization. Groote had recognized this problem, admitted it, and prepared a solution: the foundation of a monastery to which the Brethren could retire if it became impossible for them to continue living in a free community.

The Monastery of Windesheim. As early as 1387 the Deventer Brethren founded the monastery of WINDESHEIM (near Zwolle), which associated itself with the CANONS REGULAR OF ST. AUGUSTINE and soon became the center of the Windesheim congregation, which spread very rapidly; it was a sort of complement to the houses of the Brethren in that many men who favored the Devotio Moderna had been accepted into the monasteries associated with it. To Windesheim's existence is traceable the fewness of the free communities of the Brethren. Among the houses of the Windesheim congregation, the monastery of Frenswegen was an important center for the spread of the Devotio Moderna in Westphalia. It was also a focal point for religious contacts between the eastern Netherlands and Westphalia.

Scriptoria of the Brethren. An important occupation of the Brethren was the copying of manuscripts of various sorts: vitae of the saints, theological works, liturgical books. Their books were often illuminated and beautifully bound. The Deventer community, especially before the invention of the printing press, depended principally on the revenues from the copying of manuscripts and also on simple handicrafts. Other communities founded elsewhere on the model of Deventer derived most of their income from copying work as well. The monasteries of the Windesheim congregation, a product of the Devotio Moderna, had SCRIPTORIA where members of the community copied Bibles, missals, prayer books, and other ecclesiastical books, sometimes by commission; they had a good market. The Brethren wrote for their own use the biographies of Gerard Groote and the men who had been leaders in their society. Their work was unusually legible (*rotunda, fractura*); their scripts, generally used in manuscripts destined for divine service, for private prayer, and for reading in the refectory, are well exemplified in the two 1447 folios from the workroom of the master copyist Hermanus Strepel, who belonged to the Münster House of the Brethren.

Customaries. In the few *Consuetudines* that have been preserved, copying is specifically stressed as a necessary work, supplementing religious practices:

> Concerning the work of copying, note that you should order the work of your hands to the end that it may lead you to purity of heart, because you are weak and cannot be always at spiritual exercises and for this reason was handiwork instituted. Wherefore you ought to attend in your copying to three things, to wit, that you make the letters properly and perfectly, that you copy without error, that you understand the sense of what you are copying, and that you concentrate your wandering mind on the task.

There is also the regulation: ''Twice a week they [the Brethren] write for one hour in the evening for the poor, to wit from six to seven.'' Not only do the *Consuetudines* regulate the *horarium* and duties of the Brethren, they also contain description of the hours of the Divine Office and state how the members of the house are to conduct themselves externally and interiorly during Mass and what special prayers they are to add to those generally prescribed. In the *Consuetudines* are to be found the combination of individual practice and common custom. A closer investigation of the *Consuetudines* and their relation to the Devotio Moderna are problems still to be treated.

Schools and Residences. Recent research has shown that the Brethren of the Common Life concentrated on pastoral work and taught only rarely; usually the students from large city schools lived in residences managed by the Brethren or with lay families formed by the Devotio Moderna. Only in Gouda, Utrecht, and Liège did the Brethren have schools of their own *c.* 1500. Of these, the school of St. Jerome in Utrecht was by the sixteenth century the most important. The pastoral care and religious training of the young entrusted to them in their residences was generally the proper task of the Brethren.

Bibliography: Sources. J. BUSCH, *Des Augustinerpropstes Johannes Busch Chronicon Windeshemense und Liber de reformatione monasteriorum,* ed. K. L. GRUBE (Halle 1886). THOMAS À KEMPIS, *The Founders of the New Devotion, Being the Lives of Gerard Groote, Florentius Radewin and Their Followers,* tr. J. P. ARTHUR (London 1905); *The Chronicle of the Canons Regular of Mount St. Agnes,* tr. J. P. ARTHUR (London 1906). J. T. DE VOECHT, *Narratio de inchoatione domus clericorum in Zwollis,* ed. M. SCHOENGEN (Amsterdam 1908). G. GROOTE, ''The Original Constitution of the Brethren of the Common Life at Deventer,'' ed. A. HYMA in his *The Christian Renaissance: A History of the ''Devotio Moderna''* (New York 1925) 440–474. W. J. ALBERTS, ed., *Het Frensweger Handschrift* (Groningen 1958); *Consuetudines fratrum Vitae Communis* (Groningen 1959); *Consuetudines domus fratrum Embricensis* (Groningen 1965). Literature. E. BARNIKOL, *Studien zur Geschichte der Brüder vom Gemeinsamen Leben* (Tübingen 1917). R. R. POST, ''Studiën over de Broeders van het Gemeene Leven,'' *Nederlandsche Historiebladen* 1 (1938) 304–335; 2 (1939) 136–162; *De Moderne devotie* (2d ed. Amsterdam 1950). A. HYMA, *The Brethren of the Common Life* (Grand Rapids, Mich. 1950). S. AXTERS, *Geschiedenis van de vroomheid in de Nederlanden,* 4 v. (Antwerp 1950–60) 3: *De moderne devotie 1380–1550*

(1956). C. VAN DER WANSEM, *Het ontstaan en de geschiedenis der Broederschap van het Gemene Leven tot 1400* (Louvain 1958). T. P. VAN ZIJL, *Gerard Groote, Ascetic and Reformer, 1340–1384* (Washington 1963).

[W. J. ALBERTS]

BRETHREN OF THE CROSS

During the era of the Crusades, as a reflection of European reverence for the Holy Land, the site of Christ's life, death, and Resurrection, several religious communities known as bearers of the cross or brothers of the cross (*cruciferi, crucigeri*) were founded.

Order of the Holy Cross. The most renowned of these communities was the *Ordo sanctae Crucis,* canons regular of St. Augustine frequently referred to as the CROSIER FATHERS. According to traditions not yet critically studied (*Lexikon für Theologie und Kirche*, ed. J. Hofer and K. Rahner, 6:619; *Dictionnaire de spiritualité ascétique et mystique. Doctrine et histoire*, ed. M. Viller et al., 2.1:2562), the founder, Theodore of Celles (1166–1236), had participated in Frederick Barbarossa's ill-fated CRUSADE. Upon returning to Europe, he received a canonry in the cathedral of St. Lambert at Liège. Choosing to live in community, he and his four original companions took vows in the presence of the bishop of Liège on the feast of the Exaltation of the Holy Cross, Sept. 14, 1211. Their first home was the church of St. Theobald at Clair-Lieu, near Huy, a gift of the bishop. Pope Innocent III gave his blessing to the community; and Pope Honorius III, his formal approbation. Peter of Walcourt, the second superior of the order, adopted in large measure the constitutions of the DOMINICANS and secured the approval of Pope Innocent IV on May 3, 1248. During the 13th century the Crosiers spread rapidly through Belgium, Holland, France, England, and Germany. Some participated in the mission to the pagan Livonians, while others, it is said, preached the gospel to the ALBIGENSES, heretics in southern France, and established a house in Toulouse, the heart of the affected region. Joinville, the biographer of St. Louis IX of France, reports that the king gave the Crosiers a house in Paris on the ''street of the Holy Cross.'' In 1318 Pope John XXII granted the Crosiers the privileges enjoyed by the MENDICANT ORDERS. The Crosiers flourished in the 14th and 15th centuries, but they suffered greatly during the Reformation. Their houses in England and Holland were closed, and during the French Revolution they were expelled from France and Belgium. A revival commenced in the middle years of the 19th century. Today the order has three provinces, with missions in Indonesia, the Congo, and New Guinea. The master general was elected for life and since 1630 has enjoyed the privilege of using pontifical insignia. The habit consists of a white tunic and a black scapular, mantle, and hood. A cross of white and red is embroidered on the scapular.

Italian Cruciati. In Italy the former crusader Cletus of Bologna founded a community of canons regular of St. Augustine, known as *cruciferi* or *cruciati.* In 1169 Alexander III gave his approval. In 1591 they received the privileges of the mendicant orders. At its greatest extent the congregation had five provinces, viz, Bologna, Venice, Rome, Milan, and Naples, with 200 houses. Pope Alexander VII suppressed the congregation in 1656.

Portuguese Canons Regular of the Holy Cross of Coimbra. In Portugal, Tello, the archdeacon of the cathedral of Coimbra, founded the canons regular of the Holy Cross in 1131. Four years later Pope Innocent II confirmed them, and they soon spread through Portugal and Spain. The prior of Coimbra was also chancellor of the university of COIMBRA. The canons played an important role in the spiritual and political life of Portugal throughout the 16th century, but in 1833 the congregation was suppressed.

Bohemian Military Order of the Cross with a Red Star. In Bohemia the *Ordo militaris crucigerorum cum rubea stella,* or Knights of the Cross with the Red Star, was devoted principally to the care of the sick, though it also claimed to be a military order. In 1233 Princess Agnes of Bohemia gave the brethren the church of St. Peter and the hospital of St. Francis in Prague. Pope Gregory IX in 1237 approved the congregation under the rule of St. AUGUSTINE. In 1250 the papacy allowed the brothers to wear a red cross with a six-pointed red star. From their house in Breslau in Silesia the brothers established numerous hospitals. They especially distinguished themselves during the Hussite Wars and the Reformation. In the course of the Thirty Years' War the brothers fought against the Protestants, thus justifying their claim to be a military order. A general reform of the order was effected during the late 17th century. Although in 1810 the Prussian government suppressed the house in Silesia, the order still exists in the Czech Republic, with headquarters in Prague.

Order of the Holy Cross with the Red Heart. A military order organized in 1250 with its headquarters at Cracow developed especially in the 16th century. It spread into Poland, Lithuania, and Bohemia, continuing in Lithuania into the first half of the 19th century.

Bibliography: C. R. HERMANS, *Annales canonicorum regularium s. Augustini ordinis s. Crucis,* 3 v. ('s Hertogenbosch 1858). R. HAASS, *Die Kreuzherren in den Rheinlanden* (Bonn 1932). F. JACKSCHE, *Geschichte des ritterl. Ordens mit dem roten Stern* (Prague 1904). A. VAN DE PASCH, *Lexikon für Theologie und Kir-*

che, ed. J. HOFER and K. RAHNER, 10 v. (2d, new ed. Freiburg 1957–65) 6:619–621. P. A. CEYSSENS, *Dictionnaire de droit canonique*, ed. R. NAZ, 7 v. (Paris 1935–65) 4:799–814. M. VINKEN, *Dictionnaire de spiritualité ascétique et mystique. Doctrine et histoire*, ed. M. VILLER et al. (Paris 1932–) 2.2:2561–76; *Dictionnaire d'histoire et de géographie ecclésiastiques*, ed. A. BAUDRILLART et al. (Paris 1912–) 13:1042–62.

[J. F. O'CALLAGHAN]

BRETTON, JOHN, BL.

Martyr; b. ca. 1529 in West Bretton (near Barnsley), Yorkshire, England; d. April 1, 1598, hanged at York. Born into an old Catholic family, Bretton was the father of a daughter and four sons, one of whom was probably Dr. Matthew Britton, prefect and professor at Douai in 1599. An ardent Catholic, John was often separated from his wife and family, owing to the constant persecution that he suffered for his faith. He was convicted and fined several times for recusancy. In later life he was maliciously and falsely accused of traitorous speeches against the queen and condemned to death. Upon refusing to renounce his faith he was executed for high treason against Elizabeth I. He was beatified by Pope John Paul II on Nov. 22, 1987 with George Haydock and Companions.

Feast of the English Martyrs: May 4 (England).

See Also: ENGLAND, SCOTLAND, AND WALES, MARTYRS OF.

Bibliography: R. CHALLONER, *Memoirs of Missionary Priests,* ed. J. H. POLLEN (rev. ed. London 1924). J. H. POLLEN, *Acts of English Martyrs* (London 1891).

[K. I. RABENSTEIN]

BREVIARY, ROMAN

From the Latin *breviarium*, ''an abridgement.'' Historically, a book of convenience containing but a seasonal part of the Divine Office that emerged during the Middle Ages. As a condensed tome it could appear only after the contents and form of this liturgical prayer were more or less fixed and widely used, and after the obligation of daily recitation was regarded as resting upon individual persons rather than upon a religious community or local church.

In general, by the 7th century the Roman Divine Office was more or less fixed in form and content; Carolingian Europe, with its liturgical imports from Rome and its own traditions, had its Office firmly molded by the 10th century. Fixed in content, this Office rendered by community, monastic or diocesan, was solemn in form and required many books and several ministers; the congregation participated without books by reciting Psalms and responses from memory or responding to the Psalms with refrains.

The first Breviaries were choir books that gathered the Office material from many books into one. These began to appear as early as the 11th century. Portable Breviaries did not develop until the obligation devolved from the community to the individual. The first real need for the portable Breviary arose with the appearance of the mendicant orders, groups of religious who in their apostolate did not reside in a community yet desired to remain united in prayer. The need became acute with the rapid expansion of the Franciscan Order in the 13th century.

Innocent III had already approved a shortened version of the Office for the members of his curia. It was this convenient book that the Franciscans adopted. Further revised by Haymo of Faversham, general of the order in 1240, the Breviary was spread throughout Europe by his friars. And the printing press later made it easily available on a large scale, whereas the printing on a small scale of local Offices, non-Roman Breviaries, had become prohibitive.

Before the reforms of Trent this same Breviary grew cumbersome with new saints' feasts; these feast days vied with one another for prominence, obscuring the centrality of the mysteries of Christ. Pius V in 1568, in accord with the reform of the Council of Trent, imposed this Breviary universally, ruling out any Office not 200 years old. Piecemeal revisions since Trent were insufficient to address its deficiencies, making apparent the need for a thorough reform at Vatican II.

Bibliography: P. SALMON, *The Breviary through the Centuries,* tr. D. MARY (Collegeville, Minn. 1962). J. A. JUNGMANN, *Pastoral Liturgy* (New York 1962); *Public Worship: A Survey,* tr. C. HOWELL (Collegeville, Minn. 1957). P. PARSCH, *The Breviary Explained,* tr. W. NAYDEN and C. HOEGERL (St. Louis 1952). S. CAMPBELL, *From Breviary to Liturgy of the Hours: The Structural Reform of the Roman Office, 1964–1971* (Collegeville 1995). G. GUIVER, *Company of Voices: Daily Prayer and the People of God* (New York 1988). R. TAFT, *The Liturgy of the Hours in East and West: The Origins of the Divine Office and its Meaning for Today* 2nd rev. ed. (Collegeville 1993).

[R. T. CALLAHAN/EDS.]

BREVICOXA (JEAN COURTECUISSE)

Theologian; b. Haleine (Orne), France, mid-14th century; d. Geneva, May 4, 1423. He began his theological studies at the University of Paris in 1367, taught there from 1389, and was dean of the theological faculty from 1416 to 1421. His eloquence and knowledge earned for him the title Doctor Sublimis. He played an important role in bringing the Great Schism of the West to an end. Because of this, Charles VI of France in 1395 and 1396 named him ambassador to the rulers of England and Germany, respectively, in order to enlist their efforts toward putting an end to the rule of the two rival pontiffs. Courtecuisse was met by a peremptory refusal when he asked Benedict XIII to abdicate. In 1398, he became partisan to a movement to withdraw obedience to Benedict. He took part in the Council of Pisa in 1409 and in that of Rome in 1412. His panegyric of the duke of Orléans (Jan. 10, 1414) drew upon him the hatred of the duke of Bourgogne, and this led him to join the ranks of the Armagnacs. His election as bishop of Paris was confirmed by Martin V (June 16, 1421) contrary to the wishes of the English crown, which supported another candidate. The hostility of the king of England toward him was such that he had to be transferred to the see of Geneva (June 12, 1422). In his *Tractatus de fide et ecclesia, de Romano pontifice et concilio generali,* he teaches the superiority of the council over the pope.

Bibliography: A. COVILLE, ''Recherches sur Jean Courtecuisse,'' *Bibliothèque de l'École des Chartres* 65 (1904) 469–529. N. VALOIS, *La France et le grand schisme d'Occident,* 4 v. (Paris 1896–1902) v. 3-4. A. COVILLE, *Jean Petit* (Paris 1932). A. BIGELMAIR, *Lexikon für Theologie und Kirche* (Freiburg 1957–65) 5:1011-12. E. MANGENOT, *Dictionnaire de théologie catholique* (Paris 1903–50) 3.2:1984-85. G. MOLLAT, *Dictionnaire d'histoire et de géographie ecclésiastiques* (Paris 1912–) 13:953–954.

[G. MOLLAT]

BRIAND, JEAN OLIVIER

Seventh bishop of Quebec, Canada; b. Plérin, France, Jan. 23, 1715; d. Quebec, June 25, 1794. He was educated in his native Diocese of Saint-Brieuc, ordained there in 1739, and immigrated to Canada, arriving in 1741 with Bp. H. M. Pontbriand, his predecessor in the See of Quebec. Named canon, he became the bishop's assistant, confessor to the sisters, and then vicar-general. He dedicated himself to these duties during the siege of Quebec (1759) and, through his loyal obedience, gained the good graces of the new English masters. After lengthy negotiations and despite British law, he was recognized as ''Superintendent of the Roman Church.'' This permitted his private consecration as bishop in France in 1766. By his zeal and diplomacy he was able to repair the damages sustained by religious institutions during the war. To replenish his decimated clergy, he ordained 90 priests during his episcopate. He consolidated the Church's situation with the English authorities and in return exacted from his own people a deep loyalty to the British during the American Revolution. He resided at the Seminary of Quebec, contributing generously to its development. He composed a new catechism for the diocese. With approval from London, he chose L. P. d'Esglis as coadjutor with the right of succession and in 1784 turned over the administration of the diocese to him.

Bibliography: H. TÊTU, *Les Évêques de Québec* (Quebec 1889). A. H. GOSSELIN, *L'Église du Canada après la conquête,* 2 v. (Quebec 1916-17). F. PORTER, *L'Institution catechistique au Canada français, 1633–1833* (Washington 1949). M. TRUDEL, *L'Église canadienne sous le régime militaire, 1759–1764,* 2 v. (Montreal 1956-57).

[H. PROVOST]

BRIANT, ALEXANDER, ST.

English Jesuit martyr; b. Somerset, *c.* 1561; d. Tyburn, Dec. 1, 1581. While an undergraduate at Hart Hall, Oxford, in 1574, Briant was reconciled to Catholicism. He left Oxford for studies at Douai, arriving there on Aug. 11, 1577. He was ordained on March 29, 1578, and returned to England on March 3, 1579. In his native Somerset, he reconciled many to the Church, including Robert PERSONS' father. This drew Father Persons and Briant together and indirectly led to his own arrest in April by pursuivants looking for Persons. He was imprisoned first in the Counter and then in the Tower, and endured intense torture rather than disclose Persons' whereabouts. Starvation, detention in an unlit dungeon, the scavenger's daughter, the thumbscrew, and needles under the nails were of no avail. One of his torturers declared that ''this is an evident miracle, but it is a miracle of undauntable pertinacity in this Papist priest; I would not on any account anyone were here present who was not well and solidly grounded in our faith.'' He was handed over to Thomas Norton (d. 1584), the notorious rackmaster, and racked mercilessly. Although Norton boasted that he had made him ''a foot longer than God made him,'' Briant never spoke except in prayer. Even Elizabethan England was shocked. In 1583, two years after his death, the government felt it was necessary to reply in a pamphlet (ascribed to Lord Burghley) that ''a horrible matter is also made of the starving Alexander Briant; how he should eat clay out of the walls. . . . Whatsoever Briant suffered in want of food, he suffered the same willfully and of extreme impudent obstinacy.'' Briant had written from prison to the Jesuits in England, begging admission to their society; although his formal entry was not possible, he was counted as a member. On November 21, with six other priests, he was tried at Westminster Hall. Carrying aloft a rough cross he had made, he entered the court room. Charged with a fictitious plot and found guilty, Edmund CAMPION, Ralph SHERWIN, and Alexander Briant were drawn to Tyburn on Dec. 1, 1581. Briant was the last to die. He was beatified by Leo XIII on Dec. 29, 1886 and canonized on Oct. 25, 1970.

Feast: Dec. 1; Oct. 25; May 4.

See Also: ENGLAND, SCOTLAND AND WALES, MARTYRS OF.

Bibliography: A. BUTLER, *The Lives of Saints,* ed. H. THURSTON and D. ATTWATER, 4 v., (New York, 1956). B. CAMM, ed., *Lives of the English Martyrs Declared Blessed by Pope Leo XIII in 1886 and 1895* (London 1905). H. FOLEY, ed., *Records of the English Province of the Society of Jesus,* 7 v. (London 1877-82). R. CHALLONER, *Memoirs of Missionary Priests,* ed. J. H. POLLEN (rev. ed. London 1924). J. GILLOW, *A Literary and Biographical History or Bibliographical Dictionary of the English Catholics from 1534 to the Present Time,* 5 v. (London-New York 1885–1902; reprinted New York 1961). P. DE ROSA, *Blessed Alexander Briant* (Postulation pamphlet; London 1961).

[G. FITZHERBERT]

BRIBERY

A bribe is a gift or favor, given or promised, for the purpose of influencing the official decisions or conduct of a person in a position of trust. Bribery is the act or practice of giving such gratuities or the acceptance of them.

Where a public official is corrupted, bribery involves the violation not only of legal but also of commutative justice: of legal justice because it involves, presumably, the transgression of just laws and is damaging to the common good; of commutative justice, because the corrupted official is induced to violate the contractual obligation to the community that he took upon himself in accepting office. He fails to provide the public service for which he is paid. In some cases, commutative justice is also violated with respect to a private individual who suffers harm by the official's dishonesty. For example, if a judge, induced by a bribe, renders an unjust decision, he does an injury to the one who loses the case, and in compensation for this injury the loser is entitled to RESTITUTION. If the winner of the judgment refuses to restore his unjust gain to the injured man, the judge is bound to do it in his stead, even if this means giving up a greater sum than came to him through the bribe. His responsibility extends to the whole of the damage actually done by his unjust act. A similar obligation of restitution to persons suffering loss would arise in the case of a public building inspector who under influence of bribery permits inferior materials or substandard procedures to pass without correction. Other applications of the same principle are to be found in similar violations of trust.

The degree of guilt is greater where a person is induced to perform an act contrary to the duties of his office; it is less grave if it is intended as compensation for an act already performed.

In modern society it is sometimes customary for policemen and other officials to accept gifts from merchants or others who have benefited from their services. Although this practice is open to abuse, gifts of this kind are not bribes provided that they are not understood as payment for services rendered and that the citizens are not made to feel that they will not receive these services unless they make their contribution.

In cases of bribery in which no one suffers harm, it is disputed whether a dishonest official may keep money he has taken as a bribe. Some moralists hold that he may, because his act has caused no injury to others. Others hold that he has violated commutative justice and hence may not retain the money. Still, the violation of justice has been done to the community, which is paying the official for a service that he has failed to perform, and this wrong cannot be righted by restoring the bribe to the donor. If restitution is necessary, it should be made to the community.

Generally speaking, the giver and the taker of a bribe share equally in the malice of the act. If the taker violates his trust and possibly his oath of office, the giver participates in this malice by inducing him to commit the act. It sometimes happens, however, that honest individuals cannot enjoy the benefit of ordinary public services or obtain appointment to public office without paying a bribe. If the conditions necessary for permissible material cooperation are fulfilled, a person cannot be accused of sin if he pays what is demanded. He is a victim of extortion rather than a formal violator of justice.

Bibliography: F. J. CONNELL, *Morals in Politics and Professions* (Westminister, Md. 1946) 34–35, 58–61, 69–74.

[T. CRANNY]

BRICE OF TOURS, ST.

5th-century monk and bishop; b. Touraine, France, *c.* 370?; d. Tours, 444. A disciple of St. MARTIN OF TOURS at Marmoutier, Brice was at first noted for his violence and indocility. On the death of Martin in 397, Brice was elected bishop of Tours. His previous irregularities caused him to be delated before several local synods by Lazarus, later bishop of Aix (Jaffé K, *Regesta pontificum romanorum ab condita ecclesia ad annum post Christum natum 1198,* 330–331), but both the Council of Turin in 401 and Pope ZOSIMUS (2 *Epist.* dated September 21 and 22, 417) upheld Brice. Dispossessed of his see on a morals charge (*see* SIDONIUS APPOLINARIS *Epist.* 4.18), he was replaced by Bishop Justinian, then by Armentius. In

430 he pleaded his cause in Rome and in 437 was restored. He was buried in the chapel of St. Martin, which he had constructed. In the Middle Ages his cult spread throughout the West, particularly because of his biography by GREGORY OF TOURS.

Feast: Nov. 13.

Bibliography: GREGORY OF TOURS, *Historia Francorum,* ed. W. ARNDT, *Monumenta Germaniae Scriptores rerum Merovingicarum* (Berlin 1826–) 1.1:36–38; Eng. *The History of the Franks,* tr. O. M. DALTON, 2 v. (Oxford 1927). SULPICIUS SEVERUS, *Dialogus III, Patrologia Latina,* ed. J. P. MIGNE (Paris 1878–90) 20:220–222. S. HANSSENS, *Dictionnaire d'histoire et de géographie ecclésiastiques,* ed. A. BAUDRILLAT et al. (Paris 1912–) 10:670–671. L. DUCHESNE, *Fastes épiscopaux, de l'ancienne Gaule,* 3 v. (2d ed. Paris 1907–15) 2:303. A. PONCELET, *Analecta Bollandiana* 30 (1911) 88–89. H. DELEHAYE, *ibid.* 38 (1920) 124–125. R. AIGRAIN, *Catholicisme* 2:262–263. W. BÖHNE, *Lexikon für Theologie und Kirche,* ed. J. HOFER and K. RAHNER, 10 v. (2d, new ed. Freiburg 1957–65) 2:685. *Saint Martin et son temps: Mémorial du XVI*[e] *centenaire des débuts du monachisme en Gaule* (Rome 1961).

[A. DANET]

BRICEÑO, ALONSO

Chilean philosopher and theologian; b. Santiago, Chile, 1587; d. Trujillo, Venezuela, Nov. 15, 1668. In January of 1605 Briceño received the Franciscan habit in Lima and soon acquired renown as a teacher of theology. He became guardian of the Franciscan convent where he had been educated, and later, definitor of the province of the Twelve Apostles, commissary and visitor of the province of San Antonio de los Charcas and of that of Chile, and finally, vicar-general. In 1636 he was sent to Spain as procurator of the province of Twelve Apostles and was named by the Holy Office to the sensitive post of censor. Between 1638 and 1642 he published in Spain two large volumes (963 and 968 folios) of interpretations of the doctrines of Duns Scotus, the first time such material was published in Europe by an American. Briceño's study *Prima pars celebriorum controversiarum in Primum Sententiarum Joannis Scoti doctoris subtilis* was praised for its keen penetration and understanding of Scotist thought. The first volume is an apology for Scotus's doctrines; the second treats ''de scientia Dei et ideis'' and mentions a companion volume on ''voluntate et potentia Dei, de praedestinatione et Trinitate complectens caeteris controversias ad primum Sententiarum atinentes.'' In 1639 Briceño took part in the general chapter of the order at Rome, where he presided at the solemn theological convocation dedicated to Cardinal Albornoz. By special order of the minister general, he was named *Lector bis jubilatus* in theology. While in Rome he was also active in the beatification proceedings of Francis SOLANO. Briseño was appointed Bishop of Nicaragua and took possession of his diocese in December of 1646. In August of 1649 he was transferred to Caracas.

[G. LOHMANN VILLENA]

BRIÇONNET

Family name of three French churchmen of the 15th and 16th centuries.

Robert, prelate and statesman remembered for his improvement of the French fiscal system; place and date of birth uncertain; d. Moulins, June 3, 1497. Through the influence of his younger brother Guillaume (d. 1514) he received important appointments to ecclesiastical and secular positions. After serving as canon of St. Aignan and abbot of St. Vaast, he was appointed archbishop of Reims in 1493. Charles VIII made him chancellor of France (1495), an office he fulfilled until his death.

Guillaume, cardinal of Saint-Malo and principal adviser to Charles VIII; b. Tours, *c.* 1445; d. Narbonne, Dec. 14, 1514. Guillaume entered the religious life after the death of his wife and became bishop of St. Malo (1493), archbishop of Reims (1497) and Narbonne (1507). He accompanied Charles VIII on his Italian expedition from 1494 to1495, at which time he was created a cardinal by Alexander VI. In 1498 he crowned Louis XII king of France in the cathedral at Reims. During the pontificate of JULIUS II he led a movement among the cardinals, culminating in the council of Pisa-Milan, to force the pope to undertake reform. Julius summoned him to Rome, where he was stripped of his office and excommunicated. When LEO X became pope (1513) the censure was lifted and Guillaume was restored to his cardinalate.

Guillaume, bishop and advocate of church reform; b. Tours, 1472; d. Saint-Germain-des-Prés, Jan. 24, 1534. He was the son of Guillaume the cardinal. Briçonnet served as bishop of Lodève (1504) and director of the Abbey of Saint-Germain-des-Prés (1507), where he began a series of reforms. He carried out missions to Rome for both Louis XII and Francis I. Upon his appointment as bishop of Meaux (1516) he supported a reform movement through a group of intellectuals known as the ''Meaux reformers.'' Some of its members turned too favorably toward the Lutheran movement, and Guillaume was accused of heresy. The group was dispersed in 1535. Briçonnet successfully defended himself against the charge of heresy and died a Catholic.

Bibliography: P. IMBART DE LA TOUR, *Les Origines de la réforme,* 4 v. (Paris 1905-35) v. 3. A. RENAUDET, *Préréforme et humanisme à Paris pendant les premières guerres d'Italie, 1494–1517* (2d ed. Paris 1953). G. BRETONNEAU, *Histoire généalogique de la maison de Briçonnet* (Paris 1620). A. FLICHE and

V. MARTIN, eds. *Histoire de l'église depuis les origines jusqu'à nos jours* (Paris 1935–) v. 15. *Gallia Christiana* v. 6, 9. M. LECOMTE, *Dictionnaire d'histoire et de géographie ecclésiastiques* (Paris 1912–) 10:677–682. A. DUVAL, *Catholicisme* 2:263–265.

[W. J. STEINER]

BRICTINIANS

A congregation of hermits named from the hill of Brettino near Fano, Italy, on which their first monastery was built. Founded apparently between 1200 and 1215, they later (1228) adopted the rule of St. AUGUSTINE as one of those permitted by the Fourth LATERAN COUNCIL and as best suited to their purpose. Their constitutions, approved in 1235, reveal a way of life stressing bodily mortification and poverty. It was often charged that a similarity in their form of dress to that of the Franciscans occasioned their obtaining alms that would otherwise have gone to the Friars Minor. Their rapid growth in numbers seems traceable mainly to the attractive simplicity of their life; priest members of the congregation were engaged in apostolic works. In the Great Union of 1256, they and other existing hermit congregations were joined together into one Order of Hermit Friars of St. Augustine (*see* AUGUSTINIANS).

Bibliography: Sources. ''Bullarium ordinis eremitarum S. Augustini: Periodus formationis, 1187–1256,'' ed. B. VAN LUIJK, *Augustiniana,* 12 (1962) 161–195, 358–390; 13 (1963) 474–510; 14 (1964) 216–249. Literature. F. ROTH, ''Cardinal Richard Annibaldi: First Protector of the Augustinian Order, 1243–76,'' *ibid.,* 2 (1952) 26–60, 108–149, esp. 132–138.

[J. E. BRESNAHAN]

BRIDGET OF SWEDEN, ST.

Patron saint of Sweden and foundress of the BRIDGETTINES; b. Upland, principal province of Sweden, 1302 or 1303; d. Rome, 1373. The daughter of Birger, Governor of Upland, and his second wife, Ingeborg, Bridget married Ulf Gudmarsson when she was about 14 years of age. One of their eight children was St. CATHERINE OF SWEDEN. For two years Bridget was lady in waiting to Blanche of Namur, wife of King Magnus II, and attempted to win the young royal couple to holiness. After Ulf's death in 1344, she lived as a penitent near the Cistercian monastery at Alvastra. Visions and revelations, which she had first experienced in childhood, became more frequent and began to be written down.

In 1346 Magnus endowed a double monastery at Vadstena, where she established her order, and Urban V confirmed the rule of her congregation in 1370. Bridget went to Rome in 1349, and for the rest of her life remained there, except for traveling on various pilgrimages in Italy and on a long journey to the Holy Land, undertaken in 1371. Her canonization by Boniface IX (Oct. 7, 1391) was confirmed in 1415. To an Englishwoman, Margery Kempe, Bridget's maid confided that her lady had been ''kind and meek to every creature and that she had a laughing face.''

Along with her penitential practices and her charitable works for the poor and humble, she devoted herself to urging reforms within the Church. She denounced abuses of bishops and abbots and advised princes and kings on political matters. She was especially concerned for the return to Rome of the Avignon popes, and for 20 years she admonished them to do so. Revelations and prophecies frequently supported her various causes. Because of their celebrity, the written accounts and subsequent editions of her revelations have been the subject of much theological examination and textual criticism.

Feast: Oct. 8.

Bibliography: B. MORRIS, *St. Birgitta of Sweden* (Woodbridge, England 1999). J. B. HOLLOWAY, *Saint Bride and Her Book: Birgitta of Sweden's Revelations* (Newburyport, Mass. 1992). M. T. HARRIS, *Birgitta of Sweden: Life and Selected Writings* (Mahwah, N.J. 1990). J. HOGG, ed., *Studies in St. Birgitta and the Brigittine Order* (Lewiston, N.Y. 1993).

[M. S. CONLAN]

BRIDGETT, THOMAS EDWARD

Author; b. Derby, England, Jan. 20, 1829; d. Clapham, London, Feb. 17, 1899. He came from an Anglican family, and was educated at Tonbridge School (1845–47) and at St. John's College, Cambridge. In 1850 he left the College without graduating in order to avoid taking the required oath recognizing the royal supremacy over the Church of England. After attending John Henry Newman's lectures on ''Anglican Difficulties,'' he was received into the Catholic Church at the London Oratory, June 12, 1850. He joined the Redemptorists a few months later. After studying theology at Wittem, Netherlands, he was ordained (1856) and spent the rest of his life in various offices of his congregation in England and Ireland, and made his name as a missioner. From 1871 until his death he was at Clapham, where for some time he was rector. Of his books, which were mainly controversial, the two most important are: *Our Lady's Dowry* (1875), an account, based on historical and literary sources, of devotion to the Blessed Virgin in Great Britain from the introduction of Christianity to the Reformation; and *The History of the Holy Eucharist in Great Britain* (1881), which studied this subject over the same period of time.

Both books give evidence of Bridgett's considerable learning. He also wrote *The Life of Blessed John Fisher* (1888), *Blunders and Forgeries* (1890), and *The Life of Blessed Thomas More* (1891).

Bibliography: C. RYDER, *Life of Thomas Edward Bridgett* (London 1906). A. F. POLLARD, *The Dictionary of National Biography from the Earliest Times to 1900*, 63 v. (London 1885–1900) 22:267.

[L. C. SHEPPARD]

Thomas Edward Bridgett.

BRIDGEWATER, JOHN

Catholic theologian, known also as Aquapontanus; b. Yorkshire, *c.* 1532; d. probably at Trèves, *c.* 1596. He was admitted to Brasenose College, Oxford, on Feb. 4, 1552 (N.S.; 1551, O.S.), and supplicated as a B.A. of Cambridge on Feb. 21, 1555 (N.S.; 1554, O.S.). He received the degree of B.A. at Oxford on March 13, 1555 (N.S.; 1554, O.S.) and the M.A. two years later. He was the recipient of several ecclesiastical appointments that included St. Austell, Cornwall, in 1550; Yelling, Huntingdonshire, in 1554; Aldeburgh, Suffolk, in 1554; the archdeaconry of Rochester in 1560 (N.S.; 1559, O.S.); Columb Major, Cornwall, in 1559; Luccombe, Somerset, in 1563; Porlock, Somerset, in 1565; Prebend of Combell in 1564; and Compton Bishop in the Cathedral of Wells in 1572. On April 14, 1563, he was elected rector of Lincoln College, Oxford, but resigned this and his other preferments in 1574 and went abroad. It is unlikely that he ever returned to England. Pedro de Ribadaneira, Nathaniel Southwell, and Henry Foley claim him as a member of the Society of Jesus, but this is questioned. His two polemical works of theology are *Confutatio virulentae disputationis theologicae, in qua Georgius Sohn, professor academiae Heidelbergensis, conatus est docere Pontificem Romanum esse antichristum a prophetis et apostolis praedictum* (Trèves 1589) and *Concertatio ecclesiae catholicae in Anglia adversus Calvinopapistas et Puritanos sub Elizabetha regina quorundam hominum doctrina et sanctitate illustrium renovata et recognita* (Trèves 1589–94).

Bibliography: Douai, English College, *The First and Second Diaries of the English College Douay*, ed. Fathers of the Congregation of the London Oratory (London 1878) 99, 119, 128, 130, 146, 408. *A Literary and Biographical History or Bibliographical Dictionary of the English Catholics from 1534 to the Present Time* 1:294–295. *The Dictionary of National Biography from the Earliest Times to 1900* (London 1885–1900) 2:1232–33. H. FOLEY, *Records of the English Province of the Society of Jesus*, 7 v. (London 1877–82) 4:485–488.

[C. W. FIELD]

BRIDGIT, ABBEY OF

A former foundation of BRIGITTINE SISTERS, situated on Lake Vättern, Östergötland, Sweden, in the former Diocese of Linköping. It is the mother abbey of the Bridgettine Order and was built according to the directions of St. BRIDGET *c.* 1365 on the royal estate of Vadstena, which was willed to her in 1346 by King Magnus Eriksson. The first abbess was Bridget's daughter, St. CATHERINE OF SWEDEN, who reestablished the community in 1374. The work was favored by a special fee, Our Lady's pence, and in 1384 the abbey was consecrated by the diocesan bishop. According to Bridget's plan the abbey should have a nuns' and a monks' convent under an abbess as the common leader, with a general confessor at her side and visitation rights granted to the bishop of Linköping. Bridget's corpse was moved from Rome to the site in 1374, and in the later Middle Ages the tombs of the saint and her daughter became the main destination for pilgrims in Sweden. With its more than 900 estates, Vadstena was the richest abbey in Scandinavia; a large income was further derived from the Vincula (feast of St. Peter in Chains), the PORTIUNCULA, as well as the Jubilee INDULGENCES, title to which the abbey had acquired. This foundation had one of the largest libraries in Scandinavia, from which about 450 volumes are extant, housed in the University Library of Uppsala and the Royal Library at Stockholm. Among these there may be mentioned the *Diarium Vazstenense* for the years 1344 to 1545 (Codex Ups. C 89) and a copy book preserved in the State Archives in Stockholm. Great literary and artistic impulses emanated from Vadstena, and the abbey, dedicated to the Virgin Mary, became a center for the Marian devotion in Sweden. The originator of the weekly ritual of the nuns, the *Cantus sororum ordinis Sancti Salvatoris,* was Magister Petrus Olavi (d. 1378), a man of saintly reputation. The house in Rome where Bridget died was purchased by the abbey and used as a hospital for pilgrims. When the Protestant REFORMATION reached Sweden the importance of the abbey ceased, and in 1595 it was formally dissolved. The church is now used as the town church of Vadstena, and parts of the former buildings, among them the original royal estate, are still preserved.

Bibliography: R. GEETE, ed., *Jungfru Marie örtagård* (Stockholm 1895). E. NYGREN, ed., *Diarium Vadstenense* (Copenhagen 1963). H. CNATTINGIUS, *Studies in the Order of St. Bridget of Sweden* (Stockholm 1963–). T. HÖJER, *Studier i Vadstena klosters och Birgittinordens historia intill midten af 1400–talet* (Uppsala 1905). A. LINDBLOM, *Johann III och Vadstena nunnekloster* (Lund 1961); *Kult och konst i Vadstena kloster* (Stockholm 1965). L. A. NORBORG, *Storföretaget Vadstena kloster* (Lund 1958). T. NYBERG, *Birgittinische Klostergründungen des Mittelalters* (Lund 1965).

[O. ODENIUS]

BRIEUC, ST.

Monk, founder and patron of the town of St. Brieuc, Brittany (Côtes-du-Nord); b. Cardigan, Wales, 410; d. St. Brieuc, 502. Born of pagan parents, Brieuc was converted at Verulam by (St.) Germanus of Auxerre and in 429 followed him to Gaul, where he was ordained. On returning to Wales, Brieuc worked among his compatriots, but in 480 had to flee before the Saxon invasion. With about 100 Christians he crossed La Manche and established himself in Armorican Brittany not far from Tréguier. There he converted a rich chieftan, Conan, and founded at Brieuc a monastery around which the town rose. If he was consecrated a bishop, he remained a bishop-abbot in the Celtic tradition, without administering the diocese. His relics were transported to St. Sergius in Angers during the Norman invasions, but were returned to St. Brieuc in 1210. Because of his charity, he is the patron of pocketbook makers. The city was erected into an episcopal see *c.* 848 by Nominoë, King of the Bretons; its cathedral was built in the 13th century over the foundations of the chapel Brieuc erected.

Feast: May 1.

Bibliography: *Acta Santorum*, May 1:93–97. F. PLAINE, *Analecta Bollandiana* (Brussels 1882–) 161–190. H. WAQUET, *Dictionnaire d'histoire et de géographie ecclésiastiques,* ed. A. BAUDRILLAT et al. (Paris 1912–) 10:712–713. L. DUCHESNE, *Fastes épiscopaux, de l'ancienne Gaule,* 3 v. (2d ed. Paris 1907–15) 2:255, 262–263, 300–301. G. H. DOBLE, *Saint Brioc* (Cornish Saints 17; Long Compton, Eng. 1928). R. AIGRAIN, *Catholicisme* 2:267–268.

[A. DANET]

BRIGGS, CHARLES AUGUSTUS

Presbyterian biblical scholar; b. New York City, Jan. 15, 1841; d. there, June 8, 1913. He was educated at the University of Virginia, Charlottesville, and, after military service in the Civil War, at Union Theological Seminary, New York City. His study at the University of Berlin (1865–70) under Emil Rodiger and Isaac A. Dorner gave him a firm grounding in the methods of the higher criticism. Upon returning to the United States, Briggs served as pastor of a Presbyterian church in Roselle, N.J., until 1874, when he became professor of Hebrew at Union Theological Seminary.

In 1880 Briggs became editor of the *Presbyterian Review.* His articles in this periodical, republished as *Biblical Study* (1883) and *Messianic Prophecy* (1886), advocated a moderate stand between rationalistic criticism and reactionary conservatism in biblical scholarship. He opposed the Calvinist scholasticism of the Princeton school and argued against it in *Whither?* (1889), a work that directly influenced the efforts at revision of the Westminster Confession at the general assembly in 1890. In *The Bible, the Church and Reason* (1892), his inaugural address as professor of biblical theology at Union in 1890, Briggs held that theories of verbal inspiration were barriers to church unity and committed Protestantism to a superstitious bibliolatry. The immediate result was his trial for heresy, which culminated in Briggs's suspension from the ministry in 1893. He remained at Union, however, and in 1899, over the protests of Anglo-Catholics, was ordained a priest of the Protestant Episcopal Church. In 1904 he became professor of symbolics and irenics at Union.

In his later years, Briggs worked for reunion of Catholics and Protestants. He had an audience with Pius X in an effort to stave off the decrees of the Biblical Commission, which he later criticized in *The Biblical Commission and the Pentateuch* (1906). His doctrinal position was that of traditional Christianity, and he met the attacks of modernists and rationalists in *The Incarnation* (1902), *The Virgin Birth* (1909), and *The Fundamental Christian Faith* (1913). His principal work was the *Commentary on the Book of Psalms* (1906), which he contributed to the *International Critical Commentary on the Holy Scriptures*, of which he was the general editor.

Bibliography: Union Theological Seminary, Library, his correspondence and works. L. A. LOETSCHER, *The Broadening Church* (Philadelphia 1957); "C. A. Briggs in the Retrospect of Half a Century," *Theology Today* 12 (1955) 27–42.

[R. K. MACMASTER]

BRIGHTMAN, EDGAR SHEFFIELD

Philosopher, leading American exponent of PERSONALISM; b. Holbrook, Mass., Sept. 20, 1884; d. Newton, Mass., Feb. 25, 1953. The son of a Methodist minister and himself an ordained Methodist minister, Brightman studied at Brown University, at Boston University, and at the Universities of Berlin and of Marburg. His life as a professor and scholar, after early teaching at Nebraska Wesleyan University (1912–15) and at Wesleyan University in Middletown, Conn. (1915–19), was spent at Boston University (1919–53). Between 1925 and 1953 he wrote 14 books, more than 200 articles, and 300 book reviews on metaphysics, religion, ethics, and education. His scholarly and personal concern for his students was remarkable; an unusual proportion of his disciples became college presidents, deans, productive scholars, teachers, and pastors in America and elsewhere.

In B. P. Bowne's personalism Brightman found the synthesis of what had attracted his earlier loyalties to J. ROYCE and W. JAMES. Brightman grounded the theistic, pluralistic idealism that Bowne had developed from Berkeleyan, Lotzean, and Kantian roots in what he believed to be sounder experiential foundations. He argued that metaphysical, theological, and ethical hypotheses should be reasoned explanations of data immediately given in irreducible personal experience. The person, which he conceived as a complex unity of activities and capable of self-consciousness, moral purpose, and religious sensitivity, in his view should replace the scholastic notion of SOUL. The person is not a part of the personal God who created him free within limits. By contrast, physical and organic nature exist as the order of God's active Will, guided by reason and love. God Himself is omnitemporal, not eternal, and His power is limited. He is a personal Creator whose goodness and reason are the ideal guides of His will as He exerts continuous, if somewhat incomplete, control throughout cosmic evolution over the nonrational factors within His own nature.

Although Brightman's critics urged that this finitistic view of God did not meet the demands of religious experience and faith, Brightman questioned the unanimity of genuine religious experience on this point. Critics urged also that God's nature was dichotomized, but Brightman held that His metaphysical unity was not in fact jeopardized. In any case, he said, God's purpose is realized as persons actualize their individual potential in a free communitarian society that treats persons and God as ends in themselves and never as means only.

Bibliography: E. S. BRIGHTMAN, *Introduction to Philosophy* (New York 1925; 3d ed. R. N. BECK, 1963); *The Problem of God* (New York 1930); *The Finding of God* (New York 1931); *Moral Laws* (New York 1933); *A Philosophy of Religion* (New York 1940; reprint Englewood Cliffs, N.J. 1958); *Person and Reality: An Introduction to Metaphysics,* ed. P. A. BERTOCCI et al. (New York 1958). J. J. MCLARNEY, *The Theism of Edgar Sheffield Brightman* (Washington, D.C. 1936).

[P. A. BERTOCCI]

BRIGID OF IRELAND, ST.

Early Irish monastic foundress and saint; b. Offaly, Ireland *c.* 460; d. Kildare, *c.* 528. Brigid came from the Fotharta Airbrech people near Croghan Hill. Her mother was a slave-girl; but the child was acknowledged by her father and given to a foster mother to rear. Having been instructed in letters and the accomplishments of embroidery and household duties, she was sought in marriage by an eager suitor whom she rejected on the ground that she had vowed "her virginity to the Lord." After paternal objections were overcome she took the veil, the symbol of the religious state; she founded in the Liffey plain a church called Cill Dara (Kildare)—"the church of the oak"—and associated with herself a pious hermit, Conleth, who lived alone in a nearby solitude. The house for men, which he ruled as bishop and abbot, was so near the convent of women that both communities could use the same church. Kildare was thus a double monastery, the only institution of its kind in Ireland. The *Life of St. Brigid* written in the 7th century represents her as a new type of Irish woman—the Christian saint. Her likeness to modern missionary sisters is remarkable; she often left Kildare in her chariot, doing the work of the Lord's charity in distant parts. To her countrymen she was "the Mary of the Gael," and when they went as missionaries and pilgrims to the Continent of Europe they spread devotion to her wherever they settled. St. Brigid, St. PATRICK, and St. Colmcille are the three patron saints of Ireland.

Feast: Feb. 1.

Bibliography: COGITOSUS, *Vita S. Brigidae, Acta Santorum,* Feb. 1:135–155. M. A. O'BRIEN, tr. and ed., "The Old Irish Life of St. Brigit," *Irish Historical Studies* 1 (1938–39) 121–134, 343–353. C. PLUMMER et al., eds., "Vita Brigitae," *Irish Texts* 1 (1931) 2–16. J. F. KENNEY, *The Sources for the Early History of Ireland* (New York 1929) 1:356–363.

[J. RYAN]

BRIGIDINES

Popular name for the Congregation of St. Brigid (CSB, Official Catholic Directory #3735), a community of women religious with papal approval (1845, 1907), founded at Tullow, County Carlow (Ireland), in 1807 by Daniel Delaney (1747–1814), bishop of Kildare and Leighlin. The sisters profess simple perpetual vows and devote themselves to Christian education. Bishop Delaney, aware of Ireland's educational deficiencies, and himself a ''graduate'' of that country's famous ''hedge schools,'' formed the congregation with a group of six catechists whom he trained in the religious life, based on the Rule of St. Augustine. The community adopted the episcopal motto, *Fortiter et suaviter*. In the U.S., the congregation established its first community in 1953, where it is involved in education, youth ministry, counseling, and the pastoral care of immigrants. The U.S. provincial headquarters is in San Antonio, Tex.

Bibliography: M. M. DUNNE, *Watching for the Dawn* (Dublin 1963).

[M. V. DOBSON/EDS.]

BRIGITTINE SISTERS

(Official Catholic Directory #0280); the Order of the Most Holy Saviour (OSsS), commonly called the Brigittine Sisters, is an order of semicloistered nuns founded by the medieval mystic (St.) BRIDGET OF SWEDEN and first approved by Urban V in 1370. They follow the Augustinian Rule (*see* AUGUSTINE, RULE OF ST.).

Bridget felt that she had been commanded by Christ to found a new religious congregation for the reform of monastic life. In order to fulfill this divine summons, she left Sweden for Rome. She was compelled to remain there for 25 years while urging the return of the Popes from Avignon and, while awaiting the full approval of her order, she died in Rome in 1373 before her mission was fully realized. Her religious foundation, however, continued to grow. Shortly after her death, her daughter (St.) CATHERINE OF SWEDEN became the first abbess of the original monastery in Vadstena, Sweden, begun by Bridget about 1346. Other monasteries followed, none numbering more than 60 nuns. Attached to each of them was a monastery for monks who shared the same liturgical life under the government of the abbess. The discipline of the new order stressed humility and simplicity in contrast to the pride and pomp of many clerics of the period. The Brigittine Sisters contributed greatly to the culture of Scandinavia. One of the first printing presses was established in Vadstena Abbey.

Prior to the Reformation the order numbered about 80 houses, located throughout Europe. In 1595, however, the motherhouse at Vadstena was confiscated and the order was officially banished from Sweden. From the 16th century onward, the European houses were further reduced by suppression and confiscation. In modern times, there still exist four autonomous houses of nuns: Syon Abbey in Devonshire, England; Weert and Uden in Holland; and Altomünster in Bavaria. These houses follow the original rule.

In 1911, Blessed Elisabeth Hesselblad, a Swedish convert, founded a new branch of the old order. With only two postulants, she began her work of renewal in a small apartment in St. Bridget's former house in Rome, whose possession the order did not regain till 1931. In 1923 she led the Brigittine Sisters back to Sweden, after more than 300 years of exile. During her lifetime (1870 to 1957) she established houses in Italy, Sweden, Switzerland, India, England, and the United States. The first house in the United States, in Darien, Connecticut. (1957).

The order is essentially contemplative, and aims at the fullness of liturgical worship. Its members offer themselves to God in prayer and reparation, working thus for the reunion of all Christians, and in particular for the return of Scandinavia to the Catholic Church. Each Brigittine monastery maintains a guest house to which members of all faiths are welcomed. Though ancient in its history, the order is modern both in its role in the monastic revival and in its ecumenical concern.

Bibliography: H. JÄGERSTAD, *Lexikon für Theologie und Kirche*, ed. J. HOFER and K. RAHNER (2d, new ed. Freiburg 1957–65) 2:486–87. P. DEBONGNIE, *Dictionnaire d'histoire et de géographie ecclésiastiques*, ed. A. BAUDRILLART et al. (Paris 1912–) 10:728–31, especially bibliography. B. WILLIAMSON, *The Bridgettine Order* (London 1921). O. EKLUND, *A Faith Stronger than Death: The Life of Mother M. Elisabeth Hesselblad* (Rome 1962).

[A. J. ENNIS/EDS.]

BRINKLEY, STEPHEN

Printer, translator, and confessor; parentage and date and place of birth and death unknown; lost to view after 1586. Brinkley was a matriculated pensioner at St. John's College, Cambridge, in 1562, and received the LL.B. in 1570. As ''James Sancer,'' he dedicated his translation of Gaspare Loarte's *Exercise of a Christian Life* at Paris, on June 20, 1579, which was a deliberate subterfuge, since the book was really printed in London by William Carter. In 1580 a spy listed him among alleged papal pensioners ''now in England.'' Brinkley offered his services to Edmund CAMPION and Robert PERSONS after their landing in June of 1580, and he organized and supervised their secret press at Greenstreet House, East Ham. The betrayal and torture of a servant caused the press's disbandment after completing (November to December 1580) Persons's *Brief discours* and two other books. Brinkley reassembled it to print Persons's *Brief censure* (January of 1581) in a house lent by Lord Montague's brother, Francis Browne. Three more books were printed before the press was moved to Stonor Park, Henley, where Campion's *Rationes decem* was finished during June. With other work at press, Stonor was raided on the Privy Council's orders; Brinkley and four workmen were seized (August 8) and committed to the Tower. Brinkley was released on June 24, 1583. He went abroad and visited Rome with Persons and later assisted Persons's secret press at Rouen. Books issued there included his translation of Loarte—then (1584) "newly corrected by the translatour"—which had inspired Persons's *Christian Directory.* Persons suggested (September of 1585) that Brinkley should become the duke of Savoy's intelligencer at Paris. He was last described (December of 1586) as a "factor for all the Jesuyts."

Bibliography: *A Literary and Biographical History or Bibliographical Dictionary of the English Catholics from 1534 to the Present Time* (London–New York 1885–1902) 1:298–300. *Publications of the Catholic Record Society* v. 2, 4, 39, 53. A. C. SOUTHERN, *Elizabethan Recusant Prose, 1559–1582* (London 1950). A. F. ALLISON and D. M. ROGERS, *A Catalogue of Catholic Books in English . . . 1558–1640,* 2 v. (London 1956). W. R. TRIMBLE, *The Catholic Laity in Elizabethan England 1558–1603* (Cambridge, Mass. 1964).

[D. M. ROGERS]

BRISACIER, JACQUES CHARLES DE

Director of the seminary of the PARIS FOREIGN MISSION SOCIETY; b. Blois, France, Oct. 18, 1642; d. Paris, March 23, 1736. He came of an illustrious family. After his ordination he became commendatory abbot of Saint-Pierre de Neuvilliers and chaplain to Queen Marie Thérèse. Entering the seminary of the Paris Foreign Mission Society *c.* 1670, he was superior there almost continuously from 1681 to 1736. He built the church of the society in 1683, and the seminary buildings in 1732. The regulations of 1700 for the society were modified in 1716 to give the seminary a separate organization. While Brisacier was superior, 49 missionaries were sent to the Far East. He entered the controversy over the CHINESE RITES, taking a stand with the Dominicans and Franciscans against the Jesuits and the Sorbonne. Through Mme. de Maintenon, whom he counseled regarding regulations for her college of Saint-Cyr, he became involved in the dispute over QUIETISM. He was esteemed by his contemporaries for his intelligence, piety, and skill in spiritual guidance.

Bibliography: A. LAUNAY, *Mémorial de la Société des missionsétrangères 1658–1913* 2 v. (Paris 1912–16) 2:95–98. H. SY, *Dictionnaire d'histoire et de géographie ecclésiastiques* 10:758–759. M. PREVOST, *Dictionnaire de biographie française* 7:349–350. R. CHALUMEAU, *Catholicisme* 2:275–276.

[H. PROUVOST]

BRISSON, LOUIS ALEXANDRE

Religious founder; b. Plancy (Aube), France, June 23, 1817; d. there, Feb. 2, 1908. He was the second and sole-surviving child of Marie Savine (Corrard de la Noue) and Toussaint Brisson, a grocer. After studying at the minor and major seminaries in Troyes from 1831, he was ordained (1840). He then taught at the major seminary and also served as chaplain at the local convent of the VISITATION NUNS, where he came into contact with Maria CHAPPUIS, the superior and mistress of novices. At her urging, he founded the OBLATE SISTERS OF ST. FRANCIS DE SALES (1866) and the OBLATES OF ST. FRANCIS DE SALES (*c.* 1871). He also directed a successful society to promote the spread of the faith in mission territories. His spirituality was modeled on that of St. FRANCIS DE SALES. Brisson's sole extant writings are those preserved by his followers. The *Decretum super scripta* in his cause for beatification was issued in 1955.

Bibliography: K. BURTON, *So Much, So Soon: Father Brisson, Founder of the Oblates of St. Francis de Sales* (New York 1953). P. DUFOUR, *Le Très Révérend Père Louis Brisson* (Paris 1937); *Dictionnaire de spiritualité ascétique et mystique* (Paris 1912–) 1:1962–66.

[E. J. CARNEY]

BRISTOW, RICHARD

Theologian; b. Worcester, England, 1538; d. Harrow, near London, Oct. 21, 1581. He went to Oxford in 1555, received the B.A. degree in 1559, and the M.A. in 1562, being a member of Christ Church College. A brilliant scholar and speaker, he was chosen, with Edmund Campion, to debate before Queen Elizabeth I on her visit in 1566. He was a fellow of Exeter College in 1567. In his refutation of Lawrence Humphrey, he revealed his Catholic tendencies. He withdrew to Louvain and later joined William ALLEN (later cardinal) at the English College of Douay in 1569 and was its first student to be ordained (1573). There he was prefect of studies, pro-rector in Allen's absence, and daily lecturer on Holy Scripture. With Allen he revised and corrected Gregory Martin's translation of the New Testament in 1581. Allen and others wanted him for rector of the English College in Rome. But strain and fatigue compelled him to rest, so he went

Saxon Church with cemetery, Norfolk, England. (©Roger Tidman/CORBIS)

to Spa and then to Harrow, where he died shortly after his arrival. Bristow's chief writings are *A briefe treatise . . . conteyning sundry worthy motiues unto the Catholic faith* (Antwerp 1574), later called his *Motives* (new ed. 1599); *Demaundes to bee proposed of Catholickes to the heretickes* (1576); *A reply to William Fulke in Defence of M. D. Allen's Scrole of Articles and Booke of Purgatorie* (Louvain 1580).

Bibliography: *A Literary and Biographical History or Bibliographical Dictionary of the English Catholics from 1534 to the Present Time* (London–New York 1885–1902) 1:300–303.

[H. E. ROPE]

BRITAIN, EARLY CHURCH IN

The Christian faith was introduced into England and Scotland probably by commercial and military contacts between Britain and Gaul. Irenaeus in his *Adversus Haereses* (1.3), written *c.* 176, does not mention Britain in a list of Christian lands that includes the regions of the Celts. TERTULLIAN, writing shortly after 200, spoke of ''the places of the Britons not reached by the Romans but subject to Christ'' and adds that ''Christ's name reigns'' there (*Adv. Judaeos,* 7). This is the first concrete reference to the existence of Christianity in Britain, though Tertullian probably exaggerated the extent and social influence of the faith there at that time. The controversial legends of the Glastonbury mission of Joseph of Arimathea (allegedly in A.D. 63) and the request of King Lucius of the Britons to Pope ELEUTHERIUS (*c.* 167) for missionaries are without historical value.

There is sixth-century evidence (Gildas, *De excidio Britanniae,* 10; 11; Bede, *Eccl. hist.* 1.4; 5.24, using Gildas) of a persecution of Christians either in the middle of the third century or at the beginning of the fourth century; but there is strong evidence against its being an integral part of the Diocletian repression, since both Eusebius (*Hist. eccl.* 8.13) and Lactantius claim that Constantius I as emperor of the West (293–306) took no part in the DIOCLETIAN persecution. The most famous martyr mentioned for this period is St. ALBAN (Gildas, *loc. cit.;* Constantius, *Life of Germanus*); he was already reverenced as a martyr in Britain in 429.

After the so-called Edict of MILAN (313) the Church in Britain developed in security and sent three bishops to the Council of ARLES (314): Restitutus of London, Eborius (probably quite simply his title) of York (Eboracum),

Adelphius (of Lincoln or Caerleon). The conciliar decisions that bishops were not to invade dioceses other than their own and that ordinations were to be performed by a minimum of three bishops indicate that the British Church, like all those represented at Arles, was by this time a full-fledged episcopal and diocesan organization.

There is no conclusive evidence that any British bishops attended the Councils of Nicaea (325) or Sardica (343); but at least three attended Ariminum (360); according to Sulpicius Severus they were the only three to take advantage of Emperor Constantius' offer to pay bishops' travel expenses from imperial funds.

This same year (360) saw the beginning of the barbarian irruptions that were to involve Britain in the general decline and eventual collapse of the Roman Empire. The Picts and Scots attacked heavily along the northern frontier and in 367 were joined by the Saxons. Hadrian's Wall was breached and Britain's security rendered precarious. After a temporary containment of the barbarian invaders by THEODOSIUS I, the great Roman withdrawal began in 401 under Stilicho. By 409 the Britons had been told by Emperor HONORIUS I to provide their own defense. In a barbarian raid by the Irish (*c.* 405) PATRICK was carried off to Ireland.

About the same point another young Briton, PELAGIUS, began (*c.* 400) to teach a doctrine in Rome that developed into a denial of original sin. There is no record of the return of Pelagius himself to Britain after his Roman stay (405–410), but Pelagianism was probably introduced into Britain by his disciples expelled from Rome in the reign of Pope CELESTINE I (422–432). A second-rate Pelagian, Agricola, son of the Pelagian bishop Severianus, fled to Britain and seems to have been the main instrument for the introduction of heresy into the Church there. The consequent laxity became so widespread within a decade that an appeal was made to Rome, resulting in the famous missions of the Gaul St. GERMAIN (429 and 447).

During the first three decades of the fifth century St. NINIAN preached to the Picts of Galloway and can be called the first known missionary to Scotland; after his death in 432 his converts among the Picts fell away from the faith.

The Anglo-Saxon invasions of the second half of the fifth century brought a heathen agglomeration into southern and eastern Britain, and the British Church ceased to exist as a hierarchically organized institution in the more densely populated portions of the country. The continental invaders slaughtered many British Christians; others fled to Brittany; and some were fired with missionary zeal and the desire for monasticism that could better be realized abroad. A remnant in the Welsh and Cornish mountains maintained close contact with Gaul.

This remnant welcomed the newly spreading phenomenon of monasticism. C. J. Godfrey's remark is cogent: ". . . its fervent spirit was welcomed by the defeated and displaced Britons, who found in specialized 'religion' a compensation for their temporal losses.'' Important monastic foundations were that of Illtud at Hodnant or Llanilltud (*c.* 500), where a school was founded to train men for monasticism, but which also offered a liberal education; that of David at Menevia (*c.* 560); of Cadoc at Llancarvon; of Kentigern (Mungo) at a Strathclyde site named for his ''dear family'' of disciples, Glasgu (*c.* 580).

The Welsh Christians evangelized the pagan or apostate Picts and maintained constant spiritual commerce with Ireland and Brittany, but hated the Anglo-Saxon invaders for their crime of total dispossession to an extent that precluded all missionary activity to them. When AUGUSTINE OF CANTERBURY in his mission in 597 appealed to the Celts for charity to the Angles, the reply of Abbot Bangor was: ''We will never, never, preach the faith to this cruel race of foreigners who have so treacherously robbed us of our native soil'' (*Patrologia Latina,* 80:21–24).

Bibliography: BEDE, *A History of the English Church and People,* tr. L. SHERLEY-PRICE (Baltimore 1955). A. PLUMMER, *The Churches in England before A.D. 1000,* 2 v. (London 1911–12). M. DEANSLEY, *The Pre-Conquest Church in England* (New York 1961). H. WILLIAMS, *Christianity in Early Britain* (Oxford 1912). S. N. MILLER, ''The British Bishops at the Council of Arles,'' *English Historical Review,* 42 (1927) 79–80. C. R. PEERS, ''The Earliest Christian Churches in Britain,'' *Antiquity,* 3 (1929). C. J. GODFREY, *The Church in Anglo-Saxon England* (New York 1962). GILDAS, *De excidio Britanniae,* 10. *Patrologia Latina,* ed. J. P. MIGNE, 217 V., indexes 4 v. (Paris 1878–90).

[A. G. GIBSON]

BRITHWALD OF CANTERBURY, ST.

Benedictine monk, archbishop of Canterbury; b. *c.* 650; d. probably Jan. 13, 731. Neither his family nor birthplace is known but his training, presumably at the Canterbury school, earned him a reputation for ecclesiastical learning. Before 679 Brithwald (Bertwald, Beorhtwald) became abbot of the new monastery at Reculver, Kent; for in that year there is a charter—the earliest Anglo-Saxon charter in contemporary text—that records a gift of land by King Hlothhere of Kent to Brithwald and his monastery. Having been elected Theodore's successor (*see* THEODORE OF CANTERBURY, ST.) as archbishop of Canterbury on July 1, 692, and consecrated by Abp. Godwin of Lyons on June 29, 693, he was enthroned Aug. 31,

693. As archbishop he participated in several great councils and presided over those dealing with WILFRID OF YORK. His tenure of office for 37½ years, the longest in Canterbury's history, is particularly noteworthy as a period of diocesan reorganization. He was buried in the church of SS. Peter and Paul, Canterbury (*see* ST. AUGUSTINE, ABBEY OF).

Feast, Jan. 9.

Bibliography: BEDE, *Ecclesiastical History,* 5.8, 19, 23–24. WILLIAM OF MALMESBURY, *Gesta pontificum Anglorum,* ed. N. E. S. A. HAMILTON, *Rerum Britannicarum medii aevi scriptores,* 244 v., 7 (London 1870), 52, 53–55, 235–242, 376. C. J. VON HEFELE, *Histoire des conciles d'après les documents originaux,* tr. and continued by H. LECLERCQ, 10 v. in 19 (Paris 1907–38) 3.1:587, 591–596. W. R. W. STEPHENS, *Dictionary of National Biography from the Earliest Times to 1900* (London 1885–1900; repr. with corrections, 21 v., 1908–09, 1921–22, 1938; suppl. 1901–) 2:1251–52. F. M. STENTON, *Anglo-Saxon England* (2d ed. Oxford 1947) 142–145.

[R. D. WARE]

BRITHWALD OF WILTON, ST.

Abbot, bishop; d. April 22, 1045. Brithwald (Beorhtweald) became monk and then abbot of GLASTONBURY, and was elected bishop of Wiltshire (or Ramsbury) in 995. Despite his long episcopacy, there is almost no direct information on his life and work. He was remembered as a generous benefactor to both MALMESBURY and Glastonbury, where he was buried, but is chiefly famous for a reputed vision in which was foretold the succession of Ethelred II's son, EDWARD THE CONFESSOR, to the dynasty of Canute. Under his successor Hereman, the See of Ramsbury was united with Sherborne, and in 1078 the seat was permanently established at Salisbury.

Feast: Jan. 22.

Bibliography: WILLIAM OF MALMESBURY, *De gestis pontificum Anglorum,* ed. N. E. S. A. HAMILTON, *Rerum Britannicarum medii aevi scriptores,* 52 (London 1870) 182; *De gestis regum Anglorum,* ed. W. STUBBS, 2 v. *Rerum Britannicarum medii aevi scriptores,* 90 (London 1887–89) 1:272. FLORENCE OF WORCESTER, *The Chronicle . . . with the Two Continuations,* tr. T. FORESTER (London 1854) 111, 146. *The Life of King Edward . . . ,* ed. and tr. F. BARLOW (London 1962) 8–9. G. HILL, *English Dioceses* (London 1900).

[R. D. WARE]

BRITISH COUNCIL OF CHURCHES

The British Council of Churches (BCC) was an organization established in England in 1942 for the promotion of common action among the Christian churches of Great Britain. It sought to facilitate common evangelical action among the churches, to promote international friendship, to stimulate a sense of social responsibility, to guide youth work, to assist in the growth of ecumenical consciousness, and to promote Christian unity. Various conferences and groupings of the FREE CHURCHES had previously existed, but the BCC brought together the established churches of England and Scotland and the nonconforming churches. Beginning with William TEMPLE, the first president, the presidency was held by the archbishop of Canterbury. The BCC included the Church of England; the Episcopalians of Scotland, Ireland, and Wales; the English Presbyterians; the Presbyterian Church of Scotland; the Methodists; the Congregationalists; the Churches of Christ; the Baptists; the Quakers; the Unitarians; and the Salvation Army. The Greek Orthodox Church became a member in 1965. Associated with the council are also interdenominational societies such as the YMCA, the YWCA, the Student Christian Movement, the Christian Auxiliary Movement, and the Conference of British Missionary Societies.

Roman Catholics were not part of the BCC until 1990, when they were formally admitted. With the inclusion of Roman Catholics, the BCC changed its name to the *Council of Churches for Britain and Ireland*, and in 1999 they adopted the name *Churches Together in Britain and Ireland (CTBI).* In addition to building an ecumenical spirit among the member churches, the CTBI has undertaken the task of helping the churches to collaborate in common projects.

Bibliography: G. K. A. BELL, ed., *Documents on Christian Unity,* 3d ser., 1930–48 (New York 1948), No. 187, contains the articles of amalgamation of BCC. L. J. FRANCIS and K. WILLIAMS, *Churches in Fellowship: Local Councils of Churches in England Today* (London 1991).

[W. HANNAH/EDS.]

BRITISH MORALISTS

In addition to English authors, the term ''British moralists'' includes Irish thinkers such as Francis Hutcheson and Edmund BURKE; Scots such as David HUME; and Bernard Mandeville, a Dutch physician who lived in England and wrote in English. Although certain medieval scholastics and such 16th-century thinkers as St. THOMAS MORE and Richard HOOKER belong to this list, their thought is more aptly considered in relation to medieval scholasticism and Renaissance humanism, and so the term is here restricted to philosophers living in Great Britain in the 17th, 18th, 19th, and 20th centuries, writing in English, and making distinctive contributions to moral theory.

Chief among 17th-century moralists are Thomas HOBBES, Ralph Cudworth, and Richard Cumberland

(1631–1718). Hobbes and Cumberland were innovators, while Cudworth, one of the CAMBRIDGE PLATONISTS, was a spokesman for traditional doctrine. Until the 20th century, Hobbes was reviled or dismissed because of his materialistic mechanism, his rejection of any sociability or sympathy in human nature, his determinism, and his account of morality as rooted in self-seeking desires. Yet, Hobbes had an immediate and lasting effect on ethics, mainly through his political theory. For him, each man in the state of nature possessed the supreme right of self-preservation and with it all other rights; hence, society, the state, and justice result from positive agreement among men. In the controversy occasioned by *Leviathan,* Shaftesbury stressed that the chief issue should be Hobbes's ethics and his defective picture of man as dominated by ''only one Master-Passion, Fear, which has in effect devour'd all the rest, and left room only for that infinite Passion toward *Power after Power*, Natural (as he affirms) to *All Men, and never ceasing but in Death.*'' Cudworth argues for an objective and natural distinction between good and evil and for man's power to choose between them. Cumberland's *De Legibus Naturae* (1672) was the first attempt at a complete refutation of Hobbes. His use of a quantitative notion of the common good marks a break from previous treatments and anticipates utilitarianism.

Despite his religious interests, writings on the state and education, and pervasive influence on philosophy, John Locke can hardly be classed as a moralist. In *The Fable of the Bees: or, Private Vices, Publick Benefits,* Mandeville (1670–1733) shows the influence of Locke and especially of Hobbes. Claiming to be a realist concerned with what man is rather than what he ought to be, he describes man as ''a compound of various Passions, that help govern him by turns, whether he will or no.'' By nature unsociable, man has qualities such that he can be made sociable by rulers using force and cunning. Acts contrary to his natural impulses, whereby he strives to help others and conquer his passions out of a rational ambition to be good, are virtuous. Mandeville gives a repellent but effective statement of what follows from Hobbes's doctrine, and finds that debauchery, luxury, avarice, fraud, and the rest of the ''private vices'' serve the common good. Anthony Ashley Cooper, third Earl of Shaftesbury (1671–1713), author of *Characteristicks of Men, Manners, Opinions, Times,* advances a refined Stoicism. An optimist, he finds that man is naturally disposed to virtue, which is its own reward and reflects the order instituted by God throughout the universe. Love of beauty is helpful to virtue, and man possesses a moral sense, a faculty partly rational and partly aesthetic, whereby he recognizes and loves what is good. He was criticized by George Berkeley, who was particularly critical in his *Alciphron.*

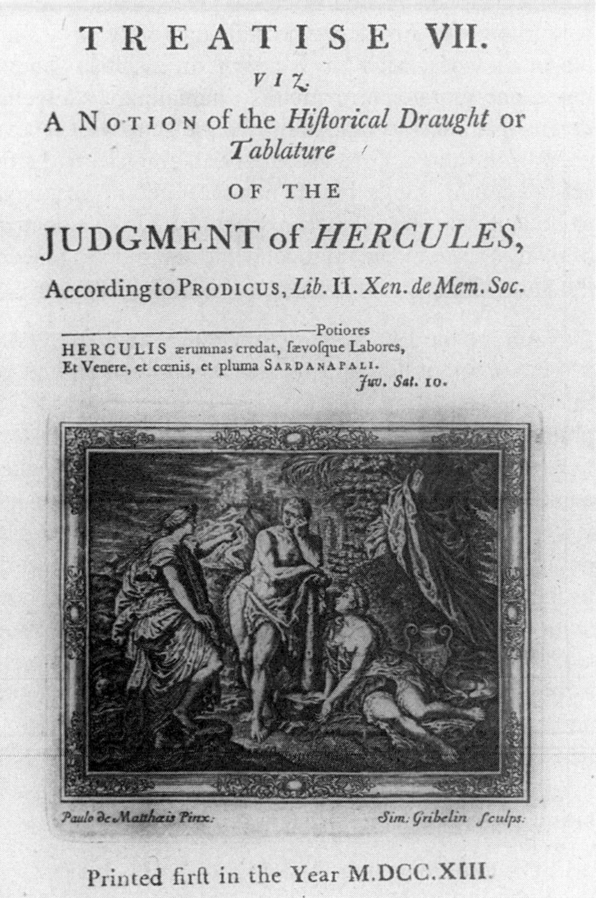
TREATISE VII.

VIZ.

A NOTION of the *Hiſtorical Draught* or *Tablature*

OF THE

JUDGMENT of *HERCULES,*

According to PRODICUS, *Lib.* II. *Xen. de Mem. Soc.*

——Potiores
HERCULIS ærumnas credat, ſævoſque Labores,
Et Venere, et cœnis, et pluma SARDANAPALI.
Juv. Sat. 10.

Paulo de Matthæis Pinx. *Sim: Gribelin ſculps.*

Printed firſt in the Year M.DCC.XIII.

Title page from ''The Judgement of Hercules,'' by Anthony Ashley Cooper (Third Earl of Shaftsbury).

A follower of Shaftesbury, founder of the Scotch school and forerunner of Bentham and the utilitarians, Hutcheson (1694–1746), in his *Inquiry into the Original of Our Ideas of Beauty and Virtue* and elsewhere, elaborates the doctrine of a moral sense, equates virtue with benevolence, and makes universal happiness the norm of morality. Joseph Butler (1692–1752) is important for his *Analogy of Religion,* where he is a powerful opponent of Deism, and for his sermons on moral subjects. A cautious thinker, he settles for probability as the guide of life. While there are ''natural appearances of our being in a state of degradation,'' man is disposed to condemn obvious vices and to approve other deeds in themselves and apart from consideration of which is ''likeliest to produce an overbalance of happiness or misery.'' Hume's greatest work, the *Treatise of Human Nature,* applies Locke's method to morality or, better, is an introduction to such application, and by it and other works he made his great impact on conduct as well as on thought. Morality is the object of feeling rather than of thought. The ''mere survey'' of certain mental qualities gives pleasure and of certain others pain; hence he calls one class virtues and the other vices. Man has a power of unselfish benevolence, and moral approbation is ''humanity,'' ''a feeling for the happiness of mankind.'' Hume's analysis is never deep or thorough. Greatest of British empiricists, he describes certain things that are but never gets at what ought to be and why. Far higher in value are Burke's doctrine of man as a social and political being and moral agent and the shrewd and solid teachings of Samuel Johnson.

Among the 19th-century thinkers, Jeremy BENTHAM, originator of utilitarianism; John Stuart MILL, who refined the utilitarian doctrine; and Herbert SPENCER, the philosopher of evolution, are the most important. Basically a utilitarian, Spencer regarded his ethics as his greatest achievement. Moral realities are subject to evolutionary laws, and ''absolute ethics'' will arrive when man and his environment are completely evolved. At the same time, he limits the powers of state and society and puts supreme value on the individual man. Henry Sidgwick (1838–1900), author of *The Methods of Ethics,* and partly a follower of Mill, the idealists T. H. Green (1836–82) and F. H. BRADLEY, and Joseph Rickaby, SJ, a neoscholastic notable for his learning, grasp of principles, originality and sureness of thought, and clarity of presentation, may also be named.

The intuitionism of G. E. Moore (1873–1958), H. A. Prichard (1871–1947), and W. D. Ross (1877–1971) dominated the early decades of the 20th century. In *Principia Ethica* (1903), Moore offered a proof that ''good'' is an indefinable attribute and therefore rejected both the utilitarian and the idealist doctrines as resting on a fallacy, which he termed the ''naturalistic fallacy.'' Morality consisted for him in simply seeing what states of affairs are good and acting to bring these about. Prichard and Ross extended Moore's analysis of goodness to obligation. In *The Right and the Good* (1930), Ross enumerated several types of duty, such as promise-keeping and gratitude, which all people immediately recognize as such. In opposition to utilitarianism, he insisted on the priority of duty over the maximization of pleasure while also denying that any duty could be absolute. After A. J. Ayer (1910–1989) applied logical positivism's theory of language to ethics in *Language, Truth, and Logic* (1936) to show that moral statements are literally meaningless, that is, incapable of being either true or false, moral philosophers devoted themselves to analyzing moral judgments. R. M. Hare (1919–) represents the mainstream in the 20th century. Against Ayer and the other emotivists, Hare argued in *The Language of Morals* (1952) that the logical positivists are mistaken in putting moral judgments in the same class as matters of taste and that this is evident from the fact that moral statements, unlike assertions of taste, have the logical features of being imperative and universalizable. In the last part of the century there has been increasing attention to the notion of virtue. Two essays published in 1958, G. E. M. Anscombe's ''Modern Moral Philosophy'' and Philippa Foot's ''Moral Beliefs,'' drew attention to the importance of character in moral reasoning and moral action. Alasdair C. MacIntyre's *After Virtue: A Study in Moral Theory* (1981), a dismissal of modern ethics as incoherent and a defense of Aristotelianism, and Iris Murdoch's (1919–1999) *The Sovereignty of Good* (1971) and *Metaphysics as a Guide to Morals* (1992), which argue that morality has its source in love for goodness, have done much to establish virtue ethics as a branch within moral philosophy.

Despite the new openness to alternative traditions of moral thought, the most influential writing in British moral theory remains as individualistic, relativist, and utilitarian (or, to use Anscombe's more precise term, consequentialist) as it was in 1965.

Bibliography: B. WILLEY, *The English Moralists* (New York 1964). W. R. SORLEY, *History of British Philosophy to 1900* (Cambridge 1965). W. D. HUDSON, *Modern Moral Philosophy* (London 1983). J. B. SCHNEEWIND, *The Invention of Autonomy: A History of Modern Moral Philosophy* (Cambridge 1998). M. WARNOCK, *Ethics since 1900* (London 1960).

[J. K. RYAN/R. P. KENNEDY]

BROAD CHURCH

A term applied originally to those members of the Church of England in the second half of the 19th century who, having no organized party, agreed in interpreting the religious formularies of ANGLICANISM in their widest sense to enable men of varied religious views to continue membership in the Church. Thomas Arnold (1795–1842), classical scholar and famed headmaster of Rugby, was a powerful influence in forming this school of thought. Broad Churchmen stressed moral rectitude and tolerance of heterodox views, but decried hierarchical organization and ritualism as unimportant. They freely accepted whatever scientific opinion seemed to say about religion and the Bible. They considered the latter a source of teaching on righteousness rather than a guide to belief. The publication by seven authors of *Essays and Reviews* (1860) made such views widely known and caused a general outcry in the established Church. The book was officially condemned and two of the essayists were punished. Their successors in the 20th century are generally referred to as modernists, but many are more easily recognizable as members of the Modern Churchmen's Union, founded in 1898 for the promotion of theological LIBERALISM in the Church of England. They advocate a continuing reformulation of Anglican beliefs as the exigencies of the times may seem to require, even when this involves discarding beliefs usually thought fundamental to Christianity.

See Also: HIGH CHURCH; LOW CHURCH.

Bibliography: J. A. T. ROBINSON, *Honest to God* (Philadelphia 1963). F. L. CROSS, *The Oxford Dictionary of the Christian Church* (London 1957) 91, 199, 287–290, 463, 910.

[E. MCDERMOTT]

BROGLIE, MAURICE JEAN DE

Bishop of Ghent; b. Broglie (Normandy), Sept. 5, 1766; d. Paris, July 20, 1821. Despite his illustrious military ancestry, Prince de Broglie chose an ecclesiastical career. After studies at the Seminary of Saint-Sulpice, Paris, he went to Germany (1790), was ordained at Trier (1792), and became a provost at Posen. Upon his return to France (1802), his candor, piety, distinction, and renowned family name won him the favor of Napoleon I. He became almoner at the imperial court (1803), then bishop of Acqui, in Piedmont (Nov. 17, 1805). When delicate health forced him to abandon this diocese, he was promoted to the See of Ghent (March 1807). At first he manifested there a certain amount of deference to Napoleon: later he opposed him at the time of the founding of the imperial university and still more during the French national synod (1811). This led to his imprisonment at Vincennes, exile to Beaune, resignation of his episcopal charge, the suspicion of his maintaining relations with the diocesan curia at Ghent, and his further incarceration at Île Sainte-Marguerite. After Napoleon's death Broglie returned to his diocese (May 28, 1814), which was henceforth incorporated into the Low Countries. He organized diocesan education, and in his *Jugement doctrinal* (1815) opposed the Fundamental Law of this kingdom, because of an unwillingness to admit the freedom of worship inscribed in it. For this he was hailed before the Court of Assizes, and condemned to deportation (Nov. 8, 1817). He fled to France, going first to Amiens, then to Paris.

Bibliography: F. CLAYS BOUUAERT, *Dictionnaire d'histoire et de géographie ecclésiastiques,* ed. A. BAUDRILLART (Paris 1912–) 10:813–818.

[A. SIMON]

BROGNE, ABBEY OF

Former BENEDICTINE monastery in Saint-Gérard, Namur, Belgium, Diocese of Namur, originally the Diocese of Liège. It was founded by GERARD OF BROGNE, who had been trained at SAINT-DENIS-EN-FRANCE. He transferred the relics of St. Eugene to Brogne and was abbot there from 923 until his death (959). The discipline of the new community attracted attention: the Duke of Lorraine asked Gerard to restore Saint-Ghislain in Hainaut; Count Arnold of Flanders solicited him to do the same for Saint-Bavon and Saint-Pierre in Ghent, for SAINT-BERTIN and SAINT-AMAND. Gerard's disciple Mainard restored the Norman monasteries of FONTENELLE, MONT-SAINT-MICHEL, and SAINT-OUEN in Rouen. Gerard, however, founded no new congregation; he only introduced his ''observance'' into older houses. In 992 Emperor OTTO III came to Brogne with Bp. Notker of Liège to meet his old teacher, Abbot Heribert. Bishop Nithard of Liège consecrated the abbey church on Nov. 14, 1038. The simoniacal abbot Guiremond, monk of Saint-Jacques (Liège), bought Brogne from Bishop Othbert, thus incurring stern reproaches from RUPERT OF DEUTZ. In 1131 Alexander of Juliers, Bishop of Liège, exalted the relics of St. Gerard (*Monumenta Germaniae Historica: Scriptores*, 4:22). Material and spiritual decline set in later: wars between Burgundy and Liège (*c.* 1425) and the conflict between the Count of Namur and the Dinantais (*c.* 1475) hurt Brogne. The Germans (1525) and the French (1554) ravaged the abbey, which, soon after the creation of the Diocese of Namur, was made part of the episcopal *mensa* (income) in 1566 and was governed by a prior who had a three-year term of office. Thus began the interminable conflict between the bishops of Namur and the monks. In 1645 the abbot of LIESSIES, Dom Gaspar Roger, restored Brogne, whose community had been reduced to six religious; he imposed the statutes of Francis Louis BLOSIUS, which were replaced in 1656 by those of BURSFELD. In 1686 King Louis XIV issued an edict that accorded the monastery a third of its revenues, the other two-thirds going to the bishop: but in 1731, the bishop of Namur had Emperor Charles VI annul this edict. The French Revolution completely destroyed the abbey, which then had 12 monks.

Brogne is one of the few monasteries in Belgium for which there is a catalogue of books prior to 1200 (MS 46). It is now in the major seminary of Namur, which contains other notable Brogne codices (MSS 43–50). Dom Eugène Massart (d. 1736), a MAURIST, was the last chronicler of the abbey.

Bibliography: L. H. COTTINEAU, *Répertoire topobibliographique des abbayes et prieurés*, 2 v. (Mâcon 1935–39) 1:510–511. F. BAIX, *Dictionnaire d'histoire et de géographie ecclésiastiques*, ed. A. BAUDRILLART et al. (Paris 1912–) 10:818–832. U. BERLIÈRE, ''L'Abbaye de Saint-Gérard,'' in *Messager des fidèles* 5 (1888) 169–181, 216–223; ''L'Abbaye de Brogne ou de Saint-Gérard,'' in *Messager de Saint-Benoît* 7 (1905). É. SABBE, ''Étude critique sur la biographie et le réforme de Gérard de Brogne,'' in *Mélanges Félix Rousseau* 8 (1958) 497–524. *Saint Gérard de*

Brogne et son oeuvre réformatrice (Maredsous 1960), also in *Revue Bénédictine* 70 (1960).

[J. DAOUST]

BROLLO, BASILIO

Vicar apostolic to China; b. Gemona, Italy, March 25, 1648; d. San-yüan, China, July 16, 1704. He became a friar at Bassano in 1666 and a priest in 1674. He followed Bp. Bernardino DELLA CHIESA to the Orient in 1680 and landed in Guangzhou (Canton), China, on Aug. 27, 1684, assuming the name Yeh Tsun-hsiao. Between 1685 and 1700, acting as Della Chiesa's provicar, he was by his initiatives and writings the main instrument by which were established the vicariates apostolic to rid the missions of the obsolescent Portuguese and Spanish patronage. Despite continual illness, Brollo, with the bishop, visited and attended the missions of Jianxi (Chiang-hsi) and Fujian (Fu-chien) (1686), Chechiang (1687), and Hu-kuang and Chiang-nan (1689); he took up residence at Nanjing (Nanking) in 1692. Named vicar apostolic of Shensi, he left for his see in June 1700. Arriving at Xi'an (Sian) with Antonio Laghi, OFM, in May 1701, he began to visit the missions of Sian and Sanyuan and Hangzhong (Hanchung) and he opened new stations at Meixian (Kai-ying) and Fengxiang (Fengsiang). In 1703 he moved to San-yüan to establish his headquarters there, but he fell ill and died. He was truly great for his learning, wisdom, zeal, and supreme charity. He left numerous mission letters, reports, and essays, as well as five Chinese works: *T'ien-chu-chiao Yao Chu-lüeh* (Compendium of Catholic Prayers and Doctrine, 1687); *Chien-cheng Shengshih Kuei-i* (Confirmation's Notion and Rite, MS, author's preface 1689); *Han Tzu Hsi I* (a Chinese-Latin dictionary arranged by radicals), MS 1694; a Chinese-Latin dictionary alphabetically arranged by transliterated phonetics (MS 1699), a model much followed and plagiarized; and *Brevis Methodus Confessionis Instituendae,* published in transliterated Chinese by Pedro de la Piñuela, OFM, in his edition of Francisco Varo, OP, *Arte de la Lengva Mandarina* (1703).

Bibliography: *Sinica Franciscana,* v. 6, ed. G. MENSAERT (Rome 1961). A. S. ROSSO, *Apostolic Legations to China of the Eighteenth Century* (South Pasadena, Calif. 1948); "Pedro de la Piñuela, O.F.M., Mexican Missionary to China and Author," *Franciscan Studies* 8 (1948) 250–274.

[A. S. ROSSO]

BRONDEL, JOHN BAPTIST

First bishop of Helena (Mont.) Diocese; b. Bruges, Belgium, Feb. 23, 1842; d. Helena, Nov. 3, 1904. He was taught by the Xaverian Brothers and attended the Episcopal Institute of St. Louis, Brussels, for ten years. Deciding to prepare for the missions, he entered the American College in Louvain, Belgium. After his ordination on Dec. 17, 1864, at Mechlin, Belgium, he joined Bp. Augustin M. A. Blanchet in the Diocese of Nesqually (now Seattle Archdiocese), Washington Territory, in November of 1866, and was appointed pastor at Steilacoom (Steilicom) on Puget Sound. From this base he organized parishes in Olympia and Tacoma, and did missionary work in Walla Walla until he was appointed bishop of Vancouver Island (now Victoria) on Dec. 14, 1879.

On April 7, 1883, he was named administrator of the vicariate apostolic of Montana and established his residence at Helena, the territorial capital. When the Diocese of Helena was created on March 7, 1884, Brondel became its first bishop. Besides transforming his territory from missionary to diocesan status, he promoted the building of schools, hospitals, and asylums; increased the number of churches from seven to 56; and added the Sisters of the Good Shepherd to the communities already staffing diocesan institutions. Development outside the city kept pace with that within: 49 churches, four hospitals, five academies, and seven parochial schools were established throughout the diocese during his episcopate. On behalf of the native Americans he made fund-raising tours in the East and founded a mission among the Cheyenne. At his request the eastern two-thirds of Montana was separated from the Helena jurisdiction in 1904 to form the Diocese of Great Falls.

Bibliography: L. B. PALLADINO, *Indian and White in the Northwest* (2d ed. rev. Lancaster, Pa. 1922). *Dictionary of American Biography* (New York 1928–36) 3:67–68.

[W. J. GREYTAK]

BRONISŁAWA, BL.

Polish contemplative; b. Kamien, Silesia, 1203; d. Aug. 29, 1259. Her father was Stanislaus, count of Prandata-Odrowaz; her mother Anna, of the noble family of Jaxa-Okolski. St. HYACINTH and Bl. CESLAUS of Silesia were her first cousins. At age 16 she entered the convent of PREMONSTRATENSIAN nuns of Zwierzyniec near Cracow. Her biographers picture her as a model of mortification and of heroic virtues. It is claimed that she had a vision of Mary bearing the body of Hyacinth, who had just died, from his Dominican priory to heaven. This experience intensified her contemplative life, and pious custom labels the hill near her convent where she retired to pray Mt. St. Bronisława. She died two years after Hyacinth. Her body, buried in the convent church, was lost during the Swedish invasion of Poland, but it was rediscovered in the seventeenth century. Her convent was rebuilt and it became a center of prayer for the Polish nation. Cracow has always considered her a saint. In 1839 Pope Gregory XVI approved her cultus. She was known as the patroness of a happy death and of a good reputation. Cardinal Hlond (d. 1948), the primate of Poland, encouraged the Poles to ask Bronisława, who had saved them from various plagues, to protect them from the danger of the worse contagion of atheism and immorality.

Feast: Aug. 30.

Bibliography: *Blogoslawiona Bronisława*, ed. J. R. BAR (Warsaw 1984). J. CHRZASZCZ, *Drei schlesische Landesheilige* (Breslau 1897). A. GONET, *Novena in Honor of Bl. B.* (Lyndora, Pa. 1936). P. DAVID, *Dictionnaire d'histoire et de géographie ecclésiastiques*, ed. A. BAUDRILLART et al. (Paris 1912) 10:841.

[L. L. RUMMEL]

BROOK FARM

A religious experiment in communal living (1841–47) at West Roxbury, near Boston, Mass. It was founded by George Ripley, a Boston Unitarian minister and Transcendentalist, and his wife, Sophia Dana Ripley, to manifest in miniature the Transcendental belief in a new world in which each man might develop his own talents according to the norms of individualism and self-reliance. Each member was to enjoy complete freedom as long as he did not trespass on the rights of others. Although it is not certain that the new association was consciously socialistic, it is clear that the founders did envisage a new attitude toward manual labor and the creation of a utopian society. As one of the Brook Farm students expressed it: "No Adventist ever believed more absolutely in the coming of Christ than we in the reorganization of society on a fraternal basis."

At Brook Farm all domestic work was divided among the members of the society. At first farming occupied most of the men, but when the land proved unproductive because of the lack of tools and skills, the community turned to manufacturing. Carpenters, shoemakers, and printers plied their trade, and Isaac HECKER worked for a while as a baker. All labor was paid at the rate of one dollar per day. Room, board, and clothing were supplied practically at cost. The work week was 48 hours during the winter and 60 hours in summer. But it was in the field of education that Brook Farm truly excelled. The curriculum of the community school was well organized and included mathematics, classics, history, literature, modern languages, philosophy, botany, drawing, dancing, and music. Faculty and students lived together, with frequent contacts between teacher and pupil. There were no specific study hours, emphasis being put on the need for personal responsibility. Each student worked at least two hours a day at manual labor, and all were called upon to work in the kitchen or wait on table. Famous visitors, including Ralph Waldo Emerson, Margaret Fuller, Orestes Brownson, Robert Owen, Horace Greeley, and Elizabeth Peabody, furthered the students' education by informal conversations, lectures, and dialogues. Many of the New England intelligentsia sent their sons there after the Harvard faculty especially recommended the Brook Farm school as an excellent place to prepare for college.

If it had concentrated on education, Brook Farm might have prospered, but its founders were more interested in universal reform. When the works of Charles Fourier, the French Socialist, were published in the U.S., Brook Farm turned itself into a Fourierist phalanx (1844), with little change in its original constitution. For the next four years it published the *Harbinger,* an important socialist paper that kept the community in debt. Meanwhile, the school was neglected as missionaries went out to teach socialism. After a fire destroyed a new and uninsured central building (March 1846), the community decided to disband and to auction all its assets to pay the heavy debts.

Bibliography: E. R. CURTIS, *A Season in Utopia* (New York 1961). K. K. BURTON, *Paradise Planters: The Story of Brook Farm* (New York 1939). A. F. TYLER, *Freedom's Ferment* (Minneapolis 1944).

[E. DELANEY]

BROOKES, JAMES (BROOKS)

Roman Catholic bishop of Gloucester (1554–59); b. Hampshire, May 1512; d. Gloucester, February of 1560. Brookes, educated at Oxford, received his doctor of divinity degree in 1546 and the following year was made master of Balliol College. He served also as chaplain and almoner of Stephen Gardiner, Bishop of Winchester. He was appointed bishop of Gloucester, replacing the deposed John Hooper in 1554. As papal subdelegate in the trials of CRANMER, RIDLEY, and LATIMER, he refrained from degrading the last two, although he zealously supported their conviction and execution. He was an eloquent preacher, a number of whose sermons appear in Foxe's *Acts and Monuments.* With the accession of Elizabeth in 1558, Brookes was deprived of his see because he refused to take the oath of royal supremacy over the Church. He was cast into prison, where he died. Since Gloucester was created a see in 1541 by Henry VIII, Brookes was the first and last bishop of Gloucester in communion with Rome.

Bibliography: T. COOPER, *The Dictionary of National Biography from the Earliest Times to 1900* (London 1885 1900)

2:1346–47. P. HUGHES, *Rome and the Counter-Reformation in England* (London 1942). L. B. SMITH, *Tudor Prelates and Politics* (Princeton 1953). *A Literary and Biographical History or Bibliographical Dictionary of the English Catholics from 1534 to the Present Time* (London–New York 1885–1902) 1:315–316.

[M. R. O'CONNELL]

BROOKS, PHILLIPS

Protestant Episcopal Bishop of Massachusetts; b. Boston, Mass., Dec. 13, 1835; d. Boston, Jan. 23, 1893. He was educated at Boston Latin School, Harvard University, and the Virginia Theological Seminary, Alexandria, Va., and was ordained in 1860. He served as rector of Holy Trinity Church, Philadelphia, Pa., before accepting a call to Trinity Church, Boston, in 1869. During this period he combated racial prejudice and advocated full citizenship rights for African Americans. At Trinity Church he won renown as a pulpit orator and frequently preached in churches of other denominations. In his sermons and particularly in the Bohlen lectures, published as *The Influence of Jesus* in 1879, Brooks stressed personal devotion and regarded dogmatic questions as of little importance. His views incited considerable opposition when he was consecrated bishop of Massachusetts in 1891.

Bibliography: A. V. G. ALLEN, *Life and Letters of Phillips Brooks,* 2 v. (New York 1900). W. LAWRENCE, *Life of Phillips Brooks* (New York 1930). J. F. WOOLVERTON, *The Education of Phillips Brooks* (Urbana 1995). S. AHLSTROM, *A Religious History of the American People* (New Haven 1972).

[R. K. MACMASTER]

BROTHER IN CHRIST

An appellation referring to the specifically Christian unity, of which Christ Himself is the center and criterion and to which the Synoptic tradition witnesses (Mk 3.31–35; 10.29–30). It is by FAITH and the doing of the Father's will that one becomes a brother of Jesus (Mt 12.46–50; 21.28–32). By His death and Resurrection Jesus has become in the fullest sense ''the firstborn among many brethren'' (Rom 8.29; *see* FIRSTBORN), reconciling divided humanity in His Body on the cross (Eph 2.11–18). It is the risen Lord who calls His Apostles truly His ''brothers'' (Mt 28.10; Jn 20.17), and in them all men without exception. This Christian concept of brotherhood is found in a strongly ecclesial context in Matthew, ch. 18 (see especially v. 15, 21, 35). To live as a brother is the specifically Christian way to live as a part of the community, to share in its common life. Brothers in Christ must show one another a tender, devoted love modeled on the sacrificial love that Christ showed His own (Jn 13.1, 15, 34–35; 15.12–13; 1 Jn 2.10–11; 3.10, 16, 17; 5.16; Rom 14.10, 13, 15; 1 Cor 6.6, 8; 8.11–13). Although the love of a Christian brother must take in all men without exception (1 Thes 3.12; 2 Pt 1.7), the visible community of the Christian brotherhood is the special field for that privileged form of love called *philadelphia* (φιλαδελφία: Rom 12.10; 1 Thes 4.9; Heb 13.1; 1 Pt 1.22–23; 2 Pt 1.7).

The early Christians soon adopted the term brother as their usual mode of addressing one another (30 times in Acts and 130 times in Paul), and the name remained in common use among Christians in general until late in the 3d century, when its use was gradually restricted to clerical and monastic circles.

See Also: MYSTICAL BODY OF CHRIST; SOCIETY (IN THEOLOGY); UNITY OF FAITH; UNITY OF THE CHURCH; EXCOMMUNICATION

Bibliography: K. H. SCHELKLE, ''Bruder,'' *Reallexikon für Antike und Christentum,* ed. T. KLAUSER [Stuttgart 1941 (1950)–] 2:631–640. J. RATZINGER, *Die christliche Brüderlichkeit* (Munich 1960).

[F. X. LAWLOR]

BROTHERS AND SISTERS OF JESUS

There are various places in the New Testament where reference is made to the relatives of Our Lord. ''Is not this the carpenter, the son of Mary, the brother of James, Joseph, Jude, and Simon? And are not also his sisters here with us?'' (Mk 6.3; cf. Mt 13.55–56). In John 2.12; 7.3, 5, 10; and Acts of the Apostles 1.14, mention is made of ''His brethren.'' St. Paul calls James ''the brother of the Lord'' (Gal 1.19). The Synoptics speak of ''His mother and His brethren'' who came to see Him as He was preaching (Mt 12.46–50; Mk 3.21–25; Lk 8.19–21; 1 Cor 9.5). In all languages the words ''brother,'' ''brethren'' and ''sister'' are used in the strict sense of blood relatives as well as in the broader sense of some one or ones united in a religious or other common bond. The same is true of the Sacred Scriptures. Our Lord Himself used the terms in reference to those who are united to Him through the fulfillment of the will of God (Mt 12.46–50). Paul and his group ''greeted the brethren,'' that is, the Christians, at Ptolemais (Acts 21.7). In the Old Testament the word ''brother'' is used by Abraham in reference to his nephew Lot (Gn 14.14). While the names of the so-called ''sisters'' are not given in the New Testament, four ''brothers'' are named: James, Joseph, Jude and Simon. Three of these names occur in the list of the Apostles (Mt 10.2–4; Mk 3.14–19; Lk 6.12–16; Acts

1.13), with one, namely, that of James, being given twice. There is little doubt that ''James of Alphaeus, and Simon called the zealot; Jude the brother of James'' (Lk 6.14–16) are the ones called the brothers of Our Lord. Paul's reference to ''James the brother of the Lord'' (Gal 1.19) is most likely to the Apostle, James of Alphaeus [*see* JAMES (SON OF ALPHAEUS), ST.].

Of these listed, James and Joseph are called the sons of Mary, one of the women mentioned in the story of the passion, death and resurrection of Our Lord (Mt 27.56,61; 28.1; Mk 15.40,47; Lk 24.10). This Mary cannot be the Mother of Jesus; some, however, identify her as ''His mother's sister'' who stood at the foot of the cross (Jn 19.25). She may thus be the same as the ''Mary of Cleopas'' mentioned in this text, as some scholars hold. It is possible that CLEOPAS, or Clopas, is another spelling of Alphaeus. If so, then the conclusion is that James and Joseph, as well as Simon and Jude (although there is more doubt about these two), are the sons of Mary and Cleopas, otherwise known as Alphaeus. Another opinion would make Cleopas the brother of Joseph, the foster father of Our Lord. There is no probability to the theory of the *Protoevangelium Jacobi,* Origen and Ambrosiaster (*Patrologia Latina,* 17:344–345) that ''the brothers of Jesus'' were the children of Joseph by an earlier marriage. The variety of opinions is an indication that the texts in the New Testament mentioning ''brothers and sisters and brethren'' of Our Lord cannot be used to pinpoint their relationship.

Sacred Scripture is very definite about Mary being a virgin when she conceived Jesus (Mt 1.18–25; Lk 1.26–27; 2.7). He is the firstborn, a term meaning the first ''to open the womb'' without any implication of other children to follow. The very definiteness with which Our Lord is called ''the son of Mary'' (Mk 6.3) would seem to point to an only son. From the cross Our Lord charged John, the beloved Apostle, with the care of His Mother, which would have been a strange action if she had other sons.

The New Testament writings are the products of men who were the first members of the Church established by Christ. They are inspired in their teaching and preaching; they reflect what the early Church believed. It is by placing these writings into the background of the Church that we are able to understand them and interpret them; in this way light is thrown on the New Testament text concerning the problem of the ''brothers of Jesus,'' which involves the perpetual virginity of Our Blessed Mother, a doctrine of the Church. The Church from its earliest days taught that Mary was always a virgin. In view of this, then, there can be no doubt that Mary did not have any other children; therefore the ''brothers and sisters'' mentioned in the New Testament cannot be the blood brothers and sisters of Our Lord.

Bibliography: F. PRAT, ''La Parenté de Jésus,'' *Recherches de science religieuse,* 17 (1927) 127–138. J. BLINZLER, ''Zum Problem der Brüder des Herrn,'' *Trierer theologische Zeitschrift,* 67 (1958) 129–145, 224–246. M. J. LAGRANGE, *Évangile selon S. Marc* (4th ed. Paris 1947) 79–93. J. J. COLLINS, ''The Brethren of the Lord and Two Recently Published Papyri,'' *Theological Studies,* 5 (1944) 484–494. *Patrologia Latina,* ed. J. P. MIGNE, 217 v., indexes 4 v. (Paris 1878–90).

[G. H. GUYOT]

BROTHERS AND SISTERS OF THE FREE SPIRIT

A name given in the 13th century to certain followers of idealistic pantheism. This ancient inheritance had received a rejuvenating impetus from the works of the Neoplatonist PROCLUS and of JOHN SCOTUS ERIGENA, and found adherents in practically every Christian country throughout the Middle Ages. The name in the above title was widely used by pantheistic groups in Central Europe between the 12th and 15th centuries. In Italy, too, the name was known, as is evident from the early 14th-century investigation conducted by UBERTINO OF CASALE in Tuscany, Spoleto, and Ancona. The link sometimes indicated between the ''brethren'' and the followers of AMALRIC OF BÈNE and Ortlieb of Strasbourg (*see* ORTLIBARII) is doubtful. However, they shared in common the central idea of the ''Free Spirit,'' i.e., a licentious intellect, incapable of any wrong, and bearing the spark of an all-pervading divinity. ALBERT THE GREAT, while serving as bishop of Regensburg, compiled a list of the main tenets of the group; all creatures are identical with the Creator; man is capable of becoming God; there is no resurrection from the dead; man transformed into God is incapable of sin. They were opposed by J. TAULER, HENRY SUSO, J. RUYSBROECK, G. GROOTE, and Jean GERSON. The doctrines of the brethren were never extinguished in some parts of the Netherlands, Germany, and Bohemia, and they may have been the origin of the teachings of the ANABAPTISTS in Germany in the early 16th century.

Bibliography: R. ALLIER, *Les Frères du libre esprit* (Paris 1905). H. GRUNDMANN, *Religiöse Bewegungen im Mittelalter* (Berlin 1935). F. VERNET, *Dictionnaire de théologie catholique* 6.1:800–809. G. MOLLAT, *Catholicisme* 4:1630. O. RÜHLE, *Die Religion in Geschichte und Gegenwart* 1:1433–34.

[B. CHUDOBA]

BROTHERS OF CHRISTIAN INSTRUCTION OF PLOËRMEL

Sometimes called La Mennais Brothers (*Institutum Fratrum Instructionis Christianae de Ploërmel,* FIC); Official Catholic Directory #0320; a religious congregation with papal approval (1891, 1910) that emerged from the union in 1820 of a group in Brittany founded by Gabriel DESHAYES in 1816 at Auray with another started by Jean de LA MENNAIS in 1819 at St. Brieuc. La Mennais administered the congregation until his death (1860), when the direction passed to a superior general and six assistants. The original apostolate of teaching in elementary schools was later extended to include agricultural, commercial, and nautical education. Secondary education was undertaken, and eventually college instruction. Missions were undertaken by 1837. The first school in the U.S. opened in Plattsburgh, NY (1903). Twenty brothers assisted the Jesuits in their work on the Native American reservations of Idaho, Montana, and Alaska from 1903 to 1910. In 1946 a separate American province was organized with headquarters at Alfred, Maine. The generalate is in Rome.

Bibliography: A. P. LAVEILLE, *Jean-Marie de La Mennais, 1780–1860,* 2 v. (Paris 1903). H. C. RULON and P. FRIOT, *Un Siècle de pédagogie dans les écoles primaires, 1820–1940* (Paris 1962).

[E. G. DROUIN/EDS.]

BROTHERS OF CHRISTIAN INSTRUCTION OF ST. GABRIEL

Popularly known as the Brothers of St. Gabriel and officially as *Institutum Fratrum Instructionis Christianae a Sancto Gabriele,* FSG; a religious congregation devoted to education. For a long time there was question whether Gabriel DESHAYES merely restored a group that had been started in 1705 by St. Louis GRIGNION DE MONTFORT or founded a new institute in 1821 at Saint-Laurent-sur-Sèvre (Vendée), France. A study by the historical section of the Congregation of Rites supported the latter conclusion [AAS 39 (1947) 240–241]. Until 1853 members were known as the Brothers of the Holy Ghost. In France, when Justin Emile Combes caused the closing of schools run by religious (1903), the bishop of Luçon suppressed the Brothers of St. Gabriel, still a diocesan congregation. After subsequent reorganization it became a papally approved institute (1910). The original apostolate of teaching in elementary schools soon came to include instruction for the deaf, mute, and blind, especially in France. Later the brothers engaged in secondary education and in teacher training. The congregation spread to Canada (1888), Belgium and Gabon (1900), Thailand (1901), England, Spain, Madagascar, and India (1903), Italy (1904), Congo (Léopoldville, 1928), Malaysia (1952), Senegal (1954), Congo (Brazzaville, 1955), Republic of South Africa (1957), Colombia (1961), and Peru (1962). The generalate is located in Rome.

Bibliography: A. BLAIN, *Institut des Frères de l'Instruction Chrétienne de St-Gabriel* (Poitiers 1897). E. GOUIN, ''Les Frères de St-Gabriel au Canada, 1888–1913,'' *La Revue Canadienne* NS 12 (September 1913) 193–206. *Nova inquisitio super dubio: An B. Ludovicus M. Grignion de Montfort historice haberi possit uti fundator . . . Fratrum Instructionis Christianae a S. Gabriele* (S. Rituum Congregatio, Sectio Historica 66; Vatican City 1947).

[E. G. DROUIN/EDS.]

BROTHERS OF THE CHRISTIAN SCHOOLS

The Institute of the Brothers of the Christian Schools (FSC, Official Catholic Directory #0330), whose members are often known as Christian Brothers, or de La Salle Christian Brothers, to distinguish them from the members of the Congregation of Christian Brothers or IRISH CHRISTIAN BROTHERS, is a congregation of lay male religious founded by St. John Baptist DE LA SALLE about 1680 in Reims, France, for the direct or indirect service of the poor through education.

Origin, Spirit, and Government. John Baptist de La Salle, born in 1651 of a well-to-do family in Reims, was appointed canon of the cathedral at Reims at age 16 and ordained to the priesthood April 9, 1678. His privileged upbringing and ecclesiastical honors were in no way a preparation for his later service in education; he was led to his lifework imperceptibly and through difficult decisions as he became aware of the educational needs of the urban poor. Once convinced that God was calling him to the work, he resigned his position as canon and gave his fortune to the poor. In 1682 he took up residence with a group of schoolteachers who had been gathered in Reims by Adrien Nyel, an energetic but inconstant founder of schools. By 1686 de La Salle formed the teachers into a community with a distinctive habit and the title Brothers of the Christian Schools. At the end of the retreat that year, the principal brothers with de La Salle took a private vow of obedience renewable annually.

The 30 years that followed saw his institute spread to all parts of France, so great was the demand for quality education by dedicated teachers for the children of the artisans and the poor. In spite of misunderstanding and opposition, both from the educational and local ecclesiastical authorities, de La Salle trusted divine Providence to prove the worth of his innovative methods in

Two Christian Brothers outside Garden of Gethsemane, Mount of Olives, Israel. (©Gary Braasch/CORBIS)

education and the unique character of his religious community of lay teachers as a new form of religious life in the Church. The rule, composed by the founder in 1694, was ratified by the brothers in a general chapter that elected him as superior, but established the principle that thenceforth the institute would remain exclusively lay. During the lifetime of the founder, the brothers took vows of association to keep gratuitous schools, stability and obedience, all centered on the educational mission. Vows of poverty and chastity were added after the founder's death when the institute won approval as an institute of pontifical right by a bull of approbation from Pope Benedict XIII Jan. 26, 1725.

As men committed to a religious lifestyle in a celibate community, the brothers consecrate themselves to procure God's glory through the work of Christian education. De La Salle made the spirit of faith the spirit of his institute. With this spirit, cultivated by meditation on the Scriptures and often recalling the presence of God, the brother is encouraged to see things as God sees them. Accordingly, children in the classroom are not to be judged by appearances, by emotional likes or dislikes, not even by ability, but as persons to be formed in the image of Christ. The spirit of faith overflows into a spirit of zeal for the salvation of those entrusted to the care of the brother in the conviction that God wills all of them ''to be saved and come to the knowledge of the truth.'' The spirit of zeal rooted in faith leads the brother to make no distinction between his personal spiritual development and his teaching ministry. In addition to the spirit of faith and zeal, the founder wanted the brothers to develop a spirit of community, manifest in the religious house where everything is done in common, and in the schools conducted ''together and by association.''

The government of the institute remained basically the same from its early development until after Vatican Council II when structures were introduced to provide for subsidiarity and wider participation by the members in policies and practices that concern them. Authority over the whole institute is entrusted to a superior general, elected by and responsible to the general chapter for a period extending to the chapter following. The general chapter, constituted as the image of the entire body of the institute, is composed of delegates, the majority of whom are elected while a limited number of the higher superiors participate by right of office. The chapter also elects a vicar general to replace the superior as need arises, as well as the members of the general council, usually six in number, who with the vicar general assist the superior general in the government and animation of the institute. The local unit of government is the community, usually composed of brothers associated in a specific educational ministry. Communities are grouped in districts or provinces governed by visitators, appointed by the superior general after consultation with the brothers. Each community is headed by a director appointed by the visitator, also after consultation. The motherhouse, located originally in France, then in Belgium, has been in Rome since 1936.

Growth and Apostolate. De La Salle's initial contribution to education was to reform the system of elementary education in France for the sons of the artisans and the poor. His brothers conducted schools as a team, using the simultaneous method rather than the tutorial approach of the isolated schoolmaster then in vogue. He pioneered in using the vernacular French instead of Latin as a vehicle for learning to read. Unlike the charity schools of the time, the Christian schools, as they were called, were known for their insistence on attendance, discipline, good grooming, good manners, and regular religious observance. Religious instruction and school prayers, frequently recalling the presence of God in the classroom, were well integrated with imparting basic skills in reading, writing, and calculation.

De La Salle gave special attention to the importance of the teacher, his training, competence, dedication, in short, transforming the once-despised function of teaching school into a profession and a vocation. On three occasions, de La Salle established teacher-training institutions, the first of their kind, to train young laymen to teach in the country parishes. To reach working teenagers who could not attend classes on school days he opened a Sunday Academy where they could learn practical subjects while receiving instruction in the truths of their religion. Since the days of de La Salle, the Christian Brothers have conducted elementary and high schools, colleges, agricultural schools, technical and trade schools, child welfare institutions, student residences, and retreat centers for students.

In 1703 de La Salle sent two brothers to establish a school in Rome. Only one of them, Brother Gabriel Drolin, remained despite his isolation and the difficulty in gaining acceptance in an educational system dominated by clerics. In 1705 Brother Gabriel was accepted temporarily as a teacher in the regional schools; it was not until 1709 that he obtained his license to teach in one of the papal schools. He remained alone as the presence of the institute in Rome until he was replaced in 1728. In the light of the antipapal Jansenism of the time, the reason that de La Salle expressed on his deathbed for sending the brothers to Rome was "to ask God for the grace that their Society be always submissive to it." It is now considered unlikely that the founder intended during his lifetime to seek papal approval for his institute. That would come only after his death.

The congregation grew rapidly throughout France. At the death of the founder (1719) there were 100 brothers in about 20 houses, some serving more than one school. By 1790 there were 123 houses and almost a thousand brothers. During the French Revolution, when the brothers refused to take the CIVIL CONSTITUTION OF THE CLERGY, they were driven from their schools and effectively suppressed. Many were imprisoned and several put to death. Brothers Solomon LeClercq, Léon Mopinot, Uldaric Guillaume, and Roger Faverge have since been recognized as martyrs and beatified. By 1798 only 20 brothers, all of them in Italy, were wearing their habits and teaching in the schools.

Pius VI, recognizing the difficulties under which the institute was laboring, in 1795 appointed Brother Frumence Herbet, then in Rome, as vicar general to act for Brother Agathon, the superior, who died in exile three years later. Under Brother Frumence a reconstruction was begun from a center in Lyon and by 1810 a general chapter could be held that elected Brother Gerbaud, giving new impetus to the reunification and revival of the institute in France. The opening in 1817 of a school on the Island of Réunion in the Indian Ocean marked the beginning of the missionary activities of the institute. The greatest expansion both in France and in mission countries took place during the generalate of Brother Philippe Bransiet, who was superior from 1834 to 1878. During the last years of the 19th century the hostile education laws in France seriously curtailed the numbers of students until the laicization law of July 7, 1904, abolished teaching by religious congregations and forced the closing of more than a thousand schools in France. The motherhouse was moved to Lembecq in Belgium, many brothers returned to secular life, while many more went to mission countries to open new foundations or to bolster those already in existence. The 20th century saw the institute expand further both numerically and geographically so that by the end of Vatican Council II in 1965 there were more than 16,000 brothers conducting schools in 80 countries.

Despite the expansion of the institute throughout the world and its implantation in a variety of cultures with extensive adaptation to new educational needs, the governmental structure, the detailed prescriptions and outdated practices of the brothers' primitive rule, little changed since the founder's day, remained in force. The global upheaval of World War II was followed by the call of Vatican Council II for adaptation and renewal in religious life. The sources were to be the Gospel as the first rule of life, the charism of the founder, and the signs of the times. In the renewal general chapter of 1966–67, the institute took bold steps to move in a new direction. The thrust of the renewal is expressed in a landmark capitular document *The Brother of the Christian Schools in the World Today: A Declaration.* This declaration provided the framework for changes in governmental structures, a complete revision of the rule, a more person-centered approach to religious and community life, new initiatives in catechetics and human education, with a strong call for a return to the service of the poor. The effective internationalization of the institute, hitherto dominated by the French, was signaled by the election in 1966 of the first non-French superior general in the person of Brother Charles Henry Buttimer, an American with a doctorate in Latin from Catholic University. At the general chapter of 1986, the revised rule, which had been in force on an experimental basis for 20 years, was reexamined, revised in the light of experience, and presented to the Holy See for approval, which was granted on Jan. 26, 1987.

The euphoria attendant upon the conciliar call for renewal and adaptation gave way in the postconciliar period to the harsh reality of dispensations from religious vows, an aging personnel, and few new recruits. This phenomenon, experienced throughout the church generally, was not without its benefits. It challenged the institute to reexamine its priorities in the allocation of personnel in favor of educational works for the poor. Lay consultants, men and women, were invited to take an active part in a general chapter for the first time in 1993, leading the institute to realize that its Lasallian mission and Lasallian spirituality were riches to be shared. In the absence of uniform rules and external signs of identity, the person of John Baptist de La Salle and a renewed interest in his life and vision, has become a bond of unity and identity for the brothers and lay partners alike. The traditional brothers' schools are now more accurately known as Lasallian schools. As with other congregations, the brothers are examining structural forms to bring their lay and clerical associates into closer relation to the institute. As of October 2000, there were 6,522 brothers, 2,692 of them active in the educational ministry in 80 countries on all six continents; there were 859,433 students, male and female, enrolled in 1,000 educational institutions staffed by 66,706 teachers: brothers, priests, religious sisters, lay women and men, constituting what is now known as the worldwide Lasallian family. While vocations to the institute have declined in Europe and North America, there are thriving formation centers in Third World countries, especially Latin America and Africa.

In addition to the founder, St. John Baptist de La Salle, canonized in 1900, recent years have witnessed many brothers formally canonized and beatified. Canonized are brothers Benilde Romancon, in 1967; Miguel Febres-Cordero, in 1984; Mutien-Marie Wiaux, in 1989; in 1999, brothers martyred in Spain: Jaime Barbal at Tarragona and the eight brothers with their Passionist chaplain at Turon. Beatified are Brothers Arnold Rèche in 1987, Scubilion Rousseau in 1989, and from Spain in 1993 the seven brothers martyred at Almería; and in 2001 the five brothers martyred at Valencia. Others causes are pending, both of brothers declared venerable by reason of their heroic virtue, or more martyrs from the Spanish Revolution.

Development in the United States. The first de La Salle Brothers to come to the United States taught in the parish school at Ste. Geneviève, Missouri, from 1819 to 1822. The three of them had been sent from France at the request of Bp. Louis DUBOURG of New Orleans but, once they were sent singly to isolated missions without a community life, they were unable to live out their vocation and left the institute. The first permanent institution in the United States was Calvert Hall school, established in the cathedral parish in Baltimore in 1845 and staffed by two American brothers who had made their novitiate in Montreal. In 1848 four brothers were sent from France to New York to open a parish school on Canal Street. In that same year Brother Facile Rabut was appointed visitator of North America to supervise the five communities and 56 brothers in Canada and the United States. In 1862 a novitiate and in 1864 a provincialate were opened in New York to serve as a center for the spread of the institute to the west and south. By 1873 five districts had been created, 76 communities had been opened, and 900 brothers were teaching in more than 100 schools. The last quarter of the 19th century was a period of unparalleled expansion guided by able leaders, among them Brothers Patrick Murphy, Justin Mc Mahon, and Paulian Fanning.

Meanwhile the bishops had been urging the brothers to move into the field of higher education in order to provide the immigrant generation of Catholics with access to the professions and to have preparatory seminaries to develop an American clergy. Christian Brothers College in St. Louis was chartered in 1853, followed by colleges in New York, Philadelphia, Ellicott City, New Orleans, San Francisco, Memphis, Santa Fe, and Washington, D.C. These ventures required a dispensation from the rule that prohibited the teaching of Latin and the classics, at that time considered an indispensable element in the college curriculum. Fearful that the American brothers were moving too far from the original mission of the institute, the French superiors succeeded in the general chapter of 1897 in having the dispensation revoked. Latin was thenceforth banned from the curriculum in all the brothers' schools. Some of the colleges were forced to close or survived as high schools, while the colleges that remained had to shift the emphasis to science, engineering, and commerce. As a punitive measure, the leaders among the American brothers were reassigned for a time to foreign countries. It is a tribute to their loyalty that they remained faithful to their vocation and were eventually returned to their districts. As a result the years from 1900 to 1925 were a period of decline with some losses and few gains. In 1923, at the initiative of Pope Pius XI, the general chapter revoked the prohibition against Latin, by which time the classical languages were no longer considered essential to a college education.

As high school education became the norm for education in the United States, the brothers entered the field with vigor and imagination so that, under new leaders, the years after 1925 saw an impressive increase in the number of brothers, schools, and students. The most significant development concerned the training of the brothers to ensure that they would be armed with a college degree before beginning their work in the classroom. At the same time brothers destined for the colleges were given the opportunity to study for advanced degrees. By 1965 there were seven districts, each with its own college, and nearly 3,100 brothers in some 158 communities teaching more than 96,000 students.

In the aftermath of Vatican II, the institute in the United States experienced the same problems of adjustment faced by religious congregations and the church universal. There are fewer brothers and fewer schools. With increasing dependence on lay faculty, the emphasis shifted from brothers' schools to Lasallian schools, many of them coeducational. There have been impressive gains in commitment to direct service of the poor through child welfare institutions and new initiatives, such as the specialized ''San Miguel'' Schools, as they are called, for disadvantaged urban youth. Cooperation at the regional level is assured by the Christian Brothers Conference, directed by the visitators of the American districts, including Toronto, and centered in Landover, Maryland, outside Washington, D.C. The conference sponsors Lasallian publications and programs in continuing formation for brothers and partners to ensure the quality education integrated with religious values and the concern for the service of the poor that are characteristic of the Lasallian educational tradition.

Bibliography: W. J. BATTERSBY, *The Institute of the Brothers of the Christian Schools in the Eighteenth Century, 1719–1798* (London 1960); . . . *in the Nineteenth Century, 1800–1900,* 2 v. (London 1961–1983); *The History of the Institute of the Brothers of the Christian Schools in the United States, 1900–1925* (Winona 1966); . . . *1925–1950* (Winona 1976). A GABRIEL, *The Christian Brothers in the United States, 1848–1948* (New York 1948). 39TH GENERAL CHAPTER, *The Brother of the Christian Schools in the World Today: A Declaration* (Rome 1967); . . . *A New English Translation* (Lincroft 1997). L. SALM, *A Religious Institute in Transition: The Story of Three General Chapters* (Romeoville 1992).

[L. SALM]

BROTTIER, DANIEL JULES ALEXIS, BL.

Priest of the Congregation of the Holy Spirit and the Immaculate Heart of Mary; b. La Ferté-Saint-Cyr (near Beaugency), Diocese of Blois, France, September 7, 1876; d. St. Joseph Hospital, Paris, France, February 28, 1936. Brottier felt called to the priesthood from his childhood. In 1887 he entered the minor seminary of Blois where he proved to be a brilliant student and an entertaining friend. In 1892 he began his study of philosophy at Blois's major seminary. After his ordination as a diocesan priest (October 22, 1899), he taught at the college of Pontlevoy. Feeling a call to the missions, he joined the Holy Ghost Fathers at Grignon-Orly (September 26, 1902), professed his temporary vows (September 30, 1903), and was sent to Saint-Louis, Senegal, Africa.

During his time in Senegal (1903–11), he demonstrated a special concern for orphans, helped found an organization for the education of girls, and published the first Catholic monthly in West Africa (1906), which ceased when he returned to France in 1911. In France, he raised the money to build Dakar's cathedral (consecrated February 2, 1936) in honor of those who had died in Africa for France. His bravery as a military chaplain in the Twenty-Sixth Infantry during World War I was rewarded with five citations, the *Croix de Guerre,* and the Legion of Honor medal. Brottier attributed his survival to St. THÉRÈSE DE LISIEUX, in whose honor he built a chapel at Auteil (1925). In 1923, the archbishop of Paris chose Brottier to administer the Orphan Apprentices of Auteuil, founded by Abbot Roussel in 1866. He undertook this work with zeal, and the number of orphans in his care rose from 175 to 1,408. Brottier was beatified by John Paul II on November 25, 1984.

Feast: February 28.

Bibliography: *Acta Apostolicae Sedis* 78 (1986): 486–89. *Au Sénégal: sûr les traces du père Brottier: jubilé de la Cathédrale du*

Souvenir Africain, 1936/1986 (Paris 1986). G. G. BESLIER, *Le Père Brottier* (Paris 1946). P. CROIDYS, *Le père Brottier, serviteur ardent de la charité* (Paris 1945). C. GARNIER, *Ce père avait deux ames* (Paris 1956); *Le père Brottier: hier, aujourd'hui, demain* (Paris 1981). J. GOSSELIN, *Daniel Brottier: visages et reflets* (Paris 1989). *L'Osservatore Romano,* English edition, no. 50 (1984): 2,12.

[K. I. RABENSTEIN]

BROU, ALEXANDRE

Jesuit spiritual writer and historian of the missions; b. Chartres, April 26, 1862; d. Laval, France, March 12, 1947. He entered the Society of Jesus in 1880, and after completing his studies, made for the most part in England, he taught literature at Canterbury (1894–97, 1907–10, 1920–23), on the Isle of Jersey (1902–06, 1911–19), and at Laval (1899–1901, 1924). He was a man of broad and scholarly interests, but his most outstanding writings were in the fields of the mission history of the Far East and Ignatian spirituality. He wrote numerous articles on St. Francis Xavier and Matteo Ricci for *Les Études,* with whose editorial staff he was associated until his death. His monograph *S. François Xavier: Conditions et méthodes de son apostolat* (Bruges 1925) illustrates his basic insight in relating spiritual principles and practical method in mission apostolate. An earlier study, *S. François Xavier* (2 v. Paris 1914), was a landmark in accurate hagiography. The same happy blend of sound scholarship and historical sense is likewise found in Brou's writings on Jesuit spirituality. His study of the Jansenist controversy, for example, in *Les Jésuites de la légende* (Paris 1906–07), is a mine of historical information. Notable among his other works are *Les Exercices spirituels de S. Ignace, histoire et psychologie* (Paris 1922); *La Spiritualité de S. Ignace* (Paris 1914), tr. W. Young, *The Ignatian Way to God* (Milwaukee 1952); *S. Ignace, maître d'oraison* (Paris 1925), tr. W. Young, *Ignatian Methods of Prayer* (Milwaukee 1949).

Bibliography: M. SCADUTO and E. LAMALLE, *Archivum historicum Societatis Jesu* 16 (1947) 223–225, with complete chronological bibliography of his works. *Index bibliographicus Societatis Iesu,* ed. J. JUAMBELZ (Rome 1938–), for works 1937–50.

[T. J. JOYCE]

BROUILLET, JOHN

Missionary; b. near Montreal, Quebec, Canada, Dec. 11, 1813; d. Washington, D.C., Feb. 5, 1884. He was educated at St. Hyacinth College, Quebec, and was ordained on Aug. 27, 1837. Ten years later he joined Bp. Augustine M. Blanchet in establishing the Diocese of Walla Walla in Oregon Territory. As vicar-general he began his long missionary career at Nesqually and established the mission of Umatilla. He was in the vicinity of Marcus J. Whitman's Presbyterian mission among the Cayuse people when they massacred the minister and his family in 1847. Whitman's associate, Henry H. Spalding, was spared the same fate by Brouillet's timely warning. Spalding, nevertheless, accused Brouillet and other Catholics of being responsible for the attack. A national controversy ensued; Brouillet was not fully vindicated for many years, in spite of his own authoritative book on the matter.

Painting of Daniel Brottier hung by the main altar inside St. Peter's Basilica, Vatican City, Rome, Italy. (AP/Wide World Photos)

Blanchet and his brother, the bishop of Oregon City, named Brouillet to settle difficulties arising from Pres. U.S. Grant's peace policy, which began in 1868. Brouillet called attention to the inequities to Catholic missions in governmental assignments and the lack of free access to Catholic natives by their missionaries. In 1872 he went to Washington as legal representative of the two bishops and early became an adviser to Gen. Charles Ewing,

Catholic commissioner for native affairs. The Grant policy was soon revised in favor of Brouillet's views. Shortly before his death he became director of the Bureau of Indian Missions, largely his own creation. Previous to this he had fostered various missionary aid associations, often in the face of apathy and militant opposition. In 1879 in Rome he won from Leo XIII a recommendation to the American bishops for the bureau's unified program. When the Third Plenary Council of Baltimore authorized an annual collection in all dioceses, continued existence of the bureau was assured.

Bibliography: P. J. RAHILL, *The Catholic Indian Missions and Grant's Peace Policy 1870–1884* (Washington 1953).

[T. O. HANLEY]

BROUNS, THOMAS

English bishop, jurist and administrator; b. *c.* 1381; d. Hoxne, Suffolk, England, Dec. 6, 1445. He was the son of William Brouns, a military tenant of the Courtenays in Sutton Courtenay, Berkshire. Thomas took the master's degree at Oxford in 1404, the licentiate in laws in 1411, and later, the doctorate. He owed his early advancement to Bp. Philip REPINGTON of Lincoln, who made him sub-dean of the cathedral (1414), a canon of Lincoln and prebendary of Welton Westhall (1416), and archdeacon of Stow (1419). He was also given the prebends of St. Botolph's (1419) and Langford Manor (1423). Then Abp. Henry CHICHELE brought him into the court of Canterbury as auditor of causes and chancellor (1425–29), in which capacity he was prominent in the Southern Convocation. In 1420 Brouns began his series of diplomatic missions on behalf of kings Henry V and Henry VI. In 1433–34 he was one of the king's representatives at the Council of BASEL and stayed on to be a member of the second English delegation to the council. In 1435 he was provided by Pope Eugene IV to the See of WORCESTER, but the King's Council preferred the young Thomas BOURGCHIER. Brouns was made bishop of ROCHESTER in 1435 and the following year accepted PROVISION to NORWICH, but he had to apologize for receiving the bull without the royal assent, later given. At Norwich he was a zealous and methodical diocesan, much concerned with securing orthodoxy and liturgical uniformity. Despite the ill will of the Norwich citizens, who attacked his palace and the priory in 1443, he remained a good friend of the municipality, interceded for it twice with Henry VI, and left money to help it pay taxation. In his will he also left a sum for maintaining six boys to study grammar and logic at Oxford.

Bibliography: Norwich Register in Norwich Public Library, Institution Books, 10; Rochester Register preserved in the Rochester Diocesan Registry. M. ARCHER, ed., *The Register of Bishop Philip Repingdon, 1405–19* (Lincoln Record Soc., 57–58; Hereford 1963). *The Register of Henry Chichele, Archbishop of Canterbury,* ed. E. F. JACOB, 4 v. (Canterbury and York Soc.; Oxford 1937–47) v. 3, 4. A. B. EMDEN, *A Biographical Register of the University of Oxford to A.D. 1500* (Oxford 1957–59) 1:281–282. E. F. JACOB, "T.B., Bishop of Norwich 1436–1445," *Essays in British History: Presented to Sir Keith Feiling,* ed. H. R. TREVOR-ROPER (London 1964).

[E. F. JACOB]

BROUWER, CHRISTOPH

Jesuit historian; b. Arnheim, Holland, Nov. 10, 1559; d. Trier, Germany, June 2, 1617. After studying humanities at the Jesuit college at Cologne, he entered the Society of Jesus on March 12, 1580. At the completion of his courses in philosophy and theology, he was ordained and subsequently taught philosophy at Trier until he was named rector of the college at Fulda. He then became rector of Trier and made this archiepiscopal see the major field of his historical research. Under the patronage of Johann VII of Schönberg and later Lothar of Metternich, archbishops of Trier, he undertook an annalistic history of the archdiocese to the year 1600, entitled *Antiquitates et annales Trevirenses et episcoporum Trevirensis ecclesiae suffraganorum.* It grew to 26 books. Because of his historical objectivity, he did not omit details that were unflattering to the archbishops, and he was accused of presenting a partisan view, especially in the conflict of the Prince Elector, Abp. Philippe Christoph de Soetern with the abbot of St. Maximin. The curial advisors of the archbishop succeeded in stopping the publication, confiscating the first 18 books already in print, and in 1626 preparing a greatly altered version. Mutius Vitelleschi, sixth general of the Society of Jesus, threatened to expose this mutilation of the original text. The Jesuits at Trier managed to obtain a copy of the first printing and the remaining manuscripts, and sent them to France. There they were enlarged by Jacob Masenius, SJ, to include events up to 1652. They were printed in their entirety in 1670 at Liège. Brouwer also published an edition of the poems of Venantius FORTUNATUS, *Venantii Honorii Clementiani opera* (Mainz 1603), and of RABANUS MAURUS, *Hrabanus Maurus poemata* (Mainz 1617); an account of the lives of some German saints, *Sidera illustrium et sanctorum virorum* (Mainz 1616); and the *Antiquitatum Fuldensium libri 4* (Mainz 1612).

Bibliography: C. SOMMERVOGEL et al., *Bibliothèque de la Compagnie de Jésus* (Brussels-Paris 1890–1932) 2:218–222. B. DUHR, *Geschichte der Jesuiten in den Ländern deutscher Zunge,* 4 v. in 5 (St. Louis 1907–28) 2.2:424–428. A. DE BIL, *Dictionnaire d'histoire et de géographie ecclésiastiques* (Paris 1912–) 10:865–866. *Die Gesellschaft Jesu einst und jetzt* 267–268.

[E. D. MCSHANE]

BROWE, PETER

Theologian and historian; b. Salzburg, Dec. 22, 1876; d. Baden-Baden, May 18, 1949. He entered the Society of Jesus in 1895 and dedicated himself to research in medieval moral and pastoral theology. He taught these subjects in the Society's houses of study at Maastricht, Valkenburg, Frankfurt, and Immensee. In time his interest turned to the medieval religious folklore. With unflagging research, he achieved an uncommon knowledge of the sources. Of lasting value are his numerous works on the historical development of Eucharistic devotion: *De frequenti Communione in Ecclesia occidentali usque ad annum circa 1000* (Rome 1932), *De Ordaliis* (2 v. Rome 1932–33), *Die Verehrung der Eucharistie im Mittelalter* (Munich 1933), *Die häufige Kommunion im Mittelalter* (Münster 1938), *Die eucharistischen Wunder des Mittelalters* (Breslau 1938), *Die Pflichtkommunion im Mittelalter* (Münster 1940). It is precisely because of his calm objectivity that his purely scientific works are of such significance, even for the practical consequences of a timely theology and liturgy of the Eucharist. He also wrote *Beiträge zur Sexualethik des Mittelalters* (Breslau 1932) and *Die Judenmission im Mittelalter und die Päpste* (Rome 1942).

Bibliography: H. TÜCHLE, *Neue deutsche Bibliographie* (Leipzig 1875–1910) 2:639. A. STENZEL, *Lexikon für Theologie und Kirche* (Freiburg 1957–65) 2:710.

[B. NEUNHEUSER]

BROWN, GEORGE

First Anglican archbishop of Dublin; b. England?, *c.* 1500; d. Dublin, *c.* 1559. Little is known of his life before 1532. As prior of the London Austin friars, Brown (Browne) leased property to Thomas CROMWELL on May 16, 1532. He was appointed provincial by Henry VIII after the breach with Rome and acted for Cromwell as one of the visitors general of all the mendicants. In 1534 Oxford awarded him the degree doctor simpliciter. After the Geraldine revolt (1534) against the new English policy and the reconquest of the Dublin area by the king's viceroys, William Skeffington and Leonard Gray, he assisted in securing the enactment by the Irish Parliament of Reformation legislation and successfully imposed on Ireland an external acquiescence to royal supremacy and the exclusion of papal jurisdiction. After the killing of Abp. John Allen of Dublin by the Irish, Brown was elected by royal direction and consecrated by Abp. Thomas Cranmer (1536). Under Edward VI he reluctantly accepted Protestantism, and he secured the primacy from Armagh when George DOWDALL abandoned the temporalities of his see rather than substitute the communion service in the Book of COMMON PRAYER for the Mass. Under Queen Mary I, Brown was deprived of his see for contracting marriage; the primacy was restored to Armagh, and Hugh Curwen was appointed archbishop of Dublin. After evidence was offered in his behalf that he had been hostile to the Edwardian changes in Eucharistic doctrines, and after his marriage was declared invalid, Cardinal Reginald POLE, as papal legate, rehabilitated Brown and dispensed him so that he could hold a benefice in the diocese.

The weakness of English power in Ireland necessitated political compromises in the Reformation even under Henry VIII. The Irish reaction to the destruction of venerated shrines and monasteries deprived Brown of any chance of permanent achievement. He was reproved personally by Henry VIII for slowness in forwarding the royal supremacy. He quarreled with the only other Reform bishop, Edward Staples of Meath, and received little support from secular authorities against the general passive resistance of the people. Later, John Bale, Protestant bishop of Ossory under Edward VI, called Brown apathetic. While prepared to use the Eucharistic controversy to defeat secular opponents, he himself was accused of opposing those who preached against transubstantiation. He attempted to save his cathedrals from secularization by advocating the foundation of a royal university.

Bibliography: R. D. EDWARDS, *Church and State in Tudor Ireland* (New York 1935). G. V. JOURDAN, "The Breach with Rome, 1509–1541," in *History of the Church of Ireland,* ed. W. A. PHILLIPS, 3 v. (New York 1933) 2:169–227; "Reformation and Reaction, 1541–1558," *ibid.* 228–291. H. J. LAWLOR, *The Fasti of St. Patrick's, Dublin* (Dundalk 1930). M. V. RONAN, *Reformation in Dublin 1536–1558* (New York 1926). F. ROTH, *History of English Austin Friars, 1249–1538,* 2 v. (New York 1961). R. W. DIXON, *The Dictionary of National Biography from the Earliest Times to 1900* (London 1885–1900) 3:43–45.

[R. D. EDWARDS]

BROWN, RAYMOND EDWARD

Sulpician priest, biblical scholar; b. New York, NY, May 22, 1928; d. Redwood City, CA, Aug. 8, 1998. He was the son of Robert H. and Loretta Brown. As a seminarian, Brown received a B.A. and an M.A. at the Catholic University of America (1948 and 1949), and an S.T.B. at St. Mary's Seminary and University, Baltimore, in 1951, when he joined the Society of St. Sulpice. Ordained a priest of the diocese of St. Augustine, FL, in 1953, he spent his first year teaching at St. Charles Seminary, the Sulpician minor seminary in Catonsville, MD. In 1954 he began his doctoral studies at Johns Hopkins University. He received an S.T.D. from St. Mary's Seminary in 1955 with a dissertation entitled *The "Sensus Plenior" of Sa-*

cred Scripture. When he finished his Ph.D. in 1958 under the renowned Palestinian archaeologist and biblical scholar William Foxwell Albright, he was awarded a fellowship for 1958 and 1959 at the American School of Oriental Research in Jerusalem, with special designation to work on the concordance of nonbiblical texts from Qumran Cave 4 then being compiled in the ''scrollery'' of the Palestine Archaeological Museum. In 1959 he was awarded the S.S.B. degree by the Pontifical Biblical Commission (and the S. S. L. in 1963).

Brown's career as a biblical scholar began in 1959 when he joined the faculty of St. Mary's Seminary, where he taught until 1971. During that time he published *New Testament Essays* (1965), *The Gospel according to John* (Anchor Bible 29, 29A [1966, 1970]), *Jesus God and Man* (1967), *Priest and Bishop: Biblical Reflections* (1970), and was one of the editors of *The Jerome Biblical Commentary* (1968). During 1967 and 1968 he became a visiting professor at Union Theological Seminary (UTS) in New York. In 1971 Brown was named professor of biblical studies at UTS and was later given the chair of Auburn Professor of Biblical Studies (1981). Until his retirement in 1990, Brown taught many seminarians of different Protestant denominations who attended UTS. For a few years he also taught Jesuit seminarians, when Woodstock College moved to New York City and became affiliated with UTS for about five years. Brown also served as a member of the newly reorganized Pontifical Biblical Commission from 1972 to 1978.

He always advocated the historical-critical method of interpreting Scripture and combined his critical scholarship with a reverence for the written Word of God and also with an ability to teach clearly. The most important of his books published during his years at UTS were *Virginal Conception and Bodily Resurrection of Jesus* (1973), *Biblical Reflections on Crises Facing the Church* (1975), *The Birth of the Messiah* (1977), *The Critical Meaning of the Bible* (1981), *The Epistles of John* (Anchor Bible 30 [1982]), and *Biblical Exegesis and Church Doctrine* (1985). He was also an editor of *Peter in the New Testament: A Collaborative Assessment by Protestant and Roman Catholic Scholars* (1973), *Mary in the New Testament* (1978), and *The New Jerome Biblical Commentary* (1990). Brown also published in this period many shorter works for a more popular readership (e.g., *An Adult Christ at Christmas* [1977], *A Crucified Christ in Holy Week* [1986]). These were part of his effort to spread solid biblical interpretation among the general public. During his tenure at UTS he became the object of much popular criticism for his biblical views. He himself called his position ''centrist,'' never advocating new, bizarre, or even particularly bold theories about the New Testament, but distancing himself from a fundamentalistic reading of it. He was among the first of the generation of biblical scholars who sought to implement the directives of Pius XII in *DIVINO AFFLANTE SPIRITU* (1943). Despite public criticism, the U.S. bishops nominated him twice to serve on the Biblical Commission (1972–78, 1996–98). He participated in dialogues with several Protestant churches: the national dialogue with the Lutherans (1965–73), Joint Commission of the World Council of Churches and the Roman Catholic Church (1967–68), and the Faith and Order Commission of the WCC (1968–93). By papal nomination, Brown served as a consultor to the Vatican Secretariat for Promoting Christian Union (1968–73) and in 1982 was appointed to the International Methodist–Roman Catholic Dialogue.

After Brown became professor emeritus at UTS in 1990, he retired to St. Patrick's Seminary in Menlo Park, California. During his retirement he continued to write and to lecture. He published a revision of *The Birth of the Messiah* (1993), *The Death of the Messiah* (two vols., 1994), and his last big book, *An Introduction to the New Testament* (1997), which was intended for the educated general reader. His popular-level books also continued; the last of them, *A Retreat with John the Evangelist* (1998), appeared a day before he died of a heart attack at Sequoia Hospital in Redwood City. He is buried in the Sulpician Cemetery in Catonsville, Maryland.

Bibliography: K. DUFFY, ''The Ecclesial Hermeneutic of Raymond E. Brown,'' *Heythrop Journal* 39 (1998): 37–56.

[J. A. FITZMYER]

BROWNE, ROBERT

First post- REFORMATION separatist from Church of England, claimed by Congregationalists in England and America as first exponent of their principle of church government; b. Tolethorpe, Rutland, 1550; d. Northampton, 1633. Browne was influenced at Cambridge by Thomas Aldrich and Thomas CARTWRIGHT, leaders of a strong puritan, presbyterian party there, and took to preaching, fervently and effectively, in London and Cambridge, without episcopal license. He denounced ordination, all Church government, and everything remotely connected with popery. For him, the Christian Church was in no sense catholic, but exclusive to the chosen few with no call to convert the wicked. Putting theory into practice, he preached in Norwich and Bury St. Edmunds to small groups calling themselves ''the church'' and known as Brownists. For this ''schism'' Browne was imprisoned, but was freed by order of Secretary Cecil, a kinsman, whose campaign at that moment to check Jesuit and Catholic activities led him to leniency toward Protestant sects. Browne and his Norwich "church" migrated in 1581 to Middelburg in Holland, where he published *A Book which sheweth the Life Manner of all True Christians* and *A Treatise of Reformation without Tarrying for Any.* This violently dictatorial man soon quarreled with his flock and left for Scotland (1583), where he carried on his denunciation of everything ecclesiastical. Having been jailed by the kirk, Browne was suddenly and unexplainably released, and he left for England. He was again imprisoned for his subversive writings, again released at Cecil's personal intervention, but he was excommunicated for contempt of the Established Church. Making a complete *volte-face,* at least outwardly, Browne submitted, was episcopally ordained (1591), and became rector of Achurch, Northants, until his death in Northampton jail, where he was sent for assaulting a police constable. Despite his mental unbalance, he had considerable influence on the development of Congregationalism.

Bibliography: C. BURRAGE, *The True Story of Robert Browne* (London 1906) with full list of his writings. A. PEEL, *The First Congregational Churches* (Cambridge, Eng. 1920). *The Oxford Dictionary of the Christian Church* 201–202. A. JESSOPP, *The Dictionary of National Biography from the Earliest Times to 1900* (London 1885–1900) 3:57–61.

[G. ALBION]

BROWNSON, JOSEPHINE VAN DYKE

Teacher, author; b. Detroit, Mich., Jan. 26, 1880; d. Grosse Pointe, Mich., Nov. 10, 1942. She was the youngest child of Henry Francis and Josephine (Van Dyke) Brownson, and the granddaughter of Orestes A. Brownson. After being educated by the religious of the Sacred Heart, she completed her training at Detroit Normal School and the University of Michigan, Ann Arbor. She began teaching in Detroit at the Barstow School in 1914, transferring ten years later to Cass Technical High School. In 1930 she resigned to concentrate on the Catholic Instruction League, which she had organized in 1916 for the benefit of children attending public schools. She outlined her method of teaching religion in *Stopping the Leak* (1926); her *Catholic Bible Stories* (1919), *Living Forever* (1928), and *Learn of Me* (1936) became standard books for catechists. In 1939 the Catholic Instruction League was incorporated into the Detroit Archdiocesan Confraternity of Christian Doctrine. That same year she was awarded the Laetare Medal by the University of Notre Dame, Ind., and was named a member of the American Social Service Mission to Venezuela. She had been earlier (1933) honored by the papal decoration *Pro Ecclesia et Pontifice* and the LL.D. degree from the University of Detroit.

Bibliography: W. ROMIG, *Josephine Van Dyke Brownson* (Detroit 1955).

[M. A. FRAWLEY]

BROWNSON, ORESTES AUGUSTUS

Preacher, journalist, editor, philosopher; b. Stockbridge, Vt., Sept. 16, 1803; d. Detroit, Mich., April 17, 1876. His spiritual and intellectual odyssey, which found him successively a Presbyterian, a Universalist preacher, a Unitarian minister, and an evangelist for his own "Church of the Future," brought him finally, at the age of 41, into the Catholic Church. During his Catholic years he became, chiefly through his editorship of *Brownson's Quarterly Review,* one of the most influential Catholic laymen of the 19th century. Yet his significance is by no means solely historical. As a protestant, Brownson was a leader in various movements for social reform. He developed an incisive and cogent criticism of the Transcendentalist movement and discussed with profundity both the foundations of authority in democratic government and the problems of an emerging industrial society. As a Catholic, he wrote essays on CHURCH AND STATE, on civil and religious freedom, on Catholic education, on the philosophy of science, and on the conflict between conservative and progressive forces in the Church. These observations not only retain their relevance but were often prophetic in their vision.

Brownson and his twin sister were the youngest of Sylvester and Relief Metcalf Brownson's six children. His father died when Orestes was a child, and poverty forced his mother to send him to live for several years with guardians in nearby Royalton. The family was reunited in 1817 and moved to Ballston Spa in northern New York, where Orestes attended the local academy and worked as a printer's apprentice. At the age of 19, he joined the Presbyterian Church. Two years later he became a Universalist and taught school in Elbridge, N.Y.; there he met Sally Healy, whom he married in June of 1827.

Early writing. From 1826 until 1831 Brownson preached in New Hampshire, Vermont, and New York, and for a time edited the *Gospel Advocate,* the chief publication of the Universalists. He soon turned to Unitarianism, and from 1832 to 1834 was a Unitarian minister in Walpole, N.H. He gave Lyceum lectures in Boston and in 1834 became the Unitarian minister at Canton, Mass. In 1836 he organized in Boston "The Society for Christian Union and Progress" to promote his "Church of the Future" and brought out his first essay, *New Views of Christianity, Society, and the Church.* In the same year he joined Alcott, Emerson, Hedge, Ripley, and others in the discussion group later referred to as the Transcendental Club.

In 1838 Brownson founded the *Boston Quarterly Review,* and for five years he personally wrote the greater part of each issue. His long, two-part essay, *The Laboring Classes*, reviewing Carlyle's *Chartism* but going far beyond Carlyle's views, condemned in the strongest terms the injustices of industrialism. The essay created a sensation; in the presidential campaign of 1840, Whig politicians used it as evidence of the socialistic leanings of the Democratic party, since Brownson had come out for Van Buren, the Democratic candidate.

The outcry against his essay led Brownson to reexamine his entire intellectual position. His Unitarian and transcendentalist assumptions gradually gave way. His study of Pierre Leroux gave him a sense of hierarchy and the doctrine of life through communion. By April of 1844 he had decided that ''either there is already existing the divine institution, the church of God, or there are no means of reform'' (*Works* 4:511). Terminating the *Boston Quarterly Review* in 1842, Brownson wrote chiefly for J. L. O'Sullivan's *Democratic Review* until he revived his own review as *Brownson's Quarterly* in January of 1844.

The Catholic journalist. Brownson began taking instruction in the Catholic faith from Bp. John B. Fitzpatrick of Boston in May of 1844 and entered the Catholic Church on October 20. Although Brownson at first considered abandoning his *Review* to study law, Bishop Fitzpatrick urged him to continue as a Catholic journalist to bring Catholic principles to bear on the great questions of the day. Agreeing, Brownson studied St. Augustine, St. Thomas, and manuals of scholasticism, and renounced entirely the eclectic modes of thought that had led him to the door of the Church. Having been in the mainstream of American Protestantism, and a leading figure in ''the movement party'' of New England, he entertained hopes of winning many of his former associates and readers to a sympathetic consideration of Catholicism. Unlike his friend and fellow convert, Isaac HECKER, he adopted a militant tone and strategy of which he was later critical. A letter of general approbation and encouragement from the American bishops appeared in his *Review* from 1849 to 1855, and Pope Pius IX favorably recognized his work in 1854. Late in 1853 Newman invited him to join the faculty of the new Catholic University at Dublin but withdrew the invitation because of the feeling aroused in Ireland by Brownson's views on the issue of AMERICANISM.

In October of 1855, because of disagreements with Bishop Fitzpatrick, Brownson moved to New York with his *Review.* He defended the Union cause vigorously during the Civil War, but in the 1864 presidential race he would have preferred to support General John C. Frémont rather than Lincoln. The disappointment at Frémont's withdrawal from the campaign, together with his own failing eyesight and the death of his two sons, led Brownson to suspend his *Review* in 1864. He revived it from 1873 to 1875. He died April 17, 1876, and was buried in Detroit; ten years later his remains were moved to a crypt in the Sacred Heart Church on the campus of the University of Notre Dame.

Brownson's achievement. As a journalist and controversialist, Brownson brought a penetrating intelligence to bear on temporal and spiritual issues. His style was vigorous and lucid, if rarely graceful. As a general critic, he wrote voluminously on religion, philosophy, society and politics, literature, and education. The central concern of his Catholic years was to clarify the relation between Christianity and civilization, and between Church and State, and to define the limits of freedom and authority. *The American Republic* is of central importance as a summation of his political philosophy. While he had rejected transcendentalism prior to his conversion to the Catholic Church, he did not abandon his reliance on intuition, and it is generally agreed that from 1842 to 1844 he was an ontologist in the sense rejected by the Catholic Church in 1861. Scholarly opinion remains divided whether he was an ontologist after his conversion.

Any just evaluation of the Catholic Brownson as a political and social thinker must recognize the fundamental changes of emphasis in various periods. From 1844 to 1854 Brownson's emphasis was conservative and traditional. In repudiating his earlier vision of an earthly Utopia, he seemed also to abandon any attempt at mediating between the Church and contemporary society. From 1855 to 1864, however, he increasingly sympathized with those European Catholic thinkers whose political and social views were liberal, as his essays on *Lacordaire and Catholic Progress* and *Civil and Religious Freedom* make abundantly clear. His return, from 1865 until his death, to a conservative position is largely accounted for by his belief that the Syllabus of Errors, published with the encyclical *Quanta cura* in December of 1864, was a condemnation of such views as he had expressed for the previous ten years. Weary and in failing health, Brownson accepted the interpretation given the Syllabus by his severest critics, and for the rest of his life did penance for his liberal period.

While Brownson at various periods of his life was denounced by liberals for his conservatism and by conservatives for his liberalism, the real task of criticism is to evaluate the dialectical relation between the conservative and liberal elements in his thought and to see both in historical context. As journalist and critic, Brownson tried to bring enduring principles into a dynamic relation with the great issues of his time. Yet he saw the Church as tied to no social or political forms merely because they were old; he stressed the Church's constant mission of renewal and the responsibilities of Catholics on the level of culture and civilization.

The Brownson papers are available to scholars in the library of the University of Notre Dame. The same university awarded its Laetare Medal to Brownson's son and first biographer, Henry F. Brownson, in 1892, and to his granddaughter, the author and catechist Josephine Van Dyke Brownson, in 1939.

Bibliography: *The Works of Orestes A. Brownson,* ed. H. F. BROWNSON, 20 v. H. F. BROWNSON, *Orestes Augustus Brownson Life,* 3 v. B. FARRELL, *Orestes Brownson's Approach to the Problem of God.* T. MAYNARD, *Oresres Brownson: Yankee, Radical, Catholic* (New York 1943). P. MILLER, ed., *The Transcendentalists: An Anthology.* F. L. MOTT, *History of American Magazines,* 3 v. (New York 1930–38). S. A. RAEMERS, *America's Foremost Philosopher: O. A. Brownson.* A. S. RYAN, "Orestes A. Brownson: The Critique of Transcendentalism," *American Classics Reconsidered,* ed. H. C. GARDINER (New York 1958); ed., *The Brownson Reader.* A. M. SCHLESINGER, JR., *Orestes A. Brownson: A Pilgrim's Progress.* T. R. RYAN, *Orestes A. Brownson: A Definitive Biography* (Huntington, Ind. 1976).

[A. S. RYAN]

BRUCE

A family of American Catholic publishers. William George, b. Milwaukee, Wis., March 17, 1856; d. there, Aug. 13, 1949. William George, the son of Augustus Bruce, a Great Lakes sailor, became a cigar maker at the age of 12 after childhood illness had limited his education to completion of the sixth grade. He later entered newspaper work and founded the *American School Board Journal* and *Industrial Arts and Vocational Education.* His firm was then incorporated as the Bruce Publishing Company. About 1927, William George turned over active management to his two sons and devoted the remainder of his life to civic activities. He was an early proponent of the St. Lawrence Seaway; for 39 years he headed the Milwaukee Harbor Commission, in addition to providing active leadership in other Milwaukee community affairs. He was named a Knight of St. Gregory and awarded the Vercelli and Laetare medals as an outstanding Catholic layman.

William C. and Frank M., sons of William George, joined the firm in 1902 and 1906, respectively, and established it as a major Catholic publishing house in the 1930s. Expansion continued with the founding of the magazine *Hospital Progress* in collaboration with the Catholic Hospital Association, and with the purchase of the *Catholic School Journal.* The firm's first Catholic books appeared in the 1920s and a program of Catholic publishing in both textbooks and trade books was set up in 1930. The *Highway to Heaven* series was a new approach to teaching religion on the elementary level. The *Science and Culture* series was a university in print. More than 300 titles, including works in biography, history, literature, education, natural science, Scripture, religion, and many other fields were published during the next 25 years. A Catholic book club, the Catholic Literary Foundation, began operation in 1943.

Frank M. was also a founder and first president of SERRA INTERNATIONAL and president of the National Association of Publishers and Church Goods Dealers. By the time of his death the firm had become one of the largest Catholic publishing houses in the U.S.

William C. was active in founding the National Catholic Educational Association and a pioneer in the field of modern school construction. He received an honorary LL.D. degree from Mt. Mary College, Milwaukee and an honorary Lit. D. degree from Marquette.

[H. SMITH]

BRUCHÉSI, LOUIS JOSEPH PAUL NAPOLÉON

Second archbishop of Montreal, Quebec, Canada; b. Montreal, Oct. 29, 1855; d. there, Sept. 20, 1939. After early studies with the Sulpicians in his native city, he continued them at Issy and Paris in France and Rome, Italy, receiving a doctorate in theology. With his illustrious fellow student Jacques Della Chiesa (later Benedict XV), he was ordained at St. John Lateran on Dec. 21, 1878. He taught dogma at the Grand Seminary of Quebec, was assigned to the department of parochial affairs, and became secretary to Abp. Edouard C. Fabre of Montreal, whom he succeeded in 1897. During his episcopate the 21st International Eucharistic Congress was held at Montreal (1910), and the branch of Laval University established in Montreal (1876) became independent as the University of Montreal (1920). Bruchési was a noted theologian and orator, known for his lofty and rich thought and elegant style. The last 15 years of his life were ones of inactivity and suffering.

Bibliography: *Mandements des évêques de Montréal,* v. 13–16. "Éloge funèbre par son successeur Mgr. Georges Gauthier," in *La Semaine Religieuse de Montréal* 98 (1939) 614–624. J. BRUCHÉSI, "La Vocation sulpicienne de Monseigneur Bruchési," *Mémoires de la Société royale du Canada* (1941); *Témoinages d'hier* (Montreal 1961) 225–301.

[L. POULIOT]

BRÜCK, HEINRICH

Ecclesiastical historian; b. Bingen, Germany, Oct. 25, 1831; d. Mainz, Nov. 5, 1903. After his ordination, he made postgraduate studies under Johannes DÖLLINGER in Munich. In 1857 he began teaching Church history at the seminary in Mainz and became a full professor in 1862. In 1885 he became professor of Canon Law there also. He was consecrated bishop of Mainz in 1899. Brück was a productive scholar and one of the first Catholic historians to study the 18th and 19th centuries methodically and comprehensively. Since this period was marked in many countries by a decline of Catholic rights and influence and by a struggle for their maintenance, a defensive attitude crept into his books. The KULTURKAMPF provided him with scholarly leisure by closing the Mainz seminary, but it also heightened the apologetical tone in his writings. His first book, *Die rationalistischen Bestrebungen im katholischen Deutschland*, shaped the Catholic outlook on the theological and pastoral implications of the ENLIGHTENMENT in Germany into the 20th century. His *Geschichte der katholischen Kirche in Deutschland im 19. Jh.* and *Die Kulturkampfbewegung in Deutschland, 1807–1900* exhibit an acute awareness of the importance of current problems, but are now outdated except for the source materials contained in them. Brück's textbook on Church history, *Lehrbuch der Kirchengeschichte,* was translated into French and Italian; it appeared in English as *History of the Catholic Church.* Brück lacked warmth in human contacts, but he had a strong energetic personality.

Bibliography: G. ALLEMANG, *Dictionnaire d'histoire et de géographie ecclésiastiques* (Paris 1912–) 10:882–883. A. P. BRCK, *Neue deutsche Biographie* (Berlin 1953–) 2:654. L. LENHART, ''Dr. Heinrich Brück, 1831–1903: Der Kirchenhistoriker auf dem Mainzer Bischofsstuhl 1900–03,'' *Archiv für mittelrheinische Kirchengeschichte* 15:261–333.

[V. CONZEMIUS]

BRUCKNER, ANTON

Distinguished symphonist and organist of the late 19th century; b. Ansfelden, Upper Austria, Sept. 4, 1824; d. Vienna, Oct. 11, 1896. His father, a schoolmaster, died when Anton was 13, and the boy was sent to the Augustinian monastery of St. Florian to continue his education. St. Florian became his spiritual home and, as he wished, his body rests under the great organ there. After a succession of lesser positions, he became organist at Linz cathedral in 1856. There the conductor Otto Kitzler introduced him to Richard WAGNER's music—a revelation that stimulated his development as a symphonist. In 1868 he moved to Vienna, where he was successful as teacher and organist but had difficulties as a composer, for he was violently opposed by Eduard Hanslick, Vienna's most influential critic, because of his Wagnerian partisanship. By the time of his death, however, he enjoyed recognition even in his own country, and through the line of descent Bruckner-Mahler-Schoenberg his influence was transmitted to composers of the later 20th century.

Bruckner's religion was the center of his life. With sincere piety he dedicated his Ninth Symphony to his *Lieber Gott.* Of his specifically sacred music, the D-major Mass, generally considered his first extended masterwork, utilizes a full symphony orchestra. In contrast, the E-minor Mass uses only wind and brass accompaniment (nonobligatory in the *Kyrie*). The F-minor Mass (1867–68, revised in 1890) represents his most triumphant essay in the symphonic Mass style. The *Te Deum,* which begins and ends in an unrestrained blaze of glorious C major, Bruckner considered a testimony to his faith. Memorable also is *Psalm 150,* with its moving violin solos and impressive fugue theme. Although fascinated by plainsong and Palestrinian tradition, he could not completely accept the viewpoint of the Caecilians, whose goal was to return church music to Palestrinian purity and eliminate the vivid orchestra of the Viennese classical Mass (*see* CAECILIAN MOVEMENT).

Bibliography: H. F. REDLICH, *Bruckner and Mahler* (rev. ed. London 1970). D. NEWLIN, *Bruckner, Mahler, Schoenberg* (rev. ed. New York 1978); ''Bruckner's Three Great Masses,'' *Chord and Discord,* 2.8 3–16; ''Bruckner's *Te Deum,*'' *ibid.,* 71–75. F. BLUME, *Die Musik in Geschichte und Gegenwart,* ed. F. BLUME (Kassel-Basel 1949–) 2:342–382. P. H. LÁNG, *Music in Western Civilization* (New York 1941). K. G. FELLERER, *The History of Catholic Church Music,* tr. F. A. BRUNNER (Baltimore 1961). M. AUER, ''Anton Bruckner als Kirchenmusiker'' *Grove's Dictionary of Music and Musicians,* ed. E. BLOM, 9 v. (5th ed. London 1954) 1:969–976. W. GRANDJEAN, ''Anton Bruckners *Helgoland* und das Symphonische,'' *Die Musikforschung,* 48 (1995) 349–368. B. VON HAKEN, ''Brahms und Bruckner: Zur Verbindung von Theorie und Geschichte in Hugo Riemanns *Musik-Lexikon,*'' *Musiktheorie,* 10 (1995) 149–157. A. HARRANDT, ''*Ausgezeichneter Hofkapellmeister:*'' Anton Bruckner an Felix Mottl,'' *Studien zur Musikwissenschaft,* 42 (1993) 335–350. C. HOWIE, ''Bruckner Scholarship in the Last Ten Years (1987–96),'' *Music and Letters,* 77 (1996) 542–554. T. RÖDER, *Anton Bruckner: III Symphonie D-moll. Revisionbericht* (Vienna 1997). R. SIMPSON, ''The Seventh Symphony of Bruckner,'' *Chord and Discord,* 2/10 (1963) 57–67. K. J. SWINDEN, ''Bruckner's *Perger Prelude:* A Dramatic *revue* of Wagner?,'' *Music Analysis,* 18 (1999) 101–124. M. WAGNER, ''Bruckner und das Problem der Zeit,'' *Musik und Kirche,* 66 (1996) 221–225.

[D. NEWLIN]

BRUNEAU, JOSEPH

Sulpician educator; b. Saint-Galmier, France, April 18, 1866; d. Evian-les-Bains, Haute-Savoie, France, Aug.

26, 1933. He studied at the seminaries of Saint-Jodard, Alix, Lyons, and Issy, and at the Institut Catholique, before being ordained on July 15, 1889. In 1894, he was sent to the United States, where he taught for two years at St. Mary's Seminary, Baltimore, Md. He was appointed superior of philosophy at St. Joseph's Seminary, Dunwoodie, N.Y., in 1904, and held the same position at Boston, Mass., and Baltimore. In addition to teaching his courses in philosophy, dogmatic theology, and Scripture, he served as director of the seminary choir at Baltimore. He gave early encouragement to the Maryknoll Missioners of his close friend Bp. James A. Walsh. Bruneau's writings included *Harmony of the Gospels*, *Our Priesthood*, and *Our Priestly Life*. As a translator, he put into French Patrick A. Sheehan's *My New Curate,* Bp. John C. Hedley's *Retreat,* and Basil W. Maturin's *Self-Knowledge and Self-Discipline;* and into English, Prosper G. Boissarie's *Healing at Lourdes* and Frédric Ozanam's *Bible of the Sick.*

[E. I. VAN ANTWERP]

Anton Bruckner. (©Bettmann/CORBIS)

BRUNEI, THE CATHOLIC CHURCH IN

Located on the island of Borneo in southeast Asia, Negara Brunei Darussalam is formed of two narrow enclaves which border the South China Sea at their north and are surrounded on all other sides by Malaysia. Comprised of rough, rocky hills to the south, Brunei has a narrow coastal region that is the source of much of its wealth. Both oil and natural gas reserves were discovered on and off-shore in this area, giving the sultanate one of the highest gross domestic products in the Third World. Most Bruneians are of Malay descent, although 15 percent of the population is of Chinese ancestry. The government subsidizes all food and housing, as well as medical services for the citizens of Brunei. Due to a dearth of arable land, agriculture production is limited to rice, tapioca and bananas; in addition there are fishing and forestry industries.

Originally part of the Vicariate of the East Indies (1842), the Catholic Church in Brunei was put under the jurisdiction of the Diocese of Miri-Brunei (1959), in Kuching (Sarawak), East Malaysia. However, in 1997 the Vatican appointed Monsignor Cornelius Sim as apostolic prefect for Brunei, still retaining the link with the ecclesiastical province in Kuching. Most Catholics living in Brunei are Chinese, Filipinos and Europeans who are temporary residents of the country while employed in technical jobs related to the country's petroleum refining and natural gas industries. The country is home to one of the largest gas-liquefaction plants in the world, although by the late 1990s efforts were underway to diversify Brunei's economy away from reliance upon its energy resources.

History. Islam entered northern Borneo in the 5th century and had become dominant by the 14th century, when Brunei King Sang Aji Awang Alak Betatar became the first sultan. In control of all of Borneo by the 16th century, the Sultanate of Brunei was gradually diminished in size as a result of piracy, wars and the colonization efforts of various European nations. By 1800 its influence reached only to the Malayan states of Sarawak and Sarah. Sarawak was lost in 1841 following a local revolt suppressed with the help of the British, who took control five years later; Sabah was leased to Great Britain in 1881 and eventually became a part of the Federation of Malaysia. After 1890 Mill Hill missionaries entered the area; their evangelization efforts were successful predominately among the region's indigenous population. In 1888, in return for his lost lands, the Sultan was granted a British protectorate, which was enlarged in 1906. In 1959 Brunei was granted internal self-rule.

The discovery of oil along Brunei's coast in 1926 greatly enhanced the region's economy, and in the early 1960s the existence of off-shore oil deposits as well as natural gas prompted pressure on the government to join

Capital: Bandar Seri Begawan.
Size: 2,226 sq. miles.
Population: 336,376 in 2000.
Languages: Malay, English, Chinese.
Religions: 6,740 Catholics (2%), 225,370 Shafeite Muslims (67%), 43,729 Buddhists (13%), 3,650 Hindus (1%), 19,887 Protestants (6%), 37,000 with other faiths or without religious affiliation.
Diocese: Miri-Brunei, with an apostolic prefecture for Brunei.

the Federation of Malaysia. That pressure was repulsed, in part by an outbreak of nationalism, and on Jan. 1, 1984 Brunei was made an independent sultanate. A state of emergency originally declared in 1962 continued to suspend the Brunei constitution of Sept. 29, 1959 and thus allowed the Sultan to rule by decree. By 2000 His Majesty Haji Hassanal Bolkiah Mu'izzaddin Waddaulah, sultan of Brunei since 1967, was named among the 350 wealthiest people in the world.

In 1991, through the sultan, the government attempted to reaffirm its commitment to Islam through the Malayu Islamic Beraja, or MIB, which dates back to the 1st century A.D.. Under the MIB the celebration of Christmas was forbidden, a decision by the government's Religious Council that supported ISLAMIC LAW (Shari'a). In addition, the two Catholic schools in the country were not allowed to teach any faith but Islam, and were also required to teach the Arabic script. Two years after the MIB was imposed, the government reasserted its commitment to freedom of religion through the Kuala Lumpur Declaration, although non-Muslim faiths remained under restrictions imposed by Shari'a. By 2000 Brunei contained three Catholic parishes and its faithful were tended by one diocecan and one religious priest. The installation of the first apostolic prefecture in Brunei was seen as a step toward a more moderate approach regarding non-Muslim faiths.

Bibliography: J. ROONEY, *Khabar gembira = The Good News: A History of the Catholic Church in East Malaysia and Brunei, 1880-1976* (1977). D. R. SINGH, *Historical Dictionary of Brunei Darussalam* (Metuchen, NJ, 1997). E. M. KERSHAW, *A Study of Brunei Dusun Religion* (Bandar 2000).

[P. SHELTON]

BRUNNER, FRANCIS DE SALES

Founder of the American province of the Society of the PRECIOUS BLOOD; b. Mümliswil, Switzerland, Jan. 10, 1795; d. Schellenberg, Liechtenstein, Dec. 29, 1859. After early training at home he was sent to the Benedictine school at Maria Stein in 1809. He entered the BENEDICTINES, changing his baptismal name Nicholas to Francis de Sales; was ordained March 6, 1819; and then spent ten years teaching and doing missionary work in neighboring areas. Because of personal spiritual problems, he left the Benedictines and joined the TRAPPISTS at Oelenberg, Alsace. When the revolution of 1830 forced his removal from French territory, he returned to Switzerland, gradually separated himself from the Trappists, and began working as a missionary in eastern Switzerland under the direction of the papal nuncio at Lucerne.

In 1838, after a chance meeting with members of the Precious Blood Society at Cesena, Italy, Brunner joined the newly founded institute. He was sent to make a foundation in Switzerland, and he gathered around him several young men at Castle Loewenberg near Llanz in Canton Graubnden, where four years earlier he and his mother had established the PRECIOUS BLOOD SISTERS. In 1843, after a brief training period and ordination, Brunner and his companions immigrated to the New World. There John Baptist Purcell, then bishop of Cincinnati, Ohio, assigned the newly arrived missionary group to north central Ohio with headquarters first in Huron and then in Seneca County. During the next 16 years, Brunner succeeded in firmly entrenching the Society of the Precious Blood in Seneca, Putnam, and Mercer counties. He established nine religious houses, all except one in Ohio. Brunner made several highly successful journeys to Europe to gather recruits from German-speaking areas; in 1858 he returned to establish a convent and a recruiting center for America in Schellenberg. His remains are buried in a crypt in the church there.

[P. J. KNAPKE]

BRUNNER, HEINRICH EMIL

Protestant theologian; b. Winterthur, Switzerland, Dec. 23, 1889; d. Zurich, April 6, 1966. An influential proponent of dialectical theology, together with Karl Barth, he led the movement away from nineteenth-century theological liberalism in favor of neo-orthodoxy.

Brunner studied theology in Zurich, Berlin, and Union Theological Seminary in New York City, and taught at the University of Zurich from 1924 until 1966. He also lectured at Princeton Theological Seminary (1938–39) and the Christian University of Japan (1953–55); because of his travels and the rapid translation of his works into English, he formed an important bridge between American and European theology. His continual concern to apply Christian theology to social problems led him from an early commitment to religious socialism to a passionate opposition to totalitarianism and communism, whose anthropological basis, according to Brunner, was atheism and the devaluation of the individual before the state. He was an ardent ecumenist, although he did not see any great value in organizational unity.

The key to Brunner's thought is his concept of the dialectical relationship between philosophy and theology, faith and reason, the gospel and the law. Philosophy does make a positive contribution to the theological enterprise by delimiting the boundaries of human reason and establishing a basis for a natural ethics. There are ''orders of creation'' that supply norms to which revelation itself testifies. But the philosophical experience of God is at best paradoxical; as Kierkegaard pointed out, no synthesis based on human reason is possible. In contrast to philosophy, revelation comes only through a personal encounter with Christ as mediated through scripture. In Jesus Christ, God discloses himself as Person whom man must acknowledge in an I-Thou relationship. Indeed, man can only be understood as a being-in-response. Man, as the image of God, is personally related and totally responsible to the holy, loving God. But man is also in revolt against God and can be saved only by the effective action of Christ the mediator who enables man to achieve integrity through personal communion with God and his fellow men.

Bibliography: E. BRUNNER, *Revelation and Reason* (Philadelphia 1946); *The Mediator* (1947); *The Divine Imperative* (1947); *Man in Revolt* (1947); *Dogmatics,* 3 v. (1950–61). C. KEGLEY, ed., *Theology of Emil Brunner* (New York 1962). R. THOMPSON, *The Function and Limits of Faith and Reason: A Critique of Brunner's Methodology* (Chicago 1970). M. G. MCKIM, *Emil Brunner: A Bibliography* (Lanham, MD 1996). J. E. HUMPHREY, *Emil Brunner* (Waco, TX 1976).

[T. MCFADDEN]

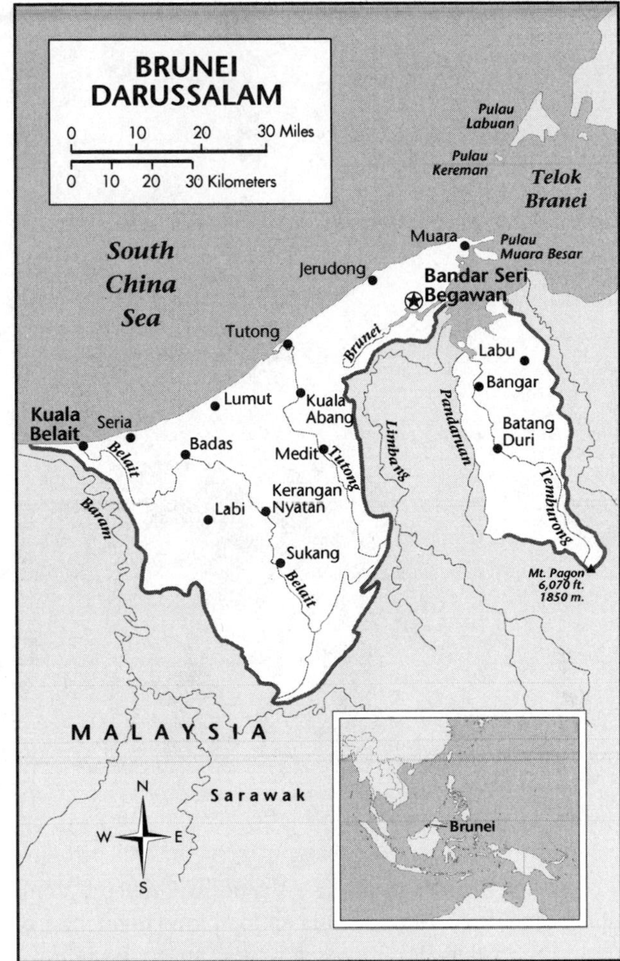

BRUNO, GIORDANO

Philosopher and poet; b. Nola, 1548; d. Rome, Feb. 17, 1600. A Dominican priest, Bruno lived until 1576 in various priories in the kingdom of Naples, where he acquired a vast knowledge of philosophy, theology, and science, and became well versed in Latin and Italian letters. He conceived culture as a single common tradition containing all religious and profane doctrines, the authentic understanding of this tradition being possible only through a philosophical interpretation known only to dominant personalities. An impetuous and intolerant love for knowledge led him to attack the supine ignorance of the unlearned and the pedantic, whom he regarded as deforming the true meaning of teachings through grotesque attempts at interpretation. His violent and imprudent criticisms against every doctrinal profession not illumined by philosophical and personal knowledge, his rejection of all authority other than reason itself, and his independent and rebellious position made him an object of condemnation and persecution in many countries and led to a tragic end.

Life and Works. Bruno fled his priory in 1576 to avoid a trial for heresy consequent upon his disrespect for current religious opinions and wandered for 15 years through many European states, testing contemporary cultures as well as various religious positions. After traveling through northern Italy in 1579, he vainly sought refuge in Calvinistic Geneva, where he was pursued by a penal lawsuit. He successfully commented upon Aristotle at the University of Toulouse from 1579 to 1581. During his consequent sojourn in Paris, he published his first important group of writings, wherein he delineated a new method for memorization and tried to develop the combinative art projected by R. LULL. After an unsuccessful attempt at teaching at Oxford, he continued his abundant literary activity in London from 1583 until 1585.

Giordano Bruno.

In his *Cena delle Ceneri* Bruno originated a completely new cosmological conception based upon the Copernican criticism of geocentricity: space is infinite, without an absolute horizon or center. This concept is amplified in his *De linfinito, universo e mondi,* innumerable heavenly bodies move through interminable space, and various living forms populate the stars. The universal meaning of life in Bruno's conception of the universe is the soul; his cosmological teaching relies upon a metaphysics of living and generating nature, which, as an image of and emanation from God, divinely forms and gathers all things into one organic totality. This manifests itself in each living thing, in which it interiorly acts and guides, as the soul does in relation to the body. The dialogue *De la causa, principio e uno* explains the principal concepts upon which his unitary view of life hinges. In *Spaccio della bestia trionfante, Cabala del cavallo pegaseo,* and *Asino cillenico*, Bruno astutely used symbols to criticize positive religions by citing superstitious aspects and advancing the idea of a purely rational interpretation of traditional teachings. In another Italian dialogue, entitled *Gli eroici furori,* he exalted Platonic love, which enables the soul of the philosopher to rise to the contemplation of God through wisdom.

Upon returning to Paris in 1586, Bruno advanced a series of criticisms against Aristotle's philosophy in his 120 articles *De Nature et Mundo adversus Peripateticos* and in his *Camoeracensis Acrotismus.* Leaving Paris to avoid the resentment aroused by some disputes, he went into Lutheran Germany, where after a vain attempt at Marburg, he gained acclaim at the University of Wittenberg. While pursuing his research relevant to the Lullian art, he continued to study Aristotle until 1588. In 1589 he made a short visit to Prague and benefited from the liberality of Rudolph II of Hapsburg. Then he stayed at Helmstdt, where his independent conduct soon brought on an excommunication enforced by the Lutheran religious authorities of the city. His sojourn at Frankfurt am Main from 1590 to 1591 enabled him to compose a series of poems in classical Latin. These, published in Frankfurt in 1591 as *De minimo, De monade,* and *De innumerabilibus sive de immenso,* manifest the power of his imagination in reference to metaphysics. Here, starting with original interpretations about the meaning of geometric figures and mathematical functions, he tried to explore what is infinitely great and what is infinitely small in the cosmos. The metaphysical synthesis entitled *Summa terminorum metaphysicorum ad capessendum logicae et philosophiae studium* he composed at Zurich; this was published there by one of his disciples in 1595.

Condemnation and Critique. Bruno's speculative work was interrupted by a tragic event. Invited to Venice by the patrician Giovanni Mocenigo, who wanted to learn the mnemonic and Lullian arts, Bruno was betrayed by his host and in 1592 given over to the Inquisition. Accused of heresy and incarcerated in Venice, then in Rome, he refused to retract his teachings and was burned at the stake in the Roman Campo dei Fiori.

Bruno's teaching cannot be separated from his impetuous, genial, and confused personality, wherein a generous love for wisdom hid under a violent and intolerant temperament. He did not know how to assume social responsibility during an era that was painfully disturbed by complex changes, during which Europe gradually overcame the torment of a religious and moral crisis. It is difficult, then, to synthesize his teaching in brief formulas, inasmuch as it is involved with polemics and affected by personal and historical circumstances. Later the name of Giordano Bruno was unduly used as a symbol for movements against the Church, and he was called the precursor of immanentistic, romantic, and scientistic positions hardly reconcilable with the historical truth about him.

Bibliography: Works. *Opere italiane,* ed. G. GENTILE and V. SPAMPANATO, 3 v.; *Opera latine conscripta,* ed. F. FIORENTINO et al., 3 v.. Literature. Copleston v. 3. A. GUZZO, *Enciclopedia filosofica,* 4 v. (Venice-Rome 1957) 1:807–820. V. SALVESTRINI, *Bibliografia di Giordano Bruno* (1582–1950) (2d ed. Florence 1958). V. SPAMPANATO, *Vita di Giordano Bruno, con documenti editi e inediti,* 2 v. (Messina 1921–23); *Documenti sulla vita di Giordano*

Bruno (Florence 1933). A. MERCATI, *Il sommario del processo di Giordano Bruno.* F. A. YATES, *Giordano Bruno and the Hermetic Tradition.* I. L. HOROWITZ, *The Renaissance Philosophy of Giordano Bruno* (New York 1952).

[A. PUPI]

BRUNO DE JÉSUS-MARIE

Carmelite writer and pioneer in the field of religious psychology; b. Bourburg, France, June 25, 1892; d. Paris, Oct. 16, 1962. Born Jacques Froissart, he entered the Discalced Carmelites in 1917, but poor health, which marked his early life, forced him to leave. After studying philosophy and theology at Rome for two years, he reentered the order in 1920 at Avon-Fontaine. From 1921 to 1925 he continued his theological studies at the Catholic University of Lille, and he was ordained in 1924. He was appointed editor of *Études Carmélitaines* in 1930, a position that he held for the rest of his life. This review became his forum for arousing interest in religious psychology, then a new field of intellectual activity. Along with his editorial work, he organized the first Congress of Religious Psychology. The congress included philosophers, theologians, and psychiatrists and, except for the war years, continued to meet annually. He also gave a series of lectures at the Universities of Vienna and Salzburg in 1935 and at that of Cairo in 1950. Among honors accorded him were the presidency of the Académie Septentrional in 1948 and the award of the Rose d'Or bestowed by the Rosati de Flandres in 1957.

His most important writings were in the fields of biography and religious psychology. They include *Saint Jean de la Croix*; *La Vie d'amour de St. Jean de la Croix*; *Madame d'Acarie, épouse et mystique*; *Le Sang du Carmel*; and *Le Livre d'amour.* His *Les Faits mystérieux de Beauring* and *L'Espagne mystique au XVIe siècle* were done in collaboration. He also edited an important work under the title *Satan.*

Bibliography: A. PLÉ, ''Le Père Bruno Jésus-Marie,'' *Vie spirituelle,* suppl. 63 (1962), 523. LUCIEN-MARIE DE ST. JOSEPH, ''Le Père Bruno de Jésus-Marie, Directeur des *Études carmélitaines,'' Foi vivante* 3 (Brussels 1962): 169–175. *P. Fr. Bruno a Jesus Maria, OCD,* in *Acta Ordinis fratrum carmelitarum discalceatorum* 9 (Rome 1964) 176–182, necrology. *Le Père Bruno de Jésus-Marie* (Paris 1964) 49–53, bibliog., various authors.

[O. RODRIGUEZ]

BRUNO OF COLOGNE, ST.

Archbishop of Cologne; b. 925?; d. Reims, Oct. 11, 965. He was the youngest son of Henry I of Germany and St. Matilda. He was educated under Bishop Balderich in the cathedral school of Utrecht, then in the court of his brother Otto, where he met the most prominent scholars of the age. In 940 he became Otto's chancellor, and sometime after receiving the order of deacon in 940, was appointed abbot of the monasteries of Lorsch near Worms and of Corvey on the Weser. He was ordained priest in 950 and in 951 accompanied Otto on the latter's first trip to Italy. He seems to have been named archchaplain in the same year. In 953, for his loyalty to his brother during the troublesome early years of Otto's reign, especially during the revolt of Ludolf, Otto's oldest son, and of Conrad, Duke of Lorraine, Bruno received the administration of the Duchy of Cologne and at Otto's wish was elected archbishop of Cologne, being consecrated on Sept. 25, 953. During Otto's second trip to Italy, Bruno, with his half-brother William, archbishop of Mainz, was coregent of the kingdom and guardian of Otto's infant son. Renowned for his personal sanctity, Bruno successfully exercised both spiritual and secular authority without prejudice to either. As abbot and bishop, he insisted on strict observance of monastic rule and devoted himself untiringly to the religious and moral training of clergy and laypeople. He is said to have made three foundations in Cologne and to have been a generous benefactor of many other churches and monasteries in his archdiocese. As statesman, he worked closely with Otto in shaping imperial policy and reformed the imperial chancery, making it a fruitful source of able administrators, especially of those prince-bishops whose loyalty to the throne made them effective instruments in the government of the empire; he established peace not only within the Duchy of Lorraine but frequently also in France. He died while returning from Compiegne, where he had gone to restore amicable relations between his two nephews, Lothaire III and Hugh Capet. The *Vita Brunonis*, written shortly after Bruno's death by his disciple Ruotger, is, despite its bombastic style, one of the best extant medieval biographies.

Feast: Oct. 11.

Bibliography: *Acta Sanctorum* Oct. 5 698–790, *Vita* by Ruotger, 765–788. *Monumenta Germaniae Historica: Scriptores* 4:252–275. P. SCHWENK, *Brun von Köln: sein Leben, sein Werk und seine Bedeutung* (Espelkamp, Germany 1995). H. SCHRÖRS, *Annalen des historischen Vereins für den Niederrhein* 87–89 (1910) 1–95; 90 (1911) 61–100; 100, 142, (1917) German text of Ruotgers *Vita,* annotated and with critical bibliog. I. SCHMALE-OTT, *Lexikon für Theologie und Kirche*, ed. J. HOFER and K. RAHNER (Freiburg 1957–65) 2:731. W. NEUSS, ed., *Geschichte des Erzbistums Köln* (Cologne 1964) 1:165–172. A HAUCK, *Kirchengeschichte Deutschlands* (Berlin-Leipzig) 3:41–46. G. ALLEMANG, *Dictionnaire d'histoire et de géographie ecclésiastiques*, ed. A. BAUDRILLART et al. (Paris 1912) 10:956–957, with bibliog. W. WATTENBACH, *Deutschlands Geschichtsquellen im Mittelalter*, ed. W. LEVISON and H. LÖWE (Weimar 1952–63) 1:321–323, 360–361.

[M. F. MCCARTHY]

BRUNO OF QUERFURT, ST.

Bishop, monk, martyr; b. Saxony, *c.* 970; d. Prussia, Feb. 14, 1009. Born into the family of the feudal lords of Querfurt in Saxony, he was educated at the cathedral school at Magdeburg under the care of St. Adalbert, first archbishop of Magdeburg and missionary to the Slavs. A man of piety and ability, Bruno, who took the monastic name Boniface, was made a canon of the Magdeburg cathedral while still young and was attached to the court of the Emperor Otto III, his close friend and, possibly, his relative. In 996 he accompanied the emperor to Rome, where he met ADALBERT OF PRAGUE and became closely associated with the Benedictine Abbey of SS. Alexius and Boniface. After Adalbert's martyrdom, Bruno decided to follow in his steps and to dedicate his life to missionary work among the Slavs and the Baltic peoples. He entered monastic life under the guidance of St. ROMUALD, founder of the CAMALDOLESE, at the monastery of Pereum, near Ravenna. Pope Sylvester II, the Emperor Otto III, and Romuald all supported his missionary plans. In 1004, after having been consecrated *archiepiscopus gentium* and having received the PALLIUM, Bruno was ready to begin his mission, but the war between Boleslas I of Poland and Emperor Henry II, Otto's successor, forced him to divert his activities temporarily to Hungary and later, in 1007, to Kievan Russia, where the ruler Vladimir welcomed him. He worked for several months among the heathen Patzinaks in the steppes between the Don and the Danube. In 1008 Bruno went to Poland and there wrote a letter to the emperor, trying to bring peace between the Poles and the Germans. At the end of the same year he and 18 missionaries went across the Polish border into the country of the Prussians, where he met a martyr's death with all his companions. The bodies of the martyrs were ransomed by Boleslas of Poland. Bruno was an outstanding hagiographer, author of a life of Adalbert of Prague, and of the martyrdom of the so-called Five Polish Brothers, a group of two Camaldolese monks and their Polish companions, slain by the heathens near Gniezno, Poland, in 1003.

Feast: June 19 (as St. Boniface) and Oct. 15 (St. Bruno).

Bibliography: THIETMAR OF MERSEBURG, *Chronicon, Monumenta Germaniae Historica: Scriptores rerum Germanicarum,* NS 9. H. G. VOIGT, *B. von Q. Cambridge History of Poland,* ed. W. F. REDDAWAY et al., 2 v. A. BUTLER, *The Lives of the Saints*, ed. H. THURSTON and D. ATTWATER (New York 1956) 2:585–586. F. DVORNIK, *The Making of Central and Eastern Europe.*

[O. P. SHERBOWITZ-WETZOR]

BRUNO OF SEGNI, ST.

Bishop, abbot; b. Solero, *c.* 1040 or 1050; d. Segni, Italy, July 18, 1123. Bruno was canon of Siena c. 1037–79. His friendship with the reforming Pope GREGORY VII, who appointed him bishop of Segni in 1079, resulted in his imprisonment by Emperor Henry IV in 1082. He was librarian of the Roman Church under Pope Victor III and later counselor to Pope URBAN II, whom he often accompanied on his journeys, notably to the Council of Clermont-Ferrand, and by whom he was entrusted with various missions. He was also a confidant of Urban's successor, PASCHAL II. In 1103 he became a monk at MONTE CASSINO and was elected abbot, in November of 1107. He publicly condemned the Concordat of Sutri, signed between Paschal II and Henry V of Germany. The pope was displeased with his action and obliged him to return to Segni, where he died. He was canonized at Segni by LUCIUS III. His scriptural commentaries mark him as an eminent representative of medieval exegesis and monastic theology.

Feast: July 18.

Bibliography: Works. *Patrlogia Latina,* ed. J P. MIGNE (Paris 1878–90) v. 164–165. *Monumenta Germaniae Historica: Libelli de lite* 2:546–562. *Spicilegium Casinense* 3 1204. B. GIGALSKI, *Bruno: sein Leben und seine Schriften.* A. DES MAZIS, *Dictionnaire d'histoire et de géographie ecclésiastiques*, ed. A. BAUDRILLART et al. (Paris 1912) 10:968–970. A. BUTLER, *The Lives of the Saints*, ed. H. THURSTON and D. ATTWATER (New York 1956) 3:140–141. R. GRÉGOIRE, *Bruno de Segni* (Spoleto 1965).

[R. GRÉGOIRE]

BRUNO OF WÜRZBURG, ST.

Bishop and imperial counselor; b. *c.* 1005; d. Bosenburg, near Linz, May 27, 1045. Bruno, son of Conrad I of Carinthia and cousin of Emperor CONRAD II, was probably educated in Salzburg. He was a member of the royal chapel, the imperial chancellor of Italy, and an intimate adviser of Conrad II and Emperor HENRY III, before being elected bishop of Würzburg. Bruno rebuilt the cathedral, constructed new churches, and improved education, to which purpose he composed an exegesis on the *Psalms,* and various catechetical writings. Under his direction the cathedral school flourished. Bruno died accidentally, en route to Hungary with Henry III, and was buried in Würzburg cathedral crypt. His cult spread in Germany, and though never formally canonized, he appears in the martyrology of 1616.

Feast: May 27.

Bibliography: J. BAIER, *Der Heilige Bruno als Katechet.* P.-W. SCHEELE, *Bruno von Würzburg, Freund Gottes und der Welt*

(Würzburg 1985). G. ALLEMANG, *Dictionnaire d'histoire et de géographie ecclésiastiques,* ed. A. BAUDRILLART (Paris 1912–) 10:972. A. BUTLER, *The Lives of the Saints,* ed. H. THURSTON and D. ATTWATER, 4 v. (New York 1956) 2:339340. T. KRAMER, *Lexikon für Theologie und Kirche,* ed. J. HOFER and K. RAHNER, 10 v. (2d, new ed. Freiburg 1957–65) 2:733.

[D. ANDREINI]

BRUNO THE CARTHUSIAN, ST.

Founder of the CARTHUSIANS; b. Cologne, Germany, before 1030; d. Santa Maria, La Torre, near Catanzaro, Italy, Oct. 6, 1101. He was of an unknown noble family; the Hartenfausts are cited, but without foundation. The 12th-century chronicle *Magister* calls him Master Bruno. Nothing of his childhood is known except that his education was carefully supervised. The chronicle says he was well-versed in letters, both profane and divine. He began his studies at St. Cunibert in Cologne and completed them at the famous schools of Reims. There is nothing to prove that he went to Paris or was ever a disciple of BERENGARIUS OF TOURS. He became a canon of Reims, where he taught the arts and theology, becoming master of the schools, and finally chancellor of the archdiocese. His students, notably the future URBAN II, praised him as an incomparable teacher.

Bruno was not content to bask in his comfortable social position and intellectual achievements. At the height of his career he chose to side with GREGORY VII in his fight against the decadence of the clergy. At Reims itself the simoniacal Archbishop MANASSES I had reached the point of openly courting scandal. It was as much through Bruno's efforts as through the zeal of the legate, HUGH OF DIE, that Manasses was finally removed. Bruno had no secular ambitions, and when the cathedral see was offered him, he refused it.

Before the end of this conflict, he had vowed to leave the world and live the life of the *pauperes Christi* or Christ's poor, the name given to groups of hermits who withdrew into the solitude of the forests to live a contemplative life of poverty and penance. Drawn to the desert, Bruno left Reims c. 1082 with two companions, although his friend Ralph refused to go. At first, with the advice of ROBERT OF MOLESME, he established himself at Sche-Fontaine, not far from MOLESME. But Bruno was not drawn to a cenobitic vocation; he set out once more in the spring of 1084 to find greater solitude. His journey brought him into the Alps, to the heart of the Chartreuse, where Bishop HUGH OF GRENOBLE helped him to establish himself. With a few clerics and laymen, he lived an eremetic life for six years in this small valley 3,500 feet above sea level, surrounded by rugged mountains and possessed of a severe climate—a site well suited to guarantee silence, poverty, and small numbers. He wrote no rule for the Carthusians and did not intend to found an order. The observance of the first Carthusians harmonized the cenobitic framework with the solitary life, without reference either to the Benedictine or to the Camaldolese practice.

"St. Bruno the Carthusian," marble sculpture by Jean-Antoine Houdon, S. Maria degli Angeli, Rome. (Alinari-Art Reference/Art Resource, N.Y.)

In 1090 Urban II unexpectedly called his former teacher to his side. Bruno obeyed, leaving Landuin in charge at La Grande Chartreuse. Urban II and Bruno were obliged to flee Rome that summer and went to southern Italy, then under Norman rule. While there, Bruno again refused the miter (he had been elected to the See of Reggio). But with the material assistance of ROGER OF SICILY he founded the hermitage of Santa Maria of La Torre. The eulogies of Bruno's mortuary rolls described him as an extraordinary soul as well as a revered teacher, a man with a profound heart. His extant works include two letters, which are veritable ascetical treatises; an authentic commentary on the Psalter; and a less certain commentary on the Epistles of St. Paul, as well as the profession of faith he dictated just before he died.

Bruno's body, buried in the hermitage cemetery of Santa Maria of La Torre, was later transferred to the church there, and still later to the church of S. Stefano. In 1514, Leo X canonized Bruno *viva voce*. His feast was introduced into the Roman liturgy in 1623.

Feast: Oct. 6.

Bibliography: Sources. *Lettres des premiers chartreux,* with the profession of faith [*Sources Chrétiennes* 88; Paris 1962] 2893. *Expositiones* (*Psalter,* etc.) in *Patrologia Latina,* ed. J. P. MIGNE, 217 v. (Paris 1878–90), 152:633–1420; 153:11–568. A. WILMART, La Chronique des premiers chartreux, *Revue Mabillon* 16: 77–142. Funeral eulogies in *Patrologia Latina,* ed. J. P. MIGNE, 217 v., indexes 4 v. (Paris 1878–90), 152:555–606. Literature. B. BLIGNY, *Saint Bruno, le premier chartreux* (Rennes 1984). *A Carthusian, Maestro Bruno, padre de monjes* (Madrid 1980). C. LE COUTEULX, *Annales ordinis cartusiensis,* 8 v. (Montreuil 1887–91) 1:iiicxviii. H. LÖBBEL, *Der Stifter des Carthäuser-Ordens* (Müster 1899). G. MURSELL, *The Theology of the Carthusian Life in the Writings of St. Bruno and Guigo I* (Salzburg, Austria 1988). U. OTTO, *Die Münsteraner Handschrift 894: Leben der hl. Hugo und Bruno* (Salzburg, Austria 1997). A. RAVIER, *Saint Bruno, the Carthusian*, tr. B. BECKER (San Francisco 1995). B. SMALLEY, *The Study of the Bible in the Middle Ages* (2d ed. New York 1952). B. BLIGNY, *L'Église et les ordres religieux dans le royaume de Bourgogne aux XI*e *XII*e *siècles* (Grenoble 1960). G. GIOIA, *L'esperienza contemplativa: Bruno il certosino* (Turin 1989). *Aux sources de la vie cartusienne* (Saint-Pierre-de- Chartreuse, France 1960). J. L. BAUDOT and L. CHAUSSIN, *Vies des saints et des bienhereux selon l'ordre du calendrier avec l'historique des fêtes* (Paris 1935–56) 10:164175. A. BUTLER, *The Lives of the Saints,* ed. H. THURSTON and D. ATTWATER, 4 v. (New York 1956) 4:4045. S. AUTORE, *Dictionnaire de théologie catholique,* ed. A. VACANT et al., 15 v. (Paris 1903–50; Tables générales 1951–), 2.2:227482. Y. GOURDEL, *Dictionnaire de spiritualité ascétique et mystique. Doctrine et histoire,* ed. M. MILLER et al. (Paris 1932–), 2.1:705776. R. AIGRAIN, *Catholicisme. Hier, aujourd'hui et demain,* ed. G. JACQUEMET, (Paris 1947–), 2:291293. H. WOLTER, *Lexikon für Theologie und Kirche,* ed. J. HOFER and K. RAHNER, 10 v. (2d, new ed. Frieburg 1957–65).

[B. BLIGNY]

BRUNSCHVICG, LÉON

French idealist philosopher and historian of philosophy; b. Paris, 1869; d. Aix-les-Bains, 1944. He was professor at the Sorbonne, president of the Academie des sciences, morales et politiques and of the Societé française de Philosophie, and founder of the Societas Spinoziana. Between the two world wars Brunschvicg served as the official representative of French philosophy at international conferences and on cultural missions. His doctrine is an IDEALISM with a strong historical orientation and with epistemological emphases. Brunschvicg viewed philosophy in close relation to the history of culture and of science, devoting much attention to physics, mathematics, and metaphysics. Philosophy, for him, is the integrating principle of knowledge and not a means of extending knowledge materially; it is intellectual activity that takes complete account of itself. Only in its critical activity can reason and science free themselves and realize themselves.

As a historian, Brunschvicg gained distinction especially through his studies of Spinoza and of Pascal. In both he saw his ideal of total mediation realized under different forms; in Spinoza through the elevation of reason to the role of total mediating principle; in Pascal through an appeal to mediating principles that outrange, without denigrating, abstract intellect.

See Also: IDEALISM.

Bibliography: Works. *L'Idéalisme contemporain*; *Les tapes de la philosophie mathématique*; *Le Progrés de la conscience dans la philosophie occidentale*. Studies. J. MESSAUT, *La Philosophie de Léon Brunschvicg*. M. DESCHOUX, *La Philosophie de Léon Brunschvicg,* extensive bibliog. C. ROSSO, *Enciclopedia filosofica,* 4 v. (Venice-Rome 1957) 1:820821.

[A. R. CAPONIGRI]

BRUTÉ DE RÉMUR, SIMON WILLIAM GABRIEL

First bishop of Vincennes, Ind. (now Archdiocese of INDIANAPOLIS); b. Rennes, Brittany, France, March 20, 1779; d. Vincennes, June 26, 1839. He was the son of Simon Bruté de Rémur, overseer of the royal domains in Brittany, and Jeanne Renée Le Saulnier de Vauhelle Vatar. Left fatherless as a child, Bruté attended local schools and then trained for the printing works inherited by his mother. During the French Revolution, young Bruté, according to his own diary, made frequent visits to imprisoned priests and nobles, smuggling messages and even the Blessed Sacrament to them. From 1796 intermittently to 1803 he studied medicine in Paris, graduating first in his class of more than 1,000. Instead of practicing, however, he entered the Sulpician seminary in Paris, and upon ordination on June 11, 1808, joined the Society of Saint-Sulpice. In 1810, while teaching theology in the Rennes seminary, he met Bishop-elect Benedict J. Flaget of Kentucky, who was seeking recruits for the American missions; that June they sailed for the United States together.

For the first two years, Bruté taught philosophy at St. Mary's Seminary, Baltimore, Md., devoting the summer of 1812 to missionary work in Maryland's Talbot and Queen Anne Counties. That September he was transferred to Mt. St. Mary's College, Emmitsburg, Md., where for another two years he taught and served as pastor to the Catholics of the countryside. Here, too, he met Mother Seton, whose spiritual director he was until her death in 1820. In 1815 he was appointed president of St. Mary's College in Baltimore, but he returned to Emmitsburg in 1818 and remained there until 1834. He was then named bishop of the new See of Vincennes and consecrated by Bishop Flaget in St. Louis on Oct. 28, 1834.

The new diocese was a frontier mission field embracing all of Indiana and a large part of eastern Illinois, with two priests, an unplastered building for a cathedral, and a widely scattered flock of about 25,000. One of Bruté's prime needs was a seminary. He visited France in 1835, gathering funds from the Propagation of the Faith, and recruiting 20 priests and seminarians. His five-year episcopate was one of unrelieved hardship: constant journeying through his diocese, preaching, teaching, composing expositions of the faith, writing to his priests when he could not visit them, and administering the Sacraments. He attended the Third Provincial Council of Baltimore, but he never fully recovered from the effects of the hard, wintry trip from Indiana. Although he published nothing, his memoranda, diaries, and letters are of historical significance, the more so since they involve prominent persons in France and America, among them H. F. R. de Lammenais, whom he tried unsuccessfully to reconcile with the Church.

Bibliography: J. W. RUANE, *The Beginnings of the Society of St. Sulpice in the United States, 1791–1829* (*Studies in American Church History* 22; Washington 1935). L. F. RUSKOWSKI, *French Émigré Priests in the United States, 1791–1815* (*Studies in American Church History* 32; Washington 1940). M. S. GODECKER, *Simon Bruté de Rémur*. J. H. SCHAUINGER, *Cathedrals in the Wilderness*.

[J. J. TIERNEY]

BRUYÈRE, JEANNE HENRIETTE CÉCILE

First abbess of Sainte-Cécile de Solesmes; b. Paris, Oct. 12, 1845; d. Ryde, Isle of Wight, March 18, 1909. Prepared for her first Communion by Prosper GUÉRANGER, abbot of Solesmes, she remained under his fatherly direction. When he decided to establish Benedictine nuns at Solesmes, he appointed Cécile Bruyère superior of the first group of postulants. After a period of novitiate, they took vows on Aug. 14, 1868. Two years later Bp. Fillion of Le Mans obtained from Pius IX the right of an abbess for the new monastery and conferred the abbatial blessing upon Mother Cécile. Under her long rule of 38 years, two new foundations were made. Exiled by the French anticlerical laws, in 1901 she settled at Ryde on the Isle of Wight. Her book on prayer, written for her daughters in Solesmes, is based on the teaching of Guéranger. Well-known and valued in monasteries in Germany and England, it was printed at Sainte-Pierre de Solesmes in 1899 as *La Vie spirituelle et l'oraison d'après la Sainte Écriture et de la tradition.*

Bibliography: *Dom Guéranger, abbé de Solesmes,* 2 v. 2:1819. J. DE PUNIET, *Dictionnaire de spiritualité ascétique et mystique* (Paris 1932–) 1:197274.

[M. M. BARRY]

BRYENNIOS, JOSEPH

Byzantine preacher and theologian; b. *c.* 1350; d. apparently *c.* 1438. Little is known of his origin and career. He was sent to Crete in 1381 to defend the Orthodox position against Roman propaganda on the part of the Venetians who then governed the island. Twenty years later he was forced to leave as a result of his criticism of the local clergy, and he became a monk at the Studion monastery outside Constantinople. In 1405 he went to Cyprus to recall the Eastern Catholics to Orthodoxy and presided over a local synod. A strong opponent of union with the Roman See, he criticized the negotiations between the Emperor MANUEL II and Pope MARTIN V aimed at reunion. After a final break with the policies of John VIII Palaeologus, he set sail for Crete and disappeared effectively from subsequent history.

A preacher of renown and a redoubtable polemicist, he was known for his erudition, but he did not produce original theological thought. In his controversies he restated the complaints of his predecessors against the Latin filioque and use of azymes. His extant writings consist mainly of homilies and controversial tracts: 21 homilies on the Trinity, three treatises on the procession of the Holy Spirit, a discourse on the union of the Churches, and reflections on the return of the Cypriots to Orthodoxy. His writings had been forgotten until Eugenius BULGARIS published some of them in 1768. A. Papadopulos-Kerameus discovered the acts of the synod in Cyprus over which he presided.

Bibliography: P. MEYER, *Byzantinische Zeitschrift* 5: 74–111, life. *Theologia dogmatica christianorum orientalium ab acclesia catholica dissidentium* v. 2. A. PALMIERI, *Dictionnaire de théologie catholique* (Paris 1903–50) 2.1:115–661. *Kirche und theologische Literatur im byzantinischen Reich.*

[P. ROCHE]

BRYENNIOS, PHILOTHEUS

Orthodox metropolitan and patristic scholar; b. Constantinople, 1833; d. Constantinople, 1914. Philotheus

Martin Buber.

studied at Leipzig, Berlin, and Munich, and from 1861 taught Church history at Chalki. He became the director of the Ecclesiastical Academy at Constantinople in 1867, and metropolitan of Serres in Macedonia in 1875 and of Nicomedia in 1877. He represented the Orthodox Church at an assembly of Old Catholics in Bonn in 1875. His fame rests on his discovery in the library of the hospital of the Holy Sepulcher in Constantinople of a Greek parchment codex that contained the text of the hitherto unknown DIDACHE, the Epistle of BARNABAS, and the Letter of CLEMENT I of Rome to the Corinthians.

Bibliography: J. QUASTEN, *Patrology* (Westminster, Md. 1950–) 1:30. J. R. HARRIS, ed., *The Teaching of the Twelve Apostles* (Baltimore 1887).

[F. X. MURPHY]

BUBER, MARTIN

Existentialist philosopher; b. Vienna, Feb. 8, 1878; d. Jerusalem, June 13, 1965. Buber's wife, Paula, was a novelist who wrote under the pseudonym Georg Munk. In 1904 Buber received a Ph.D. in philosophy and history of art from Berlin University. He then served as editor of the social-psychological monographs *Der Jude, Die Kreatur,*and *Die Gesellschaft.* In 1923 he was appointed professor of Jewish religion and ethics and history of religions at Frankfurt University, serving in this post until 1933, when he became director of the Freie Jüdische Lehrhaus in Frankfurt. From 1938 to 1953 he was professor of social philosophy at the Hebrew University, Jerusalem. He then became editor-in-chief of the *Israeli Encyclopedia of Education* and director of the Israeli Institute, a training center for teachers working among the immigrants. Buber was awarded the Goethe, Peace, Munich, and Erasmus prizes.

Thought. Buber's influence has been worldwide, especially through his translation and interpretation of the Hebrew Bible; his re-creation and interpretation of the legends and teachings of Hasidim, a popular communal mysticism of East European Jewry; and his philosophy of dialogue, in which he expounds the ''I-Thou'' relationship. Buber was a leading representative of the type of EXISTENTIALISM that begins not with the self, but with the relations between selves; through this he has influenced contemporary education, psychotherapy, ethics, and social philosophy. Buber's thought has affected Protestant, and, to a lesser extent, Jewish and Catholic theology through an emphasis on the dialogue between man and the ''Eternal Thou,'' as opposed to dealing with God as an object of knowledge.

Works. Buber's works include *I and Thou, Between Man and Man, Good and Evil, Eclipse of God, The Prophetic Faith, Two Types of Faith* (Jesus and Paul), *Pointing the Way, The Knowledge of Man, Tales of the Hasidim, For the Sake of Heaven* (Hasidic novel), *Hasidim and Modern Man, The Origin and Meaning of Hasidism, Paths in Utopia,* and *Daniel.*

Bibliography: M. FRIEDMAN, *Martin Buber: The Life of Dialogue* (New York 1960). P. A. SCHILPP and M. FRIEDMAN, eds., *The Philosophy of Martin Buber* (La Salle, Ill. 1966). D. AVNON, *Martin Buber: The Hidden Dialogue* (Lanham, Md. 1998). P. VERMES, *Buber on God and the Perfect Man* (London 1994). S. KEPNES, *The Text as Thou: Martin Buber's Dialogical Hermeneutics and Narrative Theology* (Bloomington 1992).

[M. FRIEDMAN]

BUBWITH, NICHOLAS

Bishop, ambassador, treasurer of England; b. Menthorpe, near Bubwith, Yorkshire; d. Wookey, Somersetshire, England, Oct. 27, 1424. During his career he was distinguished as a royal official and as a genuinely resident bishop. He began as a chancery clerk (*c.* 1380). He soon became such a notable provisor (Emden 1:295) that in 1399 he had to secure a pardon for obtaining papal provisions without the royal license. Under King Henry IV he received canonries and prebends in Exeter (1399),

Wells (1399), and York (1400), and the archdeaconry of Richmond (Mar. 16, 1402, which he exchanged two days later for the prebend of Driffield in York), as well as canonries in Salisbury (1400), Chichester (1402), Lincoln (1403), and Saint Paul's (1406). These offices he held while he was secretary to Henry IV (1402); he was also *custos rotulorum* (1402–05) and keeper of the privy seal (1405–06). He was provided to the bishopric of London on May 19, 1406. A year later he became treasurer of England (1407–08), then bishop of Salisbury (June 22, 1407), but he was moved to allow for Robert HALLUM, who had been provided to the archbishopric of York but had been denied the title by the king and council. Bubwith was provided to Bath and Wells on Oct. 7, 1407. While bishop of the latter see, he was appointed an envoy to treat with Scotland (May 22, 1412); in 1414 he was one of the king's ambassadors at the Council of CONSTANCE, returning in August of 1418. At Constance he and Bp. Robert Hallum induced Giovanni Bertoldi da Serravalle, bishop of Fermo, to translate the *Divine Comedy* into Latin verse with a Latin commentary. Bubwith was generous with his wealth, which was considerable. Wylie (*Henry IV,* 3: 131) states that he often returned to the Exchequer sums that he might legitimately have claimed, not least as a member of the council (£200 a year). He built the western tower and altered the walls of the church of Bubwith, Yorkshire; at Wells he contributed to poor churches and built the northern tower of the west front of the cathedral and the library above the east cloister. He also founded the Bishop Nicholas Almshouse.

Bibliography: J. H. WYLIE, *History of England under Henry IV,* 4 v. (London 1884–98) v. 3, 4. *The Register of Henry Chichele,* ed. E. F. JACOB and H. C. JOHNSON, 4 v. (Canterbury and York Society 42, 45–47; London 1937–47) 2:298–302, for his will. A. B. EMDEN, *A Biographical Register of the University of Oxford to A.D. 1500* 1:294–296.

[E. F. JACOB]

BUCER, MARTIN (BUTZER)

Protestant reformer of Strassburg; b. Schlettstadt in Alsace, Nov. 1, 1491; d. Cambridge, England, Feb. 28, 1551. At age 15 he left his poor parents to enter the Dominican house at Schlettstadt. Ten years later he was sent to study at the University of Heidelberg, where he joined the humanist movement and came to admire ERASMUS. When in April of 1518 LUTHER defended himself against Dominican opponents in a disputation at Heidelberg, Bucer was won to Lutheran theology. He obtained a papal dispensation from vows and in 1521 became a secular priest. In 1524 he was already a chief champion of Protestant divinity at Strassburg and well known as a leading reformer in Germany. As pastor at Strassburg for 25 years, he helped to introduce Protestantism into Hesse, Ulm, Augsburg, and other cities, and was as strong an antagonist of the Anabaptists as of the Catholics. In 1522 he married Elizabeth Silbereisen, a former nun; it was one of the first marriages of a priest. She died of the plague in 1541. A year later he married Wolfgang CAPITO's widow; she survived Bucer.

His chief work was *De regno Christi,* published posthumously in 1557. All his life he was a diligent writer, voluminous to a fault. A lack of brevity and clarity prevented him from leaving any book of lasting influence. But his original and powerful mind inspired several Protestant divines, including John CALVIN and Peter Martyr Vermigli. He was a peaceable man with a strong pastoral sense, laying much emphasis upon catechetical instruction. He strove to give the church authorities a due independence of the secular magistrates in spiritual things and helped to introduce the system of discipline by pastors and elders that Calvin brought to a more highly organized state in Geneva. Calvin worked as his lieutenant in Strassburg from 1538 to 1541. All his life Bucer sought to reconcile Luther with the Swiss, especially in the theology of the Real Presence. He was the chief theologian of the mediating theology known broadly as "receptionism," whereby the Body and Blood of our Lord are believed to be received by faith "with" though not "in" or "under" the elements of bread and wine. In this irenic office he expended tireless energy. He was present at the fruitless Marburg meeting of 1529 between Luther and Zwingli, and attained his main success in the Wittenberg Concord of 1536, which reconciled Luther and the Protestant churches of Upper Germany, though it was repudiated by the Swiss Protestants. These mediating efforts gained him no popularity with stern Protestants on either side. He was present at the Colloquy at the Diet of Regensburg in 1541, when Cardinal Gasparo CONTARINI sought formulas of reconciliation with the more moderate Protestants. Bucer drafted important formulas for the Cologne reformation of 1543 when Abp. Hermann of Wied tried vainly to make the archbishopric a Protestant territory. When CHARLES V enforced the Augsburg Interim of 1548, the situation of many non-Lutheran divines in south Germany became untenable. Bucer sought refuge in England. Through the influence of Archbishop CRANMER, he was made regius professor of divinity at the University of Cambridge. His criticism of the first English Prayer Book of 1549 caused Cranmer to make many alterations in the second Prayer Book of 1552. During the reign of Queen MARY I his bones were burned in the market square at Cambridge. Three years later, after the accession of ELIZABETH I, the remains were solemnly reburied in Great St. Mary's Church.

See Also: REFORMATION, PROTESTANT (IN THE BRITISH ISLES); CONFESSIONS OF FAITH, II; BOOK OF COMMON PRAYER.

Bibliography: *Opera omnia,* ed., R. STUPPERICH (Gütersloh 1960—); *Martin Bucer: Études sur la correspondance,* ed. J. V. POLLET (Paris 1958—). R. STUPPERICH, ''Bibliographia Bucerana,'' H. BORNKAMM, *Martin Bucers Bedeutung für die europäische Reformationsgeschichte* (Gütersloh 1952); *Die Religion in Geschichte und Gegenwart* (Tübingen 1957–65) 1:1453–57. H. EELLS, *Martin Bucer* (New Haven 1931). C. HOPF, *Martin Bucer and the English Reformation* (Oxford 1946). P. POLMAN, *Dictionnaire d'histoire et de géographie ecclésiastiques* (Paris 1912–) 10:1015–19. E. ISERLOH, *Lexikon für Theologie und Kirche* (Freiburg 1957–65) 2:845–846.

[W. O. CHADWICK]

BUCHEZ, PHILIPPE JOSEPH BENJAMIN

Important contributor to the formative ideas of Christian socialism in 19th-century France; b. Matagne-la-Petite, March 31, 1796; d. Rodez, Aug. 12, 1865. Buchez became a doctor of medicine in 1824 but was more interested in revolutionary activity. In 1821 he founded with Armand Bazard *Le Charbonnerie française,* which sought the overthrow of the Bourbons and the convocation of a national constitutional assembly. He was at first a disciple of C. H. de SAINT-SIMON but was converted to Catholicism in 1829. He was never a practicing Catholic because he hoped by his nonobservance to be more successful in reaching republicans with his message of social Christianity. As a philosopher, historian, economist, socialist, and deputy, he believed that the ideals of the FRENCH REVOLUTION were a development of the fundamental truths of Christianity and especially of the call to the disinterested service of one's fellow man.

His ideas were expressed in numerous publications, especially in the journals *L'Européen* (1831–32, 1835–38), *Revue Nationale* (1847–48), *L'Atelier* (1840–50); in the prefaces of the 40 volumes of his *L'Histoire parlementaire de la Révolution française* (1833–38); and in *L'Essai d'un traité complet de philosophie au point de vue du catholicisme et du progrès* (1838–40). He complemented his critique of the industrial system with proposed remedies, including associations of working men and credit facilities; these ideas were influential during the Revolution of 1848 and the Second Republic, a period in which Buchez served briefly as first president of the National Assembly.

Bibliography: A. CUVILLIER, *P.-J. Buchez et les origines du socialisme chrétien* (Paris 1948). J. B. DUROSELLE, *Les Débuts du catholicisme social en France, 1822–1870* (Paris 1951).

[E. T. GARGAN]

BUCHMAN, FRANK NATHAN DANIEL

Founder of movement known variously as Oxford Group, Moral Re-armament (MRA), and Buchmanism; b. Pennsburg, Pa., June 4, 1878; d. Freudenstadt, Germany, Aug. 7, 1961. After receiving his M.A. from Muhlenberg College, Allentown, Pa., Buchman was ordained in the Lutheran ministry (1902) and did parish work for three years in Philadelphia, Pa., where he subsequently directed a hostel for homeless boys. During a trip abroad, he experienced a ''conversion'' while listening to a sermon in an English village church. From this experience he formulated ideas that constituted a basic part of his movement: a Christian renaissance based on absolute love, honesty, purity, and unselfishness. For five years he did evangelistic work among the students of Pennsylvania State College. He spoke at youth conferences and traveled in the U.S., Europe, and the Far East. Convinced that men must be approached individually in order to be converted to God, he introduced ''house parties'' at which men might, in an informal setting, be induced to amend their lives. The first important house party was held at Oxford in 1921, hence the name Oxford Group. Buchman described the movement as a ''Christian revolution . . . the aim of which is a new social order under the dictatorship of God.'' In 1938 he renamed it Moral Re-Armament, calling it a ''God-guided campaign to prevent war by a moral and spiritual awakening.'' The activities of MRA, diminished during World War II, gained new popularity after 1945. MRA has been praised for its insistence on sincere devotion and personal commitment and denounced for its lack of emphasis on Christ. Buchman wrote extensively; among his publications are *Moral Re-Armament* (1938), *Remaking the World* (1948), and *The World Rebuilt* (1951).

Bibliography: F. E. MAYER, *The Religious Bodies of America* (4th ed. St. Louis 1961). W. G. SCHWEHN, *What Is Buchmanism?* (St. Louis 1940). W. H. CLARK, *The Oxford Group: Its History and Significance* (New York 1951).

[E. DELANEY]

BUCKFAST, ABBEY OF

Benedictine abbey in Devonshire, southwest England. Although it has been alleged that a Celtic cloister existed there from St. Pectroc's time (6th century), Buckfast actually was founded by Earl Aylward and endowed by King Canute (1018). The Domesday Book lists its possessions in detail (1086). Stephen attached it to SAVIGNY (1136), and it thus became affiliated with CÎTEAUX (1147). A new abbey was then built. Buckfast

Dining Hall of Buckfast Abbey. (©Hulton-Deutsch Collection/CORBIS)

was suppressed in the general dissolution of monasteries under Henry VIII (1538); its property was alienated, and church and abbey fell into ruin. French Benedictines from La-Pierre-qui-Vire purchased the site (1882); they were joined by German Benedictines. Buckfast became an abbey under a German abbot (1902). Under the second abbot, Anscar VONIER (1906), the rebuilding of the abbey on its ancient foundations was undertaken. The church was consecrated in 1932.

Bibliography: A. HAMILTON, *A History of St. Mary's Abbey of Buckfast* (Buckfast 1906). J. STÉPHAN, *Buckfast Abbey* (Buckfast 1923). J. M. CANIVEZ, *Dictionnaire d'histoire et de géographie ecclésiastiques,* ed. A. BAUDRILLART et al. (Paris 1912–) 10:1034–36. A. SCHMITT, *Lexikon für Theologie und Kirche,* ed. J. HOFER and K. RAHNER, 10 v. (2d, new ed. Freiburg 1957–65) 2:751. L. H. COTTINEAU, *Répertoire topobibliographique des abbayes et prieurés,* 2 v. (Mâcon 1935–39) 2:525. O. L. KAPSNER, *A Benedictine Bibliography: An Author-Subject Union List,* 2 v. (2d ed. Collegeville, Minn. 1962): v. 1, author part; v. 2, subject part, 2:193.

[J. STÉPHAN]

BUCKLAND, ABBEY OF

Former CISTERCIAN abbey on the river Tavy, Devon, England, Diocese of Exeter. Buckland, or *Locus s. Benedicti de Bochland* (*Boclan, Buglanda*), was founded by Amicia, Countess of Devon, in 1278 with monks from QUARR, Isle of Wight. Because Walter Bronescombe, Bishop of EXETER, had not been consulted about the foundation, he placed it under interdict, releasing it only on the intervention of Queen Eleanor, May 27, 1280. The abbey had two mills, one for corn, the other for fulling, but it was never rich. During the 14th century the abbots were appointed collectors of the tenth and were asked to assist the supervisors of the king's mines in the providing of fuel for smelting and to collaborate in the defense of the coast near Dartmouth. This did not free them from subsidies demanded for the marriage of Edward III's sister Eleanor to Reginald, Count of Gueldres, and for the war against France. Buckland's history was uneventful except for the quarrel between Thomas Oliver and Wil-

Exterior of Buckland Abbey. (©Dave G. Houser/CORBIS)

liam Breton for the abbacy, a struggle that dragged out for seven years (1467–73). At the dissolution John Toker, the abbot, was given a pension of £60, and 12 monks, sums of £5 or £3 according to their status.

Bibliography: W. DUGDALE, *Monasticon Anglicanum* (London 1655–73); best ed. by J. CALEY et al., 6 v. (1817–30) 5:712–715. G. OLIVER, *Monasticon dioecesis Exoniensis* (Exeter 1846). *Calendar of the Close Rolls Preserved in the Public Record Office, London (1279–1477). Calendar of the Patent Rolls Preserved in the Public Record Office, London (1272–1494).* C. GILL, *Buckland Abbey* (rev. ed. Plymouth, Eng. 1956).

[C. H. TALBOT]

BUCKLER, REGINALD

Dominican spiritual writer; b. London, Feb. 14, 1840; d. Grenada, West Indies, March 18, 1927. Both Buckler's father and grandfather were topographical artists and architects of distinction. His three elder brothers became Catholics, two of them Dominicans, before he entered the Church in 1855. The following year he entered the Order of Preachers at Woodchester and was given the name Reginald (he had been called Henry at birth). He was ordained in 1863, and during the 63 years of his priestly life he was stationed at various Dominican houses and assigned to various duties. In 1903 he received Robert Hugh Benson into the Church. He received his last assignment at the age of 71 when he volunteered for the mission in Grenada in the West Indies. Twice he held the office of novice master at Woodchester (1895–98, 1908), during which times he wrote two works on the religious life. His first and most important book, *The Perfection of Man by Charity,* a spiritual classic, was published in 1889. This was republished under the title *Spiritual Perfection through Charity* (1912), but was later published again under the earlier title (London 1954). His other principal works were *A Spiritual Retreat* (London 1907 and 1924); *Spiritual Instruction on Reli-*

Buddhist Monks collecting morning alms from Thai Buddhists, Bangkok, Thailand. (©Kevin R. Morris/CORBIS)

gious Life (London 1909); and *Spiritual Considerations* (New York 1912), which was later republished under the title *An Introduction to the Spiritual Life* (London 1957).

Bibliography: C. M. ANTONY, *Father Reginald Buckler O.P., 1840–1927* (London 1927). W. GUMBLEY, *Obituary Notices of the English Dominicans from 1555–1952* (London 1955).

[S. BULLOUGH]

BUDDHISM

The complex of religious beliefs and philosophical ideas that has developed out of the teachings of the Buddha (Sanskrit, ''the Enlightened One''), the honorific title of the founder of Buddhism, the North Indian prince Siddhārtha Gautama. Beginning as a discipline for human deliverance from pain, it came to embrace various cults and sects. Buddhism broke into various schools from an early date. Many schisms stemmed from disputes over the rules of monastic conduct, while others had to do with philosophical or ideological differences. Beginning in the first century B.C., a complex of lay and monastic movements coalesced into a new form of Buddhism that referred to itself as the Bodhisattvayāna (''vehicle of the bodhisattvas'') or MAHĀYĀNA (''great vehicle''), and to its opponents as the HĪNAYĀNA (''lesser vehicle''). Buddhism is not a strictly logical dogmatic system of beliefs and practices in the Western sense. Its adherents require of religion not that it be true rather than false, but that it be good rather than bad. The characteristic symbol of Buddhism is the ''Wheel of the Law'' (*Dharma-Cakra*).

In modern times, in part under the impact of Western thought, the rise of theosophic neo-Buddhism is to be noted. The geographic expansion of Buddhism coincided with its ideological evolution. Since the Buddhism of each country assumed various forms and characteristics, it is necessary to treat it on a regional basis.

Buddhist Peace Shrine, dedicated to the dead of WWII, Kyoto, Japan. (©Ric Ergenbright/CORBIS)

INDIA

During the lifetime of the historical buddha (*c.* 563–483 B.C.) Indian society and religion were undergoing extensive transformations. A sudden population increase, urbanization, the rise of a monetary economy, and the founding of centralized kingdoms in place of traditional tribal and clan society, led many to question the traditional religious sacrifices of the Vedas. Many began thinking for the first time about the fate of the individual after death, leading to the first formulations of the doctrine of reincarnation and karma as found in the Upaniṣads, and to the rise of many other new religious movements, of which Buddhism and Jainism are the only survivors. The proponents of these new ways of thinking were wandering mendicants who renounced the normal system of family and social ties in order to devote themselves to meditation and philosophical discourse.

Buddha. When the intellectual revolt, set forth in the Upaniṣads, had resulted in disintegration of thought and life, many wandering masters offered a way of salvation. According to tradition one of these was Siddhārtha (*c.* 563–*c.* 483 B.C.), the son of Śuddhodana and Māyā Gautama, born at Lumbinī in the Nepāl Valley. He was publicly proclaimed the sage of the Śākya clan (*Śākyamuni*) and the ''Enlightened'' (*Buddha*). At 29 he renounced his wife and child to seek deliverance from the pain of human existence. After six years of practicing deep trance meditations and extreme self-mortification, he decided to chart his own path and sat under the Bodhi Tree at Bodh Gayā and attained both enlightenment and liberation from the endless round of birth and rebirth (*samsāra*) by discovering the origin of suffering and the way to conquer it.

Before his death at Kuśinagara, Buddha formulated his doctrine and the rules for orders of monks and nuns. He taught that pain could be conquered by the knowledge and practice of the ''Four Noble Truths''; (1) Human existence is pain, which (2) is caused by desire, and (3) can

Tibetan Buddhist prayer wheels, Rumtek Monastery, Gangtok, Sikkim, India. (©Jeremy Horner/Corbis)

be overcome by victory over desire (4) by means of the ''Noble Eightfold Path.'' The Path consists in (1) right knowledge of the Four Noble Truths; (2) right resolve to curb malice; (3) right speech, true and kind; (4) right action, meaning to refrain from killing, stealing, and sexual misconduct; (5) right livelihood, which meant that one could not earn one's living in a trade that by its nature involved bringing harm to others, such as trade in weapons, poisons, slaves, livestock, and so on; (6) right effort; (7) right mindfulness, or keeping the mind at all times serenely focused on the present moment; and (8) right meditation, which consists of four steps: isolation resulting in joy, meditation causing inner peace, concentration producing bodily happiness, and contemplation rewarded with indifference to happiness and misery.

The Buddha departed from the prevailing thought of his day by affirming the reality of rebirth in higher or lower states of life based on the moral quality of one's accumulated karma, but denying that there is a self (*ātman*) that goes from body to body and life to life. It was self-contradictory, he said, to assert that the true self is an entity ensconced within the body which is eternal, unchanging, and partless but which nevertheless is affected and guided by karma. It was better not to think of the human person as an ongoing entity at all, but as a process that was ever-changing and whose relation to its own previous lives was one of continuity rather than identity. Thus, his followers came to see all living beings as aggregations of processes, both physical and mental (sensation, perception, consciousness, and mental constructions) that karma kept active just as firewood keeps the fire going, and the point of practice became to end the process (a goal called ''nirvāna,'' or ''extinguishing'') rather than to liberate an inchoate entity.

Early order and councils. Any male who was not sick, disabled, a criminal, a soldier, a debtor, or a minor lacking parental consent could enter the order as a monk. The initiation ceremony comprised the renunciation (*pabbajja*), the arrival, and the pledge to keep the four prohibitions against sexual intercourse, theft, harm to life, and boasting of superhuman perfection. The initiated was bound to observe the ten abstentions, i.e., from killing, stealing, lying, sexual intercourse, intoxicants, eating after midday, worldly amusements, using cosmetics and adornments, luxurious mats and beds, and from accepting gold or silver. Initiation, abstentions, and vows did not bind a monk for life, but only for the time he remained in the order. Daily exercises of the monks comprised

A monk carrying water to a temple, Qinghai, China. (©Eye Ubiquitous/Corbis)

morning prayers, recitation of verses, outdoor begging, a midday meal followed by rest and meditation, and evening service. Fortnightly exercises consisted in observing a day of fast and abstinence (*uposatha*) and in making a public confession of sins (*pratimoksa*).

At the entreaty of his foster mother, Mahāprajāpatī, Buddha founded a second order for nuns. Moreover, he established a third order, this one for lay people, who were obliged only to abstain from killing, stealing, lying, intoxicants, and fornication. But they were exhorted to practice kindness, clean speech, almsgiving, religious instruction, and the duties of mutual family and social relations.

According to traditional sources the primitive doctrine lapsed into heresy, and hence a council was held at Rājagrha, where the authorized version of the sayings of the Master, the *Vinaya* and the *Dhamma,* were fixed. A hundred years later a second council took place at Vaiśālī to settle ten questions concerning monastic discipline, but which led to the first major schism in the Buddhist order.

Asoka, apostle of Buddhism. Conscience-stricken at the horrors of a war for the unification of northern India, King Asoka (273–231 B.C.) embraced Buddhism. He then abolished the royal hunt and meat at his meals, engraved his precepts on stone, issued a series of edicts embodying Buddhist rules of conduct and justice, spread the Buddhist faith, governed with piety and wisdom, and convened a third council at Pātaliputra in 247. In 240 he became a monk, but without abdicating his royal office. He required his officials to give moral training to their subordinates, to promote piety among people of all sects, and to prevent unjust punishments. He sent his brother (or son) Mahinda and other missionaries to spread the faith in Sri Lanka (Ceylon) and another group to Western Asia, Macedonia, and Epirus. Only the mission in Sri Lanka was successful, but Buddhists elsewhere subsequently exerted some influence on the Gnostic and Manichaean sects. Asceticism and missionary movements left an enduring mark in India, whence Buddhism spread throughout Eastern Asia.

Rise of Mahāyāna. Northern Buddhist tradition holds that a fourth council, ignored by Pāli sources, was held at Jālandhara about A.D. 100 and authorized the addition of Sanskrit commentaries to the canon. In the first two centuries of the Christian era Buddhist believers sought a more emotional piety and more personal deities by syncretizing their faith with polytheistic Vedism, monistic Vedantism, and ritual Yoga. They also felt the influence of Zoroastrian, Gnostic, and Hellenic elements brought by Persian, Parthian, Kushan, and Greek invaders. Thus, the ideal of the *bodhisattva,* the one who sacrifices oneself to save others in a long chain of rebirths, replaced that of *Arhat,* the one who attains *nirvāna* by one's own virtue. Gautama was regarded as only one of the earthly manifestations of cosmic Buddha who did and will incarnate himself countless times. Buddhas and *bodhisattvas* were considered superbeings and deities. Hence, the adherents of the new doctrine called it Mahāyāna, the Great Vehicle to salvation, to distinguish it from the conservative Hīnayāna or Little Vehicle.

In the 2d century A.D. Nāgārjuna founded the School of the Mean (*Mādhyamika*) to develop the Great Vehicle and taught that individuals and their constitutive elements (*dharma*) were unreal and that existence was but a screen of illusory phenomena whose continuity could be broken only by the knowledge of their basic unreality. *Nirvāna* consisted in reaching the end of the chain of phenomena. The Yogācāra School, founded by Asaṅga and Vasubandhu in the 4th century, propounded that all phenomena originate in the mind through eight kinds of awareness that reveal the illusion that there is an objective world and cause all humans to acquire the wisdom whereby they unite with the ultimate. Aśvaghoṣa developed the system in a form that greatly influenced China and Japan. For him the essence of things consists in the oneness of the totality of things; ignorance of the totality results in the illusory phenomenal world, while recognition of it actualizes the only true reality, which is *nirvāṇa.* "Personality" is triple: the absolute in itself (*Dharmakāya*), the absolute as embodied in earthly Buddhas (*Nirvāṇakāya*), and the absolute as realized in heavenly Buddhas (*Sambhogakāya*). Salvation is attained by faith in the Buddha Amitābha ("having infinite light").

Decline. Buddhism became mixed with the worship of deities (*deva*), dragons and snakes (*nāga*), and Siva's consort (Devi, Durgā, Kālī, Śakti), who was confused with Tārā, Avalokita's consort. This erotic mysticism was further compounded with Tantrism, a magic ritual of spells, diagrams, sorcery, erotics, and temple prostitution borrowed from China. In the 11th century Buddhism was still strong in Kashmir, Crissa, and Bihar, but with the establishment of the Muslim power in 1193, it disappeared from Northern India, its cradle. In Western India it vanished at about the mid 12th century under the rising tide of Hinduism.

Internal and external causes account for the decay of Buddhism in India. Although Buddha taught salvation through personal effort without dependence on any god, he neither denied the existence of the Hindu gods nor forbade their worship or the rites connected with birth, marriage, and death. Under the influence of Hinduism the *Mahāyāna* sect evolved a pantheon of Buddhas and Bodhisattvas and a metaphysics of a pantheistic world soul complicated by Yoga and Tantra practices. Arising as a variation of Hinduism, this sort of Buddhism was naturally reabsorbed by it, for Hinduism, which had deeper and stronger roots in the Indian soul, in time developed a caste system with impassable social and religious barriers. This was incompatible with classless Buddhism.

SRI LANKA (CEYLON)

When Mahinda, brother (or son) of King Asoka, introduced Buddhism into Sri Lanka about 250 B.C., he met King Devanampiya Tissa at a place since called Mahindatale (now Mihintale), near the capital Anurādhapura. Having been moved by sermons and portents, the king and his subjects embraced the faith. Some days later the minister Avittha and his brothers joined the order; when Mahinda's sister arrived from India, she validly admitted many Sri Lankan women to the order of nuns. In his capital King Tissa then erected shrines and monasteries, notably the Mahāvihāra or Great Monastery, which remained the stronghold of orthodoxy for centuries. In compliance with Mahinda's directives, in order to give the faith a firm foundation, he convened the council of Thuparama so that the sacred books might be committed to memory and in turn taught by native monks.

The invasion of the Tamils from Southern India had arrested the civil and religious progress furthered by the Buddhist kings, Uttiya (207–197 B.C.), Mahāsiva (197–187 B.C.), and Suratissa (187–177 B.C.). The kingdom returned to normal only under Dutthagamani (101–77 B.C.), who expelled the invaders, reorganized the island, spread the faith, and built the Lohapaṣada and Mahāthupa monasteries, where a golden image of Buddha and statues of Māra, Brahmā, and many other Hindu gods were displayed. There ensued a period of Tamil aggression, famine, and uprisings that forced many monks to flee to India and Malaya. When the monks returned to their monasteries under King Vattagamani Abhaya (29–17 B.C.), they began to show more interest in learning than in piety. The king built the Abhayagiri monastery for

Mahātissa and his monks, who had helped to repulse the Tamil aggression, but the monks of the Mahāvihāra reproved Mahātissa for his familiarity with laymen, and a schism was enkindled in the order.

Canon and commentaries. The monks of the Mahāvihāra feared that Buddha's teachings, thus far committed only to memory, could perish with the monks in wars and the attendant miseries, or be altered through heterodox leanings in some monks. At the rival Abhayagiri monastery, in fact, the rise of a *Mahāyāna* school presaged heresy and corruption. Accordingly, 500 monks convened on neutral grounds at the Aluvihāra near Matale to write down in Pali the *Tipitaka* (Three Baskets): *Sutta Pitaka* (Buddha's sermons), *Vinaya Pitaka* (monastic rules), and *Abhidhamma Piṭaka* (treatises), the whole forming a canon of scriptural texts for the Theravāda School (one of the many schools forming the Hīnayāna) which predominated in Sri Lanka; this corpus is the basis for the present Pāli canon. The writing of the canon away from the capital and from the king bespeaks the disciplinary and doctrinal rift between the two rival monasteries. The appearance of the written canon caused controversies, the compilation of Sinhalese commentaries, and a deeper cleft between the two schools. A dispute between the two groups over the interpretation of the *Vinaya,* presided over by King Bhatiya (A.D. 38–66) and settled by a polyglot minister, gives evidence that the *Mahāyāna* school at the Abhayagiri was already using Sanskrit versions of the canon embellished with heterodox legends. Under Vohāratissa (A.D. 269–291) the schismatics upheld the *Vaipulya Piṭaka* as containing the true teaching of the Buddha, but the king thought otherwise and had their books burned. During the reign of Mahānaman (412–434) Buddhaghosa wrote the *Visuddhimagga* (The Way of Purification), a thorough exposition of *Hīnayāna* Buddhism, and translated most of the Sinhalese commentaries on the canon into Pāli.

The Tamils resumed their incursions and finally drove the native dynasty and its religion from the northern tip of Sri Lanka. But in the 11th century King Vijaya Bahu restored the dynasty and requested the Myanmar Buddhists to validate initiation in Sri Lanka to their order. In 1165 his successor called a council to stamp out schism and heresy, but again after his death the Tamils took the country. Subsequent occupations by the Portuguese (1505) and Dutch (1658) damaged the position of Buddhism, and in the 18th century the order died out. Once again it revived when the king obtained ten Thai monks to validate the succession and establish the Thai school. Finally, before the British displaced the Dutch in 1802, the Amapura school was founded through valid initiation in Myanmar.

Beliefs, order, and cult. Unlike the ethical system of the canon, which has been kept through the centuries, the religious system has become a blend of many ingredients of the rebirth tales of the late Buddhist tradition (*jātaka*) and belief in many universes, heavens, and hells on the one hand, with Hindu polytheism and demonism on the other. The Brahmās are the highest Buddhist deities recorded in the canon. Sakka of the Pali commentaries is the same god as the Indra of the Vedic pantheon. The world is protected by the Four Kings (*lokapāla*) who rule the six heavens above the human world (*mānuṣaloka*). Yama rescues people born in hell, a realm of eight divisions, each subdivided into many sections, whereas Māra, the impersonation of evil, prevents people from doing good. Four evil destinies (*apāya*) are realized in the underworld: hells, animals, hungry ghosts (*petaloka*), and giant demons (*asura*). Above the human world of sense-desire there is the abode of the Brahmās, gods in material body, and the world of no-form, which is the abode of the immaterial Brahmās, is supreme. This hybrid system began to be undermined by Christian influence after 1505 and by public education in the 20th century.

The backbone of the Buddhist faith is the order of monks. Postulants may enter the novitiate at the age of 12 through the ceremony of tonsure and investiture of the yellow robe (*pabbajja*). At 20 they make a temporary profession (*upasampada*). They spend the day in domestic work, reading the canon, meditating, begging for food, instructing children in the scriptures, healing the sick by charms and chants, and reciting protection *sūtras* (*Paritta*) to ward off the malevolence of the goblins.

The cult includes many forms of popular worship. Objects of veneration are the relics and images of Buddha. Religious celebrations are marked by offerings (*pūjā*) to Buddhist and Hindu deities and goblins and by the propitiatory recitation of the canon. Modern educated Sri Lankans associate Buddhism with the greatness of Sri Lanka's past and the national prestige of the present. Their theosophic Buddhism is only one more step away from the original path of Siddhārtha (Buddha).

[A. S. ROSSO/C. B. JONES]

CHINA

Buddhism first entered China sometime during the first century A.D., probably with foreign traders who came into China via the Silk Road or from the maritime route along the southeastern seaboard. For the first two centuries or so, it existed primarily among immigrant settlements, while slowly making its presence known among the native Chinese population. As interest grew during the second century, a few monks began translating scriptures into Chinese. Notable among these were An Shigao and Lokaksema.

With the fall of the Han dynasty in the early third century, interest in Buddhism among the Chinese increased as the unstable political situation inspired people to seek for new answers. At the same time, the division of China into kingdoms north and south of the Yangtze River gave Buddhism a different character in these two regions. In the north, greater proximity to India meant that Buddhism in this region had a greater number of Indian and Central Asian monks and meditation teachers, and so it tended to emphasize religious practice over textual study. In addition, from the early fourth century to the late sixth, the north was under non-Chinese rule. These ''barbarian'' rulers favored Buddhism and many monks served as court advisors, giving Buddhism in the north a more overtly political character.

Many of the literati had fled the troubles of the north and migrated to the Southern Kingdoms, bringing with them their emphasis on literary skill. In addition to this, the Northern Kingdoms blocked their access to the living traditions of India and Central Asia, and so the South developed a more literary approach to Buddhist study. During this time, Daoan (312–385) produced the first catalogue of Buddhist scriptures, and he and his disciples worked to produce critical editions of scriptures and treatises, and to develop principles for their translation into Chinese. It was during this period that the Central Asian monk Kumārajīva arrived in 402 and opened his translation bureau in the north, producing some of the finest translations from Sanskrit, many of which are still considered the standard. His rendering of Indian Mādhyamika texts led to the foundation of the Sanlun (or ''Three Treatise'') school that specialized in Mādhyamika philosophy. Also, the dissemination of Buddhist texts and teachings among the educated elite led to a prolonged exchange of ideas between Buddhism and Taoism, and Buddhism absorbed and modified many Taoist ideas.

Other significant figures of the Northern and Southern Kingdoms period include Daosheng (360–434) a great textual scholar; Lushan Huiyuan (344–416) and Tanluan (476–542), who helped establish the Pure Land teachings; the Sanlun master Sengzhao (374–414); and the great translator Paramārtha (499–569), whose translations of Indian Mind-only literature paved the way for the future establishment of the Faxiang school.

China was reunified by the Sui dynasty in 581 CE, but the ruling house was quickly toppled by the Tang dynasty in 618. The Tang dynasty held power for almost 300 years, and this period represents one of China's golden ages. Buddhism flourished during this period, although it also suffered severe setbacks. Increased affluence and patronage enabled many original thinkers and practitioners to establish schools of Buddhism more in keeping with Chinese cultural and intellectual patterns and less dependent upon pre-existing Indian schools of thought. Examples include Zhiyi (538–597), who founded the Tiantai school; Fazang (643–712), who consolidated the Huayan school; and the various meditation masters who established Chan as a separate school that transmitted the Buddha-mind directly from master to disciple ''outside of words and scriptures.'' Daochuo (562–645), Shandao (613–681), and others continued building up the Pure Land movement, extending Tanluan's teaching further. During this time Xuanzang (*c.* 596–664) traveled in India for 16 years and brought back many texts which he translated into Chinese. After Kumārajīva, he is considered the second of the greatest translators in Chinese Buddhist history. He concentrated on Indian Yogacāra thought, and, building on the foundation laid by Paramārtha, founded the Faxiang school.

Prosperity brought its own difficulties. As the numbers of ordained clergy increased, the government became concerned about the revenue and labor pool that would be lost due to the clergy's tax- and labor-exempt status. In addition, ever since Buddhism's inception in China some traditional Confucian scholars had decried it as a foreign religion that violated basic Chinese values, especially the loyalty that all citizens owed to the state and the filial piety that sons and daughters owed their parents. In addition, Taoists sometimes saw in Buddhism an antagonist and competitor rather than a colleague. In the past, the government instituted ordination examinations and state-issued certificates to control the size of the *sangha*, and twice during the Northern and Southern Kingdoms period the state had suppressed Buddhism (in 446 and 574). In the year 845, the Tang court was incited to suppress Buddhism once again, and for three years it pursued this policy of razing monasteries and temples, forcing clergy back into lay life or even killing them, and burning books, images, and properties. Unlike the previous two persecutions, this suppression happened in a unified China and affected all areas. Scholars are in agreement that this event marked the end of Buddhism's intellectual and cultural dominance, as the *sangha* never recovered its former glory. The Tiantai and Huayan schools experienced some revivals thereafter, but lost most of their vigor. The Pure Land and Chan schools, being much less dependent upon patronage and scholarship, fared better and became the two dominant schools of Buddhism in China thereafter. After the persecution, Chan communities experimented with new teaching methods that circumvented conventional teaching and inculcated a dramatic, instantaneous experience of enlightenment. The leading figures in this movement were Mazu Daoyi (709–788), Baizhang Huaihai (749–814), Huangbo (d. 850), Linji Yixuan (founder of the Linji school, d. 866), Dongshan Liangjie (807–869), and Caoshan Benji (840–901), the two founders of the Caodong school.

After the Tang, the intellectual vigor of Buddhism was eclipsed by the rise of Neo-Confucianism in the Song dynasty. Nevertheless, there were significant figures and movements during this time. Many figures worked to reconcile the very different outlooks and methods of the Chan and Pure Land schools, notably Yongming Yanshou (904–975) and Yunqi Zhuhong (1532–1612). The latter was also part of a revival of Chan in the latter half of the Ming dynasty that also included Cipo Zhenke (1543–1603), Hanshan Deqing (1546–1623), and Ouyi Zhixu (1599–1655). All agreed that Pure Land and Chan, though differing in method, strove toward the same goal, though Hanshan and Cipo still tended to define this goal in Chan terms. Zhixu, however, emphasized Pure Land teaching almost exclusively and came to be regarded as one of the patriarchs (*zu*) of this school.

From the Ming to the Qing dynasty, Buddhism stagnated (although it remained strong in the central eastern seaboard) until the end of the 19th century, when there was a revival of interest in it as a part of the Chinese heritage that could be brought out to counter western culture's claims of superiority. During the early years of the 20th century, figures such as Ouyang JIngwu (1871–1943) and the monk Taixu (1889–1947) sponsored new editions of the scriptures and advocated a modernized educational system that would bring Buddhism into alignment with modern currents of thought.

The Communist victory in 1949 cut short the revival of Buddhism, as the new regime tried to undercut all societal support for religion in general. The Cultural Revolution proved a catastrophe for Buddhism during the 1960s and 1970s, as Red Guards destroyed many temples and treasures, and clergy were forced to return to lay status and submit to re-education. However, after the death of Communist leader Mao Zedong in 1976 and the passing of many of his allies, the government has grown more tolerant, and many monasteries are back in operation. Currently, the Chinese Buddhist Association is a thriving organization, and Chinese universities sponsor the academic study of Buddhism. To what extent Buddhism will recover from the setbacks of the Mao era still remains to be seen.

Although formal schools did exist throughout the history of Buddhism in China as listed above, they rarely came into direct conflict with each other, being seen as alternative ''gates'' set out for practitioners of differing circumstances and temperaments. The most common form of practice is that of Pure Land, wherein Buddhists invoke the name of Amitābha-buddha in order that they might gain rebirth in his Pure Land called Sukhāvatī upon their death. With this as a basis, they might also practice Chan meditation, chanting of scriptures, and other practices in order to build up merit.

In addition, there are popular practices as well. Among these are the *fahui*, or ''dharma-meetings'' of various sorts. Some are seasonal, such as those that take place at the spring and autumn festivals, and the Ghost Festival that takes place on the 15th day of the seventh lunar month. Other events are sponsored by private patrons, such as the ''Ocean and Land Dharma Meeting'' (*shuilu fahui*), and the ''Release of the Burning Mouths'' (*yuqie yankou*), both long and very complicated ceremonies intended to better the circumstances of the patron's deceased ancestors.

JAPAN

Buddhism first arrived at the imperial court in Japan during the sixth century, when a Korean delegation brought a buddha-image and some scriptures as gifts for the emperor. During the earliest period, the court and aristocratic families understood Buddhism as a variant of their native religion, and used it primarily as a way to cure illnesses and gain supernatural protection for the nation. Prince Shōtoku (572–621) is credited with being among the first to see Buddhist teachings as distinct from the native cults and to have understood Buddhism to some degree on its own terms. He is thought to have composed commentaries to several scriptures, and he fostered a program of rapid temple construction.

The Nara Period. During the Nara period, Buddhist activity took place on two fronts: the clergy were trying to understand the newly imported texts, while the government put Buddhist rituals and organizations to work for the welfare of the state. As to the first, the so-called ''Six Schools of Nara Buddhism'' comprised groups of clergy who concentrated on the texts and thought of six different Chinese schools: (1) the Sanron school focused on Sanlun teachings; (2) the Kegon school took up Huayan studies; (3) the Ritsu school concentrated on monastic precepts and ordinations; (4) the Jōjitsu school studied Satyasiddhi doctrines; (5) the Hossō school dealt with Faxiang teachings; and (6) the Kusha school read the *Abhidharmakośa*, a ''Hinayana'' work attributed to the Indian philosopher Vasubandhu. The few scholar-monks who engaged in these studies mostly lived in the capital and were housed in the main temple there, called the Tōji. Outside of this government-sponsored establishment, a few self-ordained practitioners left society and lived in the mountains performing austeries or magical services for ordinary people. In addition to the scholarly activity in the capital, the principle activity of clergy was to perform rituals on behalf of the imperial family and the aristocracy.

The Heian Period. The Heian period saw a movement of Buddhism away from government centers and out among the people, although this movement fell far short of a full-scale popularization of the religion. During this time both Saichō (767–822) and Kūkai (774–835) journeyed to China to deepen their knowledge of Buddhism. Saichō went to study Tiantai doctrines, but while waiting for a ship to take him home, he encountered a monk who practiced esoteric (or tantric) rituals. After a short period of training and the conferral of the proper initiation, he returned to Japan and settled on Mt. Hiei, where he established the Tendai school to be a successor to the Chinese Tiantai school. However, because the real patronage came from the performance of esoteric rituals, he divided this new school's focus between the exoteric doctrines of Tiantai and esoteric ritual performance. In addition, he asked for and received permission for his school to ordain its own monks independently of the Ritsu school, making use of a set of ''bodhisattva precepts'' rather than the usual monastic precepts.

Meanwhile, Kūkai went to China exclusively to receive training in esoteric texts and rituals, and the Shingon school that he established on Mt. Kōya upon his return concentrated solely on esoteric Buddhism, and for a time outshone the Tendai school in patronage and popularity.

The relationship between Buddhism and its assembly of buddhas and bodhisattvas and the Shintō pantheon continued to concern many in Japan, and during the Heian period the theory known as *honji-suijaku*, or ''original nature and provisional manifestation,'' came to dominate. According to this theory, the local *kami* of Shintō were manifestations of various buddhas and bodhisattvas that appeared in Japan to teach the people and protect the nation. In this way, both religions could be accommodated in a single institution that incorporated both Buddhist and Shintō personnel and practices (the *jingūji*, or ''shrine-temple'').

The Kamakura Period. By the opening years of the Kamakura period, however, the Tendai school was the largest and most powerful of the eight schools in existence at that time, and its broad focus on both doctrinal and esoteric study and practice, as well as its laxity, corruption, and militancy (as seen in its infamous ''monk-soldiers,'' or *sōhei*), made it the front of reform movements and schools. The following figures emerged from Tendai to establish new schools:

(1) Pure Land: Hōnen (1133–1212) founded the Jōdoshū; Shinran (1173–1262) the Jōdo Shinshū; and Ippen (1239–1289) the Jishū.

(2) Zen: Eisai (or Yōsai, 1141–1215) founded the Rinzai school, which took its lineage of dharma-transmission from the Chinese Linjii school; and Dōgen (1200–1253) the Sōtō school, derived from the Chinese Caodong lineage.

(3) Nichiren (1222–1282) founded the Nichiren school, which asserted the primacy of the *Lotus Sutra* (*Myōhō Renge Kyō*) over all other scriptures and recommended the constant repetition and praise of its title as the sole means of salvation.

In addition to the formal establishment of these schools and their institutions, the tradition of asceticism continued under the name *shugendō*, or ''the way of experiential cultivation.'' Drawn primarily from the ranks of Tendai and Shingon esoteric clergy, practitioners lived in the mountains and practiced by fasting, repentance, esoteric rituals, and long, arduous journeys through the mountains that covered as much as 50 miles in a single day.

Ashikaga and Tokugawa Periods (1392–1868). By the end of the Kamakura Period, Buddhism was a significant presence at all levels of Japanese society. In the 15th century, Jōdo Shinshū adherents formed popular leagues called *ikkō ikki*, which rose up in rebellion against local aristocratic rule in Kaga and in 1488 took control of the province themselves. In 1571 the *shōgun* Oda Nobunaga, distrustful of the enormous landholdings and secular power of Buddhist monasteries, attacked and razed the headquarters of Tendai on Mt. Hiei, dispersing its *sōhei* once and for all, and he suppressed many other Buddhist establishments. On the other hand, the pervasive presence of Buddhist institutions could be a source of strength for the government. For instance, after the ban on Christianity in 1612 and the subsequent expulsion of Christian missionaries, the government required all citizens to register with local Buddhist temples beginning in 1640, effectively coopting these institutions as a census bureau.

Buddhism's close cooperation with and support by the government in this way led to an inevitable decline, although a few notable figures stand out as exemplars: Takuan (1573–1645), Bankei Eitaku (1622–93), and Hakuin (1685–1768) in the Zen school, and Rennyo (1415–1499) and Shimaji Mokurai (1838–1911) of the Pure Land school, to name a few. However, as the Tokugawa period drew to a close in the early 19th century, the real locus of religious vitality was in Confucianism and various intellectual and spiritual renewal movements within Shintō. In addition, the first appearance of the so-called "New Religions" such as Tenrikyō offered real competition for the loyalty of the peasants and the middle classes.

The Meiji and Modern Periods. When the Meiji emperor succeeded in restoring real political and executive power to the imperial family in 1868, one of his first acts was to abrogate the *honji-suijaku* understanding of the relationship between Buddhism and Shintō, and declared the two put asunder. He declared a persecution of Buddhism during the first decade or so of the Meiji period, but the attack galvanized Buddhists, and they successfully demanded recognition under the new constitution. At the same time, Buddhist chaplains who accompanied Japanese troops in China, Korea, Taiwan, and southeast Asia, as well as missionaries who traveled to America and Europe to participate in the 1893 World's Parliament of Religions and to settle abroad, gave Japanese Buddhism an international presence. While all schools of Japanese Buddhism came to Hawaii and the American mainland with the large numbers of immigrants at that period, Zen had the most success in making an impression on Euro-American culture. The westward expansion of Japanese Buddhism accelerated after World War II.

At the same time, social changes taking place in modern Japan have fostered the development of many Buddhist-derived "New Religions," most of which sprang from offshoots of the Nichiren school and its devotion to the *Lotus Sutra*. Examples include the Nichiren Shōshū and its now-independent lay branch, the Sōka Gakkai, and Risshō Kōsekai.

Contemporary Japanese Buddhism is a combination of the old and the new: even the most ancient of the Nara schools continues to co-exist alongside the newest of the "New Religions." The Sōtō and Jōdo Shinshū schools are the largest of the traditional schools, and Buddhism remains completely integrated as a vital part of Japanese life and culture.

TIBET

The form of Buddhism to be described here pervades the entire Tibetan cultural region, an expanse of land that stretches far beyond the borders of the area legally organized as "Tibet" by the government of China, and includes Mongolia (Outer and Inner), Xinjiang Province in China, Nepal, Bhutan, and Kalmuk and Buryat regions of the former Soviet Union.

The indigenous pre-Buddhist religion of this area is conventionally referred to as *bön*, although this term covers more than one form of religion. In older records, it indicates a kind of priest who did funerals and ancestor rites, especially for the royal houses. In later centuries, the term *bönpo* came to refer to a distinct religious tradition that, while opposing itself to Buddhism, incorporated many elements of Buddhism into its worldview and practices. The earliest records use the term *chö* to refer to the practices of the ordinary people, which included shamanistic practices and an animistic worldview, and was aimed at the propitiation of ancestors, deities, and demons that inhabited the natural world.

Inception of Buddhism and the "first dissemination." The origins of Buddhism in Tibet are not entirely clear. Legend has it that a Sanskrit Buddhist scripture descended from the sky into the court of king Tho tho rt gnyan btsan (pron. "Totori Nyentsen," b. *c.* 173 A.D.), although other sources say it arrived with a delegation from India. Better documentation is available for the importation (or, more accurately, the encompassment) of Buddhism under the great military ruler Srong btsan sgam po (pron. "Songtsen Gampo," *c.* 618–650 A.D.). Under his leadership, the Tibetan empire expanded to many areas where Buddhism was already active, and through two of his political marriages to princesses from Nepal and China, Buddhism came into the court as his wives brought their own chaplains and rites with them. It may be debated whether Srong btsan sgam po himself ever "converted" to Buddhism, but he certainly respected his wives' piety and supported their efforts to build temples.

Srong btsan sgam po also sent emissaries to Kashmir to aid in Tibet's cultural advancement. Some of the scholars he sent remained in this region for many years and devised a written script for Tibet based on the northern Indian Gupta script, and also utilized rules of Sanskrit grammar to regularize Tibetan usage. This laid the groundwork for highly accurate translations of Sanskrit Buddhist texts in the ensuing decades.

The first devout Buddhist king was Khri srong lde btsan (pron. "Trisong Detsen," *c.* 740–798 A.D.). He invited the Indian Buddhist sage Śāntarakṣita to Tibet, but upon the monk's arrival, a series of natural calamities gave the Bön priests at the imperial court an opportunity to oppose the importation of Buddhism on the grounds that it angered the local spirits and presented a danger to the country. As Śāntarakṣita left, he advised the king to call the tantric adept Padmasambhava to court, as the latter's skill in tantric ritual could pacify the local deities.

Padmasambhava arrived in Tibet not long afterward and demonstrated his ability to defeat all of the spirits and demons of Tibet massed against him. With the spirits pacified, Śāntarakṣita was able to return, and the two Indian monks and the king established the first Tibetan monastery in the capital in 775 A.D. in celebration. It was completed in 766 and consecrated in 767 with the initiation of seven Tibetans into the monastic order, an event remembered as the inception of monastic Buddhism in Tibet. After this, the king set about the task of translating Buddhist scriptures into Tibetan. He sent young monks abroad for language study, and also invited monk-scholars from India, Kashmir, and China to come and assist with translation efforts.

The presence in the court of monks from these various areas ensured that doctrinal controversies would arise, and so in 792 the king arranged for a debate to be held in Lhasa between proponents of the Indian model of practice that involved a slow and arduous process of removing defilements and errors from the mind over a long period of time, and the Chinese Chan position of ''sudden enlightenment'' that held that one attains full enlightenment all at once. While most scholars doubt that such a debate ever took place or that the issue was settled all at once, the fact remains that in the long run the Indian view prevailed, and Chinese-style Buddhism lost its foothold.

It is said that the Tibetan translations preserve many texts no longer extant in their original Sanskrit perfectly, not only because Tibetan grammar had already been systematized along Sanskrit lines, but because under the reign of King Ral pa can (pron. ''Relbachen,'' r. 815–836), the translation bureaus operating in Tibet set standards and translation equivalences and revised the grammars and scripts to facilitate the accurate representation of Sanskrit expressions and concepts. This constitutes the period of the ''old dissemination'' of Buddhism, and the texts produced in this period continue to be favored by the Nyingma School.

Ral pa can's lavish support of Buddhism, and his lack of skill in government, angered many, and he was assassinated by two ministers. His successor vigorously persecuted Buddhism, but without much success outside the immediate environs of the capital. He was assassinated in turn, marking the end of Tibet's period of empire.

The ''second dissemination.'' Local rulers maintained an interest in Buddhism, however, an interchanges with Indian monks continued. During this period, King Btsan po 'khor re (pron. ''Tsenpo Khore,'' late 10th century) of the western region of Guge, became a monk and sent many young monks abroad as well as inviting Indian monks to Tibet, thus beginning the period of the ''second dissemination.'' The greatest of the visitors was the Bengalese monk Atiśa (982–1054), who arrived in 1042. Atiśa was the foremost Buddhist scholar in India, and a master of both monastic and tantric practices. While in Tibet, his personal authority allowed him to correct deviations from Indian standards, and he also composed the treatise *Lamp for the Path to Enlightenment*, a work important for its ordering of both scholastic doctrine and tantric ritual into a single system. His disciples founded the first real ''school'' of Tibetan Buddhism, called the bKa' gdams pa (pron. ''Kadampa'') Order.

The period of Mongol suzerainty (roughly spanning the 13th century) saw the rise of Buddhism's political power as the khans looked to religious leaders such as Sakya Pandita for advice and counsel. With political power and prestige at stake, many monasteries had their own private armies, and the Mongol court often had to intervene at this time to quell violent internal disputes. The Mongol period also saw the compilation of the Tibetan Buddhist Canon.

During the late 1300s and early 1400s, the great scholar Tsong Kha pa (1357–1419) set about systematizing and reforming Tibetan Buddhism. His efforts gave rise to the dGe lugs pa (pron. ''Gelukba''), or ''System of Virtue'' school. The school's scholarly rigor and strict adherence to monastic discipline soon won it the respect of the masses and the envy of rival schools. In 1578 the dGe lugs leader bSod nams rgya mtsho (pron. ''Sönam Gyatso,'' 1543–1588) visited the Mongol chieftain Altan Khan, who was impressed with him and gave him the title Ta le bla ma, usually romanized as Dalai Lama, meaning ''Ocean Guru.'' Since that time, the Dalai Lama has been the head of the dGe lugs order, and is considered to be an incarnation of the bodhisattva Avalokiteśvara. Because of the political ascendancy of the dGe lugs Order, the Dalai Lama has been the political head of Tibet as well as the head of that monastic order, a fact that causes no small resentment among the lamas of other schools.

The latest great turning point for Tibetan Buddhism came with the Communist takeover of China in 1949, followed by the invasion of Tibet in 1951. At first the Chinese Communist Party (CCP) tried to co-opt the current Dalai Lama in order to facilitate control of the territory, but the relationship became impossible to maintain, and the Dalai Lama fled across the border into India in 1959. Since that time, Tibetan Buddhism has existed primarily in diaspora, as monks and nuns in Tibet itself have been imprisoned and tortured and monasteries destroyed. While catastrophic in its effects in Tibet itself, the self-imposed exile of the Dalai Lama and many other Buddhist lamas and leaders has also enabled Tibetan Buddhism to spread to all parts of the world, and is today one of the most widespread forms of Buddhism among European, Australian, and American adherents.

Practices. Tibetan Buddhism since the time of Tsong kha pa has been a systematic mixture of a highly visual meditation system, scholastic philosophy refined in a highly formal practice of debate and study, and tantric ritual. This latter is frequently misunderstood as consisting primarily in sexual yogas, but Tsong kha pa himself defined tantra in terms of ''deity yoga.''

This means that the student, under the supervision of his guru, associates himself with a given buddha or bodhisattva in a ritual setting, and then practices visualization techniques that enable him to generate an internal iconic image of that buddha or bodhisattva, sometimes in sexual union with a consort. This sexual union symbolizes the conjoining of wisdom and method, meaning that the wisdom that sees the ultimate non-differentiation of all phenomena and beings, is conjoined with the need to act in this world compassionately, which requires differentiation and the assignment of values. For all but the most enlightened, these two ways of relating to the world are incompatible, and the practitioner shuttles between the two, utilizing wisdom while in meditation and method while acting in the world. However, the visualization of the student's associated buddha or bodhisattva in union with his consort uses the dissolution of personal boundaries experienced in sexual union to symbolize the rupture of the boundary between wisdom and method enjoyed by the most highly enlightened beings, so that the two become like ''water poured into water,'' completely coinherent and indistinguishable. While some practitioners will realize this through actual ritualized sexual contact with a partner, in most cases it is done through symbol and visualization alone.

At the same time, the student meditates on the nature of the being so visualized, realizing that there is also no ultimate distinction between himself and that being (since the image is clearly understood as generated within the student's own mind) without collapsing himself and the buddha into a single being (since the buddha or bodhisattva also has an independent existence).

Tibetan Buddhism has also distinguished itself through the arts. There is a highly developed practice of dancing for various occasions, and Tibetan monks are widely renowned for their chanting, which employs vocal techniques that enable them to sing notes that are normally well below the human vocal range. There also exist highly refined techniques in butter sculpture and sand painting, both arts that intentionally employ perishable materials in order to emphasize the impermanence of all achievements. Finally, there are very well articulated conventions of painting and sculpture in more permanent media.

KOREA

The Three Kingdoms Period (*c.* 1–668). Buddhism was introduced into the Korean peninsula when the local tribes were first consolidating into three large kingdoms (Koguryŏ, Paekche, and Silla), and when Chinese religion, writing, calendrics, and so on were making inroads into Korean culture. Official histories give the date of Buddhism's introduction as 372 A.D., when a Chinese monk arrived in Koguryŏ bringing scriptures and images.

The Unified Silla Period (668–918). Silla came to prominence in the sixth century, and Buddhism became the official court religion under King P phung (r. 514–539), who used it as part of an ideological campaign to justify the newly established institution of kingship. He strengthened Korean ties with China and sent delegations of young men there to study Buddhism. The Unified Silla period also marked one of the high points of Korean Buddhist art.

During the early Unified Silla period, scholar-monks such as Wŏnhyo (617–686), Ŭisang (625–702), and Wŏnch'uk (631–696) took advantage of the peace and stability to travel to China and work with eminent masters and translators, returning to Korea to share the fruits of their study. Through their efforts, Korean Buddhism absorbed scholastic forms of Buddhist thought such as Huayan (K.: Hwaŏm), Consciousness-only (Ch. Weishi; K. Yusik), and *tathāgata-garbha* thought, and also took in more popular forms, most notably Pure Land (K: Chŏngt'o). Wŏnhyo in particular contributed to the systematization of scholastic Buddhism into an overarching structure called ''t'ong pulgyo'' or ''unified Buddhism,'' and disseminated Pure Land practice widely among the masses.

During this period in China, the Chan, or meditation, school was coming to prominence, and its methods and teachings began filtering into Korea during the seventh century. However, it was during the period of instability and upheaval at the end of the Silla period beginning about 780 that the Chan school, known in Korea as Sŏn, came into its own. During this period many students of Hwaŏm and other intellectual schools began traveling to China to study Sŏn while the government established a system of interlinked official temples to foster Sŏn practice.

The Koryŏ Period (918–1392). T'aejo, the founder of the Koryŏ dynasty, was a devout Buddhist and even left instructions to his heirs stating that the success of the nation depended upon the vitality of Buddhism. With governmental backing, the monasteries engaged in extensive economic activity, and even retained private armies to protect their interests. Such extensive material resources permitted the publication of the entire Buddhist canon between 1210 and 1231. When the woodblocks from this first printing were destroyed by Mongol invasions in 1232, a new set of blocks was ordered, which were completed between 1236 and 1251. Some 81,000 of these blocks remain stored at the Haein-sa on Mt. Kaya in southern Korea.

Buddhism's political and economic power led to increasing worldliness and corruption. In addition, the schools of doctrinal study and meditation had difficulty defining their unity, and often quarreled very publicly. This situation led monks such as Ŭich'ŏn (d.u.) and Chinul (1158–1210) to initiate efforts at reform and definition. The former, a prince of the royal court, remained too partial to the doctrinal schools to have much success, but the latter, through both scholarship and meditative attainment, did bring about some degree of unity. He drew upon the Chinese master Zongmi's (780–841) pioneering work to effect his synthesis and also spread the method of *kōan* practice among Sŏn adherents. Later figures such as T'aego Pou (1301–1382) continued his efforts, and strengthened Sŏn. Nevertheless, Buddhism in the latter part of the Koryŏ went into a decline as corruption and decadence worsened, and these set the scene for Buddhism's formal suppression.

The Chosŏn Period (1392–1910). The fall of Koryŏ in 1392 and its replacement by the heavily pro-Confucian Yi dynasty spelled the end of Korean Buddhism's golden age and the beginning of a period of persecution and declining influence. As time went by, stronger and stronger anti-Buddhist measures went into effect. These included a halt to new temple construction; restrictions on ordinations; the actual closing of monasteries in urban areas and their gradual isolation to remote mountain sites; and a proscription on travel by monks and nuns, which ended in their being forbidden from entering cities altogether. The panoply of doctrinal and meditative schools in existence at the end of the Koryŏ were reduced to only two: doctrinal study and Sŏn, and by the early 20th century, only the latter remained.

The Japanese annexation (1910–1945). In August 1910, the Japanese government officially annexed Korea. Ironically, this development actually helped bring to an end Buddhism's long suppression. Since the Japanese saw Buddhism as a common element with Korean culture, they demanded the lifting of many of the restrictions imposed on the clergy by the Yi dynasty. Monks and nuns could freely travel and enter cities once again, and new temples could be constructed closer to population centers. However, Japanese favor proved a mixed blessing: the Japanese also exerted pressure on Korean monks and nuns to abandon their distinct ways of life and practice in order to adopt Japanese Buddhist practices, and to give up much of their institutional independence. The most contentious issues concerned clerical marriage and the addition of wine and meat to the diet, trends that had marked Japanese Buddhist life for some time. Some monks (though no nuns) adopted the new style, while others did not, thus setting the stage for the conflicts that ensued during the post colonial period.

After the war (1945–present). With the Japanese withdrawal in 1945, conflict broke out between monks who had taken wives and abandoned many of the normal monastic precepts, and those who had not. These latter insisted upon the full restoration of celibacy and the strict enforcement of traditional rules, and they further insisted that the former group relinquish control of monastic properties. The reformers, consolidated under the now-dominant Chogye Order, eventually won out after several court battles, legislative victories, and open hostilities. Thus, after a painful transition period, married monks left the monasteries, and monastic life returned to earlier standards.

After that, the Chogye Order has overseen the revival and revitalization of Korean Buddhism. Some bitterness broke out in the late 1980s and early 1990s between Buddhists and Christians (the latter group having grown dramatically over the last century), leading to the burning of some temples, but overall, Buddhism has once again taken its place as an integral and harmonious part of Korean society.

VIETNAM

The history of Buddhism in the territory now covered by the country of Vietnam dates back at least to the second century A.D. Its territory was under Chinese hegemony through the tenth century, but materials relating the history of Buddhism during the period of Chinese dominance are scarce. Stories dating from this period show the presence of monastic Buddhism, and present tales of scripture-chanting, the erection of images, and the miraculous intervention of monks, and early records also indicate that the late Han-dynasty governor of Jiaozhou, Shi Xie (Si Nhiep) had a large number of Chinese and Central Asian monks in his entourage. Official Chinese court records speak of eminent and accomplished monks from Jiaozhou who made their way to the northern capitals, showing that there were sufficient resources there for them to receive detailed training in doctrine, scripture, and meditation, and there are also records of foreign monks who settled in Jiaozhou to carry out translation activities. The monk Yijing (635–713), a traveler and historian, mentions that several of them, having taken the southern maritime route to and from India, stopped off in Jiaozhou.

In many respects, Buddhism in Vietnam during this period was simply an extension of Chinese Buddhism. However, there was another strain of Buddhism active in the area at this time. Waves of Indian cultural exports had made their way across southeast Asia, penetrating as far as Indonesia, and Theravāda forms of Buddhism were among these. Many people in the southern part of Vietnam were more influenced by this form of Buddhism than by Chinese Mahāyāna Buddhism, and so Vietnam came to be the meeting place for the two streams: Mahāyāna going north from India along the Silk Road, down into China, then into Vietnam, and Theravāda going south along the seacoasts through Thailand, Laos, and Cambodia, and into Vietnam. Vietnamese Buddhism, as a result, is a unique mixture of Mahāyāna and Theravāda forms.

By the time Vietnam achieved independence from China in the tenth century, Buddhism had been an integral part of the cultural landscape for over 800 years. The first emperor of independent Vietnam, Dinh Bo Linh, put together a system of hierarchical ranks for government officials, Buddhist monks, and Daoist priests after ascending to power in 968 A.D. Thereafter, Buddhist monks were part of the national administration, serving the ruler as advisors, rallying the people in times of crisis, and attending to the spiritual needs of the masses.

It was the Lý Dynasty (1010–1225) that willingly coopted diverse elements in its task of constructing a national culture and identity. In this climate, many schools of Buddhism were able to exist side by side and compete in an open religious marketplace, further facilitating the intermingling of Mahāyāna and Theravāda forms. Archaeological evidence also indicates that tantric Buddhism had also made its way into Vietnam during this time (stelae with mantras inscribed on them have been discovered). During this time, Buddhism also became more widely disseminated among the common people, as monks came into villages and ''converted'' local deities, ancestors, and culture heroes to the religion and declared them now ''protectors'' of the dharma. This move worked to unify the disparate local cults under the Buddhist umbrella, and aided in the unification of the country.

In return, the Lý kings supported Buddhism lavishly: giving stipends to eminent monks, erecting and refurbishing temples, and sending envoys to eightChina in search of scriptures. In this way, new developments in Chinese Buddhism were noted in Vietnam, particularly with the importation of Chan works. This created a dichotomy between an older form of Buddhism that was highly syncretistic and incorporated many elements and practices under its umbrella, and a newer Buddhism that inclined to a purer Chinese nature, centered mostly on Chan.

Chan study and practice became more entrenched under the Tran dynasty (1225–1400), although the older forms also remained vital. Tran rulers sponsored the establishment of the first actual ''schools'' of Buddhism in Vietnam, beginning with the Truc Lam (Bamboo Grove) Chan School founded by the third Tran king. Missionary monks also arrived continuously from China, bringing both the Lin-chi and Ts'ao-tung Schools into Vietnam, and they found a ready audience among the Tran aristocracy.

In the 15th century, the Vietnamese began to conquer and absorb parts of Cambodia, strengthening the interchange between the Vietnamese Chan of the elites and the Theravāda teachings and practices of the Cambodians. The country took its current shape during the 18th century, and the country's unique blend of schools of Buddhism was fixed from that time. The French occupation of Indochina, which gave the different ethnic groupings of the land a common tongue, facilitated further interchange between different forms of Buddhism.

During the early 20th century, many educated Vietnamese began abandoning Mahāyāna Buddhism, which seemed superstitious, in favor of Theravāda Buddhism, which seemed more pragmatic and this-worldly. An instrumental figure in this evolution was Le Van Giang, who studied Theravāda meditation with a Cambodian teacher, took the name Ho-Tong, and came back to Vietnam to build the first formally Theravāda temple near Saigon. From this headquarters he began actively disseminating Theravāda Buddhism in the local language, and produced translations of the Pāli scriptures into Vietnamese. The Vietnamese Theravāda Buddhist Sangha Congregation was formally established in 1957, making what had formerly been an element dispersed throughout Vietnamese Buddhism in a diffuse manner into a formal school to rival the Chinese-style Chan schools.

During the Vietnam War, Buddhist monks were active in efforts to bring hostilities to a close, and many of them immolated themselves publicly to protest the war. Others went abroad to propagate Vietnamese Chan, notably Thich Nhat Hanh.

[C. B. JONES]

MYANMAR (BURMA)

By ancient tradition, Theravāda Buddhism was introduced into Myanmar by two of Asoka's missionaries from India. Centuries later heretical Indian teachers came via Nepal and Tibet to spread a mixture of *Mahāyāna* and *Tantra.* King Anawrahta (A.D. 1044–77), who unified Myanmar, adopted *Hīnayāna* as the state religion, curbed the heretic sect, inaugurated the era of temple building, and appointed his religious adviser as superior general of the order. Although disorganized by the Mongol occupation of 1287 and subsequent Shan raids, the order was revived by Dammazedi (1472–92), who sent monks to Sri Lanka to secure valid admission. In 1871 King Mindon Min convened the fifth Buddhist council in Mandalay, but with the British annexation of Upper Myanmar in 1885, Buddhism ceased to be the state religion.

Belief. The Burmese and the Shan Buddhists believe in the ''Four Noble Truths,'' the requital of actions, the acquisition and sharing of merits, rebirth and *nirvāna,* the canon, impermanence, and impersonality. They combine the pre-existing animistic belief system and cult of the ancestors for assistance with worldly concerns and the Buddhist belief that all gods and spirits are of no help on the journey to liberation. They propitiate the spirits of their ancestors and hostile goblins and heed good and ill omens. The Burmese, instead of adopting pure Buddhism as a philosophy of life and as an outlet for some form of social activity, take refuge in the warmer and more personal contact with the spirits to satisfy their deeper religious sense of dependence, need, and survival.

Order and cult. Burmese monarchism is organized according to that of Sri Lanka. Any male of over seven years of age may join the order as a novice (*koyin*). After initiation (*upazin*) a monk must observe the 227 monastic rules. Every morning young monks and novices go out to beg for their daily food. The monks perform certain daily exercises, assemble fortnightly for their confession chapter (*uposatha*), and in the lenten season (*wa*) make their annual retreat.

Buddhism in Myanmar has neither a formal head nor a centralized organization. Every village has a monastery (*kyaung*) with a monk (*pongyi*) in charge and a nearby pagoda. Worship at the shrines is reverential and apart from a few community exercises it is individual. Intellectual monks pray to nobody and for nothing. Devotions and private petitions to the Buddha are popular among the masses. Many pray hoping for a blessing in return, and others repeat Buddha's words with a pure heart as an infallible means of acquiring merit. The worship of images, relics, and spirits is popular. The New Year Feast (*Thingyan*) celebrates the annual visit of the king of the spirits, Thagyamin. The beginning of the lenten season is marked by devotions, floats of *nats* (spirits), and a show of Buddha's birth-stories (*zat*). The end of the season commemorates Buddha's return from the Tawadeintha heaven.

Despite the lack of a central leadership and organization, most Myanmar are devout Buddhists deeply attached to the order.

THAILAND

Theravāda Buddhism was introduced probably by Asoka's missionaries some time after 245 B.C. and superimposed on the native animism. In the first centuries A.D. the country was Hinduized and it later fell under the influence of Tantric *Mahāyāna.* Since 1057, however, a modified *Hīnayāna* has prevailed over *Mahāyāna,* at least among the educated. The stele of King Rama Kamheng of 1292 records two *Hīnayāna* schools. About 1360 Rama Thibodi, founder of the Ayuthia monarchy, believing that it was necessary to get a validation of monastic initiation, sent an abbot to Sri Lanka to enter the order and thus secure the valid succession. King Boromoraja II captured Angkor, the Cambodian capital, and brought back its statesmen and brahmans (1431). Twenty-nine years later his successor used these Cambodian leaders to reorganize the national administration and ceremonial and to establish himself as the divine Buddhist king (*Buddha rājā*), after Cambodia's divine Hindu kings (*Devarājā*). Buddhism remained the state religion, but it exhibited the marked influence of Hinduism and animism. After the fall of the Thai kingdom in 1767, its restorer, Rama I (1782–1809), upheld the national religion, showed devotion to the order, displayed zeal in temple building, promoted the revision of the canon, and published the legal corpus, *Phra Dharmaśāstra.* In its first volume appeared the Indian Code of the patriarch and seer Manu, dealing with the creation of the world, the state of the soul after death, and the customary law concerning religion, caste, and society. Rama IV (1851–68) strove to rid *Hīnayāna* of animistic, Mahayanistic, and Brahmanic accretions and reorganized the order. Rama VII (1925–35) established an ecclesiastical board within the ministry of education, and was made "Upholder of the Faith" by the constitution of 1932, a title reaffirmed by subsequent constitutional drafts.

Order and cult. Although Thai monarchism had derived inspiration, instruction, and valid succession from the order of Sri Lanka, the order had not been centralized because of the Hinduization of the country and the political absolutism dating back to 1460. However, Rama IV, initiated into Western scholarship by Catholic and Protestant missionaries, introduced a hierarchical structure into the order, patterning it after Catholic monarchism. Accordingly, authority was vested in a patriarch assisted by 15 councilors, forming together the supreme chapter. Four leaders were provided for the Mahānikaya school and four for the Dharmayuthika school, and under each there were four subdivision leaders. For each of the ten circles there was an administrator, and provincials served the 70 provinces. Superiors were constituted for the 407 districts, abbots for the precincts, and priors for the temples and monks.

Boys of 12 or more could enter the monastery as pupils. Novices were admitted at any age and for any length of time, but could not become monks before 20. Monks were exempt from military service. They received jurisdiction to initiate others, as well as titles of their own from the ecclesiastical board. Most of the temples had a monastery, and both were generously endowed by the faithful and the government. The initiation rite showed a combination of *Mahāyāna, Hīnayāna,* and animistic elements. Upon initiation each monk received a credential booklet marked with his name; in this he was to keep his own vital statistics, right thumbprint, his picture, the name of his parents, initiator, and teachers, and the records of his transfers, examinations, positions, legal charges, and laicization.

Public worship was conducted by the monks. They were to reserve the morning service to themselves, except on the four *uposatha* days set for the laity. In formal services a leader addressed an invocation to the *devatas* (minor deities) and *nāgas* (serpents) borrowed from Hinduism. The rainy season retreat (*vassa*) was marked with rites and pageantry of Buddhist and Hindu flavor. Some of the life-cycle rites (birthday, tonsure, wedding, and funeral) contained Brahmanic features but were conducted by Buddhist monks with charms, amulets, invocations for good fortune, and the sprinkling of magic water. Despite the orthodox doctrine of impermanence and impersonality, most people believed that their good deeds and Buddha's grace could be applied for the repose of the souls departed. Rites celebrating national holidays were conducted by Brahmans and Buddhists in a mixture of Hinduism and Buddhism.

Buddhist action. Thai Buddhism, which is well organized and state supported, has at its disposal the school, the press, and the state broadcasting system. It freely borrows methods of action from other religions, especially Catholicism. In 1928 the king sanctioned the *Buddhamāmaka* oath, an adaptation of Catholic confirmation, to be taken by students going abroad. The ritual, although inspired by Catholicism, is a mixture of Buddhism and Hinduism. In 1929 Buddhist religious instruction was introduced into all state schools. The Young Buddhists Association (1933), the Buddha Dharma Association (1934), and similar societies promote Buddhist action among the laity. Buddhism is rooted in Thai history, culture, and psychology and remains the soul of the nation.

CAMBODIA

After centuries of rivalry with Hinduism, the religion of the Buddha became established in Cambodia. By the 1st century A.D. the inhabitants, known as the Khmers, had been Hinduized under rulers of Indian and Indonesian descent. But *Hīnayāna,* the conservative Buddhism of Myanmar, was accepted by the Khmers in the 3rd century and flourished along with sects worshipping the Hindu deities Siva and Vishnu. Moreover, according to an inscription of 791 recording the erection of an image of the Buddhist Lokeśvara (*Avalok iteśvara*), *Mahāyāna* had been introduced into Cambodia, probably tinged with *Vajrayāna* Tantric mysticism and the influences of various Hindu cults. Jayavarman II (802–854), the founder of a kingship at Angkor, called his realm Kambudja, established the cult of the divine king (*Devarājā*), deriving his authority from Siva, and, at the expense of Buddhism, upheld a form of Hinduism based on the *Purāṇas,* or treatises on cosmogony.

Spread of Buddhism. Hinduism continued to be strong when Indravarman (877–889) began the construction of a magnificent capital at Angkor, Siva's *linga,* a phallic symbol in stone of his divine authority. His son and successor Yasovarman I (889–900) built temples for the various sects of Siva, Vishnu, Brahmanic Yoga, and *Mahāyāna.* This religious eclecticism gradually disappeared when Jayavarman VII (1181–*c.* 1200), a devout Mahayanist, turned the *Devarājā* cult into that of the *Buddharājā,* the divine Buddhist ruler. In Sri Lanka his son studied *Hīnayāna,* which he introduced into Cambodia. Because of its popular appeal and the monastic school system, *Hīnayāna* eventually became the predominant religion. After 1350 the religious life was so disrupted by Thai invasions that in 1423 Cambodian monks repaired to Sri Lanka to be reinvested, to ensure valid succession and reorganization of the order in accord with orthodox Buddhism. When in 1460 Cambodia lost its independence to Thailand, *Hīnayāna,* largely because of Thai influence, remained the dominant religion.

Belief, order, cult. Cambodian Buddhism is a fusion of the predominant *Hīnayāna* with pristine ancestor and ghost worship, Brahmanism, and *Mahāyāna.* Its Hindu cosmogony, detailed in the sacred books *Trey-Phet* and *Kampi Preas Thomma Chhean,* comprises *Prohm* (*Brahmā*), the eternal, uncreated, and uncreating absolute; the universe of countless triads of worlds (*chakralaveal*) and stars that are worshipped as deities; three categories of paradises; and great and small purgatories where the departed atone for their faults and are reborn on earth or in paradise. The pantheon contains four major Buddhas, including Gautama; *Mettrey* (*Maitreya*), the Buddha that will come at the end of time; countless Brahmanic deities; and all the heavenly beings. The universe is full of ghosts and fantastic animals that are invoked and propitiated by the Cambodians in time of need or fear. Although the core of Cambodian Buddhism is *Hīnayāna,* the monks tend toward a godless monism, and the people, while longing for a transcendent theism, syncretize all religions that have crossed the land.

The order is territorially divided into two regions and subdivided into provinces, each with from ten to 20 monasteries and temples, under the jurisdiction of a superior general. The monastic rules, exercises, and privileges are the same as those found in the Thai order. The monastery, where most Cambodian males spend some time in study and meditation, forms the center of religious and social activities. Each village has its temple. The cult includes court ceremonies, holiday rites, private devotions, propitiations, exorcisms, and conjurations against sickness and evil.

[A. S. ROSSO/C. B. JONES]

EUROPE AND AMERICA

Buddhism arrived in Europe and America in two different ways. First, there have been communities of immigrants into the United States, Australia, and the countries of Europe who have brought Buddhism with them and established communities aimed at their needs. Second, there have been westerners who have converted to Buddhism.

Immigrant groups. Chinese immigrants began coming to the west coast of the United States during the gold rush of 1848, and later to assist in building the transcontinental railroads. The companies in China that arranged for their transportation and employment also took responsibility for building temples in areas of high Chinese concentration. These temples were typically Chinese temples that encompassed the range of the ''three teachings'' of Taoism, Buddhism, and Confucianism, and the few monks who came from China generally performed more rituals for clients than study or meditation. By the end of the 19th century many buildings in San Francisco and New York as well as other cities had a Chinese temple on the top floor.

Japan had been officially closed to all foreign contact since the beginning of the 17th century, but after the forced opening of Japan by Commodore Perry in 1854, the government began allowing Japanese to travel abroad. Many went to Hawaii to work on the sugar plantations, and a Jōdo Shinshū priest arrived in 1889 to serve their needs and provide funeral services. Japanese living on the mainland at this time tended to leave Buddhism behind in an effort to adapt, but later the Jōdo Shinshū established congregations grouped under the Buddhist Churches of America, which continues to cater principally to Japanese immigrant needs. Many Japanese workers also came to South America, and the first Buddhist temple for Japanese immigrants was established in São Paulo, Brazil, in 1932.

Other groups have also established Buddhist temples and monasteries for the benefit of their people living abroad in the west, such as the Thai monastery in Bolivia, North Carolina and Vietnamese temples in the U.S., Canada, and Europe.

Western convert groups. By and large, the majority of native westerners who convert to Buddhism have embraced one of three traditions: Tibetan (mainly dGe lugs), Japanese Zen (and increasingly Nichiren), and Sri Lankan Theravāda. Western awareness of and interest in Buddhism dates back two centuries, to the colonization of India and the activities of Sanskrit scholars who began making and disseminating translations of classic texts. The ideas sparked interest among western intellectuals, such as Emerson, Thoreau, and other New England transcendentalists, and European romanticists such as Friedrich Schlegel, who were influenced by Sir Edwin Arnold's epic poem on the life of the Buddha, *The Light of Asia*, published in 1879, and the Theosophist Henry Steele Olcott's *A Buddhist Catechism*, published in 1881. Arnold himself cooperated with Anagarika Dharmapala (1864–1933) to found the Maha Bodhi Society in England and India in 1891 with the intent of reviving Buddhism in India.

A real turning point was reached when the World Parliament of Religions opened in Chicago in 1893, bringing several significant Asian Buddhist figures to America, such as Soyen Shaku and Dharmapāla. Several of them remained in America after the close of the Parliament and continued missionary activities in many major cities. Dharmapāla opened the American chapter of the Maha Bodhi Society in 1897.

Early in the 20th century, a handful of westerners became sufficiently enthusiastic about Buddhism to travel abroad to seek monastic ordination, while others remained at home and founded Buddhist societies, such as the British Buddhist Society, founded in 1924 as a lodge within the Theosophical Movement, from which it broke free within two years. In the U.S., Japanese Zen missionaries began arriving and working among non-Asian American populations, but met with little success until the 1950s, when D.T. Suzuki (1870–1966) began reaching a wide audience through his writings and talks. In Europe, the largest convert groups were to be found in England and Germany, while very small groups existed in France, Switzerland, and elsewhere.

The end of World War II marked a watershed in the dissemination of Asian Buddhism among non-Asian groups. More Asian missionaries came to the west, and westerners themselves began gaining credentials as teachers and masters within Asian traditions. At this time, Buddhism began making its first inroads into Australia as well. The swelling number of missionaries and teachers meant a growing plurality of styles of Buddhism, and more converts adopted it as a holistic religious commitment rather than as an intellectual alternative. Since the 1970s, the number of Buddhist centers and groups in western countries has risen dramatically, although it should be noted that, by approximately 1990, only in the U.S. and Australia did the number of Buddhists exceed one percent of the population among western nations listed by Baumann (2000:22–23).

Western Buddhist movements. In the late 20th and early 21st centuries, the dichotomy between immigrant and western convert groups became blurred. As the children of immigrants become increasingly westernized, and as children of converts are raised as Buddhists, the outlook of the groups tends to converge, leading to forms of Buddhism that are neither simple transplants of Asian traditions nor western appropriations of such.

Generally, Buddhist groups in the west tend to consist of educated, middle to upper class populations. Their generally modernist outlook leads them to abandon aspects of traditional Asian Buddhism that strike them as ''superstitious,'' such as rites for the dead, veneration of relics, practices intended to create merit, and the transference of this merit to improve the status of deceased family members, and even the ideas of karma and rebirth in some circles. They also have abandoned aspects of Buddhist practice that connected it with traditional communities: the alms begging round, monastic ordinations that functioned as coming-of-age rites, etc.

Buddhism has also been adapted by these groups (as well as by many that remain in Asia) for the conditions of modernity. Emphasis is more on lay practice than on the need for monastic vows, leading to the establishment of ''meditation centers'' rather than monasteries. Much attention has been given to the role of women and the bureaucratization of leadership. Even the tradition of meditation, practiced only by a minority of specialists in traditional Buddhism, has come to the fore as Buddhism serves more psychological and therapeutic needs. As a result, Buddhism in the west, and around the world, is becoming less devotional and pietistic, and more intellectual, rational, and therapeutic.

Globalization. One of the effects of the modern period with its legacy of colonialism and current ease of travel and contact is an unprecedented globalization of Buddhism. The organization of this article itself suggests that Buddhism grew in discrete geographical areas within self-contained cultures, and so indeed it has throughout most of its history. However, the modern period has seen Tibetan Buddhists interacting with Chinese Buddhists, Sri Lankan Buddhist monks traveling to Taiwan to study Chinese in order to read and translate Chinese Buddhist classics, and Japanese Buddhists living side-by-side with western Buddhists who take elements from all previous forms and add some of their own. The result has been the weakening of boundaries and the increase in mutual influence, thus creating a global Buddhism that no longer is defined by boundaries, but by openness.

Aside from the more informal cross-fertilization that modern circumstances helped to foster, this situation has also led to the establishment of Buddhist Organizations with transnational constituencies and aims. The most prominent of these is the World Fellowship of Buddhists, founded in Sri Lanka in 1950. In addition to this umbrella organization, individual Buddhist organizations, once purely local in their operations, have established branch offices and centers in other localities and other countries. Examples include Fo Kuang Shan (Taiwan), the Diamond Sangha (U.S.), and the Insight Meditation Society (Sri Lanka/U.S.).

Bibliography: M. BAUMANN, ''Global Buddhism: Developmental Periods, Regional Histories, and a New Analytical Perspective,'' *Journal of Global Buddhism*, 2 (2000) 1–43; K. CH'EN, *Buddhism in China: A Historical Survey* (Princeton 1964); R. FIELDS, *How the Swans Came to the Lake: A Narrative History of Buddhism in America* (3d ed. Boston 1992); R. GOMBRICH, *Theravada Buddhism: A Social History* (London 1988); P. HARVEY, *An Introduction to Buddhism* (Cambridge, England 1990); A. HIRAKAWA, *A History of Indian Buddhism* (Honolulu 1990); D. LOPEZ, ed., *Buddhism in Practice* (Princeton 1995); A. MATSUNAGA and D. MATSUNAGA, *Foundation of Japanese Buddhism* (2 vols.; Buddhist Books International, 1976); K. MIZUNO, *Buddhist Sutras: Origin, Development, Transmission* (Kosei Pub., 1982); J. POWERS, *Introduction to Tibetan Buddhism* (Snow Lion, 1995); K. SONODA, *Shapers of Japanese Buddhism* (Kosei Pub., 1994); J. STRONG, *The Experience of Buddhism: Sources and Interpretations* (Wadsworth, 1995); D. SWEARER, *The Buddhist World of Southeast Asia* (SUNY, 1995); M. WIJAYARATNA, *Buddhist Monastic Life* (trans. Grangier and Collins; Cambridge, 1990); P. WILLIAMS, *Mahāyāna Buddhism: the Doctrinal Foundations* (London 1989).

[C. B. JONES]

BUFALO, GASPARE DEL, ST.

Founder of the Society of the PRECIOUS BLOOD (CPPS); b. Rome, Jan. 6, 1786; d. there, Dec. 28, 1837. He was educated at the Collegio Romano and while yet a seminarian he catechized, visited hospitals, and reactivated the Santa Galla hospice for homeless men. After ordination (1808) he took as spiritual director Canon Francesco Albertini, known for his devotion to the Precious Blood, and assisted him in establishing a pious union of the Precious Blood in the church of San Nicola in Carcere. As a canon of the church of San Marco, Gaspare was summoned to swear allegiance to NAPOLEON I when the latter gained control of the STATES OF THE CHURCH. For his refusal he spent about four years (1810–14) in exile and prison. Returning to Rome, he was assigned by PIUS VII to preaching missions in the Papal States. Encouraged by the pope, Cardinal Cristaldi, and others, he established the Society of the Precious Blood (August 15, 1815) and opened its first house in the monastery of San Felice in Giano (Umbria). He also advised Bl. Maria De MATTIAS to found the Precious Blood Sisters. The rest of his life was devoted to preaching, spiritual direction, and defense of his society against the sharp objections that were made because of its title. Outstanding was his missionary activity in the bandit-infested areas of the Papal States and the kingdom of Naples. Among his friends were St. Vincent PALLOTTI and Vincenzo STRAMBI. He was beatified on Dec.18, 1904, and canonized on June 12, 1954. Pope John XXIII called him the greatest apostle of the Precious Blood.

Feast: January 2.

See Also: PRECIOUS BLOOD, III (DEVOTION TO).

Bibliography: G. DE LIBERO, *S. Gaspare de Bufalo romano e le sua missione nel sangue di Cristo* (Rome 1954). V. SARDI, *Herald of the Precious Blood: Gaspar del Bufalo,* tr. E. G. KAISER (Minneapolis 1954). G. PICCINI, *L'origine della maschera di Stenterello* (Florence 1898, rep. Bologna 1975). A. DE SANTA CRUZ, *Missionário de Sangue: São Gaspar del Bufalo* (Curitiba 1975). G. PAPÀSOGLI, *Vita e tempi di san Gaspare Del Bufalo* (Turin 1977).

[A. J. POLLACK]

BUFFIER, CLAUDE

French philosopher; b. Warsaw, May 25, 1661; d. Paris, May 17, 1737. His French parents moved to Normandy when he was a child. He studied at Rouen, entered the Jesuits on Sept. 9, 1679, and taught literature at Paris and philosophy and theology at Rouen. He was exiled in 1696 for disputing the Jansenist recommendations of his archbishop (*see* JANSENISM), but he justified himself in Rome and returned to Paris in 1701 to work on the *Journal de Trévoux* until 1731. He wrote widely on religion, philosophy, history, philology, and pedagogy, and was an original, analytical, and penetrating thinker. In his *Traité des premières verités* (English tr. 1780) he shows the influence of DESCARTES, LOCKE, and MALEBRANCHE, but does not follow them. For Buffier, first truths are propositions so evident that they cannot be proved, or refuted, by others more evident. These truths are perceived by the COMMON sense that nature has put in men so that they will judge in a uniform manner. French eclectic philosophers in the 19th century rediscovered Buffier through Thomas REID and the SCOTTISH SCHOOL OF COMMON SENSE. Buffier's successful French grammar (1709) was translated into several languages. The ENCYCLOPEDISTS excerpted extensively from his *Cours des sciences* (1732) without acknowledgment.

Bibliography: P. BERNARD, *Dictionnaire de théologie catholique,* ed. A. VACANT, 15 v. (Paris 1903–50; Tables générales 1951–) 2.1:1167–73. A. DE BIL, *Dictionnaire d'histoire et de géographie ecclésiastiques,* ed. A. BAUDRILLART (Paris 1912–) 10:1083–87. P. MAGNINO, A. MERCATI and A. PELZER, *Dizionario ecclesiastico,* 3 v. (Turin 1954–58) 1:446. L. KOCH, *Jesuiten-Lexikon: Die Gesellschaft Jesu einst und jetzt* (Paderborn 1934); photoduplicated with rev. and suppl., 2 v. (Louvain-Heverlee 1962) 277.

[M. MARTIN]

BUGENHAGEN, JOHANN

Lutheran churchman, known as ''Dr. Pommer''; b. Wollin, Pomerania, June 24, 1485; d. Wittenberg, Saxony, April 20, 1558. Bugenhagen, a Premonstratensian canon, became rector at Treptow (1504), was ordained (1509), and became a lector in Scripture and patrology at Belbuck (1517). Converted by Luther's treatise ''Babylonian Captivity'' (1520), he fled to Wittenberg in 1521 and studied theology. After his marriage (1522), he served as city pastor (1523–57) and held a professorship from 1535. Next to Philip Melanchthon, Bugenhagen was the most influential member of Luther's intimate circle: a lifelong friend, confessor, adviser, and lieutenant, endowed with Melanchthon's moderation and Luther's firmness. His works include commentaries, a Low German translation of the NT (1524) and the Bible (with colleagues, 1533), as well as polemical works against Catholics, Zwinglians, and Anti-Trinitarians. He established Lutheranism in North Germany and Denmark upon request of authorities there, writing church orders between 1528 and 1544 for Brunswick (city), Hamburg, Lübeck, Pomerania, Denmark, Holstein, Brunswick-Wolfenbuettel, and Hildesheim; these emphasized good schools, good administration of church property, good ministers, and liturgical conservatism. In 1537 he went to Denmark, where he crowned King Christian III, consecrated seven men as ''bishops'' or superintendents of the Danish church, and reorganized the University of Copenhagen.

Bibliography: J. BUGENHAGEN, *Sechs Predigten,* ed. G. BUCHWALD (Halle 1885); *Katechismuspredigten, gehalten 1525 und 1532,* ed. G. BUCHWALD (Leipzig 1909) sermons; *Briefwechsel,* ed. O. VOGT (Stettin 1888), letters. E. SEHLING, ed., *Die Evangelischen Kirchenordnungen des 16. Jahrhunderts,* 5 v. (Leipzig 1902–13). H. HERING, *Doktor Pomeranus, Johannes Bugenhagen* (Halle 1888). W. RAUTENBERG, *Johann Bugenhagen* (Berlin 1958). E. WOLF, *Peregrinatio* (Munich 1954), with sketch and bibliog. O. THULIN, *Die Religion in Geschichte und Gegenwart* (Tübingen 1957–65) 1:1504. J. ALLENDORF, *Lexikon für Theologie und Kirche* (Freiburg 1957–65) 2:761.

[R. H. FISCHER]

BUGLIO, LUDOVICO

Missionary and author; b. Mineo, Sicily, Jan. 26, 1606; d. Beijing (Peking), China, Oct. 7, 1682. He was a Jesuit by 1622, and he arrived in China in 1637. He was joined in Szechwan in 1642 by Gabriel de Megalhaens, but their missionary work was interrupted in 1643 when the bandit Chang Hsien-chung desolated the province and made them prisoners. From 1647 to 1651 they were imprisoned by the Emperor in Peking as collaborators of Chang. After further difficulties from 1659 to 1669,

Buglio at last resumed missionary work. He translated much of Aquinas's *Summa theologiae* into Chinese (30 v., Beijing 1654–79, 2d ed. 1930), wrote a treatise of moral theology in Chinese, and translated several liturgical works into Chinese. He delighted the emperor with paintings done in perspective and taught the technique to Chinese artists.

Bibliography: A. DE BIL, *Dictionnaire d'histoire et de géographie ecclésiastiques* (Paris 1912–) 10:1090–93. J. SCHÜTTE, *Lexikon für Theologie und Kirche* (Freiburg 1957–65) 2:762. G. H. DUNNE, *Generation of Giants* (Notre Dame, Ind. 1962).

[B. LAHIFF]

BUGNINI, ANNIBALE

Liturgical reformer and scholar, and titular archbishop of Diocletiana; b. Civatella del Lago (Terni), Italy, June 14, 1912; d. Rome, July 3, 1982. More than any other single person, Annibale Bugnini may be called the chief architect of the Roman liturgical reform. Beginning with his appointment as secretary of the Commission for the Liturgical Restoration by Pope PIUS XII on May 28, 1948, he occupied the critical executive position on the successive bodies of official liturgical revision: secretary of the Preparatory Commission on the Liturgy (1960–62); *peritus* (but not secretary) of the Conciliar Commission on the Liturgy, Second VATICAN COUNCIL (1962–63); secretary of the Consilium for the Implementation of the Constitution on the Liturgy (1964–69); and secretary of the Congregation for Divine Worship (1969–75). During this period he guided, coordinated, and provided continuity in the official reform of the Roman liturgy—from the pre-conciliar revisions of the 1950s and early 1960s to the constitution on the liturgy itself (1963), to the general revision of the ritual books of the Roman liturgy, including those completed only in the years following his leaving office in 1975.

Bugnini was a member of the Congregation of the Missions (Vincentians), ordained a priest in Siena in 1936. Two years later he received the doctorate, with a dissertation on the importance of the liturgy in the Council of TRENT. This was the beginning of his writings in the liturgical field, ranging from scholarly developments to popular publications, with more than 200 items in his bibliography. From 1944 to 1963 he edited the learned journal *Ephemerides liturgicae*; 1,500,000 copies of his 1950 booklet for participation in the liturgy, *La nostra Messa*, were distributed; and he was the editor of the Italian version of the French missals of Feder (1961) and Jounel (1974).

Vatican II. Bugnini's own writings and his professorial appointments at several Roman universities and institutes are of course secondary to his responsibilities in the Roman Curia. Although little heralded at the time, the commission set up by Pius XII in the wake of the encyclical *MEDIATOR DEI* on Christian worship (1947) opened the way to the later conciliar reform. It was this body, with Bugnini as secretary, that produced the reformed rites of HOLY WEEK, a major simplification of the rubrics of the Mass and office, and a revised volume of the Roman Pontifical—all issued by the Roman Congregation of Rites.

When Pope John XXIII established a series of commissions to prepare draft texts in preparation for the Second Vatican Council, Bugnini was the logical choice to direct the work of the liturgical commission, under the presidency of Cardinal Gaetano Cicognani. He was largely responsible for the planning and organization of both the working subcommissions and of the text, which was completed in January 1962. The draft was characterized by its openness to liturgical renewal and change, the influence of the recommendations from the Catholic episcopate (not so well reflected in drafts from other preparatory commissions), and the contributions of liturgical and pastoral specialists, with whom Bugnini had been closely associated in the preceding decade. The success of the enterprise is seen in its ready acceptance by the council, the only draft so accepted during the 1962 period.

In the meantime, however, Bugnini had suffered a personal eclipse. Cardinal Cicognani died shortly after the draft was completed, and his successor, Cardinal Arcadio Larraona, was out of sympathy with the projected constitution and with the preparatory commission's secretary, who was denied continuation as secretary to the conciliar commission when the council opened in October of 1962. During the refinement and amendment of the constitution's draft in the light of the conciliar debate, Bugnini played a lesser formal role as a *peritus* of the commission, but his influence was strong among the members and the other *periti.*

The Consilium. In October of 1963, before the promulgation of the constitution on the liturgy, Pope PAUL VI directed Cardinal Giacomo Lercaro of Bologna to initiate plans for its implementation. These were developed by Bugnini, who was secretary of an informal group assembled by Lercaro, and early in 1964 the post-conciliar commission or consilium was established. This had the task of revising the Roman liturgical books in accord with the conciliar mandate and at the same time promoting the liturgical renewal in close collaboration with the conferences of bishops. The directive role was Bugnini's, and he assembled a large body of consultors who worked in study groups in the preparation of instructions and other documents and above all the revised Latin liturgical books, which would be the exemplars of the vernacular ritual books.

The position of the consilium within the Roman Curia was an uneasy one, since the Congregation of Rites to which the consilium submitted its completed work was not sympathetic, nor were indeed other curial dicasteries. The support of Paul VI, however, enabled the work to go forward, and the enterprise was vastly more massive and successful than the analogous undertaking after the Council of Trent, which had also entrusted liturgical revision to the Roman See (1563). Both Lercaro, the first president of the Consilium, and Bugnini were subjected to severe criticism, often from those whose disaffection was really with the Second Vatican Council and with Paul VI himself, but the latter was determined to carry out the council's decisions faithfully and he personally reviewed each document before promulgation.

The work of the Consilium was carried out through a very broad cooperative effort and processes of consultation and experiment, all guided by Bugnini. Many compromises were needed to satisfy diverse interests, and the projects had to be completed as quickly as possible consonant with scholarly and pastoral professionalism, lest the momentum created by the council be lost. The achievement of the Consilium is best seen in the series of liturgical books, beginning in 1968 with the rites of ordination and continuing thereafter with sections of the traditional missal, ritual, pontifical, and liturgy of the hours according to the Roman rite. The best account of the work is in an exhaustive volume by Bugnini himself, *La riforma liturgica* (1948–1975), published posthumously.

The relationship of the Consilium to the Congregation of Rites was unaffected by the curial reform of 1967, but two years later Paul VI suppressed that congregation, and its work devolved upon the Congregation for the Causes of Saints and the Congregation for Divine Worship; the latter was in effect the successor to the Consilium and continued its work. Bugnini, the first and in fact only secretary of the new congregation, was ordained titular archbishop in February of 1972. His participation in the liturgical reform came to an abrupt end in June of 1975, when the Congregation for Divine Worship was merged with the Congregation for the Sacraments.

Diplomatic Work. At this point Archbishop Bugnini embarked, by papal appointment, on an entirely distinct career in the diplomatic corps of the Holy See. He was named apostolic pro-nuncio in Iran and served there until his death in 1982. During this time he continued writing, producing volumes on Saint Vincent de Paul and on the Church in Iran, as well as the account of the Roman liturgical reform mentioned above. When the U.S. hostages were held captive in Iran in 1974–76, he ministered to them, in a role that was pastoral rather than diplomatic, with visits for eucharistic celebrations whenever permitted.

The part taken by Annibale Bugnini in the 20th-century reform of the Roman liturgy can hardly be exaggerated. He brought to his several positions scholarly background coupled with pastoral experience, marked always by openness to ecclesiological and ecumenical developments. Although neither the constitution on the liturgy nor the several liturgical books can be attributed in their composition or even planning to an individual, his pervasive role from 1948 to 1975 and his impact on the liturgical life of the Church were unique. He suffered greatly from critics within the Roman Curia and from outside, but he bore this patiently as a sign of the successful accomplishment of the conciliar liturgical renewal.

See Also: LITURGICAL BOOKS OF ROMAN RITE; RITES, CONGREGATION OF.

Bibliography: A. BUGNINI, ed., *Documenta Pontificia ad instaurationem liturgicam spectantia (1903–1953)* (Rome 1953); II (1953–59). A. BUGNINI, *La riforma liturgica (1948–1975)* (Rome 1983). T. RICHSTATTER, *Liturgical Law: New Style, New Spirit* (Chicago 1977). G. PASQUALETTI, ''Una vita per la liturgia,'' P. JOUNEL, et al., eds., *Liturgia opera divina e umana: Studi sulla riforma liturgica offeri a S. E. Mons Annibale Bugnini in occasione del suo 70 compleanno* (Rome 1982) 13–28; ''Bibliografia di A. Bugnini,'' *op. cit.*, 29–41.

[F. R. MCMANUS]

BUKHTĪSHŪ'

A Christian Nestorian family prominent in medicine and in the service of the 'ABBĀSID caliphs and their successors from the second half of the 8th to the second half of the 11th century. Their public roles and academic interests were characteristic of physicians in their day. The following ten are identified and described in the literature.

Jūrjīs (George) ibn Jibrīl (Gabriel) ibn Bukhtīshū' (d. after 769) was the director of the hospital of Jundishāpūr, Iran, an institution going back to Sassanian times. He was summoned to Baghdad in 765 to cure the Caliph al-Manṣūr (754–775). His success won him the Caliph's favor. Like many of the family, he knew Greek, Syriac, and Arabic. For the Caliph he translated from Greek into Arabic. Works of his own written in Syriac were later translated into Arabic. After a few years in Baghdad he returned and died in Judishāpūr.

Bukhtīshū' ibn Jūrjīs (d. 801), son of the former, continued the direction of the Jundishāpūr hospital. He was twice summoned to court. Intrigue blocked his stay the first time, but the second time, in 787, he was named by the Caliph Hārūn al-Rashīd (786–809) physician in chief, and he kept his post until he died.

Jabrīl ibn Bukhtīshū' (d. 828), son of the preceding, had a checkered 22 years of service to the court under three caliphs. He was replaced for a while by his son-in-law. New Syriac translations of Galen were placed at his disposal, and he wrote in Arabic on medicine and logic.

Bukhtīshū' (d. 870), son of Jibrīl, succeeded his father and served the Caliph al-Ma'mūn (813–833). Exiled to Jundishāpūr by the Caliph al-Wāthiq (842–847) and recalled too late to cure this Caliph, he served under the Caliph al-Mutawakkil (847–861), only to be exiled again. He had the translation of Galen continued, and he himself wrote a text on bloodletting.

'Ubaid Allāh, probably son of the preceding, was a financial official but died, leaving a son Jibrīl, who followed the family tradition. The date of his death is unknown.

Yuḥanna, illegitimate son of Bukhtīshū', was at first physician of the brother of the Caliph Al-Mu'tamid (870–892). In 893 he became bishop of Mosul, and he was twice an unsuccessful candidate for the office of patriarch. The date of his death is unknown.

Bukhtīshū' ibn Yaḥya cannot be more particularly identified than as a member of the family. He served the Caliph al-Rāḍī (834–940) and was held responsible for the death of Prince Hārūn in 936. The date of his death is unknown.

Jibrīl ibn 'Ubaid Allāh (d. 1006), son of 'Ubaid Allāh, learned medicine in Baghdad. He served the Buwayhid Caliph 'Aḍud al-Dawla (949–983) in Shiraz, Iran, and returned to Baghdad. He went on a pilgrimage to Jerusalem. He declined the invitation to Cairo from the Fāṭimid Caliph al-'Azīz (975–996) but accepted that of the Marwānid at Maiyāfāriqīn (in modern eastern Turkey). He died there at the age of 85.

Abu Sa'id 'Ubaidallah ibn Jibrīl (d. 1058), son of the preceding, lived in Maiyāfāriqīn, a contemporary and friend of Ibn Butlan (d. *c.* 1063). His scholarly work was concerned with medicine, love, and the translation from Syriac of church law on inheritance.

'Alī ibn Ibrahim ibn Bukhtīshū', the last of the family to write, was concerned with ophthalmology. The date of his death is unknown.

Bibliography: G. GRAF, *Geschichte der christlichen arabischen Literatur*, 5 v. (Vatican City 1944–53) 2:109–112, with abundant ref. to mod. literature in Arab. and Western lang. D. SOURDEL, *Encyclopedia of Islam*, ed. B. LEWIS et al. (2d ed. Leiden 1954–) 1:1298. C. BROCKELMANN, *Encyclopedia of Islam*, ed. M. T. HOUTSMA et al., 4 v. (Leiden 1913–38) 1:614–615. E. HAMMERSCHMIDT, *Lexikon für Theologie und Kirche*, ed. J. HOFER and K. RAHNER, 10 v. (2d, new ed. Freiburg 1957–65) 2:551.

[J. A. DEVENNY]

BULGAKOV, MACARIUS

One of the most influential 19th-century Russian theologians and church historians; b. Kursk, Russia, 1816; d. Moscow, 1882. In the world he was called Michael Petrovich, but he took the name of Macarius when he received the monastic tonsure. As the son of a country priest from the region of Kursk, he studied at the Ecclesiastical Academy of Kiev. Upon completion of his studies, he was appointed to the chair of history then recently created at the academy. In 1842 he was called to the Ecclesiastical Academy of St. Petersburg to teach theology, and he became its rector in 1850. Four years later he was elected a member of the Imperial Academy of Sciences, and until his death he remained one of its most active members. He was consecrated bishop of Tambov in 1854 and was transferred to Kharkov in 1859. In 1868 he became bishop of Lithuania, and in 1879, metropolitan of Moscow. He traveled widely and expended his resources in helping students and scholars.

Besides numerous articles for religious periodicals, Macarius wrote (1843) a dissertation on *The History of the Ecclesiastical Academy of Kiev.* In 1847 the publication of his *Introduction to Orthodox Theology* earned him the title of doctor in divinity, which was rarely conferred in Russia. This was the first of six volumes of a complete course of Orthodox theology that appeared during the following years. At the same time, he was writing his history of the Russian Church. Twelve volumes were completed during his lifetime; the thirteenth was published by his brother after his death. In 1868 he published a condensed course of theology in one volume for seminarians. Besides these works, he left a *History of the Russian Schism of the Old Believers* and three volumes of sermons.

In keeping with the Eastern tradition, Macarius's theology is predominantly positive; he indulges little in speculation. He takes some inspiration from Catholic writers, particularly P. Perrone, but on controversial questions such as the procession of the Holy Spirit, purgatory, divorce, and satisfaction in the Sacrament of Penance, his views are decidedly not Catholic. Although his historical works do not always meet the standards of modern criticism, they are nevertheless a treasury of often unpublished historical documents. His compendium of theology has been translated into French and several Eastern European languages. As a consequence, his influence in the Orthodox world has been considerable.

Bibliography: M. JUGIE, *Catholicisme* 2:306–307; *Dictionnaire de théologie catholique* (Paris 1903–50) 9.2: 1443–44. *Theologia dogmatica christianorum orientalium ab acclesia catholica dissidentium* 1:612–613; v. 2–4, *passim.* J. B. FRANZELIN, *Examen doctrinae Macarii Balgakov . . . de processione Spiritus Sancti* (Rome 1876).

[P. MAILLEUX]

BULGAKOV, SERGEĬ NIKOLAEVICH

Russian economist, philosopher, and theologian; b. Livny, Orel Region, central Russia, July 16, 1871; d. Paris, July 13, 1944. He came of a family of Orthodox priests. He studied at the seminary in Orel until a religious crisis caused his transfer to a school in Elcy, where he completed his secondary education. In 1890 he entered the University of Moscow as a convinced Marxist. But his master's dissertation (written in Russian, as were almost all his works), *Capitalism and Agriculture* (2 v. 1900), questioned Marx's basic thesis because agricultural development did not substantiate it. While professor of political economy at the Kiev Polytechnic Institute (1901–06), he experienced a second spiritual crisis, as described in his *From Marxism to Idealism* (1903). He transferred in 1906 to the Commercial Institute of Moscow, where he became intimately friendly with Pavel FLORENSKIĬ and Nicholĭ BERDÎAEV. His doctoral dissertation, *Philosophy of Economics* (1912), showed the influence of the doctrine of Sophia or Divine Wisdom derived from Vladimir SOLOV'EV and Florenskiĭ. *The Unfading Light* (1917) terminated Bulgakov's purely philosophical writing. Thereafter he concentrated on theology. In 1918 he became an Orthodox priest. When the Bolshevists forced him to relinquish his professional chair, he moved to the Crimea. The government caused him to flee to Prague in 1922. From 1925 until his death he served as dean of the Russian Orthodox Theological Institute of St. Sergius in Paris. Although he steeped himself in the Fathers of the Church, he interpreted them in a very liberal fashion and was greatly influenced by German IDEALISM. His principal theological works were *The Burning Bush, The Friend of the Bridegroom,* and *Jacob's Ladder,* which form the ''small trilogy'' (1927–29); and *The Lamb of God, The Comforter,* and *The Bride of the Lamb,* which constitute his ''large trilogy'' (1933–46). His writings frequently assailed Catholic doctrines. His own doctrine on Divine Wisdom caused so much controversy among the Russian Orthodox by seeming to postulate a fourth divine person that it was condemned by the Synod of Karlovci, Yugoslavia, and by Patriarch Sergeĭ of Moscow (1935). Bulgakov submitted to Metropolitan Eulogius of Paris and declared his belief in all Orthodox dogmas. His ''sophiology'' was, he said, merely his personal interpretation of these beliefs. A popular exposition of his doctrines appeared in English as *The Wisdom of God* (1937).

Bibliography: V. V. ZENKOVSKY, *History of Russian Philosophy,* tr. G. L. KLINE, 2 v. (New York 1953) 2:890–916. N. O. LOSSKY, *History of Russian Philosophy* (New York 1951). L. ZANDER, in *Irénikon* 9 (1946) 168–185. B. SCHULTZE, *Russische Denker* (Vienna 1950). I. H. DALMAIS, *Catholicisme* 2:307–309.

[J. PAPIN]

BULGARIA, THE CATHOLIC CHURCH IN

Located in southeastern Europe on the Balkan Peninsula, Bulgaria is bordered on the north by Romania, on the east by the Black sea and Turkey, on the south by Greece, on the southwest by the Former Yugoslavian Republic of Macedonia, and on the west by Serbia. Characterized by cold, damp winters and hot, dry summers, Bulgaria is a mountainous region visited by earthquakes and landslides, its mountains falling to agricultural lowlands in the southeast and north. Natural resources include bauxite, copper, lead and coal, while agricultural crops include fruits and vegetables, tobacco, wheat, barley, sugar beets and wine grapes.

Ethnically Turco-Tatar, the Bulgarians moved into the lower Danube basin at the beginning of the 7th century and despite their small numbers, founded a large, powerful state. Intermarriage with their Slav subjects, who had previously settled there, caused the Slav strain to predominate. After a long period under Turkish domination Bulgaria became a principality in 1878 and an independent kingdom in 1908. Known as the Bulgarian People's Republic during communist rule from 1943 to 1989, Bulgaria has since become a parliamentary democracy.

Early History. While Christianity had entered the region of modern Bulgaria by 343, the date of a famous council at Sardica (modern Sofia), it almost disappeared after the Slavs migrated to the region. Bulgaria became a recognized state in 681, and Christianity was renewed *c.* 864 with the conversion of BORIS I, who was baptized by the Orthodox clergy of Constantinople. Soon after his conversion, Boris (reigned 853–889), who was eager for a status of equality with the Byzantine emperor, sought to have a patriarchate created for the Bulgarian Church. When Photius, patriarch of Constantinople, refused this request, Boris sent a delegation to Rome (866). Pope Nicholas I sent legate Bishop (later Pope) Formosus to Bulgaria and promised to eventually appoint an archbishop for the country. Dissatisfied with the papal solution, Boris took his case to the Council of Constantinople IV

Capital: Sofia.
Size: 42,830 sq. miles.
Population: 7,796,694 in 2000.
Languages: Bulgarian; ethnic languages are spoken in various regions.
Religions: 105,950 Latin-rite Catholics (1.5%), 15,590 Bulgarian-rite Catholics (.2%), 6,472,450 Orthodox (83%), 935,600 Muslims (13%), 62,375 Jews (.8%), 204,729 without religious affiliation.
Ecclesiastical organization: Bulgaria has two dioceses for the Latin Catholic Church, Nikopol (created 1789) and Sofia-Plovdiv (created 1758), both of which are immediately subject to the Holy See. The Bulgarian Byzantine Catholic Church has an Apostolic Exarchate in Sofia (created 1926). The Bulgarian Orthodox Church, an autocephalous patriarchate, has a seat in Sofia that oversees 12 dioceses in Bulgaria, two in North America, and parishes in Western Europe and Australia.

(869–870), at which the Byzantines submitted Bulgaria to the jurisdiction of Constantinople, despite the pope's protest. Bulgaria remained under Constantinople's jurisdiction and, as a result, part of the Byzantine rite and within the orbit of Byzantine civilization (*see* CONSTANTINOPLE, ECUMENICAL PATRIARCHATE OF; BYZANTINE CIVILIZATION). The issue of Bulgaria was among the chief issues in the controversy between Rome and Constantinople during the 9th century.

In 917 King Simeon the Great (893–927) proclaimed himself emperor and named the archbishop of Preslav as patriarch of Bulgaria. In 927 Constantinople recognized the first Bulgarian patriarchate, which lasted until 1018. After the Byzantines overthrew the first Bulgarian Empire (971), the patriarch left Preslav and resided in Ohrid, Macedonia. When Byzantium occupied Macedonia (1018), the Bulgarian patriarchate was reduced to the rank of autocephalous archbishopric until 1767.

Bulgaria was ruled by the Byzantine Empire until 1185. Upon regaining independence, it established its second empire (1186–1396), with Trnovo as capital. Opposition to Constantinople motivated renewed contacts with Rome. In 1204 Bulgarian Tsar Kaloian (1197–1207) asked Pope Innocent III to acknowledge him as emperor and to recognize the archbishop of Trnovo as patriarch. The pope granted the kingly crown to Kaloian and the title of primate to the archbishop, who also received the pallium from Rome. Union with Rome lasted until 1235, when Emperor John Assen II (1218–41) allied with the Greeks. In 1235 John obtained recognition of the second Bulgarian patriarchate from the Byzantine patriarch, which endured until the Turkish occupation of Trnovo in 1393. Thereafter the Bulgarian Church was incorporated into the Orthodox Church of Byzantium (*see* ORTHODOX CHURCHES).

After the occupation of Trnovo, the region fell quickly, and was part of the Ottoman Empire between 1396 and 1878. During the 17th century Franciscan missionaries entered the region and converted most of the heretical Christian Paulicians and neighboring BOGOMILS to Catholicism. As a result of this perceived effort to gain a Western foothold in Bulgaria, the Turks began a concerted effort of persecution against the Church, while allowing the Orthodox to practice their Slavic-based faith. Rising Bulgarian nationalism sparked a rebellion in 1876 during which thousands of Turks were killed. With Russian support, the Bulgarian nationalists ousted the Turks, and a treaty signed March 3, 1878 left the region independent. A vestige of Turkish occupation, Islam was the faith of ten percent of the country by 1900, most of whom were Turks, the rest being ethnic Bulgarians, or ''Pomaks.''

Catholic Rites Develop. Following independence, German nobleman Alexander of Battenburg became the prince of Bulgaria in 1879, but was forced to abdicate by the Russians due to his aggressive actions. In 1887 Ferdinand of Saxe-Coburg-Gotha was offered the crown. A Catholic, Ferdinand I gave the Church latitude in developing schools, hospitals and colleges in Bulgaria, while papal nuncio Angelo Roncalli (later Pope John XXIII) established diplomatic relations with the Vatican in 1925 and otherwise aided the efforts of Church leaders to spread the faith. Capuchins tended a growing Catholic population in the Plovdiv region, while Passionists tended those living along the Danube. In 1908, Ferdinand proclaimed Bulgaria independent and took the title of Tsar. Following defeat in the Balkan wars of 1912–13, Ferdinand abdicated in favor of his son, Boris III. The Catholic population in Bulgaria saw further increases due to refugees from Greek Thrace following the Balkan wars (*see* EASTERN CHURCHES).

The strife between the Greeks and the Bulgarians caused by the resurgence in Bulgarian nationalism also filtered down to the Orthodox Church when the Greeks refused to allow the Bulgarians their own hierarchy. In 1870, when the Turkish government granted an independent Bulgarian exarchate, the patriarch of Constantinople excommunicated the Bulgarian Church, a ban that lasted from 1872 to 1945. Controversy broke out again in 1953 when the Bulgarian Church, without Constantinople's permission, established the third patriarchate and elected Cyril (Markov) as patriarch. In 1961 Constantinople agreed to this change and settled the dispute.

After the patriarch of Constantinople denied the Bulgarian Orthodox a national hierarchy in the mid-19th century, small groups of Orthodox in Bulgaria, Thrace and Macedonia appealed to the Holy See, resulting in a formal union with Rome (1859–60) that created the Bulgari-

an rite. In 1861 Joseph Sokolski was consecrated archbishop by Pius IX, but shortly after his return to Constantinople he was seized and taken to Russia. In 1881, when the faithful totaled about 70,000, the Holy See created a vicariate apostolic for Macedonia, with its seat in Salonika, and another for Thrace, with its seat in Constantinople.

Bibliography: K. J. JIREČEK, *Geschichte der Bulgaren* (Prague 1876). S. VAILHÉ, *Dictionnaire de théologie catholique,* ed. A. VACANT et al., 15 v. (Paris 1903–50) 2.1:1174–1236. E. REINHARDT, *Die Entstehung des bulgarischen Exarchats* (Lucka 1912). G. SONGEON, *Histoire de la Bulgarie depuis les origines jusqu'à nos jours* (Paris 1913). F. DVORNIK, *The Slavs: Their Early History and Civilization* (Boston 1956); *The Slavs in European History and Civilization* (New Brunswick, NJ 1962); *Les Slaves, Byzance et Rome au IXe siècle* (Paris 1926). S. RUNCIMAN, *A History of the First Bulgarian Empire* (London 1930). M. SPINKA, *A History of Christianity in the Balkans* (Chicago 1933). R. JANIN, *Dictionnaire d'histoire et de géographie ecclésiastiques,* ed. A. BAUDRILLART et al., (Paris 1912–) 10:1120–94. D. SLIJEPČEVIĆ, *Die bulgarische orthodoxe Kirche 1944–56* (Munich 1957). M. ZAMBONARDI, *La Chiesa autocefala bulgara* (Gorizia 1960). I. SOFRANOV, *Histoire du mouvement bulgare vers l'Église catholique au XIXe siècle* (Rome 1960). M. MACDERMOTT, *A History of Bulgaria 1393–1885* (London 1962). *Oriente Cattolico* (Vatican City 1962) 191–198. *Bilan du Monde* 2:175–179.

[M. LACKO]

The Modern Era. Due to the political allegiances of its Tsar, Bulgaria joined with Germany during World War I, and as a result of Germany's loss suffered political and economic chaos as monarchists and communists fought to gain control. Bulgaria joined with the German Axis powers during World War II, but shielded its 50,000 Jewish citizens from Nazi genocide. In 1943, following the death of Boris III, the situation grew more unstable,

Sveti Georgi Church, Sofia, Bulgaria. (©Sandro Vannini/CORBIS)

despite the efforts of Boris's successor, Tsar Simeon II. A communist-led coalition government took control on Sept. 9, 1944, and adopted a policy of neutrality with regard to the war. Withdrawing from occupied territories, Bulgaria attempted to avoid further conflict, but was invaded by Soviet troops in 1944, whereupon Bulgaria surrendered to the Allied Powers.

The Church under Communism. The Communist Party swiftly took control of the government, purging itself of disloyal members, exiling the tsar and holding mock elections to establish a quasi-legitimate power base. In 1946 Bulgaria was declared a people's republic, and the following year Communist Party leader Georgi Dimitrov became prime minister. All democratic opposition was crushed, agriculture and industry were nationalized, and Bulgaria became the closest of the Soviet Union's allies.

After the communists seized power in 1945, the Bulgarian Byzantine Catholic Church and the Latin Catholic Church were oppressed as representing foreign influences, and their activities were severely limited. Under the constitution of 1947 Church and State were separated, and the government immediately forbade religious instruction in public schools. The following year, in 1948, the state confiscated all Catholic schools and institutions, and banished all religious who were not Bulgarians. The apostolic delegate was expelled in 1949, and convents of women religious were outlawed. Trials held between 1951 and 1952 resulted in convictions of treason against 60 priests. The apostolic exarch for the Byzantine Catholics, Ivan Garufalov, died mysteriously in 1951 after having strongly resisted Communist proposals for a new but unacceptable statute for the Catholic Church. Ivan Romanoff, Vicar Apostolic of Sofia and Plovdiv, died in prison in 1953. Both the Byzantine Catholic bishop for the apostolic exarchate of Sofia and the Latin Catholic bishop for the vicariate apostolic of Sofia-Plovdiv were permitted limited activity, and both attended Vatican Council II. No Catholic seminary or institutions existed.

In 1949 Dimitrov died, but the government remained in the hands of a totalitarian government. Despite the hardships imposed under communist rule, the Church remained essentially unaltered in numbers and with its basic diocesan structures and parishes intact. Despite such anti-church acts as the secret decree No. 88 of 1953 that authorized the government to confiscate all church property, the number of faithful remained steady at about 70,000, and the almost 30 priests were enough to staff the

Church with three large archways in front, Bulgaria, photograph by Cory Langley.

parishes. Moreover, the Church served as an example for those determined to resist communism: about two-thirds of its clergy suffered imprisonment and detention without making any compromises with the regime. In 1962 Todor Zhivkov took control of the government, and held power until Nov. 10, 1989, when he was deposed by members of his own party.

Following the open persecution of the early 1950s, the Church was left bereft of its bishops. Providentially, elderly Bishop Kiril Kurtev, who had resigned his position as apostolic exarch in 1941, returned to his old post. In 1963 Kurtev obtained a coadjutor, Metodi Stratiev, who had just been released from prison. However, it took until 1965 before Stratiev could be ordained a bishop. It was only in 1960, after Stalin's death, that it became possible to ordain Simeon Kokov, a Capuchin friar, a bishop for the apostolic vicariate of Sofia-Plovdiv. A serious conflict arose with the apostolic administrator, Bogdan Dobranov, whose own ordination as bishop had apparently been blocked by a Communist veto. The Holy See suggested a compromise that would divide the administration of the vicariate between the two, with the vicar Kokov, a bishop, ministering to the countryside and Dobranov, the administrator without episcopal orders, serving at the cathedral in Plovdiv. Still, the rift could not be healed. Only after Bishop Kokov died in July of 1975 did the government relent in its opposition to Dobranov and even insisted on his succeeding Kokov in the Sofia-Plovdiv see. The situation of the diocese of Nikopol remained most precarious, as its bishop, Evgeny Bossilkov, had been sentenced to death in 1952. After Bulgarian leader Zhivkov visited the Vatican in 1975 Vasko Seirekov was ordained bishop for Nikopol. Working exhaustively at his post, Seirekov died in 1976 and was succeeded three years later by Samuil Djoundrin, who had spent 12 years of hard labor in the notorious death camp of Belene. Sofia-Plovdiv was raised to a diocese in 1979.

While Bulgaria's Church leaders continued to advocate for the revival of democracy, the government recognized the Vatican as offering opportunities for contacts with the West, contacts it desired because its ties with the USSR had resulted in international isolation. The ascension of Pope John XXIII in 1958 was seen as a means to gain improved relations with the Holy See, as he had served in Bulgaria as papal nuncio from 1925–34. The pope, for his part, did not miss an occasion to recall his Bulgarian experience, even calling it ''the most vigorous ten years of my life.'' Two positive results followed for the Bulgarian Church from that special relationship with Pope John XXIII: the first was being able to reconstitute the hierarchy; the second was securing the participation of Bulgarian bishops in the Second Vatican Council.

The participation of the Bulgarian Church in Vatican II was somehow exceptional when compared to that of most other East European churches. Although half its clergy remained in prison, all three active prelates attended council sessions: Simeon Kokov in 1962, Kiril Kurtev in 1963 and 1965, and Damial Talev in 1964. G. Eldarov and I. Sofranov contributed to the work of the preparatory commissions as consultors, and the former served as a peritus on several council commissions. Shortly after the Council in 1966, Pope Paul VI appointed Eldarov, who was a professor at the Pontifical theological faculty of St. Bonaventure in Rome at the time, as visitor delegate to oversee the pastoral care of Bulgarian Catholics of both rites abroad. In 1981 Eldarov established a center for Bulgarian Church archives in Rome that came to be regarded as the best collection of books and documents relating to Bulgarian themes existing in the West. He also took responsibility for the Vatican Radio's daily broadcasts in Bulgarian.

The Church after Communism. The fall of dictator Zhivkov, in late 1989, opened up a new era promising greater religious freedom, as Bulgaria became a parliamentary democracy in 1990 and adopted a democratic constitution on July 12, 1991. The Bulgarian Orthodox Church was declared the ''traditional'' faith, while all other religious groups were required to register with the new government. The Roman Catholic, Jewish, Muslim and Bulgarian Orthodox each received financial assistance from the state. On Dec. 5, 1990, full diplomatic relations between the Holy See and Bulgaria were reestablished, and to many Pope John Paul II became a symbol of the new age rising from the ashes of Communism. The two Roman rites worked together to develop a Bulgarian-language liturgy, although the Orthodox Church still refused to establish relations with either Latin or Byzantine Catholic leaders.

In 1992, the Bulgarian Orthodox Church suffered a severe internal rift after several bishops, led by Hristofor Sabev left the synod and established their own council. In 1994 Orthodox Patriarch Maxim I's party elected its own metropolitans in most of the dioceses held by the Savev-led bishops, whereupon the new, dissident council reacted by electing its own bishops for sees loyal to Maxim, even going so far as to appointing a bishop for the capital, traditionally the see of the patriarch. Accusations that Maxim was a puppet of the communist state resulted in the appointment of a new patriarch Pimen I, by the dissident group, in 1996. The resulting rift—two full, parallel hierarchies that ruled over the Orthodox community—showed no signs of healing by 2000, despite an offer by Pimen to abdicate if Maxim would follow suit, which offer the elder patriarch refused.

An exceptional development for the Bulgarian Byzantine Catholic Church was the beatification of Bishop Evgeni Bossilkov, who died in prison four years after being imprisoned by the communist regime in 1948. Hampered by pressures initiated from inside Bulgaria, the process was restarted by Bulgarian bishops.

Into the 21st Century. In December of 1992 Bulgaria's national assembly revoked the decree permitting the confiscation of Church property. By the late 1990s the state returned religious education to Bulgaria's public schools, although Church leaders raised objections to the predominance of Orthodox educators. The country's economic woes ended in the late 1990s as businesses became privatized and the government began addressing agricultural advancement and social reforms. Despite continued unrest in the Balkans due to Serbian attempts at ethnic cleansing in neighboring Kosovo province, Bulgaria's economic outlook was bright going into the 21st century. After receiving an invitation from Bulgarian president Petar Stoyanov, Pope John Paul II anticipated a trip to Bulgaria in 2002 after a proposed visit was accepted by the Orthodox Patriarch Maxim I.

By the year 2000 Bulgaria had 53 parishes, tended by 14 diocesan and 30 religious priests. Other religious included two brothers and over 75 sisters, among them the Eastern-rite Sisters of Charity, the Benedictines and the Eucharistine nuns. Education remained a prime concern of Church leaders; not only did the University of Sofia require all students in its theology program to be Orthodox, but a 1998–99 law initiating a ''world religions'' curriculum was perceived as heavily pro-Orthodox. Latin Catholics centered near Plovdiv and in northern cities, while Byzantine Catholics lived in Sovia Plovdiv, Burgas, and villages in the southeast.

Bibliography: K.G. DRENIKOFF, *L'Eglise catholique en Bulgarie* (Madrid 1968). M.T. CARLONI, *Il silenzio della chiesa bulgara* (Urbania 1979). TREVOR BEESON, *Discretion and Valour* (London 1974). J. BROUN and G. SIKORSKA, *Conscience and Captivity: Religion in Eastern Europe* (Washington, DC 1988). F. STRAZZARI, *Tra Bosforo e Danubio* (Sinisello Balsamo 1988). I. SOFRANOV-S. MERCANZIN, *Eugenio Bossilkov* (Rome 1986). S. ELDAROV, *Uniatism and the Fate of Bulgaria* (Sofia 1994). J. ZVETKOV, *The Crucifix* (Sofia 1993). S. P. RAMET, *Nihil Obstat: Religion, Politics, and Social Change in East-Central Europe and Russia* (Durham, NC 1998).

[G. ELDAROV/EDS.]

Interior of St. Elia Church, Bozenci, Bulgaria. (©Sandro Vannini/CORBIS)

BULGARIAN CATHOLIC CHURCH (EASTERN CATHOLIC)

A general revolt in 1186 marked the end of Byzantine domination and the beginning of the second Bulgarian Kingdom, which Ivan Assen II (1218–41) brought to its greatest political expansion and which disappeared in 1396. The new capital, Tyrnovo, was also the residence of the archbishop. The first important event in this period was the return of Bulgaria to communion with the Holy See (1204) after its sad experience with Constantinople. According to the agreement between Kaloian, Archbishop Basil, and Pope Innocent III, Bulgaria returned to communion with Rome, keeping its own ecclesial and liturgical usages, while the pope granted Kaloian the title of king and Basil that of primate of Bulgaria. This title corresponded to the Eastern title of patriarch, since Basilio, invested with the pallium, obtained the right to crown the Bulgarian kings, consecrate chrism, and install metropolitans.

The union with Rome lasted until 1235. At that time relations with Constantinople (Nicaea) having been restored and those with Rome having deteriorated because of the Latin Empire of Constantinople, the Bulgaro-Byzantine Council of Blasherna was convoked, which proclaimed the autonomy of the Bulgarian Church in communion with Nicaea and separated from Rome. Bulgaria thus definitively entered the Byzantine sphere, and the union effected by the Ecumenical Councils of Lyons and Florence was rendered even less stable than it had been before.

Turkish domination. In the full flowering of its ecclesiastical, cultural, and social development, Bulgaria was struck by a new disaster—Turkish political domination (1396–1878), to which was joined Byzantine spiritual domination. This was the saddest period in Bulgarian history, when the people were reduced to actual slavery. The Ecumenical Patriarchate of Phanar, preserving a certain autonomy as mediator between the ''Sublime Portal'' (Turkish government) and the subject Christian people, devoted itself to the exploitation and Hellenization of the Slavic population. The Bulgarian bishops were gradually replaced by Greeks, and the Bulgarian language by Greek in schools and churches. The ''Phanariots'' did not hesitate to destroy even the most ancient libraries and archives.

In 1767 the Archdiocese of Ochrida, which had continued to ''represent'' the autonomous Bulgarian Church, was officially subjected to the jurisdiction of Constantinople. For almost five centuries the Bulgarian Church and state did not exist, while the people lived in the most profound ignorance and misery. Many Bulgarians were either Hellenized or totally oblivious to their national origins. The liturgy was celebrated in Bulgarian only in monasteries hidden in the mountains.

Independence. The first signs of rejuvenation came from the Catholic bishops Partehevitch, who carried on a tireless diplomatic activity, exhorting the Western powers to free Christianity from the Turks, and Stanislavov, who composed a booklet in the New Bulgarian language. The father of the Bulgarian revival, the monk Paissi, wrote the *Bulgaro-Slavic History* (1762), in which he implored the Bulgarians, ''a nation of kings and saints,'' not to forget the glorious past of their land and their Church. His ideas, taken up by Spiridon, Sofronius (bishop of Vratsa), and others, stirred up a vast national movement.

The difficult struggle against Constantinople for ecclesiastical independence was caused by two currents: the one, guided by Tsankov, proposed the union of Bulgaria with Rome, but because of the opposition of Russia, only a small group returned to the Catholic Church; the other, guided by Makaripolski, succeeded in creating an Orthodox exarchate (1870) recognized by the Turks but excommunicated by Constantinople.

Bulgarian Catholic Church. The formation of the small Bulgarian Catholic Church dates from the middle of the 19th century. Bulgarians in the Macedonian cities of the Kilkis Province sent a petition in 1859 to the apostolic delegate in Istanbul to be admitted into communion with the Apostolic See. In the following year, another group of Bulgarians similarly petitioned the Catholic Armenian archbishop of Istanbul. Joseph Sokolski was consecrated archbishop and received help from the Assumptionist and Resurrectionist Fathers. He was captured by Russian spies and was imprisoned in Kiev, where after 18 years he died. Raphael Popov succeeded Sokolski and administered the Bulgarian Catholic exarchate from 1865 to 1876. At this time there were about 80,000 Bulgarian Byzantine Catholics. The growing progress was halted due to a lack of clergy, persecution by the Russians, and the defection of Catholic Bishop Lazzarus Mladenov. Many thousands returned to the Bulgarian Orthodox Church. World War I crushed any further growth. An apostolic administrator was appointed in 1923, and in 1926 an exarchate was formed with Cyrill Kurteff appointed as the apostolic exarch. After World War II, the Bulgarian Catholic Church underwent severe persecutions, with many bishops and clergy imprisoned. Nevertheless, its lot was better than many other Eastern Catholic Churches within the communist sphere, which were forcibly suppressed and merged into their Orthodox counterparts. The collapse of communism gave the Bulgarian Catholic Church a new lease of life, with the release of imprisoned clergy and a return of expropriated church properties.

Bibliography: M. SPINKA, *A History of Christianity in the Balkans* (Chicago, Ill. 1933). V. N. ZLATARSKI, *Istoră na Bŭlgarskata Dŭrzhava,* 3 v. in 4 (Sofia 1918–40), basic work. D. TSUCHLEV, *Istorîâ na Bŭlgarskata Tsŭrkva,* 2 v. (Sofia 1910—). S. TSANKOV, *Die Bulgarische Orthodoxe Kirche seit der Befreiung bis zur Gegenwart* (Sofia 1939). I. SOFRANOV, *Histoire du mouvement bulgare vers l'Église catholique au XIXe siècle* (Rome 1960). A. CRONIA, *Saggi di letteratura Bulgara antica* (Rome 1936). R. ROBERSON, *The Eastern Christian Churches: A Brief Survey*, 6th ed (Rome 1999).

[I. SOFRANOV/EDS.]

BULGARIS, EUGENIUS

The most important Greek Orthodox theologian of the 18th century; b. Corfu, Aug. 10 or 11, 1716; d. St. Petersburg, May 29 or June 10, 1806. Bulgaris (baptized Eleutherius) studied philosophy and theology at Padua, then lectured at Janina, Greece, and entered the monastery of Vatopedi on Mt. Athos (1749) and taught there and at the Patriarchal School of Constantinople. When dismissed from his teaching assignment because his methods differed from the Oriental tradition, he migrated to Leipzig, Germany, where he encountered the Russian Marshall Theodore Orlov, who recommended him to the Czarina CATHERINE II. She brought him to St. Petersburg and gave him charge of her library (1771). He was ordained a priest in 1775, and named archbishop of Kherson (Oct. 1, 1776). There he pursued his literary activities, but he soon resigned his bishopric, returned to St. Petersburg, and composed a series of exegetical and polemical works. In 1802 he retired to the monastery of St. Alexander Nevski.

A polyglot, Bulgaris served as editor, translator, and biographer and wrote on theology, philosophy, philology, history, physics, and mathematics. He was considered a champion of Oriental Orthodoxy by his coreligionists, since he disputed both the Catholic and the Protestant positions. When the Catholics of eastern Poland were forced into Orthodoxy, he protested in favor of tolerance. One of his principal works is a dogmatic theology composed in Scholastic fashion (Venice 1872).

Bibliography: M. JUGIE, *Theologia dogmatica christianorum orientalium ab ecclesia catholica dissidentium,* 5 v. (Paris 1926–35) 1:526–527. B. KOTTER, *Lexikon für Theologie und Kirche,* ed. J. HOFER and K. RAHNER, 10 v. (2d, new ed. Freiburg 1957–65) 2:766. A. PALMIERI, *Dictionnaire de théologie catholique,* ed. A. VACANT, 15 v. (Paris 1903–50; Tables générales

1951–) 2.1:1236–41. R. JANIN, *Dictionnaire d'histoire et de géographie ecclésiastiques,* ed. A. BAUDRILLART (Paris 1912–) 10:1195–98. E. WOLF, *Die Religion in Geschichte und Gegenwart,* 7 v. (3rd ed. Tübingen 1957–65)[3] 1:1509.

[B. SCHULTZE]

BULLA

A lead seal used for authenticating documents, which for durability replaced the older wax seals. It is apparently of Byzantine origin and was used by the papal chancery from the 6th century. It was likewise employed by the royal chancelleries of Europe, with gold or silver replacing the lead on more important documents. Silken or hemp cord bindings, which became less common after the 12th century, held the document together. These cords were themselves immersed in the leaden globule, which was then impressed on the document with a circular stamping device that imprinted a double image. On one side was the signature of the pope (as this side remained empty before his coronation ceremony, such a bull was called a "half-bull"); on the other side was imprinted the papal motto and, since the end of the 11th century, the embossed facial features of the Apostles Peter and Paul, with the corresponding abbreviations S.PE and S.PA for St. Peter and St. Paul respectively.

After the 13th century the documents that were equipped with such seals were themselves called bulls. Although the expression was never officially adopted in the Papal Chancery, it gave rise to an inaccurate but common term for all documents stamped with a leaden seal.

One class of documents, called in earlier times *bullae majores* and later *privilegia,* concerned the bestowal or corroboration of rights without time limitation. In addition to the solemn preamble and conclusion ending with the monogrammed *Benevalete* as the salutation, these documents contained the signatures of the pope and cardinals. This type of bulla was discontinued in the 14th century.

A second class of documents, called *litterae* (or in earlier times *bullae minores*), dealt with matters of lesser importance. After the 12th century these less important documents were classified as: rescripts, to grant favors and promulgate decisions; or executive documents, which contained precepts and ordinances. The string bindings of such bulls were of silk or of hemp.

The dating of the bulls included the locality and the date of issue according to Roman calculation. For papal letters, usually only the year of the pontificate was given. Since 1908 the reckoning of the year, month, and day has been given according to the civil calendar.

The material on which papal bulls were written was papyrus until the end of the 10th century, but since the 11th century parchment (vellum) has been used exclusively. The language of papal bulls is Latin, and the script up to the 12th century was the so-called "curiatype writing"; from the 12th to the 14th century, the Gothic cursive script, and from the 16th to the 19th century a variation of Gothic script was employed. In the pontificate of Pope Leo XIII modern Latin script was introduced.

The different types, such as consistorial, curial, cameral, common, and secret bulls and briefs, arise from the place of origin, the classification, or the style and form of composition.

Since 1878 the leaden seals for bulls have been discontinued except for the more solemn ones. For all the other bulls, letters, and papal documents a red ink stamp with the name of the pope encircling the heads of St. Peter and St. Paul is used. Bulls are quoted or cited with the first words of the text, as encyclicals, e.g., Pope Boniface VIII's bull *Clericis laicos.*

Golden Bull. Exceptional papal, royal, or imperial acts were authenticated by a seal impressed on gold (in Byzantium, *Chrusoboullon*), in place of the usual wax or leaden seal. Thus Pope Sixtus IV attached a golden bull to his confirmation of mendicant privileges in 1479, and Clement VII when confirming the title *Fidei Defensor* to King Henry VIII in 1524; likewise two golden bulls sealed the perpetual peace between Henry VIII and Francis I of France at Amiens in 1527. The finest collection of golden bulls is that in the VATICAN ARCHIVES, with 78 examples ranging from Frederick Barbarossa to Napoleon. Antonomastically the celebrated constitution of 1356 regulating the election of kings of Germany is known as "The Golden Bull." The first part of this "Bull" was enacted on Jan. 23, 1356; the second, with much solemnity on the following Christmas Day. The constitution provided for seven electors, three ecclesiastical (archbishops of Mainz, Trier, Cologne), and four lay (king of Bohemia, count of the Palatinate, duke of Saxony, margrave of Bradenburg), granting them regalian rights over mines and salt in their own territories and the use of royal titles. The procedure endured until the dissolution of the HOLY ROMAN EMPIRE in 1806; the composition of the electoral college, until 1648.

Bibliography: J. P. KIRSCH, *Dictionnaire d'archéologie chrétienne et de liturgie*, ed. F. CABROL, H. LECLERCQ, and H. I. MARROU, 15 v. (Paris 1907–53) 2.1:1334–50. F. C. BOÚÚAERT, *Dictionnaire de droit canonique*, ed. R. NAZ, 7 v. (Paris 1935–65) 2:1126–32. W. M. PLÖCHL, *Geschichte des Kirchenrechts,* 3 v. (Vienna 1953–59) 2:65–66. K. ZEUMER, ed., *Die Goldene Bulle Kaiser Karl IV,* 2 v. (*Quellen und Studien zur Verfassungsgeschichte des Deutschen Reiches* 2; Weimar 1908). P. SELLA, *Le Bolle d'oro dell' Archivio Va-*

ticano (Vatican City 1934). G. TESSIER, *Diplomatique royale française* (Paris 1962) 197–198.

[A. H. SKEABECK/L. E. BOYLE]

BULLA CRUCIATA

A *bulla cruciata* is a papal bull or letter conceding various privileges to those who participated in or contributed to the war against the Muslims. Historically, the first concessions were issued to promote the Reconquest in Spain, the earliest known grant being that of ALEXANDER II to Ramiro of Aragon in 1063. URBAN II followed with a concession to the Count of Barcelona in 1089. Successive popes, e.g., Gelasius II (1118), Callistus II (*c.* 1123), Eugene III (1152), and Innocent III (1212) renewed the privileges for Spain. Whereas Urban II, in granting a plenary indulgence for the First CRUSADE to the Holy Land (1095), may have been influenced by previous procedures applicable to Spain, CALLISTUS II, who renewed Urban's indulgence for the East at LATERAN COUNCIL I (1123), granted to Spanish crusaders the same privileges offered to crusaders to the orient. These privileges were more clearly defined in what is commonly regarded as the first formal crusade bull, the *Quantum praedecessores* (1145), issued for the Second Crusade by EUGENE III; it included a plenary indulgence, protection of family and property, and a moratorium on interest for debts. Alexander III reissued Eugene's bull in 1165, and Innocent III's *Qui major* (1213) extended the indulgence to contributors who were unable to participate personally. Thus the Holy Land privileges became the standard for application elsewhere, not only in Spain, but for wars against the ALBIGENSES (INNOCENT III), and against the pope's political enemies in Europe (Innocent III and IV).

As crusades to the East and in Europe waned, the *bulla cruciata* (*cruzada*) came to apply exclusively to Spain or Spanish territory. A series of bulls was granted to Ferdinand and Isabella, and the bull of Gregory XIII (1573), with somewhat extended privileges, was reissued, with constant modifications, by his successors down to the present. Following the conquest of Granada (1492), the emphasis was placed on the offerings of the faithful to be used to promote various enterprises originally growing out of the Reconquest, e.g., restoration of damaged churches or building new ones, and eventually including works generally conducive to the promotion of religion. In the course of time the original requirements of support for the crusade were commuted to other religious acts, e.g., visits to specified churches and prayers. Privileges granted in lieu of the original plenary indulgence have been modified and expanded to include various dispensations for clergy and laity, notably from fast and abstinence. The bull came to apply equally to Spanish dominions, including Naples and Sicily, Latin America, and Portugal (with certain limitations), and to resident foreigners in these countries. The most recent renewals of the bull, those of Benedict XV (1915) and Pius XI (1928), were designed to bring greater precision, in harmony with the Code of Canon Law.

Bibliography: J. FERRERES, *La nueva bula de cruzada y sus extraordinarios privilegios según la concessión de Benedicto XV* (Madrid 1916). N. PAULUS, *Geschichte des Ablasses im Mittelalter,* 3 v. (Paderborn 1922–23). E. CASPAR, ''Die Kreuzzugsbullen Eugens III,'' *Neues Archiv der Gesellschaft für altere deutsche Geschichts Kunde* 45 (1924) 285–305. U. SCHWERIN, *Die Aufrufe der Päpste zur Befreiung des Heiligen Landes,* ed. E. EBERING (Berlin 1937). G. CONSTABLE, ''The Second Crusade as Seen by Contemporaries,'' *Traditio* 9 (1953) 213–279. A. WAAS, *Geschichte der Kreuzzüge,* 2 v. (Freiburg 1956). J. G. GAZTAMBIDE, *Historia de la Bula de la Cruzada en España* (Vitoria 1958). J. A. BRUNDAGE, *The Crusades: A Documentary Survey* (Milwaukee 1962).

[M. W. BALDWIN]

BULLAKER, THOMAS, BL.

Franciscan priest, martyr; known in religion as John Baptist Bullaker; b. *c.* 1602–1604 at Midhurst, Chichester, Sussex, England; d. Oct. 12, 1642, hanged, drawn, and quartered at Tyburn, London(?), or at Dorchester under Charles I. At an early age Thomas, the only son of a successful physician, was sent by his Catholic parents to the English College at St. Omer and later to Valladolid, Spain. After a period of discernment he received the Franciscan habit at Abrojo (1622), and a few years later (1627–28) was ordained priest. Upon landing at Plymouth, England, (1630) on his return, he was betrayed by the ship's captain, immediately seized, and cast into prison. Upon his liberation two weeks later, he began his 12–year ministry among the poor and sick Catholics of London. On Sept. 11, 1642 Bullaker was arrested while celebrating Mass in the house of his benefactress. He has left a partial but touching account of his arrest and trial. His cause for beatification was introduced in 1900 and completed with his beatification by Pope John Paul II on Nov. 22, 1987 with George Haydock and Companions.

Feast of the English Martyrs: May 4 (England).

See Also: ENGLAND, SCOTLAND, AND WALES, MARTYRS OF.

Bibliography: R. CHALLONER, *Memoirs of Missionary Priests,* ed. J. H. POLLEN (rev. ed. London 1924). J. H. POLLEN, *Acts of English Martyrs* (London 1891).

[K. I. RABENSTEIN]

BULLINGER, HEINRICH

Swiss Reformer, successor to Huldrych ZWINGLI; b. Bremgarten, Swiss Canton of Aargau, July 18, 1504; d. Zurich, Sept. 17, 1575. Bullinger's early schooling with the Brethren of the Common Life at Emmerich was followed by a humanistic training at the University of Cologne. His acceptance by the humanistic circle there brought him under the influence of Erasmus and of the new Reformation ideas of Calvin, Luther, and Melanchthon. Dissatisfaction with scholasticism led him to the critical study of the Scriptures, Origen, Ambrose, Augustine, and John Chrysostom. Upon his return to Switzerland, he taught at the Cistercian monastery near Cappel (1523–29). In 1528 he heard Zwingli preach at Zurich, was converted to his theology, and accompanied him to the disputations at Bern during that year. Bullinger succeeded his father as pastor of Bremgarten in 1529 and married a former nun, Anna Adlischwiler, by whom he had six sons and five daughters. On Dec. 9, 1531, he was chosen pastor of the Great Minster of Zurich to succeed Zwingli, who died in the battle of Cappel, Oct. 11, 1531. In this position, which he held until his death, Bullinger became an important voice in theological debate, particularly in his efforts to find doctrinal solutions to disputes over the Real Presence in the Eucharist that were dividing the Reformers. Together with Oswald MYCONIUS and Simon Grynaeus (1493–1541), both of Basel, he composed the First Helvetic Confession (Zwinglian in tone, but with Lutheran elements) in 1536. This was accepted by the Protestant cantons with the exception of Strassburg and Constance. The second Helvetic Confession (Calvinistic in tone with Zwinglian elements) was also the work of Bullinger and appeared in 1566 at the instance of the Calvinist Elector Palatine, Frederick III (the Pious). It was accepted in the Protestant cantons of Switzerland, Hungary, Scotland, and France (*see* CONFESSIONS OF FAITH, II.)

During his leadership in Zurich, Bullinger offered hospitality to refugees fleeing from France after the terror of the massacre of ST. BARTHOLOMEW'S DAY (Aug. 24, 1572); from Italy through fear of the Inquisition; and from England during the reign of Mary Tudor (1553–58). His special interest in England appears in his support of Lady Jane Grey in her abortive attempt to succeed to the throne (1553); his advice to Elizabeth in her opposition to the PURITANS; and his dedication of the third and fourth of his *Decadi* to Edward VI. Bullinger's theological beliefs shifted sharply away from ZWINGLIANISM to CALVINISM, especially after he collaborated with Calvin in formulating the *Consensus Tigurinus* in 1549. Bullinger was a prodigious writer, composing more than 150 works and 12,000 letters. Among his writings are a biography of Zwingli; the edition of the reformer's books; polemical treatises; the *Zürcher Chronik* and the *Diarium,* both works of historical value; and the *Hausbuch,* a popular collection of sermons and articles of faith. He was less active after the plague of 1564–65, which left him in poor health and which brought death both to his wife and to his daughters.

Bibliography: A complete collection of his writings does not exist. *Heinrich Bullingers Diarium (Annales vitae)*, ed. E. EGLI (Basel 1904); *Zürcher Chronik,* ed. J. J. HOTTINGER and H. VÖGELI, 3 v. (Frauenfeld 1838–40); *Korrespondenz . . . ,* ed. T. SCHIESS, 3 v. (Basel 1904–06). *The Decades of Henry Bullinger,* ed. T. HARDING, 4 v. (Cambridge, Eng. 1849–52). G. W. BROMILEY, ed. and tr., *Zwingli and Bullinger* (Library of Christian Classics 24; Philadelphia 1953), contains tr. ''On the Catholic Church.'' Literature. F. BLANKE, *Der junge Bullinger* (Zurich 1942). A. BOUVIER, *H. Bullinger, réformateur et conseiller oecuménique, le successeur de Zwingli, d'après sa correspondance avec les réformés et les humanistes de langue française* (Neuchâtel 1940), bibliog. T. SCHIESS, ''Der Briefwechsel Heinrich Bullingers,'' *Zwingliana* 5 (1933) 396–409. P. WALSER, *Die Prädestination bei H. Bullinger im Zusammenhang mit seiner Gotteslehre* (Zurich 1957), bibliog. G. WOLF, *Quellenkunde der deutschen Reformationsgeschichte,* 3 v. (Gotha 1915–23), bibliog. P. SCHAFF, *Bibliotheca symbolica ecclesiae universalis. The Creeds of Christendom,* 3 v. (6th ed. New York 1919). R. PFISTER, *Neue deutsche Biographie* 3:12–13. P. POLMAN, *Dictionnaire d'histoire et de géographie ecclesiastiques*, ed. A. BAUDRILLART (Paris 1912) 10:1210–11. O. E. STRASSER, *Die Religion in Geschichte und Gegenwart* 1:1510–11.

[E. D. MC SHANE]

BULTMANN, RUDOLF KARL

New Testament exegete and theologian, educator, author; b. Aug. 20, 1884, Wiefelstede, Oldenburg, Germany; d. Jul. 30, 1976, Marburg/Lahn, Federal Republic of Germany. The eldest son of the Rev. Arthur Bultmann, an evangelical Lutheran pastor, and of Helene (Stern) Bultmann, Rudolf Karl Bultmann had two brothers, Peter and Arthur, and a sister, Helene. One of his brothers was killed in World War I, the other died in a Nazi concentration camp during World War II. His paternal grandfather, a Pietist, had been a missionary in Africa, and his maternal grandfather a pastor in Baden. This family information is important for an understanding of Bultmann whose family ties, especially those with his wife and three daughters, were unusually close and influential. The classical training of his gymnasium years at the Humanistisches Gymnasium in Oldenburg, 1895–1903, developed in Bultmann a deep interest in the Greek classics, classical philology, literary criticism, and in humanistic education as such. After completing his gymnasium studies, he studied theology for three semesters in Tübingen, two in Berlin, and two more in Marburg. Bultmann was influenced in Tübingen by church historian Karl Müller, in Berlin by Old Testament scholar Hermann Gunkel and historian of dogma, Adolf HARNACK, in Marburg by New Testament professors Adolf Jülicher and Johannes Weiss, and systematic theologian Wilhelm Hermann.

After he had taught for one year in the gymnasium at Oldenburg, he accepted (1907) the position of *Repetent* in the Seminarium Philippinum in Marburg where he had a scholarship to the university. He received the licentiate in theology in 1910, after submitting his thesis *Der Stil der paulinischen Predigt und die kynisch-stoische Diatribe*, a topic suggested to him by Weiss. In 1912, he received his *Habilitation* with the thesis *Die Exegese des Theodor von Mopsuestia*, a subject proposed by Jülicher. He was *Privatdozent* in New Testament exegesis at Marburg until 1916, when he became assistant professor at the University of Breslau. It was while he was at Breslau that he began to write *Die Geschichte der synoptischen Tradition* (*The History of the Synoptic Tradition*, New York, 1968), in which he rigorously applied the methods of literary form criticism and historical analysis to the Synoptic Gospels in order to ascertain the earliest forms of that material known to the early Church and then to determine what part of that material may, with some confidence, be ascribed to Jesus. The book raised serious questions about the liberal theological conviction that the historical Jesus could be known through the Gospels and that he was or should be the central concern of Christian faith. This work was completed at the University of Giessen where, in 1920, Bultmann had succeeded Bousset as professor. In 1921, he was appointed to a professorship at the University of Marburg where he remained until his retirement in 1951.

By 1922, then, there existed for Bultmann a kind of moral imperative to formulate a theology of the New Testament commensurate with the achievements of the historical-critical method as exemplified in *Die Geschichte der synoptischen Tradition.* The catastrophic social, cultural, and religious effects of World War I evident then in Germany and Bultmann's personal and academic disenchantment with the anthropocentric naïveté of liberal theology, among other factors, led to his efforts to develop a dialectical theology in response to the program outlined by Karl BARTH in his 1919 *Commentary on Romans.* Though there is some evidence of a Neo-Kantian influence, fostered perhaps by the Marburg philosophers Cohen and Natorp, in two articles written in 1920, the dominant philosophical influence on Bultmann in formulating his theology was Martin HEIDEGGER, who taught at Marburg from 1923 to 1928 and with whom Bultmann maintained a close personal relationship and conducted a joint seminar.

In his 1924 essay, ''Die liberale Theologie und die jüngste theologische Bewegung,'' Bultmann claimed that Christian faith had to be associated with an absolute beyond the vicissitudes of history and hence that faith is not in fact necessarily related to the HISTORICAL JESUS, but is rather dependent upon the eschatological act of God in Jesus and in the Christian kerygma. In a decisive essay in 1925, ''Das Problem einer theologischen Exegese des Neuen Testaments,'' clearly employing the thematic categories of Heidegger, Bultmann holds that theological exegesis can not operate from a detached neutral viewpoint, but biblical texts are rather to be accepted as statements meant to determine the existence of the reader. The subject matter of the Bible is possibilities for understanding human existence and the object of theology is nothing other than the conceptual presentation of man's existence as determined by God, that is, as man must see it in the light of Scripture.

Bultmann's assessment of the historical Jesus may be found in his 1926 work *Jesus* (*Jesus and the Word*, New York 1934), in which he claimed that much that is known about the man is encrusted with myths that originated with the early Christians. Jesus was Jewish, an existentialist, and an apocalyptic preacher challenging his contemporaries to radical obedience in view of the imminent coming of the reign of God. Like other historical figures he challenged people's understanding of their existence, but in historical fact, he is one presupposition among others for the theology of the New Testament. Thus, the historical Jesus is not of constitutive significance for theology, for Christian faith is not a response to the message of Jesus but to the Church's message about him.

Though he eschewed political involvement, Bultmann took a determined and early stand against Nazism. In 1934, he associated himself with the Confessing Church which rejected the paganism and racial teachings of Hitler's state church and scattered throughout his articles written between 1933–60 are rejections of any exaltation of blood, nation, and race.

Although he previously had written on myth in the New Testament (e.g. in *Die Religion in Geschichte und Gegenwart,* 1930), Bultmann's lecture of Apr. 21, 1941 entitled ''Neues Testament und Mythologie,'' given before the Gesellschaft für Evangelische Theologie in Frankfurt/Main and repeated the following June in Alpirsbach, made him a controversial figure among churchmen and biblical scholars, and gave his name high prominence in the world of theology. He distinguished between the truths contained in the Gospel and the mythological language in which they are presented. He stated that if the truth of the New Testament is to influence modern man, who cannot accept myths, the New Testament itself must be stripped of its mythological trappings and restated in language that addresses man in his existential condition. A fundamental datum of that condition is that the world of nature and history is a closed world in which God cannot directly be known. The demythologization controversy that ensued is examined in detail in Bultmann's five-volume *Kerygma und Mythos; Ein theologisches Gespräch* (*see* DEMYTHOLOGIZING).

Among his other works are *Das Evangelium des Johannes* (1941; tr. G. R. Beasley-Murray, *The Gospel of John; A Commentary*, Philadelphia 1971); *Offenbarung und Heilsgeschehen* (1941); *Das Urchristentum im Rahmen der antiken Religion* (1949; tr. R. H. Fuller, *Primitive Christianity in Its Contemporary Setting*, Cleveland 1956); *Der alte und der neue Mensch in der Theologie des Paulus* (1964; tr. K. R. Crim, *The Old and New Man in the Letters of Paul*, Richmond, Va. 1967); and his most important three-volume work, *Theologie des Neuen Testaments* (2 v. 1948–53; tr. K. Grobel, *Theology of the New Testament*, New York 1951–55). Some of his moving sermons were published in the volume *Marburger Predigten* (1956; tr. H. Knight, *This World and Beyond*, New York 1960). His Shaffer Lectures given at Yale in 1951 were published in the volume *Jesus Christ and Mythology* (New York 1958), and his Gifford Lectures of 1955 were collected in the volume *Presence of Eternity: History of Eschatology* (New York 1957). Bultmann also contributed articles to Kittel's *Theologisches Wöterbuch zum Neuen Testament.*

Much honored during his lifetime by honorary degrees (St. Andrews and Syracuse), by membership in academies (Oslo, Göttingen, and Heidelberg), by the Federal Republic of Germany (Grand Cross of Merit), Bultmann received enduring tribute in the influence he has had on New Testament theologians. For whatever a theologian may think about Bultmann, his methodology and thought must be confronted by all serious scholars.

A bibliography of Bultmann's own writings may be found in R. Bultmann, *Exegetica*, E. Brinkler, ed. (Tübingen 1967). A complete bibliography is to be published soon by P. Joseph Cahill.

Bibliography: H. W. BARTSCH, ed., *Kerygma and Myth*, tr. R. H. FULLER (New York 1961); *Kerygma and Myth II* (London 1962). C. E. BRAATEN and R. A. HARRISVILLE, eds., *Kerygma and History* (Nashville 1962); *The Historical Jesus and the Kerygmatic Christ* (Nashville 1964). P. J. CAHILL, "The Theological Significance of Rudolf Bultmann" *Theological Studies* 38 (1977) 231–274. J. B. COBB, JR., *Living Options in Protestant Theology* (Philadelphia 1962). T. C. ODEN, *Radical Obedience: The Ethics of Rudolf Bultmann* (New York 1964). S. M. OGDEN, *Christ without Myth* (New York 1961). N. PERRIN, *The Promise of Bultmann* (Philadelphia 1969). J. M. ROBINSON, *A New Quest of the Historical Jesus* (Naperville, Ill. 1959). W. SCHMITHALS, *An Introduction to the Theology of Rudolf Bultmann*, tr. J. BOWDEN (Minneapolis 1968).

[T. J. RYAN]

BUNDERIUS, JAN (VAN DEN BUNDERE)

Theologian; b. Ghent, Belgium, 1481; d. Ghent, June 8, 1557. After joining the Dominicans at Ghent in 1507, he studied theology at Louvain. He taught theology for a while at Ghent and served as prior of the house there for three terms (1529, 1550, 1553), and once as provincial vicar (1550). He was appointed inquisitor for the Diocese of Tournai in 1542. He is famous for his polemics against the reformers. Among other works, he wrote the *Compendium dissidic quorumdam haereticorum atque theologorum* (Paris 1540).

Bibliography: P. MANDONNET, *Dictionnaire de théologie catholique* (Paris 1903–50) 2.1:1263–64. E. FILTHAUT, *Lexikon für Theologie und Kirche* (Freiburg 1957–65) 2:779. M. H. LAURENT, *Dictionnaire d'histoire et de géographie ecclésiastiques* (Paris 1912–) 10:1215.

[J. H. MILLER]

BUNSEN, CHRISTIAN KARL JOSIAS VON

Prussian diplomat, publicist, Protestant lay theologian, and liturgist; b. Korbach (Waldeck) Prussia, Aug. 25, 1791; d. Bonn, Germany, Nov. 28, 1860. Supporting the union of Lutheran and Reformed Churches in Prussia established by Frederick William III in 1817, Bunsen became the chief liturgist of the new church. As Prussian ambassador to the Holy See (1832–39) he played a leading role in the COLOGNE mixed marriage dispute and was, as a result, removed from Rome. He was ambassador to Bern (1839–41) and to London (1841–54). In furtherance of his desire for a rapprochement with the Anglicans, he was largely instrumental in creating the joint Anglican and Prussian Protestant bishopric in Jerusalem (1841). John Henry Newman confessed in his *Apologia* that his alienation from Anglicanism was decisively affected by this event. Despite his shortcomings as a diplomat, Bunsen served as an intellectual bridge between Germany and England. He helped impregnate Protestant theology with liberal thought. His own theology was liberal but amateurish, with a fondness for liturgy and sentiment, and a pronounced anti-Catholicism. Bunsen's books were numerous, verbose, and rarely of enduring value, ranging over such diverse fields as art history, Egyptology, patrology, ecclesiastical history, and religious philoso-

John Bunyan.

phy. They include *Das evangelischen Bisthum zu Jerusalem* (1842); *Allgemeines evangelisches Gesangbuch* (1846); *Gott in der Geschichte* (3 v. 1857–58); and *Die Zeichen der Zeit* (2 v. 1855).

Bibliography: F. BONSEN, *A Memoir of Baron Bunsen,* 2 v. (London 1868). R. PAULI, *Allgemeine deutsche Biographie* (Leipzig 1875–1910) 3:541–552, detailed but tendentious. W. HÖCKER, *Der Gesandte Bansen als Vermittler zwischen Deutschland und England* (Göttingen 1951). R. A. D. OWEN, *Christian Bunsen and Liberal English Theology* (Montpelier, Vt. 1924). W. BUSSMANN, *Neue deutsche Biographie* 3:17–18.

[S. J. TONSOR]

BUNYAN, JOHN

Puritan author and preacher; b. Elstow, England, November 1628; d. London, Aug. 31, 1688. His father was a tinker, a descendant of propertied yeoman farmers. Thus, John (like William Langland before him) became a rightful spokesman of "the common man" when he later wrote religious allegory in terms of his own life experience. His boyhood was made up of a little schooling, much hard work, games, and church-going. Village society was then becoming conscious of its political powers, while Puritanism struggled with the Established Church. When the Civil War between King and commoners broke out, Bunyan served in the parliamentarian army at a garrison in Newport Pagnell (1644–47). He then married and settled in a small house at Bunyan's End.

Bunyan had until then led what he called a "dissolute" life; he now turned to an intensely prayerful study of the Bible, seeking "the conviction of salvation." After five years of spiritual anguish, he found peace in the Baptist congregation in nearby Bedford, and, while working as a tinker, became one of the many "mechanic preachers" who spread the Gospel through the countryside. He also published controversial or devotional pamphlets, such as *Gospel Truths Opened* and *A Few Sighs from Hell.* In 1685 his wife died and he married again.

The Puritans, who had enjoyed freedom under the Commonwealth, were again persecuted after the Restoration. Bunyan refused to attend the Anglican Church services, was arrested in 1660 for preaching without a license, and, on refusing to desist, spent 12 years in Bedford prison. After his release he was named pastor of the Baptist congregation. In 1677 he was again imprisoned for six months. He died as a result of exposure while performing an act of charity, and was buried at Bunhill Fields.

Bunyan's works as a whole belong, in form and subject matter, in the flood of controversy of his day, but the best of them are marked by the observation, insight, and style of the born writer. They owe nothing to the university or to the coffeehouse, and very little to reading. From the Bible Bunyan drew doctrinal content, figures of speech, and a cadence that elevated his simple vocabulary; in his youth he had reveled in romantic chapbooks; his wife's dowry had brought him two books: the allegorical *Plain Man's Pathway to Heaven* and the devotional *Practice of Piety.* All these shaped his thought. Yet one authentic literary source, of which Bunyan was probably unconscious, may be found in pre-Reformation allegories. Their influence reached him through the living word of the pulpit tradition. G. R. Owst has shown ("Scripture and Allegory," *Literature and Pulpit in the Middle Ages,* Cambridge, Eng. 1933) that sermon figures from the poetical works of the 14th century spanned the gap made by the coincidence of Reformation and Renaissance in England and reached the Bedford tinker through sermons then still heard in rural pulpits (*see* SERMON LITERATURE, ENGLISH MEDIEVAL).

Literary achievement. Of Bunyan's 60 printed works four are most notable. *Grace Abounding to the Worst of Sinners* (1660) recounts his conversion. *The Life and Death of Mr. Badman* (1680) relates the sad end of a sinful life in the form of a dialogue between Mr. Wiseman and Mr. Attentive concerning "this deep judgement of God, . . . enough to stagger a whole world." The book exposes the evils of small-town society in a tone that anticipates the 18th-century novel. *The Holy War* (1682) is an elaborate allegory in which the town of Mansoul is recaptured from Diabolus by Emmanuel. The grandiose theme is vivid with memories of the Civil War.

The Pilgrim's Progress, Part 1 (written in prison and published in 1677) is a dream allegory in forthright prose. It has the tonal unity of a great poem and the human variety of a novel of character. It tells of the journey of Christian through ''the wilderness of this world'' to Sion, threatened by the Slough of Despond, the Valley of the Shadow of Death, Vanity Fair, and Doubting Castle, refreshed in the Palace Beautiful and the Delectable Mountains. Along the way he discourses with lively personifications of every human attitude. When he passes through the Waters of Death into the Golden City, ''they shut up the gates, which when I had seen I wished myself among them,'' says the dreamer. In Part 2 (1684) Christiana follows the same road and at last joins her husband.

The Pilgrim's Progress has been translated into almost every language; its archetypal story has a supranational theme and its psychology is perennially familiar. It spread through Europe before the end of the 17th century, and was subsequently carried by Protestant missionaries to Africa, Asia, and Oceania. Through the colonial pilgrims it entered deeply into the orthodox New England consciousness. Its most appealing interpretation may be found in the first chapter of the American classic, *Little Women,* when Marmee says: ''We are never too old for this. . . . Our burdens are here, our road is before us, and our longing for goodness and happiness is the guide that leads us through many troubles and mistakes to the peace which is the true Celestial City.'' This is the basic ethical relevance of Bunyan's greatest work.

Theological relevance. This has been both attacked and defended. Much in the book is obviously ''antipapist''—the views of an uneducated Puritan conditioned by his historical place at the storm-center of an embittered religious warfare. His picture of ''Old Man Pope'' biting his nails because he cannot get at the pilgrims passing his cave is probably as sincere as it is ludicrous. There are other repellent elements, such as the condemnation of Ignorance to Hell. A rather extreme criticism of these and of other features has been voiced by Alfred Noyes (''Bunyan Revisited,'' *The Opalescent Parrot,* New York 1929). But scholarly study and popular opinion alike form a constant tradition that recognizes these elements merely as limitations due to Bunyan's times and to his upbringing. The book is almost universally placed among the classic expressions of the Christian imagination. R. M. Frye (*God, Man, and Satan,* Princeton, N.J. 1960) claims that *The Pilgrim's Progress* has as much to contribute to contemporary Christian thought as that thought has to contribute to an understanding of the book itself.

Bunyan's ''Christian'' is perennially important; he is guided by Evangelist, he is freed from sin by the Cross of Christ, and cries in return: ''To tell you the truth, I love Him.'' Bunyan is a writer whose private experience finds a place in the long *confessio* tradition begun by St. Augustine; his universal vision follows the journey of Everyman through successive lifetimes to an abiding city.

See Also: ALLEGORY.

Bibliography: J. BUNYAN, *The Works of That Eminent Servant of Christ, John Banyan,* ed. G. OFFOR, 3 v. (London 1862), the only complete edition; *The Pilgrim's Progress,* ed. J. B. WHAREY, rev. R. SHARROCK (2d ed. Oxford 1963) definitive edition; *Grace Abounding and The Pilgrim's Progress,* ed. J. BROWN (Cambridge, Eng. 1907); *Life and Death of Mr. Badman and The Holy War* (Cambridge, Eng. 1905). J. BROWN, *John Bunyan, His Life, Times and Work,* ed. F. M. HARRISON (Tercentenary ed. London 1928). R. SHARROCK, *John Bunyan* (London 1954). W. Y. TINDALL, *John Bunyan, Mechanick Preacher* (New York 1934). O. E. WINSLOW, *John Bunyan* (New York 1961), good bibliography.

[M. WILLIAMS]

BUONACCORSI, FILIPPO

Known also by the pseudonym Callimaco Esperiente, humanist, philosopher, and political figure; b. San Gimignano (Siena), Italy, 1437; d. Cracow, Poland, November of 1496. With Pomponio Leto, he founded the Roman Academy. He took part in the plot against Pope Paul II (1468) with other members of the academy. Later exiled, he took refuge in Poland, where he became secretary to Casimir IV, for whom he performed various delicate missions (e.g., as delegate to Constantinople, Rome, Venice, etc.). He left historical works, discourses, letters, and poetry in which he gives evidence of a vast humanistic culture. He denied the immortality of the soul, called into question the distinction between soul and body, affirmed the complete independence of morality from religion, and defended the absolute sovereignty of the state. In his *Consilium Callimachi* (ed. R. Nsetecka, Cracow 1887), he went so far as to consider religion a political instrument, thus anticipating MACHIAVELLI.

Bibliography: A. SAPORI, ''Gl'Italiani in Polonia nel medioevo'' in *Archivio-storico italiano* 3 (1925) 156. G. AGOSTI, *Un politico italiano alla corte polacca nel sec. XV* (Turin 1930). G. SAITTA, *Il pensiero italiano nell'umanesimo e nel Rinascimento* 3 v. (Bologna 1949–51) 1:485–490.

[G. PANTEGHINI]

BUONAIUTI, ERNESTO

Modernist, writer; b. Rome, June 25, 1881; d. there, April 20, 1946. After ordination (1903), he taught philosophy in Rome at the Urbanian University (Pontificia Università Urbaniana de Propaganda Fide). At the Apollinaris in Rome he taught ecclesiastical history (1904–06) and acted as archivist (1906–11). Meanwhile, he became active in MODERNISM and was reputedly the author of the anonymous *Il programma dei modernisti* (1907), which was placed on the Index March 17, 1908, and was translated into English by George TYRRELL. This book, the best known of all Italian Modernist writings, endeavored to reply to *PASCENDI*, Pius X's encyclical condemning the movement. Buonaiuti maintained that Modernism was based on the results of recent biblical and historical criticism and that its primary purpose was to reconcile Catholicism with these scientific findings. According to him, the Modernists abandoned SCHOLASTICISM because it possessed no further value as a method of apologetics. Buonaiuti was presumed to be the author of *Lettere di un prete modernista* (1908; 2d ed. 1942), to which he referred in his autobiographical *Pellegrino di Roma* (1945) as "a sin of my youth." From 1905 until it was placed on the Index (Sept. 7, 1910), he was editor of the *Rivista storico-critica delle scienze teologiche,* a periodical that published articles on the history of dogmas and of the Church. While director of the bimonthly review *Nova et Vetera* (1908), Buonaiuti published his own articles under the pseudonym "P. Vinci." After the Holy Office condemned (April 12, 1916) the *Rivista di scienza della religioni,* a periodical started shortly before this by Buonaiuti, he subscribed to the oath against Modernism prescribed by Pius X. He failed to observe this and later submissions and was suspended *a divinis* in 1921. *Ricerche religiose,* a periodical he edited, was placed on the Index (Jan. 28, 1925) soon after it began publication. Buonaiuti was excommunicated *vitandus* (1925) and was forbidden to wear clerical garb (1930). In 1931 he was relieved of his post at the University of Rome as professor of the history of Christianity, which he had held since 1915 because he refused to take an oath supporting FASCISM. Another of his numerous works, *Storia del cristianesimo,* also was put on the Index (Dec. 16, 1942). All his works, *Opera et scripta omnia,* were condemned to the Index on three occasions (March 24, 1924; Jan. 28, 1925; June 17, 1944). On his deathbed Cardinal Francesco Marmaggi visited him but did not succeed in reconciling him, although Pius XII had authorized the cardinal to do so without requiring a retractation, provided the dying man expressed his belief in the Church's teachings and his disapproval of all that the Church reproved.

Bibliography: M. RAVÀ, *Bibliografia degli scritti di Ernesto Buonaiuti* (Florence 1951), with preface by L. SALVATORELLI. E. ROSA, "Il caso Buonaiuti," *La civiltà cattolica* (1925) 2:229–243; 3:220–238. D. GRASSO, *Il Cristianesimo di E. B.* (Brescia 1953). V. VINAY, *E. B. e l'Italia religiosa del suo tempo* (Rome 1956).

[F. M. O'CONNOR]

BURCHARD, DECRETUM OF

BURCHARD OF WORMS wrote his *Decretum* (*Liber Decretorum, Brocardus*) between 1007 and 1015. He profited from the help of Walter, Bishop of Spire, and Olbert of Gembloux, who was a monk of the Abbey of Lobbes. The *Decretum* is composed of 1,758 chapters divided into 20 books: the first 18 contain a complete outline of canonical prescriptions followed in that time. Book 19 (*Corrector sive Medicus*) is penitential, and the 20th (*Liber Speculationum, Speculator*) treats of dogmatic questions especially on eschatology.

Sources. The sources for the *Decretum* are mainly the Collection of Regino of Prüm (600 texts), the ANSELMO DEDICATA (300 texts), the *Dionysio-Hadriana*, the FALSE DECRETALS, the councils of the 9th century, the episcopal *Capitula* (Theodolph of Orléans, Haito of Basel, Herard of Tours), the *Collectio HIBERNENSIS* and some penitentials (Theodore, RABANUS MAURUS, Halitgaire), and finally, extracts of works of SS. Gregory the Great, Isidore of Seville, and Augustine. Texts of Roman law are rare; on the other hand, almost 90 fragments come from authentic Carolingian capitulars or from apocrypha of BENEDICT THE LEVITE.

Burchard used his sources very freely; he modified almost 600 inscriptions and even, at times, altered the substance of the documents, to adapt them to contemporary discipline or to promulgate his own ideas for reform.

Contents. Burchard's central idea is that necessary reforms must be worked out by the episcopate, aided in its task by secular power. Toward the Holy See, occupied at that time by the energetic Benedict VIII (1012–24), Burchard has the greatest respect; he recognizes pontifical primacy and the role of the pope as legislator, guarantor of councils (1.42, 179), and guide of Christianity. But this deference for principle does not prevent Burchard from defending the rights of bishops; he pretends to ignore monastic exemptions (8.66) and does not admit that the faithful have recourse to Rome to defeat the decisions of their bishops (2.80). The bishop, head of the local church, may not be judged by the secular power; it is the provincial council (not only the metropolitan one) and, on appeal, the pope, who judges such matters.

The bishop must promote the dignity of life of his clergy. Burchard condemns the marriage of clerics who have taken major orders, but does not ask the faithful to boycott the Sacraments of married priests (2.108). He condemns all forms of simony and avarice but readmits guilty clerics to the functions of their order after they have done penance and have returned to a worthy life (19.42).

Burchard attempts to ensure the morality of the Christian people by proclaiming the indissolubility of marriage (he admits, however, some cases of remarriage after divorce: 17.10, 11; 19.5). He condemns private vengeance, drunkenness, and superstition. True guide of confessors, his *Corrector* contributed to refining the moral sense and individualizing penance: *diversitas culparum diversitatem facit paenitentibus medicamentorum* (19.8).

The *Decretum* of Burchard, signed with the seal of pastoral realism, conservative and conciliating, had a large and rapid diffusion. Through the collections of IVO OF CHARTRES, his work entered the *Decretum* of GRATIAN.

Bibliography: P. FOURNIER and G. LEBRAS, *Histoire des collections canoniques en occident depuis les fausses décrétales jusqu'au Décret de Gratien*, 2 v. (Paris 1931–32) 1:364–421. J. PÉTRAU-GAY, *Dictionnaire de droit canonique*, ed. R. NAZ, 7 v. (Paris 1935–65) 2:1142–57. P. FOURNIER, ''Études critiques sur le Décret de Burchard de Worms,'' *Nouvelle revue historique de droit franç et étranger* 34 (1910) 41–112, 291–331, 564–584; ''Le Décret de Burchard de Worms: Ses caractères, son influence,'' *Revue d'histoire ecclésiastique* 12 (1911) 451–473, 670–701. O. MEYER, ''Ueberlieferung und Verbreitung des Dekrets des Bischofs Burchard von Worms,'' *Zeitschrift der Savigny-Stiftung für Rechtsgeschichte Kanonistische Abteilung* 24 (1935) 144–180.

[C. MUNIER]

BURCHARD OF WORMS

Bishop and canonist; b. Wesse, *c.* 965; d. Aug. 20, 1025. Burchard was a member of the noble family of Hesse. He studied at several schools, the most important of which was the Benedictine school at Lobbes in the Diocese of Cambrai. He entered the service of Archbishop Willigis of Mainz, who ordained Burchard to the diaconate. Burchard held the positions of first chamberlain and primate (judge) of the city of Mainz. His discretion and impartiality in fulfilling these offices brought him to the attention of Emperor Otto III, and the result was Burchard's being appointed by Otto III as bishop of Worms in the year 1000. Burchard was then ordained to the priesthood and consecrated bishop by Archbishop Willigis at Seligenstadt.

As bishop of Worms, Burchard first had to establish his authority. The rival power of an important family, supported by the Saxon dynasty, had been in complete control and were hostile to the interests of the Church. Burchard labored tirelessly for the temporal and spiritual welfare of his diocese. He erected several monasteries and churches and undertook the reconstruction of the Cathedral of Worms in 1016. He also paid special attention to the education and formation of his clerics in his cathedral school. In the interest of diocesan ecclesiastical reform, he conducted several diocesan visitations and synods.

Burchard was a leading figure in the general ecclesiastical reform taking hold in Germany at the beginning of the 11th century. He attended several provincial councils: at Thionville (1002–03), over which Henry II presided; at Frankfurt (1007); and at Seligenstadt (1023). This last council was particularly noteworthy for its reform decrees.

Burchard is also the author of one of the most important canonical collections of the Middle Ages, namely, his *Decretum collectarium* (known later as the *Brocardus*). He compiled this collection between the years 1007 and 1014 with the aid of Oldbert of Gembloux. Between the years 1023 and 1025 he promulgated a celebrated body of laws known as the *Leges et statuta familiae S. Petri Wormatiensis.* These laws were concerned principally with the impartial administration of justice, and they are a useful source for customs and conditions of the feudal society of that period (they may be found in *Monumenta Germaniae Historica I Constitutiones* 639–644).

Shortly after Burchard's death, one of his clerics wrote his biography, providing valuable historical details of his life and of the period (cf. *Vita Burchardi; Patrologia latina* 140:507–). Apparently Burchard was highly esteemed by his people, but there does not appear to have been any public cult given to him after his death.

Bibliography: G. ALLEMANG, *Dictionnaire d'histoire et de géographie ecclésiastiques* (Paris 1912–) 10:1245–47. J. PÉTRAU-GAY, *Dictionnaire de droit canonique* (Paris 1935–65) 2:1141–57. K. WEINZIERL, *Lexikon für Theologie und Kirche* (Freiburg 1957–65) 2:783–784. P. FOURNIER and G. LEBRAS, *Histoire des collections canoniques en occident depuis les fausses décrétales jusqu'au Décret de Gratien* (Paris 1931–32) 1:364–421.

[J. M. BUCKLEY]

BURCHARD OF WÜRZBURG, ST.

Bishop; b. England; d. Germany, 753 or 754. When already a BENEDICTINE monk Burchard was attracted by the great apostolate of his countryman St. BONIFACE and left England, probably *c.* 735, to become a disciple and collaborator of the Apostle of Germany. When Boniface established the hierarchy in Thuringia, he made Burchard the first bishop of Würzburg in 741 or 742. On April 21, 743, Burchard attended the first German synod and in 747 the general synod of Franconia, and he went to Rome in 748 to report on the state of the Church in Franconia. He enjoyed the esteem of PEPIN III, who sent him in 750 and 751 with Fulrad of Saint-Denis (d. 784) to Rome regarding the deposition of CHILDERIC III, last of the MEROVINGIANS, and recognition of Pepin's claim to be king of the Franks. Upon his death, Burchard was buried in the cathedral of Würzburg, but on Oct. 14, 983 Bishop Hugo (d. 990) translated his relics to the monastery of St. Andrew, founded by Burchard in 752. The account of his abdication (*Vita II*) seems to be mere legend.

Feast: Oct. 14.

Bibliography: *Vita Burchardi* I, unreliable 9th-century life, and *Vita* II, 12th century, both ed. O. HOLDER-EGGER in *Monumenta Germaniae Historica: Scriptores* 15.1:47–62. *Vita Sancti Burkardi, Die jüngere Lebensbeschreibung des hl. Burkard,* ed. F. J. BENDEL (Paderborn 1912). E. ULLRICH, *Der hl. Burkardus erster Bischof von Würzburg* (Würzburg 1877). *Bibliotheca hagiograpica latina antiquae et mediae aetatis* (Brussels 1898–1901) 1:1483–85. A. M. ZIMMERMANN, *Kalendarium Benedictinum* (Metten 1933–38) 3:177–180. W. LEVISON, *England and the Continent in the Eighth Century* (Oxford 1946).

[P. L. HUG]

BURDEN, EDWARD, BL.

Priest, martyr; b. ca. 1540 in Co. Durham, England; d. Nov. 29, 1588, hanged, drawn, and quartered at York, England. He studied at Trinity College, Oxford, before completing his theological studies on the Continent. He was ordained (1584) at Douai and returned to England in 1586 to work in Yorkshire. He was condemned for his priesthood and suffered with Fr. John HEWETT. Burden was beatified by Pope John Paul II on Nov. 22, 1987 with George Haydock and Companions.

Feast of the English Martyrs: May 4 (England).

See Also: ENGLAND, SCOTLAND, AND WALES, MARTYRS OF.

Bibliography: R. CHALLONER, *Memoirs of Missionary Priests,* ed. J. H. POLLEN (rev. ed. London 1924). J. H. POLLEN, *Acts of English Martyrs* (London 1891).

[K. I. RABENSTEIN]

BUREAU, PAUL

French sociologist and moralist; b. Elboeuf (Seine-Maritime), Oct. 5, 1865; d. Paris, May 7, 1923. After completing secondary school at Rouen, he made study tours to England in 1884 and San Francisco in 1885 and then studied law at Rouen and at the Institut Catholique of Paris. He argued few cases as an attorney. In 1891 he took charge of the course in Roman law at the Institut Catholique and then became professor of international law in 1902. He also occupied a chair of sociology at the Sorbonne.

As a sociologist, Bureau was a disciple of Frédéric Le Play, adhering at first to the school of La Science sociale, led by Henri de Tourville, from which he later withdrew. He was interested in perfecting its method, treating social facts objectively (*comme des choses*) on the condition that their character as psychological facts was respected. To the social factors considered by Tourville (geography, work), Bureau added *Weltanschauung,* thus avoiding sociological determinism and emphasizing the role of individual initiative in social development. Against Émile DURKHEIM, he refused to attribute to collective consciousness a reality anterior and superior to individual life. He prolonged the influence of Gabriel Tarde and prepared the way for Henri BERGSON. For Bureau, sociology as a science was both necessary and insufficient. He proposed the necessity of a social art, i.e., the ordering of institutions from the point of view of the reform of morals, in a period in which the reconstruction of morality was sought by rationalism and positivism. Bureau was an exacting moralist, disquieted by the sexual indiscipline and conjugal dissolution he observed. His most important works include *La Crise morale des temps nouveaux* (Paris 1907), *L'Indiscipline des moeurs* (Paris 1920), and *Introduction à la méthode sociologique* (Paris 1923).

Bibliography: G. DE LANZAC DE LABORIE et al., *Paul Bureau* (Paris 1924).

[G. JARLOT]

BUREAU INTERNATIONAL CATHOLIQUE DE L'ENFANCE (BICE)

An international network for professionals in child welfare established in France in 1948, the BICE provides a forum through which organizations and individuals can defend children's interests. It gives particular attention to the most deprived, especially disabled children, child victims of the street, war, and sex trade. In all its actions the BICE underscores spiritual growth, intercultural awareness, and the rights of the child.

Originally established to care for children affected by the Second World War, in the early 1950s the BICE expanded its focus, creating the Medico-Educational and

Psycho-Social Special Care Commission that devotes special attention to the faith development and spiritual needs of handicapped and suffering children worldwide. Further, the BICE invites other childcare groups to join in a common effort to address the special needs of children and awaken public opinion in their regard.

In 2001, the BICE's primary activities were: 1) the promotion of policies relative to childrens' rights, such as ''Poder Crecer,'' the development of strategies for the application of the United Nations Convention on the Rights of the Child for 11 Latin American countries; 2) positive approaches and supervision of particularly vulnerable children, such as those involved in armed conflict (Liberia) or those accused of ''witchcraft'' (Democratic Republic of Congo); 3) the prevention of and intervention against sexual abuse and exploitation of children, such as the protection of young girls in India; 4) alternatives and rehabilitation for children deprived of their liberty, such as imprisoned children or their families from Latvia to Senegal. Through the development and implementation of pilot projects, training seminars, educational materials, and action-oriented research, the BICE seeks to further the holistic growth of all children, to support family-based child development strategies, and to build upon the capacities of children to participate in their own development.

The BICE was instrumental in the initiation and promotion of the International Year of the Child (1979) under the aegis of the United Nations. It also established a forum to study the growing problem of street-children. A series of seminars held between 1983 and 1986 had as their theme ''The Spiritual Growth of the Child.'' It was in relation to this theme that the BICE's Special Care Commission sponsored the 1984 conference, held in Chicago, on ''Education in the Faith with Developmentally Disabled Persons.'' In September 1987 the BICE co-sponsored a seminar in Luxembourg on ''The Right of the Child to Receive the Faith.''

The BICE's General Secretariat is located in Geneva, Switzerland, where it supports the regional delegations for central and eastern Europe as well as Asia. Regional delegations are based also in Lahr, Germany (Africa) and Brussels, Belgium (Western Europe and Latin America). The General Secretariat maintains an office in Paris for finances and communications. The New York office closed in 1997, although some coordination occurs through Catholic Relief Services. Regional offices are currently located in Abidjan, Ivory Coast; Madurai, South India; Sihanoukville, Cambodia; Surkhet Province, Nepal; Montevideo, Uruguay; and Moscow, Russia. The BICE is recognized by the Holy See. As a non-governmental organization, it has consultative status with the United Nations Economic and Social Council (UNESCO), the Council of Europe, and UNICEF on child-related issues. Publications include an annual report.

[M. GARDINIER/P. J. HAYES]

BURGOA, FRANCISCO DE

Mexican Dominican chronicler; b. Antequera (today Oaxaca), *c.* 1600; d. Zaachila or possibly Teozapotlán, 1681. He was the son of Ana de Porras, but his father's name is unknown. Burgoa was a descendant of the conquistadores of Oaxaca and was related to prominent families there. He took the habit in 1618 and made his profession in Antequera in the Dominican province of San Hipólito (1620); he was ordained in 1625. Burgoa taught theology for many years and worked in various parishes. He mastered the Zapoteca and Mixteca languages, which enabled him to learn the traditions and legends of the natives of the province. He was provincial in 1649 and was named procurator of his province to the Holy See and to the master general. Eager to improve the culture of his country, he visited many libraries, museums, cultural centers, and convents while in Europe. In Rome he attended the general chapter of his order (1656) and was named definitor, officer of the Inquisition in New Spain, inspector of libraries, censor of books, and vicar general. On his return to Mexico, he was again made provincial (1662). After his term of office, Burgoa went to the convent of Zaachila, where he wrote two of his best literary works: *Palestra historial de virtudes, y exemplares apostólicos* (1 v.) and *Geográfica descripción de la parte septentrional, del polo ártico de la América, nueva iglesia de las Indias Occidentales y sitio astronómico de esta provincia de predicadores de Antequera Valle de Oaxaca* . . . (2 v.). Both these works were published in Mexico City (1670 and 1674). They were reissued by the Mexican government in 1934, along with a biography of Burgoa and a bibliography of his published and unpublished works. The *Palestra historial* is a chronicle beginning with the arrival of the Dominicans in Mexico City in 1526 and emphasizing their work in the area of Oaxaca. It is largely biographical. The *Geográfica descripción* is concerned mainly with histories of the monasteries. While Burgoa's style is extravagant and tedious, his works are irreplaceable sources for the history of Oaxaca.

[E. GÓMEZ TAGLE]

BURIAL, I (IN THE BIBLE)

In the Bible there is no complete account of burial customs. They are set out here on the basis of data gathered from isolated Biblical passages and from archeological finds. The limitations of this material must be kept in mind; much valuable information has been gathered from the several thousand graves and tombs that have been found and excavated, but only a small fraction of the millions of bodies buried in Bible lands have been brought to light.

Inhumation, Not Cremation. In Syria and Palestine during the Biblical period the common manner of disposal of dead bodies was inhumation, not cremation. Passages that speak of burning refer to ceremonial offerings of aromatic spices (2 Chr 16.14; 21.19; Jer 34.5) or to criminals or enemies (Gn 38.24; Jos 7.25; Lv 20.14; 21.9), whose remains could also be interred (Dt 21.23; Jos 8.29; 10.27). Bodies were deposited in their tombs garbed in the clothes used in life (1 Sm 28.14; Ez 32.27); the use of special burial clothes is late (Jn 11.44; Mk 15.46 and parallels). The corpse was either drawn together, knees to chin, and laid on one side, usually the left, or stretched out on its back; it was surrounded by deposits of articles used in life: dishes, bowls, pitchers, lamps, pieces of furniture, weapons, amulets, and articles of adornment.

Location of Burial Places. The place of burial was outside the inhabited area (as in the necropolises at JERICHO, Megiddo, Gibeon, and Lachish), without a preconceived plan in the layout of the graves, whether on even terrain or in tombs excavated in rocky hillsides. However, graves of individuals have been found in cities and villages and such burials are mentioned in the Bible; e.g., Samuel was buried in his house at Ramah (1 Sm 25.1), and Manasseh in Jerusalem (2 Chr 33.20). Individual graves outside the inhabited area are exceptional (Gn 35.8; 1 Sm 31.13); the more common practice was the reuse of family tombs for new burials, in some cases over hundreds of years.

Historical Sequence of Grave Forms. From the Neolithic Period to the transition from Middle Bronze to Late Bronze, the most common forms of tombs are single or connected natural caves, sometimes reshaped to better suit their use for burials. The access was direct, from above, and could be blocked by a stone and refill.

Typical of Middle Bronze and continuing into Late Bronze is the shaft grave; here the access to the sepulchral chamber is a small opening at the bottom of a perpendicular or stepped, circular or square shaft. After burial the cave was closed off by a stone and the shaft filled with excavation rubble.

The transition from Late Bronze to the Iron Age is marked by the development of burial ledges in the sepulchral caves; on reuse, the defleshed bones were gathered and deposited in an ossuary pit or in a specially prepared bone cavern.

The last development in burial chambers comes in the Greco-Roman period; a vestibule gives access to a series of burial chambers provided with niches, dug at waist height or lower, perpendicularly into the rock. These niches could be closed off by plain or inscribed coverings. When the niche was to be reused, the defleshed remains were gathered into bone boxes known as OSSUARIES. Some graves have longitudinal, arched niches in which the bodies could be placed.

The use of sarcophagi of stone, wood, clay, or lead throughout the Biblical period was an exception made in favor of especially prominent persons, no doubt because of the great cost of preparing such containers. The six so-called sarcophagi of Abraham and Sarah, Isaac and Rebekah, and Jacob and Leah beneath the *haram* in Hebron are cenotaphs erected many centuries after the burials of these people. Monuments above ground calling attention to the presence of buried bodies are late, like the Maccabean mausoleum at Modin (1 Mc 13.27–30). In earlier centuries the effort seems rather to have been to conceal the place of burial.

Interpretation of Burial Customs. The deposit of articles of daily life and, at least in the earliest period, of food and drink may indicate that, in the belief of non-Israelites, the dead were thought to live in the tombs and to have need of and use for these goods. There is nothing to show that Israelites shared this view. In their burial customs they followed the practices they found in vogue as part of the ritual of decent burial and respect for the dead, allowing themselves to be guided in their beliefs by the affirmations of their religion (*see* AFTERLIFE, 2). The late custom of collecting the defleshed bones from the niches in which they had lain and depositing them in individual ossuaries, often inscribed with the name of the dead person, may reflect the belief in bodily resurrection that arose in the 2d pre-Christian century.

Bibliography: J. VAN DODEWAARD, *Lexikon für Theologie und Kirche*, ed. J. HOFER and K. RAHNER (Freiburg 1957–65) 2:117. H. SCHMID, *Die Religion in Geschichte und Gegenwart,* (3d ed. Tübingen 1957–65) 1:961–962. R. DE VAUX, *Ancient Israel, Its Life, and Institutions,* tr. J. MCHUGH (New York 1961) 56–61. K. GALLING, *Biblisches Reallexicon* (Tübingen 1937). F. NÖTSCHER, *Biblische Altertumskunde* (Bonn 1940) 97–104. A. G. BARROIS, *Manuel d'archéologie biblique* (Paris 1939–) 2:274–323. G. E. WRIGHT, *Biblical Archaeology* (rev. ed. Philadelphia 1963) 289, index s.v. Burial of Dead. K. M. KENYON, *Archaeology in the Holy Land* (New York 1960) 321, index s.v. Burial Customs; *Digging up Jericho* (New York 1958) 272, index s.v. Tombs. J. B. PRITCHARD, *The Bronze Age Cemetery at Gibeon* (Philadelphia 1963); *Gibeon, Where the Sun Stood Still* (Princeton 1962). L. Y. RAHMANI, ''A Jewish Tomb on Shahin Hill, Jerusalem,'' *Israel Exploration Jour-*

nal 8 (1958) 101–105. R. DE VAUX, ''Fouille au Khirbet Qumrân,'' *Revue biblique* 60 (1953) 83–106.

[M. A. HOFER]

BURIAL, II (EARLY CHRISTIAN)

In the primitive Church, burial customs continued Jewish practices, as is attested by the Acts of the Apostles. As Christianity spread, however, the rites were adapted to local usages that were gradually modified by Christian belief in the Redemption, salvation, and eternal life. Christian burial stressed reverence for the body as the creation of God, the coinstrument of the soul that shared life in Christ and was destined for a glorious resurrection both personal and ecclesial. The most profound theology of burial is in Augustine's work *On the Care of the Dead,* while the most developed burial liturgy is found in the *Ecclesiastical Hierarchy* of PSEUDO-DIONYSIUS THE AREOPAGITE.

Laying Out of the Body. Upon ascertainment of death, the eyes and mouth were closed. In pagan funerals this was the occasion for the *conclamatio* or violent outcries of mourning. Christians attempted to curb this practice by singing psalms. AUGUSTINE mentions the chanting of Psalm 100, which speaks of God's mercy and judgment. After this came the washing of the body; this is attested to by the Acts of the Apostles in the case of the body of Dorcas. Tertullian witnesses to the continuation of this practice in his defense of the Christians: ''When I die I can become stiff and pale as death after being washed.'' Egyptian Christians occasionally adopted embalming, a practice witnessed to by John CASSIAN, St. Anthony, and St. Augustine, as well as by archeological remains that bear the CHI-RHO monogram or the Good Shepherd. Ordinarily, the body was anointed to preserve it before burial, a custom the pagans criticized as recorded in Minucius Felix: ''You do not grace your body with perfumes, you reserve unguents for funerals.'' Frequent mention is made of myrrh and of Arabian and Sabean spices. This anointing is not to be confused with the anointing of the deceased during the church service, as described by Pseudo-Dionysius. This was a completion of the Baptismal anointing and signified that the deceased had waged a victorious struggle.

The clothing of the dead followed the anointing. The body was wrapped in linen, since the linen of burial, like that of Baptism, signified immortality. Then the body was clothed in the toga and the outer cloak or in the garments of the deceased's state in life, e.g., emperor or monk. Usually the outer garment was dark, violet being the usual color. Constant denunciations by Eastern and Western Fathers indicate that Christians also employed precious apparel of silk or gold as burial robes and that they were berated for vain display and urged to concentrate on the garment of immortality, the resurrection. Sixth-century canonical legislation indicates that the body was wrapped in or covered with palls and cloths used for divine services. In pagan funerals, the deceased was crowned. Christianity at first rejected this custom because of its idolatrous association with the crowning of the gods; but it gradually was interpreted as presenting the crown of victory.

Les Alyscamps I, Aries, c. 1st-5th century, Allee des Sarcophagus, Aries, France. (©Paul Almasy/CORBIS)

Wake. Whenever possible there was a wake before burial, held at times in the home of the deceased. When burial occurred on the same day as death, a three-day watch was often held at the grave. The wake for one who was buried the following day took the form of a night vigil, which at times was celebrated in the church and was an occasion for friends to condole the relatives and to pray for the deceased. This custom was greatly influenced by monastic practices. The body was surrounded with candles, symbolizing the *lux perpetua* to which the deceased was called, and priests read scriptural passages dealing with death, the resurrection, and life everlasting.

Procession. The Christian funeral procession was more a triumphal march. This applied to the simple burials of the early martyrs and to the more solemn funerals after the Peace of the Church. The body, covered with an outer covering, was carried on the funeral bed, with the head raised and exposed. The Acts of the Apostles mentions special young men deputed to carry the corpse. Later there were official *lecticarii* to perform this work.

Frequently, relatives acted as pallbearers. For the funerals of outstanding persons, bishops and priests carried the body, and normally it was followed by the family and friends. In the more solemn funerals, acolytes led the procession, and deacons carrying torches escorted the corpse. In some cases the participants were arranged in such a way that the women marched with the nuns and the men with the monks. The main feature was the triumphal spirit, a feature that amazed the pagans. Pagan practices—instrumental music, hired mourners, actors and buffoons—were excluded. The entire group joyfully sang Psalms, the reason for which is given by St. John Chrysostom: ''Is it not that we praise God and thank Him that He has crowned the departed and freed him from suffering, and that God has the deceased, now freed from fear, with Himself?'' The favorite Psalms were 22, 31, 100, 114, and 115.

Eucharistic Celebration. A distinctive feature of Christian burial was the celebration of the Eucharistic sacrifice and partaking in the Eucharistic banquet. With the pagans, there was a sacrifice offered to the departed, and often a fish was used. Christianity had its own ΙΧΘΥΣ, Jesus Christ, and the sacrifice of Christ was offered for the deceased. The apocryphal *Acts of John* (*c.* A.D. 150–180) mentions the celebration of the Eucharist at the grave on the 3d day. The casual manner in which this is mentioned indicates that it was the accepted practice to offer Mass at funerals. The Eucharist was celebrated at the grave or in the church. The Mass for CONSTANTINE I and for St. MONICA was celebrated at the grave. St. Ambrose's Mass was that of Easter. St. Zeno of Verona and Pseudo-Dionysius speak of celebrating Mass in the church before the burial.

Interment. The funeral oration, if not previously delivered in the church, was spoken by a relative or friend at the grave. This was meant not only to eulogize the deceased, but to offer consolation drawn from Christian beliefs. Those of SS. Gregory of Nazianzus, Gregory of Nyssa, and Ambrose are the most famous. The relatives then approached the corpse to impart the final kiss, which was given also before leaving the house; but Pseudo-Dionysius speaks of the kiss as part of the liturgical service in the church. It indicated natural affection and the Christian belief in the sacredness of the body. This was a Christian practice, since contemporary religions considered contact with a corpse as a ritual defilement. The body, after being wrapped in linen, was placed in the grave in a lying position. The hands were extended alongside the body or folded across the chest. The body was buried facing the east, awaiting the PAROUSIA, the second coming of Christ in glory.

From the beginning Christians practiced earth burial and not cremation. In so doing, they imitated the burial of Christ and followed the Jewish practice. Originally, there was no intrinsic link between earth burial and resurrection. However, St. Paul speaks of the body being sown in corruption and rising in incorruption. Hostile pagans regarded the Christian earth burial as linked with the resurrection and often prevented burial by burning the bodies of Christians or exposing them to vultures. Through earth burial, Christianity and the resurrection became interchangeable concepts. The Christians frequently affirmed that no human intervention could thwart the divine work of the resurrection. Otherwise, Christians professed indifference to being buried or not. This was a radical change, for in contemporary non-Christian religions the proper carrying out of the funeral was regarded as vital for the repose of the soul in the land of the dead, lest the deceased become a restless and vengeful ghost. Before leaving the cemetery the participants pronounced the last farewell. The pagan departure ceremony was *vale,* a final farewell; that of the Christians was *vivas,* a prayer that the departed might live in God and intercede for the living.

Visits to the grave were frequent, and the special days for commemorating the dead were the 3d, 7th or 9th, 30th or 40th, and the anniversary. After the paschal mystery celebrated in the Eucharist, the first liturgical feasts of the saints evolved from these anniversary celebrations, which were considered prolongations of the paschal mystery, life and death in Christ being unique because of the Resurrection. In the words of St. Augustine, ''it is this belief alone that distinguishes and separates Christians from all other men.''

Bibliography: A. C. RUSH, *Death and Burial in Christian Antiquity* (Washington 1941), bibliog. Centre de pastorale liturgique, *Le Mystère de la mort et sa célébration* (Lex orandi 12; Paris 1956). H. LECLERCQ, *Dictionnaire d'archéologie chrétienne et de liturgie*, ed. F. CABROL, H. LECLERCQ, and H. I. MARROU (Paris 1907–53) 5.2:2705–15; 15.1:1266–72. J. KOLLWITZ, *Reallexikon für Antike und Christentum,* ed. T. KLAUSER]Stuttgart 1941 (1950–)[2:208–219.

[A. C. RUSH]

BURIGNY, JEAN LÉVESQUE DE

French scholar; b. Reims, 1692; d. Paris, Oct. 8, 1785. He came to Paris in 1713 and acquired an immense erudition in ancient and modern history, philosophy, and theology, and a knowledge of Latin, Greek, and Hebrew. He and his brothers formed an academy that compiled a 12-volume encyclopedia in MS. In 1720 they went to the Hague and worked with Saint-Hyacinthe on the journal *Europe savante* (1718–20). Almost all of Burigny's writings deal with religious matters and have a Gallican, even Presbyterian, slant. His treatise on the authority of the pope (4 v. in 12, 1720) is a good example of his doctrine and method. He also wrote two volumes on pagan theology (1724), a noteworthy two-volume history of Sicily (1745), three volumes on Byzantine revolutions (1750), and biographies of Plotinus, Grotius, Erasmus, Bossuet, and Cardinal J. Du Perron. In 1756 he was made a member of the Académie des Inscriptions et Belles-lettres.

Bibliography: C. CONSTANTIN, *Dictionnaire de théologie catholique* 2.1:1264–65. J. CARREYRE, *Dictionnaire d'histoire et de géographie ecclésiastiques* 10:1375–76.

[W. E. LANGLEY]

BURKE, EDMUND

British statesman and author whose writings are a main source of modern Anglo-Saxon political thought; b. Dublin, probably Jan. 12, 1729, N.S.; d. Beaconsfield, Buckinghamshire, July 8, 1797. As children of a Protestant attorney father and a Catholic mother, Edmund and his brothers were raised as Anglicans, their sister as a Catholic. Jane Nugent, whom Burke married in 1756, may have been a Catholic like her father; she conformed to the Church of England on marrying Burke.

Burke attended Trinity College, Dublin, from 1744 to 1750. He began to study law at the Middle Temple in London in 1750, but soon abandoned it to follow a literary career. In 1756 he published two works that attracted attention: *A Philosophical Inquiry into the Origin of Our Ideas of the Sublime and Beautiful* expressed a rather crudely sensistic psychology, but had an influence on aesthetic theory in England and on the Continent; *A Vindication of Natural Society* was a parody of Bolingbroke satirizing the individualistic rationalism that Burke was to combat all his life. In 1757 he became editor of Dodsley's *Annual Register*, a review of the outstanding events of each year.

In 1765 the Marquis of Rockingham, who had become first lord of the treasury, made Burke his private secretary. In the same year Burke got a seat in the Commons from Lord Verney's pocket borough of Wendover. For almost 30 years he sat in Parliament, almost always in opposition after 1766, since the Rockingham Whigs were not in favor with George III. He was elected from Bristol in 1774, an occasion he used in his *Speech to the Electors at Bristol* to expound a theory of representation that has become classic. Feeling that an attempt at reelection in 1780 was useless, he withdrew and was then made member for Rockingham's nomination borough of Malton. He held that seat until his retirement in 1794.

Position in British politics. Burke was the philosopher and spokesman for the Whig aristocracy. His

Edmund Burke.

Thoughts on the Cause of the Present Discontents (1770) exposed what the Whigs regarded as a dangerous increase in the royal power. His administrative reform plan, which he introduced in 1780, was designed to reduce crown influence in Parliament by eliminating part of the royal patronage. The East India Bill of 1783, of which Burke was at least part author, had the same object among its purposes. At the same time, Burke opposed reform of the representation in the House of Commons. Centuries of failure to reapportion representation had produced a system that allowed decayed villages to continue sending two members to Parliament while thriving new towns had none. Burke saw any change as a threat to his ideal of a constitution that maintained a careful balance among the crown, the great landowners, and a random sample of the gentry and merchants. The natural-rights ideology in terms of which parliamentary reform was usually advocated did nothing to commend reform to him, as can be seen in his *Speech on the Reform of the Representation in the House of Commons* (1782).

Generally, however, Burke was a moderate reformer who advocated criminal law reform, relaxation of the PENAL LAWS against Catholics and debtors, and the gradual abolition of the slave trade. He never favored the dissolution of the British Empire. Rather, he sought to bind the American colonies and the Kingdom of Ireland to

Britain by ties of fair treatment and mutual interest. In his great speeches on *American Taxation* (1774) and *Conciliation with the Colonies* (1775) he upheld Britain's right to tax the colonies but denounced the attempt to exercise that right as folly. Burke's policy in regard to India was influenced by considerations of party politics and by the financial interests of his relatives. But a genuine moral indignation grew in him as he delved more deeply into Indian affairs. The impeachment of the governor-general of India, Warren Hastings, with Burke as chief prosecutor, failed. But Burke's flaming oratory inspired the British public's concern for the fate of colonial peoples in the 19th century.

Opposition to the French Revolution. Burke showed his philosophical position most fully in his attack on the FRENCH REVOLUTION, which he distrusted almost from its beginning. His masterpiece, *Reflections on the Revolution in France*, appeared in February 1790. That work and the subsequent *Appeal from the New to the Old Whigs* (1791) contain the heart of Burke's philosophy. Together with *Thoughts on French Affairs* (1791), *Remarks on the Policy of the Allies* (1793), and *Letters on a Regicide Peace* (1796–97), they made him a leader not only of British but also of European public opinion against the Revolution. Burke saw the Revolution less as a revolt against intolerable conditions than as the overthrow of the social and political order by the doctrinaire devotees of an abstract theory of the rights of man. But for all his denunciations of ''theory'' and ''metaphysics'' in politics, Burke had a social and political theory and it implied a metaphysic.

Political philosophy. His conception of a divinely founded universal order, of which the state is a part, sprang from a basically Catholic philosophy. He received the medieval doctrine of NATURAL LAW through the Anglican tradition. But he insisted that although principles are necessary, they are not enough; they must be applied by PRUDENCE. Here Burke's thought is strikingly similar to the Aristotelian and Thomistic doctrine of practical reason.

He was also keenly aware of history. A good constitution cannot be struck off at a given time by the brain and purpose of man. According to Burke, ''it is made by the peculiar circumstances, occasions, tempers, dispositions, and moral, civil and social habitudes of the people, which disclose themselves only in a long space of time'' [''Speech on the Reform of the Representation . . . ,'' Works (London 1812) 10.97]. This idea is said to have influenced the historical school in Germany and to have made Burke a forerunner of G. W. F. HEGEL.

Burke saw human nature as realizing itself through an evolving and organic social order (a concept with which his laissez-faire economic theory seems inconsistent). Society, government, law, and rights satisfy natural human needs. But in themselves they are products of convention, framed not according to a blueprint furnished by an abstract law of nature but by practical reasoning and long experience. Once established, however, they have a prescriptive force and may not be abolished by appealing to a radically individualistic theory of popular sovereignty. Reform, therefore, must be accomplished by the gradual adjustment of a complex social organism to new situations, not by social revolution and only in extreme cases by political revolution.

Burke's writings are magnificent examples of the great period of British political rhetoric. Sir Philip Magnus has called them ''the finest school of statecraft which exists.'' The frequency with which they are still quoted today is evidence both of Burke's wisdom and of his style.

Bibliography: *Works*, 12 v. (Boston 1901); *Speeches of the Right Honorable Edmund Burke*, 4 v. (London 1816); *The Correspondence of Edmund Burke*, ed. T. W. COPELAND et al., 10 v. (Chicago 1958–), 5 v. pub. to date. A. P. I. SAMUELS, *The Early Life, Correspondence and Writings of the Rt. Hon. Edmund Burke* (Cambridge, Eng. 1924). Literature. D. BRYANT, *Edmund Burke and His Literary Friends* (St. Louis 1939). F. P. CANAVAN, *The Political Reason of Edmund Burke* (Durham, N.C. 1960). C. B. CONE, *Burke and the Nature of Politics*, 2 v. (Lexington, Ky. 1957–64). T. W. COPELAND, *Our Eminent Friend Edmund Burke* (New Haven 1949). R. J. S. HOFFMANN, *Edmund Burke, New York Agent* (Philadelphia 1956). J. MACCUNN, *The Political Philosophy of Edmund Burke* (London 1913). T. H. D. MAHONEY, *Edmund Burke and Ireland* (Cambridge, Mass. 1960). J. MORLEY, *Burke* (New York 1879; repr. 1928). P. J. STANLIS, *Edmund Burke and the Natural Law* (Ann Arbor 1958). The best source of complete and recent bibliographical information is *The Burke Newsletter* (Detroit 1959–). H. C. MANSFIELD, *Statesmanship and Party Government: A Study of Burke and Bolingbroke* (Chicago 1965).

[F. P. CANAVAN]

BURKE, HONORIA

Martyr, Dominican tertiery; b. Co. Mayo, Ireland, 1549; d. Burrishoole, Ireland, February, 1653. Sr. Honoria, daughter of the chieftain of Clanricard, built a convent at Burrishoole after receiving the habit *c.* 1562. She is said to have miraculously escaped capture by the English troops one time. The second time she was pursued, she sought sanctuary in a church for eight days. Additional miracles of multiplication of scarce food are attributed to her. At the invasion of Cromwell, Burke fled Burrishoole with Sr. Honoria McGaen and a servant. The soldiers caught the centenarian, beat her, and left her to die. McGaen froze to death while hiding in the hollow of a tree. The servant buried both sisters and later related the story of their deaths. Sr. Burke is expressly titled a martyr in the Acts of the General Chapter of 1656.

See Also: IRISH CONFESSORS AND MARTYRS.

Bibliography: M. J. DORCY, *Saint Dominic's Family* (Dubuque, Iowa 1963), 422–23. D. MURPHY, *Our Martyrs* (Dublin 1896).

[K. I. RABENSTEIN]

BURKE, JOHN, SIR

Martyr, married, Lord of Brittas Castle, member of the Dominican Third Order; d. 1606 (some sources say 1610). As son of the baron of Limerick's Castle Connell, Sir John was born into the Irish nobility. During the reign of ELIZABETH I of England, he ran an underground safety net for refuge priests. Upon the ascension of JAMES I, Burke reorganized the Catholics scattered under the previous monarch and openly professed his Catholic faith. Upon the arrival of Lord Montjoy in Limerick, Burke was arrested on a charge of treason and imprisoned in Dublin, where he continued to loudly proclaim his faith and to pray openly.

During a plague, he was released from prison, returned to Brittas Castle, joined the Third Order of St. Dominic, and continued to perfect his network of safety houses for priests. The castle was attacked by Montjoy's forces as a Mass was being celebrated there. Two of the three Dominican celebrants escaped; one remained in the besieged castle with Sir John.

Rather than surrendering to the English, he arranged for the priest to be secreted out of the castle. Sir John himself attacked his way out, taking with him the sacred vessels and church valuables to hide. The English continued to chase Burke, while the bounty for his capture was doubled. Two female tertieries who sheltered Burke were burned to death for refusing to disclose his location.

He was eventually betrayed, captured, and condemned to be hanged, drawn, and quartered. During his imprisonment, he steadfastly prayed and exhorted others to remain faithful. Because he wished to bequeath something to the Dominicans although his property had been confiscated, from the scaffold he dedicated his unborn child to the Order. Following his execution, he was buried in the Church of St. John, Limerick. The then-unborn daughter later entered a Portuguese Dominican convent.

See Also: IRISH CONFESSORS AND MARTYRS.

Bibliography: D. MURPHY, *Our Martyrs* (Dublin 1896). M. J. DORCY, *Saint Dominic's Family* (Dubuque, Iowa 1963), 357–60.

[K. I. RABENSTEIN]

BURKE, JOHN J.

Editor, founder of the National Catholic War Council; b. New York City, June 6, 1875; d. New York City, Oct. 30, 1936. Burke was educated in public schools and at St. Francis Xavier High School and College in New York. He was ordained June 9, 1899, after completing seminary studies at Catholic University; and he received a licentiate in sacred theology two years later. Appointed assistant editor of the *Catholic World* in 1903 and editor in September 1904, he retained the editorship until 1922. While editor, he directed the Catholic Publication Society, now called Paulist Press, and was a founder of the Catholic Press Association (1911) and consultor of the Paulist Fathers (1909–19).

When the U.S. entered World War I in 1917, Burke presented to Cardinal John Farley of New York a detailed plan for a central controlling agency to unify all Catholic war activities, especially those designed to serve men in uniform. With the approval of Cardinal James Gibbons, dean of the hierarchy, the plan was implemented in an organization called the National Catholic War Council, with Burke as director. He founded The Chaplains' Aid Association (June 1917) and became chairman of the tri-faith Committee of Six to advise the Secretary of War on religious concerns (1917–22). At the end of the war, the National Catholic War Council was formed (September 1919) into the National Catholic Welfare Council (''Council'' later becoming ''Conference,'' abbreviated NCWC). He was often called the founder of the NCWC and was praised for that work by Archbishop Hanna, chairman of its administrative board. Burke was general secretary to the administrative board from 1919 until his death.

With William Kerby he cofounded the National Catholic School for Social Service, which opened in Washington, DC, on Nov. 4, 1921. In 1928 he represented the Holy See on two trips to Mexico, working closely with American ambassador Dwight Morrow to secure a *modus vivendi* that gave some measure of relief to the persecuted Church in that country. The Congregation of Seminaries and Universities awarded him an honorary doctorate in sacred theology (1927), and he was invested as domestic prelate (Sept. 21, 1936). His published works include translations of Abbe Anger's *Doctrine of the Mystical Body of Christ* (1931), J. Duperray's *Christ in the Christian Life* (1927), and Henry Perroy's *A Great and Humble Soul* (1933).

Bibliography: W. J. KENNEY, CSP, ''The Work of Father John J. Burke, C.S.P. (1917–1922),'' unpublished M.A. dissertation, St. Paul's College (Washington, DC 1951). L. R. LAWLER, *Full Circle* (Washington, DC 1951). E. D. WHITLEY, CSP, ''Father John J. Burke, C.S.P. (1927–1929),'' unpublished M.A. dissertation

Capital: Ouagadougou.
Size: 105,869 sq. miles.
Population: 11,946,065 in 2000.
Languages: French (official language); Sudanic African languages are spoken by most inhabitants.
Religions: 1,373,796 Catholics (11.5%), 5,973,032 Sunni Muslims (50%), 438,157 Protestants (.5%); 4,161,080 follow indigenous tribal beliefs.

(Washington, DC 1951). *Catholic Action*, memorial issue (Washington, DC Dec. 15, 1936).

[J. B. SHEERIN]

BURKE, THOMAS

Dominican preacher; b. Galway, Sept. 8, 1830; d. Tallaght, Ireland, July 2, 1882. Burke entered the Order for the Irish Province in Perugia, Italy, Dec. 29, 1847. While still a deacon studying in Rome, he was appointed (1852) novice-master at Woodchester, England, by Master General Jandel. He was ordained on March 26, 1853, and then he went to Ireland to open a novitiate at Tallaght. As a result of a sermon on Church music, which he delivered at Our Lady, Star of the Sea, Sandymond, on Sept. 4, 1859, he acquired a reputation as an orator that he maintained throughout his life. Burke was prior at Tallaght (1863) and rector of San Clemente, Rome (1864). He returned to Ireland in 1867. Acting as theologian to Bishop Leahy of Dromore, he attended Vatican Council I in 1870. As visitator to the American Dominican Province of St. Joseph (1871), he gave many sermons and a notable series of lectures, refuting James Anthony Froude, who sought to justify English occupation of Ireland. In 1873 Burke returned to Ireland, where he continued preaching until his death. He is buried in the church at Tallaght.

Bibliography: W. J. FITZPATRICK, *The Life of the Very Rev. Thomas N. Burke, O.P.*, 2 v. (New York 1886). *Le Père Thomas Burke, Dominicain,* tr. P. CAVALONNE (Brussels 1899).

[J. HALADUS]

BURKINA FASO, THE CATHOLIC CHURCH IN

Formerly called Upper Volta, the Republic of Burkina Faso is located in West Africa. Bordered on the west and north by Mali, it shares its eastern border with Niger and Benin, its southern border with Togo, Ghana, and the Ivory Coast. A vast plateau, 650 to 1,000 feet in elevation, Burkina Faso has seen increasing desertification due to the encroachment of the Sahara Desert. Although natural resources include marble, gold, and manganese and zinc deposits, the country's impoverished population engages in subsistence agriculture while serving as migratory labor to surrounding nations. One of the poorest nations in the world, Burkina Faso was a French territory until 1960. The region's 160 or so ethnic groups, very unequal in size, comprise three main families. Nearly half the Burkinabe population are Mossi, who controlled the area until the late 19th century. Other tribes include the Gurunsi, Senufo, Lobi, Bobo, Mande, and Fulani.

Ecclesiastically, the Archdiocese of Ouagadougou oversees the diocese of Bobo-Dioulasso, Diébougou, Fada N'Gourma, Kaya, Koudougou, Koupéla, Manga, Nouna-Dédougou, Ouahigouya, and Banfora.

Muslim influence dates from the 11th century, when Burkina Faso was ruled by competing Mossi states. In 1897 the French entered the region and incorporated Burkina Faso first into French Sudan (now Mali) and then as Upper Volta. Catholic evangelization began almost immediately after the French arrived, when the Algerian-based White Fathers (now the MISSIONARIES OF AFRICA) traveled from Sudan and Dahomey (modern Benin) and founded missions at Koupéla (1900) and Ouagadougou (1901). The first Burkinabe baptisms were in 1905. White Sisters arrived in 1911. Conversions were most common among the Mossi, who had previously accepted Islam. A minor seminary opened in 1926, and a major one in 1942. In 1955 the Archdiocese of Ouagadougou was created and made the single metropolitan see.

Dieudonné Yougbaré was made bishop of Koupéla in 1956, the first native of West Africa to receive episcopal consecration. Another African, Paul Zoungrana (1917–2000), became archbishop of Ouagadougou in 1960 and served as cardinal from 1965 to 1995.

In 1960 Burkina Faso gained its independence, but was torn by a military coup a decade later. A succession of military dictatorships would follow until 1991, when the country held its first multi-party election and established a new constitution and a parliamentary government. In 1980 and again ten years later Burkina Faso celebrated visits by Pope John Paul II, who encouraged the region's Catholics to reach out to those of other faiths. Despite efforts at improving the quality of life for its citizens, during the 1990s the government was burdened by a failing economy and a large external debt due to its long-term reliance on foreign aid. In addition to advocating for the forgiveness of this debt, the pope aggressively addressed the threats posed by the encroachment of the Sahara through the John Paul II Foundation for the Sahel.

Beginning in 1996, Cor Unum, the Pope's private charity, donated millions of dollars to both promote irrigation and combat the poverty, hunger, and health risks caused by desertification.

Although religious groups were required to register with the government, Burkina Faso's constitution of June 2, 1991, respected religious freedom. By 2000 Burkina Faso had 115 parishes, 374 secular and 144 religious priests, 145 brothers, and 990 sisters. In addition to running several primary and secondary schools in the predominately Catholic sections of Burkina Faso, the Church operated five radio stations and published a number of evangelical periodicals. The country celebrated its first century of evangelization on Jan. 16, 2001, with the visit of a papal envoy.

Bibliography: *Bilan du Monde* 2:440–444. *Annuaire des Diocèses d'Expression Française pour l'Afrique. . .et Madagascar* (Paris 1955–). *Annuario Pontifico* has statistics annually on all dioceses, vicariates and prefectures.

[J. R. DE BENOIST/EDS.]

BURKITT, FRANCIS CRAWFORD

Orientalist, exegete, and Church historian; b. London, Sept. 3, 1864; d. Cambridge, England, June 5, 1935. Although he received his degree in mathematics at Cambridge University (1886), he soon became interested in the study of Hebrew. In 1903 he began his university career at Cambridge as instructor in paleography and religion. In 1905 he was elected a member of the British Academy. By then he had made Syriac his special field of study and was the first to recognize the importance of the Syriac PALIMPSEST from the Monastery of St. Catherine at Mt. Sinai, which he published under the title *Evangelion da-Mepharreshe* (Cambridge 1904). Although he also devoted himself to the study of the OT, his more important contributions were concerned with the NT. In this field he was one of the pioneers in England of the new trend in biblical studies, particularly by his book *The Gospel History and Its Transmission* (Edinburgh 1906; 3d ed. 1920). He made important contributions also in the field of Church history, especially in that

Capital: Rangoon.
Size: 261,000 sq. miles.
Population: 41,734,853 in 2000.
Languages: Burmese; various ethnic dialects are also spoken.
Religions: 515,660 Catholics (1%), 37,144,019 Buddhists (89%), 1,276,900 Protestants (3%), 1,669,394 Muslim (4%), 1,128,880 animist and other.
Archdioceses: Mandalay, with suffragans Hakha, Lashio, and Myitkyina (1961); Taunggyi, with Kengtung (1955), Loikaw, and Toungoo (1955); and Rangoon, with Mawlamyine, Pathein, and Pyay.

of Franciscan studies. Finally, his works on MANICHAEISM and GNOSTICISM are still of considerable value. The list of his numerous publications takes up ten pages of fine print in the *Journal of Theological Studies* 36 (1935) 337–346.

Bibliography: A. SOUTER et al., *Journal of Theological Studies* 36 (1935) 225–254. J. F. BETHUNE-BAKER, *The Dictionary of National Biography from the Earliest Times to 1900* (London 1885–1900) 124–125.

[J. M. SOLA-SOLE]

BURMA, THE CATHOLIC CHURCH IN

Also known as Myanmar, Burma is located in southeast Asia. Bordered on the west by the Bay of Bengal, India, and Bangladesh, it is bordered on the east by Thailand, Laos, and China, and on the south by the Andaman Sea. A tropical climate and large lowland region characterize this relatively poor country with its economic base consisting of agriculture, heavy industry, and energy production. Burma is also the second largest producer of illegal opium. After the imposition of martial law in 1988, Burma was renamed Myanmar by the country's new military regime; it is still known by both names. Between 1961 and 1988 BUDDHISM was the state religion.

Church Hierarchy Develops. The Burmese people are primarily of Tibetan descent, although Hindus emigrating from India settled along its southern coast. Inhabited as early as the 3rd century, it was united under one ruler 800 years later. Mogul invaders obtained power over the region from the 13th century, and several regional governments were established. The first Burmese dynasty was formed in the 16th century out of the kingdoms of Toungoo, Ava, and Pegu, and was supported through an alliance with Portuguese traders. Later conflicts with the English East India Company resulted in British occupation from 1824–85, and the region was administered as part of British India until 1937. Separated from India and made a Crown Colony in 1937, the Union of Burma gained its independence as a republic in 1948, following World War II. The country's civilian government was overthrown in a military coup in 1962, initiating a period of political instability, repression, and military rule that continued into the 21st century.

Christianity was introduced into Burma *c.* 1500 by Portuguese merchants who visited the ports and established themselves in the commercial centers. Portuguese priests (seculars, Franciscans, and Jesuits) ministered to them. The first to evangelize the Burmese was a French Franciscan, whose efforts (1554–57) were unsuccessful. In 1666 Burma had one priest, who resided in the city of Ava with 70 Catholics and who visited twice yearly 970 other Catholics dwelling in 11 localities. When the Vicariate Apostolic of Siam, Ava, and Pegu was created (1669), Bishop Laneau of the PARIS FOREIGN MISSION SOCIETY (MEP) became the Vicar Apostolic, but he lacked the personnel to staff the mission. The two missionaries whom he sent to Pegu in 1687 were murdered in 1693. Evangelization of the pagans was not undertaken again until 1721, when Carlo MEZZABARBA, the papal legate, took the initiative and sent to Ava and Pegu two Italian priests, one a Barnabite, the other a secular. In 1722 the Vicariate of Ava and Pegu was formed and confided to Italian Barnabites. They enjoyed some success in the cities of Ava, Pegu, Syriam, and Toungoo, despite the massacre of Bishop Gallizia and two priests in 1745. Paulo Nerini continued the work alone until he shared their fate (1756). New missionaries arrived in 1760, but all of them soon died except Father Percotto, an outstanding vicar apostolic (1768–76). By 1790 Rangoon had 3,000 Catholics, two parishes, and several schools. The Barnabite missionaries were withdrawn, however, as a result of the invasion of Italy by the armies of the French Revolution. The Congregation for the PROPAGATION OF THE FAITH sent other priests without delay, but a series of three wars between England and Burma ruined the mission. Oblates of Mary the Virgin came in 1842 from Turin, but in 1855 they were replaced by the MEP, to whom the mission was entrusted.

When conflict between Burma and Great Britain subsided after 1886, Bishop Paul Bigandet, vicar apostolic (1856–93), began what became the first successful effort to organize the Church in Burma. Occupied by Japanese forces during World War II, the country returned to Allied control and ultimately won independence on Oct. 17, 1947. Despite the instability of the civilian government in power following independence, the Church hierarchy was established in 1955 when Mandalay and Rangoon became archdioceses and metropolitan sees for the two ecclesiastical provinces. By the mid-20th century Burma had 187 secular and 65 religious priests, 39 seminarians, 100 brothers, 688 sisters, and 75,000 students in 367 Catholic schools.

The Church in a Secular State. After numerous attempts to unseat Burma's civilian government, military leader Ne Win took power in 1962. Establishing one-party socialist state, Ne Win was an authoritarian leader who promoted neutrality and separatism. In 1966 foreign missionaries were forced to leave Burma when work permits issued after 1948 were refused renewal by the government. Ne Win remained in power until July 1988, when a series of student and worker protests forced him to resign. The military, led by General Saw Maung, seized power in September 1988. Burma was renamed Myanmar, and martial law was imposed. Despite political inroads by the National League for Democracy led by Aung San Suu Kyi, military rule continued into the 21st century. A worsening economy and the rapid growth in illegal drug trafficking and attendant crime continued to plague the Burmese. Ethnic violence promoted by the Burmese military drew the attention of human rights organizations, as well as the Vatican, after government-dictated relocations of Karen villagers resulted in violence and forced labor. Also, in August 1999 members of a Baptist Church in northern Nagaland were reportedly coerced into renouncing their Christian faith, again drawing concern. As early as 1996 Pope John Paul II had encouraged Burmese bishops to engage in outreach with Buddhist leaders as a means of countering such ethnic and religious oppression.

By 2000, there were 263 active parishes in Burma, administered to by 446 secular and 30 religious priests. Over 1,100 sisters and 75 brothers also were at work in the country, with their duties primarily confined to social and pastoral activities.

Bibliography: L. GALLO, *Storia del cristianesimo nell 'Impero birmano* 2 v. (Milan 1862). P. BIGANDET, *An Outline of the History of the Catholic Burmese Mission, 1720–1887* (Rangoon 1887). H. HOSTEN and E. LUCE, *Bibliotheca catholica birmana* (Rangoon 1915). E. PAPINOT, ''L'apostolat des Barnabites en Birmanie (1722–1829),'' *Revue d'histoire des missions* 11 (1934) 270–86. V. BA, ''The Early Catholic Missionaries in Burma,'' *Guardian* (Rangoon; August 1962–May 1964).

[J. GUENNOU/EDS.]

BURNETT, PETER HARDEMAN

Governor, jurist; b. Nashville, Tenn., Nov. 15, 1807; d. San Francisco, Calif., May 17, 1895. Burnett spent his early life in Tennessee and Missouri, where he worked at odd jobs, edited a newspaper, and eventually studied law. In 1842 he crossed from Independence, Mo., to the Oregon Country, where he was elected to the territorial legislature and appointed justice of the Oregon supreme court. In the California gold rush of 1849, Burnett led the first wagon train from Oregon to the California gold fields and became a leader in the movement for California statehood. In November of 1849 he was chosen the state's first governor, serving until Jan. 9, 1851. Following a term on the California supreme court (1857–58), he

Ethnic Karen (Thai-Chinese cultural group) children at Mae Hla refugee camp on Thai-Burma (Myanmar) border, Mae Hla, Thailand. (AP/Wide World Photos)

became a founder and first president (1863) of the Pacific Bank in San Francisco. Burnett had joined Alexander Campbell's Church of the Disciples in the 1830s, but his beliefs were altered by Campbell's debate with Bp. John B. Purcell of Cincinnati, Ohio, and in June of 1846 he became a convert to Catholicism. He told the story of his conversion in *The Path Which Led a Protestant Lawyer to the Catholic Church* (1860); he wrote also *Recollections and Opinions of an Old Pioneer* (1880), a source for California and Oregon history.

Bibliography: W. J. GHENT, *Dictionary of American Biography* (New York 1957) 2.1:300–301.

[K. MELLON, JR.]

BURNS, JAMES ALOYSIUS

Educator; b. Michigan City, Ind., Feb. 13, 1867; d. Notre Dame, Ind., Sept. 9, 1940. Burns entered the vocational school at the University of Notre Dame, Indiana, to learn the printer's trade, but in 1883 he transferred to the college department and in 1888 entered the novitiate of the Congregation of the Holy Cross. In 1889 he was sent to Watertown, Wisconsin, where he spent two years in teaching and theological study. He returned to Notre Dame for more theology, and was ordained on July 21, 1893. Thereafter, as a teacher of chemistry at Notre Dame, he noted the general lack of preparation among Catholic college instructors and argued that they should pursue advanced studies before starting to teach.

Burns did not have a major role in promulgating this idea until 1900 when he was appointed superior of Holy Cross College, Washington, D. C., the house of studies for seminarians of the Congregation of the Holy Cross. There, in addition to directing the seminarians, he continued his own research. The Catholic University of America, Washington, D. C., awarded him the Ph. D. degree in 1906. He was instrumental in founding the National Catholic Educational Association in 1904 and became its first vice president. During his 19 years in Washington, he wrote three basic studies of Catholic education in the U. S.: *Principles, Origin and Establishment of the Catholic School System* (1908), *Growth and Development of the Catholic School System* (1912), and *Catholic Education—A Study of Conditions* (1917). In these works he sought to promote the concept of quality in Catholic education.

In 1919 Burns was elected president of the University of Notre Dame. He closed its preparatory (high school) department; reorganized the university into the four distinct colleges of arts and letters, science, engineering, and law; appointed deans and department heads in the colleges; and raised the salaries of lay professors. After increasing the enrollment, he inaugurated a campaign to match funds offered to the university by the Rockefeller Foundation and the Carnegie Foundation. In 1922 he was named president emeritus, but he continued to direct the fund raising activities of the university. In 1926 Burns was returned to the office of superior of Holy Cross College in Washington, D. C., and, in 1927, was appointed provincial of the Indiana Province of the Congregation of the Holy Cross. He was elected first-assistant superior general of the congregation in 1938.

[E. J. POWER]

James Aloysius Burns. (Catholic University of America)

BURNT OFFERING

Translation of the Greek ὁλοκαύτωμα and some similar forms, ''wholly burnt (sacrifice),'' the Septuagint (LXX) equivalent of the Heb. *minhâ 'ōlâ,* ''offering that is caused to ascend (in smoke).'' A related older term is *kālîl,* ''wholly burnt'' (Dt 33.10; cf. 1 Sm 7.9), denoted SACRIFICES, other than animal, completely consumed on the altar [Lv 6.15–16; Ps 50(51).21; Sir 45.14; cf. Dt 13.17). Similar offerings were known before Moses, but no cognate term seems to have originated in other Semitic languages. The ceremony is described in the Priestly Code (Lv 1.3–17). Perfect animals (bulls, cows, calves, sheep, lambs, goats, kids), or birds (pigeons, doves) for the poor, were selected. In the tabernacle, after the laying-on-of-hands, they were killed, cut, and placed on the altar by the one offering the sacrifice, or by the priest (assisted perhaps by LEVITES), if it was a public sacrifice. The blood was then sprinkled around the altar. The victim was completely consumed by fire; the hide was given to the priest.

There were eight obligatory burnt offerings: 1. Daily burnt offering, at the third and nineth hour, of a yearling lamb or a kid; part of morning and evening prayer, accompanied by a cereal offering and wine libation. (This was the *tāmîd,* ''routine'': Ex 29.38–42; Nm 28.3–29.39; Ez 46.13–15; Dn 8.11–14; 11.31; 12.11.) 2. Sabbath burnt offering, double the daily offering (Nm 28.9–10). 3. Feast day burnt offerings, celebrated at the New Moon, Passover, Pentecost, Trumpets, Day of Atonement, Tabernacles; here the number of victims was increased (Nm 28.11–29.39). 4. Consecration of a priest (Ex 29.15; Lv 8.18; 9.12). 5. Purification of women after childbirth (Lv 12.6–8). 6. Cleansing of lepers after their cure (Lv 14.19–20). 7. Removal of ceremonial defilement (Lv 15.15, 30). 8. Atonement offered by a Nazirite whose vow was broken (Nm 6.11, 16).

Voluntary burnt offerings could be made on special occasions (Nm 7; 3 Kgs 8.64). Gentiles, forbidden to offer other sacrifices, were allowed to make this one. Josephus says war with Rome began when Eleazar forbade Roman rulers the usual sacrificial offerings (*Bell. Jud.* 2.17.2). Burnt offerings (*'ōlâ*) were part of Canaanite cult (3 Kgs 18; 4 Kgs 5.17; 10.18–27). The price list of Marseilles (Punic inscription found at Carthage) mentions three sacrifices: *kālîl* (expiatory sacrifice), *sewa't* (communion sacrifice), and *šelem kālîl* (holocaust). Ras Shamra may have known burnt offerings (*šrp*). Its symbolism was recognized by theologians: ''This kind of sacrifice was offered to God especially to show reverence to His majesty, and love of His goodness; it typified the state of perfection as regards the fulfillment of the counsels. Wherefore the whole was burnt up: that as the whole animal by being dissolved into smoke soared aloft, so it might denote that the whole man, and whatever belongs to him, are subject to the authority of God, and should be offered to Him'' (*Summa theologiae* 1a2ae, 102.3 ad 8; cf. St. Augustine, *Patrologia Latina*, ed. J. P. Migne

[Paris 1878–90] 37: 1775; St. Gregory the Great, *Patrologia Latina* 75:577).

See Also: HOLOCAUST.

Bibliography: A. A. DE GUGLIELMO, ''Sacrifice in the Ugaritic Texts,'' *The Catholic Biblical Quarterly* 17 (1955) 196–216. R. DE VAUX, *Ancient Israel, Its Life and Institutions*, tr. J. MCHUGH (New York 1961). W. B. STEVENSON, ''Hebrew 'ōlāh and zebach Sacrifices'' in *Festschrift für Alfred Bertholet* (Tübingen 1950). L. ROST, ''Erwägungen zum israelitischen Brandopfer,'' *Von Ugarit nach Qumran* (Festschrift Eissfeldt; Berlin 1958).

[K. SULLIVAN]

BURSE

A burse is a container historically used for carrying the corporal to and from the altar. It came into use during the 11th century when the corporals, formerly large, were reduced in size. Originating probably at Rheims, the use of the burse gradually spread throughout Europe. At Mass, the burse was carried with the folded corporal inside it, on top of the veiled chalice; it was used also for Communion outside Mass and for Benediction. The burse is square, made of two cloth-covered stiff cards hinged along one edge; the corporal is placed between these. At least the upper side of the burse must be of the same color as the other Mass vestments. The name ''burse'' is given also to a small bag, of leather or other strong material, in which the clergy of some countries carry the pyx containing the Blessed Sacrament when they are taking Communion to the sick.

[C. W. HOWELL/EDS.]

BURSFELD, ABBEY OF

Former BENEDICTINE abbey on the Weser River, about eight miles from Münden (Hanover), Germany, Diocese of Mainz (patrons, SS. Thomas and Nicholas). Bursfeld or Bursfelde was founded in 1093 by Count Henry the Fat of Northeim, its first monks coming from CORVEY. Emperor Henry IV accorded it his imperial protection and the right of coinage; Abp. Ruthard of Mainz confirmed the foundation. The abbey church, a Hirsau-type structure of the 12th century, was restored in 1433 and 1589, but was drastically altered in the process; it was again restored in 1846 and shows traces of successive decoration. In 1574 a fire destroyed all the early monastic buildings. Popes Eugene III and Boniface VIII confirmed all Bursfeld's possessions and privileges. Under Abbots Henry II (d. 1334) and John II (d. 1339) discipline deteriorated, and in 1433 it was necessary for the zealous reformer Johann Dederoth, Abbot of Clus, to renew and revive the impoverished and almost extinct monastery at the insistence of Duke Otto (the One-eyed) of Brunswick. Under his successor several other monasteries amalgamated with Bursfeld into a Benedictine reform congregation; hence the beginning of the Bursfeld Congregation. Bursfeld itself flourished until the Reformation; Abbot Melchior Böddeker (d. 1601) became a Protestant. The Restitution Edict brought back two Catholic abbots (1629–80), but Protestant abbots continued to rule side by side with them. Since the 19th century the head of the Protestant Theological Faculty of the University of Göttingen has always been titular abbot of Bursfeld and receives revenues from that office. The abbey church is used for Lutheran services.

The Bursfeld Congregation was a 15th-century development. Johann Dederoth, Abbot of Clus, took over Bursfeld in 1433, uniting it in his person with Clus. On a journey to Rome he had become acquainted with the Benedictine Reform of S. Giustina (Padua), and from Abbot Johann Rode of Sankt Matthias in Trier he received two monks each for Clus and Bursfeld to initiate the new reform. Reinhausen, Huysburg, and Cismar soon joined what was to become a real reform movement. Dederoth's successor at Bursfeld, Abbot Johann von Hagen, (d. 1469) received much help and inspiration from the canon regular Johann Busch. The first general chapter of the Bursfeld Congregation as such was held from May 1 to 16, 1446, at Bursfeld, which was to remain head of the congregation until the abbey itself would become Protestant. (Clus could not lead the reform movement, as it was a proprietary monastery of the Convent of GANDERSHEIM.) Meanwhile, Pope Pius II approved the congregation in 1459, and it grew rapidly. By 1780 there were 111 abbeys (excluding convents) united in the congregation; the acts of the general chapters from 1458 to 1780 are extant. Bursfeld had its own seminary for monastic priests from 1616 to 1740 at the University of Cologne. The Bursfeld Congregation, or Union, came to an end with the secularization of 1802–03.

Bibliography: L. H. COTTINEAU, *Répertoire topobibliographique des abbayes et prieurés*, 2 v. (Mâcon 1935–39) 1:534–535. P. VOLK, *Lexikon für Theologie und Kirche*, ed. J. HOFER and K. RAHNER, 10 v. (2d., new ed. Freiburg 1957–65) 2:796–798, including list of congregation members; ed., *Die General-kapitels-Rezesse der Bursfelder Kongregation,* v.1 (Siegburg 1955) 1–5.

[P. VOLK]

BURTSELL, RICHARD LALOR

Pastor, civic leader, canonist, writer; b. New York City, April 14, 1840; d. Kingston, N.Y., Feb. 5, 1912. His parents, John Low and Dorothea (Morrogh) Burtsell, were both members of old New York Catholic families. After attending Catholic schools in New York, he began his theological studies in the Sulpician Seminary in Montreal, Canada. In 1857 he went to Propaganda College in Rome, where he obtained doctorates in philosophy (1858) and theology (1862), and was ordained on Aug. 10, 1862. From 1862 to 1868 he was assistant to T. S. PRESTON, vicar-general and pastor of St. Ann's, New York City. There, Thomas Farrell (1823–80), pastor of St. Joseph's, Waverly Place, exercised a lasting influence on him and a small group of his young priest friends.

Burtsell founded Epiphany parish (1867) and was responsible for establishing St. Benedict the Moor parish (1883), the first in the New York archdiocese for Negroes. From 1887 to 1892 Burtsell was canonical advisor and advocate for his friend, Rev. Edward MCGLYNN, supporter of the controversial single-tax theory of Henry George. At least indirectly as the result of his association with McGlynn, Burtsell was deprived in 1889 of his parish, the Epiphany. He won his appeal in Rome, and in 1890 he was appointed pastor of St. Mary's in Kingston, where he remained until his death.

In the last quarter of the 19th century, Burtsell was one of the few canonists of note in the eastern United States. As an effective parish administrator, he cleared the debt on both Epiphany and St. Mary's churches and had them consecrated. Burtsell was a contributor to the old *Catholic Encyclopedia* and wrote regularly for scholarly journals. He was also more civic minded than most pastors of his time. He was a member of the Kingston Board of Trade, a founder and onetime president of the City of Kingston Hospital, trustee of the Kingston Library, and probably the most highly esteemed citizen of the city. He was named papal chamberlain in 1905 and appointed a domestic prelate in November of 1911.

Bibliography: *Burtsell Diaries (1865–1912),* Archives, Archdiocese of New York. F. J. ZWIERLEIN, *Life and Letters of Bishop McQuaid,* 3 v. (Rochester 1925–27); *Letters of Archbishop Corrigan to Bishop McQuaid and Allied Documents* (Rochester 1946). C. A. BARKER, *Henry George* (New York 1955). S. BELL, *Rebel, Priest and Prophet: A Biography of Edward McGlynn* (New York 1937), partial to McGlynn and largely undocumented but with pertinent factual information. *Historical Records and Studies of the U.S. Catholic Historical Society of New York* (1900–) 6.2 (1912) 171, 300.

[E. H. SMITH]

BURUNDI, THE CATHOLIC CHURCH IN

A landlocked constitutional monarchy, the Republic of Burundi is located near the equator in east central AFRICA. The Nile-Congo divide runs through Burundi, which is bordered by Rwanda on the north, Tanzania on the east and southeast, Lake Tanganyika on the southwest and the Democratic Republic of the Congo on the west. A mountainous region that drops to a plateau in the east, Burundi is characterized by a moderate climate. Natural resources include nickel, uranium, peat, cobalt, platinum and copper, although the region relies primarily upon its agricultural sector, which produces coffee, cotton, tea, corn and sweet potatoes.

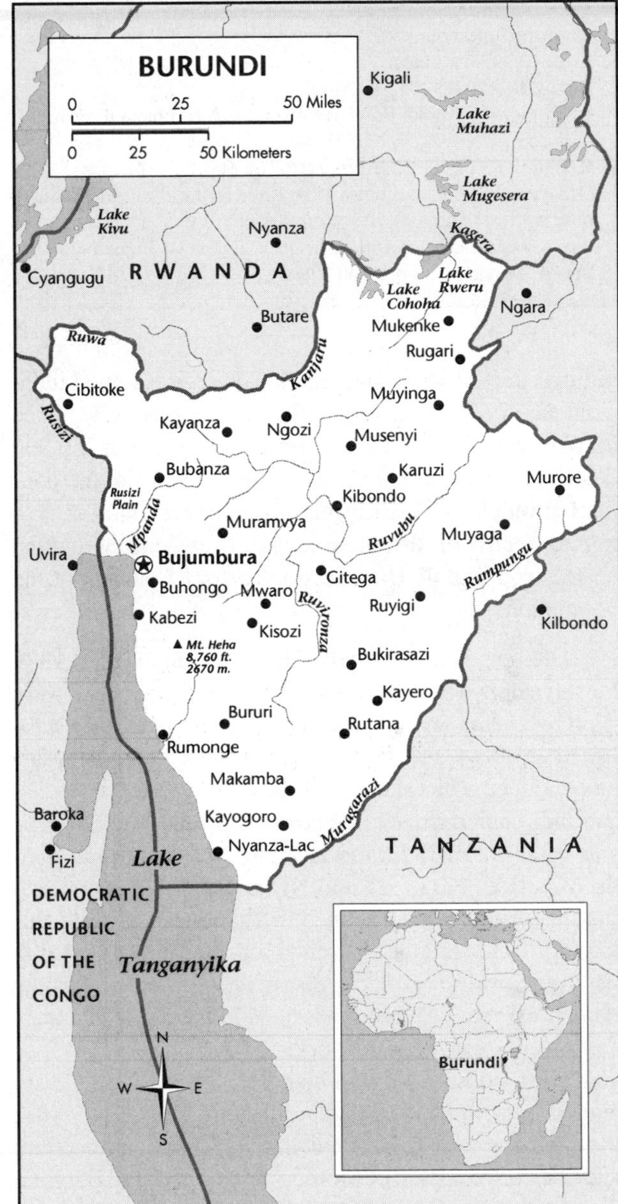

A Tutsi kingdom established in the 16th century, Burundi was incorporated into German East Africa from 1898 to 1916, and was subsequently administered by Bel-

Capital: Bujumbura.
Size: 10,747 sq. miles.
Population: 6,054,715 in 2000.
Languages: Kirunid, French; Swahili is also spoken in various regions.
Religions: 3,753,925 Catholics (62%), 600,720 Muslims (10%), 304,760 Protestants (5%), 1,395,310 follow indigenous beliefs.
Archdiocese: Gitega, with suffragans Bubanza, Bujumbura, Bururi, Muyinga, Ngozi, and Ruyigi.

gium as part of Ruanda-Urundi. The region gained independence in 1962, after which escalating ethic violence between the Hutu and Tutsi tribes culminated in 250,000 dead and 37,000 left homeless by 2000. Most of the population relies upon subsistence agriculture, and the economic health of the government is dependant on the coffee crop. Ethnic Hutu accounted for 85 percent of the population.

History. White Fathers arrived at Rumonge in 1879 but abandoned the mission when three members were slain two years later. The first permanent post was established at Muyaga in 1898. Together with Rwanda, originally under the vicariate apostolic of Kivu (created 1912), Burundi gained its own vicariate in 1922. After Bukoba was detached in 1929, the vicariate of Burundi split into the vicariates of Gitega and Ngozi (1949). The first Burundian priests were ordained in 1925, and the years following 1930 saw a multitude of conversions—1,000 baptisms a week in 1935—that made Burundi one of the most flourishing Catholic missions in the world. Conversions were based on a well-organized catechumen of four years in a population well disposed toward Catholicism and on an active lay apostolate that worked closely with the hierarchy. Two Burundian congregations of sisters and one congregation of brothers developed, and Belgian, Spanish and Italian secular priests assisted men's and women's religious orders in missionary work. Bujumbura gained a Burundian bishop in 1959 and Ngozi in 1961.

Following the country's independence on July 1, 1962, ethnic warfare broke out between the elite Tutsi minority, backed by the government army, and Burundi's Hutu rebels. Amid political upheaval, the government seized several Catholic schools in the early 1970s, and in 1979 foreign missionaries were expelled from Burundi. By the late 1980s the government further curtailed the Church, nationalizing both the major seminary at Ngozi as well as the country's six minor seminaries in 1986. A new constitution in March of 1992 established a multiparty political system; this was further broadened in 1998 in the Transitional Constitutional Act, which guaranteed freedom of religion. Church leaders were granted diplomatic status within the country and the Church was exempt from taxes.

While restrictions against the Church were lifted by 1990, the violence in the country escalated, resulting in massive emigration and a death toll in the many thousands. Burundi's first democratically elected Hutu president was murdered in 1993. Three years later Gitega Archbishop Joachim Ruhuna, an ethnic Tutsi, was murdered, and Hutu-sponsored violence against other Catholics followed, including the massacre of 46 at the seminary in Bururi. The Organization for African Unity imposed sanctions on Burundi that were objected to by both Pope John Paul II and the nation's bishops. Following a joint statement by Burundian and Rwandan bishops, this embargo was lifted in 1999.

By 2000 Burundi had 130 parishes tended by 242 diocesan and 70 religious priests. Other religious included 140 brothers and over 900 sisters who worked as teachers and administrators at Burundi's 311 primary and 25 secondary Catholic schools. With the return of those schools that had been seized by the government in the 1970s, almost all of the students in the country attended Catholic schools, and some of them also went on to attend the state university at Bujumbura (1960), the board of which was composed of government members and clergy. Most Catholics resided in the southern and central regions of Burundi. Bishops remained active in peace negotiations, ongoing since 1996. A summit held in 2001 to discuss a planned transition to democratic rule was followed by a Hutu-led attack on the capital city of Bujumbura.

Bibliography: J. R. CLÉMENT, *Essai de bibliographie du Ruanda-Urundi* (Bujumbura 1959). J. PERRAUDIN, *Naissance d'une Église. Histoire du Burundi Chrétien* (Bujumbura 1963). *Ruanda-Burundi* (Bujumbura 1963). *Bilan du Monde,* 2:179–183. *Annuario Pontificio* (Rome 1912–) 217.

[J. PERRAUDIN/EDS.]

BURY, JOHN BAGNELL

British classical scholar and Byzantine historian; b. Monaghan, Ireland, Oct. 16, 1861; d. Rome, June 1, 1927. His father, an Anglican clergyman, taught him Latin and Greek at an early age, and he had a brilliant career at Trinity College, Dublin, his principal teacher being the famous classical scholar J. P. Mahaffy. He graduated from Trinity in 1882, was made a fellow in 1885, was elected to the professorship of modern history in 1893, and was appointed regius professor of Greek in 1898. In 1902 he became Lord Acton's successor as regius professor of modern history at the University of Cambridge, a post that he held until his death. By 1891 he had acquired a knowledge of Sanskrit, Hebrew, Syriac, and several modern languages, including Russian and Hungarian. His classical training and love of ancient classical literature had a profound affect on his later work and outlook. He regarded later Roman and Byzantine history as essentially the continuation of ancient, and particularly Hellenic, civilization. Although influenced by the philosophy of G. W. F. Hegel, he was more Hellenic than Hegelian in his rationalism, opposing revealed religion and the theory of contingency in history. In 1889 he published his *History of the Later Roman Empire from Arcadius to Irene* (2 v. London); and shortly afterward, his excellent edition of the *Odes of Pindar* (2 v. London 1890–92). Between 1896 and 1900, he produced his scholarly edition of *Gibbon's Decline and Fall* (7 v. London), with introduction, notes, and appendices, which has remained standard. His *History of Greece to the Death of Alexander* (1st ed. London 1900, 2d ed. 1913) was long regarded as the best one-volume work in its field. His *Life of St. Patrick and His Place in History* (London 1905), inspired by his interest in the influence of Roman civilization, marks an epoch in critical Irish hagiography. His *Ancient Greek Historians* (New York 1909) retains a high place in Greek historiography.

Bury's profound knowledge of Byzantine constitutional history is exhibited especially in *The Constitution of the Later Roman Empire* (Cambridge, Eng. 1909) and *The Imperial Administrative System in the Ninth Century, with a Revised Text of the Kletorologion of Philotheos* (London 1911). His detailed *History of the Eastern Roman Empire from the Fall of Irene to the Accession of Basil I* appeared a little later (London 1912). Preoccupation with philosophical questions led to the writing and publication of *A History of Freedom of Thought* (London 1913) and *The Idea of Progress: An Inquiry into Its Origin and Growth* (London 1920), both books revealing a marked rationalistic bent. His last significant work was the *History of the Later Roman Empire from the Death of Theodosius I to the Death of Justinian* (2 v. London 1923). He planned the *Cambridge Medieval History*, and the first six volumes of the *Cambridge Ancient History* carry his name as one of the main editors.

Bury was one of the greatest of modern scholars in the Byzantine field. He was primarily concerned, however, with political, constitutional, and administrative history, showing too little interest in social history—and even less in religion as such. His failure to perceive the significance of religion as a dynamic and guiding force in ancient and Byzantine civilization is a weakness, above all, in his works on Byzantine history, that must be recognized.

Bibliography: N. H. BAYNES and H. LAST, *The Dictionary of National Biography from the Earliest Times to 1900* (London 1885–1900) 144–147. J. W. THOMPSON and B. J. HOLM, *History of Historical Writing*, 2 v. (New York 1942) 2:527–529. N. H. BAYNES, *A Bibliography of the Works of J. Bury . . . with a Memoir* (Cambridge, Eng. 1929).

Abbey ruins at Bury St. Edmunds. (©Philippa Lewis/CORBIS)

[M. R. P. MCGUIRE]

BURY-ST.-EDMUNDS, ABBEY OF

Former Benedictine monastery in the town of Bury-St.-Edmunds, Suffolk, England, Diocese of Norwich. Founded by King CANUTE (1020) at the shrine of King St. EDMUND THE MARTYR, the abbey was England's chief center of pilgrimage until Thomas BECKET's murder (1170). Colonized from ELY and richly endowed with lands and churches, Bury ranked among England's wealthiest and most influential monasteries throughout its existence. Bishops of Norwich failed to gain control of it, and its EXEMPTION was confirmed (*c.* 1100). Its great abbots included Baldwin (1065–98), physician and builder; Anselm (1121–48), ANSELM OF CANTERBURY's nephew; SAMSON (1182–1211), the subject of JOCELIN OF

BRAKELOND's chronicle; and Samson's successor. Hugh II of Northwold, who played an important part at the Fourth LATERAN COUNCIL (1215) and became bishop of Ely (1229–54). Since the town of Bury was a monastic borough, the abbey was continuously involved in town affairs; and since it held by the king a service of 40 knights, the abbey often quarreled with both king and tenants. Dependencies included THETFORD PRIORY (dissolved 1160) and six hospitals in Bury. Important persons were buried at the abbey; kings paid visits and sent abbots on missions; the abbot sat in Parliament, which sometimes convened there. The number of monks rose from 20 (1020) to 80 (*c.* 1260). Bury's library had about 2,000 books, including such rarities as Caesar's *Commentaries* and Plautus. The Bury Bible at Corpus Christi College, Cambridge, and the *Life of St. Edmund* in Pierpont Morgan Library, New York, are outstanding productions of its SCRIPTORIUM. Bury monks wrote annals and hagiography and started a school of monastic history (14th century); they numbered among their authors John Lydgate, the poet (1370?–1451?). Bury sent monks to Oxford, fostered the cult of Mary in England, and was a center of musical life. When HENRY VIII dissolved the abbey in 1539, there were 43 monks in the community and little sign of decay. Substantial building had taken place in the 15th century, but today little remains at the abbey site, which is designated an ancient monument.

Bibliography: *Memorials of St. Edmund's Abbey*, ed. T. ARNOLD, 3 v. (*Rerum Britannicarum medii aevi scriptores* 96; 1890–96), including Jocelin of Brakelond's chronicle. W. DUGDALE, *Monasticon Anglicanum* 3:98–176. M. R. JAMES, *On the Abbey of St. Edmund at Bury: I. The Library. II. The Church* (Cambridge, Eng. 1895). R. GRAHAM, *English Ecclesiastical Studies* (New York 1929) 146–187, 271–301. D. KNOWLES, *The Monastic Order in England*. D. KNOWLES, *The Religious Orders in England*. D. KNOWLES and R. N. HADCOCK, *Medieval Religious Houses: England and Wales* 61, 250.

[R. W. HAYS]

BUS, CÉSAR DE, BL.

Priest, catechetical apostle, founder of Fathers of Christian Doctrine (Doctrinaires); b. Cavaillon (Comtat), France, Feb. 3, 1544; d. Avignon, April 15, 1607. After studies at Avignon and a worldly life, Bus was influenced by several devout persons and began seriously to serve God in 1574. He was ordained in 1582, having already taught catechism around Cavaillon. This apostolate, needed because of the pastoral neglect and ignorance attending the wars of religion, became his main work. In it he was imitated by his converted cousin J. B. Romaillon, who was ordained in 1588. Forceful and spiritually gifted, Bus adopted a method that added to his effectiveness; it consisted of simple, lively explanations for children and clearly divided dialogue instructions for adults based on the Council of TRENT's catechism. As coworkers joined the cousins, there grew up an association of catechists, influenced by the community ideals of (SS.) Charles BORROMEO and Philip NERI. Bus directed its formal union of 1592 and the first foundation at Avignon in 1593; papal confirmation came in 1598. Despite outside criticism, the group worked well until *c.* 1600, when Bus and Romaillon differed over its structure. A painful but charitable split came in 1602. Romaillon and five others opposed to forming an institute with vows continued their work under the bishop of Aix, uniting in 1619 with the Oratory of Pierre de BÉRULLE. Bus and the rest remained at Avignon and took the vow of obedience; they soon received papal approval. Though ill and blind, Bus launched the Doctrinaires so vigorously that they survived both this split and his death in 1607 to become quite numerous and extensive. Both he and Romaillon helped establish the URSULINES IN FRANCE. As an aid for effective preaching by his disciples, he wrote the *Instructions familières* . . . (5 v. Paris 1666; last French ed. 1867). He was declared venerable on Dec. 8, 1821 by Pius VII and beatified on April 27, 1975 by Paul VI.

Feast: April 15.

Bibliography: P. BROUTIN, *La Réforme pastorale en France au XVIIe siècle*, 2 v. (Tournai 1956) 2:139–154. P. GILOTEAUX, *Le Vénérable César de Bus: Fondateur de la Congrégation des Prêtres de la Doctrine Chrétienne 1544–1607* (Paris 1961), lacks documentation. A. RAYEZ, "Spiritualité du Vénérable César de Bus," *Revue d'ascétique et de mystique* 34 (1958) 185–203. H. BRÉMOND, *Histoire littéraire du sentiment réligieux en France depuis la fin des guerres de religion jusqu'à nos jours*, 12 v. (Paris 1911–36) 2:9–31. P. CALENDINI, *Dictionnaire d'histoire et de géographie ecclésiastiques*, ed. A. BAUDRILLART et al. (Paris 1912) 10:1408–09. A. DUVAL, *Catholicisme* 2:332–333.

[W. H. PRINCIPE]

BUSAEUS (DE BUYS)

Family name of two brothers who played important roles in defense of the Church in the 16th century.

PETRUS

Jesuit theologian and editor of the catechism of Peter CANISIUS; b. Nijmegen, Netherlands, 1540; d. Vienna, April 12, 1587. In 1561 he entered the Cologne novitiate of the Society of Jesus and six years later was appointed novice master. He undertook to complete the catechism of Peter Canisius, adding, with the author's approval, the full texts of all scriptural and patristic references cited in order to demonstrate to the reformers the agreement of the catechism with the doctrine of the ancient Church.

The first edition appeared in Cologne and was entitled *Authoritatum sacrae scripturae et sanctorum patrum, quae in summa doctrinae christianae doct. Petri Canisii . . . citantur, et nunc primum ex ipsis fontibus fideliter collectae, ipsis catechismi verbis subscriptae sunt* . . . (4 v. 1569–70). The favorable reception of this work necessitated subsequent editions. Unaccountably missing from the 1571 edition by the renowned press of Aldus Minutius in Venice was the fourth volume. In 1577 the catechism was reissued at Cologne in a folio volume revised by Jean Hase, another Dutch Jesuit, under the title *Opus catechisticum, sive de summa doctrinae . . . Petri Canisii.* In 1571 Busaeus went to Vienna to lecture on Scripture in the university and teach Hebrew in the Jesuit college. He went to Rome in 1584, one of a six-member commission entrusted with drawing up a plan of studies for the entire Society of Jesus. Upon his return to Vienna he held until his death the position of rector of the College of Nobles.

Bibliography: J. BRUCKER, *Dictionnaire de théologie catholique*, ed. A. VACANT et al., 15 v. (Paris 1903–50) 2.1:1265–66. C. SOMMERVOGEL et al., *Bibliothèque de la Compagnie de Jésus*, 11 v. (Brussels-Paris 1890–32) 2:439–442. A. DE BIL, *Dictionnaire d'histoire et de géographie ecclésiastiques*, ed. A. BAUDRILLART et al. (Paris 1912–) 10:1414–15.

[M. S. CONLAN]

JOHANNES

Jesuit author and theologian; b. Nijmegen, Netherlands, April 14, 1547; d. Mainz, Germany, May 30, 1611. A younger brother of Petrus Busaeus he entered the JESUITS in 1563. He studied theology at Rome and then taught that subject successfully at Mainz for 22 years; he was also responsible during that time for the spiritual guidance of the sodality (*see* SODALITIES OF OUR LADY). Initially he produced polemic works against PROTESTANTISM: a dissertation on fasting in answer to Martin CHEMNITZ, another on the person of Christ directed against the supporters of UBIQUITARIANISM, a defense of the Gregorian calendar (*see* CALENDAR REFORM), two articles on the ROSARY and several replies to Stephen Gerlach of Tübingen on the person of Jesus. To all of these works he imparted an irenic tone rare in that age. After 1595, forsaking controversy, he edited ascetical works, such as the meditations of Fathers Bruni and Pinelli and Father Androtius's treatise on frequent Communion. Busaeus himself composed, among other works, the *Enchiridion piarum meditationum* (1st ed. Mainz 1606, numerous later editions and translations); πανάριον, *hoc est Arca medica . . . adversus animi morbos* (Mainz 1608); and *Viridarium christianarum virtutum* (Mainz 1610). Busaeus also published editions of ecclesiastical writers, most notably Peter of Blois (Mainz 1600), HINCMAR OF REIMS (Mainz 1602), the *Vitae romanorum pontificum* of ANASTASIUS THE LIBRARIAN (Mainz 1602), which he erroneously attributed to LIUTPRAND OF CREMONA, the works of Johannes TRITHEMIUS, and an abridgement of ABBO OF FLEURY.

A third brother, Gerard (1538–96) was also a theologian.

Bibliography: J. N. PAQUOT, *Mémoires pour servir à l'histoire littéraire des dix-sept provinces,* v.1 (Louvain 1763) 72–80. C. SOMMERVOGEL et al., *Bibliothèque de la Compagnie de Jésus*, 11 v. (Brussels-Paris 1890–1932) 2:416–439; 8:1949–51, complete list of works of Busaeus. H. HURTER, *Nomenclator literarius theologiae catholicae*, 5 v. in 6 (3d ed. Innsbruck 1909–13) 3:421. B. DUHR, *Geschichte der Jesuiten in den Ländern deutscher Zunge*, 4 v. in 5 (2d ed. Freiburg 1907–28). A. DE BIL, *Dictionnaire d'histoire et de géographie ecclésiastiques*, ed. A. BAUDRILLART et al. (Paris 1912–) 10:1414. J. BRUCKER, *Dictionnaire de théologie catholique*, ed. A. VACANT et al., 15 v. (Paris 1903–50) 2.1:1265. A. RAYEZ, *Lexikon für Theologie und Kirche*, ed. J. HOFER and K. RAHNER, 10 v. (2d, new ed. Freiburg 1957–65) 2:799.

[J. DAOUST]

BUSENBAUM, HERMANN

Jesuit moral theologian; b. Nottuln, Westphalia, 1600; d. Münster, Jan. 31, 1668. He taught the humanities, philosophy, theology, and particularly moral theology in various colleges, and is best remembered for his teaching at Cologne. Socius of his provincial, rector of the colleges of Hildesheim and Münster, confessor and adviser of the Prince Bishop of Münster, Christoph Bernhard von Galen, Busenbaum was known for his ardent piety, his prudence, his keen knowledge in directing souls, and his talent for teaching.

He wrote two works: *Lilium inter spinas,* written in German and dedicated to virgins consecrated to God but living in the world (Cologne 1659); and *Medulla Theologiae Moralis facili ac perspicua methodo resolvens casus conscientiae ex variis probatisque authoribus concinnata* (Münster 1650). The *Medulla* immediately achieved great popularity. During Busenbaum's life there were 40 editions; in 1670 the 45th edition appeared in Lisbon; and from 1670 to 1770, there were 150 editions published in the different countries of Europe.

By its clarity, its precision, and its methodical arrangement the *Medulla* became the classic type of manual for moral theology as taught in seminaries. The great commentaries written after the model of the *Medulla* further extended its influence. One example of such a commentary was the *Theologia Moralis* of Claude LACROIX, SJ (Cologne 1707–14). In 1757 F. A. ZACCARIA, SJ, brought out the most complete edition of it. St. Alphonsus Liguori wrote his *Theologia Moralis* as a kind of

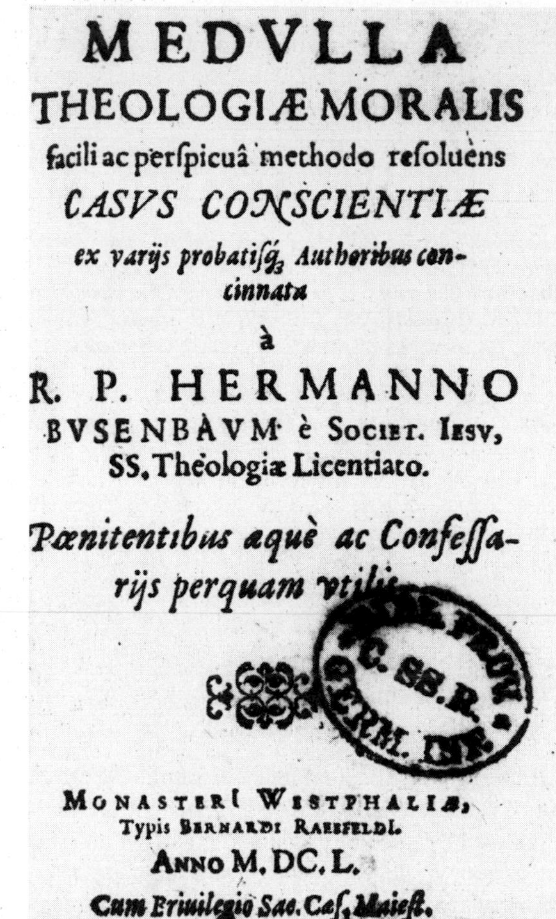

MEDVLLA
THEOLOGIÆ MORALIS
facili ac perſpicuâ methodo reſoluens
CASVS CONSCIENTIÆ
ex varijs probatiſq; Authoribus concinnata
à
R. P. HERMANNO
BVSENBAVM è Societ. Iesv,
SS. Theologiæ Licentiato.
Pœnitentibus æquè ac Confeſſarijs perquam vtilis.
MONASTERII WESTPHALIÆ,
Typis Bernardi Raesfeldi.
Anno M. DC. L.
Cum Priuilegio Sac. Cæſ. Maieſt.

Frontispiece page of "Medulla," 1650, first edition, by Hermann Busenbaum.

commentary on the *Medulla* (Padua 1737). The last great commentary on it was that of Antonio BALLERINI, the revision of which, the *Opus theologicum morale in Busenbaum medullam* (7 v., Prato 1889–93) was the work of D. PALMIERI.

Sources. Busenbaum made frequent use of the manuscript "summae" of cases of conscience written by his confreres, Hermann Nünning and Friedrich Spe, professors of moral theology. He also used the work in manuscript of Maximilien Buchier, SJ. In addition to these immediate sources, all the authors of practical moral theology who had written since the middle of the 16th century are to be encountered in the *Medulla.* It was Busenbaum's merit to have been able to discern in the mass of opinion found in his sources the views that deserved to be regarded as having permanent value. In including them in his manual, which was destined to exert so wide an influence, Busenbaum contributed effectively to the stabilization of theological opinion on a number of critical points.

Method. Busenbaum's method was strictly casuistic and analytical. It was also more rationalistic than theological, for he regarded the Decalogue as making explicit the obligations of the natural law. There is also a notable emphasis upon the idea of obligation in his writing, and this is no doubt a consequence of the purpose he had in mind in writing, which was the practical formation of confessors. Moral theology, as he saw it, was particularly necessary to enable the priest to fulfill his office of judge in the Sacrament of Penance. It is his duty to pronounce sentence, approving what is good and condemning what is not. A professional moralist should not be expected, therefore, to write a treatise on moral perfection but should content himself with producing something to help the ordinary confessor in the exercise of his judicial function.

False accusations. There was nothing startling to be found in Busenbaum's moral doctrine. A small number of his opinions were condemned as laxist by Alexander VII and Innocent XI, but there is nothing surprising in this if one considers the enormous number of matters upon which he passed judgment. Certainly he fared no worse than other reputable moralists, and his teaching on the whole is unquestionably orthodox. Nevertheless, he was vigorously denounced at one time for his teaching on two points: tyrannicide and the doctrine that the end justifies the means.

As to tyrannicide, Busenbaum actually wrote: "In order to safeguard his life or the integrity of his members, it is even permitted for a son, a religious, a subject, to defend himself, going so far even as to kill his father, his abbot or his prince, if need be, unless the death of the latter would bring about serious consequences, such as wars. . . ." (*Medulla* 3.4.1.38). This was no more than the application to a particular case of the teaching on legitimate self-defense propounded by St. Thomas Aquinas, St. Antoninus, D. Soto, D. Concina, St. Alphonsus Liguori, and many others. However, the fear of having this text exploited against them caused the French Jesuits in 1669 to ask the general of the society to have it suppressed. In numerous editions of Busenbaum's work, therefore, this proposition is missing. Opposition to the moral theology of Busenbaum reached its height in 1757 at the time of the attempted assassination of Louis XV, King of France, by Damiens. The *Medulla* was condemned and burned by the Parlement of Toulouse in 1757; it was condemned by the Parlement of Paris in 1763 and was burned in the public square. Impartial authors have recognized the falsity of the accusations cast against the *Medulla.*

As to his supposed doctrine that the end justifies the means, Busenbaum did no more in fact than affirm a truth of common sense. When a person has a right to do something, he has by that very fact the right to use the legitimate means necessary for its performance. Busenbaum himself expressly excluded violence, injustice, and, in general, the use of means intrinsically bad (*opcit.* 4.3.7.2). M. Reichmann has retraced the history of the controversies raised by this formula.

Bibliography: C. Sommervogel et. al., Bibliothèque de la Compagnie de Jésus, 11 v. (Brussels-Paris 1890–1932; v. 12, suppl. 1960). 2:444–455. WERNER, *Allgemeine deutsche Biographie* 3:646–648. T. B. BARRETT, *The Catholic Encyclopedia* 3:86–87. A. DE BIL, *Dictionnaire d'histoire et de géographie ecclésiastiques* 10:1417–18. J. BRUCKER, *Dictionnaire de théologie catholique* 2.1:1266–68. C. TESTORE, *Enciclopedia cattolica* 3:243. J. C. PILZ, *Lexicon für Theologie und Kirche,* new eds. 2:801. E. SCHWARZ, *Realencyklopädie für protestantische Theologie* 3:581. L. FENOT, *Die Religion in Geschichte und Gegenwart* 1:1534. A. BROU, *Les Jésuites de la légende* (Paris 1907). B. DUHR, *Jesuiten-Fabeln* (Freiburg 1904); *Geschichte der Jesuiten in den Ländern deutscher Zunge,* 4 v. in 6 (v. 1–2 Freiburg 1907–13; v. 3–4 Regensburg 1921–28) 2.2:389–390. M. REICHMANN, *Der Zweck heiligt die Mittel* (Freiburg 1903).

[L. VEREECKE]

BUSHNELL, HORACE

Congregationalist minister and theologian; b. Bantam, Conn., April 14, 1802; d. Hartford, Conn., February 17, 1876. After attempts at teaching and journalism he turned to the study of law, but a conversion experience in 1831 led him to the ministry. In 1833 he began a long career as Congregationalist pastor of the North Church in Hartford. In this position he developed a religious outlook that led to the preaching of the SOCIAL GOSPEL, and shaped the development of American Protestant theology during the second half of the 19th century. Bushnell adapted a contextual view of reality from German philosophic idealists, especially Friedrich SCHLEIERMACHER. This led him in his best known work, *Christian Nurture* (1847), to argue that the church is not a collection of adult individuals converted by revivals, but a community of the faithful, including children who should be educated as Christians from the time of their baptism. Bushnell believed also that men exist only in the context of social interaction, that all men are involved in the guilt of the human community, that the supernatural is consubstantial with but distinguishable from the natural, and that fallen man could not be regenerated without the moral influence of Christ's atonement. Among his writings are *God in Christ* (1849), *Christ in Theology* (1851), *Nature and the Supernatural* (1858), *The Vicarious Sacrifice* (1866), and *Sermons on Living Subjects* (1872).

Horace Bushnell.

Bibliography: M. B. CHENEY, comp., *Life and Letters of Horace Bushnell* (New York 1880). B. M. CROSS, *Horace Bushnell: Minister to a Changing America* (Chicago 1958).

[R. MATZERATH]

BUSNOIS, ANTOINE

Renaissance composer and poet (family name, De Busne); b. France, date unknown; d. Bruges, Belgium, Nov. 6, 1492. His name is first found in historical documents about 1465; he served as chaplain at the Burgundian court from 1467, but spent his final years in Bruges. He wrote Masses, motets, and Magnificats, which, although of high quality, were technically less forward looking than his elegant and sophisticated chansons. One of these, *Fortuna desperata,* was used by Josquin DESPREZ and Jakob OBRECHT as the basis for Masses, and others served Obrecht, Alexander Agricola, and Heinrich ISAAK. Obrecht based his *Missa L'Homme armé* almost directly on Busnois's Mass of that name. In one motet, *Victimae paschali,* Busnois extended the musical range upward as, in his chansons, he had extended it downward. Another, *Antoni usque limina,* dedicated to his patron saint, Anthony Abbot, includes a part for a bell (Anthony's symbol). He used much imitation (comparatively new at the time), and was extraordinarily resourceful in his treatment of rhythm. Busnois composed the texts for several of his works and corresponded in verse with the Burgundian court poet Molinet. Johannes TINCTORIS dedicated an important treatise jointly to Busnois and OKEGHEM.

Bibliography: A. BUSNOIS, *Missa super L'Homme armé in Monumenta polyphoniae liturgicae,* v. 1, fasc. 2 (Rome 1948). Compositions in *Denkmäler der Tonkunst in Österreich* (1893–; repr. Graz 1959–) 14. G. THIBAULT, *Die Musik in Geschichte und Gegenwart,* ed. F. BLUME (Kassel-Basel 1949–) 2: 515–520. G. PERLE, "The Chansons of Antoine Busnois," *Music Review* 11 (1950) 89–97. C. VAN DEN BORREN, *Études sur le XVe siècle musical* (Antwerp 1941). *Histoire de la musique,* ed. ROLAND-MANUEL, 2 v. (Paris 1960–63); v. 9, 16 of *Encyclopédie de la Pléiade,* v. 1. G. REESE, *Music in the Renaissance* (rev. ed. New York 1959). B. J. BLACKBURN, "Obrecht's *Missa Je ne demande* and Busnoys's Chanson: An Essay in Reconstructing Lost Canons," *Tidschrift van de Koninklijke Vereniging voor Nederlandse Muziekgeschiedenis,* 45 (1995) 18–32. P. M. HIGGINS, ed., *Antoine Busnoys: Method Meaning and Context in Late Medieval Music* (Oxford 1999). M. NATVIG, *The Latin-Texted Works of Antoine Busnois* (Ph.D. diss. University of Rochester 1991). M. PICKER, "Antoine Busnois," in *The New Grove Dictionary of Music and Musicians,* ed. S. SADIE, v. 3 (New York 1980) 504–508. E. SCHREURS and A. WOUTERS, "De Lierse biotoop van Antonius Busnoys en Johannes Pullois," *Musica Antiqua* 13 (1996) 106–132. R. TARUSKIN, "Busnoys and Chaikovsky," *International Journal of Musicology,* 4 (1995) 111–121.

[C. V. BROOKS]

BUSTAMANTE, CARLOS MARÍA

Mexican politician, newspaperman, historian, and editor in the independence and republican era (1805–48); b. Oaxaca, Nov. 4, 1774; d. Mexico City, Sept. 21, 1848. After being educated in Oaxaca, Mexico City, and Guadalajara, he practiced law (graduated, 1801) and became a journalist (1805). After the initiation of the independence movement, he joined Morelos in the south and later suffered many privations and imprisonments. Although he accepted a Spanish amnesty offer in 1817, he escaped and was caught and imprisoned in San Juan de Ulúa and elsewhere until ITURBIDE's triumph in 1821. Soon his opposition to Iturbide, in his paper *La Abispa de Chilpancingo,* again brought imprisonment, but from 1824 until his death Bustamante served almost continuously in congress as a deputy from Oaxaca. The Jesuit historian Mariano Cuevas has written of him: "The Church can be especially grateful to him for the defense he made of her rights, of the Society of Jesus, and of the Guadalupan Apparition" (*Historia de la Iglesia en México* 5:370). A faithful Catholic all his life, Bustamante fought for the return of the Jesuits to Mexico. He was a prolific but disorderly writer who published some 107 works of various kinds, including *Cuadro histórico de la revolución mexicana* (1843–46), *Historia del Emperador D. Agustín Iturbide* (1846), and *El Nuevo Bernal Díaz o sea historia de los anglo-americanos en México* (1847). The last title is said to reflect the depression and sadness he felt at the victory of the Americans in the war with Mexico and their occupation of the capital of the country. His editions of the historical works of Gómara, of the Jesuits Cavo and Alegre, and of Sahagún's *Historia general de las cosas de la Nueva España,* 3 v. (1829–30), the only edition of this fundamental work available for more than a century, mark him as a pioneer in modern Mexican historiography and letters.

Bibliography: C. GONZÁLEZ PEÑA, *Historia de la literatura mexicana* (Mexico City 1940; 7th ed. 1960), Eng. *History of Mexican Literature,* tr. G. B. NANCE and F. J. DUNSTAN (rev. ed. Dallas 1945).

[P. V. MURRAY]

BUTIN, ROMANUS

Marist priest, Orientalist; b. Saint-Romain d'Urfé, France, Dec. 3, 1871; d. Dec. 8, 1937. After studying at the Petit Séminaire de Saint-Jodard, he pursued his priestly studies at Dodon, Md., and was ordained a Marist in 1897. He obtained his Ph.D. in Semitic languages and literatures at The Catholic University of America, where he taught from 1912 until his death in 1937. He was the 1926 annual professor and acting director of the American School of Oriental Research in Jerusalem and a member of the 1930 Harvard-Catholic University expedition to Sinai. As an orientalist, Butin made his main contribution in placing the study of the Proto-Sinaitic inscriptions on a solid basis for the investigation of the origins of the alphabet. His doctoral dissertation was an explanation of the enigmatic "extraordinary points" of the Pentateuch. Among his other contributions were three books, 38 articles, and 21 book reviews. The founding of the Catholic Biblical Association of America was due largely to his initiative.

Bibliography: J. A. GRISPINO and R. T. COCHRAN, "Rev. Romain François Butin, S.M.," *The Catholic Biblical Quarterly* 24 (1962) 383–393.

[J. GRISPINO]

BUTLER, ALBAN

English hagiographer; b. Appletree, Northamptonshire, Oct. 10, 1710; d. Saint-Omer, France, May 15, 1773. His parents died when he was a child, and he was sent first to Ladywell School near Preston and then to DOUAI in France, where after distinguished study he was ordained in 1735. He remained at Douai as professor of philosophy and theology. In 1745 he accompanied the Earl of Shrewsbury and his brothers, the future bishops James and Thomas Talbot, on a tour of France and Italy, and then returned to Douai to continue teaching. In 1749 he returned to England to do missionary work in the Midlands and Warkworth. Bishop CHALLONER appointed him chaplain to the Duke of Norfolk and tutor to the duke's nephew, Edward Howard. He accompanied his pupil to Paris, where Howard died of a sudden illness.

After 30 years' labor, Butler completed in Paris his *Lives of the Saints*, published anonymously (4 v. London 1756–59). The work contains the lives of about 1,600 saints and has influenced English Catholics and non-Catholics. It was thoroughly revised by H. THURSTON (1926–38) and by D. Attwater (1956). In 1766 Butler was chosen president of the English College at Saint-Omer, France, from which the French Jesuits had been expelled. The bishops of Amiens and Boulogne assured him that he could with good conscience accept the office, which he held until his death. He was buried at Saint-Omer. His other works include *Life of Mary of the Cross* (1767), *Moveable Feasts and Fasts* (1774), and *Meditations and Discourses on Sublime Truths* (1791–93). He collected much material on the lives of SS. John Fisher and Thomas More. His nephew Charles Butler wrote his biography in 1799.

Bibliography: D. ATTWATER, "Lives of the Saints," *Commonweal* 66 (1957) 349–351. T. COOPER, *The Dictionary of National Biography From the Earliest Times to 1900,* 3:495–496. P. J. CORISH, "New edition of Butler's *Lives of the Saints,*" *Irish Ecclesiastical Record* 89 (1958) 195–198. H. THURSTON, "Alban Butler," *Month* 172 (1938) 52–63. A. DES MAZIS, *Dictionnaire d'histoire et de géographie ecclésiastiques*10:1439–40.

[R. J. BARTMAN]

Alban Butler, engraving by William Finden.

BUTLER, CHARLES

English Catholic lay leader; b. London, Aug. 14, 1750; d. there, June 2, 1832. He was the son of a merchant and the nephew of Alban BUTLER the hagiographer. After studying in France at Esquerchin and DOUAI, concentrating on rhetoric (1759–66), he returned to England for legal studies (1769–75). Since Catholics were banned from full participation in the courts, he practiced law as a conveyancer. After the Catholic Relief Act of 1791, he became the first Catholic lawyer to be called to the bar since 1688. In 1830 he was appointed king's counsel. Butler was active in the movement for Catholic EMANCIPATION, beginning in 1782 when he was named secretary to the committee of Catholic laymen formed to promote abolition of the PENAL LAWS. Butler's approach to the emancipation question was a controverted one, because he consistently took the position that only through concessions to the government, especially by permitting it a power of veto over the appointment of bishops, could full emancipation be attained. In this stand he met vigorous opposition from Bp. John MILNER, Daniel O'CONNELL, and the Irish hierarchy. In 1792 Butler helped to organize the Cisalpine Club, which sought to thwart the prelates who opposed compromise and favored waiting until complete freedom of religion seemed likely to be granted. After the passage of the Catholic Emancipation Act (1829), Butler retracted publicly some of his earlier statements and admitted their unorthodoxy. Throughout his life he was a devout, ascetic Catholic. Butler's writings ranged over a wide area. He published studies of Roman law, lives of 17th-century Catholic writers, and critiques of Muḥammadan and Hindu literature. His best-known work was the *Historical Memoirs of the English, Irish and Scottish Catholics since the Reformation* (4 v. 1819–21).

Charles Butler.

Bibliography: B. N. WARD, *The Dawn of the Catholic Revival in England, 1781–1803,* 2 v. (New York 1909); *The Eve of Catholic Emancipation,* 3 v. (London 1911–12). F. C. HUSENBETH, *The Life of the Right Rev. John Milner* (Dublin 1862). E. BONNEY and M. HAILE, *Life and Letters of John Lingard* (London 1911). *A Literary and Biographical History or Bibliographical Dictionary of the English Catholics from 1534 to the Present Time* 1:355–364, for Butler's writings. T. COOPER, *The Dictionary of National Biography from the Earliest Times to 1900* 3:497–499.

[A. J. BANNAN]

BUTLER, EDWARD CUTHBERT

Benedictine abbot and scholar; b. Dublin, May 6, 1858; d. Clapham, London, April 1, 1934. His father was professor of mathematics at the Irish university organized by John Henry (later Cardinal) Newman. After his school days at Downside, he entered the Benedictine novitiate (1876) and later studied and taught in the priory school at Downside. He took a leading part in a controversy in the English Benedictine Congregation that issued in the conversion of a unitary congregation devoted to missionary work into one of fully autonomous abbeys. In 1896 he became first head of the Downside house of studies at Cambridge and produced a study and text of the *Lausiac History of Palladius* (1898, 1904). He was recalled in 1904 and succeeded Dom Edmund Ford as second abbot of Downside in 1906. As abbot he was an apostle of the liturgy and an advocate of mental prayer; his lifelong guide was Augustine Baker's *Holy Wisdom.* In 1922 the frustration of his endeavors to diminish the parochial commitments of Downside led to his resignation; he moved to Ealing Priory, where he remained until his death. He produced a valuable Latin edition of the Rule of St. Benedict (1912), and *Benedictine Monachism* (1919), a series of studies on every aspect of Benedictine history, polity, and spirituality. In retirement he published *Western Mysticism* (1922), his *Life and Times of Bishop Ullathorne* (1926), and *History of the Vatican Council* (1930). Much of his work still retains its value and reflects a scholar of wide learning, sane judgment, and powerful mind. Butler lacked the common touch and some of the qualities of leadership, but his unassuming piety and patent sincerity won universal respect.

Bibliography: D. KNOWLES, ''Abbot Butler: A Memoir,'' *Downside Review* 52 (1934) 347–440, reprinted in *The Historian and Character,* ed. C. N. L. BROOKE and G. CONSTABLE (New York 1963) 264–341.

[M. D. KNOWLES]

BUTLER, JOSEPH

English theologian and bishop of Durham; b. Wantage, Berkshire, England, May 18,1692; d. Bath, June 16, 1752. Butler was the eighth and youngest child of a linen draper who reared him as a Presbyterian; he joined the Episcopal Church later and entered Oriel College, Oxford, in 1715, transferring to Cambridge on Sept. 30, 1717. He received the B.A. degree in 1718, was ordained deacon and priest in 1721 by Bp. William Talbot at Salisbury, and was appointed preacher at the Rolls Chapel, whence he delivered his famous ''Sermons on Human Nature'' (1726). In 1721 he received the B.C.L. degree and became prebendary of Salisbury. When Bishop Talbot was transferred to Durham, he gave Butler the rectory of Houghton-la-Skerne (1722) and the wealthy rectory of Stanhope (1725). In 1736 Butler was appointed clerk of the closet to Queen Caroline, who recommended his promotion in the church. In 1737 Caroline died, and George II arranged with Walpole for Butler's appointment to the impoverished See of Bristol. The sharp yet courteous letter of acceptance to Walpole indicated Butler's resentment. Butler was presented to St. Paul's attractive deanery in 1740, and made clerk of the closet to George II in 1746. He declined the primacy in 1747, explaining ''it was too late to support a falling church,'' but in 1750 accepted the bishopric of Durham, where, after delivering a remonstrance, he urged the maintenance of churches and regular services. Earlier he had offered a plan for establishing Episcopal sees in the American colonies, but it remained unheeded.

Butler's *Analogy of Religion, Natural and Revealed, to the Constitution and Course of Nature* (1736), serving as a retaliation against deistic writers who were attacking traditional theology, is widely accepted as the most solid defense of revealed religion during the 18th century. Cardinal J. H. Newman claimed that it ''formed an era in his religious opinions.'' But others, such as John Stuart Mill, regarded the *Analogy* as a retort, not an exposition, and therefore skeptical in essence.

Bibliography: *Works,* ed. W. E. GLADSTONE, 3 v. (London 1896); *The Analogy of Religion,* notes W. FITZGERALD (Dublin 1849), with introd. E. C. MOSSNER (New York 1961). A. E. BAKER, *Bishop Butler* (London 1923). E. C. MOSSNER, *Bishop Butler and the Age of Reason* (New York 1936). A. E. TAYLOR, *Philosophical Studies* (London 1934). Y. M. J. CONGAR, *Catholicisme* 2:336. J. HOMEYER, *Lexicon für Theologie und Kirche,* new eds. 2:844. *The Oxford Dictionary of the Christian Church* 211. L. STEPHEN, *The Dictionary of National Biography from the Earliest Times to 1900* 3:519–524.

[M. A. FRAWLEY]

Joseph Butler.

BÜTLER, MARÍA BERNARDA, BL.

Baptized Verena; missionary and foundress of the Franciscan Missionary Sisters of Mary Help of Christians; b. Auw, Aargau, Switzerland, May 28, 1848; d. Cartagena, Colombia, May 19, 1924. Verena, born into a Swiss peasant family, joined the Franciscan Missionary Sisters of Maria Hilf at Altstätten where she was professed as Maria Bernarda (1869) and served as novice mistress. While superior of the convent, she was invited by Bishop Schumacher of Portoviejo to establish a presence in Ecuador. Maria Bernarda left Switzerland with six sisters on June 19, 1888. In Ecuador she founded communities of the Franciscan Missionaries of Mary Help of Christians (*María Ausiliatrice*) in Chone, Santana, and Canoa Ben. Persecution in 1895 forced her community into exile in Bahia, Brazil. From there fifteen sisters traveled to Colombia, where they were welcomed by Bishop Eugenio Biffi of Cartagena. He gave the sisters a wing of the *Obra Pia* women's hospital from which Mother Maria Bernarda founded communities in Austria and Brazil. She died after serving the poor and sick for fifty-six years as a religious. A miracle attributed to her intercession was approved March 26, 1994. Pope John Paul II beatified her, Oct. 29, 1995.

Feast: May 19 (Franciscans).

Bibliography: *L'Osservatore Romano,* English edition, no. 44 (1995): 1–2, 4.

[K. I. RABENSTEIN]

BUTLER, MARIE JOSEPH, MOTHER

Religious superior, educator; b. Kilkenny, Ireland, July 22, 1860; d. Tarrytown, N.Y., April 23, 1940. After being educated by the Sisters of Mercy, she entered the Congregation of the Sacred Heart of Mary at Beziers, France, at the age of 16. Before taking her first vows, she was sent to Portugal. She was recalled in 1903 to head the congregation's second American foundation, in Long Island City, N.Y. For the next 37 years she planned an expansion program that produced 14 American schools, including six Marymounts (three of them colleges) and a New York novitiate, and 23 foreign institutions, including a novitiate in Ireland and Marymount schools in Rome, Paris, and Canada. She was foundress of an international educative program. Mother Butler's cause for canonization was officially opened in 1948. Her remains rest in the crypt at Marymount, Tarrytown.

Bibliography: K. BURTON, *Mother Butler of Marymount* (New York 1944). J. K. LEAHY, *As an Eagle: The Spiritual Writings of Mother Butler, RSHM* (New York 1954).

[F. DE S. BORAN]

BUXTEHUDE, DIETRICH

Baroque organ virtuoso and composer; b. Oldesloe, Holstein (then a Danish possession), *c.* 1637; d. Lübeck, Germany, May 9, 1707. Buxtehude studied organ with his father and played in Denmark until he succeeded Franz Tunder as organist at the Church of St. Mary, Lübeck, in 1668. In 1673 he initiated the soon celebrated *Abend-Musiken,* twilight musical services held on the five Sundays preceding Christmas. Both J. S. BACH and HANDEL journeyed to Lübeck to hear him play. He was a leader of the North German school of organ composition, with its presupposition of virtuoso technique, and his organ works exerted great influence on Bach's early compositions. Buxtehude's best organ works are those in ''free'' form, i.e., toccatas (or preludes) and fugues; his chorale preludes are not outstanding musically. His many church cantatas, some based on chorales, others freely composed, are a treasure of concerted church music. The cantatas, because of the great variety in their music, as well as the finesse with which their texts are set, are possibly even more important historically than his organ works.

Bibliography: Published music. *Sämtliche Orgelwerke*, ed. P. SPITTA, 2 v. (Leipzig 1876–77). *Complete Organ Works*, ed. J. HEDAR, 4 v. (London 1952–54). Many cantatas are pub. in modern editions. A. PIRRO, *Dietrich Buxtehude* (Paris 1913). W. STAHL, *Dietrich Buxtehude* (Kassel 1937). W. E. BUSZIN, *Musical Quarterly* 23 (New York, 1937) 465–490. F. BLUME, *Die Musik in Geschichte und Gegenwart* (Kassel-Basel 1949) 2:548–571. K. BECKMANN, ''Zur Sextole in Buxtehudes g-Moll-Präludium,'' *Ars Organi* 45 (1997) 69–77. C. BOCKMAIER, ''Buxtehudes Orgel-Chaconne in c-Moll (BuxWV 159),'' *Anuario Musical* 51 (1996) 29–38. P. REICHERT, ''Musikalische Rhetorik in den Choralvorspielen von Dietrich Buxtehude,'' *Acta Organologica* 24 (1993) 145–184. M. SCHNEIDER, *Buxtehudes Choralfantasien: Textdeutung oder ''phantastischer Stil?''* (Kassel 1997). K. J. SNYDER, *Dieterich Buxtehude: Organist in Lübeck* (New York 1987). D. YEARSLEY, ''Towards an Allegorical Interpretation of Buxtehude's Funerary Counterpoints,'' *Music and Letters* 80 (1999) 183–206.

[W. C. HOLMES]

BUXTON, CHRISTOPHER, BL.

Priest, martyr; b. Tideswell, Derbyshire, England; hanged, drawn, and quartered at Oaken Hill, Canterbury, Oct. 1, 1588. Although he was raised in a Protestant family, Christopher fell under the influence of Bl. Nicholas GARLICK, who was master of his grammar school in Tideswell. After his conversion to Catholicism, Buxton studied for the priesthood at Rheims and Rome, and was ordained in 1586. Shortly after his arrival in the English mission, he was arrested and imprisoned at Marshalsea, where he wrote a *Rituale* that is preserved at Olney, England. Although his fellow martyrs, Frs. Robert WILCOX and Edward CAMPION feared he might succumb to apostasy at the sight of their barbarous execution, he remained constant. In response to an offer of clemency in exchange for conformance to the new religion, he said that if he had a hundred lives he would willingly surrender them all in defense of his faith. He was beatified by Pius XI on Dec. 15, 1929.

Feast of the English Martyrs: May 4 (England).

See Also: ENGLAND, SCOTLAND, AND WALES, MARTYRS OF.

Bibliography: R. CHALLONER, *Memoirs of Missionary Priests,* ed. J. H. POLLEN (rev. ed. London 1924; repr. Farnborough 1969), I, 61–63. H. FOLEY, *Records of the English Province of the Society of Jesus,* (London 1877–82), I, 478, 481. J. MORRIS, ed., *The Troubles of Our Catholic Forefathers Related by Themselves,* 3 v. (London 1872–77), III, 39 ; *The Catholics of York under Elizabeth* (London 1891). J. H. POLLEN, *Acts of English Martyrs* (London 1891), 327.

[K. I. RABENSTEIN]

BUYL, BERNAL (BOYL)

First vicar apostolic of the New World; b. near Tarragona, Spain, 1445; d. place and date unknown. The name is variously spelled as Buyl, Boyl, Boil, etc. As a youth be entered the Benedictine monastery of Montserrat, and he was ordained in 1481. He became involved with governmental business and was known to King Ferdinand, serving him in various capacities, including that of ambassador to France in 1488. During much of his life as a Benedictine, Buyl lived as an anchorite in the garden and not in the monastery itself. Sometime after 1488 he left the Benedictine Order and in France joined the Order of MINIMS founded by Francis of Paula. This change in religious order gave rise to much confusion about the identity of the first vicar apostolic until Fita discovered documents on the matter. In October of 1492 King Ferdinand granted Buyl permission to found the new order in Spain and in the spring of 1493 donated to it a hermitage in Málaga. However, the king also had other plans for Buyl and on June 25, 1493, secured a papal bull appointing him vicar apostolic in the Indies. Buyl left Cádiz for America on Sept. 25, 1493, in the second expedition of Columbus; probably a dozen or more priests accompanied him. In Española Buyl quarreled with Columbus over the admiral's harsh treatment of the colonists and the native peoples. Since he considered the situation quite impossible, Buyl left for Spain while Columbus was on an expedition to Cuba and Jamaica. He arrived there Dec. 3, 1494. Even though nothing came of his assignment in America, Buyl had not lost the confidence of the king. At the end of the century, he spent three years in Rome acting as a special ambassador, at times for the king of Spain, at others as the representative of his superior, Francis of Paula. Nothing is known about the last years of his life.

Bibliography: E. W. LOUGHRAN, ''The First Vicar-Apostolic of the New World,'' *American Ecclesiastical Review* 82 (1930) 1–14. F. FITA, a series of articles in *Boletín de la Real Academia de la Historia Madrid 1877–* 19 (1891) 173–233, 267–348, 354–356, 557–560; 20 (1892) 160–178, 179–205, 573–615.

[J. HERRICK]

BYBLOS

Greek name of an ancient Phoenician seacoast town about 20 miles north of Beirut. The Greek name Βύβλος, from which the word BIBLE is derived, comes from the Canaanite (PHOENICIAN) name *gublu* (mountain, hill), with assimilation of the *g* to the following *b.* In the Hebrew Bible the name (with faulty vocalization?) appears as *g*ᵉ*bal* (Ez 27.9; see also Jos 13.5). The modern Lebanese villagers have tenaciously preserved the ancient name in the modern Arabic diminutive form Jubayl (little mount), the name of the pretty town of some 4,000 inhabitants, mostly Maronite Catholics, directly north of the ancient ruins.

Early Period. Excavations begun by the Egyptologist P. Montet (from 1921 to 1924) showed that Byblos, called *kbn* or *kpn* by the Egyptians, was a genuine Asiatic enclave of the pharaos from the earliest times. He discovered inscriptions of Nekba-Khasekhemwi of the Second Dynasty and, among the thousands of votive offerings in the Ba'al (or Ba'alat?) temple and attached rooms, scarabs of Cheops (Fourth Dynasty) and earlier pharaos (now in the Beirut Museum). Superstitious veneration of the site was perhaps connected with legends of the ''blood of Tammuz-Adonis'' at seasons when the fallen leaves turned to red the water that gushed down nearby from the famous 'Afqa spring in the mountains. In the hieroglyphic inscriptions the ''Count [*hatya*] of Byblos'' was the title of a recognized government official [see P. Newberry, *The Journal of Egyptians Archeology* (London 1914–) 14 (1928) 109]. In the Sixth Dynasty the traffic in cedars of Lebanon that were shipped from Byblos to Egypt was so flourishing under Snefru that the Egyptian word for a Mediterranean ship was a *kbnyt* (Byblos) ship. The *Admonitions* [ed. A. Gardiner (Leipzig 1909) 3.6] from the Middle Kingdom (*c.* 2040–1660 B.C.) lamented that there were no longer (after the time of Pepi II of the Sixth Dynasty) any convoys to bring back from Byblos cedars for mummy cases.

M. Dunand, who continued the excavations at Byblos from 1925 to 1966, showed that there had been a settlement on the site even from neolithic times. It was characterized by smooth plaster floors like those of neolithic Jericho and by herringbone-incision pottery like that of Sha'ar-ha Golan, as well as by other ceramic and architectural features thought to be chalcolithic.

Church of Saint John in Byblos, Lebanon. (©Paul Almasy/ CORBIS)

The temple of Ba'al (or Ba'alat?) suffered a catastrophic conflagration *c.* 2100 B.C. Above it, after a lethargy of some 400 years, was raised another temple of similar proportions, but this structure had its cult area filled with standing obelisks five to seven feet high. The excavators dismantled the later temple and reconstructed it a short distance away; they thus made it possible for visitors today to see it in its integrity, but also in striking comparison with the ground plan of the temple that had preceded it. According to Dunand a second temple for the consort divinity was built further west, and the immemorial spring of the town was allowed to gush up and form a sacred lake between the two buildings. The research of Soyez is largely in dialogue with Dunand.

Four royal tombs that were discovered by Montet in 1922 to 1923 have been shown by W. F. Albright [*The Bulletin of the American Schools of Oriental Research* 176 (December 1964) 38–46] to date from the beginning to the end of the 18th century B.C.; they reveal the close ties that Byblos had with Egypt (*see* EGYPT, 2); inscriptions of Neferhotep c. 1690 are reported on stones near Byblos. From about this time comes a West-Semitic inscription that uses 114 hieroglyphic signs that have not yet been successfully deciphered. Quite different is the alphabetic inscription on the sarcophagus of King

Ahiram of Byblos (now in the Beirut Museum), dated by Albright as *c.* 1000 B.C. (rather than Dunand's 1300) and newly deciphered by Mendenhall. It represents one of the earliest stages of the Phoenician alphabet, from which all modern alphabets are derived.

Amarna and Biblical Periods. It is strange that Byblos shows no trace of the HYKSOS, who were Asiatic rulers in Egypt (*c.* 1660–*c.* 1570), unless the sloping stone rampart is to be recognized as their handiwork. Among the Amarna Letters, however, there are 60 cuneiform letters from Rib-Addi of Byblos, from which important conclusions can be drawn regarding the HABIRU (HABIRI) marauders in Syria and Palestine in the 14th century B.C. These documents are of prime importance also for the modern knowledge of the Canaanite language as then spoken, of which the HEBREW LANGUAGE is a later dialect. [See W. Moran, ''The Hebrew language in its Northwest Semitic Background,'' *The Bible and the Ancient Near East,* G. E. Wright, ed. (Garden City, N.Y. 1961) 63.] The practices of the myth religion of the Canaanites in this period (*see* CANAAN AND CANAANITES) were, according to the much later PHILO OF BYBLOS, as brutal as those of nearby UGARIT (*see* UGARITIC-CANAANITE RELIGION).

A century after the wide-eyed visit of the Egyptian Wen-Amun to Byblos (*c.* 1060 B.C.; for the story of his journey, see J. B. Pritchard, *Ancient Near Eastern Texts Relating to the Old Testament* (2d rev ed. Princeton 1955) 25–29) the town furnished cedars and architects for the building of Solomon's temple (if the reading in 1 Kgs 5.32 is correct). However, this episode is linked rather with King Hiram of Tyre (see also 1 Kgs 5.15), who was not the same man as Ahiram of Byblos, although they bore the same name in slightly variant forms. Thereafter Byblos was eclipsed by Tyre and Sidon, and according to Ez 27.9 the shipwrights of Byblos were the servants of the Tyrians.

In the Greco-Roman period Byblos again came into prominence as an import-export center of papyri (*see* PAPYROLOGY) so that papyrus was called ἡ βύβλος or βίβλος (i.e., Byblos material) in Greek. In the Roman epoch the city was one of renewed splendor, from which a theater and a colonnade survive. The north wall of the ancient city was used by the Crusaders as the castle-crowned axis of their settlement (called Gibellet) to the north. Their cathedral of St. John is a chief surviving masterpiece, which is now used for Maronite and Latin Catholic worship.

Bibliography: L. HENNEQUIN, *Dictionnaire de la Bible*, suppl ed. L. PIROT et al. (Paris 1928–) 3:451–68. R. NORTH, ''Gebal (1),'' *Anchor Bible Dictionary* 2 (1992) 922–23 *Encyclopedic Dictionary of the Bible*, tr. and adap. by L. HARTMAN (New York 1963), from A. VAN DEN BORN, *Bijbels Woordenboek* 292–93. ''Byblos and Jericho Neolithic Floors,'' *Fifth Congress of Jewish Studies 1969* (Jerusalem 1972) 1:35–49. P. MONTET, *Byblos et l'Égypte* (Paris 1928). M. DUNAND, *Fouilles de Byblos* (Paris 1937–); *Byblia grammata* (Beirut 1945); *Revue biblique* 57 (1950) 583–603; 59 (1952) 82–90; *Bulletin du Musée de Beyrouth* 9 (1950) 53–74; 12 (1955) 7–23; 13 (1956) 73–86. R. SOYEZ, *Byblo et la fête des Adonies: Etudes préliminaire des religions orientale et romaine* 60 (1977). A. ACQUARO, ed., *Biblo simposio* 1990 (1994). G. MENDENHALL, *The Syllabic Inscriptions from Byblos* (Beirut 1985). W. F. ALBRIGHT, ''Some Oriental Glosses on the Homeric Problem,'' *American Journal of Archaeology* Concord, N.H. 54 (1950) 162–76, esp. 165; *Ensiqlopediya Miqra'it,* v.2 (Jerusalem 1954) 404–11, in Heb.

[R. NORTH]

BYRD, WILLIAM

Elizabethan Catholic composer and organist; b. Lincolnshire, 1543; d. Stondon Massey, Essex, July 4, 1623. He was organist of Lincoln Cathedral at 20 and in 1572 joined Thomas TALLIS as coorganist of the Chapel Royal, London. He had been appointed a Gentleman of the Chapel in 1570, and retained this office to the end of his life. He is important in the history of English music because of his many influential developments. Solo song, virginal music, fantasias for viols, the verse anthem, and other music for the Anglican church all benefited from his keen musical mind and unusually diversified talents. His greatest contribution, however, was to Catholic church music, which included three collections of *Cantiones sacrae* (1575, with Tallis; 1589; 1591), two books of *Gradualia* (1605, 1607), and three Masses (*c.* 1611).

As a faithful Catholic, Byrd was seldom free from worry, and an impression of his personal plight seems to emerge from the frequently despondent and penitential nature of the texts of certain of his motets. On the other hand, his professional life appears to have elicited a marked degree of respect and tolerance. Byrd is not known to have traveled abroad, and although he knew the work of some of his Continental contemporaries, his style retains a few parochial features. Yet he was a superbly capable contrapuntist, and ever sensitive to the needs of a liturgical text. His early motets include settings of hymns, responsories, and antiphons based on Sarum chants (*see* SARUM USE); later works exhibit an almost exclusive concern with the ROMAN RITE, although Catholic services could be held only in strictest privacy.

Bibliography: *Collected Works,* ed. E. H. FELLOWES, 20 v. (London 1937–50). E. H. FELLOWES, *William Byrd* (2d ed. New York 1948). P. C. BUCK et al., eds., *Tudor Church Music,* 10 v. (New York 1922–29) v. 2, 7, 9. J. KERMAN, ''Byrd's Motets: Chronology and Canon,'' *Journal of the American Musicological Society* (Boston 1948–) 14 (1961) 359–382. J. L. JACKMAN, ''Liturgical Aspects of Byrd's *Gradualia,*'' *Musical Quarterly* (New York 1915–) 49 (1963) 17–37. J. HARLEY, ''New Light on William Byrd,'' *Music* *and Letters* 79 (1998) 475–488; *William Byrd: Gentleman of the Chapel Royal* (Aldershot 1997). W. LANDOWSKA, ''English Music of the Past: At the Time of Shakespeare,'' in *Landowska on Music* ed. and tr. D. RESTOUT (New York 1964) 296–298. T. NASU, ''The Publication of Byrd's *Gradualia* Reconsidered,'' *Brio,* 32 (1995) 109–120. J. L. SMITH, ''From 'Rights to Copy' to the 'Bibliographic Ego': A New Look at the Last Early Edition of Byrd's 'Psalmes, Sonets, and Songs,''' *Music and Letters,* 80 (1999) 511–530. R. TURBET, ''More Early Printed Editions Attributed to Byrd,'' *Brio,* 35 (1998) 105; ''Horsley's 1842 Edition of William Byrd and Its Infamous Introduction,'' *Journal of the British Music Society,* 14 (1992) 36–47.

[D. STEVENS]

William Byrd. (Bettman/CORBIS)

BYRNE, ANDREW

Bishop; b. Navan, County Meath, Ireland, Dec. 3?, 1802; d. Helena, Ark., June 10, 1862. In 1820 he arrived in the U.S. from the diocesan seminary at Navan as a volunteer to work in the newly created Diocese of Charleston, S.C. After finishing his studies under the tutelage of Bp. John England, he was ordained at Charleston Nov. 11, 1827. He worked as a missionary until 1830, when he was made pastor of St. Mary's Church, Charleston. For several years he was vicar-general of Charleston, and he served as England's theologian at the Second Provincial Council of Baltimore (1833). Because of a disagreement with England, Byrne moved in 1836 to New York, where he held, successively, pastorates in several parishes. When the Diocese of LITTLE ROCK, comprising the state of Arkansas and the Indian Territory, was created in 1843, Byrne was named its first bishop. He was consecrated on March 10, 1844, in New York by Bp. John Hughes. With fewer than 1,000 Catholics in Arkansas, Byrne became active in promoting immigration to the Southwest. Twice he went to Ireland to seek co-workers for his diocese, and in 1851 he welcomed the Sisters of Mercy from Dublin. He took part in both the Sixth Provincial Council of Baltimore (1846) and the First Provincial Council of New Orleans (1856).

Bibliography: *The History of Catholicity in Arkansas* (Little Rock 1925). R. H. CLARKE, *Lives of the Deceased Bishops of the Catholic Church in the U.S.,* 4 v. (New York 1872–89) v.2. J. D. HACKETT, *Bishops of the United States of Irish Birth or Descent* (New York 1936).

[A. A. MICEK]

BYRNE, EDMUND

Archbishop of Dublin; b. probably Ballyback, near Borris, County Carlow, *c.* 1656; d. Ireland, 1723 or 1724. He was a member of the Gabhal Raghnaill branch of the O'Byrnes and a descendant of Fiach MacHugh. He entered the Irish College in Seville (1674), where he was ordained on March 18, 1679 and remained until 1681, acquiring the Spanish equivalent of D.D. At St. Nicholas outside Dublin he served as parish priest (1698). Appointed archbishop on March 15, 1707, he was consecrated on Aug. 31, 1707, in Newgate Jail, Dublin, by Dr. O'Donnelly, Bishop of Dromore, in times of appalling difficulty. He was the first archbishop actually resident since Russell's death in 1692. Although constantly fleeing the notorious priest catchers Garzia and Tyrell, he succeeded in holding a diocesan synod in 1712 to continue a precarious discipline under penal conditions. A patron of a school of Gaelic learning, he is commemorated in its versifications; he took part by his writings in public religious controversy. His difficulties were increased by the interference of the Primate, Hugh McMahon, Archbishop of Armagh. He encouraged the Dominican and Poor Clare Sisters to return to the diocese and led acceptance of Clement XI's constitution *Unigenitus* (1713) against Jansenists.

Bibliography: N. DONNELLY, *History of Dublin Parishes* (Dublin n.d.) 2:35–36, 38–48. J. J. MEAGHER in *Reportorium Novum* (Dublin n.d.) 3:378–386.

[J. J. MEAGHER]

Andrew Byrne.

BYRNE, PATRICK JAMES

Maryknoll missioner, first apostolic delegate to Korea; b. Washington, D.C., Oct. 26, 1888; d. Ha Chang Ri, Korea, Nov. 25, 1950. He was the seventh of ten children of Patrick and Anna (Seales) Byrne, and was born on the site of the present Supreme Court Building, which he referred to with typical drollery as his ''family homestead.'' He attended St. Charles College, Catonsville, Md., and St. Mary's Seminary, Baltimore, and was ordained on June 23, 1915, for the Baltimore Archdiocese. A week later, however, he entered the Catholic Foreign Mission Society (*see* MARYKNOLL FATHERS AND BROTHERS), the first priest to do so. After various administrative assignments, he founded a Maryknoll mission in northern Korea in 1923. Four years later he became the prefect apostolic of Pyongyang, with headquarters at Pengyang. He relinquished this post in 1929 when he was elected vicar-general of the society.

In 1935 he opened Maryknoll's first Japanese mission, which was soon designated the prefecture apostolic of Kyoto. He resigned from this in 1940 in favor of Rev. Paul Furuya Yoshiyuki, later first bishop of Kyoto. Byrne remained in Japan during World War II, though his mission activity was curtailed. His postwar apostolate in Japan came to an end in 1947, when he was appointed apostolic visitor, and later first apostolic delegate to Korea.

He was consecrated in Seoul as titular bishop of Gazera on June 14, 1949. With the invasion of South Korea by Communists a year later, Byrne stayed at his post, was arrested on July 16, 1950, and taken to Pengyang, the communist capital, where he was held prisoner until October 21. On that day he began a ''death march,'' with 700 other prisoners, to the Manchurian border, 100 miles north. On the way he died of exhaustion and pneumonia in the village of Ha Chang Ri and was buried in the land of his first mission.

Bibliography: R. A. LANE, *The Early Days of Maryknoll* (New York 1951); *Ambassador in Chains* (New York 1955). G. D. KITTLER, *The Maryknoll Fathers* (New York 1961).

[W. J. COLEMAN]

BYRNE, WILLIAM

Educator, author; b. Kilmessan, County Meath, Ireland, Sept. 8, 1833; d. Boston, Mass. Jan. 9, 1912. After immigrating to the United States in 1853, he attended St. Mary's College, Wilmington, Del., and Mt. St. Mary's College, Emmitsburg, Md., where he received his M.A. (1861) and taught mathematics and Greek. He was ordained on Dec. 31, 1864, for the Diocese of Boston, and was named diocesan chancellor (1866) and rector (1874) of St. Mary's Church, Charlestown, Mass. During this period, he began his lifelong activity on behalf of penal reforms, founded the Boston Temperance Missions, and edited the *Young Crusader.* At the request of Cardinal John McCloskey and Abp. (later Cardinal) James Gibbons, Byrne was elected in 1881 as the 12th president of Mt. St. Mary's College. As president and treasurer, he successfully rescued the institution from the financial difficulties that had threatened to close its doors. In 1884 he returned to Boston as rector of St. Joseph's Church, but he continued until his death as a member of the college's governing council. Byrne contributed frequently to both the secular and Catholic press, and he wrote several religious manuals in addition to a *History of the Catholic Church in the New England States* (1899). Georgetown College (now University), Washington, D.C., awarded him a doctor of divinity degree in 1881, and the library of Mt. St. Mary's College is named in his honor.

Bibliography: M. M. MELINE and E. F. X. MCSWEENEY, *The Story of the Mountain: Mount St. Mary's College and Seminary,* 2 v. (Emmitsburg, Md. 1911).

[H. J. PHILLIPS]

BYZANTINE ART

To the question "what is Byzantine art?" one might propose the following answer: Byzantine art is the art produced by and for the citizens of the empire that was centered in Constantinople from A.D. 330–1453. This answer, however, underscores the difficulty of applying any one label to the arts of Byzantium. Byzantine art is Late Antique art, Early Christian art, the art of the Eastern Orthodox Church, the art of the Eastern Roman Empire and eastern Medieval art. All of these labels are applicable, but none covers all of Byzantine art. To understand Byzantine art one must first understand the origins of the Byzantine Empire. Centered in CONSTANTINOPLE, modern-day Istanbul, Turkey, the Byzantine emperors saw themselves as heirs and continuers of the Roman Empire. In 330 the emperor CONSTANTINE I (r. 324–37) transferred his capital from Rome to the site of an ancient Greek colony named Byzantion but soon called Constantinople in recognition of its new founder (*Constantinoupolis:* 'City of Constantine'). Strategically situated on the banks of the Bosphorus, overlooking eastern Europe and western Asia Minor, the new capital granted the security necessary for the new empire to flourish. The borders of the Byzantine Empire were never stable but fluctuated over the 1,100 plus years of its existence. At its greatest extent Byzantium nearly encircled the Mediterranean, stretching from southern Spain to Italy, Greece, Asia Minor, the Middle East, and northern Africa. At its smallest, in the 15th century, the BYZANTINE EMPIRE was reduced to the area surrounding Constantinople. Our distance from this world and from the art it produced is evident in the term "Byzantine," which would be meaningless to any citizen of this empire. From the founding of Constantinople until its fall to the Ottomans in 1453 the Byzantine emperor styled himself ruler of the *Romaioi*—of the Romans. Yet, while the terms "Byzantine" and "Byzantium" are modern designations they do distinguish the unique nature of this civilization from its Roman predecessor. While Byzantium continued to recognize Roman law, it differed from Rome in fundamental ways. Where the language of Rome was Latin, the language of the Byzantine Empire was Greek. Where the Roman state supported various pagan religions, after 321 Christianity was the recognized religion of the Byzantine Empire. This singular combination of Roman law, Greek language, and Christian religion shaped the art of Byzantium.

It is usual to divide Byzantine art into three phases, reflecting major political events. Early Byzantine art encompasses that produced from the mid-4th to the mid-6th century. This is followed by a gap, as from the mid-6th until the 9th century Byzantium was caught in crises precipitated by many factors, both internal and external. The Middle Byzantine period begins in the 9th century and continues until 1204, when Constantinople fell to the army of the Fourth Crusade. The final phase of Byzantine art, the Late Byzantine period, dates from the Byzantine reconquest of Constantinople in 1261 to its final fall to the Ottomans in 1453.

An Early Byzantine work that displays Byzantium's debt to classical art and also illustrates its differences is an ivory diptych carved with the figure of the Archangel Michael. Diptychs, pairs of carved, hinged panels, are known from Rome; originally this leaf was the right-hand panel of a set. Many diptychs were produced at the end of the 4th century and display a resistance to the imposition of the Christian faith by the great senatorial Roman families. They served to announce marriage alliances and senatorial promotions, and in style and iconography they display the continuity of pagan themes and the endurance of the classical style.

The diptych of the Archangel Michael, most likely produced in Constantinople in the early 6th century, shows a shift in both patronage and iconography. The figure of the Archangel is taken from the pagan Nike, or winged victory, although in this Christian use the female Nike has become male. Other adjustments were made to fit the old iconography to the new message. Instead of a palm branch, the attribute of the Nike signifying victory, the Archangel holds an orb surmounted by a cross. The laurel wreath above Michael's head, another symbol of military victory, is here transformed into a Christian symbol of resurrection by the inclusion of a cross. The style has also undergone transformation, reflecting the new merging of classical form with Christian message. Michael's calm detached expression has its roots in classical relief sculpture, but here it serves to underscore his other-worldliness.

The precise modeling of the Archangel's form, with believably solid limbs outlined by clinging drapery, also has roots in the classical representation of the human figure. Yet despite this realistic modeling there is ambiguity in the relationship between the Archangel and his architectural setting. Michael's feet seem precariously posed on the topmost stairs, behind the square bases that support the framing columns. The rest of his body, including his wings, is in front of these columns. This spatial ambiguity reflects the new concerns of Byzantine art. While it is clear that the artist was well aware of the classical tradition of figural representation, he was not as occupied as his predecessors with naturalistic representation. This is appropriate to his subject, as according to Byzantine theology Archangels exist in both the earthly and heavenly realms.

While the Archangel ivory relies primarily on figural imagery to convey its message, another medium com-

Ivory panel from Byzantine diptych depicting archangel Michael. (©The British Museum)

"The Lamentation over the Dead Christ," fresco, in St. Panteleimon Church, Nerezi, Yugoslavia.

bined text and image in the service of defining and disseminating Christianity. Books, written by hand and illustrated with painted images, or illuminations, were popular among the clergy and the elite. While a few secular illuminated manuscripts have survived, the majority of extant Early Byzantine manuscripts are religious, comprised mainly of the Gospels and the Book of Genesis. Illuminated manuscripts were luxurious and costly objects, precious both for the skill it took to produce them and for the intrinsic value of their materials. Pages of specially prepared animal skin could be embellished by painters with gold leaf or with pigments made by grinding semiprecious gems, such as lapis lazuli. Scribes, responsible for copying the text, could write in silver or gold ink over pages dyed purple. Such so-called purple codices (codex, plural codices, is the Latin term for book) reflect patronage at the highest level. The color purple, derived from a rare organic dye and consisting of many hues of what today would be called red and blue, was reserved for imperial use throughout much of Byzantine history.

One such purple codex is the Rossano Gospel, created in Byzantium and now preserved in the treasury of the cathedral of Rossano, Italy. Its materials, style, and large size—the pages measure 30.7 x 26 cm (12 x 10.5 in.)—allow it to be dated to the 6th century. The once-purple color of the dye has faded over time to a brick-red color, and the silver used to inscribe the text has oxidized to black. One characteristic page illustrates the Last Supper and the Washing of the Feet. Above, the first scene depicts Christ and his disciples arranged around a semicircular table that resembles those painted in Pompeii or the catacombs of Rome. Christ is identified by his prominent position and larger size as well as by his distinctive dark hair and beard. In contrast, the identifying feature of the disciples is not their individual appearance but their collective number, so the artist is careful to show us 12 distinct heads while the bodies beneath merge into undifferentiated forms. Only the disciple on the far right is shown in full-figure as he reclines, Roman style, on his couch. The next scene also uses this same abbreviated style. Christ is recognizable by the replication of His form and features, and also by His halo, marked by the arms of a cross and therefore known as a cruciform halo.

What is important for identifying and understanding this scene is the interaction between Peter and Christ, as the disciple sits and allows Christ to wash his feet. Below, Old Testament authors hold up scrolls that display quotes

"Deësis with Apostles," detail of the outer reliquary of the true cross, c. 960, in the cathedral at Limberg an der Lahn, Germany.

"The Anastasis," fresco in the apse of the Parecclesion, Kariye Djami, Istanbul.

that are presented as prophesies of the events depicted above, declaring that Christ is the Messiah foretold by the Jewish scriptures. The linking of scenes from the life of Christ in the top half of the page with the Old Testament authors depicted below is emphasized by the authors' gestures, which draw the viewer's eyes up and across the page. Yet we do not understand fully the joining of the two halves of the page unless we read the text and it is this combination of text and image in the service of the message of the Gospel that is new.

The illuminations of the Rossano Gospels do not simply narrate the events of Christ's life but present arguments about the true nature of Christ. This was a topic of great controversy in the Early Byzantine period. The First Ecumenical Council, calling together bishops "from throughout the world" was convened by Constantine I in 325 in Nicaea in order to define Orthodox theology and to condemn heretics. In 451 a second council met in Chalcedon to further explicate the Orthodox position. The crux of the matter was the duality of Christ.

According to the Orthodox view, Christ was equally human and divine. After Constantine, Orthodox Christianity spread throughout the western world via Byzantium, which reached its greatest territorial extent under the rule of Justinian I (r. 527–65). After Justinian, the rise of the Islam and Slavic incursions reduced the territory held by the empire. Adding to the tensions were increasing disagreements within Byzantium about the nature of Christ. Previously the Orthodox doctrine was directed against non-Byzantine Christians, most notably the monophysites, who believed that Christ was divine in nature and when on Earth as man was therefore not fully human.

In the 8th century the theological battle raged inside the Orthodox Church, and while it touched on many aspects of orthodox theology, it centered on Christian art. Onc faction asserted that the veneration of religious im-

"The Last Supper and the Washing of Feet," in the Rossano Gospels, folio 3, 6th century.

ages facilitated the faithful, serving as a vehicle for their prayerful contemplation. The opposing side countered that religious images were idolatrous. In particular, representations of Christ were labeled as heresy, as artists could depict Christ's humanity, but not his divinity. This debate is known as the Iconoclastic Controversy (*see* ICONOCLASM), from the Greek words *eikon,* meaning image, and *klao,* to break. Iconoclasm was first decreed in 726 by the emperor Leo III (r. 717–41). The argument against religious imagery, and the persecution of those who continued to venerate or to produce such images, was intensified by Leo's successor Constantine V (r. 741–75). Constantine convened the Iconoclastic Council of 754, which decreed that there should be no representations of Christ or of any other religious figures, and that all images of religious content should be destroyed. A brief respite was provided by the Second Council of Nicaea in 787, which rejected the earlier council and reinstalled the use of religious imagery.

A second Iconoclastic period began in 815 when the Second Council was in turn repudiated and a new ban on images was imposed. This second period lasted until 843. The Byzantine Empire was shattered by Iconoclasm, and while there are numerous documents describing events and defining the ideologies of the iconophiles (image-lovers) and iconoclasts, the very nature of the contest means that little in the way of religious art survives from before or during the time of the destruction of images.

The Middle Byzantine period, beginning in 843 with the lifting of the ban on religious images, often called the Triumph of Orthodoxy, was one of great artistic production. Artists and patrons, freed from over 80 years of restrictions, sought to recapture old traditions and to forge new ways of expressing Orthodox faith. The issues raised by art of this period are still the subject of intense scholarly debate. One characteristic of Middle Byzantine art in general, and of 10th-century art in particular, is the conscious return to the style and motifs of classical antiquity. This has given rise to the term ''Macedonian Renaissance,'' indicating works of art that reflect knowledge of antique models produced under the Macedonian imperial dynasty, from Basil I (r. 866–86) to Basil II (r. 976–1025).

One of the objects that gave rise to the concept of a Macedonian Renaissance is the Paris Psalter (Paris, Bibliothéque Nationale MS gr. 139). A Psalter is book of Psalms that also contains the nine Old Testament odes and sometimes hymns as well. It was a necessary item for priests and monks, whose duties included the weekly recitation of all the Psalms. But a manuscript such as the Paris Psalter demonstrates that these books were also commissioned by, or for, the highest level of court patron

''The Pantocrator,'' mosaic, c. 1100, Daphni, Greece.

for this is clearly no mere service book. It is the largest surviving illustrated Byzantine Psalter, with fine-grained vellum pages measuring 37 x 26.5 cm (approx. 15 x 11 in.). It contains the usual Psalms and odes and also an extensive scholarly commentary. There are 14 pictures illustrating the life of David, author of the book of Psalms, and the authors of the odes. The book has been associated with the emperor Constantine VII Porphyrogenitus (r. 913–59) and his son, the future emperor Romanus II (r. 959–63), thus dating it to 950–70.

The scene of David's Repentance precedes Psalm 51, which relates David's remorse and penitence for his relations with Bathsheeba. Like all the other illustrations in this Psalter, the scene is a full-page illumination enclosed in a painted frame. We see David to the left, seated in profile on his throne, confronted with his sins by the prophet Nathan. The next figure, to the right, moves us forward in time to show David's repentance as he kneels in prayer on the ground. His name is inscribed above him, aiding in his identification, as does the replication of his facial features and royal garments. Above David is a figure turned in profile to the viewer's right, who seems oddly detached from the surrounding scenes. He is dressed in classical robes and leans pensively upon a writing desk that holds a scroll. As he gazes out of the picture frame he is linked to those around him by two details: his halo and the subtle gesture of his right hand, which gestures toward the crouching king beneath him. The accompanying inscription solves the puzzle, identifying the figure as ''penance'' (*metanoia*). This is a personification, one of many used in the Paris Psalter.

"David's Repentance," early 10th Century.

"Christ Pantocrator Between Emperor Constantine IX Monamachus and Empress Zoë," wall mosaic, Byzantine Style, mid 11th/early 12th century. (© Gianni Dagli Orti/CORBIS)

Other pages include personifications of concepts such as wisdom and clemency. There are also personifications that serve to identify the scene, such as the personification of Mount Sinai in the depiction of Moses receiving the Tablets of the Law. Such personifications were a standard element of classical art. Their inclusion in the Paris Psalter points to a renewed interest in antiquity, as does the background architecture, which does not reflect contemporary architecture but is reminiscent of that depicted in Roman art. Yet the appropriation of classical motifs is selective and not slavish. This is evident in the figure of David seated on his throne. While he is dressed in archaic robes and painted in classicizing style his pose reflects a 10th-century interest in what we today could call psychological studies. David raises his left hand to his head as if hiding Nathan's accusations while at the same time his right hand responds to the truth of Nathan's words.

This mix of antique elements with contemporary ones served to transmit in a new way a very old concept: the nature of an ideal ruler. In art and literature David had long been presented as an ideal to which earthly rulers should aspire. That is also one of the messages of the Paris Psalter. The final illumination shows David flanked by the personifications of Wisdom and Prophecy, a portrait of ideal rulership. Yet David is not shown in antique robes but in the garments and regalia of a Byzantine emperor. If, as some have argued, this work was commissioned by or for the emperor, it would have been a visual expression of the claim frequently made in Byzantine textual rhetoric, that in spirit and in fact the emperors were descendants of the ancient biblical kings, including David.

While the Paris Psalter conveyed its messages through a combination of antique and contemporary iconography and style, the enameled box known as the Limburg staurotheke (relic container) shows how similar messages could be conveyed without reference to classical art. An inscription names the emperors Constantine and Romanus, allowing it to be dated to 945–59; it is therefore contemporary with the Paris Psalter. The Limburg staurotheke is constructed of a wooden core covered in hammered gilt metal and decorated with precious gems and enamel plaques. The staurotheke was brought to Germany after the fall of Constantinople to the armies of the Fourth Crusade in 1204, and is now housed in Limburg an der Lahn, Germany. The Limburg staurotheke is a large object, measuring 48 x 35 x 6 cm (19 x 13¾ x 2⅜ in.) and was made to contain several relics, including a fragment of the True Cross and a portion of the towel with which Christ dried the feet of his Apostles.

The lid of the staurotheke contains a large square inset of enamel plaques that depict the divine hierarchy. Christ is central in the composition, occupying the most important space. His primacy is further emphasized by His size; although He is the only seated figure, He is as large as the other, standing figures. Those around Him are also positioned according to their rank in the heavenly court. John the Baptist, the proclaimer and forerunner of Christ, is to the viewer's left, while Mary, known in Byzantine theology as the Theotokos (Bearer of God), is to His left. This trio, of Christ flanked by John and the Theotokos, is a common religious image in Byzantine art. Known as the Deesis (entreaty or prayer), it is also common in painted church decorations and in manuscript illuminations. As the name indicates, the Deesis is an image of intercession. Prayers are directed to the Baptist and to the Theotokos who in turn intercede with Christ on behalf of the faithful. On the lid of the Limburg staurotheke the Deesis is expanded by the inclusion of the Archangels Gabriel and Michael who flank John and Mary, respectively. Above and below these centrally positioned figures are six enamel plaques that contain representations of the 12 Apostles. They are grouped in pairs, and while all are clothed in similar fashion each figure is given individuality through variations of facial features, expressions, hair color, and pose. And, as is the case in most Byzantine art, all figures are also identified by naming inscriptions. The cover of the staurotheke is fitted with a loop at the top, allowing it to be carried in processions, but it would usually have been displayed in one of the imperial churches of Constantinople. Set on display, it functioned like an icon, focusing the prayers of the faithful. The composition of the lid guides the viewer's eye to the aim of his entreaties. Only the figure of Christ is fully frontal, facing the viewer. The rest of the figures turn toward Him in varied degrees, or indicate His presence by word or glance.

While at first glance this object seemingly conveys only religious messages, in the 10th century it also conveyed messages of a secular nature. The lid is surrounded on four sides by an iambic inscription, prominently written in large letters, which declares the name of the patron who commissioned the piece. He was Basil, the eunuch and illegitimate son of the emperor Romanus I (r. 920–44). During the rule of Constantine VII, Basil achieved one of the most powerful positions in the imperial court. He is known to have commissioned other luxury items, including a chalice and paten, which is now in the Treasury of San Marco in Venice, Italy. The Limburg staurotheke not only conveyed Basil's piety, its gleaming gold and precious stones also spoke to his wealth, status, and artistic taste. The enamels are executed in a new variant of the cloisonné technique. While previous cloisonné enamels were small, set against backgrounds of single-colored enamel, in the early 10th century enameled images were inset in gold grounds, allowing for larger panels and greater compositional clarity. This technique displays Basil's cutting-edge taste, as does the inscription, which plays on the word ''beauty'' (*kallos*).

The Limburg staurotheke is not unique in its depiction of a heavenly hierarchy. Such hierarchy is also the fundamental organizing concept of Byzantine church decoration. Churches were embellished with a variety of media: icons, carved relief sculpture, wall mosaics composed of thousand of tiny glass or stone tesserae (cubes), and fresco paintings. Thousands of churches spread across the Byzantine Empire served a variety of functions: monastic, private, patriarchal, and imperial. While it is therefore difficult to characterize any one scheme of decoration as being typical, certain generalities can be observed.

Regardless of the media, the placement of subject matter on the walls and vaults of a church interior reflect the Byzantine concept of the celestial hierarchy. The lower walls of a church, closest to the faithful, are adorned with depictions of martyrs and other holy figures. The choice of individual saints often reflects devotion to popular local saints or reflects the preference of a donor. Higher up on the wall are narrative scenes from the life of Christ arranged in chronological order. These scenes are often referred to as festival scenes, as they represent the principal commemorations of the liturgical year. There is rarely a direct correlation with the liturgy, however, for while there were 12 major church feasts there were more than 12 narrative scenes that could be included in a church's decorative program. Those appearing most frequently include the Annunciation, Nativity, Presentation, Baptism, Transfiguration, Crucifixion, Deposition, Lamentation, and Anastasis (the Resurrection). Above these scenes, in the lower portions of the roof vaulting, are depictions of the Apostles and Archangels, with either Christ, the Deësis, or the Theotokos depicted in the apse above the main altar. The central dome, the highest point in the church, was reserved for the image of Christ, reflecting His preeminence in the celestial hierarchy. In the Byzantine church, individual scenes and portraits served as images for prayerful contemplation, while the decorative program in its entirety displayed for the faithful the theological framework promising their ultimate salvation.

Christ was depicted in many different guises in Byzantine art but one representation became particularly popular in the Middle Byzantine period, Christ as Pantokrator, or Ruler of the World. A famous Pantokrator image dating to the late 11th or early 12th century survives in the dome of the monastery church at Daphni, near Athens. The Christ at Daphni, as with all Pantokrators, is a bearded mature man with lines of care on His brow who displays a sternness not found in other portrait types of Christ. The Daphni Pantokrator, depicted in mosaic in the apex of the dome, is shown in half-length, encircled in a brilliant triple border. His left hand holds a jeweled and gilt Bible decorated with a cross, the symbol and proof of His death and resurrection. In His role of ruler and judge His right hand is raised, as if arrested in the act of bestowing a blessing approval has neither been granted nor forbidden. Robed in garments of deep purple and blue the Daphni Pantokrator is set against a shimmering gold background, interrupted only by the Greek abbreviations for Jesus Christ written to the left and right of the silver cruciform halo. Byzantine mosaicists set each individual mosaic tessera, or cube, into the plaster bedding at slightly different angles. The resulting variation in light gives Byzantine mosaics a dynamic quality that is often lost in modern restorations or in photographic reproductions. This dynamic effect was increased by the artist's awareness of the curve of the dome, evident in the foreshortening of Christ's arms, which also take into account the effects of viewing the mosaic from the floor below. The artist also manipulated the pictorial space, arranging Christ's left hand as if it is resting on the border. Visually, the Pantokrator looms over the church as if peering through a hole in the dome, ready to judge those inside.

Donors could insert themselves into this hierarchical framework of church decoration. While most donors appear with patron or namesake saints in the narthex, or entrance hall of Byzantine churches, some are depicted in the church interior, and a few bold or important donors had their portraits placed above the apse, kneeling at the feet of Christ or the Theotokos. Donors thus gave visual expression to their piety and ensured that, after their death, those who gazed on their images would pray for their souls. Some donors of modest means could fund only limited programs, perhaps a single painted panel in a rock-cut church. But we also retain portraits of imperial donors, including representations of several imperial families in the south gallery of Hagia Sophia, the Church of the Holy Wisdom, in Constantinople.

HAGIA SOPHIA was in many ways as symbolic of Byzantium as was the Great Palace complex. It was the showpiece of the empire, proudly displayed to every foreign diplomat, and was equally the object of devout pilgrims and gawking tourists. It served as the primary church of the patriarch, the head of the Orthodox church, and was the site of many of the empire's most important celebrations, including the investiture of new emperors. The scale of the building reflects it importance; throughout the Middle Ages it was the largest church in Christendom. Begun by the emperor Justinian I in 532, the great central dome rises to a staggering height of 180 feet, the largest vaulted space of any ancient or medieval building. The extent of the decoration of the building prior to Iconoclasm is unclear, but we know that there were figural images for documents attest to their removal. In 867, after the triumph of Orthodoxy, Hagia Sophia was the first church to undergo official redecoration.

The importance of Hagia Sophia to Constantinople and the greater empire also ensured that rulers would desire to leave some visible expression of their own contributions to the great church. The south gallery, on the second floor of the building, was reserved for imperial use, equipped with its own staircase. The east wall of the gallery displays a mosaic panel erected in the first half of the 11th century. It shows the enthroned Christ flanked by the emperor Constantine IX Monomachus (r. 1042–55) and the empress Zoë (*c.* 978–1050). Both emperor and empress are swathed in sumptuous jeweled regalia. Both are also equipped with haloes. This does not indicate that during their lives they were seen as saints, or even as being particularly holy. It instead reflects the carefully formulated relationship believed to exist between God and the Byzantine emperors.

There was, of course, no separation of church and state in the Middle Ages. The Byzantine emperor was believed to rule by divine right. A successful rule was the sign of divine approval, and the emperor was thus seen to have a special relationship with God, to be closer to God than his subjects. In the imperial panel the figure of Christ, larger in scale than the emperor or empress, is seated on a richly jeweled throne. He wears blue robes embellished with gold borders over an elaborately brocaded gold and scarlet tunic. He holds a richly ornamented Bible in His left hand, and raises His right hand in blessing. The emperor is shown holding a bag of coins while the empress holds a document recording an imperial donation to the church. Both the emperor and empress are shown with a relatively high degree of individuality; while these may not be portraits in the modern sense, they do attempt to convey some sense of the physical appearance of the imperial couple. At first glance this panel seems to be a straightforward image of imperial piety, but there are also messages of rank and power. The emperor's superior status vis-à-vis his wife is conveyed in several ways. He is placed on Christ's favored side, at His right hand, he is placed closer to Christ than his wife, he is larger than Zoë and he is depicted with a greater degree of frontality.

Yet the panel also displays the standardization of imperial iconography and the rather pragmatic distinction made between the title and the title-holder. Zoë was the daughter of the emperor Constantine VIII (r. 1025–28), whose dynastic legacy was imperiled by the lack of any surviving male heirs to the throne. At her father's death, Zoë thus became the conduit to imperial power. Her first husband, Romanus III Argyrus (r. 1028–34), became emperor on his wedding day. Together husband and wife made a special donation to Hagia Sophia from the imperial coffers, and it is this gift that is commemorated in the mosaic panel. Originally, the head of the emperor depicted Romanus, and the inscription above also named him. Zoë married again, to Michael IV the Paphlagonian (r. 1034–41), and on his death she adopted Michael V Calaphates (r. 1041–42) as her son and heir. He showed his gratitude by sending Zoë into exile. Michael was in turn deposed, blinded, and exiled by Constantine Monomachus, who restored Zoë to power and then became her third husband, and thus emperor. Together they gave an additional annuity to Hagia Sophia, and to commemorate this act the original donation panel was altered to its present state. The tesserae of the faces of Romanus, Zoë, and Christ were removed, as were those naming Romanus in the inscription. The new additions brought the panel up to the current standards in style, inserted Constantine's name in the inscription and replaced the head of Zoë's first husband with that of her last.

Despite the stern, even forbidding quality of the Pantokrator and the cool remoteness of the imperial portraits at Hagia Sophia, Byzantine art was also capable of representing and evoking emotion. This is particularly evident in monumental painting of the 12th century, as seen in the depiction of the Lamentation in the Church of St. Panteleimon in Nerezi, Macedonia. This church was built by Alexius Comnenus, nephew of the emperor John II Comnenus (r. 1118–43), and dedicated in September 1164. The Lamentation depicts the dead body of Christ, laid out prior to burial. His body is approached from the right by those who witnessed the crucifixion and assisted at the deposition. Nicodemus and Joseph of Arimathea kneel in sorrow, tenderly supporting Christ's feet. In front of them is the "beloved disciple" John. His agony is given clear expression: his body is bent more than 90 degrees, his face contorted in grief as he raises Christ's right hand to his cheek. The viewer's eye is then led down the line created by the extension of Christ's right arm to the figure of the Theotokos, and to the very epicenter of grief. She holds her son awkwardly in her lap, her knees emerging on both sides of His rigid form. Her left hand reaches over His body to clasp His right arm while her right hand encircles His neck, pulling His face to meet hers. Their faces converge, hers in anguished profile, His stern but calm, shown in three-quarter view. His cruciform halo overlaps that of His mother, and their conjoined rounded contours are echoed by the forms of the hills that rise behind them. Above the scene in a brilliant blue sky angels, generally so calm and still in Byzantine art, weep and tumble in grief.

It has been suggested that this new emotionality in Byzantine art reflects the extreme changes the empire underwent in the 11th and 12th centuries. A convenient starting point for a catalog of these changes is 1054, the year of the schism of the Orthodox and Latin churches, which initiated an increasing polarization of the Christian world. This was followed in 1071 by the victory of the Seljuk Turks over Byzantium on the plains of Manzikert, in eastern Anatolia. In the wake of this defeat the emperor ALEXIUS I COMNENUS (r. 1081–1118) sought aid from Western European armies and from the papacy to stop the Seljuk advance. The First Crusade was motivated in part by this request, and while it did initially end the Seljuk incursions into eastern Anatolia, it also eroded Byzantium's strength and wealth.

The crusading armies captured Jerusalem from Arab forces in 1099, establishing the first of many Latin kingdoms in the east. Byzantine trade was displaced first by Norman and then Italian commercial cities, such as Venice. To the north and west, former vassal states of Byzantium, such as Hungary and Bulgaria, became increasingly independent. While all of these factors played a role in the declining political and economic stature of Byzantium on the world stage, the event that seared the empire's soul occurred in 1204. The army of the Fourth Crusade was diverted from their stated goal of liberating the Holy Lands to Constantinople by the commercial ambitions of the Norman and Venetian leaders. As they entered Constantinople the emperor fled and the city, unprepared for attacks by a Christian army, mounted little resistance. In the days that followed, Constantinople was sacked and burned. Churches were a prime target for the looters, and icons and relics were dismembered for their jewels and gold or were carried off to adorn churches in the West.

Bronze sculptures were melted down or taken away. An example is a group of four bronze horses first brought to Constantinople from Rome and placed in the hippodrome. After 1204 they were taken to San Marco, Venice, where they can still be seen along with other booty from the imperial palaces and churches. In Constantinople a king was installed in the Great Palace of the Byzantine emperors, and the Latin Kingdom of Constantinople (1204–61) was established.

During this period multiple and competing centers of Byzantine power sprouted in Trebizond, on the Black Sea coast, and in the Greek cities of Nicaea and Epiros. In 1261 MICHAEL VIII PALAEOLOGUS (r. 1259–82) emerged from Nicaea and conducted a series of successful raids on the Latin army that culminated in the recapturing of Constantinople. He entered the city on August 15, riding behind an icon of the Theotokos, the traditional protector of Constantinople. Despite this reconquest, Byzantium never regained its stability or vigor. Geographically it was limited to the western corner of Asia Minor, northern Greece, and the southeastern edges of the Peloponnesus. Constantinople itself was mostly in ruins, and the great Orthodox churches, including Hagia Sophia, had been converted to serve the Latin liturgy. Massive rebuilding and restoration were needed. In this Late Byzantine period the patronage of significant monuments was increasingly taken over by members of wealthy aristocratic families. Theodore Metochites, a member of one such family, rebuilt what is often termed the greatest monastery of the age, the Chora monastery. Often referred to by its Turkish name, Kariye Camii, the building was transformed into a mosque during Ottoman rule and today is a museum. It contains some of the best preserved and most splendid works of Late Byzantine art.

Theodore Metochites was a scholar and statesman who held the second most powerful rank in the Byzantine court. He began work on the Chora in 1316, choosing to reconstruct a dilapidated monastery near the northern imperial palace of the Blachernai, close to the land walls of the city. From 1316 to 1321 Metochites supervised reconstruction of the vaults, the addition of an inner and outer narthex, and the construction of a *parekklesion,* a long chapel to the south of the building, which was to serve as a funerary chapel for its founder and his relatives. Metochites also oversaw the elaborate decorative program. In the main church today there remains only remnants of Metochites's original program. In contrast, the mosaics of the narthexes are well preserved, and display scenes from the Life and Ministry of Christ and from the Life of the Virgin.

The decorative program of the *parekklesion* differs in several ways from that of the main structure. Here the medium is fresco paintings, not mosaics, and the imagery reflects the funerary function of this chapel. The painted cycle of the *parekklesion* culminates in the eastern apse in the monumental painting of the Anastasis, the Resurrection of Christ. In this image we see the emotional style of the Lamentation at Nerezi taken to a new level. Christ is centrally positioned in the center of the apse and the center of the composition. He is enclosed in a brilliant *mandorla,* or body halo, which changes from pale blue to cream to white with gold stars as it emanates from Christ's body. His robes are now also pure white, indicating His resurrected state. And in contrast to representations of Christ that feature static poses, such as the Deesis or Pantokrator, the resurrected Christ at the Chora is embued with an astounding physicality. He stands atop two broken doors, representing the broken gates of Hell, around which are scattered numerous broken locks and keys. Beneath Him is a personification of Hell, a dark figure bound tightly with rope. To the left and right of Christ stand the Old Testament figures awaiting resurrection. Closest to Him are Adam, to the left and Eve, to the right, who as the first to die are the first to be resurrected. This is, however, no gentle transference to the heavenly paradise. Christ stands with feet wide apart, knees bent to brace Himself as He physically hauls Adam and Eve from their sarcophagi. Eve, presumably the lighter of the two, is shown in midair, while Adam's hair and garments flutter behind him as he too is wrenched from death into eternal life. The figures to either side are bunched together. Some look to each other in amazement while gesturing toward Christ; others are transfixed by the scene, bending eagerly toward it as they await their own resurrection. Behind them rise pale craggy mountains, set against the void of a dark blue background.

Bibliography: Sources. Texts and translations. J.-P. MIGNE, *Patrologiae cursus completus. Series graeca* (Paris 1857–66). *Corpus scriptorum historiae Byzantinae* (Bonn 1928–97). M. PSELLUS, *The Chronographia,* tr. E. R. A. SEWTER (New Haven, Conn. 1953). A. COMNENA, *The Alexiad,* tr. E. R. A. SEWTER (Baltimore 1969). P. GAUTIER, *Michel Italikos: Lettres et discours* (Paris 1972). C. MANGO, *The Art of the Byzantine Empire, 312–1453: Sources and Documents* (Englewood Cliffs, N.J. 1972). *Nicétas Magistros: Lettres d'un exile (928–946),* tr. L. G. WESTERINK (Paris 1973). J. DARROUZÈS and L. G. WESTERINK, *Théodore Daphnopatès: Correspondance* (Paris 1978). JOHN OF DAMASCUS, *On the Divine Images: Three Apologies against Those Who Attack the Divine Images,* tr. D. ANDERSON (Crestwood, N.Y. 1980). D. J. GEANOKOPLOS, *Byzantium. Church, Society, and Civilization Seen through Contemporary Eyes* (Chicago 1984). G. MAJESKA, *Russian Travelers to Constantinople in the Fourteenth and Fifteenth Centuries* (Washington, D.C. 1984). N. CHONIATES, *O City of Byzantium: Annals of Niketas Choniates,* tr. H. J. MAGOULIAS (Detroit 1984). Literature. Encyclopedias and dictionaries. M. RESTLE and K. WESSEL, *Reallexikon zur byzantinischen Kunst* (Stuttgart 1966). J. M. HUSSEY, *The Cambridge Medieval History,* v. 4 *The Byzantine Empire* (2nd ed. Cambridge 1967). W. F. VOLBACH and J. LAFONTAINE-DOSOGNE, *Byzanz und der christliche Osten,* v. 3 *Propyläen Kunstgeshichte*

(Berlin 1968). W. MÜLLER-WIENER, *Bildlexikon zur Topographie Istanbuls* (Tübingen 1977). A. KAZHDAN, *The Oxford Dictionary of Byzantium* (Oxford 1991). Journals and bibliographic studies. *Art Bulletin* (New York 1913–). *Byzantine and Modern Greek Studies* (Oxford 1975–). *Byzantinische Zeitschrift* (Leipzig-Munich 1892–). *Byzantion* (Brussels 1924–). *Cahiers archéologiques* (Paris 1945–). *Dumbarton Oaks Papers* (Washington, D.C. 1941–). *Gesta* (New York 1964–). *Jahrbuch der österreichischen byzantinischen Gesellschaft* (Vienna 1951–). *Revue des études byzantines* (Paris 1946–). Collections. S. M. PELEKANIDIS, *The Treasures of Mount Athos* (Athens 1975). A. BANK, *Byzantine Art in the Collections of Soviet Museums* (2nd ed. St. Petersburg 1985). B. DAVEZAC, *Four Icons in the Menil Collection* (Houston 1992). J. NESBITT and N. OIKONOMIDES, *Catalogue of Byzantine Seals at Dumbarton Oaks and in the Fogg Museum of Art* (Washington, D.C. 1994). J. FLEISCHER, *Byzantium: Late Antique and Byzantine Art in Scandinavian Collections* (Copenhagen 1996). *Handbook of the Byzantine Collection: Dumbarton Oaks* (Washington, D.C. 2000). Exhibition catalogs. *Byzantine Art. An European Art* (2nd ed. Athens 1964). *The Year 1200: A Centennial Exhibition at the Metropolitan Museum of Art: February 12 through May 10, 1970* (New York 1970). M. CHATZTZIDAKIS, *Byzantine Murals and Icons* (Athens 1976). K. WEITZMANN, *Age of Spirituality, Late Antique and Early Christian Art, Third to Seventh Century* (New York 1979). J. LAFONTAINE-DOSOGNE, *Splendeur de Byzance* (Brussels 1982). D. BUCKTON, *The Treasury of San Marco, Venice* (New York and Milan 1984). M. M. MANGO, *Silver from Early Byzantium. The Kaper Koraon and Related Treasures* (Baltimore 1986). *From Byzantium to El Greco: Greek Frescoes and Icons* (London 1987). G. VIKAN, *Holy Image, Holy Space: Icons and Frescoes from Greece* (Baltimore 1988). K. MANAFIS, *Sinai: Treasures of the Monastery of Saint Catherine* (Athens 1990). J. FURAND, *Byzance: L'Art byzantin dans les collections publiques francaises* (Paris 1992). D. BUCKTON, *Byzantium: Treasures of Byzantine Art and Culture from British Collections* (London 1994). *Oi Pules tou Musteriou Thesauroi tes Orthodoxias apo ten Ellada/Treasure of Orthodoxy from Greece* (Athens 1994). H. C. EVANS and W. D. WIXOM, *The Glory of Byzantium. Art and Culture of the Middle Byzantine Era,* AD *845–1261* (New York 1997). A. A. KARAKATSANIS, *Treasures of Mount Athos* (Thessaloniki 1997). *Mother of God: Representations of the Virgin in Byzantine Art,* MARIA VASSILAKI, ed. (Milano-New York 2000). General. A. GRABAR, *L'Art de la fin de l'Antiquité et du Moyen Age* (Paris 1968); *L'Empereur dans l'art byzantin: Recherches sur l'art officiel de l'empire d'orient* (repr. London 1971). O. DEMUS, *Byzantine Art and the West* (New York 1970). E. KITZINGER, *Byzantine Art in the Making* (London 1977); *Early Medieval Art* (2nd ed. Bloomington, IA 1983). J. BECKWITH, *Early Christian and Byzantine Art* (2nd ed. London 1979). H. MAGUIRE, *Art and Eloquence in Byzantium* (Princeton 1981). K. WEITZMANN, *Classical Heritage in Byzantine and Near Eastern Art* (London 1981). C. MOSS and K. KIEFER, *Byzantine East, Latin West: Art-Historical Studies in Honor of Kurt Weitzmann* (Princeton 1995). J. LOWDEN *Early Christian and Byzantine Art* (London 1997). T. MATHEWS, *Byzantium: From Antiquity to the Renaissance* (New York 1998). R. CORMACK, *Byzantine Art* (Oxford 2000). Painting and mosaic. O. DEMUS, *Byzantine Mosaic Decoration: Aspects of Monumental Art in Byzantium* (London 1948); *The Mosaics of Norman Sicily* (London 1950); *The Mosaics of San Marco in Venice,* v. 1 *The Eleventh and Twelfth Centuries* (Chicago 1984); *Die byzantinischen Mosaikikonen,* v. 1 *Die grossformatigen Ikonen* (Vienna 1991). C. MANGO, *Materials of the Study of the Mosaics of St. Sophia at Istanbul* (Washington, D.C. 1962). R. HAMANN-MACLEAN and H. HALLENSLEBEN, *Die Monumentalmalerei in Serbien und Makedonian vom 11.bis zum frühen 14. Jahrhundert* (Giessen 1963). P. UNDERWOOD, *The Kariye Djami* v. 3 *The Frescoes* (New York 1966). V. N. LAZAREV, *Storia della pittura bizantina: Edizione italiana rielaborata e amplliata dall'autore* (Turin 1967). M. RESTLE, *Byzantine Wall Painting in Asia Minor* (New York 1967). L. HADERMANN-MISGUICH, *Krubinovo: Les fresques de Saint-Georges et la peinture byzantine du XIIe siècle* (Brussels 1975). H. BELTING, C. MANGO, and D. MOURIKI, *The Mosaics and Frescoes of St. Mary Pammakaristos (Fethiye Camii) at Istanbul* (Washington, D.C. 1978). D. MOURIKI, *The Mosaics of Nea Moni on Chios* (Athens 1985). A. STYLIANOU and J. A. STYLIANOU, *The Painted Churches of Cyprus: Treasures of Byzantine Art* (London 1985). L. RODLEY, *Cave Monasteries of Byzantine Cappadocia* (Cambridge 1981). A. W. EPSTEIN, *Tokali Kilise: Tenth-Century Metropolitan Art in Byzantine Cappadocia* (Washington, D.C. 1986). C. CONNER, *Art and Miracles in Medieval Byzantium: The Crypt at Hosios Loukas and Its Frescoes* (Princeton 1991). C. JOLIVET-LEVY, *Les Églises byzantines de Cappadoce. Le programme iconographique de l'abside et de ses abords* (Paris 1991). S. GERSTEL, *Beholding the Sacred Mysteries. Programs of the Byzantine Sanctuary* (Seattle, Wash. 1999). Manuscript illumination. H. BUCHTHAL, *The Miniatures of the Paris Psalter* (London 1938). K. WEITZMANN, *The Joshua Roll: A Work of the Macedonian Renaissance* (Princeton 1948); *Studies in Classical Land Byzantine Manuscript Illumination* (Chicago 1971). C. CECCHELLI, *The Rabbula Gospels* (Olten 1959). G. GALAVARIS, *The Illustrations of the Liturgical Homilies of Gregory Nazianzenus* (Princeton 1969). S. DER NERSESSIAN, *L'Illustration des psautiers grecs du Moyen Age: Londres, Add. 19.352* (Paris 1970). A. GRABAR, *Les Manuscrits grec enluminés de provenance italienne (Ixe–Xie siècles)* (Paris 1972). I. SPATHARAKIS, *The Portrait in Byzantine Illuminated Manuscripts* (Leiden 1976); *Corpus of Dated Illuminated Greek Manuscripts to the Year 1453* (Leiden 1981); *Studies in Byzantine Manuscript Illumination* (London 1995). I. HUTTER, *Corpus der byzantinischen Miniaturhandschriften* (Stuttgart 1977–93). A. GRABAR and M. MANOUSSACAS, *L'Illustration de manuscrit de Skylitzès de la Bibliothèque Nationale de Madrid* (Venice 1979). I. FURLAN, *Codici greci illustrati della Biblioteca marciana,* v. 3 (Milan 1980). R. NELSON, *The Iconography of Preface and Miniature in the Byzantine Gospel Book* (New York 1980); *Theodore Hagiopetrites: A Late Byzantine Scribe and Illuminator* (Vienna 1991). A. CUTLER, *The Aristocratic Psalters in Byzantium* (Paris 1984). A. W. CARR, *Byzantine Illumination, 1150–1250: The Study of a Provincial Tradition* (Chicago 1987). A. J. WHARTON, *The Art of Empire. Painting and Architecture of the Byzantine Periphery* (Berkeley 1988). J. J. G. ALEXANDER, *Medieval Illuminators and Their Methods of Work* (New Haven, Conn. 1992). J. C. ANDERSON, *The New York Cruciform Lectionary* (University Park, Pa. 1992). K. CORRIGAN, *Visual Polemics in the Ninth-Century Byzantine Psalters* (Cambridge 1992). J. LOWDEN, *The Octateuchs: A Study in Byzantine Manuscript Illumination* (University Park, Pa. 1992). L. BRUBAKER, *Vision and Meaning in Ninth-Century Byzantium. Image as Exegesis in the Homilies of Gregory of Nazianzus* (Cambridge 1999). Sculpture and the minor arts. P. GRIERSON, *Catalogue of the Byzantine Coins in the Dumbarton Oaks Collection and in the Whittemore Collections* (Washington, D.C. 1966–2000). A. GOLDSCHMIDT and K. WEITZMANN, *Die byzantinischen elfenbeinskulpturen des X.–XIII. Jahrhunderts.* (repr. Berlin 1979). L. BRÉHIER, *La Sculpture et les arts mineurs byzantins* (Paris 1936). A. FROLOW, *La relique de la Vraie Croix: Recherches sur le développement d'un culte* (Paris 1961); *Les Reliquaires de la Vraie Croix* (Paris 1965). J. BECKWITH, *The Veroli Casket* (London 1962). A. GRABAR, *Sculptures byzantines de Constantinople (IV–X siècle)* (Paris 1963); *Sculptures byzantines du Moyen Age (XIe–XIVe siècle)* (Paris 1976). K. WESSEL, *Byzantine Enamels from the 5th to the 13th Century* (Greenwich, Conn. and New York 1967). A. CUTLER,

The Craft of Ivory: Sources, Techniques and Uses in the Mediterranean World: A.D. *200–1400* (Washington, D.C. 1985); *The Hand of the Master: Craftsmanship, Ivory, and Society in Byzantium (9th–11th Centuries)* (Princeton 1994). I. KALAVREZOU-MAXEINER, *Byzantine Icons in Steatite* (Vienna 1985). N. FIRATLI, *La Sculpture byzantine figurée au Musée Archéologique d'Istanbul* (Paris 1990). H. R. HAHNLOSER and R. POLACCO, *La Pala d'oro* (Venice 1994). Image-Icon-Iconoclasm. C. MANGO, *The Brazen House. A Study of the Vestibule of the Imperial Palace of Constantinople* (Copenhagen 1959). K. WEITZMANN, *The Monastery of Saint Catherine at Mount Sinai,* v. 1 *The Icons: From the Sixth to the Tenth Century* (Princeton 1976); *The Icon: Holy Images Sixth to Fourteenth Century* (New York 1978). A. GRABAR, *L'Iconoclasme byzantin: Le dossier archéologique* (Paris 1984). M. CHATZIDAKIS, *Icons of Patmos: Questions of Byzantine and Post-Byzantine Painting* (Athens 1985). A. KARTSONIS, *Anastasis. The Making of an Image* (Princeton 1986). D. FREEDBERG, *The Power of Images* (Chicago 1989). H. BELTING, *Likeness and Presence: A History of the Image before the Era of Art* (Chicago 1994). C. R. OUSTERHOUT and L. BRUBAKER, *The Sacred Image East and West* (Chicago and Urbana, Ill. 1995). H. MAGUIRE, *The Icons of Their Bodies: Saints and Images in Byzantium* (Princeton 1996). A. M. TALBOT, *Byzantine Defenders of Images: Eight Lives in English Translation* (Washington, D.C. 1998).

[L. A. JONES]

BYZANTINE CHANT

Ecclesiastical music of the Byzantine liturgical rite practiced in the Christian East, originating from the establishment of Constantinople in the 4th century, and surviving beyond the Fall of Constantinople (1453) to the present day. Included under this heading, though not part of a church service, are the acclamations addressed to the emperor and his family as a matter of courtly ceremony. These acclamations are religious in character: of purely secular Byzantine music no evidence exists save in literary references. The same may be said of instrumental music. Though instruments might accompany the imperial acclamations, they were altogether excluded from the church service proper; Byzantine musical notation, presumably the invention of clerics, was developed for the sole purpose of recording the melodies of a monophonic and unaccompanied chant. Even in this domain, the oldest surviving Byzantine musical documents can scarcely be earlier than 10th century—by which time virtually all the texts that were to figure henceforth in the standard Byzantine ritual had taken their place there, and the order of service itself had, at least in large part, assumed definitive shape. Hence, while it is reasonable to suppose that many Byzantine melodies are much older than the earliest sources preserving them, one can speak with assurance only of the textual forms of Byzantine hymnody during the period of its greatest poetical creativity.

In Eastern liturgy as in Western, the intonation of scriptural lessons and the chanting of Psalms and canticles (Psalm-like texts from other books of the Bible) always played an important part. The Byzantine liturgy, however, tended to accord a prominence to original (i.e., non-Biblical) hymnography, which the hymns, tropes, and Sequences of the Latin world never achieved. Scattered examples of hymn texts from the early centuries of Eastern Christianity still exist. Some of these employ the metrical schemes of classical Greek poetry; but the evolution of pronunciation had rendered those meters largely meaningless, and with rare exceptions when classical forms were imitated, Byzantine hymns of the following centuries are prose poetry—unrhymed verses of irregular length and accentual patterns. The common term for a short hymn of one stanza, or one of a series of stanzas, is troparion (this may carry the further connotation of hymn interpolated between psalm verses). A famous example, whose existence is attested as early as the 4th century, is the Vesper hymn Φῶς ἱλαρόν (O Gladdening Light), still a part of the Orthodox Vesper Service; another, Ὁ μονογενὴς υἱός (The Only-Begotten Son), ascribed to Justinian I (527–565), figures in the introductory portion of the Byzantine Divine Liturgy. Perhaps the earliest set of troparia of known authorship are those of the monk Auxentios (first half of the 5th century), recorded in his biography but not preserved in any later Byzantine order of service.

Development of the Kontakion. At the end of the 5th and beginning of the 6th century came the development of the first large-scale form of Greek hymnody, which only at a much later date received the special name kontakion (literally, scroll). This has been described as a kind of poetical sermon, in general setting forth the narrative theme of one of the great feasts with much rhetorical embellishment. Modern scholars have traced the derivation of the genre from Syriac prototypes. Formally, the kontakion consists of 20 to 30 or more stanzas (oikoi, literally, houses), all metrically identical (though of the characteristic irregular meter), so that each might be sung to the same music—the whole series prefixed by a metrically independent stanza known as prooimion or koukoulion. (Not only were succeeding oikoi within a given kontakion modeled on the first; it became common practice to borrow the metrical structure of a preexisting kontakion for a new poem, perhaps with the object of making use of an already well-known melody.) The stanzas were further linked together by the occurrence of a short refrain (*ephymnion*) at the end of each, and by an acrostic formed of the initial letters of each stanza, which might spell out the author's name, the alphabet, etc. (both devices are characteristic of Semitic poetry). The most illustrious composer of kontakia was Romanos (called the ''melodist''), a Syrian Jew converted to Christianity and active at Constantinople in the first half of the 6th century; to him some 80-odd poems are ascribed. But the most celebrated example of the genre itself is the anonymous AKATHISTOS hymn, the times intact with all its stanzas. Other kontakia suffered drastic abridgment with the declining popularity of the genre: by the 10th century they had by and large been cut down to the prooimion and a single oikos. Some new kontakia were written even at this late date, but in the truncated form to which the old ones had been reduced.

Development of the Kanon. It was in fact the second of the two large-scale forms of Byzantine hymnography that seems to have supplanted the kontakion in liturgical favor: the kanon, which first appeared in the second half of the 7th century. For an indeterminate time before this, a central position in the Morning Service (*Orthros*) had been occupied by the chanting of a group of nine Biblical canticles: (1) and (2) those of Moses (Ex ch. 15 and Dt ch. 32); (3)–(6) those of Anna (1 Kgs ch. 2), Habakkuk (ch. 3), Isaiah (ch. 26), and Jonah (ch. 2); (7) and (8) the Canticle of the Three Young Men, in two parts (Dn ch. 3); and (9) the Magnificat (Lk ch. 1). The kanon had its origin in the practice of interpolating a certain number of troparia between verses of these canticles, so that to each there corresponded a set of hymns, newly composed, but showing their relation to the original by textual quotation or allusion (and often combining this reference with references to the feast of the day). In time these new compositions came largely to supplant the canticles themselves in the service; and the term ''ode'' (ᾠδή)—at first simply the equivalent of ''canticle'' —was applied as well to the set of stanzas corresponding to any individual canticle. The term kanon designates the resulting non-Biblical hymnodic complex: thus a kanon has, in principle, nine odes (in fact, the second is usually omitted outside of the Lenten season); an ode in turn consists typically of three or four stanzas or troparia (several early kanons survive in which the number of troparia to an ode is much greater). Further, in each ode the successive stanzas are exact metrical reproductions of the first, so that the same music will fit all equally well; however, the model-stanzas for the different odes are, save in a few exceptional cases, metrically dissimilar. The Greek term for such a model-stanza is *heirmos,* from which derives the name of the collection containing model-stanzas (texts and, in general, music as well) for a given repertory of kanons: the Heirmologion, one of the principal types of source-book for Byzantine music. Tradition attributes the invention of the kanon to Andrew of Crete (*c.* 660–*c.* 740). While there is reason to suppose that examples of the form existed before the period of his activity, he is probably the earliest known poet to whom kanons are ascribed by the sources. Certain aspects of his work belong to the early history of the genre, e.g., the composition of an ode in a large number of short troparia: his famous ''Great Kanon'' of mid-Lent contains in sum 250 stanzas. Younger contemporaries and successors of Andrew as kanon-writers were men associated with the monastery of St. Sabas (between Jerusalem and the Dead Sea), notably John of Damascus (d. *c.* 750) and Cosmas of Maiuma. John's celebrity as hymn-writer rivals his preeminence as codifier of theology. Outstanding among his works are the Easter kanon Ἀναστάσεως ἡμέρα (Day of Resurrection) and the kanons in iambic meter for Christmas, Epiphany, and Pentecost; in general the kanons ascribed to ''John the Monk'' have a leading place among the heirmoi in each of the eight modally-divided sections of the Heirmologion. (Indeed, so numerous and varied are the kanons with this attribution in the manuscripts that a number of them must be the work of authors other than John Damascene himself.) In the 9th century the center of hymnography was no longer Palestine but Constantinople, and in particular the monastery of Studion, a bastion of the anti-iconoclastic struggle. The principal representative of this school is the Abbot Theodore (759–826), writer of kanons, kontakia, etc., who in collaboration with his brother Joseph composed many of the hymns of the Lenten season. Prominent also among the Studite hymnographers are two Sicilians: Methodios (d. 846), who was to become patriarch of Constantinople after the triumph of Orthodoxy; and Joseph (d. 883), known with special emphasis as ''the Hymnographer''—his kanons remaining today in printed Greek service-books number in the hundreds. There are a few 9th-century hymn-writers not of the Studion group who are worthy of commemoration, such as the nun Kasia, of whose work there survives a kanon for Holy Saturday and several hymns.

Other Hymn Forms. Though these hymnographers have been mentioned chiefly as writers of kanons, they composed also shorter, monostrophic hymns, some of which have considerable prominence in the service. Such troparia have a variety of denominations, specifying their liturgical function (e.g., *hypakoë* designates a short troparion of the Morning Office preceding the Gradual Antiphons, or *anabathmoi*) or their subject matter (e.g., *theotokion* designates a hymn in praise of the Mother of God). These categories are too numerous to list in detail. The most important class, in number and in variety of liturgical use, bears the name sticheron (στιχηρόν), deriving from *stichos* (psalm-verse) and showing the origin of such a hymn as appendage to a verse of a Psalm, or intercalation between verses. Thus attached to selections from the Psalter, the stichera generally occur in groups, of which the principal, throughout the year, are those accompanying the fixed set of Psalms toward the beginning of Vespers (Psalms 140, 141, 129, 116), those at the end of Vespers (called aposticha), and those accompanying the Psalms of Lauds toward the end of the Morning Service (Psalms 148–150). By the time the hymnology of the Office had reached its full development, there were proper stichera serving these functions for all the feast days of the year, for the Sundays and weekdays of Lent, and for the recurrent cycle of eight weeks in the order of the modes beginning with Easter. The music book containing these sets of stichera, together with certain other sets of troparia (such as those for special solemnities of the year, e.g., the Great Hours of Good Friday), was known as the Sticherarion; this compilation as such—unlike the Heirmologion—exists only in medieval manuscripts. If the metrical pattern and melody of a sticheron were original with itself, it was called idiomelon; if borrowed from another sticheron, prosomoion; an idiomelon, which had thus served as a model for later stichera, received the special name *automelon.* Most important among the stichera prosomoia are those in the collection composed by Theodore and Joseph of the Studion for the Lenten Office.

Significant additions were made to the Byzantine Office after this 9th-century generation of hymnographers: e.g., the eleven morning hymns (*heothina*) by Emperor Leo VI (886–912), and the eleven Resurrection hymns (*exaposteilaria*), also for the Morning Service, by his son Constantine VII Porphyrogennetus (913–959). But in general, with the 10th century the composition of new hymns within the Eastern Empire went into decline; and by the end of the 11th it had all but ceased. Hymnography flourished a while longer in the Italo-Greek world, and notably at the Byzantine-rite Abbey of Grottaferrata (near Rome)—today a leading center for the study of Byzantine music and liturgy.

The Later Byzantine Chant. With the cessation of new poetical composition, Byzantine chant entered its final period, devoted largely to the production of more elaborate musical settings of the traditional texts: either embellishments of the earlier simpler melodies, or original pieces in highly ornamental style. This was the work of the so-called ''masters'' (*maistores*), of whom the most celebrated was John Koukouzeles (active *c.* 1300), compared in Byzantine writings to John Damascene himself as an innovator in the development of chant. The multiplication of new settings and elaborations of the old continued in the centuries following the fall of Constantinople, until by the end of the 18th century the original musical repertory of the medieval MSS had been quite replaced by later compositions, and even the basic modal system had suffered profound modification under Near-Eastern influences.

To a still greater extent than Latin plainchant, Byzantine chant, as shown even in the early MSS, is formulaic in structure. Each mode is characterized by a limited number of musical formulas, ranging in length from a few notes to an entire phrase, which recur time and again, in more or less invariable form, throughout the repertory of pieces within that mode. (The greatest variation tends to occur in the middle of phrases; the most stereotyped formulas are the cadential ones.) Depending upon the literary and liturgical genre of a piece, its musical style may be more or less complex; thus, the kanons and stichera generally exhibit a simple, predominantly syllabic setting, the Communion verses a more ornamental one, while the kontakia are still more elaborate. Yet the principle of formulaic construction remains present in each style. The period of the *maistores,* however, saw the development of a new style known as ''kalophonic,'' highly florid, not reliant on the traditional preexisting formulas (though observing melodic conventions of its own), and applicable to almost all the liturgical genres—kanons and stichera as well as kontakia, etc.

It is generally agreed that Byzantine musical notation derives from the Greek phonetic signs (accents, breathings) introduced by Hellenistic grammarians. The most primitive variety of this notation is that employed by lectionary books (those with readings from the Bible for liturgical use) dating from the 9th to the 15th century. Over that period it remains essentially unchanged—a small set of signs that occur as couples (one at the beginning of a phrase, one at the end), and which presumably call for various sorts of simple cantillation formula. This notation, of which nothing more definite can confidently be said, has been named ''ekphonetic'' by modern scholars (see Fig. *a*). Almost as rudimentary are the earliest surviving examples—10th century or later—of hymn notation (see Fig. *b* lower portion, which shows several heirmoi of kanons with archaic notation). Like the early Latin neumes, these signs do not have unambiguous pitch meaning. Yet by the beginning of the 13th century, the system had been developed to the point of expressing all pitch relationships unequivocally: each sign shows the intervallic distance, up or down, from its predecessor; and a key-signature (*martyria*) shows the degree of the mode on which the piece begins.

This article has dealt solely with the hymnology of the Greek Church; but that of the Slavic Church as well might be included under the heading ''Byzantine.'' Slavic hymnology, as with liturgy in general, is in all but exceptional details simply a faithful adaptation of the Greek; even the medieval Slavic musical notation is directly based upon an early state of Greek Byzantine notation. And if specific examples of parallelism between Byzantine and Latin chant are far more the exception than the rule, nonetheless such examples in increasing number have come to the attention of scholars. Further comparative study of these relationships will be a major endeavor of future scholarship, building on the pioneering work of Wellesz and Tillyard in the Byzantine field.

Bibliography: E. WELLESZ, ed., *The Music of the Byzantine Church* (Cologne 1959). H. J. W. TILLYARD, *Byzantine Music and Hymnography* (London 1923); L. TARDO, *L'Antica melurgia bizantina* (Grottaferrata 1938). J. QUASTEN, *Musik und Gesang in den Kulten der heidnischen Antike und christlichen Frühzeit* (*Liturgiegeschichtliche Quellen und Forschungen* 25; 1930). O. STRUNK, ''The Tonal System of Byzantine Music,'' *Musical Quarterly* 28 (New York 1942) 190–204; ''Intonations and Signatures of the Byzantine Modes,'' *ibid.* 31 (1945) 339–355; ''The Byzantine Office at Hagia Sophia,'' *Dumbarton Oaks Papers,* Harvard University 9–10 (1955–56) 175–202. K. LEVY, ''A Hymn for Thursday in Holy Week,'' *Journal of the American Musicological Society* 16 (Boston 1963) 127–175. M. VELIMIROVIĆ, ''Liturgical Drama in Byzantium and Russia,'' *Dumbarton Oaks Papers,* Harvard University 16 (Cambridge, MA 1962) 349–385. E. KOSCHMIEDER, *Die ältesten Novgoroder Hirmologien-Fragmente* (*Abhandlungen der Bayerischen Akademie der Wissenschaften* [Munich 1835–] Philosophie-Historie Klasse, New Style 35, 37, 41; 1952–58). B. DI SALVO, ''L'essenza della musica nelle liturgie orientali,'' *Bollettino della Badia Greca di Grottaferrata,* New Style 15 (1961) 173–191; ''Asmatikon,'' *ibid.* 16 (1962) 135–158; ''Stichera Antiphona,'' *ibid.* 17 (1963) 37–55. The principal publication for sources and studies is the series *Monumenta musicae byzantinae,* ed. C. HÖEG et al. (Copenhagen 1935–). O. STRUNK, *Essays on Music in the Byzantine World* (New York, 1977). D. E. CONOMOS, *Byzantine Hymnography and Byzantine Chant* (Brookline, MA, 1984). B. SCHARTAU, ''Testimonia of Byzantine Musical Practice, III,'' *Cahiers de l'Institut du Moyen Age grec et latin,* no. 68 (1998).

[I. THOMAS/EDS.]

BYZANTINE CHRISTIANITY

PART I: ORTHODOX CHURCHES

Within Byzantine Christianity, there are 15 autocephalous Orthodox Churches, i.e., autonomous self-governing churches that are in communion with each other, but with internal self-government, including the right to choose its own leaders (a patriarch or a metropolitan) and to resolve internal problems. These include the four ancient patriarchates of Constantinople, Alexandria, Antioch and Jerusalem, the ten autochepalous Orthodox Churches of Russia, Serbia, Romania, Bulgaria, Georgia, Cyprus, Greece, Poland, Albania, the Czech and Slovak Republics. Of these ten, five are also patriarchates: Russia, Serbia, Romania, Bulgaria and Georgia. The status of the Orthodox Church of America is anomalous—in 1970 it was granted autochepalous status by the Moscow Patriarchate. However, the Ecumenical Patriarchate has refused to recognize it, arguing that the Moscow Patriarchate had no right to grant autochepaly to any church on a unilateral basis. In practice, other Orthodox Churches have recognized the *de facto* autochepaly of the Orthodox Church of America. The nationalism that accompanied the fall of the Soviet Union resulted in the formation of new national churches that have claimed independence from the Moscow Patriarchate. These include: the Ukrainian Orthodox Church-Kiev Patriarchate, the Ukrainian Autochepalous Orthodox Church, the Belarusan Autocephalous Orthodox Church and the Macedonian Orthodox Church. The autochepaly of these Orthodox churches have not been resolved.

Ecumenical Patriarchate of Constantinople. In the Christian East, Byzantine Christianity is the most important in regard both to the number of Christians belonging to it and to its widespread diffusion. It was the official religion of the ancient Byzantine Empire, based at Constantinople (Byzantium), which spread its influence not only throughout all of the Eastern base of the Mediterranean but also to the countries of the lower Danube and Balkan Peninsula and up into all of the Slavic countries. Through immigration, Byzantine Christianity has been brought to all parts of Europe, Asia, Australia, Africa, and North and South America, counting both Orthodox and Byzantine Catholics of various races and languages.

Once Constantine had built his ''New Rome'' along the shores of the Bosphorus, Byzantium grew from a small suffragan See of Heraclea in Thrace into the mighty ecclesiastical center for the patriarchate, which jurisdictionally coincided with the limits of the Byzantine Empire. In the Councils of Constantinople (381), Ephesus (431), and Chalcedon (451) the See of Constantinople was recognized, because it was the ''New Rome,'' as having first place of honor after the venerable See of Rome. In particular, Constantinople grew in prominence and prestige in the Christian East, especially after the Council of Chalcedon (451) declared it to be the New Rome, second to See of Rome in power, dignity and honor.

The expansion of Byzantine Christianity was intimately connected with the political ambitions of the Byzantine emperors, eager always to spread their influence throughout the Balkan and Russian lands, to Syria, the Holy Land, Egypt, and even the coasts of Italy. As Constantinople grew in power, other independent ecclesiastical centers, such as Antioch and Alexandria, diminished. In time, especially through heresies and the ravages of the Arab conquests, Alexandria and Antioch were reduced to nothing, and Constantinople stood indisputably as the supreme head of all the Orthodox Churches. This paved the way for one liturgical rite and one language (Greek) within the vast confines of the Byzantine Empire and left the non-Byzantine liturgical rites, such as the Antiochene (Syrian) and Alexandrian (Coptic), to develop only among the Oriental Orthodox Christians who modified the content and substituted their own national languages.

Outside the territorial limits of the Byzantine empire, the liturgical rite of Constantinople spread to other embryonic nations while allowing other liturgical languages. Thus Byzantine influence penetrated to the Iberian area, Georgia in the Caucasus, in the 4th century. From the 9th to the 11th century missionaries were sent from Constantinople into the Slavic countries, with Old Slavonic being used as the liturgical language in place of Greek. Later Romania with its roots among the soldiers and colonists of Trajan translated the liturgical rite into its national tongue. Western Syrians, no longer speaking Greek, used their own Syriac language from the 11th to the 17th century and then adopted Arabic. The Russian Church followed the same principle of vernacular liturgical languages in its missions.

At the time of the rupture of relations with See of Rome in the 11th century, the jurisdiction of the Ecumenical Patriarchate extended over all Byzantine churches in northern Africa, Asia Minor, the Balkan States, through all the Eastern Slavic countries as far as the Baltic Sea. In the 11th century more than 600 episcopal sees looked to the See of Constantinople for spiritual leadership. The unfortunate sequence of events that led to the estrangement between Old Rome and New Rome, culminating in the Schism of 1054 had resulted in to an estrangement that was to last for nine centuries. The Crusaders and their sacking of Constantinople in 1204 furthered the separation between the Christian East and the West, which various councils, such as the Council of Lyons (1274) and of Florence (1439) tried in vain to mend.

Moscow Patriarchate. The Christian faith came to Russian lands when Prince Vladimir in 989 was baptized by missionaries from Byzantium and then set about to convert his Kievan kingdom to Orthodoxy. The last Greek metropolitan of Kiev, Isidore, participated in the Council of Florence and accepted union with Rome, but both he and the union were rejected by the Czar Basil II. In 1459 Metropolitan Jonah was recognized as the head of the autocephalous Orthodox Church of Russia. After the fall of Constantinople to the Turks (1453), the Russians sought and obtained from the Greek Patriarch of Constantinople, Jeremias II, recognition of the Russian Church as an independent patriarchate and of Job (1586–1605) as the first "Patriarch of Moscow and of all Russia." Various internal dissensions arose, chief among which was the schism of the Old Believers (Raskolniki) who opposed the reforms of Patriarch NIKON (1654–67). They split off from the Russian Church into two groups, the Popovtsi (with priests) and the Bezpopovtsi (without priests); today they continue; the popovtsi with a fully established hierarchy of its own. Peter the Great in 1721 suppressed the patriarchate, which was later restored as a result of the overthrow by the revolutionaries of imperial Russia in 1917. Then, although the Communists suppressed it, Stalin restored it again in 1943 when he most needed the patriotic support of the religious peasant class. The Orthodox Church in Russia underwent bitter persecution until the fall of Communism. Since the early 1990s many dioceses, churches and monasteries have been restored. Abroad the Russian Orthodox are split into various jurisdictions. The patriarch of Moscow directs three exarchates for Central Europe, Western Europe, and North America. Another Western exarchate with its see in Paris depends upon the patriarch of Constantinople while another, the Russian Orthodox Church Outside Russia formerly with its see in Karlovci, Yugoslavia, now in New York, has parishes spread throughout the world.

Orthodox Church of America (OCA). The Orthodox Church of America stems from the original Russian mission to Alaska and California. In 1970 this jurisdiction, then known as the Metropolia, was granted autocephaly by the Moscow Patriarchate. It is now known as the Orthodox Church in America.

Romania. The beginnings of Christianity are not clear in Romanian history. It seems that in the early centuries evangelization was first carried on by Latin missionaries among the descendants of the Roman colonisers sent there by Emperor Trajan. When the Bulgars conquered Romania, they brought with them Byzantine Christianity, using the Old Slavonic language in the liturgy. After the fall of the second Bulgarian Empire the Ecumenical Patriarch of Constantinople gained jurisdiction and imposed the Greek language and culture. In the 17th century Romanian began to be used. Only in 1881 was Romania finally formed into a single state consisting of Moldavia and Vallachia whose national religion was of Byzantine Christianity, using Romanian as the liturgical language. After World War I Transylvania, Bessarabia, and Bucovina were added to Romania. In 1947 Romania became a republic in the Soviet sphere. The Romanian Orthodox Church was elevated to patriarchal status in 1925. In the U.S. it is divided into two different jurisdictions. The Romanian Orthodox Church and the Canonical Episcopate of America, dependent on the patriarch of Romania, has Detroit as its see; the Romanian Orthodox Episcopate of America is a diocese under the jurisdiction of the Orthodox Church in America.

Bulgaria. The Bulgarians were originally a Turco-Finnish race that settled in the Balkans in the 7th century. They fused with the Slavs who surrounded them and accepted their Slavic language. They received Christianity through the missionaries of Byzantium sent by Constantinople on request of the Bulgar Czar Boris (853–889). In 917 Czar Simeon declared the Bulgarian Church an independent patriarchate, but in 1019 it was suppressed by the Byzantine Emperor Basil II. A second Bulgarian patriarchate was set up at Trnovo in 1186 but it was destroyed under Ottoman persecution in 1393. In 1870 the Bulgars obtained from the Turkish Sultan the decree to set up their own national church free of Greek influence. The Ecumenical Patriarch of Constantinople excommunicated the Bulgarian Church in 1872, but the other Slavic Churches recognized it. Only in 1961 did the patriarch of Constantinople recognize it as an independent patriarchate.

Georgia. The early history of Christianity in Georgia is very obscure. Christianity is said to have been brought there by St. Nina, a Christian prisoner, who converted King Miriam about 320. The first missionaries came from the Patriarchate of Antioch and exercised jurisdiction until the 8th century. Byzantine missionaries entered Georgia in the 6th century, and the Georgians readily accepted the authority of the Ecumenical Patriarch, freeing themselves from the Syrian and Armenian oversight. Through the succeeding centuries Georgia became the prey of conquering armies of Persians, Byzantines, Arabs, Turks, Mongols, and finally Russians. It was annexed to Russia by Czar Alexander in 1801, and from then until the Russian Revolution of 1917 the Georgian Church was under the domination of the Russian Orthodox Church. The Georgian Church had its autocephaly recognized by the Moscow Patriarchate.

Estonia. From the 16th century nearly all Estonians were Lutheran, following the religion of their Swedish overlords. During the period from 1830 to 1848 about 75,000 Estonians and Latvians became Orthodox under the Russian Church when Russian conquered the region. In 1923 they sought and obtained approval from the Ecumenical Patriarch of Constantinople for the establishment of an autonomous Orthodox Church of Estonia, dependent on Constantinople. However, in 1940 the Soviet Union annexed Estonia and Latvia; the Moscow patriarch, not considering the autonomy granted these two churches by the Ecumenical Patriarch, assumed them under his own jurisdiction. After the collapse of the Soviet union, a dispute arose between those who wanted to remain under the Moscow Patriarchate and those who wanted to re-establish the autonomous church under the Ecumenical Patriarch. Tensions flared in 1996 when the Ecumenical Patriarch revived the 1923 arrangement. Intense negotiations between Moscow and Constantinople brought about a peaceful resolution, with parishes given the choice to elect whether to remain under Moscow or join the autonomous church. Of the 84 parishes, 50 chose to join the autonomous church, while 30 with predominant Russian membership remained with Moscow.

Albania. Christianity came to Albania from two directions, bringing Latin Christianity to the northern part and Byzantine Christianity to the southern part. After the 15th century with the occupation of the Turks, Christianity was in part suppressed, making Islamism the prevalent religion in Albania. The Orthodox Church of Albania attained autocephaly in 1937. It suffered intensely under communist rule. The collapse of communist rule rejuvenated the church, allowing it to reopen parishes and accept candidates for priesthood.

Finland. The Finns belong ethnically to the same group as the Estonians and Hungarians. In 1917 they were declared independent of Russia, but after World War II they were forced to cede a part of their southern territory to the Soviet Union. More than 96 percent of the Finns are Lutheran. The Orthodox Church of Finland received its autonomy from the patriarch of Constantinople in 1923, an autonomy that was recognized only in 1957 by the Russian patriarch.

PART II: BYZANTINE CATHOLIC CHURCHES

Historically, Byzantine Catholic Churches are known by their older designation ''Greek Catholic Churches,'' their legal name in the Ottoman and Hapsburg empires. These churches parallel their Orthodox counterparts, adopting the ecclesial, liturgical, theological and spiritual traditions of Orthodoxy, but recognizing the primacy of the See of Rome. These churches include the Melkite Catholic Church, the Ukrainian Catholic Church, the Ruthenian Catholic Church, the Romanian Catholic Church, the Greek Catholic Church, the Bulgarian Catholic Church, the Slovak Catholic Church and the Hungarian Catholic Church. There are also other Byzantine Catholic communities without hierarchies, e.g., the Russians, Belarusans, Georgians and Albanians.

Melkite Catholic Church. The word Melkite properly speaking originally designated all Byzantine Christians, both Catholic or Orthodox, of the Patriarchates of Alexandria, Antioch, and Jerusalem. The word comes from the Syriac *malka* or the Arabic word *malek* or *melek* meaning king or emperor. The term was first coined by anti-Chalcedonians in derision of those Christians who remained faithful to the Byzantine emperors in their attempt to impose the Christology taught by the Council of Chalcedon (451). But today, in its popular and limited sense, the word refers only to the Byzantine Catholics using both Greek and Arabic who through the centuries entered into communion with the See of Rome. If now all Melkites are of Arabic speaking extraction, their history was not always of such unity. Between the 5th and 12th centuries some were of Greek extraction, others of Syrian, others Egyptian. Originally they followed the Antiochene, Alexandrian, or Jerusalem liturgical rites, but with time and the centralization forced upon them by Byzantine emperors they adopted the Byzantine liturgical rite exclusively. They are now centered in three patriarchates: Alexandria, Antioch, and Jerusalem. Through the centuries, especially in the Patriarchate of Antioch, an active movement of reconciliation with Rome was developed. Beginning with the Catholic patriarch, Cyril VI (1724–59), there was an uninterrupted line of Melkite Catholic patriarchs. The Melkite Catholic patriarch resides at Damascus and bears the title ''Patriarch of Antioch and of all the East'' and the personal titles of the patriarch of Alexandria and Jerusalem. In the U.S. Melkite Catholics center mostly around New York and in New England.

Italo-Albanian Catholic Church. The Italo-Albanian Catholic Church is also Byzantine in heritage, although it does not have a direct Orthodox counterpart. Three different movements account for the origins of the Italo-Albanian Catholic Church. The first wave of Greek colonists first immigrated to Sicily and southern Italy even before Christianity was founded. The second wave of Greeks to Italy came shortly after the sacking of Constantinople by the Turks in 1453. The third migrating group was composed of Albanians. When their kingdom passed into the hands of the Turks after the death of their leader Skanderbeg (d. 1463), many fled to Italy and Sicily where they clung on steadfastly to their Byzantine heritage. At present, the Italo-Albanian Catholic Chrurch has two eparchies of equal rank: Lungro (in Calabria, southern Italy), established 1919 with jurisdiction over mainland Italy; and Piana deli Albanesi, established 1937 with jurisdiction over Sicily. The historic Italo-Greek Catholic monastery of St. Mary's of Grottaferrata, outside of Rome, founded 1004 is a territorial abbey that ministers to parishes in southern Italy and Sicily.

Ukrainian Catholic Church. The Ukrainians lay claim to being the original Russians, since the nation known as Russia today first developed in Kiev, the present-day capital of the modern Ukrainian Republic. After Russia centralized its power around the principalities of first Vladimir and then Moscow, Kiev became known as the center of ''Little'' Russia, especially for the five centuries when it was subject to Poland and Lithuania. Here a reunion of the Orthodox with Rome was effected through the Synod of Brest-Litovsk (1595–96), which set up the largest branch of Byzantine Catholics. There were many factors, political, social, and cultural, that prompted this reunion. In 1620 an Orthodox hierarchy was reestablished that paralleled the Catholic group. The Catholic Ukrainians in the West, centered in the province of Galicia, after having been under the control of Poland, came under the power of the Austrian Empire in the 18th century. One of the great names among the Galician Ukrainians is that of Metropolitan Andrew Sheptitzky who from 1900 until his imprisonment by the Soviets in 1944 ruled the See of Lvov as the primate of the Galician Ukrainians. He did much to strengthen his fellow Ukrainians amid great persecution from the Soviets and to instill in them an equal fidelity to Rome and to their Byzantine heritage. Great numbers of these Ukrainians migrated to America in two groups, the first from 1880 to 1914 and the second group during World War II. The first immigration was that of Catholics from Galicia; the second, of Western and Eastern Ukrainians. Ukranian Catholics in the U.S. are divided into the metropolitan diocese of Philadelphia, and the dioceses of Stamford (CT), St. Josaphat in Parma (OH), and St. Nicholas in Chicago.

Ruthenian Catholic Church. Ethnically different from the Ukrainians and with a language differing from the western Ukranian, the Ruthenians are called also Podcarpathian or Carpatho-Russians or Rusins. For many centuries the area they inhabited belonged to the Hungarian Kingdom, but they were Slavic. After World War I, Podcarpathia Rus was made a part of the Czechoslovakian Republic, and in 1939 it was proclaimed the Independent Republic of the Carpathian Ukraine. It was briefly returned to Hungary (1939–44) but then became part of Soviet Ukraine. The majority of its Christian inhabitants became Byzantine Catholics in the Union of Uzhorod (1646), and in 1771 the eparchy of Mukachevo was established. In America besides the metropolitan diocese of Pittsburgh there are the dioceses of Passaic (NJ), Parma (OH), and Van Nuys (CA).

Romanian Catholic Church. The beginnings of Christianity are not clear in Romanian history. It seems that in the early centuries evangelization was first carried on by Latin missionaries among the descendants of the Roman colonisers sent there by Emperor Trajan. When the Bulgars conquered Romania, they brought with them Byzantine Christianity, using the Old Slavonic language in the liturgy. After the fall of the second Bulgarian Empire the Ecumenical Patriarch of Constantinople gained jurisdiction and imposed the Greek language and culture. In the 17th century Romanian began to be used. Only in 1881 was Romania finally formed into a single state consisting of Moldavia and Vallachia whose national religion was of Byzantine Christianity, using Romanian as the liturgical language. After World War I Transylvania, Bessarabia, and Bucovina were added to Romania. In 1947 Romania became a republic in the Soviet sphere. A movement started in the 17th and 18th centuries came to a climax when a part of the Orthodox Church of Romania was united with Rome (1701). With the dissolution of the Austrian-Hungary Empire in 1918, the Romanian Catholics found themselves along with their Orthodox counterparts in a united Romania. In 1947 the Peoples' Republic put an end to the Catholic Church's organization. Before they were swallowed up through a mandate of the state by the Orthodox Church, the Catholic Romanians numbered more than one and a half million. Many emigrated to the U.S. There is now a Catholic Romanian diocese in Canton, Ohio.

Greek Catholic Church. In 1829 Greek Catholics were freed from the civil jurisdiction of the Orthodox patriarch, preparing the way for the formation of a Greek Catholic Church. This movement started under John Marango (d. 1885) in Constantinople and was transplanted to northern Greece in Thrace at the turn of the century. These Greek Catholics in Greece are under the leadership of one bishop, an apostolic exarch who resides in Athens. Relations with the Greek Orthodox Church has remained tense, which views the Greek Catholic Church as an unjustified papal intrusion in its jurisdiction.

Bulgarian Catholic Church. The Bulgarian Catholic Church began slowly in 1859, but the Balkan War (1912–13) and World War I crushed the movement. It began again, only to be throttled during World War II. Communist rule brought much hardship to the fledging church. The collapse of the Soviet communist bloc brought some relief. The Bulgarian Catholic Church regained some of its property and reopened churches. The Apostolic Exarch resides in Sofia.

Russian Byzantine Catholic Church. Russian Byzantine Catholics number only about 3,000 worldwide and owe their beginnings to the embryonic Russian Byzantine Catholic Church, established the first quarter of the 20th century under Exarch Leonid Feodorov (1879–1935). The Russian Catholics never mustered enough numbers or support to have an independent hierarchy. There are two Russian Byzantine Catholic parishes in the U.S.

Bibliography: D. ATTWATER, *The Christian Churches of the East,* 2 v. (rev. ed. Milwaukee 1961–62). F. E. BRIGHTMAN, *Liturgies Eastern and Western,* 2 v. (Oxford 1896) v.1. J. M. HANSSENS, *Institutiones liturgicae de ritibus orientalibus* (Rome 1930–32) v.2, 3. A. A. KING, *The Rites of Eastern Christendom,* 2 v. (London 1950). R. ROBERSON, *The Eastern Christian Churches: A Brief Survey,* 6th ed (Rome 1999) R. F. TAFT, *The Byzantine Rite: A Short History* (Collegeville, MN 1992).

[G. A. MALONEY/R. B. MILLER/EDS.]

BYZANTINE CHURCH, HISTORY OF

The term ''Byzantine Church,'' as used here, designates exclusively the official Church of and in the Byzantine Empire from the death of Justinian (565) to the fall of Constantinople (1453), and does not cover its Slavic offshoots nor the Melkite patriarchates of Antioch and Alexandria. The key to its history is the idea of the Christian World State, which may best be described as a Christianization of the *Pax Romana.* Rome, in conquering the Mediterranean basin, had brought peace, law, and prosperity to its variegated peoples and attempted to weld them into one by worship of the ruler. By extension, in the new Rome of Constantine the Great, worship of Christ, the Prince of Peace, would unite the various subject peoples. This conception in practice, however, made the Church an instrument of imperial policy and led to struggles for authority between emperor and pope; ecclesiastical differences became political divisions and vice versa. A state that made itself independent of Byzantium had necessarily to make its church autonomous. This mentality dominated all Europe for many centuries.

This article is divided as follows: from the death of Justinian I (565) to the accession of Leo III the Iconoclast (717); from the accession of Leo III to the Feast of Orthodoxy; from the Feast of Orthodoxy to the death of Michael Cerularius (843–1059); from the death of Michael Cerularius to the death of Michael VIII Palaeologus (1059–1282); and from the death of Michael VIII to the fall of Constantinople (1282–1453).

From Justinian I to Accession of Leo III, 565–717

With the death of JUSTINIAN I (565), medieval Byzantium rapidly assumed its characteristic features. The Jacobite Monophysites consolidated their hold on Egypt and Syria and began to break away from the empire. The papacy and Italy were left to rely more and more on their own resources. The Slavs were settling down in the Balkans. Efforts to win back the Monophysites of Egypt and Syria by a compromise creed had begun with Zeno's Henoticon, and were continued by the pro-monophysite emperor Anastasius I (491–518), Heraclius (610–641), and Constans (641–668). The last phase consisted of the formula of one will and one operation in Christ, devised by Patriarch SERGIUS I (610–638), but condemned by the Sixth General Council (680–681), and briefly revived by Emperor Philippicus (711–713).

Monophysitism, Monoenergism, and Monothelitism. The reorganization of the Jacobite Church occurred on the eve of the Persian and Arab invasions and shaped the whole course of Christianity in the Near East. At the death of Justinian, the Monophysites (*see* MONOPHYSITISM) were thoroughly demoralized by persecution and their own disagreements; they had split into more than 20 sects. But during the years of toleration granted by Emperors Tiberius I (578–582) and Maurice (582–602), they reconstituted their hierarchy; and by the end of the 6th century, Syria and Egypt were overwhelmingly Monophysite. The Monophysites had never thought of defecting from Byzantium before, but savage persecution under Emperor Phocas (602–610)—in contrast with the favor shown them by the invading Persians—disaffected them. The Persians drove out the orthodox Melkites and handed over their sees and parishes to the Monophysites. During the long enemy occupation, a cultural revolution took place. By depopulating the land, the Persians had given a mortal blow to the Greek language and ethnic element; and Aramaic rapidly became the predominant language. A new national literature of Jacobite tendencies replaced the Hellenic culture. By the time of the Arab conquest, the monophysite schism had developed into cultural, ethnic, and political antagonism, and Syria and Egypt were not unwilling to exchange Byzantine suzerainty for Arab.

Sergius and Heraclius. The cooperation of anti-Chalcedonian Armenia was indispensable to Heraclius's (610–641) strategy for the defeat of Persia. Patriarch Sergius I, practically coruler of Constantinople during Heraclius's reign, proposed a compromise formula by introducing Monoenergism, the doctrine that Christ did not have two distinct types of activity, both human and divine, but only one type, divine-human. He was supported by the sincere Chalcedonian Cyrus, bishop of Phasis, south of the Caucasus. By 633 Cyrus had made numerous converts to Monoenergism in cis-Caucasia, Armenia, Syria, and Egypt among the hierarchy and the monasteries, but not among the ordinary people.

St. Ilarion, 12th-century Byzantine fresco painting, Refectory of the Monastery of St. John, Patmos, Greece, c. 1176–1180. (©Chris Hellier/CORBIS)

The first open opposition came from Sophronius, a monk of Bethlehem, who went to Alexandria to protest to Cyrus, now patriarch of that city, and then to Constantinople, where Sergius prevailed on him not to press the matter any further. Sophronius was elected patriarch of Jerusalem (634) and in his synodal letter affirmed two energies, two types of activity, in Christ as a necessary consequence of His two natures. Meanwhile, Pope HONORIOUS I had responded to Sergius, stating that the debate about one or two energies should stop; he gave the same decision to Cyrus and Sophronius. All three patriarchs consequently agreed that the question should be debated no further and this decision was made law in a edict of Heracalius (634 or 635).

At a time when the Arab conquest was proceeding rapidly, this edict was not received well by the Monophysites. Heraclius, however, as shown by a proclamation circulated throughout the lost provinces, took for granted that he would soon recover them from the Arabs, and Emperor Constans II nourished the same hope. Consequently Hercalius published an exposition of the faith, his *Ecthesis* (638), a creed elaborated by Sergius. It presented the dogma of the Trinity and Incarnation according to the Council of Chalcedon, prohibited the expression one or two energies in Christ, and affirmed that the unique *hypostasis* of Christ had one sole will without any confusion of the two natures (i.e., the Word made Flesh). MONOTHELITISM was thus substituted for Monoenergism. The expression ''one will'' was taken from the letter of Honorius, who, however, meant that in Christ there was no conflict between reason and the flesh. This doctrine was generally accepted by the Eastern Church and the Melchite patriarchs, but not by Coptic Egypt. It was condemned by Pope John IV, and Heraclius wrote to him disclaiming authorship of the edict.

Maximus the Confessor. After the death of Heraclius, the religious battleground shifted to Africa, where Syrian and Egyptian refugees from both Persians and Arabs, mostly Monophysites, were proselytizing zealously. There MAXIMUS THE CONFESSOR took up the defense of orthodoxy, and in a debate he was able to persuade Sergius's successor, the patriarch Pyrrhus (638–641; January to June 654) who had been exiled from Constantinople. Pyrrhus then journeyed to Rome to make his submission to Pope Theodore I; this abjuration of error by a patriarch in the presence of the pope had a tremendous reaction in Italy and Africa.

Pope Theodore in a letter to Constantinople had already rejected and anathematized the *Ecthesis*. Now, he summoned Patriarch Paul II (641–653) to abjure Monothelitism, and on his refusal, he excommunicated him. He also excommunicated Pyrrhus, who, taking refuge in Ravenna, had written to the pope that he had returned to Monothelitism.

Emperor Constans II, to avoid a rupture with Rome and to settle the religious difficulties once for all, took down the *Ecthesis* from the place in which it had remained publicly posted, and issued his *Typos* or Decree (647, not 648), which forbade all discussion of one or two energies or of two wills. Pope Martin I, Theodore's successor, took action on the *Typos* by summoning a council at the Lateran (649), which condemned both the *Ecthesis* and the *Typos* and professed faith in two wills and two operations corresponding to the two natures in Christ.

Constans II arrested the pope, tried him for treason at Constantinople, and exiled him to Cherson, where he died of the cruelties and privation to which he was subjected. Maximus Confessor and two of his companions, Anastasius the Disciple and Anastasius the papal representative, were likewise arrested in Rome (653) and suffered severe hardships and cruelties for nine years. Their right hands were lopped off and their tongues cut out. Maximus and Anastasius the Disciple both died while they were in exile in Lazica, cis-Caucasia, in 662; the Roman representative survived until 666. Finally, under Popes Eugene I and Vitalian, a tacit understanding was reached; the latter sent his synodical letter to the patriarch and abstained from any condemnation of the *Typos,* while Constans II presented the pope with rich gifts and a perfectly orthodox confession of faith.

After the courageous stand of Maximus Confessor, a division occurred in the Byzantine Church. Many now believed in the importance of the issue and of finding the true solution, and discord persisted among the clergy between the followers of Maximus and the Monothelites. The latter took the offensive when Patriarch Theodore (667–679; 686–687) asked the emperor for authorization to strike the name of Pope Vitalian from the diptychs. The pope had died in 672, and neither of his successors had been added to the diptychs. Constantine IV (668–685), recognizing that Syria and Egypt were lost to the empire, not only rejected this suggestion but determined to effect a final settlement of the question by calling the Council of CONSTANTINOPLE III in conjunction with popes Donus, Agatho, and Leo II. This, the sixth ecumenical council, held 680–681 in a domed hall in the imperial palace known as the *trullo,* condemned Monoenergism and Monothelitism, but in the process listed Pope Honorius among the heretics condemned.

Quinisext Synod. In 691 Justinian II summoned another council at Trullon, now known as the Quinisext Synod, to make general laws for the Church, since the Fifth and Sixth General Councils had dealt with dogma, not with discipline. It is acknowledged as ecumenical by the Greeks, but not by the Latins. Its legislation, which is basic to Greek canon law, is characterized by open hostility to particular customs of both the Roman and Armenian Churches. Pope Sergius I (687–701) repudiated the synod, and Justinian's effort to arrest him was balked by the militia of Ravenna. The emperor then appealed to Pope John VII and, as he was anxious to have approval, finally invited Pope Constantine to Constantinople. The sources are vague as to the details for the ultimate settlement worked out principally with the future Pope Gregory II. Monothelitism was briefly revived by the Emperor Philippicus (711–713). But Pope Constantine rejected his heresy and would not recognize him.

Other Issues. Medieval Italy began to emerge after Justinian's death. The popes still regarded themselves as subjects of the empire. Gregory I (590–604) wanted a truce made with the Lombards to spare the people needless suffering. but he could not induce Emperor Maurice to accept this proposal. To save Rome in 593, Gregory concluded an armistice himself, for which he received an angry rebuke from Maurice. This episode is typical of the clash of policy that ultimately caused a total secession of the papacy. The Holy See and the Italian population became gradually more independent of Byzantium. The growth of national sentiment is dramatically highlighted by the fact (already noted) that, while Emperor Constans II did violence to Pope Martin in 653, Justinian II was prevented by a mutiny of the Ravenna militia from arresting Pope Sergius for disapproving of the Quinisext Synod (692).

Friction between Pope Gregory and Maurice developed over the title, ecumenical patriarch, regularly used in addressing Patriarch John IV the Faster. Pope Pelagius II had objected strongly and ordered his representative in Constantinople not to concelebrate the liturgy with John until the practice was abandoned. Gregory also carried out a tireless campaign against the title. Although he did not consider the issue important enough to make a break over it, he was displeased when Maurice refused to forbid the title. Later, Emperor Phocas did forbid it, but without permanent result. Scholars differ as to the significance of the issue, but it remained a bone of contention between Rome and Constantinople for centuries.

Another difference between Maurice and the pope occurred over an imperial law of 592 forbidding public functionaries to accept ecclesiastical office and barring municipal officials and soldiers from entering a monastery. The issue was ultimately resolved by a compromise: municipal officials could not become monks until they had quit themselves of their obligations, and soldiers would have to serve three years.

The primacy of Rome was taken for granted throughout this period in both dogma and discipline. When Gregory, patriarch of Antioch, was tried at Constantinople by the synod attended by the five patriarchs or their legates, the acts were forwarded to Pope Pelagius II for his approval as a matter of course. The papacy remained the center of the whole controversy over Monoenergism and Monothelitism. Maximian supported the authority of the pope over emperor and state, denying that the emperor had any role in the definition of dogma, and believed that the Church of Rome had primacy over the eastern sees. Popes exercised this primacy to a greater or lesser extent: Gregory the Great, for example, censured both Alexandria and Jerusalem for tolerating simony and rebuked Patriarch John the Faster for mistreating two priests accused of heresy. He was consulted by Kyrion of Georgia on the validity of Nestorian baptism. In general, however, the popes often struggled to remind the eastern sees and the emperor of their higher ecclesiastical authority.

From Accession of Leo III to Feast of Orthodoxy, 717–843

At the beginning of his reign, Emperor LEO III the Iconoclast (717–741) rendered a great service to Christendom. He saved it from being overrun by Islam, repulsing a massive attack of the Arabs from the walls of Constantinople. Nevertheless, following in the tradition of Byzantine emperors who believed that they were head of both State and Church, he though it his duty to cleanse the Church of images, thus beginning the iconoclast or image controversy (*see* ICONOCLASM).

This had a decisive influence on the history of Europe and of the Byzantine Church itself, and was responsible for the division between Eastern and Western Europe that exists to the present day. The Byzantine Empire thought of itself as the heir to the Roman Empire, but the iconoclast controversy precipitated the secession of the papacy and the ultimate creation of the Western Roman Empire of Germanic kings with its direct challenge to Byzantine supremacy. Leo's transfer of large territories from the jurisdiction of Rome to that of Constantinople also caused great bitterness between the see. Iconoclasm brought about a profound change in the Byzantine Church itself by impelling the monks into ecclesiastical leadership.

Iconoclasm. The iconoclast conflict lasted well over a century (726–843). Icons, a special type of religious picture, had become universal in Byzantium, not only in churches, but also in public places and in widespread private use. There is no clear-cut evidence for the origin of iconoclasm. Contemporary sources blamed Muslim influence since a decree of Omar II in 720 or Caliph Yezid II in 723 ordered the destruction of icons in all Christian churches. Yet there had always been unease in the Christian Church about the worship of an image, stemming from the prohibition in the First Commandment. At the beginning of the 8th century two bishops began to promote iconoclast views, which were accepted by Leo III. The emperor was anxious to find an explanation for God's disapproval that must surely be responsible for the loss of Byzantine territory to barbarians and a violent volcanic eruption on Thera.

Leo was opposed by Patriarch Germanus I, whom he forced to resign; Pope Gregory II; and JOHN DAMASCENE, who living in safety under Muslim rule, developed the orthodox theology of images. Leo won enough support, however, to obtain a synodal decision against images and the destruction of icons, crosses, and reliquaries ensued. Destruction was limited mainly to movable objects, however, and iconophiles were exiled or, at worst, mutilated; there are no reliable reports of martyrdoms. His successor, however, Constantine V (741–775), pursued iconoclasm more relentlessly. Iconoclasts took over all important ecclesiastical posts and in 754 he convened the Synod of Hieria, at which the cult of icons was condemned as idiolatry. Empowered by this conciliar decree, Constantine persecuted all iconophiles, especially monks, and there were many martyrdoms, including that of St. Stephen the Younger. Nevertheless, claims that Constantine also criticized relics and the intercessions of the Virgin Mary should be treated with care.

Ecumenical Council of Nicaea II. Leo IV (775–780), in his brief and milder reign, temporized on the question. Irene, widow of Leo IV and regent for the 10-year-old Constantine VI, favored icons. She invited Pope Adrian I and the Eastern patriarchs to send representatives to a general council, and Tarasius was made patriarch of Constantinople. The Seventh General Council, NICAEA II, was the last acknowledged by the Byzantine Church. It met in 787, anathematized the enemies of icons, and clarified the theology of the cult of the Blessed Virgin, the saints and their pictures.

Pope Adrian had assumed that the council would return to Rome the territory taken from it by Leo III, namely, Sicily, Calabria, and Illyricum. But Tarasius had simply suppressed this statement in the Greek translation of the pope's letter to the council. This act occasioned lasting bitterness between the Sees of Rome and Constantinople. Pope Gregory I had conditioned his allegiance to

Byzantium on its defense of the papacy and Italy. But when iconoclasts attacked and confiscated papal estates, Pope Stephen II (III) felt himself no longer bound to the Byzantine Empire, and he made an alliance with Pepin and the Franks. To Byzantium his action was an enormity. The loss of Rome, mother-city of the empire, must have been a profound shock. It is not known whether all this caused Constantinople's refusal at the council to restore the papal territories, but Pope Adrian resented the failure to do so.

The acts of this council seem never to have been submitted to Rome for approval. Tarasius had sent the pope a summary of events, and seven years later (784) the pope had still not answered. The Franks themselves did not believe in the cult of religious images; they regarded them as purely educational. Moreover, they had received a badly garbled Latin translation of the acts, which at times conveyed the opposite of the original meaning. They resented, too, the arrogance of the Byzantines in giving the name of a general council of the Church to a local Greek synod with no representatives of the West present. They reacted violently and rejected the definition of the council in favor of their own doctrine.

Charlemagne demanded that Pope Adrian repudiate the council, but the pope, who had received an authentic copy of the acts, easily answered all objections and staunchly defended the cult of icons. He was so dissatisfied, however, over the Byzantine retention of papal possessions that he offered, if Charlemagne wished, to inform the Eastern Empire that he would hold back approval of the council until restitution was made, and, if that were not done, he would declare the emperor heretical for persisting in this error. Whether such a step was ever taken is not known.

The *Filioque* and the Studite Monks. The term *FILIOQUE* first became a controversial issue at the council, which used the NICENE CREED for its profession of faith, recording it in the minutes. The Creed had been interpolated in the West with the Latin word *filioque.* The interpolation, first made in Spain in the 7th century, affirmed that the Holy Spirit proceeded from both the Father and Son. The Eastern Church maintained the original wording without the *filioque,* and the Franks, eager to prove that the Greeks were heretics, accused them of holding that the Holy Spirit proceeds from the Father alone. This doctrinal dispute provided Charlemagne with a theological reason for rejecting the acts of the council, and his letter that justified his position on the subject to Pope Adrian was the first written explanation in a polemic that was to continue for centuries. At first Adrian defended the Greeks, and by quoting statements from the great Fathers, showed that the omission of *filioque* did not necessarily imply that the Holy Spirit proceeded from God alone.

Another significant change took place at the Seventh General Council with the entrance of the monks into the government of the Church in the East. Monastic figures had taken over the leadership of the faithful during the iconoclast controversy in default of the episcopate, and this new role was now organized and consolidated in the Studite reform to which most of the monks adhered. The leading monastery was that of the Studion in Constantinople, and the leading spirit was its abbot, St. Theodore, who strove to imbue not only the Church, but also the state, layman as well as cleric, with the highest Christian ideals. He strongly opposed the claim of emperors, particularly the iconoclasts, to both priesthood and royalty, believing that the Church should be free to direct ecclesiastical dogma and discipline. Against the whole Byzantine theory and practice, he maintained that the civil ruler had no competence in matters of faith, moral, or ecclesiastical government and law. The only true head of the Church was the pope, and the papal primacy was the best safeguard of the Church's freedom. To purify society he insisted upon the strict and impartial application of the ecclesiastical canons without respect of persons.

The reform was soon put to the test in the MOECHIAN CONTROVERSY. In 795 Emperor Constantine VI (780–797) made an adulterous marriage with his mistress that was blessed by Joseph, an abbot and high official of the patriarch, and Patriarch Tarasius permitted the guilty pair to receive Holy Communion as if nothing improper had been done. The Studites condemned the emperor and broke off communion with the patriarch. Thus began the Moechian controversy, which persisted until the reign of Michael I (811–813).

Attitude toward the West. The coronation of Charlemagne on Christmas Day, 800, caused a profound change in the Byzantine attitude toward the West. Whatever the intention of Charlemagne and Pope Leo III, it was taken for granted that within a few years the Western Roman Empire represented the true heir of Eternal Rome, and that it was the Universal Empire destined to conquer and unify the world. Byzantium was but a Greek state doomed ultimately to be absorbed into the providential world-state. Henceforward, the Eastern Empire regarded every advance of the Latin Church as an advance of the Frankish kingdom.

The issue of the primacy of Rome had been raised at the Seventh General Council, when it is argued by some that in translating Adrian's letter to the council, Tarasius had simply suppressed every suggestion of the primacy of Rome. Although the primacy of St. Peter himself was not disputed in the East, there was no agreement on its transmission to his successors. Tarasius stressed Christ's role as head of the Church and council, Irene's right to summon a council, and omitted to say that Rome still exercised complete authority over the Church. The emperor Nicephorus I (802–811), Irene's successor, followed this stand; he forbade the Patriarch Nicephorus I (806–815) to notify the pope of his accession because, as the emperor said explicitly, the pope had broken away from the true Church. The patriarch, however, did write to Rome of this own accord in the succeeding reign. His letter seems equivocal on the primacy, though he firmly supported it six years later; bitter experience had taught him the necessity of some independent check on the emperor's interference in Church affairs.

Revival of Iconoclasm. Although iconoclasm had been violently suppressed by Irene, it enjoyed continued support in the empire, particularly among the army. Most of its adherents were firmly convinced that the military calamities of the times were the direct result of its suppression. The next emperor, Leo V (813–820), the governor of the Anatolikon *thema* decided to bring back iconoclasm. The iconophile Patriarch Nicephorus was deposed, as was THEODORE THE STUDITE who put up a staunch protest at the emperor's interference in doctrinal affairs. A new patriarch was chosen, the pliant Theodotos Melissenos Cassiteras (815–821). At the Easter Synod of Hagia Sophia (815), the decrees of the Seventh General Council were annulled and the Synod of Hieria was reinstated. Persecution ensued once more for five years up to Leo's death. Though many defected, a goodly number remained faithful, so that the Byzantine Church could afterwards celebrate its heroic resistance.

Michael II (820–829) granted a general amnesty but refused to reestablish the cult of icons, for at heart he was an iconoclast. He proposed a council in which both sides could exchange their views, but the orthodox bishops and abbots declared it impossible: ''If there remained in the mind of the emperor any doubt not settled by the patriarchs, he had only to submit it to the judgment of Rome, as tradition prescribed.'' When it became apparent that Michael would not restore images, the Studites became increasingly hostile, and Theodore went into voluntary exile in Bithynia. He died in 826 without seeing the triumph of the cause for which he had campaigned so long. Michael, alarmed by a dangerous rebel who posed as a champion of icons, engaged in persecution especially of monks. Anxious to restore peace to his country, he enlisted the Franks on his side (824) and asked Louis the Pious to send an embassy to accompany his own envoys to Rome to win over the new pope, Eugenius II (824–827), to a compromise with the iconoclasts. The Frankish doctrine was to provide the basis of agreement. Nothing further is known about this episode.

Michael's successor, Theophilus (829–842), resumed wholesale persecution; there was at least one martyrdom and numerous confessors, including the painter Lazarus and two brothers who were tattooed on their foreheads with verses deriding their folly. Support, however, both imperial and general, waned after the death of Theophilus. Theodora, regent for MICHAEL III (842–867), saw to the appointment of an orthodox patriarch, METHODIUS I. A synod was called that renewed the decisions of the seven general councils, declared the cult of images legitimate, and excommunicated the iconoclasts. This triumph of the true doctrine was sealed by a solemn and joyful celebration on the first Sunday of Lent. This first Feast of Orthodoxy (March 11, 843) marked the birthday of the Holy ''Orthodox'' Church, the Church of the Seven Councils.

The Pentarchy. The rule of the five patriarchs, called the Pentarchy, gained great favor in Byzantium during this period. According to this theory, the college of the five patriarchs of Rome, Constantinople, Alexandria, Antioch, and Jerusalem, in that order of precedence, governed the Church as successors to the college of the Apostles with Peter as their *coryphaeus,* or head. From the end of the Acacian schism, Constantinople had begun to feel its lack of apostolicity, a handicap in comparison to Rome. Consequently, it welcomed the pentarch theology, in which all the patriarchal sees were apostolic in the sense that the patriarchal college succeeded to the apostolic college.

The iconoclastic emperors had regarded themselves as both kings and priests, heads of the Church by divine right. The Studites fought for absolute independence of the Church from the State. The Studites won to the extent that no subsequent ruler used the title of priest. Otherwise, the emperors continued to interfere as much as ever in ecclesiastical matters.

From Feast of Orthodoxy to Death of Cerularius, 843–1059

It is during this period that the Byzantine Church became estranged from the Roman. In the 9th, 10th, and 11th centuries conflicts arose involving cultural and political elements alongside doctrinal and disciplinary issues. Neither Church ever formally excommunicated the other. They drifted apart; there is no one date on which the schism can be said to have begun. Disputes over issues of doctrine, for example, the *filioque* or iconoclasm, and the ongoing wrangling over the primacy of Rome and the pope gradually increased tension. A key period in this gradual worsening of relations was the patriarchate of Cerularius when differences in discipline and liturgy were accentuated; for example, the use of unleavened bread in the Eucharist and the enforced celibacy of priests in the West. Even this serious rift, however, was patched up, and it was not until the time of the Fourth Crusade that the Churches were truly in schism.

The Photian Affair. Shortly after the Synod of Orthodoxy occurred the celebrated affair of PHOTIUS. Michael III exiled Patriarch IGNATIUS (858), who was not deposed; he may have resigned, but it was under duress and invalid, as even his enemies tacitly admitted when they finally deposed him three years later in the synod of 861 for uncanonical promotion to the see (after he had occupied it, universally acknowledged, for 11 years). Photius was duly elected to succeed him, and he chose as one of his co-consecrators Gregory Asbestas, who was under a ban from the Holy See. Photius's election thus had two defects: the see was not vacant and he was consecrated by a suspended bishop.

Strife soon broke out between the backers of Photius and supporters of Ignatius (Studites), who included a popular following and most of the monks. Two separate meetings were held at this time, one in August 859 and one in the spring of 861; the details are as follows. When Photius sent his synodal letter to Pope NICHOLAS I (858–867), Michael III invited the pope to send legates to a general council for a second condemnation of iconoclasm. The Holy See could not participate in an affair in which Photius acted as patriarch without thereby acknowledging him as legitimate. To do so would have gone a long way toward breaking down the opposition to Photius, since the Studites had the highest respect for Rome. Many scholars think that iconoclasm was just a pretext for calling the council and gaining Rome's tacit approval of Photius. Nicholas accepted the invitation to the council but, dissatisfied with the treatment of Ignatius, insisted on reviewing the case, reserving judgment himself, and empowering his legates only to take evidence. He also requested the restitution to Roman control of Illyricum, Calabria, and Sicily. Despite his explicit instructions, the legates deposed Ignatius on the ground that he had been uncanonically elevated to the see, and pronounced Photius the lawful patriarch. Nicholas disavowed this action immediately without, however, censuring his legates. And he let it be known that he regarded Ignatius as the legitimate patriarch until proof to the contrary should be presented by Photius. There was no answer.

In 862 or 863, however, a supporter of Ignatius appeared in Rome to present an appeal. Nicholas heard his version, waited a full year to give Photius a chance to reply, and then at a synod (863), denounced Photius as a usurper and reinstated Ignatius and his followers. He censured Photius for trying to bribe the legates, disqualified all those consecrated or ordained by him and excommunicated the legates sent to the synod in 861. The verdict against Photius, however, was provisional since it had been rendered only by default, and the way was still left open for a fair trial at Rome with both parties either in person or by proxy—an offer that was repeated on several occasions and to which no answer was ever made.

The Bulgarian Question. Ecclesiastical jurisdiction over Bulgaria was fought over by Rome, Constantinople, and the Franks. At the request of Boris, the king of Bulgaria who had been baptized with the emperor Michael as his godfather, Photius had sent Greek clergy to instruct that nation. Boris wanted an autonomous Church with an independent patriarch to crown him czar, and as Photius refused this arrangement, the Bulgarian king turned to Rome in 866. Latin missionaries superseded the Greeks. Boris took a great fancy to the leader of the group, Bishop Formosus, and in 867 he decided that he wanted him named archbishop of Bulgaria without delay. But Nicholas refused.

The evangelization of Bulgaria by the papacy seemed to Byzantium to bring the Franks to their back door, and, as the Byzantines could not conquer the country by force, they decided on a religious offensive. The imperial government supported Photius as the representative of the interests of the Byzantine Empire and Church. The emperor wrote to the pope demanding the papal verdict be withdrawn and asserted the independence of the Byzantine Church. Photius then invited the Eastern patriarchs to a general council in a famous encyclical that proposed to condemn the papal incumbent without repudiating the see. Photius rejected the *filioque,* affirming that the Holy Spirit proceeds from the Father alone. The synod, presided over by the emperor, met in the summer of 867 and excommunicated Nicholas I for exceeding his authority; but the pope died in November without ever hearing of the action taken.

In September Basil I (867–886) assassinated Michael III and assumed the purple; he brought back into favor the Studites, deposed Photius, reinstated Ignatius, and restored communion with Rome. He likewise offered to accept Nicholas's offer of a fair trial at Rome for Photius and Ignatius as if the antipapal council of 867 had never existed, and he sent representatives of both prelates with his embassy to submit the affair to the judgment of the Holy See. ADRIAN II (867–872), Nicholas's successor, could hardly overlook the antipapal council; he decided that Photius and all the bishops consecrated by him should be deposed, that those consecrated by Methodius and Ignatius who had gone over to Photius should be pardoned only after signing a *libellus* that professed the primacy and condemned Photius and his adherents, and that the signatories to the acts of the council of 867 would be pardoned but would have to apply to the Holy See for absolution.

Photius's representative had died before the trial, but Adrian II nevertheless condemned Photius, presumably because he had excommunicated a pope and his guilt was clear from the acts. As a general council was being prepared in Constantinople, Adrian was determined to impose his verdict on it and instructed his legates to that effect.

The emperor, however, knew that Photius's supporters would seize upon the fact that he had been condemned without a hearing and would continue the factional strife throughout the empire. His own hold on the throne was not secure, and he was equally determined to have some sort of trial. Hence he decided to proceed with the council.

Council of Constantinople IV. The Eighth General Council was held in Constantinople (869–870) and became a conflict of wills between Roman legates and Basil's representatives. The dictatorial conduct of the legates alienated even the pro-Studite bishops, the pope's warmest supporters. In the end, however, the council finally submitted to Pope Adrian's will, but it caused further dissension between the Churches. The council was added to the list of ecumenical councils in the West, but is not recognized in the East.

In the end, however, not all decisions went in Rome's favor. At the last session, a Bulgarian embassy arrived; for Boris had turned back to Constantinople when the pope refused to give him Formosus as archbishop. The determination of the jurisdiction to which Bulgaria belonged was left to the judgment of the pentarchy, and the three Eastern patriarchs pronounced in favor of Constantinople. Though formally forbidden by the legates to interfere in Bulgaria, on their departure for Rome, Ignatius consecrated an archbishop and later 12 bishops for that country. Ignatius was about to be excommunicated by Pope John VIII (872–882) when he died; he was succeeded by Photius, who was now acceptable to all parties.

Peace was made between the two sees in the Synod of Constantinople (879–880), the Great Council of Union held in St. Sophia. John VIII agreed to recognize Photius if he apologized to the assembled bishops for his past misconduct, became reconciled with his enemies, and gave up Bulgaria. Photius refused to apologize but satisfied the other demands. It was agreed that Bulgaria should remain in the Byzantine rite, but under Roman jurisdiction. Finally John VIII absolved Photius from all censures and synodal decrees against him, including the disciplinary decrees of the Eighth General Council. The authenticity of the acts of the last two sessions, which deal with the *filioque,* has been questioned; both parties, according to the present text, came to terms on the basis of the *status quo ante,* i.e., that the addition should not be made to the Creed. Nevertheless, because Photius later quoted this as proof that John VIII taught that the Holy Spirit proceeds from the Father alone, and since papal legates could not have subscribed to that, it is difficult to know how the matter could have been resolved. Agreement was also reached as to the relative positions of Rome and Constantinople; the privileges of Old Rome were recognized, but the canonical and judicial authority of pope and patriarch were deemed to be equal. At all events, the two sees were in union at the end of Photius's patriarchate (886), though their relations in the interval did not always remain cordial. Whether minor breaks between the sees occurred under Pope Formosus or Pope Stephen VII is a matter of dispute.

Photius is a controversial figure. Older scholars held that he was the chief author of the Eastern Schism. But F. Dvornik has demonstrated that though his works became a source book for writers against the Latins, nobody singled him out as leader of schism until centuries after his death. Some maintain that he was a loyal son of the Church despite mistakes. Others, however, for various reasons think that he tried deliberately to make the Byzantine Church independent of Rome.

Photius instituted the missions to the Slavs, which won so many peoples for the Church of Constantinople. The most famous mission was the sending of the brothers CYRIL (CONSTANTINE) AND METHODIUS to the Moravians in 863. They created a new alphabet, and translated the Scripture into the language of the Slavs, but eventually had to withdraw under pressure from competing Frankish missionaries. Photius also began the evangelization of the Rhos of Kiev, marked by the conversion of Olga, princess of Kiev, and tried to win over their neighbors, the Khazars in the Crimea, to Christianity. The real conversion of the Rhos, however, came with the baptism of Vladimir of Kiev and his marriage to Anna, Basil II's sister, in 989. Bulgaria was taken over by the Byzantine hierarchy after 1025, and the Church of Kiev, in 1037. Patriarch Nicholas I Mysticus sent an archbishop to the Alans, north of the Caucasus, and kept him there by his encouragement.

Photius was forced to resign (886) by Emperor LEO VI (886–912), who wished to appoint his brother Stephen. The Studites returned to power once more but objected to the new patriarch because he had been ordained a deacon by Photius. They believed that Photius had been consecrated invalidly (or illicitly—they were not clear about the distinction), and therefore all orders administered by him were invalid (or illicit). They were willing to recognize Stephen if Rome granted a dispensation to all those promoted by Photius, and therefore appealed. The affair dragged on until Pope John IX (898–900) reaffirmed the previous papal decisions, that the correct patriarchal line was Methodius, Ignatius, Photius, Stephen, Anthony; i.e., Photius's first term did not count, but his second did. Most of the Studites accepted this settlement and were thus finally reconciled to both Rome and Patriarch Anthony II Cauleas (893–901) at a Synod of Union in 899.

Dispute over the Tetragamy. Peace lasted less than 10 years, after which the Church was torn asunder by the quarrel over the fourth marriage (tetragamy) of the emperor. The Byzantine Church had remained faithful to the early Christian attitude toward the unity of marriage; its canon law imposed a penance for a second marriage, very severe penalties for a third marriage, and absolutely forbade a fourth. In fact this legislation had been strengthened by Emperor Leo himself, who had even disapproved of a second marriage. After the death of his third wife left him without male issue, however, he took as a mistress Zoë, and in 905 she bore him a son out of wedlock, the future Constantine VII (913–959). Patriarch Nicholas I Mysticus had kept on cordial terms with the emperor, paying no attention to the love affair. He himself baptized the infant with all the pomp befitting a *Porphyrogenitus* (one born in the Purple Chamber of the palace while his father was emperor); this act amounted virtually to a legitimization of the child. He set one condition—that Leo and Zoë should separate. Two or three days after the baptism, however, Leo brought Zoë back to the palace and shortly thereafter crowned her queen; they were married by a priest, Thomas. The patriarch then forbade them to attend the liturgy or receive the Sacraments while he considered whether or not he could dispense them. At Christmas 906 and on the Feast of Epiphany 907, the emperor was turned away from Hagia Sophia. Despite the confusing nature of the sources, it seems that Leo had already appealed to the pentarchy, and chiefly to Rome—at the patriarch's suggestion, according to Nicholas's own statement.

The emperor was firmly convinced that the patriarch was engaged in treasonable dealings with a rebel in Asia Minor, and he resolved to depose Nicholas at the first opportunity, despite the patriarch's large popular following in Constantinople. Nicholas had almost decided to allow Leo and Zoë to remain in communion, but suddenly reversed his position. Several influential bishops, notably Arethas, metropolitan of Caesarea, were inalterably opposed to a dispensation, and the patriarch made the members of the synod take a solemn oath to resist the emperor's attempt at tetragamy even to the death, if need be. At last the verdict of Rome and the other patriarchs arrived. It showed the utmost respect for Byzantine usage: Pope SERGIUS III (904–911) stated that a fourth marriage was against Byzantine canon law and propriety; the dispensation, however, was granted out of consideration for the good of the state. To those who objected that a fourth marriage was adultery, Rome pointed to its own practice in this regard, and the texts of St. Paul but did not thereby intend to foist its customs on the Eastern Church. Backed by the decision of the pentarchy, Leo determined to break the resistance of the patriarch. Nicholas resigned despite the urging of Arethas and others opposed to the dispensation. Arethas thereafter always despised Nicholas, who had with great bravado led them into battle and then, by resigning, deserted them at the first sign of danger. The synod voted to accept the pentarchy's verdict, but Arethas and his companions stood their ground.

The synod then elected EUTHYMIUS I, a saintly man, in February 907. He accepted only on condition that the patriarchal representatives repeat their decision in his presence. He reconciled Arethas to the dispensation. He degraded Thomas, the priest who had performed the marriage and refused to crown Zoë in church or put her name in the diptychs. Not everybody shared Arethas's low opinion of Nicholas. Very many regarded him as the hero of Christian marriage, who had resigned rather than debauch it, and they formed the Nicholites, who were opposed by the Euthymians. The government persecuted the former, and once more strife raged.

On the death of Leo, his brother Alexander (912–913) deposed Euthymius, and reinstated Nicholas. It is debated whether Leo himself may have repented and recalled Nicholas before his death. Nicholas took savage vengeance on Euthymius and severely punished his party, particularly those who had sworn to stand by Nicholas then changed over. Nicholas maintained that he had not resigned, and, even if he had, the resignation had been motivated by fear. As Arethas put it, he had the impudence to demand that the bishops suffer anything rather than admit the validity of the resignation by which he had himself evaded what he was asking them to endure. Nicholas turned on the pope, protesting the deep humiliation inflicted on his Church; and he pretended that he had never thought of granting the dispensation himself. He berated the Holy See for approving of adultery by permitting a fourth marriage in order to curry favor with the emperor, and demanded that the pope make an example of the legates guilty of such an enormity. Then he erased the pope's name from the diptychs. Yet in 917 Nicholas was reconciled with Euthymius and attempted to bring peace between the Euthymians and the Nicholites. He succeeded partially at a synod in July 920. The two parties agreed not to condemn those who had contracted a fourth marriage and to settle the canon law on marriage by stating that a second marriage was on a par with a first, that a third was subject to stringent restrictions, and that a fourth marriage was equivalent to living in sin. An apparently strong minority demanded the intervention of the pope, however, and Nicholas finally persuaded (923) the Holy See to send legates to repeat the decision originally made by Pope Sergius III. A few Euthymians resisted and were reconciled finally under Patriarch Nicholas II (979–991) or his successor, SISINNIUS II (996–998).

Formal Schism under Sergius IV. The formal break with Rome did not come until the beginning of the 11th century. Throughout the 10th century, there remained a group within the Byzantine Church who had continued to believe in the primacy of Rome. Papal approval, when it suited, was still sought for the ordination of Constantinopolitan patriarchs, as in the case of Theophylact Lecapenus. In 933 after the death of his eldest son and heir, Christopher, the emperor ROMANUS I LECAPENUS decided to make his younger son, Theophylact, patriarch. Theophylact was only 16 years old and was known for his worldly interests, especially horses. The corrupt Pope John XI, however, was prevailed upon to send legates, who assisted at the consecration and enthroned him. As the Byzantine hierarchy did not object on doctrinal grounds, and had no rival candidate, there was no strong opposition.

In 1009, however, Patriarch SERGIUS II (1001–19) dropped the name of Pope SERGIUS IV (1009–12) from the diptychs. Even a contemporary, Peter, later patriarch of Antioch, did not know why this was done. Later Byzantine statements that it was because the pope had sent a creed containing the *filioque* must have been conjectures. As the pope's name was never restored to the diptychs, this is the only official beginning of the schism; yet, as already mentioned, neither Church ever formally excommunicated the other.

The pentarchy had developed into a theory that negated the supremacy of Rome. Peter of Antioch expounded the ecclesiology of the period in one of his epistles to Dominic, patriarch of Venice. Peter took pains to point out that there was no such thing as a patriarch of Venice; that a sixth patriarchate was unheard of; and that just as there were five senses so there were five patriarchates, Rome, Constantinople, Alexandria, Antioch, and Jerusalem. He described the pentarchy as a committee of five equals in which the majority rules. This was unequivocal; the patriarchs are all independent and the only head of the Church is its invisible Head, Christ. Peter took for granted that this was the doctrine held universally. He mentioned it incidentally as the self-evident proof for the impossibility of a sixth patriarchate, and though his correspondent was a Latin bishop, he had no doubt that they both agreed. Furthermore, Peter did not believe in the inerrancy of the Holy See; it was not only capable of error, but actually in error.

In 1024, according to a Western writer, the proposition was made to the pope by Emperor Basil II, ''whether with the Roman Pontiff's consent, the Church of Constantinople might be entitled, within its own limits, to be called, and treated as, ecumenical, as Rome was ecumenical throughout the world.'' The proposal was rejected. Some authorities maintain that this report is unreliable and the event did not occur at all; others think that it did occur, but disagree as to the meaning of the offer. If it happened, it was the first effort at reunion.

Patriarch Michael Cerularius. In 1042–43 MICHAEL CERULARIUS, a relation of the Ducas family, was appointed patriarch by Constantine Monomachus IX. Cerularius had returned to the capital after some years in exile for instigating a conspiracy against the Paphlagonian Michael IV. He enjoyed popular support in Constantinople, especially with his famous opposition to Western liturgical and disciplinary practices that he pursued vigorously, even at a time when the emperor was seeking to make an alliance with Pope Leo IX (1049–April 19, 1054) against the Normans who were gaining the upper hand against the Byzantines in South Italy. It was taken for granted as a preliminary to the political treaty between emperor and pope that religious unity would be established. But Leo, Byzantine archbishop of Bulgaria, supposedly incited by Cerularius, wrote a letter to a bishop of southern Italy, John of Trani, addressing through him the pope and the whole Western Church. He argued, while condemning many lesser points such as fasting on Saturdays, that unleavened bread (or azymes) was not valid matter for the Holy Eucharist. He continued that only Constantinople had the true faith and the true sacrifice, and that every other Church had to learn from her. Constantinople claimed Rome's own prerogative. To the Byzantines of the 11th century, the title ''Holy Orthodox Church'' meant what it said, and Orthodox was equivalent to infallible. This idea had been formulated clearly in Photius's encyclical of 867, and the synod repeated his words in its excommunication of the papal legate, Cardinal Humbert, which closed the Cerularian episode. Though Constantinople subscribed in theory to the equality of the patriarchs in the pentarchy, in fact she regarded herself as the first see. The foundation for this belief was based upon a revision (ascribed by some to Photius) of the ancient Constantinian *translatio imperii,* the claim that both the civil and the religious leadership had been transferred to Constantinople from the Old (decrepit) Rome to the New (vigorous) Constantinople by St. Andrew, the ''first-called'' of the Apostles, thus establishing the See of Byzantium.

Having heard these sentiments, Pope Leo would not agree to a treaty with the emperor. At other times, the emperor would have simply had the patriarch deposed, but

Cerularius had no intention of compromising his convictions or of resigning. His great asset was the enormous popularity he enjoyed with the common people of Constantinople, while his adversary, Emperor CONSTANTINE IX (1042–55), was quite unpopular. The patriarch closed the Latin churches in Constantinople, after desecrating their hosts to demonstrate that they were invalidly consecrated. He likewise began an intensive campaign to rouse the populace.

The papal embassy, headed by Cardinal Humbert, a staunch believer in the superiority of Rome, arrived in Constantinople to negotiate the treaty. The conditions for reunion of the Churches were the long sought-after restitution of Illyricum, Calabria, and Sicily to Roman jurisdiction and the acknowledgment of the primacy. In June, two months after the pope's death, in the presence of the emperor, Humbert insisted that one of his literary opponents, Nicetas Stethatos, repudiate his own work and in addition deliver a clear anathema against all those who denied that Rome was the first church or questioned its orthodox faith. Constantine, who realized the strong position of the Normans in South Italy, was keen that communion between the two Churches should be restored. But still Cerularius would not agree to compromise with a pope whose views he regarded as heretical: as he said, ''if the head of a fish is rotten, how can the rest be healthy'' (Angold). He therefore averred that the legates were imposters and refused to meet them, except in the patriarchal palace surrounded by the synod. On July 16, the legates in the Church of Hagia Sophia, crowded for the morning liturgy, laid a document of excommunication on the high altar. It anathematized Michael, the patriarch, and his followers; and it condemned as heretical the special features of the Byzantine Liturgy and ecclesial usages. In this way, though intended only against Cerularius, the anathema was applied to the whole Byzantine Church and aroused strong opposition. The legates had to flee for their lives, and the emperor was forced to a humiliating surrender to the patriarch. On July 24, 1054, the synod met, condemned Humbert and his companions as imposters, repudiated the *filioque,* following word for word Photius's encyclical, and defended the beards and marriage of the Byzantine priests. They made very clear that they were not excommunicating either the pope or the Western Church. The silence on unleavened bread was a stinging rebuff to Cerularius, who, after all, had commanded one of his officials to trample on the Latin consecrated hosts. Nevertheless, Michael reached a pinnacle of power never attained by any other ecclesiastic in the history of Byzantium.

The importance of incident in relations between the two Churches has been much discussed. It is clear, however, that it was not the beginning of the Eastern Schism, as has previously been argued. Popes had excommunicated patriarchs before, and Humbert's excommunication of Cerularius was of doubtful value, since the pope had died before it was proclaimed. The Byzantines made clear that they were not excommunicating the Western Church. The episode was, in fact, an unsuccessful attempt to heal a schism, though it is unlikely that an solution would have endured.

From Death of Michael Cerularius to Death of Michael VIII Palaeologus, 1059–1282

This period is marked by the succession of efforts at reunion of the Churches, culminating in the Council of Lyons. The attempts provoked a vigorous polemic over the differences between Byzantine and Latin liturgy and theology. A number of other theological controversies occurred during the time of the Comneni.

John Italus and Psellus. The case of JOHN ITALUS came to a head early in the reign of ALEXIUS I COMNENUS (1081–1118) and is of extraordinary interest. He came from South Italy to Constantinople, and became the pupil of Michael Psellus. Italus succeeded Psellus in the chair of philosophy at the university as consul of philosophers, or head of the school, and was also given responsibility for the emperor's policy of rapprochment with the Normans. His trial seems an isolated event, but it really constitutes the last act of the conflict between the Byzantine Church and the classics. While SYMEON THE NEW THEOLOGIAN argued for the idea of a mystical communion with God and the exclusive preeminence of the gifts of the Holy Spirit over all science and all authority, Psellus with his pupil Italus launched the idea that all human knowledge is a step toward God, and that dogma should be interpreted in the light of rational principles, a sort of scholasticism. This contradicted the attitude adopted by the monks since the Studite reform in the 9th century. For them the object of knowledge was revelation; all else was valueless. The only science was the insight inspired by the Holy Spirit, which comes from prayer.

Psellus had returned to the Neoplatonism of PROCLUS, not to Plato; Italus favored Plotinus, but he also learned much from Origen. Together with their contemporaries, they represented a revolutionary and rationalistic tendency, and their age had a remarkable affinity with the later Western Renaissance. In 1076–77 the movement was condemned by the synod, which mentioned no particular theologians but anathematized doctrines close to modern rationalism. One excommunicated group denied the miracles of Our Lord, the Blessed Virgin, and the saints; another considered profane literature the repository of truth to which all else must be reduced directly or indirectly. They thus placed reason above faith. Neither

Psellus or Italus held such extreme views, but their lectures were open to the public and, as they encouraged free discussion, this gave rise to serious misunderstandings. Psellus was suspected of heresy and was temporarily excommunicated by the patriarch John Xiphilinos (1064–75) until he was able to convince the patriarch that his work was not at odds with the Church Fathers. Italus's teachings, however, were believed to be not only heretical but were also in danger of corrupting his students. Eventually, in a synod of 1083, his teaching was rejected explicitly and although he retracted his views, Alexius continued to be unsatisfied and sought the condemnation of Italus's pupils.

Many reasons have been argued for the emperor's determination to secure this complete condemnation of Italus and his work. He may have been simply a victim of imperial propaganda, for the most likely explanation was Alexius's desire to be seen as restoring or cleansing the orthodoxy of the empire. The trial of Italus was held on the Feast of Orthodoxy, and the anathemas against him and his followers were appended to the *Synodicon of Orthodoxy.* The *Synodicon* became the expression of the beliefs of the Orthodox Church, and continued as a reminder of Alexius's defense of orthodoxy.

Other Controversies under the Comneni. Leo of Chalcedon accused Alexius I Comnenus of iconoclasm when, in order to save the state, he melted the gold and silver attached to icons and particularly medals stamped with the image of Christ or a saint. In 1086 the synod condemned and deposed him. Eustratius of Nicaea, who had been appointed by Alexius and had opposed Leo, was now himself condemned by a council in 1117 for heretical beliefs approximating Nestorianism during a controversy with the Monophysite Armenians; he recanted. Nilus, an unlearned but upright monk with a large following of monks in Constantinople, unwittingly became a Monophysite, after the death of Alexius, the synod condemned both him and the Monophysites to perpetual anathema (1087).

The contest between the empire and the sects of Manichaean character seems to have reached a crisis under Alexius. The Paulicians, a group that first appeared in the 7th century, believed that the whole material world was an evil creation of an evil God. They rejected the hierarchy, sacraments, and cult, and opposed images. Subject to sporadic persecution, they were favored by the early iconoclastic emperors and spread all over Asia Minor. Large numbers were transplanted to Thrace by Constantine V to counterbalance the sentiment there in favor of icons. They were reinforced by another group brought over by the emperor John I Tzimisces (969–976). They won many converts and made their center Philippopolis. By the 12th century they were absorbed into a similar sect, the Bogomils, named after the Bulgarian priest Bogomil, who in the first half of the 10th century developed a Bulgarian strain of Paulician dualism. The Bogomils believed in the fall of Satanael, the elder son of God, who made Earth habitable and tried to create man with a soul stolen from God. God sent Jesus Christ, his second son, to bring salvation. The Bogomils rejected the material world, and sacraments, and despite condemning marriage and procreation, by the 12th century they had won great popular support in Constantinople and throughout the empire. Alexius led a special expedition against Philippopolis in order to convert the heretics; two of the high officials were imprisoned for life, and their leader, Basil the Physician, was burned at the stake. Under John Comnenus (1118–43), the works of the monk Constantine Chrysomallus, which were tainted with Manichaean errors, were discovered circulating in several monasteries and were burnt by order of the synod in 1140. In the reign of Manuel I Comnenus (1143–80), two bishops were found guilty of upholding certain Bogomil tenets; Patriarch Cosmas II Atticus (1146–47) was involved and deposed, though perhaps unjustly.

During Manuel's reign two interesting discussions arose. The first concerned the meaning of a passage in the liturgy, "You are the offerer and the offered, and the receiver." Soterichus Panteugenus, titular patriarch of Antioch, decided that Christ's sacrifice was offered only to God the Father and God the Holy Spirit, and not to God the Son, since he held that Christ could not offer something to Himself. This view was condemned in a synod of 1157. Soterichus taught also that the Mass was not a sacrifice but merely a solemn and dramatic recall of Christ's Passion and death. This doctrine was repudiated. The other controversy dealt with the meaning of Christ's words, "The Father is greater than I." At least five different interpretations were proposed; the debate became embittered, and some of the views were clearly unorthodox. It required eight sessions of the synod in 1170–71 to dispose of the difficulties. Even then the emperor's interference prevented a thorough examination of the issues and the forced solution proved unsatisfactory. An attempt at revision of the synod's decisions, however, by Patriarch Michael IV Autorianus (1208–14) was blocked by opposition within the Church.

In the reign of Alexius III and Patriarch John X Camateros (1198–1206), Michael Glycas, the imperial secretary and partly blinded for plotting against Manuel Comnenus, proposed the theory that Christ's body in the Holy Eucharist is mortal from the Consecration to the Communion, just as it was at the Last Supper, but incorruptible immediately after it had been absorbed by the communicant, as it was in the Resurrection. The synod took no positive action but simply forbade anyone to read Glycas or his opponent.

Efforts at Reunion. Once the Cerularius incident had disclosed the rent between Rome and Constantinople, efforts at reunion began almost immediately, For the East, the initiative was begun by the emperor due to the special place of the civil ruler in the Byzantine Church. As a result of this situation, the popes, even when their principal end was reunion, had to negotiate politically, not religiously, and they never bypassed the monarch to treat directly with the patriarch. The popes seem to have taken for granted that once they had won the emperor, they could make the Church do anything he pleased, although this was never true of Cerularius.

These political compromises belong to the history of the Byzantine state, not the Church, which often was not even consulted. Certain episodes stand out as worthy of note. The first of this period involved Pope Urban II. He complained to Alexius I Comnenus that his name had been removed from the diptychs uncanonically and asked to have it restored. A synod summoned by the emperor had to concede the justice of the complaint, but as uncompromising as ever, decided that, for the time being, the pope should be commemorated only if he submitted a satisfactory confession of faith and accepted the Quinisext synod (which had condemned clerical celibacy). Whether the pope took any further interest in reunion is not known, but at any rate friendly relations were established between Alexius and Urban, which were, of course, ultimately to lead to the first crusade in response to the former's request for more Christian troops to fight against the Muslims.

After the death of Urban II, Alexius negotiated with his successor, Paschal II, for reunion between the churches and held debates between eastern and western theologians in Constantinople in 1112 and 1114. The primacy of Rome remained the sticking point, as did the addition of the *filioque,* which the Byzantines still rejected. Emperors remained keen to establish union. In 1141, John II wrote to Pope Innocent II saying that "there were two swords, the secular which he himself would wield, and the spiritual which he would leave to the Pope, and together they would restore the unity of the Christian Church and establish the world supremacy of the one Roman Empire" (Ostrogorsky). The emperor Manual Comnenus was also prepared to press the issue and held another synod in the 1160s or 1170s (the date is disputed). It appears that he proposed that the primacy of the pope be acknowledged, but Patriarch Michael II Anchialus replied that it was impossible to have communion with heretics; the primacy had been lost to Rome when the pope had become a heretic, and had been transferred to Constantinople; the pope was nothing but a layman.

The Crusades. Relations between the Churches of the East and West worsened during the CRUSADES. Years before this tension had been increased by the followers of PETER THE HERMIT, who looted their way across Europe in the First Crusade, and by Bohemund's seizure of Antioch, which established the Normans, the deadliest enemy of Byzantium, on both its flanks. The Byzantine Church, particularly, resented its humiliating position in the Holy Land. Meantime, the ears of the West were filled with calumnies about Byzantine perfidy principally by the Normans. The Second and Third Crusades, with their threat to Constantinople itself, strained relations almost to the breaking point. The Venetians, using their trading privileges ruthlessly were driving the Byzantines out of business in their own country and making themselves everywhere detested. Emperor Manual I Comnenus had favored the Latins, and the Greeks saw the Latins displacing themselves in high government positions. The mounting fury was unleashed in a massacre of Latins all over the empire in 1182. By this time Latin hatred of the Greeks was also intense. The climax came in the sack of Constantinople in the Fourth Crusade, when for three days the soldiers pillaged and murdered, and desecrated nuns and the altars of refuge, as well as the Sacred Species.

The Byzantine Church and empire took refuge in Asia Minor, rallying around Theodore I Lascaris (1208–22), who gathered the scattered elements of both in Nicaea. He invited Patriarch John X Camateros to join him but was refused. In 1206 Camateros died, and in 1208 Theodore assembled all available Byzantine bishops and suggested that they elect a new patriarch. Michael IV Autorianus (1208–14) was chosen, and he crowned Theodore emperor in Holy Week of 1208. Nicaea thus became the rallying point and new hope of the eastern Greeks. It had a rival, however, in the Despotate of Epirus, the cultural and political center of the western Greeks.

Innocent III. Though shocked at the outrage to Constantinople, Pope Innocent III acquiesced in the *fait accompli* and regarded the conquest as a providentially designed reunion of the Churches. The Venetians gained control of Hagia Sophia, and so of the patriarchate, and selected Thomas Morosini as Latin patriarch of Constantinople; the pope had no choice but to approve. Naturally it angered the Byzantines exceedingly to have any other than a Greek patriarch. Despite the long existence of Byzantine churches and monasteries in Rome itself and in other parts of Italy under papal control, Innocent III planned the absorption of the Byzantine Church by the Latin. This was his idea of union of Churches. But he pursued a policy of limited tolerance. When early conferences (1205–07) of Byzantine representatives with the legate Cardinal Benedict made it clear that they would not adopt the *filioque,* unleavened bread, or other Latin customs, the pope did not force them. He did insist on the oath of canonical obedience to the pope and the Latin patriarchate of Constantinople. If the bishops demurred, every effort was made to win them over before deposing them and appointing a Latin in their stead. No new bishop, however, was to be consecrated in any rite but Latin; hence the Byzantine hierarchy was doomed to die out with the existing generation.

Despite all this, the Byzantine Church survived to a certain extent. Cardinal Benedict had a winning personality, and he induced many clerics, though a minority, to take the oath of obedience. They felt that they were yielding nothing essential and their flock would still have shepherds. When some who were willing to submit to the pope found it abhorrent to recognize the Latin patriarch, since they regarded the patriarch at Nicaea as the true one, Cardinal Benedict dispensed them. The majority refused to take the oath. To those who resigned and went into voluntary exile, the empire of Nicaea offered a refuge. To those who stood their ground, it held out hope and encouragement. Many never had to take the oath because the Latin rulers refused to carry out the law, some out of sympathy and some out of cupidity, pocketing the income that should have gone either to the Latin bishop or the Holy See. Intending to put a stop to these abuses and to win over the rest of the Byzantines, Innocent III despatched a new legate, Cardinal Pelagius, in 1213 or 1214. Acting entirely contrary to the spirit of his orders, Pelagius started a persecution, manacling and imprisoning those who refused the oath of canonical obedience, sealing up churches, and driving monks from their monasteries. The Latin emperor Henry, who dealt fairly with the Greeks, released them from jail and made a compromise, according to which they need not mention the pope in the diptychs if they acclaimed the Latin emperor as political ruler after the service when they used to acclaim the Byzantine emperor. Pelagius also had been commissioned to treat with the empire of Nicaea on reunion and for political ends, and when he did that he had to stop the persecution.

Yet reunion via a general council was still possible. Among those Byzantines who had remained in the Latin-held territory was a group who believed with Innocent III that the conquest had providentially brought together under one power the two previously divided peoples. It had not, however, achieved a spiritual union of the Churches. In a letter to the pope they proposed that they should be permitted to elect a Greek patriarch who shared their views, and that then it would be possible to settle the religious differences in a general council. This move was made, apparently, with the approval of Nicaea. Innocent III would not hear of it and held to his own policy; he had proclaimed the union of Churches and to permit a general council would be to confess that the union was illusory. As a result, the conciliatory party turned its back on the Latin empire and gave its allegiance to Nicaea. The episode is variously dated 1206–07 or 1213–14.

Innocent IV. The most promising attempt at reconciliation ever made was that between Pope Innocent IV (1243–54) and Emperor John III Vatatzes in 1253–54. The immediate successors of Innocent III continued his policy, but Innocent IV abandoned it completely. He saw that the cooperation of the rising Byzantine Empire of Nicaea and union with the Greek Church offered more than the Latin Empire. John, in turn, was prepared to sacrifice the independence of the Greek Church in order to win back Constantinople. Patriarch Manuel II (1244–54), who sincerely desired an end to the schism, suggested a compromise formula, ''the Holy Spirit, who proceeds from the Father through the Son,'' instead of ''. . . and the Son,'' a formula entirely acceptable to the Latins. He succeeded in winning over the Greek Church to the following agreement: if the pope yielded the throne of Constantinople to the Greek emperor and its see to the Greek patriarch, the Greek Church would acknowledge the primacy by restoring his name to the diptychs and would take the oath of canonical obedience. Innocent accepted these terms and also consented to a general council on Greek territory to ratify the agreement. But all the principal personalities died, Innocent IV, John III Vatatzes, and Patriarch Manuel. John's successor, Theodore II Lascaris, rejected the whole plan.

Council of Lyons. Though official efforts at reunion had little success, informal exchanges between scholars contributed to a better understanding. The Latins were represented during the age of the Comneni by Peter Grossolano (Chrysolanus, to the Greeks), archbishop of Milan, and Bishop Anselm of Havelberg, a Premonstratensian, who both had occasion to visit Constantinople, and Hugo Eterianus, councilor and official theologian to Manuel I Comnenus. The Byzantines relied on Photius's work *Mystagogy,* which was written in his old age and is far from his best work. Photius had taught that the Holy Sprit proceeded from the Father alone, but Eterianus's three books on the Procession of the Holy Spirit, published in both Greek and Latin, forced on the Photians a notable revision of their patristic material. The discussion of Grossolano and Anselm induced some of the Byzantines to consider the formula ''through the Son'' instead of ''from the Father alone,'' and led others to admit the validity of the Latin position. Most of the Comnenian theologians, however, held to the Photian doctrine, and the Fourth Crusade hardly gained friends for the Western views. A chance came with the work of NICEPHORUS

BLEMMYDES during the Nicaean period. He accepted the Latin argument that unless the Son is involved in the procession of the Holy Spirit, no distinction between Son and Holy Spirit could be established. He abandoned the Photian teaching entirely. It was principally due to Blemmydes and partially to Hugo Eterianus that Patriarch John XI Beccus (1275–82), the union patriarch under MICHAEL VIII PALAEOLOGUS, owed his conversion to the Latin position. Beccus himself made an important point that ''through the Son'' was in the best Greek tradition and Photius had not done it justice.

On July 6, 1274, at the Second Council of Lyons, the union between Rome and Constantinople was sealed. Letters from Michael VIII, his son and coemperor Andronicus II, and the Byzantine hierarchy were read. The emperor recognized the primacy in a formula worded by Pope Gregory X himself. He accepted the *filioque* and the validity of consecration of unleavened bread. The Byzantine hierarchy acknowledged the primacy as it had existed before the schism and affirmed their entry into the Church, but did not repeat the formula of faith contained in the emperor's letter. A plea of the hierarchy was put into the pope's hands before they returned to Byzantium: they asked the pope to permit the Greek hierarchy to exist side by side with the Latin, and for a guarantee in writing that Greek customs would not be disturbed. The latter request was made a condition of acceptance of the union.

Michael VIII had been impelled to negotiate with the pope as the only way of saving Byzantium from destruction by Charles of Anjou. The emperor had to use pressure, but ultimately he got most of the hierarchy to sign. Patriarch Joseph preferred to resign, and John XI Beccus succeeded to the patriarchal see. Beccus had greatly aided the emperor's efforts. At first a determined foe of the *filioque,* he had been imprisoned and his reading of Blemmydes and study in jail had converted him to the Latin view.

The union was successful for a time politically, but a failure religiously. The people bitterly opposed it. To gain the throne, Michael VIII had blinded the legitimate ruler, John IV Lascaris, and had been excommunicated by Patriarch Arsenius Autorianus. He succeeded in deposing the latter (1266), but the Arsenites formed a schism and fought against both the emperor and reconciliation with Rome. After the union of Lyons, the country was divided into two hostile camps. Michael had to enforce the union to keep Charles of Anjou at bay, and he had recourse to persecution. All sections of the population were affected and the imperial family itself was divided. Finally Pope Martin IV, a friend of Charles of Anjou, excommunicated Michael VIII as a heretic (1281), and all of the West turned against Byzantium. Byzantium was saved by the Sicilian Vespers (1282), the revolt achieved by the skillful diplomacy of Michael. The Union of the Churches, however, did not survive his death and at a council held in Constantinople in 1285, it was formally rejected. A refutation of the *filioque,* drafted by the patriarch Gregory II of Cyprus (1283–89) was agreed. The Arsenite Schism ended only in 1310.

From Death of Michael VIII Palaeologus to Fall of Constantinople, 1282–1453

The high points of this period are the Hesychast movement and the Council of Florence. The latter had no influence on the Byzantine Church. The agreements made at the council, however, have ever since served as the basis for reunion, e.g., with the Melkites.

The discussions between scholars of the *filioque* continued and bore fruit. The Dominicans founded houses in Constantinople and elsewhere in the Latin kingdoms and kept up a vigorous offensive with influential publications in Greek. The union of Lyons had stimulated considerable polemic; and the controversy took a new turn with the translation into Greek of important Latin works, particularly Augustine's *On the Trinity* by Maximus Planudes, a celebrated humanist, in the reign of Michael VIII, and of the *Summa contra gentiles* and *Summa theologiae* of Thomas Aquinas by Demetrius Cydones (1355–58), completed by his brother Prochorus. These works were used extensively in the controversy over Hesychasm. Disciples and successors of Demetrius continued this activity. MANUEL CALECAS translated Boethius's *De trinitate* and Anselm's *Cur Deus Homo;* he died a Dominican in 1410. Maximus Chrysoberges (d.1430) entered the Dominicans *c.* 1390; his younger brother, known as Andrew of Crete, also a Dominican, devoted his life's work to missionary activity for union. Several Byzantines were won over to the Catholic cause at the Council of Florence, notably Isidore of Kiev and Bessarion. Most of these scholars, beginning with Demetrius Cydones, found life too difficult at Constantinople and sought refuge in Italy; they were forerunners of those who revived Greek in the West and reunited the two cultures after centuries of isolation. Theodore of Gaza, a translator of Aristotle, was a follower of Bessarion. John Argyropulos, founder of Greek philology in Italy, was famous among scholars deriving from Cydones. Both Theodore and John were staunch supporters of Florence.

The papal primacy constituted an insuperable barrier to union. To acknowledge the primacy was to admit the pope's prerogative to abolish the Byzantine Church at will. This was just what Innocent III and his successors had hoped to do. The Byzantine Church could never concede this possibility; at Lyons and Florence the unionists restricted their acceptance of the primacy correspondingly, and the popes tolerated the restriction.

Differences arose with respect to purgatory in the 13th century, and over the *epiclesis* in the 14th century. The Greeks objected to the idea of a purgatorial fire, for which they could find no proof in Scripture or the Fathers. It was the Latins who raised the question about the *epiclesis,* a prayer to the Holy Spirit in the Greek Liturgy after the Consecration: ''Send down thy Holy Spirit. . .and make this bread the Precious Body of Thy Christ, and that which is in this chalice the Precious Blood of Christ, transmuting them by Thy Holy Spirit.'' How could this petition be made after the Consecration? Neither of the objections, however, became prominent in polemic; the energies of the Greeks were entirely absorbed with the *filioque* and the Hesychastic controversies.

The debate on the azymes, which raged so hotly starting with Cerularius and continuing through the 12th century, gradually subsided thereafter. Both sides realized that the argument was of its nature incapable of settlement. Furthermore, moderate Greek churchmen found it too abhorrent to believe that the Latin Church had been deprived of the Eucharist for centuries.

Hesychastic Controversy. Although the controversy did not arise until the 12th century, hesychasm had been practiced for centuries. John Climmacus (580–650) in his *Ladder of Paradise* had already explained thus: ''the hesychast is one who aspires to circumscribe the Incorporeal in a dwelling of flesh; hesychasm is worship and interrupted service of God. . . .'' Hesychasm, following a traditionally Byzantine school of mysticism that reached its most complete development with Symeon the New Theologian (949–1022), abbot of St. Mamas in Constantinople, became associated on Mount Athos with a special technique for inducing ecstasy, and by the 12th century had become very popular. When by a life of mortification and prayer the monk had arrived at the contemplative stage, to make further progress he should adopt the following practice: sitting in the corner of a quiet cell, he should bend his head so as to rest his chin on his chest, fix his eyes on his navel, hold his breath, and repeat the Jesus Prayer, ''Lord Jesus Christ, Son of God, have mercy on me.'' Gradually sinking into ecstasy, he would see himself bathed in supernatural light, the Increate Light that the Apostles beheld in the Transfiguration on Mount Tabor. This method had only mild opposition till its orthodoxy was challenged in 1337 by the monk Barlaam of Calabria, who, besides ridiculing the peculiar procedure, contested the notion of uncreated light: what is uncreated must be God, and how could God be seen?

Gregory PALAMAS came to the defense of the monks. He accepted as fact the visionaries' belief that they saw the Increate Light of Mount Tabor and thus came into direct union with God. This new revelation made to them was implied in the New Testament as the Trinity was implied in the Old. To reconcile this doctrine with the traditional teaching about the incommunicability and invisibility of the Divine Essence, Palamas, during his debates with Barlaam, enunciated a special theory, but one incapable of logical proof, since it involved a mystery, such as the Trinity.

The Palamite controversy convulsed the Byzantine world for many years. Gregory was challenged by such scholars as Gregorius Akindynos, who argued from the Church Fathers according to the true Byzantine method, and Prochorus Cydones, who used the scholastic type of reasoning. When the question became inextricably embroiled in politics, Palamas and the monks prevailed through the backing of Emperor John VI Cantacuzenus (1347–54), who presided over a great synod at Constantinople in 1351 that condemned all opposition to Palamas. John V Palaeologus (1341–91), after the expulsion of Cantacuzenus, permitted free discussion but did not prevent the Church from imposing spiritual penalties on the anti-Palamites. The Synod of Constantinople in 1368 closed the affair so far as the Church was concerned by suspending Prochorus Cydones for life and canonizing Gregory Palamas. Hesychasm gained in popularity, especially in Bulgaria and Russia.

True union between Latins and Greeks had by now become impossible. Occasionally explorations were made by the Churches themselves, as in the conversations in 1367 between the papal legate, the imperial family, the ex-emperor Cantacuzenus, three high-ranking metropolitans of the synod, and representatives of the patriarch, in which it was agreed that a general council should debate the issues between the Churches. But the pope refused this suggestion as it seemed to put in doubt the teaching defined at the Council of Lyons. Besides, Cantacuzenus had made modifications in Palamas's theology that the Palamites would never had admitted. Generally, however, negotiations centered on the political question of the peril to Byzantium from the Turks and as time went on the chance of success diminished. In 1369 John V Palaeologus went to Rome and became a Catholic. He also promised, somewhat unrealistically, in return for Western military aid, to convert the Byzantine people to the Roman faith within six months. Pope Urban V, and after him, GREGORY XI, a true friend of the Greeks, made a ringing appeal to Europe to come to the aid of the now Catholic Byzantine emperor; but the plea fell on deaf ears. The Byzantine people became convinced that even if they changed their religion they would get no effective military help. It got to the point where schism made no real difference; the Latin principalities in Greece were by then in grave danger, and coalitions including schismatists had to be made for mutual protection. Finally in 1396, the one really strong Western effort, the Crusade of Nicopolis, collapsed.

Council of Florence. Nevertheless, John VIII Palaeologus (1425–48) decided to bring his people and the Greek clergy into union with Rome; early in 1438, on the invitation of Pope Eugene IV, he arrived in Ferrara for the General Council of Ferrara-Florence. After a thorough discussion of each point, agreement was reached on the *filioque,* azymes, purgatory, the enjoyment of the beatific vision by the blessed before the Last Judgment, the primacy, and the order of the patriarchs, Constantinople being named second after Rome. Compromises were reached: nothing was said about purgatorial fire since the Greeks did not teach it; the pope's right to call a general council was not specifically stated owing to the objection of the emperor; but the pope was acknowledged as head of the Church without prejudice to the rights and privileges of the Eastern patriarchs; and finally, the pope waived the question of the distinction between God's substance and operations, which had been the subject of controversy between the Palamites and the anti-Palamites. This question was too explosive to reopen, since it was threatening to cause a civil war in Byzantium. Eventually on July 6, 1439, the union was proclaimed in both Greek and Latin.

The only consistent dissenter among the Greeks was Mark Eugenicus, bishop of Ephesus, who alone did not sign the council's decrees. Most of the other Greek prelates agreed to the union, but with varying decrees of assent. Patriarch Joseph II, who had contributed to the outcome of the debate on the *filioque,* died before the end of the council. On the night of his death he left a note professing his faith in the *filioque,* purgatory, and the primacy.

The Council of Florence was never accepted by the Byzantine monks and lower clergy. John VIII vacillated about proclaiming its decrees, and many of the prelates who agreed to the union revoked their assent in the hostile atmosphere of Constantinople shortly after their return. But the new emperor, Constantine XI Palaeologus (1449–53), a Catholic, determined to carry out the union, and Cardinal Isidore, formerly of Kiev, as papal legate, solemnly proclaimed it in Hagia Sophia on Dec. 12, 1452, despite herculean efforts of the antiunionists to prevent it. At that moment, however, the sultan was determined to take the city by storm, and neither argument nor impassioned plea could avail against the grim fortress of Rumeli Hissar, built earlier that year by the Turks a few miles above Constantinople, which cut off help from the north. Six months later, May 29, 1453, Constantinople fell to Muḥammad II the Conqueror.

Bibliography: A. ALEXAKIS, ''The Greek Patristic Testimonia Presented at the Council of Florence (1439) in Support of the *Filioque* Reconsidered,'' *Revue des études byzantins* 58 (2000). M. ANGOLD, *The Byzantine Empire, 1025–1204* (London 1984). S. BROCK, ''An Early Syriac Life of Maximus the Confessor,'' *Analecta Bollandiana* 91 (1973). J. L. VAN DIETAN, *Geschichte der griechischen Patriarchen von konstantinopel* (Amsterdam 1972). G. D. DRAGAS, ''The Eighth Ecumencial Council: Constantinople IV (879/880) and the Condemnation of the *Filioque* Addition and Doctrine,'' *Greek Orthodox Theological Review* 44 (1999) 357–369. F. DVORNIK, *Byzantine Missions among the Slavs* (Prague 1970). W. H. C. FREND, *The Rise of the Monophysite Movement* (Cambridge 1972). N. GARSOIAN, ''L'abjuration du moine Nil Calabre,'' *Byzantinoslavica* 35 (1974) 12–27. J. GODFREY, *1204: The Unholy Crusade* (Oxford 1980). J. GILL, *Byzantium and the Papacy 1198–1400* (New Brunswick, N.J. 1979); *Council of Florence* (London 1959). P. GRIERSON, ''The Carolingian Empire in the Eyes of Byzantium,'' *Settimane* 27 (1981) 885–916. V. GRUMEL, J. DARROUZÈS, and V. LAURENT, *Les regestes des actes du Patriarcat de Constantinople* (Paris 1976–91). P. HENRY, ''Initial Eastern Assessments of the Seventh Oecumenical Council,'' *Journal of Theological Studies* n.s. 25 (1974) 75–92. J. HERRIN, *The Formation of Christendom* (Oxford 1987); ''Women and Faith in Icons in Early Christianity,'' in *Culture, Ideology and Politics,* ed. R. SAMUEL and G. STEDMAN JONES (London 1982) 56–83. J. HUSSEY, *The Orthodox Church in the Byzantine Empire* (Oxford 1986). J. N. D. KELLY, *Early Christian Creeds* (3d ed. London 1972); ''The Schism of the Franks and the 'Filioque,''' *Journal of Ecclesiastical History* 23 (1972) 97–113. V. LAURENT, *Les ''mémoires'' du grand ècclésiarque de léglise de Constantinople: Sylvestre Syropoulos sur le concile de Florence 1438–1439* (Rome 1971). V. LAURENT and J. DARROUZÈS, *Dossier grec de l'Union de Lyon (1273–1277)* (Paris 1976). K. MAKSIMOVIĆ, ''Patriarch Methodios I (843–847) und das studitische Schisma. Quellenkritische Bemerkungen,'' *Byzantion* 70 (2000) 422–446. J. MEYENDORFF, *Orthodoxie et catholicité* (Paris 1966); *Byzantine Hesychasm: Historical, Theological and Social Problems* (London 1974); *A Study of Gregory Palamas* (Leighton Buzzard 1964); *Byzantine Theology* (New York 1979); ''Byzantine Church,'' in *Dictionary of the Middle Ages* (New York 1983) II. 458–471. J. MUNITZ, ''Synoptic Greek Accounts of the Seventh Council,'' *Revue des études byzantins* 32 (1974) 147–186. D. M. NICOL, *Church and Society in the Last Centuries of Byzantium* (Cambridge 1979). D. OBOLENSKY, *The Byzantine Commonwealth: Eastern Europe 500–1453* (London 1971). G. OSTROGORSKY, *History of the Byzantine State* (2d ed. Oxford 1968). R. RIEDINGER, ''Griechische Konzilsakten auf dem wege ins lateinische Mittelalter,'' *Annuarium Historiae Conciliorum* 9 (1977) 253–301. K. M. SETTON, *The Papacy and the Levant* (Philadelphia 1976–84). P. SPECK, *Kaiser Konstantin VI,* 2 v. (Munich 1978). D. STRATOUDAKI-WHITE, ''The Patriarch Photios and the Conclusion of Iconoclasm,'' *Greek Orthodox Theological Review* 44 (1999) 341–355. F. R. TROMBLEY, ''A Note on the See of Jerusalem and the Synodal List of the Sixth Oecumenical Council, 680/1,'' *Byzantion* 53 (1983) 632–638. M. WHITTOW, *The Making of Orthodox Byzantium 600–1025* (Basingstoke 1996).

[M. J. HIGGINS/F. NICKS]

BYZANTINE CIVILIZATION

Byzantine civilization is not a term that the Byzantines themselves used for their civilization, which some

The Byzantine-Romanesque basilica of St. Cyriacus, Ancona, Italy. (Alinari-Art Reference/Art Resource, NY)

may define as a set of social phenomena (religious, social, moral, economic, cultural, aesthetic) that belong or are common to a major complex literate society. For others Byzantine civilization is the moral enterprise of a collectivity over time, including its central values and how they change, the attempt of its culture to create and realize a good society. It is its values and communities and sets of life and beliefs. It was the learned German humanist Hieronymus Wolf who invented the terminology for Byzantium and Byzantine in the sixteenth century. The ancient city of Byzantium, which CONSTANTINE I renamed CONSTANTINOPLE, was the source of the appellation Byzantine.

Byzantine civilization had periods of transition, rupture and unsettlement and remaking. The Byzantines regarded themselves as Romans. Byzantine civilization itself took recognizable form in the fourth century A.D., in the wake of the conversion of Roman Emperor Constantine I to Christianity and the rapid Christianization of the society and empire. Hellenistic civilization within the Roman Empire was already a millennium old when Byzantine civilization took on a distinct form. Earlier Greek and Hellenistic literary, philosophical, and scientific concepts, formulations, and structures created the context in which Byzantine civilization took its initial form. Urban life and structures of Greeks in the Roman Empire constituted an indispensable part of its background. It owed great debts to Latin, Coptic, Armenian, Persian, cultures and later also borrowed from Islamic cultures. But its fundamentals rested on a synthesis, which sometimes was an uneasy and tension-ridden amalgam, primarily of Hellenic and Christian elements. Critics have even labeled it an ''Orientalized Graeco-Roman civilization.'' A Roman element, however devoid of Latin (''Romanized Hellenism'' is one description), always constituted part of its identity. No one individual created this civilization, but it had taken distinct form by A.D. 400. No universal consensus exists on this issue; other modern scholars would disagree and date its beginnings to *c.* A.D. 565 (end of the age of Emperor Justinian I) or even slightly later. But such dating makes no sense in speaking of the civilization in contrast to political events and processes.

Byzantine civilization's genesis and duration resulted from the persistence of a distinctive Hellenic culture within the Greek-speaking parts of the Roman Empire. Some preferred to avoid Latinisms and other neologisms in writing in high style Greek. The relevance of this situation for the development of Byzantine civilization: a rela-

Mosaic in the arch of the forechoir, detail showing St. Gervase and St. Thaddeus (Jude), the Church of San Vitale, Ravenna, 526–547. (Alinari-Art Reference/Art Resource, N.Y.)

tively self-contained and confident Hellenic worldview and set of values and literary standards, that is, for style, vocabulary, and formal structures already existed more than a century before the disappearance of the Roman Empire in Western Europe. This self-contained Hellenic worldview permitted the relatively undisturbed continuity and survival of Hellenic culture in a Christian context for more than a millennium more, to the fifteenth century. The arbiters of its unwritten rules and assumptions resided in or traveled between Greek-speaking cities.

Orthodox Christianity became the core constituent, together with Late Antique Greek culture, in the formation of a distinctive Byzantine civilization. The Byzantines lived in a deeply religious society. Orthodox Christianity defined itself in a lengthy and acerbic process between the fourth and eighth centuries. Byzantines retrospectively regarded the eighth- and ninth-century iconoclastic crisis (*see* ICONOCLASM) as its greatest rupture. The triumph of orthodoxy, celebrated on the second Sunday in Lent to commemorate the definitive restoration of ICONS in 843, became a dominant feast day in the liturgical year. The controversy about Iconoclasm and its outcome helped to define some critical characteristics of Byzantine civilization. Only the victorious iconophiles developed a justification for miraculous images. Religious pictures and their veneration became a permanent vital part of that civilization. Devotion to Mary Theotokos (Mother of God) changed. The Virgin received less emphasis as the vessel of the divine and more for her motherhood and receptiveness to prayer. Byzantine spirituality emphasized salvation through the Incarnation itself (some scholars would specify divine condescension in the form of the Incarnation) and the doctrine of icons. Many Byzantine churches exerted a centripetal function, lifting the worshipper's gaze toward the central dome.

The failure of Iconoclasm encouraged conservatism and resistance to religious and intellectual change. Byzantines did not think of their civilization as European or Asian or eastern or western, but insisted that it was orthodox Christian. No simple distinction emerged between the political and the religious. They were not nationalist in any ordinary modern sense nor did most of them have any consciously ethnic sense of identity other than being Roman and Christian. It never required belonging to a specific ethnicity to participate in its civilization. Byzantine civilization is not the conscious expression of any Greek nationalism, for example. Some scholars argue that the Church was the primary creative element in Byzantine culture and even sharply contrast alleged ancient Hellenic rationalism with religion-based Byzantine civilization. Yet Byzantine civilization was never an ecclesiastical monopoly.

Byzantines would normally not have thought in terms of the beginnings of their civilization, but to the extent that any did, they would have conceived of its genesis with Constantine I and the birth of Constantinople, even though Graeco-Roman cultural achievements long preceded his conversion to Christianity. The notion of a beginning for Byzantine civilization is controversial in itself, for many scholars will argue that the essential quality of Byzantine civilization is the absence of any breach in continuity with Graeco-Roman antiquity. Many educated Byzantines later assumed some substantive or qualitative break or change in the early fourth century, even though others would still term the empire as Roman rather than Byzantine. Whatever the Byzantines perceived of Rome they took from Greek historians of the late Hellenistic and Roman periods (e.g., Polybius, Plutarch, Cassius Dio), not through Latin authors, whether historians or not.

The extent to which the Byzantines became self-conscious about their civilization is in dispute. Some

"Last Supper," Byzantine fresco painting in the Church of the Holy Wisdom (Hagia Sophia), 13th Century, Trebizond, Turkey. (©Adam Woolfitt/CORBIS)

would argue that in Byzantium an attitude existed toward continuity with the past (antiquity) that differed from that in the West, one that distinguishes Byzantium. But for others the Byzantine assumption that they were the unique, exclusive descendants of antiquity had tragic consequences that blinded them to achievements and potential of neighboring peoples and cultures. Ecclesiastical authors such as EUSEBIUS OF CAESAREA significantly contributed to the elaboration of ideas of the harmony of emperor, empire, and church. The concept of Constantinople as a second or new Rome emerged by the end of the fourth century. Confidence in eternity and the divinely guarded nature of Constantinople and its emperor and in eternal victory emerged only gradually, but such claims were affirmed by the end of the sixth century.

Byzantines did not specifically or consciously celebrate any superiority of their civilization against that of the West or ISLAM. There was no clash of civilizations in any ideological sense. They did not categorize in terms of civilization. However they sharply differentiated themselves from the world of Islam and, following very old norms of classical Greek literature, from the Persians and their ways or civilization. Like earlier Greeks, they differentiated themselves and their way of life from those of various other barbarians, whether Germanic, Slavic, or Altaic. Byzantine authors conceive of a different way of life inside their empire from that of nomadic peoples and other "barbarians" outside it.

Although Byzantine civilization was profoundly Christian, during its initial century significant contributors were pagan. The pagan component receded significantly by the beginning of the fifth century to a modest but vociferous minority who slowly died out in the fifth and sixth centuries. These included Emperor Julian and other members of his fourth-century intellectual circle, including the rhetorician Libanius and philosopher

Themistius. Other prominent pagan authors were the historians Eunapius of Sardis and Zosimus, the Neoplatonic philosophers Maximus of Ephesus, Hypatia, Proklos, Damascius, Isidore, Horapollon (fifth century) and the poets Claudian and Nonnus. Yet their imprint remained as well as the imprint of the conflict of Christians with pagans. The word Hellene, for a Greek, lost its meaning and normally signified a pagan, until late in the empire's history, and hence usually was avoided, except in reference to the language. The term ''Romania'' refers to a Byzantine world associated with the civilization that is not precisely coterminous with the empire's frontiers. It includes areas that lay within the cultural influence or thought-world, but not necessarily the political or military control, of the Byzantine imperial authorities. The limits of Byzantine civilization extended beyond those of the empire. The extension of Byzantine civilization beyond political borders increased after the fourth century.

Historians now interpret civilization in terms of communications instead of influences, regions instead of capital and provinces, demand instead of supply, consumption and acceptance instead of magisterial roles. These innovations are not superficial word-play, for they reflect changes in the conceptual foundations of Byzantine studies, stimulated as much by new theoretical approaches as by the discovery of new sources. Unresolved issues include whether Byzantine civilization formed from the top down or bottom up, from where did change originate, the extent to which it changed, and the intended audience of consumers for Byzantine civilization. There is much less emphasis than previously on the imperial court and its governmental structure as the creator of Byzantine civilization, whether in the form of artistic workshops or as patrons and sponsors of literature.

Although the Byzantines are said to have disliked the sea and travel, the Mediterranean provided the environment for their civilization. Most of the principal cities in which Byzantine civilization thrived are located on or near its coastline. But the Black Sea enjoyed a more important role for Byzantine civilization than for Graeco-Roman civilization, for economic activities that underlay cultural life. There was no great curiosity for individual travel even though there was some interest in the ancients' geographical knowledge.

For most Byzantines, the indispensable context for civilization was the city. Urbanity was part of being civilized. In the early Byzantine period *paideia* or education or cultivation signified civilization for elites, but that term would not be so common in later centuries. The world was the inhabited or settled world. Cities, as in Graeco-Roman antiquity, were the matrices of intellectual life, creativity and transmission of traditions. For ecclesiastics, whether the clergy or monastics, there might be other contexts, such as the isolated monastery. But Byzantine civilization is inconceivable without the city. Cities provided, at least for the few, the extra comforts of life for those who wished to enjoy the good life.

In contrast to the classical Greek and Roman city, political participation in civic or public life, that is citizenship as a decision maker, became much more passive, even though Byzantines participated actively in the defense of their cities against besiegers, or in church festivals and processions or in viewing games or public spectacles, including punishments. Cities were no longer centers of citizens' public debate and decision-making in the way that many had been in at least portions of Greek and Roman history. Public space in cities assumed different forms in the Byzantine era from that of Graeco-Roman antiquity. Public baths, for example, ceased to have as much importance in accord with changing financial realities and changing Christian attitudes towards public bathing and human body form. Some ancient cities did not entirely disappear or lose all of their economic activities, but most (outside of Constantinople) tended to become smaller and were transformed. Such changes affected Byzantine civilization. Despite ambivalence in Byzantine society and civilization the appearance of wealth persisted until almost its last century.

Although Byzantine civilization centered on Constantinople, its interests and priorities usually concentrated on nearby Asia Minor rather than the hinterlands in the Balkans, for historical reasons. As paradoxical as it seems, Asia Minor was the seat of more distinguished intellectual activity and historical reference in the past than was the Balkans, even though Byzantine civilization would exert greater lasting influence in the Balkans than in western Asia.

The physical environment outside of the cities is important for understanding Byzantine civilization and for understanding how Byzantines viewed the world and created intellectual products. But villages and the countryside also participated in that civilization. The majority of the empire's subjects, as well as adherents to the civilization who resided beyond the empire's borders, lived outside of cities, in the countryside, engaging in agricultural and pastoral activities. The topography of small isolated valleys with inadequate connections between coastal cities and interior and with main trade routes along mountain passes affected Byzantine civilization. Some Byzantines understood the mountains as a wilderness infested with beasts and robbers. They appreciated the town as a place for mild climate, potable water, arable soil and orchards, rest, pleasure and as a cornerstone of Byzantine morality, not as a center of commercial activity. Byzantines feared the mountains and the sea as well as demons and other unseen and capricious powers while they respected and gave obedience to their God, the holy family, and the saints who could intercede for them. Some distinctly Byzantine literary works represent not the city but rural or peripheral perspectives. The prose *Strategikon* of Kekaumenos and the verse epic of *Digenis Akritas* are two such works from the eleventh (the latter possibly from the twelfth) century.

The social context was equally important for Byzantine civilization, which owes much to but is not merely derivative of material and socio-economic conditions and culture. The empire's institutional continuities permitted the preservation and survival of concepts, words, and objects in some cases for more than a millennium, even though notions of meaning may have radically altered during that span. Byzantine civilization existed within a social context. Its values included respect for order, hierarchy, and tradition although there was a fascination with and horror of excess. Some Byzantinists believe that weak social ties and weak urban self-administration characterized Byzantine society and therefore implicitly its civilization, which they regard as introverted. It is not exclusively a derivative of the Byzantine imperial government and its apparatus. The centrality of the nuclear family is basic for Byzantine civilization and relevant to its sense of insecurity. Byzantine civilization existed in a world perceived to be unstable. Violence, natural disasters and poor health were part of normal experience. Ecclesiastics and their churches provided a haven of safety and peace. They were the locus of local Christian social and cultural life. Byzantine traditionalism and conformity provided security and refuge for a society of lonely, insecure individuals. Hence Byzantine civilization more often took written rather than oral form. Its literature addressed the solitary reader. Marriage was honored, but chastity, virginity, and celibacy were even more highly valued. There was concealed and open criticism of society, the imperial structure, and the church. *Oikonomia*, dispensation, allowed overstepping strict boundaries (*akribeia*).

Yet everything was not private. Byzantine civilization included spectacular processions and pomp, gaudy celebrations, which its population enjoyed. Ceremony contributed to stability, a much coveted and rarely achieved condition, and to solidarity. Court life was important but it was restricted to a very few. At court the banquet became refined to a high degree. The games, races, and other activities at the Hippodrome at Constantinople caused it to remain a vital center of public life. Public punishments were sometimes cruel spectacles. Humility and self-abasement were evident in *proskynesis*. Color and the use of semi-precious stones, use of light and its reflections on semi-precious stones, various lusters, sheens, and glitters all constituted indispensable elements of Byzantine civilization. Shades of greens, yellows, and reds and blues were all important. Sounds, scents, and fragrances as well as images and color were integral to this civilization, which expressed itself in such forms as liturgy, chants, acclamations, and music. Most conceded that its hymns, works of mystical devotion and histories and biographies constitute some of its best products. Its music brought new hymns and melodies to devotion. Its literature reflects otherworldliness as well as practical commonsense (such as treatises on warfare, mechanics, agriculture). PSEUDO-DIONYSIUS THE AREOPAGITE and Hesychast writers such as St. GREGORY PALAMAS or mystics such as SYMEON THE NEW THEOLOGIAN wrote some of its best works of devotion.

Visual culture is one of the most exiting dimensions of Byzantine civilization, whether in the dimension of painting, ivory carving, architecture, glassware, bronze casting, amulets, lamps, mosaics, or textiles. Fine glass, colored or uncolored, was an important Byzantine product. It was used for vessels, for dishes, and sometimes for receiving representations. Artistic products were created from products of local and imported provenance. The prestige and at least superficial attractiveness of Byzantine production of some objects reveals itself through the hoarded treasures of precious metalwork, textiles, and glassware that are fine examples of Byzantine workmanship. The imperial coinage itself, especially its gold coinage, symbolized Byzantine civilization and its prestige in the eyes of many.

Famous examples of Byzantine civilization on any list include: HAGIA SOPHIA in Constantinople, the Chora church or Kariye Cami, San Vitale in Ravenna, S. Apollinare in Classe, at Ravenna, the monastery complexes of MOUNT ATHOS, exquisite work in silver plate, such as the David Plates, and other ecclesiastical plate, manuscript miniature art, ivory carvings of diverse types, mosaics, beautiful reliquaries, fine silk textiles, and bindings and covers for manuscripts both secular and religious. More controversial is the imputation of ideological significance to these objects and monuments.

Church fairs (*panegyreis*) and distant and nearby pilgrimages were essential parts of daily life and devotional activity and spirituality for men and women. Byzantine civilization possessed ambivalence due to the opposition of centrifugal and centripetal forces, tensions between the impulse to asceticism and that to enjoyment of a joyful and tolerant way of life, conformity and nonconformity. Holy men were important in this society and civilization, but it is incorrect to posit a dichotomy between holy men and bishops. They are not normally represented as rivals in the literature or art. Normally they acted cooperatively or in harmony, not as mutual opponents. Byzantine hagiography describes the progress of the saint through stages of recognition, a life of perceived holiness, and the sources of saintly power, which may become manifest in personal, medical and social dimensions, including ecclesiastical, monastic, and political.

Although Byzantine civilization articulated itself primarily in the Greek language, other languages such as Latin, Armenian, Georgian, and Slavic were also mediums for its expression and elaboration. Byzantine governmental business was normally conducted in Greek after the early sixth century. Some Latin commands persisted in the army until the beginning of the seventh century and the coinage retained Latin until the eighth century. Various individuals may have spoken other languages in their childhood households and may have retained the ability to speak in that vernacular, but public discourse normally was in Greek. Because the empire drew on diverse peoples, many loan words entered the vocabulary for specialized purposes, although high-style usage normally avoided recourse to them. Only a very limited knowledge of written Latin existed after the sixth century, until the Council of Lyon in 1274 and imperatives of ecclesiastical communication with the West stimulated a modest increase in its study. By the fourteenth century Byzantine civilization was intertwined with global civilization of the Mediterranean and beyond.

Byzantium developed a set of beliefs that were not entirely coherent or consistent. It contained pluralism and diversity but its tolerance of diversity and alterity varied. There was a world of demons as well as a heavenly ideal. Rivalries and cleavages affected Byzantine civilization. One of Byzantine civilization's greatest contributions to world civilization was written in Latin not Greek: the compilation and editing of the *Corpus Juris Civilis* in the sixth century at the behest of Emperor Justinian I (527–65). Despite studied avoidance of Latinisms in high-style prose and verse, Latin maintained its prestige on certain occasions to assert and validate the empire's and its subjects' claim to be Roman. The gradual fading of the importance of Latin in the fifth and sixth century accelerated with the elimination of the requirement for Latin literacy for certain important bureaucratic offices as well as the loss of Latin-speaking areas of the Balkans and the impoverishment and subsequent loss of control of Latin-speaking north Africa and most of Italy by the beginning of the eighth century.

Located along the eastern shores of the Mediterranean Byzantine civilization drew on many varied intellectual and cultural riches of that region. A multiplicity and network of cities, including Smyrna, Ephesus, Alexandria, Antioch in Syria, Antioch in Pisidia, Prusa, Nicomedeia, Sardis, Beyrut, Gaza, Caesarea Maritima (Palestine), Gadara, Gerasa, and Jerusalem, all helped create urban contexts in which rhetoricians, artists, philosophers, physicians could develop and thrive. All this was fragile, for it depended on sufficient economic prosperity and public encouragement and enthusiasm to provide sufficient surplus to support scholarship, inquiry, discourse, and creation of artistic and architectural and musical products to embellish cities and society.

In contrast to the earliest period, in which there were multiple urban centers in which civilization and culture flourished, after the early Islamic conquests and the concomitant loss of territory in the west, Constantinople became the culturally dominant metropolis, in ways that it was not in the fourth century, when intellectuals at Antioch and Alexandria and other cities of Asia Minor competed against it and sometimes resented its rise to intellectual prominence.

Byzantine civilization communicated with the West in many different ways, with respect to liturgy, literature, and art, especially from the fourth through eighth centuries, but on to the twelfth century in visual domains. Likewise communication existed between Latin and Greek in the earliest three centuries, although most heavily with respect to law, and then again in logic and other aspects of learning in the fourteenth and early fifteenth centuries. Communication with the West never wholly disappeared. Some Byzantine pagans (e.g., the neo-Platonist Damascius) perceived that Rome had ''fallen'' and hoped that other pagans would revive or restore it. These were a shrill and untypical minority. The majority of Byzantines may well not have shared this pessimistic assessment of late Roman conditions in the West. However it is wrong to assert that no one used the verb ''fall'' in speaking of the condition of Rome. Some eastern constituencies with admitted agendas did perceive and lament what they saw as a collapse in the west.

Even in the so-called ''dark'' seventh and eighth centuries more communication and contacts existed with the central and western Mediterranean than has been hitherto assumed. Despite its lack of travelers to other societies Byzantine civilization never completely insulated itself from others. Western customs such as jousting became popular in elite circles during the twelfth century.

Byzantine and Latin civilizations or cultures were closely interrelated and even interwoven, even though each reacted against the other in rivalry and hostility. A complex process of acculturation took place. No perfect synthesis ever formed between Greek and Latin cultures. Within the civilization existed sub-groups with their own cultures, such as Jews, Armenians, Georgian, Slavs, and Christian Arabs.

The designation of periods in Byzantine civilization is necessarily subjective and controversial. Byzantine and Roman civilization overlap. Some would classify as Byzantine what others would classify as Roman or Late Antique or Early Medieval. The Age of Justinian I, the tenth century, the eleventh century, the late thirteenth and early fourteenth centuries all have claims to intellectual brilliance. One of the greatest problems is understanding what happened to Byzantine learning in the Dark Ages, between approximately 640 and 800, that is, between the end of the ages of Emperor Heraclius and Isaurian dynasty (end of reign of the iconodule Empress Irene) respectively. The silence of the sources contrasts with the evident flowering of intellectual life after 800. Presumably some intellectuals and education continued and someone preserved manuscripts but mysteries and theories abound concerning conditions and developments.

Some admirers of Byzantine civilization argue that it surpassed Latin civilization in an early phase, from the fourth through the early eleventh (others might sharply dispute that), followed by a period of confrontation from 1095 to 1261 (First Crusade to the Byzantine recovery by Emperor Michael VIII of Constantinople from its Crusader occupiers), antagonism from 1261 to 1453 (duration of the final Byzantine imperial dynasty, the Palaeologi), amalgamation after 1453 (fall of Constantinople to Ottoman Sultan Muḥammad II). Some Byzantines developed a fear of Latin cultural penetration and dominance, of cultural transformation, especially after 1095 and even more so after 1204. Latin theological dynamism and growing technological superiority stimulated fears of cultural Latinization. Opponents of reunion of the Orthodox and Catholic churches after the schism of 1054 also tended to resist Latin culture even though diplomacy concerning reunion, especially during the Council of Ferrara-Florence from 1437 to 1439, intensified cultural exchanges between Latins and Greeks. Antiunionist ranks included Mark Eugenicus, Lucas Notaras, and Gennadius Scholarius. There was an ineluctable choice between Turkish conquest or religious and cultural assimilation. These fears encouraged the careful and meticulous preservation of traditional Greek religion and culture.

Byzantine civilization's conception of antiquity drew little directly from Latin authors, whether Cicero, Livy or Tacitus, or Early Christian Latin Fathers such as Tertullian, Augustine or Jerome. It preserved memory of some Roman titulature and institutions, although sometimes in a skewed and very antiquarian fashion. Compared with what evolved in western civilization, it has a stronger admixture of Armenian, Syrian, and other west Asian and Egyptian influences. It peaked earlier than western European civilization, in most aspects excluding the visual arts and architecture—by the end of the tenth century or early eleventh. The reasons for its failure to compete successfully with the West are debatable. It lacked the vital variety of municipal contexts that stimulated many kinds of intellectual activity in western Europe from the late eleventh century. It faced greater external threats from the middle of the eleventh century that diverted its attention and material resources. But its writers and leaders coped as best they could. To some critics, it represents a case of arrested development. Others will argue that despite a devotion to the past Byzantines managed to adapt resourcefully to changing conditions and did not merely cling to conservation. Byzantine civilization was not immutable. It adjusted and evolved, however slowly due to its contacts with other civilizations, whether those of Islam or the West, especially in the fourteenth century.

Byzantine interest in Latin writers swelled in the thirteenth century. Polymaths such as Maximos Planudes translated Cicero, Ovid, Boethius, and Pseudo-Cato and other Latin authors. In the fourteenth century Demetrios Cydones and his student Manuel Calecas read and translated Latin ecclesiastical writers including Augustine and Aquinas. Another scholar who investigated Latin scholarship was Andreas Chrysoberges. This trend culminated in Cardinal Bessarion's collection and study of Greek manuscripts in the fifteenth century.

Byzantine civilization's final theological controversy was HESYCHASM. Through meditation believers sought a momentary glimpse of the uncreated divine light and a brief enjoyment of that union with God that Orthodox Christians thought every Christian could attain. Opponents led by BARLAAM THE CALABRIAN questioned the addition in devotional exercises of a new special posture, control of breathing, and repetition of a short prayer. By 1341 proponents of Hesychasm, led by St. Gregory Palamas, won definitive victory and condemnation of their opposition.

Some interpret Byzantine civilization as pluralist in its initial centuries but taking on a negative and intolerant narrow Hellenic form later. Some argue that the splendor of its classical inheritance paralyzed other cultural initiatives, causing some supposed sterility. However its civilization was never a multicultural paradise. There was always ethnic stereotyping and new inputs created backlashes. Its adherents did not cherish and value highly the diversity that actually existed within its midst.

The issue of Byzantine intolerance for intellectual diversity is complex. Several periods are candidates for a narrowing of intellectual inquiry: (1) the end of the fourth and beginning of the fifth century (2) the Age of Justinian, with the alleged closing of Platonic academy in Athens (3) the triumph of orthodoxy at the end of the iconoclastic controversy, and (4) the early Comnenian period, most notably, the trial and conviction of philosopher John Italos (1082).

Byzantine civilization existed on much of the same physical terrain that some earlier ancient eastern civilizations had occupied. Cities and towns and their fortifications and connecting routes bore the imprint of earlier peoples. Remains of ancient theaters and temples occupied many Byzantine urban sites. Byzantine fortifications occupied locations that often had served as strategic points for earlier peoples and polities. But beyond the more obvious debts to buildings, architecture and infrastructure of the classical world, there was an underlying ancient Near Eastern one, to which Byzantium owed some vague debt in manifold ways. Sealings and other techniques of control, procedures for record-keeping and internal security, many sites of habitation, symbols possibly including the double-headed eagle and even the protocol of the banquet and assassinations at lavish banquets and even *proskynesis* (prostration) have ancient eastern precedents, even though the Byzantines knew very little about most of those civilizations except through the filter of Herodotus or the Septuagint. The relationship of Byzantine practices with respect to these ancient Near Eastern practices may be very tenuous or even false, but scholars need to be mindful that precedents may not originate in the third through seventh centuries; they may have very much more ancient precedents that resurfaced after long gaps, for a variety of reasons.

The civilization owed much to its development and maturation in an already very old bureaucratic empire, which elaborated many techniques of sealing and authentication and control. We have only limited knowledge of the unwritten lore that passed down within bureaucratic circles. That secular and ecclesiastical bureaucratic culture preserved, adapted, and transmitted an intellectual heritage.

The empire's monasteries for their part also preserved, adapted and created intellectual products and a heritage. Three types of monasticism arose: eremitical (solitary), coenobitical (communal), and, especially widespread starting in the tenth and eleventh centuries, the lavriote (a combination of the above two types, with monks living in a loosely affiliated community or *lavra* under a *hegoumenos* or abbot). Prominent early monasteries included Egypt's St. Menas, White and Red Monasteries and Isauria's Alahan Monastery, all of which already existed in the fifth century. The Middle Byzantine Period witnessed the founding of St. John of Stoudion and in the tenth century both the Mount Athos complex and Hosios Loukas while Nea Mone appeared on the island of Chios before 1042. The monastery of St. John arose on Patmos early in the twelfth century. Monasticism received honor, devotion and imperial and private financial support and attention. Byzantine monastic houses were not parts of specific international orders. Although subject to the episcopate they depended on the discretion of their founders and were less strictly regulated than those in western Europe. Monks took the initiative in theology, cultivation of icons, and in shaping piety and religious priorities. At times they enjoyed a popular and even evangelical role among the populace, which enabled some of them to mobilize popular opinion effectively on religious issues. Notable monastic writers include Maximus the Confessor, Theodore the Studite, and Symeon the New Theologian, respectively in the seventh, early ninth and eleventh centuries.

Any evaluation of Byzantine civilization requires understanding of the survival, transformation, and transmission of selected parts of ancient Greek literature, philosophy, and science. The Byzantines preserved and adapted parts of that heritage in accordance with their own values and needs as their elites understood them; they developed a historiography that adapted traditional rules of historical composition in Greek to the shifted realities of a Christian world. Their use of classical Greek ethnic designations for some neighboring peoples reveals their conscious imitation of their Hellenic literary heritage.

The Byzantines preserved much ancient learning in order to use it for imitation themselves or for others to use and emulate. St. Basil of Caesarea had legitimized the utility of reading selected ancient Hellenic authors. So the propensity to imitate resulted in much selective preservation of ancient dicta, verse, and wisdom. Byzantine literary critics developed a repertory of classical Greek and early Byzantine and patristic authors who terminate in the eighth century. Later Byzantine authors of prose and verse did not become comparable models for imitation. The *enkyklike paideia* was a cycle of higher curriculum of literature and grammar. It emphasized rhetoric and philosophy, although arithmetic, geometry, astronomy, music received some, but lesser, attention. Favorite classical authors included Homer, Lucian, and Plutarch, although Isocrates, Thucydides, and Herodotus also enjoyed popularity. Some scholars argue that there is a break in the quality of classical scholarship in Byzantium after 1350.

The heritage of early Christian martyrs and patristic writing was also important. Seminal were the writings of ORIGEN, CLEMENT OF ALEXANDRIA, ATHANASIUS OF ALEXANDRIA, JOHN CHRYSOSTOM, and JOHN OF DAMASCUS. Some of the most important achievements of Byzantine theologians were formulation of Trinitarian and Christological theology in the fourth and fifth centuries.

Books were very expensive and hard to find. Parchment replaced increasingly scarce papyrus for books by the seventh or eighth century. Paper eventually, especially after the eleventh or twelfth century, spread first from northern Syria, then from Italy, as the medium for writing. Rare are the accounts that provide information about holdings in personal libraries, especially in the provinces. Private libraries were far apart and rare. Transmission and preservation of Byzantine civilization thus depended heavily on a small group of urban elite scholars, estimated to number perhaps 500 in later centuries of the empire. Constantinople provided the urban context for this civilization after the empire gradually lost control of other major Mediterranean cities. The Patriarchal school at Constantinople was a particularly important center of learning. However, it is incorrect to speak of a ''university'' in the medieval Western sense at Constantinople. There were scholars who received government salaries to offer public instruction in law, rhetoric, and grammar, but these were really schools, not universities. There was no building or grounds to house them. Caesar Bardas was an important patron of public instruction in the ninth century. The ninth century profited from the erudition of three major intellects: John the Grammarian, Leo the Mathematician, and Photios. Among its foremost philosophers were Michael Psellos in the eleventh century and George Gemistos Plethon in the fifteenth.

Educational structures for young children vanished in the course of the seventh century, although monastic schools provided some basic education to limited numbers of boys thereafter. It is impossible to estimate the rate of literacy with confidence. Memorization was a basic tool in education.

The concept of *taxis* or order or harmonious hierarchy is an important value for Byzantines. So is *mimesis*, imitation, including *theomimesis* and *Christomimesis*. Each person had a place in the order, which was an imperfect imitation of celestial order. Byzantine civilization includes but is not synonymous with a Byzantine worldview or conceptual universe or mentality. Byzantines assumed their empire was protected by God, Christ, and the Virgin Mary. From the fourth century, most Byzantines assumed the congruence of the fortunes of emperor, empire, and church, whether positive or negative. Byzantines assumed that there could be debate and dissent about ecclesiastical topics. The concept of CAESAROPAPISM, exercise of supreme authority over ecclesiastical affairs by a secular sovereign, is a modern concept that some emperors, such as Justinian I or possibly Leo III, may unconsciously have sought to implement, but it was never an explicit ideal and it was never universally accepted and adopted and was never codified in writing.

Continuity of classical forms in literature and medicine and art works persisted as late as the initial decades of the seventh century, after which the attenuation of financial means and decreased demand reduced the market. It becomes difficult to trace continuing forms of secular education and production of sumptuous objects in a classicizing style after 650. But some criticize the Byzantine impulse to perfect imitation as a tragic problem: representing itself as the exclusive and true descendant of antiquity, it became hopelessly entangled in and dulled by the process of imitation.

Intellectual activity and literary production flourished in certain categories and waned in others. Its education was based on the study of rhetoric, as was the case in the Hellenistic world. Rhetoric was important, a modified heritage from the classical past. A related form of rhetoric that elaborated itself into a highly polished form in the early Byzantine period was the sermon. The influence of sermons or public orations was probably enormous in a world of few books or other stimulants to thinking. Superb homiletic examples come from such Cappadocian Saints as Saint Basil of Caesarea, St. Gregory of Nazianzus, St. John Chrysostom. The homily had reached a perfected form by the end of the fifth century.

Distinctive literary forms include the verse form of *kontakion* (a specific form of hymn or sermon in verse, in the sixth and seventh centuries), and the Byzantine epic of Digenis Akritas (eleventh or twelfth century). Prescriptive lists of vocabulary were also important. More traditional genre included epistolography and speeches. Byzantines polished the chronicle form as well as the saints' lives. Some Byzantines composed apologias against Islam, Jews, and to a lesser degree, refutations of Latin errors. Apocalypticism and exegesis were two other forms of religious writing and thought. Byzantine lexicographers were active, including Thomas Magister in the fourteenth century. Eustathius of Thessalonica produced an important commentary on the *Iliad*. The liturgy and the related liturgical calendar were also important. Lectionaries became exquisite objects in public religious culture.

Theodore Balsamon assembled the most substantial collection of Byzantine Canon Law. Ecclesiastical canon studies flourished in the eleventh, twelfth and fourteenth centuries; however they never took the elaborate form and legal status in the Byzantine world that they developed in western Europe.

Women participated in Byzantine civilization in many ways, which included church feasts, cult of the Virgin, saints and their cults, foundation and maintenance of nunneries, monasteries, patronization of holy men, encouragement of religious pictures and their cults. One of the most important Byzantine historians was Anna Komnene (twelfth century). Nevertheless women often did lack equal access to education including literacy. Of course they encouraged and stimulated much cultural activity as well, patronizing poets and other authors. Some, like the fifth-century Empress Eudokia and the ninth-century Kassia, were poets. Women's philanthropic roles were very significant from the beginning to the end of Byzantium.

The Greek language continued to evolve. Although Attic Greek and the Second Sophistic influenced high-style writing and vocabulary and grammar, a virtual diglossy evolved that graduated separated spoken forms of the language from written Greek. There was a snobbery, which may owe something to the insecure status of many practioners. Bureaucrats were familiar with and used classicizing rhetorical language together with very technical administrative and fiscal terminology from Late Roman governmental usage. Rhetoricians were expected to say the appropriate things and use the appropriate language and style. The process had begun before the Byzantine era, but it continued unabated. The ancient Greek heritage of drama was relatively unimportant. Byzantines produced vernacular verse romances but did not develop the vernacular for prose. The resolution of linguistic difficulties persisted as a challenge into the twentieth and twenty-first centuries in Greece. Hagiography and some chronicles (e.g., John Malalas, sixth century) provide some of the most useful hints about changes in the spoken language.

At the high-style end of literary production, the Byzantine author, reader and auditor might be attentive to allusions and associations from a repertory of Greek and Biblical literature. It was possible for the educated few to know some lines from age-old Greek poets and rhetoricians and philosophers. Literary and artistic perceptions of and by the Byzantines are only partially understood today, and our perception of them differs considerably from what scholars assumed a few decades ago. Scholarship has only begun to analyze and reflect on how the Byzantines themselves visualized things and concepts. We are still trying to understand what the Byzantines saw when they contemplated a painting or architectural or sculptural detail. It is uncertain what we may be missing. The broader public seldom had an accurate understanding of the identification of surviving ancient statuary, but their interests and beliefs about it derived from different perspectives. Intellectuals competed in erudition and for literary fame at and near the court and within privileged circles at Constantinople. This competition did not involve the broader urban let alone the rural population.

Criticism and evaluation of Byzantine civilization has taken many forms and has changed. Earlier treatises on civilization often criticized Byzantine civilization as essentially the infiltration of Oriental ideas to tinge Graeco-Roman traditions, and the periodic reaction to that process, as representative of decline, decay or other negative features (corruption), but these have long since become obsolete. Those criticisms often depended on narrow and now outmoded defining criteria of classicism as the benchmark of quality and style. They criticize it as lacking creative spontaneity or for adherence to stiff conventionality. Byzantine scholars failed to construct mental systems from first principles and hence lacked systematization, they lacked specialization, and were too unadventurous and too inward-looking. Historians no longer conceive of Byzantine civilization in triumphalist fashion primarily as a medieval bulwark of Europe against Islam.

Some extreme critics call Byzantine civilization a withered and culturally impoverished entity, even a shriveled de-Romanized skeleton, and question whether survival was better than extinction, a civilization in which literature lapsed into obscurity. To some contemporaries it was a closed and arrogant civilization. For them it was and may still be an object of resentment. But it impressed many so much that that they respected and emulated it even though they disliked and resented it. Likewise there is an issue of coping with change. Byzantine civilization has been accused of extreme conservatism, but that depends on which century and which aspect is under investigation. Issues of rationality, irrationality, and intolerance are important in any evaluation of Byzantine civilization. It has attracted some as curious and strange and convoluted, confused with the concepts associated with the pejorative adjective Byzantine that has existed for more than a century in popular usage. The civilization had genuine complexity, even though modern pundits have caricatured it in clichés as excessively complicated and even convoluted.

Contributions of Byzantine civilization include preservation of the following components: (1) pagan Hellenistic culture (2) Roman tradition in law and government, including jurisprudence (3) Christian ecclesiastical Hellenistic models (4) Greek and Hellenistic language, literature, and philosophy (4) historical records and memory (5) Christian tradition refashioned on a Greek model. Beyond its role in preservation its civilization created an important missionary church with multiple successful missions, vital centers of monasticism, and seminal and lively religious art. Some argue that the civilization of

Europe is a by product of the Byzantine Empire's will to survive.

Two periods in which Byzantine civilization most energetically and most successfully extended its attractions beyond imperial frontiers were the fourth through sixth centuries, and again in the late ninth. Byzantine civilization exerted a strong attraction or pull on Serbs, Bulgars, and Russians. Armenians and Georgians has a mixed reaction to it, as did Muslims. Patriarch Photius at the beginning of the 860s encouraged the unsuccessful mission of Constantine (Cyril) and Methodius to Moravia to convert the Moravians with the assistance of a newly devised Slavic alphabet and newly translated devotional works. But their labors soon bore fruit in Bulgaria where Khan Boris' conversion to Christianity in 870 brought Bulgaria and soon other south Slavic peoples permanently into the orbit of Orthodox Christianity and Byzantine civilization. The conversion of Prince Vladimir resulted in conversion of Kievan Russia in 989, an event with enormous political and cultural consequences, even though the process of the Christianization of Russia required much time. The most significant role of Byzantine civilization in influencing others involved the Slavic world, both that of the South Slavs and that of Russia. Byzantine influences were extremely important in the Caucasus as well. Russian inventories of objects in Kiev and early Muscovy indicate the continuing local prestige of Byzantine civilization despite its waning political and military fortunes.

If one examines self-consciousness, self-reflexivity and the civilizing process rather than the civilization as a holistic entity, the Byzantines possessed no impulse or imperative to civilize let alone conquer or transform the entire inhabited world as they understood it. Their secular and ecclesiastical leaders did seek to send out missionaries to convert non-Christians. They did not however seek to convert Muslims or to hellenize western Europe. Ecclesiastical leaders did seek in specific instances and localities to extend their control and appointive power over Christian churches. Although some Byzantines possessed visions of the end of the world and their empire, there was no collective will to implement policies that would accomplish that objective.

Influential for one aspect of European thought was Byzantine military literature and science, which developed from an accumulated heritage of Hellenistic military manuals as well as from Greek ones of the Roman Empire. These preserved, adapted and transmitted lore of craft and stratagems and prudence as well as diagrams of specific formations of cavalry and infantry. Military thinkers in early modern Europe borrowed and applied some of the information from those Byzantine treatises for their own purposes. The word strategy itself in French and English traces back to the use of the concept by the late eighteenth-century French theorist Joly de Maizeroy who borrowed it from his reading of MAURICE's *Strategikon*, a Byzantine text from *c.* A.D. 600. This is a little studied and poorly known aspect of Byzantine intellectual activity, but its influence extended far beyond the borders of the empire and continued far beyond the demise of the empire. This needs to be appreciated in a broader perspective. Although a tradition of ancient Greek military manuals stimulated a continuing tradition of writing military manuals, and Byzantium inherited and transformed rituals of the military triumph from Rome, warfare and military victory were not the preeminent values for this civilization. Warfare was a common experience, yet Byzantine civilization was not overly militaristic.

Two of the most important documents of Byzantine civilization are compilations under the authority and initiative of Emperor Constantine VII Porphyrogenitus: his *De Administrando Imperio*, and his *De Caerimoniis*, respectively manuals on how to handle foreign relations with neighboring peoples, whether hostile or friendly, and a diverse group of imperial ceremonials for different ordinary and unique occasions. Both reveal some of the most distinctive aspects of Byzantine civilization. The ceremonies and pageants contain accretions from many different periods and places within Byzantine history. They display different examples of the preservation, filtering, and transmission of antiquarian lore that is elaborated for practical purposes and to bedazzle the foreign visitor, to emphasize the uniqueness and special mission of the empire and its leadership.

Excerpting and encyclopedism are other significant features of Byzantine civilization. Florilegia were important to Byzantines. Encyclopedias like the *Suda* typify some of the best accomplishments and limitations of Byzantine civilization. Others might put the *Bibliotheke* of Photios (late ninth century) among the most important Byzantine works of reference and other anthologies of ancient Greek literature and vocabulary.

Recording and understanding the past were important. Time is reckoned in indictions (15-year tax cycles), regnal years, years since creation of the world, or occasionally since the foundation of Constantinople. Although there were apocalyptic fears about the end of the world, these were not founded on any fears of millennial dating from the birth of Christ. Historiography, including ecclesiastical history and hagiography, the chronicle, narrative history in imitation of great examples from earlier Greek historical writing, are all examples of Byzantine historiography and preservation or recovery of memory.

They explain continuity and unfolding of God's purpose on earth, the Roman empire's place in universal history, divine judgment through natural and human disasters and experiences. Among its best historians are Procopius of Caesarea (sixth century), who was a superb and detailed and observant reporter, Michael Psellos (eleventh century), Niketas Choniates (late twelfth-early thirteenth century). Kinnamos, George Akropolites, and George Pachymeres wrote useful if uninspired narratives, but that of Pachymeres is vitally important for understanding the late thirteenth century. The histories of Nicephorus Gregoras and John Cantacuzenus are deeply imbedded in the political and religious controversies of the fourteenth century. None of these created any new philosophy of history or new historical method. Chronicles often had a straightforward religious purpose: to record absolute chronology, including the meaning of time in God's plan for salvation. There is a narrative with a clear plot, through it one made sense of the present. The sequence of Byzantine historical prefaces with inspiration from ancient Greek prefaces is a reasonably continuous one that stretches to the end of the empire, to Critoboulos of Imbros. The corpus of Byzantine historical writings provides a record and perspective, however imperfect, that stretches eleven hundred years. Much of it is Constantinopleocentric, and focused on the imperial court, with many omissions concerning those at the social and economic bottom, but it is an invaluable narrative from the perspective of the northeast Mediterranean. Without it historical knowledge of southeastern Europe, western Asia, and the eastern Mediterranean and Black Sea would be much poorer.

Byzantine historical memory was selective. But historical memory primarily existed for members of the learned elite and clergy, not for the majority of the population. World chronicles, which commenced with creation and evolved from very early Christian models, took a different form and simpler style, but provided more precise chronology than some narrative histories. Priorities did not lie with historical knowledge of classical antiquity, even though some of its individuals and writers acted as models for action and literary style while earlier church fathers, whether Greek, Latin, or Syrian, acted as models for religious devotion and action. The autobiographical writings of thirteenth-century authors Nikephoros Blemmydes and Gregory of Cyprus are important examples of that genre.

Byzantine civilization formed part of the intellectual environment in which Islamic civilization developed along the Mediterranean littoral. Byzantine civilization left an imprint on parts of Africa, especially Ethiopia, and related parts of the south Arabian peninsula. The role of Byzantine civilization in the Arabian peninsula, including north and central Arabia, is poorly understood and very controversial. Influences of Byzantine civilization on medieval Muslim societies may be more difficult to perceive but exist nonetheless. They range from word loans to art forms to architecture to shipping and maritime law. The process of translation and exchange of learning between the Muslim and Byzantine worlds intensified in the ninth and tenth centuries.

Humanism existed in Byzantium, especially in two periods: the ninth and tenth and again in the thirteenth through fifteenth centuries. External appreciation of Byzantine civilization expanded in the era of humanism as a limited number of Italian humanists sampled and appreciated aspects of what they considered to be ancient Greek learning, although it was difficult for them to separate out the Byzantine aspects, which they did not appreciate so much. The prestige of Byzantine civilization probably reached its nadir in the eighteenth or early nineteenth century. Mistra in the Peloponnesus (so-called Despotate of the Morea) briefly served as an important center of Byzantine civilization in the fourteenth and early fifteenth centuries, even though financial resources were limited. Scholars such as George Gemistos Plethon were active there. Painting and architecture also managed to flourish. That flowering terminated with the Ottoman conquest of Mistra in 1460. As financial resources dwindled, the dimensions of architecture whether public and secular or ecclesiastical also became more modest.

Many scholars see a breakdown in Byzantine civilization, but disagree concerning its date. The dating of an irrevocable crisis and breakdown in the Byzantine intellectuals' confidence and worldview is not an easy task. For some it is the early fourteenth century, in the writings of Theodore Metochites, for others it can be as early as the eleventh-century historian Michael Attaleiates' pessimism about conditions. Others might even find Emperor Constantine VII or his father Leo VI the Wise already recognizing and lamenting decay.

Byzantine civilization did not die on May 29, 1453, but continued to influence Greeks under Turkish and foreign rule as well as the culture of modern Greece and surrounding countries. Knowledge of Byzantine civilization is indispensable for understanding the culture of the early modern and contemporary Balkans and for understanding the culture of Greece and Greeks during the Ottoman and post-Ottoman periods. However post-Byzantine cultural phenomena cannot be the ultimate lens or benchmark by which to evaluate Byzantine civilization.

Bibliography: G. BOWERSOCK, P. BROWN, and O. GRABAR, eds., *Interpreting Late Antiquity* (Cambridge MA 2001). P. BROWN, *Power and Persuasion in Late Antiquity: Towards a Christian Empire* (Madison, WI 1992). A. CAMERON, ed., *Cambridge Ancient*

History v. 13–14;, *The Mediterranean World in Late Antiquity* (London 1993); *Byzantine Books and Bookmen* (Washington 1975). R. CORMACK, *Writing in Gold: Byzantine Society and Its Icons* (Oxford 1985). H. EVANS and W. WIXOM, eds., *Glory of Byzantium: Art and Culture of the Middle Byzantine Period* (New York 1997). D. GEANAKOPLOS, *Interaction of the "Sibling" Byzantine and Western Cultures in the Middle Ages and Italian Renaissance* (New York 1976). A. GUILLOU, *La civilization byzantine* (Paris 1974). A. KAZHDAN and G. CONSTABLE, *People and Power in Byzantium* (Washington 1982). A. KAZHDAN, ed. *Oxford Dictionary of Byzantium,* 3 v. (Oxford 1991). P. LEMERLE, *Byzantine Humanism: The First Phase,* tr. H. LINDSAY and A. MOFFATT (Canberra 1986). J. H. W. LIEBESCHUETZ, *The Decline and Fall of the Roman City* (Oxford 2001). H. MAGUIRE, ed., *Byzantine Court Culture from 829 to 1204* (Washington 1997). P. MAGDALINO, *The Empire of Manuel I Komnenos* (Cambridge 1996). C. A. MANGO, *Byzantium: The Empire of New Rome* (New York 1994). J. MEYENDORFF, *Byzantium and the Rise of Russia* (Cambridge 1981). D. M. NICOL *Church and Society in the Last Centuries of Byzantium* (Cambridge 1979). I. SEVCENKO, *Ideology, Letters and Culture in the Byzantine World* (Aldershot, VT 1982). A. J. TOYNBEE*Constantine Porphyrogenitus and His World* (Oxford 1973). K. WEITZMANN, ed. *The Age of Spirituality* (Princeton 1979). N. G. WILSON, *Scholars of Byzantium* (London 1996).

[W. E. KAEGI]

BYZANTINE EMPIRE, THE

The Byzantine Empire (*Basileia ton Rhomaion*) is the scholarly designation of the section of the Roman Empire that survived in the eastern Mediterranean after the disappearance of Roman control in its western European provinces. It takes the name Byzantine from Byzantium, the name of the city founded as a colony of the ancient Greek city of Miletus. Emperor CONSTANTINE I renamed the city CONSTANTINOPLE for himself and rededicated it in respective ceremonies in 324 and on May 11, 330. Although institutional historians may date the commencement of the empire in A.D. 284, the Byzantines themselves usually looked back to 330. Legislation from the reign of Constantine I also framed their outlook on jurisprudence, because only occasionally did they look to earlier Roman precedents and jurisprudence of eras before Christian predominance within the empire. But Byzantine imperial symbols, institutions, bureaucracy, and visual culture all have their origins much earlier. The empire's formal name remained the Roman Empire, its head of state was the emperor of the Romans (*Basileus ton Rhomaion*) and its subjects continued to call themselves Romans (*Rhomaio*). No written constitution ever existed. In a vestigial sense, legitimacy remained with the senate and people. Gradually Roman law evolved into Byzantine law. Most, perhaps 80–90 percent of the empire's population, lived in the countryside from agricultural or pastoral occupations in any period of Byzantine history. Life expectancy was relatively short, infant mortality was high. There is no accurate estimate for the empire's total population, which probably peaked in the 6th century.

Periodization is imperfect, but traditionally historians often conveniently subdivide the history of the Byzantine Empire from A.D. 330 to 602, Early Byzantine Period; 610–1025 or 1081, Middle Byzantine Period; and 1025 to 1453, Late Byzantine. Older terminology that contrasted Later Roman with Eastern Roman periods (perhaps commencing the latter in A.D. 800 or 802) has become obsolete. These are modern historical constructions, not those of Byzantines, who often conceived time in stages beginning with the creation of the world, the reign of Augustus Caesar, the establishment of Constantinople under Constantine I, followed by respective imperial dynasties. Byzantine history is not merely an extension of ancient Greek or Roman or Western medieval history. It is a subject in its own right that deserves serious investigation without imposing criteria and frames of reference from other historical periods or regions. Yet it cannot be studied in complete isolation from other fields, with which it overlaps.

In the early period, the Byzantine Empire includes regions directly under the authority of the emperor at Constantinople, not that under his colleague at Rome or Ravenna. Hence in the early period before JUSTINIAN I, its territories included Thrace, Moesia (Bulgaria), Asiatic Turkey, Syria, parts of Armenia, Jordan, Israel, Palestine, Egypt, and eastern Libya (Cyrenaica), Cyprus, islands in Aegean, and Crete. Justinian I will add Tripolitania, Tunisia, eastern Algeria, a strip of the southern Spanish coast from approximately the modern Portuguese-Spanish frontier to a point just below Valencia and the opposing northernmost tip of Morocco (Septem, or Ceuta), Sicily, Sardinia, Corsica, Italy, and the Dalmatian coast.

The Byzantine imperial archives do not survive. Only a few documents, such as laws, speeches, letters, and memoirs, however biased, remain. Byzantium was an empire that was conscious of and that used its history and the mystique of its history to maximize its prestige. It had a long memory. Its narrative historians emphasize political and military history from the perspective of Constantinople and imperial elites and often specific dynastic interests, not from the perspective of the majority of its subjects who have left us no narrative accounts of their own daily lives. We know the most about the 6th, 10th, 11th, and 14th centuries because of the quantities of written sources that have survived from these. There is nonliterary evidence. Lead seals provide a unique treasure of evidence in addition to inscriptions and coinage. Papyrology adds much new source material for the earliest period, up to the early 7th century, but mostly limited to

Hagia Sofia Byzantine Church, Trabzon, Turkey. (©David Samuel Robbins/CORBIS)

Egypt. Archaeology adds new material while its newer techniques and methodology are improving precision and raising and answering many questions.

Historical interpretation of the empire has changed in several ways. Testimonies of different historical sources are now better if still imperfectly understood. Historians, archaeologists, and art historians are now developing syntheses that take account of research in their respective specialities and those related to their own. We still need more synthesis and coordination between investigators of Late Antique and Middle Byzantine history. Historians no longer assume a monolithic and theocratic state for the Byzantine Empire. Much greater appreciation exists for the liveliness and bustling activities and changes that affected Byzantine society and culture than was the case a few decades ago. Religious controversies are not assumed to be simply expressions of social, political, ethnic, and economic interests, power, and advocacies: there may be genuine religious reasons for religious and theological disputes. More sensitivity exists for the difficulty of penetrating beneath the surface of Byzantine literary and historical texts and a greater understanding of the complexity of the codes and rules according to which they were written. More investigation is occurring for information about Byzantium in source materials from neighboring peoples, in Arabic, Syriac, Armenian, and Georgian as well as that in Latin and Greek. Muslim sources are providing much valuable information that was unknown and unappreciated for the 7th through 9th centuries. Newer techniques are being refined to utilize these sources more accurately while understanding the limits to which they can be put. Neglected questions about gender are receiving long overdue attention. Metallurgical analysis is beginning to provide more accurate information about Byzantine mining. More social and economic mobility existed in the early Byzantine period than scholars assumed.

Byzantine Chapel at Leimonos Monastery, Lesbos, Greece. (©Dave G. Houser/CORBIS)

Former interpretations of Byzantine history emphasized institutions as the key to explaining Byzantine history. A few decades ago the theme system was assumed to explain Middle Byzantine history and *pronoia* (temporary, then longer-term grant of revenues, usually from land) was the institutional fundamental device for explaining the Late Period. That is no longer the case, even though institutions are not irrelevant for a bureaucratic empire that lasted more than a millennium. Today historians do not assume that any single comprehensive social and economic reform of any single emperor created the Byzantine themes at one stroke. It is questionable how militarily efficient the thematic armies were at their height, whether they are the basic explanation for the survival of the Byzantine Empire against invasions by Muslim and Slavic and steppe invaders. Historians disagree concerning just how numerous and how efficient the Byzantine armies were at the end of the 6th century. Historians tend to assume that Byzantine field armies were relatively modest in size in the Middle Byzantine Period, that is, seldom more than 10 or 15 thousand soldiers. By the Palaeologan period Byzantium found it difficult to field armies of more than a few thousand troops. Historians no longer automatically assume that a highly centralized and regulated bureaucratic state was optimal for the Byzantine economy, society, and polity. Corporate regulation of the economy was a reality, but it is less clear that it was a blessing. More regional and municipal autonomy may have been desirable for prosperity, intellectual creativity, and political health. Historians no longer explain the dynamics of the 11th century internal history in terms of a dichotomy between a civil and military party; the reality was a far more complex domestic rivalry. Historians no longer simplistically posit a rivalry between European and Asiatic regions of the empire and they no longer consider the army to have been a monolith; familial, ethnic, and local bases created internal divisions.

Church of Panaghia Kera, 13th century, Hagios Nicolaos, Crete, Greece. (©Wolfgang Kaehler/CORBIS)

The conversion of Constantine to Christianity (312) gave impetus to the Christianization of the empire. He and his court circle encouraged the creation of a rhetoric, art, and architecture of the Christian Roman Empire. He created a senate and consuls at Constantinople, to which he moved antiques. He created precedents for imperial relations with Christian church and inspired comparison of himself not only with earlier emperors but also with Moses. He summoned and participated in the Council of NICEA, which settled issues of Trinitarian theology. But it was his son CONSTANTIUS II (337–361) in whose reign the empire settled into an institutional routine at Constantinople. He normalized diplomatic relations with various neighboring peoples and embellished Constantinople. Missionary work spread Christianity north of the Danube and south into Ethiopia. War with Sasanian Persia attracted much imperial attention under Constantius II, tempted his successor JULIAN (361–363) to a fatal and costly invasion of Persia. The outcome was humiliating defeat and the cession of valuable territory to the Persians. Julian's military debacle emboldened Christians and broke the hopes of most pagans for any restoration of their cults and privileges.

At some point in the 4th century after protracted imperial residence there the imperial bureaucracy established its norms and unwritten rules of conduct at Constantinople and began to transmit them to successors. Bureaucrats developed an understanding about the potential dynamics of power and procedures for administration from the perspective of the Golden Horn. Protocols developed for relations with imperial colleagues and their consuls and the other senate in Rome in the western Roman provinces. But controversies about the Holy Trinity rent the church and government until the definitive settlement by Emperor THEODOSIUS I in 381 at the Council of Constantinople. His legislation confirmed the unique status for orthodox Christianity and its clergy within the empire and the removal of wealth and privileges for pagan temples, cults, and their priests. Much pagan temple wealth had been confiscated and used for coinage as well as for embellishment and funding of Christian churches.

Many precedents for Byzantine ceremonies, rank, and hierarchy date to the 4th century. A gradual accretion of additional bits of ceremony occurred over the centuries. Competition for rank and office was important from the earliest Byzantine period until the end of the empire. Gradually elaborate ceremonies for a new emperor, for receiving credentials from an emperor in the west and other protocols took form and reached their ultimate recorded maturation in 10th-century documentation.

The empire's total budget or gross domestic product cannot be reliably estimated for any period. Principal treasuries in the earliest period were the Praetorian Prefecture, which assessed, collected and distributed tax revenue from land, the Count of the Sacred Largesses (mines, production, distribution of shirts to soldiers, recruitment taxes, and revenue from authenticating purity of precious metals), and the *ires privata* or Imperial Household, which administered very large accumulations of movable property as well as palaces, imperial estates, and their contents. Radical fiscal change occurred in the early 7th century, when these bureaus were reorganized and transformed. The Sacred Largesses disappeared. The Sakellarion Treasury evolved from the Praetorian Prefecture to become important in the 7th century. The Vestiarion became the imperial household's treasury, which handled the imperial family's movable and immovable wealth, in the broadest sense.

The empire lay astride the principal apertures and water corridors to the Mediterranean. Foremost was the complex of water passages of the Bosphorus and Dardanelles between the Aegean/Mediterranean and the Black Sea. It was essential for it to dominate these or face the danger of being split in half. Second was Egypt's narrow land corridor between the Mediterranean and the Red Sea, and third were the Straits of Gibraltar to the Atlantic. Both of these last two irrevocably slipped from Byzantine control by the death of Emperor Heraclius in 641. The empire's geopolitical situation made it difficult for it to wage simultaneous wars in the Balkans and in eastern Anatolia. It was difficult for it to project naval power into the Mediterranean further east than Sicily, Sardinia, or Tunisia. It wished to dominate the shores of the Black Sea but did not risk sending troops to seize the lands beyond the shores of the Black Sea. It was difficult for Byzantium to extend and maintain any effective political and military control northwest in Europe's interior beyond Belgrade.

A partial explanation for Byzantine survival lies in its ability to consult and use its accumulated hoard of ancient wisdom (Greek, Hellenistic, Roman, and earlier Byzantine) about diverse technological, geographical, political, military, and ethnological challenges. Historical contingencies also helped the empire to survive in the 5th century. In the 7th, 8th, and 9th centuries the empire profited from internal strife with the Umayyad and 'Abbasid Caliphates that it and its leaders had not conceived or created. It profited from, in much of its history, avoiding too much risky aggressive imperial overstretch. Its leaders' preference for cautious and prudent diplomacy with minimal risk of heavy casualties reduced the number of occasions in which everything was at stake in a single military expedition or battle. This reduced occasions in which ambitious military commanders or cliques or units could find opportunities to seize power or occasions in which the emperor might lose his life in combat or while on expedition. Yet prudent policies did not eliminate all conspiracies, for they were a fact of life in many centuries of the empire's history. Emperors and their advisers resorted to assassinations, and not infrequently at banquets or other moments when their opponents were caught off guard. The Byzantines preferred to use diplomacy, intrigue, and funds to persuade other peoples to wage war or exert pressure or engage in assassinations on its behalf instead of waging costly wars directly through calling up and dispatching its own troops.

The empire suffered some of its most enduring territorial losses during internal strife, in the 7th century (Levant and Egypt, North Africa), 9th century (Sicily), 11th century (most of Anatolia), late 13th (more western Anatolian regions), and 14th century (Aegean littoral and Gallipoli peninsula and Thrace).

The empire benefited from extensive trade beyond its frontiers in many directions in the early period, to Persia, Arabia, and the trans-Danubian regions, and to the central and western Mediterranean. Manufacture and export of ceramics, glass, and luxurious crafted small objects were prominent. Rare luxury items such as precious woods, fragrances, spices, condiments, and ivory were transported. Olive oil and wine were shipped in bulk. The volume of such items dropped sharply in the early 7th century. Statistics do not exist on the volume of trade or production of goods. Trade and handicrafts of commercial value contracted in towns and cities after the early 7th century but never completely disappeared. The economy quickened, especially in regions near the Aegean and Constantinople, in the 11th and 12th centuries although piracy took its toll in the 13th through 15th centuries. Anatolia and the Balkan regions both contained significant natural resources: ferrous and nonferrous metals, marble, and quarry stone. The agricultural economy's crops included grain, olive oil, wine, fruits, and nuts. The Balkans and Anatolia were suitable for raising livestock, including sheep, goats, oxen, and horses. The empire's seas yielded fish and shellfish, as well as salt that inhabitants extracted by evaporating seawater in salt pans. The empire sought some ships' timbers, furs, fragrances, amber, ivory, paper, and eunuchs from external sources.

After the contraction of its borders in the early 7th century the empire lacked navigable rivers. Maritime shipping was most efficient for bulk items. Land transportation was possible but slow, difficult, and relatively inefficient. Byzantium's economy benefited from being a crossroads for travel between Asia and Europe and between the Black Sea and Aegean and Mediterranean. Some ancient ports of Asia Minor silted up and other ports replaced them. The changed imperial borders still had their vulnerabilities. The Tauros and anti-Tauros mountain range marked southeastern limits, but no clear demarcation existed in the Balkans, despite the existence of the Rhodope and Balkan mountain ranges. Thessalonica became the empire's second largest city. Although Slavs and Avars threatened it, it did not fall to invaders until the destructive storming and looting of it by Arabs in 904, by Normans in 1185, and successive Crusader and Turkish seizures (1204, 1387, and 1430). Its inhabitants trusted to the protection of its patron St. DEMETRIUS. Slavic groups occupied much of mainland Greece in the 7th and 8th centuries but there is insufficient documentation to reconstruct a reliable narrative. Insecurity diminished but never extinguished international maritime traffic in the Mediterranean and Adriatic Seas.

By the 5th century the Byzantine bureaucracy was sufficiently strong that a weak sovereign would not dissolve the state. Germanic and other invasions overwhelmed the Roman government and its finances and military in the western provinces while the east survived. At least one minority constituency, pagans, did speak of the collapse of Roman government in the west using the verb ''fall'' (Damaskios, ''fallen Rome'') and hoped for its revival. Fifth-century imperial governments in the east attempted to help the west on several occasions but were usually unwilling to jeopardize their own existence in order to undertake risky military expeditions to the west that could cause civil war and rebellion. Byzantium succeeded in establishing internal security controls that prevented violent military seizures of power from becoming permanent. The price was restraint in international action. Governments learned to develop counterbalances to prevent any one single general or military or ethnic faction from becoming establishing a monopoly of military power.

The 4th century was one of rising population and economic prosperity for many cities and provinces in the east, in contrast to the instability and crises of the 3d century. The creation of new gold coinage the *solidus* (*nomisma*), struck at 72 to the Roman pound, contributed to financial stability although there were winners and losers with a new money. Bronze coinage circulated most frequently for ordinary purposes. The gold coinage held its value and purity until the 11th century when debasement occurred rapidly over the course of a few decades. The Byzantine economy of the 11th century has received more positive reinterpretation as one with vibrant growth and expansion, not one of stagnation and decline. A reformed coinage stabilized the monetary situation from the late 11th to the end of the 12th century, after which Byzantine coinage increasingly yielded to more desirable Italian competing coins. By the early 15th century, the eastern Mediterranean merchants and people normally preferred Italian coins in transactions. Byzantium had difficulty, as had ancient states, in raising public loans or floating public debt; there was no adequate financial mechanism for doing so, except, at the end of the empire, for seeking embarrassing and risky loans from Italian commercial powers such as Venice.

By the middle of the 5th century the imperial government found it more prudent and expedient to pay off dangerous hostile barbarians such as the Huns instead of risking costly warfare with them. Despite criticism, the populace acquiesced. The imperial government with the aid of bureaucrats succeeded in preventing powerful generals from seizing and monopolizing power. Their efforts brought decisive results. Less successful was 5th-century imperial ecclesiastical policy. The Byzantine government and its provinces managed to hunker down to escape the most violent effects of the 5th-century barbarian invasions and settlements. Its diplomacy helped, but to some degree it enjoyed luck and also benefited from its location. There was strife on at least two occasions with Sassanian Persia, which Sassanian persecution of Armenian Christians exacerbated, but the borders remained essentially stable. The eastern provinces actually received some refugees from the west. Some pagan constituencies within it deplored the condition of ''fallen Rome'' (in their terms) and hoped for its restoration or revival late in the 5th century. Plagues cut population in the 6th century although the percentage drop and significance are controversial.

Constantinople grew rapidly. Its population probably peaked in the 6th century at approximately 400,000, which required the construction of greater walls in the early 5th century (Anthemian walls) as well as an aqueduct for more adequate water supply (reign of Valens, 364–378) for its people. The city's population enjoyed a grain dole at the expense of provincial Egypt. It was a city of excitement and activity that attracted many for entertainment and hopes of advancement. Constantinople was the scene, as were numerous other cities, of horse racing. Blue, green, red, and white factions existed there, in imitation of those at Rome, although eventually it was the blues and greens that predominated. Whether these had any political or social role has been the subject of modern scholarly dispute. Constantinopolitans appreciated and expected the appearance of their emperor and empress in scheduled public ceremonies, and grew anxious when their sovereigns absented themselves from the city.

Elsewhere in the empire Alexandria was the second largest city in the east, followed by Antioch. Western Asia Minor possessed extensive urban centers, most of which had a prosperous surrounding countryside. Egypt was a populous and rich but neglected province that emperors did not visit. Certain eastern provinces such as Palestine prospered from unprecedented new imperial generosity in support of new churches, facilities for the sick, and for pilgrims. Although a Christian empire, only Heraclius visited Jerusalem while emperor.

Ecclesiastical strife concerning Christology [*see* CHRISTOLOGY, CONTROVERSIES ON (PATRISTIC)] and concerning episcopal ambitions consumed much governmental attention from the 430s on. Religious concerns were genuine in those disputes. They were not primarily vehicles of political, social, or economic pressure and protest and advocacy. But the decisions of the Council of Chalcedon in 451 made explicit definitions that led to a widening ecclesiastical cleavage that in retrospect would become permanent.

The privileges of Constantinople and its patriarch helped to make Constantinople into the de facto capital of the empire by the middle of the 5th century. Canon 28 of the Council of Chalcedon consolidated that authority. Some inhabitants of other principal eastern cities resented the rise of Constantinople to power, wealth, and prominence.

Justinian I and his advisers took advantage of vulnerabilities in several Germanic kingdoms in the west to reconquer Africa from the VANDALS, Italy from the Ostrogoths, albeit slowly, and started the never completed reconquest of Spain. These efforts brought early fame and treasures to the empire. They expended liberally to build churches and fortifications in the empire's newly liberated and old regions. But they soon overstretched imperial military and financial resources with harmful consequences for core areas of the empire, especially the Balkans, which lacked the soldiers to defend themselves from Avar attack and Slavic settlement. Byzantine military activity prompted the Persian king Chosroes I to embark on war with the Byzantines, which lasted much of the century. Justinian's conquests shifted the empire somewhat more to a more diversified population with an additional proportion of Latin-speaking population. His legislation and official rhetoric and some institutional arrangements consciously invoked an archaizing classical heritage.

LOMBARD invasions of Italy, heightened Berber raids in Africa, and intensified Gothic resistance in the Iberian peninsula deprived Byzantium of many rewards for its military efforts and increased the tenuousness of its hold on those territories.

The pace of events and developments accelerated in the early 7th century. Violent usurpation of the imperial throne by Phocas in 602 gave the Sassanian king Chosroes II (590–628) the pretext to go to war against Byzantium for a quarter century starting in 603. The successful rebellion by HERACLIUS overthrew Phocas in turn (608–610) but did not persuade Chosroes II, who was winning, to cease hostilities. Instead, his forces overran Byzantine upper Mesopotamia, Syria, Palestine, and Egypt and ravaged Asia Minor. Sassanian occupation gave the inhabitants of those lands experience of living outside of Byzantine authority. Byzantine forces evacuated their remaining territories in Spain. Only after extraordinary efforts and risking capture of Constantinople by a combined Persian and Avaro-Slav siege and blockade was Heraclius in a series of campaigns and by skillful exploitation of internal strife within Persia, able to crush Persia, overthrow Chosroes II, and impose peace terms acceptable to Byzantium. The lengthy war and aftermath involved considerable physical destruction and disruptive dislocation of populations. As it turned out, the empire had virtually no respite before new and different Muslim conquests took away the liberated territories from Byzantine control once more. Heraclius and his advisers miscalculated the Muslim threat, which constituted a different challenge from that of the Sassanian Persians. He was unable to devise techniques to divide and neutralize the Muslims. He had been an emperor who seized imperial power by means of skillful exploitation of internal strife and intrigues, and also used these methods even more than standard warfare to overcome the Persians. But he and his advisers could not find the means to bring about decisive blows against the Muslims even though he managed to extricate and spare sufficient Byzantine troops and territory such that a significant remnant of the empire could survive. Successive threats in the east prevented the government from giving attention to the deteriorating condition in the Balkans. The extensive luxury and classical literature and art and the supporting cultural infrastructure gradually disappeared with the attenuation of financial resources and urban structures.

Heraclius managed to return the captured fragment of the Cross to Jerusalem (March 630), to begin the difficult task of reconciling divided Christian churches under his favored but highly controversial Christological formula of MONOTHELITISM (one will in Jesus Christ). Harsh policies against Jews, including some instances of massacre and forced baptism, intensified Christian-Jewish strife and Jewish alienation during the reign of Heraclius in widely scattered areas of the empire: Palestine, Edessa and its region in north Syria, and in North Africa. But early in the 630s Muslims terminated Heraclius's efforts at reunification and reconstruction by invading and conquering Palestine and Syria and upper Mesopotamia. By the early 640s they also seized Egypt and then North Africa by the end of the 7th century. Their conquests resulted in enormous Byzantine losses of tax revenue, population, and resources and food and tremendous loss of prestige. The empire lost its richest and most populous and most urbanized regions, even though they included ethnically, linguistically, and religiously diverse populations. Byzantines failed to anticipate the Muslim invasions or the religious convictions that enabled these invaders to hold together.

Seventh-century military reverses compelled the empire to fall back on the security of Constantinople's walls and rely upon its territories and population and economy in Asia Minor as its heartland. Key political and military leaders and the best military units resided there. Most of southeastern Europe fell outside of the government's control. The land and maritime fortifications of Constantinople gave important protection, symbolism, and security. Many vestiges of late antique institutions, privileges, and practices disappeared.

Heraclius founded a dynasty, which historians call Heraclian, that endured tenuously until 711. A grave succession crisis at Heraclius's death in 641 exacerbated conditions. We know little about details in the reign of his grandson Constantius II (641–668), except for strong Muslim raids into Asia Minor and deeper Slavic penetration of the Balkans and the Greek mainland. Muslim raiders escalated their penetrations of Byzantine Anatolia in 662–663 by beginning to winter there, not merely engage in summer raids. Muslims blockaded and unsuccessfully besieged Constantinople between 674 and 678 during the reign of Constantine IV. Long-distance trade shrank. Monothelitism worsened the empire's relations with the Papacy and Italy. Constantine IV finally repudiated the dynasty's previous Monothelitic policies in 681.

One of the greatest puzzles in Byzantine historical investigation is explanation of the change from late antiquity to the middle period with respect to social and economic and landholding and military classes, including demography, as well as with respect to education, ethnicity, and trade and handicrafts. The paucity of primary sources contributes to obscurity. Many aspects of the continuity of Greek ethnic identity remain controversial and unexplained, but some continuing sense of Greek identity persisted. Older theses of ethnic disappearance are now obsolete and rejected.

Gradually, administrative boundaries were redrawn and reorganized within the empire during the late 7th and early 8th century, resulting in the incremental creation of military districts and their armies called ''themes'' (from Greek *themata*). This resulted from no single emperor's action, although the first four (Anatolikon, Armeniakon, Opsikion, and Thrakesion) appeared by the end of the 660s. Their relationship, if any, with social and economic reforms is unproven. The administrative rank and function lists changed substantially by the 9th and early 10th centuries from those that had existed in the 4th through 6th centuries. The Praetorian Prefecture's treasury disappeared in the 7th century in place of the General Treasury (*logothesion tou genikou*) and the Private Treasury (*logothesion tou eidikou*), which are attested to by late in the 7th century. Warehouses for *kommerkiarioi* apparently emerge as part of a new logistical support for the reorganized military, but many technical details remain unexplained. The precise steps and causes are uncertain. The imperial authorities gradually subdivided the original four themes, perhaps to reduce the potential for military unrest as well for improvement of administrative efficiency, and added additional smaller units as territorial reconquest extended control over additional regions. The government relied more heavily on Armenian talent than it had in the early Byzantine period. The basis for the funding of soldiers altered significantly from that of the early Byzantine period: soldiers received cash pay less regularly and many gradually came to subsist off of lands where they were billeted. Armies withdrawn from Syria were stationed in various regions of Anatolia where they gradually identified themselves with localities. Towns survived but often in attenuated form, concentrated around citadels for security. The social elites that dominated towns in late antiquity disappeared or receded in the 7th and later centuries. New names appeared.

Heraclius's successors managed to check and restrain Muslim raiding of Asia Minor even though the raiders inflicted much damage on the economy, communications, and demographics of the region. Use of Greek fire, an igneous petroleum mixture, helped to thwart the Muslim blockade and siege of Constantinople between 674 and 678. But the arrival of Bulgars who settled just south of the Danube added another threat in southeastern Europe, one that the Byzantines failed to dislodge. The Bulgars and Slavs remained non-Christian until the late 9th century. But by the end of the 7th century the Byzantines had developed adequate techniques to fortify and check Muslim advances in Asia Minor. Byzantines only gradually recovered effective administrative control of parts of mainland Greece that Slavs had occupied. That process terminated by the beginning of the 10th century. It is impossible to ascertain the precise extent of Byzantine territorial control in the lower Balkans and Greek mainland during many decades of the 7th through 9th century and obscurities persist with respect to Byzantine administrative control in many parts of the northern and northwest Balkans even in the late 10th and early 11th century. The second Muslim (and last ''Arab'') siege of Constantinople failed in the years 717–718.

Apocalyptic fears intensified from the middle of the 7th to the early 8th century. Muslim victories against Byzantines and others shook Byzantine confidence and contributed to religious searching and doubts. They, in addition to the negative reactions of some ecclesiastics and laity against veneration of religious pictures of sacred persons and subjects, resulted in Byzantium's greatest internal trauma, the iconoclastic controversy (*see* ICONOCLASM). It initially erupted at the end of the 720s and in 730 under Emperor Leo III, and intensified under his son Constantine V, peaking in the 760s. Its origins, nature, and significance remain controversial and inadequately documented. Only in the 750s did iconoclasm develop theological reasoning in favor of its policies. Constantine V found himself fighting strong monastic opposition, which continued to the bedrock of icon veneration through the termination of the crisis. The sources on iconoclasm are not ideal and tend to distort or obscure the motives of the iconoclasts, who have not left their own testimony for critical evaluation. Leo's daughter-in-law, Empress Irene, succeeded in reversing this dynastic policy in 787, with the aid of the Seventh Ecumenical Council that she convoked at Nicea, but more instability followed. Irene's strife with her son Constantine VI culminated in his blinding. But revulsion at his death resulted in Irene's overthrow, the end of the Syrian or Isaurian dynasty in 802, and a kaleidoscopic change of emperors until Leo V the Armenian restored iconoclasm (Second Iconoclastic Period) between 815 and 843. The abortive yet multifaceted revolt of Thomas the Slav at the beginning of the 820s was another symptom of instability. Finally Empress Theodora decisively restored veneration of icons (Triumph of Orthodoxy) on March 11, 843.

Iconoclasm contributed to the costly Byzantine loss of Italy, Sardinia, and Sicily due to local hostility to the policy and to imperial preoccupation with dealing with issues of iconoclasm. This reduced the proportion of Latin speakers to a very small minority within the empire. Muslims from North Africa also took advantage of Byzantine vulnerability in the central Mediterranean to expand and to seize Crete, thereby creating a base for piratical raiding against Byzantine shipping and coastlines.

Byzantine relations were initially difficult with the Frankish empire of Charlemagne, including concerning icon policy, which the emperor's advisers misunderstood. There were sensitivities concerning the issue of recognizing the imperial status of Charlemagne and his successors, but vulnerable Byzantines grudgingly conceded this during a crisis with the Bulgars in 812. The disastrous defeat and death of Emperor Nicephorus I at the hands of the Bulgar khan Krum in 811 was a great humiliation for Byzantium and precipitated a crisis of legitimacy and contributed to the restoration of iconoclasm.

Intellectual, economic, and political revival quickened in the 9th century. Trade intensified with Khazars (an Altaic people settled on the edge of and near the Black Sea and aperture of the Volga) and the Rus' (ancestors of the Russians). Other exchanges including diplomatic and intellectual and artistic dimensions accelerated with the 'Abbāsids in Baghdad, after they supplanted the Umayyad dynasty and moved the seat of caliphal government from Syria to Iraq. After the early 840s, Muslim raids gradually tempered against Byzantine Asia Minor. The Byzantines developed a reasonably effective system for containing and neutralizing such raiders. Byzantine military victories extinguished a heretical Paulician (a Christian sect with putative dualist theological assumptions) buffer entity at Tephrike and prepared the way for more ambitious Byzantine recovery of lost territories in the southeast.

The seizure of power by Basil I ''the Macedonian'' led to the long-lived Macedonian dynasty that endured from 867 (a traditional threshold in periodization) until 1042, the longest-lived Byzantine dynasty with the exception of its last, the Palaeologans. During it the study and revision of law thrived, commerce expanded, while institutions gained new strength and imperial armies gradually recovered territories in the east from the Muslims.

Basil I's seizure of power brought in his wake a new group of leaders, who will together with their descendants benefit from the long life of this dynasty. Many of them will profit from imperial favor and patronage and will entrench themselves in key positions and even establish dominance of specific localities. These families will extend their prominence in the 10th century. Some, however, will harm themselves through their own excessive reach for power (for example, Phocas, Maleinos families). The principal families in the 10th century were the Lecapenos, Phocas, Tzimisces, Maleinos, Musele, Argyros, Rentakius, Parsacutenos, and Scleros families. Growing centralization made aristocratic families more dependent on the government. Yet the imperial government needed aristocratic families for officers. Rebellions of the Scleros (976, 987) and Phocas (987) families represented rejection of imperial authority by a large segment of Byzantine aristocratic families. Emperor Basil II (976–1025) heavily influenced which families dominated the 11th century. The Lecapenos, Phocas, and Maleinos families were eclipsed, while the Scleros family remained important. Basil II relied heavily on a transitional group of families: Argyros, Kourkouas, Bourtzes, Abalantes, Malakinos, Nikoulitzes. But Basil II created a group of newcomers to counterbalance and dispersed power among many families: Apokaukos, Boiannes, Botaneiates, Cabasilas, Comnenos, Dalassenos, Diogenes, Ducas, Gabras, Glabas, Kekaumenos, Monomachos, Pakourianos, Peognites, Tarchaniotes, Synadenos, Taronites, Tornikios, Vatatzes, Xiphias, among others. Basil II wished to restrain new men as well as break the power of the older families. He wished to make families dependent on him. He virtually liquidated the formerly powerful office of Domestic of the Schools (commander-in-chief of armies of Asia). After 996 the major families seem to have become weaker. New families lacked familial alliances and the group cohesion of the old families of the 10th century. Imperial central power remained in the ascendancy until 1057. Familial power was erratic in the middle of the 11th century, but reemerged after 1055. Chief families remained the same between 1057 and 1081, even though their mutual strife intensified in those years.

Imperial concerns for the accumulation of excessive power in the hands of large landowners culminated in the repeated issuance of legislation to check such fiscally and militarily harmful trends (such trends tended to threaten the tax base for agricultural taxes and threaten the supply of able-bodied soldiers for military service). Legislation speaks of the powerful and the poor and indicates that military obligations had become attached to the land by the 10th century. The earliest known legislation restricting or attempting to reverse expansionist tendencies occurred in 930 but peaked under Basil II in 996. With great difficulty and after civil war, Basil II succeeded in breaking the power of several truculent families, but the problem revived and worsened after his death in 1025. But imperial legislation did check and confine the magnates to the central Anatolian plateau; it was not a total failure. One of the great magnate leaders, Nicephorus II Phocas, reconquered the strategic and valuable islands of Crete and Cyprus and the north Syrian city of Antioch. These acts stimulated economic growth and maritime activity.

The Byzantine mission under Constantine and Methodius in 863 resulted in the conversion of south Slavs, in particular conversion of the Bulgar khan Boris and his subjects in 864 and the development of a Slavic alphabet and liturgy and translation of some basic Christian texts into Slavic. But Bulgarian weakness tempted Byzantine diplomacy to exploit the situation. Bulgaria fell under Byzantine control only to throw off Byzantine control under Tsar Samuel late in the 10th and early in the 11th century. Basil II after painful and ruthless efforts and much destructive warfare reduced Bulgaria to submission by 1018. Basil II's reign witnessed the creation of a strong alliance with the Rus', whose sovereign Vladimir dispatched troops to aid Basil II. A crack imperial guard unit of Varangians will continue to exist at Constantinople even into the impoverished 14th century.

Basil II also annexed Armenian and Georgian territories and continued the policies of Nicephorus II Phocas and John I Tzimisces in expanding eastward. He annexed lands that he did not have sufficient civilian or military populations with whom to assimilate to the body of the empire. Disaffected locals in many instances resented imposition of Byzantine authority from afar. Byzantine authority over occupied regions in Bulgaria and the edge of the Caucasus was superficial and vulnerable. These were cases of dangerous imperial overstretch even though strategic logic and the desire for more fiscal revenues underlay their acquisition.

The imperial government experienced a regency at the death of Leo VI in 911. His uncanonical fourth marriage created a crisis of legitimacy in and after his lifetime. His son and legal successor, the vulnerable, young Constantine VII, found himself under the protectorate of a military commander, ROMANUS I LECAPENUS until a coup ousted the Lecapenids in 944. The Byzantines mastered international diplomacy in the middle of the 10th century to employ relatively low-cost leverage of steppe tribes such as the Pechenegs to coerce the Bulgars and other peoples to serve and respect Byzantine interests. Byzantine diplomacy reached its apogee in the middle of the 10th century. The extensive writings of and collected by Constantine VII reveal the accumulated strategic and antiquarian wisdom of the Byzantines and describe their imperial ceremonies and receptions at the moment of their greatest splendor.

Tensions between Greeks and Armenians within the Byzantine Empire divided Byzantines in the east in the middle and late 11th century, contemporary with the Seljuk Turkish invasions. Controversial is the question of conditions in eastern Anatolia on the eve of the Turkish invasions: density of population, state of the economy, ethnic and linguistic and confessional composition of the populace, and the policies for appointing and financing Byzantine officials and soldiers in those regions. Elucidation of the causes for the success of the Turkish invasions depends partially on assumptions about conditions prior to their arrival. The government did not succeed in moderating or eliminating these problems. Neglect and unraveling of older defense and muster systems together with civil war in the wake of the capture of Emperor Romanus IV Diogenes at the battle of Mantzikert in 1071 exposed Anatolia to Seljuk invasion. Within a decade the Byzantines had lost effective control of most of Anatolia. Also in 1071 Normans ejected the Byzantines from their remaining positions in southern Italy. At the end of the 11th century Byzantium found itself best by Turks in the east, by steppe raiders (Pechenegs, Cumans) to the northeast, and by Normans in the west, who threatened the Balkans from Bari and other ports in southern Italy. The imperial government resorted to more use of Latin (Frankish, Norman, Anglo-Saxon) mercenary troops as well as recruits from west Altaic peoples such as the Pechenegs and Cumans and increasingly even from eastern Turks.

ALEXIUS I COMNENUS (1081–1118) stabilized the military situation at a high price: he sought the assistance of Western military forces, who to his surprise transformed themselves into the First Crusade. Crusaders helped him recover some valuable territory and towns in Anatolia from the Seljuks, but misunderstandings and disagreements raised insoluble tensions with Crusaders who established principalities in the territories that they conquered in the Levant. He reformed coinage and the tax system, and prosecuted what some contemporaries regarded as excessively free inquiry in theology and philosophy. He established a dynasty that endured until 1185.

The CRUSADES brought increased trade and more Westerners for residence at Constantinople. Byzantine resentments soared and culminated in riots and looting directed against Latins (Venetians, Genoese, Pisans) and their property and warehouses at Constantinople in 1171 and 1182. These acts exacerbated tensions and generated Italian claims for damages and reparations. Centrifugal forces increased, culminating in the successful rebellion of Bulgars under the Asenids in 1186 while other Crusaders seized the rich and strategic island of Cyprus.

Another crisis of legitimacy struck Byzantium at the end of the 12th century. Andronicus I Comnenos managed to rebel and seize power but Isaac I Angelus overthrew and executed him in 1185. But Alexius III Angelos overthrew and blinded Isaac and set in motion a disastrous chain of events that culminated in the Fourth Crusaders' seizure of Constantinople (April 13, 1204), which terminated the Angeli dynasty. On May 16, 1204, Crusaders elected Baldwin of Hainault as Latin emperor and a Venetian patriarch after looting and massacring in Constantinople. Theodore Lascaris and many other Constantinopolitans fled to the nearby Asian countryside while David Comnenus established an independent principality in Trebizond and Michael Angelos Ducas created a despotate (principality) in remote Epiros. The most important intellectuals and political refugees clustered at Nicea to rally around Theodore Lascaris and his patriarch. The Latins failed to win over the Greek population and were disastrously defeated by Bulgars. Resentment of Greeks and other Orthodox against Latins and against ecclesiastical reunion intensified because of the Fourth Crusade and experiences under Crusader occupation or other negative experiences with Latins with respect to trade, diplomacy, or cultural contact. Negative sentiments worsened and the list of perceived Latin theological and liturgical ''errors'' lengthened. With patient diplomacy and careful military movements, Byzantines ultimately recovered Constantinople in 1261 and ejected the Crusaders, even though Venetians continued to rule many rich islands in the Aegean and Ionian Seas, Genoese gained numerous strong points and lucrative trading posts, and other Crusaders held strong points in Attica and the Peloponnesus. Crusader occupation and intervention inflicted much material and human damage but also tied Greeks irrevocably to the broader Mediterranean world and its economic and political transformations. Byzantines after 1204 fell behind innovations in the West and the Islamic world. Their ships could not effectively compete with those of the Italian maritime powers in the profitable and important long-distance trade. A tightly knit group of families, foremost of which were the Palaeologi, controlled dwindling economic and political resources.

Issues of ecclesiastical reunion bedeviled relations with the West, especially after the schism of 1054. Emperors and their ministers at Nicea held out the hope of reunion of churches, but were unwilling to implement it fully. In July 1274, to forestall another Crusade by Charles of Anjou against Constantinople, Emperor Michael VIII Palaeologus's envoy, George Acropolites, agreed to reunion on behalf of the emperor and gave on his behalf a profession of faith. But this was unenforceable. Patriarch John Bekkos consented to reunion in 1275. But the church was already rent asunder by other disaffected factions angry with the deposition and blinding of Emperor John Lascaris by Michael Palaeologus. The death of Pope Gregory, the inability of Emperor Michael and Patriarch John Bekkos to implement union fully, and political pressures for another crusade to recover Constantinople led to papal excommunication of Emperor Michael VIII on Nov. 18, 1281, not long before his death. His successor Emperor Andronikos II (1282–1328) allowed union to lapse. Each party was sure of its own superiority, showed little respect for what it knew of the other, and was ready to condemn the slightest deviation from its own norms. Old issues remained, including acceptance of Roman primacy, the *filioque,* Canon 28 of the Council of Chalcedon, the use of unleavened bread in the Latin Eucharist, prohibited degrees of marriage, the status of the just and unjust immediately after decease, and other questions. There was mutual ignorance: a complete lack of understanding and sympathy. So union was not feasible at that time. Old ecclesiastical frictions continued at Byzantium. Hence the deposition and estrangement of the ''Arsenite'' faction that supported the ousted Patriarch Arsenios. But Arsenios's successor Patriarch Joseph was also ousted because of his rejection of reunion. These factions did not reconcile themselves until 1312.

By the second decade of the 14th century plans for new crusades against Byzantium gave way to realization of the seriousness of the Turkish peril. The emergence of various Turkish *beyliks* on the former Byzantine lands in Asia Minor was a partial result of local dissatisfaction with Palaeologan overthrow of the locally popular Lascaris family. By the 2d and 3d decade of the 14th century Michael VIII's son Andronicus II and his advisers had permanently lost control of all but a few posts in Asia Minor, with grave fiscal and strategic consequences. Efforts to secure Western military assistance backfired because of the Byzantine inability to pay the mercenaries and ethnic tensions. Treacherous massacre of Catalan commanders and their bodyguards prompted remaining Catalans to retaliate by looting and ravaging the countryside and population between Thrace and Attica. They eventually seized control of Athens and the surrounding region from 1311 until 1388.

Civil war between ANDRONICUS II and his grandson Andronicus IV worsened conditions, even though intellectuals such as Nicephorus Choumnos and Theodore Metochites managed to pursue their philosophical investigations and debates. John VI Cantacuzenus took advantage of the young John V Paleologus and his mother Anna of Savoy to seize power. HESYCHASM divided Byzantines as well until its adherents triumphed by 1341. John VI supported GREGORY PALAMAS and his hesychast faction and theology and mysticism. Palamism assumed a distinctly anti-Latin tone. Meanwhile plague (Black Death 1347–48) killed many, with grave demographic and economic repercussions. The Turkish occupation of the strategic town of Gallipoli on the Gallipoli peninsula in 1354 prompted the abdication of John VI Cantacuzenus, who retired to a monastery. The Serb tsar Stefan Dushan temporarily threatened to occupy and supplant Byzantium, especially in northern Greece, claiming (1346) to be emperor of the Serbs and Greeks, but his premature death in 1355 terminated Serbia's thrust for Balkan supremacy. Ottoman occupation spread rapidly in Europe in the face of inadequate Byzantine resistance or failed coordination of defenses with other Balkan nationalities. Ottoman victories over Serbs and Crusaders in the Balkans in 1371, 1389, and 1396 confirmed Byzantine weakness. Since 1371 or 1373 Byzantium had in effect been a client of the burgeoning Ottoman empire. Although Western efforts to assist a beleaguered Byzantium were irregular and insufficient in size and scope and financing, Byzantine internal strife had crippled the empire's ability to develop any effective defensive strategy.

Emperor John V (1341–91) unsuccessfully sought aid in Italy while Manuel II visited Italy, France, and England in search of relief forces. John V experienced humiliating treatment in Italy due to Byzantium's poor credit rating. Timur's unexpected victory over Ottoman sultan Bayezid I in 1402 provided a respite to Byzantium, probably enabling the empire to survive another half-century. Towns and countryside and coastlines and monasteries suffered from depredations of plague, pirates, and land raiders during the 14th and early 15th centuries.

Byzantine leaders resorted to resourceful diplomacy, but failed to devise institutional, technological, tactical, or other innovations to enable them to resist the Ottomans successfully or compete economically and culturally with the Italian trading cities. John VIII Palaeologus (1425–48) and his brother Constantine XI (1448–53) negotiated desperately for Western assistance. John VIII agreed to reunion at the Council of Ferrara-Florence in 1439 but was unable to persuade many antiunionist clergy and laity to follow his lead. The failure of the Crusade of Varna in 1444 was the last serious hope for Western relief for the Byzantine Empire. The Ottoman sultan Muḥammad II resolved to seize Constantinople, which he accomplished by its storming on May 29, 1453, in the course of which Emperor Constantine XI died in the breach of the walls. By that time the population of Constantinople had probably fallen to 50,000 or less. The modest but intellectually vigorous despotate of the Morea (Peloponnesus) continued to remain independent under Thomas and Demetrius Palaeologus, brothers of Constantine XI, until the Ottomans overran it in 1460. The empire at Trebizond fell to Muḥammad II in 1461. Thomas Palaeologus and his family fled to Italy where their titles to Byzantine imperial rights became the object of future international claims.

The final decades of the empire require study in a larger context, for the empire's dimensions had shrunk to the size of an ancient polis. Italian humanist interest in Greek language, manuscripts, and antiquities grew and took advantage of ecclesiastical diplomacy concerning union of the churches to improve communications and contacts with individual Byzantine scholars,and in a few cases to learn something about monuments and physical antiquities.

Investigation of the Byzantine Empire is not at an end. Many historical topics still need more analysis: the Byzantine village; the Byzantine diet; Byzantium and Russia; eunuchs; mortuary practices; death and memory; Byzantine spirituality in the late 10th and early 11th centuries, including relationships with military elites and monasticism; Byzantine court ceremonial; Arabic sources on the late 7th, 8th, and 9th centuries require more exploitation; comparative analysis of Byzantine and Western European economic and technological activity, especially in the 10th and early 11th centuries; the monastery; Byzantium and the Later Crusades; and consciousness of any ethnic identity, still need a basic study. Many questions remain concerning familial alliances. The late 5th century, the late 10th and early 11th centuries, Justinian I and his legislation, Byzantine Sicily, and land tenure in Anatolia in the 4th through 6th centuries need a major review. Byzantine patristic works deserve much more intensive analysis. Many Byzantine literary, historical, and epigraphic sources still await the preparation and publication of rigorous critical editions, translations, and commentaries. These inquiries, and others that we cannot yet imagine, should amplify but also transform the historical interpretation of the history of the Byzantine Empire.

Bibliography: There is no optimal and up-to-date single-volume history of the Byzantine Empire. M. ANGOLD, *Byzantine Empire 1025–1204* (2d ed. New York 1997); *A Byzantine Government in Exile: Government and Society under the Laskarids of Nicea 1204–1261* (Oxford 1975). M. BARTUSIS, *The Late Byzantine Army* (Philadelphia 1992). A. BELLINGER and P. GRIERSON, eds., *Catalogue of the Byzantine Coins in the Dumbarton Oaks Collection and the Whittemore Collection,* 5 v. (Washington, D.C. 1966–99). C. M. BRAND, *Byzantium Confronts the West* (Cambridge, Mass. 1968). A. CAMERON, ed., *The Cambridge Ancient History* (rev. ed. Cambridge, England 2000–) v. 13–14. G. CAVALLO, ed., *The Byzantines* (Chicago 1997). J.-C. CHEYNET, *Pouvoir et Contestation à Byzance (963–1210)* (Paris 1990). G. DAGRON, *Naissance d'une Capitale* (Paris 1974). J. V. FINE JR., *The Early Medieval Balkans* (Ann Arbor, Mich. 1983); *The Late Medieval Balkans* (Ann Arbor, Mich. 1987). J. GILL, *Byzantium and the Papacy, 1198–1400* (New Brunswick, N.J. 1979). J. HALDON, *Warfare, State and Society in Byzantium 565–1204* (London 1999). M. HENDY, *Studies in the Byzantine Monetary Economy* (Cambridge 1985). R. JANIN, *Constantinople Byzantine* (Paris 1964). A. H. M. JONES, *The Later Roman Empire* (Oxford 1964). W. KAEGI, *Byzantine Military Unrest 471–843: An Interpretation* (Amsterdam 1981); *Byzantium and the Decline of Rome* (Princeton 1968); *Byzantium and the Early Islamic Conquests* (Cambridge 1995). A. KAZHDAN, *Oxford Dictionary of Byzantium,* 3 v. (Oxford 1991). T. M. KOLBABA, *The Byzantine Lists: Errors of the Latins* (Urbana, Ill. 2000). A. LAIOU, *Peasant Society in the Late Byzantine Empire* (Princeton 1977). A. LAIOU and D. SIMON, eds., *Law and Society in Byzantium, Ninth–Twelfth Centuries* (Washington, D.C. 1994). A. LAIOU et al., *Economic History of Byzantium,* 3 vols. (Washington 2002). P. MAGDALINO, *The Empire of Manuel I Komnenos* (Cambridge 1996); ed., *The Rhythm of Imperial Renewal in Byzantium, 4th–13th Centuries* (Brookfield, Vt. 1994). C. MANGO, *Byzantium and Its Image* (London 1984); *Byzantium: The Empire of New Rome* (New York 1980). R. MORRIS, *Monks and Laymen in Byzantium* (Cambridge 1995). J. NESBITT and N. OIKONOMIDES, eds., *Byzantine Seals in Dumbarton Oaks and in the Fogg Museum of Art,* 4 v. (Washington, D.C. 1991–2001). D. M. NICOL, *Last Centuries of Byzantium* (2d ed. Cambridge 1994). G. OSTROGORSKY, *History of the Byzantine State,* tr. J. HUSSEY (Oxford and New Brunswick, N.J. 1968). Out of date. E. PATLAGEAN, *Pauvrete économique et pauvreté sociale à Byzance, 4e–7e siècles* (Paris 1977). E. STEIN, *Histoire du Bas-Empire,* 2 v. (Paris 1949, 1959). P. STEPHENSON, *Byzantium's Balkan Frontier* (Cambridge 2001). A.-M. TALBOT, ed., *Byzantine Defenders of Images* (Washington, D.C. 1998); *Holy Women of Byzantium* (Washington, D.C. 1996). J. THOMAS, A. C. HERO, and R. ALLISON, eds. and trs., *Byzantine Monastic Foundation Documents,* 5 v. (Washington, D.C. 2000). W. TREADGOLD, *The Byzantine Revival* (Stanford 1984). S. VRYONIS, *The Decline of Medieval Hellenism in Asia Minor* (Berkeley, Los Angeles 1971).

[W. E. KAEGI]

BYZANTINE LITERATURE

The importance of the contribution the Byzantines made to modern civilization by protecting western Europe from barbarian invaders for more than 1,000 years and by creating a new kind of art is universally recognized. In appraising Byzantium as a cultural force, however, emphasis is usually laid on what the Byzantines did rather than on what they wrote. The customary verdict is that Byzantine literature is more significant for the information it contains than for its own sake. This judgment, though valid in general, is not altogether unassailable, and leaves out of account a number of significant facts, which are reviewed in this article.

Introduction

It should be noted at once that, except for a large number of fragments on papyrus and the *Persians* of Timotheus (which has been preserved almost intact on a papyrus nearly contemporary with its author), virtually all of our texts of the ancient Greek classics were literally saved from destruction by the diligence of the Byzantine scholars who studied them and laboriously transcribed them. If it had not been for this Byzantine interest, the pagan Greek classics would have perished long ago, and the whole shape of modern life would have been profoundly altered. Moreover, the Byzantines achieved aesthetic distinction of a high order in some areas, especially in the liturgy and in historiography.

Scope of Byzantine Literature. Strictly speaking, Byzantine literature includes the entire literary production, in all genres, of the occupants of the Byzantine Empire from the beginning of the reign of DIOCLETIAN (284) to the fall of the empire on May 29, 1453. Hence, in a survey of Byzantine literature one should presumably consider texts written not only in Greek but also in Latin, Syriac, and Arabic. Accordingly, a strong case could be made for the inclusion under this rubric of such Latin writers as LACTANTIUS (fl. *c.* 317), who was the tutor of Crispus, Emperor CONSTANTINE I's eldest son.

Similarly, it would not be inappropriate to discuss here such works as the *Corpus Iuris Civilis*, despite the fact that only one of its four major divisions (the so called *Novels,* Νεαραί) was written in Greek. For the other three parts of this extraordinary code of laws, though derived directly from preexisting Latin texts and codifications of the law, represent Byzantine legal thought and practice as reflected in the additions, omissions, and emendations made by Tribonian, Emperor JUSTINIAN I's chief adviser in such matters, and the other jurisconsults of his staff.

Nevertheless, for the sake of simplicity, this article is limited to the materials written in Greek, which was the dominant language of the empire, at least from the time of Justinian I. Even Emperor Constantine I, whose native language was Latin, used Greek in addressing the bishops at the first ecumenical council (NICAEA I, 325). Still, Latin persisted in the eastern portions of the empire as late as the time of Emperor HERACLIUS I (610–641), who apparently was the first to make Greek the official language of the Byzantine court and chancery, as it had always been of the Greek Churches in the East, which were the direct descendants of the Greek-speaking communities that had produced the New Testament, carried the Gospels to the West, and left their mark upon Rome through the first popes, all of whom had written and spoken in Greek until the time of VICTOR I (*c.* 189–198).

Byzantine Greek. The form of the Greek language that the Byzantines used varied greatly. The standard of most serious writers was the usage that prevailed in ancient Athens. That is, they were Atticizers. But not even the most determined classicists were able to reproduce this ancient language with complete fidelity, and their use of the Attic idiom invariably fell short of their ideal. Moreover, new vocabulary and usages, which are always associated with a living language, turned up regularly not only in the nonliterary texts of the years following upon the death of Alexander, but also with even greater frequency in the Christian period as a result of the birth and growth of the Christian Church.

In general, however, the intelligentsia clung to the traditional language of antiquity, so far as it was possible for them to do so. But inevitably in their hands the language underwent great changes, marked principally by the simplification of syntax that resulted from such phenomena as the disappearance of the dative case, the loss or misunderstanding of the optative and subjunctive moods of the verb, and the breaking down of the more complicated conjugations and declensions. At the same time there developed a simplification of the vowel and diphthong system which radically altered pronunciation and incidentally rendered the ancient patterns of syllable length, vital for verse composition, irrelevant. These transformations were unavoidable. At the same time, however, the determined classicism of the Atticizers, aided by the concentration of authority in Constantinople, the major cultural center of the empire, had a unifying effect linguistically, and succeeded in eradicating the ancient non-Attic dialects, which now had almost completely disappeared. Provincialisms of various kinds were always to be found, but they rarely penetrated into literary circles. Nor did they ever become truly separate types of speech that could be described as dialects.

What is called the κοινὴ διάλεκτος (the ''common language'') was essentially the neo-Attic type of Greek that resulted from the strenuous but never altogether successful efforts of writers to reproduce the idiom of ancient Athens. In the course of its history, this Atticizing language had to make concessions on a large scale to modernisms of many sorts (originating in the speech of the people, the army, imperial chancery, etc.). But the resulting changes affected syntax and vocabulary rather than morphology.

Besides their success in eliminating the non-Attic dialects, the Atticizers won another fundamental victory, for the influence of the imperial court and of the liturgy (which was always under the domination of the Atticizers), as well as the conservative instincts of the people, served to keep the Greek language as such alive, and prevented its disintegration into new linguistic creations like the Romance languages of the West (Italian, Spanish, Portuguese, and French), which came into being during the Middle Ages. Indeed, in the last three and a half centuries of its history, the very period during which the Byzantine national existence was gravely threatened (by the Crusaders and foreign enemies of all sorts who invaded and occupied its territories), the common language was strengthened by new and vigorous classical revivals. Naturally, the common language was not the spoken language of the people, but the latter never had the strength to drive out the former. In the West, on the other hand, popular usage corrupted classical Latin and made of it what was called Vulgar Latin, which then, sometime between the 7th and 10th centuries, disappeared entirely (except for the survival of the ancient idiom in the Roman liturgy and in the works of scholars), and was supplanted as a spoken tongue by the new Romance languages. In Byzantium the metamorphosis of the spoken form of Greek into anything resembling Romance never took place. Instead, there was, and remained in modern Greece officially until 1976, a duality of languages: the ''common'' or literary language (of the Atticizing writers known in modern times as the καθαρεύουσα) and, over against this, the popular or ''demotic'' language of the people. But both were, and are recognizably Greek in form and structure. *See* GREEK LANGUAGE, EARLY CHRISTIAN AND BYZANTINE.

General Character of Byzantine Literature

Though it is rarely prudent to generalize concerning an entire people, there are a few traits of Byzantine literature as a whole that may be regarded as characteristic. Above all, the medieval Greeks, like their ancient ancestors, whose literature they cherished, had a fierce sense of cultural pride that left its mark in every phase of their activity. Their emperor, who was, according to them, chosen by God himself, was the ruler of the whole of the inhabited world; and the Byzantine Church was in their sight the divinely appointed custodian and champion of the only true faith, just as their language was the sole respectable medium for communication.

In some important respects the Byzantines were the heirs of the Hellenistic age, i.e., of the Greek culture that flourished for 600 or 700 years between *c.* 350 B.C. and the middle of the 4th century of the Christian Era. It is from this period, from the school of ALEXANDRIA, that the Byzantines inherited their flair for scholarly works of all kinds—for the transcription, critical revision, and excerpting of the ancient texts; for the compilation and collection of literary materials of every description; for philological studies; for their predilection for the *ekphrasis* (a description, long or short, in prose or verse, of a person, place, object, work of art, etc.); and for the annotation, exegesis, and appraisal of ancient literature of all kinds.

Dominance of Rhetoric. Adherence to the educational practices of late antiquity led to an addiction to rhetoric, which colored everything the Byzantines said and wrote. They avoided ordinary and customary words, invented a bewildering array of new sesquipedalian monstrosities with the aid of prefixes of various kinds, and constantly strained after novel modes of expression. The result is that the modern reader has often to cut his way through tangled webs of tortuously constructed sentences, which are not always fully comprehensible.

Fortunately, a great many writers, especially in the earlier centuries, were free from this passion for rhetorical embellishment. St. Athanasius, for example, and most of the theologians of the period of the ecumenical councils cultivated a simple, unadorned style that usually offers no difficulties, and was often uninfluenced by classical standards. But more erudite authors, men such as Photius, Psellus, or Metochites, struggled so earnestly to write in the elevated manner that they became all but unintelligible.

Lack of Originality. Paradoxically, despite these frantic efforts to achieve originality of form, the Byzantines had no problems about paraphrasing or even copying out whole paragraphs and pages from the works of other authors without acknowledgment or fear of censure for so doing: plagiarism is a meaningless concept in a Byzantine context.

The Byzantine lack of sensitivity in such matters is probably to be explained by ingrained acceptance of authority, imperial and ecclesiastical, and also by the traditional convention of imitation. An emperor's decree or the dogma formulated by one of the ecumenical councils might be copied, annotated, or discussed. It could not be altered. This attitude of obeisance was transferred to literary, philosophical, and scientific texts, and is reflected in the innumerable Byzantine compendia, anthologies, excerpts, and paraphrases. It was further reinforced by an education system which, aiming at inculcating a good literary style, taught this by careful study of the masters from the past.

But few felt the need to begin afresh or to develop a new system of thought and belief. Even the neopagan George Gemistos PLETHON (*c.* 1355–1452), who sought to overthrow the Christian religion, confined himself in his scheme for a new pagan state to summarizing and weaving together a great variety of sources, mostly Platonic and Neoplatonic. He did not depart from the paths laid down in the ancient tradition.

Hence, even when they fail to cite the authors whom they copy or follow, Byzantine writers had no intention to deceive. Thus, JOHN DAMASCENE in the *Fountain of Knowledge* (Πηγὴ γνώσεως) disarmingly confesses that he was wholly dependent upon his authorities, and had made no attempt to present ideas of his own.

Being overpowered by the weight of tradition and predisposed to follow models of one sort or another, the Byzantine writers felt free to write in as many media as they chose. Before the Hellenistic Age, no writer (except Ion of Chios in the 5th century B.C., and possibly Plato, if the poems attributed to him are genuine) expressed himself in more than one literary genre. The historian confined himself to history, the lyric poet to lyric poetry, the dramatist to drama, and the philosopher to philosophy. But in Byzantium many writers tried their hands at a variety of styles, and wrote in every conceivable literary form: history, philosophy, mathematics, and poetry. As a result, the novelty they achieved was usually in expression rather than in ideas.

Theology

Byzantine civilization turned around two foci: the Church and the emperor. There is hardly a phase of Byzantine activity that can be considered apart from these two vital factors. Though the emperor dominated all phases of Byzantine life and even exerted control over the

Byzantine Church, the Byzantines felt no special urge to write about political theory or on the relation between Church and State. There are, of course, important Byzantine treatises on this subject, but they are greatly outweighed in both bulk and number by the works of the theologians, who concerned themselves with all the major problems of theology, especially those involved in the Trinitarian and Christological controversies [*see* TRINITY, HOLY, CONTROVERSIES ON; CHRISTOLOGY, CONTROVERSIES ON (PATRISTIC)]. These were the principal subjects on the agenda of the seven ecumenical councils (NICAEA I, 325; CONSTANTINOPLE I, 381; EPHESUS, 431; CHALCEDON, 451; CONSTANTINOPLE II, 553; CONSTANTINOPLE III, 680–681; NICAEA II, 787) that produced the official creeds of the Church. [*See* COUNCILS, GENERAL (ECUMENICAL), HISTORY OF.]

These documents, especially the so-called NICENE CREED (more technically described as the Niceno-Constantinopolitan Creed, to distinguish it from that of 325, which it closely resembles) and the Creed of Chalcedon provide the basic definitions of the doctrines of the Trinity and of the person of Christ, respectively, as these are understood in most of the Christian Churches throughout the world—Roman, Greek Orthodox, and Protestant.

From the point of view of the enormous influence of these creeds on the entire history of the Christian world, therefore, the theologians who drafted, expounded, and defended them deserve a place in intellectual history hardly, if at all, below that of the ancient Greek philosophers. Aesthetically and liturgically, as well as theologically, the creeds themselves merit careful study.

Moreover, on the evidence of the New Testament, in which Christ is represented both as a divine being (i.e., one who performed miracles, conquered death, and rose to heaven) and as a true man (who ate, drank, slept, wept, etc., like other men), the theological definitions contained in these creeds are logically inevitable. In other words, the heretics were not condemned because they made use of pagan philosophy, terminology, and logic, as some contend, but primarily because, in one way or another, they failed to take adequate account of the New Testament portrayal of Jesus Christ.

Antiheretical Polemics. The reasoning by which the doctrines set forth in these creeds were evolved becomes a matter of the highest interest. The earliest monuments of this doctrinal development (after the New Testament itself, the writings of the APOSTOLIC FATHERS, of the APOLOGISTS, of Pope DIONYSIUS I and DIONYSIUS OF ALEXANDRIA, and of theologians such as IRENAEUS, CLEMENT and ORIGEN of Alexandria, and TERTULLIAN of Carthage), fall outside of the chronological limits of this essay.

Within our scope, however, comes ALEXANDER, PATRIARCH OF ALEXANDRIA, and, even more significantly, his successor, St. ATHANASIUS (bishop, 328–373), the chief defender of the Nicene theology in the first half of the 4th century, to whom we owe three *Orations Against the Arians,* as well as letters and other treatises that rank among the chief sources for our knowledge of the transactions of the first ecumenical council and of much of the subsequent development down to 381. In addition, Athanasius occupies a place of importance in the history of monasticism for his *Life of St. Anthony* (251–356), the first of the great hermits and one of the spiritual ancestors of Byzantine asceticism (*see* ANTHONY OF EGYPT, ST.).

In the next phase of the Arian controversy, down to and including the second council (381), the chief authorities were the three Cappadocians, St. BASIL of Caesarea in Cappadocia (d. 379), his younger brother GREGORY OF NYSSA (d. 394), and their friend Bishop GREGORY OF NAZIANZUS (d. 389 or 390).

In his letters as well as in his works *Against Eunomius* and *On the Holy Spirit* Basil refuted the arguments of the Arians. His major contribution was the formulation and dogmatic defense of the Trinitarian formula, μία οὐσία ἐν τρισὶν ὑποστάσεσι:, one substance (or essence, i.e., one divinity) in three hypostases (i.e., three persons). Moreover, Basil was the founder of Byzantine monasticism, his regulations for which exerted influence also in the West. His nine homilies on the *Hexaemeron* (the Biblical account of creation) are noteworthy as a statement of Christian principles of cosmology, which drew freely upon pagan authorities, such as Plato, Aristotle, Poseidonius and PLOTINUS. Gregory of Nyssa carried on the attack against the Eunomians and the Macedonians (*see* SABELLIANISM; MONARCHIANISM), continued his brother's study of cosmology with a treatise *On the Creation of Man* (*De Opificio hominis*), and produced a host of works on other subjects. He relied extensively upon Plato. Gregory of Nazianzus, known as "the Theologian" because of his five theological orations, was less prolific than Gregory of Nyssa. He wrote some 400 poems and, among other things, a bitter treatise against Emperor Julian.

Another refutation of Julian's polemic against the Christians was that of CYRIL OF ALEXANDRIA (bishop, 412–444), whose chief importance, however, lay in his interpretation of the relation of the two natures (the divine and the human) in Christ. Actually, his famous Christological formula, μία φύσις τοῦ Θεοῦ Λόγου σεσαρκωμένη [one incarnate nature of God the Word (Logos)], was taken over from Apollinaris (the heretic, *c.* 310–390) in the mistaken belief that it had been enunciated by Athanasius (*see* APOLLINARIANISM). The "strict" Chalcedonians, including THEODORET OF CYR (d. *c.* 466) and NESTORIUS (fl. 428), objected that this phrase was Monophysitic and signified that Christ had only one nature instead of two. The Cyrillian theologians, in turn, insisted that, by stressing the fact that the ''one nature'' was ''incarnate,'' this formula fully safeguarded the integrity and reality in Christ of two natures, as orthodox theology required.

The chief defenders of the strictly Chalcedonian dyophysite Christology were HYPATIUS OF EPHESUS (fl. 532) and LEONTIUS OF BYZANTIUM (fl. 543), the latter of whom wrote against both the Nestorians and the Monophysites.

Taking a position midway between the strict Chalcedonians and the Monophysites were the so-called Neochalcedonians, who attempted to reinterpret the creed of 451 in Cyrillian terms. The most interesting as well as the most powerful of the theologians of this group was Emperor Justinian I (527–565), who, besides several pronouncements in the *Corpus Iuris Civilis* on theological matters, is credited in the manuscripts with three erudite doctrinal dissertations. His chief aim was to vindicate the theology of Cyril against its critics. This he succeeded in doing at the Council of 553 by interpreting Cyril's Christological formula and other aspects of the Cyrillian system, which the Chalcedonians had found objectionable, in harmony with the creed of 451.

At the same time, however, the Neochalcedonians continued to attack the Monophysites despite the fact that many modern critics fail to find much difference between Neochalcedonianism and the so-called ''MONOPHYSITISM'' of Bp. SEVERUS OF ANTIOCH (512–538), who devoted his considerable talents to the defense and exposition of the Cyrillian position. For this reason, many have doubted whether he can be properly classified as a Monophysite. Nevertheless, the orthodox prejudice against him was so great that very little of what he wrote is extant, save in Syriac translation. His chief offense, perhaps, was that he polemized against the Creed of Chalcedon, which he took to be Nestorian. On the other hand, another Monophysite of the 6th century, JULIAN OF HALICARNASSUS, is not easily defended, and was attacked even by Severus of Antioch for Aphthartodocetism.

In the conflict with Monenergism and MONOTHELITISM, the great champion of the doctrine that Christ had two energies and two wills (as set forth eventually by the sixth ecumenical council), was MAXIMUS THE CONFESSOR (580–662), the author of numerous dogmatic and polemical treatises and letters on various theological subjects, including commentaries on the PSEUDO-DIONYSIUS, an allegorical interpretation of the liturgy, and a series of so-called *Centuries.* At the end of the 7th century the struggle against heresy was continued by ANASTASIUS SINAITA (d. *c.* 700), who polemized against the Monophysites in his *Hodegos* (Guide), and wrote a commentary on the Biblical account of creation.

Despite their condemnation at the Councils of 451, 553, and 680 to 681, the Monophysites persisted in the struggle to obtain an ecumenical decision in their favor, and in the 8th and 9th centuries sought to circumvent the strict dyophysitism of 451 by calling for the condemnation of the images of Christ, Mary, and the saints, which they deemed sacrilegious (*see* ICONOCLASM). The iconoclasts were led by Emperors LEO III (717–741), CONSTANTINE V (741–775), and LEO V (813–820), but in the end they were defeated, largely through the efforts of Empresses IRENE (in 787) and THEODORA (in 843). The chief defenders of the images were Patriarch GERMANUS I of Constantinople (715–730; d. 733), John Damascene (the greatest theologian of his day; d. *c.* 753), Patriarchs TARASIUS (784–806) and NICEPHORUS I (806–815) of Constantinople, and THEODORE THE STUDITE (759–826).

John Damascene is celebrated not only for his *Three Orations Against the Iconoclasts,* a number of Biblical commentaries, and some liturgical poems of high merit, but above all for his great theological encyclopedia, the *Fountain of Knowledge* (Πηγὴ γνώσεως). John exerted great influence on theology both in Byzantium and in the Latin West (to which parts of the *Fountain* were made available in Latin translations of the 12th and 13th centuries). But he made no claim to originality and was dependent upon his sources, pagan and Christian, which he often copied verbatim.

In the second iconoclastic period (815–843), the leading figure was Theodore the Studite, an uncompromising champion of images, whose intransigence on this subject thrice drove him into exile. Besides his polemical writings in favor of images, he is known for two collections of *Catechetical Precepts* (on the duties of monks), an extensive correspondence, homilies, panegyrics, his epigrams (see below), and a notable group of liturgical poems.

Mystical Theology. Hardly less characteristic of Byzantium than the dogmatic decrees of the ecumenical councils was the Byzantine interest in mystical theology, which is closely connected with ascetical practices of various kinds. Alongside the early Biblical type of mystic union with Christ as set forth in the Pauline Epistles, the early Fathers, and Basil of Caesarea, there was the more intellectual type, which was dependent upon philosophical sources, mediated by Origen (*c.* 185–254) and EVAGRIUS PONTICUS (346–399). This latter form of mysticism is best known in its most developed form as presented by the PSEUDO DIONYSIUS thc Areopagite (fl. 500), who was deeply influenced by PROCLUS, the Neoplatonist, and served as one of the major channels by which Neoplatonic ideas were transmitted to the later Middle Ages (*see* NEOPLATONISM). Apart from heterodox variations of mysticism like that of the Messalians [combated by DIADOCHUS OF PHOTICE (d. before 486)], the Byzantine tradition was best represented by JOHN CLIMACUS of Sinai (d. *c.* 670), Maximus the Confessor (580–662), Theodore the Studite (759–826), SYMEON THE NEW THEOLOGIAN (949–1022), and NICETAS STETHATOS (fl. 1054). Finally, in the 14th century, differences of opinion on various aspects of mystical theology led to the Hesychast controversy, which ended in the triumph of the Hesychasts, such as Gregory PALAMAS and Emperor JOHN VI CANTACUZENUS, against their opponents, BARLAAM OF CALABRIA, NICEPHORUS GREGORAS, and others (*see* HESYCHASM).

After the final settlement of the iconoclastic controversy in 843, the most fruitful period in the history of Byzantine theology came to an end. The production of theological works continued as in the past. But the questions discussed after 843, though often hotly contested, were not so significant as the dogmas of the Trinity and the Incarnation, to the definition of which the ecumenical councils had addressed themselves. Even some of the earlier questions had reverberations in the later centuries, and Photius, for example, near the end of the 9th century, still found it necessary to polemize against the iconoclasts. Similarly, MANICHAEISM rose up in new forms (PAULICIANS and BOGOMILS) which called forth new refutations. But the interests and literary activity of the theologians of the later period were most actively engaged in dealing with the question of the proposed union of the Churches of Rome and Byzantium, the problem of Hesychasm, and the polemic against Islam. The proponents of union with Rome were greatly aided by the Greek translations of Latin theological masterpieces that were made by Demetrius Cydones (*c.* 1324–1397 or 1398). The most important of these were of Thomas Aquinas's *Summa contra Gentiles* and *Summa theologiae* (the latter of which was completed by Demetrius's brother Prochorus), the *DONATION OF CONSTANTINE*, and Anselm's *De processione spiritus sancti.*

In the middle of the 15th century the leading theologian, next to BESSARION (the Greek champion of union with Rome) and Abp. Mark of Ephesus (a resolute foe of the union), was George Scholarius (Patriarch GENNADIUS II of Constantinople, 1454), who was mildly in favor of union with Rome until 1443 or 1444, when he began to polemize against it. He defended the Palamites, wrote against the Jews and Plethon, and produced a number of valuable Greek translations of Latin theological classics.

Theological Encyclopedias. Appearing as compendia of the total Byzantine effort, theological encyclopedias were a favored form of synthesis, and several of them were remarkably successful. The Byzantines found this type of scholarly activity particularly congenial, and many theologians had devoted a great deal of energy to encyclopedic résumés or analyses of various kinds. (See for the earlier period, the *Stromata* of CLEMENT OF ALEXANDRIA, Eusebius of Caesarea's *Praeparatio* and *Demonstratio,* EPIPHANIUS OF CONSTANTIA's *Panarion*, Theodoret's polemic against the pagans, the 8th-century *Sacra Parallela* (Holy Parallels) and the great theological encyclopedia of John Damascene.)

In the later period the most noteworthy example of this genre was the *Dogmatic Armory* (Πανοπλία δογματική) of Euthymius ZIGABENUS, which was written to please Emperor ALEXIUS I COMNENUS, and to serve as an arsenal for orthodox theologians in their debates against the heretics. The first 22 sections are taken up with a consideration of early heresy with special emphasis on the post-Nicene era. In this section Zigabenus is dependent entirely upon quotations from the leading theological authorities of early times (Athanasius, the Cappadocians, John Damascene, Photius, etc.). But the concluding portions (bks. 23–28) in which he treats the heretics of his own time (the Armenians, Paulicians, Messalians, Bogomils, and Muslims) have independent value as historical source. Zigabenus is known also for his commentaries on the Psalms and the Gospels.

Of similar scope but different plan is the *Holy Arsenal* (Ἱερὰ ὁπλοθήκη) of Andronicus Camaterus, dedicated to Emperor MANUEL I, *c.* 1170–75. The first division of this *Arsenal* begins with a dialogue between the Emperor and the Roman *Kardenalioi* (cardinals) on the procession of the Holy Spirit, in which the Byzantine doctrine on the ''single'' procession is supported by quotations from the Bible and the Fathers, and fortified by syllogisms taken from the writings of earlier Byzantine opponents of the Latins. The second part of the work is directed against the Armenians, whom the Byzantines condemned as Monophysites, and is made up of an attack on heretical views of a Monophysitizing tendency (i.e., not only on Monophysitism itself, but also on Monotheletism, the theopaschite doctrine, and aphthartodocetism). Only a small part of the *Arsenal* has been published.

A third theological encyclopedia following those of the Comnenian period, the *Treasury of Orthodoxy* (Θησαυρὸς ὀρθοδοξίας), came from the pen of the historian NICETAS CHONIATES (brother of Michael Choniates), who supplemented the *Panoplia* of Zigabenus, and concentrated on a survey of the older heresies, which the latter had not discussed. It is probably to be assigned to the years between 1204 and 1210, when Nicetas was in Nicaea; it is still only partially published. (See history below.)

Canon Law. If Justinian's *Corpus Iuris Civilis* has been excluded from discussion on linguistic grounds, the same should not be done for the more amorphous collections of canon lay, and in particular their commentaries, all of which were written in Greek. While Byzantine civil and ecclesiastical law were never separated, civil law was subject to repeal and amendment while canon law, derived from the acts of ecumenical councils before the 9th century, was deemed immutable and remained a constant reference point. The most widely used collection was that of the *Nomocanons in Fourteen Titles*, which, combining the text of the canons with material from the secular law codes, went through several developments between the seventh and the eleventh centuries. There were two periods in which commentary flourished: the twelfth century with the work of Alexios Aristenos, John ZONARAS and Theodore BALSAMON, and the fourteenth century when the key figures were Matthew BLASTARES and Constantinus Harmenopulos, whose writings were widely disseminated. The commentaries can offer illuminating insights into contemporary problems.

Homiletics. The Byzantines produced a vast number of sermons, which are marked by their fondness for rhetorical display; many of the major theologians have left large homiletic collections. The best known of the Byzantine preachers is the archbishop St. John Chrysostom of Constantinople (d. 407), one of the most prolific authors of the Byzantine period (the author of 18 volumes in the *Patrologia Graeca*), the greater part of whose extant writings consists of sermons usually delivered in the form of commentaries on various books of the Bible. Chrysostom suffered for his outspokenness as censor of morals. But he was enormously popular with the people of Constantinople, who were so captivated by his oratory, that, to his annoyance, they often interrupted him by applause.

Of interest also in this genre, to choose only one example out of many, was Abp. Michael Choniates (Acominatus) of Athens (*c.* 1175–1204; d. *c.* 1220), whose sermons and letters illuminate the literary and cultural history of Athens in this period. Michael deplored the low state of learning in the Athens of his day, the cultural level of which had fallen so low, he complained, that his style had been corrupted as a consequence.

Hagiography. Saints' lives are a branch of literature that is peculiar. They take many forms, almost invariably in prose, and vary in length from a paragraph in a service book to a bulky volume in a modern edition. Written to edify and encourage the faithful to a more virtuous life, they range over gruesome accounts of martyrdoms, hair-raising descriptions of desert asceticism to tales of quiet monastic piety. Many are anonymous, though some notable writers, for example Theodore Prodromos, have tried their hand at the genre. Though long ignored by historians of literature, it is now appreciated that saints' lives are of undoubted interest in their own right, offer many insights into Byzantine society, and often provide valuable historical information.

History

In the field of history, the Byzantines continued the ancient Greek tradition with notable success, and produced a great historical literature. The extant texts are regularly divided into two types: histories and chronicles, though the distinction between the two is often blurred.

Historians and Chroniclers. Chronicles and histories differed from each other in many respects. The writers of chronicles, often but by no means always members of the clergy, looked upon history as a kind of homiletical exercise, by which they were enabled to justify the ways of God to man. Their chief concern was to champion their own brand of orthodoxy, making use of the most convenient sources at hand, which they excerpted freely or reproduced verbatim, with special emphasis upon the bizarre and the unusual. They had a special fondness for miracles, ice storms, comets, floods, and other phenomena that might prove interesting or edifying and exemplify God's benevolent chastisement of errant mankind.

Since the writers of the chronicles were not connected with the highly educated elite, most of them wrote in the popular idiom; and their works thus often preserved specimens of the vernacular language of their period. Though more derivative than the historians, the chroniclers are by no means devoid of significance. Many reported events at firsthand as eyewitnesses, or covered subjects, persons, and places ignored by the historians; and several have proved to be the only available sources for the information that they supply. Moreover, not a few of the chronicles, like that of JOHN MALALAS, for instance, which deals primarily with the history of ANTIOCH, preserve local information and traditions, concerning which the Constantinopolitan writers were uninformed.

The chroniclers set out to cover the entire history of the world from the creation on, and prefixed to the treatment of their own special period a section on the creation of the universe, together with a survey of ancient history, Biblical and classical. After this introductory sketch of early times, the chroniclers then went on to deal with the events of their own day. The historians, on the other hand, except for Laonicus Chalcocondyles and Ducas, made no place for the history of their remote forbears and concentrated, instead, on their own times.

Moreover, most, but not all, of the chroniclers contented themselves with a very cursory summary of each period of Biblical or ancient history, and with a short paragraph, often not exceeding a few sentences in length, for each year of later history.

In contrast with this straightforward method, the historians gave lengthy and detailed accounts of the eras with which they were primarily concerned. Most of them were laymen of high social position and excellent education, who either were themselves active participants in the events they described or were indirectly involved as ambassadors, generals, or members of the royal household. They wrote for people like themselves, often at the emperor's command, and had access to excellent sources: letters, archival material of various kinds, and texts in many languages, as well as the testimony of eyewitnesses. Though they prided themselves on their disinterestedness and undertook, like the ancient models they imitated, to investigate and expatiate upon the causal relations of the facts they reported, this claim should usually be treated with caution.

The historians were strongly influenced by the great historical writers of antiquity (Herodotus, Thucydides, Xenophon, and Polybius), whom they constantly sought to emulate in language, style, and method. For this reason, they usually avoided contemporary nomenclature and have confused modern students by insisting upon the geographical designations current in the ancient writers. [Scythians, rather than the current name, Rosoi (οἱ Ῥῶς or Ῥῶσοι) for Russians].

Similarly, in the effort to reproduce the manner and syntax of their ancient models, the Byzantine historians often used recondite words and complex constructions with the result that many sentences are so twisted as to be incomprehensible. Their attempted emulation of ancient rhetoric was often more ambitious than successful. Not all of the great corpus of Byzantine historians is extant. But from the histories that have been preserved it can be seen that the historians provided what is almost a continuous, uninterrupted account of the Byzantine world from the time of Diocletian (284–305) until the fall of Constantinople in 1453. Normally, one historian took up the thread of the narrative where his predecessor left off. Usually, whether by chance or design, there was one historian for each period, and only one. Hence, except as noted below (in the 14th and 15th centuries, in which special conditions prevailed), there were no surviving rival historians, and we have only one major authority among the historians for each chronological division.

The interpretation of history thus presented would be extremely one-sided if it were not possible, as it usually is, to compare the views of the historians with contemporary chronicles, legal documents, theological treatises, the *typika* (foundation charters of monasteries, etc.), letters, and the historical works of non-Byzantine writers (Arabic, Syriac, Armenian, Latin, and others). This generalization is applicable only to the portions of each history upon which the historian concentrated as his own special province, not to the introductory sections in which he reviewed the events of preceding years by way of preface.

Ecclesiastical History. One of the fields in which the Byzantine historians excelled was ecclesiastical history.

Eusebius. The first and greatest representative of the historians was Eusebius of Caesarea in Palestine (*c.* 263–340), who exerted an enormous influence on subsequent writers in this genre, despite his leanings toward ARIANISM and iconoclasm. His chief works were his panegyric on, or, as it is usually designated, the biography of, Constantine I and his invaluable history of the early Church (from the beginning to 324). The former (in four books), when allowances are made for its adulatory tone, is an absolutely indispensable key to the understanding of Constantine's reign, and in recent times has been strongly defended against the attacks certain modern critics had made against it.

The latter, in ten books, which is no less monumental in significance, preserves in excerpt a mass of historical records that otherwise would have perished. Eusebius is memorable also as the first to have popularized, on the basis of the efforts of Ammonius of Alexandria, an elaborate scheme for tabulating the parallel passages in the Gospels (where two or more Gospels are similar or identical) and the material peculiar to each of them by dividing the Gospels into numbered sections, which he listed under rubrics or headings, now known as the Eusebian canons or sections. These canons, which were taken over by Jerome in the Vulgate translation, are found in many medieval Gospel Books and New Testaments (both Greek and Latin), and are usually adorned with handsome representations of animals, flowers, arcades, arches, columns, and with decorative patterns of many types.

Of his numerous other works on related subjects, special interest attaches to his *Praeparatio evangelica* (*Preparation for the Gospel*), in 15 books, which is an elaborate and erudite refutation of pagan religion and mythology (based on hundreds of quotations from the classics) and a glorification of the teaching of the Old Testament. In the *Demonstratio evangelica* (*Proof of the Gospel*), originally written in 20 books, of which ten and a fraction are extant, Eusebius explained why the Christians accept the Old Testament (in which he found numerous prophecies of the appearance of Christ) but reject the Mosaic Law.

Eusebius's Ecclesiastical *History* served as the model for later Church historians in the Greek East as well as in the Latin West. RUFINUS (d. 410) rendered it into Latin and expanded it with certain, not always felicitous, additions of his own (which carried the history down to 395). More successful was St. JEROME's (d. 419 or 420) translation of the *Chronicon* (Eusebius's *Chronicle*), to which he added some new material and a supplement on the period from 324 to 378. Eusebius's work was not free from weaknesses and defects; his style is dry, humorless, and far from inspiring. Nevertheless it is doubtful whether any of his medieval successors ever attained the high standard of historical research that he set.

His Successors. His history was continued in the following century by SOCRATES THE HISTORIAN, SOZOMEN, and Theodoret, who dealt with the periods 305 to 439, 324 to 439, and 325 to 428, respectively. Some 100 years later, at the suggestion of Cassiodorus (d. *c.* 583), the renowned scholar, theologian, and adviser to King Theodoric, these three works were put into Latin and woven into a continuous narrative entitled *Historia ecclesiastica tripartita* by a certain Epiphanius. This tripartite history, in 12 books, though ineptly translated from the Greek, and unskillfully plaited together, was the principal Latin handbook of early ecclesiastical history, and circulated widely in the West throughout the Middle Ages and the Renaissance.

Epiphanius's text represents the orthodox point of view, as does Gelasius of Cyzicus, who in the last quarter of the 5th century produced an *Ecclesiastical History of the Constantinian Period,* which has little independent value except for the use of two illuminating but otherwise unknown sources.

On the heterodox side of the great theological debates of this era, however, there is not much information. Except for a few scraps, most of the heretical apologiae have fallen victim to the intolerance of the Byzantine government, which ordered them destroyed and meted out stern punishment to theologians temerarious enough to try to evade imperial proscription. Thus, for the Arian version of the Trinitarian controversy, we are reduced to the few remaining fragments of the *Ecclesiastical History* (on 300–425) by the radical Arian PHILOSTORGIUS.

Similarly, the history of Christology seen through the eyes of Nestorius's allies and written by Irenaeus of Tyre (*c.* 450–457) has survived only as quoted by the Orthodox Rusticus Diaconus (565) in his so-called *Synodicon adversus tragoediam Irenaei.* Despite this loss, we are, so far as Nestorius is concerned, the beneficiaries of the accident that has preserved the so-called *Bazaar of Heracleides,* Nestorius's minutely detailed defense of his position against Cyril, the Greek original of which was struck down by imperial decree. What we have is the Syriac version that happily found a haven in a Nestorian community, and has thus come down to the present day virtually intact.

Among the victims of imperial persecution were the valuable ecclesiastical histories of the Monophysites John Diacrinomenus (John the Heretic) and Basil of Cilicia, the former of which covered the years 429 to 518, and the latter, *c.* 450 to 540. In addition, time and accident, not the orthodox or imperial relentlessness, are responsible for the loss of many precious sources, such as THEODORE LECTOR's *Historia tripartita* (of which two out of four books have disappeared) and the same author's *Ecclesiastical History* (on the years 450–527), which circulated in a popular *Epitome* of the 8th or 9th century.

In the midst of all these losses, we are fortunate to have the Syriac translation of ZACHARY the Rhetor's *Ecclesiastical History* (in the original Greek, on 450–491), which (in Syriac) extends to 568 or 569. Zachary, who ended his days as bishop of Mytilene (d. before 553), was a convert from Monophysitism to Neochalcedonianism, and the author of a biography of Severus (the Monophysite bishop of Antioch) as well as a polemic against the pagan doctrine of the eternity of the universe. The *Life of Severus* is preserved only in Syriac; but the polemic is extant in Greek.

Evagrius Scholasticus. The fullest and best history of the Church in this period (431–593), however, is that of EVAGRIUS SCHOLASTICUS, a Syrian Greek. Despite a tendency toward prolixity, Evagrius's *Ecclesiastical History* is well written (in Greek), and imitates the ancient Greek historian Thucydides. It is a history, not a chronicle, and treats extensively of secular affairs (like the Persian wars of its times).

After Evagrius, ecclesiastical history as such seems to have disappeared almost entirely, save for that from the pen of Nicephorus Callistus Xanthopulus (*c.* 1320), who used the best sources available to him but did not, in the extant portion of his work, get beyond 610. For the later history of the Church, therefore, we have to depend upon chronicles, secular histories, the acts of councils, letters, archival records, and similar materials.

Secular History. In secular history, however, the materials are more abundant.

Early Period. For the earliest period, we have the pagan Eunapius of Sardis, whose *Lives of the Sophists* (on 270–404) is extant complete. But only fragments remain in his *Historical Memoirs* (on 270–404), as of the works by the pagan Olympiodorus of Thebes in Egypt (on 407–425), the pagan(?) Priscus of Panion (on *c.*

411–472), the Christian sophist Malchus from Philadelphia in Palestine (on the period 306 to 480), and the Christian Candidus from Isauria (on 457–491). In addition, a few extracts have survived from the *Chronicle* of Hesychius Illustrios of Miletus, who was apparently a pagan; the *Chronicle* recounted events of the period from the Babylonian Bel to 518.

More interesting is the *Historia nova* of Zosimus, an imperial fiscal officer (fl. *c.* 450–501), who set out to prove that the fall of the Roman Empire was to be ascribed to the neglect of the ancient pagan religion. The villain in this drama was Emperor Constantine I, because he granted toleration to Christianity, and the hero was Emperor Julian (361–363), who had attempted to restore paganism. Zosimus did not fail to touch upon the great Greek victories over the Persians at Marathon (490 B.C.) and Salamis (480 B.C.). But his chief emphasis was on Roman history from the victory of Augustus Caesar (31 B.C.– A.D. 14) in the battle of Actium in 31 B.C. to the accession of Diocletian in 284 (bk. 1), and from 284 to 410 (bks. 2–6).

Procopius. The best known and most important of the Byzantine writers of history was PROCOPIUS (from Caesarea in Palestine), the historian of the age of Justinian I (527–565), the most glorious era of the Byzantine Empire. Since he was (from 527) adviser and secretary to the great general BELISARIUS, it was natural that Procopius should have occupied himself seriously with the *History of the Wars* (against the Persians, Vandals, and Goths: in eight books, principally on 527–553). But he did not neglect internal history and, in his six books *On Buildings,* which he intended as a panegyric, reviewed the unparalleled program of new buildings and engineering projects of every description, which Justinian devised and brought to completion throughout the empire. In the *Anecdota* (''Unpublished Documents''), however, Procopius abandoned adulation for vituperation and gave himself up to paroxysms of rage, in which he heaped abuse on Justinian and Empress THEODORA. He not only blamed them personally for earthquakes, floods, and other natural disasters, but also berated them for all manner of debauchery and vice. Procopius's reasons for this astounding *volte face* can only be conjectured. His style, though dominated by the customary classicizing tendencies, is forceful and clear.

Agathias, Menander Protector, and Theophylactus. Procopius was followed by two historians of importance, Agathias, who put out five books on the years 552 to 558, and Menander Protector, of whose history on the period from 558 to 582 only fragments have been preserved. Agathias, whom Menander and many later writers imitated, wrote in a style with many poetic overtones and rhetorical devices. Rather more overblown was THEOPHYLACTUS SIMOCATTA, whose eight books on the reign of Emperor MAURICE (582–602) are marred by fanciful language and excessive rhetorical extravagances. Despite these stylistic defects, his history was highly esteemed by later Byzantine writers for its accuracy and objectivity.

The historical continuity was broken after Theophylactus, from 602 to 813; and the sequence of historical books was not resumed until the mid-tenth century when two writers picked up the thread again. These were Joseph Genesius, a historian at the court of Emperor Constantine VII (reigned 912–959), with his history of the empire from the time of Leo V to the death of LEO VI (813–886) and the set of anonymous imperial biographies, covering the same period and also commissioned by Constantine VII, that go under the name of Theophanes Continuatus. The reason for the interruption in the historical record between 602 and 813 has not been determined. It may perhaps be attributable to the Persian wars, the Arab invasions, or the iconoclastic controversy, which took place during this interval. But this is by no means certain; and it is not at all inconceivable that new sources may eventually come to light that will fill this gap, at least partially.

Constantine VII and the Golden Age of Byzantine Historiography. In the 10th century, however, formal historical research flourished as never before in the Byzantine Empire. The inspiration for this outburst of activity came from Emperor CONSTANTINE VII PORPHYROGENITUS, who was in his own right a classicist and historian of note. During the years that he was excluded from actual power by his father-in-law, Emperor ROMANUS I LECAPENUS (920–944), he set his subordinates the task of assembling, excerpting, and summarizing documents, while he and his most trusted collaborators collected intelligence from ambassadors, merchants, and spies. These were the materials that formed the basis for the great historical compendia he and his aides produced.

He himself was possibly the author of the *Life of Basil I* (867–886), which forms Book 5 of the collection known as *Theophanes Continuatus.* Since Constantine was writing of his grandfather, this work, although constituting a valuable source, must be used with caution because it was an encomium rather than a critical biography. More significant is his *De administrando imperio,* a manual on foreign and domestic policy intended by him for the guidance of his son and successor, Romanus II (959–963). It is a great treasury of geographical, ethnological, and historical information, written in a popular style, and therefore more comprehensible than many of the Atticizing historical works. It may be compared to a modern summary of foreign intelligence, and was undoubtedly reserved for private circulation among the most reliable members of the imperial court.

Equally official but less confidential in nature was the imperial book of ceremonies (*De ceremoniis*), an invaluable description of the rituals, religious and secular, of the imperial court. A third unit in this historical series, *On the Themes* (*De thematibus*), in two books, which outlined the geographical boundaries of the military and administrative districts into which the empire was divided, is somewhat disappointing because it was taken not from the latest information available in the imperial archives, but almost verbatim, in the typically Byzantine manner, without acknowledgment, from the geographical works of Stephen of Byzantium (fl. probably 5th century) and Hierocles (6th century). But Constantine himself (*c.* 933–934), the compiler of the first book, and an unknown hand in the second (*c.* 998) added the names of the frontiers as they were known in the 10th century.

In addition, Constantine's staff put together a vast historical encyclopedia of 53 volumes of excerpts from books of history. Constantine believed that an abridgment of this kind was necessary in order to simplify the study of history, the bulk of which, he felt, had grown to such enormous proportions that it was impossible for any ordinary person to encompass or understand it. Unfortunately, most of this great anthology has disappeared, except for 24 of the 53 titles and two printed volumes *On Embassies* (*De legationibus*), two *On Virtue and Vice* (*De virtutibus et vitiis*), one *On Plots against the Emperors* (*De insidiis*), one *On Opinions* (*De sententiis*), and a few fragments of some others. Many of the excerpts preserve valuable texts, ancient and medieval, which otherwise would have perished.

Besides engaging in these herculean projects, Constantine's associates commented on the great legal code, the *Basilica,* which was based upon the *Digest, Codex,* and *Novels* of Justinian, as compiled in the time of Basil I (867–886) and Leo VI (886–912). Their editorial activity was expended also, *c.* 950, on the *Geoponica* (a treatise on agronomy, based upon materials of the 4th, 5th, and 6th centuries); and Theophanes Nonnus, a physician at Constantine VII's court, turned out a medical handbook based upon the *Epitome,* which Oribasius had compiled *c.* 350.

None of the extant historians fills the gap between the years 886 and 959 except in part through John Cameniates's eyewitness description of the capture of Thessalonica in 904 by Leo of Tripoli. However, if the boundaries between history and chronicle are blurred, as they probably should be, then the work of Symeon Logothetes (covering 842–948 and surviving in many versions) gives valuable insights. After Constantine's death, the historical series was taken up again by LEO DIACONUS, who in ten books related the history of the empire between 959 and 976, on the basis, as he says, of his own experiences and the reports of authorities close to the events portrayed. The style resembles that of Agathias and Theophylactus.

Michael Psellus and 11th-century Historiography. After Leo Diaconus came Michael Psellus, one of the greatest of the Byzantine polymaths (1018–*c.* 1096), to whom we are indebted for a fascinating portrait of the emperors and the court from 976 to 1077. In large part, Psellus drew upon his own reminiscences of his association with the emperors, all of whom, from 1028 to 1077, were his close personal friends. He had nothing to say about foreign affairs, but compensates for this serious omission by full and accurate reporting of the lives and characters of the emperors and their families. In spite of his intimate association with the members of the royal entourage, he managed to retain his objectivity, except in regard to his pupil, Emperor Michael VII Parapinakes (1071–78), whom he could not find it in his heart to criticize.

But concerning CONSTANTINE IX (1042–55), whom he had intended to eulogize, he allowed himself to make some unfavorable observations, especially with regard to what he considered the Emperor's prodigality in utilizing the empire's resources. He did not refrain from calling attention, also, to Constantine's eccentric behavior in introducing his mistress Sklerena into the palace, crowning her empress, and persuading his wife, Zoë, not only to remain in the palace in the bedchamber next to his, but also to give written consent to this *ménage à trois* in a document witnessed by the senate.

Psellus seems not to have overlooked the tragicomic overtones in these somewhat bizarre details in the life of the Empress, who, in these unpleasant surroundings, was nevertheless able to console herself by gathering herbs and brewing fragrant unguents, while her younger sister, Theodora, who had been joint empress with her for three months in 1042, and was to be sole ruler of the empire (1055–56), amused herself, as did Zoë herself, by collecting gold coins. Psellus was one of the most brilliant of the Byzantine historians, none of whom had greater narrative power than he. But his brand of the Atticizing style is not easy to read, and his memoirs of life at the court, though scintillating and in their way unexampled, need to be supplemented at many points by other sources.

From the 11th century we have the *Strategikon* of Cecaumenus (*c.* 1071), the advice of a father to his son on how to pursue a career in the army and the imperial service. Then, after another brief interruption, the historical continuum was taken up once again by Michael Attaliates (from Attalia in Pamphylia), who wrote on the period between 1034 and 1079. His work was colored by the rhetorical, poetizing style that had become fashionable in historiography since the time of Agathias, but he was a skilled and reliable historian.

From this period, too, we have the *Synopsis historiarum* of John Scylitzes, an eminent but obscure legal official, which covers the years 811–1057 (with a continuation probably by a different author) in a technique that once again hovers between chronicle and history proper.

Anna Comnena. A new era in historical writing began with the accession of Alexius I Comnenus (1081–1118) to the throne. The Emperor's son-in-law, Nicephorus Bryennius, wrote a personal, romanticized sketch of Alexius's life from 1070 to 1079. But the court historian par excellence of the day was Alexius's daughter, and Nicephorus's wife, Anna Comnena, whose *Alexiad,* though an unabashed panegyric of her father and family (on the years 1069–1118), presents a gripping account of Alexius's rise to power and of the relations between the Byzantines and the Latins during his reign. Her style, which is heavy, pedantic, and pretentious, is often extremely difficult to unravel. Notwithstanding her passionate Byzantine patriotism and contempt for the Latins, she did not distort the facts. Nor did she minimize the victories and triumphs of the ''barbarians.'' Her zeal for the truth, which shines through in spite of her prejudices, her sense of drama, and her narrative skill make the *Alexiad* a masterpiece of medieval literature that ranks with the best.

Anna's Successors in the 12th and 13th Centuries. Anna's story was continued by John Cinnamus in his *Epitome,* which carried the history of Byzantium from 1118 to 1176. He had intended to devote his principal attention to the reign of Emperor MANUEL I (1143–80), for whom he had great admiration, but he seems never to have reached the end of his narrative. He was extremely conscientious in all matters, and did not allow himself, because of his dislike for the Latins, to misrepresent the facts. He was less learned than Anna, but his style is clearer and more intelligible.

More significant were NICETAS CHONIATES's 21 books on 1118 to 1206, which are notable, among other things, for a vivid description of the sack of Constantinople by the Crusaders in 1204 (bk. 19) and a whole book (21) on the statutes of Constantinople. (See theological encyclopedias above.)

The *Chronike Syngraphe* of George Acropolites (1217–82) has as its theme the history of Constantinople from the time the Crusaders attacked the city in 1203 until its recovery by the Byzantines in 1261 (*see* LATIN EMPIRE OF CONSTANTINOPLE). A great part of his narrative depends on his own personal observation as a general and high imperial official. He gave an objective, unvarnished account of his period in a simple if somewhat pompous style.

The continuation of Acropolites we owe to George PACHYMERES (1242–1310), who rose to high rank in the imperial service, and carried the narrative from 1261 (in part from 1255) to 1308. A man of great learning and versatility, he was the author, among other things, of a *Quadrivium* (*Syntagma ton tessaron mathematon;* i.e., on arithmetic, music, geometry, and astronomy), and an outline of the philosophy of Aristotle. He was one of the great polymaths of his age. He used many transliterations from Latin and non-Greek terms, such as κομμέρκιον and φρέριος (from *frères*). At the same time he carried pedantry so far as to use the Attic names of the months instead of the customary Christian designations.

Nicephoras Gregoras and the Last Historians of Byzantium. The next century produced perhaps the greatest scholar of the last two centuries of the Byzantine Empire. This was Nicephorus Gregoras (1295–*c.* 1359), who spared only seven out of the 37 books of his *Roman History* for the years 1204 to 1320, and lavished 30 on the 40 years from 1320 to 1359. Throughout, he focused attention upon theological questions, especially upon Hesychasm, of which he was a determined but unsuccessful opponent. He experimented with every form of literary medium and not only wrote on nearly every conceivable subject, but even, in his astronomical work, anticipated Pope GREGORY XIII's reform of the Julian calendar (in 1582).

Emperor John VI Cantacuzenus (1347–54) was a partisan of Palamism and the Hesychasts against Gregoras, for whose defeat and discomfiture he was responsible. But, when in 1354 he was forced to abdicate by Emperor John V (1341–76), whom he had himself dethroned, he retired to a monastery, as the monk Ioasaph, and there busied himself with scholarly works. The chief fruit of this activity was his four books of history (on 1320–56, with some references extending as far as 1362). He confined himself to matters that he knew at first hand, and castigated his predecessors (especially Gregoras) for deliberate suppression of the truth.

Actually, Gregoras and Cantacuzenus must at all points be supplemented by each other, not only for correction of bias but also in subject matter, since Cantacuzenus (who was an Aristotelian) limited himself to domestic history, while Gregoras (a Platonist) was concerned with foreign affairs as well. Cantacuzenus wrote clearly and forcefully. But he and his friends always occupied the center of the stage, and his history was in effect an elaborate *apologia pro vita sua.*

In 1422 Murad II laid siege to Constantinople but was unable to enter the city. His defeat was attributed to the intervention of the Virgin Mary, as we learn from John Cananus, who left an account of the siege and the repulse of the Turks in this year. In 1430, however, the Byzantines were less fortunate, and lost Thessalonica. The fall of this, the second city of the empire, was described at some length in the usual literary style of the Atticizing historians by John Anagnostes, who is to be contrasted in this respect with Cananus. The latter wrote in the idiom of the people, in simple, vernacular language, with few concessions to the classical mannerisms in which the more professional historians delighted.

The last unhappy days of the Byzantine Empire, culminating on May 29, 1453, in the collapse of Constantinople, and of the Byzantine Empire, formed the subject for four excellent historians, each of whom wrote from a different point of view. The first of these, Laonicus Chalcocondyles, was one of the few Athenians who figured prominently in Byzantine history. He paid scant attention to chronology as such but sought instead, on the basis of Turkish and Greek sources, to explain how it was that the Turks rose to power. In his ten books (on 1298–1463), to which, like the chroniclers, he prefixed a summary of universal history, it is the Turkish Empire, not Byzantium, which occupies the center of the stage. This was a most unusual approach for a Byzantine, as was also his conclusion that the Turks took Constantinople to avenge themselves for the fall of Troy. Chalcocondyles consciously imitated Herodotus and Thucydides, and in so doing sedulously avoided using foreign words and place names, which he either ignored altogether or tried to translate into the appropriate ancient equivalents.

Byzantium returned to the center of attention in the history of Ducas, who, however, like Chalcocondyles, opened with a sketch of universal history from Adam to the Palaeologi. He then paused to consider the expansion of the Ottoman Empire down to 1402. But he skimmed rapidly over these matters and the history of the second half of the 14th century in order to pass on to a more extended treatment of the reigns of the last three emperors (from 1391–1453) and of the capture of Lesbos in 1462 by Muḥammad II, with which he brought his history to a close. He wrote in the popular language, avoided rhetorical excesses, and strove after accuracy. He had a flair for the dramatic, and was able because of his own close observation to give a moving account of the empire's last days.

The third of the historians, George Sphrantzes, had been taken prisoner by the Turks in 1453 and led away with his family into captivity. He ended his days as the monk Gregorius on the Island of Corfu, on which in 1477 he completed his *Chronicon* in four books (on the years 1258–1476), the most important of which are the second (on 1425–48), the third (on 1448–53), and the fourth (on the struggles of the Palaeologi in the Peloponnesus). He wrote from deep, personal knowledge and with considerable passion against both the Turks and the Latins, the latter of whom, he complained, regarded the fall of Byzantium as punishment for heresy, although political history, in his opinion, had nothing to do with orthodoxy. He closed with an examination of ancient prophecies on the duration of the Turkish Empire. Standing stylistically between the artificial archaisms of Chalcocondyles and the simple, unadorned prose of Ducas, Sphrantzes had a fluent, easy style. He made occasional concessions to the popular language of his day, without abandoning altogether the traditional Atticizing manner of the historians.

Apparently before 1470, the fourth of the historians in this group, Critobulus, a Greek of good family from the Island of Imbros, composed a panegyrical history of the Sultan Mohammed II from 1451 to 1467. He imitated Thucydides as far as he was able in style and in the arrangement of his material, but was notable chiefly because of his subservience to the Turks. Since Critobulus, alone of the four historians, lived under Turkish jurisdiction at the time he wrote his history, it is perhaps understandable that he felt called upon to flatter the sultan and adopt the Turkish point of view.

Chronicles. The chroniclers are here listed by name, with a brief note on the extent of each chronicle:

1. John Malalas (491–578) of Antioch in Syria: Creation to 563 (probably originally went to 565 or 574)

2. John of Antioch (in fragments): Creation to 610

3. *Chronicon Paschale*: Creation to c. 627

4. GEORGE SYNCELLUS (d. 810/811); Creation to 284

5. THEOPHANES THE CONFESSOR: 284–813 (continuation of G. Syncellus)

6. Theophanes Continuatus: 813–961

7. Nicephorus (d. 829) *Historia syntomos* (the *Brevarium*) and *Chronographikon syntomon*: Creation to 829

8. Georgius Monachus: Creation to 842

9. Symeon Metaphrastes and Logothete—continued by Leo Grammaticus to 1013 (Theodosius Melitenus): Creation to 948

10. John Skylitzes: 811 to 1079

11. George Cedrenus: Creation to 1057

12. John ZONARAS: Creation to 1118

13. Constantine Manasses (in political verse): Creation to 1081

14. Michael GLYCAS: Creation to 1118

15. Joel: Creation to 1204

16. *Synopsis chronike* (of Sathas [Skoutariotes?]): Creation to 1261

17. Ephraem (in iambic trimeters, *c.* 1313): Julius Caesar to 1261

18. Michael Panaretus of Trebizond: 1204 to 1426

19. *Chronicle of the Morea* (see romance, below)

20. *Chronicle of the Tocco*: 1375–1422

Poetry

The meters of classical poetry had been based upon quantity, i.e., upon the length of vowels and of syllables. Some Byzantine poets followed the ancient prosody, mostly in iambic trimeters, less commonly in hexameters, elegiac distichs, or anacreontic verse. But even the writers who accommodated themselves to these norms took many liberties in the observance of quantity and caesura (pause), in a way which would not have been done in antiquity. They also introduced innovations, such as putting the stress accent on the 11th syllable of the iambic trimeter, which in the classical form of this meter was always unaccented.

In addition, Byzantine poets created a number of new vehicles of their own. In most liturgical poetry they abandoned the quantitative system altogether and introduced rhythm on the basis of accent. They also ignored the classical insistence on fixed limits on the length of the lines. The liturgical poets had great freedom in this respect, and imposed restraints only through the use of the *heirmos* (εἱρμός) or model strophe, which could assume almost any shape the poets wished, but which, once it was chosen, determined the pattern of all the strophes it governed; every strophe had to be identical with it, not only in the number of lines, but also in musical mode (*echos,* ἦχος), in the number of syllables per line, and in the position of the accents and caesura in each line. Thus, all strophes in a poem based upon and following the *heirmos* had to conform with it in every respect. Deviations from this arrangement of syllables and accents were not normally tolerated, and occurred infrequently.

Perhaps the most common and characteristic form of Byzantine poetry was the 15-syllable ''political'' verse. The origins of the political verse remain a matter of debate. The earliest datable examples are from the early 10th century when it was used for imperial funerary laments, while isolated instances can be observed in the kontakia of Romanos (see below). There is no agreement as to whether it is a traditional meter taken over by erudite poets or a learned innovation.

Liturgical Poetry. The practice of singing hymns in the Christian service, which began in the earliest times and made an impression on the pagans, as we learn from the Younger Pliny's famous letter to Emperor Trajan, is undoubtedly to be traced to Jewish customs. Similarly, the structure of the later Byzantine liturgical hymns is said by some to have been derived from Semitic prototypes. Hymns of various kinds are attested from every age of the Church, but in this article attention is focused on those that were built around the troparion (οἶκος i.e., stanza) in the Byzantine liturgy (*see* HYMNOLOGY).

Romanus Melodus. The greatest and most renowned of the Byzantine liturgical poets was ROMANUS MELODUS, who was born in Emesa in Syria. According to legend, he was a convert to Christianity from Judaism, and went to Constantinople during the reign of Anastasius I (491–518). He was said to have invented the kontakion and was alleged to have composed ''thousands'' of poems of this type. The kontakion, as we know it from the extant kontakia ascribed to him, consists of from 18 to 30 or more troparia. Each troparion varies in length from three to 13 lines, and all of the troparia of each kontakion follow the pattern of a model stanza (the *heirmos*).

At the beginning of each kontakion stands a separate troparion, which is metrically and melodically independent of the *heirmos* (and thus of all the other troparia of the kontakion). This separate troparion is known as the *prooimion* or *kukulion,* and is connected with the kontakion by means of the refrain (*ephymnion*) with which each of the stanzas ends, and by the musical mode (*echos*). The stanzas of the kontakion are linked together by means of an acrostic or by the successive letters of the alphabet. That is, the initial letters of the first line of each of the stanzas form a sequence either in regular alphabetical order (from alpha to omega, etc.) or spell out an acrostic. Thus, in the *Akathistos Hymnos* (the hymn sung unseated, i.e., standing), the most celebrated of all the kontakia, and one which has often been ascribed to Romanus although it is almost certainly not by him, each of the troparia begins with a letter of the alphabet from alpha to omega.

Romanus's kontakia deal with the Nativity, the massacre of the Innocents, the presentation in the Temple, Epiphany, the woman of Samaria, the man possessed by devils, the woman with an issue of blood, Pentecost, the Last Judgment, etc. They are noteworthy for their lively expression and vivid dialogues with vigorous characterization.

The kontakion was a melodic homily and was crowded out of the liturgy from about the end of the 7th century by the *kanon,* the first example of which was said to have been composed by Andrew of Crete (*c.* 660–740). The *kanon* is made up of nine odes, each of which at first consisted of from six to nine troparia (i.e., stanzas). Later on, only three of the troparia of each ode were sung in the liturgy; and there are odes of four, three, or two troparia. The nine odes of every *kanon* were patterned upon the Nine Canticles from the Scriptures, and were intended as hymns of praise or exaltation. The *kanons* usually have a different *heirmos* (or model strophe) for each ode, i.e., a total of eight or nine *heirmoi* for each *kanon.* This scheme made for great variety of structure within each *kanon*, as contrasted with the greater rigidity of the kontakion, in which all the troparia were based upon the same *heirmos.*

The most famous of the *kanons* is the *Great Kanon* of Andrew of Crete, which has 250 troparia divided into four sections. After Andrew, the leading composers of *kanons* were the theologian JOHN DAMASCENE (*c.* 675–753) and his foster brother COSMAS THE MELODIAN of Jerusalem, also described as ''of Maiuma'' in Phoenicia because of his being made bishop of that city in 743. John Damascene and Cosmas were less passionate in language and more obscure than Romanus. John delighted in elaborate poetic structure and reverted, in part, to quantitative verse in the iambic trimeters he wrote for his *kanons* on Christmas, Epiphany, and Pentecost. At the time of the second iconoclastic controversy flourished Joseph the Hymnographer (*c.* 816–886), who was born in Sicily and was then driven by circumstances all over the Mediterranean world. An earlier contemporary of his, Methodius of Syracuse, was the last poet to write a *kanon* on the basis of 12-syllable iambics.

Other Liturgical Poets. In the 9th century the great center for liturgical poetry was the monastery of STUDION in Constantinople, with which a number of important liturgical poets were associated, notably Theodore the Studite (759–826) and the brothers Theodore and Theophanes, known as ''the branded'' or ''inscribed'' (γραπτοί). The two brothers were so designated because Emperor Theophilus (829–842) was said to have punished them for their resistance to iconoclasm by having 12 iambic trimeters branded upon their foreheads. When he issued the order for this outlandish punishment, the Emperor is reported to have said, ''Don't worry if the verses are no good.'' The poems of the two poets themselves were not of the highest quality and were characterized by a fondness for neologisms created by tacking on prefixes and suffixes to ordinary words.

More distinguished than they was the poetess Kasia (b. *c.* 810), who, on being rejected as a candidate for his hand by Emperor Theophilus because of her pertness and lack of docility, founded a convent and composed a number of poems that found their way into the service books.

After the end of the 10th century, only a few writers continued to compose hymns, since the liturgy was fixed and was generally closed to new compositions. But the church historian Nicephorus Callistus Xanthopulus wrote a liturgy for the Virgin that was admitted into the *Pentekostarion.* A curiosity of the later period was a *kanon* on St. THOMAS AQUINAS, called Thomas Ἀγχίνους (the regular Greek translation for Aquinas, i.e., the ''sharp-witted'').

As inspiration and opportunity for the production of hymns declined, the commentators rushed in to fill the gap. Bishops Cosmas of Maiuma and NICETAS DAVID expounded upon the poems of Gregory of Nazianzus, and John Damascene produced a commentary on the TRISAGION. Most of these exegetical efforts were expended upon the more obscure poets, while hymnographers like Romanus Melodus, whose works offered no special difficulty, were rarely commented upon. Commentaries of one kind or another on liturgical poetry have been attributed to Theodore Prodromus (who at least regarded himself as a poet), the philosopher NICEPHORUS BLEMMYDES, and Abp. Eustathius of Thessalonica.

The modern critic occasionally has difficulties with the tediousness of some liturgical poetry, its repetitiousness and artificiality of manner. But these defects arise in part from the convention that required the poet to stretch his poetic fancy over 24 or more strophes, all of which dealt essentially with the same subject. All in all, it must be conceded that the best of the poets showed great ingenuity in adapting themselves to these requirements and commendable inventiveness in finding in the few bare facts with which tradition supplied them sufficient material for the construction of the hundreds of poems the liturgy contains on the religious festivals of the Church and the exploits of the saints.

Secular Poetry and Nonliturgical Religious Poetry. Although Byzantine literary production rarely, if ever, reached the level of the great classical writers, this was not because of lack of excellent training in ancient literature. Many Byzantine scholars acquired a great intimacy with the classical texts and knew Homer and the tragic poets almost by heart.

The theologian GREGORY OF NAZIANZUS (*c.* 330– *c.* 390) was the author of more than 400 poems, some of which are of great interest historically. But none of them has any unusual metrical, lyrical, or melodic distinction.

On the other hand nine or ten hymns of Synesius (*c.* 370–*c.* 413), the Neoplatonizing Christian bishop of Ptolemais, the author of treatises *On Kingship, On Baldness, On Dreams,* and of 156 letters, were in classical meters that exhibit intense religious feeling and a lyrical spirit of high order, expressed in a mélange of pagan and Christian symbolism.

NONNUS OF PANOPOLIS (b. *c.* 400), another pagan poet from Africa, who was later converted to Christianity, composed while he was still a pagan a work called the *Dionysiaca* in hexameters. It contains 48 books (i.e., as many as the *Iliad* and *Odyssey* combined) and is the longest extant poem in Greek. It was written in Alexandria and describes the mythical journey of the god Dionysus to India. It is very probable that the author was the same Nonnus who became a Christian and then wrote, again in hexameters, a *Paraphrase of the Gospel according to St. John* (in 21 books).

Somewhat later, Empress Eudocia (d. *c.* 460), daughter of the Athenian philosopher Leontius, and originally named Athenais (''Maid of Athens''), but baptized Eudocia at the time of her marriage to Emperor Theodosius II (408–450), produced a most extraordinary Homeric canto. She had such control over the text of Homer that, working on materials assembled by others, she composed a poem of some two thousand lines, each of which was taken almost intact from the *Iliad* and *Odyssey.* She made only minimal changes, but, nevertheless, out of the Homeric lines she had stored in her head, she wove together an impeccably orthodox treatise on theology. Her poem is divided into 50 parts: Paradise and the serpent, the Annunciation, the birth of Christ, the star and the shepherds, the Magi, Herod, the flight into Egypt, John the Baptist, the betrayal, the burial, the Resurrection, the doubting Thomas, etc.

Virtuosity of this sort with ancient Greek was not uncommon. Psellus (1018–96) had committed the whole of the *Iliad* to memory when he was 14; Anna Comnena made effective use of quotations from Homer; and Eustathius, Archbishop of Thessalonica (1175–*c.* 1194), wrote a huge commentary of seven volumes on the Homeric poems.

George of Pisidia. The best secular poet of the Byzantine period was George of Pisidia, deacon of the church of HAGIA SOPHIA, who flourished in the reign of Emperor HERACLIUS (610–641), and celebrated the latter's exploits in iambic trimeters of Byzantine style. He was so skilled in the use of iambics that in the 11th century critics could ask whether he or Euripides was the greater poet. His three historical poems dealt with (1) Heraclius's successful campaign against the Persians; (2) the Byzantine victory over the Avars, who stormed the gates of Constantinople in 626, and the Virgin Mary's protection of the city during this crisis; and (3) Heraclius's final triumph over the Persian king Chosroes (628). Of much greater length is his commentary on the Biblical account of the creation, a theological work in which, however, he found opportunity for many allusions to contemporary events. He also wrote a hexameter poem, *On Human Life.*

The Greek Anthology. In addition to the better poems of the liturgy, special mention must be made of the Byzantine compilation known as the *Greek Anthology,* which now amounts to 16 books, containing some 4,000 epigrams and approximately 25,000 lines, extending in date from the 6th century B.C. to the 10th century of the Christian Era. The Byzantine epigrams are both in the conventional ancient form (consisting of alternate dactylic hexameters and pentameters, in the so-called elegiac couplet) and in iambic trimeters.

The first major collection of poems of this kind was made by Meleager of Gadara (*c.* 60 B.C.), who brought together some of the choicest bits of ancient poetry (from the works of Archilochus, Anacreon, Sappho, Simonides, etc.). Meleager had many successors in the Hellenistic and Byzantine periods. In the age of Justinian, for example, appeared a number of epigrams by Paulus Silentiarius, who, however, was more celebrated for his two *ekphraseis* (mostly in hexameters), one on the church of Hagia Sophia and the other on its ambon. More productive in this genre was Paul's contemporary Agathias the Historian who not only wrote hexameter poems and about 100 epigrams, but also put together a collection of contemporary epigrammatists.

Of the later editions of epigrammatic poems the most indispensable for the constitution of the text of the *Greek Anthology* in its present form were those of Constantine Cephalas (*c.* 900, known from a later recension of *c.* 980, the famous *Anthologia Palatina,* so-called from the Bibliotheca Palatina in Heidelberg in which the manuscript containing it was housed) and Maximus PLANUDES (*c.* 1260–1310). Cephalas arranged the poems according to subject, and Planudes carried this division still further. The modern editions of the *Greek Anthology* consist of the *Palatine Anthology,* plus the ''Planudean Appendix'' (bk. 16) of 388 additional poems, which were derived principally, it seems, from lost MSS of Cephalas's recension and of the *Palatine Anthology.* Apart from a host of anonymous pieces (*adespota*), some 364 poets are represented by compositions primarily in epigrammatic verse but also in a great variety of other meters.

Representative Successors of George of Pisidia. Some 200 years after Agathias, the epigram was revived by Theodore the Studite (759–826) in a series of poems (mostly in iambic trimeters) on the monastic life, in which he celebrated the monastic calling itself and did not disdain to mention individually not only the *hegumenos* (the abbot) of the monastery but also the tailor, the shoemaker, the monk who awakened the brethren in the morning, the doorkeepers, the cells of the monks, the hospice for wayfarers, etc. In choice of theme and freshness of treatment Theodore was strikingly original. More conventional, but also interesting, are his epigrams on the parts of a church (in which he called attention to the altar, the gate of the narthex, the shrine, etc.), on icons, on various saints, and on himself.

Unpoetic, but historically noteworthy iambic trimeters on the state of the empire, on the Roman months, on animal fights in the circus, etc., are ascribed to Emperor Leo VI (886–912), who is said to have been the author also of peculiar palindromes, which he called crabs (καρκίνοι) because they could be read either backward or forward, like: ὢ γένος ἐμόν, ἐν ᾧ μέσον ἐγώ.

Not long after the death of Leo, Constantine of Rhodes, who held high posts in both State and Church, wrote (between *c.* 931 and 944) an *ekphrasis* in which he described the no-longer extant Constantinopolitan Church of the Holy Apostles and its mosaics. The verses themselves, in iambic trimeter, are far inferior to the poetic *ekphrasis* of Paulus Silentiarius. Constantine was endowed with neither expository nor lyric skill, but his poem is an altogether unique source, highly prized by archeologists.

More distinguished than Constantine of Rhodes was his contemporary John Kyriotes (known also as John the Geometer), who composed trimeters, hexameters, elegiac distichs, and hymns on poets, politicians, philosophers, historians, theologians, and saints, not to mention cities, historical events, myths, etc. He often managed to achieve poetic imagery of high order, but also displays the usual Byzantine addiction to plays on words and the ornate style.

One of the most elegant of the Byzantine poets was Christopher of Mytilene (*c.* 1000–1050), from whose hand we have 145 poems (14 in hexameters, the rest in iambic trimeters) addressed to the chief personages of the Byzantine court of his day, on ants, sparrows, the four seasons, the baptism of Christ, the saints, a bronze statue of a horse in the Hippodrome, a painting of the 40 martyrs, etc. His inscriptions for gravestones and riddles are better than ordinary. He even had a sense of humor, as can be seen in the complaints he made against the mice that scampered all over his house and devoured everything edible they could find, not excluding his books and papers. It was in retaliation for his verses on this subject, we may suppose, that the same creatures, or their descendants, ate up one half of the sole surviving manuscript of his poems.

In the 12th century there flourished at the court of Manuel I Comnenus and the lesser courts of the aristocrats of Constantinople *thatra*, or salons, at which well-educated young men, future bishops or secular administrators, jostled for attention and displayed their literary wares in prose and verse. A *topos* at this time was that they were underappreciated and underpaid: hence the set of begging poems by ''Ptochoprodromos'' (Penniless Prodromos), who is possibly to be identified with Theodroe Prodromos, and the constant complaints of John Tzetzes, as they sought financial assistance from the Emperor or some patron. (For Tzetzes, see section below on Byzantine scholarship and philosophy.) The Ptochoprodromic poems, in political verse, were devoted to seriocomic recitations of how the speaker suffered at the hands of his nagging wife and of two abbots in the monastery to which he had fled to find peace. He bewailed his unhappy lot as a teacher and cursed the day he first went to school.

Prodromos was a prolific and versatile writer. His chief poetic work is a verse romance in 4,614 iambic trimeters entitled *Rodanthe and Dosicles* (on which see romance and satire below). In another work of his, the *Battle of the Cat and the Mice* (*Galeomyomachia*), a parody in 384 trimeters of the Homeric *Batrachomyomachia,* the mice, led by their King Kreillos and Queen Tyrokleptes (''Cheese-thief''), snatched victory from certain defeat, when a beam fell suddenly from the ceiling and slew the all but triumphant cat. He also wrote much occasional verse to celebrate imperial military triumphs as well as domestic events at court.

Very similar to Theodore Prodromus in lively language, grim humor, and passionate complaints about poverty was Michael Haplucheir, who flourished at the end of the 12th century and was responsible for a so-called *Dramation* in 122 iambic trimeters, in which a rustic, a wise man, fate, the muses, and a chorus were the dramatis personae.

One of the most prolific of the Byzantine poets was Manuel Philes (*c.* 1275–1345), who confined himself, as did very few others, almost exclusively to this medium. Nearly all of his more than 20,000 verses were iambic trimeters, in which he sedulously avoided hiatus. In addition to poems *On the Characteristics of Animals,* and a short description of an elephant, he wrote three poems in dialogue form (two of them to console families that had suffered bereavement, one a panegyric), several on theological subjects, a number of epigrams on works of art (a marble statue of St. George, an equestrian statue of Emperor Justinian I), and a host of occasional poems soliciting favors, and expressing gratitude for gifts to leading officials and churchmen. In general Philes was a

Palaeologan reincarnation of Theodore Prodromus, whom he resembled in choice of subjects, method of treatment, and preoccupation with what he deemed his sad lot.

Approximately at the end of the 13th century appeared a moralizing poem in 3,060 political verses, written by a certain Meliteniotes, and dedicated to Moderation (*sophrosyne*), personified as the poet's guide on a long and perilous journey to a magic palace set in the midst of a fabulously beautiful garden (Paradise). The entrance to the palace was barred by seven obstacles, which represented the snares that block the path to virtue. The journey gave opportunity for all kinds of miscellaneous learning, mineralogical, mythical, and historical, which the author sedulously collected from his sources.

Romance

A phenomenon that is intriguingly parallel to that of the West, though initially independent, is the writing of romances. There were two phases, in the mid-12th century and in the late 13th to 14th centuries. Amongst the first to appear was the epic-romance of *Digenis Akritas*, of which several recensions survive, all in political verse. The kernel of the story goes back to the wars on the Arab-Byzantine frontier *c.* 860-960, though it has acquired many romantic overtones as it tells of the exploits of the hero of Double Descent (Digenis) as he wins his bride before his tragically early death.

In the 12th century, besides Theodore Prodromus's *Rhodanthe and Dosicles,* appeared Nicetas Eugenianus's *Drosilla and Charicles,* which owes much to Prodromus's romance in structure and meter. Both of these are in nine books and in iambic trimeters, and are closely related to the contemporary *Hysmine and Hysminias* (in 11 books), a romance in prose by Eustathius Macrembolites. A fourth, *Aristandros and Kallithea*, by Constantine Manassses survives only in excerpts. All are adaptations from the works of Heliodorus, Achilles Tatius, and Longus and have similar plots involving lovers who were separated, became involved with pirates, and eventually were reunited. Recent criticism has begun to see in these interesting reflections of the literary taste of the time.

More immediately comprehensible are the romances of the later period. In *Callimachus and Chrysorrhoe* (in political verse), for example, dating from the late 13th century, the hero and the heroine, after a series of adventures with a magic apple (which could kill or raise from the dead), a dragon, and a sorceress, finally triumph over adversity.

In *Belthandros and Chrysantza* Belthandros came upon an enchanted palace built of sardonyx and there, in the Castle of Love, was by magic informed that he was destined to fall in love with Chrysantza, daughter of the King of Antioch. Later on, he found her and discovered that she was the girl to whom in the Castle of Love he had presented the prize for beauty. Caught after his first tryst with her, he pretended that his intention was to pay court to her maid, whom he was then required to marry. Under cover of this marriage, he continued to make love to Chrysantza, and escaped with her to Constantinople, where they were married by the patriarch. *Lybistros and Rhodamne* (in political verse), which dates perhaps from the 14th century, was apparently influenced by both *Callimachus* and *Chrysorrhoe* and *Belthandros and Chrysantza,* or by their sources, as well as by the 12th century romances.

Very different from these three in originality and execution were Byzantine paraphrases of Western tales like *Phlorios and Platziaphlora* and *Imberios and Margarona,* both of which were written in political verse. The former, a free Greek version of the Provençal romance of *Flore and Blanchefleur,* of which several versions exist in French and Italian, dates from the late 14th century or the early 15th. Similarly, the second of these, which was derived from the old French romance *Pierre de Provence et la belle Maguelonne,* exists in several versions, both unrhymed (15th century) and rhymed (16th century).

On the other hand, the three above-named romantic tales, though apparently at several points influenced by the French *Chansons de geste,* have points of contact with Oriental poetry; and there are many features that are obviously Greek in origin. This mélange of characteristics is what might be expected of poetry produced in the latter part of the Byzantine period, when the Greeks lived in close contact with the Crusaders and their descendants, on the one hand, and with the Muslims on the other.

This same blend of culture is illustrated by the *Chronicle of the Morea,* especially in the Greek version, which was composed in the popular, nonliterary idiom, and indicates that by *c.* 1388 or so, the date of its composition, many Latins in the Morea had become Hellenophones. This *Chronicle,* which was written in political verse and exists in French, Spanish, and Italian, as well as in Greek, gives a summary of the history of the first Crusade and of the capture of Constantinople in 1204, but devotes its principal attention to the Peloponnesus from 1205 to 1292. The major Greek version, which was intended for Latins who spoke Greek, is anti-Greek in tone and includes some data on the 14th century.

A further instance of this blending can be seen in the 14th century interest in the legends of Troy. Thus the *War of Troy* (over 14,000 lines of political verse), which perhaps comes from the same environment as the *Chronicle of the Morea,* is a close translation of Benoit de Ste Maure's *Roman de Troie* (*c.* 1170).

Satire

The Byzantines were far less interested in satire, which was undoubtedly inhibited by the absolutistic character of the imperial power. But this genre was not altogether neglected. For example, in the *Philopatris,* a satire cast in the form of a dialogue, there is an exchange of views between a Christian and a pagan. The unknown author wrote *c.* 969, and was so successful in imitating the ancient satirist Lucian that the *Philopatris* was once included among the latter's works.

Another imitation of Lucian, the *Timarion,* which is also anonymous, dates from the early years of the 12th century. Taking Lucian's *Necyomantia* as his model, the author described his death, journey to the underworld, and conversations with Emperors Theophilus (829–842) and Romanus IV Diogenes (1068–71), with Michael Psellus, and many others. The *Timarion* reveals a sense of humor, which is exceedingly rare in Byzantine literature. Both the *Philopatris* and the *Timarion* direct some of their satirical shafts at the Church.

A third Byzantine imitation of Lucian, *Mazaris's Journey to Hades,* was written by a certain Mazaris (*c.* 1414–16). It is coarser and less elegant than the *Timarion,* but nevertheless a useful source for the early years of the 15th century.

Epistolography

The art of letter writing was much cultivated throughout the Byzantine period and many often voluminous collections survive. Theoretical analyses in handbooks of rhetoric recommend that letters should be modeled on an elegant conversation with a friend. However, the fact that in most cases the real message was conveyed by the messenger has ensured that elliptical density of expression prevails and many letters are extremely opaque.

Some of the most attractive and readable examples come from the Cappadocian Fathers in the 4th century while the growing numbers of the educated elite in the 11th through the 12th centuries saw an increased interest in the genre. John Tzetzes wrote a verse commentary (discussed below) to elucidate the classical allusions in his carefully arranged and edited correspondence.

Byzantine Scholarship and Philosophy

An unbroken thread of serious scholarly interest in texts from the ancient world was maintained throughout the Byzantine period. If they themselves did not produce creative works that, aesthetically considered, rival Homer and the other great monuments of ancient literature, they at least were uniquely responsible for all that have survived. They not only avidly collected these texts, but also, as we easily forget, rescued them from the fragile papyrus on which they had originally been written by copying them to the more substantial parchment. They also saw to their transcription from uncial to minuscule in the 9th to 10th centuries, when a change in writing style rendered earlier exemplars incomprehensible and obsolete. Every classical text made its debut in an edition prepared by some Byzantine editor, who corrected the errors he perceived in the work of his predecessors.

In the early centuries, many of the best scholars were pagans rather than Christian. Among the rhetoricians, the late offspring of the ancient orators and the Alexandrian grammarians, cross-fertilized by Greek philosophy, were Libanius, Himerius, and Themistius, all three of whom flourished in the 4th century. Close to this circle was Emperor Julian (361–363), who made an unsuccessful attempt to revive the pagan religion, and wrote an anti-Christian polemic (*Against the Galilaeans*), as well as a number of orations and letters.

Platonism and Neoplatonism. Greater significance attaches to the successors of PLOTINUS (*c.* 205–270), the Neoplatonist philosophers PORPHYRY (d. *c.* 304), IAMBLICHUS (*c.* 250–325), and PROCLUS (410 or 412–485), who were important thinkers both in their own right and because of the influence they exerted upon medieval philosophy in general. The PLATONISM of the Middle Ages was thoroughly Neoplatonized, and Proclus was the model for the Pseudo-Dionysius's mystical theology. The latter, in turn, was so widely read in Byzantium as well as the West (to which it was available through four medieval translations) that mysticism as a whole, medieval, Renaissance, and modern, has a Neoplatonic coloration.

The Byzantine interest in Platonism, especially in the 4th, 5th, 6th, 11th, and 15th centuries, was an important factor in the survival of the text of Plato. Similarly, much of the credit for the preservation of Aristotle belongs to the great Byzantine commentators and philosophers of the 6th century, especially to Olympiodorus, Simplicius, and JOHN PHILOPONUS, the last of whom was a Christian, not a pagan, and the author of a number of important theological treatises. Actually, Platonic and Aristotelian studies were pursued virtually without interruption through the whole of the Byzantine period.

An aberrant member of this learned circle, Cosmas Indicopleustes by name, repudiated the cosmological and astronomical notions of the ancient Greeks in favor of the Mosaic concept of the universe. According to this Biblical scheme, Cosmas believed the earth lay at the bottom of a cosmos, which resembled a two-storied house, and in which night and day, as well as lunar and solar eclipses, were caused by a high range of mountains to the north.

John Stobaeus. Scholarly activity of a somewhat different nature is associated with the name of John Stobaeus (fl. *c.* 500), who was one of the most extraordinary anthologists in history. He was a native of Stobi (hence his name) in Macedonia and compiled a huge collection of excerpts in four books known variously as the *Eclogae* or the *Anthologion.* Only about half of this work (which originally contained 208 chapters of varying length divided into four books) has survived but this portion of it fills five stout volumes in the modern edition and preserves countless texts and authors (ranging in date from Homer to Themistius) that would, but for Stobaeus, have disappeared.

Each of the chapters deals with a separate topic, and many of the topics are examined from several points of view. For example, in the section on marriage (4.22), passages are collected to show that marriage is best (4.22.1), that it is not good to marry (4.22.2), and that in marriage one should not seek high position or wealth but character (4.22.6). Stobaeus was fond of paradoxes, and he concluded his survey of this subject by reproducing a number of passages (4.22.7) that are sharply critical of the female sex, many of which were culled from Menander (342–291 B.C.), the poet of the New Comedy, who, to judge from his plays and the gnomic utterances attributed to him, was one of the most irreconcilable misogynists of all time.

The philosophical and scientific production of the school of Alexandria had continued into the 7th century under Stephen, the astronomer and polymath. Reference should be made also to Paul of Aegina and Theophilus Protospatharios, the *diadochoi* in the 7th century of ancient Greek medicine, which had been well represented by Oribasius, Emperor Julian's physician, in the 4th century, as well as by Aetius of Amida and Alexander of Tralles, in the 6th. Still, the 7th century was for the Byzantine Empire a period of tragedy, frustration, and defeat. The 8th century brought revival under the iconoclastic emperors, the importance of whose military exploits against the Arabs even the orthodox historical writers grudgingly admitted. The reverses suffered in the West at the same time, culminating in the fall of Ravenna in 751 and the loss of north Italy, seem not to have affected literary production.

Photius. The most brilliant scholar of the Byzantine period was Patriarch PHOTIUS (858–867, 877–886), whose importance in the history of literature is wholly independent of his polemical writings against the popes and the Paulicians. He was a learned exegete, a prolific epistolographer, and an erudite preacher, even if his congregation must at times have had difficulty with his highly ornate style. But he is chiefly memorable for his so-called *Myriobiblon* or *Bibliotheke* (Library), a huge corpus of Greek texts arranged in 279 sections (called codices), which contain excerpts from authors both pagan and Christian, many of whom are otherwise unknown. The *Bibliotheke* is therefore of inestimable value to students of both ancient and medieval literature, all the more interesting because of Photius's trenchant critiques of the writers from whom he made excerpts.

Almost every conceivable kind of writing, except poetry, is discussed. Photius's reading was so encyclopedic, so deep, and so varied that at nearly every turn he provides data otherwise unavailable. Of the 31 historians whose works he analyzed, for example, approximately 20 are known to us either solely or largely because of the *Bibliotheke*, and only nine of the 31 whose histories Photius had before him in their entirety and discussed in the *Bibliotheke* are extant in full today. Not more than four of the codices deal with philosophy as such, but Photius frequently referred to Plato and Aristotle, and was himself an Aristotelian. A companion volume to the *Bibliotheke* was the *Lexicon*, also compiled in the course of Photius' reading.

Photius's disciple, ARETHAS, Archbishop of Caesarea in Cappadocia (*c.* 850–944), is noted for his rich library of classical authors, and for the interesting information he provided on the cost of transcribing codices from uncial to minuscule.(*See* PALEOGRAPHY, GREEK.) In addition, he was, together with a certain Oecumenius (6th century) and Andrew (an earlier archbishop of Caesarea, *c.* 563–614), one of the few Byzantine exegetes to write a commentary on the Revelation attributed to St. John.

The Suda. One typical kind of literary activity to which the Byzantines were much addicted was the compilation of learned works and encyclopedias. The best of the encyclopedias, properly so-called, as contrasted with the anthologies and collections of excerpts, is that of the so-called *Suda*, once thought to have been a proper name, Suidas. But it seems likely that ''suda'' (meaning ditch, ''catch-all'' and thus encyclopedia) is the correct form. Aside from brief notices on lexicographical and etymological questions, often of great interest, the *Suda* includes articles on literature, history, philosophy, and science, the most significant of which, often in the form of biographies, provide data not always to be found in other sources on ancient and medieval authors and their works. The *Suda* fills many gaps in our knowledge and is indispensable for the student of Greek literature.

Michael Psellus. In the 11th century, the most active of the classical scholars was the polymath Michael Psellus (1018–*c.* 1096), who, though he complained that men of learning were scarce in his day, nevertheless succeeded in locating an excellent teacher named John Mauropus, who proved to be a thoroughly competent in classical literature. Psellus was a Platonist, but his works reflect a wide classical learning; and his universal encyclopedia, the *De omnifaria doctrina*, offers information on a great variety of subjects drawn from the major classical authorities.

The philosophical tradition also was ably represented by JOHN ITALUS, Psellus's successor as dean of the School of Philosophy (ὕπατος τῶν φιλοσόφων), who, however, in 1082 was removed from his post because, his enemies charged, he had lapsed into paganism. Actually, John Italus was a well-trained Hellenist and an Aristotelian in orientation. But there is no evidence that either he or his student, Eustratius of Nicaea (who commented on Aristotle and defended the Platonic theory of ideas), ever apostasized.

John Tzetzes and Eustathius. In the next century, the two major students of classical literature were John Tzetzes (*c.* 1112–85) and Eustathius (fl. 1175–95), both of whom, in contrast to most of the authors considered above, were concerned with poetry rather than prose. The former and less distinguished of the two was a man of insupportable vanity, who spent great energy heaping praise upon himself and denigrating his rivals. Like his contemporary, Theodore Prodromus, he overburdened his works with references to his poverty (''My head is my library, and I am too poor to buy books'': *Allegory on the Iliad*, 15.87), with interminable complaints against the universe, which had failed to recognize his enormous talents, and with abject, servile flattery of the patrons who befriended him. Nevertheless, he had had an excellent education, and he cites most of the major ancient authors.

Unfortunately, not all the references in his letters and poems are trustworthy, despite his modest avowal that no man had ever had a more tenacious memory than he (*Chiliades*, 1.277). He wrote a prose *Exegesis* of the *Iliad*, a whole volume of political verses on the allegorical interpretation of both the *Iliad* and the *Odyssey*, hexameter poems on other Homeric subjects, a long prose commentary on Hesiod's *Works and Days*, and a poem in political verse on the traditional pagan *Theogony.* Of his numerous scholia on various other authors, including some 1,700 iambic trimeters on Porphyry's *Eisagoge to the Categories of Aristotle*, the most important are the elaborate introductions and annotations he wrote on the comedies of Aristophanes.

Most astounding of all are his *Chiliades*, a poem of 12,674 political verses, which he wrote as a commentary on his own letters, and then reissued with marginal annotations in prose and verse, dedicatory letters, and supplementary poems of abuse directed against his enemies. Pompous and arrogant as he was, Tzetzes deserves further study.

Rather more interesting than Tzetzes in every way was Eustathius (*c.* 1125–1193 or 1198), who rose to be archbishop of Thessalonica. In the history of scholarship he is chiefly noted for his huge commentary on Homer. In addition, he produced exegetical works on Pindar and Dionysius Periegetes. The most valuable part of the material he assembled is his extracts from the earlier scholia and from texts that would otherwise have been lost. Modern scholarship is forever in his debt.

His learned works were written in Constantinople before he went to the metropolitanate of Thessalonica, in which he distinguished himself as a reformer of lax monastic discipline. He was subjected to much abuse by his enemies on this account, but showed himself fearless and resolute both against his personal opponents and against the NORMANS, who captured Thessalonica and held it briefly in 1185.

Nicephorus Blemmydes and Maximus Planudes. In the next century flourished Nicephorus Blemmydes (*c.* 1197–1272), a philosopher and theologian who wrote a lengthy handbook in two books on logic and physics, a treatise favoring the Latin doctrine of the double procession of the Holy Spirit, two short geographical essays, two autobiographical sketches, and several poems, one of them a very spirited and vituperative reply to slanderous charges made against him by one of his students. But he never lost the devotion of his most celebrated tutee, Emperor Theodore II Lascaris (1254–58), who was himself an accomplished scholar and the author, among other things, of a treatise on the underlying unity of nature despite appearances to the contrary, eight discourses on Christian theology, a polemic against the Roman doctrine of the Holy Spirit, and *kanons* on the Virgin Mary.

More memorable than Blemmydes was Maximus (born Manuel) Planudes (*c.* 1260–1310), who wrote poems on theological and secular subjects, essays on grammar, an *Encomium of Winter*, and an idyll in 270 hexameters in the form of a dialogue between two farmers, Cleodemus and Thamyras. Apart from his commentaries on Euclid's *Elements* and Diophantus's *Arithmetica*, his *Psephophoria* (a mathematical treatise in which he makes use of zero and the nine so-called Arabic numbers, which had occurred in Byzantium for the first time about 50 years previously), and his poems on Ptolemy's *Geography*, his major contribution was as scholiast, editor, and translator. He annotated Sophocles, Euripides, Hesiod's *Works and Days*, and Aesop's *Fables.* Of his critical editions, the most celebrated was that of the *Greek Anthology*, which he augmented and improved by the use of manuscripts that are no longer accessible.

Likewise of great interest are his critical editions of Theocritus's *Idylls* and Nonnus's *Dionysiaca.* But he himself prized above all the work he did in establishing the text of Plutarch's *Moralia*, which he published in three editions. The most sumptuous of these (*Parisinus Graecus* 1672) contains all 23 of Plutarch's *Parallel Lives* (i.e., 46 in all: 2 × 23) and the 78 *Moralia* (including all that is extant of this collection except for some fragments). He was the best Latinist of his times in Byzantium, as can be seen in his Greek versions of Augustine's *De trinitate*, Pseudo-Augustine's *De duodecim abusionum gradibus*, Boethius's *De consolatione philosophiae*, Cato's *Dicta*, Macrobius's *Commentum in somnium Scipionis*, and Ovid's *Metamorphoses* and *Heroides.*

Highly as we prize the learning and acumen of the Byzantine textual critics of the 13th, 14th, and 15th centuries, it must be admitted that in their enthusiasm they often made changes that were arbitrary, unnecessary, and erroneous. Many of their emendations indicate ignorance rather than subtlety. The scholars of the previous centuries, on the other hand, were more restrained in their methods and frequently, therefore, better witnesses to the original reading than their successors. Nevertheless, the classical scholars of the Palaeologan period (1261–1453) made important contributions, both in the exegesis of texts and in the preservation of materials, which otherwise would have been inaccessible.

Theodore Metochites, Demetrius Triclinius, and Plethon. The most important member of this group was Theodore Metochites (d. 1332), one of the leading statesmen of his day until the fall of his patron, ANDRONICUS II in 1328. His major work was the *Miscellanea philosophica et historica*, which contains 120 essays on philosophical, ethical, political, aesthetic, and historical subjects, drawn for the greater part from ancient history and philosophy. He was very much interested in mathematics and astronomy, on which he wrote a number of treatises. Most of these have not yet been published, and only the Latin translation of his paraphrase of Aristotle is available in print. Metochites's contemporary (and antagonist) Nicephorus Chumnus (*c.* 1250–1327) also deserves mention among the classicists of this period.

The best philologist and textual critic of the Palaeologan era was Demetrius Triclinius (*c.* 1280–1340), who devoted himself to the principal poets of antiquity (Hesiod, Pindar, Aeschylus, Sophocles, Euripides, Aristophanes, and Theocritus), whom he studied, annotated, and edited. Triclinius was responsible for many misguided emendations, but he nevertheless deserves the esteem of classical scholars for his great erudition and tireless activity.

Of the numerous contemporaries of Triclinius who devoted themselves to classical studies, the most noteworthy were Manuel Moschopulos and Thomas Magistros, both of whom compiled lexica of Attic usage. In the next century, on the eve of the collapse of the empire, Byzantine classical scholarship rose to an even higher level. Manuel Chrysoloras (d. 1415), the most influential of the Byzantine professors who taught Greek to the Latins, was an avid collector of Greek manuscripts and initiated the Western humanists in the art of translating from Greek into Latin.

The greatest of the students of classical literature in this period were George Gemistus Plethon, an indefatigable excerpter, teacher of many of the leading scholars of his day, and Bessarion, his disciple, who became a partisan of union with Rome and was made a cardinal (1439). Plethon visited Italy (1438–39) during the Council of Ferrara-Florence, and was credited by Cosimo de MEDICI with having inspired him with the project of founding the Platonic Academy of Florence. In the great debates on the relative merits of Plato and Aristotle, Plethon championed Plato, and was bitterly attacked for so doing by George of Trebizond, a partisan of Aristotle. Bessarion then joined the fray with his *In calumniatorem Platonis*, in which he took a mediating position in the controversy, and rebuked George of Trebizond for his abusive tone.

Bibliography: General. B. ALTANER, *Patrology,* tr. H. GRAEF from the 5th German ed. (New York 1960). H. G. BECK, *Kirche und theologische Literatur im byzantinischen Reich* (Munich 1959). H. G. BECK, *Geschichte der byzantinischen Volksliteratur* (Munich 1971). W. BUCHWALD et al., eds., *Tusculum-Lexikon griechischer und lateinischer Autoren des Altertums und des Mittelalters,* 3rd ed. (Munich 1982). *Dictionnaire d'archéologie chrétienne et de liturgie,* ed. F. CABROL, H. LECLERCQ and H. I MARROU, 15 v. (Paris 1907–53). *Dictionnaire de théologie catholique*, ed. A. VACANT et al., 15 v. (Paris 1903–50; Tables générales 1951–). *Dictionnaire d'histoire et de géographie ecclésiastiques,* ed. A. BAUDRILLART et al. (Paris 1912–). A. EHRHARD, *Überlieferung und Bestand der hagiographischen und homiletischen Literatur*, 3 v. (Leipzig 1936–39). *Lexikon für Theologie und Kirche*, ed. J. HOFER and K. RAHNER, 10 v. (2nd new ed. Freiburg 1957–65). *Reallexikon für Antike und Christentum,* ed. T. KLAUSER (Stuttgart 1941 [1950]). F. HALKIN, ed., *Bibliotheca Hagiographica Graeca* (Brussels 1957; supplements 1969, 1984). H. HUNGER, *Die hochsprachliche profane Literatur der Byzantiner*, 2 v. (Munich 1977–78). B. KNÖS, *L'Histoire de la littérature néo-grecque* (Stockholm 1962). A. KAZHDAN, ed., *Oxford Dictionary of Byzantium,* 3 v. (New York 1991). C. MANGO, *Byzantium: The Empire of New Rome* (London 1980). G. MORAVCSIK, *Byzantinoturcica,* 2 v. (2nd ed. Berlin 1958), v. 1. J. QUASTEN, *Patrology*, 3 v. (Westminster, Md. 1950). Many of the major Byzantine writers can be found in *Paulys Realenzyklopädie der klassischen Altertumswissenschaft*, ed. G. WISSOWA et al. (Stuttgart 1893–). Translations of many of the historians have been published in the series *Byzantinische Geschichtsschreiber,* ed. E.

VON IVÁNKA (Graz 1954–), and there are also many translations into English and French. For the Renaissance, the knowledge of Greek in the West, and the activity of Byzantine textual critics, see N. G. WILSON, *Scholars of Byzantium* (London 1983) and *idem, From Byzantium to Italy: Greek Studies in the Italian Renaissance* (London 1992). Prose. R. BROWNING, *Studies in Byzantine History, Literature and Education* (London 1977). G. CAMMELLI, *I dotti bizantini e le origini dell'umanesimo,* 3 v. (Florence 1941–54). J. DANIÉLOU, *Platonisme et théologie mystique* (rev. ed. Paris 1954). J. DARROUZÈS, ed., *Épistoliers byzantins du Xe siècle* (Archives de l'Orient chrétien 6; Paris 1960). A. J. FESTUGIÈRE, ed., *Les Moines d'orient* (Paris 1961–). R.M. GRANT, *Eusebius as Church historian* (Oxford 1980). R. GUILLAND, *Essai sur Nicéphore Grégoras: L'Homme et l'oeuvre* (Paris 1926). E. VON IVÁNKA, *Plato Christianus* (Einsiedeln 1964). K. KARLSSON, *Idéologie et cérémonial dans l'épistolographie byzantine* (Uppsala 1962). A. KAZHDAN and A. W. EPSTEIN, *Change in Byzantine Culture in the Eleventh and Twelfth Centuries* (Berkeley 1985). P. LEMERLE, *Le premier humanisme byzantin* (Paris 1971; English trans. Canberra 1986). P. MAGDALINO, *The Empire of Manuel I Komnenos 1143–1180* (Cambridge 1993). F. MASAI, *Pléthon et le platonisme de Mistra* (Paris 1956). L. MOHLER, *Kardinal Bessarion als Theologe, Humanist und Staatsmann,* 3 v. (Paderborn 1923–42). B. RUBIN, *Das Zeitalter Justinians* (Berlin 1960–). W. SCHMID and O. STÄHLIN, *Geschichte der griechischen Literatur bis auf die Zeit Justinians* (based on the earlier work of W. CHRIST, *Handbuch der Altertumswissenschaft,* 8 v. (Munich 1920–48). I. SEVČENKO, *Études sur la polémique entre Théodore Métochite et Nicéphore Choumnos* (Brussels 1962). B. TATAKIS, *La Philosophie byzantine,* suppl. 2 of *Histoire de la philosophie,* ed. É. BRÉHIER (Paris 1959). J. VERPEAUX, *Nicéphore Choumnos* (Paris 1959). C. M. WOODHOUSE, *George Gemistos Plethon* (Oxford 1986). Poetry and romances. R. BEATON, *The Medieval Greek Romance* (2nd ed., London 1996). H. BECKBY, ed. and tr., *Anthologia Graeca,* 4 v. (Munich 1957–58). A. D. E. CAMERON, *The Greek Anthology from Meleager to Planudes* (Oxford 1993). W. VON CHRIST and M. PARANIKAS, eds., *Anthologia Graeca carminum Christianorum* (Leipzig 1871). *Anthologie grecque. Anthologie palatine,*, ed. and tr. P. WALTZ et al., 6 v. (Paris 1928–60). R. CANTARELLA, *Poeti bizantini,* 2 v. (Milan 1948). F. CONCA, ed. and trans., *Il Romanzo bizantino del XII secolo* (Turin 1994). C. CUPANE, ed. and trans., *Romanzi cavallereschi bizantini* (Turin 1995). P. FRIEDLÄNDER, ed., *Johannes von Gaza und Paulus Silentiarius: Kunstbeschreibungen justinianischer Zeit* (Leipzig 1912). E. M. and M. J. JEFFREYS, *Popular Literature in Late Byzantium* (Aldershot 1983). E. M. JEFFREYS, ed. and trans., *Digenis Akritis: the Grottaferrat and Escorial versions* (Cambridge 1998). T. NISSEN, *Die byzantinischen Anakreonteen* (Munich 1940). P. MAAS and C. A. TRYPANIS, eds., *Sancti Romani Melodi Cantica,* v. 1, *Genuina* (New York 1963). M. PAPATHOMOPOULOS and E. M. JEFFREYS, eds., *The War of Troy* (Athens 1998). E. WELLESZ, *A History of Byzantine Music and Hymnography* (2nd ed. Oxford 1961). G. T. ZORAS, *Byzantine Poetry* (Athens 1956), selections and introds. in Greek.

[M. V. ANASTOS/E. M. JEFFREYS]

BYZANTINE LITURGY

HISTORY AND DEVELOPMENT

The evolution of the Byzantine liturgical rite shows that the Eastern liturgies did not develop in a vacuum. They were the fruit of a long and gradual formation through centuries from earlier existing rites.

St. Basil's Work. Tradition in the Church of Byzantium ascribes to St. Basil (d. 379) the oldest of its two Liturgies. It is quite certain that Basil reformed the Liturgy in use in Cappadocia. He wrote to his clergy in Neocaesarea about the complaints leveled against him because he permitted the new antiphonal way of singing the psalms (*Epist.* 207.3; *Patrologia Graeca* 32:763). Gregory of Nyssa, his brother, compared Basil to Samuel because he had given a new form to the liturgical service (*Oratio funebris*; *Patrologia Graeca* 46:808). An evolved form of the Antiochene Liturgy must have been used in Neocaesarea during the time of St. Basil, and it was this that he reformed by shortening it considerably. One ancient Antiochene Liturgy is extant, that of St. James. It seems to be the basis for Basil's order and to have prayers nearly identical with his in content and position. The oldest form of the Liturgy of St. Basil in manuscript form, located in the Barberini Library, dates from the 9th century (MS III, 55; Brightman 309–344). The text shows that from the Anaphora to the Communion the Liturgy is of his redaction; the Liturgy of the Word and the Offertory prayers came after Basil's lifetime.

Reform of St. John Chrysostom. The next point in the evolution of the Byzantine liturgy is its reform under St. John Chrysostom (d. 409). The reformed Liturgy of St. John is found in its earliest manuscript in the same Barberini manuscript that contains the 9th-century text of the Liturgy of St. Basil (Brightman 309–344). There is a tradition that St. John, when he came from Antioch to Constantinople to be its patriarch in 397, composed a shortened form of Liturgy from the Liturgy of St. Basil. Pseudo-Proclus [*Tract. de traditione div. missae* (written not before the 7th century); *Patrologia Graeca* 65:851] says: "He [Chrysostom] left out a great deal and shortened all the forms so that no one. . . would stay away from this apostolic and divine institution." A comparison of the two texts shows that the same order is followed, but abbreviations occur mainly in the Anaphora.

Brightman has attempted a reconstruction of the Liturgy as St. John Chrysostom revised it by bringing together bits and pieces from the saint's homilies. His Liturgy must have lacked the present Preparation of the Gifts (Proskomide), the Little and Great Entrances, and the recitation of the Creed. The Liturgy began with the bishop greeting the faithful with "Peace to all." There followed readings from the Prophets, the Epistles, and the Gospels. A homily was delivered and a prayer said over the catechumens who were then dismissed. Chrysostom mentions a new Offertory ritual in which the bishop carried bread and wine from the prothesis to the main altar in solemn procession, but Brightman claims that the present Great Entrance and the Hymn of the Cherubim evolved much later (Brightman 532). One should note

St. Luke (Hossios Loukas), standing in the orans posture of prayer, 11th-century Byzantine mosaic, Monastery of Hossios Loukas, Greece (©Chris Hellier/CORBIS)

that the doxology after the Our Father, ''For thine is the kingdom. . .'' was found in the New Testament codex used by St. JOHN CHRYSOSTOM (*In Matt. hom.* 19.6; *Patrologia Graeca* 57:282). Since it was in Antioch that St. John preached most of the homilies from which we can reconstruct the reformed Liturgy, it is possible that he had already shortened the Liturgy of St. Basil then in use throughout the Eastern world and brought this version to Constantinople. Various additions found their way into the Liturgy in succeeding centuries. The TRISAGION was supposedly revealed to St. PROCLUS of Constantinople (patriarch, 434–447); the Cherubim Hymn was added by Justinian II, and the Creed was ordered by him to be recited in each Liturgy (Brightman 532).

Much more recent work on the Liturgy of the Great Church has traced and elucidated more carefully the evolution of these rites. In the West the monumental work of Robert F. Taft, S.J., as well as others is available in the publications of the Pontifical Oriental Academy.

The third Byzantine liturgical service, the Liturgy of the Presanctified, is no real Liturgy, as it consists mainly in a Communion service preceded by Vespers. Legend attributes it to St. Gregory the Great. The real author of this liturgical service is unknown.

Order of the Hours. The sources of the Hours and the administration of the Holy Mysteries and other services of prayer and blessing are more difficult to discover. The basic structure may have come from Antiochene usage. It has already been seen that St. Basil introduced a new way of singing Psalms, which must have affected the Hours. In a letter to the clergy of Neocaesarea, he gave an outline of the monastic Office consisting of a nocturnal penitential watch and at dawn the reciting of Matins (*Epist.* 207.1, 4; *Patrologia Graeca* 32:762, 764). The sung Office of the Great Church of Hagia Sophia differed vastly from the monastic office of the Studite monks. Later the Studite office was heavily revised in the direction of the Sabbaitic monastic office coming from Palestine. This revised office in turn became, after the demise of the sung office of the cathedral, the standard form of the office throughout the Byzantine liturgy. Along with the other usages in the East, Byzantine Matins has the singing of the Gloria in Excelsis. The evening vesper hymn, Phôs Hilarón, is quoted by Basil (*Liber de Spiritu S.* 28.73; *Patrologia Graeca* 32:205). John Cassian in his *Institutiones* (3.4; *Patrologia Latina* 49:131) attributes the addition of First Hour to the monks of Palestine, and Basil refers to Compline as the final evening prayer of the monks (*In psalmum* 114:1; *Patrologia Graeca* 29:484). The long, complicated canons, hymns based on the biblical odes or canticles introduced into Matins were the compositions of various hymnographers, such as Cosmas, Romanos the Melode, John Damascene, and St. Theodore of Studion. As was mentioned above SS. Sabas (d. 532) and John Damascene (d. *c.* 780) are accredited with having arranged the Services for the entire year, although even after their time the Hours underwent further changes.

Rectangular gold and bejewelled reliquary with low relief figures of the Twelve Apostles, 9th–10th century. (©Elio Ciol/ CORBIS)

CHARACTERISTICS OF THE BYZANTINE LITURGY

Here will be discussed the Eucharist, called by the Liturgy, the Hours, the calendar, the Holy Mysteries, blessings and prayer services, the church building, sacred vessels and vestments, and the liturgical books.

The Liturgy. For the most part the Byzantine liturgical text remains fixed for the whole year. There were formerly many varying Anaphoras, but through the centuries, due primarily to the centralization imposed by Constantinople, these were reduced to the two Liturgies of SS. Basil and John Chrysostom and the Liturgy of the Presanctified of St. Gregory the Great. The scriptural readings in the Liturgy, from the Acts or the Epistles and from the Gospels, differ each day with continuous reading of Gospels or Epistles more or less in their canonical order. Thus in one liturgical year the whole NT is read publicly. There are small sung portions that change, such as the commemorations for each saint or feast day or day of the week, known as troparia and kontakia, along with seasonal antiphons and hymns to Our Lady for special feasts. Now the longer Liturgy of St. Basil is celebrated only ten times a year: for his feast on January 1, the Sundays of Lent or Great Fast (except for Palm Sunday), Holy Thursday, Holy Saturday, and the Vigils of Christmas and Epiphany. It is only in the Anaphora or Eucharistic Canon that there is a change to longer prayers; these are more beautiful in their poetry and theological depth than those expressed in the Liturgy of St. John Chrysostom. The Liturgy of the Presanctified can be celebrated each day during Great Lent except Saturday and Sunday; however it is usually employed on Wednesday and Friday, whereas the Hours are recited on all days. For the other Sundays throughout the year the priest celebrates the Liturgy of St. John. To show the chief characteristics, the Liturgy of St. John Chrysostom will be taken as most representative, for it contains all of the audible, external parts of the Liturgy of St. Basil.

It is divided into two parts: the Liturgy of Preparation (Proskomedia) and the Divine Liturgy proper.

Liturgy of Preparation (Proskomedia). The priest and deacon prepare themselves individually for celebrating the Liturgy by reciting prayers before the iconostasis. Entering into the sanctuary, they kiss the Holy Table, Gospel book, and cross; then they proceed to vest. They begin the initial Offertory at the side altar called the prothesis where the leavened bread and wine are prepared for the liturgical sacrifice. The bread is much larger than the Latin host and thicker. It has a special form with a mark stamped on its top. This consists of a square with a cross passing through the middle. Along the arms of the cross are printed the letters IC, XC, and below NI, KA, Jesus Christ triumphs. This square, called the lamb (amnos), is cut out and placed on the paten. With the lance the priest pierces the left side of the lamb saying: ''A soldier pierced His side and out poured blood and water'' (Jn 19.34). The deacon pours wine into the chalice, adding a few drops of water, while the priest arranges beside the lamb various particles: first, one to the left symbolizing the Blessed Lady and nine in three rows of three to the right in honor of various groups of saints. Below these the priest places further particles, commemorating in the first row the living and in the second the dead. The asterisk is incensed and placed over the diskos, then the two veils likewise are incensed and placed over the diskos and chalice, and the whole offering is covered by a large veil. The priest recites a final prayer of offering, and the deacon begins to incense the altar, icons, and faithful as he recites Psalm 50.

Divine Liturgy proper. The priest begins the Liturgy by making the sign of the cross with the Gospel book, and

Byzantine reliquary, 12th century, print. (©Historical Picture Archive/CORBIS)

the deacon leads the faithful in the Great of Litany (Ektene), a.k.a. "Litany of Peace," so-called from its various petitions for peace in the world and in the churches. After each petition sung by the deacon, the faithful or choir respond with "Kyrie eleison." A series of three antiphons sung by the choir is interspersed by two short litanies, and the priest and deacon then make the Little Entrance, in which the Gospel book is carried in solemn procession. Great respect is shown the Gospel book as representing the Divine Word, Jesus Christ Himself. When the deacon arrives at the royal doors after having passed in solemn procession accompanied by servers carrying candles and followed by the celebrant, he sings out in a loud voice: "Wisdom; let us stand erect." With a proper bow to the Gospel as to Christ Himself the deacon, followed by the priest, goes into the sanctuary where the Gospel is placed on the altar. The troparia and kontakia commemorating the feast of the saints of the day are chanted, followed by the solemn singing of the Trisagion: "Holy God, Holy Mighty, Holy Immortal, have mercy on us." During the reading of the Epistle by the lector, the deacon incenses the altar and the people. The priest blesses the deacon, who brings the Gospel to the ambo and reads it solemnly to the people. Several litanies follow with petitions for all present, all the living, the dead, and the catechumens and end with the ancient dismissal of the catechumens.

After this, two short litanies with two prayers for the faithful assisting at the liturgical sacrifice are sung. The Liturgy assumes a greater solemnity with the singing of the Hymn of the Cherubim. During this singing the priest reads a very long prayer asking to be deemed worthy by God to assist at this sacrifice for "it is really You who offer and are offered." The Great Entrance is the procession during which the priest and deacon carry solemnly before the faithful the holy gifts of bread and wine. He blesses the faithful and carries the gifts solemnly through the royal doors to place them on the main altar. The doors are closed and the curtain drawn, thus creating the atmosphere of impending mystery and solemn reverence. The deacon standing before the royal doors leads the faithful in more litanies, ending with the drawing of the curtain and the solemn chanting of the Nicene-Constantinople Creed.

Anaphora. The anaphora (or eucharistic prayer) begins with the Preface dialogue using the same exhortation as in Western liturgies: The priest urges the faithful to lift up their hearts and give thanks to God. At the end of the preface, the assembly responds by singing the Sanctus. A very short prayer of thanks for the salvation brought by Jesus Christ leads into the account of the Last Supper with the priest singing in a loud voice the words of Institution, first over the bread, then over the wine. The deacon crosses his hands above him, holding the paten and the chalice aloft while the priest sings: "We offer You Your own from what is Yours, in all and for all." The Epiclesis or prayer asking the descent of the Holy Spirit on these gifts to change them into the Body and Blood of Jesus Christ is said, and the gifts are blessed with the sign of the cross by the priest. Other prayers and litanies commemorating the living and the dead are climaxed by the solemn singing of the Our Father. After the priest raises the consecrated bread with the command "Holy things to the holy," he proceeds to break the Lamb into four parts. One part, bearing the mark IC, is placed into the chalice while the ones marked NI & KA are cut into smaller pieces for distribution at Communion. The deacon pours hot water (zeon) into the chalice signifying that in the Blood of Christ there is warmth and life; also that fervor is proper in those participating. The priest and deacon receive communion in both species. The consecrated particles are placed into the Precious Blood and presented to the people with the invitation chanted by the deacon: "Approach with faith and in the fear of God." After Communion, the priest blesses the people with the chalice and brings the Holy Gifts to the prothesis while the hymns and litanies of thanksgiving are sung by the deacon and faithful. After a prayer sung by the priest before the iconostasis, the priest gives the final blessing and the concluding prayer, the Dismissal, which commemorates the feast or saint celebrated in that Liturgy. While the deacon consumes at the side altar the remaining Holy Gifts, the priest gives the cross to the faithful to be kissed and distributes antidora, blessed particles of bread. Thus terminates the Byzantine Liturgy of St. John Chrysostom.

The Office. The Hours are almost the same as those of the Latin Liturgy of the Hours. The Office consists mainly of Psalms and liturgical hymns, litanies and prayers. So that all can be sung according to the eight tones of Byzantine chant. Each week the entire Psalter is read. It is divided into 20 parts called kathismata, which include from seven to eight Psalms each. The normal Matins and Vespers is two-fold or three-fold, and includes the commemoration of the day of the week or season of the year, the great feast in progress, as well as the saints of that day. The ferial service books comprise three parts: that of Great Lent (Triod); that of Paschal time (Pentekostarion) and the time after Pentecost, i.e., the remainder of the year (Octoechos). The Hours begins with Vespers celebrated the evening before; then Night, Midnight Office, Matins which is the equivalent of western Matins & Lauds, First, Third, Sixth, and Ninth Hours; the Liturgy is celebrated after the Sixth Hour.

Calendar. The majority of the Orthodox and some Eastern Catholics use the Julian Calendar (called the Old Style), which is 13 days behind the Gregorian. September is the beginning of the new liturgical year. The feasts are divided into four cycles. The weekly cycle commemorates each day a different mystery or group of saints: the Resurrection on Sunday; the angels on Monday; John the Baptist on Tuesday; the Holy Cross on Wednesday and Friday; the Apostles and St. Nicholas on Thursday; and all the saints and the dead on Saturday. The Holy Mother of God is commemorated each day, but in a particular way on Sunday, Wednesday, and Friday in connection with the mystery of the Redemption. The cycle of the eight weeks, Octoechos, according to the eight modes of music, begins with the week of St. Thomas immediately after Pascha and every eight weeks repeats the same eight modes. The annual cycle of movable feasts gravitates around the feast of Pascha. It includes the 18 weeks: ten of preparation before Pascha (the period of the Triod) and the eight weeks after Pascha until the Sunday of All Saints (the period of the Pentekostarion). The annual cycle of fixed feasts begins with September 1 and ends with August 31.

Sacraments. Texts for the administration of the Mysteries are found in the liturgical book called the *Euchologion*. Baptism is conferred by immersion. After the child has been anointed all over its body with blessed oil, it is immersed three times in water while the priest says the formula: ''The servant of God, N., is baptized in the

Byzantine stone reliquary, Hama, Syria. (©Michael Nicholson/ CORBIS)

name of the Father, Amen, and of the Son, Amen, and of the Holy Spirit, Amen.'' Chrismation follows immediately, and the priest is the usual minister, not the bishop as in the Latin Church. As the priest anoints with a specially prepared chrism all the senses and limbs, he recites the simple formula: ''The seal of the gift of the Holy Spirit. Amen.''

The Eucharist is usually given in both kinds with a spoon. Some Eastern Catholic churches distribute communion by intinction: The priest dips slender oblong pieces into the consecrated wine with his fingers and thus distributes it to the faithful.

Among some Orthodox there is the tradition of confessing before each reception of Holy Communion. Except for Eastern Catholic Churches who use the Latin confessional, there is usually no box used. The penitent approaches the priest who stands before a lectern or analogion on which is found the Gospel book and the cross. Standing, the penitent confesses, and the priest places the ends of his wide stole over the head of the penitent as he recites the formula of absolution.

For the Anointing of the Sick oil is blessed, oftentimes containing wine in memory of the Good Samaritan. In some places it is administered as a preparation for Holy Communion during the Great Fast or especially on Wednesday of Holy Week. The priest anoints the senses and limbs, reciting the lengthy formula beginning: ''Holy Father, You, the Physician of souls and bodies, who sent Your only Son, Our Lord Jesus Christ, who heals from every sickness and saves from death, heal your servant, N., of the bodily and spiritual sickness of which he is afflicted and give him the fullness of life through the grace of Your Christ.''

Holy Orders. In the Byzantine churches, the order of reader (lector) and subdeacon are the only two minor orders; the major orders are deacon, priest, and bishop. Orders are given in a very simple but moving rite by the bishop's imposing his hands.

Marriage is called the ''crowning'' because the spouses are crowned with two nuptial crowns with the formula: ''The servant of God, N., is crowned for the servant of God, N., in the name of the Father and the Son and the Holy Spirit. Amen.''

Blessings and prayers. These are of various kinds. Antidora are blessed particles of bread, distributed immediately after the final blessing. At the vigils of feasts and on great saints' days a special anointing occurs during Matins with an oil usually taken from a lamp that has been burning before the icon or oil especially blessed for the purpose earlier in the Vigil. The blessed grain, the kolyba, is eaten in honor of some saint or in memory of the dead. The Great Blessing of water takes place on Theophany (January 6). There are blessings for all sorts of things, the formulas of which are found in the *Euchologion.* The priest usually wears for such blessings the epitrakelion with the phelonion.

Church building. The Byzantine churches are usually constructed in the shape of a Greek cross with four arms of equal length. The Russians, besides the one central cupola above the middle of the cross, place other cupolas over the ends of the cross, surmounted on the outside by onion-shaped bulbs covered by copper or gold gilding. The building is divided into three parts, each distinct from the others: the sanctuary, the nave (naos), and the vestibule (narthex). The sanctuary and nave are separated by the iconostasis. This is a partition of wood or marble, usually high and richly decorated with images or icons of Our Lord, Our Lady, and various saints, and set facing the nave. The iconostasis is pierced by three doors, one in the middle and one at each side. The more ornate set of doors in the middle is called the royal or holy or beautiful doors. Only bishops, priests, deacons, and on occasion subdeacons can pass through these doors. Stretching behind the royal doors is a curtain that is pulled aside at certain moments of the Liturgy. The side doors to the south and north are adorned with icons of the archangels or of St. Stephen the Protomartyr or other sainted deacons or even the Good Thief. Through these pass the other clerics and servers.

Behind the royal doors is the Holy Table. It is a flat square of wood or stone, resting on four legs. There is no altar stone as in the Latin Church, but the relics besides being sealed into a fully consecrated Holy Table are also sewn into the antimension, a type of corporal, painted or stamped with the entombment of Our Lord consecrated and signed by the bishop. The Gospel book and a hand cross always rest on the altar. The eucharistic Holy Gifts are usually reserved in a tabernacle. Many small particles sprinkled with the Precious Blood and dried are kept there. Before giving it in Holy Communion, the priest dips the particle into unconsecrated wine. The Holy Gifts are renewed by many of the Orthodox on Holy Thursday but also as needed.

The sanctuary continues in front of the iconostasis by means of an elevated platform above the nave, called the solion or soleas. Here the deacon chants the litanies, and the faithful receive Holy Communion. The ambo in some churches at the left of the altar is the place from which the gospel is chanted. Usually pews are not known, except for members of the clergy and the sick and aged; others usually stand. However, in the United States among the Greeks and many Eastern Catholics pews are used. In the nave there is a lectern (called an analogion or analoy) or a small table on which the image of the saint of the day or the patron of the church is placed for veneration. The nave connects with the vestibule through several doors. In ancient churches a double division separated the vestibule into two parts, the exterior and the interior vestibule. In the interior, the monks recite canonical hours except for Matins and Vespers; here also is kept the baptismal font. In countries not under Turkish domination, bell towers are found. The Islamic governments in the name of the Qu'ran forbade the use of bells, which were replaced by wood, hit by a mallet. Such a device, called a simandron, is still used in monasteries of the Near East. The interior of churches are ornately decorated with icons painted in the Byzantine style with themes proper to each part of the church. Above the altar in the cupola of the apse is usually found a large icon of the Blessed Virgin holding the Child Jesus, while in the central cupola there is a painting of Christ the Pantokrator (the Almighty).

Vessels. The chalice is the same shape as in the West. The paten, called the diskos, is larger and often rests on a base. The lance or knife and the asterisk or star are peculiar to the Eastern liturgies. The lance, symbolizing the spear by which the centurion pierced the side of the Savior, is used to cut the leavened bread. The asterisk is made of two pieces of curved metal superimposed to form a cross. At the point of juncture a small star or sometimes a cross hangs down over the host on the paten. The asterisk is used to prevent the covering over the paten from touching the bread. Another covering is used over the chalice, and a large veil, the aër, covers the whole Eucharistic offering. These veils or covers symbolize the linen clothes and the tomb of Our Lord.

The zeon is a metal container from which hot water is poured into the chalice before receiving Holy Communion. A spoon is used to distribute Holy Communion. A small sponge is employed for purifying the fingers and the diskos.

A ripidion is a round disk made of metal fixed on a wooden pole with the image of the seraphim with six wings. The deacon waves it over the Holy Gifts at certain moments after the Consecration. During the processions two or more ripidia accompany the cross. In hierarchal Liturgies the bishop holds the dikirion, a two-branched candlestick, in his left hand and the trikirion, a three-branched candlestick, in his right hand when blessing the faithful. Usually behind the altar is a seven-branched candelabrum.

Vestments. While he is not celebrating the Liturgy, the priest wears the anterion, much like a cassock. It is generally black, but for the secular clergy no color is prescribed; often it is gray, brown, white, red, blue or purple. Over the anterion, is the rason, with ample sleeves; it is usually pleated and touches the ground, giving an air of dignity when the priest walks. Priests and deacons and sometimes lower clerics wear the kalimavkion or kamilavkion, a black cylindrical hat. Monks, archimandrites, bishops, and patriarchs cover the kalimavkion with a black veil, called an epanokalimavkion or klobuk, that falls over the shoulders. Among the Slavs and Romanians, all clerics often wear a cap called the scoufia.

Vestments worn during the Liturgy are colorful and ornate. Inferior clerics wear the stikharion, loose tunic of varying color without a cincture. The deacon wears a stikharion with the orarion, a long and narrow cloth placed over the left shoulder. The front end he holds in his right hand as he prays, while the other end falls back over his shoulder to the ground. After the chanting of the Our Father the deacon crisscrosses the orarion over his backing the manner done by subdeacons. There are five distinct vestments for the celebrating priest. The stikharion corresponds to the Latin alb; it can be of different materials and colors, usually very light. Over it he wears the epitrakhelion, a wide stole adorned with crosses; it fits over the head and falls down the front almost to the ground. It is held by the cincture (zone), which is fastened around the waist. Cuffs are worn on the wrists to keep the looser flowing sleeves of the stikarion in place. The phelonion or chasuble is of ample and supple material; it is long in front and may be folded back onto the arms for certain ceremonies. The stole, cincture, cuffs, and phelonion may be the same or contrasting color. Archimandrites, bishops, and high ranking priests wear the epigonation, a stiff, diamond-shaped material with a cross or image embroidered on the center. The priest wears it under the phelonion suspended to the height of his knees by a band from the left waist, while the bishop wears it over the sakkos, fixed by a button.

Generally the bishop wears the same vestments as a simple priest, but the phelonion is replaced by the sakkos, a large tunic with half sleeves, richly embroidered and loosely buttoned on the sides or tied by ribbons. Small bells are attached to the sleeves or sides in imitation of the high priest of the Jews. Over the sakkos, the bishop wears the omophorion, which corresponds to the Latin pallium. It is worn around the neck, forming an angle on the breast with one end falling to the ground. On the chest the bishop wears an oval medallion called the enkolpion, one or two icons of Our Lord and Our Lady, along with a pectoral cross. The headdress, or mitra, is not the usual Latin miter, but a crown, made of rigid material and adorned on top with a cross and various small pictures or icons. The pastoral staff terminates in two intertwined serpents or a curving bar, surmounted by a cross. In assisting at, or before actually celebrating, the Divine Liturgy, the bishop wears the mantle called the mandyas. It is very ample with the two parts attached in front at the neck and bottom. Along the border is rich embroidery and small bells.

From ancient times the Byzantine priests employed three liturgical colors in the celebration of the Liturgy: black for the Liturgy of the Presanctified, red for Lent and funerals, and white for all other occasions. But in modern times, the rules of color are not maintained with rigor. For the normal celebration of the Liturgy any color except black that would not shock is admissible.

Books. Many heavy books are used in the performance of the liturgical services. The *Euchologion* contains the text for the three Liturgies as well as the ritual for the administration of the Mysteries, blessings, and prayer services. Usually the priest and deacon use an extract from this volume called the *Liturgikon*. This contains their parts for the Liturgies as well as their parts at Vespers and Matins. The remaining parts of the *Euchologion* can be found in Slavic usage in the three or four volume *Trebnik*. The *Evangelion* contains the readings for each day of the gospel, and the *Apostolos* the corresponding epistles and the Acts. In the *Psalterion* are the Psalms divided into 20 groups called kathismata and the biblical canticles. The *Triodion* includes the offices for Great Lent, and the *Pentekostarion* those of Pascha up to the first Sunday after Pentecost, i.e., the Sunday of All Saints. The *Octoechos* or *Parakletiki* has services from the first Sunday after Pentecost to the Sunday of the Pharisee and Publican, the tenth Sunday before Pascha. It contains the tropars, kontakia, canons, and verses on the Vespers psalms and the morning praise psalms for Vespers, Compline, Matins, and Hours divided into eight parts, each to be sung for a week according to one of the eight tones of Byzantine chant.

The *Menaion* contain the services of the fixed feasts and of the saints for the whole year and is divided into six or 12 volumes. The *Horologion* has parts of the Hours that never change, also the ecclesiastical calendar, the apolitikia or dismissal hymns, and the kontakia for each day. The *Typikon* is a type of directory of rules to be observed for putting together the variable parts of the Liturgy and Hours for all the feasts and days of the year.

The *Archieratikon* corresponds to the Roman Pontifical and provides for the liturgical functions of a bishop. The *Theotokarion* is a collection of chants in honor of the Mother of God (Theotokos) divided into eight groups according to the eight musical tones. The *Hirmologion* is made up of strophes and melody types used as basic rhythms for the irmoi of the canons and other hymns found in other liturgical books unaccompanied by musical notation. Finally, the *Hagiasmatarion* is a collection of prayers, blessings, and offices that the priest has most need of in daily ministrations to the faithful.

Bibliography: D. ATTWATER, *The Christian Churches of the East,* 2 v. (rev. ed. Milwaukee 1961–62). F. E. BRIGHTMAN, *Liturgies Eastern and Western,* 2 v. (Oxford 1896) v. 1. J. M. HANSSENS, *Institutiones liturgicae de ritibus orientalibus* (Rome 1930–32) v. 2, 3. A. A. KING, *The Rites of Eastern Christendom,* 2 v. (London 1950). R. F. TAFT, *The Byzantine Rite: A Short History* (Collegeville, MN 1992); *History of the Liturgy of St. John Chrysostom,* v. 2, 4, 5 (*Orientalia Christiana Analecta*200, 238, 261; Rome 1978–2000); ''The Liturgy of the Great Church: An Initial Synthesis of Structure and Interpretation on the Eve of Iconoclasm,'' *Dumbarton Oaks Papers* 34; ''Mount Athos: A Late Chapter in the History of the 'Byzantine Rite,''' *ibid.* 42; *Beyond East and West* (Washington, D.C 1984); *Liturgy of the Hours in East and West* (Collegeville, MN 1993). H. WYBREW, *The Orthodox Liturgy* (London 1989). H.-J. SCHULZ, *The Byzantine Liturgy* (New York 1986). J. F. BALDOVIN, *The Urban Character of Christian Worship* (*Orientalia Christiana Analecta* 228; Rome 1987). **Liturgical Texts in English:** *Menaion of the Orthodox Church,* 12 v. (Liberty, TN 1996–2001). *The Octoechos* (Liberty, TN 1999). *The Pentecostarion* (Boston 1990). *The Lenten Triodion* (Boston 1978). *The Lenten Triodion* supplementary texts (France 1979). *The Great Horologion* (Boston 1997). *The Horologion or Book of Hours* (South Canaan, PA 2000). *The Priest's Service Book.* 2 v. (New York 1973. *The Great Book of Needs* 4 v. (South Canaan, PA 1998–99).

[G. A. MALONEY/R. B. MILLER]

BYZANTINE THEOLOGY

Byzantine theology is used here to designate the writings and thoughts of Eastern writers from the patristic age to the end of the Byzantine empire indicated by the fall of Constantinople in 1453, when it came to be called more properly Greek theology.

NATURE AND SOURCES

Byzantine theology remained faithful, generally speaking, to the dogmas defined by the first seven ecumenical councils and had great reverence for the writings of the FATHERS OF THE CHURCH. It recognized the same Sacraments and the same ecclesiastical organization and was presided over by bishops whom the Roman Church acknowledged as true successors of the Apostles. Nevertheless, Byzantine and Latin theology are profoundly different. While they treat the same matters, they deal with them diversely. What differentiates and even divides Latin from Byzantine theology is not so much the objects of belief as the manner of dealing with them. It is a question of mentality or *esprit.*

Spiritual Platonism. The Byzantine approach to theology is primarily influenced by a spiritual PLATONISM that considers the world as an epiphany or appearance of a superior world. The Gospel of John and the Platonizing Fathers of the first five centuries formed Oriental and Byzantine Christian thought. This thought insists on the separation between the visible world and the invisible world. What one sees here below are the changing, imperfect things. Behind these beings, there is the true unchanging Being that the soul will contemplate happily in immortal life. The hereafter is the sole end of man's destiny and of all worldly activity.

Visible creation is admired as the work of the Divinity, but this vision will never fully satisfy the ineffable desire of the human spirit. As long as the soul is confined to the body, it will not attain that of which it is capable. Thus, Byzantine theology considers the corporeal envelope of the senses as a prison; with the Apostle Paul, it groans for liberation from the body and considers death as an accomplishment or gain. The Fourth Gospel and Revelation express this tension of the soul in striving after Him who is the way, the truth, and the life.

The Platonizing method of Byzantine theology does not look for immanent ideas in things or a rational explanation after the fashion of the Aristotelian method; for this reason, supernatural reality, with which revelation is concerned, is enveloped in mystery. It is something spiritual and consequently not comprehensible to the soul immersed in the material as in a prison. Byzantine theology does not seek out reasons to justify the intelligibility of the supernatural in the natural order; it does not attempt to build the supernatural upon nature, nor does it consider the human spirit as naturally Christian. Speculative Byzantine theology is therefore not highly developed or sys-

"Christ Pantocrator Between Emperor Constantine IX Monamachus and Empress Zoë," wall mosaic, Byzantine Style, mid 11th/early 12th century. (©Gianni Dagli Orti/CORBIS)

tematic. It is rather mystical, liturgical, scriptural, patristic, and eclectic.

As human reason is incapable of comprehending the supernatural, or the divine side of the Christian mystery that is revelation, there are few dogmas in Byzantine theology, few rational explanations of revealed truths. There are *theologoumena,* or truths that can be accepted without being clothed with dogmatic value to be imposed as the faith for all. Byzantine theology does not admit of a well-determined, proximate rule of faith and leaves much room for belief. There is a tendency simply to identify dogma with revelation, the human and contingent expression of the revealed truth with the revealed truth itself.

In Byzantine theology, revelation is a determined sum of supernatural truths fixed from all eternity; there is little dogmatic progress in the theological science of revealed doctrine. According to Bulgakov, dogmas are the markers or limits beyond which orthodox doctrine should not strive to pass. Not having a permanent, living magisterium, Byzantine theology does not try to penetrate the revealed truths received from tradition through reason; but it tries to live them in a mystical and liturgical atmosphere. This is why Byzantine theology has not produced a powerful rational synthesis, but rather, particular treatises dealing with controverted questions, frequently merely repeating the arguments of others. ARISTOTELIANISM had more success among the Nestorians and Monophysites in the Orient. Despite his greatness, JOHN DAMASCENE, who was actually a Syrian Melkite of Damascus, did not exercise an influence on Greek Byzantine thought in any way comparable to that of THOMAS AQUINAS on Western theology.

Sources of Byzantine theology. The Byzantines admit in general two sources of their theology: Scripture and tradition. Recent Greek, rather than Byzantine, theology seems to speak of but one sole source of revelation;

this reflects the influence of Cyril Lucaris. For the canon of the Scripture, the Byzantine theologians followed the third and fourth synods of Carthage and the Council of Trullo (Quinisext 691), which with very little exception admitted Catholic teaching on both the NT and Revelation and on the Deuterocanonical books of the OT. They attributed an infallible authority to all the books of Sacred Scripture, particularly as regards faith and morals, and taught that the Church is charged with the interpretation of Scripture by means of tradition. They speak of an active tradition, by which they mean the consent of the Church, or of the piety and liturgical sense, as well as the universal consciousness of the Church. Modern authors developed and emphasized this point.

Passive tradition comprises: the CREEDS or symbols of faith, including the Nicene-Constantinopolitan, the Athanasian, and Apostles' Creeds; the APOSTOLIC CONSTITUTIONS; the first seven councils before the separation of the Churches, to which are added the Quinisext of 691 and, usually, the Photian Council of 879–880. The doctrinal authority of the councils is infallible. Some moderns, including KHOMIAKOV, also attribute this infallibility to the Church ''as already instructed.'' According to Bulgakov, the councils are merely the expression of this infallibility. The Byzantines attribute dogmatic value also to certain synods, to the Apostolic canons, the ACTS OF THE MARTYRS, the Liturgy, the usage of the ancient Church, the Fathers, and certain confessions of faith in recent theology, such as those of Dositheus and Peter MOGHILA. Among the Fathers of the Church, they venerate in particular the old, post-Nicene theologians: Athanasius, the Cappadocians, Maximus the Confessor, Pseudo-Dionysius, and John Damascene; and among the Latins, Pope Leo I and Augustine. They consider them as witnesses to tradition, and their consensus as a definite sign of the truth.

Christology. The APOSTOLIC FATHERS, such as IGNATIUS OF ANTIOCH, occupy the particular attention of the Byzantines in the discussion concerning the reality of Christ's humanity in controversy against the Docetists (*see* DOCETISM). In the 4th century, it was the divinity of Christ that had to be defended against the Arians (*see* ARIANISM), leading to a deepening of the doctrine of the hypostatic union through definitions at the Councils of EPHESUS (431) and of CHALCEDON (451).

After the constitution of the great patriarchal churches of Constantinople, Alexandria, Antioch, and Jerusalem, these patriarchal centers were at rivalry not only for ecclesiastical supremacy but also for doctrinal control. The theological school of ANTIOCH, by stressing the twofold nature of Christ, provided a foundation for NESTORIANISM, while the school of ALEXANDRIA favored the divinity of Christ, and gave a foothold to Monophysitism. The Alexandrian theologians, with their Platonizing tendencies under the guidance of Pantaenus, Clement, and Origen, attempted to reconcile Neoplatonism with an allegorical interpretation of Scripture; they tended to confuse the unity of the person in Christ with the two natures.

The school of Antioch, with its Aristotelianism and its teachers, such as LUCIAN OF ANTIOCH, DOROTHEUS, PAUL OF SAMOSATA, and DIODORE OF TARSUS, tried to reconcile Aristotelianism with a literal exegesis of Scripture, and not only did they tend to establish a division between the double nature in Christ, but they introduced this division into the person of the Savior. The schools of EDESSA and of NISIBIS were attached to Antioch. Constantinople did not develop its own theological school; only under Emperor THEODOSIUS II was a school of philosophy founded to replace the pagan academies of the Greeks.

THE AGE OF JUSTINIAN

In the Justinian age, Byzantine theology was engaged in a battle against two excesses: Monophysitism and Nestorianism. PROCLUS, the patriarch of Constantinople (434–446), had begun this controversy and inspired a group of defenders of orthodoxy in the East. He gave an orthodox explanation of the hypostatic union in his Tome to the Armenians and in his Marian homilies. LEONTIUS OF BYZANTIUM (485–543) began as a Nestorian, then combatted both Nestorianism and Monophysitism, leaning in part on Origenism (*see* ORIGEN AND ORIGENISM). His principal works, the *Three Books against the Eutychians and Nestorians* and his *Diversa Opuscula et Scholia,* employed the Neoplatonic dialectic against the Aristotelian heresiarchs and established the orthodox relations between the human nature of Christ and His divine hypostasis or person. The human nature is a true and real nature belonging to the divine hypostasis.

The concepts of nature and of hypostasis or person were finally clarified by John Damascene. Meanwhile, Byzantine writers, and particularly Emperor JUSTINIAN I (527–565), the fervent caesaropapal ruler and theologian, based their doctrine on CYRIL OF ALEXANDRIA and attacked the Monophysites; Justinian rejected Origenism and condemned the THREE CHAPTERS as Nestorian, using his own authority and that of the ecumenical Council of CONSTANTINOPLE II (553), finally bending Pope VIGILIUS to his will in this matter. While the emperor admitted the doctrine of the Roman primacy, in practice he proclaimed the ruler's right to make doctrinal and ecclesiastical decisions. His CAESAROPAPISM, particularly in ecclesiastical legislation, had a great influence on Byzantine Church development, in hierarchical structure and in disciplinary decrees for clerics and monks, as well as on matrimonial law. By inserting the famous canon 28 of the Council of Chalcedon concerning the privileges of the See of Constantinople as the second Rome, Justinian sowed the seed of discord between the churches of the Orient and that of Rome.

Patriarchal rights. The Council of NICAEA I (325) had recognized the patriarchal rights of the Sees of Alexandria and Antioch. The Council of CONSTANTINOPLE I (381) changed the order of the sees established by Nicaea I and attributed the first rank and the ''same privileges of honor'' to Constantinople after Rome. The fathers at Chalcedon (451), despite their assertion that they respected the sense of canon 3 of the Council of Constantinople I, actually gave Constantinople true jurisdiction over the Dioceses of Pontus, Asia, and Thrace: they suppressed the term ''of honor'' and added as justification the fact that old Rome enjoyed a primacy because it was the political capital. In itself, the sense of canon 28 was disciplinary and canonical; but it could easily be employed in an abusive interpretation, to concede to the See of Constantinople the same powers over the East that Rome enjoyed in the West. Hence, the papal legates and Pope Leo I rejected this canon. Before Justinian, canon 28 did not actually prevail in Byzantine theology; he gave it the attribute of law, and after him the Council in Trullo (691) and later Byzantine writers accepted it as such.

Monothelitism. Theological deviation appeared at this epoch in the guise of MONOTHELITISM that admitted but one, unique theandric operation in Christ. This doctrine was taught by the patriarch of Constantinople, SERGIUS I (610–638), and was adopted gradually by the Copts, Syrians, and Armenians. SOPHRONIUS, patriarch of Jerusalem (d. 638), was the first effective adversary of Monothelitism; he was aided by MAXIMUS THE CONFESSOR (d. 662), who during his journeys and by his contacts in Jerusalem and in Rome, particularly with Pope MARTIN I, combatted both Monophysitism and Monothelitism. In his *Florilegium,* he shows the influence of PSEUDO-DIONYSIUS and Leontius of Byzantium, as he employed Neoplatonic philosophy and dialectic to combat these errors; he employed them also to explain the double will of Christ.

The doctrine of Maximus triumphed finally at the Council of CONSTANTINOPLE III (681). Another Byzantine Melchite, John Damascene (d. 749), achieved a reputation as a great theologian in the 8th century. He is properly called the Thomas Aquinas of the East. He composed a series of ascetical, dogmatic, polemic, and poetic works. His *Fons cognitionis* (Πηγή τῆς γνώσεως) is a learned compilation of patristic authors, systematized in an Aristotelian, logical structure; it dealt with problems that later became matters of contention between the Latins and the Byzantines, such as the Immaculate Conception, the epiclesis, and purgatory. In the Christological domain, he gave clear and orthodox testimony regarding the hypostatic union, the Eucharist, and the notions of nature and person, in his *De fide orthodoxa.* John also achieved eminence with his *Three Orations on Images,* in which he defended sacred icons against the iconoclastic Byzantine emperors of the Syrian dynasty. He distinguished between the worship of latria due to God, and the worship of dulia, due to the saints and their representations in images. In this cult, it is not the material of the image that is venerated but the person of the one who is depicted.

Council of Nicaea III. Under Empress IRENE, the veneration of images was vindicated with the Council of NICAEA III (787). At the Synod of Constantinople (843), held under THEODORA (2) and Michael III (842–867), iconoclasm was definitively vanquished. As a souvenir of this event, the Sunday of Orthodoxy was established. THEODORE THE STUDITE, founder of the Studite monastery at Constantinople (798) and an ascetical and poetic writer, defended the Roman primacy and the cult of images with the same arguments as those used by John Damascene.

Carolingian controversies. During the Carolingian age, Western theologians took an interest in the iconoclastic controversy of the Byzantines. Under Alcuin, they opposed the iconophile doctrine defined at the Council of Nicaea III. In the collective work called the *Carolingian Books* (*Libri Carolini*) they attempted to achieve a *via media;* while they repudiated the exaggerations of the iconoclasts, they did not agree with the iconophiles that images were to be worshiped with the cult of dulia. This stemmed from a misunderstanding. Actually, for the Westerner the cult given to images is a relative worship, going directly to the person represented, while for the Oriental, the cult given to images is an external veneration or *proskynesis* that differs from the worship rendered to God and that given to the saints. Images, in the thought of John Damascene, possess a superior virtue because of their consecration and their quality as instruments by which God works miracles.

The Carolingian theologians also complained that the Council of Nicaea III had employed a formula proposed by Patriarch TARASIUS OF CONSTANTINOPLE concerning the procession of the Holy Spirit ''from the Father through the Son.'' They charged that this was a vague and even equivocal expression, giving the impression that the Holy Spirit was a creature. They defended the FILIOQUE formula and accused Tarasius of dogmatic error. Pope Adrian came to the defense of the patriarch by showing that the formula ''through the Son'' was well founded among the Greek fathers. Thus the filioque dispute changed terrain and became a quarrel between the Carolingians and the Romans. At the behest of Charlemagne, Alcuin defended the filioque in his *Libellus de processione Spiritus Sancto.*

Filioque. This difficulty was increased between the Byzantines and the Carolingians in 809, at a synod of Aix-la-Chapelle, when the formula ''filioque'' was introduced into the Creed in the Latin sung Mass. The Carolingians also supported the Latin monks on Mt. Olivet in Jerusalem, who defended the filioque against the Greek monks in the monastery of St. Sabas. For ecumenical reasons, Pope Leo III did not approve the use of the filioque in the Mass. ''Why approve the use of this formula without necessity,'' he asked, ''when such an addition will favor a division between the East and the West?''

Another question that came to the fore at this time was the doctrine of the pentarchy. The defenders of images were in favor of a moderate pentarchy in attributing to the five patriarchs supreme power in the Church. By this they desired to prove that the Iconoclastic Synod, presided over by only one patriarch, was not legitimate. Their chief, Theodore the Studite, recognized the full powers of the five patriarchs in an ecumenical council, but he did not desire to downgrade the Roman primacy, which, according to him, was of divine right and was provided with the charism of infallibility and the principle of unity. For the defenders of the pentarchy, the Pauline idea of the Mystical Body of Christ suggested a concept of the Church in which all the members, with their head, the Roman sovereign pontiff, are united among themselves by the intermediary of the patriarchs, who hold a rank midway between the Roman pontiff and the bishops in the direction of the Church. However, during the 9th century the Byzantines abused this interpretation of the Church to assert that it was not reconcilable with the monarchic structure defended by the Latins, and that as a consequence all the patriarchs were equal in dignity and power, including the Roman patriarch of the Latin Church.

THE PHOTIAN PERIOD: 9TH AND 10TH CENTURIES

After the suppression of the Ecumenical Academy in 726 by the iconoclastic Emperor Leo III, Michael III and his minister Bardas founded in 863 the University of the Imperial Palace of Constantinople. Profane sciences were taught at the university, and the professors were all laymen. Theology was cultivated by the monks of the Studite monastery, particularly under Theodore. Among the renowned lecturers at the university were Leo the Philosopher, Photius, and Constantine (Cyril), later the apostle of the Slavs. In the West, the secular and theological sciences were cultivated in the Carolingian Empire and in northern Italy. In Rome these studies were almost totally neglected. It was only under the Greeks in flight from the iconoclastic persecution that sacred studies began to flourish in Rome.

PHOTIUS became patriarch of Constantinople under Emperor Michael III in 858 in place of the deposed Ignatius. Because of his controversy against the Roman primate, as well as for his knowledge and virtue, Photius is held in great veneration by the Byzantine Orthodox Church. It should be remarked, however, that the knowledge of Photius was more encyclopedic than profound, and that his integrity was tarnished by his intrigues against Patriarch Ignatius and the Roman See.

Responsibility of Photius. More recently F. Dvornik has attempted to diminish the responsibility of Photius in the break between the two Churches. In his opinion, Photius would have opposed the pope only in the beginning; and his reinstallation in the patriarchal see after the resignation of Ignatius would have been approved by the pope. Likewise, in Dvornik's view, Photius lived in peace with the Church of Rome until his death. As regards his doctrine, Photius admitted the inspiration of the Deuterocanonical books; he interpreted the Sacred Scriptures in a literal and historical sense. The Fathers of the Church, from whom he omitted the pre-Nicaeans, the Latins, and even John Damâscene, are in his estimation the authentic interpreters of the Bible and witnesses to tradition. He used Aristotelian dialectic adroitly in his polemics against the Latins, particularly in the subtle questions of the procession of the Holy Spirit, not hesitating to reverse himself when the Roman-Byzantine relations took a more favorable turn for him.

In his writings before his break with the Latins (867), as in his letters to Zachary of Armenia, to King Boris Michael of Bulgaria, to Pope Nicholas I (860; containing his profession of faith), and in another letter to the same pope in 862 with his apology for his election to the patriarchate, he taught nothing contrary to the faith of the Roman Church, even though he mentioned diverse liturgical and disciplinary uses. In these letters, Photius also clearly admitted the primacy of St. Peter.

Primacy of Rome. As for the primacy of the Roman pontiffs, there is nothing explicit. While he rejected the Synod of Sardica (*c.* 13) quoted by Pope Nicholas, it seems that Photius was merely refuting the argument against the legitimacy of his own election. Besides, the allusions in the writings of Photius during this period and his whole attitude toward the pope show how much he prized papal approbation of his election. This must be said against those who would interpret his actions as being tactical rather than being dictated by conviction. But Photius tried in vain to convince the pope to confirm his election, and this certainly disposed him against the Roman See. Yet he did not immediately break with Rome. The occasion arose in the course of the conflict over Bulgaria.

Boris of Bulgaria was conquered by the Byzantines in 865 and baptized by them, but he turned toward Rome, despite the fact that Photius as patriarch sent him a dogmatic letter on the Christian faith and believed that the Byzantine Church should exercise jurisdiction over Bulgaria. Boris was motivated by political resentment against Byzantium. He maltreated and expelled the Byzantine missionaries and addressed himself to Pope Nicholas. The latter wrote his famous *Letter to the Bulgarians.* In furious reaction, Photius convoked the Synod of 867, which condemned the Latins and addressed an *Encyclical Letter to the Oriental Thronos,* inviting them to an ecumenical council called in Constantinople that same year. This council excommunicated the Latins and deposed Pope Nicholas as illegitimately elected. But immediately afterward, Emperor Michael was assassinated and his successor, Basil I the Macedonian, reestablished peace between the two Churches, reinstated Ignatius as patriarch, and expelled Photius.

After the death of Ignatius (878), Photius resumed the patriarchate until his exile in 886. During this period, a relative peace existed between Byzantium and Rome. Photius had not changed in his resentment, nor in his doctrine regarding the procession of the Holy Spirit, as is evident, for example, in his *Mystagogia,* written at this time. It is probable that he had at least a fragmentary knowledge of the Latin replies to his attacks, even though he knew no Latin. But he passed over the recriminations against the liturgical and disciplinary usages in silence and his older arguments against the Roman primacy. He made an indirect attempt to weaken the primatial authority of Rome.

The Ecumenical Council of 869–870 anathematized Photius for favoring new dogmas and for deceit. He had had predecessors who in word and deed had acted independently of the Roman See and admitted the Roman primacy when it pleased them. Before Photius, no Byzantine employed the phrase ''from the Father alone'' of the Holy Spirit, but said rather ''from the Father through the Son.'' The doctrine of Photius on the active inspiration of the Father alone is certainly contrary to the tradition of the Fathers, with the exception of one or other who used the Alexandrian formula ''from the Father through the Son,'' but limited the function of the spiriting principle to the Father, and understood ''through the Son'' to include only the temporal mission of the Holy Spirit. Duns Scotus came close to this Byzantine opinion on the procession ''through the Son'' in his work *De divisione naturae.*

Photius to Michael Cerularius. There is little evidence for the relations between Rome and Byzantium during this period. Basil I considered the quarrels between the two churches as an internal affair of the clergy and the partisans of Ignatius and Photius. Patriarch NICHOLAS I MYSTICUS anathematized Emperor Leo VI (912), who was already dead, and with him, all who had admitted the legitimacy of the emperor's fourth marriage, among whom was the pope, Sergius III. Although the Photian attacks were not repeated, his doctrinal attitudes prevailed. As the Byzantine Empire was then at the apex of its influence, the Church propagated its doctrine among the Slavs and Arabs. However, the 10th century produced no Byzantine theologian of renown, despite the writings of Arethas of Caesarea, Nicetas of Byzantium, George of Nicomedia, and particularly Emperors LEO VI THE WISE and CONSTANTINE VII PORPHYROGENITUS with their homilies, as well as patriarchs Eutychius of Alexandria and the saintly Euthymius (d. 917) of Constantinople. These authors held the procession of the Holy Spirit ''from the Father through the Son'' and favored the prerogatives of Constantinople against Rome. Yet there were Byzantine authors in this period who admitted the Roman primacy, including Nicholas of Paphlagonia, a student of both Arethas and Photius. The Byzantines were interested in defending Christianity against the Mohammedans and Jacobites. Among them were those who bore excellent witness to the Mother of God (THEOTOKOS), whom the Byzantines exalted by literary and rational arguments rather than by a profound search of revelation. In their Marian homilies, they went back to the ancient theses of the Marian feasts: her perpetual virginity, her bodily assumption, her mediation through intercession, and her holiness at the moment of her conception.

THE BREAK WITH ROME

After the formal break between the Churches of Rome and Byzantium under Patriarch MICHAEL CERULARIUS (1042–59), tension grew. During this period many popes, including Alexander II, Gregory VII, and Urban II, tried to reestablish unity, but in vain. The lower clergy and the monks in particular were opposed, as also were the patriarchs John VIII Xiphilinus and NICHOLAS III, who made use of the title ''Ecumenical Patriarch'' and tried to turn the Melkites, Nestorians, and Monophysites of the Diaspora against Rome. With the CRUSADES and the founding of the Latin Kingdom of Jerusalem (1099), matters worsened between the two Churches.

Spread of the schism. Questions were raised concerning the validity of the excommunication hurled at MICHAEL CERULARIUS and his followers by Cardinal Humbert on July 16, 1054, since Pope Leo IX (d. April

19, 1054) was dead at this time. The mutual excommunications themselves were directed at the persons and not the Churches, but unhappily the schism that resulted spread to the other patriarchates of the East, and it was further fomented by the schools. The university founded at Constantinople in 1045 by CONSTANTINE IX MONOMACHUS had faculties of philosophy and law and exercised an influence on Byzantine thought. There was also a patriarchal school for theology that held a middle position between the university and the monastery schools. In the latter two, theology was taught in a positive fashion, while at the university Michael Psellus tried to apply hellenistic philosophy to the revealed doctrines. Michael Cerularius had contributed to the separation of the churches not only by his hostile attitude toward the papal legates in his *Edictum Synodale*, read to the people on July 20, 1054, in Hagia Sophia, but also by his writings (such as his *Epistula ad Petrum Antiochenum*) on the errors of the Latins, by his *Panoplia,* and by his *Epistula Leonis Achridensis.* Michael accused the Latins of liturgical deviations and dogmatic errors concerning the azymes or unleavened bread, the Saturday fast, abstinence, Baptism, the veneration of images, lack of respect for the Greek Fathers, the filioque, and the Roman primacy; these 22 accusations in all were repeated by contemporary writers.

Hostile Influences. The Studite monk NICETAS STETHATOS, called Pectoratus (d. after 1054), left a number of works on spiritual theology and on controversy with the Jews, Armenians, and Latins (e.g., *Spiritual Paradise* and *De fermentato et azymo contra armenios et latinos*). Leo of Ochrida, the Bulgarian archbishop, accused the Latins, in a letter to John of Apulia, of liturgical deviations, such as not chanting the Alleluia during Lent. The patriarch of Antioch, Peter III, in his *Epistula ad Dominicum Gradensem* and in other writings, also brought up these questions, particularly that of the azymes. But he seemed to act as a supporter of peace, saying that he would absolve the Latins of all abuses if they would leave the filioque out of the Creed.

An anonymous *Contra francos aliosque latinos* in the second half of the 11th century brought the number of accusations to 28; this had great influence on the hostile mentality of the Byzantines and led Michael Cerularius to consider the filioque as heretical. Michael did not attack the Roman primacy directly, but he insisted on breaking with the pope, whom he considered to be in heresy, and said it was not traditional to remain in communion with heretics, even the head of a Church. If the head of the fish is rotting, he asked, how can the body be salutary? Peter of Antioch, who deplored the schism, actually held for the pentarchy, according to which the Church under one head alone, Christ, was governed by the five patriarchs as equals. But the question of unleavened bread was principal at this period. The Byzantines maintained that when Christ instituted the Eucharist, the Jews did not have unleavened bread.

Michael Psellus. Among the Byzantine theologians who tried to apply a Platonizing philosophy to the dogmas of the Trinity and Christology was Michael Psellus the Younger (d. 1078). He was a poet, historian, and philosopher. Only part of his works have been published, but he used both an Aristotelian and Platonizing approach to the Trinity and Christology and was accused by the monastic schools of Neoplatonizing. He admitted the procession ''from the Father alone,'' a certain material essence in the angels, the holiness of the Mother of God at her conception, and her mediatorship. JOHN ITALUS of Calabria (d. 1084) succeeded Psellus as rector of the university. But he had to resign his professorial chair due to the accusation of Hellenization made by the monks under Emperor Alexius Comnenus. Eleven anathemas were brought against Psellus in the *Synodicon* of the first Sunday of Lent (1082), called the Sunday of Orthodoxy. This gave a death blow to speculation in Byzantine theology.

These theologians were accused of attempting to rationalize the mysteries of the Trinity and the Incarnation. In the same current were Theodore Prodromus, a humanist rather than theologian, Euthymius ZIGABENUS, who in the second section of his *Panoplia dogmatica* furnished rational expositions for the service of theology that were fairly profound; John Mauropus, the master of Psellus; and Michael Italicus.

One of the better theologians of the time was Theophylactus, metropolitan of Bulgaria (d. 1108), disciple of Psellus, and lecturer in the patriarchal school at Constantinople. Among his writings were his *Enarrationes in 4 Evangelia; Commentaria in V. et N. Testamenta;* and *Vita St. Clementis Bulgaris.* His opuscule *De üs quorum Latini incusantur* gives an exact idea of the problems being disputed between the Latin and Greek churches. He differed with those who accused the Roman Church of heresy. He appeared to reject the Roman primacy but admitted the primacy of Peter. He said the deficiency of the Latin language was responsible for their confusion on the filioque between the ''eternal procession'' and the ''temporal sending'' of the Holy Spirit. He would allow the filioque in private usage if the Son were not considered a *principium,* or cause.

Positive Theologians. Concerning the two principal doctrines of the Trinity and Christology, the positive theologians had a better position after the condemnation of Psellus and his school. Along with Euthymius Zigabenus, whose *Panoplia dogmatica* was a new version of the Photian *Libellus* with attention to the opinions of the

Greek Fathers and some of the Latins, were Andronicus Camateros, with his *Sacrum Armentarium,* and Nicetas Acominatus and his *Thesaurus Orthodoxiae.* Both Andronicus Camateros and Nicetas Acominatus followed the official doctrine of Constantinople in the dispute with the Latins. John Phurnensis, Eustratius of Nicaea, A. Demetrakopoulus, Nicetas Seides, and Nicholas of Methone did likewise, although through their interest in the Fathers they departed from the attitude of Photius.

Nicetas of Maronia, in his *Dialogues on the Holy Spirit,* affirmed that the Holy Spirit proceeded immediately from the Son and through the Son from the Father as from a primary and original cause. He hoped to arrive at a compromise by requesting the Latins to suppress the filioque in the Creed if the Greeks would admit that the Holy Spirit proceeds from the Father through the Son, or even from the Father and the Son, understanding the *ex filio* in accord with the Fathers as *ex principio immediato*, and not *ex principio carente principio.* During all this period, however, these authors repeated the old Cerularian accusations.

Pentarchy. The Byzantine concept of the pentarchy had evolved at the end of the 12th century into a system against the Roman primacy. The canonist Theodore BALSAMON (d. after 1195) contributed to this development with his *Commentary on the Canons* and in his *Responsum de Patriarcharum privilegiis*, in which he dealt with the origin, privileges, and equality in dignity of all the patriarchs. He admitted the apostolic origin of the three patriarchates of Jerusalem, Antioch, and Alexandria. The patriarchate of Rome had its origin with Constantine I, and that of Constantinople with the Council of Constantinople I (381). This theory was sustained by the Byzantines and the Slavs, with few exceptions, until the 17th century. The other questions agitated during this period were the cult of images, as something absolute, a position that was sustained by Leo of Chalcedon, who was condemned for this reason; and the sacrifice in the Liturgy of the Mass, that is not offered to the Word (Christ offers and is offered), a position sustained by Soterichus Panteugenus of Antioch, Eustathius Dyrrachiensis, and Michael of Thessalonica, all of whom were condemned at the Synod of Constantinople of 1157. The Synod of 1166 gave an explanation of the words ''the Father is greater than I'' (Jn 14.28), which refer to Christ as man, and not solely to the humanity in Christ.

Council of Lyons. Byzantine theology in the 13th century gravitated around the Council of Lyons (1274), as a preparation or a consequence, with one nuance before the Latin occupation of Constantinople (1204–61) and another nuance after the occupation. During the Latin Empire of the East (1204–1393), the controversy with the Latins became acute under the brothers John and Nicholas Mesarites, the first a monk and exegete, and the other the metropolitan of Ephesus. The two engaged in conferences with the Latins in which the question of the Roman primacy was discussed and combatted by the Byzantines with new arguments. It was asserted that Peter was not the first bishop of Rome, but Linus; and that it was not Rome but Jerusalem or Antioch that should enjoy the primatial right. This idea is found in John Camateros of Constantinople (d. 1206) in his *Letters to Pope Innocent III.* Many authors taught the Photian doctrine on the procession of the Holy Spirit. At this period, the problem of purgatory appeared for the first time. Georgius III Bardanes, metropolitan of Corfu, denied the fire of purgatory (1231) for venial sins not expiated on earth, and he also denied immediate retribution after death. This idea became a common Byzantine teaching. The Franciscan Bartholomeus answered Georgius, and Pope Leo IV took up the question of purgatory in his letter to the legate in Cyprus (1254); Leo also brought up the problem of fornication, which the Greeks did not consider a mortal sin.

Principal Arguments. The *Tract against the Errors of the Greeks* of the Dominican Bartholomew of Byzantium (1252) gave a résumé of the principal Greek arguments and the Latin responses. After the transfer of the imperial government from Nicaea back to Constantinople under Michael Palaeologus in 1261, two tendentious factions controlled the religious thought of the capital: the zealot monks and the learned courtiers and courtesans. Michael persecuted the Zealots, who, with the deposed patriarch Arsenius, violently opposed the emperor's efforts to approach Rome.

The writings of the monk NICEPHORUS BLEMMYDES (d. 1272) contributed to the cause of union, particularly in clarifying the question of the procession of the Holy Spirit. Nicephorus did not approve the addition of the filioque in the Creed. His teaching deviated from that of Photius far enough, however, to admit the procession ''from the Father and Son'' or ''through the Son,'' admitting that the Holy Spirit was the Spirit of the Son for he pertained to the Son essentially. His critics said that the formula *per filium* in Blemmydes' thought signified the mediation of the Son in the eternal procession of the Spirit. This mediation was essential but not actual, according to V. Grumel, while Gordillo sees it as an active principle of the Holy Spirit in so far as the Son receives it from the Father. Blemmydes' doctrine, at once positive, patristic, and catholic, on the procession, had great influence on many Byzantines, including the Patriarch JOHN XI BECCUS, and it helped prepare a mentality that would affect the discussion of union at the Council of Lyons.

Rejection of the Roman Primacy. It was precisely the charge that the Latin Church taught heresy in this matter that occasioned the rejection of the Roman primacy. The council under Pope GREGORY X and Michael Palaeologus favored the Byzantine approach. Although its acts have been lost, it condemned extreme positions and decreed that the Holy Spirit proceeded not from two principles, or two spirations, but from the Father as principle, and from the Son through spiration. Accord was reached in regard to purgatory, the immediate retribution after death, and the Sacraments; mention was also made of the unleavened bread for the Eucharist and the Roman primacy.

This reunion was not brought about solely by external political pressure. Gregory Acropolites, who taught after the council, sincerely held the Roman doctrine on the Holy Spirit and the primacy, as his homily on the Apostles Peter and Paul clearly indicates. However, the monks and lower clergy, as well as certain members of the imperial family, rejected the union despite the efforts of the emperor. Pope MARTIN IV felt constrained on Nov. 18, 1281, to excommunicate the refractory Byzantines, and a synod at Constantinople under Emperor Andronicus II declared the union at an end in 1283. Andronicus expelled John Beccus from the patriarchate. Besides Beccus, Constantinus Melitiniotes, George METOCHITES, and the Dominican theologians living in Byzantium had written in favor of the union; George Moschabarus, a professor at the ecumenical Didascaleion, Patriarch Gregorius II, Maximus PLANUDES, and the followers of Arsenius had vigorously opposed it. There had been falsifications of the texts of the Fathers in the course of the controversy. Gregorius II in his *Tomus fidei* even said he had found a patristic text justifying "an eternal illumination which the Spirit received from the Son, and reflected in having his Being from the Father."

Between the Councils of Lyons and Florence. A number of theological academies were organized in the 13th and 14th centuries, of which the more important was that at the monastery of Chora which was founded by Nicephorus Gregoras. In the patriarchal school and university at Constantinople, under the stimulus of Andronicus III and Manuel II, along with jurisprudence and philosophy, theology was taught in a fashion affected by Western methods. The works of Thomas Aquinas, translated into Greek by the CYDONES brothers in the 14th century, and especially by George (GENNADIUS) Scholarius in the 15th, had considerable influence. Meanwhile, the question of Palamism became a burning issue. Besides the official theology, a current of ascetical and spiritual ideas was fomented in the monasteries. One of these manifestations could be traced back at least to the writings of John Climacus in the 6th century, author of the *Ladder of Paradise,* and a monk on Mt. Sinai. He described the rise of the soul toward God in a series of steps after the 30 steps of Jacob's Ladder. The 29th step resembles stoic impassibility and describes a state in which through asceticism the flesh has been incorruptible in the sense that all sensation has been subordinated to the reaching after transcendent Being. John is an important link binding later Byzantine spirituality to Neoplatonism as well as to the DESERT FATHERS and the FATHERS OF THE CHURCH. This current of spirituality included the works of Dionysius the Areopagite (*see* PSEUDO-DIONYSIUS), whose mystical thought was preserved in the monasteries, and the commentary on the Books of Solomon by an anonymous 8th-century author inspired by the Neoplatonism of Maximus, the disciple of Dionysius; and it was related to the thought of SYMEON THE NEW THEOLOGIAN, who maintained that mystical contemplation was incompatible with life in the world. It lead directly to Palamism.

Palamism. Gregory PALAMAS (d. 1359), a noble Asiatic educated at the imperial court, who became a monk on Mt. Athos, taught a real distinction between the divine essence and the divine operation. This doctrine occasioned a strange form of asceticism and HESYCHASM, in which the soul liberated from the passions could arrive at the sight of divine light, such as that which surrounded Christ in the transfiguration on Mt. TABOR. Under the influence of GREGORY SINAITES, author of *Quietude and Two Methods of Prayer,* of Nicephorus Haghiorita in the 14th century, and of the commentaries of Symeon the New Theologian, who wrote tracts on *Prayers and Practical Theological Chapters*, as well as *Books of Divine Love,* Hesychasm underwent a degenerating influence. Palamas maintained that the Taborite light was distinct although inseparable from the Divine Essence. It was the Divine energy or operation whose contemplation was a form of deification due to grace and the beatific vision. Barlaam of Calabria, Gregorius Akindynos, and Nicephorus Gregoras opposed the Palamite theology, and Palamism was condemned by Patriarch JOHN XIV CALECAS in 1344. Patriarch Callistus, the homily writer, condemned Barlaam in 1351, and Palamism was restored as an authentic form of Byzantine theology; Palamas himself became archbishop of Thessalonica. The condemnations against Barlaam were added to the *Synodicon* read each year on the Sunday of Orthodoxy, and Palamas was considered a saint after 1368.

Disciples of Palamas. Among the disciples of Palamas were David DISHYPATOS, author of a *Dialogue,* Nilus CABASILAS (d. 1363), successor to Palamas in the See of Thessalonica and author of *Regula theologica, De causis dissensionum in Ecclesia, De papae imperio*, and long treatises on the procession of the Holy Spirit; PHILOTHEUS COCCINUS (d. 1376), first abbot on Mt. Athos, then metropolitan of Heraclea, and finally patriarch of Constantinople, who wrote *Contra Nicephorum Gregoram, Three Dissertations* on Palamite doctrine, an *Encomium* of

Gregory Palamas, and other liturgical works (he canonized Palamas in 1368); and Theophanes, Metropolitan of Nicaea (d. 1381), author of *A Sermon in Honor of the Theotokos, Five Books on the Living Light of Mt. Tabor, Seven Books against the Jews, Against the Latins . . . , On the Procession of the Holy Spirit,* and numerous letters.

John VI Cantacuzenus (d. 1383), the emperor, wrote against the adversaries of Palamas. Nicolas CABASILAS, the nephew of Nilus Cabasilas, was the author of two well-known tracts, *Seven Books on the Life of Christ* (a remarkable ascetical work) and an *Interpretation of Sacred Liturgy;* he also wrote a pamphlet *Against the Ravings of Gregoras,* as well as three Marian homilies. Matthew Angelus Panaretus was a determined adversary of the Latins in the 14th century, who wrote some 18 works against them. Simeon of Thessalonica (d. 1429) was a writer of irenic tendencies, and he was attached to tradition; he composed a *Dialogue* against heresy and an *Exposition of the Divine Temple and the Sacred Liturgy.* He denied the infallibility of the pope but admitted the Roman primacy. Demetrius Chrysoloras (d. 1430), a friend of Michael Palaeologus, wrote some 100 letters against the enemies of Palamas and a series of dialogues (unedited). Joseph BRYENNIOS (d. *c.* 1435), a monk of Crete and of the Studion, also proved to be a determined adversary of reunion. He wrote some 49 chapters on various theological, philosophical, and moral questions.

Anti-Palamites. Of the anti-Palamite theologians BARLAAM OF CALABRIA (d. 1348), a monk who lived in Constantinople and enjoyed imperial favor, was charged with various diplomatic and religious missions. He was an adversary of Nicephorus Gregoras and Gregory Palamas. After his condemnation in 1341, he returned to his own country as a bishop and became a Catholic. In his earlier writings, he had zealously opposed the Latins and later used the same zeal and courage against the Palamites. He was the author of an *Adversus umbilicanimos* and *Adversus Messalianos,* as well as other minor writings and letters in favor of the Roman faith. Among the other adversaries of Palareas were GREGORIUS AKINDYNOS (d. *c.* 1350), who wrote against both Barlaam and Palamas and was condemned with Barlaam; and Nicephorus Gregoras (d. 1360), who wrote *Eleven Orations against Gregory Palamas, Historia Byzantina,* Marian homilies, and on the reform of the calendar. Prochorus CYDONES (d. *c.* 1368) translated the works of Thomas Aquinas and Augustine and wrote on the Divine Essence and operation and on the divine light of Mt. Thabor. He suffered much because of his ideas against Palamas. Demetrius CYDONES (d. 1400) also translated part of the *Summa theologiae* and the *Contra Gentiles* of Aquinas and wrote *On Contempt of Death.* John Cyparissiota, called the Wise, was one of the principal adversaries of Palamas and composed *Four Books of Palamitic Transgressions,* to which he added a fifth book against Nilus Cabasilas and an elementary exposition of theology. Manuel Calecas (d. 1410) was a Byzantine Dominican and author of *On the Principle of the Catholic Faith, On the Procession of the Holy Spirit,* and *Four Books against the Greeks.* Maximus Chrysoberges (d. after 1410), also a Dominican, wrote on the procession of the Holy Spirit.

While the adversaries of Palamism utilized theological information and the distinctions found in the works of Aquinas, the Palamite group repudiated this type of theological argument. In the controversy over the Holy Spirit, they refuted the Thomistic arguments in favor of the filioque. Barlaam and Nilus Cabasilas maintained that the Latins could not demonstrate the procession of the Holy Spirit by dialectical methods and appealed to the doctrine of Duns Scotus. Nilus searched for new arguments against the Roman primacy, but he recommended the convocation of a general council to put an end to schism.

Nilus distinguished two phases of papal power: that which the pope held as the bishop of Rome, and that which he held as the legitimate successor of Peter. He enjoyed power as *primus episcoporam,* which the conciliar fathers and the emperors, not Christ or St. Peter, had conferred on him. Peter had indeed received the primacy by divine right, but he had not transmitted these extraordinary powers to his successors, since he enjoyed them as a personal privilege. The bishop of Rome is the successor of St. Peter in the same manner in which other bishops are the successors of the Apostles without inheriting apostolic powers. Nilus added that the Roman pontiffs are fallible in questions of faith, as history demonstrated, and that other sees had had recourse to Rome for a testimony of mutual charity and to preserve order and unity.

Epiclesis. During this period the controversy over the Epiclesis arose. After the words of Consecration in their liturgy, the Byzantine rite employed a prayer in which the Father was asked to send the Holy Spirit to change (*transmutare*) the holy gifts into the body and blood of the Savior. According to more recent research the words *ea transmutans* in the liturgy of St. John Chrysostom are not found in the ancient Armenian translation of this liturgy (5th century) or in the codex of Grottaferatta. These words would seem to have been added in the Athens codex during the 15th or 16th centuries. However, in the 13th century an Armenian, Vartanus Magnus, mentioned the question; and in the second half of the 14th century, a Latin writer approached the Byzantines for the employment of the words of the Epiclesis in the liturgy. Nicholas Cabasilas was the first Byzantine writer to defend the legitimacy of the Epiclesis, and after Nicholas, this subject became a regular anti-Orthodox recrimination. At first, Byzantine theologians defended its place in the canon of the liturgy; later they attributed a consecratory power to the Epiclesis as completing the words of the Savior. In his book on the *Exposition of the Sacred Liturgy* (ch. 29), Nicholas Cabasilas, in answer to the Latins, said that this prayer was legitimate and useful in the liturgy, on a par with the other prayers and the other Sacraments. He claimed that the *Supplices rogamus* of the Latin liturgy was an Epiclesis. Besides, he maintained, it was necessary, because the words of the Savior achieved the Consecration not in so much as pronounced by the priest in a narrative fashion but by the priest as such provided with sacerdotal power; and this power is the grace of the Holy Spirit. It is only when the priest pronounces the Epiclesis after the words of the Savior that one becomes aware that the priest desires to use the sacerdotal power, that is, the power of the Holy Spirit who makes him a minister of the sacred mystery. While Nicholas did not enter into the problem of the exact moment in which the Consecration takes place in the liturgy, Simeon of Thessalonica, in his *Exposition of the Divine Temple,* maintained that the sign of the cross and the inclination after the Epiclesis was an indication that the Consecration took place during the Epiclesis, and he quoted the Liturgy of St. Basil as supporting this theory (ch. 87). Thus, the way was open for the Byzantines at the Council of Florence; they maintained that Consecration came with both the Epiclesis and the words of the Savior; or even through the Epiclesis alone, as the Byzantines and Greeks thought after the 17th century.

Byzantine Mariology. Since the time of Photius at least, Marian questions had been treated in homilies. The 14th century became the golden age for Byzantine Mariology. Theophane of Nicaea (d. 1381), in his *Oration for the Most Holy Theotokos,* taught that the Mother of God from the first moment of her existence possessed all creaturely perfections, particularly in the supernatural order, with the plentitude of graces. She is thus the source of man's salvation, the mediatrix between God and man. But as a Palamite, Theophane exaggerated in speaking of the relations between the Mother of God and the Divine Persons. He maintained that the Palamites excelled in extolling the privileges of Mary, such as the Immaculate Conception, the divine maternity, the perpetual virginity, the universal mediation through intercession, her bodily assumption, and her royalty.

The Byzantines taught that Marian mediation implied the cooperation of Mary in the work of man's deification. The privilege is extended to all intelligent creatures, men and angels, to whom the gifts and privileges of the ''new creature'' were accorded. With the exception of Nicholas Cabasilas, Byzantine theology did not enter into the question of the coredemption. The historian Nicephorus Callistus, in his *Synaxaria,* expressed certain doubts on the Immaculate Conception. In his explanation of the Marian hymn in the liturgy that she is worthy of all praise, he added that the Mother of God had been purified of original sin by the Holy Spirit at the Incarnation, but no one imitated him until the 16th century. On the contrary, Byzantine theologians had excluded Mary from the taint of original sin, imitating the Franciscans, who maintained that as a consequence of her original purity she was created in the state of original justice.

The Council of Florence. In preparation for the Council of FLORENCE, the emperor had assembled several theologians in Constantinople under Patriarch Joseph, for example, BESSARION, ISIDORE OF KIEV, and Marcus EUGENICUS OF EPHESUS; to the council, with representatives of all the metropolitans, he brought the lay theologians George Scholarius (later Patriarch Gennadius II) and Gemistos PLETHON for lack of well-trained ecclesiastics. Joseph's opinion before departing for the West was naïve; he felt that the Greeks would simply demonstrate the Latin errors for the Roman theologians, and that because the Orthodox teaching faithfully represented the tradition of the Fathers of the Church, their adversaries could not but be convinced.

When the debate proved otherwise at the council, Joseph showed heroic forbearance, and with the advice of Bessarion, Isidore, and George Scholarius, little by little the Greeks conceded that the two positions on the processions of the Holy Spirit, on purgatory, and on the Consecration of the Eucharist could be harmonized. The papal primacy was accepted with the provision that nothing would be done to interfere with the Oriental rites and customs. Nothing was said of moral issues such as marriage and divorce. The only dissenter at the council was Mark Eugenicus. After his return, he began a violent campaign against the union and produced innumerable theological tracts that prevailed among the lower clergy and the monks. The union was defended by Bessarion and Isidore of Kiev and some of the Byzantine refugees in the West after the fall of CONSTANTINOPLE (1453). But with that catastrophe, Byzantine theological production as such ended.

Bibliography: H. DENZINGER, *Enchiridion symbolorum. Corpus scriptorum Christianorum orientalium* (Paris-Louvain 1903). *Dictionnaire de théologie catholique,* ed A. VACANT et al. (Paris 1903–50;) Tables générales (1951) 1:1898–1919. H. G. BECK, *Lexikon für Theologie und Kirche,* ed. J. HOFER and K. RAHNER (Feiburgh 1957–65) 2:860–863. E. A. VOETZSCH and H. G. BECK, *Die Religion in Geschichte und Gegenwart* (Tübingen 1957–65) 1:1573–78. *Theologica dogmatica christianorum orientalium,* 5 v. (Paris 1926–35). M. GORDILLO, *Theologia orientalium cum lati-*

norum comparata (*Orientalia Christiana Analecta* 158, Rome 1960); *Mariologia orientalis* (*ibid.* 141, Rome 1954). A. PALMIERI, *Theologia dogmatica orthodoxa,* 2 v. (Florence 1911–13). J. MEYENDORFF, *Orthodoxie et catholicité* (Paris 1965). K. KRUMBACHER, *Geschichte der byzantinischen Literatur* (Munich 1897). H. G. BECK, *Kirche und theologische Literatur im byzantinischen Reich* (Munich 1959). J. GILL, *The Council of Florence* (Cambridge, Eng. 1959). S. RUNCIMAN, *Byzantine Civilisation* (New York 1933; pa. 1956). Important articles or studies have been pub. over many years in such periodicals as *The Christian East, Échos d'Orient, Irénikon, Orientalia Christiana periodica, Revue des études byzantines,* and *Dumbarton Oaks Papers.*

[V. MALANCZUK]

C

CABALA

A system of occult theosophy based on a mystical interpretation of the Scriptures, common not only among the Jews of the Middle Ages but also with some influence on certain medieval Christians. This article considers its rise and spread, its principal literary works, particularly the *Bahir* and the *Zohar*, and its later development, especially in Lurianic circles.

The term comes from the Hebrew word *qabbālâ,* which etymologically means a ''receiving, accepting,'' but which is used also in the sense of ''tradition,'' both actively, as a ''handing down'' of traditional lore, and passively, as the lore itself thus handed down. In rabinical writings it is used both of the post-Mosaic Scriptures and of the traditional Talmudic law. In modern Israeli Hebrew it even has the sense of ''receipt.'' But ordinarily it is used in the technical sense of the Jewish mystic lore of the Middle Ages, and this is the meaning in which the term is employed here.

Early Period. The cabala is basically a development of Jewish GNOSTICISM. As a historical phenomenon it arose toward the end of the 12th century in Provence (southern France). From here it spread at the beginning of the 13th century to Spain, where it passed through its first classical period. It arose, therefore, in Christian surroundings; only after three generations did it take root in regions of Muslim culture. Its first centers were at Lunel, Narbonne, and Posquières—all in southern France. From there it was brought by students of the Provençal Jewish scholars to Burgos, Gerona, and Toledo, and from these cities its spread to the rest of Spain.

Provençal Cabala. In the 12th and 13th centuries Provençal Judaism reached a cultural zenith. In Provence the Tibbonide family (*see* IBN TIBBON), the greatest translators of Arabic religious-philosophical works into Hebrew, were active. In this region Jews lived at the meeting place of Muslim and Christian cultures and in the immediate vicinity of the seething currents among Christians that led to the agitation for Evangelical poverty among the WALDENSES and to the Gnostic movements of the CATHARI and the ALBIGENSES. It was not by accident that the Jews who lived in such surroundings gladly welcomed ascetical tendencies and mystic-Gnostic traditions that were at that time latent in Judaism itself. The intermediaries of these tendencies and traditions were the Ashkenazic Ḥasidim (pious men), who were very influential in Jewry from the middle of the 12th century to the beginning of the 13th. There is evidence that in the circles of certain Provençal scholars people were having peculiar mystical experiences known as ''revelations of Elia.'' Such revelations were said to have been received by Abraham ben Isaac (d. 1179), the Abh Beth Din (head of the Jewish court) in Narbonne; by his son-in-law, Abraham ben David (d. 1198) of Posquières; by Jacob ha-Nazir of Lunel, a contemporary of Abraham ben David; and by Isaac Saggi Nehor (Isaac the Blind), Abraham ben David's son, who lived until the 1230s in Posquières or Narbonne. The last-mentioned was the most important personality in Provençal cabalism, and he was already using the terminology of the *sephirot* that would henceforth be customary in cabala. Thus the union of Jewish religious philosophy with Gnostic tendencies and mystical experiences among Provençal scholars led to the concrete phenomenon of cabala.

The Bahir. The first important work of the cabala was the *Book of Bahir* (Heb. *bāhîr*, taken here to mean ''bright,'' although in Jb 37.21, which is the first Biblical quotation in the book and which thus gave the book its name, the word really means ''obscured''). The work was already known by this name around A.D. 1200, but it was spread also under the names of *HAGGADAH*, *Yerushalmi*, and *MIDRASH* of Rabbi Neḥunya Ben Hakana, who is mentioned in the first section of the work as a bearer of the tradition. The text, as it has come down to us, is a collection of various literary units from different periods, some of them showing elements from an otherwise lost Jewish Gnosticism, others containing typical teachings of a date not earlier than the 12th century. Certain motifs in the *Bahir* are also found in the writings of the Ashkenazic Ḥasidim. One of the important sources that the author or editor of the book thus received and used was a book with the significant title of "The Great Mystery" or "The Great Secret"— known at first in the Orient by the Aramaic title, *Raza Rabba*, but later given the Hebrew title, *Sepher ha-Sôd ha-Gadôl.* As early as the 9th century the *Raza Rabba* was known in the East as a work concerned with divine names, angelology, and magic. Typical of the 12th century are many of the ideas that have been taken over into the *Bahir* from Judeo-Spanish religious philosophy. Thus, for instance, the influence of the teachings of Abraham bar Ḥiya can be seen in *Bahir* 2.9–10. He was the first to interpret the tohu and bohu of Gn 1.2 as meaning matter and form, and the same idea appears in *Bahir* 2.9–10. Since Abraham bar Ḥiya died around the middle of the 12th century, the *Bahir* must have been composed in Provence around A.D. 1200.

The concept of God in the *Bahir* is theosophic-Gnostic. God is the bearer of cosmic forces, which He causes to flow into the cosmic tree. The God of the *Bahir*, therefore, is similar to the God of the Gnostic myth, even though the book adheres to the principle of pure monotheism. In ch. 14 it is emphatically stated that the angels were created on the second day of creation so that they might not claim that they assisted in the creation of the heavens and the earth. In this sense, *mî'ttî*, "Who was with me [when I created the world]?" in Is 44.24, is taken, as in *Midrash Rabba* on Gn 1.4, to be *mê'ttî*, "from me, by my own power." Moreover, the *Bahir* is acquainted with the concept of the golem—a legendary human figure made of clay (ch. 136) and the doctrine of the transmigration of souls [see G. Scholem, "Seelenwanderung und Sympathie der Seelen in der jüdischen Mystick," *Eranos* 24 (1956) 55–118], which is used for solving the problem of theodicy (ch. 135).

Spanish Cabala. An important center of the early cabala in Spain was the city of Gerona, where from 1215 to 1265 many influential cabalists were active. Most of these men had studied in the Jewish schools of Provence. Some of them are known to have been disciples of Isaac Saggi Nehor. The most important one was Azriel of Gerona, who, together with other disciples of Isaac Saggi Nehor, was interested in "Platonizing" the Gnostic material contained in the *Bahir.* A sort of cabalistic catechism of his has been preserved under the title, *Sha'ar ha-Shö'ēl* (Gate of the Inquirer), later called the *Perush 'Eser ha-Sephirot* (Explanation of the Ten Sephirot) and printed as the introduction to the edition of Meir ben Gabbi's *Derekh 'Emûnâ*—"Way of Faith" (Berlin 1850). The influence of Neoplatonism can clearly be seen in this work. Another important cabalist in Gerona was Moses NAHMANIDES (1194–1270), who was likewise famous as a physician, philosopher, Talmudist, exegete, and poet. Cabalistic influence is unmistakable in his works, particularly in his commentary on the *Book of YEṢIRAH* (Jesira), since this commentary, in contrast to his other books, was primarily intended for readers interested in cabalism. The concept of God that is presented here is influenced both by the Neoplatonic doctrine of emanations and by the Gnostic doctrine of the aeons. The *'Ên Sôph* (Infinite One), as the Furthest Removed, is not the personal God of the Bible; the latter becomes manifest only through the *sephirot*, to which the divine attributes correspond.

The Zohar. The most important cabalistic work is the ZOHAR ("illumination," a term taken from Dn 12.3). About 100 years of development lie between the *Bahir* and the *Zohar.*

Authorship. The alleged author of the *Zohar* is Simeon bar Yochai, a Tanna (*see* MISHNAH) of the 2nd century, of whom it is said, in the Mishnah tractate *Sabbath* 33b, that he hid in a cave in order to escape the persecution of the Romans. This legendary anecdote is introduced into the *Zohar* in connection with its alleged authorship. Actually, the work was composed by the cabalist Moses de Leon, who was active in Spain during the last quarter of the 13th century. The whole corpus of the *Zohar* consists of five books, of which the first three are the most important. These three books contain midrashim (*see* MIDRASH; MIDRASHIC LITERATURE) on the Pentateuch: Book 1 on Genesis, Book 2 on Exodus, and Book 3 on Leviticus, Numbers, and Deuteronomy. Book 4, called *Tiqqunē Zohar* (Emendations on the *Zohar*), is a literary unit by itself, and Book 5, called *Zohar Ḥadash* (New Zohar), is made up of sections of the first four books that were missing in the manuscripts used for the first printed edition (Mantua 1558–60). With the exception of Book 4, the work consists of numerous small literary units. It is written in an artificial Aramaic, only the part called *Midrash ha-Ne'lam* (Interpretation of What Is Hidden) being written partly in Hebrew. The parts called *Ra'ya Mehemna* (The True Shepherd) and *Tiqqunē Zohar* were not written by Moses de Leon, but were added by some other cabalist shortly after A.D. 1300.

From the very beginning opinions were divided on the question of the origin of the *Zohar.* Clear evidence for it comes from the information supplied by Isaac of Accho, who migrated to Spain when the Muslims captured Accho in 1291. According to this man, Moses de Leon had indeed sworn that Simeon bar Yochai had composed the work and that he himself had merely made a copy of it; but, according to Isaac of Accho, Moses de Leon's wife had stated after his death (1305) that her husband had written the *Zohar* "out of his own head, his own heart, his own knowledge, and his own understanding,"

This statement of Moses de Leon's wife deserves the fullest confidence, for modern research has established with certainty the pseudepigraphic character of the *Zohar*. Moreover, the writings of Moses de Leon show that, in any case, he took a decisive part in the spread of the work; his own writings contain numerous Zoharic expressions at a time when the *Zohar* itself was hardly known.

The earliest citations from the *Zohar* are found in the cabalistic literature written toward the end of the 13th century. These quotations show that the writers who cited the *Zohar* at that time were acquainted only with certain parts of it. This confirms the statement of Isaac of Accho that Moses de Leon gradually spread the work in the form of separate fascicles. Quotations of greater length and from all parts of the complete *Zohar* are first made in the 3rd decade of the 14th century. Many other arguments can be adduced to show that the *Zohar* could not have been composed at the time of Simeon bar Yochai in the 2nd century. Thus, the generations of the Talmudic rabbis are frequently confused, and many Talmudic statements are wrongly understood. The author of the *Zohar* knew Palestine only from literature, and even this he at times misunderstood. The artificial Aramaic of the *Zohar* depends on the Aramaic of the Babylonian Talmud and of the Targums, and it is also influenced by the Hebrew of the 13th century. Besides, clearly in evidence is the philosophical terminology of the Hebrew philosophical literature of the 12th and 13th centuries. From the *Zohar*'s frequent changes of the modifications of the verbal roots it is clear that, for its author, Aramaic was no longer a living language. Moreover, the many later sources that are used in the *Zohar* prove that it could not possibly have been composed as early as the 2nd century. Such sources are the Targums, both Talmuds, various midrashic works, AVICEBRON's *Keter Malkuth*, Judah al-Ḥarīzī, Judah Ben Samuel Ha-Levi, Abraham Bar Ḥiyya, MAIMONIDES, RASHI, etc. Even the *Hekhalot* literature, the *Book of Yeṣirah*, the *Book of Bahir*, and the cabalistic literature from the end of the 12th and from the 13th century are used in the *Zohar*. These reasons, as well as the testimony of Isaac of Accho, justify the conclusion that the *Zohar* was composed and circulated by Moses de Leon between 1275 and 1290.

Contents. The concepts of God and creation in the *Zohar* are based upon those of the *'Ên Sôph* (the Infinite) and the ten *sephirot.* The idea of the *sephirot* and of their number, ten, comes from the *Book of Yeṣirah.* In the *Yeṣirah* the term *sephirot* (numbers) refers to the elements of creation. In cabala this term received an entirely new meaning. Under the influence of Neoplatonic philosophy the *sephirot* became the intermediaries and bases of all existence in God, yet without losing their original character as dynamic powers. In the *Zohar*, however, the term *sephirot* is found but seldom; the author, for the sake of protecting his anonymity, substitutes numerous symbolic expressions for them. The current names for the ten *sephirot* are: (1) *Keter,* ''Crown''; (2) *Ḥohkmah,* ''Wisdom''; (3) *Bînah,* ''Understanding''; (4) *Ḥesed* or *Gedullah,* ''Grace'' or ''Greatness''; (5) *Dîn* or *Gebhurah,* ''Judgment'' or ''Strength''; (6) *Raḥamîm* or *Tiph'eret,* ''Mercy'' or ''Majesty''; (7) *Neṣaḥ,* ''Eternity''; (8) *Hôd,* ''Splendor''; (9) *Yesôd* or *Saddîq,* ''Foundation'' or ''the Just Man''; (10) *Malkhût,* ''Kingdom.''

The *'Ên Sôph* is the Hidden God (*Deus absconditus*) who reveals Himself through the *sephirot.* These are not intermediate degrees between God and creations in the sense of the purely Neoplatonic degrees of emanation, but rather the self-revealing Deity Itself in jointly acting dynamic powers. Although the *Zohar* speaks of the *sephirot* as degrees in the figurative sense, they are only gradations in God Himself. Thus, in *Zohar* 3.70a it is said, as similarly in Yeṣirah 1.7, ''Come and see. The Holy one (praised be He!) brought forth ten crowns, holy crowns, above. He crowned Himself with them and bedeckt Himself with them, and He is they, and they are He, as the flame is one with burning coal, and there is no separation at all.'' The *sephirot*, therefore, do not form a fixed ontological hierarchy, as the Neoplatonic degrees of emanation do, but they are all in equal proximity to their source and unite with one another in syzygies unto mystic glory as they move up and down in the divine Organism. Very frequently the relationship of the *sephirot* to one another is presented under the form of sexual symbolism. One and the same *sephirah* can be both feminine in relationship to its source of power, and masculine in relationship to the *sephirah* depending on it. The *sephirot* are also likened to doorways through which man, by means of the right intention in his prayers and keeping of the commandments, can enter into the apprehension of the divine mysterium. Man is capable of this (only *Keter* and *Ḥokhmah* being too subtle for a direct knowledge of God) because he, like the rest of the world, has been created in the likeness of the *sephirot* and because the *sephirot* pour themselves forth as creative powers on the lower world. Thus man, like the rest of creation, becomes an image of the divine essence manifesting itself in the *sephirot.*

In the history of the cabala the *sephirot* were often portrayed in the representation of a figure, e.g., in the form of the heavenly ''protoman.'' This idea is already found in embryo in the *Abhot de Rabbi Nathan* 31, and it is met with in the later cabala (especially after Isaac Luria) in the form of *Adam Qadmon* (earlier man). For the idea of the heavenly protoman the *Zohar* uses the symbol of *Adam Dal'ela* or *Adam Ila'a* (Upper Man). Besides being portrayed in human form, the *sephirot* are presented in the form of a tree or of a circle.

The doctrine of creation out of nothing was understood to mean that the ''nothing'' was a highest ''something,'' the first externalization of God. The ''nothing'' therefore received a positive significance. It is the first *sephirah, Keter*, and thus emanated as the first activity directly from the *'Ên Sôph.* It is a ''nothing'' only subjectively from the viewpoint of the creature. It is the bridge between the transcendence of the *'Ên Sôph* and the divine creative power that reveals itself in the *sephirot.* In *Zohar* 2.239a it is said:

> Only the earliest nothing [*Keter*] brings forth a beginning [*Ḥokhmah*] and an end [Malkhût]. What is the beginning? It is the highest point [*Ḥokhmah*] that is the beginning of all things, that is hidden, and that has existence within thought. This achieved an end, which is then called the end of the thing. But there, in the *'Ên Sôph*, there is neither will, nor lights, nor lamps. All these lamps and lights depend on It, but It Itself is not known. That which the *'Ên Sôph* knows and also does not know is nothing else than the highest will, the most hidden of all, the nothing.

Under the symbol of the lamps and the lights the *sephirot* are meant.

The *sephirot* were thought of as three columns: to the right, the column of divine grace and love; to the left, that of divine rigor and judgment; in the middle, that of mercy. The *sephirah Tip'ert,* the first *sephirah* after *Keter* in the middle row, is therefore also called *Raḥamîm* (Mercy). In this way a reconciliation is made between God's goodness and His severity. Thus also, in the representation of the *sephirot* tree, the *sephirah Tiph'eret* is symbolized by the trunk; in the representation of the *Adam Qadmon*, it is symbolized by the trunk of his body. The place for hell is at the left side (*Zohar* 1.17a), an idea already present in embryo in *Bahir* 109. Evil is thus a consequence of God's power of judgment and punishment; it is God's *sitrā ăḥērā* (other side), which comes into play only when it loosens itself from the state of intercommunion with God's love and mercy and so acts on its own. As long as man does not sin, God's ''other side'' can have no power over him. If man's sin would not disturb the harmony in the *sephirot* world, the ''other side,'' the *sephirah Gebhurah*, could not develop as an evil power, but would be suspended in its quality as an evil power because of its intercommunion with love and mercy. The last *sephirah, Malkhût*, should, as the ''tree of knowledge,'' be in union with *Tiph'eret,* the ''tree of life.'' But man's sin destroys this unity and lets the powers of the ''other side'' have the upper hand. When this happens, the function of *Malkhût* as the ''tree of knowledge'' is changed into the function of a ''tree of death''.

By its position at the end of the emanation series, *Malkhût* has a double function. On the one hand, it is the last member of the *sephirot* world; on the other it is the forms that lie below it. It is thus both the channel by which the divine creative power descends to the world below and the doorway by which man can ascend to the contemplation of the *sephirot* world above. In the *Zohar, Malkhût* is frequently called SHEKINAH, God's presence, and as the mother of the lower world, especially as the mother of Israel, it is called *Matronita* (Matron). In relation to the upper mother in the *sephirah* world—the *Sephirah Bînah,* which is the ''upper'' Shekinah, *Malkhût* is also the ''lower'' Shekinah. Because Israel stands directly under the faithful protection of the Shekinah, *Malkhût* is also called, in the *Zohar*, the ''Community of Israel,'' and thus it is also the mystical archetype of Israel.

The procedure of the creation and conservation of the world within the *sephirot* corresponds to the procedure of the divine emanation and is, in particular, the work of the last *sephirah, Malkhût*. In *Zohar* 1.240b it is said, ''The act of creation proceeds on two levels, one above and one below; that is why the Torah begins with the letter Beth [the numerical value of which is two]. The lower corresponds to the upper. The one [*Bînah*] is effective in the upper world [of the *sephirot*], the other [*Malkhût*] in the lower world [of creation].'' The principal, original part of the Zohar does not present a well-developed picture of the forms of existence below the *sephirot.* But around A.D. 1300 (already in the *Ra'ya Mehemna* and the *Tiqqunim*) there appeared the doctrine of the four regions, although it was only after 1500 that its importance grew. These four regions are: (1) the world of Aṣilut (noblest) emanation, which is the world of the *Sephirot;* (2) the *Ber'îah* (creating) world, which is the world of God's throne and *Merkabhah* (''chariot'' of Ez 1.4–28); (3) the *Yeṣirah* (forming) world, in which are the angels and the celestial spheres; (4) the *'Aśîyah* (making) world, the material world. (The names of the last three regions are taken from Is 43.7: *b^erā'tîw y^eṣartîw 'ap-'aśîtîw,* ''I have created it, I have formed it, I have made it.'')

Later Cabala. After the Jews were driven from Spain in 1492, there was a strong upsurge of interest among them in the cabala. Only mysticism could give them an answer to the burning questions, why the coming of the messianic times should be so long delayed and why Jewry seemed destined for unending oppression. The center of the cabala in the 16th century was the city of Safed in Upper Galilee, which was also the home at this time of the great scholar of Jewish law Joseph CARO. The two outstanding leaders of the cabala in this period were Moses Cordovero and Isaac LURIA. Cordovero (1522–70) was the greater systematizer, who collected the products of the old cabala and arranged them in logical order. Luria (1534–72) was the more original thinker, who gave to the cabala a new impetus. Even the first major work of Cordovero, the *Pardes Rimmônîm* (Garden of Pomegranates), which was completed in 1548, was a systematic standard work on cabalism; in his later writings, too, he knew how to use his special talent for systematizing.

Lurianic Cabala. Very few of the authentic writings of Isaac Luria are preserved. Immediately after his arrival at Safed in 1569 he became a disciple of Cordovero. After the latter's death he wrote a commentary on the beginning of the *Zohar*, but most of his new teachings he set forth merely in oral fashion. His intellectual legacy was handed down by his disciple, Ḥayyim Vital (1543–1620), in the latter's two major works, *'Eṣ Ḥayyim* (Tree of Life) and *Sepher Ha-Gilgûlîm* (Book on Transmigration of Souls).

If, according to Luria, the *'Ên Sôph* is really infinite or ''without end'' (as the term literally means), outside the *'Ên Sôph* there is no place left for any emanation or any created universe. If something is to go out of the absolutely Infinite One, He must first set aside, out of Himself, a region for the finite. This self-limiting of the *'Ên Sôph* is called *Ṣimṣûm* (contraction) in the Lurianic cabala. Of His own free will God has, so to say, drawn back from an unlimited infinity to a limited infinity, and what is left over is the realm of evil, in fact, evil itself. Creation therefore necessarily presupposes the existence of evil. Yet in drawing back, God left something of His essence in the vacated space—a small remnant, which Luria calls *Reshîmô* (His trace), like the few drops left in a bottle when it is emptied. Luria describes this in his commentary on *Zohar* 1.15a, on which he must have worked shortly before his death [see G. Scholem, *Kiryath Sepher* 19 (1943) 184–199, esp. 197]. The later cabalists did not concern themselves much with the problem of the Reshîmô.

As man was conceived of as a microcosm (an epitome of the whole world), so God was regarded as a ''macroanthropos'' (man on an infinite scale). When the *Adam Qadmon*, the protoman of the *sephirot*, drew back into the *Ṣimṣûm* region, the lights of the *sephirot* were forced out of his eyes, ears, nostrils, and mouth. At first they were a unit, without any differentiation. In order to give to each *sephirah* its proper place, vessels were needed for receiving the emanations of the *sephirot.* The vessels of the first three *sephirot* were able to hold the light that emanated from these *sephirot*, but the vessels of the lower *sephirot* broke to pieces. Thus the divine light mixed with the nondivine, the divine light was caught and held in the ''cups'' of the extradivine. The rays of the divine light that are in the cups are ''in exile.'' Not only Israel, but God Himself is in exile. Corresponding to Israel's exile here below is an exile of the Deity in the cosmos.

Therefore, because the vessels of the *sephirot* were broken, and the divine rays emanated out of the broken vessels into the extradivine and mixed with it, there is need of the so-called *Tiqqûn,* ''restoration,'' of the original order. By means of the *Tiqqûn* the rays are brought back from their scattered and banished state. Since God was thought of a macroanthropos, there was need of man here below in order to complete the process of the *Tiqqûn.*

Man's decision in favor of the good is *Tiqqûn,* but by committing sin he causes a further intensification of the exile of the divine rays and sparks of light under the ''cups.'' The first Adam did not fulfill his task of completing the *Tiqqûn;* on the contrary, he committed sin and thereby again banished under the ''cups'' the sparks of light that were already on their way back. The task that Adam did not complete is now laid upon Israel, whose dealings through the covenant with God become relevant in the sense of the *Tiqqûn.* Here there is a cabalistic modification of the idea that is frequently attested to in the OT and the Talmudic literature, that Israel's fidelity brings on the eschatological consummation, whereas its sins delay it.

Israel has failed and sinned. Consequently, Israel must also bear the lot of exile, so that in the Diaspora among the Gentiles it can do its work in the sense of the *Tiqqûn.* Israel's exile corresponds to man's exile from paradise and the exile of the divine rays of light that have fallen under the ''cups.'' Because of the task that is laid on Israel in the *Tiqqûn*, it is directly entrusted with the messianic task also. The appearance of the Messiah is nothing else than the visible sign that Israel has fulfilled the task of the *Tiqqûn* that was laid on it. Israel's existence and sufferings thus received an eschatological character. In this total picture there is also a place for the trait on the transmigration of souls. Every soul receives a new existence after death until it has done its duty and completed its *Tiqqûn.*

Post-Lurianic Cabala. The two messianic movements that were founded respectively by Shabbatai Zevi (*see* SHABBATAIÏSM) in the 17th century and by Jacob FRANK in the 18th were, in a certain sense, consequences in the political sphere of Lurianic cabalism. Both movements were sparked by the thought that at last the period of the *Tiqqûn* was coming to an end and that the messianic age was about to dawn. Both movements were concerned with messianic attempts to break out of the agelong Jewish destiny. On account of the widespread popularization of the Lurianic teachings, east European

HASIDISM succeeded in controlling the messianic activity and giving the idea of the *Tiqqûn* real significance for the life of the Hasidic community.

Bibliography: A. FRANCK, *La Kabbale ou la philosophie religieuse des Hébreux* (new ed. Paris 1889). E. MÜLLER, *Der Sohar und seine Lehre* (Vienna 1932); *History of Jewish Mysticism*, tr. M. SIMON (Oxford 1946). D. NEUMARK, *Geschichte der jüdischen Philosophie des Mittelalters*, 2 v. in 3 (Berlin 1907–28). G. G. SCHOLEM, *Das Buch Bahir* (Leipzig 1923); *Bibliotheca Kabbalistica* (Leipzig 1927); *Die Geheimnisse der Schöpfung* (Berlin 1935); *Major Trends in Jewish Mysticism* (3rd rev. ed. London 1955); *Zohar, the Book of Splendor* (New York 1949); *Zur Kabbala und ihrer Symbolik* (Zurich 1960); *Ursprung und Anfänge der Kabbala* (Berlin 1962). *The Zohar*, tr. H. SPERLING et al., 5 v. (London 1931–34). G. VAJDA, *Introduction á la pensée juive du moyen-âge* (Paris 1947). R. J. Z. WERBLOWSKY, "Philo and the Zohar," *Journal of Jewish Studies* 10 (1959) 23–44, 112–135. E. BENZ, *Die christliche Kabbala* (Zurich 1958).

[K. SCHUBERT]

CABALLERO, ANTONIO

Founder of the modern Franciscan missions in China; b. Baltanás, Spain,1602; d. Guangzhou (Canton), China, May 13, 1669. He became a friar in 1618, was ordained in 1626, and entered China from Manila in 1633. He worked in Fujian (Fu-chien) and Jiangnan (Chiang-nan) but was forced back to Manila. After receiving the decrees appointing him prefect apostolic of China (1643) and forbidding certain Chinese rites as superstitions (1645), he returned to China with two companions (1649). Settling in Jinan (Chi-nan), Shandong (Shantung), he opened his first church and established stations and churches in various towns and villages, baptizing over the years some 3,000 converts and working in perfect harmony with Jean Valat, SJ. In the general persecution of 1665, he was banished with the Jesuits and Dominicans to Guangzhou. He wrote a number of reports, essays, and books. Of his Chinese books the following, written in 1653, have been published: (1) *Wan Wu Pen Mo Yo Yen* (Compendium on the Origin and End of All Things), published before 1667 and reprinted at Guangzhou, n.d.; (2) *T'ien Ju Yin* (Catholicism and Confucianism Compared), with editor's preface, 1664, published at Chi-nan: Hsi-t'ang, n.d.; and (3) *Cheng Hsüeh Liu Shih* (True Science's Touchstone), with editor's preface, 1698, published posthumously.

Bibliography: *Sinica franciscana,* v.2, ed. A. VAN DEN WYNGAERT (Quaracchi-Florence 1933). M. COURANT, *Catalogue des livres chinois . . . de la Bibliothèque Nationale,* (Paris 1910–12) v.3. A. S. ROSSO, *Apostolic Legations to China of the 18th Century* (South Pasadena 1948) 104–122.

[A. S. ROSSO]

CABALLERO Y GÓNGORA, ANTONIO

Spanish archbishop of Bogotá and viceroy of New Granada; b. Priego, Córdoba, 1723; d. there, March, 1796. He studied at the University of Granada. After ordination he was canon of Córdoba. He was consecrated bishop of Mérida, Yucatán, Mexico, in 1775. When transferred to Bogotá in 1778, he brought several young men from Yucatán with him to be educated there. He brought also his very rich library and a number of works of art, including paintings by Rubens and Murillo. During his archiepiscopate the insurrection of the Comuneros occurred (1781). The insurgents resolved to march to the capital to demand their objectives, almost all of which were of an economic nature (the repeal or reduction of certain taxes). Bogotá was defenseless. The archbishop arranged for both sides to sign capitulations that provided that the insurgents would disband and return to their homes. The viceroy, who was in Cartagena, failed to observe the terms and ordered the capture of some of the leaders who had been offered guarantees. The archbishop has been accused for not protesting these actions. Some have seen this as a betrayal on his part. However, as a Spaniard who had sworn fidelity to the king, he was acting in accordance with his principles. When Viceroy Torrezar Diaz Pimiento died, the archbishop was placed in charge of the viceroyalty. His zeal for science was responsible for the establishment of a botanical expedition, a scientific commission, headed by the priest José Celestino Mutis, that studied the flora of New Granada. About 1784 the viceroy moved his residence to Cartagena to defend the city from attack and from British armies. At that time he requested from the Holy See an auxiliary bishop to whom he entrusted the ecclesiastical administration. An earthquake occurred in 1785, and he gave generously of his own funds for the reconstruction of the churches. About 1787 he resigned from the see and the office of viceroy. Appointed bishop of Córdoba, he left South America in 1789.

Bibliography: J. M. PÉREZ AYALA, *Antonio Caballero y Góngora* (Bogotá 1951). P. E. CÁRDENAS ACOSTA, *Los Comuneros* (Bogotá 1945). G. ARCINIEGAS, *Los Comuneros* (new ed. Santiago 1960).

[J. RESTREPO POSADA]

CABASILAS, NICOLAS

Byzantine theologian, liturgist, and spiritual writer; b. Thessalonica, *c.* 1320; d. before 1391. Nicolas's surname was Chamaetus, but he preferred to use his mother's family name, Cabasilas. His uncle, Nilus CABASILAS,

Archbishop of Thessalonica, was his teacher. Nicolas served at the court of Emperor John VI Cantecuzenus in 1350, apparently as a layman; and in 1354 he was one of the three candidates for the Patriarchate of Constantinople. He was not selected, however, and remained a layman; the view that he succeeded his uncle in the See of Thessalonica is false. He is not to be identified with Michael Cabasilas, the sacellarius, nor was he a partner of NICEPHORUS GREGORAS in controversy.

Of his more important writings, *A Commentary on the Divine Liturgy* is an explanation of the Byzantine Mass; it is unexcelled as a profound and devout tract on the Eucharistic sacrifice. In spite of an anti-Latin section (cc. 29–30) that deals with the dispute concerning the words of consecration, the work has been well received in the West and was used at the Council of Trent during the deliberations on the Mass as a witness to Catholic tradition. Nicolas dealt with the spiritual life in his *Life in Christ,* composed of seven books; it is a major work on Christian asceticism. The first five books treat of the divine activity in the spiritual life, the last two, of man's cooperation. God's activity is seen to take place within the sacramental life. Thus the first book treats of Baptism, Confirmation, and the Eucharist. Man's activity is seen as a submission to the will of God, which is accomplished by prayer and meditation on the life of Jesus.

Nicolas exhibited a keen awareness of the social revolution affecting the Byzantine Empire, and particularly Thessalonica. He wrote a tract against usury and directed a memorandum to the Empress concerning the rate of interest. He opposed the policies of the religious zealots in regard to ecclesiastical property, and wrote a consideration concerning the cultivation of learning on the part of virtuous men (unedited). He wrote also a treatise on skepticism directed against the influence of Sextus Empiricus on his contemporaries.

His preaching, particularly because of its theological quality, was greatly appreciated. Among his writings are sermons on the Ascension, on the Annunciation, and on other feasts of the Blessed Virgin Mary; sermons on the sufferings of Christ; encomiums for St. Demetrius, St. Theodora, and St. Nicholas, James the Younger, and on the Three Hierarchies. He engaged in mild polemics with the West and took some part in the Hesychast controversies. He wrote religious poetry of some value and left a considerable amount of correspondence. Nicolas Cabasilas represents the tradition of the Byzantine lay theologian at its best.

Bibliography: *Patrologia Graeca* 150:368–772. M. JUGIE, ed. and tr., *Patrologia Orientalis* 19.3 (1925) 456–510, sermons. R. GUILLAUD, *Byzantinische Zeitschrift* 30 (1929–30) 96–102. V. LAURENT, *Hellenicá* 9 (1936) 185–205. R. J. LOENERTZ, *Orientalia Christiana periodica* 21 (1955) 205–231, letters and chronology. *A Commentary on the Divine Liturgy,* tr. J. M. HUSSEY and P. A. MCNULTY (Society for Promoting Christian Knowledge 1960). *Kirche und theologische Literatur im byzantinischen Reich* 780–782. S. SALAVILLE, *Catholicisme* 2:339–340; *Dictionnaire de spiritualité ascétique et mystique* 2:1–9. J. GOUILLARD, *Dictionnaire d'histoire et de géographie ecclésiastiques* 11:14–21. F. VERNET, *Dictionnaire de théologie catholique* 2.1:1292–95. H. M. BIERDERMANN, *Lexicon für Theologie und Kirche,* new eds. 7:988. G. HORN, *Revue d'ascétique et de mystique* 3 (1922) 20–45. M. I. LOT-BORODINE, *Un Maître . . . Nicolas Cabasilas* (Paris 1958).

[H. D. HUNTER]

CABASILAS, NILUS

Nilus, 14th-century Byzantine theologian and apologete, metropolitan of Thessalonica; b. Thessalonica, *c.* 1298; d. *c.* 1363. Nilus served at the court of John VI Cantecuzenus and in 1361 was consecrated metropolitan of Thessalonica, although he never took possession of the see. He was the revered professor of his nephew Nicolas CABASILAS and of Demetrius CYDONES. At first Nilus appears to have been either neutral or inclined against the Palamite teaching. He was consulted by Demetrius Cydones for clarification of the doctrines in dispute between the Latin and Greek Churches and favored efforts at reunion. He became an admirer of the writings of THOMAS AQUINAS and encouraged Cydones in his translation of the *Summa contra gentiles.* Apparently at the request of the Emperor he took an interest in the Hesychastic controversies and eventually sided with Palamas, attempting to win Nicephorus Gregoras to the Palamite position. With the Patriarch Philotheus Coccinus, Nilus composed the Palamitic tome of the Synod of 1351 and wrote an *Antigramma* against Gregoras. Realizing that the works of Aquinas posed a threat to Byzantine theology, he set about to refute the arguments of the *Summa contra gentiles* and made free use of the works of BARLAAM OF CALABRIA in his ''On the Procession of the Holy Spirit.'' Finally, he produced several other anti-Latin writings, including a refutation of the Thomistic use of the syllogism in theology, which seems originally to have been part of the work on the Holy Spirit, and tracts on the causes of the schism, another on the primacy of the pope, and one on the synod of 879–880. A work on purgatory attributed to him actually belongs to Mark EUGENICUS. His considerations on the procession of the Holy Spirit were influential at the Council of Florence.

Bibliography: *Patrologia Graeca* 148:1328–1435, *Adversus Gregoras Nicephorus;* 149:683–730, schism and primacy; 151:707–764, tome of the synod. E. CANDAL, *Orientalia Christiana periodica* 9 (1943) 245–306, Procession of the Holy Spirit; *ibid.* 23 (1957) 237–266, Palamite theology; ed., *Nilus Cabasilas et theologia S. Thomae de processione Spiritus Sancti* (*Studi e Testi* 116; 1945). F. VERNET *Dictionnaire de théologie catholique*

2.1:1295–97. H. BECK *Divus Thomas* 13 (1935) 1–22, Thomism. *Kirche und theologische Literatur im byzantinischen Reich* 727–728. M. RACKL, *Xenia Thomistica,* ed. S. SZABÓ, 3 v. (Rome 1925) 3:363–389. L. PETIT, *Patrologia orientalis* 15 (1927) 5–168. G. SCHIRO, *Studi Bizantini* 9 (1957) 362–388.

[H. D. HUNTER]

CABASSUT, JEAN

Theologian and priest of the Oratory; b. Aix, 1604; d. there, 1685. He taught Canon Law at Avignon, and was companion and confessor to the Archbishop of Aix, Cardinal Grimaldi, when the latter became Pope Alexander VII. He was well known for his writings on ecclesiastical history and was considered an authority on Canon Law and moral theology. In moral theology he was a probabiliorist and was highly esteemed by St. Alphonsus. His main works were: *Notitia Conciliorum* (Lyons 1668); *Notitia ecclesiastica historiarium, conciliorum . . .* (Lyons 1680), considered an authoritative work on the history of councils; and *Juris canonici theoria et praxis* (Lyons 1660), which went through many editions.

Bibliography: J. RAFFALLI, *Dictionnaire de droit canonique* 2:1185. *Nomenclatur literarius theologiae catholicae* 4:508. L. BATTEREL, *Mémoires doméstiques pour servir à l'histoire de l'Oratoire,* ed. A. INGOLD and E. BONNARDET, 5 v. (Paris 1903–11) 2:396–412. *Commentarium Lovaniense in Codicem iuris canonici 1* 1:541.

[J. M. BUCKLEY]

CABEZÓN, ANTONIO DE

Eminent Renaissance organist and composer; b. Castrillo de Matajudíos, near Burgos, Spain, March 30, 1510; d. Madrid, March 26, 1566. Although blind from childhood, he was appointed court organist to Isabel, consort of Charles V, in 1526 and settled in Ávila, where he married Luisa Núñez. In 1548 he became court organist to Philip II, whom he accompanied on journeys to Italy, Germany, France, England, and the Netherlands. He moved to Madrid in 1560 and remained there until his death. His son Hernando (1541–1602) succeeded him as court organist and published the most important source of his works, the *Obras de música . . . .* It contains keyboard arrangements of hymn-tunes and motets, variations (*diferencias*) on popular tunes, and *tientos,* short pieces similar in style to the Italian canzona and ricercar, all written in Spanish keyboard tablature. His music exhibits in a purely instrumental style a mastery of counterpoint and genius of conception that foreshadows Bach and ranks Cabezón among the great composers for keyboard instruments.

Bibliography: Works. *Obras de música para tecla, arpa, y vihuela,* ed. H. DE CABEZÓN (Madrid 1578); *Hispaniae schola musica sacra,* ed. F. PEDRELL, 8 v. (Barcelona 1894–98) v. 3, 4, 7, 8, only complete modern ed. of *Obras . . .;* selected organ pieces in Edition Schott, 1621, 4826, 4948, and in *Historical Organ Recital Series,* ed. J. BONNET, 6 v. (New York 1940) v. 1, 6. Literature. S. KASTNER, *Grove's Dictionary of Music and Musicians,* ed. E. BLOM, 9 v. (5th ed. London 1954) 2:3–4; *Antonio de Cabezón* (Barcelona 1952). H. ANGLÈS, *Die Musik in Geschichte und Gegenwart,* ed. F. BLUME (Kassel-Basel 1949–) 2:595–602. G. CHASE, *The Music of Spain* (rev. ed. New York 1959). G. REESE, *Music in the Renaissance* (rev. ed. New York 1959). W. APEL, ''Early Spanish Music of Lute and Keyboard Instruments,'' *Musical Quarterly* 20 (1934) 289–301. A. C. HOWELL, ''Cabezón: An Essay in Structural Analysis,'' *Musical Quarterly* 50 (1964) 18–30. For a possible kinship of Cabezón and Cavazzoni, see the following: T. DART, ''Cavazzoni and Cabezón,'' *Music and Letters* 36 (1955) 2–6. K. JEPPESEN, ''Cavazzoni-Cabezón,'' *Journal of the American Musicological Society* 8 (1955) 81–85. T. DART, *ibid.,* 148, a reply to Jeppesen. M. S. KASTNER, *Antonio und Hernando de Cabezón: Eine Chronik dargestellt am Leben zweier Generationen von Organisten* (Tutzing 1977); ''Cabezón,'' in *The New Grove Dictionary of Music and Musicians,* ed. S. SADIE v. 3 (New York 1980), 572–573. D. M. RANDEL, ed., *The Harvard Biographical Dictionary of Music* (Cambridge, Mass. 1996) 126. L. ROBLEDO, ''Sobre la letanía de Antonio de Cabezón,'' *Nassarre, Revista Aragonesa de Musicología,* 5 (1989), 143–149. M. A. ROIG-FRANCOLÍ, *Compositional Theory and Practice in Mid-Sixteenth-Century Spanish Instrumental Music: The Arte de tañer fantasía, by Tomás de Santa María and the Music of Antonio de Cabezón* (Ph.D. diss. Indiana University 1990); ''Modal Paradigms in Mid-Sixteenth Century Spanish Instrumental Composition: Theory and Practice in Antonio de Cabezón and Thomás de Santa María,'' *Journal of Music Theory,* 38 (1994) 249–291.

[A. DOHERTY]

CABRINI, FRANCES XAVIER, ST.

Foundress; b. Sant' Angelo Lodigiano, Lombardy, Italy, July 15, 1850; d. Chicago, Ill., Dec. 22, 1917. She was the last of 13 children of Agostino and Stella (Oldini) Cabrini. She completed the primary grades under her sister Rosa, the village schoolmistress, and at 13 Francesca went to the Daughters of the Sacred Heart in Arluno where, at 18, she secured a teacher's license with highest honors. At this time the annual, private vow of virginity, which she had taken for six years, became permanent. Having been a victim of smallpox in 1872, she was refused entrance to the Daughters of the Sacred Heart because of frailty and taught at Vidardo, where, in 1874, Don Antonio Serrati persuaded her to begin charitable work at the House of Providence orphanage in Codogno. Here she took the religious habit and made her vows in September 1877.

When Bp. Domenico Gelmini closed the orphanage in 1880 he made her prioress of an Institute of MISSIONARY SISTERS OF THE SACRED HEART formed from seven of the orphanage girls. The foundation was formally approved by Rome on March 12, 1888. Between 1882 and 1887 seven houses had been opened in northern Italy, and in the latter year a free school and nursery were founded in Rome. Although she had hoped from childhood to do mission work in China, Mother Cabrini nevertheless surrendered to the insistence of Leo XIII and Bp. Giovanni Battista Scalabrini of Piacenza that she go to the U.S., and on March 23, 1889, she sailed for New York with six sisters.

In New York Mother Cabrini worked among the Italian immigrants for whom she established orphanages, schools, adult classes in Christian doctrine, and Columbus Hospital, which gained state approval in 1895. In 1909 she became a naturalized citizen and in 1910 was elected superior general for life. She founded convents, schools, orphanages, and hospitals throughout the U.S. and in South America and Europe. Always frail in body, she nevertheless crossed the sea 30 times and within 35 years established 67 houses with more than 1,500 daughters. She died of malaria in Columbus Hospital, Chicago; her body is preserved in the chapel of Mother Cabrini High School in New York City.

On Nov. 8, 1928, Cardinal George Mundelein ordered an informative hearing on the merits of her cause; it was introduced by Plus XI on March 30, 1931. She was pronounced venerable on Oct. 3, 1933, and was beatified on Nov. 13, 1938. At her canonization on July 7, 1946, Pius XII said, ''Although her constitution was very frail, her spirit was endowed with such singular strength that, knowing the will of God in her regard, she permitted nothing to impede her from accomplishing what seemed beyond the strength of a woman.''

Feast: Nov. 13 (U.S.).

Bibliography: F. X. CABRINI, *Entre una y otra ola: viajes de la Madre Francisca Javier Cabrini* (Madrid 1973); *To the Ends of the Earth: The Missionary Travels of Frances Cabrini* (New York 2000). G. DALL'ONGARO, *Francesca Cabrini: La Suora che Conquisto' L'America* (Milan 1982). M. L. SULLIVAN, *Mother Cabrini: Italian Immigrant of the Century* (New York 1992).

[A. M. MELVILLE]

Mother Frances Xavier Cabrini. (UPI/CORBIS)

CABROL, FERNAND

Benedictine abbot, liturgist; b. Marseilles, France, Dec. 11, 1855; d. St. Leonard's-on-Sea, England, June 4, 1937. He was ordained at Le Mans in 1882 and taught Church history at SOLESMES, where he was prior, 1890 to 1896. In June 1896 he became prior of the newly founded St. Michael's at Farnborough, England, and from 1903 until his death was abbot, relinquishing actual rule to an abbot coadjutor in 1924. The abbey soon became known as Cabrol, and his fellow monks, especially H. LECLERCQ, continued the liturgical tradition of Solesmes. In 1900–02 Cabrol and Leclercq began the *Monumenta ecclesiae liturgica,* a collection of texts pertaining to the liturgy from Apostolic times to Constantine. Volumes 2, 3, and 4 are lacking, but M. FÉROTIN of Farnborough published as volumes 5 and 6 the *Liber ordinum* (1904) and the *Liber sacramentorum* (1912), texts and studies of the Mozarabic liturgy based on several MSS. In 1903 Cabrol and the monks of Farnborough agreed to undertake the *Dictionnaire d'archéologie chrétienne et de liturgie* (DACL), planning to make generally available exhaustive and definitive studies on archeology to *c.* 800 and on the liturgy to modern times. In 1913 Leclercq assumed major responsibility, and after his death the work was completed (1953) by H. Marrou. The *Monumenta* and the DACL have both contributed to the continuous advance of scholarship. Cabrol did a study (1895) of the liturgy in Jerusalem as seen in the *Peregrinatio Aetheriae* (*c.* 400). His *Livre de la prière antique* (1900) has been edited and translated many times. Although his writings are not definitive, they promoted popular interest in the liturgy and its history.

Bibliography: H. THURSTON, *Month* 170 (1937) 267–270. J. WARRILOW, *Irish Ecclesiastical Record* 50 (1930) 361 369. L.

GOUGAUD, *Revue d'histoire ecclésiastique* 33 (1937) 919–922. M. HARVARD, *Revue grégorienne* 22 (1937) 201–213; 23 (1938) 1–6.

[E. P. COLBERT]

CACCIAGUERRA, BONSIGNORE

Spiritual writer; b. Siena, 1494; d. Rome, June 30, 1566. As a young man he became a very successful merchant in Palermo and devoted his life to luxury and pleasure. An apparition of Christ on the cross and a series of personal misfortunes finally brought about his conversion. He disposed of his wealth, left Palermo and all its associations, and as a penitent visited the shrine of Santiago de Compostela and various cities in Italy. In 1545 he went to Rome and was ordained there two years later. His close friend and confessor, St. Philip Neri, helped Cacciaguerra secure a position as chaplain at S. Girolamo della Carità and encouraged him in what proved to be his particular apostolate, the fostering of frequent reception of the Holy Eucharist. While neither a learned theologian nor a profound thinker, he possessed a deep spiritual insight characterized by prudence and fervor. His writings were widely read, much admired by St. Francis de Sales, and repeatedly edited and translated into other languages. They include *Trattato della comunione* (Rome 1557), *Trattato della tribolazione* (Rome 1559), *Lettere spirituali* (2 v. Rome 1564–75), and others.

Bibliography: L. PONNELLE and L. BORDET, *St. Philip Neri and the Roman Society of His Times,* tr. R. F. KERR (New York 1933). P. AUVRAY, *Dictionnaire de spiritualité ascétique et mystique* 2.1:10–14. C. TESTORE, *Enciclopedia cattolica* 3:266.

[J. C. WILLKE]

CACCIOLI, ANDREW, BL.

Franciscan, early companion of St. Francis; b. Spello, near Assisi, Italy, 1194; d. Spello, June 3, 1254. These dates (*Acta Sanctorum* 1869, June 1:356–362) are to be preferred to those (1181–1264) suggested by Wadding (*Scriptores Ordinis Minorum* 1256, n. 50 and 1264, n. 11). The name Caccioli is puzzling as it can scarcely have been a family name, for at that time it was not usual to use surnames, especially in the case of mendicants. In 1223, after the death of his parents and sister, Andrew received the habit at the hands of Francis of Assisi. He was thus one of his early companions, and we are informed that he was the first priest to join the group (*inter quos fuit primus sacerdos*). He received permission in writing from Francis to win souls for Christ by preaching, and in 1226 he was present at the founder's death. His interpretation of the rule, which he shared with many of the saint's early companions, twice earned for him imprisonment under ELIAS OF CORTONA. On the first occasion he was set free by GREGORY IX on the intercession of ANTHONY OF PADUA, and the second time by JOHN OF PARMA; thus, there seem to be no grounds for asserting that he died in prison. He was present at the general chapter held at Soria in Spain in 1233. His remains lie under the altar of the chapel dedicated to his honor in the church of Saint Andrew the Apostle in Spello, and his cult was confirmed by Pope Clement XII in 1738.

Feast: June 9.

Bibliography: *Acta Sanctorum* June 1:356–362. *Martyrologium Franciscanum,* ed. ARTURUS A. MONASTERIO, rev. I. BESCHIN and J. PALAZZOLO (Rome 1939). *Il beato Andrea Caccioli da Spello*, ed. E. MENESTÒ (Spoleto 1997). O. BONMANN, *Lexikon für Theologie und Kirche*, ed. J. HOFER and K. RAHNER (Freiburg 1957–65) 1:514. *Acta Ordinis Fratrum Minorum* 69 (1950) 129. A. BUTLER, *The Lives of the Saints*, ed. H. THURSTON and D. ATTWATER (New York 1956) 2:466–467.

[T. C. CROWLEY]

CADOUIN, ABBEY OF

Former French Cistercian abbey, in the Diocese of Périgueux. It was founded in 1115 by Gerard of Sales, a disciple of ROBERT OF ARBRISSEL. In 1119, however, it was acquired by the CISTERCIANS of Pontigny. It became famous as the shrine of Christ's Holy Shroud, deposited there by the Crusaders. Between 1123 and 1175, Cadouin founded Gondon, Bonnevaux, Ardorell, La Faise, and Saint-Marcel. The monastery was magnificently remodeled by the generosity of King Louis XI (d. 1483). Cadouin declined rapidly under commendatory abbots. It joined the Cistercian Strict Observance (*see* TRAPPISTS) in 1643 and regained some of its earlier prosperity but declined again in the 18th century. The abbey was suppressed by the French Revolution (1791). Its remarkable Romanesque church and late Gothic cloister serve the local parish.

Bibliography: R. DELAGRANGE, *Cadouin: Histoire d'une relique et d'un monastère* (Bergerac 1912). J. SIGALA, *Cadouin en Périgord* (Bordeaux 1950). J. M. CANIVEZ, *Dictionnaire d'histoire et de géographie ecclésiastiques,* ed. A. BAUDRILLART et al. (Paris 1912–) 11:118–122. L. H. COTTINEAU, *Répertoire topobibliographique des abbayes et prieurés,* 2 v. (Mâcon 1935–39) 1:548–550. R. GAZEAU, *Catholicisme,* 2:348–349.

[L. J. LEKAI]

CADWALLADOR, ROGER, BL.

Priest, martyr; alias Rogers; b. 1562–1568 at Stretton Sugwas, Herefordshire, England; d. Aug. 27, 1610, hanged, drawn, and quartered at Leominster under James I. After completing his studies at Rheims (1592) and the English College at Valladolid, he was ordained priest (1593). Returning to England in 1594, he labored zealously in Herefordshire for about 16 years. Cadwallador translated Theodoret's *Philotheus, or the lives of the Fathers of the Syrian deserts.*

He and Bl. Robert DRURY were among the priests signing the loyal address of Jan. 21, 1603, in response to which the government issued the Oath of Allegiance, which was problematic for Catholics. Thereafter he was a marked man, but the authorities did not capture him until Easter Day, 1610, when he was arrested in the home of the widow Winefride Scroope.

At first he was imprisoned at Hereford in irons; then he was forced to walk in shackles to Leominster prison, where he received further mistreatment before his death. A full account of his torture and martyrdom is given by Challoner. He was beatified by Pope John Paul II on Nov. 22, 1987 with George Haydock and Companions.

Feast of the English Martyrs: May 4 (England).

See Also: ENGLAND, SCOTLAND, AND WALES, MARTYRS OF.

Bibliography: R. CHALLONER, *Memoirs of Missionary Priests,* ed. J. H. POLLEN (rev. ed. London 1924). KNOX, *First and Second Diaries of English College, Douai* (London 1878). J. H. POLLEN, *Acts of English Martyrs* (London 1891). D. DE YEPES, *Historia Particular de la persecución de Inglaterra* (Madrid 1599).

[K. I. RABENSTEIN]

Interior of Cadouin Abbey Cloisters, Dordogne, France. (©David Gallant/CORBIS)

CAECILIAN MOVEMENT

A proposed reform of church music, originating in Germany during the second half of the nineteenth century. The adjective is used also to designate the style in which the advocates of the reform composed, namely, a style polyphonic in texture, frequently unaccompanied in imitation of Renaissance polyphony but highly influenced by romanticist harmonies.

Background. The immediate roots of Caecilianism lay in church-music activity during the early decades of the nineteenth century. Prevalent at that time were two aesthetics and styles of composing: *stile moderno*, which became in the late eighteenh century a symphonic orchestral approach; and *stile antico,* the careful adherence to academic contrapuntal rules (*see* LITURGICAL MUSIC, HISTORY OF). The symphonic emphasis was especially prevalent in Germany, while the *stile antico* was represented in Rome, notably in the SISTINE Choir tradition. Chief among the Italian composers were Zingarelli (1752–1837), Raimondi (1786–1853), and Pietro Alfieri (1801–63). Their enthusiasm for the Renaissance ideal found support in Germany and Austria also and included Aiblinger (1779–1867), Schiedermayer (1779–1840), and Assmayer (1790–1862). In their concern for writing in the pure style of PALESTRINA, composers turned scholars and launched investigations into the actual music of the sixteenth century. Aiblinger traveled extensively throughout Italy, collecting works of Italian masters. The publications of Giuseppe Baini (1775–1844) and the music collection of Fortunato Santini (1778–1862), now housed in Münster, Germany, did much to enhance the prestige of Renaissance musical art—especially that of Palestrina and the Roman school—and to encourage performances of these works. Alexander Choron (1771–1834), through his *École de chant* for the study of church music and his writings, especially *Principles de composition* (1808) and *Encyclopédie musicale* (1836–38), helped bring the Renaissance ideal to France. R. J. Von Maldeghem (1810–93), another pioneer musicologist, concentrated on Flemish vocal polyphony and gave currency to much early choral music in his 29-volume *Trésor musical* (Brussels 1865–93).

It was Germany, however, that gave the movement its greatest practical impetus. Karl Proske (1794–1861) had made three trips to Italy, collecting the works of Renaissance masters. Regensburg, where his library was kept, became the center of diffusion for Germany. Here Joseph Schrems (1815–72) developed the cathedral choir into a highly proficient group and a means of implementing the polyphonic revival. Extensive work was done also by Kaspar Ett (1799–1847) in Munich; and F. Commer (1813–87), a tireless scholar and musical leader in Berlin, published several valuable collections of old music, notably his 28-volume *Musica sacra* and two-volume *Cantica sacra.* Concern for liturgical propriety brought about a reevaluation of the role of chant in the celebration of the liturgy. In the early nineteenth century, there were thus some attempts to produce a feasible version of the chant. Among the first was Ett's *Cantica sacra* (1827; last ed. New York–Cincinnati 1906), with its simplified melodies and accompaniments. His efforts were followed by those of Schiedermayer and Alfieri.

Reform Movement. It is small wonder that the contrast between the tasteless orchestral style that had predominated in Germany and the resuscitated Renaissance repertory should have moved many musicians (among them LISZT and R. WAGNER) and clergymen to seek reform. In Regensburg Bishop SAILER's reform writings and teachings found well-prepared soil. The entire milieu collaborated to bring about reform and revival in the establishment of the Caecilianverein by Franz X. Witt (1839–80) in 1868. There had been agitation for reform before this, and Witt himself had sought unsuccessfully to win approval of such an organization at a general meeting of the Catholic Society of Germany in Innsbruck (1867). At a meeting of the same society the next year, however, his ideas received more sympathy. The general objective of his movement was to improve the quality of the church music performed in Germany (and elsewhere as well). Unaccompanied polyphonic works of the Renaissance were looked upon as the consummate ideal, but the reform also embraced the use of chant, the composition of new unaccompanied works, organ and instrumentally accompanied works, and the vernacular hymn. There was no attempt to proscribe altogether the use of instruments in church, and even Witt and his colleagues continued to provide instrumental accompaniment. *A CAPPELLA* polyphony remained, however, the goal to be reached by the composer. The organization was set up under the patronage of St. Cecilia. Named to its executive body were a cardinal-protector, a general president, and local officers. The reforms were promulgated rapidly, first in Germany, then in Europe, and very vigorously in the United States. Witt disseminated his principles in the periodicals *Fliegende Blätter für Katholische Kirchenmusik* (later renamed *Caecilienvereinsorgan*, or CVO) and *Musica sacra* (which included frequent music supplements) so thoroughly that both the cathedral and the country parishes quickly adopted Caecilian reforms. Pope Pius IX gave it official sanction on December 16, 1870, in the brief *Multum ad movendos animos.*

Effects of Reform. Adherence to Caecilian standards produced a copious amount of new music intended for liturgical use. By copying polyphonic devices, cadences, and chordal declamation, composers found a stock of formulas for turning out sacred music in quantity. The rigidity of such technique brought forth many unimaginative works that produced an effect opposite from that originally intended. Whenever Caecilian reforms were spread, they were carried with somewhat dictatorial tones that triggered some opposition, such as that on the part of J. E. Habert (1833–89) in Austria, who in 1875 voiced his objection to the absolutism of the Caecilian Society. The reactionaries against Caecilian dictates favored closer collaboration with current aesthetics and a lightening of the restrictions on concert music. M. Brosig (1815–87) attempted a reconciliation of concert music and Caecilian principles. In spite of such dissatisfaction, Caecilianism grew in influence, and societies based on Witt's constitution flourished everywhere. Under the patronage of Archbishop John Henni of Milwaukee, John Singenberger (1848–1924) formally established the American Caecilian Society, which became one of the largest in the world. Its official organ, *Caecilia,* first appeared in 1874 and was still published until its merger with the *Catholic Choirmaster* in 1964.

As mentioned earlier, one of the chief objectives of the Caecilians was the restoration of Gregorian chant. Books of chant accompaniment, such as the *Enchiridion Chorale* (1853) by J. G. Mettenleiter, perpetuated Renaissance harmonic principles with little imagination. An edition of the chant itself was prepared by F. X. Haberl (1840–1910) from the Medicaean version. His *Gradualia* (1871) and *Antiphonaria* (1878), however, were based on inaccurate scholarship and were supplanted by the Vatican edition of 1903 (*see* CHANT BOOKS, PRINTED EDITIONS OF). The disqualification of this edition from the Church's liturgical books proved to be one of the death blows to Caecilianism as a society. Its reforming function, however, was fulfilled in St. Pius X's *motu proprio* on sacred music (1903). Caecilianism had generated and maintained interest in reforming Church music, in reviving the Renaissance masters, in promoting Gregorian chant, and in unifying liturgical practice—the points conspicuously emphasized in the *motu proprio.*

In the Twentieth Century. Since the society's goal had been reached, its usefulness as an organization ceased, but the style peculiar to its adherents remained. Such composers as Ravanello (1871–1938), Goller (1873–1953), and Yon (1886–1943) were composing well into the twentieth century in a style directly linked with Caecilianism, although strong romanticist sonorities predominate. Polyphonic devices frequently became nothing more than rows of clichéd patterns in the later Caecilian composers. The works of Haller (1840–1915), early Griesbacher, and Goller are among the best written in the style. Chromaticism and leitmotiv principles introduced by Griesbacher (1864–1933) created in the harmony a tendency toward Wagnerian sentimentality. In general, the ''established'' Caecilian spirit created a unique ecclesiastical style and formed a framework that, by its own inflexibility, condemned itself. The style cramped creative effort relevant to its own age, and almost none of the later efforts show originality. The spirit of the reform, however, may still be felt in the absence of orchestras in the celebration of the liturgy, the fact of a uniform edition of the chant, and the general awareness of the need for constant surveillance of the musical activity of the Church.

Bibliography: L. W. ELLINWOOD, *The History of American Church Music* (New York 1953). K. G. FELLERER, *The History of Catholic Church Music,* tr. F. A. BRUNNER (Baltimore, Md. 1961); *Die Musik in Geschichte und Gegenwart* 2:621–628. O. URSPRUNG, *Die katholishe Kirchenmusik* (Potsdam 1931). E. TITTEL, *Oesterreichische Kirchenmusik* (Vienna 1961). R. SCHLECHT, *Geschichte der Kirchenmusik* (Regensburg 1871), esp. 184–215. A. SCHARNAGL, *Die Regensburger Tradition* (Cologne 1962). G. REESE, ''Maldeghem and His Buried Treasure,'' *Music Library Association, Notes* 6 (1948) 75–117. See also the complete files of *Musica Sacra* 1–21 (Regensburg 1868–88), New Series 1–58 (1889–1928), *Caecilienvereinsorgan* 1–68 (Regensburg 1866–1937), and *Caecilia* 1–91 (Milwaukee 1874–1964). K. A. DALY, *Catholic Church Music in Ireland, 1878–1903: The Cecilian Reform Movement* (Dublin, 1995).

[F. J. MOLECK]

CAEDMON, ST.

First English poet whose name is known; fl. *c.* 670. His story is told in one of the great chapters of BEDE's *Ecclesiastical History* (5.24). He was a cowherd on lands of the monastery of Streanes Healh, usually identified with Whitby. In rustic feasts at Streanes Healh, the company used to entertain one another by singing poems to the music of the harp. Caedmon had grown old and had never been bold enough to take his turn; when the harp, passed from hand to hand, approached him, he used to steal away from the feast. One night as he slept after deserting the festival, an angel appeared to him and told him to sing of the beginning of things. ''He began at once to sing lines in praise of God the Creator, verses he had never heard before.'' Here Bede gives a Latin paraphrase of Caedmon's Creation Hymn. On awakening, Caedmon found he could compose other verses. His miraculous talent was called to the attention of the learned monks of Streanes Healh. Thereupon, they instructed him from Scripture in the events of sacred history. He meditated and composed verses until he had versified the principal events in the Old and New Testaments. Many imitated Caedmon, but none could equal him. Bede clearly regarded him as the father of vernacular Christian poetry in England.

Of Caedmon's apparently very extensive composition in English, only the Creation Hymn (nine lines) is extant. A version in Northumbrian English is found in the oldest MS of Bede's *Historia Ecclesiastica.* The translation of Bede's *Historia* made in King Alfred's time (849–899) contains a related version in West Saxon. The Biblical poems of the Junius Manuscript, *Genesis, Exodus,* and *Daniel,* can no longer be regarded as the work of Caedmon. The older portions of the poems—*Genesis*, at least, is certainly composite—may be later developments of the kind of composition based on Scripture that Caedmon introduced. In that sense, they are of his school, Caedmonian.

Feast: Feb. 11.

Bibliography: E. V. K. DOBBIE, *The Manuscripts of Caedmon's Hymn and Bede's Death Song* (New York 1937), detailed account of the versions of the Creation Hymn. G. P. KRAPP, ed., *The Junius Manuscript* (New York 1931), ed. of the Caedmonian poems. C. W. KENNEDY, tr., *The Caedmon Poems* (New York 1916). C. L. WRENN, *The Poetry of Caedmon* (London 1947), best study of significance of the Creation Hymn in the tradition of early English poetry. S. MUNDAHL-HARRIS, *Brother Caedmon* (Whitby, U.K. 1982). S. H. V. GURTEEN, *The Epic of the Fall of Man: A Comparative Study of Caedmon, Dante, and Milton* (New York 1964). G. R. ISAAC, ''The Date and Origin of 'Caedmon's Hymn.''' *Neuphilologische Mitteilungen* no. 3 (1997) p. 217.

[C. J. DONAHUE]

CAEDWALLA, KING OF WESSEX, ST.

Born *c.* 659 of the stock of Cerdic; d. Rome, *c.* April 20, 689. Caedwalla became king of the West Saxons *c.* 685–86, resigning in 688. Under his brief but fierce rule, Wessex rose to prominence and power, Sussex was subjugated, Surrey and Kent were reduced to dependency. He also conquered the Isle of Wight and extirpated its inhabitants, the last adherents of Anglo-Saxon heathenism. Probably influenced by his friend St. WILFRID, he abdicated to go to Rome, the first of several Anglo-Saxon kings to make that pilgrimage. He was baptized by Pope SERGI-

US I on Easter eve, April 10, 689; he died a few days later and was buried in St. Peter's, Rome.

Feast: April 20.

Bibliography: BEDE, *Ecclesiastical History* 4.12, 15–16; 5.7. J. EARLE and C. PLUMMER, eds., *Two of the Saxon Chronicles Parallel,* 2 v. (Oxford 1892–99) 2:31–32. W. BRIGHT, *Chapters of Early English Church History* (3d ed. Oxford 1897). F. M. STENTON, *Anglo-Saxon England* (2d ed. Oxford 1947) 68–70.

[R. D. WARE]

CAELESTIS AGNI NUPTIAS

A hymn written by Francesco Lorenzini of Florence that was formerly sung at the office of St. Juliana FALCONIERI (d. 1341), who was canonized in 1737. In 1738, the hymn was inserted in the Breviary for the Vespers and Matins of her feast (June 19). It consists of four strophes in iambic dimeter, plus the doxology. It reflects the baroque style of the period and narrates the life of the saint.

Bibliography: A. MIRRA, *Gl'inni del breviario romano* (Naples 1947). J. CONNELLY, ed. and tr., *Hymns of the Roman Liturgy* (Westminster, Md. 1957).

[J. J. GAVIGAN]

CAELESTIS AULAE NUNTIUS

A hymn formerly prescribed for the feast of the Holy Rosary. It comprises five strophes in iambic dimeter, and was composed apparently by the Dominican, E. Sirena (d. 1796), although others attribute it to his confrere, A. Ricchini (d. 1779). This hymn was first inserted in the Dominican Breviary in 1834. It was later adopted in the Roman Breviary in 1888.

Bibliography: A. MIRRA, *Gl'inni del breviario romano* (Naples, 1947). J. CONNELLY, ed. and tr., *Hymns of the Roman Liturgy* (Westminster, Md. 1957).

[J. J. GAVIGAN]

CAELESTIS URBS JERUSALEM

A hymn of nine strophes, originally in trochaic dimeter and modified to iambic dimeter under the 1632 revision of the Roman Breviary. The author is unknown, but MSS of the earlier form, the *Urbs beata Jerusalem*, suggest that it was composed no later than the eighth century, and perhaps one or two centuries earlier. It was employed in the eighth century in Poitiers (then in eight strophes) as a processional hymn to the baptismal font on Holy Saturday. From the tenth century (with nine to twelve strophes) onwards, it was used as a hymn for the dedication of churches. The hymn considers the church built on earth with her human members as a symbol of heaven. Though somewhat abstract in tone, it weaves in many references from the Old and New Testaments to present the Church as the bride of Christ.

Bibliography: A. MIRRA, *Gl'inni del breviario romano* (Naples 1947). J. CONNELLY, ed. and tr., *Hymns of the Roman Liturgy* (Westminster, Md. 1957).

[J. J. GAVIGAN]

CAELI DEUS SANCTISSIME

A hymn of unknown authorship, traditionally sung at Vespers on Wednesday in the ferial office. Written in iambic trimeter, the hymn, in a manner appropriate for the evening hour, draws a poetic picture of the varying phases caused by the Creator in the coming and going of celestial light. The first strophe of the hymn refers to the creation of light. The second, following the account of Genesis 1:14–19, describes the forming on the fourth day of the ''glowing wheel'' of the sun, and the assignment of their ordered movement to the moon and stars. The third strophe notes the use of sun and moon to begin and close the day, and to point out the beginning of the new month. The fourth makes the typical application of such hymns by asking God to expel darkness from human hearts and minds, and to free them from sin.

Bibliography: A. MIRRA, *Gl'inni del breviario romano* (Naples 1947). J. CONNELLY, ed. and tr., *Hymns of the Roman Liturgy* (Westminster, Md. 1957).

[J. J. GAVIGAN]

CAELITUM JOSEPH DECUS

The opening line of a hymn of unknown authorship, consisting of five sapphic strophes, historically sung at the Matins on the feast of St. JOSEPH (March 19). Its earliest occurrence is in a Benedictine Breviary of 1580. In this hymn, Joseph is called ''certain hope of (eternal) life,'' a reference to his importance as intercessor; ''spouse of the Virgin,'' and the man chosen by the Creator ''to be called the father of the Word.'' His place as patriarch at the end of the Old Testament and the beginning of the New is beautifully brought out in the third strophe. His rank as father of the Holy Family is described in the fourth strophe. The fifth and last is a doxology, quite different from the usual type; for it not only contains the normal praise of the three Divine Persons, but is also presented as a prayer, asking for eternal life by the intercession of St. Joseph.

Bibliography: A. MIRRA, *Gl'inni del breviario romano* (Naples 1947). J. SZÖVÉRFFY, *Die Annalen der lateinischen Hymnendichtung* (Berlin 1964–65) 2:450.

[J. J. GAVIGAN]

CAESAREA, SCHOOL OF

An offshoot of the theological school of ALEXANDRIA, stemming from the same doctrinal tradition. The school of Caesarea in Palestine possessed the most important library in Christian antiquity.

Origen. Banished from Alexandria by Bp. Demetrius (231–33) after his ordination by Bp. Theoctistus of Caesarea, ORIGEN settled in that city and began to lecture. A short while later GREGORY THAUMATURGUS and his brother Athenodorus became his disciples. Gregory's farewell address (*In Gratitude to Origen*) traced the program and pedagogic method of his master.

Teaching was given according to the divisions of the philosophy of the time. Logic, a mixture of dialectics and criticism, followed the Socratic method. Physics, which meant above all geometry and astronomy, demonstrated the work of God in His creation. Moral doctrine gave a knowledge of oneself and one's purpose in the study of virtues. Finally, theology was taught in two fashions: by readings in the philosophers and poets of all the schools except the atheists, to form a critical sense in avoiding systematic and exclusive attachments; then by the study of Scripture, for it was thought that one should attach himself only to the word of God. This method had a strong spiritual orientation, and Origen stressed the practice of virtue. Certain of Gregory's expressions that are confirmed by two fragments of letters (from Origen on Ambrose according to the 11th-century Byzantine antiquarians, George Kedrenos and Suidas; of Ambrose to Origen according to Jerome, *Epist.* 43, to Marcella) suggest a community life of the master with his Maecenas, Ambrose, and his students in prayer, the reading of Scripture, and intellectual activities.

At Jerusalem (then called Aelia) Bishop Alexander, a friend of Origen, had founded a Christian library. That of Caesarea contained from the beginning the books possessed by Origen and his own writings, particularly an original copy of the *HEXAPLA,* which Jerome consulted and which seems never to have been reproduced in its entirety; but the text of the SEPTUAGINT that it contained was copied constantly. The group of copyists that the affluent Ambrose supported for Origen followed the latter from Alexandria to Caesarea. The letter preserved in Kedrenos and Suidas shows Origen and Ambrose making a collation of the texts and verifying copies.

Pamphilus. Was the school continued after the death of Origen under the direction of an able disciple from Caesarea, possibly Theotecnus? It is not possible to affirm this. However, the library was preserved, and 40 years later (*c.* 290) PAMPHILUS was installed at Caesarea by the new bishop, Agapius, after having been the disciple of Pierius, who was nicknamed Origen the Younger, in the Didascalion of Alexandria. Ordained by Agapius, Pamphilus remained faithful to the method of Origen, taught him by Pierius. Two students, Apphianus and Aidesius, are known to have lived with him in a community together with Eusebius (*De mart. Pales.* 4.6; 5.2). The only writing of Pamphilus is his *Apologia* for Origen.

Pamphilus paid particular care to the library, which he enriched considerably (Eusebius, *Hist. eccl.* 6.33), and in the lost biography he wrote of Pamphilus, EUSEBIUS OF CAESAREA had transcribed a catalogue of the works of Origen and other ecclesiastics, which his master had assembled; the list of Origen's writings was reproduced in part by Jerome (*Epist.* 33, *ad Paulam*). He had likewise gathered a collection of more than 100 scattered letters of Origen (*Hist. eccl.* 6.36.3).

Pamphilus also employed a group of copyists to reproduce MSS that were in poor condition or those he could not acquire otherwise, as well as to furnish copies of his own holdings for others. Among the copyists was the young slave Porphyry, whom Pamphilus had brought up as a son and who desired to suffer martyrdom with him (*De mart. Pales.* 11.1.15–19). Certain MSS of the *Hexapla* Septuagint show traces of the corrections made by Pamphilus in the volume that served as a model for the copyists; thus, in the *Sinaiticus* after II Esdras there is a note: "Antoninus has made the collations; I, Pamphilus, have corrected it."

According to an interesting hypothesis of C. Martin ["Le Testamonium Flavianum: Vers une solution définitive?," *Revue belge de philologie et d'histoire* 20 (1941) 409–65], a copyist of Pamphilus and his corrector were guilty of error in respect to the testimony of Flavius Josephus (*Ant.* 18.63–64) on Jesus. Origen presents this testimony definitely as that of an unbeliever (Origen, *Contra Cels.* 1.47). Sixty years later Eusebius cited the passage in Josephus as a profession of Christian faith (*Hist. eccl.* 1.11.7–9), basing his position on the reading of the text of Josephus that he had—and which is the extant text—containing these clauses: "if he is really to be called a man," "he was the Christ," and "he appeared to them the third day, alive again, the divine prophets having foretold these wonderful things and many others about him." Martin suggests that these clauses were marginal notes, perhaps made even by Origen himself, and that between the time of Origen and Eusebius they were inserted into the text of Josephus by a careless copyist. The rest of the text of Josephus regarding the rise of Christianity is to be regarded as genuine.

Eusebius. The spiritual son of Pamphilus, Eusebius returned to Caesarea after the persecution and became its bishop, perhaps in 315. Acacius of Caesarea is supposed to have written a life of Eusebius referring to him as his master (*didascalos*), which would seem to imply that Eusebius taught at Caesarea. In any case, Eusebius used for his erudite works the libraries at Jerusalem and Caesarea, the latter of which he developed through the use of his own group of copyists. Constantine demanded 50 copies of the Bible from him for his new capital (*Vita Const.* 4.36).

Acacius and Euzoius. According to Jerome (*De vir. ill.* 113; *Epist.* 34, *ad Marcellam*), these successors of Eusebius had all the volumes recopied from papyrus onto the more durable parchment, a fact that MSS mention. Jerome frequently speaks of the library at Caesarea, where he had labored and received a good part of his learning. Regarding a visit by HILARY OF POITIERS and EUSEBIUS OF VERCELLI during their exile in the East there is no certain evidence. ISIDORE OF SEVILLE speaks of 30,000 volumes there (*Etymol.* 6.6). The destruction of the library by either the Persians or the Arabs in the 7th century was a great loss. Many of the MSS of the Bible or of Christian antiquity now known go back through copies to a volume or codex of the library of Origen and Pamphilus at Caesarea.

Bibliography: A. EHRHARD, "Die griechische patriarchal Bibliothek von Jerusalem," *Römische Quartalschrift für christliche Altertumskunde und für Kirchengeschichte* 5 (1891) 217–63; 6 (1892) 329–31. F. CAVALLERA, *Saint Jérôme,* 2 v. (*Spicilegium sacrum Lovaniense* 1922) 2:88–89. R. CADIOU, "La Bibliothèque de Césarée," *Revue des sciences religieuses* 16 (1936) 474–83. J. DE GHELLINICK, *Patristique et moyenâge: Études d'histoire littéraire et doctrinale* v.2, 3 (Brussels 1947–48) 2:259–68.

[H. CROUZEL]

CAESAREA IN CAPPADOCIA

Mazaca, capital of the kings of Cappadocia, heirs of the last Persian satrap. The area was Hellenized in the 2d century B.C. and became Eusebeia (*c.* 160), later Caesarea (12–9 B.C.) before it was annexed to the Roman Empire. The region was backward, with a primitive tribal and village economy and a few Greek-type cities, all in the south, requiring, in addition to the bishops, many CHORBISHOPS. Until the reign of Diocletian, the governor of Cappadocia had hegemony over Armenia Minor and the Pontic districts; and the See of Caesarea enjoyed a certain primacy over the central and eastern portion of Asia Minor. The Council of CHALCEDON transferred these rights to the See of Constantinople, leaving to Caesarea the title of *protothronus* (or first see). The city commanded the roads to ARMENIA and the upper Euphrates Valley; its strategic importance is reflected in its missionary activities toward the northeast, including work among the GOTHS, in the 3d century. Legend states that the see was founded by Longinus, the centurion at the Crucifixion. Christians in Cappadocia are mentioned already in 1 Pt 1.1; some of them were in Rome and elsewhere in the 2d century. Bishop FIRMILIAN OF CAESAREA (235–256) supported St. CYPRIAN OF CARTHAGE and was a representative of the theology of ORIGEN. Under Leontius I (285) there was missionary activity in Armenia. From that point on, there exists an almost certain picture of the episcopal succession. Caesarea's prestige attained its acme in the time of St. BASIL (370–379). Another great bishop was ARETHAS (907–*c.* 932), a scholar and commentator on the Apocalypse. The city was taken by the Turks in 1064, and its importance in the Church declined. There was a massacre of Armenians there in 1895; and the Greek population was deported after the Treaty of Lausanne (1923). Besides the Greek metropolitanate, it had an Armenian see and a Uniate Armenian see from 1850 to 1938.

Bibliography: R. JANIN, *Dictionnaire d'histoire et de géographie ecclésiastiques,* ed. A. BAUDRILLART (Paris 1912–) 12:199–203. A. H. M. JONES, *The Cities of the Eastern Roman Provinces* (New York 1937) 175–182.

[J. GRIBOMONT]

CAESAREA IN PALESTINE

An ancient Phoenician settlement, probably founded by Straton, King of Sidon, originally called *Straton's Tower* (*Stratonos Pyrgos*). The city came under Roman rule with Pompey and Caesar; and Augustus gave the city to Herod the Great, who improved its excellent harbor, adorned it with magnificent buildings, erected a temple to Augustus, and renamed the city Caesarea (Josephus, *Jewish Antiquities* 15.217). In order to distinguish it from CAESAREA PHILIPPI, it is referred to as Caesarea in Palestine or Caesarea Maritima. About a decade before the beginning of the Christian era it became the administrative headquarters of the Roman procurators and of the Roman garrison in Palestine. Caesarea's contacts with Christianity begin with the Apostles: Peter preached here and baptized Cornelius the centurion (Acts 10). Paul was imprisoned here under the procurators Felix and Porcius Festus until he appealed to the tribunal of Caesar (Acts 23.22–26.32). Yet the first known bishop of Caesarea is Theophilus, a contemporary of St. IRENAEUS, who presided at a council in 195 that determined that Easter must be celebrated on a Sunday (Eusebius, *Historia Ecclesiastica* 5.23). Shortly after 230 ORIGEN left Alexandria where he had incurred the displeasure of Bishop Demetrius; he arrived at Caesarea and founded the famous school where such great men as St. GREGORY THAUMATURGUS and St. BASIL came to study. Here, too, was the celebrated library that contained among other treasures Origen's *HEXAPLA,* one of antiquity's most significant works in scripture studies. Pierius and PAMPHILUS, Origen's successors at the school, expanded the library holdings to 30,000 rolls. This collection provided rich source material for the *Historia Ecclesiastica* of EUSEBIUS OF CAESAREA (*c.* 260/64–*c.* 340) but was destroyed during the Arab invasion in 638.

Caesarea was the metropolitan see of *Palestina Prima* and the scene of many councils summoned to combat ARIANISM. Until the Council of Chalcedon (451) raised Jerusalem to the dignity of a patriarchate, Caesarea was the ranking see in Palestine. Surviving the DIOCLETIAN persecution, the Church in Caesarea flourished until the inroads of the Persians in 612, and of the Arabs in 638. A brief period of reconstruction came during the crusades, notably under BALDWIN, KING OF JERUSALEM, but by 1265 the glory of Caesarea was once more in ruins.

Excavations that began at *Horbat Quesari* (ruins of Caesari) in the 1950s uncovered ruins of a Roman temple, amphitheater, hippodrome, and aqueduct. In 1961 archaeologists unearthed a Roman inscription with the name of Pontius Pilate, procurator of Judea at the time of Jesus' crucifixion. From the 1970s continuing into the 1990s archaeologists working on land and underwater discovered the contours of the harbor built by Herod the Great that made Caesarea a major port.

Bibliography: C. T. FRITSCH, ed. *Studies in the History of Caesarea Maritima* (Missoula, Mont. 1975). L. I. LEVINE and E. NETZER, eds., *Excavations at Caesarea Maritima, 1975, 1976, 1979: Final Report* (Jerusalem 1986). R. J. BULL, ed., *The Joint Expedition to Caesarea Maritima: Excavation Reports* (Lewiston, N.Y. 1987). J. P. OLESON, *The Harbours of Caesarea Maritima: Results of the Caesarea Ancient Excavation Project, 1980–1985* (Oxford, England 1989). A. RABAN, K. G. HOLUM et al., eds., *The Combined Caesarea Expeditions: Field Report of the 1992 Season* (Haifa, Israel 1993). A. RABAN and K. G. HOLUM, eds., *Caesarea Maritima: A Retrospective after Two Millennia* (Leiden 1996).

[H. DRESSLER/EDS.]

CAESAREA PHILIPPI

A city of Roman times on an ancient site long associated with fertility cults, both Canaanite and Greek. A sizeable river, the Banyasi, one of the main sources of the Jordan, issues from a nearby cave. In the 3d century B.C. the grotto was dedicated by the predominantly Greek population to Pan and the Nymphs; hence, the nearby city was called Paneas (Panion). Herod the Great received the territory in 20 B.C. from Augustus. Under his son, Philip the Tetrarch, the city was rebuilt, including, on the old sanctuary site, a new marble temple in honor of the emperor. The city was known as Caesarea Philippi or Philip's Caesarea (to distinguish it from several other Caesareas) until AGRIPPA II altered the name to Neronias (*Ant.* 20.9.4). Coins from the following centuries call the place Caesarea Paneas. The old Greek name survives in its Arab form, Baniyas, the present-day village.

Roman aqueduct in Caesarea, Israel, 37–4 B.C., created by Herod the Great. (©Richard T. Nowitz/CORBIS)

The city is mentioned in the first two Gospels as the site where Peter professed his belief in the messiah-ship and divinity of Jesus (Mt 16.13–20; Mk 8.27). According to an ancient tradition, known through Eusebius, this was the town of the woman who had been suffering from hemorrhage and was miraculously cured by touching the edge of Jesus' cloak (Mt 9.20–22). In the early Christian era, the city was a suffragan of Tyre. After its recapture by the Crusaders (*c.* 1132), it became a Latin see. Ruins of columns, capitals, hewn stones, and a city gate are still witness to the splendor it had in Greco-Roman times.

Bibliography: D. BALY, *The Geography of the Bible* (New York 1957) 194–196. C. KOPP, *The Holy Places of the Gospels,* tr. R. WALLS (New York 1963) 231–235.

[P. HORVATH]

CAESARIA, SS.

The name of two abbesses of Saint-Jean in Arles, France.

Caesaria the Elder; b. *c.* 465; d. *c.* 525. Addressed in a letter of *c.* 510 as ''holy abbess'' by her brother CAESARIUS OF ARLES (*Clavis Patrum latinorum,* [CPL] ed. E. DEKKERS L 1010, trans. Klingshirn, 129–39), she headed a small community of ascetic women, possibly in Marseille. In 507 and 508 the monastery Caesarius was building for her community outside the walls of Arles was destroyed by warfare, but it was promptly rebuilt inside the walls and dedicated on Aug. 26, 512 (*Vita Caesarii* 1.28, 35; 2.48). The rule Caesarius composed for the new foundation provided for common ownership of goods, strict enclosure, and a communal life of prayer, Bible reading, and good works (CPL 1009, trans. McCarthy). Caesaria governed the institution for more than ten years and was laid to rest in the burial church of St. Mary, dedicated in 524 (*Vita Caesarii* 1.57–58).

Caesaria the Younger, second abbess of the convent of Arles, possibly a niece of Caesarius and Caesaria; d. before 561. Probably the virgin addressed in the letter ''O Profundum'' (CPL 1011), she was educated in the monastery from a young age and in *c.* 525 became its abbess; by 542 there were over 200 nuns in her care (*Vita Caesarii* 2.47). She was instrumental in inducing Cyprian of Toulon to compose the life of Caesarius of Arles (*Vita Caesarii* 1.1) and in transmitting Caesarius's Rule to Radegund's monastery in Poitiers (Gregory of Tours, *Hist.* 9.40; Venantius Fortunatus, *Carm.* 8.3.81–84). She had many holy books, including the sermons of Caesarius and St. Augustine, copied at Arles. She is the author of a brief treatise on the monastic life addressed to Richild and Radegund (CPL 1054, trans. J. A. McNamara and J. E. Halborg, 112–18). Several sayings and burial regulations pertaining to the monastery are also attributed to her (CPL 1009, 1054). At her death she was succeeded as abbess by Liliola.

Feast: Jan. 12.

Bibliography: G. DE PLINVAL, *Dictionnaire d'histoire et de géographie ecclésiastiques* 12 (1953): 212–16. M. C. MCCARTHY, *The Rule for Nuns of St. Caesarius of Arles* (1960); A. DE VOGÜÉ and J. COURREAU, *Césaire d'Arles: Oeuvres Monastiques,* v. 1 (1988); J. A. MCNAMARA and J. E. HALBORG, *Sainted Women of the Dark Ages* (1992); W. E. KLINGSHIRN, *Caesarius of Arles: Life, Testament, Letters* (1994).

[M. F. MCCARTHY/W. E. KLINGSHIRN]

CAESARIUS OF ARLES, ST.

Archbishop of Arles (502–542); b. Chalon-sur-Saône, 469 or 470; d. Aug. 27, 542. Caesarius was tonsured in his 18th year (486–87) by Bishop Sylvester of Chalon (*c.* 485–*c.* 527) and two years later became a monk at Lérins, where he was appointed cellarer (*Vita Caesarii* 1.4–6). In the mid-490s, suffering from poor health, he was sent by Abbot Porcarius to Arles, where he was welcomed by his relative Bishop Eonius (or Aeonius, *c.* 485–*c.* 502). At the urging of local aristocrats who wished to refine his ''monastic simplicity'' (*Vita Caesarii* 1.9), Caesarius received instruction from the noted grammarian and rhetorician Julianus Pomerius. Eonius ordained him deacon and then priest, and made him abbot of a suburban monastery in 498 or 499 (*Vita Caesarii* 1.12–13). Some months after Eonius's death, probably in December of 502 (*Sermon* 231.3), Caesarius was consecrated as archbishop of Arles.

The delay in Caesarius's consecration suggests a contested election and helps to explain his continuing difficulties with the local clergy. Charged by a local cleric with conspiring to deliver Arles to the Burgundians, Caesarius was summoned to Bordeaux by the Visigothic king Alaric II in 505 and released early in 506, probably in connection with the promulgation on Feb. 2, 506, of Alaric's *Breviarium,* based on the Theodosian Code (*Vita Caesarii* 1.21–24). After Alaric's defeat by the Franks (507), Arles was besieged by Franks and Burgundians (507–8), but relieved by the Ostrogoths of Italy, who held the city until they ceded it to the Franks in 536. In these unsettled political conditions, Caesarius employed church wealth in the ransoming of captives (*Vita Caesarii* 1.32–34), thereby triggering further attempts by the local clergy to depose him. In 513 he was called to Ravenna by King Theoderic (489–526), but he was once again released, possibly through the intervention of the deacon Ennodius (*Vita Caesarii* 1.36–38; Dom Morin, *Opera omnia* 2:3–4). He then visited Rome, where Ennodius's patron Pope Symmachus (498–514) received him warmly and on Nov. 6, 513 granted him the pallium (*Vita Caesarii* 1.38, 42). The same pope named Caesarius his vicar for Gaul and Spain on June 11, 514, and he continued in this office under succeeding pontiffs. Caesarius presided over synods at Agde in 506, at Arles in 524, at Carpentras in 527, at Orange and Vaison in 529, and at Marseille in 533 (Morin 2:36–89). Of these synods, Agde is renowned for its canonical code; Orange, for its teaching on grace—approved by Pope Boniface II (530–32) on Jan. 25, 531 (Morin 2:67–70), thus vindicating Caesarius's Augustinianism against his detractors (*Vita Caesarii* 1.60)—and Carpentras and Vaison for their strengthening of rural parishes as centers of Christianization.

Caesarius's biographers praised him for his holiness (*Vita Caesarii* 1.45, 46; 2.31–35), miracles (*Vita Caesarii* 1.39–41, 47–51; 2.2–30), and preaching (*Vita Caesarii* 1.27, 54–55, 59, 61). He visited his outlying parishes regularly, instituted a full Divine Office in his cathedral of St. Stephen, and authorized the preaching of his deacons and priests. In concert with his sister Caesaria the Elder, he founded a nunnery at Aliscamps, to the southeast of the city, and after its destruction during the siege reestablished it within the city walls. It was dedicated on Sunday, Aug. 26, 512, with Caesaria as abbess. In 524 Caesarius dedicated the basilica of St. Mary, which was to serve as the nuns' burial place (*Conc. Arles*, 524; *Vita Caesarii* 1.57) and eventually as his own (*Vita Caesarii* 2.50). His *Rule for Nuns,* a composite document revised over time, was issued in its final form in 534, during the abbacy of his niece, Caesaria the Younger. The first Latin rule written specifically for women, it was adopted by Radegund's monastery in Poitiers and exercised considerable influence in early medieval Gaul and Germany. For a male community under his nephew, the priest Teridius, Caesarius also composed a *Rule for Monks* modeled on the *Rule for Nuns.*

Preeminent among works of Caesarius are 238 sermons edited by Dom Morin (*Opera omnia* v. 1, reproduced in *Corpus Christianorum,* v. 103–104) and other sermons substantiated as his (Frede, *Kirchenschriftsteller 4,* 345–47; *Clavis Patrum latinorum*1008a). A portion of his correspondence is preserved (Morin, *Opera* 2:3–32, 65, 67–70, 125–26, 134–44). So also are the texts of the councils at which he presided; his *Rule for Nuns* and *Rule for Monks,* with annexed documents; *Opusculum de gratia; De mysterio S. Trinitatis; Breviarium adversus hereticos; Expositio de Apocalypsi;* and *Testament.* The first book of the *Vita Caesarii* was composed prior to 549 by Bps. Cyprian of Toulon, Firminus of Uzès, and Viventius, the second book by the priest Messianus and the deacon Stephanus, two clerics of Arles.

Caesarius's *Sermons,* popular in his own time, have proven a most revealing source for Church life in 6th century France. Recent investigators have plumbed his moral and doctrinal teachings, his scriptural exegesis, his attitude to magic and other aspects of popular culture, and his efforts at Christianization. Though his theology is not original, his constant pastoral concern places him among the truly relevant writers of the patristic age.

Feast: Aug. 27.

Bibliography: *Opera omnia,* ed. G. MORIN, 2 v. in 3 (Maredsous, Bel. 1937–42); rev. ed. of v. 1.1–2, *Sermones,* 2 v. (*Corpus Christianorum. Series latina* 103–104; 1953). Eng. *Sermons,* tr. M. M. MUELLER, *The Fathers of the Church: A New Translation,* 31 (1956), 47 (1964), 66 (1973); *The Rule for Nuns,* ed. and tr. M. C. MCCARTHY (Washington 1960); *Life, Testament, Letters,* tr. W. E. KLINGSHIRN (Liverpool 1994). Fr. *Sermons au peuple,* tr. M.-J. DELAGE, *Sources Chrétiennes* 175 (1971), 243 (1978), 330 (1986); *Oeuvres monastiques,* 2 v., tr. J. COURREAU and A. DE VOGÜÉ, *Sources Chrétiennes* 345 (1988), 398 (1994); *L'Apocalypse expliquée par Césaire d'Arles,* tr. J. COURREAU (Paris 1989). *Clavis Patrum latinorum,* ed. E. DEKKERS 1008–19a. Literature. *Acta Sanctorum,* Aug. 6:50–83. B. KRUSCH, *Monumenta Germaniae Historica* (SRM) III, 433–501. G. TERRANEO, "Saggio bibliografico su Cesario vescovo di Arles," *La scuola cattolica* 91 (1963), suppl. bibliogr. 272–94. G. LANGGÈRTNER, "Der Apokalypse-Kommentar des Caesarius von Arles," *Theologie und Glaube* 57 (1967), 210–25. W. M. DALY, "Caesarius of Arles: A Precursor of Medieval Christendom," *Traditio* 26 (1970), 1–28. J. COURREAU, "L'exégèse allegorique de Saint Césaire d'Arles," *Bulletin de littérature ecclésiastique* 78 (1977), 181–206, 241–268. S. FELICI, "La catechesi al populo di S. Cesario di Arles," *Salesianum* 41 (1979), 375–92. L. NAVARRA, "Motivi sociali e di costume nei sermoni al populo di Cesario di Arles," *Benedictina* 28 (1981), 229–60. C. MUNIER, "La pastorale penitentielle de saint Césaire d'Arles (503–543)," *Revue de droit canonique* 34 (1984), 235–44. D. BERTRAND et al., *Césaire d'Arles et la christianisation de la Provence* (Paris 1994). W. E. KLINGSHIRN, *Caesarius of Arles: The Making of a Christian Community in Late Antique Gaul* (Cambridge 1994). K. BERG, *Césarius von Arles: Ein Bischof des sechsten Jahrhunderts erschließt das liturgische Leben seiner Zeit* (Thaur 1994). Y. HEN, *Culture and Religion in Merovingian Gaul,* A.D.. 481–751 (Leiden 1995). G. DE NIE, "Caesarius of Arles and Gregory of Tours: Two Sixth-Century Gallic Bishops and 'Christian Magic,'" in *Cultural Identity and Cultural Integration: Ireland and Europe in the Early Middle Ages,* ed. D. EDEL (Dublin 1995), 170–96. P. MIKAT, *Caesarius von Arles und die Juden* (Opladen 1996). R. H. WEAVER, *Divine Grace and Human Agency: A Study of the Semi-Pelagian Controversy* (Macon, Ga. 1996). A. FERREIRO, "Modèles laïcs de sainteté dans les sermons de Césaire d'Arles," in *Clovis: Histoire et mémoire,* ed. M. ROUCHE (Paris 1997), 97–114. M. HEIJMANS, "La topographie de la ville d'Arles durant l'Antiquité tardive," *Journal of Roman Archaeology* 12 (1999), 142–67.

[H. G. J. BECK/W. E. KLINGSHIRN]

CAESARIUS OF HEISTERBACH

Cistercian ascetical writer and historian; b. *c.* 1180; d. Heisterbach, Germany, *c.* 1240. He was educated in Cologne at St. Andrew's and at the cathedral school (1188–98). On meeting Gevard, second abbot of HEISTERBACH (S. Petrus de Monte) in 1198, he was moved to enter religious life. After delaying his entrance to go on pilgrimage to Our Lady of Rocamadour (Quercy in the Limousin), he became a monk at Heisterbach (*c.* 1199), where with a few interruptions he served as master of novices or as prior until his death.

Caesarius himself tells us the number and character of his writings. In the *Epistula catalogica,* prefaced to his homilies [ed. A. Hilka, *Die Wundergeschichte des C. von H.* 1 (Bonn 1933) 2–7], he enumerated for Peter, abbot of Marienstatt, 36 items of which today only 17 are extant. His writings include: (1) theological works, viz, homilies, *Sermones* and *Expositiones* [ed. A. Coppenstien, *Fasciculus moralitatis C. von H.* (Cologne 1615); A. Hilka 1:63–188, 3:381–390; J. H. Schütz, *Summa Mari*

Caesarius of Heisterbach at prayer, reproduced from a facsimile of a manuscript in the Stadtbibliothek, Dusseldorf, Germany.

ana (Paderborn 1908) 687–716; other works unedited]; (2) narratives, viz, *Dialogus miraculorum* [composed *c.* 1219–23; ed. J. Strange (Coblenz 1850)], *Index nominum* [ed. J. Strange (Coblenz 1857); 2d ed. 1922], and *Libri VIII miraculorum* (composed *c.* 1225–27, ed. A. Hilka 3:15–222); and (3) historical works, viz, *Catalogus archiepiscoporum Coloniensium* (composed *c.* 1225–38; *Monumenta Germaniae Historica: Scriptores* 14:332–347), *Vita s. Elisabethae* (written *c.* 1226–37 for Conrad of Marburg, ed. A. Huyskens in Hilka 3:17–50), and *Vita s. Engelberti* [written *c.* 1226–37 for Henry of Molenark; *Acta Sanctorum* Nov. 3 (1910) 644–81; Hilka 3:234–328].

From the theological and ascetical point of view the *Dialogus miraculorum* is important as a reflection of contemporary beliefs, customs, and folklore and as a continuation of the Cistercian tradition of *exempla.* Written as an exhortation to Christian perfection for his fellow religious, it presents definitions of virtues and vices, followed by supporting *exempla.* In this, Caesarius follows in the footsteps of such predecessors as Herbert de Torres and JACQUES DE VITRY. For modern tastes, these stories, culled from far and wide, along with his original contributions are "robust." The homilies, really meditations, since only the introduction and conclusion are in the oratorical manner, reflect medieval piety and belief. The purpose of the *Libri VIII miraculorum* (only three books extant) is to stir devotion to the Eucharist, confession, and the Blessed Virgin Mary. The historical works, in general, are of high quality, even by modern standards. While the *Vita s. Elizabethae* is primarily a work of edification, the *Catalogus,* when dealing with contemporaries, and the *Vita s. Engelberti* are thoroughly reliable in fact and judgment.

Bibliography: *The Dialogue on Miracles, 1220–1235,* tr. H. VON E. SCOTT and C. C. S. BLAND, 2 v. (London 1929). J. T. WELTER, *L'Exemplum dans la littérature religieuse et didactique du moyen âge* (Paris 1927). J. M. CANIVEZ, *Dictionnaire de spiritualité ascétique et mystique,* ed. M. VILLER et al. (Paris 1932—) 2:430–432. G. BAADER, *Lexikon für Theologie und Kirche,* ed. J. HOFER and K. RAHNER (Freiburg 1957–65) 2:965.

[J. M. MARIQUE]

CAESARIUS OF NAZIANZUS, ST.

Fourth-century physician; b. probably Arianzus, 330; d. Bithynia, 369. Caesarius, the son of (St.) Gregory, Bishop of Nazianzus (modern Nenizi) and (St.) Nonna, and the brother of (St.) Gorgonia and Gregory of Nazianzus, received a religious and literary formation at home with his brother, and was sent to Alexandria to complete his scientific education and study medicine. In Constantinople, during his journey home, he met his brother Gregory returning from Athens, and they traveled together to Nazianzus (354). On a second visit to Constantinople, Caesarius became a friend and physician to the Emperor CONSTANTIUS II (337–361). During the persecution of JULIAN THE APOSTATE, he was relieved of his position at court and he returned home (363). Recalled by Valens (364), he was made quaestor in Bithynia (368) and on miraculously escaping an earthquake in Nicaea, decided to follow the ascetical life, but after receiving Baptism, he died suddenly. His body was buried in the family vault in the presence of his parents, and (St.) Gregory of Nazianzus preached the funeral oration, which is the source of Caesarius's biography. He was soon honored as a saint (Nicephorus, *Hist. Eccl.* 10.19). The four dialogues that are attributed to Caesarius are certainly spurious.

Feast: Feb. 25; March 9 in Greek Church.

Bibliography: GREGORY OF NAZIANZUS, *Patrologia Graeca,* ed. J. P. MIGNE (Paris 1857–66) 35:755–788. *Acta Sanctorum* Feb. 3:501–507. A. OBERTI, *Per la storia della vaccinacione* (Pisa 1970). O. BARDENHEWER, *Geschichte der altkirchlichen Literatur* (Freiburg 1913–32) 3:174.

[F. CHIOVARO]

CAESAROPAPISM

This term expresses the conception of government in which supreme royal and sacerdotal powers are combined in one lay ruler. Although the term itself is a more recent coinage, the concept is very old and applied particularly to the kind of government exercised by the emperor at CONSTANTINOPLE. The reason for the emergence of this kind of government lay in the conception of the Roman emperor that he as supreme head of the Christianized Roman Empire had to take care of all the issues affecting it. Christianity had imparted to the Roman Empire a great strength of coherence and given it a force that bonded the various heterogeneous elements together. This consideration, together with the special functions that priests in a Christian community had, explains the efforts made by the emperors from the 4th century onward to control the Christian body politic by ordaining the faith for their subjects and by appointing and dismissing higher ecclesiastical officers, notably patriarchs and bishops.

Caesaropapism was, basically, nothing less than the transplantation of the function of the ancient Roman emperor as *pontifex maximus* to the Christian Roman emperor. The fundamental idea underlying caesaropapism was that the emperor as the divinely appointed vicegerent of divinity on earth, that is, of the *pantokrator,* was the *autokrator* who alone considered himself called upon to provide unity, peace, and order within the Christian empire. Just as only one being in the celestial order combined all power, so in the terrestrial order there was to be only one monarch.

Although signs of caesaropapism became ever clearer throughout the 5th century, it entered the sphere of practical politics in the HENOTICON of the Emperor Zeno (482), in which he unilaterally and in disregard of the Council of CHALCEDON ordained the faith for his subjects; at the same time began imperial appointments and dismissals of prelates. Caesaropapism reached its highest point in the government of JUSTINIAN I (527–565) who, imbued with the idea of monarchy, acted to all intents and purposes as king and priest. In his time it could truly be said that there was "one state, one law, one Church."

Caesaropapism remained, with modifications, the governmental principle of Byzantium throughout the millennium of its existence. The breach between the PAPACY and Constantinople was to a very large extent due to the caesaropapal form of the imperial government. It was obvious that the papacy, as custodian of the Christian idea of government, could not acquiesce in this state of affairs. Although in the West European Middle Ages caesaropapism was hardly a doctrinal possibility, the Byzantine brand of caesaropapism was continued in Czarist Russia: evidence of caesaropapism could also be detected among Protestant princes, when *cuius regio, eius religio* came to be applied. Similar observations can be made about JOSEPHINISM, FEBRONIANISM, and partly also about GALLICANISM, where the principle was adopted that the ruler had a *jus maiestatis circa sacra.*

Bibliography: K. JÄNTERE, *Die römische Weltreichsidee,* tr. I. HOLLO (Turku 1936). V. MARTIN, *Les Origines du gallicanisme,* 2 v. (Paris 1939). H. BERKHOF, *Kirche und Kaiser* (Zurich 1947). J. GAUDEMET, *L'Église dans l'empire Romain* (Paris 1958). O. TREITINGER, *Die oströmische Kaiser-und Reichsidee* (2d ed. Darmstadt 1956). H. RAAB, *Lexikon für Theologie und Kirche,* ed. J. HOFER and K. RAHNER, 10 v. (2d, new ed. Freiburg 1957–65) 6:289–295. H. RAHNER, *Kirche und Staat im frühen Christentum* (Munich 1961).

[W. ULLMANN]

CAFASSO, JOSEPH, ST.

Moral theologian, preacher, and spiritual director; b. Castelnuovo d'Asti, Piedmont, Italy, Jan. 15, 1811; d. Turin, Italy, June 23, 1860. Born of peasant stock, he entered the diocesan seminary at Chieri and became a priest in 1833. After ordination he studied at the Institute of St. Francis in Turin, which had been founded somewhat earlier by Luigi Guala for the education of young priests. Guala's teaching was strongly influenced by the doctrine of St. ALPHONSUS LIGUORI and was aimed at combating the continuing JANSENIST tendencies in northern Italy. Cafasso learned from his master well, and the same orientation characterized all his later work. After completing his studies, he became lecturer in moral theology at the institute, and upon Guala's death in 1848, he was made rector. Thereafter he labored for the intellectual and moral improvement of the young clergy from various dioceses and left his influence upon innumerable spiritual protégés. One of these was St. John BOSCO, whose spiritual progress Cafasso guided and whose vocation for the education of boys Cafasso aided and encouraged. His work also extended to tireless efforts among the laity, preaching, conducting retreats, hearing confessions, and giving spiritual direction. He was particularly noted for his concern and care for those imprisoned or condemned to death. His writings include *Meditazioni e instruzioni al clero* (Turin 1892). He was beatified in 1925 and canonized in 1947.

Feast: June 23.

Bibliography: L. MUGNAI, *S. Giuseppe Cafasso, prete torinese* (Siena 1972). N. DI ROBILANT, *Vita del ven. G. Cafasso,* 2 v. (Turin 1912). B. C. SALOTTI, *La perla del clero italiano* (3d ed. Turin 1947). A. BUTLER, *The Lives of the Saints,* ed. H. THURSTON and D. ATTWATER (New York 1956) 2:628–631.

[J. C. WILLKE]

CAGLIERO, JUAN

Missionary, bishop, and cardinal; b. Castelnuovo Don Bosco, Jan. 11, 1838; d. Rome, Feb. 28, 1926. From the age of 13, he was a favorite pupil of St. John BOSCO in Turin. He became seriously ill in 1854, and on that occasion Bosco had two visions that foretold the future of the young boy. He recovered, joined the Salesians that same year, and was ordained in 1862. He was a music teacher and composer. In 1875 he led the first ten Salesians who came to America and founded five houses in Argentina and Uruguay in less than two years. In 1877 he returned to Italy and there became spiritual director for both branches of the Salesian Society. In 1883 he was chosen vicar apostolic of Patagonia and made titular bishop of Magida. In 1885 he went to Patagonia, where he served as a missionary until 1904, when he was named titular archbishop of Sebaste and diocesan visitor in Italy. In 1908 the Pope sent him to San José de Costa Rica as apostolic delegate to Central America. He found five bishops there and raised the number to 20. In 1915 he was made a cardinal, and in 1921 he accepted the Diocese of Frascati.

Bibliography: R. A. ENTRAIGAS, *El Apostol de la Patagonia* (Rosario, Argentina 1956).

[R. A. ENTRAIGAS]

CAHENSLY, PETER PAUL

Lay leader; b. Limburg an der Lahn, Rhine province of Nassau, Germany, Oct. 28, 1838; d. Dec. 25, 1923. He was the youngest of four children of a mercantile wholesale grocery family. As preparation to succeed his father in the firm, he traveled throughout Germany, Switzerland, France, England, Belgium, and Holland, studying freight and shipping techniques. In the ports of those countries and on ships, he saw the conditions of the immigrants from Europe to the American countries during the 19th century. As an active member of the St. Vincent de Paul Society, Cahensly became a pioneer and strong advocate of welfare and care for these immigrants. He collected data regarding conditions on ships, as well as in ports of exit and entry; spoke at the annual *Katholikentage* of German Catholics; initiated social action programs to alleviate conditions; established missions and chapels at ports; and addressed petitions to governments and bishops to control the chicanery of immigration agents, lodging proprietors, local police, ticket agents, ship lines, and money changers. In 1871 the ST. RAPHAEL'S SOCIETY for the protection of German Catholic emigrants was established and was later broadened to include Italian, Belgian, French, and other European representation. Cahensly was first secretary and then president (1899) of this pioneer 19th–century lay Catholic organization, which was without clerical membership or direction and was supported by annual dues. Despite opposition from governments and vested interests, as well as from the liberal and antireligious press, the movement gained momentum. Cahensly also served in local, regional, and national political positions, including membership in the Prussian house of delegates (1885–1915) and the Reichstag (1898–1903), where he caucused with the Center party.

A daughter branch of the St. Raphael's Society was established (1883) in the United States; eight years later a turmoil broke out among U.S. Catholics concerning the rights of Catholic immigrants to their native language and customs that was termed ''Cahenslyism'' by opposition partisans. The controversy stemmed from a petition to Leo XIII in 1890, signed by 51 members of European boards of directors of the St. Raphael's Society from seven nations, requesting separate churches for each nationality, appointment of priests of the same nationality as the faithful, parochial schools where the mother tongue would be taught, and representation in the American hierarchy of the immigrant races. The petition, unacceptable to the Americanizing members of the Catholic Church in the United States, was discredited in an extended journalistic and pamphlet exchange. This Lucerne memorandum was never acted upon by the Holy See, although it continued as a partisan factor in the tension leading to the AMERICANISM controversy in the U.S. Church at the end of the 19th century. Cahensly was eventually personally vindicated and recognized internationally, with honors from church and state, under the title of ''Father of the Emigrant.''

[C. J. BARRY]

CAIANI, MARIA MARGHERITA DEL SACRO CUORE, BL.

Baptized Marianna Rosa Caiani, foundress of the Franciscan Minims of the Sacred Heart, Patroness of Tuscany; b. Poggio a Caiano, Diocese of Pistoia, Tuscany, Italy, Nov. 2, 1863; d. Montughi (near Florence), Italy, Aug. 8, 1921. Marianna Rosa worked in her family's store until after the deaths of her father Giacomo (1884) and mother Luisa (1890). In 1893, she tested her vocation at the Benedictine convent in Pistoia, but returned to Poggio a Caiano. There she founded a school (1894) and, with two companions who had left other convents, a community (1896). They formed (1905) the Minims of the Sacred Heart, who aided the wounded, sick, elderly, poor, and children of Tuscany. Maria Margherita was elected mother superior in 1915 for a term to last the rest of her life. She revised the congregation's constitution in 1920 to meet new needs and attach it to the FRANCISCANS. She was declared venerable by Pope John Paul II in 1986 and beatified by him on April 23, 1989.

Bibliography: ISTITUTO MINIME SUORE S. CUORE, *Madre Maria Margherita Caiani* (Poggio a Caiano 1969). *Acta Apostolicae Sedis* (1989): 563.

[K. I. RABENSTEIN]

CAJETAN (TOMMASO DE VIO)

Thomistic theologian; b. Gaeta, Italy, Feb. 20, 1469; d. Rome, Aug. 10, 1534.

Life. Although he was to be popularly known by the place of his birth (Gaietanus), he was baptized James de Vio. At the age of 16 he entered the Dominican Order at Gaeta, receiving the religious name of Thomas. After studying philosophy at Naples and theology at Bologna, he was sent to Padua, where he lectured on metaphysics in the priory and on the *Sentences* at the university (1493). At the general chapter of the Order at Ferrara in 1494, he held a disputation with Giovanni Pico della Mirandola. On this occasion, though only 25 years of age, he was promoted to master in sacred theology at the request of Hercules, Duke of Ferrara. At the invitation of Duke Sforza he taught at Pavia (1497–99), lecturing on the *Summa* of St. Thomas. From 1501 to 1508 he taught at the Sapienza University in Rome and served as procurator general of his Order. During this time he had occasion to preach for Alexander VI and Julius II. On the death of the master general, John Clérée, in 1507, he was appointed vicar-general by Julius II. As master general of the Dominicans (1508–18), he stressed reform, study, and the common life; settled certain difficulties involving devotees of SAVONAROLA; sent the first Dominican missionaries to the New World; and defended the mendicant orders at the Fifth Lateran Council (1512–17).

From 1508 until his death he was deeply involved in ecclesiastical affairs. When consulted about the pseudo-Council of Pisa (1511), he urged Julius II to convoke a legitimate council. Forbidding his own friars to support the schismatic council, he sent trusted friars to the scene to win over the secular clergy to the Pope's cause, and he wrote an important treatise on papal authority against French conciliarists, *De comparatione auctoritatis papae et concilii* (1511). At the Fifth Lateran Council, convoked in 1512, he defended papal supremacy, urged ecclesiastical reform, and participated in discussions on AVERROISM and the IMMACULATE CONCEPTION. He was made a cardinal priest of St. Sixtus on July 6, 1517, and was sent to

Cajetan.

Germany the following year as legate of Leo X to arouse interest in a crusade against the Turks. While there he represented the Holy See in discussions with Luther at Augsburg (1518)—which proved unsuccessful—and in the election of the new German emperor in 1519. In the latter assignment he succeeded, getting the Pope's candidate, Charles V, elected. On March 14 of that year Thomas was appointed bishop of Gaeta, his native city. He took part in the consistory of 1520, which condemned Luther, and in the conclave of 1522 which elected Adrian VI. In the following year he was made legate to Hungary, Poland, and Bohemia in the hope that he could obtain support for a crusade. After the death of Adrian (Sept. 14, 1523), he was recalled by Clement VII. Disappointed with Clement's lack of interest in reform and the crusade, Thomas devoted full time to study, writing, and examining the question of Henry VIII's divorce. During the last illness of Clement (1534) many considered Cajetan a likely successor, but he himself was gravely ill and died on the morning of Aug. 10, 1534, at the age of 66. He was buried according to his wishes at the entrance of the Dominican church of Santa Maria sopra Minerva so that the faithful might walk over his grave, but since 1666 his remains have been preserved in the sacristy.

Cajetan was a man of deep prayer and devotion to study; simple and exacting with regard to himself; broad-minded and generous with regard to others; and profoundly conscious of the needs of the Church, particularly in Biblical studies and ecclesiastical reform.

Writings. Over 150 works, long and short, came from the pen of Cajetan. Most of them can be dated accurately from his habit of indicating year, day, and place of completion together with his own age and occupation. Apart from acts and official documents, his writings may be grouped under three headings: philosophical, theological, and exegetical.

Philosophical. The commentaries and treatises were the fruit of his teaching at Padua, Pavia, Milan, and Rome between 1493 and 1507. They include commentaries on Porphyry's *Isagoge* (1497); Aristotle's *Praedicamenta* (1498), *Peri Hermeneias* (1496), *Posterior Analytics* (1496), *De Anima* (ed. 1509 from earlier notes), and *Metaphysics* (*c.* 1493); St. Thomas's *De ente et essentia* (1494–95); and five treatises, the most important of which is *De nominum analogia* (1498).

Theological. Between 1507 and 1524, while Cajetan was master general and papal legate, he wrote theological works. The most important are the commentary on the *Sentences* (1493–94, unpublished), the influential commentary on the *Summa theologiae* of St. Thomas (I, completed in 1507; I–II, completed in 1511; II–II, completed in 1517; III completed in 1520), and treatises on papal authority, confession, the Eucharist, Matrimony, Holy Orders, religious life, social questions, and Protestant errors.

Exegetical. This work filled the years from 1524 until his death. Using the Greek text of Erasmus and the latest methods of exegesis, he examined carefully the claims of Protestant reformers. In 1527 he dedicated to Clement VII a new translation of the Psalms from the Hebrew. His commentaries on the Gospels (1527–28), Epistles (1528–29), Pentateuch (1530–31), historical books (1531–32), Job (1533), and Ecclesiastes (1534) provoked much opposition, even from his own brethren. Cajetan insisted that the Latin Vulgate was insufficient for serious Biblical studies. He expressed strong doubts about the literal meaning of Song of Songs and the Revelation; the authenticity of Mk 16.9–20 and Jn 8.1–11; and the authorship of Hebrews, James, 2 Peter, 2 and 3 John, and Jude. Some of his views were censured by Ambrogio Catarini, Bartholomew Medina, Melchior Cano, and ''many theologians'' of the Sorbonne (1533, 1544).

Doctrine. Cajetan stands out as one of the most gifted and influential thinkers of the Thomistic tradition. Coming at the beginning of ''second Thomism,'' he not only helped to replace the *Sentences* of Peter Lombard by the *Summa* of St. Thomas in the schools of theology, but he also managed to influence the whole of Thomism with his views. The importance of his commentary on the *Summa* was so great that Pius V ordered its publication with the complete works of St. Thomas in 1570 (minus certain heterodox opinions expressed in the Third Part). Leo XIII ordered it to be published with the critical edition of St. Thomas's *Summa* (1888–1906). Little is known about Cajetan's intellectual formation. In his own day he was a pioneer in Thomistic studies. Undoubtedly his polemics with Averroists, Scotists, and Protestants, his sympathy for Renaissance humanism, and his involvement in practical affairs did much to shape his philosophical and theological outlook. The Thomism that he lived was not simply a restatement of St. Thomas but a Thomistic approach to problems of his day. Many of the opinions he held are not to be found in St. Thomas but are the insights that were a result of his own genius (*see* SCHOLASTICISM).

In philosophy Cajetan stressed the Aristotelianism of St. Thomas, often to the detriment of St. Thomas's originality. Constantly attacking Scotist views of being and abstraction, he presented a concept of being, which though analogical, might be considered too realistic and formalistic, depending as it does on the pseudo-Thomistic *Summa totius logicae.* In his doctrine of analogy he overemphasized the importance of proper proportionality. Thus for Cajetan the proper subject of metaphysics is attained by ''formal abstraction'' from all matter. In the metaphysical constitution of person Cajetan posited a special modality (*subsistentia*) to terminate the essence prior to existence. His doctrine of psychological abstraction, while basically Thomistic, was explained in terms of extrinsic illumination of the phantasms by the active intellect, which operates also within the thinking intellect.

The most conspicuous of Cajetan's unique positions rests on his personal view that the immortality of the human soul cannot be demonstrated by reason. In a discourse given in Rome in 1503, five years after departing from the Averroist university of Padua, Cajetan demonstrated the immortality of the human soul from the spirituality of intellectual and volitional functions, much as St. Thomas had done. Commenting on the *Summa* (1a, 75.2) in 1507, he confirmed the validity of St. Thomas's reasoning. But when preparing his *De anima* for publication in 1509, he admitted with Averroës that Aristotle had denied the immortality of the thinking intellect because of its dependence on phantasms; consequently only the active intellect is immortal and separated. However, Cajetan maintained that the immortality of the soul could be demonstrated from Aristotelian principles. Commenting on Matthew, ch. 22, in 1527, he flatly asserted that the immortality of the soul is not rationally demonstrable. He repeated this opinion in his commentary on Romans, ch.

9, in 1528, listing the doctrine of immortality with knowledge of the Trinity and Incarnation. Commenting on Ecclesiastes, ch. 3, in 1534, he asserted that no philosopher has ever demonstrated the immortality of the soul, and that this truth can be known only through Christian revelation. The reason for Cajetan's change of view is still far from certain. What is certain is that Thomists after Cajetan have unanimously rejected it as incompatible with the teaching of St. Thomas and Christian tradition.

In his commentary on the *Summa* Cajetan is a faithful expositor of St. Thomas. In the first two parts his principal adversaries are Duns Scotus, Henry of Ghent, Gregory of Rimini, Peter Aureole, and Durandus of St. Pourçain. In sacramental theology it is principally the errors of Luther and Zwingli that are criticized. The passages that Pius V had suppressed from the Third Part in no way touched the basic principles of Thomism. Rather, they were minor points that might have added coals to rampant heresies. Here his concern was to find areas of agreement between Catholic theology and Protestantism.

In Biblical exegesis Cajetan represents the best humanist tradition, faithful to the Church and to the spirit of St. Jerome; much of his criticism was far in advance of his time. While his farsightedness in Biblical theology and ecclesiastical reform were little appreciated by his contemporaries, his scholastic theology found immediate response in Italy and Spain. Even today he is found a stimulating and illuminating guide to the basic doctrines of St. Thomas; on many moral and social issues he is a very modern teacher.

Bibliography: *Scriptores Ordinis Praedicatorum* 2.1:14–21. A. COSSIO, *Il Cardinale Gaetano e la riforma* (Cividale, Italy 1902). D. A. MORTIER, *Histoire des maîtres généraux de l'Ordre des Frères Prêcheurs,* 8 v. (Paris 1903–20) v.5. *Revue thomiste* (Paris 1838–) 39.2 or *New Style* 17.2 (1934–35). *Angelicum* 11 (1934) 405–608. *Rivista di filosofia neoscolastica* 27.2 (1935). J. HEGYI, *Die Bedeutung des Seins bei den klassischen Kommentatoren des heiligen Thomas von Aquin* (Pullach-Munich 1959). *Repertorium biblicum medii aevi* 5:8207–32.9. J. F. GRONER, *Kardinal Cajetan* (Fribourg 1951).

[J. A. WEISHEIPL]

CAJETAN, CONSTANTINO

BENEDICTINE writer of the Cassinese Congregation, also known as Cajetani, Gaetani, Gaetano; b. Syracuse, Italy, 1560; d. Rome, Sept. 17, 1650. He was of noble birth and made his profession in the Monastery of San Nicolò d'Arena at Catania, Oct. 29, 1586. Constantino devoted his life to scholarship and secured a prominent position in the Vatican Archives. He was named abbot of San Baronzio in the Diocese of Pistoia and prior of Santa Maria Latina in Sicily. The Gregorian College of St. Benedict, the first Benedictine college in Rome, was founded by him. It was a hostel for Benedictine travelers in Rome and a study center for young clergy. GREGORY XV issued the bull of establishment on May 18, 1621, naming Cardinal Peretti Montalto as protector and Dom Constantino as president. When other sources failed him, Constantino requested assistance for this college from RICHELIEU and MAZARIN. Its magnificent library was eventually dispersed, and enriched, among others, the libraries of Propaganda, the Sapienza, and the Biblioteca Alessandrina. Constantino is credited with writing 26 books and about 60 manuscripts. He glorified in the achievements of the Benedictines and listed among their number St. Columbanus, St. Isidore, and even Jean Gerson, to whom the *Imitation of Christ* was often attributed. He also questioned the authorship of St. Ignatius's *Spriritual Exercises.* The writings of St. Peter Damian, edited by Constantino, were published in Rome in 1606, and in Paris in 1642. It is his finest contribution to scholarship and was reproduced by Migne. Constantino was buried in the Church of San Benedetto in Piscinula in Trastevere, Rome.

Bibliography: P. SCHMITZ, *Dictionnaire d'histoire et de géographie ecclésiastiques* 11:146–147. M. VILLER, *Dictionnaire de spiritualité ascétique et mystique* 2.1:15–16. M. ARMELLINI, *Bibliotheca Benedictino-Casinensis,* 2 pts. (Assisi 1731–32) 1:123–136. J. M. BESSE, ''Une Question d'histoire littéraire au XVIe siècle: L'Exercice de Garcia de Cisneros et les Exercices de S. Ignace,'' *Revue des questions historiques* 61 (1897) 22–51.

[B. EGAN]

CAJETAN (GAETANO DA THIENE), ST.

The leading founder of the THEATINES; b. Vicenza, near Venice, Italy, October 1480; d. Naples, Aug. 7, 1547. He was the son of Count Gaspare da Thiene. He studied law in Padua and in 1505 became prothonotary apostolic to Julius II; he was ordained on Sept. 30, 1516, and joined the Oratory of Divine Love in Rome, a group devoted to piety and charity. In 1518 he returned to Vicenza and continued his charitable activities, going to Venice in 1520 and founding a hospital for incurables (1522). He returned to Rome in 1523 and on Sept. 14, 1524, with three companions, Gianpietro Caraffa (later Pope PAUL IV), Bonifacio da Colle, and Paolo Consiglieri, founded the *Clerici regulares,* priests who took religious vows but lived in the world working for a truly Christian reform of society. By example and by exhortation they were to inspire the rest of the clergy. They were called Theatines after Chieti (Teate), the episcopal see of their first superior, Caraffa. Cajetan and the Theatines escaped from Rome in the sack of 1527 and found refuge in Venice, continuing their work. In 1533 Cajetan was made superior of a new foundation in Naples, where he labored till his death, except for a term (1540–43) as superior in Venice. In Naples he opposed the heretics Juan VALDES and Bernardino OCHINO and founded a *monte di pietá* (*see* MONTES PIETATIS) that has become the Bank of Naples. He is buried in S. Paolo Maggiore, where he resided in Naples. He was beatified on Oct. 8, 1629, by Pope Urban VIII, and canonized on April 12, 1671, by Pope Clement X.

Feast: Aug. 7.

Bibliography: B. BRAUN, *Ontische Metaphysik: zur Aktuälitat der Thomasdeutung Cajetans* (Würzburg 1995). P. CHIMINELLI, *San Gaetano Thiene, cuore della Reforma Cattolica* (Vicenza 1948). A. VENY BALLESTER, *San Cayetano de Thiene* (Barcelona 1950). B. A. R. FELMBERG, *Die Ablasstheologie Kardinal Cajetans* (Leiden 1998). G. HENNIG, *Cajetan und Luther* (Stuttgart 1966). M. NIEDEN, *Organum deitatis: die Christologie des Thomas de Vio Cajetan* (Leiden 1997). F. RIVA, *Analogia e univocità in Tommaso de Vio 'Gaetano'* (Milan 1995). P. H. HALLETT, *Catholic Reformer* (Westminster, Md. 1959). G. JACQUEMET, *Catholicisme* 4:1694–95.

[A. SAGRERA]

CALABRIA, GIOVANNI (JOHN), ST.

Founder of the Poor Servants of Divine Providence and Poor Women Servants of the Divine Providence (PSDP); b. Verona, Italy, Oct. 8, 1873; d. San Zeno, Italy, Dec. 4, 1954. When the financial situation of his nearly destitute family worsened at the death of his father, twelve-year-old Giovanni found employment as an errand boy. Despite his poverty and other difficulties, he pursued his priestly vocation. His seminary studies were interrupted by a mandatory two years of military service during which he founded an association to care for the convalescent poor. He was ordained in 1901.

Calabria's work with the poor began while he was still in the seminary when he volunteered to care for typhus victims. As a parish priest he found a young, abused runaway shivering in the cold. Taking the boy into his home, he gave him his bed. Thus began a career that earned him the title, ''the apostle of the street children.'' St. Giovanni built the *Casa Buoni Fanciulli* in 1907, the first in a series of shelters for abandoned adolescents throughout Italy. He also constructed others for the elderly and ill. His spirituality, based on Matthew 25, taught him to see the face of Christ in the suffering. It led him to found congregations for both men and women, as well as to acts of charity, like the care of chimney sweeps during the winter and the integration of the disabled into the working world. His longing for Christian unity caused him to correspond frequently with the author C. S. Lewis and others of like mind. Upon his death his remains were buried in his congregation's motherhouse at Verona.

Divine Providence brothers and sisters live in communities in Italy, Brazil, Argentina, Uruguay, Paraguay, Chile, Angola, Colombia, the Philippines, Russia, Romania, and India. In addition to those in consecrated religious life, Don Calabria's spirituality imbues several lay associations, including the Associazione ex Allievi (for former students of Don Calabria centers), Spazio Fiorito (young people and families involved in educational, spiritual, and social activities), Unione Medico Missionaria Italiana (doctors who work in lesser developed countries to train indigenous doctors and nurses and to raise funds to assist children), and Association Francesco Perez (coordinates activities of volunteers). Don Calabria's work continues through these organizations in hospitals, prisons, technical schools, drug treatment centers, parishes, and social service centers. Calabria was beatified (April 17, 1987) and canonized (April 18, 1999) by Pope John Paul II.

Feast: Dec. 4.

Bibliography: *L'Osservatore Romano,* English edition 15 (1988): 2, 5. E. BESOZZI, *Carisma e processi organizzativi* (Milan 1984). G. GECCHELE, *Biografia spirituale del servo di Dio don Giovanni Calabria* (Rome 1966). M. GADILI, *San Giovanni Calabria: biografia ufficiale* (Cinisello Balsamo [Milan], Italy 1999). C. S. LEWIS, *The Latin Letters of C.S. Lewis*, tr. M. MOYNIHAN (South Bend, Ind. 1998). G. G. PESENTI, *Storia di una integrazione affettiva* (Dolo 1974). I. SCHUSTER, *L'epistolario card. Schuster-don Calabria (1945–1954)* (Milan 1989). Vatican Information Service (April 18, 1999).

[K. I. RABENSTEIN]

CALAFATO, EUSTOCHIA, ST.

Poor Clare abbess; b. Annunziata near Messina, Sicily, Italy, March 25, 1434; d. Montevergine, Italy, Jan. 20, 1468 (or 1491?). The daughter of Bernard Calafato, a wealthy merchant, and his wife Macalda Romano Colonna, known for her holiness, St. Eustochia was named Smeralda (Smaragda, ''emerald'') because of her beauty. She overcame the opposition of her brothers and joined the Poor Clares at S. Maria di Basicò *c.* 1446, taking the name Eustochia. After eleven years she received permission from CALLISTUS III to found a community of more rigorous discipline under the Franciscan Observants. Established first at S. Maria Accomodata (1458), the community was transferred to Montevergine (1463) to house increased membership. Eustochia's outstanding qualities were love of penance and poverty, her endurance of many great interior and exterior sufferings, the miraculous efficacy of her prayers, and her devotion to the Passion, on which she wrote a tract (no longer extant). She was elected abbess when she was 30 and died when she was 35.

The cultus of Eustochia, patroness of Messina, especially during earthquakes, was confirmed as a *beata* in 1782. At her canonization in Messina (June 11, 1988), Pope John Paul II said: ''From her cell in the monastery of Montevergine she extended her prayer and the value of her penances to the whole world . . . [to] alleviate every suffering, ask pardon for the sins of all.'' Her body is venerated in the church of Montevergine. In iconography, she is commonly portrayed kneeling before the Blessed Sacrament.

Feast: Jan. 20 (formerly Feb. 16).

Bibliography: *Acta Apostolicae Sedis* (1988): 715. *Bullarium Franciscanum,* new series, 2:221. M. CATALANO, ed., *La leggenda della beata Eustochia da Messina,* 2d. ed. (Messina 1950). G. MILIGI, *Francescanesimo al femminile: Chiara d'Assisi ed Eustochia da Messina* (Messina 1994).

[M. F. LAUGHLIN]

CALANCHA, ANTONIO DE LA

Historian and chronicler of colonial Peru; b. Chuquisaca (now Sucre), Bolivia, 1584; d. Lima, Peru, March 1, 1654. At the age of 14 he joined the Augustinians and later, at the University of San Marcos in Lima, he earned the doctorate in theology. Among the offices that he occupied in his order were those of rector of the Colegio San Ildefonso in Lima and prior of the monasteries in Arequipa, Trujillo, and Lima. His fame as a preacher was considerable. Some half dozen works have been attributed to Calancha; best-known among them is the *Corónica moralizada del orden de San Agustín en el Perú, con sucesos egemplares en esta monarquia* (pt. 1 Barcelona 1638; pt. 2 Lima 1653). Part 1, the longer and more valuable volume, contains not only a history of the Augustinians in the period 1551 to 1597, but also an interesting compilation of information about the Peruvian natives, their religion, and their customs. Part 1 was later printed in an abridged form in Latin (tr. Joachim Brulius, OSA, Antwerp 1651) and in French (translator unknown, Toulouse 1653); selections from part 1 were published also in Italian (Genoa 1645) and in Spanish (Madrid 1659, Mexico City 1763, and La Paz 1939). Calancha's work, though not scientific by modern standards, is a valuable source for both history and ethnology. Another of his writings, *Historia de la Universidad de San Marcos hasta el 15 de julio de 1647,* was edited by L. A. Eguiguren (Lima 1921).

Bibliography: G. DE SANTIAGO VELA, *Ensayo de una biblioteca ibero–americana de la orden de San Agustín,* 7 v. in 8 (Madrid 1913–31) 1:487–494. A. PALMIERI, *Dictionnaire d'histoire et de géographie ecclésiastiques* 3:764–765.

[A. J. ENNIS]

CALAS, JEAN

French Calvinist executed for the murder of his son in the controversial ''Calas case''; b. Claparède, near Castres (Dept. of Tarn), March 19, 1698; d. Toulouse, March 10, 1762. From his marriage in 1731 to Rose Anne Cicibel, an Englishwoman of French Protestant origin, he had four sons and three daughters. Calas became a successful cloth merchant of Toulouse and reared his family in the Calvinist faith. Sometime in 1760 Louis, his second son, was converted to Catholicism and left his home because of his father's hostility. When Louis complained to the magistrate, Saint-Florentin, that he had been abandoned without support because of his religious views, Calas was obliged to pay the debt of 603 livres incurred by his son (Feb. 7, 1761). Then his eldest son, Marc Antoine, 28, announced his intention of renouncing Calvinism and on Oct. 13, 1761, was found hanged in his father's storehouse. The funeral became an occasion for explosive anti-Calvinist feeling. Penitents marched in procession, and the Dominicans placed a skeleton on the catafalque with a martyr's palm in one hand and the document of abjuration in the other. Jean Calas was arrested for murder, and the members of his family were accused as possible accomplices. In the interrogations (October 1761 to February 1762) Calas was often silent or involved himself in contradictions, alleging that Marc Antoine had committed suicide or was strangled by an assassin. He was found guilty by the votes of seven of the eight town councilors and 11 of the 13 members of the parlement of Toulouse, and on March 9 was sentenced to be tortured on the rack and burned. Calas suffered with courage and to the last protested his innocence. The family property was confiscated. The young girls were sent to a convent of the Visitation; the widow and her sons sought refuge in Geneva.

Opposition to the sentence grew, and when Voltaire heard of the case, he used his influence to have the judgment reversed and the family reinstated. He wrote his friend Charles Argental to acquaint the Duke Étienne de Choiseul, then powerful at court, of this *horrible aventure.* He also began a pamphlet campaign, wrote the *Sur la tolérance à cause de la mort de Jean Calas* (1763), and called Calas's widow to Paris to plead for justice. By June he had the support of Jean d'Alembert, Aimar Nicholaï, Chancellor Jérome Maurepas, and Mme. de Pompadour. On June 4, 1764, the Royal Council annulled the sentence passed by the tribunal at Toulouse and on

March 9, 1765, declared Jean Calas innocent. The property was restored and gifts of money were sent to Rose Anne Calas by Louis XV. David Baudigné, one of the magistrates at the trial at Toulouse, became demented and committed suicide. The Calas case became celebrated not only through the writings of Voltaire, but through dramas, such as T. Lemierre's *Calas ou fanatisme* (1790) and F. L. Laya's *Jean Calas* (1790), and through more than 100 books. During the FRENCH REVOLUTION the Convention voted to erect a commemorative pillar to Calas in Toulouse (25 Brumaire II). Historians have weighed the evidence, examined the qualifications of the judges, and arrived at opposing verdicts. Some are convinced that Marc Antoine committed suicide; some that if Calas were innocent, his contradictions and behavior at the trial led inevitably to condemnation; others that a solution escapes the judgment of history.

Bibliography: D. D. BIEN, *The Calas Affair* (Princeton 1960). M. CHASSAIGNE, *L'Affaire Calas* (4th ed. Paris 1929). L. LABAT, *Le Drame de la rue des Filatiers* (1761); *Jean Calas* (Toulouse 1910). A. LEFRANC, *La Grande Encyclopédie,* 31 v. (Paris 1886–1902) 8:853–854. J. DEDIEU, *Dictionnaire d'histoire et de géographie ecclésiastiques* 11:340–344.

[E. D. MCSHANE]

CALATRAVA, ORDER OF

Spanish military and religious order, founded January 1158 by King Sancho III of Castile, who ceded the fortress of Calatrava, in the modern Province of Ciudad Real, to Raymond, abbot of the Cistercian monastery of FITERO, ''to defend against the pagans, the enemies of the cross of Christ.'' Many of the warriors who came to assist in the defense assumed the monastic habit. In this way the military Order of Calatrava came into being. Six years later the order, then under the direction of its first master, obtained a *vivendi forma* from the CISTERCIAN general chapter and a bull of confirmation from Pope Alexander III. In 1187 the order was affiliated to the Cistercian Abbey of MORIMOND, whose abbots were authorized to visit Calatrava annually, to appoint the prior and to confirm the election of the master as well.

In return for its services in the Reconquest the order acquired extensive properties, especially in the central and southern regions of Castile, and also in Aragon (*see* SPAIN, 2). The loss of Calatrava to the Muslims in 1195 was a grievous blow to the order, which established its headquarters at Salvatierra until it also was lost in 1211. The recovery of Calatrava and the Muslim defeat at Las Navas de Tolosa in 1212 repaired the order's fortunes and opened the road to Andalusia. Sometime before 1221 the order moved its seat to the castle known thereafter as Calatrava *la nueva*. From this vantage point the knights were able to render significant services in the conquest of Andalusia.

Governed by a master elected for life, the order was composed of knights and conventual brethren, observing the three monastic vows and an ascetic regimen based upon that of Cíteaux. The fundamental sources concerning the order's organization and customs are the statutes enacted by the abbots of Morimond or their delegates. The military Order of AVIZ, the KNIGHTS OF ALCANTARA, and the KNIGHTS OF MONTESA were all affiliated with Calatrava.

As the Reconquest slowed to a halt, the order became involved in domestic politics, participating in the civil wars of the 14th and 15th centuries. To prevent the order's resources from being used against the monarchy, King Ferdinand V and Queen Isabella, with papal consent, assumed the administration of the order in 1489. Pope ADRIAN VI in 1523 annexed the mastership to the crown in perpetuity. The order was gradually transformed into an honorary society of noblemen, although the conventual brethren continued to adhere to the monastic observance until the dissolution of all the Spanish military orders in the 19th century.

Bibliography: F. DE RADES Y ANDRADA, *Chronica de las tres ordenes y cavallerias, de Sanctiago, Calatrava y Alcantara*, 3 v. (Toledo 1572). J. F. O'CALLAGHAN, ''The Affiliation of the Order of Calatrava with the Order of Citeaux,'' *Analecta Sacri Ordinis Praedicatorum* 15 (1959) 161–193; 16 (1960) 3–59, 255–292.

[J. F. O'CALLAGHAN]

CALCIDIUS

Neoplatonic philosopher; fl. *c.* A.D. 400. His translation of, and commentary on, the *Timaeus* of Plato is addressed to Osius, who was probably the Milanese patrician appointed, at first, chief administrator of the imperial demesne and, later, head of the imperial treasury. Although Calcidius's work shows a superficial knowledge of a few Hebrew and Christian documents, it is hardly probable that he was a Christian.

The translation and commentary covers only one-third of the *Timaeus* (31C–53C). The translation is, at times, very literal; at others, little more than a paraphrase. The commentary is expository in style and often lacks depth. It is eclectic and contains many references from Adrastus, Numenius, Galen, Porphyry, Jamblichus, Albinus, and ORIGEN (Commentary on Genesis). Aristotle is quoted with respect, especially his definition of the soul. Calcidius did not hesitate to criticize the philosophers whom he cited; usually the criticisms are in Plato's

Ruins of Calatrava Castle, Castilla-La Mancha, Spain. (©Francesc Muntada/CORBIS)

favor. The commentary is, for this reason, a valuable source of information about current philosophical interpretations. Some authors have thought Posidonius to have been the basic source of Calcidius; this, however, is unlikely.

Calcidius's influence was considerable. He is responsible for the term *silva* in place of *hyle,* or Aristotelian ὕλη. He was also an important source of Platonic doctrine throughout the Middle Ages. The authors of the hexaemeral literature of the school of Chartres make use of Calcidius in an attempt to explain philosophically and scientifically the origins of the universe. There is no evidence to show whether the commentary was an original composition of Calcidius or whether he merely translated from the Greek an already existing commentary. There are 144 known extant manuscripts of the work, most of which are complete; eight different editions have been published, the earliest in 1520.

Bibliography: J. H. WASZINK, ed., *Timaeus, a Calcidio translatus commentarioque instructus* (Corpus platonicum medii aevi. Plato latinus 4; London 1962). J. C. M. VAN WINDEN, *Calcidius on Matter, His Doctrine and Sources* (Leiden 1950). T. GREGORY, *Platonismo medievale: Studi e ricerche* (Rome 1958). R. KLIBANSKY, *The Continuity of the Platonic Tradition During the Middle Ages* (London 1939). J. H. WASZINK, ''Die sogenannte Fünfteilung der Träume bei Chalcidius und ihre Quellen,'' *Mnemosyne* 9 (1941) 65–85. W. H. STAHL, ''Dominant Traditions in Early Medieval Latin Science,'' *Isis* 50 (1959) 95–124. J. R. O'DONNELL, *Mediaeval Studies* 7 (1945) 1–20. A. C. VEGA, *Ciudad de Dios* 152 (1936) 145–164; 155 (1943) 219–241.

[J. R. O'DONNELL]

CALDARA, ANTONIO

Baroque vocal composer; b. Venice, *c.* 1670; d. Vienna, Dec. 28, 1736. His early life is obscure, but it has been established that he was a pupil of LEGRENZI. By 1690 he was composing operas to METASTASIO librettos

Antonio Caldara. (©Archivo Iconografico, S.A./CORBIS)

and oratorios to texts by Apostolo Zeno. After travels in Spain and Italy he settled in Vienna in 1716 as assistant chapelmaster to J. J. FUX under Charles VI, retaining this post until his death. Although during his early period he was esteemed as a cellist and string composer, he is known primarily for his vocal writing, particularly his mangificent 16-part *Crucifixus*, and has been favorably compared to Lotti in this sphere. In his works, which include many Masses, cantatas, and other sacred compositions, he unites the lyrical Italian cantilena with impeccable contrapuntal technique and utilizes indigenous elements that produce a valid and individual expression of the Austrian baroque. His canonic writing as exemplified in the *Missa in contrapunto canonico . . .* was said to be especially admired by Fux.

Bibliography: A. CALDARA, *Kirchenwerke*, ed. E. MANDYCZEWSKI, *Denkmäler der Tonkunst in Österreich 26*; *Kammermusik für Gesang Kantaten, Madrigale, Kanons*, ed. E. MANDYCZEWSKI (*ibid.* 75). B. PAUMGARTNER, *Die Musik in Geschichte und Gegenwart*, ed. F. BLUME 10 v. (Kassel-Basel 1949–) 2:645–650. R. EITNER, *Quellen-Lexikon der Musiker und Musikgelehrten* 10 v. (Templin 1898–). C. GRAY, ''Antonio Caldera,'' *Musical Times* 70 (1929) 212–214. K. G. FELLERER, *The History of Catholic Church Music*, tr. F. A. BRUNNER (Baltimore 1961). M. F. BUKOFZER, *Music in the Baroque Era* (New York 1947). P. M. YOUNG, *The Choral Tradition* (New York 1962). R. FREEMAN, *The New Grove Dictionary of Music and Musicians*, ed. S. SADIE (New York 1980) 3:613–616. G. KROMBACH, ''Modelle der offertoriumskompositonen bei Antonio Caldara, Johann Georg Albrechtsberger, und Joseph Preindl,'' *Kirchenmusikalisches Jahrbuch* 71 (1988) 127–136. B. W. PRITCHARD, ed., *Antonio Caldara: Essays on His Life and Times* (Aldershot 1987). D. M. RANDEL, ed., *The Harvard Biographical Dictionary of Music* (Cambridge, Massachusetts 1996). N. SLONIMSKY, ed. *Baker's Biographical Dictionary of Musicians* (New York 1992). E. R. WALTER, *The Masses of Antonio Caldara* (Ph.D. diss. Catholic University of America, 1973).

[M. CORDOVANA]

CALDEY, ABBEY OF

Cistercian house, on Caldey Island, which lies southwest of Tenby, a small town on the Pembrokeshire coast of south Wales. Celtic monks settled this abbey in the 6th century. During the reign of Henry I it became a cell of the abbey of Tironian Benedictines (*see* TIRON, ABBEY OF) then recently founded at Saint Dogmaels, near Cardigan, Wales. In July 1534 Caldey acknowledged the royal supremacy and passed at once to lay ownership. It was purchased in 1906 by a community of Anglican Benedictines, the greater number of whom submitted to Rome in 1913. The TRAPPISTS bought it in 1928, and the Benedictines moved to Prinknash Park, Gloucestershire.

Bibliography: P. F. ANSON, *The Benedictines of Caldey* (London 1940). W. DUGDALE, *Monasticon Anglicanum* (London 1655–73); best ed. by J. CALEY et al., 6 v. (1817–30) 4:129–131. W. D. BUSHELL, ''An Island of the Saints,'' *Archaelogia cambrensis,* 6 ser. 8 (1908) 237–260. D. KNOWLES and R. N. HADCOCK, *Medieval Religious Houses: England and Wales* (New York 1953) 102. J. M. CANIVEZ, *Dictionnaire d'histoire et de géographie ecclésiastiques,* ed. A. BAUDRILLART et al. (Paris 1912–) 11:375–376.

[A. BYRNE]

CALDWELL, MARY GWENDOLINE

Philanthropist who was instrumental in inaugurating the Catholic University of America, Washington, D.C.; b. Louisville, Ky., 1863; d. New York City, Oct. 10, 1909. Mamie, as she was called, was the daughter of Mary Eliza (Breckenridge) and William Shakespeare Caldwell. She and her younger sister, Mary Elizabeth (later the Baroness Moritz von Zedtwitz), moved to New York City with their father after the death of their mother. In 1874 their father died, leaving his daughters a considerable fortune. They attended the Academy of the Sacred Heart, New York City, where they first made the acquaintance of Father John Lancaster Spalding, a fellow Kentuckian on leave from the Diocese of Louisville, who was then assistant pastor of St. Michael's Church in New York and later the first bishop of Peoria, Ill. Through her friendship with Bishop Spalding, Mamie became interested in the idea of a university or higher school where Catholic clergy could be educated.

At the Third Plenary Council of Baltimore in 1884, Miss Caldwell's offer of $300,000 for the founding of a national school of philosophy and theology was made known to, and accepted by, the bishops in council, with the stipulation of the young heiress that she was to be considered the founder of the institution. Thus was inaugurated the work that later led to the establishment of the CATHOLIC UNIVERSITY OF AMERICA.

In 1896 Miss Caldwell married the Marquis Jean des Monstiers-Merinville in Paris, with Bishop Spalding officiating. Three years later the University of Notre Dame, South Bend, Ind., awarded its Laetare medal to the Marquise. However, on Oct. 30, 1904, the world learned through an Associated Press announcement that the former Miss Caldwell had renounced Catholicism. The Marquise, who died in her stateroom on the North German liner, the *Kronprinzessin Cecile,* as it lay anchored outside New York, was buried in Louisville.

Bibliography: C. J. NUESSE, *The Catholic University of America: A Centennial History* (Washington, D.C. 1990). C. W. GOLLAR, ''The Double Doctrine of the Caldwell Sisters,'' *Catholic Historical Review* 81 (1995) 372–397.

[D. F. SWEENEY]

CALÉNUS, HENRI

''First of the Jansenists''; b. Beringen, Belgium, 1583; d. Brussels, Feb. 1, 1653. Henri Calénus (Van Caelen) completed his studies at Louvain, where he established a friendship with Cornelius JANSEN, future bishop of Ypres. From 1609 to 1624, Calénus served the parish of Asse, near Brussels, as an exemplary pastor, and was also active as dean of the deanery of Alost (1613–24). After his transfer to Brussels as pastor of Sainte-Catherine and dean of the city, he displayed remarkable zeal. Having maintained close contact with Jansen, he collaborated with him and the Abbé de Saint-Cyran in introducing Bérulle's Oratory into the Low Countries. As canon (1637) and later archdeacon (1642) in Malines, he became the close collaborator of Archbishop BOONEN, and was made vicar-general.

Shortly before Jansen died, he asked Calénus to work with Libert Froidmont, a professor at Louvain, in preparing a correct edition of his work, the famous *Augustinus*. In accordance with Jansen's wishes, Calénus devoted himself to this work from 1638 to 1640. After its publication (1640) and its condemnation by Rome, he continued to defend it and strove to obtain a revision of Rome's condemnation, especially with a view to safeguarding Augustinian doctrine. In 1644, the King of Spain appointed him to the episcopal see of Ruremonde, but he was unable to obtain confirmation from Rome despite his anti-Jansenistic oath. He renounced the episcopal title in 1648; his last years were marked by illness.

Bibliography: L. CEYSSENS, ''Henri Calénus, évêque manqué,'' *Bulletin de la Commission royale d'histoire* 127 (1961) 33–128, with extensive bibliog.

[L. CEYSSENS]

CALEPINO, AMBROGIO

Latin lexicographer; b. June 2, 1435; d. Nov. 30, 1511. Ambrogio, the son of the count of Calepio, Italy, became an Augustinian at Bergamo in 1451 and devoted himself to humanistic studies. His Latin dictionary (*Reggio Emilia* 1502), a cornucopia of many years' labor, was revised by him in 1505 and 1509. Humanists reprinted and revised the work almost constantly, especially in France and Italy where *calepin* and *calepino* were added to the vocabulary. Non-Latin words were gradually added until the Basel edition of 1590 contained 11 languages. Many Latin-English dictionaries depended on Calepino's work, as did almost all Latin dictionaries before FORCELLINI's great lexicon in 1771. Calepino's vita of St. JOHN BONUS OF MILAN (*Acta Sanctorum,* Oct. 9:693–885) is unreliable. He wrote a *De Venetiarum civitatis laude* (See also P. Foresti, *Supplementum chronicarum,* Bergamo 1483).

Bibliography: A. STRADA, and G. SPINI, *Ambrosio da Calepio, il Calepino* (San Marco 1994). F. ROSSI, ''Ambrogio Calepino e il 'Maestro del 1458': un episodio di cultura di élite,'' *Arte Lombarda* (1987) 80–82.

[F. ROTH]

CALIFORNIA, THE CATHOLIC CHURCH IN

Admitted to the Union in 1850 as the 31st state, California is located on the Pacific coast, is bounded on the north by Oregon; on the east by Nevada and Arizona, from which it is separated by the Colorado River; on the south by Mexico. Sacramento is the capital, and Los Angeles, San Francisco, Oakland, San Jose, Fresno and San Diego are the largest cities. The most populous state in the United States, the population in 2001 was 33,988,545, of which 9,754,947 (approximately 30 percent) were Catholic. The only state to have two archepiscopal sees, there are twelve dioceses in all. In addition to the metropolitan see, the Province of San Francisco includes Sacramento, Oakland, Stockton, Santa Rosa and San Jose as suffragans. The Province of Los Angeles includes San Diego, Monterey, Fresno, Orange and San Bernardino as suffragans.

Archdiocese/Diocese	Year Created
Archdiocese of Los Angeles	1936
Diocese of Fresno	1967
Diocese of Monterey in California	1967
Diocese of Orange in California	1976
Diocese of San Bernardino	1978
Diocese of San Diego	1936
Archdiocese of San Francisco	1853
Diocese of Oakland	1962
Diocese of Sacramento	1886
Diocese of San Jose in California	1981
Diocese of Santa Rosa	1962
Diocese of Stockton	1962

EARLY HISTORY

The Era of the Native Missions. Although it had been discovered by Juan Rodríguez Cabrillo in 1542 and revisited by Sebastián Vizcaíno in 1602, California was not colonized until 1769, when the Church was established in the territory. The conquest, ordered by José de Gálvez, Spanish visitor-general in Mexico (New Spain), had for its purpose the protection of Mexico's northern borders against possible Russian aggression. Spain desired a bloodless conquest and from the very beginning enlisted the Franciscan missionaries of the Apostolic College of San Fernando, Mexico City, then laboring in Lower California (Mexico), to cooperate spiritually and to implant the mission system among the indigenous peoples. Gálvez and Junípero SERRA, OFM, president of the Lower California Missions, worked out relationships between the military and the missionaries in the southern peninsula. San Fernando was to supply the missionaries. The PIOUS FUND, which had been created by the Jesuits and administered by the government after their expulsion in 1767, was used to defray the expenses of founding missions and to pay the salaries of the missionaries. Two military and naval expeditions were sent to occupy the ports of San Diego and Monterey. Gaspar de Portolá was named military leader. All forces reached San Diego by July 1, and on July 16, 1769, Serra established the first mission at San Diego.

Franciscan Missionaries. Between 1769 and 1823, 21 missions were established in California, nine under Serra, nine more under Fray Fermín Francisco de Lasuén, and the last three under his successors. They were San Diego (1769); San Carlos, Monterey-Carmel (1770); San Antonio and San Gabriel (1771); San Luis Obispo (1772); San Francisco and San Juan Capistrano (1776); Santa Clara (1777); San Buenaventura (1782); Santa Barbara (1786); Purísima Concepción (1787); Santa Cruz and Soledad (1791); San José, San Juan Bautista, San Miguel, and San Fernando (1797); San Luis Rey (1798); Santa Inés (1804); San Rafael (1817); and San Francisco Solano (1823). Several submissions, such as San Pedro y San Pablo, Santa Margarita, and San Antonio de Pala, were established also. Four presidios, each with a chapel, were founded at San Diego, Monterey, San Francisco, and Santa Barbara. Three civilian colonies were established at San Jose (1777), Los Angeles (1781), and Branciforte (1797). These missions, presidios, pueblos, and intervening ranches were the only Christian settlements in California between 1769 and 1840. All were administered spiritually by the Fernandino missionaries. Serra, called the Apostle of California, experienced misunderstandings and altercations with the military authorities. Disputes arose over church asylum, clerical appointments, military guards, postal frankage, native *alcaldes* (overseers), immorality of soldiers, and a host of minor questions.

The history of the missions in California between 1769 and 1840 is understandable only in the light of the royal patronage of the Indies granted to the Spanish kings by popes Alexander VI and Julius II and the accompanying abuses that grew out of the exercise of that grant in later times (*see* PATRONATO REAL). During the 18th century especially, Carlos III and IV tended toward state absolutism in ecclesiastical affairs.

Serra's successors were Fermín Francisco de Lasuén (1785–1803), Estevan Tapis (1803–12), José Señan (1812–15, 1820–23), Mariano Payeras (1815–20), Narciso Durán (1824–27, 1830–36), José Bernardo Sánchez (1827–30), and José Joaquín Jimeno (1839–53). In 1812 the office of commissary-prefect was established whereby jurisdiction was divided between him and the president. The former was assigned the duty of transacting the business affairs of the missionaries with the territorial government, while the president attended to the disciplinary matters relating to the missionaries. Thus the commissary-prefect ranked with the president in matters pertaining to native missions, while the president held the position of vicar forane of the bishop and as such was head of the Church in the territory. The office of commissary-prefect was held by Vicente Francisco de Sarriá (1812–18, 1824–30), Mariano Payeras (1818–23), Narciso Durán (1836–46), and José Joaquín Jimeno (1846–53). Beginning in 1833 the northern missions of California were administered by the Franciscan missionaries of the Apostolic College of Our Lady of Guadalupe, Zacatecas, while the southern missions were retained by the missionaries of San Fernando College. The first commissary-prefect of the Zacatecan missionaries was Francisco GARCÍA DIEGO Y MORENO, OFM, who in 1840 became the first bishop of California; the first president was Fray Rafael Moreno.

Santa Barbara Mission. (©Phil Schermeister/CORBIS)

When California was first missionized, the territory belonged to no diocese; the nearest bishops resided at Guadalajara and Durango, Mexico. On May 7, 1779, Pius VI created the Diocese of Sonora, which included the districts of Sonora, Sinaloa, and both Californias. Antonio de los Reyes, OFM, was appointed the first bishop of the extensive territory on Dec. 12, 1780. Consecrated in 1782, he arrived in Sonora in 1783 and made his headquarters at Alamos. Neither he nor any of his successors visited Upper California. Lasuén was the first mission president who had ecclesiastical relations with the Sonoran bishops. From these bishops Lasuén and his successors received the powers of vicar forane and military vicar until 1840.

The California missions were manned by 146 Franciscans until 1840, two serving at each mission. The great majority were Spaniards, the rest of Mexican birth. The missionaries were required to give ten years of service, though many served longer. All were volunteers. Traveling expenses and supplies for the journey were paid for from the royal exchequer. Two of the missionaries, Luis Jayme at San Diego, and Andrés Quintana at Santa Cruz, were murdered by the native tribes. Four more, Francisco Garcés, Juan Barreneche, Juan Diaz, and Matías Moreno, of the Apostolic College of Santa Cruz, Querétaro, were massacred along the Colorado River at Yuma in 1781.

Missions. The Franciscan missionaries sought to attract the native peoples by kindness and gifts to Christian villages built alongside the missions, where they lived for a period as catechumens, later permanently as neophytes. Having accepted Christianity, they were required to remain at the missions and to accept the orderly regime. If they became runaways they were sought out and brought back. At the missions the natives were entirely under the jurisdiction of the missionaries except in certain criminal matters when the military took over. The Franciscans, in charge of both their spiritual and temporal formation, were to instruct, educate, and discipline their charges.

Jesuit St. Ignatius Church, University of San Francisco. (©Philip James Corwin/CORBIS)

The law envisaged a complete transformation in ten years, when the mission towns would become pueblos of freed, formed natives after the pattern of the civic entities of the Europeans.

In practice, the day-to-day working out of mission affairs was determined at three levels: locally between the governor and the mission president; at the intermediate level between the viceroy and the guardian of the College of San Fernando; and at the highest level between the commissary-general of the Franciscans at Madrid and the king and his royal Council of the Indies. Throughout the period of missionization everything was done on a cooperative basis between Church and State under the patronato real system, and thus little independent action was allowed the missionaries. The system resulted in frequent misunderstandings, conflicts, and disputes. Thus the time, the place, and the manner of founding a mission were decided both by the civil and religious arms. The name of the mission was bestowed by the viceroy.

In the beginning the missions were crude, frontier settlements composed of buildings in log-cabin style, with grass or earthen roofs and dirt floors. These originals were followed by adobe structures with tile roofs and floors. In some cases stone churches, such as those at Carmel and Santa Barbara, resulted in the final stage of building. In several cases the site of a mission was changed in favor of better economic conditions or to separate it from too close proximity to a presidio. Because of growth in the number of Christians or because of damage to a mission by physical factors, such as earthquake, a number of succeeding churches appeared, including four at Santa Barbara and seven at Carmel. Usually a mission was built in quadrangular shape to form a compound, which included the church, the missionaries' residence, a dormitory for single girls and women, workshops, and storage rooms. At first the natives, turned Christians, built their new villages by the missions in the traditional manner of native huts, which were followed by sturdier structures in the Spanish fashion. Thus at Santa Barbara there were 252 family dwellings made of adobe with tile roofs, with a door and window, built along straight streets.

The average day at a mission—and all were governed in the same manner—was regulated according to the system that had been followed earlier in Texas and in the Sierra Gorda of Mexico. The natives rose at dawn and attended Mass, during which they recited the *doctrina,* (*see* ENCOMIENDA-DOCTRINA) a set form of the principal prayers and articles of faith, after which breakfast was served and the work of the day apportioned. The noonday meal was followed by a siesta; and afternoon work was followed by prayers in church. Evenings were free for rest or amusements. The schools were primarily of a practical nature, where pupils learned trades. It has been estimated that about 50 trades were taught, the principal occupations being farming and animal husbandry. Next came the making of adobes and tiles, spinning and weaving, stonecutting and setting, tanning, shoe and harness making, the fashioning of candles and soap, and the exercise of other trades and crafts that tended to make a mission self-sustaining. Most important at each mission was the irrigation system, bringing water for domestic and agricultural purposes to the mission and its fields, by which the waters of a nearby stream were harnessed by dams, aqueducts, reservoirs, filters, and fountains. Music and choral singing were cultivated at the missions, bands of musicians being formed and taught by the padres, a type of activity to which the natives took readily. Fray Narciso Durán of San José and Santa Barbara was the greatest of the friar musicians. Other missionaries, such as Buenaventura Sitjar of San Antonio and Felipe Arroyo de la Cuesta of San Juan Bautista, became expert linguists, while Gerénimo Boscana became the ethnologist of Mission San Juan Capistrano. Francisco PALÓU of San Francisco was California's first historian and biographer. All the missions had their libraries; the central archive at Mission San Carlos, Carmel, was later transferred to Santa Barbara.

Besides participating in the functions of the liturgical year, wherein Corpus Christi and Holy Week were colorfully celebrated, the Native Americans at Christmastide produced the *Pastores,* the traditional Christmas play of Mexico. They were given frequent vacations, being allowed to visit their relatives in their native towns, and were permitted to scour the mountains for wild berries and seeds. At the missions whatever was produced was conserved for the common good and apportioned out by the missionaries according to need. Physical punishment such as the lash, stocks, and shackles was given for the serious infraction of laws.

When Mexico became independent of Spain in 1821, California became part of the republic. Meanwhile the condition of the missions deteriorated since they had to supply the military with food and clothing during the struggle and afterward, a burden that became oppressive both to the missionaries and the natives. The missions were secularized in 1833 by the Mexican Congress; temporal control was placed in the hands of lay commissioners, and the natives were emancipated. Conditions worsened until finally the missions, except for the churches and direct church property, were sold in the

Mission San Carlos Borromeo del Rio Carmelo, Carmel, California. (©Dave G. Houser/CORBIS)

1840s. Looking back to the period between 1769 and 1845, by which time most of the missions were disbanded, the missionaries baptized about 99,000 persons in California, the great majority being Native Americans. They blessed 28,000 marriages and gave Christian burial to 74,000 persons.

The Mexican Era (1821–48). With the 19th century and especially after the transition to Mexican authority, a new period began in California Catholic history. The Spanish had begun to populate their borderlands in the 18th century by giving large land grants to settlers, more than 700 grants totaling nearly eight million acres, between 1734 and 1736. Mexican officials continued the program, attracting a number of *norteamericanos* who sometimes embraced Roman Catholicism in order to gain Mexican citizenship. Many of the owners, known as *Californios*, became socially and economically prominent. Through their perpetuation of family-centered devotions and rituals as well as the acquisition of religious objects, paintings of saints or religious figures, statues, and crucifixes, they accounted for an important part of California's ongoing Catholic identity.

Organizational lines of Catholic life began to be drawn more sharply. On May 7, 1779, Pius VI created the Diocese of Sonora, Sinaloa and Ambas (both Baja and

Mission San Diego de Acala. (©Dave G. Houser/CORBIS)

Alta) Californias and in 1780 placed Franciscan Antonio de los Reyes as the first bishop. After his consecration in 1782, he took up residence in Alamos in 1783. Neither he nor his successors ever visited Alta California. They left practical administrative details to Father Fermin Lasuén, OFM, and his successors who had inherited the title of Father President of the California Missions after the death of Junipero Serra.

The next important organizational event came on April 27, 1840, when Pope Gregory XVI created the Diocese of Ambas (Both) Californias (Baja and Alta) and appointed as bishop Francisco Garcia Diego y Moreno, O.F.M. (1785–1846). Diego y Moreno was consecrated on Oct. 4, 1840 at the Shrine of Our Lady of Guadalupe in Mexico City. Diego y Moreno established his headquarters at Santa Barbara, and appointed a vicar forane to oversee affairs in Baja California. The new bishop, like many of his successors, was constantly short of both money and priests to effectively rebuild a Catholic presence in the aftermath of the secularization of the missions. The shortage of money became even more acute after Mexican government confiscated the Pious Fund that had been an important source of revenue for the Church in California. An effort to impose a system of tithing on the wealthy rancheros failed miserably. The withdrawal of the Franciscans caused a shortage of priests to minister to people in the settled pueblos and in the scattered settlements. To remedy the situation Diego y Moreno sought to bring more priests from Mexico. In 1842 he established a seminary at Santa Barbara, later moved Mission Santa Ines, that reaped a harvest of three priests in January 1846.

After Diego y Moreno's death in 1846, his assistant Jose Maria de Jesus Gonzalez Rubio O.F.M. (1804–75) tended to the administration of ecclesiastical affairs in both Upper and Lower California. That same year marked the beginning of the Mexican-American War that ended with the Treaty of Guadalupe-Hidalgo that transferred California to the United States in 1848. About the same time, traces of gold were found in the mill run of John Augustus Sutter at Coloma, and by the end of 1848 and into 1849 the Gold Rush was on. People from every corner of the world came to Northern California to strike it rich. Although few had their dreams fulfilled, the effect of this huge migration accelerated the development of California into an American province ready for admission to the Federal Union by 1850.

CALIFORNIA IN THE UNITED STATES

The Gold Rush. In the wake of the Gold Rush ''instant cities'' began to develop in the northern part of the state. San Francisco grew into a major metropolis. Sacramento, Marysville, Stockton, and other access points to the mines were soon thronged with eager argonauts, prospectors and business entrepreneurs. Although it was difficult to develop a stable presence among the transient gold-seekers, assorted priests from Oregon and elsewhere arrived to minister to people in the cities. One such, Dominican Peter Augustine Anderson, celebrated the Mass in Sacramento in August 1850. Other priests provided sacramental ministry to pockets of Catholics in the supply depot towns of Marysville and Stockton. Catholics built a new church of St. Francis of Assisi in San Francisco in 1849.

Reports from Rubio, as well as reports from various missionary priests who were sent to help the Catholic cause in California reached the ears of bishops in the East who in turn transmitted them to the Congregation for the PROPAGATION OF THE FAITH and the pope. About the time California entered the union in 1850 Pope Pius IX invited Dominican Charles Montgomery to accept an appointment as bishop of a new California diocese. When Montgomery refused, the pontiff appointed Spanish

Dominican Joseph Sadoc ALEMANY to the newly created diocese of Monterey in Upper California. Bishop Alemany arrived in San Francisco in December 1850 and for the next few years alternated between San Francisco and Monterey. On July 29, 1853, Rome appointed Alemany the first archbishop of San Francisco, making Monterey suffragan see. The boundaries of the Monterey diocese extended south from the city of Gilroy to the Mexican border, and in 1854 the Holy See appointed Vincentian Thaddeus Amat (1811–78) as bishop. Like Alemany before him, Amat quit Monterey in favor of a larger city and in 1859 he moved his episcopal residence to Los Angeles. The diocese was known as the Diocese of Monterey-Los Angeles until 1922.

The growth of Catholic life in northern California continued unabated throughout the 1850s, and as early as 1858 Alemany began to petition Roman authorities for a further subdivision of his see. After much deliberation, the Holy See created a vicariate at the city of Marysville, near the Yuba River, and in 1861 named Irish-born Eugene O'Connell (1815–91) as the vicar apostolic. O'Connell had served briefly in the San Francisco see, heading the fledgling seminary still in existence at Mission Santa Ines and later as pastor of Mission Dolores. He had returned to Ireland in 1854 and served as the dean of All Hallows College in Ireland where he sent many a young priest to the California missions. O'Connell's vicariate originally encompassed much of California and Nevada north of the 39th parallel and also extended into Utah. In 1866, the far eastern boundaries were adjusted and Utah detached. In 1868 the Vicariate of Marysville gave way to diocesan status at the hydraulic mining town of Grass Valley in 1868. O'Connell would remain as bishop until 1884. Eventually, the Grass Valley jurisdiction was transferred to Sacramento.

Personnel and financial needs were perennial problems in California where the growing population outran local resources. To resolve these problems, California's early bishops turned to the generosity of European Catholics, who sent money, church goods and decorative objects for Catholic institutions. The Society for the Propagation of the Faith in Lyons and Paris was the recipient of many of these requests and California bishops wrote regularly and visited headquarters seeking additional funds for their growing missions.

The need for money motivated Archbishop Alemany to pursue the matter of the Pious Fund which had been frozen by the Mexican government. Claiming a share of these moneys by virtue of their inheritance of the old mission churches, Alemany pressed his claim against Mexico and won an initial favorable judgement in 1875. Archbishop Patrick Riordan (1841–1914) again pressed the issue before the newly established Permanent Court of Arbitration at The Hague Tribunal. In 1902 this body decided in favor of the California bishops and a trickle of payments began but stopped again during the Mexican Revolutionary turmoil of the 1910s. A final resolution of the claim was made only in 1966.

Recruiting personnel proved to be challenging as well. Amat had only 16 priests to serve his 80,000-square-mile diocese in 1855. O'Connell had only four priests for the vast expanses of the Vicariate of Grass Valley. Alemany and Amat both had tried to establish seminaries in their respective dioceses, but the enterprises faltered. California was compelled to rely on foreign clergy throughout much of its history. All three bishops welcomed a regular flow of Irish clergy throughout the 19th century. In 1898, the Archdiocese of San Francisco built its own seminary in Menlo Park and welcomed candidates from all over the state, and thus began to reverse the tide of Irish clerical dominance in California. In 1939 the Archdiocese of Los Angeles opened its major seminary at Camarillo, California. Only the Diocese of Sacramento continued to import Irish priests as the mainstay of its clerical force down through the 1960s.

Religious orders of men and women came to supplement the ministerial contingent in California. In 1850, Italian Jesuits arrived in San Francisco and would create a popular academy and college that would establish the first stirrings of higher education for Catholics in the state. In 1851 the Jesuits began Santa Clara College, the first of a network of Catholic colleges and universities that would enhance the Catholic presence in the state. Likewise, the Christian Brothers came to California in 1868 and established St. Mary's College. Alemany's own Dominican Order established a house in Benicia. Passionist Peter Maganotto helped to build Marysville's St. Joseph Church and in 1862 brought over members of his community from Italy. The Congregation of the Precious Blood opened a popular college in Rohnerville. Vincentians entered California in 1865. German Franciscans came to California and re-established the presence and visibility of the Friars Minor as a force in California religious life. Basing themselves at Mission Santa Barbara they developed active ministries among the state's German-speaking communities. Other groups of religious men, Marists, Paulists, Claretians, Salvatorians and others added to the medley.

Religious women were also actively recruited by Alemany and his counterparts. In 1850, he brought with him Mother Mary of the Cross Goemaere who helped to establish the Dominican Sisters of San Rafael. The Sisters of Notre Dame de Namur came in 1851 and created a popular academy in Marysville and later a College in Belmont. The Daughters of Charity arrived in 1852 in San Francisco and in 1856 started a house in Los Angeles. The Irish Sisters of the Presentation came in 1854, destined for Sacramento; they decided instead to put down roots in San Francisco. The Sisters of Mercy from Kinsale, Ireland, were recruited by Alemany. Mother Mary Baptist Russell led the contingent of sisters who arrived in San Francisco in 1854. Devoting themselves to education and health care, the Sisters of Mercy soon branched out into other areas of California, establishing themselves in Sacramento in 1857 and founding an orphanage in Grass Valley in 1864. In 1870 the Sisters of St. Joseph of Carondelet also came to southern California. In 1871, the Sisters of the Immaculate Heart of Mary arrived in Los Angeles. Both of these groups were to exercise a powerful influence over the development of Catholic education on every level.

Catholic growth in San Francisco took place despite the fact that there had been anti-Catholic incidents during the vigilante turmoil of the 1850s and the election of Know-Nothing Governor J. Neely Johnson in 1856. These incidents, and other difficulties with the American Protective Association during the 1890s and the Ku Klux Klan in the 1920s, suggest a certain pattern of anti-Catholic sentiment. Catholics in California suffered comparatively mild forms of intolerance from militant Protestants. Political advancement was not barred to Catholics. The first governor of the state, Peter Burnett, was a Roman Catholic convert. The main difficulty that Catholics experienced in California was state taxation of their institutions. The legislature of 1852 had exempted hospitals, churches, cemeteries, and schools from taxes, but when Californians gathered to rewrite their constitution in 1878, this tax exemption was stripped away. In 1901, the tax levy on church buildings was lifted, and likewise taxation of private colleges was ended in 1914. In 1926 and again in 1933, Catholic Californians in union with other private school advocates sought to lift the tax burden from private elementary and high schools through the initiative process. These efforts failed at the ballot box and would not be successful until 1952.

In response to nativist and other pressures a solid tradition of Catholic journalism developed in the Golden State. In 1858, the ''Irish and Catholic'' weekly the *Monitor* made its first appearance. Initially an independent Catholic weekly owned and edited by laymen James Marks, Patrick J. Thomas and James Hamill, the *Monitor* eventually came under the control of the bishops of California, who used it as a medium for the exchange of information and the creation of a more unified Catholic identity. Heavily Irish in its orientation, it shared news of Irish conditions abroad and also information about Catholic life and growth in California. The *Monitor* would be the first of many California Catholic newspapers that would develop in tandem with the growth of various dioceses throughout the state. In 1895, the Diocese of Monterey-Los Angeles began the *Catholic Tidings,* and in 1908 Sacramento began the *Catholic Herald.*

California life in the late 19th century was decisively transformed by the advent of the Transcontinental Railroad. With its western terminus at Sacramento, the Central Pacific (later renamed the Southern Pacific) brought significant economic vitality to California. Railroad development stimulated a growing agricultural economy in the Central Valley (a 435-mile stretch of land extending from Redding to Bakersfield), and water projects stabilized and redistributed the precious water resources of the region. The railroad created new communities such as Fresno, and older towns like Sacramento, the state capital since 1854, and Stockton were revitalized. In the late 19th century, a Catholic presence began to rise in response to these new economic realities. In 1886, the Holy See approved the transfer of the Diocese of Grass Valley to Sacramento where Bishop Patrick Manogue (1829–1895) undertook the building of the mammoth Cathedral of the Blessed Sacrament, designed by architect Bryan Clinch.

There was corresponding growth in southern California beginning in the 1880s, stimulated in part by the railroad and in part by the discovery of oil. Until that point, Los Angeles still retained elements of the old *Californios* culture. Bishop Amat struggled to ''Americanize and Romanize'' his flock, insisting on uniformity and obedience to episcopal authority. In 1876, he built St. Vibiana's Cathedral near the Old Plaza in Los Angeles (the site of Los Angeles' Our Lady, Queen of the Angels Church and the center of Catholic life in the old pueblo.) The land-boom of the 1880s, however, brought large numbers of Protestants of various denominations from the Midwest who challenged the old Catholic culture. Despite the dominance of WASP elite in Los Angeles society and politics, Catholics nonetheless held their own and continued to grow.

California's Asian Catholic Missions. Ethnic diversity became a fact of life in Catholic Los Angeles and San Francisco as elsewhere in the state. Bishops, sometimes reluctantly, gave permission to establish ethnic or national parishes to accommodate the spiritual, cultural and devotional needs of newly arrived immigrants. While many of the German, Italian, Portuguese, Mexican and Filipino immigrants were Catholic, the presence of large numbers of non-Christian Asians such as the Chinese and Japanese presented a different kind of challenge for the Church. Chinese gold miners had come during the rush. Hundreds of Chinese workers had also been imported to build the railroads. After the railroad was completed, the

Workingman's Party stirred bitter anti-Chinese sentiments. The problem for the Church stemmed from fact that many of the party's members were Irish Catholics, including Denis Kearney, one of the party's organizers. Even though Archbishop Alemany sought to distance the Church from the Workingman's Party, the relationship between the Catholic Church and the Chinese was strained, if not embittered, for many years. Short-lived efforts to evangelize the Chinese were made in the early 1850s by the Chinese priest Thomas Cian, but he failed to make any headway.

In 1902, a successful mission to the Chinese was established by the Paulist Fathers in San Francisco, operating from Old St. Mary's Cathedral, located adjacent to San Francisco's Chinatown. The increasing number of Chinese who embraced Catholicism resulted in the establishment of a Chinese Catholic parish at Old Saint Mary's Cathedral, and a parochial school for Chinese Catholic students. Similar outreach to the Japanese was spearheaded by a former missionary and later bishop Albert Breton in San Francisco, Los Angeles and Sacramento.

TWENTIETH CENTURY DEVELOPMENTS

The growth of the Catholic population between 1900 and 1950 necessitated the creation of new dioceses. In the south, with the growth of the entertainment and oil industries, Los Angeles began to rival San Francisco as a commercial and cultural center. During the episcopate of John J. Cantwell (1874–1947) the Catholic population of Los Angeles soared from 178,233 in 1917 to 601,200 at his death 30 years later. Beginning in 1922, the Holy See began to subdivide the vast interior of California, creating the Diocese of Monterey-Fresno out of counties plucked from the dioceses of Sacramento and Los Angeles and the Archdiocese of San Francisco. Irish-born John B. MacGinley (1871–1969) was installed as the first bishop of the new see. In 1936, Roman authorities detached the southern part of the Los Angeles diocese to create a new diocese at San Diego, headed by Charles Francis Buddy (1887–1966). In that same year, Rome elevated the rapidly growing Los Angeles jurisdiction to metropolitan status, thereby making California the only state with two archepiscopal sees.

San Francisco's former preeminence among California dioceses was not only affected by the demographic realities of California Catholic life, but also by the disastrous earthquake and fire that nearly wiped out the city in April 1906. Twelve churches were totally destroyed, and others, including the recently opened archdiocesan seminary at Menlo Park, badly damaged. Meanwhile San Francisco provided an important forum for Irish patriots Michael Davitt, Eamon de Valera, and others who visited and collected funds to support the cause of Irish independence. A San Francisco priest, Peter Christopher Yorke (1864–1925) attained prominence in city affairs, not only as eloquent defender of Irish rights, but also as a prominent journalist and public orator. His rise to fame came during his years as the editor of the *Monitor* when he attacked the American Protective Association with vigor. Establishing himself as a friend of the working class, he supported the rising labor organizations of San Francisco in the early Progressive period. He waged vigorous public duels with Irish Catholic politicians such as James Duval Phelan and journalists like Sacramento's C. K. McClatchy, of whom he disapproved as much for their "apostasy" as their positions on issues. Yorke waded into one of the most divisive controversies in San Francisco history, when he decried the prosecution of Abraham Ruef and Mayor Edward Schmitz in the Graft Trials of 1908–10, arguing that the trials were merely a front for the force of capital to destroy working class rights. Yorke's was the most prominent Catholic voice in California for nearly a generation.

In the early 20th century the Church felt the effects of an organizational revolution brought on by a combination of new prescriptions promulgated in the 1917 Code of Canon Law and a deliberate emulation of the techniques of modern business. Catholic operations became less informal and more centralized and bureaucratized. Strong bishops like Archbishops Edward Hanna (1860–1944) and John J. Mitty of San Francisco (1884–1961), John J. Cantwell of Los Angeles, and Patrick Keane (1872–1928) of Sacramento implemented their will through equally strong chancellors and vicars general. Centralized operations headquartered in diocesan chancery offices oversaw with even greater care the day-to-day dealings of the see, the individual parishes and institutions and the activities of priests and religious. Particular scrutiny was given to financial matters and in San Francisco the Church set up an archdiocesan banking system into which they compelled parishes to place their surplus funds. Similar kinds of centralizing activity was felt in the area of Catholic Charities with each diocese establishing a central bureau to oversee the delivery of social provision and also monitoring legal issues related to child care and protection.

Growth of the Mexican Catholic Community. The restrictions placed on European immigration in the early 1920s by the United States government marked the end of one era and the beginning of another. In California, labor shortages created by the new laws and the increasing availability of reclaimed farmland due to private and government development projects led to an important increase in the number of Mexicans living and working in California. While the prospect of work in the United States was an important magnet for Mexican migration, likewise revolutionary upheavals that began in the 1910s and resumed from 1926 to 1929 had a special impact on Catholics. Many fled what they considered to be the anti-Catholic policies of revolutionary governments and among the emigres were scores of bishops, priests and religious who found sanctuary in the United States. Agribusiness welcomed these workers who performed the backbreaking tasks required to plant, harvest and process fruits and vegetables. By 1928, Los Angeles was the second largest Mexican city in the world. Mexican immigration to the United States was only slowed by the Great Depression. However in 1942, the United States government resumed the importation of Mexican laborers for farms and factories in the wake of war-time labor shortages. This *Bracero* program lasted until 1964, but Latino immigration to California continued. Statistics from the 2000 census indicate that Hispanics and people of color make up the majority of the Golden State's population.

Since most Mexicans were Catholics, efforts to provide a stable and effective ministry to them began in most California dioceses. As the contours of this ministry emerged, church leaders sought to provide religious instruction, validate Mexican marriages, provide some social services and interdict the efforts of Protestant evangelicals to convert Mexican Catholics. In Los Angeles the time-tested vehicle of the ethnic parish was used and between 1923 and 1928 twelve Mexican parishes were established. Some of them were staffed by religious orders like the Claretians who had large numbers of Spanish-speaking members. In Sacramento, efforts were spearheaded by a priest, Father Stephen Keating, who worked with two laypersons, Federico Falcon and Magdalena Martinez, to establish a structure and visibility for work with Mexicans. In San Francisco, outreach to Mexicans took similar forms along with the creation of a Spanish Mission Band to work among migrant and bracero field workers. In the training of clergy, Los Angeles seminarians were required to learn enough Spanish to administer the sacraments. In the exchange that took place between an Anglo-Irish clergy and the Spanish-speaking population a complex process of assimilation and further cultural definition took place over the years. The closeness of Mexico and other Spanish-speaking countries meant a continual replenishment of the language and culture of Latino peoples and an ever increasing demand for bilingual parishes and services. Likewise the contours of Latino spirituality: the particular forms for the celebration of religious festivals, devotion to Mary, the cult of the saints and the relationship to the more structured and bureaucratic elements of church life have also had an important effect on the development of Catholic life in California.

African-American Catholics. African-American Catholic life also began to manifest itself, especially after World War I. Archbishop Cantwell opened parishes for African-American Catholics in 1922 and 1927. In 1938, St. Benedict the Moor parish opened in San Francisco. African-American Catholics organized more slowly in Sacramento. A further influx of African-American Catholics took place as military men and women settled in California during and after World War II.

Great Depression and its Aftermath. The Great Depression hit California hard, especially after 1931. The collapse of agricultural prices in particular had created serious unemployment and privation in the state. Bands of homeless men and women roamed from place to place, with a particularly poignant stretch of tents and makeshift shelters in public view down Highway 99, which traversed the center of the Central Valley. Church charities could do little to truly alleviate the suffering. In the political radicalism of the moment, many Catholics might have been tempted to vote for the Democratic candidate for governor, Upton Sinclair, the well-known opponent of the meat packing industry and an avowed socialist, were it not for the anti-religious statements he had penned throughout his career, many of them directly attacking or ridiculing the Catholic church.

But the state rebounded. In 1936, the federal government agreed to underwrite a massive water control and power program known as the Central Valley Project. Through a complex series of dams and reservoirs, the economic life of the region was dramatically affected. In the late 1930s, as the United States geared for war, all branches of the armed forces began to expand operations in California. San Diego became the major naval port on the Pacific Coast; Los Angeles exploded with new airplane and later aerospace operations; in San Francisco, the expansion of port facilities and the opening of shipbuilding and defense-related operations in Oakland, Richmond and Daly City created a whole new booming economy. These operations rejuvenated the California economy and contributed to more growth. Between 1941 and 1961 California's population more than doubled, from seven million to 16 million. In 1962, California surpassed New York as the largest state in the union. By 1964 there were over 3.7 million Catholics in the state, and in 1991, Los Angeles topped Chicago as the single largest archdiocese in the country.

Growth, Achievements and Challenges. The immediate impact of all this was a sharp increase in both parochial and Catholic school building. In Los Angeles alone, during the tenure of Archbishop James Francis McIntyre (1886–1979), 82 new parishes were established. McIntyre directed a major portion of the archdiocese's resources to the construction of schools for the swelling number of Catholic youth. Vocations to the priesthood surged dramatically after the war. Both major and minor seminaries in Los Angeles and San Francisco were filled with youthful applicants. In 1955, the Diocese of Sacramento established its own minor seminary.

After the death of Archbishop John J. Mitty in October 1961, a major reorganization of the dioceses of northern California took place, forming the dioceses of Stockton, Santa Rosa, and Oakland from portions of the Archdiocese of San Francisco and the Diocese of Sacramento. In 1967 Monterey was separated from Fresno to create two new dioceses. In the wake of the tremendous growth of southern California, the Diocese of Orange was created in 1976 and in 1978 a new see was erected at San Bernardino. In 1981, the Diocese of San Jose was created.

Catholics were moving in large numbers to the suburban developments surrounding major cities and close to the location of military bases, aerospace plants, and commercial developments. California became more than ever an automobile society, and rates of auto ownership grew dramatically after the war. This in turn set off a massive expansion of state highways and the re-sculpting of the state and its urban centers by the interstate freeway system. As Catholics moved to the suburbs, parishes and schools followed them, creating a new environment for the heretofore largely urban community. Automobiles, private home ownership, and the general diffusion of suburban living posed new challenges to the perpetuation of Catholic identity. Likewise, as the cities emptied and freeway building and urban renewal projects began to reconfigure the urban landscape, parishes, schools and other institutions either closed, relocated or readjusted to new demographic realities created by the changing environment. The difficulties of city parishes were accentuated when Archbishop John J. Quinn of San Francisco attempted to close ten churches including the historic St. Francis Church on Vallejo Street. The public outcry compelled his successor, Archbishop William Levada, to reconsider the decision.

Perhaps one of the biggest single changes for postwar Catholicism in California came in the expansion of its school systems. Parochial schools soon became an urgent priority for rapidly growing dioceses. Successful ballot initiatives in 1952 and 1958 spearheaded by Archbishop James Francis McIntyre of Los Angeles resulted in a long-awaited tax exemption for private schools. The Catholic high school, long attached to the old academy system came into being in the 1920s and provided a clear transition for students from elementary school and a preparation for college. After the war, a tremendous demand for Catholic schools corresponded with an increase in the number of women entering convents. Religious sisters provided the bulk of parochial school teachers and their contributed services provided the low overhead that made it possible for parishes to provide them. The growth in parochial school populations eventually developed a need for additional high schools. Here too, religious orders of women and of men sponsored these institutions, which also provided them with many vocations.

The growth in the size and programs of Catholic colleges and universities was also affected by the growth generated by the war and its aftermath. Specifically, the generous education provisions of the 1944 G. I. Bill gave tuition and housing allowances to returning veterans who soon began to swamp the small network of Catholic colleges and universities that had developed in California. Older institutions like Santa Clara, St. Mary's in Moraga, the College of Notre Dame, and the University of San Francisco registered strong new enrollments. So also did Loyola University in Los Angeles.

In the expansive growth of the postwar era, Catholic life and culture seemed to flourish and a moment of particular pride for Californians came in 1953 when Archbishop James Francis McIntyre of Los Angeles was elevated to the Sacred College of Cardinals by Pope Pius XII. The conferral of the cardinal's scarlet on a prelate of California in some respects reflected the fact that the church on the West Coast had ''arrived.'' It now shared an ecclesiastical honor given to the larger and older archdioceses in the East.

Ecclesiastical power flowed to Los Angeles more than ever. McIntyre had taken a strong hand in organizing the passage of the ballot initiative securing the tax exemption. He also had worked aggressively to establish a permanent lobbying agency for the bishops in Sacramento. Pressing legislation on education, child care and the social welfare front found Catholics with the need for coordinated and effective lobbying presence in Sacramento. McIntyre took the lead in organizing the bishops in this endeavor (an earlier effort by Mitty in the 1930s had failed) and eventually a public relations executive named William Burke was appointed to lobby for the bishops in Sacramento. The California Catholic Conference was reconstituted in 1966 and was served by a number of priests who held the office of executive secretary. In 1997 Edward Dolejsi became the first layman to represent the California bishops.

Social issues regarding open housing involved the California bishops in 1964 when they took a strong stand against those who sought to repeal the Rumford Fair Housing Act. Although the repeal was approved by California voters on a ballot initiative, the fair housing provision was reinstated by the California Supreme Court.

One of the most visible recipients of Catholic support was Cesar Chavez, the organizer of the United Farm Workers. Influenced by Catholic social teaching, Chavez worked for a time with the Industrial Areas Foundation of community organizer Saul D. Alinsky. He formed the National Farmworkers Association in 1962 with the aid of Dolores Huerta. In 1965 it changed its name to the United Farm Workers. With the aid of sympathetic Catholic priests, religious and others, Chavez and his associates pressed for the recognition of his newly formed union by California agribusiness. His dramatic 300-mile march from Delano to Sacramento in 1966 culminated with an Easter Mass celebrated by Bishop Alden J. Bell (1904–1982). Chavez pressed for boycotts of various agricultural products such as table grapes and lettuce to accentuate his demands. In 1975, California passed a new Agricultural Labor Relations Act which granted the United Farm Workers the right to organize. A new Agricultural Labor Relations Board was established headed by Bishop Roger Mahon, then of Fresno.

California's reception of the changes mandated by Vatican II were in many respects similar to other areas of the country. Episcopal interpretation of various conciliar decrees varied. In most California dioceses, for example, liturgical changes such as rendering a portion of the Mass in the vernacular and celebrating the Mass *versus populi* rather than *ad orientem* were implemented by Christmas 1964 or in early 1965 in most dioceses.

Internal church struggles over episcopal authority found Archbishop Joseph T. McGucken (1902–1983) of San Francisco battling with some members of the faculty of St. Patrick Seminary. McGucken also encountered stiff opposition to his decision to erect a new modern St. Mary's Cathedral to replace the 1891 structure that had burned in 1962. Likewise Cardinal James Francis McIntyre found himself engaged in highly public disputes with one of his priests, Father William DuBay and the Sisters of the Immaculate Heart of Mary.

A Multicultural Church. The ethnic diversity of California's growing population is noteworthy in terms of its implications for Catholic life and identity. Because of the revision of immigration law in 1965, California developed an even more diverse Catholic population than at any time in its history. The largest growth is in the state's heavily Catholic Latino population, but also includes large numbers of Vietnamese, Koreans, and Filipinos. The Latino community is the fast growing Catholic community in the state, followed closely by the many Asian communities. As a result of large-scale resettlement of Vietnamese refugees in the state, California has the largest Vietnamese Catholic population outside of Vietnam, concentrated especially in Orange County and the San Bernardino valley. The Chinese Catholic community witnessed remarkable growth in the late 1990s, with an influx of immigrants from Hong Kong and the mainland. The dynamics of cultural exchange, the varying spiritualities, forms of liturgical experience and the practical realities of various cultural groups sharing one parish site continue to challenge both the leadership and the rank and file of the California Catholic Church. In recognition of this multicultural Church, Los Angeles was chosen to host Encuentro 2000, the first national convention celebrating the racial, ethnic and cultural diversity of the U.S. Catholic Church sponsored by the U.S. Conference of Catholic Bishops.

Bibliography: Archival Sources: For the missions MS materials are found in the Archives of the Santa Barbara Mission and the Archives of the Archdiocese of Los Angeles and San Francisco. The Archivio General de la Nacion in Mexico City is also an important source. Printed works. F. PALOU, *Historical Memoirs of New California,* tr. H. E. BOLTON, 2 v., (Berkeley, Calif. 1926). M. J. GEIGER, *Life and Times of Fray Junipero Serra, O.F.M.* 2 v. (Washington, DC, 1959). Z. ENGELHARDT, *The Missions and Missionaries of California,* 4 v. (San Francisco 1908–15). D. WEBER, *The Spanish Frontier in North America* (New Haven and London 1992). L. HAAS, *Conquests and Historical Identities in California* (Berkeley 1995). A. L. HURTADO, *Indian Survival on the California Frontier* (New Haven and London 1988). R. JACKSON and E. CASTILLO, *Indians, Franciscans and Spanish Colonization* (Albuquerque 1995). Mexican Period. F. J. WEBER, *A Biographical Sketch of the Right Reverend Francisco Garcia Diego y Moreno* (Los Angeles 1961). M. NERI, *Hispanic Catholicism in Transitional California: The Life of Jose Gonzalez Rubio, O.F.M.* (Santa Barbara 1998). American Period, Archival Sources. Archives of the Archdioceses of Los Angeles and San Francisco; Diocese of Sacramento, San Diego, and Fresno; Archives of the Sisters of Mercy, Burlingame; Dominican Archives, Oakland; Archives of the Christian Brothers, St. Helena; Archives of the Society of Jesus, Los Gatos. Printed Sources. W. GLEESON, *A History of the Catholic Church in California,* 2 v. (San Francisco 1872). S. AVELLA, ''Region and Religion in California,'' *U.S. Catholic Historian* 18 (Summer 2000) 28–59. J. BURNS, *A History of the Archdiocese of San Francisco,* 3 v. (Strasbourg n.d.). M. ENGH, *Frontier Faiths: Church, Temple and Synagogue in Los Angeles, 1846–1888* (Albuquerque 1992). F. J. WEBER, *Century of Fulfillment: The Roman Catholic Church in Southern California, 1840–1947* (Mission Hills 1990). J. B. MCGLOIN, *California's First Archbishop: The Life of Joseph Sadoc Alemany, O.P.* (New York 1966). M. A. MCARDLE, *California's Pioneer Sister of Mercy: Mother Mary Baptist Russell* (Fresno 1954). F. J. WEBER, *Thaddeus Amat: California's Reluctant Prelate* (Los Angeles 1964). J. T. DWYER, *Condemned to the Mines: The Life of Eugene O'Connell, 1815–1891* (New York 1976). H. L. WALSH, *Hallowed Were the Gold Dust Trails: The Story of Pioneer Priests of Northern California* (Santa Clara 1946). R. E. BONTA, *The Cross in the Valley* (Fresno 1963). F. S. PARMISANO, *Mission West: The Western Dominican Province, 1850–1966* (Oakland 1966). J. B. MCGLOIN, *Jesuits by the Golden Gate* (San Francisco 1972). R. E. ISETTI, *Called to the Pacific: A History of the Christian Brothers of the San Francisco District 1868–1944* (Moraga 1979). G. MCKEVITT, *The University of Santa Clara: A History, 1851–1977* (Stanford 1979). J. P. GAFFEY, *Citizen of No Mean City, Archbishop Patrick Riordan of San Francisco, 1841–1914* (Consortium 1976). J. BRUSHER, *Consecrated Thunderbolt: A Life of Father Peter C. Yorke of San Francisco* (Hawthorne,

N.J. 1973). R. GRIBBLE, *Catholicism and the San Francisco Labor Movement 1896–1921* (San Francisco 1993). A BACCARI et al., *Saints Peter and Paul Church: The Chronicles of the ''Italian Cathedral of the West''* (San Francisco 1985). *San Francisco Monitor,* Special Centennial Issue, Sept. 4, 1953. F. J. WEBER, *His Eminence of Los Angeles: James Francis Cardinal McIntyre,* 2 v. (Mission Hills 1997). J. P. GAFFEY, *Men of Menlo: Transformation of an American Seminary* (Washington, DC 1992). P. T. CONMY, *A Parochial and Institutional History of the Diocese of Oakland, 1962–1972* (Mission Hills 2000). J. M. BURNS, ''The Mexican Catholic Community in California,'' in J. DOLAN and G. HINOJOSA, eds., *Mexican Americans and the Catholic Church, 1900–1965* (Notre Dame 1994).

[M. GEIGER/J. B. MCGLOIN/S. AVELLA]

CALIPH

A title (from the Arabic *khalīfa,* meaning successor, lieutenant, deputy) applied to the successors of the Prophet Muḥammad. The first caliph was Abū Bakr (A.D. 632–634), and the last, the Ottoman Abdul Mejid (1923–24), the Ottoman caliphate being abolished in 1924 by Kemal Ataturk. Very early in the political history of ISLAM, controversy over the office of the caliphate divided the Islamic world, giving rise to three competing groups: the SUNNITES, the SHĪ'ITES, and the Khārijites.

The Sunnite theory of the caliphate was that the office was an elective one, thus following the custom of pre-Islamic tribes. But the candidate had to be of the tribe of Quraysh, the tribe of the Prophet Muḥammad. The Khārijites opposed this limitation, holding that the election should be truly democratic, allowing for the election of any person, even a non-Arab. The Shī'ites opposed the very principle of election, holding that God Himself made the appointment of their IMĀM, whom they regarded as impeccable.

The duties of the caliph were to preserve the religion; to establish equity; to maintain public order; to maintain penal sanctions; to equip armies for guarding the frontiers; to lead the holy war (*jihād*) against those who refused to accept Islam until they either did so or entered into the status of protection (*see* DHIMMI); to collect the alms; to divide the booty; to employ trustworthy men and appoint good advisers; and to attend personally to the supervision of the conduct of government. In order to qualify for the caliphate a person had to be an adult male of the tribe of Quraysh, of good character, free from mental and physical defects, with administrative ability, knowledge of the law, and the courage to defend the territory of Islam.

The Prophet Muḥammad died without making provisions for a successor. His sons had died before him. Abū Bakr was the first caliph, followed by three others, all of whom were elected democratically. These four caliphs, Abū Bakr, 'Umar, 'Uthmān, and 'Alī, are referred to as the''rightly guided caliphs'' (al-khulafā' al-rāshidūn). Their combined reign extended from 632 to 661, a period referred to as that of the Orthodox Caliphate, the seat of which was in MECCA, one of the two holy cities of Islam, the other being MEDINA. The succeeding period was that of the Umayyad Caliphate (661–750). Its founder was Mu'āwiya (661–680), who moved the seat of government to Damascus (*see* UMAYYADS). Henceforth, the caliphate became hereditary, though the representatives of the community still expressed their consent through the institution of the *bay'a,* symbolized by a handshake with the caliph and denoting recognition of his authority and obedience to him. This dynasty had 14 caliphs and was succeeded by the 'Abbāsid dynasty, which numbered 37 (*see* 'ABBĀSIDS). The capital of this dynasty was in Baghdad, and its downfall came with the sacking of the city by the Mongols in 1258. In Spain, the Umayyad Caliphs of Cordova reigned from 756 to 1031 (followed by minor Spanish dynasties until 1492). The rival Fātimid Caliphate of Egypt, representing the Shī'ite minority in Islam, numbered 14 caliphs who reigned from 909 to 1171 when the dynasty was overthrown by the famous Sultan SALADIN. The Ottoman claim to the caliphate was based on an alleged nomination of the Sultan Selim I (1515–20) by the last member of the 'Abbāsid dynasty, who died in exile in 1539 in Egypt. But Selim did not fulfill the necessary qualification of belonging to the Prophet's tribe of Quraysh, hence the anomaly in the Ottoman Caliphate until it was abolished.

Bibliography: T. W. ARNOLD, *The Caliphate* (London 1924). H. LAOUST, ed., *Le Califat dans la doctrine de Rasīd Ridá* (Beirut 1938). L. GARDET, *La Cité Musulmane: Vie sociale et politique* (Paris 1954).

[G. MAKDISI]

CALIXTUS, GEORG

Professor of theology and propagator of theoretical and historical bases of ecumenism; b. Medelby, Schleswig-Holstein, Dec. 14, 1586; d. Helmstedt, March 19, 1656. At 16 Calixtus (Callisen), son of a Lutheran pastor, entered Helmstedt University, where PHILIPPISM was protected. Among his professors were the humanist Johann Caselius (1533–1613) and the Aristotelian Cornelius Martini (1568–1621). With this background, his principle that ''mind is godlike and logic divine'' spelled an approach to theology in large part disdained by contemporary Lutheran theologians Although personally devoted to the AUGSBURG CONFESSION (1530), he believed a man could be saved though a Calvinist or Roman Catholic. In his concern for reunion, Calixtus appealed to spokesmen of an irenic tradition, such as St. VINCENT OF LÉRINS (d. before 456), Desiderius ERASMUS, Philipp MELANCHTHON, George CASSANDER, Georg WITZEL, and Marcantonio de Dominis. In such irenicists he found support for the idea of all churches measuring their creeds by the Apostles' Creed and the Fathers.

Calixtus's writings, though prolific, do not present a systematic theology. They consist mainly of elaborately reasoned proposals for interdenominational meetings, conciliatory tracts aiding reunion, a vast and varied correspondence, and polemical brochures. His reunion proposals were generally well received, especially by the Calvinists, partly through their wish for equal status with Lutherans within the Empire, partly because of their experience in France and the Lowlands, partly because of a lingering force of humanism. He corresponded on Protestant reunion with Franciscus Junius (1545–1602), David Pareus (1548–1622), Isaac Casaubon (1559–1614), Hugo GROTIUS, John Durie (1596–1680), Gerhardus Johannes Vossius (1577–1649), Ludwig Crocius (1586–1655), Johannes Bergius (1587–1658), and Moïse AMYRAUT, as well as with the Mt. Athos monk Metrophanes Kritopoulos (d. *c.* 1640), with whom he discussed his proposals in regard to Greek Orthodoxy.

Efforts at reunion with Catholicism foundered on the differences in the conception of the Church as a visible and continuous entity, the Petrine doctrine, Tridentine authority, and the nature of heresy. Calixtus urged Catholics to recognize man's obligation toward reason and the benefits of dialogue in mitigating bitterness. Vitus Erbermann (1597–1675), Valeriano MAGNI, Johannes C. von Boyneburg (1622–72) were among the Catholic scholars to whom Calixtus submitted his proposals. The strict orthodox Lutherans also resisted his efforts, and the conflict that ensued between them and Calixtus and his school was called the ''syncretistic controversy.'' Beginning in 1645 it continued to the end of the century. The orthodox included Coelestinus Myslenta (1588–1653), Johannes Behm (1578–1648?), Michel Behm (1610–88), and particularly Abraham CALOV. Conrad Horney the philosopher (1590–1649), Herman Conring the jurist (1606–81), and Johannes Latermann (1620–82)—all Calixtine students—defended their master's arguments. After his death, the influence of Calixtus was further extended by his student Gerard Wolter Molanus (1633–1722) and the philosopher G. W. LEIBNIZ.

See Also: CONFESSIONS OF FAITH, II PROTESTANT; GNESIOLUTHERANISM.

Bibliography: Works. *Epitomes theologiae moralis pars prima una cum Digressione de arte nova* (Helmstedt 1634); ed., *Sancti . . . Augustini De doctrina christiana libri IV: De fide et symbolo liber unus* (Helmstedt 1655); *Disputatio theologica de auctoritate antiquitatis ecclesiasticae* by J. HENICH (Helmstedt 1639). E. L. HENKE, ed., *G. Calixtus Briefwechsel: In einer Auswahl aus Wolfenbüttelschen Handschriften* (Halle 1833); *Commercii literarii Calixti* (Marburg 1835–40) fasc. 2–3. **Literature**. E. L. HENKE, *Georg Calixtus und seine Zeit*, 2 v. (Halle 1853–56), still definitive. J. T. MCNEILL, *Unitive Protestantism* (rev. ed. Richmond, Va. 1964). W. C. DOWDING, . . . *Life and Correspondence of G. Calixtus* (London 1863). R. PREUS, *The Inspiration of Scripture: A Study of the Theology of the 17th Century Lutheran Dogmaticians* (Edinburgh 1955). P. PETERSEN, *Geschichte der aristotelischen Philosophie im protestantischen Deutschland* (Leipzig 1921). H. SCHÜSSLER, *Georg Calixt, Theologie und Kirchenpolitik: Eine Studie zur Ökumenizitčt des Luthertums* (Wiesbaden 1961). H. SCHMID, *Geschichte der syncretistichen Streitigkeiten in der Zeit des Georg Calixt* (Erlangen 1846). O. RITSCHL, *Dogmengeschichte des Protestantismus*, 4 v. (Leipzig-Göttingen 1908–27). F. LAW, *Die Religion in Geschichte und Gegenwart* 1:1586–87.

[Q. BREEN]

CALL TO ACTION CONFERENCE

The Call to Action Conference, an assembly of Catholic diocesan representatives meeting under the auspices of the National Conference of Catholic Bishops (NCCB), marked the culmination of an 18-month national consultation on social justice. The Conference was held in Detroit, Oct. 21–23, 1976. The proceedings of the convocation in which 1,300 delegates, priests, religious, and laity from 152 dioceses participated, resulted in 182 recommendations, which in turn formed the basis of a five-year plan of social action for the Catholic Church in the United States.

The Call to Action Assembly was intended to mark the Catholic observance of the bicentennial anniversary of the United States. The concept for the program had its genesis in 1971 with deliberations of the U.S. Catholic Bishops' Advisory Council, a national body which provides guidance and consultation to the American bishops. The council urged the establishment of a Church-sponsored symposium on *A Call to Action*, the English title of the encyclical *Octogesima adveniens* of Pope Paul VI on the 80th anniversary of *Rerum novarum.*

A Committee of the NCCB was formed in 1973 with a mandate to prepare a conference on social justice. Cardinal John F. DEARDEN, Archbishop of Detroit, was appointed chairman of the 62-member planning committee. A program of consultation leading up to the Call to Action Conference was undertaken in 1975. At the diocesan and parish level across the country the program theme of ''Liberty and Justice for All'' formed the basis of group discussions. At the national level the NCCB conducted seven hearings, each three days in length, and held in the cities of Washington, D.C., San Antonio, Texas, Minneapolis, Atlanta, Sacramento, Newark, and Maryknoll, New York. Sixty-five bishops joined by religious, priests, and laity took testimony from over 400 persons who focused on particular areas of social need and church life. Included among the witnesses were homemakers, farmers, theologians, economists, social workers, union leaders, community organizers, feminists, unemployed persons, members of minority groups, as well as many other individuals. The consultation focused on a wide variety of topics dealing with family and neighbourhood life, economic justice, internal and political affairs, the needs of minorities, the aged, women, education, cultural pluralism, world hunger, war and peace, and a multitude of other contemporary social issues. In early 1976, the concerns and recommendations raised in the program—over one million of them—were reviewed and summarized by teams of bishops, priests, religious, and laity. A series of preliminary documents on the discussion findings were prepared for the next stage of the consultation, the Detroit meeting.

The densely written recommendations of the Call to Action Conference touch upon many areas of church life and its social mission. They range from a strong condemnation of the arms race and of nuclear weaponry to just wages for teachers in Catholic parochial schools; from a concern for the viability of the small family farm to a concern for a healthy urban neighbourhood; from the subject of the new economic order as voted by the General Assembly of the United Nations to equal rights for women in the labor market.

In their initial response to the Detroit Assembly, the bishops of the United States in a 1,400-word pronouncement, affirmed in general the findings of the Call to Action meeting and the preceding bicentennial consultation. In the statement the bishops said:

> We invited this process of structured public discussion in the Church so that we might listen to the needs of our own people and through their voices come to know more specifically and to share more intimately ''the joys and hopes, the griefs and the anxieties'' of the people of our age. Admittedly, the process of consultation was imperfect and there are some conclusions which are problematical and in some cases untenable. This has been a source of concern. Yet, this two-year process was marked by trust and respect among nearly all who took part. It gave many people a good opportunity to speak directly to church leaders. It identified issues and a number of constructive suggestions for action. It helped dramatize how the Church and its leadership are perceived by some. We are grateful to all who shared their insights with us. We affirm our commitment to the principle of shared responsibility in the contemporary Church, and we assert our intention to improve consultation with our people.

The hierarchy went on to underscore ''the direct and intimate connection between the mission of the Church and the ministry of justice,'' and pledged themselves to the establishment of a five-year program on social justice. To accomplish this the NCCB established a special committee on implementation and Archbishop John Roach of St. Paul-Minneapolis was appointed its chairman. The 31 episcopal committees of the NCCB and U.S. Catholic Conference were assigned various recommendations of the Call to Action Conference for evaluation.

Following Committee deliberations, the bishops, at their May 1978 meeting, gave final approval to a program of action designed, as the bishops themselves declared, ''to clarify and specify the implications for the Church in the United States of a social ministry at the service of the justice of God''

After the conference was concluded, many U.S. bishops gradually distanced themselves from its recommendations, disagreeing with its far-reaching reform agenda. In the early years following 1976, a group of laity and religious in Chicago who were dissatisfied with the leadership of Cardinal John Cody decided to establish a reform advocacy group based on the plan of action for church reform and other initiatives that were proposed at the conference. This fledging group adopted the name Call to Action (CTA) and met for the first time in 1978 in Chicago. Notwithstanding its name, Call to Action is an independent group that is outside the umbrella of the UNITED STATES CONFERENCE OF CATHOLIC BISHOPS, although a few bishops are members of the group.

From a local reform group in Chicago, CTA catapulted into national prominence when it invited Hans Küng to its 1981 annual conference as the plenary speaker. The publicity it received resulted in a growth in interest in the group's objectives. The next major landmark was its 1990 *Call to Reform* manifesto which, among other things, called for a more open and progressive Church that was responsive to social justice issues, issues of equality, and the needs of women and the marginalized. The various signature campaigns and resulting publicity generated by this statement resulted in renewed interest in what had been largely a local reform group. Membership enquiries came in, leading to the establishment of regional chapters and affiliates. By mid-1990s, there were 40 such regional chapters and affiliates. The establishment of a chapter in Lincoln, Nebraska, in 1996 resulted in the local ordinary, Bishop Fabian Bruskewitz issuing a blanket order excommunicating any Catholic within his diocese who joined the chapter. The latter part of the 1990s saw CTA collaborating with European reform groups to advocate for reform and renewal within the Church.

Bibliography: NCCB-USCC, *A Call to Action* (Washington, D.C. n.d.), includes Working Papers, Resolutions, Bishops' Response, Reference Documents.

[F. BUTLER/EDS.]

CALLAHAN, PATRICK HENRY

Industrialist, Catholic lay leader; b. Cleveland, Ohio, Oct. 15, 1865; d. Louisville, Ky., Feb. 4, 1940. He was the son of John Cormic and Mary Anna (Connolly) Callahan. After attending St. John's High School and the Spencerian Business College in Cleveland, he had a brief career in professional baseball as a member of the Chicago White Stockings (now White Sox) organization. After leaving baseball in 1888, he worked for the Glidden Varnish Company in Cleveland and Chicago, and on Jan. 20, 1891, he married Julia Cahill of Fremont, Ohio. The couple moved the following year to Louisville, where Callahan became manager, and later president, of the Louisville Varnish Company. In 1915 he and Rev. John A. Ryan formulated a profit-sharing plan for the company, under which surplus revenues were divided between stockholders and workers. Callahan lectured and wrote extensively on behalf of this plan. He was also active as chairman (1914–16) of the Knights of Columbus Commission on Religious Prejudices, founder (1916) of the Catholic Laymen's Association of Georgia, chairman (1917–18) of the Knights of Columbus Committee on War Activities, and helped to organize (1926–27) the Catholic Association for International Peace. After World War I he became one of the directors of the Catholic Conference on Industrial Problems (1923) and an ardent champion of prohibition, serving as general secretary of the Association of Catholics Favoring Prohibition and chairman of the Central Prohibition Commission. In 1925 he came to the aid of William Jennings Bryan in the Scopes evolution trial. He favored New Deal legislation, which he helped to administer in Kentucky, and served as a trustee of the National Child Labor Commission and vice president of the Kentucky Interracial Commission. Callahan was named to the Order of St. Gregory the Great in 1922 and awarded the Illinois Newman Foundation's honorary medal in 1931.

Bibliography: Archives, The Catholic University of America.

[R. J. BARTMAN]

CALLAN, CHARLES JEROME

Author and theologian; b. Lockport, N.Y., Dec. 5, 1877; d. Milford, Conn., Feb. 26, 1962. He received his early education in the public schools of Niagara County, N.Y., and then attended Canisius College in Buffalo. Entering the Order of Preachers at St. Rose Priory, Springfield, Ky., he was professed on Oct. 23, 1900. After ordination at Somerset, Ohio, June 29, 1905, he was sent to Fribourg, Switzerland, for further theological studies. He returned to the U.S. in 1909, and was appointed to the teaching staff of the Dominican House of Studies, Washington, D.C., as professor of philosophy arid Scriptural exegesis. He held that post until 1915, when he was sent to teach the same subjects at the newly opened major seminary of the Maryknoll Fathers, Maryknoll, N.Y. In 1916 he became co-editor with Father John A. McHugh of the *Homiletic and Pastoral Review.* The two collaborated not only in editorial work but in other writing as well. Together they wrote 16 works on theology, Sacred Scripture, and the liturgy. In addition to the works in collaboration with McHugh, Callan wrote or compiled seven books of his own, and two in collaboration with Father Thomas Reilly, on the Dominican liturgy. In 1931, Callan received the Dominican degree of Master of Sacred Theology, and in 1940 he was appointed by the Holy See as consultor of the Pontifical Biblical Commission.

Bibliography: W. ROMIG, ed., *The Book of Catholic Authors,* 2d set. (Detroit 1943). *Dominicana* 16 (1931) 148–149; 25 (1940) 246–247; 40 (1955) 284–285.

[J. COFFEY]

CALLES, PLUTARCO ELÍAS

Mexican revolutionary leader and persecutor of the Catholic Church; b. Guaymas, Sonora, Mexico, Jan. 27, 1877; d. Mexico City, Oct. 19, 1945. Calles, a descendant of Sephardic Jews from Almazón, Soria, Spain, was a natural son of Plutarco Elías Lucero and María de Jesús Campuzano. When he was four, his father died and his mother married J. B. Calles, whose last name young Plutarco took. On completing his primary education, he worked as an assistant elementary teacher. Finding this incompatible with his impulsive and authoritarian personality, he worked next in the municipal treasury of Guaymas until a small embezzlement left him jobless. After administering a hotel owned by his brother, he finally went into business for himself. The revolution of Francisco I. Madero did not affect him. However, as a commissioner of Agua Prieta—a position that he held for the benefit of his business—Calles, together with Alvaro Obregón, joined the revolution headed by Venustiano Carranza, Governor of Coahuila, when the president was assassinated. Obregón had previously fought Pascual Orozco when Orozco betrayed Madero. Calles, a captain, undertook his first attack against Naco; it was so unsuccessful Calles fled when the first shots rang out. Later he was more fortunate, and in a short time he rose to the rank of general. The revolution removed Victoriano Huerta from office and degenerated into anarchy. Since the ambitions of the *caudillos* did not bring peace to the republic, the principal revolutionary chiefs convoked a convention to find remedy. The convention, held in Aguascalientes in mid-1915, disowned Carranza and Carranza disowned the convention. Pancho Villa, in open rebellion against the commander-in-chief, was defeated by General Obregón, while Calles obtained power and influence. In August 1915 Venustiano Carranza appointed Calles governor and military commander of Sonora. There he remained nine months, during which time he first indicated his propensity toward the destruction of the Catholic Church. In Querétaro, on Feb. 5, 1917, the Constitutional Congress promulgated the new constitution in which there were included antireligious articles that served as a legal base for Calles' unleashing, as president of the republic, the most cruel religious persecution.

Carranza appointed Calles secretary of industry and commerce, a position that he left early in 1920 to follow Obregón in a new revolutionary adventure. Adolfo de la Huerta, also from Sonora, initiated the Plan of Agua Prieta, disavowing Carranza. He was seconded by a large part of the army, and the president was assassinated in a hut in Tlaxcalaltongo. Huerta became provisional president while the elections were held. Álvaro Obregón won; he took office Dec. 1, 1920, and appointed Calles secretary of war. In 1922 Calles became secretary of the interior. When Obregón's term came to an end, his secretary of the treasury, Adolfo de la Huerta, was prevented from becoming president and provoked a bloody rebellion. He was defeated and Calles became president on Dec. 1, 1924.

The first two years of his government revealed his socializing tendencies; among other things he constructed highways and irrigation projects, reorganized the army, and founded the Bank of Mexico. A man of strong passions, he first tried to divide the Catholic Church by promoting the establishment of a Mexican national church. That failing, he enforced Article 130 of the constitution and promulgated the Decree of Reforms on Transgressions of the Common Order. This meant limitation of the number of priests, prohibition of religious teaching in the schools, state control over the clergy, and suppression of religious orders. The bishops protested through the legal means at their disposal but with no effect; they were forced to suspend the public worship in churches after Aug. 1, 1926. In some states, uprisings broke out, and for three anguished years, the Mexican Catholics gave their blood to the cry of ''Long live Christ the King!'' At the end of his presidential term, two early revolutionaries, friends of Calles and Obregón, became candidates, but both were cut down by bullets. Obregón, without an opponent, was then elected, but José de León Toral assassinated him.

Plutarco Elías Calles.

Calles remained chief of the revolution. Portes Gil, the provisional president, bent to his will. He imposed Ortíz Rubio as president against the wishes of the people who were in favor of José Vasconcelos. He withdrew Ortíz Rubio and replaced him with Gen. Abelardo Rodríguez. He raised also Lázaro Cárdenas to the presidency, using the official political party created by him to guarantee the continuation of the revolutionary group in power. Calles, objecting to Cárdenas's policies, tried to intervene once more, but this time his protegé turned on him and exiled him to the United States. When in 1941, during the presidency of Manuel Ávila Camacho, he returned to Mexico, Calles remained apart from all political activity.

Bibliography: F. MEDINA RUIZ, *Calles: Un destino melancólico* (Mexico City 1960). A. RIUS FACIUS, *Méjico cristero: Historia de la ACJM, 1925 a 1931* (Mexico City 1960).

[A. RIUS FACIUS]

CALLEWAERT, CAMILLE

Historian of liturgy; b. Zwevegem, Belgium, Jan. 1, 1866; d. Bruges, Aug. 6, 1943. Callewaert studied at the episcopal college of Courtrai and took his philosophy at the seminary at Roulers. He never finished the usual course of theology at the major seminary of Bruges because his bishop sent him to study for a degree in Canon Law at Louvain. Here he also enrolled in the faculty of philosophy, studied historical criticism under A. Cauchie (1860–1922), and followed B. Jungmann's (1833–95) course in Church history. In the meantime, he was ordained on June 15, 1889.

In 1893 Callewaert was recalled to Bruges and named assistant at the cathedral. The following year he was appointed professor of Church history at the major seminary; in 1903 he was given the chair of liturgy. He was rector from 1907–34. Meanwhile, he was also professor of liturgy at the University of Louvain from 1910 to 1921. In 1929, Pius XI made him a domestic prelate, and upon his retirement he was named archpriest of Bruges. His last years were devoted entirely to study.

A historian of the first order, Callewaert made his rubrics lectures a genuine study of liturgy; they were eventually published as *Liturgicae Institutiones*, 3 v. (Bruges 1919–37). But he was not interested only in liturgical science. Conscious of the liturgy's role in the people's spiritual life, he started a liturgical study group at Bruges in 1907, an institution that was soon imitated all over Belgium. At the request of L. BEAUDUIN, Callewaert organized the Dutch liturgical week of which he retained the presidency for years.

Bibliography: The long list of his works was published in *Sacris erudiri* 1 (1948) 353–379. The greater part of his articles were reprinted in the volume *Sacris Erudiri* (Steenbrugge 1940). C. VAN HULST, *Ephemerides liturgicae* 58 (1944) 319–321.

[N. HUYGHEBAERT]

CALLINICUS, PATRIARCH OF CONSTANTINOPLE

693 to 705. His origin is unknown, but he had served in an important post at the Blachernae Church in the royal quarter of the capital city before he succeeded Paul III as patriarch of Constantinople, and frequently opposed the brutality and interference of the Byzantine Emperor, JUSTINIAN II. When the patrician Leontius mounted a revolt that resulted in the mutilation and banishment of the Emperor in 695, Callinicus supported the conspiracy and crowned Leontius as the new monarch. Another revolution placed Apsimar Tiberius II on the imperial throne in 698. Meanwhile, Justinian was preparing a return from exile, and in 705 he laid siege to Constantinople with a formidable army of Slavs and Bulgars. A surprise raid won Justinian's restoration. In the reign of terror that followed, Callinicus was blinded and exiled to Rome. The choice of Rome seems to have been dictated by reasons of security rather than of religious intrigue. Hagiographic sources report that Callinicus was immured alive—probably a typical exaggeration of the fact of his imprisonment.

Feast: Aug. 23, 24, or 30 (Eastern Church).

Bibliography: J. GOUILLARD, *Dictionnaire d'histoire et de géographie ecclésiastiques* 11:415. M. V. BRANDI, *Bibliotheca sanctorum* 3:673–675.

[R. J. SCHORK]

CALLISTUS I, PATRIARCH OF CONSTANTINOPLE

1350–54 and 1355–63, Byzantine preacher and hagiographer; d. 1363. He was a monk at Iviron on Mt. ATHOS, companion of Gregory PALAMAS, and disciple of GREGORY SINAITES, the principal proponent of HESYCHASM in the skete of Magula. Callistus signed the Hagiorite *Tome* of 1341 as a hesychastic *manifesto.* In March of 1342 he joined the Athonite delegation in Constantinople to negotiate peace between John VI Cantacuzenus and the court of Anne of Savoy; on June 10, 1350, he succeeded his former student Isidore I as patriarch of Constantinople. He presided over a synod in Blachernae palace (May to June 1351), which canonized Palamite doctrine. He was deposed after 1353 for refusing to crown Matthew Cantacuzenus Emperor.

After the abdication of John Cantacuzenus in 1354, he regained the patriarchal throne. He reorganized the parochial system under the surveillance of an exarch, excommunicated the Serbian Czar Stephen Dušan, and attempted to regroup the various Orthodox churches, particularly the Hungarian, under his patriarchate. He spread Palamite doctrine, particularly through biography, and wrote a life of Gregory the Sinaite; a life of St. Theodosius of Tirnovo; a panegyric on John the Faster, renovator of the Prodromos-Petra monastery; and many homilies, a number of which have been recently discovered.

Bibliography: O. VOLK, *Lexicon für Theologie und Kirche,* new eds. 5:1263. M. JUGIE, *Catholicisme* 2:391–392; *Dictionnaire de théologie catholique* 11.2:1789–92. *Kirche und theologische Literatur im byzantinischen Reich* 774. J. MEYENDORFF, *Introduction a l'étude de Grégoire Palamas* (Paris 1959).

[I. H. DALMAIS]

CALLISTUS II XANTHOPULUS, PATRIARCH OF CONSTANTINOPLE

Byzantine spiritual writer who reigned as patriarch in 1397. His surname indicates that he was from the monastery of Xanthopulus. With another monk, Ignatius Xanthopulos, Callistus composed the important *Century*, a tract of 100 sections on the ascetical practices of the Hesychastic monks; it was incorporated in the *Philokalia* of Nicodemus the Hagiorite and had a great influence on Orthodox spirituality. The *Century* avoided the Palamite controversy; it confined itself to practical directives based on the teachings of the Greek fathers, such as Evagrius, Maximus the Confessor, and John Climacus. At the start of his spiritual life, the monk must seek a director who will lead him to the perfection of his baptismal graces in a life of faith, hope, and charity. Obedience to the director eliminates self-will and leads to fulfillment of the commandments of Jesus. A life of continual prayer, strict self-discipline, and practice of the bodily activities of the Hesychasts are prerequisites, as is the Prayer of the Heart or the JESUS PRAYER. These means are, however, subordinate to the action of Divine Grace (c. 24). Callistus seems to have used the work of Callistus Angelicudes as a basis for this compilation. A series of ''Texts on Prayer'' is also attributed to Callistus in the *Philokalia.* Several rescripts and a confession of faith have been preserved from his reign as patriarch. The homilary attributed to him in a MS of the Chilandar monastery is not of his authorship.

Bibliography: *Patrologia Graeca* 147:635–812. E. KADLOUBOVSKY and G. E. H. PALMER, trs., *Writings from the Philokalia on Prayer of the Heart* (London 1951) 162–273. *Kirche und theologische Literatur im byzantinischen Reich* 774, 784–785.

[H. D. HUNTER]

CALLISTUS I, POPE, ST.

Pontificate: *c.* 218 to 222. According to the *Liber pontificalis,* Callistus was a Roman by birth; his father, Domitius, was from the district of Trastevere. Originally an imperial household slave of Carpophorus, Callistus is said to have engaged in banking and was accused of embezzlement. His creditors allowed him to remain free in hopes of recovering some lost funds, but Callistus got into a brawl in a synagogue on the Sabbath. He was condemned to the mines of Sardinia (*c.* 186–189). Through the influence of Marcia, the concubine of Emperor Commodus, he was released and lived in Anzio on the bounty of Pope VICTOR I, although some sources say that Victor deliberately left his name off the list of those to be freed. Under Pope ZEPHYRINUS he became deacon and was apparently given charge of the cemetery of S. Callisto. A majority elected him to succeed Zephyrinus (*c.* 217). Later, EUSEBIUS OF CAESAREA assigned a length of five years to his pontificate (*Ecclesiastical History* 6.21). The followers of HIPPOLYTUS OF ROME, however, were not prepared to accept Callistus and elected their own leader as bishop, thus making Hippolytus the first ANTIPOPE in a schism that lasted until 235. On Oct. 14, 222, in Rome, Callistus was martyred, probably in a local disturbance in Trastevere, since there is no record of a formal persecution under Emperor Alexander Severus (222–235). He was buried in the cemetery *iuxta Callistum,* possibly on the site of an earlier oratory connected with him (*titulus Callisti*).

Callistus is credited with having stabilized the Saturday fast, three times a year, decreeing abstention from food, oil, and wine according to the prescription of Zechariah 8.19. This is thought to be a source of the EMBER DAYS.

From the *Philosophumena* (9.11–12; 10.27) of Hippolytus, a prejudiced but factually correct source, we have considerable information about Callistus. His dispute with Hippolytus was primarily doctrinal. Callistus began by condemning Sabellius, the chief exponent of MONARCHIANISM that tended to overemphasize the unity of persons in the Blessed Trinity. This did not, however, reconcile him with Hippolytus, since Callistus apparently could not accept Hippolytus's theory of the Logos, which seemed to exaggerate the distinction between Father and Son and thus savored of ditheism. Since Callistus had condemned Sabellius for heresy, it is difficult to believe that he embraced the Monarchian position as asserted by Hippolytus (*Philos.* 9.12). Undoubtedly the dispute was due, in part, to inconsistencies in theological terminology, a defect that was remedied only in the course of time. Callistus also introduced a number of disciplinary changes that brought the ire of Hippolytus upon him. He authorized the ordination of men who had been married two and even three times; he recognized the validity of marriages between free women and slaves; and he maintained that the Church had authority to absolve from all sins, and should adopt a policy of mercy toward the *LAPSI* who had compromised their faith by temporary apostasy, but had repented. The last decision became a matter of controversy in the Church for years, dividing the clergy and faithful into two factions: the so-called laxists and the rigorists. Callistus was not innovator so much as a realist who accepted that the church is a community of sinners and not the rigorists' community of saints.

It is probable that TERTULLIAN'S famous sarcasm concerning a peremptory edict did not refer to Callistus: ''I hear that an edict has been published, and a peremptory one: the bishop of bishops, that is the Pontifex Maximus, proclaims: I remit the sins of adultery and fornication for those who have done penance'' (*De pudicitia* 1). This decision came to be known as the Edict of Callistus; many historians maintained that it had reference to Pope Callistus, and contained a sarcastic allusion to the PRIMACY. Contemporary scholars generally believe that it was aimed at the bishop of Carthage, but no text has survived.

Callistus is the first pope, except for Peter, whose name was commemorated as a martyr in the oldest martyrology of the Roman Church, the fourth-century *DEPOSITIO MARTYRUM* (*c.* 354). A late tradition alleged that his relics were transported to France, while another maintained that they were deposited in the crypt of S. Maria in Trastevere under Pope INNOCENT I (401–417). His tomb in the cemetery of Calepodius, on the Via Aurelia, was discovered in 1960 in the remains of an oratory erected there by Pope JULIUS I in the fourth century, and described by the seventh-century *Salzburg Itinerary.* The crypt is decorated with paintings depicting his martyrdom. The name and picture of Callistus also appear on a piece of gold glass, now in the Cabinet des Médailles in Paris. The famous catacomb of San Callisto is named after him because Zephyrinus put him in charge of the first public Christian cemetery on the Appian Way.

Feast: Oct. 14.

Bibliography: *Liber pontificalis,* ed. L. DUCHESNE, 1 (Paris 1886–92): 141–142; 3 (Paris 1938):73–74. A. FLICHE and V. MARTIN, eds., *Histoire de l'église depuis les origines jusqu'à nos jours* (Paris 1935–) 2:101–103, 404–415. E. CASPER, *Primatus Petri* (Weimar 1927). E. CASPAR, *Geschichte des Papsttums von den Anfängen bis zur Höhe der Weltherrschaft,* 2 v. (Tübingen 1930–33) 1:22–47, 572–575. C. CECCHELLI, *Tre deportati in Sardegna* (Rome 1939). J. QUASTEN, *Patrology,* 3 v. (Westminster, Md. 1950–) 2:233–235. C. DALY, *Texte und Untersuchungen zur Geschichte der altchristlichen Literatur* 3:176–182, edict. G. FERRETTO, *Biblioteca sanctorum* 3:681–689. K. BEYSHCLAG *Theologische Zeitschrift* 20:103–124. U. FASOLA, *Lexikon für Theologie und Kirche,* ed. J. HOFER and K. RAHNER, 10 v. (2d, new ed. Freiburg 1957–65) 6:20–24, tomb. E. FERGUSON, ed., *Encyclopedia of Early Christianity* (New York 1997) 1.204–205. J. N. D. KELLY, *Oxford Dictionary of Popes* (New York 1986) 13–14. A. BARUFA, *Le Cataombe di S. Callisto. Storia, archeologia, fede* (Vatican City 1992). M. MAZZA, ''Deposita pietatis. Problemi dell'organizzazione economica in comunità cristiane tra II e III secolo,'' *Atti dell' Accademia Romanistica Constantiana. IX Convenga internazionale* (Naples 1993) 187–216. A. STEWART-SIKES, ''Papyrus Oxyrhynchus 5: A Prophetic Protest from Second Century Rome,'' *Studia Patristica* 31: 196–205.

[J. CHAPIN]

CALLISTUS II, POPE

Pontificate: Feb. 2, 1124 to Dec. 13 or 14, 1124; b. Guido, date unknown. The fifth son of Count William of Burgundy, he was related to several royal houses of Europe. A member of the Church-reform party, he became archbishop of Vienne in 1088. When appointed papal legate in France by PASCHAL II, who apparently also made him a cardinal, Guido strenuously opposed Paschal's ''Privilege,'' extorted by HENRY V, which would have surrendered most of the political positions held by Church officials in the empire. After protesting the ''Privilege'' at the Lateran synod of 1112, he called and presided over a synod of French and Burgundian bishops at Vienne that denounced lay investiture (*see* INVESTITURE STRUGGLE) of the clergy as heretical, and excommunicated Henry V as hostile to the welfare of the Church. When GELASIUS II, who succeeded Pascal, refused to confirm the ''Privilege,'' the angry Henry V set up Archbishop Burdinus of Braga as antipope Gregory VIII and installed him in Rome. Gelasius was forced to spend his brief, harassed pontificate in exile and died at Cluny within a year. Some of the cardinals who had come to Cluny now elected Guido, who was crowned in Vienne on Feb. 9, 1119.

Callistus took immediate steps to establish peace with the imperial government, since both sides were tired of the long investiture struggle. Henry V favorably received a papal embassy and temporarily withdrew his support from Gregory VIII. A meeting between pope and emperor was arranged for Mousson. After presiding over a synod at Toulouse (1119), which was mainly concerned with reform of the French Church, Callistus proceeded to Reims, where he held a great council (1119), attended by some 400 prelates and by Louis VI of France. Negotiations with Henry V broke down after he came to Mousson with a large army, and papal plans to meet with the emperor were abandoned. The emperor was excommunicated again (October 1119).

Callistus then went to Rome, where he was enthusiastically received by the people, who had meanwhile driven out the antipope. He allied himself with the Normans, who aided in the capture of Gregory VIII. Gregory, who had taken refuge at Sutri, was held prisoner, and subsequently other enemies of the pope in Italy were overcome. The pope then sent a new embassy to Henry V. A preliminary understanding with a truce was arranged at Würzburg in 1121. The following year, the famous Concordat of WORMS (1122) was arrived at in a synod held in that city. Because of the pope's patience and perseverance, the concordat was a reasonably satisfactory arrangement for both sides, though a complete victory for neither, bringing peace to both empire and Church, to the great relief of Christendom. The first LATERAN COUNCIL (1123), convoked by Callistus, solemnly confirmed the Concordat of Worms and issued decrees against clerical marriage (*see* CELIBACY) and SIMONY. It provided penalties against violators of the Truce of God (*see* PEACE OF

GOD) and against forgers of ecclesiastical documents, and renewed indulgences for crusading. During his pontificate Callistus also secured from HENRY I OF ENGLAND the acceptance of his candidate THURSTAN for the archbishopric of York, transferred metropolitan rights in Spain from the ancient See of Merida (Emerita) to the popular See of SANTIAGO DE COMPOSTELA, and settled the old French rivalry over metropolitan fights between Aries and Vienne in favor of the latter.

Bibliography: P. JAFFÉ, *Regesta pontificum romanorum ab condita ecclesia ad annum post Christum natum 1198*, ed. S. LÖWENFELD (2d ed. Leipzig 1881–88; repr. Graz 1956) 1:780–821. U. ROBERT, ed., *Bullaire du pape Calixte* II, 2 v. (Paris 1891); *Histoire du pape Calixte II* (Paris 1891). C. J. VON HEFELE, *Histoire des conciles d'après les documents originaux*, tr. H. LECLERCQ (Paris 1907–38) 5.1:568–592, *passim.* A. FLICHE and V. MARTIN, eds., *Histoire de l'église depuis les origines jusqu'à nos jours* (Paris 1935) 8:378–395. É. JORDAN, *Dictionnaire d'histoire et de géographie ecclésiastiques*, ed. A. BAUDRILLART et al. (Paris 1912) 11:424–438. J. HALLER, *Das Papsttum* (Stuttgart 1959–53) 2:505–512, 623. J. LAUDAGE, *Lexikon für Theologie und Kirche* (3d ed. Freiburg 1993) 2:892. B.M. JENSEN, ''Callixtus II Consecrated the Cathedral of Piacenza in 1123?'' *Classica et Mediaevalia* 48 (1997) 389–406. *Calixte II. Pape de 1119 à 1124, archevêque de Vienne, sous le nom de Gui de Vienne de 1088 à 1119* (Vienne 1988). J. N. D. KELLY, *Oxford Dictionary of Popes* (New York 1986) 164.

[D. D. MCGARRY]

CALLISTUS III, POPE

Pontificate: April 8, 1455, to Aug. 6, 1458; b. Alfonso de BORGIA Játiva (near Valencia), Spain, Dec. 31, 1378; d. Rome, Italy. Born in the year the WESTERN SCHISM began, he studied and taught law at the University of Lérida, where he was a cathedral canon before he became a jurist in the service of his king, Alfonso V of Aragon. Pope Martin V made him bishop of Valencia in 1429 for having obtained the resignation of antipope Clement VIII (Gil S. Muñoz, who succeeded BENEDICT XIII) in Peñíscola; Eugene IV created him a cardinal for his services in separating Alfonso V from the supporters of the Council of BASEL. A man of austere life who possessed the mind of a medieval canonist, he was elected pope as a neutral, since it was impossible to elect anyone from the COLONNA or ORSINI camps.

He was not a dedicated patron of HUMANISM, as his predecessor NICHOLAS V had been, but neither was he its enemy. The policy of a balance of power in Italy that he followed had been begun by Nicholas with the Peace of Lodi, resulting in the Italian League (1454–55) of Venice, Milan, Florence, Rome, and Naples. His main goal, a crusade, made urgent after the fall of CONSTANTINOPLE to the Turks (May 29, 1453), depended on peace in Italy. Hence in 1455–56 he opposed by spiritual and military means the Sienese conquests of the condottiere Giacomo Piccinino, who was protected by Alfonso V of Aragon and (after 1442) of Naples. On Alfonso's death (June 27, 1458), Callistus asserted the rights of the Holy See to the Kingdom of Naples, which had been left by Alfonso to his natural son, Ferrante I.

The CRUSADE against the Turks was Callistus' greatest achievement. The papal legate to the HOLY ROMAN EMPIRE and to HUNGARY, Cardinal Juan de CARVAJAL, won the promise of aid from Emperor Frederick III and the complete support of King Ladislaus V of Hungary and Bohemia. John Hunyadi, exregent of Hungary, and St. JOHN CAPISTRAN, who preached the crusade, led the troops that forced the Turks to raise the siege of Belgrade. Confronted with opposition to this enterprise from German princes and prelates, who regarded the tithes to be levied as a burden on the German Church, Callistus turned to Scanderbeg (George Castriota), Prince of Albania, and to Alfonso V. After the defeat of the Turkish fleet at Metelino by the papal Aragonese fleet under Cardinal Scarampo, and after the land victory of Scanderbeg at Tomorniza (both in 1457), the pope formed an alliance with Stephen Thomas, King of Bosnia, and with Matthias Corvinus (Hunyadi), the new King of Hungary, as he was not able to rely for aid on Germany, Burgundy, France, Castile, or Portugal. At the same time, he was reconciled with the new King of Bohemia, George Poděbrad.

The Turkish threat kept Callistus from the needed reform of the Church, but his excessive nepotism was a contributing factor. The swarm of Valencians and Catalans at his court can be explained only by the animosity and ill-will shown by Italians at the election of a foreign pope and by the presence of numerous Spaniards in Naples after its occupation by Alfonso V. Some of them, however, e.g., Abp. Pedro de Urrea of Tarragona and Antoni Olzina, were more loyal to the king than to the pope. Callistus' nephews Rodrigo de Borgia (later Pope ALEXANDER VI), bishop of Gerona, Oviedo, and Valencia and vice-chancellor of the States of the Church, and Lluís Joan del Milà (bishop of Segorbe), cardinals in 1456, were known for loose and worldly lives. Rodrigo's brother Pere Lluís (duke of Spoleto and captain general of the States of the Church) had to flee Rome on the day of Callistus' death, and he himself died in nearby Civitavecchia when the Italians vented their hate against the Catalans. Callistus died on the Feast of the TRANSFIGURATION, which he had instituted to commemorate the victory at Belgrade.

Bibliography: Sources. POGGIO BRACCIOLINI, *Vitae quorundum pontificum* in *Liber pontificalis*, ed. L. DUCHESNE (Paris 1886–92, 1958) 2:546–560. Cf. C. DA CAPODIMONTE, ''Poggio Bracciolini autore delle anonime *Vitae quorandam pontificum*,'' *Rivista di storiaa della Chiesa in Itallia* 14 (1960) 27–47. *Magnum* *bullarium Romanum a beato Leone Magno usque ad S. D. N. Benedictum XIII.*, 8 v. (new ed. Luxembourg 1727) v.1. F. FITA, "Restos mortales de C. III y Alejandro VI," *Boletin de la Real Academia de la Historia* 18 (1891) 159–166. L. VON PASTOR, ed., *Ungedruckte Akten*, v.1 (Freiburg 1904) 37–91. F. MARTORELL, "Un inventario della biblioteca di C. III," *Miscellanea Francesco Ehrle*, v.5 (*Studi e Testi* 41; 1924) 166–191. J. RIUS SERRA, "Un inventario de joyas de C. III," *Analecta Sacra Tarraconensia* 5 (1929) 305–320; ed., *Regesto ibérico de C. III*, 2 v. (Barcelona 1948–58). O. RAYNALDUS, *Annales ecclesiastici*, ed. J. D. MANSI, 15 v. (Lucca 1747–56) 10:13–157. Literature. J. STEIN, *C. III et la comè'te de Halley* (Rome 1909). J. B. ALTISENT JOVÉ, *Alfonso de Borja en Lérida* (Lérida 1924). L. PASTOR, *The History of the Popes from the Close of the Middle Ages* (Freiburg 1955–) 2:315–495. J. SANCHIS SIVERA, "El obispo de Valencia, Don Alfonso de Borja (C. III), 1429–1458," *Boletin de la Real Academia de la Historia* 88 (1926) 241–313. J. RIUS, "Catalanes y Aragoneses en la corte de C. III," *Analecta Sacra Tarraconensia* 3 (1927) 193–330. P. PASCHINI, "La flotta di C. III, 1455–1458," *Archivio della Società romana di storia patria* 53–55 (1930–32) 177–254. L. GÓMEZ CANEDO, *Un español al servicio de la Santa Sede, Don Juan de Carvajal* (Madrid 1947). F. BABINGER, *Mehmed der Eroberer und seine Zeit* (Munich 1953). G. HOFMANN, "Papst Kalixt III. und die Frage der Kircheneinheit im Osten," Misc Mercati, 6 v. (*Studi e Testi* [Rome 1900–] 121–126; 1946) 3:209–237. A. M. ALBAREDA, "Il bibliotecario di C. III," *ibid.* 4:178–208. C. M. DE WITTE, "Les Bulles pontificales et l'expansion portugaise au XVe siècle," *Revue d'histoire ecclésiastique* 51 (1956) 413–453, 809–836. P. BREZZI, "La politica di C. III," *Studi romani* 7 (1959) 31–41.

[M. BATLLORI]

CALLISTUS III, ANTIPOPE

Pontificate: September 1168–Aug. 29, 1178. Known as John, abbot of Struma, a Vallambrosan monastery near Arezzo, he appears to have entered the monastery as a boy. He was a strong and early supporter of the emperor Frederick I Barbarossa (1152–90), and also supported the antipope Victor IV (1159–64). Victor named him cardinal bishop of Albano, and John served in the curias of antipopes Victor and Paschal III (1164–68). He was named successor to antipope Paschal by a small number of schismatic cardinals soon after Paschal's death on Sept. 20, 1168. Callistus was thus the third and last of the imperial antipopes during the schism (1154–78).

Callistus was in a weak position from the beginning. Frederick did not have a direct role in his election and was at the time involved in a serious challenge to his presence in northern Italy by the newly-invigorated Lombard League, which backed Pope Alexander III (1159–81). Indeed, in an effort to end the schism and decrease opposition to imperial policy in Italy, Frederick had recently proposed that both Alexander and antipope Paschal step aside for a new election. Callistus was thus little more than a bargaining chip that Frederick could use to pressure Pope Alexander when necessary. Only Rome, along with parts of the Papal States, Tuscany, and much of the Rhineland recognized him.

Little is known of Callistus's activities as antipope. He resided at Viterbo and sent a legate to Frederick at the diet of Bamberg (June 1169) to seek the emperor's support and encourage a new Italian campaign. He received Frederick's recognition and limited financial support. In 1173 Callistus again sent a legate to Germany for talks between Frederick and Louis VII of France (1137–80). Finally, in 1174 Frederick began his fifth expedition into Italy, which was effectively to end in his defeat at Legnano (May 29, 1176). At that point the emperor rightly saw that by reconciling himself with the church he might simultaneously gain the support of many German nobles (who used Alexander's condemnation of Frederick as reason to revolt), take away much of the Lombard cause against him, and even open the way to imperial influence in Sicily. Thus he came to a preliminary agreement with Alexander, at Anagni in November 1176, and then more completely in Venice (July 23, 1177). Among the terms of the truce were provisions that the emperor would recognize Alexander as pope. Callistus was to be appointed an abbot and all schismatic clergy were to be provided for in some equitable way.

Callistus refused to capitulate and remained at Viterbo, backed by the prefect of Rome, who held out against Alexander and Frederick for reasons of his own. After Alexander returned to the city in the company of Frederick's chancellor, Archbishop Christian of Mainz, Callistus was forced to flee Viterbo for Monte Albano (near Mentana). After much negotiation, Callistus agreed to surrender to Alexander. He submitted to the pope at Tusculum on Aug. 29, 1178, and was named rector of Benevento, where he died sometime between 1180 and 1184.

Bibliography: L. DUCHESNE, ed. *Liber Pontificalis* (Paris 1886–92; repr. 1955–57) 2.419–20, 439, 441, 450. P. JAFFÉ, *Regesta pontificum Romanorum* (Leipzig 1885–88; repr. Graz 1956) 2.429–30. F. X. SEPPELT, *Geschichte der Päpste von den Anfängen bis zur Mitte des zwanzigsten Jahrhunderts* (Munich 1954–59) 3.259, 266–75. M. BALDWIN, *Alexander III and the Twelfth Century* (Glen Rock, NJ 1968). K. JORDAN, *Dizionario biografico degli Italiani* (Rome 1973) 16.768–69. J. N. D. KELLY, *The Oxford Dictionary of Popes* (New York 1986) 179–80.

[P. M. SAVAGE]

CALLISTUS ANGELICUDES

14th-century Palamite and mystical writer, probably identical with Angelicudes Melenikeotes, recognized as the founder of a monastery through a patriarchal seal of 1371. He is known in Byzantine literature also as Callistus Meliteniotes or Callistus Telicudes. A. Ehrhard attributed to the authorship of Meliteniotes 30 *Logoi hesychastices paracleseos;* and to Telicudes, a tract on the *hesychastices tribes*. The latter, however, seems to be merely an abbreviated section of the first-named treatise. Both works are apparently parts of a handbook of Hesychastic doctrine.

Bibliography: *Kirche und theolgische Literatur im byzantinischen Reich* 784. G. MERCATI, "Callisto Angelicudes Meliniceota," *Bessarione* 31 (1915) 79–86, repr. in his *Opere minori,* v.3 (*Studi e Testi* 78; 1937) 415–552.

[F. X. MURPHY]

CALLO, MARCEL, BL.

Martyr; b. Rennes, France, Dec. 6, 1921; d. Mauthhausen concentration camp, near Linz, Austria, March 19, 1945. Marcel Callo, one of nine children of a working class family, attended school in Rennes until he was apprenticed to a typographer at age twelve. He became an active member and leader of the Young Christian Workers (*Jeunesse Ouvriere Chretienne* [JOC] or the "Jocistes"). He had just become engaged to marry (August 1942) when the Nazis occupied France. Marcel and his friends helped many escape the Nazis by giving them their Red Cross armbands. When the Nazis forced Marcel into labor at the Walther arms factory in Zella-Mehlis, Thuringia, Germany, he regarded it as an opportunity to evangelize. Within the labor camp he organized the JOC.

He was arrested by the Gestapo (April 19, 1944) for excessive Catholic activity after arranging for a Mass in French. He was held first at Gotha prison, then sent to Flossenbürg concentration camp, and finally, to the Mauthausen concentration camp (Oct. 26, 1944). For a time he sorted rivets for Messerschmitt aircraft at the outlying Gusen I camp, but before long (November 7) he was moved to the Gusen II, where prisoners built airplanes underground in terrible conditions with little food. There Marcel continued to encourage his fellow prisoners until he was hospitalized in the Revier at Gusen (Jan. 5, 1945). He died of malnutrition and exhaustion in the deplorable *Sanitäts-Lager* just beyond the walls of Mauthausen. Marcel was beatified by John Paul II on Oct. 4, 1987.

Feast: April 19.

Bibliography: M. FIÉVET, *Martyrs du nazisme: Marcel Callo, jociste de Rennes (1921–45), mort en martyr au camp de Mauthausen, béatifié à l'occasion du synode des évêques sur l'apostolat des laïcs, Rome, Octobre 1987 et les autres!* (Paris 1987). P. GOUYON, *Marcel Callo, témoin d'une génération* (Paris 1981); *Marcel Callo* (Salzburg 1988). A. MATT, *Einer aus dem Dunkel—Die Befreiung . . .* (Zürich 1988). R. PABEL, *Marcel Callo—Dokumentation* (Eichstaedt-Wien 1991). *L'Osservatore Romano,* English edition, no. 40 (1987): 20.

[K. I. RABENSTEIN]

CALLUS, DANIEL ANGELO PHILIP

Dominican medievalist; b. Malta, Jan. 20, 1888, the son of Paul Callus-Azopardi and Theodora, née Vella; d. Malta, May 26, 1965. He joined the order as a young man and studied at Malta, Fiesole, and Florence, where he took the degree of lector in theology and philosophy and followed university courses in palaeography, history of arts, and Semitic languages. He was ordained and did postgraduate work at the Angelicum in Rome, after which he taught as professor of theology at the Theological College of Malta from 1914 to 1921. Then came his first visit to England, where he was to make his home. He taught at the Dominican House of Studies at Hawkesyard, Staffordshire, from 1921 to 1923 and returned in 1931. He spent the intervening years as regent of studies, first at Viterbo and then in Malta. He took his degree as master of theology in 1924. In 1932 he settled permanently at the Oxford Blackfriars. Father Bede Jarrett, OP, had planned to make Blackfriars a center of scholarship that would be closely linked to the university; in Callus he found the man to realize his hopes. Callus worked under the supervision of the late Sir Maurice Powicke, then Regius Professor of Modern History, and himself became the center of a group of colleagues and pupils interested in medieval thought and learning. He received the degree of doctor of philosophy in 1938. Henceforward he regularly lectured, supervised, and examined and attended faculty meetings in the university; in addition he held the regency of studies at Blackfriars from 1942 to 1954. He read papers at many international congresses, made lecture tours in the U.S., and was visiting lecturer at the Angelicum for the last few years of his life. His researches into the history of early scholasticism took him to libraries all over Europe. The University of Malta honored him with a degree. His busy life as priest and teacher did not prevent him from publishing extensively from 1917 onward. He was the acknowledged expert on the early history of the Oxford schools, especially of Aristotelian studies and of Thomism there. A bibliography of his published work up to 1963, with an appreciation of his life and writings, is to be found in *Oxford Studies Presented to Daniel Callus* [Oxford Historical Society, New Series 16 (Oxford 1964)].

[B. SMALLEY]

CALMET, AUGUSTIN (ANTOINE)

Exegete and historian; b. Ménil-la-Horgne (Meuse), France, Feb. 26, 1672; d. Senones, France, Oct. 25, 1757. After his early studies at Breuil and the University of Pontà-Mousson, he entered the Benedictine Abbey of Saint-Mansuy in Toul and was professed there, Oct. 23,

1689. He studied philosophy at Saint-Evre in Toul and theology at Munster in Alsace and was ordained, March 17, 1696. He became in turn professor at Moyen-Moutier (1698), subprior at Munster (1704), professor at Paris (1706), titular prior of Laye-Saint-Christophe (1716), abbot of Saint-Leopold in Nancy (1718), visitator of the Benedictine Congregation of St. Vanne and St. Hydulphe (1719), president of this congregation (1727), and abbot of Senones (1728).

Calmet was one of the best Catholic exegetes of the 18th century. He endeavored to adhere to the literal sense at a time when the influence of J. B. BOSSUET had made the spiritual and mystical interpretation of Scripture supreme. Yet his exegetical works are merely conscientious compilations and lack true critical judgment. These works include his *Commentaire littéral sur tous les livres de l'Ancient et du Nouveau Testament* (26 v. Paris 1707–16) and *Dictionnaire historique . . . de la Bible* (Paris 1719). Of much greater value is his *Histoire ecclésiastique et civile de la Lorraine* (3 v. Nancy 1728).

Bibliography: P. SCHMITZ, *Dictionnaire d'histoire et de géographie ecclésiastiques* 11:450–453. P. AUVRAY, *Catholicisme* 2:392–393. P. VOLK, *Lexikon für Theologie und Kirche* (Freiburg 1957–65) 2:886. E. KUSCH, *Die Religion in Geschichte und Gegenwart* 1:1587. J. E. MANGENOT, *Dictionnaire de la Bible* 2.1:72–76. F. BECHTEL, *The Catholic Encyclopedia* 3:189.

[M. STRANGE]

CALOCA CORTÉS, AGUSTÍN, ST.

Martyr, priest; b. May 5, 1898, La Presa Ranch, San Juan Bautista del Teúl, Zacatecas, Archdiocese of Guadalajara, Mexico; d. May 25, 1927, Colotitlán, Jalisco, Diocese of Zacatecas. After revolutionaries seized the seminary in Guadalajara, he retreated to his home, then resumed his studies in a minor seminary directed by Fr. MAGALLANES. In 1919, he returned to the one at Guadalajara and was ordained (Aug. 15, 1923). He served as priest of the parish of Totatiche, Jalisco, as well as prefect of its minor seminary. He was also responsible for the surrounding ranches, founded catechetical centers, and organized a weekly social. He was arrested while helping his seminarians to escape and imprisoned with Magallanes at Totatiche. Because of his youth, he was offered his liberty, but he refused unless Magallanes was also released. General Goñi had him transferred to Colotitlán, where the prisoners were lined up against the wall for execution. His body was transferred to the parish church of Totalice (1933). In April 1952, his remains were translated to the parish of San Juan Bautista de Teúl. Fr. Caloca was both beatified (Nov. 22, 1992) and canonized (May 21, 2000) with Cristobal MAGALLANES [*see* MEXICO, MARTYRS OF, SS.] by Pope John Paul II.

Feast: May 25 (Mexico).

Bibliography: J. CARDOSO, *Los mártires mexicanos* (Mexico City 1953). J. DÍAZ ESTRELLA, *El movimiento cristero: sociedad y conflicto en los Altos de Jalisco* (Mexico City 1979). V. GARCÍA JUÁREZ, *Los cristeros* (Fresnillo, Zac. 1990).

[K. I. RABENSTEIN]

CALOV, ABRAHAM

Lutheran dogmatic theologian and polemicist; b. Mohrungen, East Prussia, April 16, 1612; d. Wittenberg, Feb. 25, 1686. He studied at Königsberg (1626–32), received his doctorate at Rostock (1637), and became rector of the gymnasium at Danzig (1643) and pastor of Trinity church. From 1650 until his death, he lived in Wittenberg, holding various academic and ecclesiastic positions. While a delegate to the Thorn Conference (1645), he came in contact with Georg CALIXTUS. From that time on, he devoted himself to polemical activity directed against what he termed the syncretism of Calixtus and his followers. In his *Historia syncretistica* (1682) he attempts, as the outstanding champion of the controversial Lutheran orthodoxy of the 17th century, to show the erroneous agreements between the doctrines of Calixtus and those of Roman Catholics, Calvinists, Arminians, and Socinians. His work in theology, *Systema locorum theologicorum* (12 v. 1655–77), is considered one of the most important productions of the period. Here, as in his *Biblia illustrata* (4 v. 1672–76), he defends Lutheran orthodoxy against the intellectual forces that were preparing the way for the Enlightenment.

Bibliography: E. L. T. HENKE, *Georg Calixtus und seine Zeit,* 2 v. (Halle 1853–56). F. A. G. THOLUCK, *Der Geist der lutherischen Theologen Wittenbergs* (Hamburg 1852). F. LAU, *Die Religion in Geschichte und Gegenwart* 1:1587. R. BÄUMER, *Lexikon für Theologie und Kirche* (Freiburg 1957–65) 2:886.

[C. J. BERSCHNEIDER]

CALUMNY

The blackening of an absent person's good name by telling a deliberate lie about him. This is sometimes called slander. The term ''blackening'' better describes the effects of calumny than do the more general terms ''unjust violation'' and ''injury.'' Just as one's good name bestows a certain luster on a person, calumny either partially blackens or totally obscures this luster. Scripture tells us that ''a good name is more precious than great riches'' (Prv 22.1). In calumny a person steals part or all of another's good name, a good to which the person possesses a right in strict justice. Besides being a violation of the virtue of justice, calumny has the added malice of a lie.

Calumnious remarks can be slight offenses; thus one who tells a lie that does only slight harm to a person's reputation would be guilty of a venial sin. If a lie seriously blackens a person's reputation, the offense is grave. In any actual instance, the extent of the harm done to a person's reputation depends on the esteem in which the calumniated person was held by his fellow men, the crime, sin, or defect falsely attributed to him, and also the credibility of the calumniator. If the person calumniated is held in high esteem, one who falsely attributes a serious crime, sin, or defect to him is guilty of a serious violation of the person's rights. If, on the other hand, the calumniated person does not enjoy a good reputation, the damage to his reputation is slight. If the calumniating person has a reputation for lying or notably exaggerating, his listeners probably do not believe him anyway. In this case, however, the calumniator's evil intention makes his action seriously sinful.

Because calumny blackens a person's good name, the offender is obliged to repair the damage he has done. If other damage, e.g., monetary damage, has been caused and this was foreseen, the calumniator is obliged to repair this also. Theologians agree that a blackened reputation can never be fully restored. The calumniator, however, is obliged to do all he can to restore the person's good name; hence he must first of all withdraw his false statements. He must also speak in a friendly manner about the person, show deference to him, etc. The awareness that a blackened good name can never be adequately restored should serve as an added deterrent to calumnious speech.

See Also: DEFAMATION; DETRACTION; REPUTATION, MORAL RIGHT TO.

Bibliography: B. H. MERKELBACH, *Summa theologiae moralis,* 3 v. (8th ed. Paris 1949) 2:423–432. K. B. MOORE, *The Moral Principles Governing the Sin of Detraction . . .* (Washington 1950).

[K. B. MOORE]

CALUNGSOD, PEDRO, BL.

Also known as ''El Visayo,'' lay catechist and martyr; b. Visayas region of the Philippines *c.* 1654–58; d. Tomhon on San Juan, Ladrones Islands (now Guam, Marianas Islands) April 2, 1672. The only documentation concerning Calungsod's life is found in the materials about his companion in martyrdom, Blessed Fr. Diego Luis de SAN VITORES. Calungsod received his education in minor seminary of Loboc, Bohol, where he learned doctrine, Spanish, and Latin.

Arriving on Guam with the first Jesuit missionaries (June 16, 1668), fourteen-year-old Pedro assisted San Vitores in the evangelization the Marianas Islands, then under the Filipino Diocese of Cebu. During the first six months, the missionaries counted 13,000 baptisms; another 20,000 natives were under instruction. For four years Pedro assisted by teaching Christian hymns and the catechism and serving at Mass until the day the priest and catechist encountered the local chieftain, Matapang and his friend Hirao. Matapang was enraged that San Vitores, at the request of the chief's wife, had baptized his daughter against his will. Pedro had an opportunity to escape, but threw himself in the path of Hirao's spear, offering himself in a fruitless effort to save the priest. San Vitores's and Calungsod's bodies were stripped, tied together to a large rock, and thrown into the Tomhon Bay.

Calungsod's cause was initiated following the beatification (Oct. 6, 1985) of San Vitores, whom he was shielding. Following the declaration of Calungsod as a martyr on Jan. 27, 2000, he was beatified by John Paul II on March 5, 2000. He is the patron of Filipino youth.

Feast: April 1 (Philippines).

Bibliography: *Father San Vitores, His Life, Times, and Martyrdom*, ed. E. G. JOHNSTON (Agana, Guam 1979). C. G. AREVALO, *Pedro Calungsod* (Manila 1999). F. GARCÍA, *Sanvitores in the Marianas*, tr. F. PLAZA (Mangilao, Guam 1980). A. DEL LEDESMA, *Mission in the Marianas: An Account of Father Diego Luis de Sanvítores and His Companions, 1669–1670*, tr. WARD BARRETT of *Noticia de los progressos de nuestra Santa Fe, en las Islas Marianas . . . desde 15 de mayo de 1669* (Minneapolis 1975). I. LEYSON, *Pedro Calungsod: Prospects of a Teenage Filipino* (Cebu, Philippines 1999). J. M. S. LUENGO, *Pedro Calungsod: The Visayo protomartyr in Tumhon, Guam* (Tubigon, Bohol, Philippines 1998). P. MURILLO VELARDE, *The ''Reducción'' of the Islands of the Ladrones, the Discovery of the Islands of the Palaos, and Other Happenings*, tr. F. E. PLAZA (Mangilao, Guam 1987). J. N. TYLENDA, *Jesuit Saints & Martyrs* (Chicago 1998), 337–39.

[K. I. RABENSTEIN]

CALVARY

The site of the Crucifixion of Jesus, identified with Golgotha and the Place of the Skull (Mt 27.33; Mk 15.22; Jn 19.17). The Greek equivalent is κρανίου τόπος, which in Lk 23.33 is given as the name of the Crucifixion site without mention of the Aramaic form Golgotha (skull). It is not known why the place was so called. Jerome suggested that the skulls of criminals lay about unburied; according to an early Christian tradition cited by Origen, it was believed that the skull of Adam was buried under the cross. But more probably the name is connected with the skull-like shape of the hill or rock.

Calvary was located outside Jerusalem (Mt 27.32; Mk 15.20; Heb 13.12) near a garden, where at least one tomb was located (Jn 19.41–42); it was a conspicuous place near the city (Jn 19.20), easily seen from a distance (Mk 15.40; Lk 23.49), and probably near a country road (Mt 27.39; Mk 15.29). The traditional site of the Crucifixion dates back to the 4th century, when the Emperor Constantine (324–337) laid bare the rock and erected there the church of the Holy Sepulcher and the Resurrection. Calvary or Golgotha is located today within the compound of the Holy Sepulcher. Until A.D. 43, this site lay outside the northern wall of Jerusalem. Under Emperor Hadrian (A.D. 117–138), Jerusalem was rebuilt and renamed Aelia Capitolina; the Calvary or Golgatha area and the Holy Sepulcher were covered with rubble and formed part of the forum of the new city. Today, sections of the original walls of the city, whose exact line has not yet been traced, can be seen. The small, modern chapel of the Holy Sepulcher is built over the bedrock on which the original tomb of Christ once stood.

See Also: SEPULCHER, HOLY.

Bibliography: C. KOPP, *Lexikon für Theologie und Kirche,* ed. J. HOFER and K. RAHNER, 10 v. (2d, new ed. Freiburg 1957–65); suppl., *Das ZweiteVatikanische Konzil: Dokumente und kommentare,* ed. H. S. BRECHTER et al., pt. 1 (1966) 4:1046–47; *The Holy Places of the Gospels,* tr. R. WALLS (New York 1963) 374–388. *Encyclopedic Dictionary of the Bible,* translated and adapted by L. HARTMAN (New York, 1963) 887–888; 1021–23. L. H. VINCENT and F. M. ABEL, *Jérusalem nouvelle,* v. 2 of *Jérusalem,* 2 v. in 4 (Paris 1912–26). A. PARROT, *Golgotha and the Church of the Holy Sepulcher,* tr. E. HUDSON (New York 1957). J. SIMONS, *Jerusalem in the Old Testament* (Leiden 1952).

[S. MUSHOLT]

CALVERT

The Calvert family played a prominent role in the establishment of an English colonial settlement that welcomed Catholics. Maryland was the center of Catholic life and culture in the 13 colonies at the time of the formation of the U.S.

George. First Lord Baltimore, founder of Maryland; b. Yorkshire, England, *c.* 1580; d. April 13, 1632. Leonard, a gentleman, and Alice (Crosland) Calvert, both Catholics, were his parents. During George's childhood, Leonard conformed to the Church of England under the pressure of penalties and the threatened arrest of his wife. At about the age of 12, George was placed under the instruction of an Anglican clergyman and was later graduated from Trinity College, Oxford, in 1597. Leonard won public office, thus opening the way for his son's subsequent career. George married Anne Mynne. After leaving college he became secretary to Sir (later Lord) Robert Cecil, then clerk of the privy council, to which office he soon succeeded. He served in Parliament from 1609 to 1624. In 1617 he was knighted and two years later became one of the principal secretaries of state, a sign of his friendship with the ruling House of Stuart. He was raised to peerage in 1625 and named Baron of Baltimore in the County of Longford in Ireland. His interests and services to the King included a commission for securing the religious pacification of Ireland through conformity; a Latin translation of the King's tract against a Dutch theologian; and support of the Spanish marriage for Prince Charles, to which some Catholic noblemen looked for relief from disabilities.

By 1620 Baltimore had become involved in colonizing activities with two Catholic families, the Arundells and the Howards. In 1628 he brought his family to his own chartered colony of Avalon in Newfoundland, and the following year visited Virginia. Baltimore's return to Catholicism had occurred not later than 1625 so his reception in Virginia was hostile. The king eased the ensuing hardships, acceding to Baltimore's desire for a colony free of religious oppression. The Maryland Charter reflected the flexibility of Baltimore in Church-State matters. He had earlier demonstrated this attitude when he signed a Catholic Remonstrance of Grievances stating that Catholics in England need not conform to what was purely disciplinary in the practices of Catholic states. The broad meaning of the charter did not require the application of discriminatory English statutes to the new colony.

Cecil. Eldest son of George, second Lord Baltimore, colonizer and proprietor of Maryland; b. London, 1606; d. London, Nov. 30, 1675. He was graduated from Oxford in 1621 and 8 years later, himself a Catholic, he married the Catholic Lady Anne Arundell of Wardour. Within a decade of his father's death, Cecil had successfully planted a colony of diverse faiths in Maryland. Before the departure for Maryland of the ''Ark'' and the ''Dove'' in 1633, he issued a memorable pamphlet, ''Objections Answered,'' which justified his experiment with the principles of religious toleration and pluralism. Baltimore commissioned his brother, Leonard Calvert (1610–47), governor of the colony, enjoining him to enforce an ''Instruction'' designed to prevent religious disputes.

Baltimore did not succeed in providing the basic laws for Maryland. The colonists themselves had set about this work shortly after their arrival in America. John Lewger, secretary of the council, then tried to impose Baltimore's own code of laws. Like similar ones in England it made reference to penalties for blasphemy and to other religious matters. Thomas Cornwallis successfully led the assembly opposition, which was also defending its right to initiate legislation. The dominantly Catholic assembly adopted the TOLERATION ACT OF 1639, which contained none of the controversial religious references of Baltimore's code. Instead, emphasis was put on the rights of Englishmen, whether Christian or not, and the state relaxed its authority over religion, in keeping with the views of English Catholics unsympathetic to the confessional-state theory.

A controversy between Baltimore and the Jesuits arose over matters related to these Church-State considerations. The original core of contention was the Jesuit title to land grants from the Native Americans. When the Jesuit Thomas Copley made dubious applications of Church law and teaching to this question, Calvert invoked the principle of the Remonstrance of the first Lord Baltimore. Henry More, the major Jesuit superior, did not support Copley's contentions and Baltimore did nothing about the legitimate basis of grievance originally stated by the Jesuits.

Although Baltimore, as a Cavalier, inevitably became an opponent of Parliamentarians and Puritans, he was not bitterly partisan. Amid the discriminatory measures that came into law during Puritan control in England, he secured passage of the Toleration Act of 1649 in Maryland. Peace did not entirely return, however, until 1660 when Baltimore's half-brother, Philip Calvert, assumed the governorship.

Charles. The third Lord Baltimore, last Catholic proprietor; b. London, 1629; d. Epson, Surrey, Feb. 20, 1715. He was the eldest son of Cecil and Anne (Arundell) Calvert and married Jane Lowe, widow of Henry Sewall of Maryland. To them was born Benedict Leonard, fourth Lord Baltimore and first Protestant proprietor of Maryland. Charles served as governor from 1661 to 1684, became lord proprietor in 1675, and interpreted proprietary authority and privilege strictly. He required property holding for membership in the lower house of the assembly, which had challenged his aristocratic rule. The policy affected Catholic freemen, who nevertheless saw in a strong proprietary party a defense of their religious freedom.

A Protestant revolution in England in 1688 was all that was needed to induce anti-Catholic feeling to support the overthrow of the Calverts in Maryland. It was effected by Coode's Rebellion and a royal colony was created, the Church of England established, and in 1718 an estimated 10 per cent of the population were disfranchised for their Catholicism. Baltimore's son Benedict Leonard conformed to the Church of England and thereby qualified for the proprietorship in 1715. Neither father nor son seemed to possess the character of the first two Barons of Baltimore. But the third Lord Baltimore had brought Charles CARROLL to Maryland during these troubled times as his attorney general, thus ensuring the continuation of Catholic tradition in Maryland's public life. Benedict Leonard survived his father by only a few months and his son Charles assumed the proprietorship while still in his minority.

John Calvin.

Bibliography: W. H. BROWNE, *George Calvert and Cecilius Calvert, Barons Baltimore of Baltimore* (New York 1890). T. O. HANLEY, *Their Rights and Liberties: The Beginnings ot Religious and Political Freedom in Maryland* (Westminster, Md. 1959). J. M. IVES, *The Ark and the Dove* (New York 1936). e

[T. O. HANLEY]

CALVIN, JOHN

After Martin Luther, the most important Protestant reformer and theologian; b. Noyon, France, July 10, 1509; d. Geneva, May 27, 1564. Calvin, influenced by Luther, with whom his background and temperament are in sharp contrast, gave Protestant doctrine its most incisive and systematic formulation. His INSTITUTES OF THE CHRISTIAN RELIGION, which first appeared in 1536, is early Protestantism's greatest theological work. Calvin's thought and influence, emanating from Geneva, where he lived without interruption from late 1541 to his death, dominated Protestantism in France, the Netherlands, and Scotland. Calvinism also became a strong movement in England and in parts of Germany and central Europe.

Early Years. Calvin was born to a prosperous family. His father, Gérard Cauvin (Calvin is the Latinized form), had settled in 1481 in the episcopal town of Noyon in Picardy, where he became a solicitor and fiscal agent for the diocese, a secretary to the bishop, and a procurator of the cathedral chapter. His mother was Jeanne Le Franc, the daughter of a retired innkeeper from Cambrai. John was the second of four sons and two daughters. His father's close relations with the bishop and with the cathedral chapter opened the way toward ecclesiastical careers for Calvin and his brothers. ''My father intended me as a young boy for theology,'' he writes in the autobiographical preface to his *Commentary on the Psalms* (1557). His early schooling was in the local Collège des Capettes where he proved a serious and able student. In 1521 he received a cathedral benefice by way of endowment for his studies; in 1527 he was given a second benefice.

Training at Paris. When he was 14, Calvin was sent to Paris with three young members of the noble Hangest family—Charles de Hangest was Bishop of Noyon—to continue his studies. For a short time he attended the Collège de la Marche, where he studied grammar and rhetoric under the humanist Mathurin Cordier and began a lifelong friendship with this scholar, who years later joined him in Geneva. He soon transferred to the austere Collège de Montaigu for theology. There he was introduced to nominalist theology under the auspices of John Major and apparently undertook the study of the early Fathers, especially St. Augustine. In these formative years he became intimately acquainted with the family of Guillaume Cop, the scholarly physician of Francis I, and formed a close association with a humanist cousin, Pierre Robert OLIVÉTAN, who had already been influenced by the Lutheran teachings. In 1528 Calvin received his master of arts degree at Paris, but about this time his father had a change of mind about theology and directed him to the study of law, which he deemed more lucrative. This change of mind has been linked to a dispute that Calvin *père* was having with the cathedral chapter in Noyon over the closing of an estate and that resulted in his excommunication. In obedience to his father Calvin proceeded to the University of Orléans, where he studied under the famous French jurist Pierre de l'Estoile. The following year, attracted by the reputation of the Italian jurist Andrea Alciati, he went on to Bourges. At both Orléans and Bourges he also pursued his humanist studies and interests, learning Greek from the German Lutheran scholar Melchior Wolmar.

The illness and death of his father in May 1531 occasioned Calvin's hurried return to Noyon and terminated his studies in law. Free now to devote himself to the literary scholarship that most interested him, he returned to Paris and attended the new Collège de France, recently founded by Francis I. He continued his Greek with Pierre Danès and studied Hebrew with François Vatable. In April 1532, he published at his own expense his first book, a commentary on Seneca's *De clementia,* a treatise in the tradition of Erasmus and Budé, intended to launch the young humanist on his scholarly career.

The Sudden Conversion. Humanist study was not to be Calvin's life work, or long remain his chief preoccupation. Sometime in late 1533 or early 1534 he underwent, in his own words, a ''sudden conversion'' and embraced the doctrines of the Protestant reformers. Neither the time nor the circumstances are known with exactness. (Discussion in Wendel, 37–44.) One event closely connected with this great turn in his life was the inaugural address that his friend Nicholas Cop, the son of the royal physician and the new rector of the University of Paris, delivered on All Saints Day, 1533. The address, borrowing passages from Erasmus and Luther, brought speedy action by the Parlement of Paris against Cop, who fled to Basel, and the others suspected of harboring heretical ideas. Calvin, who for a time was thought to have been the author of the discourse, was threatened with arrest and took refuge with a friend, Louis du Tillet, at Angoulême. There in temporary retirement, with a large library at his disposal, he gathered his thoughts and perhaps arrived at the great decision to break with the Church and devote himself wholly to the cause of Protestant reform. During these critical days he visited the famous Lefèvre d'Etaples, the humanist and scriptural scholar, then living under the protection of Marguerite of Angoulême at her court at Nérac. In May 1534 he returned to Noyon to surrender his ecclesiastical benefices, and at the end of the year, as a result of the stringent measures being taken against heretics, he left France for haven in Protestant Basel.

Publication of the Institutes. It was in Basel that his career as reformer and theologian began. In contact and correspondence with Protestant leaders in the Swiss and Rhenish cities, he undertook a formulation of the new theological ideas under debate. *See* CALVINISM; PREDESTINATION (IN NON-CATHOLIC THEOLOGY); INFRALAPSARIANS (SUBLAPSARIANS); SUPRALAPSARIANS; ARMINIANISM; JUSTIFICATION; CONFESSIONS OF FAITH II, PROTESTANT.

These ideas he published in March 1536 in *Institutio religionis Christianae* (*Institutes of the Christian Religion*), the first edition of his master work, which was to reappear in several enlarged revisions and translations during the course of his life. The *Institutes,* prefaced by a bold letter to Francis I of France, was originally intended to be a statement and defense of the beliefs of the French Protestants then being persecuted. About the time that the treatise appeared Calvin paid a visit to Ferrara to see the Duchess Renée, daughter of the former Louis XII of France and a woman sympathetic to the Protestant movement. He returned to Paris to settle some family business and in June 1536 set out again for asylum abroad. His intention was to go to Strassburg, but war between the French and Emperor Charles V obliged him to take a detour through Geneva. He planned to spend but a night in that town. However, his fellow countryman Guillaume FAREL, who had been working in Geneva to implant the new Gospel, pleaded with him to remain and help in the task. Calvin yielded to Farel's forceful entreaty and made Geneva henceforth the scene of his active ministry.

Protestantism in Geneva. When Calvin came to Geneva, he found a city of 13,000 inhabitants engaged in a struggle to maintain municipal independence against the Duke of Savoy in league with the ousted Bishop of Geneva. The neighboring city of Berne, militantly Protestant since 1528, had aided Geneva, and it was under its auspices that Protestant preachers had entered Geneva as early as 1532. Farel was the most important of these missionaries. In the months prior to Calvin's arrival he had won the city government's acceptance of the new reforms, as well as the proscription of Catholicism, but the task of firmly establishing and organizing the new Genevan church remained. This task Calvin made his own. In January 1537 he submitted a memorandum on church government to the town councils. This was followed by a *Confession of Faith* and a *Catechism.* From the start Calvin envisaged a strict unity of belief and practice and a close supervision of conduct that included the excommunication of recalcitrants.

Exile at Strassburg. The uniformity and discipline that Calvin sought evoked opposition from Catholics as well as from those alarmed at the rigid, theocratic character of the new reforms. In early 1538 the Genevan government passed into the hands of those hostile to Calvin, and in April the town councils, as a result of a dispute over liturgical forms, banished Farel and Calvin from the city. From April 1538 to September 1541 he settled in Strassburg, at the invitation of Martin BUCER, and took charge of a church for French Protestant refugees. Under Bucer's influence he developed his own liturgy in the French language, revised and published in 1539 a new edition of the *Institutes*, lectured on Holy Scripture, and in 1540 published the first of many volumes of scriptural *Commentaries.* He also attended the colloquies at Worms in 1540 and at Regensburg in 1541, convened by Emperor Charles V in an effort to end the religious schism. In 1540 he married the widow of one of his converts, Idelette of Buren, who bore him a son who died soon after birth. She herself died in 1549.

Ecclesiastical Ordinances. Meanwhile, in Geneva there continued division and contention, in the midst of which Calvin's supporters urged his recall. In October 1540, with the city government again controlled by the pro-Calvin faction, an embassy was sent to Strassburg to invite him to return. After hesitation Calvin agreed, and in September 1541 he reentered the city on Lake Leman to remain there for the rest of his life. In November he submitted to the town authorities a new constitution, the *Ecclesiastical Ordinances*, which was approved with modifications to safeguard their own civil jurisdiction. These *Ordinances* were the groundwork of the so-called theocracy in Geneva and became the charter of all future Calvinist church polity. They provided for four ministries or offices—pastors, teachers, elders, and deacons—and for a consistory of elders and pastors to maintain strict discipline in the community. Under the close and constant supervision of this latter body Geneva was intended to become a saintly city, a ''kind of huge convent for laity.'' The *Ordinances* were supplemented in 1542 by the adoption of a new liturgical formula, modeled after that of Strassburg, and the drafting of a new *Catechism* for the instruction of the young.

Conflicts and Executions. A long struggle to reach Calvin's stern ideal ensued. One of the many conflicts was the quarrel with Sebastian CASTELLIO, whom Calvin had made schoolmaster in Geneva. A dispute on certain minor doctrinal points led in 1545 to Castellio's banishment from the city. Jacques Gruet, a more extreme critic of Calvin and the consistory, was found guilty of blasphemy in 1547 and beheaded. In 1551 Jérôme BOLSEC, a former Carmelite who attacked Calvin's doctrine of predestination and defended free will, was imprisoned and subsequently banished. The most famous of all these cases is that of Michael SERVETUS (Michael Served y Reves), Spanish physician and anti-Trinitarian. In flight from France, he passed through Geneva, August 1553, was arrested on Calvin's demand, tried for heresy and blasphemy, and burned alive. Calvin faced political opposition also during these years. From 1546 the ''libertines,'' headed by Ami Perrin, a former supporter of Calvin, criticized the ecclesiastical police system and resisted the encroachments of a theocratic regime. They were overcome in 1554–55 when staunch Calvinists gained full control of the municipal government and affirmed the consistory's right of excommunication. Perrin escaped to Berne, but four other leaders, less fortunate, were caught and beheaded.

Last Years. Although polemical disputes continued with the Lutherans and Italian anti-Trinitarians, Calvin's dominance was secure. Large numbers of refugees flocked to Geneva, and efforts of evangelization abroad, particularly within Calvin's native France, were made. In

1559 the Academy of Geneva was founded at Calvin's suggestion, and Theodore BEZA, later designated as his successor, was made rector. Calvin suffered gravely from ill health in his last years, but he continued the direction of his church and the preaching of the Word as he so sternly conceived it up to the end.

Bibliography: Works. *Joannis Calvini opera quae supersunt omnia,* ed. G. BAUM et al, 59 v. (*Corpus reformatorum* 29–87; 1863–1900); *Institutes of the Christian Religion,* ed. J. T. MCNEILL, tr. F. L. BATTLES, 2 v. (Philadelphia 1960); *Theological Treatises,* tr. J. K. S. REID (Philadelphia 1954); *Commentaries . . . ,* tr. J. HAROUTUNIAN and L. P. SMITH (Philadelphia 1958), includes autobiographical preface 51–57; *Tracts and Treatises . . . ,* ed. T. F. TORRANCE, tr. H. BEVERIDGE, 3 v. (Grand Rapids 1958), includes short life of Calvin by T. BEZA. Literature. É. DOUMERGUE, *Jean Calvin,* 7 v. (Lausanne 1899–1927), the classic life. F. WENDEL, *Calvin . . . ,* tr. P. MAIRET (New York 1963). Q. BREEN, *John Calvin: A Study in French Humanism* (Grand Rapids 1931). J. T. MCNEILL, *The History and Character of Calvinism* (New York 1954). G. E. HARKNESS, *John Calvin: The Man and His Ethics* (New York 1958). P. IMBART DE LA TOUR, *Les Origines de la réforme,* 4 v. (Paris 1905–35). A. GANOCZY, *Calvin, théologien du ministère et de l'Église* (Paris 1964). A. BAUDRILLART, *Dictionnaire de théologie catholique,* ed. A. VACANT, 15 v. (Paris 1903–50; Tables générales 1951–) 2.2:1377–98. O. E. STRASSER and O. WEBER, *Die Religion in Geschichte und Gegenwart,* 7 v. (3d ed. Tübingen 1957–65) 1:1588–99. W. BOUWSMA, *Calvin* (Berkeley 1991). G. DUFFIELD, ed., *John Calvin* (Abingdon 1966). A. GANCZY, *The Young Calvin,* D. FOXGROVER and W. PROVO, Trans. (Edinburgh 1987). T. H. L. PARKER, *John Calvin* (London 1975).

[J. C. OLIN]

CALVINISM

Calvinism is the theological system elaborated by the French reformer, John CALVIN, chiefly in the *Institutes of the Christian Religion* (1536–59). (*See* INSTITUTES OF CALVIN.) This synthesis, which justifies his title as the ''theological genius of the Reformation,'' was the first systematic presentation of Protestantism as well as the doctrinal background for most non-Lutheran churches of the Reformed tradition. This article treats Calvinism under the headings: (1) Calvinism as a system, (2) doctrinal structure, (3) historical development, (4) geographical expansion.

Calvinism as a Theological System

Although Calvinism is a systematic synthesis, it is not a system properly so-called with a central idea, an articulated development, and a rigid harmony such as that of Aristotelianism, Thomism, or Kantianism. Instead Calvinism provides a reasoned and elaborated articulation of evangelical and Protestant principles that relies upon the scriptures as its primary, although not its solitary, defense. Calvin made use of the early Reformation teachings of justification by faith (sola fides) awarded by God's grace (sola gratia), the primacy of the scriptures, and the priesthood of all true believers. He forged these teachings into a new synthesis, a synthesis whose character and practice would develop very differently from the teachings of Lutheranism or Anglicanism, the other dominant magisterial reformations of the sixteenth century.

A Qualified System. Calvin was 27 when he published the first edition of his *Christianae Religionis Institutio.* His intention, as he declared in the ''Epistle to the King'' (Francis I, 1515–47), which prefaced the work, was to write an exposition, as simple as possible, of Christian doctrine by which ''those who are touched with any zeal for religion might be shaped to true godliness'' (*Library of Christian Classics,* 20:9). Throughout the rest of his life, up to the time of the definitive Latin edition (1559) and its French translation (1560), Calvin amplified his treatise, revised and polished it, until it became a complete presentation and an authoritative statement of Calvinism. Unlike many theologians, Calvin's ideas remained consistent over time. The final editions of the *Institutes* did not differ in flavor or teaching from the first 1536 edition. These later editions were distinguished by the degree of elaboration and reasoned argumentation that Calvin employed to defend his central tenets. The training in logic Calvin had received at the Collége de Montaigu and his legal education from the jurists of Orléans and Bourges are evident in the construction of his theological thought.

Central Idea. In the past the tendency has been to regard predestination as the focal point of Calvin's theology. Then the sovereignty of God, and more recently, the divinity of Christ, was proposed as the constitutive principle of Calvinism. What appears the better view today, however, is that Calvinism is not a closed system that revolves around one central idea. Rather than build his system around one pivotal abstract notion, Calvin seems to have preferred to draw together a number of Biblical ideas.

Sources. The first and indisputable source of Calvin's theological system was the Bible. Calvin read and knew the Bible thoroughly, producing commentaries on almost every book. Perhaps no other reformer had such a remarkable knowledge of the Old Testament. Calvin's use of the scriptures is idiosyncratic and bears comparison with his forebear, Martin Luther. Luther stresses that the Bible should be read with an eye toward its illumination of the principles of justification by faith, the *sine qua non* he identifies in the book's teaching. Calvin, on the other hand, argues that all parts of the scripture are of equal applicability to Christians, from the Old Testament books of law and devotion to the Pauline Epistles. The

Bible thus becomes for Calvin a book of texts that need to be read in their totality. He uses the diverse corpus of scriptures to identify a plan for the reform of individuals and society and to confirm his dogmatic positions. The Fathers of the Church form an important background for Calvin's system. He probably made contact with them for the first time at the Collège de Montaigu, and all his life he deepened his knowledge of their Greek and Latin writings (see the exhaustive index of references made in the *Library of Christian Classics*, 21:1592–1634). Though St. John Chrysostom seemed to have been his favorite at one time, St. Augustine's influence was predominant and unique. Calvin read St. Augustine constantly, quoted him frequently, and felt that he was in substantial agreement with him.

Calvin knew and drew upon scholastic authors as well. He was acquainted with the works of St. Anselm, Peter Lombard, and St. Thomas Aquinas. But it is to Duns Scotus and William of Ockham that he appears to have been particularly attracted. A number of authors have traced the Calvinist concept of God to Duns Scotus, and while this view has been questioned by E. Doumergue, A. Lecerf, and others, still the resemblance between Calvin's doctrine on God (e.g., *Institutes* 3.23.2) and Scotus's teaching is too strong to be ignored. The nominalist influence on Calvin's giving primacy to the will of God manifests itself also in his making the efficacy of the Passion of Christ (*Institutes* 2.17.1), the transmission of the sin of Adam (*Institutes* 2.1.8), and the nature of the Mediator as God and man (*Inst.* 2.12.1), all depend upon the decree of God.

Calvin was in full agreement with Luther concerning the fundamental doctrines that surrounded human salvation. After 1536, however, Calvin parted with Luther over the question of the Lord's Supper, and gradually, as Calvin developed his system, differences appeared also on matters of the canon of Scripture, predestination, the church, Christ, and the sacraments. Such differences, while making Calvinism distinct from Lutheranism, are less important than the fundamental agreement on the doctrine of justification by faith.

Philipp Melanchthon, especially through his *Loci Communes* (1531), must be looked upon as one of the sources of Calvin's thought. Calvin wrote the preface to the French translation (Geneva 1546). He, moreover, signed the Confession of Augsburg (1530) and considered that he was in full agreement with it, although he differed with Melanchthon on free will and predestination, as he declared in the preface to Melanchthon's book.

Martin Bucer and Calvin were personal friends and the accord is evident in their works. The influence of Bucer on Calvin is seen particularly in his doctrine of predestination. Calvin adopted Bucer's point of view on the definitive character of predestination and on the part played in it by vocation, justification, and glorification. At the same time, he affirmed the distinction between predestination and foreknowledge whereas Bucer fused them together (*Institutes* 3.21.5).

Doctrinal Structure

An initial general summary of Calvin's doctrines will give perspective to the more detailed study of the Reformer's principal tenets: true wisdom consists in a knowledge of God and of ourselves. Only in the light of the knowledge of God can true self-knowledge be found. God makes Himself known in a twofold revelation; as Creator through the visible universe and as Redeemer, i.e., as the saving knowledge of God, through Scripture alone. Scripture points to Christ, the sole Mediator, by whom salvation is achieved. Salvation is ours through the secret operation of the Holy Spirit and faith. Faith is necessary since by Adam's fall all men are under the blight of sin and divine judgment. Salvation is due to God's mercy, which is extended to those whom in His inscrutable will He has eternally chosen to receive it; others are justly excluded from the operation of His saving grace and suffer the consequences of their sin. Justification is by faith alone, but because of our ignorance and sloth we stand in need of such external helps as the preaching of the Gospel in His church and the administration of the sacraments of baptism and the Lord's supper. The church is both invisible and visible: the invisible church consists of all those who, by confession, example, and participation in the sacraments, profess God and Christ; the visible church has as its marks: the preaching and the hearing of the Gospel and the administration of the sacraments.

The Sovereignty of God. The *Institutes* begins with the statement: ''Nearly all the wisdom we possess, that is to say, true and sound wisdom, consists of two parts: the knowledge of God and of ourselves'' (*Institutes* 1.1.1.). To set forth all relations between God and man is the task of Calvin's entire theological structure. As Luther before him, the Genevan reformer declared that ''our very being is nothing but subsistence in the one God'' (*ibid.*). Whether Calvin intended to counteract Lutheran preoccupation with man or whether through his own firm conviction, he went beyond Luther's idea of gratuitous salvation to that of the complete sovereignty of God. God is all in the order of ends as well as of means; everything tends toward His glory. This doctrine colors his viewpoint concerning rational inquiry into the nature of God. For Calvin it is futile and even presumptuous to ask ''Quis est Deus?'' because ''His essence is incomprehensible; hence his divineness far escapes all human perception'' (*Institutes* 1.5.1.).

Thus Calvin conceives of God in terms of His supreme will that is absolute law, ". . . the truly just cause of all things" (*Institutes* 1.17.1). From it comes every decree by which all is ordered: God has "decreed what he was going to do, and now, by his might, carries out what he has decreed" (*Institutes* 1.16.8). Nor may this decree be questioned. Calvin declares: "God's will is so much the highest rule of righteousness that whatever he wills, by the very fact that he wills it, must be considered righteous. When, therefore, one asks why has God so done, we must reply: because he has willed it" (*Institutes* 3.23.2). Calvin's view of God is also connected with his view of the Bible. No one, according to Calvin, can attain to the knowledge of God unless he is taught by the Holy Scriptures (*Institutes* 1.6.2), which must be read with faith and under the enlightenment of the Holy Spirit, viz, "Therefore Scripture will ultimately suffice for a saving knowledge of God only when it certainly is founded upon the inward persuasion of the Holy Spirit" (*Institutes* 1.8.13).

The Depravity of Man. When man looks at God through the Scriptures he arrives at a knowledge of the complete sovereignty of God. When he looks at himself through the Scriptures, he sees his own total depravity. The Bible gives us this view of man's condition in the story of the Fall, where the image of God in man was not utterly destroyed, ". . . yet it was so corrupted that whatever remains is frightful deformity" (*Institutes* 1.15.4). By total depravity Calvin means the complete inability of man to institute or maintain a right relation with God by his human activity alone. Calvin's emphasis is on the order of salvation and on man's total dependence on God for justification. When Calvin turns momentarily in the *Institutes* (2.2.13) to those interests of man that belong to the present life, such as political doctrine, the mechanical arts, philosophy, and the liberal arts, he readily grants that man can do many wonderful things.

Man's will, however, is bound by the slavery of sin. If the question is raised, "Is man bound to commit sin?" Calvin answers that if man commits sin, he does so voluntarily; he has a strong propensity to sin, but he is not coerced (*Institutes* 2.3.5). Calvin also distinguishes what seems to be a denial of free will. Man's will is not destroyed, according to Calvin, but he cannot of himself will faith: ". . . free will is not sufficient to enable man to do good works, unless he be helped by grace" (*Institutes* 2.2.6.). The reformer's point is that God brings justification by His activity and not man by his. Through justification the sinner is accepted even though he is a sinner, since man is inevitably a sinner.

Faith in Christ. Man in his sinful state needs a saving contact with God. This he obtains in Christ, the sole Mediator, but he does not initiate this movement toward union with Christ. "Faith is the principal work of the Holy Spirit" (*Institutes* 3.1.4). It is "a firm and certain knowledge of God's benevolence toward us, founded upon the truth of the freely given promise in Christ, both revealed to our minds and sealed upon our hearts through the Holy Spirit" (*Institutes* 3.2.7). Even faith, however, of itself has no power nor worth. "We say that faith justifies," explains Calvin, "not because it merits righteousness for us by its own worth, but because it is an instrument whereby we obtain free the righteousness of Christ" (*Institutes* 3.18.8). Here again Calvin insists on the complete power of God and the corresponding impotency of man to do anything of himself to gain salvation. The faith that is received by man from the Holy Spirit unites him to Christ and that union is a precondition whereby ". . . we principally receive a double grace: namely, that being reconciled to God through Christ's blamelessness, we may have in heaven instead of a Judge a gracious Father; and secondly, that sanctified by Christ's spirit we may cultivate blamelessness and purity of life" (*Institutes* 3.11.1). The first of these gifts Calvin calls justification or righteousness and the second, regeneration or sanctification.

By regeneration Christ becomes man's living Lord; he is grafted into the body of Christ. The consequence of this union is that man lives by the spirit of Christ. No longer is life to be lived apart from God; the Christian life ". . . consists in the mortification of our flesh and of the old man, and in the vivification of the Spirit" (*Institutes* 3.3.5). The doctrine of justification, for Calvin, is the "main hinge on which religion turns" (*Institutes* 3.11.1). He views it under the figure of a court trial. The accused is freed or "justified" if he has a witness to affirm his righteousness. "We are sinners and therefore deserve to be condemned, but because of our communion with Christ through faith, we receive His righteousness with him" (*Institutes* 3.11.10). We are not made righteous, but simply are clothed with Christ's righteousness. God, seeing us in Christ, or rather, seeing Christ's righteousness, makes a judgment of "justification." This judicial act has two parts: the forgiveness of sins and the imputation of Christ's righteousness (*Institutes* 3.11.2). These parts are not successive, but are rather like two sides of the one action. Justification, however, is not a single act. If it were, the good works of the once-justified sinner would condemn him again since all man's works are contaminated by sin. God, therefore, not only justifies the sinner but also justifies the justified in his works so that they are not imputed to him as sins. This is Calvin's doctrine of double justification (*Institutes* 3.17.5).

Predestination. Calvin's doctrine of double predestination to election or reprobation is the result of both his logic and his doctrinal principles. Given his conviction on the absolute sovereignty of God and on man's complete inability to contribute to his salvation, the doctrine of predestination is a necessary foundation stone in his system. But practical reasons also entered into its formulation. Only by placing salvation in the divine will could the believer be freed from placing trust in merits and works for salvation. Moreover, such a doctrine was needed for Calvin's ecclesiology. ''We call predestination,'' Calvin explains, ''God's eternal decree, by which he determined with himself what he willed to become of each man. For all are not created in equal condition; rather, eternal life is foreordained for some, eternal damnation for others'' (*Institutes* 3.21.5). This decree of God is so absolute that it is independent of God's foreknowledge, and a fortiori cannot be thwarted by anyone. Grace is irresistible. Just as sinful man necessarily wills evil, so the elect or the justified man necessarily conforms to God's desires. Commenting on St. Augustine's treatise, *De correptione et gratia ad Valentinum* (*Patrologia Latina,* 44: 935, 939, 943), Calvin declares: ''. . . it is . . . grace which forms both choice and will in the heart, so that whatever good works then follow are the fruit and effect of grace; and it has no other will obeying it except the will that it has made'' (*Institutes* 2.3.13). Calvin felt obliged to affirm the doctrine of reprobation. It appalled him, but with invincible candor as well as logic he maintained that the decree of reprobation is incomprehensible but absolutely just. The reprobate is condemned justly (*Institutes* 3.21.7). The ultimate reason of the *decretum horribile* is to manifest the glory of God in the very mystery in which it is veiled.

The Church and the Sacraments. Because of man's ignorance and sloth, he stands in need of external helps to sustain and confirm his gift of faith. Therefore, declares Calvin, God, in accommodation of this infirmity, has established the church and the two sacraments of baptism and the eucharist. The church, which Calvin calls ''mother'' from St. Cyprian (*De catholicae ecclesiae unitate* 6; *Corpus scriptorum ecclesiasticorum latinorum* 3.1.214), is a divinely constituted institution and therefore is necessary. There is no salvation outside it: ''. . . away from her bosom one cannot hope for any forgiveness of sins or any salvation'' (*Institutes* 4.1.4.). The church is both visible and invisible. Under its visible aspect it is the Christian community; the invisible church includes all the elect of God and coincides with both the communion of the saints and with the body of Christ. The visible church, because it includes reprobates in its midst, is to that extent not the body of Christ. But it does not follow that two churches exist. Rather, it is one church under two aspects: invisible insofar as it is an object of faith, or as God sees it; visible as it is an object of experience and as it appears to men (*Institutes* 4.1.7). To judge the presence of the true church, Calvin, as Luther before him in the Augsburg Confession (art. 7), sets forth two objective criteria: ''Whenever we see the Word of God purely preached and heard, and the sacraments administered according to Christ's institution, there, it is not to be doubted, a church of God exists'' (*Institutes* 4.1.9).

Calvin defines a sacrament as ''an outward sign by which the Lord seals on our consciences the promises of his good will toward us in order to sustain the weakness of our faith; a testimony of divine grace toward us, confirmed by an outward sign, with mutual attestation of our piety toward him'' (*Institutes* 4.14.1). In Calvin's doctrine, the sacraments do not contain or confer grace but mirror the reality that they symbolize. The reality, promised by Christ and made effective by Him, is given at the same time that the material symbols of the sacraments are received. Thus Calvin says in regard to the eucharist: ''Now, if it be asked nevertheless whether the bread is the body of Christ, and the wine his blood, we should reply that the bread and wine are visible signs, which represent to us the body and the blood; but that the name and title of body and blood is attributed to them, because they are as instruments by which our Lord Jesus Christ distributes them to us.'' Calvin continues: ''It is a spiritual mystery, which cannot be seen by the eye, nor comprehended by the human understanding. It is therefore symbolized by visible signs, as our infirmity requires, but in such a way that it is not a bare figure, but joined to its reality and substance'' (*Short Treatise on the Lord's Supper,* 2. *Library of Christian Classics,* 22:147). Thus the effects of the sacraments are given because of the promise of Christ, are received by faith, are gained by the elect alone, and are sealed by the outward signs. They bring man into communion with Christ, from whom he receives everything that Christ gained by his death and resurrection. What are these benefits? Calvin summarizes: ''Baptism attests to us that we have been cleansed and washed; the Eucharistic Supper, that we have been redeemed'' (*Institutes* 4.14.22). In short: ''. . . redemption, righteousness, sanctification, and eternal life'' (*Institutes* 4.17.11).

Historical Development

Calvinism as a doctrinal system inevitably evolved not only into a structure of church order (generally called PRESBYTERIANISM) but also into a particular way of life, as exemplified in Calvin's reign over the city of Geneva. In this growth, Calvinism underwent structural and doctrinal modifications.

Doctrinal Disputes. The first break in the rigor of Calvinistic doctrine came in Holland. Holland had become solidly Calvinistic after the successful fight against

Philip II by William of Orange, who declared himself a Calvinist in 1573. But the very strength of the uniformity Calvinism exacted brought a reaction. The successor to Calvin, Theodore BEZA, had added to the doctrine of predestination by a position known as supralapsarianism (*see* SUPRALAPSARIANS), in which the decree of election preceded the fall of man, so that the fallen state was part of the eternal plan of God. Dirck COORNHERT, a Dutch theologian, challenged Beza's position with a doctrine of conditional predestination, or INFRALAPSARIANISM, that made the divine decree succeed the fall rather than precede or determine it. To the strongly orthodox Calvinists of Holland both of the positions differing with Beza's were heretical. In 1589 they invited Jacob ARMINIUS (Hermandszoon), once a student of Beza, to refute Coornhert and the infralapsarians. Arminius, however, found that as he studied the question, he could not defend the orthodox position and instead developed a doctrine that differed from both supralapsarianism and infralapsarianism.

Arminius was attacked by Franciscus GOMARUS, a strong supralapsarian, and had to defend himself against the charges of Pelagianism and Socinianism. In 1610 the followers of Arminius presented a remonstrance to the government for protection against the orthodox Calvinists. In the petition the REMONSTRANTS set forth five theses concerning their view of predestination. The government authorities summoned a national synod at Dort (Dordrecht) from Nov. 13, 1618, to May 9, 1619, through 154 formal sessions. It was attended not only by Dutch theologians but also by delegates from Switzerland, Germany, Scotland, and England. The synod, which took on the nature of an ecumenical council for the Reformed Church, decided against the Remonstrants. It set forth its resolutions, upholding the orthodox position on predestination, in 93 canons divided into five chapters that corresponded to the five theses of the Arminians. The synod asserted: (1) unconditional election; (2) limited atonement, i.e., Christ died for the elect alone; (3) total depravity of man; (4) irresistibility of grace; and (5) final perseverance of the saints. [Text in P. Schaff, *The Creeds of Christendom* (1877) 3.550–580]. [*See* CONFESSIONS OF FAITH II, PROTESTANT; INFRALAPSARIANS (SUBLAPSARIANS)].

Covenant Theology. Other difficulties concerning Calvin's doctrine arose, especially over a visible and invisible church, the irresistibility of grace, and an authoritarian civil government whose theocratic duty was to ''cherish and protect the outward worship of God, to defend sound doctrine of piety and the position of the church'' (*Institutes* 4.20.2). Of the new movements that modified Calvin's doctrine in seeking an answer to what seemed like intractable rigidity, the most significant was the Puritans' COVENANT THEOLOGY. Puritanism (*see* PURITANS) first appeared in the middle of the 16th century as a protest against the prescribed vestments and liturgical customs in the Church of England. The movement was essentially Calvinistic in doctrine but its main thrust was a type of piety. Concerned with man's right relation to God as a way of life and at the same time fully accepting the predestination of God as all-determining, the Puritans developed the idea of covenant. They discovered that all of salvation history had been a series of covenants between God and man. Even the government that protected the church had a covenant.

The significance of the covenants was that, while theologically upholding the absolute sovereignty of God, they made God's absolutism tractable to man's ability to conform. Man's duty was to fulfill his contract with God. Since God had made the contract, in the image of the legal and trade agreements of the time, His demands were reasonable and humanly possible of fulfillment. Thus, Calvin's God of predestination and irresistible condemnation became a Puritan God who could be served by righteous living and who would thereby consider those so living among the elect. Puritanism in this way marked the midpoint between orthodox and liberal Protestantism, between voluntarism and rationalism, between the sovereignty of God and the sovereignty of man.

Geographical Expansion

Calvinism triumphed first in Geneva where, under Calvin's leadership from 1541 to 1564, the city became the most thorough example of a community welded into a total Calvinistic society. Geneva was governed in both civil and ecclesiastical affairs by the elect.

Church Government. Basing his view on Scripture (Eph 4.11; Rom 12.7; 1 Cor 12.28) and on the practice of the early church, Calvin declared in his *Ecclesiastical Ordinances:* ''There are four orders of office instituted by our Lord for the government of his Church. First, pastors; then doctors; next elders; and fourth deacons'' (*Library of Christian Classics* 22:58). Thus, the pastors preached and administered the sacraments. To the doctors belonged the duty of teaching, a function that under Calvinistic encouragement blossomed into schools and universities. The elders shared in the enforcement of discipline; and the deacons took care of the sick and the poor. The Consistory, made up of ministers and laymen, was responsible for the corporate religious life of the city and under Calvin it became chiefly a tribunal of morality. Whenever necessary, its decisions were enforced by the Council of Geneva whose responsibility included not only the promotion of civil order but also the welfare of the Reformed Church. Geneva, under Calvin, not only became a model city to which Calvinists looked as an ideal, but also a haven for Protestant refugees through whom Calvin's ideas spread far and wide.

Switzerland. In Switzerland, Heinrich BULLINGER, the successor to Zwingli, signed a formula of faith (*Consensus Tigurinus*) with Calvin in 1549. This paved the way for the general acceptance of Calvinism throughout the cantons. In 1566 the Second Helvetic Confession, drawn up by Bullinger but heavily Calvinistic in doctrine, was published in the name of all the Swiss cantons except Basel and Neuchâtel and had wide popularity. Today about half the population in Switzerland belongs to the Reformed Church.

Germany. In Germany, Calvinism spread mostly in the Rhine region where the fierce repression of the Peasant Revolt (1524–26) cost Luther many adherents. Reformed Protestantism also appealed to the free cities, particularly Strassburg, Memingen, Lindau, and Constance. Calvinism attained great influence in the Palatinate under the Elector, Frederick III (1515–76). During his regime, the University of Heidelberg became a center of Calvinism, and a confession of faith, the Heidelberg Catechism, was compiled in 1562 by two professors, Zacharias URSINUS and Caspar Olevianus (1536–87). This Calvinistic document became the creed of the Reformed churches in Germany, and Reformed churches in Poland, Bohemia, Hungary, and Moravia were influenced by it.

France. In France, the Calvinists, who were called HUGUENOTS, were opposed from the time of their origin almost constantly, although various edicts such as the Edict of January 1562 and the Edict of NANTES in 1598 gave some official toleration. Many Huguenots fled to Holland, Switzerland, America, England, and Prussia. Finally, in 1802, full legal standing was given to the Reformed Church.

Netherlands. In the Netherlands, the Calvinists were not strong until about 1560. They gained the favor of William of Orange (1533–84), who became a Calvinist in 1573. After the declaration of independence (July 26, 1581), the Reformed Church became the established church in the northern region (Holland). In the 19th century, it became independent of the state. About 40 percent of the population now belongs to the Dutch Reformed Church.

Scotland. Scotland is the only country where the majority of the people presently belong to the Reformed Church. Nowhere else has Calvinism triumphed so well, although its history since the time of John KNOX has been one of struggle. Knox was a personal friend of Calvin and received the Genevan reformer's warm encouragement and support. In 1900 the Free Church of Scotland merged with the United Presbyterian Church to form the United Free Church of Scotland. The resulting church merged with the Established Church to form the Church of Scotland in 1929.

England. In England the Calvinist doctrine brought about a divisive struggle within the Church of England toward the end of the 16th century. One group emerged as Presbyterians with their characteristic type of ascending series of governing bodies called synods and with a confession of faith, the Westminster Confession of 1648. A further group were the Separatist and Non-Separatist Congregationalists who migrated to New England as Puritans. Today there are various free churches in England that have been influenced by Calvinism and also a relatively small Presbyterian Church.

North America. Contingents from many of the European Reformed Churches went to North America during colonial times. A number of these groups fled from persecution. In the New World they influenced the shaping of a new nation and at the same time were influenced in their religious thinking. The strict orthodoxy of old world Calvinism was slowly modified by contacts in a pluralistic society, as well as by the demands of colonial life, trade, the Revolutionary War, a new government, and a new civilization. The modification, particularly in the 18th and 19th centuries, placed more and more emphasis on man and on his power for initiative and independence. Denominations proliferated across the U.S. Today, under the stimulus of the ecumenical movement, the modification has taken a new turn toward church mergers and under the pressure of a mechanized, materialistic age, toward the sovereignty of God once again (*see* REFORMED CHURCHES II: NORTH AMERICA).

Contributions of Calvinism. In his 1902 classic, *The Protestant Ethic and the Spirit of Capitalism,* the German sociologist Max Weber identified Calvinism as a fundamentally important development in the creation of the modern world. Weber argued that Calvinism's emphasis on divine election produced a culture of ''innerworldly asceticism'' in which Calvinists hoped to demonstrate the fruits of their election through worldly involvement and enterprise. The secularization of these tendencies came to have a profound effect on the genesis of modern capitalism, as countries in which Calvinist influences were strongest became leaders in modern industry, banking, and finance. The debate over this ''Weber thesis'' dominated much twentieth-century historical writing, with strong defenders and detractors arguing over the relative merits of Weber's identification of a gene of modernity within Calvinism. More recently, scholars have pointed to traditional, even archaic attitudes toward business and finance that survived, not only in Calvin's work, but also among his seventeenth- and eighteenth-century followers. The roots of modern industrialism and capitalism are now seen to lie in forces and developments more various than the secularization of Calvin's ideas concerning human salvation. Nevertheless, during the 400 years of its existence, Calvinism as an aim and tendency has contributed significantly to the understanding of the human relationship to God. Modern followers of Calvin may not accept all of the tenets of his teaching but, within the Reformed tradition, some of the elements he expressed in his *Institutes* and other writings still recur in their discussions of human potentiality and weakness. These include Calvin's insistence on the lowly state of humankind before God's majesty, his insights into the power of divine grace, and his emphasis on biblical teaching as the rule by which Christians should seek to reform society.

Bibliography: J. CALVIN, *Opera quae supersunt omnia,* ed. G. BAUM et al., 59 v. (*Corpus reformatorum* 29–87); *Institutes of the Christian Religion,* ed. J. T. MCNEILL, tr. F. L. BATTLES, 2 v. (Philadelphia 1960); *Theological Treatises,* tr. J. K. S. REID (Philadelphia 1954); *Concerning the Eternal Predestination of God,* tr. J. K. S. REID (London 1961). J. T. MCNEILL, *The History and Character of Calvinism* (New York 1954). W. KRUSCHE, *Das Wirken des Heiligen Geistes nach Calvin* (Göttingen 1957). E. A. DOWEY, *The Knowledge of God in Calvin's Theology* (New York 1952). A. M. HUNTER, *The Teaching of Calvin . . .* (2d ed. London 1950). P. SPRENGER, *Das Rätsel um die Bekehrung Calvins* (Neukirchen 1960). F. WENDEL, *Calvin . . . ,* tr. P. MAIRET (New York 1963). J. H. FORSTMAN, *Word and Spirit . . .* (Stanford 1962). J. MACKINNON, *Calvin and the Reformation* (New York 1962). G. P. HARTVELT, *Verum corpus: Een studie over een centraal hoofdstuk uit de Avondmaalsleer van Calvijn* (Delft 1960). L. SMITS, *Saint Augustin dans l'oeuvre de Jean Calvin* (Assen 1957). W. NIESEL, *The Theology of Calvin,* tr. H. KNIGHT (Philadelphia 1956). V. RULAND, ''The Theology of New England Puritanism,'' *Heythrop Journal* 5 (1964) 162–169. M. NEESER, *Le Dieu de Calvin d'après l'institution de la religion chrétienne* (Neuchâtel 1956). L. BOUYER, *The Spirit and Forms of Protestantism* (Westminster, MD 1956). W. E. STUERMANN, *A Critical Study of Calvin's Concept of Faith* (Tulsa 1952). A. GANOCZY, *Calvin, théologien du ministère et de l'Église* (Paris 1964). O. WEBER, *Die Religion in Geschichte und Gegenwart,* 7 v. (3d ed. Tübingen 1957–65) 1:1593–99. E. W. ZEEDEN and J. MARLET, *Lexikon für Theologie und Kirche,* ed. J. HOFER and K. RAHNER, 10 v. (2d, new ed. Freiburg 1957–65) (1966) 2:891–898. A. BAUDRILLART, *Dictionnaire de théologie catholique,* ed. A. VACANT, 15 v. (Paris 1903–50; Tables générales 1951–) 2.2:1398–1422, earlier bibliog. Y. CONGAR, *Catholicisme* 2:421–424. J. QUINN, H. F. DAVIS et al., *A Catholic Dictionary of Theology* (London 1962–) 1:313–317. W. F. GRAHAM, *Later Calvinism* (Kirksville, MO 1994). E. W. MONTER, *Calvin's Geneva* (New York 1967). M. PRESTWICH, ed., *International Calvinism* (Oxford 1985). R. SCHNUCKER, ed., *Calviniana* (Kirksville, MO 1988). D. STEINMETZ, *Calvin in Context* (New York 1995).

[R. MATZERATH/P. SOERGEL]

CAMAIANI, PIETRO

Bishop of Ascoli Piceno and papal nuncio; b. Arezzo, June 1, 1519; d. Ascoli Piceno, March 27, 1579. From 1539 he was in the service of Duke Cosimo of Florence, and in 1546 he became his agent at the Council of Trent. In 1551 Pope Julius II took the able diplomat into the service of the Curia. As nuncio to Charles V (1552–53) and as nuncio at Naples (1554–55) he mediated in critical situations arising out of papal and Hapsburg policies. As bishop of Fiesole he was present at the third session of the Council of Trent. From 1566 until his death, as bishop of Ascoli Piceno, he promoted successfully the letter and the spirit of the Tridentine reforms. During his episcopate he acted as nuncio extraordinary at the court of Philip II at the request of Pope Pius V. His life and character bear witness to the movement away from the tradition of Renaissance diplomacy to the new pastoral idea of Catholic reform.

Bibliography: Short biography in *Nuntiaturberichte aus Deutschland,* Abt. 1, v.12, ed. G. KUPKE (1901) xxvi; v.13, ed. H. LUTZ (1959), his reports from the imperial court. P. VILLANI, ''Origine e carattere della nunziatura di Napoli,'' *Annuario dell' Istituto Storico Italiano per l'età moderna e contemporanea,* 9–10 (1957–58) 315ff, 411ff. L. PASTOR, *The History of the Popes from the Close of the Middle Ages* (London-St. Louis 1938–61) 8:286–289, 345–347. L. SERRANO, *Correspondencia diplomatica entre España y la Santa Sede durante el pontificado de S. Pio V,* 4 v. (Rome 1914). H. JEDIN, ''La politica conciliare di Cosimo I,'' *Rivista Storica Italiana* 62 (1950) 345–374, 477–496. G. FABIANI, *Ascoli nel Cinquecento* (Ascoli Piceno, Italy 1957).

[H. LUTZ]

CAMALDOLESE

The Congregation of Monk Hermits of Camaldoli (ErCam or OSBCam, Official Catholic Directory #0230 [ErCam], #0200 [OSBCam]), commonly known as the Camaldolese, is an offshoot of the Benedictine order (*see* BENEDICTINES). The spirit and purpose of the order are predominantly contemplative. St. ROMUALD, while remaining a Benedictine monk, imparted a unique spirit to his followers and to the many monasteries that he reformed, so that from the very beginning they began to form a separate family or institution. Romuald, however, never intended to found an eremitic order separate from the Benedictine monastic order, and the Camaldolese always pronounced their profession according to the rule of St. Benedict.

Internal Development. Romuald's activity, begun in Italy in the early years of the 11th century, was a part of the reform movement of the 11th and 12th centuries that sought to restore the more ancient monastic tradition, according to which Benedict had formulated his rule.

Monasticism, since the Carolingian era, had become overladen with formalism. The movement found different forms of expression, but most of them had a more or less pronounced tendency toward primitive eremitism, that is, greater penitential austerity, more separation from the world, and greater freedom to converse with God. Following the teaching and example of Romuald, the Camaldolese added to the Benedictine rule special regulations or customs. These were later compiled by (St.) PETER DAMIAN at FONTE AVELLANA, and especially by (Bl.) Rudolf (d. 1089) at CAMALDOLI about 1080.

Romuald organized the eremitic life by reuniting the anchorite with the monastery. In this he kept in mind the traditions of the Fathers and, in particular, the Palestinian LAURAS of SS. EUTHYMIUS and SABAS. His monastic institution was based on the following ideas. The monastery and the hermitage form one unit and complement each other. Unity is composed of three elements: rule, under a single superior; members, forming a single family; and goal, which is the ascent by degrees toward the highest summits of perfection and contemplation. Beginners reside in the monastery; the proficient and the more perfect, in the hermitage. The function of the monastery in this scheme is to prepare the monk for the solitary life. All must aspire to this, but the superior alone is to determine the suitability of the monk and the length of the preparation. He must exhort and, at the proper moment, summon the candidate to the hermitage. One may not enter the solitary life without the abbot's approval. The monastery also serves the purposes of administration, reception of guests, care of the sick and the aged, and instruction of novices. In the hermitage, the monk devotes himself solely to contemplation. Romuald summed up the rule for hermits in three things: fasting, silence, and solitude. Manual labor is encouraged to a limited degree, in conformity with the contemplative ideal.

The superior, whether abbot or prior, is the father of both hermits and cenobites (those living together in the monastery). The cenobitic family must venerate its hermit brothers, but the latter are warned against pride. In the Camaldolese tradition, the hermitage and the monastery thus take on a special character. The monastery loses some of its inflexible cenobitism, which, in Romauld's day particularly, did not allow the monk freedom to converse alone with God; the hermitage, in turn, is no longer the dangerous desert of the anchorites, but a laura where, along with the advantages of solitude, the hermits enjoy brotherly help and, above all, the blessing of obedience that preserves them from illusions and makes every good work valid. Finally, when the hermit monk has attained the highest degree of perfection, he may aspire to the apostolate of preaching the Gospel, where he may hope to offer to Christ the supreme homage of martyrdom.

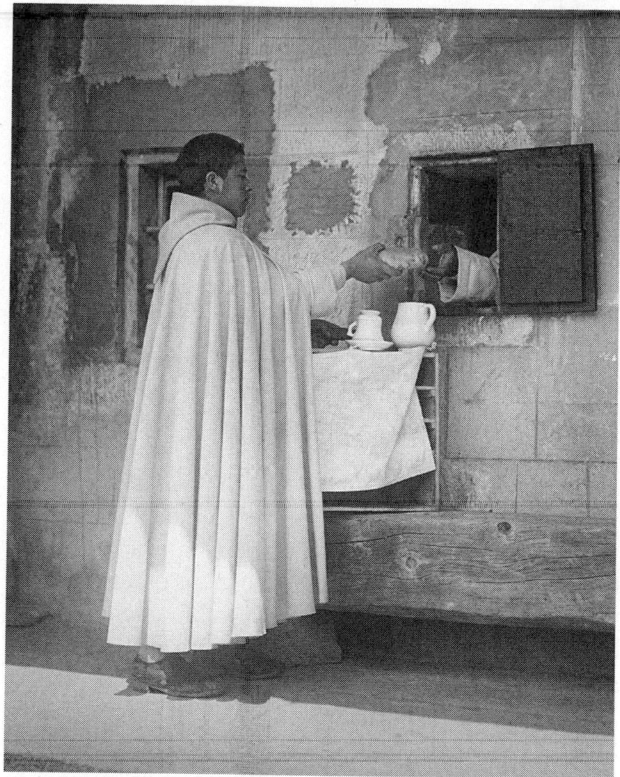

Camaldoli monk receiving food through grated opening, Apennines, Italy. (©Hulton-Deutsch Collection/CORBIS)

This ideal union of hermitage and monastery did not prove to be possible everywhere. At times Romuald founded hermitages and monasteries that were independent of one another. In such a case, the hermits were recruited from any monastery or even directly from the laity, if such candidates were sufficiently mature for the solitary life. Peter Damian also used this procedure at Fonte Avellana.

External Development. Camaldolese monasticism developed around the two principal centers in Italy, Camaldoli and Fonte Avellana. Many monasteries—some were new foundations, while others were existing monasteries that became identified with the new movement—adopted the Camaldolese rule and customs. The juridic ties between the dependent houses and the principal monasteries varied greatly, so that many monasteries were practically autonomous. The two principal centers were themselves juridically independent of one another until united by papal decree during the 16th century reform. Fonte Avellana, although it had flourished under the leadership of Peter Damian and his successors, later underwent a change in its eremitical character. Many of its monks were called to fill bishoprics in the Marches of Ancona and in Umbria. In 1325 it was converted into an abbey; the hermitage thus ceased to exist. Thereafter, the abuse of the *commenda,* whereby the abbey became the benefice of a secular cleric, hastened the decline of the monastery until Pius V, in 1569, reconstituted Fonte Avellana, and its dependent monasteries, by subjecting them to Camaldoli.

Throughout the history of the Camaldolese order, Camaldoli itself remained the chief center of vitality. Fortified by many privileges, both papal and imperial, it extended its influence over hundreds of monasteries, especially in the period between the 11th and the 13th centuries. The form of government within the order developed slowly and suffered from numerous conflicts. The chief source of difficulty lay in the very nature of Camaldolese monasticism, that is, in the tension between the twofold objective of the order, cenobitic and eremitic. The general chapter was introduced into the government of the order in the 13th century; the first chapter met at Padua in 1239. As with the other religious orders, the Camaldolese suffered from the unfavorable circumstances of the 14th and 15th centuries. In the 15th century, several reform efforts, initiated both inside and outside the order, were undertaken. One such effort, promoted by Eugene IV, was earnestly advanced by (Bl.) Ambrose Traversari, the noted Camaldolese humanist who was elected superior general in 1431.

Effective reform was not realized, however, until the following century, when the Congregation of Camaldoli and San Michele di Murano (Venice) was formed. The leaders in this movement were the then superior general, Pietro Delfino, superior from 1480 until his death in 1525, (Bl.) Paolo GIUSTINIANI, and Pietro Querini (1479–1514). Giustiniani, whose ideas were more radical than those of his confreres, led a further reform movement that came to be known as the Congregation of Monte Corona (Umbria). Under the impetus of these movements the order of Camaldoli experienced a new vitality, but the tension between the cenobitic and eremitic ideals remained. In the 17th century the cenobites separated themselves from the hermits, forming an independent group (1616). Further divisions resulted from the formation of congregations in Piedmont and in France, but both of these disappeared during the French Revolution. Finally, on July 2, 1935, the Holy See reunited the cenobites with the hermits at Camaldoli, thus reconstituting the ancient order of Romuald.

The Camaldolese have enjoyed a reputation for holiness. Their recognized saints and blesseds, however, are generally persons who became known by reason of some activity outside the hermitage, such as, SS. Peter, Archbishop of Pisa (d. 1120); John, Cardinal Bishop of Ostia (d. 1134); and BOGUMIL OF GNIEZNO. Among many blesseds, two are remembered as martyrs: Daniel of Ungrispach (d. 1411) and Angelo of Mussiaccio (d. 1485). The Camaldolese have made notable contributions to various fields of learning and of the arts. A tradition of scholarship was begun by Jerome of Prague (Johannes Silvanus, d. 1440) and the above-mentioned Ambrose Traversari. From an earlier period, however, the names of GUIDO OF AREZZO, the musician, and GRATIAN, the author of the *Decretum,* are remembered. The prior general Pietro Delfino was an outstanding humanist, and the monastery in Florence, Santa Maria degli Angeli (1294), became the meeting place for the great Florentine humanists of the 15th century. Nicolò Malermi (d. 1481) published in 1471 the first complete translation of the Bible in Italian. Fra Mauro (d. *c.* 1459) was a cosmographer of note. The historian, Giovanni MITTARELLI, published the *Annales Camaldulenses* (9 v. 1755–73). The order of Camaldoli gave to the Church many bishops, several cardinals, and one pope, Gregory XVI.

In the United States the Camaldolese began, in 1958, a foundation called New Camaldoli at Big Sur, Calif. The Congregation of Monte Corona established (1959) a hermitage at McConnelsville, Ohio.

Bibliography: G. B. MITTARELLI and A. COSTADONI, *Annales camaldulenses,* 9 v. (Venice 1755–73). A. GIABBANI, *L'eremo, vita e spiritualità eremitica nel monachismo Camaldolese primitive* (Brescia 1945). A. PAGNANI, *Storia dei Benedettini Camaldolesi* (Sassoferrato 1949). W. FRANKE, *Romuald von Camaldoli und seine Reformtätigkeit zum Zeit Ottos III* (Berlin 1913). M. BEDE, *The Hermits of New Camaldoli* (Big Sur, Calif. 1958). P. BOSSI and A. CERATTI, *Eremi camaldolesi in Italia: luoghi, architettura, spiritualità* (Milano 1993). G. VEDOVATO, *Camaldoli e la sua congregazione dalle origini al 1184: storia e documentazione* (Cesena 1994). L. VIGILUCCI, *Camaldoli: A Journey into Its History & Spirituality* (Trabuco Canyon, Calif., 1995). C. CABY, *De l'érémitisme rural au monachisme urbain: les camaldules en Italie à la fin du Moyen Âge* (Rome 1999). P.-D. BELISLE, *The Privilege of Love: Camaldolese Benedictine Spirituality* (Collegeville, Minn. 2002).

[A. GIABBANI/EDS.]

CAMALDOLI, ABBEY OF

The name of (1) the cenobitical monastery, lying at a height of 2,680 feet in the Tuscan-Romagnese Appennines, commune of Poppi, civil province and Diocese of Arezzo, and (2) of the eremitical monastery, two miles farther up (3,610 feet) in the midst of forest land. Both monasteries were built by St. ROMUALD, founder of the CAMALDOLESE congregation, on land granted by Count Maldoli to Romuald (1012–15), the name Camaldoli being formed from *Campus Maldoli.* The hermitage, with its characteristic separation of the monks' dwellings from each other by small cultivated plots of ground, served as the model for other Camaldolese eremitical foundations. Consecrated in 1027, its Romanesque-style church was

Monks from Monastery of Camaldoli, founded by St. Romualdo Abate, Apennine Mountains, Italy. (©Hulton-Deutsch Collection/CORBIS)

almost entirely rebuilt in 1220; the present baroque form dates from 1658. The once-great library was destroyed in the Napoleonic and Italian suppressions. The archives are now preserved almost intact in the state archives in Florence. The monks continue to lead a strict life of almost continuous prayer and rigorous penance and observe complete silence. The monastery proper was, like the hermitage, built by St. Romuald *c.* 1015. Originally, it was a hospice and guest house. In order that the hermit-monks might devote themselves entirely to the contemplative life, it was later organized into a cenobitical monastery. Today it consists of a 16th-century church with works by Vasari, a cloister with monks' quarters, and a section reserved for lay retreats. There is a printing press, a pharmacy, and since 1946 a workshop for the restoration of books and incunabula.

Bibliography: G. B. MITTARELLI and A. COSTADONI, *Annales camaldulenses*, 9 v. (Venice 1755–73). P. F. KEHR, *Regesta Pontificum Romanorum* (Berlin 1906–35) 3:171–185. L. H. COTTINEAU, *Répertoire topo-bibliographique des abbayes et prieurés* (Mâcon 1935–39) 1:567–569. A. GIABBANI, *L'eremo* (Brescia 1945).

[S. OLIVIERI]

CAMARA, HELDER PESSOA

Archbishop of Olinda and Recife; b. Feb. 7, 1909, Fortaleza, Cearà, Brazil; d. Aug. 27, 1999. Born into a middle-class family, the eleventh of thirteen children of Joao Eduardo—bookkeeper, journalist, committed liberal, mason—and Adelaide, primary school teacher and practicing Catholic. In 1923, Camara entered the diocesan seminary of St. Joseph, and was ordained as priest Aug. 15, 1931. He took a keen interest in social movements, playing an active role in the creation of the Young Catholic Workers, the Unionizing of Catholic Women Workers, and the League of Catholic Teachers of Ceará,

Helder Camara meeting with Pope John Paul II, Rio de Janeiro, Brazil, 1997; photo by Gregg Newton. (Reuters/Gregg Newton/ Archive Photos)

of which he became ecclesiastical assistant. Attracted by integralismo, a political and ideological movement in the mold of fascism, he was given permission by his archbishop to become a member of the new party. In recognition of his contribution to the Catholic Electoral League's victories in 1933 and 1934, he was nominated director of public instruction for the State of Ceará.

Disillusioned with the direction taken by State politics, he accepted an invitation to work in Rio de Janeiro in the Ministry of Education and Culture. His move to Rio coincided with his developing political consciousness and, on a much deeper level, in his self-consciousness of his mission as a priest. His reading of Jacques Maritain's *Integral Humanism* contributed decisively to this process. Later he became the national vice-assistant to Brazilian Catholic Action. In 1952, with the support of the Vatican pro-secretary of state, Msgr. Montini (the future Pope Paul VI), he founded the Brazilian National Conference of Bishops (CNBB), of which he became general secretary, and was ordained bishop. In 1955, he was promoted to archbishop, while remaining auxiliary to the cardinal archbishop of Rio de Janeiro. In that same year he organized, with Mgr. Larraín, bishop of Talca, Chile, the First General Conference of the Latin American Episcopate (CELAM), and served as its vice-president from 1958 to 1965.

As auxiliary bishop in Rio, Camara undertook numerous social initiatives on the local level, while as secretary of the National Conference of Bishops he was the driving force behind attempts to promote a series of ''basic reforms'' through the cooperation of the Church, the unions, and the governments, especially the federal government. He coordinated the preparation of the Emergency Plan—taken on officially by the Brazilian episcopacy in 1962—which eventually became the Collective Pastoral Plan of the Brazilian bishops.

In 1964 the government of Brazil was seized by a military coup; that same year, Pope Paul VI appointed Camara residential archbishop of Olinda and Recife. He continued his active pastoral ministry, quickly becoming ''enemy number one'' of the country's conservative forces because of his growing acclaim among the international mass media, where he was the voice of the poor and of those persecuted by the regime. He received numerous international awards during his lifetime, and was four times nominated for the Nobel Peace Prize. Among the many books he published as archbishop were *Terzo mondo defraudato* (Milan 1968), *Spirale de violence* (Paris 1970), *Pour arriver à temps* (Paris 1970), *Le désert est fertile* (Paris 1971), *Prière pour les riches* (Zurich 1972), *Cristianismo, socialismo, capitalismo* (Salamanca 1974), *Um olhar sobre a cidade* (Rio de Janeiro 1985), and *Les conversions d'un Evêque: entretiens avec José de Broucker* (Paris 1977).

He retired from his see in 1985, but continued to serve until his death in 1999, promoting the causes of peace and justice, including the world-wide campaign the Year 2000 without Misery. A brilliant orator and preacher, an efficient organizer, an indefatigable advocate of justice, a man of prayer, deeply in love with God and his creation, he became known, from the time of the council on, due to his many international conferences and sermons, as "bishop of the slums," "voice of the voiceless," "advocate of the Third World," "prophet of the Church of the Poor," "apostle of non-violence." It was for this reason he was accused by his opponents of being the "red archbishop."

Bibliography: J. DE BROUCKER, *Dom Helder Camara: The Violence of a Peacemaker,* tr. by H. BRIFFAULT (Maryknoll, N.Y. 1970). M. DE CASTRO, *Dom Helder: o bispo da esperança* (Rio de Janeiro 1978). J. L. GONZÁLEZ-BALADO, *Helder Camara: L'arcivescovo rosso* (Rome 1970). M. HALL, *The Impossible Dream: The Spirituality of Dom Helder Camara* (Belfast 1979). G. WEIGNER and B. MOOSBRUGGER, *A Voice of the Third World: Dom Helder Camara* (New York 1972).

[L. C. MARQUES]

CAMBODIA, THE CATHOLIC CHURCH IN

Capital: Phnom-Penh.
Size: 69,000 sq. miles.
Population: 12,212,306 in 2000.
Languages: Khmer, French, English.
Religions: 48,850 Catholics (.4%), 11,601,690 Theravada Buddhists (95%), 120,579 Protestants (1%), 441,187 Muslims (3.6%).
Apostolic vicariate: Phnom-Penh, with apostolic prefectures in Battambang and Kompong-Cham.

The Kingdom of Cambodia (Kampuchea), located in southeast Asia, is bound on the north and west by Thailand, on the northeast by Laos, on the east by Vietnam, and on the southwest by the Gulf of Thailand. Mountainous near its northern border as well as in the southwest, Cambodia falls to level terrain, and the country is traversed by the Mekong River that runs south to empty into the Gulf. Heavily jungled over much of its area, Cambodia has a tropical climate that brings monsoons during a rainy season lasting from May to November. Agricultural products include rice, corn, rubber, tobacco and sugar, while natural resources consist of timber, gemstones, manganese, phosphates and iron ore.

Cambodia became a French protectorate in 1863 as part of French Indochina. It became a constitutional monarchy in 1946, an autonomous state in the French Union in 1949, and fully independent in 1953. In 1975 a communist government took over the country, prompting an invasion by Vietnam that resulted in 13 years of war. The UN sponsored elections in 1993. The majority of Cambodians are ethnic Khmers, although Vietnamese, Chinese, Thais and Europeans constitute minority populations. Only 35 percent of the population was considered literate in 2000.

Early History. Although Fernando Mendez Pinto, a Jesuit, visited Cambodia in 1554, the first attempt at evangelization was by the Dominican Gaspar da Cruz in 1555. During the same period, Portuguese Dominicans and Franciscans came from Malacca; tragically, one of them, Silvestro de Azevedo, OP, was put to death in 1576. Jesuits and priests from Goa, India, also labored in the area. >From the Philippines came two Spanish Dominicans, one of whom, Father Bastide, was slain in 1588, reflecting the lack of lasting success of these early evangelical efforts. When Louis Chevreul, a priest of the PARIS FOREIGN MISSION SOCIETY (MEP), arrived in 1665, he found the Portuguese ecclesiastical "governor" Paul d'Acosta at Colompé (Phnom Penh), where he was caring for 400 Portuguese who had been driven from Makassar by the Dutch. Across the river was a group of 600 refugees from Cochin China (Vietnam), 50 of whom were Christians. Chevreul also encountered Charles Della Rocca, SJ, at Udong, where Della Rocca was occupied with 100 Portuguese and a village of 500 or 600 Vietnamese. In 1670 Chevreul was seized by a Portuguese commander, imprisoned at Macau on charges of violating Portugal's rights of padroado (*see* PATRONATO REAL), tried by the Inquisition of Goa, and finally released. Bishop Louis Laneau, MEP, the first vicar apostolic of Siam (1673–96) and administrator general of the missions in Indochina, sent one MEP to Cambodia in 1680 and two more in 1682. All three suffered greatly because of intrigues and wars, and departed for Cochin China or Siam in 1685.

For two centuries, missionary efforts focused on the Portuguese and Vietnamese. Nicholas Levasseur, MEP, was the first to specialize in the apostolate to the Cambodians, or Khmers. Between 1768 and his death in 1777 he translated into Khmer a catechism and various books. Unfortunately he had no successors. By 1842 Cambodia had only 222 Catholics and four churches. Attached to

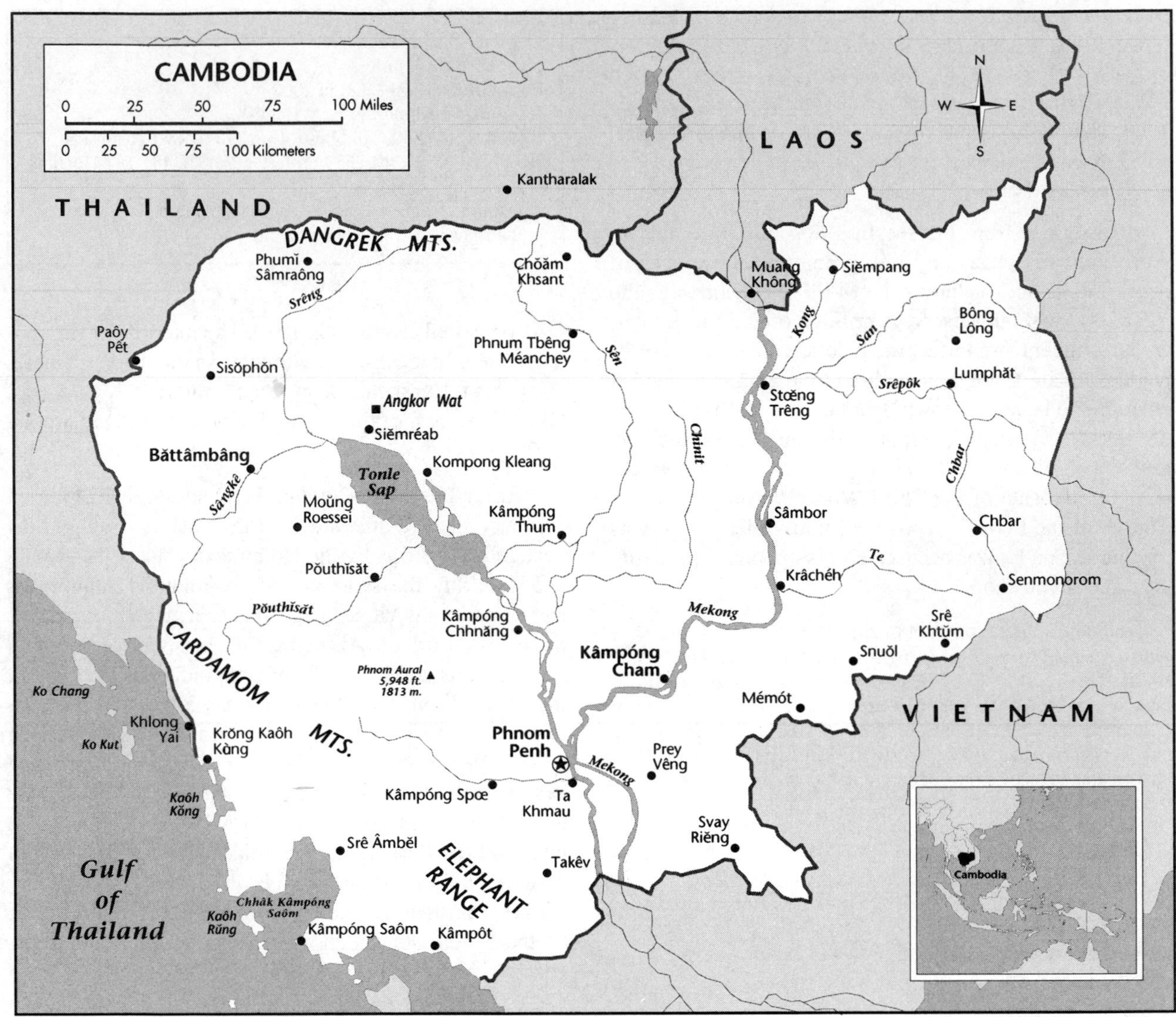

the Vicariate Apostolic of Cochin China in 1658, Cambodia, along with part of Laos, became the Vicariate of Cambodia (1850), which then numbered 600 Catholics. The French, who had established themselves in Cochin China in 1859, extended their protectorate to Cambodia in 1863. In 1865 the Vicariate of Cambodia gained jurisdiction over eight ''provinces'' of Vietnam, which then had 5,000 Christians. Thenceforth mission activity centered around these eight ''provinces,'' or on persons who were attracted to Cambodia from Cochin China by commerce and by the vast rice fields, whose value increased under the French protectorate. The name of the vicariate was changed in 1924 to Phnom Penh. On Nov. 9, 1953 Cambodia gained its independence from France and became a constitutional monarchy. Two years later the eight Vietnamese ''provinces'' were separated to form the Vicariate of Cantho, and the territorial limits of Phnom Penh were made coterminous with those of the kingdom of Cambodia. In 1968, two new apostolic prefectures were created: Battambang and Kompong-Cham. Tep Im Sotha was appointed the Apostolic Prefect of Battambang, becoming the first ethnic Khmer to occupy that position.

Persecutions. For the greater part of the 20th century, most of the Catholics in Cambodia were Vietnamese, many of them descendants of Vietnamese Catholics who had fled Vietnam during the anti-Catholic persecutions of the 1850s and 1860s. By 1970, of the approximately 61,000 Catholics in Cambodia, about 56,000 were ethnic Vietnamese, 3,000 were Khmers and 1,500 were Chinese. Ministering to the pastoral needs of these Catholics were 65 priests (45 French missionaries, 15 ethnic Vietnamese and 5 ethnic Khmers). When General Lon Nol

Four Buddhist monks, Bayon Temple at Angkor Thom, Angkor, Cambodia. (©Chris Rainier/CORBIS)

seized power on March 18, 1970 and established a military dictatorship in Cambodia, among other things he instigated a campaign to expel all ethnic Vietnamese from Cambodia. Cambodian Catholics of Vietnamese descent found themselves the target of violent attacks instigated by the military junta. From May to August 1970, more than 40,000 Cambodian Catholics of Vietnamese origin, lay and clergy alike, were forcibly deported to Vietnam. In one stroke, the Cambodian Catholic Church lost more than two-thirds of its faithful.

Life for the remaining Cambodian Catholics worsened after the collapse of the military junta of Lon Nol and the subsequent rise to power of the communist Khmer Rouge under the leadership of Pol Pot on April 17, 1975. Two days before, on April 15, 1975, Joseph Chhmar Salas became the first ethnic Khmer bishop when he was ordained coadjutor bishop for the Vicariate Apostolic of Phnom Penh by the Vicar Apostolic, Mgr. Yves-Georges-René Ramousse, MEP, who foresaw the impending expulsion of all foreign missionaries and sought to provide the Cambodian Catholic Church with local leadership. On April 30, 1975, all foreigners, including Mgr. Ramousse and other foreign missionaries, were expelled, the Catholic Cathedral in Phnom Penh was completely razed to the ground, and Bishop Chhmar Salas was arrested and deported to Taing Kauk, where he died from disease and starvation in 1976.

The Cambodian Catholic Church suffered greatly during the Khmer Rouge's reign of terror. In addition to the confiscation of all its assets, the wholesale destruction of its churches, schools and hospitals, and the expulsion of all foreign missionaries, all of the indigenous clergy and religious who remained behind were rounded up, tortured and either executed (as was the case with the monks of the Benedictine Monastery at Kep in Kampot Province, and Mgr. Tep Im Sotha) or forced into labor camps, where they later died from disease and hunger (as was the case with Bishop Chhmar Salas, and many local clergy and religious).

In the name of collective national purification and reconstruction, the Khmer Rouge implemented a massive program of radical social transformation and rewriting of Cambodia's history, abolishing all religions, money, commerce, markets and private property ownership. The country was reorganized as a single agricultural collective, with the entire Cambodian population as its labor force. The scale of human suffering was immense: between two and four million Cambodians (more than 25 percent of the total population) perished from torture, execution, forced labor, or starvation.

The Khmer Rouge regime ended when Vietnamese forces invaded Cambodia on January 7, 1979, but the situation remained desperate for the Cambodian Catholic Church under the Vietnamese-backed Heng Samrin regime from 1979 to 1990, which suppressed all forms of religious practices and prohibited all efforts to rebuild the battered Church. During these dark years, the small pockets of Cambodian Catholics who survived clung steadfastly to their faith, meeting secretly for prayer services. Living in exile, the Vicar Apostolic of Phnom Penh, Mgr. Ramousse directed the Holy See's outreach programs to Cambodian refugees throughout the world before returning to Cambodia in May 1989, after a 14-year absence. He was followed in 1990 by another French missionary, Emile Destombes, MEP, who celebrated the first Easter Mass in public since 1975. As a result of their endeavors, on April 7, 1990, the Central Committee of the Revolutionary Party issued a statement to the National Council of the Front of Solidarity, authorizing ''a place of worship for the Christian religion.'' Following this development, the Cambodian Catholic Church received permission to hold public liturgies and rebuild its churches. Foreign missionaries and representatives of religious communities were also allowed to return and reestablish their presence in Cambodia.

Renaissance and Growth. Several developments in the 1990s improved the situation for the Catholic Church in Cambodia. In 1992, Mgr. Ramousse officially resumed his responsibilities as Vicar Apostolic of Phnom Penh. The new Constitution that was promulgated in 1993 guaranteed religious freedom to all. In 1994, Cambodia reestablished diplomatic relations with the Holy See. The year 1995 marked a new milestone for the Cambodian Catholic Church, with the reopening of the seminary in Battambang, the ordination of Rev. Seila Tunlop, the first ordination of an indigenous Khmer Catholic priest in 23 years, and the first meeting in 20 years of the Catholic Bishops' Conference of Cambodia and Laos (CELAC). Two years later, in 1997, the Cambodian government formally granted official status to the Cambodian Catholic Church.

At of the beginning of the 21st century, the Catholic Church in Cambodia comprised one vicariate apostolic (Phnom Penh) and two prefectures apostolic (Battambang and Kompong-Cham). The vicariate apostolic of Phnom Penh includes the city of Phnom Penh, Sihanoukville, and the provinces of Kandal, Takeo, Kampot, Kompong Speu and Koh-Kong. The prefecture apostolic of Battambang comprises the eight provinces of Battambang, Pursat, Kompong Chhnang, Kompong Them, Siem Reap, Preah Vihear, Oddar Meanchey and Banteay Meanchey, while the prefecture apostolic of Kompong Cham covers the provinces of Kompong Cham, Kratie Prey Veng, Stoeung Treng, Mondulkiri. The Catholic Church maintains cordial ecumenical ties with other Christian churches, collaborating to produce an ecumenical Khmer-language translation of the Bible that was completed in 1997.

Bibliography: J. PLANET, *Histoire de la Mission du Cambodge* (Hong Kong 1929). B. BIERMANN, ''Die Missionen der portugiesischen Dominikaner in Hinterindien,'' *Zeitschrift für Missionswissenschaft und Religionswissenschaft,* 21 (1931) 305–327; ''Die Missionsversuche der Dominiker in Kambodscha,'' *ibid.* 23 (1933) 108–132. *Le missioni cattoliche: Storia, geographia, statistica* (Rome 1950) 270–271. 2:183–185. F. PONCHAUD, *Cambodia Year Zero* (New York 1978). F. PONCHAUD, *La cathédrale de la rizière: 450 ans d'histoire de l'église au Cambodge* (Paris 1990), by a French MEP missionary priest who was formerly the Prefect Delegate of Kompong Cham; the definitive work on the history of the Catholic Church in Cambodia, with a useful bibliography for further reading and research.

[J. GUENNOU/J. Y. TAN]

CAMBRAI, ARCHDIOCESE OF (CAMERACENSIS)

Metropolitan see since 1559, in Nord department, northern France. Cambrai's diocesan borders have changed several times, according to the political fortunes of the region, which is on France's border with the German world. At the end of the Roman Empire the see corresponded to the *civitas Nerviorum in Belgica II.* It had no bishop after the German invasions of the early 5th century. St. REMIGIUS, bishop of Reims, made St. VEDAST (d. *c.* 540) bishop of the *Netvii;* but he resided in Arras. His second successor, Vedulphus, who moved the see to Cambrai, was followed by St. GÉRY (d. *c.* 625). Until 1094 Arras and Cambrai had a common bishop, who usually resided in Cambrai. Bordered on the west by the Schelde River, the diocese expanded, along with evangelization, as far north as Antwerp.

Charles V abdicated in 1558, and Philip II moved to Spain in 1559 after the Peace of Cateau-Cambrésis. To combat Protestantism better, Mechelen and ANTWERP were in 1559 detached as dioceses from Cambrai, which, previously suffragan to REIMS, became a metropolitan, with Tournai, Arras, Saint-Omer, and Namur as suffragans. In 1790 the CIVIL CONSTITUTION OF THE CLERGY reduced Cambrai to a suffragan of Reims. It was restored as a metropolitan without authority over its former Belgian suffragans by the agreements of 1822, but no archbishop was appointed until after the death of Bishop Belmas (1841), last of the constitutional prelates. Cambrai then encompassed all of the Nord department, part of which was detached to create the See of Lille in 1913.

The bishops of Cambrai, who had regular and good relationships with the Carolingian emperors, became more powerful when the emperors gave them the *comitatus* (rights of a count) over part of the episcopal *civitas* (*c.* 941) and then (1007) over the whole county. Thus they became temporal and spiritual lords with a role in Church history under the German (Holy Roman) Empire. Trouble with the bourgeoisie caused the bishop to cede some of his rights to the commune in 1185. Under Burgundian rule (1384–1477) the bishops, who came from the highest nobility and even from the ducal family, favored the popes of Avignon in the WESTERN SCHISM; PETER OF AILLY (1396–1411), a prolific author, had a strong influence in scholastic and ecclesiastical circles. When France annexed Cambrai (1678), LOUIS XIV gained from the cathedral chapter the right to appoint bishops. Cambrai then followed the fortunes of France. François Salignac de la Mothe FÉNELON (1695–1715) was an outstanding prelate, and Auguste GRATRY (d. 1872) was a noteworthy theologian.

A rich land, the diocese has had many abbeys since the 7th century: Benedictines (11 men's and 5 women's), Augustinian (4 and 4), and Cistercians (2 and 6); 4 Premonstratensian abbeys were important during the 12th-century reform. (*See* AFFLIGEM; GROENENDAEL; LOBBES; SAINT-BERTIN; SAINT-VAAST.) There were also many houses of the mendicant orders, a Jesuit college (1563), and a university at DOUAI to train priests for England (e.g., William Allen's English College, 1568). Wars have left few monuments in good repair; the cathedral has almost been destroyed. Of note are the abbey churches of Saint-Géry, Vaucelles, and Oisy-le-Verger; and the churches of Avesnes-lès-Aubert and Saint-Géry in Valenciennes.

Arras's first resident bishop seems to have been Diogenes, perhaps a missionary, slain in the Vandal invasion (407). Early monasteries were associated with the expansion of Irish monasticism *c.* 700. The temporal power of Arras's 9th-century chapter in the *civitas* (the area around the cathedral) suffered from nearby Saint Vaast Abbey, around which grew up a prosperous community. Normans destroyed both Arras and Cambrai (879–885). When the counts of Flanders began to reside in Arras in the 10th century, the temporal power of the bishops (in Cambrai) suffered. A dispute over the episcopal succession (1092) led to the creation of the See of Arras (1094). In the 13th century, as Arras grew rich, there was a movement for evangelical poverty, and rich bourgeois founded houses of the mendicant orders. Part of Burgundy in 1369, Arras came to France in the Peace of the Pyrenees (1659); but neither its clergy nor those of Cambrai took part in the French Assembly of the Clergy. Bishop Gui Scève de Rochechouart (1670–1724) founded the seminary.

See Also: ARRAS, MARTYRS OF; ARRAS, COUNCILS OF.

Bibliography: C. J. DESTOMBES, *Les Vies des saints et des personnes d'une éminente piété des diocèses de Cambrai et d'Arras*, 4 v. (4th ed. Lille 1889). F. VERCAUTEREN, *Étude sur les civitates de la Belgique seconde* (Brussels 1934). É. DE MOREAU, *Histoire de l'Église en Belgique* (2d ed. Brussels 1945–); *Dictionnaire d'historie et de géographie ecclésiastiques,* ed. A. BAUDRILLART et al. (Paris 1912–) 7:519–756, *passim.* M. CHARTIER, *ibid.* 11:547–565. E. JARRY, *Catholicisme* 1:860–864; 2:427–434. M. DIERICK, ''La Réorganisation de la hiérarchie ecclésiastique des Pays-Bas par la bulle 1559,'' *Revue d'histoire ecclésiastique* 59 (1964) 489–499. *Annuario Pontificio* (1965) 88.

[E. JARRY]

CAMBRIDGE, UNIVERSITY OF

The origins of the University of Cambridge go back to the 13th century. There may have been schools in the town before 1200, and scholars may have come from Oxford in 1209. The university is certainly mentioned in documents of 1231.

Development. The University of Cambridge was recognized as a *studium generale* by Pope John XXII in 1318. The medieval masters and students were mostly secular clerks, but the regular clergy, both Franciscans and Benedictines, were important until the Reformation. The first college, Peterhouse, was founded by the Benedictine monk, Hugh de Balsham, Bishop of Ely, in 1284, although few students were members of colleges until the 16th century. Among the more important college foundations were King's (1441), St. John's (1511), and Trinity (1546). By 1600, however, all teachers and students were members of one of the 16 colleges then existing. In fact, between that date and the 19th century the university was little more than a loose federation of colleges.

The chief promoter of the ''new learning'' in Cambridge was its chancellor, John FISHER (d. 1535), who probably brought ERASMUS to Cambridge. The Reformation was strong there, for English Protestantism was preeminently a Cambridge movement. Under Elizabeth I theology played a more prominent part in university studies than it had done in the Middle Ages. Puritanism was flourishing, and in the following century Cambridge men played an important part in the foundation of New England and of Harvard College. During the English Civil Wars (1642–52) the sympathies of the university were largely Royalist and many of the heads and fellows of colleges were expelled by the victorious Parliamentarians. In academic studies Aristotelian and scholastic ideas remained predominant all through this period, until a new interest in scientific and mathematical studies appeared, the greatest name here being that of Isaac Newton, who was working on the theory of gravity in the 1660s. In the following century the ancient disputations were gradually replaced as the means of qualifying for a degree by a written examination in mathematics, later called the mathematical tripos.

The 18th century was not a prosperous period in Cambridge. There were, however, some distinguished men, such as the classical scholar Richard BENTLEY. After 1815 reforms were gradually introduced, although pressure from Parliament was necessary to bring about radical changes. After the appointment of a royal commission of enquiry in 1850 and the consequent reform of the university and college statutes a new age of expansion began. Numbers rose; new studies, in particular the natural sciences, were fostered; colleges for women were founded (Girton 1869, Newnham 1871), though women did not become full members of the university until 1948. The main obstacle to expansion in the later 19th century was lack of money, for although the colleges had large endowments, these were fully committed and the university had very little available for new developments. Eventually the university (and indirectly the colleges) came to depend on government grants, the first general grant being given in 1919–20. As a result another royal commission of enquiry was appointed, and new university and college statutes were made between 1926 and 1928, by which Cambridge is still governed.

Organization. The university is a common-law corporation by prescription, consisting of a chancellor, masters, and scholars. Its incorporation was confirmed by Act of Parliament in 1571. Each of the colleges is itself a self-governing body, the control of its affairs resting in the hands of its own head and fellows. There are now 20 colleges—18 for men and 2 for women. Churchill College (1960), which ranks as an approved foundation, and Fitzwilliam House for noncollegiate students (1869) both approximate very closely colleges of the normal type as does New Hall (1954), a recognized institution for women. The self-government of both university and colleges is limited only by the fact that the authority of the Queen-in-Council must be obtained for the amendment of their statutes. The interconnection between the university and its colleges is so close that one cannot be thought of without the other. It is in general not possible to be a member of one without being a member of the other, and many university officers hold college offices and vice versa. All undergraduates and research students must first obtain admission to a college; this control over admissions gives the colleges their distinctive position in the structure.

After 1871 when all religious tests for the university degree were withdrawn, residences for Catholic students attending the various colleges were established. Among these were Fisher House, named in honor of St. John Fisher, the martyred bishop of Rochester, which serves as the Catholic chaplaincy and provides a program of religious and social activities for Catholics associated with the university; St. Edmund's House, a residence for secular priests, seminarians, and laymen attending the university; and Benet House, reserved as a residence for members of the Benedictine Order. Other religious orders maintain residences for their own members, and Lady Margaret Hall is a hostel for Catholic women students, mainly foreign students residing in the city.

Administration. The ultimate governing body of the university is the senate, which consists of doctors and masters in all faculties, and of bachelors of divinity, whether resident or not. The senate has the right to confer degrees and to elect the chancellor, who is the supreme university officer but whose position is largely formal. The effective government of the university lies in the hands of the Regent House, which decides major matters of policy and consists of university and college teachers, and administrative officers who are resident in Cambridge. There is no permanent executive head like an American university president. One of the heads of colleges acts as vice-chancellor for a period of two years, and as such presides over the three main administrative bodies: the council of the senate, the general board of the faculties, and the financial board. The first, elected by the Regent House, is responsible for the general oversight of affairs and for the presentation of reports on matters of policy on which the Regent House may subsequently vote. The second is responsible for advising the university on educational policy, teaching, and research; and the third, for the regulation of expenditure.

Research and teaching are handled by 20 faculties and other independent departments. The most ancient chair, the Lady Margaret professorship of divinity, was established in 1502. Other chairs, since introduced, cover the humanities, sciences, classical and modern languages, agriculture, engineering, medicine, and Oriental and veterinary studies. In the 1850s the teaching of undergraduates was done by the colleges and private tutors, but since the early 1900s it has become more and more centralized in the university itself, particularly as a result of the rapid growth of the scientific departments. The colleges retain responsibility only for the individual teaching of their own members by college supervisors, a system that was developed during the 20th century. Many of these supervisors, but not all, are fellows of colleges, who may often hold university lectureships. The most important college officials from the undergraduate point of view are the tutors who are responsible for the welfare and discipline of the men under their charge. Although in modern times the university has become more important at the expense of the colleges, college tutoring and supervision are still regarded as very important parts of the Cambridge system.

Degrees and Examinations. All students in all subjects take the B.A. as their first degree. In the 1850s less than half the undergraduates took honors, the only road to which was through the mathematical tripos (the word ''tripos'' refers to a three-legged stool used in university ceremonies, and the word came eventually to be applied, by a devious course of events, to the honors examinations themselves). In the 19th century new tripos examinations were created in classics (1822) and in moral and in natural sciences (1848), and subsequently new triposes have been founded which cover all the main subjects of academic study, including music, architecture, and fine arts. For the B.A. degree nine terms' residence is required, and for an honors degree the appropriate standard must generally be reached in two tripos examinations. The majority of the triposes are divided into two parts, the first being taken at the end of the 1st or 2d year and the second at the end of the 3d year after a course of more specialized study. It is possible, unlike the system in most British universities, for the two tripos examinations to be taken in different subjects. Honors are classified into first, second, and third class. Within each class the arrangement is alphabetical; until 1909 mathematical honors were graded in order of merit, the first man on the list bearing the ancient title of senior wrangler. Almost all undergraduates now take honors degrees; pass degrees still exist, but they are of very little importance.

Until the 1890s there was no organized provision for graduate study. Any B.A. may be admitted to the M.A. degree without further examination after six years have elapsed from the end of his first term. The M.A. confers membership of the senate and certain privileges in the use of the university library and other institutions, but it does not represent any additional academic qualification. In the later 19th century the university began to give graduates of other universities certain credits toward the B.A. degree (at present graduates of many other universities may obtain the B.A. after obtaining honors in one tripos examination and keeping six terms' residence). In 1895 it was for the first time made possible for graduate students from other universities to obtain the B.A. by thesis, a step that inaugurated the ''research student'' in the modern sense. The Ph.D. degree was established in 1919, its supporters urging that after World War I many students, especially Americans, who had previously gone to Germany for their research work would come to England if a doctorate were available for them. The graduate studies of the university developed with great rapidity after World War II, especially in the scientific departments. Graduate students come to Cambridge from all over the world. Among the chief university institutions is the university library, which contains more than 3,000,000 works. There are other faculty and departmental libraries, and each college has a library of its own, many of these containing important manuscripts and printed collections. The university and college buildings are scattered throughout the city.

Bibliography: *The Student's Handbook to the University and Colleges of Cambridge, 1962–63* (1963); *The Annual Register, 1962–63* (1963); *Statutes of the University of Cambridge . . .* (1961); *The Historical Register of the University of Cambridge . . . to the Year 1910*, ed. J. R. TANNER (1917), with suppls.; *Alumni Cantabrigienses,* comp. J. and J. A. VENN, 10 v. (1922–54). A.B. EMDEN, *Biographical Register of the Scholars of the University of Cambridge before 1500* (Cambridge, Eng. 1963). *Cambridge University Reporter* (1870–), weekly in term. (All published by Cambridge University Press.) J. P. C. ROACH, ed., *The City and University of Cambridge* (*Victoria History of the County of Cambridgeshire . . .*, v. 3; London 1959). C. H. COOPER, *Annals of Cambridge*, 5 v. (Cambridge 1842–1908). R. WILLIS, *The Architectural History of the University of Cambridge . . .*, ed. J. W. CLARK, 4 v. (1886). D. A. WINSTANLEY, *The University of Cambridge in the 18th Century* (1922); *Unreformed Cambridge* (1935); *Early Victorian Cambridge* (1940); *Later Victorian Cambridge* (1947). (All published by the University Press.) T. D. ATKINSON, *Cambridge Described and Illustrated* (London 1897).

[J. P. C. ROACH]

CAMBRIDGE PLATFORM

Also known as the Platform of Church Discipline, it was framed by a synod held in Cambridge, Mass., in 1648. Representatives of the Puritan churches in the four New England colonies gathered to take steps against interference by unfriendly authorities in England and to formulate a common church polity based on Scripture. The WESTMINSTER CONFESSION had proposed a national church on a Presbyterian pattern, and the clergy of New England—not seeking freedom from English political rule—were determined to maintain the autonomy of their own churches. Though recognizing a bond through the covenant of grace, the leaders wanted to ensure the right of each congregation to elect and ordain a minister of its own choosing and to regulate its affairs without direction by any higher authority.

The 17 chapters of the Platform, mainly the work of Richard Mather, described carefully a system of church discipline that would regularize the practices of the New England churches, with each item supported by texts from Scripture. The synod used the word Congregational and provided for the free election of church officers by the church members. Although each church was to be distinct, the Platform recommended consultation among neighboring churches. The support of the churches by local taxation was taken for granted, but the civil authorities were to have no control, except in cases of heresy, blasphemy, profanation of the Lord's Day, and open disturbance of worship.

The Cambridge Platform established a new church order, a type of government that served the CONGREGATIONALISTS for 200 years. Its principle of the autonomy of the local church was adopted by the BAPTISTS, the UNIVERSALISTS, and other groups, so that nearly half of American Protestants belong to churches that are congregational in practice.

Bibliography: F. L. FAGLEY, ''The Narrative of the Cambridge Synod,'' in *Cambridge Platform of 1648: Tercentenary Commemoration . . .*, ed. H. W. FOOTE (Boston 1949). H. W. FOOTE, ''The Significance and Influence of the Cambridge Platform of 1648,'' *ibid.* bibliog. of editions of the Platform, *ibid.* 115–119.

[W. D. HOYT, JR.]

CAMBRIDGE PLATONISTS

A group of 17th-century English Protestant thinkers, so named because of their connection with Cambridge University and the presence of certain Platonic elements in their teaching. In religion they were ''latitude-men,'' standing, as Matthew Arnold says, ''between the sacerdotal religion of the Laudian clergy . . . and the notional religion of the Puritans,'' and in their theology they emphasized conduct rather than doctrine. Since some of them continued to hold office at the university during the time of the Commonwealth, they were considered suspect after the return of the Stuarts in 1660. However, as a contemporary account given by ''P.S.'' (Symon Patrick?) puts it, ''they were glad to conform to the Church after the Restoration.'' The same author also defends their attitude toward rites and ceremonies since ''they do highly approve that virtuous mediocrity which our Churches observe between the meretricious gaudiness of the Church of Rome, and the squalid sluttery of fanatic Conventicles,'' adding that they subscribed to the Thirty-nine Articles, were attacked by both Papists and Presbyterians and were unjustly accused of ''liberty of conscience,'' that is, licentiousness in their private lives. ''But there is another crime, which cannot be denied, that they have introduced a new philosophy; Aristotle and the schoolmen are out of request with them,'' since they had taken up with the atomical or Cartesian doctrine.

The principal representatives of the school are Benjamin Whichcote, who is generally regarded as its founder, John Smith, Henry More and Ralph Cudworth.

Benjamin Whichcote. Whichcote (1609–1683) entered Emmanuel College, a Puritan foundation, in 1626, was ordained as an Anglican priest and held high places in the university under the Puritans. After he was deprived of the provostship of King's College in 1660, he spent his remaining years as a rector, first in country places and later in London. His *Select Sermons* were published with a notable introduction by Shaftesbury in 1698 and *Several Discourses* by John Jeffrey (4 vols., 1701–07). In ''The Malignity of Popery'' he gives the essence of ''the reformed religion'' by way of contrast to asserted doctrines and practices of the Church of Rome. In various other sermons he presents what may be called a theory of natural religion, writing that ''the State of Religion lyes, in short, in this; *A good Mind, and a good Life.* All else is *about* Religion, and hath but the place of Means or an Instrument.'' He advances the teleological and moral arguments for God's existence and shows in various ways that ''it is more Knowable that there is a God, than any thing else is knowable.'' For Whichcote ''the great Rights'' are: (1) God is to be worshiped and adored; (2) there is a difference between good and evil; and (3) good is to be done, evil avoided. Elements of scholasticism are plentiful in his work, as evidenced by many particular terms, ideas and axioms and his theories of truth, objective morality, faith and reason, intellect and will and freedom.

John Smith. A philosophically more important and appealing figure is John Smith (1616–52), a student of Whichcote's at Emmanuel and later dean of Queens' College. His full development as a thinker and writer was cut off by an early death, but his posthumous *Select Discourses* (1659) show him to have been a man of wide learning, considerable intellectual power, originality of thought and expression, genuine spiritual perception and great sincerity. He stands apart from Whichcote, More and Cudworth because of the absence of bigotry and intolerance from his writing and especially from More because of his sane and rational attitude toward superstitious beliefs and practices. More truly Platonic than others in the group, Smith's cast of mind may also be described as Plotinian and Augustinian. Accordingly, he gives particular attention to the soul and advances four arguments for its immortality, namely, (1) from its incorporeity, indivisibility, powers and operations; (2) from the distinction between man's free and ''automatical'' actions; (3) from mathematical notions, which are ''the true characters of some immaterial being, seeing that they were never buried in matter, nor extracted out of it: and yet these are transcendently more certain and infallible principles of demonstration than any sensible thing can be''; and (4) from man's clear and stable ideas of truth.

On the existence and nature of God, Smith's doctrine is both ambitious and original, since he holds that he would ''not so much demonstrate that He is, as what He is.'' From a study of his own being man can arrive at conceptions of ''the most perfect mind and understanding,'' and God's omnipotence, ''almighty love,'' eternity, omnipresence and absolute freedom. Smith has many fine passages on God's nature and relations to the universe and man and on ''the Excellency and Nobleness of True Religion.'' One of the best of these is on man's true happiness as found in God. He has, or should have, a place in the history of English prose; his works are filled with memorable phrases and he may be regarded as a pioneer in the aphoristic style of writing and preaching that has been popular in more recent times. In addition to Scripture, he cites innumerable authors—Greek, Roman, patristic and medieval, as well as contemporary—and the influence of others, for example, of St. FRANCIS DE SALES, is apparent.

Henry More. More (1614–87) ranks with Cudworth as the most famous of the Cambridge Platonists. Although raised a Calvinist, he rebelled against predestinarianism while a student at Eton. At Christ's College he was a fellow student of John Milton and became a master of arts and fellow in 1639. His studies of Aristotle, Julius Scaliger, G. Cardano and others ended, he says, in ''mere scepticism'' and he turned to ''the Platonic writers, Marsilius Ficinus, Plotinus himself, Mercurius Trismegistus and the Mystical Divines.'' After taking Anglican orders, he received two benefices but gave them to friends; later he declined two bishoprics and the deanery of St. Patrick's and provostship of Trinity College, Dublin, preferring to spend his life in Cambridge. He had a wide circle of friends and many correspondents, among them Descartes, the younger Van Helmont, William Penn, John Norris, Baron Knorr and Joseph Glanvill. He was a voluminous writer on philosophy and theology and produced some verse.

Philosophy. To a basic philosophy derived from Aristotle and the scholastics More added elements drawn from Plato, the Neoplatonists and other sources. Making an early acquaintance with Descartes, he first had an extravagant admiration for his doctrine, but later showed himself to be anti-Cartesian in metaphysics and finally doubted that there is anything mechanical in nature. Incorporeal substance is for him the object of metaphysics; the universe is ''one huge Animal,'' or if it lacks sense, which lack is not proved, ''one monstrous Plant''; all nature, he says, is pervaded by ''the spirit of nature,'' or ''a plastical power''; space is an objective reality endowed with divine attributes. At the same time, he advances a doctrine of monads: bodies are composed of indivisible physical monads, and can be dissolved back into them by God's power, while spiritual substance is a ''metaphysical monad.''

In psychology and epistemology More labors to refute Hobbes and other materialists and to establish the reality of the soul, which has both preexistence and immortality. At death the soul leaves its ''terrestrial vehicle,'' ''glides into the free air,'' and enters first into an ''aereal'' and later into an ''aethereal or celestial vehicle.'' The mind is never a *tabula rasa* but possesses innate ideas; the secondary qualities of bodies are in the perceiver rather than in things. In ethics More develops a doctrine of conscience under the name of ''the boniform faculty,'' which he says is ''the best and divinest part . . . the celestial particle of the soul,'' but here as elsewhere in his ethics he has nothing new that is of value.

Theology. More's theodicy is elaborate but unreliable. Leaving undeveloped the basic proofs for God's existence, he gives first place to his statement of the *ratio Anselmi* and advances so extravagant a statement of the proof from order as to discredit teleology. Further arguments are adduced from man's innate idea of God, the nature of the soul, morality, ''miracles,'' namely, accounts of ghosts, witchcraft, demonism and the like, and man's religious instincts. In religion More is important chiefly for his strong Protestantism, in which he holds that treason against any Protestant prince or opposition to Protestantism is both civil treason and religious heresy. The Church of Rome is the kingdom of anti-Christ and ''the mystery of iniquity.'' In his attack More spares nothing: the Church's doctrine, history, claims, morals, ceremonial, members, leaders and head were all assailed. So savage is his hatred that he was found extreme even in an age when like attacks were common among such diverse groups as Anglicans, dissenters and FREETHINKERS.

More must be rated low both as a philosopher and a theologian. His work is marred by such intense bigotry and superstition as to bring injury on various valid doctrines, especially in theodicy and rational psychology. His attempts at novelty are abortive and his work must be characterized as a mélange of doctrines taken from the Greeks, the scholastics, Jewish cabalists, Protestant theology, Sacred Scripture and contemporary science. His books were read in colonial New England and helped to prepare the way for the sordid events at Salem.

Ralph Cudworth. Cudworth (1617–1688), a student and later fellow of Emmanuel College, had prestige and power under Cromwell but promptly wrote verses welcoming Charles II back home. His chief works were *The True Intellectual System of the Universe,* finished in 1671 but delayed in publication by opposition at court until 1678; and the posthumously published *Confutation of the Reason and Philosophy of Atheism* (1706); *Treatise concerning Eternal and Immutable Morality* (1731); and *Treatise of Freewill* (1838). The *True Intellectual System* is a vast work, itself a part of a vaster unfinished project, worthy—in conception at least—of comparison with some of the great systematic works of earlier centuries. It may be divided into five parts: (1) a refutation of atheism, (2) the true idea of God, (3) proofs for the existence of God, (4) the natural distinction between good and evil, and (5) freedom of will. First giving the arguments for atheism, he perhaps, as Dryden says, states them better than he refutes them. Although he rejects the Anselmian and Cartesian arguments, he gives one based on the idea of God and others from contingency, order and the character of knowledge.

Famous for his theory of a plastic nature, Cudworth describes it as a lower faculty of some conscious soul, or itself a kind of inferior life or soul, an immaterial, incorporeal substance that is the divine art embodied in nature, a shadowy imitation of mind and understanding, analogous to mental causality, acting for ends but unconscious of them. It is an instrument used by God and it operates according to laws imposed by him. Analogies to ancient theories of a WORLD SOUL and to later doctrines like those of Schopenhauer, Bergson and E. von Hartmann are evident. Certain anticipations of Kantian doctrines in theodicy and on space and time as mental forms, the categories and the unknown "thing in itself" may also be found in Cudworth.

Cudworth is almost a great philosopher. Along with pronounced intellectual abilities and immense learning, he unites many past and contemporary strains, makes some contributions of his own and anticipates certain future developments. His purposes are good, but he fails in some of his means since his great learning is often uncritical, he overuses his authorities and is at times too severe in his judgments. Instances of these defects may be found in his account of atomistic philosophy, which he traced back to Moses. If he had advanced an extremist doctrine, as did Hobbes and Spinoza in his time, he would have been a more famous and influential, but less able, thinker. As it is, Cudworth ranks with Bacon, Hobbes and Locke in 17th-century English philosophy, and in certain respects is superior to them.

Related Thinkers and Influence. Other thinkers sometimes, but incorrectly, associated with the Cambridge Platonists are Nathaniel Culverwel (1615/18–1650/51), George Rust (d. 1670), Symon Patrick (1626–1707), Joseph Glanvill (1636–80), John Hales (1584–1656), John Norris (1657–1711) and Richard Cumberland (1631–1718). In addition to their relation to Kant and Locke, the Cambridge Platonists influenced particularly the third Earl of Shaftesbury (1671–1713). In religion the effects of their teaching were away from traditional doctrine and toward RATIONALISM and a nondogmatic religion of morality. In philosophy they were dualists concerned with fundamental things—God, the soul, natural morality, free will and the epistemological problem. In some areas, they prepared the way for more radical doctrines of the 18th century.

See Also: BRITISH MORALISTS; ENLIGHTENMENT, PHILOSOPHY; PLATONISM.

Bibliography: Sources. J. SMITH, *Select Discourses,* ed. H. G. WILLIAMS (4th ed. rev. Cambridge, Eng. 1859). H. MORE, *Opera omnia,* 3 v. (London 1675–79). R. CUDWORTH, *The True Intellectual System of the Universe,* tr. J. HARRISON, 3 v. (London 1845). Literature. F. C. COPLESTON, *History of Philosophy* (Westminster, Md 1946–) 5:52–66. J. TULLOCH, *Rational Theology and Christian Philosophy in England in the Seventeenth Century,* 2 v. (2d ed. Edinburgh 1874). J. K. RYAN, *The Reputation of St. Thomas Aquinas Among English Protestant Thinkers of the Seventeenth Century* (Washington 1948); "John Smith, 1616–1652: Platonist and Mystic," *The New Scholasticism,* 20 (1946) 1–25. E. CASSIRER, *The Platonic Renaissance in England,* tr. J. P. PETTEGROVE (Austin 1953). B. WILLEY, *Seventeenth Century Background* (New York 1950). J. A. PASSMORE, *Ralph Cudworth* (Cambridge, Eng. 1951).

[J. K. RYAN]

CAMERLENGO

An Italian word that corresponds to "chamberlain" in English. In church parlance it designates the cardinal of the Holy Roman Church with specific responsibilities of treasurer and administrator during the time between the death of one pope and the election of his successor. The time period is often described as *sede vacante.* Pope John Paul II in the apostolic constitution, *Universi dominici gregis,* is the latest of five popes since St. Pius X to address this venerable office.

Appointed by the reigning pope, or elected by the College of Cardinals if the office is vacant at the pope's death, the camerlengo continues to exercise his ordinary functions of office, submitting to the College of Cardinals matters that would have had to be referred to the supreme pontiff. Upon the death of the supreme pontiff, the camerlengo must officially verify the pope's death and with those officials described by law draw up the official death certificate. He informs the dean of the College of Cardinals, who informs the cardinals and convokes them for the congregations of the college. The camerlengo seals the deceased pope's rooms of the papal apartment and the entire apartment after the pope's funeral; he informs the cardinal vicar for Rome, who informs the people of Rome of the pope's death; he notifies the cardinal archpriest of the Vatican basilica; and he takes possession of the Apostolic Palace in the Vatican and the palaces of the Lateran and Castel Gandolfo for the purpose of exercising custody and administration. As a member of the College of Cardinals to whom the government of the Church is entrusted, the camerlengo and three cardinals chosen by lot from the cardinal electors already present in Rome, form a particular congregation to deal with questions of lesser importance as compared to the general, or preparatory, congregations, which include the whole College of Cardinals and which are held before the beginning of the electoral conclave.

With the consultation of the other three cardinals, the camerlengo determines all matters of the pope's burial; and he deals, in the name of and with the consent of the College of Cardinals, with all matters that circumstances suggest for safeguarding the goods and temporal rights of the Holy See and for its proper administration. As preparation for the conclave to elect a new pope, the camerlengo reserves quarters in the *Domus Sanctae Marthae* for the cardinal electors and the areas reserved for liturgical celebrations, in particular the Sistine Chapel, making provision that a suitable number of persons be available for preparing and serving meals and for housekeeping. The cardinal camerlengo ensures, with the expertise of trustworthy technicians, that no violation of secrecy with regard to election events in the Sistine Chapel takes place before, during, and after the voting. During the actual voting of the cardinal electors, the camerlengo declares the results of each session, as well as disposes of ballots and any notes concerning the results of each ballot. The carmerlengo holds office *ad bene placitum* of the Roman pontiff.

Bibliography: *Codex iuris canonici* (Rome 1918; repr. Graz 1955) cc. 332–335; *Corpus Canonum ecclesiarium orientalium,* cc. 43–48 as modified by John Paul II, ''Universi Dominici Gregis,'' in *Acta Apostolicae Sedis* 87 (1996): 305–343.

[A. ESPELAGE]

CAMERON, JOHN

Scottish theologian, a leading divine of the French Huguenot Church; b. Glasgow, 1579; d. Montauban, France, 1625. He was educated at the University of Glasgow. In 1600 he went to France where his abilities as a classical scholar won him a professorship at the Protestant University of Sedan. From 1604 to 1608 he studied theology at Paris, Geneva, and Heidelberg. In 1608 he published the first of a series of theological tracts (*De triplici Dei cum homine foedere*), which were to make him a controversial figure in Calvinist circles. In retrospect, Cameron's theological intentions seem quite clear. He, like the Dutchman Jacobus ARMINIUS, was trying to resolve the dilemma implicit in orthodox Calvinist theology as to whether Christ had died for all men or for the elect only. Arminius, unlike Calvin, insisted that the atonement was for all—believers and nonbelievers, elect and reprobate alike. If Christ died for all, anti-Arminians charged, then nonbelievers were the victims of divine caprice and the unregenerate had a voluntary power to resist grace. In either case, significant attributes of the divine nature were impugned. Cameron contended by way of compromise that Christ's death was a universal sacrifice but that nonbelievers did not therefore have a choice of accepting or resisting grace. According to Cameron, the will of man is determined by the judgment of the mind. Men do good or evil as a result of knowledge infused into them by God, who does not move the will physically but only morally as a consequence of its dependence on human judgment. Thus Cameron believed he had removed God's ultimate responsibility for sin, preserved the irresistible nature of grace, and explained how it was that some men could seemingly accept or deny the consequences of Christ's sacrifice.

Despite his ambivalent position, Cameron held the chairs of divinity at Saumur (1618–20) and Glasgow (1622–23). Never popular with the strong Presbyterian party in the Scottish Church, he ended his days in France, where he taught briefly at the University of Montauban before his death.

Bibliography: T. F. HENDERSON, *The Dictionary of National Biography from the Earliest Times to 1900* 3:747–748. *The Oxford Dictionary of the Christian Church* 223.

[S. A. BURRELL]

CAMERON, JOHN

Bishop, educator; b. South River, Antigonish County, Nova Scotia, Canada, Feb. 16, 1826; d. Antigonish, April 6, 1910. He was the youngest son of John Cameron. After attending St. Andrew's grammar and normal school, he pursued his ecclesiastical studies at the Urban College of the Propaganda, Rome, was ordained July 26, 1853, and received the doctorate of philosophy and theology. On his return to Canada, he served as professor and director of a school at Arichat, Nova Scotia. In 1855 he was assigned as parish priest to St. Ninian's, Antigonish, where he served also as rector and professor of philosophy and theology in the newly established St. Francis Xavier College (later University) and directed its progress for more than a half-century. He was appointed to the cathedral at Arichat (1863), and was named vicar-general (1865), and coadjutor (1869). He was consecrated titular bishop of Titopolis (in Isauria) at Rome on May 22, 1870, and succeeded to the see July 17, 1887, becoming Arichat's third bishop. On Aug. 23, 1886, the episcopal see was transferred from Arichat to Antigonish. There Cameron opened new parishes, institutions, and religious schools; and under his guidance St. Francis Xavier College became the center of Catholic learning in the Maritime Provinces. In May of 1885 he was sent as papal delegate to Three Rivers, Quebec, to investigate the division of the diocese. He was regarded as one of the ablest Catholic spokesmen in Canada.

Bibliography: D. J. RANKIN, *A History of the County of Antigonish, Nova Scotia* (Toronto 1929).

[J. T. FLYNN]

CAMERONIANS

The most uncompromising Presbyterian communion in Scotland (known also as the Reformed Presbyterian Church). Though numerically small, the group is historically important. The Cameronians take their origin from those COVENANTERS who refused to follow their brethren in accepting the Revolution Settlement of the Church of Scotland (1689–90). Their reason was that the Settlement ignored the perpetual obligation incurred by the Scottish nation in the National Covenant of 1638, and by the whole of Great Britain in the Solemn League and Covenant of 1643. The name Cameronian derives from that of the principal preacher of these dissenting Covenanters, the youthful extremist Richard Cameron (1648–80), who fell in the skirmish at Aird's Moss near Auchinleck. His followers organized themselves in local societies, mainly in Ayrshire and Lanarkshire (1681). Though their three ministers entered the national church of the Revolution Settlement in 1690, the greater part of the sect, numbering several thousand, refused to conform; 16 years later (1706) they obtained a new minister, John Macmillan, whose intensive, itinerant missionary activity so strengthened the movement that the sectarians were often called Macmillanites. Under his leadership in 1743, a presbytery, known as the Reformed Presbytery, was set up, and the Reformed Presbyterians increased their numerical strength in Scotland; their ideas had considerable effect on Scottish communities overseas. They maintained, into the 19th century, the principle of "political dissent," refusing to swear allegiance to the British Constitution or to take part in any way in civil government. In 1863 a majority of the Reformed Presbyterian Synod decided to refrain from taking disciplinary action against those who exercised the franchise or took part in the civil government of an "uncovenanted" nation. In 1876 this majority joined the Free Church and were finally merged in the Established Church of Scotland in 1929.

Bibliography: M. HUTCHISON, *The Reformed Presbyterian Church in Scotland, 1680–1876* (Paisley, Scot. 1893). W. J. COUPER, *The Reformed Presbyterian Church in Scotland* (Edinburgh 1925). J. HIGHET, *The Scottish Churches* (London 1960). F. L. CROSS, *The Oxford Dictionary of the Christian Church* (London 1957) 223.

[D. MCROBERTS]

CAMEROON, THE CATHOLIC CHURCH IN

A tropical, largely agricultural country located on the coast of West Africa, the Republic of Cameroon borders Chad on the north and northeast, the Central African Republic on the east, the Republic of the Congo on the southeast and south, Gabon and Equatorial Guinea on the south, the Gulf of Guinea on the southwest and Nigeria on the west. Coastal marshes rise to a central, forested plateau region, with active volcanic mountains in the west and a plains region to the north. Natural resources include bauxite, iron ore and petroleum, while agricultural products consist primarily of cocoa, coffee, bananas, peanuts and timber. Due to its location, Cameroon is sometimes referred to as "the hinge of Africa."

A German colony after 1844, the Cameroon region became a mandate territory administered by the French and British following World War I. From 1944 to 1960 the region became a trust territory of the United Nations; in 1960 the French trusteeship became an independent republic in the French Community and was joined by a portion of the southern British trusteeship the following year, which voted to unite with it. The Cameroon population is made up of some 200 ethnic groups. In addition to the dominant Bantus, there are settlers from Sudan and immigrants from neighboring Nigeria, Chad, Benin, Togo, Senegal, Ivory Coast and Burkina-Faso. Economic and social stability has allowed Cameroon to develop a strong infrastructure of roads and communications, although politically power continued to rest within a single ethnic group. Cameroon became a member of the Commonwealth of Nations in 1995.

Early History. The region, which was originally the home of the Bantu people, was largely uninhabited at the time that the Portuguese landed on its coast in 1472. A number of small African kingdoms had become established in the region by 1800, and in the mid-19th century German traders also appeared. Methodical evangelization began in 1890, when the area was detached from the Vicariate Apostolic of the Two Guineas, and the Prefecture Apostolic of Kamerun was created and entrusted to German Pallottines, following the establishment of a German protectorate in 1911. The northern section of the region was detached in 1914 to form the Prefecture Apostolic of Adamaoua, which was confided to the German province of the Priests of the Sacred Heart, but during World War I all missionaries, except French military chaplains, were expelled. In 1916 Anglo-French forces occupied the region, and following World War I Cameroon was divided into British and French mandates—a system devised by the U.N. as a way to deal with former German territories in preparation for their eventual independence.

After 1922 the Vicariate of Cameroun was staffed by French Holy Ghost Fathers. The Prefecture of Adamaoua was transferred to Foumban, and Sacred Heart Fathers from France replaced those from Germany. Mill Hill Missionaries took charge of evangelizing the British mandate territory, where in 1923 the Prefecture of Buea was created. Thereupon the mission experienced a rapid growth: from 60,000 in 1920, the region contained almost 700,000 Catholics by 1960. In 1931 the Vicariate of Cameroon was divided into the Vicariate of Yaoundé and Prefecture of Douala. In 1947 the Oblates of Mary Immaculate were given charge of the newly created Prefecture of Garoua in the extreme north with jurisdiction over some territory in Chad until 1956. In 1949 the Vicariate of Doumé was separated from Yaoundé and was given to the Holy Ghost Fathers. The hierarchy was established in 1955, when YAOUNDÉ became an archdiocese and metropolitan see for the entire country, and continued to be revised due to shifts in population. In 1935 the first African priests were ordained in Cameroon, and in 1955 the first African bishops were consecrated. Jean Baptiste Zoa became the first African archbishop of Yaoundé in 1961, and Christian Wiyghan Tumi became the first Cameroonian cardinal in 1988.

[J. BOUCHAUD]

The Modern Era. On Jan. 1, 1960 French Cameroon was given full independence. A year later, on Oct. 1, 1961, it was joined by a portion of the British mandate territory, the remainder of the British mandate annexing to Nigeria. On May 20, 1972 these territories merged as the United Republic of Cameroon, ruled by a single party. Under the constitution of 1972, freedom of religion was protected. After widespread unrest, under President Paul Biya, other parties were eventually legalized and in 1992 the first multi-party elections were held. After several elections held the same year, Biya and his party were reelected. Although charges of fraud were leveled against him, Biya continued as president into the 21st century.

Capital: Yaoundé.
Size: 183,591 sq. miles.
Population: 15,421,940 in 2000.
Languages: English, French; numerous tribal languages are spoken in various regions.
Religions: 4,780,800 Catholics (31%), 3,701,265 Muslims (24%), 2,930,170 Protestants (19%), 4,009,705 follow indigenous beliefs.

While the reforms of Vatican II were slow in making an impact in Cameroon, after Pope John Paul II's first visit in August of 1985—he returned in September of 1995—the country's bishops began to emphasize the need for ''Africanization.'' In 1989, on the eve of the 100th anniversary of the Catholic presence in Cameroon, they issued the letter ''From the First to the Second Evangelization,'' which stated its aim as ''the implantation of the gospel in our manners and customs, namely at the incarnation of Jesus Christ thoroughly in our life.'' The 1994 African Synod, held in Rome, was a milestone on the way to that goal. The Cameroonian National Episcopal Conference (CNEC) met annually, and through communiqués addressed such matters as fairness in elections, lack of morality, the assassination of religious, harassment of parish houses, the importance of education and responsible parenthood The Catholic University of Central Africa, with its campuses at Nkolbisson and Yaoundé, was supervised by a council of bishops appointed by the Episcopal Conference of Central Africa, a group active in addressing human rights issues in the region.

Other evangelization efforts incorporated the pope's Africanization approach. Colonne de Feu, begun in 1976 by Pierre Gaby, a French layman, was popular in the Yaoundé area, as was Cana, which focused on college students. Most numerous were the Ephphata groups begun by Professor Meinrad Hebga, SJ, their success explained in part by the fact that they made a concerted effort at incorporating native languages and traditions in order to appeal to the African spirit. The Ephphata movement established a national ecumenical center for prayer, meditation and healing at Mangèn, a village 40 miles west of Yaoundé.

By the year 2000 Cameroon had 671 parishes, 660 diocesan and 480 religious priests, 200 brothers and

Archdioceses	Suffragans
Bamenda	Buéa, Kumbo, Mamfe
Bertoua	Batouri, Boumé-Abong' Mbang, Yokadouma
Douala	Bafoussam, Deéa, Eséka, Nkongsamba
Garoua	Maroua-Mokolo, Ngaoundéré, Yagoua
Yaoundé	Bafia, Ebolowa-Kribi, Mbalmayo, Obala, Sangmélina

1,660 sisters, and had established several new seminaries by the late 1990s. The Catholic population lived predominately in the former French territories of southern and western Cameroon, while former English territories were predominately Protestant; Muslims congregated in the north. The Church continued to play a crucial role in education, and operated 910 primary and 110 secondary schools in 2000. There were eight Catholic hospitals, six of which were staffed by Ad Lucem and hundreds of Protection infantile et maternelle (PMI) dispensaries. In addition, the Church published a weekly newspaper that, until the mid-1990s, was the only private newspapers published in Cameroon.

Bibliography: CONFERENCE EPISCOPAL NATIONALE DU CAMEROUN, *Assemblée plénière: de la première à la seconde évangelisation* (Yaoundé 1992); *Message of the Bishops of Cameroon for the Preparation of the Centenary* (Yaoundé 1989). J. ELA, *Ma Foi d'Africain* (Paris 1985). M. L. ETEKI-OTABELA, *Misère et grandeur de la démocratie au Cameroun* (Yaoundé 1987). M. HEBGA, *Emancipation d'églises sous tutelle* (Paris 1976); ''Universality in Theology and Inculturation,'' *Bulletin of African Theology,* 5 (1983) 179–92; ''The Evolution of Catholicism in West Africa: The Case of Cameroon,'' in *World Catholicism in Transition,* ed. H. GANNON (New York 1988) 320–32. D. LANTUM, *Recent Advances in the Healing Ministry of the Catholic Church in Cameroon* (Yaoundé 1984). E. MVENG, *L'Afrique dans l'eglise* (Paris 1986). *Bilan du Monde,* 2:186–193. *Annuario Pontificio* has statistics on all dioceses.

[M. HEBGA/EDS.]

CAMILLIANS

Popular name of the Order of St. Camillus (OSCam, Official Catholic Directory #0240), whose official title is the Order of the Servants of the Sick (*Ordo Ministrantium Infirmis*). The order was founded in Rome by St. CAMILLUS DE LELLIS about 1582 and given final approval as an order with solemn vows in 1591. To the usual three religious vows was added a fourth, that of serving the sick, including the victims of the plagues so common at that time. Camillus composed his rule with this specific character of the order in view.

The first Camillians rendered their services by visiting the hospitals of Rome, bringing the patients both physical and spiritual assistance. In 1594, however, they began founding communities housed within the hospitals, where the religious took the place of the chaplains and of the servants who were hired for nursing. Establishing itself in Naples in 1588, the order grew rapidly. At the time of the founder's death in 1614 there were 330 professed members in 15 cities of Italy. After the death of Camillus the religious began caring for the sick in their homes, gradually giving up the communities within the hospitals. By the end of the 18th century they were exercising this form of apostolate not only in Italy, but also in Hungary, Spain, Portugal, and several parts of Latin America.

The Order of St. Camillus, like other religious orders, suffered greatly from the suppressions and confiscations of the 19th century. At one point it was reduced to about 100 members, all of them in Italy. In the 20th century, however, they experienced a recovery, expanding their mission beyond Italy. In the U.S. the first foundation was made in Milwaukee, Wis., in 1924. By the end of the 20th century, the order had 11 provinces and four foundations in Europe, one province, three delegations and four foundations in Asia, two delegations and five foundations in Africa and Australia.

[P. TUTWILER/EDS.]

CAMILLUS DE LELLIS, ST.

Copatron with St. John of God of hospitals, nurses, and the sick, founder of the Order of CAMILLIANS; b. Bucchianico (Abruzzo), Italy, May 25, 1550; d. Rome, July 14, 1614. His mother, Camilla de Compellis, was nearly 60 years old at his birth and died when he was a child. His father, Giovanni, who served as a captain in both the French and Neapolitan armies, neglected the child's education. As a youth, his own inclinations were already strongly turned to the military life and to gambling. His enrollment in the army was delayed by the outbreak of an ulcer on his right foot; in 1571 it obliged him to seek medical care at the hospital of San Giacomo in Rome. When he was sufficiently healed, he stayed on as a servant in the hospital, but was dismissed for card playing. From 1571 to 1574 he fought in various campaigns of the Venetian army against the Turks. After gambling away his possessions in the winter of 1574 and 1575, he accepted employment at the Capuchin monastery of Manfredonia (Puglio).

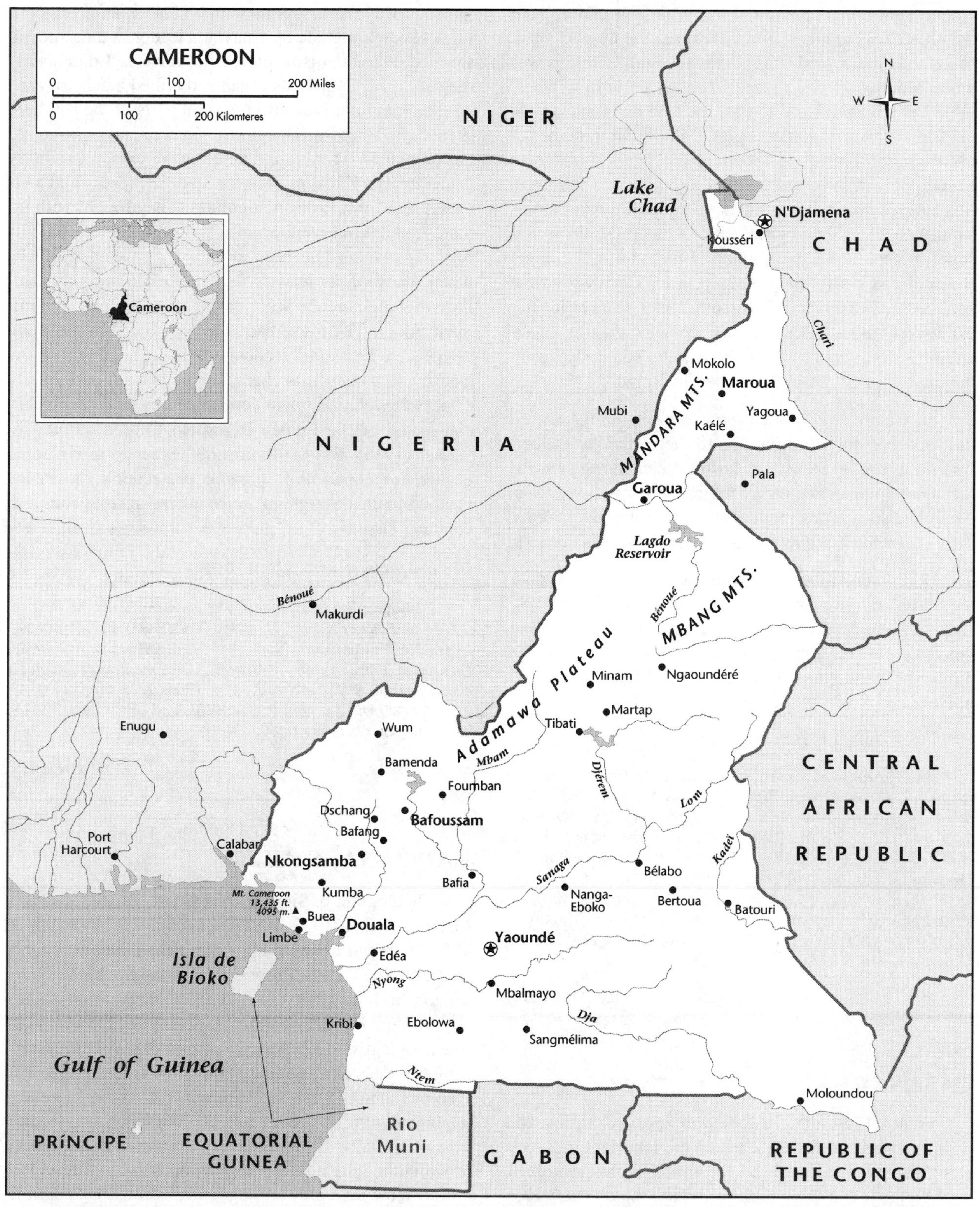

A friar stirred him to repentance on Feb. 2, 1575. He was accepted by the Capuchins as a lay brother but was dismissed from the novitiate when the old wounds irritated by the coarse garb would not heal. Camillus then returned to San Giacomo for treatment and again stayed on as a servant. He reentered the Capuchins in 1579, but the wound again opened and led to his final rejection from the order. This ailment persisted during the next 35 years of his life. Welcomed back to the hospital, Camillus was made Maestro di Casa (superintendent). He now determined to devote his life to the sick, and on the advice of his friends and his spiritual guide, Philip Neri, he began his studies for the priesthood at the Jesuit College in Rome. He was ordained in 1584 and gathered followers to share his work. He founded an order, known then as Ministers of the Sick, or Fathers of a Good Death; as first superior general he spent much of his time in the direct spiritual and bodily care of the infirm. He resigned the generalship in 1607 and devoted the final years of his life exclusively to such personal service. He died after establishing several houses throughout Italy. His body lies in the church of St. Mary Magdalen in Rome.

St. Camillus is known more for his charity toward the sick than for contributions to the technique of their care. Yet, his insistence on hospital cleanliness and the technical competence of his religious deserves mention. Notable also was his method of instructing his patients, rather than constraining them, to receive the Sacraments.

Benedict XIV beatified Camillus in 1742 and canonized him four years later. In 1886 Leo XIII declared St. Camillus and St. John of God patrons of the sick and of hospitals and inserted their names in the litany of the dying. In 1930 Pius XI extended their patronage to all nurses and to all Catholic nursing associations.

Feast: July 14, formerly July 18.

Bibliography: M. VANTI, *S. Camillo de Lellis ed i suoi ministri degli infermi* (2d ed. Rome 1958). G. DE BELLAING, *De la fureur du jeu—aux folies de l'amour!* (Paris 1982). S. CICATELLI, *Vita del P. C. de Lellis* (Rome 1624); this early life is tr. by W. FABER, *St. Camillus de Lellis* (Milwaukee 1926). E. F. CURLEY, *St. Camillus* (Milwaukee 1962). M. FISCHER, *Der hl. Kamillus von Lellis* (Freiburg 1940). C. C. MARTINDALE, *Life of Saint Camillus* (New York 1946). A. BUTLER, *The Lives of the Saints*, ed. H. THURSTON and D. ATTWATER (New York 1956) 3:134–136. *Bullarii Romani Continuatio* 1:175–176.

[P. TUTWILER]

CAMISARDS

French Protestant zealots who revolted against the government of Louis XIV early in the 18th century. They were provoked to revolt by the brutal repression of all public practice of their faith following the revocation of the Edict of Nantes (1685), and by the apocalyptic writings of certain Protestant intellectuals, notably Pierre Jurieu. They were led by a number of ecstatic, uneducated ''prophets'' convinced of their own direct inspiration and of the imminent end of the world. Their first great act of violence was the assassination in 1702 of an archpriest, François de Langlade du Chayla, a leader in the suppression of Protestantism in the Cévennes. Immediately thereafter the Camisards organized armed bands to resist government punitive action in rural parts of the southern French provinces of Dauphiné, Vivarais, and, above all, the Cévennes. They found an effective amateur military leader in Jean Cavalier and won some sympathy and a little support from Protestant nations. They fought with fanatic ferocity but were no match for the armies of Louis XIV. The revolt had been effectively crushed by 1704, when many of its leaders fled into exile abroad. Later flare-ups of violence were easily contained by government troops. The movement was repudiated by the more responsible Protestant leaders in France, notably Antoine Court, and some of its characteristic claims, particularly of direct revelation, were condemned by a secret provincial synod of the French Reformed Church of the Cévennes (1715). But the Camisards' excesses provided an excuse for continuing sporadic persecution of French Protestantism throughout much of the rest of the 18th century.

See Also: NANTES, EDICT OF

Bibliography: H. M. BAIRD, *The Huguenots and the Revocation of the Edict of Nantes,* 2 v. (New York 1895) v.2. A. DUCASSE, *La Guerre des Camisards* (Paris 1946). C. ALMERAS, *La Révolte des Camisards* (Paris 1960). F. VERNET, *Dictionnaire de théologie catholique*, ed. A. VACANT et al., 15 v. (Paris 1903–50) 2:1435–43. R. VOELTZEL, *Die Religion in Geschichte und Gegenwart*, 7 v. (3d ed. Tübingen 1957–65) 1:1603–04.

[R. M. KINGDON]

CAMPANA, EMILIO

Theologian; b. Signora (Val Colla, Ticino), 1874; d. Lugano, June 8, 1939. He completed his early education at Pollegio and Lugano. He was sent to Rome for higher studies at the Urban (Propaganda) College and won doctorates in both philosophy and theology. His teacher Alexis Lépicier (later cardinal) encouraged his pursuit of Mariological studies. After his ordination in 1897, he returned to the major seminary at Lugano to teach dogmatic theology, holding the post until his death. In 1914 he was appointed official theologian of the bishop of Lugano. From 1927 until 1932 he served as rector of the seminary at which he taught. He is known principally for his two works in the field of Mariology: *Maria nel dogma cattolico* (Turin 1923) and *Maria nel culto cattolico* (2 v., Turin 1933). The former work has been highly acclaimed by theologians throughout the world. It has gone through five Italian editions and has been translated into several languages. Besides these works Campana left two incomplete studies: one on Mary in art and the other a dogmatic-historical treatise on Vatican Council I. In addition to these monographs, he published a number of articles in various theological reviews.

[C. R. MEYER]

CAMPANELLA, TOMMASO

Dominican philosopher; b. Stilo, Calabria, Italy, Sept. 5, 1568; d. Paris, May 21, 1639. Campanella entered the religious life at an early age and was educated in the houses of studies of his order. Becoming dissatisfied with the Aristotelian teachings of his day, he favored instead the naturalistic views of B. TELESIO, whom he undertook to defend against his opponents. In 1599 he was arrested by order of the Spanish authorities and taken in chains to Naples, where he had to stand trial on charges of heresy and conspiracy. Although subjected to physical torture, he never confessed to crime or heresy and even resisted by feigning insanity. In 1602 he was sentenced to perpetual imprisonment, and, whether rightly or not, spent a total of 27 years in a Neapolitan dungeon. Released in 1626, he was again arrested and brought before the Holy Office in Rome. After regaining his freedom, he spent some time at the Dominican priory of Santa Maria sopra Minerva, but fearing further persecution, he followed the advice of Pope Urban VIII and fled to France in 1634. The 71-year-old friar ended his troubled days in the quiet of the priory of Saint-Jacques in Paris.

Campanella was an extremely prolific writer, and the critical edition of his works (ed. L. Firpo, Milan 1954) will fill many volumes. He antedated Descartes as the first philosopher to assert the need of positing a universal methodic doubt at the beginning of his system and to state the principle of self-consciousness as the basis of knowledge and certitude. His philosophy was an attempt to fuse, into a new original synthesis, the naturalistic doctrines of his time and the traditional scholastic teaching; it showed a marked tendency toward Platonic AUGUSTINIANISM. Campanella conceived being as a transcendental composition of power, knowledge, and will, which are its ''primalities'' or essential principles. This panpsychic conception of reality is matched by his theory that being and nonbeing are the metaphysical constituents of all creatures, which are thus distinguished from God who is pure being. For Campanella, to know is to be (*cognoscere est esse*), a principle that underlies his complex theory of knowledge. The central idea of his theology is Christ as universal reason. In politics he advocated a universal monarchy headed by the pope. *The City of the Sun,* his best-known work, is a political dialogue in the tradition of Plato's *Republic* and St. Thomas More's *Utopia.*

See Also: RENAISSANCE PHILOSOPHY.

Bibliography: Works. *Del senso delle cose e della magia,* ed. A. BRUERS (Bari 1925); *Epilogo magno,* ed. C. OTTAVIANO (Rome 1939); *Atheismus triumphatus* (Paris 1636); *Disputationum in quatuor partes suae philosophiae realis libri quatuor* (Paris 1637); *Philosophiae rationalis partes quinque* (Paris 1638); *Universalis philosophiae seu metaphysicarum rerum iuxta propria dogmata, partes tres, libri XVIII* (Paris 1638); *Theologicorum libri XXX,* ed. in part R. AMERIO (Milan 1936); *Aforismi politici,* ed. L. FIRPO (Turin 1941); ''The City of the Sun,'' tr. W. J. GILSTRAP, in *The Quest for Utopia,* ed. G. R. NEGLEY and J. M. PATRICK (New York 1952). Literature. R. AMERIO, *Enciclopedia filosofica* 1:866–874. N. PICARD, *Lexikon für Theologie und Kirche* (Freiburg 1957–65) 2:907. L. FIRPO, *Bibliografia degli scritti di Tommaso Campanella* (Turin 1940). G. DI NAPOLI, *Tommaso Campanella, filosofo della restaurazione cattolica* (Padua 1947). B. M. BONANSEA, *The Theory of Knowledge of Tommaso Campanella, Exposition and Critique* (Washington 1954); ''The Concept of Being and Non-Being in the Philosophy of T. C.,'' *The New Scholasticism* 31 (1957) 34–67; ''The Political Thought of T. C.,'' *Studies in Philosophy and the History of Philosophy,* ed. J. K. RYAN (Washington 1963) 211–248.

[B. M. BONANSEA]

CAMPBELL, ALEXANDER

Founder of the Disciples of Christ; b. Ballymena, County Antrim, Ireland, Sept. 12, 1788; d. Bethany, W.Va., March 4, 1866. He was the son of Rev. Thomas Campbell, a Presbyterian minister, and was educated in his father's school. After attending Glasgow University, Scotland, he joined his father's Christian Association of Washington, Pa., and was ordained in 1812. His theological views, spread by preaching tours, induced congregations in Kentucky, Ohio, Indiana, West Virginia, and Tennessee to separate from the Baptists. Campbell united these churches with the Christian churches organized by Barton Stone to form the Disciples of Christ in 1832. Denominational organization was not completed until the first national convention of the Disciples in 1849. While advocating a simplistic theology, Campbell saw the need for an educated ministry and founded Bethany College, W.Va., in 1840. He engaged in numerous debates on religious topics, including a controversy with Bp. John B. Purcell of Cincinnati, Ohio, in 1830. Besides his published debates, his thought is found chiefly in his book, *The Christian System* (1835), and in his periodicals, *The Christian Baptist* and *The Milennial Harbinger.* He held that baptism and acknowledgment of Jesus Christ as Messiah were the only requisites of Christianity.

Bibliography: J. KELLEMS, *Alexander Campbell and the Disciples* (New York 1930). W. E. GARRISON and A. T. DEGROOT, *The Disciples of Christ: A History* (rev. ed. St. Louis 1958). H. K. ROWE, *Dictionary of American Biography* (New York 1957) 3:446–448.

[R. K. MACMASTER]

Alexander Campbell.

CAMPBELL, JOSEPH

Editor, essayist, mythologist; b. New Rochelle, N.Y., March 26, 1904; d. Oct. 31, 1987. Campbell helped to create an interpretive genre in which psychoanalytical techniques were used to elucidate mythology and folklore. As Campbell pointed out in his most famous work, *The Hero with a Thousand Faces* (1949), myth stands at the interface of the human and mystery that continually beckons the human to move beyond itself. For Campbell, myths provided the human with the means for self-transformation; yet, myths themselves needed to be rediscovered by each society. His legacy as an interpreter of the inner psychological meaning of myth and symbol is a challenge to both traditional religions and clinical psychologies. His emphasis on the universal character of mythology developed out of his personal story, which brought him into the diverse stream of mythic writings.

Life. As a youth Campbell read the Arthurian legends and Native American mythology at the local library. The American Museum of Natural History in New York City further stimulated these formative encounters with Indian religious art and the ethnographic literature being collected by anthropologists. He attended Canterbury School in Connecticut and Dartmouth College before going to Columbia University for his B.A. and M.A. in literature in 1925 and 1927 respectively.

In 1927 Campbell went to Europe to prepare for dissertation work in European Romance literature. His intellectual and personal encounters during this period altered the course of his life. He studied medieval French at the University of Paris and Sanskrit at Munich. Campbell's early interest in tribal art and mythology was being echoed by such artists as Pablo Picasso and Georges Braque whose works manifested African and Native American influences. His readings in Nietzsche and Spengler gave him the critical distance he sought from which to describe the ennui and unrest of Euro-American societies. In literature Campbell entered the dream realms of James Joyce and Thomas Mann. Perhaps most important were his readings in Sigmund Freud and Carl Jung whose psychoanalytical techniques opened new questions about the unconscious structure of individual myth and the quest for a meaningful life. Jung's psychology especially influenced Campbell, who saw it as an inquiry into the collective dream of myths whereby individuals and societies aspire to integration. The variety and extent of these creative influences reoriented Campbell towards his doctoral work.

When he returned to New York in 1929 he found resistance at Columbia to his proposal to study mythical themes in literature. He abandoned his graduate program and, as the Great Depression deepened, withdrew to Woodstock, New York. For the next five years he read widely and voraciously, living on funds he had saved from a college stint as a jazz band musician.

During this period he traveled to California, where he met John Steinbeck and the biologist Edward Ricketts. On returning to the East coast he took a post teaching at Canterbury School. In 1934 he joined the literature faculty at Sarah Lawrence College, where he taught for 38 years. The unique tutorial-seminar system at this college afforded Campbell the opportunity to develop his particular interpretive style in the classroom and in personal conferences with students. Joseph Campbell's marriage in 1938 to the dancer Jean Erdman brought him into closer contact with another expression of myth and symbol.

Works. During these years of teaching and expanding his contacts with others interested in mythology, he joined with Henry Robinson to co-author *A Skeleton Key to Finnegan's Wake* (1944). This interpretive guide to Joyce's novel had been preceded by Campbell's commentary on the first volume of the Bollingen Series, *Where the Two Came to Their Father: A Navaho War Ceremonial* (1943). These two works illustrate the disparate literatures in which Campbell was able to study using his mythic analysis of themes.

In his many works on myth Campbell developed a fourfold interpretive schema that can be found in *The*

Mythic Image (1974) and also in his penultimate work, *The Historical Atlas of World Mythology: The Way of the Animal Powers* (1983). These include the mystical, epistemological, sociological, and pedagogical aspects of myth. He stressed the mystical dimension of mythology, which evokes a sense of the numinous mystery in the universe. Secondly, he pointed out the epistemological function of mythology, which gives people a comprehensive means for knowing the world about them. Campbell next stressed the sociological character of mythology—namely, its function in promoting social order and ideals. Finally, he cited as seminal the pedagogical role of myths, which enable individuals to guide themselves through the difficult passages of their lives.

This interpretation of myth by Joseph Campbell has been seen by some reviewers as being in tension with the revelations of Judeo-Christian-Islamic religion. Campbell's critical focus regarding religion hinged on the question of key teachings as being mythological or ontological. The meaning of religion for Campbell was not in the realm of ''being''; rather, he saw religion as dynamized by deeper unconscious forces that could be articulated in many forms. Campbell himself was deeply committed to the spiritual quest, and his final work, *The Inner Reaches of Outer Space: Methapor as Myth and as Religion* (1986), continued to explore the mythic meaning of words and the psychological depths in which they reverberated.

Campbell's friendship with the Indologist Heinrich Zimmer led directly to his editing Zimmer's manuscripts after his death in 1943. This work culminated in the two-volume edition of *The Art of Indian Asia: Its Mythology and Transformation* (1955). Zimmer had also introduced Campbell to the editors of the planned Bollingen series, which resulted in his eventual editing of the Jungian Conference's *Papers from the Eranos Yearbooks* (1954–68). Campbell's indefatigable editing skills also extended to such projects as *The Portable Arabian Nights* (1952), *The Masks of God* (1959–68), and *The Portable Jung* (1971).

Joseph Campbell. (AP/Wide World Photos)

Bibliography: A good guide is Robert Seagal's *Joseph Campbell, An Introduction*, which does not include his extensive audio and visual cassettes. J. CAMPBELL, *A Skeleton Key to Finnegan's Wake* with H. M. ROBINSON (New York 1944); *The Hero with a Thousand Faces*, Bollingen Series XVII (New York 1949); *The Flight of the Wild Gander: Explorations in the Mythological Dimension* (New York 1969); *The Masks of God*, v. 1 *Primitive Mythology* (New York 1959), v. 2 *Oriental Mythology* (New York 1962), v. 3 *Occidental Mythology* (New York 1964), v. 4 *Creative Mythology* (New York 1968); *Myths to Live By* (New York 1972); *The Mythic Image*, with M. J. ABADIE, Bollingen Series C (Princeton 1974); *Historical Atlas of World Mythology*, v. 1 *The Way of the Animal Powers* (San Francisco 1983); *The Inner Reaches of Outer Space* (New York 1986). J. CAMPBELL, ed., *Myth and Man Series* (London/New York 1951–54); *The Portable Arabian Nights* (New York 1952); *Papers from the Eranos Yearbooks*, tr. R. MANHEIM and R. F. C. HULL, Bollingen Series XXX (New York/Princeton 1954–68); *Myths, Dreams, and Religion* (New York 1970); *The Portable Jung*, tr. R. F. C. HULL (New York 1971).

[J. A. GRIM]

CAMPBELL, THOMAS JOSEPH

Jesuit author, educator; b. New York City, April 29, 1848; d. Monroe, N.Y., Dec. 14, 1925. He was educated in New York City in the public schools and at the College of St. Francis Xavier, where he received his M.A. in 1867; he entered the Jesuit novitiate at Sault-au-Recollet, Canada. In 1870 he was sent to St. John's College, later Fordham University, New York, where he taught classical literature for three years. After studying philosophy and science at Woodstock, Md., he returned in 1876 to St. Francis Xavier College to teach rhetoric. He then went to Louvain University, Belgium, where he studied French literature and ecclesiastical history in addition to theology. He was ordained in 1881, returned to the U.S., and spent his third year of probation at Frederick, Md., after which he became president of St. John's College. In 1888 he was appointed provincial of the Jesuits' Maryland-New York Province, a post he held until 1893. Under his administration colleges were expanded, missionary work among Italian immigrants was undertaken, a laymen's retreat movement was started, and plans were begun for a national Jesuit magazine (*America*). Campbell served briefly (1893) as vice-rector of St. Francis Xavier College, devoted two years to giving missions and retreats, and was for five years president of Fordham University. In August 1900 he was attached to the staffs of the Apostleship of Prayer and the *Messenger of the Sacred Heart* as preacher, editor, and writer. After serving from 1910 to 1914 as editor of *America,* he went to Canada for historical research and published the results in *The Pioneer Priests of North America* (3 v. 1908–19) and *The Pioneer Laymen of North America* (2 v. 1915). After filling posts at St. Francis Xavier Church (1916) and at St. Joseph's Church, Philadelphia, Pa. (1917), he returned to New York as lecturer on American history at the Fordham University Graduate School. He also completed *The Jesuits, 1534–1921* (1921), before retiring in 1925.

[V. C. HOPKINS]

CAMPEGGI, CAMILLO

Theologian; b. Pavia or Piacenza, unknown date; d. 1569. He joined the Dominicans, and after teaching theology he was inquisitor at Pavia, Ferrara, and Mantua. He was the Pope's theologian at the Council of Trent (1561–63), and became bishop of Nepi and Sutri in 1568. Besides his *De mundi fallaciis* (Venice 1562; Brescia 1563), a sermon he preached at the Council before 1561, he published only editions of texts: *De porestate papae et concilii generalis* (Rome 1563), Jean de Torquemada's sermon at the Council of Florence; and *Tractatus de haereticis* (Mantua 1567; Rome 1579) by Zanchino Ugolini (14th century). The treatise, *De primatu romani pontificis contra Matthaeum Flacium Illyricum,* which is doubtfully attributed to Campeggi, was published by J. T. Rocaberti in his *Bibliotheca maxima pontificia,* 7 (Rome 1696) 133–264.

Bibliography: *Scriptores Ordinis Praedicatorum* 2.1:201–202.

[A. DUVAL]

CAMPEGGIO, LORENZO

Cardinal and presiding judge at the court trial of Henry VIII and Catherine of Aragon, legate at the Diets of Nürnberg and Augsburg; b. Milan, Italy, 1472; d. Rome, July 25, 1539. Born of a Bolognese family that traced its ancestry to 1220 and was famous for its many lawyers, writers, and prelates, Lorenzo became a professor of law at the University of Bologna. Though a father of five children, he embraced the ecclesiastical state after the death of his wife in 1509. His advancement was rapid. He was auditor of the Rota in 1511, bishop of Feltre in the next year, nuncio to Emperor Maximilian I in 1513, and cardinal, July 1517. His first major diplomatic assignment came in 1518, when he was sent to the court of Henry VIII by Leo X to secure English support in a crusade against the Turks. Thomas Wolsey blocked his entry into England, until he himself was appointed colegate. Although the mission failed, Campeggio won honors from Henry—including a mansion (built by Bramante) in Rome, the charge of English affairs in Rome, and the bishopric of Salisbury.

Ten years later, when the annulment of Henry's marriage was being petitioned, Wolsey requested Clement VII to appoint Campeggio as judge of the legal proceedings, because of his learning and tractability. Hoping that the King's interest in Anne Boleyn would wane with time, Campeggio delayed his arrival with a convenient attack of gout. Once in England he failed to reconcile the royal couple and failed in his later attempts to induce Queen Catherine's retirement into a convent. After a series of sessions, he adjourned the proceedings of the trial, giving as his reason that the time for summer vacation had arrived. Henry's chagrin resulted in Wolsey's dismissal from Court and Campeggio's loss of prestige. As he was leaving England his baggage was ransacked at Dover, in defiance of his diplomatic immunity, for evidence of bribes from the Emperor Charles V, nephew of Catherine of Aragon, or for a decretal bull defining conditions of the divorce.

Campeggio represented Rome at the diets of Nürnberg in 1524 and Augsburg in 1530. Although he opposed any council meetings with the Protestants, believing that they could be controlled only by imperial authority, he was sent by Paul III in 1538, together with cardinals Giacomo Simonetta and Girolamo Aleandro, to convene a council at Vincenza. He died on his return to Rome in the next year and was buried in Bologna.

Bibliography: J. S. BREWER and J. GAIRDNER, eds., *Letters and Papers of the Reign of Henry VIII,* 21 v. (London 1862–1910). M. FERNÁNDEZ DE NAVARRETE, *Colección de documentos inéditos para la historia de España,* Eng. tr. and summary in *Calendar of State Papers, Spanish* (London 1856). G. FANTUZZI, *Notizie degli scrittori bolognesi* (Bologna 1783) 3:47–61. C. SIGONIO, *De Vita L. Campegi cardinalis* (Bologna 1581). J. GAIRDNER, *The Dictionary of National Biography from the Earliest Times to 1900* 3:850. H. LIEBING, *Die Religion in Geschichte und Gegenwart* 1:1606. E. V. CARDINAL, *Cardinal Lorenzo Campeggio: Legate to the Courts of Henry VIII and Charles V* (Boston 1935). A. D'AMATO, *Enciclopedia cattolica* 3:470–471. G. CONSTANT, *Dictionnaire d'histoire et de géographie ecclésiastiques* 11:633–640. P. HUGHES, *The Reformation in England* v.1. *Nuntiaturberichte aus Deutschland,* Abt. 1, suppl. 1 *Legation Lorenzo Campeggios 1530–1531* *und Nuntiatur Girolamo Aleandros 1531,* ed. G. MÜLLER (Tübingen 1963).

[E. V. CARDINAL]

CAMPIDELLI, PIUS (PIO), BL.

Baptized Luigi, known in religion as Pius of St. Aloysius, Passionist brother; b. Trebbio di Poggio Berni (near Rimini), Italy, April 29, 1868; d. San Vito di Romagna, Casale, Italy, Nov. 2, 1889. Gigino, as he was called by his family, was the fourth of the six children of poor farmers. After his father, Giuseppe Campidelli, died in 1874, an uncle came to help Gigino's mother, Filomena Belpani, with the farm. In 1877 the Campidellis became acquainted with the PASSIONISTS during a mission. Gigino entered their novitiate in the province of the Pieta (eastern Italy) that had been closed in 1866 shortly after the death of St. Gabriel POSSENTI and reopened by Bl. Bernard SILVESTRELLI in 1882. Campidelli made his profession on April 30, 1884 and received the name Pio di San Luigi. He became known for the depth of his prayer life and fidelity to his vows while studying for the priesthood. He received minor orders at San Entizio (Viterbo) prior to being diagnosed with tuberculosis in 1889. He offered his suffering for the Church and died at age twenty-one. He was beatified by John Paul II, Nov. 17, 1985 (the International Year of Youth), as a model for young people.

Bibliography: L. ALUNNO, *Pio Campidelli* (Isola 1985). G. CINGOLANI, *Pio Campidelli: la rivincita dell'anonimato* (Turin 1989). *Acta Apostolicae Sedis* (1985): 141. *L'Osservatore Romano,* English edition, no. 47 (1985): 3–4.

[K. I. RABENSTEIN]

CAMPION, EDMUND, ST.

English Jesuit priest, martyr; b. London, England, *c.* 1540; hanged, drawn, and quartered at Tyburn, London, Dec. 1, 1581. His father, a bookseller, sent him for his education to Christ's Hospital (some say St. Paul's); at age 15 he was awarded a scholarship at St. John's College, Oxford, where two years later he was appointed a junior fellow. He was an outstanding orator and was chosen to speak before Queen Elizabeth when she visited Oxford in 1566; as a schoolboy he had read an address of welcome to Queen Mary on her entry into London in 1553. He won the patronage of the earl of Leicester, and Queen Elizabeth and William Cecil both expressed interest in his future. Brilliant, popular, and the leader of an influential group, he became the most notable figure in the Oxford of his day: Cecil later referred to him as a "diamond of England."

Engraving of Edmund Campion, with knife protruding from chest. (Archive Photos)

In August 1569 Campion crossed to Dublin to assist in the foundation of a university. After writing his *History of Ireland,* a superb piece of literature (first published in Holinshed's *Chronicles,* 1587), he returned to London in 1571, witnessed the trial of Dr. John Storey and then crossed to Douai, where he was reconciled to the Church—he had taken the Oath of Supremacy and deacon's orders according to the Anglican Ordinal (1553). He was ordained subdeacon at Douai in 1573, and went as a pilgrim to Rome, where he was admitted into the Society of Jesus by Father Everard Mercurian. After his novitiate at Brünn in Moravia, he was assigned to teach in the Jesuit school in Prague, where he was ordained in 1578. At the end of the following year Campion, with Father Robert PERSONS, was chosen by Mercurian, at the instigation of Cardinal William ALLEN, to inaugurate a Jesuit mission to England. Campion set out from Rome in the spring of 1580, visiting on his way Cardinal Charles BORROMEO at Milan and BEZA at Geneva; he landed at Dover in the guise of a jewel merchant on June 25. On reaching London, where he visited Catholic prisoners, he hurriedly wrote his "Challenge to the Privy Council" (commonly called "Campion's Brag"), in which he proclaimed the purpose of his mission, namely, "of free cost to preach the Gospel, to minister the Sacraments, to instruct the simple, to reform sinners, to confute errors—in brief, to cry alarm spiritual against foul vice and proud ignorance, wherewith many [of] my dear countrymen are abused.''

Campion's winning personality, saintliness, and eloquence gave fresh heart to Catholics throughout England, but he was pursued by agents of the crown and more than once narrowly escaped capture. He wrote to Mercurian, describing his labors in Lancashire, Yorkshire, and the Midlands: ''I ride about some piece of country every day. The harvest is wonderful great . . . I cannot long escape the hands of the heretics . . . I am in apparel to myself very ridiculous; I often change it and my name too.'' At Stonor Park, Oxfordshire, he wrote and secretly printed his *Decem Rationes,* in which he openly challenged Protestant divines to dispute with him the grounds of Catholicism. On June 27, 1581, some 400 copies of this book were secretly distributed in University Church, Oxford, at the service of ''Commemoration.''

Three weeks later, at Lyford Grange, Berkshire, Campion was betrayed, arrested, and taken to the Tower of London. Attempts were made to bribe him into apostasy. He was racked several times, forced into theological debate, and finally on November 14, together with Ralph SHERWIN, Luke KIRBY, and others, condemned to death. Before sentence he addressed the court: ''In condemning us you condemn all your own ancestors—all the ancient priests, bishops, and kings–all that was once the glory of England . . . God lives; posterity will live; their judgment is not so liable to corruption as that of those who are now going to sentence us to death.'' On December 1, with Sherwin and Alexander BRIANT, he was hanged, drawn, and quartered at Tyburn. Campion was beatified by Leo XIII on Dec. 9, 1886 and canonized by Paul VI on Oct. 25, 1970 as one of the Forty Martyrs of England and Wales.

Feast: Dec. 1 (Jesuits); Oct. 25 (Feast of the 40 Martyrs of England and Wales); May 4 (Feast of the English Martyrs in England).

See Also: ENGLAND, SCOTLAND, AND WALES, MARTYRS OF; OATHS, ENGLISH POST-REFORMATION; RECUSANTS; RECUSANT LITERATURE.

Bibliography: E. CAMPION, *A Place in the City* (Ringwood, Vic. and New York 1994). L. CAMPION, *The Family of Edmund Campion* (London 1975). H. FOLEY, *Records of the English Province of the Society of Jesus,* 7 v. (London 1877–82) *passim.* L. FRENCH, *The Campion Paintings* (Melbourne 1962). T. GAVIN, *High Above the Sun: Lives of St. Thomas More and Bl. Emund Campion* (Pulaski, Wis. 1961). T. M. MCCOOG, ed., *The Reckoned Expense: Edmund Campion and the Early English Jesuits* (Woodbridge, Suffolk, UK 1996)s. E. E. REYNOLDS, *Campion and Parsons: The Jesuit Mission of 1580–1* (London 1980). R. SIMPSON, *Edmund Campion* (new ed. London 1896). M. H. SOUTH, *The Jesuits and the Joint Mission to England during 1580–1581* (Lewiston, N.Y. 1999). J. N. TYLENDA, *Jesuit Saints & Martyrs* (Chicago 1998), 415–19. E. WAUGH, *Edmund Campion* (New York 1935; Oxford and New York 1980), reprinted as *Saint Edmund Campion: Priest and Martyr* (Manchester, N.H. 1996).

[P. CARAMAN]

CAMPION, EDWARD, BL.

Priest martyr; *vere* Edwards; b. 1552, Ludlow, Shropshire, England; hanged, drawn, and quartered at Canterbury, Oct. 1, 1588. Born into a good family, possibly a Protestant one, Campion studied for two years at Jesus College, Oxford. Thereafter he was in the service of Gregory, tenth Lord Dacre of the South. Having converted to Catholicism, he studied for the priesthood at Rheims (1586–87), where he adopted the surname Campion and was ordained for service in the Diocese of Canterbury. He was arrested at Sittingbourne within months of his arrival, imprisoned at Newgate and the Marshalsea with BB. Robert WILCOX, Christopher BUXTON, and Robert WIDMERPOOL, and executed for being a priest. He was beatified by Pius XI on Dec. 15, 1929.

Feast of the English Martyrs: May 4 (England).

See Also: ENGLAND, SCOTLAND, AND WALES, MARTYRS OF.

Bibliography: R. CHALLONER, *Memoirs of Missionary Priests,* ed. J. H. POLLEN (rev. ed. London 1924; repr. Farnborough 1969), I, 61–63. H. FOLEY, *Records of the English Province of the Society of Jesus,* (London 1877–82), I, 478, 481. J. MORRIS, ed., *The Troubles of Our Catholic Forefathers Related by Themselves,* 3 v. (London 1872–77), III, 39. J. H. POLLEN, *Acts of English Martyrs* (London 1891), 327.

[K. I. RABENSTEIN]

CAMPO SANTO TEUTONICO

The oldest of the German national foundations in Rome. It comprises a church, a college for priests, and a cemetery and is situated left of St. Peter's, in the area of NERO'S circus. According to legend, Empress St. HELENA had brought some of the soil of Mt. Calvary to Rome and scattered it in the area of Nero's circus, thus the name Campo Santo (Holy Field). Under CHARLEMAGNE the *Schola Francorum* was founded there (799) with a church, a pilgrim's hospice, and a cemetery, where Frankish priests took care of their countrymen and buried their dead.

The Augustinian Johannes Golderer, later auxiliary bishop of Bamberg, founded (*c.* 1450) the All Souls CONFRATERNITY for his German countrymen in Rome; its statutes were approved by Pope Pius II in 1461. In 1519

Cemetery of Campo Santo Teutonico, Rome.

Pope Gregory XIII raised this association to the rank of an archconfraternity with headship over all other similar confraternities. It is still in existence and is the juridical body for Campo Santo.

Today the archconfraternity (*Arciconfraternità di Santa Maria della Pietà dei Teutonici e Fiamminghi*) is made up of German-speaking men and women of every class and country living in Rome. They participate in regular church services wearing their national costume. They are especially devoted to assisting at Masses for the poor souls. In the 19th century guilds of German bakers and shoemakers were included in the archconfraternity. In a small cemetery with its cypress and palm trees are graves of many famous persons, e.g., Anton de WAAL. It is visited annually by thousands of tourists from Germany, Austria, Switzerland, Luxembourg, and the Netherlands. Here likewise German Catholics of Rome celebrate the Feast of Corpus Christi, a celebration in which the papal Swiss Guard joins. November 1 is the major feast of the archconfraternity of the poor souls.

A cruciform hall church was consecrated in 1501. The paintings of the old winged altar are still preserved and are hanging in the choir. The main altar with the Pietà is the creation of Wilhelm Achtermann (d. 1884), as is the marble Resurrection altar on the left side chapel. The tombs of the Swiss Guards who died in 1527 defending Pope CLEMENT VII are in the Resurrection chapel. In the 19th century the church was repainted in the Nazarene style. The church has been enriched by various patrons: Franz Joseph of Austria (windows), Emperor Wilhelm II (organ), Pope Leo XIII (candelabra), and Pope John XXIII (a chalice). In 1959 the President of the German Republic, Theodore Heuss, donated a bronze door, which was made according to the design of E. Hillenbrand.

A college for priests was founded in 1876 by De Waal, mainly for young clerics who came to Rome to study Church history and Christian archeology. A special library of 30,000 volumes serves this purpose. In 1888 the Roman Institute of the GÖRRES-GESELLSCHAFT was founded. It provides scholarly training for the new generation and publishes source material from the VATICAN

ARCHIVES (e.g., Acts of the Council of TRENT, papal nunciature reports). In conjunction with the college it also edits the *Römische Quartalschrift für christliche Altertumskunde und Kirchengeschichte,* with supplementary issues.

The museum houses a collection of Christian antiquities, assembled originally by De Waal. It contains small articles of early Christian art, sarcophagi, inscriptions, lamps, Coptic textile fabrics, Roman imperial coins, and paintings of the Middle Ages. The association Villa Hügel in Essen arranged for the cataloguing of the museum. Displays of its holdings have been held in Essen, Mainz, Mechlin, Utrecht, and Vienna.

Bibliography: P. M. BAUMGARTEN, *Cartularium vetus Campi Sancti Teutonicorum de Urbe, Römisch Quartalschriftfür christliche Altertumskunde und für Kirchengeschichte* (Freiburg 1887–) 16. Suppl. Heft (1908). E. DAVID, *Vorgeschichte und Geschichte des Priesterkollegiums am Campo Santo* (Freiburg 1928). W. KUHN, *Frühchristliche Kunst aus Rom. Katalog,* ed. Verein Villa Hügel (Essen 1962). A. SCHUCHERT, *Lexikon für Theologie und Kirche,* ed. J. HOFER and K. RAHNER, 10 v. (2d, new ed. Freiburg 1957–65) 2:912.

[J. E. GUGUMUS]

CAMPRA, ANDRÉ

Composer of opera and church music who ranks with LULLY and COUPERIN among the masters of the French baroque; b. Aix (Provence), Dec. 4, 1660; d. Versailles, June 29, 1744. His first post was music director at Toulon cathedral in 1680. After holding a number of similar positions, he was appointed *maître de chapelle* at Notre Dame in 1694. He resigned in 1700 to devote himself more exclusively to operatic composition, since his operas were fast becoming successful. Among his important church works are five books of motets (1695–1720), a Mass (1700), and two books of psalms (1737–38). Most of these settings have orchestral accompaniment, and he is credited with having introduced stringed instruments into the services at Notre Dame. His church style can be described as a mixture of declamatory French and florid Italian techniques. As a composer of operas he is justly considered the chief link between Lully and Rameau.

Bibliography: M. BARTÉLEMY, *André Campra* (Paris 1957). R. GIRARDON, *Die Musik in Geschichte und Gegenwart,* ed. F. BLUME 10 v. (Kassel-Basel 1949) 2:730–740. A. H. WODEHOUSE et al., *Grove's Dictionary of Music and Musicians,* ed. E. BLOM 9 v. (London 1954) 2:36–39. J. R. ANTHONY, *The New Grove Dictionary of Music and Musicians, vol. 3,* ed. S. SADIE 662–666 (New York 1980). A. BAKER, *The Church Music of André Campra* (Ph.D. diss. University of Toronto, 1977). "The Church Music of André Campra: A Reconsideration of the Sources," *Recherches sur la Musique française classique* 22 (1984) 89–130. J. BOYER, "Nouveaux Documents sur la Jeunesse d'André Campra et la vie musicale à Aix-en- Provence au XVII ᵉ siècle," *Recherches sur la Musique française classique* 22 (1984) 79–88. G. GARDEN, "*Les Amours de Vénus (1712)* et le *Second Livre de cantates (1714)* de Campra," *Revue de Musicologie* 77 (1991) 96–107. D. M. RANDEL, ed. *The Harvard Biographical Dictionary of Music* (Cambridge, Massachusetts 1996) 132–33. N. SLONIMSKY, ed. *Baker's Biographical Dictionary of Musicians, Eighth Edition* (New York 1992) 289.

[W. C. HOLMES]

ISBN 0-7876-4006-9

90000

9 780787 640064